THE OXFORD COMPANION TO

CANADIAN HISTORY

EDITED BY

GERALD HALLOWELL

OXFORD
UNIVERSITY PRESS

1904 2004

100 YEARS OF
CANADIAN PUBLISHING

OXFORD
UNIVERSITY PRESS

70 Wynford Drive, Don Mills, Ontario M3C 1J9
www.oup.com/ca

Oxford University Press is a department of the University of Oxford.
It furthers the University's objective of excellence in research, scholarship,
and education by publishing worldwide in

Oxford New York
Auckland Cape Town Dar es Salaam Hong Kong Karachi
Kuala Lumpur Madrid Melbourne Mexico City Nairobi
New Delhi Shanghai Taipei Toronto

With offices in
Argentina Austria Brazil Chile Czech Republic France Greece
Guatemala Hungary Italy Japan Poland Portugal Singapore
South Korea Switzerland Thailand Turkey Ukraine Vietnam

Published in Canada
by Oxford University Press

First published 2004

National Library of Canada Cataloguing in Publication

The Oxford companion to Canadian history / edited by Gerald Hallowell.

Includes index.
ISBN-10: 0-19-541559-0
ISBN-13: 978-0-19-541559-9

1. Canada—History—Encyclopedias. I. Hallowell, Gerald

FC23.O94 2004 971'.003 C2004-902270-9

Cover & Text Design: Brett J. Miller
Cover Image: PhotoDisc/Getty Images

3 4 — 07 06 05
This book is printed on permanent (acid-free) paper ♾.
Printed in Canada

Contents

PREFACE

'. . . land so bleak and bare
a single plume of smoke
is a scroll of history.'

In some ways, F.R. Scott's description of the Mackenzie River delta stands as a metaphor for all of Canada and its history. Compared to older continents, this New World nation's past may seem no more than a puff of smoke. And yet, as Robert McGhee notes in his entry on pre-European history, people have lived in this magnificent land for thousands of years. Aboriginal peoples, with societies diverse and complex, occupied the land from coast to coast when, a millennium ago, the Norse set foot on Newfoundland's shores. No one really knows how long Europeans had been fishing off the Atlantic coast when John Cabot made landfall in the late 15th century, and Jacques Cartier in the early 16th. The origins of St John's are lost in the mists of time, though Sir Humphrey Gilbert arrived in 1583 to declare Newfoundland Britain's first overseas colony. By the early 17th century the French were establishing themselves in Acadia and the St Lawrence Valley. New France fell to the British by 1760. English-speaking people had begun to move north into Nova Scotia from the Thirteen Colonies in the mid-18th century, and after the American Revolution, with the arrival of the United Empire Loyalists, New Brunswick and Upper Canada were carved out of the wilderness. These English-speaking colonies joined French Quebec in 1867 to form a new nation, a nation whose destiny was to spread westward and northward, embracing most of the vast northern half of the North American continent. The scroll on which Canada's history is written is substantial indeed.

It could be said that Canada grew on the backs of the humble beaver. Building on the social and economic networks of the Aboriginals, and on their knowledge of the environment, it was the fur traders—the French from Quebec, the English out of Hudson Bay—who extended European influence across the continent. Later generations witnessed transcontinental railways, the spread of settlers and wheat across the plains, gold rushes in British Columbia and the Yukon. Whalers and sealers harvested the seas, ranching flourished in southern Alberta, mines of various kinds opened across the country, and Canada's huge forests were exploited.

Politically, Canada evolved from colonial beginnings to become a parliamentary democracy, the only constitutional monarchy in the western hemisphere. Evolution was slow, from the struggle for responsible government in the 1840s, through the first coming together of scattered colonies at Confederation in 1867, a gradual move towards independence within the British Empire culminating in the Statute of Westminster in 1931, the final patriation of the constitution by the Trudeau government in 1982. Political parties evolved, various ideologies from conservatism and liberalism to socialism and communism were promoted, relations between the federal and provincial governments became ever more complicated, farmers and labourers insisted on having a voice in politics, women fought for and won the vote. The First Nations and the so-called 'founding peoples', the French and the British, were joined by immigrants from many lands. Government policies of bilingualism and multiculturalism sometimes clashed, but, as John Conway remarked, Canada achieved a union in which political democracy developed based upon cultural diversity, a lesson of much value for the world.

Industrialization brought manufacturing and larger cities, the growth of factories, labour unions, and eventually the welfare state. Social reformers, inspired by the social gospel, sought to alleviate the problems of modern society, such as poverty, prostitution, and drunkenness. Attempts were made to improve education, public health, the lot in life of children and the nation's youth. Institutions as diverse as the Royal Canadian Mounted Police, banks, Frontier College, museums and art galleries, national parks, and literary societies emerged, as did newspapers, book publishing, and broadcasting.

There were darker spots too, such as the expulsion of the Acadians in 1755—an event echoed almost 200 years later by the removal of Japanese Canadians from the west coast during the Second World War—the Great Depression, shipwrecks and natural disasters, epidemics, residential schools. And there were issues that divided the country: conscription in both world wars, Aboriginal title and treaty rights, birth control and abortion, the merits of foreign ownership and 'souveraineté-association', medicare, the War Measures Act.

Militarily, Canada—a 'peaceable kingdom'—has been involved in many wars, from the imperial rivalries of European powers on the east coast in the 17th and 18th centuries, through the War of 1812, the South African War, to the worldwide conflagrations of the 20th century. There have also been internal conflicts, notably the Rebellion of 1837–8 and the North-West Rebellion in 1885. Over time the Canadian armed forces have evolved, from militiamen to international peacekeepers. The Cold War, too, has been another kind of struggle. Internationally, Canada has been a prominent member of the British Commonwealth of Nations and a strong supporter of the League of Nations, the United Nations, NATO, and other international organizations.

All of these subjects, and many more, are covered in *The Oxford Companion to Canadian History*. Obviously it is a challenge to present the history of a country in a single volume. The *Companion* attempts to do this by providing the basic details of the main events, institutions, places, and people in Canada's past. An attempt has been made to maintain a balance among the different areas of life—politics and the constitution, industry and the economy, education and religion, the law, medicine and science, transportation, social and cultural history. All time periods have been covered, from earliest recorded history to recent times, and all regions—the Maritimes, the Prairies, the North, with Newfoundland and British Columbia on opposite coasts as distinct book ends, and of course the heavily populated centre, Ontario and Quebec.

As for the people in Canada's past, an attempt has been made to include all those one would expect to find in a book about Canadian history. Individuals have been included because of their prominence—political and religious leaders, entrepreneurs and businessmen, social activists, scientists, musicians, athletes, artists, and writers. The emphasis here is on the careers of such people, the contribution they have made to Canadian history, rather than on biographical details. People are also included because they are simply interesting—a Cape Breton slave who became a successful tavern keeper; a murdered Quebec orphan, 'l'enfant martyre', whose pitiful story became embedded in the collective memory of her people; the greatest scout on the plains of the Old North-West, who helped facilitate peaceful relations between the Mounted Police and the Blackfoot. People also appear collectively: Aboriginals from different parts of the country, Acadians, Metis, explorers and missionaries, privateers, jackatars, habitants and voyageurs, farmers, feminists, merchants and miners, bush pilots, war brides and picture brides, immigrants of many nationalities, men and women in all walks of life. As in all areas and for all topics, it has been necessary to be selective, to choose representative people, since not everyone or every subject can possibly be included.

In his book *What Is History?* E.H. Carr has a passage describing how historical facts are sometimes chosen: 'The facts are really not at all like fish on the fishmonger's slab. They are like fish swimming about in a vast and sometimes inaccessible ocean; and what the historian catches will depend, partly on chance, but mainly on what part of the ocean he chooses to fish in and what tackle he chooses to use—these two factors being, of course, determined by the kind of fish he wants to catch.' The entries to be included in this *Companion* were chosen rather like that. If there are too many lowly sculpins—ugly, inedible, but endearing—and too few sleek and tasty halibut, then the general editor is entirely to blame.

Without the 527 contributors, the men and women from all parts of Canada and occasionally from abroad who wrote the entries, the *Companion* would not exist. Representing many different historical points of view and ideological perspectives, they were asked to share their expert knowledge and to provide sprightly prose descriptions of their subjects. They were also called upon to do two things with which they were likely uncomfortable. In the interests of saving space for text, they were asked not to provide sources or lists of further reading. They were also, of necessity, told to be brief. As one contributor lamented: 'brief does not come easily to us garrulous academics'. Enforced brevity can, however, lead to a clarity of definition. I thank these busy people sincerely for their contributions.

I would also like to thank the members of the editorial advisory board, who provided much good advice and support when it was needed: from west to east, Tina Loo, chair of the board, Bill Waiser, Jonathan Vance, Ian Radforth, Suzanne Morton, and John Reid. It was a great pleasure to work with them. In addition, I appreciate the special assistance of Margaret Conrad in Fredericton, Peter Gossage in Sherbrooke, and James K. Hiller in St John's.

At Oxford University Press Laura Macleod, former colleague at the University of Toronto Press and long-time friend, gave me the opportunity to do this work and encouraged me along the way. I also enjoyed working with Rachael Cayley, Ann Checchia, and managing editor Phyllis Wilson. Sally Livingston translated almost 70 entries from French into English, and Francesca Scalzo prepared the index.

There is one other person without whom the *Companion* simply could not have happened, namely my fair dinkum computer expert, Ken Bell of Lunenburg, who tweaked my programs into usable form and came to my rescue when technology failed or my limited knowledge of computers became evident. It was reassuring as well to know that I could count on the computer expertise of my friend and next-door neighbour, Judith Carey.

Two people shared the burden and the excitement more than anyone else. I have enjoyed working with Barbara Tessman, who polished our prose, helped rein in overzealous contributors when they threatened to blow the word count, and corrected our infelicities. Barbara deserves her reputation as one of the best in the business. Finally, I would like to thank Michael Browne for putting up with four years of 'snippets'.

As for the usual caveat about a book's flaws, the very British immigrant Catharine Parr Traill, in her 1868 book on Canadian wildflowers, wrote that 'Any short-comings that may be noticed by our friends, must be excused on the score of the work being wholly Canadian in its execution.' If there are imperfections in this *Companion*—unfortunate omissions, matters deemed unworthy of inclusion that somehow sneaked in—my being a fifth-generation Canadian may account for it. But I've been able to work with a wonderful community of Canadian historians, and if the book is a success it is due to their expertise and commitment to the field. We've come a long way, Katey!

In the end, why do we bother with history at all? As a character in Pat Barker's *Another World* believes: 'you should go to the past, looking not for messages or warnings, but simply to be humbled by the weight of human experience that has preceded the brief flicker of your own few days . . . '

Gerald Hallowell
Lunenburg, Nova Scotia
March 2004

NOTE TO THE READER

Entries are arranged alphabetically by headword—for example, family names, events, institutions, places. French-language institutions generally appear under the name in French. Besides looking for subjects under the headword, or title, of the entry, there are three ways to find information in the *Companion*. Cross-references to related topics are marked within entries, where possible, by asterisks in front of appropriate words. More rarely, readers are directed to subjects of related interest by the use of *See also* at the end of entries; if an asterisk has already clearly indicated a cross-reference, then *See also* is not used. Because neither of the above systems is perfect (wording does not always allow for an asterisk), the surest way to discover and explore all the various aspects of a particular topic is to consult the index.

To avoid a sea of asterisks, several obvious topics that are mentioned frequently throughout are not cross-referenced: events such as Confederation and the Great Depression; frequently used place names such as New France, Acadia, British North America, and Upper and Lower Canada, and the names of provinces, territories, and larger cities; major conflicts such as the Seven Years' War, the War of 1812, the two world wars, and the Cold War; the principal railways; the main churches; and the major political parties. These topics, which permeate Canadian history, are cross-referenced only when such a cross-reference seems particularly useful.

The word 'Aboriginal' has generally been used in the headwords to describe indigenous people. However, because other terms are also deemed acceptable—First Nations, Natives, Indians—they have been used where appropriate and where contributors preferred them. 'Aboriginal' here generally refers to the people we are used to thinking of as Indians, and does not usually include the Inuit, who, although also indigenous, are a separate people. An attempt has been made to give the most contemporary usage of Aboriginal names—for example, Kwakwaka'wakw rather than Kwakiutl, Nuu'chah'nulth rather than Nootka, Mi'kmaq rather than Micmac—but because of frequent changes it is not always possible to be accurate.

Five maps at the back of the book attempt to show the historical development of Canada: the areas generally considered to be the homelands of the various Aboriginal peoples; the eastern half of the country during the French regime; British North America from the Treaty of Paris in 1783 to Confederation in 1867; the complicated arrangement of districts in the North-West Territories in 1895, before Alberta and Saskatchewan became provinces; and the territorial evolution of the country from Confederation to the establishment of Nunavut in 1999. Five other maps—Atlantic Canada, Labrador and Quebec, Ontario, Western Canada, and Northern Canada—show the locations of many of the places mentioned in the entries. Also at the back of the book are lists of the monarchs who have ruled over Canadian territory as well as the governors general, prime ministers, and provincial premiers since Confederation. Finally, the national anthems of Canada and Newfoundland are given.

Rightly or wrongly, a decision was made, by publisher and editor, to have no sources in the entries, so as to maximize the space available for historical information. There are many other places to discover the rich bibliography concerning Canadian history. Today, sources can often be tracked down on the Internet. The contributors to the *Companion* are authorities on the subjects they are writing about and have written more extensively about their subjects elsewhere. Searching their names would likely lead the reader to many appropriate sources.

Readers who wish more information than can be presented in this single volume might consult *The Canadian Encyclopedia*, first published 1985, editor in chief James H. Marsh, and now expanded and available on line at www.thecanadianencyclopedia.com. For fuller information on individuals in Canadian history, the *Dictionary of Canadian Biography*, now covering the years from 1000 to 1920 in 14 volumes, is also on line at www.biographi.ca. Readers might also wish to consult the three-volume *Historical Atlas of Canada*. There are several scholarly journals publishing in the field of Canadian history, but the general reader would find especially attractive that fine publication *The Beaver*, Canada's History Magazine, founded in 1920 by the Hudson's Bay Company and now published by Canada's National History Society.

Almost forty years ago Norah Story published *The Oxford Companion to Canadian History and Literature* (1967). In his 1973 *Supplement* to Story's companion, William Toye referred to her work as 'invaluable and formidable . . . the impressive achievement of one person'. In 1983 *The Oxford Companion to Canadian Literature* appeared, edited by William Toye (2nd edn, 1997, ed. Eugene Benson and Toye). *The Oxford Companion to Canadian Theatre* was published in 1989, edited by Eugene Benson and L.W. Conolly. Until now there has been no separate companion to Canadian history. The study of history has changed a great deal since 1967, and much new scholarship has appeared; even in 1986, in *The Writing of Canadian History*, Carl Berger wrote of 'the vast exfoliation of historical literature over the last twenty years'. Many more layers of Canadian history have been laid down since then—new books, new scholars, even new areas of study. The present *Oxford Companion to Canadian History* is in no way related to Norah Story's pioneer volume, but I hope she would approve of it.

G.H.

CONTRIBUTORS

IRVING ABELLA
Department of History
York University
• *American Federation of Labor, Communist Party of Canada; Jews; refugees* •

ANNMARIE ADAMS
School of Architecture
McGill University
• *architecture* •

MARIANNE GOSZTONYI AINLEY
Department of History/Gender Studies
University of Northern British Columbia
• *William Rowan; E.W.R. Steacie; Alice Wilson* •

DONALD HARMAN AKENSON
Department of History
Queen's University
• (with David A. Wilson) *Irish* •

LINDA M. AMBROSE
Department of History
Laurentian University
• *Canadian Youth Commission; 4-H Clubs; Women's Institutes* •

KAY ARMATAGE
Cinema Studies and Women's Studies, Innis College
University of Toronto
• *Nell Shipman* •

CHARLES ARMOUR
Halifax
• *Marco Polo* •

KATHERINE ARNUP
School of Canadian Studies
Carleton University
• *mothers of the race; vaccination* •

LAWRENCE ARONSEN
Department of History and Classics
University of Alberta
• *Bomarc missile crisis; Cuban missile crisis; North Atlantic Treaty Organization; North Atlantic Triangle; United Nations* •

ALAN F.J. ARTIBISE
Dean, College of Urban and Public Affairs
University of New Orleans
• *urbanization; Winnipeg* •

MICHAEL ASCH
Department of Anthropology
University of Victoria
• (with Robert Wishart) *western subarctic Aboriginals* •

ALVYN AUSTIN
University of Toronto Schools
Toronto
• *foreign missions* •

DONALD H. AVERY
Department of History
University of Western Ontario
• *deportation; C.J. Mackenzie; Manhattan Project; military technology, Second World War* •

PAUL AXELROD
Dean, Faculty of Education
York University
• *education in the industrial age; public education; Student Christian Movement; universities* •

MICHIKO MIDGE AYUKAWA
Historian
Victoria
• *picture brides; Japanese Canadians* •

ROBERT E. BABE
Jean Monty/BCE Chair in Media Studies,
Faculty of Information and Media Studies
University of Western Ontario
• *Alexander Graham Bell; Bell Canada; George Grant; John Grierson; Marshall McLuhan; C.B. Macpherson; Guglielmo Marconi; Graham Spry; telecommunications; transatlantic cable* •

CONSTANCE BACKHOUSE
Faculty of Law
University of Ottawa
• *Viola Desmond; White Women's Labour Laws* •

DENYSE BAILLARGEON
Département d'histoire
Université de Montréal
• *Assistance maternelle de Montréal; gouttes de lait* •

MELVIN BAKER
University Archivist and Department of History
Memorial University of Newfoundland
• (with Aidan Maloney) *Burin tidal wave; Caribou; William Coaker; Fishermen's Protective Union; Florizel; Knights of Columbus fire; Newfoundland loggers' strike; Ocean Ranger; outport resettlement; St John's* •

WILLIAM M. BAKER
Professor Emeritus
University of Lethbridge
• *Timothy Warren Anglin* •

KAREN A. BALCOM
Department of History
McMaster University
• *Ideal Maternity Home* •

MARGARET A. BANKS
Professor Emeritus of Law and former Law Librarian
University of Western Ontario
• *Sir John George Bourinot* •

KATHLEEN BANNING
Cinema Studies, Innis College
University of Toronto
• *Studio D* •

JERRY BANNISTER
Department of History
Dalhousie University
• *Palliser's Act; mercantilism; West Country merchants; West Indies trade* •

MARILYN BARBER
Department of History
Carleton University
• *domestic servants* •

JEAN BARMAN
Department of Social and Educational Studies
University of British Columbia
• *Kanakas* •

DAVID L. BASHOW
Department of History
Royal Military College of Canada
• *William Barker; William Avery 'Billy' Bishop* •

PETER BASKERVILLE
Department of History
University of Victoria
• *colonization companies in the Canadas; life expectancy; William Price; trust companies; Victoria* •

MAURICE BASQUE
Directeur, Études acadiennes
Université de Moncton
• *Acadia; Jean-Louis Le Loutre; Prudent Robichaud* •

GERHARD P. BASSLER
Department of History
Memorial University of Newfoundland
• *Germans* •

COLIN BEAIRSTO
Whitehorse
• *Lost Patrol; Mad Trapper; Old Crow* •

BETSY BEATTIE
Fogler Library
University of Maine
• *Maritimers in the Boston states* •

THE HONOURABLE GÉRALD-A. BEAUDOIN
The Senate of Canada
• *constitutional amendment; distinct society; Drybones case; federal–provincial relations; federalism; Fulton–Favreau formula; notwithstanding clause; Tremblay Commission* •

J. MURRAY BECK
Retired, Department of Political Science
Dalhousie University
• *Botheration letters; Council of Twelve; Joseph Howe* •

JULES BÉLANGER
Gaspé, Québec
• *Gaspé* •

RÉAL BÉLANGER
Professeur titulaire, Département d'histoire
Université Laval
• *Henri Bourassa; Hector-Louis Langevin; Wilfrid Laurier; Honoré Mercier; Jules-Paul Tardivel; Louis-Alexandre Taschereau* •

JAMIE BENIDICKSON
Faculty of Law
University of Ottawa
• *canoeing; Peterborough Canoe Company* •

CARL BENN
Chief Curator
City of Toronto Museums and Heritage Services
• *Aboriginal warfare; Joseph and Margaret (Molly) Brant; Tecumseh and Tenskwatawa; Toronto* •

DAVID J. BERCUSON
Department of History
University of Calgary
• *Canadian Movement; Brooke Claxton; Korean War* •

CARL BERGER
Department of History
University of Toronto
• *Canada and Its Provinces; Canada First; George Taylor Denison; history and historians; imperialism; Harold Innis; Royal Society of Canada; Sir Daniel Wilson* •

JUDITH BERMAN
University of Pennsylvania Museum
Philadelphia
• *George Hunt* •

LITA-ROSE BETCHERMAN
Toronto
• *Ernest Lapointe* •

MARION BEYEA
Provincial Archives of New Brunswick
• *Partridge Island* •

NAOMI BLACK
Department of Political Science
York University and
Department of Women's Studies
Mount Saint Vincent University
• *Carrie Best; Elsie (Elizabeth Muriel) Gregory MacGill; Helen Gregory MacGill; Persons Case* •

MICHAEL BLISS
History of Medicine
University of Toronto
• *Frederick Grant Banting; Sir Joseph Wesley Flavelle; insulin, discovery of; Sir William Osler* •

ROBERT BOTHWELL
Director, International Relations Program
and Department of History
University of Toronto
• *Jean Chrétien; Loring Christie; C.D. Howe; Munitions and Supply, Department of; nuclear energy; Reconstruction, Department of; Trans-Canada gas pipeline debate* •

GARY BOTTING
Paetzold Fellow, Faculty of Law
University of British Columbia
• *extradition* •

ANTOINE BOUCHARD
Professeur émérite, Faculté de musique
Université Laval
• *Joseph Casavant* •

GÉRARD BOUCHARD
Département des sciences humaines,
Chaire de recherche du Canada sur la dynamique des imaginaires collectives
Université du Québec à Chicoutimi
• *Americanité* •

LYNNE BOWEN
Rogers Communication Co-Chair of Creative Non-Fiction Writing
University of British Columbia
• *Barr Colony; Robert and James Dunsmuir* •

BETTINA BRADBURY
Department of History
York University
• *families* •

LAURA BRANDON
Curator of War Art
Canadian War Museum
• *war art* •

DAVID H. BREEN
Department of History
University of British Columbia
• *Leduc; ranching* •

J. WILLIAM BRENNAN
Department of History
University of Regina
• *Assiniboia; Autonomy Bills; Regina* •

PATRICK H. BRENNAN
Department of History
University of Calgary
• *Alberta Heritage Fund; J.W. Dafoe; Robert Edwards, Blair Fraser; Arthur Irwin; journalism; Saturday Night* •

CAROL BRICE-BENNETT
Social Science Research Consultant
St John's
• *Moravian missions; Labrador* •

DAVID BRIGHT
Department of History
University of Guelph
• *Industry and Humanity (King); Mechanics' Institutes; On-to-Ottawa Trek; Rand Formula* •

GRAHAM BROAD
Department of History
University of Western Ontario
• *Wartime Prices and Trade Board* •

PATRICK BRODE
Windsor, Ontario
• *Sir John Beverley Robinson; seduction, tort of; war crimes* •

JENNIFER S.H. BROWN
Department of History
University of Winnipeg
• *Aboriginal spiritual beliefs; marriage 'according to the custom of the country'; Metis; Michif; Rupert's Land* •

P.E. BRYDEN
Department of History
Mount Allison University
• *Canada Pension Plan; community of communities; medicare; Omnibus Bill* •

J.M. BUMSTED
Department of History
University of Manitoba
• *Alexander; American Revolution; Board of Trade and Plantations; British connection; British Empire; British North America; Dawson Road; English immigrants and ethnicity; Hector; Alexander Mackenzie; Red River Resistance; Red River Settlement; Scots; Lord Selkirk; Wolseley Expedition* •

Jim Burant
Chief, Art and Photography Archives Section
National Archives of Canada
• *W.H. Bartlett* •

Christina Burr
Department of History
University of Windsor
• *printers' strike, Toronto; T. Phillips Thompson* •

Sean Cadigan
Director, Public Policy Research Centre
Memorial University of Newfoundland
• *fisheries; Newfoundland* •

Alan Cairns
Department of Political Science
University of Waterloo
• *Aboriginal Peoples, Royal Commission on; Aboriginal rights; Charter of Rights and Freedoms; Hawthorn Report* •

Agnes Calliste
Department of Sociology and Anthropology
St Francis Xavier University
• *porters* •

Gail G. Campbell
Department of History
University of New Brunswick
• *Fredericton; New Brunswick; Smashers* •

Peter Campbell
Department of History
Queen's University
• *Canadian Federation of Labour; public sector unions; syndicalism* •

Sandra Campbell
Department of English
University of Ottawa
• *Lorne Pierce* •

James E. Candow
Parks Canada
Halifax
• *Robert Bartlett* •

Jean-François Cardin
Département d'études sur l'enseignement
et l'apprentissage
Université Laval
• *Front de Liberation du Québec; René Lévesque; Parti Québécois; sovereignty-association* •

Francis M. Carroll
St John's College
University of Manitoba
• *Aroostook War; Ashburton-Webster Treaty; Jay's Treaty; Rush-Bagot Agreement* •

Sarah Carter
Department of History
University of Calgary
• *Aboriginal reserve agriculture* •

R. Kenneth Carty
Professor of Political Science, Senior Fellow,
Green College
University of British Columbia
• *party system* •

Jay Cassel
Toronto
• *Carignan-Salières Regiment; Pierre Le Moyne d'Iberville; militia, French regime; Pierre Pouchot; Quebec, siege of; Seven Years' War; Troupes de la Marine; Pierre de Troyes* •

André Cellard
Département d'histoire
Université d'Ottawa
• *penal reform; prisons and penitentiaries* •

Xiaobei Chen
School of Social Work
University of Victoria
• *J.J. Kelso* •

Carl A. Christie
Centre for Defence and Security Studies
University of Manitoba
• *air travel; bush pilots; C.H. 'Punch' Dickins; Ferry Command; W.R. 'Wop' May; Northeast Staging Route; Northwest Staging Route* •

Janet Chute
Department of Anthropology
Dalhousie University
• *Shinguakonse* •

Brian Clarke
Emmanuel College
Toronto School of Theology
• *Knights of Columbus; John Joseph Lynch* •

Daniel Clayton
Lecturer in Human Geography,
School of Geography and Geosciences
University of St Andrews, Scotland
• *Nootka Sound Convention* •

Wallace Clement
Chancellor's Professor
Carleton University
• *The Vertical Mosaic (Porter)* •

Barbara Clow
Department of History
Dalhousie University
• *alternative medicine* •

COLIN M. COATES
Canada Research Chair in Canadian Cultural Landscapes, Glendon College
York University
• *François Bigot; colonization companies in New France; Louis de Buade de Frontenac; royal colony of New France; Jean Talon; Madeleine de Verchères* •

K.S. COATES
Dean, College of Arts and Science
University of Saskatchewan
• (with W.R. Morrison) *Alaska Highway; W.C. Bompas; DEW Line; Inuvik; northern justice; northern resource development; Princess Sophia; White Pass and Yukon Railway; Yukon Field Force; Yukon Territory* •

LUCA CODIGNOLA
Dipartimento di Scienze dell'Antichità e del Medioevo
Università di Genova
• *Franciscans; Jean-Louis Hennepin; Jesuits* •

ALLAN F. COGGON
Mahone Bay, Nova Scotia
• *Aircraft Detection Corps* •

JENNIFER COGGON
Institute for the History and Philosophy of Science and Technology
University of Toronto
• *William Hincks* •

YOLANDE COHEN
Département d'histoire
Université du Québec à Montréal
• *Cercle de fermières; Yvettes* •

CYNTHIA COMACCHIO
Department of History
Wilfrid Laurier University
• *William Blatz; child welfare; industrial hygiene; youth* •

DAN CONLIN
Curator of Marine History
Maritime Museum of the Atlantic
• *Atlantic steamship disaster; Enos Collins; Samuel Cunard; Empress of Ireland; Liverpool Packet; privateers, Royal William* •

MARGARET CONRAD
Canada Research Chair in Atlantic Canada Studies, Department of History
University of New Brunswick
• *Atlantic Revolution; Ellen Fairclough; New England Planters;* (with John G. Reid) *Nova Scotia* •

TERRY COOK
Archival Studies
University of Manitoba
• *W. Kaye Lamb; George R. Parkin* •

TIM COOK
Historian
Canadian War Museum
• *C.P. Stacey* •

AFUA COOPER
Department of Sociology
Ryerson University
• *Mary Bibb; True Band Society/Provincial Union* •

JOHN C. COURTNEY
Department of Political Science
University of Saskatchewan
• (with Daniel Macfarlane) *closure; disallowance; filibuster; franchise; ombudsman; orders in council; parliamentary democracy; referendums; royal commissions* •

ROBERT J. COUTTS
Parks Canada
Winnipeg
• *Arthur Dobbs; Fort Garry; Alexander Morris; Nonsuch; Orkneymen; pemmican; Prince of Wales Fort; Red River cart; Sayer trial; Seven Oaks, Battle of; York boat; York Factory* •

MICHAEL F. CRABB
Dance critic, *The National Post*
• *dance* •

ADAM CRERAR
Department of History
Wilfrid Laurier University
• *rural depopulation* •

MICHAEL S. CROSS
Department of History
Dalhousie University
• *Robert Baldwin; Shiners' War; Philemon Wright* •

E. TINA CROSSFIELD
Okotoks, Alberta
• *Maude E. Abbott; Carrie Derick* •

TERRY CROWLEY
Department of History
University of Guelph
• *Adelaide Hoodless; Agnes Macphail* •

KEN CRUIKSHANK
Department of History
McMaster University
• *Board of Railway Commissioners; freight rates; government regulation of business; Guarantee Act; Intercolonial Railway* •

CARMAN CUMMING
Retired, School of Journalism and Communication
Carleton University
• *J.W. Bengough; Charles Dunham; Grip* •

Philip J. Currie
Curator of Dinosaurs
Royal Tyrrell Museum of Palaeontology
• *dinosaurs; J.B. Tyrrell* •

Bruce Curtis
Department of Sociology and Anthropology
Carleton University
• *census; population* •

Brian Cuthbertson
Author and former Head of Heritage
Province of Nova Scotia
• *Charles Inglis; 'Nova Scarcity'; Sir John Wentworth* •

Gurston Dacks
Department of Political Science and Adjunct Research Professor, Canadian Circumpolar Institute
University of Alberta
• *Aboriginal land claims, northern Canada; Indian Affairs and Northern Development, Department of; Mackenzie Valley Pipeline Inquiry* •

Jean Daigle
Retired professor
Moncton
• *Acadian commercial relations; Beaubassin; Nicolas Denys; Fort Beauséjour; Marc Lescarbot; Ordre de Bon Temps; Port-Royal; Théâtre de Neptune* •

Cecilia Danysk
Department of History
Western Washington University
• *hired hands* •

Regna Darnell
Department of Anthropology
University of Western Ontario
• *Franz Boas* •

Tina Davidson
Ontario Institute for Studies in Education
University of Toronto
• (with Ruth Roach Pierson) *Canadian Women's Army Corps; war brides; Women's Royal Canadian Naval Service* •

Gwendolyn Davies
Dean of Graduate Studies and Associate Vice-President (Research)
University of New Brunswick
• *Thomas McCulloch; Song Fishermen* •

Richard A. Davies
Department of English
Acadia University
• *Thomas Chandler Haliburton* •

James Delgado
Vancouver Maritime Museum
• *Roald Amundsen; Beaver; Henry Hudson; St Roch; Titanic* •

Jonathan Dembling
Department of Anthropology
University of Massachusetts-Amherst
• *Gaelic language* •

Hugh A. Dempsey
Glenbow Museum
Calgary
• *Big Bear; Crowfoot; Oldman River, Battle of* •

A.A. den Otter
Department of History
Memorial University of Newfoundland
• *all-red route; Canadian Pacific Railway; Craigellachie; European and North American Railway; Alexander Tilloch Galt; Grand Trunk Railway; Thomas C. Keefer; Newfoundland Railway; Pacific Scandal* •

Catherine Desbarats
Département d'histoire
Université McGill
• *New France* •

Kenneth C. Dewar
Department of History
Mount Saint Vincent University
• *frontier thesis; Lament for a Nation (Grant); Laurentian thesis; limited identities; A.R.M. Lower; metropolitan thesis; North, the idea of* •

Lyle Dick
West Coast Historian,
Western Canada Service Centre, Parks Canada
Vancouver
• *race to the Pole; W.L. Morton* •

Janice Dickin
Faculty of Communication and Culture
University of Calgary
• *Martha Munger Black; Aimee Semple McPherson; John Howard Sissons; Spanish influenza; venereal diseases* •

John A. Dickinson
Département d'histoire
Université de Montréal
• *diamants du Canada; Adam Dollard des Ormeaux; Antoine-Aimé Dorion; Louis Hébert; Société St-Jean-Baptiste; survivance* •

Paul Dickson
Queen's University International Study Centre,
Herstmonceux Castle
East Sussex, United Kingdom
• *H.D.G. Crerar; Sir Arthur Currie* •

René Dionne
Ottawa
• *Antoine Gérin-Lajoie* •

PATRICIA G. DIRKS
Retired, Department of History
Brock University
• *Young Men's Christian Association; Young Women's Christian Association* •

RICHARD J. DIUBALDO
Department of History
Concordia University
• *Arctic Archipelago; Canadian Arctic Expedition; Re Eskimos; Vilhjalmur Stefansson* •

ALEXANDRA DOBROWOLSKY
Department of Political Science
Saint Mary's University
• *National Action Committee on the Status of Women* •

DIANNE DODD
Historical Services Branch, National Historic Sites Directorate, Parks Canada
Hull, Quebec
• *birth control; eugenics; Helen MacMurchy; Elizabeth Smith-Shortt* •

ANNE DONDERTMAN
Assistant Director, Thomas Fisher Rare Book Library
University of Toronto
• (with Judy Donnelly) *almanacs* •

JUDY DONNELLY
Project Manager, History of the Book in Canada/ Histoire du livre et de l'imprimé au Canada, Faculty of Information Services
University of Toronto
• (with Anne Dondertman) *almanacs* •

KENNETH DONOVAN
Historian
Fortress of Louisbourg
• *Cape Breton Island; Île Royale; Louisbourg; Angus MacAskill; Marie Marguerite Rose; slavery* •

HEATHER ROLLASON DRISCOLL
Toronto
• *Samuel Hearne; Matonabbee* •

LISA DRYSDALE
English Program
University of Northern British Columbia
• *A.B. Macallum* •

KAREN DUBINSKY
Department of History
Queen's University
• *Niagara Falls; rape and seduction* •

HARRY W. DUCKWORTH
Department of History
University of Manitoba
• *North West Company* •

JACALYN DUFFIN
Hannah Chair of the History of Medicine
Queen's University
• *cholera; country doctors; epidemics; medical treatments; Wilder Penfield; scurvy; thalidomide crisis* •

RON (QUINN) DUFFY
Department of Geography
University of Calgary
• *O.S. Finnie; northern game preserves; Northwest Territories* •

MICHELINE DUMONT
Professeur émérite
Université de Sherbrooke
• *Marguerite Bourgeoys; Congrégation de Notre-Dame; education in New France; Laure Gaudreault; Soeurs Grises; Jeanne Mance; Marie de l'Incarnation; Idola Saint-Jean; Ursulines* •

PATRICK DUNAE
Department of History
Malaspina University-College
• *gentlemen emigrants* •

JEAN-CLAUDE DUPONT
Ethnologue
Université Laval
• *maple sugar industry* •

SERGE DURFLINGER
Department of History
University of Ottawa
• *G.F. 'Buzz' Beurling; Canadian army; Persian Gulf War; Scheldt Campaign* •

CARRIE DYCK
Department of Linguistics
Memorial University of Newfoundland
• *Aboriginal languages* •

KLAY DYER
Independent scholar
St Catharines, Ontario
• *Confederation Poets* •

FRANCES H. EARLY
Department of History
Mount Saint Vincent University
• *Voice of Women* •

DOROTHY HARLEY EBER
Montreal
• *Peter Pitseolak* •

WARREN ELOFSON
Department of History
University of Calgary
• *cowboys; gymkhanas; rodeos* •

JOHN ENGLISH
Department of History
University of Waterloo
• *Robert Borden; conservatism; Defence of Canada Regulations; liberalism; Lucien Rivard affair; Arthur Meighen; patronage; Lester B. Pearson; Progressive Conservative Party; Red Tories; Rowell–Sirois Commission; André Siegfried; Louis St Laurent; Pierre Elliott Trudeau; Union government; Wartime Elections Act* •

GERHARD J. ENS
Department of History and Classics
University of Alberta
• *buffalo hunt* •

ELIZABETH ROLLINS EPPERLY
Department of English
University of Prince Edward Island
• *Anne of Green Gables (Montgomery)* •

JANE ERRINGTON
Department of History
Royal Military College of Canada
• *Sir Isaac Brock; Loyalists* •

GEOFFREY EWEN
Multidisciplinary Studies Department, Glendon College
York University
• *Common Front; Confédération des syndicats nationaux; Fédération des travailleurs du Québec; Murdochville strike* •

DAVID FACEY-CROWTHER
Department of History
Memorial University of Newfoundland
• *Atlantic Charter; Beaumont Hamel* •

GEORGINA FELDBERG
Division of Social Science
York University
• *women doctors* •

MARIA VON FINCKENSTEIN
Curator, Contemporary Inuit Art
Canadian Museum of Civilization
• *Inuit art* •

JUDITH FINGARD
Department of History
Dalhousie University
• *crimping; poverty* •

ALVIN FINKEL
Department of History
Athabasca University
• *Americans in Canada; Darwinism; migrant workers; Sexual Sterilization Act; social reformers* •

KAREN A. FINLAY
Department of History in Art
University of Victoria
• *Vincent Massey* •

KEITH R. FLEMING
Department of History
University of Western Ontario
• *hydroelectricity* •

MAXWELL L. FORAN
Faculty of Communication and Culture
University of Calgary
• *Calgary; Calgary Stampede* •

MICHEL FORAND
Ottawa
• *lighthouses* •

BEN FORSTER
Department of History
University of Western Ontario
• *Edward Blake; Canadian Manufacturers' Association; customs duties; National Policy; reciprocity* •

BRIAN FOSS
Department of Art History
Concordia University
• *Miller Gore Brittain* •

RUTH A. FRAGER
Department of History
McMaster University
• *Eaton Company strikes; garment industry* •

DANIEL FRANCIS
North Vancouver
• *Arctic exploration; Joseph-Elzéar Bernier; Sir John Franklin; John R. Jewitt; maritime fur trade; national identity; Northwest Passage; George Vancouver; west coast exploration; whaling* •

R. DOUGLAS FRANCIS
Department of History
University of Calgary
• *The Great Lone Land (Butler); C.W. Jefferys; Paul Kane; 'last best West'; Frank H. Underhill* •

DAVID FRANK
Department of History
University of New Brunswick
• *Cape Breton coal strikes; coal-mine disasters; coal mining; Roscoe Fillmore; Frank slide; Goin' Down the Road (Shebib); J.B. McLachlan; Moose River mine disaster; United Mine Workers of America* •

GERALD FRIESEN
Department of History
University of Manitoba
• *communication; Manitoba; John Norquay; regionalism* •

DONALD FYSON
Département d'histoire
Université Laval
• *attorney general/solicitor general; courts of law, provincial and local; criminal law; Federal Court of Canada; riot; Roncarelli v. Duplessis* •

DAVID GAGAN
Department of History
Simon Fraser University
• (with Rosemary Gagan) *hospitals* •

ROSEMARY GAGAN
Department of Women's Studies
Simon Fraser University
• (with David Gagan) *hospitals* •

FRANÇOIS-MARC GAGNON
Director, Jarislowsky Institute for
Studies in Canadian Art
Concordia University
• *Automatistes; Contemporary Arts Society; Cornelius Krieghoff; Joseph Légaré; Jean-Paul Lemieux; Plasticiens; Refus global* •

ROBERT GALOIS
Adjunct Professor, Department of Geography
University of British Columbia
• *Maquinna* •

JEAN-PHILIPPE GARNEAU
Membre associé, Centre interuniversitaire
d'études québécoises
Université Laval
• *Quebec civil law* •

PATRIZIA GENTILE
Doctoral candidate, Department of History
Queen's University
• *Winnifred C. Blair* •

CAROLE GERSON
Department of English
Simon Fraser University
• *Waste Heritage (Baird); Woodsmen of the West (Grainger)* •

HEATHER-ANNE GETSON
Historian
Fisheries Museum of the Atlantic
• *August gales; Bluenose; Lunenburg* •

R.D. GIDNEY
Emeritus Professor, Faculty of Education
University of Western Ontario
• (with W.P.J. Millar) *common schools; high schools; law societies; medical colleges; Egerton Ryerson; Symons Report* •

EMILY GILBERT
Canadian Studies and Geography, University College
University of Toronto
• *Canada Savings Bonds; currency; metric conversion; Royal Canadian Mint* •

GREG GILLESPIE
Department of Kinesiology and Physical Education
Wilfrid Laurier University
• *Caledonian Games* •

YVES GINGRAS
Département d'histoire
Université du Québec à Montréal
• *Gerhard Herzberg; Joseph C.K. Laflamme; Brother Marie-Victorin; National Research Council; Abbé Léon Provancher* •

MONA GLEASON
Department of Educational Studies
University of British Columbia
• *home children* •

PETER A. GODDARD
Department of History
University of Guelph
• *Huguenots* •

PHILIP GOLDRING
Research Manager, Historical Services Branch,
Parks Canada
Gatineau, Quebec
• *heritage tourism* •

DAVID L.A. GORDON
School of Urban and Regional Planning
Queen's University
• *National Capital Commission* •

DEBORAH GORHAM
Professor Emeritus, Department of History
Carleton University
• *Francis Marion Beynon; Flora MacDonald Denison; feminism, second-wave; spiritualism* •

PETER GOSSAGE
Département d'histoire et de sciences politiques
Université de Sherbrooke
• *Aurore Gagnon; orphanages; revanche des berceaux* •

BARRY M. GOUGH
Department of History
Wilfrid Laurier University
• *Captain James Cook; Simon Fraser; Haida; Sir Alexander Mackenzie; Oregon Boundary Treaty; Pig War; Puget's Sound Agricultural Company; War of 1812* •

J.L. GRANATSTEIN
Toronto
• *Second World War* •

BRERETON GREENHOUS
Arnprior, Ontario
• *Royal Canadian Air Force* •

ALLAN GREER
Department of History
University of Toronto
• *charivari; habitants; Marie-Joseph-Angélique; Rebellion of 1837; saints and martyrs* •

JACQUELINE GRESKO
Department of History
Douglas College, New Westminster
• *Aboriginal missions in the West* •

JULIUS H. GREY
Associate Professor of Law
McGill University
• *citizenship* •

N.E.S. GRIFFITHS
Professor Emeritus, Department of History
Carleton University
• *Acadian deportation; French Neutrals; oath of allegiance* •

JANET GUILDFORD
Beach Meadows Research Associates, Halifax
• *Halifax* •

ELIZABETH HAIGH
Department of History
Saint Mary's University
• *Abraham Gesner* •

ANTHONY J. HALL
Coordinator of Globalization Studies
University of Lethbridge
• *Assembly of First Nations* •

DAVID J. HALL
Department of History and Classics
University of Alberta
• *immigrant recruitment campaigns; North-West Territories; Sir Clifford Sifton; 'stalwart peasant in a sheep-skin coat'* •

ROGER HALL
Department of History
University of Western Ontario
• *George Brown; Leslie M. Frost; William Notman and Sons; Ontario; Upper Canada* •

HUGH A. HALLIDAY
Orleans, Ontario
• *duelling; fires; gallantry awards; national honours; natural disasters; Quebec Bridge disasters* •

SYLVIA D. HAMILTON
Nancy's Chair in Women's Studies
Mount Saint Vincent University
• *Africville; Richard Preston; Portia White* •

WILLIAM B. HAMILTON
Former chair, Toponymy Research Committee
Canadian Permanent Committee on
Geographical Names
• *place names* •

LORNE HAMMOND
Curator of History, Royal British Columbia
Museum/Department of History
University of Victoria
• *conservation movements; environmental movements; Game Acts; great auk; Migratory Birds Convention Act; Jack Miner; passenger pigeons* •

ROBERT L.A. HANCOCK
PhD candidate, Department of History
University of Victoria
• *Marius Barbeau* •

RICHARD HARRIS
School of Geography and Geology
McMaster University
• *housing; suburbs* •

STEPHEN J. HARRIS
Chief Historian, Directorate of History and Heritage
National Defence Headquarters
• *military colleges; militia; Nile Voyageurs; No. 6 (RCAF) Bomber Group; Overseas Military Forces of Canada; Permanent Force* •

LOUIS-GEORGES HARVEY
Department of History
Bishop's University
• *Le Canadien; Guibord affair; Institut canadien de Montréal; Étienne Parent; Special Council* •

RONALD HAYCOCK
Department of History
Royal Military College of Canada
• *Sir Sam Hughes; Paris Peace Conference; Passchendaele; Ross rifle; Siberian expedition; Ypres, Second Battle of* •

ALAN L. HAYES
Wycliffe College
University of Toronto
• *Anglicans; establishment of religion; Sisters of St John the Divine* •

GEOFFREY HAYES
Department of History
University of Waterloo
• *E.L.M. Burns; CANLOAN; Dieppe; Italian campaign; liberation of the Netherlands; Normandy, Battle of* •

DAVID M. HAYNE
Emeritus Professor of French
University of Toronto
• *Les Anciens Canadiens (Aubert de Gaspé); Octave Crémazie; École littéraire de Montréal; Louis Fréchette* •

E.A. HEAMAN
Department of History
McGill University
• *exhibitions and fairs* •

KARINE HÉBERT
Université du Québec à Montréal
• *Fédération des femmes du Québec; Fédération nationale St-Jean-Baptiste; Marie Lacoste-Gérin-Lajoie* •

CONRAD HEIDENREICH
Department of Geography
York University
• *Beaver Wars; 'Canada'; Samuel de Champlain; French exploration; Huron Confederacy; Huron Feast of the Dead; Iroquois League; Louis Jolliet; René-Robert Cavelier de La Salle; Pierre Gaultier de Varennes et de La Vérendrye; mapping Canada; Pontiac* •

CRAIG HERON
Division of Social Science
York University
• *building-trades workers; Days of Action; factory work; Hamilton; industrial revolution; iron and steel industry; piano industry; steelworkers' union; unions; workers' revolt* •

BOB HESKETH
Chinook Multimedia
Edmonton
• *William Aberhart; Canol pipeline; Ernest Manning; Social Credit* •

STEVE HEWITT
Lecturer, Department of American and Canadian Studies
University of Birmingham
• *Council of Canadians; Estevan riot; McDonald Commission* •

CHARLES C. HILL
National Gallery of Canada
• *art galleries; Beaver Hall Group; Canadian Art Club; Emily Carr; Group of Seven; Louis-Philippe Hébert; Royal Canadian Academy of Arts; Tom Thomson* •

JAMES K. HILLER
Department of History
Memorial University of Newfoundland
• *Amulree Report; Sir Robert Bond; Peter J. Cashin; Churchill Falls; Edward Feild; Michael A. Fleming; French Shore; Alexander Murray; National Convention, Newfoundland; Newfoundland National Government; D.W. Prowse; Reid Newfoundland Company; Sir Richard A. Squires; United Newfoundland Party* •

NORMAN HILLMER
Department of History and International Affairs
Carleton University
• *British Commonwealth Air Training Plan; Canadian Officers' Training Corps; foreign policy; middle power; Brian Mulroney; Organization of American States; peacekeeping; Charles 'Chubby' Power; J.L. Ralston; Silver Dart; O.D. Skelton; Statute of Westminster; Suez Crisis; Third Option; United States, Canada's relations with* •

PHILIP HISCOCK
Department of Folklore
Memorial University of Newfoundland
• *mumming* •

J.E. HODGETTS
Professor Emeritus
University of Toronto
• *auditor general; cabinet; constitution of Canada; dominion; Eugene Forsey; House of Commons; judiciary; peace, order, and good government; Prime Minister's Office; Privy Council Office; Senate; Treasury Board* •

BRYAN R. HOGEVEEN
Department of Sociology
University of Alberta
• (with Joanne C. Minaker) *reformatories* •

MICHIEL HORN
Department of History, Glendon College
York University
• *academic freedom; Canadian Forum; Great Depression; League for Social Reconstruction; Leonard Marsh; Reconstruction Party; F.R. Scott* •

C. STUART HOUSTON
Professor Emeritus of Medical Imaging
University of Saskatchewan
• *Sir George Back; Hudson Bay; Sir John Richardson; Ernest Thompson Seton; Percy A. Taverner* •

CECIL J. HOUSTON
Arts and Social Sciences
University of Windsor
• *Grosse Île; Orange Order* •

COLIN HOWELL
Department of History
Saint Mary's University
• *Aboriginal games; baseball; boxing; Lionel Conacher; Edmonton Grads; W.S. Fielding; football; hockey; Matchless Six; Nova Scotia secessionist movement; Maurice 'Rocket' Richard; team sports; Gilles Villeneuve* •

CHRISTINE HUDON
Département d'histoire et de sciences politiques
Université de Sherbrooke
• *collèges classiques; shrines; Elzéar-Alexandre Taschereau; Georges Vanier; Zouaves* •

RAYMOND HUDON
Professeur titulaire, Département de science politique
Université Laval
• *bilingualism; Bloc Québécois; Cité libre; October Crisis; Ordre de Jacques-Cartier; Rhinoceros Party; separatism; Pierre Vallières* •

GEORGE HUME
President
Canadian Canal Society
• *canals* •

A.M.J. HYATT
Professor Emeritus
University of Western Ontario
• *Amiens; Mons; Vimy Ridge* •

FRANCA IACOVETTA
Department of History
University of Toronto
• *displaced persons; home missions; International Institute of Metropolitan Toronto; Italians; Cairine Wilson* •

JOSÉ E. IGARTUA
Département d'histoire
Université du Québec à Montréal
• *Alcan* •

KRIS E. INWOOD
Department of Economics
University of Guelph
• *manufacturing; Massey-Harris* •

DEAN IRVINE
Department of English
Dalhousie University
• *Montreal Group* •

ROBERT IRWIN
Department of Humanities
Grant MacEwan College, Edmonton
• *bloc settlement; dominion experimental farms; dust bowl; grain trade; harvest excursions; Peace River country* •

RUSSELL ISINGER
Department of Political Studies
University of Saskatchewan
• *Avro Arrow* •

ROGER JACKSON
Department of Physical Education
University of Calgary
• *rowing* •

CORNELIUS J. JAENEN
Department of History
University of Ottawa
• *Christian réductions in New France; François de Laval; Regulation 17; Séminaire de Québec* •

CATHY JAMES
Visiting Scholar, Centre for Women's Studies in Education
Ontario Institute for Studies in Education
University of Toronto
• *settlement houses* •

OLAF U. JANZEN
Division of Arts (Historical Studies), Sir Wilfred Grenfell College
Memorial University of Newfoundland
• *George Cartwright; J.F.W. DesBarres; Eastern Approaches* •

RICHARD A. JARRELL
Department of Natural Science, Faculty of Pure and Applied Science
York University
• *astronomy; Henry Marshall Tory* •

GREGORY A. JOHNSON
Centre for Global and Social Analysis
Athabasca University
• *Chanak affair; Halibut Treaty; Chester Ronning* •

HUGH JOHNSTON
Department of History
Simon Fraser University
• *Atlantic migration 1815–60; Komagata Maru; Sikhs* •

RUSSELL JOHNSTON
Department of Communications, Popular Culture, and Film
Brock University
• *advertising; Bertram Brooker* •

HELMUT KALLMANN
Retired chief of the Music Division
National Library of Canada
• *national anthem* •

WILLIAM KAPLAN
Barrister and Solicitor
Toronto
• *Jehovah's Witnesses; seamen's unions* •

GREGORY S. KEALEY
Department of History
University of New Brunswick
• (with Andrew Parnaby) *Canadian Labour Congress; D.J. O'Donoghue; red scare; Relations of Labour and Capital, Royal Commission on* •

LINDA KEALEY
Department of History
University of New Brunswick
• *Helena Gutteridge; Newfoundland Outport Nursing and Industrial Association; women in the labour movement* •

JEFF KESHEN
Department of History
University of Ottawa
• *censorship* •

BRUCE KIDD
Dean, Faculty of Physical Education and Health
University of Toronto
• *amateur sport; Tom Longboat; professional sport; track and field* •

GERALD KILLAN
Department of History
King's College, London, Ontario
• *Algonquin Park; David Boyle; Donnelly murders* •

STEPHEN KIMBER
School of Journalism
University of King's College
• *Angus L. Macdonald; Robert Stanfield; VE Day riots* •

Mary Kinnear
Department of History
University of Manitoba
• *Fellowship of the Maple Leaf; E. Cora Hind; Emily Murphy* •

Norman Knowles
Department of History
St Mary's College, Calgary
• *Loyalist tradition* •

Valerie J. Korinek
Department of History
University of Saskatchewan
• *Chatelaine* •

Mark Kuhlberg
Forest history consultant and
Department of History
Nipissing University
• *pulp and paper industry* •

Peter Kulchyski
Department of Native Studies
University of Manitoba
• *high arctic exiles; Inuit Tapiriit Kanatami; Nunavut* •

Nicolas Landry
Département d'histoire
Université de Moncton-Shippagan
• *Îles de la Madeleine; Plaisance; St-Pierre and Miquelon* •

Yves Landry
Directeur du Programme de recherche sur
l'émigration des Français en Nouvelle-France, Centre
de recherche d'histoire quantitative
Université de Caen Basse-Normandie
• *filles du roi* •

Paul Laverdure
Gravelbourg, Saskatchewan
• *Lord's Day Alliance* •

David Laycock
Department of Political Science
Simon Fraser University
• *Ginger Group; Preston Manning; Progressives* •

Barbara Le Blanc
Université Sainte-Anne
• *Evangeline* •

Phyllis E. LeBlanc
Département d'histoire
Université de Moncton
• *Acadian renaissance; L'Acadie l'Acadie?!?; Moncton; New Brunswick schools question; Pélagie-la-Charrette (Maillet)* •

Alvin A. Lee
General Editor, Collected Works of Northrop Frye,
Emeritus Professor of English and Emeritus President
McMaster University
• *Northrop Frye; garrison mentality* •

Renée Legris
Études littéraires
Université du Québec à Montréal
• *téléroman* •

Mark Leier
Department of History
Simon Fraser University
• *Albert 'Ginger' Goodwin; Robert Gosden; Industrial Workers of the World; Mackenzie–Papineau Battalion; riding the rods; Trades and Labour Councils* •

Douglas Leighton
Department of History, Huron University College
University of Western Ontario
• *automobiles* •

Jocelyn Létourneau
Canada Research Chair in Quebec's Contemporary
History and Political Economy
Université Laval
• *Je me souviens; mythistory* •

Andrée Lévesque
Department of History
McGill University
• *Thérèse Casgrain; Eva Circé-Côté; Jeanne Corbin; Montreal massacre; Madeleine Parent; Soeurs de la Miséricorde* •

Peter S. Li
Department of Sociology
University of Saskatchewan
• *Chinese* •

Debra Lindsay
Department of History and Politics
University of New Brunswick, Saint John
• *Burgess Shale* •

Varpu Lindström
History and Women's Studies
York University
• *Finns* •

Paul-André Linteau
Département d'histoire
Université du Québec à Montréal
• *Camillien Houde; Montreal; Quebec language laws* •

Paul Litt
Department of History and School of Canadian Studies
Carleton University
• *Massey Commission* •

J.I. LITTLE
Department of History
Simon Fraser University
• *colonization movement; Eastern Townships; Late Loyalists; Megantic Outlaw* •

ANDRÉ LOISELLE
School for Studies in Art and Culture
Carleton University
• *Les Belles-soeurs (Tremblay); Le Déclin de l'empire américain (Arcand); Mon oncle Antoine (Jutra); Les Ordres (Brault)* •

TINA LOO
Department of History
University of British Columbia
• *Barkerville; Matthew Baillie Begbie; Bute Inlet incident; Cariboo gold rush; Cariboo Wagon Road; Fraser River gold rush; Georgia Straight; hippies; miners' meetings; New Caledonia; Overlanders* •

MAUREEN K. LUX
Department of History
University of Saskatchewan
• *Aboriginals and European diseases* •

KEVIN MCALEESE
Curator (Exhibits), Archaeology and Ethnology
Provincial Museum of Newfoundland and Labrador
• *full circle* •

DOUGLAS MCCALLA
Canada Research Chair in Rural History
University of Guelph
• *public debt; public ownership; staples thesis; taxation* •

GRAHAM MACDONALD
Calgary
• *Barren Lands; John George 'Kutenai' Brown; Cominco; hardrock mining; National Energy Program; petroleum industry; Sir George Simpson* •

ROBERT A.J. MCDONALD
Department of History
University of British Columbia
• *British Columbia; Amor De Cosmos; The Inverted Pyramid (Sinclair); Vancouver* •

HEATHER MACDOUGALL
Department of History
University of Waterloo
• *abortion; Canadian Red Cross Society; poliomyelitis; public health* •

DUNCAN MCDOWALL
Department of History
Carleton University
• *banks; Sir James Dunn; finance capitalism and investment banking; investment abroad; K.C. Irving; Izaak Walton Killam* •

LAUREL SEFTON MACDOWELL
Department of History
University of Toronto at Mississauga
• *J.L. Cohen; Kirkland Lake gold miners' strike; Oshawa strike* •

DANIEL MACFARLANE
Graduate student, Department of History
University of Saskatchewan
• (with John C. Courtney) *closure; disallowance; filibuster; franchise; ombudsman; orders-in-council; parliamentary democracy; referendums; royal commissions* •

ROBERT MCGHEE
Curator of Arctic Archaeology
Canadian Museum of Civilization
• *inukshuk; pre-European history* •

FRANCINE MCKENZIE
Department of History
University of Western Ontario
• *Balfour Report; Canadian Institute of International Affairs; functionalism; isolationism; League of Nations* •

HECTOR MACKENZIE
Senior Departmental Historian
Department of Foreign Affairs and International Trade
• *Commonwealth; demobilization; External Affairs, Department of; Halifax and Sydney riots; Indochina International Control Commission; mobilization; St Lawrence Seaway agreement; zombies* •

KENNETH S. MACKENZIE
Salt Spring Island, British Columbia
• *steamships* •

LAURA MACLEOD
Senior Acquisitions Editor, Higher Education Division
Oxford University Press Canada
• *scholarly publishing* •

R.C. MACLEOD
Department of History and Classics
University of Alberta
• *Gabriel Dumont; Edmonton; Fort Whoop-Up; James F. Macleod; North-West Mounted Police; North-West Rebellion; Royal Canadian Mounted Police; Sir Samuel Steele* •

JEFFREY L. MCNAIRN
Department of History
Queen's University
• *Alien Question; Annexation Manifesto; Family Compact; Robert Gourlay; Sir Francis Hincks; Sir Allan Napier MacNab; primogeniture; representation by population; representative government; responsible government* •

LARRY MCNALLY
Canadian Archives Branch
National Archives of Canada
• *bridges; roads; tunnels* •

PETER F. MCNALLY
Graduate School of Library and Information Studies
McGill University
• *libraries* •

ALAN G. MACPHERSON
Emeritus Professor, Department of Geography
Memorial University of Newfoundland
• (with Ingeborg C.L. Marshall) *William E. Cormack* •

IAN MACPHERSON
British Columbia Institute for Co-operative Studies
University of Victoria
• *agriculture; Antigonish Movement; co-operative movement; credit unions; W.C. Good; George Keen; Alexander Laidlaw; Violet McNaughton; E.A. Partridge; Henry Wise Wood* •

KATHRYN MCPHERSON
Department of History
York University
• *nursing; Victorian Order of Nurses; wartime nursing* •

CHARLES D. MAGINLEY
Mahone Bay, Nova Scotia
• *Canadian Coast Guard* •

AIDAN MALONEY
Retired chair
Fisheries Prices Support Board of Canada
• (with Melvin Baker) *Burin tidal wave; Caribou; William Coaker; Fishermen's Protective Union; Florizel; Knights of Columbus fire; Newfoundland loggers' strike; Ocean Ranger; outport resettlement; St John's* •

S. TIMOTHY MALONEY
Head, Music Library
University of Minnesota
• *Glenn Gould* •

ELIZABETH MANCKE
Department of History
University of Akron
• *Simeon Perkins* •

JOHN MANLEY
Department of Historical and Critical Studies
University of Central Lancashire, Preston, England
• *Canadian Auto Workers; Tim Buck; Workers' Unity League* •

GREGORY P. MARCHILDON
Canada Research Chair in Public Policy and Economic History
University of Regina
• *Max Aitken; merger movement; utilities* •

SOPHIE MARCOTTE
Département de littérature comparée
Université de Montréal
• *Maria Chapdelaine (Hémon); Les Plouffe (Lemelin)* •

RICHARD MARCOUX
Département de sociologie
Université Laval
• (with Marc St-Hilaire) *Quebec City* •

GREG MARQUIS
Department of History and Politics
University of New Brunswick, Saint John
• *police; Saint John; United States Civil War* •

DAVID B. MARSHALL
Department of History
University of Calgary
• *death and dying; C.W. Gordon; George Monro Grant; muscular Christianity; secularism* •

INGEBORG C.L. MARSHALL
Institute of Social and Economic Research
Memorial University of Newfoundland
• *Beothuk; Demasduit; Mattie Mitchell; Shanawdithit; Joseph Sylvester;* (with Alan G. Macpherson) *William E. Cormack* •

MARCEL MARTEL
Department of History
York University
• *Maurice Duplessis; États généraux du Canada français; Fédération des francophones hors Québec; Jean Lesage; Padlock Law; Quiet Revolution; Union nationale* •

GED MARTIN
Shanacoole, County Waterford, Ireland
• *Colonial Office; Confederation; Great Coalition; Goldwin Smith* •

JACQUES MATHIEU
Département d'histoire
Université Laval
• *seigneurial system* •

STEVEN MAYNARD
Kingston
• *gay men and lesbians* •

ALAN METCALFE
Professor Emeritus, Department of Kinesiology
University of Windsor
• *horse racing; lacrosse* •

W.P.J. MILLAR
London, Ontario
• (with R.D. Gidney) *common schools; high schools; law societies; medical colleges; Egerton Ryerson; Symons Report* •

CARMAN MILLER
Department of History
McGill University
• *South African War* •

J.R. MILLER
Department of History
University of Saskatchewan
• *Aboriginal enfranchisement; Equal Rights Association; Indian treaties; Native–newcomer relations; Oka Crisis; residential schools; Royal Proclamation of 1763* •

MARK MILLER
Toronto
• *jazz* •

JOHN S. MILLOY
Department of History
Trent University
• *Cypress Hills massacre; Plains Aboriginals* •

ALLEN MILLS
Department of Politics
University of Winnipeg
• *democratic socialism; J.S. Woodsworth* •

DAVID MILNE
Professor Emeritus
University of Prince Edward Island and
Visiting Professor, Department of Public Policy
University of Malta
• *patriation of the constitution* •

MARC MILNER
Department of History
University of New Brunswick
• *Atlantic, Battle of the; convoys; corvettes; Fishery Protection Service; Percy W. Nelles; Royal Canadian Navy* •

K. DAVID MILOBAR
Department of History
University College of the Fraser Valley
• *Guy Carleton; Château Clique; John Molson; Montreal merchants; James Murray; Quebec Act* •

JOANNE C. MINAKER
Department of Sociology
Queen's University
• (with Bryan R. Hogeveen) *reformatories* •

DALE MIQUELON
Department of History
University of Saskatchewan
• *beaver; capitulation of Canada; conquest of New France; Great Peace; St-Maurice forges* •

WENDY MITCHINSON
Department of History
University of Waterloo
• *Richard Maurice Bucke; midwives; women and medicine; Woman's Christian Temperance Union* •

JOHN S. MOIR
Emeritus Professor
University of Toronto
• *Calvinism; Presbyterianism; Protestant ethic* •

DAVID W. MONAGHAN
Curator, House of Commons
Ottawa
• *Canadian Good Roads Association; Trans-Canada Highway* •

DAVID MONOD
Department of History
Wilfrid Laurier University
• *chain stores; department stores; Price Spreads, Royal Commission on; retail trade* •

BARRY MOODY
Department of History and Classics
Acadia University
• *Henry Alline; Baptists; governors of early Nova Scotia; Grand Pré; Neutral Yankees of Nova Scotia* •

JAMES E. MORAN
Department of History
University of Prince Edward Island
• *insane asylums* •

TOBY MORANTZ
Department of Anthropology
McGill University
• *contact; eastern subarctic Aboriginals; eastern woodlands Aboriginals* •

CARL MOREY
Faculty of Music
University of Toronto
• *Ernest MacMillan; music; opera; Jean Papineau-Couture; John Weinzweig; Healey Willan* •

CECILIA MORGAN
History of Education Program
Ontario Institute for Studies in Education
University of Toronto
• *gender; Lundy's Lane; Susanna Moodie; Laura Secord; Catharine Parr Traill* •

PETER MORRIS
Professor Emeritus, Department of Film and Video
Coordinator, Fine Arts Cultural Studies
York University
• *film industry; National Film Board of Canada* •

DAVID MORRISON
Curator
Northwest Territories Archaeology and
Curator-in-charge, Archaeology Survey of Canada
Canadian Museum of Civilization
• *Inuit culture; Inuit history* •

DAVID R. MORRISON
International Development and Political Studies
Trent University
• *foreign aid* •

JAMES H. MORRISON
Department of History
Saint Mary's University
• *Alfred Fitzpatrick; Frontier College; Pier 21* •

W.R. MORRISON
Department of History
University of Northern British Columbia
• (with K.S. Coates) *Alaska Highway; W.C. Bompas; DEW Line; Inuvik; northern justice; northern resource development; Princess Sophia; White Pass and Yukon Railway; Yukon Field Force; Yukon Territory* •

DESMOND MORTON
Department of History
McGill University
• *Canadian Brotherhood of Railway Employees; Canadian Cavalry Brigade; Canadian Corps; Canadian Expeditionary Force; Canadian Patriotic Fund; conscription; First World War; Great War Veterans' Association; Khaki University; Sir William Otter; soldier settlement; unification of Canadian forces; veterans, First World War* •

SUZANNE MORTON
Department of History
McGill University
• *gambling; Halifax Explosion; leisure; separate spheres* •

MARK MOSS
School of General Education
Seneca College, Toronto
• *Boy Scouts; cadets and the Strathcona Trust; Girl Guides* •

GORDON MOYLES
University of Alberta
• *E.J. Pratt; Salvation Army* •

ROBERT J. MUCKLE
Department of Anthropology
Capilano College
• *potlach; west coast Aboriginals* •

BRUCE MUIRHEAD
Department of History
Lakehead University
• *Bank of Canada; international economic organizations; Escott Reid; Thunder Bay* •

D.A. MUISE
Department of History
Carleton University
• *Anti-Confederation League; General Mining Association; Maritime rights movement; Sir Charles Tupper* •

TERRENCE MURPHY
Vice-President Academic and Research
Saint Mary's University
• *Canadian Council of Churches; Catholic emancipation; Paul Émile Léger; Joseph-Octave Plessis; Roman Catholics* •

HEATHER MURRAY
Department of English, Victoria College
University of Toronto
• *arts organizations; Canadian Authors' Association; literary societies* •

LAURENCE B. MUSSIO
Executive Research & Communications
Toronto
• *Sun Life Assurance Company of Canada* •

TAMARA MYERS
Department of History
University of Winnipeg
• *juvenile delinquency* •

JAMES NAYLOR
Department of History
Brandon University
• *Co-operative Commonwealth Federation; corporate welfarism; T.C. Douglas; independent labour parties; One Big Union; Regina Manifesto; socialism; Winnipeg General Strike* •

PETER NEARY
Dean, Faculty of Social Science
University of Western Ontario
• *Boundary Waters Treaty; Commission of Government; Sir John and Lady Hope Simpson; Newfoundland referenda; Joseph Smallwood; Veterans Charter* •

H. BLAIR NEATBY
Carleton University
• *Bloc populaire; five cent speech; French–English relations; W.L. Mackenzie King; King-Byng affair; André Laurendeau* •

NICOLE NEATBY
Department of History
Saint Mary's University
• *pure laine; tourism* •

WENDIE R. NELSON
Langara College, Vancouver
• *'guerre des éteignoirs'* •

DAVID NEUFELD
Yukon and Western Arctic Historian, Parks Canada
Whitehorse
• *British Yukon Navigation Steamboat Company; Chilkoot Pass; Keish; public holidays; Yukon Consolidated Gold Corporation; Yukon Order of Pioneers; Yukon River* •

W.H. NEW
Department of English
University of British Columbia
• *Tish group; George Woodcock* •

DIANNE NEWELL
Department of History
University of British Columbia
• *salmon-canning industry* •

JAN NOEL
Department of History
University of Toronto at Mississauga
• *femmes favorisées?; temperance movement* •

GLEN NORCLIFFE
Department of Geography
York University
• *Canada Cycle and Motor Company; cycling* •

SYLVIO NORMAND
Faculté de droit
Université Laval
• *legal education* •

PATRICK O'FLAHERTY
Professor Emeritus (English)
Memorial University of Newfoundland
• *William Carson; 'Come near at your peril, Canadian wolf'; Laurence Coughlan; Moses Harvey; jackatars; liviers; Masterless Men, Society of; Princess Sheila NaGeira* •

ROSEMARY E. OMMER
University of Victoria
• *Charles Robin and Company; truck system* •

MARIEL O'NEILL-KARCH
Department of French, St Michael's College
University of Toronto
• *Gratien Gélinas* •

BRIAN S. OSBORNE
Department of Geography
Queen's University
• *Kingston* •

DOUG OWRAM
Department of History and Classics
University of Alberta
• *baby boom; Henry Youle Hind; Palliser expedition; Louis Riel; western alienation; westward expansion* •

ALEXANDRA PALMER
Nora E. Vaughan Fashion Costume Curator
Royal Ontario Museum
• *fashion* •

BRYAN D. PALMER
Canadian Studies
Trent University
• *class; Knights of Labor; nine-hour movement* •

FRANÇOIS PARÉ
Department of French Studies
University of Guelph
• *Hector de Saint-Denys Garneau; Hexagone movement* •

GEORGE L. PARKER
Retired, Royal Military College of Canada
• *book publishing* •

ANDREW PARNABY
Department of History
University College of Cape Breton
• *longshoremen;* (with Gregory S. Kealey) *Canadian Labour Congress; D.J. O'Donoghue; red scare; Relations of Labour and Capital, Royal Commission on* •

DIANE PAYMENT
Historian, Western Canada Service Centre,
Parks Canada
Winnipeg
• *Batoche* •

JONATHAN PEARL
Department of History
University of Toronto at Scarborough
• *witchcraft* •

LAURA PEERS
Lecturer Curator, Pitt Rivers Museum
and School of Anthropology
University of Oxford and
Fellow
Linacre College
• *Peguis; wampum* •

STEVE PENFOLD
Department of History
Nipissing University
• *franchises* •

ROBERTO PERIN
Department of History, Glendon College
York University
• *Bishop Ignace Bourget; Paul-Napoléon Bruchési; gallicanism; Gavazzi riots; Albert Lacombe; Manitoba schools question; Alexandre-Antonin Taché; ultramontanism* •

GALEN ROGER PERRAS
National Archives of Canada
• *Canadian Army Pacific Force; Kiska* •

ADELE PERRY
Department of History
University of Manitoba
• *brideships; Chinook; John Sebastian Helmcken; Vancouver Island colony* •

DAVID PHILLIPS
Senior Climatologist
Environment Canada
• *hurricanes* •

KATIE PICKLES
Department of History
University of Canterbury, Christchurch,
New Zealand
• *Imperial Order Daughters of the Empire* •

RUTH ROACH PIERSON
Ontario Institute for Studies in Education
University of Toronto
• (with Tina Davidson) *Canadian Women's Army Corps; war brides; Women's Royal Canadian Naval Service* •

JAMES M. PITSULA
Department of History
University of Regina
• *Crown Investments Corporation of Saskatchewan* •

RICHARD PLANT
Graduate Centre for Study of Drama
University of Toronto and
Professor Emeritus
Queen's University
• *Dominion Drama Festival; theatre* •

CAROLYN PODRUCHNY
Department of History and Program in American Studies
Western Michigan University
• *canoe routes; Donnacona; pays d'en haut; voyageurs* •

ZAILIG POLLOCK
Department of English Literature
Trent University
• *A.M. Klein* •

PETER E. POPE
Archaeology Unit
Memorial University of Newfoundland
• *John Cabot; Cupids Cove Colony; English Shore; Ferryland; fishing admirals; Sir Humphrey Gilbert; King William III's Act; Sir David Kirke; Western Charters* •

CHARLENE PORSILD
Director of Library and Archives
Montana Historical Society
• *Laura Berton; Bonanza Creek; Dawson City; Klondike gold rush, L.N. 'Jack' McQuesten; Robert Service* •

ALISON PRENTICE
Emerita Professor, Ontario Institute for Studies in Education
University of Toronto
• *normal schools; one-room schoolhouse; schoolmistresses; women's education* •

W. WESLEY PUE
Faculty of Law and Nemetz Chair in Legal History
University of British Columbia
• *Canadian Bar Association; law; legal profession* •

CAMERON PULSIFER
Historian
Canadian War Museum
• *British garrison; fortifications* •

JACQUES RACINE
Faculté de théologie et de sciences religieuses
Université Laval
• *Rerum Novarum* •

IAN RADFORTH
Department of History
University of Toronto
• *bunkhouse men; Canadian Shield; Jacques & Hay; lumber industry; royal tours; square timber trade; state formation* •

KEITH RALSTON
Department of History (Emeritus)
University of British Columbia
• *Sir James Douglas* •

BILL RAWLING
Department of History
Carleton University
• *Canadian Army Medical Corps; Hong Kong, Battle of; A.G.L. McNaughton; trench warfare* •

ARTHUR J. RAY
Department of History
University of British Columbia
• *Aboriginal title and treaty rights; Aboriginals in the fur trade; 'bottom of the bay'; fur trade; Hudson's Bay Company* •

MARELENE RAYNER-CANHAM
Department of Science (Physics),
Sir Wilfred Grenfell College
Memorial University of Newfoundland
• *Harriet Brooks* •

J.E. REA
Department of History
University of Manitoba
• *agrarian revolt; T.A. Crerar; Grain Growers' Grain Company; Marquis wheat; Sir Rodmond P. Roblin; Strangers within Our Gates (Woodsworth)* •

COLIN READ
Huron University College
University of Western Ontario
• *Act of Union; Lord Durham; governors of British North America; William Lyon Mackenzie; Province of Canada; John Graves Simcoe* •

T.D. REGEHR
Professor Emeritus of History
University of Saskatchewan
• *Beauharnois scandal; Canadian National Railways; Crow's Nest Pass Agreement; Sir Sandford Fleming; Sir Herbert Holt; Hudson Bay Railway; Mackenzie, Mann and Company Limited; Mennonites; Pacific Great Eastern Railway; Donald Smith; Sir William Van Horne* •

PEARLANN REICHWEIN
Faculty of Physical Education and Recreation
University of Alberta
• *Banff; mountaineering* •

John G. Reid
Department of History
Saint Mary's University
• *Acadian civil war; Sir William Alexander; Pierre Biard; conquest of Acadia; Pierre Du Gua de Monts; imperial rivalries; Sir William Phips; Jean de Biencourt de Poutrincourt; Sieur de Roberval;* (with Margaret Conrad) *Nova Scotia* •

Bruce Retallack
Doctoral candidate, Department of History
University of Toronto
• *cartoonists* •

François Ricard
Département de langue et littérature françaises
Université McGill
• *Gabrielle Roy; Trente Arpents (Ringuet)* •

Barnett Richling
Mount Saint Vincent University
• *Diamond Jenness* •

Yves Roberge
Études françaises, St Michael's College
University of Toronto
• *Les Insolence du Frère Untel (Desbiens); joual* •

Jean-Claude Robert
Département d'histoire
Université du Québec à Montréal
• *Quebec; 'quelques arpents de neige'* •

Julia Roberts
Canadian Studies
University of Waterloo
• *stagecoaches; taverns* •

Ian Ross Robertson
Department of History
University of Toronto at Scarborough
• *Charlottetown; George Coles; fixed link; Robert Harris; Sir Andrew Macphail; Maritimes 'golden age'; James Colledge Pope; Prince Edward Island; Prince Edward Island land question; Tenant League* •

Martin Robin
Professor Emeritus, Department of Political Science
Simon Fraser University
• *fascism; Ku Klux Klan* •

Daniel Robinson
Faculty of Information and Media Studies,
Middlesex College
University of Western Ontario
• *magazines; polling* •

Charles G. Roland
Hannah Professor Emeritus, History of Medicine
McMaster University
• *Norman Bethune; Canadian Medical Association; malaria; medical schools; pasteurization; Hans Selye; smallpox; tuberculosis* •

Paul Romney
Baltimore
• *Clear Grits; compact theory of Confederation; Constitutional Act; double shuffle; founding peoples, founding nations; Sir Oliver Mowat; provincial autonomy and rights; Reformers; Union Bill* •

Ronald Rompkey
University Research Professor, Department of English
Memorial University of Newfoundland
• *Sir Wilfred Grenfell* •

Jacques Rouillard
Département d'histoire
Université de Montréal
• *Asbestos strike; French-Canadian emigration to the United States; Grande Association des Ouvriers* •

Gilles Routhier
Faculté de théologie et sciences religieuses
Université Laval
• *École sociale populaire; Vatican II* •

Patricia Roy
Department of History
University of Victoria
• *Asiatic Exclusion League; W.A.C. Bennett; Richard McBride; 'socialist hordes at the gates'; 'spoilt child of Confederation'* •

D.T. Ruddel
Director, Museums Studies Program
University of Toronto
• *museums* •

Ronald Rudin
Department of History
Concordia University
• *caisses populaires; Quebec Tercentenary* •

Norman Ruff
Department of Political Science
University of Victoria
• *David Barrett* •

Robert Rutherdale
Department of History
Algoma University College
• *home front; manhood and masculinities* •

Allan J. Ryan
New Sun Chair in Aboriginal Art and Culture,
School of Canadian Studies
Carleton University
• *Aboriginal art* •

Shannon Ryan
Department of History
Memorial University of Newfoundland
• *Atlantic fishery; Grand Banks; Abram Kean; Newfoundland sealing disaster; sealing* •

ERIC W. SAGER
Department of History
University of Victoria
• *sailing ships; seafaring labour; shipbuilding; shipping industry* •

MARC ST-HILAIRE
Département de géographie
Université Laval
• (with Richard Marcoux) *Quebec City* •

JOAN SANGSTER
Department of History
Trent University
• *Bell Telephone strike; women and the law; women's work* •

JOY L. SANTINK
Historian
Toronto
• *Timothy Eaton; mail-order catalogues* •

ROGER SARTY
Canadian War Museum
• *L.W. Murray* •

JOHN T. SAYWELL
University Professor Emeritus
York University
• *Mitchell Hepburn* •

ALBERT SCHRAUWERS
Department of Anthropology
York University
• *Quakers* •

BARBARA SCHRODT
Associate Professor Emerita, School of Human Kinetics
University of British Columbia
• *winter sports* •

JOAN M. SCHWARTZ
Department of Art
Queen's University and
Senior Photography Specialist
National Archives of Canada
• *photography* •

CHRISTABELLE SETHNA
Institute of Women's Studies/Faculty of Education
University of Ottawa
• *social purity movement* •

ADRIENNE SHADD
Consultant on Black history and culture
Toronto
• *Josiah Henson; Mary Ann Shadd (Cary); Underground Railroad* •

BRIAN C. SHIPLEY
PhD candidate, Department of History
Dalhousie University
• (with Richard White) *surveying* •

RICHARD SIMEON
Department of Political Science
University of Toronto
• *Charlottetown Accord; Meech Lake Accord* •

MICHAEL SINCLAIR
Bedford Institute of Oceanography
• *Bedford Institute of Oceanography* •

BRENT SLOBODIN
Department of Education, Yukon Territory
Whitehorse
• *Joseph Boyle; Carrothers Commission* •

HARRY SMALLER
Faculty of Education
York University
• *teachers' unions* •

ALLAN SMITH
Department of History
University of British Columbia
• *Alaska Boundary dispute; continentalism* •

DAVID E. SMITH
Department of Political Studies
University of Saskatchewan
• *constitutional monarchy; James G. Gardiner; governor general; monarchy; Rideau Hall; Jeanne Sauvé* •

DENIS SMITH
Professor Emeritus of Political Science
University of Western Ontario
• *John G. Diefenbaker; Walter Gordon; Roads to Resources; War Measures Act* •

DONALD B. SMITH
Department of History
University of Calgary
• *Deskaheh; Grey Owl; Frederick Loft; Long Lance, Buffalo Child; Mississauga missionaries* •

GORDON E. SMITH
School of Music
Queen's University
• *Ernest Gagnon* •

ROBERT W. SMITH
Department of History and Classics
University of Alberta
• *space program* •

ELIZABETH SMYTH
Department of Curriculum Teaching and Learning
Ontario Institute for Studies in Education
University of Toronto
• *education in colonial English Canada; private schools* •

James G. Snell
Department of History
University of Guelph
• *divorce; old-age pensions; Supreme Court of Canada* •

Thomas P. Socknat
Canadian Studies Coordinator, Woodsworth College
University of Toronto
• *pacifism; white feather campaign* •

Minko Sotiron
Department of History
John Abbott College and
Journalism Department
Concordia University
• *newspapers* •

John G. Stackhouse, Jr
Sangwoo Youtong Professor of Theology and Culture
Regent College, Vancouver
• *evangelicalism* •

David Stafford
Centre for Second World War Studies
University of Edinburgh
• *Camp X* •

David Staines
Department of English
University of Ottawa
• *Stephen Leacock; Hugh MacLennan; Two Solitudes (MacLennan)* •

Della M.M. Stanley
Chair, Department of Political and Canadian Studies
Mount Saint Vincent University
• *Richard Hatfield; Sir Pierre-Amand Landry; New Brunswick Official Languages Act; Regional Economic Expansion, Department of; Louis-J. Robichaud* •

Laurie C.C. Stanley-Blackwell
Department of History
St Francis Xavier University
• *leprosy* •

Philip Stenning
Professor in Criminology
Victoria University of Wellington, New Zealand
• *gun control* •

Blair Stonechild
Department of Indigenous Studies
First Nations University of Canada
• *Almighty Voice* •

David Stouck
Department of English
Simon Fraser University
• *As for Me and My House (Ross); Grain (Stead)* •

Carolyn Strange
Centre of Criminology
University of Toronto
• *capital punishment; crime and punishment; moral and social reform; prostitution* •

Veronica Strong-Boag
Educational Studies and Women's Studies
University of British Columbia
• *adoption; anti-feminism; courtship and marriage; Dionne Quintuplets; feminism, first-wave; Pauline Johnson; Dorothy Livesay; Nellie McClung; mothers' allowances; National Council of Women of Canada; women's suffrage movement* •

James Struthers
Canadian Studies Program
Trent University
• *Canada Assistance Plan; unemployment insurance; welfare state; Charlotte Whitton* •

D.A. Sutherland
Department of History
Dalhousie University
• *Lord Dalhousie; Joshua Mauger; pirates; Richard John Uniacke; John Young* •

Neil Sutherland
Professor Emeritus of Educational Studies
University of British Columbia
• *children* •

Patricia Sutherland
Curator, Archaeology Survey of Canada
Canadian Museum of Civilization
• *Norse* •

Sir Conrad Swan, KCVO, FSA
Garter Principal King of Arms Emeritus
• *A mari usque ad mare; Arms of Canada; national flag* •

Frances Swyripa
Department of History and Classics
University of Alberta
• *colonist cars; European immigration 1897–1929; remittance men; Ukrainians* •

Koozma J. Tarasoff
Ottawa
• *Doukhobors* •

C. James Taylor
Parks Canada
Calgary
• *Historic Sites and Monuments Board; national historic sites; national parks* •

Graham D. Taylor
Vice-president (Academic) and Professor of History
Trent University
• *aircraft manufacturing industry; Bombardier, Inc.; conglomerates* •

John H. Taylor
Department of History
Carleton University
• *John By; Ottawa* •

M. Brook Taylor
Visiting Foreign Professor
Master's Program of Area Studies
University of Tsukuba, Japan
• *R. MacGregor Dawson; Frederick William Wallace* •

Suzanne Taylor
Science Communications Manager,
St Andrews Biological Station
Fisheries and Oceans Canada
• *St Andrews Biological Station* •

Michel Tétu
Directeur, L'Année francophone internationale
Faculté des lettres
Université Laval
• *Francophonie* •

Julie C. Thacker
Independent scholar
Prince George
• *Isabella Preston* •

Clara Thomas
Professor Emeritus
York University
• *Robertson Davies; Anna Jameson; Margaret Laurence; Elizabeth Simcoe* •

Morley Thomas
Retired General Director
Canadian Climate Centre
• *weather forecasting* •

Peter Thomas
Retired, Department of History
University of New Brunswick
• *Albion* •

Shirley Tillotson
Department of History
Dalhousie University
• *philanthropy* •

Brian Titley
Faculty of Education
University of Lethbridge
• *Indian Act; Indian agents* •

John L. Tobias
Department of History
Red Deer College
• *Indian Claims Commission; White Paper on Indian Policy* •

P.M. Toner
Department of History and Politics
University of New Brunswick, Saint John
• *Fenians* •

Pierre Trépanier
Département d'histoire
Université de Montréal
• *L'Action nationale; Guy Frégault; François-Xavier Garneau; Lionel Groulx* •

Harold Troper
Theory and Policy Studies
University of Toronto
• *multiculturalism* •

Eric Tucker
Osgoode Hall Law School
York University
• *employment standards legislation; labour law* •

Diane Tye
Department of Folklore
Memorial University of Newfoundland
• *Helen Creighton* •

Mariana Valverde
Centre of Criminology
University of Toronto
• *liquor control; Toronto stork derby* •

Jonathan Vance
Department of History
University of Western Ontario
• *Walter Seymour Allward; The Dumbells; Generals Die in Bed (Harrison); John McCrae; prisoners of war; war memorials; The Wars (Findley)* •

Marguerite Van Die
History and Theology
Queen's University
• *Salem Bland; Chautauqua; free thought; Methodism; social gospel; theosophy* •

Odette Vincent
Historienne-consultante
Gloucester, Ontario
• *Emma Albani; Claude Champagne; chansonniers; Éva Gauthier; La Bolduc* •

Mary Vipond
Department of History
Concordia University
• *broadcasting; Canadian Broadcasting Corporation; Canadian Clubs; United Church of Canada* •

Paul Voisey
Department of History and Classics
University of Alberta
• *Alberta; dry farming; homesteading* •

NANCY WACHOWICH
Department of Anthropology
University of Aberdeen
• *Ataguttaaluk; Qitdlarssuaq; Taqulittuq and Ipirvik; Peter Tulugajuak* •

BILL WAISER
Department of History
University of Saskatchewan
• *Robert Bell; Charles Camsell; Cumberland House; Dominion Lands Act; Geological Survey of Canada; Île-à-la-Crosse; John Macoun; William Ogilvie; Jerry Potts; Poundmaker; relief camps; Sarah Binks (Hiebert); Saskatchewan; Saskatoon; wartime internment* •

P.B. WAITE
Professor Emeritus of History
Dalhousie University
• *R.B. Bennett; Donald Creighton; Sir John A. Macdonald; Sir John S. Thompson; winter* •

KEITH WALDEN
Department of History
Trent University
• *Expo 67* •

JAMES W. ST G. WALKER
Department of History
University of Waterloo
• *African Canadians; Black Loyalists; Maroons; Nova Scotia No. 2 Construction Battalion; racism* •

JEAN-PIERRE WALLOT
Department of History
University of Ottawa
• *Sir Louis-Hippolyte LaFontaine; Lower Canada; Louis-Joseph Papineau; Patriotes; Province of Quebec 1763–91* •

ROBERT WARDHAUGH
Department of History
University of Western Ontario
• *John Bracken; Natural Resources Transfer Agreement; Prairie Farm Rehabilitation Administration* •

GERMAINE WARKENTIN
Department of English (Emeritus)
University of Toronto
• *Jean-Vincent d'Abbadie de Saint-Justin; Pierre Boucher; Jean de Brébeuf; Jacques Cartier; Baron de Lahontan; Meta incognita; Pierre-Esprit Radisson* •

CHERYL KRASNICK WARSH
Department of History
Malaspina University-College
• *brewing and distilling; prohibition* •

MELVILLE WATKINS
Professor Emeritus of Economics and Political Science
University of Toronto
• *Auto Pact; 'corporate welfare bums'; economic nationalism; foreign ownership; free trade; New Left; Waffle Group* •

JEFF WEBB
Department of History
Memorial University of Newfoundland
• *William Whiteway* •

WILLIAM WESTFALL
Department of History, Atkinson College
York University
• *Children of Peace; clergy reserves; John Strachan* •

C.F.J. WHEBELL
London, Ontario
• *boundaries; local government; St Lawrence River system* •

REG WHITAKER
Distinguished Research Professor
York University and
Adjunct Professor of Political Science
University of Victoria
• *Cold War; James G. Endicott; Igor Gouzenko; immigration policy; Liberal Party; Herbert Norman; Official Secrets Act; security intelligence* •

RICHARD WHITE
Historian
Toronto
• *Sir Adam Beck; civil engineering; Sir Casimir Gzowski; Royal Engineers;* (with Brian C. Shipley) *surveying* •

ALAN WHITEHORN
Department of Political and Economic Science
Royal Military College of Canada
• *New Democratic Party* •

WILLIAM WICKEN
Department of History
York University
• *Donald Marshall, Jr; Henri Membertou; Mi'kmaq; Gabriel Sylliboy* •

WENDY WICKWIRE
Department of Anthropology
University of British Columbia
• *British Columbia Interior Aboriginals; James Teit* •

THOMAS WIEN
Département d'histoire
Université de Montréal
• *Étienne Brulé; coureurs de bois; engagés* •

JOHN WILLIS
Historian
Canadian Postal Museum-Canadian Museum of Civilization
• *postal communication* •

ALAN WILSON
Halifax
• *Thomas H. Raddall* •

CATHARINE ANNE WILSON
Department of History
University of Guelph
• *bees* •

DAVID A. WILSON
Celtic Studies and History, St Michael's College
University of Toronto
• *Thomas D'Arcy McGee;* (with Donald Harman Akenson) *Irish* •

IAN E. WILSON
National Archivist
National Archives of Canada
• *Sir Arthur Doughty; National Archives* •

JEAN WILSON
Associate Director, Editorial
UBC Press
• *McLean Gang* •

JEREMY WILSON
Department of Political Science
University of Victoria
• *Greenpeace* •

DEREK H.C. WILTON
Department of Earth Sciences
Memorial University of Newfoundland
• *A.P. Low* •

ROBERT WISHART
Department of Anthropology
University of Alberta
• (with Michael Asch) *western subarctic Aboriginals* •

DONALD WRIGHT
Department of History and Centre for Canadian Studies
Brock University
• *historical societies; '20th century belongs to Canada'* •

GLENN WRIGHT
Historian
National Archives of Canada
• *Royal Canadian Legion; Victoria Pioneer Rifles* •

MIRIAM WRIGHT
Department of History and Classics
Acadia University
• *cod moratorium; territorial waters* •

J. COLIN YERBURY
Dean of Continuing Studies
Simon Fraser University
• *Fort Chipewyan; fur trade explorers (English-speaking); Peter Pond; Thanadelthur; David Thompson* •

BRIAN YOUNG
Department of History
McGill University
• *Sir Hugh Allan; George-Étienne Cartier; Séminaire de Montréal* •

CAROLYN A. YOUNG
Architectural historian
• *Parliament Buildings* •

SUZANNE ZELLER
Department of History
Wilfrid Laurier University
• *George Mercer Dawson; Sir J. William Dawson; geomagnetism; George Lawson; Sir John Henry Lefroy; Sir William Logan; natural history; scientific societies* •

JOYCE ZEMANS
Arts and Media Administration,
Schulich School of Business
York University
• *Painters Eleven* •

THE OXFORD COMPANION TO
CANADIAN HISTORY

Abbadie de Saint-Castin, Jean-Vincent d' (1652–1707), nobleman, soldier, chief of the Abenaki. Poet Alden Nowlan vividly sketches Saint-Castin's contradictions: 'you exile from the Pyrenees,/you baron of France and Navarre,/you squaw man, you Latin poet,/ you war chief of Penobscot'. An adolescent soldier in New France and Acadia, Saint-Castin knew the woods and their Native inhabitants intimately. In 1674 *Frontenac commissioned him to ensure that the Abenaki supported France. Saint-Castin settled at Pentagouet and was adopted by the Penobscot, marrying the daughter of the great chief Madokawando. Fiercely independent, he fought and traded both as French baron and Abenaki chief, skilfully resisting military pressure from New England. Saint-Castin returned to France on estate business in 1701, dying far from Acadia before his troubled affairs were settled. GERMAINE WARKENTIN

Abbott, Maude E. (1869–1940). Dr Abbott became a world-class physician at a time when the profession did not encourage female students. Born in Quebec, she was raised by her maternal grandmother, and though financially pressed assumed the lifelong care of her invalid sister. She completed her BA at McGill University (1890) and graduated from the University of Bishop's College medical faculty (1894) because McGill initially refused to admit her. Undaunted, she pursued postgraduate training in Europe under well-known clinicians and gained international fame as a congenital heart disease specialist. She wrote more than 100 substantial research papers and several histories of medicine, and helped professionalize *nursing through the creation of special courses adopted across North America. Her interest in pathology and her curatorship of McGill's medical museum led her to incorporate the museum's collection into a teaching medium. Charming, compassionate, but often lonely, Abbott faced excruciatingly slow advancement at McGill, despite her numerous awards, honours, and 'firsts'.
E. TINA CROSSFIELD

Aberhart, William (1878–1943), Protestant fundamentalist preacher, Alberta premier 1935–43. The despair of the Great Depression of the 1930s convinced charismatic 'Bible Bill' Aberhart, western Canada's leading radio evangelist, that the Antichrist had returned to earth and the apocalypse was at hand. Politically naive, Aberhart believed that implementing Major C.H. Douglas's social credit theories would increase people's purchasing power. The individual would be released from economic bondage and be able to seek salvation in Christ. Aberhart built the populist *Social Credit Party from the ground up and decimated the governing United Farmers of Alberta in the 1935 provincial election. Unable to enact social credit without breaching the constitution, Aberhart soon lost control to his own backbenchers, who asked for Douglas's help. Under his guidance and Aberhart's nominal leadership after June 1937, Social Credit enacted several authoritarian measures that challenged the Jewish financial conspiracy Douglas believed was orchestrating world events. Douglas's policies were unconstitutional and failed miserably. Aberhart regained control by September 1938 and won the 1940 election. On his death in 1943, his great friend Ernest C. *Manning became premier. Aberhart's major accomplishments include the consolidation of local schools and province-building economic policies that often pitted Alberta against Ottawa. BOB HESKETH

Aboriginal art. The history of indigenous aesthetic production in what is now Canada is culturally and geographically diverse, dating back several thousand years. Discussion of the topic is complex and presents difficulties, as the scholarship has been shaped by the Eurocentric practice of collection, classification, and exhibition. The same object, whether an Eastern Woodlands moosehide jacket ornamented with dyed porcupine quills, or a carved and painted shaman's rattle from the Northwest Coast, might be alternately described or displayed as an exotic curio, scientific specimen, cultural artifact, or an example of 'primitive' art. Until recently the decorated jacket might have been relegated to the lesser category of women's craft, and the rattle considered male ceremonial art. The recent addition of the 'Aboriginal voice', conspicuously absent from past discourse, provides for a more culturally appropriate reinterpretation, recontextualization, and display of aesthetic materials.

Aboriginal artists and cultural scholars often argue that the term 'art' has no indigenous equivalent, in the sense of an object whose sole purpose is aesthetic contemplation. There is deemed to be no distinction between art and non-art. The term 'Aboriginal art' is no more than an arbitrary imposition of a category of aesthetic 'otherness' conceptualized in the language of the colonizer, thereby ignoring widespread cultural and geographic diversity. Among Aboriginal peoples, visual symbols and iconic images often give tangible form to cultural concepts and ideas. They are created within the broader complex of aesthetic expression: song, dance, theatrical production, and narrative oratory. It is an aesthetic that values technical mastery, innovation, creativity, and conceptual correctness.

Archaeological evidence and oral tradition suggest Aboriginal occupation of northern North America for several thousand years. Many types of ancient artistic production have been documented; among the most notable are small human effigy stone sculptures from the Fraser River in British Columbia (500 BC–AD 500), finely made Iroquoian clay pottery from southern Ontario (AD 900–1600), and numerous undatable examples of 'rock art'—images of humans and animals painted on cliff facings with natural ochres (pictographs) and incised on rock outcroppings (petroglyphs). All of these locations are believed to be sites of concentrated spiritual power and places of ceremonial practice. Like the cultures they embody, Aboriginal artistic practices are always evolving, undergoing change and refinement as new ideas, materials, and techniques are introduced and incorporated. Ancient continental trade routes confirm the active exchange of raw materials, such as fresh water pearls, shells, copper, obsidian, pipestone, and mica.

Beginning in the 16th century in the east, and the late 18th century on the West Coast, European explorers, traders, and later settlers encountered many distinct Aboriginal peoples, from east coast fishers (Mi'kmaq and Maliseet) and Great Lakes hunter-gatherers (Anishinabe) and farmers (Iroquois) to Prairie bison hunters (Plains Cree and Blackfoot) and west coast whalers (Nuu-chah-nulth). Though artistically diverse, their iconic imagery frequently shared a symbolic reverence for the Creator, respect for the spirit in all things, and acknowledgement of a relationship to the animate and inanimate world. Natural materials such as bone, hide, bark, and mineral pigments were creatively employed. Cree and Ojibwa women in the Eastern Woodlands adorned moose- and deer-hide garments with dyed porcupine-quill and moose-hair embroidery in floral and geometric designs that were also etched on birchbark containers and woven into textiles. On the Prairies, bison-hide tipis were painted with images of war exploits, and hide shields were adorned with visionary experiences of prominent leaders. Tribal histories were symbolically recorded on hide calendars called 'winter counts'. On the West Coast, towering cedar totem poles, carved in styles that evolved over several millennia, proclaimed the lineage and hereditary rights of important families living in communal longhouse villages. Family crests, portraying mythic ancestors, were painted on house fronts, woven on blankets, and fashioned into masks displayed at elaborate feasts called potlatches.

Following initial European contact, existing Aboriginal trade networks were expanded to incorporate many new materials and manufactured goods. Especially popular were broadcloth and velvet, silk ribbons, silver brooches, pearl buttons, commercial pigments, and glass beads of various sizes and colours. For many Aboriginal artisans, it was a time of unlimited aesthetic experimentation. Hybrid artforms reflected the long-standing cultural practice of incorporating new materials and ideas, contradicting the notion of a 'pristine' Aboriginal aesthetic corrupted by European trade goods and concepts.

In the wake of severe population decline precipitated by European diseases, the 19th century was a period of great social upheaval for Aboriginal peoples, characterized by political pressure, cultural marginalization, and legislated prohibition of indigenous religious ceremonies. These factors all affected artistic production, which, due to economic necessity, increasingly focused on the production of articles for the tourist trade and collectors of 'Aboriginal art'. Especially notable are the Iroquois floral beaded purses popular among visitors to Niagara Falls in the late 19th century. In earlier times, Mi'kmaq quilled birchbark trinket baskets were a poplar tourist commodity, as were Haida black slate (argillite) carvings of human and mythic animal forms. These art forms allowed Aboriginal aesthetic expression to survive.

For Aboriginal artists such as David Neel (1960–), who maintains that innovation is part of his Kwakwaka'wakw cultural tradition, it is difficult to distinguish 'contemporary' from 'traditional' art. Attempts to make this distinction trouble some scholars. Is evaluation of work based on the use of recognizable 'traditional' materials, forms, and concepts, or the proven Aboriginal identity of the artist? Who determines the criteria? Is Kwakwaka'wakw carver Mungo Martin (1879–1962), who continued to pass on traditional west coast artistic skills and knowledge into the second half of the 20th century, both traditional and contemporary? Or, is he, along with the many producers of early-20th-century tourist art, a 'transitional' artist?

By the mid-20th century a growing number of Aboriginal artists were producing works for an increasingly global market. Some were professionally trained, others self-taught. Among those who gained prominence in the 1960s and 1970s, and whose work was often perceived as being more 'individualistic' than representative of 'tribal' expression, were Alex Janvier (1935–), Daphne Odjig (1925–), Allen Sapp (1929–), Bill Reid (1920–98), and Norval Morrisseau (1931–). Together, they helped make Aboriginal art more accessible and acceptable to a broader public. The commercial success of Morrisseau's wildly colourful paintings of Ojibwa myths and legends inspired a generation of followers and imitators, while Reid is acknowledged as a major force in the revitalization of west coast Aboriginal arts. His crowning achievement, a giant bronze sculpture, *The Spirit of Haida Gwaii*, graces the reflecting pool of the Canadian Embassy in Washington, DC.

In 1992 two major exhibitions signalled institutional acceptance of contemporary Aboriginal art: 'Indigena' at the Canadian Museum of Civilization in Gatineau, Quebec, and 'Land Spirit Power' at the National Gallery of Canada in Ottawa. Featured artists, such as Carl Beam (1943–), Joane Cardinal-Schubert (1942–), Jane Ash Poitras (1951–), Bob Boyer (1948–), Edward Poitras (1953–), and Lawrence Paul Yuxweluptun (1957–), employed a variety of media—from acrylic painting, collage, photography, and installation to virtual reality. They addressed issues of Aboriginal history, political oppression, contemporary urban experience, and the struggle to regain control of self-representation. Anger was tempered with humour and hope to foster greater awareness of Aboriginal culture and facilitate cross-cultural healing. In 1995 Edward Poitras became the first Aboriginal artist to represent Canada at the Venice Biennale international exposition.

A new generation of Aboriginal artists, employing new media and metaphors, is continuing the dialogue initiated by its predecessors. Important artists on the horizon are Rosalie Favell (1958–), who explores her Metis identity through digital photo manipulation of pop-culture imagery; Marianne Nicolson (1969–), whose paintings celebrate the vitality of Kwakwaka'wakw language and heritage; and Brian Jungen (1970–), whose magnificent sculpture, *Shapeshifter*, a skeletal grey whale constructed of white plastic lawn chairs, is now in the collection of the National Gallery of Canada. ALLAN J. RYAN

See also INUIT ART.

Aboriginal enfranchisement. For Aboriginal people, enfranchisement, first legislated under the Province of Canada's Gradual Civilization Act (1857), meant more than the right to vote. As applied to male status Indians, it involved the loss of status as Indians and the acquisition of the full rights, including political rights such as voting, of British-Canadian citizens. The theory was that, as Indians became educated, they would want to shed their Indian identity and blend into mainstream Euro-Canadian society. Applied initially to adult males, the act had a direct impact on women as well. A man could apply for enfranchisement, and, after satisfying examiners that he was literate, moral, and debt-free, would qualify for a probationary period after which he would become enfranchised. Enfranchisement meant a loss of Indian status for the wife and children of such a man, but entitled the enfranchised man to a share of reserve land in freehold tenure. Additional women were affected by the Gradual Enfranchisement Act (1869), which maintained the provisions for men and required that an Indian woman who married a non-Indian (Euro-Canadian, Metis, or non-status Indian) lost her status. These provisions were incorporated into the 1876 *Indian Act, which also said that an Indian male who obtained a university degree or entered one of the liberal professions automatically lost his status. A modification in 1880 removed the involuntary aspect and made such an individual eligible for enfranchisement upon his application.

From the beginning, Indian communities resisted enfranchisement, which they correctly viewed as attempting to erode them. Men could frustrate the policy of voluntary enfranchisement by not applying for it. Or, if a band member was enfranchised, the council could resist by refusing to surrender the piece of reserve land that was supposed to go to the new citizen in freehold. Government responded to this resistance by experimenting with involuntary enfranchisement—enfranchisement at the instruction of the minister—in 1920–2 and 1933–51. Because resistance to enfranchisement was strong, most of those who lost their status were women who had married a non-Indian.

The gender discrimination in the policy was blatant and controversial: an Indian male who 'married out' did not lose his status (his non-Indian wife acquired status). After 1970, opposition to gender-based discrimination grew: first an Ojibwa woman, Jeannette Lavell, fought the discriminatory portion of the act in court, losing a Supreme Court decision in 1973; then a Maliseet, Sandra Lovelace, succeeded in having the policy branded as discriminatory by the UN Human Rights Committee (1981).

Ultimately, the passage of the *Charter of Rights and Freedoms (1982) ensured the defeat of enfranchisement. In 1985, by Bill C-31, it was removed from the Indian Act. J.R. MILLER

Aboriginal games. For Canada's First Nations peoples, sport and gaming traditions reflected the requirements of a hunting and gathering society. Various competitions such as foot and horse racing, spear throwing, and archery competitions refined hunting skills, and widely played games of chance not only provided amusement but also taught an acceptance of fate and stoicism in defeat. Stick and ball games were also popular among Aboriginal peoples across North America, and often were connected with religious ceremonies. The Native game of baggataway, or lacrosse, for example, was thought to heal sickness and exercise control over supernatural forces. By the early 19th century the proficiency of the Kahnawake players was well known, and through them the game was transmitted to the non-Native population. Other stick and ball games resembling shinny were played across the continent. On the East Coast, a ball game known as 'old fashion' was popular among the Mi'kmaq and Maliseet, and in the North the Inuit played the game of *anaulataq*, or what is now called Inuit baseball.

Physical competition also served as a way to resolve disputes. Chipewyan males turned to wrestling to settle property disputes or to win a wife. In other settings, such as among the Inuit, the ability to endure the blow of another without defending oneself was a mark of honour and a way of resolving arguments. A premium was also placed on the ability to withstand pain, as bouts of finger- and lip-pulling would suggest.

Although Aboriginal peoples now compete in a number of Euro-Canadian sporting practices, they have also promoted sport and recreation suited to their own needs and drawing upon their own traditions. Sporting events provide a way to encourage Native solidarity and sometimes include complementary activities such as powwows, cultural traditions workshops, and traditional music and dance. The North American Indigenous Games, first held in 1990, is such an event. In addition, there are attempts to revive the Arctic Winter Games, to involve circumpolar competition among indigenous peoples from Siberia, Alaska, Greenland, and the Canadian North. COLIN HOWELL

Aboriginal land claims, northern Canada. Land claims are claims that Native peoples press upon the government of Canada on the basis of their *Aboriginal rights in territories they have historically occupied. The history of these claims begins with the 1973 *Calder* decision of the Supreme Court of Canada, which ruled that *Aboriginal title to land might exist wherever it had not been formally extinguished by treaties. This decision presented the federal government with the problem that Aboriginal title and other Aboriginal rights might limit its (or the relevant province's or territory's) ability to grant mining and oil-drilling licences and logging and other land-use permits, thus frustrating the government's goal of developing northern natural resources. In 1993, it created a policy on comprehensive claims (in contrast to specific claims, which address grievances concerning land covered by existing treaties). This policy provides a process by which a First Nation or Inuit group can exchange its claim to Aboriginal rights, whose existence and benefits are uncertain, for rights and benefits that are clearly understood in conventional legal terms and constitutionally guaranteed under Section 35 of the Constitution Act, 1982. As these settlements define the boundaries of the land in which the Aboriginal group's rights apply, governments are free to promote resource development elsewhere without fear of lawsuits based on Aboriginal rights.

The claims that have been settled in the territorial North and their terms (which include wildlife-harvesting and management rights) are: the 1984 Inuvialuit Final Agreement in the western Arctic confirming ownership of 91,000 sq km of land, and providing $62.5 million to be paid over 13 years; the 1992 Gwich'in Agreement providing 24,000 sq km of land in the northern Mackenzie Valley and 1,554 sq km of land in the Yukon, $75 million to be paid over 15 years, and a share of resource royalties from the valley; the Nunavut Land Claims Agreement reached in 1993 with the Tungavik Federation of Nunavut, including 350,000 sq km of land, $1.17 billion over 14 years, the right to share in resource royalties, and a promise to create the new territory of *Nunavut by 1999; the 1993 Umbrella Final Agreement covering the 14 Yukon First Nations, providing general terms for the individual First Nations to negotiate their respective settlements, seven of which had been negotiated by 2002; the 1994 Sahtu Dene and Metis Agreement, providing 41,437 sq km of land in the Mackenzie Valley, a share of resource royalties, and $75 million over 15 years. The major settlements in the northern portions of the provinces include the 1975 James Bay and Northern Quebec Agreement, the 1978 Northeastern Quebec Agreement, and the 2000 settlement with the Nisga'a of northwestern British Columbia. The Quebec agreements include over 14,000 sq km of land, wildlife-harvesting rights over an additional 150,000 sq km, and $230 million in compensation. The Nisga'a settlement provides 2,020 sq km of land, $257 million, and institutions of Nisga'a self-government. The northern provincial agreements confirm certain wildlife-harvesting rights, and an advisory role in land and wildlife management, but not the fuller role provided by some of the settlements in the territories. Additional northern comprehensive claims continue to be negotiated. GURSTON DACKS

Aboriginal languages. About 45 First Nations languages are spoken in Canada (the estimated number depends on the classification system). The languages with the greatest number of speakers (the numbers are approximations) are Cree-Montagnais-Naskapi (60,000); Ojibwa (40,000); Inuktitut (20,000); Chipewyan (4,000–12,000); Mi'kmaq (3,000–5,000); Mohawk (3,800); Assiniboine (3,600); Slave (3,000); Babine, Dogrib, Carrier, Chilcotin, and Blackfoot (2,000 each); Gitksan and Maliseet (1,000 each); Gwich'in (500 in Canada, 700 in Alaska); and Nisga'a (700–1,000).

Aboriginal language–speakers arrived in North America between 12,000 and 35,000 years ago, and Iñupiaq-Inuktitut speakers about 2,000 years ago. There are few similarities between Aboriginal and other languages, except that the Eskimo-Aleut languages, whose speakers arrived in Alaska about 5,000–7,000 years ago, share some characteristics with the Chukotko-Kamchatkan languages of Siberia. Like other languages, Aboriginal languages are fully modern and have always been capable of expressing complex concepts.

Vocabulary lists of North American Aboriginal languages appeared as early as 1545, when Jacques *Cartier published one for (extinct) St Lawrence Iroquoian. Other vocabularies were collected, often on exploratory voyages. For example, Christopher Hall recorded a short vocabulary of Baffin Island Inuktitut on Martin Frobisher's expedition of 1576; Henry Kelsey compiled a list of Woods Cree around 1700–20; Edward Thompson (a ship's surgeon) collected a vocabulary of Chipewyan in 1742; Alexander *Mackenzie compiled a vocabulary of Carrier in 1793; and William Anderson collected a vocabulary of Nootka on James *Cook's third voyage in 1778. Grammars and dictionaries of Aboriginal languages, produced mainly by Récollet, *Jesuit, and other missionaries, appeared as early as the 1600s. For example, Joseph le Caron (Récollet) produced a Huron (Iroquoian) dictionary in 1616; around 1662, a grammar of Old Algonquin (Eastern Ojibwa, extinct) was produced anonymously; Jacques Bruyas compiled a Mohawk dictionary in 1863; and Pierre-Antoine Maillard (Catholic) produced a grammar of Mi'kmaq in 1864.

Dictionary and grammar work proper started in the 19th century, when advances in linguistics enabled accurate descriptions of the sounds and grammatical constructions of unknown languages. For example, a grammar of Saulteaux was published in 1839; a treatise on Mohawk in 1864; a dictionary and grammar of Plains Cree in 1874; a dictionary of Labrador Inuttut in 1864; a Dakota grammar in 1852; a grammar of Haida in 1895; a grammar of Tlingit in 1840; a grammar of Kwakiutl in 1889; a grammar of Nootka in 1868; and a grammar of Thompson in 1880. Linguists have been involved in this work ever since documentation was promoted as a research program by Franz *Boas, a professor of anthropology at Columbia University, 1899–1942. More recently, Aboriginal speakers have begun grammar and dictionary work on their own languages.

For written communication, Aboriginal peoples historically used culturally appropriate pictographs, petroglyphs, notched sticks, *wampum belts, and so on. Missionaries later developed alphabets (one symbol per sound) and syllabaries (one symbol per consonant-vowel combination, as in Japanese *katakana*). In 1677, Father Chrestien Le Clercq also invented a hieroglyphic system for Mi'kmaq, using ideograms, or one symbol per word. Some Aboriginals, including the Mi'kmaq, developed or modified their own alphabets upon learning the phonemic principle. Many transmitted literacy skills to family members for generations.

Today, most Aboriginal orthographies in Canada are based on either the Roman alphabet (with English, French, or German-influenced variants), the International Phonetic Alphabet, or the syllabary developed in 1841 by Rev. James Evans (1801–46), originally for the Cree of Norway House, Manitoba. For example, Western Canadian Inuktun dialects typically use Roman alphabets, while Eastern Canadian Inuktitut dialects use syllabaries, except in Labrador Inuttut, where a German (Moravian) based alphabet is used. Syllabaries are also still used in Cree and Ojibwa dialects, along with Roman alphabets.

Further documentation of Aboriginal languages is crucial, since many are endangered. Many have unrecorded oral traditions comparable to the great literary traditions of the Old World; they also preserve large bodies of knowledge about the environment and medicine, all of which could be lost without documentation. A well-rounded education should include the study of an Aboriginal language or literature, which will reward the learner with profound insights into human nature and philosophy.

ABORIGINAL LANGUAGES IN CANADA

Many language names have recently been changed by the speakers of the languages. To avoid confusion, the more traditional terms are used here. Iñupiaq-Inuktitut and Cree-Montagnais-Naskapi each form a dialect continuum; adjacent dialects are mutually intelligible, while non-adjacent ones are less mutually intelligible. The 1991 census lists a 'Yellowknife' language category: some Dogrib-speaking residents near Yellowknife refer to themselves as 'Yellowknife Dene'; their ancestors may have spoken an extinct 'Yellowknife' dialect, probably Chipewyan. *Michif is a creole or 'hybrid' dialect using Cree verbs and French nouns.

Key:
Sub-family (family); where spoken
  Language or dialect complex (=alternative name)
    Dialect (=alternative name)
Languages in italics have few if any remaining speakers in Canada.

Eskimoan (Eskimo-Aleut); Northwest Territories, Nunavut
- Iñupiaq-**Inuktitut**
  - Western Canadian Inuktun
    - Siglitun
    - Inuinnaqtun
    - Natsilingmiutut (=Netsilik)
  - Eastern Canadian Inuktitut
    - Kivalliq
    - Aivilik
    - South Baffin
    - North Baffin-Iglulik
    - Nunavik (including Itivimiut and Tarramiut)
    - Labrador (=Inuttut)

Tlingit (Athapaskan-Eyak-Tlingit); Alaska, British Columbia, Yukon
- **Tlingit** (language isolate)

Athapaskan (Athapaskan-Eyak-Tlingit); Yukon, Northwest Territories, northern British Columbia, Alberta, Saskatchewan, Manitoba
- **Babine** (=Babine Carrier or Northern Carrier)
- **Beaver**
- **Carrier**
- **Chilcotin**
- **Chipewyan**
- **Dogrib**
- *Han*
- **Gwich'in** (=Kutchin or Loucheux)
- **Nahanni**
  - Kaska
  - Tahltan
  - *Tagish*
- **Sarcee**
- **Sekani**
- **Slave** (=Slavey)
  - North Slavey
    - Bearlake
    - Hare
  - South Slavey
    - Mountain
    - Slave (=Slavey)
- **Tutchone**
- *Upper Tanana*

Haida; Queen Charlotte Islands and northward
- **Haida** (language isolate)
  - Northern Haida (Masset)
  - Southern Haida (Skidegate)

Kwakiutlian (North Wakashan); northern Vancouver Island; neighbouring mainland coast
- **Haisla**
- **Heiltsuk** (spoken by Bella Bella, Haihais), Oowekyala (spoken by Oowekeeno)
- **Kwak'wala** (=Kwakiutl)

Nootkan (South Wakashan); west coast of Vancouver Island
- **Nootka**
- **Nitinaht**
- *Makah*

Aboriginal languages

Bella Coola (Salishan); coastal British Columbia
Bella Coola (=Nuxalk)

Central Salish (Salishan); interior and coastal British Columbia
Comox
Halkomelem
Northern Straits Salish
Sechelt
Squamish

Interior Salish (Salishan); interior British Columbia
Lillooet
Okanagan
Shuswap
Thompson

Tsimshianic; coastal British Columbia, along Nass and Skeena Rivers
Coast Tsimshian
Nass-Gitksan
Nisga'a
Gitksan

Kutenai (Kootenai); interior British Columbia, along Kootenay River
Kutenai (=Kootenay; language isolate)

Dakotan (Siouan-Catawban); Morley, Alberta; Saskatchewan, southern Manitoba
Sioux
Dakota (=Santee-Sisseton)
Yanktonai
Teton (=Lakhota)
Assiniboine
Stoney (=Alberta Assiniboine)

Central and Plains Algonquian (Algic)
Blackfoot; southern Alberta
Cree-Montagnais-Naskapi; Rockies to Quebec–Labrador peninsula
Western Cree
Attikamek^{w} (=Attikamek, Tête de Boule)
(Michif)
Moose Cree
Plains Cree
Swampy Cree
Woods Cree
Eastern Cree
East Cree
Montagnais (=Innu-aimun)
Naskapi (=Innu-aimun)

Ojibwa (=Ojibwe); Great Lakes; Ottawa valley (Saulteaux also in Manitoba, Saskatchewan, British Columbia)
Northern Ojibwa
Severn Ojibwa (=Oji-Cree)
Algonkin (=Algonquin)
other dialects simply known as Ojibwa
Southern Ojibwa
Saulteaux
Odawa (=Ottawa)
Eastern Ojibwa
Potawatomi

Eastern Algonquian (Algic)
Mi'kmaq (=Micmac); New Brunswick, Nova Scotia, Newfoundland, Quebec
Malecite(=Maliseet-Passamaquoddy; St John River, New Brunswick
Abenaki
Munsee Delaware

Northern Iroquoian (Iroquoian); Southern Ontario and Quebec
Cayuga
Mohawk
Oneida
Onondaga
Seneca
Tuscarora

CARRIE DYCK

Aboriginal missions in the West. The popular perception of Christian missions to Native peoples in Canada is that they were one with the *fur trade and government activities, a colonial imposition. Historical research shows the development of missions varied according to missionary programs and the response of the Aboriginal peoples. During the early 19th century the Roman Catholic, Anglican, and Methodist churches took up the Hudson's Bay Company invitation to send clergy to serve its employees in the *Red River Settlement. Each church viewed work there as the way to begin missions further to the West.

In 1818 the Roman Catholic bishop of Quebec sent Joseph-Norbert Provencher to Red River. He drew support from French-Canadian and *Metis fur traders, but lacked priests to compete with Anglican initiatives to evangelize the nearby Saulteaux via agricultural villages. After the French Missionary Oblates of Mary Immaculate arrived in the mid-1840s, the Catholics focused on itinerant missions, building a chain of mission posts that stretched from Red River to the Mackenzie. Oblate lay brothers and the *Soeurs Grises from Montreal staffed schools and the sisters began hospitals. Two prominent Oblates, Albert *Lacombe and Bishop Alexandre-Antonin *Taché, were French Canadian, but most of the missionaries came from France. They were *ultramontanists, committed to extending a hierarchical and devotional Roman Catholic Church, but they also believed in making adaptations to Native cultures. Many Cree and Dene responded positively to Oblate projects. Although no Aboriginal men became priests, several Metis women became Grey Nuns. After the treaties of the 1870s and the rebellion of 1885, government plans for reserves and *residential schools complicated missionary efforts. Field missionaries had to become school managers and *Aboriginal languages could not be taught. By the 1900s few Aboriginal children attended residential schools. Some former students, like Assiniboine Daniel Kennedy, challenged school by promoting traditional dance gatherings.

On the Pacific Coast, as in the western interior, French Oblates became the main Catholic missionary group by the 1850s. The Sisters of Saint Ann, who came from Montreal to Victoria in 1858, founded missions, schools, and hospitals and did most of the teaching in Oblate mission schools. Bishop Paul Durieu gained fame for attempts to convert and control the Salishan peoples via a model village system in which itinerant priests were assisted by Aboriginal chiefs, catechists, and watchmen. Continuity of Aboriginal religions, competition from Protestants, and employment opportunities in new industries limited success of the system. So did the federal government requirement for English as the language of residential schools. In the 1900s Oblate initiatives for adult literacy, such as publishing the *Chinook jargon monthly *Kamloops Wawa*, declined.

Anglican missions in the West developed over the same time as the Roman Catholic efforts but differed in organization. The Church Missionary Society sent Reverend John West to Red River in 1820. He and his successors were evangelical preachers convinced that their church was the established church of the British Empire, that the fur trade 'country marriages' were immoral, and that fur traders needed to keep the Sabbath and adopt temperance. West's successors pioneered agricultural missions for Aboriginal peoples. Before he was recalled in 1823 West himself began a school for Aboriginal youth. As a result, some Anglican missions to the Cree, like the Stanley Mission in Saskatchewan, would be staffed by Native ministers. Anglican western missions also benefited from the labours of missionary wives as educators, and at All Hallows School at Yale, British Columbia, from those of an Anglican sisterhood.

The most remarkable aspect of Anglican missions in British Columbia was the career of lay minister William Duncan with the Tsimshian. Arriving at Fort Simpson in 1857, Duncan adapted the Church Missionary Society methods for African missions and began a model industrial Christian village nearby at Metlakatla. In 1887, after conflict with his bishop and the federal government, Duncan moved to Alaska, taking numbers of converts with him. The remaining Tsimshian invited other Christian denominations to send ministers, for example the Methodist Thomas Crosby. Christian Tsimshian also continued their traditional economic and social lives, as shown by the recently discovered diary of Duncan's convert, Arthur Wellington Clah.

The first Methodist missionaries who arrived to compete with Roman Catholics and Anglicans in the 1840s were evangelicals from England and, like the Anglican Church Missionary Society, were interested in preaching, teaching, and temperance. They established posts at Norway House and Edmonton. At Norway House in the 1840s James Evans developed syllabics for writing Cree and translating the Bible. The syllabics were used by Aboriginal prophet movements and other Christian missionaries. By the mid-1850s English Methodist missionaries were replaced by Canadians. They included men experienced in Ojibwa missions and, significantly, some Aboriginal ministers. In 1856 Henry Bird Steinhauer began an Aboriginal agricultural settlement at Whitefish Lake, northeast of Edmonton. Throughout the Methodist missions, women's missionary societies and the wives of missionaries supported educational work.

Although Presbyterians did not send missionaries to the Aboriginals of the West until James Nisbet went to the Cree at Prince Albert in 1866, they made interesting contributions. Like the other Protestant denominations, they benefited from Aboriginal preachers and from the work of women's missionary societies.

The Aboriginal response to Christian missions in Western Canada varied. Some Aboriginals resisted Christianity, some accepted it, some became catechists or ministers. Some, like Clah, participated while continuing their own traditions. JACQUELINE GRESKO

Aboriginal Peoples, Royal Commission on. The RCAP, chaired by Georges Erasmus and René Dussault, issued its five-volume *Report* in 1996. The overriding goal of the report was the escape of Aboriginal peoples from the colonialism inflicted on them by the majority 'settler' society. The constitutional order and the political system it sustained were considered illegitimate. The commissioners' vision of a post-colonial future was based on four fundamental principles that should inform the relations between Aboriginal and non-Aboriginal peoples: mutual recognition, mutual respect, sharing, and mutual responsibility.

The report was a passionate document of Aboriginal nationalism. The first volume, *Looking Forward, Looking Back*, provided an Aboriginal version of Canadian history in which the pre-contact setting of 'separate worlds' is followed by three stages—'contact and co-operation', 'displacement and assimilation', 'negotiation and renewal', the last dating from the defeat of the 1969 *White Paper. This volume functions almost as a 'truth commission', as it takes the reader on a pilgrimage through the 'ghosts' of history, the multiple abuses inflicted on Aboriginal peoples.

The commissioners made a number of key choices that structured the report. Although one-third of the Aboriginal-ancestry population of 1.1 million does not report an Aboriginal identity, the report ignored this group and thus the question of why, when, and how ancestry does not translate into identity. Though Indians, *Inuit, and *Metis were identified as Aboriginal peoples, the overwhelming focus was on (Indian) First Nations. Attention and analysis focused disproportionately on landed communities, although many Aboriginals live in cities. The focus on communities with a land base flowed from the commission's emphasis on 'nation' and its inherent right of self-government; neither 'nation' nor 'self-government' fitted comfortably into urban settings. These preferences implied a higher valuation of cultural survival than economic opportunity. The commission did not see its task as the incorporation of individuals into the Canadian community of citizens, but the incorporation of

Aboriginal nations into a Canada defined as a multinational polity. Finally, the report saw federalism—normally defined as a combination of self-rule and shared rule—almost entirely in terms of the former.

The public response of the federal government was lamentably inadequate. *Gathering Strength: Canada's Action Plan* (1997) ignored the constitutional vision of the report, did not respond to hundreds of recommendations, and did not mention the ambitious and expensive proposal to rebuild communities and establish a new partnership by recommending a massive 20-year 'agenda for change', accompanied by substantial and sustained increases in spending. *Gathering Strength* conveyed regret for past actions, recognized the inappropriateness of assimilation policies, and expressed sorrow for the sexual and physical abuse experienced in *residential schools. The government committed $350 million to facilitate healing. The federal response failed to engage in the public discussion merited by such a massive report and the litany of problems identified. ALAN CAIRNS

Aboriginal political organizations. *See* ASSEMBLY OF FIRST NATIONS.

Aboriginal reserve agriculture. First Nations people of the 19th century were aware that new economic accommodations were required in the face of rapid environmental and demographic changes, and many were interested in the establishment of new economies based on agriculture. For many this was not a new enterprise: some Native North Americans knew a great deal about farming long before the arrival of Europeans. Some areas had been intensively cultivated, and Aboriginal farmers had over centuries devised techniques and technologies as well as varieties of plants well-suited to their specific environments. Iroquoian people such as the *Huron of the Lake Simcoe and Georgian Bay area were primarily farmers, growing corn, beans, and squash. On the Great Plains agriculture was a far more ancient and indigenous tradition than equestrian culture. Prior to European contact, Aboriginal people practised agriculture even in the northerly stretches of the plains. Plains people, and even many of the people of Canada's boreal forest regions, were familiar with Aboriginal agricultural products through trade and travel.

There was potential for a meeting of Aboriginal and non-Aboriginal minds on the issue of agriculture in the 19th century. Euro-Canadians contended that agriculture was the key to the future livelihood of Native people, arguing that, through such work, Aboriginal people would learn the value of private property and a permanent abode, and would enjoy peace and security. A less altruistic advantage was that they would no longer require the amount of land needed to sustain an economy based on hunting and gathering. 'The Indians must farm' became a rallying cry that prevailed when non-Aboriginals sought to acquire Aboriginal land through treaties. Yet, contradicting the belief that Aboriginal people must farm was a conviction, widely shared by Euro-Canadians, that Aboriginal people were incapable of successful farming because it was foreign and distasteful to them. Thus, Aboriginal people and agriculture were seen as incompatible, often despite obvious evidence to the contrary. This was a useful notion to propagate, particularly in the late 19th and early 20th centuries, when Euro-Canadians wanted to diminish the land Native peoples retained as reserves: a people who could not farm, even though they ought to, were in need of even less land. It was a convenient myth in another sense, as economic underdevelopment of reserves could be blamed on the inadequacies of Aboriginal farmers, rather than on government neglect and indifference.

Christian missionaries were the earliest to provide assistance in establishing agricultural economies in Aboriginal communities. Missionaries believed that sedentary agriculture was essential for conversion to Christianity and assimilation to white society. In 1828 the British Indian Department announced that it would take the lead in 'civilizing' the Indians, by encouraging them to settle on reserves and take up agriculture. Native Agriculture received official support from government, but in the older provinces treaties lacked clauses that specifically included agricultural assistance. Aboriginal people welcomed agricultural assistance, although they were less enthusiastic about programs of cultural assimilation. Between 1820 and 1840, the Algonquians of southern Ontario rapidly adopted agriculture, often selling grain to Euro-Canadians.

In the 1850s the 'expansionists' of Canada West, who were determined to acquire the West for Canada, argued that Euro-Canadians had a duty to wean Aboriginal people from their hunting economy and replace this with agriculture and Christianity. Federal government and Crown representatives declared these same intentions at the making of the treaties with the First Nations of western Canada in the 1870s. Aboriginal negotiators insisted that the treaties include clauses that explicitly provided the necessities for a transition to an agricultural economy, including tools, seed, and animals.

Yet, farming failed to form the basis of a viable economy on western reserves. In the crucial 'start-up' post-treaty era, Indian reserve farmers laboured under particular disadvantages. Although their unique relationship with the federal government ought to have assisted them, it ultimately undermined their efforts. Implements and livestock promised under treaty were inadequate and substandard. Aboriginal farmers lacked proper clothing and footwear and were weak because of hunger and illness. Some of the initial obstacles were addressed through the combined efforts of reserve farmers, farm instructors, and *Indian agents, but when Aboriginal farmers in some localities began to make advances by the late 1880s, raising a surplus and acquiring the necessary machinery, non-Aboriginal residents expressed concern about 'unfair' competition in the limited markets. In 1889 the government imposed a 'peasant' farming policy that required Aboriginal farmers to reduce their acreage dramatically and to grow root crops, not wheat. The prohibitions of the *Indian Act also hampered reserve farming. Aboriginal farmers could not expand their land base, take out loans, or transact their own business affairs.

By the turn of the century agriculture did not form the basis of a stable economy on Indian reserves in western Canada. During Wilfrid *Laurier's government (1896–1911), economic viability was further eroded through the 'surrender' of valuable tracts of land on fertile reserves. Small-scale farming by a limited number of residents characterized reserve farming for much of the 20th century. An investigation of conditions in 1966 (*Hawthorn Report) described western farms as marginal or submarginal. Reserve land was leased to non-Aboriginal farmers, and farming had been abandoned on some reserves.

The trend of an initial positive response to farming, but a marked decline in the early years of the 20th century, prevailed in other areas of Canada. Although, by the late 19th century in parts of the Treaty 3 region of Ontario, agriculture was an important component of the Ojibwa economy, this activity had virtually ceased by the early 20th century, due to policies of the Department of Indian Affairs and the construction of hydroelectric projects. In reserves in the British Columbia interior agriculture was a significant part of the economy but efforts were undermined by the continued diminishment of the land base. In recent decades reserve agriculture in the West has expanded somewhat. Settling outstanding treaty land entitlements and land claims will increase land holdings and should enhance agricultural development.

SARAH CARTER

Aboriginal rights. Aboriginal people believe that Aboriginal rights were granted by the Creator and are the contemporary expression of the original sovereignty of Aboriginal peoples and their use and occupation of land before the arrival of Europeans.

In the 1980–2 negotiations that produced the Constitution Act, 1982, section 35 was the major achievement of the Aboriginal organizations and their supporters. Section 35(1) declares that the 'existing aboriginal and treaty rights of the aboriginal peoples of Canada are hereby recognized and affirmed'; section 35(2) states: 'In this Act, "aboriginal peoples of Canada" includes the Indian, Inuit and Metis peoples of Canada'. The recognition and affirmation of 'aboriginal rights', which had, of course, been previously asserted, was a major consolidation of the concept of Aboriginal rights that had received significant judicial support in the 1973 *Calder* case, in which a *Supreme Court of Canada majority recognized Aboriginal title to land (although three judges believed that title had been extinguished).

The constitutionalization of Aboriginal (and treaty) rights was a declaration that the old order of wardship and assimilation had been put to rest. Section 91(24) of the British North America Act, which gave jurisdiction over Indians to the federal government at Confederation, had been an instrument of internal colonialism. Section 35(1) was an instrument of emancipation. It was an anti-colonial, constitutional affirmation of rights, which limited federal (and provincial) authority. Constitutionalization of these rights made them part of the Supreme Law of Canada, and it necessarily followed that Aboriginal peoples possess a positive and distinct constitutional recognition by virtue of being Aboriginal.

Nevertheless, the content of Aboriginal rights—the significance of the adjective 'existing' and the interpretation of 'recognized and affirmed'—remained for future determination. This indeterminacy was underlined by sections 37(1) and (2) of the Constitution Act, which required the convening of a constitutional conference to deal with 'constitutional matters that directly affect the aboriginal peoples of Canada, including the identification and definition of the rights' of Aboriginal peoples. Ultimately, four conferences were held (1983–7) in an unsuccessful attempt to identify and define those rights. The conferences did, however, lead to the Constitution Amendment Proclamation of 1983, which in section 35(3) gave a more comprehensive definition of treaty rights and in section 35(4) guaranteed Aboriginal and treaty rights 'equally to male and female persons'. Although these were significant achievements, the conferences failed to respond to Aboriginal pressure for constitutional recognition of 'the inherent right of self-government'.

The symbolism of this failure was highlighted when federal and provincial first ministers, unwilling to agree to the 'inherent right' because of its claimed ambiguity and incoherence, agreed shortly after the fourth conference to the possibly no less vague concept of the 'distinct society' of Quebec. Aboriginal frustrations at the apparent double standard that was expressed in the 1987 *Meech Lake Accord contributed to the defeat of the accord in 1990; Elijah Harper, a Cree member of the Manitoba legislature, blocked legislative debate in the closing days of the three-year time limit for the accord's ratification.

The 1992 *Charlottetown Accord, which was defeated in a country-wide referendum, proposed entrenching the inherent right of self-government and recognized a distinct Aboriginal third order of government coexisting with the federal and provincial governments. The federal government has itself recognized the inherent right, as did the Royal Commission on *Aboriginal Peoples. Further, a 'substantial majority' of the academic legal community specializing in Aboriginal legal issues asserts that the 'inherent right' is already recognized and affirmed by section 35(1) of the 1982 Constitution Act. Strikingly, however, the Supreme Court has resisted the invitation to assert that the 'inherent right' enjoys constitutional protection under this section. In the absence of the latter, there have been numerous piecemeal moves towards self-government, including the dramatic example of *Nunavut. Sympathetic scholars agree that numerous practicalities require serious attention.

ALAN CAIRNS

Aboriginals and European diseases. Aboriginal groups throughout the Americas experienced profound population loss after contact with Europeans. Depopulation was caused by a number of related factors such as ecological disruption from the importation of new plants and pathogens including diseases; interference in Aboriginal societies by missionaries, traders, and governments; and the imposition of immigrant social organization and land use. Researchers, however, have concentrated almost exclusively on the introduction of new diseases into non-immune Aboriginal communities as the cause for post-contact (after 1492) depopulation.

One view holds that Aboriginal people were uniformly devastated by imported diseases that were carried to them through trade contacts, often prior to actual contact. Thus, recorded populations represented a fraction of once larger communities. The other, gradualist view contends that decline was more prolonged, and occurred after sustained contact and disruption. This debate hinges on the size of pre-contact populations in North America: the collapse theorists estimate from 7 million to 18 million or more; the gradualists from 1 million to 2 million. Evidence for either view is sketchy and extrapolated from very small samples. At root is an assumption that pre-contact Aboriginal people lived in a disease-free environment and thus had little immunological experience with introduced diseases. That position has been challenged recently by new research, but the scope and nature of the evidence is limited. Nevertheless, it promises to extend our understanding of pre-contact Aboriginal communities as dynamic, rather than (as so often presented) idyllic but static.

There is no reason to assume that one depopulation model can describe the history of all Aboriginal groups. The *Beothuk of Newfoundland, for instance, were the first group to encounter Europeans in the late 15th century. Estimates of their pre-contact population range anywhere from 500 to 20,000. By 1829, with the death of a young woman, *Shanawdithit, the Beothuk had vanished. They were hunter-gatherers who relied on both marine and forest ecologies, but with increasing immigration they were forced into the resource-poor interior. Although researchers have assumed that introduced disease caused depopulation, it seems more likely that starvation and isolation caused their tragedy.

Associated with the sudden collapse theory is the argument that epidemic diseases not only caused depopulation but also the death of indigenous cultures and spirituality as gods were abandoned in favour of the Christian deity. However, research on the 17th-century *Huron suggests that many adopted a veneer of Christian conversion in order to wrest economic advantages from colonial authorities. Moreover, despite a series of epidemics that swept through their communities, there is little evidence that the Huron turned to Christianity because it offered them a more satisfying form of afterlife.

On the Prairies in the late 18th and 19th centuries, epidemics of *smallpox, measles, whooping cough, and influenza erupted along trade routes. All groups, the Cree, Assiniboine, and Blackfoot Confederacy, endured *epidemics, but from 1780 to 1840 no group experienced a sustained population decline. In 1823–63 the Cree population in the southern Prairies actually grew through natural increase and immigration. Factors such as disease type, season, population density, previous immunity, and general health and nutrition mitigate the impact of epidemics. After about 1880, however, all groups suffered severe population decline with the destruction of the bison herds and the subsequent loss of food, shelter, and clothing. Treaties with the Canadian government in the 1870s failed to meet basic human needs, and new diseases of poverty and overcrowding, especially *tuberculosis, emerged. The pillars of government policy—Christianity and assimilation—suppressed Aboriginal healers and restrained economic opportunity. Until the 1950s medical care served to confine disease to the reserves, while consistently high death rates were explained as a function of Aboriginal peoples' 'stage of civilization' or their race. MAUREEN K. LUX

Aboriginals in the fur trade. Aboriginal people made the *fur trade possible. Throughout the history of the industry in Canada, they have served as the primary producers of fur, using traditional and modern trapping methods. During the expansionary phase of the fur trade, which began in the late 16th century and continued until the mid-19th century, successive groups of Aboriginal people carried the trading frontier forward, playing the role of intermediaries who obtained furs from their Native trading partners in exchange for trade goods they obtained from Europeans. In sequence, the most important intermediary groups in the land-based fur trade were the Innu (Montagnais-Naskapi), Huron, Assiniboine and Cree, and Chipewyan. On the West Coast, the Nuu-chah-nulth (Nootka) and the Coast Tsimshian of the lower Skeena River served this role for very brief periods.

Once the trading-post frontier passed, and the opportunity to serve in this capacity ceased, Aboriginal men and women established a variety of other relationships with Euro-Canadian fur traders. Groups who settled near trading posts, known as the home guard, often supplemented their hunting and trapping earnings by acting as seasonal and permanent workers for trading companies. They served in a host of capacities, most notably as skilled and unskilled general labourers, crewmen on canoe and boat brigades, and as contract and salaried hunters and fishers. By the mid-19th century, the *Hudson's Bay Company had become dependent on its First Nations and *Metis workforce. Conversely, fur-trade employment also was of increasing importance to the economic lives of these people. This was because fur- and game-depletion problems were widespread in the Canadian North by the late 19th century, which made it difficult even for the best hunters and trappers to sustain themselves in the bush.

ARTHUR J. RAY

See also MARRIAGE 'ACCORDING TO THE CUSTOM OF THE COUNTRY'.

Aboriginal spiritual beliefs. Many early Europeans thought that the Aboriginal people whom they met had no religion. They saw no churches, clerics, scriptures, or Sunday observances that conformed to their notions of religious practice. In turn, some Aboriginal thinkers have argued that 'religion' is a European construct and an inappropriate term for their beliefs and practices. Louis Bird, an Omushkego (Swampy Cree) elder from Hudson Bay, notes that the Cree translation for 'religion', *ayamihawin*, refers to speaking in a group—the missionaries' novel custom of assembling worshippers to read scriptures aloud and sing hymns. Cree traditions, in contrast—like those of many Native peoples across Canada—emphasized individual relationships with spiritual beings who, through dreams or vision fasts, proffered blessings and gifts that often included medicines and teachings to serve the recipient's community. Recipients manifested those gifts through *mitewin*, the Cree term for ritual use of medicine powers. This word is sometimes translated into English as 'shamanism', a word originally referring to Siberian spiritual practices rather different in nature.

Other imported concepts also raise translation problems and have overshadowed the world views embedded in *Aboriginal languages. No Aboriginal cosmos contained a 'hell', so missionaries translated it using terms for fire or an underground place. Clergymen likewise rendered the Ojibwa word *manidoo* (usually translated as 'spirit') as 'Manitou' or 'Gitchi [Great] Manitou' in English, to convey their notion of 'God'. Their deity, however, was male, whereas in Ojibwa, *manidoo* is grammatically animate, as distinguished from inanimate; no sex is specified. These divergent categories, as they cross linguistic boundaries, blur historical differences between Aboriginal and European conceptualizations in the realm of spiritual belief. They also reflect the effects of language displacement upon Native spiritual history: indigenous cosmologies have increasingly been filtered through newly dominant languages in which they lose nuances of meaning, even much of their content.

Generalizations about Native spiritual beliefs are risky. Nonetheless, some themes recur widely. Aboriginal beliefs were spatially focused—on ceremonial places, on rocks or mountains where spirits had made themselves known and where vision-seekers fasted, or on places such as 'Thunderbird nests' of boulders where the great birds had been seen or heard. Yukon elders stressed to Julie Cruikshank the connections—verbal, visual, and material—between places and the names, stories, and memories associated with them. Some places still hold immense spiritual significance for the communities associated with them.

As Osage scholar George Tinker has argued, Native peoples, attuned to spiritual relations focused on places, did not share the linear, progressive concept of time privileged in the Christian calendar. Aboriginal peoples had a distinctive temporal sensibility grounded in the seasons and in annual and daily cycles. Historically, the seasons structured cultural life. Northern Algonquian hunting people told their legends only after snow fell and the waters froze; individuals telling such stories in summer risked penalties from offended spirits. Legends of trickster-transformer figures such as Nanabozho (southern Ojibwa) or his more northern counterpart, Wisahkedjak, contained implicit moral teachings and explained the beginnings of features of the natural and social universe while serving to entertain listeners on long winter nights. Summer, in turn, was the time to gather at major fishing places for socializing and ceremonials, and for sharing news and stories of human interest that would not draw the spirits' attention.

Spiritual beliefs, reinforced by language, found expression in everyday activities. In Algonquian languages, Thunder is animate, construed as a large bird who manifests great power, migrates south in winter, and evokes respectful rituals during thunderstorms. Trees, many plants, animals, tobacco, and pipes are also animate. Travellers offered tobacco to calm stormy waters, and it continues to be smoked in ceremonies and offered in feasts. Good spiritual relations with animals were key to survival: hunters kept the bones of their prey away from the dogs and followed other observances; otherwise the animals would not continue to give themselves. These beliefs and practices endured longest in northern regions, where outside contacts occurred only through the fur trade and still continue in some areas.

Encounters with missionaries presented many challenges for communication and understanding. The first Aboriginal people baptized in Canada were the Mi'kmaq chief *Membertou and his family, in June 1610 at *Port-Royal. The leader of a band of about 100, he already had spiritual and political power. Although he is often described as 'converted', his interpretation of baptism surely differed from that of French Roman Catholics. For him, it doubtless implied alliance, greater prestige, and perhaps an equation with French royalty, as he and his family were given the names of the French king and queen and their children. It did not mean giving up his old beliefs and ties: when he was dying, in 1611, he distressed the *Jesuits by asking to be buried among his 'pagan' relatives rather than in the graveyard consecrated for French Catholics.

Membertou's inclusive attitude towards Christianity was widespread among Aboriginal people. He evidently saw Christian observances as enhancing the spiritual blessings he already had and as offering additional powers and gifts. European clergy, however, took an exclusivist approach. Baptism signified conversion—that is, turning to God and a new life and rejecting the old. Christian proselytizing was foreign to Aboriginal people's understandings of spiritual life and their relationships with the beings who brought help and blessings, and it conflicted with norms against coercing others to change their beliefs and behaviour. Such divergent understandings have recurred through 400 years of Aboriginal–Christian encounters.

As with intruding languages, the spread of Christian missions overshadowed older cosmologies, world views, and moral orders. At worst, governments sought to suppress Aboriginal spiritual practices: the northwest coast *potlatch and other Native ceremonies were outlawed in Canada from the mid-1880s until 1951, under laws enforced arbitrarily and unevenly. Yet many Native people also found help and solace from clergy who tried to ameliorate the dire conditions of their lives. Aboriginal Christians, like others, have ranged from the devout or the 'born-again' to non-observers. Some Native Christians have sought to harmonize their faith with traditional values. For example, the Dr Jessie Saulteaux Resource Centre (Beausejour, Manitoba), in affiliation with the *United Church of Canada, builds spiritual bridges to counter bias and mistrust, and provides culturally grounded pastoral training for workers in Native communities.

Encounters with Christianity have also generated Aboriginal movements that have either assimilated some aspect of the new religion in a novel way or rejected it to seek revivals of traditional belief and practice. Since the 1700s, several prophetic movements offering hope and renewal have swept across various regions of North America. In the early 1800s, the teachings of the Shawnee Prophet (Tenskwatawa) reached from the lower Great Lakes into southern Manitoba; at the end of that century, the Ghost Dance, founded by the Paiute Wovoka in Nevada in 1889, took root among some Dakota Sioux in Saskatchewan. In 1842–3, two Omushkego (Swampy Cree) prophets, Abishabis and Wasitek, became influential across the western Hudson Bay region, combining traditional practices with the use of texts in the Cree syllabic writing system that Methodist missionary James Evans had begun to use for printing hymns and scriptures in the Cree language. The prophets' legacy is mixed; some Hudson Bay Cree credit them rather than the missionaries with bringing Christianity to the region, while others critique their mixing of mitewin and Christian practices for their own ends.

Immensely complex and diverse relationships between Christianity and traditional Aboriginal spiritual practices still endure. Some Aboriginal people respond to poverty and substance abuse by turning to one of the evangelical churches active in many communities. Others maintain or revitalize old spiritual beliefs and practices in diverse ways. Some Native Christians find a place in the churches for pipes, sweet grass, and drumming. Others, reacting to racism, *residential school experiences or other abuses, and repression of language and culture, have rejected Christianity and revived ceremonies such as the sweat lodge, the shaking tent, and the Ojibwa Midewiwin Lodge. Adding to the cross-currents, many mainstream North Americans who used to privilege Christian converts as success stories, now seek Native traditionalists as models and teachers. The credentials of these teachers vary widely; the rise of New Age movements and of pan-Indianism (the search for a common cultural base that all can share and understand) has fuelled the rise of popular practitioners who may satisfy and profit from audience demands but may not convey or maintain the integrity of the deeply diverse spiritual traditions of older generations. This trend is reinforced by the increasing dominance of English in spiritual discourse: about 80 per cent of the approximately 200 Native languages still spoken in North America are almost extinct or are no longer spoken by children. History is being made as people adapt to countless changes and pressures; but it is daily being lost as well.

JENNIFER S.H. BROWN

Aboriginal title and treaty rights. The *Royal Proclamation of 1763 was the milestone in First Nations–European relations in what eventually became Canada. Earlier Aboriginal people tended to have economic and political relationships with European newcomers that were reflected in colonial treaties, many of which were essentially peace and friendship agreements in which Aboriginals obtained trading concessions in return for pledging loyalty to their European allies. By the time of the capitulation of New France in 1760, settlement pressures were causing serious Aboriginal dislocations that reverberated throughout the Northeast. Anticipating possible conflicts with the Thirteen Colonies, the British courted the allegiance of the First Nations with the Royal Proclamation. It reserved as Indian hunting grounds all of the land Aboriginal people had not ceded or sold to the Crown. It effectively created a great Indian reserve lying to the west of the watershed of the Appalachians and outside of Quebec and *Rupert's Land. It prohibited colonization in this vast reserve until the Crown purchased the land at a public assembly of Indians called for that purpose by appropriate government officials.

These basic land-surrender principles were followed in what is now Ontario and throughout the western interior until 1929, though the content of surrender treaties varied over time. On the West Coast, the governor of the Vancouver Island colony, James *Douglas, concluded 14 treaties in 1850–4, which encompassed less than 3 per cent of the island. Thereafter, treaty making ceased in what is now British Columbia, except for the remote northeastern corner of the province that was included in Treaty 8 (1899). Successive colonial and provincial governments have refused to recognize Aboriginal title and denied the applicability of the Royal Proclamation to the province.

This history left unanswered important questions, which became the subject of litigation beginning in the late 19th century and continue to the present. Did the proclamation create Aboriginal title, or merely protect it as an existing right? Did the British government intend the proclamation to apply to 'undiscovered' areas of North America? What is the nature of Aboriginal title on Indian reserve lands in treaty and non-treaty areas? What is the nature of *Aboriginal rights on and off reserves?

Reflecting the political climate of the times, First Nations neither initiated nor participated in the earliest landmark title litigation. The case, *Attorney General of Ontario v. St Catherine's Milling* (1888), arose as a federal–provincial dispute over Indian lands in Ontario. The original provinces retained title to Crown lands at Confederation. However, Aboriginal people had not surrendered the entire area of present-day Ontario by 1867. For example, they did not conclude Treaty 3 with the federal government until 1873. In light of this, federal officials contended that Ottawa had the right to issue forest licences to the St Catherine's Milling Company within the Treaty 3 surrender. The province objected, asserting that it owned the Crown lands in question. It believed the local Ojibwa held only a lesser use and occupancy right at the pleasure of the Crown. The litigation moved rapidly through the Canadian courts and on to the Judicial Committee of the Privy Council (JCPC) in Britain (the ultimate legal authority until 1949). That body declined to define with precision the legal nature of the Indian interest in land, except to cast it as a usufructuary (use) right, reserved by the Royal Proclamation. Although legal wrangling over Indian lands continued in Ontario, British Columbia became the focus of attention for this issue.

Before BC joined Confederation in 1871, its Indian policy involved denying the existence of Aboriginal title and unilaterally creating reserves. Colonial officials determined reserve sizes in terms of the amount of land they thought Aboriginal communities could actually use and occupy. The First Nations never accepted this policy. They petitioned and sent delegations to provincial, federal, and British officials, demanding larger reserves and recognition of their Aboriginal title. The Nisga'a of the Nass River basin and the Gitksan of the Skeena River basin were among the earliest and most persistent claimants. The Nisga'a formed the first land-rights committee in 1907. The federal government ineffectively fought for a more generous reserve policy, but it was not willing to support the First Nations' title aspirations against the province. Hoping at least to end intergovernmental wrangling over reserve issues, the two governments unilaterally created the joint McKenna–McBride Commission (1912–16). Its very creation angered BC's Aboriginal people, infuriated by its decision to reduce the size of many reserves. To fight back, Andrew Paull and the Rev. Peter Kelly helped organize the Allied Tribes of British Columbia, which flatly rejected the commission's findings and petitioned the Canadian Parliament to lay the groundwork that would enable them to take their case to the JCPC. BC politicians resented their actions, and officials at both levels of government feared how the JCPC might rule on the Aboriginal title issue in light of its recent decisions about the question in other parts of the British Empire. Accordingly, Parliament amended the *Indian Act, barring Indians from soliciting money to pursue claims cases without government approval, a notorious ban that remained in effect until 1951. By this time, the *Supreme Court of Canada had become the final arbiter of legal disputes in the country. The stage was set for a resumption of the legal battle over Aboriginal title.

In 1969, the persistent Nisga'a led the attack in *Calder et al. v. Attorney-General of British Columbia*, declaring that their title still existed. The province denied this assertion partly on the contention that the Royal Proclamation did not apply to BC. On appeal, in 1973 six of the seven presiding Supreme Court judges (one abstained) ruled that the Nisga'a had held an Aboriginal title when colonization began. Three of them also concluded that Aboriginal title had not been extinguished subsequently. This split decision convinced the Trudeau government that Aboriginal title probably survived in territories that had not been surrendered through *Indian treaties. The government established a claims process in 1974 to lay the groundwork for future land-claims settlements. It intended that the system would also address disputes arising over the interpretations and/or implementation of historic treaties. The government recognized two types of claims: comprehensive claims refer to nations' or bands' overall land claim, including title, resource rights, and self-government assertions; specific claims relate to cut-offs (lands removed from reserves) or unfulfilled treaty promises related to reserve land.

In 1987 the Gitksan and Wet'suwet'en filed the first post-*Calder* title suit. Although they failed at trial (*Delgamuukw v. the Queen*, 1991), they achieved a landmark victory on appeal when in 1997 the Supreme Court of Canada ruled the trial judge had not given sufficient weight to their oral evidence and ordered a new trial. To establish guidelines for future title litigation, the court held that blanket extinguishment of Aboriginal title had not taken place in BC. Finally, it defined the nature of Aboriginal title for the first time, characterizing it as a unique right that was blended into the common law at sovereignty. Aboriginal title is an exclusive right of occupation—an interest in the land itself—that is a burden on the Crown's title. It has to be surrendered according to the principles of the Royal Proclamation.

Well before *Delgamuukw* the federal government moved to address outstanding title issues in other non-treaty areas. The first attempt, in Quebec, resulted in the James Bay and Northern Quebec Agreement (1975) with the Cree and Inuit. Other northern Aboriginal groups demanded settlements, too, including the Dene, who were led by Georges Erasmus and issued the Dene Declaration in 1975, and the Inuit. The federal government concluded additional agreements in 1984–92, encompassing the central and western Arctic and Yukon areas. In British Columbia, fears about the likely outcome of the *Delgamuukw* litigation led successive provincial governments to seek land-claims settlements through the BC Treaty Commission, established in 1991. The failure of this process to yield timely results led the government to put the treaty issue to a controversial treaty referendum in 2002. The Nisga'a, meanwhile, had been pursuing their claim outside of the commission. In 1998 they signed the first comprehensive settlement in BC. Two years later, the McLeod Lake Sekani resolved their claim by joining Treaty 8, a treaty their ancestors had failed to sign. In this respect they were similar to the Lubicon Cree, who live in the Treaty 8 area of northern Alberta. These Cree have waged a Herculean struggle for a settlement.

Aboriginal title is the right to land itself. There are other types of rights, however, most notably the entitlement to continue traditional practices on and off reserves. Rights litigation has addressed a multifaceted central question. What practices survived until 1982 and deserve protection according to the terms of section 35(1) of the Canadian constitution, which entrenched Aboriginal and treaty rights then in existence? Most legal challenges have focused on traditional economic rights. As with title claims, BC has been the primary battleground and the place from which most precedent-setting appeals have originated. Many of them relate to fishing. In *R. v. Sparrow* (1990) regarding west coast salmon-fishing rights, the Supreme Court of Canada established two key rules. First, it held that Aboriginal rights were abrogated by legislation only when it was the clear and plain intention of legislators to do so. Legislation could curtail Aboriginal rights, but the infringement had to be justified. The court noted specifically that conservation was an example of a justified limitation. Second, it decided Aboriginal practices can be affirmed in a contemporary form rather than merely as they existed at first contact with Europeans. Six years later, in another fishing case, *R. v. Van der Peet*, concerning the Fraser Valley Sto:lo, the court elaborated on this notion by developing the 'doctrine of continuity', which says that contemporary customs are eligible for legal protection if they can be linked to pre-contact practices. It also established the principle that to be an Aboriginal right an activity must have been integral to the distinctive culture of the Aboriginal group claiming the right. Before *Sparrow* and *Van der Peet*, it was commonly believed that Aboriginal practices that had been modified through interaction with Europeans were ineligible for protection.

Undoubtedly the most controversial Aboriginal rights issue concerns the question of whether Native people have commercial harvesting rights. In *Van der Peet* the court concluded the Sto:lo had not proved their ancestors had fished commercially. In the same year, however, it ruled in *R. v. Gladstone* (1996) that the central coast Heiltsuk have a 'limited commercial right' to sell herring-roe-on-kelp in light of their ancestors' economic practices.

Commercial-rights concerns also have been central to treaty-rights proceedings beginning with *R. v. Horseman* (1990), which concerned the Treaty 8 Cree of Alberta. This is because 19th-century treaties affecting central and western Canada promised Indians the right to continue their existing livelihoods on undeveloped Crown land. By the time treaties were signed, most Natives had been engaged in commercial harvesting for the fur trade for one or more centuries. In eastern Canada, on the other hand, colonial peace and friendship treaties often contained trading concessions, such as those found in British–Mi'kmaq treaties concluded in 1760–1. In one of its most contentious decisions to date, the Supreme Court held in *R. v. Marshall* (1991) that these treaties demonstrated that the British recognized the *Mi'kmaq had a right to harvest fish and wildlife for commercial purposes. Accordingly, the court ruled they still have a right to earn a modest livelihood from fishing.

Another crucial question in treaty-rights cases concerns the matter of interpretation. Before the early 1980s, the courts relied almost exclusively on written texts. The two operating assumptions were that the Crown's negotiators had always acted honourably and generously towards Aboriginal people and had made sure the latter understood the terms. Subsequently, the Supreme Court developed two new interpretation principles in a series of rulings, most notably *Simon v. R.* (1985), *R. v. Sioui* (1990), *R v. Badger* (1996), and *R. v. Sundown* (1999). These were the notions that treaties and statutes relating to Indians should be liberally construed, resolving uncertainties in their favour, and that treaty rights, similar to Aboriginal rights, can exist in a modern form rather than being frozen in time. This means that courts now have to consider treaties in their historical context in order to understand what the various parties intended.

Another key issue that treaty rights cases have raised regarding Indians' use of off-reserve lands for ceremonial and/or subsistence purposes arises from section 88 of the Indian Act, which states that Indians are subject to all laws of general applicability except when they conflict with the terms of any treaty. Two important cases that addressed this issue were *R. v. White and Bob* (1964), concerning the Douglas Treaties in British Columbia, and *R. v. Sundown* (1999), which involved the Cree of the Treaty 6 area of Saskatchewan.

One more group of treaty claims allege that the federal government failed to discharge its fiduciary obligations arising from treaties and/or the British North America Act. Many of these claims focus on the alienation of reserve lands and the management of First Nations' assets.

ARTHUR J. RAY

See also INDIAN TREATIES.

Aboriginal warfare. Although indigenous people normally valued peace over hostilities, warfare was a part of life among the First Nations long before contact with Europeans. Their motivations for fighting varied through time and across regions, but important issues included securing lands and resources from competing peoples, fulfilling spiritual imperatives, affirming masculinity and honour, avenging deaths, and capturing prisoners who might be adopted as full members of a community or turned into slaves or sacrificed during religious ceremonies.

Influenced by novelists, the media, and earlier generations of academics, popular culture often embraces lurid notions of 'Indian massacres' and other horrors in North American history. While torture, scalping, and the murder of non-combatants did mark conflict among the First Nations and between Natives and newcomers, these practices should be understood within their cultural contexts and the brutalities experienced by Aboriginal peoples at the hands of others. An example of the first is scalping. Scalps often were 'adopted' into a victor's community to strengthen its spiritual powers, and some Natives thought scalping exalted their own dead: in 1766 Ojibwa complained to Alexander Henry when their Sioux enemies did not scalp their fallen, remarking that 'we consider it an honour, to have the scalps of our countrymen exhibited in the villages of our enemies, in testimony of our valour'. An instance of the cruelties suffered at the hands of whites occurred in the Ohio country in 1782, when American revolutionaries butchered 96 pacifist Moravian Delawares kneeling in prayer in their church at Gnadenhutten. Refugees from that atrocity moved to Canada, but US soldiers burned them and their descendants out of their new village in 1813.

There were five main commonalities in Native warfare during the great struggles for control of eastern North America between the 17th century and the end of the War of 1812. First, Aboriginal nations formed pacts with other tribes and with white powers to fulfill their own interests; they did not act as pawns of the French, British, or Americans, who often misinterpreted Aboriginal behaviour and branded Native allies as untrustworthy. Second, Aboriginal societies generally granted individuals considerable freedom to dissent from community decisions; thus people could limit their commitment to the military stance taken by their village or nation, even to the point of maintaining relationships with an enemy. Third, Native warfare changed with the introduction of European weapons and the modification of their own arms (such as the replacement of stone arrow points with metal). These innovations made combat deadlier—it took less physical energy to inflict more grievous damage. Rather than adopt white tactics along with the new technology, however, Native combat evolved within an indigenous tradition that emphasized the achievement of objectives with minimum casualties through ambush, raids, and similar techniques. Fourth, Aboriginal warriors fought under their own leaders. Finally, they wore distinctive dress that affirmed each combatant's place within his culture's traditions.

These commonalties began to break up in the East by the time of the *Rebellions of 1837. When Natives turned out (generally in support of the government) it was under their own leaders, but they were dressed and equipped much like their non-Aboriginal neighbours. Thereafter, men tended to fulfill their martial ambitions within the ranks of the Canadian military. In the West, the old ways survived for several more decades, although combat there had been affected by the introduction of horses in the 1600s and new technologies in the 1700s. An example of this East–West split occurred in the 1880s: many tribespeople on the Prairies allied themselves to the *Metis and fought government troops in the *North-West Rebellion, while, far to the east, a significant proportion of the Canadian boatmen who sailed up the Nile in the imperial adventure to relieve Khartoum were Natives from Ontario and Quebec.

Aboriginal people participated in large numbers during modern conflicts. In the Great War, 4,000 volunteered, representing 35 per cent of Aboriginal men of military age. They fought well, and the greatest sniper on the Western Front was Corporal Francis Pegahmagabow, an Ojibwa from Parry Island. At home, Aboriginal people engaged in war work and supported patriotic causes. The Second World War saw a repeat of the contributions of 1914–18, with 6,000 Native men and women enlisting. One, Milton Martin from Six Nations, rose to the rank of brigadier-general. Indigenous people continued to serve in the armed forces after 1945. Yet, in 1990 Kanesatake and Kahnawake Mohawk found themselves in a standoff with the Canadian army in a sad incident that, however, contributed to the formation of the Royal Commission on *Aboriginal Peoples.

Despite their involvement in the world wars, government treated Aboriginal veterans less generously than others, and on occasion seized reserve lands for military purposes against the wishes of their residents. Returning Native soldiers often sought changes that sometimes created conflict at home, such as occurred when Ottawa imposed an elective council on the Six Nations in 1924, justifying this unpopular measure in part on support from veterans within the community. Conversely, Natives who experienced fundamental equality while in uniform often led demands for reform in Canadian–First Nations affairs to undo the discrimination of the colonialist relationship. In spite of the prejudice Native veterans experienced in modern times and the dominant society's misunderstanding of Aboriginal warfare in earlier days, the indigenous military heritage is a proud one that contributes to the distinct identity of today's First Nations communities across Canada. CARL BENN

abortion. As many as 7–10 per cent of all pregnancies end in miscarriage or 'spontaneous' abortion, a natural form of *birth control. In addition some women, for various reasons, actively choose to terminate pregnancy. Until the late 20th century, society's disapproval of unwed motherhood led desperate women to turn to violent exercise, hot baths, douches, ergot, and easily available patent medicines. If these measures failed, they and the married women who could not afford another child turned to invasive methods such as slippery elm, knitting needles, or crochet hooks. Those with the funds turned to the infamous 'backroom' abortionists because regular doctors generally did not perform this operation.

Most British North American colonies criminalized abortion, and the procedure was labelled unethical by the *Canadian Medical Association after its formation in 1867. From the 1880s to the 1930s, the Protestant and Roman Catholic churches equated abortion with 'race suicide'. In 1892 section 179 of the Criminal Code was amended to prohibit the sale or advertisement of drugs or articles 'intended or represented as a means of preventing conception or causing abortion'.

The conflict between the goals of the legal/judicial system and the needs of Canadian women for reliable and effective fertility control contributed to a significant amount of suffering and death. Statistics from British Columbia and Ontario from the 1920s to the 1950s suggest that approximately 30 per cent of maternal deaths resulted from mishandled abortions. As hospital births and pre- and post-natal care became more common, reformers in the medical profession, the legal profession, and second-wave *feminists began to press the federal government to alter the law. In 1969 the Trudeau government repealed section 179 and replaced it with regulations governing access through hospital-based therapeutic abortion committees.

Dr Henry Morgentaler, an Auschwitz survivor and former general practitioner, became the champion of women who were unable to access abortion at local *hospitals, opening his first free-standing clinic in Montreal in 1969. Arrested in 1973 and acquitted by a jury, Morgentaler was jailed for 10 months in 1974 after the acquittal was overturned. Feminists from across Canada organized an Abortion Caravan to take the pro-choice message to Ottawa in 1974, and after his release Morgentaler opened clinics in other provinces to challenge their limited services. He was charged in Ontario in 1983 but in 1988 the *Supreme Court of Canada ruled 5–2 that hospital abortion committees were 'arbitrary, demeaning and potentially injurious'. The result has been continuing provincial differences in access and cost for a medically necessary procedure. HEATHER MacDOUGALL

academic freedom. Sometimes used to describe the autonomy that *universities should enjoy in running their internal affairs, academic freedom is more commonly applied to the freedom of professors to teach, do research, and publish; to address issues publicly without fear of institutional sanctions; and to criticize and help determine the policies of the universities in which they work. In Canada these freedoms have been gradually gained and expanded since the early 19th century.

The Canadian Association of University Teachers (CAUT), founded in 1951, holds that 'the common good depends upon the search for truth and its free exposition. Academic freedom is essential to these purposes'. Attempts to extend the concept to students have met with limited success, as have demands for academic freedom in primary and secondary education.

Major threats to academic freedom include tendencies among administrators, professors, and students to impose conformity and encourage self-censorship. The power of the purse contains a potent threat. Provincial governments, private benefactors, and the grantors of research funding have all tried at times to limit or suppress academic freedom. Executive heads and governing boards have transmitted such pressure to professors. The role of the media has been ambivalent. Usually supportive of academic freedom, they have often been hostile to its exercise in times of perceived crisis or on contentious issues.

Major incidents in the history of academic freedom in Canada include the dismissals of Salem *Bland from Wesley College, Winnipeg, in 1917; King Gordon from United Theological College, Montreal, in 1933; George Hunter from the University of Alberta in 1949; Harry Crowe from United College, Winnipeg, in 1958; and eight social scientists from Simon Fraser University in 1969. Perhaps better known than any of these is the attempted dismissal of Frank *Underhill from the University of Toronto in 1941. The Crowe affair led the CAUT to undertake its first inquiry and hastened the adoption of a statement on academic freedom and tenure. Since 1960, the CAUT's Academic Freedom and Tenure Committee has investigated and helped resolve many disputes. The CAUT's ultimate sanction is to impose censure, urging faculty members not to take employment at the censured institution.

Recent controversies have centred on 'political correctness' and research funding. Some universities, hoping to foster inclusiveness, have adopted speech codes proscribing the use of language deemed to be racist, sexist, or homophobic. Critics assert that this encourages censorship. Probably a more potent threat to academic freedom is the increasing dependence on private research funds, particularly in medicine, and the restrictions this may impose on the openness of research.

MICHIEL HORN

Acadia. Acadia got its name in 1524–5 from Italian explorer Giovanni da Verrazzano while he was mapping the Atlantic coast of North America for France. He named the region of present-day Delaware 'Arcadia' because its natural beauty evoked the Arcadia of ancient Greece. In the early 17th century 'Acadie' was claimed by the French, who established a trading post on St Croix Island in 1604. In 1605 the French crossed the Bay of Fundy and established a new settlement at *Port-Royal in what is now southwestern Nova Scotia. For most of the 17th century, Acadie designated the region of present-day Maine, the Maritime provinces, and the Gaspé Peninsula.

According to historian John G. Reid, Acadia was a marginal colony in the 17th century, less populated and in a more precarious state than the neighbouring English colonies of New England and the French settlements of the St Lawrence Valley. The first permanent French settlers arrived in Acadia in the 1630s. These settlers, who possibly originated from central-western France, transformed Port-Royal from a trading post to a prosperous, albeit small, agricultural settlement. These pioneering French families—among them, the Comeaus, Landrys, LeBlancs, and Thibodeaus—perfected a system of dykes called *aboiteaux* to reclaim the rich marshlands, thus ensuring the settlers' prosperity up to the expulsion of 1755. The ingenious *aboiteaux* system allowed the water from the salt marshes to be drained while at the same time preventing salt water from the high tides of the Bay of Fundy from inundating the fields. Other activities such as fishing and hunting complemented an agriculturally based colonial economy that was enhanced by friendly relations with the *Mi'kmaq and Abenaki First Nations. Leading Acadians, such as the Saint-Étienne de La Tour, Le Borgne de Belle-Isle, and Saint-Castin families, had close family ties with the Mi'kmaq and the Abenaki that helped cement a strong friendship between the two groups.

By the end of the 17th century, the children and grandchildren of the initial French settlers had become Acadians, a community of about 1,000 French-speaking and Roman Catholic yeomen farmers who had founded villages such as *Beaubassin on the Isthmus of Chignecto as well as *Grand-Pré, Pigiguit, and Cobequid in the Minas Basin region. Living in a colony strategically bordering New France and New England, the Acadians adopted an accommodating interpretation of allegiance to the English and French Crowns. This practice of political accommodation was rendered necessary in light of the numerous attacks launched by New England on its weaker French colonial neighbour. During the 17th century Port-Royal was attacked seven times by English raiders and soldiers. These attacks, however, did not hamper the important trading ties. Because France rarely sent supply ships to Acadie, Acadians turned to the New England traders for manufactured goods and more exotic products such as rum and molasses imported from the West Indies.

English troops put an end to French colonial rule in Acadia in 1710 with the *conquest of Port-Royal. By the Treaty of Utrecht of 1713, France ceded Acadia, Newfoundland, and Hudson Bay to the British Crown. Acadia became Nova Scotia and Port-Royal became Annapolis Royal, renamed to honour Queen Anne. France kept control of the neighbouring islands of *Île Royale—where it erected the fortified seaport of *Louisbourg—and Île St-Jean (now Prince Edward Island). Given the opportunity of removing themselves to these French possessions or remaining in Nova Scotia and becoming British subjects, the vast majority of Acadians chose the latter. Their leaders, known as deputies, devised a policy of neutrality whereby the Acadians would swear a conditional *oath of allegiance to the British monarch that would allow them to remain neutral in time of war between the French and the British or the British and the Mi'kmaq. Those who took the oath maintained the full possession of their lands and the free practice of their Roman Catholic faith. By the 1730s, British colonial authorities of Nova Scotia grudgingly tolerated these *French Neutrals, as they were called, since the British were greatly outnumbered and had no real military means of imposing an unconditional oath of allegiance. For the Acadians, the 1730s would be remembered as a time of relative peace and prosperity, a period that historian Naomi Griffiths characterized as their 'golden age'. Their numbers greatly increased; in the late 1730s there were 5,000–6,000 Acadians in Nova Scotia, and they were spreading increasingly into what is now southeastern New Brunswick. They traded their agricultural surplus with Louisbourg merchants, who were always in need of food to supply the port's local market.

This so-called golden age was short-lived. The 1740s was a decade of turmoil for Acadian villagers, who from 1744 to 1748 experienced many failed attempts by Franco-Canadian troops to reconquer Nova Scotia, including the ill-fated Duvivier expedition of 1744 and the Marin de La Malgue expedition of 1745. Each time, the vast majority of Acadians, even as they were pressed and threatened by French military officers, refused to take up arms against the British. Many French Roman Catholic missionaries strongly advised Acadians to remain neutral. However, a few of these priests, especially the notorious Abbé Jean-Louis *Le Loutre, urged Acadians to express their loyalty to the French Crown by resettling in regions still controlled by France. The establishment of Halifax in 1749 as a British counterweight to Louisbourg was a clear signal for Le Loutre and for many Acadians that it was time to leave Nova Scotia. By the early 1750s hundreds of Acadians had resettled on Île St-Jean and even more sought refuge near the newly built small French fort of Beauséjour.

Tensions between French and British military interests in Acadia were exacerbated by events taking place elsewhere in North America, as in the Ohio Valley, where in July 1755 English general Edward Braddock suffered a major defeat at Fort Duquesne at the hands of a combined French-Canadian and Native military force. Later that summer, Lieutenant-Governor Charles Lawrence of Nova Scotia, with the approval of Governor William Shirley of Massachusetts, devised a radical plan that would free his province of the 'Acadian problem'. In the summer of that year, the legislative council of Nova Scotia, in a period of official peace between France and Britain, ordered the removal of the Acadians, who were to be dispersed throughout the Anglo-American colonies of the Atlantic seaboard. The deportations lasted from 1755 to 1763. The majority of the estimated 16,000 Acadians were expelled, their lands confiscated in the name of the British Crown, their houses, churches, and villages burned by English soldiers and militiamen from New England. Several thousand Acadians fled into the woods or sought refuge in the St Lawrence Valley. Thousands died during these horrific years, either from starvation, sickness, or drowning, or by being killed. The **Grand dérangement* radically transformed Acadian life, society, and identity, and is remembered to this day by Acadians.

MAURICE BASQUE

Acadian civil war, 1640–5. Although the term 'civil war' may seem overblown when applied to events in *Acadia during the early 1640s, the intermittent hostilities between small forces deployed by Charles de Saint-Étienne de La Tour and Charles de Menou d'Aulnay Charnisay reveal much about the fragility of early colonization, and the relationship between colonization and trade. La Tour and d'Aulnay had emerged as leading colonial promoters in Acadia by the mid-1630s. They had to negotiate effectively with state officials and merchant associates to obtain the authority and the capital to establish colonies, and then recruit settlers and persuade Native leaders to tolerate the colonial presence. These tasks accomplished, the promoter could enjoy the profits of trade and the prestige of colonial leadership—or so the theory went. More often, they died frustrated and impoverished.

La Tour's father had risen from an obscure background to become a merchant and sea captain. Charles had lived in Acadia since 1610, surviving lean times through fur trading and emerging as the leader of the tiny colony in 1623. By contrast, the aristocratic d'Aulnay first came to Acadia in 1632 with an elite group led by Isaac de Razilly as royal lieutenant-general in New France. When Razilly died in 1636, d'Aulnay inherited his role and aspired to control all Acadia and its trade. La Tour held a commission as governor dated 1631, but d'Aulnay considered it to have been superseded.

For all their differences, d'Aulnay and La Tour had similar ambitions. La Tour had commercial links with the powerful Compagnie de la Nouvelle-France. With its help, he recruited colonists for his settlements, at Cape Sable and in prime fur-trading territory at the mouth of the Saint John River. The main settlement controlled by d'Aulnay was *Port-Royal, for which he gathered colonists from his family estates in Poitou, but in 1635 he also seized a New England fur-trading outpost at Pentagoet (on the Penobscot River). Commercial rivalry between the two men intensified after the French Crown made an ill-judged effort in 1638 to divide Acadia between them, attributing to each the title of lieutenant-general in half of the colony. Active hostilities began with a naval skirmish off Port-Royal in 1640. Over the next five years, the La Tour–d'Aulnay conflict was waged on two fronts. In paper warfare at the French court, the better-connected d'Aulnay was the winner by early 1641, when he received royal authority to seize La Tour and embargo his shipping. In the sporadic violence in Acadia itself, La Tour continued to hold his own through the unorthodox measure of obtaining supplies from New England. In 1643, he used Massachusetts mercenaries in a narrowly unsuccessful assault on Port-Royal. The end came in 1645. With La Tour absent in Boston and the Saint John fort commanded by his wife Françoise Jacquelin, d'Aulnay attacked in force. The fort surrendered after a bitter fight, whereupon d'Aulnay had the defenders hanged. Jacquelin was spared, but died soon after.

There were ironic sequels. D'Aulnay, deeply indebted from his colonizing endeavours, drowned accidentally five years later. La Tour married d'Aulnay's widow and set up again as governor of Acadia, only to be displaced by an English raid in 1654. He lived out his life at Cape Sable under loose English rule. In historical perspective, the civil war demonstrates clearly that the expensive business of promoting colonization in Acadia could be accomplished only through establishing control over trading profits. In this regard, the aspirations of La Tour and d'Aulnay were too similar to allow either to tolerate the competing activities of the other. JOHN G. REID

Acadian commercial relations. From its early days the economy of *Acadia was characterized by its openness to the outside world. Remoteness from Europe and lack of support and supervision from the French metropolitan government left the inhabitants a good deal of freedom, but for a population in need of goods they could not obtain from the mother country there were also great hardships. Manufactured products such as fabrics and iron implements and consumer goods like tobacco, sugar, and rum were obtained from Massachusetts. Merchants and traders from the Puritan colony, some of whom had warehouses in Acadia, delivered supplies northward. A number of Acadians and French colonial administrators were also engaged in this trade, sending south a surplus of fish, furs, and grains. The Acadian domestic economy, despite a ban on intercolonial trade, depended on external trade for its survival.

Conditions were highly favourable for the development of these trading connections. Acting as intermediaries for New England merchants, as message bearers for French officials, or as representatives arranging prisoner exchanges, the Acadians bypassed the trade restrictions of both France and England. Despite the risks, they succeeded in becoming part of the economic fabric of the time, as the activities of such men as Pierre Dubreuil, Louis Allain, and Jean Saint-Aubin suggest. These commercial ties, based on the barter system, constituted a mutual accommodation. Whenever French policy went against the economic interests of the merchants and fishers of Massachusetts, retaliation followed. While the economic activities demonstrated Acadian pragmatism and economic shrewdness, they also revealed the colony's vulnerability to outside events and decisions. The economic control of Massachusetts over the Bay of Fundy in the 17th century constitutes one of the themes of the history of Acadia. JEAN DAIGLE

Acadian deportation. The region designated in international treaties as 'Acadia or Nova Scotia' between 1621 and 1763 formed a splayed-out triangle between the northeastern edge of British colonial settlement in North America and the southeastern thrust of French colonial development. Europeans who settled there were known, by the late 17th century, as Acadians. Their political lives were essentially those of a border people and they were governed in the 17th century mostly by France but sometimes by England. In 1713 the centre of the Acadian lands, the peninsula of Nova Scotia, was awarded to Great Britain. Over the next few decades the Franco-British struggle for dominance intensified. In 1755 peace between these powers had not been formally ended but both were preparing for battle and were manoeuvring for advantage in the coming struggle. The previous year had seen bitter skirmishes in the Ohio Valley, and the government of Massachusetts as much as that of Nova Scotia was fearful of a French attack on the latter. Although Nova Scotia had been governed by the British for the last 42 years the majority of the population remained the Acadians, whose preferred language was still French and who had remained Roman Catholic. After 1730 they were often called the 'neutral French' because they had sworn allegiance to Great Britain only on the understanding that they would not be asked to bear arms against either the French or the Mi'kmaq.

After the Treaty of Aix-la-Chapelle in 1748 Acadian loyalty to Great Britain became a matter of major importance for both British and French forces. Settlement of the boundary between Nova Scotia and territory claimed by France had been left to an international commission but both empires sought to strengthen their position along the Chignecto isthmus, the narrow neck of land separating the head of the Bay of Fundy from the Northumberland Strait. France built a major fort at Beauséjour on one side of the Missaguash River, and Britain Fort Lawrence on the opposite bank. Both sides refused to give credence to the Acadian assertion of neutrality, although during the four years of fighting, 1744–8, the majority of Acadians had not taken up arms for either combatant. As a whole, the Acadians gave no important aid to the French, but both sides believed that Acadian men capable of bearing arms, estimated at somewhere between 5,000 and 6,000, could be a crucial source of strength to whomever could persuade them to fight. Further, there was a growing opinion among the British administrators of Nova Scotia, mostly military men, that anything less than whole-hearted military support for British interests was treason.

In 1755 a mixed force of 300 British regulars and 2,500 colonial troops from Massachusetts attacked and captured Beauséjour. Some 200 young Acadian men were found among its 500 defenders. In July of that year, Lieutenant-Governor Charles Lawrence and the Nova Scotia council decided to deport the whole of the Acadian population then living on lands claimed by Great Britain, sending them to the other British colonies in North America. Approximately 7,000 people in 1755 and a further 3,000–5,000 over the next eight years were embarked for varying destinations. The sea voyages were no more lethal than the norm for 18th-century journeys by ship, but this meant that the Acadians endured a mortality rate in the region of 30 per cent of those embarked. Another 20–30 per cent of the exiles died at their destination, where they succumbed to diseases such as typhoid and smallpox. Those who escaped deportation took refuge mostly along the river banks of the Saint John and the Miramichi, where cold and hunger killed many. A few survived as essentially prisoners of war within Nova Scotia. In 1764, when the proscription ended and the Acadians were granted the right to live once more in Nova Scotia, there were only 1,000 reported by the census. By 1800, that number had grown to over 8,000 in Nova Scotia alone and others had re-established an Acadian presence in New Brunswick and Prince Edward Island. A significant part of this population were Acadians who had returned from exile through their own courageous efforts. Lawrence had hoped that the deportation would see an end to a separate Acadian society. His hopes proved to be in vain.

N.E.S. GRIFFITHS

Acadian renaissance. The Acadian renaissance is associated with the rise of French-Canadian nationalism during the last decades of the 19th century, when francophone communities within the Maritime provinces began the process of adjusting to the still expanding Canadian context. This adjustment required that Acadians not only affirm—indeed, reaffirm—their collective identity, but that they also define themselves in relation to other groups with which they had some affinities, be they cultural, as in the case of Quebec, or geographic, political, and economic, as in the case of the Maritimes and Canada. Throughout this process, a number of conflicts were played out, some of these within the political realm; the New Brunswick Common Schools Act (1871) provides a case in point. The political context within which conflicts and accommodations were worked out is central to our understanding of the process of change. Thus, the Acadian renaissance can best be understood by examining the role cultural communities expected their own leaders and the state to play in supporting and nurturing identities.

Historians agree that the process of defining the basis of Acadian nationalism was undertaken by a minority of Acadians. The timing of this phase coincides with the emergence of an Acadian-born elite, comprising priests and members of the new liberal professions. These men took upon themselves the role of defining the Acadian renaissance, and they awakened Maritime francophones to the elite's own concept of nationhood.

These new leaders were educated at Acadian classical colleges. The Collège St-Joseph was founded in 1864 at Memramcook, in southeastern New Brunswick, by father Camille Lefebvre. This bilingual institution was soon followed by others: the Collège St-Louis (1877) and the Collège Ste-Anne (1890) in Nova Scotia, and in New Brunswick the Collège du Sacré-Coeur (1899) in Caraquet and the Collège St-Louis-Maillet (1946) in Edmundston. Men's classical colleges shared the common goals of providing academic training required for both secular and religious professions as well as the proper context for transmitting ideals consistent with the emerging Acadian national ideology. Women's colleges, also established at this time, provided for only two professions: religious service as Catholic sisters or domestic service (within marriage) and motherhood.

The process by which the new Acadian elite defined a distinct, collective, and essentially cultural identity is perhaps best illustrated by the symbols they adopted. These symbols were selected during national conventions held periodically from 1881 to 1927 under the auspices of the Société nationale l'Assomption. The first of these, which took place in Memramcook, debated the matter of a national (religious) holiday. Delegate support for either St-Jean-Baptiste (24 June) or the Assumption (15 August) holidays was strong. The debate was presented as a choice between the promotion of close ties and connections to French-Canadian (Québécois) nationalism through the adoption of the St-Jean-Baptiste holiday, or the promotion of a distinct, Acadian national strategy. The delegates' selection of the national holiday celebrating the ascension of the mother of Christ established the trend towards distinct national symbols, signalling the promotion of national feeling distinct from that of the rest of French Canada. At the second national convention, held in 1884 at Miscouche, Prince Edward Island, delegates supported the design of an Acadian national flag, the French tricolour blue, white, and red, adding in the upper left-hand corner a yellow papal star to symbolize Acadians' loyalty to the Catholic Church. Delegates also chose a national hymn, 'Ave Maris Stella', in recognition of Acadians' close religious attachment to the Virgin Mary.

National conventions served purposes beyond grounding the renaissance in symbolism and providing a public forum for aspiring members of the new elite. Delegates discussed themes defined beforehand, and these provided the framework for the strategies they promoted as the basis for Acadian collective survival. The Catholic Church, French-language education, and agriculture and colonization (seen as both the means of arresting the exodus of Acadians from the region and as a tool for ensuring their economic independence from Anglo-Protestant capital and the industrial, urban milieu) were first among the themes debated. The Société nationale l'Assomption, established in 1881, provided the leadership and continuity required to define the ideology of the Acadian renaissance and constituted a most effective tool for the promotion of national strategy and policy.

Demographic shifts within the Acadian population of the Maritimes occurred during the several decades following Confederation. The population grew most rapidly in New Brunswick: between 1861 and 1941 their representation increased from 16 to 35.8 per cent of the total population; by 1961 that province was home to 69 per cent of all Acadians in the region. This shift led to a corresponding adjustment to nationalist strategy, now concentrating primarily on issues relevant to New Brunswick Acadians. As Acadians' numbers and political weight grew, strategies were aimed more towards co-operation than confrontation, seeking support from local Acadian communities and the provincial government as logical partners in the process of resolving outstanding issues between cultural communities. Acadian collective strategy and, indeed, Acadian identity itself were being fragmented and redefined by provincial boundaries.

These transformations led directly to what some historians have called a second Acadian renaissance, generally dating around the time of Louis *Robichaud's election as premier of New Brunswick in 1960. This second renaissance was more political in nature than the first, leading to the creation of an Acadian political party, the Parti acadien, which called for the division of the province into two distinct territories reflecting its cultural makeup.

PHYLLIS E. LeBLANC

Acadie l'Acadie?!? L'. This 1971 *National Film Board production documents events that took place at the Université de Moncton in the late 1960s. A general student strike is called in February 1968 in support of a freeze in tuition fees. In January 1969 students occupy the Science Faculty to highlight the university's lack of core funding from the provincial government. Producers Michel Brault and Pierre Perrault interviewed several student leaders on contemporary Acadian cultural issues. Of particular import is the debate over *bilingualism, much discussed by the Royal Commission on Bilingualism and Biculturalism, acted upon by New Brunswick's Robichaud government, and rejected by Moncton city council. Support for French-language municipal services becomes a sidebar to the students' strike when the city's mayor, Leonard Jones, is presented with a pig's head symbolizing his stance against the use of French at council meetings. Students also demonstrate against the Maritime Loyalist Association and discuss their future as Acadians and their feelings regarding Quebec nationalism. This film's final word is awarded to one of the few female student leaders. Recognizing the students' failure to impose a change of mentality on New Brunswick's two linguistic communities, Irène Doiron concludes that 'L'Acadie, c'est un détail'.

PHYLLIS E. LeBLANC

Action nationale, L', Montreal nationalist monthly. With the demise of *L'Action française* in 1928, Quebec's nationalists were left without a journal. In January 1933, *L'Action nationale* was launched by the Ligue d'action nationale and its president, Esdras Minville. Though he refused the editorship, Lionel *Groulx was a regular contributor, and his influence was felt up to the 1950s. From the start, the journal blended Catholicism, traditionalism, and nationalism. After the Second World War, with contributions from younger intellectuals such as André *Laurendeau, it was set on a new course. Albeit imperceptibly at first, a wedge was thrust between its traditionalism and its nationalism. From this drift towards neo-nationalism, a crisis ensued. In 1959, a prominent rightist intellectual, François-Albert Angers, assumed editorial command and set about to restore its doctrine by fighting the secularism of the *Quiet Revolution. On the constitutional front, discontented with *provincial autonomy, the journal finally embraced outright independence, hushing its ideological divisions. Today, rethinking its understanding of the idea of nation—from cultural to territorial to contractual—it somehow strives to promote a modern nationalism in an age of triumphant free trade and globalization.

PIERRE TRÉPANIER

Act of Union. In his report on the ills of Upper and Lower Canada in the aftermath of the *Rebellions of 1837–8, Lord *Durham recommended the legislative union of the two provinces. His successor as governor general, Charles Poulett Thomson (Lord Sydenham), secured the assent of the Upper Canadian legislature, both its elected and nominated parts, and of the nominated *Special Council in Lower Canada. A statute passed by the British Parliament, which took effect on 10 February 1841, produced the union.

The Act of Union provided for equal representation of the two provinces, renamed Canada East and Canada West, in the elected legislative assembly, although largely francophone Lower Canada had 40 per cent more people than predominantly anglophone Upper Canada. French Canadians rightly saw equal representation as a device to override their interests and concerns. They were also unhappy that everyone in the new province would become responsible for the debts of the two old ones; this was manifestly unfair as Upper Canada had far larger debts. Further, although French might be used in debate, English was to be the language of record in the new assembly and legislative council. All this guaranteed that the new province would be united in name only.

COLIN READ

adoption. Child adoption, both customary and legislative, has left few families untouched in pre- and post-contact Canada. Although 'adoption' has been commonly used to describe the customary exchange of orphans and non-orphans among kin and non-kin, neither civil nor common law originally provided for the legal transfer of parental rights. Massachusetts broke with Western tradition, inaugurating the first modern adoption law in 1851. New Brunswick passed Canada's first modest legislation in 1873; Nova Scotia followed in 1896. Customary adoption—that without formal legal recognition or protection—nevertheless remained commonplace among both Native and non-Native Canadians. Canada's most famous orphan, *Anne of Green Gables, was typical: her status in the Cuthbert family was never legally confirmed. The unhappy experience of many British *'home children'—brought to Canada in a form of imperial 'rescue' by groups like the Barnardo and Miss Rye Homes, and supposedly 'adopted' by Canadians—gave ample proof that youngsters needed protection. As part of efforts to protect *children from economic and sexual exploitation and to shore up the heterosexual, nuclear, and middle-class family type that was believed to be optimal for child rearing, provinces in the 20th century increasingly employed adoption legislation: PEI 1916, BC 1920, Ontario 1921, Saskatchewan and Manitoba 1922, Alberta 1923, Quebec 1924, Newfoundland 1940. Ontario soon demanded sealed records and judicial permission for access to records. This commitment to confidentiality marked an influential policy shift in the nation as a whole. Growing determination, rooted in the optimism of 20th-century behaviouralist sciences, to sever adoptees from their past has been summed up by Canadian scholar David Kirk as 'rejection of difference'. This preference climaxed in 1957, when British Columbia eliminated the right of property inheritance from the biological family. Birth mothers were commonly stigmatized as psychologically immature or worse. Social workers and policy-makers argued that everyone in the 'adoption triangle'—which included birth mother, adoptee, and adoptive parents, but notably not the birth father—should move on with their lives as if the child had been born to the new family. With the creation of Montreal's Open Door Society to assist Black children's adoption by white families, the 1950s also introduced Kirk's 'acknowledgement of difference' approach to adoption. By the 1970s, with the Supreme Court's decree that Native adoptees retained Indian status and with lobbying by groups like AWARE (Awareness to World Adoption and Responsibility to Everyone) for international adoptions, Canadians became more willing to acknowledge, even retain, links to original communities. Growing recognition of the devastating impact of the 1960s 'scoop' that brought thousands of Native youngsters into white homes further undermined resistance to adoptees' knowledge of birth histories, just as it raised questions about the shortcomings of cross-cultural adoption. Silence was further shattered by the adoptee movement, heralded by American Jean Paton's influential *The Adopted Break Silence* (1954). By 1974 Parent Finders operated in Vancouver and by 1988 BC produced a passive Adoption Reunion registry. By the 1990s Chinese, Romanian, and Latin American adoptees, among others, made nonsense of earlier insistence on confidentiality and secrecy. In an era where domestic violence was increasingly recognized, the ideal of the nuclear family was also scrutinized more critically and various family forms were more likely to be recognized as legitimate for child rearing. BC always officially permitted adoption by unmarried women and men. New Brunswick's belated extension of this right to would-be single parents in 1987 reflected changed attitudes. By the 1990s, lesbian and gay singles and couples had begun to win the right to adopt. By the 21st century, debates about adoption, of whom and by whom, were one way that Canadians confronted shifts in both family and national ideals and realities.

VERONICA STRONG-BOAG

advertising. Mediated communication intended for mass persuasion. Culturally, advertising manipulates selected words, images, and symbols to create a favourable impression for a product or service. Economically, advertisers pay for access to the mass media; they effectively underwrite the production and delivery of media content such that audiences do not bear the full cost.

American advertising has always influenced Canadian advertising. American media products, with greater advertising revenues, are readily accessible to Canadians. The Canadian state has therefore assisted Canadian media outlets through subsidies and favourable tax laws (e.g., Bill C-58, 1976). Nonetheless, Canadians have usually competed by following American precedents in the use of new technology, media, and business practices.

Canadian advertising may be dated from the first newspaper published in what is now Canada: the Halifax *Gazette* (founded 1752). Its first issue contained ads for a grocer, printer, and tutor. For the next 140 years, most advertising in British North America was conducted by similar types of merchants, craftsmen, and professionals who used only their local papers. Such ads were modest, resembling polite invitations or business cards, and appeared in the newspaper's own typeface. By the mid-1800s, some advertisers wanted individually tailored ads. In particular, patent-medicine companies produced their own ads using distinctive typefaces and graphic designs. Use of a trademark created a uniform corporate identity for both advertising and packaging. Lithography, introduced after 1840, fostered innovation in graphic design. Etched plates were used instead of type to print images. Advertisers embraced this technology to produce elaborate cards, posters, and billboards. Such designs also translated well into magazines.

Advertising agents appeared in the 1860s. At first, they simply counselled advertisers regarding their selection of media. After 1900, agents created ads as well. Anson McKim founded the first successful agency in Canada (Montreal, 1889); J.J. Gibbons opened the first full-service agency (Toronto, 1900).

The Canadian advertising trade took its modern form between 1890 and 1920. As Canadian industry and transportation systems developed, more companies produced branded goods and services for national markets. Advertising grew in step, as did concern over its trustworthiness and efficacy. Reforms were implemented: legislation to penalize false advertising, market research to identify consumer-spending patterns, and audience research to determine the size and nature of media audiences. These reforms were led by *Marketing* magazine, the Canadian Press Association, the Association of Canadian Advertisers (all based in Toronto), and the Audit Bureau of Circulations (Chicago).

Broadcast advertising began in 1919 when XWA Montreal promoted the Canadian Marconi Company during its radio programs. By 1928, advertisers pushed all manner of goods and services on air, buying radio time just as they bought newspaper space. Instead of images and symbols, music and sound effects were employed to capture attention. Radio advertising was almost banned in 1922, due to lingering concerns over false claims and poor taste, yet listeners and legislators were reluctant to pay directly for programs. Thus, both public and private broadcasters grew dependent on advertising revenue, an arrangement that persisted after 1953, when television rapidly overtook other media as a popular source of information and entertainment. Advertisers and agents adapted film techniques to produce television commercials. Otherwise, the structure of the trade remained the same: advertisers hired agents to broker time and space in the mass media and to create ads. The popularization of the Internet in the 1990s continued this pattern. RUSSELL JOHNSTON

African Canadians. People of African ancestry have migrated from the United States and the Caribbean, as well as directly from Africa, and some have a history in Canada extending over several centuries. There is, therefore, no single African-Canadian experience, although community and cultural lives have been shaped by their encounter with Canada.

Between 1628 and approximately 1800 about 3,000 Black people were held as slaves in what is now Canada. In 1783, some 3,500 *Black Loyalists, escaping from American slavery, arrived in the Maritimes. As free British subjects, the Black Loyalists were able to establish their own communities and institutions, for self-protection and economic survival in face of discrimination from the white majority. Family and community life reflected traditions from Africa and from *slavery, adapted to circumstances in Loyalist Canada. Exploitative wages for Black workers meant that more than one income was required to sustain a family. Black women therefore entered the labour force in virtually the same numbers as men, and gained a commensurate voice in community affairs. Children were raised communally, generating a broad network of loyalty and affection. When the opportunity arose to migrate to Sierra Leone in 1792, the decision to participate was generally made by entire communities, so families and chapel congregations could remain intact.

During the War of 1812 another 2,000 former American slaves, the Black Refugees, settled in the Maritimes. Because their tiny farms prevented agricultural self-sufficiency, economic patterns set by the Black Loyalists were repeated, with similar social consequences. The refugees, too, established schools and churches in their communities, and over time internal movement and the requirements of mutual reliance brought most descendants of slaves, Loyalists, and refugees into a common society. Representative of this was the African Baptist Association of Nova Scotia, founded in 1854 as an all-Black denomination to coordinate their religious lives. Maritime Black culture incorporated a spiritual orientation, strong community consciousness, and a determination to achieve full equality.

In 1793 Upper Canada legislated the gradual abolition of slavery and provided that no new slaves could be introduced to the province. Fugitive American slaves could therefore find a safe haven: once in Canada their slave condition was not recognized by law. The term *'Underground Railroad' was coined about 1830 to describe this movement of Black Fugitives, which involved an estimated 40,000 people before the American Civil War ended slavery. The fugitives, who found themselves in discriminatory circumstances often comparable to those in the Maritimes, tended to group together for self-help and protection. Several organized communities were created in southwestern Ontario to facilitate land ownership and democratic self-direction. More generally, fugitives sought waged employment and, like their Maritime counterparts, were responsible for building a significant component of the frontier infrastructure of roads, public buildings, and, later, railroads. Some were fleeing not from slavery but from oppressive conditions imposed on free Blacks in the United States. This included about 800 people from California who migrated to British Columbia in 1858, whose volunteer militia corps, the 'African Rifles' (*Victoria Pioneer Rifles), provided the only armed defence for Vancouver Island at the time.

The Civil War ended the migration of former slaves, and the population flow was reversed for the next half-century. Then, between about 1909 and 1911 approximately 1,500 African Americans, chiefly from Oklahoma, moved to the three Prairie provinces. Their arrival provoked animosity from large segments of the white population, who feared a continuing influx of persons considered inferior by prevailing popular culture and scientific orthodoxy. A federal order-in-council in 1911 excluded further Black immigrants, but it was never implemented because informal measures proved effective, including deliberate disqualification of Black applicants on medical grounds. Those who did arrive founded farms and communities, and smaller numbers settled in the western cities.

African Canadians participated in the settlement of every Canadian region, pioneering their own communities and contributing significantly to regional development through their skills and labour. Their loyalty was demonstrated in every war fought by Canada since the American Revolution, including the First World War, when racial prejudice almost banned them from the Canadian army. *Racism formed a tragic element in the

Canadian environment that Black migrants had to confront. It established boundaries for their communities, their economic opportunities, and their social evolution. Relative isolation and residential concentration, even in cities, promoted the growth of unique cultural institutions and activities, providing support in a world of disadvantage and, occasionally, of hostility. Prejudice excluded Black people from much remunerative employment, yet designation of certain jobs as 'female'—dressmaking, basket weaving, domestic service—perpetuated a vigorous economic function, and consequent community participation, for Black women.

Since Loyalist times African Canadians have sought to improve their circumstances, through self-help and mutual assistance and through direct appeals for justice from their government. This tradition was enhanced after the Second World War, when Canada's democratic rhetoric contrasted with Black experience. Two main fields were targeted for reform: *immigration policy and discriminatory treatment in employment and public accommodations. Black delegations challenged the federal government to abandon its racist policies, contributing to the accomplishment of immigration reforms in the 1960s and permitting the subsequent arrival of over half a million new Black citizens from the Caribbean and Africa. A 1949 referendum in Dresden, Ontario, over the issue of local segregation, sparked a campaign for fair employment and fair accommodations practices acts, successful in 1951 and 1954, respectively, in Ontario, and later in other provinces. Destruction of the Black community of *Africville in 1960s Halifax revealed the limitations of protective legislation and promoted a new conceptualization of systemic racism, one that called for structural reforms and affirmative action, and thus an entirely new initiative in equity legislation.

African Canadians participated in the physical establishment of Canadian society and also in the development of Canadian democracy and equality. Black cultural contributions, including those of award-winning poets, novelists, musicians, and artists, help to define the multicultural mosaic. The Black reform movement contributed to the system of human rights protections enjoyed by all Canadians and now regarded as fundamental to the Canadian identity. Although the equality agenda has not yet been completed, the direction has been convincingly drawn. JAMES W. ST G. WALKER

Africville. Originally called the Campbell Road Settlement, Africville, which hugged the shores of *Halifax's Bedford Basin, was established in the 1840s by descendants of Black refugees from the War of 1812. Having settled earlier in Preston and Hammonds Plains, they sought improved livelihoods in the basin's fishery, in modest farming, and in the growing port city. Because racial hostility was not uncommon in Nova Scotia, Africville out of necessity became self-reliant. A church, later known as the Seaview African United Baptist Church, was founded in 1849. Large outdoor baptisms held in the waters of the basin became memorable community events, drawing supporters from neighbouring churches. An elementary school was opened in 1883. Africville, which eventually numbered over 400 inhabitants, developed a unique community and cultural identity, with core values of religious faith, family, hard work, and independence from social welfare.

A maze of external and internal pressures, characterized by racism and poverty, eventually led to the community's decline, which began after the First World War. These neglected Halifax taxpayers were denied essential city services. Substandard housing, and lack of assistance to upgrade, compounded Africville's physical deterioration. Residents petitioned a succession of city governments for help, with little success. As well, several less than desirable institutions were built nearby, including a prison, an infectious disease hospital, and a slaughterhouse. While some people found work in these establishments, their presence further stigmatized the village and its people, who, for instance, were denied car insurance because of where they lived. Railway construction, land expropriation, and the constant threat of relocation oppressed the community.

Africville became Canada's poster community for 1960s North American 'urban renewal' plans. Race and class marked the process. Between 1964 and 1970 about 80 families were moved to public housing developments in Halifax. Personal belongings were moved in dump trucks, the church and houses razed. The callous handling of the relocation and subsequent fallout remain unresolved issues for the people, who continue negotiations with Halifax officials for compensation.

Africville was designated a national historic site in 2002. Former residents, and their descendants from across North America, return each year for a community reunion in Seaview Park, the site of the original community.

SYLVIA D. HAMILTON

agrarian revolt. The so-called agrarian revolt was led by western grain growers seeking greater economic returns from the new wheat industry. Organized in their provincial associations, they enthusiastically adopted co-operative techniques for buying and marketing in their production system. They soon discovered that there were clear limits to what they could achieve by local means. The grain growers hoped to maximize returns by limiting production costs. This meant dealing with the costs of credit, transportation, and machinery—that is, the banks, the railways, and the government of Canada, which controlled the tariff rates. To pressure national institutions and policies, they needed a national political strategy. They came to this position reluctantly, convinced that political parties were the problem rather than a solution.

The first major step was taken in 1909 with the creation of the Canadian Council of Agriculture, a non-partisan lobby group to bring the farmers' concerns to the national government. The following year hundreds of angry farmers descended on Parliament Hill; the 'Siege of Ottawa' earned sensational headlines but little else. Prime

Minister Wilfrid *Laurier failed in his attempt to achieve reciprocal trade concessions with the United States and was driven from office in 1911.

Although the Great War meant increased wheat prices, in 1916 the CCA issued the 'Farmers' Platform', demanding lower tariffs, control of utilities, cheaper credit, and lower freight rates. The CCA still saw itself as a lobby group representing farmers of all parties, but there seemed little prospect of either of the major political parties taking up their cause. The farmers, as other Canadians, were caught up in the *conscription election of 1917. They gave strong support to the *Union government, which claimed to recognize the interests of the grain growers by including T.A. *Crerar of the United Grain Growers in the cabinet. Not surprisingly, as soon as the war ended the grain growers resumed their demands for tariff reduction, and Crerar made it clear he could not remain in the cabinet without concessions on the tariff. When, the following spring, the federal budget was again staunchly protective, Crerar departed for the cross benches. Around him coalesced a dozen others who began to refer to themselves as the Progressive Party.

Direct action came first at the provincial level. In 1919 the United Farmers of Ontario won a minority government but were ultimately unable to dominate in so diverse a province. In Alberta the United Farmers swept to power in 1920 and held office for 15 years. In 1922 Manitoba elected a farmer government that continued under one name or another until the late 1950s. In Saskatchewan the farmers simply took over the Liberal Party. On the Prairies the grain growers were invincible: as the primary economic interest and the demographic majority, they easily asserted control. They tended to see government as administration and wished it to be frugal and unadventurous. But they were forced to acknowledge that their most critical problems could not be resolved at the provincial level. So Crerar's little band of *Progressives were thrust into the maelstrom of federal politics.

The Farmers' Platform had been refurbished in 1918 by the CAA as the New National Policy, demanding tariff reduction, free trade with Britain, and reciprocity with the United States. Endorsed by farmers across the country, it was embraced by the new-born Progressive Party as its platform for the next election. The election of December 1921 recast Canadian politics. For the first time there was a credible third party in the field and the old two-party template was destroyed. The election of a minority Liberal government seemed a glorious opportunity for the 65 Progressives, the second largest group in the House, to take advantage of the balance of power. But that would require a disciplined and resolute cohesion, which Crerar, the erstwhile leader, failed to achieve. The only issue that bound the farmer politicians together was the tariff: beyond that, their commitment to constituency autonomy, their populist suspicion of party politics, and their sheer naïveté inhibited effective action. They achieved almost nothing on the tariff question. Pre-war transportation rates were reintroduced, but few other concessions were offered. The farmers misunderstood Parliament; their failure to seek power meant that they could be ignored. They lost interest quickly, and within two years Crerar had resigned as leader. Membership in the grain growers' associations was in decline and the farmers were grasping for a new panacea, the pooling movement.

J.E. REA

agriculture. The practices, arts, and sciences associated with cultivating the soils and rearing livestock. Its history in Canada begins with Aboriginal peoples, many of whom mingled agriculture with hunting, gathering, and fishing activities. On the prairies and in some parts of central and eastern Canada, Aboriginal peoples grew traditional crops of corn, beans, squash, and pumpkins. On the West Coast, Aboriginal people cultivated a range of plants for both food and medicinal purposes.

The earliest settlers to New France brought with them a reliance on agricultural production. *Champlain's settlers at *Port-Royal (1605) and at Quebec (1608) practised some forms of agriculture from the beginning, though Louis *Hébert is popularly credited with establishing the first 'farm' on what eventually became the Plains of Abraham. Thereafter, agriculture was vital in the life of the colony, producing both food for the colonists and, to limited degrees, for export to France. New France agriculture was diverse and included established farms on the seigneuries, smaller farm lots carved out of the woods, and a remarkable range of agricultural practice among the Acadians in eastern Canada.

The early settlers of Newfoundland, notably at *Ferryland, augmented their food supply from the beginning through gardens that replicated European practices, including gardens serving class preferences and providing a rich range of spices for their dinner table.

After the British captured Quebec in 1759, a steady migration of settlers from the south brought American agricultural practice, which was particularly suited to the opening of lands in Canada West. In the beginning, they created subsistence farms; initially, they sold relatively little to the nearby communities and towns, often not even meeting their expenses. By the 1820s, however, exporting grain and flour was becoming a major industry. Such exports contributed significantly to the economic wealth of British North America, a necessary prerequisite for the development of urban centres. The emerging grain economy went through cycles of prosperity and deprivation, the general agricultural depression of the 1830s playing a significant role in the rebellions and political reforms of that and the subsequent decade.

Agriculture was an important aspect of the expansion of Euro-Canadian peoples into the Canadian West. The *fur trade companies, particularly the *Hudson's Bay Company, encouraged agricultural production on their posts, providing many of the early experiments with different kinds of crops. French, Metis, and Scots settlers along the Red River valley relied extensively on agriculture, while the *Mennonites who came after 1870 demonstrated its potential on the plains away from the rivers.

Agriculture was profoundly affected by changes in tools, machinery, and, in the early years, livestock. The shift from sickles to scythes that took place as Europeans started to settle in the Americas was important; so too was the development of special ploughs and axes as the settlement of the forest lands and the prairies took place. The most dramatic changes commenced in the early 19th century, when the shift to more mechanized equipment began. This process would move quickly in the years ahead, altering the complex relationships among farm size, capital needs, labour requirements, and access to markets—the determinants of what was practicable. Rural historians usually refer to the agricultural changes associated with the mid-19th century as the 'Great Transformation', one that radically changed life in Canada and elsewhere, in the cities as well as in the countryside.

The Great Transformation was most dramatically obvious in the grain industry, where each stage of its annual cycle was affected: planting by multiple ploughs and drill seeders, and harvesting by reapers and then by threshing machines, powered first by animals and then by tractors. These developments made possible the opening of the grain economy and the development of over 3,000 rural communities on the prairies during the late 19th and early 20th centuries.

Less dramatically, but still importantly, the milking machine and refrigeration made possible the growth of dairying. Cheese and butter production became very important businesses in many rural communities by the end of the 19th century, and they were significant export products as well. There were over 4,000 local creameries, butteries, and cheese 'factories' in central Canada alone by 1880, before the integration of the industry concentrated the processing business in the cities. Also, early in the 20th century the development of spraying machines and the introduction of cold storage facilities made possible thriving orchards in the climatically favoured parts of the country.

Technical innovations coincided with a growing interest in 'scientific' agriculture, the applications of scientific methods and the emerging scientific disciplines—including genetics—to a wide range of agricultural endeavours. Interest in distinct breeds of cattle, horses, sheep, and poultry quickened; by 1900 the increased productivity and special qualities of new breeds—including a few that were distinctly Canadian—were transforming the economics of farming.

More generally, farmers could sustain, and often improve, their production of grains and other crops through the careful analysis of soils and the introduction of better fertilizing techniques. They could turn to new strains of fruit in the orchards of the Niagara Peninsula and the Annapolis and Okanagan Valleys. Livestock farmers developed prize herds of Holstein, Guernsey, and Jersey cattle, while horse breeders specialized in such favoured breeds as Clyde, Percherons, and quarter horses.

Experimental farms supported by the federal government and companies in the seed and implement businesses contributed much to these technical and scientific advances, as did agricultural colleges. Farmers themselves also made major contributions: each farm required its own practices, and farmers developed their own ways of surviving, often through trial and error. They had to adapt their machinery, either to make it more useful or because they had to improvise when forced to keep it beyond its optimum life.

Farm family life was being radically altered by 1900. Women's and men's work was becoming more separate, women tending to focus on house, garden, and henhouse, and men on the fields and livestock. Children's labour, while still important, was gradually declining; soon, the agricultural opportunities for many young people would evaporate as farm size grew so that more expensive equipment and a growing list of 'in-puts' could be purchased.

*Rural depopulation became a major issue in central and eastern Canada. 'Farm philosophers' from Peter McArthur to Henry Wise *Wood and William Charles *Good decried this development because they believed that agriculture, with its closeness to nature (and in the view of many, to God), as well as its emphasis on hard work, was central to a healthy nation. It was a perspective that briefly, even poignantly, gained momentum as the urban population surpassed the rural population in 1921 and as rural/farm influences on government began to wane.

As the 20th century wore on, Canadian farmers became more specialized, although the process varied across the country and was most pronounced on the prairies and in the fruit districts. This specialization made them more concerned about marketing and credit issues: they needed funds to purchase better machinery and improved livestock and poultry or to withstand the vagaries of climate and market gluts. To better themselves, they increased their participation in Farmers' and *Women's Institutes, both important institutions for developing better agricultural practice. They formed *co-operatives, both local and regional, to have better leverage in the market and to improve their production. In 1909, they formed the Canadian Chamber (after 1935, Federation) of Agriculture to have a national voice for agricultural interests.

Farmers formed political parties intensely concerned about agricultural issues, notably credit, marketing, and rural enhancement, but also about political reforms such as the initiative, *referendum, and recall. Farmer governments came to power, under different names and at different times, in Ontario, Manitoba, Saskatchewan, and Alberta from 1919 through the 1930s. The new political parties associated with the Great Depression—the *Co-operative Commonwealth Federation and *Social Credit—were built partly on the grievances and value systems of the country's agriculturalists. Even at the end of the 20th century, the Reform Party was still echoing many of the old agrarian perspectives, notably in its search for a more democratic political system.

Ultimately, farm groups focused on economic issues. They pressured governments to permit the organization of marketing pools for various commodities, especially grains, milk, and poultry. Many of them pushed for the development of marketing boards in the late 1920s and the 1930s as a way of maximizing marketing power and assuring incomes that would make the orderly transformation of the countryside possible. Marketing boards have been a controversial and often poorly understood development even though, as part of an orderly marketing process, they have helped ease the burdens of farm people.

The pace of agricultural change has been more pronounced in recent years. In fact, it has been one of the great social and economic revolutions in Canadian history, one that has taken place amid studied indifference in mainstream society. The exodus from farms has continued to increase, although, in some ways, it is offset by the growth of rural, non-farming people in areas convenient to cities. Today, there are fewer than 300,000 'genuine' farms left in Canada and the average age of Canadian farmers is over 60. The growth of larger farms, many of them corporate, continues throughout Canada, particularly on the prairies. At the same time, near many Canadian cities, encroaching suburbia consumes some of the country's best agricultural land and increases the country's reliance on imported food.

Some of these worrisome trends have been offset by continuing, increasing productivity among farmers, by all measures the sector of the Canadian economy with the most impressive productivity gains during the 20th century. As in the past, technology and science, complemented by evolving practice, continue to enhance the volume of production geared to the agro-food industries and the needs of urban consumers.

Farming is continuing to change rapidly. Computing is revolutionizing the maintenance of farm records, the monitoring of equipment, and the accessing of market information. In theory, farmers have greater choice in the kinds of crops they can grow and where they fit in within the livestock and poultry industries. In reality, more farm operations are based on contracts with processors, meaning that the farm production sector is increasingly more integrated with the processing and distribution sectors. That trend means that farmers may have fewer choices, as they have to exist within agro-food industries that are increasingly attuned to an international marketplace. At the same time, farm organizations, including some large co-operatives, are losing their capacity to speak for agriculture, since the basis of the industry has changed more rapidly than they have.

There is, however, a growing alternative to the mainstream agricultural developments of the 20th century. Across Canada, an increasing number of farmers are resisting the growth of commercial agriculture, with its emphasis on chemicals and homogenized production. Environmentally friendly food production and organic foods have become important industries, with a strong niche in the market, particularly among the more affluent urban population. Today there are over 3,100 registered growers working 340,000 ha of land and selling to more than 300 processors. Recently, too, there has been some expansion of urban agriculture, an old form of agricultural practice taking on new life through the development of community gardening as cities try to develop more sustainable food systems.

In some ways, the ethic often pervading these alternative forms of agriculture, increasingly echoed by more conscientious farmers in the mainstream agricultural tradition, recalls an earlier time when farm people tried to situate agriculture within a way of life based on a compact with Nature—a time when agriculture was not just a business concerned with short-term gain in unstable markets controlled by forces beyond local control.

IAN MacPHERSON

Aircraft Detection Corps. Formed in May 1940 by the *Royal Canadian Air Force, the ADC was the eyes and ears of Canada's home defence forces. From the Atlantic to the Pacific, 2,692 observer posts were active, decreasing in number as the war progressed. Civilian volunteers—fishermen, police officers, teachers, homemakers, lighthouse keepers, clerks of Hudson's Bay Company trading posts, boys and girls—kept watch from a sense of duty to ensure Allied victory. Corps members were given instructions, including silhouettes of enemy aircraft. At posts, which had coded names, civilians logged reports before filing them with RCAF filter centres. Corps members watched for all unusual activity, on land or on the sea, and especially noted the behaviour of strangers. As a result of this vigilance, enemy agents were captured and Nazi submarines, airplane crashes, and torpedoed ships were reported, saving many lives. At the war's end the RCAF, on behalf of a grateful government, presented some 24,000 sterling silver pins and certificates of appreciation to ADC members.

ALLAN COGGON

aircraft manufacturing industry. The Canadian government has taken a continuing interest in the affairs and health of the industry, involving either direct control or (more frequently) reliance on private sector, albeit usually foreign-owned, firms to advance Canadian policy. The industry has focused largely on two kinds of products: military aircraft and special-purpose airplanes, such as 'bush planes' capable of adapting to the challenges of flying in northern Canada, and more recently on small commercial passenger planes.

Although the first Canadian airplane, Alexander Graham *Bell's **Silver Dart*, had its premier flight in Nova Scotia in 1909, the industry did not emerge until after the First World War. In 1917 the government took over some small aircraft makers and set up a Crown company, Canadian Aeroplanes Ltd, which was closed down at the end of the war. During the 1920s, Canadian Vickers, a Montreal-based subsidiary of the British firm, developed 'bush planes' for use by the government in the northern wilderness. Its success attracted other foreign companies, including the US-owned Boeing in Vancouver and the UK-owned de Havilland in Toronto. With the Depression, the mini-boom collapsed, and the Canadian aircraft industry virtually disappeared.

On the outbreak of the Second World War, Canada joined the *British Commonwealth Air Training Plan, and C.D. *Howe, minister of munitions and supply, established two Crown corporations to produce planes. As the war ended, Howe contemplated a longer range strategy for the development of the industry, to supply both Canada's military needs and the requirements of the Crown-owned Trans-Canada Airlines (later Air Canada), selling the Crown properties to private companies that would work closely with government in sustaining a Canadian-based industry. In 1945–6, a US firm acquired the former Canadian Vickers plant in Montreal, while a UK company, A.V. Roe took over a huge plant near Toronto that had produced Lancaster Bombers for the RAF, and rechristened it Avro Canada.

Although initially intending to develop commercial airplanes, by the 1950s in the shadow of the Cold War most Canadian aircraft makers were focusing on military supply for the RCAF. Canadair and Avro produced jet fighter planes (the Canadair Sabre and Avro's CF-100), while de Havilland specialized in trainers and transport planes for use in difficult terrain (with such appropriate names as the Otter, Beaver, and Caribou).

The most ambitious military aircraft venture was Avro's CF-105 jet fighter-interceptor, the *Avro Arrow, whose cancellation by the government in 1958 marked the beginning of the end of the postwar military production boom and stimulated an enduring controversy. Canadair continued to receive military contracts while seeking to diversify its product lines and markets, but by the early 1970s it too faced termination. With its specialized aircraft, de Havilland Canada was more successful in adapting to the post-Arrow environment. But its ambitious project to develop a 'short take-off and landing' (STOL) airplane, popularly known as the 'Dash-7', initiated in the late 1960s, generated high costs that its owners were reluctant to underwrite.

With both Canadair and de Havilland threatening to follow Avro into extinction, the Canadian government bought the companies in 1974. In 1977 it backed a new Canadair project, the Challenger, a small passenger 'business' plane, seen as a potential competitor for the US Learjet, but which involved an expensive capital development commitment. In the 1980s, the two Crown-owned aircraft firms underwent 'privatization'. In 1984, de Havilland, which had developed an advanced STOL plane, the Dash-8, was sold to Boeing; two years later Canadair was sold to *Bombardier, the Quebec-based diversified transportation company. By 1992, Bombardier had acquired de Havilland as well. As the century ended, the aircraft industry was largely under the control of a single Canadian firm, which set out to develop it as an integrated unit oriented towards international markets.

GRAHAM D. TAYLOR

air travel. Although it came to Canada a little more slowly than to some other nations, air travel had a huge impact when it arrived. As in colonial days, when men in canoes had opened up the interior of North America, so in the 20th century men in airplanes opened up the vast northern reaches of the continent. The story of aviation reflects themes apparent in other aspects of Canadian history: a tension over public versus private and military versus civilian ownership, regional rivalries, difficulties in devising policies for a sprawling and disparate land, fear and admiration of the United States, concern about international image and influence, gender equality (or lack thereof), and the crucial location of the country on the great circle route between Europe and the powerful United States on the one hand and between the US and Asia on the other.

After the First World War had demonstrated the usefulness of the recently invented heavier-than-air flying machine in armed conflict, 22,000 young Canadian airmen returned home, demobilized from the British flying services. Those determined to apply their aeronautical skills to peacetime endeavours bought war-surplus aircraft and turned to barnstorming or formed companies to offer aerial services. A keen public, teased by newspaper accounts about the exploits of the knights of the air overseas and the air-training scheme at home, was only too willing to cough up a dollar or so a minute for a short flight in an airplane—a contraption most had never seen. At first no rules or regulations existed to govern aircraft or their utilization. Governments had anticipated this problem and, while assembled in Paris for the peace conference, moved towards an international air convention. In Ottawa, Sir Robert *Borden's *Union government established an Air Board to draft regulations to govern the operation of aircraft. But Canadians were already taking to the air with abandon. The increasing aerial activity, along with the proliferation of accidents and incidents involving aircraft, leant urgency to the work of the board.

Men such as J.A. Wilson, the secretary of the Air Board and formerly assistant deputy minister in the Department of Naval Service, felt that for Canada to become an air power it first had to build a strong civilian and commercial foundation. Moreover, the government did not consider the time ripe for a military aviation policy. Instead it encouraged individuals and companies to explore ways in which airplanes could be put to profitable use. With few facilities available for landplanes, attention quickly focused, as Wilson foresaw, on taking advantage of Canada's innumerable waterways as potential landing sites, or 'air harbours'.

Initially, given the rough and dirty nature of early flying and wartime genesis of the activity, only men flew the planes. Those working in aviation generally saw it as a male domain. In addition, the limited carrying capacity of most aircraft meant that few passengers were carried, and there was no passenger service per se. Some individuals—government Indian agents, forestry workers and firefighters, and prospectors—flew with *bush pilots to remote destinations, along with vital supplies and mail. Mail became a mainstay of fledgling aviation companies in more than one country. The US government used mail contracts to subsidize the development of an airline industry, which soon eyed expansion into Canada. This helped spur the Canadian government into action. In September 1924 Laurentide Air Service contracted to provide the first regular airmail service—between Haileybury, Ontario, and Angliers and Rouyn, Quebec—less than four months after launching the first regular passenger service (from Rouyn to Angliers). For the next decade, the emphasis remained cargo, not people, and a number of firms proved their worth in different regions. In March 1927 Western Canada Airways, barely four months old, airlifted almost 18,000 pounds of freight to Churchill, Manitoba, and two months later inaugurated weekly air service from Winnipeg to Long Lake, Manitoba. Before the century was half over, Canada became the first nation moving all first-class domestic mail by air. Even with these accomplishments, the prejudice of the Post Office against people and mail sharing space on aircraft, coupled with the paucity of acceptable ground facilities, limited the growth of passenger service. Such service did not really take off until the completion of a trans-Canada airway, a make-work project during the Great Depression. Workmen lived in temporary camps, building a series of airfields across the country in return for basic subsistence.

Advances in aviation technology and construction of the necessary infrastructure in many countries brought international pressure for nations to designate an airline to carry the flag on world air routes. In Canada, C.D. *Howe, the minister of the new Department of Transport, announced that he would create a new airline to represent Canada internationally. The publicly owned Trans-Canada Airlines—renamed Air Canada in 1964—commenced operation in 1937. This move antagonized those Canadians who favoured private enterprise for such ventures, especially if they lived in the West. Canadian Airways, run out of Winnipeg by James Richardson, already had a national presence and had expected to be Howe's chosen instrument. It would not be the last time a successful western-based enterprise was sacrificed on the altar of eastern-Canadian interests.

As domestic and international air travel exploded after the Second World War, the number of airlines increased. The history of civil aviation has featured succeeding periods during which small companies proliferate, flounder or flourish, then combine or go out of business. By the end of the 20th century Canada had experienced at least two such cycles and found itself served by one dominant carrier, Air Canada, which in 1999 bought its long-time rival, the financially challenged Canadian Airlines International (the last of the line that began with Western Canada Airways and had evolved as Canadian Airways, CP Air, and Pacific Western Airlines). A century after the first powered flight, Canada—and many other nations—continues to struggle with the business side of an invention that has shrunk the country and the world and introduced us all to the mysteries and joys and frustrations of air travel.

CARL A. CHRISTIE

Aitken, William Maxwell (1879–1964), financier, newspaper baron. Though born in Maple, Ontario, Max Aitken was raised in the small town of Newcastle, New Brunswick, where his father was the Presbyterian minister. Leaving school at 16, he wandered across Canada selling insurance and running small businesses including a bowling alley in Calgary. His big break came in 1900 when he met and impressed John F. Stairs, Halifax's most important financier, who soon made him general manager of the Royal Securities Corporation, providing the ambitious young man with a platform for financing industrial enterprises in Canada and utility companies in the Caribbean. Success came quickly. By 1907 Aitken had set up the Montreal Engineering Company and taken over the Montreal Trust Company, and moved to Montreal, the centre of Canada's financial universe. By 1909 he was engaged in some of the largest consolidations in Canada's first great *merger wave, including Stelco. But it was the notorious Canada Cement merger and his promotion fees that made Aitken a household name and created a backlash that damaged his reputation for life. By 1910 he took his millions in profits to England, where he soon bought his way into British politics, newspapers, and a peerage. As Lord Beaverbrook he would become famous throughout the world.

GREGORY P. MARCHILDON

Alaska Boundary dispute. Originating in ambiguities in the 1825 Anglo-Russian treaty concerning Alaska, complicated by readjustments in the relationship between Britain, the United States, and Canada, settled under trying circumstances in 1903, and giving rise to a prolonged Canadian reaction, the dispute had both a vexed history and an eventful afterlife. Hampered by imperfect knowledge of the geography of the northern Pacific coast, the 1825 negotiators defined the Alaska panhandle with reference to topographical features that did not exist. This left the panhandle's width in doubt and made sovereignty over the heads of its long inlets a matter of uncertainty: a broad definition of the panhandle would put these inlets within its limits; a narrow determination would locate them in the British territory beyond. Becoming party to the dispute as a result of its 1867 purchase of Alaska, the United States insisted on the broad view and considered the heads of the inlets American. Canada, involved following British Columbia's 1871 entry into Confederation, urged the British—who retained jurisdiction over Canada's external relations—to resist this interpretation. Following the 1897 discovery of gold in Canada's Yukon Territory, positions hardened. Canada, wanting coastal access to the gold fields through a port it controlled, put particular stress on claims that the head of the Lynn Canal and the town of Skagway were Canadian. The United States maintained its traditional stance. With the Anglo-American relationship now a factor—Britain, facing increasing rivalry from Germany, did not want complications in its ties with Washington—Canada found its position weakening. It failed to get the British support to which it felt entitled, especially in view of its assistance during the *Boer War (1899–1902). The final settlement, in which Britain supported the successful American argument, aroused strong feeling in Canada. Anti-American sentiment—President Theodore Roosevelt's aggressive tactics were especially resented—played a part in the 1911 defeat of proposals for a Canadian–American *reciprocity treaty. Disappointment with Britain contributed to Canadian desires to gain greater control of external affairs, of which the establishment (1909) of the International Joint Commission giving Canada the right to negotiate boundary and boundary-related issues directly with the United States and the creation (1910) of an embryonic *External Affairs Department were important results.

ALLAN SMITH

Alaska Highway. The Alaska Highway stretches from Dawson Creek, British Columbia, to Fairbanks, Alaska, and in its first rough version was built between April and November 1942 to provide road access from the lower forty-eight states to Alaska. Within weeks of the Japanese attack on Pearl Harbor in December 1941, plans were made to link Alaska with the southern states, since it was feared that Japanese submarines might cut the shipping route north up the Pacific coast. The highway was built by the US Army Corps of Engineers, which pushed a pioneer road through the wilderness, and by civilian contractors employing Canadian and American workers, over 35,000 in total. At the same time a pipeline (*Canol) was built to carry oil from Norman Wells on the Mackenzie River in the Northwest Territories to a refinery at Whitehorse.

The Americans paid the entire cost of both projects—about $150 million for the highway (Canada reimbursed them at war's end), and the Canadians provided the right of way and permitted the American military police to control the highway corridor. The original road, which was nearly 2,500 km long, was built very quickly, partly because construction proceeded simultaneously south from Alaska, north from British Columbia, and both north and south from Whitehorse, and partly because environmental and other concerns were ignored. The road was very rough, passable only by heavy trucks, and in 1943 much of it had to be rebuilt. In 1946 the Canadian portion of the highway was turned over to the Canadian government, which rebuilt and improved it in the 1960s. It is now a paved modern highway, quite different from the original road.

K.S. COATES AND W.R. MORRISON

Albani, Emma (Lajeunesse) (1847–1930). One of the greatest sopranos of her generation, Emma Albani was the first Canadian singer to earn an international reputation. Born in Quebec City of musician parents, she studied piano and harp, sang, composed, and played the organ. With the help of the parishioners of St Joseph Church in Albany, NY, where her family had immigrated, she left to study singing, first in Paris, then in Milan. Her debut in 1870, in Bellini's *La Sonnambula*, was a triumph. In addition to pursuing a brilliant career at Covent Garden, where she sang until 1896, she toured the great European and American stages. In time she expanded her repertoire to include French and German operas. After retiring from the stage in 1911 she published her memoirs, *Forty Years of Song*. A friend of Queen Victoria, she was made a Dame of the British Empire by George V.

ODETTE VINCENT

Alberta. The Canadian government created the province of Alberta from a portion of the North-West Territories in 1905, selecting the name in honour of Queen Victoria's fourth daughter, Louise Caroline Alberta. Although nominally a province, the new entity, like the other two Prairie provinces, did not enjoy an important cornerstone of provincial jurisdiction: control over natural resources. Ottawa wished to determine land policy and continued to direct the massive settlement boom that rapidly transformed the prairies into an agricultural society. The area encompassed by Alberta surged in population from 73,022 in 1901 to 588,454 in 1921. The majority of settlers came from eastern Canada, Britain, and the United States in roughly equal numbers. Others arrived from continental Europe: significant minorities claimed German, Scandinavian, Ukrainian, or French origins. The Native population consisted largely of Athabaskan peoples in the north, Cree in the central region, and Blackfoot in the south.

The settlers moved into the arable parkland and open plains that covered the southern and eastern third of the province, displacing the older ranching community that retreated into the foothills. Large, mechanized wheat farms soon characterized the economy, although considerable variety could be found in agriculture enterprises. In conjunction with extensive railway building, a network of cities and towns arose to service this economy, with *Edmonton (the new capital) and *Calgary emerging as dominant centres. Many coal-mining towns also appeared, and the spectacular *national parks of the Rocky Mountains gave rise to tourism. A small petroleum industry emerged from a modest strike at Turner Valley in 1914. Few newcomers settled in the vast northern woodlands, which continued to be dominated by the fur trade conducted largely by Native and Metis peoples.

The boom that prevailed through the settlement era and during the Great War ended in the late 1910s. Drought and falling wheat prices led to hardship and farm abandonment. Although the mid-1920s brought a return to prosperity, it soon evaporated with the onset of the Great Depression. These difficulties spawned new political movements. The Liberals had controlled the provincial government since 1905, but a new 'anti-party' populist movement, the United Farmers of Alberta, won the 1921 election and governed for the next 14 years. A national counterpart, the *Progressive Party, also enjoyed success, and Alberta sent a radical wing known as the *Ginger Group to Ottawa. Unable to survive the political challenge of the Depression, the United Farmers lost the provincial election of 1935 to another new entity, *Social Credit, which advocated sweeping monetary reforms. Although the courts declared its legislation unconstitutional, the party would retain power as the province underwent fundamental changes.

The transfer of control over natural resources from the dominion to the provincial government in 1930 proved fortuitous after the discovery of oil at *Leduc in 1947. Additional huge oil strikes in the 1950s soon transformed the province. Oil and gas surpassed agriculture in economic importance, and the royalties from production on Crown lands lifted the province from one of the poorest jurisdictions in Canada to one of the richest. Social Credit abandoned its anti-business rhetoric and remained in office until 1971, often winning huge majorities by expanding government services while maintaining a low tax regime. Agriculture, meanwhile, entered a new era of diesel-powered mechanization that led to expanded farm size and rural depopulation. Although the provincial population doubled between 1941 and 1971, the farm population fell, and by 1971 over half of Alberta's 1.6 million people lived in its two largest metropolitan areas.

This trend accelerated during the 1970s, when the OPEC-induced 'energy crisis' drove oil prices to record heights and launched a frenzied boom in the province. Political conflict also flared, as the new Conservative administration battled with Ottawa over energy policy. The collapse of oil prices in the early 1980s ended both the boom and the conflict, although many Albertans continued to regard the federal government with bitterness and suspicion. Alberta's tradition of political innovation found expression in the formation of the Reform Party in 1987, which garnered sufficient western support to become the official opposition in Parliament in 1997. Provincially, the Conservatives retained power by addressing Reform demands for reducing the size and cost of government.

In spite of many bankruptcies in the early 1980s, the economy recovered quickly and diversified into many areas unrelated to petroleum. That industry, meanwhile, focused increasingly on building the massive infrastructure required to exploit the oil sand deposits of northern Alberta. Meanwhile, the population diversified, as substantial numbers of newcomers arrived, many from countries like India that had contributed few people in the past. By 2001 over three million people lived in Alberta, 63 per cent of them in the Edmonton and Calgary areas.

PAUL VOISEY

Alberta Heritage Fund. In 1976, the government of Peter Lougheed established the Alberta Heritage Savings Trust Fund to finance economic diversification and cultural and social development in the province. During its early years, the fund received a portion of the province's annual oil and gas royalty revenue. By 1987, the fund peaked at nearly $13 billion. Thereafter, it slowly declined under the impact of major spending commitments, including mega-projects such as Syncrude and Kananaskis Country, seed money for innovative small enterprises, and funding for the Alberta Heritage Foundation for Medical Research and the Alberta Heritage Scholarship Fund. Albertans' attachment to the implicit economic security of the fund blocked a plan to dissolve it and pay down the provincial debt during the fiscal crisis of the mid-1990s. While critics have pointed to questionable investment strategies, the fund has achieved most of the realizable goals set for it.

PATRICK H. BRENNAN

Albion. On 11 April 1819 the brig *Albion* (166 tons; Llewelyn Davies, master) sailed from Cardigan, Wales, bound for Saint John, New Brunswick, with more than 180 passengers. Farm workers and artisans, mainly from West Wales, largely monoglot Welsh speakers, they joined a wavelet of emigration driven by post–Napoleonic War economic depression and near-famine caused by 'the year without a summer' (1816). In 1818 the brig *Fanny* had transported 112 emigrants from Carmarthen to Halifax; some, encouraged by Lord *Dalhousie, founded New Cambria, near Shelburne, Nova Scotia. Meanwhile, *Albion* had carried about 80 passengers from Caernarfon, North Wales, to Perth Amboy, New Jersey, that summer.

Albion's 1819 passage was celebrated in 'Can Sef Hanes y Brig *Albion*' (A Ballad Being the Story of the Brig *Albion*), which described a great storm, deaths at sea, and encounters with icebergs, while placing the voyage in the tradition of spiritual testing, with specifically Welsh religious and nationalistic overtones. A few passengers disembarked off Shelburne for New Cambria, but most reached Saint John on 11 June. Approximately 150 *Albion* emigrants were settled by the surveyor general, Anthony Lockwood, on forest land about 30 km from Fredericton, on the Royal Road to Stanley, naming their settlement Cardigan. By 1827 at least 30 families farmed at Cardigan, which had a dissenting church and a school, forming the first enduring Welsh settlement in British North America. Its distinct Welshness survived until the Second World War, and the Welsh language was used, in some form, into the third generation.

PETER THOMAS

Alcan (Aluminium of Canada Ltd). A multinational enterprise headquartered in Montreal, Alcan is a vertically integrated aluminum company with production and fabrication activities in 38 countries. In 1901, the Pittsburgh Reduction Company, which later became Alcoa, started making aluminum in Shawinigan, Quebec, to take advantage of the hydro power of the St Maurice River. In 1925 Alcoa built the community of Arvida, in the Saguenay region of Quebec, to house workers for a new aluminum plant powered by the large-scale hydroelectric development of the Saguenay River. The Canadian operations of Alcoa were put under a distinct corporate entity in 1928 and became Alcan.

During the Depression, Alcan sharply reduced its activities in Shawinigan and Arvida, but the company undertook a considerable expansion in Arvida during the Second World War to produce aluminum for the Allied war effort. The Arvida wildcat strike of July 1941 was ended with Canadian troops, sent at the urging of federal minister of supply and munitions, C.D. *Howe. In the early 1950s Alcan continued its expansion with a large hydroelectric power station on the Kemano River, near

Prince Rupert, British Columbia, for a new aluminium plant in Kitimat, also an Alcan-planned town.
JOSÉ E. IGARTUA

Alexander. A ship chartered by John MacDonald Glenaladale in March 1772 from John Buchanan at Greenock, Scotland, to carry Highland emigrants to his property on the Island of Saint John. The 214 passengers, chiefly MacDonalds from the mainland of Scotland, plus 55 individuals from Uist and 8 families from Barra, were all Roman Catholics. Some of those from Uist were leaving with the financial support of the Scottish Catholic Church following religious harassment by their laird, MacDonald of Boysdale. Most of the remainder were seeking more land and better living conditions in North America. The party included a priest and a physician, both MacDonalds. The passengers were collected at various points (Arisaig, Eigg, Loch Boysdale, Barra) in the weeks before *Alexander*'s departure in mid-May. After a swift passage of six weeks, marred only by the death of a child, they arrived in Charlottetown harbour around 25 June 1772 and swiftly passed on to their final destination on lot 36 on the north shore of the island. Although virtually unknown outside of Prince Edward Island, *Alexander* was the first vessel to carry an entire community of Highlanders to settle in what is now Canada. It has received far less attention than the later immigrant vessel, the **Hector*.
J.M. BUMSTED

Alexander, Sir William, Earl of Stirling (*c.* 1577–1640), Scottish colonial promoter. Alexander made his name as a poet and courtier. Under James VI (James I of England) and Charles I, he ascended steadily towards high office. Master of requests for Scotland from 1614 and royal secretary of state for Scotland from 1626, Alexander was a powerful intermediary between the British monarch and Scottish subjects. An advocate of Scottish colonization efforts in North America, he was well placed to exploit his English connections. In 1621, the Crown granted him a charter for the colony of New Scotland ('Nova Scotia' in its Latin form), encompassing the modern Maritime provinces and the Gaspé—areas already claimed by France. Efforts to develop New Scotland preoccupied Alexander and voraciously consumed his wealth. After a failed expedition in 1622–3, he persuaded the Crown in 1624 to found the order of knights-baronetcies of Scotland (or Baronets of Nova Scotia). Each knight-baronet would gain land in New Scotland, and the honour of contributing to Alexander's expenses. The response was disappointing. After another unsuccessful voyage in 1628, Alexander succeeded in establishing two settlements in 1629. One, on Cape Breton Island, was soon dislodged by the French. The other, at *Port-Royal, was more durable but was finally evacuated under the Anglo-French treaty of St-Germain-en-Laye (1632). Although Alexander continued to interest himself in North American schemes, he was a spent force. Still secretary of state but bankrupted by his colonial endeavours, he was attended on his deathbed by more creditors than mourners.
JOHN G. REID

Algonquin Park. Canada's first and most celebrated provincial park was established by Ontario in 1893 primarily to protect the headwaters of the Nipissing highlands and to create a wildlife sanctuary. Located on the Precambrian Shield between Georgian Bay and the Ottawa River, Algonquin embraces 7,725 sq km of forests, lakes, and rivers. Although the park is renowned today as an outdoor recreation mecca, recreation remained ancillary to conservation objectives until the mid-1930s, when auto-tourism was occasioned by the construction of Highway 60 through Algonquin's southwest corner. The park has also become the most important single area in Canada for biological and environmental research; beginning in the 1930s, over 1,800 published scientific papers have been generated by researchers working there. Algonquin has also inspired the art of Tom *Thomson and the *Group of Seven, some 40 books, a dozen films, and a symphony. Logging, a controversial activity, has been part of Algonquin's history since the mid-19th century, and is still conducted on a sustained yield basis by the Algonquin Forestry Authority.
GERALD KILLAN

Alien Question. A controversy in Upper Canada in 1821–8 concerning the citizenship of post-*Loyalist emigrants from the United States. Were they and their children American citizens without political and property rights until naturalized, or had they, by relocating to British territory, remained British subjects despite American independence? Complex legal issues mixed with competing visions of Upper Canada to deepen institutional and ideological conflict and to politicize settlers.

After the War of 1812, further American immigration was discouraged as governors and leading officials sought to make Upper Canada British in cultural, social, and geopolitical terms. American values and settlers were increasingly suspect. Concerns about the status of Americans already in Upper Canada came to the fore when the election to the assembly of Barnabus Bidwell (and later his son, Marshall Spring Bidwell) was challenged on the grounds of their American citizenship. The assembly refused to brand them or a large proportion of the colony 'aliens' despite the arguments of local administrators and the ruling of British courts. Instead, mounting opposition charged colonial officials with trying to dispossess and disenfranchise their detractors. Both sides appealed to Britain, which eventually capitulated by retroactively accepting the citizenship of all who held office or owned land in the colony before 1820. The Alien Question reinforced officials' sense that their vision was being undermined from within. Their opponents became convinced that the constitution and the rights of ordinary settlers were threatened by an exclusive, self-interested faction of office holders, the *Family Compact, bent on dominating the province by refusing to distinguish between dissent and disloyalty.
JEFFREY L. McNAIRN

Allan, Sir Hugh (1810–82). A member of an important Ayrshire (Scotland) merchant family, Allan came to Montreal in 1826. After training with merchant houses linked to his father's businesses, he moved to prominence in transportation, both transatlantic and to communities along the St Lawrence River; by the 1870s he dominated both the Montreal Ocean Steamship Company (the Allan Line) and the Richelieu and Ontario Navigation Company. His shipping operations benefited from government contracts to carry immigrants, military baggage, and mail. To assure traffic and to supply his steamship interests, he moved into railways, coal, rolling stock, warehousing, mining, fishing, and western land companies. Allan also understood the usefulness of monopoly in communications: his interests included telegraph, telephone, bridge, tunnel, and warehousing companies. Allan was president of the Merchant's Bank and active in a multitude of marine, fire, and life insurance companies as well as manufacturing operations that included cotton and woollen textiles, ironworks, tobacco, pulp and paper, rubber, and shoes. His position as Canada's dominant capitalist gave him huge political leverage, particularly with the Conservative Party. The most important backer of the *Canadian Pacific Railway Company, established 1872, Allan was prominent in the *Pacific Scandal of 1873, the destruction of George-Étienne *Cartier's political reputation, and collapse of the Macdonald government. A Presbyterian, his *philanthropy included the Montreal Protestant House of Industry and Refuge, Mount Royal Cemetery, and the Montreal Sailors' Institute. His 34-room mansion, Ravenscrag, remains a Montreal landmark.

BRIAN YOUNG

Alline, Henry (1748–84). The New England-born Alline moved to Falmouth, Nova Scotia, in 1761. After a profound religious experience in 1775, he immediately felt the call to preach. Defying the standards of his Congregationalist upbringing, the following year the largely self-educated and unordained farmer began his short but spectacular preaching career. A charismatic preacher, who used music extensively in his services (he wrote over 500 hymns), he made a dramatic impact on neighbouring communities, which were often starved for ministerial leadership. He eventually took his free will and often mystical theology to settlements of New England origin in the colony, touching off controversy and revival in them all. The revival often divided existing congregations and led to the establishment of new churches, although Alline himself cared little about organized churches and doctrinal distinctions such as baptism by sprinkling or immersion. His extemporaneous preaching was augmented by the publication of two works of theology, several sermons, and a book of hymns. The New Light Movement, which he touched off, led to the founding of a number of new Baptist, Methodist, and New Light Congregationalist churches and significantly altered the direction of *evangelicalism in the Maritimes. His journal account of his own conversion and preaching career circulated widely in the Maritimes and New England in both manuscript and printed form. After his early death by *tuberculosis, his work was carried on by a number of very able followers, most of whom eventually rejected his free-will doctrine but retained his emphasis on personal salvation and experiential religion. The strength of evangelical churches in the Maritimes in the 19th and 20th centuries is directly attributable at least in part to the impact of the movement led by Alline. BARRY MOODY

all-red route. The first articulated motive for building a Canadian transcontinental railway was for it to be part of a secure imperial transportation network that would encircle the globe. At the time, countries belonging to the British Empire were often coloured red on maps; thus the name signified a route from Britain to the Far East entirely by way of the empire. Early proponents included Thomas Dalton, publisher of the Toronto *Patriot*, the English poet Sir John Smythe, and British railway engineers Major Robert Carmichael-Smyth and Sir Richard Bonnycastle. For a time, its promoters hoped that Canada's *Grand Trunk Railway—completed in 1859—would form the Canadian overland link between Britain and the Orient, but eventually the *Canadian Pacific Railway—completed in 1885—fulfilled that function.

A.A. DEN OTTER

Allward, Walter Seymour (1876–1955), sculptor. Canada's greatest monumental sculptor, the Toronto-born Allward was largely self-taught. Although his work includes memorials to Alexander Graham *Bell and William Lyon *Mackenzie, Allward is best known for his *war memorials. Early in his career, he was commissioned to create monuments to the *North-West Rebellion and the *Boer War. After the First World War his style changed from the representational to the allegorical, and his memorials in Peterborough and Stratford, Ontario, feature figures whose dynamic movement contrasts strongly with his earlier, rather static sculptures. Allward's crowning achievement was his memorial on *Vimy Ridge, a striking combination of allegorical figures and architectural forms. The project consumed what might have been Allward's most productive years as a sculptor, from the mid-1920s to the unveiling in 1936, but he never questioned his single-mindedness, for he was convinced that the memorial would be the centrepiece of Canada's commemoration of the Great War. Critics have praised Allward's work, and the Vimy Memorial is widely regarded as one of the world's finest pieces of commemorative sculpture. JONATHAN VANCE

almanacs. With a pedigree stretching back to Roman times, the almanac was a mainstay of the earliest presses. After printing began in Canada in 1752 at Halifax and then made its way westward, almanacs were produced by local printers for local consumption. Rival almanacs were also imported in large numbers from Britain, the United States, and France. The first known Canadian almanac is the *Almanac de Cabinet* (Quebec City, 1765). About 400 separate series of almanacs, printed in a variety of languages (notably English, French, German, and several Native languages), were produced in Canada between 1765 and 1950, although many have not survived.

An inexpensive, essential guide for pioneer life, almanacs have been dubbed the 'weekday Bible'. As such they are a useful and often colourful resource for both genealogists and historians of urban, rural, and domestic life. Printed in large quantities in book or sheet form, almanacs contained a calendar showing holidays, astronomical information (e.g., moon's phases, eclipses), and weather predictions. The latter were sometimes satirized by the almanac makers themselves: 'whenever the moon wanes the nights will grow dark' (*Belcher's Farmer's Almanac*, 1837). Almanacs included information on postal and telegraph service, transportation, customs regulations, and laws and court schedules; offered agricultural, household, and health advice; and printed essays, poetry, and music as well as advertisements for goods and services. Among other local information, they featured lists of officials, professionals, and militia and military personnel, as well as societies and organizations.

Nineteenth-century almanac production was characterized by specialization (agricultural, commercial, mercantile, nautical, political, and religious almanacs). As communication and transportation improved in Canada, almanacs were superseded by other information sources, and by the end of the century were produced primarily as promotional items, notably by the patent medicine industry. In Quebec, however, the tradition of literary or 'family' almanacs continued well into the 20th century.

ANNE DONDERTMAN AND JUDY DONNELLY

Almighty Voice, Kitche-manitou-waya (1874–97), of the One Arrow Reserve, was young when the North-West Resistance erupted in 1885. His people were punished by having their rations cut off and other restrictions imposed. In October 1895 Almighty Voice, familiar with deprivation, killed a farmer's cow to feed a child. Arrested, he was jailed at Duck Lake. When a guard recklessly commented that the prisoner would be hanged, he made his escape. A police sergeant was shot and killed attempting to arrest the fugitive. For 19 months, Almighty Voice eluded arrest, sometimes hiding at his parents' home. His defiance was transforming him into a hero among his people, and the authorities feared this could incite others to rebellion. On 29 May 1897, after five police and civilians who had been pursuing Almighty Voice were killed or wounded, the police assembled 68 men and two cannons, and for four hours bombarded the place where Almighty Voice and two of his companions were hiding, ruthlessly crushing this symbol of Indian defiance. BLAIR STONECHILD

alternative medicine. Refers to a wide variety of therapeutic practices that often have little in common with each other beyond the fact that they are not accepted by the regular medical community or paid for by publicly funded health care in Canada. Some therapies are considered 'alternative' because they are based on ideas about health and healing that differ radically from those held by physicians. Homeopathic treatments, for instance, intensify symptoms of illness on the theory that symptoms such as fever or diarrhea represent the body's natural efforts to throw off disease; regular therapies, in contrast, work to control symptoms because these are seen to be the product of illness rather than of the body's efforts to combat disease. Other approaches to healing, such as chiropractic and rolfing, actually share much in common with approved treatments, specifically massage and physical therapy, but they have largely been rejected or marginalized as unscientific.

The phrase 'alternative medicine' first emerged in the 1960s and 1970s. Growing numbers of patients who had experienced ineffective, excruciating, or insensitive care—or who simply became interested in natural healing—turned to unorthodox practitioners. Homeopathy enjoyed a popular renaissance in this period while other therapies, such as acupuncture, took root in Canada. Critics of alternative medicine described these as 'quack' treatments that threatened the health of the public by lulling patients into a false sense of security while luring them away from the benefits of conventional care. But supporters maintained that unorthodox medicine represented an effective, credible, and, ultimately, more humane alternative to managing illness—hence the label.

'Alternative medicine', a relatively modern phrase, has been applied inappropriately to some 19th-century therapies—either because they resemble today's alternative treatments or because they do not resemble today's conventional medicine. Thomsonianism and hydrotherapy are good examples. Thomsonianism was imported into Canada from the United States in the 1820s and appears similar to herbalism or naturopathy because it revolved around the use of the lobelia plant as well as other roots and herbs to purge the body of illness. Hydrotherapy, widely endorsed at the end of the century, involved the application of water at all temperatures and in many ingenious ways: it has no current counterpart. Yet neither of these treatment systems really qualifies as 'alternative medicine' for the reason that the idea of 'orthodox medicine' did not exist during much of the 19th century. Allopathic medicine—what we now describe as the forerunner of regular medicine—was just one medical philosophy or sect among many, equally credible medical sects, including homeopathy and herbalism.

During the early decades of the 20th century, allopathic practitioners were able to assume the mantle of medical orthodoxy, but the distinctions between regular and alternative medicine remain blurred. In fact, we now appreciate that various approaches to health and healing can be blended to the benefit of sufferers and our health care system. 'Complementary medicines' may become a more meaningful label than either regular or alternative medicine. BARBARA CLOW

A mari usque ad mare, Canada's motto. Mottoes, originally battle cries, are used in many aspects of life. Aspiration, defiance, existential declaration: all are reflected.

Many are pious; others, if not impious, are impish: 'Remember the Alamo', 'Fifty-four forty or fight', 'Vive le Québec libre', 'Six into twenty will not go' (Ulster Unionist). If armorial, they are often in unchanging Latin. Other languages occur: 'Ich dien' ('I serve') of the Prince of Wales; 'Fiel pero desdichado' ('Faithful, though unfortunate'), Sir Winston Churchill's family; and the pun 'Mon nom est ma couronne' ('My name is my crown'), Sir Wilfrid Laurier.

The inspiration for Canada's motto—as established by the proclamation of George V, 21 November 1921—is Psalmis Salomonis (72:8): 'Et dominabitur a mari usque ad mare', rendered in the King James version of the Bible as 'and he shall have dominion from sea to sea'. Apparently we owe this motto to the Reverend George Monro *Grant, principal of Queen's University, who in 'powerful Presbyterian sermons' throughout the country advocated its choice. If the seed fell initially on stony ground in the East, not so in the West, being inscribed on the Saskatchewan legislative assembly's mace as early as 1906.

SIR CONRAD SWAN

amateur sport. Amateurism in sport is at once ideology, a network of sports organizations, and a system of eligibility rules. Adapted from Victorian England, amateurism melded the upper-class desire for social hierarchy with the middle-class belief in education, self-discipline, and social responsibility: the amateur ideal has always been to improve individuals and society by instilling the values of hard work, team sacrifice, and fair play and inspiring community pride with inspirational performances. The first Canadian sports organizations, such as the National Amateur Lacrosse Association (formed in 1866), embraced these ideals, and set out rules to reinforce them. The first amateur codes in mid-19th-century Canada were ascriptive, excluding workers, athletes of colour, and members of First Nations simply as a matter of status. But as sports organizations became meritocratic, they made disinterested play the measure of adherence to amateur values. By the First World War the principal test of eligibility in the Amateur Athletic Union of Canada was whether an athlete had ever accepted monetary benefit from his or her participation or had ever played with or against a professional (i.e., someone who had accepted pay for play).

At the height of its powers in the 1920s, the AAU determined who could play in virtually every major Canadian sports organization, including the Women's Amateur Athletic Federation, YMCAs, church and police athletic associations, schools and universities. The amateur code was strictly enforced. Although the prohibition against remuneration discouraged working-class participation, it encouraged those who could afford to participate to combine their athleticism with education and careers, thereby enabling many top athletes to realize the ideals and become community leaders. Not surprisingly, amateurism drew its greatest strength from the Anglo-Canadian urban middle class. It resonated with their belief in education and a system of order and it was closely linked to Canadian nationalism. The link between amateurism and nationalism was strengthened by the modern Olympics, which restricted entry to amateur athletes and became a proxy competition for nation states.

Except for men's ice *hockey and *football, which abandoned it during the Depression, most Canadian sports organizations retained amateurism as a system of eligibility until the 1970s, when the International Olympic Committee abolished it and the Canadian government began direct payments to athletes. Most sports organizations still adhere to the twin ideals of strengthening citizenship through participation and enhancing Canadian nationalism by fielding successful teams in international competition. They still enforce a system of order to encourage adherence. This was confirmed in the aftermath of Ben Johnson's disqualification for steroids at the 1988 Olympics, when pan-Canadian organizations rejected the idea of 'win at all costs' and implemented rigorous policing of performance-enhancing drugs and educational programs to revitalize 'value-centred' sport.

BRUCE KIDD

American Federation of Labor–Congress of Industrial Organizations. The AFL was founded in the 1880s by Samuel Gompers, a pragmatic New York cigar maker. It opposed the reform policies of earlier trade *unions. Winning greater benefits for its own members was its primary concern. Consisting entirely of craft unions, including many in Canada, it eschewed partisan politics, *socialism, and industrial unionism. At the 1902 conference in Berlin (now Kitchener), Ontario, of its affiliate, the Trades and Labor Congress of Canada, the AFL expelled all nationalist and socialist unions, thus ensuring its total domination of the Canadian labour movement. In the 1930s, however, workers in mass production industries, dismayed over the AFL's conservatism, defected to create the CIO. After being expelled by the TLC, these unions created their own labour centre, the Canadian Congress of Labour. Following the Second World War and changes in labour conditions, the hostility between the two centres receded and in 1956 they merged to form the *Canadian Labour Congress, a year after the AFL and CIO had come together in the United States.

IRVING ABELLA

Américanité, not to be confused with worship of the United States, is a notion that appeared in Quebec in the early 1970s to reflect a major change in francophone identity. From the middle of the 19th century to the 1950s, French Canadians in Quebec identified closely with France. They widely perceived their nation as a continuation of France in America, celebrating their French origins and modelling their intellectual life on French patterns, traditions, and norms. The cultural relationship established with France was defined in terms of submissiveness and faithfulness towards a mother country. This attitude led most of the intellectuals to borrow their culture from abroad rather than developing a thread of their own.

With the *Quiet Revolution, a new generation emerged with different views. While they acknowledged the political importance of the relationship between Quebec and France, they questioned the old cultural dependency, which they tended to view as a source of impoverishment: the constant, sterile imitation and the one-way drift of ideas marked French Canadians as inferior. The prevailing feeling was that this inhibiting framework had to be entirely redefined. The new mood conveyed the strong message that Quebec francophones were not French in America but Québécois—a different culture, a hybrid arising from an original history on this side of the Atlantic. The term *américanité* served to herald the new awareness, the new sense of belonging, and intellectuals engaged in a multifaceted endeavour to express in their own terms the experience and the sensitivity of their culture. For 20 years or so, writers, artists, and scientists indulged in unearthing their 'real self', rediscovering their roots, displaying their soul, telling their history.

This phenomenon was not unique to Quebec: it took place at some point in every society of the New World. In each case, the relationship with the motherland was, at the outset, celebrated as essentially positive, as an umbilical cord. Then, progressively, it came to be perceived as harmful, as a dependency that hindered the 'normal' growth of the new society. In all cases, the response from local elites was a protest on behalf of their roots and the 'authenticity' of their self and society. An identity emerged, fed with a strong reference to the territory, traditions, and characteristics of the new society. In parallel, the old allegiance to the motherland began to wane. This common experience received different names: *américanité* in Quebec, *americanidad* in Latin America, *oceanity* in New Zealand, *asianity* in Australia. In English Canada, intellectuals talked about their Canadianness, of which the *Group of Seven, for instance, gave eloquent expression. Thus, *américanité* appears as only a particular instance of a widespread experience in identity substitution among the societies of the New World. GÉRARD BOUCHARD

American Revolution. When Great Britain virtually eliminated the French from North America with the Treaty of Paris, which ended the Seven Years' War, it was expected that one of the major benefits would be the elimination of a military threat to the British colonies. Instead, a new threat developed as American colonists objected to various aspects of British policy, many of which were consequences of attempting to reorganize North America to incorporate the new territory. In a constantly escalating crisis, Britain and its American colonies reached the verge of military conflict by 1774, when the British Parliament passed the *Quebec Act, which was intended to stabilize the new colony. Passed at the same time as the 'Intolerable Acts'—a series of repressive measures in response to the Boston Tea Party—the act was viewed with hostility by the Americans. Within a few months, in April 1775, open warfare erupted. One of the first actions of the government organized by the rebels was to authorize the invasion of Quebec; two armies attacked that summer but retreated in the spring of 1776. The Americans mistakenly believed that the French-Canadian population of Quebec was eager to be 'liberated' from the British yoke and would quickly rise to support the invaders. A much smaller invading army came from Machias (in what is now Maine) to attack, unsuccessfully, Fort Cumberland in Nova Scotia. In Britain's northern colonies, the American Revolution was viewed, not as a movement of national liberation, but as the first American Civil War. It broke up Britain's empire on the American continent, dividing eastern North America into the United States and what became known as *British North America. Quebec, Nova Scotia, and the other northern British colonies (Newfoundland, the Island of St John) remained loyal to the British. By the Treaty of Paris in 1783, the British surrendered maritime fishing rights and the Ohio Valley to the United States. The treaty provided little solace for the *Loyalists, those American colonists who had supported the British. Unresolved issues would be settled only after the War of 1812.

J.M. BUMSTED

Americans in Canada. While Canadians have moved south in large numbers throughout their history, migration from the United States to Canada has also been extensive in most periods. Mohawk from New York, having converted to Roman Catholicism, settled in New France, with the *Jesuits establishing Kahnawake as their home in 1716. After the British Conquest, several hundred American merchants moved to Montreal to take control of the *fur trade. By then, with all of Acadia under English control, many New Englanders had begun to migrate to Nova Scotia. Before the American Revolution began in 1776, over 8,000 'Planters' had established settlements in mainland Nova Scotia, Cape Breton, the northeastern shore of New Brunswick, and on Prince Edward Island.

After the American revolutionaries seized power from the British in the Thirteen Colonies, United Empire *Loyalists began to pour into territories still controlled by Britain. Some 35,000 Loyalists settled in Nova Scotia (which included today's New Brunswick) while perhaps 12,000 settled in the old province of Quebec (which included today's Ontario, where most of these Loyalists settled). Many had little choice but to leave their homes because of the vengeance they faced from the successful revolutionaries. The Loyalists included colonists of a variety of backgrounds. Their reasons for supporting Britain varied: some members of minority religious groups, for example, feared that the revolutionaries would prove less tolerant than the British authorities; other colonists feared an interruption in trade relations with Britain; still others simply hoped to gain advantage by backing the winning side in a civil war. Once in what was left of *British North America, many Loyalists created a mythology about themselves as the only real defenders of British interests in North America. As such, they believed themselves worthy of special concessions from the colonial authorities in terms of land grants and political offices.

One group of American exiles with a special reason for leaving the new republic comprised about 3,000 former slaves of African origin who had fought with the British in order to gain their freedom. Poorly treated both by the British authorities and by white Loyalists, the American Blacks, most of whom settled in Nova Scotia, largely failed to prosper. In 1792, about 1,200 of them accepted an offer from the authorities to take free passage to Sierra Leone. Mohawk supporters of the British in the Revolutionary War, led by Joseph *Brant, were also among the Loyalists.

Immigration from the new United States of America, especially to Upper Canada (Ontario), continued apace for a generation after the revolution, with the new migrants often being referred to snidely as *'late Loyalists'. But both groups of Loyalists were often more interested in obtaining land than in living under the British flag. Angry with British authorities for failing to concede democratic institutions, many of the ex-Americans supported the American side in the War of 1812. After the war, Loyalists attempted to deprive new US immigrants of civil rights, including the franchise. Such efforts ultimately failed, and these new colonists used their franchise to express sympathy towards political radicals' demands for *responsible government. American-born Upper Canadians played a significant role in the failed *rebellions of 1837 and 1838, demanding republican status for the colony. In the 1840s and 1850s, the British, hoping to fend off total secession of their North American colonies, conceded responsible government to the various colonies.

About 2,000 ex-slaves fled the republic during the War of 1812, and the *Underground Railroad, orchestrated by free Blacks in the United States and in British North America, brought in about 30,000 freed slaves from 1840 to 1860, mostly to Upper Canada.

Americans played a large role in settling the Canadian West. About 25,000 immigrants, mostly from California, poured into British Columbia during the *Fraser River gold rush that began in 1858. After 1890, when most of the good lands in the American West had been settled, a large-scale American immigration to homesteads on the Canadian Prairies began, lasting until the First World War. American expatriates such as Henry Wise *Wood in Alberta played a large role in bringing populist ideas to the political stage in Prairie Canada. Depending on the availability of work, American tradesmen and miners often worked on both sides of the border, with many eventually settling in Canada.

About a third of immigrants to Canada during the large-scale migration from 1896 to 1914 were Americans, but by the late 1920s, with free land largely gone, only about 15 per cent came from America. One group of American immigrants who received a great deal of public attention were draft dodgers and deserters who arrived during the war in Vietnam. Although the Canadian government attempted from 1965 to the end of 1967 to prevent war resisters from making their home in Canada, public pressure forced a change in policy. Estimates of the number of American opponents of the war who settled in Canada range from 30,000 to 100,000, but there is no reliable official count of their numbers. ALVIN FINKEL

Amiens. The Battle of Amiens, 8–11 August 1918, was the only occasion during the First World War when the Australian and *Canadian Corps attacked side by side. This battle was the beginning of open warfare on the Western Front and a spectacular start for the war's last phase. To participate, the entire Canadian Corps had to move 50 km south through the French countryside and did so with a very elaborate deception plan. By the end of the first day of fighting the Canadians had advanced 13 km, and by 11 August they had advanced beyond the Australians on their left and the French on their right—a total of 22 km in four days. At Amiens the Canadians liberated 174 sq km containing 27 towns and villages. The costs were high—9,074 casualties for the Canadians—but much higher for their opponents. General Arthur *Currie, Canadian commander, calculated that the corps had faced 15 German divisions, engaging 10 of them directly. Germany's General Ludendorff would call 8 August 1918 the Black Day of the German army. Ten Canadian soldiers won the Victoria Cross for their efforts at Amiens.
A.M.J. HYATT

Amulree Report, 1933. The usual name for the *Report* of the Newfoundland Royal Commission, chaired by Baron Amulree. In 1932, the government of Newfoundland, facing a severe financial crisis, gave notice of partial default on the public debt. Alarmed at the possible consequences, the British and Canadian governments agreed to provide financial assistance on the condition that there be a royal commission of inquiry into the country's condition and prospects. The other members of the commission were both Canadians, Sir William Stavert and Charles A. McGrath.

After hearings in Newfoundland and a visit to Ottawa, the commission's report was released in November 1933. It argued that Newfoundland needed political and economic reconstruction and reform, and blamed the financial crisis on years of poor administration and misgovernment. Its proposed remedy was that Britain should guarantee and reschedule the public debt, and temporarily assume direct control of Newfoundland through the suspension of responsible government and the institution of an appointed commission. The new system was to last until the country was again 'self-supporting'. The analysis was arguably unfair, and the recommendations draconian. Nevertheless, there was little opposition. The recommendations were implemented in 1934, and the *Commission of Government lasted until 1949. JAMES K. HILLER

Amundsen, Roald Engbreth Gravning (1872–1928). A Norwegian explorer, author, and lecturer, Amundsen commanded the first expedition to sail through the *Northwest Passage (1903–6) and was the first to reach the South Pole (1911) and the first to fly to the North Pole (1926). Inspired as a child by the tales of lost explorer Sir John *Franklin, Amundsen vowed: 'I, too, shall suffer . . . in the frozen north on the way to new knowledge in the unpierced unknown'. His successful expeditions made him famous and added to our knowledge of the polar regions, but Amundsen was plagued by bankruptcy and other failed expeditions, including four attempts between 1917 and 1925 to drift in the pack ice to the North Pole in his specially built ship *Maud*. He wrote several books about his exploits, including *My Life As an Explorer*, published after his death. Amundsen perished when his plane crashed into the sea en route to the Arctic on a mission to rescue another polar explorer. Ironically, the other explorer, a rival, was rescued.

JAMES DELGADO

Anciens Canadiens, Les (1863), a historical romance set during the last years of the French regime in Canada. Written by Philippe-Joseph Aubert de Gaspé (1786–1871), the book rapidly became a classic, was translated into English three times, and remains the most popular work of the Quebec literary movement of the 1860s. The book opens with the leisurely return home from the Seminary of Quebec of Jules d'Haberville and his friend Archibald (Arché) Cameron of Locheill, accompanied by a talkative servant, José Dubé. The book then describes life in the d'Haberville manor house at St-Jean-Port-Joli before recounting events during and after the Seven Years' War, in which Jules and Arché find themselves fighting on opposing sides.

The novel is a compendium of its author's personal recollections and family traditions, and of the folklore and social history of the south shore of the St Lawrence River. Aubert de Gaspé, himself a seigneur with an English wife, idealizes the *seigneurial system, which was abolished in 1854, and presents a conciliatory view of the transfer of New France to British rule.

DAVID M. HAYNE

Anglicans. This term gained currency in the 20th century to identify persons belonging to the Anglican Church of Canada or, as it was generally known before 1955, the Church of England in Canada. In the 19th century Anglicans were more frequently called Churchmen or Episcopalians.

The Church of England identified with the Protestant Reformation in the 16th century, and the classic summary of Anglican belief, the Thirty-Nine Articles of Religion (approved in 1571), is Protestant in character. Since the 1830s, however, some Anglicans have preferred to think of themselves as Catholics of a non-Roman variety, and since the 1960s many have come to think of their tradition as a third kind of western Christianity distinct from both Protestantism and Catholicism.

Characteristic of Anglicans has been their use of a set of prescribed liturgical texts called the Book of Common Prayer. At first Canadian Anglicans used the 1662 English edition, but they produced editions of their own in 1918 and 1959. Since 1985, most Canadian Anglicans have come to worship from a Book of Alternative Services, written in an updated if somewhat bland English and reflecting a modern ecumenical liturgical theology. The 1959 BCP is still authorized.

Organizationally, the Anglican Church is divided into territorially defined dioceses, each comprehending a varying number of parishes. A parish normally comes under the spiritual care of a priest, and a diocese is administered by a bishop. The first diocese in British North America was that of Nova Scotia, created in 1787. Its bishop's jurisdiction originally included most of present-day Canada east of Manitoba, plus Bermuda. It has been subdivided many times.

In the 18th and 19th centuries, most Anglican clergy came from England, Ireland, or Scotland, and were sponsored by English missionary societies. The most important of these societies, the Society for the Propagation of the Gospel in Foreign Parts, sponsored 1,597 Anglican clergy in British North America before 1900, and continued a reduced number of sponsorships until 1940. A more evangelical group, the Church Missionary Society, focused on missions to Native Canadians. Nineteenth-century bishops sought to recruit more Canadian-born clergy and provide local theological schools to train them.

During the colonial period, Anglicans enjoyed the privileges, and chafed under the constraints, of special status. Until the 1830s, Anglican leaders such as Jacob Mountain (1749–1825) in Lower Canada and John *Strachan (1778–1867) in Upper Canada championed a full Anglican *establishment. Many Anglican lay people differed, preferring to work peaceably with other Protestants. None of the structures of Anglican special status survived Confederation. Nevertheless, some of the trappings and symbols of civic importance remained, dear to some Canadian Anglicans, and problematic to others.

About the time that British North America was receiving *responsible government, Anglican leaders were fighting for synods where the bishop, clergy, and elected lay representatives of each diocese would govern church affairs. The diocese of Toronto created the first synod in 1853, although its legality was in doubt until 1857. Synods could elect bishops, enact church 'laws' (called 'canons'), and establish budgets. For many years the ambiguity of the boundaries of authority between bishops and synods produced tensions, and sometimes lawsuits.

Following Confederation in 1867 and the completion of the Canadian Pacific Railway in 1885, Anglicans met in Toronto in 1893 to create a national organization. They called their national representative assembly the General Synod, and their national leader the 'primate', with the title archbishop. The first primate was Robert Machray (1831–1904) of Winnipeg.

From the 1880s to the 1960s, Anglicans enthusiastically supported domestic and foreign missions. Their Women's Auxiliary gained prominence for its effective mission programs, fundraising, educational ministries, and training of missionaries. By far the largest item in the church's mission budget was Indian *residential schools, although the expenditures were largely matched by grants from the federal government. Overseas, Anglicans focused their efforts on medical and educational ministries in mid-Japan, Honan, and Kangra (India). In the 1960s the Anglican mission society ceased operations. New departments began administering world relief, international development, and assistance to overseas Anglican 'partners'.

Theologically, 19th-century Canadian Anglicans argued vigorously, sometimes bitterly, over issues of church order and worship. But whether 'high church' or 'low church', they were very conservative in matters of general doctrine. Thus, in the 1860s they were overwhelmingly shocked and outraged by new critical historical interpretations of the Bible. Signs of a more liberal attitude began appearing in the 1880s, and by the 1920s modernization had become a positive goal. During the 20th century Anglicans built a reputation for considerable diversity in their theology and in their social and economic views.

Anglican church attendance reached a peak in the late 1950s. By the 1980s, declining membership and revenues were requiring significant cutbacks in the national and many diocesan offices. In the 1990s, a rising tide of lawsuits brought by victims of sexual abuse, particularly former inmates of Indian residential schools, threatened the survival of General Synod and several dioceses.

ALAN L. HAYES

See also ESTABLISHMENT OF RELIGIONS.

Anglin, Timothy Warren (1822–96). Of middle-class Irish Catholic origins, born in County Cork, Anglin emigrated to Saint John, New Brunswick, in 1849. There he founded the *Freeman* newspaper and through its pages spoke on behalf of Irish Catholics for over three decades. In 1861 he was elected to the NB assembly and eventually became a potent opponent of the *Confederation movement. As a cabinet member of the anti-Confederate government in 1865 he was subjected to a disreputable campaign that impugned his loyalty. Although embittered by the smear tactics, Anglin accepted the 1866 pro-Union electoral decision. He served as an MP (1867–82) within the emerging Reform (Liberal) Party and was speaker of the Commons during Alexander *Mackenzie's administration (1873–8). In 1883 he moved to Toronto, where his journalistic and political activities continued but his prominence declined. Throughout his life he remained an articulate, if rather priggish, participant in public life. His leadership over nearly a half-century assisted Irish Catholics in becoming acculturated within Canadian society. His son Frank became chief justice of the Supreme Court and his daughter Margaret became an internationally renowned actor. WILLIAM M. BAKER

Anne of Green Gables (1908), the first of 20 novels by Lucy Maud Montgomery (1874–1942), went through ten impressions in its first year and has sold in the millions since. Published by the L.C. Page Company in Boston, the novel appealed to such contemporaries as Mark Twain and Governor General Earl Grey. Vivacious, talkative, and red-haired, the 11-year-old orphan Anne Shirley is adopted by a staid elderly brother and sister on Prince Edward Island even though she is 'not a boy'. First translated in 1909 (into Swedish), the book has appeared in more than a dozen languages, including Japanese and Polish. The novel has been made into movies, stage and radio dramas, musicals, and television miniseries. Each year 300,000 visitors tour the Parks Canada Green Gables house in Cavendish. Anne is an icon of Canada, and in a survey by the Dominion Institute and Council for Canadian Unity Montgomery was voted one of the top 20 Canadian heroes of the 20th century.

ELIZABETH ROLLINS EPPERLY

Annexation Manifesto. Issued in Montreal amidst commercial depression in October 1849, the manifesto, with its 325 signatures, emphasized economic reasons for Canada's peaceful separation from Britain and negotiated entrance into the American republic. Its most prominent signatories were English-speaking Tory merchants from Montreal and Quebec who felt betrayed by Britain's decision to dismantle imperial trade preferences and accept the *reformers' Rebellion Losses Bill; others included radical French-Canadian nationalist disciples of Louis-Joseph *Papineau. Significant support also existed among those cities' English-speaking reformers and in Canada West, the *Eastern Townships, and New Brunswick.

A disparate protest movement, annexation appealed to a vocal minority of conservatives and reformers for political and constitutional, as well as economic, reasons. For anglophones, joining the United States would end 'French domination' of the union of 1841. For French-Canadian nationalists, it would repeal that union, create a French-Canadian republican state, and secure independence from Britain. For merchants, it spelt prosperity. For detractors of *responsible government, it offered greater democracy or republican checks and balances and the chance to overcome partisan and national distinctions inflamed in 1849. For those proud of Canada's maturity, it promised a peaceful break with colonial dependency.

The bipartisan movement quickly succumbed to economic recovery, American indifference, British condemnation, internal incoherence, government and loyalist counterattack, and lack of widespread popular support. Debate about Canada's economic and political future was, however, broadened and existing party alignments challenged. Access to American markets was achieved by *reciprocity, not annexation, while repeal of the union of 1841 through a broader federalism was achieved by Confederation. Responsible government largely survived the republican challenge. JEFFREY L. McNAIRN

Anti-Confederation League. The proposal for a union of the British North American colonies was contested when first seriously broached at Charlottetown in 1864. There was resistance to the very idea across Atlantic Canada, although the specific terms worked out at the Quebec Conference later that year provided a focal point for dissension. Prince Edward Island and Newfoundland declined to join. In Nova Scotia and New Brunswick, committed leaders such as Leonard Tilley and Charles *Tupper were determined to keep the idea of union alive, despite large-scale opposition.

Opponents of *Confederation were concerned that economic decision making would be transferred to a parliament in which the Canadians would have a permanent majority. Promises that union would lead to renewed economic development were not universally accepted, particularly among those with long-term commitments to resource extraction for sale in foreign markets—the so-called 'wood, wind, and sail economy'. They preferred more laissez-faire economic policies, with lower levels of taxation and less interference in international trade.

Anti-Confederationists also exposed a potent vein of opinion that *responsible government, only recently won, would be seriously compromised. In Nova Scotia, Joseph *Howe was recruited to lead the opposition, and his spirited attack resulted in a concerted effort to delay implementation. When Tilley stumbled in New Brunswick, losing an election in the spring of 1865, Confederation seemed dead. But continued pressure from Britain and Canada reversed that electoral defeat the following year, and delegates proceeded to London to confirm the deal. The Anti-Confederation League was formally launched during the summer of 1866. Howe led a delegation to London in an attempt to counter the initiative, but to no avail. Thwarted there, the anti-Confederates, rechristened the Nova Scotia Party, set out to demonstrate the breadth of support for their claims. The first elections after Confederation, in September 1867, gave them overwhelming majorities both federally and provincially. It would prove to be their high-water mark. Shortly thereafter, Howe and some of his colleagues were absorbed into the Conservative Party, a move that resulted in somewhat better financial terms for Nova Scotia, but led to no significant amendment to the terms of union. D.A. MUISE

anti-feminism. Anti-feminists reject women's claims for equality. 'Antis' view Canada, and Western civilization, as a battleground where they struggle against feminist demands for political and economic rights and sexual and reproductive autonomy. Like its adversary, anti-feminism ebbs and flows. Both movements engaged in influential debates during two periods of social upheaval, roughly the 1880s to the 1910s and the 1970s to the present.

Anti-feminism has inspired a few women, but leading antis have commonly been male. 'First-wave' representatives included four members of the Canadian intellectual elite. A classic 19th-century liberal, Goldwin *Smith (1823–1910), once Regius Professor of Modern History at Oxford and professor of history at Cornell, settled in Toronto to publish widely on national and international affairs. Anti-feminism, displayed in 'Woman Suffrage' in his *Essays on the Questions of the Day* (1893), informed his critique of modern life that targeted independent women, as well as Jews and Blacks. The imperialist Andrew *Macphail (1864–1938), McGill's first professor of the history of medicine and long-time editor of the *University Magazine* (1907–20), dismissed the United States as materialist and degenerate. His diatribes 'The American Woman' and 'The Psychology of the Suffragette' in *Essays in Fallacy* (1910) located feminism at the heart of American failure. French-Canadian nationalist Henri *Bourassa (1868–1952), who served in both the federal and provincial parliaments, is best known as an opponent of Sir Wilfrid *Laurier but he articulated commonplace misogyny in attacking *feminism as foreign and secular in his newspaper *Le Devoir*. In 1915, the most famous of the early antis, Stephen *Leacock (1869–1944), a professor at McGill, published 'The Woman Question', which identified female independence as a threat to civilization. Such men, arguing that feminists would consign people of European origin to degeneration, were powerful participants in discussions about the roles that modern women and men ought to play.

Anti-feminism survived suffrage victories, continuing, for example, to deny women recognition as 'persons' under the BNA Act until 1929. In the 1960s, feminist-bashing became a stock-in-trade of reactionary periodicals such as *Alberta Report* and *BC Report*, but diatribes from right-wingers like Barbara Amiel also appeared in middle-of-the-road publications. Other modern antis include William Gairdner, author of *The War against the Family* (1992), with his vitriolic assaults on feminists and lesbians and his celebration of Anglo-Celtic masculinity, and Betty Steele, author of *The Feminist Takeover: Patriarchy to Matriarchy in Two Decades* (1987), who similarly combined anti-feminism, homophobia, and racism. Opposition to women's rights to reproductive choice, freedom from violence, and equal employment inspired REAL Women (Realistic Equal Active for Life) in the 1980s. The last quarter of the 20th century saw the New Right link market economics, global racism, and anti-woman politics. Anti-feminist sentiments nourished an upsurge of violence against women, as the massacre at Montreal's *École Polytechnique on 6 December 1989 demonstrated. VERONICA STRONG-BOAG

Antigonish Movement. A movement of self-help through adult education and community economic development, usually through co-operatives. It grew out of rural conferences in Antigonish, Nova Scotia, early in the 20th century, organized by Fathers Hector MacPherson and Jimmy Tompkins. Following a 1927–8 royal commission investigating the Atlantic fisheries, St Francis Xavier University organized an Extension Department. Funded by grants from the federal Department of Fisheries and the Carnegie Foundation, the department, directed by Father Moses M. Coady, organized study clubs throughout the region in the 1930s and 1940s. The clubs encouraged people to consider issues confronting their families and communities and then use information, generally in the form of pamphlets, radio broadcasts, and films provided by the department, to envision how they might improve their lot. They usually found an answer in *credit unions and other kinds of co-operatives.

The movement achieved notable success, built on the philosophical perspectives of Coady, the activism of Tompkins, the organizational genius of Angus Bernard (A.B.) MacDonald, associate director 1930–43, and the efforts of capable field workers, a dedicated office staff, a librarian, and a writer/propagandist. Many of the women in the movement came from the Sisters of Martha, nuns drawn generally from the rural and fishing communities and close to the people the department served. Spreading quickly throughout eastern Nova Scotia, the movement reached out to the rest of the province, and to all of Atlantic Canada, primarily through the networks of the Roman Catholic Church.

Ideologically, the movement reflected Catholic social action (though it reached out to Protestants as well) and the inheritance of the international *co-operative movement. It was concerned with the 'little man' beloved by many movements in the Great Depression. It became a key success story for promoters of adult education and university extension. As it grew, the Antigonish Movement attracted social commentators and reformers trying to counteract the adversity of the Depression and the apparent failure of capitalism. From the mid-1930s onward, a steady stream of visitors and writers visited the department and local co-operatives. The *National Film Board and other organizations made films about the movement, which were widely shown throughout North America. Numerous authors wrote books and articles on the 'miracle of Antigonish'. Adult educators and co-operative leaders throughout Canada were inspired by its accomplishments, although these were exaggerated, and it started to stagnate in Atlantic Canada during the 1950s.

Moses Coady became an internationally recognized adult educator and co-operative thinker, an icon of Canadian co-operativism. His ideas were explained in numerous lecture tours and in his book *Masters of Their Own Destiny*, still in print and published in eight languages. Students from outside of Canada came to St Francis Xavier almost from the beginning. The Coady Institute, created in 1959 has trained thousands of overseas community workers. IAN MacPHERSON

architecture. The architecture of Canada is an amalgam of Native, colonial, and international forms, testifying to the country's complex relationships with the cultural traditions of its indigenous peoples and of France, England, and the United States. Sadly, Native architectural remains are rare, documented mostly in archaeological sites, drawings, and written descriptions. Our knowledge of pre-contact Aboriginal architecture is negligible, except for artifacts found in caves or excavations. Also, many post-contact architectural traditions, such as those of the Iroquoian- and Algonquian-speaking tribes, were purposely temporary. The wigwam, the Algonquian word for dwelling, was a domical or conical single- or two-family structure composed of reeds on simple wooden frames. The elm-bark-covered Iroquois longhouse was considerably larger—up to 120 m long—accommodating an extended family/clan structure.

Natives who lived on the Pacific coast have left relatively rich legacies of buildings, images, and artifacts. Each group developed versions of the plank-house—cedar buildings constructed of posts, beams, and planks that served the coastal tribes' hierarchical social structure. The Haida village of Ninstints on Anthony Island (Queen Charlotte Islands), which once accommodated 17 plank houses, is among the richest Native archeological sites in present-day Canada.

Fishers from many countries built temporary wooden dwellings, known as tilts, on the Newfoundland coast. These were composed of vertical poles chinked with moss. No buildings remain from the 17th and 18th centuries, but archaeological investigations at *Ferryland, founded in 1621, reveal a dense plan of settlement with cobblestone roads and sanitary facilities. Vernacular architecture in Newfoundland has retained its early pattern of small, rectangular, wooden houses, perching lightly on the land, as have other provinces in the Maritimes. Portability is a hallmark of many wood-framed, Atlantic coast houses.

The urban architecture of *New France followed formal traditions established in France. Both Quebec City and Montreal developed parallel to the St Lawrence River, enclosed by walls pierced by gates. The buildings were densely constructed and featured minimal setbacks, offset by a series of formal open spaces. Religious orders built monumental stone buildings organized around courtyards. These hospitals, colleges, convents, and seminaries were large, multi-storey blocks, featuring steeply pitched roofs, dormer windows, and sophisticated planning.

The *seigneurial system of land tenure was used until 1854 in the St Lawrence Valley. Seigneuries were typically divided into long and narrow lots perpendicular to the St Lawrence and other rivers. The seigneur retained a manor house, built and operated a communal mill, and provided for a church and presbytery. The dwellings of rural *habitants were typically small and rectangular, with steeply pitched, bell-cast roofs extending over a raised porch. Materials varied, including stone (typically covered with plaster-like crépi), wood, and a combination of wood and masonry. After 1665, the colonists of New France also lived in villages, which frequently included prominent parish churches. Good examples of well-preserved rural and urban French colonial masonry houses are Ferme St-Gabriel (1698) in Pointe St-Charles and Montreal's Château de Ramezay (1705, enlarged 1755). Île d'Orléans, near Quebec City, boasts an outstanding collection of French colonial typologies. The architectural traditions of New France are well documented in the work of Ramsay Traquair and Gérard Morisset.

As in England, France, and the United States, the 19th century saw a whirlwind of revival styles, some of which expressed potent ideas on both spirituality and nationalism. The most significant example of Gothic Revival architecture was the Church of Notre-Dame, on Place d'Armes in Montreal, opened in 1829. The neo-Gothic *Parliament Buildings in Ottawa, awarded by competition in 1859 to Thomas Fuller and Chilion Jones, made direct reference to Westminster. The continued popularity of Neo-Palladian architecture, illustrated by buildings such as the Saskatchewan Legislative Building in Regina (Edward and W.S. Maxwell, 1908–12), was a constant reminder of Canada's British colonial past. In general, neo-classical and Greek Revival styles were more appropriate for secular buildings, such as banks, courthouses, and post offices, and were particularly popular in eastern Canada due to stronger American influence.

Nineteenth-century Canadian architecture was marked by a growing sense of professionalism among building designers. Formal architectural education in Canada began in 1890 at the University of Toronto, followed by McGill University's School of Architecture six years later. Architects in Ontario and Quebec attained association status in 1889 and 1890, respectively; Manitoba, Saskatchewan, Alberta, and British Columbia formed organizations in the first two decades of the 20th century; and the Atlantic provinces later in the century. The Royal Architectural Institute of Canada, which held its first convention in 1907, sought to foster closer professional ties across the country.

The construction of the Canadian Pacific Railway inspired massive building projects. These included many stations and related facilities, but also lavish hotels. American architect Bruce Price designed the original Banff Springs Hotel and the Château Frontenac, Quebec City. The romantic, castle-like forms of these hotels were conceived as a nationalistic style. The Empress Hotel, in Victoria, BC, was designed by Francis Rattenbury, and made direct reference to his nearby Legislative Buildings. Another product of the industrial age was the skyscraper, first developed in Chicago in the 1880s. Canada's first building of true skyscraper construction was the Robert Simpson store in Toronto (1895) by Edmund Burke and J.C.B. Horwood.

Twentieth-century Canadian architecture reflects international trends, especially the Arts and Crafts movement, art deco, international-style modernism, and postmodernism. Despite the proximity of Frank Lloyd Wright in Chicago, early-20th-century Canadian architecture was more affected by Scottish and English ideals, especially through key figures like Percy Nobbs in Montreal, Eden Smith in Toronto, and Samuel Maclure in Victoria. All three architects made their principal contributions to the development of Canadian architecture through domestic design, emphasizing traditional forms, natural materials, and hand-crafted decoration.

In the interwar years, Montrealer Ernest Cormier emerged as a major figure, combining notions of modernism with his educational background from the École des Beaux-Arts in Paris. Cormier's major work is the main building of the Université de Montréal, a bold, brick and reinforced-concrete art deco structure situated according to Beaux-Arts planning principles. Cormier's own house from 1930–1 is also well known as the Montreal residence of Pierre *Trudeau. The *Supreme Court of Canada in Ottawa, designed by Cormier 1938–9, is an outstanding marriage of modernism and classicism. Banks and post offices across Canada were also constructed at this time in a consciously moderne, streamlined aesthetic.

Full-blown international-style modernism did not come to most of Canada until after the Second World War. Among its strongest advocates was John Bland, who with partners Vincent Rother and Charles Trudeau designed Ottawa City Hall in 1958. Bland was director of the School of Architecture at McGill, 1941–72, and was responsible for transforming its Beaux-Arts curriculum to a modern, Bauhaus-based school. His legacy also includes the establishment of the John Bland Canadian Architecture Collection. It and another at the University of Calgary are the most significant archives focusing on the subject of Canadian architecture.

*Expo 67 was a glorious moment for Canadian modernism, attracting architects and attention across the world. Its architectural legacies: the megastructure Place Bonaventure by ARCOP, the revolutionary housing experiment Habitat 67 by Moshe Safdie, and Buckminster Fuller's geodesic US Pavilion are landmarks of Canadian architecture. Yet Vancouver, not Montreal, serves as Canada's premier showcase of modern architecture. 'BC modernism' was developed in the country's youngest metropolis by a series of pioneering individuals and design firms as a unique combination of international trends and regional influences. Artist and educator B.C. Binning built his own house in 1939–42 with a frank expression of structure and flat roof. Binning and Swiss-born Frederic Lasserre, director of the School of Architecture at the University of British Columbia, were key figures in the development of the style. Perhaps its most famous disciple is Arthur Erickson, designer of Simon Fraser University (Erickson/Massey Architects, 1963), the Museum of Anthropology at UBC (1973–6), and Robson Square in Vancouver (1974–9). Erickson's work is characterized by an innovative rethinking of the program, a clear idea about structure, and an overlapping relationship between interior and exterior spaces.

Many foreign architects, too, have designed important buildings in Canada, including McKim Mead and White (dome, Bank of Montreal, Montreal), Jacques Carlu (interiors of Eaton's stores, Montreal and Toronto), I.M. Pei (Place Ville-Marie, Montreal), engineer Pier Luigi Nervi (Place Victoria, Montreal), Mies van der Rohe (Westmount Square, Montreal; Toronto-Dominion Centre, Toronto), and Viljo Revell, Toronto City Hall).

The 1970s saw the birth of a broad-based historic preservation movement, following the needless destruction of older buildings to make way for heroic modern projects. Heritage Canada was founded in 1973, about the same time that major historic districts were undergoing conservation. The Historic Properties in Halifax, Vancouver's Granville Island, the old town in Quebec City, *Dawson City, Yukon Territory, and *Lunenburg, Nova Scotia, are all notable historic districts that have attracted international attention for their conservation.

The acceptance of women by the Canadian architectural profession has been slow. Its first woman member was Esther Marjorie Hill (1895–1985), who made history when she joined the Alberta Association of Architects in 1925. Quebec had no women members until 1942. The numbers of registered women architects did not increase substantially until 1981 (5 per cent). By the 1990s the number of women had increased to about 12 per cent.

Architecture is more than individual buildings designed by famous architects. Canadian buildings that serve as significant local and international symbols might include the maritime fishing cottage, Montreal triplex, prairie farmhouses and grain elevators, the CN Tower, or even the massive 'log cabin', the Château Montebello. Fantasy-based places, like Green Gables in Cavendish, Prince Edward Island, or the West Edmonton Mall (1981–6), and even unpopular buildings like Montreal's Olympic Stadium (the Big 'O', 1973–87), also play unique roles in Canadian architectural culture, especially as tourist attractions.

Canadian architects have contributed to the international movement of postmodernism in all its variations. Whereas modern architecture shunned historical associations, postmodern buildings celebrate their immediate and historical contexts. The Canadian Centre for Architecture, designed by Peter Rose and its founding director, Phyllis Lambert, in 1989, is an essay in late-20th-century neo-classicism. Its massing and fenestration are intended to harmonize with the tradition of Montreal 'greystones' in the area. The shape of Parkin/Safdie's Great Hall at their National Gallery (1983–8) in Ottawa speaks to the nearby parliamentary library; and Safdie's Vancouver Public Library is modelled directly on the Roman Colosseum, perhaps the predecessor of all public spaces.

Multiculturalism and environmentalism, too, are much celebrated in Canadian postmodern architecture. Douglas Cardinal's curvilinear Canadian Museum of Civilization in Hull (1983–9) is intended to serve as a metaphor for the taming of a rugged, natural landscape. The architect emphasizes that these forms draw on his *Metis heritage. On a smaller scale, the architecture of Vancouver-based Patkau Architects illustrates a concerted interest in Native traditions. Their Seabird Island School (1990–1) was the first of a series of innovative schools for First Nations communities in BC.

Addressing a worldwide concern over architecture's impact on the environment, Busby + Associates Architects' One Wall Centre in Vancouver is a 48-storey elliptical tower (the tallest building in BC) that uses its own water supply to counteract wind forces. Sustainable development and 'green' architecture is a growing field among Canadian architects.

In the 21st century, the precise role of architecture in Canadian culture continues to incite debate. In 2002 Berlin-based architectural theorist Daniel Libeskind won a competition to extend Toronto's Royal Ontario Museum. His controversial proposal resembles a giant crystal. Is it a respectful nod to the museum's geological collections or a commentary on the Canadian climate? Architectural meaning is truly in the eye of the beholder.

ANNMARIE ADAMS

archives. *See* NATIONAL ARCHIVES.

Arctic Archipelago. Canada's Arctic Archipelago, now part of *Nunavut, stretches from the Arctic coast to Ellesmere Island. For over a century Canada has claimed this ice-clogged territory, ever vigilant because its sovereignty has been challenged by other nations, particularly the United States. In 1880 Great Britain transferred to Canada all territories then known to exist north of the mainland. In 1904 a confidential report warned not only that the original transfer was flawed, but also that Canada had done little to consolidate its hegemony. Other countries had made discoveries of their own, but had not put forth any specific claims. To demonstrate effective control, Canada increased its level and tempo of arctic involvement, beginning with the voyages of Captain Joseph *Bernier (1904–11), and culminating with the *Canadian Arctic Expedition (1913–18), when the last major islands were discovered. Until the 1970s at least, official Canadian maps would show that all territory and waters lying in a sector bounded by the 141st meridian and a line running from the North Pole to the waters between Baffin Island and Greenland were Canadian. During the Second World War thousands of US personnel were allowed into the North to build a series of military projects that could have undermined Canadian sovereignty. During the Cold War, with the fear that Soviet air and missile attacks would take place over the polar basin, Canada became a junior partner in continental defence, culminating with the US-dominated Distant Early Warning (*DEW) radar line. Although Canadian claims would be enhanced by the activities of the newly created Department of Northern Affairs and Natural Resources (1953), US activities went forward, sometimes unchecked. By the late 1950s US nuclear submarines were traversing under the arctic ice, and in 1969 the oil tanker USS *Manhattan* would plough through the frozen Northwest Passage. In reaction, the Arctic Waters Pollution Prevention Act was passed in 1970 to bolster Canada's claim and control. Nevertheless, American vessels, claiming the Right of Innocent Passage, continue their arctic activities, usually—but not always—notifying the Canadian government. RICHARD J. DIUBALDO

Arctic exploration. The exploration of Canada's Arctic was a long process of trial and error that went on for several centuries. It was carried out chiefly by British explorers but also by Scandinavians, Americans, and even a few Canadians. Their motives were commercial, imperial, or scientific, sometimes a mixture of all three. Each expedition, no matter how unsuccessful—and most of them were unsuccessful—added some measure of new information to the gradually developing map of the northern archipelago.

The Vikings (*Norse) were the earliest Europeans to penetrate the ice-choked waters of the Canadian Arctic. By at least the 13th century from their settlements in Greenland they were making trading forays across Baffin Bay and Davis Strait to Ellesmere and Baffin Islands.

European interest in the Arctic was reawakened in the 16th century, when mariners and merchants began searching for an open sea passage to the Orient across the top of North America—the so-called *Northwest Passage. Martin Frobisher, an English privateer, pioneered the way, leading three maritime expeditions to Baffin Island (1576–8), initially in search of the passage but subsequently to establish a colony and mine for gold. He was followed by John Davis, another English mariner, who made his own trio of voyages (1585–7) into the strait that bears his name. Along with Davis Strait, Hudson Strait seemed to offer a passage westward, and it was in this direction that explorers turned their attention in the 17th century. Henry *Hudson penetrated deep into *Hudson Bay in 1610, wintering in James Bay before his crew mutinied and left him to die. A series of expeditions—led by Jens Munk (1619–20), Luke Foxe (1631), Thomas James (1631–2) and Christopher Middleton (1741–2)—examined the eastern shoreline of the bay in a futile search for an opening in that direction. Meanwhile, Robert Bylot and his pilot William Baffin sailed to the top of Baffin Bay (1616) and located the entrance to Lancaster Sound, which many years later would be found to be the entrance to the Northwest Passage. Two overland expeditions, one by Samuel *Hearne (1770–2) and the other by Alexander *Mackenzie (1789), reached the shores of the Arctic Ocean, but at the end of the 18th century the archipelago remained almost completely unknown to the outside world.

In the 19th century arctic exploration was spearheaded by the British Admiralty and energized by a renewed search for the Northwest Passage. In 1818 John Ross sailed through Davis Strait and into Lancaster Sound, which he made the mistake of thinking was a closed bay. One of his officers, Edward Parry, returned the following year in charge of his own expedition and penetrated as far as Winter Harbour on Melville Island, where his two ships spent the winter. This voyage was notable for pioneering the use of tinned meat and vegetables, an innovation that helped to protect the crew from scurvy. Parry also pioneered other techniques for overwintering. He roofed over the decks of his vessels with boards and canvas to create a protected living space. Once the ice had closed in tightly around the hulls, snow was banked against the sides of the ships to provide insulation. During the depths of the winter total darkness descended and nobody stirred far from the ships, but once daylight returned the crews continued their explorations using sleds. Again, Parry was a pioneer of this form of transportation, which he borrowed from local *Inuit people. He made two subsequent visits to the Arctic (1821–3, 1824–5), neither of which was as successful as his initial foray. Meanwhile, John *Franklin, another naval lieutenant, led two overland expeditions (1819–22, 1825–7) that added several thousand kilometres to the map of the arctic coastline. In 1829 John Ross sought to overcome the disappointment of his first voyage. Funded by the gin manufacturer Felix Booth, Ross outfitted the first steam-powered vessel used in the Canadian Arctic. Ross sailed into Prince Regent Inlet, where he remained mired in the ice for three winters, not escaping until 1833. The highlight of this expedition was the discovery of the magnetic north pole by James Clark Ross, John's nephew, in June 1831. During the 1830s the survey of the mainland coast was extended by George *Back (1834) and the tandem of Peter Warren Dease and Thomas Simpson (1837–9), and then completed by the fur-trade explorer John Rae (1846–7).

At this point attention shifted to the search for John Franklin and his two ships, not seen since they had sailed into Lancaster Sound in the summer of 1845. The search for Franklin, carried out by several naval and land-based expeditions and lasting for more than a decade, resulted in the mapping of a vast portion of the northern archipelago. In 1853, Captain Robert McClure and his men left their ship *Investigator* iced in on the north coast of Banks Island and trekked eastward to a rendezvous with rescue vessels in Lancaster Sound, becoming the first Europeans to traverse a Northwest Passage. The official search for Franklin came to an end in 1859 when Captain Francis Leopold McClintock found artifacts, human remains, and written records on the shores of King William Island that confirmed the fate of the missing men.

With the Northwest Passage mapped, and found to be too perilous for ships to use, the emphasis of arctic exploration shifted towards the North Pole through the channels separating Greenland from Ellesmere Island. A series of expeditions—led by the Americans Elisha Kent Kane (1853–5), Isaac Hayes (1860–1), and Charles Francis Hall (1871–4), and the Briton George Nares (1875–6)—proceeded up the east coast of Ellesmere and around to Cape Columbia, the northernmost point of Canadian territory. These initiatives were followed up by members of the 'Scandinavian school of arctic exploration', characterized by the effective use of dogsleds and cross-country skis. Norwegian Otto Sverdrup surveyed the western side of Ellesmere in this way, and during an astounding expedition lasting four years (1898–1902) he and his companions were the first Europeans to reconnoitre the high archipelago west of Ellesmere. Sverdrup was followed by a second Norwegian, Roald *Amundsen, who commanded the wooden sloop *Gjoa* on the first navigation through the Northwest Passage (1903–6), completing a journey first embarked on by Martin Frobisher more than 300 years earlier.

All this activity by international explorers suggested to the Canadian government that it had better take steps to assert its claim to the arctic territory. In the 1890s it began sending regular cruises into the eastern Arctic. Some of these voyages, notably the ones led by Captain Joseph-Elzéar *Bernier (1904–11), contributed a great deal to the outside world's knowledge of the North. In 1913 the government launched the *Canadian Arctic Expedition, led by Manitoba-born anthropologist Vilhjalmur *Stefansson. Despite the loss of his ship, the *Karluk*, Stefansson spent five years exploring the northern reaches of the archipelago. He travelled some 32,000 km across the ice by dogsled and made the first recorded visits to several remote islands. With Stefansson's return, the discovery of all the significant land masses in the *Arctic Archipelago was complete and the great age of exploration in Canada's North was over. There was still much to learn about the region, its geography, and resources, but its physical contours had been added to the map of the world.

DANIEL FRANCIS

Arms of Canada. Linked from medieval times with knights, heraldic devices came to be used on seals in peacetime; they were essential for the man of affairs when literacy was considered inessential save for specialists. As medieval heads of state frequently led their armies in person, their arms soon identified not just themselves but also the sovereignty they exercised. To this tradition, Canada is heir.

Prior to the establishment of the Arms of Canada, those applicable to the arms of supreme authority were those of the relevant imperial authorities, France and then Great Britain. Following Confederation, arms were assigned for Quebec and Ontario (1868); similar Arms of Particular Purpose for the other provinces followed later. However, it was not for another half century that arms were established for federal Canada. The proclamation, dated 21 November 1921, of George V rectified this oversight. Pursuant to the *Statute of Westminster (1931) they are technically Arms of Dominion and Sovereignty of General Purpose of Her Majesty the Queen in right of Canada; briefly, the Arms of Canada.

While its uniqueness is the sole necessity—to distinguish Canadian sovereignty from any other—the actual design draws upon a rich historical inheritance. The shield is divided into five parts: four squares and a large division at the base. Usually, a blazon (technical description) is required for a heraldic design. However, with some of great antiquity a word or short phrase suffices, as with the first four elements of the design. Starting at upper left and proceeding clockwise they are: 1) *England*—red background with three gold lions (traditionally denoting determined strength), one above another, walking, viewing the viewer, right fore-paws raised, dating from Richard Coeur de Lion, 1154–99; 2) *Scotland*—gold background, a lion rampant within two parallel bands with fleurs-de-lys facing alternately inwards and outwards, all red, from the time of Alexander II, 1214–49; 3) *France Modern*—blue background, three gold fleurs-de-lys arranged two above and one beneath, from Charles V, *c.* 1375; 4) *Ireland*—blue background featuring a gold harp with seven silver strings, from James I, 1603. These four elements recall four of the early *founding peoples. The section at the bottom of the shield shows three red maple leaves conjoined on a single stem and sitting on a silver/white background. This refers to all those, Aboriginal as well as immigrant, who have contributed singularly to the development of the country. The maple leaf—quintessentially symbolic of Canada, notably in the *national flag—entered heraldry officially in the arms granted to Sir Louis-Hippolyte *LaFontaine, Baronet, when chief justice of Canada East (1854).

The animals that support the shield—termed Supporters—are inspired by the lion and unicorn of the Royal Arms of England/Great Britain since James VI and I (1603). Each holds a lance. From that of the gold lion (left to viewer) flies a Union Badge banner (often called the Union Jack), referring to the British contribution to the development of the Canadian constitution. From that of the silver and gold unicorn (a mythical pre-heraldic beast of European and Asiatic origins) a banner of France Modern flies, recalling the early settlement and exploration by the French.

The crest—the uppermost element—is a gold lion (its stance as in the first division of the shield) holding a red maple leaf. It is crowned royally. A further crown ensigns the total design, Canada being a *constitutional monarchy. The helm, upon which the crest stands, is royal: barred, all gold, and facing the viewer. The wreath of twisted silk beneath the crest, and the *parasolesque* mantling—flowing on either side from beneath the crest wreath—are of the Canadian livery colours: red and white, and thus of the national flag. Beneath the shield, a blue ribbon, inscribed in gold with Canada's motto **A mari usque ad mare*, is festooned with roses (Tudor—white on red), thistles, shamrocks, and madonna lillies, further references to early settlers. Such complete the armorial bearings.

As with West Coast totemic art, heraldry aims at quiddity, not zoological or botanical representation. Curiously, although the *beaver has long served as a Canadian symbol, it has never figured in the heraldry of colonial, provincial, or federal governments. SIR CONRAD SWAN

Aroostook War, 1839. A bloodless boundary disagreement between New Brunswick and Maine. As Maine's population grew, the state attempted to extend its jurisdiction north, particularly into the Aroostook River valley and among the Acadian settlements along the Saint John and Madawaska Rivers. *Loyalists had settled along the Saint John River and moved north through the valley, which was along the road to Quebec. The New Brunswick government considered the vital road to be threatened by American expansion. A crisis erupted in 1839 when lumbermen licensed by New Brunswick began cutting timber in the disputed area. The Maine agent sent into the region was arrested by New Brunswick authorities, but the Maine posse took into custody the New Brunswicker officials. Maine, supported by Massachusetts and the US Congress, called up the militia; New Brunswick and Nova Scotia also called up the militia, and regular army troops were sent into the region. President Martin Van Buren ordered General Winfield Scott to the border area, and he and lieutenant-governor of New Brunswick, Sir John Harvey, negotiated a truce. When the *Ashburton-Webster Treaty was signed in 1842, the lands south of the Saint John River valley, including the Aroostook River, became part of Maine.

FRANCIS M. CARROLL

art galleries. Public institutions established by collectors, amateurs, and artists for the display and collecting of visual arts to stimulate public interest in the arts. Almost all began as volunteer bodies organizing infrequent exhibitions in temporary spaces, finding permanent homes at a later date. For example, the Art Association of Montreal (Montreal Museum of Fine Arts since 1949), organized in 1860, opened its first building in 1879, and the Art Museum of Toronto (Art Gallery of Ontario since 1966), founded in 1900, built its first galleries in 1918. Specific donations have on occasion been the catalysts for the establishment of art *museums. The Bruce family's donation of paintings by W. Blair Bruce led to the establishment of the Art Gallery of Hamilton in 1914, and the Robert Harris Memorial Gallery established by the artist's widow in 1928 was the precursor of the Confederation Art Gallery in Charlottetown (1964). Established as private institutions, they now receive both private and public support and some have become municipal bodies. Only the National Gallery of Canada (1880), the Musée du Québec (1933), and the Musée d'art contemporain (1964) were founded as state institutions.

Most galleries collect both Canadian and foreign art, focusing largely on the fine arts, while others have provincial or regional mandates. Through gifts, institutions have acquired strong representations of the work of particular artists (e.g., Emily *Carr at the Vancouver Art Gallery, James Wilson Morrice at the Montreal Museum, Napoléon Bourassa at the Musée du Québec, Paul-Émile Borduas at the Musée d'art contemporain). Some (e.g., Winnipeg Art Gallery, founded in 1912, and Montreal Museum) also collect and exhibit decorative arts. The Sarnia Women's Conservation Association began collecting contemporary Canadian art in 1920 (now in the Gallery Lambton, Sarnia) but the first institution established for the display and collecting of contemporary art was the Musée d'art contemporain. Power Plant, devoted solely to the exhibition but not collecting of contemporary art, was established by a group of artists, dealers, and collectors in Toronto in 1976.

The National Gallery was the first to establish a conservation and restoration program for the collections (in the 1920s). While larger institutions now have conservators on staff, all have access to the services of private conservators. Publishing catalogues for specific exhibitions and on the collections is a major function of galleries today.

All galleries have education programs, some with a strong studio component (e.g., the Art Gallery of Toronto from 1926), and the Art Association of Montreal ran its own art school, 1883–1924 and 1934–77. The Owens Art Institution, a gallery and art school, was established in Saint John, New Brunswick, in 1886 but was sold in 1893 to Mount Allison Ladies College in Sackville, where the Owens Art Gallery is related to the fine art program. Most universities teaching studio arts and art history also have galleries, the first being Université Laval, which purchased a portion of the collection of the painter Joseph *Légaré in 1874 (now the collection of the *Séminaire de Québec on deposit at the Musée de la civilisation, Quebec). Norman Mackenzie bequeathed his collection to the University of Saskatchewan, Regina campus, in 1936, the Norman Mackenzie Art Gallery opening in 1953 and now independent of the university. The Morris and Helen Belkin Gallery at the University of British Columbia currently has an active and innovative exhibition and publishing program.

Until the 1950s artists were often active in the establishment of galleries where the annual exhibitions of artists' societies were held. Thereafter these societies became less influential. While artists have representation on a number of gallery boards, from 1967 artists established their own spaces, beginning with Intermedia in Vancouver, to control the distribution of their work and to exhibit more experimental art. These are not collecting institutions. There are now approximately 70 artist-run centres across Canada, supported by the Canada Council, where emerging artists often get their first exposure. Some of these centres are devoted to specific media, such as video, a medium in which Canadian artists have made international contributions. CHARLES C. HILL

arts organizations. It is difficult to identify the earliest arts organization in Canada: groups among the pre-contact First Nations preserved and transmitted cultural possessions such as narratives. Definition is also complicated by the variety of contemporary groups, from collectives to granting agencies, from appreciation societies to policy lobbies. To modernize and narrow the definition, 'arts organization' is here limited to groups that encourage development of arts and letters, and is differentiated from an arts ensemble itself (such as an orchestra). Using this restricted definition, the earliest society may be the *Ordre de Bon Temps, established at Port-Royal by Samuel de *Champlain in 1606–7 to encourage theatrical entertainments in the first French settlement. Military garrisons acted as cultural centres through the 18th and 19th centuries, with their band concerts, amateur theatricals, and book collections that functioned as local lending libraries. Dedicated cultural associations were first formed in the early 19th century, designed to promote learning, define taste, and develop the cultural infrastructure of the new society. Two early examples include the Society for the Encouragement of Art and Science in Canada (Quebec, 1827) and the Hamilton Association for the Advancement of Literature and Science (founded 1857, and still extant). The goal of the latter was 'the formation of a Library and Museum, the cultivation of Literature and Science, and the illustration of the History and Physical Characteristics of the Country'. Such wide-ranging mandates continued, as shown by the name of the Vancouver Art, Historical and Scientific Association (1894). Mutual instruction societies—lyceums, athenaeums, *Mechanics' Institutes—staged recitations, performances, conversaziones, and visiting lecture series that were often open to the public. More specialized societies also took root. The Halifax Chess, Pencil and Brush Club (1787) is generally considered the first artists' organization in Canada; early York (Toronto) enjoyed a public exhibition by its Society of Artists and Amateurs in 1834. Numerous literary societies, while formed primarily for readers, provided an audience and intellectual support for the writers who belonged to them.

Post-Confederation Canada witnessed some new developments. Artists' organizations such as the Art Association of Montreal (1860) and the Ontario Society of Artists (1872) organized schools of art in addition to exhibitions. This period marked the rise of women's cultural clubs: turn-of-the-century Toronto, for example, saw the inauguration of the Heliconian Club, a female counterpart to the Arts and Letters Club (1908), and of the University Women's Club, as well as branches of the Women's Art Association and the Women's Musical Club. These societies, which welcomed touring speakers and theatrical groups, curated travelling exhibitions, and promoted arts education in the schools, are all still active today.

Some early arts organizations were guilds or professional associations for their members: writers and illustrators discussed their craft at meetings of the Montreal Pen and Pencil Club (1890), for example. But by the beginning of the 20th century new organizations were formed to promote and even market the arts and to protect the intellectual and business interests of practitioners: the Canadian Handicrafts Guild (1906, later the Canadian Guild of Crafts), the Society of Canadian Painter-Etchers and Engravers (1916), the Canadian Authors' Association (1921), the Canadian Performing Rights Society (1925), the Composers, Authors and Publishers Association of Canada (1925), and the Sculptors' Society of Canada (1928). While some organizations accommodated francophone members (the Canadian Authors' Association had a separate Section française), both Quebeckers and non-urban artists were often better served by regional and provincial umbrella groups—such as the Contemporary Art Society (Montreal, 1939), the Maritime Art Association (1935), the Manitoba Drama League (1932), or the Western Board of Music (1936)—than by nominally national organizations.

Not all associations stressed professional concerns. Many promoted a specific aesthetic, as did the *Group of Seven (1920) and the *Automatistes (1941), or advanced a political position, as did the Progressive Arts Clubs (1931). The activities of music festivals and drama competitions were overarched by bodies such as the Federation of Canadian Music Festivals (1926) and the *Dominion Drama Festival (1933). The Allied Arts Council (1938), based in Toronto but with regional branches, was an ambitious attempt to connect both professional and amateur groups across all cultural sectors.

While there were many organizations active at mid-century they lacked coordination, a focus for national policy development, and established funding. This situation changed after the *Massey Commission made wide-ranging recommendations in its 1951 report. One result was the formation of the Canada Council in 1957 as a consolidated source of funding for the arts. The mushrooming of arts organizations in the 1960s and 1970s was due in part to changes in funding, but also to the new nationalisms sweeping the country and the new politicization of the art world. This period saw the rise of more activist professional associations such as Canadian Artists Representation/Front des artistes canadiens (1967) and the Writers' Union of Canada (1973). The arts in Quebec developed an increasingly separate organizational infrastructure, with parallel associations such as the Association des sculpteurs du Québec (1961).

There is now a striking proliferation of local, provincial, and national associations. An author in early-21st-century Canada could belong to the *Canadian Authors' Association, the Writers' Union of Canada, the Playwrights' Union of Canada, the League of Canadian Poets, the Writers Guild of Canada (a screenwriters' society), the Periodical Writers' Association of Canada, or the Société des écrivains canadiens. The author might belong to a Canadian branch of International PEN, or to a provincial writers' organization. Further affiliations might be to associations and collectives organized along lines of gender, sexuality, or ethnicity. Amateurs, art lovers, and audience members have their associations as well, often locally based or in affiliation with an established cultural group. Opera companies, ballet companies, and symphonies are increasingly dependent on the fund-raising endeavours of 'Friends of . . .' societies. The plethora of organizations is a sign of the diversity and vitality of the arts today but also of continuing efforts to combat the crisis in cultural funding and the weakening of a national cultural mandate.

HEATHER MURRAY

Asbestos strike. This strike, surely Quebec's best-known labour conflict, gave rise to numerous studies, including a book edited by Pierre Elliott *Trudeau. This volume was the source of the common interpretation that the conflict was a great moment in the workers' struggle and a turning point in the history of Quebec, marking the entry of francophone society into the industrial world. The conflict, which involved nearly 5,000 workers at Asbestos and Thetford, lasted more than five months, February–July 1949. Unions affiliated with the *Confédération des travailleurs catholiques du Canada demanded elimination of asbestos dust, a general increase of 15 cents an hour, and union 'consultation' on all promotions, transfers, and dismissals (the *'Rand formula'). The companies offered a general increase of 5 cents and rejected the other demands.

Because the miners stopped work without undergoing arbitration, the strike was illegal and the government suspended the union's certification. The Canadian Johns Manville Company believed itself justified in recruiting strikebreakers. Their presence provoked altercations with the strikers, who on 5 May blockaded the roads into the village. More than 200 provincial police were rushed to Asbestos and the Riot Act was read. More than a hundred arrests followed, and several strikers were roughed up by police.

As the conflict continued, it attracted a great deal of attention in the province and gave rise to a vast movement of solidarity. More than $500,000 in cash and $75,000 worth of supplies were collected by unionists of all affiliations and donated at churches, as requested by several bishops who supported the strikers and wanted the government of Quebec to back down from its overly legalistic position. Following mediation by Mgr Roy, the archbishop of Quebec, the company agreed to withdraw proceedings against the union, the government agreed to restore union accreditation, and the miners returned to work. But nothing was settled about working conditions; after negotiations failed, that issue was submitted to an arbitration panel, which granted an increase of 10 cents an hour but rejected the union's other demands.

The strike constituted a defeat for the union members involved, and it had few positive repercussions for the labour movement in the 1950s. Yet, over the longer term its effects were not insignificant: on the symbolic level the strike came to represent labour's unyielding resistance in the face of the *Duplessis government's bias in favour of employers. The interpretation given to the strike created a fund of public sympathy that provided dividends for the workers in the 1960s and 1970s, when the Quebec government proved receptive to union demands.

JACQUES ROUILLARD

As for Me and My House. This 1941 novel by Sinclair Ross (1908–96) vividly describes living through the Depression on the Prairies. There is no better fictional account of the desolation that descended on this region in the form of drought, dust storms, and crop failure, or of the demoralization from ensuing debt. The story, set in the small town of Horizon, is told in the form of a diary kept by a minister's wife who, like the land around her, is barren and who records the oppressive social reality of the false-fronted small towns riven by petty ambitions and religious hypocrisy. In the story of her husband she also conveys the frustration of a man struggling to be an artist in this suffocating environment. For its oblique narrative form (a man writing the story of a woman who is writing the story of a man) and for its genius in using setting to mirror the inner drama of its characters, *As for Me and My House* is distinguished as one of Canada's foremost modernist novels.

DAVID STOUCK

Ashburton-Webster Treaty, 1842. This treaty, negotiated by Lord Ashburton, British special minister, and Daniel Webster, US secretary of state, settled the eastern boundaries of British North America and the United States. Ambiguities in the treaty ending the War of American Independence led to disagreements about the boundary that commissions under the Jay Treaty and the Treaty of Ghent and the arbitration of the King of the Netherlands had been unable fully to resolve. Working with advice from Sir Charles Bagot, representatives from New Brunswick, and delegations from Maine and Massachusetts, Ashburton and Webster modified in Canada's favour the boundary set by the king of the Netherlands, accepted the 1774 line between Lower Canada and New York, and compromised on rival claims from the upper Great Lakes to the Lake of the Woods. Of further importance to Canadians was an *extradition clause, resolution of the *Caroline* incident, American use of the Saint John River, and a general détente with the United States.

FRANCIS M. CARROLL

Asiatic Exclusion League. From the time that *Chinese and *Japanese began arriving in the province, British Columbians opposed their presence, citing their alleged 'cheap labour', low living standards, different customs (reflecting their 'inassimilability'), and their potential to overwhelm the white population, which, in 1901, was only about 125,000. Responding to repeated protests, in 1886 the federal government imposed a head tax on Chinese immigrants; by 1904 the tax was $500. Because of the Anglo-Japanese Alliance, Anglo-Japanese commercial treaties, and Canada's colonial status, Canada could do little to curb Japanese immigration. In the first seven months of 1907, over 5,500 Japanese landed in British Columbia, and more were expected.

In August 1907, the Vancouver *Trades and Labour Council invited elected officials and anyone who believed in keeping Canada 'a white man's country' to help found the Asiatic Exclusion League. To recruit members, the league sponsored a parade and rally at City Hall on Saturday, 7 September. Several American visitors, a New Zealander, two local clergymen, and prominent Liberals and Conservatives spoke inside the hall and repeated some of their fiery speeches to the overflow crowd outside. Soon, the crowd turned into a mob that marched the few blocks to Chinatown, where they threw bricks and stones through shop windows. In neighbouring 'Little Tokyo', residents repelled the rioters but many windows were broken. News of the Vancouver riot quickly spread around the world. The embarrassed Laurier government sent deputy labour minister W.L. Mackenzie *King to investigate damage claims and labour minister Rodolphe Lemieux to Tokyo to negotiate a gentlemen's agreement whereby Japan limited emigration to Canada. Meanwhile, the league established branches in several coastal cities but had trouble maintaining its members' interest; in little more than a year it had disappeared.

In 1921, at a time of rising Asian immigration and economic uncertainty, a new, unrelated Asiatic Exclusion League emerged. It drew interest from labour and business groups and had branches in several BC cities but, after a brief flurry of activity, it too faded into obscurity. Others, notably BC's MPs and the Retail Merchants Association of Canada, took up the cause and lobbied for the passage of the exclusionary Chinese Immigration Act (1923). While both Asiatic Exclusion Leagues had short histories, their activities helped stimulate federal actions to limit immigration from Japan and to halt it from China.

PATRICIA E. ROY

Assembly of First Nations. Founded between 1980 and 1982 as part of the swirl of events surrounding the push by the federal government to patriate Canada's *constitution, the AFN is a recent manifestation of a very old process. It is the most well known and influential organization of Aboriginal peoples in Canada, but since the earliest European colonization Aboriginals have created associations and confederacies to defend their lives, their ancestral lands and waters, and their collectively held rights to self-determination.

The modern history of Indian organization, culminating in the AFN's creation, was sometimes marked by government abuse of law and the agencies of law enforcement to prevent the exercise of rights most Canadians long took for granted. Between 1927 and 1951, for instance, the government outlawed most forms of political activity whose purpose was to defend the rights, titles, and interests of registered Indians. Section 141 of the *Indian Act, the statute governing reserves as well as the Indian wards of the federal Indian Department, prohibited any unauthorized financial exchange for the advancement of a claim. This draconian provision was added to the act primarily to counter the effectiveness of the Allied Tribes of British Columbia, founded in 1916, whose main objective was to force governments to implement the provisions of the *Royal Proclamation of 1763 that required negotiation of *Indian treaties as the necessary prelude to opening new Crown lands to settlement. Many government initiatives—an early Indian Act, evocatively titled an Act for the Gradual Civilization of the Indian Tribes; the imposition of the band-council system; the federally funded system of church-run Indian *residential schools; the outlawing of Aboriginal religious ceremonies—were premised on the assumption that First Nations were terminal societies whose destiny was to disappear under federal tutelage in an accelerated transition from Indian savagery to Canadian civilization.

By the end of the First World War Aboriginal leaders mounted another organizational push to counter the concentration of so much arbitrary authority in the federal ministry of Indian Affairs. Lieutenant Fred *Loft, a Mohawk activist from the Six Nations reserve near Brantford, Ontario, was most instrumental in establishing, in 1918, the League of Indians of Canada. The league's main demand was that registered Indians should cease to be wards of the government and allowed to retain their special status as First Nations people while also sharing in the rights and responsibilities of Canadian citizenship. The government interpreted the work of the league as seditious, possibly linked to a Bolshevik conspiracy.

Before 1924 the Six Nations reserve, in recognition of its historic role as allies of the Crown in the American Revolution and the War of 1812, had not been subjected to the full repression of the Indian Act. All that changed when the RCMP on Mackenzie *King's orders broke up the reserve's Longhouse government with the aim of undermining the international effectiveness of *Deskaheh, the ambassador sent by the Six Nations to the *League of Nations in Geneva. Another target of police harassment was the Canadian operations of the League of Nations of North American Indians, led by Lawrence Twoaxe, a Mohawk from Kahnawake, Quebec, who was a resident in Oakland, California. Twoaxe worked closely with Ed Thompson of Manitoba's Peguis reserve and John Tootoosis of Saskatchewan's Poundmaker reserve. Tootoosis would emerge as one of the most influential of the Indian politicians from the Prairies, many of whom have asserted, through vehicles such as Saskatchewan's Queen Victoria's Treaty Protection Association, that their peoples' nation-to nation agreements with the Crown confirm the continuing sovereignty of their Aboriginal polities.

Federal efforts to outlaw and repress the organizational work of Indian peoples were somewhat relaxed during the Second World War. At a meeting of Indian politicians in Ottawa in 1944 the North American Indian Brotherhood (NAIB) was established, with Andy Paull, a Squamish activist, as leader. During the years when Indian politics were essentially criminalized, Paull had continued his political networking under the cover of his career as a coach of Aboriginal hockey and lacrosse teams. The government signalled that it would tolerate the work of the NAIB, but only if it excluded the activities of Jules Sioui, a Huron politician from Loretteville, Quebec. Thereafter Sioui teamed up with William Commanda of Maniwaki to establish the North American Indian Nation. Sioui's more extreme brand of sovereigntist politics would later find expression in the rise in Canada and the United States of the American Indian Movement, an organization that inspired a number of militant Aboriginal stands, including those at Anicinabe Park, Kenora, in 1974, Oka in 1990, and Gustafsen Lake in 1995. There were local roots too for these conflicts. The more militant protagonists argued that federally funded organizations, including the AFN, were too closely aligned with the structures of oppression to offer any real possibility of liberation for all but a privileged, self-serving minority.

Meanwhile, the more moderate Indian organizations represented by Paull and the NAIB led to the formation of the National Indian Council in 1961. In 1968 it divided to conform to the legal status of Native people on both sides of the rather arbitrary structures created by the Indian Act: the *Metis and non-status Indians became the primary constituency for the Native Council of Canada, while the National Indian Brotherhood took over the responsibility of providing a national political voice for status Indians governed by the act. The NIB was established just in time to become the main bastion of organized resistance to a federal initiative to eliminate all the legal and institutional edifices supporting a distinct legal status for Indian groups and individuals in Canada. That initiative, soon dubbed the *White Paper, which promoted the inclusion of First Nations in a more pluralistic model of Canadian federalism, grew from an ideological aversion of the new prime minister, Pierre *Trudeau, to nationalist movements of all kinds, especially those favouring a sovereign Quebec.

The Indian rejection of the White Paper helped Trudeau to see the potential usefulness of Aboriginal people as allies of federal authority and as natural opponents of those seeking to extend the provincial monopoly over the exploitation of natural resources. The profile of Aboriginal issues was significantly raised when the Trudeau government directed a significant flow of federal dollars not only to the NIB but to a host of provincial and territorial Aboriginal organizations, hoping to bring to the negotiations various configurations of Aboriginal political will. One of the primary laboratories for this post-1969 regime was the CCF government in Saskatchewan; from that left-leaning experiment in social democracy emerged the Federated Saskatchewan Indian Nations, a regional organization with elaborate tentacles extending far into provincial, federal, and Aboriginal politics.

The rejection of the White Paper heralded a new era of constitutional politics. The courts were key players. Their rulings affirmed the existence of *Aboriginal title in British Columbia and northern Quebec, decisions that led to the renewed application of the Royal Proclamation of 1763 in modern-day treaty deals across northern Canada. While these decisions helped to draw attention to the contemporary implications of Canada's legal inheritances from the British Empire, the election of a separatist government in Quebec in 1976 further underlined the centrality of the constitution as the main instrument of success or failure in the unfolding experiment of Canadian federalism. These developments established the context for the emergence of the AFN from the NIB. The architects of the Assembly of First Nations asserted in its founding constitution 'that the rights and responsibilities given us by the Creator cannot be altered or taken away by any other nation'. On this basis the Indian lobby intervened in Britain to try to stop the transfer without Aboriginal consent of constitutional powers, including over Indian treaties, from the mother country to Canada's governments. The Canadian constitution was patriated with a provision, section 35, recognizing and affirming the existence of Aboriginal and treaty rights. Between 1983 and 1987 a series of first ministers' conferences attempted to define these rights through a process of constitutional amendment. Like the three other Aboriginal organizations invited to these meetings, the AFN had no formal vote, but its leaders used the venue to press for expansive interpretations of section 35, insisting that its wording carved out large constitutional receptacles for the content of Aboriginal title, Indian treaties, and the inherent right of Aboriginal self-government. AFN leaders have repeated this interpretation of section 35 during the *Meech Lake controversy, in the proceedings of the Royal Commission on *Aboriginal Peoples (1991–6), in negotiations spawned by violent clashes at Burnt Church over the Aboriginal treaty right to fish off the Maritimes coast, and in recent efforts to amend the Indian Act. Prominent among AFN politicians have been George Manuel, Harold Cardinal, Billy Diamond, David Ahenakew, Sol Sanderson, Georges Erasmus, Ovide Mercredi, and Phil Fontaine.

In 1983 some Aboriginal leaders formed the Coalition of First Nations to protest the AFN's decision to sit down with the premiers in Ottawa, thereby seemingly legitimizing a provincial role in the constitutional definition of Aboriginal and treaty rights. Aboriginal women have charged that the AFN's emphasis on group rights over individual rights disguises a deep bias towards the imperatives of patriarchy. Of all the issues faced by the AFN, however, perhaps the most perplexing is the apparent contradiction between its promotion of an expansive interpretation of section 35 as the appropriate basis for the development of Aboriginal policy and its own internal structure as an organization whose leadership is derived exclusively from the votes of the elected chiefs of Canada's 633 Indian bands. In 2000 the AFN's newly elected national chief, Mathew Coon Come, implicitly recognized the centrality of this contradiction when he called for a change that would see his organization choose its leadership based on the universal franchise of all adults in Canada who are registered Indians. Even this change, however, would leave the federal Indian Act as the primary instrument for determining First Nations' citizenship.

ANTHONY J. HALL

Assiniboia. The name was first applied to the 301,600 sq km tract of land in what is now southern Manitoba that Thomas Douglas, the Fifth Earl of *Selkirk, obtained from the *Hudson's Bay Company in 1811. Selkirk's motives were partly philanthropic—he wanted to establish a colony for dispossessed Scottish tenant farmers—but also strategic: Assiniboia would provide the HBC (in which Selkirk had a controlling interest) with an assured food and labour supply and better enable it to compete in the *fur trade.

Assiniboia was also one of four provisional districts (the others were Alberta, Athabasca, and Saskatchewan) that the federal government established in the *North-West Territories in 1882. Although the subdivision was intended to facilitate mail delivery, at the time some suggested—incorrectly, as it turned out—that it might also serve as the basis for the creation of future provinces. Assiniboia had a population of 30,372 in 1891 and 67,385 in 1901. Its economy was based largely on cereal agriculture. *Regina, with 2,239 people in 1901, was its largest town.

J. WILLIAM BRENNAN

Assistance maternelle de Montréal. Founded in 1912 by Caroline Leclerc-Hamilton (1857–1945), this women's philanthropic organization was dedicated to helping needy pregnant women by providing them with material aid (bedding, layettes, food, fuel) and free medical care. In response to urgent need, in the 1920s the Assistance maternelle became the city's second most important philanthropic organization, after the St Vincent de Paul Society, and an essential part of Montreal's social and health services. During the crisis of the 1930s it assisted 3,000–4,000 mothers every year—a number representing roughly a quarter of all births in the city, or a third of all children born to French-Canadian families. But in the 1950s, with the return of prosperity following the Second World War and the shift to birthing in hospitals rather than at home, the organization declined. Still in operation, the Assistance maternelle now concentrates on distributing layettes, mainly to immigrant women.

DENYSE BAILLARGEON

astronomy. Canadian astronomical history can be divided into three phases. First, astronomy was a tool for navigation and exploration. The earliest explorers could ascertain their latitudes by using relatively simple astronomical devices, but could not measure their longitudes. Only with the development of a reliable, portable chronometer in the 18th century could explorers begin to map Canada's coasts. Canada had no need for permanent observatories or trained professionals, although navigation was taught in Canada from the late 17th century.

The second phase, beginning in the 19th century, centred upon practical astronomy, largely for land *surveying. With the expansion of telegraph lines from the 1840s, observers at two ends of a line could observe the same stars and compare their observation times, which gave the longitude difference. Astronomers were part of the survey of western Canada and of provincial and international *boundaries. Federal astronomers founded the Dominion Observatory in Ottawa in 1905 as a base for geographic and geodetic work. Accurate time-keeping was another need, first for shipping, then for railways, and finally for commerce and everyday life. In the 20th century, the Dominion Observatory provided daily time signals to the country by radio.

The third phase focuses upon astrophysics. C.A. Chant formed an astronomy department at the University of Toronto before 1920; by the end of the Second World War, Toronto trained almost all Canadian astronomers. J.S. Plaskett, at the Dominion Observatory, pioneered the study of binary stars, which became a Canadian specialty. Through his efforts, the Dominion Astrophysical Observatory opened in 1918 in Victoria, British Columbia, with the world's largest telescope. By 1935, Toronto opened the David Dunlap Observatory with the world's second-largest reflecting telescope. Work on binary stars dominated Canadian astronomy in all three observatories during the interwar years.

After the Second World War, new fields opened. Radio astronomy developed at both the *National Research Council and the Dominion Observatory; by 1960, Canada had two radio observatories—in Penticton, BC, and in *Algonquin Park. A highlight of radio astronomy was the 1967 demonstration of Very Long-Base Interferometry. At the University of Toronto, Peter Millman directed a wide-ranging meteor program from the late 1930s. This work expanded in the 1950s, especially during the International Geophysical Year (1957–8). C.S. Beals and Dominion Observatory geophysics staff began searching for and exploring ancient meteorite and asteroid craters. From the 1960s, new academic programs and new, modest observatories appeared across Canada.

The Dominion Observatory closed in 1970, the astronomers moving to the NRC, forming what is now the Herzberg Institute of Astrophysics. The Algonquin, Victoria, and Penticton facilities—opened to all Canadian astronomers—also came under its control. In 1979, Canada became a partner in the superb Canada–France–Hawaii telescope. Canadian astronomers now share land facilities with a number of countries and participate in several space-based astronomical projects.

RICHARD A. JARRELL

Ataguttaaluk (*c.* 1870–1948). *Inuit leader, born in the northern Foxe Basin region of Canada's eastern High Artic, Ataguttaaluk was renowned for her strength and courage. During an overland journey she and her young family became stranded by poor weather conditions. Unable to hunt, they ate their dogs, tent, and clothing. Ataguttaaluk watched her husband and children die of starvation. She survived by eating their bodies. Following rescue, she returned to Igloolik and married hunter Ittuksarjuat. They acted as prominent cultural brokers between Inuit and whalers, explorers, traders, and missionaries who dubbed her 'Queen of Igloolik'. Ataguttaaluk's spirit is entrenched in Inuit oral history. In Igloolik today, both schools bear her name. Ataguttaaluk died in a hunting camp called Kangiq, among her many relatives and descendants. NANCY WACHOWICH

Atlantic, Battle of the. The longest battle of the Second World War, the Battle of the Atlantic started on 3 September 1939, the day Britain declared war on Germany, when U-30 sank the liner *Athenia*; the last victim was sunk on 7 May 1945, nearly six years later. At the core of this battle was the German attempt to deny the free movement of ships essential to the Allied war effort. From 1939 until 1941 action focused primarily on efforts to knock Britain out of the war through a combined surface, subsurface, and aerial assault on its shipping. By 1941 American involvement in the war guaranteed British survival, just as the German attack shifted almost completely to submarines. From 1942 to 1945 the Germans tried to sink enough ships in the Atlantic to impede the development of Allied offensive operations based in Britain and the Mediterranean. Allied shipping losses peaked in 1942, and the high point of attacks on the main transatlantic *convoys came in early 1943, followed immediately by a crushing defeat of the U-boats. From mid-1943 until the end of the war Allied shipping and military operations moved largely unhindered.

Canada played a major role in the Battle of the Atlantic—its largest and most important contribution to any campaign in the Second World War. At the height of the battle in 1943, half of the Allied naval escorts, one-quarter of the air squadrons, and one-quarter of the aircrew in British maritime patrol squadrons were Canadian. Canada made significant contributions in command, control, and intelligence areas as well.

MARC MILNER

Atlantic Charter. In August 1941 British prime minister Winston Churchill and American president Franklin Roosevelt met aboard ship in Placentia Bay, offshore from the US naval base at Argentia, Newfoundland. It was the first and, in many respects, the most significant of their meetings, forging a special relationship that was to last until Roosevelt's death and laying the foundation for future wartime co-operation between their two countries. That meeting also produced the Atlantic Charter, a declaration of principles upon which the two men hoped to build a new world order that would govern international relations once the war was over. These principles included self-determination, liberal trade practices, improved living standards, freedom of the seas, the rejection of force, and the promotion of peace. They were later incorporated into the *United Nations Charter, giving lasting import to the Atlantic Charter and to the shared vision of these two leaders.

DAVID FACEY-CROWTHER

Atlantic fishery. The European-Atlantic fisheries originated in the late 1400s with the discovery by European fishermen of the stocks of cod fish on the *Grand Banks and around the coasts of Newfoundland. Using herring, caplin, and squid for bait, Spanish, Portuguese, French, and English fishermen caught, salted, and dried enormous quantities of cod. The industry became so significant that the terms 'fish' and 'salt fish' became synonymous with 'cod'. The English, with no source of local salt, developed a light-salted, well-dried fish that became the choice product with many consumers.

During the latter 1500s, the Spanish Empire (which included Portugal) lost a war with England, leaving only England and France to pursue the fishery in Newfoundland waters. The English fishery, now exporting fish to Spain and Portugal, was so valuable that London, Bristol, and other interests tried to establish colonies in Newfoundland in order to join in the prosperity. For various reasons, but primarily because of the short fishing season, the colonies were not a good investment and failed as business ventures, although many of the colonists joined the occasional fishermen who chose to make their homes in Newfoundland.

By the Treaty of Utrecht, 1713, France was forced to give up its claim to Newfoundland and to remove its colonists who resided on the south coast, especially in Placentia Bay. The French were allowed to establish a migratory fishery on the north and west coasts, but were prohibited from settling. This *'French Shore' became the location for a French migratory fishery.

Meanwhile, the traditional English migratory fishery underwent changes. In the beginning, it had been prosecuted on a first-come, first-served basis, with ships taking up fishing rooms (or spaces) in order of their arrival. However, necessary stages (roofed wharves), flakes (for drying fish), and cooking and sleeping facilities had to be constructed each spring. Initially, this had not been a problem because wood was plentiful right down to the water's edge. However, by the early 1600s, with the annual English fleet numbering up to 200–250 ships, convenient sources of wood had been depleted. Departing ships left few of their structures behind for fear that a competitor might reach them first the next year. As it became increasingly time consuming and expensive to acquire wood for new buildings, ships began leaving agents behind to protect their premises. They, along with the colonists and fishermen remaining on the island, became known as 'inhabitants' and carried out their own fishery in conjunction with the migratory ships from which they bought their supplies and hired their fishing servants. Additionally, ambitious fishermen who were prospering and ship owners who had lost their ships left fishing boats in the harbours and journeyed with their servants to and from Newfoundland on the migratory ships. This 'by boat' fishery became an important component of the West of England migratory fishery as well.

Inhabitants, by boats, and fishing ships (including a Grand Bank component) continued to fish throughout the 18th century, with locals prospering during wartime and the migratory fisheries prospering during the post-war depressions. Consequently, the wars with France (1689–97, 1702–13, and 1756–63) stimulated local population growth. Reluctantly, Britain provided rudimentary governance, trying in vain to maintain its migratory fishery in Newfoundland, from where so many of its naval ranks were recruited. The American Revolutionary War (1776–83) led to an expansion in the British bank fishery, but this was temporary, and the inhabitant fishery expanded until it was producing a major part of the catch. However, in many ways the inhabitant fishery was a component of the migratory fishery since it was prosecuted by planters who employed servants from Britain on an annual basis. The family-based fishery, the prominent pattern of the 19th century, was only in its infancy.

The French Revolutionary and Napoleonic Wars between 1793 and 1815 and the Anglo-American War (1812–14) eliminated all Newfoundland's market competition, and the resident fishery expanded as the demand for salt fish grew. By 1815, the local population stood at 40,000 people and included women and children. In the meantime, *sealing became important, and local sealing vessels began to sail to the unoccupied waters off the Labrador coast for the summer's fishery as the seal and Labrador cod fisheries became the mainstay of Newfoundland's northeast coast. Population levels, therefore, did not shrink in the post-war period, as had happened in the past: the Newfoundland economy had acquired its second industry and year-round habitation had become viable.

Meanwhile, the French continued to fish on the French Shore—a right that was not relinquished until 1904. After the War of Independence the United States had also received fishing rights in unoccupied harbours on Newfoundland's south and west coasts and the coast of Labrador; these had been confirmed by the treaties and the Convention of 1818. However, the Americans did very little fishing under the terms of the Convention, except in Labrador. American fishermen were most interested in fishing mackerel along the coast of the maritime British North American colonies and in catching and purchasing herring for bait in Newfoundland's coastal waters. This bait trade was stimulated by the growth in the Bank fishery in the second half of the 19th century. On the Banks, bultows or long trawl lines with many hooks could be used without the restrictions that small harbours imposed. Thus Bank fishing drew Americans,

Nova Scotians, and French away from inshore fishing. Newfoundland also engaged in this fishery but maintained its inshore fishery as well. Eventually, the introduction of steamers to the Bank fishery encouraged trawling with large nets, generating a huge amount of wasted by-catch.

In the latter years of the 19th century, the inshore fishermen of Newfoundland and Labrador began using the box-like cod trap. This became the most popular fishing technique until the widespread use of gill nets in the *fisheries of the late 20th century. SHANNON RYAN

Atlantic migration. Between 1815 and 1860, immigration from the British Isles transformed the British North American colonies. When the period began, most English-speaking British North Americans were American-born or their descendants. Some belonged to families that had migrated north before the American Revolution; others belonged to the *Loyalist influx of the revolutionary period; still others had arrived since that time. They gave British North America a Yankee flavour in speech and culture. The character of the colonies changed radically in the 19th century as transatlantic migration reached massive proportions. Such migration rose to an unprecedented level in 1832. Although it fell in the late 1830s, as a consequence of an economic downturn in Europe and North America, it reached a pre-Confederation peak in 1847, following the Irish potato famine, when nearly 110,000 immigrants disembarked at British North American ports.

Official figures show about 1.2 million immigrants arrived in the years from 1815 to 1860. These figures are imperfect because they include immigrants bound for the United States via British North America and exclude immigrants who came through the United States. The vast majority of immigrants arrived in a family group. In the 1830s about a quarter were children; by the 1840s the proportion had risen to a third. Because many of the arrivals were young families, the immigrant generation reproduced itself quickly, making the second generation a sizable element in the total population. In Upper Canada, the fastest growing colony, the immigrant generation alone made up over one-third of the population by the early 1840s. Through immigration and natural increase, British North America grew from 570,000 in 1815 to about 3.5 million in 1860.

Most of the immigrants were British, although some were German, particularly from the Rhineland. Of the British, a majority were *Irish, a third were *English, and an eighth were Scottish. Of the Irish, a majority were Protestants from Ulster and from Protestant areas in southern Ireland. Newfoundland was an early destination for Catholic Irish, but from the 1820s Catholic Irish immigration to the mainland was on the rise. It reached its zenith in the famine migration of 1847 and then fell off because the colonial economy could not absorb so many people. English immigration drew on counties from Yorkshire and Lancashire in the north to Devonshire and Cornwall in the southwest. Among the *Scots, Gaelic-speaking Highlanders predominated to 1815. Subsequently, the movement included a growing proportion of Lowlanders. Despite their smaller community base, Scottish politicians and businessmen were prominent in colonial society.

In the 1815-60 period, migration proceeded with little regulation. In the 18th century, European governments had restricted emigration because they associated a nation's wealth with its population. By the 1820s, British politicians generally agreed that emigration was a national solution for poverty and underemployment; but they were unwilling to spend public money to promote it. Voluntary, self-financed emigration had to be the answer. To make this possible, the British Parliament kept fares low by allowing crowding on emigrant ships. Between 1803 and 1828 Parliament progressively weakened the Passenger Act, increasing crowding by 50 per cent. As late as the 1840s, standards were lower than those in force at the beginning of the century. Only in 1855 did Parliament legislate a major improvement. Throughout the period, enforcement was inadequate, and many ships carried more passengers than regulations allowed. The worst conditions, and therefore the lowest fares, were allowed on ships sailing from Irish ports. This was because the British government saw emigration as a solution for Irish poverty and unrest. The most impoverished immigrants arriving in British North America came from Ireland.

Until the 1860s, wooden sailing ships, typically of 400 or 500 tons, carried immigrants. Most of these ships were engaged in the timber trade, transporting immigrants one way and timber the other. The average crossing to Quebec was six weeks. All but 2 or 3 per cent of immigrants travelled steerage because they could not afford cabin fares. In steerage, passengers were packed below the main deck in a five-and-a-half- or six-foot high space without portholes. To create this space, captains built a temporary deck on the lower beams of the ship. On a 400-ton vessel, the steerage deck would be 95 by 25 feet with tiered wooden berths along each side for 200 or 300 people. Weather permitting, passengers spent their time in the fresh air above deck. The conditions, nonetheless, invited disease. In addition, passengers ran out of provisions when the crossing was prolonged by storms or calms. The worst years were 1832 and 1847, peak years in immigrant traffic and also *epidemic years on both sides of the Atlantic. In 1847, the death rate on the Atlantic crossing was 16 per cent. In a more typical year it was about 1 per cent.

At mid-century, British North America remained overwhelmingly rural, although it was beginning to industrialize and urbanize. A majority of the English, Scots, *Germans, and Protestant Irish and nearly half of the Catholic Irish settled on farms. Although the Catholic Irish were over-represented among servants and general labourers and under-represented among merchants and professionals, every immigrant group was distributed across the occupational structure. As their numbers increased, the Catholic Irish became the targets of antagonism. Racial stereotyping, local violence involving Catholic and Protestant Irish, the rise of Orange lodges, and political division on the question of separate Catholic schools were all manifestations of the tensions produced during this period of immigration. HUGH JOHNSTON

Atlantic Revolution. A term coined by historian W.S. MacNutt in an article published in the June 1957 issue of the *Atlantic Advocate* to describe co-operative efforts by politicians, business leaders, and professional people to improve the economic conditions in the Atlantic region, which trailed behind the rest of Canada in living standards. As in Quebec, where the term *Quiet Revolution came to describe modernization trends in the post–Second World War period, the Atlantic Revolution tended to focus on the state as the vehicle for creating the conditions necessary for economic transformation. The Maritime Provinces Board of Trade set the ball of regional co-operation rolling by sponsoring a joint meeting with the premiers of the four Atlantic provinces in Moncton in September 1953, which led to the creation of the Atlantic Provinces Economic Council and regular meetings among Atlantic premiers to coordinate regional development policies. Under pressure from the poorer provinces in Confederation, the federal Liberal government established equalization payments in 1956. Two years later, the recently elected Progressive Conservative administration implemented Atlantic Provinces Adjustments Grants. Regional economic development was further advanced by the establishment of the federal Atlantic Development Board in 1962, which continued in various guises into the 21st century. Although the development projects sponsored by provincial and federal agencies failed to liberate the Atlantic provinces from their 'have-not' status in Canada, and the impact of these projects is the subject of continuing debate, the region has grown along with the larger Canadian economy, which is a victory of sorts.
MARGARET CONRAD

***Atlantic* steamship disaster**, 1 April 1873. One of the largest ships of its time, SS *Atlantic* was one of four luxurious steamships built to establish the fledgling White Star Line in 1871. En route to New York, *Atlantic* diverted to Halifax for extra coal. Despite approaching an unfamiliar coastline in darkness, the captain took few precautions and the liner struck the rocks at full speed at Lower Prospect near Halifax. The ship rolled and sank in minutes. The struggle to escape the submerged hull and make it to a wave-swept rock claimed the lives of all women, all families, and all but one child. Heroic rescue efforts by some crew members and villagers saved 370, but 562 perished, the world's worst ocean liner disaster until **Titanic*.
DAN CONLIN

attorney general/solicitor general. In the British North American colonies, the Crown appointed specialized legal officers to represent its interests: the attorneys and solicitors general. They prosecuted serious criminal cases, represented the Crown in civil cases, drafted legal documents for colonial administrations, and advised them on legal matters. The distinction between the two was not always clear, though the solicitor generalship was generally the junior position. Appointees to the lucrative posts (each service commanded a fee) were usually professional jurists, often with significant private practices. The positions were also highly political, and their holders were often active in colonial assemblies and, increasingly, executive councils. With the growth of government bureaucracies in mid-19th-century Canada, the active participation of attorneys and solicitors general in everyday legal matters declined; criminal prosecutions, for example, were increasingly left to subordinate officers. At the same time, the posts gradually became regular *cabinet positions and, with the advent of *responsible government, were filled by elected politicians rather than Crown appointees. By the end of the 19th century, attorneys and (where they still existed) solicitors general, both federal and provincial, had essentially become those members of cabinet responsible for the departments involved with justice and policing, as is the case today. DONALD FYSON

auditor general. The officer created in 1878 to assist the *House of Commons in controlling the public purse. Provinces have auditors with similar status and duties. The auditor general is appointed for a ten-year term, is removable by joint address of the Senate and Commons, and reports as an independent agent to the public accounts committee of the Commons. The traditional audit functions—reporting on the accuracy of accounts and the misuse of funds and ensuring that expenditures conform to Parliament's intentions expressed in appropriation 'votes'—were expanded in 1976 to include value-for-money audits and in 1994 an increase in the number of annual reports. Critics consider this expansion a threat to the independence of the audit. J.E. HODGETTS

August gales. The August gales and the treacherousness of Sable Island have been known to mariners on Canada's east coast since the beginning of recorded history. In 1926 and 1927 the entire eastern seaboard felt the full force of the gales. Of all communities, the port of *Lunenburg, Nova Scotia, was hardest hit, with a loss of 138 fishermen and six schooners. On 8 August 1926 the schooners *Sylvia Mosher* and *Sadie A. Knickle* were lost. On 24 August 1927, *Mahala*, *Uda R. Corkum*, *Clayton W. Walters*, and *Joyce M. Smith* also sank. The American schooner *Columbia*, with a crew that was primarily Nova Scotian, foundered as well. The greatest tragedy was the devastation felt by families in nearby small fishing communities such as Blue Rocks. Crew members were often related: Captain Warren Knickle, for instance, was lost along with his two brothers and a brother-in-law.

The gales were the start of years of mourning and financial worry. Nova Scotian families received monthly compensation cheques, graded according to the ages of the lost men. Newfoundland families, who lost fishermen aboard *Joyce M. Smith*, eventually received $100 per year.
HEATHER-ANNE GETSON

Automatistes. An artistic movement in Quebec, 1941–54. Influenced by French Surrealism, the painter Paul-Émile Borduas aimed at applying the principles of *Automatiste* writing to the visual arts, by encouraging his followers—the Automatistes—to produce their works (painting, sculpture, dance, poetry) spontaneously, without preconceived ideas, and without respect to any form of academicism. The result in painting was often non-figurative. The group, of which the principal members were Borduas, painters Marcel Barbeau, Marcelle Ferron, Pierre Gauvreau, Fernand Leduc, Jean-Paul Mousseau, and Jean-Paul Riopelle, poet Claude Gauvreau, actress Muriel Guilbault, and dancers Françoise Sullivan, Françoise Riopelle, and Jeanne Renaud, exhibited together in 1946 and 1947, both in Montreal and Paris. They had a brief showing in 1946 in New York, at Franciska Boas's dance studio, where Sullivan was studying at the time. In 1948 they collectively signed the manifesto **Refus global* to profess their conviction that the form of art they advocated was intertwined with revolutionary ideological change in Quebec society. They were often ostracized because of their ideas. Borduas lost his job at the École du Meuble, but others, like Riopelle, achieved international fame. FRANÇOIS-MARC GAGNON

automobiles. Self-propelled vehicles have long been dreamt of by human society. The ancients devised methods for moving statues over short distances during religious celebrations. Later thinkers such as Roger Bacon and Leonardo da Vinci theorized about the operational principles of such vehicles. It was not, however, until the 18th century that the recently developed steam engine was adapted to travel. The French military engineer Nicholas-Joseph Cugnot's steam-powered gun carriage of 1769 is generally regarded as the direct forerunner of the modern automobile.

Philadelphian Oliver Evans's steam-powered amphibious dredge of 1805, Cornishman Richard Trevithick's steam-powered wagon of the same period, and Englishman Goldsworthy Gurney's steam-powered omnibuses of the 1840s gave substance to these early ideas and led to steam-powered cars in the later 19th century. Sylvester Roper of Roxbury, Massachusetts, sold one to a Roman Catholic priest on Prince Edward Island in the mid-1860s. In 1867, Henry Seth Taylor of Stanstead, Quebec, demonstrated an elegantly styled steam-powered carriage to his less-than-impressed community. Unlike others built in New Brunswick and Ontario, Taylor's carriage has survived and is today on display in Ottawa. Steamers created by American firms such as Locomobile, White, Stanley, and Doble remained in production until the 1920s.

Electricity and internal combustion offered other sources of propulsion. Electricity was silent and convenient but, like steam, limited in its range of travel. An early Toronto electric car was designed by William Still and owned for some years by F.B. Featherstonhaugh, a prominent 1890s-era lawyer. By the mid-1880s the early experiments of Europeans such as Nicolaus Otto and Etienne Lenoir had led to the creation of practical internal combustion engines and their adaptation to the production of early automobiles by Gottlieb Daimler and Carl Benz in Germany. Other thinkers and inventors in the next decade, such as the Duryea brothers, Ransom Olds, and Henry Ford—Americans all—made the production of motorcars a reality.

The arrival of Ford's Model T in October 1908 ushered in the first great age of automobilization. The 'Tin Lizzie' was such a commercial success that Ford had to adopt methods of mass production, including the assembly line in 1913, to keep up with demand. Economies of scale lowered new-car prices: by 1925 a basic Model T could be purchased for $395. Charles Kettering's 1911 invention of the electric starter for gasoline-powered cars made such cars as convenient as electrics. The basic form of the modern automobile and the foundations of the industry that produced it were in place by the First World War.

Canadians shared the early enthusiasm for the automobile. Inventors such as Tom Doherty of Sarnia and George Foote Foss of Sherbrooke, Quebec, were quickly succeeded by companies like Russell of Toronto and Gray-Dort of Chatham. Individuals such as Dr Perry Doolittle of Toronto became keen automotive 'boosters'. Before his death in 1933 Dr Doolittle motored across Canada in a Ford Model T and worked constantly to secure the creation of the *Trans-Canada Highway, which was finally completed in 1962.

After the First World War, small Canadian firms found themselves increasingly dependent on American suppliers and unable to compete with larger US companies. The Ford Motor Company established its Canadian branch as early as 1904, in order to avoid high Canadian tariffs and to gain access to markets in other member countries of the British Empire/Commonwealth. Other large American manufacturers did the same thing. By 1918, McLaughlin of Oshawa, dependent on Buick for engines after 1908, had been wholly absorbed by its American partner and became General Motors of Canada. Gray-Dort collapsed when its American partner abandoned the automobile business. By 1929, independent Canadian automobile manufacturers had disappeared.

Canadian influences survived in small, but significant, ways. The Prince of Wales, later Edward VIII, had used McLaughlin-Buicks when visiting Canada and subsequently ordered one for his own use in 1935. A custom Buick Limited, incorporating the prince's own interior specifications, was constructed in Oshawa, as was a matching Roadmaster for his amour, Mrs Wallis Simpson. Delivered in London just after his ascent to the throne in 1936, these cars were used by the couple as they left England after the abdication crisis in December. As the Duke of Windsor, Edward continued to favour McLaughlin-Buicks, ordering several more from exile before the onset of war. In 1939, Ford of Canada provided a special Lincoln landaulet for the *royal tour of King George VI and Queen Elizabeth. Twenty years later, the Canadian branches of the 'Big Three'—Ford, Chrysler, and General Motors—each provided a custom-built limousine for

Queen Elizabeth II and the Duke of Edinburgh during their royal tour of 1959.

Mass-produced automobiles transformed 20th-century Canada. Cheap and readily available, they made almost everyone mobile. Car-based holidays became a normal part of family life, giving rise to leisure travel: campgrounds and trailer parks began to appear in the 1920s, motels in the 1940s. Drive-in restaurants and movie theatres became part of roadside culture. After the Second World War, suburban living depended on automobile ownership. Shopping centres and strip plazas appeared in the 1950s, to be joined quickly by indoor malls. The huge parking lots around and under these locations were occupied by the large 'fins and chrome' cars of the 1950s and 1960s, symbols themselves of this second great age of the automobile.

This opulent auto-based culture faced serious social and ecological problems. Road accidents killed and maimed thousands and caused enormous property damage. Traditional downtown commercial areas declined in the face of competition from the *suburbs, producing the familiar 'donut-hole effect' that still plagues many Canadian cities. Urban areas began to choke on their own traffic as early as the 1920s, leading to massive road-building projects, which swallowed countryside and destroyed neighbourhoods for the rest of the century. Soaring rates of fossil-fuel consumption depleted energy reserves and contributed to health problems, long-term changes in weather patterns, and economic crises caused by rising fuel prices. Yet Canadians purchased automobiles in record numbers because they offered privacy, comfort, and an unmatched sense of personal control.

Automobile technology has been a prime factor in the social and economic transformation of modern Canadian society. The automobile industry is a bellwether for the economy as a whole. The very shape of our cities, our neighbourhoods, and even our dwellings has been dictated by the presence of the automobile. At the dawn of the 21st century, we may have a love-hate relationship with this most pervasive of cultural icons, but it continues to exert a powerful influence on us all.

DOUGLAS LEIGHTON

Autonomy Bills. The creation of the provinces of *Alberta and *Saskatchewan in 1905 was the culmination of a campaign for provincial status for the *North-West Territories, which had begun in earnest in 1900. Territorial premier Frederick William Gordon Haultain (1897–1905) and his government pressed for provincial status in the belief that it would solve the financial problems the territory was then experiencing. A rapidly growing population was demanding schools, roads, and bridges, but the territorial government could not borrow money to pay for them. It could not secure any revenue from the public lands either, for these remained under federal control.

Haultain wished to see a single province created, which would have jurisdiction over its public lands and natural resources. However, the federal government of Wilfrid *Laurier decided to establish two provinces and to retain control over their lands and resources. Another controversial feature of the bills creating the new provinces was a clause Laurier had inserted to safeguard the educational rights of Roman Catholics there. Minister of the Interior Clifford *Sifton and other western Liberals objected to the wording on the grounds that it would restore clerical control over separate schools (once permitted but subsequently abolished by territorial legislation). When Sifton resigned from the government, a compromise clause was drafted to preserve the status quo with respect to minority school rights.

It might have been expected that Haultain would be offered the premiership of Saskatchewan or Alberta, but as a Conservative he was overlooked. Instead two Liberals, Alexander Rutherford and Walter Scott, were appointed to head the new governments in Alberta and Saskatchewan, respectively. Elections soon followed, and each won a handsome majority.

J. WILLIAM BRENNAN

Auto Pact. In spite of manufacturing (mostly assembling) American cars rather than its own, Canada built a large automobile industry by imposing protective tariffs that compelled production in Canada, and by taking advantage of preferential arrangements to export within the British Empire to offset imports of American parts. After the Second World War, the export arrangement broke down, and Canada faced a mounting trade deficit in autos and parts, with a relatively high-cost, inefficient Canadian industry producing a range of American cars for the smaller Canadian market. The way out of this impasse was the Canada–US Automotive Products Trade Agreement of 1965, popularly known as the Auto Pact, which allowed free trade across the border by manufacturers, thereby permitting them to rationalize the industry on a continental basis, with a proviso of a floor on Canadian production. The Canadian share of continental production dramatically increased, as did cross-border trade, and the pact was a great success for Canada. Over time the arrangement withered through the rise of offshore manufacturers, such as Japan, not covered by the pact and the erosion of protective or Canadian-content provisions by the Canada–US Free Trade Agreement (1988) and NAFTA (1992). Still, the Canadian automobile industry remained large and viable—early in the 21st century, Ontario, where the Canadian industry is centred, outproduced Michigan in this sector—albeit with the help of a depreciated Canadian dollar.

MELVILLE WATKINS

Avro Arrow. The Avro Canada CF-105 Arrow was a two-seat, twin-engine, all-weather, supersonic interceptor. The Arrow was conceived in the early 1950s as the *Royal Canadian Air Force's state-of-the-art contribution to the defence of North America against Soviet nuclear bombers. The project expanded rapidly to encompass four complex components—airframe, engine, electronics system, and missile armament—developed concurrently and domestically; as a result, costs skyrocketed and delays occurred. Sales to allies would have made the enterprise more economical, but American and British admiration never translated into orders. In 1957, Prime Minister John *Diefenbaker's government inherited the project. Diefenbaker initially temporized when confronted with the air force's ambitions, but soon he and the military reluctantly concluded that Canada could not afford the Arrow within anticipated defence budgets, especially in a time of strategic flux as the missile age dawned and the bomber threat diminished. On 20 February 1959 Diefenbaker terminated the project; all existing Arrows were scrapped. The companies involved laid off nearly 15,000 workers, with many of the best engineers leaving the country. It was a logical decision under the circumstances, but popular culture has vilified Diefenbaker for sacrificing Canada's opportunity to have a world-leading military aircraft industry. RUSSELL ISINGER

baby boom. After the Second World War the birth rate surged in the victorious countries. Such post-war booms had been seen before. The long-term trend, though, was towards a lower birth rate among industrialized nations, and the expectation was that the increase was transitory. Although this was the case in Europe, in North America the number of births increased until 1959 and then underwent a slow decline into the 1960s. By the mid-sixties over half the Canadian population was under the age of 21. This bulge has been one of the significant demographic forces of the last 50 years.

The baby boom was a cultural as well as a demographic event. The generation's influence and sense of itself may be unparalleled in modern times. Post-war affluence ensured that the boomers would be a major consumer force while new media such as television transmitted a cultural identity that spanned the vast middle classes of North America. The cultural influence of the baby boom reached its peak during the tumultuous 1960s. Generational identity, affluence, and a new level of political unrest created an outpouring of cultural, social, and ideological experimentation. Quebec nationalism, the civil rights movement in the American South, and, above all, the Vietnam War created intergenerational clashes as baby boomers actively resisted the cultural and political mores of their elders. Of course, the generational line was far from absolute, and age was crosscut by class, ethnicity, and income. As the famous phrase 'never trust anyone over thirty' testifies, however, it was an era when age was a powerful point of demarcation.

By the later 1960s baby boom politics was centred on university campuses. The decade brought an explosion in higher education. New *universities such as York, Simon Fraser, and Waterloo were created while older institutions expanded beyond all recognition. Between 1958 and 1973 university enrolment in Canada more than tripled, from 90,000 to nearly 300,000. Such growth in a turbulent decade was bound to create instability. Dozens of movements, groups, ideas, and causes sprang up. Under the right circumstances, small groups of radicals could tap the sympathies of their classmates. Old ideas of social control and paternalism gave way. New movements that would shape future decades appeared, from women's rights to environmental protection. All of this was done in a mood that employed the rhetoric of 'the revolution' freely, if vaguely.

By the mid-1970s the radicalism died. Since then the legacy of the sixties has been controversial. Certainly there was hyperbole, and much of the vaunted uniqueness of the generation was merely youthful experimentation made powerful through force of numbers. Yet the sheer size of the generation as well as at least some of the causes that were born in the efflorescence of the 1960s are likely to remain important for the foreseeable future.

DOUG OWRAM

Back, Sir George (1796–1878), explorer and artist. Back joined the British navy as a midshipman before his 12th birthday and served under John *Franklin three times, including two overland expeditions to 'put a roof on the map of Canada', 1819–22 and 1825–7. To defuse Back's rivalry with fellow midshipman Robert Hood over a Chipewyan Indian woman, Greenstockings, and to obtain additional supplies, Franklin sent Back on a five-month winter trek south from Fort Enterprise to *Fort Chipewyan. Returning overland from Franklin's summer exploration in the Arctic, and finding no food left by the Indians at Fort Enterprise, Back continued south to the camp of Akaitcho, the Copper Indian chief, and dispatched a relief party to aid Franklin and his men. In 1833–5, Back mapped the Back River, the second longest river in the Canadian North. When in 1836 his final expedition, on the wrong side of Southampton Island, was locked in pack ice, all thought of exploration was abandoned; the next summer his heavily damaged ship barely reached Ireland. Honours included knighthood, the Gold Medal of the Royal Geographical Society, fellowship in the Royal Society, an honorary DCL from Oxford University, and a retirement promotion to admiral. His sketches and painting of northern Canada illustrated four books.

C. STUART HOUSTON

Baldwin, Robert (1804–58), Toronto politician, lawyer, the architect of Canadian *responsible government. His father, W.W. Baldwin, was a flamboyant Irish liberal who carried his ideas to Upper Canada. Robert was an introverted young man but, as his father's heir, was destined for politics. Robert would have preferred a quiet life with his beloved wife, Eliza. The romance with his teenage cousin was bitterly opposed by the family, but young love won out and they married in 1827. In 1836, Eliza died as a result of complications in childbirth. Robert would suffer from depression for the rest of his life and from an obsession with rejoining Eliza in the afterlife.

He carried on despite his intense grief. He had opportunities to press for responsibility in 1836, in a brief stint in the executive council of Upper Canada, and in 1842–3 when he allied with Montrealer L.-H. *LaFontaine to form a Reform ministry in the new *Province of Canada. Governors' refusals to follow the advice of their executive councils scuttled both attempts. However, Britain came to see responsible government as the only solution to the instability of Canadian politics. The *Reformers swept the election of 1848 and the resultant LaFontaine–Baldwin ministry was recognized as a fully responsible party government. The 'Great Ministry' accomplished much, including modernizing schools and municipal government, but was bedeviled by internal feuding among Reformers. Baldwin resigned in discouragement in 1851. His later years were spent in the darkness of his depression. MICHAEL S. CROSS

Balfour Report, 1926. At the 1926 Imperial Conference, the Committee on Inter-Imperial Relations, chaired by former British prime minister Arthur J. Balfour, was given the challenge of updating the relationship between Britain and the old dominions in light of developments since the attainment of self-government. The Balfour Report was a masterpiece of nuance. It affirmed that the dominions were 'autonomous communities within the British Empire, equal in status, in no way subordinate one to another in any respect of their domestic or external affairs', a clause that representatives from South Africa and the Irish Free State could invoke to demonstrate equality with Britain. The report went on to affirm that Britain and the dominions were 'united by a common allegiance to the Crown and freely associated as members of the British *Commonwealth of Nations', a clause that representatives from Australia and New Zealand could hold up to reassure citizens that the relationship with Britain was intact. Prime Minister Mackenzie *King of Canada was well pleased with the result, which captured the two strands of his own attitude towards the *British Empire. At the same time, he was a self-proclaimed champion of Canadian sovereignty and yet was intensely loyal to the empire. As King explained: 'I believe in the larger whole, with the complete independence of the parts united by cooperation in all common ends.' The British comforted themselves that little of substance had been conceded. As Churchill once said of Balfour: 'If you wanted nothing done, A.J.B. was undoubtedly the best man for the task.' The Balfour Report was given legislative force in 1931 as the *Statute of Westminster. FRANCINE McKENZIE

Banff. Alberta town on the Bow River, 128 km west of Calgary. Archaeological sites reveal people first came here 11,000 years ago; Native peoples, including the Stoney and Kutenai, later frequented the area. Founded in 1883 as 'Siding 29', a town of 300 residents was established on a site proposed for a railway tunnel. In November 1883, CPR magnate Donald *Smith renamed it 'Banff' after his home town in Scotland. Nearby hot springs on Sulphur Mountain drew the attention of the CPR and the government of Canada, leading to modern *tourism and park development. At the urging of the CPR, in 1885 the government reserved 26 sq km around the hot springs and in 1887 decreed a larger area Rocky Mountains Park, instituting Canada's first *national park—known as Banff after 1930. In 1886, the Banff townsite moved 3 km to the present scenic location, which also became the park's administrative centre. Ottawa laid out the townsite and initiated lot leaseholds on federal Crown property. Public baths were developed at the Upper Hotsprings and the Cave and Basin, along with private ventures like the Grand View Hotel and Dr R.G. Brett's Sanitarium.

Keen on luxury resorts to generate continental passenger travel, the CPR opened the Banff Springs Hotel in 1888. The railway promoted the Rockies as Canada's Alps, emulating European spa tourism. Businesses such as Brewster's Mount Royal Hotel, Mather's Bow River Boathouse, and Harmon's drugstore were characteristic of early family-run entrepreneurship. Banff's social life pulsed with a seasonal influx of summer workers and tourists as well as annual events like Banff Indian Days (1894) and the Banff Winter Carnival (1917). In 1904, tourists arrived by car for the first time. Through wartime and depression, development was stimulated by various public works projects, resulting in road construction and attractions such as the Banff Park Administration Building and Cascade Gardens (1936). In 1933 the Banff School of Fine Arts was inaugurated by the University of Alberta and subsequently expanded as the Banff Centre. Automobile tourism grew after the Second World War, and visitor numbers escalated after the *Trans-Canada Highway reached Banff in 1958. Banff became a winter destination as the modern ski industry expanded and CP hotels geared into winter operations stimulated by the 1988 Calgary Winter Olympics.

Banff was administered by the federal government until 1990, when it was incorporated as a town. Rapid growth in urban density ensued; many historic buildings were demolished. Banff's position within a renowned national park and a UNESCO World Heritage Site guarantees ongoing debate over urban space and development in this vibrant community. Significant national historic sites include the Cave and Basin Hotsprings, Banff Park Museum, and Banff Springs Hotel; the Whyte Museum of the Canadian Rockies houses regional collections. PEARLANN REICHWEIN

Bank of Canada. The bank began operations in March 1935, following the policy of Conservative prime minister R.B. *Bennett in 1932–5 and the recommendations of the Royal Commission on Banking and Currency. The terms of the Bank of Canada Act (1934) laid out its responsibilities, which included 'to act as fiscal agent for the government in the management of public debt, regulate credit and currency, control and protect the external value of the national monetary unit and to mitigate fluctuations in the general level of production, trade, prices and employment so far as may be possible within the scope of monetary action'. The bank's first governor, Graham Towers (1935–54), proved an astute choice as he oversaw its expansion and acceptance by both Canadians and financial interests abroad. This was important, as all the major chartered *banks in Canada except the Royal (whence Towers had come) had been opposed to its creation.

The war years had a major impact on the bank. It quickly became a central institution, even though it was relieved of some of its normal functions, like setting monetary policy. It administered the Foreign Exchange Control Board (1939–51), which was given authority to control all international financial transactions in the search for American dollars. The bank also advised the government on its finances and acted as its fiscal agent, managing the public debt and arranging Canadian Victory Loan subscriptions.

Following the end of hostilities, the bank assumed normal responsibilities. The post-war period proved to be a difficult one to manage as the bank skated between the pressures of consumer demand and an official commitment to high employment. It also took a lead role in responding satisfactorily to an exchange crisis that began in the autumn of 1947, the result of increasing imports from the United States and declining cash sales in Europe. By the end of the 1940s, the bank was among the most important financial institutions in Canada. By the 1950s, it had settled into healthy young adulthood. After the Korean War (1950–3) began and an economic boom drove up employment and expectations, the bank proved to be adept at controlling inflation; in September 1950, it oversaw the floating of Canada's dollar. Towers stepped down in December 1954 and James Coyne (1955–61) took over.

Coyne's tenure began well but became increasingly difficult after the St Laurent Liberals were defeated by John Diefenbaker's Conservatives in June 1957. The bank's concern over developing inflation collided with the new government's determination to ease monetary policy as unemployment increased. The question became who controlled monetary policy, and, eventually, who controlled Coyne? The latter question was especially relevant as the governor embarked on a series of speeches decrying the dangers of *continentalism. The clash between bank and government proved damaging to the reputations of both, and, for the former, was restored only with the elevation of Louis Rasminsky to governor (1961–73) from his position as a deputy governor in charge of international financial relations. Rasminsky, one of only two Jews then in senior positions in Ottawa, proved to be an excellent choice, and during the 1960s the bank embarked upon a period of expansion and consolidation that further enhanced its reputation. BRUCE MUIRHEAD

banks. Canada's principal commercial form of financial intermediation, overseeing the taking of deposits and the lending and transfer of money, and, since the deregulation of financial services in the late 20th century, encompassing investment and some insurance functions. The Canadian banking system found its rudimentary start when in the early 19th century merchants' bills of exchange (promissory notes passed from one trader to another) and army bills (interest-bearing notes issued by the governor) were employed to facilitate colonial trade and to finance government operations. Mundane, day-to-day commerce relied on barter or the circulation of a motley assortment of foreign coins. The imperfection of this ad hoc system prompted colonial merchants to agitate for the establishment of chartered banks, regularized institutions that central Canadian and Maritime merchants associated with the efficiency and trading prowess of the British and American economies. As early as 1792 Montreal merchants created a private banking association, the Canadian Banking Company, but, without the charter right to issue its own notes, this and other early 'banks' failed. The first durable chartered banks emerged in the wake of the War of 1812. In 1817, the Bank of Montreal (chartered 1822) opened, followed by the Bank of New Brunswick (1820) and the Bank of Upper Canada (1821). From the outset the early Canadian banks were patterned on the British/Scottish branch-banking model that enabled a bank to cast its deposit taking and lending elastically over a region, thereby allowing money to be moved from areas of saving to cash-starved areas. The charters of these joint-stock banks contained a modicum of regulation—a high ratio of paid-up capital, notes that were tied to reserves of 'specie', and so on. From the 1820s onwards the colonial banks multiplied steadily; by 1867, there were 33 chartered banks in British North America. As the colonial government's banker from 1863, the Bank of Montreal—'Canada's First Bank'—spread quickest and most lucratively. Many others failed or were merged into larger banks; a sharp commercial downturn could ruin a bank with too narrow a regional or client base. In 1866, the Bank of Upper Canada failed when loans for land speculation turned sour. Others failed from a lack of probity; the Zimmerman Bank of Hamilton crashed when the free-wheeling self-lending of its founder, railroader Samuel Zimmerman, was exposed in 1857.

The strong commercial imperatives shaping Confederation placed banking securely under the control of the new federal government in 1867—banking would be a national industry falling under section 91 of the BNA Act. In 1871, the federal finance minister, Francis *Hincks, introduced a Bank Act that has served as the enduring template for Canadian banking. Most striking in the legislation was the provision that all Canadian banks hold federal charters that would be renewed every ten years after the Bank Act itself was revisited and revised. This stroke of Canadian pragmatism would allow the national banking system to be adjusted to the changing needs of Canadian society. Although the revisions have not always neatly met the decennial timetable, they have allowed the system to evolve, albeit slowly. Section 88 of the act was, for instance, frequently expanded, allowing banks to take an ever broader range of goods and crops as surety for lending, a crucial stimulant for an economy dedicated to trading.

In 1900, the Canadian Bankers' Association was chartered to carry the consensus views of Canadian bankers to Ottawa and to operate a 'clearing' system whereby interbank transactions were expedited. Thus, from the outset, unlike the diffuse, regionally based American banking system, Canadian banking was a *national* system and, as such, spread with the nation. Through the late 19th century, the number of banks increased and their web of branches spread dramatically. By 1920, a record 4,676 branches dotted the country—one branch for every 1,900 Canadians. By 1900, after many failures and amalgamations there were 35 federally chartered banks; the high-water mark had been 51 in 1873, but failures and mergers allowed a gradual concentration to take place. Despite its unfolding national character, Canadian banking maintained a strong regional differentiation. Quebec in particular supported culturally distinctive banks such as the Banque d'Hochelaga. However, as the 20th century dawned many regional banks (e.g., the Bank of British Columbia, the Summerside Bank) either failed or succumbed to mergers, which peaked in the 1900–25 period. Others followed the logic of national expansion: the Merchants' Bank of Halifax changed its name to the Royal Bank in 1900, moved its head office to Montreal in 1907, and quickly expanded westward through mergers. The Bank of Nova Scotia similarly grew, retaining its name but shifting the centre of its operations to Toronto. Montreal and Toronto became the hub of Canadian banking. At the same time, Canadian banks began to export their expertise, opening branches in the Caribbean, Latin America, and Europe.

By 1925, Canadian banking had assumed its modern corporate structure with eleven national banks. Of these, only the two Quebec banks—the Banque Canadienne Nationale and the Banque Provinciale—maintained a distinctly regional focus. After 1925, the pace of consolidation slowed, with only sporadic mergers (e.g., in 1955 the Toronto and Dominion Banks merged). Ongoing revisions to the Bank Act continued to transform the nature of Canadian banking. The banks slowly surrendered their prerogative over the nation's monetary affairs. In 1914, wartime expediency obliged Ottawa to breach the prevailing practice that the commercial banks' paid-up capital acted as the automatic regulator of the notes in national circulation. The Finance Act of that year allowed banks to exceed this ceiling, thereby stimulating economic expansion. The liquidity crisis brought on by the Depression of the 1930s finished the erosion of the notion that the commercial banks were Canada's lender of last resort. The creation of the *Bank of Canada as a federal agency in 1934 freed the chartered banks from front-line control of national credit but also deprived them of the right to issue *currency. Other significant modifications followed. At the height of the post-war building boom in 1954, banks were allowed to enter the residential mortgage field. In the 1960s, rigidly set lending rates were lifted allowing the banks to issue short-term credit: Chargex/VISA was born.

Seismic change overtook Canadian banking in the mid-1980s, when the globalization of international finance exposed the cloistered and compartmentalized nature of the Canadian financial system. Since Confederation, Canada's banks, *trust companies, investment brokers, and insurance companies had been rigidly demarcated, mainly in an attempt to prevent monopoly and self-dealing. Initially, Canadian banks managed to stay internationally competitive under these restraints, but the dramatic opening up of international finance after the energy boom of the 1960s placed Canadian financial intermediation at a disadvantage. Moreover, the 1980 Bank Act revision had allowed foreign banks access to the Canadian market. To meet these challenges Canadian banks needed to expand their asset base and to have access to a more flexible range of products. Hence the old 'four pillars' of Canadian finance crumbled in the late 1980s: banks bought into brokerage firms, began offering some forms of insurance, and began cautiously expanding into larger markets, particularly the United States. In this atmosphere, Canadian banking became more competitive; niche-playing foreign banks entered Canada. Banks came to see themselves as 'financial service groups', purveying everything from chequing accounts to mutual funds. This ethos of global bigness was nevertheless resisted by a traditional Canadian grassroots scepticism towards 'big banks'. In 2000, Ottawa blocked two proposed mergers that would have seen four of the country's largest banks become two mega-banks. The 21st century dawned with Canadian banking confronted with unprecedented change in the realms of domestic and global competitiveness, the delivery of banking services (e.g., electronic banking), and the management of public policy and opinion. DUNCAN McDOWALL

Banting, Frederick Grant (1891–1941), medical researcher. A farmer's son from Alliston, Ontario, Fred Banting struggled through high school and university, graduating in medicine from the University of Toronto in 1917. After war service and a year's training in surgery, he began practising medicine in London, Ontario. In connection with a teaching assignment at the University of Western Ontario, he developed an idea in October 1920 for research aimed at controlling diabetes. He took his idea to the better-equipped University of Toronto, and became the initiator of a team, headed by J.J.R. Macleod and also including C.H. Best and J.B. Collip, that by early 1922 had succeeded in isolating the internal secretion of the pancreas, which they named *insulin.

Insulin injections would sustain the lives of millions of diabetics around the world. Banting and Macleod shared the 1923 Nobel Prize in Medicine or Physiology for the discovery. Banting became the most famous living Canadian and the first holder of a chair of medical research in the country. In 1935 he was knighted. He died in an accidental plane crash in Newfoundland, en route to wartime Britain. His post-insulin research had not panned out. He was a talented amateur painter and a good old boy, who in later life would admit that he was 'no damned scientist'.

MICHAEL BLISS

Baptists. A Christian denomination with widespread support throughout Canada, but with particularly strong roots in Ontario and the Maritimes. Baptist beliefs came out of the Reformation in Europe and Britain, and were brought to Canada largely via the United States. A fundamental belief centres on the time and mode of baptism: baptism of adult believers by total immersion. Because of early persecution in Europe, a strong belief in the complete separation of church and state had also developed. Although Baptists came to present-day Canada in American migrations of the latter part of the 18th century, the growth of the denomination resulted largely from the revivals that periodically swept colonial communities. The first church was formed in the Maritimes in the 1760s and in Upper Canada in the 1790s. Wolfville United Baptist Church (1778) is the oldest continuing Baptist church in the country. Many of the Blacks of the Maritimes were attracted to the Baptist faith and established their own churches.

Stressing the complete independence of the individual church, Baptists only slowly established associations and conventions to carry out common aims such as educational and missionary work. Their opposition to the intrusion of the Church of England into their lives helped bring about the end of the formal ties between church and state in Canada. That same independence fostered the growth of differing theological and doctrinal positions among Baptists, which at times led to deep divisions within the broader denomination. The desire for an educated clergy and laity led to the establishment of a number of institutions of higher learning and the championing of the development of non-denominational, state-run school systems. Acadia (1838) and McMaster (1890) universities are the best-known Baptist institutions of higher learning. Both became secularized in the late 20th century. Baptists were more inclined than many in Canada to support co-education, and the first regular BA held by a woman in Canada was granted by Acadia in 1884. Support for foreign missions began in 1845 and eventually extended to Asia, Africa, and South America. In this aspect as well, women played a noted role. Baptists became strong champions of the *temperance movement in the 19th century, and were early supporters of the *social gospel in the next century.

Like many other evangelical denominations, the Baptists were significantly influenced by the fundamentalist movement of the early 20th century, causing deep divisions, especially in Ontario, where the denomination split apart. Many of the Baptist churches came together in 1944 in the Baptist Federation of Canada (now the Canadian Baptist Federation), an umbrella organization that provided unity in some areas while recognizing the continuing autonomy of the local church. BARRY MOODY

Barbeau, Marius (1883–1969), anthropologist, folklorist. Raised with the expectation that he would become a priest, Barbeau instead studied law at Université Laval. At Oxford University, as one of the first Rhodes Scholars from French Canada, he was introduced to the discipline of anthropology in the seminars of Robert Ranulph Marett. Upon his return from England Barbeau joined the staff of the Victoria Memorial Museum (now the Canadian Museum of Civilization), with which he was to be connected for his entire professional career. Barbeau's research was split between fieldwork among Aboriginal peoples (particularly the Huron and, later, the Tsimshian-speaking peoples of British Columbia) and folklore collecting in rural Quebec; his extensive work on the latter eventually led to the creation of a separate folk culture division at the museum. His ethnographic materials, particularly those collected in collaboration with William Beynon (Tsimshian), are still rich sources of data for current researchers, though his theoretical interpretations have largely been superseded. Barbeau was also interested in Canadian art, and played a role in the introduction of Emily *Carr's work to eastern Canadian audiences. He was a prolific author, writing dozens of articles and books for both academic and popular audiences.

ROBERT L.A. HANCOCK

Barker, William George (1894–1930), fighter pilot. 'Will' Barker was an exceptional First World War ace who ended the conflict with 50 accredited aerial victories. Enrolling in December 1914, he would serve in the trenches as infantry until transferring to the Royal Flying Corps in 1916. After a distinguished tour as an observer, he received pilot training, flew artillery-observation aircraft with great skill, was wounded, and became an instructor. He later became a legend in the skies over the Italian Front, flying Camel scouts, earning many decorations, and scoring the bulk of his victories. Returning to Britain to command an air-fighting school near war's end, he borrowed a Sopwith Snipe for one last tour of the front. On 27 October 1918, he had a memorable solitary engagement with 15 enemy scouts after shooting down a German observation aircraft. In the ensuing engagement, for which he would receive the Victoria Cross, he dispatched three more of the enemy while being seriously wounded three times and crashing near the lines. Weakness from his war wounds probably contributed to his death in a flying accident when he was demonstrating a new aircraft for Fairchild Aviation near Ottawa in 1930.

DAVID L. BASHOW

Barkerville. Established in 1862 and named after Billy Barker, whose claim proved to be the motherlode of the *Cariboo gold rush. The largest community in colonial British Columbia, with a transient population of 10,000, the town was rebuilt following a fire in 1868 and experienced two subsequent booms (1898–1910 and 1932–42) before becoming a heritage site in 1958. Barkerville is an example of the urbanizing and globalizing effects of gold rushes. Such events created instant communities and brought together people who otherwise would be separated by distance, culture, and experience. Where else but in a gold-rush town could Wellington Delaney Moses, 'the Black Barber of Barkerville', rub elbows with Cambridge-educated Chief Justice Matthew Baillie *Begbie, French madam Fanny Bendixon, 'a woman of undiscoverable girth', and Sing Kee, the town's Chinese herbalist?

Gold-rush societies like Barkerville also held out the promise of social mobility to working men, who dreamed of striking it rich, and working women, who hoped to capitalize on their demographic advantage. In many instances, these promises went unkept: few men shared Billy Barker's fate, and many women discovered that being a rare commodity did not mean they would be valued, much less physically safe. TINA LOO

Barr Colony. Isaac Barr (1847–1937), a charismatic but inept Anglican clergyman, promised Clifford *Sifton's Department of Immigration, anxious to import farmers to the thinly populated Prairies, that his colonization scheme would 'save Canada for the British'. The Laurier government did more than usual to ensure the safety and comfort of the 2,000 British townsfolk—bank clerks, butchers, housemaids, gardeners—who responded to Barr's call. Halfway through the 330-km trek, which took them by wagon from the railhead at Saskatoon to the 'Promised Land' west of Battleford in the dismal spring of 1903, the colonists deposed Barr and replaced him with the Reverend George Lloyd (1861–1940), another controversial man, after whom they named Lloydminster. Watched by the international press, 'the raw Englishmen loose on the plains' spent a miserable first winter in poorly built sod huts, but most proved their homesteads and eventually became successful farmers and business people. LYNNE BOWEN

Barren Lands. A vast, essentially treeless, northern tundra zone, including parts of the *Arctic Archipelago. The southern boundary runs on a southeasterly line from the Mackenzie delta towards Churchill, Manitoba, and from the Richmond Gulf, eastern *Hudson Bay, along a variable northeasterly line to Davis Inlet on the Labrador coast. This southern boundary is defined by the shifting course of the 'tree-line'. Characterized by grasses, scrub birch, willow, lichens, and mosses, the barrens host large migratory flocks of birds and herds of caribou and muskox. Archaeological sites, as at Acasta Lake, indicate a human presence perhaps as early as 8,000 years ago. The term 'Barren Lands' was coined by trader Henry Kelsey during his 1689 exploration north from Churchill. The Barren Lands functioned as a commons for many Native groups living south of the treeline as well as for Inuit peoples, some of whom, such as the Padlimuit ('Caribou Inuit') of western Hudson Bay, adopted an inland 'Barrens' way of life for many centuries. Recently, under new territorial political arrangements, tourism and resource development, including diamond mining, in the region are being linked with southern economies, leaving the fragile Barren Lands less isolated than in the past. GRAHAM MacDONALD

Barrett, David (1930–), social worker, populist, British Columbia premier 1972–5. Fired from a provincial correctional institute for his political activity, Barrett was first elected as a CCF member of the BC legislature in 1960. Following the 1969 election, he became leader of the BC *New Democratic Party and in 1972 defeated the 20-year-old Social Credit government of W.A.C. *Bennett. As BC's first NDP premier, he left a legacy that included agricultural land reserves, public auto insurance, a new labour code, and government employee collective-bargaining rights. Barrett and his government were unseated in December 1975. He re-entered the legislature in a Vancouver East by-election and remained leader of the opposition until 1983. After working as a radio talk-show host, he crossed into national politics in 1988; elected MP for Esquimalt, he became NDP trade critic. He unsuccessfully ran in the hotly contested 1989 NDP national leadership race against Audrey McLaughlin and in 1993 lost his House of Commons seat. In 1998 he conducted a BC government inquiry into leaky condominium construction. NORMAN J. RUFF

Bartlett, Robert Abram (Bob) (1875–1946). Born in Brigus, Newfoundland, to a seafaring family, Bartlett was only 17 when he captained his first schooner. He was mate on the *Windward* during Robert Edwin Peary's 1898–1902 expedition to the North Pole, then commanded the *Roosevelt* during Peary's 1905–6 and 1908–9 expeditions. He was instrumental in Peary's 'dash for the pole' in April 1909. In 1913 the Canadian government hired Bartlett to convey a scientific party to the western Arctic aboard the *Karluk*, an aging whaler purchased by expedition leader Vilhjalmur *Stefansson. On 14 January 1914, after Stefansson had left the vessel for the Alaska mainland, the *Karluk* was crushed by ice. In what has been described as 'the finest feat of leadership in Canadian marine history', Bartlett led the survivors to Wrangel Island, crossed the ice on foot with an Inuit companion to Siberia, and sailed to Alaska to organize a rescue. Between 1926 and 1940, Bartlett undertook arctic voyages aboard the *Effie M. Morrissey* for various American institutions, adding to scientific knowledge of the region. During the Second World War, the US Navy commandeered the *Morrissey* for hydrographic and supply work in the North. Bartlett died in New York but was buried in Brigus. JAMES E. CANDOW

Bartlett, William Henry (1809-54). Originator of the eponymous phrase 'Bartlett print'. Born in London, England, he was apprenticed from 13 to 20 to architect John Britton, from whom he learned to sketch architectural antiquities and landscape views for the purpose of engraving. His technical skills and draughtsmanship soon led to work with the London publisher George Virtue, and in 1832 he began collaborating with Dr William Beattie, for whom he illustrated several travel books. To support his family, Bartlett became both a writer and illustrator of travel books. His sketches in sepia pen and ink and washes, when translated into engravings, became widely popular as picturesque views. He visited North America in 1836–7, 1838, and 1841 to provide sketches for two publications by Nathaniel Parker Willis, *American Scenery* (London, 1840) and *Canadian Scenery Illustrated* (London, 1842). The 120 engravings in the latter have become ubiquitous representations, idyllic and romantic views of a still primitive society in transformation. Bartlett continued to travel widely throughout Great Britain, Europe, and the Middle East, as well as the United States. He died suddenly at sea off Malta, leaving behind a sustained legacy as a topographical artist and author. JIM BURANT

baseball. Baseball in Canada grew out of traditional stick and ball games, including English rounders and American townball, and grew rapidly in the second half of the 19th century. Although there is evidence of baseball in Beachville, Ontario, in 1838, the exact origins of the game are unclear. By the 1850s, clubs in Ontario played an 11-a-side Canadian game, while Maritimers played by 'New England' rules. In the following decade rules were standardized, allowing for interprovincial and international competition. By the time the Guelph Maple Leafs won the world semi-professional championship in 1874, baseball had eclipsed cricket as Canada's premier summer sport.

Although 19th-century critics saw the development of American baseball as weakening allegiance to the Empire, by the First World War baseball enjoyed broad support. In the interwar years professional baseball clubs operated in cities across the country from Vancouver Island to Cape Breton, and almost every small town sported a local team. The country's two most successful professional franchises were in Montreal and Toronto.

Baseball remained largely segregated before the Second World War, although barnstorming teams from the American Negro Leagues frequently toured Canada. Vancouver's Asahi baseball club (made up of Japanese Canadians), the Black Diamond club of Halifax, and the all-Black Chatham All-Stars in Ontario attested to the ethnic and colour lines that were drawn around the game. In 1946, the Brooklyn Dodgers assigned Jackie Robinson to Montreal, effectively breaking professional baseball's colour bar.

In 1969 the Montreal Expos of the National League became the first Canadian franchise in the major leagues, followed in 1977 by the American League Toronto Blue Jays. Over the years more than 100 Canadians have played major league baseball, including such notables as 19th-century star John 'Tip' O'Neill of Woodstock, Ontario, present-day player Larry Walker of Maple Ridge, BC, and Hall of Fame pitcher Ferguson Jenkins, whose father played with the Chatham All-Stars in the 1930s and 1940s.

COLIN HOWELL

Batoche. This *Metis community was founded by Xavier Letendre *dit* Batoche (1841–1901), who gave his surname to a ferry crossing he established in 1873 on the South Saskatchewan River, at the junction of the Carlton and Humboldt Trails on the main route for cart trains travelling between *Red River and Fort Edmonton. His *voyageur grandfather and Cree grandmother had lived and traded in the region in the early 1800s. By 1884 Batoche was thriving, with six trading stores, a 'stopping place', and a liquor outlet for *un pchi coup*. Letendre's trade was worth over $50,000 and several of his Metis neighbours also had successful businesses.

Most of the Metis in the surrounding region lived on river lots and pursued a seasonal mixed economy of farming, hunting, and freighting. They had come to the Northwest, in Gabriel *Dumont's words, 'in order to be free', but found the government and newcomers still would not 'leave them alone'. The fear of being dispossessed, as in Manitoba, and the determination to defend their indigenous rights as the 'new people' of the Northwest, came to the fore in 1885. Under Louis *Riel's cry of 'Justice commands us to take up arms', the Metis formed a provisional government, a move that led to armed conflict with federal forces known as the *North-West Rebellion. According to Christine Dumas Pilon, who witnessed the conflict, 'it was the government who brought war upon the poor people'. There were three engagements between the Metis and the government forces: Duck Lake, Fish Creek, and the last stand at Batoche in May 1885. The armed resistance failed, and the following years were marked by increased prejudice against the 'rebels', their exclusion from the dominant Euro-Canadian capitalist economy, and their loss of political power. Many families were unable to obtain legal ownership of their traditional lands, and scrip grants were a source of ready cash rather than a long-term benefit. Poverty forced people to move further west in search of work. Metis pride, language, and cultural traditions were kept alive by elders, but the community was marginalized and isolated from the Canadian mainstream.

By the turn of the 20th century, Batoche had lost its economic base but persisted as an enduring symbol of Metis resistance and survival. The historic village, mission, and some farms along the river are now part of the Batoche National Historic Site, and the Metis of Saskatchewan hold their annual 'Back to Batoche' days on *jolie prairie* nearby. Batoche is now a symbol of hope, renewal, and rebirth for all Metis people.

DIANE PAYMENT

Beaubassin. Some of the settlers of *Port-Royal moved to other areas of the Bay of Fundy: Beaubassin and the Minas Basin. The Beaubassin region (near present-day Amherst, Nova Scotia), at the head of the bay, was chosen in the 1670s for its tranquillity and for the large amount of marshland that could be reclaimed by a system of dikes called *aboiteau*. The salt marsh hay and good grazing supported a thriving cattle industry. Beaubassin became the capital of Acadia when Michel de La Vallière, son-in-law of businessman Nicolas Denys, was appointed administrator of the colony and settled there from 1676 to 1684. After the *conquest of Acadia in 1710, the region became the frontier of French and English possessions. In the mid-1750s France and England, respectively, built Forts Beauséjour and Lawrence on either side of the Missaguash River near present-day Sackville, New Brunswick. The fall of Fort Beauséjour in 1755 was the prelude to the deportations of the Acadians, which lasted until 1763.

JEAN DAIGLE

Beauharnois scandal, 1929–32. Promoters of a huge hydroelectric development on the St Lawrence River in the Beauharnois district of Quebec contributed more than $700,000 to the federal *Liberal Party and undisclosed large sums to Quebec and Ontario provincial politicians in 1929–30. The federal government approved their project, and provincial governments arranged contracts for the purchase of power. Parliamentary and senate inquires after the 1930 federal election were described by Liberal leader Mackenzie *King as his 'Valley of Humiliation'. He denied any personal involvement, but several key fundraisers resigned or were dismissed and changes were made in Liberal fundraising strategies. Other issues dominated the 1935 federal election, won by the Liberals.

Hopes that the Beauharnois would compete in the Montreal market with Montreal Light, Heat and Power Consolidated were dashed when its promoters could not raise the funds needed to complete the project until, in 1933, it signed a contract to sell power to its Montreal rivals. T.D. REGEHR

Beaumont Hamel. This action on 1 July 1916 was part of a major Anglo-French offensive launched against the German line north of the river Somme. The 29th Division, to which the Newfoundland Regiment belonged as a part of 88th Brigade, was assigned the task of breaking through the German front lines that ran from Beaumont Hamel southeast to the river Ancre. The division's 86th and 87th Brigades were to lead off the attack, their objectives the German first and intermediate lines. Once these were secured, the 88th Brigade was to advance against the second line on the Beaucourt Road, some 4,000 m distant. Preliminary bombardment was expected to cut the wire and weaken the enemy's defence. It would do neither. The German position in the Beaumont Hamel Valley was one of the strongest on the Somme Front. The advance by the 86th and 87th Brigades was cut short by heavy enemy fire. Confusion on the battleground left the impression that the first objective had been reached, and the 88th was ordered forward as a reinforcement. Its leading battalions, the 1st Essex and the Newfoundland Regiment, prepared to move off together, but the Essex, bogged down in its forward trenches by the dead and dying from the first wave, was delayed. As a result, the Newfoundlanders went forth on their own under withering fire. Of the 801 officers and men who left the trenches that morning only 68 answered the roll the following day. The toll was staggering: 233 dead, 386 wounded, and 91 missing. The regiment survived this terrible mauling and went on to win numerous battle honours, but Beaumont Hamel and July 1st have a special significance for Newfoundlanders and Labradorians.

DAVID FACEY-CROWTHER

Beaver. A small sidewheel steamship built for the *Hudson's Bay Company at London in 1835, *Beaver* was intended as a technological advantage to dominate the *maritime fur trade on the northwest coast of America by reaching areas not yet touched by competing Yankee traders in sailing ships. Sent, under sail in 1836, to the HBC's Columbia Department headquarters at Fort Vancouver (now in the state of Washington), where her engines were placed into service, *Beaver* became the first steamer on the Pacific coast. In a 53-year career, *Beaver* traded between Puget Sound and Alaska, charted much of the British Columbia coast, carried gold seekers in 1859–60, and served as a pioneer towboat in Burrard Inlet, site of today's Vancouver. The steamer wrecked in Vancouver harbour in 1888 due to either a strong current or strong drink. For the next four years, stranded on the rocks, the near-legendary historic vessel was stripped for souvenirs before finally sinking. Archaeologists have surveyed the wreck, and portions of the steamer are displayed at the Vancouver Maritime Museum.

JAMES DELGADO

beaver (*castor canadensis*). This large rodent of the quiet waters of deciduous woodlands is characterized by its broad flat tail for swimming and balancing, its fearsome incisors for cutting down trees, and its nimble paws for building dams and lodges. It keeps a submerged supply of edible twigs and branches near the underwater entrance of its snug lodge, where it overwinters and raises its young.

The beaver's fine fur, protected by coarse guard-hairs, is the premier raw material for making felt hats, and from the late 16th century beaver skins were traded by Indians to the French, English, and Dutch. They were the mainstay of the early Canadian *fur trade, even as it diversified after 1700 to include many other furs. The beaver's need for elaborate dams and a lodge (its 'heavy fixed capital' in the words of the economist Harold Adams *Innis) made it an easy prey for trappers, especially after iron and steel tools came into use. The beaver's existence was also threatened by 19th- and 20th-century farmers, who felled trees and drained land. The conservationist *Grey Owl campaigned tirelessly for the beaver in speeches and books such as *The Adventures of Sajo and Her Beaver People* (1935).

The beaver appears as a symbol of Canada on a medal struck by Louis XIV in 1690. Many municipalities followed the lead of the Beaver Club of Montreal fur traders in tying the image of the beaver to the qualities of industry and perseverance. The animal appeared on the first Canadian postage stamp (1851) and on many tokens, medals, and coins, notably the Canadian nickel from 1937. As a symbol, the earnest beaver fell out of favour in the mid-20th century, but it has recently made a comeback in political cartoons as a symbol of the hapless Canadian Everyman. DALE MIQUELON

Beaverbrook, Lord. *See* AITKEN, WILLIAM MAXWELL.

Beaver Hall Group. A short-lived group of artists established in Montreal in May 1920 to further modern art in that city. Inspired by the first exhibition of the *Group of Seven earlier that year, the Beaver Hall Group was established to make visible a unified message of individual expression and quality in Canadian art. Edwin

Holgate was the prime mover in its formation and A.Y. Jackson its first president. The membership consisted of 19 male and female, anglophone and francophone artists, most former students of William Brymner at the Art Association of Montreal. Holgate had left for Paris by their first exhibition in January 1921 at 305 Beaver Hall Hill, and several others followed. Four more exhibitions were organized before the dissolution of the group around 1923 due to lack of money and the absence of any driving force to keep the group together or to articulate its purpose.

The name has erroneously been associated with a number of Montreal women artists working from the 1920s. Norah McCullough's 1966 exhibition of *The Beaver Hall Hill [sic] Group*, organized for the National Gallery of Canada, included Mabel Lockerby, Mabel May, Lilias Torrance Newton, and Anne Savage, all members of the group, as well as non-members Nora Collyer, Emily Coonan, Prudence Heward, Kathleen Morris, Sarah Robertson, and Ethel Seath. McCullough's definition of the group as ten Montreal women landscape and figure painters working in high-keyed colour, within the heritage of the Group of Seven, has survived.

CHARLES C. HILL

Beaver Wars. Warfare between the *Iroquois League and their northern neighbours had been going on well before European contact. During the 1640s they intensified. The Ottawa River Algonquians were dispersed by 1647, the *Huron and Petun by 1650, the Neutral in 1653, and the Erie in 1656. Anticipating disaster, the Odawa and Ojibwa in the Lake Huron–Georgian Bay area fled westward to Lakes Michigan and Superior. With the defeat and dispersal of the northern groups after the early 1650s, the fur-trading system and French missions temporarily collapsed. These conflicts are the so-called Beaver Wars, a name that implies that the Iroquois fought their neighbours in order to conquer new territory for its furs.

Since the 1860s, historians have explained the Beaver Wars as resulting from eastern Native eagerness for European goods, which led to a rapid expansion of trade between the two groups. Adoption of these 'superior' goods led to rapid cultural change and dependency on the traders. Needing more goods, Natives expanded their trapping, especially in *beaver, the fur in greatest demand. By the 1630s the Iroquois ran short of beaver and began to raid their northern neighbours for fur. Unable to get enough through raiding, they intensified their wars in the 1640s to drive their neighbours from territories with fur-bearing animals, hence the term 'Beaver Wars'.

Recently, scholars have re-examined this theory against the increasingly available documentary record. Not only do the sources make no mention of an economic explanation for these wars, there is also no record of a beaver shortage among the Iroquois until about 1670. Moreover, both the French and English stated categorically that Natives did not fight for economic or territorial gain. The French record in particular yields a plausible alternative explanation. Following the end of *smallpox epidemics in 1641 the Iroquois intensified warfare to capture people, especially young women and children, to replace their depleted population. *Jesuits observed that, by the end of the wars, over half the Iroquois population was made up of non-Iroquois. The Iroquois also saw an opportunity to realize their long-term goal to expand by coercing their now weakened neighbours to join them. Many were killed, but most were adopted into the League. What made the Iroquois successful were their adoption practices and their ability to organize themselves into large, well-led armies equipped with some 800 Dutch flintlock muskets by 1649. Thus the term 'Beaver Wars' is a misnomer: these were not economically motivated wars, but were fought for League survival.

CONRAD HEIDENREICH

Beck, Sir Adam (1857–1925), manufacturer, civil servant, public power advocate. Born into a prosperous, entrepreneurial family in Waterloo County, Canada West, Beck received some secondary education at nearby private academies, but he did not excel and instead entered the family manufacturing business. In the 1880s he started his own firm manufacturing cigar boxes in Galt, then London, Ontario; its success soon raised him to prominence in London. In 1902 he was elected mayor and local MPP. Once in public life, Beck was drawn into the movement for publicly supplied electric power. With him as leader, the idea of a public commission to distribute *hydroelectricity, at cost, to the province's municipalities gained both popular (fairly easily) and political (not so easily) support. When Ontario created its Hydro-Electric Power Commission in 1906, Beck was named chairman, a post he held the rest of his life. The commission was opposed by Toronto's big industrial capitalists, but Beck stood his ground and for doing so became something of a legend. By the 1920s, after some well-publicized financial irregularities, his noble commission had lost its shine, but upon his death Beck was still a hero, and his name was soon memorialized throughout the region.

RICHARD WHITE

Bedford Institute of Oceanography. Established in 1962 by the federal government, the institute is a major oceanographic research facility, located on the shores of the Bedford Basin in Dartmouth, Nova Scotia. Over the last four decades it has grown to become Canada's largest centre for ocean research, providing advice and support on a broad range of issues including sovereignty, defence, environmental protection, health and safety, fisheries, and natural resources

Four federal departments are located at the institute. Fisheries and Oceans Canada is represented by its Science Sector, its Oceans Sector, the Canadian Hydrographic Service, the Aquaculture Co-ordination Office, and by technical and vessel support from the *Canadian Coast Guard. Together they provide scientific knowledge and advice on a variety of issues related to climate, oceans, the environment, marine and diadromous fish, mammals, shellfish, and plants. Natural Resources Canada is represented by the *Geological Survey of Canada (Atlantic), Canada's principal marine geoscience facility. Its research expertise focuses on marine and petroleum geology, geophysics, geochemistry, and geotechnology. The Route Survey Office of Maritime Forces Atlantic supports the Department of National Defence's ocean surveillance activities. And, in support of the Canadian Shellfish Sanitation Program, the Shellfish Section of Environment Canada conducts sanitary and water quality surveys and analyses the samples at the institute's microbiology laboratory. MICHAEL SINCLAIR

bees. In 19th-century Ontario, settlers gathered at a 'bee' to assist each other and work industriously, like bees in a hive. Making a farm required the combined strength and skills of more than one family, and people assisted each other with the understanding that they would receive hospitality and a day's labour in return. Throughout the year, farm families held bees to clear the land, raise barns, chop wood, harvest crops, butcher livestock, make rugs, quilt blankets, and even spread manure. Visiting and competitions made onerous work more pleasant, and afterwards guests enjoyed abundant food, drink, games, dancing, and courting. Everyone could find a role. At a logging bee, for example, young boys gathered up the branches, old men gave advice, newcomers learned, experienced men in their prime hoisted the heavy logs into piles to burn, and women prepared the feast—the grand finale to the day. The bee had great practical value and created an understanding of neighbourhood and one's place in it. As one contemporary claimed, the bee served as the fete, town hall, and labour convention for the whole community. Though increasingly rare, bees still take place in some communities today.

CATHARINE ANNE WILSON

Begbie, Matthew Baillie (1819–94), British Columbia's first judge and chief justice, knighted 1875. Born at the Cape of Good Hope, Cambridge-educated, Begbie practised law in London before being appointed the colony's first judge. From his arrival in November 1858, he was the legal system. Not only did he draft the colony's statutes, but he also oversaw the creation of its lower courts. He took care of the more serious legal business himself, riding thousands of miles on horseback to bring British law to the colony's interior settlements. These one-man circuits established the Begbie legend: a man with little patience for troublesome miners, he meted out a brand of justice that was harsh but remarkably blind to colour, creed, and nationality, except, perhaps, when it came to Americans, whom he viewed as unruly. To a great extent, the peace that prevailed on the colony's mining frontier was attributed to the judge's actions.

In fact, Begbie's tenure was more complex and is suggestive of the class and racial tensions in colonial society. Coloured by his paternalism, his decisions sometimes ran counter to the individualist ethos of the gold-rush colony and could be the source of disorder rather than the solution to it. As well, Begbie's supposedly liberal views on the Chinese and First Nations are belied by the outcome of the capital cases he presided over during the colonial period. The overwhelming majority of people hanged for capital crimes between 1858 and 1871 were Aboriginal. TINA LOO

Bell, Alexander Graham (1847–1922), inventor, educator, philanthropist. Bell was born in Edinburgh, Scotland. Trained by his father in 'visible speech' (a written code especially useful to the deaf, which indicates exactly how all human vocal sounds are made), he taught deaf children in London, England, and in Boston. While visiting his father in Brantford, Ontario, in 1874, he developed the idea of transmitting the human voice electrically over wire, and after much experimentation was awarded a US patent in 1876; later that year in Brantford he carried out the world's first definitive test of the telephone. Although Bell soon sold his patents, he continued to dedicate his life to invention, scientific discovery, and aiding the deaf. He carried out breeding experiments in sheep, worked on the photoelectric cell, desalinated sea water, helped invent the phonograph, contributed to the establishment of *Science* magazine, and helped organize the National Geographic Society. He died at Baddeck, Nova Scotia.

ROBERT E. BABE

Bell, Robert (1841–1917), Canada's greatest exploring scientist. The 15-year-old Bell joined the *Geological Survey of Canada as a temporary fieldworker in 1856—the beginning of an illustrious career lasting half a century. Bell conducted fieldwork throughout the young dominion, but is best remembered for his extensive explorations in northern Ontario, Quebec, and Manitoba in the 1870s and 1880s. He made notes on a wide range of topics—flora and fauna, climate and soil, Aboriginal cultures—and collected interesting specimens. It is estimated that Bell named over 3,000 geographical features, earning him the sobriquet as the father of Canadian *place names. Dr Bell earned a number of distinctions, including the American Geographical Society's Cullum Medal (the only other non-American recipient was David Livingstone). The moody Bell was never happy with his position at the GSC and believed that the directorship had been unjustly withheld from him. BILL WAISER

Bell Canada. Incorporated in 1880 by act of Parliament, the Bell Telephone Company of Canada upon inception controlled the Canadian patents for the telephone taken out by the inventor, Alexander Graham *Bell. It also possessed the right to extend its works throughout the dominion and to string lines along all public rights of way. By 1881, under the leadership of Charles Fleetford Sise, Bell acquired all other telephone properties in the country and appeared safely ensconced with a nationwide monopoly for years to come. In 1885 Bell spun off the Northern Electric and Manufacturing Company and began purchasing equipment from its new subsidiary.

Despite experiencing various name changes (Northern Electric Company, Northern Telecom, Nortel Systems), this manufacturing entity remained affiliated with Bell Canada until May 2000. Also in 1885, key patents were nullified by the patent commissioner, allowing independent telephone companies to come into existence. Some competed directly, others served rural territories that Bell deemed unprofitable and refused to serve. In 1906, amid considerable public pressure, the federal government began regulating Bell's rates. The three Prairie provinces purchased Bell's provincial operations in 1908 and 1909. By 1920, through a variety of means (refusal to interconnect, price cutting even to the point of offering free telephone service, unfavourable publicity and threats of lawsuits), all directly competing telephone companies were absorbed by Bell or put out of business, although a thriving independent telephone industry, serving territories not served by Bell, continued in Ontario and Quebec until the 1950s.

Today Bell Canada is the major holding of Bell Canada Enterprises, whose other communication operations include the *Globe and Mail*, the CTV Television Network, and Sympatico internet service. In 2000 Bell Canada accounted for $13.2 billion in revenues, provided 11.8 million telephone access lines, and served more than 2.3 million wireless telephone customers. ROBERT E. BABE

Belles-soeurs, Les. Michel Tremblay's *Les Belles-soeurs* is universally acknowledged as marking the birth of *théâtre québécois*. Extraordinary controversy surrounded its first production, in August 1968, because of its unprecedented use of **joual* (coarse French-Canadian slang) and its often scathing depiction of the French-Canadian proletariat. *Les Belles-soeurs* unfolds as a working-class housewife, Germaine Lauzon, and her sisters and neighbours paste in booklets the one million trading stamps that she has just won. Jealous of her good fortune, the women steal the stamps. As Germaine realizes what the others have done, she witnesses the disintegration of her dream for a better life. Like Gratien *Gélinas's *Tit-Coq* 20 years earlier, *Les Belles-soeurs* offers biting criticism of French Canada's endemic inability to escape its mediocre circumstances and assert itself. Combining crude naturalism with vaudeville comedy, chorus songs, and monologues, *Les Belles-soeurs* was among the first plays in Quebec theatre to escape the limits of realist drama and explore new modes of dramatic expression. Tremblay has continued to write plays, often featuring characters from the same milieu as Germaine. In addition to his dramatic output, his novels and screenplays have made him one of the most significant literary figures in Quebec.

ANDRÉ LOISELLE

Bell Telephone strike. In February 1907 about 400 women operators from Toronto's Bell Telephone exchange struck to protest the intensification of their workday from a five- to eight-hour schedule with a lower hourly rate. Few women workers at this time were unionized, and strikes by 'white-collar' female workers were rare. Arguing that their work was arduous and stressful, the 'hello girls' secured support from labour and the public, in part because Bell's monopoly was resented. However, neither successful unionization nor the operators' wage demands emerged from the strike. The conflict resulted in a federally appointed royal commission, co-chaired by Mackenzie *King. The commission was preoccupied with the medical and reproductive outcome of stressful work for Canada's future mothers and with the moral fear that low wages would lead to prostitution. King also used the report to argue for passage of the Industrial Disputes Investigation Act, while the company increasingly turned to modern management strategies of paternal care and benefits to prevent unionization.

JOAN SANGSTER

Bengough, John Wilson (1851–1923). Cartoonist, writer, and reformer, Bengough is known mainly for his satirical magazine **Grip*, but also had a prolific career as a lecturer, poet, local politician, and activist. Born in Toronto, the third child of a Scots carpenter, he was raised in nearby Whitby and worked there briefly as a printer and reporter before joining George *Brown's Toronto *Globe* in 1872. A year later he started *Grip* at an opportune time, when the *Pacific Scandal made John A. *Macdonald a prime target for cartoon attack.

Never a polished artist, Bengough compensated with energy and a keen social conscience, rooted in admiration for Charles Dickens and tax reformer Henry George. He usually sided with the Reform/Liberal Party, backing the provincial regime of Oliver *Mowat and the federal leadership of Alexander *Mackenzie, Edward *Blake, and Wilfrid *Laurier, but he was on the party's more progressive edge, supporting radical change in such areas as *prohibition, *labour law, and tax reform.

While cartooning for *Grip* Bengough launched a career as a lecturer, travelling widely to give 'chalk talks', in which quick sketches and humour backed his social messages. After *Grip* died in 1894 he drew cartoons for the Toronto *Globe* and many other publications, consistently supporting Laurier until the Liberal leader opposed *conscription in 1917. Bengough also pursued an active writing career in many forms (poetry, opera, humour, screenwriting) and served as a reformist Toronto alderman in 1907–9, pressing for prohibition, tax reform, public hydro, and free school texts. CARMAN CUMMING

Bennett, Richard Bedford (1870–1947), prime minister 1930–5. Bennett was born at Hopewell Hill, Albert County, New Brunswick, 3 July 1870, the eldest son of Henry J. Bennett, shipbuilder and merchant, and his wife Henrietta Stiles. She was a staunch Wesleyan Methodist, he an easygoing, bibulous Baptist. Henrietta Bennett's Methodism, with its strong emphasis on work, diligence, and self-denial, became the supreme law in her family. These principles—charitable to the outside world, exacting to the inner self—guided Bennett all his life.

Bennett started teaching school at age 16, saved his meagre salary, and put himself through Dalhousie

University Law School, graduating in 1893 near the top of his class. Thus began his long climb out of penury. After practising law at Chatham on the Miramichi, in 1897 he transferred to the office of Sir James Lougheed in Calgary. Despite difficulties, he succeeded through intelligence and hard work, and by the 1920s was virtually a millionaire. In Alberta, he aligned himself with the Conservative Party and in 1911 was elected MP for Calgary West. With his quick mind, commanding manner, impatience with fools, and hot temper, he was apt to be feared rather than loved. After Arthur *Meighen's 1926 resignation, Bennett was chosen leader at the Conservative convention in Winnipeg in October 1927. He then set to work with some of his own money (and that of others) to rebuild the party. His Conservatives won the July 1930 election with 137 of the 245 seats in the House of Commons.

It was not a good time to be in power. Most countries were suffering through the Depression, and Canada was more vulnerable than many. Bennett and his party hit the crisis head on. His instinct in those desperate years was to try to keep the ship of state afloat. Some changes helped. One was the *Bank of Canada, established in 1934 to shore up the Canadian financial system. It was useful and permanent, yet it could not create rain on the Prairies or export primary commodities. More radical changes suggested by Bennett—he was a *Red Tory in important ways—had been resisted by the Montreal and Toronto wings of the party, but desperation forced their hand. When Bennett's 'new deal' was announced in January 1935, it looked like a pre-election conversion.

Probably no government could have survived the first five years of the Depression. Moreover, Bennett was not well, diagnosed in March 1935 with atrial fibrillation of the heart. In the 1935 election the Conservative Party did better than many expected, receiving 30 per cent of the popular vote, but owing to the defection of Harry Stevens's *Reconstruction group, the Conservatives elected but 40 members to the Liberals' 173. After 1935, Bennett proved to be an excellent leader of the opposition, and when he resigned in July 1938 Parliament lost one of its most dynamic members. Bennett retired to England and was created Viscount Bennett by Churchill in 1941. On the night of 26–7 June 1947 he died of heart attack at his home near Mickleham, Surrey. He gave of himself, his energy, and his fortune to Canada as few prime ministers have done, and has been ill requited by history for it. P.B. WAITE

Bennett, William Andrew Cecil (1900–79), merchant, BC premier 1952–72. Born in Hastings, New Brunswick, Bennett arrived in British Columbia in 1930 and became a successful Kelowna hardware merchant. Elected a Conservative MLA in 1941, he became part of the Coalition government. As a member of the Post-War Rehabilitation Council he toured the province in 1942 and gained many ideas for provincial development. In 1951 he withdrew from the Coalition and ran as a *Social Credit candidate in the 1952 election. When, some weeks after a confusing election outcome, the Socreds were asked to form the government, the caucus chose him as premier. Taking advantage of prosperity, he extended the *Pacific Great Eastern Railway to the *Peace River, improved highways, developed hydroelectric power on the Peace and Columbia Rivers, and created new universities and community colleges. Through creative bookkeeping he 'eliminated' the provincial debt. Though he warned of *'socialist hordes', his government established the BC Ferry Corporation and took over the major privately owned electrical utility and urban transportation companies. By 1972, electors were tired of 'Wacky' Bennett, but three years later elected a Social Credit government under his son, William R. Bennett. W.A.C. Bennett died in Kelowna. PATRICIA E. ROY

Beothuk. The Beothuk or 'Red Indians' were hunters, fishers, and food gatherers who lived in small, independent bands around the island of Newfoundland. Their prehistoric ancestors can be confidently traced back to AD 400. An ancestral relationship with an earlier Indian population (AD 1–1000) is unlikely; links with the even earlier Maritime Archaic Indians (3500–1000 BC) have not yet been confirmed. At contact with Europeans the Beothuk numbered 500–700. Red ochre rubbed on face, body, and their skin clothing was a sign of tribal identity. Relying mostly on caribou, salmon, and seal the Beothuk also exploited fur bearers, birds, and other marine resources. They hunted with bow and arrow, spear, and sealing harpoon and built enclosures for caribou drives. They never adopted guns or European clothing. The Beothuk believed in life after physical death, honoured the caribou spirit in feasts, and displayed heads of slain enemies. They built multi-sided, semi-subterranean winter dwellings, constructed unique half-moon-shaped birchbark canoes, and carved stylized bone pendants and emblematic staves. The Beothuk language is probably related to the Algonkian family.

Following John *Cabot's landing in Newfoundland in 1497, Beothuk were rarely encountered. In 1612 John Guy traded with them in Trinity Bay, but increased settlements and Mi'kmaw encroachment drove them into Notre Dame Bay and the watershed of the Exploits River. Their relations with Labrador Innu remained peaceable, and strife with northern Inuit was short-lived. When settlers' hunting and fishing practices severely diminished their resource base, altercations and a vicious cycle of revenge ensued. Governors' proclamations prohibiting persecution of Beothuk were ineffective and authorities in Britain ignored their plight. Attempts at conciliation failed—Lt John Cartwright (1768) and William E. *Cormack (1822, 1827) could not find them, and Lt (later Capt.) David Buchan's expedition (1811) ended in tragedy when the Beothuk killed two marines. Offers of bounties for captives—to serve as mediators—resulted in several Beothuk being captured, among them *Demasduit (1819) and *Shanawdithit (1823). With Shanawdithit's death in 1829, the Beothuk as a cultural entity ceased to exist. INGEBORG C.L. MARSHALL

Bernier, Captain Joseph-Elzéar (1852–1934), sea captain. A native of L'Islet, Quebec, Bernier went to sea at a young age and by 17 he commanded his own transatlantic sailing ship. He developed an interest in arctic navigation and made a series of four voyages (1904–11) into the Canadian eastern Arctic in the government survey vessel *Arctic* to map the coastlines, to monitor the activities of foreign whalers and traders, and generally to lay claim to the area for Canada. His expeditions followed in the tracks of many famous explorers, and he came very close to completing a transit of the *Northwest Passage. On one of these voyages, at Winter Harbour on Melville Island on 1 July 1909, Bernier unveiled a plaque declaring that all the islands in the *Arctic Archipelago belonged to Canada. Resigning from government service, he made three private trading excursions to the eastern Arctic in 1912–17. Following the First World War he returned to government service, commanding his old vessel the *Arctic* on four more northern voyages, 1922–5, before retiring from the sea. He was the leading arctic navigator of his time and did a great deal to promote the region as a commercial and territorial frontier. DANIEL FRANCIS

Berton, Laura (1878–1967), teacher and author. Laura Beatrice Thompson journeyed from Toronto to the Yukon in 1907 to teach in the new public school in *Dawson City. Arriving well after the fabled *Klondike gold rush was over, she was witness to a community attempting to redefine itself. In 1912 she met and married a mining engineer named Francis (Frank) Berton. Their son Pierre, born in Whitehorse in 1920, became one of Canada's most famous writers. In 1954 Laura Berton published *I Married the Klondike*, a memoir detailing the social and cultural life of the Yukon in the transitional period after the rush and before the First World War.
CHARLENE PORSILD

Best, Carrie (1903–2001), human rights activist, publisher, radio personality, member and officer of the Order of Canada. Best grew up in the historic Black community of New Glasgow, Nova Scotia, the daughter of a cook and a labourer, and married a railway porter. Rejecting the limited possibilities available as a teacher, she became a crusading journalist. She founded the first Black newspaper in Nova Scotia, *The Clarion* (1946–56), and on her regional radio program she read her own poetry and fiction. Honoured for influential campaigns on behalf of groups including the Mi'kmaq as well as African Nova Scotians, she insisted that Blacks were responsible for building their own dignity and self-esteem, and that Black men should begin their liberation by showing respect to Black women. NAOMI BLACK

Bethune, H. Norman (1890–1939), surgeon, inventor, writer, artist, left-wing activist. Born in Gravenhurst, Ontario, Bethune showed an early independence of mind. He studied medicine at the University of Toronto, teaching one year at *Frontier College. After serving as a stretcher-bearer in France, he graduated in 1916, then joined the Royal Navy. After the war he studied pediatrics and surgery in England and Scotland.

Soon after setting up practice, in Detroit, he developed severe tuberculosis and was hospitalized. Later he moved to Montreal and became a prominent chest surgeon, ultimately chief of thoracic surgery at the Hôpital du Sacré-Coeur. In 1923 he married a well-to-do Scot, Frances Penney, with whom he had a tumultuous relationship: they fought, divorced, remarried, then divorced again. Much affected by the suffering he observed in Montreal during the Depression, Bethune became politically active, his socialistic sympathies gradually firming until, ultimately, though at first secretly, he became a member of the Communist Party. During the Spanish Civil War he established a mobile blood transfusion service for the Republican army out of Madrid. On his return, he faced public criticism during a speaking tour in support of the Republicans.

Early in 1938 Bethune journeyed to China and allied himself with the Communist army, serving under fire with Mao Zedong's Eighth Route Army, performing surgery on wounded soldiers and civilians. He came to be revered by the Chinese, who buried him with honours after he died of a surgical infection, having cut himself while operating, as usual, with bare hands. Bethune's Canadian reputation lagged behind that in other parts of the world, largely because of his avowed Communism. For some decades he was one of the few Westerners respected and admired by the Chinese.
CHARLES G. ROLAND

Beurling, George Frederick (1921–48). From Verdun, Quebec, 'Buzz' Beurling was the leading Canadian fighter ace of the Second World War, with a score of 31⅓ victories, 9 probables, and 3 damaged. He was already an experienced pilot when he joined Britain's Royal Air Force in 1940. Flying Spitfires, Beurling was an extraordinary aerial marksman who applied mathematical precision to the science of deflection shooting. He was also a noted individualist whose practice of breaking formation during engagements led him into conflict with his superiors. But his astonishing combat record speaks for itself. Best remembered for his spectacular role in the defence of Malta during the summer of 1942, when he downed 27 enemy aircraft in four months of intensive combat, he was shot down and wounded in October. In 1943 he transferred to the *Royal Canadian Air Force. He was awarded the Distinguished Service Order, the Distinguished Flying Cross, and the Distinguished Flying Medal and Bar. He died in an airplane crash in Rome on 20 May 1948 while on his way to fight for Israel during its war of independence. SERGE DURFLINGER

Beynon, Francis Marion (1884–1951), journalist. The Beynon family, farmers and strict Wesleyan Methodists, moved from Ontario to Manitoba in 1902. By 1908 Beynon worked in advertising (at Eaton's) and as a journalist in Winnipeg. She was active in the Canadian Women's Press Club and helped to organize the Political

Equality League of Manitoba, the province's chief *women's suffrage organization. In her column for the *Grain Growers' Guide*, where she was woman's page editor 1912–17, she took a wide-ranging view of the 'Woman Question', discussing, in addition to suffrage, women's work and the structure of marriage and the family. When war broke out Beynon took a pacifist position, opposing *conscription and working with other pacifist protesters, such as J.S. *Woodsworth. This stand, unpopular with mainstream women's organizations, forced her resignation from the *Grain Growers' Guide* in 1917. She then moved to New York City, where her sister Lillian Beynon Thomas and her brother-in-law A. Vernon Thomas had already been forced to move in 1916 because of their radical views. From New York, Beynon continued to support feminist *pacifism in Canada and published a feminist pacifist novel *Aleta Day* (1919).

DEBORAH GORHAM

Biard, Pierre (1567/8–1622), Jesuit missionary to Acadia. Pierre Biard sailed from France to *Port-Royal in 1611. His efforts to evangelize Aboriginal inhabitants reached their apex in 1613, when he and three other *Jesuits founded the mission village of Saint-Sauveur in the vicinity of Mount Desert Island. Biard had fallen afoul of the leader of the small French colony in Acadia, Charles de Biencourt, who objected to the Jesuits' thorough instruction of converts before baptism, which provided Biencourt with fewer proselytes to boast about to patrons in France. Biard hoped to free himself of Biencourt by moving to Saint-Sauveur; however, a Virginia expedition burned both settlements later in 1613. Biard was imprisoned by the English, eventually returning to France in 1614. A resourceful missionary and unbending controversialist, Biard emerged in his *Relation de la Nouvelle-France* (1616) as a perceptive writer about Native societies and the pitfalls of colonial settlement.

JOHN G. REID

Bibb, Mary (1820–77). Born in Rhode Island, Mary Miles was the first known Black woman in North America to graduate from normal school, in Massachusetts in 1843. After teaching in various states she joined the anti-slavery movement in Boston. In 1848 she married the well-known fugitive lecturer Henry Bibb, and two years later moved to Sandwich, Canada West, following passage of the American Fugitive Slave Act. In her home she established the first school for Black children disenfranchised by the Ontario Separate Schools Act. The school later moved to Windsor, where it survived until 1870. Bibb contributed to Canadian journalism by founding, with her husband, Canada's first Black newspaper, *Voice of the Fugitive*, in 1851. She founded mutual-improvement societies, taught in the Sunday school movement, helped establish a housing scheme for landless fugitives, and opened her own business, a fancy goods store. Two years after her husband's death in 1854 she married Toronto abolitionist Isaac Cary.

AFUA COOPER

Big Bear (Mistahai'muskwa), (*c.* 1825–89), Cree chief. Born to a prominent Cree-Ojibwa family, Big Bear became a chief by the early 1870s. He refused to sign Treaty 6 in 1876 because of its poor terms and a feared loss of freedom. As a result of his firm stance, government agents branded him a troublemaker. In 1882, starvation forced him to sign the treaty but he refused to take a reserve. Instead, he settled near Frog Lake and was there in 1885 when the *North-West Rebellion occurred. In April, his son Imasees and war chief Wandering Spirit precipitated the Frog Lake massacre in which nine inhabitants, including two priests, were slain. At this point, Wandering Spirit took control of the band and led it during the siege of Fort Pitt, and the battles of Frenchman's Butte and Loon Lake. Although Big Bear had not taken part in the fighting, he was convicted of treason-felony and sentenced to three years in prison. He was released in 1888 and died on the Little Pine Reserve a year later.

HUGH A. DEMPSEY

Bigot, François (1703–78). A lifelong administrator in the Ministry of the Marine, Bigot served first as financial commissary in Louisbourg, 1739–45, and then as intendant in Quebec, 1748–60. In both locations, he was in charge of colonial finances, judiciary, and civil affairs, functions he carried out capably. He nonetheless profited from his position, and his house in Quebec was renowned for the sumptuous balls he hosted. Given the rampant inflation before the fall of New France to the British in 1759–60, Bigot was accused of corruption and blamed for the colony's financial crisis. Despite the fact that many other French administrators similarly muddled public and personal financial dealings, Bigot was found guilty by the Parisian courts. He was fined 1.5 million livres and exiled from France, thus conveniently receiving much of the opprobrium for the loss of the colony. He died in Switzerland.

COLIN M. COATES

bilingualism. In response to the perception that French-speaking Canadians were being treated as a underprivileged ethnic minority, the federal government, in July 1963, appointed the Royal Commission on Bilingualism and Biculturalism to recommend the establishment of 'an equal partnership between the two founding races' in Canada, not overlooking the contributions of other ethnic groups to the country's cultural enrichment. In a view radically different from Lord *Durham's proposal that the French would be assimilated by an influx of English settlers, the commission recommended in 1967 that English and French be formally declared the official languages of federal institutions and that the provinces of New Brunswick and Ontario should act similarly. These proposals were based on the recognition of two distinct and dominant cultures embodied in distinct societies, one French-speaking and one English-speaking.

Biculturalism eventually gave way to the idea of *multiculturalism in a policy adopted by the Trudeau government in 1971. Quebec nationalists claimed that multiculturalism was intended to block the 'two nations' thesis campaigned for by the Conservatives under Robert *Stanfield in 1967–8. In 1969 the federal government passed the Official Languages Act, a policy based on three principles: the right of Canadians to access services in the official language of their choice, equitable participation and employment opportunities in federal institutions for Canadians of both language groups, and the right of federal employees to work in their chosen language in designated areas. After the election of the *Parti Québécois in 1976, nine premiers committed their provinces to provide instruction in English or French to minorities where numbers warranted. In 1982 the Canadian *Charter of Rights and Freedoms converted these government policies into constitutional guarantees. From that time, the promotion of the official languages throughout Canadian society has been a priority. In 1988 the Official Languages Act was substantially revised and took precedence over other statutes.

In their report, the B and B commissioners had found it an anomaly that the official-language minority received full recognition only in Quebec. Although Bill 101, the charter of the French language in Quebec adopted by the Lévesque government in 1977, is seen negatively elsewhere in the country, minority languages are still protected in Quebec. Some progress has been made elsewhere. New Brunswick passed its Official Languages Act in 1968 and has been officially a bilingual province since 2002. In compliance with the Charter of Rights and in some cases (Alberta, Manitoba, Ontario) following court rulings, other provinces and territories have passed legislation or have regulations protecting the rights of official minority groups, especially through different school systems. Resistance to bilingualism outside Quebec results partly from perceiving it as a burden rather than an asset. RAYMOND HUDON

birth control. Like other Western, industrialized nations in the 19th century, Canada enacted restrictive contraception legislation in reaction to falling birth rates, associated fears of 'race suicide', and the professionalizing ambitions of physicians. In an 1892 amendment to the Criminal Code, 'the advertising, sale or disposal of contraceptives' became a criminal offence. One clause, probably meant to protect physicians from prosecution, exempted those cases where the 'public good' was served.

Despite increasing evidence of birth control use, it was long associated with *prostitution and crime. Thus birth control was not advocated by reformers until 1924, when a brave group of Vancouver socialist feminists established the Canadian Birth Control League. During the Depression, the movement became more organized, but its earlier *feminism began to coexist uneasily with a socially conservative eugenicism advocated by many middle-class reformers. Mary Hawkins, who was inspired by the American birth control advocate and feminist Margaret Sanger, founded a clinic in Hamilton, Ontario, in 1932. She wanted to make safe, medically supervised birth control available to Hamilton women, but focused primarily on the relief recipients she encountered through her voluntary social welfare work. In Kitchener, industrialist Alvin Kaufman, who concluded that *poverty could be alleviated by correcting the fertility differential between the poor and the 'better classes', established the Parents' Information Bureau. Kaufman succeeded in making birth control more widely available to a large number of Canadians by innovating a system of visiting nurses who gave working-class mothers the opportunity to apply, by mail, for low-cost contraceptives. In 1936, one of these nurses, Dorothea Palmer, was arrested in Eastview, near Ottawa. Although she told the arresting officer that a woman had a right to 'control her own body', the subsequent trial was completely overshadowed by the male experts Kaufman assembled to argue the benefits of birth control. Economists, social workers, and clergymen all predicted that birth control would reduce crime, poverty, and the tax burden, and improve the quality of the race. Kaufman even suggested that the prolific French Catholic residents of Eastview were especially in need of reproductive control, adding a new wrinkle to the Canadian 'battle of the cradle'. Swayed by these arguments, the presiding magistrate acquitted Palmer and confirmed the 'public good' clause.

Ironically, although it was discredited following the Second World War, the harsh *eugenic philosophy that alienated most labour and ethnic groups helped liberalize contraception and allowing the pioneering clinics to continue their work of improving access to contraception. This had a positive impact on women's health and autonomy. With the Planned Parenthood Federation of Canada, founded in 1964, the movement campaigned against the 1892 legislation, which was finally repealed in 1969. DIANNE DODD

Bishop, William Avery (1894–1956), fighter pilot. With 72 accredited victories, 'Billy' Bishop was the highest-scoring British Empire ace of the First World War. After an academically lacklustre but socially triumphant cadetship at Kingston's Royal Military College, and a short-lived diversion to a cavalry regiment, he used his considerable brashness and charm to enter the Royal Flying Corps. Bishop successfully completed a combat tour as an observer in 1916, then trained as a pilot and returned to the front in 1917, flying diminutive Nieuport 17 scouts. Audacious and relentlessly determined to engage the enemy, he emerged from his operational tour that summer as the Imperial 'Ace-of-Aces' with 47 victories, Canada's first aerial Victoria Cross, and a host of lesser decorations. A subsequent whirlwind tour flying potent SE5a scouts at the helm of his own squadron in 1918 garnered Bishop a further 25 aerial successes. As an air marshal and highly inspirational director of recruiting for the RCAF during the Second World War, he sent the youth of the nation flocking to the enlistment depots. Several attempts in recent years to discredit his Great War record have, in the light of latest research, proven unfounded. DAVID L. BASHOW

Black, Martha Louise Munger (1866–1957). Surely one of very few persons to trek the 53 km of the Chilkoot Trail in a corset and while pregnant, Black arrived in *Dawson in July 1898. Pampered and unhappy, she had welcomed the chance to act as agent for a party seeking the elusive gold claim of a dead relative. Unable to resettle into society life upon returning home to Chicago, she divorced her husband, brought her sons north to the Yukon, and (in partnership with her brother) opened a sawmill and invested in gold claims. In 1904 she married George Black and focused on supporting his political career. In 1935–40, with George too ill to run again for Parliament, Martha campaigned over an area of 500,000 sq km and became the second woman to sit in the House of Commons. Booster of the North and an internationally recognized botanist, she lectured on both these topics while serving with the Red Cross in London during the First World War. In 1938 she dictated an autobiography, *My Seventy Years*. JANICE DICKIN

Black Loyalists. During the *American Revolution, thousands of slaves escaped from rebel 'masters' and joined the Loyalist cause, following British promises to respect their freedom and treat them equally with white *Loyalists. They served as soldiers, spies, labourers, launderers, and skilled workers, believing that a British victory would mean freedom and equality for all slaves in America. In defeat, about 3,500 Black Loyalists were evacuated to the colony of Nova Scotia.

Most Black Loyalists were located in segregated settlements, usually on the fringes of larger white towns, where they established communities and institutions, including churches and schools that became the basis for a distinct Black culture. The largest Black community was at Birchtown, near Shelburne, with over 1,500 people in 1783. Nominally free, they were tainted in the official white mind by their former enslavement and did not achieve the equality they anticipated. Most significantly, land grants to Black Loyalists were inadequate to provide subsistence. The newcomers were required to labour in the neighbouring white settlements, launching a syndrome of economic dependence and material poverty that continued for generations.

In 1790 Thomas Peters, a former sergeant in the Black Pioneer Corps, carried a petition to London addressed to King George III, complaining that the promise of equality had not been fulfilled and that *slavery continued to exist in Nova Scotia. British abolitionists sponsored his appeal to the government, resulting in an offer to transport the Black Loyalists to a new colony in West Africa. About 1,200 Black Loyalists left Halifax in early 1792 and founded Freetown, the nucleus for the modern state of Sierra Leone, where their descendants still identify as 'Nova Scotians'. Those who remained in the Maritimes formed the foundation for the African-Canadian community, which has survived for more than 200 years. JAMES W. ST G. WALKER

Blacks. *See* AFRICAN CANADIANS.

Blair, Winnifred C. (1904–?). Crowned the first Miss Canada during the Montreal Winter Carnival on 12 February 1923, Blair lived in Saint John, New Brunswick, with her widowed mother, brother, and sister, and worked as a stenographer at a custom's broker office. Winning the title made her famous across North America. The officials behind the carnival's Sports Committee were looking for a 'girl' who would symbolize 'typical Canadian womanhood', and Blair was seen to embody all the characteristics of the 'Canadian girl': pretty, charming, and unassuming. What set her apart from other beauty queens in the 1920s was her refusal to use the title as a stepping stone to a career in the movies or modelling. She preferred to continue working as a stenographer after her reign ended, and eventually married a lawyer, Harold Drummie, and had two sons. Although Winnifred Blair shunned the spotlight, her short career as Miss Canada set the tone for the future Miss Canada Pageant, incorporated in 1947. PATRIZIA GENTILE

Blake, (Dominick) Edward (1833–1912), Ontario premier 1871–2. Of Irish Anglican background, Blake gained entree to Ontario politics through his lucrative legal career, and his premiership led to federal politics. Minister without portfolio in Alexander *Mackenzie's Liberal government, he resigned after the election of 1874. High public expectation and frustrated leadership ambitions produced his liberal nationalist reform rebellion against party leadership (his famous Aurora speech, *Canada First). Returning to cabinet as minister of justice in 1875, he established the *Supreme Court of Canada. Liberals turned to him as party leader in 1880 after their 1878 *National Policy election loss. His intense reform and party-consolidation efforts led to episodic 'neurasthenic' collapse; Blake pondered resigning and, after Liberals failed to win in 1887, did. He broke with the Laurier Liberals over unrestricted *reciprocity. His legal practice, partly active throughout his political life, culminated in successful arguments before the JCPC in the 1890s for greater provincial constitutional powers. An Irish nationalist MP in the British Parliament after 1892, he laboured to resolve the Irish Question. His efforts ended in 1907 with a stroke and a return to Canada. Blake's weaknesses—nervous energy, overweening intellectuality, and gluttony for work—were also the sources of his political and formidable legal success. BEN FORSTER

Bland, Salem (1859–1950), Methodist *social gospel exponent. The intense 'prophetic' gaze in Lawren Harris's 1925 portrait captures the man who embodied progressive Christian evangelicalism and social reform in Canada. The son of a Methodist minister who rejected the hallowed doctrine of original sin, Bland was raised in an environment attuned to the social, religious, and intellectual changes then sweeping the Western world. Placements in Kingston and surroundings as a young minister exposed him to the idealistic philosophy of John Watson and the practical Christianity of Principal George *Grant at Queen's University. A voracious reader and analytical thinker, by 1903, when he accepted an appointment as professor of church history and New Testament at Wesley College, Winnipeg, Bland had become a trenchant voice for religious and social reform, and would be a formative presence within Prairie radicalism. After 1917, when his views led to dismissal, he continued to push his denomination into a more radical stance. In 1920 he published *The New Christianity*, a call to replace Protestantism and capitalism with a new social order embodying the Christian spirit of brotherhood. After retirement, he remained prominent as a powerful speaker, a writer ('The Observer') for the Toronto *Daily Star*, a supporter of the *CCF, and a critic of *fascism. MARGUERITE VAN DIE

Blatz, William Emet (1895–1964). Born in Hamilton, Blatz received a medical degree from the University of Toronto (1921) and a PhD in psychology at Chicago (1923). In 1925 he became the first director of the University of Toronto's St George's Nursery School for Child Study. By 1930, as the Institute of Child Study, the school had become a leading North American research centre in child development. Blatz's enthusiastic endorsement of 'scientific motherhood' made him the pre-eminent child psychologist in Canada. Emphasizing early training in self-control, his approach was made evident in his 1928 manual *Parents and the Preschool Child*, co-authored with Helen Bott, in which he declared that 'the kitchen timepiece is the most important tool of modern childrearing'. He was appointed chief consultant to the *Dionne Quintuplets in 1935, a role he shared with the period's foremost pediatrician, Dr Alan Brown of the Hospital for Sick Children. In 1944 Blatz summarized 20 years of research in his *Understanding the Young Child*, which served *baby boom parents as the Canadian version of Dr Spock's revered text. CYNTHIA COMACCHIO

Bloc populaire. The bloc began as a protest against the 1942 plebiscite in which the federal government asked to be relieved from its promise not to introduce *conscription. A majority of Canadians gave their approval, but in Quebec 80 per cent of French Canadians voted 'no'. The leaders of the Quebec campaign then opted to form a political party to advocate Canadian independence, *provincial autonomy, French-English equality in Ottawa, and social reform in Quebec. In the Quebec provincial election of 1944 the bloc elected only four members. As leader of the provincial party, André *Laurendeau drew attention to the problems of French-Canadian survival in an urban, industrial society, but Duplessis and the *Union nationale retained popular support by denouncing federal encroachment on provincial autonomy. Maxime Raymond, the leader of the federal wing, supported Canadian membership in the UN but advocated Canadian independence and opposed participation in NATO as a dangerous commitment to future wars. The Bloc populaire elected two French-Canadian candidates in the federal election of 1945. The party had a brief existence; it did not contest the provincial election of 1948 or the federal election of 1949. H. BLAIR NEATBY

Bloc Québécois. Following the creation of the provincial *Parti Québécois and election of its first candidates in 1970, Quebec nationalists considered how best to participate in federal politics. After much equivocation, the failure of the *Meech Lake Accord in 1990 provided an opportunity. Lucien Bouchard resigned from the Progressive Conservative cabinet and formed the Bloc Québécois with six other Conservative and Liberal MPs who believed the rest of Canada had missed its best chance to reconcile Quebec to the 1982 constitution. The BQ aimed to defend Quebec's interests within Parliament until a referendum victory could lead to Quebec sovereignty. In the 1993 federal election, the BQ won 54 seats in Quebec and, thanks to the disarray of other opposition parties, became the official opposition in the House of Commons. When Jacques Parizeau resigned as leader of the PQ following a referendum defeat in 1995, Bouchard became PQ leader and Quebec premier. In 1997 and 2000, with Gilles Duceppe as leader, the BQ won fewer seats, 44, then 38. The latter election marked a dramatic reversal in the BQ's fortunes, with the Liberal Party under Jean *Chrétien—the Bloc's main political enemy because he represented Pierre Elliott *Trudeau's uncompromising attitudes towards Quebec nationalism—winning many BQ seats. RAYMOND HUDON

bloc settlement. The Canadian government occasionally set aside lands on the Canadian prairies for the settlement of specific ethnic communities. Although considered settlement reserves in the regulations, the districts created in this manner are referred to as bloc settlements. The first bloc settlement was established in southern Manitoba for Mennonite migrants in March 1873. A second settlement in close proximity to the first was created for *Mennonites in 1876. Other settlement reserves were established near Lake Winnipeg for Icelandic settlers in 1875, along the present Saskatchewan–Manitoba border north of Yorkton for *Doukhobor settlers in 1899, and in a number of locations in Saskatchewan and Alberta for a variety of Hutterite migrants during the First World War. Restrictions on who could settle in these districts were usually lifted after the initial settlement community had established itself. The restrictions on settlement in the Icelandic reserve, for example, ended in October 1897. Yet, the areas where bloc settlements existed retain a distinctive ethnic composition. Moreover, settlers made efforts to preserve cultural traditions and values, leading to powerful critiques from nativist and assimilationist constituencies on the prairies.

The term bloc settlement is sometimes used in conjunction with the congregation of an ethnic community in specific districts through the process of chain migration. Such settlements are usually associated with *Ukrainian immigrants or the expansion of Mennonite communities from the original Manitoba reserves rather than with settlement groups such as Mormons, Norwegians, or French Canadians. Among the more significant of this type of bloc settlements are those east of Edmonton at Star, north of Saskatoon at Rosthern, and in west-central Manitoba at Dauphin. These settlements did not allow for special rights or privileges but were recognized as bloc settlements by the local population because of the traditional cultural patterns of life preserved through relative ethnic homogeneity. ROBERT IRWIN

Bluenose. Canada's famous fishing and racing schooner, *Bluenose* was launched at *Lunenburg, Nova Scotia, on 26 March 1921. Designed by William J. Roue, the vessel competed in the International Fishermen's Series between Canada and the United States. It was hoped that *Bluenose* would assuage Canadians' wounded feelings from the loss of the first international series in 1920. Under the command of Captain Angus J. Walters, *Bluenose* defeated four American schooners during the remaining races, held between 1921 and 1938. The American contenders were *Elsie* (1921), *Henry Ford* (1922), *Columbia* (1923), and *Gertrude L. Thebaud* (1931 and 1938).

As a Nova Scotian 'touring ambassador', *Bluenose* visited Chicago (1933), Toronto (1934), and England (1935). In 1937 an image of the schooner was placed on the Canadian dime. The ship had already been immortalized on a 50-cent Canadian postage stamp in 1929.

Bluenose foundered, without loss of life, on a reef near Haiti in January 1946. The historic record of the vessel is an international symbol of national pride. *Bluenose* represents the thousands of fishing schooners that sailed from Canadian ports and the best of Canada's golden age of sail.

HEATHER-ANNE GETSON

Board of Railway Commissioners. The Canadian government created the board in response to the *freight rate and service grievances of a broad coalition of merchants, manufacturers, and farmers. The Railway Act, 1903, granted three commissioners, who enjoyed the independence of judges, wide powers to review and amend freight and passenger rates, establish rules and regulations for employees, inspect new lines, require the installation of safety devices, and investigate accidents. Although judicial appeals were limited, the *cabinet could review board decisions.

The commissioners' most publicly visible activity involved freight and passenger rate regulation. Prior to 1914, the commission removed some advantages enjoyed by some shippers, and in doing so reshaped the rate structures of central and western Canada. Between 1916 and 1920 the commission, on its own or working with the government, approved a series of horizontal rate increases, intended to permit railways to keep up with rising costs. These increases led shippers and others to argue that the commission had become too sympathetic to the railway companies. Regional rate controversies in the 1920s, which could not be fully resolved by the commission, led to direct government intervention and undermined the prestige and authority of the commission.

KEN CRUIKSHANK

Board of Trade and Plantations. Established under William III in 1696, the Board of Trade was intended to bring the British colonies under closer control after years of relative neglect and both administrative and constitutional confusion. The board was a royal creation, responsible to the King rather than to Parliament, and it reported to the privy council and to the secretary of state for the Southern Department, who usually served as colonial secretary. It consisted of eight official members who were paid a salary, and eight ex-officio members (including the bishop of London) who were not. For much of the board's life, members of the mercantile community and the city of London were often denied membership in favour of representatives of the country interests, although there were always self-styled 'colonial experts' among its ranks. Its name suggested the emphasis of colonial administration, which was principally to operate a mercantilist system in the best interests of the mother country. It was also particularly responsible for reviewing colonial laws, appointing colonial councillors, and drafting instructions to governors of Crown colonies. The heyday of the board was between 1696 and 1714. Thereafter, its power was gradually reduced, as that of Parliament and the colonies themselves increased. By the 1760s a combination of the rise of Parliament and the complexities of colonial administration had virtually paralyzed the board except in the most routine matters. It was formally abolished by statute in 1782. J.M. BUMSTED

Boas, Franz (1858–1942), North America's foremost 20th-century anthropologist. Boas was born in Germany, taught in the United States, and did his fieldwork in Canada among the Baffin Island Inuit and on the northwest coast, especially among the Kwakiutl (Kwakwaka'wakw). He reoriented anthropology around collaboration between *universities and *museums, placing his students in major positions across the continent (e.g., Edward Sapir in Ottawa) from his base at New York's Columbia University. He imposed a holistic scope, including cultural, archaeological, biological, and linguistic subdisciplines characterized by an overarching cultural relativism or cross-cultural tolerance. He trained Native-language speakers to record linguistics texts, which are still useful to contemporary communities, and based his ethnography on such texts. Boas's critique of cultural evolution foregrounded diffusion and local variability: receiving cultures adapted borrowed elements to their own psychological patterns. Boas defined race, language, and culture as analytically distinct variables. His biological studies established that environment could modify heredity, with immigrant head-form changing in a single generation. Showing racial types to be arbitrary, he demonstrated that racism was a matter of cultural construction. At the end of his life, Boas applied this argument to Nazi anti-Semitism. REGNA DARNELL

Boer War. *See* SOUTH AFRICAN WAR.

Bomarc missile issue. The controversy highlights the action-reaction pattern of the Canadian–American defence relationship during the Cold War. In the aftermath of the mid-1950s bomber gap scare, American national-security planners outlined Canada's role in the defence against a Soviet attack across the polar region. The problem became more acute in February 1959 after the cancellation of Canada's *Avro Arrow Interceptor. One alternative was to equip Canadian air defence forces with the Bomarc B, a surface-to-air missile designed to intercept Soviet bombers. To be effective these missiles required nuclear warheads. Official documents indicate the Canadian government agreed to equip its NATO forces in Europe with nuclear warheads, and the American Department of Defense assumed the same for the Bomarcs. In public, however, Prime Minister *Diefenbaker wavered in the face of disagreements within his cabinet, his distrust of the Kennedy administration, and a genuine ambivalence about nuclear weapons. Sensing political mileage was to be gained, the Liberal opposition took up the cause of deploying nuclear weapons in the 1963 election and, after victory, the new prime minister, Lester *Pearson, approved their acquisition. From the benefit of hindsight there was much needless acrimony over the issue, as the Soviet bomber threat never materialized. LAWRENCE ARONSEN

Bombardier, Inc. During the 1930s, Joseph-Armand Bombardier, a largely self-taught mechanic in Valcourt, Quebec, invented a tracked vehicle suitable for travel during the winter in rural areas with unpaved roads. The *auto-neige* or snowmobile not only became popular in Quebec but also proved useful to forestry and mineral developers operating in the wilderness regions of northern Canada after the Second World War. During the 1960s Bombardier created the Ski-Doo, a popular smaller version of the snowmobile, designed for winter recreational use. When its founding father died in 1964, Bombardier was a leading manufacturer in this niche market. While the energy crisis of the 1970s affected demand for the Ski-Doo, Bombardier under the leadership of Laurent Beaudoin, Joseph-Armand's son-in-law, sought to diversify. Bombardier outbid Vickers, a UK firm, for the contract to build subway cars for Montreal in preparation for the 1976 Olympics. Its success in the home market led it further afield, building subway cars for Chicago and New York, motorail cars for Disneyland, and rail cars for the English Channel tunnel. The company also diversified into the aerospace industry, beginning in 1986 when it acquired Canadair Ltd in Montreal from the Canadian government, and developed the Challenger, a small jet oriented to business travel. In 1999 it acquired the US Learjet Corporation, and in 1992 the government sold Bombardier its other Crown-owned airplane maker, De Havilland. By this time Bombardier held a commanding position in the world's market for small aircraft.
GRAHAM D. TAYLOR

Bomber Command. *See* NO. 6 (RCAF) BOMBER GROUP.

Bompas, William Carpenter (1834–1906). Bompas was born in London, son of a prominent barrister who died when Bompas was ten. His early life was unpromising; he tried and abandoned law, then was ordained a deacon of the Church of England in 1859. Lacking money or social connections, he spent several years as a lowly curate until, in 1865, after several attempts, he was accepted as a missionary, ordained a priest, and sent to northwestern Canada. There he established a life as a priest, then bishop, in the dioceses of Athabasca, Mackenzie, and finally Selkirk (later Yukon), always moving further to the northwest. Returning to England to be consecrated bishop in 1873, he married his first cousin, Selina Cox (1830–1917). He spent the rest of his life in the Canadian North, dying in 1906 at his mission at Carcross in the southern Yukon. Bompas was devoted to the indigenous people to whom he ministered. He was less popular with the non-Native population, especially the miners in the Yukon, whose influence on the First Nations he disliked and feared.
K.S. COATES AND W.R. MORRISON

Bonanza Creek. On 17 August 1896, an American prospector named George Washington Carmack and his two Tagish relatives, *Keish and K̲áa Goox̲, discovered gold on Rabbit Creek in the Yukon. Thus began the *Klondike gold rush. Realizing that the strike was a big one, Carmack hurried to the nearest mining recorder's office at Forty Mile, where he announced his discovery and renamed the creek Bonanza. Within weeks, Forty Mile was a ghost town and the gold rush was on. Many of the most lucrative claims were located on Bonanza Creek and the adjacent Dominion, Eldorado, and Hunker Creeks, all tributaries of the Klondike. The original claims staked by Carmack and his family produced over a million dollars worth of gold. CHARLENE PORSILD

Bond, Sir Robert (1857–1927), prime minister of Newfoundland 1900–9. Born in St John's, Bond became one of Newfoundland's most respected pre-Confederation premiers. First elected to the legislature in 1882, he served as Liberal premier in 1900–9. A nationalist who believed in his country's economic potential, Bond supported the building of a trans-insular railway and opposed confederation with Canada. Instead, he believed that Newfoundland should develop economic ties with the United States. He therefore tried on two occasions (1890 and 1902) to negotiate independent reciprocity treaties. Bond achieved an unrivalled political stature when, in 1895, he negotiated loans that prevented colonial default and propped up the government Savings Bank, giving a personal guarantee to the lenders. His reputation as a patriot was further enhanced by his campaign against the grant in 1898 of what he considered excessive concessions to the railway contractor and operator R.G. Reid. As premier, Bond revised the government's contract with Reid, played an important part in establishing the colony's first newsprint mill at Grand Falls, and helped bring an end to the *French Shore dispute. His attempt to salvage the failed

1902 reciprocity treaty by imposing sanctions on American fishermen backfired, making him politically unpopular at home and abroad. Defeated at the polls in 1909, he retired from politics in 1914. JAMES K. HILLER

Book publishing in Canada slowly evolved throughout the 19th century, from modest beginnings by booksellers and printers in the last half of the 18th century. Once printing presses were brought to Halifax (1752) and Quebec City (1764) from the American colonies, the nature of publishing and distribution was shaped in response to a small population that extended for half a continent along the American border. Of lasting consequence was the early reliance by both French- and English-language readers on printed materials from abroad, a practice entrenched through Canada's political and cultural status as a colony. Canadians have always imported books and periodicals in great quantities, imperial copyright laws took precedence over Canadian ones until 1924, and the British and Americans treated the Canadian market as an adjunct to theirs. Since the 1920s, when publishers began boosting Canadian writing, they have fought against foreign control over copyrights and distribution, and over foreign ownership of domestic companies.

Nineteenth-century Canada was served by one major firm, John Neilson of Quebec, and by many small regional printer-publishers who relied on jobbing and government contracts. These companies' attempts at literary publishing were hampered by the lack of writers and by readers' preferences for British authors. Because local copyright did not favour professional authorship, the pattern set by Thomas C. *Haliburton, who dumped Halifax publisher Joseph *Howe for fame and fortune in London and Philadelphia, was followed later by Charles G.D. Roberts, Bliss Carman, and Gilbert Parker.

After Confederation, reprint publishers such as John Lovell of Montreal and the Belford Brothers of Toronto tried to stem the flood of American reprints by printing them in Canada. These efforts to develop a publishing industry—supported by Ottawa's *National Policy of protection—were frustrated by foreign publishers who used imperial copyright to maintain their hegemony; Canadians were thrust into Anglo-American conflicts over international copyright. Limited opportunities forced ambitious publishers such as George Munro and George Doran to succeed in the United States. By the 1890s three large firms—the Methodist Book and Publishing House, W.J. Gage, and Copp, Clark and Co.—had secured textbook monopolies in every province, including the recently settled Northwest (Saskatchewan and Alberta). Montreal lost its position to Toronto as the national production and wholesale metropolis, but it remained the major French-language centre.

After 1900 book publishing, slowly detaching itself from the manufacturing side, entered its most prosperous quarter century. An 1891 agreement between Britain and the United States ending international piracy stabilized the Canadian market, and New York and London opened branches and agencies with local managers in Toronto. New York and London traditionally retained world rights for their authors as well as for Canadian authors, a practice that ended only in the 1980s. With the commodification of literature came the seasonal best-sellers, written by popular Canadians such as Gilbert Parker, Ralph Connor, Robert *Service, and L.M. Montgomery. Connor had Canadian sales of 30,000–40,000 copies; there were few figures like this until the 1960s. William Briggs transformed the Methodist Book and Publishing House (founded 1829), which published religious books and periodicals, into the first successful publisher of Canadian history and literature and the first major agency house. Briggs's employees, Thomas Allen, John McClelland, and S.P. Gundy, along with C.J. Musson, themselves became publishers who carried dozens of exclusive agencies for trade and educational books. These arrangements continued among the upper-middle-class, mainly Protestant, family-owned firms up to 1970. By then the agency system had drawn the Canadian book industry into the American economic and cultural orbit.

Agency revenues provided the cash for about five locally owned firms and two branches (Macmillan and Oxford) to publish Canadian authors. In 1921, elated by Canada's war effort and by phenomenal book sales, these publishers supported the demands of the *Canadian Authors' Association for fair treatment in the new Copyright Act. One tireless promoter of Canadian writers, Lorne *Pierce of Ryerson Press (the renamed Methodist establishment), launched the Makers of Canadian Literature series and established an award for noteworthy contributions to Canadian literature. John McClelland of McClelland and Stewart augmented his roster of international best-selling authors with popular Canadian writers. The distinguished lists of Hugh Eayrs of the Macmillan Company of Canada included Mazo de la Roche, Morley Callaghan, and *Grey Owl (Archie Belaney). Graphic Publishers of Ottawa (1926–32) was the first firm devoted exclusively to publishing Canadian books, but it failed during the Depression. In the 1930s original publishing almost ceased.

The Second World War brought renewed hopes for a real publishing industry. Canadian poets established magazines and small presses to reach their readers. Despite shortages of materials and the loss of supplies from Britain (a gap filled by American books and magazines), publishers and booksellers reported heavy demand for technical and scientific books, and libraries welcomed a new audience of readers, many of them in uniform. Montreal experienced a cultural renaissance. Quebec's French-language market was long dominated by Granger Frères, Librairie Garneau, and Beauchemin, whose mainstays had been religious and devotional works and textbooks. After the fall of France, Montreal overflowed with expatriates from Europe, and the heady excitement ultimately helped to fuel Quebec's *Quiet Revolution in the 1960s. Paul Péledeau and Bernard Valiquette obtained licences to print copyrighted French works for the overseas francophone world and South America. When this activity ended in 1946, Montreal suffered a 'crise de l'édition' until Les Éditions de l'Hexagone, Pierre Tisseyre's

La Circle du Livre du France, and Jacques Hébert's Les Éditions du Jour brought Quebec audiences literary and political works of contemporary urgency.

As post-war Canada evolved into a multicultural society slowly shedding its former provincialism, Toronto publishers tried reducing their agency connections, with mixed results. Despite their own financial ups and downs, they were blessed with three generations of world-famous authors. John Gray of Macmillan published Hugh *MacLennan, Robertson *Davies, and Donald *Creighton. Jack McClelland's flair for publicity and his launch of the first quality paperback series (the New Canadian Library) brought new excitement to the industry. The pre-eminent publisher from 1950 to 1985, he published poets Earle Birney, Leonard Cohen, and Irving Layton, and novelists Margaret *Laurence, Mordecai Richler, and Margaret Atwood. While the University of Toronto Press and Les Presses de l'Université de Montréal achieved international reputations in *scholarly publishing, Harlequin Books was the only trade publisher to break into international markets.

As the nation prepared for centenary celebrations in 1967, the excellent reception of books by and about Canadians throughout the prosperous 1960s masked serious problems. Cash-flow shortages, sloppy management, over-expansion, and the decision by most provinces in 1968–70 to revamp their list of approved textbooks, the bread and butter of many firms, created the worst crisis in the Canadian publishing industry. The cumbersome agency system turned the marketing of foreign books into a nightmare. As a result, institutional libraries 'bought around' the agency-distribution network and purchased supplies from efficient, computerized American wholesalers. Canadian educational publishers, on the verge of collapse, were poised for outside takeovers.

Foreign educational companies terminated their agencies and established subsidiaries whose talented managers launched aggressive Canadian programs in English and French. Doubleday had gone this prosperous route in 1949, and in the 1960s Wallace Matheson of Prentice-Hall and Ron Besse of McGraw-Hill had similar success. In 1970 Campbell Hughes left Ryerson for Van Nostrand Reinhold. That year Ryerson was sold to McGraw-Hill and W.J. Gage to Scott, Foresman (Gage was repatriated in 1978). More shocks came in 1972: Macmillan passed to Maclean-Hunter and then to Gage (1978), and finally disappeared in 2002. McClelland and Stewart, facing bankruptcy, was bailed out by an Ontario government loan; in Quebec, Librairie Garneau was sold to Hachette.

After 1970 the industry was split by bitter debates over government aid and ownership of the cultural industries. Ottawa's help began when the *Massey Commission (1949–51) recommended the establishment of the National Library (1951), the Canada Council (1957), and funding for university research. When international conglomerates moved in, Ottawa directly intervened to provide financial aid, monitor takeovers, and promote exports abroad by ratifying international book and tariff agreements. Ontario's Royal Commission on Book Publishing (1972) recommended loans and subventions to Canadian-owned firms that published Canadian trade books and texts. Takeovers were slowed down—but not stopped—by the Foreign Investment Review Agency (1975), renamed Investment Canada in 1985. Pressure from the nationalistic Association of Canadian Publishers prompted Ottawa to create the Book Publishing Industry Development Program (1979), but even after $40 million was expended, only 20 per cent of the industry was Canadian owned in 1985.

The Baie Comeau policy (1985) called for 50 per cent ownership within two years, but very few firms were actually bought back by Canadian investors. This policy was at odds with the government's *free trade agreement with the United States, which barely exempted the cultural industries. The imposition of the goods and services tax on books and severe cutbacks in 1991, coinciding with a recession, traumatized the industry and several companies, including Lester, Orpen & Dennys, went under. Writers generally lauded government intervention, if only because official patronage allowed young writers time to mature and commercially unviable projects to see the light of day.

The other post-war transformation was the proliferation across the nation of small presses—cottage ventures with low overhead. Dissatisfaction with the Toronto houses stimulated young men and women to emphasize regional history, local issues, and avant-garde literature. Supported by arts councils, and utilizing inexpensive photo-offset technology or even old-fashioned hand presses, they gave whole communities their voice in print for the first time. Breakwater Books launched Newfoundland's cultural renaissance. Les Éditions d'Acadie revived Acadian culture. In Montreal, vlb-Éditeurs voiced Quebec's new sense of empowerment. Anansi and New Press in Toronto encouraged new authors and embraced a left-of-centre political stance. Vancouver's Douglas & McIntyre and Edmonton's Mel Hurtig broke Toronto's hold on publishing. The West Coast's thriving scene included Talonbooks with drama and Thetyus Books with First Nations writers. Niche publishers focused on women's issues, gay and lesbian writing, and third-world ethnic communities. Tundra Books and KidsCan were internationally recognized for their children's books.

Margaret Atwood, Michael Ondaatje, and Ann-Marie MacDonald are among the writers who started with small presses and moved on, often to such Canadian subsidiaries as Knopf Canada, HarperCollins, and Penguin Canada. These firms symbolize the globalization of the book market, with its Canadian centre in Toronto. If grants and subsidies helped propel writers to international stardom, they arguably hurt domestic publishers, who remained undercapitalized and were prohibited from selling more than 25 per cent ownership to foreign firms. Avie Bennett bought McClelland and Stewart in 1986; in 2000, faced with succession problems, he donated three-quarters of it to the University of Toronto and sold one-quarter to Random House Canada, whose parent is owned by international media conglomerate Bertelsmann.

In the new century crises recur like the seasons, bringing change and challenge. Anna Porter, Louise Dennys, Anne Collins, and Maya Mavjee flourish in what was once a gentleman's preserve. Traditional marketing is threatened by online bookselling and publishing. Independent retailers and many publishers were pushed to the wall by the retail chain Chapters, which was then gobbled up by arch-rival Indigo Books. Canadian houses have reinvented the agency link with foreign firms, but without its vulnerable economic dependencies. At international fairs Canadians negotiate local rights for American and British books and sell foreign rights for their Canadian authors. Publishers, fortunately, are still committed to bringing the world's print culture to Canadians and ensuring that the Canadian voice and vision endures. GEORGE L. PARKER

Borden, Robert (1854–1937), prime minister 1911–20. The last Canadian prime minister to lack a university education, Borden was, nonetheless, learned in the classics and law. A serious, even dour, public personality, he was generous and warm to those he knew well.

Borden was born in Grand Pré, Nova Scotia, where his father was a stationmaster. After teaching briefly in the United States, he articled in law and joined a Halifax law firm. A highly successful lawyer, Borden entered politics when fellow Nova Scotian Sir Charles *Tupper went down to defeat in 1896. He succeeded Tupper as leader of the Liberal-Conservative Party in 1901 but lost the elections of 1904 and 1908 to Sir Wilfrid *Laurier's Liberals.

In 1911, Borden's Conservatives were finally victorious in a controversial election fought in English Canada on the issue of *reciprocity with the United States and in French Canada on the question of how Canada should assist the British navy. His coalition of Quebec nationalists and English-Canadian imperialists was uneasy, and the outbreak of war in 1914 made his situation difficult. By 1916 the government faced strong criticism of its conduct of the war, and Borden responded by reiterating Canada's willingness to commit fully to defeating the enemy. That commitment brought controversy and extraordinary political change. Borden's announcement in May 1917 that his government would introduce *conscription caused a revolution in the Canadian *party system as conscriptionist Liberals rallied behind his announcement. He formed a *Union government of conscriptionist Liberals and Conservatives and decisively won the 1917 general election.

The coalition did not long survive the war. Borden devoted most of his remaining time in office to imperial affairs. He favoured a strong empire but one in which Canada would have an individual voice. Canada thus obtained separate representation in the *League of Nations and the International Labour Organization. Exhausted by the war and the difficult peacetime years, Borden resigned from office in July 1920.

JOHN ENGLISH

Botheration Letters. A series of editorials, published by Joseph *Howe in the Halifax *Morning Chronicle* between 11 January and 2 March 1865, lambasting the Quebec Resolutions. Forced to write anonymously because he was an imperial officer at the time, Howe charged that union with the *Province of Canada—the Botheration Scheme—would cast Nova Scotia into 'a Slough of Despond' economically, and that politically a British-type parliament could never work harmoniously with provincial legislatures in a federal system. Despite suggestions that the letters made the province anti-Confederate, they simply reinforced opinions already in evidence, especially in western Nova Scotia. J. MURRAY BECK

'bottom of the bay'. A *Hudson's Bay Company expression that referred to James Bay. That bay figured prominently in the company's history, including its inception. In 1668, Médard Chouart, Sieur des Groseilliers led the first English trading expedition there on board the **Nonsuch*. He overwintered at the outlet of the Rupert River, where he built the first English post on the bay, Charles Fort, and conducted a lucrative trade with the Swampy Cree. This success encouraged the merchants who had backed Groseilliers's venture to create the HBC. Soon after its founding, its trading operations in James Bay focused on the outlets of the Albany and Moose Rivers, which tapped vast hinterlands to the west and southwest. Fort Albany, established *c.* 1675–9, became the most important trading post on James Bay during the 18th century, serving also as the outfitting station for Eastmain post. After 1821, Moose Factory rose to prominence as the headquarters of the Southern Department of the HBC, which included most of present-day northern Ontario. Until the arrival of the railway in 1929, the settlement had a large farm, warehousing facilities, and a shipbuilding operation, known as the 'Moose works', where an Aboriginal workforce built sea-going sailing ships for the company. ARTHUR J. RAY

Boucher, Pierre (1622–1717), soldier, governor, author, and archetype of the settler ideal. Emigrating from France with his parents at 13, he married a Native as his first wife, sired a large family with his second, founded Boucherville, wrote his memoirs, and expired, aged 95, in his manor house. After a wilderness youth among the *Jesuits, Boucher became prominent in Trois-Rivières, and in 1661 was sent by the governor of New France to ask Louis XIV for soldiers to defend the settlers from Native attack. Returning, he wrote a detailed report on New France for Colbert, the king's chief minister. The *Histoire véritable et naturelle* (Paris, 1664) is brief, rich in detail, and enthusiastic; it successfully turned the French government's attention to its neglected colony.

GERMAINE WARKENTIN

boundaries. Most of Canada's major boundaries had been determined before 1871, when British Columbia joined the dominion and Canada took control of former Hudson's Bay Company territory. So-called natural boundaries—those defined with reference to topographic elements of the pristine landscape readily recognizable by travellers, traders, and fugitives—were long preferred. Precise demarcation was needed only near well-used crossing points. Eastern Canadian boundaries thus incorporate parts of many rivers, from the St Croix and Saint John, through the St Lawrence system to the Rainy. The most sweeping 'natural' boundary in the Canadian landmass was the watershed limit of *Hudson Bay, specified (in ignorance of its actual geography) by the *Hudson's Bay Company charter of 1670. It was later to form the northern limit of Quebec colony and its successor provinces until 1889 (Ontario) and 1898 (Quebec), and also mandated the southeastern limit of British Columbia along the Rocky Mountains in 1863. The 'coast of *Labrador' has also proved a troublesome concept. After many decades of uncertainty, in 1927 the Privy Council in the United Kingdom, employing mostly the drainage-area principle, awarded a large section of timbered and power-rich Canadian mainland to Newfoundland. This line has never been accepted by any government of Quebec.

The boundary between Manitoba and Ontario was briefly in doubt from competing interpretations of 18th-century proclamations. Manitoba's claim in 1880 would have included the *Thunder Bay port sites, but this was politically unacceptable to Ontario. The Privy Council decided in Ontario's favour in 1884, choosing the meridian line 95°14′ west. Other Canadian boundaries have also been astronomical lines, such as parallels of latitude and meridians of longitude, especially in the West and North. To be of any use at all, such entirely notional boundaries need to be artificially demarcated. One such is the famous 49° north parallel boundary with the United States, thought in 1818 to begin at 'the northwest angle of the Lake of the Woods', but actually lying some 40 km south of that point. Its first markers across the prairies (1872) were cairns built of cut sod. Another such is the 60° north parallel, set by British Columbia in 1863 to take in the whole Stikine River system, and after 1905 extended east to delimit the Prairie provinces.

Marine boundaries of Canada's three oceanic borderlands have been developed from baselines drawn from headland to headland along the shores: the territorial sea (at 12 nautical miles), the contiguous zone (200 nm), and others. In the 21st century, any boundary line drawn on a proper map, by whatever verbal definition, can be found on the surface by satellite location, accurately and quickly.

C.F.J. WHEBELL

Boundary Waters Treaty, 1909. In the early 20th century, the division and use of Canadian–American boundary waters—the lakes and rivers through which the long boundary passes—became important matters of negotiation between Ottawa and Washington. Eventually, as part of a general settlement of differences, an accommodation was reached in this treaty. The key negotiators for Canada were Prime Minister *Laurier and George Gibbons, a savvy Liberal lawyer from London, Ontario. Gibbons insisted that there be a 'permanent Board' to deal with boundary waters questions; to leave matters to be settled on a case by case basis through normal diplomatic channels would favour the United States. In the event, the treaty, signed on behalf of Canada on 11 January 1909 by British ambassador James Bryce, satisfied the key Canadian requirement. Article 7 provided for the International Joint Commission, and article 8 stipulated that the two countries were to have 'equal and similar rights' in the use of all boundary waters. A bruising ratification round followed, but success was finally achieved on 5 May 1910. In practice, about half the decisions of the IJC have been advisory, but the commission's mandate includes approving certain types of projects. The treaty helped pave the way for separate Canadian diplomatic representation abroad. It also fostered in Canada the appealing notion that the way forward in dealings with the United States was, as far as possible, to remove issues from power politics and make them amenable to permanent bilateral bodies acting according to agreed-upon principles.

PETER NEARY

Bourassa, Henri (1868–1952). The grandson of Louis-Joseph *Papineau, Bourassa was born in Montreal and studied mainly with a private tutor. He quickly developed a taste for journalism and politics. Mayor of Montebello at 22, he soon became editor of a Franco-Ontarian paper, *L'Interprète*. He entered the House of Commons as the Liberal member for Labelle in 1896, showing himself to be a man of principle when in 1899 he opposed Canadian participation in the *Boer War because Parliament had not been consulted. Resisting Wilfrid *Laurier and British *imperialism, he resigned and was re-elected. In 1902 he published a pamphlet, *Grande-Bretagne et Canada*, which caused a sensation. A Quebec idol was born: intellectually solid, capable of rousing the public, with a program centred on an exclusively Canadian nationalism and a Catholic-style social conservatism. This program—autonomy for Canada within the *British Empire and for the provinces within Confederation, respect and equality for the two *founding peoples, economic and cultural development for Canada by Canadians—was largely taken up by the Ligue nationaliste canadienne (1903) and *Le Nationaliste* (1904).

Mentor of the nascent nationalist movement, Bourassa attacked on every front. Having condemned in vain, as an MP, Laurier's immigration policy, and in 1905 the abandonment of the educational rights of the Catholic minority in the new provinces of Alberta and Saskatchewan, he turned to provincial politics and served in Quebec's legislative assembly 1908–12. But in January 1910, when he launched *Le Devoir*, he was once again caught up in Laurier's politics. Above all, he denounced Laurier's plan for a navy, and, allying himself with Quebec Conservatives, contributed to the prime minister's defeat in 1911. Firm in his principles, he was equally opposed to the government of Robert *Borden, especially its plan to provide naval assistance to the empire, and he supported Franco-Ontarians against *Regulation 17. Although he approved of Canada's entering the Great War in 1914, he rejected *conscription in 1917. At the height of his influence in Quebec, he was feared by Laurier and execrated in

English Canada, which regarded him as a traitor. Nevertheless, his thinking on the imperial framework triumphed in the following decade. After 1920, Bourassa chose to emphasize his social conservatism and *ultramontanism, reinforced by a private audience with the pope in 1926. He even came to denounce nationalism, thus distancing himself from his disciples, and was obliged to resign from *Le Devoir* in 1932. Re-elected to Ottawa between 1925 and 1935 as an independent, he supported the Liberals. Thereafter, apart from a few public appearances during the Second World War, he lived a secluded life in Montreal. RÉAL BÉLANGER

Bourgeoys, Marguerite (1620–1700). Devout French laywoman who dedicated herself to teaching in New France. Born at Troyes, in the Champagne region, she first heard of the Ville-Marie colony (Montreal) from Louise de Chomedey, the sister of its founder, Maisonneuve, and arrived in the colony in 1653. Able to open a school in 1658, she decided to create a group of young secular women who would devote themselves to teaching girls. In 1676, having obtained both royal and episcopal permission for her new congregation, she founded a boarding school for girls. She introduced several innovative pedagogical approaches in this institution: teaching reading from French texts, serious teacher training, no physical punishment. She also sent young women to found convents in some villages. Since the *Congrégation de Notre-Dame was a secular organization, its members were not supposed to take vows, but its founder, following the example of secular orders in France, obtained the privilege of simple vows that made them 'sisters' without the closure imposed by canon law. Marguerite Bourgeoys died in Montreal, leaving a reputation for saintliness. She was canonized by Rome in 1982. MICHELINE DUMONT

Bourget, Bishop Ignace (1799–1885). Born at Lauzon, ordained in 1822, Bourget became auxiliary bishop of Montreal in 1837 and bishop in 1840 until his resignation in 1876, when Rome made him an honorary archbishop. In promoting a French-Canadian Catholic civil society free from partisan control, he quarrelled with leading personalities and institutions, both lay and religious. The effective leader of the Canadian Catholic Church and an ardent ultramontane, Bourget organized the church into a cohesive body, an effective provider of moral direction and religious instruction. Through recruitment and foundations, he brought about the biggest expansion of religious personnel up to that time. This triggered the institutional revolution that made Quebec unique in North America because of church control of health, education, and welfare. But his influence went beyond Quebec. His priests were among the first bishops in several North American dioceses. The religious communities that he sent all over the continent were often the first to provide spiritual and temporal care to Catholics and First Nations. The new religious practices that he promoted were sensual, very public, and thoroughly Roman, and became an integral part of popular culture until the *Quiet Revolution. He was the greatest Canadian churchman of his time. ROBERTO PERIN

Bourinot, Sir John George (1836–1902), journalist, parliamentary reporter, officer of the *Senate and the *House of Commons, historian, and *littérateur*. As co-editor of the *Halifax Reporter* (1860–7), Bourinot consistently advocated a union of 'these Maritime Provinces' with their 'progressive sister colony', the Province of Canada. As clerk of the House of Commons (1880–1902), he wrote what was for many years the standard Canadian work on parliamentary procedure. Governors general and prime ministers consulted Bourinot, a renowned constitutional authority, as a plaque in Province House, Halifax, describes him, when constitutional issues or crises arose. A founding member of the *Royal Society of Canada, Bourinot played a leading role during its first 20 years (1882–1902), serving as honorary secretary throughout the period, except when he was vice-president and then president. His understanding of the administrative and financial sides of running a society and his acquaintance with scholars and government officials were of great assistance—one wonders if the society would have survived its early years without him. Bourinot wrote extensively on constitutional law, intellectual history, general Canadian history, and many other subjects. His role in the parliamentary, constitutional, and cultural life of Canada was highly significant. MARGARET A. BANKS

boxing. Boxing in Canada grew out of bare-knuckle prize fighting, which had an unsavoury reputation because of its bloody violence and its association with gambling. After the introduction of the Marquis of Queensbury rules the sport garnered a measure of respectability. Boxing was considered one of the 'manly arts', and boxers were venerated for their courage and skill. The first Canadian boxer to win national and international status was George 'Little Chocolate' Dixon, an African–Nova Scotian, who won the world bantamweight title in 1888 and subsequently became the featherweight title holder. Like many fighters of his day, Dixon fought regularly scheduled matches and other hastily arranged fights. His 800 or more matches may well have contributed to his early death at age 39. The next Canadian fighter to gain international prominence was Tommy Burns of Hanover, Ontario. Born Noah Grasso, Burns changed his name to take advantage of the popularity of the sport among Irish Canadians. Burns won the heavyweight championship of the world in 1906. Perhaps the most accomplished Canadian fighter of the first half of the 20th century, however, was Sam Langford from Weymouth, Nova Scotia. Nicknamed the 'Boston Tarbaby', Langford fought all the top heavyweights of his era. Nat Fleischer of *Ring* magazine once ranked Langford among the top ten heavyweights of all time. Yvon Durelle and George Chuvalo also challenged the world's best. Durelle lost a light-heavyweight title match to the legendary Archie Moore in 1958, and Chuvalo a heavyweight championship bout with

Muhammad Ali. Lennox Lewis, who won an Olympic gold medal for Canada, has established himself as the premier heavyweight of the modern era. COLIN HOWELL

Boyle, David (1842–1911), educator, archaeologist, museologist. Scottish-born, Boyle achieved international renown as the most important figure in Canadian archaeology before the First World War. Upon emigrating to Canada in 1856, he apprenticed as a blacksmith before becoming a rural Ontario schoolteacher and eventually principal of Elora Public School (1871–81). He was an early practitioner of the radical child-centred philosophy and methods of Swiss educator Johann Pestalozzi. Boyle was a quintessential product of British autodidact artisan culture. The common thread connecting his varied careers was a commitment to self-education and to the acquisition and imparting of knowledge. As curator-archaeologist of the Canadian Institute Museum (1884–96) and the Ontario Provincial Museum (1896–1911), he undertook the programs that laid a foundation for the development of Ontario archaeology as a scientific discipline. Boyle was also a published local historian, heritage preservationist, and author of a book of Canadian nursery rhymes. GERALD KILLAN

Boyle, Joseph Whiteside (1867–1923), entrepreneur, businessman. Dubbed 'King of the Klondike', Joe Boyle was one of the best-known mining entrepreneurs in the Yukon. Arriving in 1897, he bought into a concession near Hunker and *Bonanza Creeks, but lack of capital prevented full-scale mining. Not until he joined resources with the Detroit Yukon Mining Company in 1904 to form the Canadian Klondyke Mining Company was he able to launch his empire. The company began operations the next year, building a power plant on Bear Creek and a new dredge. Boyle worked incessantly to expand his empire. In 1910, he built the largest dredge in the world—Canadian No. 2. He ran trains between *Dawson City and the creeks, built more dredges, and in 1913 bought the Northern Light, Power and Coal Company. Boyle's aggressiveness and flamboyance often caused him trouble. His attempts to control all mining led to constant court battles with his competitors and the federal government. These battles, along with rising prices and the loss of workers during the First World War, eventually wore him down, and he left the Yukon in 1916 to help the war effort overseas. Boyle remains an entrepreneur different from others. While his competitors shipped profits outside the Yukon and hired from outside, Boyle was a Yukon booster, hiring locally and investing his profits in the region in an effort to stabilize the economy.
BRENT SLOBODIN

Boy Scouts. Launched in 1908 by Robert Baden-Powell in the aftermath of the *Boer War, with the purpose of preparing young boys to follow orders and to engage in a variety of outdoor pursuits, the first inception of the Boy Scouts was a middle-class attempt to instill patriotic and imperialistic virtues upon the 'Sons of the Empire'. The best-seller *Scouting for Boys* outlined the laws that boys had to follow in order to become loyal and obedient defenders of the empire. As a counterweight to the problems of industrialization, the scouting movement in Canada was an extremely popular youth organization that emphasized outdoor activity and good deeds as a way to create citizens of proper moral standing. Its enthusiastic reception suggests that the goals upon which it was founded spoke to the patriotic parents of a society that wished their children to have grounding in the dynamic ideals of the empire. For young boys, the appeal of the uniform, the sense of adventure, and the fraternity proved to be an attractive combination. MARK MOSS

Bracken, John (1883–1969), Manitoba premier 1922–42. Although leader of the United Farmers of Manitoba, Bracken was notably non-partisan, and his governments often held office through coalitions with the other parties. Premier Bracken was committed to the development of Manitoba's natural resources, including its pulp and paper, hydroelectric, and mining industries. He became an outspoken advocate for western Canada, particularly during the Depression of the 1930s. In 1943 Bracken accepted the leadership of the troubled federal Conservatives, but only on condition that the party's name be changed to the Progressive Conservatives. Bracken's success on the provincial stage was not duplicated in Ottawa. Failing to revive the party during a period of Liberal domination that would ultimately last 22 years (1935–57), he retired from politics in 1949. ROBERT WARDHAUGH

Brant, Joseph (1743–1807) and **Margaret** (Molly, 1736–96). The Brant half-siblings were Mohawk who came to maturity in colonial New York. They sided with the *Loyalists during the American Revolution because they believed that a Crown victory would best serve their people's interests and because of personal connections to prominent Loyalists (particularly Sir William Johnson, with whom Molly had a long-term relationship until his death in 1774). Molly encouraged the Mohawk and other Iroquois to fight; provided assistance to Native, white, and Black Loyalists; and acted as an intermediary between her people and the Crown. Joseph was a military and diplomatic leader who fought the rebels in return for guarantees that London would protect Mohawk rights and lands at the return of peace.

After the Loyalist defeat in 1783, Molly settled in Kingston and largely retired from public affairs. Joseph led 1,800 Iroquois refugees from New York to the Grand River on the north shore of Lake Erie. He then struggled against colonial officials in a failed attempt to secure clear title to the Grand River lands for his people, to assert their independence from unwanted government intrusions, and to create a pan-tribal confederacy across the lower Great Lakes to protect Native interests on the rapidly changing Anglo-American frontier. Joseph and Molly also promoted Anglicanism among the Mohawk and advocated Euro-American farming to help the tribespeople become prosperous enough to avoid dependence on white authorities, as older subsistence patterns became less viable as settlers transformed the environment of the lower Great Lakes. CARL BENN

Brébeuf, Jean de (1593–1649), priest, author, mystic, saint. Brébeuf's path to martyrdom began in Normandy. Born to a reputable family, he joined the *Jesuits at 24, briefly serving in France but living most of the next three decades as a missionary in Huronia, between Lake Ontario and Georgian Bay. Passionately devout, Brébeuf endured wilderness conditions the Jesuits abhorred to study and evangelize the *Huron, who because of his size called him 'Echon' or 'Bearer of Loads'. He planned a Huron dictionary and grammar, and wrote the Huron carol 'Jesous ahatonhia'; his *Rélations* and letters are vital ethnographic documents. The Jesuits' missionary task met frustration because the Huron preferred their own customs, and feared the 'Black Robes', whose arrival brought European diseases that mysteriously decimated their people. By the late 1640s, the Iroquois assault on Huron trade networks reached Huronia, and Brébeuf was captured. He silently endured fierce torture before his death. He and the other 'Jesuit martyrs' were canonized in 1930.

GERMAINE WARKENTIN

brewing and distilling. Brewing and distilling created many Canadian business dynasties, although the temperance movements rendered them somewhat disreputable. Yet most of these families shared class and religious values with the prohibitionists who condemned them.

Nova Scotia's most successful brewer was Alexander Keith. Born 5 October 1795 in Halkirk, Scotland, son of a prosperous farmer, Keith immigrated to Halifax in 1817. In 1820 he purchased the Nova Scotia Brewery, creating varieties of ales and porters and making the operation one of the largest in the colonies by 1836. In 1842 Keith was elected Halifax's mayor, and his death in 1873 occasioned the city's largest state funeral. Rival Oland Breweries bought Keith's in 1928. Its armistice celebration in 1945 was still remembered by Haligonians at century's end. Because of Canada's patchwork of provincial liquor laws, Keith's/Oland beers were not nationally distributed until 1996.

Hiram Walker was born a pauper in New England in 1816. Raised and schooled by friends, he left for Michigan in the 1830s to seek his fortune. With a tremendous work ethic and penurious habits, he became a successful Detroit grocer and learned to distill his own cider vinegar and whisky in 1854. Confronted by temperance agitation, he crossed the Detroit River to acquire cheap Canadian land in a more tolerant environment. Purchasing two farms upriver from Windsor, he built a distillery along the waterfront, where he used grains from his own farm. Unlike his contemporaries, who sold whisky in unmarked barrels, Walker used labelled bottles bearing his name. Walker's Club Whisky became the first Canadian brand marketed worldwide; American competitors forced the addition of the word 'Canadian'. In 1898, Hiram Walker & Sons Ltd was granted the warrant of Queen Victoria after her physician, Sir William Jenner, prescribed Canadian Club and mineral water as a more digestible substitute for claret.

Walker was a philanthropist, building St Mary's Anglican Church in Walkerville, and supporting local schools. He was also a dictatorial Victorian industrialist. While his company town provided free utilities and well-paved streets, his 600 employees were required to live in company cottages. In the 1880s he returned with his family to Detroit, buying a ferry for his private use, and built the Lake Erie and Detroit River Railroad, which transformed Walkerville into a lively town. Walker also financed the Walkerville Wagon Works, later the Ford automotive plant. During *prohibition, Hiram Walker's was sold (1927) to Harry Hatch, a Roman Catholic hotelkeeper with fewer reservations than the Walker heirs about selling to thirsty Americans.

John Molson, an enterprising 18-year-old English immigrant, correctly judged the thirst of Montrealers for mild ales when he opened his brewery in 1782. Although successful distillers (the largest in British North America in the 1840s), the Molson family abandoned hard liquor in the face of temperance agitation and diversified with, among other concerns, a sugar refinery, a steamboat line, a foundry, and a bank. In 1847 John Kinder Labatt, an Anglo-Irish immigrant, opened the forerunner of John Labatt's Brewery in London, Canada West. John Jr succeeded his father in 1866, presiding over a growing empire for 50 years. By 2003 it produced 40 per cent of all beer sold in Canada, including the most popular brand—Labatt's Blue—and had diversified with the acquisition of Ogilvie Flour Mills, Dominion Dairies, the Toronto Blue Jays, and The Sports Network (TSN).

The manufacture of liquor for export was never illegal in Canada, so many Canadians serviced the American market. The biggest fortune was made by the Bronfman brothers—Abe, Harry, and Sam—sons of poor Jewish refugees who fled the Russian pogroms and settled in Yorkton, Saskatchewan, in 1889. After their hotels were closed by prohibitory laws, the Bronfmans turned to mail-order distribution of liquor through the Canada Pure Drug Company. Harry soon became the largest liquor wholesaler in Saskatchewan, beating out the Hudson's Bay Company and others with quality, cheaper products. The Bronfmans soon began blending imported scotch whisky under their own labels, most of which was resold in the United States. Abe and Sam set up similar distribution operations throughout Canada. When Saskatchewan tightened its laws the family moved operations to Montreal, where they established Bronfman's Distillers Corp. Ltd. By 1926 they were partnered by Edinburgh's Distillers Company Ltd, which purchased the Joseph Seagram distillery in Waterloo, Ontario. The Bronfman family weathered anti-Semitism as well as harassment over charges of bootlegging and illegal activities to become the world's largest supplier of liquor. Sam Bronfman, who headed the company during its global expansion, founded Cemp Investments, which built urban institutions such as the Toronto-Dominion Centre and

Eaton Centre, Fairview Malls, and Vancouver's Pacific Centre. By the 1970s Bronfman holdings included Brascan, Noranda Mines, and a notoriously anti-Semitic American institution, Du Pont chemicals. Following the lead of earlier liquor entrepreneurs, Bronfman *philanthropy, particularly in Quebec and among Jewish organizations worldwide, has been correspondingly grand.
CHERYL KRASNICK WARSH

brideships. All Victoria flew into a tailspin when the *Tynemouth* rolled into the inner harbour on 19 September 1862. On board were some 60 young, largely working class British women intended to save the rough-and-tumble men of the backwoods from the bottle, First Nations women, and most of all themselves. The second 'brideship', the *Robert Lowe*, arrived with a cargo of 30-odd young women in February 1863. Funded and organized by a coalition of British missionaries, women's organizations, and Victoria's Anglican elite, the brideships carried women recruited from workhouses and orphanages and, to a much lesser extent, from the ranks of the impoverished and unmarried middle class. The do-gooders who organized their migration intended the women to become domestic servants, governesses, and, most importantly, settlers' wives. Historians know very little about their actual fates, but the frequency with which observers expressed disappointment in their behaviour suggests one of the reasons why the brideships are still remembered in British Columbia. ADELE PERRY

bridges. Other than short spans across streams, bridges were difficult and expensive to build in a pioneer society, and therefore they were constucted as seldom as possible. Where it was necessary to traverse a body of water, ferries were used. In the early British period, private companies were given monopolies by colonial legislatures to build multiple-span wooden bridges. In Quebec and New Brunswick numerous covered bridges were built. The only era of sustained bridge building occurred when the *Province of Canada built a network of colonization roads in the early 1840s.

With the dawning of the railway age in Canada in the 1850s, railway bridges attracted the attention of designers and builders. The greatest bridge of the early period was the *Grand Trunk Railway's Victoria Bridge, which connected Montreal Island with the south shore of the St Lawrence. When this 2,742-m wrought iron tubular bridge was opened in 1859, it was the longest bridge in the world. Other major railway bridges were built across the Niagara Gorge, over the Reversing Falls at Saint John, across the St Lawrence at Lachine, as well as numerous high trestle bridges in the Rockies. The last and greatest railway bridge in Canada was the *Quebec Bridge, constructed between 1904 and 1917.

Road bridges, though less spectacular, were slowly starting to gain importance. Prefabricated iron truss bridges were available from specialized manufacturers such as the Dominion Bridge Company from the late 1870s. By the turn of the 20th century, bridge engineers were starting to experiment with reinforced concrete as a building material. After the First World War, concrete was being used to build a wide variety of bridges, including multi-lane ones. In the 1930s bridge building was used as a public works project to provide employment. A number of spectacular suspension bridges were built: at Île d'Orléans near Quebec City, the Ivy Lea across the St Lawrence to the United States, and the Lions Gate Bridge in Vancouver.

Bridge building resumed in earnest only after the Second World War. With the development of limited-access divided highways, new bridge types became necessary. Gone were the spectacular steel truss bridges, replaced by new pre-stressed concrete bridges devoid of ornament in order not to distract motorists. In major urban areas elevated expressways were built to carry traffic above the existing street grid. Since the 1970s, few significant new bridges have been built in Canada. Instead money has gone into the maintenance and rebuilding of existing bridges in order to accommodate ever-increasing traffic. One major exception is the 13-km Confederation Bridge that links Prince Edward Island to New Brunswick, opened in 1997. LARRY McNALLY

British Columbia. Canada's westernmost province is a mosaic of diverse landscapes noted for its spectacular scenery of snow-capped mountains, pocket deserts, coastal rainforest, and scenic rivers. While 46 First Nations, through their oral traditions, date their presence in the region from the 'time the world began', archeologists assert that Aboriginal people first crossed into North America from Asia about 10,000 years ago. The arrival of Europeans dates possibly from 1579, when Sir Francis Drake is said to have reached the northwest coast, but more certainly from the 1770s, when Spanish and British explorers and maritime traders appeared. The 'historical' period is thus very recent, even by comparison with Canada's east coast, where Europeans had begun to establish a presence almost three centuries earlier.

The degree to which Aboriginal peoples were able to control the cultural and social changes that fur traders initiated—by sea in the 1780s and by land 30 years later—is a subject of considerable debate by scholars. All agree that the rush of more than 20,000 miners to the gold-bearing sandbars of the Fraser River in 1858 altered fundamentally the social and political geography of the region. In response, Great Britain, whose authority had been established during the *Nootka Sound incident of the early 1790s, added a new Crown colony, British Columbia, to another, *Vancouver Island, that it had founded in 1849, and extended British institutions of landholding, law, and governance to the mainland. At the beginning of the gold rush *Victoria prospered, but by the mid-1860s, as a second and smaller gold rush in the Cariboo wound down, the two colonies and their leading centre were in decline. The impact of this boom and bust cycle, the first of many in BC history, led the colonies to merge in 1866 under the name of British Columbia, and then to confederate in 1871 with the newly created nation of

Canada. Colonial leaders such as Amor *De Cosmos and Dr J.S. *Helmcken accepted Confederation not for any love of Canada but for the terms they could negotiate, in particular Canada's promise to assume the colony's debt and build within ten years a railway to the west coast. The national government's tardiness in fulfilling these terms created a coolness to Ottawa that remains a feature of BC's political culture.

White British Columbians then turned to province building, introducing *responsible government, creating a non-denominational public school system, denying the franchise and citizenship to people of Aboriginal (1874), Chinese (1874), Japanese (1895), and East Indian (1907) origin, and building railways to unlock the region's natural wealth. Completion of a transcontinental railway, the CPR, to Burrard Inlet in the mid-1880s tied BC more closely to Canada and led to the emergence of a new city, *Vancouver, that quickly surpassed Victoria as the province's economic centre. Coal mining on Vancouver Island, hardrock mining in the Kootenays, and salmon canning along the Pacific coast were the province's first industrial leaders, but by the early 1900s they had been overtaken by the forest sector. While services such as health care, education, and tourism became major employers, BC's prosperity remained tied to its resource industries, the latter in 2000 accounting for almost 10 per cent of the province's labour force and 80 per cent of its exports. The forest industry put its stamp on British Columbia especially after the Second World War, when government timber policies, expanding markets, and technological innovations led to its expansion from the Pacific slope, laden with Douglas fir, mountain hemlock, and yellow cedar, to the subalpine fir and Engleman spruce forests of interior mountains and plateaus. Forest industry growth reshaped the urban landscape, giving rise to many new pulp- and saw-mill communities and the emergence of Nanaimo, Kamloops, and Prince George as regional centres. The construction of an aluminum smelter at Kitimat on the north coast in the 1950s, and of hydroelectric dams on the Peace and Columbia Rivers in the 1960s and 1970s, reinforced the decentralization of the economy away from the southwest coast. Forestry has since declined sharply, threatening the economic viability of many resource-based communities.

British Columbia's non-Aboriginal residents (a majority since 1885) have usually come from elsewhere to find work and improve their economic well-being. Indeed, conservationist Roderick Haig-Brown described British Columbia as the 'profligate province', where people tended to 'test everything against a scale of dollars and cents'. This materialist ethos explains in part the organization of provincial politics along ideological lines. On the left, the Co-operative Commonwealth Federation became the official opposition in 1933. Its successor, the NDP, formed governments in 1972–5 and 1991–2001. On the centre right, coalitions emerged in four different periods—the early 1940s, 1952, the mid-1970s, and the mid-to-late 1990s—to keep the left out of power, and for the most part they succeeded. Of these coalitions one stands out—the Social Credit government headed from 1952 to 1972 by W.A.C *Bennett. These years were some of the most prosperous in BC history, when the building of roads, dams, and pulp mills generated new wealth. Under Bennett, government policies also uncharacteristically reflected the interests of the north and interior of the province rather than the more heavily populated lower coast.

Today, movements for environmental protection and *Aboriginal rights add further complexity to the often volatile and sometimes 'wacky' world of BC politics. In a province where white settlers segregated Native people onto small reserves and colonized them through church-run *residential schools, but signed only 14 minor treaties, the final passage of the Nisga'a Treaty in 1999 has given impetus to negotiations that aim to recognize Aboriginal rights and end the province's long history of colonialism.

ROBERT A.J. McDONALD

British Columbia Interior Aboriginals. The Aboriginal peoples who occupy the interior regions of British Columbia have a rich cultural history. The 'museum age' (1880–1920) played a major role in shaping this history, as British Columbia became a popular destination for museum curators, ethnologists, curio collectors, and others wanting to procure photographic images, artifacts, stories, and songs considered to be final traces of a fast 'disappearing' Aboriginal way of life. Although these early collectors set out to survey the entire province, they quickly discovered that large segments of the Interior were inaccessible because of poor or non-existent roads and trails, inclement weather, and heavy insect infestations. This led to a focus on the Northwest Coast and its culture of permanent settlements, hereditary chiefs, totem poles, potlatches, whalers, and salmon fishers. Indeed, a coastal bias became so entrenched in this early period that to this day many people attribute all things Aboriginal in the province to the coastal peoples. As the repositories of large coastal collections, museums have reinforced this perception. Through this process, Interior peoples came into public view in opposition to their coastal counterparts—that is, as transient, egalitarian, hunter-gatherers with a loose political organization who were generally lacking in rich ceremonial and artistic traditions.

The first detailed ethnographic reports for the Interior region were compiled by two men whose professions drew them across the Coastal/Interior divide. From 1875 to 1878 geologist George Mercer *Dawson travelled northward to the Nechako River to study the physical geology and glaciology of the region. An employee of the *Geological Survey of Canada (GSC), Dawson also took note of the Thompson, Shuswap, Okanagan, Chilcotin, and Carrier peoples he encountered along the way. Given his concern about the debilitating effects of European culture on these people, his portrayals were not only paternalistic but also somewhat dark in tone.

A Roman Catholic priest, Father A.G. Morice, also contributed to early Interior ethnography. Stationed at the Oblate Mission at Stuart Lake in central British

Columbia in the 1880s and 1890s, Morice wrote extensively about the Carrier peoples living in the area. Like Dawson, his work was driven by a strong sense of European superiority and religious morality. Nevertheless, Morice's descriptions of material culture and subsistence patterns are still regarded as among the most detailed for the region.

The first systematic anthropology east of the Coastal Range was undertaken by James *Teit, a Shetlander based at Spences Bridge on the Thompson River. Working under the auspices of New York-based Franz *Boas (American Museum of Natural History) and Ottawa-based Edward Sapir (Anthropology Division, GSC) between 1894 and 1922, Teit surveyed the Thompson, Lillooet, Okanagan, Shuswap, and Kutenai peoples in the south, the Chilcotin in the central region, and the Tahltan and Kaska in the northeast. A sympathetic listener who spent much of his life lobbying government officials on behalf of Aboriginal chiefs from southern and central British Columbia, Teit produced unusually sensitive ethnographic portraits.

Improved travel routes in the 1920s stimulated further ethnographic exploration, including Diamond *Jenness's work among the Carrier and Sekani in the central region.

What emerged from this early ethnographic work was a generalized profile of Interior peoples as loosely organized, nomadic or semi-nomadic hunter-gatherers who wintered in major river valleys and relied on a subsistence base of fish and extensive game and root resources. Religious traditions were fairly diverse but centred on the individual vision quest.

The region came into sharp public focus in the early 1940s, when Alfred Kroeber and George Murdock added it to their culture area maps. Based on differences between the northern and southern peoples—in particular, an Athapaskan language family in the central and northern regions and an Interior Salish language family in the south—they divided the region into 'plateau' (Lillooet, Shuswap, Thompson, Okanagan, and Kutenai in the south) and 'subarctic' (all remaining groups from the central region north). Aside from some debate over whether Chilcotin and Carrier belonged in the plateau or subarctic area, and where to place linguistic and cultural 'anomalies' such as the Kutenai language in the southeast and Cree in the northeast, as well as buffalo-hunting peoples along the eastern borders and potlatching peoples along the western borders, the Interior continues to be conceptualized according to these two culture areas. Archaeologists later assigned tangible temporal depth to the region with their discoveries of 9,000-year-old human occupation sites in the central plateau and 11,000-year-old sites in the northeast.

By the mid-1970s, historians of British Columbia began to challenge the anthropological paradigm. Rolf Knight led the way with *Indians at Work* (1977), in which he argued that an overemphasis on the pre-contact past had denied Aboriginal peoples a place in the more recent history of the province. The latter, he argued, had played a major role in the BC labour force, as cowboys, farm and cannery workers, miners, seasonal fruit and vegetable pickers, outfitters, and road and railway construction workers. Robin Fisher added to this perspective with *Contact and Conflict* (1977), which focused on Aboriginal–non-Aboriginal relations throughout the 19th century. A flurry of related work followed, covering a range of contemporary concerns, such as the history of residential schooling, Aboriginal political movements, and the Indian land question.

Today a new generation of Interior peoples has emerged. In addition to administering its own schools, social programs, cultural research projects, and political affairs, this generation is telling its own stories of the past. These cover a variety of genres, including fiction (*Slash* by Okanagan writer Jeannette Armstrong), autobiography (*Stoney Creek Woman*, the life story of Carrier woman Mary John), and visual arts (the paintings of Thompson/Nlaka'pamux artist, Lawrence Paul Yuxweluptun). These histories are constructed in opposition to the mainstream histories. For example, they reject Asian migration theories as contradicting their oral traditions, which affirm that they have occupied their territories since time immemorial. Many groups also reject the names assigned to them by their colonizers and others over the years. This is evident in the current listing of ethnic groups for the region: in the southeast the Ktunaxa (formerly Kutenai); in the south the Nlaka'pamux (Thompson), the Okanagan, the Secwepemc (Shuswap), and the St'atl'imx (formerly the Lillooet); in the south central region the Tsilhqot'in (Chilcotin); in the west central region the Wet'suwet'en (sometimes considered part of the Carrier-Dakelh); in the central region the Dakelh (formerly Carrier); in the northeast the Sekani (includes a mixture of Dene-thah and Dunne-za), Dene-thah (formerly known as Slave or Slavey peoples, who represent a mixture of Dene-thah, Kaska, Dunne-za), and the Dunne-za (formerly known as Beaver); and, in the northwest, the Tahltan. (The Saulteaux, who live on a reserve in northeastern BC, have no associations with any of the above ethnic groups.)

With the exception of the Treaty 8 peoples in the north (the Sekani, Dunne-za, Dene-thah, and Saulteaux), the Interior peoples are not covered by treaties. As a result, land claims cases are in progress throughout the region. The *Delgamuukw* case, for example, which opened in 1984, involved 12 Wet'suwet'en and 39 Gitksan hereditary chiefs, all claiming ownership of their traditional territories, right to self-government, and compensation for loss of lands. The Xeni Gwe'tin First Nation (Tsilhqot'in) are currently involved in a legal case over their rights and title to the Nemiah Valley. Although much of this negotiation has been peaceful, in 1995 one violent confrontation, concerning the rights of Aboriginal peoples to occupy a sacred site, took place at Gustafsen Lake near 100 Mile House in the Cariboo. WENDY WICKWIRE

British Commonwealth Air Training Plan. Canada's weather and open spaces were ideally suited to large-scale flying training. Under the BCATP, 131,533 Allied pilots and aircrew were trained in Canada during the Second World War, 72,835 of them Canadians. At the plan's high point in late 1943, an organization of over 100,000 personnel operated 107 schools and 184 other supporting units at 231 locations all across Canada. Flying clubs and commercial aviation companies administered many of the elementary flying schools. The BCATP trained just short of half of all the pilots, navigators, bomb aimers, air gunners, wireless operators, and flight engineers for British and Commonwealth air operations. On the third anniversary of the plan, in a message ghost written by L.B. *Pearson, serving at the Canadian legation in Washington, US president Franklin D. Roosevelt enthused that the BCATP had transformed Canada into the 'aerodrome of democracy'.

The original BCATP agreement, signed in Ottawa on 17 December 1939 (Prime Minister Mackenzie *King's 65th birthday), left unresolved the question of organizing Canadian graduates of the plan into national squadrons overseas. Although there were sufficient operational aircrew overseas for 80–90 *Royal Canadian Air Force squadrons, Britain eventually agreed to form only 35 RCAF squadrons. This reluctance to post Canadians to their own national units meant that 60 per cent of RCAF aircrew fought the war in Royal Air Force units. The slow progress in 'Canadianizing' the country's squadrons was a vexing aspect of Canada's wartime defence policy.

NORMAN HILLMER

British connection. The ties between Great Britain and Canada go back to John *Cabot and the subsequent establishment of the first English colonies in Newfoundland in the early 17th century. From 1763 to 1867 the various provinces of *British North America were all colonies of Great Britain, and not until 1949, when Newfoundland joined Confederation, was the last direct colonial government in North America eliminated. Since 1867, the British connection has existed in Canada on a variety of levels: through the presence of the Crown and the *monarchy; through the Judicial Committee of the Privy Council, which until 1949 was the final court of appeal on Canadian legal cases; through the official flag of Canada before 1965, which was the British union flag (although most Canadians would have sworn it was the red ensign); through the status of the Canadian *constitution as a creation of the British Parliament until 1982; through the membership of Canada in the *British Empire and since 1931 in the British *Commonwealth of Nations; through the strong sense of British heritage in Canada; and, finally, through the unofficial loyalty to the 'auld country' felt by millions of Canadians born in or descended from those born in the various constituent nations of the British Isles. All of these connections, official and unofficial—many of mostly symbolic importance to begin with—have either disappeared totally or lessened in importance over the years.

On the official side, the monarch has become a ceremonial and distant figure, and while there is little serious discussion in Canada—as there is in Australia—of becoming a republic, *royal tours no longer carry the cachet they did before the Second World War; when polled, many Canadians do not expect the monarchy to survive in Canada for another century. The JCPC's jurisdiction in Canada was finally abolished in 1949, the union flag was replaced by the maple leaf *flag in 1965, and in 1982 the Canadian constitution was fully repatriated. The Commonwealth at present has meaning for Canadians mainly as the ostensible presence behind the Commonwealth Games. On the semi-official level, the sense of the British heritage of Canada—the common law system of British justice, the parliamentary system of British government, the importance of British education and culture as a foundation stone of Canadian education and culture—has very nearly vanished. Even the totally unofficial connections of Canadians with Britain and the British Isles have considerably lessened in recent years, as fewer and fewer 'Brits' immigrate, as those in Canada grow older, as British prestige declines. The attraction of Britain has in some ways been lessened by the many changes that have occurred there, ranging from membership in the European Union to the unfavourable (to Canadians) exchange rate of the pound in recent years and the high cost of living and of real estate since the 1970s. Canadians still enjoy visiting and touring in Britain, but very few, even those of British origin, intend to take their pensions and retire there.

J.M. BUMSTED

British Empire. When the British Empire actually began remains an open question. The Channel Islands were dependencies of the English Crown but not part of England from 1066, and the Irish Pale was founded in 1169 as a settlement 'plantation'. By the end of the 15th century and John *Cabot's landfall in Newfoundland, the English began to think in terms of overseas colonies, particularly in North America. Martin Frobisher nearly founded a colony on Baffin Island in 1577 and Sir Walter Raleigh planted one on Roanoke Island (now part of Virginia) in 1587. The English tended to work informally through proprietors and trading companies.

Various English trading companies, beginning with the Muscovy Company in 1555, established trading factories with territorial pretensions in the East. By the 17th century, English interests were establishing settlement colonies in various forms along the Atlantic seaboard of North America, and the Crown began making some effort to oversee their administration from the mother country. A key step was the establishment of the *Board of Trade in 1696, which administered a mercantilist system that included the various colonial governments in America. Another key step was the realization that Britain's military policy and activities were international in scope, perhaps first recognized in the negotiations that produced the Treaty of Utrecht in 1713 and certainly fully accepted in the prosecution of the Seven Years' War. Most scholars would agree that, with the Treaty of Paris in 1763, Britain had created a definite North American Empire, one that had gradually developed and had been governed informally. When the mother country attempted after 1763 to regularize colonial administration, the American colonists objected, and the quarrel between the British government and the colonies rapidly escalated into open warfare by 1775. In 1783 another Treaty of Paris acknowledged American independence. Whether the period after 1783 saw the continuation of the old American Empire (minus the Americans) or the creation of a new British Empire in America is debatable.

Between 1783 and 1839, and especially after the early years of the 19th century, when the *Colonial Office was finally formed, the British attempted to reconcile overall supervision of their American colonies with colonial administrative autonomy. After the colonials in Canada rose in protest in the *rebellions of 1837 and 1838, in part against imperial constraint, three developments merged to lead the British to work towards disengagement in North America: the movement towards *responsible government, the British abandonment of *mercantilism in favour of free trade, and the settlement of most outstanding North American issues with the United States. By the early 1860s, the British were actively encouraging the union of British North America as an autonomous entity, although still in international terms a part of the British Empire. After Confederation a closer allegiance to the empire—opposed by French Canada—gradually found favour with many in both the United Kingdom and in Canada, usually in the form of imperial federation and the integration of the Canadian military into the imperial armed forces. In a series of imperial conferences held at the end of the 19th and the beginning of the 20th centuries, the Canadian government resisted both federation and military integration despite the constant wooing of its leaders with honours, while the Round Table movement (founded in 1909) advocated increased dominion involvement in imperial defence. The Laurier government, which had attempted to find middle ground between imperialists and anti-imperialists, was defeated in the 1911 election as much by its foot dragging over the construction of a Canadian navy as by *reciprocity with the Americans. The Borden government was much more openly sympathetic to the empire, and allowed Canada to be drawn into the Great War by imperial fiat. Nevertheless, Borden used Canada's substantial contributions to the war as a lever to gain at least battlefield control over Canadian military units, a place at the councils of war (the Imperial Munitions Board in 1915 and the Imperial War Cabinet in 1916), and a separate seat at the peace conference.

After the war, Canada moved gradually towards full independence. In 1926 the *Balfour Report insisted on the equality of Britain and its dominions, and in 1931 the *Statute of Westminster gave legal meaning to this equality by defining dominions and eliminating the power of the British Parliament to legislate for them except by request. The old British Empire was replaced by the British *Commonwealth of Nations. In a final obeisance to the past, the Imperial Economic Conference of 1932 attempted to resurrect some sort of imperial trading system, but all schemes failed because no dominion was willing to surrender its national interest. Although, after Versailles, the addition to the British Empire of former German territories as mandates gave the superficial appearance of growth, the clamour for self-government was increasing everywhere in the Empire. The Commonwealth still had some military meaning during the Second World War, especially in the *British Commonwealth Air Training Plan, which was one of Canada's major contributions to the early war effort, but after the war ended it became little more than a toothless voluntary association of dominions and other nations. For Canada, formal and informal associations with the United States became far more important than imperial ties. Many former dominions became republics, thus severing the final formal tie with Britain. Beginning with the withdrawal from India in 1947, the British government swiftly pulled out of most of its former colonies in Africa and Asia on the grounds that it could no longer afford to administer them. By the end of the 20th century, Britain was left with only the shards of empire in the form of a handful of small dependencies scattered around the world. As the new millennium approached, several 'settlement' dominions seriously debated the elimination of the *monarchy.

J.M. BUMSTED

British garrison. The British army maintained a garrison of regular troops in British North America from the fall of Quebec in 1763 until 1871. Afterwards, special 'imperial' garrisons remained in Halifax until 1906 and at Esquimalt 1894–1906. Before 1871, these troops were intended to form the backbone of colonial defence, assisted by the colonial *militia, against American invasion, as happened during the War of 1812. The number of troops rose and fell in accordance with the state of tensions with the United States. After 1815 their strength averaged about 7,600 a year, although occasionally it could expand to more than three times this number. Troops were mostly spread along the border from western Upper Canada to the Atlantic but were concentrated most heavily in the strategic urban centres of Kingston, Montreal, Quebec City, and Halifax. This contrasted markedly with the situation in the United Sates, where the regular army was scattered among numerous outposts on the western frontier.

Intended primarily to protect against external opponents and, as in the case of the *rebellion in Lower Canada in 1837–8, internal unrest, this force nonetheless had an important impact on the colonial civilian sphere. Its members put on stage plays and introduced sports, such as cricket, horse racing, and curling, while its bands influenced developments in local secular music. In addition, military contracts and purchases helped establish or sustain many local businesses. Officers and other ranks interacted with their respective levels of colonial society, influencing manners and helping to shape attitudes.

CAMERON PULSIFER

See also GARRISON MENTALITY.

British North America. A term used to refer to the British colonies and territories in North America after the Treaty of Paris (1783) formalized the independence of the United States. The term does not often appear formally before Lord *Durham used it in the title of his famous report in 1839 (John MacGregor's 1833 well-known survey of the region was entitled *British America*), and it had no legal meaning since there was no administrative imperial entity with that name before 1867, when the preamble to the BNA Act used the term in its title and referred to those parts of the American colonies which might later join the new confederation as 'Parts of British North America'.

As an informal collection of British colonies, British North America in 1783 consisted of the officially recognized colonies of Nova Scotia, the Island of Saint John, and Quebec, as well as the unofficial colony of Newfoundland, the territories of the *Hudson's Bay Company, and various Crown lands. Not even all recognized colonies had technically equal status. Nova Scotia and Quebec had governors, while the Island of Saint John had a lieutenant-governor responsible to the governor of Nova Scotia. Initially only Nova Scotia and the Island of Saint John had representative assemblies. New Brunswick and Cape Breton were added as separate colonies in 1784; the former was given an assembly and both had lieutenant-governors responsible to the governor of Nova Scotia. Some notion of an administrative unity for the colonies began in 1786, when Guy *Carleton was appointed governor-in-chief of them, but the term British North America does not appear in his commission. Thereafter, periodic proposals for unification of the colonies were put forward both publicly and privately, but there was no agreement on what the unified territory might be called, and the various schemes did not get very far.

In 1791 Quebec was divided into *Upper and *Lower Canada, with each new colony granted an assembly; Upper Canada had a lieutenant-governor. In 1798 the Island of Saint John became Prince Edward Island. Cape Breton was annexed to Nova Scotia in 1820. The title of governor-in-chief was revived for Lord Durham in early 1838, but his commission does not use the term 'British North America' as an appellation for the colonies he was to govern. In 1841 Upper and Lower Canada were legislatively joined as the *Province of Canada. *Vancouver Island was established as a colony in 1849, British Columbia—that is, the mainland—became a colony in 1856, and the two were joined as British Columbia in 1858. The Red River Settlement never achieved colony status. Unofficially, the various colonies and territories that remained out of Confederation continued to form parts of British North America until they joined Canada: Manitoba and the Hudson's Bay territories (1870); British Columbia (1871); Prince Edward Island (1873); and Newfoundland (1949). J.M. BUMSTED

British North America Act. *See* CONSTITUTION OF CANADA.

British Yukon Navigation Steamboat Company, 1904–55, subsidiary of *White Pass and Yukon Route Railway. The *Klondike gold discovery (1896) was a magnet for investment. While mining attracted a share, connecting the remote Yukon goldfields to world markets also drew capital. Numerous railways were proposed, but only one, from Skagway, Alaska, was started. Once the line reached Whitehorse in 1900, the rush was over and the BYN was set up to run riverboats on the *Yukon River in a hybrid, and much cheaper, transportation system.

The company's fortunes were tied to the exploitation of Yukon resources. Profits waned as traffic dwindled after 1912, when mining dredges were in place in the Klondike. However, there was a revival during the 1920s as silver and lead-zinc mines opened up on the Stewart River. During the Second World War the boats transported goods for both the *Alaska Highway and *Canol projects. This seasonal operation supplied central Yukon to mid-century, when roads extending from the Alaska Highway linked most communities.

The economic and environmental conditions of the 20th-century Yukon provided the wood-fired, steam-powered, wooden riverboats of the BYN a unique technological niche in transportation history. Three vessels of the fleet, SS *Klondike* (Whitehorse), SS *Keno* (Dawson), and MV *Tarahne* (Atlin, BC), are preserved as heritage sites.

DAVID NEUFELD

Brittain, Miller Gore (1912–68). One of many Canadians to study at the Art Students League (New York, 1930–2), Brittain grew into artistic maturity during the years immediately after the 1929 stock market crash plunged his home town, Saint John, New Brunswick, into crisis. The Depression reinforced his interest in ordinary, anonymous people, whose lives he drew and painted with sympathetic insight. This commitment to his immediate environment offered a strong regionalist vision, in contrast to the dominance of nationalist wilderness landscapes by the *Group of Seven and their followers. His works inspired by biblical subjects (1940s–50s) are among the finest Canadian religious images of the century. In the 1940s he participated in important national art projects: he attended the historic Kingston Artists' Conference, the first national gathering of arts professionals (1941); was active in the North American mural revival; and was one of Canada's 32 official war artists. His wife's death in 1957 threw him into despair, and his art subsequently became increasingly eccentric and fantasist. BRIAN FOSS

broadcasting. Canadian broadcasting began in 1919 as a marketing outgrowth of the earlier technology of point-to-point wireless communication. In the 1890s Guglielmo *Marconi had invented and begun to manufacture and sell wireless devices for sending messages in Morse code. His first transatlantic wireless message was sent from Poldhu, Cornwall, to Signal Hill in St John's, Newfoundland, in 1901. Over the next decade a number of inventors tackled the problem of radio telephony, or transmitting voices by wireless. Canadian Reginald Fessenden, working for an American electrical company, initiated the first successful sound transmission when he sent a Christmas concert from his Massachusetts laboratory to ships at sea in 1906.

During the First World War radio was used for military communication; once the war ended it was marketed by various electrical companies as a means of communication with individuals beyond reach of telegraph lines. Yet, it turned out that the most important and profitable use of radio equipment would be for sending messages not to individuals but to a large anonymous mass of listeners—for broadcasting. In Canada, the Marconi Company experimented with this practice at its Montreal factory during 1919, and in 1920 it sent a vocal concert over the air to Ottawa, where it was heard by members of the *Royal Society of Canada.

By 1922 a number of other companies, including newspapers, retailers, and electrical manufacturers, had set up radio stations mainly for promotional purposes, and they continued to proliferate through the rest of the decade. In Toronto in 1927, for example, Edward S. Rogers founded CFRB mainly to help sell the batteryless radios his company manufactured. As early as 1923 Canadian stations began using third-party advertising to help pay their costs. The radio stations, of which there were about 80 by the end of the 1920s, were regulated by the Radio Branch of the Department of Marine and Fisheries. While a few stations were financially sound, many of them struggled, particularly in the context of competition from the high-powered American stations most Canadians could easily listen to in the evening hours. By the end of the 1920s, the strongest American stations were affiliated to two networks, CBS and NBC, as were four Canadian stations.

Among other motives, the fear of increasing Americanization of Canadian airwaves led the Conservative government of R.B. *Bennett to create a public broadcasting body, the Canadian Radio Broadcasting Commission, in 1932. Wracked by political and administrative problems, the CRBC was replaced by the *Canadian Broadcasting Corporation in 1936. Both were financed mainly by licence fees collected annually from owners of radio sets. Their primary task, in addition to taking over regulation from the Radio Branch, was to construct and provide programming for a nationwide network. The CRBC and CBC, however, did not have a monopoly on broadcasting in Canada. Private stations continued to exist, and many of them were affiliated with the public network (carrying some of its programs), a practice that subsidized some of the needier private stations. Thus was established Canada's 'mixed' public/private broadcasting system. The system operated in both English and French; some strong French stations like CKAC in Montreal remained privately owned, and the CBC set up a number of French stations and a French network in eastern Canada.

During the Second World War both the public and private radio stations thrived—the CBC as the main provider of wartime news and commentary, the private stations as increasingly lucrative and powerful outlets for popular culture. The most popular American programs were relayed to Canadian listeners on both the private stations and the CBC network. As the private stations grew stronger during the 1940s, they increasingly complained that the CBC was simultaneously their 'competitor, regulator, prosecutor, jury and judge'.

Television, which had been invented well before the Second World War, hit the American market in the late 1940s. After considerable study, and influenced by the report of the *Massey Commission, the federal Liberal government decided that the CBC should be given a head start in developing television in Canada. The first two stations, in Toronto and Montreal, went on the air in September 1952. Soon a network, linked by microwave towers, spread Canadian television from coast to coast, once again through a mixed system in which the CBC owned some stations but others were private affiliates. By 1960 there were 47 television stations in Canada, providing service to most of the population. By that year as well, Canadians were spending an average of six hours a day in front of their sets: television had become the most important in-home leisure activity.

In 1957 the Conservatives came to power in Ottawa. The new government, more sympathetic to private broadcasters, almost immediately began licensing private competing television stations in the major urban centres. More importantly, in the Broadcasting Act passed in 1958 it created a new regulatory body, the Board of Broadcast Governors, to supervise both public and private stations. The new private television stations, which soon grouped into a co-operative arrangement (a de facto network) called CTV, competed with the CBC stations for popular American shows to attract advertising revenues. In 1960 the BBG introduced Canadian content rules that, while much denounced by the private broadcasters, were easily evaded.

The arrival of television did not destroy radio but permanently altered its format. Increasingly local radio stations offered weather and news reports in the morning and evening 'drive times', and popular music shows hosted by disk jockeys. Car radios became ubiquitous, as did portable transistor sets. The CBC radio network continued to exist, but as a pale shadow of its former self. Private stations evolved new programming options as the years progressed; the addition of the FM band allowed the proliferation of tightly focused music formats and of all-talk formats on the AM band.

In 1968 another Broadcasting Act replaced the BBG with a new regulatory body, now called the Canadian Radio-television and Telecommunications Commission. Under CRTC supervision Canadian broadcasting has expanded enormously. There are now four national over-the-air television networks, two run by the CBC in English and French (Radio-Canada), and two privately owned (CTV and CanWest Global). Most importantly, in the early 1970s the CRTC began to allow the importation of American channels for distribution by cable to subscribing households. Given the long-established popularity of American programs in Canada, it is not surprising that 60 per cent of Canadian homes had cable by 1982. Soon thereafter, specialty and pay-TV channels also began to multiply as part of cable subscriber packages. Now, with the addition of satellite services, most Canadians have access to a multitude of channels (if not quite the legendary 500 channel universe). The proportion of television-watching time devoted to the traditional broadcasters (Canadian or American) declined from 99 per cent in 1982 to 65 per cent in 2000. On English-language stations, the majority of the most popular drama and comedy programs continue to originate in the United States; domestic programming concentrates on news, commentary, and sports programming. French-language television stations, whether publicly or privately owned, provide a more indigenous programming mix.

Driven by the need to foster communication among a widely dispersed population, the Canadian government has developed one of the most sophisticated communication systems in the world; it has not been so successful at ensuring that its contents are Canadian. Despite the injunction of the 1991 Broadcasting Act that all broadcasters must make preponderant use of high quality programs based on Canadian creative resources, the imperatives of corporate profit making combined with the demands of Canadian audiences result in a Canadian broadcasting system that operates in both French and English, is both private and public, and is both Canadian and American. MARY VIPOND

Brock, Sir Isaac (1769–1812). In October 1812 the *Kingston Gazette* reported the death of General Brock, commander of the British forces in Upper Canada. Great Britain and its colonies had been at war with the United States since June—a war many believed could not be won. Brock's ingenuity, determination, and considerable military skills transformed the situation. His heroic action, the paper reported, 'ensured a most glorious victory' over the American invaders.

Brock had arrived in North America in 1803 and immediately set out to improve colonial defences. *Fortifications were strengthened, British troops were disciplined, and the *militia reorganized. Initially, Brock chafed at being stationed in 'this remote corner' of the empire. By 1810 the increasing threat of war with the United States made the military situation in Upper Canada precarious. When war broke out, Brock immediately went on the offensive. Quick victories at Detroit and Michilimackinac galvanized the formerly reluctant population. Brock's heroic death while leading a charge up Queenston Heights, and the subsequent roust of American forces, convinced many Upper Canadians that victory was possible. And over the next two years the colony was successfully defended. JANE ERRINGTON

Brooker, Bertram (1888–1955), artist, author, advertising executive. Born in England, Brooker moved to Portage la Prairie, Manitoba, in 1905. Influenced by contemporary physics and spiritualism, he believed the universe was unified through cosmic energy. These beliefs, as expressed through his work, placed him at the forefront of Canadian modernist expression. After settling in Toronto in 1920, he also became a celebrated copywriter. He was an early champion of market research, briefly published *Marketing* magazine, and under the pseudonym Richard Surrey wrote *Copy Technique in Advertising* (1930). He joined J.J. Gibbons Advertising in 1930, moved to MacLaren Advertising in 1940, and retired there as vice-president in 1955. Outside commercial writing, Brooker took up drawing, painting, poetry, and fiction to some acclaim. Most notably, an exhibition of his paintings in 1928 debuted the first abstracts shown by a Canadian, while his first novel, *Think of the Earth* (1936), won the first Governor General's Award for fiction.

RUSSELL JOHNSTON

Brooks, Harriet (1876–1933), physicist. Born at Exeter, Ontario, Brooks worked with Ernest Rutherford at McGill University, Montreal, and with J.J. Thomson at the University of Cambridge, England. Among her achievements, she established that the emanation from radioactive sources was a gas (we now know this to be radon), reported observing sequential radioactive decays (that one radioactive substance could decay into another radioactive substance), and discovered the recoil of the radioactive atom (later a crucial method of separating radioactive isotopes). In 1907 she travelled with the Russian author Maxim Gorky's entourage to Italy whence she went to the Sorbonne to undertake research with Marie Curie. After one year in Paris, Brooks left research to marry Frank Pitcher. They returned to Montreal, where she had three children. Brooks died at the age of 56, probably as a result of her work with radioactive materials.

MARELENE RAYNER-CANHAM

Brown, George (1818–80). Born at Alloa, Scotland, and Edinburgh-educated, Brown was much influenced by his father, a strong Whig and evangelical Presbyterian. In 1837 they emigrated to the United States and eventually Toronto, founding in 1843 the *Banner*, a Presbyterian weekly supporting Free Kirk principles and political reform. On 5 March 1844, with £250, Brown founded the *Globe*, which would become his enduring monument. Its vigorous critical editorials and broad news coverage made it the most important paper in British North America, read by supporters and detractors alike. By 1851 Brown successfully ran for parliament on the Reform ticket his paper so enthusiastically endorsed.

By 1858 Brown was the leading *Clear Grit politician and the champion of Canada West. He was as critical of Roman Catholicism as he was an advocate of political restructuring, especially 'rep by pop'. Brown and his newspaper became unceasing advocates of *federalism as the solution to Canada's sectional, religious, and ethnic differences. In 1864 he compromised with opponents to form the *'Great Coalition' that laid the foundations for Canadian *Confederation. He resigned from government in 1865. Although he continued to support Confederation, once it was achieved he became highly critical of John A. *Macdonald. His time as a politician was largely over, although in 1874 he accepted a Senate appointment.

By then his vision for Canada had crystallized and he advocated *westward expansion as well as the vigorous provincialism of Oliver *Mowat's Ontario. The *Globe* flourished, although not without problems, including a confrontational printing strike in 1872. It would be a disgruntled employee who pulled a gun on his former employer in March 1880, causing a flesh wound that became badly infected, prompting Brown's death six weeks later. ROGER HALL

Brown, John George 'Kutenai' (1839–1916). Born in County Clare, Ireland, Brown served in India after the 1857 mutiny before emigrating to Victoria in 1862. Briefly mining for gold in British Columbia, he crossed the mountains to the high plains in 1865. He ranged widely, as far east as the Red River Valley, working as a trapper, pony-express rider, whisky trader, and bison hunter. He married a Metis woman, Olivia Lyonnais, and they had three children. Following acquittal for murder in Montana in 1877, he settled permanently in Canada near the Waterton River. Following the early death of his wife, he served as a scout with a militia unit, the Rocky Mountain Rangers, during the Riel troubles of 1885. Rewarded with land for his efforts, he married a Cree woman, Isabella ('The Blue-Flash of Lightning'), and turned to *ranching and guiding before being appointed a game guardian by the Canadian government in 1901. A romantic mythology developed about Brown's past, particularly after 1911 during his tenure as the first superintendent of Waterton Lakes National Park in southern Alberta, where he is buried. GRAHAM MacDONALD

Bruchési, Paul-Napoléon (1855–1939). Born in Montreal, ordained in 1878 in Rome, archbishop of Montreal (1897–1939), this authoritarian cleric cultivated the politically powerful. His nomination as bishop at a crucial time in the *Manitoba schools question was viewed as a victory of the Quebec church hierarchy over the papal delegate who had been dispatched from Rome to mediate the issue. Although he tried to bring about an accord between Wilfrid *Laurier and Archbishop Adélard Langevin of St-Boniface on the issue of Catholic schools, Bruchési soon aligned himself with Laurier. Condemning as secular the Quebec law (1897) creating an education ministry, the archbishop used church authority to block it; when Premier Félix-Gabriel Marchand revived the measure, Bruchési turned to his new-found friend Laurier to abort it. In 1914 at the behest of federal ministers, the archbishop had the Quebec church hierarchy issue a collective letter unconditionally supporting Canada's war effort. Bruchési also publicly endorsed national registration in 1916 in return for Prime Minister Robert *Borden's fleeting promise of no *conscription. Borden's betrayal may have contributed to a protracted illness that prevented Bruchési from exercising effective authority after 1921. ROBERTO PERIN

Brûlé, Étienne (1592?–1633), the first French interpreter of the Huron (Wendat) language. Born in the Paris region, Brûlé seems to have arrived at Quebec in 1608 as a servant of *Champlain's. In 1610–11 he wintered for the first time in Native lands, most likely in Huronia on Georgian Bay, where he would acquire the skills and the connections that would make him not just a pioneering interpreter but a crucial French–Huron intermediary through the 1620s. The *Huron permitted Brûlé to travel widely; accompanying diplomats in 1615, he reached the vicinity of Chesapeake Bay before, apparently, negotiating his way out of *Iroquois (Seneca or Cayuga) captivity. During the Kirkes' brief occupation of Quebec, 1729–32, he entered English service, incurring Champlain's displeasure. With the return of French rule, his status in Huronia was problematic, even without his suspicious commercial overtures southwestward, possibly to the Senecas. Brûlé's murder at the hands of the Huron suggests that this adroit negotiator had crossed one boundary too many. THOMAS WIEN

Buck, Tim (1891–1973). Emigrating from England to Canada in 1910, Buck worked as a machinist in several North American cities before settling permanently in Toronto during the Great War. A socialist since his early teens, he joined the *Communist Party of Canada shortly after its formation in 1921, quickly establishing himself in its leading bodies. In 1929 his enthusiasm for Moscow's latest—'left'—turn helped him replace the less pliant Jack MacDonald as general secretary. However, it took his incarceration for political offences in February 1932 to cement his authority; an apparent attempt on his life by prison guards during the October 1932 Kingston riot was of immense propaganda value. Released in December 1934, Buck found the emerging Popular Front period congenial to his easygoing and emollient personal style. He and his comrades achieved their highest levels of support as anti-fascists and—after the shocking hiatus of the Nazi–Soviet pact—total war partisans. Personal charm, adroit factional skills, and Stalinist orthodoxy sustained Buck's domination through the party's Cold War decline, but he was finally elected to the post of national president in 1962. His self-serving *Reminiscences*, published unofficially in 1977, provoked an acrimonious inner-party struggle. JOHN MANLEY

Bucke, Richard Maurice (1837–1902). Bucke emigrated with his family from Norfolk, England, in 1838 and settled near London, Ontario. Orphaned at 16, he worked in the United States, returning to Canada to enter medical school at McGill University. He graduated in 1862 and then pursued postgraduate work in London and Paris. In 1865 he married Jessie Maria Gurd. After practising medicine in Sarnia, in 1876 he became superintendent of the Asylum for the Insane in Hamilton; a year later he moved to the asylum in London, where he remained until his death. Recognized by his peers, his work with the insane emphasized moral treatment and a refusal to provide alcohol and use restraint, both common in other asylums. Professionally conservative, in the late 1870s he began 'wiring' male patients (inserting a silver needle in the prepuce of the penis) to stop them from masturbating, and in the late 1890s encouraged gynecological surgery to treat some female patients. In 1872, a mystical experience while in England convinced him that 'man' could aspire to a more advanced consciousness. He was a devotee of Walt Whitman and became his friend, medical adviser, and literary executor. He wrote widely on insanity, the moral nature of humans, and Whitman. Among his writings was *Cosmic Consciousness* (1901).

WENDY MITCHINSON

buffalo hunt. The abundance of buffalo (bison) on the grasslands of North America made them very important to the *Plains Indians and *Metis, who developed a way of life that centred on their exploitation. Before the introduction of the horse, Native hunters used two techniques for communal buffalo hunting: jumps and pounds. On the northwestern plains, with both rolling terrain and rough breaks, buffalo were enticed to the edge of a cliff and then stampeded over the precipice. In those areas without steep cliffs, Natives constructed pounds, circular corrals of felled trees laid one upon the other to a height of about 2 m, usually situated at the foot of a hill. From the entrance on the hillside, sticks were set up in the form of a fence funnelling the buffalo into the kill site. These techniques were used even after the introduction of the horse, although mostly from late fall to early spring, when horses were less effective and herds smaller. Summer hunts were also conducted by surrounding a herd or stalking buffalo singly.

With the arrival of horses on the northern plains in the early 1700s, most summer hunting was conducted on horseback. Because buffalo had greater endurance than horses, and the undisciplined running of buffalo could drive herds out of the range of large Indian encampments, hunts were carefully coordinated and governed by strict rules enforced by police societies. The concentration of Plains Metis in the *Red River Settlement by the 1820s created the conditions for a Metis adaptation of these mounted communal hunts. With the large buffalo herds located south and west of the settlement, in hostile Sioux territory, Metis hunted from large, moving, armed encampments. These biannual expeditions out of Red River occurred in summer and late fall; by the 1840s the larger summer hunts could include over 1,600 men, women, and children, and 1,200 carts (one cartload comprised the dried meat and *pemmican of an estimated 8–10 buffalo). Women were crucial to the processing of the dried meat and pemmican during the hunt.

The Metis buffalo hunt was a highly organized expedition with detailed rules. Because the caravan could at any time encounter hostile Sioux or a herd of buffalo, a high level of discipline was maintained by the elected hunt captains and their soldiers. When either the enemy or buffalo were spotted, an order was given and the columns of carts, often 8 or 9 km long, wheeled to form an enclosed circle to corral the horses and protect the women and children. If buffalo were sighted, the men would mount their fastest horse and ride into the herd with their mouths filled with shot and pockets full of powder. A good hunter on an experienced horse could kill 10–12 animals on a run.

The rising demand for buffalo robes in the 1850s and 1860s increased hunting, particularly in winter, when the robes were their thickest. By the 1860s over 100,000 robes were shipped down the Missouri every year. In response to this demand, the Metis left their more permanent settlements to winter in smaller communities on the plains, and Indian groups increased the number of buffalo they killed. Overhunting, environmental factors, and disease decimated the large northern herds. By 1879 they had disappeared from the Canadian prairies, and with them a way of life.

GERHARD J. ENS

building-trades workers. Initially self-employed master artisans with a specific craft, such as carpentry or masonry. During the 19th century contractors hired many more wage-earning journeymen, likely to be members of craft *unions with 'international' headquarters in the United States. Each group closely controlled apprenticeships and work practices, and guarded craft jurisdictions against incursions from other trades. They wanted employers to hire only union members, eventually through union-controlled hiring halls run by full-time 'business agents'. Compared to most, these workers tended to be hired by smaller firms or subcontractors, moved more frequently between employers (carrying their own tools with them), and had more success in establishing collective bargaining. They were relatively well paid, but generally faced longer annual layoffs when outdoor work stopped, and even worse unemployment in serious economic downturns, since their industry was highly sensitive to business cycles. After the Second World War, they were generally covered by distinctive labour legislation and provincial regulation of apprenticeship, and increasingly participated in coordinated industry-wide bargaining.

As building technologies and materials changed, new crafts emerged—notably plumbers, electricians, and structural-iron workers—but factory-made materials and subdivision of labour could threaten others. By the mid-20th century, union membership lay principally in the commercial and industrial sectors and remained overwhelmingly male, white, and English-speaking. Developers of huge new *suburbs and apartment towers began using large numbers of recent immigrants for semi-skilled work with prefabricated components and new power tools. In the Toronto area, those workers erupted into massive strikes in 1960–1, and eventually flowed into the Labourers' International Union, which by the 1970s had developed an ethnically and occupationally diverse membership of some 50,000 in Canada, including road and tunnel construction workers. The craft unions were further weakened by charges of internal corruption and by the growth of non-union construction.

Unions in this industry had often created local building-trades councils and were always prominent in larger labour councils. Yet they opposed cross-occupational industrial unionism, and, even after merging into the *Canadian

Labour Congress in 1956, they remained the strongest supporters of highly centralized international unionism (particularly the AFL-CIO's Building and Construction Trades Department) and opponents of Canadian labour nationalism. Conflicts over jurisdictional rights led them to withdraw from the CLC to found their own *Canadian Federation of Labour in 1982. CRAIG HERON

bunkhouse men. These workers formed the large, transient labour force found on remote sites in the Canadian construction and logging industries from about the 1890s to 1929. They lived in all male work camps and performed heavy jobs in dangerous conditions. By the 1890s, in logging especially, the crude camp buildings that housed from 50–100 such men—often in squalor—had come to be called 'bunkhouses': thus the label for these workers had a pejorative ring. In their day, the men were often misunderstood and scorned by middle-class Canadians as footloose, irresponsible foreigners, capable only of grunt work. Moral reformers charged that in their isolation from family life they grew brutish and became a moral as well as a health threat to respectable society. Employers criticized them for being easily manipulated by trouble-making radicals and union organizers.

Although Canada had long relied heavily on the labour of men in camps, the economic boom of the 1900s triggered an explosion in immigration, construction, and industrial expansion that brought on the heyday of the bunkhouse men. Work opportunities in frontier regions drew men not only from Canadian farms, towns, and cities, but from abroad as well. Homesteaders on the Prairies, many of them from eastern Europe, sent men they could spare into work camps to earn much-needed cash for the family farm. Similarly, 'boys' from poor and crowded Quebec homes went north for work. Even in far-off Italy and other European countries, young men, keen to earn a nest egg and improve their rural standard of living, chose to sojourn in Canada for a season or two and seek jobs in frontier work camps. The work required a strong back, but not necessarily facility in English (or French). Transnational labour migrations, then, created a multi-ethnic workforce. It would have been more racially diverse, except that the Canadian state, concerned about building a 'white Canada', blocked the entry of most of the Asian men.

Bunkhouse men were notorious for jumping from job to job in search of better pay and tastier grub. This transiency, along with the many languages spoken in camps, made union organizing difficult. Nevertheless, some leftists believed that the raw exploitation on the job and the crude living conditions made the 'navvies' and 'lumberjacks' likely recruits for radical organizations like the *Industrial Workers of the World. They had sporadic successes. Many bunkhouse men, however, remained aloof and focused on making their 'stake' quickly so they could return home to their families.

By their hard work at dangerous, back-breaking jobs, the bunkhouse men built the infrastructure on which Canada's expansion depended. The wages they earned for doing that work helped to meet the basic needs of ordinary people scattered from Sicily to Vancouver Island.

IAN RADFORTH

Burgess Shale. The site of an important fossil bed northeast of Field, Alberta, between Mounts Wapta and Field in Yoho National Park. Particularly significant are the soft-tissue fossils from the Cambrian period (550–485 million years ago). Typically, soft tissues decompose while shells, bones, or teeth undergo fossilization, but three-fifths of the genera found here have been identified using soft tissue fossils. While there are some two dozen similar sites worldwide (e.g., in China and Greenland), the quality and quantity of fossils in the Burgess Shale—dozens of new species discovered—make the site remarkable. Additionally, the Burgess Shale is accessible (periodically) to sightseers and scientists.

Credit for the discovery of this quarry goes to Charles Doolittle Walcott, secretary of the Smithsonian Institution, who announced his find in 1909. He returned to the quarry every summer until 1927, and the 70,000 fossils collected during that period went to the National Museum of Natural History, Washington, DC. Until the 1960s, other paleontologists ignored the quarry, but once fieldwork resumed the significance of the site became apparent. In 1980 the Burgess Shale was added to the UNESCO World Heritage list. DEBRA LINDSAY

Burin tidal wave. On 18 November 1929 an earthquake registering 7.2 on the Richter scale struck Newfoundland, resulting in considerable physical and human damage. Originating 250 km south of the Burin Peninsula, the first tremors from the epicentre reached Burin about 5:00 P.M. and lasted a few minutes, creating exceptionally low water levels in the coastal areas. At 7:30 P.M. a tidal wave of 5–15 m washed ashore at a speed of 105 km per hour. The high seas lasted two and a half hours, and homes, fishing premises, boats, and food supplies were lost. The fishing season along the south coast was over for the year, but fishers and their families lost not only their winter stock of food but in many cases their boats and gears for the spring catch. Assistance came from government and donors in Newfoundland, Canada, and the United States. The tragedy, which affected 40 communities and 10,000 people, resulted in 27 deaths and property loss amounting to over $1 million.

MELVIN BAKER AND AIDAN MALONEY

Burns, Eedson L.M. (1897–1985), soldier, civil servant, diplomat, author. One of the most talented of Canada's professional army officers, this Montreal native was wounded twice and awarded the Military Cross during the First World War. He continued in the army after 1918, but found time to write for the prominent journal *American Mercury*. The five books he wrote reflected a keen mind and a wide-ranging span of interests.

Burns's operational inexperience and often stern personality overshadowed his substantial achievements during the Second World War. After briefly leading two divisions, Burns took command of I Canadian Corps in Italy in March 1944. The corps generally performed well in the difficult battles for the Hitler and Gothic Lines, but criticisms from his British commanders and Canadian subordinates led to his removal in November 1944. Burns went on to lead the first generation of peacekeepers. In 1954, he became the chief of staff of the United Nations Truce Supervision Organization in the Middle East. Two years later, he commanded the first 'classic' *peacekeeping operation, the United Nations Emergency Force in Egypt. Through the 1960s, Burns represented Canada in disarmament talks at the *United Nations. He ended his long career teaching strategic studies at Carleton University. GEOFFREY HAYES

bush pilots. Following the First World War, bush pilots quickly proved their worth in isolated communities and in opening up northern latitudes and their rich resources. Aviation made tremendous advances during the war, and many of the 22,000-odd Canadians who had served in the British flying services longed to apply their expertise to a peacetime career. Barnstorming with war-surplus aircraft evolved into more useful activities. J.A. Wilson, secretary of the federal Air Board, and others recognized that while Canada lacked ground facilities for aviation services the abundance of lakes and rivers offered natural landing sites.

Perhaps the first man to take advantage of this situation was Stuart Graham, who flew an old US Navy HS2L flying boat from Halifax to Lac à la Tortue in Quebec in June 1919. Put to work by the St Maurice Forest Protective Association and Laurentide Air Services when it took over forestry patrols, Graham and his 'H boat' demonstrated the utility of aircraft in the bush. Surveys of timber stands could be done more quickly, impressing lumber company executives, who were also attracted by the speed with which people and supplies could be flown into isolated camps and forest fires could be spotted. The planes could also deliver firefighters to danger spots on short notice.

Initially the federal government assisted the provinces and private companies by performing these services, usually for a fee. However, the clients quickly took over these functions themselves. Laurentide was followed by the creation of other firms, such as Pacific Airways of Vancouver and Western Canada Airways of Winnipeg. A publicly owned counterpart, Ontario Provincial Air Services, was established in 1924. Pilots of the infant *RCAF flew primarily as 'bush pilots in uniform' almost until the next war, concentrating particularly on aerial photography to help prepare accurate maps, putting Canada in the forefront in this field. Bush pilots continue to play a vital role moving goods and people in and out of isolated communities throughout the North. CARL A. CHRISTIE

Bute Inlet incident, 1864. This incident involved the killing of 18 whites, mostly workers building a trail from Bute Inlet on British Columbia's north coast to the *Cariboo gold fields. The alleged perpetrators, members of the Tsilhqot'in (Chilcotin) nation, were arrested and tried before Chief Justice Matthew Baillie *Begbie, who sentenced five to hang.

Though exceptional, the incident is emblematic of the colonial encounter between Europeans and Aboriginals: it involved dispossession, disease, and cross-cultural misunderstanding. The victims had trespassed on Tsilhqot'in territory in the wake of a *smallpox epidemic that had decimated the coastal Aboriginal population. With their sovereignty and lives threatened by the increased contact with the whites the road would bring, the Tsilhqot'in considered themselves under attack—and defended themselves. Asked to explain his actions, one of the accused simply said 'we were at war . . .' Although Begbie had misgivings about prosecuting men who considered themselves to be acting as soldiers, he felt public opinion demanded it. In 1999, the provincial government recognized a miscarriage of justice had occurred and granted a posthumous pardon to those executed. TINA LOO

By, John (1779–1836), military engineer. Lt-Col John By of the *Royal Engineers arrived at Chaudière Falls on the Ottawa River in the autumn of 1826, with orders to build a waterway 170 km through swampy wilderness to the British naval arsenal at Kingston, Upper Canada. The Rideau River canal and waterway were to provide a safe alternative for British soldiers and supplies should the Americans sever the vulnerable *St Lawrence River route. A Napoleonic War veteran and engineer on fortifications at Quebec City, By opened the waterway in 1832. It cost the British £800,000 and was one of the premier engineering works on the continent, consisting of 47 masonry locks and 52 dams. At its peak, 2,000 men worked on the project. Many lost their lives to construction hazards and contagious disease, including typhoid. Next to the magnificent headlocks By laid out a townsite, first named Bytown and in 1855 renamed *Ottawa, which would become the capital of the *Province of Canada and in 1867 Canada's capital. By returned to England to unproven criticisms of overspending. Though the largest landowner in Bytown, he never again saw the place.

JOHN H. TAYLOR

cabinet. The collective of members of federal or provincial legislatures holding ministerial portfolios, chosen and presided over by the prime minister or provincial premier. Constituting the government of the day, its members are individually and collectively responsible to the *House of Commons and theoretically can be brought down by a vote of no-confidence. In practice, party discipline limits this possibility and cabinet so dominates the business of Parliament and legislates increasingly by *order-in-council that concern has been expressed about cabinet 'dictatorship'. Expansion of government activities has tripled the original dozen portfolios, necessitating use of cabinet committees and the growth of such central agencies as the *Privy Council Office to service them. Such organizational arrangements and all ministerial and senior appointments are the prerogative of the prime minister, leading some to observe that cabinet dictatorship has been supplanted by prime ministerial dictatorship. However, a prime minister's cabinet making is constrained by the need in a federal state to maintain a balance of regional, linguistic, cultural, and functional interests. These collegial requirements suggest that, however powerful, a prime minister normally leads by persuasion rather than dictation. J.E. HODGETTS

Cabot, John (*c.* 1450–98), anglicized name of Zuan Cabotto, citizen of Venice (naturalized 1472), Black Sea merchant, pilot, and geographer. Cabot unsuccessfully promoted harbour developments in Valencia, Spain, then moved with wife Mattea and sons to Bristol, where merchants traded with Iceland and had backed explorations to Greenland and beyond. Like Columbus, Cabot assumed that the Atlantic was all that separated Europe from Asia. After an unproductive foray in 1496, Cabot's plan to reach Japan from the north and to establish trade was approved by Henry VII of England. In May 1497, he set sail with a crew of 18 in the 50-ton *Matthew*, likely following the old *Norse route to Greenland, and on 24 June reached North America—probably Newfoundland. If so, Cabot was first to apply new Mediterranean skills in celestial navigation to northern ideas of Atlantic geography. Although he never met Native people, he found their traces when he went ashore to plant a cross and the flags of England, the Pope, and Venice. Coasting northwards at least as far as the Strait of Belle Isle, between Newfoundland and Labrador, he then returned to Bristol, where his crew told tales of immense stocks of fish. In London, his geographic vision and trade estimates convinced Henry to invest in another voyage; several ships set sail in 1498, only to disappear. Cabot's son Sebastian became a celebrated pilot-cartographer who took credit for his father's explorations, so that for centuries John was forgotten. His memory was revived about 1897 and celebrated by British North American nationalists in Newfoundland and anglophone Canada. PETER E. POPE

cadets and the Strathcona Trust. Created in 1909 by Lord Strathcona, financier Donald *Smith, the trust funded cadet corps in order to provide expanded military training for school children. Modelled after British drill associations, the trust greatly expanded military drill in the school systems of Canada. First incorporated in Toronto in 1889 and already quite popular, the various cadet organizations throughout the country drilled and paraded at a variety of community gatherings. Through the trust, teachers were encouraged to learn and then teach the fundamentals of drill to young boys to prepare them for military duty. The patriotic goals of the trust merged with the attempt to inculcate highly honed physical responsiveness and obedience to authority. Like the *Boy Scouts, the cadet corps funded by Lord Strathcona reflected a society that deemed military education and physical fitness essential for the maintenance of a robust citizenry. After 1911, with the appointment of Sam *Hughes as federal minister of militia, the militaristic elements of cadet training increased significantly. By 1914, some 44,000 boys had drilled in the cadet corps. Some observers felt that Canada's success in the Great War was directly attributable to this development. Those who felt that the militarization of Canada's youth had gone too far met this notion with resistance. MARK MOSS

caisses populaires. In 1900, Alphonse Desjardins, a journalist and stenographer in the House of Commons, created the first caisse populaire at Lévis, Quebec. This caisse, much like the hundreds that followed, was designed as a co-operative institution that would collect the modest savings of French-speaking Catholics living within the limits of the parish. These savings were then loaned to reliable members needing funds to earn a living. Desjardins wanted each caisse to be autonomous so that local leaders, elected by the members, might assess the personal qualities of potential borrowers.

Over time Desjardins's original design has been abandoned, reflecting trends in the larger economy and the emergence of province-wide institutions serving all citizens. While Desjardins hoped to create a community-based institution, power was gradually concentrated in the hands of a bureaucracy, located symbolically at Lévis. This bureaucracy has managed the extension of the caisses into such areas as insurance to create a financial group known as the Mouvement Desjardins. Desjardins's prohibition against loans for unproductive purposes was abandoned as the caisses entered the field of consumer loans, and the institution that was designed for French-speaking Catholics was eventually made accessible to all.

RONALD RUDIN

Caledonian Games. Caledonian Societies developed in the early 1800s to assist newly arrived immigrants and to provide a forum for the expression of Scottish culture, including music, poetry, the celebration of Robert Burns Day and St Andrew's Day, and sports and athletics. The societies held annual picnics during the summer at which they showcased athletic events such as the hammer throw, stone throw, and caber toss. By the mid-19th century these picnics had become exceedingly popular, and the Caledonian Societies capitalized on the popularity of their athletics by holding separate annual games. By the 1860s, societies in Ontario, Quebec, and the northeastern United States often sent athletes to compete in each other's games. Since no standardized set of rules or regulations for equipment existed, the societies decided in 1870 to federate under an umbrella organization called the North American United Caledonian Association. During the ten years that followed, crowds flocked to the games, particularly in Montreal and Toronto.

GREG GILLESPIE

Calgary. Canada's sixth largest and third most ethnically diverse city (2000 pop. 860,749) looks westward to the Rocky Mountains, whose rugged snow-capped peaks form a natural backdrop to the city's impressive skyline. Situated on the northern edge of the short grass plains, the city's area of 721.73 sq km encompasses both prairie grasslands and rolling foothills, and straddles the valleys of the Bow and Elbow Rivers. Calgary's superb location is enhanced by a climate tempered by mild chinook winds, which help moderate the winter rigours of high-latitude climates.

Calgary, a Gaelic word meaning Bay Farm, originated as a *North-West Mounted Police post in 1875. Fort Calgary, whose main function was to deter the whisky traders operating among Native bands in the area, was situated at the confluence of two swift-flowing mountain streams. The settlement's future was assured with the arrival of the *Canadian Pacific Railway in 1883. The town was incorporated in November 1884 and nine years later became the first city west of Winnipeg in the North-West Territories. By 1896, rail links to the surrounding hinterland made Calgary the chief distributing centre in *Alberta and the urban focus of a thriving open-range beef cattle industry.

The agricultural settlement boom of the early 20th century saw Calgary's population reach almost 50,000 by 1912. Two years later, oil was discovered at Turner Valley southwest of the city, and although the field was never a major producer its presence established Calgary's primary position within the industry. Growth in the city was slow between 1914 and 1940, but accelerated during the Second World War and its immediate aftermath. Major oil discoveries at *Leduc in 1947, the development of irrigation, and a regional shift away from wheat to a more suitable mixed-farming economy combined to push Calgary to the forefront in Canada's urban hierarchy by 1960. Today Calgary is the nation's oil and gas capital and the financial centre of western Canada. The city ranks second nationally in head office locations and is a North American leader in communications, engineering research, and health sciences. Filmmaking and tourism have further diversified Calgary's economy.

Like other Canadian cities, Calgary is faced with problems associated with growth. Urban sprawl, a declining downtown retail core, widening socio-economic disparities, and the ecological disruptions consistent with urban life are urgent issues confronting planners and administrators at the millennium.

Calgary is a leading Canadian winter city. Its Alternative Level Pedestrian System counters winter's bite by allowing a comfortable 16 km indoor journey through the city's main buildings. Its two urban parks are among the world's largest and stand as a fitting tribute to a city whose urban life is always at nature's edge, winter and summer.

MAX FORAN

Calgary Stampede. The city of Calgary is recognized globally for its annual stampede, a time when the city dons its western garb, puts on its cowboy face, and treats visitors from around the world to the hospitality of the Old West. Originally a rodeo grafted onto an agricultural exhibition, the Calgary Exhibition and Stampede features one of the world's top *rodeos, and has given Calgary the most distinctive urban image in Canada. Ironically, when in 1912 the first stampede was promoted by American entrepreneur Guy Weadick, and backed financially by four Alberta ranchers, it was meant to be no more than a farewell tribute to the passing of the *ranching era. Resurrected in 1923 with the popular chuck wagon race, the stampede has become a cultural phenomenon and a powerful visible presence in the city. In 2000, over 1.2 million visitors spent $120 million enjoying the 'greatest outdoor show on earth'.

MAX FORAN

Calvinism, a Christian theological system rooted in biblical teaching, has five principles, defined simplistically as total depravity, unconditional election, limited atonement, the irresistibility of God's grace, and the final perseverance of the saints. Named for John Calvin (1509–64), French classical scholar and lay religious Reformer, the system evolved from his *Institutes of the Christian Religion* (1536), republished in expanded form in 1539 and 1559, which became a textbook of Reformed theology. Calvin eschewed too literal an interpretation of the Bible, but in reaction to rationalism he stressed the mystery of God's nature and intentions. The Bible is God's self-revelation to humankind, made recognizable by the Holy Spirit. As sovereign, creator, and sustainer, God directs all creation and foreordains all actions. Sin—willful alienation from God—can be reversed only by acceptance of Christ's redeeming death.

Calvinism holds that Scripture is the only rule of faith by which God, and one's duties to God and one's neighbour, can be known. The Old and New Testaments are of equal authority. Justification and salvation come by faith alone, rather than by good works. Calvinism presents a comprehensive view of how human life should be ordered—personally, socially, ecclesiastically, and politically—according to the will of God. Calvin believed strongly in the sacraments of baptism and communion but Calvinism, being individualistic and Word-centred, reduced their importance.

Some forms of Calvinism, concentrating on the doctrine of predestination—that God has chosen an elect group for salvation—became preoccupied with the outward signs that might identify the elect. For Calvin, however, predestination is primarily a doctrine of faith's final assurance. His work of religious reform inspired the spread of Calvinism in Canada, as well as in France, the Netherlands, Scotland, the United States, Australasia, and South Africa, and in each it indelibly influenced religious, social, and political development. From the time of Huguenot participation in New France's fur trade, Canadian Calvinists have been noted for resoluteness of will, moral perceptions, integrity, industriousness, and thriftiness, and for their strict sabbatarianism. These qualities have produced dynamic leadership in many areas, especially education and social reform movements.

JOHN S. MOIR

Camp X. Inaugurated in December 1941 outside Oshawa, Ontario, this was a Second World War training school for *security and intelligence operatives recruited in North and South America. Responsibility for developing the site—more correctly identified as Special Training School 103, or STS 103—lay with Sir William Stephenson, the Winnipeg-born head of British Security Coordination, a New York–based wartime agency operating under directives from London. The British Special Operations Executive (SOE) provided the commandants and instructors, while local staff and services were furnished by the Canadian military authorities. It also included a wireless facility, known as 'Hydra', for transmitting secret signals across the Atlantic. Briefly, after the war, it housed the Soviet defector Igor *Gouzenko and his family.

Despite its almost mythical reputation, Camp X's practical achievements, while significant, were limited. It provided introductory security courses to personnel from British-controlled factories in South America, and offered 'boot-camp' instruction to potential Canadian and American secret agents prior to more advanced training in Britain or the United States. Its historical importance lies principally in exemplifying Canada's often forgotten but crucial contribution to the making of the intelligence alliance with Britain and the United States during the Second World War.

DAVID STAFFORD

Camsell, Charles (1876–1958). Camsell went from the remote reaches of northern Canada to the halls of power in Ottawa. Born at Fort Liard in the Nahanni country of the North-West Territories, Camsell, the son of a Hudson's Bay Company trader, worked as a deck hand on barges on the Mackenzie River before pursuing graduate work in geology at Harvard University and the Massachusetts Institute of Technology. In 1900, he joined the *Geological Survey of Canada as a summer field assistant in the Great Bear Lake area. Fourteen years later, his position had been enlarged to 'geologist in charge of exploration'. Camsell was named deputy minister of mines in 1920, a position he held for almost 30 years. He was also one of the first appointees to the Northwest Territories council in 1921, eventually becoming commissioner from 1935 until his retirement in 1948. Despite his northern roots, Camsell resisted calls from the territories for self-government and saw nothing wrong with administration of the region from Ottawa. He also tried to keep the expenses of running the region to a minimum, while promoting northern development. He published his autobiography, *Son of the North*, in 1954.

BILL WAISER

'Canada'. The word first appears in Jacques *Cartier's journal of his second voyage as the expedition sailed past Anticosti Island on 13 August 1535, 'towards Canada', the home of his two kidnapped youthful Native 'informants', Taignoagny and Domagaya. Cartier used the word as if it meant the country inhabited by their father *Donnacona's people, stretching for about 50 km on either side of their principal village, Stadacona, located at the present site of Quebec City. Less commonly, he used Canada to mean the village of Stadacona. In his word-list from 'Canada and Hochelaga', Cartier indicated that Canada meant *une ville*. The Stadaconans spoke an Iroquoian language, similar but not identical to Huron or Mohawk. In Mohawk the word for village is *kanata*, while in Huron it is *andata*. As a place name, Canada became common on maps after its first appearance on a world map by Pierre Descelier in 1546. During the French regime it was synonymous with the name for the colony, Nouvelle-France. Regrettably, many writers, including modern ones, have made some remarkable nonsense out of the word, usually linking it to Spanish as in *Il capo di nada* or *cà nada*—'a cape of nothing' and 'here nothing'.

CONRAD HEIDENREICH

Canada and Its Provinces: A History of the Canadian People and Their Institutions, by one hundred associates (23 vols, 1913–17), was conceived by the publisher Robert Glasgow in 1909, and planned and edited by Arthur *Doughty, dominion archivist, and Adam Shortt, political economist at Queen's. The project, which aspired to cover the totality of Canadian history, relied on the efforts of many paid contributors and advisers, including academics, civil servants, and journalists. The editors drew a balance between the growth of Canada as a nation state and the diverse histories of its constituent parts: 12 volumes were devoted to New France, the Canadian colonies under British rule (1760–1840), United Canada (1840–67), and the dominion (its political evolution, industrial growth, and missions, arts, and letters). A further ten volumes traced the separate histories of the Atlantic provinces, Quebec, Ontario, the Prairie provinces, and British Columbia. (A final volume contained an index and bibliography.) Thanks to Shortt, considerable attention was devoted to natural resources, economic history, transportation, finance, trade unionism, immigration, and Indian policy. This comprehensive series—sold through subscription—was a major event in Canadian publishing, promoted by Glasgow, who had been sales agent for George Morang's *The Makers of Canada* (20 vols, 1903–8), a monument to the notion of history as biographies of outstanding men and a celebration of progress and self-government. In 1911, Glasgow incorporated the Publishers' Association of Canada (capitalized at $250,000) to carry through the production of *Canada and Its Provinces* and 'to open up a profitable market for the literary output of Canadian writers and investigators'. He went on to launch *The Chronicles of Canada* (32 vols, 1914–16), edited by George Wrong and Hugh H. Langton. This burst of publications on Canadian history in the first two decades of the last century attested to commercial opportunities and a genuine interest in the past during a period of unprecedented growth and national self-confidence.

CARL BERGER

Canada Assistance Plan, 1966–96. A national program through which Ottawa contributed 50 per cent of the cost of provincial social assistance. It was the product of four years of federal–provincial negotiations to develop an integrated national framework for assistance. Before CAP, Ottawa provided cost sharing for only certain 'deserving' categories of need: the elderly, the disabled, and the unemployed. CAP abolished such distinctions between the 'deserving' and 'undeserving' poor. 'The fact rather than the cause of need' became the only criterion for social assistance. CAP disallowed 'work tests' or 'residency tests' as a condition for receiving welfare. It also established the principle of a right to welfare by giving the poor the legal right to challenge denial or reduction of benefits. When CAP was abolished in 1996, national standards and the concept of a right to welfare disappeared. Work tests for the poor re-emerged in all Canadian provinces. Welfare now competes for funding with health care and post-secondary education in a single block grant—the Canada Health and Social Transfer. The product of the 1960s war on poverty, CAP ultimately fell victim to the 1990s war on the deficit.

JAMES STRUTHERS

Canada Cycle and Motor Company. Fearing the US bicycle cartel's plan to build a factory inside their protected market, and aware of the need to rationalize Canadian production, five leading bicycle manufacturers—Massey-Harris, Lozier, Gendron, Welland Vale, and the Goold Bicycle Company—merged in 1899 to form CCM. The company then accounted for 85 per cent of Canadian cycle production. In addition, CCM was briefly the Canadian agent for Ford, Winton, and Waverley cars before making its own car, the Russell (1905–15), as well as manufacturing motorcycles. After a difficult beginning, CCM was for many years the leading Canadian manufacturer of wheeled goods (cycles, wagons, children's toys), made in Weston, Ontario, and winter goods (skates, hockey equipment), manufactured near Iberville, Quebec. CCM was taken over by Levy Industries in 1962. Growing financial difficulties and strained labour relations in the 1970s led to operating losses, the company's sale in 1978 to the Cummings family of Montreal, a fleeting recovery, and then bankruptcy in 1983. The remaining assets were purchased by Procycle, located in St-Georges, Quebec, which created CCM (1983) Holdings Inc., owner of the CCM trademark worldwide, with 50 per cent held by Procycle (with a new range of CCM bicycles), and 50 per cent by Sport Maska (CCM winter goods). Both companies now use the CCM trademark.

GLEN NORCLIFFE

Canada East. *See* PROVINCE OF CANADA.

Canada First was the motto of five young men who met in Ottawa in 1868: George T. *Denison, who was lobbying for a military position; Henry Morgan, civil servant and journalist; Charles Mair, aspiring poet, who would soon move to Red River; William Foster, a Toronto lawyer; and Robert Grant Haliburton, a defender of Nova Scotia coal interests. Inspired by the recent political union of the colonies, the appeals of D'Arcy *McGee for a new nationality, and the expected acquisition by Canada of the huge *North-West Territories, they sought to invest Confederation with a patriotic spirit and national feeling by invoking, for example, Haliburton's idea of Canada as a northern nation inhabited by the descendants of hardy northern races. Their main impact, however, was in arousing Ontario opinion against the *Metis and French-Canadian Catholics who, in their minds, caused the *Red River Resistance, 1869–70, and threatened Canada's territorial expansion. The emotions they and their allies in Red River inflamed made a negotiated settlement difficult and a military expedition essential. The Canada Firsters were no less angered by the Treaty of Washington, 1871, in which Britain allegedly sacrificed Canadian interests for the sake of good relations with the United States: their reaction was to call for Canadian input into future treaty making. By 1874 the original members of Canada First dispersed, and their slogan was appropriated by a totally different group, centred in Toronto and supported by Goldwin *Smith, who formed the Canadian National Association, launched a journal (*The Nation*) and the Canada First Party. The party issued a manifesto calling for imperial consolidation and a Canadian voice in foreign policy, a national tariff for revenue, a vigorous immigration program, and electoral reform. This effort soon collapsed. The significance of Canada First lies more in what it represented and prefigured than in what it actually accomplished: it exemplified a distrust of the two political parties; an exclusive national feeling that was little more than Ontario expansionism; and, in its call for both imperial consolidation and a voice for Canada in external policy, an ambivalent attitude to empire.

CARL BERGER

Canada Pension Plan. A national pension system, funded by mandatory contributions from all employed persons and their employers, and portable from job to job across the country. The first national public pension system was introduced by W.L. Mackenzie *King's Liberal government in 1927, at the strong urging of the Progressive Party. This means-tested pension was available to Canadians who, at age 70, were sufficiently impoverished to qualify for it. In 1951 the scheme was modified to provide pensions to all Canadians over 70 who satisfied a residency requirement and to citizens aged 65 to 69 who could demonstrate need.

The introduction of the Canada Pension Plan in 1965 represented the second major revision to the system. Lester *Pearson's Liberals swept to power in 1963; pension reform was among the policies initiated during the government's first two months in office. Internal debates within the party, combined with well-defined alternative pension plans presented by both Ontario and Quebec, slowed the policy process. After several federal–provincial conferences in 1963–4, an agreement was finally reached. Based largely on the design of the Quebec Pension Plan—which was wholly compatible but administered separately—the CPP provided earnings-related benefits to retired Canadians. Taken together, the CPP/QPP offered universal, contributory, portable pensions and gave governments at both levels the opportunity to invest pension contributions. This latter quality has subsequently led to the declining benefits available under the plans.

P.E. BRYDEN

Canada Savings Bonds. Since 1946, Canada Savings Bonds have been issued every autumn. Their precursors, War Savings Certificates and Victory Bonds, helped finance both world wars and were promoted through massive media and poster campaigns. Fully backed by government, the bonds are considered to be a low-risk and reliable form of investment, but with minimum guaranteed returns. Their continued popularity is linked to their safety and security, and the ease and flexibility with which they can be purchased and redeemed. In recent years they have undergone many innovations, including the broadening of eligibility and periods of purchase, the payment of annual interest, and the convenience of online purchasing. Over one-and-a-half million Canadians currently hold Canadian Savings Bonds; recent marketing strategies have sought to broaden the consumer base by appealing to young Canadians. As a form of investment in Canada, the bonds, like their wartime equivalents, have been imbued with nationalist sentiments. Questions of sovereignty reared their head in 2001 when aspects of sales, marketing, and distribution were outsourced to an American-based computer-services company.

EMILY GILBERT

Canada West. *See* PROVINCE OF CANADA.

Canadian Arctic Expedition, 1913–16/18. This expedition was Canada's most ambitious exploration of the Canadian Arctic. At the beginning of the 20th century Canada's claim of sovereignty over the Arctic was incomplete and shaky. Other countries, especially the United States, had just as valid claims to islands in the archipelago. By 1912, to forestall further American exploration, the Canadian government under the leadership of Sir Robert *Borden persuaded the Americans to relinquish a planned arctic expedition. The Canadian government appointed a seasoned explorer, Vilhjalmur *Stefansson, overall commander; second-in-command was Rudolph Martin Anderson. Along with asserting Canadian sovereignty, and finding new lands, the goal of the expedition was to conduct the first scientific studies of the Arctic from the Mackenzie Delta westward, including hydrographical and magnetic readings, and studies of the Natives, geology and geography, marine and terrestrial biology, and the general flora and fauna. Stefansson's Northern Section would use the ship *Karluk* to explore the waters north of the Canadian mainland. Disaster struck in the early fall of 1913 when *Karluk* was crushed by the ice, causing the loss of 11 men. Stefansson continued his section of the expedition virtually alone, and by 1918 had accomplished some remarkable feats of exploration; travelling thousands of kilometres over hazardous ice, he discovered the last major islands in the archipelago and revealed the existence of subterranean canyons beneath the Beaufort Sea. The Southern Section under Anderson returned in 1916 with a wealth of scientific data that would further Canada's knowledge of the region.

RICHARD J. DIUBALDO

Canadian army. The term 'Canadian army' has long served as a generic though unofficial term describing Canada's ground-based military forces. The modern Canadian army can trace its origins to the 1855 Militia Act adopted in the *Province of Canada, which created military units staffed by part-time soldiers. In 1871, four years after Confederation, the *British garrison left Canada, and the dominion formed its first full-time, or regular, military units. This *Permanent Force was supplemented by the Non-Permanent Active Militia made up of part-time volunteers staffing second-line units. During the First World War, Canada's large army overseas was known as the *Canadian Expeditionary Force. The terms 'Permanent Force' and 'NPAM' returned to common usage with the disbanding of the CEF at the end of the war. During the Second World War, Canada again dispatched a substantial force overseas, this time called the Canadian Active Service Force. At this time, the term 'army' was increasingly applied, though not formally adopted. In 1942, Canadian ground forces overseas were organized as First Canadian Army. Here, the term refers to a field formation serving as part of the army overseas. In 1946, following the war, the 'Canadian army' officially comprised the Canadian Army Active Force, supported by a part-time Reserve Force. This nomenclature was subsequently changed to the Canadian Army (Regular) and Canadian Army (Reserve), respectively. The Canadian force dispatched to the Korean War was known as the Canadian Army Special Force.

In 1964, in a bid to avoid costly duplication of effort, Ottawa integrated most logistical and command structures of the army, navy, and air force. A year later, Mobile Command came into existence as the successor organization to the Canadian Army. In 1968, all three services were unified into the Canadian Armed Forces. By the 1980s, Mobile Command was commonly referred to as Land Forces Command, a change made official in 1992. Despite this, the military establishment continued to use the term 'army' both formally and informally.

SERGE DURFLINGER

Canadian Army Medical Corps. Although, strictly speaking, the history of the CAMC spans the period 1904–59, medical units—field ambulances and stretcher-bearer companies—had been active since the mid-19th century. In addition, many individuals served as medical officers with infantry regiments and other units in peacetime, in the northwest campaign of 1885, and in the *South African War, 1899–1902. The CAMC was, however, more than a bureaucratic hierarchy superimposed on an existing system; it provided a chain of command by which, for example, a medical officer could force a battalion commander to have his troops inoculated against typhus. With such authority the CAMC provided medical units, some as small as seven-member hygiene sections, others large enough to run hospitals with a capacity of 2,000, during both world wars. In Korea, the corps provided evacuation and treatment ranging from the front line to hospital facilities in Kure, Japan. In the post-war period, numerous individuals and small units served on peacekeeping operations. In 1959 the CAMC was amalgamated with the medical services of the navy and air force to become the Canadian Forces Medical Service. Since then, through various reorganizations, it has provided medical support to the armed forces, including a field hospital in the *Persian Gulf War, as well as to dependants and other civilians in areas adjacent to Canadian Forces facilities. BILL RAWLING

Canadian Army Pacific Force. The Sixth Canadian Division, commanded by Major-General B.M. Hoffmeister, was slated to participate in Operation Coronet, the American-led invasion of the Japanese home island of Kyushu, in 1946. That invasion did not take place, thanks to Japan's surrender in September 1945. Over 30,000 Canadian troops joined the CAPF after Prime Minister Mackenzie *King ruled that only volunteers (and not draftees) could be sent to fight in the Pacific. Following the example set at *Kiska in 1943, the Canadian force was to serve under American command, and was to be organized along American tactical lines. British attempts to attach the unit to a Commonwealth corps failed as both the Canadian army and King's government believed national interests would be better served by operating with the Americans. Indeed, the army's modest proposal of a reinforced division participating in the invasion of Japan fared much better with King than did far more ambitious Royal Canadian Navy and Royal Canadian Air Force plans to send extensive forces to co-operate with the British in southeast Asia. Still, Generals George C. Marshall and Douglas MacArthur manifested little enthusiasm for including Canadian troops in their forces. President Franklin Roosevelt intervened in autumn 1944 to ensure that the Canadian army would be invited to take part in the invasion of Japan. Had the invasion gone ahead, and had serious casualties ensued, the CAPF might have faced a manpower crisis such as the one that had plagued the Canadian army in northwest Europe in 1944.

GALEN ROGER PERRAS

Canadian Art Club, 1907–15. Established in Toronto in 1907 to advance the standards of Canadian art exhibitions and to exhibit the work of Canadian expatriate artists at home. The annual exhibitions organized in Toronto, and in Montreal in 1910, included the finest work being produced by Canadian artists. Membership included painters and sculptors and was by invitation only. Edmund Morris (1871–1913) and Homer Watson (1855–1936) were key figures in its formation and the first exhibition included work by Horatio Walker (1858–1938), working in New York since 1885, and James Wilson Morrice (1865–1924) of Paris (since 1890). Later expatriate exhibitors included Ernest Lawson (1873–1939), James Kerr-Lawson (1862–1939), and the sculptor Phimister Proctor (1860–1950). Montreal members included Clarence Gagnon (1881–1942), W.H. Clapp (1879–1954), Marc-Aurèle de Foy Suzor-Coté (1869–1937), and Henri Hébert (1884–1950).

The club sought a compromise between Old World forms or genres and New World content or themes without giving primacy to either. It promoted individual expression over any particular aesthetic, as evidenced by the late Barbizon art of Walker, the Nabis-influenced Morrice, and the impressionists Lawson and Suzor-Coté; exhibitions included European, American, and Canadian subject matter. The death of Morris in 1913, the economic effects of the war, and internal conflicts resulted in the cessation of exhibitions in 1915. CHARLES C. HILL

Canadian Authors' Association. A national body headquartered in southern Ontario, the CAA has 12 branches across Canada and is affiliated with the Société des écrivains canadiens. Approximately 100 authors first convened at McGill University in 1921 to oppose controversial copyright legislation. Prominent writers such as Bliss Carman, Stephen *Leacock, and Sir Charles G.D. Roberts were among the resulting association's founders.

A self-governing Section française was formed, and later a number of provincial and regional branches, some of which became significant organizations in their own right. The CAA initially focused on questions of literary property. It pressed for amendments to the 1924 Canadian Copyright Act, and in 1946 began a 40-year campaign for a public lending rights program (and is now represented on the executive of the Public Lending Rights Commission). It has undertaken initiatives to support new writers, reward literary achievement, and promote Canadian books. In 1936 it established the Governor General's Literary Awards (administered by the Canada Council since 1960), and has given its own CAA awards since 1975. For 36 years (until 1957) it co-ordinated Canadian Book Week, and later experimented with other forms of literary promotion including book festivals. While some of its activities were assumed by the Writers' Union of Canada (1973), the CAA continues to encourage new writers and to monitor conditions of intellectual property under changing technologies. HEATHER MURRAY

Canadian Auto Workers. Increasing disenchantment with the 'concessions bargaining' of the international leadership of the United Auto Workers led to the negotiated departure of the union's Canadian Region in 1985. Regional director Bob White led the negotiations that ended a half-century of international unity. Under his presidency, the Canadian Auto Workers was launched in 1986. Temporarily favourable markets and the Canadian state's hesitancy to embrace neo-liberalism helped it win back some of the 'giveaways' of the early 1980s, but neither White nor his successor, Buzz Hargrove, managed to stem the long-term decline of Canada's auto and aerospace manufacturing workforce. Though the CAW doubled its membership between 1986 and 2000, today barely 45 per cent of its 250,000 members are employed in its core constituency. It grew by means of mergers (notably with the Canadian Brotherhood of Transport and General Workers in 1994) and aggressive recruitment—or, as some union rivals still charge, cannibalistic 'raiding'. The CAW prefers to view itself as the true heir of Walter Reuther's 'social unionism'—the democratic vanguard of a racially and sexually egalitarian (30 per cent of its members are women) labour movement. JOHN MANLEY

Canadian Bar Association. The CBA, launched at a national conference in 1914, had grown out of the Manitoba Bar Association and largely under the leadership of Manitoba lawyers, notably founding president James Aikins. Never a regulatory body, it existed within 'civil society' as part of the network of associational life that characterized early 20th century Canada.

The CBA was a creature of reform-minded, unabashedly elite lawyers who thought law central to Canada's well-being: the founders believed that a reformed legal profession was essential if Canada's diverse, far-flung peoples were to remain united as a British dominion. The CBA sought to spur provincial *law societies (the profession's regulatory bodies) into action, gaining pre-eminence among an array of similarly minded local bar associations and law student organizations. Its leadership was widely felt, powerfully shaping emergent patterns of professionalism. A fundamental transformation of common law structures of legal professionalism (Quebec was a different matter) took place involving significant reforms in education and admission, professional ethics, the regulatory powers of professional organizations, and the assertion of a lawyer's monopoly over 'legal' services. Many of its goals having been achieved during the first two decades of its existence, after the Second World War the CBA became more committed to advancing lawyers' interests than seeking actively to contribute to state formation.

W. WESLEY PUE

Canadian Broadcasting Corporation. Canadian *broadcasting first developed in the private sector. Of the approximately 80 stations operating by the end of the 1920s, some in the larger cities were prosperous, but most were short of revenue and could provide only mediocre programs that compared unfavourably with the shows most Canadians could hear from the powerful American stations across the border. Constructing a Canadian national network was almost impossible, given the long distances and high costs of wireline connections.

Radio development during the 1920s was regulated by the Radio Branch of the Department of Marine and Fisheries. In early 1928, the branch refused to renew the licences of five stations owned by the organization now called the *Jehovah's Witnesses because of complaints about the anti-establishment sermons they were broadcasting. When the cancellation blew up into a 'free speech' issue in the House of Commons, the Liberal government hastily created a royal commission to look into the general state of Canadian radio.

The commission, comprising chair Sir John Aird along with Charles Bowman and Augustin Frigon, held several months of hearings and produced a brief report in late 1929. Convinced that a national network was needed to provide Canadian programs for Canadian listeners, and fearing the encroachment of the American networks, the commissioners made a radical recommendation: the creation of a government company to control and run all Canadian broadcasting. The private stations were to be closed down, with compensation.

Shortly after the Aird *Report* was released, the Depression began and the Liberals were voted out of office. That the new Conservative government did not file the *Report* in that great mausoleum that holds the recommendations of most other royal commissions may be credited mainly to the lobbying efforts of the Canadian Radio League. Headed by young nationalist activists Graham *Spry and Alan Plaunt, the CRL championed public ownership of broadcasting and deplored commercialized American radio. It successfully reminded the new prime minister, R.B. *Bennett, of the political potential of a national radio network, and of the dangers of Americanization. In

Spry's most famous aphorism, the choice was between 'the State and the United States'.

A government monopoly was too much for Parliament to swallow. The Radio Broadcasting Act of 1932 created a public broadcaster, the Canadian Radio Broadcasting Commission, but allowed private stations to continue to coexist alongside both it and its successor, the Canadian Broadcasting Corporation, created in 1936. The CRBC and CBC were funded until 1952 by the income from licence fees paid by each set owner supplemented by some advertising income. The total revenues were insufficient for the public broadcaster to set up a national network of its own stations; instead, affiliation agreements were worked out with many private stations whereby they carried a certain number of CRBC/CBC programs. Thus the introduction of public broadcasting in Canada, coming as it did after ten years of private-sector development, entailed a compromise that resulted in a 'mixed' system. While the CRBC/CBC ran the only national network and had regulatory authority over all stations, private radio not only survived but flourished.

The CBC came into its own during the war years, providing war news and commentary and developing innovative musical and dramatic programming. It also provided Canadians with the most popular American comedy and variety programs. A separate French network, Radio-Canada, was set up in the late 1930s, and a second English-language network in 1944. In the early 1950s the CBC was given the authority to begin the development of television stations and networks. Until 1960 only CBC-owned or -affiliated television stations were allowed to broadcast in Canada, but much of their most popular and lucrative programming, as with the old radio network, originated in the United States.

Currently, with two privately owned national networks to compete with, as well as a multitude of cable and specialty channels, the CBC has become a minor player in the Canadian television world. Struggling to define its role, and wounded by severe budget cutbacks in the 1990s, CBC television now offers almost entirely Canadian content in the prime evening hours, but attracts only about 15 per cent of the English-speaking audience. CBC Radio, commercial-free since 1975, has an audience of only 10 per cent of Canadians. French-language radio and television are somewhat healthier, but they also must battle for listeners in the marketplace. The CBC and Radio-Canada remain alternatives to the profit-oriented North American broadcasting model, but because their funding comes mainly from federal government grants, they remain vulnerable to budgetary choices made by politicians elected by people who mainly tune in elsewhere.

MARY VIPOND

Canadian Brotherhood of Railway Employees. Formed in Moncton in 1908 by employees of the federally owned *Intercolonial Railway, the CBRE found visionary leadership in Aaron R. Mosher, and bitter rivalry from US-based international railroad brotherhoods. To benefit from the organizational vacuum left by railway nationalization, Mosher moved CBRE headquarters to Ottawa, but when Frank Hall mobilized the Brotherhood of Railway and Steamship Clerks to resist, the Trades and Labor Congress was bound by its by-laws to defend internationals against Mosher's national union. In 1921, the TLC expelled the CBRE. By 1925, Mosher mustered fragments of several other national labour organizations in an All-Canadian Congress of Labour as a platform for his many ideas and as readers for W.T. Burford's vitriolic denunciations of international unions. In the 1940s, the ACCL evolved into the Canadian Congress of Labour, a Canadian wing of the Congress of Industrial Organizations. Renamed the Canadian Brotherhood of Railway Transport and General Workers, the CBRE grew to be Canada's fifth biggest union in the 1950s and then declined, with its industry. It merged with the *Canadian Auto Workers in 1994. DESMOND MORTON

Canadian Cavalry Brigade. The brigade was formed on 28 January 1915 from the Royal Canadian Dragoons, Lord Strathcona's Horse, the Royal Canadian Horse Artillery, and a British unit later replaced by the Fort Garry Horse. Command was held during most of the war by Brig. Gen. J.E.B. Seely, a former British secretary of war. It reinforced the Canadian division after the second Battle of *Ypres, and served mainly with the British 5th Cavalry Division. At Cambrai, units of the brigade engaged the German Corps; daring mounted and dismounted counterattacks slowed the German offensive at Moreuil Wood on 30 March 1918, a charge recalled in paintings by Sir Alfred Munnings. DESMOND MORTON

Canadian Charter of Rights and Freedoms. *See* CHARTER OF RIGHTS AND FREEDOMS.

Canadian Clubs. The first Canadian Club was founded in Hamilton, Ontario, in 1892, soon followed by others in cities coast to coast, and after 1909 by a parallel set of Women's Canadian Clubs. Their stated purpose was 'to foster Canadian patriotism and to stimulate intelligent citizenship'. Most of the members were young businessmen, meeting for monthly luncheons to hear addresses by local or visiting dignitaries. Forty of the clubs came together in a national organization, the Association of Canadian Clubs, in 1909. The clubs weakened during the First World War and declined further in the early 1920s as they met competition from service clubs that had spread from the United States. Prodded by prominent Winnipeg lawyer E.J. Tarr, the association reawakened in the mid-1920s, adopting a new constitution and setting up a national secretariat in Ottawa. Espousing a rather conservative British-oriented view of Canada, Tarr nonetheless advocated the promotion of national unity and identity through the spread of knowledge about Canada. The Ottawa office was given the responsibility of organizing information and speaker exchanges so that the Canadian Club movement could effectively provide leadership in moulding a national public opinion. The first full-time secretary was Graham *Spry, then a young

Oxford graduate and former employee of the International Labour Office, but later well known as a leading promoter of Canadian public broadcasting. Under his aegis the association initiated the very successful three-day celebration of the diamond jubilee of Confederation in 1927.

In 1939 the association was incorporated by the federal government, with the stated purpose of fostering an interest in public affairs and cultivating an attachment to Canadian institutions. There are now 52 member clubs, 44 of them in Canada, and the Ottawa office of the association continues to facilitate speakers' tours, publications, and a Web site. MARY VIPOND

Canadian Coast Guard. From the creation of the Dominion of Canada, the government has maintained a fleet of civilian-crewed ships. Its duties include icebreaking, servicing navigation aids, search and rescue, regulating the fisheries, hydrographic survey, scientific research, and arctic operations. Initially, these duties came under the Department of Marine and Fisheries (established 22 April 1868). By 1936, the marine service had become a branch of the Department of Transport, while fisheries and the hydrographic service were under other ministries. A major change came on 26 January 1962, when Transport Canada's fleet was renamed the Canadian Coast Guard. The change of name, and the introduction of a readily recognized red-and-white paint scheme for the ships, acknowledged the need for an organization that could further national objectives, especially in the Arctic. The Coast Guard also included ship inspection, emergency response, vessel traffic control, and radio communication branches. On 1 April 1995, responsibility for the Coast Guard, except for its regulatory functions, was transferred from Transport Canada to the Department of Fisheries and Oceans, which by then operated the fisheries and scientific vessels. The two fleets were merged, thus returning to the arrangement in force in 1868. In 2002 the Coast Guard operated 40 major ships and many smaller craft. CHARLES D. MAGINLEY

Canadian Congress of Labour. *See* CANADIAN LABOUR CONGRESS.

Canadian Corps. Formed on 13 September 1915 when the 2nd Canadian Division joined the 1st Division in France, the corps was the main fighting formation of the *Canadian Expeditionary Force. A veteran British infantry officer, Lt Gen. E.A.H. Alderson, was the first commander. A 3rd Division was formed mainly from units in France in December 1915, and a 4th Division crossed from Canada to England in August 1916. Forced out as a scapegoat for the Canadian performance at the St Eloi Craters and as a critic of the *Ross rifle, Alderson was replaced on 29 May 1916 by Lt Gen. Sir Julian Byng, a popular commander who led the corps through the Battle of the Somme and its first collective victory, during Easter 1917, at *Vimy Ridge, a success that owed much to his support of innovative tactics and painstaking preparation. Success led to Byng's promotion on 9 June 1917, and a Canadian successor, Lt Gen. Sir Arthur *Currie from the 1st Division. Currie led the corps through hard fighting at Lens in August 1917 and completion of the miserable British offensive at *Passchendaele in October and November. He resisted British pressure to create a second corps and a small Canadian army. Instead, Currie insisted on breaking up the 5th Canadian Division in England and using the men for extra infantry, artillery, and especially the nine new pioneer battalions that allowed the Canadian Corps to win the costly, decisive, and now half forgotten victories at *Amiens, the Drocourt-Quéant Line, the Canal du Nord, and Cambrai, in the last Hundred Days of the war. The corps and its four divisions, with their respective rectangular red, blue, grey, and green patches, became a defining national institution for a young country. DESMOND MORTON

Canadian Council of Churches. Founded in 1944 at a meeting of ten Christian denominations at Yorkminster Baptist Church in Toronto, the Canadian Council of Churches is a bilingual organization that exists to promote unity, coordination, and support for its member churches in areas such as education, social service, and evangelization. In pursuit of its mandate, it facilitates consultation, common planning, and action among Canadian churches; promotes ecumenical understanding; and relates to the World Council of Churches and other agencies serving world-wide ecumenism. The organizational structure of the council includes a general secretary, governing board, executive committee, and two commissions, each of which is staffed by an associate secretary. The Commission on Faith and Witness engages the churches in theological study and interfaith dialogue, while the Commission on Justice and Peace is a forum for planning and co-operation in matters of social justice and peace. The council also sponsors special initiatives and projects, and is linked to a number of faith-based agencies and advocacy groups in Canada. Since its inception, it has grown to 19 member churches, as well as a number of observer denominations, representing millions of Christians across Canada. TERRENCE MURPHY

Canadian Expeditionary Force. The CEF, which was formed by the soldiers Canada sent overseas in the First World War, was initially accepted as an 'imperial' component of the British Army, but, from September 1916, was under a minister of the *Overseas Military Forces of Canada based in London. By war's end, subject to British direction of operations, Ottawa's authority extended to its troops in France. The CEF became the army of a junior but effectively sovereign ally. Although the CEF was initially authorized to enlist 25,000 soldiers, 31,000 members sailed for England in October 1914. The 1st Canadian Division sailed for France in February 1915; the 2nd Division followed in September, forming a *Canadian Corps. The 3rd and 4th Divisions were formed in 1916, and a 5th Division was formed in England but broken up for reinforcements in March 1918. The CEF included a

*Canadian Cavalry Brigade, serving in France, Canadian Railway Troops in France and the Middle East, Canadian Forestry Corps companies cutting trees in France and Britain, and several units serving in North Russia and Siberia at the end of the war. A total of 619,636 officers and other ranks served in the CEF, of whom 142,488 were conscripted under the Military Service Act; 424,389 served overseas; and 59,544 died on active service, not counting Canadians killed with the British flying services or in other Allied forces. DESMOND MORTON

Canadian Federation of Labour. Disillusionment with the American-dominated Trades and Labor Congress led to the formation in 1902–3 of the National Trades and Labor Congress, which in 1908 was renamed the Canadian Federation of Labour. The CFL was characterized by class collaboration, opposition to strikes, and unwillingness to organize industrial unions. Struggling to maintain a membership of roughly 10,000, the CFL merged with the All-Canadian Congress of Labour in 1927. In 1982 a new CFL, based in the building trades, emerged out of opposition to the policies of the *Canadian Labour Congress. In 1997, the International Brotherhood of Electrical Workers left the CFL to rejoin the CLC; the following year the CFL failed to appear in the *Directory of Labour Organizations in Canada*.

PETER CAMPBELL

Canadian Forum. Until its demise in 2000, the *Canadian Forum* was for 80 years the foremost periodical of the arts, literature, and opinion in English Canada. Founded at the University of Toronto in 1920, the journal was, for most of its existence, edited from Toronto and co-operatively owned. Its outlook throughout was nationalist and progressive and its politics were usually leftist, so it never attracted much advertising. Because subscription revenue was not enough to keep it going, the *Forum* relied on patronage and gifts. Until 1934 the publishing firm of J.M. Dent and Sons covered the annual deficits; later the *Canadian Forum* Sustaining Fund, created by Eric A. Havelock, served that purpose for many years.

The names of editors, writers, and artists constitute a who's who of the Canadian intellectual, literary, and artistic worlds. From Barker Fairley and Graham *Spry to Robert Chodos and Denis Smith, Frank *Scott and Earle Birney to Margaret Atwood and Rudy Wiebe, Frank *Underhill and Eugene *Forsey to Abraham Rotstein and Rick Salutin, the *Forum*'s editors and contributors commanded attention. Often, though, their views were too far from the comfortable Canadian mainstream to exercise wide influence. MICHIEL HORN

Canadian Good Roads Association. The CGRA was formed in 1914 and incorporated officially in August 1917. Its purpose was to act as a clearinghouse for information relating to highway legislation as well as to encourage improved road construction and maintenance techniques throughout Canada. Its annual meetings provided an important national forum for the exchange of information and ideas among highway authorities both within and outside the country. For example, the association was instrumental in lobbying for federal funding for the construction of the *Trans-Canada Highway.

By the 1950s the CGRA undertook to develop national road-construction standards, establishing a Geometric Design Committee in 1958. The work of the committee resulted in the 1963 publication *A Manual of Geometric Design Standards for Canadian Roads and Streets*. In 1970 the association changed its name to the Roads and Transportation Association of Canada and again in 1990 to the Transportation Association of Canada.

DAVID W. MONAGHAN

Canadian Institute of International Affairs. Following the end of the First World War there was a widespread conviction that broad-based understanding of international relations was essential to prevent the recurrence of war. Organizations devoted to the study of international affairs popped up in Britain and the United States. In 1928, the CIIA was established as a non-partisan, non-political, and non-official organization with a mandate to deepen public understanding of international affairs. Its early members included luminaries from business, the media, and politics. It had 144 members in its inaugural year; Escott *Reid was the first national secretary. The CIIA continues to bring together academics, journalists, business leaders, government officials, and members of the general public to consider pressing issues in international relations, as well as Canada's role in the wider world. The CIIA's educational mandate has been developed through the John Holmes library, essay competitions, and its two principal publications: *Behind the Headlines* is a magazine devoted to topical issues, while the *International Journal*, one of Canada's leading international relations journals since its inception in 1946, publishes scholarly works. In 2003 there were 15 branches across the country and a membership of approximately 1,200.

FRANCINE MCKENZIE

Canadian Labour Congress. Founded in 1956, the CLC is a national umbrella organization of provincial federations of labour and national and international *unions, drawn from the private and public sector. Funded by its dues-paying members, the congress performs three basic tasks: pressuring governments for better labour laws; supporting its members, in cash and kind, when they are organizing, bargaining, or on strike; and providing a framework within which intra-union conflicts can be resolved. In 2002, the CLC represented 2.5 million workers, making it the largest and most influential labour centre in Canada.

The CLC resulted from a merger between two rival organizations, the Trades and Labor Congress (TLC) and the Canadian Congress of Labour (CCL). Established in 1886, the TLC represented skilled workers, such as machinists, printers, and carpenters, who belonged to craft unions. At first, the TLC's membership was a mixture of independent Canadian unions and US-based outfits affiliated with the *American Federation of Labor (AFL), the TLC's southern counterpart. By the First World War, however, the vast majority of Canadian unionists belonged to American unions, whose leaders saw Canada as simply another state. Politically moderate, the TLC faced challenges from more radical union centres such as the *Industrial Workers of the World and *Workers' Unity League. Diverse in philosophy, these organizations shared a common belief in industrial as opposed to craft unionism: all workers, regardless of skill level, needed to be unionized. The AFL was beset by similar tensions, and finally split in 1935 when the Congress of Industrial Organizations (CIO), which endorsed industrial unionism, was formed. Five years later, Canadian supporters of the CIO, many of whom had roots in the *Co-operative Commonwealth Federation and the *Communist Party of Canada, formed the CCL. Against the backdrop of the Cold War, the TLC and CCL battled each other as much as they fought hostile employers and governments. By 1954, the two rivals had formally agreed to stop poaching each others' members. They completed a merger in 1956, forming the CLC.

At the CLC's founding convention, delegates called for greater independence from the newly minted AFL-CIO. The question of participation in party politics was hotly debated too—pitting former TLC unions, which favoured a non-partisan stance, against ex-CCL organizations, which saw electoral struggles as an extension of union activity. The congress decided against backing a new labour party, but left the door open to its members to take action; many did, helping to create the New Democratic Party in 1961. Forty years later, this agonizing debate continues, complicated further by the influx of women and people of colour into the workforce, and the politics of Quebec unionists, whose strong support for *separatism has limited the CLC's presence in the province.

ANDREW PARNABY AND GREGORY S. KEALEY

Canadian Manufacturers' Association. Part of associational trends of the late 19th century, the CMA was rooted in protectionism. Antecedent organizations like the Ontario Manufacturers' Association (est. 1874) advocated the high tariffs that culminated in the *National Policy of 1879, when attempts to create a national association for tariff lobbying failed. Various organizations thereafter, including the CMA (est. 1887 but at that point Torontonian), continued sporadic tariff lobbying. Reorganized in 1900, incorporated in 1902, the CMA was no monolith dictating tariff policy. It was a flawed peak association undermined by internal friction, independent lobbying, and free riders. Defence of protectionism was delegated to the subordinate Canadian Home Market Association in the election of 1911; the CMA increasingly emphasized education on non-tariff issues to minimize internal differences. BEN FORSTER

Canadian Medical Association. Established in 1867 at a gathering of 167 doctors in Quebec City, the CMA now represents most of Canada's 59,000 physicians through affiliations with provincial and territorial associations. Dr Charles *Tupper, later prime minister of Canada, was the first president. Headquartered in Ottawa, the CMA serves scientific, ethical, and political ends; economic issues are pursued through individual provincial associations. More than 40 medical specialty bodies and scientific societies are associated with the association, which publishes the *Canadian Medical Association Journal* (founded in 1911), organizes annual scientific meetings, and provides investment and other services to its members.

CHARLES G. ROLAND

Canadian Movement. This term was used to refer to a disparate group of Canadian organizations that emerged following the First World War to promote Canadian sovereignty within the British *Commonwealth as well as Canadian national unity, culture, education, and Canadian–American understanding. The movement centred around the Association of Canadian Clubs, the Canadian League, the *Canadian Institute of International Affairs, and the League of Nations Society. Many of the leaders of the movement were war veterans whose patriotism and sense of Canadian identity had been strengthened in the trenches. Though small in numbers, the adherents were young, educated, vigorous, and generally well connected. Their ambition to influence events was not unreasonable in a Canada that was governed by a tiny political and bureaucratic establishment. Their signal achievement was the establishment in 1932 of the government-owned Canadian Radio Broadcasting Commission (later the *CBC) . D.J. BERCUSON

Canadian National Railways. CN was incorporated as a Crown corporation in 1919, when the Canadian government nationalized the financially troubled transcontinental Canadian Northern Railway system and amalgamated it with Canadian Government Railways (formerly the *Intercolonial Railway) in the Maritime provinces. In 1923 the country's largest railway, the *Grand Trunk Railway, was also nationalized and became a part of CN. The Grand Trunk system at the time included its own lines in eastern Canada, the subsidiary Grand Trunk Western Railroad to Chicago, the Grand Trunk Pacific Railway from Winnipeg to Prince Rupert, British Columbia, the government-built but Grand Trunk-leased National Transcontinental Railway from Winnipeg to Quebec City, and several smaller lines. Other railways, including the moribund *Hudson Bay Railway, were added to CN later.

Most of the amalgamated railways had received financial assistance from federal and/or provincial governments, usually in the form of bond guarantees. In return they agreed to provide services, sometimes at stipulated rates, which were not directly linked to operating costs. These obligations, combined with the massive indebtedness of the component companies, made it virtually impossible for CN to operate profitably. A further difficulty was related to the fact that construction of these various lines had proceeded without much planning.

Integrating the various lines, which had previously been competitive, required the construction of new links between the different systems, and the abandonment of duplicate lines and facilities. In addition, the work environment and culture of each system was unique, making the merging of management teams and workers difficult.

Sir Henry Thornton, who was appointed president of the amalgamated railways in 1923, worked hard to integrate the company's multifarious operations. CN also inherited from its predecessor companies numerous telegraph, township-development, land, hotel, rolling-stock, shipping, ferrying, manufacturing, and repair companies. These were further expanded in the 1920s when CN developed the country's first network of radio stations, which later became the *Canadian Broadcasting Corporation; it broadcast, among other things, programs such as *Hockey Night in Canada*. In 1937, CN also organized Canada's first government-owned airline, Trans-Canada Airlines (now Air Canada).

The company found it difficult, in the best of times, to pay the fixed charges on its enormous debt. It could not do so under the depressed economic conditions of the 1930s, even after resorting to controversial and difficult reductions in wages, the dismissal of many of its employees, and drastic cutbacks on some of its services. In an effort to streamline rail operations, the federal government passed the Canadian National–Canadian Pacific Act, which directed the two very different and fiercely competitive companies to co-operate in effecting operating economies. Even with those economies, CN escaped bankruptcy during the Depression only because the federal government paid most of the fixed charges and eventually cancelled much of the company's debt.

Under the presidency of Donald Gordon in the 1950s, CN converted its motive power from steam to electric-diesel locomotives, modernized its equipment, reduced its commitment to unprofitable passenger service, and sought authorization to abandon uneconomic branch lines. Together with other railways, CN lobbied successfully for federal financial assistance to support uneconomic services, most notably prairie grain carried under the terms of the *Crow's Nest Pass Agreement, Maritime freight carried under arrangements the federal government had made with the eastern provinces, and continued maintenance and service on unprofitable branch lines. The company formed its own trucking subsidiaries and experimented with piggy-back rail-trucking arrangements. It also initiated numerous urban real estate developments. The best-known and most visible of these were the CN tower and the convention centre complex in Toronto.

Canadian railways were built as instruments of national policy. They were expected to tie the country together along an east–west axis. But after the signing of the North American Free Trade Agreement in 1988 more trade moved along north–south lines. CN responded by strengthening its American connections through acquisitions, alliances, running rights, and traffic exchanges. It remains one of the six largest rail systems on the continent. It has, however, spun off or divested itself of most non-rail holdings. NAFTA made government transportation subsidies controversial. In efforts to resolve that problem, the federal government wrote off most of the ancient CN debts and relieved the company of many of its obligations to provide service at uneconomic rates or over money-losing branch lines. As a result, the company became profitable, and in the 1990s the federal government initiated a series of steps resulting in the privatization of Canadian National Railways.

T.D. REGEHR

Canadian Officers' Training Corps. A program to introduce university undergraduates to military life and prepare them for entry into the regular or reserve components of the army. The COTC, built on the British Army model, dated from 1 November 1912; the first contingent was formed at McGill University, followed shortly by another at Université Laval. More contingents came with the First World War, providing a cadre of junior officers available for war service. In the years after 1919, the COTC reorganized and added further contingents to a total of 25 by 1939. During the Second World War its work was harmonized with the requirements of the Officers' Training Centres at Gordon Head, British Columbia, and Brockville, Ontario. There were 26 contingents and several hundred trainees in the early 1960s, commanded by officers who were usually members of the university faculty, assisted by staff officers of the regular army. The COTC, however, did not survive that unmilitary decade. The COTC units disbanded on 31 May 1968, the military choosing to rely for its pool of young officers on its own colleges or on 'direct entry' graduates of civilian universities with no prior service experience.

NORMAN HILLMER

Canadian Pacific Railway. In the talks leading up to Confederation in 1867, politicians assumed the fledgling nation would soon annex *Rupert's Land and British Columbia and construct a transcontinental railway linking the Atlantic and Pacific Oceans. Discussed since the 1840s, the project was familiar, but colonial rivalries and jealousies as well as financial considerations had made even the eastern section through the populated Maritimes and Canadas unfeasible. To forestall more delays, the framers of Canada's constitution incorporated the *Intercolonial Railway in the British North America Act. The new government completed the project as a public work with relatively little fuss: surveys were made, contracts let, and on 6 July 1876 the first through-train from Halifax arrived at Quebec.

The western section took longer to complete. It was to be built by a privately owned syndicate with massive public assistance, but Prime Minister John A. *Macdonald had difficulty finding a politically acceptable promoter and his quest ended in the *Pacific Scandal of 1872 and the collapse of his administration. Surveys of suitable routes and piecemeal construction continued under

Alexander *Mackenzie's Liberal government. Although fiscally more cautious, the new administration's program was still ambitious. In 1875, for example, it appropriated $6 million, or one-fourth of its entire budget, for railway construction. By the end of its term, more than 4,000 km of railway were completed (including the Intercolonial, which ran from Halifax to Rivière-du-Loup), a line from the American border to Winnipeg was nearly finished, more than 91,000 km of possible routes had been examined and 19,000 km fully surveyed, a tender call for the Yale-to-Kamloops section in British Columbia was approved, and the telegraph line from near Thunder Bay to the Rockies was finished.

Macdonald's Conservatives, re-elected in 1878, acted more decisively with their second chance. In October 1880 they signed a deal with a syndicate, the Canadian Pacific Railway. Headed by several prominent Canadian businessmen, most notably the Bank of Montreal's George Stephen and the Hudson's Bay Company's Donald A. *Smith, the company also included J.J. Hill of the Great Northern Railway in the United States as well as several European bankers. Initially progress was slow, but once the company hired William *Van Horne the work accelerated. Conquering incredible geographical obstacles—muskeg, rivers, mountains—over an enormous distance, Van Horne's crews completed a rail line from Montreal to Vancouver by the late fall of 1885. On 7 November 1885 at *Craigellachie, British Columbia, Donald Smith hammered in the transcontinental's last spike.

In addition to many lives lost in accidents, the construction of the CPR came at a considerable financial cost to the Canadian people. The initial subsidy included $25 million in cash, 25 million acres of land, $35 million in completed survey costs, $38 million in existing rail lines, and a 25-year western monopoly over running rights to the United States. Later, the high cost and torrid pace of construction in Canada's rugged terrain forced the company to approach the government for further financial assistance in the form of guarantees for dividends and bonds as well as a $22.5 million loan.

Meanwhile, the company diversified its activities. It began to sell its lands, in part through a separate firm, the Canadian North West Land Company. By the turn of the century, when sales were sluggish, the CPR aggressively pursued settlers by establishing model farms, promoting dry-land farming techniques, and providing irrigation to a large block in southern Alberta. The company also developed coal, zinc, and lead mines in southern British Columbia and established an express and a telegraph service. To stimulate passenger traffic it operated dining and sleeping cars and established a chain of dining halls and tourist hotels in the Rocky Mountains, most notably at *Banff and Lake Louise. Subsequently, it built luxury hotels at major stations such as Quebec, Montreal, Winnipeg, Calgary, and Vancouver. The CPR also fostered traffic by investing in a fleet of ocean vessels that permitted the company to become a link between Europe and the Far East. Soon the company carried mail, silk, tea, and other items requiring speedy transport.

Although the young dominion's desire to have an all-Canadian transcontinental railway controlled by Canadian investors inspired the CPR, the company quickly established connections into the United States. In fact, the syndicate had emerged out of the revitalized St Paul, Minneapolis and Manitoba Railroad but, honouring its mandate, the CPR constructed an all-Canadian railroad from central Canada along the north shore of Lake Superior and across the prairies to the Rocky Mountains. After 1885, however, the board of directors set aside the government's explicit nationalist purpose and leased, bought, or constructed several branch lines in the United States, including the Short Line from Montreal through Maine to Saint John and the Soo line westward from Sault Ste Marie through Minnesota to St Paul and Minneapolis. On 3 June 1889, a through-train ran the exact route that Macdonald had approved prior to the Pacific Scandal, while a year later the CPR launched operations on a direct line from Quebec through Montreal and Toronto to Windsor, where it ferried cars across the river to be forwarded on the Wabash Railroad to Chicago. Clearly, the CPR's corporate objectives were defined by pecuniary, not nationalist, considerations.

As the pace of western settlement accelerated at the end of the 19th century, the CPR expanded its network in western Canada. First under the presidency of William Van Horne (1888–98) and subsequently under Thomas Shaughnessy (1898–1918), the company built major branch lines in southern Manitoba as well as in Saskatchewan from Regina to Prince Albert, in Alberta from Calgary to Edmonton, and in British Columbia through the Crowsnest Pass.

These massive investments were possible only because the company enjoyed the protection of a system of tariffs under the *National Policy, which encouraged the east-west flow of traffic by stimulating industrialization in central Canada and agriculture in the west. The dominion government also permitted the company to charge discriminatory *freight rates, which suppressed industrialization and diversification in western Canada in favour of agricultural production. The inequity of these policies was not lost on western farmers and, beginning in the late 1880s, they successfully attacked the monopoly clause and subsequently gained some relief on high freight rates, most notably with the *Crow's Nest Pass Agreement, which reduced grain rates to the Pacific.

The First World War, the 1920s, and especially the economic depression and drought of the 1930s forced consolidation and entrenchment. In the heady pre-war expansionist period, the dominion government had supported the construction of two new nearly parallel transcontinental railways, the Canadian Northern and Grand Trunk systems. Nationalized and merged after the war, the new heavily subsidized *Canadian National, with its express, telegraph, hotel, and steamship operations, competed directly with the CPR in a limited market. CPR President Edward W. Beatty (1918–43) met the challenge and kept the company profitable. In addition, during the Second World War he provided armaments and merchant ships to the war effort and in the last years of his presidency launched Canadian Pacific Airlines, which developed into an international carrier concentrating on South American, Far Eastern, and some European countries.

By the 1950s, years of hardship, and poor post-war management, had left the CPR in poor financial shape. Once again a strong leader, Norris (Buck) Crump (1955–64, chairman until 1972), rescued the company from the brink of disaster. Not only did Crump modernize the railway with diesel engines but he fully diversified the company, setting up various departments as fully independent bodies. He forced Marathon Realty, CP Hotels, CP Oil and Gas (until recently PanCanadian), as well as other non-transportation interests to operate on their own, allowing the parent company to concentrate on rail, air, sea, and road transport. In 1967, the company's telegraph operations merged with those of CN under the CNCP Telecommunications logo. A year later, the company devised a series of new corporate identities in transportation, such as CP Rail, CP Air, CP Ships, and CP Transport, while in 1971 it signified its broad corporate mandate with the name of Canadian Pacific Ltd. Meanwhile, it continued expanding its railway network in the United States until 2000, when that country's government stopped an ambitious takeover plan.

A.A. DEN OTTER

Canadian Patriotic Fund. A patriotic charity based on earlier funds begun during the War of 1812 and the Crimean War, the original CPF met the need for pensions, medical care, and family support for Canadian volunteers for the *Boer War, 1899–1902. It was re-established by Parliament in August 1914 solely to meet the needs of soldiers' families. Montreal MP Herbert Ames, an industrialist and social reformer, was its inspiration. In addition to collecting and distributing funds to supplement the official 'separation allowance', Ames and his Montreal coadjutor, Helen Reid, introduced a 'Third Responsibility' for soldiers' wives. Volunteer visitors provided good counsel, encouraged thrift, and punished misbehaviour. Donors were reassured that their generosity was appreciated, but families, particularly in the west, chafed under the supervision. Inflation made CPF benefits inadequate. With $47 million in donations and a frugal $38 million spent on families, the CPF had an embarrassing post-war surplus; its popularity frayed further when it reluctantly agreed to oversee the 1919–20 winter unemployment benefit for veterans. In 1939 the CPF was not revived.

DESMOND MORTON

Canadian Red Cross Society. For more than a century, the Canadian Red Cross Society has provided humanitarian assistance in military campaigns and *natural disasters. In 1885 Surgeon-Major Dr George Sterling Ryerson (1854–1925) flew the Red Cross flag on his ambulance during the Riel Rebellion and in 1896 created a Canadian branch of the British Red Cross. After supporting Canadian troops in South Africa, the society was incorporated in 1909 and became an independent member of the International Red Cross Committee in 1927.

During the First World War the Canadian Red Cross raised $35 million, provided comfort kits, recreation centres and relief supplies, and equipped six overseas hospitals. After 1918 the society supported the creation of outpost hospitals in remote under-serviced areas, funded public health nursing scholarships across Canada, and introduced Junior Red Cross courses in Canadian schools. During the Second World War the CRC provided $125 million in goods and funding as well as volunteer services for military personnel and refugees. It also prepared 2.5 million bottles of blood and dried plasma packages for Canadian troops abroad.

In 1947 the CRC responded to requests from hospital associations and provincial health departments by creating the Blood Transfusion Service, which used volunteer donations to provide free blood products until the tainted blood scandal erupted in the 1980s. The Krever Inquiry (1993–7) resulted in virtual bankruptcy for the society and refocused its activities on disaster relief, water safety programs, first aid classes, home care, and abuse prevention services.

HEATHER MacDOUGALL

Canadian Seamen's Union. *See* SEAMEN'S UNIONS.

Canadian Shield. A prominent land form, underlain by Precambrian rock, and covering nearly half of Canada. Roughly shield-like in shape, the region is centred on, and penetrated by, *Hudson Bay. Not only has the country's economic development benefited from the resources of the Shield, it has become an icon of Canadian identity. Its vast coniferous forests, countless lakes, and rugged terrain, as captured in the paintings of the *Group of Seven and in images promoting Canadian *tourism, have come to signify Canada itself.

Before and after European contact, the cultures and economies of First Nations were affected by the presence of the Shield. As agriculturalists, Iroquoian peoples settled no farther north than its southern edge, where the land became much less fertile and harder to work. To the north, the Algonquian-speaking peoples, who were hunters and gatherers, relied on the abundant animal resources of the Shield. They even made use of the exposed rock, carving on it images of spiritual significance. With the coming of Europeans and the expansion of the *fur trade, First Nations hunters who lived on the Shield trapped, transported, and sold large quantities of furs to traders from elsewhere.

Euro-Canadians long saw the Shield as both a barrier and a treasure trove. For farmers living in adjacent regions, the rocky land blocked expansion of their agrarian way of life. In the mid-19th century large numbers of farmers in Quebec and Ontario, when confronted with the infertile Shield, moved to the United States. In response, the governments of Quebec and Ontario, along with Catholic clergy, encouraged the agricultural colonization of the Shield country. Farmers succeeded only in fertile pockets. Far better economic opportunities were found in the region's forest, mineral, and water resources, and in its scenery.

As early as the 1820s, lumbering operations moved onto the Shield via the Ottawa River; by the 1850s they extended over vast forest tracts. Mining operators began prospecting on the Shield fringes of central Ontario in the mid-19th century, but their modest successes were overshadowed by the discovery of nickel and other hard metals in the Sudbury basin in the 1880s, and by the silver and gold strikes in northern Ontario and western Quebec early in the 20th century. By 1920, many mining centres had appeared. Excellent hydroelectric power sites were simultaneously developed, in some cases by the pulp and paper companies that used the power and the nearby forests to supply their northern mills. Permanent, single-industry towns developed around the mills. Only with pain and sacrifice did First Nations adjust to these intrusions into their territory. The furious pace of resource development slowed after 1930, but by then substantial and enduring industries and settlements were in place. So too were the many scars on the landscape left by decades of resource exploitation.

More Canadians today have first-hand knowledge of the Shield country because of its recreational and tourist facilities. Even in the mid-19th century the rugged landscape drew well-heeled tourists to destinations such as the Saguenay River, whose 'terrifying, haunting grandeur' could be viewed from the comfort of a river steamer. Toronto's middle class found ready access to the lakes of the Shield when railways and steamers opened the Muskoka District in the late 19th century. There, and elsewhere, resort hotels thrived for a while, but many visitors soon purchased wooded, lake-front properties from the Crown and built summer cottages. What had once been seen as a barren wilderness became a summer playground for visitors charmed by the beauty of the lakes, wind-swept pines, and rocky outcrops. A holiday in cottage country provided contact with the real Canada!

IAN RADFORTH

Canadian Women's Army Corps. The CWAC was established during the Second World War in response to army labour needs and the lobbying efforts of women's paramilitary corps. For the first time, women were recruited for military service in the *Canadian army. Corps members served predominantly as clerks to replace servicemen in non-combat duties. In spite of widespread rumours of immorality within the corps, 21,624 women volunteered for wartime service.

Basic and officer training began at Ste Anne de Bellevue, Quebec. As demand increased, additional basic training centres were opened at Vermillion, Alberta, and Kitchener, Ontario, with the original site devoted to advanced training. Most enlistees served in Canada, although many received a coveted posting abroad. The first overseas draft of 104 servicewomen arrived in the United Kingdom in November 1942, and enlistees served in Britain, the United States, Italy, France, and even India.

The CWAC began as an auxiliary service in August 1941, but was integrated into the active *militia in March 1942. Officially demobilized on 15 September 1946, it was restored to operation in 1951 during the Korean conflict, and limited numbers of women continued to serve until it was incorporated into the Canadian Armed Forces in July 1971.

TINA DAVIDSON AND RUTH ROACH PIERSON

Canadian Youth Commission. A post-war planning group created in 1943, this non-government organization, funded by private donations, recruited more than 50 volunteer commissioners for the purpose of studying the needs of 15- to 24-year-olds and making recommendations on their behalf. Supporters boasted about the broad representation of the membership. Although the commissioners represented both sexes, various regions, English and French speakers, Protestants, Catholics, and Jews, the Toronto-based group did not really represent all Canadians. Originally part of the *YMCA, the commission became independent in order to distance itself from the Y's traditional religious roots. Committed to utilizing the latest research methods, the CYC employed the newly emerging science of opinion *polling through interviews, questionnaires with individuals, and briefs submitted by youth groups. In ten reports published by Ryerson Press, the CYC recommended a full range of social welfare schemes, which were never implemented. However the CYC director, R.E.G. Davis, became director of the Canadian Welfare Council in 1948, where he continued to fight for social welfare initiatives. LINDA M. AMBROSE

Canadien, Le. Considered French Canada's first political newspaper, *Le Canadien* was founded by members of the Parti canadien in 1806. Its early editions were distinguished by a firm grasp of British constitutional principles, an early formulation of the idea of *responsible government, a defence of the Canadiens and their traditions, and professions of loyalty to the Crown. The paper's success and the electoral victories of the party it supported alarmed the colony's francophobic governor, Sir James Craig, who had its presses seized in April 1810 and imprisoned its editors. *Le Canadien* was ressurected in the 1820s and again in the 1830s, becoming extremely influential under the editorship of Étienne *Parent. Although its editor was again imprisoned in 1839, *Le Canadien* published through the rebellion period, criticized the Durham report, opposed the union, and eventually supported responsible government and the LaFontaine ministry. The paper, which usually supported moderate *liberalism, was published under various owners to the end of the 19th century. LOUIS-GEORGES HARVEY

canals. The early history of Canada is intimately tied to travel by water. Both commercial and military traffic depended on waterways. The fur-trade competition between the Montreal interests and those trading through the Hudson Bay ports led to the development of fortified settlements at strategic points along many of the rivers. The high value and relatively light weight of the cargoes allowed the use of water craft that were small enough to be carried by the men who powered them. Later, as the settlements grew and commerce in less valuable goods became important, schemes to improve the waterways were developed.

An early effort was at Lachine, the rapids southwest of the settlement at Montreal. As early as 1689 a plan for a canal to bypass the rapids was proposed. The channel was started in 1700 but never completed. After the War of 1812 a private group began again; the work was taken over by the government of Lower Canada in 1821 and completed in 1825. The work at Montreal and the lingering threat of an American invasion prompted the British government to initiate a supply route to Lake Ontario that avoided the St Lawrence River, with its proximity to US forces. The Royal Staff Corps of the British Army started work at the Long Sault rapids on the Ottawa River in 1819. They completed this Grenville Canal and its two companion canals at Carillon and Chute à Blondeau in 1834. While this work proceeded, Col John *By and his corps of *Royal Engineers laid out a route utilizing the Rideau and Cataraqui Rivers by connecting their chains of lakes. The Rideau Canal was completed in 1832. It is a testament to the builders that most of it is still in use today, utilizing the same locks and dams.

Meanwhile, a group of entrepreneurs was undertaking a bold venture to build a canal to join Lake Ontario to Lake Erie. Between 1824 and 1829 they managed to build their canal from the Niagara River just above the falls to Twenty Mile Creek on Lake Ontario. Unlike the substantial construction of the canals on the Rideau, Ottawa, and St Lawrence, the Welland Canal locks were built mainly of timber and soon had to be replaced in masonry. By 1841 the canal had been taken over by the government of the *Province of Canada. The value of the venture can be measured by the fact that it has been enlarged three times. The present fourth canal, completed in 1932, leaps up the 99 m difference in levels between the lakes in seven huge locks (plus a guard lock at the entrance to Lake Erie), whereas the original had 40 locks to get up only to the Welland River.

To join Lake Superior to Lake Huron, locks were built at Sault Ste Marie. The North West Company built the first in 1797 for its canoes. The largest lock on the Canadian side of the St Mary's River was completed in 1895, but most traffic now utilizes the larger US locks.

The combined value of electricity generation and access to the Great Lakes by ocean-going ships resulted in the *St Lawrence Seaway development. The construction along the St Lawrence from Montreal to Lake Ontario was completed in 1959. It enlarged previous works and combined with the Welland Canal and the Soo locks to provide a 3,700-km waterway from the Atlantic Ocean to the head of Lake Superior.

Smaller canals were constructed to provide or improve access locally. The Trent–Severn Canal joins Lake Ontario to Lake Huron; a group of small projects to join rivers and lakes to facilitate the timber trade was finally connected to allow the first through voyage between the two lakes in 1920. The St Peter's Canal in Nova Scotia was completed in 1869 to join the southwestern end of the Bras d'Or Lakes with the Atlantic. At the other end of the country, a lock between Marsh Lake and Whitehorse in the Yukon was completed in 1969 to facilitate navigation and bypass a dam built for electricity generation.

Over 50 canals have been built in Canada. Many are still in operation, most serving recreational traffic instead of the commercial shipping that was their original purpose. Others provide examples of what might have been. In Nova Scotia, the Schubenacadie Canal joined Halifax Harbour with the Bay of Fundy, but never solved the problem of dealing with the famous tides. Nearby, the Baie Verte Canal was intended to join the Gulf of St Lawrence with the Bay of Fundy. Supplanted by the Chignecto Marine Transport Railway Company scheme for a ship railway, neither was completed. An even more elaborate scheme, the Georgian Bay Ship Canal, would have joined the Ottawa River to Georgian Bay, providing a shorter and all-Canadian seaway route to the head of the Great Lakes.

GEORGE HUME

CANLOAN. In the fall of 1943 the Canadian army arranged to loan a surplus of its officers to the British army, then desperately short of junior infantry officers. Initially some 2,000 officers were to be a part of the CANLOAN scheme, but worsening Canadian casualty forecasts reduced the numbers. Volunteers came from those most eager for overseas service; many were surplus in other arms and accepted a reduction in rank to join the infantry. After refresher training in Sussex, NB, under Brigadier Milton Gregg, VC, the first of 52 CANLOAN officers arrived in Liverpool on 6 April 1944; many of these men led infantry platoons ashore in *Normandy two months later. By July 1944 the last of 673 Canadian officers was overseas: 622 lieutenants and captains joined 62 British infantry regiments that fought in northwest Europe; another 51 Canadian officers served with the Royal Army Ordnance Corps, 20 of them in Italy.

CANLOAN not only reflected the close ties that bound the Canadian and British armies, it also demonstrated the extraordinary dangers faced by junior officers in the Second World War. Almost 70 per cent of CANLOAN officers (465) became casualties, 128 of them were killed or died of wounds; 41 were awarded the Military Cross.

GEOFFREY HAYES

canoeing. Millions of Canadians participate in recreational paddling. This might involve a weekend camping trip or a longer venture through one of the country's wilderness parks. A small but highly dedicated group of canoeists embraces the competitive challenge, devoting countless hours to training for flatwater and whitewater events.

The attractions of recreational canoeing are varied. Elements of sport and physical activity often combine with psychic and emotional pleasures. A canoe trip may be a 'get away from it all' experience for some devotees.

Others explain their enthusiasm with reference to spiritual or even religious experience, while some are more inclined to emphasize feelings of closeness to the natural environment.

People such as the artist and filmmaker Bill Mason, Eric Morse, who revisited old fur-trade routes, or Prime Minister Pierre *Trudeau, a lifelong canoeist, helped to popularize recreational canoeing during the 1970s and 1980s, although the roots of this particular pastime are much deeper. Indeed, an association with North America's Aboriginal past is inherent in a mode of transport derived from the bark, skin-covered, and dugout watercraft of the continent's original human inhabitants. These vessels, adopted by fur traders—the *voyageurs—and early explorers, were instrumental in opening up the continent to commerce with Europe. The *canot du maître* (the Montreal canoe) and the smaller *canot du nord* could regularly be found along the corridor linking Montreal via the Grand Portage out of Lake Superior to trading posts as far away as *Fort Chipewyan on Lake Athabasca. Freighted with the past, as it has sometimes been put, the canoe conveys to Canadians a wide range of symbolic meanings, most of which are sufficiently positive that even in the age of fast cars and supersonic flight the hand-propelled watercraft continues to appear regularly in advertisements for products and services ranging from beer to banks.

Although canoeists have not been particularly organizational minded, they have nevertheless formed a number of associations to promote the cause. The Canadian Recreational Canoeing Association caters to the interests of canoe-trip aficionados and family and weekend paddlers. Competitive canoeists pursue their objectives within the general framework of the Canadian Canoe Association. Those more concerned with canoe heritage and tradition can be found within the ranks of the Wooden Canoe Heritage Association or visiting the Canadian Canoe Museum in Peterborough, Ontario.

JAMIE BENIDICKSON

canoe routes. Canoe routes comprised the major system of transportation in North America before the Industrial Revolution. Integral to the colonial enterprise of the *fur trade, several routes came to be heavily travelled and widely known. They spanned thousands of miles and connected the east, west, and northern coasts. The *Hudson's Bay Company's main route ran from *York Factory, its central depot located at the mouth of Hayes River on *Hudson Bay, up that river system to Lake Winnipeg, and then to the Red or Saskatchewan River systems. From Montreal, the *St Lawrence River connected to Lakes Ontario and Erie, which led to Lake Huron and on to Lake Superior. The shorter route to Lake Superior was to the north, following the Ottawa River to Lake Nipissing, through the French River to Lake Huron, and then along the north shore of Lake Superior to the post of Grand Portage at its western end. Later the terminus was moved 80 km northeast to Fort William. Montreal traders used this as a departure point for interior posts. They travelled west to Rainy Lake, connected to the Lake of the Woods, and down the Winnipeg River to Lake Winnipeg. The journey could then continue south, up the Red River, which led to the watershed of the Mississippi, or to the western prairies via the Assiniboine and Qu'Appelle Rivers. Northward, the journey could continue by Lake Winnipeg to the mouth of the Saskatchewan River. That river led west to the Rockies and routes to the Pacific Ocean by the Peace and Fraser Rivers, or to the Arctic Ocean by the Slave and Mackenzie Rivers.

Water levels, rapids, and especially long portages posed serious obstacles for travellers. The longest portages were located in the transition zones, referred to as 'heights of land', between continental drainage systems, such as that located 80 km west of Lake Superior, which separated the Great Lakes and Hudson Bay drainage areas. Just south of Lake Athabasca, Methy Portage, which separated the Hudson Bay drainage area from that of the Arctic Ocean, was, at almost 21 km, the longest and most difficult portage.

CAROLYN PODRUCHNY

Canol pipeline. Built between 1942 and 1944, the Canol pipeline stretched 1,000 km from an oil field at Norman Wells, Northwest Territories, to a refinery at Whitehorse, Yukon. On 7 December 1941, the US navy had lost much of its Pacific fleet when Japan attacked Pearl Harbor. The Pacific coast of North America, particularly distant Alaska, seemed vulnerable to invasion, even more so as Japan wracked up victories against the US navy and army (Wake Island, Guam) and British-led forces (Hong Kong, Singapore). The United States built the *Alaska Highway and the Canol pipeline to serve the airfields that made up the *Northwest Staging Route. The NSR was to supply Alaska and enable the United States to ferry lend-lease aircraft to its ally, the USSR. The pipeline, the highway, and the NSR fast-tracked northern development in Canada and prepared the way for more extensive exploration and mining following the war. But these projects also raised troubling questions about Canadian sovereignty, environmental degradation, and the place of First Nations peoples in Canada's changing North.

BOB HESKETH

Cape Breton coal strikes, 1920s. In the labour unrest in the last years of the First World War, Nova Scotia coal miners achieved recognition of District 26, *United Mine Workers of America (1919). Under the influence of labour radicals such as J.B. *McLachlan, they adopted plans for political and social reform, including public ownership of the coal industry. There was strong resistance from the newly established British Empire Steel Corporation (1921), which was facing difficulties in maintaining traditional markets and meeting financial expectations. As a result, for the next several years the Nova Scotia coal country was wracked by a long labour war that focused largely on wage reductions and union recognition. The confrontations were especially dramatic in the Sydney coalfield on Cape Breton Island, including a strike on the job (1922), a sympathetic strike in support of steelworkers (1923), the arrest of union leaders on sedition charges (1923), the suspension of district autonomy by the international union (1923–4), the shooting of coal miner William Davis by company police (1925), and the burning of the company stores (1925). The Canadian army was called out to support the civil power in 1922, 1923, and 1925. In 1926 an extensive royal commission investigation was completed. The labour wars did not resolve the industry's economic problems, but they secured continued union recognition for workers. Traditions of class and community solidarity have remained alive in the coal towns for several generations and are reflected in rituals such as the annual observance of Davis Day (11 June). DAVID FRANK

Cape Breton Island. After capturing *Louisbourg, the capital of *Île Royale, in 1758 the British blew up the fortifications and abandoned the town. Renamed Cape Breton, the island was mostly depopulated and became a part of *Nova Scotia. Some 250 *Mi'kmaq, the Aboriginal people who had been allies of the French, made peace overtures to the British and signed treaties at Halifax in 1760–1. By 1785 there were about 1,000 Acadians in the Isle Madame area, some of whom had been on the island since the beginning of French settlement in 1713, and 500 *Loyalists from New England in and around Sydney. In order to provide positions for the Loyalists, Cape Breton was made a separate colony that year with its own governor and executive council. Its status as a Crown colony was marked by political infighting among local politicians, difficulties that led to the island's annexation to Nova Scotia in 1820.

Cape Breton's population had grown to 55,000 by 1851, with the Scots outnumbering the Acadians, Loyalists, and Irish by two to one. In contrast to mainland Nova Scotia, the majority of Cape Breton's people were Roman Catholic and *Gaelic speaking. In 1851 there were 31,992 Roman Catholics on Cape Breton, 58 per cent of the total population. By contrast, on mainland Nova Scotia there were only 37,642 Catholics, 15 per cent of a total population of 244,125. By the 1850s Cape Breton's coastal areas had been developed and there was also considerable settlement in the interior. Large areas of forest had been cleared, and farming and fishing were the island's principal economic activities. The resource-based economy, however, failed to provide the necessary employment for young people, and their emigration contributed to the decline of Cape Breton's Scottish culture. There were 75,414 Nova Scotians of Scottish descent in 1931. Some 24,303 spoke Gaelic. Ten years later the number of Gaelic speakers dropped to 12,065, and today there are only a few hundred Gaelic-speaking people left.

The rapid industrialization of Cape Breton at the end of the 19th century helped to stem some of the outward migration. Although small in landward area, Sydney's coal field was Canada's largest producer of coal for over two centuries, the source, until 1960, of approximately one-third of the country's coal production. With over 70 mines developed in the Sydney area over the years, *coal mining touched the lives of most Cape Bretoners.

Besides providing employment for the miners, the coal mines stimulated the lumbering, shipbuilding, and shipping industries. They also led to the development of a major steel centre. Incorporated in 1904, the new city of Sydney grew up around the older colonial town. Following the establishment of the steel complex in 1900, Sydney's population expanded from 3,659 in 1891 to 17,723 by 1911. The new coal mines and steel plants stimulated large-scale immigration. Immigrants from Newfoundland and returning Cape Bretoners from the United States were joined by a few thousand people from overseas—Ukrainians, Poles, Hungarians, Italians, and Lebanese, and people of African origin from the West Indies and the southern United States.

The history of Cape Breton—and much of the Atlantic provinces—has been marked by underdevelopment. Except for the war years, 1914–18 and 1939–45, jobless figures have remained high throughout much of the 20th century. The depression after the First World War resulted in lower production in the steel and coal industries. Coal production in 1919–39 averaged 3.9 million tons per year, down from a high of 5.5 million in 1915. The problems in the coal industry in the 1920s continued apace for the next 40 years. Coal production declined from 5.2 million tons in 1940 to just over 1 million tons in 1973. Miners turned to trade unionism and labour militancy to improve wages and conditions of labour. There are now no operating coal mines or steel plants on the island.

In 2003, Cape Breton was home to 147,000 people, 16 per cent of Nova Scotia's population. Some 6,000 Mi'kmaq, most of whom still speak their Native language, live on five reserves. In the post-industrial age, efforts are underway to strengthen and diversify Cape Breton's economy to small-scale enterprise and the new information technology. With the island's rugged beauty, the world-famous Cabot Trail, and the reconstructed fortress of Louisbourg, tourism is one of the leading sectors of the new economy. Another of the island's attractions is its distinctive culture. Committed to their sense of place and their personal relationships, Cape Bretoners have grown up knowing the people around them and the genealogy of their friends. Over the past 40 years Cape Breton has experienced a cultural revival. Receptive audiences have fuelled the popularity of Celtic music, both on the island and off, and contribute to a growing appreciation of Cape Breton's special voice. KENNETH DONOVAN

capital punishment. Although capital punishment is often criticized as a sanction that reeks of the 'dark ages', it remained a potent and palatable response to *crime in Canada well into the modern era. What changed over several centuries was the extent of the death penalty's use, the crimes to which it applied, and the criminals on whom it was inflicted.

Both First Nations peoples and European colonizers agreed that some crimes called for death. Aboriginals tended to exact the extreme penalty only for offences that shattered community cohesion. In contrast the French and English defined criminal offences of all sorts as affronts to the 'King's peace'. Thus, a French royal court sitting in an 18th-century colonial town might order the execution of a servant caught stealing her master's silverware, or a farmer convicted of bestiality. Although neither offence posed a direct threat to the community, such crimes were considered serious affronts to social order and to a monarch thousands of miles away. Capital punishment provided dramatic confirmation of the monarch's power and authority. Of course, neither the French nor English king attended executions in the colonies, but colonial officials were there to represent the monarch in whose name the death penalty was carried out. Executions were presented as public ceremonies. The key official player—the hangman—was often a criminal himself, performing the distasteful job to save his own neck.

Crimes that explicitly challenged royal authority were punished with extreme violence. When American David Lane was convicted of treason in 1797, he faced a penalty that included disembowelment, decapitation, and quartering. But in a rigidly hierarchical society, servants' crimes against their masters and wives' affronts to their husbands' authority were likewise constructed as acts of 'petty treason'. Until 1829, the prescribed punishment was burning at the stake (as a small mercy the doomed were strangled first), although such punishments were rarely imposed.

Executions were nail-biting affairs, and not just for the person due to be killed. Pronouncing the death penalty did not necessarily lead to its infliction because mercy was always possible. In the 17th and 18th centuries, executions were typically carried out within hours or days of the sentence, so such sentences had to be commuted quickly. Colonial governors could commute death sentences without having to provide explanations, but privately they commented that severity had to be leavened with mercy. Under British law, the so-called Bloody Code listed scores of offences—mostly property crimes—that called for the death penalty. Had every minor miscreant been hanged, colonial officials feared that the king's justice might seem ruthless.

Starting in the 1820s, alternatives to the death penalty were sought. While some politicians argued successfully for a vast reduction in the scope of capital statutes, others advocated imprisonment as a rational alternative to the erratically administered death penalty. By the mid-19th century, most colonial statutes imposed the death penalty only for what were considered serious crimes against the state or the person (including rape, sodomy, and attempted murder). Shortly after the new dominion government assumed responsibility for the formulation of penal policy, lengthy prison terms replaced the death penalty for all serious offences except murder and treason. In 1868, Parliament declared that executions would no longer be public events.

After Confederation, responsibility for commuting sentences rested with the federal *cabinet. The *governor general granted formal approval but in reality cabinet authority prevailed. At no point was executive power more hotly contested than in the case of Louis *Riel, the Metis leader convicted of treason for his role in the *North-West Rebellion. Sir John A. *Macdonald, facing a young country deeply divided on French and English, as well as Protestant and Catholic, lines, opted to let the death sentence stand. Riel was to become the only person executed for a crime other than murder after Confederation. His execution remains controversial and inspires calls for a posthumous pardon.

Compared to Riel, the other 705 people executed since Confederation have largely been forgotten. Overwhelmingly they were the poor and the poorly defended. They included a disproportionate number of men from the country's ethnic and racial minorities—often without friends or resources. Rarely did women and youths face the hangman, no matter how horrid their crimes. By the early 20th century, cabinets effectively reserved the death penalty for adult men. In the 1960s a broad abolitionist movement gained parliamentary support. Although Canada struck it down in 1976, there continues to be significant popular support for the death penalty. CAROLYN STRANGE

capitulation of Canada, Montreal, 8 September 1760. On the evening of 6 September, the Marquis de Vaudreuil, governor general of Canada, read to his officers his proposals for the capitulation of the colony to Gen. Jeffery Amherst, who commanded the British army camped before the city. The next morning, Amherst replied to Vaudreuil's proposed articles of capitulation in terse comments in the document's wide margins. General Lévis and other French officers argued for a last stand, since Amherst denied them the honours of war. But Vaudreuil, with greater realism, signed the amended document on the morning of 8 September. The capitulation dealt in its opening and closing articles with the administrative questions involving the transportation of French officers, officials, and soldiers to Europe and the disposal of government documents. Those needed for the governance of the country were to remain, as were all maps. For Canadiens, now 'new subjects' of the British Crown, the articles of enduring importance were those concerning religion, the rights of conquered persons, and matters of law. Free exercise of the Roman Catholic religion was granted along with the property rights of the clergy, except that the rights of men's religious orders were referred to the king. Frenchmen and Canadiens retained all property rights and had the right to emigrate from the colony. Canadiens retained the right to trade. Slaves remained slaves. Indians were not to be molested for having taken the French side in the war and retained their lands and their Roman Catholic missionaries. There would be no expulsion of people as there had been in Nova Scotia in 1755. Amherst made no promises about the authority of a new bishop should one be consecrated, about the continuation of the Coutume de Paris as the law of Canada, or about Acadians who had taken refuge in Canada, since these latter were British subjects in a state of disobedience. The capitulation was more considerate of Indians than Amherst's known views would have led one to expect; it was also politic and generous in its handling of religion and was characteristic of an age and people that above all valued private property. DALE MIQUELON

See also CONQUEST OF NEW FRANCE.

Cariboo gold rush. Miners drawn to the 1858 *Fraser River gold rush soon moved upstream, making their way into Cariboo country in central British Columbia, where some struck gold in 1859 at Horsefly Creek. Word spread, and soon thousands of other fortune seekers from the distant corners of the globe followed, including the *Overlanders from Canada. Some sought gold, but others made their fortunes servicing the needs of miners from instant towns like *Barkerville. The rush peaked in 1863, when some ten metric tons of gold was shipped out of the region. All told, the Cariboo rush produced $30 million worth of the mineral in the 1860s, much of it exported via the colony's first 'highway', the *Cariboo Wagon Road.

Despite rags-to-riches stories of miners like Billy Barker becoming millionaires overnight, the Cariboo gold fields were not the land of the self-made man. In general, mining was not carried out by a solitary prospector panning for gold on a promising creekbed. Surface deposits of gold in the Cariboo were rapidly exhausted, and mining quickly became an industrial enterprise requiring large infusions of capital and labour. By selling shares, joint stock companies raised the required revenue to sink shafts into the rocky hillsides, build elaborate networks of wooden sluices, and hire miners who worked for wages to bring out the gold. It was hard and often unrewarding work, requiring, as one Overlander put it, a man to 'work like a Hottentot and live like a galley slave'.

TINA LOO

Cariboo Wagon Road. Five and a half m wide and 492 km long, the Cariboo Wagon Road ran between Yale on the Fraser River to *Barkerville in south-central British Columbia, the supply centre of the *Cariboo gold rush. Over a three-year period beginning in 1862, a contingent of British *Royal Engineers and private contractors blasted their way through the rock of the Fraser canyon, built a bridge at Alexandra, and graded long stretches of treacherous terrain so that the colony's gold fields might be supplied more readily and cheaply. A monument to the skills of both its engineers and builders, the road contributed greatly to British Columbia's mounting debt, a situation that led eventually to its union with the neighbouring colony of *Vancouver Island in 1866.

TINA LOO

Caribou. Launched in June 1925 in Rotterdam, the *Caribou* was the pride of the Newfoundland government's coastal passenger service. Put into service in November 1925 on the Cabot Strait between North Sydney and Port-aux-Basques, a route inaugurated in 1898 following the completion of a railway across Newfoundland, the ferry made three weekly crossings. The 2,200-ton ship was 81 m long, 12 m wide, and able to carry 400 passengers and 50 carloads of freight. It was designed to handle the seasonal ice conditions and heavy seas of the North Atlantic. In the early morning hours of 14 October 1942, the *Caribou*, out of North Sydney, with 238 passengers (including military personnel) and crew, was attacked and sunk by German submarine U-69. The 101 people who survived the attack were rescued by the Canadian minesweeper *Grandmère*, which had provided escort. Thirty-one of the ship's crew of 36 were lost, including the captain, Ben Taverner; 56 service personnel also died. The tragedy was seared in the consciousness of Newfoundlanders, and 'remember the *Caribou*' became a patriotic rallying point.

MELVIN BAKER AND AIDAN MALONEY

Carignan-Salières Regiment. This regiment of some 1,200 men was sent from France in 1665 to help defend the colony of Canada against *Iroquois attacks. It began by building forts to protect settlers and to serve as bases for attack. A mid-winter overland expedition led by Governor Daniel de Rémy de Courcelle suffered terribly from exposure, lost many men, and returned without striking. In October 1666 the Marquis de Tracy invaded the heart of Mohawk lands but encountered no one. The Iroquois adopted the strategy of manoeuvring away from a more powerful army (a move well known to Europeans but sometimes said to be peculiarly Iroquois). Tracy destroyed villages and crops (a move also well known to both sides). The next year, the Iroquois offered peace and Tracy accepted. He and much of the regiment returned to France in 1667. To strengthen the fledgling colony, men of the regiment were encouraged to settle; some 30 officers and 416 soldiers did so. Several famous military families grew from these origins. JAY CASSEL

Carleton, Guy, 1st Baron Dorchester (1724–1808), military officer, colonial administrator. Born in Ireland, Carleton played important roles at critical junctures of early British rule in Canada. Following his service as an officer in the Seven Years' War, Carleton won appointment as lieutenant-governor of Quebec (1766) through his connections at court. After being promoted to captain in chief and governor of Quebec (1768), he went to London to advise imperial authorities on Quebec reform in 1770. He returned to implement the terms of the *Quebec Act (1774), marking the abandonment of Britain's policy of anglicization. Sanctioning the appointment of elites to the legislative council and the judiciary, he believed that the *seigneurial system and the Catholic Church would help maintain the bond between imperial authority and Canadian society. As commander of troops defending the province from an invasion of American revolutionaries in 1775, he was disappointed with the habitants' lukewarm response to the British call to arms. After supervising the evacuation of British troops and *Loyalists from New York, Carleton returned to England, where he secured the title Baron Dorchester and the governorship of Canada (1786). He was consulted by the metropolitan government on major reforms for British North America, including the *Constitutional Act (1791), which introduced full colonial government in Lower Canada, with Catholics afforded full participation as voters and members of the elected provincial legislature.

K. DAVID MILOBAR

Carr, Emily (1871–1945), landscape painter and author. Born in Victoria, Carr studied in San Francisco (1890–3), England (1899–1904), and France (1910–11). From 1907 she committed herself to the depiction of the totem poles of the First Nations in their original sites at a time when they were being abandoned or removed by ethnologists. In 1912 she travelled to northern British Columbia villages, painting in fauvist, high-keyed colour. Carr stopped painting in 1913 due to the economic recession but in 1921 began again to paint the coastal landscape around Victoria. The inclusion of her works in the *Exhibition of Canadian West Coast Art Native and Modern* in Ottawa in 1927, when she met Lawren S. Harris, and her encounter with the Seattle artist Mark Tobey, resulted in her returning to her earlier field studies, painting them in a more geometric, sculptural style. From the early 1930s she painted the forests and skies around Victoria, in an increasingly broad manner expressive of her perception of the presence of a divine energy in nature, sketching on manila paper in oil diluted with gasoline. She began writing in the mid-1920s; her first published book, *Klee Wyck*, won the Governor General's Award for non-fiction in 1941.

CHARLES C. HILL

Carrothers Commission, established in 1965 to address the constitutional and political future of the *Northwest Territories. Until the mid-1960s the NWT was governed from Ottawa by bureaucrats and politicians, but pressure from the non-Aboriginal population for self-government forced the Pearson government to act. A distinguished academic and expert on common law, A.W.R. Carrothers was asked to head a commission to explore a range of issues, including division of the territory and provincial status. The commission travelled to many communities to observe conditions and talk directly to residents. Although most Aboriginal people were reluctant to speak, Carrothers noted the poor housing in which most lived, the diseases that plagued them, the alcohol abuse that wrecked lives, and their physical and social isolation. He also reported that the per capita income of Aboriginal people in the North was one-sixth the national average.

Despite these observations, the report released in October 1966 largely neglected the socio-economic issues faced by Aboriginal peoples, focusing instead on governance issues. Carrothers recommended that division not occur, that the seat of government be located in Yellowknife, and that a commissioner and executive council be established, along with a legislative assembly of 14 elected and 4 appointed members. Provincial status was rejected on financial grounds. He also recommended the establishment of a Department of Local Government to serve as an advisory body. To Carrothers, local governments in communities were important vehicles to help northern residents become accustomed to public institutions.

The recommendations were a compromise between local demand for self-government and Ottawa's interest in retaining control of resource development, much as it had done in 1905 with Alberta and Saskatchewan. The commission paved the way for territorial government, and over the ensuing decade most of the recommendations were implemented. Not all would work for the North: the community government models imposed, which were southern, ignored traditional Aboriginal forms of leadership and decision making and culminated in frustration and slow growth. Still, a government that was situated in the territory and allowed residents a direct say in future development was a positive step forward.

BRENT SLOBODIN

Carson, William (1770–1843), physician, agitator, reformer. A Scot, Carson studied medicine at Edinburgh University, but did not graduate. After working as a 'surgeon' in Birmingham, in 1808 he came to a prospering St John's and gave himself an MD. In 1811 he began a career as a political agitator. Newfoundland had courts, a sheriff, a grand jury, a naval squadron and military garrison, a part-time governor and other officials, but no elective government. Carson demanded the normal colonial constitution—a council, elected assembly, and year-round governor—and threatened 'revolt' if these were not forthcoming. By 1833, in part owing to his influence, all three reforms had been granted. Carson was elected to the assembly in 1833, aligning himself with an Irish underclass led by bishop M.A. *Fleming, who, with the merchant Patrick Morris and others, saw the legislature as a means of achieving greater power, if not dominance, in the community. Carson became speaker in the Irish-dominated assembly of 1837–41. His radical temperament was hardly suitable for the post, and the new legislature was dysfunctional. In 1841 the British government suspended the constitution. The year Carson died, a more easily controlled 'amalgamated' assembly was in place, two-fifths of whose members were appointed.

PATRICK O'FLAHERTY

Cartier, George-Étienne (1814–73), nationalist of both French Canada and Canada, cabinet minister, a founder of the Conservative Party. Born into a prominent merchant family, Cartier studied at the Collège de Montréal and was admitted to the Lower-Canadian bar in 1835. A *Patriote, he was forced into exile in the United States during the *rebellions of 1837. Returning after swearing loyalty to the Crown, he was soon an ally of L.-H. *LaFontaine and in 1848 was elected to the assembly. Associated with the pragmatic and non-ideological conservatism of what would become the Conservative Party, Cartier was able to bridge the often conflicting interests of railways, land, and the Roman Catholic Church. He played a key role in developing the Canadian railway system, in codifiying Quebec's civil law, and in dismantling seigneurialism in favour of a freehold land system. In 1864, he became attorney general in the coalition that negotiated federalism in Charlottetown and Quebec. He was key in manoeuvring French Canada into *Confederation and in neutralizing liberal opposition to the project in Quebec; he also facilitated the entry of British Columbia and Manitoba into Confederation. Associated with liberal Catholicism in Quebec, he was a lifelong opponent of ultramontanist Catholic ideology. Ruined by the *Pacific Scandal, he died in London. BRIAN YOUNG

Cartier, Jacques (1491–1557), navigator, explorer, merchant. His *Voyages*, probably written by others based on his ships' logs, are the earliest descriptions of the landscape of mainland Canada and Native life along the St Lawrence. Extraordinary geographical and ethnographic accounts, they unwittingly record the mutual incomprehension between Natives and French. Cartier may have visited Brazil and Newfoundland before François I sent him to the 'new lands' in search of silver and gold. His 1534 voyage coasted the Gulf of St Lawrence, already known to Europeans; he praised *Labrador's fine harbours, but saw 'not one cart-load of earth' and dismissed it as 'the land God gave to Cain'. He mapped the gulf, encountered possible *Beothuks, traded with *Mi'kmaq and Laurentian Iroquois, and, despite protests by the Native leader *Donnacona, erected a cross at Gaspé Harbour signifying French possession of the land. Donnacona agreed to send his sons Domagaya and Taignoagny to France with Cartier. Returning with him in 1535, the two directed him down the St Lawrence and past the Saguenay, reported as a prosperous kingdom of gold, silver, and copper. Below Stadacona (Quebec) mutual suspicions developed, but Cartier pressed on to the fortified village of Hochelaga, where a modern reader recognizes the ironic contrast—perceived by neither party—between Native welcoming rituals and French politico-religious ones. Increasingly suspicious of the Natives, Cartier wintered near Stadacona. His men, who were dying of scurvy, were saved by Domagaya's knowledge of Native remedies, but Cartier captured Donnacona and carried him off to France. Returning in 1541, Cartier built forts and returned to Hochelaga, but mutual distrust bred conflict; after a troubled winter he left, taking with him 'gold' and 'diamonds' that proved worthless. Donnacona died in France, reportedly 'a good Christian'; Cartier died a prosperous St Malo bourgeois.

GERMAINE WARKENTIN

cartography. *See* MAPPING CANADA.

cartoonists. Editorial cartoons have been a ubiquitous feature of Canadian popular culture since well before Confederation. In many ways, the art and the country matured together, and these comic images provide a remarkable running commentary of the nation's history. While their content has always been thoroughly political, there are aspects of the genre that also make it a fertile source of historical information about Canadian social and cultural practices. With only moments to convey their messages, cartoonists rely on a cultural lexicon of shared visual and verbal references that can be rapidly grasped, and the nature of those common references tell us much about the social and intellectual context in which they circulated.

Canada's relationship with cartooning began in 1759, when George Townshend, a British officer at Quebec, circulated caricatures of General Wolfe. But the real beginning of the Canadian cartoon tradition was the flurry of short-lived comic periodicals such as *Punch in Canada* and *Grinchuckle* that started to appear in the 1840s. These ephemeral satirical papers remained the major vehicle for editorial cartooning for the rest of the 19th century, largely because the wood-engraving technique involved was incompatible with the demands of the burgeoning daily press. These cartoons established a distinctively Canadian set of symbols, styles, and metaphors upon which subsequent generations have built. The *beaver and the maple leaf, Miss Canada and Jack Canuck, all gained their popular currency through the work of early cartoonists, as did such perennial themes as Canada–US relations, English–French conflict, and race relations. In English Canada, the dominant early figure was J.W. *Bengough, whose **Grip* magazine circulated widely among the political and social elites between 1873 and 1894. In Quebec, Jean-Baptiste Côté's rough forceful stylizations in *La Scie* and *La Scie Illustrée* set the tone for future generations of francophone cartoonists from Hector Berthelot to Roland Berthiaume (Berthio).

With the rise of the popular press and new techniques of graphic reproduction, the comic periodicals disappeared at the start of the 20th century, and cartoons migrated to their familiar position in the pages of the daily newspaper. In the process, cartoonists became more independent, professionalized, and peripatetic, moving from paper to paper as opportunity dictated. Although political partisanship still informed many of these papers, their focus became increasingly regional. Cartoonists such as J.B. Fitzmaurice, Alberic Bourgeois, Sam Hunter, C.W. *Jefferys, and A.G. Racey (who succeeded Henri Julien at the *Montreal Star*) followed suit, as did others at papers like Bob *Edwards's *Calgary Eye Opener*. Daily papers slipped into consensual propaganda during the First World War, but their sectional tendencies became even more pronounced in the interwar years. Cartoonists such as Arch Dale, Donald McRitchie, and Jack Boothe inaugurated a new visual style and a more populist approach, with the 'little guy' increasingly taking centre stage.

After an uninspired reversion to traditional boosterism during the Second World War, cartoonists of the post-war period displayed an explosion of talent that shows little sign of abatement. Under the influence of television, cartoons became simpler and more direct, with little or no explanatory text. Many well-known artists such as Ed McNally, Bob Chambers, and John Collins began their careers at this time, but the seminal figure was undoubtedly Len Norris, who inspired such successors as Sid Barron and Roy Peterson. Equally influential were the inventive craftsmanship of Duncan Macpherson and the bold caricatures of Robert LaPalme.

Cartoonists are a curiously long-lived lot, and many of the best practitioners from the 1970s and 1980s remain at their drafting boards today. They no longer jump from paper to paper, having become an integral part of their newspaper's editorial stance. With the continued tendency to regionalism in the press, many brilliant cartoonists remain unknown beyond their city limits, but most Canadians will recognize one or more of the leading names: Adrian Raeside, Dale Cummings, John Larter, Malcolm Mayes, Andy Donato, Guy Badeaux (Bado), Brian Gable, Serge Chapleau, Terry Mosher (Aislin), and Bruce MacKinnon.

At the close of the 20th century, technological changes again affected the business of cartooning, particularly in the area of digital imaging and the advent of the internet. Brian Gable now does most of his work on a computer, while the cartoonists for two Ottawa papers, Cam Cardow of the *Citizen* and Susan Dewar of the *Sun*, work from Calgary and Toronto, respectively. Social changes also influenced Canadian cartooning in this period. Dewar became possibly the first woman in Canada to make a living as an editorial cartoonist, long an all-male preserve, while Everett Soop's images added a Native Canadian perspective to the visual critique of public folly. With its editorial autonomy and aura of dissent, the cartoon still provides a popular antidote to the bland corporate dispassion of much modern *journalism, and displays, thankfully, no sign of expiring in the foreseeable future. G. BRUCE RETALLACK

Cartwright, George (1740–1819), soldier, entrepreneur, essayist. Born in England, Cartwright embarked on a military career during the Seven Years' War but debts and the return of peace in 1763 caused him eventually to seek his fortune in civilian life. In 1766 he sailed to Newfoundland where his brother, John, served on station with the Royal Navy. George became captivated by the region, for he returned there in 1768, accompanying his brother on an unsuccessful expedition to contact the elusive *Beothuk Indians. Two years later, George resigned his military commission and, for more than 16 years, he and a series of partners invested in fishing for cod, salmon, and seals as well as fur trapping. Hard luck, the fortunes of war, and tough competition forced him into bankruptcy more than once. Nevertheless, he remained positive about his experiences, writing them up in a journal after he retired to England in 1787. Published in 1792, the journal today is one of our best sources on the Native inhabitants (with whom Cartwright maintained excellent relations), natural resources, and social conditions in late-18th-century *Labrador. Cartwright died in 1819, still promoting investment in and the development of Labrador.

OLAF U. JANZEN

Casavant, Joseph (1807–74), organ builder. If the name Casavant is known around the world for the manufacture of pipe organs, it is because a certain Joseph Casavant of Maska (now St-Hyacinthe), Quebec, decided at the age of 27 to leave his blacksmith's anvil and go to study music at the seminary of Ste-Thérèse. There he found the parts of an organ that no one had been able to put together. Casavant was invited to solve the puzzle with the aid of a book, *L'Art du facteur d'orgues* (1766) by Dom Bédos de Celles. He set to work and was so successful that he turned to constructing organs. He built 14 with his own hands, among them the highly praised organs of the cathedrals in Bytown (Ottawa) and Kingston. By 1866 he was sufficiently comfortable financially to retire and oversee the continuation of his business at St Hyacinthe until his sons were old enough to take over. They did so in 1879, under the name Casavant Frères.

ANTOINE BOUCHARD

Casgrain, Thérèse Forget (1893–1980), politician, feminist. Thérèse Casgrain spent her life in politics, championing women's rights in Quebec. She ran as a Liberal in Charlevoix-Saguenay in 1942, then sat on the *Wartime Prices and Trade Board. In 1946, she joined the *Co-operative Commonwealth Federation. In 1951, as head of the CCF in Quebec, she became the first female party leader in Canada. Casgrain, best known as a suffragist, founded the League for Women's Rights in 1928. She organized lobbying on behalf of the vote for women at the provincial level, and used her influence to have the Liberals include *women's suffrage in their platform; in 1940 the Liberal government granted Quebec women the vote. Active in consumers' and civil rights organizations, in 1961 Casgrain was a founding member of the *Voice of Women, a pacifist organization protesting against nuclear armament and the war in Vietnam. In 1967, she founded the *Fédération des femmes du Québec. Nominated to the Senate in 1970, she had to resign on her 75th birthday nine months later; she then began campaigning against compulsory retirement in all occupations.

ANDRÉE LÉVESQUE

Cashin, Peter J. (1890–1977). Born into a politically active merchant family, Cashin entered politics in 1923, and served as finance minister (1928–32). His accusations against Prime Minister Richard *Squires brought down the government in 1932, and soon after Cashin left to work in Canada. He returned to Newfoundland ten years later, and was elected to the *National Convention in 1946. An outspoken nationalist, Cashin believed that Newfoundland had the resources to survive as an independent country, and strongly advocated a return to responsible government. He worked hard and spoke effectively in the convention, was a member of the London delegation, and chaired the important committee that addressed the country's financial and economic condition. He emerged as perhaps the most prominent anti-confederate leader. Being mercurial and outspoken, Cashin never achieved a dominant position comparable to that of J.R. *Smallwood on the confederate side. After Newfoundland joined Canada, Cashin was elected provincially as an independent, later becoming a Progressive Conservative, and led the opposition in 1951–3. Failing to win a federal seat in 1953, he retired from politics and was appointed director of civil defence.

JAMES K. HILLER

Catholic emancipation. The process of removing legal restrictions on *Roman Catholics in British North America unfolded between 1779 and 1830. In post-conquest Quebec, and subsequently in the Canadas, Catholics were guaranteed religious freedom under the Treaty of Paris (1763). Although this guarantee was qualified by the ambiguous phrase 'so far as the laws of Great Britain do permit', legal toleration prevailed and therefore the need did not exist for emancipation. In the Atlantic colonies, Catholics were subject to a variety of disabilities ranging from denial of religious liberty to a body of anti-Catholic laws enacted by colonial legislatures. While such provisions were often honoured more in the breach than the observance, changes were required in Royal Instructions or in local statutes before full civil liberties for Catholics were legally assured. The process of reversing official anti-Catholicism began in 1779 with an amendment to the Royal Instructions to the governor of Newfoundland, which had the effect of including Catholics in the general provision for religious toleration. In the other Atlantic colonies, the more specific restrictions on Catholics were lifted in stages. A major step came when Catholics were granted the right to vote in elections for local legislatures (1789 in Nova Scotia, 1810 in New Brunswick). In 1830, following the passage of the Catholic Emancipation Act in Britain, Catholics were enfranchised in Prince Edward Island and were deemed eligible for election to local legislatures and admission to the bar in all the Maritime provinces. Newfoundland Catholics enjoyed the franchise from the beginning of representative government in 1832.

TERRENCE MURPHY

censorship. To defend democracy, Canadian governments have often felt it necessary to curtail free expression. The most comprehensive initiatives came in wartime. During the Great War, censorship was authorized under the 1914 *War Measures Act. Under it, in June 1915, an order-in-council established a chief press censor who received authority to prohibit material criticizing military policy, 'causing disaffection, assisting or encouraging the enemy or . . . hindering the successful prosecution of the war'. The chief censor banned 253 publications, of which 222 came from a neutral America. Within the first week of the Second World War, Canada's federal government again passed the War Measures Act and, through order-in-council, the *Defence of Canada Regulations under which it could order arbitrary detention and internment, suspend jury trial and *habeas corpus*, and censor media. In October, a director of censorship was appointed; within two years 325 sources were banned, just over half coming from enemy countries and most of the rest from a neutral United States. Censorship has also been present in peacetime Canada, with attention often focusing on socialists and communists. The most notorious federal initiative was the addition of section 98 to Canada's Criminal Code. Enacted in June 1919 in reaction to the Russian Revolution abroad and the *Winnipeg General Strike at home, this legislation, which remained in effect until 1936, provided up to 20 years' imprisonment for those who printed or uttered anything that 'taught, advocated, advised or defended' the overthrow of the government or the economic system by force. Probably the most significant provincial initiative was Quebec's *Padlock Act. Passed in 1937, it permitted the closure of any meeting place used by a communist or socialist group. Even with the 1982 *Charter of Rights, the replacement of the War Measures Act in 1988 with the less draconian Emergencies Act, and the end of the Cold War, censorship remains evident. For example, in trying to protect 'community standards', the courts and Parliament have deemed it necessary to impose controls over hate literature and certain types of pornography, especially those involving children.

JEFF KESHEN

census. Early census making was affected markedly by Canada's colonial status. French and then British rulers tried repeatedly to use the census as an instrument for measuring the degree of wealth and the development of *population in the colonies. Before the first census of the new Dominion of Canada was conducted in 1871, 21 censuses had been undertaken in New Brunswick and Nova Scotia alone, many more in what became Ontario and Quebec. The censuses conducted in New France in the 1660s are among the earliest to attempt to create a nominal list of all the inhabitants of a territory. From the 1820s, colonial governors were expected to deliver a return of population as part of the annual Blue Book, but the information was not available for them to do so.

With some notable exceptions, such as the census of Montreal conducted by the meticulous Jacques Viger in 1825, early census making was largely haphazard. In British North America political representation was not apportioned according to population, as it was in the United States, and this absence removed one source of pressure for systematic procedures. Moreover, the attempt by the British government after 1840 to assimilate the French-Canadian population and to encourage English-speaking immigration politicized census making. Numbers of inhabitants, the comparative strength of religious denominations, and the rural/urban divide came to be imbued with deep cultural meanings. Growing census numbers were seen by the census agency, the Bureau of Agriculture and Statistics, as an advertising mechanism for encouraging immigration. None of the pre-Confederation censuses adopted consistent or coherent protocols. Nonetheless, many of the original manuscript returns have been preserved, providing a rich resource for researchers.

Under the terms of *Confederation, representation in both houses of Parliament was to be determined according to a complex formula that took the population of

Quebec as a baseline measure. The first post-Confederation census (1871) established a number of enduring census conventions. Censuses attempted, for example, to tie members of the population to their place of birth and 'national origin'. Until the 1990s, 'Canadian' was not among the acceptable national origins for census-making purposes. A later convention called for census informants to list their 'mother tongue'; only one response was permitted until after 1996. Canadian censuses were conducted decennially from 1871 until 1951, after which a quinquennial census period was adopted. The 1956 census was the first to make extensive use of self-reporting. By that date, census numbers were an essential part of much of governmental administration and were used in a variety of ways by non-governmental and private economic actors.

The census has long been the most extensive form of social enquiry in Canada. Census making here, as in other countries, has been the site of innovative logistical arrangements, novel data-management techniques, and shifts in statistical method. The 1871 census preparations involved the creation of detailed territorial maps. Hollerith tabulating machinery was first used in the 1891 census tabulation, and the 1961 census was an early instance of large-scale use of computing facilities by a Canadian government. Representative sampling procedures, generally accepted in social scientific practice only after 1920, were in use in the census agency in the late 1940s. Representative samples of the population now provide the basis for much of the administrative and policy work in which the census is implicated. BRUCE CURTIS

Cercles des fermières. Established in 1915 by a handful of women in the rural district of Roberval, the Cercles des fermières brought together nearly 80,000 members throughout Quebec. Attracted by the idea of modernizing agriculture, women created the first Cercles to develop their knowledge, improve the domestic economy, and acquire or gain public recognition for their skills in crafts and food production.

In a period when only a small minority of Quebec women took part in the electoral process, the Cercles generated connections between women and both the provincial state and political parties through vehicles such as grants, petitions, and banquets, allowing women to take on a new public role. The willingness of the Cercles to solicit state support drew strong reaction from the Catholic Church, which wanted them to stay under the church's tutelage. Furthermore, the church accused the Cercles of submitting to the authority of the Ministry of Agriculture, causing the organization to split in 1937. The Union catholique des fermières was founded in 1944 as the church's own organization. Thereafter the Cercles embarked on a gradual process of secularization that foreshadowed the large-scale secularization of the *Quiet Revolution. Anticipating the women's liberation movement of the 1970s, the Cercles allowed women to move into the public sphere, giving them a place to share their duties as mothers and citizens. YOLANDE COHEN

chain stores. Not incorrectly, as it turned out, many retail experts in the 1920s predicted that the 20th century would be 'the Chain Store Age'. Chains first attracted notice in large cities just after the First World War; by the Second they had become a dominating presence. At the close of the 20th century two-thirds of all retail stores were some form of chain outlet.

Unlike *department stores, which located centrally and drew customers to them with their services and selection, chains opened on main streets in residential districts and tended to concentrate on a single line of trade. The five-and-dimes—mini-department stores selling inexpensive goods—were the major exception to this. The first five-and-dimes in Canada were opened by the American entrepreneur S.H. Knox in 1897, but his stores were soon swallowed up by Frank Woolworth's retail empire. The leading American chains—Woolworth's and Kresge's—dominated the business for many decades, but in the 1960s a Montreal company, Zeller's, came to lead the discount department store business. In the food lines, big American companies like A&P and Safeway were also a strong presence through much of the century, but Canadian companies—Loblaw's, Dominion, and Sobey's—proved powerful and long-lived rivals.

Although individual businesses have come and gone, chain stores are so perfectly suited to the demands of modern industry that they have been the most adaptable of retail organizations. With identical displays, centralized advertising, and standardized pricing, chain-based merchandising is the retailing equivalent of mass production. Chain stores appealed to cost-conscious consumers and to manufacturers interested in high-volume, low-margin distribution. From the beginning industry favoured the stores with bulk buying discounts and special allowances. By the late 1920s the chains became strong enough to demand even bigger discounts from their suppliers, shifting the balance of power in the trading relationship. But so intertwined are the chains with their suppliers that frequent government investigations into discriminatory discounts, loss-leader selling, and predatory competition have failed to challenge the system.

Chain stores were ideally suited to post–Second World War urban expansion; they travelled easily with the population and became dominant in most suburban malls. The rise of the warehouse, or big-box, stores has led to the closing of many chain outlets and a move among corporations to concentrate on fewer, bigger stores. But the ongoing debate over the impact of big-box stores is really a sign of a struggle between one concept of chain selling and another, rather than a passing of the multiple-store idea. Indeed, by the end of the century most forms of retail enterprise had adopted the chain store approach: department stores had become chains in the early 20th century, and after the Second World War independent businesses increasingly organized themselves in *franchises. Truly, it remains the chain store's age. DAVID MONOD

Champagne, Claude (1891–1965), composer and teacher. Born in Montreal, Champagne studied violin and piano before completing his musical education in Paris. Returning to Canada in 1928, he devoted himself to the development of the musical life of Quebec, dividing his time between teaching, administration, and composition. A professor of harmony and composition at McGill University, he was one of the founders of the Conservatoire de musique du Québec in 1942. He introduced an entire generation of young musicians such as Clermont Pépin, Serge Garant, and Gilles Tremblay to the art of writing music. His own compositions (*Suite canadienne*, *Suite gaspésienne*) reflect the French influence and the inspiration of Canadian folklore. His work includes symphonies, concertos, choral and orchestral pieces, and chamber music.

ODETTE VINCENT

Champlain, Samuel de (*c.* 1570–1635), soldier, geographer, explorer, author, administrator, born in Brouage near Rochefort, France, to a sea-going family. After serving as a quartermaster in the army of Henri IV from 1593 to 1598, Champlain sailed in the Caribbean until 1601 for Spain. During these years he did 'important and confidential' work for the king of France, who rewarded him with a pension. In 1603, with the king's support, he joined a fur-trading expedition to the St Lawrence Valley to determine if the area was fit for colonization. He made similar resource surveys and charts of the Atlantic coast from Cape Canso to Cape Cod, 1604–7, always reporting to his superiors and the king on his return. In 1608 he returned to Canada with orders to establish a settlement (Quebec) and explore westward towards China. In 1609 he reached Lake Champlain and in 1615 Lakes Huron and Ontario, in both cases accompanying French Native allies on raids against the *Iroquois. Assistance on these raids was expected by the Natives and had been promised by Henri IV in return for their permitting French settlement. From 1612 to his death Champlain held the powers of a governor as lieutenant to various French viceroys. During his life he published four books, 23 charts and picture plans, and at least six maps.

Champlain was the first European to develop a realistic plan for the exploration of Canada: develop friendly relations with Native groups, establish permanent agriculturally based settlements, learn to operate a canoe and to live off the land, and hire Natives as geographical informants and guides. In 1615 his actions led to the introduction of Récollet missionaries to proselytize Native groups. His last act as governor, supported by the *Jesuits, was a council with the *Huron in which he proposed Native–French intermarriage, both to facilitate conversion to Catholicism and to create a people adapted to Canada. His establishment of Quebec (1608) and Trois-Rivières (1634) and his persistence in promoting and defending the colony assured the French presence in Canada and earned him the honorific 'Founder of New France'.

CONRAD HEIDENREICH

Chanak affair. A political crisis that erupted in 1922 between Canada and Britain over sending a military contingent to help the British garrison in a standoff with Turkish forces at Chanak, a small port on the Dardanelles. London asked for help on 15 September and made the request public before consulting Ottawa. Angered by what he thought was a breach of protocol, Prime Minister Mackenzie *King informed London that only Parliament could authorize the dispatch of troops. It was the first but not the last time King used this tactic to warn Britain against expecting automatic Canadian support for every British conflict.

GREGORY A. JOHNSON

chansonniers. The term *chansonnier*—literally, 'song maker'—first appeared in the 1960s; since 1980 it has been replaced by *auteur-compositeur-interprète* ('singer-songwriter'). If *La Bolduc represented a bridge between folk and popular song, the poet, novelist, and playwright Félix Leclerc (1914–88) is considered the father of the Quebec chanson. Becoming a star first in France, Leclerc sang his poetic lyrics to the accompaniment of a guitar played while standing with one foot raised on a chair—a pose that became the archetype of the chansonnier style. With him the chanson became a whole new genre, and the rising generation of young people took it for their own. The first *boites à chansons* (folk clubs) became home to a veritable cult of songs in which the emphasis was on the lyrics, structured around themes such as escape and wide-open spaces—before becoming preoccupied with matters of national identity.

The years 1960–7 were the golden age of the boite à chansons. Especially after 1970 the chanson, along with Quebec poetry, was to serve the independentist political discourse and assist in the creation of an all-encompassing 'Québécitude'. It would also symbolize Quebec's resistance to the importation of American cultural models, musical as well as linguistic. The chansonniers took great care with their lyrics and made Quebec known throughout the francophone world. In the 1970s Gilles Vigneault (*Mon Pays*) was at his peak; Leclerc (*L'Alouette en colère*) spoke out in support of independence. Claude Gauthier (*Le Grand six pieds*), Raymond Lévesque (*Bozo les culottes*), Jean-Pierre Ferland, Claude Léveillée, and Georges Dor (*La Manic*) were among the most sought-after chansonniers and appeared on such stages as Montreal's Place des Arts and the Grand Théâtre de Québec. During these transitional years, stylistic and thematic diversity was in keeping with the spirit of the times and was reflected in the musical experimentation of the group Harmonium, the urbanity of Beau Dommage and Richard and Marie Séguin, the French rock of Robert Charlebois, and the socio-political engagement of Paul Piché and Plume Latraverse.

Since 1979 the chanson has reflected the pluralistic discourse of a new generation of writers. The new guard—Michel Rivard, Jim Corcoran, and Daniel Lavoie—sing in an exportable international French, but the market for French-language chansons has dropped off. The success of Richard Desjardins, whose songs combine the language of Quebec with American musical rhythms, has given chansonniers a renewed pride in use of the vernacular. Today the chanson is returning to its original language and boîtes à chansons are again emerging all over Quebec. As Félix Leclerc used to say: 'Quebec is a divided country except when it sings.' ODETTE VINCENT

charivari. An old European custom imported into New France in the 17th century, charivari in its classic French-Canadian form was a ritual attack on a newly married couple. When the community objected to a marriage—typically because of a disparity in the age or wealth of the partners—people would gather on the wedding night to 'serenade' the couple with raucous music and abusive songs. Noise, humour, and costumes created a festive but menacing atmosphere, and the wise victim soon bowed before the storm and bought off the crowd with drinks or money. In the fall of 1837, at the time of the Lower Canadian *rebellion, the charivari form was used by *Patriotes in the villages south of Montreal to target loyal militia captains and justices of the peace in their midst. These representatives of government authority were forced to resign their positions: the turning over of an official commission took the place of the traditional surrender of money or alcohol. The charivari custom spread from Lower Canada to Upper Canada, where the term was usually pronounced 'shivaree'; Susanna *Moodie provided a description of one such event. ALLAN GREER

Charlottetown. Capital of *Prince Edward Island, named for Charlotte, consort of George III. Located inside a harbour facing Northumberland Strait, Charlottetown is at the point where three rivers meet the harbour, providing access to the interior. In the 1760s, after the British gained sovereignty over the island, a townsite was laid out on a grid pattern, with the major streets, 100 feet wide for fire protection, leading north.

As the capital after political separation of the island from Nova Scotia in 1769, Charlottetown became the seat of the legislature, courts, and government offices in general. As the centre of official power, the town was identified with elite interests. The contrast between town and countryside in Prince Edward Island was heightened by the system of leasehold tenure and the popular identification of the capital with propertied interests.

The town gained commercial importance as a market for local farmers and as the import-export centre for the colony. *Shipbuilding, *shipping, and small-scale manufacturing also took root. With the development of the colony, most cultural institutions of significance, such as academies and colleges, were in the town. The pattern was established: as the colony grew, the town grew, and it was the colony's metropolis.

In 1855 Charlottetown was incorporated and became responsible for its own governance through a mayor and councillors. They modernized municipal services over the latter decades of the 19th century. In September 1864, Charlottetown hosted the Confederation Conference. Consequently, the city has been called 'the Cradle of Confederation', a term which conveniently ignores the overwhelmingly anti-Confederate sentiment on the island in the 1860s. The coming of the railway in the early 1870s reinforced the city's role as a communications hub. New industries emerged in the 20th century, the most significant being tourism. A landmark event was construction of the Confederation Centre of the Arts to commemorate the centennial of the Confederation Conference. Conceived as a multi-purpose cultural centre, it contained a theatre, art gallery, museum, archives, and library.

After the Second World War, following a common North American trend, suburban communities emerged on the borders of Charlottetown. By the 1970s a stagnating downtown area provoked an effort to preserve and beautify 'Old Charlottetown', with some success. Six adjacent suburbs and the old city were amalgamated in 1995, forming a new, larger municipal entity, which retained the name of Charlottetown. Its political, administrative, cultural, communications, and commercial functions have ensured its continuing dominance within the province. IAN ROSS ROBERTSON

Charlottetown Accord. A set of proposed constitutional amendments agreed to by the 11 first ministers of Canada, the leaders of the two federal territories, and leaders of four Aboriginal organizations in August 1992. For the first time in Canada, the proposals were submitted to the people in a national referendum. Held on 26 October 1992, it was defeated by a majority of 54.4 to 44.6 per cent, losing in six of the ten provinces. The negotiations leading to the accord were prompted by the failure of the *Meech Lake Accord. First ministers sought to enhance the legitimacy of the constitutional renewal process by broadening participation (with a series of national conferences, parliamentary hearings, and representation of territorial and Aboriginal leaders at the bargaining table), and by widening the range of issues to be considered, to include *Senate reform, Aboriginal self-government, and other matters, in addition to the issues surrounding Quebec as a distinct society. Rejection of the accord brought to an end a long period in which Canadians had failed to agree on constitutional renewal, and demonstrated how difficult it was to find consensus on the fundamental characteristics of the Canadian polity. Subsequently, attention turned to finding more incremental, non-constitutional ways of responding to Canada's regional and linguistic diversity.
RICHARD SIMEON

Charter of Rights and Freedoms. The Canadian Charter of Rights and Freedoms, applicable to federal and provincial governments, and entrenched in the *constitution in 1982, built on and departed from the 1960 Canadian Bill of Rights. The 1960 bill, indelibly associated with Prime Minister John *Diefenbaker, was a weak instrument. It applied only to the federal government; moreover, it was an ordinary statute, and Parliament could override it by inserting a *'notwithstanding clause' in otherwise offending legislation. The courts did not see this bill as a major invitation to strike down federal statutes, which they did only once, in the 1970 **Drybones* case.

The 1982 Charter profited from the (admittedly limited) habituation to a culture of rights offered by the 1960 bill and from knowledge, gleaned from the latter, of what weaknesses to avoid. In the atmosphere following the defeat of the Quebec government's 1980 referendum on *sovereignty-association, the Charter emerged out of a titanic struggle between the federal government, supported by Ontario and New Brunswick, and eight provincial governments that initially opposed it. The Charter, which after intense bargaining and brinkmanship ultimately gained the support of all provincial governments but Quebec, had two purposes: the standard one of protecting individual rights against the state, and the political function of contributing to Canadian unity by reinforcing a pan-Canadian sense of identity based on the citizens' possession of country-wide rights. The document was the key instrument in the counterattack mounted by Prime Minister Pierre *Trudeau against provincializing trends and the independence strand in Quebec nationalism. At its deepest level, it was an instrument to nationalize the psyche of the citizenry.

The Charter protects fundamental freedoms (s. 2), democratic rights (ss. 3, 4, 5), mobility rights (s. 6), legal rights (ss. 7–14), equality rights (s. 15), and French- and English-language rights, including minority language educational rights (ss. 16–23). Further, the Charter is not to be construed as abrogating or derogating from *Aboriginal or treaty rights (s. 25); its interpretation is to be 'consistent with the preservation and enhancement of the multicultural heritage of Canadians' (s. 27); its rights and freedoms 'are guaranteed equally to male and female persons' (s. 28), and the rights or privileges of 'denominational, separate or dissentient schools' (s. 29) are protected.

Occasional criticism of the Charter as an Americanizing instrument overlooks its obvious Canadianness. In particular, the clauses dealing with official language minorities, with Canada's multicultural heritage, and with Aboriginal peoples are explicitly tailored to the Canadian scene. Canadian history, with its tradition of parliamentary supremacy, surfaces in the section 1 'reasonable limits' clause: Charter rights and freedoms are 'subject only to such reasonable limits prescribed by law as can be demonstrably justified in a free and democratic society'. Canadian history, which gave pride of place to the leading role of Parliament, surfaces again in the section 33 'notwithstanding clause', which permits Parliament or a provincial legislature to declare that an act shall apply notwithstanding the freedom provisions of section 2 or the legal and equality rights of sections 7–15.

The Charter is the most significant constitutional change since Confederation. It has overwhelming public support, even in Quebec, whose political elite has never accepted the legitimacy of the 1982 Constitution Act. The Charter has rearranged the relative status of major political institutions: legislatures, by definition, have diminished status; the federal principle based on territorial communities now confronts a rival citizen-state constitutional principle based on rights; the *Supreme Court of Canada has acquired a vastly enhanced status and recognition compared to its former self; and citizens now have a stake in the constitution that challenges the former hegemony of governments in the *constitutional amending process. By speaking directly to the citizenry, the Charter has given the constitution a popular base.

ALAN CAIRNS

Château Clique. In 1791 the metropolitan authorities divided 'Old Quebec' into Upper and Lower Canada, each colony possessing an elected assembly with Catholics obtaining full political rights. A dynamic new political elite drawn from the Canadien professional and rural merchant classes formed the Parti canadien and rose to claim its place in Quebec society by appealing to the electorate and demanding that the royal executive grant them offices to reflect their status as leaders of the Canadien majority. The Anglo-Quebec merchant elite, colonial administrators, and some of the seigneurial class came together to resist what the merchants deemed to be the anti-commercial tendencies of the Parti canadien. With the loss of control over the legislature, the English party became increasingly dependent on the governor to maintain its influence. These individuals were labelled the Château Clique because they often appealed to the governor at his official residence at the Château St-Louis. Led by Herman Ryland, members sought to assert control through a policy of anglicization of the Canadien populace. In addition, increased immigration and population growth created tensions over unsettled lands in the *Eastern Townships, which was dominated by the Canada Land Company, bringing the question of seigneurial tenure versus freehold to the fore as the English merchants and some seigneurs sought to develop new lands at the expense of the Canadien majority.

The Château Clique tried to undermine the Canadien grip on the legislature by using its substantial contacts in London to obtain legislation uniting Upper and Lower Canada, thereby diluting the Canadien majority, but a *Union Bill in 1822 failed. In this atmosphere of distrust, the gulf between the Château Clique and the Parti patriote, as it was then known, widened. The English party controlled the legislative council, but without control over the assembly governors were forced to fall back on the civil list as a means of upholding their executive powers. The merchants, who needed legislative approval to realize their aspirations for major communications projects, banking systems, and other infrastructure of an industrial/commercial society, grew increasingly restless. The unrest was not settled until *rebellions in 1837–8 drove imperial officials to unite Upper and Lower Canada in 1841.

K. DAVID MILOBAR

Chatelaine, 1928– . A middle-class women's magazine with a secretly subversive bent, Maclean Hunter's general interest periodical has been a consistent performer. Financially a proven winner for the company, it has successfully attracted a mass audience of working-class and middle-class Canadian women and men. Readers formed an 'imagined community' in which their letters to the editors, samples of which were published in each issue, applauded, challenged, and criticized the editorial content. That lively engagement between the readers and the editors provided feedback and demonstrated the importance accorded the publication, particularly for those in rural and more isolated regions. The reading community is a key reason for *Chatelaine*'s staying power and currency.

While *Chatelaine* adhered to the traditional format of a 50/50 editorial/advertising mix—with a hefty dollop of recipes, *fashion, decorating advice, and, in the pre-1970s version, fiction it also included general features. Those articles differentiate *Chatelaine* from the handful of Canadian competitors and, most importantly, their American counterparts. Not only are the features proudly Canadian, they have often introduced readers to unconventional, broadly political, fare. Pre-1945, they featured articles on prominent female politicians and professionals, championed women's ordination, and applauded women's wartime contributions. Post-1945, particularly under the direction of Doris Anderson (editor, 1957–77), *Chatelaine* popularized second-wave *feminism and took a lead role in demanding a federal commission to investigate women's status. Additionally, the magazine printed articles on a host of controversial articles, including *divorce reform, access to *abortion and the *birth control pill, child abuse, and, today, women's health advocacy.

VALERIE J. KORINEK

Chautauqua. Before cars and good roads brought the cultural attractions of large towns within reach, thousands of people flocked during the summer months to the brown tents of the Chautauqua movement for four to six days of music, drama, education, and entertainment. Originating in 1874 as a Sunday School Teachers' Assembly on the shores of Lake Chautauqua in western New York, Chautauqua was the brain child of two American Methodists, Bishop John Vincent and Lewis Miller, an Ohio farm machinery manufacturer. With an initial emphasis on study, community singing, recreation, and high Methodist standards of moral behaviour, Chautauqua was an instant success, and by the 1880s had spawned a host of independent Chautauquas, often organizing towns into circuits in an effort to extend their reach. In 1917 under the energetic leadership of John and Nola Erickson, one of these circuit Chautauquas established a Canadian headquarters in Calgary, and for the next 15 summers its Dominion Chautauquas dotted the map of the Prairies and small-town Ontario. Drawing primarily on Canadian and British musical, dramatic, and literary talent, as well as offering innovative children's programs, these unique travelling institutes offered young people valued summer employment and enlivened the cultural world of thousands of communities.

MARGUERITE VAN DIE

children. Although children have always inhabited Canada's past, only recently have historians deigned to notice them. Now, histories of childhood delineate policies affecting youngsters, and histories of children examine their day-to-day lives.

Children have always found growing up hard work. Until recent times—for Euro-Canadians, if not necessarily for their Aboriginal neighbours—the metaphor that saw youngsters as clay, needing moulding and shaping, governed their rearing. From earliest days to the middle of the 19th century most children grew up as working members of families subsisting on combinations of gathering, hunting, fishing, trapping, farming, logging, and fabricating in home workshops. Taught by elders, parents, and siblings, from infancy onward children mastered the practical, often gendered, skills needed for adulthood. By early in the 19th century, many also attended school, usually seasonally, for two or three years. Children without families were indentured to families who fostered them for the work they could do. Since families lived close to the margin, children were, especially in winter and spring, often cold and hungry.

Children attended religious services, missions, camp meetings, weddings, funerals, dances, picnics, sleighing parties, ceilidhs, and potlatches. As they took part in family and community activities, youngsters acquired both tribal and cultural lore and assumed their gender, ethnic, and religious identities. As girls and boys spent time at school or at play with other children, they entered the almost timeless world of childhood culture and their brief generation within it. There they absorbed the often crudely expressed customs, beliefs, values, social roles, and unwritten rules circumscribing relationships among peers.

Late-19th- and 20th-century modernization changed growing up. As the notion of a child as a plant needing tender care replaced the traditional metaphor, the practices of parents and others who cared for children were gradually modified. A rising standard of living permitted many families to substitute more comprehensive schooling for some child labour. To make ends meet, others sent children as young as ten to work for long hours in factories and mines. There they faced both physical and sexual abuse. Turn-of-the-century children attended school for an average of less than four years, those of the 1920s for about six, and those of the 1950s about eight. Classes for 'new Canadians' socialized the children of immigrants. Day and *residential schools for First Nations children promised to blend useful elements of European culture with Native ones; in practice they tried, sometimes brutally, to 'educate the Indian out' of their clients.

Although children were captivated by new elements of the modern world such as trains, automobiles, airplanes, motion pictures, and radio, their day-to-day lives changed little from the turn of the century until after the Second World War. Most did numerous chores, shared the happy and sad occasions of life in their extended *families, and played an active role in a childhood culture that included comic books and the Saturday movie matinee. Others were less fortunate. Although legislation ended child labour in mines and factories, children of the very poor still shared their families' desperate struggle to survive. Abused, neglected, dependent, and delinquent youngsters found little evidence in their lives of the new, more humane notions of care.

The 1950s and 1960s marked the peak of the 'traditional' family in Canadian history. The ratio of children relative to the rest of the population reached its highest point in the century. As well, a higher proportion of youngsters than ever before, or since, grew up in the care of both birth parents. Smaller families and rising living standards increased the amount of physical and emotional resources parents devoted to each child. Children were healthier, better fed, and better clothed than youngsters of any earlier generation. They lived in warmer, more comfortable homes and less often had to share beds or bedrooms. Corporal punishment declined at home and at school. Although many children received small allowances, from about age 12 they also sought out part-time work. While their earnings reduced pressures on family budgets, they increased youthful choice in clothing, school supplies, and entertainment.

Since the 1970s, changing family arrangements have affected many children. They have had to adapt to living with custodial and non-custodial parents, foster parents, adoptive parents, step-parents, same-sex parents, siblings, step-siblings, half-siblings, and foster siblings. Often, both parents worked away from the home. Although middle-class parents made satisfactory child-care arrangements, poor families made do with marginal ones, sometimes turning their children into 'latch-key kids'. Many youngsters continued to be hungry, neglected, and abused, and numerous investigations showed the pernicious effects of poverty on young lives. Others reported on how race, ethnicity, class, and gender governed how children grew up. Although residential schools were closed in the 1970s, their legacy lingered on in accounts detailing the long-term effects of abuse. The beginning of a new century still found many Native children ranking among the nation's most deprived youngsters.

In changing forms, media pervaded childhood. Both girls and boys enjoyed the products of an explosion in literature for children. As well as traditional pastimes, childhood culture included cinema, television, computer games, and the Internet. Saturday matinees gave way to videos and television cartoons that aggressively promoted expensive products.

Despite the social and economic anxieties of the closing decades of the century, continuity still characterized much of the lives of Canadian children. Virtually all of them attended school throughout their childhood and adolescence. For most children, the circle of family, school, and peers remained at the centre of their lives.

NEIL SUTHERLAND

Children of Peace. This remarkable utopian community was founded by David Willson (1778–1866), a carpenter, farmer, hymn writer, and religious visionary. Willson moved his family from New York to Upper Canada in 1801, taking up land in the *Quaker settlement near Newmarket. Deeply spiritual and charismatic, he became an active member of the Society of Friends, but his intense religious experiences clashed with the doctrines imposed by the Quaker leadership, and he was expelled in 1812. Willson and his followers then formed a new group, the Children of Peace, and set about building an ideal Christian community around the village of Sharon. The Children practised social and gender equality, developed a co-operative agricultural system, built schools, practised charity, and offered a living witness to the paths of peace. At the centre of their community was the Sharon Temple. Built by local carpenters following the biblical account of Solomon's temple at Jerusalem, the building served as an alms house and affirmed through its form many of the central beliefs of the community. It was a white frame building, three stories in height and square in dimension. When its large windows were illuminated the temple shone like a beacon in the wilderness. When David Willson died the Children of Peace went into rapid decline, but the temple has survived, a testimony to the community and its founder.

WILLIAM WESTFALL

child welfare. During the late 19th and early 20th centuries, a range of socio-economic changes, including a decline in family size, the growth of industry, urbanization, immigration, and the expansion of public schooling, led Canadians to reconsider the state's responsibilities towards *children. Earlier, state provisions were minimal and intended as the last recourse. In addition to municipal 'houses of industry', as poorhouses were known, provincial governments offered jails, reformatories, and industrial schools, some support to privately run *orphanages, and an indenture system to apprentice orphaned, abandoned, or poor children—often as young as eight years—to farmers and other employers. The state's protective role was limited to the prohibition of infanticide and severe physical abuse. The rare prosecutions for child abuse and neglect were generally lenient, as law and society upheld parental, and especially paternal, rights.

Industrialization initially led to new opportunities for child labour. Children in pre-industrial Canada had been expected to work from a very early age in order to contribute to the family's economic well-being; factory production simply meant a change in setting for many. Between 1870 and 1925, large numbers of underprivileged *'home children' were brought from Britain under various philanthropic immigration schemes to work as agricultural labourers and domestic servants. If the intention was *adoption, or at least fostering, the outcome was too often indentured servitude, with many instances of neglect and abuse. Increasing public concern about the plight of such children led to some of the earliest child welfare legislation. In 1884 Ontario became the first province to prohibit girls under 14 and boys under 12 from employment in factories, and to enforce the 10-hour day and 60-hour week for children. Similar legislation was passed in Quebec in 1885, and the other provinces thereafter. Formal schooling became more important as many traditional familial functions were transferred into the public domain. Beginning with Ontario in 1871, by

1905 all provinces except Quebec passed laws requiring children between the ages of 7 and 14 years to go to school for minimum periods.

As the economic role of children slowly shifted, new ideas about a distinct and protected childhood were formalized. Late-19th-century reformers, many operating within the auspices of a Christian activism known as the *social gospel, began to define childhood as a stage of institutionalized dependence. A variety of middle-class church and charitable organizations, with women's groups newly predominant, attempted to address child welfare issues. Women volunteers were instrumental in the establishment of institutions such as the Protestant Children's Homes, which emerged by 1860 in Montreal, Kingston, Toronto, and Halifax. Many of their residents were not orphaned but simply impoverished, often left there by parents who hoped to retrieve them in better times. By the 1880s, the Society for the Prevention of Cruelty to Animals, with branches in most urban centres, had taken on the cause of domestic violence, and was offering practical and legal support to battered women and children. The *National Council of Women of Canada, founded in 1893, brought new dynamism to a wide range of child welfare causes, including infant mortality, child labour and immigration, delinquency, and 'mental hygiene'.

The institutionalization of child welfare in the early 20th century was closely related to the rise of 'family experts' and the growing public clamour for state regulation of familial relations. The social gospel's most prominent reform association, the Moral and Social Reform Council of Canada (1907)—effectively the first national social work network—became the Social Service Council in 1913. Supported by a growing faith in the regenerative capacities of science, the new experts played a major role in identifying social problems and formulating ways to address them. The traditional assumption that parents know their children's best interests came under fire. The emerging view was that society should decide the standards for family life, and that the state should actively uphold them. Reformers advocated laws specifying minimal legal, economic, and moral criteria to ensure the necessary conditions for child welfare and to establish guidelines for the health, education, and behaviour of children.

This shift from parental rights to parental responsibilities and children's rights was facilitated by legislative departures and the creation of institutions to enforce new policies. Ontario's landmark Act for the Protection and Reformation of Neglected Children (1888) permitted courts to make children wards of institutions and charitable organizations. On behalf of neglected, abused, and abandoned children, the Children's Aid Society was established in 1891; the Ontario government sanctioned its activities with the Children's Protection Act (1893). Due in large part to the unflinching efforts of J.J. *Kelso, the first Ontario superintendent of neglected and dependent children, most provinces had joined the CAS network with enabling legislation and their own provincial agencies by 1901. By the First World War, the CAS had transformed itself from a voluntarist and philanthropic coalition of 'child savers' to a powerful regulatory agency, staffed largely by professional social workers who kept an eye on 'bad' homes and brought the law to bear on them. In 1908, the federal Juvenile Delinquents Act created the offence of delinquency and established children's courts, further enlarging the state's parental role. For the first time, a child could be legally censured for non-criminal behaviours such as truancy, wandering, and loitering and also for engaging in 'adult' practices, particularly gambling, drinking, smoking, and sex.

One of the earliest objectives of child savers resulted in a coalition of women's groups, medical professionals, public health campaigners, and various levels of government to reduce the nation's horrific infant mortality rates. Pure milk depots were established in urban areas, initially organized by local women's groups, but gradually evolving into all-round supervisory 'well baby' clinics, staffed largely by public health nurses. By 1914, urban municipal governments had taken over the clinics as the state expanded its roster of *public health work. By 1920, most provinces had a system of visiting nurses, and both provincial and federal health departments were enthusiastically publishing 'scientific childrearing' literature for free dissemination.

The Great War's casualties, and the social disruption in its wake, further legitimized state intervention in child and family welfare. Reformist and professional organizations as well as women's and labour groups demanded the creation of government agencies dedicated to assisting *families, especially children, now even more precious 'national assets'. The most important of these was the Canadian Council on Child Welfare, established in 1921. Its name change to the Council on Child and Family Welfare in 1929 reflected the more inclusive mandate that would be the legacy of the decade's family-centred reform debates and measures; it is now the National Welfare Council. Thanks in large measure to the recommendations of the Royal Commission on Dominion–Provincial Relations (1937–40), which urged state commitment to health and welfare, and those of sociologist Leonard *Marsh's *Report on Social Security for Canada* (1943), which highlighted child welfare, the Mackenzie *King government was prepared to instigate a universal family allowance (1944) as an integral component of post-war reconstruction.

Since the Second World War, the situation of Aboriginal children has come to be considered the greatest challenge facing the child welfare system. Although First Nations people account for only 4 per cent of the Canadian population, approximately 20 per cent of the children in care as the 20th century closed were Aboriginal. Until the 1970s, federal initiatives to serve Aboriginal child welfare were delivered largely through enforced residential schooling and 'placing' in foster homes, often with families outside of the children's culture. *Residential schools have been eliminated, and attempts are being made to encourage the training of Aboriginal child welfare workers and placement with families within the children's own community. Aboriginal child welfare agencies, such as First Nations Head Start and First Nations Family and Children Caring Society, are being established in many parts of the country.

Since the late 19th century, in addition to increasing government involvement and important legislative developments, Canadians have seen a shift from a volunteer to a professional child welfare system, and from institutional and protective services to non-institutional and preventive services. During the past several decades, child welfare has witnessed tremendous changes: in the classification of what constitutes neglect and abuse, in the types of services provided, and in policy, which now places legal responsibility to report suspected abuse on both professionals and ordinary citizens. Recently established by the federal government to support research on contemporary child welfare issues, in terms of both treatment and prevention, the Centre of Excellence for Child Welfare draws on a multidisciplinary panel of experts to work towards an integrated and effective program for the 21st century.

CYNTHIA COMACCHIO

See also MOTHERS OF THE RACE.

Chilkoot Pass. A 1,074-m pass between Taiya Inlet, Alaska, and *Yukon River headwaters in northwestern British Columbia. One of several passes through the Coastal Mountain range, the Chilkoot was a secondary trade route between coastal Tlingit and interior Tagish First Nations. It gained notoriety during the 1890s, when, along with the nearby White Pass, it was used by some 30,000 stampeders during the *Klondike gold rush. The pass fell into disuse when the *White Pass and Yukon Route Railway bypassed it in 1899. Considered for a major power development in the late 1940s, the idea faded when *Alcan completed its Kitimat project. The pass is now an international historic park commemorating the gold rush trail. DAVID NEUFELD

Chinese. The history of Chinese in Canada dates back to 1858, when Chinese miners from the United States came to the Fraser Valley of British Columbia following the discovery of gold. Shortly thereafter, Chinese came directly from China in response to a shortage of workers in the labour-intensive industries of the bourgeoning West. At the height of railway construction, in 1881–2, over 11,000 arrived by ship in Victoria. The Chinese quickly became the target of racial discrimination, and many laws were passed to restrict Chinese immigration and to curtail the rights of those already in Canada.

The history of Chinese Canadians can be divided into three periods. In the first 65 years after 1858 the Chinese became victims of institutional racism and were subjected to legislative controls. They were considered useful to the development of western Canada but not desirable citizens. As soon as the Canadian Pacific Railway was completed, the federal government imposed a head tax of $50 on virtually every Chinese entering the country; it was raised to $100 in 1900, then to $500 in 1903. Between 1886 and 1924, 86,000 Chinese paid a total of $23 million in head tax. In addition, British Columbia passed numerous laws after 1875, disallowing Chinese to acquire Crown lands, preventing them from working in underground mines, excluding them from admission to the provincially established home for the aged and infirm, prohibiting them from being hired on public works, and disqualifying them from voting.

The second period, the exclusion era, began in 1923 with the passage of the Chinese Immigration Act. No Chinese were admitted to Canada, and those within the country continued to face legislative exclusion and social animosity. The act required every Chinese, regardless of citizenship, to obtain a registration certificate from the government within 12 months, with a heavy penalty for failing to do so. Furthermore, every Chinese who intended to leave temporarily had to file an official notice and had to return within two years. Until its repeal in 1947 the act virtually stopped Chinese immigration. Effectively reduced to second-class *citizenship, the Chinese were denied many basic rights, including the right to pursue a living in many occupations, and were frequent targets of political demagogy. The unequal treatment further contributed to their marginal social status in Canadian society. Restrictions on citizenship rights and legal exclusion from higher-paying jobs forced the Chinese to seek refuge in service industries, notably laundries and restaurants. By 1931, about 40 per cent of the Chinese in Canada were servants, cooks, waiters, or laundry workers. The restaurant business was a survival haven for many before the Second World War, and it remained an important sector of employment and self-employment even when opportunities in professional and technical occupations became available. Another consequence of institutional racism was to retard the development of the Chinese-Canadian family. As a result of financial and legal hardships, the community remained a predominantly male society until decades after the Second World War. In 1911, among the 27,831 Chinese in Canada, the sex ratio was 2,800 men to 100 women; in 1931 it was 1,240 men to 100 women among the 46,519 Chinese—the most severely unbalanced ratio among all ethnic groups in Canada. In the absence of Chinese women, many Chinese men maintained a 'married bachelor' life—living as bachelors in Canada, separated from wives and children in China. Those who had the means would take a periodic trip to China for a sojourn with their families. Absence of women and family also meant the delay of a second generation. Throughout this period, the Chinese established many voluntary associations to address community needs, organizing social services, mediating internal disputes, and dealing with external pressures of discrimination and segregation.

In the third period, after the Second World War, the discriminatory laws were repealed and Chinese Canadians gradually gained their civil rights. However, it was not until 1967, when Canada adopted a universal point system of assessing potential immigrants, that Chinese were admitted under the same criteria as others. The Chinese population increased substantially, to 124,600 by 1971,

285,800 by 1981, 922,000 by 1996. About two-thirds of Chinese Canadians now live in Vancouver or Toronto. Slightly over a quarter were born in Canada; most foreign-born Chinese came to Canada after 1967.

It was almost 90 years after their initial immigration before the Chinese were given the *franchise and civil rights that other Canadians had long taken for granted. Throughout the 1950s and 1960s, despite the removal of legalized discrimination, the Chinese did not gain full acceptance into Canadian society. Stereotypes of the Chinese race and Chinatowns have been deeply ingrained in popular culture. Irrespective of their nationality or political allegiance, the Chinese are often seen as a foreign race with different values and customs, and Chinatown retains its Oriental mystique in urban Canada. Canada's guarded post-war *immigration policy was in part influenced by this historical stereotype and in part by Sinophobia during the Cold War. Despite financial and occupational achievements, segments of Canadian society are still reluctant to accept Chinese Canadians as full-fledged Canadians.

The new wave of immigrants who came after 1967 contributed to the growth of a new generation who were better educated, more cosmopolitan, and upwardly mobile. Their arrival, and the growth of the native-born Chinese-Canadian population, helped produce an emergent Chinese middle class, who took up professional, technical, and managerial jobs historically denied the Chinese. Further changes in immigration policy in the mid-1980s in favour of business immigrants, as well as the prospective return of Hong Kong to China in 1997, triggered another wave of immigrants with substantial wealth and human capital; many came from Hong Kong, but also from Taiwan and other parts of Asia that had experienced rapid economic growth. By the late 1980s a new affluent class of Chinese Canadians had emerged; their spending power and investment capacity stimulated a new 'ethnic' consumer market. In turn, urban Canada went through many changes: middle-class Chinese Canadians moved to traditional white neighbourhoods, Chinese businesses flourished in suburban malls, and Canadian corporations and investment houses went after the fast-growing lucrative markets created by this new wealth and social mobility. PETER S. LI

Chinook. Chinook jargon is a practical, adaptive language once spoken throughout North America's Pacific slope, including British Columbia. A version of Chinook likely existed before Europeans arrived, a common tongue designed for communication in a region characterized by remarkable language diversity. With the arrival of Europeans in the 18th and 19th centuries, Chinook became a key means of communication between settlers, traders, and First Nations people. Chinook jargon incorporates Chinookan, Salishan, and Wakashan (particularly Nuu-chah-nulth) vocabulary and grammar alongside Cree, French, and English. Its structure is simple and adaptive and its vocabulary honed to coastal environments and trading economies. It was spoken in churches, stores, and workplaces, and was the language of written as well as oral literature. It remained an important means of communication in British Columbia until the middle of the 20th century, and persists in the province's place names—including Vancouver's Siwash (Native) Rock and the interior's Cultus (worthless or bad) Lake—and in local slang including 'salt chuck' (ocean) and 'skookum' (big, strong, and good). ADELE PERRY

cholera. A disease caused by drinking water infected with the bacteria *Vibrio cholerae*, it is characterized by copious watery diarrhea, dehydration, blue discoloration of face and extremities, and cardiovascular collapse. Death can ensue within hours of onset. The first wave of 'Asiatic' cholera came to North America in 1832 during a pandemic that originated in India, where the disease was endemic. In Canada, cholera appeared at Quebec in early June 1832, then spread rapidly to all the major towns along the St Lawrence River and Lakes Ontario and Erie. Warnings from Europe had resulted in some advance precautions, but the multitude of sick taxed the existing facilities and exhausted medical personnel. New regulations and new buildings were constructed for care of the sick and quarantine of new arrivals. The bacterial cause was unknown, but its pattern of spread implied contagion from the poverty-stricken and presumably dirty immigrants. Control measures attempted to help the sick and protect the healthy, but they incorporated middle-class prejudices against poverty-stricken strangers. Newcomers, both sick and well, were crowded into sheds with inadequate hygiene, and those who were healthy soon fell ill. Moreover, the quarantine was 'permeable', and the disease spread to citizens. Estimated Canadian mortality in this first epidemic was 6,000. Subsequent waves of cholera came to various ports in 1834, 1849, 1854, 1866, and 1871. The transmission of cholera by infected water was demonstrated by John Snow (1813–58) of London, England, in 1854. The causative organism was isolated and identified in 1884 by Robert Koch (1843–1910) of Germany. Cholera responds to antibiotics, but maintaining hydration is the most important support measure. Prevention relies on water and waste management; the disease can reappear when systems for water supply and sewage are disrupted by earthquakes, floods, and war.

JACALYN DUFFIN

Chrétien, Joseph-Jacques-Jean, prime minister 1993–2003. Born into a working-class family in Shawinigan, Quebec, 11 July 1934, and educated at St-Joseph Seminary in Trois-Rivières and at Laval University, Chrétien practised law from 1958 to 1963, when he was elected to Parliament. He had the unusual fortune to be appointed parliamentary secretary to Liberal prime minister Lester *Pearson, then to Mitchell Sharp, the finance minister, who became both mentor and model. In 1967, at a very young age, he was appointed to cabinet and served in various portfolios under Pearson and his successor, Pierre *Trudeau. A strong federalist, Chrétien was the federal government's point-man in the 1980 Quebec referendum and then in the reform of the *constitution in 1982. As a result he was deeply hated by Quebec nationalists. In 1984 he ran for the Liberal leadership but lost to John Turner. After a brief and unhappy service in opposition, he left politics until Turner vacated the leadership, becoming Liberal leader over Paul Martin Jr at a convention in Calgary in 1990. In 1993 Chrétien led the Liberals to power, sweeping away the unpopular and discredited Conservatives; he repeated his success in general elections in 1997 and 2000. Chrétien led a cautious and fiscally conservative government, prudently restoring federal finances after 20 years of deficits by cutting into sensitive government programs. His time in office was punctuated by external crises, in Bosnia, Kosovo, and Afghanistan. In each Chrétien was characteristically cautious, but in the final analysis supportive of US policy.

ROBERT BOTHWELL

Christian *réductions* in New France. The *réduction* (reserve), copied from Paraguay, was introduced by the *Jesuits at Sillery in 1639 to accommodate nomadic Montagnais hunting bands. The objective was not to dispossess Natives but rather to attract them to live near French settlements, on what in the 1600s was a no-man's-land, in order to sedentarize, evangelize, and assimilate them. A *réduction* was a seigneury granted by the Crown to missionaries who had title as long as they served the Native inhabitants. The missionaries were expected to attract Native settlers but never exact annual dues from them because this would recognize a Native proprietary right.

The Montagnais did not remain long at Sillery, especially when authoritarian controls were imposed. *Huron refugees from a war with the *Iroquois in 1648–50 replaced them; the Jesuits moved the Huron to better land at Ancienne Lorette, then eventually to their present village of Lorette, near Quebec. In time the Huron learned French and traded at Quebec, and many intermarried with the French colonists, thus most closely realizing the original objective of *réductions*. Abenaki driven from their lands in Maine by New Englanders found refuge at two *réductions*—Saint-François south of Quebec and Odanak south of Trois-Rivières. In 1667, the Jesuits established a mission on the south shore for Iroquois who, to benefit from trade, were camped near Montreal. This *réduction* of Sault-St-Louis moved four times, the final time to its present location of Kahnawake. Such moves were normal for Iroquois villages but were more likely motivated by settler demands for arable land and missionary desire to distance their charges from the attractions and taverns of Montreal. The Sulpician secular clergy had several missions at the west end of Montreal island for Algonkians and Iroquois, which they consolidated at La Montagne in 1701. They moved their *réductions* twice, settling finally at Lac-des-Deux-Montagnes (Oka or Kanasatake) in 1721, with separate missionaries for the Algonkian and the Iroquois. In 1755, a number of Kahnawake Iroquois moved upstream to St Regis (Akwesasne). Four years later, the Sulpician abbé Picquet opened a mission at the fort of La Présentation or Oswegatchie (Ogdensburg). All these *domiciled* Indians, as allies of the French, were known as the Seven Fires of Canada. Kanasatake was where the French made war plans with the Three Fires Confederacy of the Great Lakes region through the Algonkian intermediaries. Kahnawake Iroquois were the intermediaries between the French and Seven Fires and the Six Nations Iroquois, who after 1701 remained neutral in international conflicts. After the British conquest and the removal of the Jesuits, all the *réductions* except Kanasatake (Oka) reverted to the Crown and became reserves as defined in British law.

CORNELIUS J. JAENEN

Christie, Loring Cheney (1885–1941). Born in Amherst, Nova Scotia, Christie attended Harvard Law School, where he was an editor of the *Law Review*. He worked as a lawyer in New York City, then in the US Department of Justice, before returning to Canada at Sir Robert *Borden's invitation to be the first legal adviser in the Department of *External Affairs. In this capacity he attended various imperial conferences with Borden and his successor, Arthur *Meighen. Christie played a large part in defining Canada's policy towards the *British Empire and the *League of Nations, hoping initially that the empire would be a viable economic and political unit. He changed his mind around 1925, having resigned from the government in 1923, and became a vigorous isolationist. Returning to External Affairs in 1935, he opposed Canadian involvement in Europe and in the empire and opposed Canada's declaration of war on Germany in 1939. He ended his career as Canadian minister to the United States, where his American connections proved valuable to the Canadian war effort. Christie died of thrombosis at his post in Washington.

ROBERT BOTHWELL

Churchill Falls. The Grand Falls (renamed Churchill Falls in 1965) in *Labrador were known to Europeans from at least 1839, and their hydroelectric potential was discussed as early as 1907. However, the falls could not be developed until the area became accessible and long-distance transmission was possible to an adequate market. The growth of iron-mining towns in the Labrador interior from the 1940s, and the construction of a railway linking them to Sept-Îles in the early 1950s, revived interest in the falls, which were enthusiastically promoted by the premier of Newfoundland, J.R. *Smallwood. In 1953 the province granted exclusive rights to the falls (among other concessions) to the British Newfoundland Company (BRINCO), which had to find markets before development could start. However, Quebec refused to participate in a national grid or to allow Newfoundland power to be transmitted across its territory. The issue was complicated by Quebec's lasting resentment at the 1927 Labrador boundary decision, which, it felt, had given to Newfoundland what was rightfully Quebec territory. The federal government refused to intervene, and Smallwood chose not to press the issue. Thus BRINCO had only one potential customer, Hydro-Québec, which also invested heavily in the development. A long-term, fixed-price sales contract was eventually agreed to in 1969, and the project was completed in 1974. The increase in energy prices since 1973 has allowed Hydro-Québec to earn substantial profits on the resale of Churchill Falls power, a lasting cause of friction between the two provinces.

JAMES K. HILLER

Church of England. *See* ANGLICANS.

Circé-Côté, Eva (1871–1949), poet, journalist. Born in Montreal, Eva Circé studied at the convent of the Sisters of St Ann in Lachine. Exceptionally gifted in music, painting, and literature, she opted for poetry and journalism. She published widely, often under various pseudonyms, including, as 'Colombine', a collection of poems and essays, *Bleu, blanc, rouge: poésie, paysages, causeries* (1903), and co-founded the literary paper *L'Étincelle* (1902). A founding member and first vice-president of the French section of the Société des auteurs canadiens, she also helped found the Montreal municipal library in 1903. Close to the literary avant-garde and to Freemasons, she was known as a free thinker. In 1909 she gave her husband, Dr Salomon Côté, a Freemason funeral and had him cremated, causing a scandal among Catholic clergy and intellectuals. From 1916, she published a weekly column in *Labor World/Le Monde ouvrier*, the organ of the Trades and Labor Congress. As 'Julien St-Michel', she wrote hundreds of columns (1916–38) on such topics as women's suffrage, local politics, education, culture, and urban life, denouncing social injustice and racism and defending modernity. In 1924, she wrote a biography of Louis-Joseph *Papineau as well as four plays. An avowed feminist, she defended women's education and the rights of married women and championed a reform of the Civil Code.

ANDRÉE LÉVESQUE

Cité libre. The magazine first appeared one year after the infamous *Asbestos strike, a landmark in the evolution of Quebec society. Some leading figures in that event played a central role at *Cité libre*. Between June 1950 and June 1959, the magazine was published 23 times, on a less regular basis at the end of the period, with a rather limited circulation. Aided by Radio-Canada, some Cité libristes gained public visibility, though the leader of the provincial Liberals at that time, Georges-Émile Lapalme, believed they had no real influence. The death of Maurice *Duplessis in September 1959 and the short-lived government of Paul Sauvé revitalized the publication, which lasted until 1966, the year after Pierre Elliott *Trudeau and Gérard Pelletier, prominent Cité libristes, became involved in federal politics. The rest of Canada discovered *Cité libre* through them and, especially after 1968, retrospectively gave it great credence. Their subsequent celebrity likely exaggerated the importance of *Cité libre* in Quebec society.

In any event, *Cité libre* was a forum for intellectuals and activists. In the 1950s various people (journalists, union activists, university professors) shared the objective of getting rid of conservative rule and the retrograde nationalism that resulted from the combined authority of the Duplessis government and the Catholic Church. *Cité libre* also occasionally welcomed in its pages women who discussed the status of women in society. On the eve of the *Quiet Revolution differences became apparent between those who opposed nationalism in general (especially Trudeau) and others who embraced the renewed Quebec nationalism (Pierre Vadeboncoeur and Fernand Dumont, for instance). Younger collaborators such as Pierre *Vallières later chose more radical action. In 1990 the failure of the *Meech Lake Accord suggested new peaks in the support for independence. Twenty-five years after *Cité libre* had ceased publication, Quebec scholars Max and Monique Nemni resuscitated it between 1991 and 2000, with the help of Trudeau and Pelletier. The impact of the revived journal remained, at best, limited.

RAYMOND HUDON

citizenship. The Constitution Act, 1982, gives jurisdiction over naturalization and aliens to the federal Parliament. This clearly implies that the power to create a separate Canadian citizenship has existed since Confederation. However, this power was not used until 1946, when the first Canadian Citizenship Act was adopted to take effect in 1947. Until then, Canadians were British subjects, and until about 1920 a strong movement existed in the English-speaking provinces to promote imperial citizenship.

Since 1947, the Citizenship Act has been amended several times, notably to permit the acquiring of new citizenship without losing the Canadian one. However, the fundamental principles remain the same. Canadian citizenship is acquired by birth—in Canada or to a Canadian parent anywhere—or through naturalization, which requires only three years' residence as an immigrant. It is lost through renunciation, and in the case of naturalized citizens can be revoked for false representations or fraud in obtaining it. The latter provision is used to deprive those suspected of atrocities during the Second World War of their citizenship.

Canadian citizenship gives full civil and political rights, as well as the protection of Canadian diplomatic missions abroad. While permanent residents have most of the economic rights of citizens, a degree of discrimination may be permitted for offices that are deemed to require particular loyalty or commitment. Otherwise, the Supreme Court case of *Andrews v. Law Society of British Columbia* established that discrimination is illegal. Citizenship can mean not only political citizenship under the Citizenship Act, but 'good citizenship' as a way of life. This concept would clearly apply to all persons in Canada, whether or not they are citizens.

The *Charter of Rights and Freedoms reserved certain rights specifically for citizenship, notably democratic rights (s. 3), some mobility rights (s. 6), and minority language rights (s. 23); other mobility rights under section 6 are reserved for citizens and permanent residents. Under both the Charter and the Immigration Act, citizens have an almost absolute right to enter or remain in Canada, but this does not prevent their *extradition under due process of law.

In recent years there has been pressure to tighten requirements for citizenship and to make it more difficult to obtain. As well, opposition has been expressed to the widespread practice of multiple citizenship. However, the varied origins of Canadians and the growing integration of world economies would make this a difficult project to realize. JULIUS H. GREY

civil engineering. The work of designing and supervising the construction of large public works, primarily for transportation (railways, *roads, harbours, *bridges) and public health (water supply and treatment), and of maintaining them once built. Facilities of this sort have been built the world over for millennia, but a profession with the name 'civil engineering'—referring to the creation of such works for strictly non-military purposes—took form only late in the 18th century.

The profession is based on several bodies of knowledge. Chief among them is the nature of construction materials, originally wood and stone but concrete and steel through much of the 20th century. Also important are the principles of statics, the strength and stability of soils for foundations, the physical nature of water and ice (both still and moving), and management techniques for handling the complex schedules, workforces, and investments that public works demand.

Civil engineering has been an essential part of Canada's commercial and industrial development since the early 19th century. Public works of a sort were built in the 18th century, under both the French and English regimes, but they were small projects, built by contractors or military engineers, and are not usually seen as works of civil engineering. The first Welland Canal, the Burlington Bay Canal at the head of Lake Ontario, the Lachine Canal on the island of Montreal, and the Shubenacadie Canal in Nova Scotia, all begun in the 1820s, are considered the country's first civil engineering projects. The Rideau Canal in eastern Upper Canada was, strictly speaking, a military undertaking, but having always served a civil purpose it is usually counted among the first civil engineering works. Engineers on these projects were few, and most did not remain in the colonies. It was not until the 1840s, when the new Board of Works of the United *Province of Canada hired dozens of engineers to supervise its program of *canal, harbour, and road construction, that Canadian civil engineering truly began. Many of Canada's notable early engineers got their start there, Casimir *Gzowski (from Poland via the United States), Hamilton Killaly (from Ireland), and Samuel Keefer (Canadian-born to Loyalist parents) among them.

The next 15 years were something of a golden age for Canadian civil engineers. The board paid well, built to a high standard, and fostered a degree of professional integrity that engineers found appealing. By 1850 railway construction offered good jobs for these early engineers, as well as for newcomers such as Sandford *Fleming. So sanguine were these men that there was talk in 1853—fanciful it turned out—of forming a Canadian engineering association.

In the decades that followed, civil engineering jobs were fewer, and salaries not so princely, but the profession matured, diversified, and became deeply embedded in Canadian life. The growth of Canadian cities brought a need for 'municipal engineers' to improve city streets, sidewalks, and water and sewer works. Engineers entered public service, as government departments of public works grew and extended their domain. Railways were built in most parts of the country, and civil engineers were called on to lay out and supervise construction of their lines and bridges.

Civil engineering education became more formalized. Until the 1870s engineering education had been by apprenticeship. Aspiring engineers obtained a secondary academic education and then set out on their own, moving from job to job until, having obtained the rank of 'assistant engineer', they could attach the label 'CE' to their name. This began to change as university-based engineering schools were established at McGill, New Brunswick, Toronto, and the École Polytechnique in Montreal. Enrolments were low at first, but within a generation university-based training had become the standard path to professional engineering practice and certification.

In 1887, after some earlier failed attempts, the country's first engineering society, the Canadian Society of Civil Engineers, was formed in Montreal. With the profession growing rapidly, it quickly gained a large membership—nearly 1,000 by century's end. It functioned as a 'learned society', not a regulating body, using its meetings for the presentation and discussion of engineering problems and techniques.

By the early years of the 20th century, civil engineering was just one of several engineering specialties. Mining, mechanical, electrical, and chemical engineering—creatures of new technologies and processes –joined civil to create a more diverse profession. Civil's share of students at engineering schools, and of members in the CSCE, declined accordingly. In 1918, the CSCE was renamed the Engineering Institute of Canada to reflect these changes.

But the older profession had not lost importance. Indeed, Canadian civil engineering accomplishments of the early 20th century, increasingly by Canadian-born and -trained engineers, are among the country's most outstanding. The CPR's spiral railway tunnel in the Rocky Mountains, built in the boom years before the First World War, was an exceptional accomplishment. So too was the extensive reconfiguration of Montreal Harbour, conceived by John Kennedy to handle increases in trade, and the remarkable Shoal Lake Aqueduct, built to carry clean water from the Canadian Shield to the insalubrious city of Winnipeg. The rapid pace of Canada's development, along with its great breadth and challenging physical environment, made civil engineers essential partners of governments and entrepreneurs in the establishment of the country and the exploitation of its resources.

As industry and commerce expanded through the 20th century, the pattern continued. Working usually for governments or large semi-public bodies, civil engineers continued to provide essential infrastructure. They laid out roads, airstrips, and hydroelectric developments for northern resource industries, expanded and improved urban water supply and sewage treatment, provided structural design for tall urban buildings, designed irrigation and drainage systems to enhance agricultural production, and built the highways and bridges to make possible safe, efficient car and truck travel. The scale of civil engineering projects increased markedly after the Second World War, as the *St Lawrence Seaway, Trans-Canada Pipeline, and northern hydroelectric projects attest.

The profession's successes should not be viewed entirely as a national accomplishment. From the St Lawrence canals to the CN Tower, Canadian engineers have drawn on international expertise, in the form of both published knowledge and individual engineering consultants. Nevertheless, they have always worked at the highest standards, and hold an international reputation as competent and fair. In the 1970s and 1980s, Canadian firms such as SNC/Lavalin (founded 1936 in Quebec), Proctor and Redfern (founded 1911 in Toronto), and others expanded into Africa and Asia, where they designed and built industrial infrastructure—sometimes amid social and environmental controversy—in several developing countries. RICHARD WHITE

class. Class is a designation of difference. It situates people in the present but also in the past according to where they are located in terms of largely material circumstances. Class in Marx's sense takes a person's relationship to the means of production as a central factor in identifying his or her place in society, bourgeois and proletarian being the two great contending classes. In other conceptions of class, ordered more by the status hierarchies of acquisition and consumption (here influences run from the European theorist Max Weber to American sociologist W. Lloyd Warner), people are located on rungs of a social ladder: upper, middle, and lower.

Historically, all systems of class categorization depend greatly on the nature of the period in which people are being studied. In industrialized societies dominated by factory production and world commerce, we would expect to see classes associated with the divide between labour and capital. Serfs, peasants, and aristocrats would be more common in feudal societies, where land was more central in determining socio-economic and political alignments. At its most general, then, class is a collective category of analysis in which people's structural place in particular political economies is assigned in various ways.

Consciousness of class complicates this notion: it is possible to be aware of and act according to one's class position or, in contrast, to have beliefs and to function in ways that seemingly defy it. People can be conscious of their class in contradictory and quite volatile ways. Historically, the more privileged the class designation, the more likely conscious class affiliation and consistent self-identification. The aristocracy of feudal Europe, despite its petty squabbles, was capable of collectively defending its class power, up to a point, and was usually able to suppress peasant revolts and the uprisings of the dispossessed. The class precipice of an economic order is reached when material contradictions come to a point of rupture, such as in the French Revolution, which ushered in the age of capital and buried the pre-industrial feudal order. A part of capitalism's staying power is its capacity to induce in its lower classes identifications with various ideologies and structures—from individualism to 'the market'—that mire them in oppression and exploitation. The bourgeoisie has always been more class conscious than the proletariat. Whether this justifies a claim that capitalism as a socio-economic order is superior to all others, timeless in its class rule, as suggested in Francis Fukuyama's *The End of History*, is debatable.

Interpreting the history of Canada in class ways is a recent undertaking. As late as 1965, one historian, Stanley Mealing, insisted that class, while it exercised an impact in Canadian history, was not likely to be a driving interpretive issue in subsequent study. Yet, across intellectual disciplines, the study of Canadian history, literature, and political economy has yielded some sturdy if often marginal overviews that were driven by class analysis: Stanley Ryerson's and Gustavus Myers's pioneering appreciations of the expropriation of Native peoples, the founding of the great fur trade fortunes, and the march to Confederation, were explorations of class inequalities, class struggles, and the victories of the class that could command and accumulate money. In a way this was also the one-class, mercantile society depicted in Donald *Creighton's account of the commercial empire of the St Lawrence or in Harold *Innis's conceptualization of the role of *staples in Canadian development, but in these better-known, mainstream accounts labour was written out of the historical process and class struggles disappeared.

From the late 1960s, historians have focused on class place as an important factor in explaining everyday life and social, cultural, and political experience. Studies of Aboriginal–white contact have suggested the class dimensions of early Canadian history, in which Native peoples were tentatively and incompletely proletarianized; the relations of clerks and *voyageurs in the fur trade are now routinely analysed with reference to class. Much historical work came to address labour decisively, and the growth of working-class history after 1975 was an important historiographic development.

As increasing attention was given to the *'limited identities' of class, ethnicity, race, region, and gender, understanding of the Canadian past grew ever more complicated. The notion of a 'peaceable kingdom' faded as accounts of strikes, radical political parties, rowdy behaviour in shanties and taverns, and rough cultures of the street took on increasing importance. The acknowledgment of class, with its persistent tensions and unvarnished inequalities, alerted Canadians to a subterranean history of violence and contention that had been swept under various interpretive carpets. No longer was the

1919 *Winnipeg General Strike the exceptional event that seemingly proved a rule of Canadian placidity in the realm of social relations. Rather, it became apparent that the experience of class had permeated labour relations in factories and mines as well as in such private realms as family life.

The 20th-century history of industrial relations, paced by the approaches of future prime minister Mackenzie *King, placed the stamp of class on both the evolution of the law and the emergence of the modern state. Welfare provisioning, as countless studies of the *Great Depression and the 1940s show (as does the dismantling of various social safety net provisions by contemporary cost-cutting governments), is about managing class discontents, at the top, middle, and bottom levels of society. Just as class interests have come to be seen as central to the making of Confederation, Quebec's *Quiet Revolution of the 1960s cannot be appreciated without reference to the opening class war in French Canada's modernization, the *Asbestos strike of 1949, or to the class dimensions of the rage of inequality articulated in Pierre *Vallière's text of revolt, *White Niggers of America* (1968). From the time of John Porter's 1965 study, *The *Vertical Mosaic*, class has been a staple of sociological analysis, and many studies now exist of 'the corporate elite' and the powerful pinnacle of class rule. But the better-read studies of ruling-class Canada tend to be written by advocates of the rich and famous, among them popular writers such as Peter Newman. Recent studies of mass culture and sexuality have shown that areas of everyday life have significant class components as well, but such subjects have yet to break into mass markets. Not surprisingly, the romance of fortunes accumulated and dissipated, and the story of massive economic power and how it is wielded, is more likely to be a saleable commodity in a capitalist society than accounts of workers' organizations thwarted or strikes defeated or difficult family strategies of survival adopted by the poor.

There is little in the vast canvas of Canadian history that is not, in some way, related to class. But the message of the importance of class divisions, inequalities, and struggles is appreciated partially and, ironically, in class ways.

BRYAN D. PALMER

Claxton, Brian Brooke (1898–1960). Claxton served in the Canadian artillery in the First World War and won the Distinguished Conduct Medal. He graduated in law from McGill University in 1921 and for most of the next two decades was a key figure in the *Canadian Movement. He helped draft the 1936 version of the Broadcast Act, which converted the Canadian Radio Broadcasting Commission into the *Canadian Broadcasting Corporation. Elected to Parliament for the Liberals in 1940, he was appointed parliamentary secretary to W.L. Mackenzie *King in 1943 and minister of national health and welfare in 1944. A sparkplug for the leftward swing of the King government in 1943–5, he oversaw the introduction of family allowances. In 1946 he was appointed minister of national defence, with a mandate to drastically cut Canada's post-war military. He did that, but also oversaw the beginning of the largest peacetime mobilization in Canadian history after the outbreak of the *Korean War and played a major role in defining Canada's post-war defence relationship with the United States and within NATO. He resigned from government in 1954, but was named chairman of the newly established Canada Council in early 1957.

D.J. BERCUSON

Clear Grits. A populist movement that emerged within the Reform Party of Canada West after its electoral triumph of 1847–8. Strongest in the western peninsula of Upper Canada, the movement represented a revival of the agrarian radicalism articulated by William Lyon *Mackenzie. Clear Grit egalitarianism encompassed American-style democracy, a radical simplification of the law and the judicial system, and the abolition of professional qualifications for the practice of law and medicine. Grits condemned as 'aristocratical' the ideal of British-style parliamentary government to which the Reform Party was committed under Robert *Baldwin, and they resented Baldwin's reluctance to secularize the *clergy reserves, a longstanding party policy.

In 1854 the party split, its leading cadre and their *bleu* allies in Quebec joining the Upper Canadian Conservatives to form a new government. George *Brown rallied the Grit rump and reconstituted the Reform party on the basis of resistance to 'Lower Canadian domination'—the supposed oppression of Upper Canada by French-Canadian clericalism and Montreal financial interests. The party's policies of parliamentary representation according to population and, from 1859 on, the federalization of the United Province of Canada were accepted by the *bleus* in 1864 and implemented three years later by the British North America Act.

The term Grit survives as a synonym for Liberal.

PAUL ROMNEY

clergy reserves. In 1791 the *Constitutional Act set aside one-seventh of all Crown lands in the Canadas 'for the maintenance and support of a Protestant clergy'. At that time few challenged the notion that the state should support a national church. Religious establishments, it was argued, secured public order (a hard lesson learned from the American Revolution) and provided important public services such as education and religious instruction. This new colonial religious *establishment was to be paid for by the colony—there would be little cost to the imperial government. Fifty years later, these Crown lands, the infamous clergy reserves, had become the Pandora's box of Canadian politics—in Lord *Durham's phrase, 'the great practical question' on which depended 'the pacification of Canada'.

Three forces challenged the policy of setting aside public land to support an established church. The first attacked the exclusive claims of the Anglican Church to these revenues. Led by the Church of Scotland, this challenge forced the Crown to divide the reserve revenue among several religious groups. Yet, this practical compromise was challenged by the rising voice of religious voluntarism, which called for the separation of church and state, the secularization of the reserves, and the application of reserve revenue to non-sectarian purposes, such as public education. The final (and most decisive) challenge came from the state itself, which concluded that the reserves were not fulfilling the purpose for which they were intended. Far from promoting order and loyalty, the clergy reserves had become the centre of intense political battles, threatening the very existence of the *British connection.

In spite of the determined efforts of John *Strachan, the bishop of Toronto, the reserves were secularized in 1854. The salaries of the clergy who were being supported from the reserves were protected, but the revenues were used to fund municipal development and local improvements, and money that had been set aside to support religion was used to finance railway building.

WILLIAM WESTFALL

closure. A procedure in a legislature that can be invoked unilaterally by the government to limit debate on a government measure. Generally employed as a remedy for *filibustering or prolonged debate, closure takes place after oral notice and a vote. A vote on the business being closed takes place by 1 A.M. of the following day. Devised in 1912 and first used in the *House of Commons in 1913 during the Naval Aid Bill debate, closure was subsequently used 18 times before 1982, including four times during the 1956 *Trans-Canada Pipeline debate. Time allocation is a gentler form of closure in which the government indicates its intention to end a debate and call a vote at some future, specified date, possibly a few days later. Time allocation is now more common: since 1982, closure has been used on 24 occasions, time allocation on 141.

JOHN C. COURTNEY AND DANIEL MACFARLANE

Coaker, William Ford (1871–1938). Born in St John's, Newfoundland, Coaker was a mercantile clerk, farmer, and telegraph operator before establishing the *Fishermen's Protective Union in 1908. He resented the mistreatment of fishermen by merchants and the exploitation of the outports by the elite of the capital. A tireless worker, he personally supervised the management of various FPU-sponsored companies. To achieve the union's economic and social reforms, he organized the Union Party, and he and seven others were elected to the House of Assembly in 1913. In 1919 the Unionists formed an alliance with Liberal leader Richard *Squires. Appointed fisheries minister, Coaker attempted to reform the fishery but met stiff resistance from city merchants. The regulations he had the legislature enact to control the sale of fish in foreign markets were rescinded in 1921. Disillusioned, he concentrated after 1924 on managing the FPU's commercial activities.

MELVIN BAKER AND AIDAN MALONEY

coal-mine disasters. The history of *coal mining in Canada is punctuated by a series of major disasters. The first of these occurred on 13 May 1873 at Westville, Pictou County, Nova Scotia, where 60 men and boys were killed in an explosion at the Drummond Colliery. The worst single mine disaster in Canadian history occurred in the Crowsnest Pass at Hillcrest, Alberta, on 19 June 1914, where 189 lives were lost. Other disasters responsible for the loss of 20 lives or more in the Alberta–British Columbia border area occurred at Fernie, BC (1902, 1917), Bellevue, Alberta (1910), Nordegg, Alberta (1941), and Michel-Natal, BC (1967). The *Frank Slide (1903) was precipitated by coal operations, but most of the victims were not miners. The largest disaster of the 19th century took place at Nanaimo, BC, on 3 May 1887, where 148 workers were killed; there were other major disasters in the Vancouver Island mines at Wellington (1881, 1888), South Wellington (1884), Extension (1903, 1909), and Cumberland (1901, 1923). In Nova Scotia major disasters occurred in Pictou County at Stellarton (1880, 1918, and 1952) and on Cape Breton Island at New Waterford (1917) and Sydney Mines (1938). Possibly the most famous Canadian mine calamities occurred at Springhill, NS. There, 125 miners died in an explosion on 21 February 1891, and two dramatic episodes in the 1950s received international media attention: on 1 November 1956, an explosion killed 39 men, but 88 survivors were rescued after several days underground; two years later, on 23 October 1958, the collapse of the roof in another Springhill mine took 75 lives, though another 19 men were rescued from the deepest levels after surviving for days underground. The most recent major disaster, at the Westray Mine in Pictou County, NS, on 9 May 1992, took 26 lives. Continuing debate over the conditions and actions responsible for the toll of lives has followed in the wake of these tragedies, and these casualties of the *Industrial Revolution are often commemorated in local song, story, and stone. A place of honour is reserved for the draegermen, the trained miners equipped with breathing apparatus who undertook underground rescue work. Despite the enormous loss of life attributed to major disasters, most of the deaths in the coal mines over the past two centuries were the result of smaller workplace accidents caused by falls, explosions, fires, floods, broken ropes, defective equipment, and other hazards that have received less attention.

DAVID FRANK

coal mining. Canada's coal resources are located in five provinces: Nova Scotia, New Brunswick, British Columbia, Alberta, and Saskatchewan. The use of coal in Canada, which was first associated with local needs, achieved national significance during the course of the *Industrial Revolution in the 19th century, and it remains important in the contemporary energy market. Coal was shipped to Massachusetts from the Grand Lake area of New Brunswick as early as 1639, but commercial development for local markets did not become significant until the early 20th century. On Cape Breton Island coal was mined at Port Morien for use at *Louisbourg during the French regime in the 18th century; large-scale operations were later established by companies such as the *General

Mining Association (1826) and the Dominion Coal Company (1893) both on Cape Breton Island and in Pictou and Cumberland Counties on the Nova Scotia mainland. On the Pacific coast, local coal supplied steamships as early as the 1830s, and the *Hudson's Bay Company opened mining operations at Fort Rupert by 1849. Major operations were later started by mining companies at centres such as Nanaimo and Wellington on Vancouver Island. In the interior, coal was mined at Fort Edmonton for local fuel supply in 1863; railway construction led to the opening of large commercial operations in the Edmonton and Lethbridge areas in the 1890s and in the Crowsnest Pass on the British Columbia–Alberta border at the end of the 19th century. The coalfields of southern Saskatchewan also began to produce substantial output for local consumption in the early decades of the 20th century.

During this era, most coal was produced from underground mines and consumed by the domestic market for fuel, energy, and metallurgical purposes. Steam-powered shipping and railways and the iron and steel industry were among the principal consumers. Although the coal industry benefited from a protective tariff under the *National Policy of the 1870s, Canada did not maintain a national fuel policy; the level of protection dropped significantly in the subsequent decades and Canadian producers had little or no access to the Ontario market for industrial coal, which was supplied from the United States. At its peak in 1949 the Canadian coal industry produced more than 17 million metric tons of coal and employed about 25,000 people. The single-industry towns of the Canadian coal country formed compact communities populated by industrial workers and families drawn from both local and immigrant populations. Often organized as company towns under the control of the mine operators, these communities also became sites of labour unrest, much of it focused on issues of union recognition, workplace safety, and community life. Their strikes and political activism attracted national attention, as did the large number of fatalities associated with underground *coal-mine disasters.

Coal production, which declined during the Great Depression, increased again during the Second World War. Yet the long-term trend towards stagnation was confirmed in the 1950s with the rise of alternative fuel and energy sources such as oil, natural gas, *hydroelectricity, and nuclear power. The international energy crisis of the 1970s encouraged new interest in coal and by the end of the 20th century domestic production exceeded 69 million metric tons per annum. This was produced mainly from open-pit mines in western Canada, and most British Columbia coal was exported to Japan and Korea. At this time Canada's domestic coal consumption exceeded 60 million metric tons per annum, mainly for the purpose of power generation. Ontario continued to rely on imported supplies from the United States; Nova Scotia and New Brunswick also imported significant quantities of coal. After a period of opening new mines in the 1970s under the supervision of the publicly owned Cape Breton Development Corporation, underground mining in Nova Scotia was pronounced uneconomical; the last of the Nova Scotia mines closed in 2001. At the beginning of the new millennium, about 19 per cent of Canada's energy supply continued to come from coal, and Canada continued to have significant coal reserves capable of supplying energy needs for the next century. Environmentalists have expressed rising concerns about the effects of sulphur dioxide and nitrogen oxide emissions from coal-fired power generation, while promoters of the industry have argued that new technologies offer continued opportunities to utilize the resource. DAVID FRANK

cod moratorium. In July 1992 federal Fisheries Minister John Crosbie announced that northern cod stocks (cod found off the east coast of Newfoundland and Labrador) were on the verge of collapse; he immediately declared a 'moratorium' on commercial cod fishing. The decimation of what was once one of the world's richest *fisheries resources would have huge consequences for Atlantic Canada—particularly Newfoundland and Labrador, where 30,000 fishers and plant workers lost their jobs. It also ranks as one of 20th-century Canada's biggest ecological disasters.

This crisis did not happen overnight. While some fisheries scientists proposed that colder than usual water temperatures in the northwestern Atlantic in the early 1990s hastened the demise, others acknowledged that cod populations had been declining for decades. While fishing has certainly had an impact over the centuries, the rise of the industrial fishery in the mid-20th century put the greatest pressure on the resource. Transformations in processing ('quick freezing') and harvesting (factory-freezer trawlers), along with rising demand for fish from growing populations after the Second World War, contributed to the emergence of large fishing companies (many of which received state support) on both sides of the Atlantic. By the early 1960s, hundreds of trawlers from a dozen countries (including Canada) were fishing off the Atlantic coast—so many that local residents claimed the brightly lit vessels looked like floating cities at night. After Canada declared a 200-mile fishing limit in 1977, the number of foreign vessels decreased, but catches remained high as the Canadian government, attempting to alleviate economic problems in the Atlantic region, supported the expansion of the domestic fishing industry. Ultimately the cod could not sustain those catch levels, collapsing in 1992. Although the government lifted the moratorium in the late 1990s, the cod have shown few signs of recovery and the future remains uncertain.

MIRIAM WRIGHT

Cohen, Jacob Lawrence (1898–1950), lawyer. A Jewish immigrant, J.L. Cohen graduated in 1918 from Osgoode Hall law school. His association with unions and the Communist Party in the 1920s and 1930s led him to specialize in *labour law, and to be an advocate for civil liberties. He became the most influential labour lawyer in Canada, and an architect of the industrial relations system. Cohen wrote *Collective Bargaining in Canada*, supporting labour's right to organize and bargain collectively. He served on the National War Labour Board in 1943; advised the Ontario government about *mothers' allowances, *unemployment insurance, minimum industrial standards, and labour legislation policies; was union counsel in the 1937 *Oshawa auto strike and the 1941 *Kirkland Lake gold miners' strike; and worked with the emerging industrial union movement and the Canadian Congress of Labour.

As a Marxist, a Jew, and a radical, he experienced discrimination. After being convicted of assault, Cohen was disbarred in 1947. Although he was reinstated in 1950, he died suddenly that year, in Toronto, at 53. The *Globe and Mail* included his own epitaph in his obituary: 'He championed all the wrong people in all the right things'.

LAUREL SEFTON MacDOWELL

Cold War. The Cold War describes international relations during the four decades between the end of the Second World War and the collapse of the Soviet Union in 1989–91. During that time, the world was divided into two antagonistic blocs of states: the Western bloc led by the United States and the Eastern bloc by the Union of Soviet Socialist Republics. The conflict was between two economic and political systems, capitalism and communism. Both blocs constructed military and diplomatic alliances to compete on a global scale. It was a 'cold' war because the possession of nuclear weapons and their delivery systems by both sides rendered direct military conflict unacceptable. Many local, or proxy, wars were fought, but were contained by tacit mutual agreement.

The immediate trigger for the Cold War was the falling out of the wartime allies over the post-war division of Europe. In 1947 the United States began Marshall Plan aid to western Europe, and in 1949 *NATO was formed. The focus of the Cold War widened to Asia—where the communists emerged victorious in China in 1949—with wars in Korea, Vietnam, and Afghanistan. The Cold War came to an end with the collapse of communism in eastern Europe and the subsequent implosion of the Soviet Union.

Canada was never at the centre of the Cold War, although the first public notice of the conflict occurred in Ottawa in 1945–6, with the Igor *Gouzenko spy affair. Sharing a continent with the US made Canada a junior partner to the Americans. Canada was a founding member of NATO, and later signed on to the NORAD pact for the air defence of North America. If often enthusiastic, Canada was also sometimes reluctant about its supportive role. Generally, Canadians were more likely to emphasize diplomacy and peaceful resolution of conflicts, while the US was more assertive about the threat, and use, of force. Canada joined the UN-led military force in *Korea (1950–3), but kept out of military involvement in Vietnam. Sometimes the question of support for the US in Cold War confrontations divided Canadians, as in the *Cuban missile crisis (1962). The controversy over nuclear warheads for *Bomarc anti-aircraft missiles in Canada (1962–3) split the cabinet and led to the defeat of John *Diefenbaker's government.

In the 1950s a Canadian Cold War consensus was widespread, although it was sometimes an enforced consensus in which dissenters were intimidated. Consensus began to break down in the 1960s and 1970s, with growing concern about the dangers of nuclear war. Very occasionally, Canadian leaders broke with 'quiet diplomacy' to voice mild concerns about American policies, as did Lester *Pearson over the Vietnam War in the 1960s, and Pierre *Trudeau with his peace mission around the world in the 1980s. These Canadian criticisms tended to be treated rather brusquely by the US. By and large, however, Canada was a faithful ally, even when Canadian society was more critical than its government.

The early Cold War was marked in the US by McCarthyism and the reckless hunt for subversives. Canadians tended to be smug about avoiding American excesses, but the record is not so clear. The Gouzenko affair received a draconian response under the *War Measures Act, which disregarded the civil liberties of suspects. In the late 1940s, the government instituted an anti-communist security screening system for public servants, defence industry workers, and for immigrants, *refugees, and citizenship applicants. Anti-communist purges took place, some in the public sector (e.g., at the *National Film Board), and some in the private sector (e.g., trade *unions). The most notorious case of McCarthyism in Canada was the diplomat and scholar Herbert *Norman, driven to his death in 1957 by accusations of disloyalty. Since his accusers were American senators, the Norman case was seen in Canada primarily as intolerable American intervention.

The Cold War was an ideological contest. It exercised considerable influence on Canadian politics, but its influence over culture was more limited, especially in its latter decades. The breakdown of the Cold War consensus was related to such phenomena as the rise of a more critical youth culture. A crucial element was the *Quiet Revolution in Quebec. In the 1940s and 1950s, conservative Quebec Catholicism was an anchor of anti-communism. The profound changes in Quebec culture and politics initiated in the early 1960s detached that province from the centre of the Cold War consensus, and then with the rise of the sovereignist movement deflected Canadian attention away from the threat to national security towards a more concrete threat to national unity.

In a real sense the Cold War was already over in Canadian society well before 1991. Yet, while it lasted, it made an indelible mark on the country, and its legacy of closer integration with the United States has long outlived the Cold War.

REG WHITAKER

Coles, George (1810–75), politician, businessman. A successful Prince Edward Island brewer and distiller, Coles became leader of the Reform Party in the mid-1840s and the colony's first premier under *responsible government in 1851. He led the most progressive of early Reform governments in the Atlantic region. His crowning achievement was the Free Education Act of 1852, which ended tuition fees and local assessment; teachers' salaries would be paid entirely from the colonial treasury. The statute, which greatly increased school attendance, was hailed as the first experiment in 'free education' within the British Empire. Coles had less success grappling with the colony's perennial problem, leasehold land tenure. He remained premier, except for a brief period in 1854, until 1859, when his party was defeated. He led the Liberals back to power in 1867, but resigned as premier in 1868 when he was beset by a form of dementia.

IAN ROSS ROBERTSON

collèges classiques. Institutions of secondary education whose programs, based on the study of Greek and Roman authors, with a gradual progression in subject matter, were inspired by the classic *cursus studiorum* developed in the colleges of Paris in the 16th century. The first Canadian collège classique was established in Quebec City in 1635 by the *Jesuits. In 1765 the Jesuits, most of whom returned to France following the *conquest, were replaced by the secular priests of the *Séminaire de Québec. They opened a college-seminary, with boarding facilities, for boys aspiring to the liberal professions as well as the priesthood. In 1773 the Sulpicians in Montreal turned a secondary school founded in 1767 into the Collège Saint-Raphaël, with structure and pedagogy inspired by the Quebec model. Classical colleges blossomed in the 19th century: a third opened at Nicolet in 1803, and a (short-lived) fourth at Saint-Denis in 1806. Over the following decades several villages acquired colleges. By the eve of the First World War the province had 33 classical colleges. Similar institutions were established in Acadia, Ontario, western Canada, and the United States. New ones continued to be established into the 1960s.

The first equivalent institution for women, the Collège Marguerite-Bourgeoys, was initially not designated a 'collège' but an 'école d'enseignement supérieur'. It opened in 1908, through the efforts of the *Fédération nationale St-Jean-Baptiste and the sisters of the *Congrégation de Notre-Dame. Offering a program similar to that for male students, it opened the door to university for girls—a door that had until then been closed.

Quebec's classical colleges disappeared in the wake of the Parent Commission (1961–6). They were replaced by the CÉGEPs, created in 1967.

CHRISTINE HUDON

Collins, Enos (1774–1871), shipowner, merchant, banker. From a family of merchants in the Nova Scotian town of Liverpool, Collins gained youthful trading and privateering experience in the Caribbean. In addition to owning the successful privateer schooner **Liverpool Packet*, he excelled at the Napoleonic War's risky trading opportunities and price speculation. Shrewdly investing his wartime earnings, he built a peacetime shipping and trading empire and married into Halifax political elites. In 1825 he was the key founder of the Halifax Banking Company (later to become the Canadian Imperial Bank of Commerce), one of Canada's first *banks. He was respected, but also feared and resented for unforgiving business dealings. Unlike many colonial tycoons, he retired not to an English estate but remained in Nova Scotia, roaring out of retirement at 90 to fiercely oppose Confederation. Upon his death, he was acclaimed as the richest man in the new nation.

DAN CONLIN

Colonial Office. The British government department responsible for the overseas empire. Founded in 1801, until 1854 it was also responsible for the army. In 1925 relations with Canada were hived off to the Dominions (later Commonwealth) Office; both were merged with the Foreign Office in 1966–8. The Colonial Office was represented in the British cabinet by the secretary of state, often an elder statesman whose career was in decline. A junior politician assisted as parliamentary under-secretary; future prime ministers Peel, Gladstone, and Churchill each obtained their first ministerial experience in this post. The senior civil servant (deputy minister) was called the permanent under-secretary, an office held by James Stephen (1836–47), 'Mr Mother-Country', among others. Other officials who dealt with mid-Victorian Canada were T.F. Elliot, an emigration specialist, and Arthur Blackwood, chief clerk of the British North America section until 1867. Colonists denounced the Colonial Office for its alleged incompetence and bureaucracy (the red tape used by the office to bundle official documents became a byword for bureaucratic entanglement). Although historians often cite 'the Colonial Office view' of Canadian issues, in reality it never aimed to become a policy-making body. Colonial secretaries usually discussed major issues not through official dispatches but in private correspondence with governors, who were sometimes personal friends. The Colonial Office operated as a glorified postbox between Canada and other British government departments. A clerk who joined in 1864 called it 'a sleepy and humdrum office, where important work was no doubt done, but simply because it had got to be done'.

GED MARTIN

colonist cars. After landing in the ports of Halifax or Quebec, late-19th- and early-20th-century European immigrants reached the western prairies by transcontinental train. The Canadian Pacific Railway reduced fares for settlers and goods, transported in third-class colonist cars in special trains sidetracked for regular passenger and freight traffic. Holding approximately 60 people, and made of wood for easy cleaning, colonist cars were basic but comfortable, equipped with benches and shelves that converted into berths (curtains provided privacy), and with water, washrooms, heaters, and stoves; travellers supplied bedding and food. Excited and fearful by turns during the three-day journey, they read, hung out the windows to watch the countryside, jumped off at station stops (risking being left behind), and prepared for arrival. Wherever possible, passengers were segregated by nationality, and an immigration agent and/or interpreter often accompanied large parties—counting heads, taking personal information, checking for illness, encouraging decisions as to final destination to facilitate dispersal from Winnipeg. To control their *bloc settlements, groups from eastern Europe were sometimes put on non-stop trains or trains with predetermined destinations.

FRANCES SWYRIPA

colonization companies in New France. One of the key features in the history of *New France is the very limited immigration from the mother country. Although some 70,000 French men and women crossed the Atlantic to New France and Acadia, over two-thirds returned to France. Given the political instability of 17th-century France and on-going economic difficulties, this failure to attract immigrants may appear surprising. Historians have sometimes blamed the French colonization companies for their inability to fulfill their duties to bring larger numbers of settlers, but other colonies in the New World experienced similar difficulties.

Like other European monarchs, French kings initially did not exercise direct control over their North American colonies. They granted the land as private fiefdoms to proprietors or companies that were supposed to bring immigrants and expand trade. As elsewhere, efforts to ensure economic growth and settlement tended to be haphazard and largely unsuccessful. In New France, the companies relied largely on private subscriptions, sometimes including subsidies from the state, and monopoly over trade to run local affairs and attract colonists.

Replacing the monopolies held by individuals such as Pierre *Du Gua de Monts, the king's chief minister Cardinal Richelieu created the Compagnie des cent-associés (or Compagnie de la Nouvelle-France) in 1627 as a way of enlarging imperial trade and acquiring greater maritime power. One hundred members were each to deposit 3,000 livres in exchange for a monopoly over the *fur trade and a 15-year monopoly over other trade, excepting the fisheries. The associates thus became the seigneurs of the French-claimed territories in North America, from Florida to the far north and from the Atlantic coast to the interior of the continent. They were supposed to populate this territory, having been instructed to bring in some 4,000 people. Despite the vast expanse of the territory nominally under their control, in practice their jurisdiction remained limited to the St Lawrence Valley.

Numerous difficulties rendered the settlement projects unsuccessful, particularly the Kirke brothers' capture of Quebec in 1629 and the consequent losses of ships. The company re-established possession of Canada in 1633, but it never managed to achieve its aims. Under Isaac de Razilly (1587–1635), the company had some success in *Acadia, displacing the embryonic Scottish settlements in Nova Scotia and establishing new forts. His actions consolidated the French control in Acadia.

By 1645 the Compagnie de la Nouvelle-France clearly could not promise a suitable financial return. It ceded the control over Canadian trade to the Communauté des habitants in exchange for 1,000 livres weight of beaver pelts per year and covering the costs of administration and immigration. Theoretically the Communauté des habitants comprised all permanent male residents in New France, but in fact it was controlled by a small coterie of families, who used the company's privileges for their own gain. It intended to attract 20 immigrants per year, although it found it difficult to fulfill even this modest goal. Ultimate administrative authority still resided in the Compagnie de la Nouvelle-France, but the Communauté des habitants played a vital role in the politics of the colony. Nonetheless, by 1652, the latter found itself in financial difficulties.

In 1663 Louis XIV revoked the grant to the Compagnie de la Nouvelle-France and assumed direct rule over the colony, but the reliance on private companies did not end. In 1664, the Compagnie des Indes occidentales was set up to administer the colony, although Louis XIV's trusted minister Jean-Baptiste Colbert maintained strong authority over the affairs of New France. The king appointed the governor and the intendant, even though theoretically the company enjoyed the privilege of appointing to the Sovereign Council. This led to conflicts over jurisdiction, and over time the importance of this company withered, the king cancelling its privileges in 1674. Thereafter, New France was under the direct control of the king and his ministers. For a brief period, the king subsidized larger-scale immigration than had previously been the case.

The expedient of administering the colony through private companies did not end with the dissolution of the Compagnie des Indes occidentales. As was the practice in France, important trade privileges continued to be farmed out to individuals and companies. The Compagnie de la colonie (1700–6) attempted to gain a monopoly over the fur trade. In other parts of French North America, private companies assumed administrative control. The Compagnie de l'Île St-Jean, for instance, was granted authority over present-day Prince Edward Island from 1719 to 1724.

COLIN M. COATES

colonization companies in the Canadas. British attitudes to emigration changed dramatically in the post-Napoleonic era. Before circa 1815, official views decreed that patriotic men should not desert their native soil. Rural land enclosures and economic downturns prompted reconsideration: emigration to the colonies seemed the answer to popular unrest. The largest colonization companies in the Canadas, the Canada Land Company in Upper Canada, chartered in 1825, and the British American Land Company in Lower Canada, chartered in 1834, hoped to profit from the new environment. John Galt, erstwhile Scottish novelist, promoted both; British capitalists provided funds; and the *Colonial Office saw in the companies a means to underwrite conservative colonial rule. Neither company fulfilled its promise and at least one private colonization effort seemed more successful.

The Canada Company purchased 1 million hectares of land for $295,000 payable to Upper Canada's appointed executive council over a period of 16 years. Half lay in the Huron tract in the west and half was Crown reserves throughout the colony. Reformers in the elected assembly correctly saw this as a move to undermine their fiscal power by providing the conservative-dominated executive council an independent source of funds. At the outset, the company focused undue attention on grandiose development in the Huron tract. The 'instant' town of Goderich became its headquarters. No paupers here: Galt solicited 'persons of substance and respectability'. Less favoured by Galt, but destined to outpace Goderich, the smaller town of Stratford also emerged, settled by working farm families. In 1829 the company refused to sell land at Wilberforce to 200 African Americans because 'present inhabitants . . . have a repugnance to [Black people] forming communities near them'.

William 'Tiger' Dunlop, an exuberant and erudite local company administrator, added an unpredictable quality to company affairs. In his promotional tract, *Statistical Sketches of Upper Canada* (1832), he asserted that Upper Canada is 'the most healthy country under the sun considering that whisky can be procured for about one shilling sterling per gallon'. Staid company directors parted ways with Dunlop in 1838. Frederick Widder, the son of a company director, arrived in 1839, moved headquarters to Toronto, instituted a leasing system and long-term payment plan, established agencies at 27 British ports, advertised throughout the Canadas, and participated in railway promotion in the 1850s. After his retirement in 1864, the company went quietly about its business, selling the last of its land in the 1950s.

Fired by the Canada Company on the grounds of sloppy administration in 1829, and put in a debtor's prison on his arrival back in London, John Galt, buoyed by literary profits, briefly reemerged as the promoter of the British American Land Company. The company purchased 343,995 hectares of Crown land in the *Eastern Townships for £120,000. As in Upper Canada, reformers railed against payments directly to the executive council, settlers chafed under strict company rule, and the company put most of its efforts into the establishment of a primary town, Sherbrooke. In 1841 the company ceded three-fifths of its grant back to the government in lieu of overdue payments. Galt's son, Alexander Tilloch, the company's bookkeeper, became local commissioner in 1844 and, as did Widder, broadened advertisements, lengthened repayments, and rationalized administration. He and his successor, R.W. Heneker, invested in railways and industrial pursuits to stimulate land sales. Indeed, Heneker saw himself less of a land commissioner and more as a 'gentleman or banker . . . I have a variety of occupations.' The company's directors had other ideas: they emphasized land sales and curbed investment activities. Henecker privileged anglophone development and regional growth centred in Sherbrooke. On his retirement in 1902 anglophones were a distinct minority, and the local economy had largely fallen under the control of Montreal. The company closed shop in the 1950s, although most of its land had been sold by 1910.

Other colonizers emerged in this period, Thomas Talbot being the most controversial. A British aristocrat, and secretary to John Graves *Simcoe, Upper Canada's first lieutenant-governor, Talbot assiduously employed official connections to amass a huge acreage north of Lake Erie. He developed his 'Princely domain' at arms length from government supervision. He kept settlement records under his control, pencilling in names and in some cases, if displeased, as quickly erasing them from the record! Despite his dictatorial ways, he provided roads for his settlers far superior to those constructed by the Canada Land Company, and by the 1830s the region he controlled was arguably more prosperous than most of the rest of the colony. PETER BASKERVILLE

colonization movement. During the pre-rebellion era, the French-Canadian settlement zone was largely confined to the seigneuries, despite their decreasing supply of arable land. Expansion beyond the St Lawrence and its two major southern tributaries was hindered by the lack of a viable transportation network through the swampy land that lay at the base of the Appalachian and Laurentian ranges, a handicap that was exacerbated by the accumulation of large land grants on the part of influential absentee proprietors. In an attempt to promote French-Canadian colonization as an alternative to emigration to the United States, Catholic priests whose missions extended into the townships adjacent to the south-shore seigneuries issued a proclamation in 1849 calling for an effective system of taxation on land held by speculators. Reform of the municipal system finally provided local communities with this tool during the early 1850s, when French-Canadian colonization spread rapidly throughout Canada East, including the remote Lac St-Jean region.

Less successful was the government's joint effort in 1848 with the Association pour l'établissement des Canadiens-Français dans les Townships du Bas-Canada. Under pressure from this short-lived society of priests and members of the anticlerical *Institut canadien, the Baldwin–LaFontaine administration offered free grants of 50 acres alongside an extensive network of colonization roads constructed in the thin-soiled townships between the upper St Francis River and Lake Megantic. This project attracted permanent settlement, but at the cost of enduring poverty ensured by the alienation of the district's most valuable resource, its forests, to an American-based lumber company.

Confederation brought renewed pressure on the provincial authorities to stem the accelerating flood of French Canadians to the New England textile towns, with the result that in 1869 large tracts of Crown land were reserved for privately funded colonization societies. Little of consequence was achieved, though the *Zouave-inspired settlement of Piopolis was established on the shores of Lake Megantic. In 1875 the province's Repatriation Act aimed at encouraging a large-scale return of French Canadians from economically depressed New England, but the only concrete result was the small settlement of La Patrie, a few miles from Piopolis. A more promising development during the same decade was the launching of Abbé Antoine Labelle's career as a promoter of French-Canadian colonization in the Laurentians north of Montreal, though even he would fail to challenge the Crown timber-lease system that marginalized settlers within their own territories. J.I. LITTLE

'Come near at your peril, Canadian wolf'. Famous line from an anti-Confederate Newfoundland ballad of 1869, written by one 'Power the poet'. Power also wrote a celebrated 'Song' (printed in the St John's *Morning Chronicle*, 15 December 1869) to accompany a procession bearing the coffin marked 'Confederation' to its burial place at the head of St John's harbour. The Canadian wolf ballad, normally entitled 'Anti-Confederation Song', seems not to have been printed in full until 1940, when it appeared (with music) in the second edition of Gerald S. Doyle's *Old-Time Songs and Poetry of Newfoundland*. P.K. Devine, however, printed two stanzas of it in 1912 and noted its connection to the events of 1869. The end of the song has this warning, later unheeded: 'For a few thousand dollars of Canadian gold,/Don't let it be said that your birthright was sold.'

Voters of Irish descent led the assault on Confederation in the 1869 election. They had used the term 'wolf' (with other abusive terms) in the 1830s to describe a Catholic who opposed their priests' political schemes. Thirty years later they transferred it to another enemy. Following 1869, having rejected Confederation, Newfoundlanders continued to be cautioned against becoming 'a prey to the gluttonous appetites of Canadian wolves' (*Evening Telegram*, 12 January 1886). PATRICK O'FLAHERTY

Cominco. Industrial conglomerate (established 1966), previously known as Consolidated Mining and Smelting Company. In 1898, the *Canadian Pacific Railway purchased the smelter, mines, and rail complex at Trail and Rossland, BC, from Montana interests. Consolidated was formed in 1906 as a subsidiary. With purchase of the Sullivan Mine at Kimberley in 1913, Consolidated commenced a growth based upon research, astute mineral exploration, progressive processing techniques, and product diversification. It conducted preliminary work in the Pine Point area, south of Slave Lake, in 1926–7, where lead and zinc potential had been reported in 1899. After 1929, gold became the main mining prospect in the Northwest Territories. Despite the depression and transportation difficulties, gold remained in demand and even rose in value, fixed in price by American president Franklin Roosevelt. Consolidated poured the first gold brick from the Yellowknife area in 1938. The company diversified into many product lines after the war. John *Diefenbaker's northern resource program facilitated completion of the Great Slave Lake Railway north from Alberta in 1964, paving the way for transformation of the Mackenzie District economy through exploitation of Cominco's Pine Point mines. The company thus became a main vehicle of large-scale regional economic and social development. Sold by the CPR in 1986 to a large consortium, it remains an important company.

GRAHAM MacDONALD

Commission of Government. The onset of the Great Depression of the 1930s quickly brought the export-oriented Dominion of Newfoundland to a financial and social crisis. By 1932–3 interest payments on the public debt amounted to 63.2 per cent of government revenue. The Newfoundland authorities first sought to deal with the mounting difficulty by borrowing more money, but credit soon dried up. Thought was also given to selling Labrador to Canada, but this scheme went nowhere. A proposal floated in the fall of 1932 to reduce and reschedule interest payments met a frosty reception in London and was quickly abandoned.

In the circumstances, Newfoundland became dependent on British and Canadian support to avoid default. In return for the help given in late 1932, the newly elected government of Frederick Alderdice had to agree to the appointment by the United Kingdom of a three-member royal commission, including British, Canadian, and Newfoundland nominees, 'to examine into the future of Newfoundland and in particular to report on the financial situation and prospects therein'. The Newfoundland Royal Commission, chaired by Lord *Amulree, began its meetings in St John's in the spring of 1933. A visit to Ottawa proved unproductive, and Canada soon after refused any further assistance, in effect abandoning its neighbour. This action left the British with a hard choice, which they made in the report of the royal commission. It recommended that the United Kingdom 'assume general responsibility' for Newfoundland's finances. In return, Newfoundlanders would give up self-government in favour of administration by a British-appointed Commission of Government, with both executive and legislative authority. The commission would give Newfoundlanders 'a rest from politics' and government with high principle. The Alderdice government and the Newfoundland legislature quickly bought into this plan, whereupon the British Parliament passed the Newfoundland Act, 1933. This legislation incorporated the understanding that *responsible government would be restored when Newfoundland was 'self-supporting' and 'on request from the people', but no procedure was specified.

The Commission of Government was inaugurated at a ceremony held in the ballroom of the Newfoundland Hotel, St John's, 16 February 1934. Under the new system, there was a governor and six commissioners, 'three . . . drawn from Newfoundland and three from the United Kingdom'. The commissioners had portfolios, but economic and financial affairs were kept firmly in British hands. The commission held 1,098 meetings and remained in office until Newfoundland became a province of Canada on 31 March 1949. PETER NEARY

Common Front. The 1972 Quebec Common Front strike was the first general strike of public sector workers in Canada. Quebec's three rival labour congresses, the *Confédération des syndicats nationaux (CSN), the Corporation des enseignants du Québec (CEQ), and the *Fédération des travailleurs du Québec (FTQ), formed a common front for negotiations on behalf of all provincial public and para-public sector workers. While the aim was to increase workers' bargaining power, events of the period had radicalized Quebec labour. In the aftermath of the imposition of the *War Measures Act during the 1970 *October Crisis, *unions were at the forefront of opposition to the pro-business government of Liberal premier Robert Bourassa. Major demands included a $100 a week minimum wage for the lowest-paid workers and wage increases that would set precedents for higher wages in the private sector. Negotiations stalled, so on 11 April about 210,000 state workers, including civil servants, teachers, hospital and social service workers, and hydro and liquor store employees, went on strike. Ten days later, the Quebec government passed back-to-work legislation. When the presidents of the three labour congresses—Marcel Pepin of the CSN, Louis Laberge of the FTQ, and Yvon Charbonneau of the CEQ—defied government orders, they were jailed for a year. This provoked a two-week wave of demonstrations and strikes that spread to the private sector. Despite the repression, unions won the minimum wage, salary increases above government guidelines, and better job security. A major consequence of the strike was to further fracture an already divided Quebec labour movement, as some union members were uneasy with militant and radical tactics. The CSN was the hardest hit, as it lost about one-third of its membership, many leaving to form a fourth Quebec labour federation, the Centrale des syndicats démocratiques.

GEOFFREY EWEN

common schools. A conventional term until the mid-19th century throughout most of the English-speaking world for a school that taught 'the common branches of an English education', such as the three Rs, to 'common people'. Although some common schools also taught the higher branches of an English education, the term tended to be juxtaposed against, for example, 'grammar school', which taught the classical languages—often along with an English education—to those who could afford a more select and extended education. Some common schools might be government-funded or tax-supported (or both), but they might also be supported entirely by private means. Such schools might be identified with one denomination or none at all.

From the mid-19th century on, the early education acts in several British North American colonies provided government funding to most common schools and organized them into fledgling systems of public education. As *high schools were integrated into public systems of education, the common school tended to restrict its curriculum exclusively to elementary studies. Nova Scotia retained the term 'common school' well into the 20th century, but elsewhere in Canada the conventional designation was changed to 'public' or 'elementary' school. In some Canadian provinces there were, and are, government-funded Roman Catholic schools established within the framework of the education acts, either through customary arrangements or as legal entities usually designated 'separate schools'. Such schools, also descended from the 19th-century common schools, are not private schools but integral parts of provincial systems of public education.

W.P.J. MILLAR AND R.D. GIDNEY

Commonwealth. The term 'Imperial Commonwealth' was first used formally during the First World War to refer collectively to Britain and the self-governing dominions of the *British Empire. After the war, Canada, particularly with W.L. Mackenzie *King as prime minister, fostered the transition from imperial unity to autonomy for the dominions in international affairs. This equality of status in the 'British Commonwealth of Nations' was acknowledged by the *Balfour Report (1926) and the *Statute of Westminster (1931). However, Canada still relied on Britain's diplomatic network for information about world affairs and to safeguard Canadian interests overseas. The King government eschewed prior commitments that supported British foreign policy, but it sympathized with the stances (notably appeasement) adopted by British governments in the 1930s and did not chart a different course.

Canada's decision to go to war 'at Britain's side' in 1939 was predictable. However, the threat posed by common foes and the stirring rhetoric of British prime minister Winston Churchill did not revive imperial sentiment. Even when Britain and the Commonwealth fought alone against Germany and Italy in 1940–1, the Canadian government resisted centralization of the Commonwealth. That tendency persisted in peacetime. Britain and the Commonwealth were no longer so vital to Canada as its own international interests and involvements diversified and expanded, but the relationship with its former imperial partners was still closer than with most foreign countries. In 1949 Canada helped to redefine the Commonwealth so as to preserve its historic links through the *monarchy even as India remained a member with a republican constitution. As decolonization in Asia and Africa transformed the Commonwealth into a multiracial group, successive Canadian governments appreciated the links that it provided to various countries around the world. One of Canada's earliest forms of development assistance came within a Commonwealth initiative, the Colombo Plan. Perhaps no episode more effectively illustrated the change in Canadian perceptions of the Commonwealth than Prime Minister John *Diefenbaker's alignment in the 1960s with African and Asian leaders who favoured expulsion of South Africa because of its racialist policies. More recently, the organization has been seen by Canadian policy-makers as a forum for advancing international policies informally and as a bridge to regions where Canada otherwise has limited interests and engagement. Yet, as the 21st century began, the Commonwealth was considerably less important to Canada—and less influential—than the empire had been at the beginning of the 20th century.

HECTOR MACKENZIE

communication. As a central organizing concept in the study of society, communication asks how ways of life are shared and how ideas are imparted or made common. It focuses on the messenger, the content of the message, the medium of transmission, the receiver of the message, and the effect of the reception. The process is 'symbolic' because it involves the transfer of models of the world from sender to receiver. Collectively, these communicative acts are central to 'cultural reproduction': they maintain a society over time, represent shared beliefs, and provide fellowship.

Several pioneering students of communication, notably Harold *Innis and Marshall *McLuhan, contributed to the development of a distinctive Canadian approach to the subject. Writing between the 1940s and the 1970s, they conjured with the notion that, in McLuhan's famous formulation, 'the medium is the message'. Innis wrote that certain media (e.g., clay tablets) possessed a bias in favour of 'time' and facilitated the transmission of allegedly eternal verities. Other societies (e.g., those where paper was used) were biased in favour of 'space'; Innis regarded their communication processes as imperial, commercial, and, in the long run, relatively superficial. He sought to make room for dissent in civilization. The burden of his message was that a 'transmission' approach to communication, which was pervasive in American scholarship, tends to reinforce monopoly. Given the increasing relevance of communication to daily life in the mid-20th century, Innis suggested that only consciousness of the 'time' dimension could enable outlying peoples to resist the hegemony of the US-led, commercially driven, globe-transforming, information system. Innis would have placed Canada among these resisting peoples because he believed that citizens who belong to nation-states outside the imperial centre could function effectively as political communities only by maintaining their own conversations. The development or downfall of these national conversations would depend on the competitive elements in and the efficiency of the communication system.

The social and cultural history of communication in northern North America begins, if one follows the Innis–McLuhan model, with the oral societies of Aboriginal peoples. These communities relied on the land itself to provide sustenance, on the human voice to conduct their daily affairs, and on stories—some of which achieved the status of 'myths'—to convey deeper truths about people and place.

This first distinct version of the dimensions of existence was eclipsed, but not erased, by a second, when Europeans arrived in the 16th and 17th centuries and when the communication technologies of their literate societies—alphabet, letterpress, print—introduced a new way of living. In northern North America, this second version of the world's dimensions was in many respects quite similar to its Aboriginal predecessor. The vast majority of residents were relatively unlettered and their communities relied on household production of natural products. Nonetheless, acquaintance with Bibles, calendars, clocks, written laws, and the international trade in staples ensured that a different perception of time and space took hold in their isolated settlements.

The trader-settler communication regime was eclipsed in the 19th and early 20th centuries by a 'print-capitalist' phase, which relied on the introduction of universal literacy as well as machines and steam power. A consequence of this technology-led regime was the creation of the nation of Canada itself, a political entity consolidated by schools, a transcontinental railway and the east-west trade it carried (including tariff-protected local manufactures), and the telegraphic communications that made possible the proper functioning of market, government, and newspaper.

In the last half of the 20th century a 'screen capitalist' civilization, which owes its distinctiveness in large part to new communication technologies, has eclipsed its predecessor. Driven by television, computers, and satellites, this communication context presents an entirely new range of challenges. Nation-states today are relatively less able than their predecessors to maintain the distinct conversations of previous generations; transnational links, both political and corporate, undermine national political control. Communication remains a pivotal issue in debate about and discovery of collective values as well as in community decision-making. GERALD FRIESEN

Communist Party of Canada. In May 1921, in a barn just outside Guelph, Ontario, 22 men and women, including one undercover police agent, met to create the Communist Party of Canada. They represented various labour and socialist groups radicalized by the First World War and the industrial unrest that accompanied and followed it. Their program, based on the writings of Karl Marx and Vladimir Lenin, and inspired by the Bolshevik Revolution in Russia four years earlier, called for revolution, the overthrow of capitalism, and the 'dictatorship of the proletariat'. Though consistently hounded by the RCMP, who saw them as a threat to Canada, the Communists established their own legal political party as well as their own trade union movement, and took over the militant Women's Labour Leagues, which organized women workers, the poor, and the unemployed and led demonstrations on behalf of women's rights.

In 1929, an English-born machinist, Tim *Buck, became the party leader. Two years later he and seven other Communist leaders were convicted of 'belonging to an illegal organization' and sent to Kingston Penitentiary. There he was shot at and almost killed by prison guards. When Buck and the other members of the 'Toronto Eight' were subsequently released, he had become a hero to many on the left and gave the party fresh impetus. Although its leadership was largely from Great Britain, the majority of its supporters were Ukrainians, Finns, Jews, and other eastern European immigrants. Throughout the Depression, party members helped mobilize unemployed men in the government *relief camps, leading the *'On-to-Ottawa Trek' of many of these men in 1935. The party also recruited some 1,600 volunteers to fight fascism in the Spanish Civil War of 1936–9. It organized thousands of workers into its *Workers' Unity League and played a key role in creating the Congress of Industrial Organizations. While they did not achieve much electoral success, Communists were elected to several municipal councils and provincial legislatures, and ultimately to the House of Commons when Fred Rose won a Montreal seat in 1943.

Because of the Nazi–Soviet alliance, Communists strenuously resisted Canada's entry into the Second World War, prompting the government to outlaw the party. Only with the German invasion of the Soviet Union in June 1941 did the party become an enthusiastic supporter of the war effort. In 1943 the party took on a new name, the Labour Progressive Party, running candidates under that banner for the next 20 years. Whatever it called itself, the party never deviated from slavishly following Soviet policies for its entire history.

Canadian Communism reached the peak of its popularity during the war because of the military achievements of the Soviet army on the Eastern Front. Shortly after the war, however, Igor *Gouzenko, a clerk in the Soviet Embassy in Ottawa, defected, disclosing the existence of a massive Soviet spy ring, which included several prominent Canadians. The most important was Fred Rose, who was convicted of espionage, jailed for six years, and then deported to Poland. These events, along with the onset of the Cold War, seriously undermined the party's credibility and influence. What ultimately destroyed the Communist Party in Canada was the Soviet invasion of Hungary in 1956 and, more importantly, the speech in that same year by the leader of the Soviet Union, Nikita Khrushchev, denouncing the brutality and anti-Semitism of the Stalin regime. These revelations shocked Communists all over the world, causing a huge rift in the movement. In Canada most members deserted the party led by the highly admired J.B. Salsberg, the party's most eloquent spokesman, a union organizer, and a long-time member of the Ontario legislature. Salsberg took with him most remaining Jewish supporters, as well as members of other ethnic groups. By the time of the collapse of the Soviet Union in the late 1980s, there were scarcely any Communists left in Canada.

IRVING ABELLA

community of communities. One of the slogans of Joe Clark's successful campaign for the prime minister's office in 1979. Extensive polling had indicated that the *Progressive Conservatives needed to develop an aura of competence and concern if they expected to wrest power from Pierre *Trudeau's Liberals. In keeping with that strategy, Clark criticized the government for creating an environment that pitted region against region and provinces against the federal government; in contrast, Clark offered a conciliatory approach to intergovernmental negotiations that would see Canada as a 'community of communities'—a decentralized view of the federation, which would include sharing jurisdiction over the *fisheries and giving provinces control over offshore resources. A Conservative alternative that stressed co-operation rather than confrontation appealed to voters, and Clark won a minority government in May 1979. A non-confidence vote in the House of Commons six months later, and the Conservative's subsequent loss of power in the February 1980 election, meant that the 'community of communities' version of Canada would not come into being.

P.E. BRYDEN

compact theory of Confederation. The idea that the founding of the Dominion of Canada expressed a compact between certain parties, who consequently possess certain rights under the Canadian constitution. In some versions, *Confederation is a compact between its member provinces, in others a compact between two founding nations: French and British Canadians. The theory's uncertainty, and its function as a challenge to the authority of the federal government, makes it highly controversial.

Traditionally, the provincial theory was invoked to support the claims of provincial governments to a determining role in the process of constitutional amendment. It was first adumbrated in 1868, when John A. *Macdonald revised the terms of Confederation in Nova Scotia's favour in order to reconcile that province to the new union. The Interprovincial Conference of 1887 cited the provincial theory as grounds for asserting that the provinces could jointly amend the constitution against the will of the federal government. This contention was later diluted into the weaker claim that major amendments required the unanimous consent of the provinces.

The national theory is likewise multifarious. As elaborated by Henri *Bourassa in the early 20th century, in response to the curtailment of francophone educational rights in the Prairie provinces and Ontario, it implied that francophones and anglophones were entitled to equal cultural facilities throughout Canada. Another version sustains Quebec's claim, as the political embodiment of French Canada, to special status within Confederation.

Every version of the theory envisaged the compact as an unwritten gloss on the British North America Act, Canada's written *constitution. The theory's uncertainty flowed partly from the unwritten nature of the supposed compact and partly from the diversity of the communities that made up the dominion. Both the provincial and the national theory were extensions of ideas that were central to the convictions of the two groups whose leaders initiated, in 1864, the process that culminated in Confederation. The one transposed to the provinces the Upper Canadian *Reformers' belief in colonial legislative sovereignty; the other originated in the belief that the French-Canadian nation possessed rights guaranteed by treaty with the British government. These ideas were potentially, though not necessarily, contradictory; the potential for uncertainty increased with the annexation to Canada of other colonies, to which both doctrines were alien. In 1900 the idea that major constitutional amendments required a provincial consensus was broadly accepted. From 1930 on, anglophones, influenced by a predominantly nationalist intelligentsia, found this idea less and less acceptable. Isolated in their devotion to the theory, Québécois authorities developed it in ways that were unhistorical and even less plausible to other Canadians—

by asserting, for example, that the Quebec government represented all francophones and the federal government only anglophones. Nevertheless, the principle of unanimous provincial consent to constitutional amendment remained politically operative until Pierre *Trudeau's *patriation initiative in 1980. PAUL ROMNEY

Conacher, Lionel (1900–54), multi-sport athlete. Born in Toronto, Conacher, unquestionably Canada's most versatile athlete, was voted Canada's greatest athlete of the half century. Nicknamed the 'Big Train', he starred in hockey, baseball, football, lacrosse, boxing, soccer, wrestling, and track and field. In addition to a National Hockey League career (1925–37), he played on the Toronto Argonauts Grey Cup championship team in 1921, played professional baseball for the Toronto Maple Leafs of the International League, was Canadian light-heavyweight boxing champion, and helped his team win the Ontario Lacrosse Association championship in 1922. A hard-nosed defenceman in hockey, Conacher played both offence and defence for the football Argonauts, and was one of the premier punters of his time.
COLIN HOWELL

Confederation. Projects to unite the British provinces in North America began with arrival of the *Loyalists in the 1780s. From the time of Lord *Durham's Report in 1839, politicians in Britain saw union of *British North America as an eventual target, although they could not grasp its scale. By the 1850s visionaries foresaw a transcontinental union, emulating US expansion to California but increasing the practical challenges. When the Cartier–Macdonald ministry in Canada tackled the idea in 1858 under pressure from A.T. *Galt, it cautiously promised to explore whether union 'may perhaps hereafter be practicable'. In any case, two opposed structures were advocated. Liberals favoured federation, on American lines, with *provincial autonomy. Tories wanted a centralized union, copied from Britain, to subordinate the French-Canadian minority. The term 'Confederation' emerged to conflate these two approaches.

Confederation became a practical option thanks to the continental crisis created by the American Civil War, but precise causal connections are hard to identify. Political union was not necessary to create a free-trade zone or to improve colonial defence. The expensive Halifax–Quebec railway meant less cash to develop the Hudson's Bay territories to the west. Upper Canada demanded increased political representation to reflect its increasing population dominance ('rep. by pop.') but a Canadian (Ontario–Quebec) federation could have achieved this. Some historians have seen Confederation as a trade-off, with the British underwriting a low-interest loan for the *Intercolonial Railway in exchange for a union that would allow them to disengage from North America. But the British had already agreed in 1862 to back such a loan to the separate provinces. The problem was that New Brunswick and Nova Scotia, poor colonies with fewer than 600,000 people, were assigned seven-twelfths (58.33 per cent) of the interest payments. Confederation with 2.5 million Canadians would shift that burden to more prosperous shoulders. Maritime leaders met at Charlottetown in September 1864 to discuss their own local union. This gathering was genially hijacked by Canada's *Great Coalition, which persuaded them to adopt the larger project. At Quebec that October, a more formal scheme, centralist in theory, federalist in practice, was drawn up in 72 resolutions. In March 1865, the Canadian assembly endorsed it by 91 votes to 33 (27–21 among francophones).

Elsewhere, reactions were negative. A mainland railway meant nothing to Newfoundland and Prince Edward Island. In Nova Scotia, only the Halifax–Chignecto corridor would benefit directly. Bluenoses had dreamed of leading a wider union but pride was affronted by this sudden Canadian-led initiative. New Brunswick was also suspicious that strategic reasons would direct the railway away from the populous Saint John Valley close to the United States. Opponents of the decade-old government of Leonard Tilley used the issue to defeat him in the March 1865 election. Although headed by an anti-unionist, the incoming ministry included some who criticized the Quebec scheme for preserving too much local autonomy. Meanwhile, the US Congress denounced the Reciprocity Treaty, and Fenian terrorists threatened the provinces with armies of Civil War veterans. New Brunswick swung back into line when *Fenians raided in April 1866. In Nova Scotia, the breadth of opposition disguised doubts and suspicions. Eventually unionist premier Charles *Tupper secured agreement to reject the Quebec scheme but negotiate a union anyway. When delegates met in England in December 1866, they ignored the first provision. Working with the *Colonial Office, the delegates, under John A. Macdonald's leadership, turned the Quebec scheme into the *British North America Act, accepted by the Westminster parliament in March 1867. Wary of American sensitivities, the British vetoed the title 'Kingdom'. Confederation came into being on 1 July 1867 as a *'Dominion'. GED MARTIN

Confédération des syndicats nationaux. A Quebec labour congress first established in 1921 as the Confédération des travailleurs catholiques du Canada (CTCC). Quebec was the only place in North America where religiously based *unions were formed. Inspired by the 1891 papal encyclical **Rerum Novarum* ('On the Condition of the Working Classes'), the Quebec church promoted Catholic and Canadian labour organizations in opposition to international unions, often affiliated with the *American Federation of Labor, which it associated with secularism, class conflict, and socialism. Catholic unions offered an alternative that promoted harmonious relations between employers and workers and support for a hierarchical social order. The threat to the AFL became real in 1917 when older national unions joined the Catholic movement. The CTCC condemned the AFL as a foreign organization and appealed to workers on the basis of French-Canadian nationalism, defending French language and culture. Despite the church's social teachings, national and Catholic unions could be combative, engaging in a number of strikes. Even among francophone workers, however, the CTCC remained smaller than the international unions.

In the late 1940s, under new leadership that included Jean Marchand as general secretary (1947–61) and president (1961–4), clerical influence declined and the CTCC became more militant. It offered sustained opposition to the repressive government of Maurice *Duplessis and engaged in a greater number of difficult disputes, including the 1949 *Asbestos strike. Ideologically it abandoned the corporatism of the 1930s for liberal humanism, an attempt to reconcile Catholicism with liberal and democratic values, calling for production based on human need and for worker co-management. In 1960 it secularized, changing its name to the CSN.

During the *Quiet Revolution of the 1960s the rise of a new progressive Quebec nationalism favoured the CSN over the rival Quebec Federation of Labour, the Quebec wing of the *Canadian Labour Congress. The CSN doubled its size, enlisting members in the public sector as new legislation allowed government workers to join politically unaffiliated unions, at a time when the QFL supported the New Democratic Party. There was growing militancy and, after mid-decade, radicalization. In 1966 the CSN embraced *democratic socialism and in 1971 issued a Marxist analysis calling for a socialist Quebec. These trends alienated the congress's more conservative members. After the 1972 *Common Front strike, the CSN lost a third of its membership, many of them private sector workers outside of Montreal who formed the Centrale des syndicats démocratiques. In the late 1970s the CSN represented about 20 per cent of Quebec union members. During the 1970s it avoided official statements favouring independence, then advocated a yes vote in the 1980 Quebec referendum. GEOFFREY EWEN

Confédération des travailleurs catholiques du Canada. *See* CONFÉDÉRATION DES SYNDICATS NATIONAUX.

Confederation poets. New Brunswicker Charles G.D. Roberts (1860–1943), his first cousin Bliss Carman (1861–1929), and two friends from Ottawa, Archibald Lampman (1861–99) and Duncan Campbell Scott (1862–1947). The term, brought into popular usage via Malcolm Ross's anthology *Poets of the Confederation* (1960), has proven justifiably elastic, expanding to include such contemporaries as William Wilfred Campbell (1860–1918) and Isabella Valancy Crawford (1850–87). Often considered the first distinctly Canadian poets, the Confederation poets are most commonly remembered for sensibilities, coloured by British Romanticism and American transcendentalism, that were particularly attuned to the aesthetic, intellectual, and spiritual possibilities of local regions, more specifically to the spirit of place. Taking their cues from long-established poetic forms (the sonnet, the elegy) and familiar cultural binaries (rural–urban, cultivated–wild, past–progress), they brought to Canadian culture a radical new emphasis. Distilling the intensities of subjective experience with a profound appreciation of the specificities of place, they recognized in nature a pathway to fuller understandings of the contours of dreams, memory, and consciousness; of the powers of imagination released from the pressures of the workaday world; and of what Lampman called the 'cosmic sympathy' connecting human culture to the rhythms of tide and season.

At times too narrowly classified as nature poets, these writers were also determined to bring to Canadian culture an appreciation for the poet as social conscience, as a political and moral guide whose affinity with the land allowed for a thoughtful interrogation of the various tensions in Canadian culture. Representative of these concerns is 'At the Mermaid Inn', an eclectic and serious weekly column written by Lampman, Campbell, and Scott for the Toronto *Globe* (1892–3). It typifies the scope of issues addressed by the Confederation group: from questions about the implications for life in a post-Darwinian world and the role of poetry in mechanized urban cultures through personal struggles with the inhumanities of war. Although closely related in important ways, these poets remain distinct political voices, with beliefs that ranged from Lampman's and Carman's open contempt for modern politics and industrial capitalism through Scott's administration of oppressive policies during his long career in the Department of Indian Affairs. Disparaged by Canadian modernists for a Victorian 'zeal for God and King [and] their earnest thought', this 'lively company', as Ross describes them, provided sustainable proof 'that we possess a poetic tradition of considerable merit and of recognizable character.' KLAY DYER

conglomerates. The term 'conglomerate' came into use in the 1960s in the United States, referring to enterprises that specialized in the acquisition of controlling blocks of shares in other companies, usually in diverse and unrelated products and services. 'Conglomerators' rationalized their strategies as providing improved management for the companies acquired and creating opportunities for unusual new products through 'synergies'.

To some extent the Canadian experience with conglomerates paralleled that of the US, but unique features reflected its smaller, more personalized financial community. Historically most large Canadian firms focused on particular industries, with some notable exceptions such as *Canadian Pacific Railway, which had significant holdings in mining, petroleum exploration, hotels, and steam lines acquired in the course of pursuing its strategy of rail expansion. Perhaps the first enterprise set up deliberately to invest in unrelated industries was Argus Corporation, created in 1945 by a group of Toronto venture capitalists led by E.P. Taylor, who had amalgamated the brewing industries in Quebec and Ontario before the Second World War. As in the case of the 1960s conglomerates, Argus was a holding company that acquired control over other companies, purportedly offering shareholders in the acquired firms the benefits of good management and improved productivity. During the 1940s–50s Argus established control over a diverse range of large Canadian firms, including Dominion Stores (retailing), *Massey-Harris (farm equipment), Hollinger Mines, and British Columbia Forest Products.

Power Corp. was founded in 1925 by the Montreal investment company Nesbitt-Thomson as a holding company to manage diverse utility firms across Canada. In the 1960s many of these utilities were taken over by provincial governments; under the guidance of Maurice Strong, Power Corp. used the proceeds from these sales to reorganize itself as a diversified 'investment and management company' with significant holdings in Laurentide Financial Co., Dominion Glass, Consolidated-Bathurst (forest products), Canada Steamship Lines, and others. In 1968, Power Corp. passed into the hands of Paul Desmarais, a French-Canadian financier who had already built up his own diversified empire of bus lines and media, real estate, banking, and life insurance companies.

While these 'proprietary' conglomerates with their colourful leaders received much media coverage, some of Canada's old-line firms joined in the trend: Canadian Pacific, under the presidency of Ian Sinclair in the 1970s, expanded into new and unrelated areas, acquiring firms such as Algoma Steel, Maple Leaf Mills, and International Paper; the word 'Railway' was dropped from its corporate title. In the following decade *Bell Canada, reorganized as a holding company, BCE, acquired a disparate range of enterprises, including Trans-Canada Pipe Lines and Dome Petroleum.

The rising tide of mergers and acquisitions, highlighted by a failed bid by Desmarais to take over Argus in 1975, aroused political concerns about conglomerates, leading to the establishment of the Royal Commission on Corporate Concentration. Its 1978 report concluded that there was little evidence that these mergers were limiting competition in Canadian industry but also observed that the financial benefits of debt-ridden conglomerates rarely met investor expectations and the promise of managerial improvements often proved illusory.

The recession of the early 1980s briefly brought a halt to the merger trend. By the middle of the decade, however, a new round of conglomerate mergers took shape, stimulated in part by the booming urban real-estate industry. Robert Campeau, a developer of high-rise office buildings and condominiums in Ottawa and Toronto in the 1960s–70s, undertook an improbable foray into the US, acquiring Allied Stores and Federated Department Stores, two of the largest amalgamations of retail stores in the country. Fellow developers, the Reichmann family of Toronto, embarked on an even more ambitious program of acquisitions, with holdings in Gulf Canada (oil and gas), Hiram Walker (liquor), and Abitibi-Price (forest products).

These far-reaching projects, along with their originators, foundered in the recession of the early 1990s. In its aftermath, more established firms such as Canadian Pacific and BCE began to divest themselves of their 'conglomerated' elements, focusing instead on their central product lines. In a general sense, the merger binges of the 1970s and 1980s were fostered by the availability of easy credit and the acquisition of large cash reserves by companies—circumstances not unlike the 'boom' eras of the early 1900s and 1920s. But the particular form of speculative growth that emphasized the benefits of 'conglomeration' seems to have been a feature of a period in which the concept of management could be rationalized to prospective investors as a set of skills transferable across a range of industries and focused primarily on financial organization rather than specialized technical or industrial capabilities.

GRAHAM D. TAYLOR

Congrégation de Notre-Dame. Founded in Montreal by Marguerite *Bourgeoys in 1658, the congregation educated girls in boarding schools (the principal one being in Montreal), in a mission to the Aboriginal people, and in the workroom of La Providence, an institution that disappeared at the turn of the 17th century. Approved by the king in 1672 and the bishop in 1676, the community had eight convents and 40 members when its founder died in 1700. The congregation continued without any major changes throughout the 18th century, receiving occasional royal gratuities, and was tolerated by the English authorities after 1760. In 1825 the superiors extended the program of study and opened English sections. They also accepted several new boarding establishments in the parishes and in 1833 took on the responsibility for many Catholic girls' schools in Montreal. Becoming an apostolic congregation under Vatican law in the mid-19th century, the congregation was able to spread into several other regions of Quebec as well as the Maritimes, Ontario, and the northeastern United States. Beginning in the 20th century, congregation educators established several more advanced programs of study—teachers' colleges, classics, and home economics, as well as an Institut pédagogique—and became the leaders in girls' education in Quebec. In 1960 their network counted an impressive total of 262 institutions in Canada, the United States, and Japan. Hurt by the decline in vocations after 1965, the departure of several professed nuns from the sisterhood, and changes in Quebec society, the congregation had to modify its original mandate. In 1988, at the end of a highly successful congress, those responsible decided to choose the 'preferential option for the poor' as their goal, disposing of most of their educational houses and organizing or financing efforts in a multitude of different areas.

MICHELINE DUMONT

conquest of Acadia, 1710–13. The military conquest of the French colony of Acadia by British forces took place in October 1710 when Governor Daniel d'Auger de Subercase surrendered the fort at *Port-Royal to General Francis Nicholson. Nicholson renamed the town Annapolis Royal—in honour of Queen Anne—and the colony Nova Scotia. The British takeover was confirmed by the Treaty of Utrecht some three years later, but its causes and consequences were complex.

The conquest originated in rival French, English, and Scottish claims to Acadia (the modern Maritime region, as well as the *Gaspé and a portion of today's state of Maine) during the early 17th century as well as in conflicts over fisheries and trade. The Treaty of St-Germain-en-Laye (1632) prompted the removal of a short-lived Scottish colony from Port-Royal in favour of the long-standing French claim. The Treaty of Breda (1667) displaced a loose English occupation of the territory that had persisted since 1654. After war resumed in 1689, the 1691 charter of the English colony of Massachusetts Bay included 'Nova Scotia' within the assigned boundaries. The Treaty of Ryswick (1697), however, reconfirmed English recognition of the French claim to Acadia.

When war was again renewed in 1702—the War of the Spanish Succession, known to English colonists in North America as Queen Anne's War—successive French governors at Port-Royal co-operated with Native allies to prompt damaging raids on New England settlements and recruited *privateers to prey on New England shipping. Retaliatory raids on Acadian settlements were effectively launched from Massachusetts in 1704, but in 1707 a substantial New England force was humiliatingly rebuffed when it attempted to seize Port-Royal. The force raised in 1710 was strengthened by including almost 400 British marines and a specially trained company of grenadiers. Backed by some 1,500 New England militiamen, the invaders quickly proved too much for Subercase's ill-equipped garrison of less than 300.

Nevertheless, the renaming of Annapolis Royal and Nova Scotia represented an act of bravado not yet substantiated by British control. The Treaty of Utrecht (1713) clarified the status of Annapolis Royal, now recognized by France as a British colonial town. The treaty also provided that 'all Nova Scotia or Acadia, with its ancient boundaries', should be ceded from France to Great Britain. Specifically excluded from this were Cape Breton Island and the Île Saint-Jean (later Prince Edward Island), but there were also ambiguities about the 'ancient boundaries'. French interpretations confined the British to, at most, peninsular Nova Scotia, while British interpretations consistently included the modern New Brunswick. Resolution would take 50 years and two more wars.

Of greater immediate concern to the few hundred British at Annapolis Royal was the numerical ascendancy of non-British peoples in Nova Scotia. The presence of the *Mi'kmaq and Maliseet was a constant reminder to the British regime that it existed on Aboriginal sufferance. The British presence at Annapolis Royal, like the French presence before it, had advantages for Aboriginal inhabitants, and was generally tolerated. Should the British stray unduly outside their accepted bounds, however, the Native rebuke could be sharp and effective. Further complicating matters was the continuing presence of rapidly growing Acadian communities around the Bay of Fundy. Under the treaty the Acadians had some obligation, albeit ill-defined, to accept the British regime or remove themselves. Most chose to stay, their uneasy relationship with British authorities spanning the years to the expulsion of 1755–62.

Thus, the military conquest of 1710 was influential in setting in motion key sequences of events, but it was no clear-cut changing of the guard. JOHN G. REID

conquest of New France. The Treaty of Paris, 10 February 1763, ended the *Seven Years' War between France and Great Britain and their allies. It brought into the *British Empire new conquests, including the colony of Canada in the St Lawrence River valley and its dependencies in the Great Lakes region. The war had turned against the French and Canadiens in 1758. In that year Louisbourg, the fortress that guarded the entrance to Canada, had been taken. In 1759 British and Anglo-American troops had savaged the settlements below Quebec, and had bombarded and captured the city. Montreal had surrendered the next year. Conquest meant colony and mother country ripped from each other, family members and friends dead, buildings and other property destroyed, the familiar patterns gone forever. Yet, when historians write of the conquest, they are more concerned with long-term consequences than with the events of 1754–63. At one time, French-Canadian historians saw their people after 1763 as a 'nation' struggling to defend its way of life: the challenge of the conquest was the challenge of materialism and of Protestantism. Many anglophone writers, Canadians and others, once saw the conquest as a triumph of progress and modernity, justifying English ascendancy in Canadian life. More recent francophone historians dreamed of might-have-beens: they lamented that the new nation they believed was being born in New France was denied the 'normal' development that would have brought it to independence and control of its state and economy. This tragic view of the past, essentially a call to action in the present, expressed dissatisfaction with the division of wealth and power between French and English in the mid-20th century. These interpretations of the past conformed to understandings of the present and served quests for power and justification. Even more recent, more 'scientific' views have not entirely escaped the claims the present makes on the past.

How can historians grasp the long term in a manner that is scientific and without illusion? One approach has been to ask whether the most fundamental structures of society and economy were damaged by the conquest or survived it with minimal perturbation. The answer has been that an authoritarian government dominated by European colonial officials, an hierarchical society dominated by priests and gentry, and a traditional agriculture practised by rent- and tithe-paying *habitants continued, while industrial capital remained marginal and the *fur trade (merchant capital) continued as the pre-eminent sector of capital formation. The great changes came after 1800.

Broad brushstrokes obscure details. After 1760, the Roman Catholic clergy maintained their position. The gentry enjoyed few military appointments and little patronage, but, in common with the habitants, they benefited from an agriculture more profitable than in the past. Most significantly, the conquest brought Canada into a business environment more emphatically capitalistic and competitive than the French Empire had been. The bourgeoisie of commercial capitalism carved out a larger place for itself than in the past in the economy and in Canadian life. English merchants were more forward in this than French-Canadian merchants, who were marginalized between 1776 and 1790. But the *American Revolution (1775–83) played an equally decisive role by encouraging the emigration of highly competitive and highly capitalized businessmen from New York to Montreal. The displacement of the French-Canadian bourgeoisie has also been attributed to the weakness of French-Canadian business before 1760, making it a result of the *ancien régime* in Canada rather than of the conquest.

Native peoples, too, were affected by the conquest, the familiar patterns gone forever. Their well-being in northeastern North America before 1763 depended in no small measure on the presence of French and British rival empires that sought the support of Indian alliances. Confronted by a single European power (Great Britain) after the conquest, Indians lost the opportunity to play off one power against the other. Again the American Revolution played its part: it pushed settlement west into Indian territory, both in Canada (the *Loyalists) and the United States. The War of 1812 made Indians only temporarily useful to Great Britain.

For the Indian allies of New France (and subsequently of Great Britain) as for the Canadiens of the St Lawrence parishes, the conquest stood at the beginning of a train of transforming events. Important as it was, it is perilous to point to it as the 'One True Cause' of the complex transformations that followed. DALE MIQUELON

conscription. Associated in Canada with the decision to force men to serve overseas in two world wars, conscription is as old as the French regime, with its requirement that all men must serve in defence of the colony. Militia laws in the British regime continued the obligation, but by the mid-19th century it was largely theoretical. Early-20th-century militarism urged universal training but succeeded only with the young. By 1914, all provinces but Saskatchewan required high school boys to take *cadet training, and a Canadian Defence League urged imposition of universal military training.

In 1914, Canadians expected a short war. Only a few opponents of the war predicted conscription; Sir Robert *Borden's Conservative government insisted that voluntarism would fill the ranks of the *Canadian Expeditionary Force. Half a million men came forward during the war, but after mid-1916 few joined the infantry. Gloomy news at the 1917 Imperial War Conference, 10,000 casualties at *Vimy Ridge in April, and conversations with soldiers convinced Sir Robert that earlier pledges had to be scrapped and conscription imposed to keep faith with the CEF and Canada's allies. On May 18 Borden told Parliament of his policy and then offered to open his government to a coalition with Sir Wilfrid *Laurier and the Liberals. To retain his influence in Quebec, which was highly opposed to conscription, Laurier refused. Borden persisted: the Military Service Act became law on 29 August 1917. Modelled on the law governing the US draft, it allowed generous exemptions and a process of appeals. Legislation gave soldiers, their wives, and mothers the vote, and struck off those considered 'enemy aliens'. Wartime patriotism persuaded many of Laurier's English-speaking MPs to back a *Union coalition. After a bitter election campaign and a promise of exemptions for farmers' sons, on 17 December1917 a divided Canada gave the Unionists power. In January 1918 call-ups began. In March, successful German offensives persuaded Ottawa to cancel exemptions. At Easter, violent conscription riots in Quebec ended in five deaths and an appeal from the church for order. By the Armistice on 11 November, of 401,882 men registered under the MSA, 124,588 men had been added to the ranks of the CEF and 24,132 had reached France. Conscription allowed the *Canadian Corps to fight all-out in the last Hundred Days of the war and to help end the war in 1918, when most expected it to last another year. However, it left Borden's conservatives with a bitter legacy in Quebec and among western farmers.

Memories of conscription helped restore the Liberals in 1921 and, like the war itself, fuelled a mood of isolation. Still, when Britain declared war on Germany in 1939, Canada followed within a week. All parties had made pre-war pledges against conscription for overseas service, and Liberals echoed the pledge in Quebec in October 1939. In 1940, as Britain's allies fell to Hitler's Blitzkrieg, Canada adopted the National Resources Mobilization Act, imposing compulsory service for home defence only. By 1941, the United States had a draft for military service already in force. In English Canada, pressure for conscription grew. Conservatives took up the cause. To defeat them in a by-election, the prime minister, W.L. Mackenzie *King, announced a plebiscite to relieve the government from its earlier pledges. The Ligue pour la défense du Canada rallied Quebeckers, and 71.9 per cent of the province voted 'No' on 27 April. Elsewhere, four-fifths of voters agreed to the government request. 'Not necessarily conscription', King announced, 'but conscription if necessary'.

Conscripts were not necessary by mid-1944, and Allied victory seemed close. However, high casualties in Italy and Normandy, the manpower wasted by fighting in two theatres, and poor casualty forecasting created a serious shortage of trained infantry. Under-strength battalions increased casualties and lowered morale. Hockey entrepreneur Conn Smythe came home wounded and spread the news to Canadians. The defence minister, Col J.L. *Ralston, went to Europe and saw for himself that men were needed. King promptly replaced him with Ralston's old enemy, Gen. A.G.L. *McNaughton, who believed he could persuade NRMA conscripts to volunteer. He failed. The government was close to a split between its English-speaking and Quebec ministers. On 22 November King changed his mind: 15,000 conscripts would go overseas. There were riots in Quebec towns and the *Bloc populaire promised to defeat the Liberals. In Terrace, British

Columbia, a brigade of NRMA soldiers went on strike, but the conscripts went to Europe. Once again, most arrived in the spring of 1945, too late for the fighting in Europe. Conservatives promptly demanded conscription for the Pacific war, but the King government refused and Liberal restraint helped King win Quebec and the election on 11 June 1945.

After the Second World War, proposals by generals for universal military training were buried. Canada's contribution to the Cold War was a small, well-paid professional defence force. The last vestiges of conscription, such as the *levée en masse*, vanished with the 1949 National Defence Act. DESMOND MORTON

conservation movements. Conservation is a deceptively simple word. To preserve from destructive forces can involve the exercise of power. The term 'Dominion of Canada' implies a biblical interpretation of human rights over all nature. Or is conservation about stewardship with nature, working with or for the land and the life that exists here? One generation conserves a forest for future use, and another argues to preserve it from use, for its intrinsic value. The debates about humans and their relationship with, or in, nature are part of Canada's history of conservation movements.

Traditional ecological knowledge (TEK) of indigenous peoples is our oldest form of conservation. Aboriginal peoples understood seasons, weather, and diverse ecological cycles through local systems of TEK. Life depended upon that knowledge. Canada's first peoples carefully transmitted between generations a practical and spiritual value system about their relationship with the world around them. TEK, the oldest conservation movement in Canada, has re-emerged in conjunction with non-Native science as part of contemporary land-management strategies for species such as caribou. However, recent scholarship cautions against creating 'new age' stereotypes of the 'Ecological Indian'.

There have always been ecological changes: peoples, plants, fish, and animals move through a landscape that is being changed by dramatic forces—climate change, fire, wind, and drought. Euroamericans contributed to and amplified the scale of that change with smallpox, traplines, dandelions, wheat, pigs, and axes. Ecological invasions spread from Viking and Basque landings and Jacques *Cartier's garden at Cap Rouge (1541). These small events marked the start of a continent-wide transformation of Canada, begun with a few seeds thousands of kilometres from the grasslands of the prairies

Sketched in the journals of dozens of explorers, from Samuel de *Champlain to Andrew Graham at Hudson Bay, Canada's flora and fauna began to be documented by generations of Linnean naturalists who would document the taxonomy of Canada's biodiversity. By the 19th century, work such as Catharine Parr *Traill's ethnobotanical studies in Ontario, John *Richardson's scientific studies in the Arctic in the 1820s, and the 1857–60 *Palliser Expedition across western Canada created a cultural identity, a bioregional map of Canada. Their work gave way to a more formalized scientific community that discussed 'Canadian' nature, through journals like *Le Naturalist canadien* (1868), founded by botanist Léon *Provancher, and the influential Ottawa Field-Naturalists' Club (1879).

By the 1880s conservation emerged in response to the transformations caused by settlement and lumbering. Confederation and a national railway made the scale of 'changes in the land' visible to all. The hegemony of dominion brought with it the bureaucrat's gaze, and what it saw were the fragile limits. The disappearance of the buffalo was a powerful symbol of loss and guilt. Nature began to be 'reserved' into parks. Even the distant North became a national concern. By the 1920s it too would fall under the administrator's gaze. Whether compassionate and benevolent or a paternalistic colonialism, the administration of nature became part of the moral duty of Canadian civil servants.

Industries worried about the future. Battles were fought on the Miramichi over sawdust dumping and its impact on salmon. The 1882 American Forestry Conference in Montreal discussed fire and deforestation. The contours of professional forestry in Canada was guided by Gifford Pinchot, Bernard Fernow, and Elihu Stewart. Canadian Forestry Association (1900) members such as Sir Henri Joly de Lotbinière talked of stewardship and replanted his lands. By the 1920s professional forestry included inventories, fire protection, nurseries, and forest entomology, all for the goal of forest conservation for future use.

Popular magazines discussed disappearing wildlife and market hunting. The buffalo, muskox, the *great auk, and the *passenger pigeon were symbols of a world that was vanishing. Maxwell Graham salvaged the last major buffalo herd in North America, buying it for Canada in 1906. Percy *Taverner worked to protect sea-bird nesting sites on the Gulf of St Lawrence. C. Gordon Hewitt framed the Canada/United States *Migratory Birds Treaty (1917). His posthumous *The Conservation of the Wild Life of Canada* (1921) summarized the work of a generation.

As cities grew, nature became a recreational refuge favoured by many, and promoted by groups such as the Canadian Alpine Club. Preservationists, intent on salvaging 'wild Canada', found friends in the federal civil service and railway, allies who saw value in the consumption of nature by tourists, all of which found full force in the parks movement. James Harkin set in place the dominion parks system, with its jewel, *Banff.

In 1909, inspired by Theodore Roosevelt, and sponsored by Clifford *Sifton, the Canadian Commission of Conservation explored Canada's natural resources through dozens of scholarly volumes. But constitutional jurisdiction in many of these areas lay with the provinces. Denied real power, dependent on political sponsorship, this grand experiment collapsed in 1922. Its legacy was the creation of provincial ministries, many of them influenced by its recommendations.

The *National Council of Women was part of the Canadian Commission of Conservation and worked on social justice issues. Urban conservation issues included sanitation, substandard housing, smoke abatement, clean streets, safe water, playgrounds, and pasteurized milk. Women activists saw these urban problems as part of the domestic sphere and their solution as creating a healthy and safe environment for children. In the interwar years Canadian children learned about conservation values through radio, film, children's books, and public lectures by figures such as *Grey Owl, Ernest Thompson *Seton, and Jack *Miner.

The 1930s drought conditions brought prairie communities together over water and soil conservation. Similar ecological disasters had occurred, but not on this scale. The state responded with agrarian science, new soil techniques, irrigation ditches, and conservation ideologies for rural communities. The farmer's view of conservation and economic hardship matured through this experience into a sense of co-operative stewardship. That spirit, which radically shaped Canadian politics, also provided for wetlands habitat-preservation groups such as Ducks Unlimited Canada (1938) and formed the early impetus for the Canadian Nature Federation (1939).

The Second World War brought destructive demands for resources. It also introduced recycling programs to aid the war. The post-war era saw a yearning for pristine land preserved from destruction. Ontario established 36 European-influenced Conservation Authorities to coordinate the multiple uses of watersheds. What was intended for flood control also created a vision of the watershed as a fragile region, a concept closely connected to the land ethic of the American writer Aldo Leopold or the sentiment of E. Newton-White's Canadian classic *Hurt Not the Earth* (1952). These views continue today in the work of various river-restoration groups and the work of the Land Conservancy.

Post-war conservation began with a tremendous faith in government and individual action. Its views were shaped by the experience of global conflict and a faith in wartime planning. In the second half of the century that faith was shaken and gave way to the activism of the *environmental movements. LORNE HAMMOND

conservatism. As in other British settler colonies, political ideas came as baggage with the first colonists. Also, pre-revolutionary France had created an intellectual environment that deeply influenced the development of political ideas among Canadians of French descent. In the case of both British and French settlers, conservative influences upon society and institutions were profound. In Quebec, conservatism became a means of defending French culture through the Roman Catholic Church and associated institutions, notably schools. Rejecting not only the French Revolution and its anti-clerical legacy but also the liberal tendencies within continental Europe, the Quebec church identified itself with the anti-revolutionary strain of European Catholicism. So strong was the anti-liberal and anti-revolutionary strain within the Quebec clerisy that Quebec Liberal Wilfrid *Laurier emphasized that Canadian *liberalism derived not from continental liberalism but from the moderate liberalism of Britain. In English Canada, the United Empire *Loyalists similarly rejected revolution and emphasized traditional values. Here the church was also significant—not only the Anglican Church but also other British congregations such as the Presbyterians and most Methodists, whose pastors expressed support for the monarch, British justice, and an ordered society. In addition to reflecting their European legacies, the beliefs of francophone and anglophone conservatives responded to their profound distrust and, on many occasions, fear of American democratic and republican ideals. In the debates surrounding Confederation, the so-called Fathers of Confederation celebrated *'peace, order, and good government' and denied the allure of 'life, liberty, and happiness'.

The creed of Canadian conservatism expressed itself in French Canada in allegiance to the Roman Catholic faith, the agrarian tradition, and the fear of modernism. In English Canada, the creed extolled the *monarchy, the *British connection, and the evil of Americanization. In two national elections, 1891 and 1911, the Conservative Party drew upon this tradition of 'the old flag' and 'neither truck nor trade with the Yankees' to obtain political victories. In 1917, francophone conservatism expressed itself in opposition to the Britishness of English Canada, while British-Canadian nationalism brought electoral triumph to a coalition that favoured *conscription and full support for the war effort. It was the greatest victory of British-Canadian conservatism but it was its last.

The collapse of the British economy after the First World War, the increasingly close links between Canadian and American capitalists, and the political success of the *Liberal Party increasingly isolated Canadian conservatives. Yet, their intellectual influence remained strong, especially in English Canada through the 1960s. George *Grant's celebrated **Lament for a Nation* was a *cri de coeur* of one who deplored the increasing American influence in Canadian life. In French Canada, the *'Quiet Revolution' swept away much of the conservative tradition, especially the close ties with the church.

Neo-conservatism in the United States deeply influenced Canadian *Progressive Conservatives in the 1970s and 1980s. Rejecting the tradition of anti-Americanism and support for an activist state, Conservative governments in Ottawa under Brian *Mulroney and in Alberta under Ralph Klein and Ontario under Mike Harris embraced *continentalism, privatization, and deregulation. By the 1990s, the roots of Canadian conservatism were mostly severed, and new sprouts deriving from American conservatism flourished. The conservative past in Canada seemed to belong to another country.

JOHN ENGLISH

Constitutional Act, 1791. A British statute to provide for the governance of the *Province of Quebec after its impending division into two new provinces, *Upper and *Lower Canada. The division of the old province was prompted by the settlement of loyalist refugees from the Thirteen Colonies in the upper St Lawrence Valley and points farther west, which were henceforth to form part of Upper Canada. The split made for more convenient administration of a sprawling territory and was also meant to accommodate the conflicting civic values of its francophone and anglophone inhabitants.

In furtherance of this policy, the act set up legislatures in both provinces, as anglophones generally desired, but established English freehold property tenure in Upper Canada only, preserving the *seigneurial system in Lower Canada until the provincial legislature should abolish it. The act also preserved the safeguards for the Catholic religion first enacted in the *Quebec Act, 1774. Other provisions aimed to prevent or moderate the sort of popular discontent that had fuelled the American Revolution. The act confirmed Parliament's renunciation in 1778 of the right to impose colonial taxes except for the regulation of trade and commerce. In a more authoritarian vein, both legislatures included an appointed upper house as a check on the elective chamber, and a proportion of the land was reserved for the support of 'a Protestant Clergy' to strengthen state religion.

The *rebellions of 1837 demonstrated the failure of this policy in both provinces, and in 1840 Parliament passed the *Act of Union. PAUL ROMNEY

constitutional amendment. The procedure for amending the *constitution of Canada, provided for in Part V (sections 38–49) of the Constitution Act, 1982, comprises five amending formulas: general, unanimous, bilateral or multilateral, unilateral federal, and unilateral provincial. The general formula, two-thirds of the provinces representing at least 50 per cent of the population, applies to every amendment not covered by the other four formulas. In particular it applies to the division of legislative powers, to the majority of provisions of the *Charter of Rights and Freedoms, and to matters specified in section 42(1). Section 38(3) allows a province to exercise its right to withdraw in the event that an amendment would reduce its legislative powers, property rights, or privileges. When a province exercises its right to opt out in matters concerning education or other cultural domains, fair compensation is provided by the federal government (section 40).

Section 41 stipulates that certain amendments require the consent of the *Senate, the *House of Commons, and the legislative assembly of each province. Five matters require this unanimous consent: the *monarchy; the right of provinces to have as many members in the House of Commons as in the Senate; the use of French or English; the composition of the *Supreme Court; and amendment of the procedure itself. Section 43 authorizes amendments to provisions that affect one or more, but not all, provinces. The consent of the province concerned is required, in particular, for changes to interprovincial boundaries or provisions relating to the use of French or English within the province. Section 44 authorizes Parliament to amend provisions in the constitution relating to the federal executive power, the Senate, and the House of Commons, subject to sections 41 (unanimity) and 42 (general formula). Under section 45 a legislature is empowered to amend the constitution of its province, subject to section 41.

Constitutional amendments, which are proclaimed by the *governor general, are ratified by resolutions of the Senate, the House of Commons, and the required number of provincial legislatures, and the same institutions may initiate the procedure. The Commons may veto any amendment proposed by the Senate or a provincial legislature. By contrast, the Senate's veto is effective only on matters covered by section 44. In all other cases, the senatorial veto is suspensive (for 180 days). Under section 39(1) of the act, an amendment does not take effect for one year, unless the legislative assembly of each province has adopted a resolution of assent or dissent. The maximum time allowed for ratification is three years for amendments made in accordance with section 38 (general formula). No time period is specified for other forms of amendment. GÉRALD-A. BEAUDOIN

constitutional monarchy. An oxymoronic term uniting contradictory ideas of power and restraint of power. In the surrogate monarchies of the *Commonwealth (Canada, Australia, New Zealand, and some Caribbean nations), as in Great Britain itself, the Crown is the fount of sovereignty, but one that since the Glorious Revolution (1688) has shared its power with Parliament. More than that, for nearly two centuries it has been accepted that the sovereign, or representative of the sovereign, will act on the advice of those who command the support of the popularly elected chamber of Parliament. Founded on convention and law, constitutional monarchy is celebrated for its adaptability. Nowhere is this more evident than in Canada. Colonial constitutions, once dominated by British-appointed governors, acquired *responsible government in the 1840s. Canada's contribution to the science of politics in 1867 was to marry parliamentary government and *federalism, a union that through judicial interpretation established the duality of the Crown at the federal and provincial levels of government. While depicted by critics as foreign, anachronistic, and a vestige of a colonial past, constitutional *monarchy, today expressed in the form of the Canadian Crown-in-Parliament, is the fundamental structuring principle of the entire system of government. DAVID E. SMITH

constitution of Canada. A combination of written documents and unwritten conventions that govern a parliamentary system of responsible *cabinet government with its union of executive and legislative powers exercised by and with the consent of the Crown's representative, the *governor general. Certain basic acts of Parliament, such as the Supreme Court Act and the Canada Elections Act, are assumed to be part of the constitution. However, Canada's true constitutional foundation is the Constitution Act, 1982, as amended.

The progenitor of this act is the British North America Act, enacted by the British Parliament in 1867, creating the Dominion of Canada by bringing together in federal union the provinces of Nova Scotia, New

Brunswick, Quebec, and Ontario and providing for the subsequent accession of future provinces and territories. The act envisaged a government 'similar in principle to that of the United Kingdom'—namely, a government that united executive and legislative branches, making the former dependent on the latter's support in order to carry out the government of the day.

The federal nature of the union was reflected in a distribution of powers between dominion and provinces, particularly in sections 91 and 92. The 29 enumerated powers assigned to the dominion by section 91 were introduced by a general power to legislate for the *peace, order, and good government of Canada. Section 92 assigned 16 enumerated powers to the provinces. Education, under section 93, was a provincial power subject to dominion remedial action where the rights of denominational schools were endangered. Section 95 provided for concurrency of powers with respect to agriculture and immigration, with dominion legislation prevailing when in conflict. Adaptation of the written constitution to meet changing circumstances has depended upon judicial interpretation of this allocation of powers and upon formal amendment of the BNA Act. For over 80 years, final adjudication of the terms of federation rested with the Judicial Committee of the Privy Council in Britain. Not until 1949 did Canada's *Supreme Court become the final arbiter for all cases.

Because the BNA Act had been passed by the UK parliament, its amendment lay beyond Canada's control. For well over a century, this became a prime source of debate, particularly among those who asserted the need to throw off the last vestiges of colonial status. The cause of the lengthy delay in finally 'domesticating' the constitution was not opposition from Britain but rather the inability within Canada to secure agreement on an acceptable amending process. The numerous amendments made to the act of 1867 were automatically approved by the British Parliament. The source of contention was in Canada: the question was the extent to which the dominion government needed to consult with and gain the approval of the provinces (how many provinces was also at issue) before sending to Britain a formal resolution of the Canadian Parliament embodying the terms of the amendment sought. When *patriation of the constitution was finally achieved with the enactment of the Constitution Act, 1982, a complex amending formula was included that reflected the debates and compromises attending the long process of bringing the constitution home.

A significant addition to the act was the inclusion of the *Charter of Rights and Freedoms. Hitherto, protection of such rights had been based on acts of Parliament and provincial legislatures, all subject to legislative change. Enshrined in the constitution, such rights could be changed only by formal amendment or in extreme circumstances by invoking a *'notwithstanding' clause, an acknowledgement of ultimate parliamentary sovereignty. Addition of the Charter has expanded the role of the *judiciary beyond the traditional task of adjudicating the constitution's allocation of powers; *courts now make decisions with respect to individuals' charter rights. Some critics view this process as potential trespass on parliamentary preserves. J.E. HODGETTS

See also CONSTITUTIONAL AMENDMENT.

construction workers. *See* BUILDING-TRADES WORKERS.

contact. This term usually signifies the arrival of the Europeans and the modifications Aboriginal societies underwent to accommodate to changed economic conditions. Such ethnocentric thinking ignores millennia of contact among Aboriginal societies: ancient trade routes, along which exotic goods and ideas flowed, crisscrossed the continent. European commerce introduced new labour-saving materials such as iron and cloth, which were welcomed, for the most part, and incorporated into local technology. European ideas and beliefs were not as readily adopted and had to await the Aboriginal peoples' loss of economic and political autonomy, which generally resulted from European settlement on their lands and the forced abandonment of a hunting way of life. Only then did it make sense for a hunting people to forsake their religion, founded on an egalitarian respect for the animal spirits, and embrace Christianity, based on salvation and acceptance of an authority that demanded a total cultural revolution in beliefs and manner of living. Such transformations of Aboriginal societies occurred earlier in the farming regions of the south or along the coasts where Europeans seized fishery resources. In the north, only in the 20th century did the mining, forestry, and transportation industries draw in southern interests.

European explorers could not have succeeded in their exploits without their Aboriginal guides and protectors. In particular, their Native women companions, often daughters of leading men, fulfilled a crucial role as intermediaries, as well as carrying out the essential domestic duties expected of women. Through the intermarriage of European fur traders and Native women there developed a class of people at the *fur trade posts who could function linguistically and culturally in the two worlds. Individuals chose with which group they would affiliate—as hunters or post employees. For women there was less choice: they most often remained within the Indian culture as wives of hunters. On the prairies, in the *Red River region, this group of people of mixed ancestry was sufficiently large and economically specialized, as suppliers to the fur trade, to become politically differentiated and coalesce into a separate nation, the *Metis.

Much of the early European writing on the Aboriginals is highly ethnocentric, describing them as ignorant and primitive, but a number of philosophers held up Aboriginal society as a mirror to their European one, depicting the Native peoples as robust, well-fed, and of generous spirit, in contrast to the ill-health, degenerate living, and poverty of the urban centres of France. There is little in the oral traditions of the Aboriginal peoples that provide their first impressions of the intruders; this may be because they did not view early contact as of great significance. In discussing their history, the Innu in central Quebec classify time not in terms of the coming of the white man ('pre-contact' and 'contact') but in terms of no longer having only hides but also cloth, not only game but flour, events of direct consequence to them.

Who were these intruders from which we date 'contact'? The Vikings who came to the northern peninsula of Newfoundland about AD 1000 stayed only a few years, so 'contact' is dated from the late 15th century, when fishermen arrived in pursuit of resources to feed Catholic Europe, which was prohibited from eating meat for more than one-third of the year. Navigators soon followed. In 1497 John *Cabot landed in either Newfoundland or Cape Breton; then a succession arrived, along with fishermen of all nations and Basque whalers. By 1519 there were as many as 100 vessels in the maritime waters. Jacques *Cartier sailed up the St Lawrence River in 1535, which led to French settlement there in 1608. In the late 16th century changes of the fashion in men's hats, made of beaver felt, brought the fur trade and settlement to Aboriginal peoples' lands. This intrusion moved inexorably across the country; by 1793 the English had passed overland to the Pacific Ocean. For the Aboriginals on the Pacific coast, a short-lived *maritime fur trade in sea otters brought the English traders there in 1778. A colony was established on *Vancouver Island in 1849. The third coast, the Arctic Ocean, inhabited by the *Inuit, was first visited by explorers seeking a *Northwest Passage in 1576. Here, this contact remained sporadic until the mid-1800s, when American whaling vessels overwintered with the Inuit, and the 1920s, when the flapper-era mania for fox furs brought in the fur traders. Thus ended the Aboriginal peoples' isolation in all regions of Canada.

TOBY MORANTZ

Contemporary Arts Society. Founded in 1939 by the Montreal painter John Lyman and modelled on a similar institution in London, the CAS, as it was called at the time, aimed at exhibiting the paintings, sculptures, and drawings of its members, promoting a better understanding of modern art, and encouraging collectors to acquire their works. Lyman saw it as a means of counteracting the influence of the *Group of Seven and a too narrow definition of Canadian art as landscape only. The CAS presented annual shows from 1939 to 1948, most of them in Montreal but some in Toronto. Paul-Émile Borduas was its first vice-president. New members were admitted on the recommendation of older members. It was an advantage for the younger painters to exhibit with their elders, but in time they became unhappy with the way their paintings were hung at the annual show; the CAS had introduced a system of double jury, one responsible for the choice of the paintings, but the other for their hanging. There were also tensions between anglophone and francophone members, but the most important frustrations were expressed by Borduas's young disciples, who wanted the society to take a bolder stand for abstract art, a move resisted by many members, including Lyman. Finally, the CAS was dissolved in 1948, Lyman not wanting to encourage such divisions in the fragile modern art milieu of Montreal.

FRANÇOIS-MARC GAGNON

continentalism. The term 'continentalism' refers to the belief—first systematically articulated by Goldwin *Smith in his *Canada and the Canadian Question* (1891)—that Canada's position on the North American continent, and specifically its proximity to a powerful and dynamic United States, is the defining feature of its cultural, economic, and strategic existence.

Two main patterns of thought and behaviour have been associated with that belief. One, generally coinciding with Smith's own ideas, identified Canada as an essentially North American society, viewed close association with American markets and capital as in its best interests, and, in time, defined Canadian security and defence as optimally provided for within the framework of integrated, American-designed military structures. Manifest in such conceptions of national identity as journalist J.W. *Dafoe's definition of Canada as an 'American nation' (1935), this view of matters has normally been taken to define the continentalist posture. It can be seen in the succession of increasingly comprehensive economic accords that culminated in the North American Free Trade Agreement of 1994, and is evident in Canada's participation in agreements on continental defence such as the Permanent Joint Board on Defence (1940), the North American Air Defence Command (1957), the North Warning System (1985), and the Northern Command (2002).

A second constellation of ideas and action rested on a similar understanding of Canada's position but entailed stronger emphasis on the use of Canadian state power to ensure that interaction with the United States yielded outcomes favourable to Canadian interests. Implementation of a variety of strategies from the *National Policy of 1879 to the *National Energy Program of 1980 was intended to make involvement with US economic strength generate balanced growth and development in the Canadian economy. State action in the cultural sphere, notably regulation by the Board of Broadcast Governors (1958) and the Canadian Radio and Television Commission (1968), put part of the profits earned from the distribution of American cultural products in Canada to work creating and diffusing Canadian music, movies, and television. Even systems for the maintenance of continental security were, in principle, rendered amenable to Canadian purposes through their formally bilateral character.

In the last decades of the 20th century, Canada's relationship with its continental neighbour was being conceptualized in a number of ways. Whether, however, observers wrote of a 'disparate dyad', a 'complex binational system', a 'hard region', a 'unique continental amalgam', or a partnership defined in terms of 'asymmetrical interdependence', their assessment was essentially the same: Canada existed as part of a highly integrated entity in which there was limited scope for independent Canadian action. A product of fundamental geographical realities, codified in terms of two distinct but complementary policy traditions, and a major element in prevailing definitions of the Canadian situation, the continentalist idea sustained a place in Canadian analysis and discussion that was at once basic, central, and definitive. ALLAN SMITH

convoys. Convoying is the ancient practice of grouping ships together so that they can be protected either by their own combined efforts or by escorting forces. In the great age of sail, ships often travelled in seasonal convoys, taking advantage of prevailing winds and the safety of numbers to get them home through war zones or in the face of *piracy.

Canada's experience with convoys is largely confined to the two world wars of the 20th century. The first soldiers sent overseas in 1914 sailed in a troop convoy under British escort, and for the rest of the war troop ships sailed in convoy or under escort. Until 1917, however, most merchant shipping did not. By then the peril of unrestricted attack by German submarines forced merchant vessels into convoys, too. By 1918 transatlantic convoys formed up and arrived at Sydney and Halifax, and the *Royal Canadian Navy developed the bureaucracy needed to control shipping and assemble convoys. That expertise was maintained after 1918, and it was invaluable during the Second World War, the high point of Canadian convoy experience.

Between 1939 and 1945 the Allies tightly controlled shipping movements and operated over 400 convoy systems world-wide—largely in response to the submarine threat. Twelve of these convoy routes were operated at one time or another in Canadian waters. Halifax, Sydney, Quebec City, and Saint John all became convoy-assembly ports. Convoys ran between these places and ports in the United States, Britain, and the Arctic. In addition, feeder convoys of transatlantic shipping joined major convoy routes offshore. Although some of these inshore convoys were attacked, they were enormously successful and provided safe passage for nearly 2,400 vessels. Canada also played a significant role in the organization and protection of the main transatlantic convoy system between North America and Britain. Halifax and Sydney were major assembly ports for the famous HX and SC series, respectively. Over 43,000 vessels sailed in these and the west-bound ON convoys; many were heavily attacked. In the end, the Allied convoy system, of which Canada was a crucial part, proved to be the bedrock of the Allied victory in 1945. MARC MILNER

Cook, Captain James (1728–79), British naval officer, surveyor, and explorer born in Yorkshire, England. Cook joined the Royal Navy in 1755, which took him to *Louisbourg and the St Lawrence River, his knowledge of the latter waterway enabling the British armada to reach Quebec in 1759, thus aiding the dislodging of the French from Canada. Following the Seven Years' War, Cook charted sections of the waters off Newfoundland and Labrador. This fostered British cod-fishing off the *Grand Banks, as well as increasing the security of shipping in and out of the St Lawrence. Cook returned to Britain in 1771 after having circumnavigated the world as well as having explored and charted both New Zealand and East Australia. In 1776, Cook accepted the challenge of finding the *Northwest Passage, and he mapped portions of Canada's west coast as well as parts of the Bering Strait and Oregon in the process. He spent April 1778 at Nootka Sound, Vancouver Island, where he collected information on the Nuu-chah-nulth Native people. In Hawaii, cross-cultural conflicts ended with Cook's death, as well as that of four of his marines, on 14 February 1779. Cook received credit as the discoverer of Nootka Sound, and, hence, the source of British claims on the northwest coast. In addition, the publication of his *A Voyage to the Pacific Ocean* (1784), with its references to the abundance of furs and sea otter pelts, created an international contest for trade and territory in the land in question. BARRY M. GOUGH

Co-operative Commonwealth Federation. Formed in Calgary in 1932, the CCF sought to coordinate the political activities of labour, farmer, and socialist groups in order to replace capitalism with a social system capable of 'the supplying of human needs instead of the making of profits'. The movement was initiated by western Canadian labour and socialist parties, but by the time the first national convention met in Regina in 1933 it included farmers' organizations from several provinces and a small group of academics from the *League for Social Reconstruction who wrote the movement's program, the *Regina Manifesto. From the outset, the CCF had a small caucus in Ottawa made up of labour MPs (including James S. *Woodsworth) and the *Ginger Group from the defunct Progressive Party.

The early CCF was a federation of disparate groups; prospective members joined affiliates whose structure and ideology varied considerably. Some, such as the United Farmers of Ontario, had little sympathy for the gradualist socialism of the Regina Manifesto and quickly left the CCF. Provincial CCF organizations were also quite autonomous. While the socialists who inaugurated the Ontario CCF were purged from the party at the behest of the national leadership, a very similar group founded and dominated the British Columbia CCF.

CCF electoral success varied greatly across the country. It quickly became the official opposition in British Columbia and Saskatchewan and elected members to legislatures and municipal offices in western Canada and Ontario. Faced with soaring unemployment and the threat of fascism, many CCFers considered that reliance on electoral action alone was too slow and ineffective. Those who felt this way often wanted to participate in actions with the *Communist Party, precipitating fierce debates within the CCF.

The Second World War dramatically affected the CCF. After a difficult debate over its attitude to the war (socialists had preferred to concentrate their fire on what they saw as the root causes of war and fascism—capitalism), the CCF backed the war effort but also campaigned for domestic civic liberties and a post-war society that would offer what Depression Canada failed to: social security. The result was rapid growth for the CCF. In Ontario, it won growing support from a burgeoning labour movement and only narrowly lost the 1943 election. A year later it won the Saskatchewan election. It held power in that province for 20 years—mostly under Premier T.C. (Tommy) *Douglas—during which time it sought to diversify the economy and provide a new level of social services, including medicare.

The decade that followed the war was difficult for the CCF. Capitalism achieved an unforeseen stability and it was difficult to repulse the ideological assault of the Cold War. The CCF vote stagnated and the party's rhetorical *socialism was muted in its Winnipeg Declaration of 1956.The party succumbed to anti-Communist sentiments on an international level, supporting the American-led Korean War and the creation of NATO. As the party's fortunes collapsed, the CCF aligned itself more closely with the *Canadian Labour Congress and 'liberal-minded individuals' to create the *New Democratic Party in 1962.

JAMES NAYLOR

co-operative movement. The co-operative movement can be understood as a set of institutions following co-operative principles and incorporated under co-operative legislation. It can also be seen as a movement whose ideology is reflected to some degree in the principles espoused by the International Co-operative Alliance, principles derived from 19th-century experience, particularly the co-operative store in Rochdale, England (established 1844) but also worker, credit, and agricultural co-ops in other European countries as well. The main principles—democratic member control, distribution of surpluses (profits) according to member use, support for education, co-operation among co-operatives, and support for sustainable community development—have been periodically revised as co-operators have adjusted to economic and social changes. Canadians played significant roles in the last revision at the ICA's 1995 Manchester Congress.

Many immigrants in the 19th and 20th centuries had experiences with European co-operatives, and many were deeply committed to co-operative philosophy. They played significant roles in the Canadian movement, although it was also shaped by indigenous traditions of mutualism. Formally organized co-operatives—consumer co-ops in Nova Scotian mining communities—first appeared in the 1860s, followed by worker co-ops in the 1880s associated with the *Knights of Labor. None survived for long, but the movement flourished in the early 20th century. In Quebec, Alphonse Desjardins studied European financial co-operatives and, with his wife Dorimène, started the *caisses populaires in Lévis in 1900. That movement spread across Quebec and some francophone communities in other provinces, meeting the needs of people ignored by the banking system, appealing to community pride, and reflecting French-Canadian cultural values. By the end of the 20th century, with 6 million members and $60 billion in assets, it was one of the world's more successful co-operative movements. Amid the adversities of the Great Depression, English Canadians also turned to financial co-operatives in the form of *credit unions, notable for flexible opening hours, good service, and local accountability. By century's end, there were 6 million members and $64 billion in assets. Both financial movements developed large insurance and *trust companies and became full-service financial systems, a significant alternative within the Canadian banking system.

Co-operatives also responded effectively to the needs of rural Canadians who needed to purchase supplies as cheaply as possible and to sell what they produced for the best prices. They required service organizations—for health, recreation, seed, hail insurance, telephone systems, petroleum supplies, electricity—to remain competitive and to have amenities that were taken for granted in most urban places. Rural Canada has seen waves of co-operative activism. Before and during the First World War the economic arm of the agrarian/Progressive movement produced supply and marketing co-operatives in grain, dairy, poultry, fruit, and mixed farming regions. Most have disappeared, although the United Farmers of Alberta Co-operative, for example, still thrives. After the war the idea of pooling swept many commodity groups, including grains, notably producing the wheat pools—bastions of rural co-operative movements until the 1990s. During the 1930s, rural people embraced credit unions and promoted the emerging insurance, consumer, and service co-operatives. More recently, they have supported New Generation Co-operatives based on large membership fees, marketing commitments by members, local value-added activities, and pursuit of niche markets.

Consumer co-operatives were developed, many in rural and remote communities, particularly in western and Atlantic Canada, where the wholesale organizations Federated Co-operatives and Co-op Atlantic became large and successful enterprises. The Calgary Co-op, one of the largest consumer co-operatives in the world, serves about 40 per cent of that city's population. The deepest penetration was in Arctic Canada, where Inuit, Inuvialuit, and Dene formed over 70 co-ops with various purposes, including art marketing and the provision of consumer goods.

The co-operative movement has generally been less effective in urban Canada. Financial co-operatives have made some inroads, except in Ontario cities—an unfortunate lacuna, given their power in shaping national perspectives. Housing co-ops made considerable progress with government support in the 1970s and 1980s but their emphasis on building economically and socially mixed communities—as opposed to ghettoized social housing—was poorly explained (and sometimes attacked) by media; they were discounted in the late 1980s by politicians committed to market solutions to housing problems. Nevertheless, the movement houses some 220,000 families. Canadians also developed co-operatives to provide health care based on preventative medical practice, a team approach to service delivery, and clear patterns of accountability to consumer members, an approach with great promise in today's uncertainties over the national health system. In addition, the worker co-operative movement started to grow in the 1970s and 1980s, particularly in the forestry, health food, and computing industries.

The largest concentration of social co-operatives—including health co-ops—is in Quebec. More influenced by the social economy traditions of France and southern Europe, Quebec co-operators have experimented with solidarity or multi-stakeholder co-operatives and have more systematically employed co-operatives in their community economic development.

Today, with two national organizations—the Canadian Co-operative Association and the Conseil canadien de la coopération—the movement has over 15 million members and $170 billion in assets, and both groups have sponsored significant overseas development programs supporting community-based responses to problems of poverty and social dislocation. Recently, the national movement has suffered when some large agriculture co-ops demutualized, although hundreds of new co-operatives have emerged, particularly among young people. Over the years a failure to educate new members has meant that most have little understanding of the movement. It has also suffered because its subtle ideology has been overshadowed in the struggles between liberalism, Marxism, conservatism, and social democracy, and it did not respond well to the various kinds of individualism common to the 20th century. As well, the educational system has virtually ignored its existence: careful analysis of its strengths and shortcomings has not materialized, and the distinct challenges of co-operative management have been ignored. Despite these shortcomings, the co-operative movement in Canada is large, generally healthy, experimenting with new forms, and providing a steadily widening range of services. IAN MacPHERSON

Corbin, Jeanne (1906–44), Communist militant. Born in Cellettes, France, Corbin immigrated to Tofield, Alberta, in 1911. At Westmount High School in Edmonton she joined the Young Communist League. After attending Camrose Normal School, she was denied a teaching job following pressures from the Royal Canadian Mounted Police. She pursued her communist education at the party's summer camp in Sylvan Lake, Alberta, in 1927 and 1928, under the direction of Beckie Buhay. From then on she devoted her life to the movement, as fundraiser for *The Worker*, as a member of the Labor Defence League, and as union organizer for the *Workers' Unity League in Toronto, Montreal, Timmins, and Rouyn-Noranda. Operating in times of severe repression, she was first arrested in 1929 at the Free Speech Conference in Toronto. In Montreal, she founded and edited *L'Ouvrier canadien* (1930–1). At the lumbermen's strike of 1933 in Abitibi she was accused of inciting riot and of illegal assembly. After serving three months in jail, she returned to Timmins to work in the Workers' Co-operative Store. Never a member of the central committee, she was highly respected in the *Communist Party and considered a 'Party heroine'. ANDRÉE LÉVESQUE

Cormack, William Eppes (1796–1868), naturalist, entrepreneur, born in St John's, Newfoundland. After his father, Alexander, died in 1803 the family moved to Scotland, where his mother (née Janet McAuslin) married David Rennie in 1806. Cormack acquired a lifelong interest in the natural sciences at university (Glasgow and Edinburgh), but pursued a mercantile career. He settled Scottish immigrants in Prince Edward Island (1818–21) and in 1822 walked across Newfoundland with a Mi'kmaw guide, Joseph *Sylvester, to explore its geology and geography, and to contact the *Beothuk. Having failed to meet them, he tried again (unsuccessfully) in 1827 and founded the Boeothick (now Beothuk) Institution. He later hosted the Beothuk woman *Shanawdithit, who provided important ethnographic information. Cormack promoted grain trade and land and resource development in the Maritimes (1830–4), farmed tobacco in New South Wales (1836–9), and attempted pastoral pursuits in New Zealand. Attracted by the gold rushes, he moved to California in 1851 and to British Columbia in 1859. An early member of the municipal council in New Westminster, BC, Cormack also acted as Indian agent and worked actively for representative government. He died there in 1868.
ALAN G. MACPHERSON AND INGEBORG C.L. MARSHALL

'corporate welfare bums'. In the federal election of 1972, David Lewis, the leader of the left-wing New Democratic Party, made this phrase the theme of his campaign. In effect, he took the pejorative term 'welfare bums', sometimes used by right-wing politicians to denigrate persons on welfare, and threw it back at them by applying the words to the corporations, which tended to support the political right. The real culprits at the public trough, Lewis argued, were 'corporate welfare bums', who received government handouts in the form of subsidies and tax breaks, particularly deferred taxes that never were paid. In the run-up to the election, Lewis regularly named corporations that he claimed got taxpayer's money, and he wrote a popular book elaborating his charges. The NDP's populist campaign helped to push Pierre Trudeau's Liberal government into a minority position in which it could govern only with NDP support. Lewis had some limited success in getting parts of the NDP's program legislated. MELVILLE WATKINS

corporate welfarism. Management strategies designed to win and maintain workers' loyalty to particular employers. Many bosses were not concerned about this. Instead they accommodated themselves to high levels of labour turnover as urbanization and immigration restocked the labour market with the unskilled and semi-skilled workers that factories and resource industries demanded.

In the First World War period, increasingly large firms faced the challenges of labour shortages, high turnover, and a more militant labour force that was organizing and demanding recognition of their *unions. Canadian employers had a couple of models to turn to. One was the 'Rockefeller' scheme developed for the American magnate in the wake of a tragic strike in Colorado that had seen state authorities set fire to a miners' tent colony, killing eleven family members of the strikers. The author of the scheme was former Canadian labour minister Mackenzie *King, who established a 'representation system' that evaded the miners' main demand—recognition of their union—and left the final say in matters of substance to the company. The other model was the Whitley system, developed in Britain, which provided unions with a formal role in some aspects of management.

Employers preferred the Rockefeller scheme, and several companies, including American-based branch plants such as International Harvester and Canadian firms such as Imperial Oil and *Massey-Harris, adopted it. Whitley schemes were rare, although one did develop in the relatively well-organized building trades in Ontario. Unionized workers dismissed Rockefeller plans as employer-dominated 'company unions' but they did provide some immediate benefits: medical insurance, housing, reading rooms, cafeterias, company sports, and more. Employee magazines such as *Stelco News*, the *Goodyear Clan*, and *At Kodak Heights* publicized the plans and tried to create a 'family feeling'. This was often appreciated by industrial workers, such as women and immigrants, whose immediate alternatives were not unionized jobs, but simply low-paying jobs without these benefits.

Corporate welfarism was somewhat displaced by the development of the *welfare state after the Second World War. Nevertheless, employee-representation schemes persist at some larger, non-union firms, such as Dofasco in Hamilton, that hoped to avoid the costs of either labour turnover or unionization. More often, the legacy of corporate welfarism can be seen in a range of 'fringe benefits' such as pensions and supplementary health care in both unionized and non-unionized workplaces. Administering such polices gave rise to the modern profession of personnel management. JAMES NAYLOR

corvettes. A class of small naval vessels, built primarily for escorting merchant ships and for anti-submarine warfare during the Second World War. Based on a whale-catcher design to simple mercantile standards, the original corvette was 205' long, 33' 1" wide, and displaced about 950 tons. All were powered by a single steam reciprocating engine giving a top speed of about 16 knots. With improved fuel storage in later designs, ranges of 3,500 miles increased to 7,500 miles—enough to cross the Atlantic with ease. Armament was basic: one gun forward, some light secondary guns, and about 100 depth charges. The final corvette variant, the radically redesigned Castle Class, was 250' long with a 9,500-mile range and carried advanced sensors and weaponry. Corvettes formed the backbone of the *Royal Canadian Navy from 1940 until 1945 and the core of the Allied escort forces in the Battle of the *Atlantic. Small, cramped, and crowded, they were exceptionally good sea-boats but were notoriously uncomfortable: it was said that they would 'roll on wet grass'. Corvettes were also the single largest class of warships ever operated and built by Canada. By 1945 Canada had built 121, and 123 had served in the RCN.

MARC MILNER

Coughlan, Laurence (d. 1784), founder of Newfoundland Methodism. A convert from Roman Catholicism, the Irish Methodist preacher Coughlan came, in 1766, once he had been ordained, to Harbour Grace, Conception Bay, where Anglicans sought a priest to help stem the tide of 'Popery'. He was permanently established there in 1767. From then until 1773 he preached to Anglicans on Sunday and went door to door looking for Methodist disciples on Monday. His facility in the Irish language attracted some Roman Catholics, but he converted not a few Anglicans too. A Methodist 'awakening' commenced and spread 'like fire' beyond Harbour Grace to Carbonear and smaller places. In 1770 Governor John Byron made Coughlan a justice, giving him power over sabbath-breakers, drunkards, and adulterers, a power he was not slow to use. Protests against him mounted, and in 1773 he appeared before the Society for the Propagation of the Gospel in London and resigned his mission. His radicalized following kept the Methodist flame burning. Coughlan's *Account of the Work of God in Newfoundland* (1776) contains a sensitive description of the people he served.

PATRICK O'FLAHERTY

Council of Canadians. In June 1985 a group of Canadian nationalists gathered to discuss strategy for dealing with the new Conservative government of Brian *Mulroney. Mulroney had made no secret of his desire for a closer relationship with the United States and had begun to dismantle policies that he saw as inhibiting trade between the two nations. The initial meeting led to the creation of the Council of Canadians, an association dedicated to resisting greater integration with the United States. Although involved in a variety of causes, the organization became a household name with its campaign against the 1987 Free Trade Agreement between Canada and the United States. Joining with a wide variety of other groups, it participated in the 1988 federal election where *free trade became the focus of the campaign. Maude Barlow, the council's chairperson, featured prominently in the ultimately unsuccessful effort to stop the agreement. Although still involved in inherently Canadian issues, by the 1990s the Council of Canadians had broadened its focus to challenging free trade on a worldwide scale in the form of globalization. The organization played a leading role in 1998 in helping to defeat the Multilateral Agreement on Investment, a piece of legislation that many argued would give multinational corporations unlimited power. STEVE HEWITT

Council of Twelve. The Nova Scotia Council of Twelve met first in July 1749 with the manifold powers conferred by the governor's commission. Chaired by the governor, it made appointments and passed minutes of council; chaired by its senior member, it had wide legislative powers; judicially it was a final court of appeal. By the 1780s the governor generally appointed councillors without interference from Britain, and, following his instructions, he chose men well disposed to government, almost all from among major provincial officers and leading merchants. Because they were mostly Haligonians, largely Church of England, and closely related by blood or in mercantile pursuits, they came to be reviled as an instrument of favouritism and monopoly. After 1790, to make government workable, the council had to make concessions to an aggressive assembly, especially in granting and spending road moneys. Nova Scotia's political awakening in the 1830 further weakened the council's position. When, in 1837, the reform majority in the newly elected assembly demanded separate executive and legislative councils, the British government reluctantly agreed and in 1838 the Council of Twelve ceased to exist.

J. MURRAY BECK

country doctors. A rural population, vast distances, and long winters mean that Canada has an established tradition of doctors working in isolation to provide diverse services. Until the 1950s, hospitals and physician collectives were found only in large cities or at remote missions, such as the Grenfell Mission in St Anthony, Newfoundland. Distinctions between surgeons and physicians were inherited from France and Britain, but further specialization was unknown until the end of the 19th century; for many decades thereafter, specialists worked in urban areas. Until 1950, then, most Canadians were treated by a country doctor or general practitioner.

The GP attended home deliveries, pulled teeth, operated on kitchen tables, set broken limbs in fields, concocted mustard plasters over wood stoves, and ventured out at night to sit with the dying. Rural practice was a small business in which accounts receivable often exceeded accounts paid. Country doctors were rarely rich, but they lived well. Notwithstanding occasional encounters with *midwives, Native shamans, and unorthodox practitioners, rural medicine was as close to the orthodox European ideal as facilities allowed. Sometimes, GPs accepted students or young doctors as apprentices. Many engaged in local politics or served on boards of health. If necessary, they performed autopsies to investigate murders.

A few found time to write about their busy lives. The following shows the years and location of some practitioners whose first-hand accounts of medicine in rural Canada were published.

1766–73	York Factory	Thomas Hutchins
1820–2	Arctic	John Richardson (1787–1865)
1821–85	PEI	John Mackieson 1795–1885)
1832–42	British Columbia	William F. Tolmie (1812–1886)
1849–89	Ontario	James Miles Langstaff (1825–1889)
1843–94	Quebec	Joseph Bettez (1818–1907)
1871–1930	Ontario	Abraham Groves (1847–1935)
1877–1912	Manitoba	Charlotte Ross Whitehead (1843–1916)
1888–1933	Saskatchewan	T.A. Patrick (1864–1943)
1893	Labrador	Eliot Curwen (1865–1950)
1885–1965	SW Quebec	H.J.G. Geggie (1896–1966)
1907–12	Saskatchewan	Hugh MacLean (1878–1958)
1912–19	Nova Scotia	Robert MacLellan
1929–31	N Alberta	Mary Percy Jackson (b. 1904)
1930s	SW Newfoundland	Nigel Rusted (b. 1907)
1933–47	Yukon	Allan Duncan (b. 1908)
1935	Aklavik, NWT	J.A. Urquhart
1924–54	Ontario	William Victor Johnston (1897–1976)

Before telephones, automobiles, and air ambulances, isolated people had to make do with one doctor for everything. By 1950, with shrinking distances and more trainees, some GPs predicted the demise of their metier. Questions of competence arose. In answer to this crisis, the Canadian College of General Practitioners was formed in 1954. The first executive director was W. Victor Johnston, a GP from tiny Lucknow, Ontario; he served for a decade. A similar body, the Fédération des médecins omnipracticiens du Québec, was created in 1963 to promote the interests of Quebec GPs. The CCGP, renamed the Canadian College of Family Practitioners in 1967, certified training programs, hosted conferences, and devised post-training evaluation systems, now widely copied by specialist groups. The movement of population from the country to the cities and the creation of a 'family specialty' from general practice, meant that the old country doctor became an urban family practitioner for whom life and work in remote areas was strange and intimidating.

To counteract the trend to city-based practice and to provide (and support) doctors for remote areas, *medical schools encouraged elective study in small centres and launched continuing education programs for out-of-town doctors. In 1992 the Society of Rural Physicians of Canada was formed 'to promote sustainable working conditions for rural physicians'. It contends 'that Canada's rural population must have access to excellent health care delivered by a stable, well-trained, well-equipped and rested medical staff'. Since 1995 the society has maintained an interactive Web site, and the first issue of its journal appeared in 1996. With new technology, the country doctor may have changed, but she has not disappeared.

JACALYN DUFFIN

coureurs de bois. These clandestine fur traders were particularly active in the Great Lakes region over the half-century beginning in the late 1660s. Until then, traders from various Native nations made the perilous journey to the French posts of the St Lawrence Valley in order to obtain merchandise for their own and neighbouring peoples in return for furs. The French who joined and all but supplanted them over three or four decades were at first known indiscriminately as *coureurs de bois* or 'wood-rangers'. In the beginning mostly footloose immigrants who would otherwise have returned to France, they traded on their own account or for that of Montreal merchants. They flaunted royal policies aimed at keeping colonists in the colony and out of the Great Lakes region, although some colonial officials were not above protecting the trade in return for a share in the profits. The practices of some of the coureurs (reneging on their debts or dealing in little else but brandy) were soon causing complaint in the colony and in Native lands. In 1681, the introduction of permits or *congés* created a legal trade around a stable minority who would become known as *marchands voyageurs*. But the turn-of-the-century glut in the French beaver market combined, paradoxically, with ordinances aimed at reducing the French presence in the interior to give the clandestine trade a new lease on life, especially in the thriving contraband with Albany, NY. Calmer conditions and more realistic policies after 1715 relegated the few remaining coureurs, supplied from French Louisiana or the British colonies, to the margins of the trade. Content to echo contemporaries' denunciations, sometimes giving them a romantic twist, historians long tended to see the coureur de bois as a veritable emblem of French colonization rather than as the transitional figure he was. Hence his prominence in popular memory, overshadowing to varying degrees his sedentary alter ego, the *habitant. THOMAS WIEN

courts of law, provincial and local. Canada's court system has always reflected the complexity of its government structures. Each British North American colony had a distinct court system. Up until the early 19th century the more established colonies had court systems that were simplified versions of the English system. Thus, most criminal offences were dealt with by justices of the peace, who were unpaid amateurs acting alone or together in Sessions of the Peace. This placed considerable power in the hands of local elites who composed the magistracy. More serious criminal cases were handled by professional judges in the higher courts, such as the Courts of King's Bench, Assizes, or Supreme Courts. As these might sit only once or twice a year, the accused could spend months in jail waiting for trial. Small civil cases were heard by justices of the peace or by local courts such as Courts of Request or Inferior Courts of Common Pleas, staffed by amateurs. More significant civil cases went before intermediate courts such as County, District, or Circuit Courts (generally but not always with legally trained judges), or the superior courts, such as the Supreme Courts, Courts of King's Bench, or Courts of Common Pleas. Most colonies also had various specialized courts—for example, Probate Courts (for inheritance issues) or Vice-Admiralty Courts (for maritime cases)—again based heavily on English precedent. Each colony generally also had a court of appeal for major civil cases; an ultimate appeal could also be made to the King and Council in England. Less established colonies often departed radically from this model. Hence, in 18th-century Newfoundland, British naval officers, along with local justices of the peace, played a central role in dispensing justice. In the West, justice was dispensed by Hudson's Bay Company officials and by the courts of Upper and Lower Canada.

From this simplified English base, colonial court systems changed dramatically through the middle years of the 19th century. Colonial legislators tinkered continually with their court systems: in Quebec, for example, the courts were fundamentally restructured no less than four times between 1840 and 1849. With the growth of the bureaucratic state, amateur judges were increasingly seen as unreliable, and their work shifted to paid professionals. Thus, professional County and District Court judges, stipendiary magistrates, and police magistrates took over most lesser civil and criminal cases, although justices of the peace and local civil courts continued to play a role, especially in rural areas. The judicial power of local elites declined correspondingly. The rise of cities also led to the establishment of Police Courts and Recorders' Courts, which were municipally based courts that generally dealt with minor crimes such as drunkenness and vagrancy, bylaw offences, and property tax cases. Because the British North America Act left the administration of justice in the hands of the provinces, Confederation brought little immediate change, although it did lead to the establishment of a federal court system and federal appointment and payment of provincial judges down to the County and District Court level.

A further fundamental change was the rise of summary justice, with cases decided by judges alone. The jury trial traditionally at the heart of the English criminal justice system was increasingly criticized by efficiency-seeking reformers. As well, crimes such as vagrancy and drunkenness, which had always been dealt with summarily, began to dominate, especially in urban courts. Finally, from the late 1860s onwards, provincial and federal legislatures began to enact 'speedy trial' legislation, which 'allowed' those accused of more serious crimes to choose between rapid trial before a judge alone and waiting (often in jail) until the next court sitting with juries. The combined effect was that by the early 20th century the vast majority of defendants were tried before a judge alone, as is still the case today. A similar decline in jury trials occurred in civil cases.

As new regions were colonized and subjected to European-style administration, they too acquired increasingly complex court systems. Thus, on the prairies west of Manitoba, HBC magistrates were replaced by federally appointed *North-West Mounted Police officers and civilian stipendiary magistrates; from 1886 the North-West Territories had a regular Supreme Court; and following the creation of Saskatchewan and Alberta in 1905 each set up its own fully fledged court system. In British Columbia a Supreme Court was created in 1853, with local courts held by stipendiary magistrates and gold commissioners; standard County Courts were added in 1867.

In the 20th century, while the legislative tinkering with the court system continued, there were two additional fundamental developments. First, progressive moves were made to simplify and rationalize the courts. For example, as provincial governments asserted their control over local justice, most provinces gradually brought their local criminal and civil courts together into a single provincial court; municipal courts also disappeared, and by the end of the century they survived only in Quebec, although Ontario has recently moved to re-establish them. In the 1970s and 1980s most provinces also abolished their intermediate (District or County) courts. The provinces and territories thus came to have their current fairly standardized hierarchy: first, an appeal court; then a superior court (Supreme Court, Superior Court, or Court of Queen's Bench) for the trial of serious crimes and major civil cases; and finally one or several provincial or territorial courts for lesser matters.

Through the 20th century, specialized courts (e.g., juvenile courts, which appeared in the early 20th century, or family courts) were created to deal with specific types of cases. These reflected contemporary concerns; juvenile courts, for example, were initially established at the urging of social reformers concerned with perceived youth crime, and subsequently became part of the developing *welfare state. Often the functions of these courts were later folded into the operations of the main courts. As well, the post–Second World War period in particular has seen the growth of provincial administrative tribunals dealing with matters ranging from labour law and human rights to the environment. Overall, these developments reflect the increasing presence of the state in the everyday lives of Canadians. DONALD FYSON

See also FEDERAL COURT OF CANADA; SUPREME COURT OF CANADA.

courtship and marriage. Most Canadians have affirmed heterosexuality through marriage, although their numbers and the rituals and relationships they have adopted have varied tremendously. Religions and, later, the state have been major players in legitimating marriage, but couples have long established meaningful partnerships in common law and according to cultural practices such as the 'custom of the country' in the fur-trade period. Marriage has been critical in linking families. Kin influence has been especially strong for younger partners in traditional societies, whether First Nations or immigrant—as among British Columbia's Carrier peoples or in early New France—but it has rarely been absent.

Courtship has traditionally been monitored by families who expected public affirmation of the union if pregnancy occurred. This pressure helps explain why so many first births occur less than nine months after marriage. The emergence of compulsory schooling and the youth culture associated with high schools, the rise of the automobile, and the growth of voluntary organization, popular entertainments, and female waged employments created historically new conditions for courtship. They widened the pool of suitors and offered greater privacy. The celebration of romantic love among the 19th-century middle classes and its perennial promotion by writers, filmmakers, and advertisers further justified individual choice. While the census reveals significant and increasing instances of intermarriage, most Canadians have courted and married within their own social and cultural communities.

Offspring have been a largely taken-for-granted product, expected to guarantee family survival. Although many women tried to control their fertility, success was limited by primitive technology, social pressure, and legal sanctions. Moreover, high infant mortality rates confronted families with the reality that not all children would survive into adulthood, thus reducing the attraction of *birth control. In settings from the family farm to the suburban bungalow, spouses have concentrated on creating viable economies. In the early 20th century, the ideal of 'companionate' marriage attempted to combine pragmatics and affection, while downplaying male power and privilege.

Husbands could be better than the law allowed, and wives could be of sterner stuff, but English common law and French civil law upheld men's marital authority in matters from violence to divorce and inheritance. Conscious of male abuse and seeking recognition for women's contribution, early feminists prioritized family law reform and egalitarian relationships. Demands by the *Woman's Christian Temperance Union and others for the 'white life for two'—with men matching women's superior sexual and moral behaviour—drew on long-standing progressive Christian traditions. In contrast, religious conservatives and others who embraced a Darwinian science, ascribing different sexual needs to women and men, rejected the 'single standard' advocated by critics such as Nellie *McClung. In the 20th century, the feminist model of marital equality founded in mutual restraint was ridiculed by both 'free lovers' and those convinced of the logic of the double standard. As the 1970 *Report* of the Royal Commission on the Status of Women confirmed, marital arrangements continued to benefit husbands. Economic disadvantage in the marketplace and responsibility for children in the home handicapped women.

Alternatives, such as Catholic and Anglican religious orders, 'Boston marriages', and other same-sex relationships have always existed. The dramatic decline in religious vocations undermined old options after the 1960s. In the late 20th century, partnerships of lesbians and gays—or, as they are sometimes referred to in First Nations communities, 'two-spirited people'—began to gain official approval, in matters from immigration sponsorship to family law. While critics such as the novelist Jane Rule dismissed marriage as an unsuitable goal, other gay and lesbian activists disagreed. New reproductive technologies, ranging from cloning to donor insemination, complicate matters further, suggesting that future courtship and marriage may vary in new ways.

VERONICA STRONG-BOAG

cowboys. In the 1830s Texans applied the term 'cowboy' to relatively wild and lawless border raiders who were in the habit of making off with Mexican cattle. After the Civil War the Texans began to utilize the word to designate ranch hands rather than rustlers. Since that time it has generally been assigned to men who make at least part of their living working on ranches. From the mid-1860s the cattle industry spread north from Texas; by the 1880s numerous cowboys were tending herds on the natural grasslands in southern regions of British Columbia, Alberta, and Assiniboia (now southern Saskatchewan). In the beginning most of them were Americans who drove in the cattle herds from Texas, Oregon, Idaho, and Montana. Their expertise was passed on to easterners and Europeans who arrived to work on the ranches and then to native-born western Canadians.

Cowboys were adept at all the skills required to tend the herds on the open range. The most accomplished were adept at breaking and training wild horses, roping cattle from the saddle while charging across the land at breakneck speed, branding newborn calves over an open fire, and wrestling grown steers to the ground. Because of their skills and their endless eulogizing by journalists, fiction writers, dime novelists, and Hollywood film producers, they were raised to icon stature in both the United States and Canada. The multitude of local *rodeos in the West, including the world-famous *Calgary Stampede, suggests that this stature is little diminished in modern times.

WARREN ELOFSON

See also RANCHING.

Craigellachie. On 7 November 1885, at Craigellachie, about 30 km west of Revelstoke, British Columbia, Donald *Smith, one of the directors of the *Canadian Pacific Railway, drove in the last spike of the just completed transcontinental. Symbolic of the company's financial position, Smith used an ordinary iron spike. After bending one, he succeeded on the second try. The short, sparse ceremony ended with the words of William *Van Horne, the company manager: 'All I can say is that the work has been well done in every way.' A.A. DEN OTTER

credit unions. A form of co-operative banking derived from the community-based co-operative banking traditions of Germany, Italy, and France. First adapted in Canada as *caisses populaires by Alphonse Desjardins in 1900, credit unions appeared in the United States shortly thereafter and spread northward to English Canada, particularly in the 1930s, promoted by the *Antigonish Movement, other co-ops, churches, and governments. They grew steadily, forming provincial and national central organizations and helping to create insurance and *trust companies. At first they were small, reliant upon volunteer labour, encouraging member thrift, and lending for 'providential' purpose. As they grew they were led by professional managers, developed a full range of financial services, and embraced technological change. They particularly helped working-class people to enter into the middle class and 'consumer society' after the Second World War. Some, such as VanCity, grew to have hundreds of thousand of members and assets of more than $5 billion, raising issues of member control, management accountability, and community responsibility. Credit unions embarked on a widespread process of amalgamation, declining in numbers from 2,000 to 700, although membership increased to 6 million and assets to $60 billion. They have become important fixtures in the Canadian financial system, an alternative to the large *banks.

IAN MacPHERSON

Creighton, Donald Grant (1902–79). Born in Toronto, Creighton was educated at Victoria College, University of Toronto, and Balliol College, Oxford. He was the son of Laura Harvie and William Creighton, the editor of the leading Methodist paper in Canada, the *Christian Guardian*. Creighton was thus a product of Methodist Toronto, earnest, intelligent, trying to be civilized. Creighton did so become, reading European and British history at Oxford. He also learned to envy British students their schools, their education, their clubs, their finish. Humberside Collegiate was not an English public school like Marlborough, and he was constantly being reminded of it. If it was good, it was but a good second class. Envy, one of the seven deadly sins, nagged him all his life.

Creighton was appointed to the History Department of the University of Toronto in 1927 and never left it. His chef d'oeuvre was his life of Sir John A. *Macdonald, published in two volumes (1952 and 1956), both of which won the Governor General's Award. The Macdonald biography permanently established Creighton's reputation as writer and historian. It is a brilliant work, elevated into literature by Creighton's writing, his research, and his remarkable eye for telling detail. A Canadian nationalist, he was long a friend of French-Canadian historians until the 1960s, when too many took up separatism. Michel Brunet tried to remind him that 'survivre n'est pas vivre', but *separatism made him angry; Mirabel airport positively enraged him.

Creighton is dead: his Macdonald lives on.

P.B. WAITE

Creighton, Mary Helen (1899–1989), folklorist. Born to an upper-class Nova Scotian family, Helen Creighton attended Halifax Ladies' College. In 1918 she chauffeured officers of the Royal Flying Corps in Toronto; later she drove an ambulance for the Red Cross in Nova Scotia and taught briefly in Mexico. In 1928, out of an interest in journalism, she began collecting Nova Scotian folksongs. She attended the Indiana University Summer Institute of Folklore in 1942, and her collecting efforts in the 1940s were supported by the Library of Congress and the Rockefeller Foundation. From 1947 to 1967 she held contracts with the National Museum of Canada. While folksongs remained Creighton's emphasis, she was less selective in collecting folklore than many of her contemporaries. Nevertheless, she has been criticized for concentrating heavily on communities of European descent and for contributing to an anti-modernist vision of Nova

Scotia. Although her significant collection of field recordings and over 80 books and articles had minimal impact on the academic study of folklore, their regional popular influence was significant. 'The Nova Scotia Song', collected in 1933 and known familiarly as 'Farewell to Nova Scotia', is the province's unofficial anthem. Creighton's Dartmouth home, 'Evergreen', is part of the Nova Scotia Museum system, and an annual festival celebrates her work and memory. DIANE TYE

Crémazie, Octave (Claude-Joseph-Olivier) (1827–79), Quebec's first important poet. Born in Quebec City on 16 April, he studied at the Petit Séminaire from 1836 to 1843 and opened a bookstore with his brother Joseph in 1844, making several business trips to France. He was an active member of the *Institut canadien, becoming its president in 1857–8. Bankrupted in 1862, he fled to France, where he lived a miserable existence, chiefly in Paris, under the name 'Jules Fontaine' until his death at Le Havre on 16 January 1879.

His first verse appeared in 1849 and he was soon acclaimed as French Canada's 'national bard' for patriotic poems like 'Le Vieux Soldat canadien' (1855), 'Le Canada' (1858), and 'Le Drapeau de Carillon' (1858). Before his exile, he published about 30 poems, including an unfinished longer piece, 'Promenade de trois morts' (1862). In prose, he left an extensive correspondence with his family and with Abbé Henri-Raymond Casgrain and a detailed diary of the siege of Paris in 1870–1. There is a two-volume critical edition of Crémazie's writings by Odette Condemine (1972, 1976) and a lavishly illustrated biographical album (1980) by the same author.

DAVID M. HAYNE

Crerar, Henry Duncan Graham (1888–1965), career soldier. Crerar was awarded a Distinguished Service Order after the *Vimy operation in 1917. Inspired by his experiences during the war, and a hefty legacy from his family's estate, he pursued a career in the *Permanent Force, enduring two decades of frustrated aspirations in the 'stagnant backwaters' of the interwar *Canadian army. As director of military operations and intelligence (1935–8) he drew up the plans that would shape the wartime army. During the Second World War, he rose rapidly, successively occupying—and often defining—the senior staff and operational positions in the army. As chief of the general staff (1940–1), he was the chief architect of a five-division First Canadian Army, outmanoeuvring the adamantly anti-army prime minister Mackenzie *King, but also committing Canadian troops to the defence of the doomed garrison at *Hong Kong. In 1942 he was appointed general officer commanding, 1st Canadian Corps, securing the use of Canadian troops in the raid on *Dieppe. Crerar emerged unscathed from both of these debacles, and was given command of First Canadian Army in March 1944. His tenure as army commander was distinguished by a fierce defence of national interests and a caution borne of inexperience. Operation 'Veritable' in February 1945 was the high point of his army command as he managed 13 Allied divisions, the largest force ever commanded by a Canadian. He retired in 1946.

PAUL DICKSON

Crerar, Thomas Alexander (1876–1975). Active in the early *co-operative movement, Crerar was president of the *Grain Growers' Grain Company and founding president of United Grain Growers (UGG) in 1917. That same year, though a Liberal, he joined Robert *Borden's Union government as minister of agriculture. He resigned in June 1919 when the government refused to lower the protective tariff.

As a rallying point for those who favoured freer trade, Crerar led the new *Progressive Party in an election in 1921 that resulted in Canada's first minority government. The Progressives accomplished little else. Discouraged by this, saddened by the death of his daughter, and under pressure from UGG to return to the company, he left politics. He returned to politics briefly in 1929 as minister of railways in Mackenzie *King's Liberal government and was defeated the next year, with the government. By 1935 the Liberals were back in power and Crerar joined what may have been the strongest *cabinet in Canadian history. He served as deputy chair of the Cabinet War Committee, which met almost daily for over four years. In 1945 he was called to the Senate, where for 20 years he extolled the virtues of self-reliance, limited government, and co-operation. J.E. REA

crime and punishment. Canada might not be a notorious world leader in crime, but it has definitely been a world leader in punishment. It was one of the first countries to build a modern penitentiary; it was at the forefront of 19th-century movements to establish separate *prisons for men, women, and children; and it kept pace with 20th-century penal innovations, such as parole. Thus, even though Canadians have historically regarded themselves as more law-abiding than their US counterparts, they have nonetheless considered crime a serious problem. Yet, over the past few centuries, the ways in which lawmakers puzzled over punishment varied significantly.

Like that of most countries in the modern industrialized world, Canada's criminal justice system transformed markedly from its indigenous origins to its contemporary character. Europeans did not come to a lawless land (although many portrayed it as such). More sensitive European observers noted that Aboriginal concepts of crime and justice were different, not absent. Every Native society had its own system of dispute resolution, but most First Nations based their sense of justice on a notion of compensation: crime was a wrong that could and had to be made right, according to customary rule. Compensation could take the form of ritual apology, offerings of material goods (food or pelts, for example), labour, or, in extreme circumstances, the perpetrator's life.

Compared to Native systems, French and English justice was inflexible and formal; in the eyes of some Native people, it was also brutal. Prior to the 19th century the English thought it perfectly reasonable to hold children fully accountable for crimes. Youths as young as 12 were executed for offences such as petty theft. Although it was rarely used, French royal justice allowed for the torture of accused criminals (those suspected of serious crimes, like arson or witchcraft) in order to extract confessions. Not surprisingly, most accused confessed rather than face torture.

Until the mid-19th century colonial authorities adhered to the belief that justice literally had to be seen to be done. *Courts were open to the public, as was the infliction of corporal and *capital punishment. In both New France and, after 1763, British North America, the law breaker's body was placed on display. Persons found guilty of morals offences (such as adultery or blasphemy) were taken to public squares and placed in stocks or pillories—wooden devices that immobilized offenders in humiliating positions. Flogging was also a public event, sometimes accompanied by parading the offender through city streets. Hangings, the only form of execution under British rule, could attract huge crowds of onlookers who were meant to absorb a brutal lesson in deterrence.

By the early 19th century, rumblings of reform were heard. Colonial politicians kept abreast of new penal approaches advocated in Britain and the United States, and Upper Canadians in particular were beginning to accept the idea that imprisonment might play a larger role in punishment. Until the mid-19th century, prisons in Canada were laughably insecure and lamentably squalid. Prison terms were short because most arrestees were minor offenders (drunks or prostitutes, for instance) who could not afford to pay fines. People found guilty of committing serious offences paid with their bodies and their lives unless they were lucky enough to see their death sentences commuted (with banishment or branding as possible substitutes). The problem with punishment, reformers pointed out, was that the existing system was both too severe and too capricious.

The symbolic shift towards a more systematic form of punishment through imprisonment appeared with the construction of the Kingston Penitentiary in 1837. Built just in time to receive persons charged with participating in the Upper and Lower Canadian *Rebellions of 1837–8, the massive stone structure asserted the power and solidity of colonial rule. But it failed to live up to its backers' lofty hopes of reform through contemplation and labour. Nevertheless, by the mid-19th century imprisonment became the standard image in most Canadians' minds when they thought about punishment.

Canadians also came to argue that different sorts of criminals required unique prisons. Women and children, generally considered to be more pliable than adult men, were the first to be plucked from general prison populations and placed in their own specially designed and managed institutions. Beginning in the 1870s, boys and girls hauled off the streets for loitering or pickpocketing were sent to industrial schools. Women found drunk or soliciting sex were shunted from local jails into women's *reformatories (the country's first being the Andrew Mercer Reformatory in Toronto). In spite of Kingston's proven failures, an evangelical faith in the restorative and moralizing powers of incarceration meant that even petty offenders served terms of several years 'for their own good'.

Experiments in non-institutional modes of correcting criminal behaviour proliferated by the beginning of the 20th century. The 1898 Ticket-of-Leave Act was a forerunner of the parole system, formally established in 1959. By offering the possibility of earning early release from prison, correctional officials hoped they could induce law-abiding behaviour among inmates. With parole came parole agents and a host of professionals assigned to monitor people assumed likely to offend. Social workers, psychologists, and medical personnel were recruited, as the criminal's mind and body became a new focus of intervention in the fight against crime. By the century's end, however, the promise of a scientific solution to the crime problem remained unfulfilled. Instead spartan 'superjails' became the new warehouses of punishment.

CAROLYN STRANGE

criminal law. The criminal law of the British North American colonies was based on English criminal law. In general, each colony 'received' the criminal law of England as it stood at various dates (e.g., 1774 for Quebec or 1858 for British Columbia) and then made such modifications as were thought necessary. English criminal law, however, was in no way systematized; it was based on common *law precedent and on thousands of laws passed through the centuries. Add to this piecemeal modifications by colonial legislatures, and the result was a legal labyrinth that few understood completely. Faced with the difficulties of such a system, many of the colonies made partial codifications of the criminal law: Nova Scotia in 1758 and 1851, for example, and the United Canadas in 1841 and in 1859. However, these 'codes' only partially replaced existing English law; as well, they were often themselves modified by other colonial laws. In the climate of rationalization and bureaucratization that characterized the 19th-century state, where legislators increasingly sought to control society through systematic regulation, the jumble of criminal law was increasingly seen as intolerable. Matters became even more pressing when, under the British North America Act of 1867, criminal law became the responsibility of the federal government, necessitating a unified criminal law for all of Canada. Various partial codifications were made, beginning in 1869; the culmination came in 1892, when John *Thompson, the Conservative minister of justice, piloted the Criminal Code through Parliament.

With the Criminal Code of 1892, Canada became the second major member of the British Empire, after India, to adopt a comprehensive national penal code. Though it did not fundamentally change existing criminal law, the code, in its 983 sections, did bring it together in one systematic enactment under the control of Parliament; among other things, this reduced the latitude judges previously enjoyed in interpreting the criminal law. In content, in addition to reflecting standard Judeo-Christian values, the code also catered to the interests and morality of the Victorian middle classes, with strict provisions on sexual morality, gambling, and so on, and detailed attention to property crime. The code dealt only with the criminal law in its narrower sense—that is, more 'serious' offences. Many other offences continued to be regulated by separate federal, provincial, and municipal legislation. For example, in Quebec the infamous *'padlock' law, used against political dissidents, and municipal regulations directed against marginal religious groups were both independent of the code. Likewise, traffic infractions, which increasingly made up the bulk of minor offences, were generally regulated by provincial or municipal laws, with the code limited to matters such as drinking and driving.

Once enacted, the Criminal Code remained largely unchanged in its general structure through the 20th century, despite a major overhaul in 1954. The code's content, though, was continually modified: between 1892 and 1927 more than 400 amendments were made; until 1970, modifications were proposed during virtually every parliamentary session. These modifications reflected the political, social, and economic context of the times. Following the 1919 *Winnipeg General Strike, for example, two articles were added that clamped down on illegal associations and seditious activity; likewise, drinking and driving provisions were added in 1921, as automobiles became increasingly common. Modifications were often at the behest of lobby groups, who benefited from having a single object (the code) and audience (Parliament) to focus on: through to the 1920s, the code's provisions on sexual morality were considerably stiffened as a result of intense lobbying by social reformers. Overall, until the 1920s the code became increasingly repressive; conversely, from the 1960s onwards, several aspects underwent liberalization, such as those concerning *birth control and *abortion. In historical perspective, it is clear that far from being a neutral and rational construction, the Criminal Code has most often reflected the desires of those with the power and presence to influence Parliament.

DONALD FYSON

crimping. During most of the 19th century, port life for merchant seamen, particularly those in the sailortowns of Quebec and Saint John, was characterized by a turbulent labour market. Governed by the market forces of supply and demand, sailor stealing, known as crimping, became prevalent when the east-bound timber trade created a need for *seafaring labour that outstripped the local sources of supply. Incoming sailors, under written articles of agreement to stay with their vessels, were eager to switch vessels for better wages at the prompting of crimps—usually ex-seamen—who facilitated the change at the expense of desperate shipmasters. The sailors paid their share of the crimp's commission by spending their advance pay in crimp-run boarding houses, which invariably sold liquor and outfitted the runaway for the new voyage. In Quebec the most notorious crimp of Champlain Street was Jim Ward, who intimidated shipmasters, violently disciplined seamen, and fixed wages at higher rates than those offered through the government shipping office. Legislation to combat crimping in the 1870s encouraged the crimps to use underlings, known as runners, to do their dirty work. Ultimately, improved employment conditions in the liner trades undermined crimping until the late 20th century, when the world's fleets became manned by third-world seamen who wanted to escape exploitative, dangerous, low-paid employment. Sometimes they found agents in ports like Vancouver to help them jump ship.

While it is true that some deserting sailors woke up in their new berths in a drunken stupor and sailed to unwanted destinations, at least they were not impressed into military service, a type of crimping that Jim Ward undertook as a sideline during the American Civil War. Merchant seamen, British 'tars' and soldiers, and even colonial civilians who were enticed into the Union army by promises of a bounty and high wages were not as unlucky as the unsuspecting men and boys impressed into the Royal Navy by press gangs in British colonial ports during the wars of the late 18th and early 19th centuries. The creation of standing, professional armies and navies eliminated this particular form of forced labour, at least until the Canadian *conscription crisis of the First World War.

JUDITH FINGARD

Crowfoot (*c.*1830–90), Blackfoot chief. As a member of the warlike Blackfoot tribe inhabiting the plains of southern Alberta, Crowfoot (Isapo-muksika) took part in 19 conflicts with enemy tribes and achieved honours as a warrior. In 1870 he became a chief of the tribe and was respected by fur traders because of his efforts to maintain peace. He welcomed the *North-West Mounted Police when they came west in 1874 and established a close friendship with their commissioner, James F. *Macleod. In 1877, he signed Treaty 7 with the Canadian government, largely because Macleod was one of the negotiators. In his acceptance speech Crowfoot said that the Mounted Police 'have protected us as the feathers of the bird protect it from the frosts of winter'. He settled on his reserve in 1881 but soon became disillusioned with the government for failing to live up to it promises. He was sympathetic to those Indians who joined the *North-West Rebellion of 1885 but kept his people out of the conflict. He died on his reserve in 1890.

HUGH A. DEMPSEY

Crown Investments Corporation of Saskatchewan. The holding company for provincial Crown corporations and portfolio investments in a variety of commercial enterprises. Its holdings in 2003 accounted for 15 per cent of Saskatchewan's gross domestic product and about 9 per cent of total employment in the province. Assets totalled about $8 billion, of which $7.5 billion was attributable to four major Crown corporations, three of which were utilities (SaskPower, SaskTel, SaskEnergy) and one an insurance company (SGI Canada). In addition to the Crowns, CIC has equity interests in industries such as heavy oil upgrading, pulp mills, fertilizer production, and food processing.

CIC's origins can be traced to 1947, when the CCF government led by Tommy *Douglas established the Government Finance Office to provide a coordinated approach to public enterprise. As Douglas explained, the holding company took a number of horses going off in all directions and got them 'working on the same line'. There were four main goals: development and diversification of the economy, generation of dividends for the provincial treasury, improvement of the quality and level of services, and public control of utilities. These continue as policy objectives in keeping with the distinctive Saskatchewan tradition of government involvement in the economy and public entrepreneurship.

JAMES M. PITSULA

Crow's Nest Pass Agreement. This agreement, dated 6 September 1897, granted the *Canadian Pacific Railway a $3.3 million federal subsidy to build a rail line from Lethbridge, Alberta, through the Crowsnest Pass into the mineral rich Kootenay region of southern British Columbia. In return the CPR agreed to reductions of approximately 15 per cent on its western freight rates. The Crow rates were undercut in 1901 by a rival railway, and suspended during the First World War due to increased costs. After much legal and political wrangling, they were restored in 1927 for shipments of grain and unprocessed grain products. This move discouraged the processing of grain in western Canada, and failed to provide sufficient revenue to cover the costs incurred by the railways, making new investments and modernization of railway grain-transportation facilities uneconomical. In 1983 the railways received authorization to charge higher, federally subsidized rates. In 1997 federal legislation rescinded the Crow's Nest Pass Agreement, but provided western farmers with compensatory federal cash payments.

T.D. REGEHR

Cuban missile crisis. After US spy planes sighted Soviet nuclear-tipped missiles deployed in Cuba in October 1962, President John F. Kennedy issued an ultimatum for their immediate removal. The confrontation threatened nuclear war and caused a dramatic rift in Canadian–American relations. Prime Minister John *Diefenbaker refused Kennedy's request for immediate support and suggested instead that the United Nations investigate the Soviet bases in Cuba before decisive action was taken. This diplomatic complication would have allowed the Soviets more time to arm their missiles. Diefenbaker exacerbated tensions when he responded slowly to fulfill Canada's NORAD commitment to place its armed forces on alert, although we now know that Defence Minister Douglas Harkness took this step without consulting the prime minister. Public opinion polls indicated that Canadians strongly supported the Kennedy administration's handling of the crisis. Thus the Diefenbaker government not only became increasingly isolated from its closest ally but lost political support at home.

LAWRENCE ARONSEN

Cumberland House. In 1774, faced with increasing competition from the Monteal-based fur trade, the *Hudson's Bay Company abandoned its century-long practice of trading from bayside and built Cumberland House, its first inland post. Company explorer Samuel *Hearne selected a site on Pine Island Lake on the Saskatchewan River system. The establishment of Cumberland House marked the beginning of a fierce, at times violent, struggle between the HBC and the *North West Company. The post served as a major supply base for country provisions to support the interior trade. A largely mixed-blood community today, Cumberland House is the oldest continuously occupied settlement in Saskatchewan.

BILL WAISER

Cunard, Samuel (1787–1865), founder of international shipping line. The son of *Loyalist shipowners in Halifax, Cunard prospered in wartime trading and by buying captured American shipping in the War of 1812. In peace, he diversified with coal, whaling, and timber ventures and held many public offices such as lighthouse commissioner. After experiments with steam in Halifax Harbour ferries and investment in the pioneer steamship **Royal William*, Cunard teamed up with Scottish shipbuilders and investors to win the Royal Mail contract in 1840. The British and North American Royal Mail Steam Packet Company, soon known as the Cunard Line, launched steam service from Liverpool to Halifax, Boston, Pictou, and Quebec. Cunard's ships established reliable and safe travel on the North Atlantic while other attempts ended in shipwreck and bankruptcy. After a difficult start, the line grew to become the world's largest and longest-serving ocean liner company. As the company expanded, Cunard spent almost all his time in Britain. His Canadian service dwindled, and soon after Cunard's death his partners dropped service to Canada entirely. DAN CONLIN

Cupids Cove Colony. Founded in 1610, in Conception Bay, Newfoundland, Cupids Cove was the original 'plantation' on the *English Shore and thus the first permanent English settlement in Canada. Sponsored by the Newfoundland Company of London and Bristol, John Guy led 39 colonists to 'secure' the local fishery, encourage a fur trade through friendly contact with the *Beothuk, and experiment with agriculture, lumbering, and minerals. After reasonable success through two mild winters, Guy brought out 16 women in 1613. The birth of the first European child in Newfoundland since the Norse infant Snorri marked a turning point for settlement. A hard winter followed, fodder for animals fell short, the pirate Peter Easton took precious livestock, and several colonists died. Following quarrels with the company, Guy withdrew in 1615, when his nephew Nicholas and Bristol investors established Bristol's Hope, at Harbour Grace. The company replaced John Guy with the experienced mariner John Mason, probably chosen for his ability to deal with pirates and migratory fishers. Interim leader Henry Crout thought the Cupids colony never properly exploited the fishery, but some *fishing admirals complained about settler competition. Mason and his celebrated Indian companion Tisquantum moved on to New England in 1621. Archaeological remains attest to the continued permanent occupation of the Cupids plantation until it burned about 1665, during the second Dutch War. The colony did not return a profit to investors but was ancestral to subsequent Newfoundland settlement not only in dispersion of colonists but in the division and disposition of proprietary rights.

PETER E. POPE

currency. Growth in population and trade in 17th-century New France increased demands for a formal currency. The legal tender, French livres, was scarce, and an assortment of coins from England, Spain, Portugal, and Spanish America was tolerated. When, in 1685, the King's ship failed to arrive, the intendant Jacques de Meulles cut playing cards into various sizes and circulated these as currency. With the surrender of Quebec to the British in 1759, the card money collapsed as inflation and corruption were revealed. Coin once again became the predominant currency, but the British were no better at supplying their colonies. Even in Nova Scotia, where the British had ruled since 1713, Spanish-American dollars prevailed; Halifax Currency, which valued five shillings local currency to one silver dollar, eventually became the accepted rating across the British North American colonies.

By the end of the 18th century, paper monies were again becoming common. Notes issued on the treasury paid for public works and were used as currency. Especially popular in the Maritime colonies, these notes also arrived in Upper and Lower Canada when General Isaac *Brock issued army bills to finance the War of 1812. The full redemption of the notes after the war helped to restore confidence in paper currencies. In 1817 the new Montreal Bank (later the Bank of Montreal) circulated the first Canadian bank notes. By 1825 note-issuing banks had also opened in Upper Canada, Nova Scotia, and New Brunswick, and bank notes quickly became the most prevalent currency. In Nova Scotia and New Brunswick the first banks held virtual monopolies over paper currency until mid-century; their notes even circulated in Prince Edward Island, which had no bank of its own until 1855. Local note-issuing banks did not arrive in Newfoundland and the colony of Vancouver Island until the late 1850s, and in the interior provinces only a couple such banks ever opened.

In those areas with limited or no banking facilities, merchant notes and tokens made up a considerable amount of the small change in circulation. From 1821 the *Hudson's Bay Company issued pound notes and metallic tokens known as 'made-beavers', denominated in fractions of beaver pelts, which could be found into the 20th century. As banking gained ground, however, restrictions on the issuing of currency grew. Counterfeiting was a legitimate concern, particularly in the early 19th century. Coins of gold and silver had always been deliberately clipped, filed, and sweated, but paper currencies were particularly susceptible to forgery and falsification.

Political integration and centralization offered other reasons for currency regulation. In 1841, with the formation of the *Province of Canada, Governor Sydenham promoted the idea of a single government currency. The banks, which stood to lose much of their income, opposed the plan. In a move towards centralization the Currency Act of 1854 established common rates of exchange, which were extended to New Brunswick later that year. Revisions to the act in 1857 legalized the sole use of dollars, and the first decimal coins were ordered from the Royal Mint. In 1858 the Province of Canada issued debentures that circulated as currency, despite being interest bearing.

Finance Minister Alexander *Galt revived the idea for government currency in the 1860s. The banks continued to resist, but the Province of Canada went ahead nonetheless. Confederation in 1867 made the notes obsolete as the new dominion acquired control over banking and currency matters. The Bank Act of 1870 rescinded the right of the *banks to issue notes under $4, as the dominion issued its own $1 and $2 notes. Demand for small currency also led to the printing of a 25¢ note, or 'shinplaster', which was so popular it persisted for 65 years. As the various colonies joined Confederation their currencies were subsumed under dominion legislation; even pre-Confederation Newfoundland came into line when its banks collapsed in 1894.

The design and production of currency became more standardized with the opening of the British American Bank Note Company in Montreal in 1866. It made nationalistic appeals for the domestic production of money, echoed in 1908 when the Royal Mint opened a branch in Canada. Further centralization and consolidation came with the formation of the Bank of Canada in 1935, which became solely responsible for the issue of paper currencies. Until that time, bank notes still comprised a significant part of the currency. In 1935 banks were ordered to reduce their notes in circulation, and in 1944 they were prohibited from issuing bank notes. Only then did Canada achieve a single national currency.

In recent years, the issuing of one- and two-dollar coins, popularly known as loonies and toonies, constituted significant changes to the currency. But it is the depreciation of the Canadian dollar that is of most concern today. From 1879 until the beginning of the First World War, and again briefly from 1926 to 1929, Canada was on the gold standard. Since then the dollar has either been fixed, as when it was pegged to the US dollar from 1962 to 1970, or has floated according to international supply and demand. Since the 1970s the dollar has fluctuated greatly. When it stalled at just over 60¢ US in 1998, calls for a North American monetary union erupted. Given the parallel rise of electronic currencies and banking, the future of Canadian currency seems far from certain. Ironically, the overtly nationalist iconography depicted on the new series of paper money gives no hint of this vulnerability.

EMILY GILBERT

Currie, Sir Arthur William (1875–1933), soldier. Currie was a respected militia officer sent overseas during the

First World War with the first contingent as a brigade commander on the strength of his experience and ties to the minister of militia, Sir Sam *Hughes. Despite some controversy surrounding his actions during the 2nd Battle of *Ypres, Currie took command of 1st Canadian Division when the *Canadian Corps was formed in September 1915. Although unmilitary in bearing and appearance, he proved a natural soldier whose attention to detail and willingness to innovate helped to professionalize the corps. In June 1917, after his division's success at *Vimy Ridge, he was appointed corps commander. His refusal to make command appointments based on political affiliation drew the ire of Hughes, who campaigned unsuccessfully to have him removed. Under Currie, the corps became one of the premier formations in the British army and a national symbol. Currie resisted attempts to break up the corps during the German spring offensives in 1918, and then commanded it as it spearheaded the final Allied campaigns in the fall. After the war, he became president of McGill University but was plagued by rumours that he had pursued national and personal glory at the expense of his men's lives, rumours quashed by victory in a libel trial in 1927. PAUL DICKSON

customs duties. Such duties (tariffs when in a schedule) are taxes on goods paid by importers and generally transferred through pricing mechanisms to secondary producers or consumers. Customs duties performed two key functions: generating government revenue and providing economic policy through differential tariffs and protectionism. They made up the single largest source of government revenue until the 1930s (61 per cent in 1911, 44.3 in 1931), when the collapse of international trade sharply reduced their importance and increased that of the income tax. After the Second World War, multilateral efforts to reduce barriers to trade through GATT caused further decline. By the late 1960s duties generated less than 10 per cent of total net federal revenue. The GST and the Free Trade Agreement reduced that further.

Customs duties, when used for protection, are levied at rates that allow for the domestic substitution of goods excluded by the duties. In the 19th century, rates of 10 per cent ad valorem were considered purely revenue generating and defensible on free-trade grounds. In A.T. *Galt's 1858 tariff, a top level of 20 per cent was established to maximize revenue; that maximum rate provided incidental protection, especially when rates were tiered depending on value added in the manufacturing process. In the process, Galt vigorously asserted independent colonial tariff policy. Confederation resulted in the centralization of tariff administration, and rates were set reflecting compromise between the low-tariff Maritimes and high-tariff central Canada. Falling transportation costs made higher maximum revenue-generating levels possible. In the *National Policy tariff of 1879, revenue was of vital importance: that tariff was not purely protectionist.

Customs duties allowed for 19th-century preferential trade policy, as instituted by Britain and modified under pressure from the Canadas. This system, the aftermath of *mercantilism, was largely abandoned by Britain with the repeal of the Corn Laws (1847) and the staggered removal of preferential timber duties. Resurgent British imperialism at the beginning of the 20th century permitted Laurier to favour preferential duties as limited free trade in a National Policy environment; R.B. *Bennett at the Imperial Conference of 1933 pressed for a return to imperial preference. Preferential trade and most-favoured-nation trade structures were also evident elsewhere, especially in the multilateral GATT.

The protectionist function of the tariff was emphasized in the National Policy tariff of 1879, and in later revisions. Rooted in nationalism, and justified on the grounds that it would generate a balanced and integrated national economy (as well as on John Rae's 'infant industry' argument), it remained evident until the aftermath of the Second World War. The National Policy played a central role in elections, particularly those of 1878, 1892, 1896, and 1911. The impact of protectionist customs duties differs by region, and they were sources of regional discontent and protest, both in the Maritimes and in the Canadian West. BEN FORSTER

cycling. Despite there being cycling enthusiasts from coast to coast, Canada has been a minor player in world cycling since the sport was launched in 1865. This is partly due to the Canadian climate, but also because North Americans have been captivated by the automobile and have built cities that, with few exceptions, are not bicycle friendly. Cycling remains somewhat peripheral to mainstream Canadian culture and sport; indeed it is above all an activity for children.

The seminal event in Canadian cycling was the founding of the Montreal Bicycle Club in 1878, with similar clubs formed in many cities in the next two decades. The coordinating organization, the Canadian Wheelmen's Association (now the Canadian Cycling Association), was founded in 1882 in St Thomas, Ontario. Highwheel bicycles and tricycles were quite fashionable in central and eastern Canada in the 1880s, but it was not until the 1890s that the first Canadian bicycle manufacturers were established. Cycling became popular in the mid-1890s among affluent Canadians, with riders venturing into the countryside and to foreign parts. A large number of bicycle-related patents were registered in this decade, most coming from overseas and from Ontario, where the major manufacturers were established. In 1899 the main bicycle manufacturers merged to form the *Canada Cycle and Motor Company (CCM), which still dominates domestic production. There are also a few high-quality artisanal makers of road, recumbent, and mountain bicycles, but the majority of bicycles now sold in Canada are made overseas.

Over the years a number of world-class cyclists have worn the maple leaf, including Archie McEachern, Torchy Peden, Pierre Gachon, Ted Harper, Jocelyn Lovell, Karen Strong, Gord Singleton, and Steve Bauer, but only rarely have Canadian cyclists had a big impact in world competition. Indeed the biggest legacy of Canadian cycling may be the snowmobile, which evolved out of the ice velocipede. GLEN NORCLIFFE

Cypress Hills massacre. In 1873 the Cypress Hills was a place in-between, in a transition from the era of the *fur trade to the new era of settlement and formal law and order—the traders not yet gone, the farmers and Mounties not yet come. The area, 500 sq km of wooded hills and valleys in the midst of far-reaching plains, sits some 65 km from the American border, straddling the Alberta/Saskatchewan boundary. A no-man's land between hostile Plains Cree and Blackfoot and therefore rich in game, it was always a dangerous resort for unwary travellers. Only *Metis hivernants (winterers) had established a semi permanent settlement. In 1870, on Battle Creek, two forts, Farwell and Soloman, were constructed by whisky sellers from Fort Benton, Montana. Such trade was illegal but there was no Canadian authority to enforce the law, and the traders, being on Canadian soil, were beyond the reach of American lawmen. On 1 June 1873 an attack on the camp of visiting Assiniboine led by Little Soldier was carried out by some of the traders. The immediate cause was a 'stolen' horse, which had actually wandered off and was found before the violence began. The fight, fuelled by alcohol, was dreadfully one-sided: the whites had repeating rifles, the Indians bows and old muskets. Forty lodges were burnt, bodies mutilated, and women held prisoner and raped. Perhaps a score of Assiniboine, including Little Soldier, were killed; one American died.

Subsequent American investigations concluded that while there was evidence of wrong-doing, the deed had taken place outside their jurisdiction. A subsequent extradition hearing, forced by the Mounties, who arrested five of the culprits in Fort Benton, resulted in the prisoners being set free. The Mounties had no greater luck when three others, captured in Canada, were brought before a court in Winnipeg in 1876. These men too were set free; the prosecution's evidence, the court determined, did not prove that these three had actually committed murder.

For the Canadian government and the *North-West Mounted Police the massacre was a nightmarish vision of what the West could become. The Mounties worked hard, and for the most part successfully, to win the trust of the *Plains tribes and thus prevented frontier violence of the sort that would trouble the American West for the next two decades. JOHN S. MILLOY

Dafoe, John Wesley (1866–1944). As editor of the Manitoba (later Winnipeg) *Free Press* from 1901, Dafoe established himself as one of the great editors of his age. Ideologically he was a liberal, and politically an independent Liberal. An admirer of Wilfrid *Laurier's masterful skills at brokering 'sunny' political compromises, he reluctantly broke with him over conscription in 1917. Dafoe's support for Laurier's successor, Mackenzie *King, was never automatic. A committed nationalist, Dafoe tirelessly advocated Canadian autonomy and full participation in collective security through the *League of Nations. A principled but lonely stand against appeasement during the 1938 Munich crisis ultimately earned him lasting respect among Canadian internationalists. Despite aspiring to be the west's voice, Dafoe was increasingly out of touch with the populist and collectivist leanings of prairie farmers. The region's gradual economic decline also undermined his national influence. Service on the Royal Commission on Dominion–Provincial Relations (*Rowell-Sirois, 1937–40) opened his eyes to grim Depression conditions and, reluctantly, the lifelong economic liberal embraced the need for a modest social *welfare state. Dafoe's commitment to journalistic independence and professionalism and his mentoring of a brilliant generation of newspapermen, including George Ferguson, Grant Dexter, and Bruce Hutchison, are his most lasting contributions. PATRICK H. BRENNAN

Dalhousie, George Ramsay, 9th Earl of (1770–1838), soldier, administrator. Although a Scottish peer, Dalhousie was compelled by money problems to pursue a career in the British army, followed by service in colonial administration. Appointed lieutenant-governor of Nova Scotia in 1816, he faced major challenges spawned by post-war recession and massive immigration from the British Isles. Among his early reforms was establishment of an interdenominational college (eventually Dalhousie University) in Halifax, an institution designed to foster enlightenment among colonial leaders. Promoted to the rank of governor general in 1820, Dalhousie moved to Quebec City, where he encountered a maelstrom of problems, highlighted by an escalating conflict between an assembly controlled by French Canadians and an administration dominated by English Canadians. Issues of language and religion, combined with the competing demands of trade and agriculture, might have overwhelmed anyone, but Dalhousie's rigid and elitist personality made him particularly prone to failure. In 1828 the London government transferred him to a military command in India. Well-meaning and energetic, Dalhousie lacked the political skills needed to cope with the challenges of an increasingly volatile British North America. D.A. SUTHERLAND

dance. Dance may broadly be described as a human behaviour characterized by rhythmic movement of the body, a seemingly instinctive response to such natural rhythms as the cycle of day and night and the continuous beat of the human heart. Dance arose from the same impulses that gave birth to *music; while dance is often, although not invariably, accompanied by music, it is unclear which came first.

People have danced for varied reasons: as a form of religious devotion or invocation, as a recreational diversion, as a mating ritual, as entertainment, as a pleasing form of exercise, as physical or psychological therapy, or simply to express something that cannot find voice in words. It is probable that as long as people have inhabited the land we now call Canada, there has been dance. Today, however, under the impact of centuries of colonization and immigration, Canada's indigenous peoples have retained but a tenuous hold on their once rich, mostly ritualistic and sacred dance heritage.

The modern history of dance in Canada begins with the implanting of European culture from the 16th century onward. The French, and later the British, brought with them their own social dances. Despite the presence from the mid-18th century of local dancing teachers in Canada's principal colonial settlements, theatrical presentations of dance were generally imported. Dance as performance emerged when particular sequences of movement became either too complex for everyone to learn or were reserved for a privileged few. It then became customary for some to dance and others to watch. In Europe, where by the 18th century dance had largely relinquished its religious and ritual functions and evolved into a form of entertainment, a further distinction arose between professional theatrical dance and dance in all its other manifestations. It is a distinction that persists and is fully reflected in the way dance has evolved in Canada.

In both its professional/theatrical and social/folkloric dimensions, dance in Canada has reflected or responded to the traditions of the country's immigrant cultures. Although born in the courts of Renaissance Italy, classical ballet as we know it took shape in France and quickly became popular across Europe. It was thus natural for Canada's French settlers to enjoy ballet. There are isolated instances of rudimentary performances occurring in New France during the 17th century and, as the art itself became more sophisticated and technically evolved, performances by itinerant troupes of dancers became popular. Louis Renault, with a studio in Montreal from 1737 to 1749, was among the first-known ballet teachers in Canada. In a 1749 letter from Montreal, Elizabeth Bégon, an aristocratic French woman, noted the enormous local enthusiasm for dancing. She further observed that it continued unabated in the face of serious opposition from the clergy, an opposition that was to endure in French Canada until the *Quiet Revolution of the 1960s.

The British Conquest of 1760 had little impact on the popularity of dance. John Durang, a versatile entertainer widely credited as America's first professional dancer, appeared with a circus troupe in Montreal and Quebec City during the winter of 1797–8. Writing in the early 1800s, the Englishman George Heriot observed: 'The whole of the Canadian inhabitants are remarkably fond of dancing.' In 1816, a performance of *La fille mal gardée,* created in Bordeaux in 1789 and still one of ballet's most enduringly popular comic creations, was given in Quebec City. Celeste Keppler, a famous French dancer, made several Canadian appearances during the 1820s and 1830s.

A pattern was established. Canada's increasingly diverse population amused itself with the social dances it had packed in its cultural baggage but was generally content to hire its professional dance entertainment from abroad. With its close proximity to the United States, Canada became an integral part of the North American touring circuit for companies such as impresario Serge Diaghilev's Ballet Russe and its various successor troupes. During the first half of the 20th century, audiences had the opportunity to see celebrated Russian ballet stars such as Anna Pavlova, Vaslav Nijinsky, Leonide Massine, and Alexandra Danilova. There were also visits by Loie Fuller, Ruth St Denis, Doris Humphrey, and Martha Graham, all pioneering exponents of the new 'modern dance'—or 'barefoot ballet', as it was disparagingly dubbed by traditionalists.

Meanwhile, the foundations of Canadian professional dance were slowly being laid by a number of gifted immigrant ballet teachers, notably Americans June Roper in Vancouver and Gwendolyn Osborne in Ottawa and the Russian émigré Boris Volkoff in Toronto. Volkoff arrived in Toronto in 1929 and initially staged dance numbers to be performed between movies at the Uptown Theatre. He soon opened his own studio and in 1936 adventurously took a group of young dancers to the Internationale Tanzwettspiele of the Berlin Olympics. In 1939, the Volkoff Canadian Ballet made its formal debut, vying for the title of first Canadian ballet company with a little group in Winnipeg established almost at the same time by recent English immigrants Gweneth Lloyd and Betty Farrally.

Both companies, professional in ambition but essentially still amateur, struggled to stay afloat through the war years but in 1948 came together in Winnipeg, along with Polish-German immigrant Ruth Sorel's modern troupe from Montreal, for the first in a series of six annual, catalytic national ballet festivals. The second, held in Toronto, combined with a stimulating visit by the British Sadler's Wells Ballet to spur a local group of ballet lovers to dream of a 'national' company. The group invited English dancer/choreographer Celia Franca to Toronto. It was Franca's artistic leadership that brought the dream to fruition. Her soi-disant Canadian National Ballet, soon renamed the National Ballet of Canada, made its debut in November 1951, much to the consternation of the Winnipeg (since 1953 Royal Winnipeg) Ballet, which, having turned fully professional in 1949, regarded itself as Canada's premier troupe. In 1952, dancer Ludmilla Chiriaeff, born to a Russian family in Latvia but raised in Berlin, settled in Montreal and soon found work choreographing for television. Les Ballets Chiriaeff made its public stage debut in 1955 and in 1958 was professionally reconstituted as Les Grands Ballets Canadiens.

These three large ballet companies, in Winnipeg, Toronto, and Montreal, still constitute the bedrock of Canadian professional dance upon which, with crucial funding from the Canada Council for the Arts, a now diverse professional dance culture was built. By the 1960s professional ballet had been supplemented by the emergence of modern troupes such as Montreal's Le Groupe de la Place Royale, Winnipeg's Contemporary Dancers, and the Toronto Dance Theatre. Like the big ballet companies, each also assumed an educational function and together contributed to a remarkable flowering of dance in Canada that coincided with an intense period of international interest in the art of dance, the so-called Dance Boom. From 1970 on, dance departments began to emerge in a number of Canadian universities, bolstering performance training with studies in dance composition, history, theory, criticism, therapy, and anthropology.

Canadian dance artists no longer had to pursue professional careers abroad. The nation earned a respected place on the international dance scene as its companies toured the world. The trail-blazing Royal Winnipeg Ballet, under its visionary director, Arnold Spohr, danced in London in 1965 and in Paris, then in Leningrad and Moscow in 1968. Canada's choreographers became noted for their often innovative ideas. As early as the mid-1960s Brian Macdonald was winning international awards and commissions, and today James Kudelka is one of the most acclaimed choreographers of his generation. Through the 1970s and 1980s, Canadian dancers such as Karen Kain, Veronica Tennant, Frank Augustyn, and Evelyn Hart, all trained at home, became internationally acclaimed ballet stars.

The modern dance scene, especially in Montreal, a city hospitable to the avant-garde, has also flourished; leading choreographers such as Marie Chouinard, Ginette Laurin, and Edouard Lock are internationally renowned, as is the great solo dancer Margie Gillis, often described as Canada's Isadora Duncan.

Although, by the early 21st century, funding problems and shifting audience preferences had dampened the growth of professional Canadian dance, the nation's dance culture had become creatively richer with the emergence and growing acceptance of dance traditions beyond the European and North American mainstream. Ukrainian, South Asian, and Afro-Caribbean dance, Spanish flamenco, and even Arab belly-dancing, have all asserted a place on the national scene. This cultural diversification has been accompanied by a growing trend among dance artists to work independently, beyond the boundaries and burdens of established companies. This new breed has grown impatient with traditional aesthetic distinctions and delves freely into a pool of creative possibilities, cross-pollinating with all types of dance, from jazz to Asian, and working collaboratively with experimental musicians, filmmakers, and designers. The resulting Canadian dance scene is truly a mosaic, the cumulative legatee of centuries of cultural importation, adaptation, and assimilation. If it has not bred anything that can truly be described as a national style, in its variety and openness to new ideas it is as vibrant and vital as any in the world. MICHAEL F. CRABB

Darwinism. From the mid-1800s, British scientist Charles Darwin rocked both the scientific and religious worlds with his writings. Although he was not the first scientist to suggest that various species existed because of evolution rather than the divine creation recounted in the Bible, he was the first to live and write in a period when the idea of evolution appeared reasonable, even irrefutable, to a large segment of the scientific establishment. In an age of scientific advance and concomitant industrial progress, scientists increasingly came to accept materialist explanations that accorded with their own experiments and studies. Rationalist Enlightenment thinking often coexisted uncomfortably with the idealist Biblical certitudes of the Christian churches. Darwin's *On the Origin of Species* (1859) offered sufficient proof to many scientists that species evolved one from the other, with some disappearing altogether as a result of natural selection, or survival of the fittest.

While many Canadian scientists accepted the findings of Darwin's massive tome, others—led by Sir John William Dawson, internationally renowned expert in geology and principal of McGill University—rejected Darwin's methodology and conclusions. Dawson argued that Darwin had failed to demonstrate empirically the actual mutation of one species into another. Holding out Francis Bacon's empiricism as the only valid scientific method, Dawson claimed that Darwin's theory was not scientific at all. But Dawson was a devout Protestant whose overriding objection to the theory of evolution was its rejection of the Old Testament story of creation and thus the foundations of the Judeo-Christian tradition. Sceptical scientists noted that creationism, even more than evolution, could not be tested by empirical methods, and that scientific discoveries of the fossil record in the 19th century, including Dawson's own work, made highly unlikely the compressed history of the world recounted in the Bible. Dawson responded that the 'days' described in Genesis were not 24-hour days but represented long eras.

With the release of *The Descent of Man* (1871), Darwinian science went a step further in undercutting long-accepted truths in the Christian world. Here Darwin suggested boldly that humans were also a product of evolution—indeed, they were scarcely more advanced than apes in their basic physical and mental structures.

Although the churches had initially denounced Darwinism as a fantastic apostasy, by the 1870s many church leaders had joined with scientists in an attempt to wed the theory of evolution to creationist thought. Rev. E.H. Dewart, the conservative editor of the *Christian Guardian*, house organ of the Methodist Church, argued that evolution was simply an example of God's plan at work in the universe and was not at odds with creation. But Christian doctrines and notions such as natural selection did not sit together easily in an age when an increasing number of Canadians, like residents of other industrializing countries, had become quite sceptical of theories that required faith rather than reasoned argument to make their case. Although it was not universally accepted, there is little doubt that Darwinian thought contributed to greater *secularism within society and to a greater willingness in the churches to entertain the possibility that everything in the Bible could not be taken at face value.

As Canadians struggled with the impact of Darwin's science on their religious views, they wondered what human societies might learn from Darwin's notion of evolution. Were there principles that should be followed in the organization of public life to ensure the better development of the species? Notions of 'social Darwinism', used to justify the domination of certain categories of people over others, conflicted with Darwin's arguments in several ways. Darwin had simply described how species adapted or failed to adapt to their environments over time. He did not present evolution as progressive or as the product of conscious interventions by particular species to gain mastery. Much less did his evidence suggest that some members of a species—a group of humans of a particular colour or resident in a particular area, for example—might advance the species by oppressing or destroying its other members. ALVIN FINKEL

Davies, William Robertson (1913–95). Born in Thamesville, Ontario, Davies was educated at Upper Canada College, Queen's University, and Balliol College, Oxford. In 1940 he returned to Canada, where he became owner and editor of the *Peterborough Examiner*. A theatre enthusiast, his literary career began with writing and directing plays, *At My Heart's Core* (1950) perhaps the best known. His weekly columns of wit and salty commentary were later published under his pseudonym, Samuel Marchbanks. A first group of three novels, *Tempest-Tost*, *Leaven of Malice*, and *A Mixture of Frailties*, all published in the 1950s, were set in the fictional university town of Salterton. In the 1970s, *Fifth Business*, *The Manticore*, and *World of Wonders* appeared, set in the small town of Deptford. Widely read and internationally known, this second group mirrored Davies's interest in Jungian psychology and magic. In 1990 Davies wrote: 'I see Canada as a country torn between a very northern, rather extraordinary, mystical spirit which it fears and its desire to present itself to the world as a Scotch banker'. He became the first master of Massey College, University of Toronto, in 1963, retiring in 1981. CLARA THOMAS

Dawson, George Mercer (1849–1901), geologist, paleontologist, anthropologist. Born in Pictou, Nova Scotia, son of John William *Dawson and Margaret Mercer, Dawson moved to Montreal when his father became principal of McGill College in 1855. Tuberculosis of the spine confined him largely to home schooling before he attended McGill (1868) and London's Royal School of Mines (1869–72). Dawson's report for the International Boundary Survey (1875) remains a classic in Canadian geology. As field geologist for the *Geological Survey of Canada, he extended broad powers of systematic reconnaissance to the Northwest, where vast mineral wealth, complex evidences of glaciation and metamorphism, impressive Native cultures, and magnificent fossil remains of *dinosaurs all caught his discerning eye. The GSC's assistant director from 1883, Dawson succeeded A.R.C. Selwyn as director in 1895. Many international honours recognized a remarkably accomplished career cut short when bronchitis attacked chronically weakened lungs further damaged by Dawson's lifelong chain-smoking. He died in Ottawa, unmarried. SUZANNE ZELLER

Dawson, Sir John William (1820–99), geologist, paleontologist, educator. Dawson imbibed Scottish culture in Pictou, Nova Scotia, where his father was an immigrant merchant and bookseller. An evangelical Presbyterian, Dawson attended Rev. Thomas *McCulloch's Pictou Academy. He then pursued *natural history, especially geology, at the University of Edinburgh, 1840–1, as Charles Lyell's *Principles of Geology* (1830–3) reshaped that science. After Dawson guided Lyell through Nova Scotia's great coalbeds (1842), Lyell became his lifelong mentor.

Dawson's scientific forte remained paleontology. With Lyell he discovered (1852) the earliest reptilian remains then known in North America. Dawson pioneered in paleobotanical researches on the Carboniferous and Devonian periods, with landmark publications illuminating the earth's climatological history. After 1859 his rejection of Charles Darwin's theory of evolution led him to prejudge the infamous *Eozoon canadense* as fossil evidence of 'the dawn of life on earth'. He remained outspoken regarding species as divine creations even while his son, George Mercer *Dawson, became a prize student of T.H. Huxley, 'Darwin's bulldog'.

Dawson contributed immeasurably to science education in Canada: as instructor at the Pictou Academy and Dalhousie College (1848–50); Nova Scotia's superintendent of education (1850); and principal and professor at McGill College, Montreal, from 1855. In 1857 and 1882 he lured to Montreal the annual meetings of the American Association for the Advancement of Science, a feat he repeated with its British counterpart in 1884. In 1871 he founded McGill's department of applied science, garnering the college's enormous private endowments from Montreal's business community. In 1881 he won the Geological Society of London's Lyell Medal, was founding president of the *Royal Society of Canada in 1882, and in 1893 was Geological Society of America president. Dawson published some 350 scientific books and articles, more than half on paleontology, in which his work retains much value. SUZANNE ZELLER

Dawson, Robert MacGregor (1895–1958). Dawson is known to generations of political science undergraduates as the author of *The Government of Canada* (five editions, 1947–70). The durability of the text, revised in the fourth and fifth editions by Norman Ward, was due to its clear and authoritative account of the development of the Canadian political system. Institutional in approach and unabashedly centralist in bias, the book eventually had its dominance shaken by methodological innovation and regionalism.

Born to an established mercantile family of Liberal conviction at Bridgewater, Nova Scotia, Dawson was educated at Dalhousie, Harvard, and London, and taught at various institutions across Canada and the United States before settling in the Department of Political Science at the University of Toronto in 1937. He produced a succession of acclaimed volumes, twice winning the Governor General's Award for non-fiction, for *The Government of Canada* and *Democratic Government in Canada* (1949). Although he was commissioned to write the official biography of W.L. Mackenzie *King, only the first volume was completed at his death. Openly Liberal in sentiment and reticent regarding King's personal eccentricities, it highlights both the strengths and weaknesses of Dawson's scholarship. M. BROOK TAYLOR

Dawson City was the service and supply centre for the *Klondike gold rush. In June 1896 the site was home to the Han First Nation, who used it as a seasonal fishing camp. By September it was populated by about 450 non-Native miners, saloon keepers, gamblers, dance-hall performers, and prostitutes. Joseph Ladue and Arthur Harper laid out the townsite on the mud flat at the confluence of the Yukon and Klondike Rivers. Before winter set in, they had sold several hundred lots and set up their own sawmill, saloon, and trading post. As news of the lucrative gold strikes spread southward, Dawson grew, peaking in the summer of 1898 at over 30,000 people, making it the largest city in western Canada for a short time. Within two years of its founding, the town boasted a judicial system, two schools, a library, over a dozen churches, and nearly 100 saloons. Dawson was also established in 1898 as the capital of the new *Yukon Territory, with a commissioner and a six-member council, all appointed by the government in Ottawa. The first wholly elected Yukon council met in 1909. As the gold rush waned, Dawson's population shrank to about 8,000 people by 1904. Since 1844, the *Yukon River had been the main transportation corridor in and out of Dawson, and thus the community was nearly cut off from the outside world from October to June while the river was frozen. Both world wars further drained the community. After the US military constructed the *Alaska Highway during the Second World War, the focus of Yukon commerce, transportation, and social life shifted south to Whitehorse, and in 1950 the federal government transferred the capital there. Today Dawson City maintains a year-round population of approximately 2,000. CHARLENE PORSILD

Dawson Road. A trail about 115 km long from Lake of the Woods to Winnipeg, part of the Dawson Route from Thunder Bay to the forks of the Red and Assiniboine Rivers surveyed by Simon J. Dawson for the government of the Province of Canada in 1858. Construction on the road began in 1868 under the supervision of John Snow; one of the early workers was Thomas Scott, who soon led a protest against working conditions. This construction was supposed to provide employment for Red River residents in a year of devastating famine, but most settlers of Red River, including Louis *Riel, saw the road as an effort by Canada to jump the gun on its takeover of Red River before consultation with the inhabitants. The road was not employed by the *Wolseley expedition in 1870, but was used in 1871 by a second contingent of Canadian volunteers headed to garrison the new province of Manitoba. Most traffic preferred alternate routes through the United States from the mid-1870s. The road is at present posted as a Manitoba heritage site. J.M. BUMSTED

Days of Action, a series of public protests organized in Ontario cities in 1995–8. When that province's new Conservative government cut taxes, social spending, the civil service, and regulatory legislation, the Ontario Federation of Labour pulled together a coalition of unions and community organizations to plan city-by-city general strikes and demonstrations. The first, in London on 11 December 1995, was followed by others in Hamilton, Kitchener-Waterloo, Peterborough, Toronto, Sudbury, Thunder Bay, North Bay, Windsor, St Catharines, and Kingston. Each brought together unionized workers, including teachers and other public sector workers, with environmentalists, feminists, seniors, students, and others affected by the government's policies. Busloads of other workers and supporters arrived from other cities. The turnouts reached massive proportions never before seen in most of these cities, notably some 100,000 marchers in Hamilton and 250,000 in Toronto. The parades featured colourful banners, costumes, puppets, and music, and converged on angry rallies. No specific political agenda united all these protests. The OFL initially resolved to call a province-wide general strike, but ultimately turned back to electoral politics instead. Despite this massive groundswell of public dissatisfaction with its policies, the Conservatives were re-elected in 1999. CRAIG HERON

death and dying. Because attitudes and rituals surrounding death and dying are connected to cultural norms, they are subject to change over time and to variations in ethnicity and religion. In the early 19th century, Christians in Canada believed death was providential: a judgmental God meted out painful or premature deaths as divine punishment. Infant diseases as well as *smallpox and *cholera and complications surrounding childbirth were responsible for high mortality rates. Rituals reflected fear and superstition. The revelry surrounding the Irish wake was designed to ensure that the dead were not angered by too much grief. Graveyards were dark and macabre places that no one wanted to visit lest the 'grim reaper' grab them.

By mid-century a more naturalistic understanding of death and disease was emerging. Death was not necessarily regarded as a reflection of God's wrath but as the result of natural forces. Moreover, with the rise of scientific medicine people thought that the process of dying could be controlled. Physicians joined the clergy in the death chamber, attempting either to forestall death or take away the pain through drugs such as morphine. Death was supposed to be 'beautiful', a release from the sinful world to a better place. This romantic view robbed death of much of its dread and horror. Death was also removed from the family and the home. Funeral directors, undertakers, and cemetery keepers assumed control of the corpse, ensuring that, if death were not beautiful, it was at least no longer horrifying. Dead bodies rested in funeral parlours. Undertakers introduced methods of embalming to delay decay. Funeral processions became displays of family status. Services could be ornate affairs, with corpses resting in expensive caskets. The pastoral yet neatly landscaped settings of cemeteries reminded mourners that there was regeneration in death.

Since the middle of the 19th century, the trend has been towards a virtual denial of death—the 'death of death'. Greater life expectancy and the conquest of numerous contagious diseases have provided a material basis for this optimism. Death could be relegated to the background of life. Mourning has also become a much less drawn out and public event. Until late in the century, women who lost their husbands wore widow's weeds for two years and circumscribed their behaviour during this mourning period. This began to change as women became less confined to the 'private sphere'. Moreover, during the First World War widows in black were depressing reminders of the deaths of young soldiers and a terrible blow to morale.

The Great War contributed to another trend—that of public memorialization. Monuments to dead soldiers ennobled their lives and celebrated their sacrifice. More general remembrance of those who died became typical of popular culture. Funeral orations were no longer occasions to warn the sinful about imminent doom but opportunities to celebrate someone's life. Numerous methods of remembering were introduced, including gravestones with messages, long obituaries in newspapers, and memorial services.

In the 20th century the denial of death continued in popular culture. Dying was taken out of the home and placed in the hospital, where it became highly medicalized and sanitized but also removed from people's view. Similarly, the modern funeral is deeply private, not a public affair. The exception is the death of someone who has touched a cultural nerve. Most commentators were surprised at the sense of loss when Pierre Elliott *Trudeau died in the autumn of 2000. That the nation came to a virtual halt from the shocking announcement of his death until the final service televised from Montreal was striking because it seemed at variance with the contemporary denial of death and the weakening of public ritual surrounding it. DAVID B. MARSHALL

death penalty. *See* CAPITAL PUNISHMENT.

Déclin de l'empire américain, Le. No other fiction film of the 1980s captured the ethos of post-referendum Quebec as accurately (and as entertainingly) as Denys Arcand's *Le Déclin de l'empire américain* (1986). The film's narrative is deceptively simple: a group of thirty-somethings, most of them history professors, spend a leisurely afternoon together. Men are cooking supper while women are working out at the gym; they all chat about their various sexual experiences. These financially successful, cosmopolitan academics enjoy a degree of material comfort, international sophistication, and self-confidence unknown to previous generations of Quebeckers. They are the beneficiaries of several years of cultural, social, and economic progress propelled in great part by nationalist fervour. However, the characters also attest to the failure of nationalist ideology. In a nation where the motto is *'Je me souviens', these historians use their education and wealth for the sole purpose of attaining personal gratification. This shift from the political to the personal is not limited to Quebec in the 1980s. In fact, one of the characters notices this change in all societies affected by the decline of the American Empire. However, as Arcand had already observed in his 1981 documentary, *Le Confort et l'indifférence*, the failure of the first referendum on sovereignty made the rejection of political commitment and the celebration of hedonistic individualism more glaring in Quebec than elsewhere in North America.

ANDRÉ LOISELLE

De Cosmos, Amor (1825–97), journalist, BC premier 1872–4. De Cosmos migrated in 1852 from his native Nova Scotia to the gold fields of California, where he worked as a photographer. Once there he changed his name from William Alexander Smith to Amor De Cosmos because, he said, it symbolized his 'Love of order, beauty, the world, the universe'. After moving to Victoria in 1858, he founded the *British Colonist*, editing it for five years before he began a 19-year career as an elected representative at the colonial, provincial, and national levels. As editor of the *Colonist* De Cosmos quickly established his credentials as a 'friend of reform' by attacking the oligarchic administration of Governor James *Douglas and his supporters among the elite of educated English civil servants and retired Hudson's Bay Company officers whom he dubbed the 'family-company compact'. As a mid-Victorian liberal De Cosmos challenged privilege, defended private property, celebrated railways and 'progress', and above all argued for *responsible government, his principal cause through the 1860s as he came to embrace British Columbia's inclusion 'on fair and equitable terms' in Confederation, achieved in 1871. Thereafter his work as a legislator, marked by an unsuccessful attempt to have the Canadian Pacific Railway establish its terminus on Vancouver Island and by racist outbursts against *Chinese immigrants, was less distinguished. Always very eccentric, egotistical, and emotionally unbalanced, the 'father of British Columbia's entry into Confederation' died in a state of 'unsound mind' on 4 July 1897. ROBERT A.J. McDONALD

Defence of Canada Regulations. The outbreak of the First World War caused the government to pass the *War Measures Act, the Canadian counterpart of the British Defence of the Realm Act. The Canadian act gave the federal government remarkable wartime powers, perhaps the greatest of any of the Anglo-American democracies. It also brought much criticism from those who believed the government abused its powers, and in 1919 courts ended the emergency powers the act had granted

The outbreak of the Second World War allowed Mackenzie *King's government to reinstate the act. The Defence of Canada Regulations were developed subsequent to the invoking of the War Measures Act; these regulations essentially passed the authority of government to the war committee of the federal *cabinet. The regulations had enormous influence in limiting free speech, suspending habeas corpus, interning suspicious individuals or groups, and confiscating property. The Canadian Civil Liberties Association developed in the mid-1940s in response to the overuse of the regulations. A meeting between the Toronto Civil Liberties League and Mackenzie King convinced the prime minister that there was danger in many of the uses of the regulations. Some were relaxed, but court judgments after the war upheld decisions made under the act. Opposition to abuse of the regulations planted seeds for the development of the movement to give Canadians a bill of rights.

JOHN ENGLISH

Demasduit, or Mary March (*c.* 1796–1820), a Newfoundland *Beothuk, was captured by settlers in March 1819 at Red Indian Lake, where the Beothuk, reduced to 31 people, were overwintering. Her husband, 'chief' Nonosabasut, and his brother were killed and her baby died shortly afterwards. Demasduit stayed in Twillingate with Rev. John Leigh, who compiled a Beothuk vocabulary. She was later taken to St John's, where Lady Hamilton painted her portrait. Her modesty and intelligence impressed citizens, who hoped she would mediate with her people. But efforts to reunite her with Beothuk on the coast failed, and Capt. David Buchan prepared a winter expedition inland to return her. However, before he could set out Demasduit died from consumption on board HMS *Grasshopper*, at Botwood, on 8 January 1820. Buchan transported her coffin to her former residence and the Beothuk later placed it in Nonosabasut's burial hut. Nonosabasut's niece, *Shanawdithit, illustrated some of these events. INGEBORG C.L. MARSHALL

demobilization. Usually refers to the disbanding of troops at the end of a conflict and the arrangements for their reintegration into the nation from which they were recruited. The term has also been applied to the overall process of converting an economy and society from wartime to peacetime purposes. These objectives and processes were most evident at the end of the two world wars of the 20th century.

The scale, impact, and human cost of Canada's involvement in the Great War was unprecedented in Canadian history, so the end of the war brought new challenges as well. Over 60,000 men had been killed and nearly three times that many wounded, with consequent demands for medical services and pensions for survivors. Beyond those casualties (more than half of those who had fought overseas), others who had enlisted required training and other assistance to re-establish themselves.

The wartime government had planned for orderly demobilization with a scheme that would have gradually released *veterans according to peacetime economic priorities, but that was shelved when soldiers who were kept waiting in England rioted in the spring of 1919. The consequent acceleration of their return to Canada compounded problems derived from an economic slump and inadequate preparation for the abrupt transition to civilian employment. A traditional way of rewarding those who had served their country was through land grants and that method was employed again, with uneven results and incomplete coverage. Considerable attention was paid by the national government to vocational training, but it was underfunded and not always linked to jobs. By international standards, the efforts of the Canadian government may have been generous and successful, but many veterans believed that authorities had not honoured their wartime pledges to provide for soldiers and their families. Economic circumstances, along with uncertainty about the appropriate role of the national government, meant that the transition to a peacetime economy was generally difficult for Canadians. Moreover, much of the onus for the success or failure of demobilization was still placed on individuals, firms, and voluntary organizations.

With the precedent of the previous conflict and its aftermath, the Canadian government was determined to take better care of returning soldiers and their dependants in the Second World War as part of a more comprehensive approach to economic management and social security. It proclaimed its good intentions in the *Veterans Charter, aims that had been backed by legislation, money, and a department of veterans' affairs. Employers were obliged to give jobs back to returning veterans, who were also given preference in hiring for the public service. Various allowances and gratuities, some geared to length of service, provided veterans with help for purchasing civilian clothing, university education or vocational training, housing or land, and other needs associated with their return to post-war Canada. Wounded and disabled veterans were treated more effectively than before as a result of lessons from past administration and advances in medicine.

Generally, the federal government assumed responsibility for the welfare of returning soldiers rather than relying on private charity or individual initiative to overcome the challenges. Political leaders, as well as military and economic planners, in Canada and other allied countries paid greater heed to the need to convert industry from military to civilian requirements even before the war was won. To ease this process of transition and reconstruction, some wartime controls (notably with respect to wages and prices) were kept in place and government expenditures were scaled back less suddenly than after the First World War. In fact, the process of demobilization was made much easier by the strength of the post-war economy.

HECTOR MACKENZIE

democratic socialism. An idea that emerged in the late 19th century, democratic socialism emphasized that legitimate *socialism must be attained through gradual, peaceful, and consensual methods. Canada's several socialisms all spoke of democracy, but this did not make them all democratic socialism. This type of socialism emphasizes parliamentary methods, and was mainly defined in contradistinction to Marxist ideas of change. Marxism, preaching the revolutionary transformation of capitalism, had a small but important following before the First World War. Early Marxists, such as those in the Socialist Party of Canada, did run for legislative office, but only to raise the political consciousness of the workers. The Bolshevik Revolution in 1917 solidified the meaning of Marxian socialism: a vanguard party would bring revolution to the workers. To this end, the Communist International was established in Moscow. The Canadian *Communist Party affiliated with it after 1921.

Another version of socialism—voluntarist, pacifist, and parliamentary—also emerged before 1917. Drawing on the British example of the Labour Party and leaders such as Keir Hardie and Ramsay MacDonald, it was labourist, Fabian, Christian, and parliamentary. In Canada, the personification of this democratic socialism was J.S. *Woodsworth, who was greatly shaped by Christian *pacifism. Change must be non-violent and voluntary to be legitimate; it was to be political and parliamentary. His intellectual course led inevitably to the House of Commons in 1921 and he went on to establish the *Co-operative Commonwealth Federation in 1932–3. Aiming to win power exclusively through the ballot box, the CCF stood firmly for economic planning and *public ownership but through democratic methods. In the 1950s, revisionism within led to social democracy. Here the emphasis was upon government regulation of the functions of private ownership, an idea well expressed in *Reclaiming the Canadian Economy*, edited by Abraham Rotstein (1970). The *New Democratic Party today is properly described as a social-democratic party, although it still includes a few democratic socialists in the tradition of Woodsworth. The *Parti Québécois is a Quebec-based, nationalist version of social democracy. Globalization has led to disenchantment with parliamentary methods. Socialists increasingly turn away from electoral and deliberative techniques in favour of extra-parliamentary ones of mass demonstrations and agitprop. ALLEN MILLS

Denison, Flora MacDonald (1867–1921), née Merrill. A feminist, journalist, and businesswoman, Denison was active in the *women's suffrage movement in Toronto from 1906. Separated from her husband and with a child to support, she ran a successful Toronto dressmaking business and a country hotel at Bon Echo, Ontario, where meals were served on dinnerware that featured suffragist slogans. Her views on religion, marriage, *temperance, *birth control, and social class, expressed through her column in the *Toronto Sunday World*, were more radical than those of most Canadian suffragists. In 1911 she became president of the Canadian Suffrage Association, but was forced to resign in 1914 because of her support for the English militant suffragettes. At the outbreak of the First World War she opposed the conflict; while she did not sustain an unequivocal antiwar position, the war deepened her commitment to thoroughgoing social and spiritual reformation. A lover of the works of American poet Walt Whitman, Denison transformed Bon Echo into a retreat dedicated to Whitmanite ideals.

Most historians have portrayed Canada's first feminist movement as dominated by conservative 'maternal feminists', solidly middle and upper middle class. Denison's public career and personal history demonstrate that there was a more radical side to women's activism in Canada. DEBORAH GORHAM

Denison, George Taylor, III (1839–1925). Immersed in the military traditions of his family, Denison was colonel of the Governor General's Body Guard and served in the *Fenian Raid, 1866, and the *North-West Rebellion, 1885. An original member of *Canada First, he glorified the martial spirit and advocated a force of mounted infantry for the defence of Canada. He gained international acclaim for *A History of Cavalry from the Earliest Times with Lessons for the Future* (1877). For three decades after the mid-1880s Denison was a major figure in the movement for imperial unity, which he identified with his United Empire *Loyalist ancestors and directed against the United States. He had sympathized with the South in the Civil War; he saw the victorious Union as unstable and bent on the annexation of Canada, sometimes, as in 1891 and 1911, aided by treasonous elements within the dominion. Denison specialized in the detection of such conspiracies. From 1877 to 1921 he served as Toronto Police Magistrate: he dispatched cases briskly, once disposing of 250 in 180 minutes. Impetuous, contemptuous of party politicians, impatient of English snobbery towards colonials, and a prickly nationalist, Denison possessed a sense of humour and an ability to laugh at himself. There were many occasions for him to indulge this latter talent. CARL BERGER

Denys, Nicolas (1598–1688), a trader, arrived in Acadia in 1632 with governor Isaac de Razilly, and spent 40 years trying unsuccessfully to develop his fishing interests in the region, notably at Port Rossignol (Liverpool, NS), in Cape Breton Island, and Nepisiguit (Bathurst, NB). Bad economic decisions and rivalry with other traders brought his business enterprises close to bankruptcy; he made several trips to France to obtain help from the Crown and metropolitan associates. In 1653, he received in concession Cape Breton Island and land from Canso to Gaspé but never fulfilled his obligation to bring settlers. Leaving his holdings to his son Richard, he returned in 1670 to France, where he published two years later his *Description and Natural History of the Coasts of North America* as an attempt to draw attention to Acadia, to justify his actions, and as a testimonial to an active life. JEAN DAIGLE

department stores. Department stores emerged in Canada in the 1880s. Toronto had several famous ones, including the T. Eaton Company and the Robert Simpson Company, but most Canadian cities had their own: Ogilvie's and Henry Morgan's in Montreal, Woodward's and David Spencer's in Vancouver, Bartlett's in Windsor. The departmentals emerged at a time when cities were growing and when road resurfacing, better policing, and streetcars were making downtowns safer and more accessible. As a result, middle-class women were more comfortable walking in business districts, and the department stores particularly targeted their custom.

In the late 19th century, when people entered a shop they confronted a counter behind which most of the merchandise was stored. The department store revolutionized shopping by inviting the public to browse at will, to admire the stock, and even to touch it, without a clerk hovering nearby. But this was not the end of the big stores' appeal. What defined a department store was the existence of many different businesses, or departments, under one roof. They were like vast and sumptuous general stores. They also featured the latest technology—elevators, telephones, electric lights—and embodied style and architectural beauty. Not surprisingly, most of their smaller, poorer competitors loathed them.

In their early years the appeal of department stores lay in their splendour and in the freedoms they provided, but those advantages were soon challenged. Smaller competitors copied their methods of advertising and display and, just after the First World War, a new rival, the *chain store, began to undercut them. In the 1920s the departmentals fought back, slashing prices and expanding dramatically by absorbing businesses in smaller centres. Their aggression paid off: by the end of the decade one-seventh of all consumer spending occurred in department stores or through their mail order services; one business, Eaton's, sold almost half that volume. But the huge cost-burden they shouldered in expansion, and the low margins they were forced to accept, hurt them when consumer spending contracted in the 1930s.

Already weakened by the Depression, department stores faced further challenges in the post-war period. The migration of people to the *suburbs, Canadians' growing dependence on cars, and the continuing competition from smaller, cheaper, departmentals like Woolco, K-Mart, and Towers, hurt the downtown stores. By 1960 department stores accounted for just 10 per cent of retail sales. In 1952 the weakest of them, Simpson's, sought new capital in a deal with Sears-Roebuck, which gave the American giant the right to use the Canadian company's name and exclusive control over all stores outside of five cities. Unfortunately for Simpson's, the reality was that retailing was reconcentrating in suburban malls with big parking lots. Only Eaton's partially bucked the trend, building glitzy shopping arcades around most of its downtown stores even as it opened new shops in suburban malls. In the 1970s sales were good, but the department stores had invested heavily in new outlets and they sought ways to control the competition and shore up profits. The most dynamic of the departmentals, the *Hudson's Bay Company, bought out one of its discount rivals, Zeller's, and then acquired control over a struggling Simpson's chain, which had marooned itself in the downtowns of a few big cities. Eaton's did less well; as populations, even in smaller places, continued to abandon their centres, they deserted the company's new shopping arcades. Eschewing aggressive price competition because it could not bear the low margins, the company closed several money-losing stores, but it was already too late: in 1998 the old giant was taken over by Sears, ending, for many, a chapter in Canadian history.

Department stores were the dominant form of retailing in an age of rising incomes, technological revolution, and urbanization. Their adaptation to the post-war era of limited store loyalty, discount shopping, and suburbanization proved painful. But through much of the 20th century they represented economic prosperity, business innovation, and the city centre. They were in many ways worthy symbols of the modern age. DAVID MONOD

deportation. Every country in the world exercises the right to expel immigrants who represent a threat to its national security, with the exercise of this power varying according to prevailing economic, social, and political conditions. In the case of Canada, deportation has long been used as a means of excluding immigrants—paupers, the mentally ill, those afflicted with serious diseases, criminals—who became a drain on public resources or violated the country's laws. During the 20th century, however, exclusion and removal for political or ideological reasons became more pronounced, particularly after the First World War and the Russian Revolution.

In the spring of 1919 the Borden government, in response to the political radicalism and social unrest associated with the *Winnipeg General Strike, enacted two draconian measures. Section 41(12) of the Immigration Act gave authorities the right to detain and summarily deport anyone advocating political revolution; section 98 of the Criminal Code established a list of prohibited activities aimed at communist and anarchist organizations that seemed to threaten Canada's national security. While both of these measures were bitterly criticized by civil liberties groups, they were extensively used by the security agencies during subsequent years, particularly during the 1930s, when fear of communism was widespread. Moreover, when the King government repealed section 98 in 1936, Quebec authorities created their own repressive system against 'dangerous foreigners' with the *Padlock Act.

Although deportation of political radicals, primarily communists, occurred during the Cold War, there were additional rights of appeal, which were eventually embodied in the Immigration Act of 1976. However, after the events of 11 September 2001 the Canadian government has once again made security screening and deportation an integral part of its immigration system, as part of its on-going war against terrorism. In this campaign there has been extensive interaction with American immigration authorities, particularly in dealing with suspected Islamic radicals. DONALD H. AVERY

Derick, Carrie (1862–1941). Colleagues called her mature, brilliant, and intellectually engaged. From her eager beginnings as a schoolteacher in Quebec, she emerged from McGill University with a BA (1890), winning top prizes in classics, zoology, and botany. She widened her knowledge by engaging in summer research projects in Massachusetts and studying at various European universities. An excellent scholar, she completed all the requirements for a PhD but at that time few such degrees were conferred upon women. Personal courage enabled her to speak up for herself, and were it not for her assertiveness at McGill, she might never have been appointed the first woman demonstrator (1882), the first woman full professor (morphological botany in 1912), and the first woman professor emeritus (1929). She pursued genetics before it was popular, gaining international recognition for her work in heredity. Social convictions included writing about science for the general public, lecturing on *eugenics, and supporting women's rights.

E. TINA CROSSFIELD

DesBarres, Joseph Frederick Wallet (1721/2–1824), soldier, surveyor, colonial administrator. Born in Basel, Switzerland, or Paris, DesBarres emigrated to England around 1752 to study military engineering. He became an officer in the Royal Americans, serving at *Louisbourg (1758) and St John's (1762), but it was his surveying skills that caught the attention of his superiors. He was commissioned in 1763 to prepare charts of coastal Nova Scotia, at a time when Samuel Holland was similarly engaged in Prince Edward Island and the Gulf of St Lawrence, and James *Cook in Newfoundland and Labrador. He eventually published *The Atlantic Neptune* in 1777, a navigational atlas primarily of his own charts but also with those of Holland, Cook, and others. Convinced of the potential of the Maritime colonies, he became first a great landowner and then lieutenant-governor of Cape Breton Island (1784), in which capacity he laid out the town and capital of the colony, Sydney. In 1804 he became governor of PEI, where he became embroiled in local politics. DesBarres was irascible and cranky, and throughout his long life he seemingly poured as much energy into personal and public disputes as he had into his greatest achievement, *The Atlantic Neptune*.

OLAF U. JANZEN

Deskaheh, or Levi General (1873–1925). An adherent of the Longhouse religion, General grew up in the non-Christian community on the Six Nations territory on the Grand River in Ontario. His first language was Cayuga. Selected as Deskaheh, one of the traditional *Iroquois Confederacy chiefs, he fought on the traditional council to protect Iroquois rights to self-government. After the federal government sought to replace the council in 1923, Deskaheh went to Geneva to argue before the *League of Nations the Six Nations' right to international recognition as a sovereign state. British objections prevented discussion of the issue. During his absence the federal government deposed the hereditary council and organized an election. Only a small minority of the community voted. The new elected council denied Deskaheh his right to speak for the Six Nations. Disillusioned and in poor health, he returned to North America. He died on the Tuscarora reservation in western New York.

DONALD B. SMITH

Desmond, Viola (1914–65), beautician and anti-racist activist. Desmond was arrested on 8 November 1946 because she was an African Canadian who insisted on sitting in an area reserved for whites in a movie theatre in New Glasgow, Nova Scotia. There were never any laws in Canada that openly enforced racially segregated seating, but the authorities utilized a provincial tax act to accomplish the same goal. Tickets for the main-floor seats reserved for whites cost more than the balcony seats relegated to Blacks, and thus Desmond was one cent short on tax. Charged with retail tax evasion, she spent the night in jail, and was tried, convicted, and fined $20 the next morning. Several efforts to have the conviction overturned before the Nova Scotia Supreme Court failed. As a legal precedent, the case shows Canadian judges at their worst, uniformly prepared to turn their backs on claims for racial equality. However, Desmond's case inspired a groundswell of support within the African-Canadian community that fostered significant further anti-racist activity.

CONSTANCE BACKHOUSE

DEW Line. The Distant Early Warning Line was begun in 1954, during the Cold War, as a series of radar stations along the arctic coast of Alaska and Canada, approximately at the 70th parallel, to give early warning of Soviet aircraft approaching North America over the Pole. Fifty-eight stations of various sizes were built, and the line was operational by 1957. Additional sites were built in the Aleutian Islands and in Greenland. Two backup chains of stations, the Mid-Canada and the Pinetree Lines, were built further south. Although the advent of intercontinental ballistic missiles and spy satellites rendered the DEW Line partly irrelevant, it operated for 30 years, until in 1987 most of it was upgraded and now operates as the North Warning System.

Building the line was a huge project, paid for by the United States, and employing military and civilian personnel from both countries. Although there have been problems with cleaning up the waste left from construction, the DEW Line did provide facilities such as modern landing strips to Tuktoyaktuk and other communities. The implications of having the American military operating in the North alarmed Canadian nationalists of the 1950s and led to a renewed interest in the question of arctic sovereignty.

K.S. COATES AND W.R. MORRISON

diamants du Canada. European navigators in the 16th century wanted to bring back something of value from their voyages, and Jacques *Cartier was no exception. During his exploration of the St Lawrence, Cartier was impressed by the rich fisheries and the agricultural potential of the land but he dreamed of more immediate wealth. During his third expedition to found a colony near Quebec City in 1541, he unearthed what he thought were gold and diamonds near the fort of Charlesbourg Royal. After the winter, he rushed back to France with barrels full of stones.The samples turned out to be iron pyrite and quartz. The episode gave rise to the saying 'false as Canadian diamonds', but also gave the name to the promontory on which Quebec City was founded: Cap aux Diamants.

JOHN A. DICKINSON

Dickins, Clennell Haggerston 'Punch' (1899–1995). A self-styled *'bush pilot', after winning a Distinguished Flying Cross during the First World War Dickins became an original member of the *RCAF in 1924. Leaving in 1927 to join Western Canada Airways, he was the first to fly over and map portions of the Northwest Territories, to deliver furs by air from northern trappers to traders in Winnipeg, to fly from Edmonton to Aklavik on the Arctic Ocean, and to fly the first prospectors to Great Bear Lake. In 1936 he was awarded an OBE. The same year, Dickins became general superintendent of Canadian Airways, which had taken over Western Canada Airways six years earlier. During the Second World War he oversaw six *British Commonwealth Air Training Plan schools and managed the Atlantic Ferry Organization for the CPR until it was militarized by the RAF as *Ferry Command. In 1947 Dickins joined de Havilland Aircraft as a director and vice-president, building a strong sales department to sell the company's new bush plane, the 'Beaver'.

CARL A. CHRISTIE

Diefenbaker, John G. (1895–1979), prime minister 1957–63. This prairie populist with a fire-breathing preacher's voice made his early reputation as a criminal lawyer and oft-defeated candidate in Saskatchewan. Diefenbaker was finally elected to Parliament in 1940 and re-elected 12 times thereafter. He established himself as a witty and coruscating front-bencher for the opposition Conservatives, an advocate of the *welfare state, minority rights, and western farmers. He sought the party leadership in 1942 and 1948 before winning it in 1956. In the 1957 election he won a minority victory against the burned-out Liberals; nine months later he won the largest majority in Canadian history after promoting his 'vision of northern development' and his belief in 'unhyphenated Canadianism'.

Diefenbaker's first 18 months in office were triumphant. The *Progressive Conservative Party grew from an Ontario rump to a reformist national party representative of all regions and elements, and progressive welfare and regional policies gave hope to the dispossessed. Diefenbaker appointed Canada's first woman cabinet minister and first Aboriginal senator, extended voting rights to Native peoples, made major wheat sales to China, and in August 1960 celebrated adoption of a Canadian bill of rights. After 1959 the government's confidence was sapped by economic recession, cabinet incompetence, and confusion in defence policy. As a dedicated Cold Warrior, Diefenbaker took Canada into a joint defence system with the United States, cancelled a costly Canadian fighter aircraft, and contracted with Washington to accept nuclear weapons. Sensing growing popular alarm over atomic war, he delayed their installation. When John Kennedy succeeded Dwight D. Eisenhower as American president in 1961, American patience faded. By the 1962 election, Conservative support was withering, but Diefenbaker retained minority power. Troubled and indecisive, he publicly hesitated in supporting the Americans during the *Cuban missile crisis, acted erratically while his cabinet splintered, was defeated in the House, and lost the 1963 election to Lester B. *Pearson's Liberals. Pearson accepted delivery of atomic weapons from the United States as promised during the campaign.

For four years Diefenbaker battled the government and his own party as opposition leader. In 1965 he held the Liberals to a second minority; in 1967 he was deposed by his own party. He remained in Parliament as a nettlesome front-bencher, brows arched, finger pointed menacingly at his foes, voice booming with sarcasm and disdain, a legendary relic revered for his courage and hated for his destructiveness. He died shortly after his 13th electoral victory, and was buried in Saskatoon after a memorial train journey from Ottawa that saw 'the population of farms, villages, and towns spread out in quiet honour along the right of way, waving, smiling, crying, saying goodbye for the last time in what had become a long festival of national communion.' DENIS SMITH

Dieppe. On the morning of 19 August 1942, two brigades of 2 Canadian Infantry Division under Maj.-Gen. Hamilton Roberts landed near the French town of Dieppe. The operation was conceived amidst Allied debates about how a 'second front' might be created in Europe. Combined Operations Headquarters planned to raid the port with flanking attacks and an aerial bombardment before tanks would support an assault on the main beach. Anxious for action, the Canadians accepted the plan in April 1942. Bad weather forced the cancellation of the original operation, codenamed 'Rutter', in early July. For reasons that remain controversial, the raid was revived (codenamed 'Jubilee') but with no aerial bombardment beforehand. The key to success was to be surprise.

Little went as planned. A German convoy dispersed the flotilla that was to land east of Dieppe. Most of No. 3 (British) Commando could not attack the coastal battery near Berneval-le-Grand. Of the 554 men from the Royal Regiment of Canada who left England to land at the narrow beach at Puys, 227 were killed or later died of wounds. To the west of Dieppe, No. 4 (British) Commando destroyed the coastal gun at Varengeville, but the South Saskatchewan Regiment and the Cameron Highlanders of Canada suffered heavily at Pourville and could not secure the heights overlooking Dieppe. With surprise lost and the flanks open, the main beach became a killing ground for the Royal Hamilton Light Infantry, the Calgary Tank Regiment, the Essex Scottish Regiment of Canada, and Les Fusiliers Mont-Royal. Only scattered parties fought past the sea wall and into the town itself.

Of the 4,963 men of Canadian units who took part, only 2,210 returned to England: 907 were killed or died in captivity; another 586 were wounded, and 1,874 became prisoners. 19 August 1942 was the costliest day for Canadian arms in the Second World War.

GEOFFREY HAYES

dinosaurs. The first dinosaur bones in Canada were reported from southern Saskatchewan in 1874. By 1910, the rich dinosaur beds of Alberta were being worked by the American Museum of Natural History (New York), sparking what became known as the Great Canadian Dinosaur Rush. By the time this flourish of activity ended in the mid-1920s, well over 400 dinosaur skeletons had been collected along the Red Deer River. These reside today in more than 35 museums around the world. A second burst of collecting activity coincided with a worldwide renaissance of interest in dinosaurs in the 1970s, and continues to this day. Most Canadian specimens are now excavated by the Royal Tyrrell Museum of Palaeontology in Drumheller. The Alberta specimens are usually from Upper Cretaceous rocks that are 65 to 80 million years old. Dinosaur Provincial Park, in Alberta, is one of the richest dinosaur sites in the world in terms of numbers of specimens found and diversity of species, and was designated as a UNESCO World Heritage Site in 1979. More than 37 species of dinosaurs, and almost 100 species of other vertebrates (from fish to mammals) that lived with the dinosaurs, are recognized from this one location. The exposures along the Red Deer River upstream from the park preserve successively younger dinosaur faunas, leading up to their extinction 65 million years ago. The last Canadian dinosaurs included the famous *Tyrannosaurus rex*, which has also been recovered close to Eastend, Saskatchewan. Dinosaur eggs and embryos were identified in 1977 at Devil's Coulee Provincial Historic

Site, southeast of Lethbridge. More than 30 sites with 100-million-year-old dinosaur footprints have been found in the foothills east of the Rockies in Alberta and in British Columbia. Other Late Cretaceous dinosaurs are known from Vancouver Island in the west to Ellesmere Island in the north, and Early Jurassic dinosaurs are collected near Parrsboro, Nova Scotia.

PHILIP J. CURRIE

Dionne Quintuplets. On 28 May 1934, Annette, Émilie, Yvonne, Cécile, and Marie, the world's first long-surviving quintuplets, were born in Corbeil, Ontario, to poor French-Canadian Catholic farmers, Oliva and Elzire Dionne. Instantly famous, they were quickly removed by the Liberal government of Mitch *Hepburn, who spotted a distraction from the problems of the *Great Depression and a source of tourist dollars. Separated from siblings and parents, the girls initially appeared to thrive in a special hospital supervised by Dr Allan Roy Dafoe, who had delivered them. As toddlers, they moved to a compound known as Quintland, where close inspection continued under public gaze. Thousands of North Americans visited, bought souvenirs, and adored the little girls, who helped them forget bad times. Featured in newsreels, talk shows, and Hollywood films, the Dionnes became symbols of what modernization promised poor children.

Their experiences represented an experiment in pediatrics that involved the nation's child-rearing experts, including Dr William *Blatz, a psychologist from the University of Toronto's Institute for Child Study, and Dr Alan Brown, a pediatrician at Toronto's Hospital for Sick Children. Quintland provided a laboratory for middle-class, English-speaking, child-rearing professionals who assumed their own superiority and the inferiority of poor Catholic farmers. Not surprisingly, conflict was often fierce. The Roman Catholic Church and Franco-Ontario nationalists campaigned to return the quints to their parents. The struggle was all the more bitter because the five girls represented a windfall for their guardians. Alienated from their family after their reunion in 1943 and ogled by the press, they never fully recovered. Émilie died in 1954; Marie in 1970; Yvonne in 2001. Unhappiness was clear when they told their story in *We Were Five* (1965) and *Family Secrets* (1995). The latter revealed sexual abuse by their father. Not until 1998 did the Ontario government admit liability with an award of $4 million.

VERONICA STRONG-BOAG

disallowance. A negative legislative power available to the federal *cabinet. Any provincial law may be disallowed by a federal *order-in-council within a year of its passage. Cabinet, on the recommendation of the justice minister, adopts the order-in-council. Disallowance has been used 112 times and against all provinces except Prince Edward Island. It was last used in 1943.

Disallowance was employed most frequently in the years following Confederation. Between 1867 and 1896 the federal cabinet disallowed, over the stated objections of the provinces, 66 provincial statutes. The gradual shift in *federal–provincial relations since then has seen the power fall into disuse. It can now be said to be effectively inoperative even though it forms part of the Constitution Act, 1867 (ss. 56 and 90). All attempts to remove the power from the *constitution have failed. The most recent failure came in 1992, when, although federal, provincial, and territorial governments agreed as part of the *Charlottetown Accord to abolish the power, the accord's rejection in the country-wide referendum meant disallowance remained part of Canada's constitution.

JOHN C. COURTNEY AND DANIEL MACFARLANE

displaced persons. When the Second World War ended in Europe in the spring of 1945, as the Allied forces overtook Germany and reduced Berlin to rubble, an estimated 12 million people who had fled or been uprooted from their mostly eastern European homelands became *refugees. Almost evenly divided between those outside Soviet-occupied Europe and inside Soviet-held territory, these displaced persons included *Jews, Balts, Poles, and others from countries that had been incorporated into Hitler's Third Reich and used as slave labour, as well as Nazi collaborators, prisoners of war, and resistance fighters. Allied personnel, the United Nations (aided by the Allied military), and local relief agencies identified, processed, and 'herded' this mass of 'human rubble' (as some called them) into hastily made DP camps or reception centres, mostly in Germany and Austria. The initial plan to repatriate everyone was partially thwarted by a million or so refugees who resisted this policy: Polish Jews keen to escape anti-Semitism in eastern Europe, and Poles, Balts, Yugoslavs, and *Ukrainians who denounced the Soviet Union and feared they might suffer the same fate as repatriated co-nationals who had been imprisoned, tortured, or murdered as war criminals. A mix of economic self-interest, international pressure, and humanitarianism led an initially reluctant Canada to participate in a plan to resettle these 'hard-core' refugees. Many came to Canada on labour contracts for jobs in mining, agriculture, logging, and domestic service. Welcomed as freedom lovers, but also seen as war casualties who might require costly support, most of Canada's 100,000 DPs set about rebuilding their lives while also influencing Canada's Cold War culture. FRANCA IACOVETTA

distinct society. Although often thought of as a contemporary concept, the notion of Quebec as a distinct society goes back to the *Quebec Act, 1774, which allowed French civil law to be maintained in Quebec, and to 1848, when the act that made English the sole official language of acts of Parliament was repealed. The 'distinct society' concept comprises, in particular, language, culture, and civil law. In these matters Quebec is distinguished from the rest of Canada: its culture is unique, it is the only province where the majority of people speak French, and it constitutes the only civil law jurisdiction in the country. Attempts to constitutionalize the concept of 'distinct society', in the *Meech Lake (1987) and *Charlottetown (1992) Accords, did not succeed. GÉRALD-A. BEAUDOIN

divorce. The early history of divorce in Canada is a tale of restriction and limited tolerance. Before Confederation, local divorce courts were established in most colonies—New Brunswick, Prince Edward Island, Nova Scotia, and British Columbia, but not in the Province of Canada. These courts were not very active, handling just a handful of cases a year. The grounds for divorce were standard across these jurisdictions: adultery. There was one exception: Nova Scotia also accepted cruelty.

At Confederation, the *constitution gave jurisdiction over divorce to the federal government. Until Ottawa passed legislation, the British North America Act provided that provincial legislation would remain in practice and thus provincial divorce courts remained active. At the same time, for couples in provinces without divorce courts resort could be had to a cumbersome legislative process in which, with the federal *Senate playing a leading role, individual couples would petition for private legislation dissolving their marriage; hearings would be held by a joint parliamentary committee, acting in a quasi-judicial fashion. Such legislation would pass through all the formal stages in both the Senate and the *House of Commons before receiving royal assent.

At the beginning of the 20th century divorce numbers were still remarkably low—just 11 divorces in the entire country in 1900, whether through courts or Parliament. At the end of the First World War the number of divorces began to climb significantly. Some of this pressure on Parliament was alleviated by decisions of the Judicial Committee of the Privy Council (*Board* and *Walker*, 1919) holding that courts in the Prairie provinces had the right to hear divorce cases. By 1920 the number of divorces, although low by modern standards, had escalated remarkably to 468 in one year.

The ground for divorce continued to be adultery, with the exception of Nova Scotia, but there was an important double standard explicit in this ground. Husbands could sue for divorce on the ground of their wives' adultery, but wives had to charge their husbands with aggravated adultery—that is, adultery compounded by some other transgression such as cruelty or desertion. In 1925 the federal government passed its first piece of divorce legislation, ending this double standard. Thereafter, simple adultery was adequate ground for divorce for either party.

The number of divorces continued to rise throughout the 1920s. Ontario, being the most populous province, contributed the largest number—over 200 a year by 1930—and this put a significant strain on the federal legislative process. In 1931, Ottawa gave the courts of Ontario jurisdiction in divorce, thus alleviating the legislative problem in part.

Divorce was still difficult to obtain, but there were a number of ways to get around the law. Some Canadians went to the United States for a divorce; others provided phony evidence of adultery so that their spouse might take legal action. For others self-divorce—desertion and bigamy—was adopted. The restricted nature of Canadian divorce was increasingly regarded as being out of touch with modern realities. Canadians came increasingly to the view that marriages ought to be happy and positive relationships, and that divorce ought to be allowed so that people could be freed to seek a new and better marriage.

In 1968 the federal government of Pierre *Trudeau passed the first comprehensive divorce act for Canada, 101 years after it had received jurisdiction in the area. The act granted jurisdiction to the superior courts of all provinces, thus ending parliamentary divorce and granting judicial divorce to the courts of Quebec and Newfoundland for the first time. The grounds for divorce changed dramatically: adultery, physical or mental cruelty, or permanent breakdown of at least three years' separation. The number of divorces exploded: 29,238 in 1970. The stigma had largely been removed from divorce, and people were intent on abandoning unhappy marriages, often in hopes of establishing another relationship that might satisfy their aspirations.

In 1985 the last major piece of divorce legislation was passed. In addition to the grounds from the 1968 act, marriage breakdown was now judged by the test of one year's separation. Again the divorce numbers rose, peaking at 96,200 in 1987 before settling at around 78,000 annually in the following years. JAMES G. SNELL

Dobbs, Arthur (1689–1765). Ulster landowner, member of the Irish House of Commons, from 1733 surveyor-general of Ireland, Dobbs actively pursued British colonial interests overseas. His 1731 tract, *Memorial on the Northwest Passage*, argued that *Hudson Bay held the key to a northern passage to Asia. Dobbs's appeals to the British Admiralty led to their sponsorship of a 1741 voyage to Hudson Bay under the command of Christopher Middleton, a former Hudson's Bay Company sea captain. After wintering at Churchill, Middleton returned to England without finding a passage and was accused by Dobbs of negligence and corruption. The resulting pamphlet war between the arctic explorer and the Irish MP lasted for years. A second expedition under William Moor and Francis Smith, this time privately financed by Dobbs and an association of merchants, was equally unsuccessful. Dobbs's 1744 publication, *An Account of the Countries Adjoining to Hudson's Bay*, attacked the stewardship of the HBC and led to a parliamentary enquiry into the heretofore private affairs of the company. In 1754 Dobbs was chosen governor of North Carolina, where he served until his death. ROBERT J. COUTTS

Dollard des Ormeaux, Adam (1635-60). A young military officer who had just arrived in the colony, Dollard was sent by Montreal governor Chomedy de Maisonneuve on a mission up the Ottawa River in the spring of 1660 along with 16 French companions and a Native contingent of 40 *Huron and four Algonquin under the leadership of Etienne Anaotaha. The objectives of this expedition have been the subject of considerable controversy. Lionel *Groulx promoted the commemoration of Dollard's sacrifice to replace Victoria Day celebrations, claiming that Dollard and his companions unselfishly gave their lives to stop an Iroquois invasion. It is more likely that he was hoping to rob *Iroquois hunters of their furs or that he was sent to escort the flotilla of Ottawa traders accompanying Médard Chouart and Pierre *Radisson back to Montreal. The group, however, ran into Iroquois hunting bands more numerous than expected. The presence of the last remaining Huron warriors among the allies drew many more Iroquois, who were eager to incorporate them. Dollard committed the blunder of firing on an ambassador seeking a truce and, during the ensuing assault, the French tried to throw a powder keg at their assailants. The keg got caught on a branch and wrought havoc within the allied fort. All the French were killed or taken to be tortured and most of the Huron died or were captured. JOHN A. DICKINSON

domestic servants. Before the First World War more Canadian women worked as domestic servants than in any other paid employment. Although almost one-third of early colonial servants were male, by the late 19th century over 90 per cent were female. Wealthy families with a large staff still included male servants, but most employers hired one or two female domestics. Until technological servants such as electric washing machines and refrigerators reduced housework labour by the mid-20th century, farm women and middle-class urban women sought human help. A servant also confirmed the higher social status of the mistress, especially in urban homes.

Canadian demand for domestic servants always exceeded the supply. Marriage opportunities in a pioneer society led to rapid turnover among female servants. With the expansion after 1870 of factory, office, and shop work for women, Canadian daughters shunned the long unregulated hours, isolation, and low status of domestic service. By contrast, immigrant women used the constant availability of domestic service as a bridge to seek a better life in Canada. As migration patterns changed, the Irish 'Bridget', the stereotypical servant of the mid-19th century, was replaced by young women from England, Scotland, and, especially in western Canada, continental Europe. Until 1924, British philanthropic societies also placed girls in Canadian rural homes that could not afford adult help.

Racial discrimination, as well as assumptions regarding women's role, structured female migration as servants. Before the 1950s, the expectation that immigrant domestics were future 'mothers of the race' severely restricted the admission of Black domestic servants. The 1955 Caribbean Domestic Scheme marked a shift in government policy. Post-war inability to recruit servants from Europe, Canadian economic interests in the Caribbean, and pressure from a multi-racial Commonwealth persuaded Canada to admit Caribbean domestic workers. By 1966, some 2,940 women came, more than all Caribbean immigrants before 1945. Racial acceptance was limited. The temporary employment authorization program, introduced in 1973, highlighted the devaluation of women's work in the home, which was not considered skilled, and increased the vulnerability of domestic workers from the Caribbean and the Philippines, who no longer entered Canada as permanent immigrants. MARILYN BARBER

dominion. The title conferred on Canada by the preamble to the Constitution Act, 1867, whereby the provinces declare 'their desire to be federally united into one Dominion under the Crown of the United Kingdom'. The title was chosen over the founding fathers' preference for 'Kingdom', allegedly to mollify Canada's republican neighbour but still represent the founding monarchical principle. Beginning in the 1950s, as an affirmation of independent status and to make a break with the colonial past, a homegrown *governor general was appointed, a *national flag adopted, and 'dominion' gradually dropped from official and popular usage. Despite the anguished protests of monarchists such as Eugene *Forsey, who saw dominion as 'the only distinctive word we have contributed to political terminology' and one 'borrowed throughout the Commonwealth', the final nail was driven by the 1982 statute changing the holiday commemorating Confederation from Dominion Day to Canada Day. Ironically, defenders of the title dominion who see signs of creeping republicanism in such changes can take comfort in the knowledge that the Constitution Act, 1982, retains the title and requires a constitutional amendment to alter it. J.E. HODGETTS

Dominion Drama Festival. Inspired by the international 'art' theatre movement, Drama Leagues in Britain and the United States, and a blossoming of the arts in Canada, the DDF was founded in 1932, in part answering calls for an organization to link the many 'Little Theatres' established since just before the First World War. The founders, Governor General the Earl of Bessborough, Vincent *Massey, and other well-placed amateurs, aimed at improving the level of *theatre, thereby enhancing the quality of life in Canada, fostering a national drama consistent with a maturing nation, and countering the overwhelming influence of American-based commercial touring. In form, the DDF was for almost four decades (1933–9; 1947–70) an annual competition in regional playoffs culminating in a week-long dominion final in a host city (first in Ottawa, 1933). Often troubled by its elitism, controversy between French and English factions, uneasy mix of social entertainment and high art aims, questionable adjudications, and financial problems, the DDF nonetheless inspired hundreds of local troupes, allowed thousands to experience theatre, and gave aspiring professionals a chance to learn. As society changed and professional theatre became established in the latter half of the 20th century, the DDF faded from existence, its final years (1971–8) as Theatre Canada unadjudicated showcases for amateur productions. RICHARD L. PLANT

dominion experimental farms. Created by Parliament in 1886, operated by the Experimental Farm Service under the guidance of William Saunders, the first five farms were in Nappan, Nova Scotia, Brandon, Manitoba, Indian Head, North-West Territories, Agassiz, British

Columbia, and Ottawa. The farms conducted experiments on subjects as diverse as grain and orchard varieties, livestock management and breeding, tillage techniques, fertilizers, and apiaries. They also became renowned as demonstration farms where farmers could witness first-hand the benefits of shelter belts, flower gardens, or new field crop production. The success of the early farms led to the creation of a series of experimental stations and substations throughout the country. Any effort to reduce or consolidate the service was fiercely resisted by farmers. As a result, in 1950 virtually every section of Canada, from Fort Simpson in the north to St John's, Newfoundland, was served by 40 experimental farms and stations. The effects of their activities can be seen in the development of *Marquis wheat (1909) and subsequent hard red spring wheats for the Canadian prairies, the development of canola (1964) and its approval for human consumption, and the development of Holstein dairy cattle and cross-bred beef cattle production. Less visible but no less important was the role of the experimental farm service in providing assistance to farmers attempting to diversify into new commodities, such as honey production in the *Peace River country. ROBERT IRWIN

Dominion Lands Act. This 1872 act described how the newly acquired North-West Territories were to be surveyed and also specified what lands were available for free homesteads, railway subsidies, educational endowment, and other uses. The grid system featured six-mile-square townships of 36 equal sections (640 acres); homesteads for prospective farmers were 160 acres, the same size as those available in the American West.

Responsibility for surveying the vast western interior fell to the Dominion Lands Branch of the federal Department of the Interior. It was a formidable task. There were roughly 1.4 billion acres under direct federal administration. This number was so large because Ottawa had retained control in 1870 of all public lands and resources in the region for what it described as 'the purposes of the dominion'. The three Prairie provinces (Manitoba, Saskatchewan, and Alberta) would not gain control of their public lands—a right enjoyed by every other province—until 1930.

The rate at which Dominion Lands surveyors measured the land was nothing short of phenomenal. By 1887, 70 million acres had been subdivided. Survey teams were able to proceed so quickly because all of the land, no matter the quality, was subject to the same standard grid system; the natural contours were completely ignored in favour of an artificial, checkerboard ordering. They also worked accurately in the field because the system was not only based on astronomical observation but uniform throughout the region. Once the system was in place and its principles understood, the location of a homestead anywhere in the Northwest was a relatively straightforward matter.

By the mid-1880s, the survey had reached the Rockies and faced the perplexing task of continuing into the mountains. In an 1887 experiment, surveyors headed to the region with cameras and took a series of panoramic views from a number of predetermined (by triangulation) stations. The photographs were then used to plot the maps in Ottawa. Over the next decade, photo-topography was increasingly improved and refined and came to be an indispensable *surveying aid in mapping the mountains and determining boundaries in the region.

BILL WAISER

Dominion-Provincial Relations, Royal Commission on. *See* ROWELL-SIROIS COMMISSION.

Donnacona. In the first half of the 16th century Donnacona was a First Nations leader at Stadacona, a village on the St Lawrence River on the site of present-day Quebec City. The people who lived in this village, called Stadaconans or St Lawrence Iroquois, are a mystery to scholars. French explorer Jacques *Cartier encountered them in the 1530s, but they had disappeared when the next Frenchman, Samuel de *Champlain, travelled up the St Lawrence in the early 1600s. Numbering about 500 in 1535, the villagers spoke a distinct Iroquoian dialect. Donnacona and his people first met Cartier on the coast of Gaspé Bay in 1534, when they objected to his raising of a French cross. Cartier seized the group and convinced Donnacona to send his sons, Domagaya and Taignoagny, with him to France to be trained as interpreters. The following year Cartier returned to Stadacona with the sons. Donnacona's objections to his plans to visit Hochelaga, a St Lawrence Iroquoian village further upriver (at present-day Montreal), led to tensions. But Cartier's survival during the harsh winter depended on Donnacona, who provided the French with a cure for *scurvy from the bark of white cedar. In the spring of 1536, Donnacona's leadership was challenged by his Stadaconan rival Agona. To gain his trust, Cartier offered to defend Donnacona, but he used the dispute as a ruse to capture him and his sons. Cartier sailed back to France with his captives, all of whom died there within a couple of years.

CAROLYN PODRUCHNY

Donnelly murders. Early on 4 February 1880 several dozen men acting as a vigilance committee, invaded the Donnelly farmhouse along the Sixth Concession (Roman Line) of Biddulph Township near Lucan, Ontario, and brutally murdered James and Johannah Donnelly, their son Tom, and niece Bridget. The vigilantes later killed another son, James, mistaking him for his notorious brother William. Notwithstanding the testimony of two eyewitnesses, the killers avoided conviction. A first trial in September 1880 ended in a hung jury; a second in January 1881 resulted in a verdict of 'not guilty'. The vigilantes were all neighbours of the Donnellys and parishioners at St Patrick's Roman Catholic Church. While apologists for the killers portrayed them as respectable citizens reacting to years of Donnelly-inspired violence against person and property, the vigilantes were motivated by more than a desire to terminate the lawless behaviour, both real and imagined, of the Donnellys.

Back of the massacre can be found longstanding family feuds, the origins of which are to be found in Tipperary, Ireland. Feelings of hatred and jealousy were also fuelled in the New World by bitter squabbles over land, resentment of Donnelly family fortunes, and by intense local political and religious divisions. GERALD KILLAN

Dorion, Antoine-Aimé (1818–91). Born into a family of reform politicians, Dorion studied law after finishing his schooling at Nicolet, and was called to the bar in 1842. In the years leading up to *responsible government, he was active in liberal clubs. Republican sympathies led him to support the *annexation manifesto in 1849, and brought him into contact with the anglophone business establishment that later played an important role in his political career. In the 1850s, he emerged as a moderate leader of the Rouge Party. He was a typical 19th-century whig, believing in a lay state, universal male suffrage, the sanctity of private property, economic development, and progress. He opposed cronyism and excessive government spending. Unlike many of his fellow liberals, however, he remained a devout Catholic and resigned from the *Institut canadien when it was condemned by Rome in 1869. He participated in three governments during the union period and became minister of justice in Alexander *Mackenzie's Liberal administration in 1873. In 1874, Dorion left politics to become chief justice of the Quebec Court of Queen's Bench. JOHN A. DICKINSON

double shuffle. Derogatory term applied to a legal contrivance whereby the Canadian ministry of George-Étienne *Cartier and John A. *Macdonald, on resuming office only four days after quitting it in August 1858, evaded the constitutional requirement that newly appointed ministers seek re-election to the legislature. It managed this by exploiting a recent statute exempting ministers who swapped one portfolio for another within a month. The ministers first assumed offices they did not mean to fill, then resumed their old portfolios the next day. As applied to this stratagem the term 'double shuffle' had a twofold meaning: besides evoking card trickery, it was the name of a vulgar nautical dance.

PAUL ROMNEY

Doughty, Sir Arthur George (1860–1936). Born in Maidenhead, England, Doughty emigrated to Canada in 1886. He was appointed dominion archivist and keeper of the records in May 1904, a position he held until 1935. He had a passion for history and sought to find and make known the original records necessary for understanding the Canadian experience. Under his leadership, the Public Archives of Canada became an active cultural institution, acquiring historical documentation in all forms, including official records, private manuscripts, art, photographs, museum objects, and transcriptions of Canadian-related records in Britain and France. Doughty promoted historical awareness through exhibitions and publications, and through his participation in the celebrations of the *Quebec tercentenary in 1908. In support of the emerging Canadian historical profession, he began a series of documentary publications, which had a significant impact on the study of history.

His own publications concentrated on the history of New France and the city of Quebec. *The Siege of Quebec and the Battle of the Plains of Abraham* (6 vols, 1901) focused on the records, while his other books were more literary. Doughty co-edited with Adam Shortt **Canada and Its Provinces* (23 vols, 1913–17), a series, W.A. Mackintosh later observed, that was not likely to be a model for the future, but one that created the future.

IAN E. WILSON

Douglas, Sir James (1803–77), *Hudson's Bay Company officer, governor of *Vancouver Island (1851–64) and British Columbia (1858–64). Born in British Guiana to the 'country' family of a Glasgow merchant, his mother a 'free coloured woman', Douglas was schooled in Scotland and apprenticed age 16 to the *fur trade. Physically imposing, a *North West Company enforcer in the struggle with the HBC, after the 1821 merger he was sent to *New Caledonia. 'Furiously violent when aroused', he came into personal conflict with resident Indians. Kicked upstairs to Fort Vancouver, he took with him Amelia Connelly, his Irish-Cree wife, by whom he had 13 children, 6 surviving to adulthood. By 1849, when the HBC western headquarters moved to Fort Victoria, he was chief factor and senior member of the Board of Management.

Governor Douglas was no democrat: he fought the Vancouver Island assembly and ruled the mainland without any representative council. His Indian policy was paternalistic, envisioning individual (though not group) advancement, in marked contrast to his settler society successors. Sober-sided 'Old Square-Toes' was nonetheless a gold rush 'boomer'. His large expenditures, especially for roads, left the United Colony of British Columbia heavily indebted, sparking demands for union with Canada. KEITH RALSTON

Douglas, Thomas Clement (1904–86), Baptist minister, Saskatchewan premier 1944–61, leader of the federal *New Democratic Party. Born in Falkirk, Scotland, Tommy Douglas spent his early years there and in Winnipeg. He was raised in a hot house of ideas: Scottish radical liberalism, trade unionism, dour *Presbyterianism, the *social gospel, and the ideological vortex of the *Winnipeg General Strike. He attended the theologically liberal Brandon College in Manitoba and later earned a master's degree in sociology. As a Depression-era minister in Weyburn, Saskatchewan, he was drawn to the new *Co-operative Commonwealth Federation. In 1935 he was elected to Parliament—in time to test the CCF's internationalist principles as the world prepared for war. The CCF grew to support the war effort while keeping an eye on violations of civil liberties and evidence of corruption at home. Accommodation combined with a desire to protect Canadians from the worst effects of unbridled militarism and capitalism marked Douglas's career. In 1944 he led the Saskatchewan CCF to power.

His 17-year-long premiership saw the modernization of the province's infrastructure and government and, in the face of vocal opposition by business and doctors, the introduction of *medicare. Douglas's attempts to diversify the province's economy were unsuccessful. Still, his record in Saskatchewan made him an overwhelming choice to lead the federal NDP from its founding in 1962 until 1971.

The NDP failed to make an electoral breakthrough, and left-wing voices, particularly the *Waffle, grew in the party. Douglas strove to unite the broadest possible movement. Although committed to the CCF and NDP programs, Douglas had accepted Social Credit support in elections and worked with the Communist-dominated League against War and Fascism in the 1930s. Four decades later he was one of the few leaders who welcomed the energy and ideas of young radicals.

JAMES NAYLOR

Doukhobors, or 'Dukho-bortsi' (meaning Spirit Wrestlers), refer to a religious group in southern Russia that opposed the usefulness of the Orthodox Church and the right of governments to wage war. As dissidents seeking social equality, justice, and non-violence, they burnt their firearms in the summer of 1895 and were severely persecuted for that act. Russian author Lev N. Tolstoy and the Quakers came to their aid and helped 7,500 of them immigrate to Canada between January and June 1899. The Liberal Laurier government saw these eastern Europeans as 'sturdy, stalwart' people who could cultivate the stubborn prairie soil, build railroads and villages, and help prevent the Americans from usurping the new Northwest. Doukhobors settled in three parcels of land in what is now southeastern and north-central Saskatchewan and built over 90 single-street Russian villages.

From their beginning in Canada, the new settlers were objects of curiosity. They were Russian and knew no English, but they had strong backs and were resourceful and self-sufficient. The women could pull ploughs, build villages when the men were away earning money, and produce high-quality handicrafts. For three decades, under a communal economic style, they established the most successful co-operative enterprise in North America, with brick factories, grain farms, and flour mills in Saskatchewan and later sawmills and three jam factories in the interior of British Columbia.

The Doukhobors experienced hardship in their new land, as in the old, due to their beliefs. A clash with the Canadian government occurred over land ownership, schooling, the franchise, and citizenship. They lost land worth $11 million in 1907 because most of them would not sign for individual ownership. In 1938 they lost $6 million property because they could not pay their debts, and the government, which was helping other farmers, refused to come to their aid. Their vote was taken away from 1919 to 1956. A 1914 Community Regulations Act in British Columbia allowed the seizure of goods and chattels of the Doukhobor community for the offences of individual members—failure to register births, marriages, and deaths; irregular school attendance; and lack of compliance with the Health Act. The legislature abolished the act in early 2002.

Today most of Canada's 40,000 Doukhobors reside in the western provinces. Their hard work, hospitality, bridge building, creativity, and self-sufficiency, and their belief in non-violence and the power of the inner spirit, continue to mark their social landscape. They are now more of a social movement than a religion.

KOOZMA J. TARASOFF

***Drybones* case**. In the landmark case *R. v. Drybones* (1970), the *Supreme Court of Canada nullified a clause in the *Indian Act (section 94(b)) for contradicting the principle of 'equality before the law' established in the Canadian Bill of Rights (1960). A lower court had convicted Joseph Drybones, a status Indian, of being in violation of the Indian Act after he was found intoxicated off reserve in Yellowknife. The Supreme Court ruled that a federal statute was inoperative if it abolished, limited, or infringed on the liberties recognized in the Bill of Rights, unless Parliament declared the statute applied notwithstanding the Bill of Rights. The court concluded that Drybones had been punished because of his race under a law that differed for other Canadians. Since 1970, this precedent-setting decision has been used in cases concerned with a wide range of issues, from Native rights to the management of Toronto's Pearson International Airport.

GÉRALD-A. BEAUDOIN

dry farming. The phrase 'dry farming' sometimes means any agricultural technique designed to address arid conditions on the prairies. Most often it refers to the practice of summer fallowing, leaving fields dormant every second or third year so that soil moisture from two seasons would be available to produce one crop. The term also has a more technical meaning, based on the ideas of Hardy W. Campbell of South Dakota. In his *Soil Culture Manual* of 1902, Campbell argued that soil moisture moved to the surface of a field by capillary action. Before seeding, he urged farmers to encourage this action by packing the subsoil, bringing moisture close to the surface where seedling roots might reach it. By maintaining a 'dry mulch' of loose soil on the surface to break the capillary action, farmers could supposedly prevent the moisture from reaching the air and evaporating. A Dry Farming Congress arose in 1906 to promote Campbell's technique, but experience demonstrated that the practice actually aggravated the problem of topsoil drifting, as high winds blew away the finely cultivated dry mulch. Agricultural scientists also discredited his theories, and by the 1930s new methods of cultivating fallow began to replace dry farming.

PAUL VOISEY

duelling. The first duel in Canada took place in 1646. In the next 200 years about 300 incidents were reported, ranging from challenges not accepted to actual swordplay or gunfire. Duels became ritualistic, with strict codes of behaviour. Principals communicated through seconds, who in turn attempted to arrange apologies or explanations that would satisfy mutual honour. Many last-minute settlements were struck as opponents stood with loaded pistols. Nevertheless, at least 8 deaths resulted during the French regime (when all such encounters were with swords) and 13 in British North America after 1760. One arose from a drunken quarrel over cards, but several were rooted in political differences—Joseph *Howe fought such a duel, but his opponent missed and he fired in the air. Still others sprang from lawyers' courtroom arguments escalating into insults, challenges, and meetings. The York (Toronto) shooting of John Ridout by Samuel P. Jarvis in 1817 was the climax of a family feud. Duels were illegal; killing an opponent often resulted in the survivor being charged with murder. However, sympathetic juries repeatedly ignored both the law and the evidence to return verdicts of not guilty, sparing their friends a public hanging. The last fatal duel in Canada occurred on 22 May 1838. Thomas Sweeney shot Major Henry Warde at Verdun, Lower Canada, after Warde sent a love letter to Mrs Sweeney. The coroner's inquest blandly reported that Warde had been killed by some person unknown. Numerous challenges and meetings took place thereafter, but they resembled theatre more than serious combat.

HUGH A. HALLIDAY

Du Gua de Monts, Pierre (*c.* 1558–1628), French trader and colonial promoter. A Calvinist who had fought for King Henri IV during the Wars of Religion, de Monts probably made his first North American visit in 1600. Three years later, gaining a trade monopoly and sweeping powers as royal lieutenant-general in North America between the 40th and 46th parallels, he undertook to colonize this vast area. Sailing in March 1604 with some 80 colonizers, including Samuel de *Champlain, de Monts explored the coastlines of l'Acadie before wintering on the ill-chosen Île Ste-Croix. The survivors—nearly half of his company had died—moved in 1605 to a new habitation across the Bay of Fundy at *Port-Royal. Here, they found accommodating *Mi'kmaq neighbours and a healthy fur trade. The rivalry of powerful French merchants, however, brought revocation of the trade monopoly in 1607 and the temporary abandonment of Port-Royal. While never visiting North America again, de Monts sent Champlain to found the trading post at Quebec in 1608 and maintained his commercial interests there for another nine years before retiring to the Ardennes. Commercially minded as he was, de Monts had taken a leading role in the foundation of lasting French settlements in both Acadia and Canada.

JOHN G. REID

Dumbells, The. In 1917, Merton Plunkett of the *YMCA assembled a concert party to entertain the troops of the 3rd Canadian Division overseas. The Dumbells (the name was inspired by the divisional insignia) were an immediate hit, with their mix of sentimental ballads, slapstick, female impersonation, and rousing singalongs. After the war, theatre promoters refused to believe that the act could attract civilian audiences, but Plunkett proved them wrong. The Dumbells, after a sold-out engagement in London, Ontario, played 16 weeks in Toronto, mounted a triumphant cross-Canada tour, and conquered Broadway in 1921 with a 12-week, sold-out show, *Biff! Bing! Bang!* Unfailingly optimistic revues like *Cheerio* and *Why Worry?* followed, but talking pictures spelled the end of vaudeville, and the Dumbells. They last toured in 1932.

JONATHAN VANCE

Dumont, Gabriel (1837–1906), was the principal *Metis military leader in the *North-West Rebellion of 1885. Dumont's first 35 years were spent in the traditional plains Metis cycle of annual *buffalo hunts. In the early 1870s, just after Canada took over control of the Northwest from the *Hudson's Bay Company, he took up land on the South Saskatchewan River and quickly emerged as the most important spokesman for the growing community there.

The main issue was land tenure. How would the narrow river-lot farms of the Metis fit into the Canadian government's square survey? The rapid disappearance of the buffalo in the early 1880s gave increased urgency to the situation. When Ottawa was unable to provide reassurance, Dumont in the spring of 1884 headed a delegation to Montana to ask Louis *Riel to return to take over negotiations. By early 1885 Riel had concluded that further talk was useless and that they must take up arms. The Metis showed little enthusiasm for such drastic measures, but Dumont's staunch support ensured that those on the Saskatchewan would follow Riel into rebellion.

When the provisional government was proclaimed 19 March 1885, Dumont was named adjutant-general. He organized the defence against the inevitable Canadian reaction by concentrating his few soldiers in entrenchments around the edges of the settlement. His forces were heavily outnumbered and, after a preliminary skirmish at Fish Creek, the Metis were decisively defeated in a three-day battle at *Batoche in May 1885. Dumont escaped capture and fled to the United States, where he performed with Buffalo Bill's Wild West Show. In 1893 he returned to the Saskatchewan, where he lived quietly until his death in 1906.

R.C. MACLEOD

Dunham, Charles A. (1832–1900). Spy, forger, and rogue journalist of the US Civil War era, Dunham had many identities but is best known for testimony claiming President Lincoln's assassination was ordered by the Confederate government and planned in Canada. His testimony came after he had spent six months in Canada, mainly in Montreal, passing among Confederate refugees as a Virginian, James Watson Wallace. At the same time he wrote for various Northern newspapers under other aliases, damaging Canada's already frayed relations with the United States by inventing stories about planned border raids. In one case he devised a scheme to destroy the Croton Dam near New York City, pressing it on Confederate officers while at the same time arranging with Northern contacts to lead raiders into ambush. Before it could be carried out, he revealed the scheme in his writing as Sandford Conover in the *New York Tribune*. In 1867 Conover was convicted of perjury after training false witnesses to implicate Confederate President Jefferson Davis in the assassination of Lincoln. CARMAN CUMMING

Dunn, Sir James Hamet (1874–1956), financier and steel magnate. Born in humble circumstances on New Brunswick's North Shore, young Dunn forsook the declining fortunes of Atlantic Canada, taking with him only a strong Presbyterian will to succeed. Like childhood friends Max *Aitken and Richard *Bennett, Dunn discerned that power emanated from the metropolitan centres that oversaw Canada's economic successes in the Laurier years. A Dalhousie law degree (1898) opened the way to the art of business promotion, first in Edmonton, then in Canada's financial capital, Montreal. Marriage into the lumber-rich Price family and a seat on the Montreal Stock Exchange positioned Dunn on the threshold of *finance capitalism with lavish profits skimmed off heady industrial development. Dunn flourished in the cutthroat world of transatlantic finance and was by 1906 a merchant banker in London. Adept at arbitrage and market manipulation, he was soon a millionaire and a prince of promotion, underwriting cutting-edge technologies ranging from 'artificial silk' to hydroelectric power. Sybaritic social and sexual indulgence, political influence, and a wartime baronetcy followed. When the Depression undermined finance capitalism, Dunn returned home and unscrupulously gained control of Algoma Steel, Canada's second-largest steelmaker, in Sault Ste Marie. From 1935 to his death, he dictatorially ruled Algoma, using the hothouse economy of war and post-war boom to modernize its plant and expand its wares. Although much favoured by C.D. *Howe, Dunn was a last breath of Carnegie-style capitalism in Canada —flinty and religiously laissez-faire. Thrice married, Dunn left an estate of $70 million, duties on which were used to establish the Canada Council.

DUNCAN McDOWALL

Dunsmuir, Robert (1825–89) and **James** (1851–1920, BC premier 1900–2), industrialists and politicians. *Vancouver Island was a new colony when Ayrshireman Robert Dunsmuir, a coal miner indentured to the Hudson's Bay Company, arrived on its shores. Backed by his wife, Joan, he parlayed hard work, intelligence, and good luck into a fortune based on his discovery of the Wellington coal seam near Nanaimo. As an influential man in a new society, he used the militia to deal with striking miners and yet won a seat in the legislature with the support of working-class votes. In return for building the Esquimalt and Nanaimo Railway for his friend, Sir John A. *Macdonald, he received an 800,000-ha land grant in 1884. He died the richest man in British Columbia, but his last will and testament pitted Joan against their son, James. As a businessman, James pursued labour policies that contributed to the present polarization of BC politics and exacerbated the volatile Asian immigration issue. As a politician, he was premier for two lacklustre years and lieutenant-governor for three. Having sold the family's mines to Canadian Collieries and the railroad to the CPR, James retired to his castle near Victoria to watch his daughters marry gentlemen of good name and little means. LYNNE BOWEN

Duplessis, Maurice LeNoblet (1890–1959), Quebec premier 1936–9, 1944–59. Elected as member for Trois-Rivières in 1927, Duplessis became leader of the provincial Conservative Party in 1933. With Paul Gouin, leader of the Action libérale nationale, he formed the *Union nationale (UN) in order to defeat the Liberals, who had been in power since 1897. The UN captured a majority of seats in 1936 and Duplessis became premier. Once in power, he brought forward legislation such as the *Padlock Law, but failed to implement needed reforms, provoking the departure of the former ALN members. He called an election in 1939, with *conscription for overseas service the main issue. When he lost, many thought his political career was at an end.

Duplessis regained power in 1944 and remained premier until his death. His government was pro-business, welcoming American investments (as did the rest of the country) and creating an economic environment characterized by low taxes and a limited role for the state. His policy of rural electrification and credit for farmers was welcomed by many. A formidable politician, he transformed the UN into a powerful electoral machine, financed by contributions from business. The use of patronage in the allocation of government contracts provoked the anger of provincial liberals and intellectuals.

Duplessis believed in conservative values and perceived Catholicism as a cohesive social and cultural force. Individuals, families, and the church, he maintained, were best equipped to deal with social issues. Nevertheless, his government aided the church financially to fulfill its educational and social responsibilities. He was praised for his aggressive defence of *provincial autonomy. His creation of the Quebec flag (the fleur-de-lys) in 1948 and a provincial income tax scheme in 1954, as well as his opposition to federal grants to universities, attracted the support of nationalist organizations and intellectuals such as André *Laurendeau and Pierre *Trudeau. His anti-union stand, however, provoked a series of bitter strikes, notably the *Asbestos strike in 1949, which forced the resignation of Montreal archbishop Joseph Charbonneau for his support of the workers. Some intellectuals compared the authoritarian and conservative Duplessis regime to *la Grande noirceur*, a period of intellectual and social darkness. During these years, however, Quebec went through a series of social and economic changes, notably the development of suburbs and consumer society, similar to those in other parts of North America.

MARCEL MARTEL

Durham, John George Lambton, Earl of (1792–1840), diplomat, politician, colonial administrator. Durham sat in the British House of Commons, 1813–28, as a prominent radical. After serving as ambassador to Russia, he became governor general of British North America in 1838, charged with investigating the causes of the rebellions in the Canadas. He arrived in Quebec in May 1838 and spent most of his time in Lower Canada. Durham's report, published in 1839, concluded that in Upper Canada an oppressive oligarchy had monopolized power and pursued narrow self-interest. In Lower Canada he had found 'two nations warring within the bosom of a single state': the progressive 'English' merchants and farmers, and the French, who pursued the dictates of a 'narrow' and 'petty . . . nationality', with all 'the unreasoning tenacity of an uneducated and unprogressive people'. In his view, reason and humanity demanded that the French be raised to the standards of the English. He urged a union of the two Canadas and the introduction of municipal institutions in Lower Canada. The first, he calculated, would ensure English control; the second would educate the French in the arts of government. He also recommended that the British government concern itself only with matters of imperial concern, among them trade and defence. He favoured the establishment of *responsible government, in which those who had the confidence of the assembly would control the executive. The introduction of these various reforms might help lead to a union of all the British colonies in North America.

The British government found the union of the two Canadas agreeable, but not the granting of responsible government. Even before his report appeared, a disgruntled Durham had left Canada, having resigned his post because London had disallowed an ordinance of his. Although tuberculosis soon cut his life short, he was to have a profound influence on the Canadas, as his report helped legitimize the efforts of those seeking political reform.

COLIN READ

dust bowl. A term, borrowed from the United States, to describe the conditions on prairie farms in the Palliser Triangle region during the *Great Depression. The 'Dirty Thirties', as prairie farmers remember the era, was a period of low grain prices, drought, high winds, and insect infestations. The aridity of the region, roughly south of the line formed by the basins of the Qu'Appelle, North Saskatchewan, and Battle Rivers, had been remarked upon as early as the 1857–60 *Palliser and Hind expeditions. Despite these warnings, farmers had moved into the district in large numbers after the completion of the *Canadian Pacific Railway and had commenced large-scale grain production. The cultivation and tillage techniques resembled those used in the sub-humid farm districts of southern Manitoba, including deep ploughing and the removal of debris and ground cover. Drought hit some parts of the district as early as 1920, leading to localized farm abandonment, and then the entire area experienced nine consecutive years of below average rainfall, from 1929 to 1937. The earlier poor cultivation techniques had pulverized the soil into a fine powder, with the result that during these years the topsoil literally blew across the prairies. Farm families had to deal with dust storms, dust drifts on roads and in ditches, and a constant film of dust in living quarters in towns and on the farms. The heat and drought provided excellent conditions for grasshoppers; huge swarms of the pests descended on any fields that had survived. The farm exodus that had begun in the 1920s increased, and by 1936 nearly 14,000 farms in the southern prairies had been abandoned. Farmers took advantage of northern settlement schemes offered by provincial governments to relocate on other marginal lands in the Duck Lake districts of Manitoba, the Meadow Lake and Carrot River districts of Saskatchewan, or the *Peace River country of Alberta and British Columbia. To stop the abandonment of farms the federal government created the *Prairie Farm Rehabilitation Administration in 1935, offering assistance in the construction of dugouts and dams to conserve water for livestock. It purchased abandoned and marginal land and turned it into community pastures. Farmers were also helped to plant trees to offer shelter breaks from the wind and to prevent soil erosion, and encouraged to implement strip-farming techniques. With the assistance of the PFRA, the farms of Palliser Triangle survived the environmental catastrophe. Today, many of the prairie dust bowl communities have developed irrigation facilities, turned to large-scale cattle production, or developed new cultivation techniques such as zero-tillage agriculture.

ROBERT IRWIN

Eastern Approaches. When John *Cabot sailed across the Atlantic in 1497, he believed that he was pioneering a new sea route to China and Japan, one that approached those fabled lands from the east. Little did he know that he had not reached Asia at all, but a world quite unknown to Europeans. In the decades that followed, dozens of explorers followed Cabot, some to determine the precise nature of this 'New Founde Land', others persisting in the belief that a transatlantic sea route to Asia could still be found. More importantly, thousands of nameless fishermen quickly responded to Cabot's reports of rich new fishing grounds. By the time Jacques *Cartier arrived in 1534, hundreds, perhaps thousands, of Europeans were already busy exploiting the natural resources that this New World had to offer.

Of course, Cabot was not the first European to reach North America. Norse Greenlanders had attempted, without success, to settle there around AD 1000. Many claims have also been made in support of those who allegedly journeyed from Europe to North America in the centuries both before and after the *Norse—St Brendan and a *curragh* of Irish monks in the 6th century AD, the Welsh prince Madoc in the 12th century, Prince Henry Sinclair, Earl of Orkney in the 14th century, and others. Belief in these legendary voyages is more a matter of faith than evidence; sometimes (as with Madoc) there is no evidence that the individual even existed. Still others have argued that Bristol merchants, or Basque or Portuguese fishermen, were exploiting the *Grand Banks for decades before Cabot, keeping the information, and the profits, to themselves. Such a view ignores how unlikely it is that a market-driven commercial fishery and trade could be kept secret. The fact remains that the European fisheries in Newfoundland sprang into existence only after 1500, and specialists in the field have a remarkably thorough understanding not only of how, and why, the discoveries took place when they did and in the way in which they did, but also of the way in which Europeans responded to opportunities in the New World.

We know, for instance, that in one sense the voyages of Columbus and Cabot were simply logical extensions of oceanic ventures that had already seen the discovery and development of Madeira, the Azores, the Canary Islands, and other Atlantic islands in the 14th and early 15th centuries. Portuguese ventures down and eventually around the African coast in the 1400s proved that such investments could be very profitable, while also demonstrating the worth of new designs in oceanic shipping, such as the caravel, which combined Mediterranean sails and rigging with northern European hull designs to create a rugged, oceanic sailer. Improvements in navigational instruments and charts came later; 15th-century seafarers relied largely on instinct and experience to judge where and how far they had travelled, which means that early explorers truly deserve to be admired, for they ventured into unknown waters despite lacking a body of experience to guide them.

Contributing to the timing of the so-called Age of Exploration was an upswing in the European economy that began in the 1400s and persisted for the next century. The availability of risk capital encouraged investment in the search for new sources of wealth. We long assumed that Muslim expansion in Turkey and the fall of Constantinople in 1453 had cut Europeans off from the overland routes by which they imported spices and silks, and had therefore triggered the search for new oceanic sea routes to Asia. Yet we now recognize that European interest in the Atlantic began long before Constantinople fell, and that pepper was not in short supply in Europe in the late 1400s. What the explorers sought was a cheaper, more efficient, and therefore more profitable route to Asia.

Cabot's conviction that he had reached Asia in 1497 appears to have been unshaken, to judge by the trade goods carried by the ships of his ill-fated 1498 expedition. Nevertheless, a flurry of exploratory expeditions over the next few years—João Fernandes in 1500 under Portuguese sponsorship and possibly again in 1501 as part of a joint English and Azorean syndicate, and first Gaspar Corte-Real in 1500 and 1501 and then his brother Miguel Corte-Real in 1502, all under Portuguese sponsorship—gradually dispelled the notion that a transatlantic voyage offered a quick route to Asia. Instead, Europeans began to realize that a land mass previously unknown to them lay in their way. It was at this point that European efforts began to turn either to finding a way through or around the New World or to finding a fortune in the New World, preferably by discovering a wealthy civilization ripe for the plundering, as the Spanish adventurer Hernán Cortés had done in Mexico in 1521.

Among those who sought a way through or around the New World was Giovanni da Verrazano; like Columbus and Cabot, he was an Italian in foreign service. Under French sponsorship, Verrazano crossed the Atlantic in 1523 in search of a route to Asia. He made landfall somewhere in the Carolinas and spent three months exploring the eastern seaboard of North America. Although he demonstrated in convincing fashion the continental proportion of the New World, he claimed to have sighted a western sea just beyond a narrow coastal strip of land. In this way, Verrazano encouraged European faith in the notion that North America could somehow be circumvented and that a direct westward route to Asia did exist. Verrazano's other legacy was to attach the name 'Arcadia' to the beautiful woodlands he discovered north of his landfall. That name survived in slightly distorted form and was later attached to *'Acadia', the first land in North America to be settled successfully by Europeans.

Verrazano was followed not many years later, in 1534, by Jacques Cartier on the first of his three voyages of exploration to North America. Like Verrazano, Cartier was seeking a route to Asia by way of a water passage through North America. That search led him into the Gulf of St Lawrence and up the St Lawrence River. Though he soon realized that this was not the hoped-for passage to the Far East, his instructions also directed him to 'discover certain islands and lands where it is said he should find great quantities of gold and other things'. This clearly reflected the belief that the New World might yield discoveries and riches such as the Spanish had stumbled across in the lands to the south. French expectations of easy wealth in the New World appear to have ended with Cartier's failure to find either a passage to Asia or wealthy civilizations to conquer. Yet wealth in abundance was being generated, albeit through difficult work. European fishermen had by then been exploiting the rich fishing grounds of North America for over a generation, and to the riches offered by fishing for cod were soon added the riches offered by hunting whales for their oil. The Basques—long familiar with shore-based *whaling in the Bay of Biscay—quickly learned that the coastal waters of Labrador teemed with humpback, bowhead, and right whales, and by the 1540s were sending fleets of ships to places like Red Bay. The industry lasted into the early 1600s, when a combination of factors, including very likely the depletion of whale stocks beyond the point where the industry could be sustained, brought the era of Basque whaling in Canada to an end.

Even after the full continental proportions of North America were understood, the dream of finding a westward sea route to Asia was not completely abandoned. As early as 1508, Sebastian Cabot—the son of John Cabot—may have sailed as far as Hudson Strait in search of a passage to Asia. Decades later, a number of serious attempts to locate a *Northwest Passage were made by English venturers. Martin Frobisher made three voyages into the Arctic between 1576 and 1578. He was followed a few years later by John Davis, whose voyages between 1585 and 1587 took him far up the strait bearing his name between Greenland and the islands of the Canadian Arctic. Henry *Hudson led several voyages in both English and Dutch service, resulting in discoveries such as the Hudson River, Hudson Strait, and Hudson Bay, all in vain pursuit of the passage to Asia. Others such as Thomas Button, Robert Bylot, William Baffin, Jens Munk, Luke Foxe, and Thomas James carried on the tradition well into the 1600s, but by then the overwhelming difficulty of the challenge, combined with the easier rewards offered by North America's proven resources, had caused European interest in an eastern approach to Asia by sea to fade, until it was revived with the advent of the 19th century and a new spirit of scientific adventure.

OLAF U. JANZEN

eastern subarctic Aboriginals. Although this geographic region of Canada, marked by northern coniferous (boreal) forests and harsh winters, extends from Labrador on the Atlantic coast to the Pacific coast, the eastern and western cultural divisions generally follow a linguistic demarcation. The eastern subarctic peoples all belong to the very large and widespread language family known as Algonquian, encompassing a number of languages and dialects. Most subarctic Algonquian societies live in Manitoba, Ontario, and Quebec, but related Western Woods Cree speakers live in parts of Saskatchewan and Alberta. This biotic zone, with its particular mix of flora and fauna, separates them culturally from closely related Algonquian speakers to the south, in the eastern woodlands and prairie regions. As resources are limited, subarctic Algonquian societies tend to share similar social and cultural practices. All were dependent on their harvest of meat and fish; plant food was of minor importance to their diet.

About 7,500 years ago, when the glaciers receded northwards, bands of hunters from the south began occupying the newly formed subarctic forests, which came to support increasing numbers of caribou, as well as fish in the abundant lakes and rivers, and later other mammals and waterfowl. Depending where people lived, some remained almost wholly dependent on caribou while others exploited a more mixed resource base of caribou, moose, bear, beaver, and a host of small mammals and birds. When animal cycles were down or climatic conditions affected hunting, fish usually sustained the family-based hunting group. As a result, subarctic peoples developed a flexible small-scale social organization that could wax and wane in size according to the seasons and availability of game. Spiritually, these peoples developed religions that displayed utmost respect for the animal spirits and an ideology of sharing. On the eve of European contact in the early 17th century, the eastern subarctic was occupied by peoples whose cultures had been fashioned over thousands of years.

The Algonquian speakers of the eastern subarctic are classified by linguists into two main branches. The northern one is Cree, of which there are a number of dialects, more or less conforming to societies known today: Western Woods Cree, West Swampy Cree, East Swampy Cree, Moose Cree, East Cree, Naskapi, Montagnais/Innu, and Attikamek. The southern branch, which is Ojibwa, comprises the dialects of Saulteaux, Severn Ojibwa, Northwestern Ojibwa, Central Ojibwa, and Algonquin. The ancestors of all these peoples were the mainstay of the European trade in beaver pelts that began at first contact and continued through to at least

the middle years of the 20th century. Despite the ongoing trade, many of the societies furthest from settled areas retained a degree of control over their social and cultural practices. In the post–Second World War era of industrialization and social welfare policies, these peoples have seen a loss of their autonomy due to greater government involvement and the encroachment and exploitation of their forests, minerals, and rivers for development by southern interests. Partaking of a more industrialized lifestyle today, they continue to retain ties to a hunting economy and its values. Many work in guiding or commercial fishing and forestry, and continue to feed their families with harvests of game and fish. They form the largest Native populations in Canada and their languages are among the very few not on the verge of extinction.
TOBY MORANTZ

Eastern Townships. Because it has never been a political entity, this region does not have clearly defined borders, but it has had a distinctive history and identity within Quebec. During the French regime, settlement was confined to the low-lying river valleys to the west, north, and east of this northern edge of the Appalachian Range, which remained the hunting territory of the Abenakis living at the mouth of the St Francis River. They used this artery to serve French imperial interests by raiding the northern frontier of New England settlement. The first settlers in the region were Loyalist refugees who fled to the Missisquoi Bay area of Lake Champlain, but Governor Haldimand forced many of them to move to the upper St Lawrence, where they would be more removed from American contact.

What would become informally known as the Eastern Townships was not opened to settlement until 1792, when Lieutenant-Governor Clarke followed Lieutenant-Governor Simcoe's example in Upper Canada, inviting Americans to expand northward. In the broadest sense, the Eastern Townships consists of the land falling under freehold tenure in the 93 townships (all of which have English names) bordered by the Richelieu-Yamaska, St Lawrence, and Chaudière seigneuries, a territory of approximately 21,400 square km. In a narrower and more culturally defined sense, the region consists of the southern band of townships originally settled by families from southern New England.

Settlers from Britain followed after the end of the Napoleonic Wars, but economic isolation and absentee proprietorship slowed development and limited the population to approximately 37,000 in 1831. The region had finally been given political representation in the legislative assembly two years earlier, and the resulting road-construction program stimulated growth to approximately 62,000 by 1844. The taxes on undeveloped land following the establishment of a township-based municipal and schools system during the later 1840s, and the concurrent construction of the *Grand Trunk Railway through the region, finally resulted in rapid growth.

Because the 1840s brought an exodus from overcrowded seigneuries, most of the new settlers in the frontier townships were French Canadians, as was the workforce in the growing industrial centres in the southern townships. As early as 1851, 36 per cent of the approximately 94,000 inhabitants were French Canadians; by 1871 they would be 58 per cent of the 168,000 total. With the abolition of the *seigneurial system in 1855, the distinction between the northern townships and the bordering parishes largely disappeared. Encouraged by the exodus of English-speaking families, the French Canadians soon began to expand into rural communities in the south, and by 1901, 72 per cent of the region's population were francophones. This transition was too rapid to result in a truly bicultural population, except for offspring of Catholic intermarriages such as Louis *St Laurent and Jean Charest. But the region was for many years characterized by political accommodation between the two cultures, if only because the French Canadians realized that they would eventually gain the upper hand. Today there are only a few pockets of English-speaking settlement left in the truncated regional municipal district officially known as l'Estrie. There are still several English-language high schools, a post-secondary college (Champlain), and a small university (Bishop's), whose student body comes largely from outside the region. The English-language population (centred in the Sherbrooke-Lennoxville area), is aging rapidly, and there is no longer an English-language radio station or daily newspaper. In short, the Eastern Townships has become largely indistinguishable culturally from the rest of Quebec.

But the region's picturesque lakes, mountains, and old New England-style villages and buildings continue to make it visually distinct, and the geography that was originally an economic handicap has increasingly become an asset because of the transportation and communications revolutions. Now easily accessible from Montreal and the northeastern United States, the Eastern Townships has become a popular tourist destination, as well as a focus of investment in technologically advanced and geographically dispersed light industries.
J.L. LITTLE

eastern woodlands Aboriginals. This designation is a geographic one that brings together societies of different linguistic origins and a variety of subsistence economies, including peoples living in the deciduous forests of coastal and inland regions. What distinguishes these societies is their dependence on intensive types of subsistence, in addition to hunting, such as maize horticulture, harvesting wild rice, and exploiting marine resources. These cultures are linked to similar ones to the south, as the woodland region extends into the United States. The northern reaches of this region are the southern limits of the coniferous boreal forest. Over millennia, boundaries have shifted, depending on climate and the vegetation cover. Also included within the eastern woodlands designation are smaller regions that, strictly speaking, are boreal forest such as the Gaspé and Cape Breton. The overall region is divided into three major woodland zones: maritime, St Lawrence lowlands, and the Great Lakes riverine area.

The peoples of the eastern woodlands first bore the brunt of successions of European invasions. Without records indicating the Native peoples' views of these aliens, one can only surmise that they suffered the consequences of aggressive greed as European fur traders pushed their way into the interior. Yet, the labour-saving devices the Europeans brought in trade evidently provided some compensation. The eastern woodland peoples first taught these foreigners how to live and travel in their lands. Had they not, the *fur trade might never have occurred, and the exploration and development of this country might have been very different.

Within the maritime zone are several eastern Algonquian-speaking peoples, one of the first subdivisions of the Algonquian-language family to have hived off and made their way to the Atlantic coast, probably several thousand years ago. However, the earliest evidence of human occupation is of an earlier Paleo-Indian culture, located on the edges of the glaciers in Nova Scotia, dated at 10,600 years ago. The tundra eventually gave way to a boreal forest cover, followed by the mixed hardwood forests known today, with easy access to the rich maritime resources of fish, shellfish, and birds. The ancestors of the present-day peoples thrived within this ecosystem. A remarkable maritime-based culture, known as the Maritime Archaic Tradition, extended from Labrador to Maine from about 5500 to 1000 BC. Several cemeteries, with burials decorated with red ochre, indicate an elaborate burial ceremonialism and have yielded tools and decorative items of exceptional quality. Made of polished stone, bone, antler, and ivory, these items indicate a mild climate and an abundance of food resources. The woodland period, which began about 2,500 years ago, is noted for the production of fine clay pottery. One burial mound site from this period—the Augustine Mound—has been discovered in New Brunswick. The ancestors of the *Mi'kmaq and Maliseet (Wulstukwiuk) peoples can be traced directly to sites that date back 2,000 years and indicate a coastal adaptation for most of the year. The *Beothuk, possibly also Algonquian speakers, lived mainly on the island of Newfoundland and suffered the earliest contact with fishermen and then settlement. They became extinct in the early part of the 19th century. Debate continues as to whether this was due to overt genocide by the settlers or to a combination of circumstances that included marginalization into less abundant regions and exposure to European diseases. Either way, the results were the same.

As peoples who could sustain relatively large, well-organized societies, the Mi'kmaq and Maliseet were able to defend their lands successfully in the 17th century when inter-societal disputes and warfare erupted as a consequence of the European fur trade and French–English hostilities. However, the end of the American revolutionary war brought thousands of *Loyalists to the Maritimes, which resulted in the dispossession of the Aboriginal peoples from their lands and led to major changes in their subsistence economy, social organization, and belief systems. These changes intensified as governments became involved and the people were settled on reserves, regulated by the *Indian Act of 1876. In more recent times, migration to the cities, Boston in particular, brought additional changes. Nevertheless, despite 500 years of living alongside their intruders, the Mi'kmaq and Maliseet have maintained a distinct cultural identity and preserved their languages.

The peoples most associated with the St Lawrence lowlands are northern Iroquoian speakers, first recorded by Jacques *Cartier in 1534–5. With their focus on maize horticulture and palisaded villages of up to 3,000 people, they are distinctive in the archaeological and archival records. Originally it was thought that the *Iroquois, coming from the south, drove a wedge between the central and eastern Algonquians, but archaeological research has shown their societies to have developed in the area of the lower Great Lakes. The prehistoric Iroquois populations took advantage of the diffusion of maize, and later beans and squash (the 'three sisters'), more than 1,000 years ago. Such horticulture sustained large populations and the development of a complex, matrilineal clan-based political organization that came together in several confederacies. The Iroquoian-speaking population of southern Ontario in the mid-1600s is estimated at 65,000. Best known among these were the *Huron, located between Georgian Bay and Lake Simcoe. *Champlain and subsequent French governors quickly latched onto the Huron, whose extensive trade networks into the interior yielded furs and allies. In 1649, however, the Huron became casualties of the hostilities caused by the fur trade and were dispersed after losing to the League of Iroquois. At the end of the 17th century, members of the Mohawk nation moved northward and settled in the St Lawrence lowlands. Throughout the next several centuries, they served first the French, then the English, as intermediaries, fur traders, militia, and most recently as the high steel workers in the construction industry of the large American urban centres.

Algonquian-speaking peoples also inhabited the St Lawrence lowlands. The Algonquins who lived along the St Lawrence were the first peoples Champlain met in 1608. Their alliance with the Huron enabled Champlain to extend the fur trade westward. However, by the mid-17th century they had been forced northward and had abandoned their middleman role for a subsistence base of hunting and fishing. About this time, the Abenaki, originally from the coastal and inland regions of the present-day state of Maine, began settling along the St Lawrence River at Becancour and St Francis, seeking a refuge from the warfare in their territory that was to last 100 years. Living as they did in the midst of settlers, the Abenaki engaged in a highly mixed economy of subsistence hunting, fur trade, and casual labour. At the end of the 19th century they took advantage of the newly developed tourist industry in Maine and New Hampshire, crafting and selling Indian souvenirs.

The Great Lakes riverine region was home to both Algonquian and Siouian peoples. The latter were the Assiniboine who occupied the territory north of Lake

Superior, straddling the woodlands–subarctic divide, until the northward migration of the Ojibwa people in the historic period. The region is culturally defined by the central Algonquians, though Indian occupation dates back, as elsewhere in the eastern woodlands, to about 11,000 years ago. This region, rich in fish and game, enabled cultures to flourish. The most spectacular occurred about 2,000 years ago, when ideas and exotic items swirled throughout the broad extent of the entire Great Lakes region. Marine shells were traded from the Gulf of Mexico, pipestone from the Ohio Valley, and copper from Lake Superior; all were used in the manufacture of implements and decorative items that have been recovered from burial mounds. Some of the mounds attained dimensions of 35 m in diameter and 8 m in height. One can only imagine the great body of knowledge, beliefs, and values that circulated as well.

The central Algonquians who came to dominate, at various times, this region's history and commerce were the Odawa, the Ojibwa, and the Nipissing. Each seized the economic opportunity when neighbouring societies faltered as a result of the 17th-century wars. Their economic base continued to be the rich resources of the Great Lakes and its surrounding forested lands, which enabled them to live part of the year in substantial villages. By the mid-1750s the Nipissing had been settled by the French, the Odawa scattered and joined with others, while groups of Ojibwa moved northward and westward to engage in the fur trade. Those who remained in the Great Lakes region, and among whom the United Empire Loyalists settled in great numbers, were the first Aboriginal peoples to be subjected to the gamut of social engineering—reserves, farming, schooling, model towns, *Indian agents, and rival missionaries—with assimilation being the goal.

Despite the over 400 years of contact and concerted attempts to assimilate or exclude them, eastern woodland Aboriginals have maintained a surprising degree of their old heritage. With population growth, political activism, economic diversity, and a degree of language retention, they have resisted assimilation and are determined their cultures will survive. TOBY MORANTZ

Eaton, Timothy (1834–1907), merchant, founder of Canada's largest privately owned *department store. After apprenticing in a general store in Ireland, Eaton followed two older brothers to Canada in 1854 and worked for a time at a store in Glen Williams, Canada West, near Georgetown. In 1856, with his brother James, he opened a small store in the Huron Tract at Kirkton, which they moved in 1860 to St Mary's, near Stratford. In 1869, convinced that change was in the air, Eaton opened his own store at 178 Yonge Street, Toronto, where he introduced Canadians to the concept of cash sales and one fixed price, as opposed to the older credit, bargain, and barter method. He displayed a sympathetic attitude towards his employees, and by the late 1880s instituted evening closing at 6 P.M. and the summer Saturday afternoon holiday. He vastly improved working conditions by creating light airy workplaces. The introduction of the Eaton catalogue in 1884 gave Canadians, particularly those in pioneer farming communities, access to a wide variety of merchandise. At his death in 1907 Eaton employed over 9,000 people in his Toronto and Winnipeg stores, in factories in Toronto and Oshawa, and in offices overseas in London and Paris. JOY L. SANTINK

Eaton Company strikes. Although the T. Eaton Company is usually remembered as a family-owned *department store, the company owned several large garment factories in the early 1900s. Despite Timothy *Eaton's attempts to portray himself as a generous patriarch who looked after his employees, Eaton's garment workers often faced gruelling conditions and low wages.

A strike of over 1,000 workers erupted at Eaton's Toronto factory in 1912 when management attempted to force certain male workers to take on an additional task that was usually performed by women. The female workers feared losing their jobs. Management refused to pay the men more for the additional work. Many of the workers were immigrant *Jews from eastern Europe, and the Jewish community strongly supported the strike, particularly as a notable example of male–female solidarity. The strikers were also protesting against poor pay, long hours, the exploitation of child labour, and sexual harassment. The factory's non-Jewish workers refused to strike, partly because of the prevalence of anti-Semitism. The strikers had to give up after four months, after which management refused to hire Jews.

Another key strike erupted in Eaton's Toronto factory in 1934 when a small group of non-Jewish women walked off the job due to abysmally low wages and harsh speed-ups. The strikers persevered despite management's attempts to exploit anti-Semitism to keep them away from Jewish union leaders. The strikers received significant support from the *Co-operative Commonwealth Federation and even from the Toronto branch of the *National Council of Women. But management was intransigent and defeated the strike. RUTH A. FRAGER

École littéraire de Montréal (1895–1935), a literary movement seeking to modernize French-Canadian literature. About 1890, young Montrealers such as Édouard-Zotique Massicotte were discovering contemporary French authors such as Verlaine, Leconte de Lisle, and Jean Richepin, whom conservative critics in Quebec immediately denounced as decadent and immoral. A few 'avant-garde' periodicals began to reprint extracts from French sources. Sensing a change in the literary climate, Jean Charbonneau and Louvigny de Montigny convened a meeting of literary hopefuls on 7 November 1895, and founded the École littéraire de Montréal.

In its first period (1895–1900), the École attracted considerable public attention. During the energetic presidency of Wilfrid Larose, four public meetings were held in 1898–9, three of them in the venerable Château de Ramezay. Already, however, conflicts between Larose and more idealistic members were affecting attendance, and after the publication in 1900 of a collective volume, *Les Soirées du Château de Ramezay*, membership dwindled. The great revelation of this initial period was the poetry of Émile Nelligan (1879–1941), whose passionate declaiming of his 'Romance du vin' caused a sensation at the public meeting held on 26 May 1899. Nelligan, undoubtedly a genius, composed some 160 poems while still in his teens, but was committed to a mental hospital in August 1899 and remained a patient for the rest of his life. His poems became known in editions published by his friend and mentor Eugène Seers (pseud. Louis Dantin).

In 1907 Germain Beaulieu undertook to revive the École by encouraging regionalist writing. Beaulieu, Charbonneau, and Albert Ferland launched a magazine, *Le Terroir*, which lasted only one year but which published excerpts from important works-in-progress by Charles Gill and Ferland. This local emphasis attracted a grant of $500 from the provincial government, but disposing of the money caused dissension. The second phase of the École (1907–13) concluded without additional achievements.

A further effort to reconstitute the École began in September 1919 with the support of Claude-Henri Grignon and Victor Barbeau. Another anthology, *Les Soirées de l'École littéraire de Montréal*, was published in 1925, but by then the more productive authors were publishing their own volumes, and several of the older members (Gill, Arthur de Bussières, Albert Lozeau, Alphonse Beauregard) had died. When Charbonneau finally published his history of the movement in 1935, the École itself was dead. DAVID M. HAYNE

École Polytechnique massacre. *See* MONTREAL MASSACRE.

École sociale populaire. Born in mid-19th-century Europe, social Catholicism was officially recognized by Pope Leo XIII in his encyclical **Rerum Novarum* in 1891. In Quebec it was first acknowledged in the essays of Eugène Lapointe, which were aimed at introducing Catholic unionism in the diocese of Chicoutimi, and in the works of Stanislas Lortie, organizer of the Société d'économie sociale et politique. Cardinal Bégin's arbitration in the shoe industry strike of 1901 lent authority to the movement, and in 1907 the Action sociale catholique was created, headed by Mgr Paul-Eugène Roy, who was to spearhead social Catholicism in Canada.

In 1911, the *Jesuits' École social populaire was founded, to interpret the church's social doctrine and prepare an elite to put it into practice. Inspired partly by another Jesuit foundation, the Action populaire de Reims (1903), its establishment cannot be separated from the Sacré-Coeur Leagues of Father Léonidas Hudon. The leagues' inquiry into labour organization led to a congress of eight dioceses, on 25–6 January, at which the ESP was founded. Entrusted to the care of Father Hudon, it was to be based in the offices of the *Messager canadien du Sacré-Coeur*, a Catholic newspaper. Its founders outlined an ambitious program. Conceived as a crossroads where people with a shared apostolic interest could come together, the ESP was to be a centre for study and training in the social doctrine of the church. The study of encyclicals was to lead to renewal of the social order. Above all, the goal was to promote the professional organization and the mutualism developed by European Catholics. The groundwork was laid by courses at the Université de Montréal, and the program was propagated by public conferences, monthly brochures, study groups, retreats, and so on. The period 1911–15 saw a proliferation of efforts to open the way for Catholic unionism in Montreal.

Under the leadership of Joseph Papin-Archambault, the ESP reached the height of its influence during the Depression. Bishops, fearing that the social turmoil provoked by unemployment would open the door to communism and socialism, wanted to propose a social project capable of competing with the *Co-operative Commonwealth Federation. It was not enough to denounce and refute the latter's program; Catholics were demanding a counter-program that would open a new path. Thus on 9 March 1933 Papin-Archambault called 13 churchmen to the training College of the Immaculate Conception, where a 13-part program for social renewal was produced. This doctrinal manifesto outlined a program of social legislation, proposed the regulation of financial operations, and envisioned some measures to control the management of public affairs. Concrete measures were put forward, including allocations for unemployment, old-age pensions, a family wage for workers, and laws regarding risks of accident and illness. Above all, the document supported the non-state corporatism promoted by Pius XI, which was based on co-operation between owners' and workers' associations in the same branch of production.

A short time later, a group of lay people under the auspices of the ESP published a second, more detailed and technical 'programme de restauration sociale', which addressed moral reform, rural renewal, the labour question, the struggle against the trusts, and financial and political reforms. Well received by *Le Devoir*, *L'*Action nationale*, and *L'Action catholique*, this program was later borrowed by the Action libérale nationale, Maurice *Duplessis's *Union nationale, and even Liberals in the 1936 election. With the approach of the Second World War and the end of the Depression, this movement for social renewal weakened, a pastoral letter on the restoration of social order (11 March 1941) being its last gasp.

GILLES ROUTHIER

economic nationalism. As long as there have been nation states there have been popular sentiments and government policies directed towards the protection and enhancement of the national economy in the pursuit of economic sovereignty—and these pass by the name of economic nationalism. While manifesting itself centrally in matters of trade and tariffs, and of policies towards foreign investment, economic nationalism is also about the capacity of the state to build national infrastructure, notably in transportation and communication, and to pursue its own fiscal and taxation policies, and its own monetary or interest rate policy, including having its own currency. For Canada, born as part of an international or global economy and manoeuvring within successive empires—French, British, American—any nationalism is bound to be muted and moderate and will be constantly tested.

Canada's first great act of economic nationalism, only a decade after Confederation, was the implementation of national policies that committed the state to building a transcontinental railway that would bind the national economy together and that brought in a high protective tariff to facilitate industrialization. These policies were highly successful in nation building and in generating economic growth. By enticing non-resident firms, particularly from the United States, to leap the tariff wall and establish branch plants in Canada, this first phase of economic nationalism was compromised and the basis laid for a second phase directed against the extent of *foreign ownership. This phase peaked in the 1960s and 1970s, culminating in the Trudeau government's short-lived *National Energy Program in the early 1980s. Since that time, the most recent era of globalization has led to the abandonment of serious concern about foreign ownership—by the 1990s the venerable Montreal Canadiens hockey team was sold to an American with nary a protest!—and to the elimination of tariffs through North American and global free trade agreements.

In Canada, the powerful pull of the United States towards *continentalism was evident in increasing talk among Canadian business people and economists in the new millennium about adopting the American dollar as the Canadian currency. The horror of the terrorists attacks on the United States of 11 September 2001 pushed Canada towards developing a common North American perimeter with the United States, at the risk of a quantum leap in the harmonization of a range of Canadian policies—security, military, immigration and refugee—with those of its larger and much more powerful neighbour. The future for Canadian nationalism, including the economic variant, is evidently problematic, although it might be presumed that Canadian governments that fail to maintain the levers necessary to create jobs in Canada do so at their peril. MELVILLE WATKINS

Edmonton. Edmonton's history has been marked by alternating periods of boom and economic stagnation. After the first *fur trade post was established in the vicinity of the modern city in 1795, Fort Edmonton emerged as the most important *Hudson's Bay Company transportation and administrative hub between Winnipeg and the Pacific Coast. With the beginnings of prairie agricultural settlement in the 1880s and the decision to move the Canadian Pacific main line south, Edmonton was for two decades in danger of remaining a small regional service centre. Shortly after the turn of the 20th century, the arrival of the Canadian Northern and Grand Trunk Pacific transcontinental rail lines, along with the decision to locate the capital of *Alberta there, set off a period of very rapid growth that led to amalgamation with the city of Strathcona, across the river, in 1912. The outbreak of the First World War brought an abrupt halt to immigration and marked the beginning of a quarter century of economic hibernation. The Second World War, in contrast, was the beginning of a half century in which Edmonton expanded from fewer than 100,000 people to nearly a million by the beginning of the new century.

One of the continuities in Edmonton's history has been its role from the 1820s onward as the principal transportation link to the western Arctic. The emergence of bush flying in the 1930s reinforced the traditional river routes. The *Alaska Highway and the *Northwest Staging Route in the 1940s extended those ties to the Yukon. The new element in Edmonton's economy after the mid-20th century was oil. Major discoveries at *Leduc and elsewhere led to important refining and petrochemical industries. In the 1970s, as conventional petroleum exploration began to wane, the huge oil sands plants at Fort McMurray came on stream to replace it. Edmonton has also benefited in recent decades from the expansion of forest products industries in northern Alberta.

Until the 1960s the University of Alberta in Edmonton was the only degree-granting institution in the province. The expansion of the university in the last four decades to one of the largest in Canada, along with the growth of the Northern Alberta Institute of Technology and an array of community colleges, has maintained the city's status as an educational centre. Perhaps because of the concentration of post-secondary institutions, Edmonton has had one of the most vigorous *theatre scenes in the country since the 1960s, with the Citadel Theatre and a number of other professional companies as well as the Fringe Theatre Festival, the first and largest event of its kind in Canada. In the last half of the 20th century Edmonton supported a highly successful symphony orchestra, a professional opera, and one of Canada's largest folk music festivals. Two of the city's professional sports franchises, the Eskimos in the Canadian Football League and the Oilers in the National Hockey League, have won more than their share of championships. R.C. MACLEOD

Edmonton Grads. It would be difficult to find a team anywhere, in any sport, as dominant as the Edmonton Grads women's basketball team. Established in 1915 and drawing its players from the McDougall Commercial High School in Edmonton, this team won every Canadian championship 1923–40, the Underwood Typewriter North American championships for 17 straight years, and every game they played in Olympic competition. Their lifetime record of 520 wins and only 20 losses testifies to their dominance in competitive women's basketball, and to the fact that basketball was the team sport of choice for most female atheletes in the first half of the 20th century. COLIN HOWELL

education in colonial English Canada. Between the end of the French regime and Confederation in 1867, a variety of educational institutions prepared the children and youth of British North America for entry into the world of work and the professions. Religious, economic, and geographic factors, and the racial and ethnic changes resulting from shifting immigration patterns, shaped the development of education in the English-speaking colonies. In this period, before the growth of a centralized system of education that would eventually control curriculum, instruction, attendance, and teacher certification, education was largely a small business or a service offered by local churches..

Parents of modest means could employ the services of local educational entrepreneurs. These included the itinerant school master, who journeyed from home to home providing instruction to individuals or small groups of children on a fee-for-service basis, or from the school mistress, a woman who offered learning for payment within her home. Other parents could elect to send their children to church-sponsored Sunday School programs that promoted literacy and numeracy.

Both Protestant and Catholic churches and the state exerted strong influences on the development of public and private educational endeavours. Tensions resulting from the push for denominationally based and nondenominational educational systems laid the foundation for the establishment of parallel, publicly funded school systems, most notably the Roman Catholic separate schools in Ontario.

Segregation and differentiated curricula based on class, sex, race, and language were features of many schools. When they were educated, Black and Aboriginal children were frequently sent to their own schools. New Brunswick's Sussex Vale Indian College accommodated both residential and day pupils. Schools such as this were partnerships among a number of institutions: the churches, independent entrepreneurs, the state, and in rare cases the Aboriginal peoples themselves. In some locations, ethnic communities came together to found schools where the language of instruction reflected their origins and cultural heritage. Sons of the wealthy attended private denominationally based or secular schools to prepare them for higher education. Class values were integrated into the overt and hidden curriculum. If they were not educated by private tutor at home, daughters of the wealthy could attend convent academies or other select schools that offered them a variety of educational experiences, from the 'accomplishments' curriculum of music, artistic expression, and foreign languages to a good preparation for higher education—had they been allowed to pursue such a goal. Generally, it was the exceptional girl, pupil of colour, or child of the poor or labouring classes who received an education beyond the basics. For youth interested in trades and some professions, apprenticeship was the norm.

By the end of the colonial period, there is evidence of the rise of the public school system of today, with its elementary and secondary panels. Central organization was winnowing out the smaller educational entrepreneurs, and standardization of curriculum was eliminating the use of the terms academy, college, or grammar school in favour of *high school or collegiate. ELIZABETH SMYTH

education in New France. In New France education was the responsibility of the church, and its objective was Christianization. Instruction was an essential part of the early French missionaries' efforts to convert and acculturate the Aboriginal people. The different approaches used by the *Ursulines, *Jesuits, and *Congrégation de Notre-Dame—seminaries, schools on reserves, catechism lessons—met with limited success, although the missionaries made a contribution to Aboriginal languages by compiling the first Native dictionaries.

The children of the French settlers were taught to read and write as part of their religious education. At the same time, the social role of education was recognized, for the civil authorities established an informal system of bursaries, gifts, and land concessions that helped the main institutions to survive. Two levels of instruction can be distinguished: primary and secondary, the latter restricted to boys. In accordance with the norms of the time, efforts were made to separate boys and girls in different institutions.

Girls were taught in boarding schools run by nuns. The first boarding school was founded by the Ursulines in 1639 at Quebec. This institution also accepted day pupils in a class for 'the poor'. In 1697 the Ursulines agreed to establish another boarding school at Trois-Rivières. In Montreal the Congrégation de Notre-Dame began teaching children in 1658. Their first school was exceptional, in that it accepted both boys and girls. Boarding facilities opened in 1676, and the congregation also opened a dozen boarding schools in various parishes. As these sisters were not cloistered, they were asked to open schools at *Louisbourg and even Detroit in the 18th century, although the latter plan could not be realized. In addition, the Hospitalières offered boarding at the Hôpital-Général de Québec beginning in 1725. Students stayed for approximately two years, the time required to prepare for their first communion. They were also taught to sew. Beginning in the 18th century, boarding institutions in Quebec City offered a more refined program, based on the goals of feminine education: mastery of the French language, the so-called gentle arts, and religious instruction. Rigorous supervision made boarders' lives very like those of nuns, ensuring their moral development.

Boys' schools were less consistent. They existed in 25 parishes, but more than 60 parishes had no schools. Some teachers were parish curés, others were sons sent into exile in New France, soldiers on leave, or adventurers of various kinds; there were few real teachers except in schools run by religious institutions, notably in Quebec City and Montreal. Boys were taught the rudiments of writing, arithmetic, and reading, along with religion. Because we know less about boys' schools than we do about girls', it has been assumed that women in New France were better educated than men. But all studies of literacy, based on the signatures of husbands and wives on marriage documents, show that the literacy rate among men was higher. We also know that the level of instruction among the general population was low.

There were no trades schools at the time; trades were learned through private apprenticeship contracts. The *Séminaire de Québec paid for the crafts training of some of the students in its schools who were not inclined towards traditional studies. In the Montreal region the Charron Brothers tried to set up a network of boys' schools after 1693, but their efforts were limited by financial difficulties the organization faced after 1720.

Secondary education began quite early, with the Jesuits opening a college for a select minority of boys in 1635. This institution, modelled on French colleges, offered courses in grammar, Latin, Greek, rhetoric, and philosophy. The full program took six or seven years to complete. The teaching faculty consisted of Jesuits from France assisted by 'regents', young novices in training with the Society of Jesus. The students, some 20 at the beginning, probably numbered 100 at the end of the 17th century. It was at this college that students at the Séminaire de Québec, founded by Mgr *Laval in 1663, went for academic instruction before beginning their ecclesiastical training. The Séminaire itself took charge of the moral and theological development of future priests. The Quebec college offered more advanced courses in hydrography and mathematics, subjects deemed essential in a colony where the navy, civil and military, played an important role. MICHELINE DUMONT

education in the industrial age. Canada's transition to an industrial society was in full swing by the first decade of the 20th century, and Canadians greeted this development with both enthusiasm and concern. They cherished the promise of occupational options, new consumer goods, and higher living standards. But many were troubled by other products of the emerging urban landscape—crowds, poverty, hazardous health conditions, wayward youth. Some lamented the erosion of rural life itself. If industrial capitalism were here to stay, could it not be made to function better? And did schooling not have a vital role to play in facilitating this end? Educational reformers thought so, and school boards, classroom, and playgrounds all felt their impact.

The rise of the *factory system eroded the position of skilled craftsmen such as blacksmiths, shoemakers, and tailors, and undermined the apprenticeship system through which young males had been trained. Employers, politicians, and school reformers argued that *public education ought to play a more active role in preparing youth for the demands of the industrial age. Manual training, which engaged boys in basic wood- and metalwork, was one popular response to the call for more practical schooling. Among its chief advocates were James Hughes, an Ontario educator, and Alexander MacKay, the supervisor of schools in Halifax, which by 1894 offered manual training in 30 city schools. The national campaign was boosted in 1899 by support from the Macdonald Manual Training Fund, established by the Montreal tobacco manufacturer and philanthropist Sir William Macdonald. Across the country, the fund initially subsidized training centres affiliated with public schools, and by 1914 manual training had become a regular part of the senior elementary curriculum in most urban communities. By facilitating hand-eye coordination, manual training was intended to strengthen those elements of the brain that contributed to orderly, precise, and analytical thinking, qualities considered essential in technical occupations. Manual training also had supposed moral value; by teaching the student to 'control himself in small actions' it would inhibit his 'passion and desires', thus discouraging antisocial, even delinquent, behaviour. These were lofty and unrealistic expectations for a program that stressed only the most elementary aspects of the mechanical arts.

Manual training was offered only to boys because, unlike girls, they were expected ultimately to work in industrial occupations. But women educational reformers, such as Adelaide *Hoodless, contended that schools were equally obligated to address the utilitarian interests of female students. A pioneer of the domestic science movement, Hoodless believed that schools should instruct girls in subjects such as food chemistry, needlework, cooking, and home management and that such domestic science courses would make mothers and wives more competent and family life more durable. By giving the practice academic and scientific credibility, schools could enhance the respectability of homemaking and discourage young women from pursuing other vocations in emerging industrial centres. The campaign for domestic education bore fruit. The subject was first included in the Ontario curriculum in 1904 and Alberta in 1912; by 1920 British Columbia had 29 domestic science centres. In the Roman Catholic schools of Quebec, the subject was made mandatory in 1921. Typically, however, the curriculum focused on cooking and sewing and, as with manual training, remained far more limited than reformers had anticipated.

However elevated the original goals, these basic courses failed to satisfy the demands of the most determined advocates of technical and industrial education. Educational and business lobbyists called for curricular provisions that would both deepen students' understanding of technology and train them for specific trades. Labour organizations, too, supported technical schooling, though some unionists feared the prospect of divisive job competition between young vocational-course graduates and older factory workers.

A technical school was established in Montreal in 1907. In the same year, Nova Scotia passed legislation that led to the opening in Halifax of the Nova Scotia Technical College, where students studied engineering. Local technical schools in other communities offered evening classes in subjects such as architectural drawing, chemistry, electricity, and surveying. Miners were encouraged to attended colliers' schools to learn the 'fundamentals' of safe mining. The Hamilton Technical and Art School was built in 1910. One year later, Ontario's Industrial Education Act augured the introduction of a range of programs, including technical departments in secondary schools, two-year general industrial schools, and, by 1914, evening industrial programs. Commissions were established to assess the need for vocational education in the Prairie provinces and British Columbia, though major developments there were delayed until the passage of the federal Technical Education Act in 1919, which authorized significant funding for provincially administered technical schooling. While vocational and technical education thus secured a significant place in school curricula, it still lacked the status of academic study, and thus reinforced social class divisions so characteristic of urban, industrial communities. Working-class youth were commonly channelled into these programs while affluent families customarily educated their children for more prestigious and lucrative occupations.

According to educational reformers, urban, industrial life also subjected children to a more sedentary lifestyle than their rural counterparts, and deprived them of adequate exercise. A number of influences combined to raise the profile of school-based physical education. Epidemics of diphtheria and *tuberculosis periodically erupted and spread quickly through poorly ventilated homes and school buildings. Physical exercise, preferably outdoors, was a recommended antidote to these conditions. Indeed in an era when social Darwinist thinkers, like the British writer Herbert Spencer, were widely cited, many educators accepted the contention that only the healthiest and fittest of the human species would survive. Physically active, able-bodied youth might also, eventually, contribute to reversing the declining birth rate in Canada, particularly among those of Anglo-Saxon origin. In light of the influx of European immigrants, fears were expressed—consistent with the racist hereditarian views that informed immigration policy itself—that the country would suffer 'racial degeneration' if its reproductive capacity were not improved. For this reason, schoolgirls were expected to avoid overexertion, which medical authorities and educators believed could damage their reproductive organs. Whereas boys partook in rugged physical competitions, as well as cadet training in the years leading up to the First World War, girls more frequently engaged in milder games such as lawn tennis and calisthenics.

By regularly examining and immunizing schoolchildren, health professionals employed by school boards addressed, in more direct ways, student health needs. Following similar American initiatives, Montreal introduced 'regular and systematic' school inspections in 1906, as did Sydney, Nova Scotia, one year later. By 1914, Toronto's School Health Department had on staff a chief medical officer, 21 physicians working as part-time medical inspectors, several dentists, and 37 full-time school nurses.

Canadian schooling responded to the industrial age with a variety of programs designed to produce not only a literate, but a disciplined and productive workforce. Manual training, domestic science, and vocational education highlighted two important elements of public schooling in the early 20th century: its concern with students' character, including their mental and physical development, and its tendency to channel youth into particular academic streams according to their gender and social class. While all children obtained more schooling than had earlier generations, both educational and economic privileges still flowed more fully to those from higher social strata. PAUL AXELROD

Edwards, Robert Charles (1864–1922). A Scottish-born journalist who earned a lasting reputation in western Canada as the maverick publisher of the Calgary *Eye Opener*, Edwards came west in 1894, launching the *Eye Opener* in High River in 1902 before moving it to Calgary two years later. His boisterous personality and hard-drinking lifestyle suited the frontier, and the paper's style assured a loyal readership. Ribald humour, caustic wit, and stinging attacks on predatory capitalists, self-serving politicians, and the socially 'respectable' were the paper's staples. Straight news coverage was always secondary. Crusading endeared him to his readers but frequently brought him into contact with the libel laws. The most notorious action, subsequently dropped, involved his dismissal of Premier Arthur Sifton as one of the 'three biggest liars in Alberta'—Edwards had characteristically named himself as the other two. Others who were stung by Edwards's pen and took him to court included the CPR and the Lord's Day Alliance. The *Eye Opener* continued to entertain and outrage until Edwards's premature death in 1922. PATRICK H. BRENNAN

employment standards legislation. Legally enforceable minimum terms and conditions of employment established by the state, these standards apply to all the workers covered by the law. Prior to 1877, a statutory master-and-servant regime prevailed in Canada, which rendered workers covered by the law criminally liable for breach of contract but which also provided workers with a simplified legal process for recovering unpaid wages. The repeal of these master-and-servant statutes in 1877 substantially decriminalized individual employment law and marked the triumph of a capitalist labour market governed by freedom-of-contract principles. This understanding ensured that in post-Confederation Canada, employment matters, including minimum standards, were seen to be largely a matter of property and civil rights, an area of provincial jurisdiction under the British North America Act.

Pressure for direct state regulation of some terms and conditions of employment occurred first in respect to hazards at work and compensation for work injuries. The push for regulation came from workers concerned about both dangerous working conditions and common law rules that prevented them from suing employers for work injuries, and from reformers concerned that factories posed a particular danger to the physical and moral health of women and children. In the 1880s, provinces began enacting protective legislation that set minimum standards for all workers, as well as special 'protections' for women and children, including limits on their hours of work. Inspectors were authorized to enter workplaces and enforce the law. At the same time, provincial legislation modified common law liability rules and, beginning in 1914, established workers' compensation systems through which workers injured in the course of employment were paid using funds collected from employers and administered by provincial workers' compensation boards.

In the 20th century, minimum standards developed in a highly gendered fashion. Federal and provincial fair-wage laws required governments to pay no less than prevailing local wages on government contract work. The first private sector minimum-wage laws, passed during and in the aftermath of the First World War, applied only to women. Minimum-wage boards were empowered to set wages on an occupational and regional basis that aimed to meet the subsistence needs of a single women living on her own, while also taking into account business conditions. In some provinces, boards also regulated hours of work for women. British Columbia was the only province to extend minimum wage and hours of work laws to men.

The Great Depression provided the impetus for a general extension of minimum wages laws to men, but few orders were issued, leaving most workers to fend for themselves under unfavourable labour market conditions. The Second World War set the stage for greater direct state regulation of labour markets and employment standards, initially through federal wage controls that limited wage increases in the face of labour shortages rather than protecting workers from unacceptable conditions. The war also led to the enactment of a long-debated and much delayed federal unemployment insurance scheme. As the war progressed and labour unrest increased, the provinces were pressured to establish additional labour standards and to address discriminatory employment practices. Vacation-with-pay legislation was first enacted in Ontario in 1944, as was the first law prohibiting racial discrimination in employment.

Employment standards proliferated in the post-war era. Fair employment laws prohibiting discrimination on an expanding number of grounds were passed by provinces in the 1950s and were transformed into human rights codes enforced by administrative tribunals in the 1960s. Among the more recent prohibited grounds of discrimination are age, sex, disability, and sexual orientation. Workplace sexual harassment was also made a human rights violation. In the 1980s, political pressure to address persistent gendered wage inequality led some jurisdictions to enact pay equity laws that required employers to take steps to ensure that women receive equal pay for work of equal value. An even smaller number of jurisdictions enacted employment equity laws that aim to eliminate barriers facing women, visible minorities, First Nations peoples, and persons with disabilities.

The range of employment standards also increased: by the 1950s it included broader minimum wage laws, overtime pay, weekend rest days, and limits on hours of work; in the 1960s, entitlements to paid public holidays, maternity leave, and notice of termination were introduced. Since then, few new standards have been added but many have been changed. Most often the standards were strengthened, although in recent years protections have been eroded in many provinces. As well, in many provinces some groups of workers, including domestics and agricultural workers, have been totally or partially excluded from protection that other workers enjoy.

A similar trend was visible in other areas of labour protection. Occupational health and safety laws were substantially overhauled in the 1970s, giving workers rights to know about workplace hazards, participate in joint health and safety committees, and refuse unsafe work, but enforcement was often problematic. Workers' compensation and unemployment insurance were strengthened in the 1970s but eroded in the mid- to late-1980s.

Finally, although the common law has never been a significant source of employment standards, since the mid- to late 19th century it has presumed that contracts of employment are of indefinite duration and can be terminated only by reasonable notice unless the employee has committed a serious breach of contract. The common law provided employees with some economic protection if they were terminated without just cause, but lower-status workers were entitled to only brief notice. Since the 1980s, the courts have adopted a more protective approach towards individual employees, including lower-status ones, increasing notice periods and making it harder to dismiss them without notice for just cause.

ERIC TUCKER

Empress of Ireland, Canada's worst ocean liner disaster, 29 May 1914. A world-class liner, *Empress of Ireland* and its sister *Empress of Britain* were built in 1906 by Canadian Pacific to attract the premier North Atlantic passenger traffic to the St Lawrence route linking CP's worldwide network of railways and steamers. In heavy fog near Rimouski, the outbound *Empress of Ireland* was struck by the coal carrier *Storstad*. An enormous hole ripped in the engine room plunged the liner into darkness. It quickly rolled to one side and sank in 14 minutes. Many passengers never made it out of their cabins, and few lifeboats could be launched. The 1,012 deaths included whole families and much of the leadership of the Canadian *Salvation Army, who were travelling to a London conference. The heavy losses, with proportionally more passengers lost than on **Titanic*, were a blow to the reputation of the sheltered St Lawrence route. However, the tragedy was forgotten by many, overshadowed by the loss of *Titanic* two years earlier and the outbreak of war a few months later. Salvage after the wreck was followed by years of souvenir hunting until 1998, when the wreck received protected status under Quebec law. DAN CONLIN

Endicott, James G. (1898–1993), missionary, peace activist. Endicott was born in China, where he returned as a missionary from Canada in 1925. An outspoken critic of the Chiang Kai-Shek regime and advocate of the Communist revolutionaries in the Chinese civil war, he resigned his *United Church ministry in May 1946. On his return to Canada he founded the Canadian Peace Congress in 1948, leading the campaign to 'ban the bomb' and promote East–West co-operation. During the *Korean War he lent support to charges that the United States was employing 'germ warfare' against North Korea and China, and was almost charged with treason by the cabinet. He was awarded the Stalin Peace Prize by Moscow in 1952. The subject of intense controversy in the 1950s, in the 1980s he was honoured by the United Church for his 'faithful and courageous contribution to the cause of Peace and Global Justice'. REG WHITAKER

engagés. In New France, two types of workers were known as engagés: male indentured servants recruited in France for service in the colonies, and canoe- and boatmen in the *fur trade. Engagés of the first kind were hired in French Atlantic ports. In return for their labour, usually for three years (hence their nickname, *trente-six mois*), they received a salary and ocean passage, usually one-way. In the St Lawrence Valley they were in relatively heavy demand from the 1650s to the early 1670s, years when a spurt of church, private, and especially royal investment created a need for both skilled and unskilled labour. While engagés continued to arrive in Canada and *Louisbourg until the end of the French regime, sea captains tended to evade regulations obliging them to transport a few engagés on voyages to the colonies, and in Canada the local population and soldiers met all but the most specialized labour needs. Only some 1,200 of the 5,000-odd engagés who made the crossing to Canada settled there. Engagés of the second sort, eventually better-known as *voyageurs, were mostly Canadian-born and increasingly of rural origin. From the late 17th century until well into the 19th they worked for fur merchants or companies, transporting merchandise and peltry on arduous trips between Lachine, just west of Montreal, and the posts of the Great Lakes region and beyond. Most participated only for a summer or two, but others were regulars, their pay rising with their skill level. Some wintered at the posts, sometimes finding a wife, usually Native, and staying for good. Over two centuries and in both its connotations, the term engagé evoked workers travelling between two worlds. THOMAS WIEN

engineering. *See* CIVIL ENGINEERING.

English immigrants and ethnicity. England is the largest and historically most dominant nation of the British Isles and, after 1707, of Great Britain. The term 'English' should be used to refer only to people born in England, and should not be confused with the more inclusive term 'British', which includes all people born in Great Britain and Ireland. Terminology is confused by several factors. First, many people assume there is a connection between the English language and the people who spoke it, as in the term 'anglais' in 19th-century Quebec. Second, the English people tend to assume that they and the British have always been virtually identical, as the study and teaching of English history in Canada have long demonstrated. Finally, it is commonly believed that the early American colonials who came to Canada before the 19th century (Yankee Planters and Loyalists) had all migrated to America from England and were thus all originally English. Only in recent years have scholars and the Canadian public come to accept the notion that the English are as much an ethnic group as *Italians or *Ukrainians, even though they often have had a superior standing and some advantages when they entered the country as immigrants. For most of Canada's history, the English have been part of the 'preferred' pool of immigrants, regarded as easily assimilable to the nation's society and economy. English immigrants, especially those of the educated classes, have found a ready welcome among the anglophilic society of Canada's elite.

In the early 17th century, people from England first settled in Newfoundland, and it remains Canada's most 'English' province. Most English emigration to Canada began following the Napoleonic Wars as part of the great movement of people from the British Isles to British North America in the 19th century. More English than *Scots came, although not as many English as *Irish. Large numbers of English tended to arrive later in the century. Because England was far more highly developed economically than Scotland, Ireland, or Wales, probably a far greater proportion of English immigrants arrived with substantial amounts of capital. Certainly large numbers of English immigrants with social pretensions arrived, mainly in two contingents. The first consisted of the half-pay officers, merchants, and colonial officials who came in the first part of the 19th century and founded little pockets of 'gentry' in places like Peterborough, Upper Canada, and Victoria, British Columbia. A second such contingent came between 1875 and the Great War and consisted of younger sons of the upper classes, often shipped to Canada and given living allowances—the so-called *remittance men—and 'distressed gentlewomen'. The remittance men had a quite negative image in Canada and were responsible for many of the notorious 'No English Need Apply' signs of western Canadian mythology. Many of these gentry were attracted to western ranches and fruit farms. Some established deliberate communities, such as Cannington Manor in Saskatchewan. They certainly created districts where an upper-class English lifestyle—private boarding schools, polo and cricket, English-style horseback riding, and the hunt—was perpetuated. The cattle country in the foothills of the Rockies was notorious for its English society: in Canada the cattle industry was dominated not by cowboys but by upper-class Englishmen.

Despite its best efforts, the Church of England was never able to establish its dominance over religion or to become the 'national church' of the English in Canada. Available data suggest that fewer than half of English immigrants were Anglican; large numbers of Methodists, Presbyterians, Baptists, and other dissenters were among the newcomers. The arrival of large numbers of English in the 19th century did enhance the position of the Church of England, particularly in the West. There, the church served something of an ethnic function; indeed, western Anglican clergymen worried that the church would be perceived as 'something for Englishmen alone'.

All English immigrants arriving in Canada, at least after Confederation, recognized that their cultural identity was quite distinct from that of the host society. Canadians spoke with American accents and often had trouble understanding the dialects and pronunciations of the new English arrivals, whether their speech reflected the cockney of the streets of London or the brogues of the industrial cities of the Midlands. English working-class immigrants were probably perceived as more 'ethnic' than the gentry. The former were, after all, accustomed to drinking thick beer in pubs, to following football (i.e., soccer) teams, to singing the songs of the English music halls, and to eating bangers and mash or fish and chips. Certainly the English immigrants who came to Canada between 1896 and the Great War formed ethnic organizations, most notably the Sons of England, which boasted over 40,000 members in 1913, and the St George's Society. Perhaps the most important aspect of this ethnic identification was the speed with which young English immigrants enlisted to fight in the 'old country's' wars. Those of English origin were clearly overrepresented among Canada's Boer War volunteers, and also in the earliest volunteer contingents of the Great War, especially those from western cities like Winnipeg, Calgary, and Vancouver.

Especially since the Second World War, English ethnic identity in Canada has been subjected to several assimilationist trends. One has been for all Canadians with ancestry in the British Isles to regard themselves as British rather than as simply members of one of the historic nations. The other has been for English cultural identity to become internationalized under the influence of the Common Market and globalization.

J.M. BUMSTED

English Shore. The east coast of Newfoundland from Trepassey in the south to Bonavista in the north. After 1565 the shore was seasonally frequented by Devon and Dorset crews fishing inshore for cod. The first proprietary colonies were at *Cupids Cove, 1610, and *Ferryland, 1621. Settlement by English fisherfolk was encouraged in 1638–51 under Sir David *Kirke, displacing native *Beothuk in the north. The area was subsequently governed only by *fishing admirals and the Royal Navy, under terms of the *Western Charters, until *King William's Act, 1699. Naval censuses in 1675–92 report resident 'planter' boat keepers, wives, children, and overwintering servants, totalling about 1,700, in about 25 harbours, joined every summer by 5,000 to 6,000 migratory fishers. The planter economy was based on salt cod, lumber, boat building, livestock agriculture, and a brisk trade in wine. In 1696–7, devastated by Canadian and Abenaki troops under Pierre d'*Iberville, who burned homes and boats, the fisherfolk embarked for England. The largest settlement, St John's (winter population about 250), was seasonally dominated by migratory fishers and effectively the capital only after British troops were stationed there in 1697. There were further French attacks in 1705 and 1708, but the regular annual rhythm of the British migratory fishery permitted rapid resettlement by English and Irish, the latter particularly after 1740.

PETER E. POPE

environmental movements. In the 1950s conservationists began to question the industrial development policy of provincial and federal governments. For author Roderick Haig-Brown, protection of trout streams meant taking stands against dam construction and aerial spraying of forests. Canadian conservationists discussed DDT on radio half a decade before American writer Rachel Carson's *Silent Spring* used examples from the Miramichi for its chapter 'River of Death'. Though few, conservationists were becoming persistently vocal.

By the 1960s, media fostered public support for environmentalism by making pollution visible and immediate. Young filmmakers used mobile cameras and colour television to show water and air pollution along the Great Lakes. Phosphate from laundry detergent and agricultural runoff threatened life in these and many other lakes. Governments seemed powerless, uncaring, and out of touch with the need to protect Canada's environment. University professors and students started citizen action groups. On the west coast, the Society for Promoting Environmental Conservation (1968) formed at Simon Fraser University. A spin-off became an early 'back to the land' movement. At the University of British Columbia a young professor, David Suzuki, became an active environmentalist. In a downtown Vancouver kitchen, concern over a planned nuclear testing at Amchitka brought the peace movement and the 'green' movement together. They became *Greenpeace, the world's most media-savvy group of environmental activists.

Elsewhere in Canada others organized for the same causes. In Quebec at Laval discussions were led by figures such as ethnobotanist and pacifist Jacques Rousseau. In Toronto Ralph Brinkhurst and Donald Chant at the University of Toronto founded Pollution Probe (1969). A young generation of wilderness converts began to oppose logging in Ontario's parks. Journals like *Alternatives* debated the environmental cost of industrial development on Canada, linking smokestacks and acid rain to the fate of lakes and forests such as Temagami. Soon they began to talk about global ecology and development. It was the age of 'heroic' environmentalism, sailing out to save the world, the whales, and the seals, and defeat incompetent government and greedy capitalism.

Yet the ascendancy of such middle-class Canadian environmentalism is only part of the story. The first nationwide meeting on pollution and the environment was held by the Council of Resource Ministers (Montreal 1966), not activists. They were concerned about air quality, safe municipal water supplies, and food-borne viruses. The International Joint-Boundary Commission studied Lake Erie and Lake Ontario pollution years before the media discovered it. However, its choice to allow industry to self-regulate phosphates failed to satisfy the public. Soon, ministries of the environment were created and government action became a visible response to the explosion of environmental issues and public demands.

In the North, Canada's extensive ecological monitoring of radioactive fallout resulted in warnings that traditional food-chain links presented health risks for the *Inuit. When Americans celebrated Earth Day in 1970, Canadian politicians passed the Canadian Arctic Waters Pollution Prevention Act in response to the passage of the US oil tanker *Manhattan* through Canada's arctic waters. Today, climate change has opened the *Northwest Passage, and reopened that issue.

Ecology and environment became a permanent part of the Canadian educational system, politics, and culture. The 1970s saw an escalation in the scale of environmental change as a wave of *hydroelectric development projects followed the 1973 energy crisis. Large areas of land were flooded. The James Bay project highlighted the impact upon Canada's indigenous peoples. Similar stories occurred under a range of political parties and provincial governments, from British Columbia to northern Manitoba and Labrador. The Berger Inquiry investigated the impact of a *Mackenzie Valley pipeline and another looked at tanker traffic on the Pacific coast.

Within these debates emerged a fledgling Canadian environmental justice movement. There had been no such advocacy for the First Nations men who died of radiation sickness after carrying sacks of uranium ore on their backs, for Canada's nuclear program in the 1940s. But, by the 1970s church groups, environmentalists, and First Nations political activists combined to defend small poor communities whose names were unknown to most urban Canadians. In 1976 Warner Troyer drew attention to the health impact of industrial discharges of mercury upstream from the Dog Creek and Grassy Narrows reserve in Ontario.

Although Canada has been slow to accept the connection between poverty, ill health, and proximity to industrial development, it is clearly evident, and not just on reserves. In the Maritimes, *Africville symbolized both the environmental marginalization of urban Black Canadians and their later dispossession by industrial development. Similarly, working-class residents of Frederick Street in Sydney, Nova Scotia, live next to tar ponds, North America's largest toxic site. To date $250 million has been spent on this legacy problem.

The last two decades have seen a continual expansion of environmenal issues: debates over budworm spraying, Canada–US negotiations on acid rain, the collapse of *fisheries, the discovery of the environmental costs of 'clean' activities such as natural gas extraction, factory farming and the water table, the state of aging nuclear power plants, the politics of genetically modified food, the protection of old growth forests, concern over links between chemicals and cancer, and the ecological impacts of global warming on Canada. Legacy problems continue to emerge, such as acid mine drainage stored in now melting permafrost, radon from old uranium mines, or the long-forgotten disposal off Canada's coasts of chemical weapons from the world wars.

Canada's environmental activist elders brought environmental values into the mainstream of culture and policy. Will their records be preserved? New scholars are doing comparative work, including examining the cultural divide between rural and urban environmental values. Canada continues to make a significant contribution to the globalization of the environmental movement.

LORNE HAMMOND

See also CONSERVATION MOVEMENTS.

epidemics. Epidemics can destroy populations and alter economic, social, intellectual, and political aspects of life. Many non-infectious diseases, such as cancer and heart disease, are said to occur in 'epidemic' proportions, but the term properly refers to intermittent outbreaks of contagious diseases. In contrast, 'endemic' diseases are continuously present with a steady incidence and mortality. Epidemic threats may be ever present, but the types change according to the ecological balance of diseases in time and space, modified by nutrition, climate, travel, and medical advances ('pathocenosis'). Present *public health practices are a legacy of past epidemics. They reflect assumptions about the presumed cause and anticipated victims; all too often informed by prejudice, greed, and fear, they sometimes fail to prevent spread of infection.

The first epidemics for which we have historical records were those transmitted to Aboriginals by contact with Europeans: *smallpox, colds, measles, and influenza. Diseases endemic in Europe annihilated entire communities of first peoples, who lacked natural resistance. Usually transmitted unintentionally, smallpox was occasionally spread to Natives deliberately.

Smallpox is caused by a virus (variola) and characterized by fever, rash, and internal lesions; mortality is high, even in populations with frequent exposure. Survivors could be disfigured and blind. After 1798, when Edward Jenner (1749–1823) proved that inoculation with cowpox (vaccinia) prevented smallpox, it slowly declined, culminating in world eradication in 1979. *Vaccination was unevenly available in Canada, and localized epidemics appeared into the 20th century. One of the largest occurred in Montreal in 1885, where riots broke out between largely unvaccinated francophone civilians and largely vaccinated, predominantly anglophone authorities.

*Cholera and typhus appeared in Canada at infrequent intervals from 1832, usually in the context of immigration. Boards of health were formed or restructured to provide care and quarantine. Because isolation sheds had few facilities for personal hygiene, cholera quickly entered the water supply to infect healthy immigrants, caregivers, and the established population. Typhus is transmitted by lice that carry rickettsia germs. Characterized by rash and fever, it attacked immigrants in the crowded, dirty holds of ships. A fierce epidemic in 1847 killed at least 6,000, mostly *Irish fleeing the potato famine. By 1832, a quarantine station had been established at *Grosse Île in the St

Lawrence River near Quebec, where approximately 8,000 graves bear witness to these epidemics. Eventually, all vessels were required to stop for inspection. Now a national historic site, Grosse Île continued as a place of quarantine for humans until 1937 and for animals until 1986.

In early-19th-century Ontario and Quebec, malaria occurred regularly in late summer and fall, causing much suffering among settlers but few deaths; it waned together with (if not because of) land reform and draining of swamps.

Localized epidemics of infectious diseases appeared yearly until vaccinations and antibiotics made them rare. Children were vulnerable to measles, scarlet fever, whooping cough, and especially diphtheria (or 'croup'). A bacterial infection of the throat, diphtheria produces a nerve toxin and causes death by suffocation. In 19th-century winters, it was an important cause of mortality in children under age 12.

*Tuberculosis was the single most important cause of adult death throughout the 19th century. It was endemic rather than epidemic among Europeans in Canada. Sanatoria were built in several provinces for isolation and treatment of active cases. In the Native population, however, epidemic tuberculosis was responsible for many deaths well into the 20th century. BCG vaccination is moderately effective against tuberculosis and has been used in targeted populations from 1925 until the present; however, most Canadians are monitored by the tuberculin skin test. Relatively controlled by the 1970s, tuberculosis returned with the advent of AIDS.

Epidemic influenza (or *Spanish flu), a viral pneumonia, killed between 30,000 and 50,000 Canadians in 1918–19, nearly 14,000 in Quebec alone. It was most severe in young adults and displayed no predilection for social class. The resultant revisions to public health measures featured respect and philanthropy, in contrast with the older, more discriminatory practices developed earlier to control suspicious foreigners.

*Poliomyelitis is a viral disease, especially of children; it attacks the nervous system and is transmitted by fecal-oral contamination. Death occurs on occasion, but most survive, often with permanent disabilities. Since the 1920s, polio appeared with increasing frequency until the largest epidemic in 1953, which saw at least 8,800 Canadian cases and dozens of deaths. Two years later, the Salk vaccine became available, followed by the Sabin vaccine in 1960. 'Innocent children' were the prime target and the life-saving technologies, such as iron lungs, were expensive. These facts enhanced the basic generosity of new public health measures and influenced decisions about national health care provision in the following decade. Polio is now in decline and the World Health Organization anticipates its global eradication.

*Venereal disease, especially syphilis, reached alarming proportions in the military services during both world wars and in large urban areas during the 1960s and 1970s. The advent of penicillin in the late 1940s brought effective treatment for both gonorrhea and syphilis, but it did little to prevent them. Social stigma fuelled the spread despite 'special clinics' and tracing contacts. Prevention included information campaigns, issuing condoms, and incarceration of infected women, as occurred in Newfoundland in 1943. Measures against the more frightening disease of AIDS have also influenced the incidence of other sexually transmitted diseases. The AIDS pandemic reached Canada in 1982. A viral disease that weakens the immune system, AIDS is spread by sex and blood. Unevenly distributed throughout the population, it first appeared in male homosexuals and hemophiliacs; now it is uncontrolled in injecting drug users and prisoners. Because transmission of AIDS is understood and because it exists in Canada, this epidemic challenges old attitudes towards health vigilance and immigration.

Epidemic scares happen regularly, and authorities move quickly to contain the problem—for example, when a high school student dies of meningitis; when an airplane arrives from an Ebola-infected country; when fecal contaminants enter the water supply, as happened in Walkerton, Ontario, in the summer of 2000, killing seven; or when a highly contagious virus arrives from Asia, as happened with Severe Acute Respiratory Syndrome (SARS) in March 2003, claiming dozens of lives, mostly in the Toronto region. Emergency treatment is often too little, too late, even for diseases that normally respond to antibiotics. The best measures are preventative: public hygiene, mass immunization, honest reporting, and, above all, clean water.

JACALYN DUFFIN

Equal Rights Association. The Equal Rights Association for the province of Ontario was a response to Quebec's 1888 Jesuits' Estates Act. The JEA resolved competing claims by the *Jesuits and Catholic bishops on the Jesuits' Estates, lands that the order had been given in the New France era to support their missions. When the British conquered Quebec and the pope suppressed the Jesuits (1773), ownership of the lands became questionable. The Crown assumed them in 1800, but the Jesuits claimed them when they returned to Canada in 1842. The JEA was designed to settle these competing claims and resolve provincial ownership of the lands by compensating the various claimants. However, to militant Protestants in Ontario, the JEA was offensive: it violated the supposed separation of church and state and had involved negotiations with the Roman Catholic Church.

The Equal Rights Association was born in Toronto in June 1889, after agitation for federal veto of the JEA had failed, and it played a minor though influential role in Ontario politics through the provincial election of 1890. It was also co-opted to some extent by a maverick Conservative member of Parliament, D'Alton McCarthy, who recruited its supporters for a campaign against *bilingualism in the West. The ERA's presence and McCarthy's rhetoric exacerbated feelings over the *Manitoba schools question and debates over official bilingualism in the North-West Territories. The ERA was both a symptom of and a contributor to the disunity of English Protestants and French Catholics that followed the *North-West Rebellion of 1885.

J.R. MILLER

establishment of religion. A religious organization is established when, by law, it enjoys the unique protection and support of the state and in some measure comes under its control. The term establishment comes from the law of England. Before Confederation the Roman Catholic Church and the Church of England displayed many of the characteristics of a church establishment in much of what is now Canada. In New France, the Roman Catholic curé and seigneur were seen as partners in shepherding their communities. Religious orders ran schools and hospitals. Parish councils (*fabriques*) functioned as local governments in both civil and religious matters. Roman Catholic religious authorities levied tithes, a right confirmed by the *Quebec Act of 1775. In 1659 the Sovereign Council prohibited Protestant assemblies, although the measure was little enforced. When the English Crown took control of Quebec in 1763, it announced its intention that 'the Church of England may be established both in Principle and in Practice'. No statute to the effect was ever passed, but some argued that the Church of England was established nevertheless, insofar as the English constitution applied to English colonies. In British North America, the Church of England was established by local statute in Nova Scotia (1758), New Brunswick (1786), and Prince Edward Island (1803).

In much of the pre-Confederation period, government officials appointed Anglican bishops and chief clergy. Protestant colonists were spared the English system of tithes, but the Anglican Church was favoured with grants from the public purse and with a substantial landed endowment, which in the Canadas included the huge but disputed *clergy reserves. Moreover, with variations from province to province, Anglican and Roman Catholic clergy enjoyed something approaching a monopoly on performing marriages. Special status began to be dismantled in the 1830s. Reasons include the politically vulnerable position of *Anglicans and *Roman Catholics, an increasing discomfort with religious discrimination, the decline of colonial dependence on England, and American immigration. Moreover, a new generation of Anglican leaders after the 1830s strongly resented the old subservience of church to state. Marriage laws were liberalized in the 1830s. In 1854 tithes in Lower Canada were ended, and the clergy reserves were secularized by an act that began, 'Whereas it is desirable to remove all semblance of connection between Church and State . . .' The end of quasi-establishment was the English judicial ruling *Long v. Gray* in 1863, which affirmed that, in English colonies, the Church of England was only one denomination among others. ALAN L. HAYES

Estevan riot. On 7 September 1931 several hundred lignite coal miners in Estevan, Saskatchewan, walked off the job. Already unhappy with poor wages and working conditions, the men chose to strike after employers were unwilling to recognize the miners' new union, the communist-dominated Mine Workers Union of Canada. Tensions grew as employers provocatively recruited local farmers as strikebreakers. A pattern of barely avoided clashes ended on 29 September. Largely inexperienced members of the *Royal Canadian Mounted Police met a parade by miners through the streets of Estevan. When a marcher jumped onto a fire truck, he was shot dead. Police bullets killed two more strikers and wounded several townspeople and miners. The strikers were blamed for firing first, and courts convicted a number for rioting. Photographic evidence demonstrated that the police had drawn their weapons earlier than was required for self-defence, and they could not prove that they had been fired upon first. Despite the crushing of the strike, the miners' spirit remained unbroken. Their dead were buried in a common grave underneath a gravestone marked with a red star and the words: 'Murdered by R.C.M.P.'

STEVE HEWITT

États généraux du Canada français. From 23 to 27 November 1967, 1,067 Quebec delegates, 167 representatives from Quebec social, labour, and cultural organizations, and 364 francophones from most of the rest of Canada attended the États généraux du Canada français in Montreal. This event marked a continuity with earlier meetings that had taken place in 1912, 1937, and 1952. Called the Congrès de la langue française, these gatherings allowed francophones from all over North America to reflect on their common experience. The 1967 meeting was special, for it occured during the 100th anniversary of Confederation. It was also the year that French president Charles de Gaulle expressed his controversial views about Quebec's status.

The meeting in 1967 marked the end of French Canada as a national reference point for all francophones. Delegates approved resolutions defining Quebec as the national territory of French Canadians and the Quebec state as the instrument for the promotion of the rights of French-speaking people where they constituted a majority—that is, in Quebec. Delegates from other provinces perceived themselves to have been abandoned by Quebec. Since then, relations between the Quebec state and Quebec nationalists and the leaders of these minority communities in the rest of Canada have been difficult, especially when Quebec's future within Canada is concerned.

MARCEL MARTEL

eugenics. The term 'eugenics', first coined in 1883 by Francis Galton, was inspired by discoveries in genetics and biology. Soon scientists, reformers, and professionals were asserting that the human race could and should be improved through the breeding out of deficiencies such as mental retardation and inheritable diseases—some even included *poverty, crime, alcoholism, and *prostitution. Voicing fears of 'race suicide' at the turn of the century, Canadian eugenicists predicted the decline of Anglo-Celtic dominance, which they blamed on the influx of immigrants and the falling birth rate of native-born Canadians. Never an organized movement, eugenics nonetheless exerted tremendous influence in the first three decades of the 20th century, particularly in the social work and health care professions. Neither was it a coherent ideology. While some conservative hereditarians sought to prevent the 'unfit' from reproducing, progressive eugenicists stressed the importance of environment. Although associated with racism, immigration restrictions, and enforced sterilization, the influence of eugenics was not always negative. It inspired early sex education programs, mandatory testing for *venereal disease prior to marriage, a relaxation of the ban on contraceptives, and the mental health movement.

Ironically, conservative 'maternalist' *feminists were among the first to advocate eugenics, despite the taunts of eugenicists that women were shirking their maternal responsibilities. Led by public health physician Helen *MacMurchy, women politicized the 'mental defective'. Early in the 20th century, they advocated the building of specialized facilities, medical inspection of schools, and auxiliary classes for the growing number of 'feeble-minded' children whom compulsory education had thrust into the schools. Offering to protect the 'feeble-minded' woman from sexual exploitation, abuse, prostitution, and unwed motherhood, maternalists also believed they were protecting society from eugenically inferior offspring and the spread of venereal disease. By the First World War, the nascent mental health movement was dominated by leading psychiatrists, two of whom, Clarence Hincks and C.K. Clarke, founded the Canadian National Committee on Mental Hygiene and established new mental health treatment facilities. In the political realm, the profession also asserted its authority by blaming social problems on the newly arrived—successfully lobbying for increasingly vigorous medical inspection of immigrants and deportation of those with mental health problems.

Once vehemently opposed to *birth control, eugenicists reversed their position in the 1930s. Abandoning hope that the middle classes would stop using contraceptives, they began promoting them among the eugenically undesirable. A.R. Kaufmann, industrialist, birth-control activist, and member of the newly formed Eugenics Society of Canada, which also included prominent geneticists and public health professionals among its members, orchestrated a 1937 trial in an attempt to liberalize contraceptive legislation. In a trial set in Eastview, Ontario (near Ottawa), with a predominantly French Catholic population, experts argued successfully that birth control could eliminate poverty, reduce expenditures for relief, quell social unrest, and address the frightening fertility differential between the eugenically fit and the unfit. Feminist and health arguments in favour of contraception were only faintly heard.

The most controversial eugenic measure was the passing of legislation in Alberta (1928) and British Columbia (1933) for the involuntary sterilization of mentally ill or retarded inmates of institutions. The Eugenics Society of Canada attempted to have similar legislation passed in Ontario; it failed due to the opposition of the Roman Catholic Church, which viewed any manipulation of human nature, including the use of birth control or sterilization, as contrary to the will of God. A sad legacy, these acts remind us of the frightening implications of mixing biology with social policy. With declining support from the scientific community, the horrors of Nazism, and Quebec's opposition, eugenics quickly declined following the Second World War. DIANNE DODD

European and North American Railway. The promoters of this railway conceptualized it as the quickest transportation link between the United Kingdom and the eastern United States. They envisioned a transatlantic steamboat service meshing with a railway across Newfoundland, a ferry across the Gulf of St Lawrence, and a railway via Cape Breton Island, Nova Scotia, and New Brunswick to the United States. Lacking capital, the railway, completed in 1860, extended only from Saint John to Shediac—about 160 km. A.A. DEN OTTER

European immigration, 1897–1929. Between 1897, following the election of a Liberal government the previous year, and the start of the Great Depression in 1929, approximately five million immigrants entered Canada. Overwhelmingly from Great Britain and continental Europe, and part of a much larger international movement, they arrived in two major periods in response to factors influencing both their own decision making and Canadian *immigration policy. While economic considerations (unremitting poverty, limited options, frustrated expectations) drove most immigrants overseas, some fled national oppression, religious persecution, and/or military conflict. Pragmatic before altruistic, Canada put nation-building needs first: settling the West, exploiting natural resources, developing agriculture and industry, and constructing and maintaining transcontinental and local infrastructures. Emphasis on manpower despite racial or cultural background, plus the newcomers' preference for English-speaking Canada over Quebec, created tensions with those who envisioned Canada's future as British and Protestant. They promoted British over non-British immigration and insisted upon assimilation of 'foreigners'.

Clifford *Sifton's term as minister of the interior responsible for immigration (1896–1905) saw his department actively recruit abroad while targeting specific types of immigrants. Keen to populate the Prairies with experienced farmers, Sifton looked beyond traditional sources in Great Britain, the United States, and northwestern Europe and solicited peasant agriculturalists from central and eastern Europe, adding a significant Slavic (especially *Ukrainian) component to Canada's population, particularly in the West. His pre-war successors, both Liberal and Conservative, encouraged British immigrants, regardless of occupation, to preserve Anglo-Celtic hegemony and values. They also responded to business pressures for labour, so that after 1907 there was a noticeable shift to unskilled peasant 'navvies', who came from not only central and eastern Europe but also, increasingly, southern Europe (e.g., Italy). In contrast to settlers on the land who saw themselves as permanent immigrants, many in this group were sojourners intending to return home once they had saved enough money.

The Great War abruptly halted immigration. When it resumed in 1923—after a further hiatus due to economic instability and inflamed nativism targeting recent enemy aliens—racial and cultural factors triumphed. British, American, and northwestern European agriculturalists were again favoured, although any occupation was welcome. British initiatives to promote imperial solidarity included assisted passage, ready-made prairie farms for veterans, and seasonal harvest work. Non-preferred immigrants, from specified countries in central and eastern Europe, were screened for occupational suitability as labourers or domestics, in which case they required sponsors, or as self-supporting farmers. The Railways Agreement (1925–30) made Canadian Pacific and Canadian National, eager to fill empty western lands and increase traffic on their lines, responsible for soliciting and settling non-preferred immigrants; Ottawa retained control over preferred sources. Even before 1929, Canadians found fault with both preferred and non-preferred schemes, complaining, for example, that Britain sent its misfits and failures and that the unemployed would-be farm workers congested the cities. FRANCES SWYRIPA

evangelicalism. In Canada, evangelicalism is rooted in the 18th-century transatlantic revivals that typically held to the unique theological authority of the Bible, believed a common core of Protestant doctrine regarding God and salvation, cultivated personal piety, and bore witness to the gospel, especially through evangelism but also in works of charity. Evangelicalism first arose in Canada in the hinterland of 18th-century Nova Scotia and New Brunswick. The 'Great Awakening' grew so strong that it stamped Maritime culture with a theologically conservative, dispositionally pious, and socially responsible ethos that has lasted to the present. In the 19th century, American Methodists brought the message of spiritual New Birth to Upper Canada. They encountered a colonial population that was generally unchurched, and also faced resistance from an establishment that privileged the Churches of England and Scotland. By 1867, however, Protestant denominations were on officially equal footing, most colonists were in church, and evangelicalism—whether among Methodists, Baptists, Presbyterians, or Anglicans—was the predominant stream of religion in the new Canada outside Quebec.

By 1900, *Lord's Day laws, temperance legislation, Protestant teaching in the public schools, and large metropolitan churches testified to evangelical dominance. Controversies over *Darwinism and the so-called higher criticism of the Bible were few and brief, and the characteristic Anglo-Canadian spirit of moderation and compromise won out over both liberal and conservative extremists in all but a few denominations (notably the Baptist Convention of Ontario and Quebec, which underwent Canada's only major fundamentalist schism in the 1920s). Yet evangelism waned in the mainline churches after the First World War, and even the surge of religious interest in the churches during the *baby boom marked merely a broad social return to traditional ways, not a deep revival of traditional doctrine and piety.

Evangelicals now make up about 10 per cent of the Canadian population and represent the largest church-going cohort in Canadian religion. Evangelicals led the way in establishing schools, from kindergarten to university, that provide alternatives to the public and Roman Catholic school systems in most provinces. Perhaps the most notable landmarks of evangelical education in Canada have been the Bible schools that currently enrol more than 7,000 students in dozens of institutions, but evangelical theological seminaries also are the largest in the land.

Immigration in the 20th century has contributed to Canadian evangelicalism. *Mennonites helped to populate Canada's vast farmlands. Reformed Christians came to Canada from the Netherlands, especially after the Second World War. Since the 1960s, East Asian Christian churches, particularly those serving Korean and Chinese populations, have grown in major cities. Most of these groups have linked up with the Canadian evangelical network. At the hub of that network is the Evangelical Fellowship of Canada (established 1964), which symbolizes a remarkable characteristic of Canadian evangelicalism: its unity despite a remarkably diverse membership. Baptist, Presbyterian, Pentecostal, Brethren, Anglican, United, and Alliance people are all in evidence, and so are Reformed, Mennonites, Evangelical Free Churchers, Salvationists, Nazarenes, and more. Among prominent Protestant groups, only the Lutherans in Canada remain largely outside of this transdenominational fellowship.

Evangelicals in the mainline denominations have felt increasingly alienated from the leadership of their own churches, which has moved both theologically and politically to the left since the 1960s. Simultaneously, most of the evangelicals on the margins have moved towards the cultural centre as their economic and educational standards have risen. Thus Briercrest (Saskatchewan) and Prairie (Alberta) Bible schools, for example, have sought formal educational accreditation and forged links with EFC and other mainstream evangelical institutions. Transdenominational evangelical schools such as Regent College (British Columbia) and Tyndale College and Seminary (Ontario), conversely, are supported in part by Anglican, Presbyterian, and other Christians that formerly looked exclusively to mainline denominational colleges for pastoral training. This confluence of evangelicals has taken place just as Canadian culture has become much more pluralized and much less Christian. Consequently, evangelicals have united in institutions such as the EFC, Citizens for Public Justice, and Focus on the Family in order to exert influence as participants in a multicultural society—neither as snipers on the margins nor as mandarins in the centre.

Fundamentalism has been of small importance in Canadian evangelicalism. Few denominations have been divided, few political campaigns have been waged, and few supporters have been found for the kind of absolutist Christianity that continues to affect American evangelicalism. Furthermore, despite the spectre of the American

'Religious Right' and the tendency of some journalists to associate evangelicals with the Reform Party and then the Canadian Alliance, Canadian evangelicals' support for political parties is not appreciably different from that of the population at large.

In the 21st century, Canadian evangelicals face the daunting challenge of re-evangelizing a country they once deeply influenced while trying to be good neighbours in an increasingly diverse society. They do so as a loosely knit fellowship of groups who recognize each other as kin, even as they typically pursue various religious, political, and social agendas.

JOHN G. STACKHOUSE, JR

Evangeline. The best-known fictitious Acadian heroine, Evangeline is the main character in the poem *Evangeline: A Tale of Acadie*, first published in Boston in 1847. Written by the world-renowned American Romantic poet Henry Wadsworth Longfellow, the tragic tale is a story of innocent young lovers, the 17-year-old Evangeline and her fiancé, Gabriel. The first part of the poem depicts the beginnings of a new nation, where the young couple grow up in the midst of peace and plenty, a terrestrial paradise, *Grand-Pré, Nova Scotia. This Eden is disrupted by the *Acadian deportation (1755–63). The couple is unwillingly separated and placed on ships that carry the deportees to the 13 Anglo-American colonies along the North American Atlantic seaboard. In the second part of the poem Evangeline spends the rest of her life searching for her true love. After many years, Evangeline, who is living in Philadelphia, becomes a Sister of Mercy, catering to the sick and aged. A smallpox epidemic ravages the city and she finds Gabriel on his deathbed. He expires in the arms of his beloved Evangeline, who herself dies shortly thereafter.

Longfellow wrote the poem to illustrate the faithfulness and constancy of woman. Inadvertently, it became an important vehicle for learning a romanticized version of the history of the Acadian deportation. Grand-Pré and Evangeline became nation-building tools at Acadian national conventions in the late 19th and early 20th centuries. Anglophone tourism entrepreneurs, especially the Dominion Atlantic Railway, used the poem's images to entice travellers to visit the heroine's homeland, the 'Land of Evangeline'. Tourists came seeking the landscape of peace, tranquillity, and simple beauty expounded in the first part of the poem.

Evangeline has become a legend, a myth, and a symbol. She symbolizes qualities of loyalty, selflessness, patience, and devotion, eliciting widespread respect and admiration because of her courage, endurance, and steadfastness in love. During the 1960s and 1970s some young Acadian writers questioned her symbolic usefulness, seeing her as silent and resigned. Resilient to such criticism, she seems stronger than ever in the 21st century. Her story represents a triumph over intolerance and rejection. She is a mythical and metaphorical message-bearer, carrying the torch of lasting love and eternal hope for struggling groups. Her durability and adaptability are due in part to her potent image as survivor. Her story, one of great happiness and sadness, provides inspiration for readers through their journey of life.

BARBARA LE BLANC

Exchequer Court of Canada. *See* FEDERAL COURT OF CANADA.

exhibitions and fairs. One challenge for the early agricultural economy in Canada was the marketing of produce. Weekly farmers' markets were soon established to meet the needs of local populations; at the larger urban markets farmers often sold their produce and livestock to merchants for shipment to more distant markets. Smaller towns attracted buyers by holding annual or semi-annual fairs. On fair day in Napanee in 1836, for example, 300 head of cattle and over 1,200 bushels of grain changed hands. Some of these fairs began as agricultural exhibitions, with friendly competitions among producers for prizes that might be sponsored by the local gentry or, increasingly, by public authorities. From the 1790s governors of the British North American colonies lent informal support to agricultural societies, and from the 1810s governments began to vote funds for agricultural exhibitions, with an eye to stimulating both the circulation of goods and the improvement of the goods circulated. Annual and semi-annual exhibitions were widely held in villages, towns, and cities across the central and eastern provinces by mid-century, when rotating provincial exhibitions were established. These were housed in crystal palaces built to imitate Paxton's Crystal Palace of 1851, which brought new glamour and impetus to the exhibition movement. Grain growers, cattle breeders, horticulturists, mechanics, and their wives would gather to display the fruit of their labours, vie for the coveted red ribbon, and enjoy a celebration amidst the amusements that exhibitions attracted: the horse racing; the oddities and spectacular displays; the stands selling machinery, handicrafts, sweets and other foods, and drink, complete with the illicit jug under the counter. When the Prince of Wales came to inaugurate Victoria Bridge in 1860, Montreal greeted him with a grand industrial exhibition. But Montreal's entrepreneurs couldn't rival the spectacular efforts of Toronto, where the self-styled 'Canadian National Exhibition' or CNE was held annually from 1879. For a few days each year, all the dizzying diversions, displays, spectacles, and amusements that modernity could conjure were crammed into a few acres on King Street West, whereupon they were packed up and carted off to the next show on the crowded autumn circuit. By this time, fairs and exhibitions were entrenched in Manitoba and had spread across the Prairies to the West Coast, where western Canada's answer to the CNE, the Pacific National Exhibition, was founded in 1907. Sponsors included farmers, merchants, civic officials, and agents of the Department of Indian Affairs. Aboriginal peoples were keen and successful exhibitors, from Cowichan to Saskatoon and Halifax, and they ran some of the most successful small fairs in the country.

E.A. HEAMAN

Expo 67. The centerpiece of centennial celebrations, Expo was intended to promote national unity and garner international status. Canada was awarded the world exhibition only after the Soviet Union backed out in 1962. The late start, aggravated by the decision to build a site on islands to be created from landfill in the St Lawrence River, led to predictions that the event would flop. The Crown corporation created by the federal government to build and run the fair delivered on schedule, and from opening day 'Man and His World' was a resounding success. During its six months' duration, about 50 million paying visitors, almost double the anticipated attendance, came to poke around the 60 government and 53 private pavilions, inspect the cutting-edge architecture and cinema, and endure an endless succession of youth choirs.

From the sexism of its theme, to the mostly unquestioned faith in progress of its exhibits, to the Cold War rivalries it encouraged, Expo was a monument to its era. In retrospect, it was also an influence in shaping the political landscape. The wildly enthusiastic response of the crowd to French president Charles de Gaulle's call, 'Vive le Quebec libre', was a revelation to many Québécois of the depth of their aspirations for distinct nationality. For other Canadians, the self-confidence generated by the fair contributed to their willingness to elect the offbeat Pierre *Trudeau as prime minister in 1968, and to endorse the ethnic dances and costumes of his brand of *multiculturalism as an acceptable part of national identity.

KEITH WALDEN

External Affairs, Department of. The DEA was founded in 1909 to bring order to the handling of international questions by the Canadian government. Initially housed above a barber shop, it began with an undersecretary of state for external affairs, Sir Joseph Pope, assisted by a small staff. Before long, other officers were added and the DEA moved to more suitable accommodation in the East Block on Parliament Hill, closer to the office of the prime minister, who took over the portfolio in 1912. In the early years, the department's functions more closely resembled those of a post office than a foreign ministry, as imperial foreign policy and the conduct of diplomacy on behalf of Canada remained British responsibilities.

That changed when O.D. *Skelton succeeded Pope in 1925. Prime Minister W.L. Mackenzie *King was determined to assert Canadian autonomy in international affairs. King supported Skelton's efforts to improve the DEA's advisory capacity and to develop a Canadian foreign service. After hesitant beginnings, with only a few missions overseas, Canadian representation abroad grew phenomenally during the Second World War and for two decades afterward. One of Skelton's recruits, Lester B. *Pearson, was a successor as undersecretary before he became Canada's foreign minister in 1948. The Nobel Prize for Peace, which Pearson earned for his efforts to resolve the *Suez Crisis of 1956, is often cited as the culmination of a 'golden age' of Canadian diplomacy.

When the DEA relocated in 1973, its headquarters was appropriately named for Pearson. That building on Sussex Drive in Ottawa served as the hub for a worldwide network of diplomatic missions. By 1982, reorganizations of Canada's representation had added officers responsible for development assistance, immigration, and trade. Within a decade, all of the additional functions except trade had left. To reflect its revised mandate, the department became known as External Affairs and International Trade Canada in 1989, though its legal name was not changed to the Department of Foreign Affairs and International Trade until 1995. Approximately 7,000 employees work for DFAIT in Ottawa and in more than 270 offices in over 180 countries abroad.

HECTOR MACKENZIE

extradition. The arrangement between or among sovereign states, either by bilateral treaty or international convention, for the delivery of an alleged criminal to face trial and incarceration for a crime where the maximum sentence prescribed by both countries is more than one year. In 1833, in the absence of a treaty, the legislative assembly of Upper Canada passed the Fugitive Offenders Act to facilitate return of fugitive slaves to the United States. This legislation was declared by the British Privy Council to be beyond Upper Canada's jurisdiction. Britain and the United States subsequently negotiated the racially neutral *Ashburton-Webster Treaty (1841), which included provisions for extradition for specified crimes, including murder. In 1861, in a case prosecuted by Attorney General John A. *Macdonald, Chief Justice John Beverley *Robinson applied the treaty to order the return to Missouri of escaped slave John Anderson, who faced almost certain death for killing a white planter. Jurists in Britain and Canada were outraged by the decision, and a lower court eventually applied a loophole in Canadian law to prevent the extradition. After Confederation, Canada's Extradition Act (1871) proved cumbersome, but more than a century passed before Canada, following the lead of the United States, streamlined extradition procedure by negotiating specific extradition treaties and implementing systems of mutual co-operation with other nations. In 1999, a new Extradition Act came into force, significantly expanding the power of the minister of justice and diminishing the discretion of Canadian extradition courts. The *Supreme Court of Canada subsequently limited the discretionary power of the minister in several cases where extradited individuals faced abuse of process or the death penalty.

GARY BOTTING

factory work. A centralized, technologically advanced system of *manufacturing based on wage labour. Before factories, goods were produced in family households or workshops of master artisans who usually served long apprenticeships before setting up shop with their own apprentices and fully trained journeymen. In the 1840s and 1850s some employers began to create 'manufactories' by hiring more craftworkers and labourers and chipping away at craft skills. To cut production costs, they forced skilled workers to specialize on fewer tasks and products, subdivided crafts into their component tasks, hired less-skilled workers (including women and children) to do simple, repetitive work, and mechanized these tasks wherever possible with steam or water power. Some industries with high-volume output made the greatest strides towards creating the new workplaces known as factories, but most 19th-century industrialists did not sell enough identical products to be able to eliminate skill or thoroughly mechanize their labour processes. They therefore had to exercise a strong paternalism to motivate and hold on to their workers, whose skill and experience were still important. They imposed strict discipline to make sure employees worked hard. Strategies included long hours (10 to 12 a day, six days a week), clocks and bells to mark off work time, authoritarian supervision by salaried foremen, and fines for tardiness, insubordination, or faulty production. At the same time, they cultivated their workers' loyalty by guaranteeing work and organizing such social activities as picnics and dinners.

Beginning in the 1890s, large new corporations in Canadian manufacturing began reorganizing work into what was soon known as mass production. More complex machinery could diminish or replace much skilled work and eliminate unskilled labour. Henry Ford's Canadian plant with its assembly line was the shining example of new possibilities. Factory owners also introduced more centralized management schemes to monitor costs and control their workers, including the so-called scientific management promoted by the American engineer Frederick W. Taylor. Most of these trends were accelerated by the development of the computer in the 1940s and 1950s, which eventually allowed more full-fledged automation of production.

By that point, factory work had incorporated another component: *unions. Skilled men had begun organizing in the 1850s and 1860s but faced strong resistance from employers. At the end of the First World War, workers in several mass-production industries organized the first all-inclusive industrial unions, which did not put down permanent roots until the 1940s. Over the next half century, these unions won much better wages and benefit packages for their members, but by the 1980s and 1990s were fighting a rearguard action against rollbacks of hard-won gains, disruptive managerial innovations, mass layoffs, and plant shutdowns. Many factories relocated to low-wage countries, where working conditions typically resembled earlier Canadian experience. CRAIG HERON

Fairclough, Ellen Louks (1905–), accountant, businesswoman, politician. Born in *Hamilton, Ontario, 28 January 1905, Ellen Cook graduated from a high school commercial program in 1921, then worked as a secretary and bookkeeper in Hamilton. She married Gordon Fairclough in January 1931. After earning her accreditation as a general accountant in 1935, she established a company specializing in office services. She was active in a variety of voluntary organizations and held a seat on Hamilton City Council (1946–9) and Board of Control (1949–50). Running as a Progressive Conservative, Fairclough won a by-election in Hamilton West in May 1950. On 21 June 1957, she became the first woman to serve in a Canadian federal *cabinet when she was sworn in as Secretary of State in John *Diefenbaker's administration. She also held the portfolios of Citizenship and Immigration (1958–62) and Postmaster General (1962–3). Following her defeat in 1963, Fairclough became corporate secretary of Hamilton Savings and Trust Association. MARGARET CONRAD

families. In all historical periods and places, families involve complex sets of lived emotional and work relationships between unequal individuals. Families are major sites of sustenance, socialization, and social relations and the location of some of the most disturbing forms of abuse. Families are institutions shaped by policy and law. And the family constitutes a powerful constellation of ideas, linked to diverse cultural identities and practices.

Different understandings of family have been at the heart of the cultural encounters involved in the peopling of Canada—between Aboriginal peoples and early Europeans, between the predominantly Catholic French Canadians and the British, and between Canadians and successive immigrant groups. Divergent lived realities and ideas about family have also characterized relations between Canadians of different classes. In these encounters, people with the most power and a conviction about their moral superiority have attempted to transform the family practices of others. Catholic missionaries in New France, and later Protestant missionaries, attempted to push First Nations men and women into church-sanctioned, lifelong marriages in which women were subordinate to their husbands and children were punished for wrongdoing. The 19th-century *Indian Acts repeatedly promoted assimilation by encouraging male family heads to own property and denying Indian status to women who married non-Aboriginals. In similar ways, middle-class charity workers in the 19th century and social workers in the 20th sought to impose their views of sexuality, child rearing, and gender roles on working-class and immigrant families. They seldom recognized that *poverty, not immorality, was the root of many families' problems.

Canadian families have always been characterized by a sexual division of labour that placed greater value on men's work than women's. First Nations men were usually responsible for hunting, warfare, and some aspects of politics, women for collecting fruits, roots, and berries or cultivation. In farming families men were usually responsible for raising cash crops and animals while women and older children gardened, made butter, and cared for the house and younger children. In Canada's first factories males constituted the vast majority of wage labourers except in industries like textiles and clothing. Farm families and working-class families expected children to work, usually at gender-specific tasks. In all but the wealthiest families, girls were important as mothers' helpers in the heavy work of cleaning, cooking, and child care that took up much of the day before running water and electricity eased these tasks. Such divisions of labour, although socially determined, were frequently considered 'natural'.

Changes in the economy after the Second World War led to growing numbers of jobs for women in the service and clerical sectors. This trend, combined with *feminists' insistence on women's right to work and on the importance of men assisting with domestic labour, provoked major changes. Married women with young children were now much more likely to work for pay, and they replaced children as the main second earners in two-parent families.

Laws governing family have varied regionally and historically. After the conquest, French Canadians struggled to maintain their own *law rooted in the Coutume de Paris while English elites attempted to impose ideas derived from English common law, which gave husbands greater power over their wives' property and over goods accumulated during a marriage. In the 19th century and earlier, marriage in common law jurisdictions led to 'civil death' for women. Husbands gained control of their wives' bodies, their labour power, and most of their goods and property: *rape within marriage was not recognized; violence against wives was frequently sanctioned by the courts; and wives could not engage in legal action without their husbands' consent. The law in Quebec differed, mostly in allowing wives a greater claim to family resources. Between the 1850s and the 1880s most provinces outside Quebec passed Married Women's Property Acts, dictating that wives would own their own property, including their wages. A century later, feminist demands and precedent-setting *divorce cases led to fundamental changes in family law in most provinces. Changes in the 1970s gave both spouses equal claims on family property. Spousal assault, including sexual assault, was recognized in criminal law. Today, husbands or wives may each be given custody of *children and required to make support payments. Yet, because women are still paid less on average than men, separation and divorce, like death in the past, create female-headed families that are predominantly poor.

Pragmatic concerns about status, economics, property, and inheritance were much more important in many people's choices of a partner in the past than were mutual attraction or emotional satisfaction. Parents could veto choices made by children who were minors, and cut off children who went against their wishes. By the 19th century growing numbers of Canadians embraced the idea that men and women should choose their own spouses and marry for love. In the 20th century the mass media spread the idea that good sex was also critical to a successful marriage.

The stress on affection and sex did not ensure that all marriages would be happy or safe places for women and children. Abusive husbands beat and even murdered their wives. Violence, drunkenness, and incest could make family life intolerable. Canadian legislators long refused to make it easy to leave such marriages. The double standard embedded in the conditions of divorce made it much easier for men to divorce their wives until 1925. Many Canadians separated informally: men walked out; women left, seeking shelter with family and friends. Rates of separation increased steadily, yet death was the major cause of family dissolution until the Second World War. Between 1901 and 1932 about 15 per cent of all families with children were headed by a single parent. Most were widows, but growing numbers were a separated or deserted wife or husband. During the 1950s and 1960s only 10 per cent of all families were headed by a single parent, rising to 15 per cent again in the 1990s. Divorce rates shot up after 1968, when new legislation made getting a divorce much simpler.

The average size of families has been dropping in Canada since the mid-19th century. Fertility rates fell long before reliable contraceptives were available. Men and women decided to have fewer children for many reasons: infant mortality was lower, children's labour became less important, raising youngsters grew more expensive, and parents were encouraged to invest more emotional energy in each child. Women born during the 1840s averaged 6–7 children each; those born 40 years later had closer to 4; by 1971 the average was only 1.7. Averages hide diversity. Among women born in the 1880s and 1890s, French-speaking women averaged 6.37 children, almost double the 3.23 average among anglophones. First Nations and immigrant families fell in between with an average of 4.7 children. These differences increased in the early 20th century as priests, politicians, and nationalists stressed the importance of the family and of high fertility as distinguishing features of French-Canadian society. During the Depression, *birth control became more widely accepted and available among Protestants, although it remained officially illegal until 1969. More reliable methods, including 'the pill', contributed to the decline in family size. Nowhere was the fertility decline faster than in Quebec, where the birth rate halved in the 1960s and 1970s until it was the lowest in the country.

While there have been major shifts in people's expectations of their spouses and of their children, families remain the locus of some of the most positive and negative emotional aspects of most people's lives. Love, nurture, and caring as well as tension, conflict, and violence continue to characterize family life. Couples increasingly expect that romantic love, friendship, and sexual satisfaction will persist throughout a marriage, whether they are formally married or not and whether they are a heterosexual or homosexual couple. When these fade, separation is both easier and more likely than in the past. Child-rearing ideas have shifted too, from regimented schedules to the more permissive patterns promoted by experts in the 1960s and 1970s. Canadians' ideas about and experiences of family continue to vary depending on whether they are men or women, adults or children, and on their cultural background, economic situation, and personal philosophies. Today, as in the past, there is no one family experience, no one meaning of family, no 'traditional' family. BETTINA BRADBURY

Family Compact. An epithet of Upper Canadian reformers for colonial leaders seen as an exclusive and nefarious faction that monopolized power illegitimately, but used more frequently by subsequent commentators, translating a party slogan into a category of analysis and referring to leading officials, or the most powerful among them, or all who opposed constitutional and political reform, or a governing social class. Such indeterminancy, while useful for a term of abuse, bedevils scholarship.

'Family compact' is better analyzed as political rhetoric than as a functioning reality in colonial government. Nonetheless there is little doubt that British constitutional forms combined with a frontier society ensured that a small number of men held the most important posts in Upper Canada and directed its affairs. Relatively few had the leisure, education, skills, manners, and commitment to the *British Empire, Britain's 18th-century balanced constitution, and state support of the Anglican Church to be eligible for high office. The slogan perhaps most aptly fits the administration of Lieutenant-Governor Sir Peregrine Maitland (1818–28) and his principal advisers, such as John *Strachan and John Beverley *Robinson, who governed with a shared sense of Upper Canada's vulnerability to the neighbouring republic and internal threats from Robert *Gourlay and the agitation over the *Alien Question. Yet the first use of the term 'family compact' in Upper Canada may have been in 1828; that is, only after the period it best describes.

William Lyon *Mackenzie's *Sketches of Upper Canada and the United States* (1833) offered the term's classical exposition: Upper Canada, despite British constitutional forms, was a despotism of office-holders. Officials maintained their positions regardless of popular will, controlled much of the public revenue, and thwarted the elective assembly through the appointive legislative council. His list of 'some of the offices, sinecures, and pensions' of 30 men interrelated by blood and marriage included members of the judiciary, executive and legislative councils, Canada Land Company, and Bank of Upper Canada. The Boulton, Sherwood, Jones, and Jarvis families figured prominently beside the usual suspects of reform demonology: Strachan, Robinson, Christopher Alexander Hagerman, and William Allan. Mackenzie concluded that 'this family compact surround the Lieutenant-Governor, and mould him, like wax, to their will; they will fill every office with their relatives, dependants, and partisans . . . they are paymasters, receivers, auditors, King, Lords, and Commons!'

It was effective rhetoric, underlining the extent of state patronage in a monarchical colony where offices were marks of royal favour and where London preferred to govern through a local elite just as it did in the British countryside. In a new colony, however, land grants and multiple offices with salaries that dazzled agricultural settlers were meant to create, rather than recognize, a local elite. Such rhetoric also traced grievances to ill-intentioned individuals surrounding the Crown rather than to the Crown itself. It suggested that reformers were the true loyalists, seeking to restore good government according to British constitutional norms. It juxtaposed the privileged, sycophantic few with the virtuous, independent many. Its family metaphor referred not to mutually supportive and affectionate kin but to a private, protective, and hierarchical network of dependants governed by paternalism and benevolence rather than the independent and public expression of reasoned arguments that reformers saw as the principal basis of good government. Such rhetoric also implied reforms that would make office-holders effectively responsible to local public opinion.

Along with its rhetorical effectiveness, Mackenzie's exposition also displayed the term's analytical weakness. By relying on family connection, Mackenzie included relatively obscure office-holders on his list and excluded more powerful ones. Indeed, Mackenzie could secure only position 29 for John Strachan as 'their family tutor and political schoolmaster'—a lame mimicry of the connections of blood and marriage that cemented the rest of the list. Moreover, he referred to 'this family connexion' as much as to 'this family compact'. Nonetheless, later commentators, like Lord *Durham and the Whig historian John Charles Dent, reified the term into the 'Family Compact' and, while jettisoning any suggestion of family ties, preserved the notion of an exclusive group of office-holders and social snobs controlling patronage and key institutions. It was neither a family nor a compact; just a self-important clique. One of many opposition slogans in several British colonies, it became a central institution of Upper Canadian government before *responsible government. JEFFREY L. MCNAIRN

farmers in politics. *See* AGRARIAN REVOLT.

fascism. Joining the chorus of protesters in Canada during the Great Depression were disparate groups of noisy fascists. Chief among them was Adrien Arcand, a Montreal-born French-Canadian journalist whose Parti national social chrétien enjoyed, in and outside Quebec, a brief notoriety before succumbing in 1940 to a government crackdown under the *Defence of Canada Regulations of the *War Measures Act. Arcand's fascist posturing began with something called L'Ordre patriotique des goglus, which advertised, in its various press organs—*Le Goglu*, *Le Chameau*, and *Le Patriote*—a fierce French-Canadian nationalism committed to heritage conservation, political purification, economic emancipation, and the liberation of the Québécois from corrupt politicians and alien exploiters. Foremost among the people's enemies were *Jews, who quickly formed the centrepiece of Arcand's burgeoning hate theology. When Arcand discovered the virtues of Italian fascism and Hitler's Nazism, the Goglus were transformed, in 1934, into the PNSC, which adopted an unabashed fascist ideology and program favouring corporatism, a Christian ethnocracy, and a one-party state. The new party's leader professed a 'moral affinity' with Hitler's Nazi party, and PNSC publications served as a clearing house for Nazi propaganda. During the mid-Depression years, Arcand's minions postured, paraded, rallied, and cheered their leader's wild speeches denouncing a Judeo-Bolshevik world conspiracy. But the fascists likely counted no more than 1,500 members at their peak. When Hitler and Mussolini went to war, the vise tightened on Canada's domestic fascists, whose organizations were declared illegal. Arcand and his cohorts, including leaders of the domestic Italian fascists and Deutscher Bund Canada, were interned.

Sharing Canada's meagre fascist stage during the Depression were other exotic groupings, shirted and otherwise. The brown-shirted Fédération des clubs ouvriers appeared, then disappeared, in the early 1930s, along with Paul Bouchard's Comité central autonomiste. In Ontario, Swastika Club members, sporting nickel-plated badges with Nazi insignias, paraded in 1933 along Toronto's Balmy Beach and Kew Gardens, to the chagrin of the Jews who fought a pitched battle with the Swastikas at Toronto's Christie Pits. There were other futile groupings, including the mean coteries of William Whittaker in Winnipeg and J.C. Farr's Ontario-based Canadian Nationalist Party, which joined with Arcand's PNSC to form, in 1938, the National Unity Party. By then Hitler and soon after Mussolini were on the path of war. Among the earliest casualties, in Canada, were the nascent fascist parties.

MARTIN ROBIN

fashion. Canadians have closely followed the major European fashion trends and attempted to remain fashionable within their local settings, and according to their income and social status. In the late 17th and 18th centuries Canadians wore the silhouettes and trends of European aristocratic dress. Because the fashionability of dress was reflected in the cloth, rather than a change in silhouette, the importation and purchase of new textiles was of great significance, while the clothes themselves were often made up locally to fit the individual, either in a domestic setting or by a professional tailor or dressmaker. In addition, the importation of ready-made gowns and petticoats for women, and breeches, coats, and shirts for men, was a significant trade. Women's late-17th- and 18th-century fashions were based upon a corseted torso that was draped with an over gown and petticoat, while men's wear consisted of coat, waistcoat, and breeches that evolved with slow stylistic changes and a shift from rich use of colour to dark hues by the early 19th century.

As the 19th century progressed the fashion silhouette changed at a more rapid rate, with clear design changes every five years. Increases in the speed of production as a result of the widespread use of sewing machines, both privately and commercially, were offset by more complex designs and the use of more fabric and trim in women's wear. In men's wear the sewing machine enabled cheaper clothing as well as a larger selection. By the mid-19th century Canada had a well-established clothing manufacturing and retailing sector. The two national *department stores, the T. Eaton Company (1869) and Simpson's (1872), produced *mail-order catalogues that made available fashionable yet moderate to low-priced clothing to large numbers of Canadians who had no immediate access to stores with such large stock and selection. In addition to department stores, in major Canadian cities fashionable women's wear was available through local stores that sold a range of imported and Canadian-made clothing. In Toronto, dry goods merchants Stitt & Co., O'Brien's Ladies Tailor, both with royal warrants, and W.A. Murray & Co. sold fashionable silks and offered dressmaking services catering to the elite, as did Montreal's leading fashion retailers, including Henry Morgan's (1845), Ogilvy's (1866), and John Murphy (1869). Women of moderate means could buy Paris-inspired styles, of varying price and quality, manufactured by less celebrated North American and European producers. Mid-range stores such as Fairweathers, Northways, and Scroggie's, established by the early 20th century, operated alongside high-end shops. Men and women also patronized local tailors and dressmakers, many of whom were European-trained and highly skilled. Seamstresses, often working out of their homes, catered chiefly to women's and children's fashion needs, while merchant tailors, who produced men's wear, were itinerant or had their own premises. During the 1920s and 1930s local designers who established reputations and custom salons across the country included Montreal's Ida Desmarais and Gaby Bernier as well as Martha of Toronto.

After the Second World War Canadian women's fashion was based upon Paris designs that were made in Europe or North America and available in a wide range of prices. By the late 1950s Canadian designers, particularly Auckie Sanft and Irving Samuels, produced high-end Paris-inspired fashions that were widely available in Canada and the United States. The Association of Canadian Couturiers was founded in 1954 to promote Canadian textiles and fashion design, achieving national recognition and representing Canada in overseas trade shows, and its member couturiers ran individual salons from Vancouver to Montreal. *Expo 67 furthered the Canadian fashion scene by profiling Canadian designers making contemporary ready-to-wear. In the late 1960s and 1970s avant-garde designers opened modern boutiques such as Unicorn, run by designer Marilyn Brooks, or Poupée Rouge, operated by Susie Rosovic, in Toronto's Yorkville area. In Montreal, designers/manufacturers such as Leo Chevalier, John Warden, and Michel Robichaud produced lines under their own labels, and the youth-oriented chain store Le Château manufactured and retailed trendy, inexpensive modern clothes.

Building on the 1960s boutique-style, more Canadian fashion designers set out to establish a successful but modest market for original designs. Avant-garde retailers such as Montrealers Nicola Pelly and Harry Parnass founded Parachute (1978), a company that sold both men's and women's forward fashions that were popular with rock stars and Hollywood celebrities. Their success led to branches in Toronto, New York City, and Los Angeles. In the 1980s a surge of new shops owned and operated by designers opened, including Hoax Couture, Comrags, and Babel (Toronto), Scandale (Montreal), and Abby Kanak (Vancouver), establishing reputations locally and across Canada. The late 20th century saw many Canadian fashion designers achieve international recognition through specialty or niche marketing. Lida Baday was known for her extensive use of matte jersey and clean, elegant styles. Albertan Brian Bailey carved out a strong business in the women's plus-size market, with success across Canada, the United States, and England. Patricia Fieldwalker developed an international market for her lingerie, and Vancouverite Martha Study for her colourful resin jewellery and household goods. In the 1990s innovative designers built on their predecessors' successes. Marie Saint-Pierre, known for Asian-influenced designs and unusual fabrics, became the first Canadian to show her collection in Paris (1995); her designs also achieved international exposure when they were worn by Governor General Adrienne Clarkson, who also patronized new designer Yumi Eto. A younger generation of fashion designers, Joeffer Caoc for Misura, David Dixon, and Crystal Siemens, each built strong businesses and reputations within specialty markets for modern innovative designs.

Canadian men's wear followed a similar pattern. The largest producer of men's clothing, Tip Top Tailors (later a subsidiary of Dylex), opened in 1911 and by 1929 had 39 stores across the country. Another important late-20th-century retailer was Harry Rosen. In the 1980s and 1990s the limited men's wear market attracted new independent designers such as Denommé Vincent and Phillippe Dubuc, who were recognized for modern, sleek tailoring incorporating unusual details.

In the late 20th century Canadian fashion designers and companies were increasingly represented within the international fashion market, though often not recognized as Canadian. During the 1980s Alfred Sung was one of the first Canadian designers to achieve celebrity status, his well-established labels resulted in licensing agreements across North America for fashion accessories, bridal wear, and perfume. He was also the original designer for Club Monaco, developed with Joseph and Saul Mimram (1985). Sung left the retail chain and continued to design under his own label, and was the first Canadian fashion designer whose company was traded on the stock exchange. Although he declared bankruptcy in 1997, Club Monaco went on to expand internationally and was bought out by Ralph Lauren in 1999. Roots opened in Toronto in 1973 with a negative-heel shoe and leather goods for men and women. In the 1980s it expanded into sweatshirts with a distinctly Canadian beaver logo and its famous wool and leather baseball jacket. In 1998 it made international fashion news with its 'poor-boy' cap worn by Canadian athletes at the Nagano Winter Olympics.

Canadian-designed fashion accessories also achieved success. Footwear designers John Fluevog, Peter Fox, and Patrick Cox each developed international markets through eponymous stores. The cosmetic company MAC (Makeup, Art Canada) Cosmetics, founded in 1985, was hailed internationally in the late 1990s for its ecologically friendly products and business strategy as well as for its sexy marketing that challenged racial and gender stereotypes. MAC, which became the main sponsor for Fashion Cares, an annual fundraiser for the AIDS Committee of Toronto, was bought out by Estée Lauder in 1998.

Canadians have also succeeded in producing fashionable sportswear. Companies with international profiles include Shan (swimwear) and Sugoi (cycling apparel). The ecologically conscious Mountain Equipment Co-op is recognized for pioneering the use of polartech fleece, a high-tech material made from recycled plastics, and produces clothing for climbing, hiking, biking that it is also widely worn as casual wear in urban centres. Fashionably hip snowboard and skiwear companies, such as Ripzone and Westbeach, have also established important leadership in high-tech wear, while Tilley Endurables (1980) has become known internationally for travel clothing.

Information about the latest fashions has been readily available since the early 19th century, when fashion plates came into common circulation. By mid-century both European and North American women's magazines featuring fashion news were widely read. Canadian magazines with reports on fashion included the *Canadian Home Journal* (1910–58) and **Chatelaine* (1928–). In the late 20th century *Flare*, Canada's first national fashion magazine (1979), was followed by a national edition of the European *Elle* (2001). Canada has also had its own fashion trade magazine, the *Dry Goods Review*, established in 1888; it reported on trends in Canada and abroad and survives today as *Style*. Most recently television has played an important role in the dissemination of fashion information and Canada has played a major role in pioneering this development. City TV's *Fashion Television* is syndicated internationally and its host, Jeanne Beker, has achieved international fame. ALEXANDRA PALMER

Federal Court of Canada. The Federal Court of Canada is the direct successor of the Exchequer Court of Canada. The Exchequer Court was part of the federal court system set up in 1875, along with the *Supreme Court, and partly in competition with provincial *courts. The Exchequer Court heard cases where the federal government was itself a party, such as revenue cases and claims for damages against government. Initially, the court had the same judges as the Supreme Court, but it became independent in 1887. Its jurisdiction was also gradually enlarged—to maritime law and intellectual property in 1891, for example. Through the 20th century, the business of the court expanded, matching the increasing complexity of relations between state and citizen. By the 1950s, much of the business of the court concerned tax matters; in the 1960s, some cases also began to call into question routine government decisions; as well, the Exchequer Court was criticized as mainly serving the interests of the federal government. As a result, in 1971, the Exchequer Court was substantially reorganized under a new name, the Federal Court of Canada. Most significantly, a division was added to hear appeals from federal administrative decisions. Since these appeals had previously been heard mainly in provincial courts, some provinces opposed this as a strengthening of the federal court system; another reorganization of the court followed in 1992, with appeals jurisdiction shared with the provincial courts. The history of the court, indeed, illustrates the continual tensions in Canada's federal system. DONALD FYSON

federalism. Federalism is the most fundamental and most discussed aspect of the Canadian *constitution. In principle, no level of government in a federation is subordinate to any other: each is sovereign in its sphere, and their activities are coordinated. The citizen is subject to two governments, two legislative authorities. Both governments act directly on the citizen.

Geoffrey Sawer, in *Modern Federalism*, enumerates six basic principles of federalism: a country that constitutes a state, a single entity in international law; a country divided into regions, each with its own political institutions; a division of legislative powers and two orders of government with authority over the same citizen; a legislative division outlined by a constitution; a rule to follow in the event of conflict; and a jurisdictional authority, such as a supreme court, to monitor constitutionality.

In 1981, when the patriation of the constitution was referred to the Supreme Court of Canada, two justices declared that there was good reason to consider federalism the 'dominant principle' of Canada's constitution. The British North America Act—now the Constitution Act, 1867—was the first to recognize Canada's federative nature, though the idea was not new. Lt-Col Robert Morse, a British military engineer, had advocated a union of the colonies as early as 1784, and Lord *Durham, in his 1839 report, spoke of a federal union in which the provinces would continue in their existing form.

The federative character of the constitution derives first from the texts. The word 'federally' appears in the first paragraph of the preamble to the BNA Act; moreover, in that act, Part V is devoted to 'Provincial Constitutions' and Part VI deals with the division of legislative powers. Paragraph 7(3) of the *Statute of Westminster (1931), which recognized Canada's independence, expressly preserved the division of powers effected by the 1867 act.
GÉRALD-A. BEAUDOIN

federal–provincial relations. Although the British North America Act (now the Constitution Act, 1867) did not provide for federal–provincial conferences, negotiations between the two levels of government have been a feature of Canadian life since the Confederation era. From the days of Ontario premier Oliver *Mowat, who defended Ontario's constitutional powers against the centralizing policies of Sir John A. *Macdonald, the provinces have been concerned with *provincial autonomy, a concept of provincial rights based on the powers defined in the BNA Act and subsequent judicial decisions and constitutional practices. Not until 1906 was the first official federal–provincial constitutional conference held, at the invitation of Prime Minister Sir Wilfrid *Laurier, who intended to ask the British Parliament to amend section 118 of the BNA Act, which provided for the federal authority to subsidize the provinces.

In subsequent years, such conferences became more frequent, and relations between the two levels of government occasionally grew acrimonious. In the 1930s, Mitchell *Hepburn in Ontario and Maurice *Duplessis in Quebec aggressively defended the powers of their respective provinces against what they perceived to be incursions into provincial jurisdiction by the federal government. Indeed, the *Rowell–Sirois Commission, spawned by the Depression and completed early in the Second World War, advised a greater centralization of power in the hands of the federal government as a necessary feature of the emergent social *welfare state. The commission helped shape post-war federal–provincial relations and paved the way for initiatives like the tax rental agreements, which further defined the taxation powers of the federal and provincial governments. This equalization of revenues through the taxation system was eventually enshrined in the Constitution Act, 1982, which also allowed the provinces to impose indirect taxes in the areas of non-renewable natural resources, forest resources, and electricity. This eliminated the long-standing constitutional provision, productive of so much wrangling between the federal and provincial governments, that the provinces could levy only direct taxes, always an unpopular form of *taxation.

Federal–provincial conferences have become part of our tradition, and they are no longer confined to questions concerning the constitution or taxation powers. On the contrary, they have come to address a wide range of issues, including Aboriginal affairs; communications, culture, parks, and sports; the internal economy; finance and revenue; immigration; infrastructure; technological innovation; international affairs; justice, public security, and civil protection; official languages; human resources; natural resources; and health and social programs. These conferences have given rise to what some have called 'executive federalism', a system decried in several quarters on the grounds that it gives too much power to provincial premiers. Some federal and provincial parliamentarians point to the United States, where federalism is highly centralized and state governors have less power than provincial premiers, to argue that the Canadian brand of federalism is not conducive to good governance. However, beyond the *constitutional amendments and judicial decisions that have determined constitutional evolution are the administrative arrangements, understandings, and agreements between the federal government and the provinces that give Canadian federalism flexibility and help it to mature. GÉRALD-A. BEAUDOIN

Fédération des femmes du Québec. The FFQ was created in 1966 following an initiative of Thérèse *Casgrain. Its founding marked the renewal of *feminism on the Quebec scene. In an increasingly secularized Quebec, the federation was essential as a coalition of women's organizations and individual members of all backgrounds and beliefs. In the beginning it defended reform-oriented feminist positions and demanded equal treatment for women and men. Although it became radicalized in the 1970s, its positions have sparked debate among its members, who represent a range of feminist positions.

To promote equality between men and women, the FFQ quickly undertook struggles in several sectors. Publishing documents, papers, and reports, it took public stands on maternity leave, decriminalization of *abortion, pay equity, education, political participation, the right to work, etc. The *Livre noir*, published in 1978, summarizes its convictions.

In 1994 the federation revised its statutes and its priorities. Although it still operates democratically, giving voices to both individual members and member associations, its new priorities are intended to represent the interests of Quebec women today: the struggles against poverty and violence against women, 'économie sociale', cultural diversity, recognition for lesbians, and a voice for young women. The FFQ supported the World March of Women (2000), which brought together thousands of women from several countries seeking the establishment of a more democratic, non-violent, pacifist society.

KARINE HÉBERT

Fédération des francophones hors Québec. Since 1967 francophone minority communities in Canada have undergone social and political changes that have altered their sense of self-identity, their relations with both the federal and Quebec states, and their political agenda. Following the meeting that year of the *États généraux du Canada français, many delegates felt a sense of abandonment, left out of the process that led to the emergence of a definition of French Canada that made Quebec the national state of French Canadians. Except for Acadians in the Maritimes, francophone minorities would base their identity on their provincial territory and their use of a common language. The terms Franco-Ontarians, Franco-Albertans, or Franco-Manitobans would replace French Canadians, and 'French Canada' ceased to be a national reference for all French-speaking people. Gradually, too, Catholicism would cease to be central to the identity of French-speaking people, due partly to the *Vatican II Council, which forced the Roman Catholic Church to rethink its role in a changing world, and the inability of the church to continue to be the prime agent in charge of schools and other socio-cultural institutions.

In 1975, delegates from every francophone provincial organization created a national body called the Fédération des francophones hors Québec (which became in 1991 the Fédération des communautés francophones et acadiennes du Canada in order to reflect diversity and the fact that francophones had ceased to define themselves in opposition to Quebec). It was the first time that francophone minority communities had set up a national organization that did not include Quebec delegates and was not Quebec-based. The FFHQ spoke officially for francophone minority groups; its strategies varied depending on leaders and the political context. At first, it tried to capitalize on the national commotion caused by the election of the *Parti Québécois in 1976. It released a document in 1977, *Les héritiers de Lord Durham*, that depicted in bleak terms the conditions they faced: linguistic assimilation, lack of services offered by provincial bureaucracies, lack of recognition of French as an official language in English-speaking provinces except New Brunswick. At the same time, the document outlined the federation's agenda for the future: French school systems administered by francophones, legislation that would make French an official language in every province, and policies to assist the socio-cultural development of francophone minorities.

During the 1980 Quebec referendum, the FFHQ remained neutral. Two years later, it tried in vain to get constitutional recognition of the notion that Canada was made up of two founding nations. It also objected to the fact that section 23 of the Canadian *Charter of Rights and Freedoms based the right to minority schools on the number of French- or English-speaking people living in a particular area. Despite their initial hesitations about the charter, section 23 on educational rights provided new ammunition for francophone minorities, allowing them to bring their provincial governments to court when they failed to offer educational systems that reflected their needs.

Relations between leaders of francophone minority communities and Quebec nationalists remained acrimonious, especially whenever the future of Quebec within Canada became an issue. The FFHQ felt left out of the *Meech Lake Accord constitutional saga (1987–90). The federation feared that acceptance of the notion of Quebec as a *distinct society would lead to the de facto recognition that it was impossible to live in French outside Quebec. Under pressure from the federal government and Quebec, the FFHQ came to support the accord. When, in 1995, Quebeckers were asked for a second time to consider their future in Canada, the federation urged them to oppose the sovereignty option.

Although francophone minority groups have made some significant gains in terms of achieving greater control over their school systems and health services—including the battle to save Montfort, the only bilingual hospital in Ottawa—many concerns remain. Assimilation continues to be a prime focus. The low birth rate, a higher percentage of marriages with non-francophones, lack of control over immigration policy, and the fact that few francophone immigrants have settled outside of Quebec, have brought new challenges. MARCEL MARTEL

Fédération des travailleurs du Québec. The largest trade union central in Quebec's highly fragmented labour movement, the FTQ represents Canadian, international, and in recent decades some exclusively Quebec-based unions. The Quebec arm of the *Canadian Labour Congress (CLC), it was created in 1957 through the merger of the Quebec Provincial Federation of Labour and the Quebec Federation of Industrial Unions, respectively the provincial wings of the Trades and Labor Congress of Canada and the Canadian Congress of Labour. Initially a weak organization representing only about a third of the CLC's Quebec membership, under the presidency of Louis Laberge, 1964–92, the FTQ became a force in its own right within Quebec labour, organizing solidarity campaigns for its affiliates and speaking out as their political representative. Raided in the mid-1960s by the *Confédération des syndicats nationaux, which claimed that the FTQ represented foreign unions, the FTQ became more nationalistic: it demanded greater independence within the CLC, which in 1973 granted it special status with exclusive jurisdiction over matters such as labour councils and union education. It has also defended Quebec union members who seceded from international unions, in 1980 establishing its own building trades organization, FTQ-Construction, a move that helped prompt international construction unions to leave the CLC to form the *Canadian Federation of Labour. In 1983 the FTQ created the Quebec Solidarity Fund, an investment tool that could protect jobs. While it recruited substantial public and para-public sector membership in the 1960s, most members worked in the private sector: it remains particularly strong in construction and manufacturing. This focus distinguishes it from other large Quebec union centrals, the CSN and the Corporation des enseignants du Québec, as does its inclination to offer electoral support to political parties. Social democratic, it backed the New Democratic Party federally in the 1960s; after 1975 it has usually supported the Parti Québécois. GEOFFREY EWEN

Fédération nationale St-Jean-Baptiste. Founded in 1907 by Caroline Béique and Marie *Lacoste-Gérin-Lajoie, the federation was a coalition of women's organizations independent of the *Société St-Jean-Baptiste. Its work was reform-oriented, Catholic, and maternalist, and its primary objective was 'to bring French-Canadian women together in order to strengthen, through union, their action in the family and in society'. A Catholic social action organization, it shared the views of the social Catholicism inaugurated by the **Rerum Novarum* encyclical (1891). As its motto 'Towards justice through charity' suggested, the federation sought to improve the conditions of life for everyone, but with the emphasis on collaboration rather than class struggle. In the opinion of its members, women could make a contribution in their capacity as potential mothers. To equip them to carry out their responsibilities, the federation focused on education as one of its principal activities.

Throughout its history the federation took part in many movements for social change, including *women's suffrage, changes in the civil code regarding married women, improved working conditions for women, protection for women and children, and charitable work. Beginning in 1913 it made its positions known through its journal, *La bonne parole*. The high point of the federation was reached under its second president, Marie Lacoste-Gérin-Lajoie (1913–33). In the early 1960s, however, it was unable to adapt to the rapid changes in Quebec society and was superseded by the *Fédération des femmes du Québec in 1966. KARINE HÉBERT

Feild, Edward (1801–76), second Church of England bishop of Newfoundland, serving from 1844 until his death. He was the architect of the institutional church in the colony, recruiting clergy in England, training others at his theological college, building churches and schools, and establishing the church's financial independence. His fine Gothic revival cathedral in St John's symbolized his High Church views and program, which provoked widespread criticism and opposition from evangelicals and their allies. Particularly controversial and divisive was Feild's determined insistence that Anglicans should have their own government-supported schools, separate from those of other Protestants. He eventually got his way in 1874, thus bequeathing to the colony a unique denominational school system. Uncompromising and ascetic, Feild was a devoted pastor who travelled extensively throughout his diocese (which included Bermuda), and in time gained the respect, if not the affection, of his flock. JAMES K. HILLER

Fellowship of the Maple Leaf. Established in 1916 in London, England, by the Reverend George Exton Lloyd (1861–1940). Emigrating to Canada in 1881, Lloyd was ordained an Anglican clergyman and after 1903 dedicated himself to promoting the church in Saskatchewan through the immigration of lay Christians from England. On a trip to England, he established the fellowship to aid in the recruitment of mainly women schoolteachers to 'Keep Canada British and Christian', the fellowship's motto. He considered teachers to be missionaries of Empire who would aid in the assimilation of non-British immigrants through 'a Christian atmosphere' and daily prayer in the schools. The fellowship provided loans to meet travel costs of qualified teachers. Once in Saskatchewan, immigrants found their own jobs. Over 400 British teachers found positions in the 1920s, but after

1930 the fellowship focused more on the recruitment of medical, welfare, and church workers who established a 'Sunday School by Post' to outlying areas. Extending its mandate to Alberta and northern Canada, the fellowship built hostels and churches while encouraging English clergy to emigrate to Canada. In the 1960s it supported the training of Aboriginal priests and still provides financial support for pioneer ministry, lay and ordained, in both Canada and Britain. MARY KINNEAR

feminism, first-wave. As a term for the politics of equal rights for women, 'feminism' did not come into use in English until the 1890s. Yet by the mid-19th century, some Canadians were describing women as a distinct social group with unequal status and were challenging patriarchal institutions and attitudes. It is convenient to label this phenomenon, which can be seen, albeit to varying degrees, in all parts of the territory north of the United States, as 'first-wave feminism'. From the beginning, the ideology was not easily summed up or categorized. Although its proponents were often middle class and European in origin, there were occasional other voices such as the African-Canadian abolitionist Mary Ann *Shadd. Some feminists found a home in radical groups such as the *Knights of Labor and the Social Democratic Party. Most pre-1920s, or pre-suffrage, Canadian feminists were, however, liberals who anticipated that institutional and individual reform rather than the overturn of class and race privilege would largely eliminate female disadvantage. A pragmatic *liberalism incorporated both those who endorsed an 'equal rights' or 'natural justice' feminism and those who embraced maternalism or essentialism, which stressed women's biologically mediated response both to children and to the world at large. Many liberals, such as Nellie L. *McClung, drew on both justifications, the emphasis influenced by audiences. Working-class feminists such as British Columbia's Helena *Gutteridge developed a class-based critique but they readily subscribed to women's essential difference. In general, middle-class Canadian feminists, such as those in the *National Council of Women of Canada, which campaigned for domestic servants and against the 1919 *Winnipeg General Strike, did not criticize class and race advantage.

Whether liberal or not, feminists were widely regarded as radical threats to the social order. They were routinely condemned as foreign imports or as infected by ideas borrowed from the 'foreign other', whether Americans or Jews or another suspect group. Visits by international feminists such as Emma Goldman and Susan B. Anthony were treated as proof of conspiracy. Indeed, Canadians were linked by personal, organizational, and intellectual ties to feminists elsewhere, especially in Britain and the United States. Quebeckers such as Marie *Lacoste-Gérin-Lajoie and Joséphine Marchand-Dandurand drew on European Catholic feminism to counter church opposition. Membership in the World *Woman's Christian Temperance Union and the Women's International League for Peace and Freedom kept many internationally minded.

Although feminists varied in their analysis, they tended to concentrate on education, law, employment, and violence. By the third quarter of the 19th century, Canadians faced demands for university admission for women, married women's property acts, protective labour legislation, and *prohibition. Dress reform, women's sports teams, and sex radicalism disturbed complacency. The 'new woman' of the 1890s, with her reputation for autonomy in employment and relations with men, embodied unrest. Women's rights were also associated with, if regularly subordinated to, other issues, such as anti-slavery, *temperance, *foreign missions, peace, imperialism, socialism, and communism.

The need to make a living caused some, like the Mohawk–English-Canadian writer and performer E. Pauline *Johnson (Tekahionwake), to curb their challenge, but resistance surfaced regularly. The problem of how to raise consciousness without prompting hostility and derision presented a recurring dilemma. Few Canadian feminists ever publicly turned to the militant tactics of the British suffragettes of the Women's Social and Political Union. Even when brutally harassed, as was Elizabeth *Smith in the first class at the Kingston Medical School for Women in the 1880s, they concentrated on keeping their temper and maintaining decorum. As liberals, they trusted that reason would ultimately prevail. Letters to the editor, such as those by Emilie Carrier LeBlanc to the Acadian newspaper *L'Evangéline* in the 1890s, joined individual appeals, petitions, parades, and theatre as preferred strategies. Novels featuring new women, such as *Roland Graeme: Knight* (1892) by Agnes Maule Machar and *The Imperialist* (1904) by Sara Jeannette Duncan, were also subversive.

While often divided on other issues, feminists by the end of the 19th century increasingly agreed on enfranchisement. As near-universal male suffrage triumphed in the 1885 federal Franchise Act, women's exclusion from electoral politics captured attention. Equal rights and maternalist arguments increasingly focused on the modern state as the solution to women's disadvantage. Female voters could usher in a new age. Feminists were not, however, unanimous in identifying which women merited the vote. As the mixed response to the *Wartime Elections Act of 1917—which enfranchised some women while simultaneously disenfranchising certain immigrants—demonstrated, class and race remained acceptable criteria for limiting the vote, even in the view of suffragists. Once the majority of women had been enfranchised, the omission of certain groups was largely ignored.

Subsequent legislative reforms, including *mothers' allowances, and elections of 'firsts' such as the MP Agnes *Macphail in 1921, owed something to the changed electorate and to the strategic response of the male-dominated party system. By the 1940s, however, when Catherine Cleverdon was interviewing suffragists for her classic text, *The Woman Suffrage Movement in Canada* (1950), disappointment was pervasive. Feminist-minded groups such as the Federation of Business and Professional Women's Clubs and the WILPF never disappeared, and a new generation of feminists, such as Madeleine *Parent, Thérèse *Casgrain, and Cairine *Wilson, arose, but common purpose largely evaporated. Canadian women did not live up to feminists' high hopes. And yet, first-wave feminists had themselves frequently forgotten non-majority group women. Racism, for example, remained a fact of life. By the 1960s, a new generation or 'second wave' of feminists was emerging. Their efforts, whether in association with the *Report* (1970) of the Royal Commission on the Status of Women, or with student, Native, nationalist, labour, and women's liberation movements, resurrected and renewed older struggles for equality. VERONICA STRONG-BOAG

See also WOMEN'S SUFFRAGE MOVEMENT; ANTI-FEMINISM.

feminism, second-wave. The revival of feminism in Canada in the 1960s and 1970s was part of an international movement now referred to as feminism's 'second wave'. The first feminist movement reached its peak in the second decade of the 20th century, when many countries, including Canada, enfranchised women. Feminist activism did not disappear during the interwar and war decades but it did diminish; moreover, after the Second World War dominant cultural voices promoted an anti-feminist ideology that encouraged women to accept the role of 'traditional' wife and mother.

The revival of feminism represented in part a response from women with connections to the first feminist movement who knew that inequalities such as discrimination in the paid workforce and in education and professional training still existed. In Canada, women's lobbying resulted in the establishment of the Royal Commission on the Status of Women in 1967. The commission held hearings in informal settings all across Canada, welcoming personal letters as well as more formal briefs, and it heard from a broad spectrum of Canadian women. The royal commission tabled its remarkable report in 1970; its recommendations were wide-ranging, its style innovative. In response, the federal government set up an Advisory Council on the Status of Women, and women activists founded the *National Action Committee on the Status of Women in 1972.

In its early years NAC represented the tradition of liberal feminism, which sought redress for women's inequalities through changes in law. In Canada, as elsewhere, there was a more radical side to feminism's second wave, typically involving a younger generation of women connected with the student *New Left, active at this time in North America in the causes of peace and civil rights. When male New Left activists refused to take women's issues seriously, women formed their own groups. From the late 1960s such groups began to define themselves as part of the Women's Liberation Movement, which advocated revolutionary change. In keeping with the New Left's commitment to participatory democracy, women's liberationists formed consciousness-raising groups and organized flamboyant public demonstrations to promote their views. In Canada their causes included the right to *abortion, an issue that was publicized through the cross-country educational efforts of the Abortion Caravan in 1970. By the mid-1970s, in Canada as elsewhere, feminists were split over such issues as heterosexism and racism. Moreover, feminists had to contend with opponents who refused to take such issues seriously or who responded with vitriol to perceived attacks on 'the family'. Despite continuing opposition, second-wave feminist activism in Canada and internationally has achieved much, even though the radical transformation in women's lives envisioned by feminists in the 1960s has yet to be realized.

DEBORAH GORHAM

femmes favorisées? Alive to the vibrant *feminist movement, late-20th-century historians devoted themselves to examining the neglected past of early Canadian women. Although wives and mothers are essential to any lasting colonization, women in *New France displayed unusual public leadership. Along with the *Jesuit fathers, nuns and laywomen spearheaded a missionary drive that energized the flagging settlement of the 1630s with workers, funds, and social services. 'Founding Mothers' indeed, they wrote some of the first historical accounts of the colony and set up hospitals and school systems that still exist today. Their contributions were analyzed by Catholic scholars of subsequent centuries, who also discovered amazons, petticoat politicians, and entrepreneurs. After 1970 a new generation re-examined this array of publicly active women. One of the first feminist interpretations of this phenomenon, 'New France: Les Femmes Favorisées', appeared in the journal *Atlantis* in 1980 and was extensively used in university classrooms for the rest of the century. It made the case that women of 17th- and 18th-century New France enjoyed a surprisingly favourable position, perhaps better than their French and American contemporaries, certainly better than their more sequestered descendants in mid-Victorian Canada. Fluid gender roles, the frequent absence of men for war and trade, and liberal inheritance practices all opened doors for these women.

Some historians find the notion of 'favoured' women too sweeping. It is problematic to discuss women ranging from slaves to chatelaines as a unified group. Aboriginal females may in fact have found their sexual and economic freedoms curtailed by the patriarchal French. Studies suggest the Coutume de Paris could be less supportive of women's claims in practice than in theory. If Canadiennes were left in charge of farms and businesses to an unusual degree, was it an opportunity or a burden? Questions remain. Lacking personal letters and diaries for this period, historians will continue to puzzle over the colony's rich baptismal and marriage data and its legal records, supplemented by the observations of travellers, nuns, and officials.

Other scholarship endorses the premise of 'femmes favorisées'. Research continues to uncover women merchants, some with transatlantic operations. Yves Landry's careful study of the famous 770 *filles du roi, the marriageable women shipped by the king, found their fecundity and their lifespan soon surpassed that of their French counterparts. It seems the air, water, and food were all better in the colony. A topic of endless fascination to students, gender in New France remains a thriving research enterprise in both languages. JAN NOEL

Fenians. In 1858 James Stephens organized the Irish Revolutionary Brotherhood in Dublin. The following year, an American branch was organized by John O'Mahoney, who named his branch the Fenian Brotherhood, inspired by the warriors of early Irish history. The word *Fenian* became a generic term to describe Irish Nationalists. Fenian ambition was to drive the British from Ireland, but the American branch eclipsed its Irish parent, recruiting Irish soldiers in the Union army during the American Civil War. When that war ended, the Fenians built their own army. The British navy made it impossible to deliver this army to Ireland, and many Fenians began to consider driving the British out of North America instead. The Canadian government was informed of these plans, but a series of false alarms and jumbled information misled authorities. During April 1866, a raid was begun against New Brunswick, then resisting Confederation. As the Fenians trickled into the border towns of Maine, the governor convened an emergency session of the legislature, forced the resignation of the government, and installed a new one favourable to Confederation. Nova Scotia's government dropped its opposition to Confederation as well. British and American troops prevented any serious Fenian action, and the raid fizzled. The Canadian government paid little attention to warnings of another raid, and when invasion came they were unprepared. Led by Col John O'Neill, a Fenian brigade landed in the Niagara Peninsula during the night of 31 May/1 June 1866. On 2 June, a Canadian brigade was defeated by O'Neill near the village of Ridgeway. Short on ammunition, O'Neill withdrew to Fort Erie, defeating another Canadian force before American authorities forced his withdrawal to Buffalo. A separate invasion into Lower Canada achieved nothing and collapsed when Canadian militia approached. The failure of two rebellions in Ireland destroyed Fenian morale, and the organization began to wither. A final gesture by O'Neill was a botched raid on Manitoba in 1871.

Confederation may have happened without the Fenians, but it was achieved in the shadow of the Fenian rifle. Ridgeway is usually dismissed as 'a skirmish', but it produced dozens of Canadian wounded and dead. It was also the only battle throughout that century in which Irish troops defeated forces of the British Crown.

P.M. TONER

Ferry Command. The generic term for the Second World War organization that, under a series of names, delivered 10,000 aircraft to the air forces of the *Commonwealth around the world. Although aircraft had not yet flown the North Atlantic on a regular basis, German successes forced the British Ministry of Aircraft Production to attempt delivering aircraft under their own power from North American factories. In the summer of 1940 a handful of experienced civilian airmen from Britain, Canada, and Australia went to work in Montreal's CPR Windsor Street station and the St Hubert airport recruiting radio operators from the Department of Transport and airline and *bush pilots, barnstormers, and crop-dusters. On 10–11 November 1940, seven Lockheed Hudson twin-engine bombers, fitted with extra fuel tanks, took off from Gander, Newfoundland, and approximately 12 hours later landed at Aldergrove, Northern Ireland. Notwithstanding a number of hurdles—such as dangerous flying conditions and inexperienced aircrew—two dozen more planes made the trip before the end of December. Lord Beaverbrook, the Canadian-born minister of aircraft production, declared the experiment a success. As the ferry scheme increased the pace of its deliveries, tragedies inevitably occurred. The first fatal crash came on 20 February 1941, taking the life of Sir Frederick *Banting, hitching a ride to Britain to meet with fellow researchers.

Once ATFERO, as the CPR-administered Atlantic Ferry Organization was known, had proven its viability, it was reorganized, first under 'Punch' *Dickins, then directly as part of the British Ministry of Aircraft Production. Finally the Air Ministry, which had initially opposed the idea, took over and provided a military veneer with the designation RAF Ferry Command. In 1943, having demonstrated the value not only of ferrying aircraft but also of carrying essential cargo and important passengers, the organization, still headquartered in Montreal, became No. 45 (North Atlantic) Group of a new RAF Transport Command. By the end of the war, 'Ferry Command' had delivered planes and people—including Winston Churchill to North Africa and Moscow—all over the world and in so doing paved the way for international air travel as we know it today. CARL A. CHRISTIE

Ferryland. From about 1500 this fishing station on Newfoundland's *English Shore was frequented seasonally by migratory Portuguese and Breton fishermen, and, after 1565, by West Country crews from Dartmouth, Bideford, and Barnstaple. It was permanently settled in 1621 as the Province of Avalon, sponsored by Sir George Calvert (1579–1632). The 1622 Patent of Avalon was the first in the New World to accept religious diversity. Calvert brought over craftsmen, under his Welsh captain Edward Wynne, to build 'a pretty street' of houses, a quay, warehouses, and harbour defences, of which impressive stone remains survive. Following political failure as James I's secretary of state, Calvert converted to Catholicism in 1625 and retired to Ireland, as First Baron Baltimore. After visiting Ferryland in 1627, he brought his baronial household of 40 to Newfoundland in 1628–9, but the cost of defence against French privateers, a slump in the fishery, and the 'sadd face of winter' drove him away, petitioning for a new proprietorship in Chesapeake Bay (eventually, Maryland). About 30 fisherfolk remained in 1629; some were still there in 1638, when Sir David *Kirke appropriated Ferryland as the centrepiece of his

'Newfoundland Plantation'. It became a transatlantic and intercolonial entrepôt and effective capital for Kirke, and, during much of the Interregnum (1649–60), for John Treworgie, a New England Puritan merchant, named commissioner for Newfoundland. After her husband's death in 1654, Lady Sara Kirke continued to manage Newfoundland's largest fishing 'plantation' at Ferryland and remained senior member of the regional merchant gentry, with her sons and her sister, Lady Frances Hopkins, a royalist refugee who had personally harboured King Charles. Following the Restoration of 1660, the Calverts briefly but ineffectively reasserted proprietorship. Despite considerable damage in 1673, during the third Dutch War, by 1677 more than 100 fisherfolk overwintered in Ferryland and nearby Caplin Bay in ten fishing plantations, many relatively large and strongly oriented to pastoral agriculture. Extensive archaeological remains survive from these later phases of settlement. Although planters were dispersed by Malouan privateers in 1696–7, Ferryland has since been continuously inhabited, becoming a focus of Irish settlement in the mid-18th century, and, as civil government slowly emerged in Newfoundland, administrative centre of the south Avalon.

PETER E. POPE

Fielding, William Stevens (1848–1929), Nova Scotia premier 1884–96. Born in Halifax, Fielding became one of the leading political figures of his generation. He began his career in 1864 as an anti-Confederate journalist with the Halifax *Morning Chronicle*, and became managing editor in 1874, articulating Liberal policy and attacking the provincial Conservative government. In 1882 he successfully contested a seat in the Nova Scotia legislature, and two years later assumed the premiership. He is best remembered for leading a campaign for repeal of the British North America Act during the 1886 election campaign. Despite winning a solid majority on the repeal ticket, the campaign for independence quickly faltered. Fielding then championed reciprocal trade with the United States. In 1896 Fielding entered federal politics as finance minister in the Laurier government, where he worked to encourage freer access to both British and American markets. In 1910 he successfully negotiated a *reciprocity treaty with the United States, but the defeat of the government in 1911 scuttled the arrangement. Despite eventual defeat in both his repeal and reciprocity campaigns, Fielding was considered a logical successor to Wilfrid *Laurier. Once more his hopes were dashed. In 1919 Fielding lost the Liberal leadership to W.L. Mackenzie *King in a close vote.

COLIN HOWELL

filibuster. The intentional use of legislative procedural tactics to obstruct and delay the consideration and passage of bills. Employed against the government to offset the opposition's numerical disadvantage, the filibuster is not a formal instrument in parliamentary procedure, but rather the term used for interference with the passage of legislation. Filibusters may be attempted through the introduction and debate of large numbers of points of order, numerous amendments, and drawn-out speeches. The 1990 debate over the adoption of the Goods and Services Tax serves as an example. NDP members of the Commons Finance Committee sought to delay referral back to the House by filibustering for 31 hours. In the end, their numerous amendments were defeated and the bill returned to the Commons, where it was approved.

JOHN C. COURTNEY AND DANIEL MACFARLANE

filles du roi. The term 'filles du roi' has been used since the end of the 17th century to refer to some 770 young French women, both never married and widows, sent to Canada, with the help of the government, between 1663 and 1673 to provide wives for the colony's male immigrants and mothers for their children. Mostly from the Paris area, Normandy, and the central-western region of France, many had lost their fathers or came from social backgrounds marked by poverty or illiteracy. The demographic behaviour of these women in Canada fulfilled the hopes placed in them: almost all married in the colony, on average a few months after arrival; they had many children, usually more than women in France; and their longevity was comparable to that of Canadian men and women in the 17th century. All in all, by arriving so early and reproducing so successfully, they made a powerful contribution to the establishment of the colony and its demographic development. Thus genealogists and geneticists give them a privileged place among the ancestors of French Canadians. In addition, because they spoke the central French of the Paris region, they ensured that French became the universal mother tongue in Canada well before 1760. The unenviable moral reputation attributed to them in the 18th century by the Baron de *Lahontan appears to be groundless, since their high and prolonged fertility was the opposite of the pattern among prostitutes.

YVES LANDRY

Fillmore, Roscoe Alfred (1887–1968). Born at Lumsden, in rural Albert County, New Brunswick, Roscoe Fillmore was a young labourer in Portland, Maine, when he was converted to socialist ideas by a street-corner speaker. He became an organizer for the Socialist Party of Canada in the Maritimes before the Great War and joined the *Communist Party of Canada in the early 1920s. A vigorous defender of radical causes, by the 1950s he was known as the grand old man of the radical left in the Maritimes. A well-regarded horticulturalist, Fillmore worked as an agricultural expert at the Kuzbas Colony in Siberia in 1923. He established a commercial nursery at Centreville, Nova Scotia, in 1924 and pioneered new hybrids suited to the Maritime climate. In 1938 he became head gardener for the Dominion Atlantic Railway, a position that included responsibility for the Grand Pré Memorial Park. He published *Green Thumbs* (1953) and other books for Canadian home gardeners.

DAVID FRANK

film industry. The business of film has three facets: production, distribution, and exhibition. Film distribution is the marketing branch of the industry and a necessary, though often resented, link between production and exhibition. It is also the most predictably profitable of the three branches, at least for the large multinational conglomerates that dominate the industry internationally. Since the early 1920s, the Canadian distribution sector has been overwhelmed by these multinationals: though there are approximately 80 Canadian distribution companies, the largest eight (all subsidiaries of Hollywood multinationals and members of the Motion Picture Export Association of America) receive about 80 per cent of total rental revenues. Although Canada is the largest foreign market for US films, most of this revenue is exported, and this has had a profound impact not only on the viability of the Canadian distribution sector (few independent Canadian companies are profitable) but also on Canadian production. Generally, distribution companies are prime sources for financing new production in a country, because of the close links established between distribution and production in the early years of the industry.

Although distribution was the last of the three branches to develop, it increasingly came to dominate the industry's economic structure. By the early 1920s the largest Wall Street–financed US distributors had acquired both production companies and theatre chains, thus creating vertically integrated combines that enabled eight major companies to dominate first the United States and then the international film industry. Although the original vertical combines were broken up after the Second World War under US anti-trust legislation, the basic operating principle continued; most Hollywood production is controlled, and usually financed, by the majors. Independent Canadian distributors, lacking significant access to the two largest chains as well as to major Hollywood films, have traditionally emphasized the marketing of independently produced films, low-budget exploitation films, and art films; they have also been the principle distributors of Canadian films. Few Canadian distribution companies survive more than a few years. The exceptions, such as Alliance Atlantis, Norstar, Cinepix, and Astral Media, have tended to follow vertically integrated models, often by financing television production and/or marketing their films to specialty TV channels (in which they often have an interest). Their market share of revenues from theatrical releases has, however, remained minimal. A federal government attempt in 1987 to strengthen the Canadian distribution sector encountered stiff opposition from the Motion Picture Export Association of America, generated intense lobbying in both Ottawa and Washington, and was eventually abandoned. Under NAFTA, it now appears that any similar proposal would be disallowed.

The consecutive patterns of vertical integration and then distributor-controlled production have seriously affected the viability of the Canadian film industry since the early 1920s. At that time, Hollywood majors acquired direct or indirect control, and through tied contracts—first with Famous Players theatres and since the 1940s with Odeon (now Cineplex-Odeon) theatres—ensured a constant flow of Hollywood films to Canadian theatres.

Exhibition has been the most lucrative branch of the Canadian industry, and Canadians such as N.L. Nathanson and Nat (Nathan) Taylor made small fortunes building up theatre chains. The two largest chains—Famous Players (established 1920) and Odeon (1941)—controlled almost 50 per cent of the total Canadian box-office gross by 1947. Independent theatres and small chains continue to thrive, especially outside the large urban centres, but they carry little weight. The two major chains continue to dominate the theatrical branch of the Canadian industry and control about two-thirds of the box-office gross.

By 1939, Canada had produced some 60 feature films and already had a reputation abroad for effective documentaries. By 1964, 60 more features had been produced and another hundred were released before the end of the decade. Since then, a range of funding and tax policies have encouraged production activity on a scale that earlier filmmakers could scarcely have imagined. Until the 1960s, film production was dominated by government agencies, especially the *National Film Board of Canada, and a small group of commercial companies primarily producing promotional and training films for industry. The Canadian Film Development Corporation (now Telefilm Canada) was established in 1967 to provide grants and loans to private Canadian feature filmmakers. Telefilm Canada has funded many critically acclaimed films, but few had a major theatrical release. Telefilm Canada is powerless to deal with the distribution and exhibition sectors of the industry.

In the 1980s, several young filmmakers (dubbed the 'New Wave in Canadian Cinema') emerged who recognised the futility of trying to compete with Hollywood. The films of such directors as Atom Egoyan, Bruce Macdonald, Mina Shum, Guy Maddin, Clement Virgo, Jean-Claude Lauzon, Patricia Rozema, Bill MacGillivray, Lynne Stopkewich, and Thom Fitzgerald have received widespread critical acclaim and have had considerable success in the marketing niche of art cinema.

While the feature film industry continues to emphasize art films, the television industry has become increasingly commercial and less identifiably Canadian in origin. Prior to the 1980s few Canadian television dramas or series were exported. Those that were tended to find their market in countries such as Britain and Australia with similar public broadcasting systems. With the advent of the Canadian Television and Cable Production Fund and its emphasis on prior sales and international co-productions, that situation changed dramatically. Companies have emerged that are now major players on the international television scene. Among them are such companies as Alliance-Atlantis Communications, Fireworks, and Paragon Entertainment. Although these companies also produce television programs aimed more directly at the Canadian market, most series are designed primarily for export. Made in Canada by Canadians, they have large budgets, employ hundreds of Canadian actors, writers, and crew and are entitled to varying degrees of financial support based on the level of involvement by Canadian personnel. The industry produces about $3 billion worth of films and television programs. It exports more than half of that, making Canada the world's second largest exporter of television programming after the United States. PETER MORRIS

finance capitalism and investment banking. Finance capitalism has both theoretical and historical meaning in Canada. In theory, it refers to the process by which capital is brought to industrial opportunity by the underwriting of securities that are then dispersed into the hands of individual investors. Merchant bankers emerged in the early-19th-century European economy as a means of satisfying the financial needs of governments and emerging industrialists. Names such as Barings and Rothschilds came to epitomize the art of marshalling the large amounts of capital needed to realize the scope and scale of the Industrial Revolution and to service burgeoning national debts. In essence, merchant bankers bridged capitalism from an era in which family-owned enterprise dominated to one in which capital and managerial imperatives dictated a broader diffusion of ownership and control. In theory, such financial capitalism should have played a passive, intermediary role, but in reality it came to assert the active primacy of financial ends (e.g., profits reaped from promotion) over industrial objectives (e.g., profits from production).

Finance capital was most pronounced in Canada's Gilded Age from the 1880s to the First World War, a period in which the nation's thin capital resources were placed under great strain by the tariff-induced industrial growth implicit in the 1879 *National Policy. Short on domestic capital, Canadian industry was obliged to look to European and American markets. Finance capitalists orchestrated the resultant deals, working largely out of Montreal, then Canada's financial hub. Aggressive young financiers like Max *Aitken, James *Dunn, and Henry Pellatt (in Toronto) connected would-be Canadian industrialists with foreign investors. Given that they operated in virtually unregulated financial markets, financial capitalists were able to manipulate their promotions through 'puffery' (biased endorsement), stock watering (inflating the actual value of the enterprise), and price manipulation, which pumped up values artificially. To ensure their sway over the enterprises they were financing, financial capitalists installed themselves on boards of directors. The profits of such operations were often spectacular. Financial capitalists came to advertise their prowess by adopting a garish lifestyle; Henry Pellatt's palatial Casa Loma in Toronto typified this trend. Canadian finance capitalism peaked in the heady *merger boom of 1909–13, when Aitken orchestrated the creation of Canada's largest steel company, Stelco, and cement company, Canada Cement. The most successful of Canada's finance capitalists, like Aitken and Dunn, migrated to London, where opportunities were wider and profits more lucrative. The return of stock mania in the 'roaring' late 1920s gave these financiers a last bout of lucrative activity but also brought on the first tentative attempts at financial regulation—for example, in 1928 Ontario began policing fraudulent investment. The Depression of the 1930s destroyed the legitimacy of finance capitalism and prompted greater regulation such as the 1934 Ontario Securities Commission. Since then, the term finance capitalism has tended to be used pejoratively, often with strong Marxian overtones to connote the exploitative nature of the 'money power'. The term merchant banker is still applied to a wide range of respectable underwriting functions such as initial public offerings and securitization. Merchant bankers (e.g., Onex Corporation of Toronto) also serve as the handmaidens of industrial restructuring, stripping ailing companies of debt and unprofitable lines of business. DUNCAN McDOWALL

Finnie, Oswald Sterling (1876–1948), northern administrator. A mining engineer in the Department of the Interior, Finnie was appointed director of the new Northwest Territories and Yukon Branch in 1920. In 1922 he inaugurated the annual Eastern Arctic Patrol, which looked to *Inuit needs, performed medical and dental services, and carried out scientific surveys. Finnie encouraged mineral exploration, fostering development of the Norman Wells oilfield and co-operating in ventures leading to the discovery of copper near Coronation Gulf and silver and pitchblende at Great Bear Lake. He was responsible for the creation of game preserves in the NWT, including Wood Buffalo Park, and in 1929 supervised introducing 3,000 reindeer from Alaska to the Mackenzie Delta to promote a herding industry for Canadian Inuit. That year he made the first flight across the Mackenzie–Yukon divide, from Aklavik to *Dawson, in a chartered plane. Finnie took a hands-on approach to northern affairs, seeking a more enlightened attitude to the territories, but was hampered by the short-sightedness of superiors. After 1931 many of his initiatives foundered when the Northwest Territories and Yukon Branch was dismantled, a victim of personality differences and budget cuts under the new Conservative government. He retired in 1932. R. QUINN DUFFY

Finns. Coming from a geographically similar country and climate, Finnish immigrants did not complain about Canada's cold winters or worry about taming the wilderness. By 1900 Finns had settled in northern Ontario and British Columbia, where the pioneers cleared homesteads, fished, trapped, and hunted. In many northern communities Finns were the first European settlers. Men found backbreaking work on the railroads, in the mines, and in the lumber camps. Finnish women, 'defiant sisters', who usually emigrated as single women, worked in lumber camps and boarding houses as cooks. As men greatly outnumbered them, the social odds were in women's favour. 'Canada is hell for men and heaven for women' became a common expression. Women were also in demand as live-in domestics in Montreal, Toronto, and Vancouver. Finns who settled in prairie sod huts often migrated later to areas where water was plentiful and forests abundant. By the Second World War, of the 41,683 Finns in Canada 80 per cent lived in Ontario or British Columbia.

A culturally close-knit group with difficulties learning English, Finns founded their own organizations. They constructed halls with stages, libraries, kitchens, and dance floors. In many picturesque parks, Finns built sports fields and staged fiercely competitive track and field events in the summer and cross-country skiing competitions in the winter. Afterwards, they relaxed in saunas and cooled off in the lake or jumped in the ice hole. Universally literate, they established newspapers, engaged in political debate, were active in temperance and suffrage movements, and became enthusiastic union supporters. Two organizers for the Lumber Workers Industrial Union, Viljo Rosvall and John Voutilainen, allegedly murdered in 1929 near Thunder Bay, became martyrs of the Canadian labour movement. Other Finnish activists were blacklisted, arrested during demonstrations, and deported. During the Depression, Finnish communities became firmly divided between the 'reds' and the conservative, mainly Lutheran 'church Finns'.

In 1901 some disgruntled miners established a utopian socialist community off the northern coast of Vancouver Island. Named Sointula ('Place of Harmony') by its charismatic leader, Matti Kurikka, the colony declared that 'men and women were equal in all respects'. In 1905, when Sointula collapsed amidst financial difficulties and discord over Kurikka's views of women's right to free love, the community had established free health care, childcare, education, and equal pay for equal work. The communal spirit continued in other Finnish communities, which started co-operatives, mutual benefit organizations, and, more recently, seniors' centres.

After a century of settlement, close to 100,000 Canadians claim Finnish heritage. Increasingly urban and English-speaking, Finns continue to love the sauna, dance tango at the hall, worship in Lutheran and Pentecostal congregations, sing Sibelius's *Finlandia* in choirs, and praise Finnish sports heroes, who now include NHL players and Formula One drivers. VARPU LINDSTRÖM

fires. Whether in forests or cities, fire threatened pioneer Canadians. Difficulties in controlling and extinguishing outbreaks were compounded by the absence of waterworks, mechanical pumps, and adequate communications. In cities, soldiers or volunteer fire brigades did what they could. Little in the countryside checked fires except rain or water obstacles. The publicity accorded such disasters varied with circumstances. Forest fires in the Saguenay district, May 1870, took at least eight lives and left 5,000 destitute, yet were scarcely reported in major newspapers distracted by *Fenian raids in the *Eastern Townships. Similar fires in the Hull and Ottawa areas in August 1870 received more coverage, occurring in settled areas with no similar distractions.

The most disastrous forest fire in Canadian history decimated New Brunswick's Miramichi district in October 1825 following a very dry summer. It burned some 15,500 square km north of the Miramichi River, destroyed Douglastown and Newcastle, and killed between 200 and 500 people. The local timber trade was crippled for many years, and logging shifted elsewhere in British North America. Northern Ontario has witnessed several disastrous forest fires. On 29 July 1916, one caused by lightning and steam locomotive sparks developed into a firestorm that consumed Cochrane, Matheson, and environs, killing at least 228. A fire that burned Haileybury and surrounding districts in October 1922 killed approximately 100 people. About this time provinces began to use aircraft to detect fires and fight many before they spread. Air patrols and firefighting techniques including water bombers and air evacuations have largely eliminated forest fires' threat to human life.

Two types of major urban fires can be distinguished: city-wide catastrophes that result in extensive material loss but relatively few casualties, and sudden fires that are confined to one or two buildings but that nevertheless kill many. Examples of the latter are the Theatre Royale in Quebec City (12 June 1846, 47 fatalities), the Laurier Palace Theatre, Montreal (9 January 1927, 78 deaths), and the *Knights of Columbus hostel, St John's (12 December 1942, 99 dead). Occurring on a ship in Toronto harbour, the burning of the cruise ship *Noronic* (16 September 1949, 118 deaths) was more akin to a hotel fire than a marine disaster. A rare tragedy was the *Halifax Explosion of 6 December 1917, which combined the forces of blast, earthquake, tidal wave, and fire to kill over 1,600 people.

Two fires in Quebec City (May and June 1845) burned almost all the suburbs, leaving 23 dead and the city smaller than at the time of the British capture. High winds fanned another fire in Quebec City in October 1866 that destroyed 2,124 homes. Two ports, St John's, Newfoundland, and Saint John, New Brunswick, seemed to compete for the number of major fires. St John's, described by some as 'built to burn', had major fires 1816, 1817, 1819, 1846, and 1892. Saint John was similarly afflicted in 1837, 1845, and 1877. Few cities escaped major conflagrations, including Toronto, Montreal, and Ottawa; yet, most were characterized by extensive destruction but relatively few fatalities. The great fire that engulfed Hull and Ottawa (26–7 April 1900) left about 14,000 homeless, yet only seven deaths were reported. Vancouver's was an exceptional case: a blaze on 13 June 1886 reduced it briefly to the status of a tent city and took at least 30 lives.

Insurance companies have supported measures to improve fire protection and firefighting methods. These extended to public education and the training of professional firefighters. Toronto and Montreal were the first cities to organize paid full-time fire departments, in 1862 and 1863, respectively. HUGH A. HALLIDAY

First World War. When on 4 August 1914 Britain's ultimatum to Germany expired, Canada found itself at war with Germany. Newspapers had told Canadians of the crisis, and the country appeared unusually united. From the opposition, Sir Wilfrid *Laurier spoke for all: in Britain's hour of danger, Canada's loyal answer was 'Ready, Aye Ready'. Everywhere, men lined up to enlist.

Canadians were better prepared than they knew. Defence spending had grown sixfold since 1897, and 60,000 militiamen had drilled in 1913. Pre-war plans safeguarded ports, canals, and bridges from surprise attack. Urged by an opposition member to 'omit no power that the Government may need', an emergency session of Parliament adopted a *War Measures Act that met the test. The minister of militia, Col Sam *Hughes, scrapped an existing mobilization plan, summoned volunteers to Valcartier, near Quebec City, and appeared in full uniform to sort out the confusion. Canadians marvelled when a convoy left for England on 2 October with 32,000 volunteers.

Most expected a voluntary effort for a short war. A *Canadian Patriotic Fund collected donations for soldiers' families. A Military Hospitals Commission created facilities for sick and wounded veterans. By 1917, militia regiments and patriotic civilians had recruited half a million volunteers. Churches, the Red Cross, and women's organizations 'did their bit', from buying machineguns to distributing *white feathers to civilian men. Patriots ended the teaching of German in schools and universities, pressed the city of Berlin, Ontario, to rename itself Kitchener, and forced Ottawa to intern 7,000 mostly harmless 'enemy aliens'.

The war proved longer and harsher than anyone anticipated. In 1915, Hughes's department swallowed up more than the entire government spent in 1913. To keep the bankrupt Grand Trunk and Canadian Northern railways operating, secret subsidies matched military costs. Sir Thomas White, the finance minister, broke tradition and borrowed in New York. In desperation, he asked Canadians for $50 million. They loaned $100 million; additional loans were also oversubscribed. In 1917, humbler citizens produced $400 million in Victory Loans, $600 million in 1918. Federal revenue grew from $126 million in 1914 to $233.7 million in 1918 but the national debt soared from $434 million to $2.5 billion. The war to end all wars would be financed by posterity.

Wartime exports of wheat, timber, and Canadian-made munitions helped lift a pre-war depression. A Canadian shell committee won $170 million in orders. Slow delivery persuaded the British to create an Imperial Munitions Board in Canada. Its manager, Joseph *Flavelle, made the IMB Canada's biggest business, with 250,000 workers (40,000 of them women) and turnover of $2 million a day. IMB factories and contractors produced ships, aircraft, chemicals, and explosives as well as shells. Food production was just as important. Ideal conditions produced an unprecedented 15 million bushels of wheat in 1915. Yields fell in later years, but prices soared.

Too late, farmers, industrialists, and governments recognized that manpower was a critical resource in wartime. By 1915 the prime minister, Sir Robert *Borden, had approved a *Canadian Expeditionary Force of 50,000 men. By summer, his target was 150,000. A transatlantic visit shocked Borden with the casual nature of British wartime leadership. To set an example of earnestness, he ignored both his military adviser, Maj.-Gen. W.G. Gwatkin, and Quebec nationalist Henri *Bourassa and raised Canada's commitment to 250,000 men. On January 1, 1916, he again doubled it.

Initially, recruiting seemed easy. When peacetime *militia regiments were exhausted, businessmen and politicians raised battalions. Civic pride, sporting links, and Highland regalia drew recruits. Clergy preached patriotism. Women wore badges inviting men to 'Knit or Fight'. British ancestry, social pressure, and traditional schooling in duty and patriotism persuaded almost a quarter of all Canadian men to enlist. Half of them were rejected as unfit. In Quebec, recruiting pressures were feeble. Militia traditions were weak and France's Third Republic repelled devout Catholics. Borden's *nationaliste* colleagues loyally backed the war, but they had won in 1911 by passionately opposing imperial adventures. Ontario refused to end its assault on French-language schools, and nativists persuaded western provinces to end minority education rights. French Canada's real enemies, claimed Bourassa, were not Germans, but their fellow Canadians. Only in 1917 did Ottawa organize Quebec recruiting, under Dr Arthur Mignault, a patent medicine manufacturer.

Sam Hughes's recruiting methods sent hundreds of battalions to Britain only to be broken up to maintain the 48 infantry battalions ultimately needed for the *Canadian Corps. He also encouraged three rival Canadian officers to claim the minister's full authority. Chaos in England led, in September 1916, to creation of a ministry in London to manage Canada's overseas forces, a statement that the CEF was part of a Canadian army, and dismissal of Sir Sam Hughes.

Canadian soldiers learned their job in the trenches and in battles made more dangerous by untrained officers and a faulty rifle. The German gas attack at *Ypres in April 1915 cost 6,035 dead, wounded, and captured. At St-Eloi, Mont-Sorrel, and in the Somme offensives Canadian divisions suffered from inexperience and poor tactics. Survivors learned that precise staff work, careful preparation, and discipline won battles and saved lives. The proof came at Easter 1917. After weeks of stockpiling, tunnelling, improved tactics, and rehearsals, Sir Julian Byng sent the four divisions of the Canadian Corps to capture *Vimy Ridge. Five days of fighting brought the Allies their first unequivocal victory on the Western Front.

Byng was British but his winning ways were inherited weeks later by his Canadian successor. Sir Arthur *Currie was a pear-shaped, pre-war Victoria real estate speculator. He had evolved into a cool, methodical soldier, open to innovation. That summer, instead of the attack on Lens demanded by his British superiors, Currie captured nearby Hill 70. When the Germans tried to retake the position, Currie's artillery destroyed them. Canadian control of its overseas forces added to Currie's authority. By 1918, the British retained little more than tactical authority over Canadian units in France. In practical terms, the war transformed Canada from a colony into a junior ally.

Pre-war Conservative opposition to a Canadian navy had left the infant service with hired trawlers barely able to protect the coasts against German U-boats. Borden also resisted forming a Canadian air force until the last days of the war, but many Canadians joined the British services. By war's end, a quarter of the Royal Air Force's pilots were Canadians. Two Canadians, Maj. William Avery *Bishop and Maj. Raymond Collishaw, ranked third and fifth among wartime air aces.

Capturing Vimy Ridge cost Canada 10,604 dead and wounded. Completing the British offensive at *Passchendaele in October 1917 cost 15,654 more. Keeping each of four Canadian divisions in action absorbed 20,000 new soldiers a year. Recruiting leagues warned that only *conscription would produce them. English Canadians blamed Quebec. The government attempted voluntary national registration to identify potential recruits. Almost no eligible registrant volunteered. At the end of 1916, David Lloyd George took power in Britain and summoned the dominion premiers. 'We want more men from them', he explained. The price was consultation. In London, Borden learned that Russia was collapsing, France's army was close to mutiny, and U-boats threatened Britain with starvation. Americans had joined the war but needed years to build an army. Meanwhile, wounded men had to return to the trenches and losses at Vimy might force Canada to cut its field army.

Borden knew that conscription was unpopular. He also saw no alternative that kept faith with Canada's soldiers and allies. On 18 May 1917, he announced selective conscription for service overseas. The conscription crisis would become one of the most bitterly divisive episodes in Canadian history. Once exemptions were cancelled, the Military Service Act found close to the 100,000 single men, 20 to 24, needed to sustain Canada's war-fighting capacity into 1919. A *Union government, created by Borden to support conscription, adopted measures made possible by wartime mobilization: railway nationalization, civil service reform, votes for women, and national prohibition of alcoholic beverages.

The last year of the war was bitter. Strains from conscription were aggravated by soaring inflation, food and fuel shortages, municipal strikes, anti-foreign riots, and the tragic aftermath of the *Halifax Explosion. Government responded with new regulations, a mild but potentially significant Income War Tax and an Anti-Loafing Law intended to force all to make themselves useful. A second National Registration included women. For the first time, the government ordered its police forces to hunt for sedition.

In France, German armies, released by Russia's collapse, attacked on 8 March. Britain's Fifth Army collapsed. More offensives followed, forcing Allied armies back. Defeat seemed possible, though Canada's army corps was untouched. At their second conference, dominion premiers predicted a war lasting into 1920. Then, quite suddenly, the war rushed to a conclusion. On 8 August 1918 Canadian and Australian divisions broke the German line near *Amiens. Tanks, aircraft, and infantry worked together. On the 11th, Currie insisted on switching fronts. A month later, Canadians broke the Drocourt-Quéant line and on 26 September the Corps crossed the Canal du Nord, taking Cambrai on 11 October. The cost was 30,802 dead and wounded. On 1 November Canadians captured Valenciennes, a key point of a new German line. By 11 November Canadians had reached Mons. There, at 11 A.M., the war ended.

The war cost Canada 60,661 dead; many more returned mutilated in mind or body. Canadians had become a deeply divided people who had inherited a staggering debt, but they had changed from colonials to allies.

DESMOND MORTON

fisheries. Until the 1950s, most Atlantic Canadian fishers worked inshore waters in household enterprises, using rudimentary technology such as traps, nets, and fishing lines in boats less than 65 feet to catch fish for salt curing. Cod was the most important commercial fish, with salmon, herring, lobster, mackerel, and other species also important in the Maritimes. In the late 19th and early 20th centuries, schooners voyaged from Newfoundland and Nova Scotia ports to fish on offshore banks, but these schooner fisheries declined relative to the inshore fisheries due to their higher overhead costs.

After Confederation (1949), Newfoundland followed Canadian fisheries modernization plans to foster fresh/frozen production for the American market. Atlantic Canadian corporations invested in huge fishing trawlers equipped with the latest technology, costly ventures that concentrated ownership in fewer hands. These trawlers ranged further out onto the offshore banks and depended on wage labour. The sector's demand for raw material allowed the survival of the small-scale fishery to ensure a stable supply of fish and diversified production in other species. Federal–provincial subsidies and loans later encouraged households to increase the scale of their investment, eroding family-based enterprises, while women's important roles in curing salt fish gave way to poor wages in the processing plants. The failure of regional industrial diversification meant that too many people continued to depend on poor earnings in the fishing industry. In the late 1950s, the Newfoundland government pressured Canadian authorities to extend unemployment insurance to fishers throughout Atlantic Canada to make up income shortfalls.

The federal government regulates the fishery for social, economic, and conservation purposes while provincial regulation governs onshore processing plants. In 1977 Canada extended its jurisdiction over coastal waters from 10 miles to 200 miles and encouraged the expansion of the Canadian industry to generate employment. Consequent over-expansion led to financial crisis in the 1980s. The Canadian government reorganized and refinanced the corporate sector but failed to address over-capacity. The resultant depletion of fish stocks led to the moratoria on east coast fishing in 1992. In Prince Edward Island, most fishers depend on the lobster fishery, and the harvesting of oysters and mussels. The territorial nature of lobster made their vulnerability to over-exploitation obvious and led fishers to accept conservation measures.

The federal government's responses to the 1992 moratoria—adjustment programs culminating in the Atlantic

Groundfish Strategy—compensated and retrained many people but failed to lessen rural dependence on the fishing industry. From the mid-1990s, fishing for invertebrate species such as shrimp, snow crab, and scallops boomed and produced higher earnings than the cod fisheries, but at the risk of over-capacity and resource depletion. Fewer people benefit from shell fisheries because of licensing restrictions and higher overhead costs. Shellfish processing fosters respiratory ailments such as crab lung, especially among women, who dominate the processing workforce.

Pacific salmon dominate British Columbia's fisheries. First appearing in the 1870s, industrial salmon fishing and canning resulted in over-capacity, ineffective regulation, and resource depletion similar to that in Atlantic Canada. The migratory nature of salmon, and the proximity of American waters, meant that international management agencies, such as the International North Pacific Fisheries Commission (1953), were important. The corresponding agency on the east coast is the North Atlantic Fisheries Organization.

On both coasts, federal regulations marginalized First Nations by not accepting Aboriginal fishing rights. In 1968, the federal Davis Plan, aimed at reducing overall fishing capacity on the Pacific coast, disproportionately targeted Aboriginal fishers, who had the least capital and greatest debt. The plan, and successive federal regulations, provoked greater demands by First Nations for recognition of their entitlements to fish. In 1990 the Supreme Court of Canada, in *R. v. Sparrow*, recognized First Nations right to fish and trade for food and for social and ceremonial purposes. In 1999 *R. v. Marshall* recognized that East Coast Mi'kmaq and Maliseet people had rights to fish and trade entrenched in their treaties.

In the freshwater fisheries of the Great Lakes and Manitoba, federal and provincial regulations similarly discriminate against Aboriginal fishers. In the Great Lakes, commercial fisheries by European settlers developed by 1800; within a century these had contributed to the extinction of Atlantic salmon. The increasing capitalization of fishing gear and vessels meant that household-based, small-scale fisheries for local markets gave way to a larger-scale industry organized for specialized American markets. Protective tariffs resulted in American capital dominating the industry. By the late 1950s, every commercial species in the Great Lakes was under pressure, and some, such as sturgeon, were commercially extinct. Manitoba's lake fisheries developed with the railway and Icelandic immigration in the 1880s. In Lake Winnipeg, harvesting of sturgeon for caviar between 1885 and 1935 led to commercial depletion and the demise of the fisheries. A Privy Council ruling in 1898 limited federal authority in fresh-water fishing to protecting fish stocks and habitat; the provinces retain proprietary licensing rights. In the Great Lakes, which share an extensive border with the United States, nine federal, provincial, and state governments make varied rules for fisheries. Agricultural, commercial, industrial, and urban development of the Great Lakes basin have adversely affected fish stocks through the destruction or pollution of habitats.

SEAN CADIGAN

Fishermen's Protective Union. Formed on 3 November 1908 at Herring Neck, Notre Dame Bay, by William *Coaker, the FPU tapped into widespread disillusionment with Newfoundland's economic and political system. It grew rapidly and by 1914 had 20,000 members (half of Newfoundland's fishermen) on the predominantly Protestant northeast coast. Membership was limited to fishers, farmers, loggers, and manual labourers. Several companies were formed to provide goods and supplies to members and to purchase fish from them for sale in international markets. The union had its own newspaper, the *Fishermen's Advocate*, and established Canada's only union-built town at Port Union near Catalina; its Fishermen's Union Trading Company eventually became one of Newfoundland's largest exporters of saltfish. Disillusioned with Coaker's support of conscription during the First World War, and his involvement in the murky world of St John's politics, membership had declined by 1924. Coaker resigned as president in 1926. The union remained in existence until 1960, mainly as a loggers' union. MELVIN BAKER AND AIDAN MALONEY

Fishery Protection Service. Founded in 1886 during a dispute with the United States, the Fishery (later Fisheries) Protection Service became a permanent federal agency in 1888. In the early 20th century a 'militarized' FPS became the foundation of Prime Minister Wilfrid *Laurier's emerging naval policy. In 1903–4 two new armed steel vessels, *Vigilant* and *Canada*, were acquired, and in 1905 the first recruits of the new 'Naval Militia' were trained. In 1908 Rear Admiral Sir Charles Edmund Kingsmill, a Canadian with a distinguished career in the Royal Navy, was appointed in command; two years later the first naval officer cadets went to sea aboard *Canada*. When the *Royal Canadian Navy was founded on 4 May 1910 Kingsmill became the first director of the Naval Service, a post he held for the next 11 years, and the FPS was transferred to the new service as a separate branch. However, by then the FPS no longer fit Laurier's ambitious plans for an ocean-going navy composed of large cruisers. In the turmoil following the election of Sir Robert *Borden's government in 1911 the navy virtually collapsed, while the FPS continued to function. It was returned to civilian control in 1920.

MARC MILNER

fishing admirals. In the Newfoundland migratory fishery, *c.* 1500–1786, fishing admirals were not naval officers but rather the first fishing masters to arrive in each harbour every spring, authorized to take first choice of 'fishing rooms' or shore space, and to settle disputes among subsequently arriving crews, on the basis of the *Western Charters, royal patents that regulated the fishery. Newfoundland historical mythology characterizes them as corrupt and cruel. After 1680, their authority was gradually displaced by the Royal Navy, particularly in matters involving resident fisherfolk. From 1729, the senior naval officer in command of the Newfoundland station was styled governor of Newfoundland. PETER E. POPE

Fitzpatrick, Alfred (1862–1936), educator, activist. Born in Pictou County, Nova Scotia, Fitzpatrick attended Queen's University in Kingston, where he was influenced by the social activism of the principal, fellow Nova Scotian George Monro *Grant. Graduating in 1892 as a Presbyterian minister, he concentrated his efforts on workers in mines, lumber camps, and railroad construction. By 1899, in Ontario, he began his work in adult literacy, founding the Canadian Reading Camp Association. He and his assistant, Edmund Bradwin, recruited university undergraduates to work during the day and teach the workers at night. By 1920, the association had become *Frontier College, and in 1922 the government awarded it a charter to provide post-secondary education nationally. Fitzpatrick wrote the first primer for teaching Canada's immigrants, *Handbook for New Canadians* (1921); his *University in Overalls: A Plea for Part-Time Study* (1920) put forth his radical ideas about society's responsibilities to the illiterate and the working poor. In 1933 Fitzpatrick resigned as Frontier College's first president. In 1934 he received the Order of the British Empire for his work in literacy. JAMES H. MORRISON

five cent speech. In February 1930 evidence of a recession was still inconclusive. When the Opposition demanded that Mackenzie *King's Liberal government should give money to provincial Conservative governments, the prime minister interpreted the demand as a partisan tactic and declared that he would not give such governments a five cent piece for the unemployed. His uncharacteristic outburst was a minor issue in the election campaign later that year. H. BLAIR NEATBY

fixed link. When Prince Edward Island joined Confederation in 1873, the government of Canada made a commitment to establish 'efficient steam service' that would guarantee 'continuous communication' with the railway system of the mainland. At the time the only means of winter travel to and from the island was by 'iceboat', a combination of boat and sled used to take mail and occasional passengers across both ice and open stretches of water between the island and New Brunswick. The early steamship service provided by the federal government was unsatisfactory; consequently by the 1880s an alternative was being discussed: a tunnel under Northumberland Strait. Instead of attempting this, the federal government eventually provided much-improved ferry service, particularly with the ice-breaking SS *Prince Edward Island*, which commenced service in 1917. After the Second World War, steadily increasing automobile traffic produced an almost constant demand for more ferry capacity. By the late 1950s another solution to the problem was proposed: a 'causeway'. This idea was eventually shelved, apparently for economic reasons. Yet, with continuing needs for new ferries, the issue re-emerged in the 1980s. This time there was organized opposition to the project, as a threat to 'the Island way of life'. Such concerns had not surfaced in earlier eras; islanders had apparently held the pragmatic view that a tunnel or causeway would simply be another transportation improvement. The government of Joseph Ghiz held a plebiscite on the principle of a 'fixed link' in 1988, and a majority of those voting endorsed the idea. After lengthy debate over the environmental implications of the actual plans, construction commenced in 1994. The Confederation Bridge opened on 31 May 1997, spanning the 14 km passage between New Brunswick and the island, an engineering marvel and reputedly the world's longest bridge over ice-covered water. IAN ROSS ROBERTSON

flag. *See* NATIONAL FLAG.

Flavelle, Sir Joseph Wesley (1858–1939), businessman. Of Irish-Protestant descent, Flavelle quit school at age 14 in Peterborough, Ontario, to learn the provision business. He specialized in hard work, rigid accounting, and earnest Methodism. In the 1890s as manager of Toronto's William Davies Company, he created Canada's first modern meat-packing enterprise and became a millionaire on profits from the firm's sales of bacon in the British market. Davies's operations apparently gave Toronto its nickname, Hogtown.

Flavelle became active in many other enterprises associated with the rise of Toronto enterprise, including the Canadian Bank of Commerce, Simpson's department store, and National Trust. He became one of Canada's leading philanthropists, responsible for rebuilding Toronto General Hospital and reorganizing the University of Toronto. 'Holy Joe' was a rock-solid pillar of the Methodist Church. As chairman of the Imperial Munitions Board during the First World War he organized Canadian munitions production, a billion-dollar enterprise. For his public service he was awarded a baronetcy in 1917, the same year he had to fight off unfounded charges of wartime profiteering. His meat-packing operations were eventually sold and consolidated to form Canada Packers Ltd. His Toronto mansion, Holwood, survives as the home of the University of Toronto's Faculty of Law. MICHAEL BLISS

Fleming, Michael Anthony (1792–1850), Roman Catholic bishop in Newfoundland 1830–50. An Irish-born Franciscan who first came to the colony in 1823, he was determined both to strengthen the institutional church and to promote the status and influence of its adherents. He actively recruited clergy in Ireland, brought over the Presentation and Mercy nuns, increased the number of parishes, and devoted himself to the building of churches, convents, schools, and a large and impressive cathedral in St John's. After the establishment of a legislature in 1832 he was active in politics, openly backing the reform-liberal party, and denouncing those members of his flock who did not. A foe of the largely Anglican ascendancy, he fought for adequate Catholic representation in the local government and bureaucracy. Fleming contributed as a result to the bitter sectarian divisions of the period, but left a stronger church and a more powerful Catholic community.

JAMES K. HILLER

Fleming, Sir Sandford (1827–1915). Born in Kirkcaldy, Scotland, Fleming, who came to Canada in 1845, was Canada's foremost railway surveyor and railway construction engineer of the 19th century. One of his most important projects included the surveying, construction, and subsequent operation, as chief engineer, of the government-owned and -operated *Intercolonial Railway from Quebec City to Halifax and Saint John. Extensive surveys of the best route for a proposed Canadian railway from Montreal to the Pacific Coast were probably Fleming's greatest achievement. His specific recommendations were not followed when the government signed a contract with the *Canadian Pacific Railway syndicate to build the railway. Later, however, the Canadian Northern Railway built a new railway along the western route suggested by Fleming.

Fleming was an ardent supporter of a communications cable between Canada and distant parts of the British Empire, including the Pacific cable laid in 1902 linking Canada to Australia. He also advocated adoption of a universal system of time keeping, which established a standard mean time and hourly variations according to established time zones. That system was adopted at an International Prime Meridian Conference in Washington in 1884 and is still in use today. Fleming also designed the first Canadian postage stamp, the three-penny beaver issued in 1851. T.D. REGEHR

Florizel. Built in 1909, *Florizel* was the flagship of Bowring Brothers' steamship company. One of the first ice-breaking ships, it was 93 m long, weighed 1,980 tons, and was equipped with submarine-signaling apparatus and wireless. The ship saw service for many years at the annual spring seal hunt off Newfoundland, and in 1914 had the honour of carrying the first 500 volunteers (the Blue Puttees) of the Newfoundland Regiment to England.

On 23 February 1918 *Florizel* left St John's on its regular run for New York, carrying 78 passengers and 60 crew. Shortly after departure the weather deteriorated. After nine hours at sea, Captain William Martin thought that the vessel had cleared Cape Race and changed course to the west. But *Florizel* was only 72 km south of St John's, and crashed upon the rocks just north of the cape. Only 44 individuals survived the disaster. Captain Martin was later exonerated of carelessness. A marine court of inquiry found that the chief engineer had contravened the captain's order, proceeding at full speed in hopes of reaching Halifax in time to spend the night with his family.

MELVIN BAKER AND AIDAN MALONEY

football. Football in Canada developed gradually. It had its roots in the game of English rugby, a popular sport in Canada for much of the 19th century and widely played in the Maritimes and British Columbia even after that. In recent years rugby has undergone a revival, and the Canadian team today is ranked among the top 12 in the world. A distinctive brand of Canadian football began to develop in the last quarter of the 19th century. Games between McGill and Harvard in 1874, and the University of Michigan and the University of Toronto in 1879, resulted in rule modifications that started the metamorphosis of rugby into Canadian football. In 1898 J.C.M. Burnside established a comprehensive rules code that would eventually be adopted across the country. Football received the royal stamp of approval when Governor General Earl Grey donated a championship trophy in 1907 to the best amateur team in eastern Canada, and which later came to symbolize national football supremacy. Major changes, including the forward pass, came in the 1920s and 1930s as American coaches made their way north to coach and play. In 1936, fearful of the drift towards Americanization, the Canadian Rugby Union placed a limit on the number of imports and established eligibility requirements for Grey Cup play. Import quotas continue, and the Canadian rules code still differs from the American in a number of respects, particularly in the size of the field and in three rather than four down play.

Canadian football grew to maturity after the Second World War, both at the intercollegiate and professional levels. The Canadian Football League established franchises across the country, except for the Maritimes, and flourished amid the growing popularity of football across North America. In addition to imported stars Canadians such as quarterback Russ Jackson, Ron Stewart, and Jim Corrigal became household names. In the 1990s the CFL fell on difficult times. In a desperate attempt to reverse its fortunes, it experimented with expansion into the United States in 1993. The league barely survived the debacle that followed, but today a commitment to fiscal responsibility and an entertaining wide-open game offers hope for a healthier future. COLIN HOWELL

foreign aid. Transfer of capital and expertise from industrial countries to developing countries through official development assistance (ODA) is a noble but flawed means of promoting economic development and overcoming global poverty. The enterprise has contended with colossal human and biophysical challenges and vastly unequal relations of wealth and power. Donor governments, buffeted by myriad domestic and international pressures, have pursued multiple and often conflicting objectives—political and commercial as well as humanitarian.

Canada has disbursed over $50 billion in ODA to countries in Africa, Asia, the Caribbean, and Latin America. Approximately two-thirds has been channelled bilaterally to recipient governments and non-governmental organizations (NGOs), and the rest to multilateral institutions—the World Bank, regional development banks, and UN agencies.

Canadian bilateral aid began after a 1950 conference that launched the Colombo Plan for south and southeast Asia. The objectives of containing communism and transforming the British colonial empire into a multiracial *Commonwealth, tempered by political caution and fiscal parsimony, resulted in modest support for new states in the Indian subcontinent. By then, limited funds had also been allocated for UN agencies engaged in refugee relief and training. A reluctant participant in the 1950s and early 1960s, Canada faced mounting pressures from the United States and the old imperial powers to shoulder a greater share of the 'aid burden'. Ottawa responded more enthusiastically to the challenge later in the 1960s, a time of optimism, idealism, and prosperity, when support for international development captured the imagination of growing numbers of Canadians. New dynamism was ensured by Prime Minister *Pearson's inspired appointment of Maurice Strong as director of the External Aid Office in 1966, and by Prime Minister *Trudeau's creation of the Canadian International Development Agency in 1968. A young, self-made millionaire, Strong served as first president of the agency, spearheading development of long-lasting policies and establishing innovative NGO and business programs to tap public energy and support. He and Paul Gérin-Lajoie, a former Quebec cabinet minister and CIDA president in 1970–7, encouraged expansion of Canadian aid to most parts of the developing world. In 1970, the government promised to meet the donor country ODA target endorsed by the UN—0.7 per cent of gross national product (GNP). By 1975–6, aid spending exceeded $900 million, the ODA /GNP ratio reached 0.53 per cent, and Canada won praise as a generous donor.

The latter half of the 1970s was marked by acrimonious 'North-South dialogue' and growing scepticism among donors about the value of aid. Neo-liberal thinking about debt, structural adjustment, and the role of the state dominated the ODA agenda in the 1980s, and programming shifted away from its earlier emphasis on infrastructure. Canada joined others in cutting assistance and seeking from it more tangible economic and political returns. The aid budget reached $3 billion in 1990–1, but the ODA/GNP ratio of 0.45 per cent was well below Scandinavian and Dutch levels, although still above the donor average. Loss of momentum was accompanied by growing bureaucratization of CIDA (symbolized by the appointment of civil servants as presidents) and, during the Mulroney years, increasing politicization as the agency began to report to a hands-on junior minister rather than to the secretary of state for External Affairs.

The end of the Cold War weakened the geopolitical case for ODA in the 1990s, and deficit reduction provided a rationale for even deeper cuts. Canada was not alone, but the fall in aid spending was steeper than in most other Western countries. From a respectable fifth among donors in ODA volume in the mid-1980s, Canada dropped to ninth out of 22 in 1999, behind the much smaller Netherlands. The ODA/GNP ratio plummeted to 0.24 per cent in 2001–2, to a point where Canada ranked 17th among donors, down from sixth in 1994. Hopes for a long-promised reversal faded in 2001 with the onset of recession and the terrorist attacks of 11 September.

The Canadian aid program has suffered from multiple objectives and a tendency to chase programming fashions rather than to stay the course. It has penalized recipients by tying contributions heavily to Canadian procurement, and its impact has been limited by a too thin spread among a large number of recipients. On the positive side, the terms of Canada's ODA have been generous and have minimized long-term indebtedness. Although deteriorating, the record on assisting the poorest countries has been better than average. Also, CIDA has been a leader internationally in responsive programming by NGOs and in gender and development. DAVID R. MORRISON

foreign missions. Canada, it is said, sent more missionaries overseas per capita than any nation in Christendom. By 1920 Canadian Protestant churches claimed responsibility for 40 million 'heathens' around the world, and sponsored 400 missionaries in China, 200 in India, and 150 in the Japanese Empire. The Methodists alone raised $1.3 million for missions, of which $300,000 went to West China, to what was reputedly the largest mission in the world, with its showplace West China Union University. Catholic missions had a different trajectory, starting a generation later and predominantly (90 per cent) French Canadian. By 1973, there were 5,300 Quebec missionaries overseas.

The first foreign missionaries from what was to become Canada were from Nova Scotia in 1844: Presbyterians John and Charlotte Geddie to the New Hebrides, and Baptist Richard Burpee to India. Among Catholics, individual Sisters of Providence joined their French colleagues in Chile in 1853, followed by Jesuits to Zambezi in 1883, Holy Cross Fathers to the Holy Land, and White Fathers to Africa. The first mission run by a Canadian church was in Taiwan, where Rev. George Leslie Mackay, sent by Ontario Presbyterians in 1872, established a successful shoe-string mission. (Known in Taiwan as the 'black-bearded barbarian', he 'went native', married a Taiwanese, and became famous for pulling teeth; he is now a national hero in Taiwan.) By 1900 Canadian Protestant churches had a patchwork of unrelated missions in India, Japan, Trinidad, Bolivia, and Angola.

With their exotic appearance and world-changing vision—'The Evangelization of the World in This Generation'—missions attracted the brightest college graduates, according to Northrop *Frye. Prominent China missionaries, for example, included Bishop William White, who collected Chinese art for the Royal Ontario Museum, Dr Robert McClure, and Rev. James Endicott, who received the Stalin Peace Prize. Many Canadian missionaries were 'Maple Leaf imperialists' who thought Canada could find its place in the world—its 'national Mission'—through its imperial connections.

As many as two-thirds of overseas personnel were women, married and single; there were very few unmarried men. The various Woman's Missionary Societies were powerhouses, with a collective membership of 200,000, at a time when the highly popular *Woman's Christian Temperance Union, for example, registered only 10,000. The slogan 'Woman's Work for Woman' justified *separate spheres, and only women could enter the zenanas of Asia. Only the most accomplished women recruits were sent to Asia, where, according to historian Rosemary Gagan, 'they flourished as professional altruists'.

By the 1920s, foreign missions were being criticized for cultural imperialism, and the Depression devastated contributions, forcing the churches to retrench or go into debt. At the same time, overseas missions were subject to famines, epidemics, warlords, civil war, riots, and rising nationalism. During the Second World War, hundreds of Canadian missionaries and their children were interned in Japanese concentration camps. After Red China expelled foreign missionaries in 1949, the mainline churches devolved their missions and became 'ecumenical partners' in world development. As liberal missions were winding down, there was a resurgence among conservative evangelicals, who still dominate Canadian non-Catholic missions.

French-Canadian missions exploded after 1920, when Pius XI internationalized the French missions of the church. The church, he declared, should 'evangelize and civilize' without national borders. French Canadians believed they had a 'providential missionary vocation', that they were a chosen people who would be 'teachers of the nations'. Between the wars, Quebec sent out at least 100 new priests, brothers, and nuns each year. By 1950 they numbered 5,000, representing 102 societies in 40 countries, figures that equalled the number of Catholic missionaries from the entire United States. Pius XI called Quebec 'the nicest garden of the church through its vocations and missionary works'. Quebec created a seamless network of agencies, congregations, and *semaines missionnaires* to sustain and propagandize missions. Huge expositions were held. 'Ville Marie Missionnaire', held in 1942 at St Joseph's Oratory to celebrate the tercentennial of Montreal, was visited by 500,000 people.

Foreign missions introduced insular Quebec to a new internationalism. Overseas missions continued to grow in the 1960s as the *Quiet Revolution was secularizing educational, medical, and social agencies at home. Religious communities had a surplus of skilled members willing to do apostolic work overseas. Some were older, strongly anti-communist, who had to adjust to post-independence Africa; others were *Vatican II liberals who identified with indigenous nationalism. Out of this 'identity crisis' emerged the gospel of liberation, in which Canadians were important links.

As the focus of Canada's foreign missions changed from evangelism to development since the 1960s, Canadian missionaries—Protestant and Catholic, liberal and conservative—have enhanced Canada's reputation as an international peacekeeper. ALVYN J. AUSTIN

foreign ownership. Foreign ownership is the result of investment by non-resident corporations in another country's companies in the pursuit of profit through control. It is incidental to the operations of transnational, multinational, or global corporations in setting up subsidiaries or branch plants. The recipient, or host, country can get the economic benefit of superior technology and management but at the possible political costs of dependency and susceptibility to foreign practice and policy.

For much of its history Canada has had, for good or bad, the highest level of foreign ownership of any country in the world—particularly high for a developed and industrialized country. This can be attributed in part to proximity to the United States, where multinational corporations are disproportionately headquartered, and to American demand for Canada's rich supply of exploitable natural resources. But it is also the consequence of conscious Canadian government policy to encourage foreign investment.

The high protective tariff of the *National Policy of 1879 helped infant Canadian firms, but it also attracted American branch plants that were already spreading nationally throughout the United States and simply spilled over its northern border. Canadian politicians boasted to their constituents about the jobs created when branch plants came to their communities. The great prosperity associated with the economic boom prior to the First World War masked the higher costs of branch plants, which lost economies of scale by producing a full range of American goods for the smaller Canadian market. Whether this inefficiency was the result of the tariff or of foreign ownership was hard to sort out since the two were so bound together.

In the first decade after the Second World War, there was another great round of American investment in Canadian resources for American consumption. For the first time, a backlash manifested itself against the extent of foreign ownership. Walter *Gordon, a prominent Canadian businessman and Liberal party guru, headed the Royal Commission on Canada's Economic Prospects, which, while admitting of the benefits, warned of the costs of foreign ownership in terms of economic and political sovereignty. The stage was set for a sustained debate on how to devise policies that would increase the amount of Canadian ownership and at the same time would increase the benefits and decrease the costs of foreign ownership. As minister of finance in the Pearson government in the mid-sixties, Gordon proposed a tax on foreign takeovers, but it generated so much controversy it had to be abandoned. The best chance to deal meaningfully with foreign ownership was lost but the issue did not go away. In 1968 a task force appointed by the Pearson government and overseen by Gordon produced a comprehensive report on foreign ownership called the Watkins Report after its chief author, economics professor Melville Watkins. It endorsed a long-standing proposal of Gordon to create the Canada Development Corporation as an instrument to increase Canadian ownership, and proposed setting up an agency to monitor the activities of foreign-owned companies to increase benefits and decrease costs. The Trudeau government commissioned another report under the direction of cabinet minister Herb Gray; his comprehensive Gray Report (1972) laid the basis for action, particularly when the Liberals found themselves in a minority government situation in 1972 and needed the support of the nationalist NDP in order to govern. The Canada Development Corporation had been created in 1971 and the Foreign Investment Review Agency was set up in 1973, though with far fewer powers than the Gray Report had recommended. In 1974 Petro-Canada was established as a

Crown corporation to facilitate the Canadianization of the oil and gas industry. Foreign ownership fell relative to Canadian ownership in the 1970s and into the 1980s. This seems, however, to have had less to do with the foreign ownership policies of government—FIRA turned out to be quite toothless—than with the increasing maturity of Canadian business.

The election of the Reagan administration in the United States and then of the Mulroney government in Canada in the 1980s precipitated a sharp about-face on foreign ownership policy. The Canada Development Corporation and Petro-Can were privatized and FIRA was given the mandate of promoting and encouraging foreign investment. Out of the long debate on foreign ownership, little of substance remained, though rules limiting foreign ownership in the media have survived. The *free trade agreements struck in the 1990s contained 'national treatment' provisions that require all firms, regardless of nationality of ownership, to be treated the same, thereby ruling out policies directed at foreign-owned firms. The Multilateral Agreement on Investment that would have enshrined globally the rights of multinational corporations failed in its implementation in the late 1990s because of global opposition organized, in part, by the *Council of Canadians.

Ironically, in the early years of the 21st century, the Canadian business community, which had mostly opposed any restrictions on foreign ownership, has expressed some concern about the tendency of American companies, in the era of free trade, to rationalize on a North American basis by closing the Canadian head-office of the subsidiary, thereby limiting decision making in Canada and eliminating some jobs. With tariffs gone, it would now seem that there may be some problems that inhere in foreign ownership itself. MELVILLE WATKINS

foreign policy. Canada was an imperfect creation, coming into being in 1867 with neither the diplomatic machinery nor the constitutional power to run a foreign policy. It acquired these incrementally, evolving to independence over many decades in the ambiguous embrace of the *British Empire. A Canadian immigration office sprang up in London as early as 1868; more followed in Great Britain, continental Europe, and the United States, and then trade commissions, beginning with Paris in 1894. The Department of *External Affairs was established in Ottawa in 1909, and it moved in the direction of a modern foreign office in the 1920s under the leadership of O.D. *Skelton, who recruited young officers such as Lester B. *Pearson and Norman Robertson and later Charles Ritchie and Jules Léger. Canada signed its first treaty without a British countersignature in 1923, and diplomatic representatives were dispatched to the United States, France, and Japan between 1927 and 1929. By the end of the Second World War Canada had 38 diplomatic missions around the world and claimed the status of a *middle power, close in stability, influence, and international commitment to the great powers, a small colonial fish no more.

From the beginning, Canadians knew what they had to have in the world. They needed close relations with Great Britain and the *United States, and also close relations between those two powers so that Canada would not get caught in the middle. But it was also imperative to have distance from both the British and the Americans, so that Canada could survive and compete on the North American continent. John A. *Macdonald's protectionist *National Policy of the late 19th century was the country's first foreign policy. It moved beyond big tariffs to become a strategy for the defence of Canadian interests against the powerful neighbour to the south.

The increasing intensity of Canadian–American relationships made it all the more attractive to Canadians to be closely aligned to Great Britain in the first half of the 20th century. Canadians fought impressively at Britain's side from the beginning to the end of both world wars. But the British connection was always controversial. The long-serving prime minister, W.L. Mackenzie *King, hid his anglophilia in the two decades between the wars, assuring the sizable francophone and ethnic populations that Canadians would choose their own diplomatic destiny. The preservation of national unity, the finding and keeping of the moderate middle ground, underpinned King's external policy, as it had that of his mentor, Prime Minister Wilfrid *Laurier.

When a European war struck in 1939, however, and Great Britain itself was threatened, King listened to what he termed the clear call of duty, which did not lie very far from national self-interest. Just as the prime minister's political strategy had tilted towards Quebec in the prologue to war, so it favoured the English-speaking parts of the country once conflict began. Fifty per cent of Canadians were of British stock, and the economic, military, and psychological links to the motherland made participation in the Second World War an inevitability. But the war fought for Britain was a war fought for Canada too, and it gave the final push to Canadian diplomatic independence.

When the smoke of the terrible war cleared, Great Britain was not what it had been, the United States was a great deal more, and a new enemy, the Soviet Union, glowered on the horizon. Canada signed on as a determined Cold Warrior, constructing a big military in the 1950s to counter communist threats in Europe and Asia. Canadian alignment shifted towards the United States, and there it has resolutely stayed.

Yet Canadians frequently had reservations about America's use of its considerable power, and Canada sought to balance alignment with activism. It joined a multitude of international institutions and led in the establishment of the *North Atlantic Treaty Organization, the General Agreement on Tariffs and Trade, and the multiracial *Commonwealth of Nations. All this diplomatic bustle was spearheaded by the Department of External Affairs, by then reputed to be among the world's best medium-sized foreign offices, and had its high point during the 1956 *Suez Crisis, when Lester Pearson won the Nobel Peace Prize and placed *peacekeeping permanently on the international agenda.

There were four major official statements about Canadian foreign policy between the end of the Second World War and the end of the 20th century. Secretary of State for External Affairs Louis *St Laurent's 1947 Gray lecture publicized Canada's newly powerful engagement in international institutions. *Foreign Policy for Canadians*, issued by the Pierre *Trudeau government in 1970, used six colourful booklets to make the time-honoured point that foreign policy ought to proceed directly from domestic aims and interests. In 1985, External Affairs Minister Joe Clark, on behalf of the Brian *Mulroney government, highlighted economic competitiveness and international security as the country's key international objectives. A decade later, the Cold War over, the government of Jean *Chrétien published *Canada in the World*, with prosperity and jobs, global stability, and the projection of culture and values as the three pillars of policy.

With remarkable consistency, all Canadian governments stressed the importance of world peace and thought Canada particularly suited to further this cause. Liberal or Conservative, they also believed that national unity was a prerequisite of policy, and so too was the projection of national values such as political freedom, social justice, and human rights. There was, however, little emphasis on the need for military power or diplomatic resources, and both the Department of National Defence and the Department of External Affairs were downgraded from the late 1960s on. *Foreign Policy for Canadians* explicitly attacked 'helpful fixing' of the Suez Crisis variety, only to find that diplomatic bridge-building was later much to Prime Minister Trudeau's taste, as demonstrated by his peace mission to damp down nuclear tensions in 1983–4.

Economics were at the centre of Canada's world view, an appropriate preoccupation for a country whose standard of living depended on trade. More and more, the business of foreign policy seemed to be business. Trudeau placed economic growth first on his 1970 list of foreign policy goals, and under his government the Department of External Affairs became the Department of External Affairs and International Trade in 1982 (the name was changed to the Department of Foreign Affairs and International Trade in 1993). The strong hint that the Conservatives would plump for *free trade with the United States was a prominent ingredient in Joe Clark's 1985 document, while Prime Minister Jean Chrétien's main international affairs gambit in the 1990s was his 'Team Canada' trade missions.

Governments specialize in generalities, even platitudes, because no overarching design drives Canadian foreign affairs. Canada has firm interests cautiously advanced and nicely masked by sincere rhetoric about principles and values. The boast that Canadians are the world's greatest joiner of international organizations, a peaceful folk with unique gifts to offer the world, has become proudly embedded in the national consciousness. But the limits of Canadian influence are clear. The events that shape external policy are usually beyond national control and are impossible to forecast. Seldom are there opportunities to plan for the future or seize the initiative. Policy tends to be responsive, its thrust defensive. Canada, in the good phrase of the Gray lecture, is a 'secondary power' that sets its foreign policy day-by-day and event-by-event.

NORMAN HILLMER

See also FUNCTIONALISM.

Forsey, Eugene Alfred (1904–91), educator, labour historian/researcher, senator, constitutional authority, civic gadfly extraordinaire. Raised in the home of his maternal grandfather, a long-time official in the *House of Commons, Forsey acquired an early interest in the processes of Canadian government that later promoted his reputation as the indisputable public conscience of the nation. His outspoken views as lecturer at McGill University, contesting with those of faculty like Stephen *Leacock, led to his termination and to a 24-year career as director of research for the Canadian Congress of Labour. A founding member of the CCF, running unsuccessfully as its candidate in three elections, he parted company in 1961 with its successor, the NDP, on a policy issue. This principled independence reappeared 20 years later when he abandoned his tenuous allegiance to the Liberal Party. His maverick nature found an outlet in letters to the press: he bombarded Canada's newspapers until his dying days, instructing, lambasting, and entertaining friend and foe alike. Such contentiousness did not stand in the way of accolades: honorary degrees, a senatorship, Companion of the Order of Canada, Privy Councillor. Above all, he remained a great humanitarian dedicated to his vision of a united Canada that would be more than a mere 'blob on the map'. J.E. HODGETTS

Fort Beauséjour. The peace terms of the War of the Austrian Succession (1744–8), which returned the fortress of *Louisbourg to France, convinced England to counterbalance the Acadian presence in Nova Scotia with English Protestant immigrants. The founding of Halifax in 1749 raised the question of the boundaries between the French and English possessions. The Chignecto isthmus at the north end of the Bay of Fundy became the scene of competing interests. In 1751 the French authorities built Fort Beauséjour in this area, persuaded the *Mi'kmaq to attack the British, and encouraged the Acadians to move to the north of the Missaguash River. In response, the British built Fort Lawrence (now Amherst) to the south of the French fort. Obtaining information from Thomas Pichon, a spy who worked as a store clerk at Beauséjour, the British attacked Beauséjour and, in June 1755, commandant Louis de Vergor surrendered to 2,000 British regulars and New England militia commanded by Robert Monckton. The fort was repaired and renamed Fort Cumberland. In 1926, Fort Beauséjour became a National Historic Site. JEAN DAIGLE

Fort Chipewyan is located at the west end of the north shore of Lake Athabasca. The old *North West Company post (built in 1788) on the south shore was used by Alexander *Mackenzie as a base for his expeditions down the river that bears his name, to the Arctic Ocean (1789) and across the mountains to the Pacific Ocean (1792). Stocked with pemmican carried down the Athabasca and Peace Rivers, it was the centre of trade for the waterways radiating throughout the North. The surrounding area eventually became an arena of intense competition between the old North West Company and its new rival the New North West (or XY) Company. The present post was established when the companies united in 1804; it became a *Hudson's Bay Company post in 1821. J. COLIN YERBURY

Fort Garry. Shortly after the *fur trade merger of 1821, the Hudson's Bay Company occupied Fort Gibraltar, the old North West Company fort at the forks of the Red and Assiniboine Rivers, renaming it Fort Garry in honour of Nicholas Garry, a member of the company's governing committee. A severe flood in the spring of 1826 destroyed the wood fort and precipitated, in the 1830s, construction of Lower Fort Garry along the Red River some 30 km north of the forks. The 'stone fort', as it was called, was situated on higher ground below the St Andrew's rapids and was intended as the HBC's administrative headquarters in *Rupert's Land. Lower Fort Garry never fulfilled this role. The forks remained the population and commercial centre of the *Red River Settlement, and the company decided in 1835 to construct a second stone fort there. Upper Fort Garry became the commercial and administrative centre and the seat of civil government for the district. During the dramatic events of 1869–70, it was the seat of Louis *Riel's provisional government. With the development of *Winnipeg after 1883, the fort's walls and buildings were dismantled; only the west gate remains today. Lower Fort Garry, the site of the signing of Indian Treaty 1 in 1871, has survived largely intact. ROBERT J. COUTTS

fortifications. Since earliest times, human communities have felt the need for defences to ward off potential predators and human enemies. Fortifications were the physical barriers they erected for this purpose. Fortifications have played an important part in Canadian military history and have served as symbols both of security and authority. From their sites have emerged many of our most important communities.

In Canada, two principal types of fortifications have been used: ones built of wood and not meant to last; the other of stone and masonry, intended to be more permanent. Fortifications predated contact. Iroquoian villages, for example, were customarily surrounded by thin poles rising vertically from the ground. In Europe, the advent of gunpowder and heavy cannon at the end of the 15th century resulted in the great age of fortification building, before the first European settlers touched foot in North America. These fortifications were square or rectangular in trace, with low-slung stone walls, surrounded by a ditch, with four-sided bastions at the corners and backed by an earthen rampart. Smaller outer works afforded additional protection.

As the great distances and tree-covered terrain made transporting heavy cannon in North America practically impossible, early European settlers were able to use the same materials as Aboriginals for their fortifications, although the traces often contained elements of European models. Fort St Louis, the first major fort begun at Quebec in 1626, was built of wood but incorporated earthen ramparts and bastions at the corners. This was also true of forts that the French built in the 1660s along the Richelieu River and of others further west along the shores of Lakes Ontario and Erie and south along the Ohio and Mississippi Rivers. Wooden fortifications have probably been the most characteristic built in Canada; fur-trading posts throughout the West continued to be constructed of wood into the 19th century, as were forts built by the *North-West Mounted Police later in the century.

Serious attention to building stone fortifications began at Quebec in the 1690s as tensions mounted with the populous English colonies to the south. Work began on a series of masonry and stone defences that by the 1740s ran across the city from south to north, closing it off to attack from the west. In 1713 the French established the town of *Louisbourg, which they enclosed with an elaborate system of stone-walled permanent fortifications backed by earthen ramparts and including numerous bastions and outworks fully in line with the latest methods in use in Europe.

The British capture of Louisbourg in 1758 and Quebec in 1759 opened the British North American era in Canadian history and perhaps the busiest time for the building of permanent European-style fortifications. The War of 1812 exposed the porousness of the border to American attack and in 1825 a commission of military officers recommended the building of an elaborate network of fortifications from which a defence could be maintained until help arrived from Britain. It inspired the building of the Rideau Canal, to allow for the safer transport of troops and supplies, and the construction of the massive stone citadels at Halifax and Quebec, built according to European bastioned systems, as well as the somewhat smaller-scale Fort Henry in Kingston.

When the British built their last fortifications in Canada across the St Lawrence from Quebec City in the 1860s, trends in the evolution of artillery and ballistics were underway that would render such large-scale fortresses obsolete. In any case, improved Canadian–American relations following the Treaty of Washington (1871) rendered them unnecessary. Thereafter, concern shifted primarily to coastal defence against attack from the sea. The British maintained powerful coastal defence systems at the two 'imperial fortresses' of Halifax and Esquimalt until handing them over to Canada in 1905. Canada maintained these during the First World War and operated an extensive network of batteries on both coasts during the Second. Since then, the only 'fortifications' built in the country were the underground 'Diefenbunker' near Ottawa and six similar but smaller facilities in other provinces, meant to maintain 'continuity of government' during a nuclear attack. These too were soon rendered obsolete by advances in the destructive capabilities of nuclear weapons. CAMERON PULSIFER

Fort Whoop-Up. In the 1840s the beginning of steam navigation on the Missouri River and the establishment of Fort Benton, Montana, led to large-scale trade in buffalo robes between the Canadian Blackfoot and the American Fur Company. The collapse of the company in 1864 opened the way for small independent traders who relied on liquor as their principal item of trade. Starting in 1869, some traders began to build forts north of the 49th parallel. The largest and most successful of the 40 or so 'whisky forts' was Fort Whoop-Up, established by a trader named J.J. Healy near present-day Lethbridge. Within a few years Healy was exporting 50,000 robes annually to the United States, and the liquor used to buy them was having devastating effects on Blackfoot society. The implicit challenge to Canadian sovereignty and the possibility of conflict with the Native population were important factors in the decision of the Canadian government to create the *North-West Mounted Police in 1873. When the police marched west in 1874 their primary goal was to shut down the whisky trade, and the forts were closed within months of their arrival. Healy and his fellow traders retreated to the United States.

R.C. MACLEOD

founding peoples, founding nations. A term used to claim political standing for certain ethnic groups within the Canadian community. The idea of two founding peoples dates from the early years of *Confederation and was fully stated in the early 20th century by Henri *Bourassa, who depicted Confederation as a compact between French and British Canadians. From this he inferred that the two language groups should enjoy equal political and cultural rights throughout Canada. The idea of two founding peoples became the cornerstone of Quebec's claim, as the political embodiment of French Canada, to a veto over amendment of the Canadian *constitution.

Since 1980 the two-nations thesis has been attacked both by opponents of Quebec's claim to special status within Confederation and by advocates of the claim of Canada's indigenous peoples to separate but equal status under the constitution. The latter perspective belittles the importance of Confederation as a founding event, emphasizing order of settlement instead. It is sometimes expressed in terms of three or four founding nations, but both numbers may seem to impose a false homogeneity on Canada's Aboriginal peoples. As Olive Dickason has noted, in the eyes of Amerindians, Canada has 55 founding nations.

PAUL ROMNEY

4-H Clubs. Rural agricultural youth organization. Originally known as Boys' and Girls' Clubs, the first Canadian group organized at Roland, Manitoba, in 1913. In these clubs rural youth learned farming and domestic science by exhibiting their own work and by training to judge exhibits at local agricultural fairs. The organization had roots in the United States, where work with children began in 1901, sponsored by agricultural organizations and schools. In 1933, the Canadian Council for Boys' and Girls' Club Work was established to coordinate provincial departments of agriculture in their sponsorship efforts. The name changed to Council of 4-H Clubs in 1952. Adopting the motto 'learn to do by doing', at weekly meetings youth recited: 'I pledge my head to clearer thinking, my heart to greater loyalty, my hands to larger service and my health to better living, for my club, my community, and my country'. Over the years, the clubs' areas of study have broadened from agriculture and home economics, and the gender-specific nature of the training has been relaxed.

LINDA M. AMBROSE

franchise. The right to vote in public elections for members of Parliament, provincial legislatures, and municipal councils. The term is derived from the Old French for 'freedom'. It was first used in England in 1790. The Canadian franchise dates from the mid-18th century. Although Canada now enjoys a franchise to be envied throughout the world, at the time of Confederation the right to vote was effectively limited to male property-owners over the age of 21. In 1867 the ability to participate in choosing a government was viewed as belonging to those who had a stake in society and were considered to be independent financially. Only about 20 per cent of the population was entitled to take part in elections between 1867 and 1891. As the secret ballot was not yet a guaranteed procedural right, many early elections saw open, public voting.

The ability to vote in provincial elections did not always mirror the right to vote in federal elections. There are several instances in Canada's history of segments of the population obtaining the right to vote in provincial but not federal elections, and vice versa. By the turn of the 20th century the traditional view that property and voting were inextricably linked had gradually been replaced by the more democratic conception of universal manhood suffrage, and the franchise was open to all male British subjects 21 and over.

Although the historical record provides several instances of women voting in pre-Confederation Nova Scotia and Lower Canada between 1809 and 1840, Canadian women were systematically and universally disenfranchised at the time of Confederation. The First World War saw female relatives of men in service, nurses, and women in the armed forces temporarily granted the franchise under the *Wartime Elections Act. In 1918 the Women's Franchise Act provided the vote to those who were over 21 and met existing property qualifications. By the federal election of 1921, the property qualifications conditions had been dropped. The Canadian electorate more than doubled with that election to 50 per cent of the total population. Women had received the right to vote in Manitoba in 1916, and almost all the other provinces had followed suit by 1925. In 1940 Quebec became the last province to give women the vote.

The extension of the vote, along with the seesawing ability to determine the franchise between the orders of government, sometimes had partisan political motivations. The *Union government, for example, admitted to partly opening the franchise to women during the First World War in order to enhance its re-election prospects.

Despite the granting of the franchise on both levels to women, several sectors of the population—those of Native and Asian descent—continued to be excluded for much of the 20th century. By 1948, Japanese Canadians became the last group of Asian descent to be permanently given the vote. Aboriginal veterans of the First World War had previously been awarded the right to vote, as had those First Nations members willing to give up their Indian status and treaty rights. The Inuit won the federal vote in 1950, but it was not until 1960 that all Canadian Natives 21 and over were ensured the right to vote. All the provinces had followed suit by 1969.

With the lowering of the voting age from 21 to 18 in 1970, only federal judges, inmates of prisons and mental institutions, and any person disqualified for corrupt or illegal electoral practices remained disenfranchised. The *Charter of Rights and Freedoms (1982) stipulates that 'every citizen of Canada has the right to vote in an election of members of the House of Commons or of a legislative assembly and to be qualified for membership therein' (s. 3). As a result, judges, the mentally incapacitated, and prisoners have successfully challenged their denial of the franchise.

By the early 21st century roughly 70 per cent of the Canadian population was entitled to vote. Virtually every Canadian citizen 18 and over can now vote in elections for any level of government. The expansion of the franchise has been due in large part to changing political and social values and to changing conceptions of Canada as a political entity, and in response to significant events, such as the world wars and social movements at home and around the world.

JOHN C. COURTNEY AND DANIEL MACFARLANE

franchises. Instead of operating its own outlets, a franchisor sold to a franchisee a licence to make or market a product in a specific area, usually in exchange for an up-front fee and ongoing royalties. In 'product franchising' (already popular in automobile retailing and beverages before the Second World War), the franchisor sold a product or process, but there was rarely ongoing contact between the two businesses beyond supplying basic materials, products, or designs. In 'business format franchising', which became popular in Canada starting in the late 1950s, franchisors sold a comprehensive business 'system' to franchisees, enforcing procedures for building outlets, making products, and even cleaning washrooms. Fast food companies attracted the most attention, but the idea was popular in many service industries.

Business format franchising typically developed in Canada along one of three trajectories. First, American companies sold single outlets to Canadian franchisees through the American headquarters or a Canadian office. Mister Donut started selling Canadian outlets from its Massachusetts headquarters in 1961 before setting up a Toronto office in 1966. Second, Canadian entrepreneurs bought the rights to a large territory from an established American company. Red Barn Systems of Canada was an early leader in hamburgers, founded in 1963 when a Toronto entrepreneur bought the Canadian rights to an Ohio-based chain, and then sold individual franchises to Canadian operators. Third, Canadian franchisors started their own companies, although many borrowed ideas from US operations. The founder of Tim Hortons based his first outlets on Mister Donut. Whatever the approach, franchising boomed in the 1980s, constituting almost half the retail dollar by the 1990s.

STEVE PENFOLD

Franciscans. At the time of the arrival of the Europeans in Canada, the Franciscans were subdivided into several branches, including Récollets, Capuchins, and Irish Franciscans. In 1897 Pope Leo XIII merged them into one central order but kept the Capuchins as a separate body.

The French Récollets were first active in Canada and Acadia between 1615 and 1629, mainly as missionaries to the *Huron and the *Mi'kmaq. In Acadia they also ministered to the small French population. Most of what we know of their early days derives from Gabriel Sagard (fl. 1604–38), a Récollet lay brother who resided in Canada in 1623–4 and wrote *Le grand voyage du pays des Hurons* (1632) and *Histoire du Canada* (1636). Following a mission at Cap-Sable, 1630–45, the Récollets did not return to Canada until 1670, an absence likely engineered by Cardinal Richelieu, who had ordered them to leave Acadia to the Capuchins. After 1670 the Récollets were employed in Canada, Acadia, and Newfoundland. Although most of them ministered to the European community, some were put in charge of Aboriginal missions. Between 1675 and 1686 Chrestien Leclercq (*c.* 1641–after 1700) ministered to the Mi'kmaq of Nova Scotia and New Brunswick. He is the author of *Nouvelle relation de la Gaspesie* (1691) and *Premier Établissement de la Foy dans la Nouvelle France* (1691). After the Treaty of Paris (1763) the Récollets, like the *Jesuits, were forbidden to receive novices in Quebec. The French Récollets returned to Trois-Rivières in 1888, becoming part of the larger Franciscan order in 1897.

The French Capuchins were active in Acadia (based in La Hève, Nova Scotia, 1632–*c.* 1635), despite Cardinal Richelieu's offer to engage in Canada. They were also in Acadia and New England, 1639–58. During this second mission, the Capuchins were as numerous as the Jesuits in Canada, but they left no printed records of their deeds. As far as we know, they devoted most of their activity to the spiritual care of the Mi'kmaq, although their overall result was modest. The Capuchins returned to Nova Scotia in 1785–1827, then New Brunswick, Ontario, and Quebec. They have been in Ottawa since 1890.

Since 1784, when James Louis O'Donel (1737–1811) was appointed prefect apostolic in St John's, the Irish Franciscans were the dominant clergy in Newfoundland. The first vicars apostolic and bishops of St John's were all Franciscans, and so were the first two bishops (from Ireland and Italy) of Harbour Grace. They were not engaged in any missionary work with the Beothuk or the Mi'kmaq, but their religious and political leadership over the Irish Catholics of the island is without question.

LUCA CODIGNOLA

Francophonie. Francophonie, with a capital 'F', is a political notion: the grouping in an intergovernmental institution of states and governments of countries that use the French language. Initially intended to promote cultural and technological co-operation, as discussed at its founding meeting in Niamey, Niger, in 1970, it also has a political vocation, affirmed in 1995 at the Cotonou summit in Benin, and especially in 1997 at the Hanoi summit, when the former UN secretary-general Boutros Boutros-Ghali was elected the first secretary-general.

Created by François Mitterand, the Francophonie summits bring together the heads of state and governments of the francophone countries (55 of them as of 2002); the first was held in Paris in 1986, the second in Quebec, 1987. Since then the summit has convened every two years. Canada has three seats—Canada, Canada–Quebec, and Canada–New Brunswick—because of the two provinces' responsibilities in the areas of language, education, and French culture. After France, Canada is the second greatest contributor to the Francophonie. The organization adds to Canada's influence abroad, particularly in African countries, which may explain why Canada spoke for Africa at the G-8 meetings in Kananaskis in 2002. In effect, Canada is able to represent the countries of both the *Commonwealth and the Francophonie without being a former colonial power, as are France and Great Britain.

In a second usage of the term, 'francophonie' refers to a notion of linguistic sociology—that is, the fact of speaking French, especially as a group of individuals or peoples, whether as mother tongue or usual language, and by extension those who speak it as their official language or language of international communication, and perhaps as a language of culture or occasional communication. Theoretically, French literature is one of the francophone literatures, but its history and prestige are such that in practice it is distinguished from that of other French-speaking countries, including Canada. In Canada the adjective 'francophone' is now replacing 'French' in references to French-language speakers and institutions. In the early 20th century people spoke of 'French Canadians' in Ontario, Manitoba, Saskatchewan, the Maritimes, and of course Quebec. Today we are more likely to say 'francophones in Canada'. MICHEL TÉTU

Franklin, Sir John (1786–1847), Arctic explorer. Franklin entered the Royal Navy at age 14 and saw action in the Napoleonic Wars, serving under Admiral Horatio Nelson at both Copenhagen and Trafalgar, but it was in peacetime that he achieved fame as one of Britain's leading explorers. He was also one of the least competent: 139 men perished on expeditions under his command, a much higher death rate than for any other Arctic explorer.

Franklin led three expeditions in search of the *Northwest Passage, all sponsored by the British Admiralty. The first two were overland expeditions aimed at surveying the continental shoreline of the Arctic Ocean. During the first (1819–22), he travelled with a party of naval officers, Orkney boatmen, *voyageurs, and Aboriginal guides from *Hudson Bay overland across the *Barren Lands and down the Coppermine River to the coast. From the mouth of the river he struggled eastward by canoe for 1,000 km before returning inland on a desperate trek marked by murder and cannibalism. It was the first successful mapping of any portion of the north coast of America, though it came at the cost of ten lives. The second expedition (1825–7) was a return visit to the Arctic coast. On this occasion Franklin travelled by boat westward from the mouth of the Mackenzie River across the top of Alaska, while his associate, the naval surgeon John Richardson, went eastward as far as the Coppermine. Together, they added several thousand km to the map of the Arctic.

Following his return to England, Franklin was knighted for his accomplishments and resumed his naval career. In 1845, he received command of two vessels, *Erebus* and *Terror*, to continue the search for the Northwest Passage. The two ships entered Lancaster Sound, by then recognized to be the doorway to the passage, and were never seen by Europeans again. Enough evidence has been gathered to reconstruct Franklin's final voyage. The two ships spent the first winter at Beechey Island near the southwest corner of Devon Island. During the summer of 1846 they sailed south down Peel Sound and into Victoria Strait, where they were trapped in the ice off King William Island. Franklin died the following spring, and other members of the expedition perished on the ships or attempting to make their way overland to safety. The ships were crushed by the ice and sank. A total of 129 men died, the worst loss of life in the history of *Arctic exploration.

The search for the missing expedition began in 1848, when the Admiralty organized a three-pronged rescue effort, dispatching ships to both the western and eastern entrances to the Arctic, as well as sending John Richardson and John Rae down the Mackenzie River. Rescuers were hampered by ice conditions and the huge area they had to cover. After initial attempts failed to locate Franklin, efforts were redoubled and in 1850 a total of 12 ships and 450 men were launched into the North. All this activity produced few results; indeed, one of the rescue vessels that had entered the search area via Bering Strait, commanded by Robert McClure, became trapped itself. In 1852 the Admiralty organized yet another relief expedition consisting of four ships under the command of Edward Belcher. This squadron did manage to find McClure and his men, trapped by ice at Mercy Bay on the north coast of Banks Island. When McClure and his surviving crewmen travelled by sled eastward to rendezvous with the rescue vessels, they became the first Europeans to traverse the Northwest Passage. But they were still not out of harm's way. Belcher's small flotilla was itself mired in the ice and in the summer of 1854 he ordered all four ships abandoned. The crews were transported home by supply vessels; Belcher faced a court martial for his incompetence but was acquitted.

Meanwhile, the search for Franklin finally met with some results. In 1854 the intrepid fur trader John Rae, on his fourth overland excursion to the Arctic coast, encountered a party of Inuit who told him that survivors of the Franklin ships had died trying to make their way to safety. Rae's report that the sailors may have indulged in cannibalism raised a storm of outrage in England, but he nonetheless received the £10,000 reward for discovering the fate of the missing expedition. At this point, the Admiralty ended the search, but Lady Jane Franklin hoped to learn more about her husband's fate. She sent Captain Francis Leopold McClintock back to the Arctic; in 1859 on the shores of King William Island he found artifacts, human remains, and written records that confirmed Rae's account.

The search for further remains of the Franklin expedition continued for many years. American explorers Charles Francis Hall (1869) and Frederick Schwatka (1879) visited King William Island, as have many other artifact hunters since. Most recently researchers have studied human remains from the expedition, confirming Rae's reports of cannibalism and suggesting that the effects of *scurvy and lead poisoning from tinned provisions must have contributed to the tragedy.

DANIEL FRANCIS

Frank slide. At 4:10 A.M. on 29 April 1903 an avalanche of limestone came crashing down from the top of Turtle Mountain in the Crowsnest Pass. In about 100 seconds more than 70 million metric tons of rock covered farms, roads, rail lines, mine installations, and parts of the town of Frank below. Prompt action by a railway brakeman stopped an oncoming passenger train in time to avert further catastrophe. From inside the coal mine, 17 men were able to dig their way to safety. Among those who died were 40 men, 7 women, and 22 children, but the number of fatalities probably exceeded 100, including an uncounted number living in tents. There was no official inquiry, but mine inspectors and geologists concluded that the coal operations undermined the stability of the limestone cliffs on the top of the mountain.

DAVID FRANK

Fraser, Robert Blair (1909–68). Canada's leading political commentator in a period of profound change for his country. Depression hardships endured while struggling to establish himself as a journalist in Montreal combined with exposure to that city's vibrant political and intellectual milieu to forge his social conscience, nationalism, and liberal-internationalism. His move to *Maclean's* as Ottawa editor in 1944 and frequent exposure on CBC radio gave him a national following. More than any political partisanship, Fraser's 'government generation' sympathies explained his apparent affinity for Liberal policies. Although averse to the *regionalism bedeviling Canada, he heroically attempted to interpret Quebec nationalism to an often uncomprehending English-Canadian audience. Frequent trips abroad enabled him to interpret international developments from his distinctively Canadian perspective. During 1960–2 Fraser served an unhappy tenure as the editor of *Maclean's*. He returned to Ottawa, but his career was clearly declining. Unlike radio, television did not suit his style, and the more confrontational—and in his view, less responsible—ethos embraced by the new generation of political journalists left him increasingly out of fashion. Fraser, whose passion was discovering the true spirit of Canada 'beyond the pavement', died in a canoeing accident in 1968. PATRICK H. BRENNAN

Fraser, Simon (1776–1862), fur trader and explorer. Born in Mapleton, Hoosick Township, New York, Fraser was the youngest of ten children whose father had joined the Loyalist forces during the American Revolution and died in prison after being captured at the Battle of Bennington. His widow fled to Canada in 1784, and Fraser began to work for the *North West Company, based in Montreal; in 1801 he became one of its youngest partners. Fraser's task was to expand the company's operations west of the Rocky Mountains, and he hoped to accomplish this by locating a route to the Pacific, thereby allowing overland transportation and thus reducing the company's transportation costs. During one of Canada's most daring explorations, he discovered the Fraser River, although its rough waters proved too dangerous for transportation. Fraser named the interior of British Columbia *'New Caledonia' and founded the first European settlements there, including a string of fur-trading forts. During the Lower Canada Rebellion, Fraser served in the Stormont Militia and damaged his knee so badly that he was reduced to a meagre government pension. He died a poor man and is buried in St Andrews, Ontario. BARRY M. GOUGH

Fraser River gold rush. In February 1858 the SS *Otter* arrived in San Francisco from Victoria carrying 800 ounces of gold. Rumours of a new Eldorado to the north began to circulate, sparking the Fraser River gold rush. The first shipload of 400 fortune-seekers arrived in Victoria in April, en route to the mainland's gold fields, and by August 10,000 miners were reportedly working the banks of the lower Fraser, in the heart of Sto:lo and Nlaka'pamux territory, an area the Hudson's Bay Company claimed as part of its fur-trading district of *New Caledonia. By year's end, the impact of the 30,000 people who passed through Victoria on their way to the mainland was discernible. What had been a fur-trading post was transformed into a culturally diverse settlement with over 225 new commercial buildings and a Chinatown.

The effects of the gold rush were not limited to urbanization, for it also led directly to the creation of a new colony. In August 1858 New Caledonia became *British Columbia by virtue of an act of the British Parliament, with James *Douglas, the governor of the neighbouring colony of *Vancouver Island, doubling as its governor. Stung by the earlier loss of the Oregon and Washington territories, Douglas and his Whitehall superiors were concerned about maintaining British sovereignty as well as law and order in a colony with a significant American presence. Schooled in California's gold fields, American miners arrived on the Fraser with well-established, extra-legal ways of dealing with each other and with the indigenous peoples they met. The British countered their bowie knives, and attitude, by implementing a centuries-old system of formal law, headed by Matthew Baillie *Begbie, the colony's first judge, in November 1858.

While Begbie's biographer credits the judge's moral authority with preserving the peace, the relative absence of violence on the Fraser River frontier was more likely due to the short-lived nature of the rush itself. Although 100,000 ounces of gold were taken out in the first year, the rush petered out quickly, leading one disgruntled American to publish a book warning prospective Argonauts not to fall victim to 'Fraser River Humbug'.

Born of the Fraser River gold rush, the myth of British Columbia's peaceful frontier is part of a larger national myth about Canada. Like all myths it has certain elements of truth, but it also obscures the violence and dispossession visited upon First Nations. From the perspective of the Sto:lo and Nlaka'pamux, who were the first to discover and mine gold on the river, the fortune seekers of 1858 were not just claim jumpers but foot soldiers in an army of invasion. The gold rush began the process of colonization, the effects of which are still being felt today. TINA LOO

Fréchette, Louis (1839–1908), poet, playwright, polemicist. Born near Lévis on 16 November 1839, Fréchette attended three classical colleges before studying law at Laval University. While still a student, he began writing poetry, composed his first play, *Félix Poutré* (1862), and published a volume of verse, *Mes loisirs* (1863). After unsuccessful attempts to open a law practice and found Liberal newspapers, he emigrated to Chicago (1866–71), working for the Illinois Central Railroad and composing virulent verses against the Canadian Confederation of 1867. Returning to Canada, Fréchette entered politics, representing Lévis in 1874–8, and married into a wealthy family. He sent his second verse collection, *Pêle-mêle* (1877), to many prominent French writers, quietly orchestrating his recognition by the French Academy in 1880. His best-known collection of historical poems, *La Légende d'un peuple*, appeared in 1887. After a final verse volume, *Feuilles volantes* (1891), Fréchette wrote almost exclusively in prose, publishing amusing portraits (*Originaux et détraqués*, 1892), polemics on Quebec education, denunciations of his rival William Chapman, memoirs, and Christmas stories. He died in Montreal on 31 May 1908. Decorated in England and France and given honorary doctorates at four universities, Fréchette was the most widely honoured Canadian writer of his time. DAVID M. HAYNE

Fredericton. Capital of *New Brunswick, shire town of York County. Ste-Anne, at the head of navigation on the Saint John River, first settled by Acadians (1731), had been attacked (1759) and largely abandoned long before the arrival of the *Loyalists in 1783–4. In 1785, New Brunswick's first governor, Thomas Carleton, selected this defensible and central site as the provincial capital, naming it after Frederick, son of George III. Structured, economically and socially, around the needs of the colonial government, Fredericton also became a military headquarters garrisoned by the British (1785–1869). Settlement extended along the river, the capital's major highway until the railway arrived in 1869.

Educational and cultural institutions reflected the hopes of the founders. The government granted land for a university in 1785, although King's College did not receive a Royal Charter until 1828. The college was secularized as the University of New Brunswick in 1859. Following the creation of the Anglican diocese of New Brunswick (1845), Bishop Medley chose Fredericton as the site of Christ Church Cathedral (constructed 1845–53), a replica of St Mary's in Snettisham, Norfolk, England. As the location of the Anglican cathedral and the legislature, Fredericton was incorporated as a city in 1848. The town's genteel aspect was somewhat marred by the lumber mills on the riverbanks and the tanneries and foundries along its back streets. Fredericton developed a vibrant manufacturing sector during the 19th century, producing goods ranging from shoes to soap and bricks, from canoes to carriages. But manufacturing waxed and waned while the business of the capital sustained the growth and prosperity reflected in the city's historical architecture: City Hall, Old Government House, the Old Arts Building, Wilmot United Church, St Anne's Chapel, the cathedral, the legislature, and many stately homes.

Since 1900, more public institutions have been established in the provincial capital. St Thomas University (founded 1910) moved to Fredericton from Chatham in 1964. Today, the universities, Beaverbrook Art Gallery, Playhouse, New Brunswick Craft College, public library, and churches sustain a rich cultural life. Between 1945 and 1973 the city absorbed the more industrial communities on the north side of the river. One of these, Marysville, is among the finest surviving examples of a 19th-century industrial town. While the provincial government remains the largest employer, since 1990 development has focused on information technologies and telecommunications. With a population of 47,560 in 2001, Fredericton provides services for an urban agglomeration of over 81,000 people. GAIL G. CAMPBELL

free thought. In the militant language inherited from the Enlightenment, 19th-century free thought opposed the claims and power of organized religion as 'priest craft and superstition' aimed at keeping society in an 'unfree' state. Free thinkers espoused a wide range of positions but were generally in agreement in supporting natural rights and reason, as well as often experimenting in a variety of ethical movements. Unlike Europe, where critical and sceptical movements were able to build on popular anticlerical sentiment and dislike of an established church, in Canada by the mid-19th century religion had become disestablished, and churches thrived as voluntary institutions. Whatever publicity free thought gained was primarily through the energetic efforts of the Christian churches to speak out against 'godless literature' and lectures by such notable American 'infidels' as Benjamin Underwood and Col Robert Green Ingersoll.

Building on the indefatigable support of a few committed individuals such as Allen Pringle, a Napanee-area farmer, and Toronto writer Phillips *Thompson, associations of free thought began to appear in Canada in 1874 with the founding of the Free Thinkers Association in Toronto. Renamed the Canadian Secular Union in 1880, it sponsored Ingersoll, amidst considerable stir in pulpit and press, to address a packed Royal Opera House. Similar free thought associations in Montreal and a number of towns and villages were equally active in outraging the respectable and attracting sympathizers by seeking to replace biblical revelation with a variety of moral schemes. Through their efforts, a newspaper *Secular Thought*, and well-staged debates between visiting lecturers and local clergy, free thought gained a certain momentum in the 1880s and 1890s. Packing town halls with well-entertained but apparently unchanged audiences, it helped motivate clergy to preach Christian truth with new vigour. While at the time the latter had the upper hand, in the long run the future would lie with the call of free thinkers for the recognition of civil marriages, the removal of religious activities such as the reading of the Bible in public schools, and the repeal of *Lord's Day legislation. MARGUERITE VAN DIE

free trade. In the closing years of the 20th century free trade became the mantra of the powerful, and deals to lessen barriers to trade, and to investment, proliferated both globally and regionally. From the Second World War forward, in the era of American hegemony, tariffs eroded globally under the General Agreement on Tariffs and Trade while the Canadian economy became increasingly interlocked with the larger American economy. The era of the *National Policy of 1879 with its high protective tariffs, and the ability of Canadian business to import from the United States but find export markets in Great Britain and Europe (the *North Atlantic Triangle), was truly over. By the 1980s Canadian business worried about guaranteed access of its resource exports to the American market and came to believe that free trade would enable its manufacturing to become more productive through access to the whole North American market. At the same time, there was a persistent undercurrent of concern in Canadian politics that too close economic integration with the United States would compromise Canadian sovereignty.

The Canada–US Free Trade Agreement was signed in 1988 by the Progressive Conservative government of Brian *Mulroney and the Republican administration of Ronald Reagan and came into effect on 1 January 1989 after a fractious election campaign pitting big business against the labour, social, and environmental movements. There had been nothing like it since the election of 1911 when Canadians had rejected so-called *reciprocity—free trade—with the United States, proposed by the then Liberal government but opposed by business. The FTA was a comprehensive agreement covering many services as well as goods, limiting discrimination against American corporations, and improving American access to Canadian energy. The United States moved quickly to add Mexico to the agreement, Canada reluctantly concurring (the Canadian and Mexican economies having little connection). The North American Free Trade Agreement came into effect 1 January 1993. This time there were side-agreements on labour and the environment, and the right of corporations to sue governments for damages for alleged trade impediments was entrenched. Attempts to replace NAFTA with a free trade agreement for all of the Americas have been tried without success.

Meanwhile, a new and more comprehensive global agreement was struck in 1995, with the World Trade Organization replacing the GATT. The effect of these agreements has been to dramatically increase cross-border flows between Canada and the United States of both trade and investment and to integrate the Canadian economy yet further into the American economy. While free trade has not led to the massive job losses that some critics of these agreements feared, neither has it resulted in the significant closing of productivity and income differences between Canada and the United States that some proponents anticipated. MELVILLE WATKINS

Frégault, Guy (1918–77), historian and high official. He taught at the Université de Montréal, 1942–59, becoming the first head of its Department of History, then at the University of Ottawa. In 1961, he was chosen by Georges-Émile Lapalme as the first deputy minister of the Quebec Department of Cultural Affairs. He was thus among the intellectuals who brought about the *Quiet Revolution. With Maurice Séguin and Michel Brunet, he put forth a new version of French-Canadian history known as the Montreal Historical School's interpretation, which secularized and radicalized the thought of Lionel *Groulx, their former professor. Contrary to Groulx's optimistic voluntarism, they viewed the consequences of the *Conquest as structural, permanent, and virtually impossible to change. At the helm of Cultural Affairs, Frégault experienced the truthfulness of this theory. In *Chronique des années perdues* (1976), he took stock of his stint as civil servant with bitter disenchantment. In *Lionel Groulx tel qu'en lui-même* (1977), he subtly settled scores with the master of his youth. The most gifted writer among French-Canadian historians of his generation, he wrote historical studies of high standard, *La Guerre de la Conquête* (1955) being regarded as his masterpiece.

PIERRE TRÉPANIER

freight rates. In a nation whose products are shipped to distant markets across the continent and the oceans, merchants, manufacturers, and farmers have been particularly concerned with the cost of transportation over land and water. Railway freight rates proved particularly controversial, because shippers saw governments providing financial assistance to railway companies. It did not help that it was difficult to determine the precise cost of carrying one particular commodity on a train that carried many different types of goods, and that used common terminal and other facilities. Many shippers experienced railway companies as monopolies, and therefore suspected those companies of extorting excessive profits. Railway managers did not see it that way. Even where direct rail or water competition did not exist, they adjusted their freight rates in order to allow their customers to compete in their destined markets, or to assist them in expanding into new markets.

Throughout the 20th century, regulatory commissions and government helped set freight rates, responding to grievances that freight rates disadvantaged certain regions of Canada. At the time of most general rate increases, lower increases were granted in regions that traditionally had higher rates. The Canadian government reintroduced the 1897 *Crow's Nest Pass rates on westbound grain and grain products in 1922, rates that remained in effect until the 1980s. The government compensated the railway companies when it ordered a reduction in Maritime rates in 1927, as it would again when it sought to encourage shipments of grain, coal, and other merchandise in the national interest, and when it froze rates in the late 1950s. Since 1967, railway managers have enjoyed more freedom in setting freight rates. KEN CRUIKSHANK

French-Canadian emigration to the United States. French and English Canadians alike took part in a vast movement of population in North America until the end of the 1920s. Between 1830 and 1930 more than a million French Canadians moved permanently to the United States, two-thirds of them settling in New England. Many of them could be found in the 'Petit Canada' neighbourhoods of industrial towns like Woonsocket, Rhode Island; Manchester, New Hampshire; and Lowell, New Bedford, Fall River, and Worcester, Massachusetts. They worked above all in the vast cotton mills, where it was easy for women and children to find jobs. Even though most of them came from rural backgrounds, they adapted relatively smoothly to the new setting, living in their own neighbourhoods and transplanting their institutions to American soil.

The attraction of the 'States', as they were called, can be explained by the difficulty of finding work in Quebec at a time of rapid population growth. Young people and families in search of a better future were attracted by the high wages. Railway transport was easy and inexpensive, and it was not hard for Canadians to cross the border. Some left for good, others just long enough to build up some savings.

Those intending to emigrate learned about work by word of mouth, from relatives, or from Franco-Americans visiting their families in Quebec. The political and religious elites of the time, worried by this hemorrhage of population, painted an unflattering picture of working and living conditions in the United States. But the migrants themselves saw their lives quite differently. In general they were satisfied, for it was easy to find work, the pay was good, and the standard of living higher than in Quebec.

The flow of immigrants almost dried up in the 1930s, when economic crisis created high unemployment in the United States. Thereafter it did not resume because American immigration laws became much more strict. JACQUES ROUILLARD

French–English relations. A distinctive feature of French–English relations in Canada has been the collective will of the French-speaking minority to survive. *Survivance has not always been easy and is still not assured. At any given time, French–English relations are shaped by the insecurity of the minority and the sensitivity of the majority to the minority's concerns.

The aspirations of the minority were given some recognition in the federal union of 1867 with the creation of the province of Quebec in which the French Canadians would be a majority and in which the government would have jurisdiction over aspects of cultural identity, including education, property, and civil rights. The central government, where English Canadians would be in the majority, would have jurisdiction over economic matters such as railways, tariffs, and banks, but since these were considered culturally neutral this was not seen as a threat to the survival of the minority.

For almost a century these arrangements were remarkably successful. In the province of Quebec the French-Canadian majority tried to protect its identity by limiting social contact with English-speaking and non-Catholic citizens. For example, the elementary public school system segregated Catholic and non-Catholic students. The French-speaking students who continued their education went to classical colleges before going on to a French-language university for a professional degree. English-speaking Quebeckers, Protestant and Catholic, followed a different path, attending public secondary schools to qualify for admission to English-language universities. This approach isolated French Canadians, especially in rural communities, from any contact with English Protestants and so minimized the risk of religious or linguistic assimilation.

French–English relations were sometimes less harmonious in other provinces where there were French-speaking minorities. The English-speaking majorities tended to use public schools to teach the language and the social values of the majority. In a series of 'schools questions', some grudging concessions were made to permit some segregation of Roman Catholic and French-speaking students.

French–English relations at the federal level depended on a uniquely Canadian *party system in which the major parties sought significant support from both English and French Canadians. English Canadians agreed, in effect, to give their French-Canadian colleagues control over the federal *patronage in Quebec in exchange for French-Canadian support for their economic policies. This collaboration was sorely tested by the issue of *Riel's execution and the *Manitoba schools question and it broke down completely in 1917 when an English-Canadian majority imposed *conscription over the objections of the French-Canadian minority. The Liberal Party restored the traditional political association of the two cultural groups after the war and its support in French Canada kept it in office until the 1950s, apart from an interlude in the 1930s.

The system broke down when French Canadians decided that economic power had cultural consequences. Instead of the policy of isolation, they looked to the provincial government of Quebec to strengthen French-Canadian participation in economic activities. This *Quiet Revolution involved educational reforms designed to assimilate immigrants. The provincial government also expropriated the private hydroelectric companies in the province, gave incentives to encourage investment in Quebec, and gave special status to the French language in the work world. This new approach to survival required greater financial resources and broader jurisdiction for the Quebec government, and French-Canadian nationalists were soon demanding special status for Quebec within Confederation.

From the 1960s French–English relations have focused on constitutional changes. Some frustrated French-Canadian nationalists concluded that English Canadians would never concede them the jurisdiction that survival required. A separatist party under René *Lévesque was elected in Quebec in 1976 but a referendum to authorize it to negotiate separation was defeated. The federal government under Pierre *Trudeau repatriated the constitution and added a civil rights charter but denied special status for Quebec. Subsequent federal governments proposed constitutional changes involving special status for Quebec but these were rejected. A second referendum in Quebec was then rejected by a very narrow margin. The controversy has altered Canadian *federalism. English Canadians accepted *bilingualism in the federal public service and an expanded jurisdiction for provincial governments but have resisted special concessions to Quebec. French Canadians in Quebec have given the French language special status in the school and the workplace and have associated survival with wider constitutional powers for the Quebec government but are divided over whether sufficient powers are possible within a federal system.

H. BLAIR NEATBY

French exploration. Although it was sporadic, exploration in North America until well into the 19th century was motivated largely by the search for a passage across the continent. During the French regime, other important motives included the expansion of Catholic missions and the *fur trade, diplomatic journeys, military campaigns, and staking territorial claims. In their exploration of the continent, the French outstripped their rivals.

Sixteenth-century exploration was sparked by Columbus's discoveries (1492), prompting England (*Cabot 1496–8) and Portugal (Fernandes 1500, Corte Real brothers 1500–2) to seek Asia by a shorter, northern route. By 1507–10 most Europeans scholars realized that western lands were neither a northern extension of Asia nor islands off Japan, but a new continent. The race was on to find a passage through this inconvenient land mass. While the expeditions of Verrazano (France, 1524), Gomez (Spain, 1525), and Rut (England, 1527) disclosed an unbroken shore, Jacques *Cartier, following fishermen's reports, discovered the St Lawrence River valley in 1534. After three major expeditions (1534, 1535–6, 1541–3), dreadful winters, scurvy, the absence of quick riches, a hostile Native population, and a St Lawrence that turned out to be a cul-de-sac for European ships, the French lost interest. Farther north the English had a similar experience with Martin Frobisher's (1576–8) ill-conceived mining venture and hostile encounters with the Inuit and John Davis's (1585–7) inability to penetrate the ice-bound coast.

By the late 16th century offshore fishing and inshore *whaling were joined by an incipient fur trade, which required permanent settlements. In 1603 Samuel de *Champlain was sent to Canada to conduct resource surveys for potential settlements. Over the next six years he formulated a strategy for exploration that carried the French across the Great Lakes, down the Mississippi, and across the plains to the Rockies before any other nation. Exploration had to be based on good relations with Natives, which were cemented by trade, aid given to Native allies in their wars, an exchange of people, conversion to Catholicism, and eventually intermarriage. To be successful the French had to solicit Native geographical information, hire Natives as guides, become proficient in canoes, and learn to live off the land. Through this strategy every French explorer knew roughly what he would 'discover' before he set out on a journey. Following his allies on raids against the *Iroquois, Champlain was the first to travel inland: Lake Champlain (1609) and the Ottawa River route to Georgian Bay and eastern Lake Ontario (1615). By 1618, he was convinced that China was only six months west of Lake Huron.

To the north, the English (Hudson 1610–11) finally penetrated into Hudson Bay. Following Button (1612–13), Bylot and Baffin (1615–16), Munk (Danish 1619–20), and especially Foxe (1631) and James (1631–2), they concluded that a northwest passage either did not exist or was impractical. Because the French were aware of English results to the north, they no longer contemplated a northern passage.

In 1634 the interior west of Montreal became a Jesuit province, traders were banned, and the *Jesuits became explorers as they sought to expand their missions. By 1654, when they negotiated a peace with the Iroquois, the Jesuits had probed the Saguenay and St Maurice Rivers, explored the upper St Lawrence and Iroquois country, and knew of all five Great Lakes. The peace made the fur trade possible again, and Médard Chouart, Sieur des Groseilliers was sent to Lakes Michigan and Superior (1654–6) to invite Natives to bring their furs to the St Lawrence. In 1659–60 he went illegally, this time with Pierre-Esprit *Radisson. Both were arrested on the governor's orders, but their geographical knowledge led to the founding of the Hudson's Bay Company (1670), increasing numbers of illegal traders (*coureurs de bois), and exploration by the Jesuits (Claude Allouez 1665–9) and Sulpicians (François Dollier de Casson and René de Bréhant de Galinée 1669–70) as they expanded their missions.

After 1670 the Hudson's Bay Company made its presence felt on French trade. The intendant Jean *Talon reacted by encouraging exploring expeditions with orders to stake French claims, keep records and maps, and persuade Native groups to trade. In 1671–2 Charles

Albanel, SJ, and Paul Denys de Saint-Simon explored the Saguenay system to James Bay; Louis *Jolliet and Jacques Marquette, SJ (1673) discovered that the Mississippi unfortunately flowed south, not west, but held out hope for the Missouri, and René-Robert Cavelier de *La Salle (1679–80) and his men completed the exploration of the Mississippi. All of these explorers traded in furs to defray their costs. In 1681, the coureurs de bois were pardoned and the interior fur trade officially opened through a licensing (*congé*) system. Increasing competition with the HBC led to the exploration of the Albany River by Jean Peré (1684) and a successful military expedition by Pierre de *Troyes (1686) down the Abitibi River, capturing HBC posts. With renegade Frenchmen as guides, the first Englishman saw Lake Ontario in 1686. The last exploratory trip of the century was Jacques de Noyon's (1688) wintering on Rainy Lake, where he heard of Spanish activities in the Southwest. In 1691 most French posts were closed to the beaver trade due to a glut on the market. During this time the English sent their first men inland accompanying Native traders, Henry Kelsey (1690–2) to the plains and William Stuart (1715–16) into the Northwest. It is not clear where they went.

Following the Treaty of Utrecht (1713) and an end to the glut in beaver, the French moved rapidly to forestall English expansion. In 1731 Pierre Gaultier de Varennes et de *La Vérendrye, with his four sons and nephew, began to explore and trade into the Northwest from Lake Superior. They reached Lake Winnipeg in 1734, the Missouri in 1738, the Saskatchewan in 1739, and the Big Horn Mountains in 1742. The location of their goal, the *Mer d'Ouest*, remained elusive. At this time Russian probes (Bering/Chirikov 1741) reached the north Pacific coast and the English (Middleton 1742, Moor 1746) renewed the search for a passage in northwestern Hudson Bay. In 1751, the last French expedition sent by Jacques Legardeur de St-Pierre wintered on the Upper Saskatchewan within sight of the 'Shining Mountains' (Rockies), proving that the *Mer d'Ouest* and a passage to the Pacific were a mirage. CONRAD HEIDENREICH

French neutrals. The name 'neutral French' or 'les français neutres' came into use after 1730, when those Acadians who had lived under British rule in Nova Scotia since 1713 took an oath of allegiance to the British Crown on the understanding that they would not be called upon for military service against either the French or the Mi'kmaq. When the Acadians were deported in 1755 to other British colonies in North America, it was the term employed to describe them by the newspapers in those colonies, such as the *New York Gazette* and the *Carolina Gazette*. N.E.S. GRIFFITHS

French Shore. By the Treaty of Utrecht (1713), France recognized British sovereignty over the island of Newfoundland. However, French fishermen retained the right to catch and dry fish in season on the coast between Cape Bonavista and Pointe Riche. This area, known to the French as 'le petit nord', was not much used by British fishermen. By the 1760s, though, the southeasterly section had become populated by settlers, and considerable friction developed between English and French fishermen. In addition, the French held that their right was exclusive, while the British argued it was concurrent. A new agreement in 1783 (part of the Treaty of Versailles) attempted a solution by shifting the boundaries of the Treaty Shore to Cape St John and Cape Ray; a supplementary British declaration guaranteed that French fishermen would not be disturbed, and that 'fixed settlements' created by British subjects would be removed. The French Treaty Shore fishery rapidly decreased after 1830 as outfitters transferred their efforts to the *Grand Banks, using *St-Pierre and Miquelon as a base. Nevertheless, France was unwilling to give up its privileges, continued to claim an exclusive right, and argued that, strictly speaking, settlement on the shore was illegal.

The French treaties, and the restrictions that they imposed, frustrated an increasingly assertive colonial government anxious to see the resources of the area developed and to build a railway across the island. The result was tension between St John's and London, and some difficult disputes on the shore itself, where British and French naval squadrons patrolled each year. A solution to this minor but complicated imperial problem was found in 1904, when, as part of the *entente cordiale*, France effectively traded its coastal rights in Newfoundland for financial compensation and British concessions in North and West Africa. JAMES K. HILLER

Front de libération du Québec. A protest movement that used propaganda and terrorist activity in its fight for a sovereign socialist Quebec. Born in 1963, the FLQ was initially inspired by the decolonization movement, but it developed in the context of the *Quiet Revolution, which, beginning in 1960, gave rise to a multitude of profound political and ideological changes in Quebec. Several protest movements emerged in Quebec in this period, but the FLQ proved to be the most radical. Over time, the anti-capitalist dimension came to predominate over the *indépendantiste* dimension: after 1965–6 independence was no longer an end in itself but a means of bringing about an anti-capitalist social revolution. With no more than a handful of very determined activists, the FLQ bore no resemblance to a centralized, hierarchical movement: it was made up of 'cells' in varying degrees of contact with one another. Its actions were illegal and generally violent; bombings (more than 20 between 1963 and 1970) soon became its trademark. From 1966 on, it became increasingly involved in the labour cause, and staged violent demonstrations during numerous strikes. In October 1970 one cell kidnapped a British diplomat, James Cross, and then a second cell seized a minister of the provincial government, Pierre Laporte, plunging the country into an unprecedented political crisis. Cross was freed but Laporte was murdered, and his kidnappers were found and tried. After 1971 the FLQ dissolved and several of its members joined Marxist groups.

JEAN-FRANÇOIS CARDIN

Frontenac, Louis de Buade de (1622–98). During his two terms of service as governor general of New France, Frontenac played a key, if contentious, role in the military history of the beleaguered colony. Irascible and keen to protect the honours he felt due to his rank, he quarrelled with many of his colleagues in the colonial administration and in the church. Often in debt, he relied on his wife Anne de La Grange's lobbying at the Versailles court and his other family connections to protect him. His first term of office lasted from 1672 to 1682, when he was recalled for his inappropriate disputes with Intendant Jacques Duschesneau. Frontenac returned to New France in 1689 and remained until his death nine years later. He is best remembered for his 1690 dismissal of a New England emissary's demand that he surrender the colony: 'I have no reply to make to your general other than from the mouths of my cannon and muskets'. The network of forts that Frontenac established greatly increased French influence in the interior of the continent. Particularly during the years when *Iroquois and New English fighters threatened the colony's survival, he dominated local politics in New France. COLIN M. COATES

Frontier College. Founded by Alfred *Fitzpatrick in 1899, in Ontario, as the Canadian Reading Camp Association, the initial impetus was to address the lack of reading and writing skills among workers in isolated lumbering, mining, and railway-construction camps across the country. Its first major innovation was to situate university undergraduates in these camps to work with the labourers during the day and to teach at night. By 1913, these 'labourer-teachers' worked in almost every province, with literacy classes, portable libraries, and, no doubt, aching backs. After the First World War the college was chartered by the government to offer university degrees across Canada, thus becoming the first and only 'national' university. Only three degrees were awarded, and by 1934, with Fitzpatrick's retirement and resistance by provincial governments and universities, the college returned to its primary focus of basic adult literacy for the isolated work camps.

In the late 1940s and 1950s Canada welcomed tens of thousands of European immigrants, and Frontier College taught many of them basic English and other subjects. As mechanization replaced manual labour in the late 1960s, the college began to work in community development with First Nations peoples, with ex-offenders, and with disabled people through individualized learning programs. In 1977 it was recognized by UNESCO for its 'meritorious work in the field of adult education'. Today, the college still seeks to bring the marginalized into the mainstream, whether working with the homeless in urban centres (Beat the Street) or by empowering university students through the Students for Literacy Program.
JAMES H. MORRISON

frontier thesis. An interpretation of American history first put forward by Frederick Jackson Turner in 1893, just as the American 'frontier' was disappearing. According to Turner, Americans continually reinvented themselves as they moved westward across the continent, shedding their European customs and institutions. A succession of frontier encounters such as trading, ranching, farming gave rise to a new American type—inquisitive, restless, and resourceful, coarse, practical, and materialistic—and a uniquely individualistic form of democracy. The idea had an immediate and long-lasting impact; it captured a mood of optimism and national self-assertion, while explaining the overall pattern of American development and distinctive aspects of the American character.

Beginning in the 1920s, a new generation of Canadian historians adapted 'frontierism' to their own needs. Reacting to the political and constitutional approaches of their predecessors, and seeking a conception of the past on which to ground a critique of British imperial rule in a time of growing national feeling, many found in Turner's thesis a means of integrating social, economic, and political history and explaining it with reference to the peculiarities of the North American environment. 'North American democracy', wrote A.R.M. *Lower, 'was forest-born'. The sociologist S.D. Clark later made fruitful use of the concept (and of the *Laurentian thesis) in his studies of social organization and political movements. Although no longer accepted in its original form by any serious historian, partly because of its narrow focus on European conquest and settlement, frontierism's influence may be found in important modern works such as R.C. Harris's *The Seigneurial System in Early Canada* (1966). KENNETH C. DEWAR

Frost, Leslie Miscampbell (1895–1973), Ontario premier 1949–61. During his political career Frost was thought to epitomize small-town virtues and values. Born in Orillia, and severely wounded late in the First World War, he became, on admission to the Ontario bar in 1921, a successful lawyer in Lindsay. He married Gertude Jane Carew in 1926. Elected to the legislature in 1937 as a Conservative, when that party formed the government in 1943 he was appointed provincial treasurer and minister of mines. In 1949 he was chosen leader and subsequently sworn in as premier and provincial treasurer on 4 May. He would retain the post until his retirement.

Frost steered the party through great social and economic changes. After the Second World War, immigration and continuing industrialization were coupled with enormous growth in the cities. Frost's sound political instincts, immense pragmatism, and cheery amiability won him many friends—and gave his party three solid election victories. The key to his success was government leadership in developing popular progressive education and health initiatives while encouraging private investment and providing sound public economic policies. Critics called him the 'Great Tranquillizer'.
ROGER HALL

Frye, Northrop (1912–91), literary critic, cultural philosopher. Frye grew up in Sherbrooke and Moncton and studied at the University of Toronto and Oxford

University. A brilliant teacher, scholar, writer, administrator, and public voice, Frye worked—for 51 years after 1939—mainly in Toronto in the Department of English at Victoria College. His subject was the human imagination as the maker of human cultures. He wrote extensively and incisively about Canada, especially in his influential Conclusion to *Literary History of Canada* (1965) and *The Bush Garden: Essays on the Canadian Imagination* (1971), but his outreach was global. Because of his wide learning, powerful uses of language, and visionary awareness of his subject, Frye became one of the 20th century's most distinguished and most frequently quoted thinkers. He lectured at more than a hundred universities in Canada and abroad.

Frye's first major book, *Fearful Symmetry* (1947), a study of the poetry of William Blake, was followed by 32 others, notably *Anatomy of Criticism* (1957), *The Great Code* (1982), and *Words with Power* (1990). Many considered Frye the finest literary mind in the Western world. His writings are available worldwide in numerous languages, and his works, including many not published while he was alive, are appearing in the 31-volume scholarly edition, the Collected Works of Northrop Frye.

ALVIN A. LEE

full circle. A thousand years ago, on the island of Newfoundland, humanity completed its encirclement of the globe. Some 99,000 years earlier our ancient ancestors, increasingly capable of living in almost any environment, had spread outward from Africa on a long and complicated journey, northeast across Asia and northwest into Europe, constantly ranging across new territories.

About AD 1000, *Norse people sailed their sturdy and graceful knarrs across the North Atlantic, eventually making landfall on the northern tip of Newfoundland at a place now called L'Anse aux Meadows. They had found the new land they were seeking and new resources for trade, and from this base they briefly explored the Strait of Belle Isle and the Gulf of St Lawrence. Twenty thousand years earlier some of the people who had migrated eastward into Siberia reached the Bering Strait and crossed over into North America. Slowly these peoples established Aboriginal hunting and fishing societies across North America, later migrations taking their descendants to its east coast. Some of them eventually became Dorset Paleoeskimoes, Inuit, Innu, Beothuk, and Mi'kmaq. The Atlantic Ocean became a barrier to further eastward expansion. It was not until Vikings and 'Skraelings'—some of whom became the *Beothuk—met at L'Anse aux Meadows, some 4,000 generations after their common ancestors had left their African homeland, that humanity had come full circle. KEVIN McALEESE

Fulton–Favreau formula, 1964. This formula, named for two successive federal ministers of justice, E. Davie Fulton and Guy Favreau, concerned *federal–provincial relations and a constitutional amending formula. To amend sections 51(a) (stipulating that no province should have fewer MPs than senators), 92 (delineating the exclusive powers of the provincial legislatures), and 133 (guaranteeing the use of French and English in the federal and Quebec legislatures and courts) of the British North America Act, and any other matter that concerned the rights and privileges of all provinces, the consent of the federal government and all provinces must be obtained. Amendments to article 93 (concerning education) also required unanimous consent (Newfoundland constituting a special case). If the matter did not affect all provinces, only those concerned must consent. Anything that did not involve provincial powers, education, or official bilingualism required the consent of two-thirds of the provinces representing 50 per cent of the Canadian population. Finally, the formula stipulated that the federal government could delegate powers to the provinces (or vice versa) after obtaining the consent of four provinces.

When Fulton–Favreau was presented in 1964, all ten premiers indicated they would accept its provisions. However, opposition soon grew, both from those who felt it gave the provinces too much power and those who felt it reserved too much for the federal government. When Prime Minister John *Diefenbaker and Quebec premier Jean *Lesage withdrew their support, the formula died.

GÉRALD-A. BEAUDOIN

functionalism. The early history of Canadian *foreign policy reflected the concerns of the new and immature political entity. From the establishment of the Department of *External Affairs in 1909 until 1939, Canadian involvement in international affairs was rooted in domestically driven objectives and circumstances. Robert *Borden, Canada's prime minister during the First World War, and W.L. Mackenzie *King, prime minister for most of the interwar years, used international affairs to advance Canadian independence from Britain. Having established Canadian authority over external policy, they rarely exercised it by formulating substantive policies. In addition, King examined international affairs through the prism of national unity. His determination to prevent discord between English and French Canadians meant that most of the time King tried to keep Canada out of international affairs.

During the Second World War, responsibility and influence supplanted status and national unity as the principal goals of Canadian foreign policy. A new generation of diplomats wanted their country to play an active role in world affairs. Canadian diplomats feared that the pattern of wartime organization—whereby Britain and the United States controlled the Allied war effort, relegating Canada to the sidelines—would persist in peacetime. Hume Wrong, a former professor of history and a disgruntled intellectual in the Department of External Affairs, articulated a philosophy of international relations to justify Canadian influence and responsibility in world affairs: functionalism. Functionalism equated capacity, contribution, and expertise with responsibility and influence on a case-by-case basis. Where a nation made a significant contribution or had particular expertise, then that nation should enjoy a commensurate influence.

Wrong, along with Norman Robertson and Lester *Pearson, made the case in Washington and London that Canada deserved to be included on the executive councils of the Combined Food Board, the Combined Production and Resources Board, and the United Nations Relief and Rehabilitation Administration. Britain and the United States were loath to share power. Canadian officials persisted, arguing that the scale of their contribution made exclusion intolerable (for instance, Canada's food contribution to the Allied war effort was second only to the United States) and threatening that Canada's exclusion would result in no material Canadian support for UNRRA. By war's end Canadian officials were included in these organizations but the norms and practices of international relations were not changed. After the war, the greatest powers continued to dominate the international community, and Canada, along with other small and *middle powers with particular capabilities and specialized expertise, had to fight for influence.

FRANCINE McKENZIE

fur trade. The fur trade, the earliest transcontinental business enterprise, was foundational to Canada. In most parts of the country it brought the First Nations and the European newcomers together for the first time, providing the institutional setting in which key elements of their on-going relationships were forged. The industry provided the catalyst for the European exploration of Aboriginal Canada. It linked the regional Aboriginal economies with the expanding global economy beginning in the early 16th century. Finally, the industry remains important to the First Nations economies in the vast Canadian North.

Exchange between Aboriginal people and Europeans began during the first half of the 16th century as a sideline of the cod fishery and *whaling industry. At that time, the fur markets of Europe were too small and fragmented to sustain fur-trading connections with North America. Fishermen and whalers, on the other hand, found that they could augment their incomes by bartering with *Mi'kmaq and Innu (Montagnais-Naskapi) people, who seasonally camped along the coasts of the Gulf of St Lawrence. Beginning in the second half of the 16th century, fashion changes in Europe, most notably the increasing popularity of the felt hat—the finest felt was made from the under wool (short hairs) of *beaver pelts—set the economic stage for the establishment of the land-based fur trade. By the time the felt-hat industry flourished, beaver had nearly been exterminated in western Europe, and merchants and manufacturers looked eastward to Russia and westward to North America for their supplies. The Aboriginal people of Canada offered them the ideal commodity—their used winter beaver coats. For maximum warmth, Natives wore these coats with the hair turned inward. In doing so, they wore off the long guard hairs, leaving behind the under wool. Because European felt makers could cheaply process these used coats into prime felt, the early coat-beaver trade represented a bonanza for Aboriginal people. Coat beaver, known to the French as *castor gras*, dominated the fur trade from its inception in the late 16th century to the end of the 17th century. Thereafter, because of changes in felt-making processes, Europeans preferred unworn pelts, known as parchment beaver or *castor sec*. Beaver, marten (known as Canadian sable), and muskrat accounted for most of the volume and value of the furs exchanged until the late 19th century. Thereafter, an ever-widening array of furs became important.

The fur trade was an industry that linked the very disparate economies of Aboriginal people and Europeans. To facilitate exchange the two parties had to accommodate each other's customs and traditions. In the Aboriginal world, social, political, and exchange relations were intricately intertwined. In order to establish and sustain the peaceful conditions that were requisite for trade, Native groups engaged in ceremonial exchanges of gifts. The gifts, which normally were of equivalent value, symbolized the good intentions of both parties. The exchange usually took place with considerable pomp and ceremony. When the parties intended to engage in long-term relationships, they often arranged marriages, which established kinship bonds. In Aboriginal society, most exchange took place between close kin who had mutual obligations to support one another. When Europeans arrived in their lands, Aboriginal people expected them to honour these traditions. French and English traders did so, and gift exchanges became a central feature of pre-trading ceremonies.

Pre-trade gift exchanges were elaborate affairs that lasted several days during the early phases of the fur trade, when middlemen groups dominated exchange. These groups, led by men whom Europeans called 'trading captains', travelled long distances. The best accounts of these ceremonies are found in the records of *York Factory, the Hudson's Bay Company post located on western Hudson Bay, which drew groups from as far west as the upper Saskatchewan River and Athabasca area. In the later phases of trade at a post, when most of the barter involved local hunters and trappers, gift exchanges were not as elaborate. Nonetheless, they persisted and remained of great symbolic importance to Aboriginal people. The practice was carried over into treaty relationships with Canada.

In most areas of the country, the fur trade had to be carried out during the relatively short open-water season. To expedite exchange, Aboriginal people and Europeans needed to develop a system that enabled them to come to terms quickly. The problem was that Aboriginal people lacked monetary systems that offered common units of value. Beaver offered the solution. Because it was the staple of the trade in most areas east of the Pacific coast until the mid-19th century, it became the accounting and bartering standard. Traders valued furs and trading goods in terms of their worth in beaver. The best record of this valuation system is contained in HBC records. They reveal that the company officially priced trade goods in terms of units of Made Beaver according to its Standard of Trade. It valued all of the furs and commodities that Aboriginal people brought to the trading posts in terms of the Comparative Standard. Traders departed from these official standards at their posts, exacting higher or lower rates of exchange depending on local competitive conditions. The fur profits they made in excess of what the official authorized rates would have yielded they termed the Overplus. Sometimes other units of value were more appropriate for local economies. For example, at Moose Factory, a Made Marten standard also was used, whereas in *New Caledonia on the Pacific slope salmon served as a point of reference.

When beaver became a staple, Aboriginal and European traders struggled to control the trade. The contest began on the north shore of the Gulf of St Lawrence near the outlet of the Saguenay River. Here the Innu traded with Europeans, bringing furs they had collected from their inland trading partners in exchange for European trade goods. Europeans competed fiercely for the trade of the Innu. In an effort to gain the upper hand, the French established their earliest settlement at Tadoussac on the Saguenay River, but it was too readily accessible to the ships of rival European nations. Accordingly, the French, led by Samuel de *Champlain and his backers, shifted their operations to the St Lawrence River. This move also enabled them to bypass the Innu middlemen and obtain furs more cheaply. The Innu had opposed the idea until Champlain concluded a treaty with them in 1603 pledging to help them in their battles against their Iroquoian enemies south of the Great Lakes. Thus, a circular and cumulative process of expansion began. Each time European traders attempted to bypass an Aboriginal middleman group, another arose to replace it. Also, to curry the favour of their Native trading partners, rival European groups entered into military-trading alliances. In this way, the fur trade became intertwined in intertribal conflicts, most notably the wars of the *Iroquois, and with Dutch, English, French, and American *imperial rivalries that continued until the conclusion of the War of 1812.

From 1600 to 1649, a succession of groups acted as middlemen in the French fur trade, which expanded up the St Lawrence River, the Ottawa River, and westward via Lake Nipissing to the eastern Georgian Bay area, where the *Huron lived. By the late 1640s, these people, who obtained their furs mostly from groups living to the north of the Great Lakes, dominated the French trading system. In 1649, the Huron were destroyed by the Five Nations Iroquois, and the French faced the challenge of rebuilding their western trading network. In the process of doing so, they set the stage for the expansion of the fur trade beyond the watershed of the Gulf of St Lawrence and St Lawrence River and into that of *Hudson Bay, which drains the whole of central Canada.

This process began in the late 1650s when Pierre-Esprit *Radisson and Médard Chouart, Sieur des Groseilliers travelled to the Lake Superior area, where they learned of the rich fur country lying to the northwest. They concluded that the easiest and safest way to reach these lands was via Hudson Bay—the 'frozen sea' to the north. After failing to enlist French support for their idea, they obtained it in England from the cousin of Charles II, Prince Rupert, and other London merchants, who founded the *Hudson's Bay Company in 1670.

The company posed a threat that the French could not ignore. In 1682 Canadian merchants organized the Compagnie du Nord to challenge the English intruders by renewing and establishing alliances with Native groups north of Lake Superior and by sending military expeditions to Hudson Bay. These efforts bankrupted the company by 1700 and failed to dislodge the HBC. In the Treaty of Utrecht (1713), which ended the War of the Spanish Succession in Europe, the French acceded to a HBC monopoly on the maritime approach to Hudson Bay. Thereafter, the French adopted the strategy of encircling Hudson Bay to cut the HBC posts off from their hinterlands and the Cree and Assiniboine middlemen who carried furs to them. This effort led the French to push westward as far as the forks of the Saskatchewan River by the mid-1750s. From the late 1720s to the early 1740s, Pierre Gaultier de Varennes et de *La Vérendrye and his sons spearheaded the French advance. Because of military exigencies in the east, the French began to withdraw from their western posts by the late 1750s. The English conquest of New France and the Treaty of Paris (1763) marked the end of the early fur trade era.

Shortly after 1763 a period of ruinous competition began, which lasted until 1821. American and British traders based on the St Lawrence River forged a series of small partnerships to reoccupy the ground abandoned by the French and to mount a new challenge to the HBC. By 1775, they made sufficient inroads into the company's business to force it to abandon its longstanding policy of 'sleeping by the frozen sea' and move inland and confront them head on. To meet this threat, and to expand northwestward into the Mackenzie River basin, the St Lawrence River–based traders operating in Saskatchewan country pooled their resources and formed the *North West Company in 1779. Soon the NWC and the HBC were locked in a no-holds-barred contest. In the prairies and parklands, the two companies built competing networks of posts to gain access to the dried meat, *pemmican, and grease that the buffalo-hunting First Nations produced. This food was essential for the canoe and boat brigades that supplied the burgeoning networks of trading posts.

In the northern woodlands, the NWC pushed westward up the Peace River and into the interior of British Columbia, a land the Scottish-born Nor'Westers called New Caledonia. Alexander *Mackenzie provided them with their first direct knowledge of this region in 1793, when he made his overland trek to the Pacific coast near Bella Bella. By 1806 the NWC operated a network of posts in New Caledonia. Meanwhile, the Nor'Westers blocked the HBC from following them up the Peace River. By 1820 the two companies were financially exhausted, and their unbridled competition had depleted fur and game throughout most of the boreal forest country between James Bay and the Peace River. Also, the excessive use of alcohol in the trade had seriously disrupted First Nations societies. Ruinous financial losses and political pressure from British politicians, who were concerned about the welfare of Aboriginal people, forced the two rivals to merge in 1821.

While this contest played itself out in the interior, a lively trade in sea otter pelts developed on the west coast following Captain James *Cook's visit in 1778. Cook's crew discovered that the Chinese prized the sea otter coats the Nuu-chah-nulth (Nootka) had given them as presents. As word of this bonanza spread, British and American ships began to ply the coast. Also, the Russian America Company, which was created in 1799, expanded southeastward from the Aleutians into the Alaskan panhandle area. The demand for sea otter was so great that most areas of British Columbia were seriously depleted by 1821 and the trade was in steep decline.

From 1821 until the 1870s the reconstituted HBC held sway, being seriously challenged only along the American border, particularly in the Prairie region. Here the American Fur Company, which John Jacob Astor founded in 1808, expanded up the Missouri River and into the upper Red River basin, to engage in the buffalo-robe trade. To discourage Americans from entering its domain, the HBC encouraged Aboriginal people to trap out the lands on the south side of the American border to create a fur desert. In the depleted forestlands of central Canada it introduced a beaver-conservation program. Meanwhile, it expanded trading operations in the Mackenzie Valley and New Caledonia. Throughout the North, it eliminated the trading of alcohol, in compliance with the terms of its 1821 trading licence.

In the late 19th century the fur trade changed substantially in response to global industrialization and rapid advancements in transportation and communication systems. These developments facilitated the mass marketing of furs to the growing middle class. The construction of railways before the First World War, and the increasing use of bush planes immediately thereafter, opened the North to a host of challengers to the venerable HBC. Revillon Frères of Paris proved to be one of the most formidable. It operated in Canada from 1899 until 1926, when the HBC bought their interests. American traders also reappeared in the North. The unbridled competition of the industrial age once again threatened fur stocks. This time, provincial and federal governments introduced conservation legislation to address the problem.

ARTHUR J. RAY

See also ABORIGINALS IN THE FUR TRADE.

fur trade explorers (English-speaking). In the early 17th century, European ships explored the Arctic, searching for a northern passage to the western ocean. Their crews considered *Hudson Bay and its hinterland a desolate, uninhabited wilderness. French *coureurs de bois, however, had learned from Indians that 'the Bay of the North Sea' was the source of their furs. Unable to convince Quebec fur merchants that the centre of trade was far north of Lake Superior, French traders *Radisson and Groseilliers turned to London (1665). Their actions led to the voyage of the **Nonsuch* in 1668 and the grant of a royal charter to the *Hudson's Bay Company in 1670. They also laid the grounds for the rivalry between the St Lawrence and Hudson Bay approaches to fur country, which lasted for the next 150 years.

In the following decades, conflict between the English and French around the bay allowed only sporadic expeditions. Only one inland expedition, Henry Kelsey's, in 1690–2, was historically remarkable. Kelsey, 'a very active Lad, Delighting much in Indians compa.', left York Fort with instructions 'to call, encourage, and invite, the remoter Indians to a Trade with us'. He travelled with his Indian guides along the Saskatchewan and northern plains, southwest across the Saskatchewan and Red Deer Rivers, and on to the prairies proper. Despite these contacts, the policy of attracting Indians to bayside posts continued for nearly 50 years with only one more notable journey of exploration. The enterprising *York Factory governor James Knight sent William Stuart inland in 1715–16 to explore for gold and the western ocean. Using only a compass, Stuart crossed the barrens, reaching the area of Great Slave Lake. To lure to the bay the Chipewyan and other Dene groups Stuart encountered, Knight established a post at the mouth of the Churchill River in 1717. Returning to England, Knight persuaded the HBC to outfit an expedition to search for a passage to find gold and furs. After his vessels, the *Albany* and *Discovery*, were trapped in the ice along the shores of Marble Island in 1719, his entire crew perished. The company again became reluctant to venture from bayside posts.

Further exploration came as fears of French territorial expansion grew. In 1743, in his 'Observations on Hudson's Bay', James Isham echoed the criticisms of Ulster MP Arthur *Dobbs, writing 'what is the most Concer'n is to see us sitt quiet & unconcern'd while the french as an old saying, not only Beats the Bush but run's away with the Hair also'. Eventually Anthony Henday (1752–5) was sent to persuade Indians to trade at the bay. He travelled with Cree guides to the Lower Saskatchewan and across the south branch of the Saskatchewan. Moving west and southwest, he met mounted members of the Blackfoot near the Red Deer River.

After the Seven Years' War, formidable new British- and American-backed 'pedlars' took over many French posts. In 1772–3, when the HBC sent Matthew Cocking inland, he found Canadian traders active everywhere he travelled. Persuaded by the reports and maps of York Factory factor Andrew Graham, the London Committee decided to compete aggressively. In 1774, Samuel *Hearne, who had just returned from his Arctic expedition, established *Cumberland House 60 miles from The Pas. At first, it hardly affected Canadian traders like Alexander Henry, Peter *Pond, and Alexander *Mackenzie. But over a half-century of direct and often violent competition, the HBC established a long line of inland posts, still relying on cheap sea transport to deliver goods to Hudson's Bay posts.

Just as Hearne had been seeking a navigable passage to the Dene and Inuit, 'pedlars' continued to seek cheaper and shorter supply routes and to expand their territory westward. Pond's 'Old Establishment' (1778) on the Athabasca River and Roderic Mackenzie's *Fort Chipewyan (1788) on Lake Athabasca became sites for trade along the waterways radiating throughout the north. Alexander Mackenzie used Fort Chipewyan as a base for his expeditions to the Arctic Ocean and across the mountains to the Pacific Ocean; his adventures and discoveries were described by the fur trader and novelist R.M. Ballantyne (1872).

In 1797, the Nor'Wester James Finlay followed Mackenzie's path up the Peace River to Finlay Forks and explored both the Finlay and Parsnip Rivers. David *Thompson explored the Columbia River system (1807–10) for the North West Company 'to extend their Fur Trade to the west side of the Rocky Mountains, and if possible to the Pacific Ocean'. Simon *Fraser's fame lies in the three-year period (1805–8) in which he explored and extended trade along the Fraser River and in what is now British Columbia. The *North West Company's long and expensive overland *canoe routes were not sustainable and, ultimately, the company amalgamated with the HBC. With the union of 1821, the HBC enjoyed an era of continental fur trade dominance. J. COLIN YERBURY

Gaelic language. Massive social upheavals in the Scottish Highlands launched a wave of emigrant Gaelic-speakers to British North America from 1770 to 1850. The earliest and largest settlements were in eastern Nova Scotia, Prince Edward Island, and Glengarry County, Ontario. Later communities were established in every province, with significant populations in southwestern Newfoundland, the Eastern Townships in Quebec, much of Ontario (in particular Bruce County), and southern Manitoba.

At Confederation, Gaelic was Canada's third most widely spoken language, and the first two prime ministers are reputed to have been native speakers. In 1890, Senator Thomas Robert MacInnes introduced a bill to make Gaelic the third official language. Jonathan G. MacKinnon of Whycocomagh, Nova Scotia, published the weekly *Mac-Talla* ('Echo'), 1892–1904, the longest run of any Gaelic newspaper in the world. The dynamic character of Gaelic society in Canada and its vibrant oral culture were reflected in songs that told of the beauty of Cape Breton's hills and Manitoba's plains, the joys of maple sugaring, and the corruption of local politicians, among other topics.

Gaelic began to lose ground in the late 19th century. Heavy outmigration and intense assimilationist pressures led to a sharp drop in speakers. By the mid-20th century virtually all parents were raising their children in English. The decline spurred calls to protect the language, but early efforts suffered from tokenism or submerged Gaelic in a pastiche of cartoonish Highland pageantry. Universities offered occasional classes but otherwise did their best to anglicize their Gaelic students. The Gaelic College of Celtic Arts and Crafts, founded in 1939 in St Anns, Nova Scotia, championed the language while alienating many locals with its 'tartan circus' atmosphere. Later revivalists, more sympathetic to Canadian Gaelic culture, generated increased activity at the grassroots and institutional levels. Gaelic was introduced in a few schools and universities, and the Gaelic College placed more emphasis on the language. St Francis Xavier University in Antigonish established a Gaelic studies chair in 1983. Gaelic societies operate in cities from Halifax to Vancouver, and revitalization efforts continue in many of the original strongholds, particularly Cape Breton.

JONATHAN DEMBLING

Gagnon, Aurore. Victim of a widely publicized case of child abuse, ten-year-old Aurore died in Fortierville, Quebec, 12 February 1920, battered and neglected by her recently remarried father, Télesphore Gagnon, and by her stepmother, Marie-Anne Houde. Both were tried for murder in Quebec City. Aurore's father, whose brand of corporal punishment involved whips and axe handles, was convicted of involuntary manslaughter, but served only five years of his life sentence. It was Houde who was portrayed at trial as the true villain. Prosecutors demonstrated that, among other outrages, the stepmother had bound and beaten Aurore and had branded her with a hot poker. They also claimed that she had enlisted her husband's participation with sinister lies about the girl's misbehaviour. Houde was convicted and condemned to death by hanging, a sentence that was commuted to life in prison on 29 September 1920, two days before the scheduled execution.

In 1921, Léon Petitjean and Henri Rollin used these widely reported events as the basis for *Aurore, l'enfant martyre*, one of the most successful plays in Quebec during the interwar years. This popular melodrama inspired scores of retellings of Aurore's tragic tale, the best-known being Jean-Yves Bigras's classic 1952 film, *La petite Aurore, l'enfant martyre*. Retold on stage, screen, and in popular fiction, Aurore's pitiful story became embedded in the collective memory of several generations of francophone Quebeckers. Why was this so? Some have argued that Aurore's 'martyrdom' touched a political nerve and offered a handy domestic metaphor for Quebec's historic sense of victimization under British and Canadian rule. More likely, these narratives simply resonated with one of the most enduring archetypes in Western folklore: the cruel stepmother. In exploiting widely held prejudices around stepmothers, these texts articulated dominant ideologies of family life by holding up for public condemnation an inverted example of the prescribed maternal role.

PETER GOSSAGE

Gagnon, (Frédéric) Ernest (Amédée) (1834–1915). Gagnon received a classical studies education at Joliette College, then studied music in Montreal and Paris. During his European travels, he met some leading musicians of the day, including Rossini and Verdi. He spent his professional life in Quebec City, where he was organist at the basilica and music teacher at the École normale Laval, the Petit Séminaire de Québec, and for the *Ursulines. From 1903, he was a civil servant with the Quebec government. A virtuoso organist and a composer, Gagnon is also remembered for his folk-song collection *Les Chansons populaires du Canada*, first published in the mid-1860s. His historical writings include a biography of the

17th-century explorer Louis *Jolliet. Gagnon played a crucial organizational role in the composition of 'O Canada' by Calixa Lavallée (words by Adolphe Routhier) in 1880, and introduced into North America 'Minuit Chrétien'—'O Holy Night'—by French composer Adolphe Adam.

GORDON E. SMITH

gallantry awards. Traditionally, military officers distinguishing themselves in the field received a variety of honours, including special medals or swords presented by grateful parliaments and legislatures. For example, the legislative assembly of Lower Canada presented Jean-Baptiste Rolette with an engraved sword for his services on the Great Lakes during the War of 1812. Conspicuously brave non-commissioned personnel could expect little—promotion during wartime and land grants afterwards. Civilian rewards for bravery were chiefly from private sources. Abigail Becker, who saved the lives of mariners shipwrecked off Long Point, Lake Erie (1854), received £50 from Queen Victoria, $500 from seamen in Buffalo, New York, plus medals from the New York Life Saving Benevolent Association and the Royal Humane Society. Mariners rescuing people at sea were often rewarded with cash, sextants, and spy glasses.

National medals specifically for bravery evolved in the 19th century. France and Germany led the way during the Napoleonic Wars. The earliest British gallantry award, the Indian Order of Merit, was created by the East India Company in 1837, followed by a Sea Gallantry Medal (1855) and the Victoria Cross (1856). Canadians were entitled to all British honours. The prestigious Victoria Cross was presented to 94 Canadians out of 1,351 awarded, commencing with Alexander Dunn for gallantry during the Charge of the Light Brigade. An Irish soldier, Timothy O Hea, won his VC in 1864 in Canada during the *Fenian Raids; he fought and extinguished a fire in a rail car loaded with munitions. The Albert Medal, created in 1866 for civilian gallantry, was awarded to 22 Canadians, including CPR conductor Thomas Reynolds for saving lives following a 1910 train wreck in northern Ontario. Numerous other awards for both civilians and military personnel evolved over the years, particularly during the First and Second World Wars.

Although some distinctive Canadian campaign and service medals appeared between 1885 and 1949, no unique gallantry awards were created until 1967, when the Medal of Bravery was struck. It became obvious that one medal could not recognize different degrees of hazard and bravery, and the original medal was never awarded. In 1972 a hierarchy of gallantry awards was created: the Cross of Valour, Star of Courage, and Medal of Bravery. These have been bestowed on both civilians and military personnel. Part of René Jalbert's Cross of Valour deed (calming and ultimately disarming a gunman in Quebec's National Assembly) was filmed by TV cameras that normally recorded legislative debates. The Star of Courage and Medal of Bravery have been awarded with generosity verging on profligacy. In 1993 three new gallantry medals were struck for combat situations: a Canadianized Victoria Cross, Star of Military Valour, and Medal of Military Valour. None of these has yet been awarded.

HUGH A. HALLIDAY

gallicanism. As a set of legal principles and practices upholding royal rather than papal supremacy or the national church's corporate rights, gallicanism did not take hold in Canada. Under French rule, the diocese and clergy of Quebec were separate entities from the church of France; ecclesiastical leaders worked closely with colonial rulers to reinforce each other's authority; and Rome accepted the Quebec church's heavy financial and administrative dependence on the Crown. After the *Conquest, official efforts to use gallicanism to turn the church into a tool of statecraft were abandoned as contrary to British interests in the insurrectionary 1830s. Occasionally in the 19th century individuals and groups seeking to further their own interests advanced gallican claims with public support from prominent politicians. They contended that the state had the right to review decisions taken by the church. Thus, the Sulpician Seminary, sole ecclesiastical authority in Montreal since 1657, contested Jean-Jacques Lartigue's nomination as bishop in 1821. The Sulpicians, as perpetual pastors of Montreal, also had their lawyer, Attorney General George Étienne *Cartier, block Bishop Ignace *Bourget's plans to divide their enormous parish in 1865. This triggered the *Programme catholique*, which reaffirmed the autonomy of religious authority in the spiritual realm. The most celebrated affirmation of gallican ideas occurred during the *Guibord affair. Louis-Antoine Dessaulles and Rodolphe Laflamme, both prominent members of the *Institut canadien, succeeded in having the courts force Bourget to bury renegade Catholic Joseph Guibord in Montreal's only Catholic cemetery. As an expression of anticlericalism, gallicanism survived for some time longer, but it had no lasting impact on Canadian jurisprudence.

ROBERTO PERIN

Galt, Alexander Tilloch (1817–93), politician, contractor, diplomat. Born in London, England, Galt immigrated to Lower Canada in 1835 as a clerk for the British American Land Company. He rose quickly through the ranks and in 1844 became the company's commissioner in Canada. He promoted the St Lawrence and Atlantic Railway, which, connected to the American-built Atlantic and St Lawrence, gave Montreal access to the Atlantic Ocean at Portland, Maine. Also in the early 1850s, Galt and his associates built the Toronto to Sarnia portion of the *Grand Trunk Railway. Thirty years later, Galt arranged British financing for a large coal-mining, railway, and irrigation complex in southern Alberta.

Galt was a prominent politician. Elected in 1849 to the legislature of the United Canadas, he became inspector-general in 1858. A year later, he introduced a tariff that not only increased revenues for public works but was also deliberately protectionist. The new strategy, also directed against Great Britain, became the model for the *National Policy tariff of 1879. Galt was actively involved in the *Confederation conferences and became Canada's first minister of finance, serving only a few months. In 1879, the newly re-elected government of Sir John A. *Macdonald appointed him Canada's first high commissioner in London. A.A. DEN OTTER

gambling. Gambling is a popular leisure activity and business that has ranged from thoroughbred horse racing and any kind of sport to specific card and dice games, lotteries, sweepstakes, bingo, and slot machines or video lottery terminals (VLTs). Particular forms of gambling have been linked to specific locations and communities: Faro, a card game linked with the *Klondike gold rush; barbotte, a dice game associated with Montreal in the 1940s and 1950s; and fan tan, a guessing game linked with early Chinese-Canadian neighbourhoods. Gambling has been a cause of concern among opponents, who believed it undermined values such as the work ethic, thrift, and divine providence. More recently gambling's critics have adopted the language of addiction.

Legislation in 1856 forbade all types of lotteries in Canada East and West; the Canadian Criminal Code of 1892 prohibited lotteries and gambling houses. Before 1969, most forms of gambling where a third party made a profit were technically illegal, even if the law was unevenly enforced. Exceptions were made for charities, religious organizations, and agricultural fairs, since the public was thought to benefit. Federal legislation in 1910 permitted parimutuel betting for *horse racing at government-chartered tracks during a limited number of racing days. This encouraged the growth of illicit off-track bookmakers, who were often tied to organized crime syndicates.

Notwithstanding their unlawful status, lotteries were widely popular among Canadians. Regional contests such as British Columbia's Salmon Sweepstakes predated the First World War, while the 1968 Montreal Lottery drew participants from outside the city. The most popular draw was the international Irish Sweepstakes, whose tickets were available everywhere in Canada from 1930. After sections of the 1969 *Omnibus Bill permitted governments to operate or license lotteries, all the provinces, territories, and the federal government entered the arena. In 1969, Quebec established the Société des loteries et courses du Québec, which was followed by the Western Canada Lottery Foundation in 1974 (BC went on its own in 1985), the Ontario Lottery Corporation in 1975, and the Atlantic Lottery Corporation in 1976. In 1973 the Olympic Lottery Corporation of Canada, under licence of the federal government, sold tickets to fund the 1976 Calgary Olympics. Loto-Canada, established in 1976, initiated a constitutional dispute between the provinces and the federal government that was settled in 1979 when the federal government withdrew from lotteries in exchange for quarterly payments. This division was enshrined in a 1985 amendment that excluded the federal government from conducting lotteries and legalized video machine gambling, slot machines, and the numbers game keno. Canada's first legal casino opened in Winnipeg in 1989; in 1990 New Brunswick became the first province to introduce VLTs. SUZANNE MORTON

Game Acts. Aboriginal game management was embedded in the cultural and ecological knowledge of elders. In comparison, new colonial societies were suddenly freed of Europe's restrictive game laws. Early wildlife law included bounties on wolves (Nova Scotia, 1796), closed seasons for deer hunting (Upper Canada, 1830), and networks of game wardens (Halifax, 1854). Immigration, habitat change, and railway-based hunting increased pressure on wildlife. Provinces like Ontario began to exercise their constitutional jurisdiction over wildlife, first with a royal commission (1890) and then a department (1907).

Federal wildlife laws were created for the new territories in the West and the North. The near extinction of the buffalo resulted in a series of Game Acts enforced by the *North-West Mounted Police (1877, 1883, 1896, 1906) aimed at preserving wildlife as an Aboriginal food source. Aboriginal leaders objected that closed hunting seasons contradicted their treaty rights, beginning a long dispute. Provincial status for the Prairies meant federal constitutional jurisdiction over wildlife shifted to *national parks and the North. The salvage of North America's last buffalo herd, the Pablo herd (1906), marked the move to a parks policy of preservation of wildlife for its own sake. In 1917 Gordon Hewitt revised the Northwest Game Act to save the caribou and the musk-ox from the buffalo's fate, while supporting subsistence hunting. The Thelon Game Reserve was created and wildlife inventories followed. The 1947 establishment of the Canadian Wildlife Service launched a fascinating blending of science, conservation, and traditional ecological knowledge, evolving into today's successful co-management with Inuit and Dene stakeholders. LORNE HAMMOND

Gardiner, James G. (1883–1962), Saskatchewan premier 1926–9, 1934–5, farmer, relentless Liberal. Archetypal regional minister, Gardiner sat an unprecedented 22 years (1935–57) as minister of agriculture in the federal Liberal governments of Mackenzie King and Louis St Laurent. First elected to the Saskatchewan legislature in a by-election in 1914, he served as backbencher, then highways minister, before serving as premier after an interval as leader of the opposition. He entered federal politics in 1935. Thoroughly partisan, Gardiner became a by-word for intensive party organization, political *patronage, and electoral cunning. A passionate advocate of what he called the 'British system of representative, responsible government', he fervently opposed minor parties for the debilitating effect they had on decisive government. Regions such as the Prairie West could best make their case, he maintained, from within rather than from outside the governing caucus. Viewed as a chieftain of another age, the Liberal Party under Lester Pearson, as well as the voters of western Canada, rejected his counsel.

DAVID E. SMITH

garment industry. By the early 1900s the shift to factory-made clothing was dramatic. In earlier times, most clothing was homemade, by the woman of the house, and skilled tailors produced custom-made clothing for the wealthy. The development of the clothing industry depended on the rationalization of production, particularly once the sewing machine was developed. Clothes were produced in standardized sizes, and the labour process changed radically. In most sections of the industry, the tasks involved in making a garment were divided up into many small operations, which were then parcelled out to individual workers each of whom was to repeat his or her particular task over and over again. One person would make button holes all day long while another sewed only pockets.

Concentrated in Toronto, Montreal, and Winnipeg, the clothing industry had become one of the country's major industrial sectors by the beginning of the 20th century. In contrast to the many sectors that employed only males, this labour-intensive industry provided jobs for women as well, although female garment-workers were generally confined to low-paid jobs that were deemed less skilled than those done by men. The early-20th-century garment industry employed many Jewish immigrants from eastern Europe. Male and female *Jews congregated in this sector partly because local anti-Semitism ensured that many other occupations were closed to them. The ethnic composition of the labour force changed dramatically with the entry of new kinds of immigrants after the Second World War. By the late 1900s, female immigrants from Asia constituted a key source of low-wage labour in this sector.

Historically, working conditions in the needle trades were notoriously bad, and intense competitive pressures squeezed wages. At the turn of the 20th century, subcontractors could rent a few sewing machines and set up shop in their own small apartments. Workers in these sweatshops often toiled late into the night for meagre pay. Even in the large garment factories there were often major problems. Speed-ups sometimes led to nervous breakdowns; other occupational hazards included kidney problems, skin irritations, and the dreaded 'tailors' disease'—*tuberculosis.

Activists in the garment industry struggled to protest against these notorious conditions, and numerous strikes erupted in the early 20th century. The workers formed the International Ladies' Garment Workers' Union, for men and women who made women's clothing, and the Amalgamated Clothing Workers, for those who made men's clothing. These unions made important gains. More recently, many of these gains have been eroded in the context of the massive shift of clothing production to regimes with low labour standards in the global South. The ILGWU and the ACW merged to form UNITE (Union of Needletrades, Industrial and Textile Employees), which has become very active in the global anti-sweatshop movement. RUTH A. FRAGER

Garneau, François-Xavier (1809–66), historian and poet. A notary and city clerk living in Quebec, Garneau decided that writing his people's history was his patriotic duty. Despite his sense of mission, he never compromised truthfulness or historical method. Without the benefit of a formal classical education and burdened by his livelihood, he devoted every spare minute to his self-imposed mission. He became French Canada's national historian and gave French-Canadian literature its first masterpiece. *Histoire du Canada depuis sa découverte jusqu'à nos jours* was published in three volumes from 1845 to 1848 (2nd and 3rd editions in 1852 and 1859). A response to the conqueror's haughtiness, it was erudite, eloquent, and timely. In the aftermath of the tragedy of the 1837–8 rebellions and the union of the Canadas, it touched his compatriots' hearts and souls, strengthening their will to survival, and providing them with a clear consciousness of their historical rights. In the first volume, liberalism and nationalism vied for prominence, but he later muffled some judgments the clergy had frowned upon. In any case, his liberalism stressed national liberty over individual freedom. His nationalist appeal to tradition attracted later intellectuals such as Lionel *Groulx.

PIERRE TRÉPANIER

Garneau, Hector de Saint-Denys (1913–43), poet and essayist. Considered one of the most important writers of 20th-century Quebec, Garneau was born in Montreal. Early on he contributed poems and art reviews to the avant-garde literary magazine *La Relève* and to *L'Action nationale*. *Regards et jeux dans l'espace*, a selection of poems, was published in 1937. Distressed by the indifference that greeted publication of this first book, Garneau did not attempt to publish further writings. The 1949 posthumous publication of his *Poésies complètes* affirmed for the first time his privileged position within Quebec's literary canon, putting his search for affirmation at the centre of a new modernist consciousness. Garneau's diary, personal letters, and collections of unpublished poetry have appeared more recently. In the 1970s, his sense of ascetic revelation and his split persona were said to embody the state of cultural alienation and dissociation affecting French-Canadian society. Later studies of his work emphasize his striving for autonomy and formal experimentation in a deeply conservative society.

FRANÇOIS PARÉ

garrison mentality. A metaphorical image used provisionally by Northrop *Frye in the 'Conclusion' to *Literary History of Canada* (1965) to help identify how Canadian culture has developed. The image of the garrison is from the earliest maps of Canada, where the only human settlements are forts. The first Canadian novel, *The History of Emily Montague* (1763), is by Frances Brooke, a British clergyman's wife living in the garrison town of Quebec. Such facts symbolize the enclave culture dominant in early Canada but continuing psychologically well into the 20th century: isolated human communities surrounded by a vast, indifferent natural world; groups of people with narrow, inward-turning mental habits and loyalties. Such a society obeys the officers of the garrison, whether political, religious, moral, or economic, and whether or not the physical garrison still exists. What there is of culture is highly derivative from the imperial centres. As with all good metaphors, contradictions are possible within the garrison mentality. Frye extended the image in a positive direction, to identify the culturally conscious individual who makes 'the steep and lonely climb into the imaginative world', and so helps form a vital, creative minority, a 'revolutionary garrison' of knowledge and understanding, within urbanized, multicultural Canada.

ALVIN A. LEE

Gaspé. A 21,000 sq km peninsula in southeastern Quebec that extends like a finger into the Gulf of St Lawrence, Gaspé takes its name from the Montagnais word 'Gespeg' ('land's end'). Gaspé is also the name of a town situated at the extreme eastern end of the peninsula that marks the place where in 1534 the French navigator Jacques *Cartier claimed the land that would become Canada on behalf of François I.

History planted in the Gaspé a variety of peoples, from whom the current population of some 100,000 are descended. Approximately 90 per cent are francophones. Aboriginal people have lived in the region since 4000 BC. In the 16th century French fishermen set up a seasonal base there, and later several attempts were made to establish permanent settlements. A few hundred of the Acadian families deported by the English in 1755 moved to the south shore of the peninsula. After the conquest of Canada, in 1760, a number of British traders and discharged soldiers settled in the region. Beginning in 1767 merchants from the French-Norman Channel Islands found their way to this new British territory to exploit the cod fishery. Bringing with them many of their countrymen, they established a commercial empire on the Gaspé coast that would continue into the first quarter of the 20th century. At the time of the American Revolution, hundreds of *Loyalists immigrated to the Gaspé between 1775 and 1785. Throughout the 19th century, Canadians from the Lower St Lawrence travelled to the north coast of the Gaspé to fish in the summers, gradually making their homes there.

Besides the fishery, the main pillars of the Gaspé's economy are the forest and tourism industries. Distance from the country's industrial centres largely explains the region's economic difficulties and high unemployment rates. Nevertheless, the geographic situation of this territory, at the entrance of the St Lawrence and on the route linking the industrial centres of Canada and Europe, does have a strategic value. Indeed, in the 18th century Governor Charles de Beauharnois de la Boische and his intendant, Gilles Hocquart, had called the peninsula the 'Key to Canada' and recommended that the king fortify the site of the town of Gaspé.

JULES BÉLANGER

Gaudreault, Laure (1889–1975), Quebec unionist. Born at La Malbaie, she became a teacher in 1916, discovering the miserable conditions under which women teachers in rural areas lived. In response to deteriorating conditions during the Depression of the 1930s, Gaudreault established the Association catholique des institutrices rurales, and the following year she transformed it into a 'federation'. She published a union journal, *La petite feuille*, 1937–46, and worked tirelessly to improve salaries and pensions for rural women teachers. Her energetic role in the union was recognized in 1946, when three teachers' unions merged to form the Corporation des instituteurs et institutrices catholiques de la province du Québec—the predecessor of the powerful Centrale de l'enseignement du Québec—and Gaudreault was named vice-president. Yet, as a result of this merger the influence female teachers exercised in the teachers' union movement was reduced for nearly a quarter of a century, although they outnumbered their male counterparts.

MICHELINE DUMONT

Gauthier, Éva (Ida Joséphine Phoebe) (1885–1958), avant-garde singer. Born in Ottawa, Gauthier left to study in Europe and there met Emma *Albani, who assisted her. She devoted herself to the art of the recital and gradually made a name as an unconventional artist specializing in little-known works by celebrated composers, 'Oriental' songs, and new works by contemporaries, earning herself the title 'high priestess of the modern lyric art'. Settling in New York, in 1923 she presented a recital of works by George Gershwin, who accompanied her at the piano. Her mezzo-soprano voice was celebrated above all for its intensity of expression. A founding member of the American Guild of Musical Artists, she was a tireless supporter of contemporary vocal music in America. She was survived by the Eva Gauthier Society for Living Song.

ODETTE VINCENT

Gavazzi riots, 1853. Alessandro Gavazzi (1809–89) broke with Catholicism when Pius IX failed to support Italian unification after becoming pope in 1846. The expriest's speeches in England and North America, which were violently anti-papal, sparked rioting by Irish Catholics on 6 June in Quebec City and 9 June in Montreal. In the latter city, ten people were killed and more wounded as troops fired on an unruly crowd outside the church where he had spoken. Sectarian disturbances continued for several days. These events were part of a larger conflict resulting from Protestants' determination to uphold their ascendancy in the face of the heavy influx of Irish Catholics to North America in the 1840s. The riots also reflected political tensions in the united Canadas, when evangelical Protestants failed to stop state support for Catholic schools. Although sectarian collective violence soon abated, conflict based on religion would continue to disrupt Canadian politics for many years to come.

ROBERTO PERIN

gay men and lesbians. 'A conspiracy of silence has robbed lesbians and gay men of their history', boldly declared the Canadian Lesbian and Gay Archives in 1977. Decades later, that silence has been broken, and it is now possible to sketch the broad contours of Canada's lesbian/gay past.

Cases of same-sex activity date from the first centuries of exploration in the territories that would become Canada. The journals of Hudson's Bay and North West Company fur traders reveal that long before the arrival of Europeans many First Nations cultures carved out a special place for those believed to have 'two spirits'—Aboriginal women and men who crossed genders and engaged in same-sex behaviour. References to sodomy have turned up in the Jesuit journals and legal documents of New France from the 1600s and 1700s, while indictments for buggery among soldiers, apprentices, and elite men reflected the social strata of Maritime and Upper and Lower Canadian societies during the early 19th century. What is important to note about this early period is the relatively sporadic use of the law to punish transgressors, and an understanding of same-sex relations not as 'homosexuality' but as a sin or crime against the procreative imperative of colonial life.

By the second half of the 19th century, moral reformers and newspapers began to report the existence of 'Oscar Wilde types' in communities from Medicine Hat, Alberta, to Truro, Nova Scotia. The shift from 'sodomy' and 'buggery' was telling: same-sex activity increasingly became associated with distinct 'types' of people. This emergence of homosexual identities was matched by more extensive regulation. Parliament introduced the offence of 'gross indecency' into Canadian criminal law in 1890: it made any sexual contact between men a crime, paving the way for intensive police surveillance and legal persecution. In turn-of-the-century British Columbia, for instance, prosecutions for homosexual offences fell disproportionately on the province's South Asian communities, revealing the entwined roles of racism and sexual policing.

For much of the 19th and early 20th century, sexual relations between women escaped the purview of the law. Thus, in contrast to the public, legal records central to gay men's history, what we know about lesbians comes primarily from private letters and diaries. The personal nature of lesbian history sources reflects, and women's unequal access to financial resources and public space helps to explain, the fact that much about lesbian life during these years remained private in character. However, as the early 20th century unfolded, lesbian identity would gain greater public circulation, in bohemian, artistic circles (poet Elsa Gidlow in Montreal) and with the spectacular 1929 trial over the censorship of Radclyffe Hall's novel *The Well of Loneliness*, a formative event covered in *Canadian Forum* and other national magazines.

During the Second World War, the Canadian military grappled with same-sex relations within its ranks, and men and women explored the possibilities of same-sex desire in the gender-segregated worlds of military service and wartime production. After the war, lesbian/gay subcultures emerged as visible features of many Canadian cities and towns. Oral histories and sources such as the tabloid press detail the fascinating culture of working-class lesbian bars in the 1950s, and the extensive sexual world of gay men, one revolving around lively lunch counters, darkened theatres, and public washrooms. But the Cold War climate also prompted purges of gay men and lesbians—deemed threats to national security—from the federal public service, as well as the development of Canada's infamous 'fruit machine', a failed, government-funded experiment to develop a machine to detect homosexuality.

Resistance to state and other forms of regulation in the post-war period took a variety of shapes. In Ottawa, individuals refused to co-operate with the *RCMP's efforts to ferret gay people out of the civil service, while Jim Egan, dubbed Canada's 'pioneer gay activist', embarked on a one-man letter-writing campaign to counter homophobic messages in the tabloid press. In the mid-1960s the Vancouver-based Association for Social Knowledge, along with Canada's first gay magazines, *Two* and *Gay*, signalled the advent of homophile organizing. Meanwhile, many gay men and lesbians led courageous sexual lives, circumventing 'sexual psychopath' laws and a powerful psychiatric profession bent on 'curing' homosexuals of their 'illness'.

With the social and political upheavals of the late 1960s came the contemporary lesbian/gay liberation movement. In 1969 the struggle for law reform resulted in the partial decriminalization of homosexual relations between two consenting adults (so long as such business remained confined to the bedrooms of the nation). Gay and lesbian groups sprang up across the country: the Vancouver Gay Liberation Front (1970), the Gay Community Centre of Saskatoon (1973), the Lesbian Organization of Toronto (1976), Montreal's Front de libération homosexuelle (1971), and the Gay Alliance for Equality in Halifax (1972), to name only a few. In August 1971 Canada's first public gay demonstration took place on Parliament Hill, followed a few months later by the first issue of *The Body Politic*, an influential voice for gay liberation. Throughout the 1970s and beyond, lesbian/gay communities in Canada grew sophisticated and strong, rising to the challenge of Toronto's infamous 1981 bathhouse raids and the conservative backlash of the 1980s and 1990s.

In its 1977 manifesto, the Canadian Lesbian and Gay Archives wrote that 'a sense of continuity which derives from the knowledge of a heritage is essential for the building of self confidence in a community'. The centuries-long history of homosexuality in Canada has been one of gradual transformation from sodomitical acts to homosexual identities and lesbian/gay communities, parallelled by a movement from sin to crime, sickness, and affirmation. Animating this historical change has been the ongoing dialectic between regulation and resistance. So sweeping have the changes been that the archives' notion of a singular community can no longer capture the diversity and many differences among lesbians, gay men, bisexuals, and transgendered people. But as we enter a new century of lesbian/gay experience in Canada, a sense of continuity and the knowledge of a heritage—that is, history—will continue to be of lasting importance.

STEVEN MAYNARD

Gélinas, Gratien (1909–99), playwright, founder of La Comédie Canadienne, chairman of the Canadian Film Development Corporation. The creator of Fridolin, a simple, warm, and whimsical revue character, Gélinas is best known for his four plays. *Tit-Coq* (1948) brought fame to the author (who also played the title role on stage and screen) and marks the beginning of modern Quebec *theatre. An illegitimate young soldier believes that his fiancée, Marie-Ange, and her parents are ready to welcome him into their family. But a great war, a wide ocean, and meddling relatives intervene. Tit-Coq, whose quest is thwarted by social (read political) forces, was seen as a symbol of Quebec. In his second play, Gélinas again focuses on an outcast. *Bousille et les justes* (1960) shows how a family can become so perverted that an innocent man is obliged to perjure himself to save a perfect bounder from richly deserved punishment. A rather different view of society comes out of *Hier les enfants dansaient* (1968), which deals with the growing separatist movement. Finally, in his last play, *La passion de Narcisse Mondoux* (1992), Gélinas comes full circle, when the title character is joyfully reunited with the woman from whom he has been separated for 40 years.

MARIEL O'NEILL-KARCH

gender. The use of the term 'gender' as a category of analysis in Canadian history can be traced to the body of work in women's history in Canada but it has also been influenced by debates in feminist theory and history outside of Canada. From the 1970s feminist historians argued that women historically had different experiences than men, in areas such as education, paid labour, the law, the state, the family, and local communities. Their work also pointed to women's different records of activism in various arenas: religion and social reform, *woman's suffrage, *unions, political parties, and organizations representing ethnic and racial-minority communities. This rich body of scholarship inspired scholars to employ the term 'gender' as a way of analyzing how Canadian society, and thus Canadians' experiences, have been structured by differences between women and men.

As well as examining women's position and different experiences, Canadian historians also have turned their attention to explorations of masculinity, as a set of ideologies and practices shaped in relationship to those pertaining to women. This work largely examines the workplace and the family from the late 19th century until the post–Second World War period, particularly as a way of furthering our understanding of changes brought about by industrialization and urbanization. Much of this scholarship has been influenced by materialist and/or Marxist theories and approaches; it seeks to understand how social and economic structures and processes, such as the growth of industrial capitalism and the state, have shaped women's and men's lives and have resulted in unequal relationships within the paid labour force, the union, or the home. But in keeping with both women's history and with other kinds of social history, scholars working in this area seek to document how women (and sometimes men) have attempted to challenge and change dominant models of femininity and masculinity and whether these challenges brought about changes in society.

Historians also have used 'gender' as a means of investigating areas where women were not present in an official capacity, such as the armed forces or 19th-century electoral politics, but where the absence of women has been an important means of securing masculine power and privilege. This scholarship has pointed to the different ways in which ideologies that rely on gendered imagery and symbolism—such as notions of men being effeminate—have been used to legitimate certain types of masculine behaviour and to exclude others. Some of this work has been influenced by cultural historians' and theorists' insights on the importance of language and discourse in shaping meaning in the past. Others influenced by feminist philosophers have drawn our attention to the importance of seeing how Canadian society's understanding of 'woman' or 'man' might have had different meanings in different historical contexts, particularly prior to the advent of industrial capitalism and democratic government.

Another development that has shaped the direction of work in Canadian gender history has been the desire to see how notions of 'gender' have differed according to a number of other relationships and factors. Canadian historians have identified most frequently *class, ethnicity, race, language and culture, religion, and sexuality as influencing the way in which individuals and groups have experienced masculinity and femininity. Others, such as age and marital status, have also been significant.

While there is not complete agreement about the 'best' way of exploring these questions, most historians of women and gender agree that gender has been an important structural feature of Canadian society. Canadians' historical experiences cannot be comprehended fully without understanding the influence of gender relations.

CECILIA MORGAN

General Mining Association. The company was formed in 1826 in London to take advantage of a monopoly over Nova Scotia's mineral resources granted to the Duke of York. The principals, jewellers to whom the duke owed a great deal of money, took on the monopoly in lieu of debts owed them. Actively traded on the London Stock Exchange, the company enjoyed a 30-year monopoly until it was rescinded following negotiations with the government in 1857. It continued to be one of the largest coal operators in Cape Breton County until 1900, when its interests were sold to the Nova Scotia Steel and Coal Corporation.

The General Mining Association was instrumental in the transfer of British technology for deep-pit *coal mining, and largely responsible for introducing steam technology and railways to Nova Scotia. However, controversy surrounded the monopoly exercised by the company, who argued it was necessary to overcome the expense of sinking deep shafts and operating within a volatile New England market. But the determination of colonial governments to control their own natural resources would not permit the continued exercise of such an imperial privilege. The company's determination to profit through opening New England markets gave force to the notion that outside capital was a prerequisite for developing resources for outside consumption, a legacy that lives on in many other aspects of Canada's economic development. D.A. MUISE

Generals Die in Bed. The most famous Canadian novel of the First World War was written by a native of Philadelphia who served in the Canadian infantry. After the war, Charles Yale Harrison worked in Montreal before moving to New York City, where he wrote the novel. Extracts from it appeared in print in 1928, but the entire manuscript was rejected by various American publishers; it was eventually published in England in 1930. Reviews were mixed, and the book was widely condemned in Canada for alleging that Canadian soldiers had pillaged towns and murdered prisoners. According to former Canadian Corps commander Arthur *Currie: 'There is not a single line in it worth reading, nor a single incident worthy of record . . . I have never read . . . a meaner, nastier and more foul book.' Harrison went on to write other books, though none had the power of his first. He died of heart failure in 1954. JONATHAN VANCE

gentlemen emigrants. One of Canada's most colourful immigrant groups consisted of well-born, well-educated settlers from Great Britain, the 'gentlemen emigrants'. Their ranks included retired military officers and youthful graduates of elite British public schools. Some came in search of wealth or adventure, some to escape scandal, and most emigrated because they were unable to find suitable careers at home. Many remained emotionally attached to the Old Country and so considered themselves British emigrants, not Canadian immigrants. They were prominent in the West, where they invested in the *ranching industry and urban real estate, and established libraries and theatres in many frontier communities. Despite their economic and cultural contributions, they were not universally admired. Their tendency to affect mannerisms and attitudes associated with the British aristocracy exasperated many Canadians. *Remittance men, who received regular stipends from their families in Britain and devoted themselves to leisure activities instead of physical labour, were particularly resented.

Cannington Manor near present-day Moosomin, Saskatchewan, was a haven for these settlers. Founded in 1882, it was renowned for its hotel bar, race course, and jockey club. But the convivial settlement failed to develop an economic base and collapsed in 1902. Walhachin, in the Thompson River valley of British Columbia, was the same kind of place. Established in 1910 as a horticultural centre, it was better known for its dance hall and hunt club. For a variety of reasons, orchards never flourished and the community was abandoned by its genteel residents after the First World War. PATRICK DUNAE

Geological Survey of Canada. In 1842, the United Province of Canada established the Geological Survey of Canada to develop a geological profile of the country in order to facilitate the fledgling mining industry. This emphasis on economic geology would become a defining feature of the survey under its first director, Montreal-born William E. *Logan, and ensure its survival into the 20th century as a permanent government institution. Logan, with a small budget and equally small staff that included the pioneer geochemist T. Sterry Hunt, identified and mapped the province's major geological features, in particular the Precambrian Shield. This fieldwork formed the basis of Logan's *Geology of Canada* (1863), and provided specimens for several impressive mineral displays at international exhibitions in the mid-19th century. It also helped secure the young agency's reputation in the world scientific community.

The GSC's field of inquiry expanded exponentially with Confederation in 1867 and the transfer of *Rupert's Land and the northwestern territory three years later. It also faced enlarged duties. The wide-ranging field activities that the survey was required to perform in the Northwest transcended the bounds of traditional geology; most areas, for example, required general exploration and topographical surveys, let alone detailed geological mapping. The survey met this challenge as best it could, but its financial and staff resources were entirely disproportionate to the task at hand. Much of the survey's success depended on the energy and initiative of a handful of scientists working in difficult and often hazardous conditions in remote areas.

The GSC's new assignment coincided with the appointment of a new director, Dr Alfred Selwyn. The British-born geologist, who headed the survey for almost a quarter century, realized that his officers would initially have to concentrate on description and collection in the Northwest—in other words, on 'inventory science'—as opposed to specialized fieldwork. He also recognized that the government agency had been founded in the belief that scientific knowledge was to be used for practical and immediate results. There would consequently be no testing of the celebrated British naturalist Charles Darwin's theory of natural selection in the vast natural-history laboratory of the western interior; instead, scientific exploration would be essentially Baconian in approach in an attempt to discover possible uses for the region's many resources.

Although the GSC did not neglect Ontario, Quebec, and the Maritime provinces in the 1870s, the majority of its field endeavours were concentrated in the Northwest. Given the vastness of the new territory and the amount of general reconnaissance work that was required, Dr Robert *Bell, George Mercer *Dawson, and R.G. McConnell (all future directors) concentrated on collecting data, including specimens, on a wide range of topics and indicating areas that merited future in-depth study. The tackling of geological problems generally had to wait for another day. It was a respectable start, as evidenced by the fact that the GSC was made a permanent branch of the

Department of the Interior in 1877 and renamed the Geological and Natural History Survey of Canada, with responsibility for examining the flora and fauna of the dominion. Four years later, the survey and its museum were relocated from Montreal to Ottawa, so that it could be placed directly under federal control and supervision.

The increased duties were accompanied by more federal funding in the early 1880s. Selwyn used the improved financial situation to hire better-educated and more highly specialized officers. He also embarked on one of the most ambitious and longest-running programs in GSC history—the production of a geological map of Canada on a scale of one inch to four miles. This systematic mapping of Canada's geology was initially confined to known areas in central and eastern Canada that were readily accessible and capable of immediate development. The West, however, was not neglected. In response to the rerouting of the *Canadian Pacific Railway main line across the southern prairies, a series of regional surveys were conducted in present-day southern Alberta and Saskatchewan.

The GSC also continued to send out general reconnaissance surveys, particularly into subarctic and arctic regions, into the 20th century. In 1884, for example, A.P. *Low made the first of what would be a two-decade survey of central Quebec and Labrador. Three years later, the survey's field operations extended beyond the Arctic Circle for the first time, when Selwyn dispatched a three-pronged expedition (Dawson, McConnell, and dominion land surveyor William *Ogilvie) to explore and map the Yukon Territory. Perhaps one of the most celebrated trips during the period was J.B. *Tyrrell's 1893 crossing of the *Barren Lands. Some critics questioned the value of these expeditions, but the GSC could not in good conscience leave the distant regions unexplored, especially when these areas might provide invaluable scientific information. Survey officers were also usually the first representatives of the federal government in remote areas.

Another important consequence of the reconnaissance surveys was the vast array of geological, ethnological, and *natural history objects that survey officers gathered in the field each season. These collecting efforts had an unanticipated effect on institutional development in Ottawa. In the course of retrieving specimens, the GSC soon became the custodian of what was generally acknowledged as a magnificent national collection. But survey headquarters had no place to store or display the material adequately. The beautiful Victoria Memorial Museum (renamed the National Museum of Canada in 1927) was consequently built in downtown Ottawa in 1912 to showcase these treasures. At the time, it was argued that a new national museum would be a wonderful advertising medium for the resources of the country—it was not enough to justify the building on the grounds of science alone.

By the start of the Great War, the great GSC explorations that had been performed under government auspices since the mid-19th century began to be replaced by more specialized surveys by more highly qualified personnel. This new emphasis on detailed geological work was reflected in the GSC's transfer to the new federal Department of Mines in 1907 and then Mines and Resources in 1936. It did not mean, though, that the agency's natural history research came to an end; the GSC would retain responsibility for the museum and its associated work until after the Second World War. Nor did the survey completely abandon economic geology; it continued to assist and encourage mineral development, especially in the 1930s and 1940s.

Since the end of the Second World War, the GSC has gone through another major transformation. Thanks to motorized transportation, the nature and amount of fieldwork has been dramatically altered. There has also been a new emphasis on scientific research for its own sake. The most revolutionary and far-reaching innovation, however, has been the development of electronic systems for measuring distance. The GSC has become a recognized world leader in remote sensing—the collection and processing of natural resource and environmental information using imagery secured by airplanes and spacecraft. It is also a pioneer in geographical- and land-information systems. Although it took a century and a half, the GSC has ably met the challenge of Canada's having 'too much geography'. BILL WAISER

geomagnetism. Although knowledge of the earth's magnetic properties dates back to ancient times, European interest intensified with early modern overseas exploration. The Scientific Revolution linked scientific observation to material progress, and dreams of confirming a *Northwest Passage to the riches of the Orient remained unfulfilled because of the compass's unreliability in northern navigation. William Gilbert's famous treatise on the theory of magnetism, *De Magnete* (1660), inspired long-term co-operation between the Royal Society of London and the Royal Navy towards systematic collections of geomagnetic data relating three components of magnetism: declination (variation), the horizontal angle between geographic and magnetic north; dip, the vertical angle between a suspended needle and the horizontal plane; and intensity in the earth's magnetism to various points in time and place on the earth.

Interest in pinpointing the north magnetic pole focused scientific and navigational investigations on the arctic region beyond the settled parts of the British North American colonies. The peace of 1815 left a superabundance of military officers with scientific training, opening a new era of *Arctic exploration, including expeditions led by John Ross (1818), William Parry (1919), and John *Franklin (1821, 1825), with geomagnetic readings conducted for Ross and Parry by Edward Sabine, Royal Artillery (RA). James Clark Ross located the north magnetic pole on Boothia Peninsula (1831). Motivated by the German scientific traveller Alexander von Humboldt, Sabine persuaded the Royal Society and British Admiralty to establish a worldwide network of imperial geomagnetic observatories, including one at Toronto (1839). He assigned John Henry *Lefroy, RA, who was directing observations on the island at St Helena, off the coast of

Africa, to undertake an overland arctic geomagnetic survey in North America. With one assistant and co-operation from the Hudson's Bay Company, Lefroy spent an arduous winter (1843–4) taking regular readings as far north as the Arctic Circle. The resulting isogonic lines on Sabine's maps completed a previously suspected elliptical pattern that varied with time, weather, and the appearance of the aurora borealis. Lefroy directed the Toronto observatory until 1853, when his recall persuaded the Canadian government to take over its oldest scientific institution. Lefroy's international scientific reputation included expertise on the aurora and co-operation with American scientists to instigate a continental telegraphic storm-warning system. Canada participated in the International Polar Year (1882–3) with Lefroy's remarkable record of geomagnetic observations, a tradition continued by the *Geological Survey of Canada and the institutional antecedents of Environment Canada.

SUZANNE ZELLER

Georgia Straight. Established by a group of Vancouver poets, this bimonthly newspaper was a response to the mainstream media's 'campaign against the youth culture'. As befitted an 'underground' publication, the first issue was published in a Kitsilano neighbourhood apartment in May 1967. In less than six months it achieved a circulation of 60,000.

While the local press detailed the wayward ways of youth, the *Straight* took aim at the values underlying mainstream opinion. With a combination of idealism, humour, and outrage, its writers addressed topics ranging from personal hygiene and homophobia to Hendrix and hallucinogens. Its support of 'dropping out' notwithstanding, the newspaper's hallmark was its political engagement—something that won it both supporters and enemies. In its first two years, the publication's licence was suspended and several municipalities banned its sale. It faced charges of criminal libel and obscenity, and of 'inciting to commit an indictable offence' for printing instructions on marijuana growing.

Despite harassment, it flourished. The only Canadian underground publication from the 1960s remaining today, and one of a handful in North America (it predates *Rolling Stone*), the *Straight* is a mainstay of the alternative media, its success especially remarkable in the context of media concentration and 'convergence'. TINA LOO

Gérin-Lajoie, Antoine (1824–82), journalist, writer, lawyer, and public servant, born at Yamachiche, Lower Canada. As a student at Nicolet College he wrote the poem 'Un Canadien errant' (1842) and *Le Jeune Latour* (1844), the first Canadian tragedy. He was a founding member and president of the *Institut canadien, a journalist for *La Minerve* (1845–7), and the author of *Catéchisme politique* (1851). He was a translator to the assembly of the Province of Canada and, later, from 1856 to 1880, assistant librarian at the Library of Parliament. He helped found the literary magazines *Les Soirées Canadiennes* and *Le Foyer Canadien*, of which he was the leading figure. His most famous work is a two-part novel, *Jean Rivard, le défricheur* (1862) and *Jean Rivard, économiste* (1864), which extols the virtue of clearing uncultivated land in Quebec as a means of ensuring survival of the French-Canadian nation. Part of his *Mémoires* and an important historical work, *Dix ans au Canada, de 1840 à 1850*, were published after his death in Ottawa in 1882.

RENÉ DIONNE

Germans. People of German-speaking background have migrated to Canada from the beginning of European settlement. By 1991 every tenth Canadian acknowledged German ethnic origin. Almost two-thirds of Canada's estimated 400,000 German-speaking immigrants from 1650 to 1950 were from lands other than Germany; only among the 380,000 migrants from 1950 to 1994 have natives of Germany predominated. From their homelands and history of previous migrations, immigrants transplanted a mosaic of German cultures, including ancestral traits that had died out in Germany.

German migrations to Canada can be divided into six major waves: the arrivals from the 1650s to 1776; the influx generated by the American Revolution, 1776–1830s; the Ontario settlers, 1830–80, the colonizers of western Canada, 1874–1914; the immigrants between the world wars; and the post–Second World War influx.

Prior to 1760, Germans came to New France primarily in the service of the French military forces. German Swiss guards were members of the first French expedition to Acadia in 1604. In Quebec settlers from Germany are recorded from the 1660s on. Following the British conquest, Germans came with the British militias and rose to prominence in Quebec as businessmen, doctors, surveyors, engineers, silversmiths, and furriers. Canada's oldest German settlement developed in Nova Scotia in 1750–3, when 2,400 Protestant southwest German farmers and tradesmen with their families landed in Halifax. They were recruited by British agents to strengthen Britain's position vis-à-vis the French. In 1753, 1,400 of these Germans started the nearby community of *Lunenburg. Although arriving with no marine skills, they became expert fishermen, sailors, and boatbuilders by the next generation.

The American Revolution triggered the migration of *Loyalists, among whom Germans were the largest group of non-British descent, constituting an estimated 10–20 per cent of the refugees fleeing to Canada by 1786. To suppress the revolution, Britain contracted some 30,000 auxiliary troops in Germany. Of these so-called Hessians, 12,000 were stationed on Canadian soil in 1776–83 and an estimated 2,400 remained. On their heels arrived *Mennonites from Pennsylvania. These pacifist farmers fled the fervour of American nationalism and sought land for their growing population. Preferring cohesive settlement, they acquired a huge tract in Waterloo County, Upper Canada. Through chain migration, they transplanted their families, co-religionists, and Pennsylvania German culture. Between the 1830s and 1850s they also attracted some 50,000 newcomers from Germany to their colony. Its capital, named Berlin (renamed Kitchener in

1916 in response to anti-German fervour during the First World War), developed into an area of concentrated German settlement. From there, German settlers spread to the surrounding Perth, Huron, Bruce, and Grey Counties. In the 1860s the American Civil War diverted America-bound Germans to the agriculturally marginal wilderness lands of the upper Ottawa Valley, where a population of 12,000 Germans from Prussia settled by 1891.

Of the 152,000 German pioneer settlers in western Canada by 1911, more than half came from eastern Europe. Some 7,000 Mennonites, who in Russia were losing their exemption from military service, blazed the trail 1874–9. Their East and West Reserves in Manitoba demonstrated that farmers from the Russian steppes adapted well to prairie farming and that ethnically and denominationally homogeneous *bloc settlement proved a viable strategy for colonizing the West. They attracted a continuous flow of co-religionists from Europe and the United States to the Canadian Prairies. In 1918, Canada admitted 1,000 Hutterites and 500–600 Mennonites fleeing intense American intolerance towards pacifists. All but one of the 18 Hutterite colonies in the United States settled in western Canada and were granted immunity from military service. In May 1919, however, Canada prohibited the entry of Hutterites and Mennonites until 1921, and nationals of former enemy countries until 1923.

From 1924 to 1930, 52 per cent of Canada's 100,000 German immigrants came from eastern Europe and 18 per cent from the United States. The immigration from Europe was organized by agencies of the Canadian railways (CPR and CNR) in co-operation with Mennonite, Baptist, Lutheran, and Catholic immigration boards. Some 21,000 Mennonite refugees from Soviet Russia, barred from the United States by quotas, were Canada's largest group of ethnic German immigrants in the 1920s. In the 1930s, Canada denied sanctuary to most Jewish refugees from the Third Reich, except for 972 from a group of 2,300 sent in 1940 from British to Canadian internment camps. Many of the 972 later made outstanding contributions to Canadian cultural life. The only other German refugees admitted in 1939–40 were 1,043 Sudeten German Social Democrats. From 1947 to 1950 Canada admitted some 15,000 *volksdeutsche* (east European ethnic Germans) as *displaced persons. The readmission of German nationals in 1950 opened the flood gates to a quarter million German newcomers by 1960, about one-third of them ethnic German refugees from eastern Europe.

Diversity of origins has not prevented German-speaking immigrants from interacting as a single community throughout Canadian history. From eastern to western Canada, German communities composed of immigrants from every possible German-speaking background formed the predominant pattern of German settlement, as well as of membership in churches and voluntary ethnic associations. However, the trauma of being stigmatized as enemy aliens in two world wars caused many German Canadians to camouflage or jettison their German identity. GERHARD P. BASSLER

Gesner, Abraham (1797–1863), geologist, chemist, entrepreneur. Born in the Annapolis Valley, Gesner studied medicine in London in 1825–6. Between 1836 and 1846, he published geological surveys of Nova Scotia, New Brunswick, and Prince Edward Island. While serving as NS Indian commissioner, he prepared *New Brunswick with Notes for Emigrants* (1847) and *The Industrial Resources of Nova Scotia* (1849). While experimenting with cracking coals, Gesner extracted a superior illuminating gas, dubbed kerosene, using as a raw material some bitumen located in Albert County, NB. His attempt to secure the mineral rights to that albertite seam ended disastrously for him in major lawsuits in Halifax and Fredericton. In 1853, he moved to New York to work as a chemist manufacturing kerosene fluid. He described the process in his influential *A Practical Treatise on Coal, Petroleum and other Distilled Oils*. He died weeks after being appointed to the chair of Natural History at Dalhousie College.

ELIZABETH HAIGH

Gilbert, Sir Humphrey (*c.* 1537–83), soldier, early proponent of a northwest passage and British colonization of Ireland and America. Although reputed 'of not good happ by sea', he promoted schemes for expeditions to Norumbega (New England) and finally set sail, in 1583, with an ill-equipped piratical fleet of five ships, intending to rendezvous at St John's, Newfoundland, for provisions. There he found French, Portuguese, and English migratory fishing crews, who rescued him when he ran aground, and from whom he then extorted supplies and rents, after claiming Newfoundland for Britain by erecting a lead plaque. He sailed onwards towards Sable Island for further provisions with three ships but, with the largest lost in a storm, turned back with his remaining captain, Edward Hayes, who last glimpsed Gilbert on the deck of his tiny bark *Squirrel*, shouting 'We are as near to heaven by sea as by land'. Though among the first to suggest English colonization of America, Gilbert achieved little. He followed the wake of fishermen to Newfoundland, claimed authority there he could not sustain, and drowned before he reached the North American coast he had promoted for colonization. Histrionic to the end, he remains an Elizabethan celebrity: famous for being famous.

PETER E. POPE

Ginger Group. The name given to a faction of Progressive MPs elected in 1921 who demonstrated their opposition to *Progressive collaboration with Mackenzie King's Liberal cabinet in 1924 by refusing to caucus with other Progressive MPs. They believed such a collaboration implied acceptance of what they considered the undemocratic practices of old party 'machines', and that it would involve abandoning their defence of economically beleagured prairie farmers and their support of a distinctive, anti-capitalist co-operative economic philosophy. The Ginger Group included Robert Gardiner, E.J. Garland, G.G. Coote, D.M. Kennedy, J.T. Shaw, and H.E. Spencer from Alberta, M.N. Campbell from Saskatchewan, W.J. Ward from Manitoba, and Preston Elliot, W.C.

*Good, and Agnes *Macphail from Ontario. Most of these MPs went on to be leading figures in the early years of the *Co-operative Commonwealth Federation; in fact, their co-operation in Parliament with Labour MPs J.S. *Woodsworth and William Irvine was a crucial step in the creation of the CCF's farmer-labour political alliance.

DAVID LAYCOCK

Girl Guides. Founded in 1909 by Robert Baden-Powell's sister Agnes as the sister organization to the *Boy Scouts, their purpose was to include young girls in the program of forging patriotic and loyal youth. Doing good deeds, helping out, and acquiring badges were all part of the program, as was the seminal dictate 'Be prepared'. Less militaristic then its male counterpart, the Girl Guides provided girls an outdoor outlet and a refreshing opportunity to move beyond the bounds of a traditional girlhood and to explore new options. At the same time, the Girl Guide structure was in no way radical and sought to instill very traditional notions about the role of women in society. Despite the oppressive pedagogy of its charter and rules, it nonetheless served to introduce young women to the wonders of nature and the freedom of physical activity.

MARK MOSS

Goin' Down the Road (1970). Made on a low budget by a young filmmaker, Donald Shebib, *Goin' Down the Road* told the story of two likeable working-class youths from the Maritimes seeking opportunity and advancement in the Toronto of the late 1960s. Memorably acted by Doug McGrath (Pete) and Paul Bradley (Joey), the young men encountered misadventures that were more tragic than comic in their implications. The film captured a classic experience of outmigration from the Maritimes and portrayed the underclass of working poor in the big city with compassionate appreciation. William Fruet's screenplay and Richard Leiterman's camera gave the film the authenticity of a documentary. A strong supporting cast included Jayne Eastwood. Bruce Cockburn provided a musical score. The film enjoyed both critical and commercial success and is frequently identified as one of the finest Canadian films ever made. It was re-released in 1999. Like Claude Jutra's **Mon Oncle Antoine* (1971), *Goin' Down the Road* is considered one of the turning points in the history of Canadian film because it helped encourage public support for Canadian filmmaking and a new wave of feature films on Canadian themes in the 1970s.

DAVID FRANK

Good, William Charles (1876–1967), farmer, politician, co-operative leader. Born near Brantford, Ontario, Good was raised on a farm called Myrtleville, where he resided most of his life. Influenced by Methodism and involvement in social and political questions as a student at the University of Toronto, he became a key agrarian leader. Serving on the executive of the Farmers' Association, he encouraged its amalgamation with the Dominion Grange in 1907. He helped prepare the Canadian Council of Agriculture's constitution and found the United Farmers of Ontario and the United Farmers Co-operative. A *Progressive member of the House of Commons (1921–5), deeply interested in the limits of democratic practice, he was an expert on proportional representation and an advocate for economic democracy through co-operatives. As president of the Co-operative Union of Canada (1921–45), he helped define the Canadian *co-operative movement in its formative years. In his retirement, he became the movement's beloved elder statesman.

IAN MacPHERSON

Goodwin, Albert 'Ginger' (1887–1918). Born in Yorkshire, England, Goodwin participated in the coal mine strikes of Glace Bay, Nova Scotia (1909–10) and Vancouver Island (1912–14.) Blacklisted, he moved to Trail, BC, to work at the Cominco smelter. He was a Socialist Party of Canada candidate in 1916 and held positions in the International Union of Mine, Mill and Smelterworkers (Mine-Mill) and the BC Federation of Labour. Goodwin opposed the First World War and was declared medically unfit for service—until Mine-Mill struck *Cominco. Then he was re-examined and miraculously found fit. A draft-dodger wanted by police, he headed to Cumberland, Vancouver Island. On 27 July 1918, Goodwin was shot and killed by a Dominion Police constable who claimed self-defence. Many believed Goodwin was ambushed, and on 2 August Vancouver workers launched Canada's first general strike in protest. Today his rough-hewn tombstone remembers Goodwin as 'A worker's friend'.

MARK LEIER

Gordon, Charles W. (1860–1937). Born on Indian lands, Glengarry County, Canada West, Gordon studied theology at Knox College in Toronto after graduating from the University of Toronto. The Presbytery of Calgary ordained him to the ministry in 1889 and he began missionary work among miners and lumbermen in the Banff region. His concern for adequate resources for mission work in the West motivated him to write fictional accounts of heroic missionary activity, under the pseudonym Ralph Connor. He wrote 24 novels, a biography of his mentor in western missions, James Robertson, numerous devotional pamphlets, a dramatic account of the life of Jesus, and his memoirs, *Postscript to Adventure*. In the latter he suggested that the 'authentic picture' of western Canada and the religious motif of his stories accounted for their enormous appeal. Gordon also believed that the Christian gospel should be applied to social conditions. He was an exponent of *temperance and Sunday observance and served as a labour mediator. Believing that the First World War was a Christian crusade, he enlisted as a chaplain and served overseas. In 1922, he became moderator of the General Assembly of the Presbyterian Church. He successfully encouraged the church to resume negotiations to enter union with the Methodists and Congregationalists.

DAVID B. MARSHALL

Gordon, Walter Lockhart (1906–87), public servant, politician. Gordon attended Royal Military College, joined the family accounting firm in 1927, and became a partner in 1935. He served as adviser to two public enquiries in the 1930s, and during the Second World War was three times seconded to the *Bank of Canada and the Ministry of Finance. In 1955–7 he chaired a major royal commission on Canada's economic prospects. His growing anxiety over Canada's economic independence drew him into close association with new Liberal leader L.B. *Pearson after 1958, and in 1963 he became finance minister in the Pearson government. Gordon's first budget faced severe criticism, and parts of it were withdrawn under pressure. Never a complacent partisan, he resigned from cabinet after the 1965 election, returning briefly to supervise the Watkins task force on Canadian industry, 1967–8. In the 1970s he inspired creation of the Committee for an Independent Canada with Peter Newman, Abraham Rotstein, Jack McClelland, and Claude Ryan, promoting a series of nationalist measures later adopted by Ottawa. Gordon published an autobiography and books on Canadian economic independence, and actively advocated nuclear arms control and disarmament during a public life of integrity. DENIS SMITH

Gosden, Robert Raglan (1882–1961), labour activist, police spy. Born in England, Gosden went to sea at an early age. In Prince Rupert by 1911, he was imprisoned for his role in a road construction workers' strike instituted by the *Industrial Workers of the World. Later he wrote newspaper articles advocating revolution and sabotage, and was imprisoned in the United States. He returned to British Columbia to participate in the Vancouver Island coal miners' strike, where he advocated sabotage and suggested that assassinating the premier might be a useful tactic. By 1919, however, Gosden was disillusioned with the labour and radical movements; he became the notorious 'Agent 10' of the *RCMP and spied on *unions during the wave of general strikes. In one of his reports, he advocated 'disappearing' labour leaders as a way to crush the labour revolt. Exposed as a spy, he worked as a gardener and general labourer before retiring to Gibsons, BC. MARK LEIER

Gould, Glenn Herbert (1932–82). A musical phenomenon who earned an associate diploma at the Toronto Conservatory of Music at age 12, he made his Toronto Symphony debut at 14 and was performing throughout Canada by 19. His American debuts in Washington and New York in 1955 were critically acclaimed and resulted in an exclusive contract with Columbia Records. His 1955 recording of J.S. Bach's *Goldberg Variations* was an enormous critical and popular success, gaining him invitations to perform in the world's finest concert halls and with renowned conductors. He toured internationally for only nine years, however, ceasing all concertizing in 1964 and devoting himself thereafter to recording and writing music, and producing radio and TV documentaries.

Ranked among the 20th century's finest keyboard artists, he is celebrated for his mastery of contrapuntal music—notably that of Bach, although his repertoire was broad—and for his deeply original insights into musical interpretation and recording. His technical virtuosity, intellectual brilliance, and musical iconoclasm, coupled with personal eccentricities such as chronic overdressing, avoiding physical contact with others, and total seclusion in his later years, provoked controversy during his life and led to the posthumous conclusion that he had Asperger's syndrome, a form of autism. S. TIMOTHY MALONEY

Gourlay, Robert (1778–1863). An agrarian radical who distrusted authority and believed in the widest possible distribution of property ownership, Gourlay was a prolific author with a flair for invective and self-aggrandizement. Born in Scotland, he came to Upper Canada in 1817, was twice acquitted of seditious libel in 1818 and was banished from the colony for sedition in 1819. He was preoccupied with vindication until his death. In Upper Canada to repair his fortunes by promoting British emigration, Gourlay called township meetings to answer a questionnaire. Results appeared in his *Statistical Account of Upper Canada* (1822). Capitalizing on local discontent after the War of 1812, he moved from information gathering to escalating charges of colonial mal-administration, heaping abuse on leading colonial figures, and calling for mass petitioning of Britain. Fearful of his unprecedented use of print and public meetings, colonial leaders turned to the courts to silence Gourlay, but they created a martyr by zealously pursuing the case despite his deteriorating mental health. JEFFREY L. McNAIRN

gouttes de lait. Part of the struggle against infant mortality, these 'drops of milk', which began as centres providing clean milk to poor mothers who were not breast-feeding, became clinics where doctors and nurses taught women how to take care of their babies. They took their name from France, where similar clinics had been created in the late 19th century. In Quebec the first *gouttes de lait* was founded in Montreal in 1901. After 1910 the centres multiplied, first in Montreal, then in Quebec City (from 1915), Sherbrooke (1922), and other cities. Parish-based, they were often initiated by groups of middle-class women. In Montreal, beginning in 1919, the municipal heath service created its own 'baby consultation' network with the same objective, but by then the name *goutte de lait* had become so well established that women used it for the municipal clinics as well. The *gouttes de lait* disappeared in the 1960s, after nearly 60 years in the forefront of social-health services in many Quebec cities. DENYSE BAILLARGEON

Gouzenko, Igor (1919–82). Born in the Soviet Union, Gouzenko was appointed cipher clerk in the Soviet embassy in Ottawa in 1943 as a member of GRU, Soviet military intelligence. On 5 September 1945 he took documents from the embassy indicating a Soviet spy ring operating in Canada. After initial failed attempts to defect, and an abortive Soviet attempt to seize him, he was taken into protective custody two days later. His defection was kept secret for five months, but on 15 February 1946 suspects were swept up and held for interrogation. The news of the spy ring created an international sensation, signalling the public beginning of the Cold War. Fearing Soviet retribution, Gouzenko and his family were kept hidden and he himself appeared in public wearing a trademark bag over his head. He published an autobiography, *This Was My Choice*, in 1948, and in 1954 he won the Governor General's Award for a novel, *Fall of a Titan*. He continued to warn of the Soviet threat, and launched lawsuits against writers who questioned his behaviour.

REG WHITAKER

government regulation of business. Government regulation aims to shape the economic behaviour of private firms, particularly their decisions with respect to prices and the kinds of services they offer to the public, or decisions about production that are determined to have negative consequences for society. Historically, Canadian governments have relied on a broad range of regulatory instruments. During the 19th century Canadian governments adopted legislative rules, and expected them to be policed through the court system, sometimes with the assistance of specialized inspectors or other officials. Governments also placed conditions on businesses in exchange for access to public funds, Crown resources, or licences. In the 20th century governments increasingly chose to establish only broad standards in legislation; they granted specialized officials working in departments, boards, or agencies the power to develop and enforce more precise rules that derived from and were consistent with those standards. At the same time, governments acquired and operated some firms within economic sectors, ostensibly to use these public enterprises to set standards, offer competition, and provide a behavioural model for the remaining private firms. Particularly after the Second World War governments also used the *taxation system to encourage or deter certain kinds of private business decisions.

Regulations of various kinds were most often applied to businesses that were deemed to be public *utilities, such as transportation, communication, and energy companies. Canada's first national regulatory agency—the *Board of Railway Commissioners—was granted broad powers by the government in 1903 to regulate disputes between railways and shippers over matter such as rates and conditions of carriage, and between railways and communities over issues such as safety and property. Three years later the commission gained similar authority over disputes arising from the operations of *Bell Telephone, although some provinces and municipal governments opted for *public ownership or for their own regulatory commission in order to control local telephone development. Hydroelectric companies increasingly were subject to local utility commissions, but Ontario chose control through public ownership as early as 1906. Coal and later oil and gas companies remained relatively free of these kinds of controls, although British Columbia imposed some controls in 1937, and Alberta created a regulatory board in 1938 to determine the optimal use of oil and gas fields. In 1959 the Canadian government created the National Energy Board to regulate the rates charged by interprovincial pipeline companies, to approve energy imports and exports, and to advise the government on national energy requirements. As this last example suggests, whereas earlier regulatory agencies tended to focus on policing behaviour and resolving disputes, increasingly in the 20th century they were given mandates to plan, or provide planning advice, for the economic sector they governed.

KEN CRUIKSHANK

governor general. The Constitution Act, 1867 (section 12), refers to but does not create this office, which represents the sovereign in Canada. That was done by Letters Patent issued in 1878. In 1947, new Letters Patent made a complete delegation of all the sovereign's powers so that the governor general, acting on Canadian advice, could legally exercise all prerogative powers. These include, among others, the power to summon, prorogue, and dissolve Parliament; to see that there is always a prime minister (and, by extension, a government), to sign *orders-in-council and other state documents; and to give royal assent to bills passed by both houses of Parliament. Within the provinces these powers, as they relate to matters of provincial jurisdiction, are exercised by the ten lieutenant-governors.

Today, the governor general is the Crown in Canada. As such, it is commonly asserted that the office symbolizes the unity of the country, a claim supported by the governor general's extensive domestic travel, maintenance of residences in Ottawa (*Rideau Hall) and Quebec City (the Citadel), and by a pattern of appointment that acknowledges Canada's bilingual and multicultural heritage. Symbolic representation should not disguise the pragmatic role the office has played in Canada's political evolution. *Monarchy remains the last constitutional link with Great Britain, but its Canadianization confirmed the country's autonomy from London and its independence in the eyes of others. Since 1926 the governor general represents the sovereign alone and no longer the government of Great Britain. Beginning with Vincent *Massey (1952), only Canadians have been appointed to the office by the sovereign on recommendation of the Canadian government.

DAVID E. SMITH

governors of British North America. Governors were important people in the *British Empire, typically standing at the head of colonial government and society. Most were appointed by the Crown, some by individuals or companies holding colonial charters. After the *American Revolution (1775–83) most of Britain's remaining colonies on the North American continent had governors sent out by the British government; Red River settlement, 1811–70, and Vancouver Island, 1849–59, had governors selected by the *Hudson's Bay Company.

The first provincial government established by the British in the territory that was to comprise Canada was in peninsular Nova Scotia, formerly the heartland of Acadia, which had been acquired from the French as a spoil of war in 1713. Here imperial officials established a governor and council, to which they later added an assembly. A Nova Scotia threatened by France needed a decisive chief executive. A succession of military men seemed to fit the bill. One, Charles Lawrence, has often been thought responsible for the decision of 1755 to expel the Acadians from the colony, lest they aid the French in retaking it. Many suffered grievously, as has Lawrence's reputation, though Admiral Edward Boscawen seems to have been the principal architect of the scheme.

When the English took New France in 1760, a conquest recognized in 1763, they continued to enlist military men as governors. To improve the temper of the mainly French inhabitants of the new colony, Governor Guy *Carleton recommended a series of propitiatory measures, including recognition of the Catholic Church. His plans were capped by the *Quebec Act of 1774. When the *habitants failed to support Britain enthusiastically against the Americans and their former French compatriots during the American Revolution, a disillusioned Carleton felt betrayed. In 1786 as Lord Dorchester he returned as governor of Quebec—indeed, as governor general of Britain's remaining possessions in North America. In this latter capacity he, and later governors general, followed the practice of the French regime, which had seen the governor of Quebec the superior of the governor of Acadia and Île Royale (Cape Breton). In both the French and English regimes, however, the governors general exercised at best a shadowy authority over their supposed inferiors, who in the British colonies bore the title 'lieutenant-governor'. Confusingly, governors general and lieutenant-governors both were commonly referred to as 'governors'. Occasionally, the governor general at Quebec did call subordinates to heel, as Dorchester did with Lieutenant-Governor John Graves *Simcoe of Upper Canada, who sought to pursue a virtually independent military and diplomatic policy vis-à-vis the Americans.

The governor general at Quebec was joined by a lieutenant-governor, who helped with day-to-day affairs and acted for the former when he was away. These two officials and the lieutenant-governors in the other colonies exercised civil authority, appointing a host of functionaries, most notably the various councillors as well as local magistrates. They reserved legislation for the consideration of the British authorities when they felt that it needed review. In short, they were, or could be, virtually their own prime ministers. Unsurprisingly, many became embroiled in partisan politics. In Lower Canada, for instance, long and bitter financial battles with the assembly were fought by governors George Ramsay, Earl of Dalhousie; Sir James Kempt; and Matthew Whitworth, Baron Aylmer. There the governor general came to be seen as the head of the *Château Clique, a group of mostly English-Canadian functionaries representing commercial interests mixed with some French-Canadian office-holders and aristocrats.

A similar situation developed in Upper Canada, where politics were also embittered and where successive lieutenant-governors were seen by the *Reformers as creatures of the *Family Compact, which, in its narrow power base and pursuit of special interests, resembled the Château Clique. Both Upper and Lower Canada experienced *rebellions in 1837 and attendant troubles thereafter. The British government despatched a civilian, John George Lambton, the Earl of *Durham, as the new governor general to investigate discontents and propose remedies. His 1839 report made two key recommendations: he implicitly suggested the grant of *responsible government, which came to be understood as the control of the administration by the dominant party in the assembly, and he explicitly advocated the union of the Canadas (though he actually preferred a union of all British North America). The British government could agree to the second but not the first, feeling it incompatible with colonial status.

The United Canadas were locked in a furious battle over responsible government for the better part of a decade. Successive governors arrived with instructions to be conciliatory but not to concede responsible government. Two in particular, Charles Poulett Thomson (later Lord Sydenham) and Charles Metcalfe, were excoriated by the Reformers for their obduracy, but they were the prisoners of their instructions—though, in truth, granting responsible government accorded with neither's personal predilections. When responsible government came in the Canadas, it did so under the governorship of James Bruce, the Earl of Elgin, whose instructions allowed him to be magnanimous. He was able to let the Reformers, victorious in the elections to the assembly, remake the administration by sacking Tory office-holders and appointing their own supporters. Sir John Harvey, lieutenant-governor of Nova Scotia, and former lieutenant-governor of New Brunswick and Newfoundland, had a few short weeks before he acted in accordance with the principles of responsible government, and with directives from London, by letting victorious Liberals assume the reins of government from defeated Conservatives.

Before leaving his post, Elgin further adorned his reputation. In the 1840s Britain had helped produce a depression in much of British North America by moving to free trade and abandoning the preferential tariff system, which had all but guaranteed markets for colonial products in Britain. Elgin was instrumental in negotiating and securing acceptance in Washington of a *Reciprocity Treaty that allowed for the expansion of trade in natural products between the republic and the colonies to the north. This agreement, in force in 1855–66, heralded a new era of prosperity for British North America.

American determination to end the Reciprocity Treaty, announced in 1865 and to take effect the following year, helped spur on the *Confederation movement. Here, Britain's vice-regal representatives played an important and, at times, controversial role. On 24 June 1865 Colonial Secretary Edward Cardwell sent a circular letter from London to the Maritime lieutenant-governors enjoining them to support Confederation actively. Arthur Hamilton Gordon of New Brunswick, an advocate of Maritime union, proved reluctant to do so. Governor

General Charles Stanley, Viscount Monck was much more in step with imperial thinking. At the Charlottetown and Quebec conferences of 1864, which laid the basis for Confederation, he, like Elgin before him, adroitly practised the arts diplomatic in a round of parties that went some distance to paving the way to Confederation. On the other hand, lieutenant-governors Sir Anthony Musgrave of Newfoundland and George Dundas of Prince Edward Island found the opposition to Confederation so strong that they were unable to smooth its path.

Rarely did governors so disagree with the British government on matters of policy that they rebelled or resigned, though that did happen, most notably when Lord Durham quit Quebec after the British government disallowed an ordinance of his. Durham, a civilian, had less the habit of obedience than the mostly military men who had preceded him. Yet military figures were increasingly out of fashion as administrative, political, and diplomatic issues, rather than military ones, demanded the governors' attention. Besides reflecting and implementing official British policy, these imperial appointees were vital sources of information for their superiors in London. Even Elgin's grant of responsible government did not make them redundant. Little wonder, then, that the new Canada agreed to carry them forward into the new written *constitution adopted in 1867. COLIN READ

governors of early Nova Scotia. The early government of British Nova Scotia involved a bewildering array of offices and men, with overlapping and often conflicting powers and responsibilities, reflecting an uninformed and negligent government in London. On the surrender of *Port-Royal (renamed Annapolis Royal) in 1710, the town was placed under the military governorship of Samuel Vetch, one of the individuals responsible for the successful assault on the French fort. Francis Nicholson, with his strong Tory connections in London, was able to displace Vetch in 1712 and became responsible for the entire colony when it was ceded to Britain in 1713. Each man heaped abuse on the other, trading accusations, probably with cause, that the other manipulated the finances of the colony for his own advantage. With the Whig ascendancy in 1715, Vetch was able to dislodge his old enemy and resume the governorship. Since neither man spent much time in the colony (Vetch did not return for his second term), beginning in 1711 a lieutenant-governor—first of the fort and town, and in 1713 of the colony—was appointed to carry out the actual administration. The men who held these offices were charged with the impossible task of regulating the Acadian inhabitants and attempting to extract an *oath of allegiance, as well as defending the colony with few men and scant resources. Most of them performed far better than an indifferent British government had any right to expect. Thomas Caulfeild, 1711–17, and John Doucette, 1717–26, usually filled both roles; the latter continued as president of the council when Lawrence Armstrong was appointed lieutenant-governor in 1725.

In 1720 yet another layer of bureaucracy was added with the creation of a governing council to oversee civilian affairs. In the frequent absences of Governor Richard Philipps, 1717–49, the role of president of the council assumed considerable importance, especially during frequent disputes over exactly who ought to hold that office. In addition, from 1726 to 1742 the offices of lieutenant-governor of the fort and town and lieutenant-governor of the colony were split, with Alexander Cosby, brother-in-law of the governor, assuming the former, causing great bitterness and confusion in the almost constant absences of the governor. It was only with the death—ostensibly suicide, but probably murder—of Armstrong in 1739 and the death of Cosby in 1742 that any real order was brought to Nova Scotia. Paul Mascarene, as president of the council but without the title (or pay) of lieutenant-governor, served effectively and efficiently for the crucial decade of the 1740s, which saw the colony brought to the brink of defeat and seizure by the French. In 1749 a new governor, Edward Cornwallis, was appointed, and Annapolis Royal was displaced by Halifax as capital of the colony. A new and more stable era in Nova Scotia's government had arrived. BARRY MOODY

Grain, a 1926 prairie novel by Robert J.C. Stead (1880–1959) that focuses realistically on the problems of the farm and its mechanization in the early 20th century. On the one hand it portrays farm work for many young people as a heavy and soul-destroying way of life from which the Great War is a welcome escape, but on the other it tells the story of Gander Stake, an awkward, inarticulate youth who is too shy and frightened to enlist and who is attached to the land and its traditional labours. The novel describes vividly the daily life of a farm family, a boy's experiences as a harvester and farm hand working with animals, his first sexual stirrings, and the accumulating tensions between father and son. It also portrays the lighter moments of prairie life—hunting, dancing, and baseball games. But the larger sociological interest turns on Gander's conviction that 'the war must be won by wheat' and his acceptance, finally, of the inevitable coming of tractors and threshing machines.

DAVID STOUCK

Grain Growers' Grain Company. In July 1907, at the first annual meeting of the Grain Growers' Grain Company, T.A. *Crerar was elected a director and offered the presidency. He would guide the fortunes of the company, and its successor, the United Grain Growers, until 1929. The GGGC was a farmer-owned marketing agency, intended to free the producer from the exploitation of private grain-dealers. Its farmer members would receive patronage dividends based on the amount of grain they sent to the company. A commission of one cent per bushel would cover the expenses of the company, build up a reserve fund, and finance the acquisition of grain elevators.

From the outset, the GGGC was bedevilled by the privately dominated Winnipeg Grain Exchange, through which all grain was traded. Threatened with loss of trading privileges, the company was obliged to compromise its co-operative principles, when, at the insistence of the exchange, they had to pay dividends based on stock held rather than patronage. For one year, the exchange challenged the very existence of the GGGC by suspending all commission houses. The survival of the company depended entirely on the loyalty of its thousands of members. By the beginning of the Great War, the GGGC was securely established and paying annual returns to its members. There were also annual grants for education made to the three provincial grain growers' associations. To further the cause, the company sponsored the publication of the *Grain Growers' Guide* through its wholly owned subsidiary, the Public Press, which was also a successful job printer. To avoid the large international grain dealers, another subsidiary, the Grain Growers' Export Company, was created in 1911 to market grain directly in Europe. It was reorganized in 1914 with an English connection. The Great War inflated demand and price for western grain and the company seemed to go from strength to strength.

It had always been the hope that the three Prairie provinces would market their grain through the company. At a meeting in 1916 the provincial grain growers' associations expressed interest but the Saskatchewan Cooperative Elevator Company demurred. They handled 50 per cent of the prairie crop and had no wish to sink their identity in the new enterprise. In the end, the GGGC and Alberta Co-operative agreed to form United Grain Growers in 1917. It survived the pools, the Depression, and served its farmer owners until it went public in 1992.

J.E. REA

grain trade. A complex system of interdependent components in the handling, marketing, transportation, inspection, and export of grain. Many farmers complained that the trade was prone to corruption, collusion, and monopolies, and that the marketing system was hindered by the practices of the railway companies, grain-buying agencies, and regulators. They complained about the spread between 'street' prices (the price for grain sold at the local delivery point or grain elevator) and 'track' prices (the price in railway car lots ready for shipment to the market). They complained about shortages in the weights and measures of their deliveries and collusion on price and grade offered by local grain buyers. They complained about the grading system, the inability of railways to deliver the grain to market in a timely fashion, and the manipulation of prices by speculators active on the futures market organized by the Winnipeg Grain Exchange. Between 1899 and 1943, the trade was the subject of five federal royal commissions and numerous provincial inquiries. During this period farmers organized large-scale co-operative grain-handling corporations and marketing agencies; the provincial governments financed and supported farmer-based co-operatives; the federal government first regulated the grain trade, then intervened directly in the marketplace, and finally took complete control of the trade through the establishment of the Canada Wheat Board.

Before the Second World War most grain was delivered during the harvest season, roughly September to November. With few provisions for storage, most farmers needed to sell their grain to meet financial commitments in the form of operating loans. The delivery of such large volumes in a short period resulted in shortages of elevator space and railway cars, often 'plugging' the system and resulting in lower grain prices. To address their concerns, farmers created large co-operative grain-handling and marketing agencies. The *Grain Growers' Grain Company, established in 1906, and the Saskatchewan Cooperative Elevator Company, 1911, became two of the largest grain-handling and -buying businesses in Canada. Neither of these companies could address the farmers' concerns regarding futures trading and price fluctuations, so in 1923 farmers created the Prairie Wheat Producers Cooperatives or wheat pools. These businesses required farmer members to contract to the pool for the delivery of their crop. They received an initial price upon delivery, and the grain was then pooled and delivered into the market, where it was sold to European buyers. At the end of the year, the pool was reconciled and final payment made to farmers based upon their patronage of the pool. By 1926, the wheat pools entered the grain-handling business as well, building their own elevator networks. In Saskatchewan, the pool purchased the Saskatchewan Cooperative Elevator Company. The pooling system, however, collapsed in the Depression as markets disappeared, prices fell below the initial delivery price, and the pools found themselves with outstanding liabilities and millions of bushels of unmarketed wheat.

The federal government had entered the field of grain trading in 1900 through passage of the Manitoba Grain Act, amended and broadened in 1912 as the Canada Grain Act. This act addressed farmers' concerns by regulating the businesses of handling, marketing, and transportation as well as making provisions for the inspection of grain products by federal authorities. During the Great War, the price of wheat inflated dramatically, leading the government to take control of the trade through the Board of Grain Supervisors. After the war, as prices fluctuated dramatically, the government formed the Canada Wheat Board. The first board was disbanded in 1920 and grain prices fell dramatically. Many farmers associated this decline with the government withdrawal and a long campaign to re-establish the board began. The failure of the prairie wheat pools during the Depression led to more intense demands from some farm organizations and in 1935 the government created a voluntary board as a method of price stabilization. In 1943, in the context of inflating wheat prices, the government made the Canada Wheat Board a mandatory pool for prairie wheat marketing, a situation that continues to this day. The board establishes delivery quotas for wheat and barley sold for export, offers farmers an initial delivery payment, controls transportation to the market, monitors quality, and sells internationally. Oilseeds such as flax and canola, and grains such as oats and barley not delivered for export are marketed through the Winnipeg Commodity Exchange in an open market system. The wheat pools, meanwhile, reorganized as grain-handling concerns after the Depression. Today Saskatchewan Wheat Pool and Agricore are two of the largest grain-trading companies in Canada. The merits of the Canada Wheat Board system continue to be debated among farmers. Groups such as the Western Wheat Growers' Association and the Alberta Barley Growers' Association with the support of the Alberta government have challenged the board-marketing system in the court of law and public opinion. Thus far the wheat board has survived and continues to be the monopoly marketer of Canadian wheat and barley for export.

ROBERT IRWIN

Grand Banks. These raised submarine plateaus include three smaller banks—Burgeo Bank, St Pierre Bank, and Green Bank—off the south coast of Newfoundland, and the largest—the Grand Bank of Newfoundland—off the south and east coasts. They cover over 93,000 sq km, with water between 36 and 185 m deep. The warm Gulf Stream flows north over the large Grand Bank, meeting the cold Labrador Current and thereby producing thick fog, but also food for marine life. Beginning in the late 1400s, the Grand Banks provided fishermen from Britain, France, Spain, and Portugal with vast supplies of cod. In later centuries, Newfoundland, Canada, and the United States took up this fishery, followed, after the Second World War, by other nations as well. Canada extended its control 320 km (200 miles) from its coast in 1977 and enclosed all the Grand Banks, except the 'nose and tail', which lay beyond. However, the cod stocks declined, and in 1992 the cod fishery was closed. Since then other species, especially crab and shrimp, have been utilized, and most fishers hope that the cod stocks can be rebuilt.

SHANNON RYAN

Grand dérangement. *See* ACADIAN DEPORTATION.

Grande Association des Ouvriers. The Grande Association was founded in 1867 by Médéric Lanctôt, a Liberal lawyer, member of the *Institut canadien, and opponent of Confederation. He became interested in the conditions of the working class after a trip to Europe, where he was struck by the misery of the workers and the revolutionary agitation to which it gave rise. To assist in the workers' cause, he launched the idea of a Montreal league of trade associations, which was organized 6 April 1867 at a meeting of some 3,000 people. A federation of 26 trades, the association aimed to curb immigration, work towards the well-being of workers, and promote collaboration between capital and labour. It set up bakeries and co-operative stores. Under the flag of the *Patriotes, on 10 June more than 8,000 workers belonging to the association marched through Montreal in a vast demonstration of solidarity, an event that prefigured the Labour Day marches of later years. But the Grande Association did not endure. One by one, the co-operatives closed their doors, and Lanctôt directed his energies towards federal politics, standing for election in Montreal East in September 1867 against George-Étienne *Cartier, a Father of Confederation and minister of militia and defence.

JACQUES ROUILLARD

Grand Pré. Acadian district/village on the Minas Basin. The area was first settled by Europeans in 1680, when two Acadian families from *Port-Royal were attracted by the huge expanse of salt marsh—the great meadow (over 1,200 ha) from which the region derived its name. In the 18th century, after miles of dykes were constructed to protect the marsh from the extremely high tides, it became the most prosperous of the Acadian regions. Although the inhabitants were reluctant to commit themselves in the ongoing struggle between the imperial powers of France and Britain, conflict nonetheless sometimes intruded into their lives. In February 1747 New England soldiers billeted in Acadian homes were attacked by French forces. Over 80 New Englanders were killed in the 'Grand Pré Massacre'.

Only one of the centres from which Acadians were deported in the late summer of 1755, Grand Pré has become the best known due to the influential poem **Evangeline*, published by Henry Wadsworth Longfellow in 1847. In 1760 the area was resettled by New Englanders, although the Acadian name was retained. Today it is an attractive village of largely 18th- and 19th-century homes, with a national historic park commemorating the story of the Acadians.

BARRY MOODY

Grand Trunk Railway. Running from Quebec to Sarnia, the Grand Trunk Railway was intended to carry international freight between the Atlantic Ocean and the American Midwest. The government of the United Province of Canada, inspired by its finance minister Francis *Hincks, vigorously promoted the venture as a means of stimulating the economy. The London banks of Glyn, Mills, and Company and the Baring Brothers provided the financing while the British firm of Peto, Brassey, Jackson, and Betts and the Canadian contractors Gzowski and Company built the line. Completed in 1859, the 1,760 km Grand Trunk was the longest international rail way at the time. Although the provincial and many municipal governments provided substantial bond guarantees and subsidies, the Grand Trunk was never profitable due to high construction costs, corruption, poor line location, and competition with Canada's canals and the railway system of the United States.

Over the years, the Grand Trunk absorbed a number of railways, including Canada's first, the Champlain and St Lawrence, a portage line between La Prairie and St Jean, Quebec, that opened in 1836 and merged into the Montreal and Champlain Railroad; the Grand Trunk leased it in 1864 and bought it in 1872. The Grand Trunk also purchased the St Lawrence and Atlantic and leased its American counterpart, the Atlantic and St Lawrence, to provide it with an Atlantic harbour at Portland, Maine. In 1882, the company absorbed the Great Western, a 1,280-km network in southern Ontario. Planned as early as 1834, as a connector between Niagara Falls and Windsor and promoted by Isaac Buchanan, a leading wholesale merchant and ardent advocate of protective tariffs, the Great Western was not completed until 1854. Like the Grand Trunk, it could not compete with American railways and quickly ran into financial difficulties, which continued even after its amalgamation with the Grand Trunk in 1882.

Although one of the Grand Trunk presidents, Edward Watkin, was an active promoter of Confederation, the annexation of *Rupert's Land and British Columbia, as well as the construction of a transcontinental railway, the company failed to seize the initial opportunity in the 1860s and 1870s to expand to the Pacific. In 1903, however, urged on by the dominion government, the Grand Trunk incorporated the Grand Trunk Pacific. Completed in 1914, the subsidiary gave the mother company access to the Pacific Ocean, thus forming another transcontinental railway in Canada, alongside two competitors, the Canadian Pacific and the Canadian Northern. The outbreak of the First World War, scarcity of capital, a crippling debt load, and ruinous competition contributed to the failure of the Grand Trunk system. In 1923, the Canadian government nationalized the railway, merged it with the Canadian Northern, and formed the *Canadian National Railways. A.A. DEN OTTER

Grant, George (1919–88), political philosopher and professor at Dalhousie and McMaster Universities. While a student at Oxford during the bombing of London in the Second World War, Grant served as an Air Raid Precautions Warden, giving rise to profound trauma. He underwent spiritual and intellectual transformations, becoming a devout Christian and a Red Tory. Grant defined philosophy as 'faith seeking understanding', and faith as 'intelligence enlightened by love'. Believing that humanity participates in an order greater than itself, he was contemptuous of *liberalism, which proposes automatic betterment through individual initiative and technological change. Reflecting critically on the writings of Heidegger, Nietzsche, and other existentialists, Grant maintained that 'technological society', which he termed also 'the age of progress', is ultimately nihilistic because it recognizes no values or criteria to guide or constrain applications of ever-increasing raw technological power. Grant's most famous work, **Lament for a Nation*, described the erosion of Canada's founding hopes and principles—namely, to build an egalitarian community within North America with a 'stronger sense of the common good' than was possible under American-style individualism. For Grant this erosion was due to rapid technological change, corporate power and greed, and encroachments of American liberal ideology into Canadian consciousness through media and the educational system.

ROBERT E. BABE

Grant, George Monro (1835–1902). Born in Pictou County, Nova Scotia, Grant became minister at St Matthew's Presbyterian Church in Halifax. In 1872, joining Sandford *Fleming's CPR survey expedition, he travelled across Canada and gained a deep appreciation of the potential of the new Canadian nation, especially the West. His observations and adventures were published as *Ocean to Ocean* (1873). He was a firm Canadian nationalist and a fierce opponent of annexation to the United States; rather, he felt, Canada's destiny rested with its connections within the *British Empire. In 1877, Grant was appointed principal of Queen's University in Kingston, Ontario. He led successful endowment campaigns, promoted the rise of the sciences, fostered the mining and medical schools, and protected the university's autonomy. In the controversies surrounding higher criticism, he argued that Christianity could withstand the challenges of doubt and reform. Critical inquiry led to a clearer understanding of Scripture. He rejected narrow dogmatism and schismatic denominationalism and supported church unions, anticipating a national church. A harbinger of racial and religious tolerance, Grant eschewed the politics of Protestant-Catholic antipathy and refused to get involved in popular Protestant crusades like *temperance. He also opposed efforts to exclude *Chinese immigration. His progressive outlook was expressed in *Religions of the World in Relation to Christianity* (1894), in which he pointed out that non-Christian religions had much to offer Christianity. DAVID B. MARSHALL

great auk (*Pinguinus impennis*). After 10,000 years these birds became extinct in Canada (1841 or 1852). Penguin-like, they flew only underwater and were easily killed on land. Their bones are found in Native midden sites along the Atlantic coast. They were eaten by the *Norse, Basque, and Portuguese, and recorded by Jacques *Cartier (1534). By 1785 they were hunted for the feather trade and boiled for oil. Funk Island, Newfoundland, named for its smell, was the largest colony of auks fishing the *Grand Banks. LORNE HAMMOND

Great Coalition. Formed in June 1864 in the *Province of Canada under the leadership of elder statesman Étienne Taché, the Great Coalition united George-Étienne *Cartier and his conservative Bleus and their Upper Canadian allies led by John A. *Macdonald with a section of the Reform (Liberal) Party represented by George *Brown, William McDougall, and Oliver *Mowat (soon replaced by W.P. Howland). Other ministers included Hector Langevin, A.T. *Galt, and D'Arcy *McGee. Although remembered for initiating Confederation, the Great Coalition was primarily committed, at Brown's insistence, to create an Ontario–Quebec federation by 1865, with possible extension to other provinces. In essence, Brown and Cartier struck a deal that—with or without the Maritimes—recognized Upper Canada's numerical preponderance (*'representation by population') within a structure protecting the distinct identity of Lower Canada. On Taché's death in July 1865, Brown forced Macdonald to renew the commitment to the smaller Canadian federation, and Narcisse Belleau took over as compromise premier. In December 1865, Brown resigned over trade talks with the United States, but without consulting fellow Reformers Howland and MacDougall. Although the Great Coalition formally ended with Confederation in 1867, Macdonald, the first dominion prime minister, claimed he led a cross-party cabinet until 1872. GED MARTIN

Great Depression. Images of the Great Depression in Canada include breadlines, *relief camps for single men, protest marches, and dust storms sweeping over the western plains. Perhaps no image is more poignant than the 'Bennett buggy' (named after Prime Minister R.B. *Bennett), an automobile without engine turned into a horse-drawn carriage. Poverty compelled this technological step backwards. The 1930s witnessed many such defeats.

During the downswing that began in 1929 and ended in the spring of 1933, GNP fell by 29 per cent in constant dollars. Industrial activity in the first quarter of 1933 was 57 per cent of the 1925–9 average; national income in 1933 was barely over half of what it had been in 1929. The recovery was uneven, leaving out wheat farmers altogether, and ended in a renewed slump in 1937. Only the war that began in September 1939 brought full recovery.

The Depression had external and domestic causes. Economic dislocations resulting from the Great War lingered. Great Britain was unable to resume its pre-war role of stabilizing an inherently unstable world economy. The United States would not replace Britain in that role; instead, it joined other countries in reducing imports when prices fell, seeking to protect domestic markets against foreign competition. American banks cut long-term lending abroad at the same time that long-term lending at home declined. As well, these banks restricted short-term credit. These actions intensified the shocks to the international system resulting from an overproduction of cereals and several other commodities, and from the stock market crash of October 1929.

Canada was among the hardest-hit countries. Exports declined while the terms of trade turned against Canada, as prices for wheat, fish, lumber, and base metals fell more steeply than the prices of imported manufactured goods. Expansion during the boom of the later 1920s had led to excess capacity in agriculture, fish processing, pulp and paper, mining and smelting, transportation, construction, and automobile manufacturing. In the context of heavy public and private debt, with interest rates staying high well into the 1930s, falling prices prompted a 'credit crunch' of unprecedented severity. Corporate profits fell or vanished; many enterprises went into bankruptcy.

As business firms and individuals cut back, unemployment grew. By the late winter of 1933 more than a quarter of Canadian workers were unemployed. Others were on short time or had seen their wages and salaries cut. In the absence (until 1941) of *unemployment insurance, some 1.5 million Canadians (15 per cent of the population) received direct government relief. Dependency remained a problem through the decade: in 1938 there were still 1.1 million relief recipients, including 200,000 people living in drought-stricken southern Saskatchewan.

Among the consequences of the Depression were declines in the number of marriages and in the birthrate, and increased interest in contraception. Between 1929 and 1939 the long-established movement from the country to the towns and cities all but ceased. So did immigration, as Ottawa sought to protect the jobs of Canadians. Among those routinely excluded were Jewish refugees from Nazi Germany. Thousands of recent arrivals from Europe were deported, a few because of their 'radical' views but most because they had become indigent.

The Depression did not hit all regions and groups with equal force. Blue-collar workers suffered more than white-collar workers; farmers in western Canada more than those in central Canada and the Atlantic provinces. Fishers suffered whether they lived in British Columbia or the Atlantic region, but gold mining boomed, as gold maintained its price and then rose. Pensioners and others on fixed incomes saw real incomes grow as the Consumer Price Index fell by 23 per cent from 1929 to 1933.

The Depression brought a crisis in public finance. Seeking to balance budgets, all levels of government raised taxes while trying to cut costs. Fixed debt charges, guarantees made to the bondholders of the *Canadian National Railways, the rising costs of relief, and growing municipal tax arrears brought continuing deficits that undermined the solvency of many municipalities and all four western provinces. By 1932 the western provinces avoided default only by means of 'loans' from Ottawa.

The Conservatives, led by Bennett, were elected in 1930 but defeated in 1935. Led by W.L. Mackenzie *King, the Liberal government sought to gain control over provincial borrowing. Alberta, which opposed the attempt, defaulted on an interest payment in early 1936. The implications for Ottawa's own credit rating prompted King to bail out the other three western provinces, but the federal government established a Royal Commission on Federal–Provincial Relations to determine whether the fiscal capacity of the provinces was equal to their responsibilities.

Politically, the Depression gave impetus to new parties seeking economic and social change—the Co-operative Commonwealth Federation, Social Credit, and the short-lived Reconstruction Party. Political power changed hands not only in Ottawa but in most of the provinces. Even in Alberta, though, where Social Credit, led by William *Aberhart, took office in 1935, there was little real change. Debts and deficits discouraged experimentation and reinforced caution. The dominant wish was less for change than for a return to a past bathed in the golden glow of nostalgia. The Depression also came to be seen as something to be avoided in the future at almost any cost. For three decades that attitude influenced the Canadian people, their political leaders, and the country's social and economic policies. MICHIEL HORN

Great Lone Land, The (1872). William Butler's book was the most popular of a sizeable body of travel literature written about the Northwest on the eve of large-scale settlement that followed the building of the *Canadian Pacific Railway. Its title captured the image of the region as a pristine wilderness, uninhabited except by a few Native people whom Butler depicted as 'noble savages'. Highly romantic, exuberant and melodramatic in style, the book depicted a West where, in the 'solitude of a night-shadowed prairie', amidst its 'glorious sunsets', one could find God and live in harmony with Nature. Such romanticism appealed to a British public eager to escape the drudgeries of urban and industrial England by travelling vicariously to exotic and far-flung regions of the empire. Ironically, the popularity of *The Great Lone Land* was one of the factors contributing to settlement. In this respect, the book served as a eulogy for a region about to be transformed, while today it captures a popular image of the Canadian West in the mid-19th century.

R. DOUGLAS FRANCIS

Great Peace of Montreal, 1701. Hector de Callière, governor of New France, sought to ensure the cohesion and French dominance of the long-standing alliance between Canada and the Great Lakes peoples and to establish peace between them, Canada, and their mutual enemy, the Five Nations *Iroquois. In 1700 Callière negotiated a treaty among these peoples on the basis of a mutual return of prisoners and an agreement that he and his successors as governor would lead a police action against any nation that broke the peace. On 4 August 1701 the treaty was ratified at the Great Peace by Callière and 31 distinct Indian groups. The governor exhorted the signatories to settle their disputes concerning hunting grounds amicably. By two separate instruments, the Iroquois agreed, in return for access to Great Lakes hunting grounds, to be neutral in French–English wars. Six decades of conflict had ended.

DALE MIQUELON

Great War Veterans Association. Formed in Winnipeg in April 1917 to unite scattered local associations of largely disabled returned soldiers, the GWVA supported *conscription, condemned 'enemy aliens', and urged members to forget rank and address each other as 'Comrade'. Some members organized anti-alien and racial riots 1917–19. When able-bodied veterans returned in 1919, membership soared to 350,000 and *The Veteran* became the largest circulation magazine in Canada, but demands for a billion dollars in bonuses for lost earnings led to a split. More radical members created a Grand Army of United Veterans. Moderate leaders like future CCF MP C. Grant MacNeil made the GWVA a voice for pensioners and the disabled and won a royal commission in 1924 that responded to many grievances. However, loss of members and scandals over the Poppy Fund and other efforts to finance its programs led to further fragmentation. The GWVA's decline led to its replacement by the Canadian Legion in 1926.

DESMOND MORTON

Greenpeace. This organization was founded in Vancouver in 1971 by members of the Don't Make a Wave Committee, a small group of activists opposed to US nuclear testing at Amchitka Island. Described by one insider as incorporating 'hippies, draft dodgers, Tibetan monks, radical ecologists, rebel journalists, and Quakers', this group subsequently protested whaling, the seal hunt, and French nuclear testing. Through a complex and at times trouble-plagued process, the Vancouver founders spawned an international organization. By 2002 it claimed 2.5 million supporters and had offices in more than two dozen countries. With an estimated 100,000 members, Greenpeace Canada focuses on issues including climate change, preservation of ancient forests, and genetic engineering. The approach underlying the initial protest voyage—'bearing witness' through innovative, non-violent, media-savvy direct action—has remained a cornerstone of Greenpeace strategy, but throughout its history it has employed diverse tactics. It now emphasizes science-backed lobbying, diplomacy, and public education.

JEREMY WILSON

Grenfell, Sir Wilfred Thomason (1865–1940), medical missionary, social reformer. A heroic figure in Newfoundland and Labrador at the beginning of the 20th century, Grenfell was born at Parkgate, Cheshire, and after training at the London Hospital Medical College was appointed superintendent of the Royal National Mission to Deep Sea Fishermen. At the invitation of the merchant community at St John's, he surveyed the Labrador coast in 1892 and returned the following summer to build two small wooden hospitals for the support of itinerant fishermen. What began as a modest medical mission turned eventually into an international cause after Grenfell founded the International Grenfell Association, a network of supporting associations, in 1914.

Not content with treating debilitating illnesses like tuberculosis and beri-beri, Grenfell devoted his energies to eliminating the social problems that permitted such diseases to flourish. He founded fishermen's co-operatives and home industries, farms and gardens, an orphanage, interdenominational schools, and a chain of hospitals and nursing stations. When his modern concrete hospital was opened at St Anthony in 1927, he was made a knight of the Order of St Michael and St George. Though his most productive years were behind him he spent the rest of his life raising funds to support what he had created.

RONALD ROMPKEY

Grey Owl (1888–1938), conservationist. Born Archibald Belaney and raised by two maiden aunts in Hastings, England, as a lonely young man Belaney fantasized about North American Indians, longing to join them. At 17 he emigrated to Canada. Apart from two years of service in England and France during the First World War, he lived in northern Ontario for the next 20 years. The Ojibwa of Temagami taught him their language and his first lessons in First Nations ways. In 1910 he married an Ojibwa woman, but a year later, lacking any model of a normal family, he abandoned her and their infant daughter. As early as 1912 he claimed to be part Aboriginal. Upon his discharge at the end of the war he returned to northern

Ontario and, disgusted with 'civilization', continued to learn Ojibwa and Aboriginal ways. His Iroquois wife Anahareo convinced him to work for the *conservation of the beaver and to write. Anahareo believed his story that he was the son of a Scot and an Apache woman. The federal parks service in western Canada hired him as what today would be called a beaver conservation officer. Through his articles, books, and lectures in North America and Britain, as well as films featuring him in his role as beaver protector, Grey Owl emerged in the mid-1930s as Canada's most famous 'Indian'. He became one of the most eloquent voices for the environment in 20th-century Canada. Only after his death were his English origins discovered. DONALD B. SMITH

Grierson, John (1898–1972), filmmaker, propagandist. With the Empire Marketing Board in England in 1929, Grierson wrote, directed, and edited *Drifters*, a documentary film of the Scottish herring fisheries, which for the first time brought workers to the British screen with dignity. Many of the other films for which Grierson was responsible also focused on—in his own words—'the ardour and bravery of common labour'. In Canada in 1939 he set up and became first commissioner of the *National Film Board, responsible thereby for much of Canada's propagandistic war effort. He not only trained a generation of Canadian filmmakers and launched the NFB's reputation for documentaries, he also published widely and controversially on the relation among democracy, media, education, and propaganda. At the war's conclusion, Grierson was unjustifiably accused of being a communist, which ended his aspirations to produce films in the United States. In 1957 in his native Scotland, he launched a critically acclaimed television series that had an 11-year run. Towards the end of his life Grierson lectured at McGill University, attracting up to 700 students to his introductory film course. ROBERT E. BABE

Grip (1873–94). A journal of political satire and cartoons produced mainly by John W. *Bengough, *Grip* served as an effective critic of John A. *Macdonald's governments. Its much-reprinted cartoons have also shaped the perceptions of later generations on Macdonald policies, especially in the *Pacific scandal, the *North-West Rebellion, and the Jesuits' estates question.

While often supporting Reform/Liberal policies, the magazine flirted with more 'progressive' ideas and third parties, notably on *prohibition, tax reform, women's rights, and free trade. In 1876 it briefly espoused Macdonald's protective *National Policy. In the late 1880s it joined the virulent Toronto-led campaign against Roman Catholic influence in Quebec politics and the Macdonald government, then veered sharply to champion Wilfrid *Laurier's policies of moderation. Through swings like these, Bengough's cartoons offer insights into the shifting public views on political and social issues.

Much of *Grip*'s most radical material, especially in the late 1880s and early 1890s, was produced by T. Phillips *Thompson, a noted socialist writer who probably inspired the magazine's strong anti-imperialist, anti-capitalist phase. Listed as associate editor starting in 1890, Thompson became editor at least briefly when business associates squeezed Bengough out in 1892. The new managers and Thompson's radicalism combined to destroy what Bengough had built up in two decades, and in mid-1893 *Grip* lapsed. Bengough tried to revive it with a new company, but the attempt lasted only a year. CARMAN CUMMING

Grosse Île. An island in the St Lawrence River 50 km downstream from Quebec City, a quarantine station, 1832–1937. The mid-river isolation, hospitals, barracks, and cemeteries of Grosse Île defended Canada from disease and vermin on ships bound for Quebec. At the island, ships with sickness were quarantined, diseased passengers taken ashore to infirmaries, and the dead buried. In most years quarantined passengers were few, but in the 1832 *cholera season and in the 1847 Irish Famine emigration, the island's facilities were overwhelmed. In 1847, 38 hospital staff and 4 Catholic and 2 Anglican priests died tending the sick. The disease and mortality that year moulded the island's image and its heritage designation as 'Grosse Île and the Irish Memorial' National Historic Site. In 1847, the worst year of the Great Famine (1845–50), about 80,000 *Irish sailed to Quebec. Almost 5,000 perished at sea, from typhus and dysentery, and 4,300 died at Grosse Île. Another 9,000 died inland. Among the survivors, about 50,000 crossed the border to the United States. Only 10,000 settled in Canada.

In the Irish diaspora, Grosse Île is hallowed ground and it assumes passionate meaning for Irish nationalists bent on blaming England for the moral devastation of the famine. In 1909, on Grosse Île's highest bluff, the Ancient Order of Hibernians in America erected a 14-m Celtic cross proclaiming that 'Thousands of the children of the Gael were lost on this island while fleeing from foreign tyrannical laws and an artificial Famine in the years 1847–48'. Through that message, Irish nationalists appropriated Grosse Isle's symbolic power.

In the 1990s Heritage Canada planned to make the island a national site to celebrate immigration and nation building. The intention to submerge the meaning of the 1847 events outraged Irish Canadians and unleashed an international cultural controversy. Canadian-Irish nationalists with American and Irish support pressured the government to make Grosse Île the 'Irish Island' and symbol of English culpability. Ultimately, although Heritage Canada refused to include the term 'famine' in the historic designation, Grosse Île is now clearly the Canadian and North American memorial to the Irish Famine. CECIL J. HOUSTON

Groulx, Lionel (1878–1967). Roman Catholic priest, university professor, and nationalist leader, Groulx is the most famous French-Canadian historian of the 20th century. No intellectual figure in Quebec has drawn more admiration, even adulation, than the little peasant of

Vaudreuil; none has stirred as much controversy, owing to his leaning towards separatism and his criticism of the Jewish community. His passing was marked by national mourning in his home province.

One of the co-founders of the Association catholique de la jeunesse canadienne-française while teaching at Valleyfield College (1900–15), he showed a lifelong interest in youth, hoping the younger generations would make up for the shortcomings of their parents. Speeches, poems, short stories, and novels were specially directed at them. At the helm of *L'Action française*, he rose to the status of social mentor, exerting up to the Second World War a profound influence upon those who felt threatened by industrialization and the modern world. He offered the solace and the challenge of a nationalism that combined a renewed sense of the importance of the Quebec government, a quest for economic emancipation, an acute awareness of the province's responsibility towards the French-Canadian diaspora, and the firm belief that a discerning loyalty to tradition, both religious and cultural, was the key to an exciting future. Never in Quebec were traditionalism and nationalism merged and expounded with such fervour and reasoning. Though critical of parliamentary failings, he supported both the Action libérale nationale and the *Bloc populaire canadien. Towards Maurice *Duplessis and his Union nationale, his attitude was one of disappointment and disgust.

Like François-Xavier *Garneau's, his writing of history blended workmanship and passion. To his readers, he was a prophet as well as a scholar. These qualities are evident in his masterpiece, *Histoire du Canada français* (1950–2). The historical profession owes much to his teaching at the Université de Montréal and his founding of the Institut and the *Revue d'histoire de l'Amérique française*. He lamented the radical and pessimistic interpretation given to his beloved people's history by his students who succeeded him in the history department.

PIERRE TRÉPANIER

Group of Seven (1920–33), a group of primarily landscape painters established in Toronto in 1920, although the movement began in that city before the First World War. Convinced of the necessity to create a uniquely Canadian art expressive of the country, they insisted that the northern (a relative term in their arguments) Canadian landscape was the only unique feature of the country and that this landscape was having a determining effect on the formation of a new Canadian identity. By exploring the full range of landscapes and revealing it to the public through their art, they would further the growth of Canada as an independent nation. The nationalist argument, developed in reaction to the colonialism of other Canadian artists and of the Canadian elite, was stimulated by the war. The members were J.E.H. MacDonald (1873–1932), Lawren S. Harris (1885–1970), Frank H. Johnston (1888–1949), and Franklin Carmichael (1890–1945) of Toronto, A.Y. Jackson (1882–1974) from Montreal, and Arthur Lismer (1885–1969) and Frederick H. Varley (1881–1969), both from Sheffield. Tom *Thomson (1877–1917) played a key role in the early development of the movement, although he died before its formation.

The artists came together in Toronto between 1910 and 1913, several working for the commercial art firms of Grip and Rous & Mann. In 1914 Harris and Dr James MacCallum, professor of ophthalmology at the University of Toronto, financed the construction of the Studio Building as both living and working quarters for the artists. During these years they painted around Toronto, on Georgian Bay, and in *Algonquin Park. Dispersed by the effects of the First World War (Jackson and Harris enlisted, Lismer moved to Halifax to teach, MacDonald suffered a physical collapse), the artists came together again in Toronto after the war; in response to the opposition to their work, they decided to form their own society to articulate their ideas and create a distinctly Canadian modern art based on the landscape of the near and far north. Together or individually they painted in Algoma and later on the north shore of Lake Superior, the Rockies, the Skeena River, and eventually around Great Bear Lake and in the eastern Arctic. Both MacDonald and Harris painted in Nova Scotia, and Jackson throughout the 1920s painted on the north and south shores of the Lower Saint Lawrence.

The artists organized almost annual exhibitions in Toronto and exhibited their work across Canada and in the United States. They were aggressive propagandists for the Canadian arts, including painting, *theatre, literature, and *music, and supported artists across the country, inviting many younger painters to exhibit with them. Their nationalist goals were consistently supported by the National Gallery of Canada through purchases and inclusion of their works in exhibitions.

Johnston dropped out of the group in 1920, moving to Winnipeg, and A.J. Casson (1898–1992) replaced him in 1926, the year Fred Varley, primarily a figure painter, moved to Vancouver to teach. In an effort to expand their membership outside Toronto, Edwin Holgate (1892–1977) of Montreal was made a member in 1929 and LeMoine FitzGerald (1890–1956) of Winnipeg in 1932. The death of J.E.H. MacDonald and the need to solidify, in the face of conservative opposition, the informal network of modern artists they had developed across the country resulted in the dissolution of the group and the formation of the Canadian Group of Painters in 1933. Through the 1940s, the new society included most of Canada's leading artists; they organized almost annual exhibitions until 1967. However, due to its unwieldy national structure and lack of a cohesive aesthetic and ideology, it found itself surpassed in influence by smaller, more focused groups.

CHARLES C. HILL

Guarantee Act, 1849. Railway construction projects cost more money than was available in North America, and several private promoters in the Canadas failed to interest British investors in their projects during the 1840s. The government intervened to make investment more attractive. The 1849 Guarantee Act promised that, if any of the colony's four largest private railways failed to pay the promised 6 per cent interest on their bonds, the government would honour much of what was owed investors. In 1851 the government agreed to guarantee the principal as well as the interest of those bonds. In two related acts the government also guaranteed the interest (1850) and then the principal (1852) of any bonds issued by local municipal governments to support smaller, local railway projects. These initiatives, combined with improved international economic conditions, fuelled the expansion of the Canadian railway network, from about 100 to over 2,800 km. Unfortunately, they also nearly bankrupted the government, which borrowed money in order to bail out those municipal governments and private railway companies that could not pay their debts.

KEN CRUIKSHANK

'guerre des éteignoirs'. The government of Lower Canada established publicly funded elementary schools between 1841 and 1849. This process triggered a rancorous debate because poor and rich landowners objected to the imposition of school taxes, and parents believed that control over schools was being wrested from them and turned over to those with ties to the central government. Resistance, in the form of petitions and evasion of property taxes, resulted in the government imposing new penalties on those who obstructed the school system. Pent-up frustration burst forth in the winter of 1850 as opponents of the school laws rioted, burned schools, and intimidated school supporters. Seen as attempts to snuff out the light of knowledge, these events were labelled the candle snuffers' war (guerre des éteignoirs) by government supporters. In fact, small farmers very much wanted schools for their children, but were incensed by taxes they could ill afford and by their loss of control over school matters. Ultimately, and perhaps not surprisingly, the government prevailed. WENDIE R. NELSON

Guibord affair (1869–75). Part of the epic struggle between Quebec liberals and ultramontanes over the temporal role of the Catholic Church. Joseph Guibord, a printer, was a member of the *Institut canadien of Montreal, which had been condemned by the bishop of Montreal, Mgr Ignace *Bourget. Because members of the institute were refused the sacraments and faced excommunication, Guibord, at his death in 1869, was considered unfit for burial in the plot he had purchased within the consecrated ground of the Catholic cemetery in Côte-des-Neiges. In what became one of the most famous court cases in 19th-century Quebec, the institute sued the church for breach of contract and finally won its case after numerous appeals, which eventually reached the Privy Council in England. Guibord was finally buried in his plot on 16 November 1875, but Bishop Bourget later deconsecrated the small area in which his mortal remains rest to this day. LOUIS-GEORGES HARVEY

gun control. The early British settlers in Canada shared Sir William Blackstone's view that the 'right to bear arms' was one of the 'fundamental liberties' of an Englishman. Private ownership of firearms was regarded as essential for both personal and national security. The vulnerability of the young colonies to external aggression and internal rebellion spawned a legislative ambivalence towards the private ownership of firearms, which persisted throughout the 19th century. There was a clear recognition that maintenance of a well-armed, trained, volunteer civilian militia was vital to the defence of the colonies. But there were also legitimate concerns that such training could facilitate those who sought to overthrow the established government. Following the Mackenzie rebellion in 1837, the government passed An Act to Prevent the Unlawful Training of Persons in Military Evolutions, and the Use of Fire Arms, and to Authorize the Seizure of Fire Arms Collected for Purposes Dangerous to the Public Peace. This legislation was re-enacted by the new federal Parliament in 1867.

In the 1870s the focus of gun-control legislation turned to the role of firearms in everyday crime. The Act to Make Provision against the Improper Use of Firearms, enacted in 1877, generated heated controversy. Despite concerns about disarming those who may need firearms for their protection, the act was passed, and in 1892 provision was made for justices of the peace to issue 'certificates of exemption' to carry handguns. During the first half of the 20th century, numerous gun-control measures were passed by Parliament, aimed primarily at ensuring that 'aliens' and subversives were denied access to firearms. Following the lead of the United States, Parliament introduced mandatory registration of handguns in 1933. With the Second World War, fear of 'enemies from within' led to a short-lived (1940–5) requirement for universal registration of all privately owned firearms. These measures were all directed at the protection of national security rather than suppression of firearm use in 'ordinary' crime. In the 1930s and 1940s, strict controls over fully automatic firearms were introduced, despite a lack of evidence of their use for criminal purposes in Canada.

From the 1960s onwards the rationale for gun controls in Canada shifted from national security to reducing the role of household firearms in crime, suicides, and accidents. Some measures introduced during the last quarter of the 20th century had been tried before but their efficacy in preventing or reducing 'ordinary' criminal and other misuses had not been persuasively demonstrated. Despite a long history of firearm regulation in Canada, therefore, public ambivalence towards such legislation persists, and the efficacy of such measures in preventing and reducing 'ordinary' civilian misuse of firearms continues to be much disputed. PHILIP C. STENNING

Gutteridge, Helena (1879–1960). Born in working-class London, Helena went to work at 14. After emigrating to Vancouver in 1911 and finding work as a tailor, she joined the Journeyman Tailors' Union of America in 1913, soon becoming vice-president of her local and a delegate to the Vancouver Trades and Labour Council. She joined the BC Political Equality League, a suffrage organization, and the Vancouver Local Council of

Women. To attract working women to the cause she founded the BC Woman's Suffrage League and wrote a suffrage column in the *BC Federationist*. With the outbreak of war, Gutteridge formed the Women's Employment League to assist unemployed women, and continued to champion women's and labour causes, supporting mother's pensions and a minimum wage. After the war she married and moved to a small farm in the Fraser Valley. When her marriage ended, she returned to Vancouver, where she joined the CCF; with their backing she became the first woman councillor in the city in 1937 and led the fight for low-income housing. During the Second World War Gutteridge became a welfare supervisor in a Japanese relocation camp. LINDA KEALEY

gymkhanas. The gymkhana is a competition that originated in Britain and India during the 19th century. The term comes from *gym*, for athletic events, and the East Indian word *khana*, meaning court or an area where events are held. Gymkhanas might offer a number of athletic and/or equestrian competitions. In Canada, where the equestrian type has predominated, they emerged in places where numbers of British people settled. The object is laughter as much as competition. Usually a dozen or more races are held in which riders and mounts negotiate a straight, wavy, or circular obstacle course under various circumstances. For instance, they might be required to ride one horse and lead another, or pick up a ball while galloping past a certain point and then deposit it into a bucket, or ride to a water trough, pick up a potato with their teeth and carry it that way to the finish line. WARREN ELOFSON

Gzowski, Sir Casimir Stanislaus (1813–98) civil engineer, construction contractor. Born into the minor Polish gentry in Russian Poland and schooled at an elite academy, at 17 Gzowski joined the Imperial Military Engineers. After participating in a revolt against Russian authorities in 1831 he was exiled to the United States. In 1842 he moved to Upper Canada to join the new provincial Board of Works as a civil engineer, and there gained the skills, contacts, and reputation that would carry him through a long, successful career. His two most notable projects were the western section of the *Grand Trunk Railway (1850s) and the International Bridge over the Niagara River (1870s). Gzowski was also active in Canada's early military affairs and an avid Anglican churchman. Although more a contractor than engineer, his success and background made him a paragon of the early professional engineer. He served as an early president of the Canadian Society of Civil Engineers (1889–1892). To this day the Gzowski Medal is the society's highest professional distinction. RICHARD WHITE

habitants. Originally used in the early years of *New France to designate any French colonists permanently resident in Canada, 'habitant' gradually acquired a more specific, agricultural sense. The habitants of French Canada were the rural settlers or peasants, and from the 17th century to the 19th, they constituted the majority of the population of the St Lawrence Valley. Habitants generally owned their own farms, each one a long rectangular plot with a house, barn, and stables fronting on a road or on the river and with grain fields, pastures, and perhaps a wood lot stretching out behind. Each family enjoyed a high degree of economic self-sufficiency, producing the wheat, milk, meat, and vegetables needed for food from the farm; firewood, building materials, and, in some cases, wool and flax were also domestically produced. The family supplied the labour in this household economy, men usually handling the fieldwork while women took charge of the house, garden, and barnyard. When markets for Canadian wheat opened up in the 18th century, many habitants profited from the sale of surplus grain, while still maintaining their self-sufficiency.

In most basic respects, the situation of the French-Canadian habitant resembled that of other North American settlers of the colonial period. They were, however, subject to *seigneurial tenure, meaning that their land was subject to annual rents and to various restrictions, such as the requirement to grind their grain at the landlord's mill. This regime, which prevailed through most parts of Quebec through the middle of the 19th century, implied some affinity between the habitants and the peasantries of western Europe.

The habitants were never an undifferentiated mass. By the late 18th century, some were quite prosperous, able to employ 'servants'; others were impoverished and despaired of providing lands for their children. Although some could read and write, the majority was illiterate. Through the institution of the Catholic parish, habitants took an active part in the political and religious life of their respective rural communities. ALLAN GREER

Haida. Canada's most famous warship, last of the Tribal-class destroyers worldwide. Built by Vickers-Armstrong Ltd in Newcastle, England, the ship was launched on 25 August 1942. HMCS *Haida*'s first commanding officer was Commander H. DeWolf, who employed the ship dynamically during the Second World War, in D-Day, the Arctic, the English Channel, and Bay of Biscay operations, where *Haida* was part of the 10th Destroyer Flotilla. It also served in Korea in 1952–3. Acquired by Ontario in 1971 as a naval memorial to the Second World War, *Haida* is now owned by Parks Canada and berthed in Hamilton harbour. The ship may be considered the northern dominion's equivalent to HMS *Victory*.

BARRY M. GOUGH

Haliburton, Thomas Chandler ('Sam Slick'), (1796–1865), jurist, historian, politician, writer. Born in Windsor, Nova Scotia, a member of the local assembly 1826–9, he created *The Clockmaker* series (1837–55) and other works, the most interesting being *The Old Judge* (1849). He claimed himself to be a supporter of railways, steamships, and Yankee innovation. His *General Description of Nova Scotia* (1823) promoted Nova Scotia to prospective immigrants. However, his acclaimed *Historical and Statistical Account* (1829) eulogized a cultivated province with established gentry and yeoman classes that needed no immigrants. His polemical *The Bubbles of Canada* (1839), much of it reused in *Rule and Misrule of the English in America* (1851), damaged his reputation by its reactionary and prejudiced politics. So did successive politically charged sequels to *The Clockmaker*. An old-fashioned Tory, Haliburton believed that the abolition of slavery was a species of political cant. From 1840 onwards, he ignored his North American (Yankee) heritage. Literary success eventually lured him to England in 1856, where he sat as a member of Parliament in 1859–65. One British MP described him as a 'remnant of a past age'. In an 1862 speech, he vehemently attacked the Yankee side in the American Civil War. The Confederates, he said, 'are our cousins'. He died in Isleworth, London.

RICHARD A. DAVIES

Halibut Treaty. An agreement signed by Canada and the United States on 2 March 1923 to regulate the nearly depleted halibut fishery in the North Pacific Ocean. Although Canada had negotiated commercial agreements, this was the first treaty Canadian statesmen negotiated and signed independent of Great Britain. London was initially opposed to Canada signing alone but gave in when Prime Minister Mackenzie *King threatened to open a Canadian legation in Washington. The treaty was an important milestone in constitutional development; King believed it rid Canada of another 'badge of colonialism'. Together with the *Chanak affair, the treaty established a new direction in Canadian foreign policy away from *imperialism and towards autonomy. GREGORY A. JOHNSON

Halifax. In 1749 the British, under the leadership of Governor Edward Cornwallis, established Halifax as a civilian town and military fortress on a large deep harbour mid-way along the seaward coast of *Nova Scotia to counter the power of the French fortress of *Louisbourg, built after the Treaty of Utrecht in 1713. Nova Scotia's *Mi'kmaq population viewed the development of Halifax with foreboding as Cornwallis refused to acknowledge Mi'kmaq sovereignty, and three years of intermittent conflict ensued. During the Seven Years' War, 1756–63, the town's military purpose was fulfilled. In 1758 a naval yard was established, fortifications on Citadel Hill were improved, and 22,000 military personnel crowded into Halifax in preparation for the final and successful assault on Louisbourg. After a brief decline at the end of the war, the American Revolution (1776–83) revived Halifax's fortunes. By the end of the war the city had taken in 1,200 Loyalist refugees, including a significant group of people of African descent who had gained their freedom from slavery by fighting for Britain. In 1794, Prince Edward, Duke of Kent after 1799, rebuilt the town's fortifications. His architectural legacy includes the Town Clock built on the eastern slope of the Citadel and St George's Anglican Church.

In the first decade of the 19th century Halifax began to emerge as a dynamic centre for trade. Both imperial and commercial interests were stimulated by the War of 1812. While the British navy played the decisive role in the war at sea, *privateers—privately owned, armed vessels licensed by the Crown—brought home many prizes and earned an important place in Nova Scotian folklore. The most famous prize of the war was USS *Chesapeake*, captured off Boston by HMS *Shannon*; the arrival of the vessels in Halifax triggered mass euphoria.

From 1814 to 1914 Halifax enjoyed a century of peace. Although it continued its role as base for the Royal Navy's North Atlantic fleet, and until 1906 as a *British garrison, civilian society assumed greater importance as the city developed its commerce and expanded its role in the international carrying trade. A *reciprocity agreement with the United States, 1854–66, and the American Civil War increased trade with that country. Railway construction, begun in the early 1850s, strengthened commercial relations with the interior of British North America. Confederation, however, was not popular in the city as Haligonians remained committed to international trade. Industrial production was stimulated by the protective tariffs of the *National Policy of 1879. Halifax also became a centre of political, social, and intellectual life in the region. Relatively harmonious relationships between Protestants and Catholics, especially by the 1860s, were a notable feature of political and cultural life.

The First World War revived Halifax's earlier naval and military roles, but strained the city's resources. Halifax was Canada's major troop port and a convalescent centre for returned soldiers. *Convoys of merchant ships formed in Bedford Basin awaiting naval escort across the Atlantic. The war's most dramatic impact on the city was the explosion caused by the collision of the inbound *Mont Blanc*, a French munitions ship, and the outbound *Imo*, a Norwegian vessel chartered for Belgian relief, in the narrows of Halifax Harbour on 6 December 1917. It killed nearly 2,000 people on both sides of the harbour; 9,000 were injured and 6,000 left homeless. Enormous amounts of relief were required, with Massachusetts leading the international relief effort.

Between the two world wars Halifax lived with severe unemployment and widespread poverty. While labour unions tried to protect their members and reformers reorganized private charity and lobbied governments to provide for the needs of the poor, many people simply gave up and left the city to find work in the United States. The bright spot in the period was the modernization of port facilities, including a new immigration facility at *Pier 21.

Halifax played an enormous role in Canada's Second World War effort, and as the city's population doubled, resources were stretched to the breaking point. Once again convoys formed in Bedford Basin for naval escort across the Atlantic and the city was the major port for troop embarkation and an important ship repair centre. Shortages of goods and services severely strained social relations in the city, and on 8 May 1945, *VE Day, the pressure erupted in two days of rioting and destruction causing $5 million damage. While all Canadians made sacrifices to support the war effort, Haligonians lived with the war in more immediate ways than did Canadians in other cities.

After the war Halifax embarked on a vigorous program of urban renewal, including the destruction of the old Black suburb of *Africville, which quickly became an important symbol for the human rights struggles of African Nova Scotians. In the late 1960s an urban heritage movement successfully prevented the demolition of waterfront buildings and a heritage preservation district was created. Although Halifax remained a navy town, it also became a regional and national centre for health care, research, post-secondary education, and the arts. In 1996, the old city of Halifax joined with other municipalities in Halifax County to form the Halifax Regional Municipality.

JANET GUILDFORD

Halifax and Sydney riots. During the First World War the ports of Halifax and Sydney both had to contend with large numbers of sailors and soldiers on leave. In Halifax there were serious incidents in February and May 1918, in which large crowds of soldiers and civilians destroyed some stores and restaurants. On the latter date, a mob attempted to burn down City Hall. An outraged *Halifax Herald* likened the actions of 'Hoodlums in Halifax' to those of 'the Huns in France and Belgium'. By comparison, the end of the war was marked more peacefully in that city.

In Sydney the major wartime disturbance was sparked by a clash between police and American sailors over two nights at the end of August 1918, with Canadian sailors and civilians joining the fray on the second night. Eventually, an agreement with American naval commanders on payment for damages settled most claims. A large victory parade in Sydney on 12 November was marred only by a minor clash between returning soldiers and American sailors. Meanwhile, in more sedate Sydney Mines, the highlight of the celebrations on the same day was apparently an interfaith thanksgiving service at the Presbyterian church. No arrests were reported on that occasion.

HECTOR MACKENZIE

Halifax Explosion. On 6 December 1917, the accidental collision in the Halifax Harbour narrows of the *Mont Blanc*, a French munitions ship carrying a 2.9-kiloton cargo of explosives, and the *Imo*, a Norwegian steamer carrying Belgian relief supplies, resulted in the largest man-made explosion to take place in an urban centre before Hiroshima. The brutal reality of the First World War was brought to the home front. The force of the explosion, damage from flying debris, and the ensuing fires as wooden structures collapsed on stoves resulted in the complete devastation of 2.5 sq km in the Halifax north end suburb of Richmond and caused considerable damage on the Dartmouth side of the harbour. Official totals claimed that 1,963 people were killed while an estimated 9,000 were injured, and 6,000 lost their homes completely. At the time, Halifax had a population of close to 50,000 while Dartmouth was home to around 6,500.

As Canada's primary wartime port, Halifax benefited from immediate military leadership. Response to the disaster was widespread. Of particular note was the assistance of Americans, especially Bostonians, who quickly sent supplies and medical assistance. The US Red Cross brought its disaster relief experience gained in the 1907 San Francisco earthquake; this expertise was combined with local knowledge about mass mortuaries acquired after more than 200 bodies were landed from the **Titanic* disaster of 1912.

In January 1918, the federal government issued an order-in-council under the *War Measures Act and the Enquiries Act to create the Halifax Relief Commission. The incorporated commission did not dissolve until 1976, when responsibility for those still receiving pensions was transferred to the Canada Pensions Commission. The three men originally appointed to the commission, T. Sherman Rogers (chairman), William B. Wallace, and Frederick L. Fowke, were vested with the power to receive all unexpended moneys (almost $30 million), to reconstruct the devastated area, to investigate losses, damages, and injuries, and to award compensation. The commission reflected contemporary progressive ideology, which attempted to apply efficient business-like principles and scientific management to social organization. Its most enduring legacy was the redevelopment of 130 hectares with the consultation of urban-planning expert Thomas Adams, then of the federal Commission on Conservation. He conceptualized a plan, realized by Montreal architect George Ross, to construct a garden suburb housing project, the Hydrostone, named for the fireproof cement blocks used in its construction. This scheme was intended to serve the dual purpose of providing decent housing for the homeless and generating long-term pension income for those unable to support themselves. Following the explosion, Halifax was briefly at the forefront of Canadian public health services with the establishment of the Halifax-Massachusetts Health Commission, an agency charged with promoting community health and serving the needs of explosion victims.

SUZANNE MORTON

Hamilton. Canada's largest city devoted primarily to industrial production. The first inhabitants at this site on the plain below the Niagara Escarpment (locally known as Hamilton Mountain) at the western end of Lake Ontario were Neutral Indians, who established agricultural villages in the area. As a result of European disease and hostile attacks from the Iroquois, they had departed by the mid-17th century, and the first white settlers who arrived more than a century later found the area unoccupied. A town was first laid out in 1816 as a land-development project by wealthy landowners. Much of the commerce in the area by-passed the town until a permanent channel was cut through the land bar separating Burlington Bay from Lake Ontario in 1827. Montreal merchants soon saw Hamilton as the best regional centre for servicing the growing agricultural hinterland. The booming port was incorporated as a town in 1833 and as a city in 1846. The town's commercial elite competed with Toronto merchants for control of trade in the region, and, in 1850 brought the city its first railway, the Great Western, to extend their reach into southwestern Ontario and the American Midwest. A financial depression in 1857 brought disaster to the railway project and to Hamilton's dreams of commercial hegemony.

Meanwhile, the local economy had been expanding as an industrial centre. Back in the 1830s, iron moulders had established the first foundries to produce stoves and other iron products. In the 1850s many local firms also started manufacturing goods for the railways. Over the next 40 years, many more factories opened, turning out diverse consumer goods, although iron products, especially stoves, remained pre-eminent. Hamilton's industrial life began to focus more narrowly on *iron and steel production after the opening of a blast furnace in 1895 and, through a series of mergers, the creation of the Steel Company of Canada (Stelco) in 1910. Basic steel production attracted many large American corporations and smaller metal-working firms, among them Canadian Westinghouse and International Harvester. With the boost of production from two world wars, Hamilton became the country's leading steel-making centre. Primary textiles (especially knit goods) and clothing constituted a second major industrial sector until the 1950s.

Despite the arrival of McMaster University in 1930, employment in the so-called Lunch Bucket City was overwhelmingly in factories. The population reached 52,000 in 1901 (twice what it had been in 1871), doubled by the First World War, climbed over 150,000 by the 1930s, and doubled again by the 1970s. Many newcomers were migrants from the British Isles and, after 1900, southern and eastern Europe, especially Italy and Poland. Class distinctions became sharply defined as large new working-class communities grew up in the north and east ends, and the wealthy withdrew into their own neighbourhoods in the south and west. Much of the city's social, cultural, and political life was shaped by workers' traditions of militancy and collective organization on the job and in politics. After hard-fought strikes in three large industries in 1946, Hamilton became widely known as a union town. As the steel industry boomed and *unions negotiated a better standard of living, the city enjoyed three decades of relative prosperity after the Second World War, symbolized by the rapid expansion of new suburbs on the mountain. Starting in the 1970s, many companies began to lay off workers, curtail production, and eventually close completely. Manufacturing became proportionally much less important: in the 1990s half the city's workers had jobs in health care, environmental services, and education. CRAIG HERON

hardrock mining. Mineral extraction procedures in which significant subsurface landscape modification is required to obtain concentrated 'lodes' of minerals. This may be distinguished from two other forms. The first, called placer mining, occurs where small fragments of minerals (gold, silver, tin, etc.), have been deposited in streams as a result of erosion of local base materials, and are taken by panning and sluicing methods. The Yukon gold rush was based on placer mining. The second type involves shallow surface or strip quarry mining of stone and shale-type products (coal, limestone, talc, gypsum, asbestos, etc.). Nova Scotia, the Eastern Townships of Quebec, the Prairies, and Vancouver Island have been important centres for these kinds of extraction.

There are five geological regions of Canada: the Precambrian Shield; the Western Cordillera; the interior plains (which extend into the western Arctic); the Appalachians of eastern Canada; and the islands of the central and eastern Polar Margin (Innuitian) region in the Far North. All favour hardrock mining by degree. The ancient shield zone provides the host rock for many of the most important mines. Gold, silver, iron, cobalt, uranium, nickel, zinc, and copper are characteristic. In Canada, at least 45 industrial mineral products are won by hardrock mining.

The quest for minerals in Canada is as old as New World exploration itself. Queen Elizabeth I's encouragement of Martin Frobisher's voyages of the 1570s into the eastern Arctic were motivated by the search not just for a northern route to Cathay but also for mineral wealth en route. The ores taken from **Meta incognita*, as Elizabeth called Frobisher's zone of contact around Baffin Island, helped justify subsequent voyages. Much confusion surrounded the assays, by reputable metallurgists, of the ores brought back to England. As a result, it may be said that fraudulent mine claims became an early feature of Canadian history. Metallurgical and mining science in Europe advanced rapidly in the 16th century, particularly in Saxony, and navigators maintained their quest for New World resources. Royal patronage was stimulated by the economic effects of South American precious metals entering Spain, producing the European 'price revolution'.

During Canada's long colonial period, mineral extraction remained modest compared with production in furs, fish, timber, and agriculture. Interest was occasionally shown in local lodes of bog iron, as at the *St-Maurice forges in Quebec, or in surface finds of copper around Lake Superior noted by 18th-century fur traders. Systematic work began only after the 1840s, stimulated by growth in settlement and by the mid-century gold rushes in western North America. In colonial Canada the potential value of the geological patrimony was understood, and the *Geological Survey of Canada was founded in 1842. Its first chief officer, native-born William *Logan, was well-versed in both geology and mining, having studied in Edinburgh before supervising his uncle's copper mine in Wales. The GSC became a permanent contributor to the mining industry through exploration and documentation of Canadian lands.

The middle decades of the 19th century saw several important advances in mining technology practices. Deep-drilling bore tools, which could confirm the presence of minerals far underground, were steadily improved, culminating in adaptation of French engineer Rodolphe Leschot's diamond drill in the 1860s. This new method was used in tracing the rich Silver Islet strike near Thunder Bay, Ontario, in the early 1870s. Another great advance came in the late 1860s with the practical adaptation of compressed air to mining techniques. Steam power had, to that time, only limited uses in mining, but this invention transformed extraction work at the deepest levels, affecting hewing, draining, hauling, and support-machinery capacities.

Confederation in 1867 became the occasion for subsequent territorial expansion requiring on-going landscape appraisal. Railway enterprise became a main vehicle of this expansion, one in which hardrock mining opportunities were also furthered. Railway building was often an act of geological exploration, occasioned by the blasting of bedrock. In addition, every railway worker was a potential Sunday surveyor. The first discovery of copper at Sudbury came about in this way. Between 1880 and 1930 many railways systems were completed, giving access to previously isolated parts of Canada.

Mining geologists distinguish two main classes of mineral ores. Syngenetic types were formed at the same time as the ancient host rock in which they are found. Epigenetic types were deposited long after the host rock was formed, usually with the assistance of hydrothermal fluids and gases introduced into the host rock and filling cavities. The *Canadian Shield is a rich source of minerals owing to its great age, having been eroded into low rounded hills where outcrops of ancient epigenetic deposits are exposed. 'Greenstone belts'—rocks of igneous (or volcanic) origin that often hosted other igneous 'intrusions' sometimes called 'plugs' or 'batholiths' running to a great depth—were much sought by prospectors of the shield. Other intrusive rocks are called 'dykes' or 'sills', the former usually standing vertical to the prevailing stratigraphy, while the latter are flat-lying and run parallel with the local stratigraphy. A famous sill underlies the Cobalt camp in northern Ontario, the rich silver veins being located on the upper side of the sill. From smaller mid-19th-century beginnings in the 'Frontenac Axis' shield country of southeastern Ontario, many important mine districts developed across the greater shield country from Lake Athabasca to northern Quebec. Interest in new prospects was high in regions such as Great Bear Lake, Flin Flon, Red Lake, Kirkland Lake, Timmins, Noranda, and Val d'Or until the financial crash of 1929 affected all operations.

West of the Great Divide, American miners had penetrated southern British Columbia from Spokane and northern Idaho in the early 1880s, searching the Kootenays for the silver and lead long reported by fur traders. With Canadian railway advances into southern British Columbia after 1885, hardrock mining commenced more systematically in a number of areas. The development of branch lines, such as the Kaslo and Slocan Railway, gave access to minerals in high mountain country. The geology of the Western Cordillera is of a very different kind from the shield, and the lodes were seldom of the magnitude of shield veins. This was not uniformly the case, however, as indicated by the great open-pit copper operations in the Boundary Mining district or the Britannia Copper Mine on the lower mainland coast. Gold, of the non-placer type, has also been taken in the long term at sites such as Bralone near Lillooet. Recurring difficulties in separating ores from the Cordilleran host rock in an economic fashion led to the establishment of the Zinc Commission in 1906 and a BC Geological Survey regional office in 1918. Railways into southern BC helped stimulate developments in smelting, notably at Granby, Greenwood, Revelstoke, Nelson, and Trail. With the CPR's purchase of the Trail smelter in 1898, one of the great integrated Canadian mining companies was established, the Consolidated Mining and Smelting Company (*Cominco). On the other hand, the extensive smelters in the Boundary region fell silent after the First World War, victims of cyclical demand for copper and stock-piled wartime production.

Before the Second World War, iron ore production in Canada was modest. In the 1890s, at Sydney, Nova Scotia, small-scale processing traditions based on local coal were enhanced by ores from Bell Island, Newfoundland. After 1900, steel production at Sault Ste Marie started, based on mines on the east coast of Lake Superior. War demand and exhaustion of ores in the American Mesabi range stimulated new Canadian extraction. Cyrus Eaton developed Steep Rock's open-pit operations near Atikokan, and in 1949 a consortium, the Iron Ore Company of Canada, established Schefferville at the iron lodes on the Quebec-Labrador border, along with the Sept-Iles Railway. Other post-war developments included new resource communities at Thompson, northern Manitoba, based on extensive nickel deposits. Elliot Lake and the Blind River area of Ontario became important uranium centres as did Uranium City in northern Saskatchewan.

Hardrock minerals have long been subject to boom and bust cycles, but the industry has been a major employer and contributor to national wealth and regional growth. Diversification, research, technological improvement, and long-term planning are important elements for an industry with high preliminary investment requirements. Finding uses for base metals within the new materials and electronic information economies is now an important business aspect. The establishment of a diamond industry in the Yellowknife area in the 1990s is a recent addition to Canadian mining diversity. New political arrangements in the North and improved transportation have done much to link that area with southern Canada. Frobisher's early attempts in the eastern Arctic were, perhaps, not totally misguided, for the lead-zinc mine on Little Cornwallis Island (Polar Margin) is now the most northerly mine in the world.

GRAHAM MacDONALD

Harris, Robert (1849–1919), artist. A native of Wales, Harris moved with his family to Prince Edward Island when he was a child. After studying art in Boston, London, and Paris, he took up residence first in Toronto, then Montreal, where he remained after 1885. Harris is best known as a portraitist, having done hundreds of studies, including that of Sir John A. *Macdonald. Commissioned in 1883 to portray the Fathers of Confederation at the Quebec Conference, he worked from photographs, interviews with participants, and questionnaires, completing the work in the following year. It received an enthusiastic response from the public but would be destroyed in 1916 when fire swept the *Parliament Buildings in Ottawa. Aside from his portraiture, Harris produced a wide range of art, such as *A Meeting of the School Trustees*, which illustrated a young female teacher in a confrontation with four stern male trustees.

IAN ROSS ROBERTSON

harvest excursions. Before the introduction of mechanized combine threshers, harvest on the Canadian Prairies was a time-constrained, labour-intensive operation. From September to November, thousands of men were required to cut, stook, and thresh the wheat crop. Authorities tried to time the arrival of new immigrants to coincide with the harvest. They extended school holidays and furloughed soldiers. Most notably, from 1890 to 1928 they organized harvest excursions. Harvesters were recruited throughout eastern Canada and, on occasion, from British Columbia, Britain, and the United States. At their peak in 1925, the harvest excursions moved some 55,000 men to the Canadian Prairies. The railway companies offered these harvesters special reduced fares, and after 1900 ran special 'harvest trains' from Ontario, Quebec, and the Maritimes. The harvest trains utilized the notorious *'colonists cars', which made few stops at population centres along the route, leading to numerous complaints about conditions. The labour market for these workers upon arrival was haphazard, and harvesters were often greeted in Winnipeg by a carnival-like atmosphere as agents competed to get the harvesters to travel to their district. Wages were high, hours were long, the work was backbreaking and tedious, the living conditions often substandard. Demand for labour, like the prairie weather, was unpredictable; in some years, thousands of harvesters remained unemployed in the Prairie's urban centres, and the competition for work drove wage rates down. In the most notorious example, thousands of British harvesters recruited in 1928 found themselves unemployed and destitute. To avoid violence, the Canadian authorities had to intervene and return the workers to Britain at government expense. The onset of the Depression and the poverty of prairie farmers brought the harvest excursions to an end. ROBERT IRWIN

Harvey, Moses (1820–1901), cleric, journalist, scientist, historian. Irish-born of Scottish descent, Harvey became a Presbyterian pastor in St John's in 1852. He was soon lecturing and writing as well as preaching. In 1878 he left the ministry and devoted himself to literature. In his numerous articles for the foreign press he was an indefatigable booster of Newfoundland. He championed signs of 'progress': telegraphy, confederation, railways. He looked hard for improvement and, sometimes improbably, found it. To scientists he is best known for his work on the giant squid (which he identified with the 'mythical devilfish'). His most impressive book was a history of Newfoundland (1883), co-authored with the English journalist Joseph Hatton (Harvey wrote most of it). He was always more inclined to ponder Newfoundland's future than to brood on its gloomy past. In his history he slid over the ugly sectarian conflicts of the early to mid-19th century. 'Happily the strife has long since ended', he wrote. But in 1883, as if to refute his claim, there occurred the bloodiest affray between Catholics and Protestants in Newfoundland history.

PATRICK O'FLAHERTY

Hatfield, Richard Bennett (1931–91), lawyer, New Brunswick premier 1970–87. While in power, this Progressive Conservative premier expanded on the cultural, economic, and social policies of the preceding Liberal administration. Believing New Brunswick could be the model for national unity and dual linguistic equality, Hatfield fully implemented the *NB Official Languages Act and pursued the objectives of the Program of Equal Opportunity. His government introduced single-member electoral ridings, launched extramural hospitals, streamlined government contracting, passed conflict-of-interest legislation, modernized natural-resource industries, encouraged writers and artists, oversaw bicentennial celebrations (1984), and created advisory councils on women and youth issues.

A passionate believer in national unity, Hatfield actively endorsed Prime Minister Pierre *Trudeau's *patriation of the constitution and *Charter of Rights and Freedoms package. He was instrumental in seeing the principles of equalization and linguistic equality enshrined in the 1982 constitution. Controversy constantly dogged Hatfield: allegations of influence peddling and fundraising kickbacks, pesticide spraying, creation of a Highway Patrol Force, financing of the Bricklin car fiasco, building of the Point Lepreau nuclear power plant, and charges of illegal possession of marijuana (on which he was acquitted). This colourful, globe-trotting man who loved politics fell victim to his own ego, losing all 58 seats to the Liberals in 1987. He died shortly after his appointment to the Senate.

DELLA M.M. STANLEY

Hawthorn Report. *A Survey of the Contemporary Indians of Canada: Economic, Political, Educational Needs and Policies* (2 vols, Ottawa 1966–7), edited by Harry B. Hawthorn, was undertaken following a 1964 request by the federal government to the University of British Columbia. The overall philosophy of the report was captured in the phrase 'Citizens Plus'. Indians should be regarded as 'charter members of the Canadian community'. Indian peoples, who had often been deprived of many of the benefits of standard *citizenship, particularly *welfare state benefits, should have a plus component added to their citizenship. The contents of 'plus', some of which were found in treaties, were to be worked out in future political processes. 'Plus' was justified, among other reasons, because Indians 'once occupied and used a country to which others came to gain enormous wealth in which the Indians have shared little'.

The Liberal government of Prime Minister Pierre *Trudeau rejected the report, especially its 'plus' component, and proposed a contrary policy in its 1969 *White Paper. The Indian Association of Alberta led the successful counterattack against the White Paper with its own document, entitled *Citizens Plus*. ALAN CAIRNS

Hearne, Samuel (1745–92), fur trader, explorer. Soon after joining the *Hudson's Bay Company in 1766, Hearne volunteered to travel overland to locate rumoured northern copper mines. After two failed attempts, the HBC secured *Matonabbee, a Chipewyan trading captain, to lead the expedition. After reaching the mines, Hearne determined that they were of no value; moreover, he found the only water route to the area was frozen, even during the summer. Despite these disappointing results, the HBC was impressed with Hearne, eventually promoting him to chief factor of Churchill, a key northern post. Hearne managed the post for over a decade before retiring to London in 1787. During his time at Churchill and in London he drafted a manuscript chronicling his experiences as a fur trader, including his famous journey to the Arctic Ocean, published in 1795 as *A Journey to the Northern Ocean*.

HEATHER ROLLASON DRISCOLL

Hébert, Louis (*c.* 1575–1627). Ties to the *Poutrincourt family apparently enticed the Parisian apothecary, Louis Hébert, to Acadia in 1606–7. He returned in 1611, but his second sojourn was cut short when English ships from

Virginia forced the French to abandon the colony in 1613. In 1617 Hébert was lured by the promise of a good salary to sell his house in Paris and embark for Quebec with his family. The merchants, however, changed the conditions of his contract, forcing him to work two years in their service and then sell all his agricultural produce to the monopoly company's storehouse at current French prices. Despite these misunderstandings, Louis Hébert and Marie Rollet became the first married couple to settle definitively in Canada and farm their land. An initial grant in 1623 was enlarged and made a noble fief in 1626. A century after Hébert died, over 1,000 descendants had been born in Canada. JOHN A. DICKINSON

Hébert, Louis-Philippe (1850–1917), Canada's national sculptor at the turn of the century. His monuments can be found from Halifax (Joseph *Howe, 1904) to New Westminster (Simon *Fraser, 1911), and especially in Ottawa (four monuments on Parliament Hill, 1884–1901), Quebec City (including seven figures and groups on the façade of the Quebec legislature, 1889–94), and Montreal (including de Maisonneuve, 1895; Mgr *Bourget, 1902; and King Edward VII, 1914). He began as a carver of religious sculptures in wood for the cathedrals of Notre Dame in Ottawa and Montreal, among others; his first bronze monument was that of Charles de Salaberry in Chambly, Quebec, unveiled in 1881. Because of the absence of art foundries in Canada, he worked frequently in Paris. A superb technician and excellent portraitist, Hébert enhanced his monuments through the inclusion of allegorical figures and narrative reliefs. Early in his career he produced plaster statuettes of politicians and historical figures, sometimes related to his larger commissions, which were widely distributed. He later sculpted bronze statuettes drawn from the history of New France. CHARLES C. HILL

Hector. A vessel chartered by John Ross, an agent for the Philadelphia Company, to carry a party of Highland emigrants from Lochbroom to Pictou, Nova Scotia. Most of the passengers, who were Protestants, came from land administered by the Board of Forfeited Estates, a progressive Highland landlord. A passenger list later reconstructed showed 99 passengers above the age of eight and 68 below that age, plus 9 (and a child) 'from the Clyde'. The party included a piper but neither a physician nor a clergyman. The voyage was a disaster from start to finish. It left Scotland in early June, too late to catch favourable winds, and was nearly 14 weeks at sea. Provisions and water went bad or ran low, while *smallpox and dysentery carried off 18 children. The passengers complained that the vessel was old and rotten. They complained further when they were set ashore in a densely forested site not prepared for their arrival. In 1923, an extensive celebration sponsored by the government of Nova Scotia commemorated the 150th anniversary of the arrival of *Hector* as the first contingent of Scots settlers to Canada, thus ignoring the earlier and more successful voyage of **Alexander*, which carried Roman Catholic Highlanders. J.M. BUMSTED

Helmcken, John Sebastian (1824–1920). Helmcken spent his childhood in Whitechapel, London, where his family kept a public house. He qualified as a physician in 1848, and became the Hudson's Bay Company surgeon at Fort Victoria, *Vancouver Island, a year later. This upwardly mobile, working-class Englishman quickly made the backwoods colony his home. In 1852 he married Cecilia Douglas, the mixed-blood daughter of Governor James and Amelia Connolly *Douglas. Cecilia died in 1865, leaving Helmcken a single parent of four young children. His career as a doctor—first in the service of the HBC, later in private practice—was rivalled only by his career as a committed if somewhat ambivalent representative of the colonial state. First elected to the Vancouver Island assembly in 1856, he capped his political career by helping to negotiate British Columbia's entry to Confederation in 1871. Thereafter Helmcken devoted himself to his children, practising a rough style of medicine and the fine art of reminiscing. He died in 1920, having been both participant in and witness to British Columbia's transition from fur trade territory, to settler colony, to Canadian province. ADELE PERRY

Hennepin, Louis, baptized Antoine (1626–*c*.1705), *Franciscan Récollet Roman Catholic priest, explorer, author, polemicist. Born in Ath, Belgium, he moved to France, joined the Franciscan Order around 1644, and in 1675 was appointed to the Canadian mission. Between 1678 and 1681 he took part in the explorations led by French explorer and trader René-Robert Cavelier de *La Salle towards the Great Lakes. He claimed that in 1680 he had travelled to the mouth of the Mississippi, a claim most historians have disputed. He left Canada in 1681 and subsequently lived in Belgium, Holland, and Italy. Hennepin is best known for the three books that derive from his experience in North America: *Description de la Louisiane, nouvellement decouverte au Sud Oüest de la Nouvelle-France* (1683), *Nouvelle decouverte d'un tres grand pays* (1697), and *Nouveau voyage d'un Pais plus grand que l'Europe* (1698). Although very successful, Hennepin's books were controversial even when first published; historians now agree they must be used with care. LUCA CODIGNOLA

Henson, Josiah (1789–1883), fugitive slave, preacher, Black leader. An important figure in the African-Canadian community of the 19th century, Henson escaped Kentucky with his wife and four children and established a communal settlement named Dawn, near Dresden, Ontario, in the 1840s. This settlement set up Black families on 200 acres of land, upon which a sawmill, gristmill, and a manual-labour school, the British American Institute, were erected. Because of indebtedness and mismanagement, the experiment was never the success it could have been. Henson's notoriety as the real life 'Uncle Tom' from Harriet Beecher Stowe's *Uncle Tom's Cabin* is perhaps his most enduring legacy. Travelling widely throughout the northern United States and Great Britain on fundraising and speaking tours, Henson cemented his reputation as one of the best-known Black leaders of his day. ADRIENNE SHADD

Hepburn, Mitchell Frederick (1896–1953), Ontario premier 1934–42. One of the flamboyant politicians of the interwar years, 'Mitch' sat in the Commons in 1926–34 and was elected leader of the Ontario Liberals in 1930. Often portrayed as an unprincipled, right-wing demagogue, Hepburn was a populist who allied with the *Progressives, advocated inflation to increase purchasing power in the Depression, sought justice for Catholic schools, repudiated the Quebec power contracts, made the *pasteurization of milk compulsory, made the *Dionne Quintuplets wards of the state, and brought order to provincial finances. Often portrayed as an enemy of labour, he more accurately should be seen as opposed to the increasing Communist dominance in some trade *unions. It was the Communist dominance in the CIO that led him to intervene in the famous GM strike at *Oshawa in 1937.

Hepburn's career was marred from the outset by his relations with Mackenzie *King, who resented his outspokenness and his popularity within the party, and detested his private life. Hepburn became an outspoken and at times vicious critic of King—particularly his prewar foreign policy, his limited war effort, and his opposition to *conscription. The feud was partly responsible for Hepburn's resignation in 1942. He returned as leader in 1945 but lost both the election and his seat, and retired to his farm near St Thomas. JOHN T. SAYWELL

heraldry. *See* ARMS OF CANADA; NATIONAL FLAG.

heritage tourism. Canadians absorb much of their knowledge of the past from historic sites, landscapes, buildings, and plaques. Heritage tourism is both an activity pursued by travellers and a component of a major service industry. It mixes travel and recreation with learning about the past and the celebration of national, regional, or ethnic identities.

Travellers have visited Canada's historic places since the 18th century, but the deliberate conservation and interpretation of sites began in the mid-19th century, especially on the battlefields of the War of 1812 and the scenes of Anglo-French imperial struggle in Quebec and the Maritimes. Individual sites, notably forts, were conserved by local effort from the 1880s onwards. In 1919 Interior Minister Arthur *Meighen recruited some of the local leaders onto the *Historic Sites and Monuments Board, which was to advise the National Parks Branch. While the branch acquired over a dozen battlefield memorials and redundant forts, most of the recognized sites were evocative landscapes, where local effort and a federal plaque would encourage knowledgeable civic pride and stimulate *tourism. The number of tourists grew steadily through the 1920s with the development of better roads and publicity. At this time most federally administered historic sites were in Quebec and the Maritimes. In Ontario, the province managed equivalent properties until the 1960s.

The Depression saw governments loosen their purse strings to develop heritage infrastructure. Ontario restored Fort Henry in Kingston, Toronto reconstructed Fort York, and National Parks built six new 'fireproof' museums. In a modest shift towards recognizing historic homes, the federal government rebuilt a house of William Lyon *Mackenzie's at Queenston and acquired Wilfrid *Laurier's boyhood home in St-Lin. In Manitoba, *Prince of Wales Fort was restored after the railway reached Churchill, and in Nova Scotia the *Port-Royal 'Habitation' was reconstructed. In 1938 a special illustrated section of the *Canada Year Book* listed all the federally marked sites, extolling them as a 'great national heritage'.

Stimulated by the Depression then stifled by war, tourism rebounded as a major earner of foreign exchange dollars (second to pulpwood exports) and thus as a component of post-war reconstruction. An alliance of business and governments marketed historic attractions aggressively, excusing them from strong benefit-cost analysis because they had 'a strong appeal to the visitor as well as contributing to our national identity'. The cornerstone of this strategy, which became the federal blueprint for heritage tourism, was public investment in reconstruction and interpretation in order to rescue and market history that was 'entombed in the dry rot of textbooks'.

In the 1950s and 1960s the Parks Branch acquired numerous historic properties (especially urban *fortifications) from other federal departments and from private or provincial owners. Provinces were also active, and economic change—both expansion and decline—created heritage opportunities. When Ontario Hydro inundated the St Lawrence Valley below Morrisburg, the best of the region's historic buildings were collected into an imaginatively reconstructed *Loyalist settlement, Upper Canada Village. New Brunswick met the same challenge a decade later at King's Landing, and British Columbia revived the former gold-rush town of *Barkerville. This was an era when politicians would boast about how much they were spending on heritage. It was therefore also the era of the heritage megaproject, with large developments—from *Dawson City, Yukon, to *Louisbourg, Cape Breton—occurring far from any local market that could justify the scale of investment. Other major sites—Lower *Fort Garry, Manitoba, Fort William and Sainte-Marie-among-the-Hurons, Ontario, the *St-Maurice forges in Quebec, the Halifax Citadel—served a local market as well as appealing to travellers. Although tourism sparked the heritage boom, historical and archaeological research became an essential part of it, not least to ensure a quality product for the visitor. Presentation of sites became more sophisticated. In 1962 federal institutions announced a major shift away from uniformed guides and towards interpreters in period costumes.

The boom in new investment waned by 1978. Apart from the Canadian Museum of Civilization in Gatineau, Alberta's Head-Smashed-in-Buffalo Jump, and *Pier 21 in Halifax, recent developments have mainly been local in their impact (such as Heritage Canada's successful Main Street Program) or address niche markets—for example, through learning travel and Aboriginal heritage tourism, and the emergence of isolated attractions accessible only by water, such as Herschel Island, Yukon, and Battle Harbour, Labrador.

Today, tourists wanting to experience Canada's heritage have a wider choice than in 1950, but the blueprint adopted then is recognizable still. Several heritage megaprojects have international appeal. *Museums define and market regional identities, though only a few achieve the status of tourist destinations. Festivals and gatherings like the Antigonish Highland Games or the *Calgary Stampede draw the expatriate and the tourist to celebrations of ethnic or regional identity. Winnipeg's Folklorama, Toronto's Caribana, and the Irish Festival of Miramichi are newer celebrations of heritage, growing out of the centennial celebrations of 1967.

Heritage tourism in Canada is heavy on forts and trading posts but also strong on pioneer life and local history. Obsolete infrastructure continues to be converted to provide learning opportunities and employment. Diversity is a strength of the system. Canada's dual French and British heritage was celebrated from the beginning, and sites of contested meaning like *Batoche and *Grand Pré were developed relatively early. The heritage tourist today receives a reasonably balanced view of the historical inheritance Canadians share. PHILIP GOLDRING

Herzberg, Gerhard (1904–99). Herzberg left Germany in 1935 as a refugee and taught for ten years at the University of Saskatchewan. After some time at the University of Chicago, in 1948 he accepted a research position in the laboratories of the *National Research Council in Ottawa and worked there for the rest of his career, retiring officially in 1995. His major discoveries were recognized in 1971 with the Nobel Prize in Chemistry, awarded 'for his contributions to the knowledge of electronic structure and geometry of molecules, particularly free radicals'. His laboratory was the world leader in the field of molecular spectroscopy. His memory is preserved through eponymous prizes and institutions such as the Herzberg Institute of Astrophysics, created in 1974, and the Gerhard Herzberg gold medal for science and engineering, awarded each year since 2000 to an outstanding Canadian scientist by the Natural Sciences and Engineering Research Council of Canada. YVES GINGRAS

Hexagone movement. Gaston Miron (1928–96), born in Ste-Agathe-des-Monts, founded the important literary movement and publishing house L'Hexagone in 1953. First conceived as a literary 'meeting place', the movement attracted an entire generation of Quebec poets and artists, including film makers Gilles Carle and Louis Portugais, playwright Jean-Claude Rinfret, graphic artist Hélène Pilote, and poets Olivier Marchand and Jean-Guy Pilon, galvanizing the cultural and political energies around the issue of Quebec's independence. For the next 30 years, Miron would remain L'Hexagone's most visible public figure. He published poetry and short essays in various nationalist newspapers and literary magazines, including *Le Devoir*. His complete works appeared in 1970 under the title *L'homme rapaillé*. Miron was involved in almost all of the significant artistic ventures of this crucial period in Quebec history, including the founding of the influential magazine *Liberté* and the organization of Montreal's unique Nuits de la poésie, an international gathering of poets, songwriters, and musicians. In his essays, using the writings of Frantz Fanon and Albert Memmi on colonization, Miron and other Hexagone members developed the widely accepted view that francophone Quebec had been and continued to be a deeply colonized society in need of social and political liberation. According to the group, the French language itself, as it was spoken in Quebec, revealed the extent of the cultural alienation experienced by the Québécois. These views shaped a powerful nationalist discourse that still underlies Quebec society as a whole. They prepared the ground for the Quebec government's linguistic legislation in the late 1970s. For Miron, the decolonization process would come through language, and literature was bound to play a seminal role in denouncing inequalities and past oppression. Although members of L'Hexagone did not advocate violence, many of them, including Miron himself, were arrested in the aftermath of the *October 1970 FLQ crisis. Upon Miron's death in 1996, the Quebec government granted to one of Canada's most influential writers the unusual privilege of a state funeral, underlining both his literary and political contributions.
FRANÇOIS PARÉ

high arctic exiles. In 1953 the Canadian government 'experimented' to see if the problems *Inuit faced in southern parts of the Arctic could be solved by moving them into unoccupied areas farther north. Seven families from Port Harrison (now Inukjuak) on the eastern shore of Hudson Bay were moved to Resolute Bay and (ultimately) Grise Fiord, along with three families from Pond Inlet to help the more southerly Inuit adjust. The move came to be seen as a fiasco: the people likely did not know how far they were being moved; promises of return were next to impossible to keep; material support was ludicrously insufficient; the families did not know they were going to be separated until one group was being offloaded; Resolute Bay was chosen because it was near a US airforce base, but it was poor hunting territory. As well, ecological conditions in the High Arctic were vastly different than what the families had been used to: fewer species could be relied on for subsistence and winters were longer and darker. Inuit at Resolute Bay have bitter memories of foraging through the air-base garbage dump for food scraps. Although the families at Grise Fiord were better situated, they too reported severe hardship. There was also concern among the Inuit that one of the reasons for the relocation was to secure Canadian sovereignty in the region. The high arctic exiles, as they became known, engaged in a decades-long struggle: a royal commission, a human rights report, and three books supported Inuit claims that an injustice had been done. The issue became a *cause célèbre* among Inuit people and eventually led to a government-sponsored compensation package.

PETER KULCHYSKI

Highland Games. *See* CALEDONIAN GAMES.

high schools. One of several traditional terms—others include 'grammar school', 'academy', and 'collegiate institute'—identifying schools that taught subjects beyond the rudiments of the three Rs. Although in British North America the most common term was grammar school, the designation 'high school' was familiar to Canadians, if only because of the distinguished reputation of Scotland's Edinburgh High School (George *Brown was a student there). These schools did not offer what we now think of as secondary education. Rather, they taught everything beyond the rudiments to university-entrance subjects (in Canada, the phrase 'grammar school' was never applied to schools that taught only the rudiments). In the second half of the 19th century, government-funded academies and grammar schools were reorganized into a distinctly secondary sector—that is, intermediate schools between elementary school and university—and, as in Ontario in 1871, the generic term high school was increasingly adopted. During the 20th century, that designation tended to replace all other terminology and be synonymous with secondary education, although schools might still have titles like vocational school, collegiate institute, or grammar school. For most of the 19th century, grammar and high schools were intended to educate that minority of boys entering mercantile or professional life; they offered a curriculum heavily weighted towards the classical languages. However, in order to remain economically viable, they often had to admit girls. Increasingly in the 20th century the high school was transformed into a school for all adolescents.

W.P.J. MILLAR AND R.D. GIDNEY

Hincks, Sir Francis (1807–85). Irish-born, Hincks gained prominence by founding the Toronto *Examiner* in 1838 to rejuvenate post-rebellion reform and by reaching out to Lower Canadian reformers to achieve the paper's motto, 'Responsible Government'. Elected to the assembly in 1841 and holding executive office from 1842, he resigned with other *reformers to protest Governor Charles Metcalfe's interpretation of *responsible government in 1844. Hincks founded another newspaper, the Montreal *Pilot*, to fight Metcalfe's supporters, triumphantly returning to office in 1848 as inspector general in the first fully responsible cabinet. He succeeded to the co-premiership on Robert *Baldwin's retirement in 1851, but his administration was marred by procrastination on key reform causes and allegations of personal corruption. Increasingly preoccupied with the province's credit and railroad construction, Hincks chose economic development and continued co-operation with the Lower Canadian majority over accommodation with Upper Canada's more radical reformers. He believed that their principles threatened both development and sectional harmony. His government defeated in the assembly, Hincks joined like-minded conservatives in the coalition of 1854. Viewed more favourably in Britain than Canada, Hincks was appointed to colonial governorships in the Caribbean from 1856 until 1869, when he was knighted and returned to Canada as John A. *Macdonald's finance minister, retiring from politics in 1873.

JEFFREY L. McNAIRN

Hincks, William (1794–1871), naturalist, clergyman. Before emigrating to Canada West from Ireland in 1853 at age 59, Hincks edited a Unitarian journal in London and taught *natural history. Due to the influence of his younger brother, Francis *Hincks, then premier, he secured a professorship at the new University College (later University of Toronto) over candidates including T.H. Huxley. A passionate botanist, Hincks discovered two rare ferns in the Owen Sound area in 1857. He was an editor of the *Canadian Journal of Industry, Science and Art*, for which he wrote many papers and reviews, and was president of the Canadian Institute for two years. He began the plant and animal collections of the Royal Ontario Museum and amassed many stuffed birds. To counter the new theory of Darwinian evolution, he promoted his own revision of a discredited taxonomic system called quinarianism, which arranged all plants and animals into groups of five in a circle. Although Hincks was industrious, kindly, and professionally ambitious, his work had little impact on colleagues who conducted field research from a biogeographical perspective.

JENNIFER COGGON

Hind, E. Cora (1861–1942), agricultural journalist, women's activist. Orphaned as an infant, Hind moved from Grey County, Ontario, to Winnipeg with her aunt in 1882. Thwarted initially in her ambition to become a journalist, she operated one of the first typewriters in the city, first at a law office and after 1893 as an independent stenographer. Actively working for temperance reform in the *Woman's Christian Temperance Union, and for female suffrage, she became well known for predicting wheat crops on the basis of in-field surveys, which she undertook dressed in her hallmark high boots, buckskin coat, stetson hat, and cane. In 1901 J.W. *Dafoe, new editor of the *Winnipeg Free Press*, appointed her agricultural editor, and until her retirement in 1937 Hind enjoyed international fame as an agricultural expert.

MARY KINNEAR

Hind, Henry Youle (1823–1908). Born and educated in England, Hind is best known for his role in an evolving Canadian nationalism. He attended Cambridge but did not graduate. Emigrating to Canada in 1846, he found that his education was sufficient for him to be appointed a professor of chemistry at Trinity College, University of Toronto. He was to be an important figure in Canadian academic life. He brought a strong enthusiasm for scientific enquiry and founded the first scientific magazine in Canada, the *Canadian Journal*. By the age of 29 Hind had become a leader in the Canadian scientific community. The high point of Hind's career came in 1857 when the government of the Province of Canada appointed him to undertake an expedition to assess the value of the vast territories of the *Hudson's Bay Company. The resultant work, *Narrative of the Canadian Red River Exploring Expedition*, was influential in shaping initial Canadian thinking about the West. Specifically, the idea of a 'fertile belt' of land shifted perceptions of the region as a fur trader's wilderness. However, Hind was ultimately forgotten. His seemingly enthusiastic assessment would eventually be set aside for even more enthusiastic voices. He became embittered with the lack of recognition, and died in Windsor, Nova Scotia, having lived to see the West transformed into an agricultural power. DOUG OWRAM

hippies. The term used to identify a group of young people who in part defined the counterculture of the 1960s in North America and western Europe. Vancouver's Kitsilano and Toronto's Yorkville districts were the best-known hippie centres in Canada.

Predominantly white, middle class, and urban, hippies rejected the affluence, materialism, technophilia, and conformity of Western society. Instead, they practised voluntary poverty, embraced the experiential over the rational, and insisted on the value of 'doing your own thing' and disengaging from the mainstream. Hippie ideas manifested themselves aesthetically—in long hair, androgynous clothing, and communal living—and explain their fascination with hallucinogens and Eastern religions, as well as their liberal attitudes towards sex and sexuality. Their non-conformity captivated the media, which spent a great deal of time musing about exactly what a 'hippie' was. For some civic officials, the answer was clear: they were trouble. Not only did their presence bring property values down, but their aggressive idleness, lack of personal grooming, and drug use were an affront to common decency, a threat to public order, and a potential drain on the public purse.

While many Canadian municipal councillors and mayors at the time saw hippie culture as a radical rejection of the mainstream, later commentators are not so sure, seeing the hippies' insistence on doing their own thing as an expression of the individualism they purported to reject. Others, using gender analysis, ask if men and women were equal participants in 'free love', and whether patriarchy was still a part of hippie culture. Finally, those attentive to the status of the hippies see 'dropping out' as both an outcome and luxury of their class and race privilege. Regardless of how radical the hippies were, their sheer numbers (a product of demography—the *baby boom—as much as ideology) ensured their influence. TINA LOO

hired hands. Waged agricultural labourers, predominantly men, whose principal occupation was outside farm work. Their skills encompassed every farm task—from tedious, back-breaking ditching to exhilarating, finely skilled horse-breaking—and required strength, resourcefulness, and wide-ranging expertise. Agricultural labour offered variety, independence, and an avenue to farm proprietorship, but was onerous, dangerous, and poorly paid.

Working conditions varied enormously, determined by an individual employer's economic position, farming practices, and character. Ethnic stereotyping handicapped those minorities deemed undesirable by the majority. Living conditions were equally diverse, with some farm hands enjoying good meals, comfortable beds, and warm welcomes while others endured unpalatable food, straw bedding in leaky sheds, and ostracization. For most, these conditions were secondary to developing skills and earning a bankroll to begin farming. In such an apprenticeship, hired hands experienced a rough equitability with their employers, sharing work and living standards, and making crucial contributions to the agricultural economy and rural community.

Membership in the dominant agrarian culture made hired hands unlikely candidates for labour organizers, who focused instead on migrant workers, competitors for high seasonal wages. Operating independently, hired hands could parlay experience and labour shortages into choice positions and higher wages, wielding labour's ultimate weapon of walking off the job. Historically, hired hands' advantages were short-lived, found only when land was abundant and labour in demand. As farm lands were occupied or consolidated and as farming costs soared beyond farm wages, hired hands became proletarianized. Their low wages and long hours continued, but their increasing refusal to work under such conditions hastened mechanization and the growth of commercial *agriculture. Currently, union organization is the most promising avenue to improved working and living conditions, yet it was only in 2001, in a Supreme Court of Canada decision, that farm workers gained a qualified right to inclusion in collective bargaining legislation. CECILIA DANYSK

historical societies. Founded in 1824, the Literary and Historical Society of Quebec is Canada's oldest historical society. Its mandate included the collection, preservation, and dissemination of historical material relating to the early history of Canada. Its members were educated men, but they were not historians as we now understand that term: history may have been a passion, but it was not yet a profession. On the occasion of its centenary in 1924 the society claimed to be 'the senior learned society in the whole of the British Empire overseas'. This boast betrays the society's membership. Although a handful of French Canadians participated in the society's activities, its members were for the most part English-speaking. French-speaking intellectuals gravitated towards the *Société St-Jean-Baptiste (1834) and the *Institut canadien (1844). The tradition of two solitudes in historical societies continued throughout much of the 20th century.

The patriotic surge following Confederation in 1867 and the emergence of an urban middle class led to a dramatic increase in the number of regional and local historical societies. These included the New Brunswick Historical Society (1874), the Nova Scotia Historical

Society (1878), the Historical and Scientific Society of Manitoba (1879), the Ontario Historical Society (1888), and the Women's Canadian Historical Society of Toronto (1895). By 1900 there were some 20 historical societies across the country. The existence of a historical society of their own might suggest that women were excluded from the historical project in the late 19th and early 20th centuries. It is true that women were not members of the Literary and Historical Society of Quebec, but this was the exception, not the rule. When understood as an exercise in patriotism, preservation, and commemoration, history was open to both men and women.

Located in Ottawa, the Historic Landmarks Association (1907) set out to save the country's natural and physical landmarks from neglect and encroaching development. Although a national association in name, it was an English-Canadian association in fact. When the federal government created the *Historic Sites and Monuments Board in 1919 to advise it on matters relating to preservation and commemoration, the HLA became redundant. Three years later, the HLA adopted a new constitution, a new mandate, and a new name—the Canadian Historical Association. Modelling itself after the American Historical Association, the CHA quickly became an association for the community of professional historians located in the country's universities. In addition to organizing an annual meeting at which scholars presented their work, it published an academic journal and lobbied governments and archives. Because professional history defined itself as an objective and therefore supposedly masculine discipline, women were notably absent from the ranks. And, like its predecessor, the CHA was rooted largely in English Canada. This fact, coupled with changes to the practice of history within Quebec, led to the creation of the Institut d'histoire de l'Amérique française in 1946. The IHAF would be to French Canada what the CHA was to English Canada—a home for academic historians.

Against the backdrop of the *Quiet Revolution in Quebec and in the context of the social history revolution from the bottom up, the CHA has changed. Now fully bilingual, it houses a variety of sub-groups, including the Canadian Committee on Women's History, the Canadian Committee on Labour History, and the Canadian Committee on the History of Sexuality.

DONALD WRIGHT

historic sites. *See* NATIONAL HISTORIC SITES.

Historic Sites and Monuments Board. A federal advisory board, constituted by the minister responsible for *national historic sites, to identify people, places, and events of national historic significance. The board's authority derives from the Historic Sites and Monuments Act of 1953. An amendment to this legislation further empowers the board to recommend the designation of buildings as national historic sites for their architectural significance. The Heritage Railway Stations Protection Act (1995) also authorizes the board to recommend the designation of heritage railway stations.

The board consists of representatives from each province, plus the Yukon, Nunavut, and the Northwest Territories along with the national archivist and a representative from the Canadian Museum of Civilization. Ontario and Quebec each have an additional member. The board works closely with the National Historic Sites Program of Parks Canada; administrative and research support is provided by this program. The board usually meets twice yearly to consider submissions originating with the public, non-government organizations, and Parks Canada.

The history of the board dates to 1919, when a group of historical scholars was convened by the commissioner of *national parks. Through the 1920s and 1930s the board was dominated by Ernest Cruikshank, Benjamin Sulte, James Coyne, Clarence Webster, and Frederic Howay, distinguished members of the Canadian cultural elite but for the most part amateur historians. Beginning in the 1930s professional historians began to be named to the board, with the appointment of D.C. Harvey from Nova Scotia and Fred Landon from Ontario. By the 1950s prominent academic historians such as Donald *Creighton and A.R.M. *Lower were participants. These members shared an interest in using historic sites to instruct rather than in preserving sites as relics of material culture. Their approach tended to be didactic and they consequently focused on a program of erecting plaques and monuments. In the 1950s heritage communities showed greater interest in recognizing and preserving historic architecture. This trend began to influence the composition of the board, with the appointment of architects and planners who were more interested in the buildings themselves than in the ideas behind them, although erecting plaques continues to be the main function of the board. In recent years there has been interest in appointing members from diverse backgrounds to better represent the multicultural mosaic of Canada.

C.J. TAYLOR

history and historians. The earliest histories of the colonies that would form Canada were written by promoters of settlement and investment to confirm and measure material and political progress or, in the case of the most influential history in French by François-Xavier *Garneau, to defend French Canada against Lord *Durham's dismissal of its past. Annals published in the Victorian period were often local, antiquarian, and celebratory, notable for their vast bulk and the industry of their compilers. William Kingsford's *History of Canada* (1887–98) comprised ten volumes. The collection, preservation, and publication of historical documents was furthered by 'amateur' historians, local historical societies, the Public Archives of Canada, founded in 1872, and the *Royal Society of Canada. In the 1890s professional historians in universities attempted to upgrade standards of historical writing, especially impartiality, factual accuracy, and ample documentation, through the annual *Review of Historical Publications Relating to Canada* (1897, ed. George M. Wrong). Academics and men of letters contributed to *The Makers of Canada* and **Canada and Its Provinces*, and established the *Canadian Historical Review* in 1920, and the Canadian Historical Association in 1922.

The pre-eminent theme in the first two decades of the 20th century was the advance of self-government: historians fixed upon the friction between elected assemblies in the colonies and imperial officials, which led to the rebellions in the Canadas, Lord Durham's Report, the attainment of *responsible government in the late 1840s, and onwards to the recognition of dominion autonomy after the Great War. Chester Martin's *Empire and Commonwealth* (1929) extolled responsible government for reconciling nationhood with continuing membership in the British *Commonwealth. This history as the unfolding of self-government hinged on the political co-operation of French and English moderates, an angle highlighted by Thomas Chapais and challenged by Lionel-Adolphe *Groulx, who, in order to inspire self-respect and fortify their resolve in the present, used history to remind French Canadians of the struggles of their ancestors for survival. In *Notre maître le passé* (3 vols, 1924, 1936, 1944) Groulx attributed the liberties French Canadians enjoyed to their own unremitting efforts rather than to bicultural collaboration or a beneficent empire.

Political and constitutional history was increasingly eclipsed in the interwar years by economic history and an accent upon the country's physical environment, a trend exemplified by Harold *Innis, Arthur *Lower, and Donald *Creighton, whose *The Commercial Empire of the St Lawrence* (1937) treated the waterway as the inspiration to a merchant class and a base for transcontinental dominion. While Innis and Creighton accentuated the distinctive geographical and economic elements in Canada's development, the Carnegie Series on Canadian-American relations (25 vols, 1936–45, ed. James T. Shotwell and John Bartlet Brebner) depicted a common North American experience, the interplay of economic activity and population movements, as well as diplomatic history. Brebner's summary, *North Atlantic Triangle* (1945), nicely balanced Canada's continental and transatlantic links.

The two decades after the Second World War saw a vitalization of political history and biography. Most influential was Creighton's life of John A. *Macdonald—*The Young Politician* (1952) and *The Old Chieftain* (1955)—a masterpiece of narrative history that presented through Macdonald's eyes the nation-building achievements of Victorian Canada: Confederation, the incorporation of the West, the completion of the CPR, and the *National Policy, all of which depended upon British support against American competition. Biographies of others followed, including George *Brown (J.M.S. Careless), J.S. *Woodsworth (Kenneth McNaught), Mackenzie *King (R. MacGregor *Dawson and H. Blair Neatby), and Louis *Riel (George F.G. Stanley). Even when historians did not write about the careers of politicians, they concentrated upon attitudes, ideas, and political convictions, often reflected in newspaper sources, as did P.B. Waite on *Confederation and Ramsay Cook on the journalist John W. *Dafoe. Notable histories of provinces also appeared—W.L. *Morton's *Manitoba* (1957), Margaret A. Ormsby's *British Columbia* (1958), and W.S. McNutt's *New Brunswick* (1963). The summation of a generation's view of history as narrative political history was the Centenary Series, edited by Morton and Creighton, completed in 19 volumes, 1963–88. Meanwhile, the first volume of the *Dictionary of Canadian Biography* came out in 1966.

Post-war French-Canadian historiography followed a different path. Groulx's legacy, apart from his *Histoire du Canada français depuis la découverte* (4 vols, 1950–2), was the establishment of the Institut d'histoire de l'Amérique française (1946), and the journal *Revue d'histoire de l'Amérique française* (1947). His successors, trained in the social sciences, were concerned with the abnormal character of French Quebec in which the economy was controlled by outsiders. Guy *Frégault and Michel Brunet explained the traditional dominance of agriculture and the church as the result of the *conquest, which disrupted the colony's business and commercial evolution. This view was rejected by Fernand Ouellet in the first major Canadian work in quantitative history in the French *Annales* tradition: *Histoire économique et sociale du Québec, 1760–1850* (1966). According to Ouellet, the economic inferiority of French Canadians was due more to internal weaknesses, especially the failure to respond positively to commercial opportunities in the early 19th century and the espousal of a reactionary nationalism. Though not addressed directly to the dispute about the impact of the conquest, Louise Dechêne's *Habitants et marchands de Montréal au XVIIe siècle* (1974) offered a comprehensive statistical picture of the demography, social classes, landholding, agriculture, families, and religious life in early New France. These books by Dechêne and Ouellet signalled a profound shift in French-Canadian historiography towards a clearer recognition of conflicts of groups within the community and interest in basic social and economic structures.

The early 1970s saw a vast expansion in the numbers of academic historians, an explosion of research and publications, and the rise of new fashions in history writing that rejected political narratives and biographies in favour of accounts of the experiences of ordinary people and explorations of *gender, *class, ethnicity, and region. Women's history, a by-product of the feminist activism of the late 1960s, aimed at writing women into history, in tracing the links between traditional domestic ideology and reform movements, and, most importantly, popularizing the notion of gender as a social construct that defined the expectations of women—past and present—and accounted for their oppression (Veronica Strong-Boag, Joy Parr). The conclusions of specialized studies in this field were synthesized in Alison Prentice et al., *Canadian Women: A History* (1988; 2nd ed. 1996). Labour studies were once almost exclusively focused on *unions, legislation, left-wing politics, and strikes. Some labour historians turned to workers' control of practices on the shop floor and involvement in politics (Gregory S. Kealey) and to associations beyond the work place and to the development of 'working class culture' (Bryan D. Palmer). Neo-Marxist historians regarded the integration of workers into society as misdirected, a deflection of revolutionary potential, a theme that was central to many articles in *Labour/Le Travail* and in Palmer's overview, *Working Class Experience* (1983; 2nd ed. 1992).

One of the most rewarding insights of social historians concerned the family as a malleable, vital social unit. In statistical micro studies of transiency and social structures in Hamilton and Peel County, Ontario, respectively, Michael B. Katz and David Gagan uncovered striking patterns in the composition of households, fertility, and childhoods. In *Working Families: Age, Gender, and Daily Survival in Industrializing Montreal* (1993), Bettina Bradbury examined the ways in which some working-class families compensated for inadequate wages and unemployment. Gérard Bouchard, *Quelques arpents d'Amérique: population, économie, famille au Saguenay, 1838–1971* (1996), emphasized how much French-Canadian family strategies resembled what prevailed in other parts of North America.

Historians corrected a long-standing neglect of Native peoples. After 1970, issues once thought settled were reopened—unfulfilled treaties, Aboriginal land claims, and the reckoning with Canada's internal colonialism. A practitioner of ethnohistory, Bruce Trigger, in *Natives and Newcomers: Canada's 'Heroic Age' Reconsidered* (1985), demonstrated how Natives had adapted and changed before the arrival of Europeans and how in the contact period rational and economic calculations dominated their behaviour. Publications on fur-trade society by Arthur J. Ray, Robin Fisher, Sylvia Van Kirk, and Jennifer S.H. Brown all highlighted the autonomy and agency of Indian participants. Canadian Native policy in the 19th and 20th centuries was considered an unmitigated failure by J.R. Miller and Sarah Carter.

The history of ethnic groups was carried to a new level of sophistication by Donald Harman Akenson, Bruce S. Elliott, Cecil J. Houston, and William J. Smyth in revisionist investigations of 19th-century *Irish immigration and settlement. Once stereotyped as Catholic famine Irish who gravitated to cities, these immigrants were now presented as mainly Protestant and successful farmers. Accounts of *Italians (John E. Zucchi, Franca Iacovetta), *Jews (Gerald Tulchinsky), and *Ukrainians (Orest Martynowych) conveyed the gender, class, and political differences within these communities as well the foundations of separateness. Studies of the host society's attitudes to some groups, especially Jews (Irving Abella and Harold Troper) and Asians (Patricia E. Roy), uncovered deeply rooted racialist traditions.

Regional and provincial histories flourished, supported by such periodicals as *B.C. Studies*, *Acadiensis*, and *Prairie Forum*, and often imparted highly critical assessments of the effects of national policies on the Maritimes and the West. The best provincial/regional histories—Gerald Friesen, *The Canadian Prairies* (1984), *The Atlantic Region to Confederation* (1994, ed. Phillip A. Buckner and John G. Reid), and *The Atlantic Provinces in Confederation* (1993, ed. E.R. Forbes and D.A. Muise)—devoted more space to Natives, minorities, women, and class conflicts than to politics. The Ontario Historical Studies Series, conceived in 1971 as biographies of premiers, became more diverse with books on schooling (Robert Stamp, Alison Prentice and Susan Houston), economic history (Ian M. Drummond, Douglas McCalla), religion (John Webster Grant), and social policy (James Struthers).

Historians in general were sensitized to the importance of ethnicity, class, and gender in historical experience even when they wrote histories of higher education (A.B. McKillop, Paul Axelrod) or the history of sport (Bruce Kidd, Colin Howell), or religion and church going (Lynne Marks). Though the sub-departments of social history were often discussed in splendid isolation, some excellent books—for example, Robert A.J. McDonald, *Making Vancouver, 1863–1913* (1996)—escaped categorization altogether.

Historical writing about Quebec in the early 1970s exhibited two trends: increased attention to the century after 1850 and an emphasis on the modernization of society through *urbanization, industrialization, and differentiation of classes. This 'normalization' of the Quebec past—stressing how its experience resembled that of other places—drew upon studies of the labour movement (Jacques Rouillard), French-Canadian developers of a Montreal suburb (Paul-André Linteau), US investment in the province (Yves Roby), religion and popular mores (Serge Gagnon), and Normand Séguin's unidealized *La Conquète du sol au 19e siècle* (1977), and was presented in a cogent synthesis, Linteau, René Durocher, and Jean-Claude Robert's *Histoire du Québec contemporain* (2 vols, 1979, 1983). The focus on economic structures and social history in both English- and French-Canadian historical writing brought a convergence but not a fusion of the two traditions.

The burst of new ways of doing history did not supplant traditional forms of historical writing. Biography thrived with books by Michael Bliss on Joseph *Flavelle, Frederick *Banting, and William *Osler, David Frank on the Cape Breton labour leader J.B. *McLachlan, and John English on Lester *Pearson. Two prolific historians carried on the legacy of C.P. *Stacey in war studies: Desmond Morton published profusely on labour and military history, including *When Your Number's Up: The Canadian Soldier in the First World War* (1993), surpassed in output only by J.L. Granatstein, who wrote over three dozen books on military and political history, mainly on the King era, among them *Canada's War: The Politics of the Mackenzie King Government, 1939–1945* (1975). Political history claimed the attention of political scientists—Reg Whitaker on the organizing and financing of the Liberal Party and Canada and the Cold War, and S.J.R. Noel on the political culture of Ontario. Journalists such as Pierre Berton and James Gray enjoyed a popular readership far beyond that of most academics.

At a time when it seemed that there were no unchangeable signposts in the past it was perhaps inevitable that history as public memory would be treated as contested ground. The selectivity of memory and the manipulation of the past were central elements in Ian McKay, *The Quest of the Folk: Antimodernism and Cultural Selection in Twentieth-*

Century Nova Scotia (1994), Jonathan F. Vance, *Death So Noble: Memory, Meaning, and the First World War* (1997), and H.V. Nelles, *The Art of Nation-Building: Pageantry and Spectacle at Quebec's Tercentenary* (1999).

Despite this vast elaboration of Canadian history in all its richness and complexity, many observers (especially academics) detected a malaise, a sense that what had once been a coherent story of nation building was fragmented beyond repair, and an awareness that to the public history seemed to matter less and less. This was understandable, for much scholarly history told of oppression, victimization, and injustice, and was presented in a graceless formulaic fashion with jargon, graphs, statistical tables, and copious footnotes, and much on the shortcomings of predecessors. Historians who did not find it enlightening to learn of the role of taking in other people's laundry in the family economy of the working class accused social historians of trivializing history and subverting its 'mission' in forging national unity. Pronouncements about the death of Canadian history were premature, however, as the popularity of the CBC's television series, *Canada: A People's History* (broadcast 2001–2), indicated. It should provide some small comfort to note that the development of Canadian historiography since 1970 mirrored the growth of modern history writing everywhere.

CARL BERGER

hockey. Although it is widely held that hockey in its modern form originated in a game played by McGill students in 1875 under rules brought to Montreal by Haligonian J.G.A. Creighton, earlier forms of stick and ball games on ice had been played for decades, especially in the Maritimes and at military garrisons in Quebec and Kingston. Whatever its origins, hockey quickly spread from coast to coast. In 1893, Lord Stanley, Canada's governor general, donated a trophy to the champion senior team in the country, and teams from the Yukon to Nova Scotia competed for the prize. During the first two decades of the 20th century, an exclusively amateur brand of hockey in Canada increasingly gave way to emerging professional teams and leagues, beginning with the International Hockey League (1904), the Eastern Canadian Hockey League (1906), the National Hockey Association (1909), the Pacific Coast League (1912), and the National Hockey League (1917).

Without a doubt the NHL was the premier professional hockey league in North America, and by the Second World War was solidly ensconced in Montreal, Toronto, Boston, New York, Chicago, and Detroit, often referred to as the 'original six'. Sporting new arenas such as the Montreal Forum (1924) and Maple Leaf Gardens (1931), competing for the Stanley Cup, and taking advantage of new technologies such as radio broadcasting, NHL hockey established itself as a major league sport. Foster Hewitt's *Hockey Night in Canada* radio broadcasts, and later those of Danny Gallivan and French-language broadcaster René LeCavalier, also helped make hockey an important element of Canada's national identity. A first generation of hockey heroes quickly emerged, including defenceman Eddie Shore of the Boston Bruins, speedy forward Howie Morenz of the Montreal Canadiens, and goaltender Georges Vezina, after whom the NHL's Vezina Trophy for the best goals against average is named. They would be followed by the incomparable Maurice 'Rocket' *Richard, Gordie Howe, a rugged right-winger for the Detroit Red Wings, and gentlemanly Jean Beliveau of the Canadiens. During the 1960s the NHL followed baseball and football in a program of expansion that would ultimately result in a league of continental proportions.

Canada has always been a power in international hockey, dominating Olympic and world championship events from the 1920s until the 1950s, when the Swedes, Finns, Czechs, and Russians began to challenge for international supremacy. The most dramatic of the international encounters came in 1972: Canada eked out a victory in an eight-game series with the Soviet Union when Paul Henderson scored with 34 seconds left in the final game. Canadians also cheered as Wayne Gretzky and Mario Lemieux led Canada to victory in the 1986 Canada Cup series. A particularly notable triumph came in 2002, with Olympic gold medals for Canada's men's and women's hockey teams.

COLIN HOWELL

holidays. *See* PUBLIC HOLIDAYS.

Holt, Sir Herbert (1856–1941). Born in Geashill, King's County, Ireland, Holt was a Canadian railway contractor and capitalist who became a dominant force in Canadian hydroelectric, banking, and other economic developments. He came to Canada in 1873 and worked with several small Ontario railways before becoming superintendent of construction on the Canadian Pacific Railway's Mountain Division in 1884. He subsequently held other construction contracts, including some to electrify Montreal's street railways. His involvement in the merger of several electrical companies resulted in his election as president of Montreal Light, Heat and Power Consolidated. In 1901 he was named president of the Royal Bank of Canada—formerly the Merchants Bank of Halifax—which became Canada's largest bank. Active in numerous corporate mergers in the 1920s and early 1930s, Holt resigned as president of the Royal Bank in 1934.

T.D. REGEHR

home children. Between 1869 and the mid-1920s, thousands of British children were sent to Canada to benefit from a better life. Orphaned, abandoned, or left by families too poor to care for them, they were represented by over 50 philanthropic organizations in Britain and Scotland. In total, nearly 100,000 children would make the journey across the Atlantic.

In October 1869, Maria Rye, an English woman, accompanied 68 children from London's streets and workhouses to Canada. Rye established a 'distributing centre' in Niagara-on-the-Lake that placed the children on Canadian farms. Between 1870 and the 1920s, Annie Macpherson and her sisters, Louisa and Rachel, sent nearly 14,000 children to Canada. Many religious and philanthropic societies in Britain sent children, but the largest agency involved was the Barnardo Homes, founded by Dr Thomas J. Barnardo. By his death in 1905 at age 60, Barnardo had established a network of children's homes throughout the British Isles. At the beginning of the 20th century, almost every second immigrant child in Canada was from a Barnardo Home.

Once in Canada the children were to be placed in suitable homes. The placement system was intended to benefit both the children, who received the support of a new family, and farmers, who found suitable work for them. Children 9 years of age or younger were considered placed for *adoption, although the law did not govern such arrangements until the 1920s. Depending on the laws of individual provinces, older children were indentured to farmers to the ages of 16, 18, or 21.

Not surprisingly, many home children suffered various forms and degrees of abuse in their new homes. Promises of a modest allowance and an education were often not delivered. Placements were rarely monitored and abuses went unchecked. Four years after the emigration movement began, a visiting British commissioner complained about the placement laxities. Little was done, because the home children represented much-needed cheap farm labour. By the 1920s Canadian reformers such as Charlotte *Whitton and J.S. *Woodsworth echoed the concerns of British officials over the exploitation of home children. As a result, by 1924 only older teenagers were brought to Canada. Yet the schemes were ended only by the Great Depression and objections from labour movements, not by enlightened child-saving.

MONA GLEASON

home front. With innocent enthusiasm, cheering and parading crowds in virtually every Canadian city and town with a newspaper office greeted the outbreak of the First World War in 1914. As recruitment of the *Canadian Expeditionary Force commenced, civilian volunteers in the *Canadian Red Cross, the *Imperial Order Daughters of the Empire, *Women's Institutes, Next-of-Kin Associations, the *YWCA and *YMCA, and the *Canadian Patriotic Fund, among others, initiated war relief efforts, from sock-knitting drives to collecting funds to support soldiers' families.

The *War Measures Act, unanimously passed by Parliament on 14 August, gave Ottawa sweeping powers deemed 'necessary for the security, defence, peace, order and welfare of Canada'. The federal government imposed *censorship measures and market regulations, and required that all citizens of Germany, Austria-Hungary, or the Ottoman Empire, about 100,000, register as enemy aliens. An internment operations branch of the military detained a total of 8,579 enemy aliens, mostly young immigrants who could neither enlist by law nor hold down jobs in the face of public opinion.

Prime Minister Robert *Borden created the Imperial Munitions Board to increase shell and armaments production, the Wartime Purchasing Board to administer procurements, and the National Service Board to rationalize labour. Wartime production soared to $2 million a day, with 600 factories employing 150,000 workers—one in five were women—producing shells, ships, aircraft, and other military supplies. Women's labour, at lower rates of pay than men, also eased wartime shortages in transportation and agriculture. Wheat sales came under the Board of Grain Supervisor's control. A Food Controller oversaw gas, coal, and wood burning, with 'fuelless days' imposed monthly. The sale of Victory Bonds and war savings certificates supplemented wartime financing. Total wartime expenditures never exceeded 10 per cent of the GNP, though government loan debts grew to $2 billion. In 1916 the federal government imposed a war profits tax, and the following year a personal income tax, destined to become a key revenue source only after the war.

*Conscription became the most divisive home front measure, driving a deep wedge between French and English Canada. A major riot in Quebec City on Easter weekend left four civilians dead and ten soldiers wounded. Parliament passed the Military Service Act in July 1917, enabling the draft. Many farmers opposed conscription of their sons and resented the humiliation of local service board hearings. A general election in December 1917 gave the wartime *Union government, comprised of Conservatives and pro-conscription Liberals, a mandate bolstered by the *Wartime Elections Act. Following recent gains in *women's suffrage in some provinces, soldiers' wives, mothers, and sisters were granted the vote, while enemy aliens and pacifists were disenfranchised. Ottawa also imposed liquor *prohibition in the final year of the war, in the wake of anti-drink measures adopted in the provinces.

Twenty years later, in September 1939, the Second World War came on the heels of the Great Depression. A total war, involving the full *mobilization of resources, began, and more than a half million workers rapidly gained employment. The National Resources Mobilization Act required the registration of all men and women, aged 16–60. Once again, women filled non-traditional jobs, about 250,000 in factory work, in addition to the new women's auxilliaries for each of the armed service branches. A heated economy led to inflation, wage-and-price controls, and the sale, once again, of Victory Bonds. The War Measures Act was applied to hundreds of German and Italian Canadians, but the most drastic measure was the evacuation of 22,000 *Japanese Canadians (nearly three-quarters of whom had been born in Canada or naturalized) from coastal areas in British Columbia.

Conscription also returned to challenge Mackenzie *King's Liberal government. King's reluctance to send conscripts overseas until near the end of the war was guided by concerns over national unity. His decision in 1942 to hold a plebiscite, releasing his government from a promise to deploy only volunteers, underscored the French-English split. *'Zombie' conscripts drafted under the National Resources Mobilization Act remained on Canadian soil until November 1944.

Ottawa also adopted order-in-council PC 1003 in 1944, providing a framework for collective bargaining that outlasted the war. The federal government implemented *welfare state reforms, including family allowances and the creation of the departments of reconstruction, veterans affairs, and national health and welfare. The expansion of the interventionist state that began with the war continued in a post-war society characterized by consumer-based domesticity and relative conservatism and preoccupied by security seeking, child bearing, and family-based modernization. ROBERT RUTHERDALE

home missions. In the early 20th century, Canada experienced a mass influx of immigrants, many of them continental Europeans who settled in cities and became associated with the social and urban ills of the day including spreading poverty, slums, and infant mortality. Reform-minded, middle-class Canadian men and women became involved in a variety of social reforms intended to ameliorate the conditions of the working classes, including immigrants, and thus prevent social and moral decay. Motivated by a mix of Christian ideals (particularly the *social gospel movement), by notions of racial and moral superiority, and by anxieties about the dangers of unbridled industrialization and urbanization, Protestant Canadians, led by the Methodist and Presbyterian churches, incorporated the immigrants into their churches' expanded home missionary field and administered to them directly through local missions and *settlement houses based in poor neighbourhoods.

At the Fred Victor Mission in Toronto, Methodist minister J.S. *Woodsworth's All People's Mission in Winnipeg, and settlement houses in Montreal and other major cities, immigrants were offered social and recreational services, including sewing classes for women and girls and sports for boys, as well as nursing and medical help for babies and sick children. The immigrants were also exposed to English and civics classes, health lectures, and Canadianization programs intended to inculcate bourgeois Canadian values and standards and to transform the immigrants, or at least their children, into largely assimilated and morally proper Canadian citizens. Reform-oriented women such as suffrage leader and maternal feminist Nellie *McClung were particularly active in the social gospel and in home mission work. On a darker side, some reformers were also influenced by theories based on *eugenics, which assumed a racial hierarchy of peoples that placed themselves at the top, and race suicide, the fear that the (non-British) 'foreign-born' were procreating at a faster rate than Anglo-Celtic Canadians. FRANCA IACOVETTA

homesteading. Homesteading occupies a cherished place in the mythology of the prairie region. It remains a staple of both popular and scholarly histories, as well as published reminiscences, diaries, letter collections, and works of fiction. In many of these accounts, homesteading not only transformed the Prairies from an untamed grassland to a settled, agrarian society, but taught the settlers self-reliance, perseverance, neighbourliness, and other sterling virtues that shaped the western character.

Technically, homesteading refers to the legal process of 'proving up' a quarter section of western Canadian land (64 ha) available from the dominion government for a nominal registration fee, under the *Dominion Lands Act. Commonly, however, the term refers to agricultural pioneering in general, even if a settler purchased raw land from a railway company or other institutional seller. Although pioneering occurred in parts of the West throughout the 19th and 20th centuries, homesteading is usually associated with the great settlement boom of 1898–1914. Most settlers were young adults, single men, or couples with small children. They often selected homesteads located near friends or relatives from their former communities. Some selected land with physical features that reminded them of home, but many paid little attention to such important criteria as soil quality and distance from a railtown. Settlers commonly arrived in the West by railway and hauled their possessions to homesteads by horse and wagon. Although the sod hut acquired notoriety on the treeless plains, most settlers lived in tents until they could build one-room shacks. Those who survived subsequently built frame houses, including pre-fabricated models purchased by catalogue. Other duties during the first season including drilling a water well, erecting fences and outbuildings for livestock, breaking sod with a horse and walking plough, planting a garden, and seeding grain. Married couples enjoyed an advantage over their bachelor neighbours in sharing this work, and many women shouldered duties normally performed by men. Bachelors, who faced domestic chores in addition to field work, often found the labour overwhelming. Many soon visited their home communities to search for brides.

Since pioneering involved considerable costs before a profitable farm could be developed, settlers often left their homesteads in winter to seek employment income. Few could afford to buy all the machinery or supply all the labour they needed, so neighbours often shared their time and equipment. Local contractors carried out some duties, especially well drilling and grain threshing. Co-operative efforts also prevailed to build community institutions like schools, churches, and meeting halls.

The nature of homesteading depended on the time and place of settlement, and on the national, ethnic, and religious origins of the settlers. Pioneers along the northern fringes of the arable prairie devoted considerable time to clearing trees before land could be broken. Europeans from peasant cultures often preferred parklands with wood and water. They used little machinery, but much labour, to develop small, mixed farms designed more for self-sufficiency than commercial profitability. By contrast, some wealthy, business-minded pioneers from eastern Canada and the United States bought vast tracts of flat, treeless land on the southern plains and launched bonanza wheat farms that utilized considerable machinery and hired labour. In most cases, pioneers began with a quarter-section homestead and later expanded by adding one or more additional quarters. In some arid districts, irrigation gave rise to yet another pioneering experience.

American Mormons were often involved in these projects, while other ethnic and sectarian groups arrived with their own visions of Utopian communities. Some English settlers hoped to replicate the life of a landed aristocracy, while communal groups like the Russian *Doukhobors owned land and machinery in common, worked their farms co-operatively, and lived in centralized villages.

Some settlers wished to develop farms to support their families indefinitely, while others intended to speculate, selling out at various stages of development, and often homesteading again on another frontier. Many pioneers failed as a result of drought, hail, early frosts, grasshoppers, fires, or wheat rust, or because of ill-chosen locations, poor soils, inadequate financing, weak management skills, or lack of agricultural knowledge. Many more succeeded in spite of these difficulties. All contributed to the mammoth task of creating both an agrarian society and a regional mythology. PAUL VOISEY

Hong Kong, Battle of. One of the worst catastrophes, in terms of percentage of losses, the Canadian army suffered in the course of the Second World War was at Hong Kong, a colony of the British Empire to which Canada decided to contribute two battalions in late 1941. Given a lack of documentation, the reasoning behind making such a contribution is rather obscure, but for the troops of the two battalions concerned, the Royal Rifles of Canada and the Winnipeg Grenadiers, such issues were less important at the time than the fact that they had been posted to an exotic locale. Neither unit had been properly trained for combat, but both were deemed suitable for garrison duties.

Arriving in Hong Kong in November 1941, they found themselves, whether tactically skilled or not, in the thick of fighting after Japanese forces, following the attacks on Pearl Harbor and elsewhere of 7–8 December, invaded the British colony. Along with four other battalions from various points in the empire, the Canadians fought for several days, but were constantly forced to withdraw as Japanese units outflanked them. It is a mark of the two units' lack of tactical training that the enemy was, almost without exception, able to capture high ground before the Royals or Grenadiers could occupy it, forcing the latter to engage in near-hopeless counterattacks.

The colony surrendered on Christmas Day. Having lost 290 men in the fighting, the Canadians would lose another 268 in Japanese prison camps. Put to work in various industries in Japan, they suffered fatality rates ranging from 4.5 per cent in one group to 20 per cent overall. When liberated in 1945 nearly all suffered from diseases and conditions directly attributable to their incarceration. In the years that followed, veterans of the battle for Hong Kong sought compensation, achieving only partial success some 50 years after the war ended. The Royal Rifles of Canada and the Winnipeg Grenadiers were the only two units of the Canadian army to lose 100 per cent of their strength in a single battle. BILL RAWLING

honours. *See* GALLANTRY AWARDS; NATIONAL HONOURS.

Hoodless, Adelaide Sophia (1858–1910). Born in Brant County, Ontario, Adelaide Hunter married furniture manufacturer John Hoodless in 1881 and moved to Hamilton. In 1890 she became president of the city's *Young Women's Christian Association, and organized the founding of the national YWCA in 1893–5. She also helped establish the *National Council of Women of Canada, where she served as treasurer.

Deeply troubled that urban industrial employment robbed young women of traditional domestic skills, Hoodless campaigned locally for the introduction of domestic science into public schools. Ontario's minister of education, George Ross, hired her on contract to promote the curricular innovation. A speech she made at the Ontario Agricultural College in 1897 led directly to the founding of the Ontario *Women's Institutes. The institutes eventually spread around the world as rural women's organizations, but Hoodless served more as inspiration than instigator. When the school of domestic science and art that she began at the Hamilton YWCA in 1900 failed to raise sufficient money to continue, Hoodless worked with OAC president James Mills to secure a large donation from tobacco magnate William Macdonald. This fund built the Macdonald Institute at Guelph, where Hoodless moved her school in 1903. Operated in conjunction with the OAC, the institute continued to graduate home economists, nutritionists, and dietitians until 1970.

TERRY CROWLEY

Hope Simpson, Sir John (1868–1961), colonial administrator; **Lady Hope Simpson**, née Mary Jane Barclay (1870–1939). After a career in the Indian Civil Service, the Ministry of Labour, the United Kingdom Parliament (1922–4), and the League of Nations, Hope Simpson was appointed in 1934 to the Newfoundland *Commission of Government. Based in St John's until September 1936, the Hope Simpsons travelled extensively in the country by car, train, and boat. Sir John and Quita (as Lady Hope Simpson was called) recounted their adventures in detailed and lengthy letters to their two sons and three daughters in England. They gave Newfoundland society mixed reviews but rhapsodized over the landscape. The Cambridge-educated Quita had a particular flair for description of natural wonders. Though written from the perspective of officialdom, their letters constitute a rich source for understanding both the workings of the Commission of Government and the social history of Newfoundland in the 1930s. Excerpted in *White Tie and Decorations: Sir John and Lady Hope Simpson in Newfoundland, 1934–1936* (1996), the letters read like an epistolary novel and are part of the *Schwanengesang* of the *British Empire. PETER NEARY

horse racing. Racing horses has been a part of Canadian life from the time of the earliest settlers. The habitants of New France raced horses on the ice. Settlers in the Maritimes and Upper Canada raced at the agricultural fairs that sprang up during the first half of the 19th century. However, as a sport with an organizational infrastructure the beginning was in 1860, with the running, in Toronto, of the first Queen's Plate. During the 1860s and 1870s the plate was run on different tracks. In 1881, a small group of wealthy Ontarians formed the Ontario Jockey Club to bring some focus and control to the thoroughbred scene. The social elite's control of horse racing was solidified when Parliament passed an act restricting betting to their tracks. In fact, they dominated racing; the horses of Joseph Seagram, of distillery fame, won 20 Queen's Plates between 1891 and 1935. A thoroughbred-racing calendar was established in limited locations: Toronto, Montreal, Winnipeg, Vancouver, Victoria, and Calgary. However, one of the highlights of 20th-century horse racing occurred in 1920 at the Devonshire Track in Windsor, Ontario, when Man O' War beat Sir Barton in front of 32,000 spectators. Another far more pervasive and popular form of racing was harness racing. Locally based circuits, for ice racing during the winter and at commercial tracks and agricultural fairs during the summer, developed from Halifax to Victoria. Central to both forms of racing were the opportunities for *gambling. Gradually, betting shifted from the thoroughbred scene to harness racing. By 1971, the latter attracted $177 million in betting, eclipsing the $115 million bet on thoroughbreds. By 2000 harness racing was dominated by 33 commercial tracks across the country. ALAN METCALFE

hospitals. The hospital arrived in Canada in the 17th century when Roman Catholic religious orders established the Hôtels-Dieux for the medical treatment and care of the sick poor in the principal settlements of New France. For the next 250 years hospitals, as medical charities, were restricted to a few major urban centres, where they provided custodial care for sick and injured persons without familial support networks, and coincidentally furnished, in the Victorian era, clinical subjects for medical education and research. These institutions were popularly regarded as warehouses of death because of the prevalence of deadly infections before the acceptance of germ theory and the imposition of aseptic environmental regimes at the end of the 19th century. Since no invasive surgery was performed in hospitals except as a last resort, and the threat of puerperal sepsis discouraged hospital births, these institutions were medically irrelevant. They did, however, manifest the moral and social benefaction of the comfortable classes (who preferred to be treated at home by their personal physicians) towards the 'deserving poor'.

The modern hospital for the scientific diagnosis of, and medical intervention in, acute illnesses among all social classes emerged between 1890 and 1914 from the convergence of several historical developments. One was the advent of the new science of *nursing. Following the Nightingalian nursing revolution in the 1860s and 1870s, the hospital-based nurses' training schools that proliferated in the 1880s produced a new profession of female caregivers whose scientific education complemented the assumed natural domesticity and moral authority of middle-class Victorian womanhood. Student nurses also proved to be a vast source of cheap labour for financially challenged hospitals. A second development was the medical profession's gradual acceptance, between 1870 and 1890, of germ theory and its application within the hospital to create a contagion-free environment conducive to safe surgery and childbirth. At the same time, the laboratory sciences—chemistry and biology—that had spawned the bacteriological revolution became the essential handmaidens of medical diagnosis through serology, urinalysis, and tissue pathology. Similarly, technology, particularly Roentgen's discovery of the diagnostic and therapeutic potential of X-rays in 1895, also enhanced the reputation of the new scientific medicine over the claims of the myriad medical sects, irregular practitioners, and quacks who had hitherto competed successfully in the medical marketplace. These developments converged in the general hospital, which very quickly after 1890 became the exclusive community source of medical science and, more particularly, the surgeon's workshop—a 'factory whose product is health'.

The advent of hospital-based scientific medicine made the hospital medically essential for all social classes. The result was an era of unparalleled hospital construction between 1890 and 1930 as communities large and small sought to acquire this essential new public utility, whether it was a 25-bed cottage hospital in Birtle, Manitoba, or a 500-bed model teaching and research facility like Toronto General (1912). Amid such variants as civic, confessional, and specialist (women's, children's, lying-in) hospitals, the most common institution in Canada was the voluntary public general community hospital, a charitable trust managed by a board of citizen volunteers. The sick poor continued to constitute a significant community burden, partially supported by public charity in the form of provincial and municipal per diem maintenance grants. Hospital boards were expected to fund the balance of indigent care costs from private charity. In fact, they increasingly depended on the income from the fees they charged to paying patients to balance their operating budgets, to expand capacity to meet demand, and to keep abreast of medical innovation. The urban middle classes not only were able to pay for hospital treatment and care, but eagerly sought hospitalization differentiated from the public wards, which were contaminated by historical association with pauperism. Hospitals were no longer one-class institutions; they were socially structured around the patient's ability to pay for the degrees of luxury represented by private, semi-private, and semi-public accommodation. The 'patient of moderate means' who could pay the full cost of differentiated hospitalization quickly became the object of the hospital enterprise whose insatiable appetite for income was recognized even before the First World War as the Achilles heel of scientific progress and of medical and social responsibility.

Early intimations of financial fallibility turned to reality in the 1920s as economic dislocation, growing social structural inequality, and demographic change escalated the costs of meeting the demand for hospitalization, especially among the indigent and chronically ill. For example, it was estimated that in 1920 half of the population of British Columbia could not afford medical care, hospital care in particular, at any price. The Great Depression exacerbated these trends and added others. The ability of the middle classes to sustain, through perpetually increasing hospital charges, the unmet costs of indigent hospitalization had been exhausted. It was estimated that a three-week hospital stay would effectively bankrupt a typical white-collar worker. Second, a rapidly increasing incidence of lifestyle diseases would drive the post-war upsurge in hospitalization and the new costs associated with an epidemic of cancer and cardio-pulmonary and respiratory diseases. Finally, the discovery of penicillin on the eve of the Second World War anticipated the pharmacologically based therapeutic revolution and the incalculable costs of realizing its potential. Meanwhile, hospital deficits accumulated dangerously; some community hospitals were forced to close their doors (33 in Saskatchewan alone); doctors and nurses, unable to earn a living, migrated out of small communities.

To many Canadians, the solution to this crisis was a system in which the cost of health care was not borne by the sick alone, or subsidized by the middle-class patient, but was shared by all members of the community. The first successful attempt at creating a publicly funded health care scheme in Canada was the hospital insurance program initiated by the CCF government in Saskatchewan in 1944–7. Its success in providing hospital accessibility throughout the province, in improving the quality of medical care, in attracting health professionals to Saskatchewan, and in stabilizing doctors' incomes, undoubtedly encouraged the other nine provinces, beginning with Ontario in 1957, to adopt the federal government's model of jointly funded, provincially operated contributory public hospital insurance programs. They have now been folded into comprehensive provincial health insurance programs. But the uncontrollable hospital costs associated with insatiable demand stimulated by the promise of scientifically mediated immortality remains.

DAVID GAGAN AND ROSEMARY GAGAN

See also MEDICARE.

Houde, Camillien (1889–1958). Born in Montreal, Houde studied at a commercial high school and was a bank employee and an insurance salesman before devoting his career to politics. First elected to Quebec's legislative assembly in 1923, in 1929–32 he headed the provincial Conservative Party opposing Premier Louis-Alexandre *Taschereau, but resigned after he lost the election of 1931. Houde was most famous as mayor of Montreal (1928–32, 1934–6, 1938–40, 1944–54). During the Depression he tried to help the city's unemployed through numerous public-works projects. He also tried to improve the battered city's finances by initiating a sales tax, a novelty in the province. In 1940 he rejected the National Resources Mobilization Act and was promptly arrested and sent to an internment camp. Released in 1944, he returned to Montreal and was re-elected mayor. He was also elected to the House of Commons as an independent (1949–53). Though relatively well educated and relishing an expensive lifestyle, Houde was a populist in politics and stressed his humble origins. His style and discourse were very popular among the Montreal working class.

PAUL-ANDRÉ LINTEAU

House of Commons. The lower chamber of Canada's bicameral legislature established by the Constitution Act 1867. Known familiarly as Parliament, its 310 members (in 2002) are elected by universal *franchise in single-member constituencies, each designed to be as equal in population as Canada's varied geography permits. Constitutionally, Parliament must have annual sessions but cannot continue beyond five years. Prorogation brings a parliament to an end, clearing the slate for a new parliament whose composition and leadership are the outcome of a general election. Timing of the decision to prorogue is controlled by the prime minister, who seldom waits for the expiry date. Parliament creates its own procedures and now elects from its own membership a speaker, who is not only the impartial arbiter of proceedings but also, with the help of an expert staff, the chief administrative officer. Such self-regulation under its own independent officer is vital to the preservation of Parliament's role as open forum for scrutinizing the government's conduct of the nation's business. The influence of Parliament as the nation's talk shop depends upon how its proceedings are reported. Historically, a daily record of proceedings, a so-called Hansard, has been published; more recently televised records have also been maintained. The media's reporting of parliamentary activity determines the image of Parliament in the public's mind, often a distorted image created by what reporters deem newsworthy. The business of the House, concluded in short order in earlier times, has increased to require it to remain in permanent session with three set adjournment vacations each year. Resort to standing and special committees has enabled MPs to contend somewhat with an expanding agenda. Despite procedural reforms, criticism of Parliament is rampant, based not only on generally negative appraisals by the media but also on misconceptions of its true role. That role is often described as governing; yet, it is the *cabinet that governs, assisted by the non-political career public service. The House does not initiate but acts as the 'focus group' for the government's proposals, debating general policy, questioning its detailed application, and generally enforcing transparency in the formulation and conduct of the nation's business. Even Parliament's traditional role as controller of the public purse, assisted by the *auditor general, is limited to post facto commentary. Indeed, its ultimate power to bring government to heel by a vote of no-confidence is effectively controlled, as are all other proceedings, by party discipline, which remains in the hands of cabinet and prime minister.

J.E. HODGETTS

housing. In terms of the size and quality of their homes, Canadians are among the best-housed people in the world, but lower-income people still face a housing problem. Until the 1960s this took the form of poor and inadequate dwellings; where these were clustered in urban areas they were known as slums. In the past 30 years, as minimum housing standards have been enforced, the housing problem has become one of affordability and homelessness. Today, on average, Canadians spend almost 30 per cent of their income on housing; a century ago they spent about half that.

Lower-income households have usually been housed through a process of filtering down, by which homes built for the affluent deteriorate and become cheaper. In the process, structures become unsound or, when subdivided, overcrowded. Poor housing was once associated with inadequate public services: piped water and sewers were standard in middle-class areas by the 1880s, but many workers' districts still lacked these in the 1920s. There were risks from water-borne diseases such as *cholera, while women and children hauled water to cook and clean. During the reform era of the 1890s to the 1920s, middle-class observers fretted about the moral implications of overcrowding, where children of both sexes shared bedrooms or where families took in lodgers. The passage and later enforcement of building regulations, and from the 1930s of occupancy and housing (maintenance) bylaws, raised minimum standards. In the 1950s and 1960s slum-clearance programs eliminated the worst urban housing. These efforts, and the gentrification of many inner districts since the 1970s, eliminated affordable housing and helped create homelessness.

As artifacts, houses help define the Canadian landscape, both rural and urban. Materials and architectural styles once distinguished cities and regions: painted wood in the Atlantic region, plexes with outside iron staircases in Montreal, gabled row houses of polychromatic brick veneer in Toronto, and variations on the bungalow, sometimes stuccoed, out west. From the 1940s to the 1970s redevelopment and suburban growth occurred in a generically modern idiom. Since the 1980s, local and regional styles have again become popular.

The varied character of Canadian houses reflect the changing social relations of production, ownership, and use. Houses have been built by owners for their own use or by professionals who have either built for specific clients or on speculation. Most families that built homes did so from necessity, erecting modest structures that they improved over time. Custom builders were hired by those who could afford distinctive, often architect-designed homes. Speculative, or 'merchant', builders occupied the large and growing middle ground, erecting larger numbers of standard homes for a predictable market. To this day, most builders erect fewer than five homes a year, using materials and techniques that have evolved steadily, but slowly, over the decades. The main development in the past century has been the growth of offsite production, first of windows and doors and then of roof trusses.

In Canada, as opposed to Europe, most housing has always been privately owned. Public housing—that is, housing built for state agencies and rented at subsidized rates—has been built since the late 1940s, and 'third sector' (mostly co-op) housing was built in significant numbers from the 1970s. Today, more than nine in ten homes are still privately owned, whether owner-occupied or rented. In urban areas until the early 20th century about a quarter of all housing units were owner-occupied; although few acquired homes before reaching their forties, a small majority of families were eventually able to acquire a home. Owner-occupancy rose during the urban boom of 1900–30, because of owner-building by workers and immigrants. After falling during the Depression, it increased from the early 1940s as mortgage financing became available on easier terms. Today more than two-thirds of homes are owner-occupied. Almost all home buyers have required credit, although until the 1930s it was usual for households to save until they had a down payment of about half the purchase price. They often borrowed the balance from a family member or a wealthy widow. Lending institutions played a role from the mid-19th century, but became the main source of mortgage finance only in the 1950s. In the 1930s the Dominion Housing Act, later folded into the National Housing Act, encouraged 'approved' lenders to make long-term, amortized loans. The state taught home buyers to acquire homes by taking on prodigious debt.

The growth of owner-occupancy among households has been impressive because more people have been able to form their own households. Until the 1920s it was normal for young people to stay at home until they married, and sometimes after. Elderly parents were cared for in their children's homes. Until the 1950s, families 'doubled up', or took in lodgers, which both enabled unwaged women to earn income and supplemented the household's revenue. At first most lodgers boarded, taking meals with their hosts. By the 1920s, rising incomes and changing standards of privacy were reducing lodging to a mere rooming arrangement. Booms in apartment construction in the 1920s and 1960s enabled young married couples, and then single people, to set up housekeeping, although recent problems of affordability have compelled some young adults to remain in, or return to, their parents' home.

Homes have enabled family life to turn inwards. After the 1920s new homes lacked verandahs, semi-public spaces for observing and visiting with neighbours. Radios and gramophones created new forms of home entertainment that were later extended by television and home computers. New spaces accommodated them, and homes became more important for recreation. As dwellings became larger and families smaller, it became common for each family member to have his or her own room. Canadians have not reached the limit of private space they are willing to pay for. RICHARD HARRIS

Howe, Clarence Decatur (1886–1960). Born in Massachusetts, and a graduate of MIT, Howe came to Halifax to become a professor at Nova Scotia Technical College, and stayed to work for the Canadian Board of Grain Commissioners. He decided in 1915 to launch into private enterprise, and by the late 1920s the C.D. Howe Company had become the world's leading builder of grain elevators, but the Depression flattened Howe's company. In 1935 he won election to Parliament as a Liberal, becoming minister of railways and canals (later minister of transport) in the Mackenzie King government. A successful wartime stint as minister of munitions and supply and then minister of reconstruction established Howe not just as a prominent politician but as a leader of the Canadian business community. In the 1950s, as minister of trade and commerce in the St Laurent government, he directed the Canadian economy via his personal connections and through megaprojects such as the St Lawrence Seaway and the Trans-Canada Pipeline. Renowned for his administrative skills, Howe was scarcely less famous for his abruptness and impatience; by the mid-1950s he had become a political liability, contributing to the Liberal defeat in 1957. Losing his own seat, Howe moved to Montreal for a few frantic years as a corporate tycoon.

ROBERT BOTHWELL

Howe, Joseph (1804–73). A decade after acquiring the *Novascotian* in 1827, Joseph Howe, a man of restless vitality, had made it the province's most influential newspaper. After publicizing the corruption in local government, he used his oratorical powers to defend himself successfully in the province's most celebrated libel suit. Using the *Novascotian* to the full, he secured almost single-handedly a majority of reforming assemblymen in 1836. As a conservative reformer he was the driving force in achieving *responsible government in 1848 without a pane of glass being broken. After 1850 he promoted visionary but unachievable projects such as building an intercolonial railway and revamping the empire to permit colonials a share in its government. He got only his 'poor bantling', the railway from Halifax to Windsor, and the uninfluential position of imperial fishery commissioner. When finally he became premier in 1860, provincial politics was a stagnant pool, lacking the great themes on which he liked to expound. Arguing that Nova Scotia should not be forced into a scheme of dubious economic benefit without its consent, he opposed *Confederation and led the 'Antis' to overwhelming victories in the provincial and federal elections of September 1867. Finding repeal unattainable and no longer trusting British politicians, the Briton became Canadian and accepted the situation. Using patronage skilfully, he reached an accommodation with the Nova Scotian Anti MPs and pacified a dangerous situation. His health broken by a mid-winter by-election campaign, he served only three weeks as lieutenant-governor before his death in 1873. Some, like Angus L. *Macdonald, called Howe the greatest Nova Scotian. Howe believed that a leader should, 'neither be afraid of the saddle by day nor the lamp by night [but] in advance of the general intelligence . . . should lead the way to improvement and prosperity'.

J. MURRAY BECK

Hudson, Henry. The ill-fated explorer who left his name on Canada's great inland sea is best known for the mutiny that cast him and a small band of followers adrift in *Hudson Bay in June 1611. The London-born Hudson's early life is unknown. A master mariner and an intrepid explorer, he was not a leader of men; his voyages were marked by discord and near-mutiny, and he was the architect of his own death thanks to indecisiveness and failure to assert control over an unruly crew. Hudson's achievements, nonetheless, were remarkable. In just five years (1607–11) he charted a portion of the Northeast Passage across the top of Europe and opened the Svalbard Arctic whale fishery to commercial exploitation. He also, often in defiance of orders from his private employers, pursued the *Northwest Passage. His 1609 voyage in *Half Moon* surveyed the American eastern seaboard and charted the Hudson River (and the future site of New York City) in a vain quest for the passage. His final voyage of 1610–11 led into the great bay. While not the entrance to the Northwest Passage, Hudson Bay proved to be the gateway to Canada's rich fur trade and the foundation of a great mercantile enterprise, the *Hudson's Bay Company, founded in 1670.

JAMES DELGADO

Hudson Bay, 'land of fog and bog', is the world's largest sea (637,000 sq km) within the boundaries of one country. The west shore is composed of lowlands while the east shore has steep margins. Twice-daily tides, highest on the west shore, can reach nearly 4 m at Churchill. The bay freezes in winter; ice persists until June. The boundary between the arctic and boreal climatic regions falls between *York Factory and Churchill, roughly coincident with the tree line, continuous permafrost (60 m deep at Churchill), and with the 100 C summer isotherm. The tree line has moved north since the Little Ice Age (AD 1450–1850). Cree Indians reside on James Bay and the southwest coast of Hudson Bay. Inuit occupy the west coast from 60 degrees north and the east coast north of 55 degrees. The bay and the waters draining into it were assigned by royal charter in 1670 to the *Hudson's Bay Company and not relinquished until 1870. During its first century the HBC operated posts only on the bay, notably Churchill, York Factory, Severn, Albany, and Moose Factory. At these posts, fur traders kept weather records over a longer period than anywhere else in North America (810,735 data points for York Factory and Churchill combined), and collected bird species for Linnaeus to describe in 1758, exceeded in number only by Catesby's collections from South Carolina. William Wales observed the transit of Venus at Churchill in 1769, helping to determine the distance from the earth to the sun. Christopher Middleton studied the effects of cold, and Dr Thomas Hutchins determined the congealing point of mercury, both efforts earning the prestigious Copley Medal. In 1929, the *Hudson Bay Railway reached Churchill, a shorter route than the Great Lakes for grain shipments to Europe. Churchill is a popular birding destination because of the juxtaposition of freshwater lakes and saltwater, boreal forest and subarctic tundra.

C. STUART HOUSTON

Hudson Bay Railway. Prairie grain farmers, frustrated with the *freight rates charged by Canadian railways, dreamed of a competitive railway paralleling the old and shortest trade routes from western Canada to British and European markets—through Hudson Strait and *Hudson Bay. To build along this route, two rival companies were chartered in 1880; they amalgamated in 1883 and the first 64 km were built in 1888. Promoters of the Canadian Northern Railway took over the project in the 1890s. They opted for an alternative route but failed to build northward beyond Hudson Bay Junction in Saskatchewan. *Canadian National Railways completed construction of the line to Churchill, Manitoba, in 1929. Since then the *grain trade through Churchill has been limited by obsolete grain-handling facilities, high marine insurance rates due to ice hazards along the northern shipping lanes, and a roadbed that cannot accommodate the heavier modern grain hopper cars. Northern mineral deposits generate some local traffic. T.D. REGEHR

Hudson's Bay Company. One of the oldest joint stock–trading companies in the world, the HBC received a royal charter from Charles II on 2 May 1670 granting it monopoly trading rights and title to the vast territory drained by rivers flowing into the Hudson Strait. Ironically, two Frenchmen, Médard Chouart, Sieur des Groseilliers and Pierre-Esprit *Radisson, first proposed the idea of creating a company to operate in this region. After failing to obtain French support, they travelled to the court of Charles II, where they persuaded his cousin, Prince Rupert, and an influential group of courtiers to back their scheme. The success of the initial voyage to the region in 1668 encouraged the financial backers to form a permanent trading company.

From its inception to the modern era, the company was managed from London by the 'Governor and Committee', which was elected from among the shareholders at the annual general court. Until the 20th century, members of the committee did not visit Canada. Rather, they managed by correspondence from London. Canadian management was the responsibility of senior commissioned officers, the post commanders or chief factors. During the first 100 years of the company's operations, the directors restricted trading-post operations to the shores of Hudson and James Bays, a strategy the company's critics dubbed 'sleeping by the frozen sea'. The commanders at *York Factory and Fort Albany were in charge of the operations of their respective regions. After the 1770s, when the company moved inland, a more complex organization was needed to meet the opposition and minimize competition between its own posts. It divided the country into trading districts, each of which had a senior officer who acted as a manager. In 1810 the HBC grouped the districts into two departments: the Southern (essentially present-day northern Ontario) and Northern (the Prairie provinces and the Northwest Territories), each of which had a governor. After the merger with the *North West Company in 1821, George *Simpson was appointed head of the Northern Department, which temporarily was expanded to include *New Caledonia (mainland British Columbia). In 1839 he was placed in charge of all of the company's Canadian operations as governor-in-chief of *Rupert's Land, a position he held until his death in 1860. He added the Montreal Department (mostly present-day Quebec) in the 1840s. Chief Factor John McLaughlin directed the Columbia District in Oregon country, formerly a North West Company domain, until 1845, when the HBC created a board of management consisting of three district heads. Although the company underwent many organizational changes in subsequent years, the spatial management structure remained fundamentally the same.

The company's labour force was markedly hierarchical, with three groups of employees. The uppermost level consisted of commissioned officers, most of whom were recruited in Europe, especially Scotland, until the mid-20th century. After 1810 the company gave them a share in the trading profits in addition to their salaries. Below the officers were contract servants consisting of two groups: skilled tradesmen, and unskilled workers and apprentices. Until the late 18th century the company recruited most of these men in Europe, initially from England, and subsequently from Scotland. Beginning in the late 18th century the company also recruited in Canada and hired increasing numbers of workers of mixed Aboriginal-European descent. The lowest echelon of the workforce consisted of seasonal workers, most of whom were of First Nations and mixed ancestry.

In addition to fur trading, the company was involved in two colonization schemes. The first of these was at Red River, where in 1834 it took over control from the Selkirk estate the settlement (Assiniboia) established by Thomas Douglas, the 5th Earl of *Selkirk, in 1812. On the west coast the British government granted the company a charter for the *Vancouver Island colony in 1849. It held this charter until the creation of the colony of British Columbia in 1858.

The HBC began to change in fundamental ways after 1863, when the International Financial Society bought control primarily to gain the company's title to Rupert's Land. Until that time a small group of shareholders who were interested in the *fur trade owned the company. The new shareholders anticipated receiving a quick bonanza on their investment through the sale of the company's title. This was not to be. In a complex agreement signed in 1870, Canada bought the company's title to Rupert's Land for $1.5 million, a figure far less than what the shareholders expected. The company retained the developed land around its posts and a 1/20th share of the prairie West. In 1870 the shareholders gathered in London to chart the company's future in light of this sale. The Governor and Committee put forward a diversification plan that envisioned the company remaining active in the fur trade, while developing its remaining real estate holdings and expanding its retailing activities. Reluctantly, the shareholders agreed. The stage was set for the development of the modern company, which became involved in real-estate development, resource extraction (most notably oil and gas), transportation, wholesaling and retailing (department and northern stores). It remained active in the fur trade until 1986, when it sold its fur-trading interests. This was a time when the company also retrenched from other activities to focus on its *department store business. ARTHUR J. RAY

Hughes, Sir Sam (1853–1921). First a teacher then a journalist-editor in Lindsay, Ontario, Hughes was the quintessential militiaman and politician who believed implicitly in Sir John A. *Macdonald's Conservative Party and the moral duty of the volunteer citizen-soldier to be the first line of Canada's defence. He was intelligent, very ambitious, pushy, opinionated, and proof that Canadian history is not dull. He had all of the national pride and optimism of the Confederation generation. Elected to Parliament in 1892, Hughes was a talented campaigner and a powerful federal Tory party organizer and loyalist during their lean opposition years. With victory in 1911, Hughes was rewarded with the Borden government's militia portfolio. With great flare and greater controversy, Hughes set about shaping the *militia into his citizen-soldier image with more armouries and equipment, but little for professional force development. When war came in 1914, Hughes was rightly applauded as the person who rallied the nation to war, established the munitions industry, and, some say, kept the Canadians together as an national force. But by late 1916 his increasingly chaotic administration, bristling nationalism, *Ross rifle and shell scandals, and increasing tendency to flout responsible government, finally forced the prime minister to fire him. RONALD HAYCOCK

Huguenots. French Protestants who followed the teachings of John *Calvin in the 16th-century Reformation were for obscure reasons called 'Huguenots'. They made up 10 per cent of the French population in 1560, before a series of civil wars arrested their growth. Huguenots obtained limited religious toleration with the 1598 Edict of Nantes, but their rights were eroded over the course of the 17th century and finally suppressed by Louis XIV in 1685.

French Protestantism was concentrated in the west of France, notably in the port towns of the Atlantic coast, including La Rochelle. Huguenot merchants were key participants in early colonial ventures, including failed attempts to establish Protestant colonies in Brazil (1555) and Florida (1562–4). Pierre *Du Gua de Monts, together with Pierre Chauvin, established a Huguenot presence at Tadoussac (1600) and *Port-Royal in Acadia (1604), events chronicled by the Huguenot sympathizer Marc *Lescarbot, author of *Histoire de la Nouvelle-France* (1609).

Huguenots were barred from New France from 1625 onward, as colonial governors pursued a policy of religious orthodoxy. In the eyes of authorities, Huguenots were not simply heretics but, insofar as they shared the religion of England and Holland, likely traitors as well. Charters of monopolistic commercial companies such as the Compagnie des cent-associés founded in 1627–8, specifically excluded Huguenots, who were also denied any opportunity to spread their creed through mission in New France. In 1664, French chief minister Jean-Baptiste Colbert, seeking to boost the economic fortunes of France's Atlantic colonies, sought to encourage Huguenot participation in the new Compagnie des Indes occidentales. Yet such plans made little headway against the prevailing official hostility towards Huguenots. Its small population, strict church surveillance of orthodoxy, and relative isolation ensured that New France would never become a religious refuge for French Protestants. PETER A. GODDARD

Hunt, George (1854–1933), ethnographic fieldworker. Born in Fort Rupert, British Columbia, Hunt was the son of Mary Ebbets, a Tongass Tlingit noblewoman, and Robert Hunt, a Hudson's Bay Company employee and later postmaster at Fort Rupert. In 1872 George Hunt married Lucy Homiskanis, with whom he had a large family. After Lucy's death in 1908, he married Francine, who survived him. Both women belonged to the Kwakwaka'wakw (Kwakiutl) of coastal BC. In his adolescence and young adulthood Hunt was employed as an HBC fur buyer. In 1879, he began a second, highly productive career as a fieldworker for a series of museum collectors and ethnographers. Through this labour Hunt became one of the most important fieldworkers in the history of Native North American ethnography.

Hunt's most significant professional relationship, lasting from 1888 until his death, was with pioneering US anthropologist Franz *Boas, who hired him to collect material culture and to provide him with linguistic, ethnographic, and folkloric information. Boas published some 15 books based on their collaborative Kwakwaka'wakw research; 11 of the volumes consist largely or exclusively of Hunt's Kwak'wala-language texts. While this work was not without flaws, probably no single ethnographic enterprise has documented a Native North American group as completely and from as many different angles. JUDITH BERMAN

Huron Confederacy. The Huron comprised five tribes joined in a defensive alliance against their common enemy, the *Iroquois League. Except for mutual aid in war, each tribe was largely independent. Collectively the Huron called themselves Ouendat (Islanders), Huron being their French nickname meaning 'boar's or bristly head' (*hure*) after the ridge of hair on the men's heads. The five tribes were the Attignawantan (Bear People), Attigneenongnahac (Cord Makers), Arendaronon (Rock People), Tahontaenrat (Deer People), and Ataronchronon (Swamp People).These tribes shared a common culture, spoke mutually intelligible Iroquoian dialects, and lived in adjacent territories. Today, these five territories are called Huronia (northern Simcoe County, Ontario), but originally there was no special name for the area. The Bear and Cord claimed that their alliance went back to the mid-15th century; the Rock joined them about 1590 and the Deer about 1610, while the Swamp people seem to have formed during the 1630s. Before the others joined the

Bear and Cord, they lived to the south and southeast. The reason for the movement into Huronia seems to have been warfare along the southern frontier. Before the epidemics accompanying European contact (1636–41), the Huron population was about 25,000 in 20 villages. By 1640, a Jesuit census yielded 9,000 in 23 villages.

Individual Huron saw themselves first as members of an extended family and clan, secondly of a village and tribe, and lastly of the confederacy. The most important economic and decision-making level was the extended family, a collective of nuclear families presided over by an elderly matron who lived in her longhouse with her married daughters, their spouses and offspring, and unmarried daughters and sons. Her married sons would live with their wives in the houses of her lineage. Next in importance to the extended family was membership in one of eight clans. Clan membership was inherited at birth through the female (mother's) line, ultimately to a mythical ancestor. Clan members treated each other like cousins and were prohibited from marrying each other. All discussions and decisions filtered through these kin structures before they came to the village councils, made up of the older men appointed by the clans and presided over by a respected chief. Unlike among the League Iroquois, Huron women had no overt political role. Periodically the village councils would meet at the tribal level and at least once a year at the confederacy level. At such meetings friendships were renewed and plans made for the ruination of common enemies. These councils were presided over by a venerable chief in whose territory the council was held. Government at the confederacy level was weak. Consensus was sought through debate and voting, but pronouncements were only expressions of majority opinion and not binding on anyone. With the rapid Iroquois onslaught in the 1640s, the tribes could not act together and were defeated piecemeal.

CONRAD HEIDENREICH

Huron Feast of the Dead. The most solemn religious ceremony of the *Huron. During the life of a village those who died were placed in temporary graves below ground or on scaffolds. Periodically a village had to be moved to fresh soil and firewood. Just before the move, the graves were open, the bodies removed, the bones cleansed of flesh and packed into individual bundles. When the feast was announced, each family brought their bundles to a large common grave (ossuary). Here the bundles were opened, and men with long poles stirred the bones together, symbolizing union in death as in life. Sometimes several villages from a tribe shared this ceremony. After the feast the village site was abandoned, leaving it and the surrounding old corn fields to the spirits of the dead. CONRAD HEIDENREICH

hurricanes. Each year in the Atlantic, hundreds of thunderstorms begin over the tropical waters near the equator, but fewer than ten become hurricanes. Tropical disturbances are classified by their maximum sustained wind speed. If winds reach over 118 km/h, a tropical storm attains hurricane status. Hurricanes are divided into five categories, ranging from minimal to catastrophic.

The North Atlantic hurricane season extends from June through November. Storms reach their greatest fury and frequency in September, when the surface ocean temperature warms to over 27°C. A third or more make their way up the east coast of North America to New England and eastern Canada. As they leave the tropics, they are caught up in the prevailing westerlies and curve to the north and northeast. Their forward speed increases, often quadrupling, to as much as 80 km/h. At such speeds, they can move from the Carolinas to Atlantic Canada in less than 24 hours.

After travelling north some 15,000 km, most tropical storms have lost much of their sting, weakening rapidly over cooler waters or as they pass over land. Sometimes, however, a dissipating hurricane is rejuvenated by interacting with a mid-latitude storm. In eastern Canada, the heaviest rains in hurricanes (or their remnants) often shift to the left side of the storm track, while the strongest winds are found on the right side—generally good news for Canada since the often beneficial rain falls over land but the damaging winds and high waves stay out to sea.

When hurricanes form in the western Pacific Ocean, they are known as 'typhoons'. Although tropical storms from the Pacific seldom stray into Canada, because the coastal waters are too cold to sustain hurricane intensities, occasionally one does make landfall. The remnants of typhoon Freda struck southern coastal British Columbia on 12 October 1962, killing seven people.

Hurricane Hazel is the most remembered hurricane in Canadian history, striking the Toronto region on 14–15 October 1954, leaving 81 dead. Over 300 million metric tons of rain fell on Toronto, submerging whole streets, washing out bridges, and marooning hundreds of people on drifting roof-tops and floating debris. Other less famous but more deadly hurricanes have reached Canada. The Independence Hurricane struck Newfoundland on 9 September 1775. The storm drove vessels onto the *Grand Banks, drowning several thousand British sailors. Another deadly hurricane was the Great Nova Scotia Cyclone of 25–6 August 1873. The storm destroyed 1,200 fishing vessels and killed 1,000 people. Weather forecasters in Toronto knew a day in advance that the hurricane was heading to the Maritimes, but no warning was raised because the telegraph lines to Halifax were down. Prompted by the public outcry, federal politicians voted $37,000 for the development of a national weather-warning system. Four years earlier, a hurricane generated the highest storm surge ever recorded in the Maritimes. The famous Saxby Gale struck western New Brunswick on 4 October 1869, tearing vessels from moorings, driving some boats ashore and badly damaging others. At Moncton, tides were 2 m higher than previous records. On 11 September 1995, the remnants of Hurricane Luis slammed Newfoundland's Burin Peninsula. Luis is the only hurricane with winds above 200 km/h to make landfall in Canada in the last 100 years. The storm tossed around yachts and airplanes, trashed piers and shacks, and crumpled satellite dishes. One wave set a record, as the world's largest—29 m. DAVID PHILLIPS

hydroelectricity. Generated by the kinetic energy of falling water, hydroelectricity was the earliest and is still the largest source of electrical power in Canada. By Confederation in 1867, low capacity (1,000 h.p. and less) waterwheels and turbines were a common sight across the settled regions of the country, a result of Canada being richly endowed with rivers suitable for hydroelectric development. Only Prince Edward Island lacked significant hydro power resources. The widespread harnessing and utilization of Canada's hydro wealth followed a series of technological breakthroughs in the 1870s and 1880s, including the commercial application of direct-current generators and Thomas Edison's invention of an electric incandescent lamp. Soon thereafter, Canada's urban residents were enjoying such conveniences as electric street lighting and streetcars and were eagerly equipping their homes, businesses, and industries with an expanding array of labour-saving electrical appliances and equipment. Most farm and rural families, by contrast, were required to wait until after the Second World War to share in these benefits, for only then did rural electrification become a priority for most provincially owned electrical *utilities.

Although much of the technology associated with hydroelectricity originally was imported from the United States, Great Britain, and Europe, its subsequent application was a testament to the ingenuity, nerve, and foresight of Canadian entrepreneurs and public officials. Committed to squeezing ever greater economies of scale from the enormously capital-intensive generating facilities and transmission grids traversing the country, Canada's hydro pioneers constructed some of the world's largest and most complex hydroelectric networks. In 1897, for example, Canadians completed construction of the first long-distance high-tension (11 kV) transmission line in the British Empire, spanning 27 km between St-Narcisse and Trois-Rivières, Quebec. Knowledge that the industry's long-term viability depended upon harnessing rivers far removed from population centres prompted the design and construction in 1903 of what was then the world's longest high-voltage (50 kV) transmission line, linking Shawinigan and Montreal, a distance of 136 km. Once operational in 1921, Ontario's 500,000 h.p. Queenston-Chippawa generating station at Niagara Falls was the world's largest. Half a century later, when thermal energy was becoming increasingly important, Canada remained an international leader in hydro power technology. This claim was best exemplified by the completion in the 1970s and 1980s of the 5,428 MW *Churchill Falls (Labrador) project, the largest underground hydroelectric generating station in the world, and the multi-phase 15,800 MW La Grande (James Bay) facility in Quebec.

As public awareness of the immense economic, social, and political ramifications of hydroelectric development increased in the early 20th century, most provincial governments enacted legislation nationalizing private electric companies, thereby ensuring that the benefits of hydro power flowed to their tax-paying electorates rather than to utility owners. Moreover, there was a consensus among policy-makers that hydroelectric generation and distribution systems, being so capital intensive and technologically complex, needed to be treated as 'natural monopolies'. Consequently, it was not deemed to be in the public's interest to have competing power companies duplicating electrical systems within and between municipalities. As a result, Canada's hydroelectric industry came to be centralized under *public ownership, both municipal and provincial. By guaranteeing capital debt and foregoing profit taking, provincially owned utilities promised to deliver reliable supplies of electrical power at affordable and roughly uniform rates, benefits not hitherto associated with investor-owned utilities. Every province except Alberta and PEI eventually withdrew from privately owned utilities responsible for hydroelectric generation and distribution.

The enormous financial and technical complexity of hydroelectric development was matched in human terms by the towering and occasionally ruthless ambition of some of the country's first hydro 'barons', among whom Sir Adam *Beck (1857–1925) in Ontario and Sir Herbert *Holt (1856–1941) in Quebec loom large. Beck, a successful London manufacturer, mayor, and MPP, promoted with evangelical fervour the idea that cheap Niagara Falls–generated power, if placed under public rather than private ownership, was the key to provincial economic prosperity. His maxim 'power at cost' became the rallying cry for a coalition of municipalities that successfully pressured James Whitney's Conservative government into creating the Hydro-Electric Power Commission of Ontario in 1906. North America's first nationalized public utility, the HEPC became chairman Beck's personal satrap. Indeed, political accountability was the first casualty in Beck's unrelenting campaign to ensure that his beloved HEPC met soaring demand for electricity in the province, a recurring challenge for the publicly owned utility in the decades that followed. Nevertheless, the legacy of Beck and his successors at the helm was a fully integrated, if debt-ridden, utility producing hydroelectricity at most economically viable water-power sites in the province, and distributing energy directly to urban municipalities and rural customers alike. In 1974 the HECP was transformed into a Crown corporation, Ontario Hydro.

Whereas Beck's mission was to spread his province's hydro wealth fairly among Ontario's domestic power users, Herbert Holt regarded Quebec's bountiful hydroelectric resource as a means for personal enrichment. Holt, who was arguably the most powerful Canadian capitalist of his day, presided over a host of utility and industrial ventures, including the Montreal Light, Heat and Power Company. By 1907 he had orchestrated a loose alliance of interconnected power companies, thereby acquiring a virtual monopoly over the lucrative Montreal electricity market. While Beck's HEPC earned public favour by subsidizing domestic electricity rates with relatively higher priced industrial power sales, Holt took the opposite tack, curbing any enthusiasm Quebec's politically influential business community might exhibit for a publicly owned power system by assessing bulk power users the lower rates. Not until 1944, three years after Holt's death, was public resentment towards Quebec's 'electricity trust' sufficient to impel Adélard Godbout's Liberal government to nationalize Montreal Light, Heat and Power, creating the Quebec Hydro-Electric Commission (later Hydro-Québec). The process was finalized in 1963, when René *Lévesque, minister of natural resources in the Liberal government of Jean *Lesage, spearheaded Hydro-Québec's expropriation of the province's remaining privately owned electrical utilities. Hydroelectricity still accounts for over 95 per cent of Hydro-Québec's energy production. Across Canada, 61 per cent (585 TW.h) of all electricity generated in 2000 was hydro power, followed by thermal (27 per cent) and nuclear (12 per cent) power. KEITH R. FLEMING

Iberville, Pierre Le Moyne d' (1661–1706). Son of a prominent Canadian family, Iberville joined Pierre de *Troyes in the capture of *Hudson's Bay Company posts on James Bay in 1686. In these raids he revealed a penchant for aggressive attacks and an extraordinary ability to fight well on both land and water. In 1690 he led a midwinter overland expedition that destroyed Schenectady, New York, killing two-thirds of its settlers. In 1694 he sailed to Hudson Bay and seized York Fort. In 1696 he helped destroy Fort William Henry (Pemaquid) on the disputed boundary between New England and Acadia. Then he and the governor of *Plaisance, Jacques-François de Mombeton de Brouillan, destroyed St John's; terror raids across Newfoundland wiped out 36 English settlements in 1696–7. In Hudson Bay in September 1697 his ship sank two English vessels and drove off a third. During a brief peace, Iberville was sent to help establish the colony of Louisiana; he explored the Mississippi delta and built a fort at Biloxi Bay (1699). Illness reduced his activity until 1706, when he devastated Nevis in the West Indies. Iberville's attacks were bold, not systematic: he took forts by assault and intimidation, not siege. He was notorious for harsh treatment of opponents and prisoners.
JAY CASSEL

Ideal Maternity Home. A maternity home and adoption service in East Chester, Nova Scotia, operated by William and Lila Young in 1928–46. By 1945, the home housed 80–125 infants at any one time. Unwed mothers paid up to $600 for shelter, medical care, and discretion. Adoptive parents from eastern Canada and the northeastern United States paid 'fees' or made 'donations' ranging from less than $100 to a reported $10,000. The Youngs did not investigate adoptive parents, flouting professional standards in adoption practice. Rumours persist that they deliberately murdered 'imperfect' children who were difficult to 'sell', but these allegations are unproven. There is substantial proof of serious deficiencies in sanitary conditions, nutrition, and medical care. Children who died were buried in wooden dairy boxes and were commonly referred to as 'Butterbox Babies'. Through the 1930s, provincial officials had no legal authority to regulate the home. Changes to the Adoption Act (1943) and a new Maternity Boarding Houses Act (1940, 1945, 1946), aimed at the Youngs, led to legal convictions forcing closure in 1946. The scandal helped modernize the provincial child welfare system.
KAREN A. BALCOM

Île-à-la-Crosse. One of Saskatchewan's oldest communities, its name derives either from its lake, which is shaped like a bishop's staff, or from the marathon *lacrosse games played by Native peoples on the lake's largest island. Located where the Churchill and Beaver Rivers meet, the site was originally a favourite Aboriginal meeting place. During the *fur trade, Île-à-la-Crosse served as a major supply depot on the route between the Churchill and Athabasca river systems. In 1846, the Oblates of Mary Immaculate established St-Jean Baptiste mission, leading to the Roman Catholic domination of the northwestern half of the province. Over the next half century, Île-à-la-Crosse became known as the 'Bethlehem of the North', especially after the arrival of the Grey Nuns of Montreal in 1860 and the building of a convent, orphanage, and school. It was also called the 'nursery of the bishops' because four future bishops (Laflèche, Taché, Grandin, and Faraud) did missionary work there. Today, Île-à-la-Crosse is a largely mixed-blood community and regional service centre.
BILL WAISER

Île Royale. Although French fishermen had been coming to *Cape Breton since the 16th century, the island was permanently settled by the French only after 1713. The colony of Île Royale, which included Île St-Jean (Prince Edward Island) as well as Cape Breton, was founded after the War of the Spanish Succession (1702–13) resulted in France's loss of Acadia and Newfoundland. The French renamed Cape Breton Île Royale and established *Louisbourg as the capital of the colony. In 1717 they began construction of the massive fortifications at Louisbourg, the largest of their type in North America.

The French fishery in Île Royale became highly successful. By 1720 approximately 150,000 quintals of dried codfish were caught (one quintal equals 50 kg), and throughout the 1720s and 1730s the figure ranged between 120,000 and 160,000 quintals annually. Île Royale cod production in the first half of the 18th century accounted for one-third of all the cod caught by the French in North American waters. By the 1740s Île Royale was selling up to 40,000 quintals per year in the West Indies, particularly in St Domingue. The colony also became a entrepôt for Caribbean products. Shiploads of sugar, molasses, and rum were brought in and immediately re-exported, primarily to the British American colonies. So extensive was the trade in rum and molasses that by the 1750s the value of Île Royale sugar products rivalled the value of the colony's codfish production. New

England traded extensively with Louisbourg, providing foodstuffs and building materials and returning with cod, French manufactures, and molasses. Île Royale traded with Quebec and Acadia as well, and foodstuffs and manufactured goods were also imported from France.

By the late 1750s Île Royale's population, including soldiers, approached 10,000. The society was stratified, dominated by colonial officials, officers, and successful merchants, categories that were not mutually exclusive. On a descending social scale, merchants, innkeepers, and artisans served the garrison, port, and fishery. The society was also multicultural, as each summer migrant Basque, Norman, and Breton fishermen swelled the population. Hundreds of Irish Catholics came from Newfoundland and New England seeking religious freedom. A German-speaking, Swiss-based Karrer Regiment, composed of 150 men, served at Louisbourg from 1722 to 1745. Finally, there were at least 266 slaves, mainly Blacks, but also 24 Aboriginals (*panis*). In 1758 Louisbourg fell to the British and Île Royale once more became Cape Breton.

KENNETH DONOVAN

Îles de la Madeleine. These islands in the Gulf of St Lawrence, visited much earlier by Basque fishermen, were granted first to Nicolas *Denys in 1653, then to François Doublet (1663), Denys de Fronsac (1667), and finally the Comte de Saint-Pierre (1719), but no permanent settlement occurred. Deported Acadians took refuge there after 1755, and by 1761 some were hunting walrus for Col Richard Gridley, a New York merchant. Other settlers joined them later. In the 18th century land grants were often given as compensation to deserving officers of the British military. Isaac Coffin (1759–1839) of London, a successful naval officer, persuaded the Quebec legislative council that Americans were exploiting the islands' fisheries and that if they belonged to an individual the illicit trading would be halted. In April 1798 the islands were granted to Coffin as a seigneury. Thereafter, the Acadians preferred to make their living from the sea rather than from the land, which no longer belonged to them. Agriculture became a matter of family subsistence. In 1792 Coffin tried in vain to deport, as enemies of England, 22 French families who had arrived from *St-Pierre and Miquelon. Coffin made his only visit to the property in 1806. As in Prince Edward Island, with its absentee proprietors, few English-speaking colonists were attracted. Beginning in 1822 Coffin tried unsuccessfully to sell or lease the islands to the United States. Not until 1895 would a Quebec law permit the Madelinots to own their lands. The population grew from 1,757 in 1831 to 6,200 in 1901.

NICOLAS LANDRY

immigrant recruitment campaigns, 1867–1914. The young Canada that became transcontinental in the period 1867–73 was little more than a geographic expression. From Atlantic to Pacific, its settled communities were bound together with hope and promise. By 1885 governments had ensured that railways were in place to provide the physical backbone to a transcontinental, all-Canadian economy and communications network. Protective tariffs were intended to enable fledgling Canadian industries to flourish in the face of international competition in the domestic market. The hope for the future also depended upon people: a settlement population for the Prairies, workers to construct infrastructure and staff expanding factories, servants for the growing middle and upper classes who could afford them. Yet, before 1900 Canada was losing a larger number of people to the wealthier, rapidly growing United States than it was able to replace by immigration. By the turn of the century it was estimated that one Canadian-born person in five was resident in the United States, while many immigrants simply used Canada as a port of entry to America.

In the 1870s the federal government assumed primary responsibility for promotion of immigration. Initially its efforts were directed at repatriation of Canadians, especially French Canadians, resident in the United States. Beyond that, it sought to attract immigrants from Britain and Europe and made provision for *bloc settlements in the West for various ethnic or religious groups such as the Icelanders and *Mennonites. It also relied on land companies and transportation companies to recruit potential settlers and labourers (a method that had limited success). Recruitment was highly competitive: prospective emigrants from Europe were confronted by aggressive agents from the United States, from South American countries such as Argentina, and from British colonies such as Australia and South Africa, as well as Canada.

After 1896 Clifford *Sifton, minister of the interior in the Laurier administration, energized recruitment. He placed agents on commission, blanketed England, Europe, and the United States with propaganda, paid commission to shipping agents who delivered agricultural settlers to Canada, and formed land companies that were more successful than in the past. He also encouraged the migration of *'stalwart peasants' of eastern Europe—*Ukrainians, *Doukhobors, Poles. Improved economic conditions, better strains of grain and techniques for dry-land farming, and the end of the American frontier of free land all contributed to the record numbers of immigrants pouring into the country. Frank Oliver, who succeeded Sifton in 1905, introduced restrictive legislation in 1906 and 1910 to strengthen the powers of the department to exclude or deport those deemed undesirable. Despite that, the numbers of immigrants continued to grow, reaching over 400,000 in 1913. The former relatively open-door policy was curtailed, but the newcomers were both fulfilling the dream of Confederation and changing the face of Canadian society.

DAVID J. HALL

immigration policy. From earliest colonial times, immigration was an integral part of trade and economic development. Ships bringing in colonists brought out fish, fur, and timber. There was, however, a persistent flow-through of people from British North America to the more prosperous United States to the south. In the

Confederation debates, encouragement of immigration to open up the western frontier was touted as one of the benefits of the union of the colonies.

In the BNA Act of 1867, immigration was a concurrent jurisdiction between the federal and provincial governments. The provinces shortly lost enthusiasm for this role, leaving the federal government with *de facto* responsibility. The first federal Immigration Act (1869) re-enacted colonial controls over entry and conditions on immigrant vessels. Sir John A. *Macdonald's *National Policy (1878) saw an important positive role for immigrants, both as farmers for the western agricultural frontier and workers for the protected industries of central Canada. Yet western expansion was largely a failure for the first three decades of Confederation, with emigration to the United States continuing to outdistance immigration.

The federal government in the 19th and early 20th centuries left much responsibility for immigration to the private sector, particularly the Canadian Pacific Railway and other transportation companies, which had an economic stake in encouraging settlement. The CPR had its own Department of Colonization and Immigration and promoted and assisted emigration to Canada from Europe and the United States.

The Liberal government of Sir Wilfrid *Laurier (1896–1911) marked a turning point in immigration. New winter wheat strains and better farming techniques combined with a rise in world wheat prices to stimulate settlement of the West. Laurier's first minister of immigration, Clifford *Sifton, proved an effective promoter of peasant farmers from central and eastern Europe, and successfully encouraged farmers from the United States to move to the Canadian frontier. He also modernized and centralized the bureaucratic structures of his department. By the early 20th century, record numbers were pouring into the Prairies. After 1905 and Sifton's replacement as minister, Ottawa, in response to a growing racist backlash against 'the foreigner', began a partial withdrawal from its open door policy. Particular alarm was sounded about non-white labour. *Racism was especially rife on the West Coast against Asians, who made up a quarter of the British Columbia labour force in the early 20th century. By the First World War such fears were compounded by xenophobia about enemy aliens, thousands of whom were interned during the war, and, after the Russian Revolution of 1917, alarm about Bolshevism among the 'dangerous foreigners'. Immigrant groups became subject to sometimes intensive police surveillance, and foreign-born labour 'agitators' were subject to *deportation.

The 1920s witnessed a return to high pre-war immigration levels, at the insistence of business. The Empire Settlement Act (1922) assisted 100,000 British immigrants, but the Chinese Immigration Act (1923) virtually halted immigration from China. In 1925 the government capitulated to pressures and passed the Railways Agreement, under which eastern and southern Europeans who qualified as 'bona fide agriculturalists' would be placed on the same footing as those from western Europe. This agreement, run largely by the private sector, brought 185,000 to Canada.

Rising racist opposition to immigration in the late 1920s would have forced modifications, but the Great Depression of the 1930s put a virtual halt to migration to Canada. In the early 1930s, many previously landed were deported as either indigents or subversives. The late 1930s also saw the notorious barring of Jewish *refugees from Nazi Germany. During the Second World War racism reached new heights, with the mass removal of the *Japanese-Canadian population of the West Coast to camps in the interior, and a plan, never implemented, to deport the entire community to Japan at war's end.

After the war, Canada moved into a new era of mass immigration. First were 100,000 *displaced persons from the European war, who began arriving in the late 1940s. European immigration continued on a large scale through the 1950s, backed by the general approval of the public as well as groups, such as trade unions, that had previously been critical. The contribution of immigrants to post-war prosperity was widely acknowledged. A Canadian Citizenship Act (1946) for the first time defined Canadian *citizenship as distinct from status as a British subject. In 1950 a new federal Department of Citizenship and Immigration was created. As various immigrant communities grew in size and confidence, they formed an influential pro-immigration lobby. The government's encouragement of 'sponsored' or family-class immigration in the early post-war era accelerated this trend.

The 1952 Immigration Act enshrined a strict control-oriented policy with heavier emphasis on who would be excluded. It dealt with pro-immigration pressures by giving the minister and senior officials an excessive degree of discretion to get around the rules in specific cases. It also maintained a hierarchy of acceptability, beginning with those from the United Kingdom, white *Commonwealth, United States, and France, followed by other western Europeans, then southern and eastern Europe, and finally a restricted category for Asians. The minister described the act as a 'prohibition act with exemptions'.

Canada accepted on ministerial permit 37,000 Hungarian refugees in 1956–7 after the crushing of the Hungarian revolt by the Soviet Union, and a smaller number from the failed 'Prague Spring' in Czechoslovakia in 1968. Behind the scenes, refugee policy was being run along the lines of the Cold War. Refugees from Communist countries were welcomed, but security controls were quietly being imposed on refugees and immigrants with Communist pasts or left-wing associations. The Cold War bias was exemplified at the end of the 1970s and early 1980s, when Canada, despite its dishonourable past of anti-Asian racism, welcomed 100,000 'boat people' from Southeast Asia who were fleeing Communist rule. By contrast, the government was reluctant to open its doors to refugees from Chile who were fleeing bloody right-wing repression in the 1973 military coup against the democratically elected leftist government.

As racial discrimination fell into disrepute, the Conservative government in 1962 enacted regulations admitting applicants according to their skills and means of support, rather than their national origins. In 1967 the Liberal government went further, establishing a colour-blind points system for assessing applicants. With the return of European prosperity, the era of European immigration was effectively over. Canada would require skilled immigrant labour that would more and more come from Asia.

After widespread public consultation, a new Immigration Act was passed in 1978, more liberal and positive than its predecessors. It opened with a declaration of the contributions of immigrants to Canada, insisted on non-discrimination, and recognized Canada's humanitarian obligations to refugees. It also provided for continuing participation in policy making by interested parties, such as business, labour, advocacy groups, and the provinces. The latter assumed a growing responsibility in this area in the late 20th century, although the only province to assume its full constitutional jurisdiction is Quebec, with its particular interest in attracting francophone immigrants. Agreements have been struck between the federal and Quebec governments on immigration that have proved effective.

In the late 1980s Canadian attitudes towards refugees began to harden, with huge backlogs, well-publicized evidence of bogus claimants, and the unwelcome arrival of 'queue-hopping' boatloads seeking asylum. In 1987 the Immigration Act was amended to make asylum harder to attain and deportation of failed claimants easier. Restiveness about high levels of immigration at a time of high unemployment, revived (if now somewhat covert) racism, and a backlash against *multiculturalism all contributed in the 1980s and early 1990s to pressures on government to become more restrictive. Countering this was a well-established pro-immigration and pro-refugee lobby and the Canadian *Charter of Rights and Freedoms, which was helping liberalize the political culture. Finally, government was armed with demographic statistics indicating that a declining birth rate threatened an inverted age pyramid in the 21st century, with too few people of productive years to sustain pensioners—unless sustained immigration righted the imbalance.

The Mulroney government (1984–93) tried to maintain high levels of annual immigration, while bowing in the direction of anti-immigration sentiment by becoming more restrictive towards refugees. It also began the practice of encouraging business or entrepreneurial immigration and discouraging family class, thus signalling that economic motives were uppermost. By the mid-1990s the majority of new immigrants were in the economic class (business and skilled worker categories), while sponsored immigrants accounted for less than a third, a sharp drop.

Economic recovery under the Liberals in the 1990s deflated much of the anti-immigration and anti-multicultural sentiment of the 1980s. However, security concerns, heightened after the terrorist attacks of 11 September 2001, led to a renewed emphasis on tighter controls over refugees. A new and more stringent act to cover refugees emerged in 2001. In 2002 the Canadian and American governments jointly agreed on a 'safe third country' provision for asylum seekers that was interpreted by refugee advocates as highly restrictive.

Canada, it would seem, is a country of immigrants that has never quite made up its mind about immigration.

REG WHITAKER

imperialism. Imperialism—imperial unity in the Canadian context—was a resolve to strengthen the connection with Great Britain through economic, political, and military means; a hope that Canada could attain national stature by acquiring an influence over imperial policy; and a conviction that only with British support could Canada maintain a separate existence in a North America dominated by the United States. The organized movement for imperial unity began with the founding of the Imperial Federation League in London in 1884 and the establishment of Canadian branches that became centres of opposition to free trade with the United States and the threat of eventual political absorption. Growing in vitality and amplitude in the 1890s, the movement was led by George T. *Denison, military enthusiast and proponent of the United Empire *Loyalists as the first imperialists; Rev. George *Grant, principal of Queen's University, whose religious idealism was expressed in the notion of the British Empire as an immense force for uplift in the world; and George *Parkin, headmaster of Upper Canada College, Toronto, whose *Imperial Federation* (1892) played upon the special capacity of the Anglo-Saxon race for progress and self-government, and laid out clearly the strategic and geopolitical rationale for imperial solidarity. The most committed and vocal supporters came from the urban middle class of English Canada, especially Ontario, and were educators, intellectuals, Protestant clergy, journalists, and politicians (from both parties, though Conservatives tended to be more enthusiastic), and women in the *Imperial Order Daughters of the Empire, founded in 1900. Imperial sentiment was cultivated in the schools through Empire Day observances, and—in time—the presence in all classrooms of a map of the world with the empire in red, Canada at the centre. In 1898, to mark the beginning of imperial penny postage, Canada issued a stamp picturing such a map with the caption: 'We hold a vaster empire than has been'.

The *British Empire—which eventually encompassed one-quarter of both the earth's surface and population—provided Canadians with a sense of belonging to and participating in a great world power that stood at the summit of civilization and embodied cherished freedoms and the rule of law. Canadians were 'British subjects' (there was no category of Canadian *citizenship till 1947) and Canada was a 'British country', with 57 per cent of the population in 1900 tracing origins to the British Isles. Feelings of identity were strengthened by the exuberant celebration of Queen Victoria's Diamond Jubilee (1897), royal visits, and the bestowing by the Crown of knighthoods and other honours on Canadians. The supporters of imperial unity advocated imperial tariff preferences, which Canada extended to Britain in 1897, and forced the Laurier government to provide 7,300 volunteers to support the empire in the *South African War (1899–1902) and in 1909 to commit Canada to help maintain

British naval supremacy (upon which Canada's security depended). *Laurier's 1910 naval bill—seen by imperialists as an unsatisfactory compromise—created a small naval force that could be put at the disposal of Britain in wartime.

The zenith of imperial solidarity was Canada's participation in the Great War, 1914–18: the country's huge military contribution, its prime minister's involvement in imperial councils, and the promise of recognition of autonomy and a voice in imperial affairs in the post-war years seemed a realization of Anglo-Canadian nationalism and imperialism. The human and material costs of the war and the bitter internal divisions it intensified, however, impaired the cause, and in the interwar years Mackenzie *King insisted on the clear separation of Canadian and imperial interests and policies. The imperial idea had many enemies: inertia and satisfaction with the status quo in imperial affairs; reluctance of those at the centre to take seriously the claims of colonial upstarts; indifference among labour and farming communities; incisive liberal critiques of imperialism by Goldwin *Smith, who dismissed it for—among other reasons—denying the North American affinities of Canada, and by Henri *Bourassa, who articulated French Canada's opposition to the prospects of being dragged into endless conflicts by imperial economic interests and by fellow Canadians who had a dual loyalty. Yet the ideological and emotional elements that had sustained the movement for imperial unity long outlived it. In 1939 Canada decided on its own to enter the Second World War at Britain's side, for reasons of sentiment. CARL BERGER

Imperial Order Daughters of the Empire. Canada is home to the largest and longest-surviving female imperialist organization in the British *Commonwealth. The Federation of Daughters of the British Empire was founded in 1900 by Margaret Clark Murray, journalist, philanthropist, and wife of an influential McGill professor. After returning from a visit to London during the *South African War, Margaret decided to act upon the Anglo-Canadian patriotism that she sensed about her. She had ambitious plans to form an empire-wide federation of imperial women, but in 1901 the rival Victoria League began in London and demanded that Murray confine her efforts to Canada. The national headquarters was moved to Toronto from Montreal in 1901, the name changed to the Imperial Order Daughters of the Empire, and president Edith Nordheimer promised not to expand outside of Canada. Thereafter, although the IODE was largely confined to Canada, small satellite chapters existed in pre-confederation Newfoundland, the United States, Bermuda, the Bahamas, and India.

The symbols of the IODE reflected its view that the way to a strong Canada was through a strong *British Empire. The motto was 'one flag, one throne, one Empire'. The IODE badge cast imperial foundations in metal, with a crown symbolizing the monarchy, the Union Jack flag for Britain and empire, and a seven-pointed star, one point for each of the major territories of the empire. The IODE's objectives were to stimulate patriotic sentiment, to foster a commitment to unity among women and children throughout the empire, to care for the dependants of military personnel, and to preserve the memory of brave and historic deeds. Such objectives were pursued through hard work on projects in education, health, and welfare. The IODE published its own quarterly magazine, *Echoes*, edited by a long-serving series of women journalists, in particular May Kertland and Agnes Mary Pease.

Officially non-partisan and non-sectarian, provincial, municipal, and primary (local) chapters were set up in every part of Canada. The IODE grew most rapidly in Ontario. National membership peaked during the First World War at 50,000 members. Among the members were many women who achieved political 'firsts', from mayor Charlotte *Whitton, to lieutenant-governor Pauline McGibbon, to federal cabinet minister Ellen *Fairclough. Members Wilhelmina Gordon, first woman lecturer at Queen's University, and Mary Bollert, first dean of women at the University of British Columbia, both used their expertise to implement IODE war memorial scholarships, which are still in existence.

KATIE PICKLES

imperial rivalries, 1613–1763. For 150 years, the territory later known as Atlantic Canada was intermittently fought over and repeatedly negotiated for by European imperial powers. The region's proximity to rich fishing grounds formed one imperial attraction, and its strategic positioning vis-à-vis the Gulf of St Lawrence and the New England colonies became important over time.

The 16th-century North *Atlantic fishery had an international character, as Basque, English, French, and Portuguese vessels coexisted. During the decades surrounding the beginning of the 17th century, however, imperial claims to territory became explicit. Newfoundland was claimed by England and France. Acadia or Nova Scotia (overlapping terms applied to today's Maritime provinces and adjoining areas) was claimed by those two powers and by the Netherlands and Scotland. Active intervention by the Netherlands was confined to a single raid in 1674. The Scottish presence consisted primarily of a settlement at *Port-Royal from 1629 to 1632, although the Scottish claim to Nova Scotia remained an element of Great Britain's territorial pretensions.

The outbreak of imperial violence in the region came in 1613, when a Virginia expedition destroyed French settlements in Acadia. This set a pattern that persisted until 1690, by which time hostilities consisted largely of occasional sea-borne raids on small colonial settlements. While they were 'imperial' in that raiders used the terminology of imperial claims, there was little or no European coordination. No imperial troops were deployed, and naval involvement was rare. Many of the ventures were privately organized and financed, and allegations of *piracy often had more than a grain of truth. Even though these episodes could have serious consequences for the lives and property of those directly affected, they had limited overall significance. Aboriginal nations generally stood aloof from such petty goings-on, while colonial populations endured them as best they could. Insofar as control of settlements changed hands, international treaties such as those of St-Germain-en-Laye (1632) and Breda (1667) repeatedly restored the status quo ante.

When the War of the League of Augsburg embroiled England and Scotland with France in 1690, a transitional phase began that ended with the Treaty of Utrecht (1713). Increasing settler populations in colonies such as Canada (the French colony in the St Lawrence Valley) and New York gave boundary disputes a more practical significance. Harassment of New England fishing and merchant vessels by French *privateers raised the economic stakes. Aboriginal nations such as the Wabanaki, concerned by English territorial encroachment, were increasingly though still intermittently willing to ally themselves with the French, as were the *Mi'kmaq and Maliseet.

Interrupted by the Treaty of Ryswick (1697) and resumed in 1702 in the War of the Spanish Succession, the conflicts became bitter and recurrent. Raiding warfare remained the norm, but forces were larger and strategic aims were explicit. Sir William *Phips's attacks on Port-Royal and Quebec in 1690 involved substantial New England militia armies and represented a failed effort to expel the French from North America. More nearly successful was the French effort to evict the English from Newfoundland during the 'Winter War' of 1696–7. Although the attempt fell short when a key naval squadron was redeployed to Hudson Bay, only two tiny English outposts survived the assault. French overland raids on northern New England towns, and retaliatory English raids on Acadian villages, were also destructive. Most decisive of all was the English *conquest of Acadia in 1710 by a force that included naval vessels and a contingent of British marines, although its success was offset by the humiliating failure of the Walker expedition of 1711 to seize Quebec.

In the Treaty of Utrecht, France and Great Britain attempted to settle their territorial differences. Newfoundland, save for certain fishing rights, was assigned to Great Britain. Acadia/Nova Scotia was also to be British, except for the French islands of Cape Breton and Saint-Jean (later Prince Edward Island). More problematic was the absence of any agreed definition of the boundaries of Acadia/Nova Scotia, and the lack of consent from powerful Aboriginal peoples including the Mi'kmaq and the Wabanaki. Even so, major conflicts might have been avoided if a diplomatic rapprochement between Great Britain and France had persisted beyond the early 1730s. It did not, and outright imperial warfare threatened. Land and sea battles between 1744 and 1748 as part of the War of the Austrian Succession, and the Treaty of Aix-la-Chapelle (1748), proved indecisive. France and Great Britain accordingly strengthened their fortifications throughout the region. The *Seven Years' War, declared formally in 1756 but under way in North America by 1754, brought bloody and destructive fighting that involved regular imperial troops and naval vessels. The fall of *Louisbourg in 1758 was a prelude to the British capture of Quebec (1759) and Montreal (1760). The French capture of St John's (1762) caused British alarm but proved short-lived.

The Treaty of Paris (1763) signalled the end of active imperial rivalry in the region. Even though the Mi'kmaq and Maliseet retained military potential, they chose to enter into a treaty relationship with Great Britain. For many generations of Aboriginal and colonial inhabitants, however, imperial conflict had been a threatening if intermittent reality. JOHN G. REID

independent labour parties. From the onset of Canadian industrialization, 'labour' candidates often contested elections to all levels of government. They spoke to a growing sentiment that governments composed of businessmen and lawyers would not protect workers' interests. Nevertheless, the lure of power and *patronage was strong, and labour candidates were often drawn back into the Liberal or Conservative Parties. By the early 20th century, proponents of labour political action were forming local independent labour parties—sometimes but not always called the Independent Labour Party—to provide an organizational base for autonomy from the old parties.

Although a national phenomenon, this movement was decentralized despite an attempt to form a Canadian Labour Party in 1917. During and after the First World War, workers' anger at 'autocratic' governments that catered to 'profiteers' prompted a revolt against the established parties. From Cape Breton Island to Vancouver Island, local labour parties elected municipal governments. After the *Winnipeg General Strike, the Dominion Labour Party won half the seats on the city council and elected 11 members of the legislature (several still serving prison sentences). In British Columbia, the Federated Labour Party competed with the socialists for working-class allegiance. In the fall of 1919, the Ontario ILP elected 11 members to form, in alliance with the farmers' movement, the provincial government.

The ideology of this movement—labourism—was vague. Labourists fought for democratic reforms and championed an egalitarianism based on the dignity of manual labour, but they were able to herald few concrete measures. In the 1920s labourism lost its predominance in the labour movement. In BC, it was eclipsed by a more sharp-edged *socialism. Elsewhere, particularly in Ontario, the Canadian Labour Party housed a range of labourist, socialist, and communist currents and succumbed to infighting. By the 1930s, the *Co-operative Commonwealth Federation incorporated most of the remnants of this political labour movement.

JAMES NAYLOR

Indian Act, 1876. A federal statute that governs the affairs of those Canadians legally recognized as 'Indians', the act had its origins in legislation, passed in 1850 in Upper and Lower Canada, that vested Native lands in the Crown. Paternalistic in tone, these acts assumed that Indians required protection from land speculators and careful tutelage to become self-reliant, Europeanized Christians. The Gradual Civilization Act of 1857 furthered this idea by specifying that an adult male Indian of good character and free of debt would be eligible to remove himself from the protective care of the Crown and acquire full citizenship in a process known as enfranchisement.

At Confederation the federal government acquired responsibility for 'Indians and lands reserved for Indians'. It inherited the Indian Department and the policies and assumptions inherent in the colonial legislation. Building on these practices, it resolved to extend the system to newly acquired provinces and territories while rationalizing and consolidating the legal and administrative framework. This was accomplished by the Indian Act of 1876, which incorporated and refined earlier legislation and applied it more or less uniformly across the country. The act attempted a clearer definition of 'Indian': in effect, an Indian was someone officially registered as such under the act. Those so classified were relegated to being wards of the state, forbidden to vote or consume alcohol. The relinquishment of Indian status (*Aboriginal enfranchisement) was still allowed for, involving a three-year probation period. Indian women who married non-Indians were automatically enfranchised.

Under the act, Indians were given some say in the conduct of their affairs. While reserve lands were still vested in the Crown, they could be sold when a majority of adult male band members agreed to do so. Chiefs and councils could provide for the maintenance of roads, bridges, and public buildings and make regulations for the suppression of 'intemperance and profligacy'. These measures were designed to encourage an elective system of self-governance while undermining traditional concepts of leadership. Local political initiative was stymied by regulations that placed ultimate control in the hands of the federal minister known as the superintendent-general of Indian affairs. Little could be done on a reserve without the approval of his representative, the *Indian agent. The assertion of state authority over Native communities was the ultimate purpose of the act. With such control in place, Indians could be subjected to a forced apprenticeship in the ways of the white man; schools, religion, and agriculture (where possible) were seen as the principal means in this process.

The Indian Act was amended frequently over the years, usually to render it more effective as a coercive instrument of assimilation. After much agitation by missionaries, an amendment in 1884 forbade the *potlatch in British Columbia. In 1895 the prohibition was extended to features of the prairie Sun Dance. These clauses proved difficult to enforce, but convictions and jail sentences for celebrants did result. The pressure to assimilate was conducted on many fronts. While enfranchisement was encouraged, the process was cumbersome and rarely occurred. In 1920 the act was changed to allow the superintendent-general to enfranchise Indians against their will if he thought it desirable. Native protests and a change of government led to the repeal of this clause, but it was reintroduced in a modified form in 1933. School attendance was made compulsory for Indian children aged 7–15; a 1930 amendment authorized Indian agents to keep children in *residential schools until age 18.

The protection of Native lands had been one of the principal features of the act but by the 20th century reserves were seen to hamper economic growth, and these protective features were weakened. New clauses in 1911 allowed municipalities to seize reserve lands for roads and public works and allowed for the removal of Indians from reserves adjacent to towns. During the 1920s militant Native organizations were agitating for greater political autonomy and the settlement of land claims and other grievances. In conducting these campaigns they sometimes employed the services of lawyers, much to the annoyance of the government. An amendment in 1927 preventing lawyers from collecting funds from Indians was designed to put a stop to the agitation.

A parliamentary inquiry in 1946–8 exposed the shortcomings of Indian policy and led to a major revision of the act in 1951. The more repugnant prohibitions such as those on alcohol, Native ceremonies, and the engagement of legal services were removed. Greater initiative was given to band councils, and the power of the Indian agent was weakened. A notable feature was the increased application of provincial laws and standards to Natives with a view to ending their isolation from mainstream society. Yet the revised act dealt mainly with details; its historic rationale was not questioned. Assimilation—now more palatably termed 'integration'—remained the goal, but it would rely on persuasion rather than coercion. The 1951 act remains largely in place. One notable change since that date was Bill C-31, passed in 1985, which repealed the clause that deprived Indian women of their status upon marrying a non-Indian. By 1989 almost 67,000 women and their children had regained their status because of Bill C-31.

The Indian Act is a curiously 19th-century statute, a reminder of the difficult historical relations between First Nations and Canadian settler society. BRIAN TITLEY

Indian Affairs and Northern Development, Department of. Also known as Indian and Northern Affairs Canada, and DIAND, the department carries out Canada's responsibilities for First Nations and Inuit and the three northern territories. The first governmental agency responsible for Indian affairs in what is now Canada was a unit of the British army established in 1755 to maintain military alliances with Indians. Since then, the portfolio has shifted among several government agencies, including the Office of the Secretary of State, and Citizenship and Immigration, until the creation of DIAND in 1966.

Until the mid-20th century, Canadian Indian policy, administered by DIAND 's predecessors, centred on assimilating Indians, and controlling those who did not assimilate so that they would not impede non-Native development of Canada's hinterland. The policy included treaties extinguishing First Nations' title to the lands they formerly occupied, the creation of reserves, the establishment of *residential schools designed to assimilate—

sometimes forcibly—Native children, and the use of the paternalistic *Indian Act to control the affairs of First Nations. The emphasis of the department has evolved away from these policies and from delivering such services as education, health care, and social assistance. While controversy surrounds the pace, direction, and adequacy of funding, the department now focuses on fostering the self-sufficiency of First Nations by developing their economic strength, improving social conditions on reserves, and settling comprehensive and specific land claims. The department also promotes the self-determination of First Nations by devolving program and service-delivery responsibilities and funding to them, and by developing the institutions of governance and the pools of skilled and profession Aboriginal workers that will enable First Nations to successfully exercise their inherent right of self-government, which the government of Canada has recognized since 1995.

The department's role in the Yukon, Nunavut, and the Northwest Territories has undergone similar changes. Once responsible for delivering government services to the North, DIAND has devolved authority to the territories, which now enjoy almost the full span of jurisdiction and degree of governmental autonomy possessed by the provinces. GURSTON DACKS

Indian agents. These agents made their first appearance in the mid-1700s as emissaries of the British military entrusted with forging alliances with Indian nations. By the 1830s this military need no longer existed, and Native peoples became subjected to a policy of assimilation. Agents joined with Christian missionaries in directing cultural change. After Confederation they became the principal field officers of the federal Indian Department and were located on reserves that formed part of their 'agencies'. Agents were often of military or police background. A knowledge of agriculture was also valued, since farming was considered the surest road to self-sufficiency for Natives. The position was viewed as a well-paid sinecure, and political patronage was not unusual in making appointments.

Indian agents played key roles in asserting state authority. Their powers under the *Indian Act enabled them to regulate a detailed range of social, political, and economic activities. Withholding rations was an important weapon used to impose their will on their wards. An amendment to the act in 1881 made agents justices of the peace for their reserves. An 1894 amendment clarified that these powers applied only to the Indian Act and certain sections of the Criminal Code. In effect, the agent became investigator, prosecutor, and judge in a specific range of offences—an extraordinary use of judicial power.

Agents called and supervised band council elections. They attended council meetings and, while they couldn't vote, could influence deliberations. Their recommendations respecting band affairs were usually heeded in Ottawa, including recommendations to depose chiefs and councillors for incompetence, intemperance, or immorality. Despite their power, agents were often isolated and sometimes faced organized opposition on the reserves, especially when they tried to enforce repressive features of the Indian Act, such as the prohibition on traditional ceremonies. In the Northwest during the 1880s, there were many tense confrontations over the harsh work-for-rations policy. When rebellion broke out in 1885, one agent was killed; several others, fearing for their lives, sought refuge in nearby towns.

Lacking in resources and constructive directions from Ottawa, agents pursued economic policies that brought stagnation to reserves. Agriculture, where it was possible, rarely rose above subsistence level. By the 20th century, agents seemed less optimistic about assimilation. Their aims became more limited: keeping costs down, minimizing trouble, and retaining control. Theirs was a custodial rather than a developmental role and was deeply resented. Major changes to Indian policy and the Indian Act following the Second World War gave greater initiative to Native communities. By the 1950s the department began to move its agents off reserves. Many of them became managers of newly created district offices, where they were joined by education and social welfare personnel. Indian agents and their autocratic rule had come to an end.

BRIAN TITLEY

Indian Claims Commission, 1969–77. A product of the 1969 *White Paper on Indian Policy, the commission, and Commissioner Lloyd Barber, had no authority to deal with issues that Aboriginal peoples believed had to be the basis of any government–Indian relationship, namely treaty and *Aboriginal rights. Moreover, it was given no power to settle any claims; it could only receive and study claims and recommend how they could be adjudicated. As a result, Aboriginal peoples refused to deal with it. In 1973, however, the commission gained credibility when its mandate was changed to allow it to receive and study 'comprehensive claims'—claims that dealt with rights of traditional occupancy and use of lands. In its short life the Claims Commission helped Indians and the government understand one another, and it helped make the public aware that effective resolution of claims had to provide resources and political powers to Aboriginal peoples on a level that would assist them to be independent.

JOHN L. TOBIAS

Indian treaties. The earliest agreements between First Nations and Europeans in Canada were between fur traders and Natives engaged in fur commerce. Because many of these pacts were informal, no written record of them remains. From *Hudson's Bay Company sources, however, it is known that the company instructed its representatives in the region around James Bay to make agreements, solemnized according to the religious practice of the Indians, to secure permission to operate in indigenous territory. It is also clear that European and Canadian fur traders followed Native protocols—such as formal welcomes and gift exchanges, smoking the ceremonial pipe, and speech making—as part of fur-trade practice. Such behaviour is consistent with a formal relationship within a commercial pact.

The next type of treaty making—diplomatic and military treaties—is better recorded in both Aboriginal and European sources. The first of these agreements was the *Great Peace of Montreal of 1701, by which the *Iroquois Confederacy and some other nations ended decades of guerrilla warfare against New France by means of a treaty of peace and friendship that also recognized an Iroquois right to remain neutral in the event of war in North America between Britain and France. At the same time, the Iroquois made a peace treaty with the British in New York, thereby positioning the confederacy to avoid entanglement in war between the European powers. The Great Peace is commemorated in archival documents and likely also in a wampum belt, the First Nations method of recording significant events.

The Great Peace of 1701 was the first of many treaties of peace and friendship concluded during the 18th century, the period dominated by diplomatic rivalry and warfare in the eastern half of North America. Also important, both at the time and for later judicial decisions, were a series of treaties between the British and the *Mi'kmaq of Nova Scotia. Of these many Maritime pacts, two of the most important were the Treaty of Boston (1725), also known as Mascarene's Treaty, and the 1852 Treaty of Halifax. Both were treaties of peace and friendship that also contained guarantees of continuing Mi'kmaq rights to harvest the land's resources and to trade. These provisions have had important judicial consequences, most recently in the *Marshall* decision of the Supreme Court in 1999.

Treaty making began to shift to land-related treaties following the *Royal Proclamation of 1763. In part the reason for the shift was that diplomacy and warfare were becoming less important after the defeat of the French, although the American Revolutionary War and the War of 1812 would revive many of the old alliances between Natives and newcomers. The other reason for the emergence of land-related treaties was that growing numbers of agricultural settlers began to immigrate to British North America, especially after the end of the War of 1812. Following the prescription of the Royal Proclamation, representatives of the Crown made a series of treaties in what was to become Ontario to secure peaceful entrance for settlers onto Ojibwa lands. (Parallel treaty processes did not occur in Quebec and the Maritimes because First Nations in those colonies were either located away from the expansion of settlement, as in Quebec, or so marginalized that their land rights were ignored by settlers, as in the Maritimes.) The process of making land-related treaties culminated in 1850 in the Robinson Superior and Robinson Huron treaties between the Crown and the Ojibwa in lands east and north of the two upper Great Lakes. The Robinson Treaties established a pattern—they covered large tracts of land, guaranteed First Nations reserves and annuities, and recognized the Aboriginal signatories' continuing right to hunt and fish—that would be applied elsewhere.

After Confederation the Robinson pattern was employed in the Prairie West in seven numbered treaties concluded between 1871 and 1877. Prairie practice was in stark contrast to colonial British Columbia, where, except for 14 small treaties on Vancouver Island negotiated by Governor James Simpson in the early 1850s, most of the region was not covered by treaty. On the Prairies Crown representatives negotiated with the Saulteaux, Cree, Assiniboine, and Blackfoot for access to land in exchange for initial per capita payments, annuities, reserves, assistance with farming and education, and continuing rights to hunt and fish. The first seven numbered treaties ensured peaceful access for Euro-Canadian settlers in a region stretching from the Lake of the Woods to the foothills of the Rockies, and from the international boundary to a point midway up what are now the three Prairie provinces.

After 1877 Canada was reluctantly drawn into making more treaties only when southern Canadian economic interests expressed a desire for Indian lands. To ensure peaceful access to mining territories, Treaty 8, covering the northeastern corner of British Columbia, northern Alberta, and northwestern Saskatchewan, was negotiated in 1899–1900. Treaty 9 in northern Ontario was negotiated in 1905, at a time when southern mining and forest interests were eyeing northern resources. The same motivation largely explained Treaty 10 in 1906, dealing with northern Saskatchewan. Finally, when oil was discovered at Norman Wells, Northwest Territories, in 1920, Canada was motivated to negotiate Treaty 11 the following year. Thereafter, treaty making ceased for half a century, largely because the federal government wished to avoid financial commitments to other Aboriginal groups.

Modern treaty making began in the 1970s because of greater Native assertiveness. The resistance of the James Bay Cree in Quebec to hydroelectric power development on their lands led to the James Bay and Northern Quebec Agreement of 1975; Indian assertions of unsurrendered Aboriginal title to lands in BC and the North were a factor in Ottawa's creation of a claims-resolution office in 1974 to deal with disputes. Comprehensive claims settlements, which resolve disputes arising from assertion of *Aboriginal title, are modern treaties. To date several have been concluded in the North. Finally, the *Nunavut agreement (1990) in the eastern Arctic and the 1996 Nisga'a agreement in northern BC are two separately negotiated treaties. Large areas of British Columbia, the North, Quebec, and Atlantic Canada still remain uncovered by treaties.

J.R. MILLER

Indochina International Control Commission. Canada was one of three members (with Poland and India) of the International Commissions for Supervision and Control, which were established at the Geneva Conference of 1954 to oversee implementation of the settlement that ended the war between France and its former colonies in Vietnam, Laos, and Cambodia. The Canadian government reluctantly accepted an unexpected invitation to monitor indefinitely a problematic armistice where Canada had limited interests and no previous diplomatic representation. In their reports and decisions, the commissioners divided along Cold War lines, with Canada's representatives more sympathetic than their colleagues to complaints from South Vietnam about actions by North Vietnam. As the conflict in Indochina deepened and broadened, particularly with escalating American intervention, the commissions became even more ineffective and irrelevant. With vague and unhelpful terms of reference and increasingly bitter internal divisions, the commissions were not mourned when they were superseded as part of a peace agreement between the United States and North Vietnam by the International Commission of Control and Supervision. The latter body proved to be no better than its predecessors, and Canada withdrew from participation in it after only six months. That ended two decades of frustrating involvement for Canadians in Southeast Asia. HECTOR MACKENZIE

industrial hygiene. The origins of industrial hygiene, now referred to as occupational health and safety, can be traced to the late-19th-century development of heavy industry and *manufacturing. Its key objective is the identification, evaluation, control, and prevention of health and accident risks associated with exposure to chemical, biological, and physical dangers in the workplace. Since the Second World War, industrial hygiene has taken in such health and environmental issues as indoor air quality; the use of pesticides and other contaminants; air, water, and soil pollution; hazardous-waste disposal, and a wide variety of workplace human stressors.

Although the federal government has developed consultative agencies through its health and labour departments since the First World War, and also oversees the health and safety of federally employed workers, industrial hygiene and workers' compensation are constitutionally under provincial jurisdiction. The initiatives of Ontario, the most industrialized province, have been widely imitated, beginning with the Ontario Factories Act of 1884, the first example of 'protective' legislation in Canada. When the Workmen's Compensation Act was passed in 1914, followed by similar legislation in every province, the basis was laid for expanded state efforts in health education, disease control, accident prevention, and workplace safety. Increasingly, public health authorities recognized that certain health problems were particular to the specific conditions of employment. Pneumoconiosis (black lung), silicosis, asbestosis and other asbestos-related diseases, and lead poisoning were common ailments among miners and *factory workers of the early 20th century.

In 1914, with commitment to both industrial and military support for the Great War, the federal government created the Honorary Advisory Council for Scientific and Industrial Research, the forerunner of the *National Research Council. Imitating British efforts to gauge the relationship between industrial efficiency and workers' health, the council devised an Associate Committee on Industrial Fatigue in 1919. 'Fatigue' originally referred to the physiological changes leading to muscular inefficiency, but its meaning soon expanded to allow for the scientific delineation of optimum hours and conditions of work. The committee operated out of the University of Toronto's Department of Physiology, home of its chair, Dr J.J.R. Macleod. The university's School of Hygiene began to offer instruction in industrial hygiene in 1919. By the 1920s industrial fatigue had become the leading area in applied physiology. When the committee ceded responsibility for research in this field to the dominion health department in 1924, the Industrial Health Branch was established under the direction of Dr J. Grant Cunningham. The branch's investigation, research, and active promotion of prevention and early recognition of occupational diseases, and its training of industrial health professionals, provided crucial support for the provincial bodies constituted during the interwar years, commencing with the Ontario Board of Health's industrial hygiene division in 1920. A separate federal division of industrial hygiene was created in 1938.

Across Canada, provincial divisions turned their attention almost exclusively to the prevention of occupational disease and accidents. The most important outcome was a combined medical/state lobby that resulted in provincial legislative amendments to require the reporting of occupational diseases, the procedure to be followed in their medical control, and the mechanical control of dust, fumes, and specified toxic chemicals. The principal goal was medical supervision in mines and factories, ideally through a physician specializing in industrial hygiene, more commonly through part-time employment of a public health nurse. The Royal College of Physicians and Surgeons of Canada also recognized occupational medicine as an area of specialization.

Following the Second World War the scope of industrial hygiene widened. Provinces enacted laws regarding the detection and control of asbestos-related diseases and silicosis, the use of pesticides, protection against exposure to radiation, and the regulation of environmental pollutants. Specialists established the Occupational and Environmental Medical Association of Canada. Current research indicates the continued high incidence of certain occupational health and safety hazards, despite historic changes in the structure of the economy, the composition of the workforce, and the nature of production.

CYNTHIA COMACCHIO

industrial revolution. A term describing a process of social and economic change that brings the production of goods and services into more concentrated units with centralized management and increasingly sophisticated technology. In Canada industrialization has most often taken place under private ownership and has been driven by a desire to extract higher profits by increasing the volume of output, intensifying work, and reducing production costs, especially labour input. That has generally meant some combination of undermining the labour markets for craft skills, subdividing labour into narrowly specialized tasks, hiring cheaper, less skilled workers (women, children, recent immigrants), mechanizing production processes, and imposing strict workplace discipline and increasingly bureaucratic management. It has generally also involved geographical concentration in urban areas and some government promotion and protection (notably tariffs).

Using the term 'revolution' to describe this process could be misleading, in that all industries were not transformed at the same time or pace, and there was considerable unevenness in industrial development. Nonetheless, industrialization in Canada, as in other countries, evolved through distinct phases (one starting in the 1840s, a second in the 1890s, a third in the 1940s, and a fourth in the 1970s), each of which can be usefully described as a new 'industrial revolution'. Each time, the accumulated changes in production and in society amount to a marked departure from the preceding phase.

Industrialization has never been a simple top-down process, but has involved negotiation and accommodation to the needs of workers as well as capitalists. Craftsmen and coal miners were the first to organize, but *unions remained weak in Canadian industry before the 1940s. At that point, they established stable collective bargaining in mass-production, resource, and transportation industries, which brought industrial workers a better standard of living. Over the 20th century, unions also convinced the state to provide legislative protection against workplace accidents, unemployment, and discriminatory hiring practices and to guarantee minimum employment standards (such as the eight-hour day). After 1975, however, many of these negotiated and legislated gains were eroded. CRAIG HERON

Industrial Workers of the World. Created in Chicago in 1905 as a revolutionary industrial union, the IWW and its members, nicknamed 'Wobblies', organized minorities, immigrants, women, and unskilled workers ignored by conservative craft *unions. But its ultimate aim was a revolution that would create a new society with neither bosses nor government. This revolution would be brought about by direct action, sabotage, and the general strike, not the ballot box. Thus the IWW was closer to anarchism and *syndicalism than to *socialism or communism.

The IWW was most successful in British Columbia, where it organized 8,000 railway navvies in strikes in 1912, and among loggers in northern Ontario. Famous Wobbly organizers such as Big Bill Haywood, Elizabeth Gurley Flynn, and Joe Hill often came to Canada, and IWW songs such as 'Solidarity Forever' and 'Where the Fraser River Flows' remain labour anthems.

The IWW was declared illegal during the First World War and was in disarray by the time of the 1919–20 labour revolt. Yet its ideas shaped the strike wave, and former Wobblies helped create the *One Big Union, the *Communist Party of Canada, and the industrial unions of the 1930s and 1940s. The IWW exists today, though in much-reduced form. MARK LEIER

Industry and Humanity. Written by William Lyon Mackenzie *King and published in 1918, this rather odd book mixed history, industrial relations, and philosophical inquiry, reflecting King's years of experience as federal minister of labour in Canada and as consultant to the American Rockefeller Foundation during the First World War. 'The existing attitude of Capital and Labor toward each other is too largely one of mistrust born of fear', opened *Industry and Humanity*. 'This attitude must be changed to one of trust inspired by Faith.' The next 300 or so pages elaborated this notion, arguing for a balance among capital, labour, management, and society, to be achieved through the scientific investigation of workers' grievances.

Unfortunately for King, the book's plea for industrial harmony fell on deaf ears, as the years 1918–19 marked Canada's greatest outburst of labour unrest to that time. However, King's views did shape Canada's evolving industrial relations legislation during his tenure as prime minister. DAVID BRIGHT

Inglis, Charles (1734–1816), bishop. From a Scotch-Irish clerical family, Inglis became a Church of England missionary to colonial America. He rose to become rector of Trinity Church, New York, the most sought-after preferment in the colonial church. At the onset of the American Revolution, in reply to Thomas Paine's *Common Sense*, he wrote *True Interest of America Impartially Stated*. A modern assessment of *True Interest* calls it the 'greatest loyalist pamphlet of the war'. For his loyalism he was consecrated Bishop of Nova Scotia, with episcopal jurisdiction over British North America, thereby becoming the first overseas bishop in the Church of England. As bishop he is best remembered as the chief founder of King's College, Nova Scotia, the inspiration and directing force behind the construction of over 40 churches, and his episcopal tours during which he confirmed over 4,300 individuals. Throughout his ministry and episcopate, he held steadfastly to his belief that the king, as the supreme head of the Church of England as the national church, governed its proceedings. The alliance of church and state was for him essential, because only religion could provide the ultimate and necessary sanction for the laws and institutions of Christian society. BRIAN CUTHBERTSON

Innis, Harold (1894–1952), economic historian, pioneer in communications studies. Innis, whose entire teaching career was spent at the University of Toronto, explained Canada's economic and institutional development as the result of the exploitation of a succession of staple commodities (fish, fur, timber, wheat) to satisfy external markets. In *The Fur Trade in Canada* (1930), he traced the trade's relentless expansion across northern America in terms of European demand, the character of the beaver, the network of rivers and lakes, and the transport technology, and concluded that the fur traders laid out the boundaries of modern Canada. Canada emerged because of geography, not in spite of it. The country's dependence on staple exports accounted for its strong ties to Britain as well as vulnerability to shifts in demand. The development of mining and pulp and paper in the 20th century accentuated north–south economic links and weakened east–west coherence forged by fur and the wheat economy. Though Innis was a poor stylist, mixing arresting epigrams with a mass of undigested detail—as in *The Cod Fisheries* (1940)—the *staples idea was a dominant influence on historians and political economists from 1930 to 1960. In turning to pulp, paper, and the press, Innis veered into speculations about the ways mediums of communication bias cultures towards time or space. While *Empire and Communications* (1950) and *The Bias of Communications* (1951) inspired Marshall *McLuhan, they had little impact on the social sciences in Innis's own day. Innis was by temperament and conviction an intense individualist, anti-statist and anti-bureaucratic; he prized detachment and made the search for bias and an escape from obsessions with the present major aims of the social sciences. He had only scorn for academics venturing into politics or pontificating on public issues. CARL BERGER

insane asylums. Insane asylums were introduced into Canada in the first half of the 19th century. The earliest were provisional asylums established in makeshift institutions, most notably in the basement of a converted cholera hospital in Saint John (1836), on the third floor of the Montreal Jail (1839), and in the renovated Toronto Jail (1841). Within a decade, many of these proto-asylums had been replaced by a first generation of purpose-built institutions, in New Brunswick (1848), Quebec and Ontario (1850), Newfoundland (1854), and Nova Scotia (1859). Although the mad were also managed and cared for in hospitals, jails, and family households before and subsequent to the establishment of asylums, over the course of the 19th century the insane asylum gained pride of place as an increasingly specialized response to madness.

The underlying treatment philosophy was moral therapy. It asserted that the architecture of a properly built asylum would in itself be a curative force for its patients. Asylums were therefore built away from urban centres, in a symmetrical architectural style that would foster mental orderliness, in surroundings that were conducive to mental and physical recovery, and on a relatively small scale to allow for maximum medical attention. Moral therapy also included a highly organized round of daily activities, again with an eye to re-establishing order in disordered minds. Of central importance to this therapeutic strategy was work. It was firmly believed that the physiological improvements resulting from physical work, along with the repetitive and orderly nature of the activity, would greatly improve the insane condition.

Moral therapy came to be seen as best practised in a state-organized institutional system, although the Beauport Asylum, Quebec's first permanent institution, was privately run on a 'farming-out' system. Classification of the insane was usually based on three categories: mania, melancholia, and dementia. Although sedatives and stimulants were used in 19th-century asylums, on the whole drug therapy was but a minor aspect of moral therapy.

Although most first generation asylum physicians in Canada joined their European counterparts in anticipation of high cure rates, the philosophy of moral therapy proved difficult to put into practice. Buildings generally grew too large and it was impossible to make the architecture work for large patient populations. Families tended to base the committal and retrieval of their relations on their own needs and understandings of madness, often in defiance of doctors' orders. This frustrated psychiatrists like Joseph Workman, who complained that his institution looked more like a 'giant poorhouse' than an asylum.

It was also difficult to maintain moral therapy in the face of a high patient/attendant ratio, which often ran into the 30:1 range. Moreover, attendants were notoriously poorly remunerated and overworked, making their job more a drudgery than an occupation. This led to the creation of asylum 'subcultures' based on relations among attendants and patients that challenged the official medical strategies of the institutions' medical directors. These difficulties were not helped when 'degeneration theory' started to supplant earlier more optimistic ideas about the curability of madness. Finally, the gap between the ideals of moral therapy and the realities of the insane asylum was partly the result of fiscal constraints placed on asylum infrastructure by government legislators.

By the end of the 19th century the treatment of patients in insane asylums was being challenged by clinical therapies offered by neurologists and psychotherapists. These challenges led to the development of new treatment strategies including drug therapy, and more aggressive physical treatments like insulin coma therapy and electroconvulsive therapy. JAMES E. MORAN

Insolences du Frère Untel, Les. Written by Jean-Paul Desbiens, a Mariste brother (born in 1927 in Métabetchouan), and published in 1960 by Les Éditions de l'Homme, the book (in English, *The Impertinences of Brother Anonymous*) was based on letters sent by Desbiens to the newspaper *Le Devoir* in 1959. It attacked the Quebec school system and criticized the Catholic Church's hold on that system, arguing that it resulted in a general atmosphere of fear among the Quebec people, reflected at all levels of society, politics, and culture. Desbiens argued that what he considered the poor quality of spoken French (**joual*) showed a lack of free will by people too subdued and fearful of the civil and religious authorities to promote their own freedom. *Les Insolences* is often recognized as having contributed to the *Quiet Revolution. With over 100,000 copies sold in one year, it became the first best-seller in Quebec. YVES ROBERGE

Institut canadien de Montréal. The institute was founded in 1844 with a view to creating a literary association and Montreal's first French-language circulating library. Although the project initially attracted wide support, the subjects of lectures and debates held at the institute became more radical and its administration fell into the hands of liberals associated with the republican, democratic, and anti-clerical Parti rouge. This, and the institute's growing collection of books that circulated freely in the city and thus escaped clerical censure, led Mgr Ignace *Bourget to issue three pastoral letters in 1858 dealing with literary associations, the last of which specifically condemned the institute and forbade Catholics from becoming or remaining members and from frequenting its library, threatening them with excommunication or refusal of the sacraments.

These condemnations led to the very public resignation of one-fifth of the institute's members and to negotiations with Bourget. The main issue was the circulation of books on the church's *Index* of banned works; the association briefly considered separating such titles from the rest of its collection. By 1865 the negotiations had broken down, and 17 members of the institute launched an appeal to Rome, claiming they had been unfairly treated by the bishop. In 1869 Rome upheld Bourget's action, added its own condemnation of the institute, and placed its 1868 *Annuaire* on the *Index* of prohibited books. At the same time, the Parti rouge was being wiped off the electoral map, its younger members adopting a more moderate tone, ironically identified by the label *violet*. The institute thus found itself in debt and isolated by the early 1870s. It was also embroiled in the *Guibord affair, a conflict with the bishop concerning the burial of one of its members. Paradoxically, its library, now free, was more popular than ever, catering to skilled workers and clerks and to those members of the elite who dared to brave the clerical condemnations. Regardless of class or gender, the library's patrons read mostly romantic literature and favoured popular French novelists such as Alexandre Dumas and Eugène Sue, whose works were banned by the *Index*. Dedicated to freedom of choice in a society increasingly subject to ultramontane censure, the institute was forced to close its popular library in 1880. For all intents and purposes, this marked the end of the association and of the radical liberalism it had supported.

LOUIS-GEORGES HARVEY

insulin, discovery of. In 1889 it was first postulated that an internal secretion of the pancreas regulated metabolism, enabling the body to absorb the nutrients in its food. A massive search for the internal secretion proved fruitless until a team at the University of Toronto announced in early 1922 that they could extract a hormone, insulin, from animal pancreas (the name derives from the pancreatic islet cells) and use it to control the symptoms of diabetes mellitus.

Frederick Grant *Banting, a young medical doctor, initiated the insulin research by proposing to J.J.R. Macleod, professor of physiology, that Banting investigate an idea involving pancreatic duct ligation and islet-cell transplant. Macleod supervised the research and assigned Banting a student assistant, Charles Best. Banting and Best worked largely on their own in the summer of 1921, then with the help of a trained biochemist, James B. Collip, who was assigned to the project at Banting's request. Banting's initial research idea was discarded, and the team's critical successes came only after Collip improved their technique of making extracts of pancreas. While the discovery process was gradual, the most important single event was the successful trial of Collip's extract on 14-year-old Leonard Thompson in Toronto General Hospital on 23 January 1922.

Insulin produced therapeutic miracles, near-resurrections, on starved, dying diabetic children. Its discovery was honoured almost instantly, as Banting and Macleod were awarded the 1923 Nobel Prize in Physiology or Medicine. Banting shared his prize money with Best, Macleod shared his with Collip. The glory of insulin was tarnished by the personality conflicts and rivalries that had irreparably fractured the insulin team—at one point Banting and Collip came to blows in the lab. Canada's two Nobel laureates did not speak to one another. In later years Best attempted to rewrite history to increase his recognition.

Insulin was discovered in Canada because of a combination of serendipity, improvements in blood-sugar monitoring, and the fact that a world-class research capacity had been developed at the University of Toronto. Two of the early patients, who had come within days of death from their diabetes, outlived all the members of the discovery team.

MICHAEL BLISS

Intercolonial Railway. The Intercolonial was constructed and operated by the government of Canada to fulfill its 1867 constitutional commitment to join the Maritime provinces to central Canada. The British government, anxious to unite the colonies and hopeful that new railway construction would restore the value of private Canadian railway bonds held by British investors, assisted in the project. While the Canadian government hoped a private company would take over operations of the railway, the Intercolonial remained publicly owned.

To meet the British government's desire that the railway be safe from American attack, and in order to connect existing population centres, the Intercolonial followed a circuitous route from Halifax or Saint John to Quebec City via the north shore of New Brunswick, through the Matapedia Valley, and then along the south shore of the St Lawrence. By 1900 the line had been extended west to Montreal and east to Sydney.

Between the completion of the railway in 1876 and 1914, a tenfold increase in freight and passenger traffic did not translate into financial success. The railway was never expected to pay its capital costs, but in 19 of its first 40 years operating expenses outstripped revenues. Critics at the time argued that government ownership was inherently inefficient. Defenders of the railway argued that the public railway granted unusually low *freight rates to help promote economic development and trade between the regions. The Intercolonial disappeared as an independent entity between 1918 and 1923, as it was incorporated into the *Canadian National Railways system.

KEN CRUIKSHANK

international economic organizations. Organizations like the International Monetary Fund and the General Agreement on Tariffs and Trade were given form and substance in the post–Second World War period. Their negotiation marked the high water point of international co-operation in financial and commercial matters designed to reduce impediments to the freer flow of goods and services.

Discussions relating to the IMF began between the Americans, led by Harry White, and the British, headed by John Maynard Keynes, in 1942, and quickly included the Canadians, and especially Louis Rasminsky, who was to be Canada's IMF executive director in 1946–61. Clashing Anglo-American philosophies over the form of the future organization animated these discussions, but the American view prevailed and the fund, given shape at the Bretton Woods conference of July 1944, came into existence in March 1946. Its purpose was simple—to maintain exchange rate stability among its membership and prevent the competitive devaluations that had plagued the 1930s. That was provided for via the par value system, where all currencies were pegged to the US dollar, and US$35 would purchase one troy ounce of gold. It was also designed to provide short-term loans to countries that were experiencing payments disequilibria. This system prevailed until 1973, when it collapsed following intolerable global financial pressures and, in particular, difficulties experienced by the American economy. Countries went from pegged to floating currencies, and the IMF cast about for another purpose, eventually becoming the lender of last resort, primarily to developing countries.

The International Bank for Reconstruction and Development was almost an afterthought as the IMF was under discussion. It was not until 1943 that the United Kingdom and the United States turned their attention to a world bank. Its charter evolved very quickly and while it too was approved at Bretton Woods, it was very much the lesser known twin of the Bretton Woods organizations. In its original incarnation, it was dedicated to reconstruction in Europe and much less to (third world) development. It was also designed to provide long-term funds to members in need. By the 1950s, it was evolving into the World Bank Group, comprised of the International Finance Corporation, the International Development Association to disburse low cost loans, and the World Bank.

The GATT, based on a system of multilateralism and non-discrimination that had first been promoted by the American secretary of state Cordell Hull, promised to free international trade, which had been hindered in the 1930s by high tariffs. Originally designed to be one element of the four-part International Trade Organization, it became a stand-alone institution when the ITO charter died at the hands of the Truman administration following their reluctance to submit it to Congress for a vote in 1950. As a result of its truncated nature, the GATT relied almost exclusively on moral suasion to enforce its rules.

As befitted its status as a country heavily reliant on international trade for domestic prosperity, Canada was intimately involved in the negotiations leading to the GATT's establishment by 1947, and became known among the contracting parties as one of the 'Big 3' along with Britain and the United States. Of the first three tariff rounds undertaken at Geneva (1947), Annecy (1949), and Torquay (1950–1), the first was the most successful and marked the high point of international co-operation in reducing tariffs. As the so-called post-war transition period stretched out far longer than anyone had anticipated, the commitment to reducing tariffs diminished during the 1950s.

The GATT did not benefit Canada as had initially been intended. Given the myriad of non-tariff barriers to trade and currencies among Canada's putative trading partners, the only country able and willing to absorb the billions of dollars of exports upon which Canadian prosperity depended was the United States. Canadian policy could be described as multilateral by preference and bilateral by default. Later rounds were more successful, but they also favoured Canada's trade with the US. The Kennedy round (1964–7) in particular was critical in terms of tying Canada into a continental economy in that about CAN$2.5 billion of its trade with the US was freed by lower tariffs. The Tokyo (1973–8) and Uruguay (1986–93) rounds accelerated the process.

The World Trade Organization came out of the Uruguay round and is a much more powerful institution than the old GATT, having the power to enforce its decisions among members. The WTO launched a new tariff round at Doha (2001) focusing on agricultural subsidies and financial services. BRUCE MUIRHEAD

International Institute of Metropolitan Toronto, 1956–74. A social agency that promoted immigrant integration, interaction between new and old Canadians, and a modest form of cultural pluralism. The institute belonged to a network of private and public social services that included family, children's, and ethnic agencies and served mostly non-English-speaking immigrants. Its work included hosting educational and social activities such as banquets; classes in English; for women, the operation of powered sewing machines; and cultural nights showcasing refugee musical talent. Professional and volunteer social workers, some of them also newcomers, provided support ranging from job placement to personal counselling for those dealing with (often war-related) emotional problems and family crises.

The institute had two precursors: St Andrew's Memorial Friendship House evolved out of the Hart House Group (University of Toronto professors who gave aid to refugees); the New Canadians Service Association was funded by the Toronto Junior League. When these institutions amalgamated to form the institute in 1956, its board included wealthy philanthropists and leading social workers.

The history of the institute sheds light on key issues of the early post-war era, including national reconstruction and campaigns to promote bourgeois family values, the elimination of variously defined political and social threats such as communism and the ethnic Canadian left-wing press, and the fostering of patriotism and citizenship.

FRANCA IACOVETTA

Inuit art, a phenomenon of the second half of the 20th century, has developed out of the exchange between two cultures. Canada's vast North had remained largely untouched by Western civilization until the Second

World War. The inhabitants, the Inuit (formerly referred to as Eskimos), had experienced sporadic contact with other cultures, first during the 19th century when the lucrative bowhead whale-hunt induced annual northern excursions by *whaling companies. Once the whales were depleted, traders from the *Hudson's Bay Company set up small trading posts, and were followed by missionaries. However, the nomadic lifestyle of the Inuit, based on travelling by dogsled in winter and by kayak in summer, remained largely unchanged.

During the 1950s and 1960s dramatic changes were to alter life in the North forever. The Canadian government, driven by sovereignty issues and concern for the welfare of its most remote citizens, established small settlements around the trading posts and began to deliver services such as education and health that were available to other Canadian citizens. Administering a nomadic group of people became unmanageable, and Inuit were pressured and induced to abandon their nomadic lifestyle and live in the nearest settlement. It soon became apparent that the Inuit, unilingual nomads, had few useful skills for a cash economy. They did, however, have remarkable manual skills: they carved all their tools, built their sleds, and sewed their skin clothing. Channeling these skills into arts and crafts was the obvious strategy. James Houston, a young artist from Toronto, had recognized this as early as 1948. With the assistance of the Canadian Guild of Crafts and the Hudson's Bay Company he developed a distribution system for small sculptures and sewing items, finding instant success in Montreal. The government of Canada soon followed suit. Arts and crafts officers were sent north. While sculpture was a familiar medium—Inuit had traded small ivory sculpture ever since the first foreign ship landed—other skills such as printmaking had to be taught. The Inuit acquired these skills with remarkable ease.

Out of these unique historical circumstances a new art form was born. Unfortunately, the term 'Inuit art' tends to be used for the cheapest little carving produced in a hurry as well as for the most exquisite stone sculpture, executed with great care and forethought; the more accurate term would be 'arts and crafts made by Inuit'. Inuit art has made its greatest impact through sculpture. This particular art form has been most easy to integrate into a mixed economy. It does not involve a commitment to a regular workplace or set hours and it allows flexibility and draws from natural local materials. To this day, many male Inuit go hunting whenever possible and carve during winter or whenever the weather does not permit treks. The cash from carvings allows for rifles, gas, and other hunting provisions. Although there are female carvers, women in general tend to do textile arts such as appliqué wallhangings and woven tapestries or are involved in printmaking.

The main themes of both prints and sculpture have remained constant: Arctic wildlife, the family, camp life, hunting and fishing, and shamanism. Although missionaries have turned shamanism into a taboo subject it seems safe to express it through art. The materials used for carving range from antler and weathered whalebone to ivory, although stone is the dominant medium. The local green-blue serpentine on Baffin Island lends itself to exquisitely carved animals, birds, and dramatic hunting scenes; the dull grey stone from Nunavik is often treated with shoe polish to give it lustre. Whalebone, with its distinct organic shapes, is used for multi-media assembled pieces.

Over time, producing arts and crafts for an outside market has become much more than a source of revenue. Art has played a crucial part in helping one of the last remaining hunter-gatherer societies to make the difficult transition from camp life to settlement life. It has developed into an important vehicle for Inuit to express pride in their culture and to record ancient customs and legends in visual form before they slip into oblivion. Most importantly, it has helped Inuit to maintain a sense of cultural identity during a time when their lives were overtaken by another, technologically superior, society. Says Andrew Karpik from Pangnirtung: 'The drawings I do are for people who suffered and struggled for their lives—for food and clothing. What strength was used by our great-grandfathers in their livelihood!'

MARIA VON FINCKENSTEIN

Inuit culture. The Inuit are the most widespread and perhaps the most well-known Aboriginal people on earth. The Native inhabitants of the entire North American Arctic, they live from the west coast of Alaska to the east coast of Greenland, and have close cultural relatives living south of Bering Strait and in eastern Siberia. Occupying so vast an area, the Inuit go by a variety of regional and local names, including Inupiat in north Alaska, Inuvialuit in the western Canadian Arctic, Inuit in the rest of Arctic Canada, and Kalaallit in Greenland. Until recently, all were called Eskimos by the outside world, a term many now consider impolite.

All modern Inuit—or their immediate ancestors—share a common language. Sometimes called Inuit-Inupiaq (Inuktitut) by linguists, it consists of a continuum of local dialects spoken by small communities across the top of North America. Although classified as a single language, there are strong dialect divisions within Inuit-Inupiaq, making it difficult—but not impossible—for people living half a continent apart to understand one another. Most Inuit now also speak a second language; English (in Alaska and most of Canada), Danish (in Greenland), or occasionally French (in Arctic Quebec). Inuit also share, or shared in times past, a common traditional culture, again with regional variations, and are physically distinct in various subtle ways from their Native and non-Native neighbours.

This entry describes traditional Inuit culture as it existed prior to significant contact with Europeans and Euro-North Americans in the 19th and early 20th centuries. Many people imagine that this culture was timeless, even primordial, because it was Aboriginal and somehow 'in tune with nature'. This is not true. As we know from archaeological and other evidence, Inuit culture changed dramatically, even in the distant past. And of course, Inuit culture has continued to change over the past hundred years. The Inuit are now a modern people, and like almost everyone else in the world, no longer live the way their ancestors did.

Inuit culture was never entirely uniform, since neither the environment nor historical circumstances were everywhere the same. We can begin by examining those aspects of the traditional culture that were broadly shared, before looking at some of the differences. With few exceptions the Inuit were (and are) a people of the sea coast—maritime hunters depending for their livelihood primarily on seals, walrus, and whales. Land mammals such as caribou and muskox were also hunted, but were generally of lesser importance, as were fish and various small game. The Inuit were superb hunters, perhaps the best in the world. Inevitably, they moved with the seasons, harvesting different resources as they became available.

Many Inuit lived with as little government as any people on earth. Communities were comparatively small and sometimes transitory, while the independence and self-reliance of the individual was highly prized. The nuclear family was everywhere the basis of society, and both men and women brought a different set of skills to the marriage. Men did most of the hunting, and made most of the family's tools and weapons; women cooked, looked after children, and did the sewing—their most skilled and perhaps most important task. The division of labour was not foolishly strict, however, and women enjoyed a relatively high social position. Marriages were generally quite stable, at least after the birth of the first child. Polygyny (the taking of more than one wife) was limited to the few men wealthy enough to support an extra wife, and the many children that might result. In most areas, nuclear families existed within a larger web of extended family relationships.

The Inuit believed their world to be inhabited by dangerous spiritual forces, which had to be placated through various rituals and by observing a number of taboos. In the Canadian Arctic, it was considered unwise to mix the products of land and sea—to cook caribou and seal meat in the same pot, for example. To do so would offend Kannakapfaluk, the Mother of All Sea Creatures, who would exact revenge by letting people starve, by causing storms, or by splitting the sea ice so that people drowned.

Traditional spiritual life focused on the shaman, or *angiguk*. This person, either a man or older woman, had special powers derived from the spirit world. These powers were usually the gift of spirit helpers who visited the shaman while he or she was in an ecstatic trance, often induced by rhythmic drumming. With the aid of these helpers, the shaman could fly through the air, visit the underworld, or turn into an animal. Shamans were not priests, but did often charge for their services. Some used their powers for evil, and were much feared, while others worked for the benefit of others.

The Inuit enjoyed one of the most elaborate and sophisticated tool kits of any hunting people on earth. They made literally hundreds of different kinds of tools, including many kinds of harpoons and floats for sea-mammal hunting, backed compound bows, large and small skin-boats (umiaks and kayaks), several kinds of dogsled, elaborate sewing paraphernalia, bow drill gear, and complex arrays of tools for carpentry, animal butchering, and hide preparation. Warm, light, and serviceable clothing was perhaps their greatest achievement. It was generally made of caribou hide for warmth, or sealskin when waterproofing was important. For protection against the bitter arctic winter, it has not been surpassed by even the best modern clothing.

Anthropologists generally divide the seamless realm of the traditional Inuit into three main geographic areas. Cultural differences in large part reflect relative differences in the natural wealth of each area, as measured by its wildlife.

The Western Inuit of northwest Alaska and western-most Canada—Inupiat and Inuvialuit—were the most prosperous, and the most settled. Typically, they lived in large coastal villages of several hundred people, where they spent their summers hunting sea mammals, and their winters—as much as possible—living on the stored surplus. Winter houses were made of driftwood and sod, and social life was relatively elaborate. Extended families were led by semi-hereditary chiefs called *umialit* ('rich men'), who through influence and family position were able to acquire considerable wealth. In the early 19th century there were about 30 independent Western Inuit 'polities' or bands, with a total population of about 9,000–10,000. Each had its own defined territory and, often, a main or capital village. Small-scale warfare between neighbours was not uncommon. The relative wealth of the western Arctic was based on fish, several inland caribou herds, and particularly on its abundant sea life: bowhead whales, belugas, walrus, and various seal species.

In traditional times, the Central Inuit, who lived in the central Canadian Arctic, were materially the poorest of all Inuit. Most sea mammal species are absent from the ice-bound waters of the region, and in many areas subsistence was limited to caribou hunting and fishing during the summer, and the hunting of small ringed seals through the sea ice during winter. Leadership positions were poorly developed, communities were fluid and often inchoate, and the population was sparse and thinly spread, numbering no more than about 3,000–3,500 people in traditional times. Permanent architecture was lacking; instead people lived in snowhouses ('igloos') during the winter and skin tents in the summer. Important regional subgroups include the Copper Inuit (living around Victoria Island), the Netsilik (in the Queen Maud Gulf area), the Caribou Inuit (living inland west of Hudson Bay), and the Igloolik Inuit (living along the coast between northwestern-most Hudson Bay and northern Baffin Island). The Sadlermiut, a small and rather aberrant group living on Southampton Island, went extinct after an epidemic in 1902.

The Eastern Inuit live along the eastern and southern coasts of Baffin Island, the arctic shores of the Quebec-Labrador peninsula, and in coastal Greenland. Here the standard of living was once again relatively high, supported by abundant small seals, belugas, and in many areas walrus, narwhal, and bowhead whales. Communities were relatively settled, particularly in Greenland, with well-defined territories. Leaders, known as *ishumataq* (literally 'he who thinks'), enjoyed considerable influence, if less wealth than some of the Western Inuit. Winter houses were made of wood, stone, or even whalebone, insulated with sod; snowhouses were used mainly when travelling. It was in western Greenland that kayak hunting was most developed, including the ability to do the famous 'Eskimo roll' (whereby the kayaker is able to flip his kayak upside down in the water, and then right himself). The Eastern Inuit were among the first Native North Americans to meet Europeans, beginning with the Greenlandic *Norse (Vikings). It is estimated that about 13,000 people lived in the eastern Arctic prior to 1800, most of them in Greenland. DAVID MORRISON

Inuit history can be traced back almost 2,000 years, to an ancient culture called Old Bering Sea by archaeologists. As the name indicates, archaeological sites representing this culture are found around the shores of the Bering Sea, in westernmost Alaska, and easternmost Siberia. The Bering Sea is a rich hunting area, and Old Bering Sea people seem to have made some adjustments and inventions that made it possible for them to prosper there. Principal among these were the invention of harpoon float gear and of sophisticated watercraft that allowed—for perhaps the first time anywhere—the efficient hunting of sea mammals in open water. By about AD 1000 the Thule culture descendants of these people had colonized all of arctic Alaska, and were poised for great things.

Beginning about 1,000 years ago, these Thule Inuit began to move east. By AD 1250 they were in northwestern Greenland, and within another century or so had taken possession of the entire North American Arctic, from their Bering Strait homeland to eastern Greenland. In so doing, they seem to have completely supplanted the original inhabitants of arctic Canada and Greenland, the so-called Dorset people, whose ancestors had lived there for 4,000 years before the arrival of the Inuit. Early Inuit pioneers also met farmers and hunters from the Norse colonies in southwestern Greenland. By the 15th century, both the Dorset and the Greenlandic Norse had disappeared.

Little is known about the details of these events. Outright violence does not seem to have played a large role in the Inuit triumph; indeed archaeological evidence seems to suggest that they and the Dorset people, at least, avoided one another whenever possible. Inuit oral tradition suggests that the Dorset—called *Tunit* by the Inuit—may have been pushed into marginal areas, where they found it progressively harder to make a living. There is little evidence that modern Inuit have any significant Dorset ancestry.

The Thule period in arctic North America, between about AD 1000 and 1500, was something of a golden age. The Thule Inuit were skilled fishermen and superb hunters, able to harvest everything from caribou and ringed seals to walrus, muskoxen, polar bears, and even the great bowhead whales, 15 metres or more in length. In areas where whales were abundant, Thule Inuit were able to live in large coastal villages of several hundred people. Houses were solid and well-built, framed with driftwood or whalebone and insulated with sod. Villages were smaller in areas where whales were less abundant, but everywhere archaeologists have found evidence of a rich and vibrant culture.

This, however, was not the situation that greeted early European explorers, at least in arctic Canada. Areas of the High Arctic where Thule Inuit had once flourished had been abandoned and whaling as a systematic activity and focus of Inuit life had largely ceased. People lived in temporary snowhouses on the winter ice, not in the warm sod houses of the Thule period, struggling to make a living by hunting ringed seals. In many areas, tool kits had been simplified and the whole way of life was impoverished compared with what it had been. A cooling climate, for which there is abundant evidence, was at least partially responsible. It has also been suggested that European infectious diseases may have ravaged the Arctic at a date earlier than we can document. The nature of this transition between the Thule culture of ancient times and the 'historic' or 'traditional' culture of the 19th century requires further clarification.

Contact between Inuit and Europeans dates to the Viking period, for *Norse trade iron and other materials are found widely in eastern Arctic archaeological sites. By at least the 16th century, later European explorers were venturing into eastern Arctic waters; by the 18th century the *Hudson's Bay Company was engaging in fairly regular direct trade out of *Prince of Wales Fort (Churchill, Manitoba) and at the Savage Islands (in Hudson Strait). It was the 19th century before Europeans began to have an obviously profound impact on Inuit life and culture, or to learn much about them. One important event in this process was the search for a *Northwest Passage, and particularly for the missing third Franklin expedition, during the 1850s. Dozens of private and Royal Navy ships were involved, and Inuit were contacted everywhere across arctic North America.

Of far greater effect was the commercial *whaling industry. In the 1820s, commercial whalers based in Britain and New England began hunting in eastern Canadian waters, particularly along the Baffin coast, into Lancaster Sound, and later, in northwestern *Hudson Bay. By the 1850s they had profoundly altered traditional Inuit life almost everywhere in the eastern Arctic. Hundreds of Inuit were hired or otherwise supported by the whalers, the men as commercial hunters and crew members, the women as seamstresses, wives, and mistresses. European infectious diseases were introduced, along with vast quantities of manufactured goods, such as firearms (which revolutionized hunting), fabrics, and even tea and flour. The process was repeated in the western Arctic, beginning in the 1850s. By 1900, many western Inuit populations had decreased by as much as 90 per cent due to epidemic outbreaks of infectious diseases such as measles and influenza.

It is difficult to summarize the history of the Inuit during the 20th century, so complex and varied was its course. By 1910 the whaling industry was dead, the victim of depleted whale stocks and the invention of commercial substitutes for whale oil and baleen. The *fur trade moved north to take its place; by 1925 almost all Canadian Inuit enjoyed fairly easy access to a trading post. White fox furs became a staple trade item. The Canadian government extended its hand north at the same time, opening police detachments and enforcing Canadian law. The Anglican and Catholic Churches were actively involved in missionary work, and *residential schools were opened in many areas to teach literacy, English, and the other values of Western civilization. Often all three institutions—the RCMP, the church, and the Hudson's Bay Company—were located side by side, offering each other support and serving, in one way or another, a largely nomadic population that still supported itself by hunting and trapping.

The 1950s and 1960s saw major changes. The Canadian government, embarrassed by serious incidents of starvation in the Keewatin and at Garry Lake, decided to end an arctic policy based on (relatively) benign neglect. The Inuit were actively encouraged to settle in new 'micro-urban' villages, often located around the nucleus of the old RCMP post, HBC store, and mission. Prefabricated housing was made available, along with government assistance and services such as schools and nursing stations. The old life on the land was ended, with little to replace it in the way of meaningful wage labour.

Democracy came to the Canadian Arctic during the 1960s, when federal constituencies were organized in the Northwest Territories. During the 1970s and 1980s a second tier of responsible government was established as the governing body of the Northwest Territories evolved from an appointed commissioner to an elected assembly. In 1975 the Inuit of arctic Quebec signed a final land claim agreement; in 1984 the Inuit of the western Arctic (Inuvialuit) followed suit. Finally, in 1999 the Inuit of the eastern and central Northwest Territories signed their own land claim agreement in conjunction with the creation of a new federal territory, called *Nunavut ('our land'). The Inuit are once more the political masters of their own lands. But they still face huge economic and social problems. Chronic unemployment is a fact of life in most communities, and until a viable economic base is created, the Arctic—and the Inuit—will remain at least partially dependent on southern tax dollars.

DAVID MORRISON

Inuit Tapiriit Kanatami, formerly the Inuit Tapirisat of Canada, is the main organization representing about 41,000 *Inuit people. The phrase roughly translates as the Inuit 'Friends' of Canada. The impetus for its establishment came in part from Tagak Curley, an Inuit representative of the Indian/Eskimo Association of Canada; at his request the association sponsored a meeting in Kugluktuk (then Coppermine) in 1970. Broader conferences were held later in Toronto and at Trent University. Incorporated in 1972, the ITK originally attempted to represent Inuit on all issues, including land claims, but within a few years it became clear that regional bodies would take the lead in claims negotiations and ITK would engage in broader political lobbying. It now represents Inuit from regional bodies, many of which have taken on more of a corporate structure after the settlement of land claims. These regional bodies include the Labrador Inuit Association; the Inuvialuit Regional Corporation; Makivik Corporation, representing Inuit of northern Quebec (Nunavik); and Nunavut Tunngavik Incorporated. As well, the Inuit Circumpolar Conference (ICC), the Inuit women's association Pauktuutit, and the National Inuit Youth Council are represented in ITK, which itself is a member organization of ICC. From its head office in Ottawa, ITK has worked on a broad range of issues, including environmental protection, law and justice, health care, social and economic development, and promotion of Inuit culture and rights.

PETER KULCHYSKI

inukshuk. In the language of the *Inuit, *inukshuk* refers to an arrangement of boulders that resembles a human figure. Most are simple cairns or vertically placed slabs built as part of drift-fences to guide caribou towards hidden hunters, or to mark the location of a trail, a good fishing-spot, or other significant site. A more elaborate form with 'arms' and a 'head' has become an arctic icon and is featured on the flag of *Nunavut. It is associated with the area frequented by European vessels during the 17th to 19th centuries, and may have been designed to attract the attention of potential European trading partners. This form may have originated in stone crosses that were built on the Baffin Island coast by Martin Frobisher's 1578 expedition.

ROBERT McGHEE

Inuvik ('place of man' in Inuktitut). Located on the east channel of the Mackenzie Delta 1,100 km northwest of Yellowknife, Inuvik is the main access point for the western Arctic and the Beaufort Sea. Established in 1954 after a serious flood severely damaged the older community of Aklavik, the administrative centre of the western Arctic, it was the first community in the North that was planned rather than being allowed to grow haphazardly. Accessible by road from the south via the Dempster Highway from the Yukon (except during the freezing and breakup of the Mackenzie River), Inuvik attracts tourists who admire its igloo-shaped church or enjoy cruising the river or experiencing *Inuit cultural activities.

K.S. COATES AND W.R. MORRISON

Inverted Pyramid, The (1924). A scathing critique of the social and ethical character of speculative capitalism in British Columbia before the First World War. Its Scottish-born author, Bertrand Sinclair (né William Brown Sinclair), for seven years a ranch hand in Montana, had published his first story in 1902 and was well established as an adventure-story writer before settling permanently in BC in 1911. Before becoming a licensed salmon fisherman in the mid-1930s, Sinclair produced 15 novels, dozens of novelettes, and hundreds of short stories, which mostly followed a pulp yarn formula but also integrated fiction with well-researched descriptions of ranching, logging, and salmon fishing. Sinclair loved the 'green timber' and 'running water' of BC, saw dignity and pride in working people, and abhorred pretentious elites and soulless corporations. One of his two most literary novels, *The Inverted Pyramid* documents the class tensions, rapacious destruction of coastal forests, and uncritical acceptance of individualist and materialist values that characterized pre-war British Columbia.

ROBERT A.J. McDONALD

investment abroad. Global flows of investment capital generally take two forms: indirect and direct. Indirect or fixed connotes investing in the bonded debt of another country or foreign corporation. Such debt provides a contractually defined and relatively safe investment; it does not afford the lender any control beyond a lien on the borrower's assets. Direct or portfolio entails buying into the equity of a foreign enterprise; such investment has no fixed value and fluctuates with the fortunes of the enterprise. It is a livelier form of investment, giving the investor an opportunity to control the enterprise, influence its policies, and share in its profits. Unlike the fixed nature of indirect investment, portfolio investment is more footloose; shares can be sold at the owner's whim. Each form of investment carries implications for national sovereignty. A high bonded indebtedness can restrict a nation's freedom of economic action, placing it at the mercy of foreign bankers (and more recently such agencies as the International Monetary Fund). Portfolio investment can divorce a nation from control over its industrial base and its ability to generate technology and to nurture its own managers and workers. As a country chronically short of capital, Canada has historically been crucially dependent upon steady inflows of fixed and portfolio investment. Its late-19th-century railway boom was sustained by bonds and shares sold in London and New York. Portfolio inflows fed the *National Policy industrialization, thereby creating 'made in Canada' products under the aegis of a branch-plant economy. To this day, Canadians are mindful of the bond rating given them by foreign bankers, while our governments try to mitigate the effects of too great a reliance on foreign direct investment. From 1973 to 1985, the Foreign Investment Review Agency, a federal tribunal, 'screened' new foreign investment entering Canada to ensure that it was of 'significant benefit'. Since 1985, Investment Canada has exhibited Ottawa's friendlier attitude to foreign investors.

Less well known is the fact that Canada has pumped its own portfolio investment into other countries. The pattern began in the late 19th century when *finance capitalists detected an opportunity to use Canada's established reputation as a destination for foreign investment to promote investment in other, less developed nations. Drawing on the technological and managerial expertise built up in Canadian railway and utility development, Toronto and Montreal financiers sought out utility and railway concessions in the Caribbean, Mexico, Latin America, and Spain. These long-term, lucrative concessions reflected the eagerness of cities like Rio de Janeiro and Barcelona to acquire the trappings of modernity. These 'traction' companies were incorporated under Canadian laws and boasted Canadian expertise but were largely conduits for American and European investors to pump money into the developing world. The best known of these companies was the Brazilian Traction, Light and Power Company, formed in 1912 to consolidate Canadian utility companies in Rio and Sao Paulo. This would be Canada's largest overseas investment until it was bought by the Brazilian government in 1979. Other such companies in Mexico and Latin and Central America succumbed to revolution and nationalization.

Since the Second World War Canadian manufacturing companies have 'gone global' by opening their own branch plants and acquiring assets in other countries. *Alcan and *Bombardier have used direct investment to establish themselves abroad in transportation equipment and aluminum products while other Canadian companies like Trizec-Hahn have invested heavily in real estate in the United States. Food processors like McCain and media companies like Quebecor have also spread internationally. In some years, outflows of Canadian direct investment have exceeded inflows.

DUNCAN McDOWALL

Irish. The Great Famine of 1846–51 looms largest in popular images of the Irish in Canada. This perspective views Irish migration in terms of impoverished, starving, and disease-stricken Catholics forced out of Ireland by heartless landlords, crowded into coffin ships, dying in their thousands at the *Grosse Île quarantine station, and enduring severe discrimination within a hostile and alien Anglo-Protestant, English-Canadian culture.

Like all stereotypes, there are elements of truth in this picture. Of the more than 100,000 Irish immigrants who arrived in Canada in 1847, probably 80 per cent were Catholics. Although most of them were not from the poorest stratum of Irish society, they were prone to diseases such as typhus, which spread rapidly in the unsanitary conditions of the transatlantic ships. At Grosse Île, over 5,000 Irish immigrants died in the summer of 1847, making the island the largest Irish Famine graveyard in the world. And it is clear that Irish Catholics in Canada were over-represented in the urban labour force, and under-represented in the country's political institutions, from the municipal to the federal levels. Nevertheless, this view presents a distorted image of the overall Irish-Canadian experience. The events of 1847 were the exception, rather than the norm, and most of the Famine Irish moved right through Canada to settle in the United States. In fact, the majority of Irish Canadians were Protestant, and arrived in British North America before the famine. In Ontario, Irish Protestants outnumbered Irish Catholics by two to one; this ratio remained constant before and after the famine. Both Protestants and Catholics were voluntary migrants, who came to Canada in search of a better life for themselves and their children, and generally found it.

The roots of Irish migration to Canada can be traced back to early-18th-century Newfoundland, where seasonal fishery workers from Waterford and Wexford clustered into long-term communities. There were also pockets of Irish settlers in late 18th-century Nova Scotia, Cape Breton, and New Brunswick. But the really large-scale Irish migration got under way after the end of the Napoleonic Wars in 1815; in the pre-famine period, Irish immigration to British North America averaged just over 22,000 each year. Most of the immigrants settled in Ontario, with Quebec a distant second and New Brunswick a close third. The numbers continued to climb during the famine, but dropped quickly after 1854, and have remained at a trickle ever since. Largely because of the pre-famine migration, the Irish became the single largest ethnic group in English Canada from the 1830s to the 1880s; in 1871, almost a quarter of all Canadians were of Irish ethnicity.

With their ethno-religious divisions, their separate points of origin in Ireland, and their diverse experiences in the different regions of British North America, the Irish were highly heterogeneous; any attempt to define a distinct Irish community is bound to fail. Among the Irish Catholics, a small but significant minority joined the Irish revolutionary nationalist Fenian Brotherhood; a hard core of Irish-Canadian *Fenians went further still and supported the various invasion attempts of American Fenians between 1866 and 1870. But they faced the opposition of the Catholic Church, the hostility of liberal-conservative politicians such as Thomas D'Arcy *McGee, and the indifference or pragmatic neutrality of most Irish Catholic settlers. After the failure of the third Fenian invasion in 1870, Irish-Canadian Fenianism faded away, although many Irish Catholics kept in touch with events in the Old Country, and were generally sympathetic to Irish constitutional nationalism.

Irish-Canadian Protestants, in contrast, were among the most enthusiastic supporters of the *British Empire, and expressed intense loyalty to the Protestant Crown. Their views found institutional expression in the *Orange Order, which Irish Protestants such as Ogle Gowan transmitted to British North America in 1830. In the conservative, loyal, and Protestant atmosphere of 19th-century English Canada, the Orange Order expanded beyond its Irish origins to embrace all sections of Canada's Protestant population. By 1900, one-third of all Canadian Protestant adult males had become Orangemen. In the long run, the Irish-Canadian experience had more to do with Protestantism and the Orange Order than Catholicism and Grosse Île.

As a militantly anti-Catholic organization, the Orange Order injected overt sectarian prejudices into Canadian life; among Irish-Canadian Catholics, anti-Protestant prejudice generally assumed a more clandestine character. From the 1820s to the 1860s, there were sporadic Orange and Green riots, triggered by traditional parades, taking a highly ritualized and theatrical form, and sometimes resulting in loss of life. Gradually, though, such ethno-religious violence became much less intense than in Ireland. With fewer people and more resources, Canada was not characterized by the bitter Protestant-Catholic competition for land, work, and housing that occurred in Ireland. And in political terms, the complex tactical alliances within and between Canadian conservatives and reformers during the 19th century militated against a straightforward Protestant-Catholic division, and made some degree of accommodation possible.

Another reason for the diminution of Protestant-Catholic conflict within Irish Canada was that both groups were rapidly becoming acculturated to Canadian norms. By 1871, Canadians of Irish ethnicity matched the overall population in terms of residency, occupation, and occupational success. Most of the ethnic Irish lived in the countryside, and became farmers; the proportion of those who were merchants, manufacturers, professionals, and artisans was virtually identical to that of the population at large. There were important regional and social differences; Irish Protestants, for example, had a significant edge over Irish Catholics in the Maritimes, and Irish Catholics were more likely than Irish Protestants to be unskilled labourers. But the degree of convergence between Protestant and Catholic, and between Irish and Canadian, is more striking than the differences. The process of acculturation accelerated during the 20th century, to the point at which the Irish blended in so well with Canadian society that they became almost invisible. Nothing could be greater testimony to their success in adjusting to their Canadian environment.

DONALD HARMAN AKENSON AND DAVID A. WILSON

iron and steel industry. The industry has used varying forms of heat and intense pressure to transform iron ore into usable commodities. In Canada it developed in four phases. The first began in New France with the opening of the *St-Maurice forges in 1730. By the mid-19th century, several more small iron works had appeared across the colonies near the sites of iron deposits, though many had closed when they found the available iron difficult to smelt. In their primitive blast furnaces, they combined ore with charcoal and limestone to produce molten iron, which then hardened into 'pigs'. Moulders in foundries then used this pig iron to make cast-iron goods, while blacksmiths hammered it into more flexible wrought iron.

New markets in the emerging age of steam and rail opened a second phase after 1850. Blast furnaces got bigger, but ore quality was still a problem, and, when some ironmasters began replacing charcoal with coke, they also found Canadian (mostly Nova Scotian) coal difficult to use. Industrialists on the finishing end of iron production were often so dissatisfied with the quality and supply of Canadian pig iron that they used imported iron instead and convinced the federal government not to give tariff protection to the primary sector under the *National Policy in 1879. Primary iron production was consequently a weak, fragmented, technologically antiquated part of Canada's industrial structure at the end of the century, while production of secondary products expanded. In the large new foundries, moulders cast a wider variety of consumer goods, often becoming specialists in stoves or agricultural implements. Huge steam-powered rolling mills (such as those that opened in Hamilton, Toronto, Montreal, and Saint John) produced wrought iron bars, plates, and other basic shapes. Several spin-off industries turned out nails, screws, and other hardware.

The third phase began in the 1890s and was marked by consolidation, technological innovation, and expansion of output. American and European producers already had large factories for turning iron into steel, a more serviceable product with higher carbon content. An ambitious project in the 1870s to make steel at the Londonderry ironworks in Nova Scotia had failed, but a small iron forge company at Trenton spun off a new enterprise known as the Nova Scotia Steel Company, which began producing the country's first steel on a small scale in 1883. It used an open-hearth furnace to turn pig iron into molten steel. No other company followed suit until 1900. Meanwhile, the Nova Scotia firm set out to integrate all stages of production—a railway in 1890, a blast furnace and coke ovens at Ferrona in 1891, iron mines on Bell Island off Newfoundland in 1894, and coal mines in Cape Breton in 1900. A year later the firm was rechristened the Nova Scotia Steel and Coal Company. In 1904 it shifted its blast-furnace and open-hearth production to a more convenient location at Sydney Mines. Trenton remained the site for diverse finishing operations, an associated railway-car plant (opened in 1912), and a shipyards and munitions factory during the First World War.

A group of entrepreneurs followed a similar path at Hamilton, Ontario, a good location for bringing in raw materials from the United States and selling to metalworking firms in southern Ontario. They launched the Hamilton Blast Furnace Company in 1895, which merged with the local Ontario Rolling Mills in 1899 to create the Hamilton Steel and Iron Company. This firm opened a small open-hearth steel plant the next year. After a decade of cautious expansion, it merged with two large Ontario companies in the finishing end of the industry and two in Montreal in 1910 to create the huge new Steel Company of Canada (Stelco). The primary plants at Hamilton were soon expanded and modernized, and the wartime demand for munitions allowed further development, along with vertical integration into iron-ore and coal-mining operations in the United States.

In contrast to these business strategies of servicing a diversity of secondary producers, two other newcomers to the industry decided to concentrate on the mass production of steel rails for the country's rapidly expanding railway system. In 1899 an energetic American businessman, H.M. Whitney, spearheaded the creation of the Dominion Iron and Steel Company, with a huge new steel plant at Sydney, Nova Scotia. Two years later the Algoma Steel Company emerged in Sault Ste Marie, Ontario, as part of a massive corporate empire in the region known as the Consolidated Lake Superior Corporation, pulled together by another flamboyant American-born entrepreneur, Francis Hector Clergue. Both ambitious projects quickly ran into trouble as a result of unwise investment decisions and poor management. They had to scale back their grandiose plans but by the First World War had stabilized as major producers. Both used wartime production as an opportunity to expand and modestly diversify. A few other steelmaking firms existed alongside the big four, but none competed on the same scale.

The industry was in crisis by 1920. Algoma, Dominion Iron and Steel, and, to an increasing extent, Nova Scotia Steel had relied too heavily on sales to the railways, whose expansive phase was over. Algoma limped on through the next 20 years at far less than capacity production. A more ambitious plan unfolded in Nova Scotia. In 1920 a group of British and Canadian investors brought together the two eastern steel companies, all the coal operations, and the Halifax Shipyards in a huge new conglomerate known as the British Empire Steel Corporation, which promptly closed Nova Scotia Steel's operations in Sydney Mines and scaled back its Trenton works. This corporate giant proved disastrous. It squared off in major battles with coal miners and steelworkers in the early 1920s and went into receivership in 1926. The new Canadian owners kept the Sydney plant running on a hand-to-mouth basis through the 1920s and 1930s. Meanwhile, Stelco seemed better able to respond to the new market demands of the automobile and consumer-goods producers in central Canada, though it too had to curtail production during the Depression of the 1930s.

The Second World War put most of the Canadian steel industry back on its feet and opened a fourth phase of development. Wartime production, subsidized by generous government tax policies, allowed for expansion and modernization and brought a new major player into the front ranks—Hamilton's Dominion Foundries and Steel Corporation (Dofasco), which had started as a small steel foundry in 1912, had a fully integrated steel plant by 1951, and quickly became the country's second largest steelmaker. The post-war boom in manufacturing, which was disproportionately concentrated in southern Ontario, gave Stelco and Dofasco the markets to grow dramatically. The opening of the St Lawrence Seaway in 1959 gave them access to new iron ore deposits in Labrador. Hamilton became the undisputed centre of the industry, turning out 70 per cent of the country's steel by the 1970s. Production in Sault Ste Marie and Sydney never enjoyed such a thorough revival. When in 1967 the British owners of the Sydney plant announced its closing, public protest forced the Nova Scotia government to take it over. But its production facilities were never adequately modernized and were steadily scaled back until its final shutdown in 2001. In 1988 Dofasco purchased Algoma, but four years later sold it back to the company's employees, who struggled to keep it open during the 1990s.

The steel industry's rapid growth since the beginning of the 20th century had brought together an occupationally mixed, ethnically diverse workforce that generally saw Anglo-Celtic workers in most skilled and unskilled positions and newcomers from southern and eastern

Europe and from Newfoundland as poorly paid labourers. Until the 1930s, most of these men worked 12-hour days, seven days a week, under harsh, authoritarian supervisors. The owners envisioned no place for *unions, and, until the late 1930s, steelworkers' efforts to organize (notably at Sydney in 1902–4 and in most plants at the end of the First World War) had been defeated. Post-war expansion had to take unions into consideration after the United Steel Workers of America won stable collective bargaining following a long but successful industry-wide strike in 1946. The exception was Dofasco, which remained a high-profile bastion of anti-unionism and *corporate welfarism, but which nonetheless matched the higher wages and benefits won by unionized workers in the post-war decades.

The 1970s marked another major turning point for the industry and its workers. In the face of growing competition from low-wage, technologically innovative foreign producers and from new, more specialized 'minimills' (which used electric furnaces to melt scrap metal), Canada's integrated steelmakers, like their American counterparts, saw their market share begin to shrink. The deep economic slump of the early 1980s and the arrival of North American *free trade in 1989 created more uncertainty. During the 1980s and 1990s the companies dramatically reduced their workforces, restructured management to amalgamate jobs and introduce more 'flexibility' and 'teamwork', and launched a series of major technological innovations, notably basic oxygen furnaces and continuous casters, which eliminated the open hearth and other steps in the production of ingots. (Stelco opened a new state-of-the-art plant at Nanticoke on Lake Erie in 1980, but eventually decided to introduce these innovations into its Hamilton operations as well.) In 1985, the companies and *steelworkers' union began meeting together in the Canadian Steel Trade and Employment Congress to discuss common problems and to lobby for government support. CRAIG HERON

Iroquois League. The word 'Iroquois' was in use before European contact but its origin and meaning are obscure. Originally the Iroquois League comprised five tribes, Mohawk, Oneida, Onondaga, Cayuga, and Seneca. Metaphorically the league called itself 'people of the extended house'—in Mohawk *rotinohsyoni* and Seneca *hotinohsyoni*—with the central Onondaga as 'fire keepers' (seat of the council) and the Mohawk and Seneca as 'guardians of the eastern and western doors'. They spoke an Iroquoian language with marked tribal (regional) dialects. The aim of the traditional founders of the league, Deganawida and/or Hiawatha (both Mohawk), was to establish a 'Great Peace' among all nations. After considerable negotiation, the five tribes ceased fighting each other and formed a league against those who opposed them. Seneca tradition places the event in 1451 during an eclipse of the sun. The laws of the league were recorded in detail in the 19th century. The pre-epidemic Iroquois population was about 25,000 in 11 villages. By 1656, following huge population losses due to *smallpox and measles, the Iroquois had attacked and absorbed remnants of the *Huron, Petun, Neutral, and Erie. In 1723, the league was joined by the Tuscarora, who had been driven out of North Carolina by English settlers.

Like other Iroquoian societies, the maternal extended family was the primary social, political, residential, and economic unit. Individuals were born into their mother's clan and formed a village clan segment with members of the same clan. These combined with related clan segments in other villages and tribes into one of the ten Iroquois clans. The clans were grouped into moieties, and since members of the same clan and moiety regarded themselves as siblings, individuals had 'family' across most of the league. The clan and moiety system distributed economic risk and engendered social and political cohesion. Decision making originated within the clan segment and moved upward through the clan structure to village, tribal, and league councils. The clan mothers (senior matrons) were very important, heading the extended families and therefore the clan segments. Their councils appointed and removed the civil chiefs who represented the clans at the councils. The women were therefore consulted by the chiefs on all important matters. Through the control women exercised over their families and the civil chiefs, they could declare war and peace. The operation of a campaign was, however, the prerogative of the war chiefs, appointed on the basis of merit by the men.

The Iroquois League functioned well when threatened by common enemies, although occasionally members followed different courses of action. Permanent fractures occurred when the Iroquois were forced to take sides in the Seven Years' War (1754–61), the Revolutionary War (1776–83), and the War of 1812. Today the league councils have only a ceremonial function.

CONRAD HEIDENREICH

Irving, K.C. (Kenneth Colin) (1899–1992), industrialist. Born into New Brunswick's declining wood, wind, and water economy, Irving flirted with university education and wartime service before latching onto the 1920s automobile revolution. An Imperial Oil gas station and a Ford franchise led to profit and the intuition that greater profits could be reaped by wresting control of such growth industries from central Canada. The 1927 creation of K.C. Irving Gas and Oil Ltd. sowed the seed of vertical and horizontal expansion that would allow Irving to capture monopolistic economies of scale. Tankers, oil refining, shipbuilding, pulp and paper, trucking, busing, radio (later TV), and newspapers soon made Irving the 'Paul Bunyan of New Brunswick'. Headquartered in Saint John, the Irving empire was both loved, as the largest provincial employer, and hated, as a monopoly, by New Brunswickers. Austere and secretive, K.C. eventually withdrew to Bermuda to avoid Canadian taxes. He was ranked in the 1980s by *Forbes* as one of the world's richest men. DUNCAN McDOWALL

Irwin, William Arthur (1898–2000). As editor of *Maclean's*, Irwin almost single handedly launched the magazine into its golden age as a forum for post-war

Canadian culture and nationalism. After honing his skills at several Toronto newspapers, Irwin was hired by Horace Hunter in 1925 as part of an effort to revitalize Maclean Publishing's flagship publication. Irwin became associate editor the following year, and in 1942 managing editor. Even though he had been functioning as de facto editor for some time, management did not formally hand him the position until 1945. If Hunter wanted a respectable, interesting, and profitable publication, Irwin was bent on nothing less than transforming *Maclean's* into an indispensable nationalizing force to promote his personal brand of self-confident Canadianism and progressively minded *liberalism. On a slim budget, he set about recruiting a group of talented, and like-minded, young journalists including Ralph Allen, Blair *Fraser, and Pierre Berton. Under Irwin's dynamic editorial direction, circulation grew steadily until it surpassed all competitors. Readers were treated to superb writing, whether political commentary, general interest features, or fiction. Even the covers displayed original artwork on Canadian themes. Despite the magazine's success, seemingly constant battles with management exacted their toll. When senior civil service friends approached him in 1949 to undertake the politically sensitive but pressing task of dealing with rumoured communist involvement in the *National Film Board, he resigned the editorship. After cleaning up NFB—by all accounts a task he undertook humanely—he settled into a diplomatic career.

PATRICK H. BRENNAN

isolationism. Canada made its first notable international appearance during the First World War. After the war, Prime Minister Robert *Borden fought for direct representation at the *Paris Peace Conference, independent ratification of the Treaty of Versailles, and full membership in the *League of Nations. Having eventually secured recognition as an independent member of the international community, Canada retreated into isolationism, shunning active participation and obligations in world affairs for the next 20 years.

Canada's isolationism reflected an underlying sense of the country's moral superiority over, as well as physical detachment from, Europe. As a North American state and a member of the New World, Canada was suspicious that Old World conflicts would embroil it in war. By contrast Canadian–American relations were a model of peace and co-operation. Canada's inexperience as well as its inability as a small state to influence international affairs reinforced its isolationism. Ottawa's refusal to endorse the Locarno agreements of 1925—multinational agreements that were supposed to make Germany's boundaries with France and Belgium more secure—and repeated calls to expunge or dilute the collective security clause from the covenant of the League of Nations were manifestations of isolationism. Senator Raoul Dandurand's 1924 'fire-proof house' speech to the League of Nations exposed the many layers of Canadian isolationist sentiment. Dandurand pointed out to the general assembly that 'in this association of mutual insurance against fire the risks assumed by different states are not equal'. He added that Canadians 'live in a fire-proof house, far from inflammable materials'. Although his speech is usually cited as the definitive expression of Canadian isolationism, Dandurand was no isolationist. He was committed to the League of Nations as an arbiter of international disputes and urged the Canadian government to support the organization. His personal commitment resulted in his election in 1925 as president of the league's general assembly, with the support of 41 of the 47 member countries.

The onset of the Great Depression and the intensification of international tensions throughout the 1930s strengthened isolationist currents even though these events confirmed how misguided was insularity. Although the expression of Canadian isolationism was a product of factors particular to Canada, isolationism was a worldwide phenomenon.

FRANCINE McKENZIE

Italian campaign. In April 1943 British officials asked the Canadian government to commit its soldiers to operations in the Mediterranean. Canadian soldiers had then been serving in England for over three years, and the government quickly agreed. Time was short. While 1st Canadian Infantry Division and 1st Armoured Brigade trained in Scotland for an 'opposed landing', the troops were introduced to new weapons, including Sherman tanks. Infantry battalions were reorganized, and the first of five Canadian general hospitals was readied for dispatch. Only when the last of the convoys carrying the Canadians departed Britain on 1 July 1943 did they learn their destination: Sicily.

Ten days later the sandbars near Pacino posed the Canadians' worst opposition. They soon gained a reputation as the 'mountain boys' of the British 8th Army as they captured the heavily defended heights of Leonforte and Assoro—in the latter instance by a spectacular night climb by the Hastings and Prince Edward Regiment. Sicily fell in 38 days.

The 8th Army crossed onto the toe of Italy on 3 September 1943; six days later the country surrendered, leaving German forces to slow the Allied advance. The Canadians captured Potenza on 20 September, and with the Americans at Salerno there was hope that Rome would soon fall. But the Canadians faced stiffening resistance through the Fortore and Biferno River valleys in October. The fighting intensified at the Moro River near Ortona on the Adriatic Sea, where the Loyal Edmonton Regiment and the Seaforth Highlanders of Canada spent Christmas fighting through the town's ruined streets. In church ruins the cooks served Christmas dinner to the fighting troops.

The Canadians remained on the Adriatic through the winter of 1944, reinforced by another Canadian armoured division and a corps headquarters. The British wanted neither, which made life difficult for the corps commander, General E.L.M. *Burns. But the 5th Armoured Division proved itself in the stiff fighting through the Hitler Line in May. Rome beckoned, but it fell to the Americans on 5 June. The *Normandy invasion began the next day; henceforth those in the Mediterranean proudly called themselves the 'D-Day Dodgers'.

The Canadians were near Florence by summer's end. As Winston Churchill looked on, the Canadians, British, New Zealanders, South Africans, and Greeks punched through the Gothic Line. But the weather, mountains, and determined Germans stopped a pursuit farther north. Burns was replaced as corps commander in November, and as the Canadians fought slowly towards Ravenna the prospect of another Italian winter loomed.

The Canadians were not in on the final victory in Italy: by March 1945, First Canadian Corps troops had joined First Canadian Army in northwestern Europe. Nonetheless, the Canadian contribution to the Italian campaign was remarkable: almost 93,000 served in Sicily and Italy, more than a quarter suffered casualties, including 5,400 dead.

GEOFFREY HAYES

Italians in Canada. The first Italian to arrive on Canadian shores was likely John *Cabot, but there were also early adventurers, Jesuit missionaries (including the ill-fated Father Francesco Giuseppe Bressani), and military troops (*Carignan-Salières soldiers). Until the First World War, however, Italians came mainly as sojourning men. Transoceanic emigration, following established patterns of internal migration and sojourning throughout Europe, rose sharply after Italian unification in 1861. At first South America, particularly Brazil and Argentina, was the main destination, but after 1900 immigrants favoured a rapidly industrializing North America, especially the United States. The numbers entering Canada were comparatively small, but significant.

Italians left to escape poor soil, high rents, over-population, heavy taxation, a land tenure system that protected privileged interests, and industrial polices that favoured the north over the south. Young men from small farms, displaced agricultural labourers, and underemployed rural craftsmen (shoemakers, tailors, butchers) dominated the overseas migration in the early 20th century. Employers recruited thousands of Italians for the mixed-ethnic work gangs that toiled in northern Ontario's resource industries, built and repaired railway track across the West, and entered the mines and steel factories of eastern Canada. About 80 per cent were young men, three-quarters from southern Italy. Their wages helped to support families back home, buy land, build a better house, or finance a sister's dowry. Women who stayed behind played an important role; wives and mothers influenced decisions to send men overseas, maintained the family plot, took products to market, and joined seasonal work gangs.

A commerce of migration developed around Italian immigrants. Shipping lines, steamship agents, and labour recruiters (padrone) hired by big Canadian employers like the CPR benefited from the importation of cheap foreign labourers. The padrone, who earned fees from both employer and workers, was the classic middleman, needed but distrusted by both sides. His role declined in the early 20th century as contacts with earlier migrants and kinship ties increasingly fulfilled the same function.

Chain migration included political exiles but also artists and artisans who hailed from specific towns or regions. Fresco painters, decorators, and sculptors, as well as stonemasons and mosaic workers, did fine work in wealthy homes, churches, and public institutions. They were joined by itinerant statue-makers, street musicians (including the much ridiculed organ-grinder), animal trainers, and indentured child entertainers. Some immigrants, many originally railway navvies, turned to mining and farming, including in the orchards and vineyards of the Niagara Peninsula, while others became merchants, barbers, hoteliers, and small businessmen.

The First World War marked a transition from sojourner to settler, as 46,000 Italians became permanent residents, mainly in Montreal and Toronto. Although migration resumed after wartime disruption, new restrictions on southern and eastern Europeans reduced the number of Italian immigrants after 1921 to a few thousand each year. Mussolini's rise to power in 1922, which resulted in restrictions on emigration, and the onslaught of the Great Depression firmly closed the doors until after the Second World War.

Those who came after 1945 and settled permanently were generally humble people from rural areas, especially the impoverished regions south of Rome. The massive exodus from Italy was fuelled by familiar factors plus wartime devastation and high levels of post-war unemployment. More than half a million came to Canada, a major magnet for emigrating Italians. Most were young men and women (average age 23 in the 1950s, and by 1971 the sex ratio was almost equal). With employers clamouring for workers to fill acute labour shortages in agriculture, logging, mining, and construction, the government reluctantly opened the doors. Most post-war newcomers arrived under the family sponsorship admission system. With economic recovery and social reforms in Italy and restrictions in Canada on family sponsorship, immigration declined during the 1960s and the 1970s; by the 1980s it had dwindled to a trickle.

Mainstream labour leaders have often depicted Italian workers as poor, ignorant dupes of capitalists who subjected them to sub-standard wages and working conditions and used them as strikebreakers, but Italian workers engaged in labour militancy and were involved in syndicalist movements such as the *Industrial Workers of the World. Some seasoned radicals were active in militant unions like the *United Mine Workers of America. Italians were active in the Jewish-led garment unions, and after 1945 Italian immigrant women, fed up with exploitative wages and conditions, joined certification drives. A tunnel disaster at Hogg's Hollow in Toronto in March 1960, when five Italian tunnellers (sandhogs) were killed, triggered two massive organizing drives among Italian construction workers.

In the 1970s Italians began to move up in the construction industry, becoming employers, contractors, developers, and union officials. Italians became increasingly upwardly mobile, with women moving into clerical, sales, and service jobs, and men into business, especially contracting companies. Home ownership, a favoured immigrant strategy for attaining security, remains very high.

Italians transplanted many of their clubs, customs, and rituals to Canada. Among the earliest were mutual benefit societies, where modest resources were pooled to deal with injury, illness, or death. National and provincial organizations emerged after the First World War, most importantly the Order of the Sons of Italy. With Canada's entry into the Second World War, community organizations were crushed or went underground, Italian storefronts were smashed, and about 600 Italians were interned for their supposed fascist connections. Renewed immigration after 1945 led to the resumption of community associations and to tensions between the largely Canadianized 'old timers' and the less well-off Italian-speaking newcomers. An important new social agency was COSTI (Centre for Italian Schools), created in 1961, which provided retraining and rehabilitation for injured workers. Professional groups such as the Canadian Italian Business and Professional Association reflected the growing interest of middle-class Italians in national politics. The National Congress of Italo-Canadians (1974) launched a partially successful redress campaign over wartime internment that resulted in 1990 in an apology, but no compensation, from Prime Minister Brian *Mulroney.

Most Italians are Roman Catholics, although their continued commitment to the madonna and saints cults, an important part of rural peasant folklore, frustrated the Irish- and Anglo-Catholic church fathers they encountered. Conflict between parish priests and congregations arose over the pagan-influenced *feste* (religious festivals, with parades, picnics, and games) organized in honour of patron saints. By the late 1960s the church hierarchy effectively gave up its opposition to the *festa*. Perhaps the greatest impact of Italian culture on the wider society has been in the realm of food: strong and smelly cheeses, spicy cold cuts, and tiramisù. FRANCA IACOVETTA

jackatars. The common English term for a sailor, 'jack tar', became 'jackatar' or 'jack'o'tar' in Newfoundland and took on a new meaning. By the mid-19th century settlement on the island's west coast was markedly different from the English–Irish mix in the more populous east. In the west, Highland Scots, who had begun coming from Nova Scotia in the 1840s, were living next to Irish, Acadian French, 'pure French from the motherland'—deserters from the French fishing fleet that came annually to the region—English (some of Jersey descent), Mi'kmaq, who were settled on St George's Bay since the 1760s, and even one Hawaiian islander. There was yet another group, of mixed French and Mi'kmaq descent: these were colloquially, and no doubt often derisively, termed jackatars. They lived mostly on St George's Bay, where the principal settlement was Sandy Point. Their darker skin distinguished them to some extent from their neighbours, though even descendants of English and Irish on the east coast were by 1840 sufficiently brown, to one observer, to merit the description 'copper-coloured'.

PATRICK O'FLAHERTY

Jacques & Hay. This Toronto firm became Canada's pre-eminent furniture-maker in the mid-19th century. The partnership, formed in 1835, brought together two immigrant cabinet-makers: John Jacques (1804–86) of London, England, and Robert Hay (1808–90) of Perth, Scotland. Initially, their King Street shop had only two assistants, but by the 1870s their waterfront factory employed nearly 500 people. Theirs is a classic case of artisans who became self-made industrialists by staying in their trade and investing in new factory methods. In the 1850s the firm added operations 45 miles to the north, where pine and hardwoods were harvested, sawn, and shipped by rail to the Toronto factory. Much of Jacques & Hay's output was for a mass market, but its quality hand-carved suites graced Canadian mansions. At international exhibitions, the firm brought distinction to industrial Canada by winning prizes for design and craftsmanship. In 1870 Jacques retired and the firm reorganized; in 1885 Hay retired, closing the business. Today, in the antique furniture trade, factory-made Victorian pieces are casually called 'Jacques & Hay' (in fact, because its furniture was seldom signed or stamped, attribution is difficult). And so, the name lives on as a reminder of a firm at the forefront of Canada's industrial revolution.

IAN RADFORTH

Jameson, Anna Brownell Murphy (1794–1860). Born in Dublin, Jameson was an ambitious, clever, and self-reliant girl with a flair for languages and an adventurous nature. At 16 she left home to become a governess. In 1826, because of the success of her first book, *The Diary of an Ennuyée*, a fictionalized travel memoir, she became the lioness of the hour in literary London. Her *Characteristics of Women* (1832), a study of Shakespeare's heroines, incorporated her concern for the education and emancipation of women. In 1836 she reluctantly travelled to Canada to join her husband, Robert Jameson, who had become attorney general of Upper Canada and was about to become its chancellor. The marriage had been unhappy from the beginning. In September 1837, she left Canada and her husband for good. Her legacy to Canada was the lively, informed, and opinionated *Winter Studies and Summer Rambles in Canada* (1838). *Sacred and Legendary Art*, a massive six-volume compendium, was the major work of her last two decades, establishing her as the first notable female art critic.

CLARA THOMAS

Japanese Canadians. Japanese immigrants began to arrive in Canada in the late 19th century. Like most pioneers they struggled for survival, but as Asians they also experienced racism. The Japanese experience is unique. During the Second World War their possessions were confiscated, they were deprived of their rights for over seven years, and their community was completely destroyed. Some 4,000 were deported to Japan, the rest forced to relocate throughout Canada. Not until 1949 were they free to live where they wished and allowed to vote. Before the war 23,000 people of Japanese descent lived in Canada; in the 1996 census they numbered 77,000, of which one-third were of mixed parentage.

The first Japanese immigrant to Canada is reputed to have been Manzo Nagano, who jumped ship in New Westminster, British Columbia, in 1877, but Japan did not permit emigration until 1885, when the Japanese government allowed peasants to work in sugar-cane plantations in Hawaii on three-year contracts. They were classified as *dekasegi* ('to go out to work') and were expected to return, but many did not. Some Japanese migrants ventured farther west to North America.

The first immigrants to British Columbia were ambitious, learned English, and later returned to Japan to recruit other male immigrants. By 1907, after the United States closed its doors to the Japanese, the influx to

Canada numbered in the thousands. This aroused the ire and fears of many whites, resulting in the formation of a BC branch of the US *Asiatic Exclusion League. An exclusionist rally on 7 September 1907 led to a riot through Vancouver's Chinatown and the Japanese district on Powell Street. In 1908, the Lemieux-Hayashi Gentlemen's Agreement came into force, limiting male immigrants to 400 per year. Since family members were not included in this number, the demography began to change. Many teenage sons arrived, while bachelors of marriageable age brought in wives, many as *picture brides. The continuing fear of many British Columbians about the burgeoning Japanese population led to revisions to the agreement in 1923 and 1928. The latter limited total immigration to 150; by the 1930s, Japanese immigration levels declined to 50 per year.

Due largely to the 'boss' system of hiring, where English-speaking Japanese labour contractors negotiated jobs and arranged housing, the Japanese lived in isolated communities, working in sawmills, lumbering, and fishing. Since their wages were lower than those of white workers, the latter feared being displaced and were angry and resentful. Japanese workers were occasionally used to break strikes. In 1920 they formed the Japanese Labour Union, but it was not until 1927 that it was accepted as a branch of the Vancouver–New Westminster *Trades and Labour Council and became known as the Japanese Camp and Mill Workers Union, Local 31.

With the arrival of women, families grew. The Nisei (second generation) attended Canadian schools, but even university graduates could find work only as labourers. By government decree many professions were closed, and due to social discrimination Japanese Canadians were not hired by mainstream employers. There were a few white-collar jobs within the community, but facility in the Japanese language was necessary and many Nisei had to attend Japanese-language schools. By the 1930s, the Nisei were organizing; they sent a delegation to Ottawa to seek the right to vote. Later, they began an English-language newspaper, the *New Canadian*. At the same time, military aggression by Japan added to their ostracism by the mainstream populace. The bombing of Pearl Harbor in December 1941 led to a shocking climax: the seizure of the property of all those of Japanese descent (75 per cent were Canadian-born or naturalized citizens) and their expulsion from the West Coast to 'ghost towns' and hastily built 'shack towns' in the BC Kootenays and to sugar beet farms in Alberta and Manitoba. Although the Nisei were eager to prove their allegiance by enlisting in the armed forces, it was not until January 1945 that 150 were accepted in the Canadian Army Intelligence Corps. In the spring of 1945 all Japanese 16 years and over were ordered either to apply for 'voluntary repatriation' or move immediately east of the Rockies. Ten thousand signed, often just to remain in the camps for the immediate future. Many tried to cancel their applications, but 4,000 were deported in 1946 before the orders were finally rescinded in January 1947.

In April 1949 Japanese Canadians were granted the right to vote and allowed to return to the West Coast. By this time, the original pioneer immigrants were aged, had lost all their savings, and were struggling to survive in an alien world. The majority of these elders had never learned to speak English, having lived in segregated company towns or in the Japanese community on Powell Street in Vancouver. The Nisei worked hard and cared for their elders. Struggling with their identity, many rejected their heritage, ashamed of the havoc their ancestral land had caused on the world scene. Living in suburbia, they raised their children in a mainstream middle-class environment. One result has been that 95 per cent of new marriages are now with people of non-Japanese descent.

Over time, the acute hurt diminished, and in 1977 Japanese Canadians from coast to coast rallied to celebrate the centenary of Japanese immigration. The third generation, the Sansei, began asking questions as they learned of the past. Having been raised in a freer, more tolerant environment, they had more self-confidence than their elders. With Nisei activists they began the long battle for redress of wartime wrongs. On 22 September 1988, Prime Minister Brian *Mulroney delivered an official apology in Parliament. Individual monetary compensation, a community fund, and the creation of the Canadian Race Relations Foundation in 1997 helped ease the psychological damage and contributed to rebuilding the community, including promoting awareness of racism.

The descendants of the early pioneers are now predominantly urban and highly educated. Many—David Suzuki, Thomas K. Shoyama, Joy Kogawa, Raymond Moriyama, Paul Kariya, to name a few—have become prominent in the public service, arts, science, and sports. Changes to Canada's immigration laws in 1967 have resulted in a small influx of well-educated, self-confident, middle-class Japanese immigrants. Their culture is far removed from the Meiji heritage of the descendants of the early pioneers. Today, the differences between the 'old' and 'new' immigrants are diminishing. Meanwhile Canadians have also become more worldly and tolerant.

MICHIKO MIDGE AYUKAWA

Jay's Treaty. Signed in London by John Jay, chief justice and special envoy for the United States, and Lord Grenville, British foreign secretary, on 19 November 1794. Relations between the two countries, still fragile after the War of Independence, deteriorated steadily in the 1790s over matters of trade, maritime rights, *Loyalist claims, boundary disagreements, British forts in American territory, and Indian warfare. The outbreak of war in Europe over the French Revolution, together with growing American military strength on the frontier, led the British to settle their differences with the Americans. The treaty had an important impact on British North American relations with the United States. British troops were removed from the seven frontier forts, though British subjects (fur traders) were permitted to continue operations south of the boundary and to have free access to the

Mississippi River. Native people and their goods were to have unrestricted passage across the boundary, a right still claimed. Commissions were to arbitrate pre-war commercial debts and spoliation claims, to identify the St Croix River boundary, and to survey and determine the boundary between Lake of the Woods and the Mississippi (the latter was not acted upon). These commissions revived arbitration for dispute settlement in international relations in modern times. The treaty provoked protest in the United States because it failed to grant desired trade and neutrality rights and it appeared to undercut relations with France, but more importantly it averted war for 18 years.

FRANCIS M. CARROLL

jazz. Developed during the first years of the 20th century by African-American musicians in New Orleans, jazz was introduced to Canada by vaudeville acts, notably the Creole Band in 1914, and by groups that performed in cabarets and dance halls, particularly in Vancouver—where pianist Jelly Roll Morton worked in 1919—and Montreal. Duly inspired, Canadian musicians took up the new music's syncopated rhythms and improvised melodies for themselves before 1920. Jazz in Canada would continue to mirror developments in the United States throughout the 20th century, following the successive innovations of swing, bebop, the avant-garde, and fusion at a respectful delay. Canada's most celebrated jazz musician, pianist Oscar Peterson personalized elements of swing and bebop with his electrifying technical facility. Trumpeter Maynard Ferguson drew on similar resources to even more flamboyant effect. Two other major Canadian figures, pianist Paul Bley and trumpeter-composer Kenny Wheeler, have worked cautiously in the avant-garde. While Peterson has remained a Canadian resident, Ferguson and Bley went to the United States early in their careers, and Wheeler to England; a later generation of expatriates also moved stateside, led by pianist Renee Rosnes and singer-pianist Diana Krall.

At home, jazz has survived in the hands of musicians given to a pragmatic conservatism, including clarinetist-composer Phil Nimmons, flutist Moe Koffman, guitarist Ed Bickert, trombonist-arranger Rob McConnell (with his big band, the Boss Brass), tenor saxophonist Fraser MacPherson, and pianist Oliver Jones. Latterly, this mainstream approach has been resisted by modernists of varying stripe, among them guitarist Sonny Greenwich, trumpeter Freddie Stone, pianist Paul Plimley, and flutist-saxophonist Jane Bunnett. Equally, it has been challenged by the more venturesome programming of summer jazz festivals established during the 1980s in Montreal, Vancouver, and many other Canadian cities.

MARK MILLER

Jefferys, Charles William (1869–1951), artist, historical illustrator, teacher. Born in England, Jefferys emigrated with his family in 1875. In 1888 he joined the newly founded Toronto Art Students' League, an organization committed to creating an indigenous Canadian art. In 1892 he produced the first of a series of 12 annual illustrated souvenir calendars. He moved to New York in the 1890s to work as a newspaper artist-reporter. Inspired by the northern landscape paintings in a Scandinavian gallery and the French impressionist paintings at the 1893 World's Columbian Exposition in Chicago, Jefferys returned to Canada permanently in 1901 to paint the country's northern and western landscapes from a new Canadian perspective.

Jefferys is best known for his prairie paintings, which conveyed his love for the region and captured the lure and power of its landscape. Of particular note are his canvases, *Western Sunlight*, *Lost Mountain Lakes*, and *Prairie Trails*. Such works have been heralded as setting the groundwork for the *Group of Seven and their followers. In later life, Jefferys devoted his time to a 'visual reconstruction' of Canada's history. Ryerson Press published all six volumes of his historical illustrations, *Dramatic Episodes in Canada's Story* (1930); *Canada's Past in Picture* (1934); and a three-volume compilation of some 2,000 images, *Picture Gallery of Canadian History* (1942, 1945, 1950).

R. DOUGLAS FRANCIS

Jehovah's Witnesses. A religious sect that believes that God's plan for humanity is revealed in the Bible, through which they interpret human history and predict the future. The Bible teaches the faithful how to prepare for Armageddon, which, Witnesses believe, is imminent. Their history in Canada has been marked with conflict, particularly with the Roman Catholic Church. In 1940, following the intervention of the cardinal of Quebec with a federal government anxious to placate French Canadians, the Witnesses, along with the *Communist Party of Canada and various fascist organizations, were declared illegal. Overnight, it was unlawful for Jehovah's Witnesses—or Bible Students, as they liked to call themselves—to meet, worship, and proselytize. Witness children who refused to stand up in school when 'God Save the King' was played were removed from their parents' care and placed in foster homes. Eventually, the ban was removed but it, along with Quebec premier Maurice *Duplessis's 'War without Mercy' against the group, galvanized Jehovah's Witnesses into alerting the Canadian people to the need for formal legal mechanisms for the protection of fundamental rights and freedoms, a process that culminated in the *patriation of the constitution and the entrenchment of the *Charter of Rights and Freedoms.

WILLIAM KAPLAN

See also RONCARELLI V. DUPLESSIS.

Je me souviens. This phrase served as Quebec's motto from 1883, but was not included in the province's arms until 1939. Attributed to Eugène-Étienne Taché, architect of the Quebec legislature, and inscribed on Quebec licence plates since 1976, the expression remains largely enigmatic. For some, it is the first line of a poem expressing the ambivalent allegiance of Canadiens to France and Great Britain: 'I remember I was born under the lily and grew under the rose'. For others the motto simply translates Taché's personal view of the history of Quebec as a distinct province within Confederation, reflecting his desire to make the façade of the legislature into a pantheon honouring the great figures in the country's history.

Although few Quebeckers know the origins and possible meanings of their motto, those of French-Canadian heritage respond easily to its call, remembering all the historic moments which remain in the collective franco-québécois memory like imperfectly healed wounds: the *conquest, the *rebellions, the *Act of Union, the *British North America Act, the *conscription issue, and, more recently, the *patriation of the constitution without Quebec's consent. JOCELYN LÉTOURNEAU

Jenness, Diamond (1886–1969), anthropologist. New Zealand–born and Oxford-educated, Jenness came to Canada in 1913 as a member of Vilhjalmur *Stefansson's *Canadian arctic expedition. His two years (1914–16) at Coronation Gulf resulted in a wealth of information about the Copper Inuit, a people whose traditional life was then in the earliest throes of contact with whites. Following combat service overseas, he joined the staff of the Victoria Memorial (later National) Museum in Ottawa and embarked on a 50-year career dedicated to studying the past, present, and possible futures of the country's Aboriginal peoples. His numerous scholarly contributions included documenting social customs, beliefs, and oral traditions among Carrier, Coast Salish, and Sekani peoples in British Columbia, Sarcee in Alberta, and Ojibwa in Ontario; identifying two previously unknown prehistoric arctic cultures, Dorset Eskimo and Old Bering Sea; and writing *The Indians of Canada*, for years the standard reference on this vast subject. His expertise also found practical application, most notably in gaining government protection of archaeological sites in the Northwest Territories and in urging change in education policy and other aspects of Canada's Native affairs administration. Retiring in 1947 after several years devoted to wartime and post-war intelligence work, Jenness turned again to Aboriginal issues. His last major project, a five-volume comparative history of Inuit-state relations in Alaska, Canada, Greenland, and Labrador, concluded with an appeal to Canadian policy-makers to provide the Inuit with the educational and economic opportunities necessary to regain control of their own destiny. BARNETT RICHLING

Jesuits. The Society of Jesus, a regular order of the Roman Catholic Church, was founded in 1534 by Ignatius de Loyola and approved by the bull *Regimini militantis ecclesiae* (1540) issued by Pope Paulus III. In the 17th century the order had missions all over Europe, besides those in Asia (begun in 1541), Iberian America (1566), Acadia (1611), Canada (1625), and Maryland (1633). The Jesuits were in present-day Canada from 1611 to 1800. After the Treaty of Paris (1763), the Jesuits, like the *Franciscan Récollets, were forbidden to receive novices in Quebec. Moreover, the order was suppressed by the brief *Dominus ac Redemptor* (1773) issued by Pope Clement XIV. When he died, Jean-Joseph Casot (1728–1800) was the last of the early Jesuits in British North America. The order returned to Canada in 1842, following the bull *Sollicitudo omnium ecclesiarum* (1814) issued by Pope Pius VII, which restored the Society of Jesus.

In the first half of the 17th century, the Jesuits, who came almost invariably from France, devoted most of their efforts to the conversion of Aboriginal peoples. They were reasonably successful among the *Huron north of Lake Ontario, among whom they claimed conversions by the thousands. Unfortunately, their 16-year-long missionary effort coincided with the end of the century-long conflict between the Huron and the *Iroquois, who came from present-day upstate New York. The defeat and successive dispersion of the Huron nation in 1649 represented the end of the Jesuits' major missionary project in North America. Between 1642 and 1649 eight Jesuits, priests and lay brothers, were killed by the Iroquois. Since they were judged to have died for their faith, they were canonized by the Holy See in 1930 and are known as the Canadian Martyrs. Among them were proficient linguists such as Jean de *Brébeuf (1593–1649) and writers such as Isaac Jogues (1607–46). In spite of their emphasis on missionary work and their comparatively small number (only 77 of them left France for Acadia and Canada between 1611 and 1658), their weight in early Canadian society is undeniable. Traditionally, English-speaking historians have depicted theirs as a stifling influence over the development of New France. More recently, others have suggested that until the 1650s the colony's survival was made possible by the presence of the church, of which the Jesuits were a great part.

From the 1660s onwards the Society of Jesus carried on its missionary activity among the Aboriginal peoples along the St Lawrence, in the Great Lakes region, and along and west of the Mississippi River; they continued to do so after their return in 1842. Some members, such as Charles Albanel (1616–96), Claude Allouez (1622–89), Jacques Marquette (1637–75), and Pierre-François-Xavier de Charlevoix (1682–1761), helped explore the New World and describe it to Europeans. The order's main emphasis, however, was in the field of education. The Jesuits opened a school in Quebec as early as 1633 and the Collège de Québec in 1635, the earliest institution of higher education in the New World outside of Iberian America. Later, they continued to teach and to manage educational institutions at all levels. Their considerable estates, whose destiny was debated at length after the Treaty of Paris, were finally settled through the Jesuits' Estates Act (1888), which provided monetary settlements for all interested parties, including Protestant institutes of higher education and Université Laval (founded 1852).

One of the most modern features of the Jesuits was their recognition of the importance of internal and external communication. From the founding of the order, the circulation of written information among its members was meant to excite the missionaries' zeal, control their activities in distant places, and build knowledge of their world-wide endeavour. The printing of a carefully selected corpus of missionary reports was intended to elicit general lay support for the Jesuit missions. The *Annuae litterae*, published between 1583 and 1658 (34 vols.), the *Lettres édifiantes et curieuses, écrites des missions étrangeres* (1702–76, 34 vols), and the *Jesuit Relations* of Canada (1632–73, 41 vols) fall into this category. The latter are the most important corpus of primary printed sources relating to the early contact era in the history of French and English North America. They deal with language, warfare, food, climate, religiosity, migrations, and values, and with intersocietal and gender relations. The ethnohistorical information they contain, both on the Aboriginal peoples and on the missionaries themselves, is invaluable. LUCA CODIGNOLA

Jewitt, John Rogers (1783–1821), blacksmith. In 1802 he sailed as an armourer aboard the *Boston*, an American fur-trading vessel bound for the northwest coast of North America. The following March in Nootka Sound on the west coast of Vancouver Island the vessel was attacked by Nuu-chah-nulth people, perhaps in retaliation for some insult, and all the crew was killed except for Jewitt and another man. The two survivors were held as captives and slaves at Nootka for two years. Following his rescue Jewitt ended up in New England, where he published a book about his experience, *Narrative of the Adventures and Sufferings of John R. Jewitt* (1815). The book was a unique account of the Nuu-chah-nulth people based on first-hand experience, and has been republished many times. Jewitt was briefly a celebrity, but soon sank into obscurity and died poor and forgotten. DANIEL FRANCIS

Jews. There has been a Jewish presence in Canada almost from the beginning of European settlement. Although no Jews were allowed to enter New France, it appears some did, perhaps by hiding their origins. According to some historians, a French Jewish merchant, Abraham Gradis, helped finance, feed, supply, and keep afloat Quebec settlers in the 1740s and 1750s even though he and his family were barred from New France.

Thus, it was with the arrival of the British that Jewish settlement in Canada began. In 1749 about a dozen Jews arrived in Halifax from the New England colonies at the invitation of the new British governor. Most did not stay for very long. The first permanent Jewish settlement was in Montreal, where a handful of Jewish suppliers accompanied British troops in 1760 following the victory over the French at the Plains of Abraham. Most became merchants and fur traders and helped open up large parts of uncharted Canada. Almost all fought to repel the American invasions of Canada in 1776 and 1812. Some fought so gallantly that they became the first Jewish military officers in the British Empire. Perhaps in gratitude, the Lower Canada legislature emancipated its Jewish community, allowing it equal rights with the majority English community, long before the British Parliament followed suit. So open was Canada that in the 1840s, although fewer than 500 Jews lived in the colony, there were several Jewish bank presidents, a dean of medicine, some judges, many municipal officials, and even a chief of police.

It was not until well after Confederation and the arrival of tens of thousands of Jewish refugees from the pogroms in Russia that anti-Semitism took hold in Canada. Incited in Quebec by Catholic clergy and in English Canada by Goldwin *Smith, a prominent writer and intellectual, a campaign was launched against the admission of Jews and to ostracize those already in the country. Yet by the 1920s there were almost 150,000 Jews in Canada. Although some had settled on the Prairies, in about a dozen Jewish farm settlements, most headed for the slums of Montreal, Toronto, or Winnipeg and took jobs in the myriad of sweatshops that dominated the *garment industry at the time. Their lives were not pleasant. For the first half of the 20th century Canada was a country permeated with xenophobia and anti-Semitism. For Canadian Jews, quotas and restrictions were a way of life. Most professions were closed to them; universities restricted their admission; many hotels and beaches posted signs warning them away, large areas of cities and towns had restrictive covenants on properties that prevented them from being sold to Jews. Jews were denounced from church pulpits and by various politicians as threats to Canadian society.

To protect itself and to represent its interests to the government, the Jewish community created the Canadian Jewish Congress in 1919. It took the lead in combatting anti-Semitism and, in the 1930s, in lobbying Canadian officials to admit Jewish *refugees desperately attempting to escape the Nazis. Although headed for 25 years by the wealthy and influential Samuel Bronfman, the founder of the Seagram's liquor empire, it achieved little. So engrained was anti-Jewish sentiment in Canada that the government allowed in only a tiny handful of the refugees. Indeed, of all the world's democracies, of all the immigration countries, Canada had arguably the worst record in providing sanctuary to European Jewry during the Holocaust. No more than 5,000 Jews made it to Canada, compared to the 22,000 allowed in by Argentina, 85,000 by Great Britain, 100,000 by tiny Palestine, or 20,000 by penurious Mexico.

Following the Second World War, anti-Semitism receded. With the help of newly sympathetic politicians and courts, the community successfully lobbied for anti-discrimination legislation. With astonishing rapidity, Jews, together with other Canadians of good will, tore down these barriers, thus opening up Canadian society not only for themselves but for other immigrant and ethnic groups as well. Out of these changes, a new, open, diverse, multicultural Canada was born, a Canada that included a Jewish premier, a Jewish chief justice of the *Supreme Court, a Jewish governor of the *Bank of Canada, Jewish ambassadors, university presidents, cabinet ministers—positions that would have been closed to Jews in a previous generation.

Canadian Jewry has come a long way over the past 50 years. At 365,000, its population makes it the fourth largest Jewish community outside of Israel, and the fastest growing. According to every survey, Canadian Jews are among the most integrated, most affluent, and most educated communities in the country. They have social, financial, and political clout they have never had before. There is no area in Canadian society in which they do not play an important role. Canadian Jews give more per capita to charities, schools, hospitals, and the arts than any other group in Canada. Ironically, the new openness and absorbency of Canadian society, for which the Jewish community struggled long and hard, may pose a real threat to Jewish survival. Today's Jewish leaders worry as much about the rate of assimilation as about anti-Semitism. Together, the decline in fertility and the increasing frequency of intermarriage could create a demographic disaster for Canadian Jews. IRVING ABELLA

Johnson, Emily Pauline (1861–1913), Mohawk-English performer and writer, best known for the poetry collection *Flint and Feather* (1912) and *Legends of Vancouver* (1911). By law and by sympathy, Tekahionwake, as she called herself in Mohawk, was Indian. Like her parents, George Henry Martin Johnson and Emily Susannah Howells, she favoured an on-going Native-European alliance. Northwest tribes and *Metis in the 1885 rebellions won her sympathy in 'A Cry from an Indian Wife' (1885). Hopes for an interracial partnership spurred her exploration of a brighter future in prose such as 'Among the Blackfoots' (1902). By the end of her life, however, *Legends* suggested failing hopes. Johnson also articulated a doubled vision: 'I am a Redskin, but I am something else too—I am a woman'. She forged ties to the Anglo-imperial world, including feminists such as Nellie *McClung. Her commitment to gender equality drew on Native traditions, making her a remarkable New Woman. She nevertheless resembled other imperialists: Canada should be led by virtuous elites, notably great men and motherly women—both English-speaking and Native. Her funeral on 13 March 1913, organized by feminists and occasioning a civic day of mourning with Indians and whites lining Vancouver streets, aptly commemorated her life.
VERONICA STRONG-BOAG

Jolliet, Louis (*c.* 1645–1700). A perceptive, intelligent, courageous, and talented man, Jolliet combined the roles of explorer, fur trader, cartographer, seigneur, and teacher. In 1656 he entered the Jesuit College at Quebec, took his minor orders, but left in 1667 to become a fur trader. In 1672 he was chosen by the intendant Jean *Talon to determine whether the Mississippi, known from Native accounts, flowed south or west to the Pacific. Accompanied by Father Jacques Marquette, S.J., a gifted linguist, and five others, the expedition reached the Arkansas River in mid-July 1673, far enough to establish that the Mississippi flowed into the Gulf of Mexico. On their return they explored the Illinois River and Lake Michigan. In 1679 Jolliet was awarded a fur-trade concession at Mingan and Anticosti Island. The same year he explored the route from Tadoussac to James Bay. Thereafter he developed the fur trade and fisheries at his concession but was raided and burned out by the English in 1690 and 1692. In 1694 he surveyed the Labrador coast to Zoar (56°8′ N). His request for a trade concession to the coast and the Inuit was denied. In recognition of his talents as cartographer and navigator he was appointed (1697) teacher of hydrography at the Jesuit College.
CONRAD HEIDENREICH

joual. From the French word *cheval* (horse), '*joual*' is the general term used to refer to the most colloquial variety of popular Quebec French, characterized by extensive lexical borrowing from English as well as distinguishing features of pronunciation. It is widely assumed that André *Laurendeau created the term in an opinion letter sent to the newspaper *Le Devoir* in 1959, although similar uses have been attested in Quebec as early as 1930. This creation is most likely based on an old French expression 'parler cheval' (to mumble). The real birth of the term in its current meaning can be traced to the publication by Jean-Paul Desbiens in 1960 of *Les *Insolences du Frère Untel*, a caustic condemnation of the Quebec education system. It appears that *joual* provided a sort of anchor for the affirmation movement launched by the *Quiet Revolution. Used in literary works, mostly in theatre (Michel Tremblay), poetry (Gérald Godin), and songs (Robert Charlebois), in the second half of the 1960s, *joual* became a symbol of Quebec culture and a tool to promote Quebec identity in distinction from France and to the rest of Canada. Since the mid-1970s, active language-planning efforts have resulted in a more secure position for the French language in Quebec. This led to questions regarding norms of language in Quebec. Language remains the defining component of Quebec culture, and the language issue has evolved largely along two axes: maintenance and quality. Today, the term *joual* has a strong negative connotation and is used mostly to refer to the variety of French spoken by the lower socio-economic classes in Montreal.
YVES ROBERGE

journalism. The first *newspapers, and journalists, arrived in Canada with British conquest and settlement. Utterly dependent for revenue on government *advertising, they loyally endorsed their patrons and reported little else. By the early 1800s, however, the combination of commercial advertising and far-reaching court decisions that began to establish true press freedom, meant that emerging entrepreneur-publisher-editors such as William Lyon *Mackenzie, Joseph *Howe, and Étienne *Parent were more able to speak their minds. Journalism became more contentious and outspoken, advocating popular causes like *responsible government. From mid-century onward, rapid urbanization and rising literacy led to an explosion in mass-circulation daily newspapers. Publisher-editors such as George *Brown of the *Globe* dominated the journalistic landscape. Reporters were largely anonymous, self-taught generalists whose careers were transient and viewed as slightly disreputable. Journalism's focus remained intensely partisan politically, with newspapers and journalists alike serving as little more than party auxiliaries.

By 1900, the daily newspaper's emergence as the 'Victorian authority'—a monopolistic source of local and national developments—was complete. The need to appeal to an ever wider array of reader interests ensured openings for journalists with more specialized expertise in areas from business and agriculture to sports and 'women's issues'. Journalism was swept along in the contemporary wave of professionalization as journalists sought greater respect in the community. An increasingly literate readership was demanding a less emotional and more objective press. The determination of editors such as John Willison, J.W. *Dafoe, Joseph Atkinson, and Henri *Bourassa to meet these demands by separating news fact from editorial opinion and by simultaneously raising the standards of journalists' training went a long way to establishing journalism as a profession in Canadians' eyes. With journalism's emergence as a respectable profession, it became one of the first careers open to women, and talented women such as Violet *McNaughton, Cora *Hind, Francis Marion *Beynon, and her sister Lillian Beynon Thomas met with success in the field.

The trials of the Great Depression brought an unprecedented seriousness to Canadian journalism and a steady decline in old-style political partisanship. Many of the younger, better-educated journalists embraced the progressive ideology of the 'government generation', with the result that their newspapers and magazines became forums for 'recruiting the nation's mind'. Aided by the establishment of formal journalism programs, the first at Carleton College in 1945, 'objective' journalism continued to make inroads after the Second World War. The 1940s and 1950s also witnessed the emergence of political pundits—Blair *Fraser, Ken Wilson, Bruce Hutchison—who had a national audience. Their intimate (critics said too intimate) understanding of the inner workings of government policy-making, gained by equally intimate access to bureaucratic insiders, established their credibility. The post-war years witnessed the golden age of general interest *magazines, most obviously B.K. Sandwell's **Saturday Night*, and *Maclean's* under the direction of a pair of brilliant editors, Arthur *Irwin and Ralph Allen. Around mid-century, two new mass media emerged that would challenge the supremacy of print and transform the practice of Canadian journalism. Both the English- and French-language services of CBC radio (1936) and television (1952) embraced public affairs as a central mandate, and by 1958 were covering national and international politics directly with their own journalists.

By the 1960s, objective journalism, so long the standard, was being vigorously challenged in both the print and electronic media by a new generation of journalists who rejected it as neither attainable nor especially desirable. The blending of American-style investigative journalism, the treatment of news as drama, and the blurring of news and editorializing were epitomized in CBC television's sensational *This Hour Has Seven Days*. Print journalists had no choice but to respond to the challenge of the electronic media, mimicking their approach. Henceforth, the journalist as adversary would be the template, and a deep cynicism—a culture of 'disparagement'—would characterize media coverage of the establishment, especially the political establishment. These years also saw the emergence of a left-liberal and nationalist conventional wisdom among the majority of anglophone journalists. The abandonment of objectivity as a goal, and the blurring of opinion and fact were particularly pronounced in Quebec, where francophone journalists such as André *Laurendeau, Gérard Pelletier, and René *Lévesque were drawn into the maelstrom of the *Quiet Revolution. The 20th century ended with a growing reaction against the unaccountability of contemporary journalism, and yet a recognition that it was indispensable to gaining a thorough understanding of an ever more complex society. PATRICK H. BRENNAN

judiciary. The third branch of government, comprising the *courts of law and the judges and lesser officials who deliver justice through interpretation and application of unwritten common law and legislated criminal and civil law. Criminal law is created by Parliament but civil law is enacted by both dominion and provincial legislatures, Quebec alone following a European heritage of a civil code. Under the *constitution Parliament creates appelate courts (*Supreme Court and *Federal Court) while the provinces organize their own courts, which administer both provincial and dominion law. However, appointment of all major provincial court judges is a federal responsibility, leaving provinces to appoint judges of minor courts and other officials such as magistrates. This arrangement preserves the integrity of a single judicial system within a federal state, unlike the United States where dual hierarchies of courts and laws prevail. The principle of an independent judiciary is assured by appointments with fixed tenure, dismissal requiring a joint resolution of both legislative chambers. Independence is essential where judicial determinations affect the rights of citizens, an especially important role after the arrival of a *Charter of Rights and Freedoms. Such independence is also essential where courts adjudicate disputes over the division of powers in a federal state. J.E. HODGETTS

juvenile delinquency. Before the 19th century, the criminal justice system did not recognize *children. Those under seven were not held accountable for their crimes and those over seven were treated like adults. A crusade launched by middle-class reformers at mid-century to rescue children had by the beginning of the 20th century succeeded in creating reform schools, legislative change, and a separate court system.

The first special treatment for *youth involved the creation of separate reformatory prisons in the Canadas in 1857. In the following decades new facilities called reform schools opened across the country, charged with the segregation and rehabilitation of youth. The Youthful Offenders Act (1894) extended these ideas by separating youth from adults at the time of arrest and trial and prohibiting publicity about the event. The same act permitted Children's Aid Societies' involvement in the disposition of cases. A lack of systematic application across the country subsequently led *child welfare advocates, including William L. Scott and J.J. *Kelso, to demands for a comprehensive juvenile justice system. Their aspirations were realized in the Juvenile Delinquents Act (1908). This federal law gave exclusive jurisdiction over young offenders to juvenile courts. The act standardized a definition of juvenile delinquent as any child under 16 (later 18 in many jurisdictions) who had violated any provision of the Criminal Code, dominion or provincial statute, or municipal bylaw or ordinance; it also included any child liable for committal to industrial or reformatory schools according to provincial acts. The act called for informal, summary trials in which publicity regarding the offender and family remained strictly prohibited. Dispositions included reprimand, fine, foster care, and institutionalization, though probation—where both child and family could be observed—was advocated as the most modern method of rehabilitation.

Driving the juvenile justice system was the idea that youthful offenders were children to be treated, not criminals to be punished. Under the *parens patriae* philosophy of the Juvenile Delinquents Act the state ostensibly acted in the delinquent's best interests and was cast, as W.L. Scott said, as 'superparent . . . of those unable to protect themselves'. Beyond processing delinquent youth, the new juvenile courts also held jurisdiction over neglected and abused children and prosecuted adults for promoting delinquency and neglecting children. This seemingly gentle justice system expanded the offences for which an adolescent could be brought to court, far beyond adult crimes. The juvenile courts were inundated with highly subjective cases of incorrigibility and uncontrollability, the definitions of which were inscribed with gender, class, and race biases. Further, in 1924 the act was amended to include 'sexual immorality or any similar form of vice' in its definition of delinquency, which largely targeted adolescent girls. Eventually the act fell under intense criticism for this loose definition of delinquency and because the courts typically overlooked children's legal rights and representation and were often staffed with judges who lacked legal training. The arbitrary nature of juvenile justice came under attack in the mid-20th century and was eventually overhauled and replaced with the Young Offenders Act, which came into force in 1984. TAMARA MYERS

Kanakas, a word meaning 'persons' in the Hawaiian language, was the term long used to name indigenous Hawaiians and other Polynesians. Numerous Kanakas men worked in the *maritime fur trade to the Pacific Northwest from the 1780s. In the first half of the 19th century, 500–600 were employed in the land-based *fur trade, recruited mostly by the Hudson's Bay Company in Honolulu on three-year contracts. Almost all of them labourers, these men were stationed at coastal trading posts across the Pacific Northwest. Other indigenous Hawaiians jumped ship along the west coast of North America or arrived on their own initiative. While most eventually returned home, a minority remained. Upwards of 100 settled along the British Columbia coast, on the Gulf Islands, or in the Fraser Valley. Transferring their loyalty to Canada, they took seriously their responsibility as British subjects and soon got themselves on voting lists. The descendants of their families with Aboriginal women are very much part of British Columbia society.
JEAN BARMAN

Kane, Paul (1810–71), artist. Born probably in Mallow, Ireland, Kane immigrated to York (Toronto) with his parents in 1819. He worked as a sign painter, furniture decorator, and portrait artist in York and Cobourg before going to the United States and then to Europe in 1841 to study the 'old masters'. In London, he met George Catlin, the famous American painter of the Indians of the American plains, and was inspired to do the same for the Indians of the Northwest. Kane made three trips west between 1845 and 1849, the most famous being the one to the West Coast 1846–8, upon which his *Wanderings of an Artist among the Indians of North America* (1859), now known to be ghostwritten, was based. He made over 700 sketches from which he later composed many of his oil-on-canvas paintings. Art critics note the discrepancy between his more 'realistic' depictions of Indians and the western landscape in his sketches and the more 'Europeanized' renditions in his oil paintings. Still, Kane's paintings are the best pictorial record of the early Canadian West, making him the first great painter of the region.
R. DOUGLAS FRANCIS

Kean, Abram, sometimes Abraham (1855–1945). Born on Flower's Island, Bonavista Bay, Newfoundland, at 17 Abram married Caroline Yetman and started a family. In 1879, they moved to the nearby coast and founded the community of Brookfield. Kean became a sealer at a young age, advanced through the ranks, and in 1889 received his first command of a steamer, *Wolf*. In a record-setting 11 days, he brought in 26,912 pelts and established his reputation as 'high-liner' seal killer. When he retired from his *sealing career at the age of 81 in 1936, he had commanded nine steamers and had brought in over one million seals. Meanwhile, he had been elected to the legislature and had moved his family to St John's. He enjoyed a successful political career and served as the first minister of the Department of Marine and Fisheries (1898–1900) and as a member of the Legislative Council (1927–34). An inquiry absolved Kean of any blame for the **Newfoundland* sealing disaster of 1914 in which 78 men died, but his reputation has always suffered from his role in that tragedy.
SHANNON RYAN

Keefer, Thomas Coltrin (1821–1914), one of Canada's most eloquent engineers and an enthusiastic advocate of early railway construction in Canada. As a propagandist, Keefer wrote *The Philosophy of Railroads*, in which he linked railway technology with the 'moral and material progress of man'. He argued that railway construction was a prerequisite for national economic progress because it would stimulate desirable urbanization and industrialization. Educated at Grantham Academy in St Catharines and Upper Canada College, Keefer learned his profession as an apprentice on the Erie and Welland Canals. His first engineering assignment was a timber slide and river improvements at Bytown (Ottawa) in 1845. He also surveyed the Montreal-to-Kingston and Kingston-to-Toronto railways in 1851, but when the *Grand Trunk took over these lines, it did not hire him as its engineer. In 1852–6, he designed and supervised the construction of the Montreal municipal waterworks. Subsequently, he worked in a number of municipalities. Disappointed at never receiving a railway commission, Keefer published *A Sequel to the Philosophy of Railroads* in which he criticized railway managers.
A.A. DEN OTTER

Keen, George (1869–1953), law clerk, salesman, co-operative leader. Born in Stoke-on-Trent, England, Keen immigrated in 1904. He helped establish the Brantford consumer co-op in 1906 and the Co-operative Union of Canada, serving as its secretary from 1909 to 1943. Steeped in the British consumer tradition, he advocated organizing society through intelligent consumption in local co-operatives, which would jointly own the means of production. He gradually enlarged his view to include agricultural and housing co-operatives and *credit unions as integral parts of the movement. From Brantford he advised local societies, edited a journal, and travelled frequently across Canada on railway passes. He was the most consistent and best-informed *co-operative leader in Canada in his time, largely defining the movement's orthodoxy in its formative years. IAN MacPHERSON

Keish (*c.* 1860–1916), Tagish trader. Born into the Dakl'aweidi clan of the Wolf moeity in the Tagish/Inland Tlingit community of southern Yukon, Keish (Skookum Jim Mason) traded with coastal Tlingit. His packing feats through coastal passes gained him renown, hence Skookum (strong). His family connections and spiritual beliefs shaped his life and legacy. His sister, Shaaw Tláa (Kate), married George Carmack, a white trader and prospector. A few years later, Keish underwent a spiritual experience with Wealth Woman and was directed north to find riches. In 1896 he headed north with his Tlingit wife Daakuxda.éit' and two nephews, Kootseen (Patsy Henderson) and Káa Goox (Dawson Charlie), to find his sister and brother-in-law. They met at the Klondike River and prospected for gold. On 17 August, Keish found gold. Carmack staked the discovery claim while Keish and his nephews staked adjacent claims on what became *Bonanza Creek. Back home the *White Pass and Yukon Route Railway also negotiated with him for a right-of-way over his family's traditional lands. However, riches did not make Keish's life easier: his wife returned to her family as he fell into drink; Káa Goox drowned in 1906; Carmack abandoned Kate, kidnapping their daughter to return to the United States. Kootseen survived and was Tagish chief during the 1950s. Keish established a trust fund for the education of Yukon Indians, evidenced today by the Skookum Jim Friendship Centre in Whitehorse.

DAVID NEUFELD

Kelso, John Joseph (1864–1935). A prominent figure in social and child welfare movements in Canada. His first major reform activity was his leadership in founding the Toronto Humane Society for the Prevention of Cruelty in 1887, which initially attended to both animals and children. His primary interest in 'child saving' came from Christian missionary aspirations and the belief in the connection between cruel or negligent treatment of *children and immorality and crime. In 1891 Kelso led the incorporation of the Toronto Children's Aid Society and was elected its president. His resignation shortly afterwards attested to his uncomfortable position as one of the emerging middle-class reformers in an environment of old-fashioned private *philanthropy. Kelso's subsequent lifelong career as the superintendent of neglected and dependent children for Ontario (1893–1934) coincided with the broader transformation of philanthropy to professional social work. His profound influence on Canadians' ideas about children, especially child welfare legislation, foster care, *adoption, juvenile court, and fresh-air activities, went far beyond Ontario's borders.

XIAOBEI CHEN

Khaki University. Canada's adult education program for soldiers overseas near the end of the First World War was a model for British and American allies. In 1917, chaplains and YMCA officers in England and France claimed an insatiable appetite among Canadian soldiers for books, courses, and ideas about post-war life. The YMCA sought advice from an old friend, Henry Marshall *Tory, president of the University of Alberta, who visited England and France and in six weeks devised his 'Khaki University': battalion schools would teach basics; 'khaki colleges' organized advanced courses; a correspondence branch dealt with individuals. During demobilization, a central college would offer two years of an arts program. Backed by Canadian generals, and Sir Robert *Borden, and $500,000 raised by the YMCA in Canada, Tory's scheme was largely realized. An order-in-council in September 1918 put Tory in command of educational services for the General Staff. Across England, 14 khaki colleges operated by the Armistice and, on 1 December, Ripon in Yorkshire opened for programs for soldiers in subjects ranging from arts to theology. Through the program, 300 Canadians found places in seven British universities. Battalions managed libraries, organized reading groups, and tried to overcome illiteracy. Of course, soldiers in 1918–19 had their minds on demobilization, not studying, and education standards varied widely. However, more than 650,000 veterans attended lectures, 50,000 enrolled in classes, and 2,000 registered at Ripon.

DESMOND MORTON

Killam, Izaak Walton (1885–1955), financier. Born into a family of shipowners and merchants in Yarmouth, Nova Scotia, Killam joined the exodus of ambitious young men from the economically faltering Maritimes. A clerkship in a Halifax bank brought him into the orbit of Max *Aitken, a bumptious securities promoter who soon lured Killam to Montreal as his acolyte. Sent to London in 1913 to manage Aitken's Royal Securities Corporation, Killam became Royal's president by 1915, bought out his mentor in 1919, and then used Royal Securities to assemble an empire of Canadian and foreign industrial and utility holdings. Killam's International Power, for instance, gave Canada a prominent role in Caribbean and Latin American power generation. In Canada, he invested heavily in pulp, power, construction, and film-making. Among Canada's wealthiest men, Killam was secretive and austere. Although often described as a 'mystery man of finance', Killam never attracted the opprobrium of other moguls of Canadian capitalism. Death duties on his 1955 estate were used as seed money by Ottawa to establish the Canada Council, and Killam's widow, Dorothy, in turn generously endowed Canadian education and medical research upon her death in 1965.

DUNCAN McDOWALL

King, William Lyon Mackenzie (1874–1950), prime minister 1921–6, 1926–30, 1935–48. 'In a country like ours', according to Mackenzie King, 'it is particularly true that the art of government is largely one of seeking to reconcile differences'. Reconciling differences did not lead to radical or innovative politics but in King's case it was very successful; he was leader of the federal *Liberal Party for 30 years and prime minister for 21.

As a young man King was interested in labour relations. He became the first deputy minister of labour in 1900. Eight years later he went into active politics and became minister of labour. In 1919 he was chosen as Sir Wilfrid *Laurier's successor as leader of the Liberal Party. King inherited a party deeply divided by *conscription and *agrarian revolt. The Liberals won a bare majority in the 1921 election but King's courting of the *Progressives, a farmers' protest party, had limited results and the Liberals lost their majority in the election of 1925. King stayed in office with Progressive support until his government was defeated over a scandal in the Department of Customs. In the ensuing election King deflected attention from the scandal by alleging constitutional interference by the governor general and was returned to office with a stable majority in 1926. King reduced taxes but by 1930 the economic recession made his careful stewardship less popular than the Conservative promise to use higher tariffs to create jobs. R.B. *Bennett won the election but had no effective response to the Depression. In 1935 the Liberals won a record majority with the slogan 'King or Chaos'. King negotiated trade agreements with the United States and Great Britain but these had little economic impact and the country remained deeply divided.

The threat of involvement in a European war was an additional complication. King promised to make no commitment in advance to support Britain, leaving it to the Canadian Parliament to decide when the time came. This policy made it difficult to prepare for war but it did reassure Canadians that they would make the decision. In 1939, when Great Britain declared war, Parliament met and voted almost unanimously to participate. The government provided effective wartime leadership. It enrolled over a million people in its armed services, and Canadians played important roles on the Atlantic, in the air over England and western Europe, and in the campaigns in Italy and northwest Europe. Canada also produced a wide range of munitions and trained most of the air crew for the Commonwealth. King avoided a potential division over conscription by a series of compromises and half measures; eventually some conscripts were sent overseas. He also introduced a series of social measures, including unemployment insurance, collective bargaining, and mothers' allowances. These measures, and the grudging admiration in both English and French Canada for his honest and competent wartime administration, led to a narrow electoral victory for the Liberals in 1944.

After the war Canada reverted to a peacetime economy with surprisingly little economic disruption. Canada also played an important role in post-war international agreements and sided with the United States in the early stages of the Cold War. King was persuaded to retire in 1948 and died in 1950. It was only after his death that Canadians learned that this apparently dull man believed in the immanence of the spirit world. King needed emotional support. When he could not get it from the living he turned to the dead. The assurance he found there had given him the strength to survive the stresses of his lengthy political career. H. BLAIR NEATBY

King-Byng affair. In the election of 1925 the Liberals under Mackenzie *King won fewer seats than the Conservatives. When the House of Commons met early in 1926 the Liberals stayed in office with the support of the *Progressives, an agrarian protest party. Late in the session, however, the Progressives threatened to withdraw their support because of a scandal in the Customs Department. King asked Governor General Byng for a dissolution. Instead Byng called on Arthur *Meighen, the Conservative leader, to form a government. Meighen was then defeated on a no-confidence motion and Byng granted him a dissolution. In the ensuing election campaign King alleged that Byng, with Meighen's co-operation, had interfered in Canadian politics. Byng's decisions had been constitutionally correct but King's argument did draw attention away from the customs scandal. Enough moderate Progressives preferred the low-tariff Liberals to the high-tariff Conservatives to give the Liberals a stable majority. H. BLAIR NEATBY

Kingston. Following the exploration of the region in 1615 by Samuel de *Champlain, in 1673 the French constructed a fort and trading post on the site, initially known as Cataraqui, which developed into an elaborate establishment built by the French, Fort Frontenac. Intended as a military outpost against the *Iroquois and the British, it was also a trading centre and a base for explorations to the west along the Great Lakes. Captured by the British in 1758, Fort Frontenac and the region were ceded to the British in 1763 by the Treaty of Paris.

In 1783, following the *American Revolution, the British negotiated with the new First Nations occupants of the region, the Mississauga, for lands to accommodate refugees from the former British colonies. The *Loyalists were settled on the site at Kings Town, which became the administrative centre for the new townships laid out along the Upper St Lawrence and eastern end of Lake Ontario. The nascent urban centre, Kingston, was stimulated by the significant naval and military presence during the War of 1812 and subsequent development of a large garrison centred on Fort Henry. From a permanent population of about 2,000 just after the War of 1812, the city grew to almost 12,000 by mid-century. By this date, Kingston had emerged as an important commercial centre involved in transshipping outgoing lumber and grain and incoming merchandise and passengers. This role was consolidated in 1832 by the completion of the Rideau Canal, which bypassed the strategically vulnerable St Lawrence and linked Montreal with the Great Lakes. Kingston became the largest town in Upper Canada and served briefly (1841–3) as capital of the *Province of Canada.

By mid-century, Kingston's fortunes were affected by a weakening of the Laurentian grain trade; improvements in navigation of the St Lawrence, which allowed vessels to bypass Kingston; the arrival of the *Grand Trunk Railway in 1856 as a competitor to water transport; and the increase in the size of ships, which posed problems for Kingston's harbour. Another economic blow was dealt by the departure of the imperial garrison in 1871. The relative decline continued throughout the second half of the 19th century, as Kingston failed to industrialize. Textile factories were established in the 1880s, but the city's economy continued to be dominated by commerce and such ancillary industries as the locomotive works and shipyards. Consequently, Kingston's rate of growth fell behind that of the rest of the province, attaining a population of only 14,000 by 1881 and 30,000 by 1941.

With the onset of the Second World War, the city attracted new industries such as *Alcan Aluminium and DuPont Nylon and the population increased to some 50,000 by 1952, while that of the Greater Kingston area approached 113,000 by the close of the 20th century. With the relative decline of former industries, Kingston's society and economy have a distinctive institutional base dominated by the military (Fort Henry, Royal Military College, National Defence College, Canadian Army Staff College, Royal Canadian School of Signals, Royal Canadian School of Electrical and Mechanical Engineers), federal penitentiaries, and education (Queen's University, Royal Military College, St Lawrence College). Because of its lakeside amenities, historical heritage, and small-town ambience, Kingston is currently experiencing growth as a centre for historical-cultural tourism. The cityscape of the 'Limestone City' reflects its past as a 19th-century commercial-institutional town, with a remarkable concentration of buildings of historical or architectural significance: Kingston City Hall, Customs House, Post Office, Market Square, Bellevue House, St George's Cathedral (Anglican), St Andrew's (Presbyterian), St Mary's (Catholic), and Sydenham (United) churches, Grand Trunk and Kingston and Pembroke railway stations, and the military complex of Fort Henry and the Martello towers. Accordingly, the city looks to a future in which its educational, institutional, and cultural features underpin its development as a 'smart-growth' environment. BRIAN S. OSBORNE

King William III's Act to Encourage the Trade to Newfoundland was passed in 1699 to clarify administration of the *English Shore by revising the *Western Charters. The act repeated traditional controls over ballast dumping, fishing stages and cookrooms, forestry practices, observance of sabbath, and echoed the 1676 charter in requiring that a fifth of crews be new to the fishery. Although in Newfoundland historical mythology another impediment to settlement, it actually confirmed resident 'planter' boat-keepers' rights to property enclosed before 1685 or not used by migratory fishing crews, who retained their rights to self-regulation by their own *fishing admirals. This compromise between pro- and anti-settlement interests epitomized the political situation in Newfoundland after 1680. The new power given fishing admirals 'to determine differences between masters of fishing ships and inhabitants' was rendered increasingly irrelevant after 1729 by the gradual development of local courts and the increasing administrative dominance of the Royal Navy. PETER E. POPE

Kirke, Sir David (1597–1654), privateer, entrepreneur, royalist governor of Newfoundland, and first resident fish merchant, blamed by some Devon merchants and *fishing admirals for facilitating settlement. In 1629, with his brothers Lewis and Thomas, and the help of Montagnais allies, Kirke seized Quebec and its fur trade from *Champlain. When the 1632 treaty restored Quebec to France, Kirke returned to the wine trade with brothers John, James, and partner William Barkeley. In 1637, Charles I gave Kirke and three aristocratic associates a patent for Newfoundland with rights to tax French and Dutch ships fishing or trading. In 1638, as governor of the *English Shore, settled with his wife Sara in *Ferryland, he developed a transatlantic trade in fish and wines with the American colonies. Following the execution of Charles and two of the Newfoundland patentees in 1649, the Commonwealth recalled Kirke to London in 1651 to account for profits concealed from his fellow patentees and the Crown. Imprisoned at the suit of Cecil Calvert, he died, leaving his Ferryland fishing interests in the hands of his wife and their sons. PETER E. POPE

Kirkland Lake gold miners' strike. Conducted in a harsh northern winter, from 18 November 1941 to 12 February 1942, the strike was one of the most important industrial disputes in Canadian working-class history. The issue of union recognition was central to the dispute. Both in the local community and on the national stage, this work stoppage in eight mines united the Canadian labour movement around the demand for collective-bargaining legislation. The strike was a microcosm of national wartime developments, which produced unprecedented union growth, serious industrial unrest, a hostile management response, and generally antagonistic labour-government relations. Locally, the dispute polarized the community, a one-industry town whose miners were dominated by the operators' paternalistic approach to labour relations. The churches split over the issue of union recognition and collective bargaining, and a sympathetic public learned of the miners' poor working and living conditions through public-conciliation proceedings.

The strike was lost, even though the vast majority of the miners supported the union, which went through every hurdle—government investigation, conciliation, strike votes—to try to gain union recognition from the intractable mine operators; when that failed it conducted a legal strike. The union's defeat clearly revealed the inadequacy of existing labour policy and united unions and other supporters to change it. Collective-bargaining legislation was finally won in 1944 with the federal government's proclamation of war order PC 1003. Collective bargaining remains central to the industrial relations system created in the war years.

LAUREL SEFTON MacDOWELL

Kiska. On 15 and 16 August 1943, some 5,000 troops in the 13th Infantry Brigade, or Greenlight Force, along with 30,000 American personnel, assaulted the Aleutian island of Kiska. Several hundred Canadians in the elite First Special Service Force also participated. Although Japan's garrison had covertly evacuated the island on 29 July, dense fog and nervousness led to numerous casualties from friendly fire. Four Canadians died on Kiska: two were killed by Japanese mines, two perished while mishandling enemy munitions. C.P. *Stacey, the army's official historian, branded the operation a fiasco, but it marked the first time home defence conscripts served in a combat zone in the Second World War. It was also the first time that Canadian troops served directly under American operational control. GALEN ROGER PERRAS

Klein, Abraham Moses (1909–72). One of Canada's leading modernist poets, Klein, born in Ukraine, was also the first major Canadian author from a Jewish, or indeed from any ethnic minority, background. His books include *Hath Not a Jew* (1940) and *Poems* (1944), which draw heavily on Jewish cultural traditions; *The Hitleriad* (1944), a satire on Nazism; *The Rocking Chair* and Other Poems (1948), an affectionate, though not uncritical, portrait of Quebec, which won the Governor General's Award; and *The Second Scroll* (1951), a symbolic treatment of the Holocaust and of Zionism. Klein was active in a wide range of activities: he was a lawyer; a public speaker on Jewish, Zionist, and literary themes; an editor and columnist for the *Canadian Jewish Chronicle*; a visiting lecturer at McGill; a speech writer and public relations consultant for Samuel Bronfman; and, in 1949, an unsuccessful candidate for the Co-operative Commonwealth Federation. In the early 1950s he began to show symptoms of psychological distress, and soon after gave up public activities and ceased writing altogether. ZAILIG POLLOCK

Klondike gold rush, 1896–1901. The gold rush brought tens of thousands of men and women from around the world to the Yukon, establishing it as a separate Canadian territory with *Dawson City as its capital. It began when an American prospector named George Washington Carmack, his Tagish brother-in-law *Keish (Skookum Jim Mason), and his nephew K̲áa Goox̲ (Dawson Charlie) discovered gold. The three men were prospecting along what they dubbed *Bonanza Creek, a small tributary of the Klondike River, when they made the most significant gold discovery in Canadian history. Within weeks of their 17 August 1896 discovery, more than 400 other miners, traders, and camp followers arrived in the area from other points along the *Yukon River, intending to spend the winter at the new diggings. By the summer of 1897, Bonanza and the neighbouring creeks had surpassed the miners' wildest dreams; dozens of them headed for the ports of Vancouver, Seattle, and San Francisco laden with literally a ton of gold dust and nuggets. George Carmack and his Tagish relatives extracted more than $1 million worth of gold from their Bonanza Creek claims. Others, especially those who arrived early in the rush, also made their fortunes. Clarence and Ethel Berry's claim on Eldorado Creek produced $1 million, while that of Thomas and Salome Lippy produced $1.5 million. Less spectacular claims brought individual miners $100,000 or more and were bought and sold at a fantastic rate.

Between the fall of 1897 and the spring of 1898, tens of thousands of people caught 'gold fever' and began preparations for their journey to the Klondike. Getting there was an expensive and complicated ordeal, whether an individual came from Canada or farther afield. The main route began by sea, with steamers leaving from Vancouver, Seattle, or San Francisco daily in the summer of 1898 bound for the Alaskan coast. The majority of these let off their passengers on the southern coast of Alaska, at the end of the Lynne Canal at a bustling boomtown called Skagway. From there, travellers offloaded their goods (they were required to carry a year's provisions), packed them into bundles, and began the climb over the *Chilkoot Pass. Once over the pass—and through the Canadian customs at its summit—Klondikers proceeded to Lake Bennett, the headwaters of the Yukon River. There they built a boat, or hired someone to do so, and floated the remaining 500 miles downstream to Dawson City.

Historians estimate that in the 'Stampede Summer' of 1898 over 50,000 individuals attempted some portion of the route to the Klondike. About half of them made it. Of those who arrived in 1898, most were disappointed to find that nearly all the available mining claims had been staked. Many turned around and left the same year. Other would-be miners became boat builders, freighters, carpenters, cooks, bartenders, waitresses, teachers, nurses, and clerks, filling the many needs of the growing community and ever hopeful that they would be ready for the next big strike.

The discovery on Bonanza Creek changed the course of Yukon history. Relations between Natives and non-Natives deteriorated as 400 non-Native miners and their friends were joined by at least 40,000 others—all intent on making their fortunes regardless of whose homeland they had wandered into. These newcomers dug up every available creek and gulch within reach; disrupted salmon and greyling runs; caused innumerable forest fires; hunted and consumed vast numbers of caribou, moose, and other big game; and cut vast numbers of trees for firewood and building materials. The federal government directed its handful of officials in the Yukon to 'enter into no treaties' with the Yukon Indians for fear that once treaty rights were established in a given area gold would be discovered there. Thus, Yukon Indians retained sovereignty (albeit largely unacknowledged) over the entire Yukon until their comprehensive land claim was settled nearly 100 years later. CHARLENE PORSILD

Knights of Columbus. A Catholic lay organization, founded in the United States as an alternative to the mainstream fraternal organizations such as the Masons, which Catholic men were forbidden to join. First introduced to

Canada in 1897, the Knights of Columbus quickly acclimatized themselves to Canadian circumstances, and by 1910 they had established councils from coast to coast in Canada's major urban centres. The organization was especially popular among middle-class laymen, who responded to its rich ceremonial life, comprehensive medical and life insurance program, and fervent support for the church and its teachings. The Knights' English-speaking branches became well known for their Anglo-Canadian nationalism and patriotic service, most notably during the two world wars, when the Knights' army huts became popular recreational centres among enlisted men of all faiths. BRIAN CLARKE

Knights of Columbus fire. On Saturday, 12 December 1942, St John's experienced its most serious loss of life by fire when tragedy struck the Knights of Columbus Canadian Army Huts. The hostel was a major recreation centre for servicemen and that night it was the location for a local radio broadcast of the *Barn Dance*. As a Canadian soldier, Edward Adams, sang 'Moonlight Trail' to the crowd of about 500 people, the building became engulfed in flames. In the confusion 100 people died and another 107 were injured. A subsequent judicial report suggested the fire was likely a result of arson, but there is no evidence to prove the popular view that it was the result of enemy sabotage. MELVIN BAKER AND AIDAN MALONEY

Knights of Labor. Formed in the United States in 1869, the Knights aimed to organize all workers (except Chinese) in a broad movement of social reform. Part trade union, part fraternal society, part labour educational society, part political party, the order was unrivalled, by the 1880s, as the most significant workers' organization of the late 19th century.

Entering Canada in 1881, at Hamilton, the Knights eventually chartered 450 local assemblies across the country, mostly in Ontario and Quebec. Their high point was roughly 1886 in south-central Ontario, but they also reached in the 1890s to the lumber mills of the Ottawa Valley and industrial Quebec. In Toronto they were associated with the street railway strike in 1886, while in Victoria they were closely linked to anti-Chinese agitations of the 1880s. Newspapers such as the west coast *Industrial News* or the Toronto-Hamilton-based *Palladium of Labor* publicized their particular brand of eclectic radicalism, while prominent Canadians such as T. Phillips *Thompson, D.J. *O'Donoghue, and Alexander W. Wright wrote articles, spoke, and organized assemblies on their behalf.

The Knights of Labor survived into the 20th century but were finally vanquished in 1902, expelled from the Trades and Labor Congress that many of their founding figures had helped to build in the mid-1880s. *American Federation of Labor head Samuel Gompers dictated that no unionist could belong to both a craft union and a local assembly of the Knights, and he wanted no rivals to his craft union-based organization. Quebec workers, attracted to the Knights because they offered workers a space to organize regardless of skill level or language, refused for the most part to be drawn in to the AFL-affiliated TLC, and instead formed their own French-speaking Catholic unions. The vision of the Knights, one big union of all workers, would be embraced by radical labour in the post–First World War upheavals and by industrial unionists in the 1930s. BRYAN D. PALMER

Komagata Maru. The 1914 voyage of the converted freighter *Komagata Maru* represented a notorious but unsuccessful challenge to discriminatory Canadian immigration regulations. It was also a minor episode in India's freedom struggle. The freighter's 376 passengers were Indian Punjabis: 24 Muslims, 12 Hindus, and 340 *Sikhs. Seeking work in British Columbia despite Canadian regulations that had excluded immigrants from India since 1908, they boarded at Hong Kong, Singapore, and Yokohama. Their leaders believed that Canadian regulations were open to court challenge. They also saw their effort as part of India's struggle for independence, and they believed that Canadian refusal to admit the ship's passengers would instigate anti-British protest in India. The ship arrived in Vancouver on 23 May; none of the passengers was allowed to land, except 20 who had previously established domicile. After some delay, the passengers secured a hearing in the BC Court of Appeal but lost their case. On 23 July, following tense negotiation, the ship and its passengers were escorted out of Canadian waters by the cruiser *Rainbow*. On 29 September the *Komagata Maru* reached Budge Budge in Bengal, and a riot, provoked by police efforts to arrest their leaders, led to the death of 20 of the passengers. HUGH JOHNSTON

Korean War, 1950–3. At the end of the Second World War Korea, a former colony of Japan, was divided into Russian and US zones of influence with the 38th parallel as the dividing line. In the northern half of the peninsula, the Soviets established a Communist government headed by Kim-il Sung. In the southern half, the Americans sponsored a nationalist and anti-Communist government led by Syngman Rhee. On 25 June 1950, Kim's Soviet-equipped and -trained military, accompanied by Russian advisers, launched a surprise attack across the 38th parallel with the aim of unifying the peninsula by force. The southern forces, the ROK (Republic of Korea) army, virtually collapsed. Much weaker militarily than the North and with very limited US aid, the ROK army retreated south in great haste, abandoning Seoul, the capital city.

Although the United States had indicated prior to the attack that South Korea was not considered a vital US defence interest, President Harry S. Truman quickly changed his mind, ordered US jets based in Korea to impede the North Korean attack, and sought *United Nations support for a combined military operation to restore the 38th parallel boundary. Canada supported the US initiative in the overall belief that Communist aggression must be resisted but also due to Ottawa's suspicion, shared in other Western capitals, that Soviet leader Josef Stalin was testing the resolve of the new *NATO alliance.

Canada's determination to help defend South Korea was strengthened when the UN Security Council acceded to US requests and sought the participation of UN member nations' military forces to fight under command of US General Douglas MacArthur. It did so because the Soviet Union was, at the time, boycotting the council over the UN's refusal to oust representatives of Nationalist China from its councils and assemblies and replace them with representatives of the new Communist government. Canada's initial contribution to the UN 'police action', as Truman dubbed it, was three destroyers and a squadron from the *RCAF's Air Transport Command. The former were sent to patrol Korean waters under the ultimate command of the US Navy while the latter was ordered to help airlift men and supplies from the west coast of the United States to Japan for eventual shipment to Korea. But as the military situation deteriorated in South Korea in late July 1950, pressure mounted on Ottawa from Washington, London, and UN headquarters in New York for Canada to send a substantial contingent of ground forces as well.

On 7 August 1950, Prime Minister Louis *St Laurent announced that Canada would send a brigade group, consisting of a brigade headquarters, three infantry battalions, an armoured regiment, a field artillery regiment, and support troops as appropriate including medical, engineering, and logistics units, to Korea. The government intended to save time in training and preparing this contingent by focusing on the recruitment of Second World War veterans where possible and filling out senior ranks with *Permanent Force personnel. The brigade would receive the bulk of its training at Fort Lewis, Washington. The formations that made up the brigade would consist of newly created 2nd battalions and regiments of existing Permanent Force formations. The contingent was named the Canadian Army Special Force, later becoming the 25th Canadian Infantry Brigade. Despite some considerable teething problems in supply, recruitment, and training, the 2nd Battalion of the Princess Patricia's Canadian Light Infantry (2 PPCLI) left for Korea late in the year, arriving in December 1950 in the midst of a strong Chinese Communist offensive. The only partly trained Canadians stayed out of the line until February 1951, when they joined 27th British Commonwealth Infantry Brigade (BCIB) to help spearhead a major UN counterattack against the Chinese.

The Chinese intervention in the Korean War began in November 1950 after MacArthur's forces had outflanked the North Koreans by landing at Inchon, on the west coast not far from Seoul. Caught by surprise from the rear, the North Koreans began a long retreat virtually to the Yalu River, the border between North Korea and China. MacArthur's forces followed, but the Chinese entered the war before the UN troops could chase the Communists totally out of Korea. Chinese intervention virtually guaranteed a long and costly war. Thus, Canada sent the rest of the Special Force to Korea. It arrived in May 1951, but only after 2 PPCLI and the rest of the 25th BCIB had helped stem a major Chinese attack in April 1951 at Kap-yong, to the northeast of Seoul. The Patricias were awarded a US Presidential Unit Citation for their role in the defence of Kap-yong, the only Canadian military unit ever so honoured.

In July 1951 the Special Force joined with British, Australian, and New Zealand troops and Indian medical personnel to form 1st Commonwealth Division. The division fought under overall American command in an offensive that succeeded in pushing the Chinese and North Korean troops back across the 38th parallel. In the fall of 1951 armistice talks began, dragging on for close to two years until the war finally ended on 27 July 1953. In that time Canadian troops and Canada's destroyers twice rotated home.

Canada sent the fourth largest UN contingent to the war—26,791 soldiers, sailors, and airmen. Canadian casualties totaled 1,588 with 516 killed in action or dead on active service. D.J. BERCUSON

Krieghoff, Cornelius (1815–72). Born in Amsterdam, Krieghoff enlisted in the US Army in New York in 1837 to fight the Seminoles in Florida. He was in Canada by 1840, where he advertised himself as an artist, first in Toronto (1844), then in Montreal (1846), and finally in Quebec City (from 1854), and married a French Canadian, Marie (Émilie) Gauthier dite Saint-Germain (1820–1906). Represented for 13 years by John Budden, a Quebec auctioneer, Krieghoff then joined his daughter Emily in Chicago, where he died four years later. Known as a painter of French-Canadian life and of Aboriginal subjects, his approach contrasts sharply with contemporaries such as Joseph *Légaré, Antoine Plamondon, or Théophile Hamel. He painted scenes of everyday life rather than official portraits. Some critics found his view of French Canadians in paintings like *Chez Jolifou* and *Merrymaking* disrespectful, but he was taking their side against the strictness of the church. He painted beautiful autumn landscapes, usually with Indian hunters, showing them as the 'free men of the forest'. He had some of his works lithographed during his lifetime.

FRANÇOIS-MARC GAGNON

Ku Klux Klan. The KKK entered Canada in the early 1920s, following its rebirth in the United States during the First World War. The original American Reconstruction Klan, a regional organization centred in the South during the post-Civil War years, directed its anger and hatred at the newly emancipated Blacks and their perceived friends. The born-again Klan, which spread in the interwar years across wide regions of the United States and into Canada, added Catholics, Jews, and immigrants to the hate list of aliens thought to be un-American—or un-Canadian.

A tame version of the American organization, the Canadian Klan enrolled a tiny membership across the country—with the exception of Saskatchewan. Klansmen burned occasional crosses, distributed incendiary hate literature, and pressed the issues of selective immigration and restriction of French- and minority-language rights, in defence of a white, Protestant Canada purged of alien influences. Only in Saskatchewan did the message resonate, albeit briefly. At its peak in the late 1920s, the Saskatchewan Klan signed up over 20,000 members, contributing to the defeat of the Liberals in the 1929 election. But support for Saskatchewan's hoodless day-riders quickly dissipated, and during the early Depression years klansmen there followed their colleagues elsewhere in the country into an enduring obscurity. MARTIN ROBIN

La Bolduc (Mary Rose-Anne Travers) (1894–1941), popular singer and songwriter. Born at Newport in the Gaspé, to an Irish father and a French-Canadian mother, she learned to play the fiddle, the harmonica, and small accordion when she was very young. At 34 she made her first professional appearance, as a musician during the *Veillées du Bon Vieux Temps* at the Monument-National in Montreal, under the name Madame Édouard Bolduc. She was an instant success. She sang songs like 'Ça va venir découragez-vous pas' and 'La Gaspésienne pure laine', which sketched a humorous portrait of ordinary life at the time, inventing a distinctive 'turlutage'—a technique using nonsense syllables (not unlike the 'tura-luras' or 'diddle-dum-dees' of traditional Irish songs)—as a refrain. Her records and tours through Quebec and New England made her Quebec's most popular singer.

ODETTE VINCENT

labour law. The regulation of collective bargaining and worker collective action. Its history can be roughly divided into four periods: master and servant (settlement–1872), liberal voluntarism (1872–1907), industrial voluntarism (1907–43), and industrial pluralism (1943–present).

In the master-and-servant regime, the legal status of worker combinations or trade *unions was uncertain. Some Canadian workers were convicted of criminal conspiracy because of their strike activities, but none for simply acting in concert to improve their conditions. Striking workers were far more likely to be prosecuted under master and servant law. The question of the legality of trade unions came to a head when Toronto printers were charged with criminal conspiracy in 1872. Before the case came to trial, the Canadian government enacted the Trade Unions Act, 1872, granting workers immunity against prosecution for simple combinations, inaugurating the period of liberal voluntarism. While workers were free to join a trade union, they did not enjoy a protected right to do so, since employers were also free to refuse to employ trade union members. A significant element of direct state coercion was also part of this regime. Strike-support activity, such as picketing, was closely regulated. The criminal law provided police with ample justification for intervening in strikes and, when required, the *militia was called up in aid of the civil power. Yet, state coercion alone proved insufficient to reduce labour conflict, and many provinces also enacted state-sponsored conciliation schemes that, for the most part, depended on the willingness of the parties to submit their disagreement voluntarily to tripartite panels authorized to make non-binding recommendations. These mechanisms were little used.

As Canada entered the 20th century, the potential for labour disputes to disrupt the national economy became more worrisome. In response, the federal government established a department of labour and enacted a series of laws culminating in the Industrial Disputes Investigation Act of 1907. The law, which applied to 'public utilities' including mines and railways, required the parties to submit their disputes to a process of investigation and conciliation before resorting to economic sanctions. This new regime of industrial voluntarism helped stabilize industrial relations in some sectors (e.g., railways) but not in others (e.g., coal mining). Employers continued to have access to earlier forms of coercion, including the militia, but also found a new source of legal assistance in the courts, which began granting injunctions to limit picketing and other strike-support actions on the basis that they interfered with employers' freedom of contract and enjoyment of private property.

During the First World War trade unions grew stronger and more militant. The government responded by supporting collective bargaining with responsible unions and by strengthening its own coercive powers. In the post-war period, many workers demanded a labour regime that recognized their right to form unions, while many employers insisted on a return to the pre-war situation. Conflict grew, culminating in the 1919 *Winnipeg General Strike. Its defeat led to the restoration of industrial voluntarism. A period of relative calm followed, during which the courts determined that the constitutional jurisdiction to legislate in respect of labour relations rested primarily with the provinces.

During the Great Depression unemployed workers organized to protest their conditions, and many workers were attracted to new, militant industrial unions. Again, the state responded with a mixture of increased repression aimed at radicals and some ameliorative measures, including increases in relief and the enactment of provincial industrial standards legislation in the mid-1930s. Such legislation provided a mechanism for groups of organized workers to negotiate standards that would become binding minimum standards for all workers in an industry and region, provided there was a group of employers who were willing to engage in this kind of joint regulation. These schemes were effective for only a minority of workers. The federal government belatedly introduced a package of 'New Deal' legislation in 1935, but the courts ruled it unconstitutional. A surge of industrial union growth, another strike wave in 1937, and the establishment of a new, labour friendly political party, the Co-operative Commonwealth Federation, prompted nearly every province to pass legislation prohibiting employer interference with trade union formation; a few, beginning with Nova Scotia in 1937, enacted statutes that required employers to bargain with unions that enjoyed majority support. None provided an effective enforcement mechanism.

The Second World War precipitated the final crisis of industrial voluntarism. Early efforts to address labour unrest, modelled on the mix of exhortation and coercion adopted in the First World War, failed. In 1944, faced with a mounting strike wave and growing support for the CCF, the federal government, exercising its wartime powers, issued order-in-council PC 1003, which established a regime of industrial pluralism. Its principal elements were: prohibitions on unfair labour practices; compulsory recognition of unions enjoying majority support; a prohibition on strikes or lockouts over union recognition, prior to conciliation or during the life of a collective agreement; and establishment of labour boards empowered to enforce the scheme. Disputes over the interpretation and application of a collective agreement were to be resolved through grievance arbitration. As federal jurisdiction waned in the post-war period, the question of the future of collective bargaining was resolved through a series of major strikes that further institutionalized responsible trade unions. The federal government's 1948 Industrial Relations and Disputes Investigation Act adopted the main features of PC 1003 and became the model for the various provincial collective-bargaining laws that were subsequently enacted.

Although courts continued to restrict the scope of lawful picketing and other strike-related activities and to narrow labour board powers, trade unions representing predominantly male workers in core sectors of the economy thrived under industrial pluralism in the 1950s. In the 1960s another wave of union militancy led to the strengthening of its institutions and their extension to the public sector, albeit in modified form. This trend continued in the 1970s—as most provinces raised the floor of rights for unionized workers and enhanced the remedial authority of labour boards—but began to reverse in the 1980s, when wage and price controls were frequently imposed on public sector workers and their right to strike was often suspended. Many provinces also amended their private sector collective-bargaining laws to make it more difficult to unionize and to engage in collective action. This pattern continued into the 1990s at the same time that changes in the labour market, including the growth of part-time and self-employment and employment in small business, threatened the continued viability of industrial pluralism. Ironically, the courts may be becoming its defender.

ERIC TUCKER

Labrador. Historic maps dating to the 16th century show Labrador as the name for the entire northeastern peninsula of the North American continent. In 1912 the northwestern and Ungava Bay areas were annexed to the Canadian province of Quebec, after which the territory was often described as the Labrador-Quebec peninsula. Labrador was under the jurisdiction of the Dominion of Newfoundland. A dispute over the interior border separating Quebec and Labrador was arbitrated by the Judicial Committee of the Privy Council of Great Britain. Ruling in Newfoundland's favour in 1927, it determined that the boundary extended northward from 52° latitude following the crest of the watershed flowing into the Atlantic Ocean. This decision accounts for the uneven line forming most of the boundary on modern maps. A straight line along the 52nd parallel dipping south to Blanc Sablon was established in 1825 as the southern boundary by the British North America Act. Quebec authorities have never accepted the 1927 decision, considering instead that the border should follow a narrow strip of land along the coastline.

European discovery of Labrador is officially attributed to John *Cabot in 1497, but the southern coast was likely already known to Basque and Breton fishermen for its rich cod stocks and migration of bowhead whales in the Strait of Belle Isle. There, in about 1540, Spanish Basque merchants established land stations for processing whale blubber into oil for export to Europe, creating the first major industrial enterprise in North America. *Whaling ventures ceased by 1620 due to fewer whales and the bankruptcy of the Spanish economy following the defeat of the Armada in 1588. Many Basque stations were then used for fishing cod and seals by Quebec and French fishermen. Their legacy is several French place names for modern communities in the Strait of Belle Isle, such as Forteau and L'Anse au Loup.

In 1763 French interests in Labrador were ceded to Britain under the terms of the Treaty of Paris ending the Seven Years' War, with the territory's administration assigned to the governor of Newfoundland. British merchants assumed control over fisheries development but they were thwarted in opening new stations by Inuit travelling from the northern coast to obtain ironware and other European goods through trade or raids at fishing posts. Such journeys declined after 1771, when *Moravian missionaries opened trade stores at northern stations established to convert Inuit to Christianity. Seasonal fishing posts began expanding along the southern Labrador coast, and gradually people originating from Britain and Newfoundland became permanent settlers. After 1860 fishing fleets from Newfoundland regularly harvested cod stocks off the Labrador coast until a moratorium on the fishery was declared in 1992.

Historical knowledge of Labrador was confined largely to the coast until the 19th century, when Hudson's Bay Company agents and explorers began venturing inland to areas traditionally occupied by Innu (Indian) bands. The central interior consists of a barren plateau formed by glacial erosion and known geologically as the *Canadian

Shield. Its rugged terrain of 'stones and rocks' compelled Jacques *Cartier in 1534 to describe Labrador as 'the land God gave to Cain', a view since dispelled by the discovery of valuable mineral deposits.

Geologist A.P. *Low, conducting surveys in central western Labrador in 1893–5, found massive quantities of iron ore, which were developed after 1960 by two mining communities, Labrador City and Wabush. A majestic waterfall cascading from the plateau at Grand Falls (renamed *Churchill Falls) was transformed into a hydro-electric-generating facility in 1972, forming another modern community. Uranium and other minerals have been found, notably a huge nickel deposit in 1995 at Voisey's Bay on the northern coast, bringing worldwide attention to Labrador and prospects for future mining enterprises.

In 1942 the flat terrain at the head of Hamilton Inlet in central Labrador became the site for a military airbase, called Goose Bay, to refuel aircraft involved in the Second World War. Canada's NATO allies have used the base since the 1980s as a training centre for low-level flight exercises. Together with its adjacent civilian community, Happy Valley–Goose Bay is now the administrative capital of Labrador. The resident population consists mostly of people of Inuit and Metis ancestry who left coastal villages to find wage work in the area. An Innu community, Sheshatshit, is located 30 km away.

Covering approximately 290,000 sq km, Labrador is more than twice the size of the island of Newfoundland, but has a sparse population of about 30,000 inhabitants, over half of whom live in four industrial communities. Twenty-six coastal villages range from less than 100 people to about 1,400 residents at Nain, the largest and northernmost community. In 1949 Newfoundland with its Labrador dependency became the tenth Canadian province. In 2001 Labrador was added to the province's official name—now Newfoundland and Labrador—in recognition of its significant historic and economic role.

CAROL BRICE-BENNETT

Lacombe, Albert (1827–1916). Born at St-Sulpice in Quebec, ordained in 1849, the celebrated missionary was closely identified with the early history of the Canadian Prairies. Viewing as inevitable and necessary the transition from *Hudson's Bay Company rule to white settlement that caused the collapse of their way of life, Lacombe encouraged Plains Amerindians to become sedentary, educated, and Christian. His pronounced social skills made him an intermediary among increasingly desperate and aggressive tribes and between Aboriginal and white societies. He fought for Louis *Riel's amnesty after the uprising of 1869; persuaded angry Blackfoot to renounce treaty land selected by the CPR for the railway; lobbied for Aboriginal industrial schools, establishing one at Dunbow, Alberta; dissuaded Amerindians from joining the second Riel uprising (1885); and published dictionaries, catechisms, and New Testament translations in Aboriginal languages. Although a firm believer in Canada's bicultural character, his efforts to attract French-speaking immigrants to the West were unsuccessful. With fellow Oblate Alexandre-Antonin *Taché, archbishop of St-Boniface, and his successor, Adélard Langevin, Lacombe played a critical role in the *Manitoba schools question, lobbying hard for remedial legislation despite partisan and public accusations of Conservative bias. His encounters with the rich and powerful never deterred him from the simple lifestyle of an early Prairie missionary.

ROBERTO PERIN

Lacoste-Gérin-Lajoie, Marie (1847–1945). From the late 19th century to the 1930s, Marie Lacoste-Gérin-Lajoie was an important figure in the French-Canadian feminist and Catholic social action movements. Concerned about the social issues troubling Montreal, she joined the Montreal Local Council of Women, but her religious convictions led her to dream of a federation for French-Canadian women. Thus in 1907, with Caroline Béique, she founded the *Fédération nationale St-Jean-Baptiste, and from 1913 to 1933 served as its president.

She campaigned for several causes in the course of her career, including *women's suffrage and women's access to higher education, and her daughter, Marie Gérin-Lajoie, was the first female graduate of Université Laval à Montréal, in 1911. She also was known for her efforts to improve the legal status of married women. Having taught herself law, she published a manual on the civil law, *Traité de droit usuel* (1922), which went through numerous editions. Although women were not yet admitted to the bar in Quebec, she was the first woman to obtain a teaching position in the Faculty of Law at Université de Montréal.

KARINE HÉBERT

lacrosse. In 1994 Parliament declared lacrosse one of Canada's two national sports. The game emerged in the 1850s, when the anglophone middle class of Montreal adopted the Indian game of 'baggataway', which was a violent game played by the Native population of eastern North America. The 1860s witnessed the emergence of the first lacrosse powerhouse, the Montreal Shamrocks—Irish, Catholic, 'horny-handed sons of toil'. During the 1870s and 1880s their bloody confrontations with the middle-class Montreal and Toronto Lacrosse Clubs revealed the basic problem that was to plague the game to the present day—violence. Field lacrosse spread across the country with the tide of anglophone settlers from Ontario and Quebec. By the early 1890s it could claim to be the most popular summer game in Canada. Rivals, in particular the New Westminster Salmonbellies, emerged to challenge the supremacy of the eastern clubs. The early 1900s were the golden years of field lacrosse, culminating in the emergence of two professional leagues. The popularity of the professional game is reflected in Con Jones's paying 'Newsy' Lalonde the staggering sum of $6,500 in 1911 to play 16 games for Vancouver. Escalating violence led to the collapse of the professional leagues in 1914. The great days of lacrosse were over. While it continued to be played in the 1920s, its base of support was limited to Montreal, small-town Ontario, Victoria, Vancouver, and New Westminster—it was not a truly 'national' game. Its failure to gain a firm foothold was due in part to the lack of an organizational infrastructure and also to the fact that it was never adopted by schools and churches.

In 1931 the game was revived by some ice hockey arena owners in Ontario with the new game of box lacrosse. Though eagerly adopted in the strongholds of the game, it was still plagued by violence, as was reflected in eastern perceptions of the 1933 Mann Cup: 'Trench warfare such as occurred in France was actually no worse than what our boys had to put up with in their invasion of the west.' Periodically professional box lacrosse leagues, located in urban centres in Canada and the United States, flourished briefly. Field lacrosse was resurrected in 1998 when some Ontario universities included it in their women's athletic programs; university women now played the game once associated with Canadian masculinity.

ALAN METCALFE

Laflamme, Joseph-Clovis-Kemner (1849–1910). Trained as a priest at the *Séminaire de Québec, Laflamme devoted his life to the teaching and promotion of science at Université Laval. He became professor of geology and mineralogy in 1870 and also taught physics from 1875 to 1893, the year he became rector of the university. His *Éléments de minéralogie et de géologie*, published in 1881, was re-edited many times and used by college students. Laflamme also did geological research, exploring the Quebec region on behalf of the *Geological Survey of Canada. As a rule, his publications are more popularizations than specialized research, and through his lectures and contributions to magazines he made known to many the new technologies of his time such as electric light, telephones, and X-rays. A founding member of the *Royal Society of Canada, Laflamme represented his country at many international scientific meetings. He can be seen as the ambassador of French Canada in the Canadian scientific community during the last quarter of the 19th century.

YVES GINGRAS

LaFontaine, Sir Louis-Hippolyte (1807–64), politician, judge. Admitted to the bar in 1828, in 1831 LaFontaine married Adèle, the daughter of Amable Berthelot, a rich lawyer and political figure. Elected representative of Terrebonne, he strongly supported Louis-Joseph *Papineau and the Parti patriote, but balked at violence. Although briefly arrested in 1838, he was not accused. He negotiated with both the government and imprisoned rebels, gaining the respect of both sides; he was already arguing for a general amnesty and compensation for innocent victims, a program he would eventually implement by 1849. A few Canadien radicals, including Papineau after his return, still centred their energies on an impossible repeal of the *Act of Union (1841). LaFontaine, although initially opposed to the Union, was supported by most Canadien reformers in concluding an alliance with Upper-Canadian reformers to work for *responsible government and fair treatment of Canadiens in the union, which actually functioned more like a federation. The solid links between English and French reformers eventually pushed the British government and the governor into granting responsible government in 1848, a decision facilitated by England's shift to free trade. This victory—internal self-government—would be referred to for many generations as the embodiment of the Canadian duality ('LaFontaine and Baldwin', later 'Cartier and Macdonald'). Tired of politics, facing a more vocal radical wing (the *Clear Grits, in Canada West), plagued by ill health, LaFontaine resigned on 26 September 1851. He became chief justice of the Queen's Bench in 1853.

JEAN-PIERRE WALLOT

Lahontan, Louis-Armand de Lom d'Arce, Baron de (1666-1715?), nobleman, soldier, philosopher. Lahontan spent only ten years in North America, but his narratives, letters, and dialogues were eagerly read by Europeans in the 18th century. Soldier son of an illustrious family, he came to Canada in 1683, serving widely in the interior, learning Algonquian, and accumulating an expert's knowledge of the landscape and Native life. At Michilimackinac Lahontan met the survivors of *La Salle's ill-fated expedition to the Mississippi; later he fought against Sir William *Phips at Quebec. Provoked by a hostile governor at *Plaisance, the witty aristocrat fled to France in 1693, spending his remaining years as a wandering intellectual at European courts. Lahontan published three volumes of voyages, 1702–3. Mingling closely observed experiences with a possibly imaginary journey up 'la rivière Longue' (the Missouri), they were quick best-sellers. His fictionalized philosophical dialogues with the Native Adario (Kondiaronk) address typical Enlightenment questions of religion, law, happiness, medicine, and marriage.

GERMAINE WARKENTIN

Laidlaw, Alexander Fraser (1908–80), teacher, *co-operative leader. Born in Port Hood, Nova Scotia, Laidlaw graduated from St Francis Xavier University (1929) and became principal of Port Hood Academy (1929–40). An educational reformer, he subsequently became a school inspector (1941–2) and bureaucrat in the NS education ministry (1943–4). He served as associate director of extension, St Francis Xavier (1944–56), general secretary of the Co-operative Union of Canada (1958–68), and co-operative housing expert, Central Mortgage and Housing Corporation (1968–80). He headed a royal commission on co-operatives in Sri Lanka and undertook development assignments in several southern countries. His book *Co-operatives in the Year 2000* (1980), written for the International Co-operative Alliance, is a major document in 20th-century co-operativism, profoundly affecting the international movement's recent development.

IAN MacPHERSON

Lamb, William Kaye (1904–99). Kaye Lamb significantly shaped Canada's cultural landscape. As provincial librarian and archivist of British Columbia, 1934–9, he founded the *British Columbia Historical Quarterly*, blending thereby his lifelong passion for regional history and archival management. As chief librarian, University of

British Columbia, 1940–8, he directed the library's substantial post-war expansion. Appointed fourth dominion archivist in 1948, he launched microfilming projects of overseas historical records, inaugurated the systematic management of government records, and improved the archives' public services. In 1953 he became Canada's first national librarian, creating the National Library of Canada and a Canadian Legal Deposit system, the national bibliography, and the Canadian union catalogue. In 1967 the Public Archives–National Library building opened in Ottawa under his proud sponsorship. His scrupulous historical writing focused on west-coast shipping, the Canadian Pacific Railway, and early exploration of his beloved Pacific Northwest. He published many volumes of writings by Simon *Fraser, Alexander *Mackenzie, John McLoughlin, and, in a culminating magisterial work, George *Vancouver. TERRY COOK

Lament for a Nation. No political tract in modern times—perhaps in all of Canadian history—has had a wider influence than *Lament for a Nation: The Defeat of Canadian Nationalism* (1965) by George *Grant. A short book (97 pages), it was written in response to the victory of the Liberal Party in the 1963 federal election, and the subsequent acquisition of nuclear warheads for *Bomarc anti-aircraft missiles. Conservative leader John *Diefenbaker opposed acquisition, even though his government had acquired the missiles, and his opposition had precipitated its defeat. Grant was no great admirer of Diefenbaker, but he was a pacifist, and the warheads decision enraged him. With extraordinary intensity, he argued that it symbolized the Liberals' historic role in subordinating Canada to the United States, whose interests nuclear weapons chiefly served; more broadly, *liberalism was the ideology of capitalism, technology, and modernity, in the face of whose universalist homogenizing force no small society could sustain its particularity. 'The impossibility of *conservatism in our era', he wrote, 'is the impossibility of Canada.' Ironically, in lamenting the defeat of Canadian nationalism, Grant gave it new force, while his deeply conservative evocation of a vanished past found resonance on the political left. The book's powerful articulation of *'Red Toryism' gave rise to vigorous debate and even, it might be said, to modern Canadian political theory.
KENNETH C. DEWAR

Landry, Sir Pierre-Amand (1846–1916), teacher, lawyer, politician, judge. Born in Memramcook, Landry was a man of firsts: son of New Brunswick's first Acadian MLA; first NB Acadian lawyer (1870), provincial cabinet minister (1879), judge of the county court (1890), judge of the NB Supreme Court (1893), chief justice King's Bench (1913), and knight (1916). He was also a key participant in the first Acadian National Convention (1881) and successful lobbyist for the appointment of the first Acadian senator and bishop. Throughout his life, this tactful, urbane gentleman fostered ethnic harmony, French–English linguistic equality, national unity, and Acadian advancement. Fluently bilingual, he emerged in the late 19th century as a spokesperson for the *Acadian Renaissance—the political and cultural coming of age of the Acadian population. DELLA M.M. STANLEY

Langevin, Hector-Louis (1826–1906). Born in Quebec City, Langevin became a lawyer and journalist, but it was his 40-year political career that made him well known. A moderate reformer and then a liberal-conservative of the George-Étienne *Cartier school, he was primarily interested in national politics even while serving as alderman (1856) and mayor of Quebec City (1858–61).

Elected to the legislative assembly of the *Province of Canada in 1857–8, he served as solicitor general, then as postmaster general. One of the Fathers of Confederation, he played an active part in the conferences at Charlottetown and Quebec in 1864 and London in 1866, arguing the necessity of a strong central power and defending the interests of Catholic French Canadians. After 1867 his life as an MP was not always easy, but through the important functions he performed in John A. *Macdonald's cabinet he helped to build the new country. By turns secretary of state and superintendent general of Indian affairs, minister of public works, and postmaster general, and as head of the Quebec wing of the Conservative Party following George-Étienne Cartier's death, he exercised genuine influence on the government. In 1885 he accepted Macdonald's position in the celebrated Riel case. His reputation in Quebec suffered, but the internal divisions and scandals within his party ended his career. He retired, in disgrace, in 1896. RÉAL BÉLANGER

Lapointe, Ernest (1876–1941), lawyer and parliamentarian, Mackenzie *King's Quebec lieutenant. It was Lapointe who secured King's election as Laurier's successor at the 1919 Liberal leadership convention. With the Liberal victory in 1921 Lapointe became minister of marine and fisheries, and in 1924 minister of justice. A Canadian nationalist, he helped Canada come of age when he signed the 1923 *Halibut Treaty with the United States without a British co-signatory. At the imperial conferences of the 1920s, he was a leader in obtaining dominion autonomy, which culminated in the 1931 *Statute of Westminster. In 1937 he was named to the imperial Privy Council. An appeaser in the 1930s, he repudiated the Canadian representative at the *League of Nations who proposed oil sanctions against Italy in the Ethiopian crisis. As justice minister, he favoured his home province, refusing to challenge the constitutionality of Duplessis's notorious *Padlock Act but disallowing Alberta's debt legislation. He championed *bilingualism and jobs for Quebeckers in the federal government. In 1939 Quebec's anti-war stance threatened to split the country; Lapointe won Quebec's support for the war by promising, with King's approval, that there would be no overseas *conscription—a promise that was broken after his death.
LITA-ROSE BETCHERMAN

La Salle, René-Robert Cavelier de (1643–87). Born in Rouen, La Salle, once a Jesuit novitiate, came to Canada in 1667. Hoping to discover the Ohio River and a route to China, he joined the Dollier/Galinée expedition (1669), saying he could speak Iroquois; on reaching the Seneca they learned he had lied, and parted company. Through the influence of Governor *Frontenac, he received letters of nobility (1673) and the grant of Fort Frontenac (Kingston, Ontario), where he initiated an illegal fur trade. In 1678, he received permission to explore westward to the Pacific. He built a series of trading posts from Niagara to the Illinois River and the ship *Griffon* (1679) to trade on Lakes Erie and Michigan. In 1683 he reached the Mississippi delta and persuaded Louis XIV to let him establish a colony there. Early in 1685, through a series of errors, his four ships with about 500 colonists missed the delta and came ashore at Matagorda Bay, Texas, with the loss of most supplies. As the ill-prepared colony was dying, the increasingly erratic La Salle stumbled eastward through the wilderness in search of the Mississippi. Desperate, some of his men assassinated him. La Salle could be persuasive and charming; he had considerable courage and stamina, but his paranoia, erratic behaviour, and ill-considered decisions destroyed him.

CONRAD HEIDENREICH

'last best West'. A popular image of, and phrase used to describe, the Canadian West in immigration pamphlets issued roughly between 1896 and 1914. The term was used to appeal to immigrants from the British Isles, Europe, and the United States. The phrase was so popular that it became the title of one of the most frequently reissued immigration pamphlets, published yearly with new information and a new cover but the same appealing title. To overseas immigrants, the phrase was a reminder that the American frontier was closed, but good cheap land was still available in Canada. To American farmers, drawn to their own west by the spirit of the frontier, it depicted the Canadian West as an extension of that frontier. To Canadian farmers who had emigrated south a generation earlier due to inadequate transportation facilities in the Canadian West, the phrase was designed to bring them back 'home' to the 'last best West'.

R. DOUGLAS FRANCIS

Late Loyalists. A term used for those American settlers in Upper and Lower Canada who failed to conform to the definition of United Empire *Loyalist, including the requirement that they had left what became the United States by the end of the Revolutionary War, or soon thereafter. Rather, the so-called Late Loyalists responded to invitations in 1792 by Lieutenant-Governor *Simcoe to settle in the newly created colony of Upper Canada, and by Lieutenant-Governor Clarke of Lower Canada when he declared the region north of the Vermont border open to colonization. Most of these settlers were attracted by relatively inexpensive and accessible land, as well as low taxes, but they were required to take oaths of allegiance before receiving titles to their land—hence the term, Late Loyalist. It conformed to Simcoe's belief that many people in the new republic remained loyal to Great Britain, while many others could be won back to their old allegiance. These settlers rapidly outnumbered their Loyalist predecessors, causing concerns for the loyalty of Upper Canada and the *Eastern Townships during the War of 1812.

J.I. LITTLE

Laurence, Margaret Wemyss (1927–87). Born in Neepawa, Manitoba, Laurence lived in England, then Africa, with her husband, Jack, who had been employed by the British government to build dams. From her years in Africa, she published a translation of Somali poetry, a novel and stories set in Ghana, and a memoir. In 1964 *The Stone Angel*, the first of her Manawaka novels, proclaimed her as a major novelist of international stature. In 1962 she moved to England with her children. In the next decade she published *A Jest of God*, *The Fire-Dwellers*, and *A Bird in the House*. *The Diviners* (1974) completed the Manawaka cycle for which she is best remembered. She returned to Canada in 1973, settling in Lakefield, Ontario. A founder of the Writers' Union of Canada, she was active in many causes devoted to international peace and understanding. She won two Governor General's Awards and was chancellor of Trent University, 1980–3. She also wrote *Long Drums and Cannons*, a study of prominent Nigerian writers; three children's books; and her autobiography, *Dance on the Earth* (1989).

CLARA THOMAS

Laurendeau, André (1912–68), journalist. Laurendeau was a French-Canadian nationalist, committed to the survival of French Canada in the modern industrial world. As a young man he was influenced by the social Catholicism of Emmanuel Mounier. In 1942 he played a prominent role in the Ligue pour la défence du Canada, campaigning for a 'no' vote in the plebiscite over *conscription. The success of this campaign in French Canada led to the formation of the *Bloc populaire, with Laurendeau as the provincial leader. After his election to the assembly in 1944 he criticized the *Duplessis government for its lack of interest in social reforms. Laurendeau resigned in 1947 to join the editorial staff of *Le Devoir*, where he became the editor-in-chief in 1958. Here he helped to redefine French-Canadian nationalism in response to the needs of an urban, industrial society. He continued to believe that French-Canadian survival was possible within the Canadian federal system, and as co-chairman of the Royal Commission on *Bilingualism and Biculturalism from 1963 he played an important role in recommending measures for linguistic and cultural duality.

H. BLAIR NEATBY

Laurentian thesis. The Laurentian thesis responded to the continentalist implications of the *frontier thesis by arguing that Canada was founded on an east–west axis—at the heart of which was the *St Lawrence River transportation system—and on the European exploitation of peculiarly northern resources, especially fur. 'The present Dominion emerged not in spite of geography but because of it', wrote H.A. *Innis in his seminal work, *The Fur Trade in Canada* (1930). The Laurentian thesis did for Canada what the frontier thesis had done for the United

States: it offered a compelling vision of the past that appealed to both the intellect and the imagination, and it offered a framework within which historians, economists, sociologists, literary critics, and others could pursue meaningful research for decades to come. It also provided a geographic basis of nationhood, which D.G. *Creighton transformed into a Romantic ideal in his hugely influential study of commerce and politics, *The Commercial Empire of the St Lawrence, 1760–1850* (1937). The dream of western commercial empire, he wrote, 'rose, like an exhalation', from the great river itself.

Like frontierism, however, the Laurentian idea conceived too narrowly of the nation whose history it sought to explain. It virtually ignored the Maritimes, except when it assumed the guise of its intellectual cousin, the *staples thesis. From a western perspective it seemed less an account of nation making than a justification for central Canadian imperial ambitions. Its influence waned as attention turned to more *'limited identities', and as historians everywhere grew sceptical of transcendent governing ideas. KENNETH C. DEWAR

Laurier, Wilfrid (1841–1919), prime minister 1896–1911. Born at St-Lin, Canada East, Laurier entered law school at McGill College in 1861 and practised law in Montreal until 1866. This period had a powerful influence on his future: he met his wife, Zoé Lafontaine, and formed strong links with the *Institut canadien, the literary circle and centre of the Montreal *rouges*, ardent defenders of radical liberal ideas. As first vice-president of the institute, 1864–6, he took on the ultramontane bishop Ignace *Bourget, who was so opposed to *liberalism. In 1867 Laurier began to practise law in Arthabaskaville. Adopting a moderate liberalism and rallying to Confederation—a cause he had earlier opposed—he was elected as a Liberal to the provincial assembly in 1871. He resigned in 1874 to stand for election to the House of Commons, where he remained for 45 years.

On 26 June 1877, in Quebec City, Laurier delivered a memorable speech on political liberalism that was intended to calm the Catholic clergy and improve his party's position. His argument for English-style moderate liberalism was so effective that the following October he was named minister of inland revenue in Alexander *Mackenzie's government. In 1885 the hanging of Louis *Riel gave him the opportunity to defend the cause of the Metis leader and at the same time promote his vision of a Canada founded on the union of and respect for different peoples following a moderate, tolerant path. Recognizing his value, Edward *Blake proposed that Laurier succeed him as leader of the *Liberal Party in June 1887. Grounded in two ideals—national unity and the unity of his party—he would retain this position, which he did not want, until his death.

Laurier set to work immediately. In 1891 he suffered a searing electoral defeat when John A. *Macdonald passionately opposed his plan for unlimited commercial *reciprocity with the United States. But a successful convention in Ottawa in 1893, together with the weakness of the Conservative Party and the controversy surrounding the *Manitoba schools question, carried him to power on 23 June 1896, at a time when the country was experiencing serious ethnic tensions. Laurier became Canada's first French-Canadian prime minister; he was to continue in office for 15 years.

In autumn 1896 Laurier settled the schools issue in Manitoba. In the Laurier–Greenway accord—a dangerous precedent—separate schools were not returned to the Catholic minority and only a few crumbs were conceded concerning the teaching of religion and language. In 1897, having put in place a tariff policy giving priority to imperial preference and begun his great project to develop the West through immigration, he travelled to England and received a knighthood. Then he frustrated imperialists by opposing any military, economic, or political federation of the empire, a policy he continued until 1911, although in 1899 he agreed, amid controversy, to send Canadian volunteers to the *Boer War in South Africa, to the disgust of nationalists in his party, including Henri *Bourassa. In 1903 he proposed the construction of a second transcontinental railway (later to prove a financial failure). His glory at its height, he won the election of 1904, and in 1905 established two new provinces, Alberta and Saskatchewan. A reflection of the West's development, the project nevertheless disregarded the rights of the Catholic minority, effectively putting an end to any hope of a bicultural country while once again provoking Quebec nationalists. Laurier carried the elections of 1908 despite accusations of scandal and an overly timid attempt at social policies. Guided, in effect, by his 19th-century conservative liberalism, he lacked sufficient understanding of the transformations his country was undergoing. He was finally driven from power on 21 September 1911 by two policies—the creation of a navy and limited commercial reciprocity with the United States—that brought together against him both imperialists and nationalists.

Effective in opposition, before 1914 he vigorously attacked the government of Robert *Borden, including its project of naval aid to the empire in 1912–13. During the Great War he staunchly supported Canada's voluntary participation, but firmly opposed *conscription and *Union government, and as a result was defeated in the dramatic elections of 1917. RÉAL BÉLANGER

Laval, François de (1623–1708), vicar apostolic of New France and bishop of Petraea (1659–74) and first bishop of Quebec (1674–88), was educated at the Jesuit colleges in La Flèche and Paris, renounced his seigneurial rights in 1647, and as a young priest embarked on a life of extreme asceticism and self-denial through association with zealots of the Société des bons amis and retreats at the Hermitage of Caen. He remained intolerant of non-Catholics and jealous of ecclesiastical authority in community affairs, and he favoured the *Jesuits over other religious communities. The political influence he wielded under the rule of the Compagnie de la Nouvelle-France in the colony was curtailed by Royal officials. In 1674 Louis XIV nominated him to the bishopric of Quebec created by Rome.

His episcopacy was marked by a long and unsuccessful campaign to prohibit brandy trafficking, restrict women religious to cloisters, and encourage frequent communion. He organized the *Séminaire de Québec to train colonial secular priests, enforced tithing, and promoted missionary work. He resigned in 1688 because of ill health and retired to the seminary. He died on 6 May 1708 and was buried in the cathedral; his remains were removed to the seminary chapel in 1878.

CORNELIUS J. JAENEN

La Vérendrye, Pierre Gaultier de Varennes et de (1685–1749). Born at Trois-Rivières, La Vérendrye fought in Canada and in France, where he was seriously wounded (1709). He returned to Canada (1712), married, and settled as a farmer and part-time fur trader. In 1726 he became partner to his brother Jacques-René, commander of the *poste du nord*, a fur-trade district on the north shore of Lake Superior. Pierre succeeded his brother (1728) and revived the dream of discovering the vast sea rumoured to exist in the western interior of Canada. To defray the cost of exploration he received (1731) a fur trade monopoly for the area northwest of Lake Superior, optimistically named the *Mer d'Ouest*. Progressing at a snail's pace, La Vérendrye's men reached Lake Winnipeg three years later, prompting orders to do less trading and more exploration. In December 1738 he reached the Missouri. The following year his son Louis-Joseph explored Lakes Manitoba and Winnipeg to the lower Saskatchewan River, and in 1742–3 Louis-Joseph and brother François crossed the American plains to the Big Horn Mountains. Expectations for a major discovery were high; with continuing negative results La Vérendrye was forced to resign in 1743. He was reappointed in 1746 but died in Montreal before he could take up his command.

CONRAD HEIDENREICH

law. The history of law in Canada involves two stories. The first concerns a succession of legal regimes, each gaining ascendancy over time but never entirely expunging its precursors. The other is about law reform and legal change within the dominant legal system. First, however, some definitions.

Canada's dominant legal system is called a 'common law' system. It is derived from English law. The laws regulating government and crime (together these are called 'public law') are based on common law. So is the rest of the law in 11 of the 13 provinces and territories: Quebec retains a legal system derived from its French heritage, while *Nunavut seeks to create a legal system blending Inuit and common law legal understandings. Common law is 'judge made': fundamental rules of law are articulated and found in the decisions of the *courts rendered in actual legal disputes ('cases') rather than in a legal code (as in 'civil law' systems) or in custom (as in many First Nations communities).

Confusingly, the term 'common law' is used in several different ways. Sometimes it denotes those laws standing apart from ecclesiastical law, customary law, and that part of the law traditionally administered by the Courts of Equity. Both church law and equity were once administered by separate courts as important, parallel, legal systems. Although equity no longer exists as a separate system, it remains a conceptually distinct field of law, and lawyers sometimes speak of law and equity as different things. Similarly, lawyers sometimes distinguish between common law (in the sense of judge-made legal rules) and statutory law (legal rules created by statute).

Historically, the law was said to be 'common' because it reflected the common customs of the realm rather than the peculiar local customs of particular places. Local custom is a recognized source of law, and customary law is valid provided it conflicts neither with statutes nor with fundamental common law principles. In practice, however, customary law is rarely encountered in the 21st century. The major exception concerns the laws of First Nations peoples: wherever strict legal tests relating to continuity of custom can be met, First Nations customs are accorded legal recognition. This is so as a matter of common law principle, but also under the express terms of Canada's written *constitution (s. 35 of the Constitution Act, 1982, protects 'existing aboriginal rights'). Areas in which customary law may be especially significant include marriage, inheritance, child custody, resource allocation, property rights, and self-governance.

'Civil law' also has several meanings, again depending on context. Civil law systems—as in Quebec, all of continental Europe, and much of the world outside the former British colonies—rely on a written code as the source of law, placing little emphasis on judge-made legal rules. Civil law is also sometimes used to refer to state law, as opposed to international law, church law, local customary law, or universal principles of legality. Confusingly, common law lawyers sometimes use the term 'civil law' to refer to the body of laws governing property, contract, and various private relationships. So used, it stands in contradistinction to 'public law', which is generally understood as encompassing constitutional law, the law regulating government (administrative law), *criminal law, and, in earlier times, the law of empire.

Three waves of law have swept over Canada. The laws of the various First Nations were in place before Europeans arrived, other legal systems finding foothold only as French and British colonization advanced. Because no new legal system ever entirely replaced its predecessors, strong elements of British, French, and Aboriginal legal heritages persist.

Shortly after the conquest, the 1774 *Quebec Act established that French law would govern private matters relating to such things as property ownership, employment, contract, and inheritance. As a British colony, of course, Quebec's public law followed English legal principle. When Upper Canada separated, it adopted English private law as it stood in 1792. This basic pattern was to persist thereafter. The empire and, later, federalism provided a public law framework, while matters relating to private law—'Property and Civil Rights in the Province', in the words of section 92(13), Constitution Act, 1867—were left to the separate colonies or provinces.

The most important historical development in public law has been the story of European imperialism and the subsequent movement from colony to independent state. Key markers along this path included the establishment of *responsible government, Confederation (1867), subsequent territorial expansion of the dominion, gradual development of independent *foreign policy, the creation of Canadian *citizenship (1947), the appointment of a Canadian-born *governor general (1952), and the adoption of a *national flag (1965). In the legal realm, three moments of constitutional development stand out as especially important: the *Statute of Westminster (1931), immunizing Canada from British legislation; abolition of appeals to the (British) Judicial Committee of the Privy Council (1949), making the *Supreme Court of Canada the country's highest court; and the Constitution Act, 1982, which 'patriated' the constitution, established an all-Canadian amending formula, and enacted a *Charter of Rights and Freedoms.

Many other important changes have taken place elsewhere in the public law realm. Criminal law in Canada is based on the English system. The constitution places jurisdiction over criminal law with the central government. The real world is messy, however. Provinces can prohibit things and some prohibitions can look like criminal law (e.g., impaired driving laws and other highway traffic offences).

Although it rarely happens, any private individual can begin a criminal prosecution. In practice, prosecutions are now most commonly begun by police officers and conducted by Crown attorneys (whose duty is said to be to see justice done, not to obtain a conviction at all costs). Long-standing legal principle establishes that an individual is to be treated as innocent until proven guilty 'beyond all reasonable doubt'. The common law heritage requires public trials (to prevent the abuse of secret tribunals) and that trial by jury be available in serious cases.

Canada enacted a Criminal Code in 1892, expressing a large number of common law principles in statutory form. Of the many amendments since that time, few have been fundamental. The most significant of these include the abolition of killing as state punishment (the 'death penalty'), numerous (mostly ill-advised) legislative enactments criminalizing psycho-active drugs, and a large number of reforms introduced in the early 21st century either as part of the 'war on drugs' or in response to the terrorist threat that became apparent with attacks on the United States on 11 September 2001.

In administrative law, there was a notable growth in state institutions and regulatory apparatuses from the mid-19th century onward. It was recognized that an increasingly mobile, complex, and inter-connected world required state coordination. Legal doctrine moved from outright hostility to state administration early in the 20th century to an approach more accepting of government—always within the framework of the rule of law—during the Depression and in the years following the Second World War.

The decades following that war also saw significant legal developments aimed at protecting human rights within Canada. These included Supreme Court of Canada rulings protecting an 'implied bill of rights' (1950s), Prime Minister John *Diefenbaker's Canadian Bill of Rights (1960), the enactment of both federal and provincial human rights codes, and the adoption of the Canadian Charter of Rights and Freedoms (1982). (Legislation introduced in the aftermath of the aforementioned 11 September terrorist attacks profoundly warps Canadian law in the opposite direction.)

In the private law realm, Canadian common law has by and large 'tracked' wider movements within the common law world. The common law as we know it is a systematized body of legal principles derived from court decisions over the centuries. It was significantly reshaped during the 19th century as scholars reduced inchoate legal principles to systematically arranged expositions of the law (called the 'textbook' tradition), as law reporting became established on a professional basis, as *legal education became formalized, and as concerted efforts were made to reform the law by modernizing it and tidying up some of the messiness of a system that had accreted over centuries.

Major changes in private law over Canada's history have included the fusion of 'law' and 'equity'—the two great systems of judge-made law—into one. Canadian colonies/provinces followed English statutory reforms of 1875, each at different times. Ontario's Judicature Act merged the two court systems in 1881. An expansive law of negligence was created starting in the 19th century and developing explosively from the 1930s onward. The simple principle that a person owes a duty to avoid injury to anyone who might foreseeably be harmed by his or her actions has swept aside many fine categories of civil wrong-doing that had developed piecemeal. The last two centuries have seen a concerted effort (hotly contested at times) to remove a number of legal disabilities attaching to women, particularly married women.

Property law became increasingly rationalized and simplified, rendering land a more liquid asset than it had been. The Torrens system of land registration (introduced in Manitoba in 1885, the North-West Territories in 1887) and other statutory systems of land registry have replaced much more complex common law approaches to land law.

The law of contract moved powerfully toward laissez-faire ('freedom of contract') principles during the 19th century, but this in turn was balanced somewhat later as both consumer protection legislation and new judge-made legal doctrines emerged to prevent abuse.

Increasing recognition that people's private lives are their own has produced a virtual revolution in the laws regulating marriage, *divorce, and sexuality (areas governed by a mixture of federal and provincial law). The direction has generally been towards greater rights for women and towards greater correspondence with the principle enunciated by Justice Minister Pierre *Trudeau (1967–8) that 'There's no place for the state in the bedrooms of the nation'.

W. WESLEY PUE

See also QUEBEC CIVIL LAW; LEGAL PROFESSION.

law societies. The organizations of lawyers that govern the *legal profession in each province and territory of Canada. Created by ordinance or statute, there are now 14 of them; the first to be established, in 1797, was the Law Society of Upper Canada in what is now Ontario; the most recent is the Law Society of Nunavut (1999). In Quebec there are two governing bodies: the Chambre des notaires du Québec, and the Barreau du Québec. Elsewhere in Canada, the legal profession has been unified; lawyers must belong to the law society in their particular jurisdiction.

The law societies regulate admission to membership in the profession, set professional standards, and discipline members. Traditionally, they provided *legal education but, from the late 19th century on, university law schools gradually took over this function. Dalhousie Law School, founded in 1883 in Nova Scotia, was the first to supplant the provincial law society in this respect; in Ontario the law society did not give up its law school until 1957. The law societies still require a period of articling, followed usually by a bar-admissions course and examinations, before a licence to practise is conferred. The provincial law societies are autonomous but since 1926 they have met in a national umbrella organization, now titled the Federation of Law Societies of Canada. This group attempts to set standards for national uniformity in legal education, admission requirements, and so on.

W.P.J. MILLAR AND R.D. GIDNEY

Lawson, George (1827–95), botanist. Lawson was born in Fife, son of Alexander Lawson and Margaret McEwan. His life in the Scottish countryside tinged his love of nature with a Baconian penchant for organizing people and disseminating information. From 1848 at the University of Edinburgh he served as an officer of the Botanical Society of Edinburgh and a demonstrator in J.H. Balfour's botanical laboratory, imbibing Balfour's pioneering biogeographical approaches to northern plants.

In 1858, with a DPhil from Giessen, Germany, Lawson became professor of chemistry and natural history at Queen's College, Kingston, promoting science as experimentation, observation, and application. In 1860 he founded the Botanical Society of Canada, publishing its *Annals* in 1861. In 1863 Lawson left Queen's to become professor of chemistry and mineralogy at Dalhousie University, Halifax, where he helped organize the Technological Institute and joined the Central Board of Agriculture of Nova Scotia. A charter member of the *Royal Society of Canada and president in 1887, he founded the Botanical Club of Canada in 1891 to encourage plant collecting throughout the country's vast territories. Never able to collate a complete catalogue of Canadian plants, Lawson nevertheless inspired a generation of Canadian contributions in botany's transition to a modern science.

SUZANNE ZELLER

Leacock, Stephen (1869–1944). A dedicated university professor and internationally recognized public speaker, Leacock contributed to Canadian letters in a number of ways, including countless essays on economics, history, and political science. An avid amateur historian, he contributed a volume on *responsible government to the important Makers of Canada series in 1907 as well as three volumes in 1914 to the heavily promoted Chronicles of Canada series. He also wrote two popular biographies: *Mark Twain* (1932) and *Charles Dickens: His Life and Work* (1933). Despite his success as a skilled essayist, he is best remembered as Canada's most celebrated humorist, and, as he openly declared in the autobiographical preface to his best-known work, *Sunshine Sketches of a Little Town* (1912), he was a writer who 'would sooner have written Alice in Wonderland than the whole Encyclopaedia Britannica'. A book that deals determinedly with questions of perception and self-knowledge, *Sunshine Sketches* introduces readers to what becomes a familiar constellation in Leacock's writing: a deftly managed combination of subtle ironies, genial satire, and kindly humour deployed in support of what critics have generally described as Leacock's tory-humanist vision. Distinct from the more rigid Tory *conservatism, his is a view of the world that underscores the value of tradition, order, and a sense of social responsibility.

DAVID STAINES

League for Social Reconstruction. The first organization of left-wing intellectuals in Canada, the LSR was founded during the winter of 1931–2, mainly as a response to the *Great Depression. Chiefly the brainchild of University of Toronto historian Frank H. *Underhill and McGill University law professor Frank R. *Scott, it began among academics in Toronto and Montreal. Quickly spreading beyond the universities, by early 1933 (the high point) the league had 20 branches from Montreal to Victoria and perhaps 600–700 members, no more than 50 of them professors. The Montreal and Toronto branches were largest and survived longest, and all six national presidents—Underhill, Scott, Leonard *Marsh, Louise Parkin, W. Jarvis McCurdy, and G.M.A. Grube—were drawn from them.

Never formally linked with a political party, the LSR made its sympathies clear by electing the socialist MP James S. *Woodsworth its honorary national president. After 1932 the league informally associated itself with the new party led by Woodsworth, the Co-operative Commonwealth Federation, whose *Regina Manifesto (1933) was drafted by several LSR members led by Underhill. The league's social-democratic ideas, succinctly stated in a ten-point manifesto (1932), found fullest expression in the books *Social Planning for Canada* (1935) and its abridgement, *Democracy Needs Socialism* (1938). These volumes called for a planned and socialized economy, for greatly improved social services, and for a foreign policy that would elevate local Canadian interests above the obligations resulting from membership in the British Empire and the League of Nations. LSR members also stated their views in booklets on current topics that appeared at irregular intervals from 1934 to 1941, and in the monthly **Canadian Forum*, which the league came to control in 1936.

Its strength waning even before war began in Europe in September 1939, the LSR ceased to exist in 1942. By this time the needs of the resurgent CCF seemed more pressing than the survival of a little band of intellectuals. Its influence on the CCF was substantial; its influence on the development of a *welfare state in Canada is still open to debate. MICHIEL HORN

League of Nations. In 1919 at the *Paris Peace Conference US President Woodrow Wilson outlined his vision of an international institution with a mandate to prevent war: the League of Nations. Prime Minister Robert *Borden wanted Canada to join, but there was some question about whether the British government represented Canada through the British Empire seat as well as whether Canada was eligible for election to one of the non-permanent seats of the council of the league. In the end Canada assumed its seat in the general assembly as an independent member.

Once in, Canada had neither interest nor faith in the potential of the League to maintain peace. Canadian representatives objected to Article X, the collective security clause of the league covenant, lest it embroil Canada in war. Throughout the 1920s Canada proposed that Article X be abolished or diluted. Nonetheless, there were some positive signs of commitment. In 1925 Walter Riddell was appointed Canada's permanent representative to the League of Nations. However, Canada's mission in Geneva was chronically under-staffed and under-funded. As international tensions mounted in the 1930s, Canada remained unwilling to support the league's increasingly fruitless efforts to keep the peace. In 1935 Riddell suggested adding oil, coal, iron, and steel to the list of sanctions to be applied to Italy in light of its unprovoked attack on Ethiopia. The international press dubbed the ban on oil 'the Canadian proposal', and Canada briefly found itself in the international spotlight. The glare was too much for Mackenzie *King, re-elected in the midst of the crisis. He wanted to fire Riddell, but in the end was satisfied with a rebuke. In 1936 King led a delegation to Geneva and announced to the general assembly that collective security had failed. Canada was not an upstanding member of the League, but then neither was any other country. At least Canada was a member—unlike the United States, which never joined the organization it had forced on the rest of the international community.

FRANCINE McKENZIE

Leduc. The dramatic eruption of oil, belching flame, and smoke at Imperial Oil's Leduc No. 1 well south of Edmonton on 13 February 1947 signalled that Alberta's long-anticipated oil boom was under way. American capital poured in and Alberta was transformed. Within six years, 16 new oil fields were discovered. By 1960, the value of oil and gas products exported from the province surpassed the returns earned from agriculture, and regional economic power began to shift from Winnipeg to Calgary and Edmonton, the industry's rapidly growing refining and administrative centres. The burgeoning oil industry also reinforced Alberta's American orientation, inherited from the earlier cattlemen's frontier, and strengthened its longstanding desire for a larger voice in national affairs. DAVID H. BREEN

Lefroy, Sir John Henry (1817–90), soldier and scientist, born and died in England. Graduating from the Royal Military Academy in 1834, Lefroy joined the Royal Artillery. In 1839 he helped staff a worldwide network of British observatories organized by Edward Sabine, RA, and the Royal Society of London to study the earth's magnetism. After a stint at St Helena, Lefroy directed the Toronto observatory from 1842. With one assistant he surveyed *geomagnetic variations northwest to the Arctic Circle in 1843–4, publishing important scientific results in 1855. Lefroy also undertook detailed magnetic and meteorological observations at Toronto, introducing photographic and self-registering instruments to ensure a continuous record of change as settlement progressed. Active in Toronto society (he married John Beverley *Robinson's daughter in 1846) and its institutions, he evinced an evangelical zeal for education. Returning to England in 1853, he persuaded the provincial government to continue the Toronto observatory—and Egerton *Ryerson to require daily weather observations of grammar school headmasters. Internationally respected as a specialist on the aurora borealis who also pioneered a continental weather-warning system, Lefroy never elaborated the general geomagnetic theory that he sought. He capped his distinguished scientific career as a military adviser and colonial administrator. SUZANNE ZELLER

legal education. The training of practitioners of the *law in Canada long depended on articling. A clerk would sign on with a practitioner who would transmit the essential elements of professional legal practice. Much time was spent drawing up and writing various procedural actions and attending to court business. In addition, the clerk was invited to explore in depth the great legal authors and textbooks. At the end of this period, an examination would authorize admission to the bar.

Legal education was introduced into Canadian *universities in a limited way in the middle of the 19th century. In Quebec, McGill and Laval welcomed their first candidates for the baccalaureate in law in 1848 and 1854 respectively. In the common law provinces, Dalhousie was the first to offer a complete law program, in 1883. These faculties and those that followed developed slowly and often haltingly. Until the mid-20th century the professorate consisted essentially of lawyers who lectured on specific topics. Only a few brave career professors, such as Frederick Parker Walton at McGill and Augustus Henry Frazer Lefroy at Toronto, distinguished themselves.

For many years completion of a program in a law faculty was optional. Outside Quebec, articling remained the usual method of training until the Second World War. Clerks attended professional institutions such as the

Osgoode Hall Law School in Toronto or the Vancouver Law School rather than university faculties. Quebec universities—no doubt because of the province's civil law tradition—succeeded more rapidly in establishing themselves as the privileged sites for the training of legal practitioners. After the war, the faculties sought to obtain greater autonomy with respect to the bars and to establish better-structured programs. Dean Cecil Augustus 'Caesar' Wright of the University of Toronto waged a memorable, ultimately successful, battle against the powerful Law Society of Upper Canada to confirm the university's role in legal training.

The study of law has long been seen as contributing to the establishment of a social elite. Professional schools and law faculties have served as nurseries for politicians and business leaders. The difficulty that women experienced gaining admission to legal training and practice was typical of the obstacle course that minorities in general faced.

In the second half of the 20th century, the development of a career professorate facilitated the evolution of instruction and research. Whereas the faculties had been confined to an essentially professional perspective, they now opened up to new fields of interest—*labour law, for example—and approaches influenced by the social sciences. Such shifts were often regarded with suspicion in professional circles unfamiliar with socially engaged research. Greater sensitivity to social change has nevertheless become an important part of legal education, reinforced by the Canadian *Charter of Rights and Freedoms, which came into effect in 1982.

SYLVIO NORMAND

legal profession. In many societies legal work is done on behalf of other people by many individuals, only some of whom are known as lawyers. Today's law work is undertaken by, among others, accountants, patent agents, realtors, immigration agents, barristers and solicitors, notaries public, and notaires under *Quebec civil law. Because boundaries were even less clear in the past, I focus here on the origins of the *organized* legal profession—the people most commonly called 'lawyers'—in common law Canada.

Outside of New France/Quebec/Lower Canada, early British North American authorities assumed that as the colonies flourished their legal structures would come to resemble professional structures in England. England had three legal professions of consequence in the 18th century. Barristers (the 'bar' or 'upper branch' of the legal profession) enjoyed exclusive rights of audience in the superior courts. Attorneys and solicitors constituted the 'lower branch': the former acted as agents in *courts of law; the latter as agents in the courts of chancery. All three gave legal advice but only barristers had right of audience in the Superior Court. The bar enjoyed privileges of self-governance through ancient guild structures (the Inns of Court), while the lower branches were regulated by the courts and, sometimes, by statute. The professional associations of solicitors or attorneys were entirely voluntary.

Because the embryonic legal and social systems of new settler colonies could not sustain complex structures of professionalism, 'lawyers' were at first accorded formal recognition by colonial governors and then by the courts. When Upper Canada was created, its chief justice, William Osgoode, created an English-style judiciary by his Judicature Act, 1794. This clearly required an English-style legal profession—something a 'bush' colony, however staunchly Loyalist, could not readily provide. The immediate gap was filled by Upper Canadian legislation of 1794 authorizing Governor *Simcoe to license up to 16 lawyers during the next two years. Thereafter, Upper Canada reverted to the more common colonial practice whereby suitably qualified individuals were called to the bar by the chief justice.

In 1797 Upper Canada's assembly passed the Law Society Act, creating the Law Society of Upper Canada and making it a new type of governing body of lawyers. This was a radical departure from both colonial and British practice. The Law Society of England and Wales would not attain similar status until decades later and, although some Upper Canadian lawyers imagined themselves governed by an 'Inn of Court', they were more than a little pretentious in so thinking: ancient guilds could not be legislated into existence.

Three principles established in 1797 came to serve as a model for most subsequent professional development in British North America. First, admission was to be determined in the ordinary circumstance by the organized profession itself. Second, all lawyers were required to be members of the Law Society and all would be governed by it. There would not, in other words, be either ungoverned lawyers or separate institutions of governance for 'barristers', 'solicitors', and 'attorneys' (most Canadian lawyers became both barrister and solicitor, the title of attorney falling into disuse during the 19th century). Third, the organized legal profession was mandated both to improve itself and to protect the profession.

Many leading Canadian lawyers conceived of professional organizations as having a central role to play in protecting British constitutionalism, the rule of law, orderliness, and good government. Although the American and French Revolutions had revealed that radical lawyers could cause considerable trouble, colonial lawyers viewed the legal profession in a more positive light, as crucial to the task of building the social cohesion on which colonial, dominion, or national unity was founded. The organized profession sought to contribute to this as a proactive agent of state building.

Archdeacon John *Strachan advocated such a role for lawyers in 1826, a call taken up by the Law Society of Upper Canada in reforms that immediately followed his intervention (these included building Osgoode Hall as a centre of lawyers' education). The 'mission' of organized professionalism was transformed. Reimagined, its purpose was to guard against the admission of inadequately socialized individuals (the conceits of a masculinist profession made it particularly difficult for women to gain a professional foothold until well into the 20th century); to expose neophytes to educational and socialization processes directed towards forming lawyers who could embody British constitutionalism; to ensure the ethical conduct of lawyers once admitted; and to expel those who failed to live up to their calling. Similar missions attached to the work of the *Canadian Bar Association during the first half of the 20th century. Following the Second World War, however, the organized legal professions came to view their tasks in more narrowly technocratic terms. Rapid development of higher education, the confirmation of the university (rather than professional apprenticeship) as the exclusive route of entry to the legal profession, and significant demographic and economic transformations profoundly altered the composition and ethos of legal professions across Canada. W. WESLEY PUE

Légaré, Joseph (1795–1855). An 'artiste engagé', Légaré was much involved in the political life of his troubled times. Known as a *Patriote, he was imprisoned in Quebec in 1837 but released shortly thereafter. In 1849 he joined *Papineau's Annexation Party, which proposed union with the United States, but he ended his life as a legislative councillor in Quebec. Légaré was self-taught as an artist, learning his craft by copying the paintings of the Desjardins Collection, a group of religious paintings imported from France after the revolution. In his paintings he documented the main events in the life of the people in Quebec: *Cholera Plague in Quebec* (1832), *The Fire at St Roch* (1845), *Scene near Château Richer* (1849). He painted many landscapes; his *Landscape with Wolfe Monument* (*c.* 1840) at the Musée du Québec is probably his best-known painting. Lord Elgin, George III, and Queen Victoria were also his subjects. His own collection of paintings and engravings, which he declared in 1833 'the richest ever known in Canada', is now part of the Quebec Seminary Collection. FRANÇOIS-MARC GAGNON

Léger, Paul-Émile (1904–91). Born in Valleyfield, Quebec, Léger was educated in Montreal and Paris and ordained in 1929 as a member of the Sulpician Order. His early years in the priesthood were spent in Paris and in Fukuoka, Japan, where he established a Sulpician seminary. Returning in 1939, he taught briefly and then served seven years as vicar-general of Valleyfield before leaving Canada again to become rector of the Pontifical Canadian College in Rome.

In 1950 Léger began a distinguished career as archbishop of Montreal. Elevated to the rank of cardinal in 1953, he built a reputation for commitment to social justice, ecumenism, and educational reform. His increasingly progressive views made him a sympathetic supporter of the church reforms associated with the Second *Vatican Council. He served as a member of the influential preparatory commission of the council, 1959–62, and was a leading Canadian participant in the council's proceedings, 1962–5. In 1967 he retired from the archbishopric of Montreal and went to Cameroon as a missionary to lepers and the physically disabled, returning occasionally to raise funds for his work. In 1979 he retired to Montreal, although he remained active in relief work, especially among Southeast Asian refugees. TERRENCE MURPHY

leisure. Intimately connected with work, and dependent on a large number of variables—including gender, class, age, ethnicity, health, season, and moral values—leisure is a relative idea. As paid labour became the norm, leisure and work were separated, and each took on a formal meaning. Leisure has been experienced as enjoyment and community building, but also as struggle—to gain the *nine-hour day in the 19th century, for example, or the five-day work week in the 20th. It has been a site of generational conflict and the redefinition of gender behaviour, as the uproar caused by young women riding bicycles attests. Leisure has also served to create and reinforce social ties around ethnic groups, schools, voluntary associations, and workplaces.

Forced idleness during the long months of winter long ago led to organized entertainment to counter boredom. During his first winter at *Port-Royal (1606–7), Samuel de *Champlain founded the *Ordre de Bon Temps, a dining society. Later, fur traders in the **pays d'en haut* held their own 'grand rendez-vous'. Throughout the 19th century Canadians found informal ways to battle *winter, through visiting, dancing, *music, eating, and, for the intemperate, the pleasures of rum or ale.

The promotion of respectable or 'improving' leisure was the aim of the late-19th-century middle classes who, through the rational recreation movement, sought to lure working men away from the pleasures of alcohol, sex, and violence by promoting leisure activities connected to self-improvement, personal health, and values that would create good workers. Rational recreation was fiercely resisted by those who preferred the *tavern, the brothel, and the streets, but the movement helped shape ideas about class-appropriate leisure.

Religion and ethnicity also influenced notions of leisure. Once a week, well into the second half of the 20th century, Sabbath observance and leisure time often seemed incompatible: some Protestants' very strict notion of proper Sunday activity clashed with the only day most employees had free, while Saturday night, with its connection to payday and sleeping in, held particular pleasure for many workers. The calendar year brought some feast days unique to Canada. From 1880 Acadians celebrated the Feast of the Assumption of the Blessed Virgin Mary on 15 August, since 1834 French Canadians have celebrated St-Jean-Baptiste Day on 24 June, and the Mi'kmaq Feast of Ste Anne has been held on 26 July since 1633. Other national days were celebrated, such as the English St George's Day (23 April), the Irish Catholic St Patrick's Day (17 February), and the Scots St Andrew's Day (30 November). Irish Protestants and their anti-Catholic sympathizers in the *Orange Order paraded and picnicked on 12 July, a leisure activity that could lead to violence clashes with Catholic neighbours.

With increased separation between work and play, and with paid vacations and the establishment of *public holidays such as Christmas, New Year's Day, and Labour Day, leisure time became more regulated. While the rhythms of work in an agrarian society might be determined by nature, and the interconnection of work and leisure continued in the form of *'bees', in urban industrial centres a wage connected to the clock separated labour and spare time. With *urbanization leisure became more formal, as organized activities, clubs, and associations were established among prosperous city dwellers, the Montreal Curling Club (1807), for example, and the Royal Montreal Golf Club (1873), the first golf club in North America. Urban male elites adopted Native activities such as *lacrosse, while also enjoying *rowing, racing, thoroughbred *horse racing, and *team sports. Snowshoeing was enjoyed by both men and women. In the late 19th century *baseball was probably the most popular spectator sport but *hockey was gaining popularity, especially among the middle and upper classes. Watching *professional sport continues to be one of the most popular forms of leisure for Canadian men.

Leisure time could be spent publicly or within the home. Singalongs using sheet music and accompanied by parlour piano and ukulele were particularly popular. In the Depression of the 1930s, hobbies and board and card games gained in popularity as unemployment increased the time available for 'leisure' but economic conditions limited options. More publicly, circuses, travelling fairs, annual events such as winter carnivals and *exhibitions, provided leisure. *Theatre, though not universally condoned, was popular. Canadians saw both local amateurs and professional touring companies from Britain, France, and the United States. The first building specifically for theatre opened in Halifax 1846.

For *children, leisure often meant playing on their own with toys and games, or they could take advantage of the playgrounds and parks that had been established in the late 19th century to keep them safe. Adolescents sometimes had access to the YMCA and the YWCA and later, in cities such as Toronto, Montreal, Winnipeg, and Sydney, the Young Men's Hebrew Association.

In the 20th century leisure was increasingly marked by commercialism and the role of technologies such as *automobiles, airplanes, radio, movies, television, computers, and video recorders. The first movie theatre in Canada was probably Vancouver's Schulberg Electric (1902). By 1914 cinemas were showing silent pictures across the country. These films were especially important to adolescents, who were increasingly likely to spend their spare time apart from their families. In doing so, they created a *youth culture identified with leisure: dancehalls and roadhouses, and eventually drive-ins, fast food, rock 'n' roll, and video and computer games.

Somewhat ironically, transportation technology opened up wilderness for recreational use. Growing urbanization led many Canadians to seek nature through *canoeing, camping, hiking, and skiing. Trains, and later automobiles, revolutionized transportation patterns, and middle-class Canadians visited the vacation areas of Muskoka, the Laurentians, or the Rockies. Working-class families might spend a week in a rooming house at *Niagara Falls, take the ferry for a day trip to Toronto Island, or visit the amusement parks of Sohmer and Dominion Park in Montreal or Sunnyside in Toronto. Ultimately, rising standards of living and cheaper air travel opened the possibility of winter vacations in the south.

Not all the new technologies took Canadians outside the home. Radio was likely to be experienced by the whole family. The association of hockey and Saturday night began in 1931 with the first NHL broadcast. Television, introduced in 1952, kept people at home, thus having a serious impact on movie theatres and other forms of recreation. Observers in the 1960s commented that only bingo was holding its own.

Commercial recreation in the form of films, radio, and television raised concerns about Americanization, as did the magazines and comic books that crossed the border. Reflecting this unease, the *Massey Commission (1949–51), with its elite notion of culture, put forth a perhaps unrealistic vision of how Canadians should be spending their leisure time. Earlier governments had also become involved in citizen's leisure activities with the establishment of national and provincial parks. After 1945, this role expanded in the nascent *welfare state as leisure activities, at least briefly, were regarded as a means to promote democracy and active citizenship. Attempts were made to integrate immigrants and marginal communities through organized sports and crafts.

Although much leisure is now commercialized, it would be a mistake to ignore the continuing importance of family and associations. Leisure continues to have a fluid definition. Activities that once would have been considered work—gardening, fishing, hunting, baking, sewing, woodworking—can now often be seen as leisure pastimes. The promise of a post-industrial leisure-rich society, much vaunted in the 1960s, has not yet come to pass; instead, many Canadians suffer stress from either too much work, or too little. SUZANNE MORTON

Le Loutre, Jean-Louis (1711–72), French priest and missionary. Le Loutre studied at seminaries in Paris and was ordained in 1737. The same year, he arrived in Louisbourg and shortly thereafter was living among the Mi'kmaq of Cape Breton in order to learn their language. In 1738, the abbé Le Loutre began his much-contested work as missionary of the Mi'kmaq of mainland Nova Scotia; British authorities and even some of his French contemporaries saw him more as an agent of French military interests rather than a missionary of the Roman Catholic Church. Knowing that he was a key player in French plans to recapture Nova Scotia, the British authorities wanted him dead or alive. No great friend of neutrality, Le Loutre fiercely encouraged the ongoing war between the Mi'kmaq and the British in Nova Scotia and even threatened Acadians with religious sanctions if they did not remove themselves to French-controlled territories near Fort Beauséjour. Captured by the British in 1755, he was jailed and released at the end of the war in 1763. He died in Nantes in 1772 after spending several years helping

Acadian families that had settled in Brittany as a consequence of the *Grand dérangement. MAURICE BASQUE

Lemieux, Jean-Paul (1904–90). After studies at the Montreal School of Fine Arts and the Colarossi Academy in Paris, Lemieux taught painting, first in Montreal but mainly at the Quebec School of Fine Arts (1937–65). In paintings such as *La Fête-Dieu à Québec* (1944), he commented ironically on the deeply Catholic and conformist society of Quebec in the 1940s. A Canada Council grant gave him the opportunity to travel in France in 1954–5, and when he returned he saw the Canadian landscape as no one had seen it before him: vast expanses of snow, a small prairie with 'a road that leads nowhere', low horizons, grey sky. But Lemieux insisted that he was not only a landscape painter. He loved to paint the people of Quebec, sometimes in front of the vast spaces in his landscapes. Immensely popular, Lemieux was much honoured during his lifetime, with retrospectives at the National Gallery of Canada in 1967 and the Musée du Québec in 1991.
FRANÇOIS-MARC GAGNON

leprosy. Leprosy's origins in Canada are enveloped in speculation and folklore. Some sources claim the disease arrived in New Brunswick in the early 1800s from a French vessel run aground near Caraquet. Others identify a fugitive from a Norwegian leper hospital as the original source. Still others allege that the Acadian diaspora returning to the Maritimes from Louisiana carried the bacillus.

Leprosy first made inroads in northern New Brunswick during the 1820s. Escalating public panic led to the construction of a lazaretto on Sheldrake Island in 1844, relocated to Tracadie in 1849. More custodial than curative, this facility was humanized by the arrival of the Religious Hospitallers of St Joseph in 1868. Along with the lazaretto's physician, Dr A.C. Smith, who became an international authority on leprosy, they pressed for major reforms.

In the late 19th and early 20th centuries, Canada's response to leprosy took on exaggerated proportions when the disease appeared in British Columbia. In 1891, the D'Arcy Island leper colony was established for a preponderantly Chinese patient population, doubly stigmatized by leprophobia and anti-Asian sentiment. Harsh conditions were eased in 1924, when the more humanely run Bentinck Island replaced the earlier colony. Leprosy in Cape Breton was confirmed in the 1880s, and in 1897 several Icelandic immigrants in Manitoba were diagnosed. By the 1940s and 1950s patients in Tracadie came from China, Malta, Russia, and Lithuania. Yet, numbers steadily declined, and the Bentinck Island lazaretto closed in 1957, Tracadie in 1965. In 1998 there were only three reported cases in Canada.

Canada boasts historic links to leprosy in both the mission field and laboratory. The Mission to Lepers (now the Leprosy Mission) established its senior national auxiliary in Canada in 1892. Quebec-born Armand Frappier (1904–91) promoted the study of leprosy at the Institut Armand-Frappier, founded in Montreal in 1938. Both agencies continue to operate, a legacy of Canada's brief encounter with one of humankind's most myth-laden diseases. LAURIE C.C. STANLEY-BLACKWELL

Lesage, Jean (1912–80), Quebec premier 1960–6. Elected a member of the federal Parliament in 1945, Jean Lesage became the leader of the provincial Liberal Party in 1958. The death of Maurice *Duplessis in 1959, the sudden death of the new *Union nationale leader, Paul Sauvé, on 2 January 1960, and the inability of his successor, Antonio Barrette, to rally his party, helped Lesage lead the Liberals to victory in the 1960 provincial election. Under his government Quebec society went through a period of political, social, and economic change known as the *Quiet Revolution, and the provincial state became the principal agent of change. With the slogan 'Maître chez nous', Lesage received a second mandate as premier in 1962 and went ahead with Hydro-Québec's plan to take over the hydroelectric power companies outside of Montreal. He presided over important social reforms such as the creation of the Ministry of Education and the Quebec Pension Plan; inaugurated the Maison du Québec in Paris on the advice of George-Emile Lapalme, who believed that Quebec should develop closer relations with France; and developed relations with francophone minority groups. Lesage lost power during the 1966 election but remained head of the Liberal Party until the election of Robert Bourassa as leader in 1970. MARCEL MARTEL

Lescarbot, Marc (*c.* 1570–1642), lawyer and author. Lescarbot came to Acadia in 1606 and remained until the following summer. Travelling widely, he came to understand the colonization and commercial opportunities offered by the colony. He studied the ways of life of the Aboriginal people, whom he considered more civilized than Europeans. His findings and ideas were recorded in various publications. His *Histoire de la Nouvelle-France*, published in 1609 (reprinted in 1907–14 by the Champlain Society), gave an account of the natural and human resources of the colony. This first historian of North America criticized the search for instant riches by the European countries and promoted colonization based on the resources of the land. Lescarbot is known also as a poet and a playwright. His **Théâtre de Neptune*, the first theatrical production in North America, was presented in *Port-Royal in 1606 and put both Europeans and Aboriginals on stage. Upon returning to France, he resumed his law practice. JEAN DAIGLE

Lévesque, René (1922–87), Quebec premier 1976–85. While working as a liaison agent in the American army during the Second World War, Lévesque discovered the horrors of the Nazi extermination camps, which contributed to his aversion to extremism and anti-democratic regimes. Thereafter he worked as a journalist, first on radio, then television, where he displayed his ability as a communicator. The Radio-Canada strike of 1959 brought out his nationalist convictions. Entering politics, in 1960 he became a minister in the Liberal government of Jean *Lesage and played an active role in the *Quiet Revolution. In 1962 he persuaded the government to nationalize the private electricity companies. In the course of his work he found Quebec's powers within the Canadian federal system too limited. Following an unsuccessful proposal that the Liberal Party opt for *sovereignty-association, in 1968 he founded the *Parti Québécois, dedicated to achieving that goal, and in 1976 he led the party to victory. His government adopted a number of progressive reforms, among them a law to make the financing of political parties more democratic and transparent, and Bill 101, making French the official language of Quebec. In the referendum of May 1980, 60 per cent of voters rejected sovereignty-association. Re-elected in 1981, Lévesque had to manage a difficult economic situation, which led him to take a firm stand against the state employees then on strike. In 1984, after the election of Brian *Mulroney's Conservatives in Ottawa, Lévesque announced that sovereignty-association would not be an issue in the next election, sparking a crisis in his own government. Following the resignation of several of his ministers, and despite the support of party members, an exhausted Lévesque resigned in June 1985 and returned to journalism. His death on 1 November 1987 generated a large wave of emotion and sympathy.

JEAN-FRANÇOIS CARDIN

liberalism. Canadian liberalism derives from the intellectual and political tradition of liberalism in Europe and the United States. Historically identified with the rise of the bourgeoisie or the middle class, liberalism rejected aristocratic and theological institutions and emphasized the rights of the individual. Both the American and French Revolutions drew upon the arguments of John Locke and Scottish Enlightenment figures in rejecting aristocracy and restrictions on individual rights. In Canada, the conquest occurred before the end of the French monarchy, but liberal ideas did cross the Atlantic and become part of the political debate in Quebec after 1776.

In English Canada, American settlers did not reject the *monarchy but they did bring with them North American notions of individual rights, ones that were quickly expressed in the debate about the *Family Compact in Upper Canada. In Lower and Upper Canada, foes of the established order used arguments for liberty derived from the French and American Revolutions and the British liberal tradition. The last of these, British liberalism, became an increasingly powerful force in the politics of British North America as hundreds of thousands of British immigrants influenced by the lively debates about individual liberties settled in Canada. Claims of aristocratic privilege, whether from church or state, landed on harsh soil in North America. In Quebec, the Parti rouge emerged as a liberal force while other liberal elements took form in other parts of British North America.

In the first decade of Confederation, a *Liberal Party congealed that incorporated the Parti rouge of Quebec, agrarian free traders from Ontario, and others who opposed the high public works expenditures of the Macdonald Conservatives. In Quebec, Wilfrid *Laurier, a former *rouge*, carefully separated his liberalism from the anti-clerical and radical clericalism of France and identified himself with the tradition of the British liberals such as John Bright and Richard Cobden. Liberalism in Canada favoured lower tariffs, a broader *franchise, agrarian interests, modest expenditures on defence, and, often, a closer relationship with the United States.

In the 20th century, Canadian liberalism followed its Anglo-American counterparts in shedding its opposition to broadened state activities. The influence of political thinkers such as T.H. Green in Britain and politicians such as Franklin Roosevelt in the United States altered the shape of Canadian liberalism. By the 1960s liberals strongly supported a *welfare state and, increasingly, individual rights. The Canadian *Charter of Rights and Freedoms reflected these changes in the 1980s as did the decisions made by judges thereafter. Liberalism in Canada did not endure the intellectual assault against it that so diminished its force in the United States after 1980. Nevertheless, the resurgent *conservatism and doubts about the efficacy of state action troubled liberals at the beginning of the 21st century, and they began to define their old doctrine anew.

JOHN ENGLISH

Liberal Party. The most successful national political party from the late 19th to the early 21st century, holding office for over 70 per cent of the time since 1896, the Liberals have been called Canada's 'Government party'.

The party's origins reach back to the pre-Confederation period, to the *Clear Grits in Upper Canada and the *rouges* in Lower Canada. Dominated by Sir John A. *Macdonald's protectionist and centralist Conservatives in the first two decades of Confederation, the Liberals supported freer trade and led the cry for provincial rights. After Wilfrid *Laurier became leader in 1887, the party gradually built wider bases of support in both English and French Canada, holding office from 1896 to 1911. The Liberals not only appropriated many of their Conservative predecessors' policies, they extended them, including large-scale immigration to settle the West. In 1911 the Liberals negotiated *reciprocity with the United States, but lost the subsequent election. During the First World War, the issue of *conscription split the party, with many English-Canadian Liberals joining the Conservatives in the *Union government, while Laurier remained in opposition.

Liberals met in a national convention in 1919 to determine Laurier's successor. Their choice, Mackenzie *King, a former bureaucrat and minister under Laurier, reconstructed the alliance between English and French Canada and modernized the party, responding to the challenges of industrialization. The 1921 election that brought King to power signalled the end of the two-party system, with the emergence of the largely western-based *Progressives, which King proved adroit in co-opting.

Defeated in 1930 in the Depression, and facing a number of new parties, the Liberals' slogan in their return in

1935 was 'King or Chaos'. War in 1939 restored full employment, but presented new challenges. The Liberals skilfully defused a conscription crisis, and at war's end headed off the rising threat posed by the CCF with a reconstruction program that leaned on interventionist Keynesian economics. King retired after 29 years at the helm, to be succeeded by Louis *St Laurent, who won easy majorities in 1949 and 1953. The Liberals of this era benefited from post-war prosperity while steering Canada into a new international role, both at the UN and as a Cold War partner of the United States. Twenty-two years of uninterrupted Liberal rule came to an abrupt halt in 1957, with the surprise victory of John *Diefenbaker's Conservatives.

Six years later, the Liberals were back. The governments of Lester *Pearson, 1963–8, expanded the *welfare state with *medicare and the *Canada Pension Plan. In 1968, Pierre *Trudeau succeeded Pearson, presiding over a turbulent decade and a half marked by the threat of Quebec sovereignty, the *patriation of the constitution, and the creation of the *Charter of Rights and Freedoms.

After an interlude from 1984 to 1993, the Liberals returned under Jean *Chrétien, who won three consecutive majority governments against a highly fragmented and ineffective opposition. The Chrétien Liberals faced down a renewed sovereignist threat in Quebec, and preempted a new challenge on the right from the Canadian Alliance by reversing a huge budgetary deficit bequeathed by its predecessors. In 2002, the architect of Liberal fiscal policies, Paul Martin Jr, was fired as finance minister and began an open challenge to Chrétien's continued leadership, forcing the prime minister into retirement. In the fall of 2003, Martin was nominated at a national convention as only the eighth Liberal leader since 1887.

The Liberal Party has always been a classic centrist party, one of the most successful in the Western world.

REG WHITAKER

liberation of the Netherlands. The bright tulips that bloom in Ottawa every spring are a gift from the people of the Netherlands. They remind Canadians of the many bonds that grew between the two countries during the Second World War.

After the fall of the Netherlands in May 1940, Queen Wilhelmina's only daughter, Princess Juliana, the future queen, chose to live in exile in Ottawa. She delivered her third daughter there in January 1943. The hospital room was placed temporarily outside of Canadian law so that Princess Margriet, named for a flower worn as a symbol of Dutch resistance, might hold exclusively Dutch citizenship.

Until September 1944, and again near war's end, the Royal Netherlands Brigade (Princess Irene's) fought under First Canadian Army. From 1 October to 8 November 1944 Canadian troops fought into the Netherlands to clear the approaches to the *Scheldt estuary. Among the many Dutch villages the Canadians liberated was Eede, where Queen Wilhelmina returned from exile in England. From November 1944 until February 1945, the Canadians stood watch in the province of North Brabant, south of the Maas River. After the battles for the Rhineland, First Canadian Army returned to the Netherlands as liberators. First Canadian Corps captured Apeldoorn on 17 April 1945 and reached the Zuider Zee two days later; operations soon began to relieve those starving in the western Netherlands. Second Canadian Corps fought into the northern provinces; Delfzijl fell after a stiff fight on 2 May 1945. The war in Europe ended three days later.

The euphoria of liberation continued through the summer of 1945. By the fall, most Canadian soldiers had left the Netherlands to return home. Over 1,800 Dutch *war brides would follow. The Canadian war cemeteries at Bergen-op-Zoom, Groesbeek, and Holten remind the Dutch people of the cost Canada paid to free the Netherlands from tyranny.

GEOFFREY HAYES

libraries. Libraries are knowledge and literacy systems that exist for the collective ownership of textual publications. Their emergence in Canada coincides with the arrival of Europeans and literacy. Begun as vehicles for the transmission of European culture and values, libraries have become integral to all aspects of Canadian life.

The first permanent library on the continent, north of Mexico, was at the Jesuit College in Quebec City (1632). During the French regime, libraries were limited to urban centres and existed under the jurisdiction of the Roman Catholic Church and its educational and medical institutions. Commercial lending libraries also existed. With the British regime, and the introduction of the printing press, other types of libraries began to appear. Legislative libraries emerged in the Maritime colonies and Upper and Lower Canada, following their being granted legislative assemblies. Social libraries emerged when member-owned subscription libraries were established in Quebec City (1779), Montreal (1796), and Niagara-on-the-Lake (1800). Lending libraries continued to be popular. The largest library in Canada in 1800 would have been that of the *Séminaire de Québec, which held 5,000 volumes.

Between the end of the Napoleonic Wars (1816) and Confederation (1867), there was a great flurry of library activity. Legislative libraries emerged as the leading libraries, serving both legislators and local communities. Academic libraries remained small, but plentiful, as institutions of higher learning developed. Precursors of public libraries emerged. *Mechanics' Institutes became endemic throughout English-speaking British North America, beginning with the first in St John's, Newfoundland (1827). School and township libraries also appeared. A problem with both types of libraries was their emphasis upon worthy books rather than the popular literature that people wanted. Even so, these libraries fulfilled an important function. Within francophone Quebec, libraries became a source of great controversy, with the library of the secular *Institut canadien de Montréal being in direct competition with the clerically based parish libraries. After the *Guibord affair, the parish libraries won the day and dominated Quebec's local library scene until the 1970s.

Following Confederation library development assumed new directions, which remained constant for many decades. Although the federal government spoke of creating a national library, and made some moves towards having the Library of Parliament assume such a role, nothing came from the initiative. All the provinces passed public library legislation, with Ontario being the first, in 1882, and Quebec the last, in 1959. Academic libraries emerged as substantial entities with the opening of specifically designed buildings at the University of Toronto (1892) and McGill University (1893).

From 1900 to 1945 Canadian library development was dominated by American philanthropy. Andrew Carnegie spent $2.5 million building 125 public libraries, of which 111 were in Ontario, one east of the Ottawa River, and none in Quebec. Canada's unique contribution to public library development, the regional library, first appeared in the 1930s in British Columbia's Fraser Valley and in Prince Edward Island, thanks to Carnegie Corporation support. The corporation and the Rockefeller Foundation, individually and collectively, supported and encouraged the development of graduate library education at McGill (1930), and national institutions such as the Canadian Library Association (1946), and the National Library of Canada/Bibliothèque nationale du Canada (1953).

During its first 50 years, the National Library has used its legal depository privileges, as well as transfers from the *National Archives and the Parliamentary Library, to build the world's largest collection of Canadian publications. Various bibliographical projects, such as *Canadiana*, the national bibliography, have been invaluable to the country's scholarly and publishing activities. Many national and international co-operative projects have emerged from the library. Its Amicus electronic catalogue contains references to 24 million books and journals. The Bibliothèque nationale du Québec, which was created in 1967 out of the Bibliothèque St Sulpice, formerly the parish library of Montreal, possesses joint depository privileges within the province.

As the 21st century begins, Canada's library network is one of the most extensive in the world, with thousands of school, public, academic, government, and specialized libraries. Thanks to information technology, they provide access to a wide range of publications within and beyond their walls—in paper, microform, and electronic formats. Although in some circles there are dire predictions of the demise of libraries, their use continues to outstrip their resources. Major building projects have characterized Canadian libraries in recent decades, including Metropolitan Toronto Public Library (1977), Vancouver Public Library (1995), and the Grande bibliothèque in Montreal (2004). The National Library plans to build a new structure during this century's first decade.

PETER F. McNALLY

life expectancy. How long might people expect to live? The skeletal remains of a small band of Aboriginal people who lived in what is now southern Ontario in 1000 BC suggest that the average age of death was in the mid-30s. By 1801 little had changed: for Canadians, life expectancy at birth was 39 for women and 38 for men. The main reason for short life expectancy was the high probability of death at a young age. Nearly one in five of Canadian children born in 1801 died before their first birthday. Of those who survived, one in seven died before age five.

Infant and childhood mortality did not decline sharply until the late 19th and early 20th century. The case of Toronto is revealing. In 1909 the city's infant mortality was at the rate it had been for Canada 100 years earlier. During the next decade the city stopped dumping untreated sewage into the city's water supply; imposed more rigorous standards in its milk-inspection program, restricting sales to only pasteurized milk; and put more resources into its Board of Health. Infant mortality fell and general life expectancy rose. By 1998 only one in 200 Canadian children died before age one, and life expectancy for women had risen to 81.5 and for men to 76.1.

Life expectancy for poor people has always been lower than that for the relatively rich. In Hamilton, Ontario, for example, people living in areas with the highest per capita property values in 1900 had the lowest mortality rates. In 1970 infant mortality rates for the poorest people in urban Canada were double that for the richest. In 1998 infant mortality in Nunavut was 3.5 times higher than the Canadian average. Yet historical studies suggest that economic differentials cannot explain all the variation in death rates. In Belleville, Ontario, and Montreal in the late 19th century infant mortality was lower for Catholics than for Protestants in similar class levels. Apparently Catholic mothers protected their infants from contaminated water and unpasteurized milk by breast-feeding for a longer period than did Protestant mothers.

PETER BASKERVILLE

lighthouses. With coastlines on three oceans and four of the five Great Lakes, as well as numerous inland waterways and countless islands, reefs, and shoals, Canada needed many lighthouses to meet the requirements of navigation. After a slow beginning, the development of the fishing industry, commercial shipping, and steamer passenger services in the 19th century led to the establishment of large numbers of light stations, channel markers, and harbour lights.

Although unlighted beacons almost certainly marked Canadian shores from the early days of settlement, lighthouse construction began slowly. The first recorded tower, built by the French at *Louisbourg in 1733, was severely damaged during the siege of 1758. That year, the British established Sambro Island light at the entrance to Halifax Harbour—Canada's oldest surviving lighthouse. Other Atlantic colonies subsequently acquired their first light towers: New Brunswick in 1791 (*Partridge Island), Newfoundland in 1810 (Fort Amherst), and Prince Edward Island in 1840 (Point Prim).

In 1809 Quebec Trinity House, Canada's earliest lighthouse authority, built the Green Island (Île Verte) lighthouse, the first of many structures to mark islands and shoals in the St Lawrence River. In the upper reaches of the river, between Quebec City and Kingston, the constant silting, shifting, and dredging of channels required numerous 'range' lights to guide the growing maritime traffic. On the Great Lakes the first recorded lighthouse, erected in 1804 at Point Mississauga, on the west side of the Niagara River, soon gave way to military *fortifications as war with the Americans loomed. Gibraltar Point light, established in 1808 on an island near York (Toronto), is the oldest surviving lighthouse on the lakes. Hundreds of lighthouses were built between Fort William (Thunder Bay) and Kingston.

The pace of construction quickened in the mid-19th century, with British Columbia acquiring its first two towers in 1860 (Fisgard and Race Rocks). The most active building period began soon after Confederation, when lighthouse responsibility was centralized under the Department of Marine, and lasted beyond the First World War. By 1914 Canada boasted more than 1,400 lighthouses on the Atlantic and Pacific coasts, in the St Lawrence/Great Lakes system, and on many rivers (Saint John, Saguenay, Richelieu, and Ottawa) and lakes (Bras d'Or, Memphremagog, Nipissing, Simcoe, the Muskokas, Lake of the Woods, Winnipeg, Winnipegosis, and Kootenay). The coasts of Labrador and the Arctic regions as well as the northern waterways (the Mackenzie, Great Slave Lake, Lake Athabasca) were also provided with unwatched navigational aids in the 20th century. Lighthouse administration was transferred to the Department of Transport in 1936, and later to the *Canadian Coast Guard under the Department of Fisheries and Oceans.

Originally fuelled by oil, then acetylene, lighthouses began to be electrified in the 1890s, a process completed after the Second World War. Automation had already started, gaining momentum in subsequent decades. More recent technological advances, such as the 'global positioning system', made lighthouses all but obsolete and, combined with a succession of budget cuts, put pressure on the Coast Guard to dispose of unneeded assets. Although many structures have been demolished since 1950, protests by mariners and local groups have succeeded in slowing down the process in recent years. In early 2003, of the few hundred active lighthouses that remained, only 52 were staffed—27 in British Columbia and 24 in Newfoundland and Labrador, as well as New Brunswick's offshore Machias Seal Island Light Station, which had retained its keepers primarily because sovereignty over the island is contested by the United States.

The future of lighthouses in Canada remains uncertain, but prospects for their preservation are improving. In the 1990s and early 2000s, the Coast Guard implemented a divestiture program to determine the fate of lighthouses under its responsibility, in consultation with local and regional interests who seek practical uses for them as museums and interpretive centres while preserving their heritage value. MICHEL FORAND

limited identities. Less an interpretative scheme than an affirmation of value, 'limited identities' began life as a phrase tossed off by Ramsay Cook at the end of a disgruntled review of several books concerned with the perennial problems of national unity and identity (*International Journal*, 1967). Cook proposed that, instead of lamenting their lack of a single *national identity, Canadians ought to examine their 'regional, ethnic and class identities'; they might discover in doing so a more pluralist version of 'Canadianism' than those prescribed by 'over-heated nationalist intellectuals'. J.M.S. Careless gave the idea something like systematic formulation (*Canadian Historical Review*, 1969). Rejecting the 'teleological cast' of national history, he called for an acceptance of variation, particularly among regions, whose histories were often shaped by the *metropolitan role of cities. Still, this was a conception that continued to assume a national framework within which regions (and other forms of community) found 'articulation'. In the event, much of the historical practice that found legitimacy under the umbrella of 'limited identities'—Marxist, feminist, regionalist, postmodernist—departed entirely from the national approach and rejected the very pluralism that Cook and Careless sought to encourage. As Cook himself later observed, the fact that such a wide variety of endeavours gathered under the banner of so imprecise an idea was indicative of the 'interpretive vacuum' in historical studies of the time. The 'theses' of earlier decades—*frontier, *Laurentian, *staples—had exhausted their organizing force. For better or worse, history had broken its tie to the fate of the nation. The result was a fractured community of historical scholars, at odds with one another over the purpose and proper subject matter of their discipline, and alienated from the general reading public—though it, too, had ceased to be a singular entity.

KENNETH C. DEWAR

liquor control. *Prohibition was a divisive issue in Canada from the mid-19th century until the First World War. With the war, a combination of moral-patriotic fervour and new justifications for government economic intervention resulted in the imposition of bans on nearly all alcohol sales. In Canada, as in the United States, prohibition was quickly undermined by bootlegging, corruption, and a notorious overuse of the 'medical prescription' exception. Returning *veterans were key in the emergence of a post-war compromise between the failures of prohibition and the purported excesses of the old, unregulated pre-war saloon. That compromise was government liquor control.

The first government liquor stores opened in British Columbia in 1921. Throughout the twenties, provincially owned liquor (and also beer) stores were opened in other provinces. This was followed by the sale of beer by the glass, first allowed only in hotels and later in bars called beer parlours or *taverns. Such places were subject to myriad regulations, very few of them set out in legislation. Also, provincial liquor inspectors had—and to some extent still have—tremendous discretionary powers to demand specific changes to decor, interior design, opening hours, food items sold, and entertainment. Neither the regulatory power of the new provincial bureaucracy nor the unprecedented economic power of the government wine and liquor importers were subject to challenge. The industry tried to keep inspectors and licensing board members happy for fear of losing their licence—until the late 1980s a licence was legally considered a privilege, not a right. And the public tolerated intrusive regulations, perhaps because of a Protestant unease about 'the demon rum'.

The close supervision of the leisure activities of Canadians—especially working-class male Canadians—from the 1920s to the 1970s or 1980s was much more concerned with moral and racial improprieties than with health risks. Beer prices were uniformly low, and while liquor inspectors told hotel owners what musical instruments were or were not allowed, little was done to encourage healthier drinking habits; indeed, food was positively banned from beer parlours for many years.

Government liquor control—a system later adopted in many American states and in Scandinavian countries—is, for good or ill, one of the great Canadian administrative inventions of all time. Well before the United States repealed prohibition in 1933 and moved towards local and state control, Canadian provincial governments had implemented a system for regulating and taxing 'vice' that ensured both fiscal health and an orderly, closely supervised space for revelries. That drinking—and later, other 'vices' (mainly *gambling)—could be legalized but in a highly regulated and fiscally beneficial manner was the historic bet first made by Canadian politicians in the post–First World War period. This bet is perhaps representative of a distinctively Canadian approach to pleasure, consumption, and state power. MARIANA VALVERDE

literary societies. An important form of cultural, educational, and social organization in early Canada and the forerunners of modern book discussion clubs, literary societies took 'literature' to mean belles-lettres and rhetorical study broadly defined: book discussion, debate, essay reading, dramatic performance, and recitation. Unlike more recent clubs, which focus on a single text, literary societies often included musical interludes and current events discussions in their programs. Many groups undertook cultural promotion or civic improvement projects.

The earliest literary societies drew upon several models: the antiquarian and bibliophile societies established by Scottish and European gentlemen in the late 18th century; the *Mechanics' Institutes, initiated in England in 1827; and the public lecture lyceums of the eastern United States. French literary-political societies of the 18th century provided a further model for francophone Quebec. Once they were implemented, their fate was mixed. While the Literary and Historical Society of Quebec (founded 1824) developed impressive cultural facilities (and remains in existence today), the exclusive York Literary and Philosophical Society (Toronto, 1831) suffocated under the pretensions heaped upon it by *Family Compact patrons. Societies with a practical mandate and more open membership stood a greater chance of success: the Halifax Athenaeum (1834), the Toronto Athenaeum (1843), the Fredericton Athenaeum and New Brunswick Literary and Scientific Association (1847), and the St John's Athenaeum (1861), are four such examples. The Mechanics' Institute movement took a firm and early hold, with a branch in St John's in 1828, Montreal the following year, and York in 1830—a total of 43 in Canada by mid-century. While the *Institut canadien (Montreal, 1844), an organization that developed some 60 branches, is better known for its left-nationalist activities, as a literary society it developed lecture series and a library collection, and was a crucial agent in Quebec cultural development.

While some societies were focused in their interests—as with the Shakspeare (*sic*) Club of Toronto (*c.* 1835) and the Montreal Shakspere (*sic*) Club (*c.* 1845), others were more varied, as witnessed by the name of the Western District Literary, Philosophical and Agricultural Association (Amherstburg, Ontario, 1842). It was not uncommon for a literary society to piggyback on a scientific or agricultural society, to which government grants were given. Conversely, a scientific society, such as the Canadian Institute (now Royal Canadian Institute), might have a literary division, since cultural and practical pursuits were judged equally necessary for the development of a new nation. At mid-century, many societies assumed a more public presence and attempted to establish reading rooms, libraries, lecture halls, and museums.

Literary societies were normally confined to men until the late 1870s (with women offered occasional admittance to open meetings and conversaziones), although there must have been women's reading circles for which no records exist. An exception is in the early African-Canadian community; Black fugitives appear to have developed both the first women's societies and the first mixed-sex societies. Groups such as the Windsor Ladies Club (1854) and the Chatham Literary Society (*c.* 1875) in Ontario assisted their members to gain literacy and cultural skills, acted as centres of mutual assistance, and initiated early civil rights mobilization. Among the European-descent settler population, women's societies began in the 1870s and mushroomed in the closing decades of the 19th century. Women saw these societies as a form of higher education. The groups stressed oratorical skills and mastery of the rules of order, to prepare women for public life, and approximated a liberal arts education with an 'eclectic' program of study. Women's groups often undertook various forms of public service as well, such as sponsorship of scholarships and essay competitions, and local history and preservationist activities. Mixed-sex societies became popular in the 1880s as well, especially among young men and women who enjoyed the socially sanctioned opportunity for entertainment and courtship. Literary societies also took hold in religious denominations: while these were most frequently attached to Methodist congregations, there were societies for Roman Catholic men, young men, and young women, as well as mixed-sex societies among the Hicksite branch of the Society of Friends. In addition, by the end of the century 'lits' could be found in most colleges, collegiates, and universities.

The late 19th century saw some new models for literary society organization. Beginning in the 1880s, and well into the 20th century, hundreds of Chautauqua Literary and Scientific Circles followed the four-year course of correspondence education laid down by the *Chautauqua Institution in New York State. These circles became especially popular in rural or remote areas where a cultural infrastructure was otherwise lacking: by the late 1880s, such circles had spread to Manitoba and Saskatchewan, and as far west as Bella Bella. More specialized forms of literary organization evolved, following the late-19th-century vogue for the study of Shakespeare and Browning. Other systems developed for groups torn between the desire for a broad or liberal program and the need for more orderly or systematic study. The 'travel club' became popular at this time, organized according to study of the literature, culture, history, and even cuisine of a different country annually.

The literary society movement reached a crescendo in the late 1880s and early 1890s, with the development of collegiate and congregational societies, and the spread of literary societies to small towns and rural areas. The First World War caused the disbanding of many literary societies, and the conversion of others to societies for charitable and war work. The post-war period brought the development of new forms of reading circles and book clubs: men's public-speaking societies, which were an outgrowth of earlier debating societies; clubs for the promotion of Canadian literature; clubs co-ordinated by the Canadian Home Reading Union; 'great books' circles; and the sorts of book-discussion groups common today. But a number of the groups established on the older 'literary society' model proved to be remarkably enduring. The Eclectic Reading Club (Saint John, 1869), the Baconian Club (London 1885), and the Tuesday Reading Club (Woodstock, Ontario, 1896) are some of the venerable literary societies that have persisted into the 21st century.

HEATHER MURRAY

Liverpool Packet, War of 1812 *privateer schooner. The most successful privateer vessel in Canadian history, this tiny schooner captured over 50 American vessels. Originally a slave-smuggling Baltimore Clipper–style schooner, it was captured by the Royal Navy in 1811 and bought at auction in Halifax by Enos *Collins and Joseph Alison. Less than 18 m long and mounting only five guns, the *Packet* was remarkably fast. Its unpredictable movements and daring captures caused panic and anger in American ports. It was captured by a larger American privateer in 1813 but was soon retaken by the British and went back to hunting American shipping with its original owners. After peace arrived, the *Packet* was sold to Jamaican owners in 1816; its eventual fate is unknown.

DAN CONLIN

Livesay, Dorothy (1909–96). Born in Winnipeg, the progressive daughter of writer Florence Randal Livesay and journalist J.F.B. Livesay, Dorothy Livesay won two Governor General's poetry awards, for *Day and Night* (1944) and *Poems for People* (1947). Her autobiographical *Right Hand, Left hand* (1977) recollects her life at the University of Toronto and the Sorbonne and later as a social worker and communist in the 1920s and 1930s. She co-founded the League of Canadian Poets, Amnesty International Canada, the Committee for an Independent Canada, and the poetry magazines *Contemporary Verse* and *CVII*. From 1959 to 1963 she taught English in Northern Rhodesia (Zambia), where children's desperate plight proved further inspiration. As a writer-in-residence at various universities and a prolific poet who mixed the erotic and the political, she was widely celebrated as an outspoken champion of feminism, socialism, nationalism, and the elderly.

VERONICA STRONG-BOAG

liviers. The word 'liver', meaning simply inhabitant, is found in British authors, but in 19th-century Newfoundland and its dependency Labrador it acquired a special significance. Until 1904 the French had seasonal fishing rights, which they argued were exclusive, from Cape St John, the western extremity of Notre Dame Bay, to Cape Ray, Newfoundland's southwest corner. Despite their claims and presence, settlement on this coast had occurred. Between Bay of Islands on the west coast and Cape St John, that settlement was particularly sparse, and by the late 1850s those who permanently inhabited that region were called (and called themselves) 'livers'. This was meant to distinguish them from the French and others who came temporarily to the coast to trade or fish. By the 1850s the word was also applied to permanent dwellers on the Labrador coast, to differentiate them from the thousands of migratory fishermen and their families, and others, who came to that coast each summer. As decades passed the word 'liver' was replaced by the more euphonic 'livier', sometimes spelled 'livyer', and attached itself more to Labrador than to the island. It is now sometimes loosely applied to outport residents to distinguish them from cottagers.

PATRICK O'FLAHERTY

local government. The Canadian municipality may be defined historically as a 'body corporate and politic', self-governing through a local council that is elected on a resident ratepayer (or broader) franchise and that exercises fiscal and legislative powers ('by-laws') for its inhabitants' 'security, health, comfort and good order'. Rural municipalites are a peculiarly Canadian development of the mid-19th century. In 1800, local government in all four mainland colonies of *British North America was effected through an ancient English institution, the justices of the peace, who received no salary and were appointed by executive authority from the substantial landholders of a county. As the Court of Quarter Sessions (QS), JPs shared in managing the county's public business—public buildings, roads and bridges, poor relief, licences, property rates and audits, appointing constables, regulating markets, and other local government matters.

The first counties were five erected in Nova Scotia in 1759 as constituencies for the first provincial assembly.

The territory that became New Brunswick in 1784 had been a single county (Sunbury) of Nova Scotia. In both provinces the QS continued its administrative roles until the 1870s, when elective county councils were instituted. In 1764 the new English government at Quebec created two judicial districts, commissioned JPs, and ordained QS local government within the province. Five additional districts were proclaimed in 1788 to accommodate the settlements of *Loyalists, and in 1791 the four districts inland of Montreal were separated to form the new province of Upper Canada. In Upper Canada, some township-meetings of householders had begun before 1792. In 1793 this unofficial institution was commandeered by Governor *Simcoe to legitimize property taxes. The district QS set the rates and disbursed the taxes. New districts and electoral counties were occasionally created by partition. In Lower Canada, the town-meeting tradition was lacking, and few new districts were created, although counties proclaimed in 1792 were superseded in 1828 in a reapportionment of legislative seats.

True municipalities first appeared in the Canadas when the cities of Montreal and Quebec (1832) and Toronto (1834) obtained legislative charters. A number of towns were allowed elective Boards of Police, with powers to make rules and regulations for their civil government. During the 1840s numerous cities and towns were incorporated, but mayors were nowhere popularly elected until after 1850.

The concept of rural municipality was introduced into Canada in 1840–1 as part of the reforms of the Union. In 1836, the *Colonial Office had decided upon the use of elective 'subordinate legislatures' for imposing punitive taxes on absentee owners of wild lands. Governor C.P. Thomson, applying this concept, in 1840 ordained for Lower Canada a novel set of 22 districts with elective councils; in 1841 (now Lord Sydenham) he finagled the new assembly into creating the same institution in the 20 districts of Upper Canada. Each corporate district council was to be comprised of qualified representatives from lower-tier units (parishes and townships), under an appointive head (warden), and was to assume all the civil-administrative powers of the QS. In the Lower province, the francophone population refused to participate, and these districts were abolished in 1845. By 1855, a substitute system had been established.

The district municipalities worked well in Upper Canada: although Robert *Baldwin's Municipal Corporations Act (1849) abolished the district system, it devolved many of its functions to the constituent townships, with their own elective councils. The act also standardized the incorporation of cities, towns, and villages. County councils made up of the heads of township and village councils (the 'reeves') exercised power over selected county-wide matters. Baldwin's system (although often amended) served Ontario until well after the Second World War.

After 1870, Manitoba experimented with parts of the Ontario system but found it unsuited to the sparser population of the plains. In 1883, the province created a tier of local units called 'Rural Municipalities' (RMs) made up of blocks of eight or more of the Dominion Land Survey (DLS) standard (93.6 sq km) townships. The elective headman of an RM was titled 'reeve'. Winnipeg was incorporated as a city in 1873 by legislative charter. Under North-West Territory ordinances Local Improvement Districts (LIDs) were created in the 1890s, each of a few DLS townships. By 1905, five cities and many towns and villages had been incorporated. The successor provinces followed the LID idea by creating standard territorial units (nine DLS townships), Saskatchewan in 1909 and Alberta in 1912; these might progress from 'unorganized' status to LID to RM (headed by a 'reeve') as population and wealth increased. Alberta amended its system in 1950 to convert the more heavily settled RMs into larger municipal 'counties', a concept unrelated to the historic county of eastern Canada. In British Columbia, where the population is very scattered, both rural and urban municipalities might be proclaimed as expedient under an 1872 act, the wording of which is reminiscent of the Baldwin act.

Economic and demographic trends of the later 20th century have put municipalities under severe stress: rural entities from loss of population and tax base; larger urban ones from the sheer rapidity of their growth and the consequent pressure on their infrastructures. By 2000, drastic restructuring of local government had become endemic.

C.F.J. WHEBELL

Loft, Fred (1861–1934), First Nations political leader. Loft, or Onondeyoh, was born on the Grand River Six Nations territory into a family of Christian Mohawk, then the majority religious group there. After attending primary school at Grand River and high school in neighbouring Caledonia, he became a lumberjack, timber inspector, newspaper reporter, bookkeeper, and, ultimately, Ontario civil servant. In Toronto he and his Canadian wife of British descent led a busy middle-class life. He enlisted in the First World War, and after service overseas as an officer he returned determined to increase the autonomy of the First Nations. In December 1918 he founded the League of Indians of Canada to work to persuade the Canadian government to improve the standard of education it offered Aboriginals. The league expanded from Ontario to western Canada, but the Department of Indian Affairs' continual opposition and Loft's poor health hampered its further growth. By the time of his death the first pan-Indian political organization in Canada had become effectively defunct. DONALD B. SMITH

Logan, Sir William Edmond (1798–1875), geologist. Born in Montreal to Scottish immigrants William Logan and Janet Edmond, Logan attended Alexander Skakel's school in Montreal, Edinburgh High School, and the University of Edinburgh. Employed by his uncle in London from 1817, he managed the Forest Copper Works, Swansea, South Wales, from 1831. Logan's cross-sectional maps of regional coal seams raised the standard of precision for the Geological Survey of Great Britain. His theory of coal's in situ formation, presented to the Geological Society of London in 1837, earned further recognition from leading geologists.

Logan visited Montreal in 1841, when the provincial government began to fund the *Geological Survey of Canada. Combined with his experience in locating coal deposits, his ties to the Montreal business community won him the GSC directorship. In 1843 Logan began his survey with one assistant. Despite his devastating verdict that the province possessed no workable coal, Logan's faith in the colony's economic future secured continued funding. He cultivated political support, collaborated with British and American scientific counterparts, and earned accolades at the London (1851) and Paris (1855) exhibitions, including a knighthood and France's Cross of the Legion of Honour. Acquiring capable field and laboratory assistants, Logan illuminated Laurentian and Huronian formations in Canada's Precambrian Shield (1857). His career culminated in a magnum opus, *Geology of Canada* (1863), which won him the Royal Society of London's Gold Medal (1867). When Logan retired (1869), his GSC had expanded with Confederation, soon to extend from sea to sea. He died in Cilgerran, Wales.

SUZANNE ZELLER

Longboat, Tom (1887–1949), celebrated runner from the Onondaga Nation of the Six Nations Reserve in Ontario. Before the First World War, Longboat held every Canadian amateur record from one mile to the marathon, and won most of the major distance races in the United States and Europe. He was the headline attraction wherever he raced. In 1999 *Maclean's* magazine voted him the top Canadian sports figure of the century. Despite pressures to assimilate, Longboat spoke proudly of his Aboriginal heritage, and today he is revered by the First Nations as a symbol of Aboriginal athletic prowess. The Tom Longboat Award, established in 1951 and now administered by the Aboriginal Sports Circle, annually recognizes the outstanding male and female Aboriginal athletes in Canada.

BRUCE KIDD

Long Lance, Buffalo Child (1890–1932). Born Sylvester Long, of European, Native American, and possibly African ancestry, he was classified as 'colored' in his hometown of Winston-Salem, North Carolina, but used his 'Indian' appearance to escape segregation. In 1909 he gained entrance into Carlisle Indian School in Pennsylvania as a Cherokee. As Long Lance he served in the Canadian Army in the First World War. Upon discharge in Calgary he reinvented himself again, as Chief Buffalo Child Long Lance, Blackfoot. In the mid-1920s he wrote for newspapers and magazines on North American Indians and boxing, a sport at which he excelled. His 'autobiography', *Long Lance*, about his Blackfoot childhood, was published in New York in 1928, and in 1930 he starred in *The Silent Enemy*, a feature film. But fear of exposure remained constant and in Arcadia, California, he took his own life.

DONALD B. SMITH

longshoremen. Derived from the phrase 'along shore', the word 'longshoremen' refers to port workers who load and unload ships. It is often used interchangeably with 'stevedores', 'dockers', 'lumpers', and 'wharfies'.

Throughout the 19th and early 20th centuries, longshoring in Canada, as in the rest of North America, was a casual affair. Waterfront workers were often unskilled and available at any time to load and/or unload vessels. In this context, work came in fits and starts, earnings fluctuated, and competition between men was intense. Typically, hiring was conducted on the wharf in a 'shape-up', a large ring of men that formed daily around a foreman. Employers argued that this method of hiring provided maximum flexibility; longshoremen contended that it allowed foremen to accept bribes, hire and fire at whim, and ban union organizers. The waterfront workplace was shaped by complex occupational structures as well. Organized into gangs, some men worked on ship, others on shore; in both categories men stressed different abilities to improve their chances in the shape-up. Divisions of skill and specialization often mapped cleavages of race and ethnicity. In the early 1900s, for example, Halifax's African-Nova Scotian longshoremen usually handled the most arduous and poorly paid cargoes.

The casual nature of longshoring and the shape-up method of hiring made the waterfront ripe for union activity. Between 1889 and 1935 Vancouver's longshoremen organized a variety of *unions—from the conservative to the communist—and fought at least 18 strikes, some of which were bloody, all-or-nothing affairs. In Vancouver and elsewhere, control over the waterfront labour market was the pre-eminent issue. Since the 1960s, however, the introduction of containers—large rectangular boxes that hold cargo—to the *shipping industry has revolutionized longshoring. The number of men required on the docks has plummeted; cranes, not strong backs and arms, are used to move containers; and unions, generally, are on the defensive.

ANDREW PARNABY

Lord's Day Alliance. Influenced by biblical sabbatarianism, *social gospel principles, and the rise of industrialism in Canada, denominational, provincial, and locally based, voluntary, Sunday-observance organizations reorganized in 1901 as branches of a federal, non-denominational, lobby group called the Lord's Day Alliance. The Presbyterian minister John George Shearer, with mainly Methodist and evangelical Anglican allies, led the alliance to its greatest success, the drafting and passage of the federal Lord's Day Act of 1906. The act, which came into force in 1907, outlawed a number of business and manufacturing activities on Sunday, but left implementation of the act in the hands of provincial attorneys general in order to safeguard different Sunday afternoon customs, mainly in Quebec.

Under Methodist minister T. Albert Moore, the alliance grew into a powerful inter-denominational lobby group, with provincial field secretaries reporting on Sunday activities and prosecutions and instigating Sunday controversies in each province. After the First World War,

French-speaking Roman Catholics in Quebec organized their own Ligue du dimanche, and joined labour groups and Baptists to give stronger support to the alliance's attempts to give everyone one day's rest in the week. With the formation of the United Church of Canada in 1925, however, Lord's Day Alliance members became preoccupied either with the establishment of the new church or the continuation of the Presbyterian Church, and social gospel activities were curtailed. By the time denominational boundaries settled, the Depression and then the Second World War brought manufacturing and other interests to plead industrial necessity. After the war, the alliance found itself fighting a rearguard action against an increasingly affluent society developing commercial Sunday leisure activities to supplement, and then supplant, traditional Sunday religious activities. The alliance lost a key 1950 plebiscite in Toronto, the traditional heart of English Protestant sabbatarianism, and commercial baseball games began on Sunday. Provincial alliance branches closed as donations fell off and older sabbatarians died or moved to other causes. The smaller Roman Catholic sabbatarian league disbanded shortly after the Second Vatican Council (1962–5).

The specifically Christian religious lobby group was not attracting non-Christian support in an increasingly secular nation adopting American principles of the separation of church and state in a Canadian *Charter of Rights and Freedoms. Accordingly, in 1982 the Toronto-based alliance changed its name to 'People for Sunday' and became a mainly Ontario-based lobby group with some organized labour support for its watered-down defence of a quiet Sunday. It helped establish the Coalition against Open Sunday Shopping and similar lobby groups. The Lord's Day Act, however, was struck from the statutes in 1985 as unconstitutionally infringing religious liberties. Although meeting sporadically, the Lord's Day Alliance ceased activities shortly thereafter.

PAUL LAVERDURE

Lost Patrol. The Lost Patrol of the Royal *North-West Mounted Police perished on a trip from Fort McPherson, Northwest Territories, to Dawson City, Yukon, becoming the most famous and tragic of hundreds of such patrols that crossed northern Canada for decades. Mountie patrols performed vital roles in the North: confirming sovereignty, checking on remote trappers, traders, and families, and carrying the mail between distant communities and detachments. Charged primarily with this last task, the four men and three dog teams of the Lost Patrol, led by the respected veteran of northern travel Inspector Francis J. Fitzgerald, departed Fort McPherson on 21 December 1910, on the 765-km trail. Travelling south on the Peel River and then into the Richardson and Wernecke mountains, the men faced multiple trail hazards compounded by high winds and sub-40°C temperatures for days on end. Unable to locate a key side stream on the trail, they spent valuable days searching, began retracing their route, and were again struck by gales and extreme temperatures. In mid-February 1911, exhausted and starving, they died within a day's travel of their starting point, three of exposure, one of a self-inflicted gunshot. A loss still remembered by Mounties, the tragedy added to the reputation the force sought as iron lawmen of the North.

COLIN BEAIRSTO

Louisbourg. When the Treaty of Utrecht (1713) established British control of mainland Nova Scotia and confirmed British title to Newfoundland, the French moved to *Île Royale (Cape Breton) and built their capital at Louisbourg. The town was intended to replace *Plaisance in Newfoundland as the headquarters for the fishery and to serve as a haven for trading ships. By 1718 Île Royale had become a thriving French colony.

As capital and commercial centre, Louisbourg depended on the fishery, the military, and trade. Residents and migrants both practised an inshore boat fishery, and much of Île Royale's fish was marketed in Europe and the Caribbean. Although Louisbourg started out as a simple base for the cod fishery, it prospered and developed into a major entrepôt, one of the most important ports in New France. By the 1730s more than 150 ships were sailing into the town, making it one of the busiest seaports in North America. Louisbourg's permanent population was 633 in 1720, 813 in 1724, 1,463 in 1737, and 2,960 in 1752, figures that do not include the garrison, fishermen, or other transients who were there on a seasonal basis.

Besides its economic and commercial importance, Louisbourg was the capital and administrative centre of Île Royale. By 1734 the town was basically completed. Fishing properties—most with landing stages, drying platforms, and a few buildings—surrounded the harbour. In Louisbourg's newly formed society, people tended to change occupations more readily than in France but, because almost all manufactures were imported, their occupational choice was narrow. As in small French towns of the day, people of different status lived side by side. Regional backgrounds were unusually diverse: most of the women had been born in the New World; the majority of men were from western France but all French provinces and other European countries were represented among them.

Louisbourg became the main French military stronghold in the Atlantic region. Begun in 1717, its massive fortifications were based on the geometric style of Sébastien Le Prestre de Vauban (1633–1707), the chief engineer of Louis XIV. As a fortress, Louisbourg resembled a European fortified town: it was enclosed by walls and had batteries and outer works. This fortified town ranked among the most heavily defended in North America. Although intended to resist attack from the sea, Louisbourg was twice attacked from the rear, where its defences were vulnerable. Following a siege, the town surrendered to a combined force of 4,000 New Englanders and British in 1745; its citizens were deported to France, and the town was occupied by an enemy army. Four years later, after the Treaty of Aix-la-Chapelle (1748) gave Île Royale back to France, the French returned.

In 1758, following another siege, Louisbourg again surrendered to a combined British force of 30,000 men. In both sieges Louisbourg put up a spirited defence against superior forces during a six-week period. It held out as long as Vauban had calculated that his fortresses could withstand a massive assault. Ultimately, whoever controlled the seas and supply lines would gain victory in siege warfare. Once more, the French soldiers and settlers were sent back to France. With Louisbourg eliminated as a strategic force and naval base, the British moved on to conquer Quebec (1759) and Montreal (1760). The Treaty of Paris in 1763 established that New France had become part of British North America.

Although many have remarked on the expense of fortifying Louisbourg, the total spent by the French in any one year never exceeded the cost of outfitting a large warship for a six-month patrol of the coast of New France. In return, France got a naval port, a base for the fishery, and a commercial centre that brought much wealth to the mother country. Expenditure on the fortifications from 1714 to 1758 was slightly over 4 million livres or roughly £200,000 in English currency during that era.

The fall of New France spelled the end of Louisbourg as a fortified town. The once formidable bastion faded quickly from the world scene. The British systematically demolished its fortifications in 1760 and withdrew the last of their garrisons in 1768. For the next century, Louisbourg was little more than an isolated fishing village, remarkable for its 'heaps of stones'. In 1961 the federal government began the partial reconstruction of 18th-century Louisbourg to provide work for unemployed coal miners and to stimulate the Cape Breton economy. With over 60 reconstructed buildings, together with the fortress walls, the Fortress of Louisbourg National Historic Site is Canada's most ambitious attempt at preserving its history.

KENNETH DONOVAN

Low, Albert Peter (1861–1942), geologist and explorer. Born in Montreal, Low graduated from McGill University (1882) and was appointed to the *Geological Survey of Canada. Known for his explorations in northern Quebec and Labrador, from 1893 to 1894 he travelled by canoe from Lac St Jean to Kuujjuaq (formerly Fort Chimo), then sailed to Rigolet on the Labrador coast, canoed up the Churchill River around Lake Michikamau (now Smallwood Reservoir) into the Ashuanipi River of western Labrador, thence southwards to the north shore of the St Lawrence River. Low estimated this trip at over 8,700 km of which 4,700 km were by canoe, 1,600 km by vessel, 800 km by dog team, and 1,600 km on foot. He discovered and documented the vast iron ore ranges of western Labrador, now the mining operations at Labrador City–Wabush. Low was appointed GSC director in 1906, but was stricken with meningitis in 1907, the consequences of which were so debilitating that they caused him to leave the civil service entirely by 1913. DEREK H.C. WILTON

Lower, A.R.M. (1889–1988). Arthur Reginald Marsden Lower was educated at the University of Toronto and Harvard, where he received his PhD in 1929. Active in an era when *history and historians (*Creighton, *Groulx, *Morton, *Underhill) were at the centre of intellectual life, Lower preached (and practised) high standards of professional scholarship while believing in the necessity of engagement in the public life of the nation. He made his scholarly reputation with close studies of the timber trade, carried out within the framework of the *staples thesis, yet with a frontierist's eye to its human dimension. His opinionated general history, *Colony to Nation: A History of Canada* (1946), won him a wider audience (and a Governor General's Award). He wrote seriously about *French–English relations, which he called the 'primary antithesis' of Canadian history, and about political ideas; *This Most Famous Stream: The Liberal Democratic Way of Life* (1954) won him a second award. Looking back, he wrote that his scholarship had been governed chiefly by the question of how and with what effect a civilization transferred itself from one place to another. He has been called the most nationalistic of English-Canadian historians, yet like others of his generation his ultimate quest was for answers to large questions on the boundary between history and philosophy. KENNETH C. DEWAR

Lower Canada, 1791–1841, a British province in the southern part of present-day Quebec. The *Constitutional Act (1791), which created Lower Canada, provided the Canadiens with a majority in an elected assembly, which they would use to preserve and promote their laws, their French language, and their institutions. The *seigneurial system discouraged settlement by the British, and, except in cities, the Canadiens eventually occupied the whole of the seigneurial zone in the St Lawrence Valley.

In the new assembly the 'British party' and the Parti canadien clashed regularly as early as 1793. The former promoted British colonization, trade, and assimilation of the Canadiens, the latter their national and social interests as well as democratic ideals. The two were locked in multiple levels of conflicts: a constitutional struggle between imperial sovereignty and nascent colonial aspirations aimed at more internal autonomy—control of finances, patronage, *responsible government, an elected legislative council; a social opposition between the British minority, with its placemen controlling the aristocratic councils defending imperial authority, and the representatives of the mass of the population in the assembly, fighting for local autonomy; divergent economic strategies, the former favouring international trade and expansion, the latter local investments and agriculture. In addition, religious, legal, cultural, and ethnic or 'racial' conflict was rife. Each side vetoed the other. The British party publicly fostered assimilation of the French, notably in the Quebec *Mercury*, founded in 1805. In *Le *Canadien* (1806), the Parti canadien agitated for more power and the development of the 'nation canadienne'. These issues came to a head under Governor James Craig, who in 1810 imprisoned many leaders of the Parti canadien suspected of nationalism and 'democratic' tendencies. During the War of 1812 Canadiens demonstrated their loyalty, and the conciliatory attitude of the new governor, Sir George Prevost, towards them lowered tensions. Meanwhile, society and the economy were restructured and modernized through the intrusion of market forces: a lumber boom, the proliferation of villages and urban growth, the construction of the Lachine canal, and the rise of the first corporations, insurance and investment companies, unions, banks, and so on.

Despite growing prosperity, inequalities were deepening, and political conflicts resurfaced after 1818. The near paralysis of colonial government, the unpopular *Union Bill of 1822, the failure of the mother country to initiate reforms, the creation of a land monopoly in the townships when good land was growing scarce in the seigneuries, the rejection by England of the assembly's demands, all led to the radicalization of the Parti canadien into the Parti patriote. The *Patriotes' Ninety-two Resolutions (1834), a summation of all the Canadiens' frustrations, were answered by the Russell Resolutions (1837), which rejected French colonists' demands and even condoned the use of public funds without the assembly's authorization. Many Canadien leaders were preaching independence and republicanism; at the same time, British colonists opposed any concessions and threatened to take up arms or even join the United States. This maelstrom exploded in the *Rebellions of 1837–8. Sent by London to investigate the situation, Lord *Durham identified constitutional and 'racial' problems in Lower Canada. In his report (1839), he recommended granting responsible government and uniting the Canadas in order to assimilate the Canadiens. The constitution had already been suspended in 1838. In 1840 the *Act of Union was passed in Britain, and in 1841 Lower and Upper Canada became the united *Province of Canada. However, the Canadiens numbered more than 500,000, and assimilation was impossible. JEAN-PIERRE WALLOT

Loyalists. Between 1781 and 1784 tens of thousands of colonists who had supported the British cause during the *American Revolution were forced to leave the Thirteen Colonies. These Loyalists became political refugees who had to seek asylum in other parts of the *British Empire. As they waited to be transported to their new homes—in Nova Scotia, Quebec, or as far away as the Caribbean or Great Britain—many were bewildered by rapidly changing circumstances and apprehensive about the future. They sought confirmation that their allegiance to the Crown had not been in vain. They also shared a determination to recoup their losses and a desire to rebuild homes in peace and safety.

The Loyalists were not a cohesive, homogeneous group. Although some were men and women of property and standing, most were farmers, labourers, and tradespeople. Reflecting the diversity of American society, they spoke a variety of languages, belonged to different ethnic groups, and represented many religious faiths. And, as soon became evident when they reached their new homes, they held widely divergent, often conflicting, understandings of what it meant to be loyal.

For some, loyalty had been a conscious and principled position that was not merely a conservative reaction to revolutionary fervour. Many government officials, merchants, lawyers, and other professionals had shared the patriot disquiet with British colonial policies and had publicly denounced ministerial corruption. Yet, they believed that the relationship between the Thirteen Colonies and Great Britain must not be severed: it could and should be reformed, for, they argued in pamphlets, newspapers, and broadsides, only the British constitution could guarantee liberty.

When war broke out, a few leading Loyalists went into exile confident that the British government would soon put down 'the madness of the multitude'. Other colonists (about 19,000 in total) joined provincial regiments to fight for the British cause. Most residents tried to carry on with their lives, and for many of them loyalty was situational and often contingent on their personal circumstances. Those who lived outside the mainstream of colonial society—recently arrived Dutch, German, and Scottish immigrants, for example—looked to the Crown for protection from assimilation. Sir John Johnson's Scottish tenants in the Mohawk Valley of New York remained loyal to their landlord when he fled north to escape imprisonment. Most women found loyalty thrust upon them as a result of their marriage to Loyalist men. African-American slaves declared their loyalty, encouraged by promises of freedom and land. The Mohawk and other Native Americans supported the British because they believed the Crown would secure their territory.

Many Loyalists were shocked by the British defeat at Yorkton in 1781; they were appalled two years later by the terms of peace, which provided no guarantee of compensation for their losses. Although in some instances Loyalist sympathizers were able to put aside their differences with patriot neighbours, those whom Committees of Safety had identified as 'tory' traitors, or who had fought in the bitter guerrilla war on the northern frontier, could not and often did not want to return home.

Throughout 1783 and 1784, British authorities scrambled to organize convoys to transport refugees from the last Loyalist strongholds in New York and Charleston and to ensure that they were adequately housed, fed, and resettled. Almost half of those who left relocated in the West Indies and Great Britain. A few went to Cape Breton. Somewhat more than 30,000, often organized into associations or still in their regimental units, embarked for Nova Scotia. Between 6,000 and 8,000 made their way overland to Quebec.

The new and inexperienced governor of Nova Scotia, John Parr, had limited resources and very little time to prepare for the influx of refugees. As boatloads of families, former slaves, and disbanded soldiers landed at the mouth of the Saint John River, or at Port Roseway (Shelburne), Guysborough, and other settlements along the peninsula, colonial authorities quickly began to survey land and to extend contracts for the enormous quantities of food, timber, and equipment needed. Inevitably tensions mounted among refugees living in tents, rough huts, and ships' holds. Colonial officials were charged with ineptness. Loyalists resented Nova Scotian neighbours who had not suffered the privations of war and exile. Moreover, many feared that they were not getting their rightful share.

The 14,000 or so who had landed at the Saint John River felt particularly aggrieved and isolated from the halls of government in Halifax. Influential and articulate Loyalists, such as Harvard-educated Edward Winslow, believed that as the natural leaders of their communities they should be recognized for their rank and that their loyalty deserved special compensation. Fifty-five 'of the most respectable' merchants and professionals therefore petitioned for 5,000-acre grants each. Resistance from 'ordinary' Loyalists and authorities in Halifax encouraged Winslow to press for the creation of a Loyalist colony—an asylum that could become 'the envy of the American states'. In 1784 Nova Scotia was partitioned. Colonel Thomas Carleton, brother of Sir Guy *Carleton, governor general of British North America, was appointed governor of the new colony of New Brunswick, and the Loyalist elite there set to work to establish a respectable, agricultural society, one that accepted the 'natural order' and hierarchical notions of good government. The Loyalist majority continued to challenge Winslow's vision.

Similar tensions between colonial authorities, second- and third-generation Nova Scotians, and Loyalists persisted in Nova Scotia, exacerbated by the difficulties of eking a living from poor land. By 1800 thousands of disenchanted Loyalists had made their way back to old homes in the United States; others left their land in search of work; and many trekked west to the new Loyalist colony of Upper Canada. The situation was particularly difficult for former slaves, who made up a significant proportion of the Nova Scotia refugees. Despite promises of freedom and land, African-American Loyalists were the last to be resettled, and many received no land at all. In a colony in which *slavery was still legal and some white Loyalists owned slaves, discrimination was condoned and segregation accepted. Not surprisingly, nearly half of all *Black Loyalists eagerly accepted a plan in 1792 to relocate to Sierra Leone.

An increasingly attractive destination for American refugees was the interior of the continent. After 1781 a growing number of colonists from New York, New Jersey, and Pennsylvania made their way north to Quebec—to join provincial regiments, to seek safety from threatening patriot neighbours, or, for many women, to be reunited with Loyalist husbands and fathers. The arrival of a fleet of evacuees from New York in 1783 forced Governor Haldimand to decide quickly how and where these Loyalists should be resettled. The upper country of the Great Lakes region was the most practical. After allocating lands along the Grand River to the Six Nations—who under the leadership of Mohawk Joseph *Brant and his sister Molly had been valuable allies during the war—surveyors began to mark out lands north of Lakes Ontario and Erie.

Loyalist settlement in the interior was organized in military fashion. Each Loyalist group that travelled up the St Lawrence River in 1784 was led by former officers, who then supervised the allocation of grants. The Crown helped to build saw and grist mills, provided each family with rations and farming tools, and promised continuing aid and protection. Members of the Loyalist elite chafed at being subject to civil law and not British common law, however, and British-American Loyalists objected to the absence of a representative assembly. The situation was rectified when the *Constitutional Act of 1791 partitioned Quebec into Lower Canada (the older settled portion on the St Lawrence River) and Upper Canada (now Ontario). The appointment of former British officer John Graves *Simcoe and not Loyalist Sir John Johnson as lieutenant-governor highlighted the growing divisions with the colony. The new governor hoped to create a little Britain in Upper Canada. The Loyalist elite considered themselves British Americans and wanted to recreate a variant of their old homes south of the border. The rank-and-file majority, who attended Methodist camp meetings and pressed for town government, wanted a more egalitarian society than the conservative hierarchical institutions that were established in Upper Canada.

Although there was no single, shared Loyalist vision for British North America, within a generation political refugees had become resident settlers. Those living in the colonies continued to swear allegiance to the King, and their governments and societies reflected the basic conservative views of the Loyalist elite. For later generations, the legacy of the Loyalists was increasingly tied up with the mythology of the Loyalist experience. Rather than a disparate group of political refugees, the Loyalists were mythologized by nascent 19th-century English-Canadian nationalists as valiant crusaders who had consciously rejected the revolution and republicanism and eagerly defended the Crown and the far superior notions of *peace, order, and good government inherent in the British constitution. The idea of the 'tory touch' remains a powerful touchstone in English-Canadian national identity. JANE ERRINGTON

Loyalist tradition refers to a cluster of related ideas and beliefs about the *Loyalist refugees who settled in Canada following the *American Revolution. According to this tradition, the Loyalists were a highly principled and well-educated elite who chose to sacrifice comfortable lives and endure the hardships of a northern wilderness rather than sever their ties to the British Crown and Empire and submit to republican institutions. United by their ideology and suffering, and motivated by a divine sense of mission, Loyalists, it was claimed, formed a closely knit community founded on conservative social and political values and characterized by an unwavering fidelity to the empire and an intense dislike of all things American.

The Loyalist tradition has frequently been identified as one of the defining elements of English-Canadian identity, but the traditional portrait of the Loyalists as aristocratic imperialists and anti-American anglophiles bears little relationship to historical reality. They were in fact a diverse group of people of generally modest means whose 'loyalty' arose from a wide range of motives and interests. Divided and discontented, Loyalist settlers resisted efforts to transform the Canadian wilderness into a 'little Britain' and quickly re-established ties with the new American republic. The traditions surrounding the Loyalists were invented in the century following their arrival by a variety of different groups who sought to construct usable pasts to further particular interests and causes. These groups included Loyalist settlers intent on furthering claims to compensation and maintaining their social status and political influence, filiopietistic descendants seeking to honour their forebears and to share in their accomplishments, nationalists and educators determined to produce an inspiring and unifying official history, and imperialists promoting closer ties between Canada and the *British Empire.

The tradition peaked in the aftermath of the 1884 Loyalist centennial celebrations, when the changes accompanying urbanization and industrialization created both a sense of anxiety about the present and a nostalgia for a simpler, more stable past. The influence of the tradition declined in the years following the First World War as ties to the empire weakened, anti-American sentiment waned, and the middle class embraced an ethic of progress and development. Invented rather than inherited, the tradition was often the subject of controversy as different groups and interests debated the meaning of the Loyalist past and competed to control its use.

NORMAN KNOWLES

Lucien Rivard affair. Lucien Rivard would belong to history's dustbin were it not for his suspicious escape from jail in 1965, on a warm night when he was sent out to create a skating rink. Using the waterhose, Rivard apparently scaled the wall and had freedom for four months. He was facing *extradition to the United States on drug-smuggling charges, but the controversy derived from the interventions on his behalf by senior officials in the federal Liberal government. Several assistants to Liberal ministers, including a special aide to Justice Minister Guy Favreau and an executive assistant to the minister of citizenship and immigration, had interfered in the Rivard extradition proceedings. A royal commission was appointed to investigate the affair, and its report was extremely damaging to the government and to Favreau in particular. He resigned but was given another position in the government. His prestige greatly diminished, he died in 1967. Rivard was extradited to the United States and given a 20-year sentence. He served nine years and returned to Canada.

JOHN ENGLISH

lumber industry. No manufacturing industry has had a longer or larger impact on as many parts of Canada as the lumber industry. Sawmills and retail lumber outlets have peppered the country since the beginning of European settlement. In several regions of Canada in the mid-19th century, giant sawmills began devouring forest resources to produce vast quantities of sawn lumber for export. A basis was laid for one of Canada's largest export industries, one that has been fundamental to economic development in several parts of the country, from Nova Scotia to British Columbia. Its impact on the natural landscape has been equally significant.

The locally oriented branch of the lumber industry has the longest history. In the settlement era, small, water-powered sawmills were ubiquitous. Under the civil law of French Canada before the 1850s, the seigneur enjoyed a monopoly right to own and operate a sawmill on his seigneury. Elsewhere entrepreneurs built sawmills to process local timber and to meet the local demand for lumber. Although the output of each mill was small, the sum total of their production was considerable when seen in the context of pre-industrial colonial economies. In time, some small mills grew to serve urban markets in Canada and abroad, but locally oriented sawmills and lumber yards remain a feature of many rural districts today.

The history of the export-oriented part of the business is best understood on a regional basis. Substantial lumber firms emerged in Nova Scotia in the mid- and late 19th century, but in comparison with the New Brunswick industry they were more apt to be family-run, community businesses that drew on private rather than Crown forests. Lumber exports to England greatly assisted economic development in Nova Scotia, but the industry never dominated the provincial economy in the way that it did in New Brunswick. There the lumber-export business grew out of the venerable trade in *square timber. Beginning in the 1830s British and American capital built large mills that used gang saws to produce thick, pine planks (known as 'deals') for export to England. Provincial policies favoured well-financed firms, which acquired rights to harvest Crown forests at bargain prices. In the 1860s and 1870s changing markets in Britain and the depletion of high-quality pine in New Brunswick reduced the province's exports of square timber and caused the expansion of sawmilling. Increasingly the big mills, which were now steam-driven, produced both spruce and pine lumber cut to dimensions ready for use in the British construction industry. In the 20th century the region's export lumber trade gradually declined in significance as suitable forests were cut over, but it never disappeared.

Developments in Quebec and Ontario only partly mirrored those to the east. As in New Brunswick, the deal mills of William *Price's empire on the Saguenay River remained oriented towards British markets after mid-century, and they too increasingly produced sawn lumber ready for the British building industry. On the other hand, companies in the Ottawa Valley (on both sides of the river) supplied American lumber markets as early as the 1830s. From the 1860s to the 1920s, American hunger for lumber of almost any quality was insatiable, and new railways enabled Quebec and Ontario lumber firms to feed that demand. American investment in Ottawa Valley and Georgian Bay lumbering was considerable. When Michigan producers ran short of timber in the 1890s, they moved their logging operations to the north shore of

Lake Huron and Georgian Bay, towing giant booms of logs to mills in the United States. In a successful bid to protect jobs, Ontario passed regulations requiring that timber cut on Crown land be sawn in the province. Job losses were much more catastrophic during the Great Depression, and, because the forest resources of Ontario and Quebec were by then so depleted, the industry never resumed its earlier vitality. Yet the lumber business lived on, sometimes in new form. By the 1970s, integrated forest products corporations produced both lumber and *pulp and paper for Canadian and American purchasers.

From the 1840s to the 1940s, logging methods and sawmill technology remained remarkably stable in eastern and central Canada. The large mills used integrated processes from the start, and by 1870 they relied on steam power. In logging, however, hand tools prevailed and power came from the muscles of men and horses. It was not until after the Second World War that bush operators introduced mechanized equipment and developed a less seasonal workforce.

On Canada's west coast the lumber-export business got its start in the 1860s at Burrard Inlet, where Vancouver later grew. Attracted by the magnificent cedar and Douglas fir growing close to sheltered water, British and American investors built huge mills to saw lumber for export around the Pacific rim. Mill owners gained ready access to Crown timber, but only trees growing near tidewater could be handled by existing logging methods. Coastal logging expanded massively after 1900, when mechanical methods, including logging railways, made it possible to log vast Crown forests and supply lumber to the Canadian Prairies and to markets abroad. Eastern Canadian and American lumbermen, having exhausted forests in their home regions, invested heavily in coastal lumbering. Labour demand continued so strong that woods and sawmill workers managed to unionize in 1919. The Depression brought staff layoffs and mill closings, but British demand during the Second World War revived the industry. In the post-war period, depleted forests drove the province to introduce new forest-management policies and forced forest operations inland and to the north. Lumbering remained crucial to the British Columbia economy during the late 20th century, even as American protectionism threatened the industry's main market and the environmental movement discredited certain logging practices, such as logging old-growth forests and clear-cutting.

Regional differences aside, the lumber industry has a long and proud record of contributing to Canada's economic well-being, most notably as a top earner of foreign currency. Lumbering's longstanding approach to the forest resource—'cut and run'—has left behind a much less attractive record: devastated forests, mill and community closings, criticisms from angry conservationists, and belated attempts at redress by the industry.

IAN RADFORTH

Lundy's Lane. Fought between British and American forces 25–26 July 1814, this still-disputed battle was part of the American invasion of the Niagara Peninsula during the War of 1812. The fighting was brutal, marked by strategic errors of both commanders and the fatigue of the British troops. There also was much confusion on both sides, since the battle took place in the dark between soldiers who, because of similar uniforms and a common language, could not always distinguish friend from foe. Three hundred died as a result, surviving soldiers were left severely weakened, and both commanders, British general Sir Gordon Drummond and American Major-General Jacob Brown, were badly wounded. One survivor, British Lieutenant John Le Couteur, wrote that he 'never passed so awful a night'. CECILIA MORGAN

Lunenburg. In June 1753, some 1,453 'foreign Protestants' arrived on the peninsular shore of the new community of Lunenburg. The township was the second British settlement in Nova Scotia, following Halifax (1749). Named in honour of the king of England, whose titles included Duke of Brunswick-Lunenburg, the town was created to balance the presence of French Catholic settlements elsewhere in Nova Scotia.

The settlers came from Germanic states, with a smaller number from France and Switzerland. They were farmers, attracted to Nova Scotia by the promise of free land, supplies, and limited freedom from taxation. They soon discovered that their future required a change from harvesting the land to harvesting the sea. With a strength of will that was to become Lunenburg's trademark, they became shipbuilders and fishermen. The new enterprise was established by 1760.

Lunenburg endured times of hardship, but in the 1870s the success of dory schooners led to an economic boom. Larger Lunenburg vessels sailed to international ports, taking salt fish and returning with fine clothing, materials, food, and of course rum. The beginning of the 20th century saw the highest population, at 5,000. Newfoundland fishermen had joined the fleet and their families became a vital part of the community. During the century the economy followed the rise and fall of the North Atlantic fisheries. With typical pluck, industry adapted. The town continues to have a vibrant working economy, with the inclusion of heritage and tourism-related themes.

Original settlers would recognize 21st-century Lunenburg, with its intact grid pattern of settlement, as first laid-out by the British military. The grid, combined with architecture spanning the life of the town, led to the UNESCO designation of Old Town Lunenburg as a World Heritage Site in 1995. HEATHER-ANNE GETSON

Lynch, John Joseph (1816–88), Roman Catholic archbishop. Born in Ireland, Lynch joined the Lazarist order to become a missionary priest. After serving as an itinerant saddle-bag priest in Texas and a seminary superior in Niagara Falls, New York, in 1860 he became the third bishop of Toronto, a city whose Roman Catholic minority was mostly of *Irish origin. Following the creation of Ontario, with Toronto as its capital, Lynch was elevated to archbishop, the metropolitan of the province's English-speaking hierarchy.

A fervent Irish nationalist, ardent defender of the Catholic faith, and inveterate political activist on behalf of Catholic schooling and government patronage for members of his flock, Lynch was a controversial figure. Among the Protestant majority, these challenges to the status quo often provoked fierce resistance. Likewise, many lay Catholics chaffed at their bishop's quest to exercise such wide-ranging and undisputed leadership. Even Lynch's lay opponents, however, admired his efforts to build a comprehensive system of Catholic benevolent institutions that made possible the creation of a distinctly Catholic subculture in Toronto. BRIAN CLARKE

Macallum, Archibald Byron (1858 1934). Born in Belmont, Canada West, Macallum is recognized as one of the founders of Canadian science. He began lecturing in biology at the University of Toronto in 1886, before completing his education. He received his PhD from Johns Hopkins in 1888 and his medical degree from Toronto in 1889, and was the recipient of many other degrees and academic honours. He was elected a fellow of the Canadian Royal Society in 1901 and the Royal Society five years later. Macallum held professorships in the physiology and biochemistry departments at Toronto before joining the biochemistry department at McGill University. He spent three years involved in the founding of the *National Research Council of Canada and played a key role in establishing the Ontario Library Association. His contributions to scientific theory are significant; he also played an integral role in the inclusion of biochemistry in the premedical curriculum in Canada. LISA DRYSDALE

MacAskill, Angus (1825–63), the Cape Breton giant. Born in Harris, Scotland, one of 13 children, MacAskill emigrated with his parents to St Ann's in 1831. An enormous man, he was 7′ 9″ tall and weighed 425 pounds; he measured 3′ 8″ across the shoulders, the palm of his hand was 12″ long and 6″ wide. His feats of strength became legendary—he was reputed to have lifted a 2,700-pound anchor on his shoulder. At the age of 24 MacAskill joined a travelling show and toured Quebec, the United States, the West Indies, and Cuba, from 1849 to 1853. He also had an audience with Queen Victoria. Upon returning to Cape Breton he opened a store and a grist mill. He died of 'brain fever' at St Ann's. KENNETH DONOVAN

McBride, Richard (1870–1917), lawyer, BC premier 1903–15. Born in New Westminster, McBride was very much a British Columbian. After the fifth administration in five years collapsed, the charismatic McBride formed a Conservative administration in June 1903 and introduced party lines and stability. His fight with Ottawa for 'Better Terms' was locally popular; so too were his expansionist policies that reflected the speculative fever that gripped the province after 1907. He promised to guarantee bonds for the Canadian Northern Pacific, *Pacific Great Eastern, and other railways, made plans to build the University of British Columbia, and encouraged investors. After the economy weakened in 1912–13, his enemies accused him of giving away provincial resources, the new railways had financial problems, and British Columbians were demanding reforms such as female suffrage and prohibition, for which he had little sympathy. Give this situation and his failing health, McBride resigned on his 45th birthday to become British Columbia's agent general in London. His rise and fall echoed the boom and bust nature of the BC economy. PATRICIA E. ROY

McClung, Nellie L. (1873–1951). A leading liberal feminist and popular author of 19 volumes, McClung contributed significantly to *franchise and *prohibition victories during the First World War. Her essays in *In Times like These* (1915), capture the spirit of first-wave *feminism in North America. Born Helen Letitia Mooney in Grey County, Ontario, she and her Methodist Scots-Irish family joined the Manitoba land rush in 1880. A school teacher (1890–6), she married pharmacist Robert Wesley McClung in 1896; they produced five children. A member of the *Woman's Christian Temperance Union, she trusted suffrage would banish the bar and protect the family. Well-known for her best-seller *Sowing Seeds in Danny* (1908), she joined Winnipeg's Canadian Women's Press Club and the Political Equality League. In 1914 she parodied Manitoba premier Rodmond *Roblin in a mock parliament to promote *women's suffrage. In 1916 that province became the first to enfranchise white women. Elected an Alberta Liberal MLA in the 1921 campaign won by the United Farmers, she struggled to be non-partisan and attributed her 1926 defeat to 'liquor interests'. In 1925 she joined the new *United Church of Canada and campaigned for women ministers. In 1929, as one of the 'Famous Five', she secured the Judicial Committee of the Privy Council's recognition of women as 'persons' within the constitution. In 1936 she became the first female member of the CBC's board of governors and in 1938 a delegate to the *League of Nations. She died in Victoria. VERONICA STRONG-BOAG

McCrae, John (1872–1918), poet, doctor, soldier. Born into a military family, the author of the best-known poem of the First World War joined the *militia at age 14 and later studied medicine at the University of Toronto. McCrae served as an artilleryman in the *Boer War, but in 1904 put aside soldiering to concentrate on medicine and became a popular teacher at McGill University. He re-enlisted in 1914 as a surgeon, and in May 1915, after a friend was killed by shellfire, a grieving McCrae snatched 20 minutes' respite from his duties to compose 'In Flanders Fields'. He thought little of the poem until a fellow officer persuaded him to submit it for publication; one editor rejected it, but *Punch* published it in December 1915 to immediate acclaim (although the press rarely spelled either his name or the poem's title correctly). McCrae took his fame in stride, and went about his medical duties. On 24 January 1918, he was appointed consulting physician to the First British Army, but four days later he died of meningitis and pneumonia. He is buried at Wimereux, France. JONATHAN VANCE

McCulloch, Thomas (1776–1843). Born in Fereneze, Scotland, McCulloch graduated in logic from the University of Glasgow (1792) and was ordained a Secessionist Presbyterian clergyman in 1799 after studying theology. Sailing to Pictou, Nova Scotia, in 1803 en route to Prince Edward Island, he accepted the call to be Pictou's dissenting Presbyterian minister in 1804. Here, in 1816, he established Pictou Academy, an influential interdenominational institution of higher learning; became a catalyst for theological debate in the province (publishing *Popery Condemned*, 1808; *The Subjects and Mode of Baptism Ascertained from Scripture*, 1810; *The Prosperity of the Church in Troublous Times*, 1814); and assembled bird and insect collections that earned him honorary degrees from Glasgow and Edinburgh (and the friendship of John James Audubon, who visited him in 1833). In the view of critic Northrop *Frye, McCulloch's satirical Mephibosheth Stepsure letters (*Acadian Recorder*, 1821–3), with their 'quiet, observant' humour based on 'a vision of society', have deservedly earned McCulloch a reputation as 'the founder' of 'genuine Canadian humour'. Although an Edinburgh publisher rejected the Stepsure letters because of their pungency and Swiftian humour, another printed McCulloch's moral emigrant tales, *Colonial Gleanings: William and Melville*, in 1826. McCulloch assumed the presidency of Dalhousie University in Halifax in 1838, continuing to endorse until his death the views on liberal education (including scientific instruction) that had informed his life as an educator and on which he had published in Halifax, in 1819, *The Nature and Uses of a Liberal Education Illustrated*. GWENDOLYN DAVIES

Macdonald, Angus L. (1890–1954), Nova Scotia premier 1933–40, 1945–54, federal cabinet minister. Born in Dunvegan, Cape Breton, Macdonald, a stirring orator, was only one-quarter Scottish but developed an image as 'a Scot, first, last and all the time', and 'a gentleman in the tradition of the Scottish chieftain'. Educated at St Francis Xavier, Dalhousie (law, 1921), and Harvard (PhD, 1929), he won the first ever provincial Liberal leadership convention in 1930 and led the party to victory three years later. During the Second World War he was recruited to Ottawa to serve as minister of national defence for naval service. He returned to Nova Scotia in 1945 and, running under the slogan 'All's well with Angus L', was swept back into power with the largest mandate in the history of the province. His government developed a modern highway system, including a one-mile causeway to link Cape Breton to the mainland and a suspension bridge between Halifax and Dartmouth, which was named for him after he died unexpectedly of a heart attack at age 63. More than 100,000 Nova Scotians lined the streets for his funeral procession. He was, as one newspaper noted, the 'most beloved Nova Scotia statesman and scholar since Joseph *Howe'. STEPHEN KIMBER

Macdonald, Sir John Alexander (1815–91), prime minister 1867–73, 1878–91. Born in Glasgow, son of Helen Shaw and Hugh Macdonald, who brought him to Kingston with three other siblings in 1820. Hugh Macdonald was feckless, friendly, and fond of the bottle, but with the stiffening and energy of Helen Macdonald, young John managed to get an education and was called to the bar in 1836. He had early success as an ingenious defence attorney, but soon focused on corporate law. In 1843 he married his cousin, Isabella Clark. Sadly, she became chronically ill; her two pregnancies were difficult, and only one of the children, Hugh John (born 1850), survived. Isabella herself died in 1857.

Macdonald was elected to the *Province of Canada assembly in 1844 as a Conservative. He was a genuine one, opposing *responsible government not on principle but as premature. In cabinet in 1847–8 he proved an adroit administrator; his conservative bent did not prevent him from accepting new and useful ideas. By 1854, when he became attorney general, he had established friendly relations with French Canadians; these were the basis of the future success of his party. His advice in 1856 to the editor of the Montreal *Gazette* was shrewd: 'No man in his senses can suppose that this country [the Province of Canada] can for a century to come be governed by a totally unfrenchified government . . . [You] must . . . respect their nationality. Treat them as a nation and they will act as a free people generally do—generously. Call them a faction and they become factious.'

Macdonald opposed *Confederation when the idea first took concrete shape in the spring of 1864; the American Civil War (1861–5) proved that federations were dangerous and divisive. But his empirical mind ultimately concluded that 'federal' could cover several possibilities. Under a federal constitution, one could centralize where it mattered (and with Macdonald that covered a great deal of ground) and decentralize where it didn't—that is, when one needed to dissipate regional prejudices or cosset regional differences.

In 1867 Macdonald emerged as the prime minister of the government of the new Dominion of Canada. He had considerable political strengths: ductility, perceptiveness, a knack for the right word in the right place, an infinite capacity for remembering names and faces. He was no beauty; his face was hewn on rugged Scottish principles, a full mouth, and a generous nose. He was tall, slim, and nonchalant; he moved through the world like an 18th-century gallant, well primed with poetry, political and military biography, a wicked sense of humour, and a decided capacity for drink. He believed in manners, but he looked to the man or the woman behind them. Though he believed troubles and worries were inevitable, he had his father's tendency to drink when the going was really rough. He lost all of his money in 1868 as a result of his law partner's bankruptcy and was rescued by his mortgaging everything, by loans, and by friends; what was worse, in 1869 his second wife, Susan Agnes Bernard, whom he had married in 1867, gave birth to a hydrocephalic daughter, Mary. Although she would never walk or play, she lived until 1933, and her father was devoted to her.

Macdonald was prime minister from 1867 to 1873, when he was defeated by the *Pacific Scandal, and from 1878 until his death in 1891. His main accomplishments were the protective tariff of the *National Policy, the CPR, and Confederation itself. He was no saint; elections and loyalties were won by *patronage. He loved old even gamy friends and acquaintances and could be tender and generous to them in adversity. He was a patient man who listened to everyone, and seemed to enjoy his métier. When he died in June 1891, Canadians mourned for him as if he had been taken from their very households.

P.B. WAITE

McDonald Commission. In July 1977 the government of Pierre *Trudeau announced the establishment of a three-member royal commission to investigate wrongdoings by the Royal Canadian Mounted Police Security Service. Nicknamed the McDonald Commission after Justice David McDonald, its head, it represented a partially pre-emptive strike by the Trudeau government against a provincial foe. One month earlier, Quebec's *Parti Québécois government had launched its own investigation of the same issues.

For nearly three years the commission listened to the testimony of a wide variety of witnesses, in Ottawa and across Canada, and accessed thousands of pages of secret RCMP security files. In the process, a litany of illegal activities by Canada's national police force, including break-ins, thefts, smear campaigns, and even the burning of a barn, would be revealed. The result of the commission was three volumes of findings and recommendations. The first appeared in 1979, the remainder in 1981. The final volume was the most controversial, primarily because it appeared (rightly, as evidence would later reveal) to step back from assessing the full extent of the federal government's knowledge of the illegal activities by its police force as they were occurring. In its most significant recommendation, the commission suggested the creation of a new civilian intelligence service that would operate free of the *RCMP. The government accepted this proposition and in 1984 created the Canadian Security Intelligence Service. Ironically, this 'new' outfit was staffed primarily by former members of the RCMP Security Service.

STEVE HEWITT

McGee, Thomas D'Arcy (1825–68), politician, journalist, poet, historian, orator. Born in Ireland, McGee moved to the United States in 1842, where he distinguished himself as an outstanding journalist. He returned to Ireland in 1845, joined the Young Ireland movement, and participated in the abortive 1848 rising against Britain. Disguised as a priest, he escaped to America, where he proudly proclaimed himself a republican revolutionary and traitor to the British Crown. But he rapidly became disillusioned with anti-Irish and anti-Catholic sentiments in the United States, and in 1851 embraced a deeply conservative form of Catholicism. Convinced that Irish Catholics were much better off in Canada, he moved to Montreal in 1857, where he launched the *New Era* newspaper and became a member of Parliament for Montreal West. In Canada, McGee supported separate schools for Catholics, fought against both the militant Protestant *Orange Order and the *Irish revolutionary *Fenian movement, and became an early, energetic, and eloquent supporter of Confederation. He advocated a 'new nationality', characterized by western expansion, economic growth, protective tariffs, a distinctly Canadian literature, and the entrenchment of minority rights. His uncompromising attacks on the Fenians alienated a significant section of his Irish Catholic constituency and resulted in his assassination in Ottawa in 1868.

DAVID A. WILSON

MacGill, Elsie (Elizabeth Muriel) Gregory (1905–80), feminist activist, pioneer in applied science. She was the first woman to earn a BSc in electrical engineering at the University of Toronto (1927) and her MSE in aeronautical engineering (University of Michigan, 1929) was the first awarded to any woman anywhere. Partially disabled by *poliomyelitis in 1929, she nevertheless carried on an active career as an aeronautical engineer, recognized by many public honours. In 1943 she married E.J. Soulsby, a widower with two children. As an engineer, she is best known for her role in producing the Hawker Hurricane fighter planes during the Second World War. Her feminist activism included the national presidency of the Business and Professional Women's Clubs (1962–4), during which she encouraged the group to take an active political role. A member of the Royal Commission on the Status of Women (1967–70), she wrote for its *Report* a separate statement that advocated taxing women as individuals and decriminalizing *abortion. Later, with the Ontario Committee on the Status of Women, she lobbied for the application of the royal commission's recommendations. Indomitable and loveable, she was a major inspiration to the second wave of the Canadian women's movement.

NAOMI BLACK

MacGill, Helen Gregory (1864–1947), feminist reformer and judge, first woman graduate of Trinity College, University of Toronto (BA and MA). As a young reporter MacGill travelled alone across the Canadian West to Japan, marrying her first husband en route and moving with him to the United States. Widowed young, with two young sons, she married James MacGill in 1903 and moved to Vancouver, where her two daughters were born. Her mother before her had been active in the women's movement as her daughter Elsie Gregory *MacGill would be; she herself was influential in feminist groups such as the Women's University Club. Without any formal legal training, she served for 23 years as a judge of the Juvenile Court of Vancouver, the first woman appointed judge in the region (1917) and the third in Canada. The court itself had been created because of the pressures for reform exerted by women's groups in which she had been active. Typical of her generation, this much-honoured Canadian did not consider herself a career woman, in spite of a lifetime of public service, writing, and publishing. NAOMI BLACK

Mackenzie, Sir Alexander (1762–1820), fur trader, explorer, born near Stornoway, Scotland. Mackenzie moved from New York to attend school in Montreal, and in 1779 he entered the fur-trading firm of Finlay and Gregory, which merged with the *North West Company. Mackenzie became a partner at the post on Athabasca River, where he helped establish *Fort Chipewyan, setting out from this point in 1789 to test Peter *Pond's theory that Cook's River (Alaska) provided a travel route to the Pacific from Great Slave Lake. Mackenzie discovered that the river (later named after himself) led not to the Pacific, but to the Arctic. Undeterred, Mackenzie headed west on a second expedition, from Fort Fork on the Peace River 9 May 1793. He arrived at the Fraser watershed, where he was advised by Natives to continue to the Pacific overland. The last stretch Mackenzie completed via the Bella Coola River, reaching Mackenzie Rock, Dean Channel, British Columbia, on 22 July. This feat represents the first crossing of North America by a European north of Mexico. Mackenzie returned to England in 1799, where he was knighted and his *Voyages from Montreal* (1801) was published. He married in 1812 and retired to Scotland. BARRY M. GOUGH

Mackenzie, Alexander (1822–92), prime minister 1873–8. Born near Dunkeld, Scotland, Mackenzie came to Canada in 1842 to work as a stonemason. An injury on the job led him to enter the construction business in the Sarnia area with his brother. He subsequently began a career in politics as a crusading newspaper editor and was elected to the legislative assembly of Canada in 1861 as a *Reformer. Mackenzie supported Confederation, but was one of those politicians who sat in both the federal and provincial legislatures until the practice was abolished in Ontario in 1872. Early in 1873 he became leader of the federal *Liberal Party; soon after he became the second prime minister of Canada. Mackenzie was a dour, hard-working, penny-pinching Scot (in both his personal and public life). He was often criticized for attempting to serve as his own finance minister. Perhaps his chief contribution to Canada was an administration demonstrating that political life went on after Sir John A. *Macdonald and that a different political vision from that of the first prime minister was possible. His government's major achievement was probably the creation of the *Supreme Court of Canada in 1875. Mackenzie refused a knighthood and other honours after his retirement from politics in 1880 due to ill health. J.M. BUMSTED

Mackenzie, Chalmers Jack (1888–1984). Best known as Canada's chief defence scientist during the Second World War, C.J. Mackenzie had a varied and notable career. Born in Nova Scotia, he attended Dalhousie University until the Great War, when he enlisted in the Canadian army, serving with distinction on the Western Front. After the war Mackenzie pursued his engineering career, in the private sector and as dean of this faculty at the University of Saskatchewan. During the 1930s he established close connections with the *National Research Council and its president, General Andy *McNaughton, who subsequently recommended that Mackenzie be his wartime replacement. This appointment continued until Mackenzie's official retirement in 1961.

During the Second World War most of Canada's defence science contributions came about within the framework of the Anglo-American military alliance, which allowed Canadian scientists to participate in various research and development projects. These included radar equipment, high explosives, proximity fuses, chemical weapons, biological agents, and components for the US atomic bomb project. For Mackenzie, the post-war years posed many challenges. First was his successful attempt to extract the NRC from defence research, while at the same time drawing upon the expertise gained by its wartime atomic program to develop the acclaimed CANDU reactor system. Another priority was his attempt to prevent scientific 'brain drain' to the United States by convincing federal and provincial governments to fund long-term scientific research. Unfortunately, at the time of Mackenzie's death, Canada still lagged behind other industrialized nations in this commitment.

DONALD H. AVERY

Mackenzie, William Lyon (1795–1861), journalist and politician. Mackenzie settled in Upper Canada from Scotland in 1820. Publishing the *Colonial Advocate*, he championed reform, outraging a group of tories, who ransacked his York (Toronto) press. This helped him win election to the assembly in 1828, where tormented opponents manufactured reasons for expelling him. He took a host of complaints to England in 1832, receiving a sympathetic hearing there, but not satisfaction. Back in the assembly in 1834, he compiled a massive report on grievances. The heated election of 1836 saw him and many other reformers lose their seats. When rebellion broke out in Lower Canada in November 1837, he published a draft constitution based on American models, then helped rally some 500 men on the outskirts of Toronto, having repeatedly told the insurgents that a peaceful display would win the day. Government supporters put the rebels to flight on 7 December. Escaping to Buffalo, Mackenzie helped institute a series of raids; American authorities eventually imprisoned him for breaching neutrality laws. Granted an amnesty, he returned to the province in 1850, where he sat as an independent in the assembly, 1851–8, acting as a strident critic of the new political and economic order attendant on industrialism. COLIN READ

Mackenzie, Mann and Company Limited. Mackenzie, Mann was a railway-contracting partnership and financial holding company created by William Mackenzie and Donald Mann, who built and promoted Canada's third transcontinental railway, the Canadian Northern Railway. Mackenzie and Mann, who were railway contractors with the *Canadian Pacific Railway in the 1880s, both secured construction contracts on the CPR's line across the state of Maine in 1888. Since their contracts were contiguous, they merged their operations to form an unincorporated company in which they owned almost all the shares. The partnership was incorporated in 1902 as Mackenzie, Mann and Company Limited.

New contracts to build independent western railways were negotiated in the 1890s. Mackenzie and Mann declined payment beyond actual expenses incurred, taking shares in the newly built railways instead. Those railways were amalgamated in 1898 to form the Canadian Northern Railway, which was gradually extended to become Canada's third transcontinental railway. Mackenzie and Mann also organized or acquired and then turned over to Canadian Northern numerous ancillary enterprises, again taking shares in return for their services. Canadian Northern encountered serious financial problems during the First World War. The federal government provided interim assistance after Mackenzie and Mann surrendered 40 per cent of the Canadian Northern shares. Further difficulties resulted in a 1918 arbitrated settlement that provided Mackenzie and Mann with compensation for these shares. It barely covered their indebtedness to the Canadian Bank of Commerce. Both men were knighted in 1911. T.D. REGEHR

Mackenzie–Papineau Battalion. In 1936 Republican Spain elected a Popular Front government of liberals, democrats, socialists, communists, and syndicalists. Its reform program was violently opposed by industrialists, landowners, the Catholic Church, and fascists. Led by General Francisco Franco and supplied by Nazi Germany and Fascist Italy, these opponents launched an insurrection against the government, and the Spanish Civil War broke out. The Republican government issued a plea to the western democracies for political support and much-needed food and arms. All refused; only the Soviet Union gave limited aid.

Although governments did nothing, people from around the world came to the aid of the republic. Thousands left their homes to join hastily formed volunteer military units called the International Brigades. In Canada, enlistment was largely organized by the *Communist Party and supported by the *CCF, trade *unions, and progressives. Over 1,500 Canadians, including the author Hugh Garner and Dr Norman *Bethune, went to Spain. Many had endured the unemployment, poverty, and *relief camps of the Great Depression. Denied much democracy at home, they were keen to fight for it abroad. By spring 1937 they had created their own unit, the Mackenzie–Papineau Battalion (Mac–Paps), named after the leaders of the 1837 *rebellions in Upper and Lower Canada. Canadians fought in many of the important actions of the war, including Fuentes de Ebro, Teruel, and Gandes, always outnumbered and out-gunned by the well-supplied Fascists.

In September 1938 the Republican government repatriated the International Brigades, in the hope that Franco would send home his Italian and German troops. To no one's surprise, he did not, and the Spanish Republic fell to the fascists in March 1939.

Half of the Mac–Paps were dead or missing in action; many of the survivors were wounded. They returned to a hero's welcome in Canada, but the Canadian government labelled them 'premature anti-fascists' and treated them as potential subversives; many were blacklisted. With the outbreak of the Second World War in September 1939, the government would finally heed the warning the International Brigades had issued three years earlier. Official recognition of their sacrifice and commitment to democracy would not come until 2001 with the unveiling of a national monument to the Mac–Paps in Ottawa. Even then government support was subdued: funding for the monument came from private donations. MARK LEIER

Mackenzie Valley Pipeline Inquiry. In 1974, Canadian Arctic Gas Pipeline Limited sought the government of Canada's permission to construct a pipeline through the Mackenzie Valley to connect reserves of natural gas in the Beaufort Delta with southern markets, and a pipeline across the northern portion of the Yukon to feed Alaskan natural gas into the Mackenzie Valley pipeline. The government appointed Justice Thomas Berger to conduct the Mackenzie Valley Pipeline Inquiry to recommend conditions that should be imposed on such a project. Berger interpreted his mandate broadly: he examined not just the single application but also the cumulative effects of all the development that would accompany the pipeline; he recommended not only how but, more fundamentally, whether a pipeline should be built. His exhaustive hearings in the northern communities to be affected, and in southern Canada, attracted much media attention, educated Canadians about the circumstances of northern Aboriginal people, and built support for their land claims. The inquiry's 1997 *Report* recommended that, for environmental reasons, no pipeline should ever be built across the northern Yukon. While it judged an energy corridor along the Mackenzie Valley to be environmentally feasible, it recommended that no pipeline be built for at least ten years to provide time for the Native peoples of the region to negotiate and implement their land claim settlements. This would enable them to gain the resources and self-determination necessary for meeting the economic, social, and cultural challenges that Berger anticipated would accompany the pipeline. The inquiry itself did not kill the pipeline proposal, but the scepticism it generated led the government to favour a pipeline—never built—along the *Alaska Highway. The legacy of the inquiry was Canadians' enhanced understanding of northern Aboriginal peoples and of how properly to assess large-scale resource-development projects.

GURSTON DACKS

McLachlan, James Bryson (1869–1937), coal miner, labour leader. Born at Ecclefechan in the south of Scotland, McLachlan went into the Lanarkshire pits at ten years of age. As an immigrant to industrial Nova Scotia in 1902, he brought contemporary ideas about labour unions and social reform to the Cape Breton coalfields. There he became a member of the Socialist Party of Canada and an organizer of District 26, *United Mine Workers of America, which achieved recognition from employers in 1919. In the dominion election of 1921 McLachlan swept the mining districts in and around Glace Bay, polling 8,914 votes, but was not elected. In 1923 the international union removed him from office for supporting a sympathetic strike; the same events resulted in his conviction on charges of seditious libel. After his release, he edited the *Maritime Labor Herald* (1924–6) and the *Nova Scotia Miner* (1929–36). A member of the *Communist Party of Canada from 1922 onwards, he became president of the *Workers' Unity League in 1930 and was known across the country as a spokesman for labour radicalism. McLachlan is remembered in the coalfields as the uncompromising champion of the miners and is commemorated with a monument in Glace Bay bearing his plea for working-class history: 'I believe in telling children the truth about the history of the world, that it does not consist in the history of Kings and Lords and Cabinets, but consists in the history of the mass of the workers, a thing that is not taught in the schools.' DAVID FRANK

McLean Gang. Celebrated in song (Ian Tyson, Bill Gallaher) and fiction (George Bowering), the McLeans caused much trouble in British Columbia in the 1870s. Living in the Nicola Valley, the 'gang' consisted of Allen (age 24), Charlie (17), and Archie (15), sons of the ruthless Hudson's Bay Company fur trader Donald McLean, and their friend Alex Hare (17). Their mixed-blood status made them all social outcasts. They achieved notoriety in December 1879, when they killed Johnnie Ussher, a provincial policeman, and later a second man. This violence provoked fears throughout the province of an Indian uprising. The gang fled to a cabin on Douglas Lake, holding out there for three days and three nights before surrendering on 13 December. Although their first trial was declared a mistrial, they were all convicted at a second, and on 13 January 1881 the four young men were hanged in New Westminster. Archie McLean was the youngest person ever hanged in British Columbia. JEAN WILSON

MacLennan, Hugh (1907–90). Born of a Cape Breton family, he took his degrees in classics, completing his PhD at Princeton University in 1935. Returning to Canada, he settled in Montreal. The first major English-speaking author to attempt to delineate Canada's national character, he tried his hand at two unpublished novels before deciding to set his books in Canada. *Barometer Rising* (1941), his first published novel, is a compelling romance set against the horrors of wartime and the catastrophic *Halifax explosion of 1917. **Two Solitudes* (1945), his second novel, treats English–French tensions in Quebec. His seven novels as well as his many essays and travel books present a chronicle of a Canada that often mediates between the old world of its European cultural heritage and the new world of American vitality and materialism. A cartographer of Canadian society, he performed a service of inestimable value to the development of Canadian fiction: he mapped the terrain of Canada and enabled later novelists to turn directly to the character novel and its exploration of human lives. DAVID STAINES

Macleod, James F. (1836–94), mounted policeman, judge. Macleod's family emigrated from Scotland in 1845 and settled near Toronto. Educated at Upper Canada College and Queen's University, Macleod began a legal career at Bowmanville in the 1860s. After militia service during the *Trent* crisis and the *Fenian raids, he participated in the Red River Expedition of 1871. In 1873 he was appointed superintendent in the newly created *North-West Mounted Police, and the following year was made assistant commissioner.

Macleod rode west with the NWMP in the summer of 1874. That fall he established Fort Macleod, the first police post in the North-West Territories, remaining there in command of the majority of the NWMP for the next year. In 1876 he was appointed commissioner; in his four years in that position he made the cultivation of good relations with the Cree and Blackfoot his first priority. His influence was important in the negotiation of Treaties 6 and 7. He resigned from the NWMP in 1880 to take up an appointment as stipendiary magistrate for the Bow River Judicial District, a post that also made him a member of the NWT Council. In 1887 he was appointed puisne judge in the Supreme Court of the NWT. He died in Calgary. R.C. MACLEOD

McLuhan, Marshall (1911–80), world-renowned communication theorist, professor of English at University of Toronto. Born in Edmonton, McLuhan, as a student at Cambridge, studied 'practical criticism' under literary theorist I.A. Richards, who proposed that words are best understood in terms of 'effects', often subliminal, as opposed to their dictionary definitions. In his mature writings on communication McLuhan applied practical criticism to nonverbal artifacts, which he termed 'media', and speculated on media's effects, of which, he cautioned, people usually are unaware. Every artifact, according to McLuhan, extends or amplifies some part of the body; he contrasted particularly media extending the eye (e.g., print) with those extending the ear (e.g., speech and electronic media). He argued that because they rebalance the senses, such media affect individual perception and thereby the organization of society. McLuhan coined his famous aphorism, 'the medium is the message', to indicate that the means of communication are more important than the ostensible messages they carry.

Near the close of his career McLuhan devised four laws of the media: every medium enhances, accelerates, or makes possible something; every medium pushes aside something or renders it obsolescent; every medium retrieves something; and, when pushed to the limit, every medium reverses into something else. He coined his most famous phrase, the 'global village', to emphasize that, through electronic media, distances cease to be a barrier to communication. His writings are filled with profound insights, but also with hyperbole, puns, satire, and inconsistencies, making him at once provocative, entertaining, and difficult. ROBERT E. BABE

MacMillan, Ernest Campbell (1893–1973), musician. Born in Mimico (Toronto), MacMillan was the most dominating musical figure in Canada in the mid-20th century: principal of the Toronto (now Royal) Conservatory of Music (1926–45), dean of music at the University of Toronto (1927–52), and conductor of the Toronto Symphony Orchestra (1931–56) and the Toronto Mendelssohn Choir (1942–57). He was frequently a guest conductor of orchestras in Canada and abroad. He composed a few works of conservative but polished craftsmanship, and in his early career he toured as a virtuoso concert organist. Serving on most national musical and cultural organizations, MacMillan used his extraordinary abilities and prestige unsparingly on behalf of Canadian musical development. He wrote, lectured, agitated, petitioned, and performed unceasingly over 40 years. By the late 20th century there was little in Canadian musical life that had not in some degree been influenced by him. CARL MOREY

MacMurchy, Helen (1862–1953), physician. Daughter of the principal of Toronto Collegiate Institute, MacMurchy taught literature at her father's school for two decades before realizing a lifelong ambition to become a physician. In 1901 she graduated from the University of Toronto with first class honours in medicine and surgery. Allying with conservative feminist organizations such as the *National Council of Women, MacMurchy became an advocate for *public health, maternalist, and *eugenic reforms. As the Ontario government's Inspector of the Feebleminded (1906–19) and as author of three influential studies on infant mortality (1910–12), she called for improved social, educational, and health care resources for the mentally ill, the 'feeble-minded', infants, and mothers. Her 1920 appointment as chief, Child Welfare Division, of the newly formed federal Department of Health, signalled government recognition of women's health advocacy and improved support for health care. Well remembered for her little Blue Books, later amalgamated into *The Canadian Mothers' Book*, which provided health advice to thousands of Canadian mothers, MacMurchy also produced a major study, *Maternal Mortality in Canada* (1928), during her years in Ottawa. She retired in 1934, and returned to her native Toronto, where she continued to promote health reform and women's professional development. DIANNE DODD

MacNab, Sir Allan Napier (1798–1862), lawyer, land speculator, railway promoter, politician. MacNab is usually associated with Upper Canada's Tories. He tried repeatedly to expel William Lyon *Mackenzie from the assembly in the early 1830s, resisted *responsible government, supported the *clergy reserves, led the military campaign against the rebellion, rejected union with Lower Canada, and was horrified by the Rebellion Losses Bill. Yet, based at Hamilton and heavily involved in regional banking, railway, and land schemes, MacNab was never considered part of the *'Family Compact'. He sought to restrict institutions based in the capital and closely tied to its leading families, lacked the anti-American and anti-Catholic sentiments of some fellow conservatives, was elected speaker of the assembly in 1837 as a non-partisan, and was critical of the composition of the legislative council. Nonetheless, after the *rebellion, MacNab was isolated politically, too closely identified with discredited Toryism. Despite campaigning in Britain against the Rebellion Losses Bill, he opposed the mob protests, the *Annexation Manifesto, and conservative republicanism that ensued. Emerging as a moderate conservative leader in the early 1850s, when he claimed that 'all my politics are railroads', MacNab helped form the coalition of 1854 with moderate reformers. He led it fitfully until 1856. JEFFREY L. McNAIRN

McNaughton, Andrew George Latta (1887–1966). Born in Moosomin, Saskatchewan, McNaughton, after studying electrical engineering at McGill, joined the university as an instructor. He also pursued a career in the militia, joining in 1909 and going overseas with the outbreak of war in 1914. Twice wounded as an artillery officer, he was awarded the Distinguish Service Order. A brigadier-general by war's end, he remained in the army and was appointed chief of the general staff in 1929. Never losing interest in things scientific, he left the army in 1935 to become president of the *National Research Council, where he remained until the outbreak of the Second World War. Appointed commander of the Canadian contingent, he was promoted several times. Yet, having focused on the expansion of the *Canadian army, he neglected his development as a general and was forced to relinquish command in December 1943. He retired from the army in September 1944.

After a brief stint as minister of national defence (1944–5), McNaughton served as chair of the Canadian section of the Canada–US Permanent Joint Board on Defence (until 1959), and was also chair of the International Joint Commission, 1950–62. He served on the UN Atomic Energy Commission, as president of the Atomic Energy Control Board of Canada, as Canadian permanent delegate to the *United Nations, and on the UN Security Council. BILL RAWLING

McNaughton, Violet Clara (1879–1968), farmer, writer, feminist, co-operative leader. Born in Borden, England, Violet Jackson joined her family on a Saskatchewan homestead in 1909, married John McNaughton, and became active in the Saskatchewan Grain Growers' Association. She was the early driving force behind the Women's Grain Growers, the SGGA's women's section, concentrating particularly on suffrage and health issues. Active on both the SGGA and WGG boards, she attacked the patriarchy of the agrarian movement. She was president of the Interprovincial Council of Farm Women and an important leader in the Farmers' Union of Canada, ultimately promoting its amalgamation with the SGGA (1926). She edited the 'Mainly for Women' page in the *Western Producer* (1925–50). She helped develop egg and poultry co-operatives, particularly important to farm women, and was active in the International Co-operative Women's Guild. A clear, decisive, and eloquent leader, McNaughton was a central figure in Prairie feminism, politics, and co-operativism.

IAN MacPHERSON

Macoun, John (1831–1920). Irish-born, Macoun tried almost single-handedly to roll back the *natural history frontiers of Canada. After he emigrated to Canada West in 1850, the farmer-turned-schoolteacher's interest in the local flora developed into an obsession with Canadian botany. Devoting every spare moment to plants and his herbarium, he soon became a leading authority with a growing international reputation. Between 1872 and 1881, the federal government hired Macoun to investigate the potential of the western interior; he concluded, largely on the basis of natural vegetation, that the region was an agricultural Eden. He was rewarded for this work with an appointment to the *Geological Survey of Canada, first as dominion botanist and later as survey naturalist. Over the next 30 years, he spent as much time as possible in the field, tramping thousands of kilometres in search of new specimens. Macoun believed his duty was to work up an inventory of Canada's great natural history heritage. His fieldwork had a profound impact on the development of life sciences. Thanks to his activity, natural history research came to be regarded as a legitimate concern of the GSC. His enormous collections also figured in the establishment of the National Museum of Canada.

BILL WAISER

Macphail, Agnes Campbell (1890–1954). Born on a farm in Grey County, Ontario, Macphail overcame her family's resistance to education for girls and graduated from high school and normal school. While teaching in rural Ontario and Alberta (1910–21) she became an organizer for the United Farmers of Ontario. In 1921 she gained the UFO nomination in Southeast Grey and went on to become the first woman member of Canada's Parliament.

Macphail, a superb populist speaker, expressed the righteous indignation of beleaguered farmers and subjected women. During the 1920s, as the only woman in the House of Commons, she spoke forcefully for equality between men and women. Actively involved with the Women's International League for Peace and Freedom, she became the first woman to represent Canada abroad as a delegate to the *League of Nations in 1929. The Depression directed her attention to the Ontario CCF, which she headed in 1932–4. Later she threw herself into a campaign for penal reform that succeeded in changing the country's brutal and archaic prison system. A Farmer/Labour candidate until defeated in 1940, Macphail then moved to Toronto. In 1943 she secured York East for the CCF and became the first woman in Ontario's legislature. Prior to retiring in 1951, she campaigned for pay equity for women.

TERRY CROWLEY

Macphail, Sir Andrew (1864–1938). A native of Prince Edward Island, Macphail graduated in arts and medicine from McGill University, and practised medicine in Montreal, becoming McGill's first professor of the history of medicine in 1907. By this time he had emerged as a prominent man of letters, especially as an essayist. An outspoken supporter of *imperialism, he articulated a conservative, anti-industrial ideology, and criticized forcefully such modern social movements and trends as *feminism and utilitarian education, which he tended to link to American influences. He also edited and financed the *University Magazine*, a highly successful quarterly, 1907–20, except for the years of the First World War, when, although middle-aged, he insisted on serving as a physician at the front. Well-known within his profession, he was founding editor of the monthly *Canadian Medical Association Journal* (1911 to the war). He published several collections of essays, a novel, a play, and the official history of the wartime Canadian medical services, but his most enduring work was *The Master's Wife* (1939), a semi-autobiographical memoir of his youth in rural Prince Edward Island. This beautifully crafted book has made Macphail an icon of rural life for many islanders.

IAN ROSS ROBERTSON

McPherson, Aimee Semple (1890–1944). Born in Salford, Ontario, Aimee Kennedy Semple Hutton McPherson—one of the most famous women of the 1920s and 1930s—has been the subject of (mostly scurrilous) plays, books, songs, and newspaper columns but rarely of serious consideration. She was an early convert (1907) to Pentecostalism, an American religion, and was the major factor in its institutionalization as part of mainstream culture. Angelus Temple, established in Los Angeles in 1923 by McPherson and her mother, Minnie Kennedy, is the central administration for the International Church of the Foursquare Gospel, which claims to be the world's fourth largest Pentecostal sect. Claimed by her followers not only as founder but as prophet, McPherson was interested less in increasing the power of her church than in seeking and making visceral God's word to a rapidly secularizing population. Her scandalous disappearance in 1926, which she claimed was a kidnapping by 'white slavers', is generally seen as the end of her glory days but she in fact spent her last two decades productively exploring the ability of dramatic techniques, including operas, to accomplish an emotional connection with God.

JANICE DICKIN

Macpherson, C.B. (Crawford Brough) (1911–87), political philosopher, University of Toronto professor. Macpherson secured an international reputation with publication of *The Political Theory of Possessive Individualism*

(1962), where he reinterpreted Thomas Hobbes and John Locke, critiquing their views of property and human nature, and lauded the 'morally superior' views of John Stuart Mill. Hobbes and Locke justified both private property (defined by Macpherson as the right to exclude others from use or benefit) and unlimited individual accumulation of wealth on the premise that humans are by nature acquisitive and selfish. Mill, by contrast, argued for a developmental view of human nature, insisting that people by nature are users, developers, and exerters of their talents and skills—a position favouring common property (that is, the right not to be excluded from some use or benefit, including the means of production). Macpherson saw private ownership as undemocratic because ever-increasing concentrations of wealth bar more and more people from accessing on an equitable basis the means of production. His association of private property with autocracy and common property with democracy remains poignant for many areas of social life, including media studies, in the 21st century. ROBERT E. BABE

McQuesten, Leroy Napoleon 'Jack' (1836–1909), trader, outfitter. McQuesten was a Yukon legend. A native of New Hampshire who arrived in Alaska in 1872, he established, with Arthur Harper and Alfred Mayo, a sequence of small trading posts up and down the *Yukon River. His first post was at Fort Reliance, near the confluence of the Klondike and Yukon Rivers. Hearing rumours of gold, he turned his mercantile efforts away from trading furs with the Indians and into grubstaking miners, offering them food and supplies in return for a share of the proceeds from their claims. He was known to be a generous grubstaker, providing supplies even when prospects were dubious, which earned him the moniker 'Father of the Yukon'. Trusted as a trader, in 1883 he was elected the first mining recorder, the person trusted to record all other claims in the area. In 1887 he left Fort Reliance for a new gold camp 40 miles downstream. Ironically, McQuesten's abandoned trading post was almost on top of what became *Dawson City, and when the *Klondike gold rush occurred a decade later McQuesten himself arrived too late to stake a claim. CHARLENE PORSILD

Mad Trapper. The Mad Trapper, also known as Albert Johnson, was a recluse who, after interfering with a neighbouring trapline on the Rat River in northwestern Northwest Territories in December 1931, led pursuers on what was perhaps Canada's most dramatic manhunt. Over the following two months, he repeatedly eluded pursuers, led them on an arduous chase, and died in a final shootout in the northern Yukon. His incredible strength and savvy kept him ahead of a very capable posse, which, but for resupply by airplane, might never have caught its quarry. Along the way Johnson killed one of his pursuers, an RCMP constable, and seriously wounded two others. Evidence suggests Johnson used the name Arthur Nelson in northern British Columbia and the Yukon between 1926 and 1931 but otherwise his origins are unknown.
COLIN BEAIRSTO

magazines. Like many of its early followers, Canada's first magazine, the *Nova-Scotia Magazine and Comprehensive Review of Literature, Politics and News*, proved short-lived. Published by John Howe, 1789–92, it covered mainly British public affairs for some 200 subscribers. Samuel Neilson's bilingual monthly, the *Quebec Magazine/Le Magasin de Québec*, ran from 1792 to 1794. Magazines did not match colonial newspapers in growing more resilient during the early 19th century. One of the most successful, Michel Bibaud's *La Bibliothèque canadienne*, managed a five-year run, starting in 1825. High production costs, low circulation, and poor transportation systems impeded magazine publishing in British North America.

Population growth, the spread of railways and the telegraph, and improved printing technology helped rejuve nate magazine publishing after Confederation. George Desbarats's *Canadian Illustrated News* (1869–83) pioneered photoengraving methods while promoting the views of emerging Canadian nationalism. Goldwin *Smith, a controversial figure supporting closer economic ties to the United States, edited the influential *The Week* from 1883 to 1896. Other prominent magazines included *Canadian Monthly and National Review* (1872–82) and *Canadian Magazine* (1893–1939). John W. *Bengough's weekly **Grip* (1873–94) served up political satire, animated by Bengough's cheeky cartoons. Journalist Edmund Sheppard founded what would become Canada's oldest magazine: **Saturday Night* (1887–) combined moral crusading with social and political reporting to appeal to upscale readers. These magazines shared relatively small readerships comprised of political and social elites; revenues derived mainly from subscriptions, not advertising; and content centring on Canadian political, economic, and social issues.

A different model of magazine publishing surfaced in the United States during the 1890s. Publishers like Frank Munsey and Cyrus Curtis slashed cover prices for magazines like *Munsey's*, *Cosmopolitan*, and *Ladies Home Journal* in order to boost circulation. In contrast to literary magazines like *Harper's*, which had few ads and whose primary purpose was reader edification, Munsey and Curtis advanced a first principle of commercial media: it was more profitable to sell readers to advertisers than magazines to readers. With the input of advertisers, their magazines promulgated a consumerist ethos, with illustrated advertising appearing throughout. This model was taken up in Canada in the early 1900s. When John Bayne Maclean launched *Maclean's* magazine in 1911 (earlier versions were called *Business Magazine* and *Busy Man's Magazine*), the first issue carried 115 pages of illustrated advertising. *Canadian Home Journal* (1905–59) and *Everywoman's World* (1914–22) offered a steady diet of housekeeping tips and buying advice to women, the advertiser-anointed 'family purchasing agents'. *Canadian Homes and Gardens* (1924–62) and Maclean-owned titles like *Mayfair* (1927–61) and **Chatelaine* (1928–) broadened the class reach of consumer magazines.

Consumer magazines presented a formidable problem by the 1920s: sales of US titles like *Saturday Evening Post* and *McCall's* far outnumbered Canadian ones, by a ratio of 8:1 by 1925. The absence of Canadian material in these American titles, which offered a mix of entertainment, service information, and sports, did not impede sales north of the border. Magazine owners fought back. They formed the Magazine Publishers Association, attacking US imports for their sometimes scandalous tone, their detrimental economic impact on the domestic publishing industry, and their erosion of national culture and civic life. Cultural, economic, and political arguments were used to lobby the federal government to impose tariffs on imported consumer magazines. When the Liberal government proved unresponsive, the MPA turned the tables and sought, ultimately successfully, lower customs duties on imported printing materials used by Canadian publishers. Improved postal subsidies were also secured.

The Conservative government elected in 1930 assumed a different approach. It implemented a sliding-scale tariff pegged to a publication's advertising volume. From 1931 to 1935, US magazine sales fell by 60 per cent, much of which was absorbed by Canadian publications. The Liberals returned to power in 1935 and scrapped the tariff as part of an unrealized effort to secure a free trade agreement with the United States. Predictably, US magazine circulation levels in Canada rose threefold between 1935 and 1940. This situation continued into the 1950s. By 1954 American titles constituted 80 per cent of the Canadian magazine market. The Canadian editions of *Time* and *Reader's Digest* (so-called split-runs—modest additions of Canadian content to US editions sold in Canada) alone accounted for 37 per cent of all general-interest magazine ad revenue in 1955.

Canadian magazines faltered. *National Home Monthly* folded in 1950, followed by *Canadian Home Journal* in 1958, and *Mayfair* two years later. The Liberal government responded, in 1956, with a 20 per cent tax on advertising in the Canadian editions of foreign magazines. Two years later the Diefenbaker Conservatives repealed the tax. But the issue would not go away, and in 1960 the government appointed a Royal Commission on Publications, chaired by Senator Grattan O'Leary, a former newspaper editor. His report heaped criticism on foreign control of the periodical market. American publishers leveraged favourable economies of scale to produce split-run editions offering cut-rate pricing to Canadian advertisers, effectively 'dumping' their product in Canadian markets. The report recommended that advertising expenditures in foreign-owned, split-run editions be ineligible as a tax deduction. The Pearson government implemented this proposal in 1965, but it exempted Time and Reader's Digest, the two largest split-run publishers, owing to US political pressure. The half-hearted measure meant that the US share of magazine ad revenues endured, rising from 43 per cent in 1956 to 56 per cent in 1969.

A turning point came in 1976, when the Trudeau government defied US pressure and implemented Bill C-58, which rescinded the *Time* and *Reader's Digest* exemptions. Shortly thereafter, the Canadian magazine industry experienced a renaissance. *Maclean's* adopted its current weekly format in 1978. *Harrowsmith* and *Report on Business* were launched in 1976 and 1984 respectively. Ad revenues at Canadian magazines jumped 66 per cent between 1976 and 1980. Circulation rates for Canadian magazines rose from 30 per cent of the total in 1971 to 68 per cent in 1992. Only one US publication—*National Geographic*—ranked among the top 12 selling magazines in Canada in 1987. DANIEL ROBINSON

mail-order catalogues. Catalogues evolved from services that had existed earlier on a purely informal basis as rural customers wrote to urban stores seeking goods not available locally. Recognizing the existence of a new customer base, the Eaton store in Toronto distributed its first 32-page catalogue at the 1884 annual Industrial Exhibition. It was also sent to post offices and regular customers in western Canada, which was then undergoing settlement. The attraction offered by such services was the enormous variety of merchandise and the reliance on cash sales and one fixed price, in contrast to the smaller rural stores that still relied on credit, bargain, and barter. Many of the latter gradually lost their customers and, for some, ultimately their businesses. By the turn of the century Eaton's mail-order sales totalled close to $2 million; by 1919 these rose to over $30 million. The development of suburban malls in the 1950s gradually ate into these sales figures, and by the 1980s most large mail-order services had been discontinued. JOY L. SANTINK

malaria. In Canada, endemic malaria—'fever and ague' in the 18th and 19th centuries—afflicted chiefly what is now southern Ontario. Its existence depended on the conjunction of three conditions: four species of Anopheles mosquitoes, which transmit the disease; large quantities of standing water in swamps; and importation of carriers of active disease. The first two conditions existed naturally; then the British army transferred disease-ridden troops from Caribbean stations to recuperative assignments in Canada and malarious *Loyalists arrived from southern American states. By 1800, Elizabeth *Simcoe, wife of the lieutenant-governor of Upper Canada, could report that almost no one, including herself, escaped the disease. Malaria hindered combatants on both sides during the War of 1812 and ravaged the men constructing the Rideau Canal from Kingston to Ottawa (1826–32). The latter constituted the northernmost occurrence of malaria in Canada. Because cultivation of land eliminated marshes that were mosquito breeding-grounds, malaria had largely disappeared by the 1850s. Occasional localized outbreaks occurred in Ontario into the 20th century. Now, malaria occurs only among travellers returning from malarial countries. CHARLES G. ROLAND

Mance, Jeanne (1606–73), co-founder of Montreal. Born at Langres, she heard in 1640 about New France and met members of the Société Notre-Dame de Montréal, which wanted to establish a settlement in America. She was adroit at finding investors among the devout to finance settlement, and in 1642 she arrived at Montreal (Ville-Marie) with Paul Chomedy de Maisonneuve. That autumn she undertook to build a hospital, the Hôtel-Dieu. In 1649, learning that serious financial difficulties threatened to destroy the foundation of the settlement, she travelled to France to oversee the situation. In 1657 she again returned to France and brought back three nursing sisters, of the Hospitalières de la Flèche, to take charge of the Hôtel-Dieu. She went to France again in 1662 to negotiate the replacement of the Société Notre-Dame de Montréal by the company of the priests of St-Sulpice, as owners of the island of Montreal. She died at Montreal. MICHELINE DUMONT

Manhattan Project. The atomic bombs that destroyed the Japanese cities of Hiroshima and Nagasaki in August 1945 were developed by scientists associated with the US Manhattan Project. These two weapons, one based on enriched uranium, the other using the new element plutonium, killed over 210,000 people with their massive explosions and intense heat, and many others died from radiation poisoning. The subsequent development of even more powerful thermonuclear bombs meant that the existence of humankind was in question.

During its four years of existence the Manhattan Project mobilized over 120,000 people—including most of the United States' physicists, chemists, engineers, doctors, and technicians, along with a small group of outstanding German/Austrian refugee scientists—into 37 top-secret installations. It also co-operated with the Anglo-Canadian Montreal Atomic Laboratory, established by the *National Research Council during the fall of 1942, which developed a heavy water reactor process for obtaining plutonium. After the war, however, Canada decided against developing nuclear weapons and concentrated its efforts in the peaceful use of *nuclear energy. DONALD H. AVERY

manhood and masculinities. In the summer of 1793, while en route with a crew of French-Canadian voyageurs west of Lake Superior, North West Company clerk John Macdonell described the symbolic moment in which he became a 'North man' through a ceremony of baptism unique to the Montreal-based fur trade, one that combined Aboriginal and Christian customs. These rituals marked, according to historian Carolyn Podruchny, 'the passage into a new state of occupation and manhood' for these men. For Canadian historians, they become part of a greatly expanding set of windows through which to view the complex histories of manhood and masculinity, which appear whenever and wherever gendered social relations can be detected, from the earliest records of Aboriginal–European contact to the present day.

Manhood, as a comparatively new field of historical inquiry that considers how men lived, perceived, and expressed their lives, does not take sexual difference as a natural, predetermined endpoint; rather, it considers particular patterns of masculinity expressed by specific men, as groups or as individuals, as the historically constituted outcomes of their gendered activities. This recognition has launched new studies of manhood and masculinities across an enormous span of periods and contexts in Canadian history, from early colonization to the rise of contemporary consumer culture. It has led to new research questions that usually draw on rather than depart from feminist theory to examine men's places in constructions of patriarchy and other forms of gendered power relations. Its enormous scope as a field of inquiry has produced a diverse array of new research, from studies of traditional masculine behaviours in pre-industrial settings to examinations of working-class manhood, of gay/queer cultures, or of fatherhood and masculine domesticity in the near-contemporary period.

The gendered attributes that defined men in many roles have been examined not only in relation to ethnic, class, and other social differences but also as a vehicle to examine particular periods, places, and human experiences. Studies of childhood, for example, have considered age-based relationships in examining how Canadian boys grew up within the gendered cultures of childhood and youth. Studies of transitions from peace to war have considered how men of all ages responded to the expression of manful assertiveness in wartime Canada. As well, studies of women and breadwinning recognize the fluid relationship between gendered regimes in family life, where the forces of public activities impinge on the private lives of both sexes. The ongoing enterprise of examining manhood and masculinities in Canadian history holds enormous potential, challenging the perspectives that have equated men in history as history itself.

ROBERT RUTHERDALE

Manitoba. Developing canola and curling champions, introducing polar bear and aurora borealis tourism, discovering the Rh factor in blood, passing Canada's first legislation giving women the vote—all belong in the historical capsule of the 'keystone province'. Manitoba's Aboriginal origins include Cree, Ojibwa, Dakota, Dene, and Inuit peoples. When it entered Confederation in 1870 as Canada's first new province, nearly 10,000 of its 12,000 inhabitants were *Metis—that is, of mixed Aboriginal–European parentage. Manitoba played a central role in a number of national dramas, including epochal French–English, Protestant–Roman Catholic, and worker–capitalist confrontations. It raised its share of national heroes—Louis *Riel, Nellie *McClung, J.S. *Woodsworth, Graham *Spry, Gabrielle *Roy, Margaret *Laurence, and Baldur Stefansson (the developer of canola)—and provided a home for others in their adult years, including J.W. *Dafoe, Carol Shields, John Hirsch, and Evelyn Hart.

The Manitoba Act, creating the first new province of the dominion, came into effect on 15 July 1870, formally marking the end of the *Red River resistance waged by the Michif- and French-speaking Metis led by Louis Riel. The tiny postage-stamp province was increased in size in 1881, 1884 (by judicial ruling), and 1912, when it assumed its present dimensions. By the early 1880s the *fur trade, which had been conducted in these lands for two centuries, was eclipsed by agriculture and especially the export of wheat. In 1890, when the official use of the

French language and Roman Catholics' right to public financing of their school system were abolished (the anti-French law was declared illegal by the courts in the 1970s), the province appeared to be an outpost of Ontario. However, its nascent pluralism was resoundingly reinforced by waves of immigrants from Britain and Europe in the next generation.

Development of the new economy and the struggle between French and English and Roman Catholic and Protestant preoccupied political leaders in the first generation after 1870. Between 1900 and the 1930s, how to integrate the 'foreigners' and to distribute the rewards of the burgeoning economy were at issue. The completion of the Panama Canal (1914), which permitted the three western-most provinces to establish distinct economies, and the wrenching six-week general strike in 1919, contributed to the eclipse of Winnipeg as regional metropolis. Thereafter, the province diversified slowly and steadily, adding hydroelectricity, mines, and forests to its agricultural, manufacturing, financial services, and communications industries.

A farm protest movement won control of the provincial government in 1922 and, by governing cautiously and slowly co-opting opponents, remained in power until 1958. A left–right ideological divide, typical of many western democracies, emerged in the 1960s and has formed the strongest pattern ever since. The New Democrats have opposed the Conservatives in each of the nine elections from 1969 to 1999, the two parties dividing equally the years in office. The former leaned to social investment and state intervention in the economy, the latter to reduced government activity and reliance on the private sector.

Two significant social trends have affected the province in the 20th century, rural depopulation and multicultural accommodation. An extensive network of rural communities was developed in the half-century before 1930, then faced an economic crisis during the Great Depression, and, slowly but surely, was dismantled thereafter. The acreage of farmland has not declined and agricultural production has increased substantially, but rural society has been decimated by this out-migration. Northern Manitoba was an Aboriginal and fur trade world before 1930. Then, the completion of a railway to *Hudson Bay and the development of resource industries introduced Euro-Canadians in numbers equal to the Aboriginal population. The north, too, has sustained environmental crises and significant out-migration in recent decades.

Manitoba and its capital city, *Winnipeg, were the sites of noteworthy 20th-century Canadian experiences in multicultural integration. The British, French, German, Ukrainian, Aboriginal, Polish, and Filipino communities each number 40,000 or more, and several dozen other ethnic and religious groups have sufficient numbers to make their presence felt in community affairs. Because fully two-thirds of the provincial population resides in Winnipeg—Canada's third largest community when the First World War commenced and its eighth largest today—the concentration of numbers and cultures also constitutes a noteworthy provincial social characteristic.

In 2001, Manitoba contains about 6 per cent of Canada's land and just under 4 per cent (1.1 million) of its people. It offers cultural treasures ranging from the archives of the *Hudson's Bay Company, the exhibits of the Manitoba Museum, and the collections of the Winnipeg Art Gallery to the presentations of the Royal Winnipeg Ballet, Folklorama, and music festivals. Some of its most fortunate families—Richardson, Moffatt, Asper, and others—and many ordinary citizens have donated millions to the development of community institutions. Its greatest natural resource is its supply of fresh water: six major rivers and a hundred thousand lakes, including three very large ones, represent an exceptional storehouse, including potential for hydroelectric power.

GERALD FRIESEN

Manitoba schools question (1890–1916). This was a complex, drawn-out conflict with significant ethnic, religious, political, and constitutional implications. In the wake of the second Riel uprising (1885), the Jesuit Estates controversy (1888–9), and massive non-British immigration before 1914, Anglo-Protestants reinforced Canada's British character through education, among other means. In 1890 the Manitoba Liberals substituted a uniform school system for the dual religious and linguistic structure copied from Quebec and entrenched in the Manitoba and British North America Acts in 1870. Among the Catholic minority, those directly affected were mainly anglophones living in mixed, especially urban, areas and constituting over a quarter of Catholic pupils. In the countryside, where compact French-Canadian communities controlled local school boards and municipalities, little changed. Finding scant support for their cause in Ottawa, the aggrieved parties turned to the courts, which ruled in favour of provincial over minority rights, further eroding federal politicians' will to intervene. In the federal election of 1896, French Canadians ignored their bishops' collective letter obliging Catholics to back only candidates committed to remedial legislation. They rejected a badly divided Conservative Party, which lacked credible leaders in Quebec, and handed a decisive victory to Wilfrid *Laurier, a native son and proponent of the politically more lucrative policy of persuasion. Ethnicity, however, was no gauge of political conduct, and Laurier sought to neutralize the church. His complaints of clerical meddling in politics prompted Rome to dispatch an apostolic delegate, but when Archbishop Raphael Merry del Val arrived in Canada, he was presented with a fait accompli—an agreement reached between Laurier and Premier Thomas Greenway that largely sanctioned the status quo. Even so the prelate shared Laurier's assessment of the situation and determined Rome's action. Unfairly accused of ethnocentrism, the only body determined to restore Catholic schools, the Quebec hierarchy, was silenced. The encyclical *Affari Vos* underlined that Pope Leo XIII sided with English-speaking Catholics, content to accept the Laurier–Greenway agreement in the vain expectation of future improvements. Archbishop Adélard Langevin of St Boniface, leader of Manitoba's Catholic minority, was isolated in his struggle against formidable political forces. In 1916 in a climate of wartime hysteria the Manitoba Liberals abolished the small concessions regarding bilingual instruction and teacher training made since 1896. Although meeting Anglo-Protestant demands for 'national' schools, the crisis strengthened French-Canadian allegiance to Quebec as a national space. Churchmen realized that the Canadian Catholic Church did not share their view of Canada as a partnership between two equal peoples. The fight between francophones and anglophones over control of western dioceses (1910–29) and the Ontario schools question (1912–18) further emphasized that French-Canadian aspirations were best promoted through Quebec institutions.

ROBERTO PERIN

Manning, Ernest Charles (1908–96), Protestant fundamentalist preacher, Alberta premier 1943–68. Manning, following in the footsteps of his religious and political mentor, William *Aberhart, was the first graduate of Aberhart's Calgary Prophetic Bible Institute, served in Aberhart's *Social Credit cabinet (1935–43), and became premier when Aberhart died in 1943. Following the 1947 *Leduc oil discoveries, Manning instituted oil and natural gas policies that put provincial concerns ahead of national ones, filling his government's coffers with royalty revenues. Surviving controversies over highways contracts and Treasury Branch loans that almost derailed his government in 1955, Manning introduced new blood into his cabinet. The changes set the stage for another 15 years of Social Credit rule that saw Manning fight socialism, the welfare state, and medicare, while Alberta prospered. After his retirement, Social Credit, appearing stodgy and old-fashioned, lost power in 1971 to Peter Lougheed's youthful, urban Conservative Party. Brilliant and hard working, Manning later served as a Canadian senator (1970–83) and became an icon of the political right. His social conservative beliefs strongly influenced his son, Preston *Manning, and the Reform Party.

BOB HESKETH

Manning, Ernest Preston (1942–). Born in Edmonton, son of long-serving Alberta Social Credit premier Ernest *Manning, Preston was active in Social Credit as a teenager. In 1967 he co-authored, with his father, *Political Re-Alignment: A Challenge to Thoughtful Canadians*. Between the late 1960s and the mid-1980s he was a business consultant in Alberta but kept in close contact with various conservative organizations and activists for whom the federal Progressive Conservative Party was too centrist, too wedded to Canada's *welfare state, and too solicitous of Quebec.

In 1987 Preston Manning was the principal architect of the Reform Party, which expressed his western *regionalism, his promotion of an anti-elitist populism, his conservative Christian evangelical faith, and his commitment to New Right free market economics. After 1992 this blend attracted substantial support in most of the West, and huge support in Alberta. After just three federal elections, Reform had 60 seats and official opposition status, but was stuck in the West. Manning, who had always wished to recast the western Reform Party into one capable of forming a national government, pushed strenuously for this from 1998 to 2000. He then lost the leadership race for the new Canadian Reform and Conservative Alliance Party to the telegenic Stockwell Day, whose subsequent political ineptness led to serious internal party troubles, MP defections, and decline in public support.

Manning's Reform Party pushed the federal Liberal government into accepting conservative fiscal policies and major tax cuts, and popularized ideas concerning business deregulation and social service and tax cuts that were adapted by Conservative regimes in Alberta and Ontario in the 1990s. Retiring from party politics in 2002, Manning accepted a 'scholar in residence' position with the Fraser Institute, a New Right think-tank in Vancouver.

DAVID LAYCOCK

manufacturing. The transformation of natural resources and materials derived from them, manufacturing includes a wide range of activities. The early inhabitants of Canada, both European and Aboriginal, milled grain in order to be able to bake with it. Animal skins were tanned in order to provide the raw materials for the manufacture of shoes, industrial belting, harnesses, saddlery, and so on. Farmers burned limestone to make potash that would be used to produce soap, fertilizer, and chemicals. Mineral-bearing ore was smelted, after which the metal was melted and cast into particular shapes, or forged so that it might be hammered, drilled, and polished. A great deal of metal, both cast and forged, would end up as a component of machinery used to manufacture other materials. The most common manufacturing material before the 20th century, however, was wood. Water-driven mills took in logs and sawed them into rough planks and square timber, which secondary mills processed into staves, shingles, lathing, and finished wood for construction and a variety of other purposes. Some of the wood was exported in a semi-finished state, but much of it was sawed, trimmed, shaped, turned, planed, carved, hammered, heated, bent, burned, dissolved, and gassified in domestic workshops.

These examples hint at the diversity and complexity of manufacturing. From the earliest times until the present day, Canadian industry has produced many thousands of manufactured goods from hundreds of different kinds of wood, minerals, grains, and other materials. Some kinds of manufacturing, such as crushing stone and sawing construction wood, involved only one or two stages of processing. In other cases, a single workshop or factory would submit diverse raw materials to both hand- and machine-based techniques in multiple stages of production. The small rural blacksmith and the country furniture-maker each used a wide range of tools to produce a surprisingly diverse array of products. Their internal complexity, albeit on a small scale, rivalled that of the large factories and multi-plant businesses. Ontario farm implement manufacturers such as Massey (in Newcastle) and Harris (in

Brantford) operated multi-process factories long before they merged to create the well-known *Massey-Harris Corporation. Firms selling machinery and transportation equipment, such as Canadian Car and Foundry based in 19th-century Montreal, routinely passed materials from one factory to another in a complex chain of production that spanned long distances, diverse technological processes, and a variety of work environments.

The various kinds of manufacturing contributed, in total, about one-quarter of all income earned by Canadians in the later 19th century. Of course there was considerable regional variation in the importance of manufacturing. Montreal, Toronto, Hamilton, and Saint John emerged as early industrial centres. Many manufacturing industries tended to locate in towns and cities, in order to be close to their markets and to transportation infrastructure, although the resource-processing industries provide numerous examples of large industrial establishments situated in relatively remote locations.

The sheer size and diversity of the manufacturing sector make it difficult to generalize about the Canadian experience. We do know that manufacturing was the fastest growing economic activity in Canada throughout the 19th century and much of the 20th. Already by 1891 nearly 400,000 Canadians earned most or all of their livelihood from manufacturing, and many others combined manufacturing with *agriculture or other activities. The rising importance of manufacturing, which is part of a phenomenon known as industrialization, continued until the expansion of service activities in the later 20th century finally overtook manufacturing as the fastest growing sector.

The experience of industrialization in Canada as elsewhere owes a great deal to organizational and technological changes that originated in western Europe during the late 18th and early 19th centuries and became known as the *Industrial Revolution. The Europeans who arrived in Canada before the Industrial Revolution manufactured with pre-industrial techniques that relied on wind, water, animals, and human power. The reliance of these energy sources on products of the land, principally wood, effectively limited the potential for economic growth. In the pre-industrial world a natural expansion of population eventually would be checked by a local capacity for forest growth and the ability of local agriculture to feed both people and livestock. During the 18th and 19th centuries, according to the influential interpretation of E.A. Wrigley in his book *Continuity, Chance and Change*, Europeans and their overseas settlements gradually learned to harness first coal, then petroleum, electricity, and eventually more ambitious sources of energy in an ever-widening range of industrial processes. The resulting Industrial Revolution eased a powerful constraint on economic growth and transformed many aspects of social and economic organization.

Small markets and the abundance of raw materials in thinly settled Canada allowed pre-industrial techniques and organization to survive late into the 19th century. We have especially detailed information about manufacturing in 1871, in which year more than 40,000 firms operated. Durable goods of wood, metal, and leather accounted for more than three-fifths of all output. The wood-using sector by itself contributed one-third of output and an even larger share of labour. Secondary iron and steel production was growing very quickly, although in 1871 it was still much smaller than wood. Of course, many establishments used both metal and wood. Fewer than one in ten industrial establishments used steam power, although those that did employed, collectively, more than one-third of all industrial workers and generated an even larger share of industrial production. The most common organizational form was the personal proprietorship or the partnership. One striking characteristic of the Canadian manufacturing sector during the 19th century is what we do not see. The new industries of the second industrial revolution (chemicals, electrical equipment, cheap steel, and non-ferric metal) came more slowly to Canada than to the United States, Britain, and continental Europe.

Canadian industry continued to evolve in a way that reflects the growth of a small and fragmented local market. We can trace the progress of the Industrial Revolution in Canada through the building of steam railways and *shipping, the import of cheap manufactures from Britain and the United States, and the eventual adoption by Canadians of new technologies, larger factories, and entirely new industries. Probably the most important of the new industries in eastern Canada was *steel and *coal production. Primary production in Nova Scotia's Pictou County and in Cape Breton used local coal and Newfoundland iron ores. By the early 20th century Quebec manufacturing was beginning to restructure around abundant *hydroelectricity and the fast-growing *pulp and paper industry. Ontario's early strengths in agricultural implement, carriage, and machinery production led to primary steel production at Hamilton and automobile manufacturing at several locations. In western Canada the chain of technological innovation made possible a boom in the *petroleum and natural gas industries during the second half of the 20th century.

The seemingly endless stream of technological advances by manufacturers in other countries has created a constant competitive pressure for Canadian manufacturers. As early as the 1870s workers and investors sought respite from foreign competition in the form of a system of protective tariffs. The Conservative Party administration of Prime Minister John A. *Macdonald obliged by introducing in 1879 Canada's first protective tariffs of substance. Henceforth, imports would be taxed so that the foreign goods would have to be sold at a higher price in the Canadian market.

This policy of industrial protection inaugurated a debate that continues to this day. Historians have had difficulty identifying industries that took advantage of the import tariffs and other subsidies to expand more than they would otherwise have done. One possible beneficiary was the steel industry. Companies based at Sault Ste Marie, Ontario, and Sydney, Nova Scotia, probably would not have existed without industrial protection. Companies at other locations such as Hamilton, Ontario, undoubtedly earned higher profits, and they too may have grown more quickly as a result of Conservative industrial policy.

The Canadian preference to subsidize manufacturing enterprise at the expense of other industries continued into the 20th century and remains one of the more contentious issues in Canadian politics. The level of Canadian manufacturing tariffs declined during the Liberal administrations of the 1960s and 1970s as part of an international movement to reduce trade barriers. The first truly substantial change, however, was made after the Progressive Conservative Party won the 1988 national election on a platform of abandoning its traditional commitment to industrial protection and negotiating a free trade agreement with the United States. The Conservatives successfully negotiated *'free trade', first with the United States and then with Mexico, leading to heated debate in the 1980s and 1990s that paralleled that of the 1880s and 1890s. Today we remain uncertain about the precise effects of these great fluctuations of national economic policy. Nevertheless, provincial and federal governments continue to support important Canadian manufacturing companies such as *Bombardier, the maker of transportation equipment, to the extent that is permitted by international law. Other industries, such as textiles and footwear, face increasingly intense international competition with diminishing public assistance.

Government regulation and support for manufacturing have frequently been linked to the participation of foreign investment in Canadian manufacturing. At the end of the 19th century, for example, some American manufacturers responded to the raising of Canadian tariff barriers by establishing branch plants inside Canada. An American trade surplus between the 1920s and 1950s led to a recycling of US dollars into another wave of investment in branch plants in Canada and elsewhere. Heated public debate about the merits and disadvantages of this process led to the creation of the Foreign Investment Review Agency by the federal Liberal government of Pierre *Trudeau. Ironically, the attempts to limit American investment in Canada gained momentum just as a growing American trade deficit limited that country's ability to invest internationally. During the 1970s and 1980s Japanese investments, especially in automobile production, increased in importance. National policy at the beginning of the 21st century seems to have reverted to an earlier paradigm of encouraging foreign investment, and the issue of foreign investment, like that of protective tariffs, has largely disappeared from public debate.

KRIS E. INWOOD

maple sugar industry. The sugar maple (*Acer Saccharum*) can reach 25 m in height. Its five-lobed leaves are part light and part dark green and turn red in autumn. Maples are abundant in the forests of eastern Canada and the northeastern United States. When the sunlight increases in early March the trees thaw and the sap begins to rise. This is the sugar season, a period of roughly 40 days when the trees are tapped and their sweet sap is collected and transformed into syrup or sugar.

Before the arrival of Europeans, Aboriginal people tapped the trees and boiled the sap in birchbark containers into which they placed hot stones. Because they were not able to generate enough heat to make granulated sugar, they produced loaves of soft sugar.

In the past, making maple sugar was a manual occupation, but today the sap travels through a plastic vacuum tube to the 'sugar shack', where it is transformed into syrup by a gas- or electric-powered evaporator controlled by a computer. Quebec, which has 25,000 maple plantations (*sucreries*), supplies 90 per cent of Canada's production and nearly 70 per cent of the world total: some 9 million litres of syrup annually.

The sugar season is always festive, even though it no longer marks the end of the period of fasting and privation respected by Catholics in the past. Pinewood sugar moulds are no longer sculpted into the shapes of churches, houses, hearts, and fish, but the custom of holding parties at the 'shack' continues, with traditional food and an intoxicating drink called 'caribou', made of whisky, wine, and hot syrup. JEAN-CLAUDE DUPONT

mapping Canada. The earliest map showing any part of Canada is the 'Cantino' (1502) chart. It originated with the Portuguese Gaspar Corte-Real expedition (1501) along the southern tip of Greenland and the east coast of Newfoundland. To avoid problems with Spain, these new discoveries were fraudulently placed about 13° east of their true position in waters given to Portugal under the Treaty of Tordesillas (1494). Within a few years they appeared on maps as islands off the coast of Japan, or more commonly as the eastern extremity of a vast northern extension of Asia (on maps by La Cosa 1500–8; Contarini 1506; Ruysch 1507). In 1507 a world map by the geographer Martin Waldseemüller first proposed that these western discoveries might be a new continent. As this concept gained credibility, expeditions returned from searches through this inconvenient continent with charts of an unbroken Atlantic coastline from Florida to Greenland (Ribeiro 1529; Ramusio 1534; Santa Cruz 1541–5). Jacques *Cartier's expeditions (1534–42) resulted in the first manuscript charts of a recognizable east coast from the Strait of Belle Isle to Cape Breton and inland to the Lachine Rapids (Rotz 1542; Desceliers 1546 and 1550; 'Harleian Map' 1547; 'Vallard Map' 1547). Of the printed maps of this time, only the world map by Gerard Mercator (1569) deserves consideration. It shows eastern Canada based on Cartier material and introduced the Mercator projection, on which straight lines are lines of constant compass bearing. This useful feature, as well as the cessation of further exploration in the Atlantic coast and St Lawrence area, assured that the map was copied to the end of the century. To the north Martin Frobisher's expeditions (1576–8) produced the first maps of the Arctic coast (Beare 1578; Best 1578; Lok 1582). These were so poor that contemporaries wondered where Frobisher had been. John Davis's three voyages (1585–7) resulted in the first charts of a recognizeable coastline from Baffin Island to Newfoundland (Mercator 1595; Wytfliet 1597). Maps of the 16th century were produced from rapid reconnaissance surveys. They were based on few calculations of latitude, rough estimates of distance, and compass bearings rounded to the nearest point (11°15′), often uncorrected for declination. Achievements in this century were best summed up by Edward Wright and Richard Hakluyt in their world map of 1599.

Early in the 17th century, motives for mapping changed to settlement, safe navigation, and exploration inland. Between 1603 and 1607 Samuel de *Champlain charted the St Lawrence Valley and Atlantic coast to Cape Cod. His charts of harbours and summary map *Carte Geographique . . . 1612* were published in *Voyages, 1613*, the first modern-looking maps of Canada. These were followed by maps in 1613, 1616, and 1632 documenting the beginning of *French inland exploration. All his maps were based on good latitude readings, estimated distances, and triangulation of features through compass bearings. To the north English mariners charted the coast of *Hudson Bay, leading to printed maps by Gerritsz (1612), Briggs (1625), James (1633), and Foxe (1635).

After 1650, the first printed maps of the Great Lakes (e.g., Sanson 1650, 1656; the beautiful map by Bressani 1657; Du Creux 1660), and the first maps of Lake Superior (Allouez and Dablon 1672) and the Mississippi (Marquette 1673), began to appear, all made by *Jesuits or based on Jesuit mapping. Cadastral surveys of the St Lawrence settlements began in 1641 with those by Jean Bourdon east of Quebec. In 1709 the maps by Jean-Baptiste Decouagne show in detail the extent of settlement and names of the settlers. Hydrographic charting of the St Lawrence began in 1685 by Jolliet, Franquelin, and Deshayes. Jean Deshayes's map, which was printed in 1702, became the standard chart of the river, although military surveyors continued mapping to the end of the French regime. The maps by Coronelli (1688) and Delisle (1703) best sum up the century.

Map compilation was put on a systematic basis by Intendant Jean *Talon. In 1666 he appointed Martin Boutet to the Jesuit college in Quebec to teach navigation and surveying, and in 1670 he ordered all explorers to file reports and maps when they returned from the interior. Four years later, Governor *Frontenac appointed Jean-Baptiste-Louis Franquelin to compile up-to-date maps from those reports and in 1686 he became the first official cartographer for New France. To the end of the French regime, this position was consistently filled by capable men, creating a well organized channel of information to the cartographers in the Ministry of the Marine, Paris.

Map accuracy was greatly improved over the 17th century. Observers were better trained, had better instruments, and made more observations over increasingly familiar territory. Attempts to measure longitude between Europe and Canada were begun by the Jesuits in the 1630s through observations of eclipses. In 1685 the hydrographer Jean Deshayes recorded the first accurate fix on the longitude of Quebec through a lunar eclipse. His observations permitted Guillaume Delisle to produce the first map of Canada (1703) with a fairly accurate grid of latitude and longitude.

During the 18th century, the settled areas of New France, the strategic lower Great Lakes, and the Atlantic coast were mapped with increasing precision by military surveyors and engineers. On the expanding frontier, the *La Vérendrye expeditions produced rough maps of the newly explored West, while the Jesuit Father Laure produced maps of the Quebec interior. All of these maps were based largely on Native mapping. The maps drafted in Canada were transmitted to Paris and transformed into published maps by Bellin, D'Anville, and others. British mapping during this period was confined to the west shore of Hudson Bay by Middleton (1743), Wigate (1746), and Ellis (1748) and the east shore by Coats (1749). On the Pacific coast, probes by the Russians Chirikov and Bering (1741) found their way onto a French map by Buache in 1752. The last published map of the French regime summarizing European knowledge of Canada was Jacques-Nicolas Bellin's *Carte De L'Amérique Septentrionale* (1755).

Following the British Conquest, the St Lawrence Valley and east coast were mapped in detail by army (Holland and *Desbarres) and navy (Cook) surveyors. When the *Loyalists arrived (1783), land surveyors began the painstaking task of township and cadastral *surveying. In 1815 the admiralty undertook hydrographic surveys of the Great Lakes under William Owen and Henry Bayfield, while in the West, the *Hudson's Bay Company and *North West Company started to map the interior river systems. Maps by Samuel *Hearne (1795) and Alexander *Mackenzie (1801) showed that there was no east–west passage from Hudson Bay. Mackenzie's map also linked for the first time the mapping of the East with the emerging mapping of the Pacific coast under James *Cook (1784) and George *Vancouver (1798–1801). Of all the inland surveyors, the one who contributed most was David *Thompson. Between 1784 and 1812 he crisscrossed and surveyed some 20,800 km of Canadian territory between Lake Superior and the Pacific. Although none of his maps was published, they were conveyed to professional cartographers such as Aaron Arrowsmith. The Arrowsmith maps are the best tool for studying the evolving cartography of Canada after 1795. Most of the maps produced in the late 18th century were incomparably more accurate than any that came earlier. British training of their military and civilian surveyors was excellent and the instruments they were equipped with, such as Hadley's octant, the sextant, and with Cook's and Vancouver's voyages the marine chronometer, were the best British technology could offer. By the 1820s, except for a great deal of infilling and charting of the High Arctic, Canada had emerged on maps in its modern form.

CONRAD HEIDENREICH

Maquinna (m'okwina) is a hereditary name, or title, among the Mowachaht, a Nuu-cha-nulth people inhabiting the Nootka Sound area of Vancouver Island. The best-known holder of this name was active in the sea otter trade that developed following James *Cook's visit in 1778. Between 1785 and 1795 European and American trading vessels made *Nootka Sound their primary supply and trading location; establishment in 1789 of a Spanish fort at Yuquot, the site of Maquinna's summer village, augmented this role. Maquinna (*c.* 1760–*c.* 1825) used his strategic location to influence operations of the sea otter trade, controlling the access of other Nuu-chah-nulth groups to the traders and drawing furs from neighbouring territories. This situation changed in 1795. Closure of the Spanish fort and declining fur returns prompted traders to concentrate their activities farther north, and Nootka Sound became an economic backwater. This abrupt decline likely contributed to Maquinna's capture (described by John *Jewitt) of one of the few subsequent visiting vessels, the *Boston*, in 1802. When last encountered by Europeans, in 1825, Maquinna was in good health and between 60 and 70 years of age.

ROBERT GALOIS

Marconi, Guglielmo (1874–1937), inventor, born in Bologna, Italy. Reading about experiments with electromagnetic waves conducted by physicist Heinrich Hertz, the youthful Marconi in 1894 set up equipment on his parents' estate. He received the first British patent for wireless telegraphy in 1896. In 1899 he sent a message by radio across the English Channel. Attempting to attract attention and capital to his invention and company, and with support from naval armaments companies and newspaper groups, Marconi established the first transatlantic radio-telegraph communication on 12 December 1901. At Signal Hill in St John's, Newfoundland, using a kite with an aerial, Marconi received the letter 'S' in Morse code dispatched from Cornwall, England, 3,470 km away. Hitherto, the furthest distance a wireless message had been sent was about 130 km. Soon ships were routinely using Marconi equipment for ship-to-shore and ship-to-ship communication. Marconi's invention pushed back the limits to global communication in a world already profoundly altered by undersea telegraphic cables. His work also contributed to the development of radio broadcasting. In 1909 Marconi was a joint recipient of the Nobel Prize in physics.

ROBERT E. BABE

Marco Polo, a ship of 1,625 tons, was built by James Smith at Courtney Bay, New Brunswick, launched 17 April 1851, and registered at Saint John. A year later it was sold to James Baines for the Black Ball Line, registered at Liverpool, and refitted for the Australian emigrant trade. On the first voyage, the ship sailed from Liverpool on 4 July 1852, with 930 emigrants and a crew of 60. The captain, famous James 'Bully' Forbes, boasted he would be back within six months. They arrived at Port Phillip Head on 18 September, achieving a record time of 68 days. The return voyage, via Cape Horn, was made in 76 days, arriving in Liverpool on 26 December. The round trip had taken a record time of 5 months, 21 days, and the vessel was proclaimed 'The Fastest Ship in the World'. *Marco Polo* continued to make good passages and remained in the Australian trade for another 15 years. Registered at South Shields in 1872 and sold to Norwegian owners in 1880, it was wrecked on Cape Cavendish, Prince Edward Island, on 22 July 1883.

CHARLES ARMOUR

Maria Chapdelaine, a novel by French native Louis Hémon (1880–1913), published posthumously in Montreal (1916) and Paris (1921). Translated into over 25 languages and adapted for the screen, theatre, and television, Hémon's 'regionalist' novel captures the French-Canadian way of life during the early 20th century in the Lac St-Jean region, several hundred kilometres north of Quebec City, where the author lived for a short period of time. The novel explores the eternal conflict between the nomad and the settler. To ensure the survival of the race, the young have to pursue their community's and parents' dreams and hopes—to be faithful to their homeland, their mother tongue, and God. For 19-year-old Maria, this means remaining in the region and living the same life her father and mother led. After the death of François Paradis, the lumberjack and trapper she was supposed to marry, Maria chooses the life offered by her neighbour Eutrope Gagnon, with whom she will pursue her parents' work, and rejects Lorenzo Surprenant's proposal, which would have meant emigrating to a city in New England.

SOPHIE MARCOTTE

Marie de l'Incarnation (1599–1672). Founder of the *Ursuline order in New France, Marie de l'Incarnation is known for her letters and mystical writings. Born Marie Guyart in Tours, she married Claude Martin and had a son before she was widowed in 1619. Some years later she felt a religious vocation, and in 1631 she joined the Ursulines in Tours, abandoning her son. After reading the *Jesuit Relations* she decided to establish a convent at Quebec. From her arrival in 1639, her life was closely tied to the colony: she built a convent, a boarding school for young girls, and a 'seminary' for Aboriginal women. She kept up a large correspondence (more than 13,000 letters) and wrote several other works that bear witness to an extraordinary mysticism. She died at Quebec in 1672, by which time the convent was solidly established. She was beatified by Rome in 1980.

MICHELINE DUMONT

Marie-Joseph-Angélique, a Black slave convicted of arson and executed at Montreal in 1734. A domestic servant, Angélique objected to the abuse she suffered at the hands of Madame de Francheville, her mistress. She tried to escape to New England with a French-Canadian servant who was probably her lover, but she was captured and returned. Filled with hatred towards her mistress (and perhaps towards the institution of slavery), and fearing she would be sent to the West Indies, she set fire to the house. A strong wind carried the blaze across much of the city, and 46 buildings were reduced to ashes. Angélique was arrested, tried, and sentenced to be burned at the stake, although the executioner was secretly ordered to strangle her before throwing her body on the flames. The records of Angélique's trial shed light on the otherwise obscure history of *slavery in early Canada. Thousands of Black and Native people were brought to the colony as slaves, most of them in the 18th century to work as domestic servants. ALLAN GREER

Marie-Victorin, Brother (1885–1944), born Conrad Kirouac. Professor of botany at the Université de Montréal, 1920–44, Marie-Victorin is well known for his major book *Flore laurentienne* (1935; 4th rev. ed. 1997) describing the plants of the various regions along the St Lawrence River, as well as their use and cultural significance. His public fame is justly associated with the creation in 1929 of the Montreal Botanical Garden, but his major influence on the development of science in Quebec was through his vigorous and active promotion of scientific culture in many public discourses and newspaper articles. He played a central role in organizations like the French-Canadian Association for the Advancement of Science (1923) and the Cercles des jeunes naturalistes (1931). These activities were based on his conviction that to break the vicious circle of the lack of scientists in Quebec society one had to work at both extremities of the spectrum: in elementary schools (through the CJN), in order to stimulate interest in science, and in universities, to train specialists and contribute to the advancement of knowledge. Today, he is remembered through the many buildings, roads, and prizes named after him.
YVES GINGRAS

maritime fur trade. When James *Cook's third expedition to the Pacific put in at Canton, China, on its way home to England from the northwest coast in 1779, a few of the sailors took the opportunity to sell some of the sea otter pelts they had acquired on the coast. Word got out that Chinese merchants were willing to pay generously for the skins, and a number of sailing vessels began visiting what is now coastal British Columbia to trade for otter pelts from the First Nations people. The first British trader to arrive was Captain James Hanna in his brig *Sea Otter* in 1785, trading furs in Nootka Sound that fetched over $20,000. But Britons were soon superseded by American traders known as 'Boston Men' since they came mainly from that New England port. Between 1793 and 1825, when the fur business was past its peak, just over 400 trading voyages were made to the coast; of these, 75 per cent were made by American vessels. The pelts they traded were exchanged in China for tea, silk, porcelains, teak, and sugar. Coastal First Nations were experienced at trade and drove a hard bargain, bartering their furs mainly for guns, metalware, cloth, and liquor. Relations between traders and Aboriginals were often strained, and there were instances of violence on both sides. The trade expanded the wealth of the coastal people, and seems to have stimulated a burst of ceremonial and artistic activity, but contact with the traders also introduced diseases such as *smallpox, which led to drastic decreases in population. The maritime trade also had a dramatic impact on the sea otter, which was wiped out except for remnant populations in Alaska. By the 1820s the trade was in decline and the land-based fur trade carried out by the *Hudson's Bay Company was taking over from the seagoing traders. DANIEL FRANCIS

Maritime rights movement, 1922–7. This movement was contrived to convince Canadians that the Maritime region had declined under the policies of the federal government. While offering a broad critique of federal economic and transportation policies, it could also be seen as an attempt by Nova Scotia and New Brunswick Conservatives to overthrow the Liberal hegemony that had persisted both at provincial and federal levels for much of the preceding three decades.

Collapse of the Maritime provinces' urban/industrial economy, largely set in place over the decades preceding the First World War, was intensely felt, especially in the face of the post-war economic recovery in the rest of Canada. Within a few years of the war's end, half of all Maritime manufacturing jobs had disappeared, as local companies failed to adjust to peacetime demands or were absorbed by bigger competitors from central Canada. That process of national consolidation had been evident on the eve of the war, but had been interrupted by brisk wartime demand for all products.

The sense of crisis evinced by the urban middle classes, who counted on continued prosperity to sustain the large infrastructure investments in their towns, spawned one of the most intense regional political movements of the century. In the process, central Canada's perspective on the Maritimes was recast to that of a have-not region within Canada, eventually leading to a somewhat sympathetic viewpoint demanding that its economic and social problems be addressed through federal action.

Politically, discontent with the region's gradual loss of parliamentary representation was a critical issue, especially following the 1921 census, when yet another round of redistribution threatened to reduce further the region's representation in the *House of Commons. However, near universal support outside the region for strict adherence to the British North America Act's call for representation by population as the only fair and equitable system in a democratic society drove Canadians to oppose any concessions to Maritimers.

Transportation issues revolved around restoration of the *Intercolonial Railway's role as an instrument for economic development and integration, mostly discussed in the framework of re-establishing preferential *freight rates, which had skyrocketed following the formation of the CNR system. Directing Canadian goods through Canadian ports and improving Halifax and Saint John facilities for handling freight were additional elements in this renewed economic strategy. Higher tariff protection for specific Maritime industries such as coal and steelmaking and increased federal subsidies to the provincial governments were more problematic.

Working primarily through Boards of Trade and an informal network of Maritimers' clubs throughout Canada, the movement strove both to improve the region's image and to impress the seriousness of its economic collapse on the rest of the country. A variety of means were used to achieve this awareness, including speaking tours, editorial campaigns, and a massive delegation to Ottawa in 1925, calculated to impress the federal government with the unity of the region.

Maritime Rights finally bore fruit when, following Liberal reverses in the region in the 1926 federal election as well as in provincial elections the preceding year, Prime Minister Mackenzie *King appointed a Royal Commission on Maritime Claims, to be chaired by British industrial expert Sir Arthur Rae Duncan. While broad sympathy for regional problems was expressed, there was also relief in Ottawa when, after extensive hearings and submission of various provincial briefs, the commission's recommendations proved palatable to the rest of the country. The most important single recommendation was that the federal government provide additional subsidies to provincial governments in the region so that they might maintain a level of services commensurate with some national standard, the beginning of a decisive new trend in *federal–provincial relations. The report, however, made few concrete recommendations about the two most contentious issues: tariffs and freight rates. The onus for rate adjustments, which regional spokespeople had seen as a continuous barrier to their competitive participation in the economy, was transferred to the *Board of Railway Commissioners. Tariff questions were dismissed as outside the commission's scope. Nevertheless, the federal government would maintain that it had listened and responded to Maritime grievances.

In spite of good intentions and practical solutions offered by the commissioners, a sudden Liberal cabinet backlash in 1927 led to modification and dilution of the response to the commission and neglect of the region. While attempts were made to regain the momentum of the Maritime rights movement in subsequent years, by the end of the decade regional political agitation had quieted. The Depression of the 1930s would raise many of the same issues at the national level. D.A. MUISE

Maritimers in the Boston States. Between 1860 and 1930 nearly 500,000 Maritimers left home to work in the United States or other parts of Canada. This out-migration took place at a time when the Maritime provinces were struggling to build an industrial base to replace a dying mercantile economy based on ocean trade and wooden-ship building. The migration also occurred when Maritime agriculture faced growing competition from larger farms in the fertile American and Canadian prairies.

Most who left the region were young, single men and women who sought better-paying jobs in more prosperous parts of North America. Some headed west, but the majority went no farther than eastern New England, especially the Boston area, often called the 'Boston States'. Both men and women looked for occupations that were familiar to them. Men found work in mining, the fisheries, lumbering, skilled trades, or farming, while women took jobs in domestic service and the needle trades, work that required skills they had learned at home. Young men and women had different motives for leaving home. While most sons were free to earn money for themselves as future breadwinners, most daughters were expected to send money home to help support parental families. Only in the latter years of out-migration, when jobs like office work, nursing, and sales offered women occupational choices beyond the domestic sphere, did it become common for them to go to the US in pursuit of a career and financial independence.

The period of greatest migration to the US ended in the 1930s, when anti-immigration sentiment and Depression-era unemployment made it difficult for Maritimers to find or keep a job in that country. Maritimers again began leaving their home provinces after the Second World War, but by then they were more likely to head to central and western Canada than to the Boston States. BETSY BEATTIE

Maritimes 'golden age'. Myth or reality? The Maritimes, and especially Nova Scotia, are often said to have experienced a 'golden age' preceding Confederation. 'Golden ages' are invariably situated in the past and represent periods following which there has been deterioration. In this instance, the perspective is post-1900, and refers to an earlier era of economic, political, and cultural dynamism. The notion is associated with a review article Lawrence Burpee, a federal civil servant born in Nova Scotia, published in the *Queen's Quarterly* in 1929.

What is the evidence? All three Maritime colonies experienced a boom in *shipbuilding, which made the region a leading supplier of ships to Great Britain and a major owner of ships in its own right; a Nova Scotian, Sir Samuel *Cunard, dominated transatlantic steam navigation. Politically, Nova Scotia was the first colony to win *responsible government, and its Reform leader, Joseph *Howe, was intensely proud that his countrymen had done it without rebelling (unlike the Canadas). Culturally, Thomas *McCulloch and Thomas C. *Haliburton, both Nova Scotians, were the founders of English-Canadian literature. All this occurred during a time of widespread optimism and local patriotism. By 1900 the region did not have the same sense of progress; shipbuilding had disappeared, and although some new industries had taken root, out-migration was an undeniable fact of life. By the 1920s many of the new industries were in deep trouble following the national government's destruction of the *Intercolonial Railway, the one major economic benefit that Confederation had offered the region. In this context, Maritimers began to view the past with longing as a 'golden age'. Such views are inevitably partial, and ignore the underside and the inequalities of society, but it is easy to understand why such an interpretation would emerge when it did, particularly when it corresponded so well with reality. IAN ROSS ROBERTSON

Maroons. The name, which derives from the Spanish-American term for runaways, was applied to fugitive slaves in the Caribbean who maintained free communities separate from the European settlements. Fearing their influence on the slave population, the British attacked the Maroons in the Jamaican interior and deported a group of more than 500 to Nova Scotia in 1796. Lieutenant-Governor John Wentworth offered them employment reinforcing the Citadel, and settled them at Preston on the outskirts of Halifax. The proud Maroons insisted on an independent life in a tropical country, and in 1800 British authorities removed them to Sierra Leone in West Africa. Their legacy was the 'Maroon Bastion' on Citadel Hill, and an example of successful defiance for the African-Canadian population in Nova Scotia.

JAMES W. ST G. WALKER

Marquis wheat. A hybrid strain developed in response to the difficulties of growing wheat on the Canadian prairies. The popular Red Fife variety had a long growing season, which made it vulnerable to early frosts. Beginning in 1892, Charles Edward Saunders and his fellow agronomists of the Central Experimental Farm in Ottawa experimented with various crossbreeds. The most promising was a cross of Red Fife and Hard Red Calcutta wheat from India, dubbed Marquis wheat by Saunders. Tests that began in Ottawa in 1907 indicated its high bread-making strength. Field trials in Indian Head, Saskatchewan, and Brandon proved that Marquis wheat was more rust resistant than Red Fife. It yielded a remarkable 42 bushels per acre, 10 per cent greater than Red Fife, demonstrated excellent colour and baking strength, and ripened six to ten days earlier. The development was timely, as increased immigration to the Prairies and the inflated demand for wheat during the Great War led to a dramatic increase in wheat production. J.E. REA

marriage. *See* COURTSHIP AND MARRIAGE.

marriage 'according to the custom of the country'. The phrase—*mariage à la facon du pays* in French—is commonly used to describe unions of fur traders and Native women that were not formalized by Christian rite or European law. By the late 1700s, such relationships were widespread in the **pays d'en haut*—the upper country around the Great Lakes—and in the Hudson's Bay Company territory of *Rupert's Land. Traders formed such unions for several reasons: because they were lonely or needed aid, and because there were no white women in the fur trade country. They were also responding to strong Aboriginal pressures. Native trading partners saw kinship ties as key to building trust and friendship; strangers could be enemies unless linked to their host communities. A trader might be adopted as a son or brother, or assimilated as a son-in-law, husband, and, by extension, kinsman to his wife's relatives, who expected him to be generous and to fulfill his new familial obligations. In turn, he received support, protection, and, most important for business, furs from his new relatives and their connections. The Aboriginal women in these unions became critical to the trade: they processed furs, made moccasins and other clothing, netted snowshoes, and gathered and processed a variety of foods, and were essential to the traders as guides and interpreters as well as mothers to the often large families that these unions produced.

In Native terms, these relationships were marriages, often formalized by gift-giving and other ceremonies, such that writers sometimes equate 'custom of the country' with Native marital custom. Traders and other outsiders treated these unions in loving, abusive, or dismissive ways that echoed their own life experiences and changing times, as European and Canadian settlers and Christian missions increasingly penetrated the Northwest. Some, like James *Douglas, who had a large Native family, treasured 'the *many tender ties*, which find a way to the heart'. HBC governor George *Simpson, in contrast, considered such ties convenient and agreeable in the short term, but expendable; in 1830, he left his fur trade wife to marry his cousin Frances Simpson while on furlough in England. Later court cases such as that over the estate of trader William Connolly in the 1860s in Montreal highlighted the contested status of these unions, even though Connolly's Cree wife and children were declared legitimate. In sum, individual and community definitions and understandings of the custom varied over time and in different contexts; the phrase obscures the diversity of relationships gathered under this descriptive umbrella.

JENNIFER S.H. BROWN

Marsh, Leonard Charles (1906–82), social scientist and music lover. Born in England, Marsh joined McGill's political economy department in 1930 and was director of its Social Research project from 1931 until 1941, when McGill declined to renew his contract. He presided over the *League for Social Reconstruction (1937–9) and co-authored its books *Social Planning for Canada* (1935) and *Democracy Needs Socialism* (1938). He also wrote several scholarly books, the most important being *Employment Research* (1934) and *Canadians In and Out of Work* (1940), the first comprehensive study of social class in Canada. Upon leaving McGill, he became research director for the federal Committee on Post-War Reconstruction and wrote the *Report on Social Security in Canada* (1943). Drawing on his own work at McGill and on Great Britain's Beveridge Report (1942), Marsh produced a blueprint for a post-war *welfare state. Chiefly designed to enhance family income and to increase financial security for the lower half of income earners, the report was generally well received. But there were concerns about costs, and the only recommendation to find its way quickly into legislation was one for universal family allowances. The report's influence on social policy lingered into the 1960s.

After the Second World War, Marsh worked for the United Nations Relief and Rehabilitation Administration before joining the University of British Columbia Faculty of Social Work in 1948. He moved to the Faculty of Education in 1964 and retired in 1973. A fine amateur cellist and a devotee of cats and classical music, he wrote several books about these subjects and about education in the broadest sense. MICHIEL HORN

Marshall, Donald, Jr (1954–). Born and raised in Membertou, a *Mi'kmaq reserve on the outskirts of Sydney, Nova Scotia, Marshall was convicted in 1971 of killing Sandy Seale. Despite insisting that he was innocent, Marshall spent 11 years in prison. He was released in 1982 after a new RCMP investigation showed that Roy Ebsary had killed Seale. Marshall's wrongful conviction led to the appointment of a royal commission in 1987 to investigate the justice system. Its report, issued in 1989, led to the establishment of the Public Prosecution Office, the Indigenous-Black Law Program at Dalhousie University, better professional police methods, and other reforms of Nova Scotia's justice system. In 1996, Marshall was convicted of selling fish without a commercial licence, a conviction overturned by the Supreme Court in 1999. The court's decision resulted in the federal government granting commercial fishing licences to Mi'kmaq communities throughout Atlantic Canada. WILLIAM WICKEN

Massey, Charles Vincent (1887–1967). Born in Toronto, heir to the *Massey-Harris farm implement manufacturing empire, and best-known as Canada's first native-born *governor general (1952–9), Vincent Massey was a passionate Canadian nationalist. Raised in a strictly Methodist family, he attended the University of Toronto (1906–10) and Balliol College, Oxford (1911–13). As one of the trustees of his grandfather Hart Massey's estate, he masterminded the creation of Hart House (1919) at the University of Toronto, an innovative undergraduate student centre (for males only until after his death) in which the fine arts occupied a central place. President of Massey-Harris, 1921–5, he resigned to serve briefly in the federal Liberal cabinet, but failed to win a parliamentary seat. From 1932 to 1935, he acted as president of the National Liberal Federation. He was appointed the first Canadian minister to Washington (1927–30) and high commissioner to London (1935–46). Both experiences hardened his conviction that Canada must resist the growing sphere of American influence. He believed that Canada needed to foster multilateral relationships and champion its own diversity, regionally and ethnically, in order to combat the relentless conformist tendencies of totalitarianism, mass consumer society, and cosmopolitanism (now globalism). He became an ardent believer in the importance of culture in the sovereignty of a nation, and as chair of the *Massey Commission he strongly endorsed an enlarged federal presence in cultural matters. KAREN A. FINLAY

Massey Commission. The Royal Commission on National Development in the Arts, Letters, and Sciences (known after its chairman, Vincent *Massey) drafted a blueprint for a national cultural policy for post-war Canada. Its recommendations covered matters as diverse as filmmaking, historic sites, and UNESCO, but it is best remembered for recommending an arts funding body, the Canada Council. On the strength of this and other proposals for an expansive federal cultural policy, it is celebrated as one of the most effective royal commissions in Canadian history.

The commission was established in 1949 by the Liberal government of Louis *St Laurent to diffuse political heat from two issues: *broadcasting regulation and university funding. The CBC was then regulator as well as broadcaster in Canada's public radio system, but its authority was challenged by private station owners who wanted the same freedom to make money enjoyed by their American counterparts. The impending arrival of television raised the stakes. The federal government was also looking for ways to finance *universities, which were short of money and besieged with expectations following the war. Since education was a provincial responsibility, the government equipped the commission to sneak into the field by instructing it to investigate the feasibility of federal scholarships. National cultural institutions, both existing and anticipated, were included in the commission's mandate, in part to camouflage the government's agenda on broadcasting and universities, and in part because they badly needed attention.

The commissioners (who, besides Massey, included social scientist Rev. Georges-Henri Lévesque, historian Hilda Neatby, university president Norman MacKenzie, and engineer Arthur Surveyer) did not limit themselves to the specifics of their mandate, but launched a broad investigation of Canada's cultural condition. In public hearings across the country they were supported by education and cultural groups, opposed by Quebec nationalists and private broadcasters, and portrayed by suspicious journalists as highbrows with a self-serving agenda. The commission trumped its critics by exploiting the nationalist mood of post-war Canada. The Massey Report, tabled in June 1951, linked culture to the nation's aspirations for international recognition and an independent identity. It positioned high culture as an antidote to antidemocratic threats such as fascism and communism by crediting it with the cultivation of the independent, critical-thinking citizen required to make liberal democracy work. Conversely, it equated popular mass culture with the United States, characterized it as an invasive, threatening force, and promoted a distinct Canadian culture as the best defence against it.

The Massey Report called for perpetuation of the existing public radio system, its extension to television, secure funding for the CBC, new government cultural institutions, better support for existing ones, and, jurisdictional niceties notwithstanding, federal funding for universities. The government acted quickly on its broadcasting and university recommendations and sat on most of the rest. Nevertheless, the commission's vision of a broad-ranging federal cultural policy would be realized, in scale if not in design, within the following two decades. PAUL LITT

Massey-Harris. The origins of the Massey-Harris Company lay in a typically Canadian combination of American influence and Canadian government policy designed to limit American competition. Daniel Massey immigrated to Upper Canada from Vermont but returned to the

United States for schooling and later to purchase machinery for his farm. By 1850 Massey had an agricultural foundry in Newcastle, Ontario, which profited from farm mechanization by importing, selling, and repairing American machinery. His son Hart, also US-educated, took over the business and began to produce American-designed equipment under licence. The use of American materials, designs, and many American links did not stop Hart from lobbying for higher tariffs to limit import competition. By the 1880s Massey operated Toronto's largest factory and sold throughout Canada and in the British, Argentine, and Australian markets. A merger in 1891 with the Harris firm of Brantford consolidated Massey's role as Canada's largest implement maker. Favourable tariffs facilitated the firm's export sales throughout the British Empire. Massey-Harris and its successor, Massey-Ferguson, remained a Canadian business icon for much of the 20th century.

KRIS E. INWOOD

Masterless Men, Society of. Newfoundland's Robin Hood fable. The story is that around 1750 one Peter Kerrivan, a Royal Navy deserter, led a group of male fishing servants, mainly Irish, from settlements on the Southern Shore—the coast south of St John's—into the woods and barrens of the hinterland near the tolt called Butter Pot. There they lived free from labour, subsisting on such food as the wilderness offered, sometimes trading with fishermen on the coast, and cunningly eluding the authorities. Eventually, they drifted back to the coast and settled to 'live out their lives in peace'. How close was the legend to reality? There were certainly discontented and overworked Irish servants in 18th-century Newfoundland as well as deserters. Some of the servants who overwintered, living in primitive tilts on the fringes of settlements, were from time to time a menacing presence. Their English masters needed them but feared them too. The masterless men fiction was perhaps a reflection of this anxiety, or of the exploited Irishmen's longing for liberty.

PATRICK O'FLAHERTY

Matchless Six. Before the First World War the Olympic Games were exclusive competitions, reserved for the most part for the 'gentleman' athlete. Women competed in international competitions only in a handful of sports that were regarded as suitable illustrations of feminine behaviour, refinement, and beauty. In 1928 the Olympics opened *track and field competition to women, and Canada's women's Olympic contingent, led by Fannie 'Bobbie' Rosenfeld, captured the overall point title, surpassing favoured teams such as the United States. The leading Canadian female athlete of her day, Rosenfeld remains one of the finest all-round athletes of the 20th century. The Canadian contingent at the 1928 games was dubbed the Matchless Six. That squad, which included Rosenfeld, Jean Thomson, Myrtle Cook, Ethel Calderwood, Ethel Smith, and Jane Bell, won two gold medals, a silver, and a bronze. Calderwood won gold in the high jump, and Rosenfeld, Smith, Bell, and Cook took the 4 x 100-m relay. Rosenfeld and Smith won silver and bronze respectively in a disputed 100-m final. Rosenfeld appeared to have nipped American Betty Robinson at the tape, but without a photo finish the decision fell to a committee dominated by American judges, who not surprisingly gave Robinson the nod.

COLIN HOWELL

Matonabbee (1736/7–1782/3), trading captain. Born to Chipewyan parents nearby the Hudson's Bay Company's post at Churchill on Hudson Bay, Matonabbee began work as a hunter around 1752. He later brokered peace between the Chipewyan and Cree near Lake Athabasca, which allowed the HBC to begin trading in that region. He had also drawn a map of the route to the northern copper mines for the company and was the obvious choice to guide Samuel *Hearne to these mines in an 18-month trek that ended in June 1772. Upon their return, the HBC proclaimed Matonabbee chief of all the Chipewyans. In late 1782, by then one of Churchill's most prominent traders, he discovered that the post was abandoned and destroyed by the French. Around the same time a *smallpox epidemic killed the majority of his people. That winter, with the HBC inexplicably gone and his people dead, Matonabbee hanged himself.

HEATHER ROLLASON DRISCOLL

Mauger, Joshua (1725–88), merchant, power-broker. Born in the Channel Islands, Mauger emerged in the late 1740s as a military contractor operating in the Maritimes as that area became drawn into the protracted Anglo-French struggle for North American empire. Resident at Halifax during the 1750s, he acquired enormous wealth and power through sales, especially of rum manufactured at his Halifax distillery, to the large *British garrison stationed in Nova Scotia. Overcoming charges of smuggling and graft, Mauger became the dominant figure in local trade, including sales of slaves. After moving to London in 1760 and buying his way into Parliament, Mauger retained an interest in Nova Scotia. As creditor to most local officials, he exercised indirect control of the colonial government for most of the next two decades and used his influence to protect his business interests, which included vast holdings of real estate. The debt, dependency, and economic underdevelopment spawned by Mauger's rapacious grip on Nova Scotia likely contributed to why, in the mid-1770s, at least some outport residents rallied in support of the American Revolution.

D.A. SUTHERLAND

May, Wilfrid Reid 'Wop' (1896–1952). On 21 April 1918, during his second combat flight, May almost became the 81st victim of the infamous Red Baron, Manfred von Richthofen. Instead, just as the Luftwaffe ace had the young RAF pilot in his sights, he himself was killed. Lieutenant May recovered from this frightening introduction to air warfare, eventually claiming 15 aerial victories and winning the Distinguished Flying Cross. On demobilization, May turned his aerial know-how to earning a living. Flying out of Edmonton, he became one of Canada's best-known pioneer *bush pilots. Some of his mercy flights, and his role in the RCMP's capture of the *'Mad Trapper' (Albert Johnson) caught the interest of the world press and helped earn him an OBE. During the Second World War, May managed the *British Commonwealth Air Training Plan's No. 2 Air Observer School in Edmonton. Troubled by the loss of pilots when aircraft crashed in the wilderness, he formed his own search-and-rescue (SAR) organization. Before the end of the war, its members were absorbed into the *RCAF's new para rescue trade, the forerunners of today's SAR technicians.

CARL A. CHRISTIE

Mechanics' Institutes. Originally voluntary associations of working men in England, seeking to improve themselves through learning and education, the institutes began in the 1820s, providing evening lectures, lending libraries, and reading rooms. They soon spread to British North America, where the first Canadian Mechanics' Institute was formed in Montreal in 1828. By the mid-1800s they could be found across Canada, but were most numerous in Ontario, where the industrial revolution was beginning to take hold. By the end of the century, there were more than 300 individual institutes in Ontario, with a combined membership of over 31,000. By this time, however, their importance was beginning to wane, as the rise of public education, public libraries, and trade union activities provided alternative routes to personal advancement.

Mechanics' Institutes provided an important bridge between the past and present during Canada's era of industrialization. Whether they were primarily middle-class organizations, in terms of leadership and the values they espoused, or part of an emerging working-class culture, teaching lessons of solidarity, is a point on which Canadian historians remain divided.

DAVID BRIGHT

medical colleges. Colleges of medicine are self-governing bodies of medical doctors in each province, known as Colleges of Physicians and Surgeons (in Quebec, Collège des médecins). There are three exceptions: in Newfoundland a medical board still regulates practice, and in the Northwest Territories and Yukon the equivalent authorities are departments of government. In all cases, however, doctors who wish to practise in a particular jurisdiction must be registered with and have their qualifications recognized by the respective regulatory body.

The colleges were created out of the struggle by medical practitioners for legislative authority to govern their profession. In most provinces, colleges were preceded by government licensing agencies or medical regulatory bodies—often called medical boards or councils—with limited powers; it took the colleges themselves many years to achieve full self-government. The first college to be established was in Lower Canada (Quebec) in 1847, but the first college with full control over terms of entry and practice was not established until 1869, in Ontario. As practitioners organized in other provinces, a series of medical acts gave other colleges similar powers.

Though the colleges were composed of all the practitioners within a jurisdiction, the executive work was performed by small elected bodies called medical councils. The main business of these councils was to set educational and admission standards for entry to the profession, confer the licence to practise, prosecute illegal practice, and ensure ethical practice, including discipline of members. The examining functions of the colleges gradually devolved upon the universities. Since each province is autonomous in medical regulation, in order to facilitate interprovincial licensing the Canada Medical Act in 1912 created the Medical Council of Canada, which examines and issues a licentiate to provide Canada-wide certification. Other examining bodies exist, such as the Royal College of Physicians and Surgeons of Canada, established in 1929 to oversee the medical education of specialists and conduct certifying examinations. Until the second half of the 20th century, the governing councils of the colleges were composed almost entirely of practitioners; though practitioners are still in the majority, a number of non-practitioner, 'public' members now sit on these bodies.

W.P.J. MILLAR AND R.D. GIDNEY

medical schools. Formal medical education, gradually supplanting apprenticeship, began in 1824 in Quebec. Modelled on the Edinburgh School of Medicine, in 1829 the Montreal Medical Institution merged with the fledgling McGill College. In Upper Canada, after a short-lived school in St Thomas, John Rolph created a proprietary school (owned by teachers and operated for profit) in Toronto in 1831, which functioned until Rolph fled Canada after the *rebellion of 1837. In 1843, he returned and opened the Toronto School of Medicine. Simultaneously, the Anglican Upper Canada Medical School, later King's College Medical School, which required adherence to articles of faith, was created in the same city. After legislators prevented sectarian schools from receiving public monies, King's College became the 'godless' University of Toronto, with King's medical school as the university medical school, although it was later supplanted in this capacity by the Toronto School of Medicine.

By mid-century, competition among medical schools was fierce. In Toronto, another Anglican university appeared and established Trinity Medical School. In Quebec, the first francophone medical school was at the Université de Montréal—the École de médecine et de chirurgie de Montréal, founded in 1843. In Quebec City, the École de médecine incorporée de la Cité de Québec (ultimately the Laval Faculty of Medicine) was founded in 1847. Queen's University in Kingston began medical teaching in 1854. In 1866 the faculty left the university, becoming the Royal College of Physicians and Surgeons of Kingston; this separation lasted until 1892, when the college became the Medical Faculty of Queen's University. In Halifax, medical teaching began in 1868 at Dalhousie University. Two additional medical schools were created later in the century: the London Medical College (later joining the University of Western Ontario) in 1882, and the Manitoba Medical College, affiliated with the University of Manitoba, in 1883.

Although the Toronto School of Medicine and Queen's University reluctantly admitted a few women in the 1870s, the experiment was difficult for the women and unsatisfactory for the schools. In 1883, two women's medical schools opened, Kingston Women's Medical College and Women's Medical College of Toronto. The Kingston school closed in 1894, its students transferring to Toronto to the renamed Ontario Medical College for Women, which in 1906 was absorbed into the Faculty of Medicine at the University of Toronto. Today, at least 50 per cent of students at most medical schools are women.

The Flexner Report of 1910, based on surveys of North American medical schools, forced revisions upon Canadian schools to provide adequate laboratory facilities and libraries. Over the course of the 20th century, new medical schools were located at the universities of Alberta, Saskatchewan, Ottawa, British Columbia, Sherbrooke, McMaster, Memorial, and finally Calgary. Until McMaster opened in 1969, lectures dominated teaching, especially in the first two years of training. McMaster pioneered problem-based, self-directed learning by small groups of students assisted by a tutor. Subsequently, many schools adopted similar approaches.

CHARLES G. ROLAND

medical treatments. Therapeutic preoccupations reflect the major causes of death. Until the early 20th century the most important fatal diseases were fevers, including *tuberculosis, pneumonia, post-partum fever, and diphtheria. By the mid-20th century heart disease and stroke were the leading causes of mortality; at the time of writing, their impact is slowly being overtaken by cancer.

In keeping with humoral theories of disease, 19th-century fever therapy entailed bleeding, blisters, head shaving, foot warming, and strong drugs—mercury, antimony, emetics, cathartics, opium—with multiple side effects. By 1900 these drastic remedies were displaced by milder, more focused treatments: digitalis, sedatives, electrotherapy, and aspirin. The change was prompted by new anatomical views of disease and by purification of active ingredients in plants; competition with gentler alternative practices, such as homeopathy, may also have stimulated the change.

With the triumph of the germ theory of disease in the 1880s, therapy for fevers, thought of as 'infections', took two paths: first, prevention by immunization and quarantine; later, treatment with new drugs intended to kill germs. *Public health rules for quarantine were revised, and from the 1920s to the 1960s new vaccines and antitoxins were applied against the scourges of diphtheria, tetanus, polio, whooping cough, measles, mumps, and rubella.

Surgical practice was revolutionized in the 19th century by the discoveries of anesthesia (1846) and antisepsis (1867). Used in Canada within a few weeks of their first reports from the United States and Britain, these new techniques were disseminated by publications and word of mouth. Canadian Archibald E. Malloch (1844–1919), who had worked with Joseph Lister, returned to develop a system of aseptic surgery. Similarly, X-rays, discovered by W.C. Röntgen in late 1895, had found applications in Kingston, Ontario, by February 1896.

Control of the major obstacles of pain and infection invited surgeons to imagine anatomical solutions for disease. For example, appendicitis (or perityphilitis) became a 'new disease' in this period. From modest beginnings, Canadian contributions to surgery grew in number and type. William Canniff (1830–1910) wrote the first Canadian textbook of surgery (1866). Operating on a kitchen table, Abraham Groves (1847–1935) of Fergus, Ontario, performed the country's first appendectomy in 1883. Norman *Bethune (1890–1939) invented surgical instruments and established a mobile unit for transfusion during the Spanish civil war. Neurosurgeon Wilder *Penfield (1891–1976) developed operations for focal epilepsy. Postwar rehabilitation of soldiers with spinal cord injuries improved with an interdisciplinary collaboration between Toronto neurosurgeon E.H. 'Harry' Botterell (1906–97) and physiatrist Albin Jousse (1910–93). Congenital abnormalities of the heart were analyzed by Montrealer Maude *Abbott (1819–1940); her work paved the way for surgical correction of these problems. The anticoagulant heparin, developed in the Toronto laboratory of C.H. Best (1899–1978), was applied to open heart surgery by D.W. Gordon Murray (1894–1976). Another cardiac surgeon, Wilfrid G. Bigelow (b. 1913), pioneered operative hypothermia. Later Canadian innovators include William T. Mustard (1914–87), who devised repairs for congenital heart disease, and Robert B. Salter (b. 1924), who invented an operation for congenital hip displacement and methods for joint healing. In the 1980s, the University of Western Ontario established a multi-organ transplant centre.

The drug remedies of vitamins, hormones, and antibiotics were developed in the 20th century. Called 'magic bullets', they were designed to 'kill' disease without harming the patient. The most famous and durable of Canadian discoveries was the hormone *insulin, used to manage diabetes. It was isolated by J.B. Collip (1892–1965) for Frederick *Banting (1891–1941) and Charles H. Best in the Toronto laboratory of J.J.R. Macleod (1876–1935). They shared the Nobel Prize in 1923. Another hormone, human prolactin, was discovered in 1970 by Winnipeger Henry Friesen (b. 1934).

In the realm of cancer care, Canadians contributed to chemotherapy, radiotherapy, and their provision. From early in the century, various schemes supplied expensive radium, X-rays, and, later, chemotherapy without charge. In 1958, vinblastine was isolated from the Madagascar periwinkle by Charles Beer (b. 1915) in the London, Ontario, laboratory of Robert Noble (1910–90). It and related drugs are still widely used. Canadians also developed radium and Cobalt 60 radiotherapy.

In obstetrics, doctors attended at least half of all births by the late 19th century, but most deliveries took place at home until the late 1930s. Stillbirths were the single most common type of death during the 19th century, and childbed fever killed many new mothers. With better understanding of labour, hygiene, and safe methods of intervention, Canada lowered maternal and infant mortality rates. Nevertheless, geographic differences are still apparent, and Caesarian rates are considered high. Canada was slower than Europe to integrate midwifery into obstetrics. Having worked in the country for centuries, *midwives could not find formal training and regulation in Canada until the 1990s.

With changes in social attitudes to children, pediatrics emerged as a specialty. Infants succumb quickly to infections that adults easily survive; the mainstay of child care was prevention through nutrition and immunization. Dispensaries for milk and information on feeding were founded by several cities. The federal government published advice literature on child rearing by Dr Helen *MacMurchy (1862–1953). These well-intended booklets now appear biased in terms of race, class, and gender. Specialized pediatric hospitals were built in Toronto (1875), Montreal (1907), Winnipeg (1909), and other cities, where research resulted in discoveries, especially in genetics and surgery. A method for preventing Rh-disease of the newborn (erythroblastosis foetalis) was developed in Winnipeg in the laboratory of Bruce Chown (1893–1986).

From the mid-19th century asylums were constructed to care for the mentally ill. Run on the principles of humane care by erudite physicians such as Joseph Workman (1805–94) and Richard Maurice *Bucke (1837–1902), these places have been characterized by historians as sites of so-called incarceration. Psychoanalysis came to Canada in 1908 with Ernest Jones (1879–1958), who had studied with Sigmund Freud and was hired to Toronto by Charles Kirk Clarke (1857–1924). In 1954, Heinz Lehmann (1911–99) of Montreal pioneered the major tranquilizer chlorpromazine, for schizophrenia. With the 1960s success of psychoactive drugs, treatment for the mentally ill shifted from in-patient talking to out-patient medication. By the late 20th century, many psychiatric hospitals were closed in so-called cost-saving measures that are criticized for increasing the number of homeless people. JACALYN DUFFIN

See also ALTERNATIVE MEDICINE; INSANE ASYLUMS.

medicare. A system of government-funded health insurance available to all Canadians. Some type of health insurance had been on the Liberal Party's agenda since 1919, when Mackenzie *King included it as part of his platform. The programs that existed at the time were minimal in their coverage, limited in their availability, and exclusively private. During the Depression of the 1930s, insurance companies lobbied the government to enter into the health care field in order to provide some security for insurers unable to collect premiums from a destitute public; however, the general prosperity of the post-war period silenced the insurance companies, and the Liberals pushed health insurance to the back of the agenda, where it had been most of the time since 1919.

The socialist *Co-operative Commonwealth Federation was far more committed to the idea of providing state-sponsored medical insurance. When Tommy *Douglas formed the first CCF government in Saskatchewan in 1944, he did so with a promise to introduce hospital insurance, the first step on the way to full health coverage. Saskatchewan's Hospital Services Plan, which came into effect in 1947, was one of the factors pushing Ottawa to respond with a similar national plan that shared with the provinces the cost of diagnostic services and hospital-operating costs, available to all Canadians by 1961.

For a system of full health insurance, however, Ottawa again waited for Saskatchewan to take the initiative. Liberal politicians and strategists at the federal level had been designing a health care system while in opposition, 1957–63, but a full legislative agenda and the difficulties of negotiating with the provinces forced a delay in dealing with the issue until 1965. That allowed Saskatchewan another chance to be the test case for the nation. A 1959 inter-departmental committee of the Saskatchewan government concluded that a system of universal, pre-paid and government-sponsored health insurance would best suit the provincial environment. The re-election of the CCF the following year seemed to endorse the provincial plan. With some hurrying, the government, by 1961 under the leadership of Woodrow Lloyd, passed legislation establishing a comprehensive, universal, pre-paid health insurance plan that would see physicians remunerated on a fee-for-service basis. It was to become operational on 1 July 1962.

Doctors in Saskatchewan had other ideas. Unwilling to accept the public scheme, they threatened to withdraw medical services if the act was not repealed. Initially, the highly organized Saskatchewan College of Physicians and Surgeons attracted widespread support both within the province and across the country; when last-minute negotiations failed to achieve a deal, however, and the physicians walked off the job, the tide of public opinion quickly turned against them. Three weeks later, the doctors were forced to accept the principle of public, compulsory health insurance in Saskatchewan. The victory on the Prairies boded well for a national health insurance scheme.

Further pressure to act came from the Royal Commission on Health Services. Established by Prime Minister John *Diefenbaker in late 1960, the Hall Commission issued its report in June 1964, significantly rejecting the possibility of a voluntary health insurance system and endorsing a universal and compulsory program jointly funded by the federal and provincial governments.

Lester *Pearson's Liberals thus had volumes of their own studies, the experience of Saskatchewan, and the report of the royal commission at their disposal when they entered into negotiations with the provinces in 1965. They also had a considerable amount of experience in the intergovernmental arena. Discussions went smoothly, as the premiers were offered a simple proposal: each province that implemented a health insurance program that was universal, compulsory, portable, and publicly administered would have half the costs covered by the federal government. In December 1966, the federal government passed the enabling legislation, allowing it to transfer funds as soon as conditions were met. There followed, however, a period of intense debates within the federal government over when it could afford to begin payments, and within at least some of the provinces over whether they would allow their own priorities to be manipulated by federal spending power. Ultimately, the Liberals accepted a start date of 1 July 1968 for payments to begin under the Medical Services Act; all provinces ultimately accepted the offer and met the federal criteria, starting with Saskatchewan in 1968 and ending with New Brunswick in 1971. The system, quickly nicknamed 'medicare', was finally, and universally, available to Canadians. P.E. BRYDEN

Meech Lake Accord. A set of proposed constitutional amendments agreed to by the prime minister and the ten provincial premiers in April 1987. It was designed to bring Quebec back into Canada's constitutional family following the constitutional amendments of 1982, which had not responded to Quebec's desire for constitutional recognition as a 'distinct society'. The accord proposed to add a clause to the Constitution Act, 1867, requiring that the *constitution be interpreted so as to 'recognize that Quebec constitutes within Canada a distinct society' and to affirm the role of the government of Quebec to preserve this 'fundamental characteristic of Canada'. Other provisions were designed to constitutionalize Quebec's role in immigration policy and its representation on the Supreme Court of Canada, to ensure a Quebec veto on future constitutional change, and to provide a provincial role in Supreme Court and Senate appointments and some limits on the scope of the federal 'spending power' in areas of provincial jurisdiction. The amending procedure for the Constitution Act, 1982, required that the accord be adopted by all 11 Canadian legislatures, within a three-year period, before it became law. Between initial agreement and the final deadline, widespread opposition developed. Some objected to the recognition of Quebec as a province with distinct powers, others to a perceived weakening of federal influence, especially in social policy, and yet others to the 'elitism' of a constitutional amendment agreed to by first ministers meeting behind closed doors. An extraordinary federal–provincial conference, in April 1990, failed to rescue the accord, and it died when two provinces, Newfoundland and Manitoba, did not ratify it. RICHARD SIMEON

Megantic Outlaw. Donald Morrison (1858–94) was born into an isolated Gaelic-speaking, Presbyterian community in the mountainous district between Quebec's upper St Francis Valley and Lake Megantic. In 1885 he sued his parents for refusing to transfer to him the family farm in which he had invested two years' labour and $482 earned during his seven years as a cowboy in the American West. A sheriff's auction produced only $300 after debts, and Morrison lost an additional $465 in lawyers' bills in his futile attempt to cancel this sale. He then turned to a campaign of intimidation against the farm's purchasers, culminating in the shooting of the man deputized to arrest him. Morrison's fame as the Megantic Outlaw grew as the local community helped him to evade arrest, despite the efforts of the Montreal police force and American Pinkerton agents, the promise of a $3,000 reward, and the arrest of those accused of harbouring a fugitive. Only when a truce was declared to discuss terms of surrender was Morrison shot and captured. He was sentenced to 18 years for manslaughter and died in jail five years later after intermittent refusal to eat or to take medication. Morrison continues to symbolize heroic resistance to unjust laws and state oppression, with the family conflict that initiated the incident suppressed by popular mythology. J.I. LITTLE

Meighen, Arthur (1874–1960), prime minister 1920–1, 1926. Born at Anderson, Ontario, Meighen moved to Manitoba after graduation from the University of Toronto. A lawyer in Portage la Prairie, he quickly demonstrated a remarkable memory and a sharp tongue. He became an MP in 1908 and in 1913 was appointed solicitor general in Robert *Borden's Conservative government.

Meighen had gained attention for his efforts to support *conscription and to defend the controversial *Wartime Elections Act. When the *Union government was formed in 1917 he became minister of the interior, and in the next two years, as Borden and others were preoccupied with imperial matters, he became the most influential domestic minister. His popularity with the caucus was not reflected among ministers, who found his approach too aggressive. Nevertheless, he became Borden's successor as prime minister in July 1920, but was defeated in the general election of December 1921. In June 1926 he briefly regained the office after the governor general called upon him to form a government in a minority government situation; he called an election on 2 July and was defeated in December. He resigned as party leader and was appointed to the Senate in 1932.

Memory of his wartime advocacy persuaded many Conservatives to ask him to accept the party leadership in the Second World War. However, he lost a by-election in 1942 and his political career ended. JOHN ENGLISH

Membertou, Henri (*c.* 1530s–1613), *Mi'kmaq leader. Membertou was the sakamaw (chief) of the Mi'kmaq community living along the Annapolis Basin in southwestern Nova Scotia when Samuel de *Champlain, a French trader, built a trading post there in 1605. Membertou's political influence extended over a larger area as he was able to assemble a war party consisting of Wulstukwiuk, Passamaquoddy, and Montagnais warriors to fight the Armouchiquois, who lived in what is now southwestern Maine. During the early 1600s, Membertou established strong ties with French traders and missionaries. He was baptized in 1610 by the French priest Jessé Fleché. Today, many Mi'kmaq believe that by this baptism the Vatican became the political and religious protectors of the Mi'kmaq. This agreement, known as the Mi'kmaq Concordat, was formalized in a *wampum belt. Although thought to be lodged at the Vatican or somewhere else in Europe, the belt is yet to be found. WILLIAM WICKEN

Mennonites. Mennonites are a Protestant religious-cultural group with origins in 16th-century Anabaptist movements. Their name derives from a former Dutch priest and religious leader, Menno Simons. They believe that true Christian life requires a mature adult commitment to follow the teachings of Jesus, which is symbolized by adult rather than infant baptism. They are religious radicals in the sense that they believe that Jesus's teachings should be applied holistically to all aspects of a believer's life. That includes, among other things, Jesus's admonition that his disciples should not hate or kill their enemies: they should love those who hate them and do good to those who do them harm. Before 1950, many Mennonites thought it was easier to follow those ideals in relatively separated rather than in open secular communities.

Mennonites came to Canada in five major migrations. After the American Revolution approximately 2,000 came from the United States, mainly from Pennsylvania, to present-day Ontario in search of religious freedom and fertile but inexpensive land. They were followed after the Napoleonic Wars by approximately 1,000 Amish Mennonites from Europe who were eager to escape the ravages of war and were attracted by the promise of good, and inexpensive land. In the 1870s, more than 7,000 Mennonites in Russia, unhappy with that country's reformist policies, migrated to Manitoba. They were followed in the 1920s by more than 20,000 Mennonites who had suffered harsh treatment at the hands of Russian revolutionaries. About 7,700 more Mennonite refugees from the Soviet Union and eastern Europe came to Canada after the Second World War.

The Canadian government granted Mennonites and other religious dissenters special privileges and exemptions from military service because these were people who could provide much-needed pioneer economic services. During both world wars, notwithstanding administrative and bureaucratic difficulties, Mennonite claims to exemption from combatant military service were generally respected. Most Mennonite young men were, however, obliged to provide non-combatant alternative service during the Second World War.

Mennonites became an increasingly urbanized people after the Second World War. They have developed world-renowned social service, relief, rehabilitation, and aid programs that, through the Mennonite Central Committee, enjoy the support of almost all Mennonite groups. Two of the largest Mennonite conferences have integrated their activities in recent years, but Mennonites remain a divided and schismatic people with two large and numerous smaller Canadian conferences. T.D. REGEHR

Mercantilism refers to a set of policies used to regulate colonial commerce in the 17th and 18th centuries. Mercantilist policies were designed to maximize the economic benefits accrued to the imperial government from its colonial possessions. Based on the belief that the economic health of a nation depended on achieving a favourable balance of trade and a surplus of gold bullion, the British government sought to make its imperial system as self-sufficient as possible. Consequently, both public promotion of private enterprise as well as protection against foreign competitors became central tenets of colonial expansion. Governments regularly granted chartered companies a range of incentives, including monopoly trading rights and large tracts of land in North America. In the mid-17th century England decided to intervene more directly to protect its imperial interests. The United Provinces of the Free Netherlands, which was the leading maritime power during this period, threatened to usurp England's position in colonial trade. The English Civil War had disrupted commercial networks, providing an opportunity for the Dutch to expand their North American trade. In response, the English Parliament passed a series of Navigation Acts (in 1651, 1660, 1663, 1673, and 1696), which formed the statutory basis of mercantilism and the embodiment of mercantilist thought. The first act directed that all commodities imported into England could be transported only in English ships. This was designed to ensure that the revenue from the carrying trade remained exclusively in English hands. The act of 1660 stipulated that certain enumerated commodities produced in English colonies and territories, particularly sugar and tobacco, could be exported only to England or to another English territory. To augment this policy, the act of 1673 sanctioned the creation of a system of duties and customs officers in the colonies to enforce imperial authority. From London's perspective, the colonies were mere extensions of the metropolis, parts of a single managed economy. The Navigation Acts acknowledged the right of colonial merchants to participate fully in imperial trade and to compete with English merchants in commodity markets. Mercantilism may have closed the *British Empire to Dutch, French, and Spanish traders, but it also presented new opportunities for colonial merchants, who were quick to exploit the system to their advantage. Although the Navigation Acts placed significant restrictions on trade by favouring metropolitan interests, they also contributed to the growth of the first British Empire by giving colonial enterprises access to capital and markets. With several notable exceptions, such as the smuggling of molasses and rum from foreign colonies in the West Indies, the mercantilist system functioned largely according to its design from the early 18th century to the outbreak of the American Revolutionary War. JERRY BANNISTER

Mercier, Honoré (1840–94), Quebec premier 1887–91. Born at St-Athanase, Lower Canada, Mercier was a brilliant student in the classical program at the Collège Ste-Marie de Montréal, 1854–62. A journalist and lawyer in St-Hyacinthe, he entered politics and in 1883 became leader of the Quebec Liberal Party. He fought for provincial autonomy and passionately supported the cause of Louis *Riel, the Metis leader hanged in 1885. Championing the unity of his compatriots in the face of the contemptuous attitudes of many English Canadians, he formed the Parti national, bringing together Liberals and dissident Conservatives moved by Riel's death. On 29 January 1887 he took power in Quebec.

Mercier's government was marked by his authoritarian, flamboyant, and efficient style. From the outset he proposed civil recognition of the *Jesuits and in 1888 he settled the long-standing question of their estates. In 1887, to strengthen the *provincial autonomy that had become the political expression of his nationalism, he called the first interprovincial conference since Confederation. He encouraged railway construction, created a ministry of agriculture and colonization, managed forestry concessions, modernized the road network, opened night schools for workers, permitted the establishment of public libraries, and was concerned about child labour. He was also the leading French-Canadian nationalist, defending his people's right to exist, their cultural attributes, and their union against attacks by English Canada, and affirming the state of Quebec, although respecting the federal principle outside the framework of an imperial federation. Easily re-elected in 1890, the triumphant Mercier headed for Europe in 1891, where he received honours and decorations. His glory was ephemeral. Following the Baie des Chaleurs railway scandal, his government was removed at the end of 1891. Although cleared of the accusations, Mercier was ruined. He was engaged in a crusade for Canada's independence from the empire when death intervened. He remains one of the legendary figures of French-Canadian nationalism.

RÉAL BÉLANGER

merger movement. Canada's first merger wave appeared at the height of the prosperous Laurier boom, one full decade after similar merger waves in the United States and Great Britain. From 1909 until 1913 the country's industrial landscape was fundamentally reshaped by over 70 mergers, 55 of which were multi-firm consolidations, swallowing up almost 200 existing, and in many cases, long-standing firms.

There were many reasons for the mergers, including the technical and administrative economies of scale that could be obtained, almost overnight, through multi-firm consolidations in certain industries; the huge profit incentive offered to Canadian financiers if they could create attractive new opportunities for investors; and the ability to deal with gluts in industries where competition had led to over-production and severe price-cutting. All three reasons were at play in many of the mergers. The first was both understandable and acceptable. The second created an envious backlash against 'get-rich-overnight' financiers who flaunted their new wealth. And the third fuelled a political fire that would not be extinguished until the decline of the *Progressive Party two decades later.

Many mergers were efforts to create 'combines' in which the firms consolidated or combined in order to fix prices. Some succeeded in controlling production and hiking up prices in the short term, but many failed as monopolies in the longer run. Even with the prohibitive tariffs of the period, which locked out foreign companies, there was enough domestic competition from new firms (including the new branch plants of American firms) that competition could not be locked out permanently. However, this was cold comfort at the time. Immediately following the infamous Canada Cement merger, for example, the price of cement rose 25 per cent in some areas even though Canada Cement never succeeded in creating a permanent monopoly.

Such price hikes in the wake of mergers created an outcry in the country. To defuse the controversy and to avoid having it become an election issue, Wilfrid *Laurier's Liberal government decided to act. In December 1910 the government's new minister of labour, W.L. Mackenzie *King, introduced the Combines Investigation Act in the House of Commons. There were high expectations for the new legislation, particularly among MPs from western Canada, where the anti-monopoly sentiment was strongest. King's bill would disappoint, however. The convoluted process of laying a complaint, combined with the way in which the new law differentiated between a 'good monopoly' and a 'bad monopoly', guaranteed that it would be rarely deployed. Instead of lancing the boil of political protest, the new law simply served to highlight the weakness of the Laurier government, one of many reasons leading to its defeat in the famous *reciprocity election the following year.

GREGORY P. MARCHILDON

Meta incognita. 'The Unknown Shore', the name given by Elizabeth I to Baffin Island, encountered by the privateer Martin Frobisher (*c.* 1535–94) in 1576 while searching for a northwest passage to China. Frobisher's chief investor, Michael Lok, concluded that an ore sample contained gold, and a second exploratory trip in 1577 impressed courtiers and merchants, who financed a third expedition in 1578. Frobisher assembled seamen, assayers, labourers, even a prefabricated house, in an attempt to establish a settlement, but a month after his storm-battered ships arrived, faced with bad weather, internal dissension, and fear of Inuit aggression, he sailed home. Frobisher's 'ore' proved worthless and the disillusioned Lok was jailed. The expedition produced rich documentation, including an Inuit oral account recorded by the American Charles F. Hall in 1861. The Elizabethan house foundations on Kodlunarn Island mark the first English attempt to settle in the New World. Today 'Meta Incognita' names the peninsula forming the southern shore of Frobisher Bay. The 'Meta Incognita Project' (1990–9) was an international multidisciplinary study of Frobisher's expeditions and the frigid, isolated site itself.

GERMAINE WARKENTIN

meteorology. *See* WEATHER FORECASTING.

Methodism. An offshoot of the Church of England, Methodism became the largest Protestant denomination in 19th-century Canada and would continue for decades thereafter to shape the country's 'Victorian' morality. In 1738 its founder, John Wesley, an Oxford don and Anglican priest, underwent an assurance of salvation and became convinced that this conversion was the core of true religion. Known for his 'methodistic' religious practices, Wesley, until his death in 1791, established within the Church of England a far-flung, highly structured movement of spiritual renewal, organized around an itinerant ministry and religious societies consisting of small groups or class meetings. Convinced that actual sinlessness, or 'Christian perfection' was possible in this life, he encouraged Methodists 'to spread scriptural holiness over the land'.

Although Wesley intended to keep his movement within the Church of England, he organized a separate Methodist Episcopal Church in 1784 to meet the needs of his followers in the new American republic. Among a cluster of New York City Methodists who entered Upper Canada in the 1770s were Loyalists Barbara Heck and Philip Embury, who organized the colony's first Methodist class in Augusta Township, near Brockville. Until the War of 1812 brought its American connection into suspicion, the Methodist Episcopal Church sent scores of itinerant preachers north to preach and organize new societies. Especially effective in evangelization (though seen as boisterous and 'enthusiastic' by critics) were its camp meetings. Lasting several days, and held in sylvan settings, such as at Hay Bay, near Picton, Ontario, in 1805, these reputedly drew large numbers from the scattered population and invariably resulted in stirring tales of sinners saved and scoffers confounded.

In the Maritime colonies, Methodism was more closely linked to its parent body in Britain, the more conservative Wesleyans, who shortly after their founder's death withdrew from the Church of England to form a separate denomination. In Newfoundland, Anglican priest Laurence *Coughlan in 1766 introduced an unconventional form of Methodism. Here, as in Nova Scotia, which contained a group of Yorkshire Methodists under the leadership of William Black, the movement soon turned to the British Wesleyans for support.

In central Canada it took many years before rivalry between the Methodist Episcopals and the Wesleyans ended, and not until 1884 did these two, and most of the other, smaller Methodist offshoots, unite to form a single denomination. By that date, Methodists, attuned to the social and intellectual changes of the century, had replaced their earlier revivalistic exuberance with a more staid piety that emphasized Christian nurture, social and moral reform, and the need for a college-educated ministry. Part of this task was carried on by a thriving book and periodical industry, but also by educators such as Egerton *Ryerson, who in 1846 became Ontario superintendent of education, and by institutions like Victoria College in Cobourg (which in 1891 moved to enter into federation with the University of Toronto), as well as by ladies' colleges dedicated to providing the graces and accomplishments of refined womanhood.

Increasingly as their interests expanded to social reform on a regional and national scale, Methodists availed themselves of voluntary societies, from *temperance movements to sabbatarian reform. Long interested in work among the country's Aboriginal population, they also became heavily committed to *foreign missions, opening a field in Japan in 1872, followed by another in West China, which would eventually become the world's largest single Protestant mission. As overcrowding and poverty arising from immigration and industrialization began to call for more intervention, Methodists established city missions such as All Peoples' Mission in Winnipeg and the Fred Victor Mission in downtown Toronto. Sponsored by the wealthy Massey family, the latter was only one of the many institutions and buildings that reflected the denomination's happy combination of lay piety and entrepreneurial wealth. However, proponents of the *social gospel, who were especially strong within Methodism, were not enamoured by this congruence between the church and wealth, and questioned the denomination's ability to reach the working classes and bring about systemic changes. As a result, in 1918 the church's main legislative body, the General Conference, accepted an unusually radical statement rejecting the capitalist system and calling for a complete reconstruction of the economy to serve the needs of all, not merely a few. Within the denomination's older hierarchy, General Superintendent Samuel D. Chown, while concerned about the danger of class conflict, was one of the strongest supporters of this new expression of practical Christianity. Like many of his generation who could look back to a tradition of co-operation among Canadian Protestants in revival and moral reform, he was eager also to further the social gospel's goal of greater Christian unity. In 1925, after several decades of negotiations, the Methodist Church joined with the Congregationalists and a majority of Presbyterians to form the *United Church of Canada. MARGUERITE VAN DIE

Metis. In 1982, Canada's Constitution Act conferred federal recognition on the Metis, specifying that the Aboriginal peoples of Canada include 'the Indian, Inuit and Metis peoples'. 'Metis', which has appeared on Canadian census forms since 1981, has become the term widely applied to people of mixed Aboriginal-European origin, but the category is not defined in the constitution and has been variously applied in different times and places. The term derives from an old French word meaning 'mixed'. In older Canadian French usage, *métis* referred generically to persons of mixed ancestry; it did not denote a sociopolitical or ethnic group. This article uses *métis* for that generic category, and Metis when referring to the distinct ethnic identity that emerged in the fur trade context of the early 1800s. Biologically, *métissage* or racial mixing, has gone on since earliest contact between European and Aboriginal people. But vast numbers of people have combined Aboriginal and European ancestry without being Metis. Some status Indian groups in eastern and central Canada have European genetic admixtures ranging from 20 to 40 per cent, while many North American families identified as European have some Aboriginal ancestry, often hidden or forgotten. Ethnicity is a function of cultural, political, economic, and other factors and is not predetermined by 'blood' or parentage.

Along Canada's Atlantic seaboard, the unions of European fishermen and traders with Native women from the 1600s on produced uncounted children who grew up as 'Indians' among their mothers' relatives. Some among the Maliseet became known as 'Malouidit' because so many of their fathers came from the French port of St-Malo.

Others served the French governors as cultural brokers and interpreters because of their dual connections. But they did not coalesce as an ethnically distinct group. The same was true of the *métis* progeny of those few French-Native unions that were solemnized as Christian marriages. Those children and their mothers were baptized with French names and were recorded only with reference to their French fathers and husbands. Samuel de *Champlain told his Native allies in the early 1600s, 'Our young men will marry your daughters and we shall be one people.' He was not, however, thinking of a *new* people; for the colonizers, the resulting families were without question French. New France itself, then, did not furnish a niche for the rise of a distinct Metis population; its first traces appeared around the Great Lakes in the mid to late 1700s.

As the French extended their claims westward, they built military and fur-trading posts at strategic sites such as Detroit, Michilimackinac, and Chicago. Their Ojibwa, Ottawa, and other Native trading partners valued kinship ties as foundations for trust and reciprocity, and often drew the newcomers into *marriages according to Native custom, sometimes termed *à la façon du pays* ('according to the custom of the country'). Catholic priests who sojourned at these settlements solemnized some of these unions and baptized family members, documenting the rapid rise of a mixed population. These *métis* were often multilingual, skilled interpreters, guides, and provisioners to the *fur trade, and sometimes small-scale farmers as well; the term *bois-brulés* ('burnt wood'), by which they were sometimes known, is usually taken to refer to complexion, but may also allude to their slash-and-burn method of clearing small fields. Many of them, like some of their *canadien* fathers, stayed in the **pays d'en haut*, the upper country, after completing their fur trade employment contracts. These *gens libres* ('free men') and their descendants formed an important demographic base for the spread of the Metis from the Great Lakes to the western plains.

In the 1700s, the Hudson's Bay Company's territory of *Rupert's Land became home to growing numbers of people of mixed descent, as English and Scottish traders formed families with Native, mainly Cree, women. In its first century (1670–1770), the company forbade such unions. The Cree, however, like the Native people around the Great Lakes, relied on kinship to build good relations; and the HBC men, unable to bring families from Britain, had both personal and tactical reasons to ally themselves with the people whose skills and help with trade, travel, fur processing, and the providing of local or 'country' foods, winter clothing, and other equipment made their survival possible. The company eventually recognized that it could not prevent such unions. By 1800, it began to see their progeny as 'a colony of very useful hands' with valuable skills and ties to Native communities. But both its fur trade focus and the boreal climate around *Hudson Bay worked against allowing permanent settlements such as those around the Great Lakes. To avoid expense and interference with trade, the company shipped its retired servants home, generally without their Native families. These families usually rejoined their Native relatives while maintaining ties and intermarrying with later HBC traders, a fact that explains the many Scottish and English surnames found in Cree communities today. The assimilation of these families among the Cree and the lack of an HBC class of 'free men' meant that no mixed ethnic group was recognized in Rupert's Land before about 1815. HBC writers before that time had no vocabulary for people of mixed descent; they subsumed them under 'Indians' or 'natives of the country'.

The founding of *Red River set the stage for the historic emergence of the Metis. In 1811, Thomas Douglas, Earl of *Selkirk, a major HBC shareholder, received HBC support to settle landless Scottish and Irish farmers around the confluence of the Red and Assiniboine Rivers; the company also saw the colony as a home for its former employees and their Native families. This enterprise aggravated hostilities with its fur trade rival, the Montreal-based *North West Company. Agriculture would displace the Red River bison herds that supplied the *pemmican that fed the NWC canoe brigades on their long trading journeys to the far Northwest. The Red River buffalo hunters and processors were largely Metis, as were many younger NWC *voyageurs and clerks such as Cuthbert Grant, Jr. Conflicts peaked with the Battle of *Seven Oaks in June 1816; Robert Semple, governor of the new colony, and 20 other settlers were killed in a confrontation with Grant and other NWC Metis who were trying to bypass the colony with provisions.

Some observers of these events began to introduce to Rupert's Land ethnic terms from older colonial contexts (*métis* from French Canada, and 'halfbreed' from the American English colonies, where it was first used in the 1700s) and to apply them to these newly visible people. Nor-Wester William McGillivray, in a letter of 14 March 1818, affirmed Metis distinctiveness most strongly: 'they one and all look upon themselves as members of an independent tribe of natives, entitled to a property in the soil, to a flag of their own, and to protection from the British government'. Further, 'the half-breeds under the denominations of bois-brules and metifs [alternate form of *métis*] have formed a separate and distinct tribe of Indians for a considerable time back'.

The merger of the Hudson's Bay and North West Companies in 1821 brought relative peace to the fur trade. By 1870, Red River had grown to a population of about 10,000, nine-tenths of whom were of mixed Aboriginal-European descent. In this period, 'Metis' referred to persons of Native and Canadian-French ancestry who were commonly francophone and Roman Catholic. Anglophone, Protestant mixed-bloods, usually of HBC families, were often known as Scottish or English 'half-breeds', a term used pejoratively by HBC governor George *Simpson in the 1830s and later increasingly rejected, although mixed-descent people who do not identify themselves historically with the Metis still choose it in some contexts. Red River historians have disagreed on the extent of separation between the two biracial groups but all these families born of the fur trade have become remarkably intertwined in a vast network of descendants.

Whatever their genealogies, Red River people shared many concerns as the bison herds shrank and as they searched for a stronger economic base. By the mid-1800s, the Metis of the Red River region and their American relatives to the south were challenging the HBC monopoly and control over Red River governance. In 1849, Pierre-Guillaume *Sayer was charged with privately trading furs. The court, impressed by a vocal crowd of armed Metis outside the building, found him guilty but did not impose a sentence. The cry went up, 'Le commerce est libre!' ('Trade is free!')—and so it became.

In the next 20 years, eastern Canadians seeking new lands and resources increasingly looked west, encouraged by Henry Y. *Hind's glowing survey accounts (1857–8) of prairie agricultural possibilities. In 1869, the British arranged to transfer Rupert's Land to the new Canadian confederation. But its residents were scarcely consulted, and when surveyors arrived to map grids across the landscape with little regard for prior occupants' claims, Louis *Riel and his followers, comprising many Metis and some 'halfbreeds', resisted vigorously. Riel's provisional government initiated the bargaining with Ottawa that led Canada to create a new province, Manitoba, in July 1870. The Manitoba Act provided that land titles be confirmed for holders of lots along the Red and Assiniboine Rivers, and that 1.4 million acres (566,580 hectares) be reserved for the children of the 'halfbreeds' (the generic term used in English at the time). The promised lands were largely lost under the pressures of incoming settlers and land speculators, while changing government regulations, language barriers, and lack of communication made it difficult for Metis to establish claims to lands they thought they owned. Many moved west to the Saskatchewan River or to Catholic missions in the Edmonton area; others went to the United States, as did Louis Riel when Red River came under Canadian control in 1870. The Metis communities of St Laurent and *Batoche on the Saskatchewan River repeated Red River history, settling river lots, trying to confirm land titles, establishing a provisional government under Gabriel *Dumont, and, when land issues went unresolved, turning again to Louis Riel, who returned from Montana in 1884. The *North-West Rebellion of 1885 ended in Metis defeat at Batoche in May, and in the trial and execution of Riel in November.

As the major western *Indian treaties were negotiated, officials tried to distinguish 'Indians' destined for reserves from 'halfbreeds' eligible for land under the Manitoba Act and later provisions. Many mixed-descent people who were initially assigned treaty status later opted out, sometimes under government pressures to reduce the numbers of 'Indians'. Others received scrip—certificates granting blocks of surveyed land to individuals. Scrip was often given in transferable form as 'money scrip'. Its recipients commonly thought cash more useful than undeveloped farmland, and sold their scrip at a discount to 'scrip hunters'. During Treaty 8 negotiations, speculators paid $70–$130 for Metis scrips worth $240, and resold them at considerable profit.

In 1896, Father Albert *Lacombe tried to counter Metis landlessness by founding St-Paul-des-Métis in Alberta on land leased by the government; the colony failed as Quebec migrants moved in. In the 1930s, two Metis socialist activists, Jim Brady and Malcolm Norris, organized petitions and delegations to the Alberta government to secure land rights for Metis squatters on Crown lands. Their efforts led to the appointment of the Ewing Commission to 'make enquiry into the condition of the Half-breed population of Alberta' and to the Metis Population Betterment Act of 1938. The main result was the founding of ten Metis settlements on leased land. Despite problems, eight still survive as Metis homelands that have no parallel in other provinces; as organized communities they have mobilized to negotiate land and resource rights.

Since the 1960s, Metis political organizations have sprung up across Canada, accompanying renewed attention to culture, heritage, and, notably, family history as Metis people recover ties and memories lost in the displacements and racial discrimination experienced after 1885. From 1970 to 1983, Metis and non-status Indian interests were represented by the Native Council of Canada (now the Congress of Aboriginal Peoples), whose president, Harry Daniels, secured constitutional recognition of the Metis as one of the Aboriginal peoples of Canada. After the 1983 First Ministers' Conference, where both NCC seats went to non-status Indians, the Metis National Council was formed to represent the people of the 'Metis Homeland', defined as the western Canadian home of the descendants of Louis Riel's Metis Nation. The Congress of Aboriginal Peoples, defining 'Metis' more inclusively, continues to represent 'off-reserve Indians and Metis people living in urban, rural, and remote areas throughout Canada'. In the 1996 census, 220,740 people identified themselves as 'Metis'.

JENNIFER S.H. BROWN

metric conversion. The program for metrication was set out in the *Trudeau government's 1970 White Paper on Metric Conversion. Although the metric system had been legal in Canada since the first Weights and Measures Act of 1871, the imperial system was far more prevalent. Following the 1970 recommendations to bring Canada in line with international trading partners who were rapidly converting to metric, an aggressive campaign for full conversion was begun in 1971, under the aegis of Metric Commission Canada.

In 1974 toothpaste became the first consumer product to be sold in grams. In 1975 temperatures were reported in degrees Celsius. In 1977 speed-limit signs across the country were changed to kilometres/hour. By 1979 almost all gasoline stations were posting prices per litre. Although it was expected that conversion would be complete by the 1980s, legal challenges prompted a moratorium on enforcing the use of metric. When Brian *Mulroney's government came out in 1984 in favour of voluntary conversion, the program was further eroded; Metric Commission Canada was disbanded the following year.

Metric conversion in Canada has been only partial. Gasoline and milk are sold in litres, but houses are sold by the square foot, while grocery stores give prominence to prices per pound. Given that the United States, Canada's largest trading partner, is one of three countries worldwide that has not embraced metric, it is likely that Canada will continue to straddle both systems for some time to come.
EMILY GILBERT

metropolitan thesis. An approach to Canadian history articulated by J.M.S. Careless in the early 1950s (*Canadian Historical Review*, 1954) as an alternative to the *frontier and *Laurentian theses, although also used earlier by D.C. Masters (*The Rise of Toronto, 1850–1890*, 1947). Frontierism, it said, got the process of historical causation backwards, at least in the case of Canada, which had been shaped more by old-world traditions and institutions than by new-world innovations. Akin to the Laurentian and *staples theses in its emphasis on transatlantic trade and communications, metropolitanism focused more specifically on the rise of cities and their influence over surrounding (and distant) 'hinterlands'. Fundamentally economic in approach, it conceived of towns and cities as evolving through successive stages as marketing, manufacturing, transport, and financial centres. Yet the process of metropolitan growth and influence extended into other spheres as well: for example, the intellectual influence of a city newspaper such as the Toronto *Globe* might be assessed by tracking the extent of its circulation; or the power of urban elites might be revealed by studying their role in political parties, government, and wider business networks. Careless applied the concept in this way in his masterly biography of the *Globe*'s editor George *Brown (*Brown of the Globe*, 2 vols., 1959, 1963) and in numerous other books and essays. Historical geographers have been especially adept in their use of the metropolitan thesis (e.g., *Heartland and Hinterland: A Geography of Canada*, ed. L.D. McCann, 1982).
KENNETH C. DEWAR

Michif (or Mitchif, Metchif) is a distinctive language that arose in certain Plains *Metis communities in the old Hudson's Bay Company territory of *Rupert's Land before it became part of Canada. The name is a variation on the word 'Metis' (referring to people of mixed Aboriginal-European descent). Observers formerly dismissed Michif as bad French or as a disorderly mix of languages, but linguists now recognize it as having a syntax and structure consisting largely of Plains Cree verbs with some Ojibwe elements, and French nouns: for example, 'I like fish'—*Li pwesoon nimiyaymow*.

Michif is thought to have developed from about the 1820s to 1860s in small Metis buffalo-hunting communities that wintered on the Plains around Pembina, North Dakota, the Qu'Appelle Valley, Turtle Mountain, Wood Mountain, the Touchwood Hills, and Cypress Hills. By the late 1900s, when scholars began to study Michif as a language with its own grammar, the number of speakers, largely among descendants of these settlements, was estimated to be about 1,000 and declining. In 2000, the Metis National Council initiated a Michif revival strategy to promote survival of the language through teaching, recording, and other means.

Many Metis never spoke Michif; those who lived in larger and more diverse communities were commonly multilingual, often serving as translators and interpreters in trade contexts. Michif speakers used the language orally among themselves, not with outsiders, and were not necessarily fluent in French or Cree. In contrast, those Metis who spoke Cree or Ojibwe fluently might incorporate French elements learned from church or school, without speaking Michif. Other northern people of mixed descent spoke mainly Canadian French or English. Many descendants of old Hudson's Bay Company Scots-Cree families spoke a Cree-influenced English dialect known as Bungee (from an old term for Ojibwe traders who visited the HBC posts). Once common in the Red River region, it combined elements derived from Cree and from the Scottish dialect spoken by the many HBC employees who were hired from the Orkney Islands in the 1700s and 1800s, and to lesser extents from Gaelic, French, and Michif. Unlike Michif, Bungee did not become a distinct language. By the 1980s, its few remaining speakers were all elderly, and only traces of the dialect remain among descendants.
JENNIFER S.H. BROWN

middle power. A term associated with activist and mediatory Canadian diplomacy in the post-1939 era. Before the Second World War no one would have argued that Canada was anything but a small power; by 1947, still in the flush of the country's enormous wartime economic and military contribution to the Allied victory, the Department of *External Affairs was claiming that Canada was in the international middle, situated nearer to the world's powerful than it was to marginal states. 'The Middle Powers', ran External's post-war definition, 'are those which by reason of their size, their material resources, their willingness and ability to accept responsibility, their influence and stability are close to being great powers.' Middlepowerhood had its definitive moment during the 1956 *Suez Crisis, but the concept has persisted as a description of the intent and direction of a Canadian *foreign policy emphasizing multilateralism, conflict management, and moral suasion.
NORMAN HILLMER

midwives. Well into the 19th century, midwives in Canada remained unregulated and numerous. Some had formal training; others apprenticed with an experienced midwife; still others were helpful neighbours or women with a reputation for healing. The care provided by midwives was excellent and, before the advent of antibiotics, safer than care by physicians. Midwives intervened less than physicians and saw childbirth as natural and generally unproblematic. The assistance they gave after birth was significant, staying or visiting for 9–10 days to care for mother, newborn, and the larger household.

By the end of the century their numbers had declined. Many physicians viewed midwives as competitors and obstacles to their entree into family practice and so encouraged legislation to circumscribe midwifery. Neither was midwife work attractive—it was poorly paid, physically difficult, and time consuming. Midwives were not organized and had few powerful advocates. In addition, many Canadian women came to prefer physician care and its alignment with science. The rise in hospital births in the interwar period solidified the control of physicians. Nonetheless, midwives survived among First Nations, the poor, newly arrived immigrant groups, and in isolated areas.

Legislation regulating midwifery is a provincial responsibility. By the end of the 19th century legislation existed limiting where and under whose control midwives could practise. By the 1940s midwifery was either illegal or licensed and controlled by the medical profession. Midwife revival began in the 1970s. Criticism of doctor/hospital-managed birth increased, focusing largely on childbirth intervention and lack of choice for the birthing mother. The women's movement provided a powerful base for such criticisms and support for the home birth movement, which by its very nature used midwives rather than physicians. In recent years, some jurisdictions in Canada, such as Ontario and Alberta, have legalized midwifery. WENDY MITCHINSON

migrant workers. Canada's early industrialization benefited from the labour of immigrant European workers, primarily from southern and eastern Europe, many of whom had been forced to leave home because of deteriorating agricultural conditions. Railway-construction camps, coal and metal mines, and urban employers of construction workers and day labourers hired immigrants, often at the barest subsistence wages. They believed that the immigrants, who usually spoke neither English nor French, were more willing than Canadian-born workers and English-speaking immigrants to accept exploitative wages and dangerous working conditions.

Many of these workers, particularly the *Italians, were sojourners: their goal was to earn money in Canada and then return to their villages. Coming mainly from southern Italy, where big landowners shamelessly exploited peasants, sojourners hoped to earn enough money to buy a small plot of land of their own, pay off debts, or pay for a dowry for a daughter's or sister's marriage. Once in Canada, both sojourners and those workers hoping to establish a life in their new country often migrated frequently. Migrancy had two causes. First was the temporary character of many jobs: once track was laid in a particular area, the work ended; mines laid off workers when markets disappeared; urban construction jobs lasted only as long as a particular project was in progress. Second, low wages and poor working and living conditions convinced workers to seek better conditions elsewhere. They were often labelled 'blanketstiffs' because they rolled their few possessions into the blankets they carried with them as they roamed about in search of work. The search for better conditions was often fruitless: particularly in construction work, competition among companies was often based solely on success in keeping labour costs down. Railway companies subcontracted the building of track to the lowest bidder, and the companies doing the bidding kept bids low by paying their workers little, housing them cheaply, and making few outlays on equipment that might make the work go easier.

Immigrant workers did not long accept such exploitation by railway companies, subcontractors, and mines. They often organized collectively to demand better treatment. Many joined the radical *Industrial Workers of the World in order to stand up to the bosses. Sojourners were exploited not only by bosses but also by padrones, middlemen of Italian background who acted as labour agents linking employers and workers. While sojourning was common in the 1880s and 1890s, by the early 20th century many of the migrant workers had settled in cities, where their efforts at collective self-help and better working conditions often made it more attractive to stay in Canada than to return to the old country. ALVIN FINKEL

Migratory Birds Convention Act. By the end of the 19th century North Americans knew about the extinction of the *great auk, *passenger pigeon, and Labrador duck. They were concerned by the dramatic decline of populations of trumpeter swan, whooping crane, and wood duck, and the rapid disappearance of the Eskimo curlew. Farmers saw a surprising decline in numbers of songbirds, caused by hunting and the loss of habitat as swamps and marshes were filled in. Women activists from the Audubon Society criticized the use of plumage on women's hats, which were advertised in the 1902 Eaton's catalogue. State and provincial officials found themselves powerless to protect birds who left their jurisdiction on the great spring and fall migration flyways.

By 1913 the debate in the United States inspired officials in Ottawa. They knew the federal government had no constitutional jurisdiction over birds, but it did have the power to make treaties. Dominion biologist Maxwell Graham calculated the tremendous cost to agriculture of crops lost to insects, because of the loss of insectivorous songbirds. Supported by this evidence and Canada's Commission on Conservation, Dominion Parks Commissioner James Harkin met with provincial and US counterparts to draft a treaty to protect migratory birds. It received final assent in 1917. Entomologist Gordon Hewitt claimed it protected a thousand species. However, problems emerged as the dates in the treaty denied spring hunting in New Brunswick and Prince Edward Island. Relations between Ottawa and the Maritimes remained cool and these provinces left enforcement to Ottawa. British Columbia and then other provinces did match their legislation to meet the treaty's terms. Forgotten, or perhaps deliberately ignored, Aboriginal bird-hunters found their traditional seasonal activity had been made illegal. The treaty was upheld against early constitutional challenges in both nations as a necessary extension of federal powers for the common good. LORNE HAMMOND

Mi'kmaq. An indigenous people of eastern Canada whose identity as a distinct community can be traced back at least 4,500 years. At the time of first sustained contact with Europeans, about 1600, the Mi'kmaq inhabited Cape Breton Island, mainland Nova Scotia, Prince Edward Island, the eastern coast of New Brunswick—including all those river systems flowing into the Gulf of St Lawrence—the Gaspésie, and the Magdalen Islands. By the early 1700s, a Mi'kmaq community also occupied southern Newfoundland. They called their territory *Mi'kma'ki*, or land of the Mi'kmaq

Before the 1800s, the Mi'kmaq lived principally by fishing, hunting, and gathering wild plants. Some communities in southern areas also cultivated corn and tobacco, perhaps even before 1500. They were a semi-nomadic people who migrated to exploit resources as necessary. During summer, families lived together in coastal areas. These villages may have held 300 or more people. In winter, families lived in groups of 10 to 50 people, the size depending upon local circumstances. Population estimates vary. Before 1500, there were probably 10,000–12,000; these numbers declined as Europeans diseases took their toll, and by 1760 there were perhaps 4,000–5,000.

Mi'kmaq diplomatic relations with Europeans were varied. The French were the first to build permanent settlements in Mi'kma'ki, from about 1632. Thereafter, the Mi'kmaq built a strong relationship with the French that continued until the defeat of French forces at *Louisbourg in 1758. After Great Britain conquered Acadia in 1710, various Mi'kmaq communities signed treaties with the British in 1726, 1749, 1752, 1760–1, and 1779. Later treaties built on earlier agreements. These treaties are now protected by the 1982 constitution. Two Supreme Court decisions—*R. v. Simon* (1985) and *R. v. Marshall* (1999)—focusing on these treaties have influenced how treaty rights for Canada's Aboriginal population should be defined.

Beginning with the *Loyalist emigration of the late 1770s, the Mi'kmaq's ability to live by fishing and hunting became more difficult. In 1820, the Nova Scotia government established reserves in areas traditionally occupied by communities. Similar moves were made by the other colonies except Newfoundland, where the Mi'kmaq were not recognized until 1982. Few families lived on reserves on a year-round basis. With Confederation, responsibility for Indian affairs was transferred to the federal government. Currently, there are 31 inhabited Mi'kmaq reserves—13 in Nova Scotia, 1 in Newfoundland, 1 in Prince Edward Island, 13 in New Brunswick, and 2 in Quebec—and 1 is currently being negotiated.

As the 1900s progressed, families experienced more difficulty providing for themselves. Provincial game laws interfered with hunting, and more restrictions were placed upon community fishing. Meanwhile, people's attempts to work outside the reserve were constrained by racial prejudice and the fact that for most English was a second language. In part because of these problems, the federal government in 1942 attempted to centralize the entire Mi'kmaq population of Nova Scotia on two reserves. Resistance to the initiative led to its abandonment in 1949. In the 1960s and 1970s, Mi'kmaq communities formed political organizations to deal with federal and provincial agencies on Aboriginal title and related issues: in Nova Scotia the Union of Nova Scotia Indians and the Confederacy of Mainland Micmacs, in New Brunswick the Union of New Brunswick Indians and Mawiw, and in Quebec in 2000 the Mi'kmawei Mawoimi.

WILLIAM WICKEN

military colleges. Post-secondary educational institutions that prepare young men (and now young women) for careers as officers in the armed forces. Following British and American precedent, Canada opened the Royal Military College of Canada at Kingston, Ontario, on 1 June 1876 to provide a corps of educated officers for the Canadian *militia and *Permanent Force as well as engineers to assist in the development of Canada's industrial infrastructure. A Royal Naval College of Canada opened at Halifax, Nova Scotia, in 1911, moving to Esquimalt, British Columbia, after the 1917 Halifax explosion, but closed its doors in 1922. A new naval college, Royal Roads Military College, opened at Esquimalt in 1942 to help meet Second World War needs. Collège militaire royale opened at St-Jean, Quebec, in 1952 for mainly francophone officer cadets for all three branches of the service (RMC and Royal Roads became 'tri-service' in 1948). The curriculum at all three colleges combined academic and military subjects, and RMC in particular has always been known for its engineering program. All three colleges became degree-granting institutions (RMC in 1959, CMR in 1971, and Royal Roads in 1975) and all three opened their doors to women (RMC and CMR in 1980, Royal Roads in 1984). Although never able to supply all the officers required by the armed forces, military college graduates have nevertheless always seemed to do better than their 'direct entry' colleagues in obtaining senior staff and command appointments; it is often argued that the belief and behaviour patterns inculcated into military college cadets form the basis of the ethos, beliefs, and behaviour pattern of the armed forces as a whole. Cutbacks in defence spending and the size of the armed forces led to the closure of Royal Roads and CMR in 1995. As a consequence the Royal Military College/Collège militaire royale at Kingston became a bilingual institution. It has also substantially expanded its mandate, offering postgraduate degrees (including doctorates) in selected fields as well as a distance-learning program aimed at increasing the basic education profile for all ranks.

STEPHEN J. HARRIS

military fortifications. *See* FORTIFICATIONS.

military technology, Second World War. The Second World War was a unique global conflict waged on the back of industrial and technological resources, the terrifying wonder weapons produced by scientists on both sides. In part, this was an extension of developments during the First World War, when new technologies such as the airplane, submarine, and gas warfare assumed a minor role in determining the war's outcome. But the global conflict of 1939–45 was much more of a scientist's war: the creation and development of advanced weapon systems was regarded as crucial in achieving military supremacy. As a result, thousands of scientists were recruited for laboratory rather than combat service.

Radar and the proximity fuse, for instance, represented challenging new technologies that very rapidly became essential to Allied military victory. In contrast, RDX explosives, chemical weapons, and biological warfare did have First World War legacies; between 1939 and 1945, however, the potential killing power of these devices increased dramatically. But the most fearsome weapon of mass destruction was the atomic bomb, which the United States used against Japan in August 1945 with devastating results.

While Germany developed many important weapons, notably jet aircraft, sophisticated submarines, and the V 2 supersonic missiles, the United States achieved the most spectacular results in harnessing its scientific and industrial communities behind the war effort. By 1945 the country had become an awesome weapons factory capable of producing every form of military technology, with the most spectacular achievement being the *Manhattan Project's nuclear bomb program that ended the war. Canadian scientists contributed to this undertaking through the Montreal Atomic Laboratory, a joint Anglo-Canadian venture that provided the basis for post-war nuclear opportunities: the British pursued their own atomic/thermonuclear weapons, while Canada opted for the peaceful use of atomic energy.

Under the direction of the *National Research Council, Canadian scientists were involved with a variety of other important weapon systems within the Anglo-American military alliance. In 1940–1 the greatest need was for the development of a variety of radar systems for defensive and offensive purposes, along with proximity fuses that greatly enhanced the accuracy of artillery shells. The high explosive RDX, used in bombs and depth-charges, was greatly improved through the efforts of Canadian chemists, who were also involved in the massive chemical weapons operation at Suffield, Alberta. Although battlefield chemical warfare did not occur during the war, most Allied experts believed that it was imminent, thereby requiring a massive retaliatory capability and extensive defensive measures. Even more horrifying was the prospect that Germany and Japan would deploy biological weapons such as anthrax, plague, and *botulinum* toxin, fears that Nobel laureate Sir Frederick *Banting raised in the late 1930s. By the end of the war Canada had acquired considerable expertise in both chemical and biological weapon systems, which it retains today.

Some critics have admonished Canadian scientists, past and present, for being involved with weapons of mass destruction and other forms of military technology. The counter-argument is that Canada and its allies could defend themselves only by having a retaliatory capacity; it was, therefore, their duty as scientists to ensure their country's survival. Given the appearance of even more frightening types of weapons, the debate is as relevant today as it was in 1939. DONALD H. AVERY

militia. Currently, the reserve element of Canada's land forces (army). Historically, the militia was a citizen army of part-time soldiers that could be (but was not always) trained, equipped, uniformed, and paid for its military service. In colonial times, militias provided local home defence, both in New France and in British North America. Although British regular troops were largely responsible for success in the War of 1812, Canadian defence policy for the next 140 years was influenced by the 'militia myth', the idea that the country needed no large professional regular army to defend itself. Militia companies, battalions, and regiments, formed throughout the country in small towns and cities, were the recruiting and mobilization base for Canada's overseas armies in both the First and Second World Wars as well as the Korean conflict. It was only with the coming of the Cold War in the 1950s that the regular professional army supplanted the part-time (and partially trained) reserve as the mainstay of Canada's land forces. At its peak in 1913–14, the Canadian militia comprised some 74,000 officers and men. By 2002, despite a much larger population, it numbered fewer than 20,000, and its primary operational role was to provide individual soldiers to augment the regular army at home and abroad. However, because its battalions and regiments were still located in towns and cities throughout the country, the militia provided the regular army with a national 'footprint', and many who joined the latter did so after part-time service in the reserve. STEPHEN J. HARRIS

militia, French regime. From the 1640s, settlers in Canada had to defend themselves against *Iroquois attacks. In 1669 Louis XIV formalized the service, obliging men 16 to 60 to serve both in military operations and on public works (*corvée militaire*). Selection was based on aptitude, possession of a musket (many did not have one), and physical condition. It was also restricted by the need to sustain essential economic activities. Militiamen formed a substantial part of most military operations, but the *Troupes de la Marine provided most of the officers leading them. Operations were few and as the population grew the number of militiamen who saw action declined. A core of experts, often men associated with the *fur trade, gave Canadiens a formidable reputation as guerrilla fighters. Many militiamen assembled to defend Montreal and Quebec against the British, but faced combat only in 1759–60. Their performance was variable, but the core proved its worth as sharpshooters and in *la petite guerre*. During the winter of 1759–60 militiamen retrained under François de Lévis as light infantry proved outstanding in the Battle of Ste-Foy. JAY CASSEL

Miner, Jack (1865–1944), conservationist. This popular author from Kingsville, Ontario, learned to read and write at age 34, after his brother died in a hunting accident. Born again from tragedy as an evangelical conservationist, he made the family home a bird sanctuary, lecturing literally for bird feed. Jack banded the legs of Canada geese with religious scriptures to map their migrations and promoted the Canada goose as Canada's national bird. Yet he hated hawks, owls, and 'vermin' crows. Kingsville was a popular Sunday drive for thousands of visitors and many more knew 'Wild Goose Jack' through radio, books, and his articles on the pollution of the Great Lakes and the negative impact of automobile tourism. Like *Grey Owl and Ernest Thompson *Seton, Miner drew attention to our relationship with wildness, and dedicated himself to nature education. A working-class conservationist, he received the Order of the British Empire in 1943. LORNE HAMMOND

miners' meetings. Ad hoc, extra-legal, democratic tribunals used to resolve disputes among miners. They were not peculiar to Canada, but part of the 19th-century working-class culture of the gold fields in the United States, Australia, and New Zealand. Miners in a given locale called meetings to present their disputes to those assembled, who voted on a solution. The range of issues dealt with was wide, and the decisions were aimed at ensuring the ongoing security of the community rather than punishing the offender. In British Columbia and the Yukon, meetings dealt with conflicting claims, theft, and—rarely—homicide.

Anxious to establish a monopoly on legal authority, governments worked to limit the power of these tribunals by establishing a system of law that mimicked them. British Columbia's gold commissioner's courts functioned largely as meetings did, except that the government-appointed gold commissioner was not bound by the opinion of the miners in his district. In the Yukon, the Mounties practised the same kind of 'forward-looking justice' the miners had, and thus facilitated the acceptance of formal Canadian law. TINA LOO

mining. *See* COAL MINING; HARDROCK MINING.

Mississauga missionaries. In the mid-1820s a remarkable phenomenon occurred in southern Ontario: over 1,000 Ojibwa-speaking First Nations people adopted *Methodism. Peter Jones (1802–56), or Kahkewaquonaby ('Sacred Feathers'), son of an American surveyor and his Mississauga wife, served as the catalyst. Raised by his mother among her people to the age of 16, then on his father's farm until 21, Jones became the badly needed cultural go-between after his own conversion at a Methodist camp meeting in 1823.

From the Credit River mission immediately west of Toronto, Jones and Native mission workers reached out to surrounding communities anxious to adjust to European-style farming and a settled way of life. Jones assembled a remarkable team of Ojibwa-speaking allies. John Sunday (*c.* 1795–1875), or Shuwundais ('Sultry Heat'), became one of the most dedicated. This hardened veteran of the War of 1812 apparently knew only three words of English before his conversion to Christianity: pint, quart, and whisky. Once converted he studied to become an ordained Methodist minister, and won back his community's respect he had lost through years of abusive alcoholism. Henry Steinhauer (*c.* 1820–84), a young Ojibwa from Lake Simcoe, also became a prominent Methodist church worker. The mission school graduate served as a teacher in the Northwest and later as an ordained Methodist preacher. Eventually he established a successful farming settlement in Alberta.

Not all the early Native preachers retained the church's respect. George Copway (1818–69), or Kahgegagahbowh, a Mississauga from Rice Lake near Peterborough, became probably the best known to fall from grace. Caught embezzling band funds in the mid-1840s, he was expelled by the church. He went immediately to the United States, where he became a highly successful author and lecturer. Between 1847 and 1851 he published three books: an autobiography, a history of the Ojibwa, and an account of a journey he made to Europe in 1850.

A split in the Methodists' ranks, the cold response of some non-Native Methodists, and the declining zeal within the Canadian church for Aboriginal missions, all weakened what had been from the late 1820s to the 1840s a strong Native Methodist church. DONALD B. SMITH

Mitchell, Mattie (Matthieu Michel) (1846–1921), guide, prospector. Born at Halls Bay, Newfoundland, Mitchell was a renowned Mi'kmaw hunter and sought-after guide. In 1904 he took H.C. Thomson, a world traveller, through the Northern Peninsula and assisted in mapping this area; Lake Michel was named after him. In 1908, he led a small party with 50 reindeer through difficult terrain and blizzards from St Anthony to Millertown. Employed as prospector by the Anglo-Newfoundland Development Company, Mitchell is credited with discovering in 1905 the massive ore body that later became the basis of the Buchans Mining Company. He died in Corner Brook.
INGEBORG C.L. MARSHALL

mobilization. Usually refers to the preparation of armed forces for involvement in a possible war. With the advent of 'total war' and the consequent importance of the *'home front' to military success, the term has also been applied to expansion of an economy in wartime. The mustering of Canada's personnel and resources in two world wars provides a considerable contrast in approach, though ultimately the country contributed significantly to victory in both conflicts.

Pre-war planning meant that government departments and the military leadership knew generally what was expected when war was declared in August 1914. Unfortunately, the militia minister, Sam *Hughes, scrapped careful preparations for a Canadian overseas contingent of 25,000 soldiers and substituted an unlimited patriotic appeal for volunteers. That then necessitated an improvised response to larger recruitment.

Ultimately, that initial chaos hardly mattered. The scale, intensity, character, and duration of the conflict were unexpected. Canada's military and economic commitment escalated. In military recruitment and many aspects of production, voluntarism eventually gave way to compulsion or direction. The approved strength of the *Canadian Expeditionary Force in January 1916 was

20 times greater than first envisaged, with enlistments usually obtained by a decentralized network of recruiting offices. To support that army in the field and to meet other requirements necessitated an exceptional expansion and redirection of Canada's industrial and agricultural output. Most of that was achieved by persuasion rather than coercion. Under the *War Measures Act of 1914, the government possessed exceptional powers to control daily life and work in Canada, but it generally relied instead on patriotic zeal and voluntary compliance. Even so, government played a major role in Canada's economy and it was held accountable for the war effort. In wartime, Canada's economy grew by about two-thirds over its former level, with manufacturing almost tripling in value. The federal government's revenues more than doubled, but its expenditures nearly tripled.

When the Second World War began, the Canadian government initially attempted to pursue a policy of 'limited liability', including orderly recruitment and organization of army units for overseas service. Some aspects of economic activity were immediately regulated, but a gradual approach to mobilization prevailed. After the fall of France in June 1940, however, that changed. The Canadian armed forces expanded considerably, as did Canada's effort at home and the role of the government in maximizing output for the common cause. Controls were imposed on production and consumption (including rationing). Canadian labour and resources, it was hoped, would be used efficiently to defeat the enemy.

A shift from voluntary enlistment to *conscription for overseas military service took place in stages. The expansion of the Canadian army took place in spite of uncertainty about prospective casualty rates and replacement requirements. Meanwhile, Canada assumed a greater role in the war at sea and in the air than before, with those branches of the armed forces relying exclusively on volunteers. In fact, one of the more problematic aspects of mobilization was the allocation of manpower between military and civilian purposes.

In the circumstances, the federal government assumed a much greater role in the national economy than it had done in the previous war. Still recovering from the Great Depression when war began, Canada's economic output more than doubled in six years. As for the national budget, it grew more than sevenfold during the war.

HECTOR MACKENZIE

Molson, John (1763–1836), entrepreneur. Born in England, Molson arrived in 1782 in Montreal, where he became involved in various commercial endeavours. His activities anticipated the profound changes that would alter the economic landscape of the colony in the 1790s. In 1786, when the fur trade was at its zenith, Molson established a brewery. He showed a keen awareness of rising channels for investment in timber, agriculture, industry, and communication. His early investments in a steamship service connecting Quebec and Montreal led to the creation of the St Lawrence Steamship Company. In 1831 he was one of the first investors in the Champlain and St Lawrence Railroad. Molson served as an assemblyman, but his most significant political activities were in the legislative council, where his presence on committees for commercial, banking, and financial policies highlighted his abiding interest in the commercial life of the colony.

K. DAVID MILOBAR

monarchy. Among the cardinal characteristics of Canada's constitution—*federalism, parliamentary government, and *bilingualism are others—monarchy is the oldest. The only monarchy in the western hemisphere, Canada has never had any other governmental form since the arrival of European settlers. Today, that form takes expression as a *constitutional monarchy, with this caveat—the sovereign does not reside in Canada but is represented by a *governor general appointed on the advice of the prime minister. Monarchy's singular features of heredity and permanence are diluted for Canadians by successive selection and turnover, its pageantry and ceremony derivative rather than direct.

Despite the cult of celebrity and the intrusion of electronic media into the lives of royalty, modern monarchy is an institution first and a matter of personalities second. The lessons of the English Civil War and the Glorious Revolution were codified in the Declaration of Rights (1689) and the Act of Settlement (1701). Together, they limited the prerogative power of the Crown when acting alone and established the principle that ministers should be responsible for acts of the sovereign. This formula has rendered the powers of the sovereign largely theoretical and monarchy a facade—so much so that a century ago Great Britain was already being described as a counterfeit republic. But if modern monarchy were no more than a matter of form, it would not have survived.

All monarchies, whether of ancient Egypt or China, pre-revolutionary France or modern Britain, depend upon as well as sanction religion. The coronation ceremony at Westminster Abbey resembles the ritual at Rheims, where the kings of France were crowned. Oaths, prayers, and regalia sanctify the act and signify the dedication of the anointed to serve the nation. The English Reformation, which saw Henry VIII place himself at the head of a state church, exaggerated the link between religion and monarchy; it did not create it. Monarchs might lay claim to sovereign power, but all have acknowledged spiritual obedience. They are forced to act justly. The phrase 'the king can do no wrong' requires the sovereign to practise justice. From this understanding other attributions flow: the monarch as protector, redresser, succour, and servant. These qualities identify monarchy with the people, and it is in performance of actions embodying them that monarchy becomes relevant.

Another, now largely historical, bond between monarchy and the people is through battle. The warrior king or queen has metamorphosed into Trooping the Colour on the Queen's birthday or, in Canada, the governor general's designation but inactivity as commander-in-chief. Once, the kings of France and England personified their nations in the field, an image depicted in art and literature.

Out of uniform, monarchs symbolized national identity—in the case of the Sun King in the exaggerated grandeur of Versailles and its immense court or, half a century before, in the form of Scotland's James VI, who ascended England's throne as James I and thus personified the union of the two kingdoms. More than symbolism was involved, however. Public administration in France begins under Louis XIV, radiating from Versailles then but centralized in Paris now. In Britain today the regulation of the civil service remains based largely on Crown prerogative, its clerks and letter carriers working for the nation as servants of Her Majesty. Similarly, in the making of law (the Crown in Parliament) and its enforcement (through the Queen's Courts), monarchy plays a practical yet pervasive part in the lives of subjects.

Today, monarchs and governors general represent the nation to itself. Through awards and orders, they recognize on behalf of all the people outstanding demonstrations of valour and the excellence of a few. Through their own performance of public duties, they reflect and enhance the national character. DAVID E. SMITH

Moncton. The site that became Moncton was well known to, and sometimes inhabited by, both Mi'kmaq and Acadian peoples, but it was the shipbuilding industry of the mid-19th century—attracting specialized labour and commercial capital—that led to its greatest leap in development. The boom was short-lived, over by the 1870s.

Moncton was incorporated as a town in 1875 and as a city in 1890, its growth in these years owing much to its having been chosen, in 1870, as headquarters of the *Intercolonial Railway. The city acquired administrative responsibilities as well as all technical and mechanical functions. The 1880s witnessed the effects of the federal government's new national economic policies. Implementation of protective tariffs encouraged the multiplication of industries, and in Atlantic Canada these developed particularly well in towns and cities where commercial capital could be reinvested in industry. Between 1881 and 1891 capital invested in Moncton industries more than doubled, from $530,000 to $1,134,000, and this upward trend continued through the first decades of the 20th century. Moncton's population grew as a result, from 4,810 people in 1871 to 22,763 in 1941. Workers came mostly from the surrounding areas of Westmorland and Kent; since these counties contained a large number of Acadians Moncton's francophone population grew quickly, representing 15.5 per cent of the population in 1871 and 34 per cent by 1941.

By the end of the Great War, industrial and financial consolidation and centralization had eroded the progress of industrialization throughout the Maritimes. Moncton city council, chambers of commerce, and other elites developed strategies to redirect, yet again, the city's economic future. Moncton's geographic location as 'the hub of the Maritimes' and, more prosaically, its railway facilities were used to promote the city's warehousing and distribution functions. The economic outlook throughout the next decades was more positive than expected, setting a trend that continued during the more prosperous years after the Second World War. In the 1960s the railway still employed 3,000 people, but two decades later the CN shops—the last vestiges of the city's extensive railway infrastructure—were abandoned by the government, initiating a crisis in employment and a general fear of prolonged economic hardship.

The last decades of the 20th century, however, saw rapid growth of employment opportunities in the service sector, within the more traditional wholesale and retail trades, and in new technology and teleservice industries, reflecting Moncton's reputation as a bilingual city. In 1996 Greater Moncton (including Moncton, Riverview, and Dieppe) had a population of 84,000 people, of whom more than a third were francophone.

PHYLLIS E. LeBLANC

Mon oncle Antoine. Hailed by critics as the best film ever produced in Canada, Claude Jutra's *Mon oncle Antoine* (1971) focuses on the coming of age of Benoît, a teenage boy living with his aunt and uncle in a small mining town in Quebec. Set during the *Duplessis era (1940s–50s), the film has been interpreted as an allegory for French Canada's own maturation from a state of passivity and dependence to a position of resistance and rebellion. Released in 1971, at a time when nationalist sentiments in Quebec and Canada informed artistic production, it has been praised as the quintessential Canadian film. Shunning Hollywood formulas, this feature adopts a distinctly Canadian style combining elements of documentary realism—achieved primarily through Michel Brault's cinematography—with an engaging narrative and solid performances by some of Quebec's best actors, including Jean Duceppe, Hélène Loiselle, and Jutra himself. More accessible than his previous feature, *A tout prendre* (1963), and more emotionally compelling than his later work, *Kamouraska* (1973), *Pour le meilleur et pour le pire* (1975), *Surfacing* (1980), and *La Dame en couleurs* (1984), *Mon oncle Antoine* represents the high point in a remarkable career that came to a tragic end in 1986 when, suffering from Alzheimer's disease, Jutra committed suicide.

ANDRÉ LOISELLE

Mons. The Battle of Mons in 1918 was the last action of the First World War on the Western Front for British Empire forces. Mons was also the location of the first contact between German and British forces in 1914. Immediately after the war the former Canadian minister of militia and defence, Sir Sam *Hughes, accused the commander of the *Canadian Corps of 'recklessly sacrificing' Canadian lives in a vainglorious attempt to take Mons before the armistice. The claim was without any evidence. General Arthur *Currie had ordered that there should be no large-scale attack and every effort made to minimize casualties. Moreover, soldiers of the Royal Canadian Regiment and 42nd Battalion had freed Mons by daybreak on 11 November, well before the official ceasefire order was received. There were 16 casualties in the entire Canadian Corps on that day. The only fatality occurred in the 28th Battalion when a Canadian soldier in the village of St Symphorien ignored warnings by Belgian civilians and was shot by a sniper moments before the armistice. A.M.J. HYATT

Montreal. In 1535 French explorer Jacques *Cartier visited the Iroquoian agricultural village of Hochelaga located on the slopes of Mount Royal. St Lawrence Iroquoians had lived in the area for a few centuries but disappeared towards the end of the 16th century. Montreal, also called Ville-Marie in the early period, was founded in 1642 as a missionnary colony by Paul de Chomedey de Maisonneuve and about 40 settlers. The early years were marked by constant warfare between the *Iroquois and the French and their Native allies; although a military expedition in 1665–6 eased the pressure, tensions did not disappear until the *Great Peace of 1701. Montrealers were involved early in the *fur trade, the main staple of New France. Their city became the headquarters for commercial expeditions and journeys of exploration to the interior of the continent. The population grew slowly, from 50 in the 1640s, to 1,000 by 1700, to 4,000 in 1760. The townsite expanded accordingly, protected by a wooden palissade (1688) and later by walls (1744). Six religious orders established themselves in the city.

In 1760 the city surrendered to British troops without a fight. British merchants, notably Scots, soon took over the fur trade. A new thrust of western exploration expanded Montreal's hinterland to the Pacific coast and into the Arctic, but the city lost its long-standing role as leader in the fur trade when the Hudson's Bay Company took over in 1821. In the meantime, Montreal found a new role as the metropolitan centre for the expanding agricultural frontier of Lower and Upper Canada, its business elite dominating the import–export trade and transportation on the St Lawrence River. Population grew rapidly from 9,000 in 1800 to 58,000 in 1852, and Montreal passed Quebec as the most populous city in British North America. British immigration (the Irish being the most numerous) fuelled that growth, and anglophones became the majority around 1831. The old town walls were demolished in the early 19th century and British architecture transformed the urban landscape. A city charter was granted in 1832, the first council being elected the following year; although it lapsed in 1836, municipal administration resumed in 1840 after the rebellions.

By the 1850s Montreal was Canada's leading mercantile centre and a major gateway of the *British Empire. It also became the largest industrial centre in the country, its manufacturers turning out a variety of consumer and durable goods. Railway construction strengthened its function as the major transportation hub: both the *Grand Trunk and the *Canadian Pacific established their administration and main shops in the city. Industry spurred migration from the countryside, allowing francophones to regain the majority around 1865. By Confederation, the population had reached 100,000.

The beginning of the 20th century was a time of tremendous growth. The harbour was transformed to handle huge quantities of wheat from the Prairies. Wholesalers and manufacturers expanded their facilities. Banks and other financial institutions expanded their networks across the country. Montreal was at the apex of its dominance, and Old Montreal was bustling with thousands of office workers. By 1911, the population had reached more than half a million, thanks to the influx of immigrants, many of them part of a new wave of eastern European *Jews, *Italians, and other groups. Urban expansion took place chiefly in the suburbs, most of which were annexed by the First World War. Slowed down by the war, urbanization resumed during the 1920s, pushing up the metropolitan population to 1 million by 1931. When the Depression struck, unemployment rose, construction nearly stopped, and poverty abounded. The Second World War put an end to bad times, with factories running at full capacity and employment plentiful.

The post-war years were synonymous with prosperity. New investments poured in, services expanded, and the standard of living rose significantly. European immigrants came in droves and, with the *baby boom, fuelled growth to 2 million by 1961. New *suburbs in the 1950s led to urban sprawl. The good times continued into the 1960s, climaxing with *Expo 67, which gave Montreal new international stature.

During the last third of the 20th century, Montreal experienced three major changes. First, its economy was dealt severe blows. Toronto took over as Canada's leading financial metropolis, triggering the transfer of numerous enterprises and their staff. The old industrial base crumbled rapidly. Towards the mid-1990s the city emerged from a long and painful adjustment with a modernized and buoyant economy geared to high-tech and export-led activities. The second change came in the wake of Quebec's *Quiet Revolution with the rise of new francophone elites who took over as leaders in all areas. The French language became pre-eminent in the city's public life. Finally, the changing patterns of immigration, with the substantial rise of non-European newcomers, transformed the ethnic, cultural, and social fabric of the city. At the beginning of the 21st century, with a population of 3.4 million, Montreal had become a thriving francophone and multicultural metropolis.

PAUL-ANDRÉ LINTEAU

Montreal Group. The group comprised a number of writers and editors, including A.J.M. Smith, F.R. *Scott, John Glassco, A.M. *Klein, Leo Kennedy, and Leon Edel. The majority attended McGill University as undergraduates in the 1920s. Owing to its early institutional affiliation, the group is alternately known as the McGill Movement.

Four periodicals were founded and edited by the Montreal Group: the *McGill Daily Literary Supplement* (1924–5), the *McGill Fortnightly Review* (1925–7), the *Canadian Mercury* (1928–9), and the *McGilliad* (1930–1). The first of these was issued as a weekly supplemental section of the McGill undergraduate society's newspaper, the *McGill Daily*, and was edited by Allan Latham, A.P.R. Coulborn, and A.J.M. Smith. They were joined by Scott, Glassco, and Edel as editors of the *McGill Fortnightly Review*, the most important of the group's periodicals, which announced itself in November 1925 as 'an independent journal of literature, the arts and student affairs edited and published by a group of undergraduates at McGill University'. First Klein and later David Lewis edited the *McGilliad*, the lesser-known successor to the *Fortnightly*. The *Canadian Mercury* was the first periodical produced by the Montreal Group without affiliation to McGill, financed by Montreal businessman Leo Schwartz and edited by Jean Burton, Felix Walter, Scott, and Kennedy. The three student periodicals published poems, short stories, reviews, and articles by McGill undergraduates (the majority of which came from the editors themselves, writing under their own names and under pseudonyms), but the *Mercury* solicited contributions from a broader group of Canadian (and expatriate Canadian) writers and aimed at audiences beyond McGill and outside Montreal. After the departure of key figures such as Smith, Glassco, Edel, and Kennedy from Montreal in the late 1920s, four of the poets from the Montreal Group (Smith, Kennedy, Klein, and Scott) reunited for the publication of the anthology *New Provinces: Poems by Several Authors* (1936).

Among literary critics and historians of the 1920s, the Montreal Group is not only defined by its 'little magazines', which catered to innovative prose and poetry influenced by contemporary movements in British and American modernism, but also by its belated inheritance of a *fin-de-siècle* poetics from the aesthetic and decadent movements in Europe. The Montreal Group is recognized chiefly for the early writings of its poets who later established themselves among the major Canadian modernists of the 20th century. DEAN IRVINE

Montreal massacre. By the end of the 1980s, feminism faced a backlash from those who believed that women's equality came at the expense of opportunities for men. This had tragic consequences for students at the École polytechnique in Montreal, where women formed only 19 per cent of the student body. On 6 December 1989, 13 women students in engineering and a secretary were shot dead by a young man. First separating the women from the men, he then announced 'You're all feminists. I hate feminists.' After killing and wounding 23 students, he committed suicide. With him was a list of 15 prominent Quebec women he intended to kill. This tragedy was an extreme example of the misogyny that is still an unfortunate feature of much of Canadian society.

ANDRÉE LÉVESQUE

Montreal merchants. Occupied the border between the Atlantic trading world and the equally vast continental North American frontier. During French rule Montreal served as a beachhead for a fur-trade empire ranging from the territories south of the Great Lakes to within sight of the Rocky Mountains. Montreal merchants also engaged in an illegal clandestine trade with British subjects in what became upper New York State.

The cession of New France to the British in 1763 brought Montreal into the orbit of the British Atlantic world, and British and American traders sought to avail themselves of the opportunities afforded by the newly acquired colony. Anglo-Scottish merchants moved to establish connections with Canadien traders and re-establish the pre-conquest fur-trade networks, aggressively expanding the trade westward to the Athabaska River, the Rocky Mountains, and the Pacific. Many of these merchants reflected the link between the commercial revolution that characterized the 18th-century British Atlantic Empire and the role of the Scottish diaspora in shaping that world. They were part of a network of transatlantic merchants who maintained strong ties with their native Scotland as well as London.

By the late 18th century Montreal was beginning to assert itself as the pre-eminent metropolis for the interior of British America. As the *fur trade began to wane in importance, merchants such as James McGill and George Moffatt represented a transition to the new world of an Anglo-Scottish merchant class engaged in a wider range of economic activities. By the 1790s McGill was increasingly focused on investment in land and exporting *squared timber, and showed an interest in early efforts at establishing banking. Similarly, Moffatt shifted from the fur trade to investment in the Canada Land Company and insurance, and was an investor in the newly established Bank of Montreal. The canal- and railway-building booms of the first half of the 19th century allowed a new generation of Anglo-Scottish merchants to leave their mark on the fast-growing city. Canal construction provided fresh opportunities for the next wave of entrepreneurs to diversify into new activities, including industry and banking as well as processing agricultural and timber products. It is no surprise that early industrialists—such as John Redpath, who constructed a major sugar refinery on the Lachine Canal, and the brewer John *Molson—also invested heavily in finance and transportation. The merchants used their extensive contacts in Britain to connect Montreal directly to the trading world of the British Empire. Perhaps the most dynamic example was Sir Hugh *Allan. Using his family contacts in Britain, by the 1850s he had established a regular steamship line with a number of ports in Britain as well as railway networks that connected Montreal to Canada West, the Maritimes, and the United States.

The commercial elites of 19th-century Montreal reflected the broader social and cultural values of the world in which they lived. In the late 18th and early 19th centuries their direct involvement in politics was sporadic: it took time from their commercial activities. As the century progressed they increasingly become engaged. In one sense this reflected the needs of capitalists operating in an increasingly industrialized society. Sir Hugh Allan's activities demanded that he develop close associations with policy-makers in Canada East as well as in Britain. His steamship lines required government assistance in the form of subsidies; railroads and banks required charters that were granted by the local assembly. But it also reflects the degree to which Montreal's Anglo-Scottish merchant community was developing its sense of identity as part of a British North American elite. Their role in contributing to charitable and cultural institutions bears this out. James McGill contributed to both the Protestant and Catholic churches and was integral in the establishment of the university that bears his name. John Molson was an active supporter of the Montreal General Hospital. The many philanthropic activities of John Redpath, a devout Presbyterian, including the Montreal General Hospital, Montreal Presbyterian College, the Protestant House of Industry and Refuge, and the French-Canadian Missionary Society, to name a few. In this way Montreal's merchant class came to see itself as rooted in a distinct community instead of as sojourners in a world far from their Anglo-Scottish roots. K. DAVID MILOBAR

Moodie, Susanna Strickland (1803–85), writer, British immigrant, literary symbol. Born into a middle-class family from southern England, Moodie and her sisters began writing for publication after their father's death in 1818 left the family with little income. In 1831 she married a Scots half-pay officer, Lieutenant John Dunbar Moodie, and emigrated to Upper Canada, where the family began farming near Cobourg. The Moodies abandoned farming in 1839 and moved to Belleville, when John was appointed sherriff of what would become Hastings County. Although Susanna had continued to write for publication since her arrival, in Belleville she became more prolific, writing poetry, serial novels, and editing the educational journal *Victoria Magazine*. She also began the sketches of 'pioneer life' that developed into *Roughing It in the Bush* (1852), a complex book that combines elements of travel guide, autobiography, fiction, and social analysis. While Moodie followed with other tales of life in Upper Canada, *Life in the Clearings* (1853) and *Flora Lynday* (1854), *Roughing It in the Bush* is her best-known work, the book that led 20th-century Canadian literary critics and nationalists to claim her as both an important literary figure and an archetypal 19th-century British 'gentlewoman' immigrant. CECILIA MORGAN

Moose River mine disaster. This event occupies a unique place in the history of mine disasters: a relatively small incident that attracted international attention. On Easter Sunday, 12 April 1936, three men were trapped 141 feet underground in an abandoned gold mine in rural Halifax County. Two were Toronto investors, the third a local employee. Rescue efforts were slow, but by 19 April it was learned that the men were alive. Two days later J. Frank Willis, regional director for the Canadian Radio Broadcasting Commission in Halifax, began live reports by telephone line from the site, which continued until completion of the rescue on 23 April. Although the CRBC at this time had no stations of its own in the Maritimes, Willis's short, dramatic reports were carried by more than 400 radio stations across North America, amply demonstrating the power of radio to provide up-to-the-minute coverage of developing events. In the history of *journalism, the event contributed to the emergence of radio as a significant news medium. One of the trapped men, Toronto lawyer Herman Magill, did not survive the ordeal, but by the standards of the time Moose River was not a major disaster. Sixteen men were killed in other mine accidents in Nova Scotia that year. DAVID FRANK

moral and social reform. The Victorian age was an optimistic period in Canadian history. For every problem, there was a solution. And from the point of view of Canadians concerned about the moral foundations of the new nation, there were plenty of problems to be solved, particularly in light of urban growth and Canada's changing demographic mix.

Religious authorities, as well as family and community members, had traditionally regarded moral training and regulation as their province. With the rise of industrial cities over the mid to late 19th century, formal means of building moral citizenship began to emerge. The first major organization to pursue that challenge was the *Woman's Christian Temperance Union. Drunkenness and the saloon industry were the principal targets, but the WCTU also took on a range of issues, from juvenile smoking to wife beating. *Prostitution was another major concern, and by the 1890s the *National Council of Women of Canada added its voice to those castigating the 'social evil'. If Canada wanted to step on to the world stage it would have to undertake thorough moral housekeeping. And who better to do it than women?

By the late 19th century the *social purity movement was in full swing, as membership in Canadian women's clubs grew. Men began to play a more prominent role as well. Through organizations such as the *YMCA and the *Boy Scouts, male leaders tried to steer young men away from the physical and moral laxity of city life towards the healthy pleasures of manly sports. Impure thoughts led not only to prostitution but also to masturbation, a practice that doctors and psychiatrists associated with neurosis and insanity. Replacing lusty ideas with noble ideals required the most intimate scrutiny of personal habits.

Canadian social purity groups believed that individual morality was the foundation of social morality. Evangelical fervour fired the movement and dictated its pulpit-thumping style, but it also committed campaigners to work with politicians to close down saloons and brothels and to impose tighter restrictions on sexual imagery (such as posters of actresses in flesh-tone tights). The links between personal and social purity had to be managed carefully in an increasingly urban and heterogeneous world that beckoned with sinful pleasures.

Social purity adherents were convinced that certain sorts of people were more likely than others to require moral guidance. Those notions were saturated in racialized, gendered, and class-based prejudices that were commonly held in turn-of-the-century Canada. Social purity leaders, all of them white, middle-class, and most of them

Protestant, believed that respectable Anglo-Celtic men and women possessed the self-restraint and moral backbone of the ideal Canadian. All others, particularly non-British immigrants, who arrived by the hundreds of thousands under the national scheme to people the West, were inferior. So were the poor. And the Aboriginal. And the non-Christian. Just as Protestant missionaries criss-crossed the globe, looking for heathens to convert, so the advocates of social purity set out to bring light to the darkest corners of Canadian civilization.

The most ambitious and successful purity organizations were formed in the early years of the 20th century by Methodist and Presbyterian clerics. With Methodist minister T. Albert Moore, Presbyterian Dr John Shearer established an umbrella organization in 1907 to coordinate the Protestant churches' separate campaigns to oversee the moral improvement of Canadian society. Called the Moral and Social Reform Council of Canada, its headquarters were in Toronto 'the good' but its regulatory reach was national. At the top of its agenda was 'white slavery', the supposed traffic in innocent maidens for the purposes of sexual enslavement. Fears of the traffic circulated throughout the industrialized world in the early 1900s. Women's and social purity groups were sure that Canadian girls were at risk, particularly from 'foreign' men. Law enforcement officials were unconvinced. Nonetheless social purity advocates successfully lobbied Parliament to pass legislation prohibiting the seduction of women for the purposes of prostitution. At the local level, they pressed police forces to crack down on pimps and madams. Local police bowed to the pressure but white slavery rings were never uncovered.

The enthusiasm and vast ambitions of social purity began to wane by the 1920s. Campaigners against the demon rum achieved only partial victories in provinces that passed temperance legislation. Some purity advocates turned to the new field of sex hygiene, an early form of sex education, which aimed above all to reduce the high rates of *venereal disease reported during the First World War. Others interested in furthering the moral improvement of Canadian citizenship took a more drastic turn, advocating the sterilization of the 'unfit'.

Social purity, a movement born in the Victorian age, had an antiquated ring by the jazz age. With the rise of professional agents of moral regulation, such as social workers, truancy agents, and female police officers, the evangelical thrust of purity work was largely secularized.

CAROLYN STRANGE

Moravian missions. In 1771 missionaries of the Protestant Moravian Church established a station at Nain on the northern *Labrador coast to convert *Inuit to Christianity. An attempt in 1752 to begin a mission failed after Inuit murdered seven expedition members. Knowledge of the Inuit language and customs from Moravian stations operating in Greenland since 1732 gave later missionaries more success in approaching Labrador Inuit. Moravian contact with Inuit bands increased after two more stations, Okak (1776–1919) and Hopedale (1782), were erected, each station with a trade store offering ironware, household utensils, and other European items in exchange for seal oil, fox pelts, and other wildlife resources. With direct access to trade articles, Inuit gradually ceased travelling to southern Labrador, where they previously obtained goods, and an Aboriginal exchange network circulating European items to far northern populations was eliminated. An annual supply ship, typically called *Harmony*, conveyed goods between England and the Labrador stations.

Inuit resisted abandoning their traditional spiritual beliefs until a widespread religious movement in 1804, called the Great Awakening, endorsed greater stability in social relations provided by Christianity. Moravian congregations increased and more mission stations were established, including Hebron (1830–1959), Ramah (1871–1908), Zoar (1866–94), Makkovik (1896), Killinek (1904–24), and Happy Valley (1957). Until the early 20th century, missionaries originated mainly from Germany, where mission policies were directed by officials based at Herrnhut, Saxony. Later missionaries came from Britain.

Financial difficulties after 1900 led to the closure of several stations, while an epidemic of influenza in 1918 decimated the Inuit population at Okak. In 1926 the Moravians leased their trade operation to the *Hudson's Bay Company, which managed community stores until 1942. The government of Newfoundland assumed responsibility for economic affairs, and operated retail stores until 1995 when they were sold to private enterprises. Surviving Moravian communities are Nain, Hopedale, and Makkovik.

CAROL BRICE-BENNETT

Morris, Alexander (1826–89). Born in Perth, Upper Canada, Morris was educated in Scotland, studied law in Kingston under John A. *Macdonald, and attended both Queen's College and McGill University. A leading Canadian imperialist, he advocated the annexation of *Rupert's Land. After a career in politics, in 1872 he was appointed the first chief judge of the Manitoba Court of Queen's Bench, although just five months later he resigned to become lieutenant-governor of Manitoba and the North-West Territories. As the administrator of federal monies in the West, Morris had responsibility for Indian affairs. Between 1873 and 1876 he played a pivotal role in the negotiation of *Indian Treaties 3, 4, 5, and 6, which encompassed a huge portion of land between Lake Superior and the Rockies, and helped revise Treaties 1 and 2. Though he recognized *Aboriginal title, he nevertheless viewed treaties as the first step towards gradual assimilation. As the federal representative, Morris failed to protect the *Metis lands that had been guaranteed under the Manitoba Act. Moreover, he was himself an active land speculator. In 1878 he moved back east and won the Toronto East seat in the Ontario legislature.

ROBERT J. COUTTS

Morton, William Lewis (1908–80), educator, historian. A native of Gladstone, Manitoba, he studied at St John's College, Winnipeg, and Oxford University as a Rhodes scholar, and taught at Brandon College, the University of Manitoba, and Trent University. Morton was a prolific writer of historical works and was an important early exponent of regional studies in Canadian history. His major early works included the essay 'Clio in Canada' (1946), *The Progressive Party in Canada* (1950), and *Manitoba: A History* (1957). By the mid-1950s, a perceived Americanization of Canadian culture prompted Morton to embrace a more centralist view of Canadian history. Between 1955 and 1980 he was executive editor of the Canadian Centenary Series. In his own series volume, *The Critical Years* (1964), and other writings, he emphasized Canada's northern geography and European cultural inheritance in defining its distinctive history. Born into a family with a tradition of elective service under the Liberal Party, he turned to the Progressive Conservatives in the 1950s in search of a vehicle for maintaining a separate 'Canadian identity', the subject of one of his books. Morton's principal achievement was to give voice to a regional—specifically, a prairie—perspective in Canadian historiography. LYLE DICK

mothers' allowances. Provincial payments to impoverished mothers first appeared during the First World War. Private charities such as *orphanages and poor-law institutions had been the first response to such poverty. By the late 19th century, such solutions were deemed inadequate by maternal feminists, who, with professional and social reform allies, argued that women's responsibilities for caregiving and child rearing, while natural, were undervalued. Mothers and motherly women constituted good citizens, just as men met civic obligations by wage earning and military service. A nationwide child-welfare movement that initiated Children's Aid Societies in the 1890s articulated the related conviction that children needed protection and did best in families under women's supervision. Organized labour, wishing to advantage male breadwinners, and nationalists who favoured public policies that might transcend class differences and promote higher birthrates also endorsed the 'endowment of motherhood'. Needy mothers themselves insisted on their right to non-stigmatizing aid. By 1910 sympathetic charities experimented with subsidizing impoverished mothers who were without male breadwinners. During the war the allowances offered by patriotic societies to the dependent wives and children of servicemen affirmed that female-led families deserved state support. In 1916 Manitoba's Liberals, newly elected with feminist support, introduced a Mothers' Allowance Act. Saskatchewan followed in 1917, Alberta in 1919, British Columbia and Ontario in 1920. Provinces favoured applications from impoverished but respectable white women with more than one child. Where reform forces were weaker, legislation was slower: Nova Scotia and New Brunswick in 1930, Quebec in 1937. British Columbia's program, designed to promote Anglo-Celtic families, included, for a time, higher rates of payment than elsewhere; it also included some divorced, deserted, and unwed mothers, but not Natives and Asians. Applicants everywhere proved more numerous than anticipated; the 1930s brought brutal cuts, and the new war exposed further desperation. As the social security system evolved, it seized on male unemployment and largely rejected motherhood as a legitimate basis for state support and social citizenship. In 1944 federal family allowances showed superficial similarity to mothers' allowances but their preoccupation with post-war consumption as the key to full employment asserted the particular commitment of the new *welfare state to male breadwinners. VERONICA STRONG-BOAG

mothers of the race. During the early decades of the 20th century, population concerns led governments in Europe and North America to identify motherhood as a social problem. The declining birth rate among native-born Canadians coupled with increasing non-British immigration bred fears that Anglo-Saxon dominance was in peril. Recruitment for military service caused alarm, when two-thirds of applicants were rejected as unfit. That fact, compounded by the losses of war and by high infant and maternal mortality rates, led officials to declare a national health crisis.

Infants and young *children were particularly at risk. Despite developments in medical technology and sanitation and discoveries in bacteriology and immunology, infant mortality rates continued to rise. Although infant mortality had always existed, attitudes were changing: nations could no longer afford to squander its citizens. Children were a 'national asset' to be preserved and protected at all costs. The key to their preservation lay with mothers. To increase the birth rate, women—especially Anglo-Saxon middle-class women—were exhorted to become 'mothers of the race'. Although women were 'naturally' equipped for pregnancy and childbirth, they lacked the specialized knowledge motherhood required. Thus, through films, radio talks, and a massive output of advice literature, experts bombarded mothers with detailed instructions on pregnancy and infant care. Experts promised that careful adherence would secure children's health. Failure could result in serious illness or even death.

Women were willing participants in this enterprise. Fears engendered by infant mortality, coupled with an acute shortage of medical care, led many mothers to seek expert advice. Separated from their own mothers and lacking experience with young children, women welcomed the information about the latest scientific discoveries, available only from a physician, public health nurse, or advice manual.

During the 1920s and 30s, child-rearing experts advocated regimentation in all aspects of a child's life. From the minute the baby was born, a rigid schedule was to be established for activities ranging from toilet training to sleeping. Manuals such as the popular *Canadian Mother's Book*, by Dr Helen *MacMurchy, chief of the federal Division of Child Welfare (1920–33), provided detailed instructions, with requirements far beyond the reach of the average Canadian family. While the advice may have had some salutary effects, it also engendered considerable confusion and guilt. Although women might have enjoyed their status as 'mothers of the race', this role provided neither autonomy nor self-determination. Mothers' behaviour was closely monitored by physicians and other child-rearing experts. Measured against middle-class standards of scientific motherhood, many mothers found themselves wanting. Nonetheless, they continued to do their best for their children in a society that provided little concrete assistance. KATHERINE ARNUP

mountaineering. Canada's mountaineering birthplace, in the 1880s, was Glacier House in Rogers Pass, British Columbia. A golden age of mountaineering and first ascents in the Rockies followed swiftly on the heels of Philip Abbot's fatal fall from Mount Lefroy near Lake Louise in 1896. To enhance tourist climbing near its mountain hotels, the CPR hired professional Swiss guides, starting in 1899 with Edouard Feuz and Christian Hasler. European guides, such as Austrian-born Conrad Kain, played a formative role in Canadian mountaineering. In 1906, Arthur Oliver Wheeler and Elizabeth Parker founded the Alpine Club of Canada in Winnipeg. It promoted mountaineering, exploration, literature, art, science, conservation, and 'Canada's mountain heritage'. Open to men and women, with sections in cities across Canada and abroad, the ACC held annual mountaineering camps, built alpine huts, and published the *Canadian Alpine Journal*, promoting Canada's mountain terrain to international climbing enthusiasts. Its Alpine Clubhouse in *Banff opened in 1909. During the Second World War, the ACC offered mountain warfare training to Allied troops in Jasper. Today the ACC is based in Canmore, Alberta.

The first ascents of monumental Canadian peaks such as Robson (1913), Logan (1925), Alberta (1925), Waddington (1936), and Asgaard (1953) led to more difficult routes and northface ascents. Changing styles and equipment expanded from classic alpine mountaineering to technical climbing, ice climbing, ski touring, free climbing, and sport climbing. Canada was slow to adopt climbing techniques involving carabiners, pitons, and bolts, though immigrant European and British climbers moved this style of technical climbing to the forefront after the war. Hans Gmoser was one of these leaders. Along with the ACC, they helped found the Association of Canadian Mountain Guides (1963), dedicated to ensuring safety via professional certification and licensing and later instated to the Union International des Associations des Guides de Montagne in 1976.

Canadian mountaineers have established an international reputation. As early as 1921 Edward Oliver Wheeler's survey around Mount Everest laid the groundwork for British expeditions. In 1982, Laurie Skreslett became the first Canadian to reach the summit of Everest, and in 1986 Canadian Sharon Wood was the first North American woman to reach the summit.

PEARLANN REICHWEIN

Mowat, Sir Oliver (1820–1903), lawyer, Ontario premier 1872–96, noted for his successful defence of Ontario's constitutional powers and territorial claims against John A. *Macdonald's centralizing policies. Nationalist historians condemned him as small-minded or even perfidious, since, as a delegate to the Quebec Conference, he had helped to design the supposedly centralist scheme of *Confederation. Even less openly nationalist writers have dismissed his arguments as retrospective rationalizations, if not outright lies. In reality, though, Mowat was throughout his career a leading exponent of that strand of the Upper Canadian reform tradition that exalted *responsible government as a means to local autonomy, and he was a loyal follower of George *Brown, who led the Reform Party into Confederation to secure Upper Canada's autonomy. These political credentials, a reputation for probity, and his remarkable political finesse enabled him to retain power through six general elections despite the steady weakening of his party's agrarian political base. His success rested on a knack for alliance building that embraced trade unionists, Ontario's Catholic hierarchy, and ultimately even his party's favourite whipping boy, the province of Quebec. This alliance building helped to launch the Liberal Party's rise to federal electoral dominance in 20th-century Canada.

PAUL ROMNEY

Mulroney, Martin Brian (1939–), prime minister 1984–93. A fluently bilingual Quebec lawyer born in Baie-Comeau, business executive, and political activist with Irish roots, Mulroney won the leadership of the *Progressive Conservative Party in 1983 without ever having held elective office. His period as prime minister began with a massive victory of 211 of 282 House of Commons seats in the general election of 1984, followed by a solid second mandate four years later (169 of 295 seats), making Mulroney the first Conservative chief in decades to head two straight majority governments. His government negotiated the Canada–US Free Trade Agreement and the North American Free Trade Agreement, but failed to get approval for the constitutional reforms contained in the *Meech Lake and *Charlottetown Accords. Mulroney's internationalist foreign policy included a campaign against South African apartheid and the dispatch of unprecedented numbers of Canadian peacekeepers all over the globe. He was a bold and innovative leader, but a combination of his controversial prime ministerial style and the divisions caused by constitution making and closer ties with the United States generated intense animosities. By the end of a difficult second term, with a faltering economy and the introduction of an unpopular Goods and Services Tax (GST), the electorate had deserted him and his party had split into regional factions. He resigned, leaving the Conservatives to Kim Campbell and returning to Montreal for a lucrative career as a lawyer and public speaker.

NORMAN HILLMER

multiculturalism. On 8 October 1971, Prime Minister Pierre *Trudeau stood in the House of Commons to proclaim Canada's policy of multiculturalism. As pronounced by Trudeau, 'There is no official [Canadian] culture, nor does any ethnic group take precedence over any other. No citizen or group of citizens is other than Canadian, and all should be treated fairly.' While English and French remain Canada's two official languages, Trudeau dismissed the notion that Canadians of British or French heritage retain any custodial right to define the boundaries of Canadian identity. Rather, Canadian identity must be seen to embrace the contributions of all Canadians. Multiculturalism promised more than just passive recognition of cultural pluralism. The policy pledged government assistance to Canadians in developing and sharing the nation's diverse cultural richness. Furthermore, the government reaffirmed its support for the removal of all cultural or racial barriers to full and equal citizen participation in Canadian society.

In some ways the Trudeau statement heralded a major public policy reversal. It was long assumed that becoming Canadian meant that non-English-speaking immigrants needed to discard their home cultures. In English Canada this was understood to mean that immigrants and their children should be compelled to cast aside ethnic identity and assimilate into Anglo-Canadian culture. But, in spite of the best efforts by government officials, educators, social workers, and other gatekeepers, ethnicity persisted and even flourished. In the liberal spirit of the 1960s, with the children and grandchildren of working-class and under-educated immigrants increasingly urban, affluent, educated, politically active, and proud of their cultural heritages, the assimilationist crusade withered. Faced with demands for recognition of the cultural mosaic as a true reflection of Canadian identity, the federal government delivered multiculturalism.

While most Canadians of the day supported the federal policy initiative, others attacked it. In English-speaking Canada some protested that multiculturalism was divisive, dividing Canadians from one another. Some in French-speaking Canada protested that multiculturalism was little more than a federal scheme designed to downgrade Quebec's national aspirations to the level of other ethnic groups. Still others argued that multiculturalism's focus on culture and identity distracted Canadians from larger pressing issues such as economic inequality. None of these fears derailed multiculturalism, and as Canada's population has changed since 1971 so too has federal multicultural programming. In response to increasing numbers of immigrants of non-European-origin, multicultural programming has turned from its earlier focus on cultural celebration towards championing anti-racism and citizen-participation initiatives. Multiculturalism has also been enshrined in the Canadian *Charter of Rights and Freedoms and again by Parliament in a 1988 Multiculturalism Act as a defining feature of Canadian society.

HAROLD TROPER

mumming. Examples of mumming—customary traditions of masking, usually involving parading or house visiting—are found in many parts of Canada. Mummering and belsnickling use visual and oral disguises to hide the mummers' identities and make them 'strangers'. Their visits to the homes of neighbours, friends, and relatives usually entail an informal game of hosts guessing who they are. The modern fear that mummers might be real strangers is often stated as a reason for the decline of the practice. In Nova Scotia, belsnickling derives from German traditions. Often thought to have disappeared after the Second World War, the tradition continues in areas such as Riverport. Similarly, Newfoundland mummering (and wren boys) has often been declared dead, but it never quite stopped, and the 1980s saw a revival in the wake of the popular 'Mummers' Song' by Simani.

Francophone communities in Quebec, Acadia, and elsewhere have marked Mardi Gras (in Shrovetide, just before Lent) and *mi-carême* (mid-Lent) with masked visits and celebration. In francophone Newfoundland until the mid-20th century a parade of single men took place on la Fête de la chandeleur (Candlemas Day, 2 February). Centring on visits to single women's homes and the decoration of a beribboned stick along the way, the procession gathered food for a party that night.

Being nearly coincident with the Julian New Year, Malanka, celebrated in Alberta and Ontario, is often called the Ukrainian New Year. Its origin is in the feast of St Melania, venerated in the Eastern Orthodox Church. Disguise and cross-dressing, music and dancing mark the celebrations, now usually held in halls but once including house-to-house carolling. In modern Makkovik and Nain, Labrador, Inuit children gather at a hall to meet masked nalujuks; later the maskers question and threaten them in the streets. A localized tradition of Christmas Eve carolling in Newfoundland can be seen as a species of mummering even though no disguises are worn.

Historically, most mumming was connected to Christmas and Shrovetide, but as the customs were exploited for tourism these connections get looser. The 'Downhomer Mummers' performed summer musical entertainment for tourists in St John's in the late 1990s; in 2001 staff on the Nova Scotia–Newfoundland ferry 'mummered' while the ship's musical group performed Simani's song. Tourist shops in Newfoundland sell cards and posters showing Christmas kitchen scenes with mummers and musical instruments, while 'Mummers' Beer' has become a popular brand. Since the 1970s the Newfoundland Mummers' Troupe has performed traditional mummers' plays for public and private audiences. In Acadia, *mi-carême* masks are sold through the year as tokens of Acadian culture.

PHILIP HISCOCK

Munitions and Supply, Department of. Established in April 1940 by the authority of the Munitions and Supply Act passed by Parliament in September 1939. The delay between the passage of the act and its implementation occurred because of the King government's uncertainty as to whether Canada would be asked to produce much in the way of munitions for the Allied war effort, and because the government hoped that a War Supply Board, staffed by businessmen, would prove sufficient. The board, however, caused more problems than it solved, so in April 1940 King formally established a munitions department and placed C.D. *Howe, the minister of transport, at its head. Howe lost no time in recruiting a group of senior executives such as Henry Borden, H.R. MacMillan, and E.P. Taylor to organize Canadian industry for war. Many of these individuals were paid a token dollar for their services and became known as 'dollar-a-year-men'. The problem of orders for Canadian goods was solved when the British army lost most of its equipment at Dunkirk in June 1940; thereafter the British would take everything the Canadians could supply. The department was surprisingly effective in establishing war industries such as aircraft manufacture and shipbuilding, and in increasing Canadian production of strategic goods such as lumber and minerals; the gravity of the war crisis and the possibility of defeat undoubtedly contributed to public acceptance of Munitions and Supply's drastic powers to commandeer civilian supply and even to expropriate, for the purposes of the war, private property, including whole factories. The department was also unusually scandal-free, although its record—in the production of uranium, for example—was not without blemish. Through 'DM&S' Howe established a durable link between the Liberal Party and the Canadian business community, which up to that point had been overwhelmingly Conservative and anti-King in its sympathies. The department was wound up at the end of the war and passed out of existence at the end of 1945; its remaining functions were assumed by the Department of Reconstruction and Supply, also headed by Howe.

ROBERT BOTHWELL

Murdochville strike. The strike began on 10 March 1957, pitting about 1,000 members of the United Steel Workers of America against Gaspé Copper Mines, a subsidiary of Noranda. This dispute raised public awareness about how anti-union legislation and the pro-business bias of Premier Maurice *Duplessis' government could prevent workers from forming a union. Over the previous five years, the company used a number of tactics to thwart organizing drives. While Noranda used court action to delay certification for 14 months, it was the firing of the local union president that sparked the walkout. Without certification the strike was illegal; the company, which secured an injunction against picketing, continued operations using strikebreakers protected by provincial police. Government support for the employer prompted Quebec's rival labour movements to form a united front against the Duplessis regime. The leaders of the *Canadian Labour Congress, the *Fédération des travailleurs du Québec, and the Confédération des travailleurs catholiques du Canada all participated in a march on Murdochville during which they were attacked by strikebreakers while provincial police watched from the sidelines. After seven months the strike was defeated, a company union was installed, and the USWA was later forced to pay more than $1.5 million in damages. The USWA was certified as the miners' bargaining agent only in 1965, following the enactment of a new labour code with better guarantees for union rights.

GEOFFREY EWEN

Murphy, Emily (1868–1933), writer ('Janey Canuck'), magistrate, and legal reformer, published *The Impressions of Janey Canuck Abroad* (1901) based on her experience living in Europe with her two daughters and husband, Arthur Murphy, an Anglican minister. Moving to Manitoba in 1903 and Alberta in 1907, she published the best-selling *Janey Canuck in the West* (1910), *Open Trails* (1912), and *Seeds of Pine* (1914), books that captured the multicultural adventure of western Canada. In Alberta Murphy campaigned for legislation, culminating in the 1911 Dower Act, to protect the wife's share of a husband's property. For seven years (1913–20) she served as president of the Canadian Women's Press Club and pursued reforms on behalf of women, including suffrage, which was achieved in Alberta in 1916. In 1922 her book *The Black Candle* blamed Chinese immigrants for the Canadian drug trade. In 1916 Murphy was appointed a police magistrate for Edmonton, the first woman magistrate in the British Empire. Her authority was challenged on the grounds that a woman was not a 'person'. In 1929 Murphy, with the support of four other Alberta women, succeeded in having the Judicial Committee of the Privy Council in England declare that women were persons within the meaning of the British North America Act. Murphy retired from the bench in 1931.

MARY KINNEAR

Murray, Alexander (1810–84). A Scot, Murray emigrated to Canada in 1837 after service in the Royal Navy. In 1843 he became one of the original members of the *Geological Survey of Canada and carried out numerous geological surveys over the next 20 years, mainly in Canada West. He worked on the north shores of Lakes Superior and Huron, finding the Murray Fault in 1858; traced the southern boundary of the *Canadian Shield; and produced the first accurate maps of some parts of the province. In 1864 Murray moved to Newfoundland, where he became the first director of the colony's own geological survey. Assisted from 1868 by James P. Howley, Murray began the first systematic surveys of the island's interior and sections of its coastline. He drew the first complete geological map of Newfoundland, published in 1873. The annual geological survey reports, invariably optimistic in tone, were published in collected form in 1881. These helped convince local politicians that the island contained valuable land-based resources that should be made accessible by building a railway—a controversial project that Murray backed with energy and enthusiasm. He retired to Scotland in 1883.

JAMES K. HILLER

Murray, James (1721–94). Born in Scotland, Murray was an army officer and governor who introduced British military and civilian rule in post-conquest Quebec. He represents the growing influence of Scottish interests in the administrative as well as commercial life of the empire. He served as an officer in the Seven Years' War at the siege of Louisbourg (1758) and upon Wolfe's death commanded the defence of Quebec. He became a military governor of the District of Quebec (1760) and was made civilian governor in 1763. Despite initial misgivings about the loyalty of the Canadiens, he realized the British policy of anglicization as laid out in the *Royal Proclamation of 1763 was counterproductive; he tried to mediate between the realities of governing a Catholic French-speaking colony with often contradictory and confused instructions from metropolitan policy-makers. His attempts to reconcile the demands of the local Anglo-merchants for full British constitutional institutions with the need for a system of governance and law supporting Canadien property rights and the Catholic Church largely failed. Undermined by London's insistence on separating civil and military command and by complaints from the British merchant community, Murray was recalled in 1766. K. DAVID MILOBAR

Murray, Leonard Warren (1896–1971), rear-admiral, *Royal Canadian Navy. Born at Granton, Nova Scotia, Murray was the only Canadian to hold an Allied theatre command during the Second World War. He joined the RCN in 1911, served in British and Canadian warships during the First World War, and played a key role in directing mobilization of the navy at the beginning of the Second. In June 1941 he took command of the newly created Newfoundland Escort Force and provided leadership to the small Canadian and British warships that protected merchant ship *convoys against German submarine attack across the difficult North Atlantic passage to Britain. On 30 April 1943 he was appointed commander-in-chief, Canadian Northwest Atlantic, an Allied theatre of war created by Britain and the United States in recognition of the expanding Canadian navy's ability to control convoy operations in the western third of the north Atlantic. Murray's brilliant career ended tragically. With news of Allied victory in Europe in May 1945, naval seamen played a leading part in riots that caused severe damage to downtown Halifax; a royal commission found Murray responsible as the senior commander present. He retired from the navy in early 1946 and emigrated to England, where he began a new career as a lawyer.
ROGER SARTY

muscular Christianity. A form of liberal Christianity that emphasized masculine exertion and healthy living, enjoyed its heyday in the late 19th and early 20th century. Competitive sports and physical exercise were celebrated as a means to create the ideal Christian man. This doctrine of activist Christianity was suited to the age of missions that demanded young men who could confront the most challenging conditions in home and *foreign mission fields. It was also designed to attract boys and young men to the churches, a direct response to what many clergy, having observed that church pews were filled by women, considered to be the 'young men' problem. Other institutions adopted muscular Christianity as a means to make Christianity appealing to male culture. The *Young Men's Christian Association adopted sports and gymnasium programs, such as Canadian James Naismith's game of basketball, as a healthy Christian alternative to the vices of drink and gambling that young men were exposed to on the streets. In the wake of the First World War, activist missionary outreach was reconsidered and a pacifist-minded Christianity that opposed the ethic of competition emerged. Muscular Christianity's popularity waned, though an institutional legacy has remained in the YMCA, *Boy Scouts, and gymnasiums in church basements. It has enjoyed a resurgence recently, finding currency in evangelical institutions such as Campus Crusade for Christ and Athletes in Action, an organization that boasts the commitment of Paul Henderson, the hero of the 1972 Canada–Russia hockey series. DAVID B. MARSHALL

museums. The inspiration for museums in Canada originated in 19th-century Europe and was based on Eurocentric assumptions and practices concerning progress, beauty, and truth. Before the electronic age and universal instruction, museums provided visitors with displays of curiosities and high art, along with moral and intellectual training. Traditional museum functions included acquiring, preserving, and conducting research on objects and diffusing knowledge about them through exhibitions and publications. During the latter years of the 20th century, the focus gradually shifted from research and collections to education and leisure activities.

Museums in rural areas and villages, often founded to preserve artifacts and traditions important to local families and communities, included historic sites that belonged to notable inhabitants, pioneer villages, and institutions based on religion or on economic activities such as farming, fishing, sealing and whaling, mining, logging, or transportation. This has resulted in unique regional institutions that have developed according to the evolution of different parts of the country.

Museums in larger centres developed from different collecting traditions, including those of *mechanics' institutes, scientific and religious organizations, and private collectors. In Atlantic Canada the Halifax Mechanics' Institute (established 1831) became part of the Provincial Museum of Nova Scotia in 1862, and the collection of New Brunswick's first Museum of Natural History, displayed in the Saint John Mechanics' Institute in 1842, found a permanent home in the new provincial museum in 1934. Scientific organizations like the Natural History Society of Montreal (1827), the *Geological Survey of Canada (Montreal 1842), and the Canadian Institute (Toronto 1851) laid the groundwork for important *natural history, archaeological, and ethnological collections in 19th-century central Canada. The GSC's collection ultimately became an important part of Ottawa's natural history museum, which opened in the Victoria Memorial Building in 1911. McGill University's Redpath Museum (1882) included the distinguishing characteristics of the period's modern facility: a showcase of Victorian science where the grand architecture of the universe could be discovered.

Museums in Canada imitated the approach of British and European institutions in demonstrating superiority over natural environments and other cultures. The construction of typologies in the study and display of exotic flora and fauna from Africa, Asia, and Latin America, of art and artifacts of ancient civilizations, and of scientific instruments and technologies, was an organizing principle of imperial institutions that found resonance in former colonies like Canada. According to this rationale, museum professionals in the Western world felt it was their responsibility to own, preserve, display, and interpret the art and artifacts of other peoples and countries. One of the underlying assumptions was the superiority of European traditions over local Aboriginal communities. Non-Europeans represented in imperial institutions were often seen as part of the early phases of human development, with Europeans at the summit; similarly, indigenous peoples in North American museums were depicted as primitive populations on the verge of extinction. In both instances, no links were made between the past and present of groups and cultures being exhibited, nor was there much explanation given for studying other peoples' histories while neglecting that of European immigrants living in former colonies like Canada and Australia.

Professors, clerics, and members of religious orders who acquired objects for teaching classified them according to the academic disciplines of the Western world. In some instances these efforts led to the creation of early collections in 18th-century religious institutions, in *universities in the 19th century such as the collections at Laval, McGill, and Dalhousie, and occasionally to significant provincial facilities in the 20th century such as the University of British Columbia's Museum of Anthropology (1949) in Vancouver and the Art Gallery of Newfoundland and Labrador (1961) in St John's. Although they continued to support *art galleries, universities were more interested in furthering scientific discoveries than in managing museums. Thus, McGill University not only failed to maintain its collections, it also closed its Ethnological Museum (1926) in 1940 and turned the McCord Museum (1921) over to a private board in 1987. The Royal Ontario Museum (1912) is one of Canada's best examples of an imperial model. Inspired by the collecting activities of curators at institutions like the British Museum, curators at the ROM set out to acquire artifacts from ancient civilizations and specimens from overseas. Although relegated to a secondary role, furniture, textiles, and historical illustrations were collected, as well as Aboriginal artifacts. In 1968 the University of Toronto allowed the ROM to become a separate entity.

Instead of building collections from other countries, federal and provincial professionals concentrated their efforts on acquiring national and regional holdings. In federal institutions like the Canadian Museum of Nature (1911) curators collected the country's natural specimens while their counterparts at the National Museum of Man (1968) sought archaeological remains and artifacts of the country's First Nations. Thinking that folk traditions and artifacts from people of European origin also needed to be preserved, specialists started collecting them as well.

Although provincial museums in British Columbia, Alberta, Manitoba, Nova Scotia, and New Brunswick included both natural and human history in the same structures, art was stored and displayed separately. Canadian supporters of art museums shared the imperial practice of reinforcing their status by promoting high art. Canada's early art museums originated when prominent citizens of Montreal founded what was to become the Montreal Museum of Fine Arts in 1860 and their counterparts in Toronto established the Art Museum of Toronto in 1906 (renamed the Art Gallery of Ontario, 1966). Until the last half of the 20th century, folk, popular, and *Aboriginal art were largely excluded from the country's major art museums. Even in some instances today it is still displayed in spaces that are separate from European or 'Canadian' art and devoid of contextual explanations that would help visitors understand the people and environment from which the art stems.

Early art museums like the National Gallery of Canada (1880) in Ottawa and the Musée du Québec (1933) in Quebec City were built to demonstrate the growth and importance of Canadian and Quebec art and to inspire pride in its production. They also served to promote an understanding of the world's artistic achievements. Opened in 1965 in Kleinberg, Ontario, the McMichael Canadian Art Collection was dedicated to Canadian art and particularly to the art of the *Group of Seven. This emphasis on regional artists has been embraced by most provincial art galleries from St John's to Victoria.

Government support for history has traditionally been linked to the promotion of Canadian identity and prestige, and after the 1960s it was increasingly tied to national unity and regional development. Thus, during the 1970s the secretary of state decided to increase Canadians' access to their heritage by supporting travelling exhibits and establishing new policies and programs, including the National Museums Act, the Museums Assistance Program, the Canadian Conservation Institute, the National Inventory Program (now the Canadian Heritage Information Network), and the Cultural Property Export and Import Act. Other federal initiatives that affect museums include the Canadian Multiculturalism Act (1985) and the Canadian Digital Cultural Content Initiative (2000). Seeking to encourage regional economic development, most provincial governments developed similar museum and heritage programs.

Canada's centennial celebrations and *Expo 67 led to the growth of interpretation centres and museums across the country, including the Manitoba Museum of Man and Nature and the Provincial Museum of Alberta. Seeking ways to attract more visitors, provincial museums in the West adopted British- and American-style streetscape designs, a model employed, for example, in Saskatchewan's pioneer village at North Battleford (1966) and during the early 1970s in Winnipeg's Museum of Man and

Nature and in British Columbia's Provincial Museum in Victoria. Streetscapes reached their national apogee in the 1990s with the opening of the new Canadian Museum of Civilization building in Hull, Quebec. Dubbed 'Disney North' because of the use of gimmicks, replicas, and idealized and nostalgic scenes, it featured large reconstitutions of building facades from Aboriginal villages and from town and city streets. Conforming to the federal government's emphasis on *multiculturalism, the new building also included space for celebratory exhibitions about the country's cultural communities.

In 1987 the Quebec government opened the last of Canada's major provincial museums of the 20th century. Employing techniques and organizational principles borrowed from Parks Canada and science centres, the new Musée de la civilisation in Quebec City used a large exhibition budget to support regional and international shows. The 1980s also saw the growth of municipal museums, such as Montreal's Palais de la civilisation, the Centre d'histoire, and in 1992 the Pointe-à-Callière archaeological and historical centre.

After the launch of the Soviet Union's first Sputnik in 1957, the Canadian government, like the American, increased science education by supporting the development of science centres and museums. Whereas the National Museum of Science and Technology in Ottawa (1967) followed the trend in industrial museums to have staff operate machinery and involve visitors in educational activities, the Ontario Science Centre in Toronto (1969) used current themes and interactive exhibits to interest visitors who pushed buttons and pulled levers, or watched machines and models work. Examples of other facilities employing the 'interactive' model include Vancouver's Science World (1982), Sudbury's Science North (1984), Montreal's Science Centre (1997), Shawinigan's Cité de l'énergie (1997), and Sherbrooke's Musée de la nature et des sciences (2000).

Building on the success of participatory approaches, museums of every description began integrating interactive exhibits, science galleries, and children's centres into their existing structures. Based on thematic approaches that are not dependent on collections, a sense of history, or original research, these new centres emphasize educative and entertaining shows to attract visitors. By providing an abundance of information, games, and activities set in comfortable environments, science centre professionals aim to help the public understand science and technology.

Despite the disappearance of numerous collections and museums throughout the 19th and 20th centuries, financial insecurity, and undependable government support, museums continue to multiply and those in large urban centres continue to grow. The Canadian Museum Association estimates that these facilities have increased from 161 in 1951 and 838 in 1972 to 2,300 in 2002. They receive approximately 55 million visitors annually and are staffed by over 24,000 employees and 55,000 volunteers.

Seeking to attract new visitors and to make artifacts more accessible, museums now host a variety of activities outside their buildings and create 'virtual' exhibitions and 'searchable' collections on their Web sites. Museum professionals also negotiate with members of cultures whose histories they are exhibiting and publicize information about art of dubious provenance. Described as centres of debate about redefining identities, encouraging alternative narratives, and including new voices, museums continue to struggle with the challenge of presenting the histories, ideas, and artifacts of women, First Nations, and recent immigrants. D.T. RUDDEL

music. Among Native peoples, before the arrival of Europeans, music existed as an integral element in daily activities and rituals. While the number and variety of distinct societies and languages—from the Inuit in the North to the diverse nations in the Southeast—make generalities about Native music virtually impossible, it can be said that singing and a vast number of drums and rattles make up the primary musical resources, and that much of the music depends on subtle and sophisticated interplay of rhythms. Many repertoires have been lost over time, and all Native musical cultures have been influenced by encounters with Western music, whether the hymns of missionaries or popular music of the later 20th century; but it is equally true that many musical traditions have been maintained, both in form and in the cultural integration of music in Native societies.

The earliest sustained encounters between Europeans and Native peoples were in French settlements in the 17th century. By mid-century missionaries were teaching elementary music and were adapting their hymns as part of their approaches to converting indigenous people, who were attracted to European music. Surviving records suggest that music in New France was primarily religious but evidence of secular music can be inferred, usually from condemnation of singing and dancing. The first original secular piece was a masque written by Marc *Lescarbot, *Le Théâtre de Neptune*, which was performed at Port-Royal in 1606 and which contained a trumpet call and a song. A few string instruments appear to have been available, and by 1661 an organ, the first in North America, was in use in Quebec City.

Clerics and administrators brought to New France music from the rich musical culture of 17th- and early-18th-century France, but the focus on the *fur trade and the political instability brought about by the struggles between France and England were hardly conducive to the growth of music, or indeed any kind of cultural life. After the Treaty of Paris (1763), by which England obtained New France, and the influx of thousands of *Loyalists, who moved to the British colonies after the American Revolution (1776), the population and the political and economic conditions provided a basis for the development of musical life. Towards the end of the 18th century musical activity grew quickly in Halifax, Quebec, and Montreal with performances of popular musical works including operas, the appearance of teachers, and the beginning of a music trade with the importation of instruments. During the first half of the 19th century in the flourishing Upper Canadian towns of Kingston, Toronto, and Hamilton halls and theatres were built, performing societies were formed, and the music trades developed for the manufacture, printing, and sale of music and instruments.

Throughout the 19th century the principal performing groups in most cities were choirs. Several factors combined to make choral music central to most communities: the British choral tradition, the emphasis in Protestant churches on choral and congregational singing, the large choirs that were a musical characteristic of the century—and the fact that almost anyone can sing. Next to choirs, bands were the most common musical organizations. They were often attached to British regiments, but community bands and bands supported by business firms were also popular. Among the oldest still active at the end of the 20th century were those in Newmarket, Ontario (1843) and Nanaimo, British Columbia (1872), as well as several bands maintained by Native people in BC.

Orchestras were much slower to develop. Choral societies frequently assembled an orchestra from local resources (bands provided an important nucleus) or later engaged famous orchestras from the United States for their concerts, but the absence of a large enough aggregate of players, especially of string instruments, made the formation of permanent orchestras difficult. The first independent orchestra was the Société symphonique de Québec (1903), followed by the Toronto Symphony Orchestra (1906).

Famous touring musicians began to visit eastern cities early in the 19th century. After mid-century a network of railways linked the towns from Windsor to Montreal with each other and with the United States. A similar if less extensive system extended eastward from Montreal. Many of the greatest musical performers of the era made trips to North America and they usually included the Canadian provinces in their tours. Among them were the sopranos Jenny Lind, Adelina Patti, and Henriette Sontag, the violinists Wieniawski and Sarasate, and the pianists Thalberg and Anton Rubinstein. Not only individual musicians but entire companies appeared regularly on the eastern circuit, performing operas and symphony concerts in any town that was on a railway line and had a theatre to accommodate them.

Westward expansion in the later 19th century replicated patterns already established in the east. The transcontinental railway (the CPR began operations in 1886) transformed trading posts into cities. Populations increased, visiting artists began to travel westward, and musical organizations and teachers sprang up in the first years of the 20th century. Permanent orchestras were the last to be established—in Vancouver (1930), Winnipeg (1948), and Calgary (1949)—but soon after mid-century every major city in Canada had an orchestra with a regular season of concerts. This expansion saw not only the establishment of orchestras but also *opera companies and, in general, an active musical life. Towards the end of the 20th century Canadian musicians joined the increasing interest in historical performance, exemplified in the Vancouver Society for Early Music, the Tafelmusik orchestra and Opera Atelier in Toronto, and the Studio de musique ancienne in Montreal.

Publishers, merchants, and instrument makers established their trades in the 19th century and in many cases survived well into the 20th: the *piano manufacturers Heintzman, Lesage, Nordheimer, and Mason and Risch; the organ builder *Casavant Frères, one of the great international builders; and the merchant Ed. Archambault—the latter two still active.

Schools and conservatories such as the Royal Conservatory of Toronto (1886), the Maritime Conservatory of Halifax (1887), and the McGill Conservatorium of Montreal (1904) provided formal and professional musical training. In 1942 Quebec founded the unique government-supported Conservatoire de musique et de l'art dramatique. After about 1950, *universities undertook the training of upper-level students in all musical fields; the Canadian Association of University Schools of Music, formed in 1965, had 40 institutional members in 2002.

Original composition had tentative beginnings in the 17th century, but only in the 19th century was a significant body of locally composed music created, primarily songs or piano music in the popular styles of the day, destined mostly for personal use at home and reflective both of popular taste and the ability of local publishers and merchants to supply material. The few large-scale works tended to be for choir, again reflective of interests and resources of the time. In the first half of the 20th century the principal composers were Claude *Champagne and Healey *Willan, important as teachers but also as composers of large-scale serious music ranging from symphonic works and opera to solo and chamber music. In 1951 the Canadian League of Composers was founded to provide a collective voice for the growing number of composers and to advance the cause of contemporary musical composition. In 2002 the league had about 300 members.

Condemnation of dancing in New France in the 17th century, the denunciation of itinerant fiddle players in Upper Canada in the 19th century, and the market for sheet music of polkas and quick-steps are sufficient evidence that popular music has always been part of musical life. In the early and mid-20th century bandleaders such as Guy Lombardo and Percy Faith became international stars; they reflected the large number of dance bands that were staples in most Canadian cities. The 1950s and 1960s saw the rise of a host of varied popular singers, including Félix Leclerc, Gordon Lightfoot, Neil Young, Joni Mitchell, as well as rock bands. Winnipeg was home to a number of bands in the decade 1960–70, among whom The Guess Who was the most famous. In Quebec in the 1960s the *chansonniers, building on a lively folk tradition that went back to New France, produced vital and distinctive popular songs. *Jazz had been prominent since the 1920s, especially in Montreal and Vancouver, but flourished widely after 1950. In popular music, among the many artists are vocalists Ginette Reno, Anne Murray, Bryan Adams, Céline Dion, and k.d. lang, violinist Ashley MacIsaac, and the vocal quartet The Nylons. Classical artists who have had international careers include violinist Kathleen Parlow, pianists Glenn *Gould and Louis Lortie, and a host of singers such as Jon Vickers, Teresa Stratas, and Maureen Forrester.

From the 1930s the *Canadian Broadcasting Corporation/Radio-Canada has had a tremendous impact on music in Canada. On both French and English radio networks (and on television after 1952) the corporation has broadcast most major musical events, commissioned new works, sponsored artists, and presented concerts in public halls as well as in its studios. Recordings had been issued from the 1940s but in the 1980s the CBC vigorously entered the commercial recording field with LPs and later CDs of concert music performed and frequently composed by Canadian musicians. Apart from the CBC the last two decades of the 20th century saw a notable increase in the Canadian recording industry for all kinds of music.

CARL MOREY

mythistory. Although it rests on a body of concrete facts, history—the story given to us of what was—is also a representation of the past. Circulating at any given time within a society are several representations of the past, which may complement or contradict one another. Informed representations of the past, notably those developed by historians, are not always the ones that take precedence in the general vision of the past entertained by their contemporaries. This vision is usually fed by several stories that combine to form a sort of great collective story that often is a story of identity for those who choose to use it to situate themselves in the space and time of the group they belong to. Thus between the historical narrative, the collective identity, and the memory of the collective self, there is often an epistemological unity, which has extraordinarily powerful structuring effects on individual and collective imaginations. To describe the strength and significance of the narratives and references that, amalgamated in the form of metahistorical visions of ourselves, construct the identities and imaginations of collectivities, we may use the concept of *mythistory*.

From the beginning, Canada as a symbolic space was constructed on a framework of mythistories that have become literally the country's identity narratives. An historian of the imagination, Daniel Francis, has shown how one formerly dominant representation of Canada, given particular credence in anglophone circles, was based on a body of stories and icons that include Aboriginal space, the heroism of the builders, the cult of nordicity, Anglo-Saxon superiority, and the infantilization and obsolescence of French Canada. In Quebec, the national identity story was for a long time constructed on a stock of references depicting the French-Canadian collectivity as the unfortunate victim of the Other, and its destiny as consisting of finding the means to survive through the protection and expansion of the specific attributes of its identity.

The same exercise of identification, and deconstruction, of mythistories could be undertaken for every group that has inhabited the country and that has, in order to exist—that is, to define itself against and express itself to an archetypal Other—staged its own history in the theatre of the past.

The richness and breadth of historians' work have not yet erased these representations from the country's cultural landscape. Today in Canada there still exists a repertoire of mythistories, only partially updated, through which anglophones, francophones, and First Nations in particular, conscious of a heritage to be handed down, like to display themselves to the world and to themselves.

JOCELYN LÉTOURNEAU

NaGeira, Princess Sheila (also spelled NaGira, Nagueira, Maguiela, etc., the name perhaps derives from an Irish air called 'Sheela Na Guira'), legendary Irish princess, said to have come to Newfoundland in the early 17th century. She is an invention of recent vintage: the earliest mention of her name in print appears to have been in 1910. Details about her soon accumulated. Harold Horwood called her 'a little Irish princess from the County Connaught'. It remains unclear how he determined her stature—and there is no County Connaught. Legend has it that her ship, on its way to France, was attacked by the Dutch, and she was taken prisoner. The Dutch ship was then attacked by an English vessel commanded by Peter Easton, later a notable pirate, who was headed for Newfoundland. En route Sheila fell in love with and married a man named Gilbert Pike. Sheila lived to 105. Her gravesite in Carbonear, Conception Bay, has become a 'historic' park. PATRICK O'FLAHERTY

National Action Committee on the Status of Women. Established in 1972, NAC is a national umbrella organization for over 700 women's groups including radical collectives and more traditional associations ranging from rape crisis centres to church and farm groups. To advance women's equality it lobbies government and engages in research and public education, tackling a policy spectrum from child care and reproduction to economic and constitutional change.

NAC grew out of women's mobilization around the Royal Commission on the Status of Women. In 1966 the Committee for the Equality of Women was formed to pressure the government to study the plight of women. In response, the state appointed the royal commission. Its *Report* (1970) included a call for a federal women's advisory council. Wary of being too closely tied to the state, the CEW called for the creation of an organization that would be more autonomous than an advisory council. Thus, the National Ad Hoc Committee on the Status of Women was formed to ensure that the commission's recommendations were met. In 1972, this coalition of approximately 40 member groups, mostly from Toronto, transformed into NAC.

During its early years, NAC's leaders had associations with parties of the right (Laura Sabia, Progressive Conservatives), left (Lynn McDonald and Judy Rebick, NDP), and centre (Lorna Marsden and Chaviva Hošek, Liberals). But the organization became increasingly sceptical of partisan politics. Its tactics altered from collaboration to confrontation, reflecting its changing relations with the state and efforts to build a more inclusive women's movement. Actions such as lobbying, meeting with officials, and preparing briefs were replaced by citizen mobilization, coalition building, and protest-oriented strategies. Originally led by white, middle-class women, NAC became increasingly diverse. It also worked to become more regionally representative. In 1986, Louise Dulude was the first non-Torontonian to become president; since the early 1990s most NAC presidents have been women of colour (Sunera Thobani, Joan Grant-Cummings, Denise Andrea Campbell), including an Aboriginal woman (Kudooka Terri Brown).

In the 1980s and 1990s, NAC's increasing radicalism was evident in its notable—perhaps even notorious—efforts in relation to trade, the constitution, and poverty. NAC was one of the first groups to speak out against Canada's *free trade agreements with the United States. It also raised public awareness about the exclusive nature of the *Meech Lake and *Charlottetown Accords, showing how they jeopardized women's equality rights and helping to sink both deals. By 1996 NAC was instrumental in organizing hundreds of thousands in a cross-Canada trek against poverty. NAC has been ahead of public opinion on an array of important issues, influencing Canadian politics and women. Yet, because of representational concerns and dramatic reductions in federal funding, its future is uncertain.
ALEXANDRA DOBROWOLSKY

national anthem. National anthems, as symbols of nationhood, are distinguished from other patriotic songs by having official recognition, through either legislation or a tradition of performance at public occasions. In Canada from the late 18th century, the British anthem 'God Save the Queen [or King]' was sung on ceremonial occasions. The writing or adaptation of pieces intended as national songs dates back to the first half of the 19th century. A favourite was 'Vive la Canadienne' (words and music anonymous), which appeared in *Literary Garland* in 1840 as 'The Canadian: A French Air' and was recognized in an 1859 publication as a 'mélodie nationale canadienne'. Also popular were 'Un Canadien errant', an old French tune, with new verses by Antoine *Gérin-Lajoie (1842); 'Le Drapeau de Carillon: légende canadienne' (1858), words by Octave *Crémazie, music by Charles Wugk Sabatier; and 'La Huronne', words by Pierre-Gabriel Huot, music by Célestin Lavigueur (*c.* 1861). Isidore Bédard's 'Sol canadien, terre chérie' (1827) was first 'arranged' and then set to new music, both by Theodore Molt (1859). 'O Canada! Mon pays! Mes amours!' with words by George-Étienne *Cartier was sung either to a traditional tune (published 1860) or to a new melody by Jean-Baptiste Labelle (by 1868).

Signifying the growth of Canadian nationalism, the maple leaf was considered the emblem of Canada as early as the 1830s. James Paton Clarke wrote 'The Emblem of Canada' (*c.* 1850). 'The Maple Leaf For Ever' (1867) must be considered the first unofficial national hymn. With words and music by Alexander Muir (1830–1906), it was popular into the 20th century, although it suffered from its lack of reference to French Canadians. Muir made two important changes to the words in 1894: he added a reference to the lily, Quebec's flower, and he provided a new five-stanza text, changing the opening from 'In days of yore, from Britain's shore, Wolfe the dauntless hero came' to 'In days of yore, the hero Wolfe Britain's glory did maintain', but this revision never caught on.

After Confederation, patriotic songs in either English or French were produced in some quantity, culminating in the first decades of the 20th century. By the end of the First World War some 200 had appeared as sheet music, some as sound recordings. 'God Bless Our Wide Dominion' by Arthur Sullivan, commissioned in 1880 by the author of the text, Governor General the Marquess of Lorne, was not popularly accepted. Nor was 'Canada' by another British composer, Edward German (1904).

'O Canada' (1880) by Calixa Lavallée (1842–91), with words by Adolphe-Basile Routhier (1839–1920), was commissioned for the Fête nationale des Canadiens-français by the *Société St-Jean-Baptiste. It was first performed by a band in Quebec City on 24 June 1880 in the presence of the governor general and other dignitaries, and first sung at St Roch Church by the choir of the Société Ste-Cécile on 29 June 1880 in Quebec City. Immediately popular among French Canadians, by 1900 the song was embraced in other provinces. Many sheet music editions appeared, some re-harmonizing the tune. An English text by Thomas Bedford Richardson received performances by the Toronto Mendelssohn Choir; some 350 others were submitted in a contest in 1909, but Justice Robert Stanley Weir's text, written in 1908 (to celebrate the 300th anniversary of the city of Quebec), became the most popular. In 1964 Prime Minister Lester *Pearson proposed selecting an official national anthem. A committee of both houses of Parliament recommended 'O Canada' in 1967, but the song became the official national anthem only on 1 July 1980. At the same time 'God Save the Queen/Dieu sauve la Reine' was designated the royal anthem. Over the years, some of the lyrics of 'O Canada' have been severely criticized, particularly the Weir text's reference to 'all thy sons' (amended by Weir in 1914 from his original 'true patriot love thou dost in us command') and 'our home and native land' (also not in the 1908 version). The repetition of 'We stand on guard for thee' has been lessened by substituting the words 'From far and wide' once and 'O Canada' once (in the penultimate line). Six private members' bills had been introduced by 1994 to change the words. In 2002 Senator Vivienne Poy introduced a bill to change 'all thy sons' to 'all of us'.

Several provincial or quasi-national hymns should be mentioned, including 'Ode to Newfoundland' by Sir Hubert Parry (1902) and 'Farewell to Nova Scotia'. Bobby Gimby's centennial song 'CA-NA-DA' (1967), though achieving widespread popularity, cannot be considered a national anthem. Gilles Vigneault's 'Mon pays' (1964) and 'Gens du pays' (1975) have had great success both within and outside Quebec. HELMUT KALLMANN

National Archives. Established by the federal government in June 1872 as the result of a petition from the Literary and Historical Society of Quebec. In the Canadas in the 1840s and 1850s, efforts had been made to collect and preserve historical documents, but no formal archives had been created. In Nova Scotia, Thomas B. Akins (1809–1891) was appointed commissioner of public records in 1857, very much in the mid-19th-century tradition found in the Canadas and in the United States. Copies of documents were acquired from repositories in Britain and France to form the basis of an archival collection.

Douglas Brymner (1823–1902) was appointed archivist in June 1872 and devoted the next 30 years to the collection of documents and publications relating to Canadian history. He concentrated his efforts on the copying by hand of Canadian-related documents in London and Paris. Brymner was a strong believer in the need for an archives, even though he was hampered by a small staff, few resources, and lack of adequate accommodation. A rival operation within the government, the Keeper of the Records, created confusion and hindered any real progress towards the creation of a national archives. By the time of his death, Brymner had succeeded in establishing archives as an essential government service and responsibility, thus providing the foundation upon which the archives would expand in the 20th century.

Brymner's successor, Arthur G. *Doughty (1860–1936) emphasized the cultural role of archives. Appointed in May 1904, he convinced the government to provide the archives with a new building, more staff, and a larger budget. In 1912, the Public Archives Act created the Public Archives of Canada and provided much-needed legislative authority. Doughty encouraged the use of archives—by the emerging historical profession as well as by teachers, students, and ordinary Canadians. By the mid-1920s, the archives was the focal point for Canadian historical studies. It had a summer school for graduate students, and staff members were involved with the founding of the Canadian Historical Association and the *Canadian Historical Review*. With its extensive and rapidly increasing collection of historical documents, the PAC nurtured the emergence of the historical profession, providing the raw material that allowed history to be studied, taught, and written.

Doughty embarked on an ambitious acquisitions program at home and abroad, expanded the work of the archives' offices in London and Paris, and for the first time acquired documentary art, photographs, and museum artifacts. During the First World War the PAC was also responsible for the collection and distribution of war trophies. Many of the museum objects are now with the Canadian War Museum and the Canadian Museum of Civilization.

The Depression of the 1930s had an adverse effect on the PAC. Staff and budgets were reduced and no new initiatives were undertaken, a situation that would persist through most of the war years. Doughty, long identified with the archives and its fortunes, retired in 1935 and was succeeded in 1937 by Gustave Lanctot (1883–1975), a respected historian of French Canada and an employee of the archives since 1912. Although many traditional activities were curtailed during the war (the office in Paris was closed), new opportunities arose, including responsibility for the preservation of historical government records. Lanctot retired in 1948.

With the appointment of W. Kaye *Lamb (1904–99), archivist, librarian, and historian, the archives once again entered a period of renewal and growth. A systematic acquisitions program was established, finding aids were published and distributed, and, for the first time, new technology was used—microfilm in the 1950s, computers by the mid-1960s. Under Lamb, the archives assumed a more active role in the selection, disposal, and retention of federal government records. He wore two hats: in addition to being dominion archivist he was also Canada's first national librarian, 1953–68, and in 1967 the archives moved into new quarters shared with the National Library.

During the past three decades, the archives has been transformed from the least to the most accessible heritage resource in the country. Under archivists Wilfred Smith (1920–98), Jean-Pierre Wallot (b.1935), and Ian Wilson (b. 1943), the archives has embraced technology as a means of disseminating information about its collections to users throughout Canada—from the greater use of microfilm and computerized indexing in the 1960s and 1970s to digital imaging and the Internet in the 1990s.

The archives has been a leader in the Canadian archival community, in professional development, and in making original documentation and records available for the study of Canada's past. The first active cultural institution established by the new federal government following Confederation, its unique holdings, gathered over 130 years, constitute an incredible inheritance as the essential evidence for constitutional evolution, human rights, social justice, even Canadian sovereignty. Archives are the original source of our stories and our collective memory as a nation.

In 1987 new legislation renamed the PAC the National Archives of Canada, and it is expected that the NA and the National Library (est. 1953) will be combined in 2004 to create the Library and Archives Canada with a broad mandate to provide Canadians with easy and integrated access to their documentary heritage and to promote knowledge about Canada. The LAC will continue the traditional roles of both institutions, seeking to acquire information in all media that reflects the diversity and complexity of the Canadian experience while addressing the difficult issues posed by modern technologies and electronic records. The LAC will support and assist archives and libraries throughout Canada and will be responsible for the Portrait Gallery of Canada and the Canada History Centre. IAN E. WILSON

National Capital Commission. A federal Crown corporation created in 1959 to plan and build a capital that is a meeting place for Canadians, the NCC is the successor to the Ottawa Improvement Commission (est. 1899 by Wilfrid *Laurier) and the Federal District Commission (est. 1927 by Mackenzie *King). The NCC built most of the parks, parkways, bridges, and greenbelts that grace the national capital. A 1903 report by landscape architect Frederick Todd planned a regional parks system. Edward Bennett's 1915 report for the Federal Plan Commission was perhaps Canada's first comprehensive city plan, but little was built beyond Gatineau Park. The NCC's 1950 plan, prepared by French urbanist Jacques Gréber, was quickly implemented, transforming *Ottawa and Hull from dreary industrial towns to an attractive and functional national capital. The NCC was a leader in re-establishing Canadian urban planning after 1945 and a historic preservation pioneer. Its planning power waned after Ontario and Quebec established regional governments in the 1970s, but it still acts as a planning bridge across the Ottawa River. Since 1988, it has emphasised the cultural and symbolic dimensions of the capital, producing popular events like Canada Day and Winterlude and plans for the historic core. DAVID L.A. GORDON

National Convention, Newfoundland. At the end of the Second World War, the British government decided to deal with the anomalous position of Newfoundland, administered by an appointed *Commission of Government since 1934. At that time, it had been agreed that *responsible government would be restored when the country was again self-supporting, and the people requested it. That Newfoundland was self-supporting was clear, but in order to ascertain what people wanted, and to ensure that they made an informed choice, the British government decided to establish a National Convention that would 'examine the position of the country' and recommend the 'possible forms of future government to be placed before the people at a national referendum'. The election of the 45 delegates took place in June 1946, and the convention met on 11 September. It then divided into ten committees to investigate various aspects of the country's economy and government, a process that was to precede discussion of forms of government. Debates were broadcast over the government radio station.

On 28 October Joseph R. *Smallwood interrupted this program by moving that a delegation should be sent to Ottawa to investigate confederation with Canada. Though the motion failed, an emotional debate clearly showed that the central issue would be whether Newfoundland should return to responsible government or become a Canadian province. In the spring of 1947, a largely anti-confederate delegation visited London to ascertain what assistance might be available under responsible government. It received no encouragement from a frosty Dominions Office, which favoured confederation. In June, another delegation, dominated by Smallwood and his ally F. Gordon Bradley, travelled to Ottawa. After some hesitation, the Canadian government agreed to discuss draft terms of union, which were settled by the end of September and presented to the convention in November. Smallwood dominated the lengthy debate that followed. The delegates then considered their recommendations, agreeing unanimously on 22 January 1948 that both responsible and commission government should be on the referendum ballot. Smallwood moved that confederation should be added. After an impassioned debate lasting until 28 January, the motion was defeated by 29 votes to 16. The convention dissolved the next day.

Though the British government placed confederation on the ballot anyway, the convention had not been a waste of time. It served, as intended, as a means of political education, it turned confederation into a viable political option, and it launched the careers of a new generation of politicians. JAMES K. HILLER

National Council of Women of Canada. The NCWC was created in 1893 as a federation, or parliament, of women's organizations. Its federal structure, composed of Local Councils of Women (LCW) from coast to coast and Nationally Organized Societies (NOS), including the Girls' Friendly Society and Women's Art Association, made it larger than the *Woman's Christian Temperance Union, previously Canada's most numerous women's group. Unlike the WCTU, the NCWC adopted a moderate *feminism, typified by its adoption of the 'golden rule'—'Do unto others as you would have them do unto you.' The first president, Ishbel Gordon, Marchionesse of Aberdeen and Temair, the wife of the governor general (1893–8) and longtime president of the International Council of Women (1888–1939), was influential. A liberal internationalist and suffragist, she feared religious and racial hatreds and pressed the NCWC to negotiate a sufficiently moderate course to include French and English, Catholic, Protestant, and Jewish women. She won a fierce battle in favour of silent prayer in 1893 but the evangelical Protestant WCTU and *YWCA rejected this compromise. The council's refusal to endorse *women's suffrage until 1910—despite the enthusiasm of many LCWs, such as Montreal and Victoria, and the adherence of the Dominion Women's Enfranchisement Association as an NOS—was also intended to keep conservatives and progressives in the same room. Fierce opposition to even moderate initiatives, such as the council's endorsement of the *Victorian Order of Nurses in 1897, confirmed Aberdeen's caution. Her ecumenical orientation was only partially successful: French Canadians were rare and Protestant liberals dominant. Nor did inclusion often extend to workers, Native peoples, or non-charter cultural groups. As its enthusiasm for *domestic servants and opposition to *unions suggested, the council often succumbed to racism and classism. To be fair, however, no other organization of Canadian women or men did any better, and most far worse. The NCWC also focused on research and reports from standing committees, NOS, and LCWs. Annual meetings heard lectures on key issues, including *public health and education, criminal justice, suffrage, citizenship, maternal mortality, immigration, and peace. While urban middle- and upper-class Anglo-Celtic elites controlled key offices and spoke at the international council, other voices sometimes surfaced, testifying to the breadth of activism. The council—as its publication for the Paris Exposition, *Women of Canada* (1900), suggested—was a major generator of data on women. Female professionals in education, health care, social work, and law and the first generation of university-educated women demonstrated their talent in meetings and publications, contributing significantly to the NCWC's creation of a national middle-class, reform-minded female elite. It survived into the 21st century, although an aging membership reflected its difficulty in capturing the spare moments of Canadian women who more than ever juggled paid and unpaid responsibilities.

VERONICA STRONG-BOAG

National Development in the Arts, Letters, and Sciences, Royal Commission on. *See* MASSEY COMMISSION.

National Energy Program. Federal energy policies initiated in the 28 October 1980 budget. Prior to 1947, Canada was highly dependent on *coal and *hydroelectricity. Post-war discoveries of oil and gas resources at *Leduc and Redwater in Alberta were complicated by isolation of eastern Canadian markets from the supply, by US market restrictions, and by cheap import prices. The stormy pipeline debate of 1956 led to establishment of the National Energy Board in 1959. Given regulatory and advisory powers over interprovincial pipeline development, pricing, marketing, and import and export of fuels, including electricity, the NEB helped develop the National Oil Policy of 1961. Import restrictions were imposed west of the Ottawa Valley line, stimulating western development, but cheaper foreign oil was still allowed to reach eastern Canadian refineries. With sharp price rises imposed by OPEC in 1973, policy determination shifted to the Department of Energy, Mines and Resources and cabinet. In 1978, domestic prices were lower than world prices by about $3 a barrel, but the Iranian Revolution of 1979 raised world prices 150 per cent. In 1980 the Trudeau government legislated the National Energy Program, reinforcing policy directions in place since 1973, including those of the short-lived 1979 Clark administration. Assuming that world prices would continue to rise, the NEP sought to achieve lower domestic prices through subsidization, conservation, and new discoveries of domestic supply. Increased nationalization was facilitated by the Canadian-owned company, Petro-Canada. Increased tax revenues went to Ottawa and exploration on northern lands were encouraged through the Petroleum Incentives Program. Federal–provincial agreements were eventually signed in 1981 following modification of the original terms. When world prices declined, high national debt remained, the ironic result of the Canadian industry having been nationalized and developed during historically high prices. The NEP was dismantled between 1984 and 1986 by the Mulroney administration.

GRAHAM MacDONALD

National Film Board of Canada. Following a report by John *Grierson on government film activities, the NFB was founded 2 May 1939 under the terms of the National Film Act; Grierson was appointed the first film commissioner in October 1939. The act was revised in 1950, primarily to separate the NFB from direct government control, with a mandate to interpret Canada to Canadians and other nations. For the first two decades of its history, the NFB was the principal focus for Canadian film activity. It pioneered developments in social documentary, animation, documentary drama, and direct cinema, and has been a continuing initiator of new technology. Having produced about 10,000 titles, the NFB has won hundreds of international awards, including 10 Oscars among its 66 Academy Award nominations.

Although it was originally designed as a modestly staffed advisory board, the demands of wartime production, together with Grierson's personality, led the NFB to a shift into active production by absorbing (1941) the Canadian Government Motion Picture Bureau (formerly the Exhibits and Publicity Bureau, established in 1919). By 1945 it had grown into one of the world's largest film studios (with a staff of 787), an animation unit had been set up, non-theatrical distribution circuits established, and many young Canadian filmmakers trained.

In the post-war years budgets and staff were reduced and the NFB came under attack for allegedly harbouring left-wing subversives and as a monopoly that threatened the livelihood of commercial producers. A new film commissioner, Arthur *Irwin, calmed the storm, initiated a new National Film Act (1950), restructured the NFB along modern bureaucratic lines, and planned to move the NFB from Ottawa to Montreal.

Production expanded into new areas in the post-war decade: the first dramatic films were made, new techniques in animation were explored (inspired by Norman McLaren), and the information film and production for television was initiated. Filmmakers paid more attention to style and technical polish, and new approaches emerged, more intimate in tone than the earlier didactic approach.

In Quebec the NFB was viewed for some years as a federalist agency that denied Quebec's cultural aspirations. French-language production was minimal until the late 1950s, when the demands of television and the move to Montreal provided catalysts for expansion. Many young Quebec filmmakers who were hired played seminal roles in the later flowering of Quebec cinema, both within and outside the NFB. After a series of protests by filmmakers, the appointment of the first French-speaking commissioner, Guy Roberge, initiated a series of changes that culminated (1964) in a total separation of production along linguistic lines.

Women filmmakers made major contributions during the war years but were then virtually absent from active production until the early 1970s. Encouraged by such series as En tant que femmes and Working Mothers, and the development of *Studio D under Kathleen Shannon, women have since made significant contributions both as directors and technicians. Native peoples objected for many years to the folkloric and condescending images of themselves projected in NFB films. Only in the late 1960s did a truer portrait emerge. At the same time, Aboriginal people were given access to NFB equipment to produce their own films. Through the 1970s this initiative was extended into broadly based regional production.

Production of dramatic feature films for theatrical release began in 1963–4 and continued for about three decades, despite debate about the appropriateness of such production within a state institution. Many NFB feature films have won international awards and have had wide release, including, in the 1980s, a number of intensely realist social dramas and comedies produced at modest cost.

The once dominant role of the NFB has been significantly reduced in recent decades by the growth of the commercial *film industry and the expansion of television production. Severe cuts to its budget have further eroded its position, forcing it to eliminate many programs. The NFB now places more emphasis on co-productions with independent producers, especially of documentaries intended primarily for television. The animation section is one of the most admired in the world and continues to encourage new talent. The NFB has continued to attract talented new filmmakers, to emphasize high qualities of production, and to maintain its position as the world's most widely respected national film agency.

PETER MORRIS

national flag. The first flag to fly in Canada, raised by John *Cabot in 1497, was the Royal Banner—*France Modern* quartering *England* (*Arms of Canada). The Royal Banner of France (*France Modern*) did duty from 1534, when it was raised on Gaspé by Jacques *Cartier, to 1759. British North America and then the Dominion of Canada have been served by the Union Jack—first in Newfoundland after 1603 and since 1964 as a symbol of Canada's membership in the *Commonwealth and its allegiance to the Crown—and the Canadian Red Ensign (the British Red Ensign with an heraldic shield for Canada in the fly). Until 1965 the Canadian Red Ensign flew on Canadian registered ships (from 1892), on government buildings abroad (from 1929), and on government buildings at home (from 1945).

Following Confederation, the idea of a national flag for Canada was 'an unflagging debate', as E.M. Chadwick titled his article in the *Canadian Almanac* (1896). Being so, successive federal governments considered it prudent not to become embroiled. As late as 1964, Col John Matheson, MP for Leeds and parliamentary private secretary to the prime minister, in the famous debate in the Commons in June of that year, had to remind the House that the country still 'does not have an official national flag'. As Canada approached the centennial of *Confederation (1967) the matter could no longer be shelved. When it became known that Ottawa favoured the establishment of a national flag, the 'Great Flag Debate' swept the country. Hundreds of designs—excellent, good, bad, and terrible—to be considered by an all-party committee, poured into room after room of the Parliament buildings. Matheson, the éminence grise, had the collaboration of the then Rouge Dragon Pursuivant of Arms (a Canadian) of the College of Arms department of the Royal Household, who provided heraldic and vexillological expertise. The designs were whittled down to that of the present national flag: three vertical stripes ('pales' in heraldry)—one white between two red and on the white a red maple leaf. In the process, Rouge Dragon added to the heraldic vocabulary a new term, 'a Canadian pale', in order to specify that the central division be *square*, as desired, and not a vertical one-third of the total design as otherwise technically required by such a design. With matters finally settled, the national flag of Canada was established by the Queen by a proclamation dated 28 January 1965, effective 25 February.

SIR CONRAD SWAN

National historic sites are designated by the federal government on the advice of the *Historic Sites and Monuments Board of Canada. They commemorate events, activities, people, and *architecture considered to be of national significance. They also include *canals. Parks Canada administers the program, providing research, planning, conservation, and other professional support, and is also responsible for erecting and maintaining commemorative plaques and monuments. Only a small proportion of the sites are actually owned by this federal agency; the rest, owned by individuals, corporations, other levels of government, and non-government organizations, are the responsibility of the owners. There are no legal obligations or restrictions implicit in a national historic site designation, unless stipulated in a cost-sharing agreement with Parks Canada.

Most of the 145 national historic sites managed by Parks Canada have been developed as public attractions. They typically include some combination of a visitor orientation centre, restored buildings, archaeological remains, exhibits, and costumed guides. Examples include L'Anse aux Meadows, Newfoundland; the Halifax Citadel; the *St-Maurice forges in Quebec; Bellevue House in Ontario; Lower *Fort Garry, Manitoba; Bar U Ranch, Alberta; and the Gulf of Georgia Cannery in British Columbia. Similar developed national historic sites operated by other agencies include Fort Henry, Ontario; Head-Smashed-In Buffalo Jump, Alberta; and McLean Mill in Port Alberni, BC.

Designated historic sites, national and otherwise, comprise two elements: the place itself with its in situ resources, such as archaeological remains, buildings, or other physical relics, and the significance attached to the place. These two elements usually enhance each other, but in some instances, as at the Fortress of *Louisbourg National Historic Site, they are in stark contrast. This former French fortress guarding the entrance to the Gulf of the St Lawrence had been completely demolished by British troops in 1758. The significance of the place was recognized early by the Historic Sites and Monuments Board, which wished to commemorate the role of Louisbourg in the French and British imperial rivalry of the 18th century culminating in the fall of New France. The siege and destruction of Louisbourg was viewed as a chapter in the development of Canada as a British colony. There was a parallel interest in the ruins as a portal to appreciating a past way of life, inspiring a campaign to partially restore the former French settlement. This proposal was encouraged by a wish to build a major tourist attraction in Cape Breton. Through the 1960s a multimillion-dollar project led to the reconstruction of several key buildings. Subsequently, more buildings have been reconstructed and today there are more than 50, which, along with over 100 costumed guides, present Louisbourg as it might have appeared in the summer of 1744. Just beyond the public view, the remains of the British siege works have become overgrown by the surrounding forest.

National historic sites can have meaning on more than one level, their significance can change over time, and they can resonate differently in different segments of the population. Competing interpretations can be attached to many sites; those commemorating the 1885 rebellion have presented a special challenge. At *Batoche National Historic Site, Parks Canada has attempted to present multiple voices, showing the significance of the site to Anglo Canadians, French Canadians, Metis, and Cree. More recently, the historic sites program has sought to articulate an official statement of national significance and heritage character through the preparation of an approved commemorative integrity statement. This has brought needed focus to presentation programs at a number of sites.

C.J. TAYLOR

national honours. Often associated with *gallantry awards, national honours are also bestowed for long-term services. Although often linked to military careers (such as the Order of St Louis, awarded to some 300 persons in New France, or the Companion of the Bath—CB—given Charles de Salaberry in 1816), many were granted to Canadians for peaceful contributions. The highest British honours were knighthoods and baronetcies, allowing recipients to be styled 'Sir', and rare peerages, admitting them and their heirs to the House of Lords. Two examples of many knighthoods are those to William *Logan, founder of the *Geological Survey of Canada, in 1856 and Matthew Baillie *Begbie, a famous British Columbia judge, in 1875.

Some people have thought formal honours were undemocratic and should be abolished. In 1918 and 1919 the House of Commons passed resolutions calling for cessation of hereditary and titular honours. Formal state honours were revived in 1933 by Prime Minister R.B. *Bennett, who nominated some 200 Canadians for

British awards including 15 knighthoods. This ceased when his government was defeated in 1935. In 1942, the House of Commons passed a resolution endorsing formal state honours if they did not include knighthoods and titles. Thus, many Canadian civilians were decorated for wartime services, including A.Y. Jackson, consultant to the official war artists program (Companion, Order of St Michael and St George or CMG), and Marcel Ouimet, CBC war correspondent (Commander, Order of the British Empire, or CBE). These awards ceased after 1 July 1946.

In 1866 Lord Monck proposed establishment of a distinct Canadian Order of Chivalry, which he suggested be called the Order of St Lawrence. The idea was periodically revived, supported by governors general, military officers, the *Royal Society of Canada, a parliamentary committee, and the *Massey Commission. However, Canadian prime ministers were either enamoured with British awards (Bennett), terrified of short-lived egalitarian forces in the nation (Borden), philosophically suspicious of honours (King), or indifferent to them (St Laurent). The sole attempt at a Canadian order was creation of the Canada Medal (1943), which was then awarded to no one.

The approach of Canada's centennial encouraged patriotism. Prime Minister L.B. *Pearson was determined to forge Canadian unity by adopting unique national symbols (the Maple Leaf *flag, recognition of 'O Canada' as the *national anthem, renaming the national airline). In 1966 he proposed to cabinet that distinctive Canadian honours be created, in April 1967 he reported their institution, and on 1 July 1967 the first appointments to the Order of Canada were announced. The statutes of the Order of Canada were revised in 1972; the original two grades became three (Companion, Officer, Member). A corresponding Order of Military Merit was also created. Another tier of awards (the Meritorious Service Decorations) was established in 1984 and revised in 1991; it now exists in Military and Civil divisions, each with a Cross and Medal. The insignia of the Order of Canada, designed by Bruce Beatty and patterned upon a snowflake, is one of the most beautiful among global decorations.

HUGH A. HALLIDAY

national identity. An elusive concept that Canadians have debated for generations, national identity is a phrase that has been used in at least two different ways. First, it has referred to a set of individual characteristics that are said to describe a Canadian personality type. For example, Canadians are deferential to authority; Canadians are naturally ironic; Canadians are afraid of the wilderness; and so on. The problem is that for every Canadian who exhibits any one of these characteristics, another does not. Canadians, like the inhabitants of most countries, are too diverse for a single personality profile. Second, more promisingly, national identity has referred to a set of characteristics that describe Canadian society. For example, Canada is a *constitutional monarchy with a democratic electoral system; it was occupied by Aboriginal people long before the arrival of European colonists; the original colonists came principally from France and Great Britain; subsequently the country was settled by successive waves of immigration from many different countries. Taken together, these characteristics, which have emerged from our historical experience, give Canada a unique character in the world of nations and may constitute a national identity. Sometimes they seem to be crystallized in specific public policies or institutions that Canadians believe express something basic about the country. Publicly funded health care and the CBC are two examples.

The issue of national identity naturally emerged following Confederation in 1867. The short-lived *Canada First movement was the first attempt to articulate a 'new nationality' for the new dominion, one based on a bracing northern climate and an Anglo-Saxon racial and political inheritance. The first prime minister, John A. *Macdonald, spoke for generations of English-speaking Canadians when he declared: 'I am a British subject, and British born, and a British subject I hope to die.' Canada was considered to be a British country, tied to the mother country by bonds of sympathy, history, and culture. Some people found these bonds constraining, but for most they helped to bolster self-confidence and clarify a distinct national destiny. At the same time French-speaking Canadians were developing their own sense of identity based on the three pillars of French language and culture and the Catholic religion. On matters of cultural identity, the two language groups seldom agreed, living, as novelist Hugh *MacLennan famously put it, as 'two solitudes'.

As time passed English-speaking Canadians began to express a more autonomous identity as ties with the mother country frayed and then unravelled. The literary critic Northrop *Frye described a Canada 'so long apologetic for being so big an obstacle on the way to somewhere more interesting, yet slowly becoming a visible object in its own right'. One source for this new identity was the wilderness landscape, as expressed, for instance, in the paintings of the *Group of Seven and the writings of *Grey Owl. Sometimes Canadians have revelled in the wilderness; sometimes they seem to be threatened by it; regardless, the link to the land appears to be a defining national characteristic. As well, several landmark historical events contributed to the break with a colonial mentality; these included Canada's participation in the world wars, the passage of the Citizenship Act in 1946, the creation of a *national flag in 1965, and the upwelling of national pride that accompanied *Expo 67. Perhaps most importantly of all, with the easing of immigration restrictions after the Second World War Canada's population swelled with newcomers of all ethnic backgrounds. During the 1950s, 75 per cent of all Canadians were of either British or French background. By 1991 that figure had dropped to 40 per cent and the downward trend has continued. Canada had become an ethnically heterogeneous society. The metaphor used to describe this change was the mosaic—Canada was a mosaic comprised of 'tiles' from many different ethnic and cultural backgrounds—compared to the Americans, who were said to constitute a melting pot where cultural differences were boiled down to a single, homogeneous norm. The mosaic was translated into law in 1971 with the announcement by Prime Minister Pierre *Trudeau of his government's policy of official *multiculturalism.

Paradoxically, while cultural diversity provided Canadians with a new way of describing their society, it also made a single national identity increasingly problematic. Not only do French- and English-speaking Canadians rarely share the same understanding of their country, neither do Aboriginal Canadians, with their own history on the continent, or Canadians of non-European origin. Add to this the profound regional identifications across the country, not to mention differences of social class and gender, and it becomes evident that in Canada, national identity is a contested concept, and that attempts to imagine or impose a single identity can be misguided, even destructive. For this reason, perhaps more than many other nationalities, Canadians have learned to live with a comparatively loose definition of themselves. ('I suppose that a Canadian is someone who has a logical reason to think he is one', writes the author Mavis Gallant.) Some people worry that this is not enough to hold the country together, especially given the seductive influence of the United States next door; others argue that it is the only realistic option for a society as diverse as Canada.

DANIEL FRANCIS

national parks. It is generally believed that national parks began with the 1885 order-in-council reserving the Cave and Basin Hotsprings in what is now *Banff, Alberta, from private development. Parks Canada selected this date in determining its centenary celebration, and the designation of the Cave and Basin as a national historic site is based largely on this association. But the 1885 order-in-council did not really articulate the idea of a national park. This came later. George Stewart, who had been charged with surveying the hot springs reservation, identified an area of about 260 acres which the Rocky Mountains Park Act of 1887 established as Canada's first national park. This act stated that the area's purpose was to be 'a public park and pleasure ground for the benefit, advantage and enjoyment of the people of Canada'. Changing policies as well as subsequent legislation in 1911, 1930, and 2001 were gradually to change the way parks are viewed. Before 1911 a number of other parks were established, largely concentrated in the Rockies (Jasper, Kootenay, Yoho, and Waterton Lakes) and in the Columbia Mountains (Mount Revelstoke and Glacier).

The establishment of Rocky Mountains Park reflected broad concerns, emerging at the turn of the century, for the conservation of natural resources, part of a constellation of ideas that has been termed the *conservation movement. A growing acceptance that natural resources were no longer in limitless supply was tied to the notion that resources could be effectively managed to provide long-term benefits to society as a whole. The conservation movement was dominated, at least in its official manifestations, by a doctrine of usefulness. Forests were to be managed to allow for sustainable development, parks were to be developed to maximize public access and enjoyment. Coexisting with this practical business approach was a sentimental side to conservation. A wide body of opinion, represented in the United States by John Muir, and well-articulated in Canada by nature writers such as Ernest Thompson *Seton and Charles G.D. Roberts, held that wilderness areas should be protected for their own sake. Joined to this perspective was an even larger body of opinion that held that spectacular wilderness areas such as those found in the Canadian Rockies were important as scenery. Just the appearance of the mountains, glaciers, forests, and streams, populated with charismatic animals such as deer, elk, and bears, could uplift the spirit. These supposedly sublime qualities were also seen as useful because they attracted tourists. The practical and sentimental strands of the conservation movement influenced the approach to national parks at the turn of the century. National parks were promoted according to a doctrine of usefulness, as a national resource to be exploited for the common good. Yet, the appreciation that sublime scenery was important for the enjoyment of the people served to promote its protection. Early programs of park management were therefore aimed at managing scenery, satisfying both the mercenary and aesthetic ends of the program.

Attitudes towards national parks became more complex as conservationists placed more emphasis on understanding natural processes and ecological systems. By 1930, when the new National Parks Act was passed, the commissioner of national parks, J.B. Harkin, wrote: 'The primary purpose of National Parks is not recreation as it is understood by the advocates of regionally distributed National Parks, but rather that they are the outdoor museums of the finest in primitive conditions.' This perspective influenced the establishment of national parks, such as Wood Buffalo and Elk Island, whose objectives were to preserve species at risk. The conservation objectives of national parks were enshrined in an ideal that Commissioner Harkin termed 'the principle of inviolability'. This meant that, while tourist development would be tolerated, other industrial activities such as hydroelectric projects, mining, and logging would not. Although enforcing this principle has been problematic, it still distinguishes national parks from many provincial parks, which have often allowed 'multiple use', combining commercial and industrial activities with recreation.

By the 1920s it was a stated objective to have at least one national park in each region, and by the mid-1930s five new parks were established: Prince Albert, Saskatchewan; Riding Mountain, Manitoba; Georgian Bay Islands, Ontario; Cape Breton Highlands, Nova Scotia; and Prince Edward Island. The manner in which these parks were developed indicates that *tourism was still a main objective for the national parks program. Using Depression relief money, the parks branch created new townsites at Prince Albert and Riding Mountain, employing the services of its influential Architecture and Town Planning Division to establish suitable rustic design motifs. The new parks received highways, golf courses, and beach facilities courtesy of the government.

The years 1968–78 were an extraordinary period of expansion for the program as ten new parks came on stream: Kejimkujik, Kouchibouguac, Pacific Rim, Forillon, La Mauricie, Gros Morne, Pukaskwa, Kluane, Nahanni, and Auyittuq. New parks established in settled area caused some social upheaval: properties were expropriated, residents evicted, and traditional activities suppressed. Vitriolic local protests and long-lasting bitterness at places such as Kouchibouguac, New Brunswick, led to the realization that the establishment of new parks needed to be more flexible and sensitive to local concerns. At the same time, established national parks such as Banff experienced unprecedented pressure from developers, both within and outside the organization, to accommodate burgeoning tourist demands. Highways, resorts, campgrounds, and other facilities mushroomed in the parks during this period. The development ethos was challenged at a number of points but nowhere more fiercely than over the proposed scheme to greatly enlarge the ski resort at Lake Louise. Originally approved by Parks Canada, this scheme was cancelled by the minister in 1972 following massive nationwide protests. This action brought about a sea change in the culture of national parks, away from development and towards principles of environmental conservation. Park expansion of the early 1970s identified many new areas for protection, including the North, which had previously had no representation, and in the Prairies. In order to manage the many issues surrounding the expanding system, Parks Canada instituted formal planning studies. The systems planning manual, first issued in 1971, divided Canada into natural regions and 'formalized the goal of establishing a system of national parks representing each of these regions'. Individual park management plans were instituted to balance local concerns with wider public concerns and to address issues of sustainable use and resource management and protection.

In the last decades of the 20th century national parks have continued to face the same issues they confronted at the beginning of the century. New national parks have continued to be established to represent diverse geographic areas—Gwaii Haanas on the Queen Charlotte Islands, Grasslands in Saskatchewan, and Aulavik on Banks Island, Northwest Territories. The South Morseby Agreement, which led to the proclamation of Gwaii Haanas, incorporated a clause stipulating co-management in partnership with the Council of the Haida Nation. The protected heritage area of Grasslands was implemented slowly to allow the gradual phasing out of ranching in the area. Meanwhile, development pressures have continued to haunt popular destinations such as Banff. The Banff–Bow Valley study, completed in 1996, documented serious environmental pressures in the park and raised questions about the ecological integrity of other national parks. The findings of this and subsequent studies influenced the wording of the revised legislation. The National Parks Act of 2001 states that 'maintaining ecological integrity, through the protection of natural resources and natural processes, shall be the first priority of the minister when considering all aspects of the management of parks'. C.J. TAYLOR

National Policy, when capitalized, refers to the protective tariff policy instituted by the Conservative government of Sir John A. *Macdonald in 1879, which centred on whether protection could create a diversified and integrated economy. While protectionism had significant origins in the later 1850s with A.T. *Galt, the demand for the 1879 policy emerged out of the depression of 1873–9 in the aftermath of a failure to win renewed *reciprocity through lobbying, the Treaty of Washington negotiations (1871), and the George *Brown-led trade negotiations of 1874–5. The election of 1878 saw a struggle between the protectionist Conservatives, with their allies in business, commerce, and labour, and those who favoured free trade and a revenue tariff, largely allied with the Reformers (Liberals) led by Alexander *Mackenzie. Using tariff protection to generate nationality and diversified economic growth was progressively abandoned only after the Second World War. While the protective tariff was revised on a number of occasions, with business interests such as the *Canadian Manufacturers' Association having some influence, the chief challenge to its long reign as the major device of economic policy came in the election of 1911. Then the Liberal government of Wilfrid *Laurier, which had resigned itself to keeping the NP after taking office in 1896 despite underlying free-trade predilections, decided to challenge the policy's tenets and pursue a trade agreement with the United States, partly persuaded by hostility to the NP from a now politically vigorous agrarian West. Central Canadian business interests, however, helped the Conservatives to victory, and the NP remained Conservative policy through to R.B. *Bennett.

When in lower case, 'national policy' refers to an integrated system of economic policies intended to foster national growth, but in this instance it is an heuristic device rather than a precisely articulated government policy with integrated legislative presence. The policies most commonly combined are a triumvirate of tariff protectionism, western settlement, and transcontinental railway construction. Historians have stressed the dynamic interrelations of these three elements; late-19th-century politicians and businessmen had a poorer comprehension of these matters and, with few exceptions, tended to partial, self-interested, and pragmatic views. BEN FORSTER

National Research Council. Created in 1916 by the federal government as the Honorary Advisory Council on Scientific and Industrial Research, the NRC played a central role in the construction of a Canadian system of research. In 1917 it created programs of research grants for university researchers and fellowships for graduate students in science and engineering. In order to promote the results of Canadian scientific research it created in 1929 the *Canadian Journal of Research*; after the war, this journal would be replaced by over 15 disciplinary journals, including the *Canadian Journal of Physics*, *Canadian Journal of Botany*, and *Canadian Journal of Chemistry*. The NRC also played an important role in the management of information through the foundation of the National Science Library in 1927, which became the Canadian Institute for Scientific and Technical Information (1974). In 1932 an attractive central research laboratory was opened in Ottawa; active in basic as well as applied science, it grew and diversified its activities over the years as the NRC took charge of new fields of research, notably atomic energy during the Second World War and biotechnology and space science in the 1970s. Major research facilities are now in British Columbia, Saskatchewan, Alberta, Manitoba, Ontario, Quebec, Nova Scotia, and Newfoundland.

The NRC served as an incubator for many of the organizations that now form the basis of the Canadian research system. In the 1950s, the growth of the atomic program led to the creation of Atomic Energy of Canada Ltd; space science led to the creation of the Canadian Space Agency in 1987. Medical research was also covered by NRC until the creation in 1960 of the Medical Research Council. Finally, in 1978, the NRC's role in managing research grants and fellowships was transferred to a new agency, the Natural Sciences and Engineering Research Council. The NRC now concentrates its activities on the management of its own laboratories and on helping industrial research through various programs like the Industrial Research and Application Program, created in 1961. It also continues to play a central role in funding major research facilities like particle accelerators and telescopes. YVES GINGRAS

Native–newcomer relations. The complex history of relations between Natives and newcomers can more easily be understood if organized into several phases: co-operation, coercion, and confrontation.

When Europeans first arrived in Atlantic Canada in the 16th and 17th centuries, they came for reasons that did not threaten the territorial interests of the indigenous peoples. Europeans sought fish, fur, exploration, and evangelization, four goals that required the forbearance, if not the co-operation, of the Native people. Primarily because they desired access to European goods through trade, First Nations in the eastern woodlands tolerated explorers and missionaries. While the initial commercial relationship was not untroubled—epidemic disease and alcohol being two serious consequences—in general relations between Natives and newcomers were co-operative. The co-operative phase arrived at different times in various parts of the country. In the east the beginning occurred in the 1530s, in the western interior in 1670 with the establishment of the *Hudson's Bay Company, on the Pacific in the 1770s when Spaniards landed on the west side of Vancouver Island, and in the far north in the 18th century when whalers began to visit. *Whaling activity intensified in the 19th century in both the western and eastern Arctic.

In the eastern half of the country, the period 1700–1814 was characterized by a distinct phase of the co-operative stage. This was the century-long era of diplomacy and warfare, as British and French—and later Americans and British Canadians—squared off for control of land. Both sides sought First Nations allies, and Indians for their part either remained neutral or chose their allies according to their calculation of their advantage. While this diplomatic-military phase obviously caused conflict, relations between individual First Nations and their European allies were co-operative.

The end of the military relationship ushered in a period of coercion of First Nations by Euro-Canadians, which dominated from the end of the War of 1812 until 1969. The second stage was caused by Euro-Canadian motives and activities that threatened the territorial security of First Nations. Immigrants were interested in levelling forests and creating farms or in developing mining, all enterprises that interfered with the hunting-gathering economies of First Nations. The consequence of this changed relationship was a sharp deterioration in relations between Natives and newcomers, as well as Euro-Canadian initiatives that drastically affected indigenous peoples.

The most important newcomer activities in the coercive phase were land treaties and programs of assimilation and attempted control. Following the procedures of the *Royal Proclamation of 1763, the Crown began to negotiate treaties with First Nations to obtain access to Aboriginal lands for settlers, miners, and other entrepreneurs. The consequence of this treaty making was that First Nations gave up their control of large portions of the Canadian land mass in return for modest annual payments and reserves. Although promised continuing rights to hunt and fish by most treaties, First Nations found the guarantees hollow when newcomer expansion interfered with their harvesting activities. The final indignity was the loss of large portions of prairie reserves by often fraudulent means during the period of heavy settlement, 1896–1913. The consequence of these changes was that, when First Nations' populations soared in the 20th century, their communities lacked a land base to accommodate them.

The other major product of the coercive phase was a series of programs pursued by governments and Christian churches to modify First Nations' behaviour and control them politically. These activities ranged from efforts to change reserve land-holding from communal to individual, controls on reserve band governments, interference with spiritual ceremonies such as the *potlatch, encouragement of loss of Indian identity through *Aboriginal enfranchisement, and coercive educational programs such as *residential schools that were designed to remake Native society. All these aggressive programs failed to achieve either assimilation or control, but they had a long-term demoralizing impact on First Nations.

Although First Nations had always attempted to resist coercion, by approximately 1969 their efforts became sufficiently sustained and successful to justify labelling the period since then the era of confrontation. Political organization was critical to sustaining Native resistance, as was notable in the activities and successes of bodies such as the National Indian Brotherhood. In the period of confrontation First Nations pushed for greater control of their own affairs through self-government and for redress of grievances such as land claims. They also contributed with a spectacular flourishing of Aboriginal art, music, and performance. Although Natives have enjoyed success in this third phase, Canada still finds itself in the confrontation stage. J.R. MILLER

natural disasters. Disasters involve two essential elements: traumatic events and people to experience them. In the absence of the latter, the former go unrecorded and affect no one. An example is a spectacular earthquake that rocked the St Lawrence Valley from Gaspé to Lake Ontario on 5 February 1663. It precipitated landslides, created waterfalls in some streams, obliterated them in others, and levelled a hill near Baie St Paul while creating a small island nearby. Natives and scattered French settlers were terrified, but no deaths or injuries were recorded. At the time it was a curiosity noted in missionary journals; three centuries later it would have been a catastrophe in a densely populated and industrialized area.

Although spectacular in lives lost, major Canadian disasters have seldom altered the nation's history. The worst shipwreck (**Empress of Ireland*, 1,105 fatalities), worst mine accident (Hillcrest, Alberta, 189 fatalities), and worst seal fishery disaster (77 men frozen to death, 173 missing on a vanished steamer), all occurred between 31 March and 19 June 1914, yet none had effects even remotely comparable to the assassination of an Austrian archduke on 28 June of that year. An exception may be the outcome of a failed British invasion in 1711. A fleet commanded by Admiral Sir Hovenden Walker entered the St Lawrence River but lost its bearings in heavy fog on the night of 23 August. Several ships blundered onto rocks near Île aux Oeufs (west of Sept-Îles), drowning an estimated 950 men. The expedition was abandoned, leaving New France to flourish for another two generations.

Some disasters have become the focus of legend and exaggeration. The August gales (24 August 1873) that struck the Maritimes have been blamed for in excess of 1,000 fatalities. Careful analysis of marine losses puts the figure closer to 300, principally fishermen in schooners. Others have inspired authors and playwrights. The 'Yankee Gale' of October 1851, named for the large number of American fishing schooners wrecked near Prince Edward Island, claimed 150 lives. It also became central to the musical *Ballade*, produced many times at the Charlottetown Festival. Modern *weather forecasting has lessened but not eliminated the chance for such tragedies. As recently as 20 June 1959 the fishing fleet of Escuminac, New Brunswick, was hit by a storm that sank 22 boats and drowned 35 men. Ships have not been the only victims. The storm-induced sinking of the offshore oil rig **Ocean Ranger* 265 km east of Newfoundland (15 February 1982) was Canada's first tragedy of this nature; 84 men were lost.

Inland waters have also witnessed fierce storms resulting in marine disasters. Georgian Bay, not noted for wrecks, saw the steamer *Asia* driven onto rocks in a sudden gale (14 September 1882); 92 perished and only 2 passengers survived. On 7 November 1885, fierce storms drove the CPR steamer *Algoma* onto Greenstone Rock, Lake Superior, drowning 48 passengers and crew. Modern media and folksinger Gordon Lightfoot have immortalized the sinking of the *Edmund Fitzgerald* in Lake Superior (10 November 1975, 29 fatalities). Nevertheless, this pales when compared to the storm that swept the Great Lakes on 9–10 November 1913. It claimed four Canadian ships (80 lives) plus nine American vessels (182 lives). A storm in November 1905 had drowned approximately 50 sailors.

Tornadoes feature in several Canadian tragedies. The most deadly was that which ripped into Regina on 30 June 1912. The newly built limestone Legislative Building stood, but the city, still largely a clapboard frontier town, took a beating. Described by some as 'a mammoth elephant's trunk' and by others as 'an awful cornucopia', the storm claimed at least 28 lives immediately; perhaps 13 more later succumbed to injuries. Some, estimating the toll at 65, accused city officials of minimizing losses so as not to discourage a land boom. More recent storms have included the Edmonton tornado of 31 July 1987 ('Black Friday') that killed 27 people, 15 of whom inhabited a trailer park (4 of them members of one family). On 14 July 2000 a campground near Red Deer, Alberta, was struck by a tornado one km wide and packing 300 km/hr winds; 10 people died and scores were injured.

The impact of floods has varied with circumstances. Manitoba's Red River has flooded many times, most notably in 1826, 1948, 1950, and 1997. Snowfalls and the meandering nature of the river allowed forecasting of river levels, and loss of life was minimal. Property damage and personal inconvenience was extensive, however. The 1950 inundations forced the evacuation of more than 100,000 people from Winnipeg. A large floodway bypass around the city prevented a similar occurrence in 1997, but rural areas were still vulnerable; the 1997 floods caused at least $150 million in damages, temporarily drowned 180,000 hectares of land, and led to the evacuation of 30,000 citizens.

Flash floods, usually following unexpected storms, have been far more deadly. Toronto remembers Hurricane Hazel (15 October 1954) but it was water, not wind, that caused the greatest losses. After the storm dumped over 100 mm of rain on Toronto in 12 hours, swelling rivers burst their banks, leading to 81 deaths and extensive property damage. Similarly, unseasonably heavy rains in the Saguenay–Lac St Jean area on 20–21 July 1996 led to the evacuation of 12,000 people and seven deaths. Flooding of a different sort followed an earthquake in the Gulf of St Lawrence (18 November 1929). A 4.6 m tidal wave struck Newfoundland's *Burin Peninsula, sweeping away houses, boats, and fish stages, causing $1 million in damages and killing 27 people.

Avalanches and rock slides have also featured in Canadian disasters. Persons living on Champlain Street, Quebec City, built their homes close to 100 m cliffs. Rock falls warning of the hazards were ignored. Ultimately, a huge rock slide on 17 May 1841 demolished eight homes and killed 32. People continued to live in the area, although smaller slides continued, including one that killed eight. Although authorities resorted to cement, chains, and a retaining wall to prevent further casualties, on 19 September 1889 a murderous rain of boulders flattened homes and warehouses. Many inhabitants were absent, attending two wakes (the community was largely Irish at the time), but the death toll was still 45. The worst rock fall in Canadian history involved *Frank, Alberta, close to Turtle Mountain. For several years coal mine shafts were driven under the mountain, disregarding signs of geological instability. On 29 April 1903 the face of the mountain collapsed, burying much of the town. At least 70 were killed, but transients and newly arrived immigrants may not have been included in this total.

Snow avalanches are usually associated with skiing and mountain-climbing accidents. On 5 March 1910 a total of 62 men were buried alive by such an occurrence. They had been clearing snow from CPR tracks in Rogers Pass, deposited by an earlier snow slide, when a second overwhelmed them. More recently (18 February 1965) an avalanche destroyed a portion of a mining camp 30 km northwest of Stewart, BC, and buried 68 men. Heroic rescue efforts with bare hands and shovels saved 42.

In terms of social impact, the most significant natural disaster in Canadian history was the drought that ravaged the Prairies in 1930–7. Although the nation was spared the famine that often accompanies such events elsewhere, repeated crop failures and topsoil losses impoverished thousands. Many farms were abandoned, some families moving to northerly districts such as the Peace River and others leaving the Prairies altogether. Those who remained were radicalized, launching new political parties (Social Credit, the Co-operative Commonwealth Federation). Municipalities and provinces were bankrupted providing humiliating social assistance known as 'relief'. A royal commission subsequently recommended constitutional changes that would enlarge federal social responsibilities. Author Ralph Allen (*Ordeal by Fire*) observed that the global economic disaster known as the Depression was an abstraction to many, but the drought was 'a constant physical presence'.

Technology has both shielded Canadians from natural forces and made them more vulnerable. Two massive ice storms in eastern Canada—one in January 1947, the other in January 1998—were almost identical in their severity. The former closed down streetcar systems when overhead wires became caked with ice, but most affected persons were inconvenienced rather than put at risk. The 1998 storm, by contrast, wrecked the electrical power grids upon which even rural dwellers had come to depend for water pumps and milking machines. This time the brunt of effects fell outside the cities (which experienced power losses of less than a week, and sometimes less than an hour). The Canadian Armed Forces mobilized troops and aircraft to assist the civil authorities, while power companies across the continent rushed workers and equipment to help restore electricity to the affected areas.

HUGH A. HALLIDAY

natural history. Science, the rational study of nature, forms a long-standing component of the Western heritage. While its perspectives, approaches, and practices have changed over time and place, an analytical interest in nature's workings trace back to ancient Greek philosophy. This 'natural philosophy' tradition can be differentiated from popular interest in nature's animal, vegetable, and mineral kingdoms, or 'natural history', which took root in Renaissance humanism during the 15th century, intensifying during the 17th-century Scientific Revolution. In England, Sir Francis Bacon (1561–1626) articulated a powerful utilitarian ideology touting science to improve the material conditions of life. In this way, the thirst for natural knowledge encompassed the growing interest in natural resources, which motivated overseas exploration and the establishment of colonial empires in Canada and elsewhere. The writings of Canada's earliest explorers, including the reports of Jacques *Cartier and the Jesuit *Relations*, contain detailed natural history descriptions of natural phenomena and resources.

Enlightenment culture in the 18th century adopted these utilitarian claims as a rational basis for the Agricultural and Industrial Revolutions. The much-admired Prussian scientific traveller Alexander von Humboldt (1769–1859) reinforced Bacon's conviction that scientific knowledge could best be accumulated through international co-operation among the widest array of collectors and analysts, legitimizing Britain's 'amateur naturalist' tradition as part of this larger project. Humboldt emphasized exploration as the rational search for discernable patterns in the geographical distribution of natural phenomena, including natural resources, over all the earth, especially in unexplored territories, including Canada.

By the 19th century, the practice of natural history in the Baconian/Humboldtian mode had spread among Britain's educated classes. The end of the Napoleonic Wars in 1815 saw the resurgence of state-supported exploration in search of a *Northwest Passage to the Orient by way of the Canadian Arctic, with voyages staffed by military officers trained in science, including natural history. Three further developments encouraged interest in systematic observations of nature: the Linnaean system of classification brought widespread consensus and a rational overview to the understanding of plants, animals, and minerals; the publication of Gilbert White's *The Natural History of Selborne* (1788) raised interest in the regular observation and recording of nature's local and seasonal variations; and William Paley's *Natural Theology* (1802) added religious justification to natural history as evidence of the existence of God, its Creator, as argued by Design.

British and Loyalist immigrants to British North America shared the appreciation for natural history that came to characterize Victorian culture. In particular, the Scottish Enlightenment conveyed natural history's ideas and values abroad through an army of Scottish-born or -educated settlers and sojourners. Among them, William Dunlop surveyed the Canada Company's Huron Tract during the 1820s by applying his Glasgow scientific training; and Edinburgh-educated David Chisholme, as editor of the *Montreal Gazette*, advocated state-supported scientific inventories of colonial natural resources. The pioneer

Catharine Parr *Traill emulated Gilbert White in her writings and sent plant specimens back to British collectors. Traill and others applied natural history to comprehend an otherwise bewildering new environment, taking comfort that their contributions of New World information enhanced Old World knowledge. They demanded public schools, universities, libraries, and other institutions to 'diffuse useful knowledge', including organized nature walks, collections of specimens, and natural history societies.

Over time, natural history splintered into growing specializations in botany, entomology, zoology, mineralogy, and so on. The publication of Charles Darwin's *The Origin of Species* (1859) marked the end of its heyday, overshadowing the amateur naturalist tradition with an evolutionary paradigm whose internal logic rejected natural history's basic assumptions. Yet the love of nature persists in amateur birdwatchers, specimen collectors, and their respective organizations, all interesting vestiges of this classic natural history tradition. SUZANNE ZELLER

Natural Resource Transfer Agreement. On 15 July 1930 the Canadian government transferred control of the natural resources of the three Prairie provinces (Manitoba, Saskatchewan, and Alberta) to the respective provincial governments. By this time, however, the 'natural resources question' was a long-standing source of friction between Ottawa and the Prairie region.

According to the British North America Act of 1867, control of natural resources lay within provincial jurisdiction. But when the West was opened for development in the 1870s, the dominion government maintained control in order to administer its railway and homestead policies. In the meantime, Manitoba (and Saskatchewan and Alberta in 1905) was provided a subsidy in lieu of the resources. It was understood by all parties that once development was complete, the resources would be transferred to provincial control. By 1912 pressure was building in the West for Ottawa to surrender control of the resources, but controversy arose as to a suitable compensation package. Finally in 1929, after prolonged negotiations with each province individually and the appointment of a royal commission to deal with the compensation issue, an agreement was reached and the resources transferred. ROBERT WARDHAUGH

Nelles, Percy Walker (1892–1951), naval officer. Born in Brantford, Ontario, Nelles joined the first class of Canadian naval cadets in 1908, transferring to the *Royal Canadian Navy upon its founding in 1910. He served overseas with the Royal Navy during the First World War. After briefly commanding HMS *Dragon* in 1929 when the captain took ill, in 1931 Nelles assumed command of HMCS *Saguenay*, the first warship built for Canada. By 1933 he was the youngest commodore in the British Empire and in 1934 became chief of the naval staff. Nelles was the architect of the navy's growth through the late 1930s and its phenomenal wartime expansion from 1939 to 1945. An able if colourless leader, he took on assignments that the RCN was barely able to sustain but that proved essential to Allied victory in the Battle of the *Atlantic. He also used the war to build the basis of a powerful post-war navy. Tired and ill by 1943, Nelles fell out with the naval minister, Angus L. *Macdonald, over the fleet's inability to sink submarines and was sent to London as a liaison officer in January 1944. He retired in January 1945. MARC MILNER

Neutral Yankees of Nova Scotia. By 1775 recently arrived New Englanders constituted approximately two-thirds of the population of the old colony of Nova Scotia. The outbreak of the *American Revolution left many Nova Scotians confused and uncertain. Tradition and loyalty bound them to Britain; economics and family ties pulled them towards New England. Some openly showed support for their fellow colonists, but most maintained an uneasy neutrality—probably a neutrality of action, not of sentiment. BARRY MOODY

New Brunswick. The first peoples arrived in the region after the retreat of the ice circa 7000 BC. Further climate change brought a shift from hunting to woodlands cultures. Hunting, fishing, and gathering sustained the First Nations peoples who penetrated the region's dense forests over 3,000 years ago. While the *Mi'kmaq of the eastern shore moved from coast to interior to coast with the seasons, the Maliseet and Passamaquoddy of the southwest lived in semi-permanent coastal villages, their winter migrations inland likely reflecting disruption wrought by Native–European contact.

Apart from an abortive French settlement on Île Ste-Croix (1604–5) and short-lived settlements along the Saint John River (1690s), in the 17th century the territory that would become New Brunswick remained the preserve of Native peoples and European fur traders. Acadian settlements in peninsular Nova Scotia pushed northward by the 1650s, though scarcely beyond the Chignecto Isthmus at the southern end of the great arc of wilderness separating Acadia from New France.

By the Treaty of Utrecht (1713) the English gained the ill-defined area known as Acadia, but the forests of the interior remained contested territory. When the English expelled the Acadians from their settlements around the Bay of Fundy (1755), many fled to the Saint John Valley and to the coasts of the Gulf of St Lawrence. Most were driven even from there in 1758–9. Planters and merchants from the American colonies and small numbers of British immigrants moved onto the Acadian lands. Returning Acadians settled along the eastern coast. European settlement remained sparse until the end of the *American Revolution (1783) brought such an influx of displaced persons loyal to the British king that Native peoples lost control of territory traditionally theirs. In response to Loyalist demands for land, place, and privilege, New Brunswick was established as a separate colony in 1784. Approximately 14,000 *Loyalists occupied lands in the Saint John and St Croix River valleys. To the north,

Canadiens drifted across the line, settling the Madawaska region, although the boundary with the United States remained in dispute until 1842.

Trade began to boom in 1810, when a shortage of wood led Britain to give preference to timber imported from its North American colonies. After 1815 a burgeoning economy and cheap land attracted waves of immigration from the British Isles, changing the demography of the colony. The poorest immigrants, fleeing famine in Ireland, arrived in 1847, just as Britain began dismantling the preferential tariffs that had promoted the province's seaward economy. Trade soon revived, stimulated by a *reciprocity treaty with the United States (1854). The timber trade fostered shipbuilding (1840–70) and the colony flourished as New Brunswick ships plied world trade routes, and New Brunswickers became cosmopolitan.

Defeated at the polls in 1864, proponents of *Confederation gained the ascendancy when an anti-Confederation government failed to renegotiate the reciprocity treaty. At Confederation, New Brunswick (with 8.1 per cent of the population of the new country) emerged as the 'keystone of the arch', linking the Maritime provinces to Canada. New Brunswickers served as finance ministers during the long Conservative hegemony (1867–74, 1878–96). Confederation and the transition from sail to steam signalled political and economic transformation. The *Intercolonial Railway created new patterns of distribution, dashing hopes that *Saint John, Canada's third largest city at Confederation, would become Canada's winter port. *Moncton, at the hub of the railway system, emerged to challenge the hegemony of Saint John and *Fredericton. The completion of the Intercolonial (1876) coincided with a worldwide recession. Young people began leaving the province, although after 1879 some found work in cotton mills, sugar refineries, and other manufacturing enterprises established by local entrepreneurs taking advantage of Canada's *National Policy. But such initiatives lost momentum as control of finance and industry became centralized in Montreal and Toronto.

After 1900, expansion of staples industries brought the rise of pulp and paper, fish processing, coal mining, oil refining, and, after 1950, potash, zinc, and lead production. Yet between 1881 and 1931 uneven outmigration continued, changing the province's demographic profile, with the Acadian population rising from 18 to 33 per cent. The Depression threw economic, geographic, and cultural differences into stark relief. After the Second World War, government replaced forestry as the leading employer. Like other Canadians, New Brunswickers benefited from federal social programs. Once equalization payments began in the 1950s, the province sought to redress internal disparities between rural and urban, north and south, French and English. The Equal Opportunity Program (1965) brought administrative centralization of services. The Official Languages Act (1969) and Bill 88 (1981) made New Brunswick Canada's only officially bilingual province.

Providing equal opportunity and extending it to the First Nations peoples, the fastest-growing population cohort, posed major challenges for later governments. Optimism about the province's ability to meet such challenges is tempered by the knowledge that a slow growth rate, coupled with the continued export of educated youth, means that with a population of under 730,000 in 2001 (2.4 per cent of the Canadian population), New Brunswick is losing ground. GAIL G. CAMPBELL

New Brunswick Official Languages Act, 1968. To ensure the linguistic survival of French-speaking Acadians in the midst of an English-speaking majority, the Liberal government of L.-J. *Robichaud unanimously passed this statute giving equality of status and equality rights to the French and English languages. In 1981, the government reaffirmed its protection of the unique cultural character of the province, passing An Act Recognizing the Equality of the Two Official Linguistic Communities in New Brunswick. A year later it supported the enshrinement of the equality of the two official languages, and the right to receive government services in either language, in the *Charter of Rights and Freedoms. In 1984, the Poirier-Bastarache Task Force studying the status of both official languages in the province reported that much was lacking. To address the problems of uneven delivery of quality linguistic services, New Brunswick adopted an Official Languages Policy and set up an Office of Official Languages in 1988. In 2002, the Office of Official Languages Commissioner was created and the act was expanded to govern municipalities and bilingual services. DELLA M.M. STANLEY

New Brunswick schools question. Catholics in New Brunswick—including Acadian francophones—believed that under article 93 of the British North America Act the right to provincially funded Catholic schools was guaranteed, because these schools had been established prior to Confederation. In 1871, New Brunswick decided to establish a system of publicly funded, non-confessional schools, signalling the end of provincial grants to confessional schools. The proposal met with resistance from New Brunswick's Catholic minority, because this prohibited any form of religious teaching or symbols in provincially funded schools. Between 1871 and 1874, the issue ran its political course: from discussion and debate within the provincial assembly to legislation (the Common Schools Act, 1871); from requests by New Brunswick's Catholics that the federal government disallow the legislation to a submission to the Judicial Committee of the Privy Council. In the end, the federal government and the Privy Council upheld the right of the province to define publicly funded education.

The debate, however, did not end there, and public outcry against the law was followed by public disobedience. In Acadian communities, where Catholic education was synonymous with French-language education, Catholics employed a variety of strategies to circumvent the law: refusing to pay school taxes, using self-imposed parallel taxes for the maintenance of private Catholic schools, and hiring clerics to teach their children in publicly funded schools, although this was in clear defiance of the law.

In 1875 the situation came to a head in Caraquet. Following weeks of resistance to the law, an armed confrontation between local militia and Acadians resulted in the death of one Acadian, Louis Mailloux, and one militiaman, John Gifford. A number of Acadians were arrested. At this point, the provincial government stepped in with a compromise, which essentially allowed the teaching of catechism in publicly funded schools after regular school hours, as well as the display of religious symbols and the wearing of religious habits. The compromise tacitly strengthened French-language teaching, which had never been a specific target of the 1871 legislation.

PHYLLIS E. LeBLANC

New Caledonia. On seeing the area that would become *British Columbia for the first time, fur trader Simon *Fraser named it 'New Caledonia' because it reminded him of his mother's descriptions of Scotland—a land he had never seen. A separate department of the *Hudson's Bay Company, New Caledonia was amalgamated into a reorganized Columbia Department in 1828, and with the *Fraser River gold rush (1858), it became a colony. Because France possessed a colony of the same name, Queen Victoria dubbed her new creation 'British Columbia', a name the Duke of Newcastle deemed 'neither very felicitous nor very original'. TINA LOO

New Democratic Party. The NDP was created in 1961 as a joint effort by its predecessor the *Co-operative Commonwealth Federation and the *Canadian Labour Congress. Seeking to reinforce the pillar of political rights by creating a foundation for social rights (e.g., public education, health care, and housing) and economic rights (a secure job and safe working conditions), NDP supporters hope to build a more viable democratic society. The NDP believes in a moderate form of *socialism with government planning and public ownership. It seeks to reduce social inequalities by programs such as universal medicare, old-age pensions, unemployment insurance, and affordable child-care. It supports higher taxes on corporations and the rich, while improving workplace conditions for labour. The party opposes Canada's involvement in NATO and NORAD, dominated by the US, and is critical of the high rate of foreign, particularly American, ownership of Canadian industry.

Tommy *Douglas, the first federal NDP leader (1961–71) was the Saskatchewan premier who had launched medicare. He was followed by David Lewis (1971–5), a former CCF national secretary, labour lawyer, and NDP architect. Ed Broadbent was the longest-serving NDP leader (1975–89) and led the party to its greatest levels of support. Under Audrey McLaughlin, a former social worker and the first female leader (1989–95), the party suffered its largest losses. Former Nova Scotia NDP leader Alexa McDonough (1995–2003) guided the federal party to electoral gains in Atlantic Canada. In 2003, Jack Layton, a Toronto city councillor and former president of the Federation of Canadian Municipalities, was elected leader in a direct ballot of party members. Since its creation, the NDP has averaged about 15 per cent of the vote and usually placed third in seats, enough to give voice to left-wing ideas in Parliament, particularly during minority governments. The party has been more successful at the provincial level, where it has formed the government in Saskatchewan (under Tommy Douglas, Woodrow Lloyd, Allan Blakeney, Roy Romanow, and Lorne Calvert), Manitoba (Ed Schreyer, Howard Pawley, and Gary Doer), British Columbia (Dave *Barrett, Mike Harcourt, Glen Clark, and Ujjal Dosanjh), and Ontario (Bob Rae). The federal NDP has suffered in recent years from its association with the unpopularity of some of its provincial governments. Increasingly, the NDP is seen as one of the old parties and is now confronted by the right-wing populist Alliance Party in the West.

Currently, the NDP is trying to rebuild its left-labour coalition while responding to new social movements such as feminism, environmentalism, and anti-globalization. Political activists continue to debate the future electoral prospects for social democracy and the NDP.

ALAN WHITEHORN

New England Planters. The largest immigrant group to settle in the old province of Nova Scotia (now Nova Scotia and New Brunswick) before the arrival of the *Loyalists, the New England Planters settled in the Maritimes between 1759 and 1775 and their descendants remain a significant component of the region's cultural mosaic.

The old English term for a colonist who took up land in new settlements, 'planter' is also used specifically to describe settlers recruited by private and public agencies to occupy areas of the *British Empire. As used in the 18th century, the term was general enough to include everyone from West Indies sugar plantation owners to Newfoundland settlers who conducted a shore-based fishery.

The approximately 8,000 New Englanders who settled in the old province of Nova Scotia were planters in both senses of the word. They were part of a frontier movement typical of the land-hungry Yankees and they were specifically recruited by Nova Scotia's governor Charles Lawrence to settle the lands recently vacated by the deported Acadians and still claimed by the indigenous *Mi'kmaq and Maliseet. Through proclamations issued in 1758 and 1759, and circulated widely in New England, Lawrence offered free land and attractive terms, including freedom of religion for dissenting Protestants, an elected assembly, English legal institutions, and exemption from land taxes for ten years. Indeed, the timing of the introduction of representative institutions in the colony (the first in the area of present-day Canada) was in large measure due to the reluctance of the liberty-loving New Englanders to settle in the area without them. In the spring of 1759 advance parties arrived in Nova Scotia to see what was on offer and by 1760 ships carrying New England immigrants, their effects, and in some cases even their dismantled houses, could be found in many harbours along the south shore of Nova Scotia and around the Bay of Fundy. The tide of New England immigration receded as the western frontier reopened for settlement in the late 1760s, but by that time western areas of old Nova Scotia had become a new New England.

Technically, the New Englanders cannot lay exclusive claim to the term planter, even in the Nova Scotia context. Yet the term has stuck to the New Englanders, in part because they are difficult to distinguish from other English-speaking immigrants, who are often lumped together under the unhelpful term 'pre-Loyalist'. The Planters arrived too early to be described as Loyalists, but they became Loyalists by default when Nova Scotia remained in British hands following the American Revolution. In recent years scholars, genealogists, and those interested in public history have revived interest in the New England Planters, whose impact on their Maritime homeland and further afield is evident in the fact that their descendants include major educators, theologians, inventors, industrialists, social reformers, politicians, and at least two Canadian prime ministers (Charles *Tupper and Robert *Borden). MARGARET CONRAD

Newfoundland. Until contact with Europeans in the 15th century AD, various prehistoric cultures in this area, beginning with the Maritime Archaic, bridged the gap with the people of the historic era—the Innu and Inuit of Labrador and the *Beothuk of Newfoundland. *Norse explorations of the 11th century led to no colonization. John *Cabot's voyage of discovery in 1496–7 produced little immediate interest as the English preferred fishing in Icelandic waters. The Basques were the first Europeans to exploit local marine resources through whaling and cod fishing. Although France, Spain, and Portugal had migratory fishing fleets in Newfoundland waters by the mid-16th century, the English became the dominant imperial power. English official proprietary colonial adventures in the 17th century failed: mercantile and aristocratic backers found Newfoundland's ecology unsupportive of other commercial activity except fishing. By allowing only a naval government and refusing colonial recognition, English policy favoured West Country merchants' migratory fisheries, although limited settlement was accepted to counterbalance the French at *Plaisance.

The Innu and Inuit survived contact by developing trade with Europeans. The Treaty of Utrecht (1713) ended the French presence, except for fishing rights in coastal waters from Cape Bonavista to Pointe Riche. West Country merchants relied on settlers and overwintering fishing servants to protect their seasonally abandoned premises from the Beothuk, who pilfered them for iron and nets. Consequent conflict led the Beothuk to retreat into the interior, where resources were insufficient to maintain their population; they became extinct by 1829. French fishers continued to use the south and west coasts, and some settlement ensued. Mi'kmaq from Cape Breton settled at Conne River.

As a result of the loss of American supplies during the American Revolution, the fishery relied more on local supplementary farming; consequently British merchants and officials accepted more settlement. The Napoleonic wars and the War of 1812 ended the migratory fishery, but produced a boom in fish prices. This prompted Irish immigration and the expansion of a resident fishery supplemented by a spring seal hunt. The end of the wars saw the boom and immigration collapse. At the same time, colonial reformers in *St John's, Harbour Grace, and Carbonear pressed for more self-government. The result was a representative House of Assembly in 1832 and *responsible government in 1855.

Despite some interest in Confederation in the 1860s as a means of economic diversification, Newfoundland decided to pursue its own railway development, interior resource development (including gaining control over the *French Shore by 1904), and protected manufacturing. The attempt to diversify failed and increased public debt by the eve of the First World War. Wartime expenses aggravated Newfoundland's financial problems, even as the military tragedy of *Beaumont Hamel stimulated national pride. Outport fishing people supported the war effort less than did people in St John's. Indeed, controversy among fishers about the *Fishermen's Protective Union's support for conscription in 1917 helped undermine the FPU as Newfoundland's only significant third-party and populist political movement.

Newfoundland's Great Depression began with collapses in post-war fish prices. Financial problems and scandals about officials' misuse of funds destabilized politics in the 1920s. Mounting unemployment and government retrenchment reinforced the 1924 Hollis–Walker inquiry's suggestion of rampant political corruption. Riots over cuts in relief spending in 1932 precipitated a crisis. The British government assisted the Newfoundland government on condition of an external investigation by the *Amulree Commission, which recommended the suspension of responsible government. Newfoundland would be governed by a British-appointed commission composed of three British and three Newfoundland commissioners, and a British-appointed governor.

The *Commission of Government (1934–49) was unable to revitalize the economy, although the Second World War brought relief through employment prompted by American and Canadian military-base construction. In 1946 the commission arranged for Newfoundlanders to elect delegates to a *National Convention, which would debate the country's future. J.R. *Smallwood led the fight for Confederation within the National Convention, making it the cause of fishing people against the old commercial and political dominance of St John's business interests. Despite stiff opposition from a St John's-based Responsible Government League, and with British and Canadian assistance, Confederation won by a narrow margin in a referendum in 1948.

Newfoundland became Canada's tenth province on 31 March 1949. As premier, Smallwood advocated modernization and improved living standards based on federally funded social programs, but his small-scale manufacturing schemes of the early 1950s failed. Smallwood turned to industrial staple projects characterized by natural-resource rights giveaways and substantial provincial financial support. To court foreign investment, his government became more hostile towards organized labour, notably in the premier's battles with the International Woodworkers of America, 1956–9. Smallwood's fisheries-modernization plans recommended centralizing the industry in a few large communities. Rural resettlement to these communities would supposedly make it cheaper to deliver public services, while assembling labour pools to attract other industry. Between 1954 and 1975, *outport resettlement produced rural dislocation and dependence on government assistance, but little economic development.

Smallwood fell to Progressive Conservatives' promises of greater democracy and provincial control over natural resources under Frank Moores in 1972. Moores's successor, Brian Peckford, inspired neo-nationalists with his fight for provincial control over offshore oil, renegotiation of the *Churchill Falls hydroelectric-development agreement, and promise of rural revitalization. The failure of these fights, a deepening economic recession, and growing public debt led the electorate back to the Liberals in 1989, under the strong federalist and fiscally conservative leadership of Clyde Wells and his successor, Brian Tobin. Roger Grimes followed as Liberal premier in 2001 when Tobin returned to federal politics, but was defeated by Conservative Danny Williams in 2003.

Throughout the 1970s and 1980s provincial and federal governments encouraged more investment in *fisheries. This expanded capacity, in combination with the expansion of the 200-mile limit and foreign fishing in the late 1970s through the 1990s, contributed to the present *cod moratorium in the east-coast Canadian fishing industry. Offshore oil development fuels economic growth, but Newfoundland's economy continues to be based on limited industrial-staple extraction and overcapacity in fisheries. SEAN CADIGAN

Newfoundland loggers' strike. In 1956, the International Woodworkers Association sent H. Landon Ladd to Newfoundland to organize a local. Ladd's efforts quickly met with success and included loggers from existing unions. In 1958, the IWA was certified as a bargaining agent, but Ladd's strident militancy in asserting better working conditions and higher wages for loggers raised concerns with both Premier Joseph *Smallwood's government and the province's two pulp and paper companies. When he failed to negotiate a contract with one of the companies, Ladd called a loggers' strike effective 31 December 1958. Smallwood considered Ladd a serious threat to his political dominance and the economic viability of the forestry industry and, in a province-wide radio address on 12 February 1959, appealed to local patriotism in branding the union a subversive outside influence. The speech had the desired effect: the IWA became increasingly unpopular and the death of a police officer on the strikers' picket line convinced Ladd that the loggers' only alternative was a return to work. In a general election held later in 1959 Smallwood easily won re-election and had legislation enacted decertifying the IWA. Loggers then joined a government-sponsored union.

MELVIN BAKER AND AIDAN MALONEY

Newfoundland National Government. Formed in July 1917, the Newfoundland National Government was a coalition of the People's Party administration led by Sir Edward Morris, in power since 1913, and the two opposition parties, the Liberals and the Fishermen's Protective Union. Up to this point, the war effort had been the responsibility of the Newfoundland Patriotic Association, a non-partisan, non-denominational body that had established the Newfoundland Regiment and orchestrated a remarkable volunteer effort. However, by 1917 the NPA was unable to maintain a sufficient level of voluntary recruitment and was widely criticized. At the same time, the Morris government was becoming unpopular, and faced probable electoral defeat. Morris therefore postponed elections until after the war and engineered a national government that contained a new Ministry of Militia to replace the NPA. From January 1918 the government was led by W.F. Lloyd. It addressed shipping and food-supply problems, and legislated conscription, which was widely unpopular outside St John's. Income and profits taxes were imposed for the first time.

By the spring of 1919 old political antagonisms were beginning to surface, and on 20 May the National Government collapsed when, in a bizarre scene, Lloyd seconded a motion of no confidence in his own administration. In the difficult years that followed, Newfoundland would arguably have been better served had the coalition survived; instead it experienced political fragmentation and uncertain leadership.

JAMES K. HILLER

Newfoundland Outport Nursing and Industrial Association. NONIA was founded in April 1924 to help place qualified English nurse-midwives in outports along Newfoundland's coast, where there were few medical facilities or doctors. Lady Elsie Allardyce, wife of the governor, assembled a committee of the elite citizens of St John's to garner support for her plan: outport women would produce local handicrafts and their sale would contribute to the salary of a community nurse. Drawing on a similar program in the Scottish isles, NONIA provided nursing services and employment in several dozen communities in the 1920s and 1930s. Moreover, knitting, weaving, and mat-hooking activities spread far beyond those communities seeking to support a nurse, reaching up to 50 communities. By 1934, however, only eight nurses remained and the new *Commission of Government took over responsibility for the nursing service. Questions immediately arose as to the future of the handicraft work. Lady Walwyn, wife of the governor and president of NONIA in 1935, worked with manager/designer Marguerite Beckett (1931-40) to revitalize the work and the number of centres rebounded. In pre-Confederation Newfoundland, NONIA not only provided health care but also contributed to economic self-sufficiency and the preservation of local craft traditions. By 1956 NONIA became involved in the wholesale market and in 1965 incorporated the crafts produced by the Jubilee Guilds and later other craft producers. LINDA KEALEY

Newfoundland Railway. In 1881, the Newfoundland government chartered the Newfoundland Railway Company to build a railway across the island. Over the next three years, the American-owned firm completed about 100 km from St John's to Harbour Grace, Conception Bay; by then it was bankrupt. In the late 1880s the government built a branch-line to Argentia, Placentia Bay. In the 1890s, it reorganized the company and chartered Robert G. Reid of Montreal to extend the line to Port-aux-Basques in exchange for generous land grants, a task he completed by 1897. Over the next quarter century, the heavily subsidized, yet indebted, Newfoundland Railway remained a recurrent, hot political issue. In 1923, disenchanted with the Reid monopoly, Newfoundland bought the rail and steamship services. It operated the system, including the famous 'Newfie Bullet' renowned for its slow runs over the curvy narrow-gauge rail-line, until 1949, when *Canadian National took over the system and introduced diesel locomotives and modern rolling stock. In 1970, CN discontinued trans-island passenger service and in the late 1980s ended rail service altogether. A.A. DEN OTTER

Newfoundland referenda, 1948. In 1934, hit hard by the Great Depression, Newfoundland gave up self-government in favour of administration by a British-appointed *Commission of Government. The coming of war in 1939 revived the Newfoundland economy and led the British to prepare for constitutional change. In December 1943 the United Kingdom announced that, after victory in Europe, it would provide Newfoundlanders with machinery to decide their own constitutional future. In 1945 the British announced that a *National Convention would be elected in Newfoundland to advise them on constitutional choices to be decided by referendum. Prior to this announcement, they had reached an understanding with Canada that the two countries would work behind the scenes to promote Newfoundland's entry into Confederation. The British favoured this option but could achieve it only through the ballot box.

The National Convention was duly returned and its members, all male, began meeting on 11 September 1946. The convention sent delegations to London and Ottawa, and the Canadian government sent draft terms of union for its consideration. Ultimately, the convention recommended the following referendum choices: 'Responsible Government as it existed prior to 1934' or 'Commission of Government'. The British, who had carefully kept the last word to themselves, decided that the referendum would feature three choices, given in law as follows: 'Commission of government for a period of five years', 'Confederation with Canada', or 'Responsible government as it existed in 1933'. They justified the inclusion of the second option on the democratic ground that the issues involved in union with Canada had been 'sufficiently clarified' to enable the people to pronounce on them. Given three choices, the British ruled that a second referendum would have to be held if a first did not produce a majority among those voting. The second ballot would drop the option with the lowest number of votes in the first round.

In the hard campaign that followed, Joseph Roberts *Smallwood and F. Gordon Bradley led the forces for confederation. Peter *Cashin was the heavyweight champion of responsible government. The St John's businessman Chesley A. Crosbie campaigned for economic union with the United States but faced the difficulty that this option was not on the ballot. In reality, Washington had no reason to undermine the policy of the United Kingdom and Canada. When the issue was put to the electors on 3 June 1948, the result was 69,400 for responsible government, 64,066 for confederation, and 22,311 for commission of government. This outcome necessitated a second referendum, held on 22 July 1948. In this vote 78,323 supported confederation and 71,334 responsible government. Following the negotiation of final terms of union Newfoundland became a province of Canada on 31 March 1949. PETER NEARY

***Newfoundland* *sealing disaster**. In 1914, the aging SS *Newfoundland*, under Westbury Kean, took part in the annual seal hunt. The owners had removed its wireless to save money, but Westbury's father, Abram, commanding the newer SS *Stephano*, had arranged to signal Westbury with his ship's derrick when seals were spotted. On 30 March, with no seals on board, Westbury was relieved to see the signal from the *Stephano*, and the following morning ordered his men, under second hand (first mate) George Tuff, to proceed to his father's ship, seven miles away. Westbury assumed that his men would stay on Abram's steamer overnight as there was a snow storm brewing, but instead, Abram carried the men to the seals and ordered them to return to their own ship after the kill. This miscommunication proved fatal. The men became lost in the storm and when rescuers found them 53 hours later, 77 out of 132 men had already died; one more succumbed in hospital. SHANNON RYAN

New France. New France first appears as a place name in Gerolomo da Verrazano's 1529 world map, due north of the waters beyond the outer banks of North Carolina, which the Italian mapmaker believed to be the Pacific. Norman and Breton cod fishers had reached the North Atlantic coast earlier, but official French interest began in 1524, with the Verrazano brothers' royally sanctioned entry into the race for the East. Their tantalizing *Nova Gallia* promised riches and easy access to those of Asia.

For the next two and a half centuries, beginning with Jacques *Cartier's 1534 voyage up the St Lawrence River, French kings claimed the largest empire in North America, typically after seeking apparent, ambiguous approval from Native populations. Proprietary *fur trade companies first established year-round settlements in peninsular

Nova Scotia or *Acadia (intermittently held between 1604 and 1713) and Canada (roughly today's province of Quebec, 1608–1760). By the late 17th century fur traders and explorers had reached Hudson Bay, circled the Great Lakes, and found the Mississippi's mouth. New France contracted after the Treaty of Utrecht in 1713, when Louis XIV ceded Acadia, Hudson Bay, and his Newfoundland colony of *Plaisance (established 1670) to Britain. But with the founding of Louisiana in 1699, and *Île Royale (Cape Breton Island) in 1713, French spheres of influence arched strategically around British North America, from the Gulf of St Lawrence to the Gulf of Mexico. By the mid-18th century Frenchmen had reached Santa Fe and the foothills of the Rockies. Even so, geographic ignorance and Native control beyond enclaves of French settlement kept New France's boundaries ill-defined and contested.

Part administrative fiction, the *royal colony of New France encompassed separately run colonies, far-flung posts, and connecting rivers, theoretically under the aegis of a single governor general, and, after 1663, an intendant, stationed at Quebec. In practice, however, outside Canada high-ranking officials within the naval department reported directly to France. State sovereignty was exercised most effectively over colonial towns and rural farmsteads and was legitimized with the help of counter-Reformation clergy, who preached respect for worldly authorities and social hierarchies.

Few left France, the most populous European country, for New France. Protestants, in particular, were officially barred from this Catholic colony. Even Canada, home to some 80 per cent of New France's population, attracted only about 27,000 migrants (mainly male indentured servants and soldiers) between 1600 and 1760. Just a third would stay. Total migration to maritime regions numbered in the hundreds. Roughly 7,000 French men and women travelled to Louisiana between 1717 and 1721; slaves of African origin arrived in similar numbers between 1718 and 1731. In both cases, only half survived. On the eve of the Seven Years' War (1756–63), fewer than 100,000 colonists lived in New France, mainly in the St Lawrence Valley, Illinois Country, and Lower Mississippi, as well as at Détroit on Lake Erie, and in the fortified town of *Louisbourg on Île Royale. Although confined to the eastern seaboard, British North Americans outnumbered them roughly 20 to one.

New France's trade was equally modest. As a group, Canadian peasants grew enough wheat and peas to pay tithes and seigneurial dues to their social superiors, and to feed themselves, soldiers, fur traders, fishermen, and urban consumers, leaving only a modest surplus for export in years of good harvests. Canada's 18th-century fur exports and Île Royale's dried cod each hovered around 2 million livres. Louisiana tobacco fitted into a single vessel. The costs of colonial rule always exceeded state revenues collected from such activities. From the late 1740s onward, government military needs tended to crowd out private shipping and compromised the harvests of those increasingly taxed with militia duty. Frequent war reinforced the harshness of absolutist rule, even as it created opportunities for colonial suppliers.

Although epidemics killed over half the indigenous population in New France, as elsewhere, Bourbon monarchs could never tax or impose their laws on the survivors, who still outnumbered Frenchmen and on whom New France's fur trade and security depended. Not even those baptized by *Jesuits in the St Lawrence Valley's Native villages, such as Kahnawake, could be treated as subjects. New France's intendant legalized the use of Native slaves within Canada in 1709, but the system remained tributary to Native captive-taking traditions. Overall, the Crown's envoys were enmeshed in more or less hegemonic alliances that had to be renewed constantly according to Native cultural norms. In exchange for offering appropriate presents, and for mediating conflicts, including those arising among Native villagers, colonial officials gained trading partners and essential military allies. Ultimately, such alliances lent credibility, at least in Europe, to France's unwieldy imperial claims.

War was frequent in New France. Between 1609 and the *Great Peace of Montreal in 1701, the French were embroiled in conflicts with the *Iroquois. From 1689 onward, European dynastic struggles pitted French colonists against British North Americans. When Frenchmen failed to act as generous mediators, whether from ignorance or an urge to coerce, their own alliances cracked. Unwillingly at war against the Fox between 1712 and 1740, the French were also attacked in 1729 by the Natchez, and in the 1740s by the Miamis. Repaired alliances were crucial to New France's early victories in the Seven Years' War, which overlapping claims to the Ohio Valley helped ignite. Ultimately, the unprecedented resources channelled into North America by William Pitt after 1757 prevailed. By the Treaty of Paris in 1763, France ceded most of New France to Britain, reserving trans-Mississippian claims for Spain, and the small islands of *St-Pierre and Miquelon for itself, thus retaining an enduring national stake in the valuable North Atlantic fisheries.

CATHERINE DESBARATS

New Left. The 1960s was a time of protest that was sufficiently novel and pervasive, in terms both of issues and countries, to garner the name New Left. The New Left was the 'third way' of its time, rejecting the old left paradigms of communism and social democracy as repressive and hopelessly bureaucratic. It thought electoral politics was a spent force and that what was needed was extra-parliamentary politics centred on organizing people and communities and engaged in direct action. Very much a politics of youth, it flourished on university campuses. By the late 1950s and early 1960s politics was spilling out on the streets. The risk of nuclear annihilation at the height of the Cold War led to Ban the Bomb protests and the activist Student Union for Peace Action. Canadians went south to join Americans demonstrating for civil rights for Blacks. Two long-lasting movements of fundamental importance, those for women's liberation and the environment, took on fresh significance that has carried down to the present day. The issue that came to dominate the 1960s was the American war in Vietnam; the turmoil it created on American campuses spread to Canada with teach-ins and anti-war protests. Students organized the Canadian Union of Students and, supported by a minority of faculty, pressed for democratization of the universities. New Left students in the 1960s later became professors, giving impetus to the scholarship of dissent. Two radical left magazines that first appeared in the 1960s have survived, *Canadian Dimension* and *This Magazine Is About Schools* (now *This Magazine*). The Canadian content of the New Left is to be found in demands inside Quebec for Quebec's independence and support for that in the rest of Canada. MELVILLE WATKINS

newspapers. This medium developed later in Canada than in Great Britain or the United States. Vast distances, a harsh climate, rugged terrain, and a sparse population initially limited the spread of the printing press. Yet, these factors made the development of this communications medium a pressing necessity during Canada's nation-building period.

Historians debate whether there was a printing press in New France, but certainly there was no newspaper. It was left to immigrant printers from the American colonies to start the first English-language newspapers. In 1752, two Boston printers, Bartholomew Green and John Bushell, imported the first printing press to Nova Scotia and started the *Halifax Gazette*. Almost immediately after the British Conquest, two Philadelphia printers brought a press into Quebec, and, with the help of their French-speaking apprentice, the bilingual *Quebec Gazette* was born in 1764. Slowly other small four-page news sheets came into being elsewhere; their content mostly reflected the official needs and deeds of the governors of the British colonies. An exception was the Montreal *Gazette du Commerce et Littéraire*, which was founded in 1778 by Fleury Mesplet, a protege of Benjamin Franklin, in a failed attempt to persuade the French-speaking population to join the American Revolution. By the early 19th century, the *Gazette* became solely an English-language publication and today vies with the *Hartford Courant* as the oldest continuously publishing newspaper in North America.

The end of the War of 1812 spurred economic development, immigration, and the growth of newspapers. A more feisty, opinionated press appeared. Journalists debated the form of British rule, the rights of French Canadians, and the merits of *'responsible government'. Often editor-publishers were politicians, as was the case with William Lyon *Mackenzie (*Colonial Advocate*) and Étienne *Parent (*Le *Canadien*). These two men and other journalists were in the forefront of the failed *Rebellions of 1837. In the papers of these men too we see the origins of the popular perception that the press had a civic function—providing a public forum for different political opinions.

Canada had its first freedom-of-the-press judicial case in 1835. Joseph *Howe, editor of the *Novascotian*, published an anonymous letter accusing the governor of corruption. The British Crown charged Howe with seditious libel, a treasonous offence. Howe successfully defended himself, establishing the Canadian precedent of truth being a defence against libel and also the right of a jury to determine guilt or innocence. Howe's example furthered the popular idea of the newspaper as a defender of the rights of people against arbitrary government authority.

A daily newspaper first appeared in 1833 in Montreal. Population growth in the late 1840s and 1850s led to a permanent, and extremely partisan, daily press in Montreal, Toronto, and smaller cities. At Confederation, virtually every one of the country's 291 newspapers allied themselves with a political party. Not only editorials but news stories openly championed party causes. When the party won power, allied newspapers benefited from the patronage of government printing, advertising contracts, and even the release of government news.

Yet, as Canada industrialized, change was coming to the newspaper-publishing world. George *Brown, the founder of the Toronto *Globe*, was a transitional figure in the development of a more business-oriented and thus independent news press. Brown was a prominent partisan politician and a 'Father of Confederation', and his newspaper became required reading even for people who hated his political views. Constant innovations at the *Globe* meant that it printed more news faster than its competitors. It was the first to use a powered press, the telegraph, and other technological developments. Brown successfully gambled that such investments, more features and reporters, would provide greater circulation, resulting in more advertising revenue.

By the 1870s, a new breed of publisher, such as Hugh Graham (*Montreal Star*), John Ross Robertson (*Toronto Telegram*), and later Trefflé Berthiaume (*La Presse*), founded newspapers modelled on the American 'penny press'. Partisan politics gave way to a greater emphasis on local news—crime, scandal, and corruption—often reported in a sensational manner. Entertainment began to supplant the informative and persuasive purpose of news reporting. Changing the news emphasis forced publishers to pay as much attention to the financial bottom line as to editorial content. The features, technological innovations, increasingly specialized journalists, and printing technicians necessary to persuade more people to buy a newspaper were expensive. With the price of newspapers dropping significantly, *advertising edged out subscriptions to provide eventually 80 per cent of pubishers' revenues. Newspaper publishers became businessmen and made their publications independent of control by political parties.

The largest of the big city dailies provided their proprietors with fame, fortune, and influence. Publishers such as the *Toronto Telegram*'s Robertson and the *Toronto Star*'s Joseph Atkinson influenced politics from choosing mayors to advising prime ministers. The *Montreal Star*'s Graham parlayed his clout to become, literally, Canada's first press baron, Lord Atholstan, in 1908.

The content of newspapers became increasingly diverse. To capture different groups of readers newspapers added more features, including serialized novels, science columns, sports news, women's pages, and comics. These newspapers were more reflective of the population at large. In addition, an ethnic press emerged during the early 20th century to serve Canada's broadening social mosaic. By 1900, the Canadian newspaper world was a lively place where even small cities had several competing papers. But as newspaper readership became saturated, competition grew fierce. Helped by the expanding postal service and railroads, newspaper publishers invaded other locales.

Other competitive techniques were used. The Southam family began Canada's first chain of newspapers. First expanding from Hamilton to Ottawa (the *Citizen*) near the turn of the century, the family added another three dailies in the West by 1911. The First World War caused more consolidation and concentration in the industry. The overall number of newspapers dropped from a high of 138 French and English dailies to a low of 90 in 1940. This situation improved somewhat with the post-war boom. The Southam chain continued to expand. Other chains formed to meet the challenge, such as the Federated Press and the Thomson organization. The number of single-newspaper cities rose, and by the late 20th century the independent daily was swallowed by larger corporate entities. Leading the way was Roy Thomson, later Lord Thomson of Fleet, who added newspapers to a chain of radio stations and other properties from the late 1930s.

The issue of concentration of ownership and the decrease in independent editorial voices worried the public. In 1970, the government established the Special Senate Committee on the Mass Media, better known as the Davey Committee, which concluded that 'diverse and antagonistic sources' of information, central to free and open debate, were threatened. However, its recommendations to halt concentration were never carried out. Ten years later, a new round of consolidation occurred when the Thomson organization and Southam Press eliminated the *Winnipeg Tribune* and the *Ottawa Journal*, respectively, to create monopolistic local markets. The ensuing uproar caused the government to set up the Royal Commission on Newspapers (Kent Commission) to study the implications of the newspaper industry being in progressively fewer hands. None of its recommendations to safeguard a diversity of opinion were acted on either.

Concentration has become more intense not only in the daily field but also among community weeklies, the 'underground' press of the late 1960s, and the 'alternative' free press of the late 20th century. In a bewildering series of developments around the turn of the second millennium, such dominant newspaper establishments as Thomson Newspapers and the Hollinger chain (led by Conrad Black) divested themselves of their holdings. Today most Canadian (French and English) newspapers are controlled by non-journalistic enterprises such as CanWest Global, BCE, Quebecor, and the Power Corporation.

MINKO SOTIRON

See also JOURNALISM.

Niagara Falls. It is difficult to imagine a pre-tourist era of Niagara's history, yet the tourist industry at Niagara Falls dates from only the early 19th century. Tourist entrepreneur William Forsyth built Niagara's first hotel on the Canadian side of the falls in 1822. He also promptly fenced in his property, restricting the magnificent view to paying hotel guests. The battle between commerce and nature has been raging ever since. Canals, railways, and bridges brought more tourists in the 1830s and 1840s, though the industrial potential of the waterfall was the motivation for most of this investment. For much of the 19th century manufacturing plants and tourists jostled more or less comfortably along the Niagara River. The waterfall was the main attraction, but sideshows such as cave tours, steamboat rides, museums, and bathing palaces have been part of the tourist landscape since the beginning. Spectacles, promotional gimmicks, and a stream of celebrity tourists—from Charles Dickens and Sarah Bernhardt to Oscar Wilde—made the falls an icon, a canonical sight of the New World.

Everyone agreed that the waterfall was sublime, but not all visitors went away happy. It seemed to many that 'the very pick of the touts and rascals of the world had assembled here', as one visitor put it in the 1860s. By the 1870s the fashionable shrine to nature resembled a rowdy carnival: working-class excursionists frolicked next to Native souvenir-sellers and Black tourguides, all treating the waterfall like a gigantic aquatic toy. The wrong sort of commerce had established itself, and through the 1880s governments in the United States and Canada stepped in to save Niagara from itself. The famous landscape architect Frederick Olmsted was hired to design parkland surrounding the waterfall, and the carnival was pushed some discreet distance away, where it remains.

The 20th century witnessed several developments, especially automobile travel and paid vacations, that entrenched Niagara as a mass tourist destination. Mass travel exploded after the Second World War, but Niagara possessed two geographical advantages: the waterfall and proximity to post-war North America's industrial heartland. After the Marilyn Monroe film *Niagara* was released in 1953, 13 million people trooped to the falls. Never again was Niagara to feel the spotlight quite so intensely. By the late 1960s Niagara's star had faded. Its status—two centuries in the making—as a honeymoon destination seemed a bit antiquated in the sexual climate of the 1960s, and mass airline transit gave vacationing North Americans plenty of options. Yet Niagara remains tremendously popular with people from other parts of the world, and periodic schemes to revitalize the tourist industry—most recently through a casino—suggest that Niagara's ability to reinvent itself will continue.

KAREN DUBINSKY

Nile Voyageurs. Throughout the 19th century Canadian politicians were more than happy to rely upon Britain as the ultimate guarantor of Canadian security. The reciprocal idea, that Canada was obliged to help the Mother Country defend its empire, was less welcome. Thus,

when British Major-General Charles Gordon was besieged at Khartoum by the radical Muslim forces led by the Mahdi early in 1884 and London looked to Canada to assist in his relief by providing experienced boatmen, Prime Minister John A. *Macdonald wanted no part of the 'wretched business' because, he believed, the fundamental security of Britain was not at stake. On the other hand, he could not refuse altogether. Accordingly, with government approval (but not financial support) the governor general, Lord Lansdowne, was able to recruit 386 backwoodsmen (including Aboriginal volunteers from the Six Nations) to serve under Canadian militia officers (Lt Col Fred Denison, of Toronto, was in command) as a paramilitary component of Gen. Sir Garnet Wolseley's relief force. Paid by the British, the 'voyageurs' spent six months moving Wolseley's boats up the Nile. They arrived in Khartoum on 26 January 1885, two days after the Mahdists had overrun the city and killed Gordon.
STEPHEN J. HARRIS

nine-hour movement. A shorter work day was a major aspiration of 19th-century craftsmen and labourers. Gaining prominence internationally in the 1860s, the movement first appeared in organized form in Canada in 1872. Beginning in Hamilton, the demand for the nine-hour day (some workers were expected to toil 12 hours and more) spread quickly to Toronto and Montreal. Echoes of the movement were heard in small-town Ontario, and as far east as Halifax. Nine Hour Leagues were formed, an articulate labour leadership emerged, and union and non-union workers were brought together. Strikes broke out, most notably in the printing trades in Toronto. In May 1872 workers formed the Canadian Labor Protective and Mutual Improvement Association. With Great Western Railway mechanic James Ryan at their head, Hamilton workers led a protest procession of 1,500 through city streets on 15 May, demanding shorter hours for all. As employers resisted and many workers urged reliance on paternalist political figures in the mainstream Grit and Tory parties, the fight to win the shorter working day foundered and died. But it led to some ambiguous legislation, widely perceived as establishing the beginnings of collective bargaining rights for Canadian workers (the Trade Unions Act of 1872), and prefaced the formation of wider organization in the Canadian Labour Union of the later 1870s, a forerunner of the Trades and Labour Congress of Canada.
BRYAN D. PALMER

Nonsuch. The *Nonsuch*, with French fur trader Médard Chouart, Sieur des Groseilliers aboard, sailed from England in June 1668. The voyage was sponsored by Prince Rupert, a cousin of King Charles I, to exploit the fur-trade potential of the *Hudson Bay hinterland (a second ship, the *Eaglet*, carrying Pierre *Radisson, had been forced to turn back). The crew spent the winter of 1668–9 at the mouth of the Rupert River on James Bay. In October 1669 the ship returned to England loaded with furs, and on 2 May 1670 a royal charter was granted to the 'Company of Adventurers of England Trading into Hudson Bay', or the *Hudson's Bay Company. In 1968 a full-scale replica of the *Nonsuch* was built in England and installed at the Manitoba Museum of Man and Nature.
ROBERT J. COUTTS

Nootka Sound Convention, 28 October 1790. A legal agreement between Britain and Spain ending a bitter dispute over territorial rights and commercial access to the Pacific. The dispute stemmed from an obscure incident on Vancouver Island when a Spanish naval commander, Estevan Martínez, instructed by the Viceroy of Mexico to occupy Nootka Sound to safeguard Spain's imperial claims and a lucrative trade in sea otter pelts, in 1789 arrested three British trade vessels as legal prizes for trading in Spanish waters. When the news reached London, a diplomatic row ensued. At the core of the dispute was a centuries-old disagreement between these two imperial powers about the legal foundations of empire. The Spanish claimed they had exclusive rights to the entire Pacific littoral by virtue of numerous treaties, royal proclamations, and acts of discovery from 1493 to the 1770s. The British, relying heavily on the claim made by a British trader, John Meares, that he had occupied land in and around Nootka Sound before Martínez, asserted that occupation was the only principle upon which questions of territorial jurisdiction could be based. Neither party granted Native people a stake in the law of nations. Faced with the possibility of a disastrous war against a militarily superior Britain, Spain capitulated over exclusive sovereignty. Article 3 of the convention stipulated that British subjects could trade up to ten leagues from parts of the American coast already occupied by Spain and could form settlements, for the purposes of trade, in unoccupied areas.
DANIEL CLAYTON

normal schools. Normal schools were the major institutions for training and certifying common, then elementary, school teachers from the mid-19th to the mid-20th century. Earlier, academies had supplied some training, as had a few schools for the poor, but most teachers simply taught as they had been taught. Normal schools emerged with the development of standardized state schooling: teachers would be instructed in proper methods of teaching and school governance, using prescribed texts. Anglophone normals were chiefly co-educational, while francophone schools were segregated and governed by nuns or clerics. Everywhere, the schools brought pupil teachers to urban centres and taught not only officially sanctioned norms of teaching but the gendered norms of urban, middle-class life, usually featuring a male in charge and women subordinates. Some rebelled against such stereotypes and eventually the schools were closed down or absorbed into colleges or universities. For a century, however, they were the only higher education available to many and, for both the women and men involved, a source of professional authority and income.
ALISON PRENTICE

Norman, E. Herbert (1909–57), scholar, diplomat. Norman spent his childhood in Japan, and was educated at the University of Toronto, Cambridge, and Harvard. His book, *Japan's Emergence as a Modern State* (1940), is regarded in both Japan and the West as a classic. Appointed to the Canadian embassy in Tokyo, he was interned following the outbreak of the Pacific war in December 1941, released in mid-1942. For the remainder of the war he served as head of the Japanese intelligence section in the *External Affairs department. From September 1945 to January 1946 he was seconded as adviser to US General Douglas MacArthur, the 'proconsul' of the American Occupation. Norman was recalled from Japan in January 1950 for the first of two security investigations prompted by US charges of 'communism'. In 1956, as ambassador to Egypt, he played a key role in the UN peacekeeping negotiations following the *Suez crisis. In 1957, after public revival of charges by a US senate committee, Norman committed suicide in Cairo, precipitating a strong anti-American reaction in Canada. An official report in 1990 cleared him of disloyalty. REG WHITAKER

Normandy, Battle of. Canadians played a role in the Battle of Normandy out of all proportion to their numbers. Canadian-manned vessels, from destroyers to landing craft, represented 7 per cent of all Allied vessels committed to the Normandy landings. *No. 6 (RCAF) Bomber Group flew in support of the invasion; another 16 RCAF fighter squadrons formed No. 83 Group to assist 2 British Army. On the morning of 6 June 1944 (D-Day), 1st Canadian Parachute Battalion landed to the east of the invasion beaches as part of 6th British Airborne Division.

Later that day, men of 3 Canadian Infantry Division under Maj.-Gen. Rod Keller, supported by 2 Canadian Armoured Brigade, stormed the heavily fortified beaches codenamed 'Juno'. Over 1,074 Canadians suffered casualties on 6 June, including 359 who were killed or died of wounds. In the weeks following, Canadians withstood repeated attacks by 12 SS Panzer division, whose troops murdered an estimated 156 Canadian prisoners.

One day after Caen fell to the British and Canadians on 10 July 1944, Second Canadian Corps became operational under Lt-Gen. Guy Simonds. The corps' first battles south of Caen were grim introductions for 2 Canadian Infantry Division. Its losses in Operation 'Spring' on 25 July were second only to those it suffered at *Dieppe. Simonds's reputation was made in August, when his infantry used improvised carriers to punch through the German defences south of Caen. By 16 August the remnants of two German armies began their retreat across the Canadian front. Three days later, Maj. David Currie led a small force into St-Lambert-sur-Dives to close what was then the last German escape route from Normandy. Currie won the Victoria Cross for his gallantry. The price of victory that summer was high: from 6 June to 23 August 1944 the Canadian component of 21 Army Group suffered 18,444 casualties, of which 5,021 were fatal.

GEOFFREY HAYES

Norquay, John (1841–89), Manitoba premier 1878–87. Born near St Andrews, *Red River settlement, child of a fur trade family of mixed European and Aboriginal background, Norquay was raised on a farm by grandparents. He won a scholarship provided by the Anglican bishop and became, in succession, teacher, fur trader, and farmer. He ran successfully in Manitoba's first provincial election in 1870 and was appointed cabinet minister a year later. The *Free Press* described him in 1878 as 'able, educated, a native of the country and a half-breed, and of Conservative leanings'. Premier for nine years, he is associated with successful negotiations in Ottawa to extend the provincial boundary in 1881 and with increased federal subsidies granted in lieu of provincial control over public lands. Norquay's opposition to the 'monopoly clause' in the federal government's contract with the Canadian Pacific Railway prompted Prime Minister Macdonald to double-cross him in 1887, causing the fall of Norquay's administration. He died of a sudden illness two years later while serving as leader of the provincial opposition.

GERALD FRIESEN

Norse. Europeans began their westward expansion across the North Atlantic during the Viking Age, establishing farming settlements on the Shetland and Faeroe Islands and in Iceland by the 10th century AD. Icelandic sagas report that Greenland was discovered by Eirik the Red during the late 10th century and that settlements were soon founded along its southwestern coast. The Norse Greenlandic colonies quickly grew to 2,000 or more people, and existed until some time during the 15th century. Greenland was the base for Norse exploration, trade, and attempted settlement in northeastern North America.

The vague and confusing saga accounts, which were written a few centuries after the events, report that at least four voyages were made to what is now eastern Canada, most of them associated with the family of Eirik the Red: Leif Eiriksson, his brothers Thorvald and Thorstein, and his daughter Freydis. The explorers discovered and named three lands to the south and west of Greenland: Helluland, a desolate stony land; Markland, a land of forests; and Vinland, a land of wild grapes and self-sown wheat. At least one attempt at settlement of Vinland is reported, undertaken by the merchant Thorfinn Karlsefni and his wife Gudrid, and abandoned after two or three years due to fear of attack by Native people, whom they referred to as skraelings.

Archaeology has recently begun to add to our knowledge of Norse activities in America. In 1960 the Norwegian explorer Helge Ingstad was shown traces of ancient houses at the fishing village of L'Anse aux Meadows at the northern tip of Newfoundland. During the following years, excavations by his wife Anne Stine and by Parks Canada archaeologists revealed the remains of several turf-walled structures similar to those built by the Norse in Greenland. Artifacts found at the site are similar to those used by the Norse; related finds suggest that the structures were occupied for a few seasons at most. L'Anse aux Meadows is located on a bleak coast beyond the limit of wild grapes, but the recovery of butternut shells from the site indicates contact with regions to the south. The northern limit of butternuts and wild grapes in Norse times was probably along the western coast of the Gulf of St Lawrence, in eastern New Brunswick and northern Nova Scotia. Vinland probably lay in this region, and the settlement at L'Anse aux Meadows was established at the northern Strait of Belle Isle entrance to Vinland, a spot that could be easily located by Greenland voyagers and that lay beyond the region of dense Indian occupations to the south.

There is no evidence to indicate that the Norse explorations of Vinland were more extensive than the tentative 11th-century voyages that are mentioned in the sagas. However, a historical record suggests that the Norse continued voyaging to Markland until at least the 14th century, probably to obtain timber from Labrador. A variety of archaeological finds indicate other activities to the north, in the region the Norse named Helluland. Fragments of smelted metal and other objects of European manufacture are widely distributed in the remains of early Inuit settlements dating from the 13th and 14th centuries in arctic Canada. It has been suggested that the Inuit established trading relationships with Norse Greenlanders who occasionally visited or were storm-driven to arctic Canada. More intriguing are elements of European technology associated with settlements of the Palaeo-Eskimos, the people who occupied arctic Canada before the arrival of the Inuit. Lengths of spun cordage and wooden objects similar to those from Norse Greenland, as well as apparent portrayals of European faces by Palaeo-Eskimo artists, suggest a relationship based on more than occasional trade. These finds hint at a significant Norse presence in the eastern Arctic during the centuries around AD 1000, a presence not mentioned in historical accounts and not previously suspected. PATRICIA SUTHERLAND

North Atlantic Treaty Organization. Canada played an important role in the creation of NATO. In February 1947 diplomat Escott *Reid acknowledged the collapse of the wartime alliance with the Soviet Union and the possibility of a Soviet invasion of western Europe. Multiplying Cold War crises forced the Liberal government to create a strategy through which a *middle power like Canada could respond to the perceived threat. A distinctive position on collective security emerged that reflected a mixture of liberal internationalism and national self-interest. The *United Nations with continued Soviet membership remained central to Canada's international policies; a new multilateral regional defence organization consistent with the UN Charter would contain communist aggression. As minister of external affairs Louis *St Laurent actively promoted this idea, and international crises gave the concept greater force. Shortly after the communist coup in Czechoslovakia in February 1948, Canada joined Britain and the United States in secret talks in Washington. Canada pressed for a multilateral alliance that promised both collective security and a means to balance the excesses of US Cold War policies; it also insisted that NATO's charter include an article (Article 2) calling on members to co-operate to strengthen democratic institutions internationally. In April 1949 nine other countries signed the charter along with Canada, the United States, and Britain: France, the three Benelux nations, Denmark, Iceland, Italy, Portugal, and Norway.

Economically, NATO worked for Canada. Defence production exports increased dramatically, most notably the export of F-86 fighter interceptors to European allies. Culturally and militarily, it never fulfilled Canada's hopes. Article 2 quickly vanished into irrelevance. Nor did NATO allow Canada or other middle powers to shape allied defence strategy. After the outbreak of the *Korean War, NATO commitments instead shaped Canada's armed forces. Overall, Canada deployed 10,000 soldiers and airmen in Europe as a first line of defence against a Soviet invasion; the navy was assigned to protect convoys that would supply Europe in the event of war from submarine attacks. These conventional forces, however, were secondary to NATO's nuclear strategy, dictated by the United States, which threatened the first use of nuclear weapons to deter the Soviet Union. NATO membership made Canada's desire to reject nuclear arms impossible. During the *Diefenbaker years (1957–63) the acquisition of nuclear weapons became a domestic political controversy, but under Lester *Pearson Canada's NATO commitment remained unquestioned. The turning point came with Pierre *Trudeau's succession in 1968. The new leader, who had no experience in military or international affairs, believed that US assessments of the communist threat were exaggerated. Under his leadership Canada gradually watered down its support for NATO, halving its European force to 5,000, and seriously considered withdrawing from the alliance altogether. The end of the Cold War seemed to condemn NATO to irrelevance, but events in the Balkans demonstrated its continued usefulness.

LAWRENCE ARONSEN

North Atlantic Triangle. The title of a 1945 book by historian J.B. Brebner, 'North Atlantic Triangle' describes the Canadian conception of a special political, cultural, and military relationship between Canada, the United States, and Great Britain in the 20th century. Co-operation on matters related to the defence of the North Atlantic and weapons production reached a highpoint during the Second World War. After 1945 the historical reality never matched the perfect symmetry of a triangle. Although the countries continued to share obvious cultural similarities, Canada's economic relations shifted dramatically away from Britain towards greater trade and investment with the United States. As for military ties, the growing threat of an atomic attack over the polar region led to the establishment of a continental air defence system under the 1957 NORAD agreement. Free trade agreements with the United States and Mexico suggest that by the end of the 20th century the triangle had been superseded by a trilateral North American relationship. However, in response to crisis situations, such as the terrorist attack on America in

2001, the special relationship between the United States and Britain has remained intact. LAWRENCE ARONSEN

Northeast Staging Route, sometimes known as the Crimson Project, essentially three Second World War air routes through the eastern Arctic that met in Greenland. Originally conceived by the US government in 1941 as an alternative to other transatlantic airways, especially the crowded direct one through Gander, Newfoundland, this route was designed to facilitate the ferrying to the British Isles of single-engine fighters and other short-range aircraft via Greenland and Iceland. Motivated by this American vision, Canada built a large airport at Goose Bay, Labrador, as an alternative western air ferry terminus to Gander, and either built or co-operated with the United States in constructing other facilities, most notably at Regina; The Pas and Churchill in Manitoba; Mingan and Fort Chimo (christened Crystal 1 by the Americans) in northern Quebec; and several in the Northwest Territories—Crystal 2 at Frobisher Bay (now Iqaluit) on Baffin Island, Crystal 3 on Padloping Island, and Coral Harbour on Southampton Island. In the end, the route was little used during the war, but its network of radio and meteorological facilities as well as landing strips left Canada a useful infrastructure for the Cold War and for post-war development. CARL A. CHRISTIE

northern game preserves. Federal legislation aimed at wildlife conservation in the North dates to the 1890s. Later, when traders and trappers, attracted by high fur prices after the First World War, flooded northwards with modern firearms, restrictions to protect Native interests became imperative. In 1923 the Northwest Territories Council established the Yellowknife, Slave River, and Peel River preserves, where hunting and trapping were restricted to Indians, *Inuit, *Metis leading the Native life, and white trappers already working in the areas. Other preserves followed, from the largest, the Arctic Islands Game Preserve (1926), to the smallest, the Yukon's McArthur Game Sanctuary (1948). The former, incorporating the Banks and Victoria Islands preserves, covered 114 million ha and included almost the entire archipelago, except eastern Baffin Island, plus portions of the mainland north of Keewatin. As NWT commissioner O.S. *Finnie, said, 'The creation of this Preserve . . . has a bearing on British Sovereignty in the North and serves to notify the world-at-large that an area between the 60th and 141st meridians of longitude, right up to the Pole, is owned and occupied by Canada.'

By 1948 reserved lands covered more than 233 million ha; then the process went into reverse, not least from white Canadian antagonism. That year, the federal government transferred power over the 'preservation of game' to the NWT Council, then still headquartered in Ottawa. The council mandated hunting licences for Natives and, five years later, began dismantling the game-preserve system, starting in 1953 with Mackenzie Mountain. Yellowknife and Peel River followed in 1955, the Arctic Islands in 1966.

Still in existence, the 5.6 million ha Thelon Wildlife Sanctuary is the continent's largest tract of untouched, fully protected wilderness, and Canada's oldest surviving preserve. Stretching across eastern Mackenzie and into Keewatin, the sanctuary is crossed annually by 400,000 Beverley-herd caribou, and is home to 20,000 muskoxen, a remarkable recovery for an ancient mammal hunted almost to extinction. Discovering muskoxen in the Thelon Valley in 1925 hastened establishing the sanctuary two years later. Since 1956 mining companies have encroached into Thelon, and after the discovery of uranium in the Thelon Sandstone, mineral staking has reached the sanctuary boundary, raising pressure to open the area to mineral exploration. In 1999 a new boundary through the sanctuary, demarcating Nunavut's western border, divided Thelon into an eastern portion, managed by Inuit, and a smaller western portion administered by Dene in the NWT. R. QUINN DUFFY

northern justice. There was no law enforcement north of the 60th parallel until the government sent a detachment of *North-West Mounted Police to what is now the Yukon in 1895 to demonstrate Canadian sovereignty. The government's initial desire was to spend as little money in the North as possible, and to leave the indigenous people to follow their own customs unless they threatened newcomers, which very rarely happened. However, demands from missionaries and traders forced the government to take action. In 1903, detachments were set up in the western Arctic at Herschel Island and Fort McPherson, and at Cape Fullerton in Hudson Bay, for the purpose of enforcing customs and other laws on the *whaling crews. After the First World War, other posts were established along the arctic coast and on Baffin Island, and as far north as Bache Pensinsula on Ellesmere Island, for the purpose of 'showing the flag' in an era when Canadian sovereignty in the Arctic was somewhat in doubt.

In the Yukon after 1900 the law was enforced in much the same way as in the rest of Canada. But in the Northwest Territories, where almost all the population was indigenous before 1945, some allowances were made for the fact that these people knew little of Canadian law and customs. Three murder cases between 1912 and 1922 show a change from tolerance to harshness. When two explorers, Radford and Street, were killed in June 1912 by *Inuit in revenge for ill-treatment, the authorities investigated but did no more than warn the Inuit; when two missionary priests, Fathers Rouvière and Le Roux, were killed for the same reason in 1913, the killers were arrested, tried, and given light sentences. But when in 1922 a Mounted Police corporal was the victim, the Inuit killer was tried and hanged.

The modern era of jurisprudence in the NWT began with the appointment of J.H. *Sissons as first resident justice in 1955. Both he and his successor, W.G. Morrow (1966–76), applied common sense solutions to northern justice in the era when the hunting-gathering way of life was giving way to life in settled communities. More recently experiments such as community policing and sentencing circles have been made in an attempt to adapt justice to northern conditions.

K.S. COATES AND W.R. MORRISON

northern resource development. Resource development in northern Canada falls into two periods: one up to about 1970, when the region was considered a storehouse of treasure to be used for the advantage of southern Canada, and no consideration of indigenous rights or environmental concern entered into plans; and the more recent era, when First Nations and the environment have been at the top of any plan for development.

The exploitation of the gold resources of the Klondike region in 1898 was typical of the first period: to get the gold, the indigenous people were brushed aside or ignored, the country stripped of trees, the creeks ravaged, the rivers polluted. It was only briefly a 'poor man's' opportunity: the era in which wealth could be dug from the ground with a shovel lasted only a few years. By 1900 big capital had arrived in the person of the 'concessionaires'—men who got government permission to buy up claims on the creeks and build expensive hydraulic systems to mine them on a large scale. Later, even more expensive dredges chewed up the old creek beds, employing only a few men where recently thousands had worked the diggings by hand.

Forty years later, the *Alaska Highway and the *Canol project were built with the same disregard for the environment, nor did any environmental-review process accompany the development of the gold mines at Yellowknife (capital intensive because they required *hardrock mining) or the radium mines at Great Bear Lake in the 1930s. Ghost towns such as Clinton Creek, an abandoned asbestos mine west of Dawson City, and Cassiar in northern British Columbia, are relics from the days of impermanent mining communities. In 1974 a lead-zinc mine was opened at Nanisivik ('the place where one finds things') on northern Baffin Island. The second most northerly mine in the world, it was established as a joint venture between government and a private company, and has operated successfully despite a bitterly harsh climate and fluctuations in world prices.

A turning point in northern resource development came with the proposal for a pipeline to carry natural gas from the newly discovered Beaufort Sea deposits to southern markets via a pipeline to be built along the Mackenzie River. The newly emerged power of the Dene people and the sympathetic support of the Trudeau government led to a 1975 royal commission headed by Thomas Berger, which effectively stopped the project in its tracks. When the federal government began to negotiate comprehensive claims with the First Nations, a key demand was for control over resource development. New resource development in the North, therefore, must proceed with the approval and under the partial control of First Nations people, whose vigilance for environmental concerns is constant. Where agreements cannot be reached among First Nations and other interests—for example in the Voisey's Bay region of Labrador, where a huge nickel project was stalled for years by disagreement among the stakeholders—development does not proceed.

Probably the most exciting modern resource project in the North is the development of diamond mines north of Yellowknife. Here the Ekati mine is producing 4 per cent of the world's output of diamonds, a second mine will soon begin operations, and a third is proposed. The three mines have $24 billion in diamonds underground, and it is believed that the region holds still more. As well, the *Mackenzie Valley pipeline project has been revived, this time potentially with the approval of the First Nations, who now see themselves as participants in the project rather than victims of it.

K.S. COATES AND W.R. MORRISON

north magnetic pole. *See* GEOMAGNETISM.

North Pole. *See* RACE TO THE POLE.

North, the idea of. The North has a place in the Canadian imagination comparable to that of the West in the American: a place of mystery and possibility, a repository of value, and a point of orientation. Neither 'out west' nor 'down east' evokes as powerful a cluster of feelings and expectations as 'up north', much less 'the true north, strong and free'. Yet 'the idea of north' (as Glenn *Gould entitled one of his radio documentaries) is not fixed, either geographically or historically. It can refer to the High Arctic, the tundra, the Laurentian Shield, the 'North West', or all of Canada, and its meaning has changed over time, from Jacques *Cartier's dismayed reaction to the rocky coast of Labrador in 1534—'I am rather inclined to believe that this is the land God gave to Cain'—to Zacharias Kunuk's mesmerizing film of the Inuit legend of Atanarjuat (*Atanarjuat* [*The Fast Runner*], 2000). Explorer and filmmaker both describe a recognizable reality, but their meanings and the myths they inscribe are embedded in the circumstances and attitudes of their times, including, in Cartier's case, prior European perceptions of mythic and faraway places, and, in Kunuk's, previous representations of North, since Cartier, and a renewed assertion of Aboriginal legitimacy.

The mythification of the North dates especially from the mid-19th century, when poets, essayists, scientists, and politicians found in it a means of promoting the creation of a Canadian nation, unifying its founding European peoples, British and French, and distinguishing them from their American neighbours to the south. In 1869, Robert Grant Haliburton, son of Thomas Chandler *Haliburton and a founding member of the nationalist *Canada First movement, delivered an address to the Montreal Literary Club entitled *The Men of the North and Their Place in History*. Canadians were a northern race, he said—'*We are the Northmen of the New World*'—a mixture of Celtic, Teutonic, and Scandinavian elements, and embracing the Norman French as well. They were inheritors of a northern tradition of law and liberty, which they were destined to sustain and enrich in the crucible of their own demanding northern environment. Southerners, by contrast, were prone to effeminacy and degeneration. This was a highly gendered and racialist conception of nationality; neither women nor Aboriginal peoples—no matter how northern their origin—were included in Haliburton's formulation. Nevertheless, it began an intellectual and cultural assimilation of the northern wilderness that led down through Ernest Thompson *Seton and the *Group of Seven to Jean-Paul Riopelle, Margaret Atwood, and Glenn Gould, and even, perhaps, through the anthropology of Diamond *Jenness, to the huge success of *Atanarjuat* as well.

'The idea of North' permeated much of Canadian historical thought in the 20th century, finding expression in both the *Laurentian and *staples theses. The historian who incorporated it most explicitly in his thinking about the nation's past was W.L. *Morton, who argued in *The Canadian Identity* (1961) and elsewhere that Canada was defined in large part by its 'northern character'. Far from being a pale reflection of American history (as liberals and frontierists seemed to think), the history of Canada was 'rather an important chapter in a distinct and even an [sic] unique human endeavour, the civilization of the northern and arctic lands'. Morton conceived of the North as a physical region—the territory north of commercially arable land—as well as an idea, and called for empirical study of its economy, society, and influence on national development, as well as for an acknowledgement of its symbolic significance. The idea of a northern nationality has faded, however, as historians have turned their attention to more *limited identities, though a vigorous regional history has emerged (e.g., in the Yukon-based *Northern Review*) while literary critics have sought to deconstruct the semiotics of 'North' (e.g., Sherrill Grace, *Canada and the Idea of North*, 2002).

KENNETH C. DEWAR

North West Company. After the conquest, British traders quickly re-established the *fur trade into the Northwest, the vast area of western Canada reached by canoe from Montreal by way of the Great Lakes. The distances and money involved made partnerships essential. One, involving the brothers Benjamin and Joseph Frobisher, the firm of Isaac Todd and James McGill, and others, was called La Grande Compagnie du Nord Ouest as early as 1770. The trade limped through the American Revolutionary War, and in January 1784 the first long-term North West Company agreement was signed by a coalition of Montreal suppliers and 'wintering partners', men actually engaged in the fur trade.

The architect of the 1784 NWC, along with the Frobishers, was Simon McTavish (1750?–1804), who quickly became its guiding genius. In 1787, all the company's Montreal business, with its valuable commissions, was assigned to his firm, McTavish, Frobisher & Co. In 1791, a London company was created to buy the trade goods and market the furs. McTavish saw the northwest fur trade as his own monopoly, and there were frequent struggles with excluded rivals. The first opposition firm, Gregory & McLeod (active 1785–7) was quickly ruined and absorbed; from it the NWC acquired the intelligent and ambitious Alexander *Mackenzie. Under the company's auspices, Mackenzie made two celebrated voyages of exploration—to the Arctic Ocean in 1789 and to the Pacific in 1793. He probably hoped to head the NWC himself, but McTavish was grooming his nephew, William McGillivray (1764?–1825), as his successor. In 1799 Mackenzie quit the NWC, was knighted in England in recognition of his explorations, and returned to Canada to add weight to the latest opposition. This enterprise, the XY Company, consisted of fur traders and suppliers whose business had dried up with the handover of Detroit and Michilimackinac to the Americans in 1796. The XY rivalry, characterized by trickery and violence on both sides, ended in 1804 with McTavish's death. The two companies then joined in a new partnership, with McGillivray at its head.

At its peak, soon after the amalgamation, the NWC operated almost 100 posts, mainly between the Great Lakes, the Pacific, and the Arctic tundra, and employed perhaps 1,500 men, especially *voyageurs recruited in Quebec. Most of the trade goods and furs passed through the company's depot on Lake Superior—Grand Portage till 1802, and Fort William after that. McGillivray's 17-year rule was marked by increasing expense and declining fur prices. Competition with the London-based *Hudson's Bay Company, once a minor factor in the Northwest, escalated into a death-struggle, marked by thievery, kidnapping, starvation of rivals, and murder. A more sophisticated NWC tactic, manipulation of the political conscience of the emerging mixed-blood population, provided the context for the slaughter of 20 HBC men by Metis at Red River in 1816. As the demoralizing war dragged on, McGillivray shored up the business with capital left in his hands by the wintering partners, who never saw most of their money again. Finally, in 1821 a union was negotiated—effectively a takeover of the NWC by the HBC, with the end of the fur trade in Montreal.

As a business enterprise, the NWC left little permanent mark on Canada. What money was made ended up in Britain and was not reinvested in the growing colony. The company's most important contribution was in exploration. Wintering partners, especially Peter *Pond, Alexander Mackenzie, Simon *Fraser, and David *Thompson, defined the geography of the Canadian Northwest, and this knowledge was made available to European mapmakers. As the employer of voyageurs, the NWC introduced hundreds of young Quebeckers into the Northwest, where some founded mixed-blood families with Native wives. Thus began the *Metis nation, an NWC legacy, and a continued cultural and political presence in western Canada today. HARRY W. DUCKWORTH

North-West Mounted Police. In order to maintain control of the huge area it acquired from the *Hudson's Bay Company in 1870, the Canadian government decided to create the NWMP in 1873. Recruited largely from Ontario and Quebec, the first 300 men of the force left Manitoba in June 1874 to eliminate the liquor trade in what is now southern Alberta. The epic march across the unmapped prairie resulted in many hardships but by October the police were established in their first western post, Fort Macleod.

Because the failure of the original transcontinental railway slowed agricultural settlement until the late 1880s, the NWMP, for its first decade, was able to concentrate on establishing good relations with the Native population of the Prairies. This enabled them to facilitate the negotiation of Treaty 6 with the Cree in 1876 and Treaty 7 with the Blackfoot in 1877. These relations were also important for the force's ability to meet several serious challenges in this period. In 1876 Sitting Bull and about 3,000 followers came north to Canada. They remained peacefully in the Cypress Hills area under the supervision of Superintendent James Morrow Walsh until their return to the United States in 1883. The rapid disappearance of the great buffalo herds in the early 1880s created conditions of near starvation among the plains bands, a situation the NWMP countered with the widespread distribution of food.

The most serious crisis for the police came in the spring of 1885 when a group of *Metis living under the leadership of Louis *Riel along the South Saskatchewan River took up arms against the government. Police warnings of imminent trouble in the area had been ignored by Ottawa. Apart from a small scouting unit organized by Superintendent Sam *Steele, the NWMP took relatively little part in the fighting during the rebellion. Their real importance was illustrated by the fact that only a few hundred Cree and Metis outside the South Saskatchewan valley joined the rebels.

When gold was discovered in the Yukon in mid-1890s, the NWMP moved in to keep order among the thousands of miners and camp followers. They succeeded admirably. Whitehorse and Dawson City at the height of the rush were as law abiding as Toronto. Just as the gold rush was abating, the outbreak of war in South Africa drew in many volunteers from the NWMP. Their contribution to units like Lord Strathcona's Horse resulted in the force becoming the Royal North West Mounted Police in 1904. With the creation of the provinces of Alberta and Saskatchewan in 1905, the RNWMP took over provincial policing under contract. In 1920 the RNWMP and the Dominion Police were amalgamated into a new national police force called the *Royal Canadian Mounted Police.

R.C. MACLEOD

Northwest Passage. The search for an open waterway linking the Atlantic and Pacific Oceans across the top of North America motivated several generations of arctic explorers. The search began in the 16th century when European navigators began seeking a northern sea passage to the Orient and the precious goods that these exotic lands possessed. A sequence of voyages by Martin Frobisher (1576–8), John Davis (1585–7), and William Baffin (1616) revealed the general contours of Davis Strait and Baffin Bay and located the entrance to Lancaster Sound, the channel that eventually would prove to be the doorway to the passage. Other explorers—Henry *Hudson (1610–11), Jens Munk (1619–20), Luke Foxe (1631), Thomas James (1631–2), and Christopher Middleton (1741–2)—probed the shoreline of *Hudson Bay in a futile search for an opening in that direction. In the late 18th century, the voyages of James *Cook (1778) and George *Vancouver (1792–4) tested the theory that an opening to the passage existed along the west coast of the continent, the fabled Strait of Anian. Meanwhile fur traders Samuel *Hearne (1770–2) and Alexander *Mackenzie (1789) made the initial overland treks by Europeans to the continental shoreline of the Arctic Ocean.

The search for the passage picked up impetus in the early 19th century, the British Admiralty rationalizing the project more for scientific research and national glory than for economic gain. Voyages by John Ross (1818, 1829–33) and Edward Parry (1819–20, 1821–3, 1824–5) penetrated deep into the heart of the *Arctic Archipelago. At the same time, naval lieutenant John *Franklin carried out a pair of overland expeditions (1819–22, 1825–7) that surveyed thousands of kilometres of the Arctic shoreline. In 1845 Franklin led a third expedition, this one by sea. Following his disappearance, the search for the Northwest Passage became incidental to the search for Franklin and his men, but one result of the rescue effort was the discovery of a passage. In 1853, when their ship *Investigator* was caught on the north coast of Banks Island, Robert McClure and his men trekked eastward across the ice to rescue vessels in Lancaster Sound, becoming the first Europeans to traverse a northwest passage.

The actual navigation of the passage had to wait another half century, until 1903–6, when it was finally accomplished by the Norwegian adventurer Roald *Amundsen, who followed a southerly route that hugged the continental shoreline. By this time it was clear that the passage was not suitable for commercial shipping; despite the advent of modern icebreakers, it still isn't. Nevertheless, other vessels made the crossing, including the RCMP patrol vessel **St Roch* (1940–2, 1944). By the end of the century the passage was being traversed by adventurers in sea kayaks and tourists in comfortable cruise ships.

DANIEL FRANCIS

North-West Rebellion, 1885. In the early 1880s the *Metis living along the South Saskatchewan River around the settlement of *Batoche were finding life difficult because of the bad weather conditions that ruined their crops and the disappearance of the buffalo herds. Some had unsettled land claims from the Manitoba settlement of 1871 and all were concerned that the government survey would not recognize their existing river lot farms. Lack of action by Ottawa on the latter grievances led them to send a delegation to Montana to ask Louis *Riel to return to Canada to lead their cause. Riel agreed, and in July 1884 began to try to arrange an alliance between the Metis, the white settlers, unhappy because the Canadian Pacific Railway had shifted its main line south, and the Cree and Blackfoot, near starvation because of the lack of buffalo and at odds with the government over the allocation of reserve lands.

At first it seemed that Riel might succeed in drawing the various groups into a political alliance as he had 15 years earlier at *Red River, but his religious ideas had become increasingly eccentric over the years and he now believed that he was a prophet with a mission to reveal God's plan for Canada and that the Metis were the new chosen people. These heretical views deprived him of the support of the Oblate missionaries, who were influential among all the groups in the Northwest. Support among the white settlers waned in early 1885 when Riel began to talk about armed rebellion rather than the letters and petitions that had been the substance of earlier protests. With few exceptions the First Nations leaders had a much more realistic grasp of the potential military power of the Canadian state than did Riel and had no interest in confrontation.

With strong backing from Gabriel *Dumont, Riel decided to push ahead and on 19 March 1885 declared a provisional government and ordered all representatives of the Canadian government out of the North-West Territories. A governing council that Riel called the 'Exovedate' was established and Dumont was appointed military commander. The first military encounter took place on 26 March at Duck Lake when a force of *North-West Mounted Police and civilian volunteers from Prince Albert led by Superintendent Leif Crozier met Dumont and the Metis. A dozen were killed on the government side and half that many of their opponents. Its defeat in the skirmish led the NWMP to abandon its largest post in the area, Fort Carlton, and retreat to Prince Albert.

Ottawa reacted decisively as soon as the telegraph brought news of the uprising. The country had only a handful of professional soldiers but militia regiments were hastily mobilized. There was great enthusiasm for the expedition even in Quebec where battalions from Quebec City and Montreal were given rousing public send-offs. Although the CPR was incomplete through northern Ontario, the troops could bridge the gaps on foot or by sleigh. Within a month 3,000 troops from as far away as Nova Scotia reached the Prairies. Almost 2,000 were recruited in the West. The British officer in command of the militia, Maj. Gen. Frederick Middleton, put together a staff who quickly improvised transport, medical services, and all the supplies the little army needed to take the field.

Middleton's original plan was straightforward. His entire force would leave the railway at Qu'Appelle, march north to the centre of the uprising at Batoche and defeat the rebels. By the time the troops began to arrive on 10 April, events had forced a change in plans. A large group of Cree, mostly from *Poundmaker's reserve, moved into the territorial capital, Battleford, prompting the residents of the town to take shelter in the NWMP fort. The Cree did not cut the telegraph wire and the refugees bombarded Ottawa with demands for rescue. On 2 April some warriors from *Big Bear's Cree killed the Indian agent, two priests, and half a dozen other whites at Frog Lake. Word of these incidents led to further pressures from Calgary and Edmonton for military protection. Middleton responded by sending a column of troops under Lt. Col. William Otter north from Swift Current to Battleford. He sent the Quebec troops, whom he distrusted, to Calgary, where they became the largest element in the Alberta Field Force under the command of Gen. Thomas Bland Strange, a retired British officer who was ranching near Calgary. Strange left the 9th Voltigeurs as a garrison to calm the fears of Calgarians and marched north to Edmonton with the 65th Mount Royal Rifles, the Winnipeg Light Infantry, and an improvised group of local volunteers and mounted policemen called Steele's Scouts. From Edmonton the force would proceed downriver in pursuit of Big Bear's Cree.

Middleton remained convinced, correctly as it turned out, that the Metis force constituted the most serious threat and that if they were defeated the rebellion would be over. With about 900 men he marched cautiously north towards the Metis settlements on the Saskatchewan. Under the leadership of Dumont, the Metis had been preparing for the attack. On 24 April Middleton's soldiers ran into the southernmost Metis position, which the Metis called Tourond's Coulee but which appeared on the surveyor's maps as Fish Creek. After a fire fight that lasted most of the day, both sides pulled back, the government forces having suffered heavier casualties. Middleton decided to wait for reinforcements before going further. While Middleton was waiting, Otter's force reached Battleford without incident. As soon as they did so, the Cree and Assiniboine in the town dispersed. Although his instructions from Middleton were to avoid confrontation, the absence of resistance tempted Otter to take the offensive. On 1 May he marched west to Poundmaker's reserve and on the following day ran into a well-prepared force led by the war chief Fine Day at Cut Knife Hill. Otter's force was quickly surrounded and was fortunate to be able to retreat after six hours' fighting with just eight fatalities.

By 9 May Middleton was ready to attack the main Metis positions at Batoche. His plan included the use of a Hudson's Bay Company river steamer, the *Northcote*, as an improvised gunboat. Lack of coordination with the troops attacking on shore led to the failure of that plan; the *Northcote* was put out of action when the Metis used the ferry cable to knock down its smokestacks. Middleton's force retreated at the end of the day. On 10 and 11 May Middleton directed cautious attacks at the Metis lines but was unable to break through. On the morning of 12 May, some of the militia officers, tired of their commander's apparent indecision, charged the Metis lines without orders. The Metis force by this time was exhausted and running low on ammunition. The attack succeeded at the cost of eight killed on the government side and perhaps as many as 50 of Riel's followers. Riel surrendered on 15 May but Gabriel Dumont escaped across the border. The rebellion was essentially over after the defeat at Batoche but the pursuit of Big Bear by Gen. Strange's force dragged on for another six weeks. There were minor skirmishes at Frenchman Butte on

28 May and Loon Lake on 3 June. Big Bear surrendered on 2 July.

Louis Riel was tried for high treason at Regina in August and was quickly found guilty. There was little controversy about the facts of the case or of the application of the law. Riel's defence team realized that the only possible argument was one of insanity based on his religious delusions. Riel refused to go along and made an eloquent statement that convinced the jury of his ability to understand the illegality of his actions. He was condemned to death, the only possible sentence for high treason. Appeals to higher courts upheld the verdict. At this point pressure began to build in Quebec for the government to commute the sentence to life imprisonment. A medical commission examined Riel and reported that he met the legal definition of sanity, although there was sufficient latitude in the report to justify commuting the sentence had the government wanted to do so. Riel's hanging on 16 November 1885 at Regina gave Wilfrid *Laurier and the Liberal Party in Quebec their first real opportunity to break the Conservative hold on the province.

Eight of the Cree who had participated in the Frog Lake killings were convicted and executed for murder. Most of the other Metis leaders along with Big Bear and Poundmaker were convicted of treason-felony and served short jail terms. Perhaps the most significant feature of the rebellion was the fact that most of the Native population declined to participate. The rapid and decisive defeat of the rebellion meant that the Canadian government's policy of clearing the way for white settlement by treaties and confining Indians to reserves was dramatically confirmed and the possibility of further resistance eliminated.

R.C. MACLEOD

Northwest Staging Route, an airway to Alaska from Great Falls, Montana, with principal Canadian airfields at Lethbridge, Calgary, Edmonton, and Grande Prairie, Alberta; Fort St John, Beaton River, and Fort Nelson, British Columbia; and Watson Lake, Teslin, Whitehorse, and Snag, Yukon. Originally conceived by the US War Department to reinforce Alaska in the event of war in the Pacific but ultimately used primarily to ferry American-built aircraft to the Soviet Union, it is also known as the Alaska airway or the ALSIB route, since Soviet pilots collected the planes in Alaska and flew them to Siberia. During the Second World War almost 8,000 lend-lease aircraft were delivered via this route. In the end, Canada assumed ownership and control of what quickly became an important asset, particularly for Yukon and the western Arctic. The many post-war users and beneficiaries of these facilities owe a debt to the pioneer airmen and the military construction workers who built the airway—although they were called American invaders at the time. Furthermore, it is possible to trace the development of an international system of air traffic control to the co-operative systems worked out by the US and Canadian air forces operating in western North America, starting with the Northwest Staging Route. As an aside, the Mackenzie River air route and the *Canol project linked up with this airway at Edmonton and Whitehorse, thereby magnifying its significance in wartime strategic thinking.

CARL A. CHRISTIE

North-West Territories, 1870–1905. Following negotiations with the British government and the *Hudson's Bay Company, and the events of the *Red River Resistance of 1869–70, *Rupert's Land and the North-Western Territory passed to Canadian jurisdiction on 15 July 1870. Except for the tiny province of *Manitoba, established at the same time, the vast region included the *Hudson Bay drainage basin to the north of the original boundaries of Quebec and Ontario, west to the Rocky Mountains, and north to the Arctic Ocean. This would be known as the North-West Territories. In 1880, when the British transferred the Arctic islands to Canada, they too became part of the North-West Territories.

Initially the region was governed under the Temporary Government Act of 1869, which was replaced by the North-West Government Act of 1871, and then by the North-West Territories Act, from 1875 to 1905. Ottawa's intent was to treat the region as a dependency or 'colony' modelled on the experience of Britain's rule of its colonies, with a gradual evolution towards democratic parliamentary institutions and eventually full provincial status, as the growing population justified such change. From the beginning Ottawa established highly centralized control. The *Dominion Lands Act (1872) was designed to encourage both agricultural settlement and railway construction. The *North-West Mounted Police, established in 1873, were intended to maintain a peaceful settlement frontier and to establish British and Canadian social values. Aboriginal title to the transportation corridors and settlement lands was extinguished by seven *Indian treaties negotiated between 1871 and 1877. All this, as well as surveying the land and encouraging immigration, was the responsibility of the Department of the Interior (created 1873), through which Ottawa funded most of the expenses of the local government and kept tight control of the purse strings.

At first the territories were governed from Winnipeg by the lieutenant-governor of Manitoba and an appointed council. In 1876, as a small settlement population began to emerge, the federal government moved the capital, first to Battleford (1876–83), and then to Regina. In 1882 the settlement area was divided into four provisional districts: *Assiniboia, Saskatchewan, Alberta, and Athabaska. The territories had their own lieutenant-governor. As the population grew, elected members were gradually added to the appointed council, beginning in 1880. By 1884 some were beginning to advocate full *responsible government and eventual provincial status; by 1888 the legislative council was almost wholly elective, and was renamed the legislative assembly. In 1891 it gained an executive committee, in 1897 full responsible government was finally granted, and provincial status was achieved with the creation of *Saskatchewan and *Alberta in 1905. In 1887 the territories elected their first members of Parliament (4), and the first senators (2) were appointed.

None of this was achieved without struggle. Ottawa successfully promoted settlement, but failed to provide the funding necessary for local services such as schools, roads, and bridges. Leaders such as F.W.G. Haultain succeeded in raising popular enthusiasm for local control of the annual grant the territory received from Ottawa and provincial status to enable local government to carry out its responsibilities. DAVID J. HALL

Northwest Territories. In 1870 the vast interior of Canada, granted to the *Hudson's Bay Company in 1670 and known as *Rupert's Land, together with the largely unknown North-Western Territory, were transferred to the new Dominion of Canada and became the *North-West Territories. The 5,560-ha province of Manitoba was carved from the territory to accommodate settlers in the *Red River colony. When agricultural settlement spread north out of Manitoba, the District of Keewatin was created in 1876 to handle its administration.

On 31 July 1880, all British territories in North America and all adjacent islands were annexed to Canada. Including the *Arctic Archipelago in this acquisition greatly extended the area of the NWT, but the enlargement of Manitoba, Ontario, and Quebec in 1881, 1889, and 1898 reduced this area again. After 1881, the NWT were divided into administrative districts: the more populous Athabaska, Alberta, Saskatchewan, and *Assiniboia in 1882; Yukon, Mackenzie, Franklin, and Ungava in 1895. Yukon and Mackenzie occupied the territory between Alaska and Keewatin; Franklin included the Arctic Archipelago and the Boothia and Melville peninsulas. Yukon was detached from the others, first as a judicial district, then as a separate territory by acts in 1898 and 1901.

The biggest changes came on 20 July 1905, when a federal statute created the provinces of *Alberta and *Saskatchewan. That same year Keewatin—a truly northern region of ice-smoothed hills and lake- and swamp-filled basins, occupying the eastern mainland and the *Hudson Bay islands—was reincorporated into the NWT. Because Alberta and Saskatchewan extended to 60° N, Manitoba, Ontario, and Quebec all claimed extension to the same latitude. Granting this in 1912 removed Ungava from the NWT, leaving only Mackenzie, Keewatin, and Franklin.

In 1921 a Northwest Territories Branch was established within the Department of the Interior. The deputy minister of the interior, as commissioner, exercised overall control with the advice of a six-member council. Director of the Northwest Territories Branch, renamed the Northwest Territories and Yukon Branch in 1923, was O.S. *Finnie. A resident of Yellowknife, a gold-mining boom town, was admitted to the council in 1947, when the federal franchise was granted to non-Native residents of Mackenzie. In 1950 the franchise was extended to all Natives in the NWT. In 1951 an amendment to the Northwest Territories Act changed the composition of the council to three appointed members and three elected by the Native and white residents of Mackenzie. It also provided for the summer session of the council to meet in the NWT and the winter session in Ottawa.

In 1958 the constituency of Mackenzie was widened to include the whole NWT, but the Inuit of Franklin and Keewatin were unable to vote in territorial elections until 1966. At that time the *Carrothers Commission rejected a proposal to split the NWT into Mackenzie, potentially a future province, and a territory called Nunasssiaq, but it did recommend moving the seat of administration of the NWT from Ottawa to Yellowknife, the future 'capital' of the NWT. In 1976 the Electoral Boundaries Commission advocated division of the huge constituency of the NWT into two ridings: Mackenzie to become Western Arctic, and Franklin and Keewatin together to form Nunatsiaq. An administrative restructuring of the NWT, which could ease the way to later division, amalgamated the districts of Franklin and Keewatin into Arctic District, separated from Mackenzie by a northward extension of the Manitoba–Saskatchewan border. Mackenzie contained most of the populated centres: Yellowknife, Fort Smith, Port Radium, posts along the Mackenzie River, and Aklavik. It also contained most of the operating mines, the Great Slave Lake fishery, the inland waterways leading to the Arctic Ocean, the Norman Wells oilfield, the Pine Point mine, some timber, small areas of arable land, trapping regions, and potential mineral wealth. Mackenzie could thus expect to attain provincial status sooner than the less well-endowed Arctic District.

By the end of the 1970s the fully elected executive council, by then referred to as the legislative assembly, was persuaded to consider political division of the NWT. Meanwhile residents of Mackenzie, predominantly white and Indian, invoked the right of self-determination, but only to claim greater autonomy within the NWT. In a plebiscite on 14 April 1982, a majority of Mackenzie residents voted against dividing the NWT, but they were outnumbered by those, predominantly Inuit, in Franklin and Keewatin. In November the federal government announced its willingness in principle to divide the NWT, thus paving the way for the establishment of *Nunavut on 1 April 1999. R. QUINN DUFFY

Notman, William, and Sons. Canada's most celebrated 19th-century photographers, the Notman firm was established in Montreal in 1856 by William Notman (1826–91), a Scots emigrant who had dabbled in photography in Glasgow. Notman, whose particular skill was portraiture, became Montreal's most fashionable practitioner, although he was careful to keep his prices competitive to assure a broad clientele. He built an international reputation through promotion, his record of the construction of the Victoria Bridge in 1858, and his presidency of the Centennial Photographic Company, created to record the Philadelphia Centennial Exposition of 1876. The firm specialized as well in colourizing photographs, in composites where individual portraits were assembled against a painted background, and in photographic records of trans-continental journeys taken on behalf of organizations such as the Canadian Pacific Railway. Notman exhibited in numerous international competitions. Moreover, he established branches throughout Canada and the United States, staffed by either his brothers and sons or photographers trained in the Montreal office. As a result, Notman photographs, wherever they were produced, had a similarity of style and technique. Eventually there would be 23 associated studios, 16 in the United States, where the firm was directed from Albany, New York. Some 400,000 photos are preserved at the McCord Museum in Montreal. ROGER HALL

notwithstanding clause. This clause, or override power, is provided for in section 33 of the Canadian *Charter of Rights and Freedoms. It allows a province or the federal government to ignore certain rights and liberties (fundamental liberties, judicial guarantees, equality rights) for a period of five years (which may be renewed). It cannot be used to override voting, mobility, or minority language education rights. In the *Ford* case (1988), the Supreme Court of Canada declared that a section 33 declaration is sufficiently explicit 'if it refers to the number of the section, subsection or paragraph of the *Charter* which contains the provision or provisions to be overridden'. To date, recourse to the override has not been common. Only three provinces have invoked the notwithstanding clause: Quebec to mark its opposition to *patriation of the constitution and in certain cases relating to education and commercial signage between 1988 and 1993; Saskatchewan to protect back-to-work legislation introduced during a 1986 dispute with government employees; and Alberta to prohibit same-sex partner marriage.
GÉRALD-A. BEAUDOIN

'Nova Scarcity'. An epithet of derision bestowed on Nova Scotia by disillusioned American *Loyalists. In the wake of the American War of Independence over 16,000 Loyalists arrived on Nova Scotia's shores, doubling its population. They had become political refugees because they had no other choice. Embittered by their fate, they felt betrayed by a peace that virtually disowned them. Nova Scotia was grossly ill-prepared to receive such a sudden, massive influx. Most of the good lands had been granted a generation earlier to *New England Planters. Getting the Loyalists settled on their lands and giving them the means to begin a new life proved a daunting task. By the 1790s, though many Loyalists had left disenchanted with 'Nova Scarcity', those remaining were making significant contributions in politics, education, religion, architecture, literature, law, and commerce. In John *Wentworth, former royal governor of New Hampshire, they had one of their own as the colony's governor. The prosperity brought by the long war with Revolutionary France also did much to turn Loyalists into Nova Scotians. BRIAN CUTHBERTSON

Nova Scotia. Human habitation in this area dates back at least 10,600 years. As glaciers receded, early hunting societies gave way some 2,500 years ago to an 'eastern woodland' culture. These fishing-hunting-gathering peoples were the direct ancestors of today's *Mi'kmaq nation. Sustained interaction between Mi'kmaq and Europeans began around 1500. The rich fisheries in the region attracted Europeans, and from the 1580s there was a regular fur trade. French settlement at *Port-Royal in 1605, after an earlier failure at Île Ste-Croix, marked a sustained effort to colonize the territory that France named *Acadia. By the 1650s several hundred settlers lived in the region, ancestors of a growing population of Acadians.

French territorial claims were hotly contested. The name Nova Scotia (Latin for 'New Scotland') originated in a 1621 Scottish colonial charter. Despite a brief Scottish occupation of Port-Royal in 1629–32, the term was used only intermittently before the final British conquest of Acadia in 1710, confirmed by the Treaty of Utrecht in 1713. Until 1763, the boundaries of Nova Scotia were disputed by France, but for a time thereafter they encompassed all of what is now the Maritime region of Canada. Nova Scotia was diminished by the creation of Prince Edward Island (1769), New Brunswick (1784), and, briefly, Cape Breton (1784–1820) as separate colonies.

During the 18th century, Nova Scotia saw major population disruptions. Most Acadians were expelled between 1755 and 1762, and the Mi'kmaq, although recovering from epidemic diseases brought by early Europeans, were increasingly pushed to unpromising reserve lands by waves of immigration. *Halifax was founded in 1749. 'Foreign Protestants', *New England Planters, British settlers, and returning Acadians quickly occupied other areas. The migration of nearly 35,000 *Loyalists to the Maritime region in the wake of the American Revolution (1776–83) doubled the existing population and included the first substantial numbers of African Nova Scotians. Immigration from the British Isles, especially Scotland and Ireland, filled up the remaining unsettled regions of the colony, which hosted a population of about 277,000 in 1851.

By this time Nova Scotia was entering a period of impressive economic growth and social development. Rural economies were based on agriculture, fish, timber, and mining. *Shipbuilding and merchant shipping characterized ports large and small. As a financial and administrative centre, Halifax was the focus for a province-wide intellectual awakening characterized by literary output, scientific discoveries, and the founding of several universities. The first colony in what is now Canada to be granted *representative government (1758), Nova Scotia was also the first British colony to win *responsible government (1848).

Nova Scotia became a founding province of the Dominion of Canada in 1867. Convinced that the terms of *Confederation were inimical to the colony's well-being, many Nova Scotians supported a brief but intense repeal movement. The tide of anti-Confederation sentiment gradually receded in the 1870s but has remained an undercurrent of political life in the province.

Notwithstanding a flurry of investment following the passage of the *National Policy tariff in 1879, most notably in iron and steel production in Pictou and Cape Breton counties, Nova Scotia fell behind Ontario and Quebec in the race for industrial development. Out-migration reached crisis proportions between 1871 and 1931, draining the province of population. As a result, Nova Scotia's representation in the House of Commons declined. Federal grants, calculated on a per capita basis, failed to keep up with burgeoning demands on provincial coffers. In the 1920s, Nova Scotia took the lead in a coordinated effort, known as the *Maritime Rights Movement, to secure redress from Ottawa, but the movement failed to effect the deep policy changes necessary to reverse the downward economic trend. Meanwhile, industrial collapse, the lack of immigration, and the growth of the tourist industry led to a focus on the region's pre-Confederation history, most notably its seafaring heritage and folk culture. Enduring symbols such as the **Bluenose*, the Scottish bagpiper, *Evangeline, and Glooscap became the stuff of promotional literature, and inspired a variety of cultural industries.

The implementation of *welfare state measures and regional development programs in the post–Second World War period helped to shore up the province's economy, though at the expense of increasing dependency on Ottawa. By the end of the 20th century, the Free Trade Agreement of 1989 and growing hostility to state intervention had forced the province to adjust to dramatically new conditions. While rural areas of Nova Scotia had difficulty meeting the challenge of public and private centralizing tendencies in the global age, Halifax thrived, emerging as not only the capital of Nova Scotia but also a regional centre for the Atlantic provinces. The home of corporate headquarters, government offices, and social agencies serving the entire region, as well as more than a third of Nova Scotia's population of nearly 950,000 in 2001, Halifax serves as a signal that the problems posed by the industrial age may at last be receding.

MARGARET CONRAD AND JOHN G. REID

Nova Scotia No. 2 Construction Battalion (Coloured). In 1914 young African Canadians volunteered to fight for Canada, but most were excluded by racially prejudiced recruiting officers. Despite insult and rebuff, many Black men persisted, believing that by contributing to the war effort they would gain respect and equal rights for their community. As the war worsened in 1916, authorities relented and established an all-Black construction battalion, headquartered in Nova Scotia but authorized to recruit across Canada. With white officers, except chaplain William White, in March 1917 the 603 enlisted men of the No. 2 went overseas, where they served as a labour company attached to the Canadian Forestry Corps in the Jura region of France. They faced segregation and discriminatory treatment—and even violence from white soldiers during a riot at Kinmel Park in England in January 1919. Their experience illustrates the extent of racial stereotyping among Canadians during the First World War.

JAMES W. ST G. WALKER

Nova Scotia secessionist movement, 1880s. Nova Scotia entered Confederation in 1867 despite widespread public reluctance. Anti-Confederates, led by Joseph *Howe, swept both the provincial and federal elections later that year. Secessionist sentiment waned in the 1870s, only to revive in the following decade. The secessionist movement of the 1880s was fuelled by the transition from a traditional sea-based economy to a new industrial order. As industrial centres along the railroad prospered, the sea-based economy faltered. Lumbering and shipbuilding were in crisis, and markets for fish and agricultural products in the West Indies and the United States constricted. For those regions tied to the older Atlantic economy, independence was attractive. Secessionist feeling was particularly strong within the provincial Liberal Party. Responding to the party's secessionist faction led by James A. Fraser of Guysborough County, Premier William S. *Fielding guided his party to an election victory in 1886 on a platform calling for repeal of the British North America Act. Liberals did particularly well in rural areas, in fishing communities along the eastern and southern shores, and in communities such as Yarmouth and Halifax that depended heavily upon sea-borne commerce. It soon became clear, however, that the election results were ambiguous and that many had supported repeal in hopes of squeezing better terms out of the federal government. This was made obvious in the 1887 federal election, when Prime Minister John A. *Macdonald's Conservative Party trounced its Liberal opponents in Nova Scotia, effectively bringing the secessionist movement to an end.

COLIN HOWELL

nuclear energy. The potential of a nuclear chain reaction to create energy has been recognized since at least the 1930s. As far as Canada was concerned nuclear energy became a serious possibility only during the Second World War, when the British located a reactor design project in Montreal, later transferred to Chalk River, Ontario, in 1945. The Chalk River laboratory was originally intended to produce plutonium for the US Atomic Energy Commission, but from the beginning there was always the possibility of designing a reactor to produce electricity. Under the idealistic leadership of Dr W.B. Lewis, Chalk River concentrated more and more on the design of power reactors and by the mid-1950s had come up with the prototype of what would later become the CANDU—a specifically designed Canadian reactor that would draw on Canada's own resources of natural uranium and not require enriched uranium supplies from the United States.

Chalk River was converted into a federal Crown corporation by C.D. *Howe, with the primary mission of proving the viability of nuclear power. In co-operation with Ontario Hydro, Atomic Energy of Canada Limited (AECL) designed and built reactors at Rolphton, Douglas Point, and Pickering. These reactors used natural uranium fuel and a heavy water moderator and featured on-line refuelling in a 'calandria' with multiple fuel bundles that could be exchanged one by one without having to power down the reactor.

The Pickering reactor in particular proved very successful in the short term. Ontario Hydro was encouraged to 'go nuclear' in a big way, and Quebec and New Brunswick joined Ontario in building CANDUs or CANDU-variants. India also acquired CANDU technology via Canada's foreign aid program. Nevertheless, the CANDU did not become the dominant reactor design around the world and by the 1970s Canada was virtually alone in promoting heavy water reactor technology. Despite its limited appeal, the CANDU in the 1970s was regarded as a reliable, safe, and economically viable technology.

The later history of nuclear power was less encouraging. There were a number of well publicized scandals as AECL attempted to promote its CANDUs in a fiercely competitive and certainly unethical world marketplace. Although there were some reactor sales, for example to Korea, there were not enough to keep the Canadian nuclear industry at full production. Spectacular reactor accidents, including the Chernobyl incident in the Soviet Union, stimulated public dread of nuclear technology. At the same time, nuclear power proved to be much more expensive than its earlier advocates had believed, as Ontario demonstrated in the building of a very expensive reactor in the 1980s at Port Darlington. Worse, the Ontario reactors began to suffer frequent breakdowns and in the late 1990s several of the older ones had to be taken out of service altogether. Ontario Hydro by the late 1990s had accumulated a spectacular debt without securing a reliable, Ontario-based, source of power.

The future of Canadian nuclear power at the dawn of the 21st century is therefore in serious question. The economics of nuclear power had proved to be more chancy than first believed, while the CANDU technology had not worked as well as its proponents had hoped. On the other hand, so much money had been invested in nuclear power that the province of Ontario had not completely abandoned hope of making the technology work.

ROBERT BOTHWELL

No. 6 (RCAF) Bomber Group. Formed on 1 January 1943 from the seven Canadian squadrons then serving in other Second World War Bomber Command formations, No. 6 (RCAF) Bomber Group was part of the effort to 'Canadianize' the country's contribution to the air war—that is, to ensure that as many Canadian air and ground crew as possible served on Canadian (RCAF) squadrons in Canadian formations. Commanded by an RCAF officer (although still under the control of RAF Bomber Command), No. 6 Group would grow to 14 squadrons by war's end, 10 per cent of the Bomber Command total. The formation of the group was not entirely welcomed by British authorities, who feared losing operational control of Canadian squadrons committed to the strategic bombing offensive against Germany and worried that inexperienced 'colonials' could not manage such a large military formation. The former was never a problem, but 6 Group's early months seemed to bear out the latter: limited experience led to inadequate training and leadership and, subsequently, ill-disciplined flying that cost lives and produced inaccurate bombing. Or so it appeared. But once 6 Group's squadrons routinely flew the same aircraft type from the same permanent home base, conditions lacking at the outset and beyond Canadian control, the casualty rate fell and bombing accuracy improved to the point that, statistically, their performance was better than the Bomber Command average. Bombing was nevertheless risky. Throughout the war, 44 per cent of bomber aircrew were lost on operations or during training. For its part, No. 6 Group flew 40,822 sorties (dropping some 90,000 tons of bombs) at a cost of 4,000 lives, while another 5,000 RCAF aircrew died serving on non-RCAF squadrons. Although there is dispute over the effectiveness of the strategic bombing offensive against Germany, there is no doubt that the operations conducted by Bomber Command (and therefore No. 6 Group) shortened the war by at least several months.

STEPHEN J. HARRIS

Nunavut. A territory in northern Canada carved out of the *Northwest Territories, Nunavut was established on 1 April 1999. Its population of about 28,000, in 26 communities, is 85 per cent *Inuit. The name means 'our land' in Inuktitut.

Proposals for dividing the NWT were circulated in the mid-1960s, primarily by politicians from the western Arctic concerned that the comparative political underdevelopment in the east was impeding their ability to move towards provincial status. These efforts failed, but the idea was resuscitated in the late 1970s, this time by Inuit from the eastern Arctic, partly inspired by the development of Greenland home rule earlier in the decade. When Inuit, Dene, and Metis leaders took control of the NWT territorial government in the 1979 election it became possible for Inuit to have official support for their initiative. Several attempts were made to negotiate division, including the development of parallel constitutional bodies, the Western and Eastern Constitutional Forums. A tentative agreement in the late 1980s, the Iqaluit Accord, foundered over Dene and Metis renegotiation of their comprehensive land claim.

At the same time, a land claim was being negotiated by Inuit in the eastern Arctic through a body called the Tungavik Federation of Nunavut. A version of the claim had originally been submitted in 1976 by the *Inuit Tapiriit Kanatami but it was withdrawn and the TFN formed for the explicit purpose of negotiating the claim. Creation of a new territory was a critical part of the agenda but little progress was made. Partly concerned about the failure of a global Dene and Metis claim in the western Arctic, the federal government moved to salvage its land-claim policy by giving Inuit in the east what they had long pushed for, their own territory. In an NWT-wide plebiscite in 1992 voters favoured dividing the territory. Article 4 of the Nunavut Final Agreement stipulated that the territory of Nunavut would be created, effective 1999. The TFN dissolved upon signing the agreement and was reconstituted as the Nunavut Tungavik Incorporated, which oversees implementation of the land claim. A separate body, the

Nunavut Implementation Commission, operated for four years to make recommendations about the structure and nature of the new government. John Amagoalik, chair of the commission, is seen as one of the 'fathers' of Nunavut. Voters considered two issues. Iqaluit on Baffin Island was eventually selected as the capital, but a proposal that gender parity among legislators be achieved through male and female representatives from each riding failed to generate enough support. In 1997 NIC completed its work and an interim commissioner, Jack Anawak, was appointed to continue the work of forming the new government.

Elections were held in February 1999 for the 19 seats. Paul Okalik was eventually selected by the other members as the first premier of the territory. A dramatic, televised first session of the new government showcased Inuit culture. Although the territory is beset with serious problems—rapid population growth, high cost of health, education, and social services, critical social difficulties—the ingenuity of Inuit leaders, partly demonstrated in the creativity and patience they used in negotiating Nunavut itself, offers many observers hope that Nunavut will succeed. PETER KULCHYSKI

nursing. Nursing has played a vital part in Canada's evolving health care system. Until the late 19th century, most Canadians relied on the nursing care of female kinfolk or neighbours, some of whom combined midwifery skills with extensive knowledge in what was generically termed 'sick nursing'. Equally important was the attendance provided by religious orders devoted to nursing the sick. One of Canada's earliest *hospitals, Montreal's Hôtel-Dieu, was founded in 1642 by the devout Catholic Jeanne *Mance, while orders like the Sisters of Charity (*Soeurs Grises) established hospitals across Canada.

Nursing underwent a significant reorganization late in the 19th century. Canadian hospitals, eager to integrate new scientific practices like antiseptic surgery, wanted to create a more skilled, disciplined, and respectable nursing workforce. Beginning in 1874 with Mack's General and Marine Hospital in St Catharines, Ontario, many Canadian hospitals established nursing schools, where young single women laboured for two or three years on the wards in exchange for room, board, training, and certification as 'graduate nurses'. This apprenticeship system was often termed the 'Nightingale' system, after the famous British reformer and social scientist.

Upon completion of their education, most graduate nurses worked in private duty providing home care, while a small minority staffed *public health programs such as the *Victorian Order of Nurses. These professional nurses were easily recognized for their distinctive uniforms, which earned them safe passage as they traversed urban neighbourhoods and rural communities. Still, many families continued to rely on less well-trained practitioners, who were cheaper and perhaps more accessible and familiar than the graduate nurse in her starched apron and hat. In response to this competition, graduate nurses formed provincial associations, which, along with the national body, the Canadian Nurses Association (CNA), lobbied for legislation that would define legal and educational standards for the professional nurse. The battle for public recognition was won during the First World War, when graduate nurses served, and died, with Canadian forces overseas. By the 1920s, all provinces had passed legislation outlining the educational requirements of a graduate or 'registered' nurse (RN).

These political victories reflected the increasing importance of professional nurses to scientific medicine. Apprenticing students were grilled in the germ theory of disease and in the many rituals designed to maintain aseptic or 'germ-free' conditions at the bedside, during procedures, and in surgeries. By the 1920s, even the smallest of institutions relied on inexpensive and efficient apprenticing students to treat the growing number of patients choosing institutional over home care. Each year, large numbers of new graduates swelled a shrinking private duty market, a tension that was brought into focus in the 1930s, when, during the nation-wide depression, many nurses, like doctors, were paid in pigs, poultry, or garden produce in lieu of fees.

The outbreak of the Second World War reversed this downward economic spiral, quickly absorbing the 'surplus' of RNs into military and civilian work. After the war, massive hospital-construction projects, many funded by the federal government, prompted a dramatic rise in institutional employment of RNs and a national nursing shortage. Married women were encouraged to resume their nursing careers—so much so that nursing was no longer the preserve of single women—while the recruitment of immigrant nurses significantly diversified the racial and ethnic composition of an occupation that had once welcomed only white women. More men joined the occupation too, but by the 1970s they still comprised less than 10 per cent of the RN workforce. During these years, nursing education slowly shifted out of hospitals and into university and community college programs. Many RNs also earned bachelor degrees in nursing science (BSc Nursing).

As medical procedures became increasingly complex in the post-war hospital, RNs assumed many duties previously assigned to doctors, while many personal and bedside care nursing tasks were reassigned to new categories of institutional workers, such as practical nurses and nurses' aides. By the 1970s these diverse strata of nurses, including RNs, had formed unions through which they could negotiate improved salaries, hours, and working conditions. These unions became increasingly embattled during the 1980s and 1990s as provincial and federal governments reduced health care funding, and as staff shortages led to 'burn out' among nursing staff. At the national level, leaders like Dr Helen Mussalem and the CNA have worked hard to represent nursing's interests to the federal government and its various commissions investigating the status of Canada's health care system.

KATHRYN McPHERSON

See also WARTIME NURSING.

oath of allegiance. The British demand for an oath of allegiance from the Acadians followed swiftly on the Treaty of Utrecht (1713), which had transferred the region then known as 'Acadia or Nova Scotia' from French to British control. Demands by governments for such oaths were common throughout Europe at the time, so this request was a normal enough procedure. However, the Acadian lands had served as the border between French and English territorial claims in eastern North America since 1612, and throughout the 17th century the Acadians had been governed first by one imperial power then the other. They wished no further part in the wars of empire. So in response to the demand for an unequivocal oath of loyalty—to George I and, on his death in 1725, to George II—the Acadians offered a variety of oaths that contained some sort of provisions for the right not to bear arms against the French and the Mi'kmaq. In 1726 Lieutenant-Governor Lawrence Armstrong accepted the oath offered by the settlers in the Annapolis Royal region on the condition that they were to be exempt from bearing arms—that exemption, the minutes of the council noted, 'to be writt upon ye Margent of the french Translation in order to gett them over by Degrees'. By 1730 the majority of the Acadian men had sworn an oath under these conditions; thereafter the Acadians were often called 'the Neutrals' or 'the neutral French'.

This accommodation served the Acadians well until the Franco-British struggle for North American dominance reached its climax after 1748. At that point, the British officials administering Nova Scotia demanded an unequivocal oath of loyalty. Sir Edward Cornwallis, who arrived in the colony as governor in 1749, and his successor Peregrine Hopson, temporized when the Acadians refused to take any oath that did not allow them to remain neutral. Colonel Charles Lawrence, however, who took over as lieutenant-governor in 1753, decided that the Acadians were to be forced to take an unqualified oath of allegiance. He made their refusal to do so grounds for their deportation in 1755. N.E.S. GRIFFITHS

Ocean Ranger. In 1980, Mobil Oil Canada Ltd contracted the Japanese-built rig—the largest self-propelled, semi-submersible offshore drilling unit in the world when it was launched in 1976—to drill the Hibernia oil field on the *Grand Banks off Newfoundland's east coast, where the ice floes, high winds, and seas of the North Atlantic can be very dangerous. During the night of 14 February 1982 a severe storm hit, capsizing the rig and killing all 84 members of its crew. Of the 69 Canadian crew members, 56 were Newfoundlanders, a fact that struck local society hard. A subsequent royal commission investigating the tragedy found that there were design weaknesses and inadequate safety measures and that insufficient training was available to the crew.

MELVIN BAKER AND AIDAN MALONEY

October Crisis, 1970. The October Crisis, one of the most disturbing episodes in post-war Canadian history, was the culmination of a long series of terrorist acts over nearly two decades by the *Front de libération du Québec, a group inspired by decolonization movements in the Third World, especially Algeria and Cuba. Beginning in 1963 with only four people, Félquistes undertook a series of about 100 bomb attacks against symbols of 'colonial' presence: mailboxes deemed anglo and royalist because of the post office logo, monuments for anglophone heroes, factories owned by 'foreign' capital and affected by labour conflicts, and so on. Activities were financed in part by robbery. By the end of the 1960s the organization had become a little more sophisticated, and its members thought the time had come for more radical action. On 5 October 1970 James Cross, a British trade commissioner in Montreal, was taken hostage. Quebec City and Ottawa rejected most of the FLQ's demands. On 7 October a manifesto encouraging the Quebec people to revolt was aired by a private radio station, and by Radio-Canada the next day. As negotiations stalled, on 10 October the FLQ kidnapped a Quebec government minister, Pierre Laporte. Sensing that the FLQ had some public support, Ottawa invoked the *War Measures Act on 16 October. Over 31,700 searches were made. More than 500 people were detained; 467 were freed before being accused. The next day Laporte was found dead in the trunk of a car. Cross was freed on 4 December, hours after his kidnappers had flown to Cuba. On 28 December, with the help of Jacques Ferron, Laporte's kidnappers gave themselves up to the armed forces. At the height of the crisis, officials suggested that FLQ membership numbered about 3,000; later it was determined that it was only about 35. In the end, fewer than 20 people were convicted. Violence continued sporadically until the beginning of the 1980s, but it had totally lost credibility following the trauma of October 1970. RAYMOND HUDON

O'Donoghue, Daniel John (1844–1907). Once called the 'father of the Canadian labour movement', O'Donoghue immigrated from County Kerry, Ireland, with his family in 1852. At the age of 13 he apprenticed as a printer in Ottawa. After achieving journeyman status, he organized Local 102 of the National Typographical Union in 1866. During the 1870s and 1880s, a period of great working-class activism, he emerged as a high-profile labour leader. He battled for the *nine-hour work day and the legalization of *trade unions; he also won a seat in a provincial by-election in 1874—the first independent labour candidate in Canada to do so. He was a reformer, not a radical, an ideology his contemporaries called Liberal-Labour, or Lib-Labism. After moving to Toronto in 1880 O'Donoghue played a pivotal role in founding the *Knights of Labor, the Toronto Trades and Labor Council, and the Trades and Labor Congress of Canada. A husband, father, and journalist, he finished his political career as a civil servant in the newly created federal Department of Labour, where, among other contributions, he tutored the young bureaucrat W.L. Mackenzie *King.

ANDREW PARNABY AND GREGORY S. KEALEY

Official Secrets Act. Introduced in 1939, the act was modelled on the 1911 British act of the same name. The draconian federal statute combined two separate types of offence: espionage (unauthorized disclosure of classified information to a foreign power) and 'leakage' (unauthorized disclosure to the press or public). Information disclosed did not have to be harmful, merely unauthorized. A conviction could be based on the 'known character' of the accused. The burden of proof was shifted from the Crown to the accused. Trials could be held *in camera*. The act was used extensively in the 1945 *Gouzenko espionage affair, but rarely thereafter. Two high-profile leakage prosecutions, against a public servant and a journalist, failed in the 1970s. By the 1980s the Crown doubted its ability to secure convictions, and it became a dead letter. After the terrorist attacks of 11 September 2001, the government repealed the Official Secrets Act as part of its anti-terrorist legislation and replaced it with a modernized Security of Information Act that exempts 'whistleblowers' who release information in the public interest.

REG WHITAKER

Ogilvie, William (1846–1912). Ottawa-born, Ogilvie began work as a Dominion Land Surveyor in 1869 and for the next two decades measured land in the western interior. But in 1887, because of the large number of American miners entering the Yukon Territory, he was dispatched to the far Northwest to locate the 141st meridian, the boundary between Alaska and Canada. After determining that the mining community of Forty Mile fell within Canadian territory, he continued his survey down the *Yukon River and then over the mountains into the Mackenzie River basin. In the mid-1890s, Ogilvie, who was one of only a few Canadian government representatives in the Yukon, was widely known for his honesty and fairness. During the 1896 *Klondike gold rush, he surveyed claims in the gold fields at the request of the miners and did the formal survey of the *Dawson City townsite. In 1898, because of his experience and popularity, he was named Yukon commissioner; he lasted less than three years before he was encouraged to resign because of wrangling with Ottawa. Ogilvie's *Early Days on the Yukon* was published in 1913, a year after his death. In 1966, the mountains northwest of Dawson City were named in his honour.

BILL WAISER

oil and gas industry. *See* PETROLEUM INDUSTRY.

Oka crisis. The immediate cause of the Oka crisis was an early morning entry in force by a large party of Quebec provincial police into a wooded area known as The Pines in July 1990. However, the long background to the Oka dispute stretched back more than two centuries. In the late 18th century Indians settled at a Sulpician mission there began to demand recognition of their land rights. Repeated requests between 1781 and 1961 were ignored or evaded by government, and a decision by the highest court in the British Empire in 1911 also failed to secure vindication for the Mohawk. In 1961 a protest was provoked by the construction of a nine-hole golf course on lands claimed by the Mohawk. When the town of Oka proposed expanding the course to 18 holes, the Mohawk, who now referred to their lands as Kanesatake, promised resistance. Since there was no Warrior Society in Kanesatake itself, volunteer warriors were recruited from two other Mohawk reserves, Kahnawake and Akwesasne, to staff a roadblock in The Pines. Two injunctions ordering the blockade removed were ignored by the Mohawk, leading to the police attack on 11 July that resulted in the death of a policeman by gunshot.

The confrontation between Mohawk Warriors and police turned into a stalemate that lasted 11 weeks. Before it was over both sides were reinforced, the Mohawk by mainly Native sympathizers from across the country, and the police by 2,500 soldiers. Confrontation also spread to Kahnawake, where the Mohawk blockaded the Mercier bridge to Montreal, a measure that provoked violence towards Natives by non-Native residents. The crisis ended on 26 September, when the Mohawk and supporters walked out to the waiting army. Responsibility for the policeman's death was never established, and the land dispute that provoked the crisis is still unresolved.

J.R. MILLER

old-age pensions. With increasing life expectancy in the 20th century, old age increasingly became a social phenomenon associated with retirement and leisure time, but it had not always been so. In the past many elderly, particularly those with fewer economic resources or ill health, found old age a difficult time. Prior to the early 20th century, retirement was usually something to be avoided. People worked as long as they could in paid labour, often 'stepping down' to less onerous work as their physical capacity or stamina diminished. Retirement came when paid work became impossible, either because of poor health or because increasingly impersonal employers were unwilling to make adjustments for elderly workers. Forced retirement frequently meant that an elderly person or couple had to resort to family members for support. Families were expected to provide assistance for elderly parents, and usually did so, taking them into their homes where necessary. Those without families able to assist them were thrown on charitable aid. Charities to help the poor sprang up across the 19th century. Though charities' work was usually not age specific, the elderly poor made up a large portion of their clients. To supplement this charitable work, houses of refuge and houses of industry—commonly known as the local poor house—were established, usually by local counties and municipalities. By the second half of the century such institutions were common across the country. Local jails also often acted as places of temporary refuge.

With industrialization and urbanization the elderly poor became increasingly visible. By 1900 pressure began to build for the state to respond to what was perceived to be a developing social problem. In 1908 the federal government established an annuities program aimed at encouraging individuals to save for their old age, but the program was successful only among a small portion of the middle class who had motive and opportunity to participate. That same year the province of Nova Scotia appointed a royal commission to investigate the possibility of old-age pensions, but the scheme was too expensive to establish. In 1911 Newfoundland began a limited old-age pension program. In 1921 in Ontario, and in most other provinces in succeeding years, filial responsibility laws (also known as parents' maintenance acts) were passed, forcing adult children to support destitute parents wherever possible.

Finally in 1927 the federal government adopted an old-age pension scheme in which the federal and provincial governments share the costs equally. British Columbia was the first to pass complementary legislation, and other provinces adhered to the scheme over the next decade—made easier by the fact that the federal government paid 75 per cent of the costs after 1931. The first old-age pension (OAP) was a limited program, paying a maximum of $20 per month to those elderly aged 70 or more with assets and income producing no more than $120 annually. Administrators tried to force families to take responsibility for their elderly members in preference to relying on the OAP. Families and elderly in turn manoeuvred their way through the system, reshaping it to help as many elderly as possible. The OAP reshaped how the elderly thought about themselves, leading many to begin to call themselves by a collective name—pensioners—and to begin to form associations for the elderly. Older persons were coming to think of themselves as an identifiable group.

In 1951 OAP legislation was modified. Support became universal for all those over 70, and the means-tested pension was available beginning at 65. More and more people were being forced into mandatory retirement and private pension plans became increasingly common for employees of large companies. In 1965 the *Canada Pension Plan was established (with a parallel scheme in Quebec) and another level of assistance for elderly persons was thus added by the state. At the same time the OAP was made available without a means test to those aged 65.

The elderly of the second half of the 20th century had acquired a collective identity. Associations for pensioners and retired persons were formed. Many elderly used their more secure income base to support themselves in retirement, increasing numbers living independently. Retirement homes and care facilities became more prevalent as families tended to provide complementary support rather than primary care.

JAMES G. SNELL

Old Crow. A Gwich'in settlement at the confluence of the Porcupine and Old Crow Rivers in northern Yukon. While Old Crow began as a settlement only around 1900, Gwich'in peoples, part of the Athapaskan language group, have inhabited an area stretching from the lower Mackenzie River region in the Northwest Territories to the headwaters of the Koyukuk River in Alaska for centuries. Old Crow, population 284 in 2001, represents the settling of much of the Vuntut Gwitchin and Takudh Gwich'in portions of the Gwich'in in permanent settlements, growing gradually through the first half of the 20th century. Before that time, family groups moved seasonally through their traditional territory. By about 1950, when a day school opened in Old Crow, most families had their permanent homes there, though they still spent considerable time on the land throughout the year. The Vuntut Gwitchin First Nation signed land claims and self-government agreements with the federal and territorial governments in 1993. With regular access to the community by air only, Old Crow's economy relies heavily on First Nation, territorial, and federal government programs and facilities.

COLIN BEAIRSTO

Oldman River, Battle of. In the spring of 1870, a combined force of some 800 Assiniboine and Cree attacked camps of enemy Blood and Peigan near the confluence of the Oldman and St Mary Rivers, within the boundaries of present-day Lethbridge, Alberta. The attacking force under Chiefs Piapot and Big Bear struck a small Blood village at dawn, not realizing that there were large camps of Peigan nearby. The Peigan and Blood then drove the enemy into a narrow coulee, where spirited fighting took place for several hours, until the Assiniboine and Cree were forced to withdraw. As they waded across the Oldman River, their retreat became a rout and many were killed in the water. When it was over, an estimated 173 attackers and 42 Blood and Peigan had been killed. This proved to be the last major Indian battle on Canadian soil.

HUGH A. DEMPSEY

ombudsman. A public official who acts as the citizens' defender against government. The ombudsman has its origins in 19th-century Scandinavia. The office has since proliferated throughout Western democracies. In Canada, ombudsmen are appointed by and accountable to the legislatures of the relevant province. An ombudsman investigates and reports on citizens' complaints, and makes an annual report, although the recommendations are not binding. Alberta appointed Canada's first ombudsman in 1967. Every province, with the exception of Prince Edward Island, has created such an office. There is no federal public ombudsman comparable to those in the provinces.

JOHN C. COURTNEY AND DANIEL MACFARLANE

Omnibus Bill. A series of broad-ranging amendments to the Criminal Code, first introduced in December 1967 and given final assent in the spring of 1969. Pierre *Trudeau had been appointed minister of justice in April 1967, little more than a year after he was elected a federal member of Parliament. He jumped into his new position determined to begin with the most difficult tasks then confronting the department. Among those were a series of reforms to existing social legislation that had long been contemplated by the bureaucrats of the Department of Justice. In December, Trudeau introduced in the House of Commons a divorce-reform bill and a series of amendments to the Criminal Code dealing with homosexuality and *abortion. He then proceeded to capture both the public imagination and the new spirit of modernity by explaining to the press that 'there's no place for the state in the bedrooms of the nation'. This unknown minister of justice was catapulted onto the national stage with his profoundly modern campaign to legalize homosexuality between consenting adults and legalize abortion in cases where a three-doctor panel approved. The development of his national reputation could not have come at a more propitious time, as Prime Minister Lester *Pearson had just announced his intention to retire and Trudeau soon found his name being bandied about as a potential successor. Three months and four hard-fought ballots later, Trudeau had parlayed his state and bedroom pronouncement into victory at the Liberal leadership convention.

The Criminal Code reforms were lost in the madness of the leadership campaign. However, Trudeau's successor in the justice portfolio, John Turner, reintroduced the amendments in December 1968 as part of the Omnibus Bill. It had a difficult run through Parliament, including as it did the changes to the criminality of abortion and homosexuality, in addition to gun controls, the introduction of the use of breathalyzer tests, amendments to the Parole Act, the Penitentiary Act, and over 120 pages of changes to the criminal and penal law. There was something for almost everyone to distrust, with the changes to abortion law eliciting the greatest opposition. Nevertheless, the bill passed final reading in May 1969, with 149 Liberals, Conservatives, and New Democrats voting in favour, and 54 Conservatives and Créditistes and one Liberal opposed.

P.E. BRYDEN

One Big Union, a western-based radical labour organization that emerged after the First World War. Like earlier movements, such as the *Industrial Workers of the World, it hoped to unify all workers, skilled or not. This contrasted with the dominant labour organization in Canada, the Trades and Labor Congress, which was based on the division of workers into craft-based unions. When attempts to make the TLC a more inclusive, militant body failed, western workers decided to meet separately to decide on a plan of action. The Western Labour Conference that met in Calgary in March 1919 was an extraordinary event. Highly representative of unions across the region, it enthusiastically identified with revolutionary movements in Russia and Germany, proposed general strikes over several issues, including the six-hour working day, and planned to secede from the TLC to form a new One Big Union. It elected as its leaders unionists with a history of radicalism, members of the Socialist Party of Canada.

In the midst of a general strike movement that climaxed in Winnipeg in May and June 1919, a referendum was held on seceding from the TLC. The OBU carried this vote handily in the West, and there were pockets of supporters elsewhere in Canada and in the United States. Despite OBUers' fierce loyalty, the organization faced a united opposition of employers, governments, and the TLC-affiliated craft unions (for whom employers seem to have found a new and temporary appreciation). OBUers were divided over the structure of the organization and growing numbers of radicals—particularly the new *Communist Party of Canada—argued that it was a mistake to abandon members of TLC unions to their conservative leadership. A tiny organization after the early 1920s, the OBU persisted (led by R.B. Russell) to 1956, when it joined the *Canadian Labour Congress.

JAMES NAYLOR

one-room schoolhouse. The one-room schoolhouse deservedly evokes much in the Canadian imagination, both good and bad. But what was this famous institution? Emerging from the schools that early teachers ran in their own homes, one-room schoolhouses were free-standing buildings in which tax-supported schooling was carried on by a single teacher. Such schools existed nearly everywhere in Canada from the beginning of publicly supported education early in the 19th century, but eventually mainly in non-urban areas. The community built the school, and the teacher taught all grades and ages, and usually—but not always—both boys and girls. Teachers might be very young or very old, and pupils' ages ranged widely, as did their numbers—from a handful to a hundred. Parents complained that older male pupils were virtually excluded if a 16-year-old girl taught the school, and they justifiably raged about bias if teacher or trustees exhibited prejudice against a particular religious or racial group. Trustees complained if teachers failed to make it through the school year, refused to sweep the floor or build the fires, or later in the 19th century were not skilled in running the Christmas concerts that became traditional in most school communities. Taxpayers muttered about the costs, even burning down some schools.

The one-room schoolhouse was characterized by surprising architectural variety. As Jean Cochrane has noted, 'early log' (probably with an outhouse) was a style 'preserved by poverty' through the 1930s, while wealthy communities boasted schools made of stone or brick, with separate entrances for boys and girls. The teacher usually boarded in the community but sometimes lived right in the school. A 19th-century Quebec schoolhouse plan shows an adjoining room for the teacher, while the film *Don't Shoot the Teacher*, set on the Prairies in the 1930s, has its teacher living in the school basement. In northern Ontario, some schools were set up in railway cars, while coastal British Columbia boasted schools on barges.

By the mid-20th century school consolidators deemed one-room schools backward. Increasingly, rural children were bussed to schools that conformed more closely to the urban ideal: a hierarchically organized, graded school, with many rooms and many teachers. ALISON PRENTICE

Ontario. The country's most populous and second largest province, Ontario has generally been considered the heart of English Canada and has been the provincial leader in terms of economic strength and wealth-production. Its geography, topography, and climate are the most diversified of any province, a factor that explains much of its history. 'Old Ontario', the region of first settlement, refers largely to temperate agricultural lands lying immediately north of the lake of the same name and occupying the 'Ontario Peninsula', between Lakes Erie and Huron and Georgian Bay. The most distinctive geographic feature of the rest of the province, arrayed in a huge arc stretching from Quebec to Manitoba, is the great mass of Precambrian rock known as the *Canadian Shield. A zone of trees, lakes, and streams, it is richly endowed with a large variety of minerals. Parts of this region, opened to settlement and exploitation in the late 19th century, were frequently referred to as 'New Ontario'.

European penetration of what would become Ontario began with *Champlain's explorations in 1615 and continued with the development of the *fur trade, which was reliant upon Native partnerships. English sovereignty replaced French after the Seven Years' War, but European settlement did not really commence until the influx of American *Loyalists following the Revolutionary War. A blueprint for the future was seen in the *Constitutional Act (1791), which gave the area a fledgling British government and a new name: *Upper Canada. Tory–Loyalist domination was strengthened by the War of 1812. In the aftermath of the *Rebellions of 1837–8, imperial authorities saw the need for restructuring, out of which came the union of Upper and Lower Canada into the new *Province of Canada. This initiative failed despite the achievement of *responsible (cabinet) government and the beginnings of financial autonomy. In 1867, Ontario became one of Canada's four founding provinces. By that time, the agricultural lands of 'Old Ontario' were largely taken up (first by wheat and then with mixed farming), the region was knitted together by an expanding band of railways and canals, and the beginnings of industrial growth were seen in developing cities, especially the provincial capital, *Toronto.

Post-Confederation political developments were, at the national level, characterized by battles with the federal government over defining provincial and federal constitutional rights and responsibilities—especially concerning control of natural resources and the extension of Ontario's boundary westward to the Lake of the Woods (1889). A long period of Liberal control, chiefly under Oliver *Mowat, showed tendencies that would characterize Ontario politics in the future: social pragmatism, sound economics, a wedding of rural and urban interests, and an abiding concern with development of natural resources, all served up in brokerage-style governments where the ruling party anticipated the wants of the electorate. With the building of transcontinental railways through the Canadian Shield, much attention shifted to northern development, particularly exploitation of mineral deposits, which, to the chagrin of the northern population, were sent elsewhere for refining. One mineral missing from Ontario's storehouse was coal—essential in *manufacturing and in powering southern cities. Beginning in the decade before the First World War, the gap was filled by extensive *hydroelectric development under state direction. The government by this time was formed by James Pliny Whitney's 'Progressive' Conservatives, which continued the practical brokerage system. Change—slow, deliberate, and calculated—addressed new challenges as the province became more urban than rural, more industrial than agricultural, more secular and less strictly religious. Loyal to the *British connection, Ontario intransigently opposed teaching French in schools. When, in 1914, the empire found itself at war, Ontarians marched off enthusiastically. Not all of that fervour came back from the trenches.

The impact of the war on Ontario, like the rest of Canada, was profound. Although provincial politics were largely suspended for the duration, government grew in size and influence, industrial output soared, women worked in increasing numbers, racial and ethnic tensions multiplied, *temperance became a religion and religion became less temperate. Discontent erupted in 1919 with the surprising election of a farmer–labour government. The moral accounting demanded by this inexperienced group did not sit well, and in 1923 they were turned out for the more familiar Tories who, under the practical Howard Ferguson, moved back to centrist concerns, temporizing volatile issues like temperance by introducing the Liquor Control Board and reintroducing more French in schools.

During the Depression, Mitchell *Hepburn's Liberals ostensibly shifted to the support of the common people, but in reality Hepburn battled unions and also his federal counterpart, W.L. Mackenzie *King. The Tories took over the government in 1943 and held onto it for the next 42 years. Their success was based on a powerful combination of the old pragmatism and brokerage politics, splits in the opposition between Liberals and the CCF-NDP, and unprecedented prosperity for most of the period. That prosperity began in the war years, and not a little could be traced to closer economic ties with the United States. Some feared this proximity might lead to political integration, but the post-war years exhibited a strong resurgence of Canadian cultural nationalism, backed and informed by federal and provincial support.

When the Tories finally bowed out to a Liberal–NDP alliance in 1985, it appeared as though an era had ended. But most successive governments were measured by the extent to which they adhered to Ontario's centrist pragmatism. Liberal excesses saw them turfed out in 1990, followed by an NDP government that jerked first left and then right, losing its footing and credibility, and finally in 1995 by the triumph of neo-conservative Tories with Mike Harris's 'Common Sense Revolution'. Re-elected in 1999 less because of policies than a buoyant global prosperity for which they took credit, the Tories by 2002, under a new premier, Ernie Eves, were addressing growing unpopularity by abandoning tax-cuts, privatization, and user-fees. It was back to the comfortable, conservative centre—the balance of interests that had characterized Ontario since the coming of the Loyalists more than two centuries before. ROGER HALL

On-to-Ottawa Trek. The trek began in the unemployment *relief camps of British Columbia in June 1935 and culminated in the Regina riot of 1 July that year. Its original purpose was to petition the federal government of R.B. *Bennett about conditions in the camps and to protest recent cuts in relief pay. As it made its way eastwards, however, it became a focal point for a broader public anger at Bennett's failure to deal with the *Great Depression.

In April 1935, 1,500 inmates of federal relief camps in British Columbia went on strike to protest conditions. Organized by the *Workers' Unity League and led by WUL official Arthur 'Slim' Evans (1890–1944), the men took their protest to Vancouver, where they staged demonstrations and questioned civic and provincial politicians. The latter claimed unemployment relief to be a federal responsibility and refused to offer any new assistance. Thus twarted, Evans and other WUL members proposed the On-to-Ottawa Trek. On 3 June 1,000 strikers boarded CPR freight trains to 'steal' rides east. The trek wound its way over the Rockies through Kamloops, Field, Golden, and Calgary, at each stop receiving food and funds raised through 'tag days' organized by local labour councils, women's organizations, and other groups. At the same time, more and more unemployed men joined the procession, eventually doubling its original size.

Bennett viewed the trek as an insurrection and, by the time it reached Regina, ordered that a federal ban on riding freight cars be enforced. This effectively stranded the trek, so Evans led an eight-man delegation to Ottawa to meet with Bennett and negotiate a solution. It was an angry meeting—Bennett called Evans a thief, Evans called Bennett a liar—that ended in acrimony. Further conferences with provincial leaders followed the delegation's return to Regina, but Bennett had decided to act. On the evening of 1 July he ordered a combined force of RCMP and city police to break up a gathering of strikers and citizens. A violent clash ensued, with police firing revolvers and tear-gas bombs, and trekkers fighting back with stones and sticks. By the end, hundreds had been wounded, 130 were arrested, and one police officer lay dead.

A federal enquiry into the riot placed the blame on the trek's leaders. The people of Canada, however, cast their own verdict that year when they threw Bennett and his government out of office. DAVID BRIGHT

opera. Although a few operatic performances were heard in Halifax, Quebec, and Montreal in the 18th century, it was only from the mid-19th century that the towns and cities in Lower and Upper Canada heard opera on a regular basis, thanks to touring companies that mostly originated in the United States. By 1900 opera had become genuinely popular entertainment in Ontario and Quebec and by the mid-20th century Montreal and Toronto were familiar with most of the standard repertoire. The CPR marked the completion of the transcontinental railway by building the Vancouver Opera House, which opened in 1891 with Wagner's *Lohengrin*, and the railway brought travelling companies to Winnipeg and Edmonton in the first decade of the 20th century. The first lasting company was the Canadian Opera Company in Toronto (1950), which until 1990 regularly sent a touring group throughout the country. By the 1980s most of the major cities had permanent production companies with regular, if often short, seasons.

The first opera composed in New France was *Colas et Colinette* (1790) by Joseph Quesnel. Throughout the 19th century composers made sporadic attempts at opera but the country's meagre resources offered few opportunities for performance. During the 20th century a growing number of composers of original works included Alphonse Lavallée-Smith, Healey *Willan, Maurice Blackburn, Jean Vallerand, Harry Somers, John Beckwith, Raymond Pannell, Claude Vivier, André Gagnon, and Randolph Peters. R. Murray Schafer has written a number of theatrical pieces that have been performed in unconventional surroundings, from Toronto Union Station to a wilderness lake at dawn.

The first Canadians who were prominent in opera internationally were the sopranos Emma *Albani (1847–1930) and Marie Toulinguet (1867–1935); the latter, who was born Georgina Stirling, adopted her stage name from her birthplace of Twillingate, Newfoundland. In the course of the 20th century Canadian singers rose to great prominence, among them Edward Johnson, Raoul Jobin, Léopold Simoneau, Maureen Forrester, Louis Quilico, Teresa Stratas, Lois Marshall, Jon Vickers, Michael Schade, Richard Margison, and Ben Heppner. Other important figures include conductors Wilfred Pelletier, Mario Bernardi, Yves Abel, and Bernard Labadie and stage directors Irving Guttman and Robert Carsen.

CARL MOREY

Orange Order. Irish Protestant fraternity and secret society, renowned in Canada for antipathy towards the Catholic Church and French Canadians, bigoted treatment of Catholics, and active support of conservative political parties. The Orange Order is a voluntary association of 'lodges' of Protestant men, organized in a hierarchy of local, county, provincial, and national Grand Lodges in a manner like Freemasons. Its tenets include the correctness of the Protestant faith, loyalty to the English Crown, and maintenance of the traditions of William of Orange. At lodge, members don regalia and perform rituals that promote secretiveness and mysteriousness. They also share in convivial fellowship and conversation. Giving aid to brethren in distress is a central feature of lodge activities and in the late 19th century the order established sickness and death benefit insurance schemes.

The Loyal Orange Association arose from the revolutionary turbulence of Ireland in the 1790s. To defend their 'liberties' (privileges), Protestant farmers in Ulster formed local clubs dedicated to the 'pious and immortal memory' of William of Orange. In 1688, the English Parliament had invited William to replace his Catholic father-in-law, James II, and sustain the Protestant succession. The armies of William and James fought four battles in Ireland, and William's victories secured both the Protestant succession and the privileged position of the loyal Protestant minority in Ireland. The siege of Derry in 1688 and the battle at the Boyne River on 12 July 1690 became epics of Protestant folklore. Each 12th of July Orangemen are pledged to parade in commemoration of William's Boyne victory.

*Irish immigrants established lodges in early Canadian settlement districts. Although authorities tried to proscribe them because of Orange–Catholic riots and violence, the lodges flourished, attracting farmers, labourers, timbermen, artisans, shopkeepers, and local leaders. In 1830 Ogle Gowan, an immigrant from Wexford, convened the first Grand Lodge of British America at Brockville. The Grand Lodge provided Gowan with a platform and a network for organized political activity. That political base grew through Irish immigration, the enculturation of immigrants' children, the acceptance of Orangeism by other Protestants in both rural and developing urban areas, and the deep anti-Catholic sentiment of Canadian Protestant society. The order became most prominent in Newfoundland, New Brunswick, Ontario, and the Prairies. It was at its height during the 1920s, and commenced serious decline in the 1950s.

The history of the order in Canada includes a nasty record of anti-Catholic bigotry, neighbourhood violence, social exclusion, and sectarian riots. But that record overlays a century and a half of social and political relevance. Orange lodges and their traditions served the interests of many conservative and colonial Protestant communities loyal to the English Crown and trying not to become American. CECIL J. HOUSTON

orders-in-council. Formal instruments through which several types of executive actions or orders can take place. Orders-in-council are used to formalize appointments and nominations, to establish regulations fleshing out statutes, to issue special warrants under statutory authority, and to proclaim legislation once it has passed royal assent. An order-in-council is technically an order given by the *governor general or the lieutenant-governor on the advice of the Privy Council. By convention, such orders are formulated by the *cabinet, or cabinet committee, and formally approved only by the governor general or the lieutenant-governor. Between 1990 and 2001 an average of 2,327 OCs per year were passed by the federal cabinet.

JOHN C. COURTNEY AND DANIEL MACFARLANE

Ordre de Bon Temps, or the Order of Good Cheer, was the first social club established by Europeans in North America. The French in Acadia had to adapt to a harsh environment. In the winter of 1606–7, Samuel de *Champlain devised a plan to entertain the men during the long, cold winter months and to raise their spirits. Each person was, in turn, to provide food for the day's banquet and prepare the menu for the next day. The Ordre de Bon Temps led to competition between the men and was instrumental in maintaining their morale and improving their diet. The government of Nova Scotia now uses the order's theme of revelry to promote tourism.

JEAN DAIGLE

Ordre de Jacques-Cartier. Commonly called *La Patente,* the order obtained its letters patent in October 1927, a year after a group of 17 people with shared concerns had met in Ottawa. It is difficult to be exact about the secret society's membership and its actions. However, some of its members believed that it set in motion every positive development in French Canada, even the *Quiet Revolution. Supporters and opponents agree that it was very influential in Quebec society for more than three decades. As a group the OJC played an important role in many matters in various spheres and at different levels. It created, pressured, or was involved in politics (the *Union nationale and *Bloc populaire, municipal councils), education (school boards, curricula and textbooks, Département de l'Instruction publique, teachers' communities, leisure activities and playgrounds), economics (caisses populaires, co-operatives, insurance companies), the media (particularly at *Le Devoir*), and trade unions. Described by fierce adversaries as a French Catholic Ku Klux Klan, it promoted Catholic values and French-Canadian traditions. Because the order failed to adapt to the declining power of the church and the modernization of Quebec nationalism, its influence lessened and it was officially disbanded in 1965. RAYMOND HUDON

Ordres, Les. The events of October 1970 in Quebec have been brought to the screen in three very different films. Robin Spry's *Action* (1973) is a thoughtful documentary that provides the 'official' history of the *October Crisis. Pierre Falardeau's *Octobre* (1994) fictionalizes the events from the perspective of the kidnappers and focuses on the ideological and ethical conflicts experienced by members of the *Front de Libération du Québec. Michel Brault's *Les Ordres* (1974), the most critically acclaimed of the three, abstains from both Spry's authoritative commentary and Falardeau's subversive discourse to show the effects of the *War Measures Act (decreed on 16 October 1970) on the hundreds of innocent people who were arrested and incarcerated without just cause. Based on interviews with actual victims of the act, *Les Ordres* mixes documentary style with fictionalized narrative to achieve a high degree of authenticity while transcending the limits of local history to reflect on the impact of authoritarianism on ordinary people. Recipient of the esteemed Best Director Award at Cannes in 1975 for *Les Ordres*, Brault has devoted his entire career as a fiction filmmaker, documentarian, and realist cinematographer to giving a voice and a face to those ordinary people whose place in Quebec history has been overshadowed by the public scuffles between federalists and separatists. ANDRÉ LOISELLE

Oregon Boundary Treaty, 1846, a settlement between the United States and Great Britain that divided the area farthest west of the Rocky Mountains between the two powers along the 49th parallel. The division ended at the coastal straits, leaving all of Vancouver Island to the British. Although the name 'Oregon' now refers to a US state, during the early to mid-19th century it applied to a much larger area west of the Rocky Mountains. During the earlier part of the century, the *Hudson's Bay Company was virtually uncontested in its domination of 'Old Oregon'. Sir George *Simpson, who saw the region as useful due to the availability of furs, had established a number of forts, including Fort Langley near the mouth of the Fraser River, and British control of the Pacific coast was evident. However, US interest in the area also began to increase; by 1846 the number of American settlers numbered about 6,000. President James Polk, who came to power in 1845, famously declared '54 40 or fight', demanding all of the land up to the Russian boundary. However, the Americans became distracted by a war with Mexico, and did not wish to fight on two fronts. The British, sensing this, withdrew all land claims south of the Columbia River, and the treaty was signed on 15 June 1846. The British won the right to navigate the Columbia River, although the water boundary was often confused as the treaty did not take into account the fact that the strait breaks into several channels, in which ownership of the islands was often contested. The Treaty of Washington (1871) aimed to deal with this issue as well as other Canadian–US disputes, although final resolution came only in 1872 when the arbitrator, the German Emperor Wilhelm I, decided upon Haro Strait as the boundary.

BARRY M. GOUGH

Organization of American States. The OAS, an association founded in 1948 and now consisting of North American, Latin American, and Caribbean countries, includes Canada, the United States, Mexico, Brazil, Argentina, and more than 30 other states. Although it had permanent observer status at OAS headquarters in Washington from 1972, Canada did not join until 1990; the long period of ambivalence towards membership reflected the low standing of hemispheric affairs in official and public thinking and scepticism about an institution where the United States was inevitably at the centre of things. Canada is the second largest contributor to the OAS budget, and takes a particular lead on security issues and on the promotion of democracy, human rights, and freer trade beyond the North American Free Trade Agreement. Nevertheless, Caribbean and Latin American relationships, apart from those with Mexico and Brazil, remain on the periphery of Canadian *foreign policy concerns. NORMAN HILLMER

Orkneymen. In the early 18th century the *Hudson's Bay Company began recruiting servants—mainly boatmen and labourers—from the Orkney Islands, located off the north coast of Scotland. Hardier than the company's English servants, Orkneymen comprised approximately 80 per cent of the labour force by 1800 and continued to be recruited well into the 20th century. With their fishing and farming ancestry, they were well suited to the work at bayside factories and inland fur posts. While most occupied the lower levels of the HBC hierarchy, some like John Rae and William Tomison rose to prominent positions in the fur trade. Many Orkneymen returned home after the expiration of their contracts, but some stayed in the West and married Native women. Today, many Canadian families can trace their ancestry to these early Scottish fur traders. ROBERT J. COUTTS

orphanages. Institutional care for *children has a long history in Canada. An early example is the Crèche d'Youville, established in Montreal during the 1750s by Grey Nuns' founder Marguérite d'Youville to shelter exposed and abandoned infants. Well into the 20th century, the crèche collected babies abandoned anonymously on doorsteps, in church pews, or by unwed mothers who had given birth in the maternity hospital run by the *Soeurs de la Miséricorde. In contrast to foundlings, *orphans* did not attract a specific institutional response until the second half of the 19th century. In the earlier period, children whose parents had died were more likely to be raised by friends or relatives than placed in an institution. But the later 19th century saw the growth of industrial capitalism, and with it the problem of urban poverty. Many working-class families, especially immigrants, lacked the kin and community networks that provided a safety net for orphaned children in rural, pre-capitalist societies. Reform-minded religious and voluntary groups began to see the proliferation of young 'waifs and strays'—to say nothing of *juvenile delinquents and child prostitutes—as a major social problem deserving a specific response.

Canada's network of orphanages was built in this context, with a view to 'saving the children' by substituting enlightened institutional care for parental guidance and support. In the decades after 1850, local committees instituted Protestant Orphans' Homes in cities from Halifax to Victoria. At the same time, the Catholic Church established a parallel network of denominational orphanages, including St-Alexis in Montreal, Mount Cashel in St John's, and homes named after St Patrick in Ottawa, Quebec, and many other cities. Meanwhile, between Confederation and the mid-1920s a Canadian *'home children' movement flourished. Agencies such as the Barnardo Homes channelled some 80,000 British children into Canada, most of whom were indentured to rural families as agricultural labourers or domestic servants.

Canadian orphanages had their heyday between the 1870s and the 1950s. Their clientele was always much broader than a narrow construction of the term 'orphan' would suggest. Poor families in crisis used the orphanage as a temporary refuge for children they could not support, and only one-third of the British home children sent to Canada were orphans. As the state began to provide families with the means to keep children at home despite unemployment, illness, and widowhood, and as the thinking around children and social welfare turned away from the 'asylum' and towards foster homes, institutions like the British Columbia Protestant Orphans' Home lost their raison d'être. Founded in Victoria by Reverend Edward Cridge in 1873, this orphanage closed in 1969, having sheltered some 1,600 needy children over the course of its history.

Life for children in Canadian orphanages was highly structured, with a strong emphasis on rules, routines, and discipline. Whether large or small, purpose-built or converted from other uses, the buildings typically featured dormitories, classrooms, workshops, a dining area, and spaces reserved for worship and exercise. Accounts vary widely, but some young Canadians clearly took comfort in the routine and predictability offered by the institutional setting. 'I felt greater security there than at home, where my family was disrupted by poverty, illness, and death', writes Lionel Allard of the years he spent in Quebec City's Nazareth Orphanage in the early 1920s. Recent scandals, however, have left a bleak impression of life in these institutions. Accounts of physical and sexual abuse at Mount Cashel first emerged publicly in 1989. The orphanage was closed later that year; and a painful public inquiry in 1990 led to the arrest and conviction of several Christian Brothers and the payment of $11 million in compensation by the Newfoundland government. In the early 1990s, a group called Les Enfants de Duplessis began seeking compensation for the treatment they had received while inmates of Quebec's child-welfare institutions in the 1940s and 1950s. Many had been falsely classified as 'mentally deficient' and transferred from crowded orphanages and crèches to a potentially much more damaging environment: the province's psychiatric hospitals.

PETER GOSSAGE

Oshawa strike. The 16-day strike at General Motors' Oshawa plant in April 1937 was the first successful organizing campaign in Canada's manufacturing sector by an industrial union, the United Automobile Workers. This dispute over the right to organize and bargain collectively gained support across the country and from American autoworkers, particularly after Premier Mitchell *Hepburn intervened, objecting to the local's affiliation with the militant Congress of Industrial Organizations, branded by the Canadian press as foreign and communist-inspired.

Faced with wage cuts, speedup on the line, and layoffs, the auto workers formed their union by secret organizing, sporadic shutdowns, and then by open support, wearing union buttons. When the company refused to negotiate, the strike began. Hepburn asked the federal government for RCMP, and sent in the provincial police and 'specials', called by the strikers the 'sons of Mitches'. He instructed the welfare department to refuse relief to strikers, even though they received no strike pay. Cabinet ministers Arthur Roebuck and David Croll resigned, protesting Hepburn's actions. Despite having no financial assistance from the UAW, the local union held on. A brief economic upturn convinced the company to produce cars, and finally it negotiated a collective agreement, which, at Hepburn's insistence, made no reference to the UAW, even though the local publicly reaffirmed its UAW connection. The workers won their demands. The CIO issue polarized the province and helped Hepburn win re-election in 1937, but workers, buoyed by the victory in Oshawa, organized other unions and increasingly supported the Co-operative Commonwealth Federation, while Hepburn's anti-labour position lessened the Ontario Liberal Party's support among the growing ranks of organized labour.

LAUREL SEFTON MacDOWELL

Osler, Sir William (1858–1919), physician. One of the several high-achieving sons of an Anglican circuit-rider in backwoods Ontario, Willie Osler took a medical degree at McGill in 1874, completed his training in Europe, and settled down as a McGill faculty member, prolific publisher of pathological studies, and part-time practising physician. In 1884 he became professor of clinical medicine at the University of Pennsylvania and in 1889 was appointed physician in chief and professor of medicine at the Johns Hopkins Hospital and Medical School in Baltimore. In 1892 he published *The Principles and Practice of Medicine*, which became the Bible of medical education throughout the English-speaking world.

At Hopkins in the 1890s Osler became the great American physician, idolized by students and colleagues for the breadth of his knowledge, his boundless enthusiasm for the medical calling, and his kindliness and personal charisma. A great bedside teacher as well as an inspiring essayist, he introduced the clinical clerkship into American medical education and, in the brilliant dawn of modern medicine, came to personify the role of the physician as healer. In 1905 he accepted the Regius Professorship at Oxford, dying there in 1919 in the aftermath of the influenza epidemic. His only child, Revere, was killed in France in 1917.

Osler lives on in medical memory as the patron saint of clinical medicine. He is commemorated by the Osler Library at McGill, many Osler societies, medals, and lectureships, and a major hospital in Toronto. His career exemplifies the role Canada once played as a conduit of

Anglo-European professional values to the new world, and, to a degree, the Canadian 'brain drain' to the United States. MICHAEL BLISS

Ottawa. Canada's capital city. Ottawa has changed often since it emerged in 1826 from a beaver swamp on a high bluff above the Ottawa River, some 200 km west of Montreal. That year a British engineer, Lt.-Col. John *By, arrived to build a waterway along the line of the Rideau River to the British naval arsenal at *Kingston, to thwart the invasion plans of the restless Yankees. 'Bytown' began as a construction camp alongside the valley leading down to the Ottawa River, in which the headlocks of the Rideau Canal were located. Two small townsites were soon marked out, intended for 'tradesmen and artificers' to service the canal. Like most cities in Canada, Bytown had a military beginning, but soon the little canal town began to service an emerging trade in *squared timber and the nearby farms, soon becoming a rough frontier town of merchants, tradesmen, professionals, and the itinerant workers of the timber trade, who moved through the town in the fall to the bush shanties and back again in the spring with the rafts of squared timber. It was also divided: the Lower Town a commercial place embracing many French and Irish Catholics, the Upper Town of Protestant professionals. Soldiers defending the canal often kept the two factions apart.

In 1855 Bytown was transformed into the city of Ottawa. It had acquired a rail and telegraph link to the St Lawrence Valley via the Ottawa and Prescott Railway, and mills powered by the massive Chaudière Falls began to saw *lumber for the American market. With squared timber and sawn lumber, Ottawa emerged as one of the largest wood-based cities in the world. At the end of the 1850s, Ottawa was chosen capital of the *Province of Canada, and in 1859 work began on the government buildings on Barracks Hill. In 1867, the provincial capital became the capital of the Dominion of Canada, and Barracks Hill became Parliament Hill.

Until the end of the century the woods industries, including *pulp and paper, dominated the city. Ottawa in 1900 was a working-class town. The lumber town steadily lost ground to government, and by the end of the Second World War the public service, numbering some 30,000 employees, was clearly dominant. Prime Minister Mackenzie *King was determined to make a worthy capital and, guided by the Gréber Plan of 1950, Ottawa was transformed into a modern white-collar city. Business travel and *tourism became the second industry. Ottawa also became much larger: in 1950, a massive annexation increased the area of the city over four-fold, to control development and provide land for it.

Not only did government continue to grow, but in 1961, with the *National Research Council and the Defence Research Board in place, Computing Devices was born in the private sector and Bell Northern Research (now Nortel) moved its operations to Ottawa. They provided the seedbed for a high-tech industry, now approaching in size the 70,000 employees of government. People and businesses spilled over the boundaries of the enlarged city of 1950. It was no longer a population divided along the old Catholic and Protestant or French and English lines, though the school system continues to reflect that reality. Small Jewish, Italian, Asian, and German communities from the early 20th century grew apace, and were joined after the Second World War by an Arabic-speaking community and more recently by an East African and Vietnamese community. Currently visible minorities account for 15 per cent of the population. English is still the dominant language at 65 per cent, but French, at 15 per cent, has fallen behind those who speak neither English nor French, at 19 per cent. To deal with the growth, a regional government was created in 1968, but on 1 January 2001, the 'old' City of Ottawa, ten area municipalities, and the regional government merged to form a new city that now embraces about 800,000 people. Its economy and society is centred on government and advanced technology, each sector among the largest in the nation. JOHN H. TAYLOR

Otter, Sir William Dillon (1843–1929), a veteran Canadian soldier, sometimes called the Father of the Force. Born near Clinton, Canada West, Otter worked as a clerk in the Canada Company's Toronto office while building a reputation as an athlete and as an officer in Toronto's Queen's Own Rifles. He survived the Battle of Ridgeway in June 1866 and commanded his regiment from 1875 to 1883, when he joined the *permanent force. He led the Battleford Column to Cut Knife Creek in the 1885 campaign, commanded central Ontario's Military District No. 2, and, from 1893, the Royal Canadian Regiment, grouping permanent force infantry. In 1899, he was the logical choice to command the first Canadian contingent to the *South African War. His insistence on strict discipline and hard training was unpopular with subordinates but prepared his men for their demanding battle at Paardeberg in 1900. In 1908 the Laurier government made him the first Canadian-born chief of the general staff and later inspector general but his career ended in 1912 after his old enemy, Sam Hughes, became minister of militia. Otter commanded Canada's internment camps 1914–20. The British knighted him in 1913 and in 1922 he became the second Canadian soldier (after Sir Arthur *Currie) to reach the rank of general.
DESMOND MORTON

outport resettlement. Beginning in the mid-20th century, organized efforts were made to centralize the population of Newfoundland. In his efforts to promote industrial development, Premier Joseph *Smallwood had to deal with the rising expectations for a standard of living concomitant with Newfoundland's status, since 1949, as a province of Canada. The challenge for government was to get public services into many of the small isolated communities. At a conference in 1956 Smallwood told delegates that 1,000 of the province's 1,300 scattered outports should be eliminated so that more people could live in fewer settlements and have a better life (as late as 1961,

815 of the province's then 1,104 communities had fewer than 300 inhabitants). During the 1950s a program was initiated to encourage residents to move voluntarily. Launched in 1954 and lasting until 1965, the province's first resettlement program saw over 110 communities and some 8,000 people resettled. Provincial assistance of $150 was available for each household (later increased to $600), but only if everyone in the community agreed to move. In 1965 both the federal and provincial governments initiated a program specifically designed to move people to larger towns designated as growth centres. The federal government hoped to rationalize and modernize a fishery that was based on offshore fishing and processing plants located in larger urban centres. Between 1965 and 1970, 116 communities were resettled, involving 3,242 families (16,000 people). A community was resettled only when 90 per cent (lowered to 80 per cent in 1966) of residents agreed to move to one of the approved reception centres. The head of a household received a basic grant of $1,000 towards the cost of moving and $200 each for other family members. Most of the growth centres were located on the south coast, where several towns had a strong economy based on the modern offshore fishery. Resettlement remains a strong, emotional issue that tugs at the hearts and souls of those who were directly affected.

MELVIN BAKER AND AIDAN MALONEY

Overlanders. The name given to the 350 Canadians who travelled to the Cariboo gold fields between 1858 and 1863, the first immigrants to do so by land. From Canada, they travelled first to *Red River, where their trek really began. The main contingent of 250 (including four women and five children) left in 1862, after dividing itself into three groups based on route as well as religion, friendship, temperance, and nationality. Regardless of their path, the Overlanders discovered the road to riches was tortuous. What was supposed to be an easy five-week excursion turned into a gruelling expedition through the Yellowhead Pass, across the Rockies, and down the Fraser, which lasted four months, killed ten men, and convinced others to abandon their dreams of striking it rich. The majority of Overlanders made it to the Cariboo, but mining made few of them wealthy. Nonetheless, many went on to gain positions of influence in British Columbia. The presence of the Overlanders distinguished the *Cariboo gold rush from the earlier, American-dominated *Fraser River one, and shaped the colony's political culture. Caribooites strongly supported Confederation and—perhaps remembering their own difficult journey across Canada—a transcontinental railway.

TINA LOO

Overseas Military Forces of Canada. Not yet independent, Canada was at war because Britain was at war in August 1914, but the Canadian government (and particularly militia and defence minister Sam *Hughes) was adamant that Canadian soldiers serve together in Canadian units and formations under (wherever possible) Canadian command and that Ottawa be responsible for their care and custody. Hughes took on the latter task with enthusiasm, but was dismissed in November 1916 because of erratic behaviour that, Robert *Borden especially believed, had impeded the efforts of the *Canadian Expeditionary Force. To maintain Canada's control of its army, the prime minister took the unusual step of setting up an overseas department of government headed by a full cabinet minister permanently resident in London. Under Sir George Perley and, subsequently, Sir Edward Kemp, the Ministry of Overseas Military Forces of Canada brought order to the administration of the CEF and steadfastly supported *Canadian Corps commanders Sir Julian Byng and Sir Arthur *Currie in their efforts to enhance and protect the fighting abilities and cohesiveness of their formation. Training in England was geared to front-line requirements; officers were appointed and promoted on the basis of merit; and, in March 1918, OMFC stood behind Currie when he resisted British efforts to break up the corps following a massive German offensive. While Sir Arthur Currie and his divisional and brigade commanders provided the military leadership that made the Canadian Corps a great field army, the OMFC provided the administrative and political support that allowed Currie's leadership to flourish.

STEPHEN J. HARRIS

Pacific Great Eastern Railway. This British Columbia railway received its charter and substantial provincial bond guarantees in 1912. It had authorization to build from North Vancouver via Squamish and Lillooet to a junction with the Grand Trunk Pacific Railway at Fort George (later Prince George). In 1914 it received additional bond guarantees to build an extension from Fort George to the *Peace River country. Construction proceeded slowly, and the company became embroiled in political scandals and financial difficulties. In 1918 the provincial government acquired all its capital stock. The line was operational only between Squamish and Quesnel when construction was halted in the 1930s. Freight was carried from Squamish to North Vancouver by barge. In 1952, 40 years after its incorporation, the railway reached Fort George. The line from Squamish to North Vancouver was opened for traffic in 1956, and the extension to the banks of the Peace River at Fort St John in 1971. A branch to Dawson Creek provided a much needed connection with the Northern Alberta Railways.
T.D. REGEHR

Pacific Scandal, 1873. The scandal resulted from the Liberal-Conservative Party's accepting election campaign contributions from individuals seeking the contract to build a railway to the Pacific. Although the Canadian government, under the leadership of Sir John A. *Macdonald, was committed to building a transcontinental railway, the prime minister could not muster a politically acceptable company to undertake its construction. He was torn between the Canada Pacific, under the leadership of Sir Hugh *Allan, a Montreal-based shipping magnate, and the Inter-oceanic, under the management of David L. Macpherson, a Toronto-based businessman. His attempt to amalgamate the two companies failed, as did his bid to form a government-appointed board of directors. Unfortunately for Macdonald, Allan's proposal had the backing of the Northern Pacific, an American-owned railway that planned to traverse the continent south of the Great Lakes and then head across the Canadian prairies and Rocky Mountains. Although he initially approved the American involvement, public opinion forced Macdonald to veto the Northern Pacific connection when he finally awarded the contract to Allan's Canada Pacific. Outraged, the jilted Northern Pacific management leaked documents that exposed Allan's financial contributions to the Liberal-Conservative Party during the closely fought 1872 election campaign. When a royal commission implicated Macdonald and his lieutenant Sir George-Étienne *Cartier, the prime minister was forced to resign in November 1873. The first attempt to award the contract for the western portion of the transcontinental railway had failed. A.A. DEN OTTER

pacifism. A belief, based upon either religious or humanitarian ideals, that war and social violence are immoral, inhuman, irrational, and therefore wrong. In Canada there are two pacifist traditions: sectarian pacifism and liberal pacifism.

Sectarian pacifism is represented by the historic nonresistance of religious sects, such as the Society of Friends (*Quakers), *Mennonites, Hutterities, and *Doukhobors, which hold as a tenet of their faith the refusal to bear arms. Upon entering Canada these groups received official guarantees that they could live according to their pacifist beliefs; exempt from military service during the two world wars, they formed the nucleus of conscientious objectors in those conflicts.

Liberal pacifism is based on the pacifist teachings of Jesus as well as a faith in the power of human reason to settle disputes without recourse to violence. Largely inspired by the Protestant *social gospel, it surfaced at the beginning of the 20th century in the progressive reform movement, which emphasized international arbitration and conciliation as the best way to preserve world order and peace. Before the outbreak of the First World War nearly all church, farm, labour, and women's groups endorsed this principle, and the Canadian Peace and Arbitration Society, the first secular peace group in Canada, organized a small peace campaign.

With the outbreak of war, however, the liberal peace movement disintegrated, leaving only a small but vocal contingent of committed pacifists such as J.S. *Woodsworth and William Ivens, renegade Methodist ministers who openly broke with their church in opposition to conscription, and Laura Hughes, Alice Chown, and Francis Marion *Beynon, outspoken feminists of the day. It was particularly embarrassing to the authorities that Hughes was the niece of the minister of militia and defence, Colonel Sam *Hughes, and Chown was the cousin of the superintendent of the Methodist Church, Samuel Dwight Chown, but before the end of the war even these voices of pacifist dissent had been effectively silenced.

By the mid-1920s there was a resurgence of liberal pacifism, partly out of disillusionment with the last war and partly out of support for the *League of Nations and disarmament. As Woodsworth and Agnes *Macphail pressed the peace issue in Parliament, and the Canadian branch of the Women's International League for Peace and Freedom conducted a campaign to abolish *cadet training in schools and militarism in textbooks, an inter-war peace movement took shape. By the 1930s it represented a broad coalition of religious and political groups that staged peace rallies and torchlight parades. Yet, this common front was short lived, and with increased fascist aggression by the mid-1930s social radicals deserted the peace movement for the fight against fascism. Once the Second World War began even the CCF abandoned its neutralist foreign policy, leaving only J.S. Woodsworth to voice his pacifist position in Parliament.

Except for the Quakers, who helped organize the popular peace movement, sectarian pacifists remained withdrawn from mainstream society throughout these years, but they also remained committed pacifists and, as in the first war, they formed the bulk of conscientious objectors (approximately 12,000). Support for liberal pacifism was reduced to a small core of Christian pacifists organized through the Fellowship of Reconciliation. Their most dramatic protest came in October 1939, shortly after the war began, with the publication of a pacifist manifesto signed by 68 (ultimately 75) *United Church ministers. Otherwise, official constraints limited pacifist activities, as they had in 1914–18.

The atomic bombing of Hiroshima and Nagasaki at the war's end increased the urgency and popular appeal of pacifism with a new focus on nuclear disarmament and the easing of Cold War tensions. The Canadian Peace Congress, headed by James G. *Endicott, took the lead in organizing a 'ban the bomb' campaign in the early 1950s but its ties to Soviet communism severely weakened its popularity. In the 1960s the Canadian Campaign for Nuclear Disarmament and the *Voice of Women generated wider public support for disarmament while opposition to the Vietnam War produced a renewed interest in pacifism. By the 1980s both sectarian and liberal pacifists were swept up in a broad anti-nuclear campaign in response to heightened tensions between East and West, but the collapse of Soviet communism also meant the collapse of the popular peace movement. Nevertheless, pacifism, whether based on sectarian or liberal humanitarian beliefs, remained an important ingredient in anti-war protests. THOMAS P. SOCKNAT

Padlock Law. Anti-communist legislation passed by the Quebec government in 1937. During the Great Depression, various groups defined communism as a threat to Christianity and humanity, and for a time the *Communist Party of Canada was banned by the federal government. In the context of the Spanish Civil War (1936–9), many in Quebec felt that state repression was the most legitimate way to deal with the communist threat, and the Catholic Church, and particularly Quebec City archbishop Rodrigue Villeneuve and other right-wing nationalists, promoted this idea. The newly elected Quebec premier, Maurice *Duplessis, brought forward legislation called an Act Respecting Communistic Propaganda. It defined communism broadly and gave police the authority to close, for one year, any building suspected of being a communist propaganda centre. It also made illegal the printing and distribution of communist material. Despite pressure from the Co-operative Commonwealth Federation and other groups concerned with freedom of expression and the dangers of state abuses, the federal government refused to disallow the Padlock Act. In 1957 it was struck down by the Supreme Court of Canada.

MARCEL MARTEL

Painters Eleven. A group of Toronto-based abstract painters, Painters Eleven had a major impact on the Toronto art scene in the 1950s and were instrumental in developing a new respect for contemporary art. Formed to create a common platform for the exhibition of abstract art, the group began when William Ronald (1926–98) mounted the 1953 exhibition 'Abstracts at Home' in the furniture-display area of Simpsons department store. The seven artists represented—Ronald, Jack Bush (1909–77), Oscar Cahén (1916–56), Tom Hodgson (b. 1924), Alexandra Luke (1901–67), Ray Mead (1921–98), and Kazuo Nakamura (1926–2000)—were later joined by Hortense Gordon (1887–1961), J.W.G. (Jock) Macdonald (1897–1960), Harold Town (1924–90), and Walter Yarwood (1917–97) to form Painters Eleven.

Members held no single idea of the nature of abstraction. Their work varied from the expressionist bravura of Ronald and Hodgson to the subtle paintings of Nakamura, who found a premise for his art in the structures and patterns revealed by the physical sciences. Their sources were varied: Macdonald, who had been exploring abstraction since 1934, introduced Luke to surrealist automatic painting in Banff in 1945 and would later teach and inspire Ronald at the Ontario College of Art. Mead trained in England; Cahén in Europe; Luke, Gordon, Macdonald, and Ronald worked with Hans Hofmann in Provincetown, Massachusetts. Influenced by international developments and particularly by the New York School, they were also aware of the work of their Montreal counterparts, especially the *Automatistes.

Exhibitions were held annually in Toronto from 1954 to 1958, first at the Roberts Gallery, then at the newly opened Park Gallery in 1957 and in 1958 ('Painters Eleven with Ten Distinguished Artists from Quebec'). In 1956 they showed at New York's Riverside Museum with the association of American Abstract Artists. In 1958, Macdonald wrote that he believed the group's objectives had been achieved: critics were championing their work and new galleries supporting contemporary work had opened. In 1960, the year of Macdonald's death, Painters Eleven voted to disband. JOYCE ZEMANS

Palliser expedition. Captain John Palliser, whose name is forever linked with the Canadian Prairies, was a member of the 19th-century Irish gentry. He was instrumental in the process that brought the vast western *Hudson's Bay Company territories into the new Dominion of

Canada. In 1857 the British government commissioned Palliser to head an expedition to the North-West Territories to assess its agricultural potential. Behind the decision was the Province of Canada's growing interest in the region. The British government also had to decide whether to renew the HBC's exclusive licence to trade in those territories outside the original charter. Though Palliser was not a scientist, he surrounded himself with individuals of impeccable training, including British army officer Thomas Wright Blakiston and Edinburgh medical graduate James Hector. The result was a group of considerable ability.

Palliser's expedition began in the summer of 1857 and continued through 1859. The group travelled extensively, going through the upper Great Lakes to Red River and traversing much of the Prairies and the Rockies. The resultant topographical and botanical reports did much, along with the parallel work of Canadian Henry Youle *Hind, to alter British and Canadian understanding of the region's potential for settlement. One observation in particular became an indelible part of the lexicon of Canadian geography. There was a section of land, noted the report, 'forming a triangle, having as its base the 49th parallel from the longtitude 100 degrees to 114 degrees W., with its apex reaching the 52 parallel of latitude'. This triangle was, Palliser concluded, an extension of the 'Great American Desert' and unsuited for agriculture. His conclusion created controversy, especially among later promoters of immigration. By the 1880s authoritative writers had dismissed it and during the turn of the century boom much of the area was settled. The triangle seemed a relic of history. Yet droughts in the triangle after the First World War and during the Great Depression of the 1930s confirmed the original assessment of Palliser and his expedition. DOUG OWRAM

Palliser's Act. Passed by the British Parliament in 1775, the Act for the Encouragement of the Fisheries Carried on from Great Britain reflected the official view of Newfoundland as a seasonal fishing station. What was popularly known as Palliser's Act, in honour of Governor Hugh Palliser, did not actually bar settlers from coming to Newfoundland but rather prohibited fishing servants from staying after their contracts had expired. It codified the local custom that the salt fish produced each summer was liable first for the payment of servants' wages. Following broader trends in imperial law, Palliser's Act also criminalized breach of contract. Servants who willingly absented themselves without permission, or neglected or refused to work according to the terms of their covenant, were to be fined two days' pay for each day of absence or neglect of duty. Those who absented themselves without leave for five days were deemed a deserter and forfeited all of their wages to their master. Convicted deserters were liable to be publicly whipped as vagrants and shipped back to their country of origin. JERRY BANNISTER

Palliser Triangle. *See* DUST BOWL.

Papineau, Louis-Joseph (1786–1871), lawyer, seigneur, politician. Born in Montreal, Papineau was exposed to the Enlightenment by his father, who sold him the seigneury of Petite Nation in 1817. Elected to the assembly in 1808, he eventually became leader of the Parti canadien, and later of the *Patriotes. His oratorial skills and passion energized French-Canadian nationalism. Initially, as a moderate, Papineau admired British institutions, but frustrated by disputes with the *Château Clique and by the unmoveable colonial stance of the British, he became increasingly radical. By 1832, this complex man considered himself a 'republican', a political reformist, and a 'democrat', yet at the same time he was a 'social conservative', defending the *seigneurial system. Although anti-clerical and a non-believer, he viewed the Catholic clergy as a pillar of the nation. Only his nationalism, his constitutional positions on financial control and decision making in the colony, and his oratory held together a party comprised of traditional and liberal elements. In the Ninety-two Resolutions, Papineau and others put forward their demands for control of revenues by the assembly, *responsible government, and election of the legislative council. Rejected by the British, some advocated violence.

Historians debate whether Papineau planned the *Rebellions of 1837–8. Though plans certainly existed, government action prevented their execution. It can be argued, too, that Papineau, although radical in his pronouncements, did not approve of violence. But when public rallies gathered steam in 1837, he lost control to the more radical and revolutionary elements in the party preaching violence and a social revolution. Fleeing to the United States, Papineau disagreed with the other exiled leaders and remained aloof from the 1838 rebellion. In 1839 he left for Paris, where he stayed until 1845. Pressured by friends, he returned to politics in 1848 and found himself fighting Louis-Hippolyte *LaFontaine over the union of the Canadas and responsible government: he loathed the first and preferred annexation to the 'illusion' of the latter. Gradually, between 1852 and 1855, he withdrew from politics, busying himself with the administration of his seigneury. JEAN-PIERRE WALLOT

Papineau-Couture, Jean (1916–2000), composer, teacher, administrator. Born in Montreal, Papineau-Couture was one of the most important musicians in Canada, and especially Quebec, during the second half of the 20th century. Many of his students at the Université de Montréal (1951–87) subsequently became notable musicians and composers; as a member of organizations for the support of *music and the arts (Canada Council, Canadian Music Centre, Canadian League of Composers, Conseil des arts du Québec, etc.) he influenced the course of musical life throughout Canada as well as in his city and home province. His music is sensitive and often richly expressive but always with an intellectual control of form and technique. Throughout his career he explored many varied stylistic challenges of composition but his music consistently reflects a distinctive and original personality.

He wrote extensively for orchestra, chamber ensembles, voice, and keyboard instruments. CARL MOREY

Parent, Étienne (1802–74), journalist, member of the assembly, civil servant. Appointed editor of *Le *Canadien* at the age of 20, Parent became an important and influential supporter of the Parti patriote and its republican program before dramatically breaking with Louis-Joseph *Papineau in the fall of 1836 over what he saw as the movement's annexationist tendencies. His moderate stance allowed *Le Canadien* to continue publishing through the rebellions, but did not protect him from being jailed for criticizing the government's policy of violent repression. Parent continued to write from his cell, advocating *responsible government, criticizing *Durham's Report and proposals to assimilate the French Canadians. Initially opposed to the Union Act, Parent was elected to the legislature in 1841 and in 1842 began a 30-year career as a senior civil servant with the Canadian government. A series of remarkable lectures in the 1840s and 1850s, most notably *L'Industrie considérée comme moyen de conserver notre nationalité* (1846), urging French Canadians to participate in the new industrial economy, cemented his reputation as a forward-looking yet moderate liberal. Many historians consider Parent an important exponent of a moderate liberal tradition that would find its fullest expression 30 years later in the thought of Wilfrid *Laurier.

LOUIS-GEORGES HARVEY

Parent, Madeleine (1919–), trade unionist. Born in Montreal, Parent graduated from McGill University in 1940 and devoted most of her life to the trade-union movement. She organized textile workers in Montreal, then in Valleyfield, where she led and won a major strike in 1946. In 1947, as organizer of a strike in Lachute woollen mills, she was arrested and charged with seditious conspiracy. Premier Maurice *Duplessis carried a personal vendetta against her, and by the time she was acquitted in 1955 her trial had been the longest in Quebec history. A staunch champion of Canadian *unions, as opposed to American-affiliated ones, in partnership with her husband Kent Rowley she founded the Canadian Textile and Chemical Union and the Council of Canadian Unions in 1969, later the Confederation of Canadian Unions. In Ontario, she was at the forefront of a number of strikes in the 1970s and 1980s. A founding member of the *National Action Committee on the Status of Women, she fought for equal pay for work of equal value, and championed the interests of Native women. An active defender of women's rights, especially those of immigrant women, she is a vocal critic of neo-liberalism and American imperialism. ANDRÉE LÉVESQUE

Paris Peace Conference. From the First World War's armistice until June 1919, Prime Minister Robert *Borden fought hard to gain Canada separate recognition first within the British Empire delegation and then as a state represented at the Paris Peace Conference that led to the treaties levied on Germany and its allies. The United States was particularly resistant, but with 60,000 Canadian dead on European battlefields, it was a hard case to deny. Helped by other dominions' statesmen, Borden won. On 28 June, dominion delegates signed the Treaty of Versailles separately as well as part of the empire—the first time that Canada did so for a multilateral international treaty. Clearly, Canada's primary interest at Paris was in securing its own national status both in the world and in the empire rather than making the world safe. As C.P. *Stacey has written, these events established Canada and the other dominions as 'international persons in their own right . . . combining the status of small independent countries with the solid advantage of association with a great power'. Certainly such events laid the basis for Canadian participation in the *League of Nations, for the British *Commonwealth, and for Canadian independence manifest in the *Statute of Westminster 12 years later.

RONALD HAYCOCK

Parkin, George Robert (1846–1922), educator, imperialist, author. Parkin was the best known of Canada's imperial nationalists from 1880 to 1920. An influential teacher in New Brunswick, 1868–89, reforming headmaster of Upper Canada College, 1895–1902, and first organizing secretary of the Rhodes scholarships, 1902–20, he was throughout a tireless advocate for closer unity within the *British Empire. This was not slavish colonialism, but Canadian national pride. Geopolitical position in an age of railways and steamships, and moral strength bred of northern climate, *Loyalist roots, and idealist values, ensured for Canada a 'keystone' imperial role. Through such influential books as *Imperial Federation* (1892), *Round the Empire* (1892), *The Great Dominion* (1895), and *Sir John A. Macdonald* (1908), Parkin advanced a two-pronged historical interpretation: that Canada was increasingly pan-Britannic in orientation, and that (anticipating the *Laurentian thesis) the east–west geographical features of Canada resisted north–south continental integration.

TERRY COOK

parks. *See* NATIONAL PARKS; ALGONQUIN PARK.

parliamentary democracy. One of two major forms of government (the other being the presidential-congressional model) used in liberal democratic states. Canadian parliamentary democracy has its roots in the British, or Westminster, model. As such, its principal institutions include a bicameral legislature, made up of an elected lower house (*House of Commons) and an appointed upper house (*Senate), periodic elections of members of Parliament, and a *cabinet accountable to the Commons and, ultimately, the electorate.

The monarch, represented in Canada by the *governor general, remains head of state in Canada's parliamentary democracy. In reality, this executive officer plays a largely symbolic role. Joining the Crown in forming the executive branch are the prime minister and cabinet, the two offices in which the greatest concentration of power resides, and the permanent administrative wing of government.

British parliamentary institutions and practices evolved over hundreds of years. The gradual development of traditions, conventions, and rules continued in Canada after Confederation. Many of them are now unique to this country. Together they ensure the widespread acceptance of such fundamental principles of parliamentary democracy as *responsible government, by which the cabinet as a whole and its individual ministers are responsible to the Commons for their actions and policies, and majority government, by which the cabinet must enjoy the support on critical issues of confidence of a majority of MPs either from a single party or from two or more parties.
JOHN C. COURTNEY AND DANIEL MACFARLANE

Parliament Buildings, Ottawa (1859–76; numerous alterations and additions), home of Canada's government and prominent symbol of Canadian nationhood. For its scale, national profile, leading-edge style, and breadth of influence, this monumental group of imposing High Victorian Gothic buildings was unquestionably the most significant Canadian architectural project of the Victorian age and deserves greater recognition in international studies of Gothic Revival architecture.

Thomas Fuller (1823–98), recently arrived from England, and Chilion Jones (1835–1912), of Gananoque, Canada West, designed the Centre Block and its semi-detached polygonal library, Thomas Stent (1822–1912) and Augustus Laver (1834–98), both English immigrants, the departmental buildings, known as the East and West Blocks. In an enormously creative enterprise that reflects the peculiarities of the Canadian context, the architects married a gritty urban European style with the backwoods of Canada. Unlike most national buildings that form part of grand urban schemes, our 'national palace' was adapted to its dramatic 29-acre site 'on the banks of a wild river, almost at the back of Canada'. The symmetrical facade of the Centre Block, with its tall central tower and rhythmically positioned pavilions, emphasized the formal nature of the parliament square and gridiron plan of Ottawa, while the picturesque riverfront, dominated by the broken outline of the library crowning the cliff, echoed the informal landscape setting. This fusion captured the dichotomy of the site and the eclectic essence of the new style, and underlined the complex nature of the emerging Canadian nation.

The Parliament Buildings are outstanding examples of the 1850s union of utilitarianism and romanticism. They reconciled the 19th century's disparate passions for progress and for history by combining rational planning, modern technology, and a historically inspired style to develop a truly contemporary idiom. These buildings rapidly became the basis for a new Canadian public architecture and their style was spread 'from sea to sea', most notably through federal post office design.

The fire of 3 February 1916 devastated the Centre Block. The library was spared largely because of librarian Alpheus Todd's (1821–84) 1859 specification that it be isolated from the main building. John A. Pearson (1867–1940) and J. Omer Marchand's (1872–1936) replacement structure (1916–27) abstracted the essence of the earlier building, stylizing it in a 20th-century vein and creating a national icon.
CAROLYN A. YOUNG

Parti Québécois. A political party dedicated to political sovereignty for Quebec. The PQ was born in October 1968 under the leadership of René *Lévesque, a former minister in the Lesage government. Advocating *sovereignty-association, the party soon brought together the various sovereignist forces. In the elections of 1970 and 1973 the party saw its vote increase from 23.5 to 30.8 per cent. In the elections of 15 November 1976 the PQ was elected, shocking English Canada. It then adopted a series of progressive meaures: Bill 101, making French the official language of Quebec; democratization of political party financing; preservation of agricultural lands, and so on. As promised, the government held a referendum on sovereignty-association in May 1980 and lost, its option attracting 40 per cent of the vote. Re-elected in 1981, it had to manage a bad economic situation, and internal dissension increased. In 1982 the government experienced another failure when Ottawa repatriated the constitution without the agreement of Quebec. In 1984 several PQ ministers resigned when Lévesque announced that the sovereignty option would be put on the back burner. Lévesque resigned in turn, and the party, led by Pierre-Marc Johnson, lost the elections of 1985. Profiting from the wave of Quebec nationalism provoked by the failure of the *Meech Lake Accord (1990), in 1994 the PQ returned to power under Jacques Parizeau. On 30 October 1995 a second referendum on sovereignty was held and again the PQ lost, but with a very narrow margin, obtaining 49.4 per cent of the vote. In January 1996 Lucien Bouchard became party leader and premier. A former minister with the federal Conservatives, he had resigned in 1990 in order to promote sovereignty. Like René Lévesque, he took a moderate stand on sovereignty and was very popular with the public. Putting off a third referendum, his government devoted itself to balancing the budget. Believing that he could not lead Quebec to sovereignty, Bouchard resigned in January 2001 and was replaced by cabinet minister Bernard Landry, a militant from the earliest days of the party, but the PQ lost the 2003 election to the Liberals.
JEAN-FRANÇOIS CARDIN

Partridge, Edward Alexander (1862–1931), farmer and agrarian leader. Born in Whites' Corners, Ontario, Partridge homesteaded near Sintaluta, North-West Territories, in 1884 and joined the militia during the Riel Rebellion. A key agrarian leader in the 1890s and central figure in the 1902 'Sintaluta' case (questioning the CPR grain-car allocation practices), he led the farmer attack on the Grain Exchange. First president (1906–10) of the *Grain Growers' Grain Company and first editor of the *Grain Growers' Guide*, he helped found the Canadian Council of Agriculture. Resigning the presidency of the Grain Growers because of institutional politics, his own limitations, and pressures from Thomas *Crerar, he organized the Square Deal Grain Company and promoted the Union Bank. He was devastated by their failures and the death of a daughter and two sons in the war. Reemerging in the 1920s amid the pooling campaigns and the formation of the Farmers' Union of Canada, he wrote *A War on Poverty*, advocating a new western nation, Coalsamao. Written as an extended pamphlet, it mystified many and failed to gain support. He died in 1931, probably by suicide. IAN MacPHERSON

Partridge Island. This 12.5 ha island at the mouth of Saint John Harbour was set aside as a quarantine station for immigrants with the incorporation of the city in 1785. Permanent facilities, constructed in the early 1830s to house individuals in quarantine, along with a resident physician proved inadequate for the approximately 16,000 sick and destitute *Irish fleeing the potato famine detained there in 1846–52. A Celtic cross was raised in 1927 in tribute to the 2,000 who died. The station operated until 1942. A memorial to Jewish immigrants was erected at the site in 1985. New Brunswick's first lighthouse was built there in 1791, and the world's first steam-operated fog alarm in 1852. The island served as a major fortification site to protect the harbour and port, with the first military works completed in 1800. Defences were activated and augmented in the face of military threats of the War of 1812, post-Civil War America and the *Fenians in 1866, and both world wars. MARION BEYEA

party system. In Canada, a country founded by party politicians, the shape and character of party competition has always been critical to the definition of the country as a democracy. The first common Canadian experience was a general election, and from it grew a pair of parties defined by their parliamentary caucuses and distinguished by their desire to appeal to as many voters as possible, rather than to articulate and advance the views of distinctive social or economic interests. Practising a 'brokerage' style of politics, the Conservative and Liberal Parties have provided a long string of one-party governments.

The continuity and stability of Canadian politics suggested by the continuing dominance of the Liberals and Conservatives mask important ruptures in the party system, the character of the parties, and the electoral equations that have governed Canadian politics. Long periods of stability were broken by periods of political upheaval in which the structure, leadership, financing, and operations of political parties were refashioned as they struggled to mobilize new coalitions of supporters. Out of each of these episodes came new party systems in which the Liberals and Conservatives succeeded by transforming themselves in response to popular demand.

The original party system managed a *patronage-based politics of a small-town and rural society. Fiercely competitive, the parties organized both federal and provincial politics, as they directed the state-building activities that expanded the country across the continent. This politics collapsed in the aftermath of the First World War, unable to cope with the modernizing demands of merit-based government administration or the country's shifting demography. The parties moved to organize extra-parliamentary organizations, strip leadership selection from the caucus, and establish new patterns of financing. The old parties survived, but shared the system with a series of minor parties (Progressives, Social Credit, and the Co-operative Commonwealth Federation) that drew most of their support from the newly emergent West.

The Liberals dominated this second party system, for a realigned electorate shut the Conservatives out of Quebec and off the Prairies. However, these same voter shifts separated federal and provincial political life so that the party system no longer integrated the politics of both: distinctive party systems came to organize politics in the provinces. Throughout the years 1921–62, the parliamentary caucuses continued to speak for the party, although were themselves easily led by leaders content to practise a nation-building style of accommodative politics. Quebec's *Quiet Revolution, the development of governance by executive *federalism, and the Conservative's capture of the West overturned this party system and led to the emergence of a third one in the 1960s.

Although the Liberals and (by then) Progressive Conservatives again transformed themselves, the new party system included the social democratic New Democrats. Active party organizations now accorded members the right to fire (as well as choose) leaders and soon came to depend on substantial public funding for their electoral activity. New voting patterns swept aside the political equation that had long guaranteed Liberal pre-eminence. With a Conservative West and a Liberal Quebec, elections turned on Ontario, as the centre came to dominate the peripheries. In one sense, this new equation did not matter, for all three parties practised a pan-Canadian politics of accommodation in a newly bilingual Canada.

In the early 1990s, Canadians, unhappy with the (lack of) choices offered, again overturned the party system in the most volatile democratic election seen anywhere during the century. With voter turnout in sharp decline, the parties are struggling to reassert their legitimacy and the centrality of the party system to democratic competition. The process of building the (fourth) system is still underway, but it appears that it will be one with more—and more diversified—parties engaged in more regionalized competition for an increasingly fragmented electorate.

R. KENNETH CARTY

Passchendaele, 1917. Part of British Army Commander F.M. Haig's futile hopes for the elusive break-out to win the war in 1917, this series of Flanders battles started in late July. For the next two months the British and Anzac troops of General Gough's 5th British Army vainly and with enormous human cost tried to capture the village of Passchendaele and the ridge beyond. Their assault stopped when heavy rains and constant shelling turned the ground to bog. Convinced that the attack had to continue to keep the French armies from collapsing and to waste the enemy by attrition, Haig solicited the *Canadian Corps, commanded by Arthur *Currie, to finish the job. A reluctant Currie accepted but only if the corps could fight as a whole and not in a British army whose commander he thought incompetent. He also insisted on freedom to plan and on having vital reserves and munitions. Typical of Currie were careful staff work and his belief that mass artillery firepower in creeping barrages supporting the infantry saved lives and gave the only chance of success. Between 26 October and 10 November, in terrible rain and mud conditions, the corps' three-phase assault won all the objectives. The cost was terrible, with 15,654 casualties. Nevertheless, the competence, confidence, and maturity begun in 1915 at *Ypres a short distance away, and so evident at *Vimy Ridge earlier that spring, again confirmed the reputation of the Canadian Corps as the finest fighting formation on the Western Front.

RONALD HAYCOCK

passenger pigeons (*Ectopistes migratorius*). Now extinct, flocks of millions once blackened the sky. They were found west of the Rockies, but primarily in the deciduous forests of Central Canada, feeding on mast (acorns). Elizabeth *Simcoe's 1793 diary describes knocking them from the air with sticks. Commercial net hunters took millions, but hunting and loss of habitat do not completely explain their rapid disappearance after 1880. The 1914 death of Martha, the last passenger pigeon, motivated Canadian conservationists to lobby for migratory protection for birds. LORNE HAMMOND

pasteurization. In France, Louis Pasteur created his eponymous process in the 1860s, first to prevent wine and beer spoilage, later to preserve milk. Without pasteurization, milk is subject to enzymatic action, microbial souring, and contamination by pathogens such as the *tuberculosis and brucellosis bacilli. Pasteurization is effected by applying heat to milk. In Canada, pasteurization was introduced piecemeal. The Hospital for Sick Children in Toronto installed the first milk-pasteurization plant in Canada in 1908. In 1915 Toronto passed a by-law requiring pasteurization of all milk sold in the city. Finally, in 1937, the process became mandatory in the province of Ontario, with a subsequent dramatic decrease in the number of children afflicted with bovine tuberculosis. Recently, irradiation has proven effective in sterilizing milk, providing lengthy shelf-life in sealed containers at room temperature. CHARLES G. ROLAND

patriation of the constitution. The word 'patriation', a genuine Canadian invention, refers to Canada's final 'bringing home' of its *constitution from Westminster, with full patriotic fanfare, on 17 April 1982. Although Canada enjoyed sovereignty since at least 1931, it nonetheless continued to depend on requests to the United Kingdom Parliament for making amendments to its constitution. The reason for this anomaly was clear: Canadian governments had proved unable to agree on an internal amending procedure by which legal changes to the constitution could be made at home without having recourse to Britain.

Replacing the old colonial procedure proved difficult because an amending formula, specifying what level of governmental consent was needed for changes, was thought to require the unanimous consent of the government and Parliament of Canada, together with that of all the provinces. Unanimity among the negotiating governments had not been achieved since 1927, except briefly at the Victoria Conference of 1971, a short-lived triumph that lasted a matter of days before Premier Robert Bourassa of Quebec withdrew his consent. Not only were the issues themselves complex and politically contentious, but movement on the amending formula, in the 20 years prior to patriation, became linked to the satisfaction of governments' other constitutional goals. Indeed, the negotiations got caught up in the political struggle over Quebec independence, Western regionalism, and Prime Minister Pierre *Trudeau's constitutional plan to reform and modernize Canada's constitution with a new *Charter of Rights and Freedoms.

As the constitutional agenda expanded and became entwined in the fierce battle to reshape Canada's future, the political fight became the most drawn-out, far-reaching, and publicly acrimonious in Canada's history. Constitutional conferences on patriation and other subjects began in earnest in 1968, and continued with brief respites for the next 14 years. It was only after the defeat of the Quebec referendum on *'sovereignty-association' in 1980 that Trudeau decided to proceed with patriation, with or without the consent of the provincial governments. After the collapse of intergovernmental talks in the summer of 1980, Ottawa decided to act unilaterally in requesting that the UK Parliament amend Canada's constitution for the last time, and affix to it a domestic amending formula and a Charter of Rights and Freedoms. Hence, a large and important set of constitutional changes was contained in the federal 'patriation package'. This unilateral action was opposed by eight provinces, tagged the 'Gang of Eight', with the governments of only Ontario and New Brunswick supporting Ottawa.

For the next two years, unilateral patriation of the Canadian constitution, as a matter of politics and of law, was ferociously debated within Canada, its courts of appeal, and at Westminster. When the *Supreme Court of Canada on 28 September 1981 ruled that Ottawa's patriation initiative, while strictly legal, nonetheless offended constitutional convention, all the governments returned to the bargaining table in a last effort to reach an agreement. The court had held that the package of amendments could constitutionally proceed with 'substantial' (not unanimous) provincial consent. During the course of intergovernmental negotiations, 2–5 November 1981, the Gang of Eight alliance of provincial premiers began to break up. On 5 November, the 'Night of Long Knives', agreement was reached between all federal and provincial negotiators in the absence of separatist premier René *Lévesque and his officials. This negotiated package included patriation, an amending formula favoured by the Gang of Eight, a Charter of Rights and Freedoms advanced by Ottawa, stronger provincial powers over natural resources, and constitutional entrenchment of the principle of equalization payments to have-not provinces. These proposed amendments were subsequently endorsed by all first ministers except Lévesque.

The proposed changes to Canada's constitution proceeded through the Houses of Parliament at Westminster, despite the strong objections of Quebec, and a final unsuccessful appeal by its government to the courts, on the basis of a distinct Quebec right of veto over constitutional amendments. The amendments, which formed the Constitution Act, 1982, were signed into law by Queen Elizabeth II in Ottawa on 17 April 1982, ending any application of UK law to Canada. These amendments applied as law from that date to all of Canada, including Quebec.

The glaring omission of Quebec's consent to these fundamental changes laid the basis for future rounds of constitutional talks, in the 1980s and early 1990s, aimed at healing the profound political rupture with Quebec left by patriation. A decade later, following failure of the *Meech Lake and *Charlottetown Accords, modern 'mega-constitutional' talks finally came to an exhausted and dispirited stop. DAVID MILNE

Patriotes. Founded by reformers in 1792, the Parti canadien promoted a program that would strengthen French-Canadian interests within British constitutional and parliamentary apparatus. Its first leader, Pierre Bédard, pursued objectives such as a strong Canadien majority in the assembly, financial control by the assembly of public expenditures including the civil list, a 'responsible ministry' (an executive drawn from the majority in the assembly and responsible to it for its advice to the governor), and protection of the language, laws, and institutions of the maturing Canadien nation. When Louis-Joseph *Papineau gained control of the party by 1820, he remained close to Bédard's positions, but the main focus shifted to financial control because of the leverage it would give the assembly.

Radical changes occurred. By 1826 Papineau changed the party's name to the Parti patriote, in response to various issues: Great Britain's underhanded proposal in 1822 of a union of both Canadas; Britain's interference in internal matters (the laws of 1822 and 1825 authorizing the commutation of tenure to the British freehold system, subject to English common law); obstruction by the legislative council in matters such as finances, education, reform of the *seigneurial system; a lengthy and unproductive study by a parliamentary committee in London of Lower Canadian complaints; the nastier tone of confrontations between British colonists and Canadiens; increased immigration from the United Kingdom; and British refusal to create new seigneuries in the townships and the creation of a British monopolistic land company. By 1828, the British proposed reforms, but apart from a weak compromise in 1831, rejected by the assembly, they would not be implemented.

By then the Patriotes—comprised mostly of Canadiens with some moderates such as John Neilson and radical English-speaking reformists such as E.B. O'Callaghan and Wolfred Nelson—directly blamed the British, who were seen as the armour protecting the *Château Clique and as a threat to the 'nation canadienne'. Moderates, including Neilson, left Papineau's party, which in 1834 called for radical reforms (elective legislative council, control of finances, responsible executive, and reforms to land tenure, administration of justice, and the employment of Canadiens in the administration), couched in the Ninety-two Resolutions, with thinly veiled threats of independence. The Parti patriote, with Papineau outnumbered by more radical elements (such as the Nelson brothers, C.-H.-O. Côté, E.-E. Rodier, A. Girod, T.S. Brown), maintained its dominance until the failed *Rebellions of 1837–8, when it gave way to the Fils de la liberté, Frères chasseurs, and, later, reformists. JEAN PIERRE WALLOT

patronage. At the beginning of the 20th century, Sir Wilfrid *Laurier considered patronage to be 'the most important function of government', the one that bulked largest among correspondence and that brought most visitors to his office. A hundred years later, journalist Jeffrey Simpson described Prime Minister Jean *Chrétien as the friendly dictator because so much power of appointment and favour was concentrated in his office.

The importance of patronage in the development of Canadian political parties and government was clear in the earliest years, when the elected assemblies sought to limit the appointed colonial governors' power to select advisers and officers of the state. With *responsible government, the elected ministers gained the right to choose who should deliver the post, run the customs house, and publish government notices in newspapers. In the United States, a so-called spoils system developed, where a new administration fired the public servants of the past administration and replaced them with their own followers. In British North America, such blatant practice was limited by the tradition of non-partisan public service that was part of Canada's British heritage. Nevertheless, when positions came open, the governing party's friends usually got them.

Following reforms in Britain, Canada introduced the merit principle into the civil service in the first two decades of the 20th century. Competitive examinations and special skills were required for many posts, but differences among provinces persisted, with virtual spoils systems existing in parts of the Maritimes, Quebec, and elsewhere. The creation of the coalitionist *Union government broke down the old system at the federal level during the First World War. Competitive examinations for the federal pubic service created an outstanding diplomatic corps and several pockets of excellence in the bureaucracy. Yet new difficulties appeared. The examinations favoured graduates of anglophone universities, and by the early 1950s the number of francophones in the public service was one-third of the figure it had been at the turn of the century. Remedial action was required and taken.

Patronage is an important glue for a party system, and political leaders are extremely reluctant to give it up. The

*Senate, for example, is a useful reward for party service and the many order-in-council appointments induce loyalty to the leader. Simpson claims that the Canadian prime minister possesses more 'direct, unchecked power' than any other leader in a *parliamentary democracy. One may debate the argument but still recognize that the power flows mainly from the discipline of reward and patronage.
JOHN ENGLISH

pays d'en haut. Translating literally as 'the country up there' or 'upper country', the term referred to areas 'upriver' where French speakers from the St Lawrence Valley trapped and traded furs. In the early years of New France, the term referred to the area north of the St Lawrence River, in present-day Quebec, and west of Montreal, in present-day Ontario. By the late 17th century, it came to be widely used for the *fur trade territory mainly around the Great Lakes. After the mid-18th century, the boundaries moved farther west and north, following the reaches of the fur trade to the prairies around the Mississippi, Missouri, and Assiniboine Rivers, to the northern parkland along the Saskatchewan River, and even to the Subarctic around Lake Athabasca. Today the *pays d'en haut* generally refers to the northwestern part of the province of Quebec. CAROLYN PODRUCHNY

peacekeeping. The use of an impartial force of specialized personnel to ease tension and maintain stability between states or within a state; a major activity of the post-1945 Canadian military, one that became a potent symbol of national identity. Although peacekeeping predated the Second World War, the term became synonymous with the efforts of the *United Nations to manage conflict, and in 1988 the UN's peacekeepers were awarded the Nobel Peace Prize. Canada, one of the founders of UN peacekeeping, took great pride in its record of participation in almost all of the world body's missions. Peacekeeping suited the internationalist objectives of Canada's *foreign policy and assisted its allies, the United States not the least. The public, meanwhile, was apt to think of peacekeeping as a moral endeavour in an immoral world.

Canada's first UN peacekeepers were sent to Kashmir in 1949. Four reserve army officers joined a military observer group sandwiched uncomfortably between India and Pakistan. Brigadier H.H. Angle, who took over as the group's commander in 1950, was killed in a plane crash later that year, the first Canadian to die on a peacekeeping mission. In 1954 Canada began its long involvement in Middle East peacekeeping with a contribution of observers to the United Nations Truce Supervisory Organization (UNTSO); General E.L.M. *Burns was soon appointed its chief of staff. That year Canada also became a member of non-UN International Control Commissions in Vietnam, Laos, and Cambodia, engagements that lasted until the 1970s and turned the Canadians who served with them into fervent anti-Communists.

UN peacekeeping entered a new phase with the *Suez Crisis of 1956, which led to the formation of a United Nations Emergency Force (UNEF), several thousand strong and big enough to act as a buffer between Arabs and Israelis. L.B. *Pearson's Nobel Peace Prize–winning diplomacy was instrumental in the forging of UNEF, and General Burns was chosen to lead it; Canada provided logistics, signals, and reconnaissance personnel, specialities that became a common Canadian contribution to peacekeeping missions. After UNEF came UN missions to the Congo in 1960 and Cyprus four years later, both substantial multinational forces with Canadian contingents. The Congo operation was costly and controversial, Egypt dismissed UNEF from its country in 1967, and the Cyprus commitment dragged on and on. Peacekeeping, however, became entrenched in international practice as a stopgap between conflict and diplomacy: it took place with the consent of all the parties, used force only in self-defence, and was delivered by *middle powers like Canada. Canadians, indeed, came to see themselves as the supreme practitioner of the art. Canada did not miss a single UN peacekeeping turn from the early 1950s until the late 1980s.

The end of the Cold War made peacekeeping's constricted rules seem outmoded. So much more was surely possible. Expectations exploded, along with missions to accompany them. Observer missions like UNTSO, and UNEF-style forces that interposed themselves between parties who had agreed to a ceasefire, were called 'traditional' peacekeeping to distinguish them from 'second-generation' operations, which could involve civilians (like the *Royal Canadian Mounted Police) and range from humanitarian assistance to nation-building and sometimes stray into the enforcement of UN Security Council resolutions. The Mulroney government embraced the sometimes dangerous post–Cold War peacekeeping with enthusiasm: in February 1993 there were more than 4,700 Canadian peacekeepers stationed around the world.

Changes of government did not change the urge to peacekeep. 'We will always be there', Prime Minister Jean *Chrétien boasted in 1999, 'like the Boy Scouts'. His government despatched peacekeepers to the Middle East, Africa, Latin America, Europe, and Asia, more than 40 missions in all, as well as pushing for reforms in the UN peacekeeping system. Some significant Canadian peacekeeping operations of the period were not under the auspices of the UN; one notable example was the *North Atlantic Treaty Organization's Stabilization Force (SFOR) in the former Yugoslavia. The Canadian military, paradoxically, had to do all this in the face of puny budgets and governmental indifference. Not for the first time, the politicians valued peacekeeping more than they did the peacekeepers who carried it out. NORMAN HILLMER

peace, order, and good government. Key phrase of section 91 of the Constitution Act, 1867, signalling the intent of the founding fathers to create a powerful central government for the new *dominion. For greater certainty, but not so as to limit this comprehensive assignment of power to Parliament, 29 classes of enumerated powers are listed. Section 92 assigns 16 classes of subjects to the exclusive jurisdiction of the provinces. Disputes over this division of powers—the essence of the federal system created in 1867—have been adjudicated by the *judiciary. Until 1949, when the *Supreme Court of Canada was made the final arbiter, the Judicial Committee of the Privy Council in the United Kingdom had the final word. Over time, the latter's decisions tended to modify the centralist intentions of the founders by favouring the provinces' jurisdiction over 'property and civil rights', leaving the residual power to legislate for the peace, order, and good government of Canada to apply only in a national crisis or in an emergency such as war. Since 1949, although domesticated review has reaffirmed the primacy of the clause, Supreme Court interpretations are not likely to promote high-handed trespass on provincial terrain by the central government. J.E. HODGETTS

Peace River country. Roughly defined as the area drained by the Peace River and its tributaries in northwestern Alberta and northeastern British Columbia, between 55 and 59° north latitude, the Peace River country, isolated from the southern prairies by the rugged Athabasca River watershed, is the northern-most grain-growing region in Canada. First described by Alexander *Mackenzie during his 1793 expedition to the Pacific coast, it is a zone of spruce, aspen, and willow forest interspersed with open prairies. Maintained primarily by fires, these prairies provided excellent habitat for deer and buffalo, game the fur traders used for provisions. The prairies, which existed both north and south of the Peace River, varied in size from the large Grande Prairie to the smaller Spirit River prairie. Debates over the country's agricultural potential commenced in the 1870s following exploration by the *Geological Survey of Canada. The area was considered as a possible candidate for the route of the Canadian Pacific Railway, and its agricultural potential was a primary topic of enquiry in an 1888 Senate committee study. Klondike-bound prospectors travelled through the district in 1897 and 1898, leading to the making of Treaty 8 with the Cree and Dunne-za population in 1899. Agricultural settlement began in the prairie sections after 1900, and the Peace River country became an important grain- and livestock-producing district, attracting settlers from the drought-stricken southern prairies. As agriculture expanded, settlers cleared the forests to obtain new crop and pasture lands. The primary agricultural commodities today are wheat, canola, hay, and cattle. The Edmonton, Dunvegan, and British Columbia Railway, re-named the Northern Alberta Railways following its sale to the CPR and Canadian National in 1927, provided connection to Edmonton by 1916 and reached as far west as Dawson Creek, BC, by 1930. Despite vigorous campaigns to create a direct rail link with the rest of British Columbia, the link did not materialize until 1957, when the *Pacific Great Eastern reached Dawson Creek and Fort St John from Prince George. The district became the staging area for the construction of the *Alaska Highway during the Second World War. After the war, oil and gas development joined agriculture as a major economic activity; in the last 20 years, hydroelectric production, forestry, and pulp and paper have become important regional industries. Urban development has accompanied this new industrial activity; major urban centres anchor the district at Grande Prairie, Fort St John, Dawson Creek, and Peace River.

ROBERT IRWIN

Pearson, Lester Bowles (1897–1972), prime minister 1963–8. Pearson was born at Newtonbrook (Toronto), the son and grandson of prominent Methodist ministers, both parents of Irish Protestant background. His studies at the University of Toronto were interrupted by the First World War. When he turned 18 he joined the *Canadian Army Medical Corps, serving in Salonika. Bored, he returned to England for training, first for the infantry and then for the Royal Flying Corps. In learning to fly, Pearson crashed and, in a later incident, was hit by a bus. His health collapsed, and he returned to Toronto in April 1918. He completed his undergraduate degree in 1919, tried law, then tested the business world in Chicago. Dissatisfied, he decided to study history at Oxford in 1921. After only two years of study, he returned in 1923 after the University of Toronto offered him a lectureship. He met his wife, Maryon Moody, taught history, and, more famously, coached football and hockey.

Sensing limited opportunity at Toronto, in 1928 Pearson joined Canada's small Department of Foreign Affairs, where his quick intelligence, clever wit, and considerable charm brought increasingly prominent roles. He went to London in 1935 as the European continent lurched unsteadily towards war. Initially hesitant about a Canadian commitment to a European war, Pearson became convinced in 1938 that Hitler was a menace and Britain the only hope to stand up to him.

He was fortunate again when he was moved to Washington in June 1942, just as the centre of action was shifting to the United States. A baseball and movie fan, Pearson fitted in well in Washington political society, and his international experience was enormously useful in the creation of the new *United Nations system. He served as the interim chair for the new Food and Agriculture Commission. He was appointed Canadian ambassador to the United States in January 1945; one year later, he returned to Ottawa as undersecretary of state for external affairs. In 1948 he left the bureaucracy and became minister of external affairs. Between 1945 and 1957, Pearson was one of the pre-eminent diplomats in the world. Only a Soviet veto, twice-exercised, kept him from becoming UN secretary-general, although he did serve as president of the General Assembly. He was a key to UN policy in Korea, Indo-China, and especially the Middle East. His deft handling of the 1956 *Suez Crisis, where he separated the warring countries through the creation of a United Nations Emergency Force, won him the Nobel Peace Prize in 1957.

That triumph, however, was accompanied by many troubles. The *Liberal Party lost office in 1957. Pearson became its new leader, but his weakened party suffered its worst defeat in 1958. Never a good parliamentarian, he decided to emphasize a highly progressive platform, to recruit excellent candidates, and to create a new and stronger role for French Canada. On 22 April 1963 the Liberals won a minority government. During the next five years of tumultuous government until his retirement in 1968 Pearson created a considerable legacy: the Canada Student Loan plan, the *Canada Pension Plan, a new *national flag, colour-blind immigration, *medicare, *bilingualism and biculturalism, and new regional development schemes. Many deplore the costs of the programs, but their endurance testify to their popularity with most Canadians. JOHN ENGLISH

Peguis (1780?–1864). Peguis's Ojibwa band had its main camp near the mouth of the Red River at Lake Winnipeg, and Peguis became known as the 'Colony Chief' for the nearby *Red River settlement. He protected settlers during attacks by the *North West Company in 1815, and ceded land along the Red River from Lake Winnipeg to the Forks in the 1817 Selkirk Treaty. Traders, settlers, and missionaries turned to him to make decisions on behalf of his band, and he used the authority accorded him by Europeans to negotiate opportunities for his people. Peguis was not a war chief, but a civil chief and talented statesman. After long resisting missionary attempts to convert him, he became Christian in 1840, perhaps as much to maintain assistance from missionaries as for personal spiritual reasons. He became increasingly concerned to preserve land rights for his band, refusing bribes to sell land and complaining for decades (locally and in England) of settlers' failure to respect Ojibwa land rights or to pay promised compensation for ceded lands. LAURA PEERS

Pélagie-la-Charrette. Antonine Maillet's 1979 novel, published by Leméac, was awarded that same year the prestigious Prix Goncourt. The novel's heroine, Pélagie LeBlanc, daughter of Théotiste Bourg, packs her children and goods into a cart pulled by oxen and, 15 years following her expulsion from *Acadia, leaves Georgia for her native land. This trek takes ten years to complete, and ends (as does the novel) with the heroine's death.

Wrapped in symbolism, the novel's themes deal with the reality of Acadia, despite its disappearance from formal political geography. Consequently this novel speaks to the continuity of national feeling. The novel also speaks to Acadian women's perseverance and strength, their particular sense of both self and community, and their response to the incredible pull of homeland.

A variety of tales, humorous, sad, and thoroughly human, entertain the reader throughout this journey through history, itself represented mostly accurately, though sometimes renegotiated to fit the telling of the story. Maillet concocted a tale worthy of its stated objective: a celebration of the 375th anniversary of Acadia.

PHYLLIS E. LeBLANC

pemmican. A word derived from the Cree word *pimikan*, meaning 'manufactured grease', the dietary mainstay of the western *fur trade in the 18th and 19th centuries. A highly nutritious and portable food that kept for many months, pemmican was most often manufactured from dried and pounded buffalo meat to which melted fat was added. Berries were often used for flavouring, and the resulting mixture was sown into buffalo-hide bags, each containing approximately 40 kg of preserved meat. Buffalo-hunting plains First Nations and Metis peoples manufactured the enormous quantities of pemmican required for the expansion of the fur trade throughout the West. ROBERT J. COUTTS

penal reform. One hundred years after the first Canadian penitentiary opened in Kingston in 1835, the federal government was forced to admit that its whole penitentiary system was in need of a major shake-up. A series of riots, which contributed to the sudden increase in the number of inmates (66 per cent) at the beginning of the economic crisis in the 1930s, forced the government to establish a royal commission to investigate the state of the penitentiaries and to recommend ways to overhaul the prison system. The Archambault Commission, set up in 1934, condemned the conditions of detention and recommended considerable reform. Among the findings of the Archambault Report (1938) was that the primary purpose of incarceration turned out to be not rehabilitation—the original intention—but punishment. Inmates not only had to remain silent but spent an average of 16 hours a day locked alone in their cells, with only a half-hour for recreation. Communication with the outside world was limited and, when released, prisoners returned to society with only the personal effects they had when incarcerated, along with what little money they had been able to earn in prison if given the opportunity to work.

With a view to completely revamping the system, the commission made a total of 80 recommendations, including significant improvements to the conditions of imprisonment. It also focused on rehabilitation and returning inmates to society, recommending that more highly skilled staff be hired and that specialists, particularly mental health professionals, should become attached to the prisons; that there should be a better system for classifying prisoners; that educational programs be introduced, along with a better system of vocational training. The report also aimed at encouraging the reintegration of offenders through rehabilitation programs and improvements in the post-incarceration system, particularly through a reform of the parole system.

With the outbreak of the Second World War, the momentum that the royal commission had hoped to create was slowed considerably. A few reforms and improvements to prison conditions were made following the war, but it was not until the Fauteux Committee (1953–6) that penal reform became a priority once again. The Fauteux Report, which advocated scientific treatment of inmates and criticized the obsolete penitentiary machinery, was followed by two others, the Ouimet Report (1969) and the McGuigan Report (1977), both of which alluded to the growing feeling of failure with respect to the use of imprisonment and cast doubt on the ability of *prisons to rehabilitate inmates. Indeed, the authors of the McGuigan Report—on behalf of the federal minister of justice of the day—agreed that the penal system was a failure with respect to its main functions, rehabilitation and the protection of society. ANDRÉ CELLARD

Penfield, Wilder (1891–1976), neurosurgeon, scientist, writer. Born in Spokane, Washington, Penfield pursued athletics at Princeton and medicine at Oxford. Influenced by William *Osler and Charles Sherrington, he chose neuroscience and completed his degree at Johns Hopkins University, Baltimore, in 1918. Recruited from New York City to Montreal in 1928, he became the founding director of the Montreal Neurological Institute in 1934. Penfield's surgical creativity led to special operations for focal epilepsy and contributed to neuroscience. Under local anesthetic, his patients described sensations, feelings, and memories or they made gestures in response to electrical stimulation of the brain. The results generated an anatomical 'map' of human brain function. Penfield corresponded with scientists in many countries and travelled widely, including to the Soviet Union in 1943. Much honoured during his lifetime, he took up writing and social causes in his later years. In his readable but dated novels, *No Other Gods* (1954), about the biblical Abraham, and *The Torch* (1960), about the young Hippocrates in love, Penfield expressed his interest in religion and the history and philosophy of medicine. JACALYN DUFFIN

Perkins, Simeon (1735–1812). In the 1760s approximately 7,000 Yankees settled in Nova Scotia, among them Simeon Perkins, a merchant from Norwich, Connecticut. He established himself as a prominent leader in Liverpool, serving in numerous public offices, including justice of the peace, magistrate, member of the legislative assembly, colonel in the militia, and judge of probates. As a merchant, Perkins owned a sawmill, commissioned local shipwrights to build vessels, contracted with fishing masters for their catch, and sent cargoes of lumber and cod to the Caribbean. During wartime, he invested in outfitting *privateers.

Perkins's diary, ranging over five decades, richly documents Nova Scotia's place in a fractured Anglo-Atlantic world. Outport merchants, such as Perkins, forged commercial ties with Halifax, while nurturing family and economic ties with New England. Perkins sent his nine children to visit family in Connecticut and welcomed their cousins in Nova Scotia. Politically, however, Liverpool reoriented itself to the new imperial order, and most residents, including Perkins, remained loyal during the *American Revolution and cast their lots with the British Empire. ELIZABETH MANCKE

Permanent Force. Canada's professional standing army—confusingly named Permanent Active Militia until 1940, when it became the *Canadian Army (Regular)—as well as its full-time navy and air force. The first regular army units date from 1871, when two artillery batteries were formed to man the guns in the fortresses at Quebec and Kingston and to provide training to the Non Permanent (part-time) Active Militia. Cavalry and infantry units were added in 1883, and other corps and branches (Engineers, Medical, Signals, Service Corps, etc.) from 1903, but the number of regulars remained very small (3,000, all ranks, in 1914) because Canada was content to rely on its volunteer part-time citizen soldiers and the British armed forces for defence. A full-time *Royal Canadian Navy was created on 4 May 1910, and a permanent *Royal Canadian Air Force on 1 April 1924, but, because there was no obvious direct threat to Canadian security and defence spending could be kept low, they too were small. Providing only a fraction of the million men and women who served during the Second World War (the permanent navy numbered 1,585 in 1939, the army 4,200, and the air force 2,200), Canada's regular sailors, soldiers, and airmen were nevertheless fully engaged in the fighting, and, because of their superior training and experience, regular officers dominated the wartime staff and high command structure of all three services.

The regular forces remained relatively small after the Second World War (40,000, all ranks), but after fighting broke out in Korea, and with the full flowering of the Cold War, in the 1950s they were vastly expanded to provide front-line defence and deterrence against the Soviet Union in Europe and North America. By 1962 the full-time RCN (21,500 strong) manned 50 modern warships, the Canadian Army (Regular) comprised 52,000, all ranks, and the RCAF (53,000) maintained 19 modern jet-fighter squadrons along with transport and maritime patrol units. Regular sailors, soldiers, and airmen also contributed to *United Nations *peacekeeping operations around the world, making it a Canadian specialty.

The separate navy, army, and air force disappeared when the Canadian Armed Forces were unified in 1968. Difficult economic times and a changing international situation have seen a continuous diminution of Canadian Forces regular force strength. By 2001 the permanent force establishment had shrunk to fewer than 60,000, all ranks, and peacekeeping (and other overseas) commitments were such that the regulars could no longer fulfill such tasks without the assistance of reservists.

STEPHEN J. HARRIS

Persian Gulf War. On 2 August 1990 Iraq invaded oil-rich Kuwait. The *United Nations promptly placed an embargo on Iraq while the United States organized a multi-national coalition to impose it. The UN subsequently approved the use of force to liberate Kuwait. The ensuing hostilities (17 January–28 February 1991) resulted in a complete coalition victory and the restoration of Kuwaiti independence. Canada immediately committed military forces to support these UN mandates. The government of Prime Minister Brian *Mulroney dispatched three warships to the Persian Gulf, 26 CF-18 fighter-bombers, and an air-to-air refuelling aircraft to Qatar, a headquarters unit to Bahrain, and a military field hospital to Saudi Arabia. Canada's naval force organized the Combat Logistic Force to ensure resupply of the vast coalition fleet. The CF-18s undertook a variety of roles including escorting coalition bombing missions and, at war's end, mounting ground-attack missions against enemy targets. Although Canada's forces were under overall coalition command, Ottawa approved the nature of their combat operations. Approximately 4,000 Canadians served in the war. They suffered no casualties. SERGE DURFLINGER

Persons case. A constitutional ruling establishing women's right to be appointed to the *Senate, the case became symbolic of women's legal equality. By the time a uniform federal *franchise was instituted in 1920 the Senate was the only part of the federal government to which Canadian women did not have access on the same terms as men. Women's groups that had sought the vote to bring about social change now wished to have women appointed to the Senate to continue their campaigns. Two successive prime ministers claimed that women were not among the eligible 'persons' specified under the British North America Act since women had no independent legal identity in Britain when the act was passed in 1867.

Edmonton feminist Emily *Murphy, whose actions as the first woman magistrate in the British Empire had been challenged on the grounds that she was not a 'person' under the BNA Act, was the preferred Senate candidate of national women's groups. Along with four other prominent women activists—Henrietta Muir Edwards, Nellie *McClung, Louise McKinney, and Irene Parlby—Judge Murphy persuaded the government to direct the *Supreme Court to rule on whether women were indeed 'persons'. The court ruled in the negative, but on 18 October 1929 the Judicial Committee of the Privy Council in England, then the final appeals court, ruled in the women's favour.

Judge Murphy was not appointed to the Senate. Nor has it proved an effective platform for feminist reform. The decision in the Persons case was significant, however, as a victory achieved by women through the machinery of the existing system. Second-wave feminists in the 1970s adopted 'personhood' as a symbol of women's legal equality and made the decision's anniversary into an occasion for celebrating the achievements of women activists. Several Canadian governments annually give 'Persons Awards' honouring prominent women. NAOMI BLACK

Peterborough Canoe Company. Renowned for the canvas-covered vessels that helped, by combining low cost and durability, to popularize *canoeing in Canada from the turn of the century through the 1940s, this company emerged from the ashes of the Ontario Canoe Company, a thriving manufacturing venture destroyed by fire in 1892. Like its predecessor and its most prominent Canadian rival, the Chestnut Canoe Company of New Brunswick, as well as numerous smaller enterprises, Peterborough supplied watercraft to surveyors, prospectors, the burgeoning recreational market, and a surprising number of paddling afficionados in the United Kingdom and Europe. The typical canvas-covered canoe, whose lines echoed Aboriginal bark watercraft, was approximately 4.8 m long and about 30 cm deep with a .75 m beam. To facilitate shipping, canoes of various sizes were built to nest within each other.

In the early 1920s a network of small builders, sometimes individual craftsmen, gave way to a handful of dominant firms, including Peterborough and Chestnut. Control of these two enterprises was consolidated in 1923 through a holding company, Canadian Watercraft Limited. The Canadian Canoe Company joined the consortium in 1928, although all three businesses continued to manufacture under their own names. Competition from large-scale aluminum and fibreglass builders following the Second World War put pressure on the traditional canoe companies. These eventually foundered, but the canvas-covered Peterborough-style canoe, still available from small specialized builders, remains a sentimental favourite.
JAMIE BENIDICKSON

petroleum industry. The organized discovery, recovery, processing, and marketing of raw oil and gas. The chemical constituents of all petroleums are hydrocarbons. Despite some contrary theories, the consensus favours petroleum (literally, 'rock-oil') having an organic origin, based on decayed plant and living matter subjected to heat and pressure during sedimentary rock formation beneath ancient seas. Over time, the organic elements of these layered rocks turn to coal, liquefy, or turn gaseous. Oil and gas then migrate upward out of the porous host rock and become trapped beneath overlying impervious rock. Important types of petroleum-bearing formations in Canada are frequently associated with old carbonate 'reefs' of Devonian and Cretaceous age, or traps created along fault lines. The main sources in Canada are on the western and arctic prairies and in some shallower offshore regions.

While oil has been known for millennia through surface seepages, and had ad hoc uses, the systematic use of oil and gas required certain breakthroughs in recovery and industrial chemistry. Advances in both were afoot in mid-19th-century North America. In 1854, Abraham *Gesner, former provincial geologist of New Brunswick, patented kerosene, based on his experiments with Nova Scotia asphalt. Kerosene was more controllable than coal oil, but both were expensive and the source rock for kerosene was rare. Cheap domestic and public lighting remained the direction of attention until the early 20th century, when demands for engine fuels and diversified products started to emerge.

The history of the Canadian industry may be identified in four distinct phases. The first commenced in Lambton County, Ontario, in 1858. Charles N. Tripp's 'discovery well' at Oil Springs preceded the famous, and ultimately more significant, Drake find in Pennsylvania by only a few months. The find at Oil Springs was based on Tripp's knowledge of Sterry Hunt's *Geological Survey of Canada report on 'mineral springs' (1850). Tripp remained preoccupied with the asphalt potential of the area, and fell upon hard financial times. It fell to J.M. Williams and Co. to bring in the first oil production in Lambton County. The underground methods employed were adapted from ancient Oriental, European, and American artesian well- and salt-drilling techniques, particularly those in use in West Virginia. By 1866, Jacob Englehart had established a refinery at nearby London, having sensed the obvious need to transfer whisky-distilling technology to petroleum. This was useful with respect to the second, but water-rich, strikes at Petrolia made in 1865. Englehart consolidated with other refiners in 1880 as Imperial Oil, adjourning to Sarnia in 1883. In 1890 Imperial was absorbed by the American-owned Standard Oil Trust. Modest extraction continues in southwestern Ontario.

The second phase focused on southern Alberta. In 1874, geologist George M. *Dawson asked the veteran frontiersman 'Kutenai' *Brown to ask local Indians to be alert for signs of oil in the vicinity of Waterton Lakes. Seepages were reported in 1884 and by 1902 a discovery well was in place along Cameron Creek, developed by local entrepreneurs and drillers from Petrolia. The geology was not productive of substantial pools, but this failed rush helped stimulate other more productive searches. The Medicine Hat Bow Island project of 1909 marked the beginning of the western natural gas industry. Gas in the area had been discovered accidentally by railway crews drilling for water. Eugene Costa had brought in the first gas field near Windsor, Ontario, in 1889. Now in the West he and his persistent driller, W.R. 'Frosty' Martin, brought in 'Old Glory', leading to establishment in 1912 of the Canadian Western Natural Gas Company, which innovated the piping of gas overland to supply the urban markets of Calgary and Lethbridge. (It is worth noting that 1909 was also productive in New Brunswick, where at Stoney Creek near Moncton a still-active gas field was brought in.)

In May 1914 excitement erupted in Calgary owing to a strike of wet gas (naphtha-laden light oil, capable of being burned in automobiles without processing) in the heavily faulted anticline geology around Turner Valley. The Turner Valley gas fields suffered from diverse technical difficulties but oil was finally struck in 1936. So much gas had been burned off and wasted, however, in the effort to draw off the naphtha, that the pressure of the entire oil field below the gas was seriously lowered, rendering capture difficult. The Second World War resulted in federal assistance to exploit the field, and its production peaked in the early 1940s. The Alberta government's attempt to impose guidelines on the industry failed in 1932, but in 1938 the Alberta Petroleum and Natural Gas Conservation Board was created, partially as a response to the damage done to the Turner Valley field. Quotas, well spacing, conservation, engineering standards, inspections, and many other items were regulated by the board, which is known today as the Energy Resources Conservation Board.

Between 1914 and 1939, the *automobile transformed the North American economy. Americans led the way in production of cars and gasoline refinement but there was a high degree of ownership integration between the United States and Canada. Smaller players such as K.C. *Irving of New Brunswick and Charles Trudeau of Montreal (father of the future prime minister) made personal fortunes by carving out regional niches as oil and gas distributors.

The Second World War stimulated an interesting, if short-lived, experiment in the Far North. Oil developed in 1920 at Norman Wells on the Mackenzie River was too far from most markets for significant distribution. Yet by 1942, with US fuel supplies an important security issue, the *Canol project was initiated, taking oil from Norman Wells by pipeline to a new refinery at Whitehorse. Product was then sent via new links to Skagway and Prince Rupert. Massive financing was involved but when production came on stream in April 1944 the military significance of the project was uncertain. In 1947, the refinery at Whitehorse was dismantled, shipped to Edmonton, and reconstructed there by Imperial Oil.

Canada's third phase also focused on Alberta, but in two parts. The first was south of Edmonton, following the great strike made at *Leduc in 1947 by Imperial Oil. Subsequent production from these Devonian reefs led to many other finds in northeastern British Columbia, central Alberta, Saskatchewan, and southwestern Manitoba. New refineries were built in Edmonton by McColl-Frontenac (Texaco) and British-American (Gulf)—and in Saint John, NB, by Irving. Much upgrading of earlier refineries also took place. The availability of western petroleum quickly induced demand for new pipelines and a need for market regulation, leading to establishment of the National Energy Board in 1961. The second part concerned attempts to develop the heavy oil or bitumen resources of the Alberta 'tar sands'. These resources represented a vast potential in world terms but required much research and processing to exploit. Several firms became established around Fort McMurray in the 1960s. With the sharp increase in world oil prices in 1974, resulting from the control of supply enforced by OPEC, production from strip-mined deposits of northern Alberta was stimulated by the Syncrude consortium, an important tool of national policy by 1979.

A fourth phase of development concerned off-shore strikes in the western Arctic and the Atlantic region. The 1968 Prudhoe Bay discovery on the north slope of Alaska proved to be one of the largest oil fields in North America. Panarctic Oils, a consortium in which the federal government was the major shareholder, was founded in an effort to tie together diverse groups active in the Arctic since the late 1950s and to strengthen Canadian sovereignty. The Bent Horn field on Cameron Island sent oil to market in 1988. Canadian exploration of the Mackenzie delta and Beaufort Sea fostered diverse pipeline proposals for the Mackenzie Valley, and elsewhere, to take product south. While an all-American route for Alaskan oil was selected, Canadian requirements have been subjected to lengthy hearings, the results of which are still coming to fruition.

On the east coast, three shelves have been of interest: the Scotian, the Grand Banks, and the Labrador Shelf. Initial drilling commenced in 1943 off Prince Edward Island. Attention shifted to Sable Island over the next two decades, indicating that many off-shore Cretaceous finds involved high pressure gas fields. The cold and iceberg-laden Labrador Shelf received attention after 1971, but economic conditions restrained interest. The greatest attention has been on the *Grand Banks at the Avalon and Jeanne d'Arc Basins, where exploration commenced in 1966. The Hibernia strike of 1979 has been filled with promise, as have the discoveries at White Rose and Terra Nova.

The petroleum industry is complex, drawing on a widening range of specialists and labour skills. The economics of extraction and production are costly and complicated by short-terms shifts in international supply and demand. The controversial *National Energy Program introduced by the Trudeau government in 1980 was merely the most dramatic of several episodes in which attempts have been made to balance the free flow of production with an assured supply, equitable consumer costs, and rational distribution. GRAHAM MacDONALD

philanthropy. The story of philanthropy has typically begun with the financing of the early missionary orders of New France. However, we might more accurately begin with the First Nations peoples' practices of giving and sharing. The reciprocal gift giving of hunter-gatherer societies, for example, belongs in the tradition of mutual aid that, in later Canadian history, included organizations such as insurance co-operatives, fraternal societies, community doctor schemes, and burial clubs. Without the history of mutual aid, working-class philanthropy would largely be overlooked.

Nonetheless in New France we do find the first instance of an important theme in the history of Canadian philanthropy—immigrant aid. The benefactors of the missions of New France were Old World actors, seeking to solve European problems by exercises in New World colonization. In the 17th century, poor spinsters in Paris found themselves exported to New France as wives, for their own good as well as in aid of the French colonial effort. Similarly, in the early 19th century, emigration from the British Isles was organized to relieve British taxpayers and to give British paupers a chance for prosperity in the colonies. This enterprise led to organizations such as the Montreal Emigrant Society, which helped find work for dazed and disoriented immigrants and sometimes provided treatment for the sick or food for those unable to work. As the immigrant 'frontier' became increasingly urban, immigrant aid continued, and continues, to be an important part of Canadian philanthropy.

In immigrant aid—as well as in relief for widows, orphans, the sick, and the elderly—the helping hand was often that of a co-religionist or an ethnic brother or sister. Such identities were understood to give people a claim on others of their 'kind', and the better-off members understood that the reputation of their religion or ethnic group would be hurt and possibly members lost if they ignored their obligations to care for their own. In organizations such as the St Vincent de Paul Society, charity was not just a social duty, but also an aspect of worship. Even so, social purposes were important in this and many other kinds of charitable fundraising and giving. Dances, strawberry socials, bazaars, bingo tournaments, and a host of other charity benefit events brought people together and marked social boundaries. By the mid-20th century, attempts to raise money from the community as a whole, emphasizing common citizenship, led to the United Way and other national charities.

Common identities may have warmed the cold hand of 19th-century charity, but the widening distances between the flourishing business classes and the ill-paid factory worker gave such philanthropy a rather censorious tone. The storms of international economic depressions shipwrecked ordinary families, but to prosperous philanthropists it seemed likely that the unemployed were simply lazy. British ideas about the corrupting effect of indiscriminate charity encouraged the benevolent founders of homes for the poor to require hard physical labour of their inmates. Many 19th-century institutions (including homes for unmarried mothers or for the blind, and *residential schools for Indians) were to some measure self-supporting businesses, financed by their inmates' work. By the 1870s most were to some extent also 'public charities', supported in part by grants from provincial governments.

Philanthropy has rarely been entirely independent of government support. Whether through grants-in-aid or income tax exemptions, governments have endorsed the private donation of funds for social purposes. The 20th century saw a noticeable expansion in governments' contributions to the relief of *poverty and the provision of health care. The wars of that century, both hot and cold, played a major part in creating need (disabled *veterans, soldiers' dependants, *refugees) and inciting generosity (the Canadian Patriotic Fund, the Canadian Legion, Red Cross blood donations). Although war-related philanthropy dates back to the War of 1812, the mass scale of 20th-century wars was a major factor in exposing the limits of private charity. In the usage of the day, 'public charities' and 'social legislation' were called upon to support the efforts of philanthropists, who, by the 1940s, were not just the wealthy few, but the mass of working-class Canadians too. SHIRLEY TILLOTSON

Phips, Sir William (1651–95). Son of a Maine blacksmith, William Phips became a Boston sea captain and found wealth in 1687 by salvaging a Spanish wreck off Hispaniola. In spring 1690 he commanded a Massachusetts expedition that seized *Port-Royal, in French Acadia, holding the town long enough for systematic plundering. He was immediately commissioned to command an assault on the tougher target of Quebec. This campaign was disastrous, for reasons not wholly attributable to Phips. The weather was bad, and overland support from New York proved feeble. Phips's retreat down the St Lawrence lost many lives to shipwreck and disease.

Nevertheless, he became governor of Massachusetts in 1691. Making powerful enemies, he was recalled to London, where he died. Phips was a brash and often foul-mouthed opportunist, yet he understood clearly the fluidity of English–French–Native relations in northeastern North America and boldly attempted to capitalize on it. JOHN G. REID

photography. Modern Canada developed within the photographic era. From the union of the Canadas onward, photography grew from a curiosity to a commonplace, with photographers—amateur and professional, government and commercial—producing an extensive record of people, places, and events. More importantly, these images played a role in shaping individual and collective notions of landscape and identity, history and memory, nationhood and empire, helping to make British North America seem a smaller, more familiar place.

News of inventions by Daguerre in France and Fox Talbot in England reached British North America in the spring of 1839. The first known daguerreotypists were amateurs and itinerants, but by the summer of 1841 commercial studios had opened in major Canadian centres. Over the next decades, photographers in garrison cities and colonial capitals supplied British military men and government administrators with souvenirs of their tours of duty. Immigrants, fortune seekers, and genteel travellers took photographs and purchased others from commercial photographers who operated in the larger cities and towns. Smaller centres and outlying districts were served by travelling photographers, who announced their arrival in the newspaper and set up shop in the local hotel.

As technology advanced and the daguerreotype process (which produced a unique image) gave way to the wet-collodion process (which permitted multiple paper prints from a single glass negative), the role of photography in the recording and shaping of Canadian history changed. Increasingly part of the rituals of public and private life, the professional photographer recorded ceremonial occasions, commemorative events, and celebratory gatherings, as individual and group portraits were adopted as a way to mark life passages, record historic meetings, symbolize social cohesion, and express corporate pride. Landscape photographs compiled in albums and stereoscopic views, issued in series and viewed through a hand-held device to give the realistic impression of three-dimensional space, were a source of education and entertainment.

Beginning in the late 1850s, photography was used to document the construction of monumental public works and feats of civil engineering—University College (Toronto), the Victoria Bridge (Montreal), and the *Parliament Buildings (Ottawa). During this same period, Humphrey Lloyd Hime, Charles Horetzky, Benjamin Baltzly, and the *Royal Engineers struggled with heat and dust, overturned carts and upturned canoes, bulky equipment and messy chemicals to produce a remarkable record of people and places in conjunction with the boundary, geological, and railway surveys in the Canadian West. Stiff poses and dour expressions in portraits bear witness to the technological limitations of the wet-plate era. Before flash photography using magnesium powder came into general use late in the 19th century, studio photographers were forced to use skylights, long exposures, posing stands, and head clamps to overcome the difficulties posed by low indoor light levels. Hand-tinting and overpainting were used with varying degrees of delicacy and success at a time when photography in full colour remained an elusive goal.

Although photography throughout the 19th century was largely a male pursuit, some women established successful businesses; others worked as camera operators, darkroom assistants, and print retouchers, some in the Montreal studio of William *Notman (1826–91). When 'Mrs Fletcher' arrived in Quebec City from Nova Scotia in 1841 she announced herself as a 'Professor and Teacher of the Photogenic Art' and encouraged women to take up photography as a means of securing independence in an 'honourable, interesting and agreeable' profession. Other women professionals included Hannah Maynard (Victoria), Élise L'Heureux-Livernois (Quebec City), Alvira Lockwood (Ottawa), and Rosetta Carr (Winnipeg).

Although primarily practised by professionals at first, photography was a topic of popular interest, scholarly discussion, and amateur experimentation, with information exchanged through professional associations, academic communities, and social circles, in particular the Art Association of Montreal and the Canadian Institute in Toronto. One of the most active pockets of early amateur photography was the Hudson's Bay Company post at Moose Factory, where a group of employees, which included Bernard Rogan Ross, Charles Horetzky, and George Simpson McTavish, produced a photographic record of Aboriginal and company life around Hudson and James Bays during the 1860s and 1870s. Francis Claudet, son of noted London daguerreotypist A.F.J. Claudet and manager of the government assay office and mint at New Westminster (1860–73), was typical of amateurs who practised photography while on a colonial posting.

The advent of the dry plate in the 1870s freed photographers from carrying portable darkrooms and opened up new applications, particularly for exploration and travel. During his extensive travels for the *Geological Survey of Canada in the West after 1876, George Mercer *Dawson used the dry-plate process as an integral part of his field work. Technological advances towards the end of the 19th century profoundly changed the way photographs were taken and viewed. Shortly after George Eastman released his first Kodak in 1888, amateur photographer Robert Reford, son of a Montreal shipping magnate, set out across Canada by train, carrying a hand-held, point-and-shoot 'box' camera pre-loaded with a 100-exposure roll of celluloid film. Its simplicity and portability, coupled with the availability of commercial processing, separated the now simple act of taking a picture from the more complex task of developing and printing it, opened up new opportunities for amateur photography, and put cameras into the hands of women and children. With subsequent 20th-century advances in equipment, films, and processing, and as cameras became smaller to transport, cheaper to buy, and easier to use, photography became increasingly popular as a recreational pastime and a personal form of visual communication, artistic expression, and autobiographical record.

Appearing for the first time in 1888, the *Dominion Illustrated* (Montreal) heralded the modern era of photomechanically reproduced illustrations. Previously, photographs had circulated in limited numbers as original prints, as engravings based on photographs, and as albumen prints pasted onto the pages of modest pamphlets, government reports, scholarly journals, tourist guides, instruction manuals, popular biographies, and lavish art books. However, the halftone screen-printing process, pioneered by William Augustus Leggo and George Desbarats in the *Canadian Illustrated News* as early as 1869, overcame earlier technical problems and finally allowed photographs to be reproduced cheaply and accurately in text-compatible form. This new form of pictorial illustration, first in black-and-white and later in colour, added veracity and immediacy to published images, and was enlisted to nurture a new sense of Canadian nationhood. The strong tradition of photo-journalism, which began with photographs of the aftermath of the Great Western Railway disaster at the Desjardins Canal in March 1857, continued in the work of staff photographers supplying images to major newspaper and wire service agencies throughout the 20th century. Those who have achieved national and international recognition include Kryn Taconis, Sam Tata, Duncan Cameron, Horst Ehricht, Chris Lund, and Ted Grant.

Interest in fine art as well as amateur photography was nurtured, during the late 19th and early 20th centuries, through camera clubs and salon competitions, and a number of Canadian photographers, most notably Sidney Carter and John Vanderpant, achieved international standing in fine art photography circles for their pictorialist work. The Canadian International Salon of Photographic Art, organized by the National Gallery of Canada between 1934 and 1941, and the wartime photography of the *National Film Board validated and fostered interest in fine art and documentary photography, respectively. In the years that followed, the increasing interplay of photography, film, and television nurtured a growing awareness of the power of visual communication, which assumed new intellectual proportions with Marshall *McLuhan's identification of medium and message.

The last decades of the 20th century witnessed a rise in interest both in the history of photography and in photography as a fine art, with the publication of Ralph Greenhill's *Early Photography in Canada* (1965), the establishment of the photography collection at the National Gallery (1967), and the creation at the *National Archives of Canada of the Historical Photographs Section (1964) and the National Photography Collection as a separate division (1975). The Canadian Museum of Contemporary Photography, created in January 1985 as an affiliate of the National Gallery, traces its origins to the Second World War and the work of the Still Photography Division of the NFB. The Photographs Collection of the Canadian Centre for Architecture was begun in 1974, the same year that the Photographic Historical Society of Canada—with its publication, *Photographic Canadiana*—was founded in Toronto 'to advance the knowledge of and interest in the history of photography, particularly of photography in Canada'.

Technical, fine art, commercial, and critical periodicals that have fostered popular and scientific interest in photography since the short-lived *Canadian Journal of Photography* first appeared in 1864 include *Photo Life* (Vancouver/Toronto), *Photo Sélections* (Montreal), *Photo Communiqué* (Toronto), *OVO* (Montreal), *Blackflash* (Photographers Gallery, Saskatoon), and *The BC Photographer*. This literature serves a diverse audience of photographers, collectors, curators, and critics, and supports the study and criticism of photography now taught at a number of colleges and universities across Canada. *Mois de la Photo*, Montreal's major international biennale, and *Contact*, Toronto's annual photography festival, reflect and promote current interest in photography in Canada.

Canadians have made significant but little-known contributions to the history of photography. Pierre Gustave Gaspard Joly de Lotbinière (1798–1865), a Swiss-born French-Canadian seigneur, was the first to photograph the Parthenon in Athens; his daguerreotypes of Egypt, Nubia, and Syria were published and circulated as engravings in France. William Augustus Leggo (1830–1915) invented a photo-lithographic process and patented a number of improvements to the photo-electrotyping process during the late 1860s and early 1870s. Edouard Deville (1849–1924), surveyor-general of Canada, perfected the first practical method of photographic surveying, wrote one of the first English-language texts on the subject, and transformed photogrammetry with his use of a survey camera and stereoscopic plotting instrument for mapping in the Rockies and along the Alaska–BC boundary between 1886 and 1923.

Over the last 150 years, photography has been used by individual, corporate, and government interests to construct notions of landscape and identity, define the cultural Other, promote travel and tourism, sway political opinion, regulate immigration, prompt social reform, and chronicle progress. Thomas Coffin Doane's daguerreotype of Louis-Joseph *Papineau; George Ellisson's enigmatic portrait entitled *Grey Nuns*; the Royal Engineers' record of North American Boundary Commission sappers marking the 49th parallel; group portraits of the Fathers of Confederation; Frederick Dally's views along the *Cariboo Road; driving 'the last spike' at *Craigellachie; Ivor Castle and William Rider-Rider's remarkable record of Canadian military involvement in the First World War; the marine views of Nova Scotian Wallace R. MacAskill; the commercial photography of Saint John's Isaac Erb; images of the developing West by the Calgary firm of Boorne and May and its successor, Edmonton photographer C.W. Mathers; Yousuf Karsh's classic portrait of a defiant Winston Churchill; wire service photographs of Robert

*Stanfield's football fumble or Charles De Gaulle's 'Vive le Québec libre' speech; Roloff Beny's photographic glimpses of the art and architecture of faraway, exotic places; Ted Grant's record of Ben Johnson's infamous Olympic victory—these and other photographs have been part of the way Canadians have explored and articulated their relationship to the world around them. While traditional film-based photography has always had the power to filter our realities and configure our memories, digital imaging is raising new concerns about photographic truth in the post-photographic era. Where the box camera and commercial processing helped to democratize the means of image creation, digital cameras and scanners now help to democratize the processes of image manipulation and, with them, the power of the medium to shape and reshape Canadian reality and Canadian history.

JOAN M. SCHWARTZ

piano industry. The industry began in craft workshops in Quebec City, Montreal, and Toronto in the first half of the 19th century to supplement imports from Europe. After 1870, manufacturers opened larger factories to produce, principally, upright pianos, which became affordable for many families and popular in many public places. The roughly 100 firms that appeared over the next half century continued to include craft workshops as well as such large producers as Toronto's Heintzman and Nordeimer factories, Oshawa's Dominion works, and Guelph's huge Bell plant, which by the turn of the century each turned out hundreds of pianos per year (as well as many organs) and cultivated a mass consumer market through aggressive advertising. In the early 1900s they also introduced the novelty 'player piano'. Most manufacturers were located in Montreal and southern Ontario, many in small towns, but had retail outlets across the country and a substantial export market. Several won international prizes for their instruments. The industry declined over the 20th century in the face of competition from other forms of home entertainment, such as phonographs, radios, television, and stereos, and eventually from cheaper imports. The last Canadian piano factory closed in Clinton, Ontario, in 1988. CRAIG HERON

picture brides. *Japanese immigration to Canada began in the late 1800s and was predominantly male. An anti-Asian riot in Vancouver on 7 September 1907 led to the Lemieux–Hayashi Gentlemen's Agreement between Japan and Canada that limited male immigrants to 400 annually but allowed entry to family members. Approximately 6,000 Japanese women arrived between 1908 and 1926, usually as picture brides. Subsequent agreements virtually stopped this influx of women.

The picture bride custom was a practical adaptation of the Japanese tradition whereby marriages were arranged by household heads through intermediaries. Extensive investigation of the backgrounds of both families ensured social compatibility. Most picture brides were adventurous and were often better educated than their husbands. Since face-to-face meetings were not possible, photos were exchanged, and marriages were conducted by proxy, then registered in the village records. After a six-month period, passport applications were made and the brides joined their husbands. Although some brides refused to honour their marriage commitment, the majority settled into the 'arranged' union, awakening to the reality of a hard life, making extraordinary sacrifices, and helping to create stable homes and communities for the next generation, the Nisei. MICHIKO MIDGE AYUKAWA

Pierce, Lorne Albert (1890–1961), publisher, editor, writer. For over 40 years, Pierce championed Canadian literature. Born in Delta, Ontario, ordained a Methodist minister in 1916, he served churches in Ottawa and elsewhere, punctuated by wartime army enlistment. In 1920 he joined the church-owned Ryerson Press as literary adviser, serving as its editor from 1922 to 1960. An ardent cultural nationalist, he launched the pioneering bicultural Makers of Canadian Literature critical anthology series, the Ryerson Chapbook poetry series, and the landmark Canadian Art series. He personally conceived nationalistic elementary and high school textbooks, including the Canada Books of Prose and Verse, which dominated the market from about 1930 to 1960. Pierce's own writings include studies of William Kirby and Marjorie Pickthall, and a critique and an anthology of Canadian literature. His philanthropy included donating important literary Canadiana to Queen's and the Lorne Pierce Medal to the *Royal Society of Canada in 1926; spurred by his own deafness, he was a key founder of the Canadian Hearing Society in 1940. SANDRA CAMPBELL

Pier 21. Completed in 1928, Pier 21, situated on Halifax Harbour, was designed as a modern immigration complex. With almost 600 feet of seafront and within walking distance of the Canadian National Railway terminal, it was well suited to welcome the flood of expected immigrants. However, the worldwide depression slowed the flood to a trickle and it was not until the Second World War that Pier 21 became a bustling hub of activity as half a million Canadian service personnel departed for Europe. With war's end, all returning men and women came through Pier 21, many of the men accompanied by *war brides (some 50,000). After the war, *refugees and *displaced persons from wartorn Europe entered Canada through Pier 21 and were dispersed across the country. Almost a million immigrants passed through its doors before they were closed in March 1971. By then, immigrants were arriving by airplane.

In 1991, the Pier 21 Society was formed with former immigration official John LeBlanc as president. He, and later president Ruth Goldbloom, gained public and private financial support to save the structure and to build within it a high-tech exhibit and resource centre that would convey the emotional experiences of the immigrants who had passed through. The new Pier 21 was opened to the public on 1 July 1999.

JAMES H. MORRISON

Pig War. A controversial border dispute between Great Britain and the United States, erupting in 1859 during the British Columbia gold rush. Partly a result of ambiguous wording in the *Oregon Boundary Treaty of 1846, the contested land was San Juan Island, east of southern Vancouver Island. The *Hudson's Bay Company under James *Douglas claimed ownership of the island, while US authorities based in Whatcom County, Washington Territory, did the same. The quarrel reached a crisis in 1859 when an American squatter shot a marauding pig that belonged to the HBC—hence the title of the dispute. Under George E. Pickett 60 American troops were sent to occupy the island; although British war vessels were sent, no armed conflict resulted. The island was placed under joint Anglo-American occupation until 1872, when Emperor Wilhelm I of Germany, acting as arbitrator, decided upon Haro Strait as the boundary. Thus, the entire San Juan archipelago became US territory. Historical data, based upon discussions prior to the Oregon Treaty, have revealed that the British were primarily concerned with Vancouver Island and not so interested in maintaining control of the surrounding islands.

BARRY M. GOUGH

pirates. The folklore of east-coast Canada is rich in stories about buccaneers. Perhaps most famous are those who allegedly buried a fortune in gold at Oak Island, located on Nova Scotia's Atlantic shoreline. While that episode remains shrouded in mystery, other incidents are well recorded. For example, in 1612 renegade English sea captain Peter Easton conducted a series of raids against foreign and English fishing stations, as well as the fledgling settlement at *Cupid's on Newfoundland's Avalon Peninsula. Easton's main goal was acquisition of loot, which if accumulated in sizeable enough amounts could be used to buy a pardon from one's home government. Easton made such a success of piracy that eventually he retired to a life of ease on France's Mediterranean coast.

Pirates usually invoked patriotism as a cover for their actions. Thus in 1613 when Samuel Argall raided the French settlement at *Port-Royal in Nova Scotia, he claimed to be asserting English title to frontier territory. Typically, Argall's actions were essentially negative, featuring theft and arson rather than investment of capital and labour. Throughout the 17th century both Newfoundland and the Maritimes were vulnerable to hit-and-run forays conducted by an array of English, French, Dutch, and New England freebooters. Few deaths occurred, but the raids caused major losses of property and thus contributed to the chronic instability that plagued European enterprise within the region. Pirates persisted in Atlantic Canada until 1713, when a comprehensive territorial settlement negotiated between the English and the French ushered in peace and led to the establishment of garrisoned bastions at Annapolis Royal for the English, and Louisbourg for the French.

D.A. SUTHERLAND

Pitseolak, Peter (1902–73), South Baffin Island photographer, artist, writer. In the early 1930s he took his first photograph—for a white man afraid to approach a polar bear—and in the early 1940s he acquired a camera himself. Through experiment he and his second wife, Aggeok, became accomplished processors of film. On hunting expeditions they developed film in igloos on top of the sleeping platform using a three-battery flashlight covered with red cloth; they printed by the light of oil lamps in their small wooden hut at the Cape Dorset fur-trading post. With his camera Pitseolak caught the last days of *Inuit camp life, consciously leaving a record 'so my grandchildren will know what went on while I was alive'. From the 1950s to the early 1970s, as Inuit gave up life on the land, he contributed drawings depicting Inuit material culture, stories, and legends to the print-making program of Cape Dorset's West Baffin Eskimo Co-operative, but most celebrated are the watercolour drawings of fur trading created for John Buchan, second Lord Tweedsmuir, an HBC trader in Cape Dorset during his father's term as Canada's governor general. Pitseolak's account of his life was published posthumously in 1975 as *People from Our Side*. After his death the Department of Secretary of State bought 1,623 negatives and some original prints from Aggeok.

DOROTHY HARLEY EBER

place names. Towards the end of the 19th century Canada established an agency to make decisions on toponyms, or geographical names, their spelling and application. Before this, the assigning of place names was largely accidental. The oldest, and among the most interesting and euphonious, Canadian place names can be traced to Amerindian sources. Then came explorers and cartographers, pioneers and politicians, all of whom played a part in haphazard naming. Following Confederation the need to avoid duplication became apparent. The evolution of a postal service, advent of the railway, and westward expansion of the country, all provided incentives for the use of distinctive place names.

On 18 December 1897 an order-in-council was passed by the Laurier government to establish the Geographic Board of Canada. It directed that all questions concerning place names be referred to the board, and that 'all Departments shall accept and use in their publications the names and orthography adopted by the board'. In 1899 a further order-in-council granted the provinces and territories the right to name representatives to the board. Since 1948 the board has undergone three name changes. In that year, a new designation, the Canadian Board on Geographical Names, came into effect. The Canadian Permanent Committee on Geographical Names was adopted in 1961, to be replaced in 2000 by the Geographical Names Board of Canada.

Early in their history, the provinces were invited to provide advice on the use, spelling, and application of names, and in 1961 formal responsibility for naming was transferred to the provinces. Since 1979 the authority for place names on Indian reserves, in national parks, and military reserves has been held jointly by the appropriate federal department and the province or territory concerned.

The GNBC now has a membership of 27, with the chair being appointed by the federal minister of natural resources. In addition to representatives from the provinces and territories, there are members from federal departments concerned with mapping, archives, defence, translation, Indian reserves, national parks, and statistics. Included are the chairs of the four GNBC advisory committees: Toponymy Research, Nomenclature and Delineation, Digital Toponymic Services, and Names of Undersea and Maritime Features. Decisions to adopt or change place names are sent to the GNBC secretariat, provided by Natural Resources Canada, for entry into the Canadian Geographical Names Data Base (CGNDB) to be made available to cartographers, the media, and the general public through the GeoNames Web site. In addition to coordinating information that may be required by the data base, the secretariat arranges all GNBC meetings and those of its various committees, organizes workshops and seminars, and undertakes the production of GNBC publications. To keep the public informed concerning all aspects of toponymy and place-name research, the secretariat publishes the journal *Canoma* twice yearly. Beyond these formal activities, it also maintains contact with international agencies involved with place naming. Within Canada, the secretariat encourages the use of approved names and the development of standard policies. The GNBC also provides information on place names to School Net, which then makes it available to educational institutions and others over the internet.

It has been estimated that the CGNDB contains well over 500,000 geographical name records. However, in a country the size of Canada there remain many locations and physical features for which names may be known in oral tradition but have not yet been recorded. Also, each year, as a result of amalgamation of municipal units, new and revised names must be added to the CGNDB. Notwithstanding the efforts to give widespread publicity to the GNBC's policies and procedures, name controversies do arise, often resulting from lack of consultation with GNBC members and the secretariat. Two of the most heated disputes are cited as examples. In 1946 Prime Minister Mackenzie *King decided to rename Alberta's Castle Mountain as Mount Eisenhower, for the famed Allied commander in the Second World War. For over 30 years a 'war of words' ensued condemning this change. The matter was finally resolved in 1979 when the Clark government reinstated Castle Mountain and applied the name Eisenhower Peak to the summit. In 2000 Prime Minister Jean *Chrétien announced that Mount Logan in the Yukon would be renamed Mount Trudeau in honour of former prime minister Pierre Elliott *Trudeau, who had recently died. Mount Logan, the highest peak in Canada, was named for Sir William *Logan (1798–1875), noted geologist and founder of the *Geological Survey of Canada. A public outcry resulted in the announcement being revoked.

From ocean to ocean to ocean, Canada possesses a rich heritage in place names. Thanks to the guardianship of the Geographic Names Board of Canada, this inheritance is being preserved and enlarged for posterity.

WILLIAM B. HAMILTON

Plains Aboriginals. The Canadian Plains, the northern region of the Great American Plains, remain a distinct region of the West, geographically and historically. Now the heartland of wheat, beef, and oil and gas production by the descendants of Euro-Canadian settlers, the plains, stretching southward from the north branch of the Saskatchewan River, were for many millennia the homeland of a range of unique and complex Aboriginal cultures. From those cultures evolved, in the 18th century, what became known as the Plains Indians.

Prior to the arrival of Europeans, Aboriginal people, both agricultural and hunting and gathering, had harvested the resources of the plains for centuries, particularly during the *buffalo hunt. Permanent villages based upon corn, bean, and squash cultivation grew up in the fertile valleys of the Missouri River and the Red and other rivers emptying into Lake Winnipeg. Hunting and gathering people, some using canoes and others moving on foot with dogs pulling travois, visited the plains in the summer and retreated in the late fall to the protective fringe of woodlands or to sheltered river valleys. These plains inhabitants developed a variety of co-operative methods for killing buffalo, notably the wooden pound (corral) into which buffalo were driven for slaughter and the 'jump', a cliff over which the herd was stampeded. The meat, often wind-dried, pounded with saskatoon berries and mixed with fat, could be stored for winter consumption. *Pemmican was a valued part of the diet of European fur-traders, particularly when they needed to move quickly over long distances.

While each of the region's communities had its own recognized territory, these communities were not isolated one from another; rather they were engaged in a complex of trade and military networks that saw the exchange of the produce of the hunt for that of the garden, as well as an array of other goods such as handicrafts, pipe-stone, and beaded clothing. The most extensive such network, based on the Mandan villages near the elbow of the Missouri River, included goods from as far south as the Gulf of Mexico, west from the Pacific, and north from Hudson Bay. Setting out from Hudson's Bay Company posts, established on the bay side between 1668 and 1688, Cree and Assiniboine (a group that had broken away from the Sioux far to the southeast) traders, middlemen as they are known, carried European goods inland along the extensive waterways, exchanging them for prime fur and then returning to the bay. By the mid-18th century, they traded annually with the Blackfoot along the south branch of the Saskatchewan River.

Some markets were specialized, like the Cheyenne–Arapaho horse market and the Shoshone rendezvous south of the Missouri River. Horses, along with buffalo numbering in the millions, were the most critical elements in the region's history over the next two centuries. Originally from Spanish colonies in the far south, wild horses were redomesticated by Indians. That act sparked a cultural revolution.

On the Canadian plains horses began to appear in the 1720s, years before whites arrived, and by the end of the 18th century the plains nations had evolved from the long-resident woodland communities: the Plains Cree, the Assiniboine, and the largest group, the Blackfoot Confederacy, composed of the Siksika (Blackfoot proper), Blood, Peigan, and Sarcee. Over the next 75 years the human geography continued to change. New groups appeared: the Canadian Plains Ojibwa (Bungee) left behind woodland and canoe, and the Young Dogs, an amalgam of Plains Cree and Assiniboine, evolved. Similar migrations and ethnic transformations took place along the Missouri and to the south.

Although these new plains communities bore the memories of a past life in their languages, stories, songs, beliefs, and arts, they were unique as well. Old forms were amended. The horse was a useful addition to the pound and dead-fall techniques, and now buffalo could be chased on a valuable 'buffalo runner' and killed with the plainsman's short bow or musket. A valued servant, but horses were masters too. The camp moved constantly to ensure adequate pasturage, and winter camping sites were chosen with an eye to the availability of fodder. Younger boys tended the horse herd like wary shepherds on the lookout for strays or enemy horse-stealing raiders.

But the effect of the horse was much more profound. It gave the band a much expanded range and carrying capacity that was the foundation for communities of considerable size and social complexity. A band, sometimes as large as 200 people, passed most of the year together travelling, hunting, trading, and, when necessary, launching war parties. Often in mid-summer, bands came together for tribal meetings. These were social and political occasions, times of song, story, and dance, and most importantly the setting for the annual sun dance, an elaborate ceremony in a specially built lodge, calling upon the Creator to bring health and good fortune to the community over the next year.

The comfort of family and friends, a rich and plentiful life, were for decades the hallmark of plains life, but there were challenges as well. More populous communities underlined the need for social order, and differences in abilities, ages, and needs demanded the development of a range of social institutions. In a plains band there was a permanent government of chief and councillors and a number of societies, or lodges, for men and women. The soldiers' lodge protected the community, guarded the line of march when travelling, and enforced discipline during co-operative buffalo hunting. These men also carried out important social functions. Men strove to be rich in war records and in horses, but such success brought responsibilities. To achieve real status in the band, rich men had to be open-handed. Generosity was the key virtue; thus, they had to distribute meat, horses, and other goods to those less well off and to the sick and aged. Women, too, particularly the wives of wealthy men, had similar caring duties. Boys and girls, educated by parents and grandparents in the necessary hunting and household skills and in their duties to family and community, sought spirit guides and protectors to help them through their lives. Plains life was free but it bound individuals in bonds of duty even while applauding and rewarding them for their achievements.

These plains communities flourished in the first three quarters of the 19th century. The population of the northern plains soared to well over 35,000, although travellers' and traders' estimates are, at best, guesses and often contradictory. It is certain that over the century the numbers fluctuated, rising and falling, thinned by that other persistent and deadly European migrant—infectious diseases. *Smallpox hit hard in 1737, 1781, 1837, and again in 1870. The impact could differ. The Plains Cree escaped the worst of the 1837 epidemic; the Mandan were virtually wiped out by it. Measles, whooping cough, and chickenpox were common, almost annual, experiences and common causes of death. *Tuberculosis lurked as the major killer at the end of the century, driving the population down until just before the Second World War. Thereafter rapid growth returned and has been sustained since then.

During the last quarter of the 18th century the plains population was augmented by Europeans, and the Plains people entered into a new relationship with them and with the buffalo. Initially, the plains world was an Aboriginal world with Europeans confined to the margins. But in 1774 the Hudson's Bay Company established *Cumberland House on the Saskatchewan River in answer to competition from Montreal-based traders. Before the two sets of traders amalgamated in 1821, they opened a line of posts along the Saskatchewan and into the Rocky Mountains. The Americans, too, came west in the guise of the Missouri and then the American Fur Company, establishing posts along the length of the Missouri system. By the mid-1820s every plains tribe had a post on its doorstep and direct access to European goods. The days of the middleman were over.

Tragically, soon the days of the disappearance of the great buffalo herds began. Pressure on the herds had increased with the growth of the Aboriginal population, but it escalated even more dramatically when American traders with an eastern market and bulk transportation by steamboat raised the price of buffalo robes. The HBC, to counter the competition, raised its prices too. In the subsequent decades well over 100,000 robes a year were traded on the Missouri. Special brigades of non-Aboriginal hunters, some hired to feed railroad crews, others to acquire robes for sale, conducted large-scale hunts. By the 1870s buffalo could be found in Canadian territory only in the extreme southwest close to the mountains. More eastern plains tribes, the Cree and Assiniboine, pressed into that territory, the homeland of their traditional enemy the Blackfoot, in a desperate and often violent attempt to find food. By 1879 the herds were gone, and so, too, was the traditional life of plains people.

At their back, to the east, a new set of Europeans appeared: Canadians—more particularly, treaty makers with a vision of a new West and a new relationship with plains people. The treaties signed between 1870 and 1877 confined the bands to reserves in exchange for a recognition of their rights and promises of economic assistance and education. Such promises were never effectively met and the education provided, mainly in *residential schools, did widespread injury to the language and culture of plains communities. Poverty and disease replaced the comfort of the old days; despite this, the warrior survived. In the two great wars of the 20th century young Indian men volunteered in the thousands to protect Crown and country. JOHN S. MILLOY

See also CYPRESS HILLS MASSACRE.

Plaisance. In the 1660s Louis XIV of France and his minister for the colonies, Jean-Baptiste Colbert, decided to establish a civil administration and a garrison at Plaisance (Placentia), on the south coast of Newfoundland. Although this harbour had been frequented by Portuguese, French, and Basque fishermen since the beginning of the 16th century, it was only after 1660 that fishermen began to settle there permanently. The first official census, from 1671, counted 71 persons. In later censuses the permanent population of the capital itself never exceeded 250, but in the summer fishing season fishery workers and vessels from metropolitan France raised the numbers to more than 1,000.

Although it had to face English attacks beginning in the 1690s, Plaisance was never conquered; rather, it was ceded to the English in the Treaty of Utrecht (1713). Until 1691 the colony was vulnerable and its administration questionable, especially under Governor Antoine Parat. The arrival of Governor Jacques-François de Monbeton de Brouillan that year was an improvement; at the same time, the metropolis provided a little more money in order to erect fortifications. Plaisance became the preferred harbour for several French corsairs during the first two imperial wars between France and England.

Living conditions could be precarious for the fishermen-settlers, and they continued to depend on provisions brought by merchant ships from France. Nevertheless, they succeeded in exporting their cod to international markets. In the early 18th century Plaisance played an important part in France's North American account books. Its port, which was accessible almost year-round, provided a welcome rest stop for vessels travelling to and from Canada.

Despite all the difficulties the colony and its settlers faced, the garrison and the French corsairs, assisted by the militia, managed to repel numerous attacks, and with the help of Canadien and Aboriginal allies they even succeeded in taking St John's. Following the Treaty of Utrecht, the garrison, the officers, and the majority of the inhabitants moved to *Port-Royal, the new capital of the French fishery in America. NICOLAS LANDRY

Plasticiens. Quebec painting movement. The *Automatiste vogue created the mood for a return to a better-controlled and more orderly form of painting. A manifesto written by Rodolphe de Repentigny, painter, photographer, and art critic, and also signed by Louis Belzile, Jean-Paul Jérôme, and Fernand Toupin, launched the new movement in Montreal in 1955. Very different from the Automatistes' **Refus global*, this manifesto dealt only with aesthetics and abstained from politics. It marks the beginning of geometric abstraction in Quebec. De Repentigny, who painted under the pseudonym Jauran and died prematuraly in 1959 in the Rockies during a climbing excursion, used Mondrian and other pioneers of abstract art as models. The Plasticiens' movement soon encouraged other young painters to go even further. In 1956, Guido Molinari and Claude Tousignant proposed a much more radical form of painting and, especially in the case of Molinari, resumed the polemical inclinations of the Automatistes, but this time against them. Molinari claimed that they were still attached to the three-dimensional space inherited from the Renaissance and advocated complete detachment from any form of realism and bidimensionality. FRANÇOIS-MARC GAGNON

Plessis, Joseph-Octave (1763–1825). Born in Montreal, Plessis received his formal education at the Suplician primary school, the Collège Saint-Raphael, and the Petit Séminaire de Quebec. In 1780 he was tonsured and three years later began a 15-year term as secretary to successive bishops. He was ordained in 1786, appointed pastor of Notre-Dame in Montreal in 1792, named coadjutor to Bishop Denaut in 1797, and became bishop of Quebec in 1806. In 1817 he was appointed to the legislative council.

Plessis's episcopate coincided with a period of transition and uncertainty in the life of the Quebec church. In facing the challenges that confronted him, he navigated skilfully between principle and pragmatic accommodation. His major accomplishments include building up Catholic educational institutions, achieving civil recognition as Roman Catholic bishop of Quebec, and effectively devolving authority in his vast and diverse diocese to local bishops. At his death, the Diocese of Quebec was much stronger from both an institutional and pastoral point of view, and a modus vivendi had been achieved with the British authorities, removing much of the legal uncertainty that had surrounded the Catholic Church in Quebec. TERRENCE MURPHY

Plouffe, Les. Novel by Roger Lemelin (1919–92), published in 1948. After *Au pied de la pente douce* (1944), in which Lemelin describes life in the *quartier populaire* of Quebec, his native city, the young author wrote this second novel, whose action takes place in the city's *basse-ville*, in 1938. Through the story of the Plouffe family (Théophile, the father; Joséphine, the mother; and their four children Napoléon, the athlete; Ovide, who seems destined for the monastery; Guillaume, the baseball player; and Cécile, who is in love with a married man), Lemelin offers a faithful description of the transformation of the French-Canadian family's typical values during the Great Depression, and on the eve of the Second World War, as well as a portrait of Quebec's political and religious evolution. *Les Plouffe* was to be astonishingly successful. Adapted for radio and television in the 1950s—in French and in English—it was adapted to the screen in 1980 by Gilles Carle. SOPHIE MARCOTTE

police. Policing in Canada reflects the nation's diversified historical and regional development. In the era of New France, law and order was the preserve of the community, although the larger urban centres had watchmen, and the military was available to aid the civil power. In 18th-century Nova Scotia, and in Canada following the British conquest, the English model of part-time justices of the peace and constables and ad hoc urban watchmen was instituted. This amateur, reactive police system prevailed over most of rural British North America in the 19th century.

The shift to municipal incorporation after 1815 brought gradual police reform to centres such as Halifax, Saint John, and Montreal. Full-time, salaried constables, who patrolled a beat and wore uniforms, appeared in the 1840s and 1850s. In theory their proactive patrols and expanding legal arsenal revolutionized public order. The degree of political control and police corruption varied from one town to the next. By mid-century the police worked with police magistrates, either mayors serving in an ex officio capacity or legally trained stipendiary magistrates. In addition to enforcing the vagrancy and public order laws and regulating working-class leisure, the 'new' police provided rudimentary welfare services. Their record in enforcing morality laws was mixed. Some historians stress the anti-labour tactics of the local police, but this remains to be clarified by detailed research. Colonial government innovations in law enforcement following the 1837–8 rebellions included the short-lived Quebec and Montreal police and Lower Canada's Rural Constabulary. The latter's political role echoed British measures in Ireland. Special constabularies were created in Canada West and East in the 1840s to counter collective violence among canal navvies. Two specialized forces to survive Confederation were the Quebec and Montreal harbour police.

Until the creation of the *North-West Mounted Police as a temporary expedient in 1873, the premier government constabulary was the Dominion Police, tasked with guarding federal buildings and enforcing certain federal statutes. This force, which controlled the national criminal identification system, was absorbed into the new *Royal Canadian Mounted Police in 1920. Provincial governments and independent Newfoundland developed detective branches that broadened into 'territorial' forces to deliver rural police services. Other than the Royal Newfoundland Constabulary, only the Ontario Provincial Police and Sûreté de Québec remain. Starting in 1928, an expanding RCMP invaded the field of provincial policing. A final innovation, first evident in Ontario, was the creation of regional police forces.

Responding to urbanization, industrialization, and immigration, and the stinging criticism of moral and social reformers, Canada's police attempted to professionalize after 1900. The major vehicle for this defensive reaction was the Chief Constables' Association of Canada, which held conventions, published a journal, and lobbied the federal and provincial governments on crime-control issues. Although welcoming RCMP members, the CCAC represented the professional aspirations of municipal and provincial police. Police managers supported a military model, the insulation of policing from 'politics', improved recruitment, training, and pay standards, and the use of technology such as signal systems, automobiles, and radios. Their crime-fighting message masked the complex reality of policing and the use of technology by senior officers to save on labour costs. The rank and file, which experienced a wave of unionization in the 1910s, became more powerful following the Second World War with the spread of collective bargaining. At the national level, its interests came to be represented by the Canadian Police Association.

Following the Second World War, police forces embraced mobile patrol, rapid response to citizen telephone calls, and traffic enforcement. As society became more individualistic and pluralistic and crime rates rose in the 1960s and 1970s, the police came under unprecedented scrutiny and criticism. Police hawks called for more aggressive enforcement, resisted civilian oversight, and campaigned against reforms to *capital punishment and parole. Police doves turned to legitimization strategies such as community policing and the recruitment of women, minorities, and college graduates.

GREG MARQUIS

poliomyelitis. Polio is a filterable virus that can cause paralysis and death if it attacks the central nervous system. Between 1916 and 1960 polio epidemics occurred with frightening regularity in most Canadian provinces between June and September. Ontario had 2,544 cases with 109 deaths in 1937 while Manitoba experienced 1,011 cases and 20 deaths in 1941. The most extensive national outbreak occurred in 1953 with 8,000 cases and 481 deaths. In the late 1940s and early 1950s Paul Martin Jr and Neil Young were stricken with 'infantile paralysis'. Polio generally infected children aged 1–14 and prompted immediate quarantine in the home or local isolation hospital. Schools were closed, beaches and amusement parks were deserted, and parents watched anxiously for symptoms.

Throughout the 1930s and 1940s scientists in the United States and Canada searched for vaccines or sera to prevent or treat the disease. Connaught Laboratories in Toronto provided convalescent serum and zinc nasal spray in the 1930s but these did not work. All of the provinces introduced rehabilitation facilities to assist victims to regain use of their limbs and return to productivity. Severe epidemics in the 1940s and early 1950s prompted further research, and in 1953 Dr Jonas Salk of Pittsburgh announced the creation of a killed-virus vaccine. Connaught Labs developed and provided Medium 199, the culture in which the vaccine was grown. In 1954, 44 American states, 2 Canadian provinces, and Finland conducted a successful clinical trial of the vaccine; one year later mass immunization of Canadian children began.

The last major epidemic occurred in Montreal in 1959; in 1962–3 most Canadian provinces shifted to the Sabin oral vaccine to prevent the disease. Recently some polio survivors have experienced a return of the debility they experienced during their bout with the disease, and post-polio syndrome has become a reminder of the human cost of *epidemics. HEATHER MacDOUGALL

polling. The origins of opinion polling in Canada reside in consumer research and the activities of American pollsters. Sample surveys of consumers were first conducted in Canada in the late 1920s by ad agencies, notably Cockfield, Brown & Co. and J. Walter Thompson Co., seeking to demonstrate advertising's effectiveness to manufacturers and media owners. By 1940, these surveys were a familiar feature of Canadian marketing. In the mid-1930s, US consumer researchers such as Elmo Roper and George Gallup harnessed this technique to the citizenry. In 1935, Gallup formed the American Institute of Public Opinion, referred to as the Gallup Poll, to poll nationally and sell the results to subscribing newspapers. Gallup championed polling as a democratic innovation. By amplifying the voices of ordinary citizens, polls weakened lobbyists, economic interests, and the party brass.

In 1941, Gallup set up a polling operation in Toronto. Like its American parent, the Canadian Institute of Public Opinion polled nationally, bundling the results in columns for newspaper sponsors. Federal officials, stung by French Canada's rejection of overseas conscription in a recent plebiscite, soon seized on polls, secretly sponsoring Gallup surveys in a bid to reverse Quebec's lukewarm support for the war. Ottawa's Wartime Information Board commissioned CIPO polls to design information campaigns and bond drives. The federal Liberals were the first party to use polling, testing campaign slogans and conducting surveys in 43 Ontario ridings in 1944.

The CIPO was the only national polling operation during the 1940s and 1950s, during which time relatively little political polling occurred. This changed in the 1960s when the Liberals recruited Democratic Party pollsters Lou Harris and Oliver Quayle. A journalist covering the 1962 election heralded it as a turning point, when 'advertising experts and pollsters' superseded the 'age-old talents of politicians'. The Tories soon joined forces with Republican pollster Robert Teeter and, in the 1970s, the Canadian Allan Gregg. Martin Goldfarb was the Liberal Party pollster during the 1970s and early 1980s, when the charge 'government by Goldfarb' reflected the Trudeau government's dependence on polling.

Polling grew more sophisticated and ubiquitous in the 1980s. Computer-assisted telephone interviewing systems reduced the cost while advancing the speed of survey research. Other advances include tracking polls, focus groups, and psychographic analysis. During the 1988 election, a record 24 national polls were sponsored by media outlets. Today, most parties and provincial and federal governments lean heavily on polling when shaping campaign positions and public policies. Polling, ironically, has become the lifeblood of the very groups—parties, interest groups, governments—whose power it was initially meant to diminish. DANIEL ROBINSON

Pond, Peter (1740–?1807), fur trader, explorer. Soon after the end of the Seven Years' War, Pond, who was born in Connecticut, became a trader based in Detroit and later at Michilimackinac. His first expedition (1775) to the Saskatchewan River and success with the Natives interested Simon McTavish and the Frobishers, rivals of the *Hudson's Bay Company, who encouraged his next expedition into the Athabasca region (1777–9). The success of these ventures helped precipitate the formation of the *North West Company, which Pond eventually joined. His first post, Old Establishment, on the Athabasca River (1778), remained his headquarters for ten years. He was the first white man to see the tar sands and to open trade in the arctic watershed. In 1785 he presented one of his maps to the lieutenant-governor of Quebec and the US Congress. It and his later sketch-maps were used by Alexander *Mackenzie and are still a source of trade history. Pond's volatile temper was a source of trouble: he was implicated in the murders of two rivals, Etienne Waden in 1782 and John Ross in the winter of 1786–7. He sold his NWC shares in 1790 and returned to Milford, Connecticut, to spend his final years. J. COLIN YERBURY

Pontiac (*c.* 1720–69). Born at the Odawa village opposite Détroit, Pontiac (Obwandiyag) was a respected, charismatic Odawa war chief who organized the last war of the Great Lakes Natives against the Europeans. As their loyal ally, he fought for the French during the Seven Years' War. When the war ended, General Jeffery Amherst discontinued the French custom of distributing annual presents and forbade the sale of powder and shot to Natives, even though these were necessary for hunting. Pontiac and his followers had regarded the presents as a form of rent for the land occupied by settlers and forts. Fearing seizure of their lands by the flood of English settlers, Pontiac and his allies decided to organize armed resistance. During the summer of 1763, they captured all British forts west of Niagara and laid siege to Fort Pitt and, under Pontiac's leadership, Détroit. Pontiac's hope of French support was dashed when he got news late in October that the French and British had signed a peace. *Smallpox, spread on Amherst's suggestion during the winter, ended Native resistance. During the peace negotiations Pontiac insisted that the interior lands still belonged to the Natives, a condition the British accepted. Continuing English settlement of Native lands and Pontiac's decision to honour the peace he had negotiated led to his isolation and subsequent murder by a Peoria Native at Cahokia.

CONRAD HEIDENREICH

Pope, James Colledge (1826–85), Prince Edward Island premier 1865–7, 1870–2 (coalition), 1873. A successful entrepreneur in several sectors, particularly *shipbuilding, Pope entered politics as a Conservative, becoming premier three times, and in 1873 led the island into Confederation. The decisive factor was the building in the early

1870s of a railway the colony could not afford. Pope's second government had undertaken this project, and the anti-Confederate opposition had argued that it would be the means of dragging the island into Canada. Whether Pope had this motive is uncertain; it seems likelier that as a businessman strongly committed to transportation improvements, he supported the railway project for economic reasons, and was willing to contemplate Confederation as a by-product. Afterwards, he supported Sir John A. *Macdonald's party, eventually serving as minister of marine and fisheries. In the early 1880s, overtaken by a form of dementia, he withdrew from politics.

IAN ROSS ROBERTSON

population. No generally agreed upon accounts exist of the numbers of inhabitants of what is now Canada in the period before European colonization. The timing of the first migrations and the migration paths also remain subject to debate. Yet, clearly several species of very large mammals were hunted to extinction some thousands of years ago, and the variety of material conditions contributed to a high degree of cultural diversity. Massive construction projects, such as the serpent mounds in Ontario, show that groups with complex forms of social organization and widespread trading networks existed well before the arrival of Europeans.

Although attempts at European colonization on the east coast around the first millennium were unsuccessful, later contact with European populations in the 15th and 16th centuries may have improved the conditions of life among some Aboriginal peoples by introducing new technologies such as the horse and iron implements. But sustained contact from the 17th century onwards transformed local economies and had a devastating impact on the indigenous population. French observers, settled at Quebec and Montreal in the 1600s, wrote with astonishment of the disappearance of Indian groups along the Great Lakes watershed. Several groups in eastern Canada had vanished by the 19th century, victims of European diseases rather than of sustained wars of extermination. Later Canadian governments would pursue policies of 'aggressive civilization', but, in contrast to the situation in the United States, such policy was not conducted as a military campaign.

From small initial settlements in the east and west of the country, European immigration to Canada began in earnest in the wake of the American War of Independence. From perhaps 100,000 Europeans in 1760, there were as many as 400,000 in 1800, about 2.5 million in 1850, and 3.7 million in 1870. After Confederation and the extension of Canadian territory to the Pacific, systematic efforts were undertaken to attract European settlers to the West, while sharp limitations were placed on *Chinese. Yet there was a net out-migration to the United States for much of the second half of the 19th century and population growth was modest. Waves of religious persecution, war, and revolution that affected European countries, as well as hopes of economic prosperity and the attraction of free land, changed matters dramatically after 1890. Hundreds of thousands of immigrants from northern, western, and eastern Europe arrived before the First World War and in the first decade following it. Official population counts were 5.3 million inhabitants in 1901 and 8.8 million in 1921. After the Second World War there was a further influx of people displaced by the war and of economic immigrants, especially from eastern and southern Europe. From 11.5 million in 1941, the official population reached 14 million in 1951, 18.2 million in 1961, and 21.6 million in 1971. After 1970, increasing numbers of immigrants came from south and east Asia. In the first decade of the 21st century, Canada's population is well over 30 million.

Nineteenth-century observers confidently predicted the disappearance by extinction or assimilation of the Aboriginal population, and English policy-makers also aimed at the assimilation of the French. Yet, while disadvantaged economically and subjected to controversial government policy and a reserves system, Indian populations remain vibrant and a renewed pan-Indian identity as 'First Nations' peoples works against assimilation. French-Canadian nationalism, tied initially to a pronatalist Catholic agrarian vision, and followed by secularizing liberalism in Quebec, created the institutional basis for the survival of the French fact. Canadian government policy since the 1970s, not without its critics, has explicitly favoured a vision of ethnic diversity called *'multiculturalism', and substantial cultural diversity in the Canadian population is celebrated in official policy.

BRUCE CURTIS

porters. From the 1880s to the 1960s Canadian railway companies employed Black men as porters because they were cheaper and had traditionally been assigned physically demanding and service roles. White dining-car employees collaborated with Canadian National Railways to exclude Blacks from higher-paying, higher-status jobs, especially during the contraction in the industry after the First World War. The *Canadian Brotherhood of Railway Employees, formed in 1908 to represent non-operating railway employees on the Intercolonial Railway, restricted membership to whites. Porters on the Canadian Northern, which became part of CNR, organized the Order of Sleeping Car Porters in 1917 and applied for membership in the CBRE. In 1919 the exclusionary clause was removed and the OSCP was given segregated status within the brotherhood. The CBRE and CN used the segregated porters' and dining-car locals to establish a seniority system that 'locked' Blacks into portering.

The OSCP—the first Black railway union in North America—worked to organize all sleeping car porters across Canada, negotiating contracts on the Canadian Northern and Grand Trunk Railways in 1919–20. Labour legislation protecting workers' right to organize (1939) gave Canadian Pacific porters some freedom to organize. The American-based Brotherhood of Sleeping Car Porters was certified to represent porters on CP (1942) and the Northern Alberta Railway (1946). The Canada Fair Employment Practices Act (1953) gave CN and CP porters

the leverage they needed to combat discrimination in railway employment. In 1955 CPR porters won the right to promotion to the position of sleeping-car conductor.
AGNES CALLISTE

Port-Royal. Fishermen and fur traders had already visited the coast of *Acadia and traded with the Aboriginal people, but in 1604, anxious to discover a route to Asia and gold, the French government gave Pierre *du Gua de Monts a ten-year fur-trade monopoly in the lands situated between the 40th and 46th latitudes. De Monts and Samuel de *Champlain were part of an expedition of about 80 men who settled on the island of Sainte-Croix in the Baie Française (Fundy). After a disastrous winter, they relocated to Port-Royal at the mouth of the Dauphin (Annapolis) River. There, the first social club in North America, the *Ordre de Bon Temps, was created by Champlain during the winter of 1606–7 and the first play, **Théâtre de Neptune* by Marc *Lescarbot, was performed.

From the beginning, the settlement's progress was hampered by internal and external strife. Its geographical situation, as a pivot between rival colonies of French to the north and English to the south, hampered its growth. Prior to its final conquest by British forces in 1710, Port-Royal suffered seven attacks. The settlement was attacked and burned by Samuel Argall in 1613 and its few colonists, all males, were scattered. In 1621, the Crown of Scotland claimed Acadia and renamed it Nova Scotia. Scottish settlers arrived in 1629, although three years later the colony was returned to France. In 1632, the governor Isaac de Razilly brought 300 men to La Hève on the south shore. At his death in 1635, most of the colonists resettled in Port-Royal under the guidance of Governor Menou d'Aulnay, who was responsible for the arrival of 20 families in the 1640s, mostly from south of the Loire River in France. The colonists, experienced reclaimers of wetlands, drained the marshlands with a system of dikes. Combined agricultural, fishing, hunting, and trapping activities provided them with a fairly high standard of living. In 1654–67, Acadia again passed to the English. The census of 1671 listed more than 400 colonists, of whom 375 lived in Port-Royal. The settlement's insecurity and the desire to find new marshlands led families to relocate in the 1670s to *Beaubassin and in the 1680s to *Grand-Pré (Minas Basin); by the 18th century these settlements were larger than Port-Royal.

Port-Royal was attacked again in 1690, 1704, 1707, and finally in 1710. Although the defence was successful in 1704 and 1707, in the end the small garrison and the inadequate fortifications were no match for the opposing forces. The colonists received little help to maintain French control. Having to rely on their own resources they did not hesitate to trade with the New England colonists against the wishes of the French authorities. English merchants came to Port-Royal to sell manufactured products while Acadians sent fish, grain, and furs to New England. Powerless to control their future, the Acadians tried to satisfy contradictory demands. By not taking sides in the Anglo-French rivalry, they thought their 'neutrality' would spare them a military backlash.

The population of Port-Royal stagnated after the migration to the new settlements. The 1701 census recorded 500 colonists, not counting the small garrison of soldiers. The Treaty of Utrecht in 1713 signalled the decline of French power in North America and the Nova Scotia peninsula became a British territory. Port-Royal was renamed Annapolis Royal after Queen Anne and remained the administrative centre of the British colony until the founding of Halifax in 1749. JEAN DAIGLE

Portuguese White Fleet. Portuguese interest in Newfoundland dates from as early as 1500–2, when the Corte-Reals explored the region. Soon Portuguese fishermen were fishing on the *Grand Banks. This fishery ceased after 1585, however, because of wars between England and Spain/Portugal, and Portugal became a market for Newfoundland salt cod. Only in the 1830s was the Portuguese–Newfoundland cod fishery re-established. The 19th-century Portuguese cod fishery grew slowly because the Portuguese government restricted its size. After regulations were lifted in 1901, the fleet expanded from 8 ships to 70–80 vessels by the post–Second World War period. By this time, most ships were painted white, and the fleet became known as the 'White Fleet'. It became a familiar sight in St John's, where it often found shelter and purchased supplies. In 1986, after disputes about overfishing the nose and tail of the Grand Banks and Portugal's refusal to allow Canadian observers on board their vessels, Canada denied landing rights to the White Fleet except in an emergency. Thus ended Portugal's historic connection with Newfoundland. SHANNON RYAN

postal communication. We begin with an apparent paradox. There was no formal postal service in New France, yet men and women successfully exchanged letters throughout the colony and across the Atlantic. Ocean-going ships regularly carried mail between New France and the mother country. Because it took up little space, captains agreed to store mail aboard their ships; mail also travelled with crew and passengers. Merchants residing in port cities on both sides of the Atlantic took mail on and off the ships for friends, acquaintances, and clients. Within New France itself mail was carried to recipients as a favour, by travellers moving between Quebec and Montreal, aboard canoes paddled by *voyageurs heading for or returning from the **pays d'en haut*, or perhaps in the bags of smugglers, or *Iroquois messengers working on their behalf, running errands and furs between New France and Albany in the English colonies. Natives were regularly hired to carry messages, helping to spread the news contained in written dispatches or that learned by word of mouth.

New France's postal heritage was twofold. First, a custom of letter writing was firmly established, even in an age when correspondents had to overcome the stringent seasonal contingencies of sending letters, when navigation and hence ocean-going transport were paralyzed for six months of the year. Second, a geographical knowledge of North America was gained, and various types of transportation were developed to overcome the challenges raised by the vast distances. This legacy provided a foundation for postal communication in the British era.

Following the conquest of New France in 1763 the British established a formal postal service in Canada. Mail was carried along a designated route, the King's Road, built originally by the French to connect Montreal, Trois-Rivières, and Quebec City. A postmaster was appointed in Quebec City. After the conclusion of the American war of independence, the position of deputy postmaster general was created to oversee the colonial mails from Quebec City. For better or for worse, this official worked under the authority of postal officials in London.

During the 1760s and the 1780s year-round routes were opened in the direction of Halifax and New York. These new routes were especially important for the exchange of mail with the rest of the Atlantic world. Because mail could be circulated from these ports 12 months in the year, merchants and others residing in Montreal or York (Toronto), the capital of the new province of Upper Canada, could have access to overseas news and the current prices of commodities much more quickly than their counterparts in the days of New France. Beginning in the late 18th century and well into the following one, New York served as British North America's postal window on the world.

Despite the establishment of the post office, the custom of sending mail by favour persisted. Mail travelled informally by *stagecoach, steamboat, and in winter by sleigh. As the means of transportation multiplied around and between the principal urban centres of British North America, so did the opportunity to carry mail, both officially and unofficially. In fact, the postal service often helped to underwrite new means of transportation. Mail transport contracts to individual steamboat or stagecoach companies were intended to help foster transport links for goods and passengers as well as mail along stretches of road or coastline.

The postal service continued to expand throughout British North America. New post offices in Upper and Lower Canada were on the increase, as were new way offices—a place where mail was left for subsequent pickup—in the Maritimes. Beginning in the 1840s new mail routes were opened in the West, between the Red River colony and St Paul, Minnesota, for example. This route remained the quickest way of getting mail to and from the colony at the time of the first Riel Rebellion of 1869–70.

The colonial postal service was to some extent a victim of its own success. The volume of mail in circulation exceeded by far the capacities of the post office. Newspapers and colonists criticized the service, finding it slow and costly. After years of protest, postal responsibility was devolved to the individual colonies. In 1851 the governments of Nova Scotia, New Brunswick, and Canada formally took charge of their domestic postal affairs. Prince Edward Island and Newfoundland would soon follow suit. Each issued a postage stamp and initiated improvements in service. Their experiences set the stage for the founding of the dominion Department of the Post Office in 1867.

In the century after Confederation the Post Office expanded in all directions, largely because of developments in transportation and increased demands for the service. The Railway Mail Service, first established in the 1850s, was reorganized as a formal branch of the department in 1897. A host of trucks, cars, and horse-driven and hand-hauled vehicles of all sorts carried the mail over shorter distances. Snow, mud, and freezing temperatures as well as a dispersed population proved to be enduring challenges. Sailing vessels and later steamships served the extensive Pacific and Atlantic coastlines as well as the inland waterways.

Home delivery began in the cities as early as the 1870s, and the seemingly ubiquitous letter carrier came to personify the operation of the Canadian postal service. Out in the country, a network of post offices distributed mail to small towns and villages. Rural mail delivery, introduced gradually from 1908, brought the post office to the farmer's door. Canada's largest cities were among the first to benefit from the introduction of airmail in 1928; during the next two decades airmail brought the farthest reaches of the Canadian North more firmly into the postal picture.

The volume of mail rose precipitously during the 20th century, from 230 million articles in 1901 to 9.2 billion in 1998. Business was primarily responsible for the increase. *Newspaper dailies and weeklies depended on the post, as did the mail-order operations of large *department stores like Eaton's, Simpson's, Dupuis Frères, and Woodward's. Indeed, the extensive use of the *mail-order catalogue from about 1900 to 1930 created an entire postal dimension within the burgeoning consumer economy of the nation.

The growing stream of mail created new challenges, which were eventually addressed by the reorganization of work and technology. The advent of the postal code in 1971 signified Canada's entry into the modern age of mechanized mail-processing. It also helped initiate a unique period of labour conflict; never before, or since, have labour relations within the Post Office been so acrimonious.

Since the 1970s the Post Office, or Canada Post as it became known in 1981 following its re-establishment as a Crown corporation, has experienced at least two generations of technology, and more change is on the way, with the prospect of a fully automated system of mail processing including parcels as well as first-class mail. Meanwhile the post is turning to electronic mail as a means of expanding business. No doubt the volume of private e-mail communication has cut into the business of Canada Post, as did the advent of the telephone. However, it remains to be seen how this will affect our ingrained habit of exchanging written messages, a custom that began when the French reached our shores four centuries ago.

JOHN WILLIS

potlatch. A ceremony practised by *west coast Aboriginals in which guests receive a gift for witnessing an event of social significance, such as a person's formal assumption of the role of chief. By accepting the gifts, guests legitimize the event. Feasting, dancing, and the reciting of oral history are other common elements of a potlatch. Besides validating events, potlatches give groups an opportunity to put on public record all important changes in a group such as births, marriages, deaths, and the transfer of rights. Archaeologists speculate that potlatching has been practised for about 4,000 years. The federal government banned the potlatch in 1884; although some people were imprisoned, potlatching continued underground and resurfaced publicly in the 1950s when the prohibition was lifted. ROBERT J. MUCKLE

Potts, Jerry (*c.* 1840–96). Jerry Potts (or 'Bear Child') was arguably the greatest scout in the Old North-West. Born to a Blood Indian mother and Scottish-American fur-trader father, Potts had one foot in each culture. A fierce, sometime reckless, warrior who participated in the Battle of *Oldman River in 1870 (the last great Cree–Blackfoot skirmish), he was working in the Alberta–Montana whisky trade in 1874 when he was hired by the *North-West Mounted Police as a scout. At home on the open prairie, he helped the Mounties establish themselves in southern Alberta and facilitated peaceful relations between the police and the Blackfoot. His translation work was noted for its brevity, and many a great Indian speech was reduced to a few words. Despite being a notoriously heavy drinker, he remained with the force until his death. BILL WAISER

Pouchot, Pierre (1712–69), military engineer. Son of a Grenoble merchant, Pouchot rose by talent, not birth. In 1755–6 he redesigned Fort Niagara with enormous regular defenceworks (still standing); as commander, he proved adept at diplomatic relations with the Aboriginals. He also participated in French victories at Fort Oswego (1756) and Carillon (1758). He defended Fort Niagara tenaciously against an Anglo-American army that used heavy cannon in a European-style siege (1759), and led the defence of Fort Lévis, on Lake Ontario east of Prescott, against a fierce bombardment by Jeffery Amherst's army in August 1760, the last battle in the campaign to conquer Canada. Pouchot left many maps and architectural drawings, as well as his extraordinary *Memoirs on the Late War in North America* (1781). His observations on Aboriginals are remarkable for his sympathetic stance, insightful observations, and wealth of detail. JAY CASSEL

Poundmaker (c.1842–86) was the son of an Assiniboine father and Cree mother, and the adopted son of *Crowfoot, head chief of the Blackfoot. Although respected for his diplomatic talents, he was an outspoken critic of Treaty 6 (1876) and tried to continue to hunt buffalo near the international border. He later entered the treaty and took a reserve near Battleford, Saskatchewan, where he farmed with limited success. During the 1885 *North-West Rebellion, Poundmaker travelled to Battleford in late March to declare his allegiance to the Queen and secure rations, but his hungry followers ransacked the abandoned village. The Canadian army later attacked his camp near Cut Knife Hill in early May, but he held back the Indian warriors and prevented a massacre of the retreating troops. Despite surrendering to Canadian authorities and pleading his innocence, Poundmaker was found guilty of treason-felony at his Regina trial and sentenced to three years in Stony Mountain penitentiary. He was released after less than a year and died shortly thereafter, a broken man but a hero to his people. BILL WAISER

Poutrincourt, Jean de Biencourt de (1557–1615), French colonizer. From a landed family, Poutrincourt fought for Catholicism in the French Wars of Religion. When King Henri IV became Catholic in 1593, Poutrincourt began to attain office and honours. In 1604 he sailed to Acadia with Pierre du Gua de Monts, returning to France with a shipment of furs that autumn. Poutrincourt set out again in spring 1606 and took command of the settlement at *Port-Royal, for which he also received a seigneurial grant. The colony was abandoned in 1607 after losing its trading monopoly, but Poutrincourt still wished to develop his seigneurie. He returned in 1610 to re-establish the tiny settlement. His eldest son, Charles de Biencourt de Poutrincourt (known as Biencourt, *c.* 1591–1623) assumed command when Poutrincourt departed for France in 1611 to deal with discontented patrons. Biencourt was eventually forced to leave Port-Royal in 1613 when it was burned by an English force, although he remained in Acadia to head a small group of fur-trading colonists and died there. His father revisited Acadia briefly in 1614, before being killed in civil strife in France. Poutrincourt and Biencourt, while experiencing repeated frustrations, contributed to establishing a continuous French presence in Acadia. JOHN G. REID

poverty. The experience of poverty in Canada is defined by three historical periods: the years before the *welfare state (until the 1940s), the years marked by the flowering of the welfare state (1940s–1970s), and those since the welfare state began to crumble (1980s–present). Whereas unimaginable privation was a fact of life for the lower classes in the first period, the social legislation of the second took the edge off the worst features of poverty. The third period has been characterized by the plight of such socially marginalized groups as Native people and inhabitants of the streets. Throughout, poverty has existed in tandem with inadequate responses by church, state, and society.

Colonial views of poverty reveal a masculinist, Utopian perspective. By proclaiming that no settler in a land of opportunity need be destitute, observers overlooked the scores of women and children without providers. They also failed to reckon with the vicissitudes of the Canadian climate, particularly the impact of harsh winters on men's employment patterns and commodity prices. More prosaically, at the community level poverty was acted upon either as a problem or an opportunity. The problem was posed by the undeserving, who were considered feckless, drunken, or dishonest, and by the cyclically (often seasonally) unemployed for whom some means of 'less eligible' employment must be found, which usually meant gruelling manual labour at non-competitive wages. Opportunity, on the other hand, especially for the sweet pleasure of exercising charity, was presented by the deserving and unemployable—helpless widows and the young, aged, sick, and maimed. Together they were considered a class of permanently poor that inspired churches, philanthropists, and the emergent 'helping' professions to establish health and welfare institutions, relief organizations, and special funds for targeted groups.

A variety of local practices developed: auctioning off the poor to the lowest bidder/caregiver in Nova Scotia's rural poor districts, issuing licences to beggars in Quebec, and everywhere imprisoning debtors, most of whom had little chance of expunging their debts. Although only the Maritimes adopted English-style Poor Laws, many of Canada's chronically poor people, wherever they lived, ended up in poorhouses or almshouses, houses of refuge or industry, or local jails. These primitive welfare homes were run by either the municipalities or religious organizations. When inhabitants of coastal or country areas suffered privation because of environmental disaster, emigration or starvation were their choices. At the same time, the arrival in Canada, beginning in the late 18th century and continuing until the mid-20th century, of *refugees—American Loyalists, ex-slaves, dispossessed immigrants from overseas, and people displaced by modern warfare—increased the incidence of poverty, particularly in urban areas. Slum districts of the major cities and towns were clearly identifiable by the second half of the 19th century, stimulating the organization of Catholic parish relief, Protestant city missions, and municipal public health measures, and prompting the publication of books such as Herbert Ames's *The City below the Hill* (1897), a graphic description of living conditions in Montreal.

Canada's industrial age introduced the spectre of the working poor, who drew wages insufficient to support their families. The ideal, promoted by reformers, of the family wage earned by the male breadwinner was another gender-biased notion that overlooked the increasing numbers of low-paid working women with family responsibilities. The more provident poor people looked to forms of self-help—collective bargaining, life insurance, and savings banks—to try to overcome the worst disadvantages of the capitalist system. Degrees of poverty produced a variety of ways of measuring it. Trade *unions, for example, were among the first to estimate the 'poverty line' in terms of the cost of living, a recurrent theme later taken up by governments. In the early 20th century the state began to intervene in the form of totally inadequate workers' compensation, *mothers' allowances, and minimum wages.

Nationwide poverty was at its most stark during the *Great Depression of the 1930s. Parsimonious though relief was at all levels, the continuing suspicion of the able-bodied jobless reached paranoic levels. Families suffering from desperate want wrote heart-wrenching letters to politicians, especially to Prime Minister R.B. *Bennett, begging for help. Many of the destitute died of untreated diseases or suicidal despair. The high rates of unemployment and illness stimulated the search for political solutions.

The resulting state welfare program in post-war Canada redefined poverty. Giving the poor the means to maintain a degree of independence signalled the end of Poor Laws and institutionalization. When, by the late 1960s, a combination of measures such as *old-age pensions, *unemployment insurance, family allowances, social assistance, and *medicare had still failed to prevent poverty, the federal government appointed a senate committee, which issued its report, *Poverty in Canada*, in 1970. Many of the problems encountered by people in want were aggravated by the division of authority not only between Ottawa and the provinces but also between municipalities and the provinces and among the departments of health, welfare, labour, and economic development. Other problems related to race and ethnicity, whereby systemic discrimination made matters worse. Still others reflected new forms of the feminization of poverty, as the number of single mothers and elderly women increased. For the underprivileged trapped by 'the culture of poverty', self-help took the form of 'rights' movements to address historic wrongs.

Arguably, the welfare state produced high levels of welfare dependency. Even in wealthy Ontario it was not unusual to find 15 per cent of the population on social assistance. For those who fell through the cracks, 'new' post-welfare state practices emerged such as food banks—the late-20th-century equivalent of the Victorian soup kitchen—and traditional begging or panhandling, often by people released into the streets when traditional welfare and chronic care institutions closed or reduced their residential facilities. The major concern of the new millennium is child poverty, the most recent example of the long-standing tendency of neo-conservative governments and welfare agencies to fail to address the root causes of poverty. JUDITH FINGARD

Power, Charles Gavan 'Chubby' (1888–1968). Born in Sillery, a French-speaking Irish Canadian, Power inherited his businessman father's Liberal sympathies and his Quebec City seat in the federal Parliament, which the young Power won in 1917 after wounds sustained at the Battle of the Somme brought him home from the First World War. His career, marked by an exuberance for politics and a profound sympathy for French Canada, was damaged by his alcoholism and independence of spirit. Power was minister of pensions and national health (1935–9), postmaster-general (1939–40), and minister of national defence for air (1940–4). He resigned from the Mackenzie *King cabinet in November 1944 because of the imposition of *conscription for overseas military service, fearing an uncooperative francophone population 'with a deep sense of injury . . . prey to the worst elements amongst them, and, worst of all, hating all other Canadians'. Remaining in the House of Commons, he was appointed to the Senate in 1955; he published his superb memoir, *A Party Politician*, in 1966. Power ran unsuccessfully for the Liberal leadership in 1948, thinking he would make a poor prime minister but a rousing leader of the opposition. NORMAN HILLMER

Prairie Farm Rehabilitation Administration. This agency was a Depression-era measure enacted by the federal government in 1935. It provided specifically for the rehabilitation of the areas stricken by drought in the Prairie provinces, most particularly in southwestern Manitoba, southern Saskatchewan, and southeastern Alberta, an arid region known as the *Palliser Triangle. Its immediate task was to promote the conservation of surface water resources on farms and to encourage practices designed to combat the serious soil drifting that resulted from the prolonged drought of the early 1930s. This included offering aid to farmers to control soil drifting; to construct dugouts to catch the spring run-off for livestock, gardens, and household use; to regrass their lands; and, on occasion, to move to more suitable land. The financial appropriation for work covered the years 1935 until 1940, by which time it was hoped that the crisis would have ended.

Over the next several years the PFRA was amended to reclaim approximately 800,000 ha of ruined farmland. Experiments in Manitoba had provided scientists with possible methods of controlling grasshoppers and overcoming crop rust through resistant strains of wheat. Soil scientists were confident that wind erosion could be controlled with time, money, and machinery. The federal Department of Agriculture was authorized to purchase, lease, or sell lands coming within the scope of any project. The PFRA urged farmers to withdraw from cereal cultivation of sub-marginal lands and regrass them for ranch land or community pastures. ROBERT WARDHAUGH

Pratt, Edwin John (1882–1964), poet, man of letters. The son of a Methodist parson, Pratt spent his maturing years in Newfoundland, steeped in its ritual and romance. At 25, a candidate for the ministry, he pursued studies at the University of Toronto, where he completed a doctorate in 1917. Deflected from a clerical profession by his graduate studies, Pratt began teaching literature at Victoria College and, under the tutelage of Pelham Edgar, began a writing career that would see him acknowledged as one of Canada's foremost modern poets. Beginning with *Newfoundland Verse* (1923), continuing through to *Towards the Last Spike* (1952), but most memorably in such lyrics as 'In Absentia' (1921) and 'Erosion' (1931), Pratt successfully bridged the gap between the romantic verse of the 19th century, exemplified in the work of Carman, Roberts, and Lampman, and the new realism of the 20th, emerging in the work of writers such as A.J.M. Smith, Leo Kennedy, and Dorothy *Livesay. His influence in establishing a new realism in Canadian writing was widely asserted through his editorship of *Canadian Poetry Magazine* (1936–43). His Newfoundland themes helped place that province on the literary map of Canada. R.G. MOYLES

pre-European history. The human history of northern North America began during the last Ice Age, when most of the region was covered by continental glaciation. The amount of water trapped in glaciers lowered sea levels by 100 m or more, exposing a broad plain joining eastern Siberia and Alaska. The Bering Land Bridge and adjacent areas of northeastern Asia and northwestern North America, which were relatively free of ice, supported a rich variety of animals. Paleolithic hunters from Asia expanded their range throughout this area, without realizing that they had discovered a new continent.

The earliest evidence of this occupation comes from the Bluefish Caves, a small set of limestone caverns in the northern Yukon. Animal bones excavated from the caves show traces of cutting and chopping by humans and are radiocarbon dated to more than 20,000 years ago. Later hunters, living around the end of the Ice Age, left chipped-stone tools in the caves. At the time Bluefish Caves were first occupied, the region was essentially an extension of Asia, isolated from the remainder of North and South America by hundreds of kilometres of glacial ice. As the glaciers melted, routes to the south opened; by at least 15,000 years ago humans began to move southwards through the mountain valleys of northwestern Canada or along the Pacific coast. No convincing evidence of this movement is at present known in northwestern North America, but humans appear to have reached the southern portion of South America by at least 14,000 years ago.

By about 12,000 years ago the glaciers that had covered most of Canada were melting rapidly, forming huge meltwater lakes and raising sea levels. Hunting peoples moved northwards following herds of caribou, bison, horses, mammoths, and other Ice Age animals into the tundra environment of what is now southern Canada. These people are known to archaeologists as Paleoindians, big-game hunters who were the first widespread occupants of North America to have left significant archaeological evidence. Archaeological sites related to the Paleoindian tradition are sparsely scattered across southern Canada from Nova Scotia to eastern British Columbia, while there is evidence of a distinctive and more poorly defined human occupation of Pacific coastal regions.

Over the following millennia Paleoindian big-game hunting cultures expanded northwards across the prairies and into the region west of Hudson Bay, almost reaching the Arctic coast at about 9,000 years ago, when the last Ice Age glaciers disappeared from the area. Others moved north along the Atlantic coast, following the arctic-like environment left by the retreating ice and learning to exploit the rich sea-mammal resources of the region. About 8,000 years ago one of these groups buried a child beneath a large mound of boulders near L'Anse Amour in southern Labrador; the deeply excavated tomb contained several stone spear heads, red ochre and graphite paintstones, a walrus tusk and a decorated ivory handle, a harpoon head, a bird-bone flute, and evidence of ceremonial fires. A burial of this scale and complexity, which is unusual for such an early period, hints at the unexpected economic and spiritual wealth of these early hunters.

As the low-latitude tundras and the associated herds of large herbivores diminished, hunters across the continent quickly adapted to the development of environments similar to those of the present day. These adaptations across eastern and central North America are known to archaeologists as Archaic cultures, including all those that existed between the end of the big-game hunting traditions of the Paleoindian period and the beginning of agricultural economies of the past few millennia. The Maritime Archaic tradition of Atlantic Canada, which focused on the coastal resources of the region, is remarkable for a rich complex of burial practices of which the L'Anse Amour burial is an early example. The Laurentian Archaic tradition shows similar patterns of development in the Great Lakes region and is distinguished by the widespread use of tools and ornaments made from copper mined from the Lake Superior region. Bison-hunting cultures developed across the plains, their use of bison jumps and pounds continuing to the historic period. Related groups adapted to the caribou and fish resources of the northern forests. Along the Pacific coast and in the adjacent river valleys local cultural traditions that had existed in earlier millennia expanded markedly from 5,000 years ago, apparently at a time when sea levels stabilized and populations of Pacific salmon became established. Permanent villages began to be marked by the growth of shell middens, while evidence of trade and warfare suggests an increase in the complexity of social and economic patterns.

Although most of the Aboriginal inhabitants of the Americas may be descended from the hunters who crossed the Bering Land Bridge during the Ice Age, several peoples of northern and northwestern Canada may be related to later arrivals. The forested interior of Alaska and northwestern Canada is occupied by people speaking languages of the Dene (Athabaskan) family, and groups speaking related languages are scattered from the interior of British Columbia to Arizona. The ancestry of the Dene can be traced to early Alaskan cultures around the end of the Ice Age, using technologies characterized by microblades—small razor-like flakes of flint or obsidian made by a specialized technique used by northern Asiatic peoples of the time. Some of these groups may have been among the last Asian hunters to move across the Bering Land Bridge before it disappeared about 10,000 years ago.

A more recent immigration of Siberian peoples is seen in the Arctic, where the remains of a unique cultural tradition known as Paleoeskimo appear from Alaska to Greenland around 5,000 years ago. The Paleoeskimos must have crossed Bering Strait in boats, or more likely on winter sea ice, and brought with them important elements of Asiatic technology—the bow and arrow and finely tailored skin clothing—that made arctic life possible. Their descendants, the Dorset culture people—noted for their fine miniature sculptures of humans, animals, and spirits—were the primary occupants of arctic Canada until displaced by the Inuit a few centuries ago.

Beginning around 3,000 years ago, cultural traditions across southern Canada began to develop more rapidly than they had during earlier Archaic times. This period saw the adoption of the bow and arrow, which had probably been introduced through contact with Paleoeskimos in the North. Ceramic technology, which had been invented much earlier in South America, spread northward and produced a very important technological change in the cooking and storage of food. Agriculture was an even more significant southern invention that was gradually spreading northwards from Central America, as food plants such as maize, squash, and beans were slowly adapted to shorter growing seasons. Although effective agriculture was not established in southern Canada until the first millennium AD, an increasing interest in local plant resources combined with the use of pottery to store and process seeds or roots led to population growth and an increase in sedentary settlement from southern Ontario to the Maritimes.

Between about 2,500 and 1,500 years ago these same areas were significantly influenced by cultural traditions centred in the Ohio Valley. This influence is especially apparent in the spread of a mortuary complex involving mound burials, which included specific forms of elegant artifacts made from materials that came from the Ohio Valley region. In the West, a distinct but similar expansion of southern influence saw the establishment of pit-house villages in the interior valleys of British Columbia, apparently associated with an increased emphasis on the use and storage of root-plants as a supplement to salmon resources. The period also produced a florescence in stone carving and the production of other decorated objects among the peoples of the Pacific coast, together with larger permanent settlements and evidence for development of the elaborate social patterns that characterized the area in the historic period.

By about 1,000 years ago a form of maize had been developed that would grow as far north as the southern Great Lakes, and the Iroquoian-speaking people of southern Ontario and the upper St Lawrence Valley were engaged in a fully agricultural economy that produced an expanding population. The cultures and religious beliefs of these groups were influenced by the major civilization that had by this time developed in the central Mississippi Valley. Although the political power of Mississippian civilization was relatively local, the influence of its wealth and cultural complexity spanned much of the continent from the mountains to the Atlantic Ocean. Bison-hunting peoples of the prairies were involved in trade that extended down the Missouri Valley to the Mississippi, and the construction of large burial mounds in the area indicates that religious ideas as well as agricultural products were moving northwards. By this time, most of the peoples of southern Canada were part of a continent-wide network involving the exchange of economic products, exotic or precious materials, and ideas that filtered northwards from the civilizations to the south.

The centuries after AD 1000 saw the appearance of two new peoples in Canadian history: the *Inuit and the *Norse. By 1,000 years ago Alaskan Inuit, who had developed efficient technologies for hunting marine mammals and surviving the arctic environment, had expanded their occupation into the western portion of arctic Canada. At the same time, Norse Icelanders extended their agricultural-based occupation to subarctic Greenland and began to make at least occasional forays along the eastern coasts of arctic Canada, reaching as far south as the Gulf of St Lawrence. The presence of the Norse as a potential source for valuable metal products may have attracted the Inuit expansion across arctic Canada, an event that seems to have occurred around AD 1200. Norse contact and trade with the Aboriginal peoples of arctic Canada appears to have continued sporadically over the following three centuries, setting the stage for subsequent European ventures across the North Atlantic. ROBERT McGHEE

Presbyterianism. A system of church government sometimes described as corporate episcopacy because the governing regional unit, the presbytery, exercises through its collective membership approximately the same powers as a bishop does over a diocese. Regionally associated congregations are ruled by the Court of Presbytery composed of the minister (teaching elder) and one of the elected (ruling) elders from each congregation's Court of Session. Two higher representative levels of courts, the larger regional synod and the annual General Assembly of the denomination, are subject to a system of checks and balances through referenda and initiatives that leaves essential power ultimately in the hands of the presbyteries. This concentration of control has produced the jibe derived from the slogan of the Russian communist revolution, 'All power to the presbyteries'.

This presbyterian form of corporate government developed after the Reformation in reaction against what was seen as excessive power held by individual bishops under the long-established pattern of church government by bishops in dioceses. Presbyterianism achieved its modern shape in Scotland in the late 16th century under Andrew Melville (1542–1622), who provided this form of church polity to compliment the Calvinist theology introduced there by the Genevan-trained Reformer John Knox (1513–72). With some variations the same form of church government is used by other denominations sharing the Reformed tradition of Protestantism in France, the Netherlands, Hungary, Switzerland, South Africa, the United States, and Canada, and through missionary contacts in Korea and Japan. Presbyterianism and *Calvinism played a significant role in the ideology of the American Revolution, sometimes dubbed the 'Presbyterian Revolution', which may explain why Presbyterians were a minority among the United Empire *Loyalists.

Presbyterianism became a dominant element in the Canadian denominational scene because of the heavy Scottish immigration to Nova Scotia and Upper and Lower Canada in the century after the British Conquest. By the early 20th century Presbyterians formed the largest Protestant denomination in Canada, but in 1925 approximately two-thirds of its members entered the newly formed *United Church of Canada. After this, Presbyterians made up only 8 per cent of the Canadian population, a proportion that did not vary much even during the rapid revival of church attendance after the Second World War but that has decreased fairly consistently since the 1970s because of immigration. At the beginning of the present millennium less than 4 per cent of Canadians are Presbyterian. Because of Canadian Presbyterianism's predominantly Scottish roots, and partly as a defensive reaction against the union of 1925, the Presbyterian Church in Canada retains and promotes numerous ethnic characteristics, even though a considerable portion of its membership has Dutch, Hungarian, and Korean, and other Protestant origins.

Because of those Scottish cultural associations Presbyterian attitudes and practices have become the subject of jokes that stressed the frugality, puritanism, and conservatism of Presbyterians, despite the fact that, in the late Victorian and Edwardian period the Presbyterian Church in Canada was the most vocal and active Protestant denomination to support the reform movement known as the *social gospel. That movement urged social activism and reform on a host of public issues, including alcoholism, penology, urban working conditions and hours, political corruption, poverty, the environment, housing and public health measures, child welfare, and women's rights. Much of this Presbyterian energy and organization was absorbed by the United Church at the time of union in 1925, but social gospel ideals have remained a strong component of the ideology of the Presbyterian Church in Canada. JOHN S. MOIR

Preston, Isabella (1881–1964), horticulturist. Born in Lancaster, England, Preston studied briefly at Swanley Horticultural College and emigrated to Canada in 1912. On arrival, she enrolled at Ontario Agricultural College and worked part-time in the greenhouses. In the spring of 1913, she left formal horticultural studies to manage Professor J.W. Crow's experiments and teach herself about hybridization. In 1916 she became Canada's first women hybridist with her historic lily cross and major breakthrough in lily hybridization 'George C. Creelman'. In 1920 Preston entered the federal civil service, becoming a leading expert in ornamental horticulture. Specializing in lily, lilac, rose, Siberian iris, and flowering crab-apple hybrids, she created over 200 Canada-hardy (zone 2 and 3) varieties. As a writer, Preston was known for her helpful and empathetic responses to enquiries, and she published many articles, plant bulletins, and two books. One—*Garden Lilies* (1929)—was Canada's first book on lily cultivation. JULIE C. THACKER

Preston, Richard (1790–1861). Preston was born into slavery in Virginia. After buying his freedom, he sailed to Nova Scotia in search of his mother, who had migrated as a War of 1812 refugee. A preacher during his days in Virginia, Preston became the leader of the Black Baptists after studying and being ordained in England in 1832. While there he joined the British abolitionists. A skilled orator, he lectured against *slavery and later set up an abolition society in Nova Scotia. In revival services Preston preached and recruited members for the African Baptist churches he founded in rural Black villages throughout the province.

By 1854 there were 12 churches, which Preston organized into the African Baptist Association during an inaugural meeting at Granville Mountain. Now called the African United Baptist Association, this organization followed its founder's philosophy of attending to the members' spiritual and social needs. Its annual meeting rotates among member churches and is a significant religious and community event for African Nova Scotians.

SYLVIA D. HAMILTON

Price, William (1789–1867), lumber merchant, plank manufacturer. Born in London, England, Price arrived in Quebec City in 1810, where, after working in the import-export sector, he entered the timber-export trade in the 1820s. Profiting from British Admiralty contracts, Price diversified into deal and plank manufacturing. By 1850 he owned at least 40 sawmills, most acquired by foreclosing on debts owed him by smaller saw millers. Some 2,000 colonists and 2,000 workers in the Saguenay region of Quebec were tied to the fortunes of Price's enterprises. Price worked his men from dawn till dusk, fined them if they were ill too often, required them to provide their own tools, and paid them in company scrip redeemable at the company store at exchange rates established by Price himself. He brooked no opposition. He typified many other successful Lower Canadian rural entrepreneurs, acquiring, like his seigneurial counterparts, the trappings of feudal status: manor houses, landed property, a subservient workforce, and a statue, overlooking Chicoutimi, dedicated to him from the people of the Saguenay.

PETER BASKERVILLE

Price Spreads, Royal Commission on. In the early 1930s Prime Minister R.B. *Bennett was challenged by some in his caucus, who hoped he would set a more radical course. One of the most important critics of his ride-it-through approach to the Depression was the minister of trade and commerce, Harry Stevens. To contain Stevens's challenge to his leadership, Bennett appointed him in 1934 to head a parliamentary investigation into business practices (later reconstituted as the Royal Commission on Price Spreads) in order to determine whether the system really needed reforming. Stevens's belief was that the Depression had been caused by price deflation, which had happened because big businesses were attempting to create monopolies and were driving down prices to squeeze out rivals. The impact of deflation could be seen in falling wages for workers and in the ruin of thousands of smaller companies that could not compete with the giants. The commission found the strongest evidence of predatory competition in the retail sector and its major targets were the chains and *department stores. Although it did find some of the evidence it was searching for, Bennett refused to act on most of its recommendations. As a result, Stevens founded the *Reconstruction Party, split the right-wing vote in the 1935 election, and helped produce the decade-long debilitation of the Conservative Party.

DAVID MONOD

prime minister's office. Relatively late to develop, this office was formalized during Lester *Pearson's prime ministership, although his successor, Pierre *Trudeau, is deemed the architect of the present office, which has grown from a handful of advisers to a highly organized staff of 80–120 persons. Unlike the *Privy Council Office, the other central agency serving the needs of prime minister and cabinet, staff of the PMO are temporary political appointees, not permanent public servants. Their role is to help the prime minister carry out functions as head of his or her political party rather than parliamentary, public policy functions as head of government. Duties associated with this role include handling correspondence, speaking itineraries, and relations with media, party, and caucus; providing political intelligence from the regions; and advising on *order-in-council appointments. Beyond these functions, senior staff engage in crisis management, guard the gateway to the prime minister, and push his or her agenda. In the process, the line separating politics from administration blurs, raising the prospect of overlap and conflict with career civil servants in other central agencies.

J.E. HODGETTS

primogeniture. A principle of English common *law whereby the land of those dying without a valid will descended to the eldest son or his heirs. Although other British North American colonies had adopted more egalitarian rules of descent, primogeniture came to Upper Canada when the common law was imported wholesale in 1792. Despite a prominent and persistent campaign against it, primogeniture survived until 1851, when the first fully reform government legislated equality for all children.

Critics argued that primogeniture was an aristocratic device inappropriate for a more egalitarian North America, was unfair and contrary to parental wishes, and would concentrate land and therefore political power in fewer hands. Supporters countered that monarchical government and a British cultural identity required aristocracy and the common law and that primogeniture prevented yeoman farms from being subdivided into subsistence plots. Eighteen bills were introduced in the assembly to abolish primogeniture, many by Marshall Spring Bidwell, but the legislative council ensured its survival until the advent of *responsible government. Thus the debate was as much about the ideal constitution and social structure as inheritance laws.

JEFFREY L. McNAIRN

Prince Edward Island. The island was known as Abegweit ('resting on the waves' or 'lying parallel with the land') or Minago (simply 'the island') to the *Mi'kmaq, who were present at the time the first Europeans arrived. Jacques *Cartier sighted the island in 1534, and the French named it Île St-Jean. The first permanent French settlers did not arrive until 1720. The French-descended population grew slowly until the period after 1748, when many Acadians, anticipating another war between England and France, left the mainland hoping to avoid the conflict. But after war came and *Louisbourg fell in 1758, the British expelled most; virtually all the rest left in order to avoid expulsion.

By the Treaty of Paris (1763) France relinquished to Britain its claim of sovereignty. The British used the name St John's Island until 1799, when they chose the name Prince Edward Island, after Prince Edward, the future father of Queen Victoria. The imperial government divided almost the entire island into 67 townships, and in 1767 distributed all but one to individuals and small groups by a lottery. This gave the island a neo-feudal system of land tenure, which made it unattractive to many potential settlers. Struggles over the *Prince Edward Island land question dominated public life in the colonial period and gave rise to considerable social and political conflict. Yet it was thanks to the lobbying of proprietors that the island gained political autonomy from Nova Scotia in 1769.

The colony won *responsible government in 1851, after a protracted struggle spearheaded by George *Coles, leader of the Liberal Party, and Edward Whelan, a brilliant journalist. The Coles government gave the island the first system of 'free education' within the British Empire but failed to end leasehold tenure. When the Confederation issue arose in 1864, most islanders were opposed, in good part because the Quebec terms did not include a plan to deal with leasehold. The construction of a railway in the early 1870s by the island government of James C. *Pope precipitated a financial crisis resulting in acceptance of Confederation; the new terms agreed to in 1873 included compelling the landlords to sell their properties.

Like the rest of the Maritimes, the island did not prosper as a result of Confederation. The population peaked with the census of 1891 and began a lengthy decline that was reversed only in the 1930s. The decreasing population resulted from out-migration, first flowing towards the New England states. Eventually, as Canada developed, the migrants headed westward within the country, mostly to central Canada. The small population of the province meant a decline in political influence within Canada as a whole. Representation in the House of Commons fell from six in 1873 to four in 1904.

In addition to suffering from out-migration, the island did not succeed in attracting immigrants. Consequently, the mix of ethnic origins remained fairly stable. The largest single group has been the Scots, followed by the English and Irish. There has also been a significant Acadian minority. Despite the relative lack of diversity, the province was the first to elect as premier a person of non-European origin—Joseph Ghiz, a Lebanese Canadian, who served 1986–93.

Agriculture has always been at the centre of the economy, which led to the island's designation as the 'Garden of the Gulf'. With the 20th century, the potato increasingly dominated, and the island established a place for itself as a major producer of both table stock and seed potatoes. A second traditional industry, fisheries, focused on shellfish, particularly lobster. Tourism became a major factor within the economy after the Second World War. Tourists have been drawn to the province by its beaches and temperate summer climate, the major limiting factor the shortness of the summer season.

The island remains the smallest Canadian province, and islanders are acutely aware of their identity. In 1973 the centennial of entry into Confederation, combined with an exuberant promotion of tourism, prompted considerable soul searching about the first century within Canada and what it had meant. The question of identity arose again because of the promise, made in 1873, of 'continuous communication' with the mainland, which led, after generations of ferry boat service, to a proposal for a *'fixed link' in the 1980s. It proved divisive: some feared that easier access would lead to irreversible and undesirable changes. Yet, in a plebiscite held 18 January 1988 a majority voted in favour of a fixed connection. The result was construction of the Confederation Bridge, completed in 1997. IAN ROSS ROBERTSON

Prince Edward Island land question. After Prince Edward Island was transferred from France to Britain by the Treaty of Paris in 1763, the British government divided almost all of it into 67 townships of about 20,000 acres. Four years later a lottery held in London distributed all but one of these, the smallest, to individuals or small groups. Typically, the new owners were military, political, or commercial persons who had performed services during the war with France, or who had good connections to those in office. The British government seems to have expected them, or some of their family members, to live in the colony, constituting a landlord class. The lottery determined that there would be virtually no Crown land for settlers to acquire; consequently, most would become tenants. One of the first acts of the landlords, or 'proprietors', was to petition successfully for political separation from Nova Scotia so as to protect their interests from an assembly potentially dominated by people committed to the yeoman ideal of freehold tenure. The autonomy that resulted in 1769 was their most enduring contribution to the island.

The proprietory system never worked as intended. In the first instance, there was the uncertainty of the American Revolutionary years, which made it risky to attempt to fulfill the most crucial condition of the land grants: to settle one person per 200 acres within ten years. The lack of settlers meant that little rent was paid, a fact that led most proprietors to default on another important condition, namely payment of quitrents to finance the local administration. By 1800 it was clear that no proprietor had fulfilled all the granting conditions. The supposed penalty for non-fulfillment was the feudal remedy of escheat or resumption of land by the Crown. In their defence the proprietors pointed out that everyone had greatly underestimated the costs of settling a densely wooded area and the time required to make it productive; further, many townships had changed ownership, some more than once, and it was argued that purchasers should not be punished for the failures of the original grantees. The remoteness of the colony and lack of amenities also meant that few proprietors resided on the island; the interests of the absentees were in the hands of middlemen—often lawyers or public officials—known as land agents, who formed the basis of the local elite, centred in Charlottetown.

The island was settled in a significant way only after 1815. Within a generation a popular movement of working farmers, both tenants and squatters, arose demanding escheat. Their expectation was that once the Crown owned the land, it would be granted free to the actual occupiers. The movement won a smashing victory in the assembly elections of 1838, but the British government made it clear that it would not contemplate such a radical solution. The reasons behind the rejection were twofold: the undoubted access proprietors had to those who held political power in Britain, and the unwelcome precedent escheat would set by depriving a propertied class of its property without compensation.

After the failure of the escheat movement, a more moderate Reform or Liberal Party arose, led by George *Coles and the young Irish-born journalist Edward Whelan. The Liberals argued that *responsible government was necessary in order to resolve the issue. Once in office after 1851, the Liberals introduced a number of measures to liquidate leasehold tenure gradually and to palliate its workings in the meantime. Their success was limited, primarily by the unwillingness of many proprietors, such as Sir Samuel *Cunard, the shipping magnate, who owned one-sixth of the colony, to sell or to surrender any of their prerogatives. A royal commission report in the early 1860s and a subsequent delegation to London accomplished little. A new organization, known as the *Tenant League, arose more or less spontaneously in 1864, its members committed to resist collection of rent. The movement successfully defied the civil authorities, leading the island government to call upon British troops in 1865 to assist the sheriff. The league disintegrated in the face of this use of force, but with the disturbances, many landlords, including the Cunard heirs, appeared to lose heart and voluntarily sold their estates to the local government for resale to occupiers. A political consensus became apparent that the system, now faltering, was doomed. The Confederation terms of 1873 provided for compulsory sale of the remaining estates, which was accomplished through legislation passed in 1875.

IAN ROSS ROBERTSON

Prince of Wales Fort. To attract the fur trade of Dene and Inuit peoples, James Knight of the *Hudson's Bay Company established a post near the mouth of the Churchill River in 1717. Known simply as Churchill River Post until 1719, when it was renamed Prince of Wales Fort, this location was also used by the HBC as a base for a whale fishery along northwestern *Hudson Bay. In 1731, as part of a plan to defend company possessions against seaborne attack, the HBC began construction of a massive stone fortress at Eskimo Point at the mouth of the Churchill. Also called Prince of Wales Fort, this bastioned, star-shaped fortress, which used locally quarried stone, took four decades to build. Despite its 40 cannons, it was surrendered in 1782 to a French force under Comte de Lapérouse, who mined the walls and ramparts and spiked the cannons. ROBERT J. COUTTS

Princess Sophia. Launched in 1912, the 74.6 m *Princess Sophia* was a member of the 'Princess' fleet of Canadian Pacific Steamship vessels, carrying passengers and freight between Seattle/Vancouver and Skagway, Alaska. As such it was a vital part of the route linking the entire *Yukon River valley, both Canadian and Alaskan, with the south. Late on the night of 23 October 1918, the ship left Skagway with 353 passengers and crew on board, carrying Alaskans and Yukoners leaving the North as the Yukon River was freezing for the winter. At 2 A.M. on the 24th the ship ran onto Vanderbilt Reef in the Lynn Canal 50 km north of Juneau. It seemed in no immediate danger and, since strong winds made removing the passengers risky, the ship remained on the reef throughout the day while another vessel was sent north. But in the early evening of the 25th the wind rose, drove the ship off the reef, and sank it. All on board were lost, in the worst maritime disaster in the history of the north Pacific coast.

K.S. COATES AND W.R. MORRISON

printers' strike, Toronto. In the spring of 1872 George *Brown, editor and owner of the Toronto *Globe*, spearheaded the organization of the Master Printers' Association to mobilize employer resistance to the movement for the *nine-hour working day. In addition, Brown used his editorials to challenge the credibility of the nine-hour activists. To press their demands in the face of such resistance, members of Toronto Typographical Union, Local 91, went out on strike for the nine-hour day on 25 March 1872. In response, Brown used a 1792 English law against combinations of workmen to have the printers in his employ prosecuted for conspiracy to combine. This action created enormous hostility among Toronto's unionized printers and precipitated one of the key events in Canadian labour history. In an attempt to secure the votes of working men in the upcoming federal election, John A. *Macdonald came to the rescue of the indicted printers. Immediately following their arrest, Macdonald introduced a Canadian version of the British Trade Union Act. On 14 June 1872 Canada's Trade Unions Act was passed, protecting union members against prosecution for criminal conspiracy. Ultimately, the nine-hour movement failed, but it gave organized workers a glimpse of their potential strength. CHRISTINA BURR

prisoners of war. 'For you the war is over'. The phrase, which came into use in the 1940s, has come to represent in popular culture the transition from soldier to prisoner of war. For the thousands of Canadian servicemen and women who have experienced captivity in wartime, the transition from fighter to prisoner may have removed them from the battlefield, but it scarcely ended their exposure to danger.

In Aboriginal society, captured warriors were used for ritual torture or human sacrifice (which occasionally involved cannibalism), and in other cases were enslaved or assimilated into the captor society, particularly when wars or disease had reduced its population. The fact that Native societies treated white prisoners the same way had a striking impact on the European mind. Colonial society in North America became obsessed with captivity stories, eagerly devouring the hundreds of books that described either gruesome torture or the adoption of white prisoners by Native communities.

The Europeans brought their own institutions of captivity to Canada, most notably the principles of parole (allowing a prisoner to gain release upon swearing to take no further part in hostilities) and exchange (by which the warring sides agreed to swap prisoners, usually on terms of numerical equality, so they could return to action). These practices were employed extensively during the War of 1812, when the exchange of paroled prisoners was often a subject of intense negotiations at the highest levels of government.

In the late 19th century Canada's soldiers began to come under the influence of international agreements intended to protect prisoners of war, particularly the Hague Conventions of 1899 and 1907 and the Geneva Conventions of 1929 and 1949. Ironically, the codification of international law was accompanied by a general deterioration in the treatment of POWs. Despite being used to good effect during the First World War, when overage and long-term Canadian prisoners were released into neutral hands as part of an exchange agreement between Britain and Germany, parole and exchange fell from favour. During the Second World War, only 237 of the most grievously wounded and desperately ill Canadian POWs were released from captivity on medical grounds. The vast majority of the 9,700 Canadians in enemy hands during that war gained release only through death or the conclusion of hostilities. Furthermore, although the German military and government were willing to abide by international law when it suited their purposes, there is no indication that the Geneva Convention had any effect in ameliorating the horrific conditions endured by the 1,700 Canadian POWs (including two military nurses captured in *Hong Kong) held by the Japanese. Nor did the notion of reciprocality have a significant impact. The tens of thousands of German prisoners in Canada were treated with a solicitude that often irritated people who lived near prison camps, but this enviable treatment rarely encouraged the government in Berlin to act with equal generosity towards Canadian captives.

The experience of the 33 Canadians captured in the *Korean War, who were subjected to blatant attempts at political indoctrination, suggested that the nature of captivity was changing. Later, Coalition prisoners became objects of public spectacle during the *Persian Gulf War, and Canadian peacekeepers were used as human shields in Bosnia. Clearly, any future Canadian prisoners of war will find that their treatment is determined, not by international law or human sympathy, but by whatever advantage their captors believe can be gained from them. JONATHAN VANCE

prisons and penitentiaries. In most Western countries the second quarter of the 19th century was a period of vast prison-reform projects, and denunciatory sentences that focused on physical punishment were replaced with a period of custody intended to reform prisoners. Subject to influence from both Europe and the United States, Canada would become part of the movement when it decided to build its first penitentiary in Kingston in the mid-1830s. The main building, in the shape of a cross, at the centre of which was a dome, consisted of three wings of 270 cells each and also housed an infirmary, a refectory, and a chapel. Modelled on the system used in Auburn Prison in the United States, inmates worked together in silence during the day and were isolated at night in tiny cells. The purpose of this practice was to prevent penitentiaries from turning into schools for crime through talk among inmates; at the same time reformers hoped to encourage solitary meditation leading to improvements in the prisoners. After the *Act of Union, Kingston Penitentiary began to receive prisoners from Lower Canada. In 1843 the government specified that it would henceforth accommodate only those prisoners sentenced to more than two years of imprisonment. Small district prisons—called common jails—built early in the century were to be used for those with lesser sentences.

In 1841 Saint John, New Brunswick, built an institution that would soon become the provincial penitentiary; Halifax did the same in 1844. Both institutions were modelled on the penitentiary in Kingston: prisoners worked together during the day and were kept in solitary confinement at night.

Following Confederation in 1867 provincial governments became responsible for common jails, still used to incarcerate those sentenced to less than two years of prison. The federal government, responsible for the administration of sentences of more than two years, decided to establish a network of penitentiaries, adding St Vincent de Paul in Quebec (1873), Stoney Mountain in Manitoba (1876), New Westminster in British Columbia (1878), and Dorchester in the Maritimes (1881) to replace the Saint John and Halifax penitentiaries; later penitentiaries in Alberta (1906) and Saskatchewan (1911) were added.

In the 20th century a string of provincial and federal investigations and reports were increasingly critical of the ability of a prison setting to rehabilitate inmates. In the 1970s these reports went so far as to say that prison had failed, causing more harm than good to Canadian society. Despite such assessments, by the early 1990s Canada had

167 prisons administered by the provinces and 58 by the federal government. ANDRÉ CELLARD

See also PENAL REFORM.

privateers. Privately owned warships frequently used in colonial warfare, privateers were licensed by the state to attack enemy shipping in wartime, and their crews were entitled to keep most of what was captured. Often confused with lawless piracy, privateering was an accepted and often admired wartime trade and, for most of Canadian history, well regulated by a specialized system of vice-admiralty courts.

The colonial settlements that became Canada were often the victim of privateer attacks, especially from aggressive New Englanders. However, privateers also provided colonists with a measure of defence and the means to strike back. In New France, which was deprived of an effective naval force for most of its history, privateers were particularly important. The French settlement at *Port-Royal in Acadia proved a busy base for French privateers in the 1690s, including Pierre 'Baptiste' Maisonat. Quebec privateers mounted effective raids on Newfoundland settlements in 1704. Later, privateers based at *Louisbourg in Cape Breton made such impressive attacks on New England shipping that they were a critical factor in support for the New England attack on Louisbourg in 1745. In the last days of New France a privateer frigate hired to run supplies to Quebec, the *Machault*, was scuttled on the Restigouche River in 1760. The wreck has proved a valuable underwater archaeological site.

English-Canadian privateering, which began out of Halifax during the Seven Years' War, included the notorious *Mosquito*, the commander of which was convicted of torturing a neutral Dutch crew. In the American Revolution, Atlantic Canadians were at first reluctant to launch privateering against their American cousins. Soon, goaded by relentless American raids, they embraced the practice with gusto. In the French Revolutionary Wars, ambitious squadrons of vessels from Nova Scotia, especially the small town of Liverpool, scoured the Caribbean and even captured small Spanish islands. Canadian privateering reached its climax in the War of 1812: over 50 vessels, including the famous **Liverpool Packet*, sailed from Nova Scotia and New Brunswick to capture over 250 American vessels.

Britain and most Western nations abolished privateering with the Declaration of Paris in 1856. Although often misunderstood, the practice offered not only economic reward amidst the hardship of war but also a locally controlled military force. Privateers retain a romantic fascination, amplified in recent years by the Stan Rogers song 'Barrett's Privateers', a rousing anti-war ballad of a fictional privateer. DAN CONLIN

private schools. Independent schools (the current preferred label) are well integrated into the fabric of Canadian education, providing an alternative to the provincial public school systems. Given that education is a provincial responsibility, the administrative and financial relationships between private schools and provincial ministries of education have varied widely across time and across Canada. At present, what may be an independent school in one province may be fully or partially funded by the state in another. Ontario, for example, has two parallel fully funded state school systems, Roman Catholic and non-denominational, while some other provinces offer parents the opportunity to apply their taxes to alternative schools. As with virtually all schools in Canada, religious, economic, and geographic factors, as well as changing immigration patterns, have influenced the development of independent schools, which have evolved into two broadly defined categories: elite schools catering to the children of the wealthy, and alternative schools established to meet an array of theological, philosophical, and pedagogical orientations.

The first elite private schools were founded by men and women religious to educate the children of New France. These schools prepared boys for careers in business and the church and girls to be wives and mothers. Throughout the 19th and 20th centuries, convent schools were a popular choice for parents of all denominations. They became much more than finishing schools. Many adapted their curriculum to meet provincial standards and actively competed for top academic honours. One convent school, the Sisters of Charity's Mount St Vincent Academy in Halifax, evolved into a teacher education institution and ultimately a women's university. Communities of Anglican women religious, such as the *Sisters of St John the Divine, also established convent boarding schools.

Although some elite independent schools for both boys and girls, such as King's-Edgehill School (Windsor, Nova Scotia, 1788) and Bishop Strachan School (Toronto, 1867), were initially affiliated with the mainstream Protestant churches, others were non-denominational from their inception. In the course of the 20th century, significant changes occurred. Church influence waned. Convent boarding schools virtually disappeared, a function of the declining numbers of women religious. Many boys' schools became coeducational, although some, like Toronto's Upper Canada College (1829), retained their single-sex clientele. While student bodies became more reflective of the cultural mosaic of Canada, the elite schools retained their English public school traditions—especially those associated with extracurricular activities.

Alternative schools dot the history of Canadian education, their heyday being in the 1960s and 1970s. Some were short-lived; others integrated into public school systems. Independent education experienced a revival in some provinces in the 1990s because of growing parental dissatisfaction with the public systems and demands of immigrants for culturally appropriate options. Independent education remains a viable option for 5.6 per cent of school-age children. ELIZABETH SMYTH

Privy Council Office. Originally the PCO was little more than an agency for preparing and registering decisions of *cabinet. In 1940, with the assignment of the permanent head of the office—the clerk, as secretary of the cabinet—the office has evolved into the administrative department of the prime minister (not to be confused with the *Prime Minister's Office). Its secretarial role has expanded to embrace the committees of cabinet and extends beyond the mere keeping of minutes to include research, planning, and advisory services that keep the prime minister apprised of policy issues and problems likely to require cabinet attention. As the liaison between prime minister and government departments, the clerk of the PCO in 1993 received statutory designation as 'head of the public service'. This is an unusual instance of a legislative base for the PCO's powers; in the main, its important duties rest, as do those of the prime minister, on the unwritten, conventional prerogative powers of the Crown.

J.E. HODGETTS

professional sport. Professional sport involves two distinct but interrelated practices: the awarding of prize money to and/or the hiring of athletes, coaches, and other personnel, and the commodification of sport spectacles for private profit. The two have become synonymous in the most popular forms of sport today, but they developed in different ways. Although both were enabled by the growing 19th-century urban markets for leisure, the popularity of sports in the mass media, and the 'representational status of play' that conferred 'bragging rights' to the communities whose names champions bore, athletes who sought to gain financially from their efforts were often in bitter conflict with the entrepreneurs who sought to profit from their performances. There was rarely enough revenue to share. All of the fully professional, for-profit teams and leagues in pre-First World War Canada failed. Those early professional athletes who did earn livelihoods competed in individual sports, like *rowing or distance running, where they could manage their own careers, or they played for community-based teams where profit was not an issue. The successful early entrepreneurs were facility owners who staged games involving amateur teams.

The first fully professional, for-profit sports organization in Canada to succeed was the National Hockey League, in the 1920s. To do so, it had to expand to the United States, forge tight control over all North American *hockey, suppress players' salaries, and establish a national radio network through the *Canadian Broadcasting Corporation. More recently, it has established a transatlantic labour market. The only other fully professional Canadian sports organization to succeed has been the Canadian Football League, which began as a community-based association in 1958. The CFL, too, briefly experimented with expansion into the United States in the 1990s, and relies heavily upon American players. The other major corporations in Canada—Major League Baseball, the National Basketball Association, the National Lacrosse League—operate as extensions of a largely American enterprise. Few of the players in *baseball and basketball are Canadian.

Today, through the controlled expansion of franchises, the spectacular growth of television, and the public subsidization of stadiums and arenas, the sport corporations take super profits, while the best players, through unionization and collective bargaining, earn multi-million-dollar salaries. Outside this well-financed sector, Canadian athletes earn modest incomes in individual sports like golf and tennis or eke out their livelihood on the Athlete Assistance payments they receive from the government of Canada.

BRUCE KIDD

Progressive Conservative Party. This party's curious name reflected its attempts to define its purpose in a nation that had broken away from its foundations. The Conservative Party of British North America reflected its British parliamentary origins. It stood strongly for the imperial connection, established institutions, and a deferential society, and gained support among conservative British Canadians, especially Anglicans, and among conservative French Canadians fearful of the revolutionary and liberal ideas that threatened their institutions in the mid-19th century.

A Scot, John A. *Macdonald, crafted a political vehicle that maintained parts of the British tradition while recognizing that North American democracy made arguments for deference politically difficult. In 1854, in the United Canadas, he created a Liberal-Conservative coalition that became the Liberal-Conservative Party that established *Confederation. A separate *Liberal Party soon emerged and the Liberal-Conservatives became popularly known simply as Conservatives or even Tories. A political genius, Macdonald emphasized moderation and economic growth based on the *National Policy of tariffs, immigration, and railway building. His was the dominant party for the first 25 years of Confederation.

The death of Macdonald after the 1891 election caused disarray that was reflected in the party's four leaders before defeat by the Liberals in the 1896 election. The party's Quebec strength weakened greatly after the hanging of Louis *Riel and the choice of Wilfrid *Laurier as Liberal leader. Simultaneously, the new European *imperialism created tensions as Canadians of British origin increasingly called for closer co-operation with the Empire.

Robert *Borden became leader after Charles *Tupper's defeat in 1900 but lost two elections, 1904 and 1908. In 1911, however, Borden used two issues, *reciprocity with the United States and a naval contribution to Great Britain, to defeat Laurier. The country had a British-Canadian majority that responded to anti-American appeals and to support for the Motherland. In Quebec, ironically, nationalists opposing Laurier made common cause with Borden who had promised a referendum on any contribution to the British navy.

The referendum was never held, and the influence of French Canadians in Borden's government became progressively weaker. When war came, Borden initially promised no *conscription but high casualties made him reverse his decision in 1917. He called upon conscriptionist Liberals to join with him in a coalition. Many did, and in December 1917 the Unionist coalition won a decisive victory.

That victory was the last for British-Canadian nationalism. As the Unionist coalition came undone after the war's end, the Conservatives found themselves with much diminished support among French Canadians, German Canadians, and other non-British groups. Borden's successor, Arthur *Meighen, appealed to traditional Conservatives with an emphasis on the *British connection and the tariff, but the party came third behind the new Progressive Party in the 1921 election. Although he restricted Mackenzie *King to a minority in 1925, he lost in 1926. The Depression did bring the Conservatives to power under R.B. *Bennett, but they went down to their worst defeat in 1935.

Recognizing their weakness in the West the Conservatives turned to Manitoba Progressive John *Bracken in 1942, but the newly-named Progressive Conservatives were unable to break the Liberal hold on power until 1957. John *Diefenbaker, elected leader in 1956, ignored Quebec in 1957 relying on the Conservative bastion of Ontario and taking many western seats. In 1958 he swept the country winning 208 seats. His government was more progressive than conservative, and Diefenbaker did establish a strong western base for the party. Nevertheless, erratic government, lack of understanding of Quebec, and personal animosity undermined the Diefenbaker government, which collapsed in 1963.

The Conservatives seemed to be a perennial opposition party, and there was talk of a 'Tory Syndrome'. They did take power very briefly in 1979 under Joe Clark but lost it in early 1980. Turning to Brian *Mulroney, a fluently bilingual Quebec businessperson, the Conservatives won the greatest victory in Canadian federal history in 1984 with strong strength in the West and Quebec. His uneasy coalition lasted through the 1988 election when, in a reversal of historic political stands, the Conservatives won on *free trade with the United States. Mulroney's troubles, however, came with Quebec. He tried to remake the Canadian *constitution to satisfy Quebec nationalist demands, but his *Meech Lake and *Charlottetown accords were not accepted. The leadership passed to Kim Campbell for the 1993 election, and the governing Conservatives won only two seats.

The future of the party became unclear after the 1993 disaster. It was the fourth or fifth party in the House of Commons, and its electoral support was too diffuse to obtain many seats. Canada's founding party saw its roots wither, its branches weaken, and its core become soft. Although the party continued to retain support of about one in five Canadians in polls, it won few seats under Joe Clark. Upon his resignation, the party turned to Peter MacKay, a young Nova Scotian, in 2003. Despite a written promise to progressive leadership opponent David Orchard that he would not merge with the Alliance Party, MacKay began negotiations with the Alliance soon after his leadership victory. In December 2003, Progressive Conservative Party members voted to dissolve their historic party and to create a new Conservative Party. A few Progressive Conservatives, notably former Prime Minister Joe Clark, refused to join the new party. The Conservative Party's future was uncertain; the fate of Progressive Conservatism, however, was clear. JOHN ENGLISH

Progressives. The Progressives arose as a political force in 1921, in the middle of a major recession in the post-war agricultural economy, and on the heels of provincial political successes by the United Farmers of Ontario (1919) and the United Farmers of Alberta (1921). With 23 per cent of the popular vote, federal Progressive candidates won 65 seats in 1921: 24 in Ontario, 12 in Manitoba, 15 in Saskatchewan, 11 in Alberta, 2 in British Columbia, and 1 in New Brunswick. The Progressives were not a normal political party: although they won the second highest number of federal seats, they did so without a national leader, a national campaign, or a national organization; they rejected the role of official opposition in Parliament, choosing instead to vote on each issue on its perceived merits, and to emphasize 'constituency autonomy' rather than centralized party control in their political action.

Progressives wanted to end the 'protective tariff' that benefited central Canadian business at the expense of farmers and served as the major source of 'old party' financing and political corruption. They generally supported more government regulation of banks, nationalization of railways and hydroelectric power, campaign-spending reforms, and use of direct legislation (the initiative, referendum, and recall) to hold elected officials accountable or to impose the public will against party preferences. They advocated proportional representation, progressive income taxes and inheritance taxes, equal voting and legal rights for women, and *prohibition of alcoholic beverages. Finally they wanted federal and provincial governments to do more to give *co-operative enterprises—including farm-marketing and consumer associations—a strong position in the rural economy.

From the outset the Progressives were torn between two factions. The initially dominant faction was led by ex-Liberals from southern Ontario, Manitoba, and Saskatchewan who wished to prod the federal Liberal Party into keeping its 50-year-old promise to bring in free trade and to cut their close ties with big business. By contrast, Alberta MPs elected in 1921 became the core of what emerged in 1923 as the *Ginger Group, a resolutely anti-party faction within the Progressive caucus. The federal UFA representatives advocated a more left-wing economic policy and radical democratic alternatives like 'group government' and 'delegate democracy', both designed to give greater power to grassroots, class-based organizations.

The Progressives' impact in national politics dropped rapidly between 1923 and 1926, as many of their MPs returned to the Liberal Party. Progressives won 24 seats (9 per cent of the popular vote) in 1926; by 1930 they had been reduced to a rump of 12 seats in Alberta. But by demonstrating that regionally concentrated parties could break old monopolies on political representation and present a regional voice in national politics, the

Progressives paved the way for later western parties with more staying power and more radical challenges to the status quo—the *Co-operative Commonwealth Federation and *Social Credit. DAVID LAYCOCK

prohibition. From the early 19th century the *temperance movement tried to curb excessive alcoholic consumption by founding temperance societies, urging people to pledge abstinence, and attempting to close *taverns and saloons. Depressions in the 1870s and 1890s acted as catalysts for a new and more powerful wave of reform as temperance advocates increasingly lobbied for legislation to achieve their goals and ameliorate social problems. The aim was 'prohibition'—the criminalization of all manufacture, sale, and transport of alcoholic beverages. This goal was never achieved.

The first federal prohibitory legislation, the Scott Act of 1878, allowed for local option; each county could vote to be 'dry' or 'wet', leading to a checkerboard of policies and the anomaly of alcohol-free counties facing a row of pubs across the road. In 1891, the Dominion Alliance for the Total Suppression of the Liquor Traffic and the *Woman's Christian Temperance Union lobbied the Conservative government into establishing the Royal Commission on the Liquor Traffic. Its 1895 report opposed prohibition, citing national divisions. The prohibitionists subsequently pressed the new Liberal government of Wilfrid *Laurier into holding a plebiscite, which revealed, as Laurier feared, a nation divided by language, class, and region. While the prohibitionists won a simple majority, cities, immigrant counties, and the province of Quebec voted no, and Laurier would not legislate prohibition.

Canada was scarcely 'wet', however. The division of powers under the British North America Act allowed the provinces to regulate the sale of liquor, although manufacture and export were under federal jurisdiction. Ontario, for instance, maintained stricter liquor laws than Quebec and British Columbia. Between 1915 and 1917, all the provinces voted 'dry' except Quebec, and in 1918 national prohibition became part of the *War Measures Act, in response to popular sentiment for wartime domestic reform.

Provincial adherence varied. Because of loopholes in the legislation (liquor sales for 'sacramental' or 'medicinal' purposes remained legal), many physicians had a lucrative practice on the side prescribing 'medicinal' pints, while ritual use by Catholics and Jews only flamed the racist rhetoric of evangelical Protestant prohibitionists. By 1920 the 'wet' forces were organizing and seizing the moral ground with their enlistment of *veterans, who had earned the right to commiserate about Ypres in Legion halls. The hypocrisies and violence associated with prohibition's enforcement also reduced its popularity. Bootleggers and moonshiners selling concoctions charitably termed 'rotgut' were rampant, and the enforcers themselves had imperfect loyalties to the unpopular measure. British Columbia's prohibition commissioner, W.C. Findlay, was convicted of bootlegging, while Maritime temperance inspectors were instructed that too many arrests would put them out of work. Municipal judges and police found frequent summary convictions and fines both to fatten local coffers and generally keep the peace. Where inspectors (particularly temperance agitators) were more diligent, violence occasionally erupted. In 1920 Inspector Rev. J.O.L. Spracklin shot and killed hotel proprietor 'Babe' Trumble during a raid in Ontario; in 1922 an Alberta constable was killed in a shoot-out with 'Mr Pick' Picariello. Revolted by such events and the reports of greater violence in the United States, voters soon accepted the arguments of the Moderation League for stringent provincial liquor-control laws rather than prohibition. Provincial governments also wanted to replace the municipal fines (which ended up in local coffers) with liquor taxes that could be diverted into social programs and public works.

The provinces also wanted their share of the American trade. Prohibition in the United States, which was legislated by the 18th Amendment to the Constitution (the Volstead Act) in 1920, would remain until repeal in 1934. The combination of the vast undefended continental border and provincial liquor laws made servicing the American thirst a major export industry for Canadians from the Maritimes to the Great Lakes, across the Prairies, and on the west coast. Via rowboats, trains, and the newfangled motor cars, booze was legally exported to the American border, by, among others, the Bronfman brothers, the Hudson's Bay Company, and Hiram Walker's, and illegally smuggled and sold on the other side by miscreants like Dutch Schultz and Al 'Scarface' Capone, who ferried Canadian whisky, rum, and beer over the Detroit River and south from the Prairies to Chicago.

Depending upon the province, the manufacturers faced different challenges. Neither Molson's Breweries in liberal Quebec nor Calgary's Cross family, owners of Calgary Brewing and Malting, faced much regulation. In London, Ontario, the respectable Carling Brewery was sold to Harry Low and his band of rum-runners, while fellow Londoners, the Labatt family, left the unsavoury side of the operations (but not all of the profits) to its Catholic manager, Edmund Burke, who built himself a mansion complete with zoo and resident mistress. Atlantic Canada kept a lively trade from Nova Scotia to New England, with rum-running seen as an occupation of last resort for unemployed fishers. Caribbean rum, whisky, and wines were shipped through the French free port of *St-Pierre and then rerouted through the Maritimes to the New England ports known as 'Rum Row'. On the Pacific coast, liquor labelled for export to Mexico landed in San Francisco or ports near Seattle. Both in New Brunswick's and British Columbia's interior, the new public highways became the rum-runners' domains; motor cars like the McLaughlin Six Specials or the 'whisky sixes' rumbled through the Crowsnest Pass from Fernie to Alberta and points south.

Even the most venerable corporations got into the (Volstead) act and used the railroads to lure Americans northward. Advertisements in chic magazines like *Vogue* for the Canadian Pacific Railway and its hotels, including

Quebec City's Château Frontenac, touted skating and cocktail parties for affluent, thirsty Americans. Montreal's vivid nightlife peaked during the 1920s, and other provinces turned envious eyes at such profitable tourism, further fuelling the flames for temperance's repeal.

CHERYL KRASNICK WARSH

See also LIQUOR CONTROL.

prostitution. Prostitution may be the world's oldest profession, but the ways in which it has been practised and policed have varied significantly. In Canada, a general pattern of limited tolerance began to break down by the mid-19th century. Two factors account for this shift: first, the rising influence of moral reform lobby groups; second, changing legislation and *police tactics. Nevertheless, the informal laws of supply and demand proved resilient. By the mid-20th century prostitution transformed rather than disappeared.

Prostitution was a highly visible feature of urban life in Canada's earliest cities. In towns like Halifax, the naval garrison and the citadel drew women who earned their keep by selling sexual services to sailors and soldiers. In more industrialized cities, such as Montreal and Toronto, the sex trade flourished where men worked, lived, or passed by—train stations, theatres, wharves, and boarding-house districts. In the dynamic towns of the West, prostitutes operated on the wrong side of the tracks, plying their trade in saloons and dancehalls, or using cheap rooming houses for assignations with customers. To be ignorant of prostitution in 19th-century Canadian cities would have required blinkers.

Respectable citizens and church folk had always defined prostitution as sinful. But in mid- to late-19th-century Canada they began to organize to fight it. Women were at the forefront of these campaigns. Through the *Woman's Christian Temperance Union, a group that lobbied for government restrictions on and self-control over drinking, women found a public voice on a range of troubling social issues. Although the WCTU considered alcohol abuse a scourge on modern society, reform advocates defined prostitution as 'the' social evil of the age. By the 1880s, the battle against commercialized vice, and prostitution in particular, had begun in earnest.

In the early phases of this campaign the prostitute was portrayed as a victim who had been led into sin through a poor home life and inadequate religious training. Left to drift in the swirl of city life, weak-willed women became the targets of unscrupulous men. Seeing prostitution as a moral failing, rather than an economic issue, well-meaning advocates set out to reform prostitutes in houses of refuge or institutions known as 'magdalene' homes (named after the biblical repentant prostitute). The trouble was that most women who sold sex were not interested in repenting. If the path to redemption was a poor-paying job in *domestic service and an endless round of prayers and hymns, most preferred to take their chances on the streets.

By the early 20th century, as fears of 'white slavery' (the sexual enslavement of innocent women) began to circulate throughout the Western world, Canadian women's groups agreed that more punitive tactics were called for. But when they urged officials to enforce existing laws they discovered that most Canadian police forces informally tolerated prostitution within certain urban districts. Formal inquiries in Winnipeg, Calgary, and Vancouver revealed long-standing patterns of bribery and corruption. Under the glare of unfavourable publicity, police forces stepped up their patrols of red-light districts and raided brothels, hauling in both women and customers. Over the 1910s pimps and brothel operators faced stiffer penalties. During the First World War, when the fighting fitness of Canadian manhood was of prime concern, arrests peaked. But evil 'white slavers' were never nabbed; those most likely to be arrested were the women (and a comparatively small proportion of male customers). By the 1920s, aspirations to reform prostitutes had disappeared. Street sweeps and brothel raids reduced the visibility of prostitution, but fining and arresting prostitutes failed to stamp out the sex trade.

CAROLYN STRANGE

Protestant Ethic. The belief that work is a virtue that brings spiritual rewards as well as economic superiority and prosperity. Although the theory can be traced to Reformation times, the term itself was coined by German sociologist Max Weber in his 1904–5 essay 'The Protestant Ethic and the Spirit of Capitalism'. Weber examined the relations between religion and economic and social life in post-Reformation culture to discover what psychological conditions led to the development of modern capitalist society. He concluded that this change stemmed from Calvinist doctrine that, by emphasizing individualism, promoted bourgeois capitalism as an economic system based solely on financial profit instead of such customary or traditional values as the medieval concept of the 'just price'.

Because Weber viewed capitalism as the social counterpart of *Calvinism, he defined work as no longer an economic means but a spiritual end or calling, an exacting enterprise to be chosen and pursued with a sense of religious responsibility. Since the individualistic element in Calvinism rejected any interference in business by both state and church, Weber suggested the result would be an orgy of materialism. His hypothesis was virtually unknown outside Germany until American sociologist Talcott Parsons published an English translation of the essay in 1930. Although Parsons admired Weber as an original theorist, some scholars criticize the theory as being too simplistic.

In Canada Protestant denominations with a Calvinistic background traditionally emphasized work as a godly calling with its own rewards, lauding the work ethic as the cause of economic and technological dominance of Protestant religions. This emphasis on individualism began to wane in the late Victorian era when the worst social results of capitalism, industrialism, and urbanization fostered the *social gospel of collective responsibility for the quality of life.

JOHN S. MOIR

Provancher, Léon (1820–92). A self-trained naturalist, Provancher's main contributions to Canadian science have been in botany and, more importantly, entomology. His career as a parish priest was brief; he retired at the age of 49 and had ample time to devote himself to his passion. A prolific author, he published, among other books, *Traité élémentaire de botanique* for college students in 1858 and, four years later in two volumes, his *Flore canadienne*, the first major book on Canadian flora. A staunch anti-Darwinian, he founded *Le Naturaliste canadien* in 1868, the oldest French-Canadian scientific journal. His international reputation among naturalists was acquired through his *Petite faune entomologique du Canada*, published in 1877, followed by many additions and corrections, and describing more than a thousand new species of insects. Through his work he also built an important collection of insects still extant at Université Laval. Strongly conservative in religion, he founded *La Semaine religieuse* in 1888. He also published books on his travels: *De Québec à Jérusalem* (1888) and *Une Excursion aux climats tropicaux* (1890).

YVES GINGRAS

Province of Canada. The United Province of Canada, created in 1841 from the union of Lower and Upper Canada, consisted of Canada East (present-day southern Quebec) and Canada West (southern Ontario). Despite Canada East's larger population, both sections were represented equally in the assembly. The proscription of French as a language of record, the imposition of the western half's large debts upon the union, and the selection of *Kingston as the capital, all helped ensure the hostility of most francophones in Canada East to the new creation. Many anglophones, especially those associated with commercial interests, were well-disposed towards it, believing that it would promote continued canal construction and economic development.

Robert *Baldwin realized that if the moderate reformers of Canada West joined with their counterparts in Canada East the two could control the agenda of the legislative assembly. He engineered an alliance with Louis-Hippolyte *LaFontaine and his reform brethren in the eastern province. Reform attempts to produce *responsible government—which had come to mean that the majority grouping in the assembly would name the executive councillors, who oversaw governmental administration—were ultimately successful when Governor General Lord Elgin accepted the reformers' position after they won the elections of 1847–8.

By 1852 the population of largely anglophone Canada West had outstripped that of largely francophone Canada East. As the main source of immigrants was the British Isles, that imbalance was destined to increase. Voices in Canada West—particularly that of influential newspaper publisher and politician, Scottish-born George *Brown—demanded that representation in the assembly be based on population. 'Rep by pop' became a compelling political slogan, its underlying grievance aggravated by a series of political-religious issues involving the conviction that French-Canadian politicians were winning undue privileges for the Catholic Church. By the late 1850s two major political groupings had emerged: a liberal-conservative party and a looser reform grouping. The opposing forces came into delicate balance. By 1864 the union was in political deadlock until a constitutional committee, inspired by George Brown, advocated a union of *British North America.

While the union of 1841 might seem a failure, it produced a political framework for the Canadas for over a quarter century and foreshadowed the dominion's federal experiment, since governmental departments often operated on a dual basis. The union also witnessed the elaboration of municipal bodies and the growth of other state institutions, particularly those related to schooling in Canada West. Equally, the union saw the development of state-owned canals, which were essential to commerce, and legislation designed to facilitate the construction of railroads, often by letting developers dip into the public purse. Generally, the union was on a sound economic footing, though like other parts of British North America it had to reorient much of its economy with the British movement to free trade in the mid-1840s. A limited free trade agreement with the United States, 1855–66, helped generate prosperity, and the union was an economic, if not a complete political, success. COLIN READ

Province of Quebec, 1763–91. By the *Royal Proclamation of 1763, following the Seven Years' War, Great Britain carved a narrow trapezoid 'Province of Quebec'—primarily the inhabited portion of New France—out of what was Canada. It was to be settled by British Americans following the introduction of English laws, tenure, anti-Catholic oaths, and a promised House of Assembly; meanwhile, an appointed council advised the governor. A vast Aboriginal reserve was established in the western and northern part of the old territory of Canada.

The first governor, Sir James *Murray, could not implement the proclamation: the expected British immigration did not occur, and there was little danger that 200 British merchants would crush the 80,000 Canadiens reported by Murray. He allowed the consecration of Mgr Jean-Olivier Briand as Catholic bishop (1766) and provided lower courts where Canadiens could be jurors and lawyers. A rift between Murray and the British merchants over an assembly and concessions to the French led to his replacement by Sir Guy *Carleton in 1766. But the concessions remained, and Canadiens requested laws and ordinances in French. Agitation in the Thirteen Colonies in 1765–9 convinced Carleton that a rebellion would occur and that it would be supported by France. Thus he needed to rally the Canadiens, who were destined to remain the majority in the province. His aristocratic ideals meshed well with the *seigneurial system. This dynamic led to the *Quebec Act (1774), the 'magna carta' of French Canadians: re-establishment of French civil laws and tenure (inside the seigneurial zone), an oath of loyalty replacing the anti-Catholic oaths, authorization for Catholic parishes to levy tithes, a very limited religious tolerance, an appointed council with some Canadien seigneurs, and expansion of the territory, including administration of the Indian reserve. The Quebec Act rooted Canadien nationalism and helped secure quasi-neutrality during the American invasion of Canada (1775–6).

In the 1770s and 1780s, conflicts raged in the colony. The British colonists pointed to the arrival of 6,000 *Loyalists and to economic realities and clamoured for an assembly, which they thought they would control. The Canadien bourgeoisie also agitated for an assembly, but they expected to dominate it. Given the seigneurs' opposition, the two groups formed an opportunistic coalition to pressure London. Meanwhile, the Loyalists demanded a separate colony with an assembly, English laws, and tenure. These combined pressures pushed London to adopt the *Constitutional Act (1791), splitting the colony into Upper and Lower Canada, each with an assembly and appointed legislative and executive councils. The idea was to douse 'racial' strife, ensure the levy of local taxes, and reinforce the aristocratic and imperial mould. Each colony would choose its civil laws and tenure, although the seigneurial regime was frozen in Lower Canada. For British prime minister William Pitt, Jr, the assimilation of Canadiens would be the preferred outcome, but that could be accomplished only through the use of English institutions, not by force.

JEAN-PIERRE WALLOT

provincial autonomy and rights. The idea of provincial rights emerged soon after Confederation in response to John A. *Macdonald's drive to establish the dominance of the dominion government. From 1872 to 1896, Ontario premier Oliver *Mowat led a campaign to limit Ottawa's powers under the British North America Act and confirm the provinces' possession of executive and legislative powers that were either substantively important or emblematic of sovereignty. Mowat's campaign rested on an assertion of the provinces' constitutional equality, if not superiority, to the dominion government, which they had, in a sense, created. By contrast, provincial autonomy denotes a conception of provincial rights that is based, not on the provinces' inherent constitutional status, but on their powers as defined by the BNA Act, judicial interpretation thereof, and Canadian constitutional practice. Its rise reflects the strengthening of anglophone Canadians' sense of national identity since the First World War and the concomitant weakening of provincial allegiances. French Canadians' fear of Canadian nationalism has made the province of Quebec the most consistent champion of provincial rights. Beyond Quebec, the principle has appealed particularly to the wealthiest provinces, which have often invoked it against federal schemes to redistribute wealth to the less prosperous. Until the 1960s, Ontario often joined Quebec in resisting apprehended federal encroachments on the provincial sphere. Since then, the strongest advocates of provincial rights outside Quebec have been Alberta and British Columbia.

Controversy over provincial rights has arisen in relation to four main issues. One is amendment of the Canadian *constitution. Until 1982, relations between the federal and provincial governments were formally defined by the BNA Act, a British statute that made no provision for Canadian participation in its amendment. Quarrels periodically erupted between those who asserted that Ottawa alone had authority to speak for Canada and those who claimed that provincial governments could at least veto changes affecting provincial powers. The other major bones of contention have been economic: authority over intraprovincial commerce and fields of *taxation and the ownership or regulatory control of natural resources. Conflicts over taxation and resources, as major sources of revenue, intensified between the wars as the provinces' administrative responsibilities outstripped their fiscal capacity. During the Great Depression, centralists cited the provinces' fiscal plight as a reason for increasing Ottawa's constitutional powers, while provincialists assailed the federal income tax as an encroachment on provincial taxing powers and a threat to provincial autonomy. The conception of provincial autonomy as a fundamental principle that trumps Ottawa's statutory powers is illustrated by its current invocation against Ottawa's use of conditional financial grants to impose national standards in fields of provincial jurisdiction such as health care. The notion's effectiveness in this regard, which depends on public opinion rather than the courts, has varied. It was effective in the 1880s against Ottawa's power to disallow provincial legislation and in the 1980s against the *National Energy Program.

PAUL ROMNEY

Prowse, Daniel W. (1834–1914). Best known now as the author of the magisterial *History of Newfoundland from the English, Colonial, and Foreign Records*, first published in 1895, Prowse was in his day also well known as an energetic (and idiosyncratic) government official, magistrate, and essayist. A lawyer, he sat in the House of Assembly during the 1860s and supported Confederation. He served as judge of the Central District Court in St John's, 1869–98. In addition to carrying out a wide range of duties for the government, he sat on numerous boards and commissions. He defused a protest in Conception Bay against the railway (1880), organized the enforcement of the Bait Act (1888), and reported on the 1892 St John's fire. In 1877, Prowse published a *Manual for Magistrates . . .*, which guided outport justices of the peace for many years; his *The Newfoundland Guide Book* appeared in 1905. His *History* has become something of a period piece: it presents a traditional, patriotic, and romantic view of the Newfoundland past and reflects a now-forgotten imperial pride. For its time, however, it was remarkably comprehensive, and it remains essential reading for the student of Newfoundland history.

JAMES K. HILLER

public debt. Public debt is debt owed by government. An essential element in public finance at the federal, provincial, and municipal levels, it derives from borrowing on capital account to finance improvements of a long-term nature; from deficits on annual operations; and from government guarantees of the debts of others, including Crown corporations, private enterprises, and individuals. The latter are termed indirect, or contingent, debts. Much of governments' direct debt is in the form of bonds, but it also takes other forms, such as treasury bills—notes running for less than one year, issued by the federal government. Such securities may be held within or outside Canada. Although parts of the public debt are formally accounted for in distinct 'funds', related to specific taxes and/or offset by assets, these distinctions blur in reality. To interpret published data, it is essential to know the definitions behind them.

The creation of a local public debt began with the development of autonomous colonial and municipal governments in British North America. By the 1830s colonial governments could sometimes borrow in London on their own credit. Since Confederation, the national debt has tended to expand, although not necessarily in relation to the economy's ability to carry it. As measured relative to GNP, it has fluctuated in distinct waves, which peaked in the mid-1890s (at over 20 per cent of GNP), shortly after each world war (the all-time peak coming in 1946, at over 100 per cent), and at the depth of the Depression. After falling to 15 per cent by 1974, the national debt surged to almost 60 per cent of GNP by the early 1990s.

Provincial and municipal public debts are not as consistently documented, but in total have amounted to less than the federal debt. For much of the post-war period, however, they tended to grow more rapidly than the national debt. DOUGLAS McCALLA

public education. Formal schooling in Canada owes its origins to a variety of social forces, including religious commitments, immigration patterns, nationalism, democratic movements, social class and gender relations, and local community needs. In the early 19th century the inhabitants of the British North American colonies were preoccupied with making a living. Most parents expected their children to contribute to the family economy, which left them limited time to pursue formal schooling. Still, education was far from absent in the pioneering communities. Religious denominations took the initiative in establishing schools, where children were taught to read the Bible and to deepen their commitment to Christianity. The Catholic Church oversaw a small but culturally significant network of schools and *classical colleges in French-speaking Quebec. Similarly, Anglican clergy and teachers provided religious instruction in a variety of English-Canadian schools. As the population of Canada grew and diversified, 'evangelical' Protestants, such as Methodists and Baptists, opened Sunday schools as well as a number of religious colleges for the training of clergy. The evangelical movement, which was especially influential in the Atlantic region and Upper Canada, enthusiastically promoted conversion and repentance rituals; religious schools aided the evangelical mission. At the same time, risk-taking entrepreneurs established 'private venture' schools in the hope of securing contracts from parents for the instruction of their children. In addition, schooling within private households—conducted by tutors, governesses, or parents themselves—was not unusual. Finally, academies, seminaries, and colleges, a minority of which received partial state funding, attracted children from middle class families. The young women who attended these institutions would study the 'ornamental' subjects, including art, music, and modern languages. Males, usually in separate institutions, would study the classics in preparation for careers in medicine, law, or government service.

Limited state funding for *common schools was available in the provinces, though educational facilities were generally rudimentary and the schools normally required families to pay tuition fees. Common schools provided a basic English education, as opposed to instruction in the prestigious classical subjects of Greek and Latin. Advanced education, where students would learn the classics, was provided in state-aided grammar schools, attended largely by the sons of privileged families. The allocation of educational funding from provincial and local governments was frequently a contentious political issue, complicated by competing religious loyalties and social class divisions. Thus, throughout the colonies, educational opportunities were available on an uneven basis, most often to the relatively affluent, in the first half of the 19th century.

Intent on promoting the cause of public schooling and meeting the growing demand for it, educators, politicians, and other committed citizens undertook a campaign for free and compulsory elementary education that led to important legislative measures between the 1840s and 1870s. During this period, the colonies were enveloped by political and social change. The rebellions of 1837 and 1838 and the heavy influx of immigrants from the British Isles had led to concerns in elite circles about the problem of social stability. Leading educators, such as Egerton *Ryerson, the superintendent of Ontario schools in 1844–76, believed that education had a critical role to play in helping to ensure social peace. He contended that schools should prepare youth for 'their appropriate duties and employments of life, as Christians, as persons of business, and also as members of the civil community in which they live'. Education should attend especially to the children of the lower classes, who were perceived as a potential social menace. According to this view, mass education stressing discipline, morality, manners, and respect for private property would prevent, or at least control, delinquency and lead to class harmony and a safer community.

Elite groups also expected schools to cultivate students' sense of citizenship by teaching them to respect the authority of the government and to regulate their own behaviour even in the absence of direct state intervention. *Loyalists in Ontario and the Maritimes believed that the British *monarchy deserved the fidelity of all Canadians and that schools had a key role to play in promoting its legitimacy. While Canadians generally admired the United States for its economic and educational progress, writers frequently portrayed American culture as too individualistic, materialistic, aggressive, and disorderly, characteristics symbolized by the prolonged Civil War of the early 1860s. In the interests of nation building, schools should curb the spirit of political dissent, avoid American textbooks, and promote the 'civility' of British culture and traditions.

Public schooling could also help resolve the ever-present problem of religious conflict by stressing the bonds that linked Christian communities instead of the doctrines that divided them. Drawing from taxes paid by the general population, state-funded schools would free individual denominations from the burden of financing education directly. At the same time, basic Christian morality could be taught in virtually every Canadian school. If the nation's children were exposed to a common spiritual message, then the moral foundations of the country could be buttressed in a period of uncertain social change. While controversial clerical creeds would have no place in the public school classrooms, scriptural readings, the Lord's Prayer, and the Ten Commandments were both acceptable and required.

Although most denominations accepted a common state-regulated school system, Catholic educators, both English and French, opposed the growing authority of the secular state in education and were determined to preserve independent school systems. This issue was crucial to the act of *Confederation in 1867. The British North America Act assigned to the provinces the legislative and administrative responsibility for schooling, but so concerned were religious minorities that their legal rights would be withdrawn by intolerant provincial governments that the *constitution guaranteed these rights. Where denominational schools existed in law at the time of a province's entry into Confederation, they would endure, and the federal government had the power to restore a denomination's educational privileges if they were threatened by provincial initiatives. Separate (Catholic) schools persisted in Ontario; Quebec preserved a publicly funded dual system of Protestant and Catholic schools, as did Manitoba when it entered Confederation in 1870. British Columbia and Prince Edward Island joined Canada with single non-denominational school systems, and in Nova Scotia and New Brunswick arrangements were made during the 1870s to preserve religious instruction on the basis of local community initiatives. In Nova Scotia, for example, Roman Catholic educators followed the provincial curriculum but were able to provide religious instruction in public school classrooms after regular school hours.

Those unpersuaded by the loyalist, nationalist, or religious arguments could find other reasons for supporting the extension of public schooling. Reformers, such as Joseph *Howe in Nova Scotia, who favoured *responsible government, believed that education would improve the quality of political life by producing a more informed and enlightened citizenry. Education was not to be the exclusive prerogative of the affluent. Indeed, in Prince Edward Island, tenant farmers had agitated for public schooling in order to strengthen their ability to negotiate contracts with absentee landlords.

If democracy could be served by the spread of schooling, so too might one's standard of living. Historians have found evidence that farming families, wanting to prepare their children for an uncertain future, made provisions in their wills for the education of one or more of their offspring. They hoped that such training would enable the young person to secure economic competency through other occupational pursuits. If schools were built in rural communities, children could obtain their training without moving long distances from home. Even for those planning to remain on the farm, knowledge of accounting and the basics of mechanization would be useful in the world of commercial agriculture. Thus, many farmers were predisposed to the campaign for public education. Even without the propaganda from prominent school promoters, they could see the value of state-supported schooling. So too could an increasing proportion of urban working-class Canadians, though their children often found it economically impossible to attend school on a regular basis. More and more, the level of one's education reflected one's status in the community.

Schools could also contribute to the socialization of children according to prescribed gender roles. Fearing the sexual precociousness of youth, educators sought, where feasible, to segregate boys and girls in separate classrooms. Moreover, once children of both sexes had mastered the basics of reading and writing, the curriculum diverged. Boys learned mathematics and bookkeeping—skills that might prove useful in the workforce. Girls were taught needlework, penmanship, and drawing—skills intended to highlight the importance of cultural refinement and household duties.

Throughout the 19th century, local school districts had increasingly employed the 'local option', which permitted them to fund their schools from property taxes in order to reduce or eliminate tuition fees. Ontario was the first province, in 1871, to legislate compulsory attendance. Children between the ages of 7 and 12 were required to attend school for at least four months per year. With the exception of Quebec and Newfoundland, which delayed such legislation until the early 1940s, Canadian provinces all had introduced mandatory attendance laws by 1916. It is important to note, however, that Canadian families were inclined to send their children to school even before provincial laws compelled them to do so.

By assigning provinces control over education, the BNA Act not only acknowledged the country's denominational distinctions but also signified the importance of regional cultures in the governance of schools. Provincial school authorities generally favoured and employed centralized decision making, but they were often compelled to negotiate with, and even defer to the will of, local communities in the administration of school policy.

In subsequent decades, the forces of industrialization and urbanization, religion and secularization, war and depression, governmental authority and community interests affected the course of Canadian public schooling. These changes arose on educational foundations built in the 19th century. PAUL AXELROD

public health. From colonial times to the present, Canadians have attempted to deal with sanitation problems and communicable disease outbreaks through legislation, inspection, and public policy measures. Drawing on European and American models, early-19th-century Canadian towns and cities created temporary local boards of health to respond to outbreaks of *cholera, typhus, and *smallpox from 1832 to 1885. Because contemporary medical theory claimed that rotting garbage produced miasmatic vapours that caused disease, thorough cleansing was usually the first measure introduced at the onset of each epidemic. Gradually this was accepted as an essential part of urban life, and by the 1880s large cities such as Toronto, Montreal, and Hamilton had permanent staffs of sanitary inspectors. These men were responsible for ensuring that 'nuisances' such as overflowing privies, unsanitary stables and slaughterhouses, and contaminated food supplies were inspected, their owners counselled about required standards, and the premises reinspected until the problem was resolved or court action undertaken. Persuasion rather than coercion was and remains the hallmark of sanitary inspection. Developing and maintaining potable water, healthy food supplies, and effective waste-disposal practices required not only co-operation from the public and various industries but also legislation and administration by all three levels of government.

By the 1860s the miasmatic theory was being challenged by the germ theory. Positing a single bacterial cause for cholera, *tuberculosis, diphtheria, gonorrhea, and syphilis, researchers such as Louis Pasteur and Robert Koch revolutionized public attitudes to disease control and the role of government. In contrast to the earlier period, when citizens believed that disease outbreaks represented the will of God, the bacteriological revolution suggested that humans could master disease organisms and hence control and prevent communicable diseases. From the 1830s on, local and provincial authorities developed standard disease-control procedures that called for notification, in-home quarantine if possible or isolation in purpose-built facilities, and disinfection of the premises and the disease sufferer once the outbreak was over. Using the force of law if necessary, local medical health officers and their slowly growing staffs worked to educate the public to obey isolation and quarantine orders. For hourly paid workers and their families, in-house quarantine was often impossible, but the role of the state in providing food, fuel, and medical or nursing assistance prompted debate in cost-conscious city councils. Gradually each Canadian province passed legislation requiring the creation of local boards of health and outlining their sanitation and communicable disease–control duties. In 1919 a federal health department was finally created; it took over external quarantine and inspection of immigrants and sick mariners.

Effective prevention, however, required vaccines, which took many years to develop. Smallpox vaccination provided a model preventive measure after it was introduced in 1796. But as francophone opposition to vaccination in Montreal in 1885 demonstrated, the public had to have faith in the efficacy of the procedure if mass immunization programs were to succeed. The quality of vaccine supplies and scrupulous cleanliness during *vaccination were essential. As Canadian cities grew between 1880 and 1920, the rising death rates from typhoid, diphtheria, and tuberculosis challenged disease-control practices. The failure of tuberculin to prevent TB led to anti-spitting ordinances to control the spread. Typhoid was eradicated through chlorination of water supplies and milk inspection, although Canadian troops were immunized in the First World War. Diphtheria toxin–anti-toxin treatment was used from 1896 to the 1920s. Although the introduction of diphtheria toxoid in the 1920s and 1930s resulted in a marked decline in cases in the 1940s, it was quickly superseded by *poliomyelitis. Public immunization programs using the Salk and Sabin vaccines in the 1950s and 1960s eliminated this scourge, but left Canadian children vulnerable to measles and hepatitis C. Periodic outbreaks of meningitis and the recent SARS outbreak serve to remind us that consistent surveillance and well-trained public health staff are essential to control the spread of epidemic disease.

By 1900 attention shifted to health education. Voluntary groups such as *Women's Institutes, the *Woman's Christian Temperance Union, evangelical Christian associations, and local and national women's councils helped to organize milk depots and well-baby clinics in urban and rural Canada. The purpose was to educate girls and women in the best methods of child rearing beginning with infant-feeding practices and moving on to child and adult nutrition, household sanitation, and personal hygiene. As urban health departments expanded, many of the nurses who worked for these groups were added to city staff. They not only continued to organize the well-baby clinics at which infants were weighed, measured, and offered immunization against childhood diseases, but also became responsible for home visits. These enabled them to see whether the family needed assistance from social welfare agencies or if educational visits were sufficient. Although local doctors occasionally expressed discontent about the loss of patients, the families who attended the out-patient clinics often did not have a general practitioner. Several provinces, including Alberta and Ontario, created travelling clinics to provide medical examinations, immunization, and specific treatment such as tonsillectomies and dental care to families living in remote, under-serviced areas. The federal government contributed to child health by creating a Division of Child Health in 1920 and preparing series of booklets outlining pre- and post-natal care as well as the best methods of infant hygiene.

Public health reformers also focused attention on school children. Copying British and American cities, Hamilton, Montreal, and Edmonton introduced school medical inspection in the early 20th century. Initially the service was designed to identify children suffering from communicable diseases or problems such as myopia, dental caries, hearing difficulties, and developmental challenges. The public health nurses gradually became involved in health education, providing posters, height and weight charts, and dental honour rolls, and teaching little mother's classes because they assumed that training future homemakers and their spouses in basic health practices would improve the health of the next generation. The privations of the Great Depression and the two world wars demonstrated the importance of prevention, because so few families could afford the full cost of medical or hospital care. The introduction of national hospital insurance in the late 1950s and medical services insurance in the late 1960s eliminated the need for community-wide services and programs and led to a focus on high-risk children and adults—usually the poor, the homeless, the mentally ill, and non-English-speaking immigrants.

After 1945 public health experts recognized that chronic diseases had overtaken communicable diseases as the leading killers. Heart disease, cancer, and lifestyle problems such as addiction came to prominence as did the needs of the elderly. In the early 1950s smoking was identified as a leading cause of heart disease and cancer but concerted action started only in the 1960s. Initially the problem was medicalized, but in the 1970s behaviour modification and health promotion became the norm. Today smoking is no longer socially acceptable, and health-education activities are supplemented by increasingly stringent local and regional by-laws. This cultural shift reflects the effectiveness of education campaigns and the reality of the high personal and medical costs of disease and debility produced by smoking. From controlling *epidemics to identifying new environmental threats and arguing for attention to the social determinants of health, public health workers since the 1830s have attempted to protect and promote Canadians' health.

HEATHER MacDOUGALL

public holidays. These holidays and celebrations are important elements in the construction of community identity. As events sanctioned by government, community, or group they commemorate elements of a shared past, promote selected values, and provide individuals with a sense of membership in a collective with a common present—and future. Public holidays generally reinforce the existing social order and establish boundaries for membership. However, they have also been used by new groups wishing to forward their aims. In Canada holidays celebrate our faith, our *national identity, our culture, and our class. The diversity of public holidays reflects the many different types of communities to which we belong.

The public celebration days recognized as statutory holidays in Canada almost exclusively reflect the heritage of the Western European Christian founders of the Canadian state. Although religious celebrations such as Christmas, Feast of St Stephen (Boxing Day), Good Friday, and Easter Monday are noted in legislation, the calendar of Canadian secular holidays is influenced by the same cultural roots.

The earliest continuing public holiday in Canada, albeit a British import, is Thanksgiving. The first was proclaimed by the Crown in January 1799 to celebrate British military victories over the French in Europe. Generally celebrated in late fall through the 19th and early 20th centuries, the holiday's purpose also included the King's health, abundant harvests, and the ending of *epidemics. In 1921 Armistice Day (Remembrance Day) and Thanksgiving Day were combined as a single legal holiday on 11 November. Ten years later a distinct Thanksgiving Day, 'For general thanksgiving to Almighty God', was established in mid-October.

In the 1830s the francophone population of Lower Canada developed the first Canadian holiday. The *Société St-Jean-Baptiste, established in 1834 to develop the French-Canadian cultural and linguistic heritage, organized activities, generally with Catholic overtones, for 24 June. This became Quebec's fête nationale in 1922. In the 1960s the holiday was secularized and became linked with Quebec nationalism. In 1845 the English majority of the United *Province of Canada responded with an official patriotic holiday—Victoria Day. In 1901 Parliament made this a legal holiday to commemorate Queen Victoria's death and as a reminder of the imperial connection to Britain. It was known as Empire Day until the late 1940s, thence simply as the Queen's Birthday.

Confederation in 1867 prompted Governor General Lord Monck to proclaim 1 July as the anniversary of the nation in 1868. Dominion Day became a legal public holiday in 1879, but the first official public celebrations took place only in 1917, when the Centre Block of the new Parliament Buildings was dedicated to the Fathers of Confederation and the valour of Canadian troops in France. Since 1958 the federal government has arranged for a national observance of the holiday, with a special royal celebration for the centennial in 1967. Over the last 40 years the holiday has transformed to recognize *multiculturalism (1968) and, since 1980, community-based celebrations. In 1982 Dominion Day became Canada Day, coincident with the *patriation of the constitution and the Canadian *Charter of Rights and Freedoms. In Newfoundland and Labrador 1 July is also commemorated as Memorial Day in remembrance of their heavy losses on the first day of the Battle of the Somme in 1916.

The Canadian labour movement originated labour day when on 15 April 1872 the Toronto Trades Assembly paraded to protest against Canada's anti-union laws. Annual picnics and parades to highlight trade union interests were held in major cities through the late 19th century, usually in summer. In 1894, 1 September was enacted as a national labour holiday. Workers' organizations continue to identify 1 May, associated with the Chicago Haymarket protest of 1886, as an unofficial labour day. The social tension surrounding the commemoration of labour remains in the contemporary celebration of Davis Day in Nova Scotia. William Davis, a *United Mine Workers of America member slain on 11 June 1926 during a vicious strike at a Sydney colliery, is remembered by mining unions as a symbol of their ongoing struggle. The Nova Scotia legislature, in a proposal acknowledging Davis Day, noted it as mine workers safety day.

The August civic holiday is now recognized in most provinces as a regional heritage day. The oldest of these is Discovery Day—the third Monday in August—a legal holiday in the Yukon since 1912. Discovery Day celebrates the discovery of *Klondike gold in 1896 and the subsequent industrial development of the territory. Its focus upon newcomer achievements has led to the recognition of National Aboriginal Day (21 June) as a legal holiday by Yukon First Nation and some municipal governments in recent years.

Ethnic groups across the country have organized public events to gain broader public recognition of their existence, although these are not recognized as legal holidays. Winnipeg hosts one of the largest of these festivals, Folklorama. Originally a part of the Manitoba centennial celebrations (1970), the festival runs for two weeks every summer, featuring almost 50 different ethnic communities. Gay and lesbian communities across the country have similarly taken their interests to the streets, with Pride parades and picnics in many cities, usually in late June.

The Christian, Western European heritage of the settler society shaping Canada through the 19th and most of the 20th centuries established the present set of recognized public holidays. These holidays were powerful social tools forwarding the interests and values of the dominant groups in Canadian society. Changing patterns of immigration, the evolution of Canada's social structures, and broader recognition of regional, sectarian, and ethnic interests have all contributed to the transformation of the lively public celebration of Canada and its people.

DAVID NEUFELD

public ownership. Refers to government ownership of enterprises that sell goods and services and might be imagined as for-profit businesses. This is usually distinguished from governments' ownership of buildings and land for their own activities; of institutions such as schools, hospitals, and prisons; and of roads, harbours, arenas, parks, and other infrastructure. Yet any of these can also be privately owned. Ultimately, decisions on what the state should own are political. Acquisition of an existing company by the federal or a provincial government is generally called nationalization; government disposition of a company is privatization. Public ownership of an asset can also be combined with private management or development of it; thus, although provincial governments own most natural resources, exploitation has usually been left to private businesses.

Governments promote, regulate, and otherwise participate in business in many ways, of which public ownership is by no means the most common. Even so, it has encompassed enterprises in many sectors, created by governments at all levels, of varying ideological orientation, and typically with support from within the business community. On occasion, under farmer or socialist provincial governments and when the left has had leverage on the federal government, socialist theory and populist distrust of capitalism have also helped determine the choice of public ownership.

The principal aim has been development, notably providing—and maintaining—what was understood to be essential infrastructure. Thus, all four Atlantic provinces built railways, beginning with Nova Scotia and New Brunswick in the 1850s; the federal government constructed the *Intercolonial; and Ontario later built a line to foster northern development. More often, public ownership followed state efforts to achieve development by other means. For example, when the Welland Canal Company was nationalized in the early 1840s, the state was already its largest financier by far. Similarly, the failure during the First World War of railways that had been heavily aided by the state led the federal government to organize the *Canadian National Railways. At the same time, Alberta and British Columbia took over failed rail ways into their north.

Another motivation, which could be closely linked to development promotion, was to control what were understood as strategic sectors. Thus, in the 1930s, the federal government took responsibility for developing national broadcasting and a national airline. Electrical generation and transmission, begun in private hands, came in most provinces to be provincially owned. The model was Ontario Hydro, established in 1906. Hydro-Québec began in 1944; the province's nationalization of the remainder of the system in 1962 was represented as a way for the people of Quebec to determine their own destiny. The almost simultaneous nationalization of electricity in British Columbia by a pro-business Social Credit government did not carry the same symbolic weight. Cities and towns regularly had to consider questions concerning control of local *utilities. Almost everywhere, water services came under municipal ownership, and many towns and cities later decided to own their electricity-distribution and transit systems. Edmonton owned its telephone system, as did all three Prairie provincial governments after 1908.

During the Depression and the Second World War, liberal theories of the role of the state that encompassed public ownership as a policy tool gained increasing authority. Thus, the *Bank of Canada was established, then nationalized; the Canadian Wheat Board was re-established; and the federal government created or acquired companies in high technology sectors important to the war, including the production of aircraft, synthetic rubber, and uranium. Late in the war it began to create companies to help manage the post-war economy, and many provinces subsequently joined this trend. Just in the financial sector, governments at one or both levels went into housing finance, credit for farms, small businesses and exporters, and crop and automobile insurance. In the 1960s, Quebec created its Caisse de dépôt et placement to invest public pension funds and to play a strategic part in the development of francophone enterprise. Several provinces created companies to promote development, and rising economic nationalism helped to justify Ottawa's creation of the Canada Development Corporation in 1972.

Municipal utilities often were governed by autonomous commissions. At the federal and provincial level, a common organizational form was the Crown corporation, control of which was delegated to a board and management. Even so, such enterprises were subject to government policy and influence; many were also subject to regulation by other public agencies. That is, none were wholly removed from politics.

No single, simple theory can encompass all the variations on the theme of public ownership in Canada. Although public ownership has sometimes been seen as the expression of a distinct public enterprise culture in Canada, that argument exaggerates the ideological element in Canadian policy making and makes the United States—actually a highly stylized United States—into the standard of measurement. In fact, Canadians have hardly been alone in believing that the state should foster development and control behaviour deemed monopolistic. Moreover, the state itself has been a tool that business, regional, and other interests, including the managers of publicly owned enterprises themselves, have sought to use to their advantage. DOUGLAS McCALLA

public sector unions. In Canada these unions trace their roots to the late 19th century. Growth was slow before the Second World War; the Canadian state considered strikes or even opposition by government employees a form of treason. Members of the Western Federation of Postal Employees learned this firsthand during the *Winnipeg General Strike of 1919, when many of them lost their jobs.

The *Co-operative Commonwealth Federation, elected in Saskatchewan in 1944, took a major step forward by including public sector workers in its Trade Unions Act, which gave workers the legal right to bargain collectively. By the early 1960s salaried public employees constituted 20 per cent or more of the Canadian workforce. In 1963 the merger of two existing unions created the Canadian Union of Public Employees, which represented hospital, social, and municipal workers, and university employees. When the Public Service Alliance of Canada, the major federal employee organization, was formed in November 1966, it immediately became the country's third-largest union. This dramatic growth impelled the passage of the Public Service Staff Relations Act in February 1967. Thereafter, strikes were possible in the federal civil service, many restrictions and conditions notwithstanding. Yet, legislative changes did not halt public hostility to workers in 'essential services' going on strike, as members of the Canadian Union of Postal Workers repeatedly found out.

Provincial public sector workers proved that they were no pale imitation of workers in the private sector. In Quebec in 1972, 200,000 public sector workers participated in the largest strike in Canadian history, forcing the government to legislate them back to work. In British Columbia in 1983, teachers and social workers were front and centre in BC Solidarity's escalating protests against *Social Credit cutbacks. In the early 1990s, Ontario's public sector workers led the charge against the NDP's social contract. In the 1980s and 1990s, public sector workers in all regions of the country found themselves fighting restructuring, downsizing, privatization, and the abrogation of collective agreements.

The rise of public sector unionism shifted the power base in the Canadian trade union movement from American- to Canadian-based unions; it also dramatically altered its gender composition. Sixty per cent of CUPE's half million members are women, and the union's social activism reflects that reality. The ability to organize women, young workers, and workers of colour will be crucial to the continued growth of public sector unions in the 21st century. PETER CAMPBELL

See also COMMON FRONT; TEACHERS' UNIONS.

Puget's Sound Agricultural Company. Established in 1839 by the parent *Hudson's Bay Company to develop agriculture in Oregon to help sustain the *fur trade and to promote trade with the Russians in Alaska. The establishment of farms also helped promote permanent settlement. After the Treaty of Washington, 1846, which established a boundary between US and British possessions west of the Rocky Mountains, the headquarters of the company moved from Fort Vancouver to Fort Victoria. Until the British Columbia gold rush of 1858, the company and its parent concern controlled the land, immigration, labour supply, capital, and import and export duties, and dominated the society of Vancouver Island. Gardens were developed on the island near various forts. Ranching occurred along the Thompson and Nicola Valleys, and some permanent farming emerged; however, production tended to lag behind demand as people were drawn to gold. Large-scale farming flourished in the Cariboo and Similkameen districts; smaller specialized industries thrived in the Okanagan and Fraser Valleys. The introduction of the railway system created valuable markets for agricultural products, but it destroyed British Columbia's wheat industry, which could not compete with prices of prairie wheat.

BARRY M. GOUGH

pulp and paper industry. During the 20th century, the pulp and paper industry came to be established in every province in Canada but Prince Edward Island. While it started from humble beginnings—it was a tangential part of the country's economic and social fabric in the early 1900s—within short order it grew to be Canada's most important modern staples industry.

Before Confederation the technology used in manufacturing paper dictated that it was generally a small-scale enterprise. Paper was produced using large amounts of power to grind up rags. Consequently, most paper plants were located along major waterways, which could be tapped with waterwheels for their hydraulic energy, and near urban centres, from which sufficient supplies of rags could be obtained and where paper was sold. Output was small and paper a relatively costly product.

Beginning in the mid-19th century, paper production underwent a major transformation. New technology permitted paper makers to process wood, which was relatively abundant, instead of rags, and generate far greater quantities of energy from waterways. These developments precipitated a dramatic rise in the productive capacity of paper mills and caused a steep decline in paper prices. This was particularly true for newsprint in North America: its price fell from roughly $300 per ton in 1867 to $36 per ton 30 years later.

As the 20th century dawned, many parts of Canada were ideally suited to producing vast volumes of inexpensive newsprint. Black spruce, the best species for making newsprint, is predominant in the boreal forest region, a broad band of woodland that comprises most of the forested area of Canada east of the Rockies. British Columbia's forests supported large quantities of hemlock, the western species of choice for pulp and paper. These regions are also punctuated by numerous large rivers, which could be tapped to provide the sizable quantities of energy needed to grind timber into pulp and paper. The construction of the Canadian Pacific Railway in the mid-1880s, and two new transcontinentals in the early 1900s, rendered many of these timber and water-power resources (particularly those in northern Ontario and Quebec) accessible to mill developers. The railways also provided a means by which paper makers could ship their product to market.

Because Canada's capacity to manufacture pulp and paper was immense compared to domestic demand, from very early on the industry was highly dependent upon export markets, principally the United States. Consequently, American tariff policy played a significant role in shaping the development of Canada's industry. For example, Canadian newsprint production was growing at a healthy rate in the early 1900s despite a hefty duty imposed by the United States on this type of paper; however, the elimination of this tariff in 1913 triggered a dramatic expansion of the dominion's newsprint industry. By the mid-1920s Canadian mills were supplying more than half the American demand, and this percentage continued to rise. At the same time, the United States maintained prohibitive duties on other pulp and paper products. This fettered the diversification of the Canadian industry into such things as kraft papers (used for cardboard and packaging) and fine papers. For most of the 20th century the industry has been overwhelmingly dominated by newsprint production, and the country has been by far and away the world's largest supplier.

Changing technology had spurred the establishment and remarkable growth of the industry, and this same force had a dramatic influence on the lives of the workers involved. Pulp and paper mills consumed immense quantities of trees and initially required thousands of employees to harvest and deliver this wood from the forest to the mills. At the turn of the 20th century, logging was a seasonal, labour-intensive, and highly dangerous activity, and the rhythmic life of the 'lumberjack' was romanticized in Canadian folklore. The fall was the time for advance parties to erect the rudimentary bush camps in which the gangs of cutters would be housed and to cut the trails along which the wood would be hauled. Winter was the season during which the cutters would migrate to the 'bush' to harvest the timber. They took the trees down with hand saws, and teams of horses would draw the wood to water's edge, where it would be piled awaiting the spring thaw. When the ice and snow melted, the timber would be skilfully river-driven or boomed to the mill pond to be processed, a method of delivery that often took more than one season to complete. By mid-century, working conditions had changed radically. An acute labour shortage and the often irresistible attraction of urban life in post–Second World War Canada compelled companies to improve both the quality of life for bush workers and their productivity. Harvesting wood became a year-round activity carried out by cutters who either commuted to the bush from town or lived in comfortable, semi-permanent bush camps equipped with modern conveniences. In most instances, the process of cutting timber was mechanized: tractors or 'skidders' replaced horses, chain saws and giant mechanical 'feller-bunchers' replaced hand saws, and trucks, not waterways, transported logs to mills. While bush workers still required a high degree of skill to carry out their tasks, most were now operating machinery instead of carrying out physical labour.

Changes in the pulp and paper mills were far less dramatic. Only gradually did increasing mechanization reduce the number of hands required on production lines. In the early 1900s paper plants employed several thousand workers to handle supplies and the finished product and to carry out the maintenance work that large-scale industrial enterprises required. By the eve of the 21st century, thousands of mill jobs had been eliminated through the introduction of computer-automated production and maintenance.

Although the pulp and paper industry remains a central cog in Canada's economy and a major contributor to the country's balance of trade, it has maintained this status only by overcoming a string of challenges, many of which it continues to confront. Concerns about diminishing fibre supplies compelled many producers to develop means of maximizing their utilization of traditional, and processing non-traditional, pulpwood species, and led them to introduce forest-management programs. Most producers became integrated with sawmills, whereby they processed the waste slabs and chips from lumber manufacturers. Since at least the late 1960s, the industry has also dealt with increasing public criticism of the manner in which it manages both its primary raw material (wood) and the by-products of its manufacturing processes (air and water pollution). In response to this pressure from the environmental movement, the industry dramatically improved its practices in these areas. Canada's pulp and paper makers continue to confront intense competition from established producers in places like the southern United States and Scandinavia, and from new rivals in Latin America and the Far East. More recently, First Nations have been asking for greater influence over the management of many timber limits, which they view as their traditional areas of land use. This has forced the industry to recognize Aboriginal rights in this regard and to negotiate agreements under which the mills would continue to enjoy cutting privileges.

While many predicted that the advent of the computer age would lead to the 'paperless society', quite the opposite has occurred. Paper seems to be in greater demand than ever, a trend that augurs well for the future of Canada's pulp and paper industry. MARK KUHLBERG

pure laine. 'Pure laine' Quebeckers are direct descendants of French pioneers who established themselves in New France. The expression also describes Quebeckers faithful to traditional values or those who profess a Québécois nationalist pride. More recently, pure laine has referred to an exclusionary form of nationalism, invoked to contrast the descendants of pioneers with allophones or immigrants. Although *Québécois de souche* has now become the preferred alternative, identifying this category of Quebeckers remains a controversial endeavour.

NICOLE NEATBY

Qitdlarssuaq (*c.* 1795–*c.* 1870), *Inuit shaman, leader, born in North Baffin region of the eastern High Arctic. After hearing from explorers and whalers about the existence of Greenlandic Inuit across the waters of the Davis Strait, Qitdlarssuaq (Qitdlak) led more than 40 Baffin Islanders on an 1860–3 expedition across Ellesmere Island to northwestern Greenland. Some of Qitdlarssuaq's group settled among the Polar Inuit and reintroduced to the region previously lost hunting technologies such as the bow and arrow, fishing spear, and kayak. Others began an ill-fated journey back to Canada, during which some perished. Although such epic Inuit migrations rarely appear in Western annals of *arctic exploration and discovery, they dominate Inuit oral tradition. Inuit in the contemporary settlements of Pond Inlet in Nunavut and Qaanaaq, Greenland, still consider themselves related and regularly organize exchanges. NANCY WACHOWICH

Quakers. The Religious Society of Friends ('Quakers') was founded in England in the 1650s as a protest against the formalism of the Established Church. The movement emphasized spontaneous ministry, egalitarian organization, pacifism, and 'plainness'. Within the decade, the message had traversed the Atlantic and was firmly established in New York, New England, and Pennsylvania (the 'Quaker State'). A small offshoot of Quaker whalers from Nantucket established themselves in Dartmouth, Nova Scotia, about 1786, but the majority of Quakers migrated from the United States to Upper Canada in the first three decades of the 19th century, a part of a general westward migration in search of farms. The Canadian meetings were deeply influenced by contentious theological debates then emerging among urban elites in the major American port cities. Canadian Quakers were thus torn by schism in 1812, with the separation of the *Children of Peace, in 1828 with the Hicksite-Orthodox separation, and in 1881 with the Gurneyite-Wilburite separation. These schisms greatly weakened the society. The surviving three branches reunited in 1955, after decades of rapprochement in the field of shared 'service'. It is for this service that Friends are now best known; the Canadian Friends Service Committee has been instrumental in providing relief (for groups such as the *Doukhobors) and peace education (Grindstone Island Peace Centre) and in the formation of ecumenical groups to further these causes (Canadian Save the Children Fund, Project Ploughshares). The society is now a largely urban denomination with meetings in most Canadian centres. Numerically small, its influence has been disproportionate to its size.

ALBERT SCHRAUWERS

Quebec. Since 1867 Quebec has been Canada's largest province. Descended from *New France, through *Lower Canada, and Canada East in the United *Province of Canada, it remains the heartland of French Canada.

In 1865–6, although the anglophone minority in the province was largely in favour of Confederation, francophones were sharply divided. In the end, George-Étienne *Cartier's conservatives won the debate. The new *constitution, it was argued, would bring political stability and solve the problem of a French-Canadian nation in the midst of a growing British-American nation. French Canada would accept a minority status, but there would be official *bilingualism in the federal government and a provincial government in Quebec in which a francophone majority would control social and cultural development. The Roman Catholic Church was pleased by the new constitution.

Archaeological records indicate that the land that is now Quebec was slowly populated by Aboriginal people after the last glaciation, which lasted until approximately 15,000 BC. At the time of Confederation most of the St Lawrence lowlands was occupied by descendants of European settlers. Only a few Aboriginal reserves bordering the river remained, although the *Canadian Shield and the north were occupied mostly by Innu and Inuit. In 1851, 75 per cent of the population was of French origin; by 1901 that figure had grown to 80 per cent, with sizeable British minorities concentrated mostly in the cities (indeed, between 1832 and 1867 the majority of Montreal was English speaking). After 1850, and until 1920, an important out-migration took many French Canadians to the United States.

Quebec's economy has long depended on natural resources. Towards the end of the 19th century lumber and pulpwood replaced timber; later *hydroelectricity, hydrometallurgy, and mining became important. For a long time, the economy was based on *agriculture. This was true for Canada as a whole, but agriculture gained a renewed importance during the second half of the 19th century in Quebec, when French-Canadian elites proposed that the divine mission of the people was to be Catholic and rural. Of course there was always a gap between this discourse and reality: a sizeable commercial agricultural sector developed around milk production, but at the same time people were moving to the cities, either in Canada or the United States. Nevertheless, expansion of agriculture at all costs, sometimes regardless of realities, was pursued up to 1939.

Industrial development came early. In 1848, when the enlarged Lachine Canal was reopened, it became the birthplace of modern industry in Canada, with factories lining its banks and using water power created by the locks. This first phase occurred mostly in *Montreal, but there were industries throughout the countryside. This first industrial sector was linked to the Canadian market: large-scale wheat milling, saw mills, foundries. A second phase included the development of hydroelectricity, which brought factories into the countryside. The St-Maurice Valley and the Saguenay–Lac St-Jean area are almost textbook cases. When in 1898 Shawinigan Water and Power began constructing its dam the venture was intended to sell electricity in Montreal. However, the company also needed customers in the vicinity of its power plant, and new technologies for paper making and electrometallurgy made this possible. In the Saguenay, development stemmed from the rise of demand for aluminium and the fact that raw materials could be brought in by boat. As new regions opened to industrialization, opportunities for jobs were created and the agricultural sector was stimulated. Today, Quebec's industrial sector is varied, building on its traditional strength and diversifying with entreprises like aerospace, transport, and electronics, and expanding its markets outside Canada.

Politically, crises in the late 19th century—school questions, the hanging of Louis *Riel, the extinction of French-language rights in the West—reinforced the importance of the Quebec government as the only one French Canadians could trust. The sad ending to Wilfrid *Laurier's political career seemed to demonstrate the limits of French-Canadian influence in Ottawa. Within the province, debate centred on development and modernization. The Liberal Party, in power between 1896 and 1936, wished to develop the economy, aided by foreign investment. A rising nationalist movement, with a strong clerical following suspicious of urbanization, sought to reinforce traditional and rural values and accused the Liberals of squandering the province's natural resources. During the Depression, Maurice *Duplessis's Union nationale claimed to achieve both aims. Duplessis focused on economic growth and his own power, leaving social and cultural development to chuch-run institutions. In the 1950s, however, the church became overwhelmed by such tasks, especially in education, given the effect of the compulsory education act (1942) and the *baby boom. The *Quiet Revolution of the 1960s brought a series of reforms that helped to modernize society. Debates took place on ways to develop a modern francophone society. On the one hand Quebec asked for more power from the federal government, while on the other the idea of independence gained prominence and became a political project. Attempting to relegitimize the federal government's role in developing both Canadian and Québécois society, Pierre Elliott *Trudeau proposed a third alternative. The debates continue.

In the meantime, the population of the province was undergoing changes. At the beginning of the 20th century a new wave of immigrants arrived, for the first time introducing significant numbers of non-French and non-British people. The most important early groups were Russian Jews and Italians, who settled in the cities, mostly in Montreal. At the same time, the British group began to dwindle. Urbanization increased over the century, and Quebec began to offer two different faces: a countryside massively French speaking and rural, and a multicultural metropolis that, while 60 per cent francophone, still appeared to be very English. Such English dominance continued because Canada's English-language bourgoisie lived largely in Montreal and because the ethnic and linguistic division of labour saw francophones largely confined to unskilled work while people of British origin held the better-paying jobs. Immigrants became quickly anglicized, because of economic opportunities and because the French public education system was closed to non-Catholics.

After 1960 there were more changes, both socio-political and demographic. Montreal's bourgeoisie lost its relative importance, the traditional division of labour was no longer accepted, and there was a determination to obtain a better place for francophones in the Quebec economy. With the advent of the service economy, language became more important as a working tool. Both Canada and Quebec enacted language laws to try to cope. The federal Official Languages Act (1969) was meant to create a bilingual environment. In contrast, the *Quebec language laws were aimed at consolidating the predominance of French in Quebec by promoting the use of that language in the workplace and in the schooling of immigrant children. The French-Canadian birth rate, already in decline, plunged remarkably. Immigration also changed. Migrants came increasingly from Asia or the Caribbean, further transforming the population. In contrast to the rest of Quebec, a multicultural and multiracial French-speaking society has been emerging in the Montreal region since the 1980s. JEAN-CLAUDE ROBERT

Quebec, siege of, 1759–60. General James Wolfe and Admiral Charles Saunders led 41 warships and 140 transports, 18,000 sailors, and 8,750 soldiers up the St Lawrence River towards Quebec in June 1759. Despite forewarning of this threat, Governor Pierre de Rigaud de Vaudreuil had only recently prepared the city's defences. The French abandoned outer areas and defended the north shore of the St Lawrence tenaciously with 3,200 regular soldiers and marines, 11,500 militia, 1,460 sailors, and 900 Aboriginals. Trenches and batteries lined the Beauport Flats between the St Charles and Montmorency Rivers, and batteries and infantry posts guarded the cliffs west of Quebec. The English quickly took Île d'Orléans and the south shore, and added a fortified camp east of Montmorency on the north shore. Cannon across the river at Point Lévis bombarded Quebec from 13 July to

4 September, reducing many buildings to rubble but scarcely weakening the city's fortifications. English vessels eventually slipped past Quebec, but the French shadowed them, repulsing three landings. Frustrated, the English torched settlements in the areas they controlled. When Wolfe tried one last landing in the west to cut supply lines and force a battle, inept guards at Anse-au-Foulon and poor communications made it possible for British forces to scale the cliffs. On 13 September, 4,829 redcoats formed a thin line across the Plains of Abraham. General Louis-Joseph de Montcalm, with 4,500 men and 800 skirmishers, planned to break it with a column flanked by lines that forced the British to maintain formation. Inexperienced in such combat, the French militiamen and marines broke and the regulars fled. Both Wolfe and Montcalm were killed. Vaudreuil summoned François de Lévis from Montreal, then hastily abandoned Quebec. Lévis regrouped the army and rushed back to the city. Meanwhile, Jean-Baptiste-Nicolas-Roch de Ramezay, the Canadien left in command of Quebec, surrendered. Lévis counterattacked in the spring of 1760, and the Franco-Canadian forces won the Battle of Ste-Foy on 28 April, almost forcing the British commander, James *Murray, to capitulate. Lévis then besieged Quebec. However, the British won the naval race to relieve the city, and Lévis withdrew. JAY CASSEL

See also CAPITULATION OF CANADA.

Quebec Act, 1774. The act represents the official abandonment of the policy of anglicization that had dominated imperial policy in post-conquest Quebec. In the euphoria of the *conquest, metropolitan statesmen had naively believed that the Canadiens would be eager to convert to Protestantism and embrace British constitutional institutions, and that British administration of the frontier would introduce trading practices enhancing both security and trade. By the mid-1760s it was apparent that these assumptions were incorrect. The need to reconcile treaty guarantees of Canadian property and religious rights with the *Royal Proclamation of 1763's promise to introduce British institutions in a timely fashion drove the North ministry in London to accept the reality that Canadiens were not about to embrace British constitutional or religious values wholeheartedly. To ensure metropolitan control while allowing a system of governance sensitive to local issues, the Quebec Act created an appointed council including Catholic Canadiens. Clauses confirmed French custom in civil law and English criminal law. The right to practise religion freely, subject to the King's supremacy, was guaranteed, as was the legally enforceable right of the Catholic Church to collect tithes from its adherents. Reducing the burgeoning cost of administering the frontier, providing justice for fur traders and Indians, would be achieved by restoring Quebec's boundaries to their pre-Proclamation lines. When extending Quebec's boundaries, Whitehall policy-makers had in mind the failure of more than one ministry to obtain revenues from the American colonies and their inability to check western migration.

By allowing Catholics to participate in the colony's governance the North ministry recognized that the post-1763 empire was a polyglot in need of flexible local government subject to metropolitan control. Popular reaction to the Quebec Act highlights how far it represented a departure from traditional practice. Anglo-Quebec merchants felt that allowing Catholic participation in an appointed council was a threat to their economic and constitutional liberties and a betrayal of the promises made in the 1763 Proclamation. American colonists denounced the Quebec Act as further proof that the King in Parliament sought to undermine their constitutional liberties. In Britain radical politicians outside of Parliament placed the act in a pantheon of issues that provided evidence of a 'popish plot' and the dangers of ministerial corruption. The Quebec Act had little direct impact on the majority of Canadien *habitants other than representing a flawed attempt to recognize the reality of the world in which they lived. K. DAVID MILOBAR

Quebec Bridge disasters. Construction of a bridge across the St Lawrence River near Quebec City was considered from 1852 onwards, but only in 1900 was a cornerstone laid. The principal contractor, the Phoenix Bridge Company, used a design drawn up by P.L. Szlapka and approved by Theodore Cooper, consulting engineer to the Quebec Bridge and Railway Company, which would own the finished bridge. Work on approach spans occupied three years, after which construction began on the central portion. Although by June 1907 there was evidence of buckling plates, workers remained on the site. On the afternoon of 29 August the bridge collapsed, killing 75 men. A royal commission concluded that the disaster sprang from a defective design, compounded by errors in judgment on the part of the engineers. The need for a bridge remained, however, and the Canadian government took up the task using a new design. The centre portion was being lifted into place on 12 September 1916 when an attachment broke and the span dropped into the river. Twelve workmen were killed. A new span was built, and the bridge was finally completed in 1917. Although Canada has witnessed several bridge disasters, those involving the cantilever bridge at Quebec City were the most deadly. Their only rival was the collapse of the Point Ellice Bridge in Victoria, in May 1896, which claimed 55 lives. HUGH A. HALLIDAY

Quebec City. Located at the head of the St Lawrence estuary, Quebec City was founded by Samuel de *Champlain in 1608. Visited by Jacques *Cartier in 1535 and the site of tentative settlements later in the 16th century, Quebec ('narrow' or 'straight' in the Algonquian language) was established first as a trading post but rapidly became the head of an emerging French empire based on the St Lawrence River; except for a few years, it has been a capital—colonial French or British, Canadian, French-Canadian, Québécois—ever since. The post's founding was made possible by diplomatic efforts that led to alliances with many First Nations, but also to wars against some others, among them the *Iroquois who threatened the whole colony until the *Great Peace of 1701. Strategically dominating the river from Cap aux Diamants (Upper Town), Quebec's forts (the first built in 1620) controlled the gateway to the whole *St Lawrence system. The city's key location made it the goal of many military expeditions, by Great Britain before 1760 and by the United States thereafter.

Shortly after Quebec City's founding, its administrative functions were reinforced by the establishment of several religious institutions (in addition to secular clergy, male and female orders devoted to health, education, and, of course, Christianization). Surrendered in 1759, the city became capital (1783) of the British Empire in North America. As well as administration and trade, the city was a centre of *shipbuilding and maritime transportation from 1665 to the mid-19th century. The years 1800–60 were particularly prosperous. Thanks to the timber trade the harbour was very active, and it was also the port of entry for the rapidly growing colony. Despite deadly *epidemics, population increased steadily from 8,000 in 1800 (only slightly more than in 1760) to 57,000 in 1861. By that time, Quebec had become a cosmopolitan city by contemporary Canadian standards (60 per cent French Canadians, 20 per cent Irish Catholics, 20 per cent British Protestants).

The second half of the century was much tougher. Shipbuilding virtually collapsed in the 1860s; a large part of the Atlantic harbour activities transferred to Montreal; continental railroad development took place on the south shore of the St Lawrence, leaving the capital without any rail link until 1879 (Canadian Pacific); Confederation in 1867 left the city with a lesser role as a provincial capital; and the Citadel's *British garrison embarked for home in 1871. Industrialization occurred slowly, with labour-intensive activities such as leather processing, shoe factories, and food, tobacco, and clothing industries. Meanwhile, *tourism began to emerge, the unique architecture of the city and its symbolic cityscape attracting thousands of American and British tourists, many of them staying at CP's luxurious Château Frontenac hotel (1893). As economic activity migrated westward, population followed; thousands left the city, and growth almost ceased between 1860 and 1900. Along with massive out-migration, rural migrants from the surrounding countryside created dramatic changes in the social and cultural fabric of the city, the French-Canadian proportion of the population reaching 85 per cent in 1901.

The city's economy was partially relieved by the consolidation of its hinterland in the northeastern regions of the province through railroad construction, an objective facilitated by the erection of the Quebec Bridge (1917). Thanks also to the second Quebec industrial revolution, and the expansion of established industries, the city's economy improved notably and demographic growth recovered and kept on steadily for the first half of the 20th century. At the same time there was a growing affirmation of French-Canadian self-consciousness as a national collectivity. Cradle of French North America, and progressively seen as the capital of French Canada, Quebec City hosted numerous cultural events and institutions promoting French and Catholic culture (the latter up to the 1950s). The city's architectural heritage was developed with preservation laws and by-laws covering the Old City. Efforts to restore Place Royale, in the Lower Town, were recognized in 1985 when UNESCO declared the Old City a World Heritage Site. With the *Quiet Revolution and the modernization of French-Canadian institutions in the 1960s, and the emergence of the Québécois identity, Quebec City has been increasingly perceived as a national capital. It has amalgamated with 13 surrounding towns to form a city of about 510,000 people (2001).

MARC ST-HILAIRE AND RICHARD MARCOUX

Quebec civil law. In Quebec, anyone who takes the trouble to go to a bookstore can find a copy of the civil code. Anyone with the patience to scan its 3,168 articles can boast of having consulted the essentials of Quebec civil law (though not necessarily of having understood all its subtleties). The code is the most tangible aspect of Quebec's judicial particularity in a Canada characterized by the common *law—a system historically reluctant to codify its rules, which were first developed by the *courts. Faithful to the tradition of continental Europe, Quebec's civil law is distinguished by its form (codification), but also by its content, which originated in old French law. The legacy of French colonization in North America, civil law gained its Québécois character through four centuries of history.

Because the pioneers of New France brought their law with them, the history of civil law could begin with the colony itself (1608). But it was in 1664 that King Louis XIV chose one of 300 different 'customs', the Coutume de Paris, to be the common law of his subjects in America. The 362 articles of this text, drawn up in 1580, deal with matters such as property law, matrimony, and succession. The product of a society both feudal and patriarchal, the Coutume de Paris also regulated seigneurial law (spelling out the privileges due to the seigneur and the obligations of his *censitaires*) and the dower right of widows (the right to a certain part of their husbands' estate). A number of French royal ordinances, certain elements of ancient Roman law, and prescriptions of the Catholic Church were combined with the Paris text to form the civil law of New France.

In the same period the monarchy created the Sovereign Council to administer justice and apply French law in the colony. Presided over by representatives of the king (the governor and intendant), with some 'Canadien' members, the council served primarily as a court of appeal. In their judgments, these magistrates, who generally had no legal training, sometimes adapted French law to North American conditions. It should be noted that lawyers (already victims of their reputation) were forbidden to reside in New France and had to wait until 1765 to practise among the Canadien population. Before that date, notaries handled everything, representing the settlers before the courts and directing their transactions. A figure typical of the civil law tradition, the notary is still a part of the legal profession in Quebec (which, incidentally, women first entered only a few decades ago).

The British Conquest and military regime (1760–4) were followed by a period of uncertainty, owing to the introduction of English law in the *Province of Quebec (1764–74). But in 1774 the British Parliament passed the *Quebec Act, which re-established the Laws and Customs of Canada with respect to property and civil rights. This measure covered the *seigneurial regime, the law of succession, and real estate transactions conducted in front of a notary, but excluded the rules governing the business transactions so important to the British. It was on the basis of this vague compromise that a mixed legal system was constructed that has no parallel anywhere: civil law of French origin combined with public law and criminal law in the English tradition.

The dividing line remained in flux, for private law became a frequent object of political struggle in Lower Canada until the 1840s. Two great legal traditions stood in opposition to one another not only within a politicized judicial system but in the legislative sphere, where, from the creation of the assembly in 1791, the British leaders crossed swords with the Canadiens or *'patriotes'. More than one anglophone saw the Coutume de Paris as outmoded and difficult to use, an obstacle to the advance of mercantile or industrial interests of the colony and the empire. The French-Canadian elites, however, saw it as a bulwark in the defence of a society and identity that they perceived as threatened. In the mid-19th century, some deplored the 'legal Babel' that prevailed in Lower Canada, the product of a patchwork of laws and the hybridization of two legal traditions.

In the second half of the century, law reform sorted out the confusion and paved the way for a more rational and accessible—although still unique—common regime of law. With the triumph of *liberalism, most of the archaic elements of the old French law were abolished, in particular the seigneurial regime. At the same time, elements of a modern legal system were put in place (legislation was recast, the magistrature depoliticized, the legal profession organized, etc.). Above all, in 1866 the province gave itself a civil code (and in 1867 a civil procedural code). Long after France (where the Napoleonic Code dates from 1804), Quebec gave new life to a civil law tradition that was running out of steam. Although inspired by the French model, the civil code of Lower Canada included some novel features, including a text in two languages, commercial law and a registration system for property title, both influenced by the English tradition.

In the context of the Canadian federation, the civil code quickly became a symbol of French-Canadian nationality. It has retained its symbolic value to the present day, being one of the elements of the *'distinct society' debated by politicians in recent years. Despite the growth of regulation in modern society, the civil code remains at the heart of Quebec's law. Completely revised and corrected in 1992, the Quebec Civil Code has been able to renew itself by integrating fundamental reforms, such as the legal recognition of women.

JEAN-PHILIPPE GARNEAU

Quebec language laws. A series of laws adopted under Quebec governments to improve the status of the French language, the legislation was crafted in reaction to growing public pressure from francophone groups who felt that French was being relegated to second-class status, especially in Montreal. Various issues were at stake, particularly the status of the French language as the dominant language, its use in the workplace and in public life, the language of instruction in the schools. Opinions spanned from the advocacy of a French unilingual society to the support of free choice in a bilingual environment. Governments had to balance individual and collective rights, promote the use of French, and protect the anglophone minority.

A crisis was sparked in the late 1960s by disagreement between French- and Italian-speaking communities regarding the language of instruction for immigrants' children. Under the *Union nationale government of Jean-Jacques Bertrand, the legislature adopted Bill 63 (1969), which maintained free choice for the language of instruction. A commission of inquiry (Gendron) was set up to study the condition of the French language and linguistic rights. In 1974 the Liberal government of Robert Bourassa, acting upon the Gendron commission's proposals, introduced Bill 22, which made French the official language of Quebec and promoted its primacy in the workplace and in public life. Access to English-language public schools was restricted: only those children who could pass an English test were admitted. René *Lévesque's *Parti Québécois government, in power from 1976, went a step further. Bill 101, the charter of the French language, was adopted in 1977. Admission to English-language public schools was allowed only for children whose parents had attended such schools in Quebec (later in Canada). Generally, the measures to increase the use of French at work and in public, which were mostly voluntary in Bill 22, became compulsory. The use of languages other than French was banned on public signs. Courts later struck down some of the provisions of Bill 101.

In addition to these bills, various other laws contributed to the evolving Quebec language policy. In conjunction with significant social and demographic changes, language laws helped reshape the image of Quebec. At the same time, Quebec governments recognized the importance of protecting the anglophone minority's right to its own educational system and to health and social services in English.

PAUL-ANDRÉ LINTEAU

Quebec tercentenary, 1908. At the beginning of the 20th century, countries across the Western world were staging large-scale commemorative celebrations. In Canada, the most significant such event was held at Quebec City to mark the tercentenary of its founding by Samuel de *Champlain. While French and English Canadians had their own reasons for feting Champlain, the most significant promoter of the tercentenary was an Englishman, Governor General Earl Grey. He wanted to bring French and English Canadians together to celebrate their common allegiance to the *British Empire, which was in need of Canadian support in the years leading up to the First World War. Grey had little interest in Champlain's deeds, turning instead to historical moments that might encourage co-operation between francophones and anglophones. He saw the tercentenary as the pretext for turning the Plains of Abraham, upon which France had been defeated in 1759, into a park that might celebrate the coexistence of former enemies, now united under British rule.

Grey's scheme met with considerable resistance among French Canadians. The prime minister, Sir Wilfrid *Laurier, dragged his feet in providing support, fearing negative political effects in Quebec. Still other Quebeckers were bothered when Grey tried to bring France into the fete to cement the Anglo-French alliance against Germany. France had recently severed ties between church and state, thus making itself unpopular among some French-Canadian leaders, mostly clerics, who refused to participate in events attended by representatives of the Third Republic.

Although some French Canadians were reluctant to embrace the tercentenary, over the last two weeks of July a city of 70,000 became home to more than 100,000 visitors, the most prestigious of whom was the Prince of Wales. The fete was built around his schedule, thus further annoying Quebeckers who saw Champlain recede from the scene. Champlain's marginal status was particularly visible in the most dramatic event of the fete, the pageants staged upon the Plains of Abraham. Thousands of local residents were dressed up in period costumes to tell a history of Canada beginning with the arrival of Jacques *Cartier and closing with the generals from the battle on the Plains of Abraham, Wolfe and Montcalm, along with their armies, entering the stage as allies. Although the spirit of co-operation between the two linguistic communities was central to the celebrations, the tercentenary brought out divisions between those two communities as much as it brought them together.

RONALD RUDIN

'quelques arpents de neige'. This disparaging expression was used by Voltaire (1694–1778) in his novel *Candide* (1759) to ridicule the war between England and France for Canada. He was a steadfast opponent of colonial ventures in Canada, preferring the consolidation of Louisiana, which had for him more value. In his various writings, he mutliplied his sarcasm about Canada, remarking on its cold temperature, its wild beasts, and its waste of public money. In the past his attitude was viewed in French Canada as the explanation for the abandonment of New France by the mother country. While recent research has mitigated this view, the expression is still very potent and frequently used. It has become a reference point indicating a certain misjudgment relative to the development of French Canada.

JEAN-CLAUDE ROBERT

Quiet Revolution. A phrase describing the relatively non-violent nature of the rapid political, institutional, social, and cultural changes that occurred in Quebec in the 1960s. Though the changes began with the defeat of the *Union nationale and the election of the provincial Liberals under Jean *Lesage in June 1960, historians disagree about the precise moment that marked their end, since they continued beyond the unexpected Liberal defeat in 1966.

The Quiet Revolution was characterized by a change of perception about the role of the state. The prime movers for change were members of a new middle class who advocated a more progressive form of nationalism and perceived the Quebec state as an instrument to implement social and economic reforms. They challenged the Catholic Church, which had been having difficulties coping with its social and educational responsibilities, and aimed for increased francophone control over the economy. State activism and new attitudes towards religion contributed to the decline in the church's status and influence. With the creation of a Ministry of Education in 1964, massive investment in the educational system assured greater access. Several social programs, such as the Hospital Insurance Program and the Quebec Pension Plan, were implemented, and the province took a more active role in the economy through state-owned enterprises such as Sidbec, an integrated steelmaking facility, and Hydro-Québec, which took over control of electrical utility companies outside Montreal. State financial institutions, such as the Caisse de dépôt et de placement—a deposit and investment fund—and the Société générale de financement, were aimed at increasing the degree of francophone control over the economy.

The Quiet Revolution had a huge impact on Quebec society, and its effects reverberated across the country. It led to the emergence of a new sense of self-identification among French Canadians and a new definition of the French-Canadian nation. Quebec nationalists, who gradually came to focus on Quebec alone, no longer felt they shared a common national identity with all of French-speaking Canada. They saw themselves as part of an emerging identity based on a common language, French, and a precise territory, Quebec. Given the importance of the French language in the Quebec identity, conflicts were triggered over strategies to protect and promote its use. The Quiet Revolution stimulated the process of nation building. The new definition of the Quebec nation altered the nature of relations between French and English Canada. Quebec came to be defined as the nation state of one of the two founding nations, and Quebec, not French Canada, became the nation state of francophones in Canada. This change in the nature of the Canadian duality triggered a new wave of conflicts between the federal government and Quebec over the division of powers, Quebec's status in Confederation, and its role in world affairs.

MARCEL MARTEL

race to the Pole. Between 1850 and 1925 the race to the North Pole prompted the European exploration of Canada's most northerly region, the Queen Elizabeth Islands of Nunavut. Initially, the polar quest derived from efforts of European commercial interests to find a *Northwest Passage to the Orient. Following the Napoleonic Wars, Britain's Royal Navy revived the search through an ambitious program of exploration in the Arctic Archipelago. By mid-century, the focus shifted to the North Pole as the United States sought to continue its own imperial expansion. The race intensified around 1900 through a developing rivalry between Norway and the United States, and culminated in a series of expeditions by Americans Robert E. Peary and Frederick Cook. Peary, using relay teams across the pack ice from Ellesmere Island, claimed to have reached 89°57′ in April 1909. Cook professed to have discovered the Pole a year earlier, striking out from Axel Heiberg Island. Peary emerged victorious in the ensuing public relations battle. By the 1920s, advances in the technology of fixed-wing aircraft set the stage for renewed efforts to reach the Pole by air. In 1925, the American Richard Byrd, flying from Etah, northern Greenland, and passing over Ellesmere Island, tried to find the Pole; he claimed to reach it the following year.

Following these attainments, interest in the North Pole began to wane, although it has been revived in recent decades by adventurers attempting to reach it using distinctive techniques. Among the important consequences of polar exploration was the initiation of contact between European and Inuit cultures. Canada did not participate directly, but the race to the Pole played a role in nation building, as federal authorities responded to foreign incursions by sending expeditions and establishing *RCMP detachments to assert sovereignty over the High Arctic. LYLE DICK

racism. When Canadians imagine a racist society, they probably think of the segregated American South, South Africa under apartheid, or Nazi Germany. By contrast, Canada seems to have had no 'race' problem at all, an idea reinforced by the historical fact that American slaves sought refuge here. But for most of our history, Canadians accepted an ideology of 'race'—that is, an understanding that human beings belong in biologically defined categories that determine their character, values, and behaviour. According to this world view, it was possible to identify people's suitability to participate in Canadian life simply by observing their physical traits, or phenotypes.

'Race' doctrine derives from European imperial expansion and the stratification of the world's peoples to serve European power and wealth. Imperial rule and the functions assigned to subject populations gave genuine economic, social, and political significance to anyone's place in the phenotypical hierarchy, most abruptly through the institution of *slavery. Empires were colour-coordinated; 'race' acquired meaning, and its measure was skin colour and other genetic features. Nineteenth-century science gauged the distinctions between 'races', but the underlying hypothesis that 'race' determined character remained untested. 'Scientific racism' legitimized differential treatment of people because of their 'race'.

Global racial mythology was transferred to Canada through membership in the British Empire and neighbourhood with the United States. Popular culture taught the validity of racial stereotypes, and our mentors exemplified the management of 'inferiors' through legal and other restraints. English law was directly implemented, both as precedent for Canadian courts and through decisions by the Judicial Committee of the Privy Council in London, Canada's final appeal court until 1949. These various lessons were, however, applied in distinctly Canadian ways, to suit domestic requirements and federal political structures.

The *Indian Act of 1876 and related regulations were predicated on the assumption of inherent differences and evolutionary stages. Aboriginals were legally defined as 'minors' requiring the supervision of a more advanced civilization. *Immigration policy was another conspicuous application of racial doctrine. Persons deemed genetically incapable of assimilating to Canadian norms were barred completely or admitted only to perform a narrow range of economic functions. For example, *Chinese were welcomed to construct the CPR, but its completion in 1885 brought exclusionary 'head taxes', culminating in absolute rejection in 1923. Quotas, secret agreements, and subterfuge were utilized against Japanese, Indians, West Indians, Africans, and African Americans. The Immigration Act of 1910 specifically authorized the federal government to restrict immigration on grounds of 'race'. Until the 1960s, immigration preferences reflected 19th-century racial categories, with heightened barriers for Asians and especially Africans.

Domestic restrictions perpetuated marginalization for minority Canadians. Overt laws, or private prejudices upheld by law, dictated exclusion from many employment opportunities. Economic restriction had consequences for social status and for access to quality housing and health care. Federal Indian policy prescribed primitive agricultural methods for Aboriginal farmers. Canadian conditions, therefore, added substance to stereotypes and expectations of racially differentiated behaviours. Aboriginal children were consigned to federal boarding schools, and some provinces maintained segregated schools for *African Canadians until the 1960s. Usually, separate education was inferior, so the syndrome of disadvantage continued over generations. Residential segregation was legally enforceable into the 1950s, while hotels, restaurants, and resorts could select their clientele by 'race'. 'Race' was a qualification for civil rights such as the vote and jury service. Even during the recruitment crisis of the First World War, Canada spurned certain minority volunteers, showing that racial mythology prevailed over national interest.

Throughout Canadian history, minority groups challenged these conditions, through petitions to government, court cases, and appeals to fellow citizens. Their campaigns had modest impact until the majority population became sensitive to issues of racial discrimination. Scholars gradually undermined the scientific validity of 'race', and then the Second World War and its identification as a crusade against Nazi racism discredited discriminatory practices. Wartime treatment of *Japanese Canadians evoked, eventually, an awareness that Canada had participated in the problem. Post-war dissolution of European empires further weakened international structures upon which racial doctrine had been built. Canadian society and government became more receptive to minority protests. Nevertheless reform was not automatic, and protracted campaigns were necessary before effective protection was legislated, beginning in the 1950s. Since then provincial and federal governments have introduced measures against racism, including the *Charter of Rights and Freedoms. Distinctions on grounds of 'race' are no longer legal, though the legacy of past policies, evident in income statistics and other indicators, has still not been eliminated from life in Canada. JAMES W. ST G. WALKER

Raddall, Thomas Head (1903–94). Born in England, Raddall grew up in wartime Halifax, joined the merchant fleet, was wireless operator on Sable Island, and began writing short stories. After 1923, as a paper mill bookkeeper, he became a skilled woodsman and naturalist, ranging Queens County's historic Mi'kmaq and pre-Loyalist forests. After 1928 his stories appeared regularly in *Blackwood's*, *Maclean's*, and *Saturday Evening Post*, and in radio and TV scripts.

His best work, set in the French and Napoleonic wars, celebrated the legends of the sea and regional folklore. In 1942, with *His Majesty's Yankees*, he began a series of romantic novels developing Nova Scotia's imperial role, its West Indies connections, Yankee idiom, and sea-bound culture. The best of these, *The Nymph and the Lamp*, was set in Sable Island; the liveliest, a biography of the courtesan Fanny Wentworth, *The Governor's Lady*. His 70 short stories and 11 novels were complemented by a memoir and five histories, including the popular and colourful *Halifax, Warden of the North* and the authoritative *West Novas: A History of the West Nova Scotia Regiment*. Exploiting character and eccentricity, Raddall relied on meticulous research in folkways, costume, dialect, and pioneering skills. He wedded historical accuracy to a colourful imagination, and greatly helped Nova Scotians and other Canadians to recognize themselves in their roots.

ALAN WILSON

Radisson, Pierre-Esprit (1640?–1710), and **Médard Chouart, Sieur des Groseilliers** (1618–95?), explorers and fur traders. Their early vision of Canada's potential gave the British an important foothold in the northern part of North America. Groseilliers—a shrewd strategist—came to New France about 1641 and served the *Jesuit missionaries in Huronia, where his eyes were opened to the country's trading potential. In 1654 he began exploring in earnest, possibly to the headwaters of the Mississippi. Radisson, the ingenious master of every situation, arrived around 1651 and was promptly captured by Mohawk. He lived with the Mohawk for two years, during which time his half-sister became Groseilliers's second wife. Radisson brilliantly recounts the explorers' 1659–60 journey to Lake Superior. Returning to Quebec with a treasure in furs, they were treated as outlaws, so they took their ideas for exploiting the interior to England, where investors, eager to avoid taxation in New France, welcomed their proposal of a northern route via Hudson Bay. The *Hudson's Bay Company was founded in 1670, and Radisson and Groseilliers served it for five years. Disillusionment led them to France, but in 1682 they returned with investors from Quebec. Radisson writes vividly of his own masterly handling of the ensuing conflict for control of the fur trade between English, French, and New Englanders. In 1684 he and his followers switched allegiance to England. The two adventurers probably never met again after 1685: Radisson retired in 1686 to London, where his burial record calls him 'a decay'd gentleman'; Groseilliers died somewhere in New France. GERMAINE WARKENTIN

Ralston, James Layton (1881–1948). Born in Amherst, Nova Scotia, Ralston was a decorated battalion commander in the First World War. Liberal minister of national defence, 1926–30, he won expenditure increases for all three services and compliments from antimilitarists Agnes *Macphail and J.S. *Woodsworth. During the Second World War he was a towering figure in the Mackenzie *King government: a parsimonious finance minister, 1939–40; a detail-minded defence minister, 1940–4. At the outset of the war, King saw the conscientious Ralston as his successor, calling him 'the most unselfish man, I think, that I have ever met'. But the relationship between the two men soured as they clashed over the issue of *conscription of men for overseas military service, a measure King desperately wished to avoid. On 2 November 1944, with pro-conscription sentiment at fever pitch, King forced Ralston's resignation and brought in General A.G.L. *McNaughton as defence minister for one last, ultimately futile, attempt to find volunteers for the war in Europe. NORMAN HILLMER

ranching. The arrival of the *North-West Mounted Police at *Fort Whoop-Up in the autumn of 1874 coincided with the cattlemen's advance on to the grasslands of the North American West and hastened the expansion of the ranching frontier into Canadian territory. It was soon apparent to the police and others that the foothills country around the new police post at Fort Macleod was prime grazing land. Abundant nutritious grass, well-watered and sheltered valleys, combined with the region's characteristic Chinook winds that regularly melted the snow and exposed the grass for winter pasture, made this an exceptionally attractive grazing territory.

Certain Montana and ex–Hudson's Bay Company traders resident in the area were quick to take advantage of the market and security provided by the police and establish small herds in the vicinity of Fort Macleod. The surrender of Aboriginal land title along with the Canadian government's assumed responsibility, under Treaty 7 in 1877, to supply the Blackfoot with beef expanded the local market, giving a further boost to the region's nascent cattle industry. Witnessing the arrival of the first herds between 1874 and 1877, many enlistees in the NWMP, especially those from stock-raising districts in Ontario and Quebec, decided to go into the cattle business at the conclusion of their three-year contracts. Their example was followed by others and the annual incorporation of discharged police into the ranch community over the following two decades exerted a powerful influence upon the region's social development and helped to foster the law and order ethos that distinguished the Canadian ranching frontier.

Assisted by reports in financial journals of the great profits being made by western cattle ranchers, news of the region's ranching potential spread quickly. Policemen and their eastern friends were soon joined by scores of English gentlemen and aristocrats who seemed attracted by a perceived lifestyle as much as a business opportunity. Once the promise of a transcontinental railway was confirmed in 1881, a host of well-connected Canadian businessmen, led by Senator Matthew H. Cochrane and Sir Hugh *Allan, rushed to establish cattle companies and jockey for preferred western grazing lands.

The emerging social character of the Canadian cattle kingdom was shaped primarily by the operating structure of the traditional cattle ranch combined with the character of the population drawn to ranch country. Ranching, unlike farming, required political preferment to obtain a coveted grazing lease as well as substantial capital to purchase a herd, prerequisites that tended to eliminate those on the political and economic margins. Furthermore, the operational structure of the cattle ranch, which rested upon a paid work force of *cowboys managed by a foreman who, on larger ranches, might be supervised by a ranch manager, was well suited to support the style of the English country estate. In contrast to farming, cattle ranching could more readily support imported social values and a lifestyle that helped to set the ranch community apart from the social development of the larger agrarian frontier. Along with the Anglican churches in the foothill valleys, outward manifestations of the cattle country's social character included hunt and polo clubs, winters abroad or on the West Coast, and, for the rancher doing business in Calgary, the comforts of the Ranchmen's Club.

Two other groups had a marked influence on the social and economic development of the foothill cattle kingdom: American and First Nations cowboys. American cowboys, many of whom were hired initially to drive the first cattle herds north into Canada, brought with them vital stock-management skills and a rodeo culture. First Nations people were part of the ranch labour force almost from the beginning. Young men from the Blackfoot and Stoney tribes much more readily identified with the masculine cowboy culture of the ranch country than with the sodbusters' frontier. They soon became skilled participants in the cattlemen's enterprise.

Erosion and transformation of the cattlemen's empire began in the mid-1890s. With defeat of the Conservatives by the Laurier-led Liberals in the 1896 federal election, the ranchers lost their political preference. Spurred on by an aggressive immigration and settlement policy, homesteaders poured into ranch country. While struggling to cope with the sodbusters' advance, the cattlemen suffered an unexpected natural calamity. The winter of 1906–7 locked the region in a deep freeze that lasted for months. Without the indispensable chinooks, range cattle perished by the thousands, often along the settlers' new fence lines. The disaster completed the break-up of most of the remaining large cattle companies into smaller units. Economic transition brought demographic and social change, which was accelerated by the impact of First World War enlistments and casualties sustained by the British ranching class. Greatly altered, the western cattle industry entered a new phase in the interwar period. DAVID H. BREEN

Rand Formula. The Rand Formula provided for the collection of union dues from all employees of a bargaining unit, regardless of whether they were union members or not. Also known as 'compulsory check-off', it was named for a ruling by Supreme Court Justice Ivan Rand (1884–1969) in January 1946, following his arbitration of a strike at the Ford motor plant in Windsor, Ontario. Rand's ruling embodied three central beliefs: that strong trade *unions were crucial to economic and social stability; that the government should accept and assist the role of unions in collective bargaining; and that in return unions should be responsible to and accountable for their members, by, for example, holding secret ballots and rejecting wildcat strikes.

The Rand Formula soon spread and became the model for post-war industrial relations. As such, it completed the formal legalization of unions in 1872 and the expansion of collective bargaining during the Second World War. It may also be viewed as part of the Canadian *welfare state that emerged after 1945. DAVID BRIGHT

rape and seduction. When disputed, the line between coercive and consensual heterosexuality is notoriously difficult to judge. Historically, vastly different understandings of male and female sexual and gender identities made this distinction even more complicated. The history of rape raises vexing questions about social and individual definitions of sexual rights and wrongs.

In a social context in which women could not, for example, vote or own property, ideas about the inviolability of the female body were necessarily different than they are today. So while rape was considered a serious crime in the 19th century, adjudicating stories of sexual conflict brought before the criminal courts was often an exercise in stereotyping. Good women were by definition chaste and sexually innocent. Men, on the other hand, smouldered with sexual passion, but good men—the Anglo middle-class sort—kept their instincts in check. In this climate, sexual disputes between women and men were never straightforward. Even force or violence was not necessarily a reliable indicator of sexual coercion, because some laws, such as that of 'seduction', criminalized voluntary sexual activity. Such offences traded heavily on the distinction between 'good girls' and 'bad girls', or, to use the language of the times, 'maidenly girls' and 'designing women'. These prosecutions served as much to cement a parent's hold over a delinquent daughter as to punish an errant young man.

Ironically, plenty of social institutions and relations were in fact sexually harmful, chiefly to women and children, but have rarely become the subject of intervention, commentary, or criminalization. Over time various bogeymen—especially the dangerous foreigner and the mysterious stranger—have caught the public's attention. Yet as many *domestic servants, daughters, nieces, and wives have learned, patriarchal and hierarchical households were often the source of danger and exploitation. Cultural stereotypes of dangerous men or situations left vast areas of 'private' life unexamined and unsafe. Yet historical studies of sexual crime and the courts indicate that conviction rates decrease dramatically according to the degree of intimacy between the victim and perpetrator. Sexual conflicts between strangers were much more likely to be punished than those between friends or family members.

Historically, rape has been a shameful topic, and it did not find its way onto the feminist or social reform agenda until relatively recently. The often humiliating treatment of rape complainants by the legal system, coupled with the emergence of a revived woman's movement, helped to politicize the issue in the 1960s. A new era of support services for victims of sexual violence, as well as demands that complainants be treated with respect by the legal system, has changed the pubic discourse of sexual crime dramatically in recent decades. KAREN DUBINSKY

Rebellion of 1837–8. From the autumn of 1837 to the early months of 1839, Upper and Lower Canada experienced a major political upheaval, with recurrent outbreaks of violence in both provinces. Historians have traditionally deconstructed these events and analysed the separate fragments—hence the popularity of the plural phrase 'Rebellions of 1837–8'—but I argue that the various episodes of rioting, constitutional breakdown, military confrontation, and martial law are best understood as interconnected elements of a single revolutionary event. The Canadian Rebellion was a characteristic phenomenon of the Age of Revolution when, around the Atlantic world, established regimes were being challenged in the name of 'the people' and of 'the nation'.

For several years before 1837, tensions had been building in both the Canadas. Politics were most polarized in Lower Canada, where the Parti patriote, led by Louis-Joseph *Papineau, called for constitutional changes that would give the elected assembly and the voters of the province greater control over governmental affairs. The various Upper Canadian factions that rallied under the banner of 'Reform' had a different list of grievances (their concern focused on the clique of office holders known as the *Family Compact), but their broadly democratic stance was in harmony with that of the *Patriotes. Indeed, the most radical Reformer, William Lyon *Mackenzie, was distinguished partly by his staunch support for the Papineau party. Yet clear differences separated the opposition movements of Upper and Lower Canada, the French-Canadian nationalism of the Patriotes setting them apart most obviously from their counterparts in the upper province. Moreover, public opinion in Upper Canada was far less supportive of radical reform than in Lower Canada, where an overwhelming majority gave consistent support to Papineau's party.

Simmering conflict in Lower Canada came to a head in May 1837, when word reached the colony of Lord John Russell's Ten Resolutions, by which the mother country not only rejected Patriote demands, but actually rolled back the financial powers of the elected assembly. *Representative government had by then ceased to function and, as popular protests proliferated across both provinces, troops were brought in from the Maritimes to reinforce colonial authority. In the rural districts around Montreal, the *habitants were becoming active. By October, insurgent militias were forming and loyalist officers and magistrates were being forced to resign in favour of popularly elected local leaders. Agrarian issues—particularly opposition to tithes and seigneurial rents—were coming to the fore as peasants imposed a radical social agenda on the middle-class Patriote movement.

Armed conflict broke out when General Colbourne sent troops to crush the rural 'sedition' and arrest the Patriote leadership. Habitant militiamen successfully defended St Denis (23 November 1837), but the British later scored decisive victories at the Battles of St Charles (25 November) and St Eustache (14 December). Meanwhile, Mackenzie felt the time was right for a sympathetic rising in Upper Canada. Taking advantage of the turmoil, and wanting to take some pressure off the Lower Canadian insurgents, he led a march down Yonge Street towards Toronto (5 December). Loyal militia units easily routed the attackers. By the end of December, the revolt had been defeated and most of the leaders from both provinces were refugees in the United States.

In the months that followed, while much of Canada remained under military occupation, the border states emerged as the main centre of revolutionary activity. Americans and Canadian exiles formed secret societies—'Hunters' Lodges' or 'Frères chasseurs'—dedicated to overthrowing British rule and setting up independent republics in the Canadas. Several cross-border incursions occurred in Upper Canada, the most serious at Prescott ('Battle of the Windmill'). A Patriote invasion of Lower Canada led by Robert Nelson, coordinated with rural risings across the southern district of Montreal, resulted in considerable loss of life before it was defeated in November 1838. Widespread arrests and detentions followed in the wake of this second round of fighting; 14 men were hanged and 108 transported to Australia. British regulars and loyal militia burned hundreds of homes.

The bloodshed and property damage tell only part of the story of 1837–8. Along with the suspension of parliamentary government and the setting aside of civil liberties, they are symptomatic of a fundamental breakdown in legitimate rule. The republican-inspired opposition was decisively defeated in both provinces, so this can hardly be called a revolution. Nevertheless, it was a revolutionary event, and one with important and lasting consequences. Alerted to the severity of popular discontent and to the striking ineffectiveness of colonial government, the British authorities engineered a thorough overhaul, rationalizing and strengthening the Canadian state.

In his famous *Report*, Lord *Durham concluded in 1839 that the conflict had not really been about politics at all; rather, it had been a matter of 'two nations [i.e. French and English Canadians] warring in the bosom of a single state'. The phrase was clever, the analysis highly misleading (the ethnic strife he witnessed was mainly the result, not the cause, of political conflict). He suggested that Upper and Lower Canada be united as a first step towards the anglicization of the French Canadians. This measure, instituted in 1841 under the *Act of Union, failed to achieve the assimilation of the French Canadians, but it did help to foster the impression that the amalgamation of Upper and Lower Canada was a punitive measure designed to bring about the political marginalization of French Canada. ALLAN GREER

reciprocity. The Reciprocity Treaty, 1854–66, permitted near free trade in a narrow defined list of primary or slightly processed products (e.g., lumber, fish, and grains), created zones of mutual access to fishing grounds between Atlantic British North America and the United States, and nominally provided some free canal access for both parties. The treaty grew out of the apparent needs of the British North American colonies to replace preferred admission to British markets lost by the removal of the Corn Laws, the Navigation Laws, and ancillary elements of British policy during commercial depression in 1847–9. Resultant annexationist sentiment in British North America made reciprocity the obvious alternative. Several years of debate and government-subsidized, purportedly private, cross-border lobbying led to the treaty as formally negotiated for the colonies by the governor general of the Canadas, Lord Elgin, as British plenipotentiary. The treaty created a one-time increase in trade and fostered a 'trade of convenience' but did not cause structural economic change. Nonetheless, it held mythic power, and the US Senate's abrogation in March 1865 caused considerable distress in the colonies. The treaty's end, rooted in northern US hostility to some British North American support for the Confederacy during the Civil War, and the colonies' failure to pursue reciprocity in manufactured goods, came one year later. Canadian Confederation, with its creation of a national commercial market, was seen as compensation for the abrogation. After all, the 1854 treaty had permitted a common market in the listed primary products among the colonies.

The issue figured in John A. *Macdonald's negotiations leading to the 1871 Treaty of Washington (when proposed 'national policy' tariff increases were unsuccessful in budging Americans towards reciprocity), and again in informal negotiations in Washington led by George *Brown in 1874. Liberal advocacy of 'unrestricted reciprocity', an economic cure-all of ill-defined substance, was successfully painted as disguised annexation to the US by Conservatives in the election of 1891. Reciprocity then faded as a central political issue until 1910, when, after American initiative, Laurier sought to satisfy growing free-trade sentiment in agrarian Canada by advocating a broad free-trade agreement to include many manufactured goods. A resultant protectionist furore helped to defeat his government in 1911. Notions of reciprocal *free trade with the US have found formal contemporary expression with the *Auto Pact (1965) and the controversial Free Trade Agreement (1989).

BEN FORSTER

Reconstruction, Department of. The embodiment of the Mackenzie King government's policy for the conversion of the Canadian economy from war to peace at the end of the Second World War. Established by statute in October 1944 as the Department of Reconstruction, it became the Department of Reconstruction and Supply on 1 January 1946. It was finally wound up in January 1950. The central idea behind the department was to apply planning to the economy so as to combat an anticipated economic slump like the one at the end of the First World War. Not everyone agreed with this notion; among the dissenters was the department's first (and most powerful) minister, C.D. *Howe. Accordingly, Howe reshaped the department in his own optimistic image. Its planning functions remained rudimentary; its main importance was to offer incentives to industry to convert to civilian production in an orderly and politically palatable fashion. However, the department's existence reassured a nervous public opinion, as did the government's promises to maintain 'a high and stable level of employment', in the words of a White Paper Howe issued in April 1945. In November 1948 Howe left the department to a more junior minister, Robert Winters, whose main function was to keep it nominally in business until a new departmental structure more suited to a stable peacetime economy could be developed. ROBERT BOTHWELL

Reconstruction Party. Founded in July 1935 to contest the federal election in October, the party gained 390,000 votes and almost 9 per cent of the popular vote, but only its leader, Henry Herbert Stevens, won a seat in the House of Commons. In 1939 he returned to the Conservative caucus; his party had fizzled out well before then.

The party originated in a split that developed between the small- and big-business wings of the Conservative Party as the *Great Depression deepened. Hurt by the allegedly predatory purchasing and pricing practices of department stores, supermarkets, canners, fish processors, and tobacco manufacturers, entrepreneurs such as the clothing manufacturer Warren K. Cook gained the sympathy of Stevens, a Vancouver businessman who was minister of trade and commerce in R.B. *Bennett's Conservative government. A parliamentary committee appointed to investigate the business practices of large firms led in turn to the Royal Commission on *Price Spreads. The evidence presented to these bodies caused Stevens to criticize monopoly power in business and then, in October 1934, to resign from the cabinet. The party formed in 1935 was an unpromising gamble whose chief consequence was to increase the Liberal electoral majority. Fatally injured by the Depression, the Conservative government had been doomed anyway.

MICHIEL HORN

Red River cart. Often traced to *North West Company trader Alexander Henry, the Red River cart first appeared around 1801 at Pembina in the Red River Valley. The style of the cart, constructed entirely of wood and fastened with leather, originated in French and Scottish traditions and soon became indispensable to overland freighting on the Prairies. The high, well-dished wheels provided stability and could be removed to float loaded carts across waterways. *Metis peoples used the cart to haul goods and furs, or meat and robes from the *buffalo hunt. Brigades of carts, often numbering in the hundreds and pulled by oxen or horses, travelled the trails between Red River and St Paul, Minnesota, as well as the Carlton Trail between *Fort Garry and Fort Edmonton. Renowned for the loud squeal of their ungreased wheels—the poet Charles Mair wrote that 'a thousand of these wheels all groaning and creaking at one time is a sound never to be forgotten'—the Red River cart was eventually replaced by steamboats and later the railway.

ROBERT J. COUTTS

Red River Resistance. Less than six months after the new Dominion of Canada was proclaimed a nation, Parliament debated seven resolutions designed to set the stage for expansion of the fledgling country across the vast prairies to the Pacific Ocean. William McDougall, the MP from Lanark, Ontario, who had shepherded those resolutions through Parliament, subsequently accompanied Sir George-Étienne *Cartier to London to arrange the transfer of the territories of the *Hudson's Bay Company to Canada. The HBC agreed to sell, the arrangements were completed in March 1869, and the Canadians returned home to administer the transfer, scheduled to occur on 1 December 1869. None of the parties to the deal—Canada, the British government, the HBC—felt any need to consult with either the Council of *Assiniboia (the government of the *Red River settlement) or the residents of Red River at any point in the proceedings. The Canadians intended to administer Red River and the North-West Territory as a colony, with a lieutenant-governor and an appointed council. Few other details of the new administration were set out in advance. William McDougall was appointed lieutenant-governor, and he was given a small suite of appointed councillors, none of whom had ever set foot in the region. Thus was set in motion a chain of blunders that would end with Canadian intentions in tatters.

The Canadian government had already dispatched to Red River an unpopular team opposed by the Metis of the settlement to build the *Dawson Road, and compounded its mistakes by sending in advance of the transfer a team of surveyors. The local government in Red River warned the surveyors that 'as soon as the survey commences the Halfbreeds and Indians will at once come forward and assert their rights to the land and probably stop the work'. This is exactly what happened in October 1869, when Louis *Riel led a group that stood on the surveying chain and told the surveyors to stop. Soon after, Joseph *Howe, the Canadian secretary of state for the provinces, arrived in the settlement on a fact-finding expedition. Howe discovered a settlement with a functioning political and legal system and consulted with many residents. He did not talk with Riel or any of the *Metis, who were already organizing to keep McDougall out of the country. The lieutenant-governor designate was so informed when he arrived at Pembina. As secretary of the National Committee of the Metis, Riel subsequently told the Council of Assiniboia that his people objected to a new government that had not consulted with them and had not outlined the terms and conditions under which it would administer the country. He added that the Metis expected to be joined by 'their English-speaking fellow countrymen' in defence of their 'common rights'.

In early November the Metis occupied without opposition the HBC fort at Upper *Fort Garry. They then invited the anglophone mixed bloods to meet with them to 'consider the present future state of this Country and to adopt such measures as may be deemed best for the future welfare of the state'. The two groups met several times in November to debate policy. They could agree on the need to set terms before the Canadians—and even on the terms—but disagreed on whether this should be done before or after McDougall was admitted into the territory. In the end, the Metis refused to budge from their position that Canada had to come to the bargaining table with the necessary rights embodied in an act of Parliament as a preliminary to negotiation. When the mixed bloods refused to accept this stance, Riel told them, 'We are going to work and obtain the guarantee of our rights and yours. You will come to share them in the end.'

Because of the unrest, the Canadian government had decided to postpone the transfer of the territory until it was pacified. Unfortunately, the impatient McDougall was not informed of this decision, and he improperly proclaimed the extension of the Queen's writ to Red River on 1 December 1869. McDougall's proclamation set into motion the Canadian Party, a relatively small number of local residents and Canadian officials who fully supported the government of Canada and the transfer. An armed party of these individuals, led by Dr John Schultz, barricaded themselves in Schultz's store, were forced to surrender, and were taken prisoner to Fort Garry on 7 December. The next day Riel issued a 'Declaration of the People', announcing the creation of a provisional government to replace the Council of Assiniboia. The Canadians continued to compound their blunders. Instead of sending emissaries empowered to negotiate terms, Ottawa sent a team of representatives with instructions only to reassure the local populace of Canada's good intentions. The people remained sceptical.

Two mass meetings with Canadian emissary Donald A. *Smith, held outdoors in the bitter cold on 19 and 20 January 1870, resulted in Smith's agreement to take back to Canada a statement of what Red River regarded as essential to its acceptance of Canadian rule. Louis Riel proposed a convention of 40 delegates, equally divided between the two language groups, to prepare a 'List of Rights' to be debated and ratified. In early February the Canadian prisoners who had not escaped were released, and three delegates were appointed to go to Ottawa to negotiate admission of Red River to Confederation. At this point, the Canadian Party again stirred itself into action. A force of Canadian-born settlers, led by Maj. C.A. Boulton (one of the surveyors) and including Thomas Scott, left Portage la Prairie to join up with Schultz at Kildonan. The goal of this action was to get the prisoners liberated; when they were released, the armed parties disbanded reluctantly. On 17 February, a group of these men on their way back to Portage was arrested and imprisoned by Riel's men. To this point Riel had orchestrated his moves brilliantly. He had kept his Metis and the mixed bloods together under the aegis of the provisional government, and terms for the entrance of Red River to the Canadian union had been generated. Meanwhile, uncertain of the outcome of events in Red River, the Canadian cabinet prepared a military force, to consist of British regulars and Canadian volunteers, that could be employed if necessary.

At this point Louis Riel made an error of judgment. He allowed one of the prisoners, Thomas Scott, to be tried by a Metis tribunal and sentenced to death, for reasons that have never been properly explained. Scott was subsequently executed on 4 March 1870. Riel apparently did not think much about this fatality, the first that had occurred in the course of Red River's resistance. But the treatment of Scott would have enormous repercussions in Ontario, which had been searching for some excuse to punish Riel and Red River for its refusal to accept Canadian manifest destiny without dispute. Although nobody in Red River knew that Scott had been a member of the *Orange Order, a dominant force in Protestant Ontario, this connection was used in the East by a secret society called *Canada First to stir up public reaction against the Metis. Soon the entire province of Ontario was up in arms about the dastardly 'murder' of an innocent Orangeman for his loyalty to Canada. By the time the Red River delegates arrived in Ottawa, large portions of Canada were inflamed against Riel and his provisional government.

Canada refused to meet officially with the delegates, led by Abbé Noel Ritchot, or to recognize the provisional government. Negotiations were conducted privately. Most of the List of Rights brought forward by the delegates were accepted and embodied in the Manitoba Act. A small area around Winnipeg to be called *Manitoba was granted provincial status. A large amount of land (1.4 million acres) would be set aside for the Metis, and bilingual services were guaranteed. On the other hand, the Red River negotiators had been carefully instructed not to enter into discussions with Canada unless an official amnesty was granted for all acts committed during the unrest. The Canadians managed to persuade the Red River people, without putting anything in writing, that such an amnesty would be forthcoming. Whether the Canadians would keep any better faith over its land guarantees to the Metis was another matter. The prospects were not good for, despite the passage of the Manitoba Act, the government insisted on sending its military expedition to Red River, led by Colonel Garnet *Wolseley. The expedition entered Red River in late August of 1870 as a conquering army, with punitive intentions against the members of the provisional government, including Louis Riel, who was forced to flee Winnipeg. On 6 September 1870 Adams Archibald was formally installed as lieutenant-governor of Manitoba. Whether or not Manitoba was an autonomous province or one effectually occupied and controlled by the Canadian military was another matter entirely, as was the question of whether the Metis were to be fairly treated by the Canadian government. J.M. BUMSTED

Red River settlement. The establishment of a settlement at the forks of the Red and Assiniboine Rivers was one of the reasons that Lord *Selkirk, a Scottish peer, gave for accepting a grant of 116,000 square miles from the *Hudson's Bay Company in 1811, over the strenuous objections of the partners of the *North West Company. The settlement, physically begun in 1812 by a small party of servants headed by its 'governor', Miles Macdonell, never became a formal colony of Great Britain. Its early years were fraught with conflict, as it inevitably became involved in the fur trade war between the HBC and the NWC for control of the West. The problem of feeding the settlers Selkirk was shipping to Red River from the Highlands of Scotland led Macdonell to prohibit the export of *pemmican from the region in 1814. This action led the NWC to entice most of the settlers, who were extremely unhappy with the primitive conditions under which they lived, to move to Upper Canada in 1815 and to drive the remainder out of the area. Led by the fur trader Colin Robertson, a rump of settlers returned to the forks in August 1815 and were joined in September by another contingent from Scotland led by Governor Robert Semple.

After almost a year of sparring, a party of armed settlers met a party of mounted *Metis horsemen at *Seven Oaks in June 1816; in the ensuing melee, most of the settler party were killed and the remainder were again driven from the area. An armed expedition of Swiss mercenaries restored the settlement by force to Selkirk in January 1817. He visited it later that year and granted land to those few Scots settlers who had returned and to a number of the mercenary soldiers who accompanied him. Selkirk also purchased land rights from the resident First Nations. In return for an annual quitrent of 200 pounds of 'good merchantable tobacco', the chiefs granted to the King an area extending six miles in all directions from Fort Douglas and Fort Daer, as well as land extending two miles from the banks on either side of the Red and Assiniboine Rivers.

After 1817, the settlement was beset by a series of natural disasters that hampered its growth. An invasion of grasshoppers began in 1817. A party of 200 Swiss settlers arriving in 1821 found that conditions continued to be extremely primitive. The problems of the Swiss led the Selkirk estate to decide to people the settlement with redundant fur trade employees, chiefly mixed bloods. The Swiss and most of the other European settlers abandoned Red River after a disastrous flood in 1826, leaving behind a handful of original Scots settlers, a few HBC employees, and increasing numbers of mixed bloods, both francophone and anglophone. The Roman Catholic Church had sent its first missionaries in 1818 and the Anglican Church followed in 1820. By 1830 both denominations had established churches and schools throughout the settlement.

In 1835 the Selkirk family sold its interests in the settlement to the HBC, which established a formal government and judicial system in a series of steps beginning that year. The Council of *Assiniboia was separate from the HBC, although its members—intended to represent the broad constituency of the settlement—were appointed by it. Revenue came from import duties irregularly collected at *York Factory. A fully developed judicial system was also in place after 1839, supplementing the establishment of the General Quarterly Court of Assiniboia in 1835 with a 'recorder' serving as chief judicial officer and a series of magistrates courts. Cases were heard before a 12-man jury of six francophones and six anglophones. The Earl of Southesk in 1859 described the centre of the settlement, the village that would become Winnipeg, as an important and bustling administrative place. It became more important when the *Nor'-Wester* newspaper was founded in late 1859. The economy relied heavily on the *fur trade.

Although in its early days Red River had been extremely difficult to access from the outside world, steamboat transportation service from the south was begun in 1859. By the early 1860s the settlement was less than 400 miles from a railhead in Minnesota, and a regular postal service run through the American post office worked extremely effectively. By the time Canada purchased the West from the HBC the settlement had a population of over 12,000 (10,000 of them mixed bloods, fairly evenly divided between francophone and anglophone) with a fully articulated political and cultural life that the Canadians attempted to ignore to their peril.

J.M. BUMSTED

red scare. In the aftermath of the Russian Revolution of 1917, the Western world, including Canada and the United States, was gripped by a 'red scare'—a widespread belief that communists, or communist sympathizers, were working to undermine domestic security. Spurred on by the stress and anxiety of the Great War, the red scare placed a premium on loyalty, making dissent of any kind suspect, even treasonous. In Canada, for example, the federal government created the RCMP in 1920 to investigate and, if necessary, repress suspected subversives.

Although the red scare waned as a mass phenomenon during the 1920s, anti-communism, which remained an article of faith for conservative unions and the Canadian and American governments, surged again during the Great Depression and the Second World War. Allies during the war, the United States and the Soviet Union became bitter antagonists afterwards, as each country tried to remake the world in its own image. Known as the Cold War, this rivalry reshaped international relations and domestic life on both sides of the 'Iron Curtain' for nearly five decades. Canada was swept up in the Cold War, and experienced a renewed red scare of its own—developments captured graphically by the *Gouzenko affair (1946) and the suicide of Canadian diplomat Herbert *Norman (1957). During this time, the RCMP subjected bureaucrats to intense security vetting, and spearheaded efforts to exclude homosexuals from the civil service; their sexuality, the Mounties feared, made them easy targets for blackmail by Soviet agents. Public policy was shaped by the red scare too. By the late 1940s Ottawa routinely tested new immigrants for communist sympathies, despite having lifted most restrictions on Nazi war criminals and their collaborators. In other areas of political life, the red scare was more virulent. During the 1940s and early 1950s the Canadian Seamen's Union, a strong, national union with a left-wing leadership, was beaten into submission by the combined efforts of mainstream *unions, employers, and governments in Ottawa and Washington. Other unions, like the International Woodworkers of America, were torn apart by internal battles bent on ousting 'red' members.

By the late 1960s and early 1970s the red scare's stranglehold on political discourse was starting to loosen. In the United States, campaigns for civil rights, women's emancipation, and Black power were gaining momentum; so, too, was the student movement, which opposed the Vietnam war. In Canada, similar organizations emerged, although they often came with a nationalist twist: to them, the federal government's support for the Cold War, and the red scare that came with it, was as much about the erosion of civil liberties as it was about the erosion of the nation's sovereignty. As questions of loyalty waned, questions of American dominance came to the fore.

ANDREW PARNABY AND GREGORY S. KEALEY

Red Tories. The 'Red Tory' is a curious political specimen. It appeared in Canada in the mid-20th century as the British Empire/Commonwealth declined and its legacy appeared increasingly uncertain. The concept of 'Red Toryism' derived its strength from the domination of federal Canadian politics by the *Liberal Party, whose conservative approach to social welfare and reluctance to participate in British Commonwealth/Empire activities irritated intellectuals, church leaders, and journalists in English Canada.

The socialist Gad Horowitz traced Red Toryism to the *Loyalists, who, he claimed, brought to Canada a belief in an organic society and a rejection of American individualism. Horowitz was less influential than George *Grant, scion of a distinguished Canadian family and a bitter foe of the post-war Liberal governments. Grant argued in several books, notably **Lament for a Nation*, that Canada's identity derived from its monarchical, British, and conservative tradition. Without such an identity, Canada would vanish as if in a dream.

The Red Tory tradition deeply influenced many Canadian conservatives. Red Tories such as Dalton Camp, Joe Clark, David Macdonald, and others argued that the 'Tory tradition' was fundamentally different from the right-wing conservatism of the United States. In the 1980s, those arguments influenced the Mulroney government in its approach to social welfare, South Africa, and international politics. However, the rise of the Reform Party/Canadian Alliance shattered the Conservative Party and the Red Tory tradition. It has little force in Canadian politics in the 21st century. JOHN ENGLISH

Re Eskimos. In 1939 the *Supreme Court of Canada declared that Eskimos (Inuit) were Indians and thereby the responsibility of the Canadian government. Throughout the early 20th century the legal status of *Inuit was uncertain. In 1924 an amendment to the *Indian Act made the Indian Affairs Branch their overseers, but the government refused to act directly on their behalf, fearing the cost implications, and worried about repeating the follies of the Indian Act. Health, education, and relief were basically left to the trading companies and the missionaries; Inuit within Quebec were considered the responsibility of that province. With the onset of bad economic times in the North, exacerbated by the Depression, the plight of Inuit worsened. When the Quebec government approached Ottawa for reimbursement of Inuit relief monies, as it had successfully done in the past, it was rebuffed. The Canadian government argued that these Inuit were citizens of Quebec and thus the province's responsibility. Quebec took the matter to the Supreme Court, arguing that Eskimos were Indians under the British North America Act, section 91(24), and thus wards of Canada. The court ruled in Quebec's favour. Canada all but ignored the 1939 decision, and would ultimately take the position that Inuit were ordinary Canadians requiring special attention.

RICHARD J. DIUBALDO

referendum. A device for referring an important question of public policy to the voters. It is one of the several ways of involving the larger public in government decision-making. Imported into western Canada from the United States at the beginning of the 20th century by supporters of American populism, the referendum can be traced back to 16th-century Switzerland. Support for referendums has generally been strongest among supporters of parties such as *Social Credit, Reform, and Alliance. Since the debate over Quebec sovereignty entered the Canadian political agenda in the 1970s, the province of Quebec has given strong support to referendums as a tool for gaining public support of government-approved constitutional policies.

The referendum is a direct democracy device that clashes with the principles of parliamentary responsible government. It is often a risky venture for a government to hold a referendum as there is no assurance that the electorate's view will match the government's. The 1995 defeat, by a narrow margin, of the *Parti Québécois-supported question on an independent Quebec is a case in point.

Only three national referendums have been held in Canada: over *prohibition (1898); concerning *conscription (1942); and on the *Charlottetown Constitutional Accord (1992). In the 1942 vote the Mackenzie King government took the issue of conscription to the nation. Freed from their campaign promise not to introduce conscription during the Second World War, the Liberals were then in a position to adopt, as they did in 1944, such a policy. The Charlottetown Accord of 1992, which resulted from an agreement approved by the federal, provincial, and territorial governments to fundamentally alter the *constitution, was rejected nationally by a 55 to 45 per cent margin.

Technically, Canada's three national referendums were in fact plebiscites, as the returns were not legally binding on the governments. For any government to have ignored the results of the votes, however, would have been politically unwise and a major affront to accepted democratic practice.

Referendums have more frequently been employed at the provincial level to help resolve questions of primarily local interest. There have been provincial referendums on such diverse questions as the introduction of agricultural marketing boards, prohibition of sales of alcoholic beverages, and acceptance of daylight saving time. A 1948 referendum in Newfoundland resulted in that province joining Confederation. Quebec has employed referendums in two critical votes, in 1980 and 1995, on the future of that province in Canada. Prince Edward Island held a referendum in 1980 on whether a fixed link with mainland Canada should be established, and in 2002 the province of British Columbia held a controversial referendum on Aboriginal treaty rights.

JOHN C. COURTNEY AND DANIEL MACFARLANE

See also NEWFOUNDLAND REFERENDA.

reformatories. Before the mid-19th century prisoners in Canada were not classified or segregated by age, gender, character, or *crime. Consequently, men, women, and young people were detained together in local jails, where violent offenders mixed with drunkards, prostitutes, the insane, and habitual deviants. Nineteenth-century prison reformers such as Inspector J.W. Langmuir and the Prisoners' Aid Association argued that such mixing reinforced promiscuity among females, confirmed idle habits among boys, and permitted the sexual abuse of women. Growing scepticism about the practice of incarcerating youth and women alongside hardened male offenders led reform-minded individuals to favour American- and European-style reformatories. Separate reformatories and industrial schools for boys, which preceded government attempts to reclaim women and girls, were most prevalent in Ontario.

In 1857 an Act for Establishing Prisons for Young Offenders authorized the creation of 'reformatory prisons' in Upper and Lower Canada, where deviant boys could be 'detained and corrected, and receive such instruction and be subject to such discipline, as [was] most conducive to their reformation'. By 1859, two reformatories had been built, the first in Quebec at Île-aux-Noix, the second at Penetanguishene, Ontario. Their allure was a promise to save young boys from a life of crime by separating them from the damaging influence of hardened adult criminals and providing them with education and religious instruction. Discontent among child savers about Penetanguishene's location, operation, and treatment program led to its closure and provided the impetus for the creation of industrial school legislation in the 1870s. Established to mould boys into law-abiding Christian citizens, industrial schools taught deviant working-class youth the virtues of self-control, industry, and bourgeois civility. Modelled after a well-regulated family, they employed a five-pronged plan of educational, physical, social, economic, and religious training.

Reform institutions had been working to reclaim Ontario's boys for over half a century before the first reformatory for men was erected in 1916 near Guelph. Accepting young men up to the age of 20, the institution attempted to instill good work habits in inmates. Shortly after it opened its doors, however, the initial enthusiasm that surrounded the reformatory turned to disdain.

The emergence of the Andrew Mercer Reformatory for Females in 1874 in Toronto reflected growing sentiment that women required a different kind of reformation. Mercer, the first institution devoted solely to women and the first to be called a 'reformatory', adopted a program of motherly supervision and maternal guidance directed towards first-time and non-serious offenders. Religious, domestic, and moral training, along with strict discipline and restraint, characterized the program, the goal of which was to instill continued dependence and submission. The goals of reformers for separate institutions for women were soon thwarted by short sentences and inadequate facilities.

BRYAN R. HOGEVEEN AND JOANNE C. MINAKER

Reformers. The name adopted by critics of the authoritarian political order prevailing in Upper Canada under the *Constitutional Act, 1791. Populist reformers such as Marshall Bidwell and William Lyon *Mackenzie favoured US-style democracy; an elitist wing, led by William and Robert *Baldwin, preferred British-style *responsible government. The populists were ascendant during the 1830s, but after Mackenzie's rebellion the Baldwinites prevailed and campaigned during the 1840s for responsible government under the Union of 1840. Success in 1848–9 revived the Reform movement's latent populism in the form of the *Clear Grit movement, and a schism in 1854 saw most Baldwinites unite with the Conservative Party. George *Brown then assumed leadership of the Clear Grits and channelled their populism into a campaign against 'Lower Canadian domination'—the supposed oppression of Upper Canada by French-Canadian clericalism and Montreal financial interests. In 1864 Brown joined George-Étienne *Cartier, leader of the *bleus*, in a proposal to establish Upper and Lower Canada as autonomous provinces within the United *Province of Canada. This project was achieved in expanded form in 1867 as the Dominion of Canada. After Confederation, the Reform movement thrived politically as Ontario's champion against the supposed domination of Quebec and its Ontario minions led by John A. *Macdonald.

PAUL ROMNEY

refugees. Historically, Canada's refugee policy has been anything but consistent. For much of its history Canada closed its doors to those attempting to escape persecution in their homeland. More recently, it has been among the most receptive of nations in welcoming those seeking sanctuary. Its response has always been motivated by the prevailing economic and political conditions in the country.

Canada's first major wave of immigrants, the United Empire *Loyalists, was perhaps also its first refugee contingent, although many historians believe they were not refugees but rather settlers from the Thirteen Colonies who preferred to live under their old British flag rather than the new American one. The second wave of refugees comprised the 30,000 fugitive slaves who made their way north on the *Underground Railway.

For the first 50 years following Confederation Canada had no refugee policy. It did not need one. Anyone who wanted to come to Canada could come, so long as he or she was of white, European background. Blacks and Asians were, for the most part, barred. In 1914 the Canadian government even forcibly turned around a ship, the **Komagata*

Maru, full of some 375 *Sikh and Hindu refugees after a two-month siege in the waters outside Vancouver.

In the 1930s, Canada turned its back on the hundreds of thousands of German *Jews fleeing the Nazis. Bowing to the pressure of pervasive anti-Semitic attitudes and the mounting economic crisis, Canada admitted only 4,000 Jewish refugees, a dismal number that was a mere fraction of those granted sanctuary by other Western democracies. Efforts by pro-refugee lobby groups such as the Canadian National Committee on Refugees fell on deaf ears because the Liberal government of Mackenzie *King believed that allowing in Jewish refugees would alienate Quebec and disrupt Canadian unity. Following the war Canadian policy changed. With a booming economy and a need for workers, Canada accepted 100,000 refugees from the *displaced persons camps dotting Europe, and in 1957 it admitted 37,000 Hungarians fleeing the Soviet invasion of their country. By the 1980s Canada had become perhaps the most generous of nations in allowing in refugees: American draft dodgers, Czechs evading Soviet troops, Ugandan Asians deported by the notorious Idi Amin, Chileans running from a military dictatorship, and, most striking, nearly 100,000 Vietnamese 'boat people' fleeing for their very lives. Although many Canadians feel their country's refugees policy is too liberal and open to abuse by bogus claimants, and although the government has imposed some restrictions, Canada still admits more that 20,000 refugees every year. IRVING ABELLA

Refus global. Launched at the Librairie tranquille in Montreal on 9 August 1948, and signed by 15 members of the *Automatistes group, the principal essay of this manifesto was written by the painter Paul-Émile Borduas, with texts by Bruno Cormier (later a psychoanalyst), poet Claude Gauvreau, painter Fernand Leduc, and Françoise Sullivan (then a dancer), and illustrations of their works by members of the group. *Refus global* not only challenged the traditional values of Quebec ('To hell with the holy-water-sprinkler and the *tuque*!') but also fostered an opening up of Quebec society to international thought. It strongly advocated the need for liberation, if not 'resplendent anarchy', and anticipated the coming of a 'new collective hope'. These sentiments were enough to cause the authorities to have Borduas removed from his post at the École du Meuble, where he had been teaching since 1937. The press echoed the government. By January 1949 no fewer than a hundred newspaper and magazine articles had condemned the manifesto, though some voices, Claude and Pierre Gauvreau in particular, came to its defence. In each decade since its publication the manifesto's importance has been underlined in Quebec. In 1998 especially, marking its 50th anniversary, major Canadian museums, the press (*Le Devoir* published a 'cahier spécial'), and publishing houses celebrated the event with special exhibitions and publications. FRANÇOIS-MARC GAGNON

Regina. Founded in 1882 when the *Canadian Pacific Railway main line reached Pile of Bones (Wascana) Creek, Regina was named in honour of Queen Victoria. The CPR chose the site of the town, subdivided the land into a simple rectangular grid, and determined the location of Regina's downtown business district by the placement of its station and freight yards. At the same time the federal government moved the capital of the *North-West Territories from Battleford to Regina and established the headquarters of the *North-West Mounted Police there (until 1920). The town grew slowly at first, but in the early 20th century newcomers began to arrive in substantial numbers. Regina became a city in 1903, and the interim provincial capital of *Saskatchewan two years later. It gained the permanent honour in 1906, beating off a strong challenge from Saskatoon. A handsome legislative building was soon after erected on the bald prairie south of Wascana Lake (an artificial body of water created by damming the creek of the same name).

Cereal agriculture dominated the economy of the new province and of its capital city. Regina became a major shipping and distribution point, particularly for farm implements. Most major banks and trust and insurance companies established their provincial head offices there. By 1911 Regina (population 30,213) was Saskatchewan's largest city. The boom mentality of the period survived the destruction wrought by a 1912 tornado, which claimed 28 lives and caused $1.2 million worth of property damage. However, an economic depression in 1913 and the outbreak of the First World War temporarily halted Regina's growth. Through the war years and the two decades that followed, the city alternated between periods of hard times of increasing severity and periods of modest prosperity. It took another world war to bring real prosperity to Saskatchewan agriculture and hence to Regina. Retail and wholesale trade rebounded as commodity prices and farm incomes rose. Since the Second World War Regina has enjoyed steady though unspectacular growth. Its population more than doubled from 71,319 to 164,313 between 1951 and 1981, in part through immigration from outside the province but more from a general population shift from farm to city within Saskatchewan. This period also witnessed a substantial influx of Native people to the city.

The provincial government continues to be a major factor in Regina's economy, and took the lead in creating Wascana Centre, a 920-ha park in the heart of the city. The most significant federal government presence is the *Royal Canadian Mounted Police, whose training facilities have been located there since 1885. With a population of 178,225 in 2001, the city of Regina is also the most important retail, distribution, and service centre in southern Saskatchewan. J. WILLIAM BRENNAN

Regina Manifesto. The program of the *Co-operative Commonwealth Federation adopted at its founding convention in Regina in July 1933. Its 14 points outlined a planned social order in which 'production, distribution, and exchange' would be regulated to ensure 'the supplying of human needs and not the making of profits'. While Canadian socialist parties had previously been overwhelmingly working class in composition, the Regina

Manifesto was written by academics led by historian Frank *Underhill of the *League for Social Reconstruction. It proposed a key role for experts who would guide the economy, run 'socialized' industries, and address social problems under the watchful eye of a socialist government. An array of socialists, farmers, and middle-class people supported the manifesto, although some socialists on the left wing of the CCF charged that it evaded difficult questions of how to challenge capitalism. Ironically, as the CCF evolved to support a 'mixed economy' that would include significant capitalist participation, those who most identified themselves as socialists in the party clung to the manifesto and its declaration that 'No CCF Government will rest content until it has eradicated capitalism.' The 1956 Winnipeg Declaration that supplanted the Regina Manifesto made no such claim.

JAMES NAYLOR

Regional Economic Expansion, Department of. The 1960s saw a proliferation of federal programs to reduce regional economic disparity. The first was an Act to Provide for the Rehabilitation of Agricultural Lands and the Development of Rural Areas in Canada (1961), renamed in 1966 the Agricultural and Rural Development Act. Its federal–provincial, cost-shared projects helped small farms increase productivity, sought alternative uses for marginal land, and created agriculture-related jobs. In 1966, the focus shifted to non-agriculture projects like infrastructure and industrial incentives, particularly in five areas designated by the Fund for Rural Economic Development. This shift continued under the Regional Development Incentives Act, whereby incentives and monies were provided for projects in urban 'growth poles' promising economic growth potential. To coordinate these efforts the Department of Regional Economic Expansion was set up in 1968. In 1973 DREE abandoned the 'growth poles' concept as too restrictive and centralized in favour of General Development Agreements designed for urban and rural areas demonstrating viable 'developmental opportunities'. Special ARDA programs were also introduced to encourage commercial ventures. In 1982, DREE was replaced by the Ministry of State for Economic and Regional Development, overseeing a wider range of highly centralized agreements. Although ARDA remained on the books, it became inactive.

DELLA M.M. STANLEY

regionalism. 'Region' is an intermediate category, a medium-sized unit between the large and the local. 'Regionalism' usually implies action or analysis based on a person's identification with a particular place. Canada has been described as a country of regions. By this, observers mean that the component parts of this vast territory differ profoundly in landscape, economy, historic settlement pattern, voting pattern, and culture. The result has been the popular embrace of six 'traditional' regions—Atlantic, Quebec, Ontario, Prairie, British Columbia, and the North—and a popular assumption that territory-based secession is an appropriate response to 'national', economic, and cultural disputes.

Canada's scholarly disciplines, ranging from geography and economics to history and literature, have employed regional concepts to convey a sense of difference within the nation-state, as is suggested by such phrases as the Prairie novel, the southern Ontario auto industry, and the *Maritime Rights movement. Recently, reference to trans-national regions such as Cascadia (the Pacific Northwest) and the Circumpolar Arctic have come into vogue. Region is increasingly associated, too, with the largest urban centres, implying that the city proper and its immediate hinterland are part of a system.

The differences in Aboriginal cultures and in European relations with these Aboriginal peoples ensured that a pattern of regional difference was entrenched in northern North America during the 17th and 18th centuries. Then, the distinctive settlement experiences associated with the export of different staples—fish, fur, timber, and wheat being the original trades—and with the fortunes of the French and British Empires were superimposed on these community identities. European settlement in the scattered arable patches was disjointed and discontinuous, in the words of geographer Cole Harris, because the larger zones of agricultural land such as the St Lawrence Valley and the prairies of the western interior were separated by hundreds of miles of rock. Thus, in the Canadian experience, region predated nation.

When the Fathers of Confederation decided to create a federal state, they allocated a number of increasingly important responsibilities, notably education and the administration of health and social services, to the provinces and thereby established *federal–provincial relations as a key forum for contests over public policy. French-speaking descendants of Canada's first large European-origin empire faced unique obstacles to continued linguistic and cultural survival and, eventually, the province of Quebec became their bastion. John A. *Macdonald's *National Policy, which sought to establish Canadian *manufacturing for a Canadian market, encouraged regional economic specialization and, as subsequent struggles over tariffs and *freight rates suggest, core–periphery conflict. Immigrants, especially Asian-origin peoples in British Columbia, continental Europeans on the Prairies, and people from everywhere who settled in southern Ontario, also distinguished regional societies one from another. In this sense, French–English, federal–provincial, core–periphery, and multicultural–charter group tensions all reflected regional differences. They also increased the tendency of Canadians who challenged the national consensus to do so in the name of 'regionalism'.

GERALD FRIESEN

Regulation 17, Ontario, 1912–27. Bilingual schools were first organized in Canada West by Egerton *Ryerson in 1857. Franco-Ontarians first favoured public schools but moved to the separate school system after 1885 to continue to offer instruction in French. In 1890 the law required all instruction be given in English, unless that language was not understood. Unsatisfied, after 1900 both the *Orange Order and Irish Catholics protested the teaching of French in separate schools. In 1912 the minister of education issued Regulation 17 limiting French as a language of instruction to the two first years of primary school. Prominent Quebec leaders came to the support of the Franco-Ontarians. In Ottawa, the newspaper *Le Droit* was launched to give a voice to the protesters, and 7,000 people gathered to protest the action of the 'Ontario Prussians', as Henri *Bourassa called them. Intervention by the Senate and even the pope failed to end the dispute, and bitterness lingered, influencing Quebec's rejection of *conscription during the First World War. As late as 1923, a teacher in Pembroke was fired for teaching in French, an incident that gained national prominence. Legal redress was never forthcoming, especially after the imperial Privy Council refused to invalidate the regulation. But anglophone Protestants formed a Unity League that gradually influenced the authorities to ignore the offensive regulation. The controversy created a new solidarity between Quebec and Ontario francophones, increased the profile of organizations such as the Association d'education française de l'Ontario, and gave rise to the secret *Ordre de Jacques-Cartier and the fraternal Clubs Richelieu.

CORNELIUS J. JAENEN

Reid, Escott (1905–98), diplomat, official, scholar. Reid was a graduate of the University of Toronto and Oxford, where he held a Rhodes scholarship. Upon his return to Canada, he became the national secretary of the *Canadian Institute of International Affairs, a position he held for eight years. His social democracy increasingly clashed with the views of some on the institute's board, leading him to join the Canadian foreign service in 1939, where he served until 1962. During that time he held many senior positions, including those of assistant undersecretary of state for external affairs (1947), acting undersecretary (1948–9), deputy undersecretary (1949–52), high commissioner to India (1952–7), and ambassador to Germany (1958–62). In 1962, he joined the World Bank as a senior administrator, the director of the South Asia and Middle East department, until June 1965. He retired from active employment in 1969, having been the first principal of Glendon College of York University. His writings include *Envoy to Nehru*, *A Time of Fear and Hope*, and *Radical Mandarin*.

BRUCE MUIRHEAD

Reid Newfoundland Company. With considerable experience in building bridges and railways elsewhere in North America, the Scottish-Canadian contractor Robert Gillespie Reid (1842–1908) undertook in 1890 to complete the railway from St John's to Hall's Bay for the Newfoundland government. In 1893 he agreed to continue the railway to Port-aux-Basques, and operate it for ten years. Reid completed the railway in 1897, and then entered into negotiations concerning the future of the railway and the Reid interests in Newfoundland. After years of controversy and confrontation, a deal concluded in 1901 extended the railway-operating contract to 1941, confirmed Reid ownership of approximately 10,500 sq km of land, and allowed the Reids to operate a coastal steamer service, the Cabot Strait ferry, and the dry dock and street railway in St John's. These and other assets were transferred to the new Reid Newfoundland Company.

Controlled by R.G. Reid's sons, the company and its subsidiaries played an important role in the country's economic and political affairs. It built four branch railways for the government (1909–14) and was heavily involved in the development of the forest industry, playing a central role in the promotion of the Corner Brook newsprint mill. After 1918 the company shed all its undertakings to concentrate on land development. Rather than making money, it ran heavily into debt and was placed in receivership in 1931.

JAMES K. HILLER

Relations of Labor and Capital, Royal Commission on. Conceived by Prime Minister John A. *Macdonald in 1886, the commission heard testimony from approximately 1,800 people in Ontario, Quebec, New Brunswick, and Nova Scotia on working and living conditions in late-19th-century Canada. Its origins were, essentially, political. The 1870s and 1880s witnessed intense working-class activism: strikes proliferated, *unions grew, and labour candidates sought public office. As new political options emerged, the ruling Tories feared they were losing their grip on working-class voters. Politically astute, Macdonald created the commission to shore up his credentials as a 'friend of the working man' and, in the process, forestall any major legislative concessions while drumming up support for his beloved *National Policy.

Although the formation of the royal commission sheds light on the character of Canadian politics in the 19th century, its true significance is found in the testimony of the employers, employees, and *social reformers who appeared before it. At the hearings, wages, hours of work, and working conditions were spoken of often; so, too, were the ways in which working families made ends meet, what their neighbourhoods looked like, and how gender relations were starting to change as more women worked for wages. In short, the testimony painted a vivid picture of the country's transition to industrial capitalism: populations were on the rise, cities were getting bigger, technology was revolutionizing the economy, and working people were bearing the brunt of it all. It was no wonder, more than one witness stated, that organizations such as the *Knights of Labor, which promised to 'make the world anew', were so popular.

The commission delivered its report in 1889. No substantive legislative changes followed, but the very creation of the inquiry attested to politicians' new interest—however modest and politically motivated—in the proper role of government in industrial relations. The agitation that prompted the inquiry persisted, surfacing again in the early decades of the 20th century, when the next widespread working-class challenge to the political and economic status quo took place.

ANDREW PARNABY AND GREGORY S. KEALEY

relief camps. On 8 October 1932, the Conservative government of R.B. *Bennett established a national system of work camps for the tens of thousands of men who were roaming the country in search of work during the *Great Depression. The camps, to be administered by the Department of National Defence, were intended to feed, clothe, and shelter the single, homeless unemployed. The initiative was universally applauded, but the camps quickly came to symbolize all that was wrong with Ottawa's handling of the unemployment crisis and ultimately put the government and relief workers on a collision course.

The relief camp scheme had a modest beginning: during the winter of 1932–3, some 2,000 men repaired the Halifax and Quebec citadels and cleared landing fields for Trans-Canada Airways in eastern Canada. But as depression deepened, the program was rapidly expanded to include military and road-building projects in every province except Prince Edward Island. By 1936, when the program ended, 167,171 men had provided over 18 million man-days of relief work on 144 projects.

Life in the camps was monotonous and often bleak. In the interests of providing work for as many as possible as cheaply as possible, the men were required to do as much as they could by hand. This menial work, together with the demeaning 20-cent daily allowance, aggravated the men's sense of hopelessness. It also made the camps ideal breeding grounds for the communist-affiliated Relief Camp Workers' Union, which organized a number of disturbances and strikes. In April 1935, the union called a mass walk-out of the British Columbian camps to demand a 'work and wages' program. When the Bennett government refused to negotiate, 1,000 men left Vancouver by freight train in early June to lay their demands directly before the prime minister. By the time the *On-to-Ottawa Trek reached the prairies, it had nearly doubled in size, prompting the federal government to order the *Royal Canadian Mounted Police to stop the men in Regina. On Dominion Day, the police arrested the trek leaders at a peaceful rally, provoking a riot that left one dead, hundreds injured, and thousands of dollars of damage to downtown Regina. A provincial inquiry later exonerated the Mounties, but the Bennett government was punished in the next general election. BILL WAISER

remittance men. Between the end of the Napoleonic wars and the outbreak of the Great War, British gentlemen flocked to the outposts of empire. Many, lured by adventure (like shooting game in the western interior), visited Canada only briefly. Those living on reduced incomes at home—first pensioned officers, but increasingly non-inheriting sons under *primogeniture and young men ill prepared by their public-school education for a meritocratic industrializing society—stayed longer or emigrated permanently. Initially, attracted by land grants, they favoured the backwoods of Upper Canada; later they went to British Columbia, forming enclaves in places like the Cowichan and Okanagan Valleys, and to the Prairies, where cattle *ranching was popular. However strange to outsiders, their pastimes typified those of their class: cricket, afternoon tea, polo, fox (or coyote) hunting. Ideologically conservative and imbued with a sense of duty to public service and empire, some left their mark on Canadian politics, education, and economic development. Yet, they tended to be lumped together with the disreputable in their ranks, derisively referred to as 'remittance men'. Having left home under a shadow, and paid a regular allowance, or remittance, by their families to stay away from Great Britain, they acquired a reputation for unwarranted arrogance towards 'colonials', impracticality, laziness, and a fondness for gambling and alcohol. Many redeemed themselves in 1914 when they, like other *gentlemen emigrants, returned home to fight. The remittance man's lifestyle is perhaps best epitomized by the short-lived farming experiment at Cannington Manor (established 1882) in southern Saskatchewan.

FRANCES SWYRIPA

representation by population. With the achievement of *responsible government, radical colonial reformers campaigned for equal constituencies—the democratic principle of one man, one vote—to ensure that assemblies better reflected the will of the electorate. When the two Canadas were given equal representation at their union in 1841, despite Lower Canada's greater numbers, a sense of injustice fuelled French-Canadian demands for sectional representation by population. The census of 1851, however, revealed that Upper Canada had surpassed Lower Canada. The demand was taken up by George *Brown and his supporters to end 'French domination'. It was a demand for justice (now that numbers were in Upper Canada's favour) but also a claim to cultural superiority—that the 'progressive' section should not be dominated by a different culture. Such arguments deepened sectional hostility. For French Canadians, acquiescence in representation by population required minority protection. Confederation brought the former to the *House of Commons, while the latter brought equal regional representation to the *Senate and the creation of a province in which French Canadians were the majority.

JEFFREY L. McNAIRN

representative government. A system where part or all of the deliberative and law-making process is conducted by popularly elected representatives. It implies that at least some people have a right to participate in government or the belief that they have relevant ideas or interests best brought to bear by electing their own representatives.

There was little room for such rights or beliefs when New France became a *royal colony in 1663. Beginning in 1647, leading colonists had elected syndics for the three towns, but by 1673 all offices were filled by royal appointment. France's colonial minister reminded the governor of the basis of absolutist monarchy: it was 'good that each person speaks for himself alone and that no one speaks on behalf of all'. Unauthorized meetings and the circulation of petitions were banned in 1677.

British colonies were usually granted representative institutions with various powers in response to the growth of populations thought sufficiently loyal and capable, local lobbying against appointed officials, the migration of United Empire *Loyalists accustomed to popular participation in government, and British constitutional conventions, especially that only local governments with elective legislatures could raise their own taxes. Nova Scotia was granted the first representative assembly in 1758, Prince Edward Island in 1773. New Brunswick and Cape Breton were carved out of Nova Scotia in 1784 but only the former was granted an elective assembly. Cape Breton was reunited with Nova Scotia in 1820 rather than be given representative institutions. When the *Province of Quebec was divided into Upper and Lower Canada in 1791, both were granted representative institutions. Newfoundland followed only in 1832, Vancouver Island in 1856. After Confederation, elective assemblies were created by federal statute for the dominion's territories and new provinces. Only with *responsible government, however, was representative government transformed into a form of democracy. JEFFREY L. McNAIRN

Rerum Novarum. In 1891, the year Pope Leo XIII published this encyclical on the subject of labour, Canada's bishops were deeply divided over the *Manitoba schools question and how to protect Catholic and French-language education. Consequently, little attention was paid to the encyclical.

Nevertheless, as early as 1891 Abbé D. Gosselin, director of the 'Semaine religieuse de Québec', published a 'popular catechism' in which he presented the contents of the encyclical, using questions and answers to facilitate comprehension. French-Canadian priests studying in Rome at the time of the encyclical's publication were enthusiastic adherents and set out to promote it when they returned home. One of them, Eugène Lapointe, tried to introduce Catholic unionism in the diocese of Chicoutimi, while in Quebec City his colleague Stanislas Lortie established a Société d'économie sociale et politique and introduced the teachings of Leo XIII in his *Cursus philosophicus*.

In 1902, during a strike by workers in the shoe-making industry in Quebec City, Cardinal Bégin intervened at the request of the employers' and workers' organizations. His decision as arbitrator was inspired largely by *Rerum Novarum*. One clause in the agreement required that the union's American advisers be replaced by Catholic chaplains. This decision, together with parallel efforts in Chicoutimi, Trois-Rivières, and Hull, led to the creation of Catholic *unions, which in 1921 came together in the *Confédération des travailleurs catholiques du Canada. In Montreal Mgr *Bruchési arbitrated strikes by tramway employees in 1903 and carters and plasterers in 1905. He also attempted to destabilize the neutral unions.

Alongside the birth of Catholic unionism, other direct fruits of *Rerum Novarum* included the establishment of the Desjardin *caisses populaires (1901) and the Coopératives agricoles (1903), the founding of the Action sociale catholique (1907) and the Jesuits' *École sociale populaire. The influence of *Rerum Novarum*, consolidated by *Quadragesimo anno* (1931) during the Depression, would mark the Catholic Church in Canada until the Second World War. JACQUES RACINE

residential schools. Native residential schooling was part of Canada's history since New France, when both Catholic missionary orders and the Crown unsuccessfully promoted such institutions. New France's schools were short-lived because of strong First Nations opposition to them. The second phase of residential schooling developed in British North America once the era of agricultural settlement began. In New Brunswick in the 1780s, the New England Company, a non-denominational Protestant missionary body in England, sponsored what it called an Indian College. This enterprise, too, was a failure as a result of exploitation of students by nearby settlers to whom some students were assigned to learn agriculture. The NEC next opened a residential school known as the Mohawk Institute in Brantford, Ontario, in 1829 to minister to the Six Nations. The Anglicans also undertook residential schooling in the colonial phase with a short-lived school run by John West in Red River in the 1820s. Finally, in the middle of the 19th century Roman Catholics, principally the Oblates and several female religious communities, initiated schools in Ontario and British Columbia. This preliminary phase was completed in 1873 when the Church Missionary Society, the Anglican evangelical arm, opened a school in Sault Ste Marie.

Residential schooling as a policy of the Canadian government was born in 1883, when Canada created three industrial schools in Saskatchewan and Alberta. Industrial schools, which could also be found housing marginalized non-Native youths in eastern Canada and the United Kingdom, were conceived with ambitious educational goals. The early industrial schools were relatively well funded, located well away from reserves, and had an ambitious pedagogical regime for both academic and vocational instruction. Industrial schools took their place alongside a few small boarding schools that existed prior to the government initiative. Boarding schools were smaller, less ambitious, and more poorly funded than industrial schools. Both industrial and boarding schools grew steadily from the 1880s until the 1920s, when at their height they numbered 80 institutions operated jointly by Christian churches and the government. Roman Catholics ran about 60 per cent of them, Anglicans a third, and Methodists and Presbyterians the remainder. The distinctions between industrial and boarding schools eroded over time as government pulled back from funding the former; in 1923 the two were combined into a single category thereafter known as residential schools.

Residential schooling had many problems, which stemmed from characteristics inherent to the system and from governmental neglect. First, residential schools operated on the half-day system, meaning that students spent half the day in the classroom and half at work in or around the school. The theoretical justification was that the half-day system provided students with practical training that would help them earn a living after leaving school. In reality, especially because government constantly sought to restrain funding and the churches could not make up the shortfall, the half-day system extracted labour from students to support the schools' operation. Overwork and inadequate training were part of residential schooling until the late 1950s, when funding improved and the half-day system was abolished. Second, residential schools were conceived as crucibles in which to forge Christianized and Europeanized Indians. Particularly because of governmental insistence, the use of Native languages—known colloquially as 'talking Indian'—was vigorously discouraged, even though many missionaries favoured the use of *Aboriginal languages when evangelizing. Preaching also frequently disparaged Aboriginal spirituality, calling it devil worship. Throughout their school experience, students were subjected to the denigration of Aboriginal identity and the promotion of Euro-Canadian values and practices.

Schools also failed because of neglect and abuse. Poor funding resulted in inferior teachers and childcare workers, inadequate diet, poor clothing and equipment, and, in general, neglect of the children's educational and physical welfare. Many students complained later of a lack of emotional support, and blamed their inability as adults to relate well to marriage partners or children on the coldness of the environment in which they were raised. Severe corporal discipline, general throughout residential schools, became abuse at the hands of ill-qualified workers whose mistreatment was not checked by church or government oversight. In too many cases, residential school children were the victims of sexual predators, both staff and older students.

Although the federal government decided to close the schools in 1969, their malign legacy lives on. The 1996 report of the Royal Commission on *Aboriginal Peoples detailed the problems with the schools and called for a public inquiry into them. The federal government in January 1998 issued a formal apology to former students and established a $350 million fund for community healing. School survivors have initiated litigation claiming damages for various forms of abuse, the legal actions involving 11,500 people by October 2002. It will be some time before Canada is finished with residential schools.

J.R. MILLER

responsible government. Shorthand for reforms to the executive branch of colonial governments. Before the 1840s the governor's principal advisers in each colony, the executive council, were appointed by and thus answerable to him and the British government. By the 1830s, reformers argued that these advisers were effectively responsible to no one; they frequently had security of tenure and were too few in number, too distant, and too in control of the flow of information to be effectively monitored from Britain. Resentment of appointed officials fuelled demands that power be exercised only by individuals the colonists could themselves hold accountable. The term 'responsible government' was ambiguous, encompassing a variety of potential reforms to achieve such accountability. Who, after all, was in favour of irresponsible government?

Increasingly, however, the term was used in the more limited sense of ministerial responsibility, or parliamentary government whereby the executive council was to become a cabinet of ministers collectively responsible to the assembly and retaining office only as long as it had the support of the assembly's majority. Governors were to choose their ministers from among those who commanded such support and to accept their advice, withdrawing from day-to-day politics. Ministerial responsibility promised to end conflict, endemic by the 1830s, between appointed executives and elected legislatures, and to achieve local self-government. For moderate reform leaders such as Robert *Baldwin in Upper Canada and Joseph *Howe in Nova Scotia, one of its appeals was that it mimicked evolving British practices, thus avoiding the American model of elective offices. It could also be championed as an issue of justice, extending the rights enjoyed by British subjects in Britain to fellow subjects elsewhere in the empire. Britain's desire to disentangle itself from local conflicts and its adoption of free trade in 1846 encouraged it to surrender control over the internal politics of established colonies that had predominantly Euro-American populations.

In 1847, Britain instructed the lieutenant-governor of Nova Scotia to choose his advisers from among those who commanded a majority in the assembly. After the election that year saw reformers victorious, the first 'responsible' colonial administration took office in 1848. The following year Canadian reform leaders Robert Baldwin and Louis-Hippolyte *LaFontaine led a ministry after reformers secured the majority of seats in the 1848 election. The principle was extended to the other Atlantic colonies by 1855. Responsible government transferred authority from Britain and local elites to a broader segment of the colonial population, encouraged the growth of political parties, and concentrated power in the hands of executive office-holders far more than under the old colonial system.

JEFFREY L. MCNAIRN

retail trade. Trading in Canada is as old as human settlement, but retailing is of much more recent provenance. Before the mid-19th century, business people did not specialize in resale: they manufactured and wholesaled as well as retailed goods. Artisans ran many of the stores people shopped in, while the bigger stores were operated by wholesale merchants who imported consumer goods and exported natural resources. Not until industrial production was so concentrated that manufacturers required multiple outlets did retailing assume its contemporary form.

The character of shops and shopping changed dramatically over the succeeding 150 years. In the mid-19th century stores tended to be long and narrow, with windows at the front. Counters typically ran down the three walls, and most of the retailers' goods were kept behind them, with male clerks serving each customer individually. This labour-intensive approach was suited to an age where goods were scarce, precious, and expensive and when little cash was available. Almost all buying was done on credit: customers paid their tab when it was convenient; retailers had to judge the honesty and affluence of their clientele.

This type of retailing gradually disappeared for a variety of causes. Rising incomes allowed some merchants in the late 19th century to experiment with selling only for cash. Credit remained central to distribution, particularly in rural areas, but it was less likely to be carried by the retailer. From the 1920s an increasing share of the burden of financing sales was assumed by third-party creditors—such as Household Finance or, after the 1950s, by credit card companies—or by the consumer-finance departments operated by the suppliers of the item being bought.

While rising incomes gradually transformed the business of paying for goods, pre-packaging, manufacturer-generated advertising, and resale price maintenance revolutionized the delivery of products. Retailers were in the front line of the struggle that saw centralized manufacturers obliterate local artisans. Factory-made products cost less than those produced by local craftsmen, but quality and competition were often problems. In order to establish the value of their wares in the public mind and differentiate their goods from those of rivals, manufacturers started labelling, advertising, and suggesting retail prices for their products. This greatly reduced the demand for clerks in stores, as customers soon became adept at comparing brands and prices for themselves. Retailers reduced their staff, opened their shelves to self-service, and hired cheap female labour.

The proliferation of factory-made pre-packaged goods empowered consumers, who were able to compare prices, and dramatically increased competition. *Chain and *department stores grew strong by cheapening the costs of distribution and increasing the range of goods available to consumers. Retail margins became tighter in the 20th century, and small firms, which had higher costs, were steadily driven out of business. By the 1990s, independent stores were selling only a third of the shoes and clothing bought by Canadians and less than 40 per cent of the groceries. Only one store in three was owner-operated, and a large percentage of these were *franchises. Franchise businesses first emerged in the 1920s, when they were called 'voluntary chains', but their popularity grew dramatically in the inflationary years after 1970. Franchising allowed independent merchants to buy stock at lower prices and to save costs on advertising and display, making them more competitive.

After the Second World War the dramatic growth in Canada's population, its rising affluence, and suburbanization further refined these changes. Chain and department stores followed the population outside established residential areas and in the 1950s began locating in shopping malls. The triumph of the car over other forms of transportation all but eliminated expensive services, such as home delivery, by the 1960s. Increasing price consciousness and people's willingness to drive long distances to save money, led, in the 1980s, to the emergence of huge chain stores that emulated warehouses. Rival retailers, unable to match the bulk stores in selection or price, experimented with innovative layouts, coupons, and frequent-buyer plans to keep customers. Others tried to reach more consumers by selling over the Internet, although the greatest success of on-line shopping has been in areas where product identification is so pronounced that consumers feel secure in what they buy.

Since retailing's emergence as a distinct occupation in the mid-19th century, two great forces have shaped its development: consumer consciousness and the demands of suppliers to reduce distribution costs and increase the flow of goods. Both have pressed retailers to lower margins and adopt standard methods of advertising and display. While this has served to make goods more affordable and available, it has also homogenized trading's character and assured the domination of the corporate chains and department stores. DAVID MONOD

'revanche des berceaux' ('revenge of the cradles'). A term first used by the Montreal Jesuit Louis Lalande in a 1918 speech later published in *Action française*, it describes the traditionally high French-Canadian birth rate—marital fertility in Quebec was about 50 per cent higher than in Ontario at the end of the 19th century—and underlines the role of natural increase in maintaining the demographic importance, and thus the political influence, of Quebec in Canada.

Lalande was aware of the irony embedded in a trope that associated confrontation and revenge with the 'innocent, frail, smiling image of an infant in its silent alcove'. Yet, his speech furnished the slogan for a conservative nationalist discourse that extolled the fertility of French-Canadian women and exhorted them to resist economic pressures to limit family size. The expression gained currency in the 1920s and has since been used to describe historic fertility differentials between Quebec and English Canada. During the *Quiet Revolution, however, fertility in Quebec fell precipitously to the lowest levels in Canada. Since that time, provincial governments have tried to simulate the birth rate, not least through generous baby bonuses and inexpensive, universal daycare. In the end, perhaps, any 'revenge' belongs to the generations of women who resisted pressure to adhere to a narrowly defined maternal role and who gained vastly greater reproductive freedom in the decades since 1960.

PETER GOSSAGE

Rhinoceros Party. Founded by Montreal doctor and writer Jacques Ferron (1921–85) to satirize Canadian federal politics, the Rhinoceros Party entered nearly 400 candidates in successive federal elections, mostly in Quebec (although a baseball pitcher ran as a Rhinoceros candidate for the American presidency). The eldest son in a wealthy family, Ferron was deeply committed to the most humble; he eventually embraced Quebec nationalism and is sometimes considered close to the *Front de libération du Québec. His party, which counted many famous singers, writers, and actors among its number, greeted politics with derision; a basic party tenet was to take lightly its own hare-brained electoral promises. The Rhinoceros Party disappeared when the candidature filing fee was increased from $200 to $1,000. For three decades it had made it possible for cynical citizens and unconditional Quebec nationalists to participate in federal elections. RAYMOND HUDON

Richard, Maurice 'Rocket' (1921–2000). Born in (St Denis) Montreal, Richard is one of Canada's true sporting icons. He played 18 years for the Montreal Canadiens, 1942–60, scoring 544 regular season goals and 82 more in playoff competition. Known for his dashing style of play, his intensity, determination, and goal-scoring abilities, Richard astounded the *hockey world during the 1944–5 season, when he became the first 50-goal scorer in the history of the National Hockey League, doing so over a 50-game schedule. Over his career, Richard was named to the NHL All Star team 14 times, won the Hart Trophy as league MVP, and led the Canadiens to eight Stanley Cups. Richard identified with his French-Canadian origins and was idolized by his supporters. In March 1955 NHL president Clarence Campbell suspended an aggressive Richard, precipitating a riot that spilled over into the streets of Montreal, an event that many consider the opening volley of Quebec's *Quiet Revolution. Richard's stature did not diminish over time. After his death over 100,000 paid their respects as his body lay in state; thousands more lined the streets in a state funeral procession that wended its way through the streets to Old Montreal. COLIN HOWELL

Richardson, Sir John (1787–1865), explorer. The foremost surgeon-naturalist in British history, Richardson spent nearly eight years in Canada: during the War of 1812; as surgeon-naturalist to the first two *Franklin Arctic expeditions, 1819–22 (which was rescued by Coppermine Indians) and 1825–7 (during which he mapped Great Bear Lake and 863 miles of arctic coastline); and as leader of the first overland expedition (1849–50) in search of the missing third Franklin expedition. Proficient in geology, lichenology, botany, and mammalogy, he learned ornithology in America. On the Saskatchewan River he made the most complete pre-settlement inventory of *natural history in North America. He was also an administrator, author (*Fauna Boreali-Americana*), and scholar (abstracting words from writings of his friend Robert Burns for what was to become the *Oxford English Dictionary*). He was knighted in 1846. His name is perpetuated in Canada by Richardson mountains, islands, river, bay, and cape, in addition to a ground squirrel, owl, and merlin. C. STUART HOUSTON

Rideau Hall, the Ottawa home of Canada's *governors general. Constructed in 1838 as a private villa, it was purchased by the government of Canada in 1868. Situated in gardens and parkland, the enlarged structure is recognizable today because of its imposing, pedimented west front (1913). Rideau Hall's significance lies less in its architecture than in its long identification with the country's history through the involvement of governors general in Canadian life. DAVID E. SMITH

riding the rods. The romance of the Canadian railway makes much of the hobo who travelled in boxcars seeking freedom and adventure. In fact, riding the rods was a dangerous necessity before the Second World War when workers sought employment on farms and logging, mining, and construction crews across the country. Wages and working conditions were often terrible; many workers found their pay docked for grossly overpriced tools, food, and supplies at the company store. Canada's industrial development and the fortunes of railway, logging, and mining barons were based on this exploitation. As a result, the work camps were fertile grounds for the *Communist Party and for radical *unions such as the *Industrial Workers of the World and the *One Big Union. These unions showed that this workforce could be unionized and could engage in industrial action to improve conditions. However, it was difficult to fight for better conditions. Many of the workers were recent immigrants who did not speak English or French and did not have the vote. Union organizers were fired and even kidnapped and beaten.

The Great Depression forced a new generation to ride the rods looking for work and relief. Hoboes would panhandle for money and food on city streets, then head to 'jungles' on the outskirts to cook and sleep. Later they formed unions of the unemployed and organized protest marches, rallies, and demonstrations. In June 1935, a thousand unemployed workers decided to ride the rods in the *On-to-Ottawa Trek to take their issues directly to the federal government.

After the Second World War, the wider availability of automobiles meant that riding the rods was less necessary. Migrant workers, however, have not disappeared, as Canadians still leave regions of high unemployment for those with more chance for jobs. MARK LEIER

Riel, Louis (1844–85). Riel is one of the most controversial of Canadian historical figures. He has been termed a traitor, a heretic, the founder of a province, the hero of a people, a false god. The myth and man have blended together so as to make it impossible to reach any conclusions that all would accept.

Born in the *Metis settlement of St Boniface, he went to Montreal to study for the priesthood. He returned to St Boniface in the later 1860s and came to prominence during the resistance to Canadian expansion in 1869–70. His decision to execute a troublesome Canadian, Thomas Scott, forced Riel into exile when the transfer of the *Red River territory was completed. Well before the age of 30, he had become a leader of the Metis and an object of hatred for many Canadians. The subsequent years were troubled ones. He was elected to Parliament but was unable to take his seat because of charges related to Scott. He suffered a mental breakdown in the mid-70s and spent time in a Quebec asylum. He also began to exhibit extreme religious ideas that pictured a new Catholic church arising in North America. The later 1870s and early 1880s were spent in exile in the United States.

In the meantime the situation of the Metis was deteriorating. An influx of Canadian settlers, the failure of the buffalo, and bad weather all hurt the economy of Metis settlements. Grievances against the federal government remained unresolved. By 1884 the situation had reached a crisis point and a delegation visited Riel, asking him to return and press their case with Ottawa. Riel's religious extremism and mental state worked against him. By the spring of 1885 his exasperation with the federal government and his sense of religious messianism led him to take drastic steps. In March he declared a provisional government, as had been done in 1869–70. This time there was no power vacuum, however, and the Metis soon clashed with a local Mounted Police detachment, leaving 18 dead. As violence flared in nearby Native tribes the Canadian government moved swiftly, sending a military force westward. By 15 May Riel was under arrest, charged with treason. His lawyer attempted a plea of insanity but Riel rejected this approach. He was convicted and after a series of appeals was hanged at Regina on 16 November 1885.

While interpretations vary, Riel's importance in Canadian history is undisputed. His actions affected key fault-lines of our society: French–English; east–west; European–Aboriginal. In a history emphasizing consensus and compromise he symbolized another road. DOUG OWRAM

See also RED RIVER RESISTANCE; NORTH-WEST REBELLION.

riot. Despite Canada's reputation as a 'peaceable kingdom', its history is rife with instances of riot, from the burning of Parliament in Montreal in 1849 to the 1990s Stanley Cup riots. Many riots involved groups excluded from formal power, such as mid-19th-century canal workers, anti-conscription rioters in Quebec, or penitentiary inmates; before Confederation, election riots were also common. Other riots expressed intolerance of minorities, as in anti-Catholic riots in 19th-century New Brunswick or anti-Asian riots in turn-of-the-century British Columbia and Alberta. Others might be directed against the houses of individuals who had violated community norms. Faced with such threats to public order, or to the state's monopoly on violence, local officials 'read the Riot Act', calling on rioters to disperse, and could then use force. Through most of the 19th century large-scale riots often led to military intervention, and sometimes resulted in deaths when troops fired on the crowd; from the later 19th century police forces increasingly took over. Although riots have declined overall through the 20th century, they remain part of Canada's culture.

DONALD FYSON

roads. Canada is one of the most difficult places in the world to build roads. Besides the problem of great geographic distances between population points, there is also a severe climate to contend with. In many parts of Canada an abundance of coastline, lakes, and rivers provided transportation and mitigated the need for roads. Roads, which were very expensive to build and maintain, were constructed only when there was no alternative. The typical way to get over swampy land was to build a corduroy road made from the trunks of small trees laid at right angles to the direction of the road, which might or might not be covered with earth.

The first Canadian road was built in 1606 by Samuel de *Champlain from *Port-Royal to Digby, Nova Scotia (16 km). In Quebec up to 1832 the *grand voyer* was the chief figure in road building since he decided on routes and arranged for construction. The major highway was the 267-km Chemin de Roi between Montreal and Quebec City, opened in 1734. In Upper Canada the first roads were built as military works: Yonge Street from Toronto to Lake Simcoe in 1796 and Dundas Road from Toronto to London. The first government appropriation for road building was in New Brunswick in 1801, followed by Upper Canada in 1804. By 1820 increased immigration created a demand to link places not connected by waterways. Roads could be built by individuals or companies that received a monopoly from colonial legislatures to build toll roads. Lower Canadian examples include the Chemin Chambly and the Upper Lachine Road in Montreal. In the 1830s plank roads were seen as the answer to road-building problems, but high maintenance costs limited their usefulness.

In the early 1840s the Department of Public Works of the newly created *Province of Canada sponsored a brief burst of road building. New long-distance colonization roads such as the Garafaxa and Opengio were built. After the money ran out in the mid-1840s, the roads were transferred to local authorities. However, this coincided with the beginning of the railway age in Canada. In the 1850s, railways were seen as the engine of economic development, and all available resources went into their design and construction. Roads merely served to link people to the nearest railway station.

With Confederation in 1867, responsibility for public works, such as roads, was given to the provinces, but they had few resources and roads were left to municipalities. Growing cities were constrained by the lack of suitable material for constructing streets. Continual attempts were made to develop pavements from wood blocks, cobblestones, concrete, and various types of asphalt. As rural areas became more settled, engineers built better roads by lowering crowns in the middle of roads, widening road surfaces, improving drainage, and using gravel made by portable rock crushers. Canadian society was also changing. The rapid growth of *cycling in the 1890s created a demand for better roads. The spectacular growth of *automobiles after 1900 created even more demand. However, it was only when provincial governments intervened to create highway departments and province-wide highway systems that the situation improved. The first provincial highway department was created in Quebec in 1912, quickly followed by other provinces. The first stretch of hard-surfaced road was an 11-km concrete road from Montreal to Laval in 1910. A concrete road from Toronto to Hamilton was built in 1914–17. Other provinces began to pave their highways, especially those that started at the American border, in order to attract tourists. The federal government made one of its brief forays into road building in 1919, when it offered subsidies up to 40 per cent to the provinces to improve roads that were part of a designated highway system.

Automobile growth pushed road construction in both urban and rural areas in the 1920s. Urban streets were constructed with either concrete or asphalt. During the Depression of the 1930s, projects to upgrade existing roads or to link remote areas to the existing road system were used as make-work projects. Continued high levels of traffic, especially during the Second World War, seriously degraded the existing road system. After the war, provinces began to pour large sums of money into roads to ensure economic growth as more material started to move by truck rather than by rail. Multi-lane roads were built in major cities to speed up the traffic flow. These became the limited-access urban expressways of the 1960s and 1970s whose construction often severely damaged the existing urban milieu. Multi-lane, limited-access, divided highways—descendants of the Queen Elizabeth Way from Toronto to Niagara Falls (1939), one of the first divided highways in the world—became the standard for inter-urban travel in Canada. The Macdonald–Cartier Freeway (Highway 401) was constructed in Ontario from Windsor to the Quebec border (831 km) in the 1950s and 1960s. Other provinces followed suit. The construction of the *Trans-Canada Highway between 1949 and 1965, heavily subsidized by the federal government, greatly aided the creation of a modern highway network.

By the 1970s the highway system in Canada reached its zenith. Most major Canadian cities were linked by limited-access divided highways. Urban streets and expressways were well designed and paved. But the number of cars and trucks continued to rise, creating traffic chaos. Most road construction came to halt in the 1980s and 1990s as provincial and municipal governments devoted their budgets to maintaining an over-burdened road system. It has yet to be determined how the road system is going to advance and be financed. LARRY McNALLY

Roads to Resources. When Conservative prime minister John *Diefenbaker opened the 1958 federal election campaign, he proclaimed his 'vision of northern development', a romantic pledge to complete Canada's creation through exploitation of the vast northlands of the *Canadian Shield, the Yukon, and the Northwest Territories. Diefenbaker foresaw a doubling of the country's population by the year 2000, to be sustained above all by the still-to-be-exploited riches of the North. To reach these isolated regions, he promised that Ottawa would fund a program of 'Roads to Resources' involving mapping, surveying, prospecting, mining, and eventual settlement. Opposition leader Lester *Pearson ridiculed the plan for roads 'from igloo to igloo', but Diefenbaker's boldness caught the public mood, and he was returned to power with an overwhelming parliamentary majority. Over the next five years more than 6,400 km of roads, at an estimated cost of over $300 million, were built in the territories and the northern areas of the provinces, although mining and petroleum exploration resulted in little development or settlement during the same period. The first of the 'Roads to Resources' was the Dempster Highway—following a dramatic 640-km route from *Dawson in the Yukon to *Inuvik on the Mackenzie Delta—constructed between 1959 and 1979. Other projects in the program included the Pine Point Railway in northern Alberta, a highway bridge in the prime minister's constituency of Prince Albert, and a striking restoration of the 18th-century fortress *Louisbourg on Cape Breton Island. DENIS SMITH

Roberval, Jean-François de La Rocque, Sieur de (*c.* 1500–60), French lieutenant-general in Canada. A military officer and impoverished noble, La Rocque de Roberval was an influential courtier of King François I despite having converted to Protestantism. Appointed lieutenant-general in Canada in early 1541, he was granted sweeping powers. With merchant associates, he also received a commercial monopoly for the St Lawrence region. Desperately short of funds, Roberval set sail only in the spring of 1542—a year after the departure for Canada of his guide, Jacques *Cartier. When the two met by chance in St John's harbour, Cartier rejected Roberval's order to sail with him up the St Lawrence. Roberval pressed on with his party of some 200 and re-occupied Cartier's short-lived settlement at Stadacona (Quebec). The winter of 1542–3 proved disastrous, with harsh weather, disease, and dissension among the colonists. Although Roberval explored upriver as far as Hochelaga (Montreal) during the summer of 1543, the entire enterprise was then abandoned. The survivors returned to France, where Roberval strove for many years to fend off his creditors. He was killed by Catholic assailants in a street skirmish in Paris at the beginning of the French Wars of Religion. JOHN G. REID

Robichaud, Louis-Joseph (1925–), New Brunswick premier 1960–70. Three themes dominated in the decade that New Brunswick's first elected Acadian premier held power: social responsibility, ethnic equality, and industrialization. Liquor laws were liberalized, the civil service modernized, and the hospital premium tax eliminated. Starting in 1965, economic disparity in the rural, often predominantly Acadian, areas was addressed through an ambitious, controversial reform package, the Program of Equal Opportunity. It centralized government funding and administration of schools, hospitals, and social assistance; abolished poll and personal property taxes and county governments; and standardized property assessments. The government sought to revitalize natural resource industries, particularly mining and forestry, through outside investment, in spite of opposition from local industrialist K.C. *Irving. The charismatic Robichaud became the symbol of Acadian maturity, appointing a largely francophone cabinet, establishing the Université de Moncton and the École Normale, and passing an Official Languages Act. This era of social and cultural ferment, political change, and urbanization brought New Brunswick into the 20th century. After serving as co-chair of the International Joint Commission (1971–3), Robichaud was appointed to the Senate.

DELLA M.M. STANLEY

Robichaud, Prudent (*c.* 1669–*c.* 1756), Acadian deputy, merchant. Probably born in *Port-Royal, Robichaud profited from the British *conquest of Acadia in 1710 by becoming one of the leading Acadian suppliers of foodstuffs and wood to the English garrison of Annapolis Royal. At the same time, he was chosen by the local inhabitants to become their representative in his capacity of *syndic* and, after 1720, as one of the group of deputies that Acadians elected each fall as their spokesmen. In 1727 he became justice of the peace; in 1733 the British authorities of Nova Scotia again expressed their confidence in him by naming him collector of fees and dues. One of the most influential and prominent Acadians of his time, Robichaud maintained close ties with the French at *Louisbourg as well as with the *Mi'kmaq. However, his extensive business, family, and political networks did not prevent him from being deported in 1755. It is reported that he died the following year along the banks of the Saint John River as he was trying to find refuge in New France.

MAURICE BASQUE

Robin, Charles, and Company, Channel Island merchants. Established formally by Charles Robin at Paspébiac, *Gaspé, in 1786, this firm grew out of the earlier Robin, Pipon and Company, a Jersey cod-fishing enterprise based at Isle Madame. Over the next 100 years the firm expanded until it became the pre-eminent fishing firm in the Gulf of St Lawrence, operating a 'merchant triangle' in which the ownership apex resided in Jersey, production took place in a series of fishing stations on the eastern coast of Canada with headquarters at Paspébiac, and markets (in the Mediterranean, Brazil, the Caribbean, the Baltic, and London) were controlled through family agents in the various locations. The firm operated its vast cod-fishing enterprise through the use of a *truck system to control access to the fish and its Canadian labour force, coupled with indentured service for the skilled labour it brought from Jersey. It brought wealth to Jersey merchants, shipbuilders, and artisans, and opened Gaspé to settlement, but left it under-developed. In 1886, the original company failed for complex reasons including the crash of the States Bank of Jersey. The firm continued in Gaspé, with new ownership and a simplified business structure until the depression of the 1930s. A remnant exists today as a series of department stores.

ROSEMARY E. OMMER

Robinson, Sir John Beverley (1792–1863). If any one individual personified the *'Family Compact' of early Ontario, it was Robinson. During the War of 1812 he served with distinction and, thanks to the patronage of Justice William Powell, was made acting attorney general in 1813. He capably handled a number of difficult situations, including the treason trials of Canadian raiders. After the war, he was sent to England and studied law. Upon his return in 1818, he was appointed solicitor and then attorney general. Elected to the assembly in 1820, he became the voice of the lieutenant-governor's administration and directed several important measures for public development. But since his war years he had distrusted Americans and saw disloyalty behind every criticism of the government. His approach to settling the issue of alien (American) property rights brought him many enemies and encouraged a determined reform movement. W.L. *Mackenzie subjected Robinson to a tirade in his radical newspaper, the *Colonial Advocate*. Despairing of politics, Robinson was appointed chief justice in 1829. Robinson's last foray into public affairs occurred in 1840, when he travelled to England to lobby against the Durham Report. He wrote a conservative treatise on the future, *Canada and the Canada Bill*, and although he gained the support of the Duke of Wellington his campaign ultimately failed. Robinson remained chief justice until 1862.

PATRICK BRODE

Roblin, Sir Rodmond Palen (1853–1937), Manitoba premier 1900–15. Roblin, descended from Dutch Loyalist stock in Prince Edward County, Canada West, arrived in Manitoba in 1877, farmed successfully at Carman, and developed business interests in Winnipeg. Ambitious and locally popular, he entered the Manitoba legislature in 1888 as an independent. He supported Liberal premier Thomas Greenway's attack on the CPR 'monopoly', but otherwise criticized the government, especially for its violation of the language and educational rights of the Franco-Manitoban minority. He assumed the leadership of the provincial Conservatives and in 1900 became premier. In power, Roblin proved to be a Conservative reformer. He conjured a deal with the Canadian Northern in which the railway accepted government control of freight rates in return for an alternate route to the Lakehead. He nationalized the Bell telephone system, introduced workers' compensation laws, and established corporation taxes in Manitoba, although he resisted the establishment of women's suffrage. He was fiercely partisan, deftly using patronage to build an unassailable government. In 1915, the building of a new legislature and other public facilities mired his government in scandal and he resigned.

J.E. REA

rodeos. A rodeo is a set of competitive events in which people demonstrate their ability when pitted against livestock. Many rodeo events such as riding bucking broncos, wrestling steers, and roping calves originated as the skills required by *cowboys in western North America during the late 19th century. The first rodeos occurred rather spontaneously during roundups when cowboys, horses, and cattle from numerous ranches were brought together. In time, some of the competitions were organized and outsiders invited to attend. This marked the beginning of the modern rodeo, which by the early 20th century had proliferated all the way from Texas to the Canadian West. In Canada the most celebrated rodeo is the *Calgary Stampede.

WARREN ELOFSON

Roman Catholics. From the time that Christianity came to Canada from Europe, Roman Catholics have played a prominent, at times dominant, role in the religious life of the country. During the French colonial era, the European population was almost exclusively Roman Catholic, a monopoly officially supported by the French monarchy from 1627, and Catholic missionaries were active in proselytizing among the Aboriginal peoples. Attempts at conversion led in some cases to lasting, if by no means untroubled, attachment to the Catholic Church among some First Nations, such as the *Mi'kmaq of Atlantic Canada.

The British Conquest brought a major change in the mid-18th century in that waves of English-speaking settlers, both Catholic and Protestant, followed. The growing English-speaking Catholic population comprised mainly *Irish and *Highland Scots, whose distinctively ethnic forms of Catholicism often brought them into conflict with the French-Canadian church and sometimes with each other. Episcopal appointments and later the educational rights of linguistic and religious minorities were among the chief bones of contention. The conflict between French- and English-speaking Catholics was at its height in the second half of the 19th and early part of the 20th centuries, when both groups embraced the authoritarian principles and intense popular devotions associated with *ultramontane Catholicism. Despite many parallels between their religious evolution, French- and Irish-Canadian Catholics harnessed ultramontane Catholicism to their peculiar ethnic and national aspirations in a manner that placed them sharply at odds, while also heightening tensions between Catholics of both linguistic groups and increasingly evangelical and militant Canadian Protestants.

From the early 20th century, large-scale immigration of western and eastern European populations, especially from Ukraine, Poland, Germany, and Italy, added a third major element to the Canadian Catholic population. Although European Catholics were concentrated in the West, pockets of such newcomers could be found from coast to coast. The eastern rite *Ukrainians were the single largest group, and the one that posed the greatest challenge to established Catholic authorities and institutions. In many cases, European Catholics created their own religio-ethnic institutions, including ethnic parishes. These distinctive parishes and other church-based social and cultural institutions played a crucial role in the transition of such immigrants to their new homeland. By this time, however, English-speaking Catholics were increasingly integrated into mainstream Canadian society and assimilated to the imperial British view that Canada was destined to be an English-speaking country. Reflecting this view, which was also supported by the ecclesiastical authorities in Rome, they engaged in aggressive, though not entirely successful, attempts to assimilate European immigrants to the English-speaking church. These efforts to make the church an essentially English-speaking institution exacerbated conflict with French-speaking Catholics.

Over a period of four centuries, Roman Catholic institutions in Canada evolved from rudimentary missionary structures to complex, interlocking networks of social and religious institutions that included dioceses, schools, colleges, hospitals, and social welfare agencies. This evolution occurred at a more rapid pace among different segments of the population, and was already advanced in Quebec when Irish and Scottish Catholics began to arrive in British North America. The appointment of resident bishops (beginning with the appointment of Jean-François *Laval as vicar-apostolic in 1658 and titular bishop of Quebec in 1674) was a crucial step, as was the arrival of numerous religious orders, including dozens of orders of female religious, who staffed schools, hospitals, and orphanages. The strengthening of Catholic institutions was generally accompanied by a growing rate of conformity among the laity to official religious norms. As late as the 1950s, the rate of attendance at weekly Mass was over 80 per cent.

Since the 1960s, secularization has resulted in declining rates of participation (33 per cent weekly attendance in 1990), a shift of responsibility for many social institutions from the church to the state, and a dramatic decline in the number of clergy and members of religious orders. At the same time, with the immigration of non-Christian and non-Western peoples, the Roman Catholic percentage of the Canadian population has dropped. Despite growing cultural and religious diversity, Roman Catholics still constitute by far the largest Christian denomination in the country, and in 1991 formed approximately 45 per cent of the total population. The Roman Catholic Church, although nowhere near as powerful a force as it once was, nevertheless remains an important institution in Canadian society. TERRENCE MURPHY

Roncarelli v. Duplessis, 1946. *Jehovah's Witnesses had proselytized actively and publicly in Quebec since the 1920s. Given their pronounced anti-Catholic message, they faced stiff opposition from Catholic clergy and municipal authorities, who often had them arrested. Banned throughout Canada during the Second World War, the Witnesses began campaigning again directly after the war. In Montreal and Quebec, municipal authorities rigorously applied bylaws that prohibited the distribution of pamphlets without police permission. Frank Roncarelli, a Montreal restauranteur and fervent Witness, provided bail for almost 400 Witnesses charged under these bylaws. Quebec's premier, Maurice *Duplessis, like most Quebec francophones, was incensed by what he considered the Witnesses' seditious propaganda, attacking his administration, his religion, his ally the Catholic Church, and Quebec as a whole. Part of his response was to have Roncarelli's liquor licence revoked in 1946, thereby ruining his business. After Roncarelli sued Duplessis personally, the premier launched a 'war without mercy' against the Witnesses; up to 1953 almost 1,700 prosecutions occurred against them, ranging from bylaw infractions to blasphemous libel and sedition. Although the lower courts in Quebec generally ruled against the Witnesses, the

*Supreme Court of Canada favoured them. For example, in 1953 the court exempted religious pamphlets from the bylaws, and in 1959, in Roncarelli's case against Duplessis, the court found the premier personally responsible and ordered him to pay almost $50,000 in damages. The Supreme Court's judgments in these and other similar cases, which often pitted its anglophone majority against its francophone minority, helped lay the basis for the Canadian Bill of Rights in 1960. DONALD FYSON

Ronning, Chester Alvin (1894–1984). Although he was a cowboy, school administrator, politician, pioneer, teacher, veteran of both world wars, and even a choirmaster, Ronning's primary contribution was as a diplomat. Born in China to Lutheran missionaries, he came to Canada in 1909 following the death of his mother. Educated in Alberta and Minnesota, he trained as a sapper and cadet-for-pilot during the First World War. In 1918 he married Inga Horte and in 1922 returned to China as a school administrator. Ordered out in 1927, he became principal of Camrose Lutheran College, also serving as a United Farmers member of the Alberta legislature, 1932–5. In 1942 he enlisted in the RCAF; after wartime service as head of an intelligence unit, he joined the Department of *External Affairs. He held several important posts: China, 1945–51; Ottawa, 1951–4; ambassador to Norway, 1954–7; high commissioner to India, 1957–64. In 1966 he was called out of retirement to try to mediate an end to the Vietnam War. He recounts this unsuccessful mission and other aspects of his life in *A Memoir of China in Revolution* (1974). GREGORY A. JOHNSON

Rose, Marie Marguerite (1717–57). A native of Guinea in Africa, Rose was a slave belonging to *Louisbourg officer Jean Chrysostome Loppinot. Purchased in 1736, she worked in the Loppinot household for 19 years, helping to prepare meals and to raise 12 children, as well as her own son. After being freed in 1755, only two years before her death, she married Jean-Baptiste Laurent, a Mi'kmaq, and together they opened a tavern. Although a slave for most of her life, Rose acquired considerable business skills. As well as managing a tavern, she was a cook and seamstress, she could knit, dye, and iron clothes, and she made her own soap and preserves. An inventory of her possessions at her death is unique in Canada, since it tells the story of a recently freed slave woman. As a gardener, Rose had vegetables worth 40 livres, the most valuable item in her estate. KENNETH DONOVAN

Ross rifle. Much rated, hated, and debated, the Ross rifle was Canada's first sally into munitions procurement. Adopted in 1901 by Laurier's administration to cure chronic shortages of, and dependence on Britain for, militia weapons, it was an accurate, advanced rifle designed by Scottish aristocrat Sir Charles Ross and made in Quebec City. It soon fell victim to partisan politics. Stubbornly championed by Sam *Hughes, Canadians took it to war in 1914. By the time rectifiable problems occurred in battle, the weapon was so controversial that troop confidence was destroyed, forcing the rifle to be withdrawn in late 1916 and Ross's factory expropriated early the next year. A well-intended policy gone wrong. RONALD HAYCOCK

Rowan, William (1891–1957), world-renowned zoologist and nature artist, born in Switzerland, educated in England. As a ranch pupil he observed wildlife on the Canadian Prairies (1908–11), then studied zoology at University College London. At the University of Alberta (1920–56) he taught zoology, conducted pioneering research on bird migration, and investigated the embryology and cyclic fluctuation of animals. Beginning in the 1920s, his weekly radio broadcasts on conservation reached a wide audience across the Prairies, and after the war his concerns about scientists' responsibility to society were published in the popular press. A lively, colourful person with a flare for publicity, 'Doc Rowan' had a major impact on his colleagues, students, and the general public. MARIANNE GOSZTONYI AINLEY

Rowell–Sirois Commission, 1940. The Royal Commission on Dominion–Provincial Relations, established in 1937 to respond to the economic and constitutional crisis created by the Depression, is popularly known as the Rowell–Sirois Commission because of its successive chairs, Newton Rowell and Joseph Sirois. It held hearings across Canada and attracted considerable attention. It commissioned important research, and some by scholars such as Donald *Creighton and J.A. Corry was of outstanding quality.

Although several provinces were deeply suspicious of the commission's work, it did set out some important principles that would become part of Canadian *federalism in the future. Its three-volume report, which appeared in 1940, became part of the wartime debate about jurisdiction and responsibility. The recommendation that the federal government take responsibility for unemployment insurance was quickly accepted, and the principle that the federal government should equalize revenues through the tax system was enshrined in the 1982 Constitution Act.

The commission's report appeared during the Second World War, when the major concern of Canadians was the nation's security. As a result, the centralizing aspects of the report attracted the most attention. Careful scrutiny reveals a balanced document that responded sensitively to the concerns of regions and special interests. Nevertheless, the report did permit the federal government to argue persuasively that wartime required a more effective and co-operative federal system.

The dominion–provincial conference called to discuss the report ended in chaos, but the lack of agreement permitted the federal government to act decisively on its own. The report also shaped discussion of post-war *federal–provincial relations. JOHN ENGLISH

rowing. One of the earliest recorded rowing competitions occurred in Halifax Harbour in 1811 between the *British garrison and a visiting Royal Navy warship. By the mid-1830s, rowing had developed in Maritime communities and west into Ontario, promoted by the desire of the working class to participate in popular British sporting traditions.

The oldest continuous sporting event in what is now Canada is the St John's Regatta, held since 1816 on Quidi Vidi Lake. Canada's first victory in international competition was by a Saint John four-oared crew that won a double victory in 1867 at the Paris Exposition. In the 1860s and 1870s, a fisherman named George Brown of Herring Cove, NS, became one of Canada's earliest successful rowers, winning stake races in Canada and the United States. The 1870s and 1880s were the golden age of 19th-century rowing, with the proliferation of clubs across the country. The Canadian Association of Amateur Oarsmen was formed in 1880, partly in response to the problems of betting and professional rowers, and to organize the sport nationally. Rower Edward (Ned) Hanlan was Canada's first national sports hero. He became champion of England and the world, defeating the Australian Edward Trickett on the Thames in 1880. Hanlan died in 1908, having won more than 300 races. In 1904, Lou Scholes of the Don Rowing Club won the Diamond Sculls at the English Royal Henley Regatta, as did Joe Wright Jr and Jack Guest in the 1920s.

Canada's international success was not to be seen again until the 1950s and 1960s, when the University of British Columbia/Vancouver Rowing Club crews were first in the fours and second in the eights at the 1956 Olympic Games, and won Canada's only medal, a silver, in the eights at the 1960 games. At the 1964 Olympics, UBC/VRC rowers Roger Jackson and George Hungerford won Canada's only gold medal, in the coxless pairs event. Canada won its first gold medal in the eights and five other medals at the 1984 Olympic Games, and four gold medals (women's pair, fours, and eights, and men's eights) and a bronze medal in the women's single by Silken Laumann at the 1992 games. Canada's rowers brought home six medals from the 1996 games, confirming them as the most significant rowing power in the world in the 1990s. Derek Porter of Victoria is perhaps Canada's best-ever oarsman. He stroked the men's gold medal eight in Barcelona, was first and third at the 1993 and 1999 World Championships in the single skulls, and was second and fourth in singles at the 1996 and 2000 Olympic Games.

ROGER JACKSON

Roy, Gabrielle (1909–83), novelist. Born and educated in Manitoba, where she worked as a teacher, Gabrielle Roy left for Paris and London in 1937. On her return she became a freelance journalist in Montreal and found international success with her first novel, *The Tin Flute* (1945); set in the Saint-Henri neighbourhood of Montreal at the beginning of the Second World War, it revealed the urban hell in which proletarianized French Canadians lived. After a second period in Europe she lived quietly in Quebec City and Petite-Rivière-St-François. Her work, which was recognized with the highest honours, varied between novels centred on solitary individuals (*The Cashier, The Hidden Mountain, Windflower*) and stories inspired by her life in the Canadian West (*Where Nests the Water Hen, Street of Riches, The Road Past Altamont, Garden in the Wind, Children of My Heart*), before concluding with her great posthumous autobiography, *Enchantment and Sorrow*. Well known in both linguistic communities, read and studied by the public as well as literary specialists, her work is distinguished by a simple and personal style, themes and settings closely tied to Canadian history and culture, compassion for the humblest characters, and an acute sense of human diversity and community.

FRANÇOIS RICARD

Royal Canadian Academy of Arts. A national art society established to enhance the status of artists, to unite artists in various regions through the organization of annual exhibitions, to further art education, and to establish a national gallery. At the request of artists and art societies and with the support of Governors General the Earl of Dufferin and the Marquess of Lorne, the Canadian Academy was established in 1880. Membership consisted of associates and 40 full academicians and included painters, sculptors, designers, and architects. The first president was Lucius O'Brien (1832–99) and the first female academician (1880) Charlotte Schreiber (1834–1922). In 1933 Marion Long became the second woman academician. The diploma works, exemplary of the academicians' talents, submitted to the government as a requirement of membership, formed the core collections of the National Gallery of Canada. Prevented from setting up art schools because of provincial jurisdiction, the academy funded life classes in various cities, promoting art based on sound draughtsmanship and art of the past. Annual exhibitions were held in Montreal, Ottawa, or Toronto, and occasionally elsewhere, and the academy selected the representation of Canadian art for international expositions until 1911. Control by mostly elderly academicians led the academy to become a conservative force in Canadian art in the 1920s. Since the presidency of George Reid (1860–1947) in 1906–7, the academy has on occasion promoted decorative architectural projects uniting the talents of the member professions. Until the Second World War its membership was largely drawn from Quebec and Ontario and its influence was greatest in these regions. It now includes workers in all the visual arts from across Canada, all full academicians. Inadequate funding and the lack of an established headquarters or building and school have prevented the academy from fulfilling its initial national mandate.

CHARLES C. HILL

Royal Canadian Air Force. The RCAF came into being on 1 April 1924, its ancestors being the British flying services of the First World War. It was initially a component of the Canadian army, answerable to the chief of the general staff, but most of its tasks, like its aircraft, were essentially civilian in nature. Forestry patrols took pride of place, followed by aerial photography, fisheries protection, and the occasional 'mercy' flight. In 1925 only 73 out of 5,111 hours flown were devoted to military training.

In the first 15 years of its existence the RCAF's most notable achievement was probably the Hudson Strait expedition of 1927–8 to study ice and weather conditions with a view to opening up Churchill, Manitoba, as a port from which to export prairie grain to Europe. Its worst moment probably came in 1932, when cuts in the defence budget left it with a strength of less than 800. Growing tensions in Europe led the government to increase appropriations from 1935 on, and the air arm, which became an independent service with its own chief of air staff in 1938, was the primary beneficiary. On the eve of the Second World War, in August 1939, the RCAF numbered 8 Permanent Force and 12 Auxiliary squadrons, with 8 Hawker Hurricanes its only battle-worthy aircraft. That soon changed. Of the 250,000 men and women who served in the wartime RCAF, 94,000 served overseas, 60 per cent of them with Royal Air Force units.

The RCAF reached its maximum strength at the end of 1943 with 39 squadrons serving overseas and 38 on the Home War Establishment (HWE). Overseas strength peaked at 47 squadrons in February 1945, when the HWE had dropped to 24. The HWE consisted of Eastern and Western Air Commands engaged primarily on maritime reconnaissance and anti-submarine operations, and Training Command, responsible for the implementation of the *British Commonwealth Air Training Plan, which graduated 131,553 aircrew, of whom 72,835 were Canadians. Overseas squadrons served in northwest Europe, Italy, North Africa, India, and Burma, the largest formation being *No. 6 RCAF Bomber Group, formed in January 1943 and commanded initially by Air Vice-Marshal G.E. Brookes, followed (from February 1944) by AVM C.M. McEwen. At its peak strength, 6 Group numbered 14 squadrons. One bomber squadron, No. 405, moved to the elite No. 8 (Pathfinder) Group in April 1943 after a brief sojourn in Coastal Command. Twenty-four day and night fighter and army co-operation squadrons served in Fighter Command, the Air Defence of Great Britain, and/or 2nd Tactical Air Force at one time or another (but never in more than wing strength), while one day fighter squadron, No. 417, operated with the Desert Air Force in North Africa and Italy. Excluding No. 405, six squadrons contributed to Coastal Command, three on maritime reconnaissance, and two on maritime strike duties.

Twelve reconnaissance and strike squadrons of the HWE's Eastern Air Command patrolled the western side of the Atlantic, and nine Western Air Command (WAC) squadrons guarded the Pacific coast at one time or another. Two fighter squadrons and one bomber reconnaissance squadron from WAC participated directly in the Aleutian campaign in 1942, guarding Anchorage against the remote possibility of Japanese bombing raids and strafing Japanese positions on *Kiska, where Squadron Leader K.A. Boomer shot down one Japanese aircraft—the HWE's only air-to-air victory. One maritime reconnaissance squadron, headquartered in Ceylon, monitored remote areas of the Indian Ocean from 1942 onwards, and three transport squadrons—one of which had earlier participated in the ill-fated Arnhem operation of September 1944—air-supplied the British 14th Army in Burma during 1945.

The first women to serve in the RCAF were the 12 who initiated the RCAF Nursing Service (which peaked at 395 in October 1944) in September 1940. In July 1941 a Canadian Women's Auxiliary Air Force was authorized, subsequently designated RCAF (Women's Division) in February 1942. Initially, members were employed only as cooks, clerks, drivers, telephone operators, waitresses, and such customary women's work. After 1942 they were admitted to all trade classifications other than aircrew and many served overseas in the United Kingdom. Over the course of the war, almost 17,000 (including 260 from Newfoundland) were enlisted in the RCAF (WD), 50 of them being decorated. The last members of the Women's Division were demobilized by March 1947, but on 21 March 1951 the cabinet authorized the recruitment of women into the regular RCAF.

By the end of 1947 RCAF strength had dwindled to 12,200 and all its combat aircraft were obsolescent. For the *Korean War (1950) the air force could offer only a long-range transport squadron, although 26 RCAF fighter pilots flew with USAF squadrons. However, the onset of the Cold War put the RCAF on an upward path once again. Early in 1951 an air division of 12 squadrons of modern jet fighters was committed to *NATO duties in Europe, a figure that sank to six by 1964. Several squadrons of four-engined maritime patrol aircraft monitored Canada's coastlines and the western Atlantic. Through the 1950s and 1960s another nine fighter squadrons were deployed in Canada, assigned to *NORAD after its institution in August 1958, when the RCAF mustered over 55,000 airmen in its ranks. NORAD also involved the RCAF in ground radar chains—the Pinetree Line (constructed in the early 1950s), the Mid-Canada Line (mid-1950s), and the Distant Early Warning Line (late 1950s).

In the post-Korean War era, the RCAF participated in *UN operations, airlifting troops and equipment to major 'hot spots' such as Cyprus and the Congo and delivering observers to many out-of-the way places such as Yemen and New Guinea. A new National Defence Act, passed in April 1967, led to the *unification of the Canadian armed forces from 1 February 1968 and brought an end to the RCAF. BRERETON GREENHOUS

Royal Canadian Legion. The organization was incorporated in 1926 as the Canadian Legion of the British Empire Service League, the result of the amalgamation of the *Great War Veterans Association, the largest veterans' organization in Canada at the time, and several smaller associations that had been created during and after the First World War. It assumed responsibility for *veterans and their dependants by lobbying the federal government on pensions, health care, vocational training and education, land settlement, and other benefits, and was especially active during the Second World War to ensure that programs designed for veterans and their families were properly organized and implemented. The legion is also dedicated to the commemoration and remembrance of the contribution of Canada and Canadians to past wars, through 11 November ceremonies, annual poppy campaigns, and the tomb of the unknown soldier. After shortening its name to the Canadian Legion in 1958, it received permission from the Queen in 1960 to add the term 'Royal'. Since the 1970s the legion has assumed a more activist role in the community, with programs for seniors and youth. With headquarters in Ottawa, in 2002 it had a membership of about 450,000, organized into provincial commands and some 1,600 branches.

GLENN WRIGHT

Royal Canadian Mint. On 1 December 1931 the Ottawa branch of the British Royal Mint was transferred to Canadian jurisdiction to become the Royal Canadian Mint. From its opening in 1908, the Royal Mint had been responsible for the production of Canadian coins. Modest demand, however, meant that the mint was often idle. Orders from the Bank of England during the First World War pushed the mint into over-production, but by the 1920s demand had again dissipated. Relations between the Royal Mint and the Canadian government became increasingly strained. It was up to Winston Churchill, then the British chancellor of the exchequer, to suggest that a transfer of jurisdiction might help relieve some of the tension. Soon after his election in 1930, Prime Minister R.B. *Bennett met with Churchill, and plans for nationalization gained some headway; within the year a bill to establish a domestic mint was passed in the House of Commons.

The Royal Canadian Mint quickly expanded after 1931. A new refinery opened within five years and further upgrades were undertaken during the economic expansion of the Second World War. An additional production facility opened in Winnipeg in 1976. Since becoming a Crown corporation in 1969, the mint has kept a keen eye on its profits, actively seeking to diversify its products, at home and abroad. Domestic requirements increased with the introduction of one- and two-dollar coins, in 1987 and 1996 respectively, but medals and commemorative coins also constitute a significant part of its business.

EMILY GILBERT

Royal Canadian Mounted Police. In 1920 the Royal *North-West Mounted Police absorbed the Dominion Police to form the RCMP; the headquarters of the new force moved from Regina to Ottawa. The Dominion Police had been Canada's first *security and intelligence service from their creation in 1869 and in 1901 organized the national fingerprint bureau. The amalgamation of the two forces was a result of security concerns growing out of the final years of the First World War and the *Winnipeg General Strike of 1919. The new RCMP was to gather intelligence on potential subversives and to act as a mobile reserve for local *police forces across the country. In fact, the activities of labour groups like the *One Big Union and political organizations with revolutionary agendas declined very rapidly in the early 1920s. The RCMP survived attempts to disband it and spent most of the decade doing administrative work for various government departments and policing the Yukon and Northwest Territories.

In 1928 the government of Saskatchewan requested a return to the arrangement that had existed in 1905–17 by which the RNWMP had carried out provincial police duties under contract. Ottawa agreed; four years later the RCMP took over provincial policing in Alberta, Manitoba, New Brunswick, Nova Scotia, and Prince Edward Island. Newfoundland, on joining Confederation in 1949, also acquired the provincial services of the RCMP; the following year British Columbia joined the majority, leaving only Ontario and Quebec with their own provincial forces. In all provinces where it does provincial policing, the RCMP also contracts to do municipal police duties in many towns and even some large cities. There has been occasional tension about which level of government controls the RCMP in particular circumstances but only one serious open dispute. During a logger's strike in Newfoundland in 1959, the federal government refused a request for RCMP reinforcements, which led to the resignation in protest of Commissioner L.H. Nicholson.

Under the leadership of Commissioner Sir James MacBrien (1931–8) the RCMP underwent extensive modernization. Among other things, the first national crime laboratory was opened at Regina in 1937 and an aviation section was established the same year. In 1935 the force began sending officers to university for training and in 1938 an RCMP Police College in Ottawa began offering courses to members of all Canadian police forces.

The Second World War directed the priorities of the RCMP once again to security and intelligence. Members of pro-Nazi and fascist organizations were rounded up and interned at the start of the war, as were many communists until the German invasion of the Soviet Union in 1941. Although the RCMP was wholly successful in preventing sabotage and rounding up the few German spies landed by submarine, until the defection of Igor *Gouzenko in September 1945 they failed to detect the large spy ring organized and run from the Soviet embassy in Ottawa. The Cold War meant a great expansion of security checks for government employees and others but there were no more public revelations about espionage until the comic-opera episode involving some Conservative cabinet ministers and a German woman named Gerda Munsinger in the mid-1960s. With the rise of Quebec *separatism in that decade the attention of the RCMP security service turned to domestic threats. Several clumsy attempts by the force to infiltrate the movement turned embarrassingly public and led to the appointment of the *McDonald Inquiry into Certain Activities of the Royal Canadian Mounted Police. The commission recommended a separate security organization, and in 1984 the Canadian Security and Intelligence Service took over from the RCMP in such areas. The misadventures of the late 1960s suggested that the RCMP was out of touch with a rapidly changing Canadian society. As a result, in the

1970s the force began to recruit women for the first time as well as beginning an aggressive program to attract visible minorities. R.C. MACLEOD

Royal Canadian Navy. The Canadian navy was founded on 4 May 1910, when the Naval Service Act became law. Wilfrid *Laurier intended that the navy should grow from a militarized *Fishery Protection Service, but the arms race in Europe prompted a parliamentary appeal for something larger. The result was Laurier's Naval Service Bill of 12 January 1910 and a plan for a fleet of ocean-going cruisers. In 1910 two aged British cruisers, *Niobe* and *Rainbow*, were acquired for training purposes, and in August 1911 the new service became the Royal Canadian Navy.

Laurier's naval scheme was almost stillborn. Cruisers were more than anti-imperialists would support and less than imperialists wanted. When Robert *Borden's Conservatives won the 1911 election they tried to retract Laurier's legislation. They introduced a Naval Aid Bill in 1912 to build battleships for the imperial fleet, but by 1914 Borden's bill was stalled in the Senate and Laurier's navy was moribund: only *Rainbow* was active, doing fisheries patrols.

The First World War did little to redeem the RCN, although it demonstrated that only Canadians cared about defence of the Canadian coast. By 1918 the navy consisted of small patrol vessels, a couple of submarines, and 9,000 personnel—not enough to respond effectively to attacks by German submarines in Canadian waters that year. Post-war schemes to rejuvenate the navy collapsed amid hard times and disarmament. Drastic budget cuts in 1922 reduced the RCN to a couple of ships, a few hundred personnel, and two small bases. In response, Commodore Walter Hose, director of the Naval Service, established the RCN Volunteer Reserve, with divisions in 15 Canadian cities. It proved to be a highly successful scheme. Although in the late 1920s the first proper warships were built for the RCN, *Saguenay* and *Skeena*, the government nearly abandoned the RCN in the Depression. Hose fought for his budget and won. By 1939 the navy comprised six modern destroyers and 1,800 personnel.

The Second World War was Canada's formative naval experience. With shipping under attack from German submarines, the RCN helped establish and operate *convoys in the North Atlantic. This role was suited to rapid expansion, local construction of vessels, and the reservists whom the navy recruited. By the end of 1942 half of the escorts for the main North Atlantic convoys were Canadian, and in the spring of 1944 the whole system came under RCN escort. By the end of 1944 the RCN peaked at over 400 armed vessels and nearly 100,000 personnel. The professional service also used the war to acquire cruisers, aircraft carriers, and a naval air service. In 1945 the RCN was briefly the third largest navy in the world.

The RCN maintained the core of its new fleet after the war. However, the government was a reluctant supporter and the fate of the RCN was secured only by the advent of the Cold War. Warships were the first Canadian forces committed to the Korean crisis in 1950. With a renewed western alliance (NATO), the RCN slipped back into the escort and anti-submarine role. By the end of the 1950s it was a world leader in anti-submarine warfare, building innovative warships of the St Laurent class, pioneering the use of helicopters, variable depth sonars, and integrated data-processing systems. Strength peaked at about 100 ships and over 20,000 personnel. Thermonuclear weapons and skyrocketing costs brought conventional forces into question by the early 1960s and forced the Canadian government to economize. The result was armed forces integration, announced in 1964. Under this scheme, which was bitterly contested by senior naval officers, the RCN ceased to exist as an institution on 1 February 1968, when the Canadian Armed Forces (CF) came into being.

The navy survived integration as Maritime Command (MARCOM), which for a while included the maritime squadrons of the former *Royal Canadian Air Force. In 1970 the navy was also forced to adopt the standard CF green uniform, a major blow to identity and morale. Through the 1970s MARCOM was starved of resources, and the fleet and its equipment deteriorated rapidly. Concern about a decline in conventional deterrence prompted a rebuilding in the 1980s and early 1990s. This scheme permitted diversion of modern equipment to the old fleet, which fought the Gulf War 1990–1. Since then 12 'Canadian Patrol Frigates' and 12 small Maritime Coastal Defence Vessels have been built, four Tribal-class destroyers modernized, and four ex-RN submarines acquired. The new fleet and its 9,000 personnel have deployed around the world from the Balkan crisis, to Somalia, East Timor, and the war on terrorism.

By the end of the 20th century the navy was modern and highly capable. In 1985 it reverted to blue uniforms and by the 1990s it was common to talk of 'the navy' once again. This was affirmed by reorganization of the CF along traditional service lines, with the navy—still officially MARCOM —now under the chief of maritime staff. MARC MILNER

royal colony of New France. In 1534 Jacques *Cartier claimed territory in eastern North America in the name of the French king. By the early 1600s, French influence stretched from the shores of Newfoundland through large parts of the present Maritime provinces into the St Lawrence Valley. Nonetheless, the French population in the New World remained very small, even long after Samuel de *Champlain's establishment of a fortress at Quebec in 1608. French monarchs devolved effective control over the area called *New France to private companies, which were expected to bring settlers to the New World. However, in 1663 Louis XIV established direct royal rule over the colony; henceforth it came under the authority of his minister of the marine.

More than most other French colonies in the New World, New France not only replicated features of the absolutistic government structure of the mother country, but even improved on them. In France, many officials, with the major exception of the intendants, purchased their offices and held them as personal property, selling or bequeathing them. As a result, the king lost direct control over many of his officials. In contrast, in New France, all office-holders (with only one minor and brief exception) were appointed by the king and could be fired by him.

As in the French provinces, the governor was the chief regal representative, in charge of military and diplomatic matters. The second most important public figure was the intendant, Jean *Talon being the first to take up his position in New France, in 1665. Through his control over finances and policing in the broadest sense of the word, the intendant exercised a great deal of power. He played a key role in ensuring the king's control over the colony, providing detailed censuses of the population, and overseeing the provision of justice. He presided over the Sovereign Council (renamed the Superior Council in 1703), the body of local notables that registered the king's edicts, promulgated regulations, and served as an appeal court. Civil government was thus greatly improved once the king assumed control. In 1663 the tithe was given legal sanction, although the burden of the tithe remained lower than in many parts of France, at 1/26th of the annual production of grain. In 1664 the Coutume de Paris became the sole juridical code in force in the colony.

As in France, patronage networks played a very important role in the exercise of power. The governor and the intendant often fought over jurisdictions and patronage, and a number of the leading figures had to be disciplined, sometimes recalled to France for their misdeeds.

Jean-Baptiste Colbert, chief minister to Louis XIV, perceived the economic and, more importantly, military potential of the colony. Despite this recognition, successive ministers wished the colony to be as self-sufficient as possible; consequently French financial support always remained limited. The brief flurry of royal investment, including sponsored immigration, under the direction of Intendant Talon was essentially finished by 1672. From that point, the king's attention focused much more on military matters in Europe. Still, the *fur trade and the natural growth of the colony provided catalysts to further growth. The population grew from some 3,000 in 1663 to around 20,000 by 1713, ultimately reaching about 75,000 at the time of the British *Conquest in 1759–60.

New France became the most 'French' of the French colonies in the Americas. In theory, Protestants and Jews were not permitted to immigrate, although some found a place as important merchants in the trading community in Quebec during the liberal years of Louis XV's reign, which began in 1715. Aboriginal settlements grew on the outskirts of the major towns, and trade and contact continued between the French and the First Nations, but relatively few intermarriages resulted from these connections. The Catholic basis of the colony was largely unchallenged, even if the local church hierarchy was not always able to control the colony's morals as much as it would have wished.

As was the case in northern France, land in New France was distributed under *seigneurial tenure. Until the revocation of its charter in 1663, the Compagnie des cent-associés exercised the privilege of distributing land to seigneurs. After that date, the intendant and the governor jointly distributed land along the St Lawrence River and some its major tributaries. About one-quarter of the land under seigneurial tenure was owned by church communities. In other seigneuries, the local lord often occupied a place of great social prestige. The seigneur granted land to the *censitaires*, often called *'habitants' in the documents of the time. These peasants owed certain tributes to the seigneur, just as the seigneurs were expected to offer homage to the king when called upon to do so. The burden of the *censitaires* remained relatively low in the early years, though it increased as settlement pressures developed in the 18th century.

Although New France remained an underfunded colony through much of its history, its military significance was understood, and the king did send troops and ships for defence. Other state initiatives bolstered modest economic growth. In 1737 the colonial government completed the royal road that linked Quebec and Montreal. Colonial authorities supported the *St-Maurice ironworks, one of the few large-scale enterprises. The extended period of relative peace from 1713 to 1744 is considered by some as the 'Golden Age' of New France.

New France's colonial status meant that it was involved in dynastic and international struggles. Colonists often found themselves in conflict with their Anglo-American neighbours from Massachusetts and the other British colonies. They also fought many wars against different First Nations, including the *Iroquois Confederacy through much of the latter 17th century and the Fox, Chickasaw, and others in the 18th century. Governors such as Louis de Buade de *Frontenac, Philippe de Rigaud de Vaudreuil, and Charles Beauharnois de la Boische provided effective military leadership to the embattled colony.

New France suffered from the precarious finances and military defeats of metropolitan France. The Treaty of Utrecht in 1713 spelled the loss of Acadia, Newfoundland, and the French Hudson Bay posts to British control. Although under the official control of the governor at Quebec, Acadia, Île Royale (Cape Breton), and Louisiana had largely developed separately from the St Lawrence Valley settlements. Nonetheless, the capture of *Louisbourg, given its important role in protecting shipping access to the St Lawrence, was of considerable concern to the colony centred on Quebec. First captured in 1745 and later rebuilt, Louisbourg fell for a second, and last, time in 1758.

The fortress at Quebec itself was captured by the British in 1759, and authorities at Montreal surrendered in 1760. In 1763 the Treaty of Paris ceded control over New France to the British. Only the small islands of *St-Pierre and Miquelon off the Burin peninsula of Newfoundland today remain under French control, remnants of the French empire that once extended through much of North America. COLIN M. COATES

royal commissions. Ad hoc, advisory organizations of one or more commissioners appointed by a *cabinet. The task of a royal commission is to investigate, conduct research, and report upon a matter assigned to in its terms of reference. The power and authority granted to royal commissions for the conduct of their investigation is contained in the relevant federal or provincial Inquiries Act. A government is not bound to accept any of the recommendations presented in a commission's report. With the presentation of its final report, the commission ceases to exist.

Several large-scale royal commissions had major impacts on federal social or economic policy in the 20th century. Generally named after their chairpersons, these have included the Laurendeau–Dunton Commission (1967), whose call for official *bilingualism was acted upon by the Trudeau government, and the Macdonald Commission (1985), whose call for *free trade was accepted by the Mulroney government. But not all commissions see their recommendations turned into public policy. Recent examples of reports not yet acted upon include the Lortie Commission on Electoral Reform and Party Finance (1991) and the Royal Commission on *Aboriginal Peoples (1996).

JOHN C. COURTNEY AND DANIEL MACFARLANE

Royal Engineers. A branch of the British military that played a brief but important role in mid-19th-century British North America. The Corps of Engineers ('Royal' in 1787) had a presence in Canada from the time of the British Conquest, but it was following the War of 1812, amid tense Anglo-American relations, that they left their greatest mark, building several important defensive works through the 1820s and 1830s that remain Canadian landmarks—the Halifax Citadel, Fort Henry in Kingston, Ontario, and the Rideau Canal. This last, Lieutenant-Colonel John *By its chief engineer, ranks among the finest early engineering accomplishments in North America. In 1858, two contingents of the corps were dispatched to the Pacific coast to establish civil order in the British fur trade territory then being flooded with gold seekers. One surveyed the international boundary on the 49th parallel from the Pacific to the Rockies. Another, under Colonel R.C. Moody, laid out townsites and built public facilities, chief among the latter being the *Cariboo Road from Yale to Quesnel. Their major works, paid for from the public purse, were built to standards private entrepreneurs could never have matched, and some stand to this day as telling vestiges of non-commercial ideals.

RICHARD WHITE

Royal Proclamation of 1763. Although the Royal Proclamation of 1763 has become known as 'the Indians' Magna Carta', its origins were prosaic. It was issued by Britain's King George III on 7 October 1763 to establish the boundaries and governmental institutions of new territories that Britain had acquired at the end of the Seven Years' War. As a result of the Peace of Paris, 1763, British rule was extended to Quebec, Florida, and Grenada. The proclamation set the western boundary of Quebec west of the Ottawa River, annexed Prince Edward Island and Cape Breton to Nova Scotia, and struck the Appalachian Mountains as the western limit of the Thirteen Colonies. It also promised representative assemblies and the establishment of a legal system 'agreeable to the Laws of England'; in the case of Quebec an assembly was not granted until after the creation of Lower Canada in 1791, and the legal system remained a blend of British and French practice.

Since Native affairs were matters of great importance when the proclamation was issued, the document contained a number of elements that addressed these issues. When the proclamation was being prepared, their importance was heightened by an Indian rising against British rule, led by the Odawa chief *Pontiac, by First Nations south of the lower Great Lakes who had fought with the French in the Seven Years' War. Their capture of British forts and slaughter of some 2,000 soldiers and settlers made Britain anxious to conciliate First Nations and secure their acquiescence in British rule. The clauses aimed at First Nations have given the proclamation lasting influence in Canadian law and its nickname.

The proclamation's elements related to Native concerns were several. First, establishing the western boundary of the Thirteen Colonies severed a rich agricultural hinterland from the seaboard American colonies. These provisions were intensely resented in the Thirteen Colonies, which looked to the western lands for future development. Furthermore, the proclamation ordered anyone who had located on lands west of Quebec or the Thirteen Colonies to 'remove themselves' forthwith. No one was to enter these western territories to trade with the Indians without a licence from the governor. This closing of the western regions was intended to placate First Nations, who feared that a British victory would mean an influx of settlers into their lands.

What made the proclamation of lasting significance for Canadian Native affairs was what it said about lands west of the boundaries specified. First, the proclamation, while assuming that all lands in the eastern half of North America were British, specified that lands west of Quebec and the Thirteen Colonies were Indian territories. They were 'reserve[d] under our Sovereignty, Protection, and Dominion, for the use of the said Indians'. Second, it said that no individual could negotiate with Indians for purchase of these lands that were reserved for their use, but, if the Indians wished to dispose of their territorial rights, they could do so to the Crown 'in our Name, at some public Meeting or Assembly of the said Indians, to be held for that Purpose by the Governor or Commander in Chief of our Colony'. The purpose of these restrictions was to avoid upsetting the Indians by allowing individual entrepreneurs to negotiate for land purchases, a practice that in the earlier history of the Thirteen Colonies had often led to conflict between Indians and settlers.

These rules for acquiring First Nations' land—only by the Crown, and only at a public meeting called for that specific purpose—became the basis of Canadian treaty making. In the future southern Ontario this procedure was followed in a series of *Indian treaties after 1783. Later in the West, even though the proclamation had explicitly exempted *Rupert's Land from its scope, the

Canadian government followed similar practice in negotiating 11 numbered treaties between 1871 and 1921. By the late 20th century, it was generally held in both political and judicial circles that the Royal Proclamation's dictates about Aboriginal lands applied everywhere in Canada. A reference to the proclamation was even included in the Constitution Act, 1982. Although the immediate purpose of the Royal Proclamation of 1763 was limited and practical, some of its clauses dealing with Indian lands have acquired great legal import and practical policy relevance. In light of that transformation it is not surprising that the document is still part of Canadian law. J.R. MILLER

Royal Society of Canada. Founded in 1882 by Governor General Marquess of Lorne to advance scholarship in the sciences and humanities, recognize intellectual achievement, and provide a focus for dispersed individuals and institutions. It was organized into four sections with 20 members (fellows) each: I. littérature français, histoire, archéologie; II. English literature, history, archaeology; III. mathematical, physical, and chemical sciences; IV. geological and biological sciences. In its first half century the society was supported by some of the country's major scholars and its annual *Proceedings and Transactions*, exchanged with hundreds of similar organizations abroad, reflected a wide slice of Canadian intellectual activity. These stout volumes contained a profusion of factual detail—historical documents, descriptions and classification of natural history specimens, and results of laboratory experiments. They also carried accounts of such government agencies as the Geological Survey, Experimental Farms, and Tides and Currents Survey. The strength of the sciences was mirrored in the steadily expanded membership: in 1938, 200 of 305 fellows were in the science sections.

Increasingly, however, developments inside and outside the society sapped its vitality and stimulated a feeling of ineffectuality. Inadequate funding had crippled its ability to support research, although private initiatives enabled it to award prizes and medals for merit in virtually all fields. The appearance of specialized periodicals and the *National Research Council supplanted the *Transactions* as an outlet for publication. Members had always displayed an uneven commitment to the society: a minority tried to make it a working organization of influence; others were content with the cachet of fellowship as an end in itself. There were few contacts among the semi-autonomous sections and no significant interchanges between the French- and English-speaking groups. Finally, the society never fully realized an early ambition to become a source of expert advice to governments. After mid-century it was reorganized into Académie des lettres et des sciences humaines (academy I), Academy of Humanities and Social Sciences (academy II), and Academy of Science (academy III). Determined efforts were made to assert a role as Canada's National Academy in representing the country abroad and in evaluating research programs, enhancing public awareness of science, sponsoring independent research into such matters as lead in gasoline and the safety of nuclear power reactors, and advancing the status of women in scholarship. CARL BERGER

royal tours. From time to time since 1860 Canadians have welcomed members of the royal family on state visits. The purpose of these royal tours has been to bring Canadians closer to the *monarchy, to legitimate authority, and to reinforce imperial/Commonwealth ties.

In 1860 Albert Edward, Prince of Wales (later King Edward VII), made the first royal visit to Canada (various members of the royal family had visited in their professional capacities as soldiers or administrators, but this was the first state visit). The 18-year-old son of Queen Victoria came in response to an invitation from the Province of Canada legislature to open the Victoria Bridge in Montreal. Everywhere he went, from St John's to Sarnia, vast crowds welcomed him and took part in the elaborate festivities. There was trouble, however, in ultra-loyal Kingston, where Orangemen sought royal recognition, and the prince, on advice from the colonial secretary, refused to give it. Demonstrations and heated debates ensued, which the international press closely covered, to the embarrassment of authorities. It was a lesson for the future: royal tours would need to be closely choreographed.

A few of the later tours stand out. The 1901 coast-to-coast tour made by the Duke and Duchess of Cornwall and York (later King George V and Queen Mary) was one leg of a global tour of the empire. Set against the backdrop of the *South African War and Britain's desire for colonial support, the tour had a jingoistic tone and an explicit military purpose. Military matters figured prominently in the 1919 tour made by Edward, Prince of Wales (later Edward VIII). In the Great War, the dashing prince had served in the Grenadier Guards and had been stationed alongside Canadian troops on the Western Front. Delighted to welcome a prince and a comrade, recently returned soldiers mobbed Edward. Like every royal visitor to Canada, the prince took part in ceremonies with Aboriginal peoples, reinforcing the tie between the monarchy and First Nations. Edward showed a particular interest in the *rodeo and on impulse bought a ranch in Alberta, to which he returned on private visits.

The grandest tour was made in 1939 by King George VI and Queen Elizabeth (later 'the Queen Mum'). As war clouds gathered in Europe, the young royal couple distracted people from their anxieties about the Depression and Hitler. To the delight of countless Canadians, resourceful journalists covered all the pomp and ceremony. It was no accident that the tour—the first by a reigning monarch—enhanced the ties of affection between Canada and England at a crucial time.

In 1951 Princess Elizabeth and Prince Philip visited Canada for the first time, making a five-week, cross-country tour. Public interest ran high, not least because Canadians had been following the couple's romance and the royal wedding celebrations. Elizabeth came to Canada as queen in 1957 for a five-day visit to open Parliament, the first of many short visits made practical by air travel.

The queen and Prince Philip made more extended tours on occasions such as Canada's centennial in 1967 and Elizabeth's golden jubilee in 2002. IAN RADFORTH

Royal William, pioneering steam vessel. The construction of this paddle wheeler in 1831, with a hull built in Quebec and engines from Montreal, was an impressive but short-lived Canadian milestone in steam navigation. Its intended service on the St Lawrence for the Quebec and Halifax Steam Navigation Company was disrupted by *cholera quarantines and weak colonial trade. By 1833 its owners decided to send it to Britain to find a buyer. Carrying a cargo of coal and some passengers, the vessel crossed in 25 days entirely under steam, making the first genuine steam crossing of the Atlantic (an honour often claimed by the American *Savannah*, whose 1819 crossing was mostly under sail). Sold for coastal European trade, *Royal William* was later bought by the Spanish government and renamed *Ysabel Segunda*. In 1836 it became the first *steamship to fire a shot in anger. A year later it became a storage hulk. DAN CONLIN

Rupert's Land. The territory held by the *Hudson's Bay Company from 1670 until its transfer to Canada in 1870. Defined by royal charter as comprising the lands draining into *Hudson Bay, it originated in the context of European political and fur trade rivalries. Two trader-explorers of New France, Médard Chouart, Sieur des Groseilliers and Pierre-Esprit *Radisson, had a major role in its creation. Finding their colonial government oppressive, they brought their fur trade knowledge to England, which, having just taken New York from the Dutch, looked forward to extending its domains to the northern perimeter of New France. On 2 May 1670, King Charles II conferred on his cousin Prince Rupert and 17 other courtiers and businessmen 'the sole Trade and Commerce' of the entire Hudson Bay watershed, claiming it as 'one of our Plantacions or Colonyes in America'. The 18 HBC proprietors received monopoly trade rights to a territory larger than anyone realized. Until 1818, when the 49th parallel was declared the northern boundary of the United States, Rupert's Land extended into seven present-day Canadian provinces and territories (Quebec, Ontario, Manitoba, Saskatchewan, Alberta, Nunavut, and the Northwest Territories) and portions of Minnesota, North Dakota, and South Dakota. The estimated size of the watershed is over 3.8 million sq km.

Rupert's Land was home to an Aboriginal population speaking mainly Algonquian, Athapaskan, and Siouan languages; many Cree, Ojibwe, Assiniboine, and Dene communities played major roles in the *fur trade. They were not consulted when Rupert's Land was created, although early HBC traders were instructed to make treaties of friendship with local groups on whose lands they built their forts. The early HBC did not seek to govern or to change the cultures of Native peoples; rather, it depended on them to continue (and intensify) their traditional fur harvesting in exchange for its trade goods, and to provide the aid, knowledge, and local resources or 'country provisions' that made the newcomers' survival possible. Although the HBC charter had directed it to colonize as well as trade, its first colonial initiative came late: the founding of *Red River under the aegis of Thomas Douglas, Earl of *Selkirk, in 1812.

In the 1860s, the decline of the fur trade and bison herds and growing eastern Canadian interest in prairie agricultural land and territorial expansion were among many factors leading to the annexation of Rupert's Land by Canada. Its residents, including thousands of *Metis, were consulted almost as little about its demise as they had been in its founding. The result was the *Red River Resistance in 1869–70, which led to the creation of the province of Manitoba. JENNIFER S.H. BROWN

rural depopulation. Canada was an overwhelmingly rural place at Confederation, but as early as the 1870s and 1880s people began emigrating from the established country districts of Ontario, Quebec, and the Maritimes faster than they were replaced by childbirth or immigration. The contemporaneous growth of the populations of towns and cities meant that by 1921 census takers could report that the country was predominantly urban. That many Canadians described this development as rural 'depopulation'—a word previously used to describe the clearance of pasture lands in Britain and the effects of plague, locusts, and war—suggests their ambivalence about the emerging urbanization of the country.

The sources of Canadians' anxiety about these shifts in *population were diverse and not always complementary, but they generally reflected their concerns about aspects of the modern world and Canada's place in it. Non-farmers and farmers alike worried variously about electorates dominated by dependent employees rather than independent property-owners, the association of cities with immigrant populations, the fate of young urban-bound farm women free of the patriarchal family, and the social health of a nation populated by downtrodden factory workers and sedentary clerks rather than men and women made vigorous by life on the land. Farmers feared a loss of power to the burgeoning cities, and organized co-operatives and political organizations as a partial solution. The United Farmers of Ontario became the first third-party government in Canadian history in 1919, in part because the *conscription of farmers' sons in the First World War convinced many farm people of the need for an agrarian response to growing urban political dominance.

Although these concerns were deeply felt, 'rural depopulation' is itself best seen as a kind of migration rather than as a social devastation wrought by anti-farm attitudes. In Ontario, where the rhetoric of rural decline was fiercest, there was no dramatic attrition of family farms prior to the 1940s. Before then population losses consisted largely of a non-farm population of craftsmen and tradesmen unable to compete with urban factories and retailers, and of non-inheriting farm children without new local farming opportunities. Those children, when they left, were less inclined to migrate abruptly than to do so in stages, with the home farm providing a resource until they could support it and younger siblings yet to be established. Some left farm life by choice or necessity, but others recreated it on the western prairies.

Canadians' concern about rural emigration faded after the Second World War, a sign less of a recovery and triumph of rural life than of the actual decline of farming opportunities through widespread consolidation, and the attendant loss of farmers' political power and place in Canadian culture. ADAM CRERAR

Rush-Bagot Agreement, 1818, part of an attempt to resolve a number of Anglo-American difficulties after the War of 1812. Decisive naval engagements on inland lakes during the war (Put-in-Bay and Plattsburgh) led to extensive naval building during the first years of peace. At the initiative of Secretary of State James Monroe, the US minister to Britain, John Quincy Adams, opened talks with the foreign secretary, Lord Castlereagh, to limit the size and number of naval vessels on inland waters. The talks were shifted to Washington, where the acting secretary of state, Richard Rush, and the British minister, Charles Bagot, worked out the final details of a convention, ratified in April 1818. The provisions of the agreement allowed each nation one ship of 100 tons with one gun on both Lake Champlain and Lake Ontario and two ships of similar displacement on the upper Great Lakes. This was an early example of a naval arms limitation agreement, although land fortifications continued in place along the border until the 1870s. It ended the naval-building competition on the inland lakes; although the agreement was violated (during the Rebellions of 1837 and the Civil War) and the United States threatened to abrogate the convention, it has held. In modern times the agreement was amended to allow for training and naval shipbuilding. FRANCIS M. CARROLL

Ryerson, Egerton (1803–82). Born into a *Loyalist family in Upper Canada and raised by a deeply religious mother, Ryerson was one of five brothers who became Methodist preachers. Gradually, as the author of letters and pamphlets defending Methodism and especially as editor of the widely read and influential Methodist newspaper, the *Christian Guardian*, he emerged as a leading spokesman for his denomination on secular as well as religious issues. These activities also involved him in the turbulent politics of the era; with the advent of a moderate coalition, he agreed in 1844 to become superintendent of Upper Canadian *common schools. In this position, which he held until 1876, Ryerson shaped a developing system of elementary and grammar schools administered by local school boards, supported by parents, taxpayers, and government grants, and loosely bound by central policies and statutes. He established effective administration of the schools through a strong central Education Office, a body of administrative procedures, and a system of local inspection to ensure the implementation of provincial policy; he also sought to improve the program of studies and textbooks, and to establish a well-trained teaching force. He extended the common school system to include grammar schools, the predecessors of *high schools. Universal access to elementary education for all Upper Canadians was achieved with the School Act of 1871, which made the elementary schools tuition free and introduced the first steps towards compulsory education. Few of Ryerson's ideas were original, nor was his vision without flaws. But Ontario's school system, as he shaped it, became a model for most of English-speaking Canada and one that endured well into the 20th century. W.P.J. MILLAR AND R.D. GIDNEY

sailing ships. Sail power preceded the arrival of Europeans in the northern half of North America: some Aboriginal people attached simple sails to waterborne craft. Eventually, long after the first European arrivals, colonists adapted European technology and erected shipyards on Canada's eastern shores for the construction of wooden-hulled, sail-powered vessels. The first sailing ships were built in Acadia and New France in the 17th century, but the great boom in sailing ship construction and ownership occurred two centuries later. The 'golden age' image is a romantic and sometimes ideologically driven myth, especially if it implies general prosperity and a free-market heyday. It is true, however, that the colonies possessed substantial *shipbuilding and *shipping industries. For a few years in the 1860s and late 1870s, official tonnage figures suggest that Canada had the fourth largest merchant marine among maritime nations, although tonnage figures were questioned at the time and since.

The sailing ship industries grew under the protection of British navigation acts and preferential tariffs. In the Maritimes settlers of the 1760s and 1770s built sloops and schooners for coasting, fishing, and the *West Indies trade, and by 1778 more than 270 vessels were on registry. The Napoleonic Wars and protection for colonial wheat and timber set off an unprecedented shipbuilding boom. Between 1815 and 1860 more than 2.2 million tons of shipping was built in the three Maritime provinces, and another 800,000 tons was built in Upper and Lower Canada (a ton here is a measurement of internal space in a ship, roughly 100 cubic feet). Much of the tonnage was transferred to Britain, and the colonies became major suppliers of shipping for British shipowners. By the middle of the century the British North American colonies accounted for almost half of all new tonnage being built in the British Empire.

A sudden increase in net capital formation in shipping occurred in the 1850s, as a result of decisions by merchant-shipowners to retain newly built sailing ships for several years prior to resale to British or European owners. The 'golden age' that followed was short-lived: tonnage on registry peaked around 1879, and the collapse that followed was exceptional and rapid. Between 1880 and 1900 merchant shipping tonnage (much of it sail-powered) increased in almost all maritime nations; in Canada tonnage declined by 3.38 per cent a year. An old explanation for the decline emphasizes the obsolescence of wind power and wooden hulls. This explanation is unsatisfactory, because disinvestment in Canada preceded the decline in sailing ship tonnage elsewhere. Some Canadian shipowners shifted capital into iron, steel, and steam; most decided not to do so. Their decisions occurred in the context of national policies that emphasized landward development. Capitalists and the Canadian state acted together in building a great coastal nation with a small merchant navy. ERIC W. SAGER

St Andrews Biological Station. In 1908 the Biological Board of Canada opened Atlantic Canada's first permanent marine research station in St Andrews, New Brunswick. Located at Brandy Cove, the site was chosen for its proximity to the rich and diverse waters of Passamaquoddy Bay and railway service from Montreal. Rumour has it that the local amenities (e.g., a first-class golf course) played a deciding factor as well. In the early years, the station was open only during the summer months, generally from May to September, and was the home for university researchers. In 1928 it began operating year-round. A fire destroyed the station and its valuable library collection in 1932. With little money forthcoming during the Depression, the director, Dr Archibald Huntsman, ensured its rebirth by transferring funds from its operating budget, including the scientists' salaries.

Fisheries and Oceans Canada now operates the Biological Station. Its scientists have gained international recognition for their pioneering research on oceanography, aquatic ecology, chemical toxicology, and commercially important species, including stock-assessment methodology. Since the 1970s, research has expanded to include aquaculture. Indeed, the $200 million salmon aquaculture industry in New Brunswick began as a station project. Research continues to support this industry, including methods to increase profitability and to diversify to other species. SUZANNE TAYLOR

Saint-Jean, Idola (1880–1945), Quebec feminist. Born in Montreal, she made her living teaching elocution. Attracted to volunteer work, she worked with an assistance committee during the *Spanish flu epidemic of 1918, gave hundreds of lectures on hygiene, and, beginning in 1922, was mobilized by feminist demands. In 1928 she founded the Alliance canadienne pour le vote des femmes du Québec; the next year she took on a regular column on women's demands for the *Montreal Herald*; in 1930 she ran in the federal election; and from 1933 she published the magazine *La Sphère féminine*. Saint-Jean appeared on every panel on women's demands, on the radio, and in front of federal and provincial commissions. Commitment to her beliefs made her a courageous feminist who denounced the 'sexual aristocracy' in Quebec society.

MICHELINE DUMONT

Saint John. Located at the mouth of the Saint John River, the site was known to both the *Mi'kmaq and the Maliseet. A generation following the visit of *Champlain in 1604, French traders were active in the area, but French settlement was sparse even by the early 1700s. The British military arrived in 1758 and stayed. In the 1780s American *Loyalist refugees formed the communities of Carleton, Parr Town, and Portland. The former two were incorporated by royal charter as the city of Saint John in 1785.

During the early 19th century the city benefited from British *mercantilism and its control of *New Brunswick's import-export trade. Exports included square timber, sailing vessels, and eventually lumber, and the city was home to a thriving artisan culture. Although primarily a commercial centre, it experienced industrialization starting in the 1850s. The locally owned fleet of merchant vessels, which specialized in bulk cargo, was competitive into the 1870s. A rail link with the Gulf of St Lawrence by the 1860s failed to produce a larger through route to New England. As a result of Confederation-era political manoeuvring, the city was hooked up to the *Intercolonial Railway in 1876. The *CPR arrived in the 1880s. The modernization of port infrastructure, which included grain elevators, aimed to make Saint John the nation's winter port.

As in other 19th-century communities, class, ethnic, and religious tensions were apparent, with Anglo-Celtic Protestants dominating business, political, and social life. Beginning in the 1820s British immigrants, including Irish Protestants and Catholics, supplied much of the population increase. Protestants and Catholics practised forms of social apartheid that extended to schooling. In 1849 religious and ethnic tensions culminated in a bloody riot between Orangemen and Irish Catholics. After 1850 there was little further immigration; two decades later, out-migration to the United States was a major issue. A small African-Canadian community faced considerable discrimination. Small Jewish and Lebanese communities took root by the early 1900s. Persons of Acadian descent were rare until the mid-20th century.

A typical Victorian amalgam of elite residences, well-appointed commercial buildings, and working-class tenements, the city experienced forced urban renewal following the Great Fire of 1877. The rebuilding of the commercial and residential South End produced an architecturally interesting cityscape with heritage appeal. The amalgamation of Portland in 1889 began a merger process that eventually included Simonds parish and the town of Lancaster by the 1960s.

Following the First World War Saint John experienced the same economic doldrums as the rest of the Maritime region, although business and political interests succeeded in interesting the national government in port modernization. However altered by economic and technological forces such as the expansion of the service sector, streetcars, and automobiles, the city remained a cluster of distinct neighbourhoods and its Protestant–Catholic divisions shaped social life.

Following the Second World War, Saint John was affected by industrialization, transportation infrastructure changes, and urban renewal. Entire neighbourhoods of substandard housing, and tightly knit urban enclaves, disappeared. The upwardly mobile moved into new suburban neighbourhoods to the east and west, the less fortunate into public housing or private apartments and flats. Industry, with its demands on water, air quality, and aesthetics, came to dominate the skyline of eastern Saint John. Heavy industries, which gave the city a blue-collar sensibility, included a major oil refinery, a deep-water petroleum terminal, a dry dock, two pulp and paper mills, and a container terminal. Although home to a campus of the University of New Brunswick and a regional hospital, Saint John has a relatively small public sector and has been hit hard by federal job cuts. Typical of the region, the modern city has depended on megaprojects such as the expansion of the Irving oil refinery in the 1970s and late 1990s, the construction of a nearby nuclear power plant in the late 1970s, and construction in the 1980s of patrol frigates for the Canadian navy.

As older industries have disappeared in recent years, much faith has been invested in tourism and information technology. Despite attempts since the 1980s to rejuvenate the downtown core, including restoration of the classic Imperial Theatre, Saint John lost population in the late 20th century. Much of its workforce resides in surrounding Charlotte, Kings, and Saint John counties.

GREG MARQUIS

St John's. According to popular legend, the city of St John's takes its name from the discovery of the harbour by John *Cabot on 24 June 1497, the feast day of St John the Baptist. Deep and landlocked, the harbour from the early 1500s has been a haven and supply base for European fishermen because of its close proximity to the rich cod fisheries on the *Grand Banks. By the early 1700s St John's was probably the largest settlement in *Newfoundland, with about 700 permanent inhabitants. Along with its military role in protecting the English fishery, it became the administrative and judicial centre for the island by the early 18th century. The French Revolutionary and Napoleonic Wars brought major structural changes to the fishery between 1790 and 1815, leading eventually to the displacement of the migratory fishery by a resident one that required a larger permanent population. During this period there was substantial immigration to St John's from both Ireland and the west of England. By 1795 the town's permanent population stood at over 3,000, two-thirds of whom were Irish. Within another decade its winter population was over 5,000, occupying over 700 wooden houses. From approximately 43 per cent of shipping trade to Newfoundland in 1790, the town's share had increased to 63 per cent in 1805 and to 78 per cent by 1811. With commercial development came population growth: by 1815 St John's had a permanent population of over 10,000.

In 1824 the town's pre-eminence in Newfoundland was once more enhanced with the establishment of the Supreme Court, followed in 1832 by the colony's first legislature. Although also dealing with broad issues affecting all the island, the legislature to a large extent served as a form of municipal government. In 1888 the city achieved elected local government, so that the burden of civic improvements could be borne by residents rather than by the colonial government. In July 1892 fire destroyed much of the city core—as it had in 1816–17 and 1846—leaving 11,000 people homeless and destroying property estimated at about $13 million. Just two years later, the city's two commercial banks collapsed, wiping out the savings of many. Financial stability was eventually restored with the establishment of branches of three major Canadian banks. Structural changes in the fishery and in the banking system strengthened the economic hold the city held over the outports.

The Second World War greatly changed the face of the city. After 1940 Canada and the United States established major military facilities, with military personnel stationed in St John's reaching over 10,000 by 1944. 'Newfyjohn', as the city became known to military people, was also visited by thousands of Allied seamen in Atlantic *convoys. The military presence made for an infusion of cash, while base construction attracted many men and women from the outports. Until its closure in 1960 the American Pepperrell base continued to contribute substantially to the city's economy, while the military personnel greatly influenced the city's social and sporting life.

Newfoundland's entry into Confederation in 1949 had a devastating effect on the city's secondary industries, while greatly enhancing its position as a service centre. The removal of protective tariffs and the subsequent introduction of cheaper Canadian goods resulted in the collapse of many long-established industries. The city also lost its traditional role as the export centre for Newfoundland. As the major merchant houses withdrew from the salt-fish trade, St John's became an import-service centre with emphasis on Canadian goods and the servicing of local and international fishing fleets. Indeed, many of the old established firms, such as Bowring Brothers, turned their attention to the growing consumer retail trade. Following the completion of a paved highway across the island in the mid-1960s, goods and supplies for many parts of the province were imported either through the port of Corner Brook or by truck through the marine terminal at Port-aux-Basques. Since 1949 St John's has owed its economic and physical growth to public sector employment and to the establishment of major post-secondary institutions and other provincial facilities. In 1994 the provincial government was the largest employer, followed by Memorial University. The growth of the university has also played a large role in the city's becoming more culturally and ethnically diverse.

Between 1951 and 1971 the population grew rapidly, from 52,873 to 88,100. The discovery of offshore oil on the Grand Banks in 1979 and the subsequent development of several oilfields since the mid-1990s, especially the Hibernia oil field, have spurred a revival of the economy and offer much hope for future prosperity for the city's approximate 100,000 residents.

MELVIN BAKER AND AIDAN MALONEY

St Laurent, Louis Stephen (1882–1973), prime minister 1948–57. Born in Compton, Quebec, St Laurent became an outstanding corporate lawyer and gained national recognition as president of the *Canadian Bar Association and counsel to the *Rowell–Sirois Commission. When Ernest *Lapointe died in 1941, Mackenzie *King needed a new Quebec lieutenant and St Laurent was his choice despite the latter's complete lack of political experience. He served as minister of justice during the Second World War and quickly gained the respect of King and his colleagues. In 1946 he became minister of external affairs and on 15 November 1948 he succeeded King as prime minister, having been elected Liberal leader.

Distinguished in appearance, completely bilingual, and gracious, St Laurent was a surprisingly attractive candidate in the 1949 election in which he became 'Uncle Louis', the personification of the comfortable post-war attitude. He promised little that was new, but assured Canadians that a Liberal government would guarantee continued prosperity. His accomplishments were many: the accession of Newfoundland to Confederation, better pensions, hospital insurance, a highway across Canada, and a St Lawrence Seaway. He won the 1953 election easily.

After the election, some of the better ministers left. His opposition to the British–French–Israeli invasion of Suez in 1956 offended some English Canadians. Moreover, he was tired and his powerful legal mind no longer rallied to partisan challenge. He won the most votes in the 1957 general election but John *Diefenbaker garnered the most seats. After some hesitation, St Laurent resigned in January 1958. His defeat was ignominious, but his record was excellent. Those who served in his cabinet ranked him highly as a prime minister. His times were good, but his stewardship reflected his excellent personal qualities.

JOHN ENGLISH

St Lawrence River system. For over four centuries, movers and shapers of the Canadian polity have taken an intense interest in the St Lawrence River and its many tributaries, especially the Great Lakes. The Great Lakes Basin (GLB) alone, at some 670,000 sq km, is one-quarter larger than mainland France. The other tributary basins totalling over 500,000 sq km add the equivalent of Spain to the resource-rich lands accessible to whoever has held the chief maritime entrepôt at Quebec and its subsidiary at Montreal.

Imagine the GLB as divided along the 45th north parallel into two parts, roughly equal in size but greatly dissimilar in physical character. The northern part is characterized by thin soils over hard, mineral-rich rocks, supporting a mixed vegetation profuse with conifers, and laced with fast, turbulent rivers. Since 1818 most of this portion has been within Canada. The southern part is based upon extensive cultivable soils over sedimentary bedrock, with native hardwood forests and mature, navigable rivers. It lies within the United States, except for—most importantly—peninsular Ontario.

During the 17th century the French, exploiting the St Lawrence River system, learned that its water channels and low-gradient land routes led some 3,000 km into the continent, with easy connections to other major rivers of the interior. Their vast fur-trading network was gradually supplanted after 1763 by Scots and English traders with similar ambitions. For much of the 19th century, timber dominated the downstream movement of staple exports, and immigrants the upstream. After 1854, agricultural commodities became increasingly important.

Venturers into the St Lawrence system have had always to cope with three major constraints: sheer distances and the relative time-costs of travel; the many falls, rapids, and shallows necessitating costly break-bulk transfers and portages (except for most timber, which moved only downstream); and winter, the most intractable of the three because it is inevitable, protracted, and expensive. These constraints were progressively reduced during the 19th and 20th centuries by constant innovations in transportation—in ship size and motive power—and in epochal routeway improvements: *canals, railways, and motorways. These, cumulatively, have effected huge economies of scale in both the size of vehicle payloads and the number of trips in a given period, or season (the 'throughput').

Major railways (e.g., the *Grand Trunk), appearing in the 1850s, supplemented the rebuilt canal system and mitigated the costs of winter. They also drew the expanding Canadian West into the trading sphere of the St Lawrence. A century of urban-industrial growth along the Quebec City–Windsor corridor before the Second World War accelerated with new postwar freeways. At the end of the 20th century this corridor contained about half of Canada's metropolitan clusters, including the largest two, for a total of some 13 million persons. Trucking on the freeways had by then eclipsed the railways, while direct overseas shipping had also relatively declined, despite the St Lawrence Seaway (1959). Following trade agreements in 1965 (the *Auto Pact) and 1993 (NAFTA), the main focus of this huge economic system was becoming realigned more towards the southwest, to the US interior, than towards its historic Atlantic connection.

C.F.J. WHEBELL

St Lawrence Seaway agreement, 1954. Though the Great Lakes had long been linked to the Atlantic Ocean by a series of shallow draft *canals, it had been a persistent Canadian objective to secure American agreement to rebuild the system to permit commercial transit by larger vessels. By 1932 the Welland Canal between Lake Erie and Lake Ontario had been deepened, but the critical and most expensive section was that which would link Lake Ontario to Montreal. After years of frustration, the threat that Canada would construct a seaway and associated hydroelectric power-generation facilities entirely within Canadian territory persuaded the US Congress to approve an international project in 1954. As a consequence, farmland, villages, and towns in eastern Ontario were flooded, necessitating resettlement of communities and relocation of infrastructure, including roads and railroads. Not only was the St Lawrence Seaway a formidable engineering and construction challenge, but it also involved a significant and controversial financial outlay. The seaway had already been in use for two months when it was formally opened by Queen Elizabeth II and President Dwight Eisenhower on 26 June 1959. Perhaps the greatest immediate impact of the new waterway was that it made economically viable the development and shipment of iron ore from deposits in Labrador and Quebec to the American industrial heartland. Iron and steel are still the most valuable commodities transported via the seaway. However, grain shipments (mainly for export) represent about 40 per cent of current traffic by volume.

HECTOR MACKENZIE

St-Maurice forges. When closed in 1883, the forges on the St Maurice River near Trois-Rivières were obsolete and small according to the standard of the time. But when the blast furnace was first lit on 20 August 1738 the iron works was the most advanced in North America, where the primitive bloomery forge was the norm. Canadian entrepreneurs under the patronage of the intendant, Gilles Hocquart, brought iron workers from France and located them in Canada's first company town. Technical shortcomings and cost overruns plagued the forges, which were taken over by government in 1743. Investment and technical innovation continued under the British Crown, which leased the forges to a series of syndicates and individuals: the most colourful, Christophe Pélissier, made cannonballs for American invaders and fell from favour; the most successful, Andrew Bell, held the lease from 1799 to 1845. Iron bars were the first product of the forges, although various moulded items and cannonballs were also made. The forges became justly famous for cast iron box stoves, first made in 1744 on the model of Dutch stoves. The forges became a National Historic Site in 1973.

DALE MIQUELON

St-Pierre and Miquelon. These French islands off the south coast of Newfoundland played an important role in the cod fishery. From the mid-1660s they were under the administrative authority of *Plaisance, the capital of French Newfoundland. Thinly populated, they were exposed to attack by the English and by pirates. The residents lived in small cabins, hired fishermen every year from the merchant fishing ships, and traded with the metropolitan ships in exchange for provisions, clothes, salt, and so on.

Following the Treaty of Utrecht (1713) the islands were transferred to the British, along with *Acadia and Plaisance. Although the islands were under British control, many Acadians took refuge there after the deportation of 1755. Under the Treaty of Paris (1763), the islands were returned to France, the sole remnant of the French Empire north of the West Indies. Some 350 people arrived from La Rochelle and St-Malo, many of whom had been merchants and fishermen on *Île Royale (Cape Breton), and 216 Acadians came directly from Île Royale and New England.

During the American and French Revolutions, the islands were attacked and pillaged by the British. Some 300 Acadians left Miquelon for the *Îles de la Madeleine in 1793, but in 1796 the French fleet attacked Miquelon, expelling the English fishermen. British attacks continued, disrupting the French fisheries, but after the defeat of Napoleon at Waterloo the French regained possession permanently.

In 1817 St-Pierre had 173 inhabitants and Miquelon 280. The population grew to 6,482 by 1902, but thereafter maritime disasters and poor fishing caused many people to depart. Disaster also struck in 1844, 1865, and 1867, when fires destroyed large parts of the town of St-Pierre. In the 1930s the islands were central to the illegal liquor trade with the 'dry' United States, and in 1941, after the fall of France, they were occupied by General de Gaulle's Free French forces. In 1976 the islands gained the status of a French department overseas, but in 1985 they became a territorial collectivity of the French Republic. Despite disputes with Canada in recent years over fishing rights in the Gulf of St Lawrence, fishing remains important. Today some 6,316 people live on the islands, mainly on St-Pierre. NICOLAS LANDRY

St Roch. Arctic supply and police vessel built in North Vancouver for the *RCMP in 1928. Under the command of Norwegian-born Henry Larsen (1899–1964), *St Roch* made annual voyages into the Arctic to deliver supplies to police detachments in isolated settlements before 'freezing in' for the winter. Small but sturdy, *St Roch*'s hull is shaped like an egg. While this shape makes it difficult for ice to grip and crush the ship, it wallowed in heavy seas and made the crew violently seasick. For much of its 20-year career *St. Roch* spent a great deal of its time frozen into the pack ice and serving as a police detachment in areas without a government presence. Larsen's dream, to follow in Roald *Amundsen's path as an explorer, came true in 1940–2, when *St Roch* became the second ship to navigate the *Northwest Passage, a feat repeated in 1944. No other vessel had made it through the passage since Amundsen's *Gjoa* four decades earlier, and the wartime feat made both *St Roch* and Larsen famous. Retired from the Arctic and sent via the Panama Canal in 1950 to Halifax, *St Roch* became the first ship to circumnavigate North America. Returned to Vancouver in 1954, *St Roch* inspired the creation of the Vancouver Maritime Museum in 1958, and was subsequently restored by Parks Canada as a National Historic Site. JAMES DELGADO

saints and martyrs. In 17th-century Europe, Canada was more famous for its saints than for its furs. Catholic France drew inspiration from the lives of pious nuns, missionary saints, and heroic martyrs, slain for the True Faith. Jesuit writings, mined by historians for their chronicles of events and their ethnographic description, were, to a significant degree, composed as 'sacred biography' (or hagiography), an ancient Christian genre with distinctive conventions and principles of selectivity.

Following the lead of earlier writers in Latin America, the New France *Jesuits pursued a version of life-writing that might be called 'colonial hagiography'. It was 'colonial' in that it focused on the exploits of Europeans in a 'savage' New World setting. Natives entered the narrative as secondary figures, representing either deadly danger or, if they converted, proof of the missionary's effectiveness. It was 'hagiographic' in that it stressed resemblances between the subject and established saints of earlier centuries; moreover, the texts tended to be organized more as a catalogue of virtues than as a narrative of events.

The majority (eight out of ten) of official saints canonized for exploits in Canada were Jesuits (and Jesuit assistants) killed in the 1640s in the wars that pitted the French and their Native allies against the *Iroquois of the Five Nations. There was Father Isaac Jogues (1608–46), who, along with the Jesuit lay employee René Goupil (1608–42) and a group of *Huron, was captured by the Mohawk and tortured. After escaping, he returned to the Mohawk and was executed, as was his lay companion, Jean de la Lande. Jean de *Brébeuf (1593–1649) and Gabriel Lalemant (1610–49) were tortured and killed when the Iroquois overwhelmed the Huron country where they served as missionaries. Antoine Daniel (1600–48), Charles Garnier (1606–49), and Noel Chabanel (1613–49) were also killed in this same general conflagration and each has been recognized as a martyr. Thousands of Huron, Iroquois, Tionnontaté, and Algonquin people died in these same wars, many of them displaying great fortitude amid terrible suffering, but Jesuit hagiography conferred on the eight European deaths great religious significance. The martyr narratives were shaped so as to recall archetypical stories of bloody self-sacrifice from ancient times, when Christians faced torture and death at the hands of persecuting Roman emperors.

Two recent canonizations made saints of Marguerite *Bourgeoys (1620–1700) and Marguerite d'Youville (1701–71), respectively the founders of the *Congrégation de Notre-Dame and of the Sisters of Charity (*Soeurs Grises). Other women, including the famous Ursuline mystic *Marie de l'Incarnation (1599–1672), have been beatified, making them 'blessed' but not yet saints.

Canonization is very rare and usually occurs long after the subject's death. The first Canadian saints, the Jesuit martyrs, were canonized only in 1930. However, unofficial veneration of religious heroes began long before that, and the list of 'uncanonized saints' in New France included many more individuals than the ten who were eventually recognized by the Vatican. French settlers and Native Catholics cherished the relics of Father Brébeuf, and others, and prayed to them for help in times of illness and distress. In the 17th and 18th century, hospital nuns at Quebec used pulverized martyrs' bones mixed with a hot liquid to cure the sick and to make Protestant patients convert to Catholicism. The popularity of colonial saints was one of the ways in which colonists expressed their identity as Canadians.

Above all, believers wrote hagiographic biographies of religious exemplars. In 1672 Paul Ragueneau published a life of Catherine de St-Augustin (1632–68), a Quebec City hospital nun famous for her austere life and her ability to cast out devils. Catherine predicted the earthquake of 1663 after experiencing a vision of demons holding the four corners of the country and shaking them vigorously.

One of the most intriguing instances of colonial hagiography is one that overturned the characteristic colonialist configuration and cast a Native in the starring role. The Mohawk convert Catherine ('Kateri') Tekakwitha (1656–80), came from the Five Nations country to live at the mission community of Kahnawake near Montreal. There she joined a group of young women determined to pursue the most demanding program of ascetic penances, fasting, and renunciation of sex and marriage in order to gain the spiritual empowerment they felt the French clergy possessed. After her death at the age of 24, a cult developed, with pilgrimages to her grave and stories of miraculous cures for those who drank a solution of dust from her tomb. In 1980 she was beatified by Pope John Paul II. ALLAN GREER

salmon-canning industry. In British Columbia the canning of salmon for export was continuous from 1871, becoming part of the largest salmon industry in the world. Dozens of companies, several hundred canneries, and many thousands of Aboriginal and Asian shore workers and fishers were involved. The creation of such a competitive, highly seasonal, scattered industry with mostly isolated locations along the coast, removed from the centres of industry and product markets, and faced with scarcities of industrial labour, capital, and materials, was considered a great triumph of 19th-century entrepreneurship. The growth of the industry affected provincial politics and social life as well as labour, commerce, shipping, and fisheries science.

After 1900, the BC fishing industry accounted for more of the volume and value of Canada's total fishery production than any other province; by 1905, because of the growth of salmon canning, the BC salmon fishery ranked first in the dominion. Canning was an intrinsically industrial solution to the problem of food preservation because it depended on tinplate production and full-scale factory organization. Canning (putting food in a container, sealing it, and subjecting the sealed container to the heat of boiling water) made possible the distribution of salmon on a worldwide basis and contributed to its popularity as a food. Canning is a French process dating to the 1790s; as a means of transporting fish to market it began in the 1830s in Scotland, then spread to North America.

Important differences in the life cycles, size, spawning habits, and quality of the various species of Pacific salmon (genus *Oncorhynchus*) influenced developments in the growth and spread of the BC salmon-canning industry. The extreme perishability of fish, seasonal and cyclical variation in yield, regional and total limits in volume of supply, and the existence of a cheap, flexible production system (the 'Chinese Contract') meant that productive capacity was increased primarily by moving into new geographical areas and species of salmon, and by processing other fish, rather than by increasing the size of individual plants. BC salmon-cannery operators adopted key mechanical innovations from the early 1880s to the late 1920s. These involved mainly straight transfers of American techniques developed in other branches of the food-processing industry. An American fish-butchering machine, commonly known as the 'Iron Chink', was the only significant invention to originate in the salmon-canning industry. DIANNE NEWELL

Salvation Army. Born in the slums of London, England, in 1865, the army was a fulfilment of William and Catherine Booth's desire to address the spiritual and physical impoverishment of the city's 'submerged tenth'. Espousing a Wesleyan doctrine, adopting a military style (soldiers, uniforms, flags, and marching bands), and engaging in a practical 'soup to salvation' mission, the army was, by the 1880s, the fastest-growing evangelical movement in Great Britain. By 1882, it had invaded such foreign domains as Switzerland, France, India, the United States, and Canada.

It was brought to Canada by emigrants—English Salvationists such as Jack Addie and William Freer—who, fired by the Booths' zeal, began to hold impromptu meetings in the streets of Toronto and London, Ontario, in the early months of 1882. Encouraged (or perhaps forced) by the boldness of his emigrant-soldiers, in June William Booth sent Thomas Moore from the United States to officially launch the Salvation Army. The 'new-fangled' religion spread across Ontario like wildfire. Attracted by the zealotry of young women (who comprised 50 per cent of its officership), by the novelty of soldiership, by religious worship freed from ritual and formality, and by preaching adapted to the lower classes, thousands flocked weekly to the army's barracks. By the end of 1884 the army had established 73 corps (stations) across Ontario; by 1887 it had planted its flags from St John's (January 1886) to Victoria (June 1887).

It was by its social work that the Salvation Army became a respected institution. Even after the evangelical fervour had abated, the army's 'hand-to-man' service continued to affect the Canadian community. Rescue Homes for 'fallen women', established in 1886, were augmented by Prison Gate Homes for released convicts in 1891, and shortly thereafter by children's shelters, men's hostels, and prison farms. By the beginning of the 20th century every major Canadian city had its 'Sally Ann' hostel. In 1904 the army opened its first Grace Hospital in Winnipeg; by 1927 it had 11 such maternity hospitals throughout Canada. In 1905 it commenced its emigration service, eventually bringing to Canada as many 150,000

British settlers. So effective was the army's social outreach that during the Second World War it was chosen by military officials as an Auxiliary Service. The army's Red Shield set up hostels and canteens across Canada, and sent more than 200 volunteers to serve the troops in Britain and on the front lines in Europe. Such service entrenched an image of the army as a Christian social agency. Although today it maintains its evangelical outreach (with about 90,000 members), its Thrift Stores, Rehabilitation Centres, Sunset Lodges, and Red Shield Services define the Salvation Army. R.G. MOYLES

Sarah Binks, the sweet songstress of Saskatchewan, was the literary creation of Paul Hiebert (1892–1989), a University of Manitoba chemistry professor. Born in Pilot Mound, Manitoba, Hiebert was raised in nearby Altona, where his father ran a general store. Hiebert began writing poetry and prose as a young boy to pass the hours; it was a passion that was central to his life and served to balance his professional career in the physical sciences. In 1947, Hiebert published his first novel and pseudo-masterpiece, *Sarah Binks*, a satirical biography of a fictional figure. The late Sarah, who died tragically young from mercury poisoning from a cracked thermometer, immortalized the heady settlement days of Saskatchewan through her dreadful poetry: 'Spring is here, the breezes blowing/Four inches of topsoil going, going'. Hiebert published several other works, but none enjoyed the success of *Sarah Binks*, which won the Stephen Leacock Award in 1948. Hiebert later confessed that he based Sarah on a woman he met while teaching in the Dante school district, near Leader, Saskatchewan, in 1913–14. BILL WAISER

Saskatchewan. Saskatchewan's earliest societies consisted of hunters-gatherers who followed a seasonal pattern dependent on the resources in the province's three major ecological zones (northern boreal forest, prairie parkland, and southern grasslands). First Nations responded to the coming of the Euro-Canadian *fur trade in the 18th century by serving as trappers, trading intermediaries between the posts and outlying bands, or provisioners. Fur-trade activity was confined largely to the Saskatchewan and Churchill River corridors. By the mid-19th century, northern Saskatchewan was the scene of an intense rivalry for Aboriginal souls; the northwestern side of the province became a Catholic stronghold, with Anglicans dominating the east side, thanks to the building of Holy Trinity Church at Stanley Mission, the oldest existing structure in the province.

After Canada assumed control of the western interior in 1870, Anglo-Canadian settlers initially occupied the prairie-parkland district, but when the *Canadian Pacific Railway located its main line across the open prairie, development was reoriented to the southern half of the province. Settlers from Great Britain and continental Europe homesteaded in record numbers in the early 20th century when economic and climatic conditions improved and an earlier maturing wheat was introduced. Between 1901 and 1911, the population jumped five-fold, from 91,000 to 492,000; over 80 per cent lived on farms or in rural areas. This exponential growth spawned the building of several thousand kilometres of railway, as well as a network of urban centres. *Saskatoon grew from a hamlet of 113 in 1901 to 12,000 by 1911. The rapid settlement initiated political change, and in 1905 Saskatchewan joined Confederation as a province, with *Regina as the capital.

The provincial wheat economy became firmly established by the Great War. In 1915 alone, Saskatchewan produced over 60 per cent of the wheat crop for the three Prairie provinces. Such harvests overwhelmed the grain-handling and -marketing system and led to the creation of the Saskatchewan Co-operative Elevator Company in 1911 and the Saskatchewan Wheat Pool in 1924. Wheat production continued to climb through the 1920s—reaching a third of a billion bushels in 1928—in response to strong international demand and increased farm mechanization. Saskatchewan was hit hard during the *Great Depression of the 1930s, when wheat prices plummeted to a 300-year low and sent shock waves through the economy. A prolonged drought, combined with poor tillage practices, compounded the crisis, reducing the southern part of the province to desert-like conditions. Thousands of farm families migrated north to lands along the edge of the boreal forest or simply left the province.

The election of the *Co-operative Commonwealth Federation in 1944, Canada's first socialist government, was a direct consequence of the Depression. Under populist leader Tommy *Douglas, the CCF sought to lessen the impact of another agricultural depression through the development of a manufacturing sector and resource exploitation. Many of the government's experiments with Crown corporations enjoyed little success, and the provincial economy remained largely dependent on *agriculture until the 1970s. The other bold initiative in the post-war period was the introduction in 1962 of a province-wide *medicare system.

Since the 1970s, successive provincial governments have sought to bring some stability to the agricultural sector in the face of growing production costs and international subsidies. Farmers have responded by turning to specialty crops, but agriculture's once dominant position has slipped, accelerating the demise of the family farm. Agriculture today accounts for less than 10 per cent of the provincial GDP, while only 5 per cent of the population works in agriculture.

Other resources, such as heavy oil and potash, have offered greater promise. In 1975, the government established the Potash Corporation of Saskatchewan and bought controlling interest in the industry. But this kind of interventionist activity has done little to solve the problems inherent in a resource-based economy. The few bright spots in an otherwise stagnant situation over the last decade have been the controversial mining of some of the world's richest uranium deposits in northern Saskatchewan, large offshore sales of potash, and a booming biotechnology industry in Saskatoon. The University of Saskatchewan is home to the Canadian Light Source, the only synchrotron in Canada.

Saskatchewan faces many challenges. It needs to develop a stable mix of economic activities if it is to stem the outward flow of population, particularly among its young people. It has to contend with conflicting demands, especially between a growing urban population and a rural society in decay. Finally, it has to find a way to end the isolation and poverty of its Aboriginal peoples, who will constitute almost half the provincial population in 2045. A step in this direction was the 1992 signing of the landmark, though controversial, Treaty Land Entitlement Agreement, which was designed to settle all treaty-related land obligations. BILL WAISER

Saskatoon. Founded by the Temperance Colonization Society of Toronto in 1882, Saskatoon derives its name from the Cree word for a local berry (misaskwatomina). The community, located on the east bank of the South Saskatchewan River, limped along until 1890, when a railway was pushed north from *Regina into the prairie parkland. But the rail line, by running along the lower, western side of the river, created a second community that soon rivalled the original settlement.

Saskatoon boomed in the first decade of the 20th century. A mere hamlet of 113 in 1901, it grew to a city of 12,000 in just ten years—a whopping hundredfold increase. Even then, Saskatoon boosters disputed the 1911 census figures and conducted their own head count, including people staying in hotels or passing through on trains. The city's transformation was so remarkable—it promoted itself as the 'Wonder City'—that it might have become the capital of the new province of *Saskatchewan if not for the intervention of the first premier.

Saskatoon's spectacular growth was attributable to three major railways (Canadian Pacific, Canadian Northern, and Grand Trunk Pacific) that ran through the city by 1908—hence the nickname, hub city. It also secured the provincial university in 1909. What made the city, however, was a building binge, the likes of which went against Saskatoon's teetotaller beginnings. Indeed, the city could not build fast enough to keep pace with the demand.

The boom ended with the start of the Great War in 1914. The city was just beginning to recover in the late 1920s when it was walloped again, this time by the Great Depression. But by then, Saskatoon's place as a major regional trade and distribution centre was secure. Higher agricultural prices, coupled with strong world demand for potash, revived the city's fortunes in the 1950s and 1960s. Servicing the northern mining industry and the development of an innovative local biotechnology sector have helped sustain growth in the past few decades.

Today, Saskatoon's temperance beginnings are part of the distant past. It is the largest city in the province and a leading educational and service centre. It has also made a conscious effort, since the creation of the Meewasin Valley Authority in the 1970s, to incorporate the river into development plans (seven bridges now span the South Saskatchewan). Saskatoon may not be widely known, let alone appreciated, beyond the region, but according to the lyrics of a Tragically Hip song, it's the 'Paris of the Prairies'. BILL WAISER

Saturday Night. Launched in 1887 to cover Toronto 'society', *Saturday Night* enjoyed its finest reputation, and greatest commercial success, during the editorial regimes of Hector Willoughby Charlesworth and particularly B.K. (Bernard Keble) Sandwell. Appointed in 1926, Charlesworth was an established Toronto newspaperman and arts critic who successfully broadened the magazine's appeal by emphasizing ideas and commentary with a Canadian, if consistently conservative, bent. Sandwell assumed the editorship in 1932, and it was during his 19-year tenure that *Saturday Night* really blossomed both critically and financially, no mean feat during the difficult depression and wartime years. The British-born Sandwell's Canadian nationalism remained firmly rooted within the imperial connection, and he shared most of his intellectual contemporaries' instinctive anti-Americanism. But his progressively-minded social views and commitment to civil liberties set the magazine's tone as well. Sandwell quickly transformed *Saturday Night* into a critical and opinionated review of political and cultural issues of broad interest to Canadians—in effect, a magazine for the liberally minded 'highbrow'. He supplemented his own superbly written contributions by drawing on a host of promising—and mostly Canadian—writers. By 1938, *Saturday Night* could claim the third highest advertising lineage of any general interest magazine in North America and an enviable critical reputation. Unfortunately, after Sandwell's retirement in 1951, the magazine lost much of its lustre as his successors and their publishers tinkered erratically with its publication frequency, format, and content. PATRICK H. BRENNAN

Sauvé, Jeanne (1922–93), journalist, politician, *governor general. Labelled during her life as a woman of firsts—first female French-speaking cabinet minister (1972–9), speaker of the House of Commons (1980–4), governor general (1984–90)—Jeanne Sauvé had a career more substantial than implied by those accomplishments. A popular broadcaster with Radio-Canada, at a time when the *Quiet Revolution and the feminist movement began to command attention, she proved an attractive political candidate. Possessing strong administrative skills and committed to preserving a united Canada, she served first as minister of the environment and then communications, areas ripe for jurisdictional conflict. As minister, she displayed modest parliamentary skills, a weakness again evident during her time as speaker, when relations between parties and respect for the chair deteriorated.

DAVID E. SMITH

Sayer trial. The 1849 trial of *Metis trader Pierre-Guillaume Sayer for trafficking in furs outside the monopoly of the *Hudson's Bay Company was a watershed in the long-standing Metis challenge to the power of the HBC.

Sayer and three other traders were arrested in the spring of 1849 by Red River chief factor John Ballenden, who hoped to use the company's 1670 royal charter to back its claim to exclusive trading rights. The trial, held at the General Quarterly Court of *Assiniboia on 17 May 1849, attracted a large number of armed Metis incensed by HBC attempts to curtail free trade in the district. Sayer, who was represented by the respected English-speaking Metis James Sinclair, was found guilty. He was released by the court, however, because he legitimately believed his activities to be legal. Charges against Sayer's three companions were dropped. With the HBC unable to provide the force that would support its claim to exclusive trade, Sayer's release represented the symbolic end to the company's monopoly in the West. ROBERT J. COUTTS

Scheldt Campaign. Waged by the First Canadian Army to clear German forces from both banks of the 80-km-long Scheldt River estuary in Belgium and the Netherlands. The goal was to open a channel to the port of Antwerp, needed by the Allies to supply their drive on Germany. In early October 1944 the Canadians struck north from Antwerp to capture the South Beveland Peninsula, accomplished by 31 October after vicious fighting. Simultaneously, Canadian forces crossed the Leopold Canal and cleared the flooded lowlands of the heavily defended Breskens 'pocket' on the south bank of the Scheldt. They were supported by a Canadian amphibious assault into the pocket from across the Braakman inlet. The Canadians cleared the area by early November, capturing 13,000 prisoners. The final phase of the campaign was the invasion of the strongly fortified island of Walcheren, dominating the North Sea entrance to the Scheldt. Canadian units suffered heavy losses as they advanced along the causeway linking South Beveland to Walcheren. British marines landed on the island following a devastating aerial bombardment. The enemy surrendered on 8 November, and the first Allied supply ships entered Antwerp on 28 November. The campaign cost Canada more than 6,300 killed and wounded.

SERGE DURFLINGER

scholarly publishing. The publishing of *books by academics for academics began in Canada in the early 20th century, the primary vehicle being the university press. Before the establishment of such presses, scholars published their work in Britain or with American presses. Large universities also had internal publishing programs, with series such as the University of Toronto's 'University Studies' as an outlet for original Canadian scholarship.

The earliest university press in Canada was the University of Toronto Press, founded in 1901. Initially, Toronto printed mainly examination papers. Its publishing program began in 1912 with the publication of *A Short Handbook of Latin Accidence and Syntax* by J. Fletcher, head of the Department of Classics at University College. This indigenous press was soon joined by a university press 'branch plant', when Oxford University Press opened an office in Toronto in 1904. In its first decade the office was largely a distribution centre for Oxford's British bibles and music, but in 1913 the first book to bear the Oxford Canada imprint was published, *The Oxford Book of Canadian Verse*, an anthology edited by the poet William Wilfred Campbell and scholar John D. Logan.

These two firms dominated scholarly publishing until after the Second World War, supplemented by a small number of private commercial firms—W.J. Gage, Macmillan, Clarke Irwin, McClelland and Stewart, The Ryerson Press—that often published the work of academics, particularly historians, literary scholars, and political scientists. Canada's only bilingual university press, the University of Ottawa Press/Les Presses de l'Université d'Ottawa, was established in 1936.

The years after the war saw a huge expansion in publishing. The first French-Canadian university press was founded at Laval in 1950. It was during this period that the University of Toronto Press solidified and expanded its publishing program, examining other models of university publishing as part of that process. Despite its anglophile traditions, the press turned to the business models of American university presses such as Harvard and Chicago in shaping its program.

A greatly expanded academic market coincided with the flourishing of Canadian universities in the 1960s. The 1960s and early 1970s saw the creation of seven new university presses: Les Presses de l'Université de Montréal, Manitoba, McGill, which shortly thereafter become the joint press McGill-Queen's, Alberta, British Columbia, University College of Cape Breton, and Wilfrid Laurier. The last to join was Calgary, in 1981. These presses, while showing variations on a theme, all followed a pattern similar to that developed by Toronto in the 1950s: publishing first the works of faculty members and then expanding their lists to include works by scholars from other institutions. The lists of Canadian university presses focused on the humanities and social sciences: virtually all Canadian academic writing in the sciences was published either in journals or outside of Canada.

The growth of scholarly publishing in Canada was boosted by government funding. In the early post-war period the Canada Council was the prime source of funding; later, money came from the Aid to Scholarly Publications Program, an agency of the main academic funding body, the Social Sciences and Humanities Research Council of Canada. The availability of these funds, tied to individual books rather than to publishing houses, has allowed scholarly publishing to flourish in a very small market. This in turn has encouraged the development of mature scholarly disciplines devoted to the study of Canada—history, political science, sociology, literary studies—which may otherwise have found the dissemination of their research confined to journals.

LAURA MACLEOD

schoolmistresses. From the late 18th century until the early 20th, the paid work most typically undertaken by young women, apart from their employment as servants, was teaching. Traditionally this work took place in families. A girl might be engaged to help with the children even in modest households; in grander settings she came to be called a governess. Well into the 19th century the line between teaching and domestic service was blurred for both women and men. Male tutors, too, had the status of upper servants in more prosperous households.

The shift from private to public service in teaching occurred in the 19th century. With the development of state school systems, teaching gradually moved out of the household. Like service, teaching was a stage in the life cycle. A girl might live at home and teach in the local school, or move around from school to school and board with local families, before settling down to marriage and a family of her own. Of the surviving five daughters of the McQueen family of Pictou County, Nova Scotia, all but the eldest became schoolmistresses, beginning in the 1870s. They taught near home, in other rural school sections, and one taught in Halifax before she married. The two youngest, Jessie and Annie, crossed Canada to teach in rural British Columbia soon after the completion of the CPR, the latter eventually settling there to raise a family. Jessie sojourned in BC, moving from one community to another and sending money home from her teaching wages, before finally returning to the home farm in Nova Scotia to care for her widowed mother and ailing eldest sister.

Like Jessie McQueen, many women chose not to marry and instead developed careers in teaching. Denominational colleges had long provided lifetime employment for such women. Mary Electa Adams was principal of the Ladies' Department of Mount Allison, as well as of several Methodist academies in Ontario, during an influential career lasting from the 1840s to the 1890s; her sister Augusta taught in at least three of her schools. Ladies' college and secondary school teaching eventually led to university teaching careers, a field that would develop slowly for women in the 20th century.

Schoolmistresses at all levels struggled with lower wages than those of schoolmasters, with considerable opposition to their paid employment in the first place, and an informal bar against their continuing to teach after they married. Career elementary-school teachers founded the first women teachers' associations in Montreal and Toronto in the 1880s; 90 years later women teachers and their associations would be among the strongest supporters of second-wave *feminism.

ALISON PRENTICE

scientific societies. Scientific societies grew from traditions in Western culture that had stimulated science—the rational study of nature—since the ancient Greeks. Natural philosophy and *natural history had found encouragement in the 17th-century Scientific Revolution, whose spokesperson, Sir Francis Bacon, promoted science as key to material improvement. This utilitarian purpose inspired a Baconian revival in Britain during the Agricultural and Industrial Revolutions. Bacon's call for wide-ranging co-operation, including scientific institutions, to facilitate the acquisition and dissemination of scientific knowledge resonated widely after salons and coffee houses expedited the exchange of rational ideas in 18th-century Enlightenment culture, providing fertile ground for formally organized literary and scientific organizations in the decades that followed.

Three prototypes offered models for scientific societies in Canada: the Royal Society of London, found in 1660 as an elitist organization, helped to shape state scientific policy; the British Association for the Advancement of Science, founded at York in 1831 as a more democratic organization, met peripatetically and funded scientific investigations of particular interest; and local natural history societies, including those specializing in botany, entomology, geology, astronomy, reflected the remarkable popularity of the amateur naturalist tradition in Victorian culture. In an age when intellectual life rested largely upon conversation, these latter groups met for lectures and conversaziones, assembling lending libraries and museums, organizing excursions, producing a published record, and disseminating knowledge among less-privileged classes.

The Literary and Historical Society of Quebec (founded 1824) centred on Lieutenant-Governor Lord *Dalhousie and his wife, both amateur naturalists, and their entourage of military officers and other social elites. Similar groups, including physicians and other professionals, established the Natural History Society of Montreal (1827). The Beothick [*sic*] Institution (1828) and the Literary and Philosophical Society of Upper Canada (1830) were short-lived because, as frontier towns, St John's, Newfoundland, and York (Toronto) lacked critical masses of dedicated members. In contrast, the Pictou Literary and Scientific Society (1834), founded by Rev. Thomas *McCulloch, formed a kernel for the Nova Scotia Institute of Natural Science and its New Brunswick counterpart during the 1860s. The Canadian Institute, established at Toronto (1849) by Sir Sandford *Fleming and other engineers, and obtaining a royal charter in 1852, emphasized physical sciences before broadening its purview to attract more members, with H.Y. *Hind editing its *Canadian Journal of Science, Industry, and Art* from 1854. The Natural History Society of Montreal inaugurated its *Canadian Naturalist and Geologist* in 1856. Specialized societies included the Botanical Society of Montreal, founded in 1856 by James Barnston, who died tragically soon thereafter, and the Botanical Society of Canada, founded in 1860 by George *Lawson at Queen's College, Kingston. Both founders emulated the Botanical Society of Edinburgh, having studied there under J.H. Balfour. Lawson published a set of *Annals* (1861), with BSC members proudly appending the group's letters to their names. One member, J.C. Schultz, organized the Institute of Rupert's Land, Red River (1862). The Entomological Society of Canada, founded at Toronto by William *Hincks and others (1863), sprouted London and Quebec branches, as well as a rival association, the Toronto Entomological Society, founded by William Brodie (1877). The Astronomical Society of Canada, organized by eight amateurs at Toronto (1863), obtained a royal charter (1903) and soon expanded to the national level. The Ottawa Field-Naturalists' Club, established in 1879, followed the trend of attracting both scientists and amateurs.

New developments—including Charles Darwin's evolutionary theory (1859), Canadian Confederation (1867), and the professionalization of science—favoured the establishment of an elite academy: hence, the *Royal Society of Canada, founded by Sir J.W. *Dawson and Governor General Lord Lorne at Ottawa (1882), and eventually an offspring of the British Association for the Advancement of Science, the Association canadienne-française pour l'avancement des sciences, in Quebec (1923). The rise of the research ideal and industrial research in science, with the *National Research Council of Canada founded in 1916, helps to explain the increasing dominance of professional scientific associations after the First World War. SUZANNE ZELLER

Scots. One of the ethnic peoples of Canada, Scots trace their origins to Scotland, a historic nation of the British Isles, which maintained its independence until 1707 when its parliament was merged with that of England. Scotland has managed to maintain cultural identities distinct from England, which have been perpetuated by Scots in British North America and Canada. Most Scots would regard the Ulster Scots of northern Ireland as Irish. Scotland has historically been divided into a number of separate regions, of which the most important were the Highlands, a highly traditional Gaelic-speaking area dominated by the clans, and the Lowlands, which spoke Scots, a variant of English, and was more highly developed economically and closer to England.

Scotland has been a country with a limited amount of arable land that has long been under the control of a small group of landlords. The pressures for emigration have thus been severe. Scots began emigrating to Canada in noticeable numbers in the early 1770s, and the flow has been both considerable and steady ever since. Most Highland emigration came before 1880, while Lowland emigration has increased markedly since the 1850s. Scots have come in substantial numbers to every province but Newfoundland. The province with the highest proportion of Scots has been Prince Edward Island, the lowest Quebec. Those of Scottish origin are equally distributed between urban and rural areas. Scots have been disproportionately successful in Canada, probably because they have always been 'preferred' immigrants.

Settlement in Canada can be divided into five periods: before 1815, 1816–70, 1871–1918, 1919–45, and 1946 to the present. Before 1815, Scots Highlanders established community settlements in all the colonies of British North America, but especially in the Maritime region. Highland Scots became extremely visible in the *fur trade, and were a substantial proportion of *Loyalist refugees. Between 1791 and the end of the Napoleonic Wars, most Highland emigrants came from the western Highlands and islands. From 1816 to 1870, the extent of Scottish emigration increased markedly from both Highlands and Lowlands. Most of the Highlanders departed their homes during the 'clearances' because of a combination of demographic pressure and declining economic opportunity especially after the famines of the 1840s. In the Lowlands, agricultural improvement and industrialization created redundant populations. Scots were eager for land, and most at least initially settled in agricultural circumstances in Canada. In the period 1871–1918, the substantial flow of emigrants from the Highlands ended abruptly after 1880, although some notorious crofter settlements would be established with government assistance at the end of the century. Most emigrants, many of them females, came from the Lowlands to find jobs in domestic service and the industrializing cities. Many Scots settling on farms in western Canada were not recent immigrants. Between 1919 and 1945, Scots participated in soldier and empire settlement schemes. Canada was interested mainly in putting experienced farmers on the land, and it targeted immigrants with agricultural backgrounds. After the Second World War, Scotland continued to be a major source of immigrants, especially before 1970, when conditions of austerity in the British Isles led many to leave for North America. With the exploitation of North Sea oil, improved economic conditions in Britain have reduced the attraction of Canada.

While many Scots have become farmers, the Scottish contribution to Canada is most notable in commerce, business, and labour organizations. In the 1880s, a full 20 per cent of the Canadian industrial elite had been born in Scotland, and another 28 per cent had Scottish-born fathers. Scots were well represented in all aspects of economic activity, bringing an intense work ethic and much experience in industrial enterprise to the Canadian business world. Since the First World War labour leaders of Scottish origin, trained in Scotland's extensive industrialization and often highly militant, have been increasingly prominent.

From the beginning, Scots have been preferred newcomers, often privileged over those from other British nations. They have been held desirable chiefly because of their work ethic. On the negative side, they have often been criticized for their 'clannishness', which is another way of saying that they have maintained a public sense of their own identity and have often assisted fellow Scots in a variety of ways. A number of Scottish societies—the St Andrew's Society, the Highland Society, the Robert Burns Society—were founded to perpetuate Scottish ethnicity, frequently by invented traditions such as the emphasis upon kilts and haggis. Like most ethnic traditions in Canada, that of the Scots is heavy on nostalgia and sentimentality for a frozen and mythologized culture of the past, increasingly labelled 'tartanry' by its critics. Tartanry has been deliberately employed by tourist boards, especially in the Maritime region, to turn Canada's ethnic heritage to commercial purposes, as well as by the Canadian military.

One of the most important contributions of the Scots has been the importation and development of various Scottish sports, including curling, golf, early versions of *hockey, and the *Highland Games. The early Highland emigrants also brought the *Gaelic language and culture, and by 1850 Gaelic was probably the third most commonly spoken European language in British North America. Gaelic would decline partly because of the reduction of its usage in Scotland after the mid-19th century, but mostly because of the failure of the Gaelic speakers of Canada to insist on the perpetuation of Gaelic-speaking schools after the introduction of free *public education. The Scots took the lead in the introduction of public education, and the Scottish system of education, especially at the college or university level—with its emphasis on practical subjects of vocation value—has dominated in Canada.

In religion, most Scots have been *Presbyterian, although the Presbyterian Church in Scotland experienced numerous schisms in the 18th and 19th centuries, and there has been a strong Catholic minority, especially in the Highland regions. In the 19th century, Highland Scots tended to support the Conservatives, Lowland Scots the Liberals. Scots in contemporary Canada have reached an almost total accommodation with the larger Canadian society, and their Scottishness has become increasingly ceremonial. J.M. BUMSTED

Scott, Francis Reginald (1899–1985). Poet, political activist, civil libertarian, and legal scholar, F.R. Scott was born into an old Anglo-Quebec family. Educated at McGill, where he began to write poetry, and at Oxford, he taught history before turning to the study of law. He joined the faculty of McGill in 1928, the year he married the painter Marian Dale, and taught there until his retirement 40 years later. The 1930s Depression and the repression of protests by the unemployed sparked Scott's interest in civil liberties and *democratic socialism. National president of the *League for Social Reconstruction (1935–7) and the *Co-operative Commonwealth Federation (1942–50), he stated his socialism most clearly in *Make This YOUR Canada* (1943, with David Lewis).

He was critical of Quebec's authoritarian premier, Maurice *Duplessis, and became associated in the 1950s with legal actions whose outcome constituted major victories for freedom of speech and association—*Switzman v. Elbling* (the *Padlock case) and **Roncarelli v. Duplessis* (the *Jehovah's Witnesses case). Perhaps paradoxically, he supported the use of the *War Measures Act to meet the 1970 crisis created by the *Front de Libération du Québec. An expert on constitutional law, he served on the Royal Commission on Bilingualism and Biculturalism. His dislike of ethnically and linguistically based nationalism had an influence on younger intellectuals such as Pierre Elliott *Trudeau. It also led Scott to oppose Quebec's language legislation in the 1970s. His *Essays on the Constitution* (1977) received the Governor General's Award for non-fiction. He also received the Governor General's Award for poetry for *Collected Poems* (1981). Although much of Scott's poetry was lyrical, some of his satirical poems are better known. He translated French-Canadian poets Anne Hébert and Saint-Denys *Garneau. MICHIEL HORN

scurvy. A bleeding disease caused by a lack of vitamin C (ascorbic acid). Ancient remains show that Aboriginals suffered from it during food shortages. Scurvy also plagued sailors on long voyages, arctic explorers, fur traders, and early settlers wintering in Canada. That cases occurred in clusters made the disease appear contagious; however, most observers suspected a dietary cause. Scurvy affected the colony of Jacques *Cartier at Stadacona (Quebec) in 1535–6. A Native, Domagaya, directed Cartier to a traditional cure, a tea made from the 'aneda' plant. Samuel de *Champlain tried in vain to find the same plant when scurvy ravaged *Port-Royal in Acadia in 1604–5. By the late 18th century the British navy carried citrus juices for prevention, as recommended by Sir James Lind (1716–94). In central Canada fresh meat and dried fruit served this purpose. Several plants are rivals for the identity of 'aneda', the leading candidate being white cedar (*Thuja occidentalis*). This theory must contend with several problems: first, translations of the Native word are uncertain; second, vitamin C is altered by heat; and, finally, white cedar contains little vitamin C. The exact identity of Domagaya's plant is still unknown.

JACALYN DUFFIN

seafaring labour. Since the beginning of human settlement in the northern half of North America seafaring peoples have used waterborne craft for many purposes. Merchant *shipping, referring to the waterborne transportation of goods or people for commercial profit, was a relatively recent development that followed the arrival of Europeans.

Following their 'discovery' of fish stocks in the western Atlantic in the late 1400s, migratory Europeans began fishing in these waters in a variety of craft, including French bankers and English dorries. Most sailors were seasonal arrivals from Europe, one of the first large groups of wage labourers to pass through colonial settlements. Among settlers, until the 18th century at least, specialist sailors were a minority among seafarers, most of whom were occupational pluralists: they were fishers, hunters, lumbermen, and farmers who took to fishing or coastal seafaring on a seasonal basis, often to convey their own produce to local markets. In fishing and coasting trades, resident fishers and mariners were employed as indentured servants, waged workers, or co-venturers in a share system, as in the seal hunt.

As the merchant marine of the eastern provinces grew during 19th century, the proportion of seafarers paid monthly wages increased and so did the proportion specializing in the occupation of 'seaman'. During peak mid-summer shipping activity in the late 1870s, the deep-sea merchant marine of Atlantic Canada employed as many as 10,000 seafaring workers; another 5,000 worked in coastal vessels. Although the majority of deckhands in ocean-going vessels were born outside the colonies, and most would have considered their home to be in Britain or continental Europe, the majority of ship's masters were local men. Most seafarers went to sea as young men and stayed for a few years before taking up other occupations in their late twenties or early thirties. Of all sailors hired in ocean-going vessels registered in major ports of the Maritimes in the late 19th century, only one in every 238 was a woman.

For a few years during the 1860s and 1870s, Canada possessed the fourth largest merchant marine among the maritime nations of the world, according to official tonnage figures. In the early 20th century Canada's merchant marine declined, but seafaring employment remained an alternative for many in Canada's ports. The first Canadian woman to earn a master's certificate was Molly Kool of Alma, New Brunswick (1939). The two world wars saw rapid expansion, and employment in Canadian merchant shipping increased from a mere 3,600 in 1939 to over 75,000 in 1943. Merchant mariners were critically important to Canada's war efforts, and it is estimated that 1,466 Canadian merchant mariners lost their lives in the Second World War. The struggle to secure veterans' benefits for wartime merchant seaman continued into the 1990s; they were not recognized officially as veterans until 1992. The Canadian-flag merchant marine declined again in the post-war decades, although coastal and lake shipping remained vital to Canada's export trades. By the end of the 20th century there were only about 6,000 deck and engine crew employed in all water transportation in Canada.

ERIC W. SAGER

See also CRIMPING.

sealing. Although harvesting seals had always been important to the coastal peoples of the northern shores of North America, the development by Newfoundland fishermen of a commercially viable seal hunt by the 1800s was the direct result of the rising demand for traditional oils like whale, seal, and rape seed oil, which was created by the Industrial Revolution. Increasing amounts of oil were needed for lubricating machinery and for the currying process to feed a growing middle-class demand for leather products. Most importantly, developments in oil-lighting technology (beginning with the Argand lamp in the 1780s) led to a revolution in lighting, and the demand for traditional oils soared.

During the Revolutionary and Napoleonic Wars (1793–1815) English and Irish migratory fishermen adapted to living in Newfoundland year round. By augmenting their income from the summer cod fishery with the spring seal hunt, they could support themselves and their families. The population expanded from less than 20,000 in 1800 to about 40,000 in 1815 and 125,000 in 1857. The sealing industry became established in the capital, St John's, and in the old fishing harbours, and soon towns grew up in Harbour Grace, Carbonear, Brigus, and Bay Roberts. Meanwhile, sealing ships also sailed to the Labrador coast to fish for cod during the summer months, adding another considerable area of fishing grounds to those being exploited along Newfoundland's coasts.

During the latter years of the Napoleonic Wars, about 100,000 seals were killed annually. The harvest rose to more than 600,000 in 1831 and peaked at about 700,000 in the 1840s. By the early 1830s 8.5 million litres of seal oil were exported annually. Throughout the 1830s and 1840s, about one-third of Newfoundland's economy was dependent on seal-oil exports. Although production peaked in the 1840s, investment continued to grow until in 1857 it crested at 370 ships employing 13,600 men.

The refining of petroleum, the expansion of gas lighting, the introduction of electricity, and the adoption of the kerosene lamp soon reduced the demand for seal oil. Meanwhile, over-harvesting reduced the size of the herds. The industry tried to compensate by investing in steamers, which were much more effective than sailing vessels, but decline continued. By 1900, sealing accounted for only about 5 per cent of the colony's economy and employed only 3,000–4000 men in 18 to 20 steamers. By this time, the ordinary sealers were receiving about $30 per trip, compared to $100–$150 in the 1830s and 1840s. However, captains received huge rewards, often amounting to thousands of dollars per trip. Sealing had become very competitive because only so many mammals were accessible each spring. The men drove themselves hard; moreover, both ships and men were driven by their captains, who, in turn, were pressed by the large firms that employed them. The result was the loss of human life and many wooden steamers. In 1898 the SS *Greenland* lost 48 men at the icefields; in 1914, the SS *Southern Cross* sank with 173 men on board and 78 men of the crew of the SS **Newfoundland* lost their lives. The steam seal fishery was effectively over as a significant activity by 1914, but it struggled on, offering some little income to sealers, especially through the post-war depression and the Great Depression. During the Second World War, sealers, among others, found more lucrative employment in wartime construction. The hunt was revived after the war but participation was much reduced; by the time the industry ended in the 1980s because of mounting public protest, it was being prosecuted by only a handful of dedicated captains and sealers.

In the early 1800s, sealing was the engine of growth that changed Newfoundland from a cod fishery—prosecuted by migratory crews from England, Ireland, and the Channel Islands—into a colony. SHANNON RYAN

seamen's unions. Under the leadership of a former ship's cook, J.A. (Pat) Sullivan, the Canadian Seamen's Union was established in 1936, and from the outset was under the control of the *Communist Party of Canada. Although Sullivan was interned during the early part of the Second World War because of his Communist Party activities, the CSU was able to achieve impressive gains for its membership, and after the Soviet Union was attacked and the conflict transformed in red circles from an 'imperialist war' to a 'just anti-fascist crusade', it made a tremendous contribution to the war effort. The union could not, however, survive the peace. Two key strikes—on the Great Lakes in 1946 and the 1949 deep sea strike, both directly benefiting international communism—gave the rival American Seafarers' International Union the excuse it needed to take on the CSU. In a bloody and brutal confrontation, masterminded by an American ex-convict named Hal Banks, the

SIU was able to roust the CSU and take over the bargaining rights of Canadian seamen. It was a classic Cold War battle that left the communist leaders of the CSU—except Sullivan, who had turned on his former comrades—running for cover. Once in charge, Banks ran his union with an iron fist, eliminating all opposition, real and imagined, through his notorious 'Do Not Ship List'. Eventually, Banks's brutal and outlandish tactics could no longer be ignored by either organized labour or the federal government, both of which had supported him against the CSU. A commission of inquiry was held under the auspices of a distinguished jurist. Banks's methods were publicly revealed. Convicted of perjury, he fled to the United States. Although extradition was ordered by an American court, the US secretary of state refused to allow the committal, having been privately asked by a Canadian cabinet minister not to return Banks. The SIU was placed under trusteeship for a number of years before being returned to the control of the same old gang, except for Banks who, living like a bum, died alone in 1985 aboard the *Malabar*, a dilapidated ship moored in the San Francisco marina.

WILLIAM KAPLAN

Second World War. Canada entered the Second World War on 10 September 1939, when King George VI, on behalf of the Canadian government, declared war on Germany. Fighting had been under way for ten days, and preparations had begun in Canada in the last week in August. The Mackenzie *King government, acutely conscious of Quebec's concerns about *conscription, had earlier pledged that there would be no compulsory overseas service, a pledge repeated on the outbreak of war and in the Quebec election that resulted in the defeat of Maurice *Duplessis's Union nationale in October. At the outset, the government's policy was 'limited liability' war, a controlled effort that would not bankrupt the nation, produce high casualties, or strain the delicate balance between French and English Canada. Mackenzie King's policy choice was confirmed by the electorate in the general election in March 1940.

By that point, the war effort was just getting under way. The government had agreed in December 1939 to join a *British Commonwealth Air Training Plan, operate its bases in Canada, and pick up a large proportion of the costs. Events turned the scheme into a huge operation, one that by 1945 produced over 131,000 aircrew, almost 73,000 of whom were Canadian, cost Canada $1.6 billion of a total cost of $2.2 billion, and employed 104,000 Canadians in airbases across the land. The *Royal Canadian Air Force, with a regular strength of some 3,000 at the onset of war, had its hands full operating the BCATP and used civilian instructors to get the plan up and running. The regular RCAF's aircraft were, except for a few Hurricanes, obsolete. The *Royal Canadian Navy, 2,000 officers and men and a small reserve force in September 1939, had a handful of destroyers and smaller craft, but it went to war stations at once. The army, with 4,500 in the *Permanent Force and some 50,000 ill-trained *militia, had almost no modern equipment, and the prime minister initially had no intentions of sending troops overseas. By mid-September, however, King agreed that an infantry division could be raised. Commanded by Gen. Andrew *McNaughton, the division, still untrained and partially equipped, went to Britain in December.

The domestic war effort also took time to gear up. The government hoped that the war would spark an end to the Depression, but the British were slow to place orders in Canada. Despite C.D. *Howe's leadership, planning for war factories began slowly. Discussions over wheat sales to Britain were similarly difficult.

The disasters of spring 1940 changed everything. The German assault on Denmark and Norway in April and the unleashing of the blitzkrieg against the Low Countries and France in May 1940 shook Canadians. The French surrender put British survival in doubt, and Canada rushed another division to Britain, sent all its ships and planes, and ended financial constraints. Fortunately for the services, they were not caught up in the debacle. An infantry brigade went to France after Dunkirk but did not come in contact with the enemy. The navy's small fleet had a limited role in British waters, and one RCAF fighter squadron played a gallant, costly role in the Battle of Britain.

The task after June 1940 was to prepare larger forces and a major industrial-agricultural effort. This required the complete mobilization of Canadian society. In June the government passed the National Resources Mobilization Act, which authorized home defence conscription, and men soon began to be called up for 30 days training, then 90, and finally for the duration of the war. The army gradually expanded to three infantry and two armoured divisions, all in Britain by 1943 as part of First Canadian Army, commanded by McNaughton. Other formations served in North America. In August 1940, King and President Roosevelt established the Permanent Joint Board on Defence, tying Canada and the United States together. The Hyde Park agreement the next year linked the two economies. The industrial effort, soon marked by controls over labour, rationing, and strong bureaucratic control from Howe's ministry, began to churn out vast quantities of goods, as did the nation's farms. Women who chose not to join the armed forces entered the workforce in huge numbers, and tens of thousands moved from rural and small-town Canada to work in factories. By 1942 cash-strapped Britain could no longer pay for goods, and Canada, richer by the day, began a Mutual Aid program that gave away billions in armaments and food to the UK and other allies. The industrial war effort cost $22 billion.

The war, however, was not progressing well for the hard-pressed allies. Japan's attack on Pearl Harbor on 7 December 1941 brought the United States into the war, but it led to the surrender of *Hong Kong on Christmas Day, with a brigade of Canadians taken prisoner. The whole Pacific seemed open to Japanese invasion. Fears in British Columbia about the loyalty of the 22,000 Japanese Canadians there led to demands that Ottawa evacuate the community inland. Although some in Ottawa did not agree, the anti-Japanese sentiment was too strong to be resisted. Seven hundred Japanese Canadians were interned, while the rest were housed in camps in the BC interior; over the next months, many Japanese Canadians moved east, facing discrimination almost everywhere.

After Hong Kong, the next action for the army came in a raid on *Dieppe, France, on 19 August 1942, when 5,000 men from the Second Division ran into strong enemy defences. The result was a disaster: very few who got ashore were able to escape death, wounding, or capture. The army's First Division had better luck in July 1943 when it participated in the invasion of Sicily and soon after in the attack on the Italian mainland. The division's most notable struggle was at Ortona in December, a fierce battle. The First was joined in late 1943 by Fifth Canadian Armoured Division and participated in cracking the Hitler and Gothic Lines as allied armies moved slowly up the Italian boot.

At sea, the RCN found its primary role in the *convoy war on the North Atlantic. With the navy's force increased to 100,000 men, its little *corvettes fought the U-boats, crews learning on the job. Initial failures bred later successes, and the RCN, the third largest navy in the world by 1945, escorted half of all ships to Britain. By war's end, the RCN had aircraft carriers, cruisers, large destroyers, and an array of smaller vessels.

The RCAF, enlisting 250,000 men and women, created 77 squadrons at home and overseas and provided, in addition, a quarter of the Royal Air Force's aircrew. The RCAF's *No. 6 Bomber Group played a major role in the campaign against Germany, and RCAF squadrons and aircrew served everywhere from Ceylon to Iceland to North Africa.

For First Canadian Army, two of its divisions in Italy, the war did not begin in earnest until the invasion of France on 6 June 1944. The Third Division participated in the assault and by late July the army, now commanded by Harry *Crerar, was in operation. The Canadians played their part in closing the Falaise Gap, clearing the Channel ports, and in opening the *Scheldt Estuary, the latter a desperate struggle in autumn 1944 fought in mud and cold. Heavy casualties meant that reinforcements fell short of keeping units up to strength, and the army staff told the government that the only source of trained men was now the 60,000 home defence conscripts. With victory near, King was most reluctant to upset Quebec and impose conscription. He had won an April 1942 plebiscite giving him authority to use conscripts overseas, but Quebec had voted massively 'non'. King sacked Col Layton *Ralston, the conscriptionist defence minister, and appointed Gen. McNaughton in his stead. McNaughton proved unable to persuade conscripts to volunteer for overseas service and King, facing revolt in his cabinet and with the army brass restive, did a volte-face and decided to send 16,000 conscripts overseas. That resolved the political question, and the military reinforcement shortage disappeared when the army overseas was largely out of action for three months. The move of the Canadians from Italy to northwest Europe early in 1945 also helped. The army soon fought its way into the Rhineland and liberated the Netherlands in April and May 1945, earning that country's eternal gratitude. The price of victory for all services was high: out of the 1.1 million who served, Canada lost 42,042 men in action with 54,414 men wounded. Fortunately, Canada did not have to participate in an invasion of Japan—a division was readying for that task when Tokyo surrendered in August 1945.

The nation's war effort had been extraordinary for a nation of just 11 million, but politics went on as usual. In the June 1945 election, the Conservatives called for conscription for the Pacific, which almost none favoured, and the Co-operative Commonwealth Federation fell victim to a vicious anti-socialist campaign. Running in Quebec on its careful management of manpower and across the country on its war record, social reform policies, and generous program of veterans' benefits, King's Liberals secured a narrow victory. J.L. GRANATSTEIN

Secord, Laura Ingersoll (1775–1868), War of 1812 participant, national symbol. Emigrating with her family from Massachusetts to Upper Canada in 1795, she married James Secord, a Queenston merchant from a *Loyalist family, around 1797 and spent the rest of her life in the Niagara Peninsula villages of Queenston and Chippawa. In 1813 members of the Secord household overheard American plans to ambush British forces at Beaverdams. Laura carried the news to the British, walking approximately 32 km over rough terrain. Her contribution to the war went largely unrecognized until the Prince of Wales's 1860 visit to Canada, when she received £100. Late-Victorian and Edwardian Canadian nationalists and imperialists memorialized Secord and her story in sculpture, art, and history textbooks. Despite some scepticism about her significance, her story continues to be told today, particularly in children's inspirational stories. Perhaps her most enduring commemoration, though, was Frank O'Connor's use of her name and signature for his candy company founded in 1913. CECILIA MORGAN

secularism, or secularization. This complex and much disputed concept generally refers to disestablishment, the separation of church and state. In the colonial era, the Church of England was granted special privileges by the state, including lucrative *clergy reserves. Disestablishment took place in the 1840s and 1850s because a growing majority of colonists in the English-speaking colonies were members of the non-established denominations—Methodists, Presbyterians, and Baptists. These dissenting Protestants called for voluntarism, whereby each church or religion would rely on the voluntary contributions of the faithful. In Quebec, secularization has occurred differently. The Roman Catholic Church, which was the major institution providing education, welfare, and health care, was at the core of the French-Canadian identity and way of life. During the *Quiet Revolution of the 1960s, the close ties between church and state unravelled. A modern state-run educational system also emerged, and the church could no longer afford to attend to the welfare of a growing urban-industrial population.

There are other forms of secularism, which are more controversial and difficult to document. A loss of a sense of awe or mystery about the world is also involved. Beginning in the late 19th century, uncertainty about the existence of the supernatural increased. Religious institutions and ideas began to lose their central place in society, and religious beliefs became relatively peripheral. The causes of this disenchantment were rooted in both intellectual and social change. Science and critical inquiry, in particular, relegated the supernatural and mysterious to a marginal position. A myriad of social changes—industrialization, urbanization, entertainment, leisure, and consumerism—also contributed to secularization. The historic Christian churches in Canada faltered. Weekly attendance declined, especially since the Second World War. The churches are no longer dominant institutions in the moral and social fabric of Canadian life. Many choose to worship in non-institutional settings. Despite the powerful forces of secularism, however, religious belief has not disappeared. Polls suggest that substantial numbers of Canadians believe in God and that many engage in religious activities such as prayer. The persistence of religious belief and practice has called the theory of secularization into question.

DAVID B. MARSHALL

security intelligence. The systematic gathering of information about threats to national security from espionage, sabotage, foreign-influenced activities, and subversion. Sometimes it also includes attempts to counter such threats through covert state actions. It is also referred to as 'political policing'. In liberal democratic societies, such activities are inherently controversial. They are, however, sanctioned by all Western states, usually in conjunction with forms of accountability and democratic oversight.

In Canada there has been a federal agency responsible for security intelligence since the early 20th century. Under various names, it is generally referred to as the 'security service'. It began within the *Royal Canadian Mounted Police in the aftermath of the *Winnipeg General Strike (1919) and the fear of Bolshevism spreading from Russia. During the Great Depression of the 1930s the security service was extensively involved in policing trade *unions and strikes. In the Second World War the service identified and rounded up for internment Nazi and fascist sympathizers from the German and Italian communities, as well as communists until the Soviet Union became an ally in 1941. It also took charge of the first security screening of federal civil servants.

The *Gouzenko affair of 1945–6 and the coming of the Cold War strengthened the position of the security service and confirmed its perception of communism as the main threat to Canadian security. In the late 1940s the government began a systematic Cold War program of security screening of public servants, workers in defence industries, and immigrants, *refugees, and citizenship applicants. The security service developed ever closer links with its allied counterparts, especially in the United States and the United Kingdom. Throughout the 1950s and early 1960s its activities in the political policing of Canadian society remained relatively uncontroversial, but as the Cold War consensus began to break down in the later 1960s there was more criticism. A royal commission on security reported in 1969, recommending that the security service be detached from the RCMP. This was successfully resisted by the RCMP.

In the 1960s and 1970s violent Quebec *separatism began to pose a more serious security problem. The *Front de libération du Québec carried out a terrorist campaign, culminating in October 1970 with the kidnapping of a British trade commissioner and the kidnapping and subsequent murder of the Quebec minister of labour, Pierre Laporte. The federal government invoked the *War Measures Act against an 'apprehended insurrection'. The security service was later blamed for allegedly inadequate intelligence, and then given a blank cheque to counter and eliminate the violent separatist movement. It embarked on a no-holds-barred campaign that extended to break-ins, barn burnings, intimidation, and illegal and unauthorized acts, which eventually became public scandals. There was also well-founded concern in Quebec that distinctions were not being drawn between violent separatists and the peaceful *Parti Québécois, elected in 1976 as the government of Quebec. In fact, the second most important figure in the PQ, intergovernmental affairs minister Claude Morin, was a paid RCMP informant.

The *McDonald Commission on RCMP wrongdoing reported in 1981, recommending the 'civilianization' of the security service. In 1984 the Canadian Security Intelligence Service Act created a new security service. Unlike its RCMP predecessor, CSIS has a specific legislative mandate that prescribes what it can and cannot do by way of domestic spying. 'Lawful advocacy, protest and dissent' were henceforth to be off-limits. An independent watchdog agency was created to monitor and report on CSIS compliance with its mandate. In 1986 the government ordered CSIS to close its counter-subversion branch, thus bringing to a close the service's most controversial Cold War activity, which in the 1970s had led it to accumulate files on 800,000 Canadians.

By the end of the Cold War in 1989–90, CSIS had shifted attention away from espionage to other threats, especially terrorism (the notorious Air India bombing in 1985 cost 329 lives, yet criminal proceedings against those responsible did not begin until 2003). The terrorist attacks of 11 September 2001 in the United States confirmed the important role CSIS was to perform in tracking and checking terrorist groups. Anti-terrorist legislation provides new powers, and expanded resources have been made available for counter-terrorism in close co-operation with the United States and other allies. There are also new concerns expressed by Arab and Muslim communities about being targeted unfairly. After almost a century of operation under different names and mandates, and after the disappearance of the old communist adversary, the security service is once again at the centre of Canadian government, and controversy.

REG WHITAKER

seduction, tort of. Pursuant to the tort of seduction, which British North America inherited from English common law, a father could sue his daughter's seducer for the loss of a servant. Babe in arm, a woman would be called to the witness stand to point out the deceiving lover. The one hurdle to a successful seduction claim was the plaintiff's obligation to show a 'loss of service' arising from his daughter's pregnancy, a serious obstacle that was partially remedied by the 1837 Seduction Act of Upper Canada. This statute was in stark contrast to developments in England, where amendments to the Poor Law placed greater emphasis on making the unwed mother solely responsible for her predicament. Despite this reform, successive court decisions eviscerated the act and upheld the loss-of-service requirement.

By 1890, scores of these claims were adjudged, and the families of the seduced gained public vindication. However, with the waning of the Victorian age, the tort was not often invoked. Social welfare statutes after the First World War enabled the state to exact support payments from putative fathers, and seduction faded from the legal scene. It made one dramatic reprise in the 1934 case by a secretary, Vivian MacMillan, against Alberta premier John Brownlee. The seduction tort was formally repealed in most provinces as a result of family reform acts of 1978 (Ontario) to 1990 (Saskatchewan). Ultimately, the courts held that the equality provisions of the Charter of Rights quashed this feudal relict, which held that women were mere chattels of their father. PATRICK BRODE

seigneurial system. This system began in *New France with the letters patent given to Jean-François de la Roque de *Roberval in 1541 and the mandate to grant lands as fiefs and seigneuries. However, this kind of colonization was not solidly established until after 1627. The seigneurial regime was officially abolished in 1854, but certain elements would survive for another century.

Although inspired by the feudal system, which was based on the *censitaire*'s (tenant's) dependence on the seigneur, and despite the survival of certain symbolic elements, in New France the seigneurial system had more to do with the distribution and occupation of space, and the authorities in France even wanted to make it a way of peopling the colony. The system was controlled by a body of laws and rules outlining rights and obligations on both sides. The state granted large portions of land to individuals, who became seigneurs and in turn were supposed to allocate the lands among commoners by providing grants to those habitants who requested them, although usually not before reserving vast sections for themselves. The seigneur was supposed to render 'fealty and homage' to the king's representative as a symbol of the vassal's subjection to the lord from whom he held his fief. He was also supposed to maintain a residence and make concessions of land. In return he enjoyed rights both onerous and honorary. He could carry a sword and take precedence at church and in various ceremonies. Within his seigneury he could establish a court of justice, receive the homage due to his rank in ceremonies, erect a mill, organize common pasture, and reserve to himself the right to hunt, fish, cut wood, or exploit any mineral deposits, as well benefit from several days' work every year on the part of his tenants.

Tenants were supposed to inhabit and improve their land. Every year tenants were expected to pay the seigneur the *cens*, a small fee recalling the feudal origins of their dependent status. They also paid an annual *rente*, either in cash or in kind, which was the equivalent of several days' work. In addition *censitaires* had to grind their grain at the seigneur's mill and pay, as a fee, a part of their production, not to mention the various fees due for other privileges such as fishing rights, access to the common pasture, and so on.

Seigneurial lands played a major role in the history of the Laurentian valley. In their time they accounted for approximately 80 per cent of the colony's population. In all, more than 10,000 families, distributed over some 200 seigneuries, made their living practising agriculture, initially at the subsistence level.

The seigneurial system left an indelible mark on both the landscape and mindset in Quebec. It created a ribbon of population along the St Lawrence that overflowed to its principal tributaries. The long, narrow strips into which the land was divided, perpendicular to the river—the principal means of communication at the time—can still be seen. The seigneurial system has also survived in the collective memory as a historic symbol of the traditional mode of settlement followed by the French colonists in North America and as an institution that promoted the survival of the nation that shaped and occupied that space.

JACQUES MATHIEU

Selkirk, Thomas Douglas, Fifth Earl of (1771–1820). Born in Kirkcudbrightshire, fifth son of the Fourth Earl of Selkirk and Helen Hamilton, he was educated at Palgrave School and the University of Edinburgh, leaving without taking his degree. Young Thomas spent several years in revolutionary France and travelled in Europe before returning to Scotland in 1797 to become heir to the title, which he inherited in 1799. The very profitable sale of several estates his family had 'improved' provided him with capital for several ventures in transporting Highland emigrants to lands in Prince Edward Island and Upper Canada. The result was a book published in 1805, *Observations on the Present State of the Highlands*, which advocated emigration as a solution to the problems of the Highlands and was well received by political economists. Elected to the House of Lords in 1806 (as a representative peer of Scotland), Selkirk became involved in 1809 with the *Hudson's Bay Company. In 1811 he acquired from the HBC a tract of 116,000 square miles of land on both sides of the eventual international border, upon which he attempted to plant a colony. The *Red River Settlement became intimately involved with a fur trade war between the HBC and its rival the *North West Company, which resulted in the death of many settlers at the Battle of *Seven Oaks in 1816. Selkirk spent years and much of his remaining health and fortune attempting unsuccessfully to bring to justice those he regarded as the perpetrators of that disaster. At Selkirk's death in France in 1820 the future of the settlement was still most uncertain.

J.M. BUMSTED

Selye, Hans (1907–1982), physician and researcher. Of Austro-Hungarian parentage, Selye graduated as MD (1929) and PhD (1931) from the German University of Prague, Czechoslovakia. In 1932 he came to Montreal to do research and never left. First at McGill (1932–45) then the Université de Montréal (1945–82), his research extended from his early observations on the general signs and symptoms common to all human disease, to what he called the General Adaptation Syndrome. This led to his description of the crucial role of stress in human physical distress as well as in daily existence. Any demand put on the body creates stress or strain. The response is non-specific and has three phases: alarm, resistance, and exhaustion. In addition to this work, which produced both praise and controversy, Selye performed productive studies on allergies, ulcers, inflammation, and several hormones. He published 33 books and 1,600 papers.

CHARLES G. ROLAND

Séminaire de Montréal. Part of the French religious order the Séminaire de St-Sulpice, the seminary was prominent in the Montreal region in establishing preparatory colleges and training Roman Catholic priests, and in working with Natives particularly at its seigneury of Two Mountains. The mother house was founded in Paris in 1641 as one manifestation of the Catholic Counter-Reformation. The interest in New France of the Sulpicians, as their members were known, dates from the founding of Montreal. Four Sulpicians came to Canada in 1657, and in 1663 the Séminaire de Montréal was named seigneur of the Island of Montreal and its priests were granted control of the parish of Montreal. By 1755, the seminary had 45 members, all born in France.

Unlike the *Jesuits, the Sulpicians were permitted to remain in Canada after the British Conquest and to retain their seigneuries and Indian mission. In the 19th century the seminary was one of the most powerful Roman Catholic institutions in Quebec, controlling the parish of Montreal and establishing schools, convents, and hospitals. On social and religious issues it spoke from a liberal or gallican perspective, often contesting the ultramontane approach of Ignace *Bourget, bishop of Montreal. Today, after three and a half centuries in Canada, the Sulpicians remain active, working from their seminary adjacent to Notre-Dame, the parish church of Montreal. They remain the parish priests of the city, continuing to educate young people at the Collège de Montréal and to train priests at the Grand Séminaire.

BRIAN YOUNG

Séminaire de Québec. In March 1663, Bishop *Laval instituted the seminary 'for the formation of young secular priests in the service of God, teaching them the proper administration of the sacraments, how to catechize and preach moral theology, church ceremonial, and Gregorian chant'. It was affiliated with the Séminaire des Missions-Etrangères in Paris, which provided some funding and teachers. In October 1668, a Petit Séminaire for the education of Native and colonial youth was added. After 1730 the seminary began to fulfill its mission of training a colonial clergy drawn mostly from the urban middle classes. Twenty years later most rural parishes were served by its graduates, who had a moderate level of literacy and theological training. Affiliation with the Paris seminary was cut off by the British administration in 1763, but two years later the Séminaire de Québec resumed teaching and eventually took over the Jesuit college, which the British had shut down. The seminary expanded greatly between 1822 and 1850 in response to a growing demand for priests to serve a rapidly increasing population. In 1852 Laval University was founded to provide a broader scope of post-secondary education. The seminary was extensively damaged and rebuilt on several occasions: by fire in November 1701; in the siege of Quebec in 1759; and again by fire in 1865 and 1888. It survived all these disasters and stands proudly today on the campus of Laval University in Sainte-Foy, the old buildings a historic site in the Upper Town of Quebec.

CORNELIUS J. JAENEN

Senate. The upper chamber of the legislative branch that functions in conjunction with the *House of Commons and the *governor general as the Parliament of Canada. Under the Constitution Act, 1867, senators are appointed by the governor general on the advice of the prime minister, originally for life but after 1967 until age 75. Equal representation of the provinces/regions in the Senate was the compromise that enabled *Confederation to succeed, allaying the less populous provinces' fears of being dominated in the elective (rep-by-pop) lower house. However, the protection of regional interests originally intended by this membership formula has, in practice, been assumed by the *cabinet, where the prime minister seeks to accommodate such interests.

The Senate was conceived at the outset as a court of sober second thought to act as a restraint on the presumed vagaries and passions of the popularly elected Commons. For this purpose it was assigned legislative powers equal to the House of Commons, save for the initiation of money bills, which can be introduced only on recommendation of ministers of the Crown in the lower house. By the Constitution Act, 1982, the Senate was given a suspensive veto of 180 days over any *constitutional amending legislation but otherwise retained its absolute veto over all other legislation. Almost from its creation, the Senate has been the focus for reform proposals. Once high on the agenda of parties of the left, the extreme remedy of outright abolition has in more recent times been displaced by a medley of proposals that, during the 1990s, have been assembled under the slogan 'Triple E Senate', standing for equal, elected, and effective. The demand for equality expresses the concern, particularly of the western provinces, that the allocation of seats should be changed to represent more fairly their current status. An elected

Senate has been a consistent remedy proposed by those who see the body as an unrepresentative and irresponsible agency, an anachronism in a truly democratic polity. An effective Senate is seen to be the outcome of implementing the first two 'Es', more particularly to provide a proper voice for the provinces at the federal level. Since the Constitution Act, 1982, all such reform proposals involving the allocation of seats, appointments to, and powers of the Senate must face the burden of meeting formidable amendment requirements that require the approval of Parliament and not less than seven provinces having at least half the population of Canada. J.E. HODGETTS

separate spheres. The prescriptive 19th-century ideology found in popular culture, medical science, and religion that assigned men and women to distinct public and private spheres and duties based on attributed 'natural' character, physical traits, and divine will. This sex-role framework delegated women to the private sphere or household, whereas men were given responsibility for the public sphere of war, economy, and politics. This division reflected the reproductive roles and the sexual division of labour of the emerging Euro-American middle class after many kinds of production were removed from the household. It also echoed *liberalism's preoccupation with keeping private and public affairs discrete. This ideological framework was so pervasive that even human characteristics or personality traits were classified along public/private lines, so that women were generalized as moral, emotional, submissive, and nurturing, while men were labelled rational, intellectual, and courageous.

Separate spheres offered women authority in areas such as domestic responsibilities, child rearing, and moral and religious education, but excluded them from so-called male areas such as the economy, law, politics, and sexual passion. The complementary roles this framework gave men and women did not reflect how real people ordered their lives: men had rich domestic lives, and women were never confined to their homes—especially working-class women, who increasingly sought paid work, and middle-class women, who engaged in social reform activities. But this powerful idea, about the overarching way things should be organized, excluded women from participation in some important aspects of public life and provided the most important rationale behind women not having the vote or access to institutions of higher learning. The exclusion of women from political and economic life assigned them to dependent and subservient roles. Paradoxically, female reformers at the beginning of the 20th century justified their participation in public campaigns for *temperance, urban reform, and *social purity through the authority granted them by this ideology as women and mothers. Some suffragists argued that women needed to vote precisely because they were different from men and Canadian society and politics needed these so-called feminine traits. SUZANNE MORTON

separatism. The idea of creating a separate and sovereign political entity for French people in North America has a long history. In February 1838, after the defeated rebellion, a Déclaration d'indépendance to make Lower Canada a republic was addressed to newspapers by expatriates in the United States; both French and English would be used in the new state's public affairs. At the end of the century, an American-born journalist, Jules-Paul *Tardivel, promoted in his *La Vérité* the creation of an independent Catholic republic that might include parts of the northeastern United States and eastern Canada. In the mid-1930s, another newspaper, *La Nation*, led by Paul Bouchard, became a vehicle for promoting independence, an idea supported or debated by a number of other groups (Jeune-Canada, Les Jeunesses patriotes) and publications (*Vivre, L'Unité nationale*). Bouchard introduced separatism to Raymond Barbeau, the founder of the right-wing Alliance laurentienne (1957) and author of *J'ai choisi l'indépendance* (1961). The idea had also occasionally been evoked within political assemblies. In the aftermath of the *conscription crisis in 1917, Joseph-Napoléon Francoeur, a Liberal member of the Quebec assembly, tabled a motion stating that Quebec would be ready to break from Confederation if the rest of Canada believed its own development was obstructed by that province.

At the end of the 1950s and especially at the beginning of the 1960s the threat of separatism developed as a serious concern for Canadians and a plausible option for Québécois. Three years after the birth of the Alliance laurentienne, a left-wing organization was founded, Action socialiste pour l'indépendance du Québec. More importantly, in September 1960 the Rassemblement pour l'indépendance nationale appeared, with André d'Allemagne as its president. At its first national convention, in October 1961, Marcel Chaput replaced him, one month after publication of his *Pourquoi je suis séparatiste* and fourteen months before the launch of the first separatist party, the Parti républicain du Québec. In March 1963 the RIN became a political party; within days it had to make clear its distance from the first violent actions of the *Front de libération du Québec. In 1964, a faction separated from the RIN and formed the Rassemblement national, later joining Créditistes to form the Ralliement national. Together RIN and RN candidates in the 1966 election got nearly 9 per cent of the popular vote; the *Union nationale was a surprising winner with its motto 'Égalité ou indépendance'.

A few attempted reunifications of the separatists met with failure until the creation of the Mouvement souveraineté-association in October 1967, following the split between René *Lévesque and the Quebec Liberals. One year later the MSA was joined by the RN to form the *Parti Québécois; the RIN also dissolved, inviting members to join the new party. Under Lévesque's leadership, and following the momentum gained from Charles de Gaulle's 'Vive le Québec libre' speech in July 1967, the independence option—in practice, the word 'separatist' was declared taboo—gained increasing support. In subsequent elections (1970, 1973, 1976), the PQ got 23.1, 30.2, and 41.4 per cent of the vote, winning the 1976 election with a commitment to hold a referendum before opening independence negotiations with the rest of Canada. Federalists won the May 1980 referendum with 59.6 per cent of the vote, but in April 1981 the PQ returned to power with near-majority support (49.3 per cent). After two electoral defeats in 1985 and 1989, the PQ won the 1994 election with 44.8 per cent (only 0.4 more than the Liberals) and the 1998 election with 42.9 per cent (trailing the Liberals by 0.7 per cent). In the meantime, a second referendum had been held in 1995 with very close results: 49.4 per cent voted to make Quebec sovereign on condition of a partnership accord with the rest of Canada. The belief spread that victory was within reach. However, in the 2003 Quebec election, the PQ was defeated, with 33.2 per cent of the vote compared to the Liberals' 40 per cent. In two subsequent federal by-elections, the *Bloc Québécois lost two seats to the Liberals. Nonetheless, the suddenly increased support (up to more than two-thirds) following the failure of the *Meech Lake Accord in 1990 should serve as a warning against any premature writing of a death certificate for separatism. RAYMOND HUDON

Service, Robert (1874–1958), poet, 'Bard of the Yukon'. Service was a Scottish-born bank clerk who went to the Yukon in 1904 as an employee of the Canadian Bank of Commerce. Arriving after the heyday of the *Klondike gold rush, he heard many tales of the roaring days. Although he worked long hours at the bank, he spent his spare time penning rhymes that captured the hyperbolic nature of Yukon story telling. His poems were full of colourful Klondike characters, rollicking adventures, and gruesome details. 'The Cremation of Sam McGee', 'The Spell of the Yukon', and 'The Shooting of Dan McGrew' were among the poems in his first published collection, entitled *Songs of a Sourdough* (1907). In its first year, the volume went into ten printings in England, Canada, and the United States. Two years later, the royalties were enough for Service to quit the bank and pursue a full-time writing career. Ironically, although Service arrived in *Dawson City well after the Klondike gold rush had subsided, his name became synonymous with the event.

CHARLENE PORSILD

Seton, Ernest Thompson (1860–1946), naturalist, author, artist, public speaker. Following high school in Toronto, Ernest Thompson studied art in London, England, for two and a half years before he assumed the ancient family surname of Seton. In 1882–4 he studied nature in Manitoba, filed on a homestead near present-day Runnymede, Saskatchewan, and was the first person to discover nests of the Philadelphia vireo and the Connecticut warbler. His observations from this period appeared in *Birds of Manitoba* (1892) and *Trail of a Sandhill Stag* (1899). *Wild Animals I Have Known* (1898), never out of print in the subsequent century, was the first and most successful of his 40 popular nature books. Stung by nature essayist John Burroughs, who unfairly called him a 'nature faker', Seton responded by publishing scientific studies, the two-volume *Life Histories of Northern Animals*, dealing with Manitoba mammals (1909), and the medal-winning four-volume *Lives of Game Animals* (1925–8). Using the North American Indian as a model, Seton wrote *Two Little Savages*, the basis for the League of the Woodcraft Indians (1902) and the Boy Scouts of America (1910); he was chief scout in 1910–15 but quit when the organization chose to pursue the British military model advocated by Lord Baden-Powell. Seton's superb sketches illustrated his own books and those of others. He was a gifted public speaker. He lived in the United States from the late 1890s, but did not become an American citizen until 1931.

C. STUART HOUSTON

settlement houses. In 1902 Sara Libby Carson, an American settlement worker, established Evangelia House, Canada's first social settlement, in a working-class neighbourhood of Toronto. By 1914 Toronto had six settlements, and there were six others in cities from Vancouver to Montreal. By the 1930s the total had grown to 20, several of which still exist today.

Canadian settlements were part of an international reform movement that was particularly influential in the early 20th century. Advocates argued that the best way to tackle social problems was to encourage well-educated young people to live in working-class communities and interact with the poor and the immigrant as neighbours and friends. They hoped to promote tolerance and a sense of community by encouraging rich and poor, as well as members of different ethnic, religious, or cultural groups, to see each other as peers. They distinguished the settlement approach from traditional, religiously based charity and mission work, which they criticized as narrow, judgmental, and divisive. Yet many settlement workers were profoundly inspired by religious idealism, especially the *social gospel. Moreover, several missions adopted many settlement programs; of these, Toronto's Fred Victor, Winnipeg's All Peoples', and Halifax's Jost Missions are the best known.

Canada's early settlement leaders implemented an ambitious program of community education and civic reform. They organized self-governing, age-graded clubs for neighbourhood children and adults, hoping through these groups to teach subtle lessons in citizenship. Club members paid small annual membership fees and weekly club dues, and organized their own activities. Settlements also offered a wide variety of classes, including English, vocational, music, and matriculation courses. They established numerous community programs—including athletics, daycares, supervised playgrounds, and amateur theatre groups—and instituted a number of neighbourhood services, including housing surveys, well-baby clinics, district nursing, and children's libraries. Many of these programs were later taken over by government agencies.

The settlements relied heavily on students and graduates in post-secondary institutions. University-educated women were the movement's strongest supporters, comprising roughly three-quarters of all settlement residents and volunteers. Men joined the movement too, but in much smaller numbers. Many of Canada's first professional social workers began their careers in the settlements. The settlements enthusiastically championed the professionalization of social work, actively participating in the creation of the first Canadian school of social work at the University of Toronto in 1914.

Ultimately, the settlements did not realize their goal of transforming Canada into an ideal society through neighbourhood work. They have, however, helped hundreds of people in the past century, including immigrants, *displaced persons, and *refugees, as well as needy families and the elderly, by promoting cohesive neighbourhoods and positive social reform, and by working to bridge the social and economic divisions in Canadian society.

CATHY JAMES

Seven Oaks, Battle of. This battle remains an important, if controversial, event in the history of western Canada. The death of 21 settlers and one Metis in this battle was the outcome of the Pemmican Wars, which characterized plains life in the early 19th century. On 19 June 1816 Selkirk settlers clashed with a party of *Metis traders under the leadership of *North West Company clerk and trader Cuthbert Grant.

The battle had been foreshadowed by rivalry between the fur trade companies and the establishment of the Selkirk colony at *Red River. The Pemmican Proclamation of January 1814, which *Assiniboia governor and Selkirk agent Miles Macdonell hoped would ensure an adequate supply of food for his settlers, forbade the export of *pemmican from the area and was viewed by the Metis as a threat to their economic way of life. Open conflict soon erupted; settlers' crops were burned in the summer of 1815, Colin Robertson of the HBC destroyed the NWC's Fort Gibraltar at the forks the following spring, and the HBC's Brandon House was seized by the Metis under Grant in early June 1816. A few weeks later, transporting a supply of pemmican from the upper Assiniboine River to Nor'Wester canoe brigades on Lake Winnipeg, Grant and a large party of Metis freighters travelled overland hoping to avoid the HBC-controlled forks. North of Fort Douglas, however, in an area known as la Grenouillère (Frog Plain, or Seven Oaks in the English tradition), Grant was intercepted by a party of settlers under the command of colony governor Robert Semple. The resulting battle led to the temporary abandonment of the colony, the 1817 capture of the NWC depot at Fort William by Selkirk and his private army, the Coltman inquiry of 1818, and ultimately the union of the two fur-trading companies in 1821.

Differing interpretive traditions have long characterized the historiography relating to Seven Oaks. In one, the incident is viewed as a 'massacre' in the context of a struggle against the 'forces of barbarism', while in another it is considered in tragic terms, the inevitable outcome of a mercantile war among rival fur-trading concerns in which the Metis were the pawns of the North West Company. A more current analysis sees Seven Oaks within the struggle for Metis independence, the resistance of a marginalized people against economic domination, and the emergence and consolidation of the Metis nation in the West.

ROBERT J. COUTTS

Seven Years' War, 1756–63. Britain's main aim in this war was to destroy French naval power and seize its colonies. In North America, fighting broke out between the British and the French in 1754 over the disputed Ohio Valley. Subsequently, the British launched four attacks: against Fort Beauséjour in Acadia, Fort St Frédéric on Lake Champlain, Fort Niagara, and Fort Duquesne on the Ohio River. Only the attack on Fort Beauséjour was successful; it fell in 1755 and the British began deporting most of the 10,000–12,000 Acadians.

In May 1756 Britain formally declared war on France. French strategic thinking in North America was divided. Governor Pierre de Rigaud de Vaudreuil favoured defending the full extent of French claims by combining guerrilla warfare with attacks on English bases to blunt invasion efforts. General Louis-Joseph de Montcalm pointed to limited manpower and resources and favoured reducing the territory actively defended. His position, though later adopted by Versailles, was ignored by Vaudreuil. Each year the British persevered with attacks against Canada and *Louisbourg on Île Royale. Montcalm frustrated the the British by destroying Fort Oswego on Lake Ontario (1756) and Fort William Henry on Lake George, south of Lake Champlain (1757). Aboriginal attacks on settlers in the west and guerrilla raids by marines, miltiamen, and warriors all along the frontier intensified British and American desires to conquer New France rather than trim its limits. In 1758 Louisbourg succumbed to a large amphibious attack. At Carillon (Ticonderoga) a second attack, by 15,400 troops under Maj.-Gen. James Abercromby, was defeatd by Montcalm, who had only 3,850 men. Later, John Bradstreet's army destroyed Fort Frontenac, at the eastern end of Lake Ontario, along with its fleet (left in port), crippling French operations in the west. Canada suffered from the immense strain of supporting an army nine times its former size while contributing record numbers of militiamen. Currency problems and the corrupt practices of Intendant François *Bigot and the munitionnaire Joseph-Michel Cadet further undermined the economy. In 1759 Gen. Jeffery Amherst invaded the Champlain Valley, taking Forts Carillon and St Frédéric. Fort Niagara, recently redesigned by Pierre *Pouchot, also fell. The same year, the British captured Quebec. In 1760 the Chevalier de Lévis counterattacked but failed to retake the capital. Amherst entered Montreal in September, completing the British *Conquest. The colony of New France was ceded to Britain at the Treaty of Paris in 1763, but the terms of surrender gave French colonists certain rights that became the foundation for their efforts to retain their identity. The war established Britain as the dominant colonial and maritime power. France was excluded from the North American mainland, retaining only the islands of *St-Pierre and Miquelon off the Newfoundland coast.

JAY CASSEL

See also CAPITULATION OF CANADA.

Sexual Sterilization Act, Alberta, 1928. Social *Darwinism and long-standing racist attitudes combined to promote *eugenicist ideas throughout Canada. In western Canada, the United Farmers of Alberta government spoke of the need to 'cull the stocks'—to prevent mentally deficient folk, particularly in rural areas, from reproducing. In 1928 it passed the Sexual Sterilization Act, which established a Eugenics Board with the power to order the sterilization of Albertans it determined to be mentally defective. The board remained in place for 43 years through UFA and Social Credit administrations, and was abolished only in 1972 by the Progressive Conservative government of Peter Lougheed. During that time, the board ordered the sterilization of 2,822 Albertans, mostly children who were in turn committed to a school for those labelled mentally defective. The grounds for sterilization orders varied from low IQ to apparent promiscuity. Some boys with Down's syndrome had one testicle removed for the benefit of a researcher into the causes of Down's.

As adults, many of the victims sued the Alberta government for violation of their human rights. In 1996, the Court of Queen's Bench awarded compensation of $750,000 to one of the victims, Leilani Muir. This case and public pressure forced the government to provide a compensation package for all remaining victims in 1998. Ultimately, it became clear not only that the victims had suffered gross violations of their human rights but that many of them were highly intelligent: the board's means of determining so-called mental defectiveness were themselves defective. ALVIN FINKEL

Shadd, Mary Ann (Cary) (1823–93), teacher, newspaperwoman, abolitionist, lawyer, suffragist. A key figure in 19th-century African-Canadian history, Shadd was among the first Canadian women to establish, edit, and write for a newspaper. Born of free parents in the slave state of Delaware, she taught in schools for Black children throughout the northeastern United States. She came to Canada after the passage of the Fugitive Slave Act of 1850, which allowed whites to arrest any African American, whether escaped or free, without warrant or trial. She established a school in Windsor, Ontario, and published *A Plea for Emigration*, a tract that sang the praises of Canada as an ideal place of settlement for Blacks. She founded the *Provincial Freeman* (1853–60), an anti-slavery newspaper that she published out of Toronto and then Chatham. During the Civil War, she recruited Black soldiers for the Union army. Later, after relocating to Washington, DC, she became the second Black woman attorney in the United States. Whether fighting for emigration, abolition, equal rights, or women's suffrage, Shadd blazed a trail for generations of women.

ADRIENNE SHADD

Shanawdithit, or Nance, Nancy April (1800/3–29). In April 1823 this last-known Newfoundland *Beothuk and her mother and sister were found by settlers in starving condition in Badger Bay. The mother and sister soon died. Other close kin had already perished; only 13 Beothuk were left. Shanawdithit was taken into the household of John Peyton, Jr, on Exploits Island, where she assisted with housework and children. In September 1828 the Boeothick (now Beothuk) Institution transferred her to St John's to the home of William E. *Cormack, who described her as intelligent, high-spirited, and proud. Cormack obtained from her a Beothuk vocabulary, a population census since 1811, and information on Beothuk artifacts, practices, and beliefs, as well as on encounters with Englishmen—including Lt (later Capt.) Buchan's expedition in 1811—which she elucidated with sketches and maps. In January 1829, Shanawdithit joined Attorney General James Simms's household but died of consumption on 6 June. She was buried in St John's.

INGEBORG C.L. MARSHALL

Shiners' War (*c.* 1835–45), a conflict between Irish and French-Canadian timberers that produced widespread disorder in the Ottawa Valley. The Shiners were *Irish immigrants; the name may have come from their occupation—*chêneurs*, or cutters of oak—or from the shiny silk hats worn by the newcomers. They became an organized force under Peter Aylen, an Irish immigrant who had become a major timber operator. He hired only Irish and employed them not only to cut wood but to drive out competition. The Shiners began in 1835 to attack and demolish timber rafts manned by French Canadians, who, in retaliation, ambushed rafts owned by Aylen. The war spread into the settlement of Bytown (Ottawa), where Shiners defied authority by assaulting their foes, burning down a tavern owned by an enemy, and disrupting public meetings.

Townspeople tried to resist the Shiners by organizing the Bytown Association for the Preservation of the Peace in October 1835. The association had some success by establishing nightly armed patrols, but the Shiners were effectively controlled only when, in the spring of 1837, the government supplied troops to guard prisoners and convey them to jail. Sporadic outbreaks of violence by gangs who called themselves Shiners continued until at least 1845. However, Aylen moved to Aylmer, Lower Canada, where he carried on legitimate and peaceful business. Irish labourers, who had won some of the jobs they had fought for, integrated into the larger society.

The Shiners' War had made apparent the lack of social controls on the frontier. One response was the Upper Canadian Master and Servant Act of 1847. It provided fines and imprisonment for labourers who defied their employers or absconded from their jobs. Its sponsor, Henry Smith, said it was specifically intended to bring order to the timber trade. MICHAEL S. CROSS

Shingwaukonse (1773–1854), Ojibwa chief. Born south of Lake Superior, Shingwaukonse moved to Garden River (Kitigon Sibee), just east of Sault Ste Marie, in 1836. Exposed to various Christian missions, he converted in 1835 to the Church of England, as did two of his sons, Augustine and Buhkwujjenene. Native beliefs continued to inform his thoughts and actions, however. In earlier years he had risen to prominence as a member of the Midewiwin, or Grand Medicine Society, which until the 1830s promoted regular contacts among Ojibwa leaders. Recognizing that communication with the encroaching settlers was necessary, Shingwaukonse travelled during the winter of 1832–3 to York hoping that Sir John Colborne, lieutenant-governor of Upper Canada, might provide a school, an Anglican missionary, and agricultural implements for his people. In 1841 he moved to the Anglican mission at Manitowaning on Manitoulin Island, but finding government restrictions on his band's economic and social activities burdensome he returned to Garden River. In his later years Shingwaukonse became a leading advocate of Native resource rights, including access to revenues from mining and logging on Aboriginal lands.

JANET CHUTE

shipbuilding. An old industry among European newcomers to the northern half of North America. Small sailing craft were built in Port-Royal, Acadia, in the first decade of the 17th century, but the first substantial shipyard dates from 1732, when the French government established a shipyard on the St Charles River. The French also built a number of vessels on the Great Lakes. Following the conquest, English shipwrights appeared in Quebec City and elsewhere, and other settlers began building small coasting and fishing vessels in the Maritime colonies and Newfoundland.

A rapid expansion of shipbuilding occurred during and after the Napoleonic Wars, when the timber trade to Britain created an unprecedented demand for bulk cargo carriers. British shipowners discovered the advantages of building or buying vessels in the colonies: a plentiful supply of timber and low vessel prices more than compensated for the short average life of the softwood hull. Between 1815 and 1860 about half of all tonnage built in British North America ended up on registry in the United Kingdom.

Canadian and Maritime shipyards expanded again when local merchant-shipowners increased their own interest in the Atlantic carrying trades in the third quarter of the 19th century. Canadian-built *sailing ships carried a range of cargoes from US ports, including cotton, wheat, and petroleum. The square-riggers of the 1870s and 1880s—mainly three-masted ocean-going vessels (barques, ships)—were larger, faster, and more durable than their predecessors earlier in the century. The wooden ship acquired more metal over time: iron knees, iron strapping, copper sheathing, chains, windlasses, and pumps. Shipyards also changed, from simple artisan workshops on the beach to large factory-type operations including a blacksmith's shop, joiner's shop, moulding loft, sawpits, steam engines, timber booms, warehouse, and wharf.

Canadian builders had long experience with steam engines, beginning with the steamboat *Accommodation*, built in Montreal in 1809. Iron and steel vessels were built in various locations on the Atlantic coasts and the Great Lakes, but the first great boom in steel-ship construction occurred during the First World War, when some 60 steel cargo ships were built. On a much larger scale was the building of both merchant ships and naval vessels during the Second World War. Some 398 merchant vessels, operated mainly by the Park Steamship Company, and 393 naval vessels were built during the war, and for a brief time Canada was one of the major shipbuilding nations in the world. Shipbuilding declined after the war, but shipbuilding and ship repairing remained important in many ports. Canadian shipbuilders specialized in vessels for Canadian waters: lake carriers, icebreakers, car ferries, tugs, log barges, and research vessels. By the end of the 20th century, employment fluctuated at around 7,000 workers.

ERIC W. SAGER

Shipman, Nell (1892–1970). Born Helen Foster-Barham in Victoria, British Columbia, Shipman began writing for films and directed her first one-reeler in 1913. She became a star for Vitagraph Films, playing leading roles in a dozen feature films. After *Back to God's Country* (1919), a magnificent adventure set in the Canadian North, she formed her own company, writing, producing, directing, editing, and starring in feature films, independently produced. She was known for her zoo of wild animals, wilderness consciousness, and proto-feminist representation of courageous womanhood. Her company, Nell Shipman Productions, went bankrupt in 1924, along with many of the other independents of the silent era. She continued to write and pitch projects until her death, in Cabazon, California. Her extant films include *Back to God's Country*; *Something New* (1920); *A Bear, a Boy, and a Dog* (1921); *The Grub-Stake* (1923); a series *Little Dramas of Big Places*: *Trail of the North Wind* and *The Light on Lookout** (1923) and *White Water* (1924); *The Clam-Digger's Daughter/The Story of Mr Hobbs* [fragment] (1947).

KAY ARMATAGE

shipping industry. European settlement in North America depended on successful navigation of the North Atlantic. The *Norse, beginning around AD 1000, were the first Europeans to carry goods and people to and from Canada's eastern shores. They were followed in the 16th century by English and European fishers, Basque whalers, and explorers. In the 1600s the French began the regular carriage of goods to their settlements across the Atlantic; by the 1660s La Rochelle merchants were sending 1,000 tons of shipping a year to New France. Canadian-owned ships were crossing the Atlantic by the 1730s, but the transatlantic trade was still dominated by ships from La Rochelle and Bordeaux. The Seven Years' War witnessed a substantial increase in shipping: 199 ships totalling 45,322 tons departed France for Quebec between 1755 and 1760.

English merchants ran sailing ships across the North Atlantic long before the conquest, carrying supplies to fishing stations in Newfoundland and to fur traders in Hudson Bay. In the early 1800s colonial exports of timber and wheat caused an unprecedented boom in transatlantic shipping and encouraged the growth of locally owned fleets in such major ports as Quebec, Saint John, Halifax, Yarmouth, and Charlottetown. Timber carriers often returned to the colonies carrying passengers. Voyages in both directions were extremely dangerous in the era of wooden *sailing ships: in the 1830s hundreds died in the North Atlantic every year.

Shipowning became one of the important elements in the diverse investment portfolios of merchants in Canada and the Maritimes. Samuel *Cunard of Halifax, who in 1840 established the transatlantic service that developed into the Cunard Company, was one of many colonial merchants with substantial investments in the Atlantic carrying trades. By the third quarter of the 19th century Canadian shipowners were deeply committed to the shipping of bulk cargoes (wheat, cotton, petroleum) from eastern US ports to Britain and Europe.

Although some Canadian shipowners (Cunard, Hugh *Allan) established liner companies and put *steamships into the transatlantic trades, by the early 20th century the overwhelming majority of vessels in Canada's export trades were owned and registered in other countries. The two world wars saw renewed Canadian involvement in *shipbuilding and shipowning: the Canadian Government Merchant Marine Limited was an outgrowth of the First World War; during the Second World War another Crown corporation, the Park Steamship Company, was vital to Canada's connection to Britain. The domestic merchant marine declined again after the war, and by the 1970s few Canadian-flag ships were operating in deep-sea routes. Amendments to tax regulations in the 1980s offered some incentive to investment in international shipping, but most domestic routes and transatlantic shipping continued to be dominated by vessels registered elsewhere.

ERIC W. SAGER

shrines. Canada has a number of pilgrimage sites. One of the oldest shrines, Ste-Anne-de-Beaupré, east of Quebec City, is also one of the most popular. The first church was erected there in 1658. It attracted sailors, who went to honour their patron, St Anne, with the sick and infirm seeking a miraculous cure. That pilgrimage experienced a surge in popularity in the 19th century, with the introduction of the steamship. The Redemptorists took over the shrine's management in 1879. Construction of the present basilica, which began in 1923, was not completed until 1962.

Around 1880, thanks to the development of the cult of Mary and ultramontane piety, the first pilgrims began travelling to Notre-Dame-du-Cap, near Trois-Rivières. The Oblates took charge of this shrine in 1902. The present basilica was completed in 1964, nine years after construction began.

The most popular of all the urban shrines, St Joseph's Oratory, was the product of the particular devotion of Brother André, a Ste-Croix brother who installed a statue of St Joseph in an oratory erected in 1904. The miracles attributed to Brother André soon attracted large crowds. The crypt on which the basilica stands was constructed in 1917. The great basilica was begun in 1924 and finished in 1967.

Other shrines with a more limited influence and in some cases a more ephemeral life span appeared in the 19th and 20th centuries. They reflect popular devotions to the Virgin, St Anne, and St Joseph as well as the Sacred Heart and Calvary.

CHRISTINE HUDON

Siberian expedition. In the closing months of the First World War, from October 1918, nearly 5,000 Canadian troops under Canadian Major General J.H. Elmsley served around the Siberian port of Vladivostok as part of a larger Allied Force commanded by the Japanese and including American and British units. The Siberia force had a precedent in the smaller Canadian commitment to North Russia around Archangel and Murmansk a few months earlier. Originally, both actions were attempts to keep resources away from Germany and its allies and to reopen the Eastern Front after Russia left the war following the Bolshevik Revolution. Pressured by the British to participate, Prime Minister Robert *Borden had visions of future economic opportunities for Canada. Ottawa sent two infantry battalions, some field artillery, machine gunners, and HQ and other troops. A British battalion was also under Elmsley's command. Supposedly they were to keep open supply lines on the Trans-Siberian Railway and to protect the 100,000 Czech troops then trying to get back to Europe to fight against Austria-Hungary.

When the European armistice came, the expedition's rationale disappeared and the situation rapidly became confused. The Canadians' task shifted: to train Admiral Kolchak's White Russian forces in the fight against the Bolsheviks. Siberian involvement was never popular in Canada: war weariness, demands for quick demobilization, and a revulsion against great power rivalries, especially between the Japanese and Americans in Siberia, added to Canadians' growing isolation. By early 1919 the Canadian cabinet decided Elmsley's force would stay out of domestic Russian affairs and remain around Vladivostok. Frustration and boredom rapidly set in. 'Fight or home' was the slogan reflecting evaporating troop morale. With the increasingly bloody and chaotic Russian civil war, disunity in the White forces, and no promise of economic advantage, it all seemed senseless to most Canadians. Finally, amid strong British objections, Ottawa ordered the troops home. The first left in April 1919, the last in June. Siberian involvement was a muddled failure but it did demonstrate that the price of Canadian maturity was likely to be more international responsibility.

RONALD HAYCOCK

Siegfried, André (1875–1959). Siegfried was a young French sociologist who toured Canada in 1904 and observed the Canadian general election in that year. Only 29, he had earlier written an important study of New Zealand and would later publish in the 1920s an influential work on American democracy. His ambition was to understand the settler colonies, which he knew would be increasingly important in the 20th century.

Siegfried's Canadian study was immediately recognized as an extraordinarily perceptive analysis of Canadian politics and, in particular, the relationship between French and English Canadians. Well-written, occasionally witty, invariably shrewd, *The Race Question in Canada* appeared in English in 1907 and received abundant and favourable notice. His argument that 'in the absence of ideas or doctrines to divide the voters, there remain only questions of material interest, collective or individual' influenced many generations of Canadian political commentators. Canadian elections, in his opinion, mattered little on the national level but were extremely significant on the local level, where the spoils were divided. Siegfried identified the tension in the *party system that caused its breakdown in the First World War. JOHN ENGLISH

Sifton, Sir Clifford (1861–1929), lawyer, entrepreneur, politician, newspaper publisher. Born in Ontario, Sifton practised law in Brandon from 1882 and was elected to the Manitoba legislature in 1888. Appointed attorney general in the Liberal government of Thomas Greenway in 1891, he became the principal defender of the government's controversial legislation of 1890 to create a 'national' school system. In 1896 he became minister of the interior and superintendent-general of Indian Affairs in the government of Sir Wilfrid *Laurier. He reformed the immigration system, advertising Canada aggressively in the United States, Britain, and continental Europe, attracting large numbers of agricultural settlers, and bringing new efficiency to the settlement process. He was responsible for government policy in the Yukon during the gold rush that began in 1897, and was Canadian agent-general during the *Alaska Boundary Tribunal of 1903. Sifton resigned in 1905 during a dispute with Laurier over educational policy when the provinces of Alberta and Saskatchewan were created. He opposed the reciprocity agreement of 1911, siding with the victorious Conservatives under Sir Robert *Borden. Sifton supported *conscription and aided in forming the *Union government in 1917. He headed the Canadian Commission of Conservation, 1909–18. He was also owner of the *Manitoba Free Press*. DAVID J. HALL

Sikhs. The Sikhs are an ethno-religious community from the Indian state of Punjab. They are notable emigrants, with about 6 per cent living outside India. After the United Kingdom, Canada has the second-largest population in the Sikh diaspora. Sikhs have been in Canada since 1903–4, when the Canadian Pacific Steamship Company began to recruit Sikh passengers to make up for lost Chinese traffic. Sikhs celebrated a Canadian centenary in 1997, and possibly some came as early as 1897, or earlier, but their presence is not documented. The original immigration was small: 5,000 up to 1908, half of whom went immediately to the United States. In Canada, Sikhs arrived originally in British Columbia. They dispersed across the country only with a large immigration after 1967, settling in all major cities. Even so, British Columbia remains the home of half of Canada's Sikhs.

The early immigrants came from rural villages and most were members of the Jat farming caste. They were typical sojourners: men arriving without families, seeking whatever work they could get, remitting home as much of their savings as possible, and intent on returning to Punjab. Through legal and illegal immigration, men circulated between Canada and Punjab for decades. In British Columbia these men found work mostly in saw mills and shingle mills; the *lumber industry remained their main employer for more than 60 years. Because Canada excluded immigrants from India from 1908 to 1918, and then allowed only sponsored wives or children up to 1953, the Sikh population grew slowly until the 1960s and included few women and children. Only through the immigration of the last 35 years have Sikhs acquired the numbers to assert a political presence and to demand respect for their distinctive religious emblems, particularly the turban and the kirpan (ceremonial sword). Recently, their community has produced a BC provincial premier, Ujjal Dossanj, who served for 15 months in 2000–1, and a federal cabinet minister, Herb Dhaliwal, first appointed in 1997. Canadian Sikhs have been involved in the struggles of Punjab, where political developments dating from British rule have contributed to heightened religious nationalism. Sikh separatism destabilized Punjab for more than a decade, following Indian army action in June 1984 against Sikh militants occupying the Sikh Golden Temple in Amritsar. The separatist issue and questions of orthodoxy still divide Sikhs in Canada. HUGH JOHNSTON

See also KOMAGATA MARU.

Silver Dart. The 'aerodrome' that made the first powered, heavier-than-air machine flight in Canada was built under the auspices of the Aerial Experiment Association, formed by Mabel and Alexander Graham *Bell. The machine's designer and pilot was Canadian John A.D. McCurdy, who flew it 11 times in the United States in 1908 before shipping it to Baddeck, Nova Scotia, the Bells' summer home. On 23 February 1909, 390 kg fully loaded, the silver-winged craft was tugged onto the ice of Bras d'Or Lake by horse-drawn sleigh. 'The machine rose . . . after travelling about 100 feet', recalled McCurdy, 'and flew at an elevation of about ten to thirty feet directly east for a distance of about half a mile . . . The speed I should judge to be about forty miles an hour.' Hoisting his glass of homemade raspberry drink, Bell toasted Canada's entry into the aviation age, and the first flight by a British subject anywhere in the British Empire. After more than 200 flights, the *Dart* crashed at Camp Petawawa, 2 August 1909, only its 8-cylinder, water-cooled engine surviving. NORMAN HILLMER

Simcoe, Elizabeth Posthuma Gwillim (1762–1850). Born in Northamptonshire, Elizabeth married John Graves *Simcoe in 1782. With inherited wealth she bought a 5,000-acre estate near Honiton, where the Simcoes lived until her husband was appointed lieutenant-governor of Upper Canada in 1791. They spent the first winter at Quebec, a year at Niagara-on-the-Lake, then moved to York (Toronto) in 1793. After returning to England in 1796 they settled on their Devon estate, where Elizabeth brought up her children, 13 in all. She enjoyed her adventuring years in Canada and recorded them in a series of diaries, illustrated with many sketches. Numerous watercolours also commemorated Canadian scenes. She wrote at least three versions, commenting on flora and fauna, on the medical uses made of them, on Native people and their customs, and on vignettes of Canadian life. First edited and published by John Ross Robertson in 1911, reprinted in 1934 and 1973, they were edited and published as *Mrs. Simcoe's Diary* by Mary Quayle Innis in 1965. CLARA THOMAS

Simcoe, John Graves (1752–1806), soldier and colonial administrator. Simcoe served the British army with distinction in the American Revolution before being invalided home in 1781. He came with his wife, Elizabeth, to Upper Canada in June 1792 as the province's first lieutenant-governor. He wanted to make the province a beacon of rational liberty on the North American continent and to attract Americans discontented with republican excesses. The colony's well-ordered, monarchical, Church of England–centred regime, and its good land, would appeal to them. Soldiers would build roads, farm, and help establish urban centres. Naval vessels would sail the Great Lakes. Diplomacy among the western Natives would stiffen their resistance to American encroachment. Few of Simcoe's ambitious plans were implemented, and several involved him in controversy with Lord Dorchester, the governor general of British North America.

Plagued with ill health, Simcoe left the province in 1796 to recuperate, resigning his governorship in 1798, but not before also serving as governor of St Domingo (Haiti). Appointed commander-in-chief in India, he died in 1806 before taking up his post. His most lasting mark came in Upper Canada, where, however fanciful his dreams, he had considerable success in establishing the province's day-to-day administration. COLIN READ

Simpson, Sir George (*c.* 1786–1860), overseas governor, *Hudson's Bay Company. Born out of wedlock in Scotland, Simpson was raised by his father's family and sent to London in 1800 to work with his uncle at Graham and Simpson, sugar brokers. Merger with Wedderburn and Company in 1812 opened opportunities in the *fur trade, as Wedderburn's sister, Jean, was married to Lord *Selkirk, an important shareholder of the HBC. Selkirk's influence led to violent competition with the *North West Company and after his death in 1820 the company sought amalgamation with its rivals. Simpson, untainted by the conflicts, was sent to oversee the fusion of the work forces. Quickly gaining a reputation for efficiency and strategy, he was made effective North American governor of the company in 1826. He expanded trade across the mountains and his prodigious travel focused on zones of competition with America and Russia. Simpson was knighted in 1841 for his support of arctic exploration. With ratification of the *Oregon Treaty in 1842, he oversaw withdrawal of HBC interests located south of the 49th parallel to lower mainland British Columbia and Vancouver Island. After 1839, Simpson's personal business interests expanded towards transportation, settlement, banking, and mining. He died a wealthy and prominent citizen of Montreal. GRAHAM MacDONALD

Sissons, John Howard (1892–1969). Born in Orillia, Ontario, Jack Sissons worked his way through Queen's and then articled in Alberta precisely so that he could be a pioneer. He practised 25 years in the *Peace River country and was a Liberal MP, 1940–5, before being appointed to the bench in southern Alberta in 1946. In 1955 he accepted the post of first judge of the territorial court of the Northwest Territories. Beyond the age when many retire, Sissons and his wife Frances started over in Yellowknife. Never secretive about his disdain for bureaucrats, Sissons fought to establish his vision of common law as necessarily created within the context of individual cases. He insisted on taking his court on a vast circuit and on utilizing Inuit and Dene values and customs in his rulings. His most famous case, involving charges of murder and child abandonment, was covered by *Time* magazine. Dying in Edmonton within three years of his retirement, Sissons left behind not only a legal tradition but memoirs (*Judge of the Far North*, 1968) and a collection of sculptures commissioned to represent his cases.

JANICE DICKIN

Sisters of St John the Divine. The first permanent Canadian *Anglican religious order, organized in 1884–5. The mother foundress was Hannah Grier Coome (1837–1921), a descendant of two elite Upper Canadian families. After the death of her husband from cancer in 1878, she began considering the religious life and was persuaded by others to organize a Canadian sisterhood. She prepared for this task by entering a sisterhood in Peekskill, New York, in 1882. She opened her first house in Toronto in 1885, ignoring those Protestant-minded critics who denounced the venture as 'papist'. The SSJD has administered hospitals, homes for the elderly, missions to the poor, shelters for women, Sunday School by Post, care for the mentally handicapped, and other ministries across Canada and in New York State. ALAN L. HAYES

Skelton, Oscar Douglas (1878–1941). The son of an Ontario teacher and small businessman, Skelton was a Queen's University professor and administrator, 1909–25, doubling as a public intellectual, writing fluidly and critically about politics and the economy. He was a passionate Liberal, publishing an admiring biography of Sir Wilfrid *Laurier and catching the eye of W.L. Mackenzie *King, who brought him into the public service as his chief foreign policy adviser. Skelton's decision to leave Queen's was a difficult one, but in his words 'the possibility of doing something effective & on a big scale for the country' was irresistible. As deputy minister of the Department of *External Affairs, 1925–41, he built a modern Canadian foreign office and became Ottawa's indispensable bureaucrat, close even to the mercurial Conservative prime minister R.B. *Bennett. The great cause of Skelton's life was Canada's independence from Britain. In a 1931 comment on an American professor's question, 'Does the future of Canada lie with the United States or the United Kingdom?' Skelton responded in his dry way: 'It does not seem to have occurred to the gentleman . . . that the future of Canada might perhaps lie with Canada.'

NORMAN HILLMER

slavery. Before the arrival of Europeans, hundreds of people were enslaved by Aboriginals along the northwest coast. Slaves were usually, though not always, captured in war. Valued for their labour and as items of exchange, they were central to the hunting and fishing cultures of the Northwest. Aboriginal slavery continued there until the 1880s.

Slaveholding after European contact was part of a broader phenomenon that began when the first slaves were brought from Africa to America. The French enslaved Black people in Canada as early as 1608. By 1759, the end of the French regime, there were 3,604 slaves in Canada, 1,132 of whom were Black. The majority of slaves were *Panis*, a term derived from the Caddoan tribes of the Great Plains, and included members of more than 20 Aboriginal societies such as the Fox, Sioux, Iowa, Kansa, Chickasaw, Blackfoot, and Comanche. By 1750 the French name *Panis* had become a generic term for an Aboriginal slave.

There is little evidence that slavery in Canada during and after the French regime differed much from that in New England and the Middle Atlantic colonies of British America. Throughout the northern colonies, unlike the plantation economies of the South, living conditions mitigated the harshest aspects of slavery. Employed on farms throughout the countryside and as domestic servants in towns, slaves lived in close proximity to whites. Owning only one or two slaves, most slaveholders remained confident of their hegemony, and hence slaves were allowed a certain degree of autonomy. Slaves in Canada represented less than 1 per cent of the population; thus, Canada was a society with slaves, not a slave society.

During the Revolutionary War (1775–83) Black slaves in the American colonies were offered refuge by the British if they left their rebel owners. Some 3,550 *Blacks eventually migrated to Nova Scotia. United Empire *Loyalists also brought their slaves, and 1,232 Black people, 34 per cent of the Black immigrants, remained slaves. During the late 18th century practically every town and village in mainland Nova Scotia had slaves, a story that remains to be told. Recent research has revealed that there were also more than 400 slaves in Cape Breton. Hundreds were also brought to Ontario and Quebec by their Loyalist owners. Although legislative and judicial measures had restricted its development, slavery remained technically legal in British North America until abolished by the imperial Parliament in 1833.

KENNETH DONOVAN

smallpox. An especially repulsive and frightening disease, smallpox ravaged Canada from its introduction from Europe in the early 17th century. Lacking immunity, Native people in the St Lawrence Valley, and ultimately across the country, were heavily infected. Major epidemics occurred throughout the 18th and 19th centuries. In a crude attempt at germ warfare, the British military gave smallpox-contaminated blankets to Aboriginal opponents during the *Pontiac Uprising in 1763. The last serious epidemic occurred in Montreal in 1885. The disease swept through the city, especially poor neighbourhoods, aided by a strident anti-vaccination campaign largely by francophone residents. This issue, plus anger over the execution of Louis *Riel, led to rioting that had to be put down by militia. Smallpox killed more than 3,000. Strict quarantine prevented the disease from spreading outside Montreal.

The smallpox virus is highly infectious. Although it is commonly conveyed by droplets spread by coughing or sneezing, the virus is sturdy and can be acquired by handling infected clothing and bedding. A victim develops fever, severe headache, extreme malaise, vomiting, and an often widespread rash of skin lesions filled with pus, which frequently left survivors with disfiguring facial scars. Even among European Canadians from areas where there was some acquired immunity, the death rate could reach 20 per cent; epidemics among members of the First Nations could kill as many as 90 per cent of patients.

Variolation was introduced into England from the Middle East early in the 1700s. Under this practice, a healthy person would be inoculated with smallpox pus in hopes of inducing a mild case of the disease, resulting in immunity to further attacks. The risk of serious disease in the patient, and its spread to others, made the process risky. Then, in 1798, Dr Edward Jenner observed that milkmaids who developed cowpox from milking infected cows never had smallpox. He experimented with inoculating cowpox pus instead of smallpox pus—the procedure later called *vaccination—and found that this much safer process still created immunity. The procedure was introduced into Canada early in the 1800s though use was at first sporadic.

After the world's most successful public health campaign, mass vaccination conducted by the World Health Organization, smallpox was officially declared eradicated in 1979. No case has occurred since. However, the threat of the disease being spread by terrorists has raised fears of recurrence in the 21st century. CHARLES G. ROLAND

Smallwood, Joseph Roberts (1900–91), Newfoundland premier 1949–72. Smallwood was born in the Newfoundland outport of Gambo but grew up in St John's. Leaving school at age 14, he became an apprentice printer, then worked as a journalist. In the 1920s he mixed in leftist circles in New York and London. He ran for the Liberal Party in the Newfoundland election of 1932 but was defeated. After the introduction of the *Commission of Government in 1934, he promoted co-operative activity among fishermen and was the subject of police reports. In 1937 he published the two-volume *Book of Newfoundland* (four more volumes 1967–75). Also in 1937 he began broadcasting 'The Barrelman', a program of Newfoundland history and lore, over VONF, a St John's radio station. In 1941 he briefly edited *The Express*, which mercilessly satirized the Commission of Government. In 1943 he moved to Gander, a wartime boom town, where he ran a pig farm.

His career to this time had been decidedly mixed, but he knew how to write, debate, and organize, and had an established radio voice, assets he used to great advantage following the Second World War. In 1945 the United Kingdom announced that a *National Convention would be elected in Newfoundland to advise it on constitutional choices to be put to the people by referendum. Smallwood was elected to the convention and seized the opportunity to become the leading proponent of confederation with Canada. He carried this cause in two hard-fought referendums in 1948. Subsequently he was premier of Newfoundland from 1 April 1949 to 18 January 1972. As premier, he promoted economic development, championed the *welfare state, and attracted a national following. Politically defeated, he published memoirs, *I Chose Canada* (1973), and masterminded the *Encyclopedia of Newfoundland and Labrador*, three volumes of which were published in his lifetime (1981–91). PETER NEARY

Smashers. New Brunswick Reformers emerged in the 1840s, governed briefly in 1855, lost support by endorsing prohibitory liquor legislation, regained power in 1857, and maintained ascendency until the *Confederation debate splintered the party in 1864. Although the first government in British North America to introduce the secret ballot and voters' registers, the Smashers did not prove as radical as their opponents' characterization implies. Their assessment franchise was a modest reform. While other colonies abolished legislative councils, the Smashers increased representation by increasing appointments. Their revision of the Common Schools Act omitted compulsory assessment in support of schools. Comprised mainly of evangelical Protestants, the party rejected a proposal to publish the synoptic debates in French as well as English. It opposed the privileges granted the Church of England, and transformed King's College into a secular provincial university. Forward looking and in tune with the times, the Smasher government presided over a period of economic prosperity.
GAIL G. CAMPBELL

Smith, Donald, 1st Baron Strathcona and Mount Royal (1820–1914). Born at Forres, Scotland, Smith was a fur trader and railway entrepreneur. He joined the *Hudson's Bay Company in 1838 and worked his way through the ranks to become its chief executive officer in 1889. He successfully represented the company in the difficult negotiations of 1869–70 and served as a member of the Manitoba legislature (1870–4) and as an MP (1871–8). In the latter capacity he voted against the government of Sir John A. *Macdonald in the *Pacific Scandal. In 1873–4 Smith joined his cousin George Stephen and others in acquiring the depreciated bonds of the St Paul, Minneapolis and Manitoba Railway. Both Smith and Stephen became partners in the *Canadian Pacific Railway syndicate formed in 1881. Smith, who was a driving force behind the building of the CPR, drove the last spike of that railway's main line at *Craigellachie on 7 November 1885. Serving from 1896 until his death in London as high commissioner for Canada in the United Kingdom, he was elevated to the British peerage in 1897. T.D. REGEHR

Smith, Goldwin (1823–1910), political commentator. Smith was an unlikely figure in Victorian Canada. Although professor of history at Oxford University, he was a journalist rather than scholar. Sympathetic to the North in the American Civil War, in 1862 he argued for the independence of Canada. He moved to the United States, and in 1871 settled in Canada. Marriage in 1875 made him owner of the Grange, an English-style country house in Toronto. He sponsored the *Canada First movement, but in 1877 declared that the movement for nationality had failed and that annexation to the United States was 'morally certain'. However, he then backed the *National Policy, before denouncing Macdonald for corruption. In 1891 he published *Canada and the Canadian Question*, again arguing for union with the United States. The key to Goldwin Smith lies in his pen-name, 'A Bystander'. Although he lived in Canada, his heart remained in Britain, which he visited often. His views on Canadian–American relations were coloured by his opposition to provincial-style self-government for Ireland. He condemned Canadian *federalism as a failure and argued that small countries were destined for absorption by their larger neighbours. Famous for his limp, bony handshake, he was also kind to his cat. GED MARTIN

Smith-Shortt, Elizabeth (1859–1949), physician and feminist reformer. Elizabeth was born in Winona, Ontario, to Sylvester Smith and Isabella McGee Smith of E.D. Smith jam fame. Nurtured by a feminist mother, she taught briefly before challenging the male monopoly on medicine. Enrolling at Queen's University, she became, in 1884, one of the first women to graduate from a Canadian medical school. Her evocative diary depicts the harassment she experienced at the hands of hostile instructors and students, and a threatened strike by male medical students, which led to the founding of separate women's medical schools. Conducting a private practice before her marriage to civil servant Adam Shortt, Elizabeth later combined family duties with leadership in maternalist and public health reforms. DIANNE DODD

Social Credit. Social Credit formed provincial governments in Alberta (William *Aberhart, 1935–43; Ernest *Manning, 1943–68; Harry Strom, 1968–71), and British

Columbia (W.A.C. *Bennett, 1952–72; William R. Bennett, 1975–86; Bill Vander Zalm, 1986–91; Rita Johnston, 1991) but never grew beyond third party status in federal politics. The national party sprang into existence following Social Credit's stunning August 1935 election victory in Alberta. With scant time to organize before the fall federal election, Social Credit nonetheless won 18 seats, 16 of which were in Alberta. The inability to achieve more than regional popularity would plague Social Credit until its demise in the 1980s. Disunity within the party, already evident in 1935, would also mark its history.

Under its first national leaders, Alberta MPs John Blackmore (1935–44) and Solon Low (1944–61), the party relied heavily on Alberta Social Credit for its philosophy, policies, and finances. The national and provincial parties also split internally along the same fault line. Influenced heavily by the Great Depression, most party MPs believed an international conspiracy was orchestrating world events in order to eliminate individual freedom and establish a dictatorship. Some supported fundamentalists Aberhart and Manning and their gradualist strategy of increasing purchasing power to release the individual from the conspiracy. Others backed social credit founder Major C.H. Douglas, who urged an immediate assault on the conspiracy and its lackeys, the banks, governments, and courts. The division between the two factions became untenable by 1946, when the national convention adopted Douglas's positions. With anti-Semitism, always at the dark underbelly of Social Credit, gaining voice in the party's national newspaper and the speeches of some MPs, Manning finally acted. He cut off funding to the paper and excised the most visible of the Douglasites from the national and provincial parties. A chastened Low, himself a Douglasite, returned to the mainstream of the party, championing fiscal conservatism and provincial rights. Adopting Aberhart/Manning rhetoric, but with a bitter twist of McCarthyism, through the remaining years of his leadership Low attacked the *welfare state and the socialist-communist conspirators behind it.

Under Blackmore and Low, Social Credit never won more than 19 seats. Attempts to create a viable national presence (the 1940 New Democracy movement and the 1941 Democratic Monetary Reform Organization) were miserable failures. In John *Diefenbaker's Conservative sweep of 1958, no Social Credit candidate claimed victory. Seemingly on its deathbed, Social Credit staged an unlikely recovery by allying with populist Réal Caouette's Quebec-based Ralliement des créditistes. Although Caouette lost the leadership contest to Alberta's Robert Thompson (1961–7), his fiery, anti-finance brand of Social Credit won support in rural Quebec, where the party elected 26 MPs in the 1962 election. With Diefenbaker's government reduced to minority status, Social Credit briefly held the balance of power. Thompson and his pro-federalist Quebec lieutenant Caouette, however, proved to be uncomfortable allies. The party was once more split into two camps. By 1963, Caouette was gone, as was the party's influence when Lester *Pearson's minority Liberal government assumed power. The party was again wiped out in Pierre *Trudeau's Liberal sweep of 1968. By then, even Manning had given up on the national party. He called for the creation of a new social conservative movement. Caouette returned to lead Social Credit from 1971 until his death in 1976, but, in terms of electoral success, the party was by then a Quebec-only phenomenon. Since 1980, fleeting attempts to revive Social Credit, whether in the Manning or Douglas image, have failed. BOB HESKETH

social gospel. Usually referred to as the 'social gospel' in North America and as 'social Christianity' in Britain, this form of liberal Protestantism emerged at the end of the 19th century at a time of widespread social, theological, and intellectual change. Traditional Christianity no longer seemed adequate to address the insights of the new Biblical criticism, Darwinian evolution, large-scale industrialization, immigration and urbanization, and growing labour unrest. Building on the religious activism and belief in moral improvement that were characteristic of 19th-century evangelicalism, the social gospel went beyond conversion of the individual to call for the renewal of all of society to reflect more clearly Jesus' teachings on the kingdom of God. In the spirit of the age, it included among the marks of the kingdom the eradication of social inequality, the abolition of capitalism, the end to denominational divisions, and the promotion of *social purity and altruism.

In Canada proponents tended to be ministers and members of the Methodist, Presbyterian, Baptist, and Anglican denominations. Some were already familiar with the social Christian thought of British writers such as F.D. Maurice and William Booth, the American social gospel theologian Walter Rauschenbusch, and the neo-Hegelian thought of T.H. Green in England and John Watson in Canada. Increased international travel had also publicized innovative social programs such as those of Methodist Hugh Price Hughes in London and Jane Addams's Hull House in Chicago. In Canada, social gospel spokespersons such as J.S. *Woodsworth and Salem *Bland, and novelists Ralph Connor (the Rev. Charles *Gordon) and Nellie *McClung reflected in their speeches and writings the prevailing optimism of a young country, as well as the national culture-building role of mainline Protestant denominations. Together with old-style evangelicals, those drawn to the social gospel organized a range of interdenominational reform groups such as the *Lord's Day Alliance (1888), which unleashed a campaign that in 1906 culminated in the federal Lord's Day Act regulating business activities and public events on Sundays. As well, by 1916, as province after province except Quebec voted for *prohibition, a dry Canada had almost come within reach thanks to the concerted efforts of the *Woman's Christian Temperance Union and the Dominion Alliance.

Committed to the new theological teaching that God was immanent within the cultural process, social gospellers drew on insights from sociology and science on the importance of environment in understanding social problems, and on the need to engage in systematic collection and dissemination of facts. Their wide-ranging concerns allowed for extensive co-operation with progressive civic reformers in the promotion of *child welfare, *public health, slum clearance and model housing, city parks and urban beautification, and the suppression of *prostitution. Through publications, congresses, and study groups, they were instrumental in broadening the social awareness of the people in the pews. Although several of the more radical advocates encountered opposition on occasion, the extent of denominational support is noteworthy, for many co-religionists were troubled by the growing misery of the poor and were willing to consider some of the new implications of a practical Christianity.

Among the more visible signs of the impact of social gospel thought were the progressive declarations of major denominations, drawing attention to systemic economic injustices and endorsing such correctives as an eight-hour working day, a living wage, *old-age pensions, compulsory arbitration in industrial disputes, and public ownership of *utilities. Formidable too were the networks put in place to publicize and carry out this reform program. In 1907, led by Presbyterian J.G. Shearer and Methodist Albert Moore, an interdenominational Social Service Council of Canada was organized to coordinate the reform activities of religious groups and labour and farm organizations. When in 1914 the council sponsored the first national council on social welfare in Ottawa, its huge success was seen by many as a vindication of the social gospel's claim to make Christianity a vital force in shaping 20th-century Canada.

The war that followed, while contradicting the idealism that had fuelled the movement, also raised expectations of an outcome favourable to its ideals. During the 1920s, however, the repeal of prohibition belied those hopes. So too did the fracturing of Protestantism, first in 1925 when a third of the Presbyterians, undermining the social gospel's call for Christian unity, refused to join the new *United Church of Canada, and then in 1927 when a belligerent fundamentalism split the Baptist Convention of Ontario and Quebec. Nor by the 1920s, as secular forces that had long affected older countries became more evident, could one continue to speak with confidence of the 'Christian Canada' that had once fed social gospel enthusiasm. By the 1930s, new forces and inner contradictions led to the demise of the social gospel and its supersession by a new movement, the Fellowship for the Christian Social Order. MARGUERITE VAN DIE

socialism. Canadian socialism emerged at the end of the 19th century in the context of growing discontent with the inequities and hardships of industrial capitalism. Many of its proponents were veterans of earlier radical causes, including the *Knights of Labor, the agrarian Patrons of Industry, the 'single-tax' reform movement of American Henry George, and the 'nationalism' prompted by the popular utopian novel *Looking Backward* by Edward Bellamy. Socialists argued that only the collective and democratic control of the economy could replace a society based upon greed and competition with one based on co-operation and the full development of the capacities of all.

Socialism in Canada was overwhelmingly a working-class movement, and its self-declared task was to 'make socialists' through education. The first efforts to build a socialist organization in Canada were made by the Socialist Labor Party, led by American Marxist Daniel DeLeon, but it maintained a self-imposed isolation from the broader labour movement. More successful, at least numerically, was the Canadian Socialist League. The CSL's ethical socialism was a broader and less demanding movement than the SLP, rooted in Protestant morality and more open to reforms and half-measures that, it was felt, would lead in the general direction of socialism. Differences between such reformers and the revolutionaries who argued that meaningful reforms were impossible under capitalism would continue to divide the movement.

Socialism was strongest on the West Coast, where the Socialist Party of British Columbia made an electoral impact in mining communities (and to a lesser extent in Vancouver) shortly after its formation in 1902. This was all the more significant because—they claimed—they had run on the most 'uncompromising statement of the principles of revolutionary socialism that had ever been drafted in any country'. The SPBC rallied socialists across the country to form the Socialist Party of Canada in 1904 on the basis that capitalism could not be reformed and that the 'wage system' needed to be abolished. The SPC program contained no 'immediate demands' or reforms. Rather, it sought to educate working people about the nature of capitalist society and the need for its abolition. Its commitment to revolution has been seen as the product of capitalist development in the West, where the harsh and dangerous environment of mining camps and company towns provided little evidence that the system could reform itself. But it also appealed to many British-born workers in urban Canada, as well as to significant numbers of Ukrainians, Finns, Italians, Jews, and other immigrants who, in many cases, organized their own SPC locals.

Not all socialists shared the SPC's views. Many looked to the apparent successes of more gradualist movements, such as the Labour Party in Britain, and wanted to work more closely with non-socialist reformers. As well, many of the non-British locals of the party felt alienated by the apparent inflexibility of the SPC. After 1910 such socialists formed the Social Democratic Party of Canada. There was more uniting the SPC and the SDPC than dividing them. During the First World War they both denounced what they saw as the imperialist slaughter and they both celebrated the victory of the Bolsheviks in Russia. While the SDPC put more weight on winning reforms, there was a general recognition that these were ephemeral gains compared to the cultivation of a solid 'scientific' class consciousness among workers.

As the most active and articulate spokespersons of the dramatic events of 1919, socialists (particularly SPCers) played key roles in the general strikes in Winnipeg and elsewhere, and in the *One Big Union. Ironically, they were uncomfortable in this role, feeling that the emancipation of workers had to be taken collectively by workers themselves—no leaders could guide them to socialism. Nor did they feel that the general strike was necessarily advancing the cause of revolution. Without a solid education in Marxist historical materialism, workers would be subject to demagogues and peddlers of panaceas who would only perpetuate class society.

The formation of the *Communist Party and the *Co-operative Commonwealth Federation between the two world wars again divided socialists. For some, these new parties offered a more effective strategy to power, either by revolution or by the ballot box. Many old-time socialists stood aloof, feeling suspicious of parties that claimed to 'lead' the working class rather than to educate it. During the 1930s, an attempt was made to re-create the old SPC, based mostly in British Columbia, but this older tradition was absorbed into the dominant political organizations of labour, the Communists, and the CCF.

JAMES NAYLOR

'socialist hordes at the gates'. Since adopting party lines in 1903, British Columbia's legislature has had at least one socialist member. In 1933, a new socialist party, the *Co-operative Commonwealth Federation, became the official opposition; it traditionally got about a third of the popular vote. Beginning in 1952, W.A.C. *Bennett successfully presented his *Social Credit Party as the champion of free enterprise against the CCF and its successor, the *New Democratic Party. On 21 August, nine days before the 1972 election, an uneasy Bennett warned again that 'the socialist hordes are at the gates'. This time, British Columbians ignored his battle cry and elected the NDP under David *Barrett. PATRICIA E. ROY

social purity movement. A movement for social purity—a euphemism for sexual chastity—first arose in England in the late 1880s. It took root easily in Canada over the next decade, the ground having been cultivated by the *social gospel and fertilized by fear of urban decay, working-class unrest, and the decline of the Anglo-Saxon race.

A loose network of educated lay and professional white, middle-class, evangelical Christians, social purists were intent on eradicating *prostitution and the double standard of morality. The movement became synonymous, however, with the moral regulation of all non-reproductive sexual activity. It was directed mainly by social purity feminists in organizations like the *Salvation Army, the Moral and Social Reform Council of Canada, and the Canadian Purity Education Association. Blaming male sexual vice for racial, national, and imperial degeneration, such feminists essentialized women as sexually passive *'mothers of the race'. But all women were not viewed as equal: because of their superior evolutionary heritage, women of Anglo-Saxon origin, it was claimed, were best suited to assume a leading role in purifying society.

Moral regulation occurred on three fronts: the redemptive, the punitive, and the preventive. Rescue workers encouraged prostitutes to train as domestics in female refuges. Legal reformers lobbied to raise the age of consent for girls and penalized male homosexual activity. Sex education advocates demanded that boys and girls be taught about social purity. By the beginning of the 20th century, sex education outstripped rescue work and criminal law reform in popularity. The public health threat of *venereal disease, combined with the belief that robust white *children were the lynchpins of the regeneration of society, led social purists and physicians to join in a tenuous alliance in favour of sex education as a medico-moral prophylactic.

Social purists spawned numerous guides to help mothers, as the centre of the home, to instruct children about sex. American texts about dispelling ignorance in children, by Drs Mary Wood-Allen and Sylvanus Stall, were part of the best-selling *Self and Sex* series in Canada. Mothers were to teach children reverence for parenthood by informing them in vague terms about the reproduction of flora and fauna, but the detail most obscured was sexual intercourse. The mother's other task was to protect her children from the most pernicious of all non-reproductive activity, masturbation. Vitalist theory, widely accepted in medical circles, held semen to be the most potent form of vital energy. Semen loss was detrimental, especially for Anglo-Saxon males; it retarded the growth of their complex moral, mental, and physical faculties, thereby dooming them to venereal wards, mental institutions, and cemeteries. Yet, while agreeing on the need for sex education, social purists believed that mothers—particularly if backward immigrants—were reluctant to provide such instruction.

The Ontario *Women's Christian Temperance Union, known for its educational campaigns for children against alcohol and tobacco, hired Arthur Beall, a former YMCA missionary, as a 'purity lecturer' primarily to public school boys. Beall compared children's bodies to living temples and encouraged them to reject the double standard. His lectures to adolescent boys cautioned them in frightening terms against masturbation and its consequences—illness, castration, and death. He also urged them never to have 'smutty' thoughts about girls or—in an overt allusion to homosexuality—play with another boy's penis. Beall concluded his lectures with standard social purity fare: 'I see a new Ontario, a new Canada, a new British Empire, a new Earth—in which shall dwell Righteousness, and Peace, and Joy in the Holy Spirit.' Responses to Beall's lectures ranged from horror to gratitude, and to curiosity about masturbation. In 1912, as a result of intense lobbying by the WCTU, the Ontario Department of Education hired Beall. Later, styling himself as a social hygienist, he published the highly regarded *The Living Temple: A Manual on Eugenics for Parents and Teachers* (1933).

During the First World War, a social hygiene movement dominated by male physicians concerned with a rise in venereal infection decried social purity as old-fashioned and unscientific. These 'experts' blamed prostitutes, not profligate men, for VD. Moreover, they sidelined social purity feminists' contribution to sex education by invoking a caricature of the spinster whose attack on male sexual vice sprang from her prudish—and likely lesbian—dislike of sexual relations with men. Unlike their American counterparts, organizations such as the Canadian social hygienists did not support sex education in schools, worrying that it would pique students' sexual curiosity. Social purity feminists' support for sex education had signalled their faith in the individual's regenerative abilities. By contrast, social hygienists opted more often for repressive *eugenic measures such as mental hygiene testing and sterilization. The social purity movement declined in the late 1920s, but its influence on sex education was evident in *public health campaigns that talked of birds and bees and that scared audiences with graphic depictions of individuals with VD. During the Second World War, when VD rates skyrocketed again, social hygienists finally endorsed school-based sex education, but the contribution made by social purity feminists was entirely forgotten.

CHRISTABELLE SETHNA

See also MORAL AND SOCIAL REFORM.

social reformers. In pre-Confederation British North America, opinion leaders regarded individual lack of morality rather than the social system as the cause of *poverty. While organized charities and spontaneous community solidarity were regarded as legitimate ways of helping widows with young children and the severely ill, who clearly could do little to help themselves, few advocated state action to create greater social equality. Still fewer questioned whether the capitalist economic system was the best means of organizing economic and social life.

In the late 19th century several factors led to a debate regarding both the causes of poverty and the best remedies for it. Within a generation, industrialization had doubled the percentage of city dwellers, challenging Canadians' notions of their country as rural and agricultural and characterized by small land-holders. Destitution and class divisions in the cities led to class conflict and to middle-class questioning of the social order. Such questioning was also encouraged by the debates that became common among educated Christians regarding the meaning of religion in the wake of Darwin's theory of evolution. Increasingly, those who had become more sceptical about the literal truth of the Bible found solace in forms of religion other than conventional Christianity and/or in programs of social reform that might create a Kingdom of Heaven on earth. Social gospellers believed that poverty was the result of greed promoted by an economic system that extolled profits. They wished to reform society by using the state either to regulate or eliminate capitalism. They wanted to ensure that workers received living wages, and that society supported the unemployed, allowing them to remain in their own homes rather than being forced into dreaded workhouses.

Not all advocates of state intervention to deal with poverty were *social* reformers. Conservatives called for controls over *individual* behaviour rather than state help for the poor as the solution to poverty. Opponents of social reform believed that the state's goal should be to ban the sale of alcohol and prevent the poor from breeding. Even among those who advocated social change, there was a continuum of thought, from those who supported radical social change to those who advocated tinkering with the existing system or combining social change with changes to the behaviour of individuals.

Agnes Maule Machar, a novelist and popular historian, serves as an example of one wing of the progressive reformers. Although unwavering in her adherence to Christianity, she believed in a social Christianity that caused her to espouse in particular the cause of better pay and shorter hours for industrial wage-earning women. She believed that the state must intervene in relations between labour and capital for moral reasons, but she warned the churches that if they failed to defend workers' interests, the workers would reject Christianity and turn to communism. By contrast, journalist T. Phillips *Thompson, who shared Machar's solid middle-class background, embraced *free thought and *socialism. Thompson made common cause with the fledgling labour movement in Canada, and argued in favour of an evolutionary socialism that would eventually eliminate capitalism. Thompson regarded Jesus as a worker and a socialist, and claimed that organized Christianity had emptied Christ's thought of its revolutionary egalitarianism. Like many others who were disillusioned by the churches' close ties with and cheery defences of wealthy capitalists, Thompson dabbled in non-Christian religious movements such as *spiritualism and *theosophy. The mixture of social reformism and religious liberalism of writers such as Thompson and Machar had a significant impact on early-20th-century reformers such as socialist J.S. *Woodsworth and Mackenzie *King, a reform-minded liberal and a future Liberal prime minister.

Alexander Peter Reid, a medical doctor and asylum and hospital superintendent in the Maritimes, represented a somewhat more conservative strand of social reform than Thompson and Machar. He found much to criticize in the existing social order, but he rejected unregulated capitalism less from a consciously moral standpoint than from the perspective of a scientist interested in rationality and efficiency. He supported not only a variety of *public health measures but also state action to reduce conflicts between capital and labour. In keeping with many advocates of state legislation to ensure that citizens had clean water, pure milk, and knowledge of how to avoid diseases, Reid believed that cadres of professional experts employed by the state could best protect the interests of all citizens. Reid's 'scientific' perspective on how society should be organized included advocacy of eugenics and marriage control to prevent the 'degeneracy' of the Canadian population.

The wide embrace of *eugenics among late-19th- and early-20th-century reformers—as well as some of their conservative opponents—owed a great deal to the influence of social *Darwinism, preached in particular by the English philosopher Herbert Spencer. Spencer used Darwin's ideas in ways not advocated by that scientist to argue for the preservation of laissez-faire economics. The consequent social inequalities would be no more than a reflection of the survival of the fittest, a desirable state of affairs that, Spencer argued, mirrored Darwin's findings in the natural world. While non-radical reformers such as Alexander Reid clearly believed that the state should act to ensure the survival of what he regarded as the fit members of society, many reformers opposed the idea of having social benefits determined by the free market alone. Yet, Spencer had many intellectual defenders in Canada. William Dawson LeSueur, who embraced free thought in religion as enthusiastically as did Phillips Thompson, rejected the latter's socialism, convinced that the scientific truth of evolution applied to human affairs as much as to the development of nature.

Within the churches, debates about whether society or individuals most required reform were evident in the different priorities for legislative action put forward by various factions. Conservatives focused on having the state prohibit the production and consumption of alcohol, claiming that money wasted on drink caused poverty and that alcoholism destroyed family life. Social gospellers, while often willing to support bans on alcohol, insisted that low wages were the root cause of poverty and that poor working and living conditions drove working men to drink. Much of the same debate persisted in Canada during the first half of the 20th century. Eventually the severity of the Depression of the 1930s and the radicalization of working people and farmers during both the Depression and the Second World War weakened the impact of conservatives' arguments, allowing *'welfare state' programs that reflected *social gospel thinking to be implemented. ALVIN FINKEL

See also MORAL AND SOCIAL REFORM.

Société St-Jean-Baptiste. In 1834, journalist and *Patriote politician Ludger Duvernay hosted the first St-Jean-Baptiste feast in honour of the French-Canadian nation. The 1837–8 rebellions put a damper on such festivities, but in 1842 Quebec City nationalists formed the Association St-Jean-Baptiste to organize a public celebration. The following year the Société St-Jean-Baptiste was formed to unite all Canadiens and to promote their national and economic interests. A government charter was granted in 1849. Apart from an annual parade to demonstrate solidarity, the society was active in promoting the French language, commemorating historical events and heroes, erecting monuments (such as the Monument aux braves in Quebec City and the illuminated cross atop Mount Royal), and providing pension plans and life insurance for its members. In its heyday, at the end of the 19th century, associations could be found throughout Quebec and in Ontario, Manitoba, and a dozen northern states. In 1907 a women's wing—the *Fédération nationale St-Jean-Baptiste—was formed. Although the federation promoted change to the Civil Code, its outlook on gender relations was largely conservative. In recent years, the society has been vigilant in denouncing non-compliance with the Charter of the French Language (Bill 101) and in promoting Quebec independence. JOHN A. DICKINSON

Soeurs de la Miséricorde. In 1845, Rosalie Cadron-Jetté (1794–1864), a Montreal widow and mother of 11 children, opened the Hospice Sainte-Pélagie for single pregnant women. In 1848, she answered Bishop *Bourget's call to open a home 'to welcome fallen women, bring them to a better life, insure baptism [of] and a Christian education for their children'. Three years later, Cadron-Jetté and seven midwives founded a religious community, the Soeurs de la Miséricorde, and later her hospice became the Hôpital de la Miséricorde. For 125 years, this institution served as a shelter and maternity home for thousand of single mothers. There they worked for up to six months before and after their deliveries. When in 1862 a papal decree prevented the sisters from performing deliveries, lay midwives, doctors, and medical students took over the obstetrics. In the 20th century, the hospital opened its doors to married women, keeping the single wards totally segregated. With changes in attitudes, more tolerance for unmarried mothers, and the secularization of hospitals, the institution closed its doors in 1974. The Soeurs de la Miséricorde extended their services to pregnant women and their children in Canada, the United States, Africa, and Latin America.

ANDRÉE LÉVESQUE

Soeurs Grises (Sisters of Charity). This religious congregation, founded in Montreal in 1738 by Marguerite d'Youville, took over the operation of the Hôpital-Général de Montréal, which had been founded by the Charron Brothers in 1693. To this initial responsibility, d'Youville soon added caring for foundlings, visiting the poor, and more, but the nuns were able to pay off the colossal debts accumulated by their predecessors. The congregation quickly obtained the support of the French authorities, and after the conquest the new English ones. Following their founder's death in 1771, the Grey Nuns of Montreal became a pillar of private charity in the city, taking on a multitude of new responsibilities: orphanages, hospices, shelters for working-class children, the blind, and so on. The significance of their charitable work is confirmed by their invitation to undertake similar efforts in other dioceses: St-Hyacinthe (1840), Ottawa (1845), Quebec City (1849). At the same time the Grey Nuns were responsible for important missionary endeavours in the Canadian West, starting in 1844. At the beginning of the 20th century they developed expertise in the hospital field, opening numerous hospitals and becoming leaders in the training of nurses in Quebec, establishing a nursing program affiliated with the Université de Montréal in 1934. In 1960 the congregation was responsible for a vast network of charitable and educational works, which it gradually adapted to the new social circumstances of Quebec. The Accueil Bonneau, a shelter for homeless people in old Montreal, remains this congregation's best-known project. MICHELINE DUMONT

soldier settlement. From the disbanded companies of the Régiment *Carignan-Salières to the old soldiers of the Royal Canadian Rifles, pre-Confederation Canada was often settled by veterans. After the British Conquest in 1760, Fraser's Highlanders brought Scottish blood to rural Quebec; German, English, and Swiss regiments colonized the St Lawrence lowlands. 'Military bounty', as the land grants were termed, was a cheap way to pay off an army. Few old soldiers prospered; most sold their land to speculators. Canadians cursed the tradition but repeated it after sending volunteers to the Northwest in 1870 and 1885. In 1908 the last military bounty, 2.3 million acres, was given to 7,340 South African veterans. Only 657 even tried to become settlers.

The grants far exceeded the supply of good agricultural land in Canada but the tradition of military bounty was so established that *veterans of 1914–19 were confident of receiving land grants, and Military Hospitals Commission chairman Sir James Lougheed did his best to oblige. The *Great War Veterans Association demanded 320 acres per soldier, to be taken from railway grants, Indian reserves, and 'enemy aliens'. A Soldier Settlement Act was drafted in 1917 and a Soldier Settlement Board was appointed in 1918. By 1918, a tough-minded future prime minister, Arthur *Meighen, was in charge of the issue. Meighen wanted a practical scheme to produce successful settlers. Applicants needed experience and physique suited to the robust demands of Canadian farming. The SSB approved full-scale farms, refused garden plots, and rejected disabled veterans, city dwellers, and women. Qualified settlers chose their land under supervision, paid 10 per cent down, and borrowed up to $4,500 from the SSB, plus $2,000 for stock and equipment and $1,000 for 'improvements', normally a shack, a shed, and fencing. A sixth of soldier settlers found homestead land; most purchased land from a farmer. Some provinces and many farmers transferred unsuitable land. *Doukhobor land was taken; Indian reserves were mostly protected, though some bands yielded to pressure. The SSB discouraged colony schemes and exempted few from the down payment (and noted that most of the few failed). Some officials were crooked or incompetent. In Winnipeg, a notorious 'St. Regis Ring' manipulated land prices to the detriment of Manitoba veterans.

Wartime wheat prices of $2.02 a bushel made soldier settlement seem like a bounty. By 1920, wheat at 80 cents killed optimism. By 1923, a fifth of the 30,604 soldier settlers had walked away from their farms. Veterans' organizations spoke of a national calamity and called for revaluation. Ontario's Kapuskasing scheme collapsed completely. So did some British Columbia soldier settlements. Manitoba veterans and politicians who had insisted on northern land could not make a go of it. By 1927, after years of campaigning, organized veterans won revaluation: of 10,907 soldier settlers still on the land, 8,301 emerged with debt reduction totalling $7.4 million. Others failed during the Depression years. Except for a lucky, hard-working few, soldier settlement was no bounty.

DESMOND MORTON

Song Fishermen. Originally coalescing as an informal group of poets interested in sharing their love of poetry and the Atlantic coastal region, the Song Fishermen between 1928 and 1930 organized lectures and recitals in Nova Scotia, produced broadsheets (illustrated by artist Donald MacKay), nurtured emerging poets (such as Charles Bruce), maintained contact with writers from the Maritime provinces who were living outside the region, published a memorial to Bliss Carman after his death, and produced mimeographed *Song Fishermen's Song Sheets* sent to aficionados around North America.

Including poets Sir Charles G.D. Roberts, Bliss Carman, Charles Bruce, Kenneth Leslie, James D. Gillis, Andrew Merkel (the Halifax animateur of the group), Joe Wallace, and Robert Norwood, the Song Fishermen often struck an anti-modernist note at a time when rural values and the oral tradition were being threatened in the Maritimes by economic decline, out-migration, and rapid change. After J.F.B. Livesay of the Canadian Press closed off their publishing outlet, they disbanded in September 1929 after a two-day celebration of poetry and friendship, including piping, Highland dancing, reciting, and a marine excursion to East Dover, Nova Scotia. Attempts to continue publishing in 1930 with Theodore Roberts's Saint John *Acadie* were short lived. The Song Fishermen remain a uniquely anachronistic literary group in a 1920s Canadian field otherwise dominated by the modernist movement.

GWENDOLYN DAVIES

South African War. Canadians were divided on their country's participation in its first official military expedition abroad, a war in South Africa between Britain and the South African Republic (supported by the Orange Free State), which began on 11 October 1899. Before the war ended on 31 May 1902, more than 7,368 adventurous young Canadians (officially aged 22–40, though some as young as 15) served with British troops. The first unit, the 2nd (Special Service) Battalion Royal Canadian Regiment, contained 1,000 infantrymen. Those that followed were artillery and mounted men, formed into units such as the Royal Canadian Dragoons, the Canadian Mounted Rifles, the Royal Canadian Field Artillery, the Strathcona's Horse, and a Canadian component of the South African Constabulary. Perhaps another 300 Canadians joined irregular British forces such as the notorious Howard's Canadian Scouts. Canada also sent 23 artificers, a 64-person hospital unit, 12 nursing sisters, 12 instructional officers, 6 chaplains, and 5 postal clerks.

Canada's three most celebrated battles were at Paardeberg, Liliefontein, and Hart's River. At Paardeberg, the Royal Canadian Regiment's first and costliest battle consisted of two engagements, nine days apart. Both were designed to surround and capture the Boer force of some 4,000. On 'Bloody Sunday', 18 February 1900, at Paardeberg Drift, a poorly planned British assault left 18 Canadians dead and 63 wounded, Canada's bloodiest battle since the War of 1812. The second engagement occurred on the 19th anniversary of Britain's humiliating defeat by the Boers at Majuba Hill. Placed on the front lines, the

Canadians led an early morning assault on the demoralized Boer fortifications, bringing the Canadian troops exaggerated credit for the spectacular surrender, Britain's first major victory of the war. On 7 November 1900, at Liliefontein, the Royal Canadian Dragoons, supported by the Canadian Mounted Rifles and two guns from the Royal Canadian Field Artillery, earned unqualified admiration at home and abroad for their courage, ingenuity, and stamina, covering a British retreat. Two Canadians were killed and 11 wounded in the battle; 3 won the Victoria Cross, an unprecedented number of Canadians to have won this award in one battle. At Hart's River, on 31 March 1902, the 2nd Canadian Mounted Rifles provided another example of Canadian heroism, which left 13 men dead and 40 wounded, the second most costly Canadian battle of the war, and one that for a time made the names of Bruce Carruthers, William Knisley, and Charles Napier Evans symbols of Canadian martial courage.

Some 270 Canadians were buried in South Africa; over half fell victim of disease. Another 252 were wounded. Some, like the Ottawa trooper L.W.R. Mulloy who lost both eyes, remained a living monument to the human cost of Canadian participation in this distant conflict that threatened no vital Canadian interest, from which Canada derived no apparent gain, and which created a bitter reference point in English- and French-Canadian relations.

CARMAN MILLER

sovereignty-association. The main political option of the movement for a sovereign Quebec that led to the creation of the *Parti Québécois in 1968. Its principal designer and promoter was René *Lévesque, an influential reformist minister in the Liberal government of Jean *Lesage and a leading figure in Quebec's *Quiet Revolution. In the course of his duties he became increasingly critical of the federal regime, which he saw as a straitjacket limiting the range of political activity available to the Quebec government. Beginning in 1966, Lévesque's nationalism—which was more political than cultural—led him to envision a Quebec that would be sovereign with respect to political powers while remaining economically linked to the rest of Canada. In October 1967, after the provincial Liberals rejected his option, Lévesque and others founded the Mouvement souveraineté-association and published a manifesto, *Option Québec*, in which he defined his project of political sovereignty and economic association with Canada. In 1968 the Parti Québécois was created around this option. The party was to become the rallying point for the majority of Quebec's sovereignist forces.

The idea of sovereignty-association has continued to be the subject of debate and dissent between 'radical' and 'moderate' sovereignists. The central issue in this debate has been the nature of the economic association with Canada. Should it be inseparable from the sovereignty project? What would happen to the sovereignty project in the event that Canada did not agree to economic association? In the elections of 1970, the PQ did not present economic association as an essential condition of sovereignty. In the referendum of 1980, which the PQ lost, Lévesque declared that the two were inseparable and must be achieved simultaneously; economic association would call for a common currency and central bank, a free-trade zone, free circulation of goods and persons, and a bipartite council to resolve disputes. In 1984–5 sovereignty-association was temporarily set aside by the PQ, but in 1995 sovereignty was accompanied by an offer of 'partnership' with the rest of Canada. In that referendum, 49.4 per cent of the Quebec electorate supported this proposal.

JEAN-FRANÇOIS CARDIN

space program. Canada's space activities initially centred on scientific studies supported by the *National Research Council and, from its establishment in 1947, the Defence Research Board. Cosmic ray studies were an early focus of the NRC, together with the investigation of the interaction of high-energy particles and the Earth's upper atmosphere. The DRB funded space research at several universities and established the Defence Research Northern Laboratory at Churchill in northern Manitoba. Examinations of the aurora were conducted from Churchill employing rockets developed by the DRB at Valcartier, Quebec.

The DRB had also founded the Defence Research and Telecommunications Establishment in 1947. When NASA came into being in 1958 in the wake of the Sputnik crisis, non-US researchers were invited to construct scientific payloads to be launched by US rockets. The opportunity was seized by scientists at DRTE, who built a satellite to 'sound' the ionosphere from above. Thus in 1962 Canada became only the third country in the world to develop and fly its own satellite, *Alouette I*. The success of *Alouette* led to a follow-on program of scientific satellites. Canada also fashioned satellites for resource management and communications. *Anik A1*, for example, was launched in 1972, and Canada thereby became the first country to have a satellite in geostationary orbit for domestic communications.

Long discussed, the Canadian Space Agency/Agence spatiale canadienne was established by the federal government in 1989. Its charge was to manage directly a variety of space program activities as well as coordinate other Canadian space efforts, and so simplify the variety of government organizations and committees that had previously been involved in space enterprises. Since its founding, the agency has overseen Canadian participation in a wide range of projects for scientific and commercial benefits. Perhaps most importantly these have included Canada's involvement with the International Space Station program, the key element of which is the $1.4 billion 'Space Remote Manipulator System'. This followed on the success of the 'Canadarm', a robotic arm that has flown on numerous NASA space shuttle missions and that was developed initially by the NRC and Spar Aerospace Ltd. as the prime contractor. The Canadarm was first tested on the shuttle *Columbia* in 1981.

Several Canadian astronauts have flown into space, the first being Marc Garneau, a commander in the Canadian navy, who was a payload specialist in 1984 for mission STS-41G aboard the space shuttle *Challenger*.

ROBERT W. SMITH

Spanish influenza. During the fall and winter of 1918–19, Canada (including Newfoundland and Labrador) suffered approximately 50,000 deaths in a pandemic of influenza that took approximately 21 million lives worldwide. Thought at the time to have originated in Spain, the disease probably started in Canton, was carried to Europe by Chinese trench diggers, and was spread to North America by soldiers returning from the Great War. Flu flourished in army camps and rapidly spread across the continent along all transportation routes. Despite attempts at quarantine, no part of the country escaped infection. The isolated communities along Labrador's coast were probably the hardest hit, losing perhaps a third of their population. There were no effective drugs for either prevention or cure.

Statistics on the Spanish flu are poor for a variety of reasons. At the beginning of the epidemic, flu was not a reportable disease; by the end doctors were too inundated to comply with newly legislated reporting requirements. Households hid infection for fear that they would be isolated and wage earners kept from work. Symptoms could be so mild that some sufferers were never diagnosed, and the death certificates of many others would have listed as cause not flu but the pneumonia that followed it.

Epidemics of influenza are common but not usually serious. The disease tends to kill only the very old and the very young. The pandemic of 1918 was anomalous (as was the pandemic of 1890) in that it tended to take those in the prime of life. Soldiers were at particular risk, due to the crowded and unsanitary conditions of army camps, but the death rate among childbearing women was also high, due to reduced immunities during pregnancy.

Even those uninfected found their lives disrupted. Private businesses such as theatres were shut down and public services such as streetcars suspended. Schools were closed and turned into hospitals; some teachers were forced to take up nursing duties to replace disrupted income. Masks were obligatory in public, and public gatherings banned. The flouting of both these edicts in impromptu celebrations of the Armistice on 11 November caused a resurgence of the disease. Although the influenza strain stayed around for two or three more years, it never again reached epidemic status.

The Spanish influenza was a factor in the timing of Germany's surrender but not in the final outcome of the war. Both sides suffered at home and in the trenches, but Germany had no more reserves to call upon. The epidemic had real and long-standing effects that have never been factored into the examination of history: families decimated, businesses destroyed, some remote communities entirely eradicated. The lasting legacy, in many countries, was a centralized department of health established to face such emergencies.

JANICE DICKIN

Special Council, Lower Canada, 1838–41. In the aftermath of the *Rebellions of 1837–8, the British government adopted a policy of repression in Lower Canada. In addition to military campaigns, pillage, and the burning of farms at the hands of British regulars and loyal volunteers, the government suspended the legislature, judging French Canadians incapable of participating in their own government. In order to preserve a semblance of constitutional government, Parliament replaced the legislature with a Special Council comprising an indeterminate number of members to be named by the colonial governor. Although 44 councillors were appointed, not more than 26 attended any one session of the council. Most prominent and influential were councillors representing the views of the Montreal Constitutional Association, which had organized militias and rifle clubs to oppose the Patriotes before 1837. During its brief existence, the Special Council met for only six short sessions under three different governors, mainly to rubber stamp legislation needed to expedite the trials and punishment of Lower Canadian rebels. The council did attempt some reforms along the lines long advocated by the Montreal merchant elite and, once it acquired the authority in August 1839, laid new taxes in support of the creation of municipal infrastructures and police forces. For this reason, some historians now consider that the council facilitated the transition to a form of government more in keeping with the emergence of commercial capitalism in the St Lawrence Valley.

LOUIS-GEORGES HARVEY

spiritualism. The belief that it is possible for the living to contact the dead had many adherents in the 19th and early 20th centuries. In North America and Britain it frequently attracted well-respected, reform-minded men and women whose religious beliefs were heterodox. They saw spiritualism as a rational replacement for orthodox religion. Such individuals were often attracted as well to *theosophy, Swedenborgianism, and other alternate forms of belief.

Although many spiritualists were men, women outnumbered men as mediums (individuals who, it was believed, could contact the spirit world). Moreover, many male and female adherents supported the women's rights movement, and some espoused radical views on marriage.

In Canada, spiritualism was often linked to social reform. For example, Dr Richard Maurice *Bucke (1837–1902), mental health reformer and superintendent of the London asylum, was a major participant in the Whitmanite movement. Even before his death in 1892, the American poet Walt Whitman was a folk hero, a prophet with a vibrant vision of freedom and democracy and an inspiring love of nature. His followers believed that his benevolent presence lived on after his death, and a Whitmanite movement flourished, spreading from the United States across the world, including Canada.

Flora MacDonald *Denison (1867–1921), feminist activist, journalist, and businesswoman, was another Canadian spiritualist and, like Bucke, a Whitmanite. Denison grew up in a family that rejected orthodox Christianity, but accepted spiritualism, especially after the death in 1880 of Flora's sister Mary. Flora and others believed they could communicate with her spirit, and much later Denison would publish *Mary Melville: The Psychic* (1900), a book loosely based on her sister's life, which linked spiritualism with social reform. By early adulthood, Denison discovered Walt Whitman. She treasured her copy of *Leaves of Grass*, and espoused Whitman as a spiritual guide to true democracy, the equality of the sexes, and reverence for nature. After 1916 her involvement with spiritualism, the Whitmanite movement, and theosophy became the centre of her life. Instrumental in the founding of the Canadian Whitman Fellowship, she turned her country hotel at Bon Echo, near Tweed, Ontario, into a Whitmanite shrine. In her magazine, *The Sunset of Bon Echo*, she emphasized Whitman and spiritual concerns. Her contributors included A.E. Smythe, founder in 1919 of the Theosophical Society in Canada.

Bucke, Denison, and Theosophists like Smythe, and suffragist mother and daughter Dr Emily Howard Stowe and Dr Augusta Stowe-Gullen, were part of an important group of reform-minded Canadians who were attracted to alternate forms of spirituality. To 21st-century readers the combination may seem odd. It did not seem so to the participants, who firmly believed that spiritualism rested on rationalism and sound scientific evidence.

DEBORAH GORHAM

'spoilt child of Confederation'. Scholars do not agree on the origin of this expression, but Sir John A. *Macdonald wrote of 'the spoilt child of the Dominion' in 1883 in reference to continuing conflict with British Columbia over railway and other problems, even though the *Canadian Pacific Railway was then rapidly being constructed. Since Margaret Ormsby used the phrase as a chapter heading in her *British Columbia: A History* (1958), historians and political scientists have adopted it as a synonym for British Columbia's persistent habit of boasting of its natural wealth while demanding better financial terms and other considerations from the federal government.

PATRICIA E. ROY

Spry, Graham (1900–83), diplomat, journalist, political activist, Canadian *broadcasting pioneer. In 1930, with Alan Plaunt, Spry formed the Canadian Radio League, a voluntarist association dedicated to establishing public broadcasting in accordance with recommendations of the 1929 Aird royal commission. For Spry and the league, broadcasting was to be an instrument for cultivating an informed public opinion and for educating, not merely to be a vehicle for advertising and transmitting American programs into Canadian homes. In the early 1930s Spry coined his famous and effective aphorism, 'It is a choice between the State and the United States', to emphasize that in the face of commercial pressures Canadian broadcasting could not survive without government support and guidance. Although the league's activities were concentrated in the heart of the Depression, and despite Prime Minister R.B. *Bennett's declared policy at the time of cutting back expenditures to balance the federal budget, Spry succeeded in convincing the government to establish in 1932 the Canadian Radio Broadcasting Commission, forerunner of the *Canadian Broadcasting Corporation, as Canada's public broadcaster. In addition to radio activism, Spry was publisher of the *Farmer's Sun* (1932–4) and of the **Canadian Forum*, which he purchased for one dollar in 1935, rescuing that periodical from bankruptcy. In 1948 Spry was appointed agent general for Saskatchewan in Britain; among other activities while in that office he recruited medical personnel from England to help neutralize the 1962 doctors' strike opposing the introduction of provincial *medicare.

ROBERT E. BABE

square timber trade. One of early Canada's great staples industries, this trade did much to strengthen Canada's link with Britain in the 19th century, to drive economic growth, especially in New Brunswick and the Ottawa Valley, and to shape social and political life both in the timber-producing regions and in the port cities of Saint John and Quebec, from where most of the wood was exported.

'Square timber' refers to high-quality wood exports, bound for Britain, that remained in a semi-processed state at the point of export. The name denotes the shape of the main product. Immediately after felling and branching a tree, woodsmen wielding broadaxes hewed it, removing the round edges and turning the trunk into square pieces of timber. With the help of oxen or horses, woodsmen skidded the timber out of the forest along snow- or ice-covered trails and then in spring and summer floated or rafted it down river to export centres. There the timber could be loaded into the holds of ships for transatlantic travel. Choice pine (red or white) and oak were the preferred species, and timbers had to be least one foot square at the tapered end. Often included as 'square timber' were 'deals'—that is, long, thick planks that had been sawn in large, steam-powered mills that specialized in the product. Once the timber arrived in the United Kingdom, square sticks and deals alike were sawn into dimensions suitable for use in the construction, shipbuilding, moulding, and other industries.

The square timber trade took off early in the 19th century. Before that, including during the French regime, modest amounts of wood were exported from Canada, but only exceptionally fine timber, such as that for ships' masts, could be sold in France or England at prices competitive with those of nearby Baltic suppliers. Napoleon's 1807–9 blockade of European ports starved Britain of timber needed by the Royal Navy and war industries. As a result, Parliament provided financial incentives for British timber merchants to develop alternative sources of reliable supply in the colonies. Overnight the Canadian industry boomed, and in the post-war decades a policy of 'colonial preference' provided protection in the

UK market, notwithstanding the high cost of transatlantic shipment. The policy gave a material basis to Canada's ongoing ties with England. So firmly was the industry established in Canada that even when Britain moved towards free trade in the 1840s, colonial wood competed effectively in the English market. The trade remained vital until the 1880s, when Britain turned to other forms and sources of wood imports. By then, choice timber in the more accessible forests of New Brunswick and the Ottawa Valley was seriously depleted.

The trade had its greatest impact in New Brunswick, where timber dominated the export sector and stimulated the growth of the province's other leading industries: *shipbuilding, *shipping, and agriculture. The link to shipbuilding is obvious: the timber trade required ships to carry the wood to Britain, and in an era of wooden ships New Brunswick had the essential material for constructing them. Local investors leapt at the opportunity to own ships and profit from the carrying trade. The *Cunard family made a fortune by lumbering in the Miramichi River basin, but the family business became world famous for its fleet of ocean-going ships. Agriculture in New Brunswick also benefited from lumbering. Outgoing ships carried wood, incoming ones brought immigrants. Settlers sold timber from their farm lots (and from nearby Crown forests that they trespassed), gaining a much-needed cash crop. In wintertime farmers and their sons found jobs working for timber firms, providing the industry with its main source of labour and earning wages that supplemented the family economy during the agricultural off-season. Nevertheless, contemporary observers criticized the timber business for distracting the agriculturalist from farm work, with deplorable consequences for the morality of the province. Critics contrasted the stability of farm life, rooted in the soil and based on the family, with lumbering, a highly risky business that relied on a mobile labour force of men who worked far from their families. Lumbering gained yet more critics because so many politicians in the province were lumbermen. Timber barons had the prestige and clout to win office, and it was in their interest to do so not least because of their need to gain access to valuable Crown forests. Even though the timber interests fought to keep down the charges they paid the Crown for the use of its forests, the provincial government gained a vital source of revenue from the industry.

For the first two-thirds of the 19th century, Canada deserved its reputation as 'Great Britain's woodyard'. Although cast in the role of 'hewers of wood' for the metropole, many Canadians—businessmen, craftsmen, mill workers, woodsmen, and raftsmen—found ways to make a living, support families, and build communities as a result of the opportunities opened up by the transatlantic trade in square timber. IAN RADFORTH

See also LUMBER INDUSTRY.

Squires, Sir Richard A. (1880–1940), prime minister of Newfoundland 1919–23 and 1928–32. Squires's name became synonymous with the supposed misgovernment and corruption that some contemporaries thought caused the suspension of responsible government in 1934. Squires entered politics in 1908, becoming minister of justice in 1914. At the end of the Great War he formed what was effectively a new party, which, allied with the *Fishermen's Protective Union, won the 1919 election. The government's main achievements were to settle a serious dispute with the *Reid Newfoundland Company over the future of the railway and to negotiate the establishment of a newsprint mill at Corner Brook. In 1923 Squires retired temporarily from politics, faced with accusations of petty corruption, which were later upheld. He returned to power in 1928, only to face the onslaught of the Depression. As the crisis deepened he and his government became increasingly unpopular, and corruption charges were again levelled against him. He barely escaped angry rioters who invaded the legislature on 5 April 1932. Defeated in the June 1932 election, Squires was the scapegoat for the failures of the Newfoundland political elite, rather than the sole architect of the country's collapse. JAMES K. HILLER

Stacey, Charles Perry (1906–89). C.P. Stacey was Canada's pre-eminent military historian of the 20th century. After a prolific academic career at Princeton in the 1930s, Stacey became the Canadian army's historical officer during the Second World War. In that position he ensured the creation of war records while also preparing, with a number of talented junior officers, draft narratives for post-war official histories. Following the war, the Army Historical Section, which he headed, published three first-class army official histories. These works of enormous synthesis and compilation laid the foundation for future understanding of that conflict. With his retirement from the army as a colonel in 1959, Stacey became professor of history at the University of Toronto, specializing in military and diplomatic history, penning numerous works, including a controversial biography of W.L. Mackenzie *King.

Throughout his life Stacey published an astounding number of reviews, articles, and books, leaving his indelible mark not only on military history but also on the canon of Canadian history. In the process, he infused Canadian military history with academic rigour and respectability. TIM COOK

stagecoaches. Public vehicles travelling regular, long-distance routes, with scheduled stops. Each stop marked a stage of the journey. Pulled by four horses, typical coaches held nine persons on three bench seats, the middle one pivoting to let passengers in and out. Suspended on leather straps, the body was closed front and back; curtains covered the open side windows when needed. Racks top and rear carried luggage and mail. In winter, runners replaced wheels. A good day's travel, pre-dawn to dusk, in dry conditions, was 95 km. Planked roads permitted speeds up to 16 km per hour. Like English coaching inns and American ordinaries, Canadian *taverns facilitated stagecoach travel. There, horses were stabled and changed; passengers booked seats, met coaches, and paused for refreshment or sleep. Expensive and slow compared to waterways, stagecoaches carried a minority of travellers; these were typically very mixed, by sex, age, ethnicity, and class. Before 1800, Halifax, Quebec City, Montreal, and Newark had intra-regional stages. The Montreal–Kingston–York route connected Ontario and Quebec in 1817. In combination with steamboats, stage travel peaked in the 1840s, giving way gradually after 1853 to railroads. Stages remained important away from the rails. The Edmonton–Calgary stage line, for instance, opened for business in 1883. JULIA ROBERTS

'stalwart peasant in a sheep-skin coat'. In April 1922 Sir Clifford *Sifton published 'The Immigrants Canada Wants' in *Maclean's* magazine. He wanted the government to return to the policies he had pursued as minister of the interior, 1896–1905, actively seeking 'quality' peasant farmers suited to the difficult life of opening up Canada's remaining, often marginal, farm lands: 'I think a stalwart peasant in a sheep-skin coat, born on the soil, whose forefathers have been farmers for ten generations, with a stout wife and a half-dozen children, is good quality.' Such people, he claimed, were to be found in Scandinavia, Belgium, Bohemia, Hungary, and Galicia (Ukraine). 'These men are workers. They have been bred for generations to work from daylight to dark.' Abandoning the principle of selectivity after 1905 had led to 'a considerable portion of the off-scourings and dregs of society' entering Canada, 'and some of them and their children have been furnishing work for the police ever since.'

Sifton would have considered his views practical, not racist. Indeed they have been praised by some historians, particularly of *Ukrainian immigration, for flying in the face of popular opposition and giving eastern Europeans the opportunity to prove their value in the developing Prairies. DAVID J. HALL

Stanfield, Robert (1914–2003), Nova Scotia premier 1956–67, leader federal Progressive Conservatives. Scion of a famous Nova Scotia business and political clan, he was born in Truro, earned a BA from Dalhousie University (1936) and a law degree from Harvard (1939). After a stint at the Wartime Prices and Trade Board, Stanfield set about resuscitating a moribund provincial Progressive Conservative Party that had held power for only 12 of the 89 years since Confederation. Despite a reputation for shyness and a halting speaking style, Stanfield led the Tories to power in 1956 and became the first Conservative in the province to win four majority governments in a row. As premier, Stanfield invested heavily in education. He also established Industrial Estates Ltd., an industry-seeking agency that attracted successful international companies like Volvo and Michelin Tire, but its spectacular failures, including a heavy water plant and a television-manufacturing venture, cost taxpayers millions and damaged his party's reputation. In 1967, two years after joking he had considered running for his party's federal leadership 'the same way I have considered ski-jumping', Stanfield ran and won the leadership. Though he failed in three attempts to become prime minister, he became a much-admired elder statesman, considered by many 'the best prime minister Canada never had'. STEPHEN KIMBER

staples thesis. The staples thesis is a theory of unbalanced, export-led growth: it sees development as a process led by a strategic, export-oriented sector that drives the entire economy. In Canada, such sectors are understood to have been based on natural resources for which there was demand from metropolitan markets in Europe and, from the mid-19th century, the United States. This approach was pioneered by W.A. Mackintosh, whose 'Economic Factors in Canadian History' (*Canadian Historical Review*, 1923) drew on Guy Callender's interpretation of American development, and especially by Harold *Innis, who gave the idea its fullest Canadian shape, for example in the frequently cited conclusion to his *The Fur Trade in Canada* (1930). They told a story of the search for and exploitation of an overlapping sequence of staples, from cod and beaver to pine timber, wheat (at times a farm staple, but not a resource product), sawn lumber, gold and other minerals, pulp and paper, and petroleum.

The staples thesis embodied one of Canadians' fundamental myths—that their economy depended essentially on a rich endowment of natural resources. Positing a distinctive development pattern for Canada based on its specific northern geography also fit well with other elements in Canadian nationalism in the interwar period. Hence the idea was widely accepted and shaped subsequent research and the selection of events and issues thought to constitute the essential narrative of Canadian history. At the end of the 20th century, it remained the core of the economic history in virtually all English-language surveys of Canadian history, economic history, and historical geography. Reformulated by Mel Watkins in terms of the theory of economic development in a 1963 article, it also was basic to an influential left-nationalist Canadian political economy and sociology. Analogous approaches, sometimes explicitly grounded in Innis and/or Watkins, have been taken by some students of other settlement societies, including the United States, and even of some export-oriented third world economies.

As an explanation of how the Canadian economy actually developed, however, the staples thesis has substantial limitations, both theoretical and empirical, as scholars such as Kenneth Buckley, Vernon C. Fowke, and John Dales long ago pointed out. It is particularly inadequate as an account of the balanced, diversified economies based on mixed family farming that characterized parts of the Maritimes and what became the Canadian heartland, the St Lawrence axis from Quebec to Windsor. That the latter story is still often depicted in terms of staples is evidence of the power of established interpretations to subsume competing accounts.

DOUGLAS McCALLA

state formation. A term used by some historians of Canada when referring to the processes by which governance changed, particularly in the 19th century, in connection with the coming of *responsible government, the growth of public institutions, and the strengthening of the regulatory powers of governments and their agencies. Whereas earlier schools of history represented such matters as advances made by nation-builders, historians of state formation, writing in the late 20th century, critically assessed the measures from the standpoint of the governed as well as the government.

Of course, in Canada state power was both significant and varied in its forms long before the mid-19th-century transitions. The British ruled early Newfoundland by means of the Royal Navy, whose officers interpreted law and passed judgment on the people of the fisheries. In the early part of the 17th century, the French state delegated power over its distant colonial possessions in Acadia and along the St Lawrence River to private fur-trading companies. Only in 1663 did the absolutist state of Louis XIV adopt a policy of direct rule. Even then, the top colonial administrators (the governor and the intendant) shared authority with the Roman Catholic Church (the state church) and officers in the French army. In the Northwest, the hand of the state rested lightly on the Aboriginal people and fur traders. Yet many traders worked under regulations imposed by the *Hudson's Bay Company, a firm that enjoyed a state monopoly under the terms of its royal charter.

The conquest brought somewhat greater conformity to the colonies, which came under the authority of one imperial state, but both the forms of state power and its reach still varied greatly across regions. In the hope of gaining public consent to their rule, British authorities retained parts of the apparatus of the French state in Quebec, notably the civil law, with its provisions for seigneurial tenure and various institutions established by the Catholic Church. In the other colonies, state structures more closely resembled those of England. The great innovation of the era was the introduction of *representative government. The British North American colonies that gained elected assemblies in the 18th century were Nova Scotia (1758), New Brunswick (1784), Prince Edward Island (1773), and the Canadas (1791). Thereafter, political struggles pitted elected representatives, eager to enhance the power of the assemblies, against Crown-appointed officials. In 1837–8, in the Canadas, the state endured a crisis of legitimacy that saw popular movements forcibly challenge colonial rule and develop alternatives to it.

When confronted with *rebellion, authorities moved aggressively to restore order and buttress the colonial regimes. The aftermath of the rebellion was a moment of state formation par excellence; it brought, for instance, the birth of a state police force, the suspension of representative government in Lower Canada and its reintroduction in a new form under the *Act of Union, massive public works projects, experiments in municipal government, and administrative reform on a broad front. Even in the provinces where rebellion had not erupted, imperial and local authorities undertook intensive state-building programs during the 1840s. Jails and prisons sprouted, public schooling grew quickly, and the introduction of responsible government brought with it new systems of accountability and regulation even as it legitimized and strengthened the executive. The momentum continued, as the agencies grew and as new crises triggered new institutional responses. *Confederation itself, which introduced a federal state structure, can be seen as a climax to this process of state formation. It was also a beginning.

IAN RADFORTH

Statute of Westminster. A British law of 11 December 1931 and the founding document of the *Commonwealth, establishing the supremacy of the Canadian Parliament and conferring on Canada and the other British dominions of Australia, New Zealand, South Africa, and the Irish Free State as much legal independence as they wished to exercise. Canada had no war of national liberation, no revolution against imperial rule; it evolved into independence within the structure of the *British Empire, step by cautious step and over many decades. Before the passage of the statute, the imperial (that is, United Kingdom) Parliament retained a vague and ultimately overriding authority over Canadian legislation. Under the 1865 Colonial Laws Validity Act, any Canadian law that conflicted with legislation of the Parliament in England was, to the extent of the conflict, null and void. The Statute of Westminster swept away the CLVA and declared that Canada had the full power to enact laws having extraterritorial operation. At Canada's request, the repeal, amendment, or alteration of the British North America Acts, 1867–1930, were specifically excepted from the statute. It took another half century for the federal government and the provinces to agree upon an amending formula, allowing the *constitution to come home in the Constitution Act, 1982. The Statute of Westminster was the result of pressure on the British from the Canadians, South Africans, and Irish in the 1920s; historian C.P. *Stacey has called it the closest approximation of a Canadian declaration of independence. NORMAN HILLMER

Steacie, E.W.R. (1900–62). Born in Montreal, Steacie studied chemical engineering at McGill University. Influenced by Otto Maas, he changed fields, obtained his doctorate in chemistry (1926), and became a lecturer and research fellow in physical chemistry at McGill, where he conducted groundbreaking investigations in chemical kinetics. In 1939 he was appointed director, chemistry division, of the *National Research Council, becoming its vice-president, scientific (1950) and president (1952). Although these roles and his wartime activities concerning nuclear science often removed him from hands-on research, Ned Steacie never forgot that, in spite of its political implications, scientific research could be fun. An eminent scientist and, in spite of his shyness, a persuasive advocate for both Canadian science and the integrity of research, he became an excellent scientific administrator, received numerous honours and awards, and, in 1961, became the first Canadian president of the International Council of Scientific Unions.

MARIANNE GOSZTONYI AINLEY

steamships. Canada and the age of steam approached maturity together. The application of steam propulsion was a critical factor in taming the country's vast open spaces. While Canadians have paid homage to the way the land was conquered by steam railways, little remembered is the similar role played by steamboats in the interior and on the fringes of Canada, and by steamships extending the country's reach on the world's oceans. A railway president in 1924 remarked favourably on the interdependence of 'wheel and keel', but the 'keel' has all but been forgotten. Yet at one time Canada and Canadians were in the forefront of steamship development in North America. Canadians launched the first purpose-built steamship to steam across the North Atlantic: the **Royal William* left Quebec City in 1833 on this pioneering voyage. Three years later the British-built **Beaver*, owned by the Hudson's Bay Company, was the first steamship to operate on the west coast of North America. Samuel *Cunard's pioneering steamship, the little *Unicorn*, was a much-loved institution as it plied its business on the waters of the river and gulf of St Lawrence, 1840–9. Venturing as far as Pictou and Halifax, *Unicorn* linked the Cunard Royal Mail service with British North America.

Steamships did not feature prominently in Canadian waters again for some 20 years. Although steamboats—many of them belonging to the renowned Canada Steamship Line (established 1839)—had navigated the St Lawrence since 1809 and had gradually pressed their way into many of the nooks and crannies of Canada's inland waterways, scheduled steamship service was not established until 1853, from Liverpool to Montreal in summer, and to Portland, Maine, in winter. This effort was short-lived, designed as a stop-gap until Hugh *Allan was able to get his regular service under way. Four steamships were the minimum requirement for a biweekly mail route to Britain; his line, the Montreal Ocean Steamship Company (better known as the Allan Line), finally went into operation in 1856. Ultimately, his ships became the benchmark against which steamships serving Canada on the North Atlantic were gauged.

Steamships played a special role as the British North American colonies moved towards union. When the Canadian Fathers of Confederation crashed a Maritimes political gathering in Charlottetown in 1864, they wended their way from the Canadas in the aptly named *Queen Victoria*. When Confederation was settled upon and links were cast to bind the new country together, a steamship company did the binding. The Quebec & Gulf Ports Steamship Company linked the founding provinces with a scheduled service from Quebec City to Pictou. After the completion of the *Intercolonial Railway in 1876, the company's *Miramichi* and that ship's successors faithfully maintained a single-ship service well into the 20th century.

By the 1870s steamships were regular visitors to Canadian east coast ports. It was the 1890s before similar service became available on the west coast. Then, the *Canadian Pacific Railway completed the Pacific section of its *all-red route to the Far East with its fabled 'White Empresses'. Alternatives to the Allan Line service developed on the North Atlantic in this period, led by the Beaver Line and the Dominion Line, both Canadian companies. In the heyday of steamship travel to Canada, the lines plying the route owned ships that caught the imagination of travellers. The best example in the 19th century was Allan's *Polynesian*. Although the ship had an unfortunate tendency to roll in the slightest weather (perhaps the reason Allan pioneered the use of bilge keels on passenger ships on the North Atlantic), many chose to take the 'rolling poly'. In similar fashion, the Beaver Line's *Lake Superior* and the Dominion's *Vancouver* made their mark with a loyal following. It was not unusual, at the end of a voyage, for disembarking passengers to present the captain with a memorial in praise of his and his crew's skill, or even money for the local seamen's hospital. Whole fleets were sometimes similarly patronized. The CPR 'White Empresses' and 'Princesses' on the west coast, and their 'Empress' and 'Duchess' counterparts on the east, and *Canadian National Railways' 'Princes' and 'Lady Boats', west and east respectively, had their own loyal followings.

Steamship travel—literally the only way to go—held the edge until after the Second World War. Now, although Canada's major ports are among the busiest in North America (thanks in part to excellent rail connections), the ships serving them are no longer steam-driven—and are rarely Canadian. Indeed, the last significant steamship operations in Canada were carried out by the fleet of steam-driven warships on both coasts. The *Royal Canadian Navy has been updated, and its vessels are either gas-turbine or diesel driven. A very few heritage steamships (or engines that have been removed from them) form the core of maritime museum displays: even fewer heritage steamboats are operated on inland waterways. Steamships are now part of our maritime past.

KENNETH S. MACKENZIE

Steele, Sir Samuel Benfield (1849–1919), mounted policeman, soldier. Born and raised near Orillia, Ontario, Steele came to the *North-West Mounted Police by way of the *militia and the Red River Expedition. He was one of the original members in 1873, enlisting as staff constable. He rose quickly through the ranks to inspector in 1878 and superintendent in 1885. In 1883–5 he supervised construction of the CPR across the prairies and into British Columbia. When the *North-West Rebellion broke out in 1885 he organized Steele's Scouts from ranchers and mounted policemen in Alberta. The unit carried out reconnaissance for the Alberta Field Force during the pursuit of *Big Bear. In 1898 and 1899, he commanded the NWMP in the Yukon at the height of the gold rush. In 1900 Steele left the NWMP to command Lord Strathcona's Horse in the *South African War. After helping Lord Baden-Powell organize the South African Constabulary, he returned to Canada in 1907 as a colonel and was appointed to command Military District No. 10 (Alberta). In 1915, then a major-general, he was given command of the 2nd Canadian Division. Judged too old to lead the division in combat, he was appointed to command the Southeastern District of England in 1916. He died in London. R.C. MACLEOD

steel industry. *See* IRON AND STEEL INDUSTRY.

steelworkers' union. The United Steelworkers of America is the largest 'international' union in Canada and one of the largest in the private sector. It began in the United States in 1936 as the Steelworkers' Organizing Committee (renamed the United Steel Workers of America in 1942) to sign up unorganized American steelworkers. Previously independent unions in Sydney and Trenton, Nova Scotia, and Hamilton and Sault Ste Marie, Ontario, soon joined, along with new locals in other metal-working industries. Collective bargaining with two of the three primary steel companies began before the Second World War, but it took renewed organizing efforts during the war and a national steel strike in 1946 to consolidate the union's right to negotiate for the industry's workers. After the war it added miners to its membership, including, in 1967, after many years of bitter rivalry, locals of the International Union of Mine, Mill, and Smelter Workers in Sudbury, Ontario, and Trail, British Columbia. By the 1990s, mergers with other unions and recruitment of workers in white-collar and service jobs had resulted in a diverse membership of 190,000, 20 per cent of which were women. The Canadian members have their own national office in Toronto and one divisional and three district offices. From 1984 to 1994 a Canadian, Lynn Williams, served as president of the international union; beginning in 2002, another Canadian, Leo Gerrard, filled the same post. The union has always strongly supported the New Democratic Party and the Parti Québécois.

CRAIG HERON

Stefansson, Vilhjalmur (1879–1962), explorer and ethnologist. Stefansson was one of Canada's greatest arctic theorists and promoters. He was born in Arnes, Manitoba, of Icelandic parents who soon left for the Dakotas. He began his arctic exploration in 1904, but his first taste of fame came with his controversial discovery of the so-called Blond Eskimos in 1910. This led to his command of the *Canadian Arctic Expedition (1913–18) where he distinguished himself by record-breaking treks across the ice and, among other things, discovering the last major land masses in the *Arctic Archipelago. He returned south full of visionary ideas. The Arctic was not a bleak and forlorn wasteland, but a 'friendly' place in which Canada could become a major player in the 20th century. The Canadian Arctic could become a commercial and political polar Mediterranean: submarines beneath the ice-clogged waters, the use of airplanes via the Great Circle Route, and the tapping of yet-to-be discovered riches. His misguided occupation of Wrangel Island (1921–3) north of Siberia, which he claimed for Canada, and the tragic loss of life that ensued, caused an embarrassing diplomatic incident. Thereafter, he spent most of his time in the United States lecturing and promoting the North to an American audience. RICHARD J. DIUBALDO

Strachan, John (1778–1867). Strachan was 21 when he arrived in Kingston in 1799 and began his career as a tutor in a private home. He went on to become an outstanding teacher, and his grammar schools in Cornwall and York drew to his care the future leaders of the colony. His growing reputation led to his appointment in 1822 to the presidency of the General Board of Education, where he created the colony's first system of education, and he was instrumental in the founding of McGill University, King's College (Toronto), and the University of Trinity College. A gifted and hard-working missionary, he was ordained in the *Anglican Church in 1803, became archdeacon of York in 1827, and bishop of Toronto in 1839. He skilfully led his church through the painful transition from state church to self-governing denomination.

Strachan's political career was long and controversial. As a member of both the executive and legislative councils he was determined to use the power of the state and his own administrative abilities to implement his vision of an hierarchical and carefully ordered British society, secured by an established church. By the time he left office in 1840, his political role had become largely defensive, holding on to elements of an old order (most notably the *clergy reserves) that very few in Canada or Britain were prepared to preserve. WILLIAM WESTFALL

Strangers within Our Gates. When J.S. *Woodsworth published *Strangers within Our Gates* in 1909, he made clear the apprehension with which western Canadians viewed their future. Political structures, social institutions, and the school system were all recast to ensure the dominance of the Anglo-Protestant majority. But the agricultural promise of the West required more immigrants, and the Canadian government sought out the peasantry of Europe to cultivate the Prairies. Government accorded little regard to the social consequences of this new immigration. But for Woodsworth and the English majority, the sudden influx of Slavs and *Jews posed a social threat. His compassion for the plight of the newcomers succumbed to the ethnocentrism he shared with the majority. If the Anglo-Protestant vision for western Canada was to be realized, the threat posed by the immigrants must be neutralized. Woodsworth was convinced that this would be in the interests of the newcomers as they were brought up to the norms of the superior majority. Political parties, the Protestant churches, the public schools, the *YMCA, *Frontier College, were all bent to this purpose. His book was meant to justify and dignify the process.

J.E. REA

Strathcona, Lord. *See* SMITH, DONALD.

Student Christian Movement. Begun in 1921 amid a post-war quest for permanent peace and moral order, the SCM was a creature of the *social gospel, a Protestant reform movement 'seeking to realize the Kingdom of God in the very fabric of society', as Richard Allen wrote in *The Social Passion*. The SCM was the most important and enduring element of the Canadian student movement during the 1930s, drawing the active involvement of some 5 to 10 per cent of English-Canadian students. Inspired by the activities and writings of reformist theologians such as Reinhold Niebuhr and J. King Gordon, it convened chapters on most campuses, sponsored talks by controversial speakers, raised relief funds for war victims in China, and campaigned for peace and social justice. Along with those in other left wing activist groups, SCM members were subjected to surveillance by the RCMP, but the organization's political moderation and righteousness earned it a secure place on Canadian campuses. University presidents frequently supported campus chapters by becoming honorary members.

In the post–Second World War period the SCM focused on public service and the promotion of personal religion, though it experienced tension between these two roles. Some members emphasized theological discussion and personal salvation while others sought to expand the organization's political and social agenda. The latter became especially significant during the student and youth protest era of the 1960s. The SCM supported the 'ban the bomb' movement and opposed the Vietnam War. While other activist organizations subsequently disappeared, the SCM survived as a small national organization. In 2000, it had chapters on five Canadian university campuses. Its mission, reflecting its historical roots, was the promotion of 'spirituality and progressive social justice issues'.

PAUL AXELROD

Studio D, 1974–96. The women's unit of the *National Film Board owed its founding to international struggles for gender equity as well as to the specific frustrations of female NFB employees. Women at the NFB were largely relegated to the roles of editor or production assistant and blocked from career advancement, while proposals dealing with women's content were generally refused. These issues prompted lobbying for a separate film unit that would be operated by women and deal with women's experiences.

The gaps between male-authored cinema and the reality of women's lives precipitated demands for women to take control of film production. Two exceptional 1972 series, Working Mothers, from the NFB's path-breaking *Challenge for Change* program, produced by Kathleen Shannon, and the pioneering En tant que femmes, produced by Anne Claire Poirier for Quebec's Office national du film, the French side of the NFB, helped to strengthen the case for Studio D's formation. These private portraits of women's lives, focusing on issues such as abortion, love, marriage, and balancing children and paid work, anticipated the form and subject matter of subsequent Studio D films. The Royal Commission on the Status of Women in 1970 and the impending International Women's Year of 1975 also served as catalysts. In 1975 Shannon was appointed to head the new studio, the first woman executive at the NFB.

During its early years Studio D was poorly funded, relegated to basement offices. Until 1979, productions were allocated to freelancers, but an Academy Award for Beverly Shaffer's *I'll Find a Way* (1978) helped elevate the studio's profile. Indeed, several of Studio D's films achieved widespread recognition (*Not a Love Story*, 1980; *If You Love This Planet*, 1982). A variety of documentary forms were honed. Gail Singer's *Portrait of an Artist as an Old Lady* (1982), about Paraskeva Clark, is a prototype portrait film, a form arising out of a feminist, revisionist imperative of documenting the lives of outstanding women. Anne Wheeler's *Augusta: Great Grand Mother* shares some of these features, while Bonnie Klein's *Patricia's Talking Pictures* (1978) focuses on an 'ordinary' woman who eventually finds the determination to change her life.

In 1987 Rina Fraticelli succeeded Shannon as executive producer. The priorities of Studio D began to shift, and its stable of filmmakers was dismantled. Two feature films were produced: a documentary/drama hybrid, *The Company of Strangers* (1990), by long-time Studio D director Cynthia Scott, and a history of lesbian life in Canada, *Forbidden Love* (1992), by independents Lynne Fernie and Aerlyn Weissman. Challenging the universalism of women's experience, films began to examine differences among women, with a focus on issues of race, ethnicity, and sexual orientation. The studio produced several documentaries on the lives of African-Canadian women, including *Black Mother, Black Daughter* (1989), *Older Stronger Wiser* (1989), and *Sisters in the Struggle* (1991)—all by Black filmmakers. In its last years, Studio D became more accountable to women filmmakers throughout the country, gave more assistance to independent women producers, and established outreach programs for immigrant women and women of colour. KATHLEEN BANNING

suburbs. In the first half of the 20th century Canada became an urban nation; in the second half, for better or worse, it became suburban. Suburbs have existed since almost the beginnings of urban settlement, became extensive in the 19th century, and are now the most common type of place in which Canadians live. Although they have always been criticized, suburbs embody the desire of most Canadians for a home of their own, and for space in which to raise a family.

A suburb, like a city, is a generic place that exists in many locations. For Americans, suburbs must be distinct political jurisdictions; the British view them as places that lie towards the edge of the built-up area; both think of suburbs as largely or even purely residential districts of single-family homes, with low densities coupled with high levels of owner-occupation. Canadians blend these criteria in equal measure. Apart from such physical features, suburbs involve a manner of living, one that values privacy and is centred upon the family. They are a way of life and a state of mind as much as a physical presence.

suburbs

Two developments made it possible for suburbs to become extensive. First, the decentralization of manufacturing enabled people to work and live near the urban fringe. This trend occurred in waves from the mid-19th century. Where suburban factories were isolated they fostered self-contained industrial satellites. When built at the urban fringe, in planned or unplanned districts, they stimulated the formation of industrial suburbs. Second, better transportation enabled people to commute further, settling in purely residential districts far from downtown offices or suburban factories. A crucial innovation was the electric streetcar, adopted everywhere in the 1890s. Faster and cheaper than its horse-drawn predecessor, the electric car was the first form of mass transit. When rapid urban growth resumed after the depression of the 1890s, land speculators laid out subdivisions along radial lines, which became 'streetcar suburbs'. Noisy, crowded, and smoky, streetcars were soon unpopular, especially among women. From the 1920s, they were supplemented and replaced by buses, while rising car ownership enabled people to settle the interstices of the radial streetcar lines, and then beyond their termini. After the Second World War, cars became common and suburbs were developed at densities that make the provision of unsubsidized transit impossible.

Until the 1950s, Canadian suburbs were socially diverse, including immigrants as well as the native born, workers as well as the middle and upper middle classes. Diversity was made possible by the political fragmentation of territory beyond city limits. The developers or residents of some areas, such as Westmount (Montreal), Shaughnessy (Vancouver), and Forest Hill (Toronto), made their suburbs exclusive by incorporating and enacting regulations that mandated materials and standards that were unaffordable to all but the elite. Others, such as Toronto's Earlscourt, did not incorporate or require high standards of building and service provision, since residents wished to occupy modest homes and pay minimal property taxes. Such suburbs were more common in Canada than the United States, and lacked public transit. They became hostages to fortune. As unregulated districts filled out, piped water and sewers replaced wells and privies; these were more expensive to install after houses had already been erected. Taxes rose and owners fell into arrears; when the Depression set in, many lost their homes while suburban municipalities, including all but two of those around Toronto, went bankrupt.

The political fragmentation and social diversity of Canadian suburbs reached their zenith in the first half of the 20th century. Until then, cities had annexed areas at the fringe since this appeared to add to their stature. In the early 1900s, many baulked at the cost of servicing previously unregulated suburbs and, with the most notable exception of Hamilton, annexation slowed. Following the fiscal difficulties of the 1930s, after 1945 provincial governments began to amalgamate the functions of cities and suburbs, creating varied, metropolitan levels of governance in most large urban centres.

Since the 1930s suburbs have become more uniform. In the 19th century, land subdividers sold lots on a piecemeal basis. Buyers took the risk that neighbouring properties might develop in undesirable ways. Slowly, subdividers realized they could charge a premium in areas where minimum building standards were required, though at first few actually built homes. By 1900, privately imposed building and zoning controls were the norm in better suburbs; they later diffused down market. During the 1930s the federal government encouraged financial institutions to become more involved in mortgage markets by offering mortgage insurance. After 1945, it tied insurance to homes and subdivisions that conformed to federal guidelines. Lenders, allied with a new breed of entrepreneur who took responsibility for all stages of land development from subdivision through construction to marketing, helping to create standardized, packaged suburbs. At the same time, provincial governments introduced planning controls that made unregulated development uncommon. Thus, as the fashion in subdivision layout changed from the grid to curvilinear designs, the modern suburb was made.

In the 1950s and 1960s, the homogeneity of cookie-cutter suburbs gave visible expression to new concerns about the blandness of suburban life and the conformist mores of the 'suburbanite'. Canadians began to speak in generic terms about 'the suburbs'. Conformity was also apparent because, after two decades of depression and war, so many couples were starting families. Soon, because few families had two cars, feminists began to express concerns about the isolation of suburban women. Since the 1960s, the demography of suburbs has become more diverse, while more women work for pay and use cars. Today the most common criticism of suburbs is that their sprawling form costs too much to service, and encourages a privatized way of living that is environmentally irresponsible. RICHARD HARRIS

Suez Crisis, 1956. This crisis, the high point of Canadian diplomacy in the 20th century, resulted in the first of the large United Nations *peacekeeping forces and a Nobel Peace Prize for External Affairs Minister L.B. *Pearson. In July 1956 Egypt nationalized the Anglo-French Suez Canal; in October the British and French, plotting with Israel, invaded Egypt to retrieve what they thought of as lost property. The American and Canadian governments were horrified by the Anglo-French aggression, especially since the ensuing crisis coincided with the ruthless repression of Hungarians struggling to get free of the grasp of the Soviet Union, the West's Cold War adversary. Pearson coolly forged an international consensus behind a United Nations Emergency Force to secure and supervise peace in the Middle East. Not everyone was pleased. Howard Green, a future foreign minister, captured a frequent sentiment with his complaint that the government had deserted Britain and France, Canada's mother countries. In 1957 Pearson's Liberals lost the federal election, but he won the Nobel Prize. NORMAN HILLMER

Sun Life Assurance Company of Canada. The company began modestly in 1871 as a business venture floated by M.H. Gault and his Montreal syndicate. Despite fierce competition, it vaulted to prominence, first in the Canadian life insurance market in the first decade of the 1900s, then internationally in the ensuing two decades. Under the leadership of Robertson Macaulay and his son, Thomas Bassett (T.B.) Macaulay, Sun Life became one of the world's great life insurance companies, spanning the globe by 1929. Heavy investments in US common stock in the 1920s almost led to disaster after the Great Crash of 1929. Management suffered a 'near-death' experience, avoided taking chances (or innovating) thereafter, and quit many international markets. In the 1950s, Sun Life's restored health attracted US takeover attempts, which led management to mutualize its operations after 1958. In 1978–80, the company moved its head office from Montreal to Toronto, plunging it into the national unity debate. In the 1980s and 1990s, the company embraced new activities and global markets, demutualizing its operations in 1999 and attempting a radical transformation of its operations to face 21st-century challenges.

LAURENCE B. MUSSIO

Supreme Court of Canada. Founded in 1875 as a judicial component of the federal structure that had been established with Confederation in 1867 and was still in the process of formation. First drafted by Sir John A. *Macdonald's government, the legislation was introduced by the government of Alexander *Mackenzie. The new court consisted of six members, of whom two had to be from Quebec (respecting the distinctive civil law traditions there). Access of cases to the court was relatively easy. Appeals could be taken to the Judicial Committee of the Privy Council, rendering the court not 'supreme' in the country; indeed, appeals to the JCPC could be taken directly from provincial appellate courts, bypassing the Supreme Court entirely. The jurisdiction of the court was thus weakened from the beginning.

From the court's inception, its personnel followed a regional pattern of distribution. The first court was led by Chief Justice Sir W.B. Richards of Ontario, who was soon followed in 1879 by Sir W.J. Ritchie of New Brunswick. The decisions of the court in these early years were not generally intellectually powerful, and there was a tendency for the JCPC to overturn Supreme Court rulings, particularly in cases involving constitutional matters, where the centralizing tendencies of the Ottawa court were reversed in favour of the provinces. Many observers regarded the court as useful in minor issues but weak and ineffectual when it came to important legal issues.

In the early decades appointment to the court was regarded as a patronage plum. Cabinet ministers would, for example, retire to the court. In 1902 the former minister of justice, David Mills, joined the court, and in 1906 Sir Charles Fitzpatrick moved directly from the cabinet to the position of chief justice. The result was that the best legal minds in the country, regarding the court as weak and a tool of *patronage, were reluctant to join; indeed, they were often not asked. Issues of representation, regional and otherwise, often militated as well against the appointment of the best possible candidates. Justices such as Pierre Mignault and John Armour were some of the exceptions to this tendency.

In 1906, Lyman Poore Duff joined the court, succeeding to the position of chief justice in 1933. His career offers a good example of the political uses to which the court could be put by the federal government. In 1916 Duff was part of a two-man royal commission to investigate the politically charged controversy regarding the Shell Commission. In 1917 he was named the sole central appeal judge to hear appeals regarding *conscription under the Military Service Act; the issues involved great bitterness and ethnic animosity, and the government was happy to be able to use an apparently neutral judicial figure to deal with such politically sensitive issues. In 1933, Duff—now Sir Lyman—became chief justice, but his willingness to act as a political instrument did not falter. He was a commissioner for the Transportation Commission in the early 1930s and in 1942 accepted appointment as a one-man royal commission to investigate the politically contentious decision to dispatch Canadian troops to *Hong Kong just before that colony surrendered to Japanese forces. Duff serves merely as an example of the frequent political use of the Supreme Court justices to handle difficult or sensitive political problems.

The history of the Supreme Court took a new turn in the late 1940s. A new, impressive building was opened, occupying a prestigious position on Parliament Hill. In 1949 appeals to the JCPC were ended, making the Supreme Court the final court in the Canadian judicial hierarchy. The quality of appointments also improved, and leading figures from the bar or bench were more willing to join. Ivan Rand, for example, a leading figure in *labour law, joined in 1943. In 1954 Patrick Kerwin was named chief justice and led the court through an important era in which it began to assert its voice in Canadian *law. He was followed by Robert Taschereau in 1963–7. Scholars have noted the rising intellectual quality of the court's decisions in the 1950s. *Boucher v. The King* (1951), *Saumur v. Québec* (1955), and **Roncarelli v. Duplessis* (1959) were all leading decisions in establishing the legal foundation for individual rights.

In 1970 one of the leading legal scholars in the country, Bora Laskin, accepted appointment. He was the first Jewish member of the court and in 1973 was elevated to chief justice. Though he often found himself in dissent on important cases, Laskin challenged his fellow justices on the intellectual quality of their decisions. The barrier against women was broken in 1982 with the appointment of Bertha Wilson. In 1984 Laskin was replaced by Brian Dickson, who demonstrated a strong ability to shape a more unified court. After the 1960s the court found itself sitting securely at the top of the Canadian judicial hierarchy, with a respected membership and handing down leading decisions in Canadian law. The government tended to involve the court less in political controversies. In 1974 appeals to the Supreme Court as of right ended, allowing the justices henceforth to decide what cases contained legal issues worthy of further judicial consideration. After 1982 the court began hearing an increasing number of cases involving the *Charter of Rights and Freedoms. JAMES G. SNELL

surveying. The science of determining the exact location of points on the Earth's surface—both natural formations and artificial boundaries—so that they can be represented on a map. Unlike exploration, it seeks to increase the quality rather than the quantity of geographical knowledge, and it generally took place just in advance of settlement rather than, as with exploration, on the frontiers of European expansion.

The first European known to have surveyed any part of Canada was Samuel de *Champlain, the skilled navigator and cartographer who founded New France. Using only an astrolabe to measure latitudes, he produced detailed harbour charts and maps of the region from the Atlantic coast inland to the eastern Great Lakes. Longitude was more difficult to calculate precisely in Champlain's time, and his maps contain inaccuracies as a result. It could be determined only by crude estimates of the east–west distance travelled or, more scientifically, by making precise lunar observations and comparing them to European data. Such calculations were possible throughout the French regime thanks to the *Jesuits at the *Séminaire de Québec, whose mathematical skills were put to use in the ongoing charting of the St Lawrence region. 'Cadastral', or property boundary, surveys also served an important function in New France; using a fixed length of chain, a compass, and trigonometric tables, surveyors located and recorded *seigneurial property lines throughout the colony.

British army and naval officers arriving after the Conquest (including the young James *Cook, who charted Newfoundland and Labrador) brought a new level of precision to Canadian surveying. They benefited from mathematical training, and utilized superior instruments like the sextant and the artificial horizon to improve latitude determinations. They also brought the newly invented marine chronometer, a timepiece so accurate that longitude could be quickly and accurately determined. Colonial Surveyor-General Samuel Holland oversaw the laying out of *Loyalist settlements in Canada after the American Revolutionary War, and in the early 19th century British surveyors in special commissions conducted traverse surveys of the contested Canada–US border. In the decades prior to Confederation, tireless British specialists like hydrographer Captain Henry Bayfield and geologist Sir William *Logan made important contributions to early Canadian surveying—the former by precisely mapping miles of Great Lakes shoreline, the latter, using telegraph connections between astronomical observatories, by fixing the longitude of several cities in north-eastern British North America.

Canada expanded rapidly to the north and west in the later part of the 19th century, presenting new surveying challenges. The *Hudson's Bay Company had conducted scientific surveys of the interior, which had eventually reached the Pacific and Arctic shores but, having little interest in settlement, the company had conducted no systematic land survey. With passage of the *Dominion Lands Act in 1873, this vast undertaking began. The act called for rapid surveying of the western plains to make way for settlers and the transcontinental railroad, and the job was accomplished with remarkable speed. The surveying was not without conflict, however, for the *Metis and Native peoples quite rightly saw it as the first step in the Canadian appropriation of their land, and they openly objected. Grievances over land surveys played no small part in the rebellions of 1869 and 1885.

The early 20th century saw the emergence and eventual union of three federal topographical agencies and the beginnings of comprehensive trigonometric surveying, long the standard elsewhere. After the Second World War, the rapid development of aerial photography and related 'photogrammatic' image processing made possible expansive surveys of remote Arctic districts, while air-borne radar surveys allowed precise mapping of land elevations and contours. By the end of the 20th century, satellite-based positioning systems had further improved the speed and accuracy of surveying, rendering yet another generation of technologies obsolete. In each era, Canada's size and terrain have challenged surveyors, but diligence and ingenuity have met the ever-increasing demands to know and control the land.

BRIAN C. SHIPLEY AND RICHARD WHITE

survivance. The survival of a French Catholic minority in Anglo-Saxon North America was a persistent theme in French-Canadian public life for two centuries. At the time of the French Revolution, clerical elites in Lower Canada preached that Divine Providence, through the *conquest, had saved French Canada from the horrors of anticlericalism to preserve a purer Catholicism in North America. Liberal reformers at the beginning of the 19th century, who were less enthusiastic to embrace submission to Britain, also fought to affirm a distinct French-Canadian identity. As the motto of Quebec City's reborn *Le *Canadien* newspaper implied in the 1830s, survival depended on the preservation of 'Our Language, Our Religion, Our Laws'. During the years of clerical hegemony (1840–1945), the Catholic Church portrayed itself as the best guarantor of survival by setting an intellectual, Catholic tradition in opposition to the materialism of Protestant America. It used its control over education to reinforce an idealized view of New France's rural heritage as a model for the present, and considered that language and religion reinforced one another in preserving agriculturalism and in isolating French Canadians from the mainstream. After the Second World War, however, lay elites were tiring of accepting mere survival. They wanted French Quebeckers to share fully in the benefits of economic prosperity and to take their place in the modern world. Survival was no longer enough: an independent lay state was seen as the only way to ensure the economic and social development of a vibrant francophone community in North America.

JOHN A. DICKINSON

Sylliboy, Gabriel (1875–1964). A *Mi'kmaq born at Whycocomagh, a reserve in southern Cape Breton Island, Sylliboy succeeded John Denny as grand chief of the Grand Council in 1918, a position he maintained until his death. The Grand Council is the political organization uniting Mi'kmaq throughout Atlantic Canada, though its influence in the 20th century was greatest in Nova Scotia. In 1927, Sylliboy was charged with hunting muskrats out of season. In his defence, he argued that the treaty of 1752, signed by his ancestors with the British, made statutory regulations on hunting inapplicable to the Mi'kmaq. A number of elders testified in the case, recounting what their fathers and grandfathers had told them about the treaty. Sylliboy was found guilty. The court case, *R. v. Sylliboy*, was used by the federal government to argue that status Indians throughout Canada were subject to provincial game laws. WILLIAM WICKEN

Sylvester, Joseph, today also called Sylvester Joe (fl. 1822), guide. A noted *Mi'kmaw hunter from Bay d'Espoir, near Weasel Island, he was William E. *Cormack's guide when crossing the unmapped interior of Newfoundland in 1822. The two men left Random Bar, Trinity Bay, on 5 September and arrived at Flat Bay, St George's Bay, on 2 November, having collected much information on Newfoundland's geography, geology, and fauna. The successful completion of their journey was due in part to Sylvester's survival skills in the wilderness and his knowledge of the country. A landmark mountain north of Fortune Bay was named Mount Sylvester.
INGEBORG C.L. MARSHALL

Symons Report. Appointed to a one-man commission by the Association of Universities and Colleges of Canada to report on 'the state of teaching and research in various fields of study relating to Canada at Canadian universities', T.H.B. Symons produced *To Know Ourselves* (the Symons Report, 4 vols) in 1975. He tapped into a rich vein of debate over Canadian studies, receiving over 1,000 briefs and almost 30,000 letters with widely varying recommendations. The report reflected a profound concern over what was perceived as neglect of Canadian studies. It concentrated on the humanities and social sciences, but also contained sections on science and technology, the professions, Native peoples, and the state of scholarship on Canada within and outside the country. Its recommendations advocated more attention, and better funding, to the entire field.

Perhaps the most controversial part of the report concerned the issue of non-Canadians teaching in Canadian *universities. The recommendation that Canadians should become more self-reliant in producing qualified scholars brought to the boil a simmering debate over the number of Americans who had been hired by fast-expanding Canadian universities. The resulting outburst of nationalism gradually subsided under the influences of fiscal restraint, increasing production of Canadian-trained scholars, and, perhaps as a result of the Symons Report, more attention to Canadian studies. Though only part of a much larger movement, the report provided a forum for existing concerns, and helped to reinforce the notion that it was both respectable and responsible for Canadians to study their own country.
W.P.J. MILLAR AND R.D. GIDNEY

syndicalism. In Canada, syndicalism has become synonymous with the *Industrial Workers of the World, organized in Chicago in 1905. Espousing direct action and the general strike, the IWW reached out to low-paid, unorganized workers alienated from the electoral system and the mainstream labour movement. The advocacy of 'striking on the job', rather than 'striking at the ballot box', appealed to labourers who questioned all forms of leadership and top-down authority. Constantly, and often inaccurately, associated with Georges Sorel and the advocacy of violence, syndicalism envisioned a mass, economic-based general strike that made non-violent revolutionary transformation possible. In the 1910s through the 1930s, syndicalism, as much a form of worker self-expression as an 'ideology', inspired British Columbia bush workers, rail workers, and longshoremen and Finnish bush workers in northern Ontario. The spirit of syndicalism, largely divorced from its union origins, lives on in the anti-globalization protests of the early 21st century.
PETER CAMPBELL

Taché, Alexandre-Antonin (1823–94). Born in Rivière-du-Loup, Quebec, ordained in 1845, bishop (1853–71) and archbishop (1871–94) of St-Boniface, he was a legendary figure in his own time, arriving in the Northwest in 1845 and travelling extensively as an Oblate missionary before white settlement. The Canadian government recalled him from the Vatican Council in Rome to help quell the Riel uprising (1869), promising amnesty to the insurgents. Taché publicly condemned Ottawa's failure to honour this commitment and its negligence in handling *Metis and Aboriginal land claims, which triggered a second Riel uprising (1885). He helped craft the Manitoba Act (1870), although its linguistic and religious balance would quickly be overturned by massive Anglo-Protestant immigration. His sustained efforts to bring sufficient numbers of French speakers and Catholics to settle the Prairies having failed, Taché was not surprised when Manitoba created a common school system in 1890. Although he fought hard to have Ottawa disallow the legislation, he also missed a golden opportunity to focus attention on it during the federal election of 1891, confident that politicians would do the right thing. Taché's dream of a bilingual West comprising Aboriginal, North American, and European peoples endowed with equal opportunities and rights remained unfulfilled.

ROBERTO PERIN

Talon, Jean (1626–94). Despite the brevity of his two stays in New France (1665–8 and 1670–2), Talon is usually credited with being the most active and visionary intendant in the history of the colony. In the evolution of French government, the creation of the office of the intendant represented a key development, as it allowed the king and his ministers to control affairs in their realm. The intendant, directly controlled by the king, had a great range of powers over civil, judicial, and economic affairs. As the first intendant to reside in New France, Talon used his position to foster demographic and economic growth and improve the structure of the colonial government. He oversaw one of the few periods of intense immigration to the colony. He aimed to ensure an agricultural basis for the colony, and at the same time diversified economic activities by establishing a brewery; supporting the search for iron, coal, and copper mines; and encouraging the coastal fishery, domestic crafts, and intercolonial trade. On his return to France, Talon was appointed first valet of the king's wardrobe and secretary in his privy chamber, a recognition of his successful tours of duty in New France.

COLIN M. COATES

Taqulittuq (Hannah Tookoolito, *c.* 1839–76) and **Ipirvik** (Joe Ebierbing, Eskimo Joe, *c.* 1839–*c.* 1881), *Inuit guides, interpreters, culture-brokers. Born in the Cumberland Sound region (near Pangnirtung) during the high point of eastern arctic *whaling, this multifaceted wife-and-husband team first appears in the written record around 1853, when they journeyed to England for two years with a British whaler and were invited to dine with Queen Victoria and Prince Albert. Returning to Baffin Island, they met American explorer C.F. Hall in 1860. Hall's diaries portray the couple as mentors retained during his arctic travels (1860–2 and 1864–9) and investigations of the missing *Franklin expedition. Taqulittuq and Ipirvik accompanied Hall fundraising around the United States (1862–4 and 1869–71) and settled temporarily in Groton, Connecticut, before joining Hall's 1871 *Polaris* expedition. Mutiny left Hall dead from arsenic poisoning early in this expedition, and resulted in the couple keeping 19 *Polaris* crew members alive while drifting for 190 days (and almost 3,200 km) on an ice-floe. The US press recognized them for their heroism and they returned to Connecticut, where, in 1875, their adopted daughter Puna died of pneumonia. Taqulittuq died of *tuberculosis the following year. Ipirvik eventually returned north with the 1878–80 Schwatka expedition and died among his people.

NANCY WACHOWICH

Tardivel, Jules-Paul (1851–1905). Born in Covington, Kentucky, to a French father and a British mother, he attended college in St-Hyacinthe, Quebec, in 1868. There he discovered his life's leitmotifs: defence of the papacy and of Catholicism and glorification of French Canada. Beginning in 1873 he devoted himself primarily to journalism, ultimately founding *La Vérité*, the weekly that became his life's work, in Quebec City in 1881. He pursued his two obsessions with such zeal that he became one of the most widely recognized interpreters of Quebec *ultramontanism and a dominant figure in French-Canadian nationalism. He advocated the ideal of a very conservative, mainly rural, and agricultural society, under the complete control of the Catholic Church, rejecting liberalism, socialism, democracy, and freemasonry. The hanging of Louis *Riel in November 1885 pushed him to favour Quebec's separation from the rest of Canada and to propose the creation of an independent Catholic French-

Canadian republic. The father of Quebec separatist thought, in 1895 he published a synthesis of his thought in the novel, *Pour la patrie*. At the cultural level, he prepared the way for Henri *Bourassa and Lionel *Groulx.
RÉAL BÉLANGER

Taschereau, Elzéar-Alexandre (1820–98). The first Canadian cardinal, Taschereau was born at Ste-Marie-de-la-Nouvelle-Beauce and died in Quebec City. Following studies at the *Séminaire de Québec, he was ordained on 10 September 1842. Beginning as a professor at the seminary, he soon assumed administrative responsibilities at the institution and took part in the establishment of Université Laval in 1852. Director of the Petit Séminaire in 1856–9, and the Grand Séminaire in 1859–60, he became superior of the seminary and rector of the university in 1860, continuing in those roles until 1866. On 24 December 1870 Rome named him archbishop of Quebec. He obtained the title of cardinal on 7 June 1886. His episcopate was more notable for consolidating existing institutions than creating new ones. It was also shaken by disagreements and confrontations with Mgr *Bourget, bishop of Montreal, and the more radical ultramontane fringe on several subjects, among them the teaching of classical authors in the colleges, the establishment of the Université de Montréal, elections, and reform of the civil code. CHRISTINE HUDON

Taschereau, Louis-Alexandre (1867–1952), Quebec premier 1920–36. Born into the judicial elite of Quebec City, Taschereau made a name for himself as a lawyer. In 1900 he was elected to Quebec's legislative assembly as Liberal member for Montmorency, which he represented until 1936. His intellectual abilities, judgment, and sense of duty led Lomer Gouin to give him a portfolio in 1907 and, when he resigned as premier in 1920, to entrust the succession to him. Taschereau's government was characterized by financial management centred on a balanced budget; support for education, highways, and industrialization based on the massive entry of foreign capital; and support for big business. Agriculture suffered, to the displeasure of French-Canadian nationalists, and, disregarding accusations of anticlericalism, in 1921 he created the liquor commission and introduced the public assistance law, thus greatly troubling the clergy. A partisan of *provincial autonomy, he resisted the erosion of the province's powers and followed a moderate policy on national unity. The Depression of the 1930s nevertheless brought down his government amid accusations that, among other things, it was corrupt and too closely tied to the trusts. Taschereau was unable to adapt his predominantly classic *liberalism to the new situation; for example, he rejected socio-economic reform and nationalization of hydroelectricity. His party split and lost several promising young members, who founded the Action libérale nationale in 1934. RÉAL BÉLANGER

Taverner, Percy A. (1875–1947), ornithologist, author, conservationist. Born in Guelph, Ontario, but educated in Michigan, Taverner practised architecture in Chicago and Detroit from 1902 to 1911, when his self-taught avocations of taxidermy and ornithology gained him an appointment at the National Museum of Canada in Ottawa. An intense stammer impeded public speaking and encouraged writing. Through building the museum's collections and publishing *Birds of Eastern Canada* (1919), *Birds of Western Canada* (1926), and *Birds of Canada* (1934), he helped lay the foundation for scientific ornithology in Canada. Some of Taverner's descriptions of bird life are classics that have not been improved upon. His successor, W.E. Godfrey, maintained the pre-eminent standard for national bird books set by Taverner, with revisions of *Birds of Canada* in 1966 and 1986. A warm-hearted person, Taverner carried on extensive correspondence with people across the country and helped increase interest in birds, their distribution and behaviour. He was influential in the establishment of Point Pelee National Park in 1918.
C. STUART HOUSTON

taverns. Places open to the public and licensed to sell beer, wine, and spirits by small measure, offering meals and lodging for a charge. These establishments were also called inns or public houses. The term 'saloon', which in its British sense indicated quality establishments, was also used by early Canadians; later it took on the Wild West connotations it still bears. Frontier taverns were notorious in travellers' tales for terrible food, bad whisky, and promiscuous sleeping arrangements. More commonly, patrons experienced decent, even excellent, accommodations in numerous minor public houses and in principal public houses (sometimes called hotels) in big towns and resorts. Barrooms, dining rooms, and larger meeting rooms offered public sociability; parlours and sitting rooms gave more seclusion. Minor houses had, minimally, three beds, but not always in separate rooms; principal houses offered private chambers. Taverns were stocked with all manner of alcohol. Minor houses served 'meat-and-potatoes' meals while principal establishments advertised haute-cuisine. Tavern keepers lived in their establishments with their families. Men held over 90 per cent of tavern licences; because almost all owners pursued other occupations, women's household work included attending to patrons. Principal houses employed staff to do so.

Taverns had a mixed clientele from all walks of life. White men dominated the space, but women were also patrons; so too, on occasion, were people of colour, although Blacks faced racist challenges to access, and First Nations people, after 1835, could not buy spirits. Women, who had earlier enjoyed tavern going with male relatives or friends, found that Victorian morality pushed them out by 1840, unless they were travelling. As cities emerged, some taverns catered to particular classes or political or ethnic groups. In Ontario, taverns numbered approximately 1 per 325 persons from 1801 until after Confederation—very thin compared to European and US cities. Today there are half that number.

Historically, taverns supported a range of public activities. Crucial to *stagecoach travel, they remained valuable to local travellers into the railway era. People went to auctions, listened to political speeches, attended courts, mustered for *militia training, or met in voluntary and working-men's associations in taverns. In towns, specialized buildings eventually usurped these roles, but taverns remained important in undeveloped areas. Taverns also encouraged good fellowship. Companions bought each other liquor, usually sharing a gill (four ounces), taken with water. People who had had a couple of drinks were reckoned sober, but tavern goers disapproved of habitual drunkards. Violence sometimes erupted, especially in disreputable taverns, but usually tavern keepers and patrons co-operated to maintain 'good order'. JULIA ROBERTS

taxation. The imposition of taxes, which are compulsory payments imposed by a government on individuals and corporations to raise government revenues and to serve other purposes (e.g., redistribution of income or stimulation or deterrence of various economic activities). Highly charged politically, especially when new taxes are proposed, taxation is influenced also by considerations of theory, administration, and competition among jurisdictions.

Initially imposed under French and then British authority, taxation became increasingly a matter for local determination as Britain devolved control to its North American colonies. The main colonial taxes were *customs duties, levied on goods coming into the country, supplemented later by excise duties on selected locally produced goods, especially alcohol and tobacco. After 1867, these remained the principal forms of taxation for the federal government until the Great Depression. In 1920, the federal government imposed a sales tax, which from 1924 was levied at the manufacturing level. These were all indirect taxes, imposed on a producer or middleman and passed along to the consumer in the price of the goods taxed.

The demands of war finance, and calls to conscript wealth as well as men, led the federal government to introduce direct taxation (i.e., tax collected directly from the taxpayer), notably the personal and corporate income tax begun in 1917. Income tax in modern form dates from the Second World War, when it became the largest single source of federal revenues. Its administrative and conceptual complexities and the need to share the field with the provinces challenged the state to develop much more sophisticated understanding and management of fiscal policy. No major new federal tax followed until 1991, when the Goods and Services Tax, a value-added tax applying to a wide array of transactions, replaced the manufacturers sales tax.

Under the 1867 Constitution Act, the provinces were confined to direct taxes. All imposed succession duties, taxes on businesses, and, by 1940, personal income tax. During the 1920s, all found a rapidly rising new source of revenue in taxes on gasoline. The first provincial retail sales taxes dated from the late 1930s; in the 1950s and early 1960s they were adopted by all provinces except Alberta. Most provinces had substantial non-tax revenues from natural resources, fees (such as for motor vehicle licences), and services (such as liquor sales, which all provinces made a government monopoly when *prohibition was abandoned).

Although subordinate to the provinces, municipal governments collectively accounted for more taxation than the provinces until the modern era. Here taxation came to be based largely on the assessed value of real and personal property. In the West, induced by rapidly rising real estate values after 1900, most cities fully or partially exempted improvements to land from tax. Among the rationales for this was Henry George's 'single tax' theory that land rents, because they were created collectively, could legitimately be taxed and would yield enough revenue to replace all other taxes. After the land boom ended in 1913, the approach proved unsustainable.

DOUGLAS McCALLA

teachers' unions. The historical development of teachers' unions in Canada has been determined by two dominant themes. First, until relatively recently primary and secondary school teachers have been individually employed by the myriad of local (mainly rural and small) boards of education, thus greatly limiting possibilities for combining collectively. Second, state officials have strongly promoted the ideology (if not the reality) of 'teacher professionalism'. Indeed, the first 'teachers' associations' in many provinces (as early as the 1860s in Ontario and anglophone Quebec) were founded and controlled largely by state education officials wishing to imbue centralized schooling systems with 'professionalism'. Although local teachers sometimes banded together in the late 19th century to gain better salaries and benefits (often expressing hostility to the 'official' teachers' groups), these unions were usually short-lived, given the opposition of the state and the difficulties of organizing in rural areas. It was well into the 20th century before voluntary independent provincial unions began to form, with the express purpose of improving the material conditions of teachers.

By the 1950s all provincial governments had reasserted their formal involvement with teachers' unions by passing Teaching Profession Acts. These required public school teachers (except Quebec's Catholic teachers) to belong to official provincial unions, which in turn were restructured and governed (directly or indirectly) by statutory legislation and regulation. Virtually all union leaders have lauded the advantages of these arrangements, although close links with the state have often influenced the decisions and actions of these organizations. In the 1990s British Columbia became the first province to rescind mandatory membership legislation. In spite of dire predictions, voluntary union membership remained strong, and many believe that the BC Teachers' Federation became even more committed to the interests of its members. Several provincial teachers' unions have recently joined the *Canadian Labour Congress, following the example of Quebec Catholic teachers who, during the *Quiet Revolution of the 1960s, founded the Corporation des enseignants du Québec and affiliated with the province's *Confédération des syndicats nationaux. HARRY SMALLER

team sports. Such activities developed in Canada with the coming of industrialism and the growth of cities and towns in the mid-19th century. As they developed, team sports gradually overwhelmed rural sporting practices, many of which were characterized by the close association between humans and animals. The development of team sports in Canada also reveals the influence of the *British Empire. Soldiers at imperial garrisons and immigrants from the British Isles brought games such as *football, rugby, curling, and cricket, and a fondness for *rowing competitions of various sorts. Britons considered these sports important ingredients of good health, hardiness, and respectable manliness, and a Christian alternative to 'blood sports', such as cock-fighting or animal baits, that involved inhumane treatment of animals. Many of those who called for team sports adhered to the idea of *'muscular Christianity', a blend of spiritual discipline and physical hardiness, which they contrasted with an effete and overly intellectualized approach to Christian life. Promoters of British sporting traditions also considered team sport, especially *amateur sport, useful in developing gentlemanly characteristics. Supporting vigorous hard-knock competitiveness, advocates of team sport encouraged respect for opponents and the umpire, and espoused an ethic of fair play that they considered a hallmark of British life.

Team sports also reflected the spatial and temporal realities of the new industrial and urban order. As factory production developed, a more disciplined approach to time emerged. Seeking to increase productivity, factory owners introduced scientific management techniques, and the factory time clock became the symbol of workplace discipline. The new industrial age witnessed a sharper separation of work and leisure time, and sporting activity reflected the new order. Players, organizers, and spectators alike preferred regularly scheduled matches played in a relatively confined amount of time outside working hours. Some games—particularly *hockey, football, and basketball—even made use of the time clock.

Unlike earlier rural sporting traditions that took place in relatively unbounded spaces, team sports tended to be played in confined spaces in urban communities (in parks, arenas, or enclosed fields). Such places emerged for two reasons. First, merchants opposed games being played in city streets because they interfered with their businesses. Second, enclosed athletic grounds provided an opportunity for sporting entrepreneurs to make a profit from competitions. Team sports were especially prone to commercialism. In addition to capitalist promoters, who regarded sport as a potentially profitable business, community teams often employed highly skilled professional players to help them compete against teams from neighbouring towns. Professionalism was particularly widespread in *baseball and *lacrosse and became commonplace in hockey after the turn of the century. Defenders of 'gentlemanly amateurism' often denounced the willingness of professionals to play for money rather than a supposed love of the game.

Team sports often involved petty *gambling as well. Wagering and prize competitions could affect individual sports such as rowing and *boxing, to be sure, but the significant community allegiances and rivalries that emerged around team sports led fans to demonstrate loyalty to their teams, and hopefully win a little money, by placing bets.

Although the first generation of team sports revealed the influence of British sporting practices, later generations would turn increasingly to North American games. By the last quarter of the 19th century baseball and lacrosse had supplanted cricket as Canada's most popular summer sporting activities. Hockey, which began as a form of shinny or hurley on ice, but which dates from the mid-1870s in its organized form, rapidly asserted itself as the country's dominant winter sport at the end of the century, spreading across the country from the Maritimes, Quebec, and Ontario into the western territories. Rugby underwent a gradual metamorphosis into Canadian football, beginning with intercollegiate matches between McGill and Harvard in 1874 and the University of Toronto and the University of Michigan in 1879. Basketball, invented by Canadian James Naismith in 1891, grew rapidly in schools and colleges at the turn of the century and in gymnasia of the *Young Men's Christian Association. Before the First World War basketball and softball were the most popular participation sports for women.

Today hockey, baseball, softball, football, and basketball are the major team sports in Canada. Women are actively competing in most of these sports, as witnessed by the gold medal performance of Canada's women's hockey team in the 2002 Salt Lake City Olympics. Of the British sports, soccer is perhaps the most widely played, although Canada has recently fared well in rugby at the international level. Curling remains a widely played winter game, but cricket has been relegated to the margins of Canadian sporting life. In recent years, individual sports have grown in popularity. These include not only individual sports with a lengthy pedigree, such as golf, paddling, and *track and field, but the new 'extreme' sports such as snowboarding and rollerblading.

COLIN HOWELL

Tecumseh (*c.* 1768–1813) and **Tenskwatawa** (1775?–1836), Shawnee brothers from the Ohio country. Horrified at the loss of land to settlers and the consequent devastation of indigenous independence and social cohesion, they formed a pan-tribal confederacy in 1805 to oppose the United States in the 'Old Northwest' of today's Michigan, Indiana, and neighbouring regions. Their objective was to create an independent homeland where Native societies could evolve on their own terms. Tenskwatawa was a prophetic religious figure, while Tecumseh served as the movement's political and military leader.

Aboriginal–American hostilities broke out at Tippecanoe in 1811, which led the tribesmen to ally with the British at the outbreak of the War of 1812 to fight their common enemy. Tecumseh fell at the battle of Moraviantown in October 1813, and Tenskwatawa lost most of his influence threreafter. Their dream of an Aboriginal homeland died as well because the victory gave the Americans dominance on the Detroit front. This made it impossible for the British to demand that the United States give up land for the tribes without continuing hostilities, which was not in the interests of Britain or its colonies. However, they convinced the Americans to restore Native rights to their 1811 status, in the Treaty of Ghent, but the benefit was only temporary: the United States continued to take Native land and force tribespeople further west after 1815. CARL BENN

Teit, James Alexander (1864–1922). Teit emigrated from the Shetland Islands to Canada in 1884. He spent most of his life at Spences Bridge, British Columbia, where from 1894 until his death he worked for the eminent New York–based anthropologist Franz *Boas. Teit's legacy is huge. Among the best-known of his monographs are *The Thompson Indians of British Columbia* (1900), *The Shuswap* (1909), and *The Salishan Tribes of the Western Plateau* (1930). After 1908 he combined his ethnographic work with political lobbying on behalf of the Interior Tribes of British Columbia, the Indian Rights Association, and the Allied Tribes of British Columbia. Teit also worked as a hunting guide in remote regions of the province, eventually earning the title 'premier guide in the province'. WENDY WICKWIRE

telecommunications. Literally 'communicating over distance', the term is now usually confined to electronic modes of transmitting and receiving messages on a point-to-point basis, encompassing the telegraph, telephones, satellites, and computer communications, but excluding *broadcasting, which is offered on a point-to-mass basis. For decades telecommunications has been of central interest to Canadian policy makers, undoubtedly on account of the vast and often rugged geographic space and low population density characterizing the country.

In North America invention of the telegraph in the 1840s signalled the advent of modern telecommunications. The telegraph is usually attributed to Samuel F.B. Morse, who took out a US patent and developed the Morse code. Morse's patents were not applied to Canada, where the telegraph was introduced mainly by businesses, such as railways, newspapers, and retailers, who saw it as a useful adjunct to their existing operations. The first telegraph company, the Toronto, Hamilton & Niagara ElectroMagnetic Telegraph Company, was founded in 1846. The Canadian industry underwent rapid growth, experiencing direct and often cutthroat competition followed by consolidation and cartelization. By 1920, it became essentially a duopoly under the control of rival railways. In 1980, *Canadian Pacific and *Canadian National formed a partnership (CNCP Telecommunications, now AT&T Canada) to provide a broad range of telecommunications services beyond the moribund telegraph service. It is a rival of companies founded on the telephone for a wide range of telecommunications services.

In 1877, for one dollar, the inventor of the telephone, Alexander Graham *Bell, turned over to his father, Alexander Melville Bell, the Canadian patent, thereby inaugurating the Canadian telephone industry. After a brief period of rivalry with the Montreal and Dominion telegraph companies (which were offering telephone service under competing patents), the elder Bell sold his Canadian patent in 1880 to American interests, and left to join his son in Washington. National Bell, the US company that purchased the Canadian patent, promptly hired Charles Fleetford Sise to oversee the consolidation of the Canadian telephone industry, and within a year possessed not only the parliamentary charter for the Bell Telephone Company of Canada, but also all Canadian telephone facilities and patents. When the original Canadian patent was declared void in 1885, the door was opened once again to rival companies. Direct competition in some localities persisted until the early 1920s, and even today in *Bell Canada's territories of Ontario and Quebec there exist a handful of small, independent telephone companies. The more general pattern had been that of province-wide monopolies, although recent consolidations have taken place among them: Telus, for example, represents an amalgamation between the British Columbia Telephone Company and AGT (Alberta Government Telephones), while Aliant represents the merger of the four phone companies that had served the Atlantic provinces. Other major providers in Canada include Manitoba Telecom Services, now partly owned by Bell Canada, and Saskatchewan Telecommunications, owned by the provincial government.

The Canadian government too has been active in telecommunications development. With the launch of Alouette I by NASA on 29 September 1962, Canada became the third nation in *space and the first country in the world to place a domestic geostationary satellite into commercial service. That satellite, used exclusively for scientific experimentation, was designed by the Canadian Defence Research and Telecommunications Establishment, later renamed the Communication Research Centre. In 1969 the Telesat Canada Act created a private telecommunications corporation, with the government, the terrestrial telecommunication companies, and ultimately the general public each to own one third of the shares. Between 1972 and 1976 Telesat launched three Anik A satellites to provide television networking as well as voice and data communication services. In 1991, the Telesat Canada Reorganization and Divestiture Act provided for the continuance of the company and the divestiture of the government's shares. (The general public was never afforded the opportunity of purchasing the one-third interest, as set out in the original legislation). Today Telesat Canada is owned by BCE Media, a subsidiary of BCE Inc., the company that also owns Bell Canada and such other communication entities as the *Globe and Mail*, the CTV Network, and Bell ExpressVu, a direct broadcast satellite company. Telesat operates a fleet of satellites that provide broadcast distribution and telecommunications services throughout the Americas. The Anik F1 satellite, launched on 21 November 2000, is the newest member of the expanding fleet, inaugurating Telesat's next generation and sixth series of satellites.

ROBERT E. BABE

téléroman. Central to the history of media in Quebec, the téléroman's cultural importance is all the greater because of its location on the borders between literature and theatre, using audio-visual techniques close to those of film. It has been almost a daily fixture of television programming since 1953. Originating in a concept of radio production that recognized the effectiveness of narrative continuity and systematic reminders of elements such as characters, location, and décor, the téléroman has become an economic motor in the structure of programming because it allows for the insertion of advertising and at the same time, as a serial, it guarantees a loyal audience.

The first téléroman, the novelist Roger Lemelin's *La Famille Plouffe* (1953), created a craze for the genre, in which the humour derives from the depiction of contemporary life and the creation of character types. The audience discovered in the genre a diversity of dramatic languages, comic and tragic. Depicting a variety of social settings, the téléroman created dynamic images of the Quebec bourgeoisie with André Giroux's *14 Rue de Gallais* and of Montreal's diversity of cultures and classes, including the bourgeoisie of Robert Choquette and Françoise Loranger's *La Pension Velder*, the magnificent version of *Sous le Signe du lion* with Ovila Laré, Marcel Dubé's *De 9 à 5*, and Jean Desprez's *Joie de vivre*. The lower middle class found humorous expression and plenty of drama in Michel Faure's *La P'tite semaine*, Jean Filiatrault's *Le Paradis terrestre*, Claude Jasmin's *La Petite patrie*, and Jeannette Bertrand's *Quelle famille*. The working class saw itself in Mia Riddez-Morisset's *Rue des pignons* as well as Victor-Lévy Beaulieu's *Race du monde*. Regional and rural life, well represented in the dramatic fiction of the téléromans, found its apotheosis in the great television classics: Germaine Guèvremont's *Le Survenant*, Claude-Henri Grignon's *Les Belles Histoires des pays d'en haut*, Guy Dufresne's *Cap-aux-sorciers*, Réginald Boisvert's *Montjoye*, and Beaulieu's *L'Héritage*. Several historical téléromans revealed parts of Quebec's history: Dufresne's *Les Forges du Saint-Maurice*, Fernand Dansereau's *Le Parc des Braves* and *Shehaweh*, Pierre Gauvreau's *Le Temps d'une paix*, and Beaulieu's *Montréal PQ*. The recent téléromans *Virginie* and *Caserne 24* tried to give a contemporary vision of teaching and firefighting. Similarly, Réjean Tremblay's *Urgence*, *Lance et compte,* and *Scoop* explored various situations in a hospital setting, sports, and journalism, with writing techniques that renewed the genre's aesthetic, drawing more from made-for-TV movies than drama series.

RENÉE LEGRIS

temperance movement. Temperance was the most passionate of all reform movements in 19th-century Canada, and the most tenacious. Part of the passion sprang from the movement's origins in millennial religion, fostering utopian projections that *crime, *poverty, disease, and domestic violence would disappear as dry mankind attained perfection. Another invigorating force was the movement's genuine success in curbing alcohol abuse. Methodists, Baptists, Presbyterians, and Congregationalists spearheaded the voluntary or 'moral suasionist' campaign in the first half of the 19th century, and remained active throughout the century. After 1850, influenced by the more secular approaches of fraternal societies and lobby groups, the movement threw its weight behind the drive for *prohibition.

The modern temperance movement originated in early-19th-century America in response to abuses arising in new settlements where it was more profitable to distill grain for local sale than to ship it to distant markets, and where *taverns were the prevalent social institutions. Such conditions also affected settlements in Canada West and Red River, while the Atlantic colonies and Canada East were inundated with cheap imports of rum from the British West Indies. Moreover, it was widely believed that workers, travellers, nursing mothers, and even children needed alcohol to keep up strength, ward off cold and heat, and as all-purpose medicine and tonic.

British North Americans received temperance publications and heard the word from various preachers, religious and lay, American and Canadian. The first known Canadian society was founded at Russelltown, Lower Canada, in 1822 by Presbyterian Mrs John Forbes, who was troubled by inebriate teachers and pastors. Some 30,000 pledged temperance in Nova Scotia in the 1830s, and the Maritimes gradually became the driest region of the country. Political tensions interfered with work in the Canadas until 1840, when Scottish and Canadian mercantile families in the Montreal Temperance Society financed a campaign to unite people of all persuasions in a mighty Temperance Reformation. Travelling agents preached abstinence to audiences at chapels, schoolhouses, and crossroads from Gaspé to Lake Huron. In 1844 the *Canada Temperance Advocate* was able to report over a 100,000 teetotallers in the united province and a drop in workplace drinking. By the end of the decade there were higher liquor taxes, more tavern restrictions, and many other community-gathering places besides taverns.

Catholics too awoke to the cause in the 1840s. In the final years of the decade, a crusade led by the charismatic Father Charles Chiniquy addressed fears raised by heavy British immigration. Some 400,000 French Canadians pledged abstinence, assured it would make them sufficiently industrious and progressive to survive on an anglophone continent. Chiniquy fell from grace by pursuing female converts, literally. In Quebec, Atlantic Canada, and the West, Catholic temperance remained parish-based throughout the century.

Among Protestants the campaign became more secular around 1850. The Sons of Temperance and other fraternal groups offered inducements such as insurance schemes, clubrooms, and colourful parades. The Sons spearheaded the drive for prohibition, a measure narrowly defeated in the Province of Canada but briefly in effect in New Brunswick in 1855. The movement tended thereafter to focus on winning local option elections, though there were serious problems with enforcement. The Canada Temperance Act (Scott Act) of 1878 established common standards for municipal and county votes on whether to license the sale of liquor. Though the

North-West Mounted Police were desultory in enforcing stiff liquor laws west of Red River, vigorous nationwide activity came from the *Woman's Christian Temperance Union (1874) and the Dominion Alliance for the Total Suppression of the Liquor Traffic (1876). They secured a mighty victory in a 1898 national plebiscite, when every province save Quebec voted for prohibition. Prime Minister Wilfrid *Laurier snatched it away by declaring the margin too narrow and the turnout too low, leaving prohibitionists to await nationwide enactment as a wartime measure in 1917. Temperance and prohibition have been excoriated as wellsprings of underground activity. Historians nonetheless acknowledge that they did reduce alcohol consumption and its associated physical and social ills.

JAN NOEL

Tenant League. The Tenant Union of Prince Edward Island, a grassroots movement founded on 19 May 1864, and popularly referred to as the Tenant League, represented a new strategy in attempting to solve the land question. Members refused to pay rent or arrears of rent, and supported others who resisted, in order to pressure landlords to sell freehold title to the farmers who occupied their lands. The movement soon claimed 11,000 members in a colony whose population was between 80,000 and 94,000. Two sales, together exceeding 10,000 acres, occurred according to the prescription of the league, but most owners were defiant. By the summer of 1865 leaguers were preventing the sheriff of Queens County from doing his job; typically, members were summoned by horns or trumpets to obstruct service of writs. When the island's Conservative government called upon the British military to assist the civil authority, leaguers did not resist the troops, and the organization melted away. Yet the league cannot be judged a failure. In the wake of the disturbances, many proprietors lost heart and sold their estates to the local government for resale to occupiers, thus hastening the end of leasehold tenure.

IAN ROSS ROBERTSON

territorial waters. By the mid-20th century, coastal states around the world, including Canada, found that the existing territorial sea boundary measured three miles from shore was no longer adequate for the protection and development of ocean resources. In Canada, there was pressure to extend jurisdiction to limit fishing by foreign fleets on both the Atlantic and Pacific coasts, which had increased dramatically in the 1950s and 1960s. The United Nations Law of the Sea Conference, a series of negotiations held between 1973 and 1982 to establish an international agreement on ocean policy, addressed the issue of extended jurisdiction. One of the provisions of the 1982 agreement allowed coastal states to claim a 200-mile Exclusive Economic Zone. In 1977, before the deal was ratified, Canada declared a 200-mile Exclusive Fishing Zone. While this gave Canada jurisdiction over most of the offshore fish stocks of the Atlantic coast, it did not include areas of the continental shelf outside the boundary (the 'nose' and 'tail' of the *Grand Banks; the Flemish Cap) where fish populations spent at least part of their lives, leaving them vulnerable to international fleets.

By the mid-1980s, the Northwest Atlantic Fisheries Organization, the body created in 1979 to manage the fishery outside the 200-mile limit, found it impossible to enforce its catch quotas. After the collapse of the northern cod stocks off Newfoundland in 1992, the Canadian government, in addition to declaring a moratorium on commercial cod fishing inside the 200-mile limit, introduced legislation to monitor the area outside the boundary. In March 1995, in one of the more dramatic uses of this new legislation, Canadian fisheries officers seized a Spanish vessel, *Estai*, and arrested the captain for catching Greenland halibut (turbot) contrary to NAFO regulations. The 'Turbot War' aroused anger on both sides of the Atlantic, with Canadian federal Fisheries Minister Brian Tobin sparring with European Union officials about Canada's right to protect, as he called it, 'the last, lonely . . . little turbot, clinging by its fingernails to the Grand Banks'. The government later dropped the charges, but the incident raised public awareness of the difficulties in managing fish in international waters.

MIRIAM WRIGHT

thalidomide crisis. Developed in the 1950s, thalidomide is a sedative drug with immune effects. Within a year of its licensing in Canada, limb abnormalities (phocomelia) appeared in infants of German women who had taken thalidomide in early pregnancy. It was withdrawn from the Canadian market on 10 April 1962, five months after the initial reports linked it to birth defects. The first affected Canadian was born in Saskatoon in February 1962; the second, in June. The full scope of this tragedy was not known until nine months after withdrawal of the drug. Worldwide, approximately 5,000 victims survived childhood; many others died in infancy, and countless pregnancies ended in miscarriages. The Thalidomide Victims Association of Canada was founded in 1987, under the leadership of Randy Warren. It represents the 125 surviving 'thalidomiders' in Canada. Of normal intelligence and eager to participate in society, they and their families faced huge difficulties without compensation until September 1992. Because the drug had been licensed, the Canadian government was held liable in court, not the pharmaceutical industry that had manufactured and sold it, nor the doctors who had prescribed it. Since 1992 thalidomide has been cautiously reintroduced as treatment for diseases that benefit from its actions on the immune system or on the growth of blood vessels. In 1998 the US Food and Drug Administration approved strict guidelines for its use in the management of *leprosy, certain cancers, and autoimmune conditions, including graft-versus-host disease, which, ironically, is a doctor-caused (iatrogenic) problem caused by the medical intervention of bone-marrow transplant.

JACALYN DUFFIN

Thanadelthur ('marten shake'), a Dene/Chipewyan woman, *Hudson's Bay Company guide, interpreter, and peace negotiator (1714–17). Known as 'Slave Woman', she escaped from the Cree and arrived 'Allmost Starv'd' at York Fort in November 1714. Governor James Knight needed a Chipewyan interpreter to encourage their trade and negotiate their passage through Cree territory. Thanadelthur was guide and 'Chief promoter and Acter' on the successful peace-making mission Knight sent out under William Stuart in 1715, which 'causd respect to her, & Carry'd Allso a Great Sway among the Indians'. Her death, on 5 February 1717, was 'very Prejudiciall to the Company's Interest'. J. COLIN YERBURY

theatre. 'Theatre' has often been used to describe performative activities among Aboriginal peoples both before and after Europeans arrived. Much First Nations storytelling, dance, and ritual uses narrative devices, impersonation, visual illusions, self-aware dialogue and characters, as well as performance settings given heightened significance. The sacred and profane often co-mingle in a manner unlike European 'theatre', which separates religious ceremony and 'art', but this Aboriginal performance tradition grew to be sophisticated, utilizing fire, smoke, elaborate painting, costumes, masks with mechanical transformational properties, and other theatrical devices.

That Native and European traditions interpenetrate is evident, although the extent is largely unstudied. European-based activities began with the arrival of explorers, who brought shipboard entertainers (as early as 1583) and staged plays. The first European-style play in Canada, Marc *Lescarbot's masque *Le Théâtre de Neptune*, was staged at *Port-Royal (1606) and published in France (1609). Among its characters are 'Indians' (enacted by Frenchmen); its dialogue incorporates Amerindian words. Throughout the 17th century and until the British Conquest, records indicate that French theatre was persistent, if sporadic. The first known actor, Martial Piraubé, arrived in 1636 as Governor Montmagny's secretary; the first known actress, Françoise-Marie Jacquelin, in 1640. Among important records for early years are the *Jesuit *Relations*, ironically so given the opposition to theatre expressed by the church. Yet theatre proved a successful tool for Christianizing Native people, and in *Ursuline and Jesuit collèges for teaching the classics. It also somewhat inadvertently fostered playwriting as well as stage performances in schools and beyond. As early as 1640 the *Relations* record a 'mistère' (mystery play?) and a 'tragi-comédie' performed for the Dauphin's birthday. Subsequent *Relations* speak of 'réceptions' (formal dramatic pieces welcoming dignitaries to new offices), classical plays, and locally written pieces. Recurrent demands by clerics that parishioners avoid theatre confirm performances outside the colleges. The most famous such instance pits Archbishop Saint-Vallier against Governor *Frontenac, who staged plays at his Quebec residence and proposed the controversial *Tartuffe* in 1694. The intrigue—which set church against state, involving personality clashes between Saint-Vallier and Frontenac, personal opposition to the church, and financial gain—ultimately kept the play off the Quebec stage for two centuries.

Theatre became more common around the mid-18th century as the number of British troops and settlers increased. By 1773 in Halifax and 1774 in Montreal—where British officers pointedly staged two Molière plays in French—and until the regiments were recalled in 1871, garrison theatricals entertained the officers, troops, and civilians, and served as important social occasions, subtly inculcating British ways in the population. The French also had had garrison theatricals, as Montcalm himself testifies, citing *Le Vieillard dupé*, written by one of his officers, performed in 1759 at Fort Niagara. Among civilians, troupes of 'Gentlemen Amateurs' (women still generally avoided the stage except as professionals) formed in the new towns, staging a popular English repertoire shaped by rudimentary production conditions. Influential British North American playwriting began with George Cockings's *The Conquest of Canada or the Seige of Quebec* (1766), which likely had several Canadian showings, and Major Robert Rogers's *Ponteach, or the Savages of America* (1766). In Halifax (1774) a garrison production of *Acadius* (anonymous) traced a Black servant disguised as a woman, searching for his lover who was transported to England as a slave. In Quebec *The Village Festival* by Sieur Lanoux, 'famous Canadian poet', was performed in 1765 by 'Canadian village women, new subjects of His Britannic Majesty'. *Jonathas et David*, staged in Montreal (1776), became the first play printed in Canada. Another anti-theatre attack by a Quebec priest fortunately failed to stop performances of Joseph Quesnel's *Colas et Colinette* (and seven other plays) by the Théâtre de société, which Quesnel formed in 1790.

Those activities were amateur, but in 1765 the Quebec engagement of Pierre Chartier's troupe in *Le Festin de Pierre* foreshadowed short commercial stays by professionals, more so among the English, who were less troubled by church opposition. Towns along waterways (in 1825 the Erie Cannel facilitated tours from New York, Boston, Philadelphia) began to see not only the adaptation of existing buildings into performance venues but the occasional purpose-built theatre. One of the most striking was Montreal's Theatre Royal, with its classical pilasters, erected in 1825 by Montreal businessmen, including John *Molson. Its resident company was augmented by visiting stars, including the tragedian Edmund Kean in 1826.

By mid-19th century many small centres had at least makeshift theatres and were occasionally visited by small troupes, some regionally based. Larger centres, (e.g., Halifax, Saint John, Toronto, Hamilton) were beginning to benefit from professional resident stock as well as local amateurs and tours. Companies from France began to travel to Montreal and Quebec, while playwriting, focused on French-Canadian issues, led to notable dramas, such as Antoine *Gérin-Lajoie's *Le Jeune Latour* (1844) and L.-H. *Fréchette's *Félix Poutré* (1862). A somewhat similar nationalism was arising in English Canada, evident in criticism that *Fiddle, Faddle and Foozle* (1853), Toronto's first play by an Upper Canadian, was not Canadian enough. *The Female Consistory of Brockville* (1856), *The King of the*

Beavers (1865), and *Dolorsolatio* (1865) were among plays attacking corruption in Canadian institutions.

From the 1870s the growth of arterial railways, industry, and urban population supported the establishment of Canadian stops on the touring circuits that dominated North America until the First World War. The extent of this commercial enterprise is evident in the more than 300 companies, almost all American, touring in Canada in 1899–1900, and the 36 theatres holding 1,000–2,000 people built between 1873 and 1892 across the country. Civic pride and entrepreneurship led many to be called 'Grand Opera Houses', although not always 'grand' and rarely offering opera. Like television today, they featured melodramas, domestic dramas, comedies, and the occasional Shakespeare. Over the years, hundreds of foreign luminaries appeared on these circuits and hundreds of Canadians found theatre careers. Some, like Margaret Anglin, became stars, but almost all had to work from the United States. Only a handful of companies (Harry Lindley, Ida Van Cortland, the Marks Brothers) and producers like theatre owner Ambrose Small were based in Canada. The formulaic scripts had to 'play in Peoria', but Canadians wrote hundreds during the circuit years. English-Canadian dramatists of the period also wrote works dealing with 'Canadian' subjects, such as *Tecumseh, Laura *Secord, national politics, or *women's suffrage, which appeared in satires, musicals, and poetic tragedies, and were sometimes staged locally. A few, such as *HMS Parliament* (1880) and *Leo, the Royal Cadet* (1889), were successful in commercial houses. Parallel to this, a sort of mini-'golden age' occurred in Montreal in the 1890s. Over 1,000 performances were given in 1898–9 alone, almost all imported plays. But after the war changing economic conditions caused a decline in both English and French touring. In interwar Quebec, variety and burlesque vied with movies, and led to a legion of sketches and improvised plays. One in particular, *Aurore, l'enfant martyre* (1921), based on the tragedy of the young Aurore *Gagnon and her brutal step-mother's trial, met phenomenal success, being staged hundreds of times until the early 1950s.

Throughout Canada a strong amateur theatre arose after the First World War, in part reacting against commercial dross. Influenced by the 'art' theatre movement in Europe and the United States, 'Little Theatres' expressed a nationalistic spirit, like other arts (e.g., the *Group of Seven), and joined that serious aim, sometimes uneasily, with the social aspects of amateur theatre. The *Dominion Drama Festival (1932–78) served as 'Canada's national theatre', holding an annual, often controversial, competition of winning performances by Canadian 'Little Theatres'. A flurry of patriotic playwriting in Quebec during this same period contributed several DDF winners (e.g., Arthur Provost's *Maldonne*, 1938) as well as the first Canadian play performed in Paris (Jean-Aubert Loranger's *L'Orage*, 1925) and many others for college productions. Father Émile Legault's Compagnons de St-Laurent, among several troupes, worked to expand the repertoire and train performers in Quebec. Through the 1930s a vibrant Workers' Theatre also developed, staging left-wing political plays that challenged Depression-era worker exploitation. Through amateur theatre, thousands in Canada were exposed to stage productions.

Post-Second World War rebuilding and increased material wealth, as well as theatre experiences overseas and in Canadian universities, were forces supporting many people's urge to earn a living in theatre. The DDF restarted, flourishing through the 1950s, when Robertson *Davies was English Canada's leading playwright. Simultaneously, drama on CBC radio, and then television, offered artists professional fees. Between 1946 and 1957, when public funding urged by the 1951 *Massey Commission arrived with the Canada Council, several dozen professionally oriented stock companies were set up. Gratien *Gélinas's *Tit Coq* (1948) and playwrights such as Marcel Dubé led Quebec into a new era of theatre. Le Théâtre du rideau vert (1948), Le Théâtre du nouveau monde (1951), and the Stratford Shakespearean Festival (1953) highlighted the founding of large-scale companies in a burgeoning professional scene. During the 1950s and 1960s experimental 'théâtres de poche' offering some Quebec plays were matched in English Canada by small coffee houses and repertory companies introducing a foreign avant-garde repertoire. These were followed by the 'regional' movement, inaugurated by the Manitoba Theatre Centre in 1958–9, which resulted in a large-scale professional theatre in most major cities. Despite contributing to increased production standards, the 'regionals' were heavily criticized for failing to offer Canadians lead roles, directing assignments, or Canadian plays. In Quebec, through the 1960s and 1970s, culture focused on the *Quiet Revolution, giving rise to a new theatre urging a 'Quebec for the Québécois' with artists such as Michel Tremblay at the forefront. In English Canada a second generation of small, anti-establishment ('alternative') theatres (e.g., Factory Theatre, Theatre Passe Muraille, Tamahnous, Northern Lights) championed a nationalist focus and/or denounced society's materialism, its leaders' affinity for war, and its hypocritical moral stance especially in regard to sex and human relationships. As the millennium closed, Canadian playwrights, designers, and companies, and new forms of theatre such as the image-based work of Robert Lepage, were receiving international acclaim. A thriving 'Fringe' theatre had developed in many cities; in contrast, a Broadway-style musical scene had arisen in Toronto, by then North America's second largest theatre producer.

Further developments in the past two decades focused on society's marginalized areas, a movement led by feminists, gays, lesbians, and First Nations artists. Over the years, a tendency for immigrants of a similar background to stay together allowed culturally specific theatre to be part of each community. Consequently, there are long histories of theatre among African-Canadian, Chinese, Finnish, Italian, Japanese, Jewish (in Yiddish), Polish, Ukrainian, and other immigrants, as well as shorter but vital histories of more recent ones. These were inaccessible to those without the specific language but now, in a more multicultural country, there are plays often in two or more languages, about and by First Nations people, as well as Southeast Asian, African, Caribbean, and other cultural groups. RICHARD L. PLANT

Théâtre de Neptune. The first documented Western-style drama performed in Canada, *Théâtre Neptune de la Nouvelle-France* was written by Marc *Lescarbot and played in *Port-Royal in November 1606 to celebrate the return of Jean de Biencourt de *Poutrincourt and Samuel de *Champlain from an expedition of exploration. Written as an entertainment, it showed Neptune, the mythological god of the sea, welcoming the travellers home. A mixture of music, recital, and choral song, it featured Indians and mythical figures as well as glorias to the King of France, cannons, and trumpets. It was performed by 70–80 Frenchmen and *Mi'kmaq. After the author's return the piece was published in France in 1609 as part of a collection of poems entitled *Les Muses de la Nouvelle-France*. In 1963, a professional theatre was founded in Halifax and named Neptune Theatre in honour of Lescarbot. JEAN DAIGLE

theosophy. Born out of the ferment of science and religion in the late 19th century, and claiming a more profound knowledge than either could offer, theosophy in Canada attracted a surprising number of artists, writers, feminists, scientists, and social reformers during the period 1890–1940.

The Theosophical Society was formed in 1875 in New York by a Russian aristocrat, Helena Blavatsky, and Henry Steel, a New York lawyer and journalist. In her major writings, *Isis Unveiled* (1877) and *The Secret Doctrine* (1888), Blavatsky sought to investigate the spiritual laws of nature and the universe by bringing together aspects of the Western occult tradition and of Hindu and Buddhist thought with the contemporary belief in evolution and progress. Central to her complex teachings was the conviction that outward forms express inner spiritual realities, and that there exists a monistic cosmos grounded in Consciousness, in which through a cyclical pattern universes, worlds, civilizations, and individuals are evolving. Reflecting much of the spiritual optimism of the age, theosophy considered humanity in all stages of its development to be governed by a universal brotherhood based on the essential identity between the individual and Consciousness. To hasten this realization was the task of the Theosophical Society.

In 1891 this hope was transferred to Canada with the founding of the Canadian Theosophical Society, an autonomous lodge under charter from its New York parent. Organized first in Toronto, under the committed leadership of a recent Irish immigrant and journalist, Albert E. Smythe, who until his death in 1944 edited its monthly, *The Canadian Theosophist*, it quickly became a major cultural force. At its height in the 1930s the society counted over 20 lodges and nearly 1,000 members. Especially effective in applying theosophical principles to aesthetics were artists Lawren Harris and Bertram *Brooker. Others influenced by the social and intellectual reform impulses of the movement included scientist Frederick *Banting, psychologist Richard *Bucke, physicians Albert Durrant Watson, Emily Stowe, and Augusta Stowe-Gullen, their fellow suffragist Flora MacDonald *Denison, Hart House Theatre director Roy Mitchell, and well-known socialists and nationalists William Arthur Deacon and Phillips *Thompson.

MARGUERITE VAN DIE

Third Option. A policy of the Pierre *Trudeau government aimed at reducing Canadian dependency on the United States. In late 1972, days before a federal election and noting a critical edge in Canadian public opinion towards the US, External Affairs Minister Mitchell Sharp issued a document outlining three options for the future of the Canadian–American relationship: 1) the status quo; 2) closer ties with the US; or 3) 'a comprehensive, long-term strategy to develop and strengthen the Canadian economy and other aspects of our national life and in the process to reduce the present Canadian vulnerability'. Trudeau and Sharp chose the third option, attempting to diversify Canada's export trade through economic co-operation agreements with Europe and Japan, both signed in 1976. But the Japanese and Europeans, although polite, were not enthusiastic adherents, nor was the Canadian bureaucracy, business, or public. The prime minister himself was easily distracted, and the economic integration of the North American continent continued apace. 'Lots of luck, Canada', said an American official in hearing news of the Third Option plan. The pessimism was warranted.

NORMAN HILLMER

Thompson, David (1770–1857), fur trader, explorer, geographer. Apprenticed to the *Hudson's Bay Company in 1784, after learning surveying skills from Samuel *Hearne and Philip Turnor, Thompson mapped large parts of western Canada before joining the *North West Company in 1797. From his station at Rocky Mountain House on the North Saskatchewan, he concentrated on finding a route to the Pacific. He crossed Howse Pass in 1807 and travelled to the source of the Columbia. He established Kootenae House nearby and lived there with his family as he explored southeastern British Columbia and the adjoining states. In 1810, in an effort to forestall American traders, he continued exploring the Columbia River system, starting from Athabasca Pass. He reached its mouth four months after John Jacob Astor's Pacific Fur Company. Settling in Montreal, he produced an exceptional map of the West in 1812–14. On it, he named the Fraser after Simon *Fraser, who in 1808 had given Thompson's name to a major tributary. He worked 20 more years, 10 of them for the US–Canadian boundary commission (1816–26). Financial failures and blindness left him living in obscurity and dependent on his family. He received little recognition until J.B. *Tyrrell discovered his manuscripts and called Thompson the 'greatest geographer who ever lived'. J. COLIN YERBURY

Thompson, Sir John Sparrow David (1845–94), prime minister 1892–4. Born in Halifax, Thompson, who came from a modest family rich with Irish memories and poetry, carried a wealth of intelligence, integrity, and decency. He had a passion for justice and hated cruelty, especially to women and children. He served as a lawyer, then as Halifax alderman, attorney general of Nova Scotia, and briefly its premier. In 1882 he was appointed to the Supreme Court of Nova Scotia. In September 1885 Sir John A. *Macdonald's government in Ottawa was in trouble. With the results of the *North-West Rebellion still echoing, the fate of Riel pending, and the CPR nearing completion but at huge cost, the government badly needed strengthening. Macdonald was told he needed John Thompson as minister of justice. Thompson, happy in Halifax, was reluctant to accept, but he soon proved indispensable in Ottawa.

After Macdonald's death in June 1891, Sir John Abbott became prime minister; when he left office a year later, Sir John Thompson (he'd been knighted in 1888) reluctantly took up the prime ministership. He passed the new Criminal Code, set up Labour Day, and made substantial efforts to resolve problems with the United States. On *reciprocity, the aggressive American secretary of state, James G. Blaine, wanted a complete customs union, but Thompson was too much of a nationalist to risk such a union with an expansionist US.

The hardest domestic issue was the *Manitoba schools question. In the midst of that tangle, Thompson, only 49 years old, died of a heart attack at Windsor Castle in England, on 12 December 1894. Canadians mourned his loss, said the Saint John *Sun*, especially 'the onward look of that untrammelled mind'. P.B. WAITE

Thompson, T. Phillips (1843–1933), journalist, labour reformer, radical, socialist. Phillips Thompson's first major assignment as a correspondent for the *Globe* was to cover the Irish Land League agitation in 1881. The plight of the Irish tenants aroused his sympathies and he devoted the rest of his life to the struggles of voiceless peoples. Thompson's trip to Ireland coincided with that of Henry George, whose book *Poverty and Progress* was making inroads among the membership of the Land League. George's cure for the prevailing state of affairs was a taxation policy, popularly known as the 'single tax', that would give society the unearned increment currently pocketed by landlords. Thompson embraced the single tax as one of his many causes. In Toronto, supporters of the single tax banded together in numerous organizations, including the *Knights of Labor, the Anti-Poverty Society, the Single-Tax Association, the Nationalist Clubs. Thompson believed that land monopoly was only part of the problem. He identified the broader problem as one of monopoly from above combined with competition among wage earners from below. Edward Bellamy's 1887 publication *Looking Backward* also had an impact among Canadian reformers, and led Thompson to abandon the single tax and embrace *socialism. CHRISTINA BURR

Thomson, Tom (1877–1917), landscape painter. His depictions of the rugged landscape of the Near North had a great influence on the artists who formed the *Group of Seven in 1920. Born on a farm near Claremont, Ontario, Thomson grew up at Leith, near Owen Sound. He first worked in the commercial arts in Seattle (1901–*c.* 1904) and Toronto (1905–13). With no formal training as a painter, he learned from his painting associates, including J.E.H. MacDonald, A.Y. Jackson, and Lawren S. Harris. He began painting in oil in 1911 and defined his style in 1914 when he was able, through the support of his patron, Dr James MacCallum, to leave commercial art and paint full time. He then worked as a fishing guide and fire ranger in *Algonquin Park. He sketched in oils in the park from late winter to late fall, painting his canvases in his Toronto studio. He sold his first canvas to the government of Ontario in 1913 and subsequently three paintings to the National Gallery of Canada. He was an exceptional colourist with a keen sensitivity to the changing light of the seasons. He drowned in Canoe Lake in Algonquin Park in July 1917, leaving approximately 450 designs and sketches and 45 canvases.

CHARLES C. HILL

Thunder Bay. Fort William was established in 1803 as the inland headquarters of the *North West Company. Following NWC amalgamation with the *Hudson's Bay Company in 1821, the settlement fell on hard times as the fur frontier moved north. It was revived in the 1880s by railway construction and in 1907 was incorporated as a city, then home to almost 16,000 people. Nearby Port Arthur (12,000 souls in 1908) also became a transportation hub, first because of its position at the head of the *Dawson Road—the rough track that led through wilderness to Winnipeg—and later as the Canadian Northern terminus.

Given their proximity in a region of Ontario comprising wilderness and scanty human settlement, competition soon developed, often descending into downright hostility. While Port Arthur observed daylight saving time, Fort William did not, thereby inconveniencing many labourers. Streetcar systems ended at municipal boundaries and their schedules were not designed to provide continuous service between the towns.

Both cities boomed in the years after 1900, but they suffered mightily during the Great Depression, largely because of their dependence on resources. *Pulp and paper, a major employer, both in the mills and in the forest, was hit especially hard. Ship construction at Port Arthur Shipbuilding Company, which had the largest drydock in Canada in the 1920s, ground to a halt. N.M. Paterson Shipping (still based in the city) was also badly affected. Finally, the tidal wave of *grain that had poured through elevators from 1886 slowed to a trickle. Although the twin cities revived briefly during the Second World War, even being represented in Parliament by C.D. *Howe, the 'minister of everything', could not slow the fundamental change adversely affecting them.

Since 1955 the Lakehead has genteelly declined. The opening of the *St Lawrence Seaway in 1959 did little to reverse its economic misery. Grain shipments fell off year after year, the railways hired fewer and fewer men as diesels took the place of the old steam engines, and mechanization in the forest industry slashed that workforce. A forced amalgamation of the two cities in 1970 by the minister of municipal affairs, Darcy McKeough, failed to ensure the co-operation between the renamed North Ward and South Ward that was needed to plan for the future.

Thunder Bay continues to struggle against the odds as its economy and population continue to decline. Aboriginal people from the region are increasingly moving into the city and may prove to be its salvation. Too far—1,600 km by road—from the provincial capital, it is also distant psychologically from the corridors of power.

BRUCE MUIRHEAD

***Tish* Group** refers to several young Vancouver-based poets who in 1961 began publishing the literary journal *Tish* at the University of British Columbia. The word 'tish' was intended both to imitate breath sound and (because these poets saw themselves as artistic rebels who rejected the discreet romanticism of conventional Canadian lyrics) also to resonate scatalogically. Until it folded in 1969, *Tish* was edited at different times by Frank Davey, George Bowering, Fred Wah, David Dawson, and Jamie Reid. It attracted collaborative contributions from Daphne Buckle (Marlatt), Lionel Kearns, Gladys (Maria) Hindmarch, Peter Auxier, David Cull, and Robert Hogg, while, from across Canada, poets John Newlove, David McFadden, and others were also drawn to the journal's theory and practice. The writers' collective experimentation with open form—treating units of breath as poetic lines, as in Kearns's theory of 'Stacked Verse'—reveals the influence of the school of Projective Verse as practised by the American poets Robert Creeley, Robert Duncan, and Denise Levertov. These 'Black Mountain' poets—named for Black Mountain College in North Carolina—found 'ideas' only in 'things' (i.e., grounded their intellectual concerns in the exact perception of the material world). In 1961, Creeley, Duncan, and Levertov participated in a poetry conference that the critic Warren Tallman organized in Vancouver and that Davey, Bowering, and other young poets attended. Attacked by some critics at the time as unpatriotic, in that they adapted their poetics from conventions current in the United States, the *Tish* Group, over subsequent decades, came to be hailed as innovators in technique and the forerunners of a postmodern sensibility in Canada. Through Raymond Souster's Contact Press, Black Mountain aesthetic principles also influenced such Ontario poets as Margaret Avison. Literary historians see Davey's *Open Letter*—and his later 'electronic journal' *Swift Current*—as *Tish*'s successor.

W.H. NEW

Titanic. The most famous wreck of the 20th century, *Titanic* collided with an iceberg off the *Grand Banks of Newfoundland on the night of 14 April 1912 and sank early the following morning. The ill-fated liner had many links to Canada other than that the fatal iceberg probably drifted into the North Atlantic from Canadian waters. Of the 2,228 people aboard, 130 were bound for Canada, the most notable being Charles Melville Hays, president of the *Grand Trunk Railway, Montreal millionaire Harry Markland Molson, president of Molson's Bank and the family brewery, and Toronto millionaire Arthur Godfrey Peuchen, president of the Standard Chemical Company. Lost with *Titanic* were 1,523 men, women, and children, among them Molson and Hays. In all, 75 of the ship's passengers bound for Canada died. The disaster was strongly felt throughout Canada, particularly Halifax, where most of the bodies recovered after the sinking were landed and where 150 victims were buried. A number of artifacts, recovered adrift in the North Atlantic in 1912, ultimately made their way into Halifax's Maritime Museum of the Atlantic.

JAMES DELGADO

Toronto. People have lived in the Toronto region on the north shore of Lake Ontario for almost 11,000 years. Direct contact with Europeans occurred in the 17th century, and the French built small trading posts there during the 18th, but the birth of the urban community did not occur until the British regime. In 1787 the Toronto area was alienated from the Mississauga; then, in 1793, John Graves *Simcoe, lieutenant-governor of Upper Canada, established a military post and civilian town to improve the colony's defences during a period of threatened American invasion. He named his settlement York and moved the provincial capital there from the vulnerable border village of Niagara.

York grew slowly, to only 720 people by 1814, and faced numerous blows in its early years, including American attacks and occupations during the War of 1812. Nevertheless, the settlement expanded quickly after 1815 because of its importance as the colonial capital, which attracted institutions with province-wide interests, such as banks and schools. At a time of expanding trade and improving transportation, it was geographically well positioned to serve the commercial needs of a newly settling hinterland. When the province incorporated the town as the City of Toronto in 1834 (to provide mechanisms to meet the needs of an urbanizing population), the community was Upper Canada's largest with 9,250 souls. This population continued to grow, reaching 30,775 in 1851 on the eve of the railway era. However, various tribulations threatened the city: the economy suffered serious downturns at various times, rebellion sundered Toronto in 1837–8, *cholera ravaged the population in 1832, 1834, and 1849, and typhus struck in 1847–8. Yet, by 1853, the year the first trains pulled out of Toronto, a recognizably modern city had taken shape, with distinct residential and commercial neighbourhoods, gas lighting, piped water, and such notable public buildings as St Lawrence Hall and St James' Cathedral.

Industrialization, beginning modestly in the mid-19th century, expanded greatly after Confederation, and contributed significantly to shaping the city's environment and prosperity. By 1901 this industrial, commercial, financial, and institutional centre had a population of 208,000, which rose to 667,500 by 1941. During these years, Toronto began to compete with Montreal as the nation's premier centre, not only economically, but also culturally, as exemplified by the founding of the Royal Ontario Museum (1912) and the Toronto Symphony (1922). However, Toronto's overall character was provincial, as captured in Francis Pollock's 1938 novel, *Jupiter Eight*, which described the city as 'a slow place, a dull place, where English snobbery met American vulgarity and each thrived on the other'. Toronto's population surpassed Montreal's in 1976, by which time the city had become Canada's most important economic and cultural engine.

As late as the 1940s, Toronto's population was largely Protestant (72 per cent in 1941) and fundamentally British (78 per cent, but mainly Canadian-born). As might be expected given these statistics, the world wars saw Torontonians flock to the colours with particular fervour compared to other parts of Canada. The wars contributed to dramatic increases in the city's economic, industrial, and technological enterprises as well as to breaking down social barriers. Torontonians faced numerous other challenges during the 20th century, ranging from the poverty suffered by many families across the generations to the shorter-term disaster of the Great Depression.

A great shift in the spirit of the community began with the numerous waves of immigrants after 1945. By 2001 Toronto had become one of the most multicultural cities on the planet, where 152 languages and dialects were spoken in an atmosphere of comparative harmony. According to that year's census, more than half of Toronto's 2.5 million residents were born outside Canada, and a million people belonged to visible minorities. These post-war decades also saw the compact city of 1945 burst its boundaries in a typically North American orgy of urban sprawl that consumed some of Canada's best farmland, both within Toronto's 632 sq km boundary, and far beyond into the bedroom communities of Ontario's 'Golden Horseshoe'.

Despite its many attractions and enviable quality of life compared to other cities, Toronto's future at the beginning of the 21st century is unclear. Globalization's impact on the city is mixed, and the municipality's taxation and administrative powers compared to those of other large North American centres are inadequate, but higher levels of government—particularly that of *Ontario—have withheld the legal and financial resources that Toronto needs to meet its challenges. CARL BENN

Toronto stork derby. When Toronto lawyer Charles Millar died in November 1926, he left most of his considerable estate to the Toronto mother who would in the subsequent ten years give birth to the most children. This caused headlines, with the *Toronto Star* suggesting the will might be against the public interest and hence void, in part because it did not specify that the children need be legitimate. The province introduced a bill to invalidate the will, but popular opinion forced the government to backtrack, and the 'stork derby' proceeded. Ten years later, a judge had to decide what constituted a child for the purposes of the will. Along with the medical details of various births, the legitimacy of some children was investigated in the public courtroom. Eventually the case was appealed to the Supreme Court, which decided that a woman who had had five children by her husband and five by another man was ineligible. In the end, the half million dollars was split among four other mothers who had all had nine children within ten years.

MARIANA VALVERDE

Tory, Henry Marshall (1864–1947). Born in Port Shoreham, Nova Scotia, Tory was perhaps the most significant educational institution builder and promoter of scientific research of the 20th century. Following his father's example, he became a Methodist clergyman, serving briefly in Montreal. With a McGill doctorate, he taught mathematics at that university, though undertook little research. In 1905, McGill despatched him to reform its affiliate colleges in Vancouver and Victoria, work that prepared the way for the University of British Columbia. In 1908, the provincial government of Alberta appointed him first president of the University of Alberta. He took leave in 1917 to organize the *Khaki University. Back at the university, in 1919 he created the first provincial research council in Canada. In 1923, Tory joined the *National Research Council of Canada, leaving Alberta in 1928 to become the first full-time NRC president. His greatest achievement was building the National Research Laboratories during the Depression. Tory retired in 1935, but became involved in organizing Carleton University, serving as professor and president from 1942 till his death.

RICHARD A. JARRELL

tourism. From its early days Canada has attracted many people, mainly settlers or immigrants, but pleasure-seeking travellers also set foot in Canada as early as the mid-17th century. These were mostly isolated adventurers, but by the 1820s large numbers of British, American, and European urban middle- and upper-class tourists developed the habit of taking an annual holiday and embarked on the Northern Tour, the equivalent to the European Grand Tour. Canal building in the 1820s and 1830s opened up the Canadas and the Great Lakes region, with *Niagara Falls as its main attraction. These excursions into the Canadian wilderness allowed relatively wealthy individuals to escape from pressures encountered in their increasingly industrialized and urbanized homelands. The further expansion of steamer and railroad service during the 1850s made it possible to include the St Lawrence in the tour. Although transportation in the Maritimes and the West expanded later, these areas attracted a growing share of the tourist population with their much-appreciated hunting and fishing opportunities and the spectacular grandeur of their coastlines, the prairies, and the Rocky Mountains.

Although some tourists valued Canada's untamed nature specifically for what it had to offer hunters and anglers, many others simply appreciated the fact that by coming to Canada one could still expect to find vestiges of an uncivilized world or of a distant past. The hope to see Indians epitomized this; travelling companies obliged by hiring Aboriginals on their steamers, making them available as guides to sportsmen, or scheduling stopovers at Native reserves such as the popular village of St Regis (Akwesasne). The French-Canadian *habitants were also popular, perceived as primitive and charming incarnations of the past still living as did their 17th-century ancestors. By the early 20th century, Nova Scotia's transportation companies were promoting the Annapolis Valley by labelling it the *Evangeline region, once again conjuring up images of the past—this time the Acadian past—to draw the tourist dollar.

After the First World War, Canada benefited from the new mass tourism. Largely composed of Americans, it was mostly the result of affordable *automobiles being made available to a growing number of working-class families. This was also the time when workers were granted an annual holiday. Furthermore, provincial governments became increasingly involved in tourism promotion. They started by opening up otherwise inaccessible areas of the country by building roads. During the difficult economic times of the 1930s and following the recommendations of the Senate Committee on Tourist Traffic (1934), the federal government also carved out a niche for itself in the industry, recognizing tourism's economic contribution to the nation's wealth. The Canadian Travel Bureau (1934) was set up to coordinate, among other things, a tourism-promotion campaign.

An even more significant tourist boom occurred following the Second World War. Post-war prosperity meant that an ever larger proportion of the public in North America and Europe could travel for pleasure. During the 1940s the majority of public and private sector employees had gained paid vacations. Increasing amounts of money were spent by governments and the private sector to make the country more attractive to growing numbers of tourists. In the 1950s several marketing campaigns were launched and the decade experienced a motel-building boom. By the 1960s governments realized the economic benefits of encouraging their citizens to visit their own country; today Canadians are the country's largest tourist population.

Over time, many tourist attractions in Canada have proven constant and appealing to visitors, if for different reasons, while other features of the country have lost some of their initial charm. The appeal of Niagara Falls has not subsided but it increasingly has had less to do with its connection to wilderness. The lure of the Quebec habitant gradually subsided by the 1960s, accelerated by the impact of *Expo 67; the province gradually was marketed more as a sophisticated and cosmopolitan place were one could partake of a wide range of epicurean pleasures. By the 1940s Nova Scotia was increasingly being marketed as the home of the fisherfolk. Native cultures are still well represented among Canadian tourist attractions, but contemporary social and economic conditions and changing attitudes have made it difficult for today's tourists to project their fantasies onto the First Nations in the way their predecessors had done.

NICOLE NEATBY

See also HERITAGE TOURISM.

track and field. Also known as athletics, track and field consists of individual competitions in walking, running, hurdling, jumping (high jump, pole vault, long and triple jumps), throwing (shot, discus, javelin, and hammer), multiple events (heptathlon, decathlon), and team relays. In Canada, the sport grew out of the running and throwing contests of the Aboriginal peoples, colonial tests of strength at rural fairs and work bees, the *Caledonian Games of Scottish immigrants, competitions staged by the *British garrisons and the sports clubs of the urban, male middle class. By Confederation it was thriving, although increasingly tainted by fixed races and gambling stings. In 1884, clubs from Montreal, Ottawa, and southern Ontario created the Amateur Athletic Union of Canada to bring honesty and order to the sport. The AAU and its successors, the Canadian Track and Field Association (after 1969) and Athletics Canada (after 1990), have governed track and field ever since, in affiliation with the International Amateur Athletic Federation, now the International Association of Athletic Federations, established in 1912.

Since the 1920s, track and field has enjoyed a broad, grassroots following in schools, colleges, universities, and community clubs and fitness programs. It draws inspiration from the performances of the best Canadian athletes in international competitions such as the modern Olympics. Every generation has had influential stars. None brought more recognition to the sport than the members of the 1928 Olympic track team in Amsterdam. Vancouver's Percy Williams won the 100- and 200-m races, Saskatoon's Ethel Catherwood the high jump, and Fanny 'Bobbie' Rosenfeld, Jane Bell, Ethel Smith, and Myrtle Cook the 4 x 100-m relay. The *Matchless Six (as the women's team was called) scored more points than any other nation. Their accomplishments added athletic respectability to the Canadian proposal for a new international event, the British Empire (now Commonwealth) Games, and their celebrity ensured the success of the first games in Hamilton in 1930.

Track and field remained an *amateur sport in Canada until the 1970s, and Canadians fell behind countries where the best athletes were subsidized to train full-time and sport science research and sometimes banned performance-enhancing drugs were used to aid performance. Some Canadian athletes began to take drugs to catch up, but that practice was exposed, to national embarrassment, when sprinter Ben Johnson was disqualified for steroid use after a world record 100-m win at the 1988 Olympics in Seoul. After a damning royal commission and calls by other coaches, athletes, and the public for ethical, drug-free sport, Athletics Canada toughened its anti-doping policies and procedures. The sport's reputation was redeemed when Donovan Bailey won the 100-m dash and the relay team of Bruny Surin, Gilroy Gilbert, Robert Esmie, and Bailey won the 4 x 100-m relay at the Atlanta Olympics in 1996. BRUCE KIDD

Trades and Labor Congress. *See* CANADIAN LABOUR CONGRESS.

Trades and Labour Councils. Many of the first Canadian *unions were made up of workers in a particular craft or trade. Construction workers, for example, would not be organized into a single union but into several craft unions—carpenters, glaziers, ironworkers, labourers, electricians, plumbers, and so on. These unions proved successful at winning improved conditions within the trade. When it came to larger political questions, however, they needed to work together to press their common concerns. Thus trades and labour councils—labour centrals of affiliated unions—soon sprang up as workers needed to support each other in strikes, elect working-class candidates to legislatures and city councils, and rally for political issues that required more support than an individual union could muster.

One of the first of the labour councils was the Hamilton Trades Assembly, formed by 1863. Toronto followed in 1871. These early labour councils were crucial in the 1872 battle for the *nine-hour day. Attacked by employers and hurt by a depression, there were no functioning labour councils or trades assemblies by 1881. In that year, however, Toronto workers created the Trades and Labour Council, and workers in other cities soon followed. By 1890 labour councils could be found from Vancouver to Saint John.

The labour councils were active in local and provincial politics, education, and the creation of working-class newspapers and labour halls. They were also the forum for intense battles within the labour movement as unions hammered out strategies and tactics. Between 1910 and 1919 they took up questions of political action, general strikes, resistance to the First World War, and *syndicalism. The Vancouver Trades and Labour Council split over the question of affiliation to the *One Big Union, and for a time two rival councils vied for support. In the 1940s and 1950s the labour councils were sites for the battles between the *Communist Party and the *Co-operative Commonwealth Federation. Today, while private and public sector unions sometimes differ, anti-labour governments and corporations have reinforced the importance of the solidarity labour councils were first formed to foster.

MARK LEIER

Traill, Catharine Parr Strickland (1802–99), writer, botanist. With her sister, Susanna *Moodie, Traill is often seen as an archetypal 19th-century British 'gentlewoman' immigrant. Born into a middle-class family from southern England, she and her sisters began writing for publication after their father's death in 1818 left the family with little income. Traill's life took a dramatically different turn when she married the Scots half-pay officer, Lieutenant Thomas Traill in 1832 and emigrated to Upper Canada, settling in the Peterborough area. Between the 1830s and 1850s Catharine's work was published on both sides of the Atlantic. Her best-known book, *The Backwoods of Canada*, is both a memoir of her family's life on a bush farm and a practical guide for fellow countrywomen considering emigration. In this and other works, her cheerful practicality and determination to overcome adversity have often been contrasted with Moodie's more acerbic style. Yet her optimism was needed to cope with both a depressed husband unsuitable for backwoods farming and the many hardships they encountered, such as the deaths in infancy of two of their nine children. CECILIA MORGAN

transatlantic cable. In 1851, Fred N. Gisborne, an English emigrant, secured from the colonial government an exclusive 30-year right to construct telegraph lines in Newfoundland. After an unsuccessful attempt to link Newfoundland, Prince Edward Island, and New Brunswick, he began planning for an Atlantic cable. In New York he broached a young millionaire, Cyrus W. Field, who promptly organized the New York, Newfoundland, and London Electric Telegraph Company and acquired Gisborne's charter for Newfoundland. Field attained exclusive rights from the Newfoundland and PEI legislatures to land cables along their coasts. After several failed attempts at laying a transatlantic cable between England and Newfoundland, Field met with brief success in August 1858, and arranged for Queen Victoria to send the first transatlantic message. Three weeks later, the cable snapped. The transatlantic connection was not successfully restored until July 1866. That cable, however, remained in service for nearly a century.

Competing with Field's east coast venture was an enterprise backed by Western Union, which, in 1864, won a concession from the tsar of Russia to build a 11,000-km telegraph facility to link Moscow and the Pacific. In 1865 Western Union set up the Collins Overland Telegraph Company to join New Westminster, British Columbia, via the Bering Strait with Russia in the north, and through the California State Telegraph Company with San Francisco to the south. However, when news arrived in August 1866 that the Atlantic cable had been laid successfully, all work on the Collins Overland line stopped abruptly; tons of wire and other materials were abandoned to rust or rot in the forests and mountains, although some lines were eventually purchased by the dominion government beginning in 1871.

Yet a third venture to link continents—a Pacific Cable—was envisaged as early as 1879 by Sandford *Fleming, who wished to connect 'the outer empire' (Canada, Australia, and New Zealand) with England and the rest of Europe. There was much opposition, particularly from the private enterprises enjoying a monopoly connecting Australia through Asia and eastern Europe to England, and the 'Red Cable' became operational only on 31 October 1902. On that night, Fleming sent messages both east and west, and discovered that whereas it took over 5 hours for messages from London to reach Australia by the eastern route, the 'all-red line' required only 18 minutes. ROBERT E. BABE

Trans-Canada gas pipeline debate. The 'Pipeline Debate' was one of the classic parliamentary/political confrontations in Canadian history. At stake was Trade and Commerce Minister C.D. *Howe's vision of a secure, domestically sourced Canadian energy supply. When oil and natural gas were discovered in large quantities in Alberta in the late 1940s, it became possible to supply the central Canadian and British Columbia markets by oil and gas pipelines from Alberta. For natural gas Howe envisaged an all-Canadian route across sparsely populated northern Ontario. Although he had hoped the pipeline could be built by private capital (mainly American), the northern Ontario portion required an infusion of public funds, for which, in 1956, Howe turned to Parliament. Unwisely tying his project to strict deadlines, Howe created an opportunity for the opposition in Parliament to *filibuster the financing bill. Howe and the Liberal government cut off the debate by resorting to *closure, which in the 1950s was almost never used in Parliament or legislatures. The Liberal majority carried the bill, but the government suffered a severe defeat in Canadian public opinion, which contributed to the defeat of the government, and Howe personally, in the general election of 1957. ROBERT BOTHWELL

Trans-Canada Highway. The federal government enacted the Trans-Canada Highway Act on 10 December 1949 as part of its post-war employment plans. Funding was provided on a 50/50 basis with provincial governments for the construction of a two-lane, hard-surfaced, modern highway from St John's, Newfoundland, to Victoria, British Columbia. Ottawa's maximum contribution was set at $150 million and the target date for completion was 1956.

Despite widespread support, the project, which was overly ambitious and under-funded, was beset with problems from the beginning. Not all provinces agreed to the terms and some initially refused to participate. Rising construction costs, unanticipated major engineering works through the Rocky Mountains, and conflicting provincial priorities resulted in major construction delays. Only a small portion of the highway was completed by 1956.

In subsequent agreements Ottawa increased its share of expenses to encourage provincial interest. Nevertheless, when Prime Minister John *Diefenbaker officially opened the approximately 8,000-km highway in Rogers Pass on 3 September 1962, large sections remained unpaved. The entire route was paved by 1966, and the act terminated in 1970. Having cost approximately $2 billion, the Trans-Canada Highway is one of the longest continuous *roads in the world. DAVID W. MONAGHAN

Treasury Board. Created in 1868 as the only statutory committee of *cabinet, the board initially consisted of ministers heading the largest-spending departments and was chaired by the minister of finance. It was empowered to issue minutes (TBMs) regulating in detail departmental expenditures. Largely a paper tiger until the Depression of the 1930s, the board progressively assumed its current status as the key central agency responsible for the government's overall expenditure budget. Headed since the 1960s by its own minister (president) and served by a large secretariat, the board approves departmental spending plans, establishes through regulations the frameworks within which departments manage finance and personnel, obtain supplies, make contracts, and acts as employer in collective bargaining with associations. Faced with mounting complexity of government, the board has modified the draconian exercise of its legal authority and now delegates many of its powers to departmental managers.

J.E. HODGETTS

Tremblay Commission, 1956. Appointed by the government of Quebec, the Royal Commission on Constitutional Problems, headed by Judge Thomas Tremblay, was set up to study the issue of tax sharing among the federal, provincial, and municipal governments and school boards; to examine federal intervention in the field of direct taxation, particularly taxes on revenue, corporations, and inheritances; to consider the consequences of these interventions for the province's legislative and administrative system and for its people; and, more generally, to examine constitutional problems of a legislative and fiscal nature. Published in four volumes in 1956, the commission's report, emphasizing that the federal government is a creation of the provinces, considered that the role of the political system established in 1867 was to create an infrastructure within which the English- and French-speaking communities could benefit from federalism. It advocated greater *provincial autonomy, proposing that social programs be in the hands of the provinces. It also recommended extensive fiscal reform, very different from the recommendations proposed by the *Rowell–Sirois Commission (1940) on federal–provincial relations. The Tremblay report is generally considered a classic analysis of the Quebec nationalist vision of federalism.

GÉRALD-A. BEAUDOIN

trench warfare. Although for centuries armies had relied on trenches in order to take cover from enemy fire, the war of 1914–18 brought trench warfare to the public imagination. Following huge clashes in France and Belgium in 1914, German forces on one side and French, British, and Belgian armies on the other dug in, neither being able to outflank or destroy the other. Trench works of one form or another formed a thick line from Switzerland to the English Channel; in a sense, both sides settled into a mutual siege. The result was not just a set of defensive positions but something akin to a city below ground, with communication trenches—leading from the rear to the front—acting as main thoroughfares, with dugouts providing shelter for headquarters, medical units, and other facilities, and with sanitation requirements that equalled those of a large metropolis.

In early 1915 the Canadian contingent, raised in Valcartier in August 1914, entered this atmosphere. The Canadians faced three main challenges. The first was simply to live in conditions that included choking dust in summer, clinging mud in winter, and rats and lice year-round; artillery, machine guns, and snipers provided their own distinct hazards. The second, so-called minor operations, comprised trench raids designed to capture prisoners, destroy portions of the enemy's defences, and gather information. These began in earnest within the *Canadian Expeditionary Force, as it came to be called, in the latter part of 1916, and would punctuate trench life until the major offensives of 1918.

The third main challenge was the one that has stuck in the public mind: 'going over the top' in a major offensive. After the failure of artillery to destroy enemy defences on the Somme in 1916, leading to 24,000 Canadian casualties, commanders and staff officers worked out a tactical doctrine that operated at two main levels. First, artillery would 'creep' forward, allowing infantry to follow along behind and, it was hoped, enter German trenches before defenders could emerge from their dugouts. Second, the platoon of about 30 men was divided into sections, each of which would support the others to attack specific positions, such as machine-gun posts or pillboxes. Canadians fought the trench warfare of 1917 and 1918 with such tactics. The result was that casualties, which had eaten up a third of the Canadians' strength each time they fought a major battle in 1915 and 1916, were reduced to 15 or 20 per cent in the last two years of the war. In the end, however, trench warfare claimed over 53,000 Canadian lives, more than all other wars and military operations put together, including the Second World War.

BILL RAWLING

Trente Arpents. Published in Paris in 1938 and translated two years later as *Thirty Acres*, the first novel by Ringuet (the pseudonym of Philippe Panneton, 1895–1960) is a classic of Quebec and Canadian literature. Set in an 'old parish' in the agricultural region of the St Lawrence Valley between roughly 1880 and 1930, the story follows the life of Euchariste Moisan: his establishment as a farmer, his prosperity, his misfortunes, and his final exile in a New England town. Influenced by the naturalist aesthetic and reflecting meticulous observation, the novel offers a powerful picture of a traditional French-Canadian way of life, grounded in rurality, the family, and conservative values. But the vision it suggests is marked by its ironic realism. Believing himself to live at the centre of an unchanging idyllic universe, the farmer in fact becomes the slave of his land and is increasingly alienated by the social and economic changes of the modern world. Describing, with lucidity and compassion, both the grandeur and the decline of a way of life, this magnificent novel is a perfect marriage of regional inspiration and universal relevance.

FRANÇOIS RICARD

Troupes de la Marine. Infantry companies raised for service in French ports and colonies and on French ships. The first units came to New France in 1683 to help fend off Iroquois attacks. By 1689 there were 1,400 men. Their strength was much reduced between 1699 and 1749, but was raised to 1,800 in 1750. Marine officers provided leadership for large-scale operations, small war-parties, and patrols. Soldiers fought alongside the Canadien militia and Aboriginals, sometimes in formation but usually blended together in smaller parties. These troops formed a third to a half of the men in the large forces that went on the attack against targets in Iroquoia, New York, and New England, and a variable number in smaller operations. Officers increasingly came from the Canadien aristocracy, which provided many of the most successful commanders, serving in forts across the interior and playing a major role in diplomacy and trade with the Natives. These troops came to specialize in small-scale surprise attacks on forts and hit-and-run raids typical of *la petite guerre* (guerrilla warfare) both in Europe and North America. Lack of attention to training and drill compromised their ability to fight in large formations and they could not undertake a European-style siege. Sensing that marines would not suffice to oppose British regiments during the Seven Years' War, Versailles raised their strength to 2,200 in 1756 and added battalions of regular infantry from the French army between 1755 and 1757.

JAY CASSEL

Troyes, Pierre de (d. 1688). A captain in the Troupes de la Marine, Troyes arrived in New France in 1685. Governor Brisay de Denonville considered him 'the most intelligent and the most capable of our captains'. In 1686 Troyes led 35 troops and 65 militiamen from Montreal overland to James Bay, where they seized three HBC posts. His journal records the arduous journey and reveals the ability of Frenchmen to adapt to Canadian conditions. The expedition benefited from aggressive fighting by three Le Moyne brothers, notably Iberville. Troyes joined Denonville's expedition against the Seneca and fought at Gannagaro in July 1687. He then served as commander of the rebuilt Fort Niagara. Surrounded by Iroquois in the winter of 1687–8, he and most of his garrison died of scurvy.

JAY CASSEL

truck system. Initially described by G.W. Hilton in his definitive work *The Truck System* (1960) as 'a set of closely related arrangements whereby some form of consumption is tied to the employment contract', in the New World the system has come to refer to the credit mechanisms employed by merchant staple firms (including fur, fish, timber, tobacco, cotton, and coal) in regions where specie was scarce and/or where distance, along with settler poverty, made barter transactions between the firm and its labour force the easiest way to conduct business. It had benefits for both management and labour. As a wage and credit mechanism, it permitted purchase of store goods by employees against future payment in kind in lieu of wages. It thereby oiled the wheels of a commerce that would otherwise have been severely restricted. It also gave the labour force indirect access to distant markets. However, control of the staple good accrued to the merchant firm, which 'purchased' it from the producing worker through a truck system arrangement. The system also had disadvantages for both parties. For labour, it incurred the risk of 'tying' a worker to one firm through bonds of indebtedness, since the cost of goods purchased and the price paid to a producer for the staple were both set by the merchant firm. For management, it incurred the carrying of risk over a period of time until payment could occur (usually harvest time), making them vulnerable to bad harvests, to poor prices at market, and to the possibility of workers changing from one firm to another. Indebtedness of the labour force was one strategy employed by some firms to minimize those risks; low pricing of payments for the staple and high pricing for store goods was another. It is from the excessive use of such strategies that the truck system has acquired its rather infamous reputation. ROSEMARY E. OMMER

Trudeau, Pierre Elliott (1919–2000), prime minister 1968–79, 1980–4. Born in Montreal to a Scottish mother and a francophone father, Trudeau learned to speak unaccented English and French. His father's wealth gained him entrance to the best educational institutions in the world—Jean de Brébeuf, Université de Montréal, Harvard, Paris, and the London School of Economics. He did not serve in the Second World War.

Upon returning to Canada in 1949 he became active against the Duplessis government in Quebec, notably through support of the unions during a strike at *Asbestos. With other activists he founded the influential anti-Duplessis and anti-clerical journal **Cité Libre*, in which he set out his arguments for individual rights and against restrictive nationalism. After the election of the Lesage Liberals, Trudeau was a frequent media commentator. He increasingly worried that the old nationalism of *Duplessis was being replaced by a new nationalism that could end in *separatism. Believing that *Lesage had lost control of the radicals in his government, Trudeau decided to stand for election as a federal Liberal in 1965 with his friends Jean Marchand and Gérard Pelletier.

Trudeau did not immediately join the cabinet, but in 1967 he became minister of justice, gaining attention quickly when he introduced reforms to laws governing *divorce, *gambling, *abortion, and homosexuality. His brilliant performance at a constitutional conference won him attention and the Liberal leadership on 20 April 1968.

Apart from King and Macdonald, Trudeau served longer than any other prime minister. His early years in government reflected the wide range of his interests. He tried to make government more participatory and to shift Canada away from the American orbit militarily and economically. His strong belief in equality led to programs that sought to redistribute income between regions and individuals. He presented his vision of Canada as 'the Just Society'. The economic changes of the early 1970s made policy-making difficult. Trudeau almost lost the election of 1972, although his performance during the *October Crisis had been popular. He shifted towards the left to maintain New Democratic support in his minority government, 1972–4, and managed to win another majority in 1974. By this time, the situation in Quebec was preoccupying him, and his personal life was difficult.

René *Lévesque was Trudeau's nemesis, and they fought bitterly after the victory of the *Parti Québécois in the 1976 Quebec election. Trudeau flirted with new constitutional schemes, appointed committees, developed special programs for Quebec, and vigorously promoted *bilingualism and biculturalism. Nothing seemed to work, and he lost the election of 1979 to Joe Clark's Conservatives. Clark, however, was politically maladroit and allowed his government to be defeated in December 1979. Trudeau, who had announced his retirement, agreed to return as leader. He won another majority government in February 1980. Lévesque had called a referendum; Trudeau challenged him directly and, in what many believe to be his finest hour, Trudeau and the federalists won. During the referendum campaign he promised that Canadians and Quebeckers would have a new *constitution and bill of rights. In a bitter fight, Trudeau constructed the Canadian *Charter of Rights and Freedom, which was proclaimed on 17 April 1982. Still controversial, the charter nevertheless has the support of the large majority of Canadians and has enormously strengthened individual rights. It is Trudeau's major legacy.

When Trudeau left office, he was highly unpopular, especially in the West because of his *National Energy Program. He seldom made public appearances, but those he did had great impact. His opposition to the *Meech Lake Accord and the Charlottetown agreements did much to undermine those initiatives. When Trudeau died on 28 September 2000 public opinion polls indicated that he had become the most popular and respected Canadian political leader. His funeral was unparalleled in Canadian history. His impact on Canada came not only through the legislation his government passed but, perhaps even more, from the fiercely individualist stands that he took and the brilliant personality he possessed. JOHN ENGLISH

True Band Society/Provincial Union. The True Band Society and the Provincial Union, founded by Black men and women, were organizations dedicated to the elevation of Ontario's Black communities during the mid-19th century. Toronto-based abolitionists Thomas Cary and Wilson Abbott organized and led the Provincial Union. Although it had branches in Chatham and London, it remained focused on Toronto. The True Band Society was born in Amherstburg, with Levi Foster and Major Stephens as two of the leading lights behind its formation. Branches were eventually established in most of the province's major towns, and membership ran into the hundreds. Both organizations had similar objectives. The Provincial Union sought to unite all Black Ontarians and encouraged them to found their own businesses. While the True Band also encouraged Black unity, it was vehemently against 'begging' agents, who raised funds on behalf of fugitives from slavery, believing that such agents misrepresented the conditions of the fugitives by portraying them as incapable of looking after themselves. Both groups did much to foster Black economic empowerment and political strength. AFUA COOPER

trust companies. Emerging in the 1870s, trust companies supplanted individuals as executors and trustees of personal and business estates. Catering to the wealthy, 14 trust companies operated in Canada in 1900; none were among the ten leading financial institutions. By the 1930s trust companies were one-tenth the size of *banks but included three of the top ten financial institutions. By 2000 only one ranked in the top ten.

In theory, trust companies—one of the four pillars of the Canadian financial sector besides banks, insurance, and securities—operated separately from banks. In practice they operated in tandem. In the early 20th century, for example, a wealthy Toronto businessman, George Cox, had all four types of institutions under his personal control. Interlocking directorships were not disallowed until 1967. Well before that date trusts had taken advantage of weak and divided regulation—trust companies are administered at both the provincial and federal levels—to engage in business very similar to that of banks. Legislators gradually caught up to practice and in 1967 began to dismantle the 'firewalls' between trusts and banks and to consolidate regulation, a move sparked by a public run on weak trust companies in 1966. Nevertheless, 14 trust companies, many tightly owned by a close-knit few individuals, failed in a span of five years in the 1980s.

In the 1990s interprovincial competition for financial institutions and international competition led to further deregulation and fuelled mergers, the biggest being that of Canada Trust, the nation's largest trust company, and the Toronto-Dominion Bank in 2001.

PETER BASKERVILLE

tuberculosis. Throughout history tuberculosis has been a major killer. In Canada, the disease has had four phases: pre-sanatorium, ending about 1900; physical treatment, up to 1950; antibiotic, tainted by disillusion in the 1980s; and resurgent, which continues. Until a century ago, most Canadian families included at least one person with tuberculosis. Most commonly, it affected the lungs. Symptoms were weight loss, decreasing energy, cough, shortness of breath, and bloody sputum, with heavy bleeding from the lungs often the terminal event. Other forms of tuberculosis affect the bones, kidneys, and lymph nodes.

The first useful therapy, beginning late in the 1800s—when tuberculosis killed one in every ten dying in Canada—was the sanatorium rest cure, often made available through volunteer movements. The rationale was that injured lungs would heal better if rested; patients lay abed or sat in easy chairs, ideally breathing pure country air. But such 'cures' required months or years of bed rest. Often, those supposedly cured relapsed, necessitating further treatment. Absences for years, particularly if the patient were the breadwinner, were often destructive to the family. When Aboriginal patients—including thousands of Inuit who were treated in sanatoriums between the 1920s and the 1960s—returned home after years away, they often lacked the skills to resume their lives. During the First World War many men recruited into the Canadian forces had tuberculosis, and the government provided free sanatorium care when they were discharged. Such care rapidly came to include the men's families and, ultimately, the general public, beginning in Saskatchewan in the 1920s. Between the wars, surgical therapy became popular, particularly techniques to collapse or compress, and thus rest, lung tissue. Also in the 1930s a controversial vaccine, the Bacille-Calmette-Guérin (BCG) was tested, especially in Quebec.

Bovine tuberculosis was found in the 1870s to result from drinking milk from tubercular cattle. Many children acquired bovine tuberculosis, leading to efforts early in the 1900s to eliminate the disease in cattle, to assure germ-free milk supplies, and to improve school health examinations.

After 1950, antibiotics revolutionized treatment, curing most patients, and many sanatoriums closed. Yet before the end of the century the tubercle bacillus developed resistance to drugs. While the incidence of tuberculosis is much lower than a century ago, the disease has become difficult to treat. It affects the poor and malnourished, especially Native Canadians. Individuals who have deficient immune systems, including those with HIV, are commonly infected with tuberculosis, often lethally.

CHARLES G. ROLAND

Tulugajuak, Peter (*c.* 1870–*c.* 1935), *Inuit hunter, whale-boat leader, shaman, Anglican catechist, trader, culture broker. Born in the Cumberland Sound region (near Pangnirtung on Baffin Island) when *whaling was at its height, this prominent hunting leader and minor shaman, to the delight of frustrated Anglican missionaries, converted to Christianity in 1902 and began acting as a lay preacher in Inuit camps and whaling stations. The combination of his status and persuasive proselytizing converted most of the Cumberland Sound Inuit and lay the foundation for the spread of Christianity across the eastern High Arctic in the 1920s and 1930s. In the historical record Tulugajuak is also remembered as a strong leader and for a notable letter of protest he filed in 1922 with the Northwest Territories commissioner on behalf of the Pangnirtung Inuit, impeaching the morality of Hudson's Bay Company traders. In the Inuit oral tradition, stories still venerate Tulugajuak as a generous man and prominent hunter. NANCY WACHOWICH

tunnels. Tunnels for transportation were so expensive and took so long to dig that Canadian engineers generally preferred to go around obstacles rather than through them. However, when the *Grand Trunk Railway needed to cross the St Clair River from Sarnia, Ontario, to Port Huron, Michigan, a bridge was not feasible, so it was decided to build a tunnel. Joseph Hobson, a Canadian engineer, built the 1.8-km tunnel in 1889–91. A second tunnel was built in 1995–8 by *Canadian National Railways parallel to the earlier one.

When the *Canadian Pacific Railway first built its line through the Rockies in the 1880s, it avoided tunnelling. Later, to increase efficiency tunnels became necessary. The famous twin Spiral Tunnels in Kicking Horse Pass were opened in 1909. In order to reduce excessive gradients, the CPR also built the 8-km Connaught Tunnel under Rogers Pass in 1916. In 1988 the CPR opened the 14.7-km Mount MacDonald Tunnel to further improve this route.

Canadian railways have built short tunnels to give better rail access to urban areas. The first tunnel in Canada was built by the Brockville and Ottawa Railway under the city of Brockville so that trains could get from the railway yards behind the city down to the waterfront. The 518-m tunnel, which opened in 1860, is still in existence. Similar tunnels were built in Quebec City, Montreal, and Vancouver.

The first major tunnel for automobiles was the Detroit–Windsor Tunnel underneath the Detroit River. When it opened in 1930, it was only the third automobile tunnel in North America and one of the very few international tunnels. The six-lane, 1.4-km Lafontaine Tunnel (1967) was built to link Montreal Island to the south shore of the St Lawrence. Short tunnels have been built to increase traffic flow in major urban areas by going under built-up areas or to carry traffic under canals and railway yards.

Another major use for tunnels is for subway lines in major urban areas. The first subway in Canada opened in 1954 in Toronto. Only the downtown section is underground, the rest is on the surface like a standard electric railway. However the Montreal Metro, based on the one in Paris, is entirely underground. Since its opening in 1966, the Montreal system has been extended to 66 km. Other Canadian cities such as Vancouver, Edmonton, and Calgary have rapid transit systems that go underground only near the city core. LARRY McNALLY

Tupper, Sir Charles (1821–1915), prime minister 1896. Descended from prominent *Loyalists and *New England Planters, Tupper studied at Horton Academy in Wolfville, Nova Scotia, then at the University of Edinburgh, where he took a medical degree in 1843. After practising in Amherst, Cumberland County, he entered Nova Scotia politics as a Conservative in the mid-1850s and immediately assumed a prominent role in the party. The Conservatives held office tenuously in the late 1850s; under Tupper's leadership they won a more decisive victory in 1863. He implemented expansive railroad and education policies and advocated intercolonial union, initiating the call for the conference in Charlottetown that eventually led to Confederation. He was one of the principal authors of the political and constitutional framework enshrined in the *British North America Act.

His role in national politics spanned more than 30 years. He served as principal regional counsellor to John A. *Macdonald and held several key cabinet posts, including a brief stint as prime minister in the dying days of two decades of Conservative rule in 1896. He sought to protect Canada's economy and especially the Maritime fishery from the United States, at the same time advancing the idea of a co-dependent empire, arguing that British military and diplomatic power was central to maintaining Canadian independence. As high commissioner to Britain throughout much of the 1880s, he was a stalwart advocate of Canada's interests. Defeated in 1896 he led the party in opposition until 1900. He died in England. D.A. MUISE

'20th century belongs to Canada'. 'I think that we can claim that it is Canada that shall fill the 20th century', boasted Prime Minister Wilfrid *Laurier in an 18 January 1904 address before the Ottawa Canadian Club. Laurier's optimism was not unfounded: immigrants were peopling the Prairies, industries were running full steam ahead, and the government had committed itself to supporting the construction of not one but two more transcontinental railways. Of course, the 20th century did not belong to Canada; it belonged to the United States. Nonetheless, the century was not unkind to Canada. The United Nations and the Organization for Economic Co-operation and Development have consistently placed Canada atop their lists of key economic, demographic, and social indicators. In this sense, the 20th century belonged to Canadians. DONALD WRIGHT

Two Solitudes. Published in 1945, Hugh *MacLennan's second novel focuses on Athanese Tallard, a reasoning, passionate man whose mind constantly thinks of the future, not the past, of his culture. In the Quebec village of St-Marc-des-Érables his opponent is Father Beaubien, who embodies the traditional, agrarian, authoritarian Catholic Quebec. When the setting moves to Montreal, Athanese strives to assist English financiers, only to see them desert him and negotiate directly with the local bishop. Despite his vision of a peaceful Canada with French and English united through understanding, Athanese belongs to the old world; he must be content to remain a prophet, a voice of intelligence ahead of his time. Athanese's son Paul and Paul's beloved Heather Methuen become the hope for Canada. Addressing the central problem of the nation, the dialectic between the French and the English, the novel offers a happy resolution to the national tension.

As his epigraph makes clear, MacLennan drew his title from Rainer Maria Rilke's reflection: 'Love consists in this, that two solitudes protect, and touch, and greet each other'. The phrase 'Two Solitudes', in contrast, entered Canadian vocabulary as an expression for the inability to connect across the two national languages. DAVID STAINES

Tyrrell, Joseph Burr (1858–1957). Born in Weston, Ontario, the son of a wealthy stonemason, Tyrrell did well at the University of Toronto despite poor eyesight and impaired hearing. He left geology to study law, but after becoming sick he decided to take a job working outdoors with the *Geological Survey of Canada. As a field assistant in 1883, he explored large areas of western Canada. The following year, he led an expedition to study coal resources near present-day Drumheller. Using rather primitive techniques, he and his assistants collected the first *dinosaur skull in Canada. It took a week to take the specimen by wagon across the unbroken prairie to Calgary. In Ottawa, it was studied by some of the most famous paleontologists of the era. In 1905, the year Alberta became a province, the dinosaur from which the skull came was named *Albertosaurus*. Although Tyrrell never worked on significant fossils again, he became famous for his exploration of northwestern Canada. Moving to Dawson City during the *Klondike gold rush, he eventually became president of the Kirkland Lake gold mine. In Alberta and British Columbia, Mount Tyrrell, Tyrrell Creek, Tyrrell Lake, and the Royal Tyrrell Museum of Palaeontology were named after him.

PHILIP J. CURRIE

Ukrainians. Ukrainian immigration to Canada has occurred in four waves. The largest, 1891–1914, brought 170,000 peasants from the Russian Empire and Austria-Hungary (especially Galicia and Bukovyna). Poverty and land congestion following the abolition of serfdom, plus national oppression, spurred emigration. Lured by Canadian officials seeking experienced farmers, most settled in the prairie West, establishing informal blocs marked by a distinct agricultural lifestyle, folk traditions, and architecture. Male labourers on resource frontiers, railway gangs, and construction projects, as well as female domestics and waitresses, created Ukrainian pockets in urban centres, northern Ontario, the Rockies, and Cape Breton Island. Another 68,000 individuals arrived in the 1920s, when the Railways Agreement solicited prairie farmers, agricultural labourers, and domestics from 'non-preferred' countries in eastern Europe; interwar immigrants also included intellectuals, professionals, and political émigrés. Again they came primarily from western territories, at the time divided among Poland, Romania, and Czechoslovakia; the new Soviet state absorbed the larger east. The third wave, 1947–54, comprised 34,000 *displaced persons forced to work in Nazi agriculture or industry, who chose resettlement abroad over repatriation to the Soviet Union, which then controlled all Ukraine. Highly politicized, socio-economically and geographically diverse, some two-thirds chose Ontario or Quebec, many initially contracted to northern resource towns or hydroelectric projects. Changes in eastern Europe in the 1980s and 1990s inaugurated a fourth wave, still in progress. The major sources were Poland, thanks to the Solidarity movement; Yugoslavia, dominated by Bosnian refugees; and Ukraine itself, particularly after independence in 1991. As the 20th century closed, Ukrainians, overwhelmingly native-born, resided across Canada, although the Prairies, where they constituted one-tenth of residents, remained their heartland. Ontario and Alberta were favoured provinces, Edmonton, Winnipeg, and Toronto favoured cities. In 1996 over a million Canadians reported Ukrainian ancestry (331,680 single origin, 694,790 multiple origin); 3.6 per cent of the population, they formed the third largest 'non-charter' immigrant group.

Welcomed for their labour but criticized for their peasantness, clannishness, and Ukrainian consciousness, Ukrainians endured Anglo-Canadian prejudice and assimilatory pressures. During the Great War, when unnaturalized subjects of Austria-Hungary became enemy aliens subject to registration, restrictions, and internment, approximately 5,000 (of 8,529) detainees, most unemployed workers, were Ukrainians. During the Second World War, Ukrainian loyalty was again questioned, as pro- and anti-communist factions contended with the Soviet Union, first as Canada's foe and then its ally, and with Hitler's contradictory policies for Ukraine. The Cold War legitimized the agenda of nationalist Ukrainians and ostracized communists. Decreasing socio-economic and cultural differences encouraged and reflected ongoing integration. After 100 years, ethnicity little affected younger generations, who spanned the occupational spectrum and voted like others of their class or region.

Political representation beyond the local level began with the election in 1913 of Andrew Shandro (Liberals) to the Alberta legislature; the first member of Parliament was Pennsylvania-born Michael Luchkovich (United Farmers of Alberta) in 1926. Both represented heavily Ukrainian constituencies. No Ukrainian received prestigious Senate or cabinet appointments until the 1950s, evidence of persisting prejudice and imperfect integration. Stephen Juba (Winnipeg) and William Hawrelak (Edmonton) have been prominent Ukrainian-Canadian mayors; Roy Romanow was premier of Saskatchewan (NDP), 1991–2001; and in 1990 Ramon Hnatyshyn became the second non-British, non-French *governor general. Over the decades Ukrainian-Canadian politicians and community activists have lobbied for a variety of causes: state bilingual schools, support for Ukraine, admission of Ukrainian displaced persons, federal *multiculturalism, and redress for *wartime internment.

Religion has been a defining feature of Ukrainian-Canadian life. Emigration magnified Galician (Byzantine-rite Catholic) and Bukovynian (Orthodox) confessional differences, temporarily legitimizing Roman Catholic and Russian Orthodox missionary activity, and permitting proselytization by Anglo-Protestant Methodists and Presbyterians. The Ukrainian Catholic Church acquired an independent hierarchy in 1912; six years later individuals disturbed by its centralization and latinization established the rival Ukrainian Orthodox Church. Their popularity peaked in 1941, when 50 per cent of Ukrainian Canadians reported Ukrainian Catholic and 29.1 per cent Ukrainian Orthodox affiliation. Once pivotal to preserving language, culture, and ethnic identity, the two churches have lost members. By 1991 under 10 per cent of multiple-origin Ukrainians, the product of increasing intermarriage, belonged; among single-origin Ukrainians,

23.2 per cent were Ukrainian Catholic and 18.8 per cent Ukrainian Orthodox.

Beginning in the 1920s the Ukrainian-Canadian community was ideologically polarized around nationalists and communists operating through nation-wide organizations. Communists supported exploited workers and farmers under Canadian capitalism and the Soviet regime in Ukraine. Popular because of the Great Depression, they were hurt by Stalinist excesses in the homeland, opposition from the third immigration, the Cold War, and the fall of the Soviet Union. Today their remnants stress social justice and world peace. Nationalists coalesced around Catholic and Orthodox laity, who desired integration into Canadian society, retention of their language and culture, and sovereignty for Ukraine, and second-wave monarchists and republicans from Ukraine's failed revolution, whose first priority was the homeland. In 1940, to aid Canada's war effort, nationalists formed a coordinating superstructure, the Ukrainian Canadian Committee (now Congress); augmented by organizations from the third wave and Canadian born, it became the group's 'official' voice. Although most Ukrainian Canadians have never belonged to community organizations, their sympathies have been broadly nationalist and in 1991 they celebrated Ukraine's freedom and the centennial of their own settlement in Canada.

Ukrainian-Canadian identity remains strong and on the Prairies has infiltrated mainstream culture. Onion dome churches and the paintings of William Kurelek epitomize the settlement era, a regional music combines country and Ukrainian folk elements, and towns like Vegreville with its gigantic Easter egg boast Ukrainian tourist attractions. Contemporary Ukrainian-Canadian symbols are largely non-linguistic, with food and dance most popular; the latter involves thousands of participants across Canada, including semi-professional ensembles that perform experimental as well as folk pieces and tour both nationally and internationally. The pagan-Christian practices of peasant life have disappeared, but other traditions persist in personal rites of passage, religious holidays, and, for the organized community, commemoration of homeland events. FRANCES SWYRIPA

ultramontanism. Of medieval origin, 19th-century ultramontanism stressed the pope's absolute power within the *Roman Catholic Church, the latter's autonomy from the state or primacy in common areas of jurisdiction, as well as standardized Roman religious practices and education. In Canada the church as a whole was ultramontane; its keenest advocates were Bishops Michael Anthony *Fleming of St John's (1792–1850), Ignace *Bourget of Montreal (1799–1885), and Louis-François Laflèche of Trois-Rivières (1818–98). The hierarchy, except for two Maritime bishops, were early champions of papal infallibility, which the First Vatican Council (1869–70) proclaimed a dogma of faith. They promoted denominationally-exclusive social relations in education, marriage, and associational life. Although supporters of industry and material progress, they endorsed the *Syllabus Errorum* (1864), Pius IX's condemnation of modern ideas including *liberalism and rationalism. They did not question Bourget's censure in 1869 of the *Institut canadien, a literary society and hotbed of liberalism, or his refusal to give a deceased lifelong member, Joseph Guibord, a Catholic burial. The *Guibord affair led to a protracted legal challenge and decision in 1874 by the highest court in the empire ordering Bourget to permit his burial in a Catholic cemetery.

Dissent erupted in Quebec not over ultramontanism as a pervasive religious outlook, but its application. Bourget became disillusioned with political leaders' failure to uphold what he regarded as the church's higher interests. He encouraged lay professionals, many intimately involved in his struggles against powerful foes, to publish the *Programme catholique* in 1871. Viewing politics exclusively in ideological terms, the manifesto neither unconditionally supported an established party nor advocated a Catholic one as opponents charged. Rather, through independent journalism and political action under church sponsorship, it sought to fashion a Catholic rights lobby on recent controversies, including Louis *Riel's amnesty and the *New Brunswick schools question. With Rome's support, political and church leaders accustomed to quiet diplomacy marginalized this potentially populist and nationalist movement. Bourget was retired in 1876, his only episcopal ally, Laflèche, reined in by Bishop George Conroy, apostolic delegate to Canada (1877–8). When Laflèche persisted in disrupting relations with political leaders, Rome punished him by dividing his diocese in 1884. Lacking episcopal support and clear direction, the Programmistes became a restless rump within a fractious Conservative Party. Denouncing politics as corrupt and unprincipled, *Le Pays, le Parti, le Grand Homme*, a pamphlet published in 1882 under the pseudonym Castor (Senator F.X.A. Trudel and the priest Alphonse Villeneuve), expressed their profound alienation. Although individual Castors would exert influence in forming the Parti national after Riel's hanging in 1885 and in the *Manitoba schools question, the movement was already a spent force. Yet, its legacy of independent journalism and political action, represented in the 20th century by Henri *Bourassa, would remain. ROBERTO PERIN

Underground Railroad. One of the most spellbinding periods in the history of African people in the Americas was the era of the Underground Railroad (late 1700s–1860s). Coined in the early 1830s, the term was a metaphor for the series of secret routes used by slaves escaping their masters in the American South to the northern free states and Canada. Its more popular usage, however, referred to the loosely organized network of abolitionists who hid, transported, or otherwise aided escaped slaves on their trip northward to freedom. Once escaped slaves reached a free state, they could receive assistance at 'stations' or safe houses presided over by 'station masters' or abolitionists. 'Conductors' might transport this human 'freight' in wagon compartments or carriages, by boat, or on actual trains. Some escapees were disguised as slaves travelling with their masters, who were actually Underground Railroad activists. Men dressed as women, women as men, and light-skinned Blacks might be disguised as white slave-owners to throw the slave catchers off the scent. Some ingenious freedom-seekers even had themselves boxed in crates and shipped northward on trains.

Whether or not they later received organized assistance, slaves usually had to escape their masters and make their way through dangerous slave territory completely on their own, fighting hunger and cold, and evading vigilantes. To avoid recapture, fugitives hid by day and travelled only by night, following the 'drinking gourd' (Big Dipper and North Star). Given the tremendously arduous and perilous journey, most of the fugitives—about 80 per cent—were men. It was far more risky for women, particularly if accompanied by children, to escape successfully.

Upon reaching freedom in Canada, a number of brave individuals risked their lives to return and conduct others out of bondage. Perhaps the best-known conductor was Harriet Tubman. After successfully escaping from Maryland, Tubman took an estimated 19 trips back into slave territory and rescued 300 people. Although a wanted woman, she was never caught. At least 30,000 Blacks reached Canada as a result of the Underground Railroad.

ADRIENNE SHADD

Underhill, Frank Hawkins (1889–1971), historian, political commentator, social critic. Born in Stouffville, Ontario, Underhill served in the British, then briefly the Canadian, army during the First World War, and taught history and political science at various universities. He was a public intellectual, involved in left-wing activities in the interwar years. He wrote for **Canadian Forum* and served on its editorial board. In 1932, he founded, along with Frank *Scott, the *League for Social Reconstruction, which served as a think-tank for the *Co-operative Commonwealth Federation. Underhill drafted the party's platform, the *Regina Manifesto, and was one of the authors of the LSR's socialist study, *Social Planning for Canada* (1935). In 1940–1, he was threatened with dismissal from the University of Toronto for his anti-British imperialistic and socialistic views. He faced down the challenge in a landmark case that identified him as a champion of *academic freedom. By the 1940s, he had abandoned his leftist position, becoming an admirer of Liberal leaders Mackenzie *King and Lester *Pearson. Internationally, he uncritically supported American foreign policy in the Cold War. Still, he continued his tradition as an outspoken critic. He published several collections of essays including *In Search of Canadian Liberalism* (1960) and *The Image of Confederation* (1964).

R. DOUGLAS FRANCIS

unemployment insurance. UI represented the federal government's most important response to the *Great Depression, even though it was enacted only when the Second World War began. Throughout the 1930s Ottawa had insisted that relief of the jobless was primarily a local responsibility. This policy evasion bankrupted hundreds of municipalities as well as four provinces, and condemned hundreds of thousands of Canada's jobless to uncertain and woefully inadequate levels of support. The Conservative government of R.B. *Bennett did attempt to pass an unemployment insurance act in 1935, but the legislation was ruled unconstitutional because consent of the provinces had not been obtained. Mackenzie *King, winner of the 1935 election, promised that his Liberal government would enact a constitutional scheme. Over the next four years, though, King delayed acting as long as unemployment and budget deficits remained high. War galvanized King into action. UI became an essential tool for alleviating public fears about another depression when the war ended. By linking UI to the war effort King also dissolved lingering provincial opposition to the scheme. The 1940 Unemployment Insurance Act represented the only exclusive transfer of jurisdiction from the provinces to Ottawa in Canadian history. UI also signaled the arrival of a new activist federal role in social policy, which would be reinforced by the creation of universal family allowances in 1945 and old age security in 1951.

UI had its limitations. The 1940 legislation covered only 42 per cent of the workforce. Built around an insurance metaphor, UI concentrated only on the 'good risks'. Seasonal workers and domestic servants were left uncovered. So too were married women, since UI was designed to reinforce the male 'breadwinner ethic'. Benefits also mirrored the inequalities of the marketplace, not family need. Despite these limitations, UI became a keystone of the post-war Canadian *welfare state and helped to solidify the Liberals' hold on power. As King sagely told his cabinet in arguing for UI, '[I am] anxious to keep Liberalism in control in Canada, [and] not let third parties wrest away from us our rightful place in the matter of social reform'.

JAMES STRUTHERS

Uniacke, Richard John (1753–1830), lawyer, office-holder, farmer. Irish-born Uniacke came to Nova Scotia in the mid-1770s. After flirting with sedition early in the American Revolution, he retreated to political orthodoxy and in 1781 emerged, through family influence, as solicitor general of Nova Scotia. Uniacke excelled as a lawyer, building up the largest legal practice in the colony; he also gathered lucrative fees from his position as officer of the Vice Admiralty Court, which controlled the confiscation and sale of enemy goods during the long war against France and later the United States. Wealth, wit, and gregariousness made Uniacke hugely popular in Halifax high society. After 1800, as the influence of rival American-born Loyalists waned, he moved to the forefront of Nova Scotia's ruling oligarchy. Although he had become an arch-Tory, critical of democracy and religious dissent, Uniacke supported innovations such as abolition of slavery, free trade within the empire, and the political integration of British North America. He also championed agricultural improvement, and his estate at 'Mount Uniacke' became a showpiece of innovation and extravagance.

D.A. SUTHERLAND

unification of Canadian forces. A uniquely Canadian experiment in a single-uniform armed force lasted from 1967 to 1985. Unification grew out of a search for economy and the frustration of successive defence ministers due to inter-service rivalry and the conflicting priorities and practices of Canada's navy, army, and air force. In 1922, George Graham merged separate Militia and Naval Service departments into a single Department of National Defence and promised a 'snappy' and economical result. In 1946–54, Liberal Brooke *Claxton unified the forces' military law and *military colleges, but the Cold War mobilization deterred progress. In 1957–62, the Conservatives merged medical, dental, and chaplains' services, but lacked a coherent defence policy. Rival services acquired weapons systems requiring nuclear warheads and ignored orders during the *Cuban missile crisis. Victorious in 1963, Lester *Pearson's Liberals promised a searching review of security policy and chose Toronto businessman Paul Hellyer as defence minister. Hellyer's 1964 report featured adjectives like 'mobile', 'flexible', and 'imaginative' and favoured *peacekeeping. One line promised 'a single unified defence force'. A few months in office wrestling with three service chiefs, scores of lobbyists, and 200 inter-service committees convinced Hellyer. On 7 July 1964, he merged separate service establishments at National Defence Headquarters; 11 months later, six functional commands replaced all navy, army, and air force commands. On 1 May 1966, army camps, air force stations, and the navy's land-based ships became 39 Canadian Forces bases.

Many officers favoured integration but expected Hellyer to cool plans for unification. However, Hellyer's choice as the first chief of defence staff, General Jean-Victor Allard, endorsed unification as a means to eliminate some British traditions and strengthened the minister's resolve. Protests by senior officers ended in their early retirement. Tories forced a long rancorous debate over Hellyer's reorganization, but Social Credit and the NDP backed the Liberal plan in 1967. In 1968, Canadian Forces members appeared in new green uniforms, modelled on those of the United States Air Force.

It was largely appearances that changed. Old rivalries reappeared in the new 'environments'. Hellyer promised more spending on weapon systems as a reward for accepting change, but inflation and procurement delays devoured savings from unification. When Pierre Elliott *Trudeau, not Hellyer, replaced Pearson, he cut Canada's NATO contribution in half, ordered the Canadian Forces to become functionally bilingual, and promoted 'civilianization', policies that increased civil service influences and administrative policies within the forces. Insiders regarded this as a more fundamental change than Hellyer's unification.

Back in power in 1984, Progressive Conservatives kept an old promise to restore three distinct service uniforms. Functional integration remained, but separate maritime, land forces, and air commands soon emerged in Halifax, Montreal, and Winnipeg. In 1995 they moved to Ottawa. In the 1990s, Canada's three services were largely restored. The integration experiment was imitated, with variations, by most of Canada's NATO and Commonwealth allies.

DESMOND MORTON

Union Bill, 1822. A British proposal to reunite Upper and Lower Canada to the grave detriment of French-Canadian political power. It was introduced by the British government on the assurance of agents of Montreal's anglophone merchant community that it would not be opposed. Widespread opposition in both colonies prompted the bill's withdrawal. In Lower Canada, Britain's move to repeal the *Constitutional Act, 1791, without prior consultation rallied francophones behind Louis-Joseph *Papineau and the Parti patriote; in Upper Canada it boosted the growth of a provincial political consciousness. It also evoked the earliest extant statement in both colonies of a 'compact theory' of the Constitutional Act. This idea bore connotations of local autonomy that were to find expression decades later in the *compact theory of Confederation. PAUL ROMNEY

Union government. In 1917 Robert *Borden's Conservative government was highly unpopular. Its war policies had irritated many Canadians, and scandals gave the Liberal opposition easy targets. When the war began Borden had promised no *conscription and had reiterated that pledge until the fall of 1916. The war itself was going badly, and Canadian casualties exceeded enlistments. In spring 1917 Borden travelled to Britain, where he learned that the Germans were to make their greatest assault on western lines that summer as the Russians left the war and the unprepared Americans entered. The Canadian victory at *Vimy Ridge moved him deeply, and he returned to Canada determined to introduce conscription in order to maintain full Canadian strength at the front.

Having announced his intention to introduce conscription, Borden asked Sir Wilfrid *Laurier and the Liberals to join with him in a 'Win the War' coalition. Laurier hesitated briefly but then said no. Borden then began to seek out other Liberals to join a new government committed to full prosecution of the war. His pursuit of these Liberals was considerably assisted by the *Wartime Elections Act, which deprived citizens of enemy birth naturalized after 31 March 1902 from voting unless they had a son, grandson, or brother in the military. The Military Voters' Act had already assisted the pro-war faction. On 12 October 1917 a coalition 'Union Government' was announced, with significant Ontario and western Canadian Liberal representation. It was overwhelmingly British Canadian in composition.

Borden called an election for 17 December. The campaign was bitter. A German-Canadian crowd in Kitchener, Ontario, prevented Borden from speaking. The Unionists did not campaign in French Quebec. The result was an overwhelming Unionist victory, but the coalition lost every francophone seat decisively. The country divided bitterly.

Unionism did not survive the war. The Liberals returned to their old party, where German, French, and some other groups joined them. The Conservative Party was the major victim of the coalition Borden created to continue the war. JOHN ENGLISH

Union nationale. This political party, which emerged in Quebec during the Great Depression of the 1930s, resulted from the merger of the provincial Conservative Party, led by Maurice *Duplessis, and the Action libérale nationale, a new party of dissident provincial Liberals led by Paul Gouin, the son of a former Quebec premier. The goal was to defeat the Liberal Party, which had been in power since 1897. In 1935, Duplessis became leader of the Union nationale and won the 1936 election, becoming Quebec premier. Once in power, the Union nationale did not implement several key reforms promoted by the ALN, including the nationalization of electricity. In 1939 it lost to the Liberals, who campaigned on the *conscription issue, reminding francophones that Liberals were their best insurance against forced overseas service.

The Union nationale regained power in 1944 and kept it until 1960. A right-wing conservative party, it came to dominate the political scene as party organizers such as Gérard Martineau, party treasurer, and Joseph-D. Bégin transformed it into a powerful political machine. It remained an important vehicle for conservative and nationalist supporters throughout the 1960s, regaining power in 1966 under Daniel Johnson, who was succeeded by Jean-Jacques Bertrand until he lost power in the 1970 provincial election. Despite a comeback in 1976, the Union nationale would quietly disappear.

MARCEL MARTEL

unions. Organizations of wage earners intended to promote solidarity among their members, to better their terms and conditions of employment, and, often, to bring about supportive government action. The first in Canada were craft unions to protect apprenticeship and work practices in specific trades and often to run mutual-benefit funds. They insisted that only union members should practise the craft. In the 1850s, many of these local unions began to join larger 'international' unions in the United States, eventually affiliated with the *American Federation of Labor (AFL), to establish common standards of employment across North America for each craft. They also co-operated across occupational boundaries in local trades and labour councils, the national Trades and Labor Congress (TLC) of Canada (founded 1886), and, by the First World War, a few provincial federations. Challenged by employers, who wanted to reduce their reliance on skilled men, craft unions resisted any changes they believed would disrupt work routines, lower wages, or threaten unemployment. By the turn of the century, most shared the AFL's cautious industrial-relations strategy of stable, orderly collective bargaining with signed contracts, but few industrialists were interested. By the 1920s, craft unions had been driven out of most workplaces other than printing and construction.

Some labour organizations had tried recruiting all workers in one workplace, an approach eventually known as industrial unionism. In the 1880s the American-based *Knights of Labor chartered some all-inclusive 'local assemblies' of factory workers. In coal-mining communities, unions of skilled hewers founded in the 1870s (notably the Provincial Workmen's Association in Nova Scotia) were including most mine workers by the turn of the century. In western Canada, more radical variants appeared, notably the *Industrial Workers of the World (founded 1905) and the *One Big Union (1919). Employers and the state defeated these radical organizations with the help of craft unionists. New centres of industrial unionism emerged between the wars: the All-Canadian Congress of Labour (ACCL) (founded 1927), the Communist-led *Workers' Unity League (1930–5), and, finally, after 1935, the Canadian branches of the Committee for Industrial Organization (renamed the Congress of Industrial Organizations when it was expelled from the AFL in 1937 and the TLC in 1939). These organizations reached out primarily to blue-collar workers in mass production, resource industries, and transportation, but in Canada they had limited success before the Second World War. In 1940 the ACCL united with the Canadian CIO unions to create a new national centre of industrial unionism, the Canadian Congress of Labour (CCL), with its own local and provincial branches. Another source of tension came from a brand of conservative unionism sponsored by the Catholic Church in Quebec, with both craft and industrial branches under close clerical control. After 1921 they had a labour central known as the Confédération des travailleurs catholiques du Canada.

Until the Second World War, most unions in Canada did not last long as effective organizations. Many employers not only broke strikes, blacklisted activists, and maintained espionage networks on the shop floor, but also set up company welfare programs to win their workers' loyalty. In the 1920s and 1930s some also experimented with more direct alternatives to unions in the form of industrial (or works) councils of elected workers and management representatives, or in the later 1930s with employee associations backed by employers and generally known as 'company unions'. The state was rarely sympathetic either. Aside from the Trade Unions Act of 1872, which had decriminalized unions, governments introduced no legislation to protect unions. Courts were generally hostile, and strikers frequently faced police or militia. Some unionists believed workers had to elect their own representatives to legislatures, but labourist, socialist, and communist candidates had limited electoral success.

In the 1930s, renewed labour militancy prompted some provinces to introduce relatively weak collective-bargaining legislation. Then, in 1944, a large strike wave and the soaring popularity of the social democratic Co-operative Commonwealth Federation prompted the federal Liberal government to introduce a wartime measure known as PC 1003, modelled to some extent on the 1935 American Wagner Act. It enabled unions to be certified as legal bargaining agents by labour relations boards and compelled employers to negotiate with such unions. Post-war provincial and federal labour legislation made this industrial-relations model permanent. Unions thus got more legal rights, but also the responsibility to keep their members from striking while collective agreements were in force. Their activities became more legalistic and bureaucratic.

During the war, many craft unions had opened up to less skilled members, and their differences from industrial unions had diminished. In 1956 the TLC and the CCL merged to form the *Canadian Labour Congress (CLC). Many unionists continued to believe that they needed to engage in politics as well and helped to found the New Democratic Party in 1961 and support it in subsequent decades. In Quebec the Catholic unions had also become steadily more like other labour organizations and shed their religious affiliation in 1960 to become the *Confédération des syndicats nationaux. Thereafter, along with branches of mainstream unions in the province, they plunged into support for Quebec nationalism.

In the 1960s white-collar workers finally became unionists. Most public sector workers had turned their old employees' associations into more effective unions and over the next decade won collective-bargaining rights. Although some were denied the right to strike, others, including a province-wide *'Common Front' in Quebec in 1972, waged long, bitter strikes. By the early 1980s public sector organizing had pushed union membership in Canada up to 40 per cent of the non-agricultural workforce, and their unions made up half the CLC membership. They also brought in many more women.

Beginning in the 1970s, unions faced a chillier climate. Employers demanded rollbacks of collective-bargaining victories and used widespread unemployment and the threat of layoffs to curb union demands. Governments passed wage-control programs, particularly aimed at public sector workers, as well as back-to-work legislation and other measures to weaken unions' bargaining power. Unions in various parts of the country responded by working in coalitions with other social movements to protest a broad range of government policies. Since the 1970s, they have also reorganized internally by loosening or completely cutting their links with American unions and by merging many different unions into single large units (such as those that joined the *steelworkers' or autoworkers' unions). Older blue-collar unions have also responded to the decline of employment in their traditional base by reaching out to previously unorganized workers in the private service sector, most of whom remain unorganized. At the close of the 20th century, outside the building-trades organizations, unions typically had large, diverse memberships. CRAIG HERON

See also LABOUR LAW.

United Church of Canada. The United Church of Canada was created on 10 June 1925, a union of the *Methodist and Congregational Churches in Canada, and about 70 per cent of the *Presbyterians. All of these national churches were themselves products of unions among different streams that had occurred in the late 19th and early 20th centuries. In 1968 one section of the Evangelical United Brethren Church also joined the United Church.

The initial union was the culmination of years of discussion among the founding institutions about how best to serve a rapidly changing Canada: immigrants and settlers in the West, growing inner-city population, and overseas missions all needed to be ministered to both spiritually and physically. The church's founders believed they could most efficiently spread the word of God and create 'His Dominion' in Canada by sharing resources. The church's dual goals were well summed up in the name of one of its central departments, 'Evangelism and Social Service'.

The doctrines of the United Church were laid out in the 1925 Basis of Union, elaborated in 1940 by the Statement of Faith. While accepting the guidance of traditional Christian beliefs and considering the Bible a key resource, the church tolerates a wide variety of personal interpretations of Christianity. Generally the United Church is known for its liberal public stance on many social-justice issues, although a more conservative wing also has considerable strength.

The church's governance represents a balance between central authority and congregational autonomy. The highest body is the General Council, which meets every two years; the moderator is elected for the same two-year term. The church began ordaining women in 1936, although there were not a substantial number of women clergy until the 1970s. The first lay moderator was elected in 1968; the first woman moderator in 1980.

Although it is still Canada's largest Protestant church, as with other mainstream churches the number of United Church members, adherents, and worshippers has been declining steadily since the 1960s. In the last decade or so the church has been embroiled in difficult controversies concerning the ordination of homosexuals and the legal claims of Aboriginal peoples who were students in the *residential schools the church ran for many years. Throughout its history, the church's greatest challenge has been to combine its diversity, its social and evangelical impulse, and its desire to be both a united and uniting church. MARY VIPOND

United Empire Loyalists. *See* LOYALISTS.

United Mine Workers of America. Organized in 1890 to represent workers in all branches of the coal industry, the UMWA became one of the largest labour organizations in North America in the first half of the 20th century. Canadian miners originally formed local unions such as the Provincial Workmen's Association (1879) in Nova Scotia and the Miners' and Mine Labourers' Protective Association (1890) on Vancouver Island. After the turn of the century they turned to the UMWA, establishing District 18 (1903) in Alberta and British Columbia (and later Saskatchewan), District 26 (1909) in Nova Scotia (and later New Brunswick), and a short-lived District 28 (1911) on Vancouver Island. Often regarded as a model of industrial solidarity and political activism, the UMWA assisted

Canadian workers in struggles to achieve union recognition and improve wages and conditions. The international union was accused of imposing bureaucratic rule on the districts, and organizations such as the Mine Workers' Union of Canada (1925–36) and the Amalgamated Mine Workers of Nova Scotia (1932–8) offered challenges to the UMWA. Although its numbers have been severely reduced by the decline of traditional underground operations, the UMWA is associated with the lasting importance of unionism in the *coal industry.

DAVID FRANK

United Nations. Conceived as a successor to the *League of Nations, the United Nations was actively supported by the liberal internationalists in the Mackenzie King government. Although Canada did not sit as a permanent member on the Security Council, it played a key role in the UN General Assembly, in the drafting of key articles of the Charter, and in the operation of the UN Relief and Rehabilitation Administration and the UN Economic and Social Council. John Humphrey, a Canadian who served on the UN Secretariat, became the principal author of the 1948 Universal Declaration of Human Rights. Drawing on historical experience, Canadian diplomats such as Lester *Pearson believed that balance of power politics would not maintain international stability; only a viable international organization with the authority to implement collective security could do so. Despite their discourse of liberal internationalism, Canadian officials also pursued national economic self-interest, as reflected in their active support for UN-sponsored negotiations between the wartime allies to create a new international trade organization.

Until the onset of the Cold War in 1947, the Canadian government was cautiously optimistic that the United Nations could be the last best hope to resolve international disputes. Despite the polarization of international politics into two rigid blocs, Canada continued to support UN social and cultural initiatives. Above all, *peacekeeping became Canada's distinctive contribution. Canadian troops deployed under the UN flag during the *Korean War (1950–3) and were a major component of the United Nations Emergency Force (UNEF) created to resolve the 1956 *Suez crisis. Canadian peacekeepers served the UN in New Guinea and Yemen in 1962 and for more than three decades in Cyprus beginning in 1964. Peacekeeping suffered a major setback when Egypt demanded the removal of UNEF troops from the Suez before its 1967 attack on Israel. Canada continued to honour UN requests for peacekeepers; thereafter, however, successive governments paid more attention to UN agencies such as the World Health Organization and the UN High Commission for Refugees.

The commitment to peacekeeping further deteriorated with the Somalian fiasco of the 1990s. Questions have recently been raised in the media about the moral authority of the UN, at least on matters involving dispute resolution among nations. The nomination and likely appointment of Libyan dictator Mu'ammer Gaddafi to the Human Rights Commission and the denunciations of Israel and the United States at the UN-sponsored Durban Conference of Racism (2001) are recent examples of UN failings. Some critics have suggested that Canada reconsider its historic commitment to the UN, strengthen NATO ties, and focus on North American regional security.

The Canadian government's support for UN-sponsored social and cultural initiatives remains strong among liberal internationalists. Throughout the 1990s Canada's ambassador to the UN, Stephen Lewis, worked tirelessly to promote the cause of international children's relief. In 1995 he became head of UNICEF. His next step up the UN ladder was appointment as director of the Joint United Nations Program on HIV/AIDS (UNAIDS). In this capacity he has lobbied for funding to counteract the AIDS crisis devastating many African countries. Ottawa has offered financial support for UNAIDS, and recently gave $4 million as well to the UN Fund for Population and Development. The Canadian government was also actively involved in the World Summit on Sustainable Development (June 2002) and the UN Special Session on Children.

The UN continues to attract modest attention in the Canadian media and on occasion in Parliament. However, the most active support for UN organizations comes from liberal internationalists in the education sector and churches. According to polling data, most Canadians pay little attention to such issues, and Foreign Affairs Minister Bill Graham's announcement of 24 October as United Nations Day generally went unnoticed.

LAWRENCE ARONSEN

United Newfoundland Party. The First World War effectively destroyed the pre-war political party structure in Newfoundland. Parties were replaced by factions that could be roughly characterized as either outport and populist in orientation, or St John's and 'establishment'. After the collapse of the national government in 1919, power alternated between Richard *Squires, who represented the former, and coalitions of St John's-based 'Tories'. In the early 1930s, the Tories began to mobilize against the Squires government, which seemed helpless in the face of the Depression. On 5 April 1932, a march they organized to the legislature turned into a serious riot. An election followed on 11 June. Squires's party was nearly obliterated by a Tory coalition named the United Newfoundland Party, led by F.C. Alderdice. One of its promises was to examine the desirability of government by commission, subject to electoral approval.

The new government proved to be as impotent as its predecessor, and possibly more affected by the prevailing panic. Alderdice cut spending and announced a partial default on debt payments. This prompted the intervention of the British and Canadian governments, and the appointment of a royal commission. The government cooperated, endorsing the *Amulree Report's recommendation that commission government be imposed. Little attempt was made to bargain for terms and conditions, and there was no consultation with the voters. Instead, the recommendation was pushed quickly through the legislature in November 1933, as the British government wanted, and implemented in February 1934. Alderdice was rewarded with a seat on the commission.

JAMES K. HILLER

United Province of Canada. *See* PROVINCE OF CANADA.

United States, Canada's relations with. The Canadian–American border is the world's longest frontier between two countries, stretching for 8,893 km—5,061 km on land and 3,832 km over water. Most Canadians, nine out of ten, live a short distance from the United States, and the ties near 'the line' between the cities, towns, and villages of southern Canada and the northern United States are extensive. More than a quarter of a million North Americans cross the border daily. Each country is the other's best trading partner, and each invests heavily in the other's economy.

Canadians celebrate the border. The staple boast of politicians and publicists for generations has been that the only guards along the frontier are neighbourly respect and honourable obligations, standing as an example to others and a pattern for a harmonious international future. Yet a uniquely peaceable Canadian–American past is pure mythology. From the 1830s to the 1860s there were repeated confrontations and occasional violence along the border. During the American Civil War, 1861–5, Canada built military *fortifications on the frontier. Fear of invasion from the south helped propel the British North American colonies towards Confederation in 1867. The 1871 Treaty of Washington ushered in an era of good relations, but Canada prepared seriously for war as late as 1895, when mother country Britain and the United States jousted over colonial and commercial interests in South America. The United States had armed warships on the Great Lakes at the turn of the 20th century, violating a decades-old disarmament agreement, and the Americans dispatched troops to Alaska in the midst of a spat over the *Alaskan boundary and access to the Yukon goldfields.

The metaphor for the early-20th-century relationship was not a dispute about the boundary but an institution created to watch over the waterways along the border. The International Joint Commission, which had equal numbers of Canadian and American members, began its useful jurisdictional and environmental work in 1912. Its mandate was narrow and its authority limited, but the IJC gave the impression that North Americans did their business in superior ways. Why couldn't other countries get along the way Canada and the United States did?

By the time the IJC came into being, the United States was on its way to becoming a great power and a great friend. But Canadians were determined to remain apart, even as the two countries came together. Canada specialized in moral superiority, which slid easily into anti-Americanism. Wanting to remain British and keep their fragile east–west economy intact, Canadians rejected free trade with the United States in 1911, as they had in 1891. All the while, commercial and cultural ties grew apace. In the 1920s the United States surpassed Britain as Canada's major trading partner and the leading external investor in the Canadian economy. During the same decade, nationalists called on the federal government to protect Canadian magazines and build a national radio network. 'The state or the United States' was the cry of the effective chief lobbyist of the Canadian Radio League, and the *Canadian Broadcasting Corporation provided the desired result.

Military links were few until the Second World War, but then they came with a vengeance. The Permanent Joint Board on Defence was established in 1940 after the fall of France to Hitler, and an intimate military partnership expanded and deepened as the Second World War was replaced by the Cold War. The 1957 North American Air Defence Agreement (NORAD) consolidated the air defences of the continent into a single package, and the Defence Production Sharing Agreements of 1959 and 1963 gave Canadian business access to the US military procurement system. Polls from the 1940s to the early 1960s demonstrated the confidence Canadians had in American policies and leadership. A 1963 survey revealed that 50 per cent of Canadians believed that dependence on the United States was beneficial.

Yet, even in this most pro-American period in Canadian history there was unease about the United States. The report of the Royal Commission on National Development in the Arts, Letters, and Sciences (the *Massey Commission) fretted eloquently in 1951 about the flood of American magazines, broadcasting, and film into Canada, while the mid-1950s Royal Commission on Canada's Economic Prospects, under Walter *Gordon, drew attention to high levels of US investment and extensive American control of Canadian business. John *Diefenbaker rode to power in the federal elections of 1957 and 1958, promising a true north strong and free from the United States. The *Cuban missile crisis and the controversy over the acquisition of nuclear weapons for the Canadian military caused dark days in the relations between Washington and Ottawa in 1962–3.

A 20-year period of scepticism about the United States followed, when Canadians could think that all their long-held stereotypes about America's violence and corruption were confirmed. The Vietnam War led some Canadians (and some Americans) to believe that the US was an evil empire. President John Kennedy, his brother Robert, and Martin Luther King, Jr, fell to assassin's bullets, and racial problems erupted on America's streets and campuses. Richard Nixon was toppled by the Watergate scandal. Ronald Reagan, a tough-talking anti-communist who promised to face down the Soviet Union, was elected president in 1980. In response, the proportion of Canadians who said that Canada and the United States were 'getting further apart' went from 8 per cent in 1966 to 49 per cent by 1982.

Walter Gordon was the personification of a movement aimed at Canadianizing an economy that nationalists claimed had been too long Americanized. The *Trudeau government, aware that it was good politics, promised the *Third Option policy to diversify Canadian trade, ended the privileged perch of *Time* and *Reader's Digest* in the Canadian magazine market, and invented the Foreign Investment Review Agency, Petro-Canada, and the *National Energy Program. During Trudeau's last period in office, some Canadians began to worry about a relationship in disrepair. Enter Brian *Mulroney, whose government's outlook and strategy were very different. The Trudeau package of nationalist reforms was scrapped, and a Canada–US Free Trade Agreement was signed in 1988. Exports to the United States had been a staggering three-quarters of the total, even as Mulroney took office. The FTA was a final recognition of Canada's inevitable destiny as a North American nation.

By century's end, the post–*free trade integration of the two economies gave rise to commentaries on a vanishing Canadian–American boundary. The 11 September 2001 terrorist attacks on New York and Washington, and the subsequent tightening of border security, did not deter North American leaders from regularly insisting that their frontier joined as well as separated them. Speaking in Detroit one year after 11 September, Prime Minister Jean Chrétien enthused about the 'longest undefended border in the world', repeating the ancient and durable cliché that spoke to shared experiences, values, and goals, and to the utter interdependence of the continental relationship. NORMAN HILLMER

United States Civil War. The American Civil War (1861–5) not only consumed more than 600,000 lives and eradicated slavery but also influenced the nature and timing of British North American *Confederation. The doctrine of states' rights, which fed Southern secession, convinced the colonial framers of the British North America Act (1867) to favour a strong central government. The demands of the Northern war economy for raw materials more than countered any temporary disruptions to trade. The abrogation of the 1854 Reciprocity Treaty by a protectionist Congress in 1865 undermined the economic platform of opponents of Confederation, notably in the pivotal New Brunswick election of 1866. The war also encouraged elites to contemplate the economic and constitutional future of Canada and the Maritime colonies in geo-political terms. Britain's policy of official neutrality towards both sides in the American conflict created an awkward situation for its colonies. Animosity and diplomatic conflicts between the Union government and Britain highlighted the strategic and economic vulnerability of the North American colonies. Colonial opinion at first supported President Lincoln's attempts to preserve the Union, but relations soured in late 1861 when the US navy interfered with the British steamer *Trent*. Britain's rushed reinforcement of colonial garrisons underscored the need for an intercolonial railroad. Slavery notwithstanding, many British North Americans sympathized with the Confederacy's military capability and underdog status. The North resented colonial involvement in blockade running and the harbouring of Confederate refugees, and the depredations of the rebel cruiser *Alabama*, built in Britain. Issues directly relating to British North America included the seizure of the Northern steamer *Chesapeake* by New Brunswick supporters of the Confederacy, the Halifax visit of the Confederate commerce raider *Tallahassee*, and a Confederate raid on the Vermont border town of St Alban's in 1864. After robbing three banks and killing one citizen, the Southerners fled into Canada, where they were arrested and examined by a magistrate, but released. The reaction in the Northern states forced the Canadian government to institute controls over aliens. Ironically, although public opinion in the colonies sympathized with the Confederacy, roughly 50,000 BNA-born men served in the Union army and navy against the rebels. GREG MARQUIS

United Steelworkers of America. *See* STEELWORKERS' UNION.

universities. Canada's original universities were founded by religious communities, which required trained ministers and community leaders who could raise the status and disseminate the doctrines of their respective denominations. Advanced education, exclusively for males, was offered first in the Jesuit Collège de Québec (established 1635), the Grand *Séminaire (1663), and the Petit Séminaire (1668). Middle- and upper-class youth seeking general classical training, or certification for the priesthood, attended these institutions. The first degree-granting university, King's College, was founded by Anglican *Loyalists in Windsor, Nova Scotia, in 1789. Modelled on Oxford University, it was expected to train Anglican clergymen who would provide religious and moral leadership to their communities.

Inspired by competing Christian commitments and visions, other universities took root in the 19th century, including McGill (Montreal), Laval (Quebec City), Dalhousie (Halifax), and King's College (Toronto). The University of Toronto began as a non-denominational institution in 1850. Aspiring clergymen, doctors, lawyers, and other 'gentlemen' could enrol in these institutions to receive the classical training, including Latin, that was required for admission to the learned professions. Yet, in 1871, a select group of only 1,561 students attended Canada's 17 universities. The largest, McGill, registered 323; 10 other campuses had enrolments of 50 or fewer.

Traditionally expected to explore the world through the perspective of Christian theology, university students and faculty confronted the intellectual challenge of *Darwinian science in the late 19th century. At first fiercely debated, the idea of evolution was incorporated, along with other scientific subjects, into university curricula by the end of the 19th century. As intellectual agents of 'progress' in an industrializing era, universities soon proposed to serve society in ways that were not exclusively religious. Professional training in medicine, engineering, education, pharmacy, dentistry, social work, and law were situated increasingly in universities. Biblical knowledge and fluency in Latin were no longer the dominant symbols of middle-class respectability, though they were still venerated components of the arts curriculum. The study of

English and modern languages assumed growing importance and was augmented by courses in Western philosophy, political economy, and history. Universities were intent on cultivating among their (mostly male) students esteemed middle-class values that would, they hoped, contribute to the cultural enhancement of Canadian life.

The end of the century also witnessed the admission of women to higher education. Long considered ill equipped for the strains of advanced intellectual life, women had proven themselves in high school, frequently outperforming male classmates and demonstrating their academic potential. The cultural refinement that educated women might bring to middle-class communities further impressed some previous sceptics, as did the example set by American universities, which enrolled women earlier than did their Canadian counterparts. Universities also came to understand the economic advantage of boosting enrolments with female students. Finally, individual women who campaigned persistently for admission to higher education helped to break down the resistance of university authorities. By the end of the 1880s, all English-Canadian institutions admitted women, though not into all professional programs, and full gender equality in universities was still a distant prospect.

The promotion of middle-class ideas constituted the core of the university's mission in the 1920s and 1930s. Drawing students primarily from the families of professionals, businessmen, and white-collar employees, universities were expected to prepare their graduates for respectable social and occupational positions. Fulfilling these expectations in the midst of the Great Depression was challenging, and many students were unable to find professional—or any—work upon graduation, though most did realize their occupational goals over the following two decades.

While attending university, students were exposed to a liberal arts curriculum that combined the elements of genteel culture and utilitarianism. Outside of French Quebec, English was the core subject and featured the literary icons of British civilization. American and Canadian writers received minimal attention. History courses stressed the European and British experiences, but with the growth of Canadian nationalism following the First World War, some influential historians looked more to North America and less to Britain for the sources of Canada's identity and character. The social sciences—psychology and sociology—took root during the 1920s and 1930s, though critics considered these subjects bereft of intellectual and cultural merit and overly influenced by American academic currents. Students in professional courses, the most prestigious of which was medicine, learned to respect the authority of science, specialized knowledge, and the market value of those with professional credentials.

In 1939 university life was disrupted by the Second World War. Educational authorities modified academic programs in order to meet the demands of war. Universities ceded autonomy to the government and favoured the training of doctors, scientists, and engineers over arts graduates. Male students in both secondary and post-secondary schools were required to take cadet and military training, while female students participated in Red Cross activities. Universities conducted war-related research under the direction of the *National Research Council. Freedom of expression, always subject to some limitations in universities, was further constrained by the political environment of the 1930s and 1940s. The RCMP conducted extensive surveillance of students and professors who were considered potentially subversive; academics who publicly questioned Canadian foreign policy, the British connection, or the capitalist system were harassed and in some cases ousted from their universities.

At the end of the war, Canadians turned their attention to family life and the prospects for prosperity and security. The number of marriages reached a historic high in 1946, helping to spawn the *baby boom generation. Thousands of veterans, benefiting from a plan that provided them with free tuition, doubled university enrolments in 1944–8, straining institutional resources. The *Massey Commission (1951) hailed the university's role in the nation's cultural and economic life. The theory of 'human capital', which held that higher education would improve the country's standard of living, underscored this view and was widely embraced. Direct funding to higher education followed, except in Quebec, which regarded Ottawa's financing of universities as an unwarranted intrusion into provincial jurisdiction. The Quebec government's position changed in the 1960s, facilitating the rapid growth of the university sector. In 1964, the federal government introduced a national student loan plan. Provincial funding of higher education, including community colleges, reached unprecedented levels throughout the decade; by 1970 the country had 48 degree-granting universities.

A growing proportion of young people, especially women, participated in higher education. While the full-time enrolment of men rose by 100 per cent between 1960 and 1970, that of women increased by 240 per cent. For their evident contribution to social and economic progress, universities elicited broad public support, and governments were praised for spending bountifully on the system. In the late 1960s, attitudes suddenly changed. Student activists, in Canada and elsewhere, issued sweeping critiques of the social order, including schools and universities. They condemned universities for failing to fulfill their lofty humanistic promises. While boasting of higher education's devotion to *academic freedom, university administrators periodically employed paternalistic rules to deny students freedom of expression. Some university scientists conducted research funded by the American military and were accused of supporting the protracted war in Vietnam. Students called for reformed, 'relevant' liberal arts curricula that addressed social problems.

Faculty, too, wanted a greater say in the governance of universities, a position that was supported in a 1966 study sponsored by the Association of Universities and Colleges of Canada. Cultural nationalists, who were increasingly vocal in this period, criticized the recruitment of large numbers of non-Canadian, particularly American, faculty. Universities, it seemed, were no longer bastions of respectability and consensus. Amid the unrest, some politicians openly questioned the value of the educational investment.

While rejecting the radical ideology of the student movement, universities did make significant changes at the end of the 1960s. Social science and humanities courses now covered a broader range of subjects, including communications, poverty, and developing societies. Canadian themes in history, literature, and sociology courses received increasing attention. Examinations were de-emphasized and campus residence rules were liberalized as students secured more autonomy in both their academic and extracurricular lives. Faculty obtained more power on university senates, higher salaries, and clearer tenure procedures.

From the 1970s on, Canadian universities grappled with a variety of social and economic challenges. Enrolments rose constantly during this period; by 1991, the participation rates in higher education of 18–24-year-old Canadians surpassed those of all Western countries. More women than men enrolled as undergraduates, though the reverse remained true at the graduate levels and women were still a minority in science and engineering.

Notwithstanding the demand for higher education, including a greater interest in part-time learning, funding restraints were imposed on universities and other public institutions by governments reeling from cyclical recessions, ballooning deficits, and a growing intolerance for higher taxes. Universities coped with the problem of inadequate revenue by increasing class sizes, extending their reliance on part-time instructors, and turning to the marketplace for alternative sources of income. The most successful among them secured contracts and partnerships with private corporations, especially in the areas of biotechnology, information services, and microelectronics. 'Strategic' research grants—even in the humanities and social sciences—were targeted increasingly to projects designed to promote employment and economic growth. The relative autonomy that universities traditionally enjoyed was eroded by accountability-driven policies like 'performance indicators', which tied funding to such factors as student satisfaction and the employment rate of graduates. Critics worried about the impact of market-driven educational policies on the tradition of 'pure' scholarship and on the integrity and continuing breadth of the liberal arts. By the beginning of the new millennium, higher education, always exposed to external pressures, was again in transition. PAUL AXELROD

Upper Canada. A political entity created by the *Constitutional Act (1791), and evidently so named because it was located adjacent to the upper reaches of the Ottawa River. In broad terms this new English-speaking colony, which existed until 1841, might be considered a political failure, having begun in the aftermath of revolution (American) and ended in that of rebellion (Canadian). By other measures, however, the nascent community achieved considerable success and held within its borders and collective experience the social and economic nucleus for what would later become the province of *Ontario.

Originally conceived as a refuge for *Loyalists from the American Rebellion, the settlements north of Lakes Ontario and Erie were characterized by an abiding political conservatism in terms of both local and imperial appointments. The Constitutional Act promoted *representative government, but its cautious imperial architects were keen to avoid too much power being given to a local assembly, so there were more checks than balances with hierarchical vetoes designed to truncate popular legislation. Whiggish opposition emerged in the decade before the War of 1812, but the triumphant patriotic fervour that accompanied that conflict ensured the chief definition of loyalty thereafter would be a Tory one. Efforts at political liberalization during the 1820s met sharp antagonism from a tight band of provincial Tories clustered around sympathetic lieutenant-governors who controlled power and patronage. Chief among them was the Anglican archdeacon of York (Toronto), John *Strachan. Their most vociferous critic was journalist-politician William Lyon *Mackenzie, whose frustrations would eventually lead him to sponsor political rebellion in the late 1830s. A more moderate, deliberate, and temperate course was practised by the Toronto Reformer Robert *Baldwin.

Insurgence caused the imperial government to investigate and resulted in the celebrated visit of Lord *Durham to the Canadas in 1838. His report contributed to a change of policy that saw the upper colony reunited with its twin, *Lower Canada, in an imperial act of 1840. But another of Durham's recommendations, *responsible government (where the cabinet is responsible to the assembly rather than to the Crown), long-championed by Baldwin and seen to be the panacea for most of the colony's political ills, would take another decade.

Substantial progress had been made in other directions. Population had grown from a few thousand scattered over a rough uncultivated territory to more than 400,000 people inhabiting growing towns and villages and successfully pushing back the agricultural frontier to its climatic and geological limits. Public works projects such as the Welland Canal and financial organizations such as the gigantic Canada Company projected richer opportunities for the future. But religious factionalism too often blocked educational advance, the presence of the British military provided too much of the social and artistic activity, and even cities such as Toronto lacked the confidence to do anything but ape fashions and traditions from abroad. Nevertheless, the core of a potentially prosperous and successful society had been created.
ROGER HALL

urbanization. Canada's first urban settlement, Quebec City, is almost four centuries old, yet the image the country evokes is still that of an immense, unsettled wilderness. On postcards home, visitors write about the fresh air, the wide open spaces, the clean water, the magnificent natural scenery. Despite its reputation as the world's largest country, however, where wilderness landscapes are commonplace, it is in Canada's villages, towns, and cities that one can best discover the nature of the country.

Urbanization is a complex process that results in increasing numbers of people living in organized human settlements. As urbanization occurs, a society is transformed from one organized around rural activities such as hunting and farming to one organized by urban activities (manufacturing, trading, banking, etc.). A simple measure of this transformation is the proportion of the population living in defined urban areas. This process began early in Canada's history. In 1871 over 18 per cent lived in urban areas; by the 1920s over half the population was urbanized; by 1996 the figure was 78 per cent. It is noteworthy that by 1996 only 2.5 per cent of the country's population was rural farm, a decline from 50 per cent in 1921. Today Canada is one of the most urbanized nations in the world.

Urbanization in Canada has passed through four major phases. The earliest began with the founding of Quebec in 1608. Urban development was mercantile or colonial in nature and was characterized by imperial (French and British) control over location, function, and growth. Functionally, urban places, notably Quebec City, Montreal, Halifax, and St John's, tended to be administrative or military centres. Economically, they were entrepots, collection agencies for colonial staples and distribution centres of manufactured goods from the mother country. The second phase began in the early 1800s and was marked by the increasing control of commercial interests. Interregional trade increased, as did small-scale manufacturing related to the commercial role. The third phase, which began with industrialization in the 1870s and lasted until the 1920s, saw the development of a national urban system that tended to concentrate power in major central Canadian cities, notably Montreal and Toronto. The fourth phase, which began in the 1970s, was characterized by suburbanization and slowing rates of central city growth.

The urbanization process expressed in percentage terms says little about the changes in people's lives. This can be better understood by examining the sizes and distribution of cities and towns. In 1921, Canada had only six cities with populations of 100,000 or more; the average Canadian lived in a village, town, or small city. By 1961, the number of places with over 100,000 residents had grown to 18, and two, Montreal and Toronto, had over a million. By 2000 there were 25 metropolitan regions with over 100,000 residents, four with over a million. The average Canadian now lives, works, and plays in a large urban area, a very different experience from previous generations. Indeed, over 36 per cent of Canadians now live in one of four metropolitan areas—Toronto, Montreal, Vancouver, and Ottawa-Hull. ALAN F.J. ARTIBISE

Ursulines. Founded in Italy in 1534 by Angèle de Mérici, the Ursulines were originally secular, but had to submit to cloistering after the Council of Trent. Established in Quebec in 1639 by *Marie de l'Incarnation, they founded the first boarding school for young women and took charge of teaching the girls of Quebec in a school adjoining the convent. These two institutions are still in existence. For several decades they took Aboriginal students in a 'seminary'. They were supported by land concessions and royal gifts, which they administered successfully. The convent gradually became more 'Canadian' after the end of the 17th century. The Ursulines of Quebec established the foundations of girls' *education in New France: intense religious training, mastery of the French language, and practise of the gentle arts. Among the surviving examples of their many talents are scores of sacred music, paintings on bark, and liturgical decorations. After 1760 they accepted clients of English origin while respecting the boarders' Protestant faith. This strategy ensured the school's material survival. Although their expansion was limited by their status as cloistered nuns, the Quebec Ursulines nevertheless contributed to the foundation of several autonomous convents: Trois-Rivières (1697), Roberval (1882), Stanstead (1884), Rimouski (1908), Gaspé (1924). In 1857 they accepted responsibility for the first teacher's college for women in Quebec. Despite competition from new teaching congregations, they were able to maintain their reputation for excellence, especially in Quebec City. In 1953 new canonical rules changed their status, and all the offshoots of the Quebec City convent were united. Since *Vatican II the Ursulines are no longer cloistered, and they have had to adapt to the province's new social reality. MICHELINE DUMONT

utilities. Utilities are companies that provide basic infrastructure services to the public. In Canada, such companies have supplied water, gas, telegraph, telephone, and, most importantly, electricity to cities and towns, farms and factories. Historically, urban transportation services such as electric railways were considered utilities. Initially, while most utilities were privately owned, over time a large number came to be publicly owned, some by municipal authorities, others by provincial governments. More recently, utilities in some sectors and some parts of the country have been deregulated or privatized.

While much of the initial technological and managerial know-how initially came from the United States, the innovations were adopted, and expanded upon, more quickly in Canada than in Europe. Over time, Canadian utility entrepreneurs and engineers created a niche for themselves in exporting their technological know-how and organizational methods to the rest of the world, especially Latin America and the Caribbean. In particular, the revolution wrought by electricity allowed for cities and factories to be brightly illuminated and powered around the clock. Electric streetcars radiating far from the centre of cities encouraged the urban sprawl that would eventually come to characterize the 'typical' Canadian city. And the emergence of *hydroelectric power, along with the desire to see these utilities operated in the public interest, would create two of the largest public corporations in 20th-century Canada—Ontario Hydro and Hydro-Québec.

Toronto and Montreal were the first cities to undergo extensive electrification. In 1883, J.J. Wright incorporated the Toronto Electric Light Company and tried to win the concession for street lighting from an existing gas company. Wright had previously worked with Professor Elihu Thomson, one of the leading electrical engineers and entrepreneurs in the United States. Although the City of Toronto gave Wright only half a concession, keeping the other half with the existing gas company to hedge its bets, electricity soon proved its superiority. Around the same time, Thomson's American company in association with some prominent Montreal capitalists formed the Royal Electric Company to introduce electricity to the city of Montreal. Royal Electric emulated the much larger Thomson-Houston Electric Company south of the border by manufacturing electric power plants and equipment, and was soon responsible for selling hundreds of small, thermal power plants throughout Canada.

By 1890 electricity had arrived in most Canadian cities in the form of street lighting provided by one or more suppliers as well as hundreds of small, independent thermal plants illuminating individual factories, office buildings, warehouses, and train stations. Electricity was also moving into the hinterland, beginning to illuminate mines, sawmills, and lumber camps. The diffusion of urban railways powered by electricity was more gradual, for two reasons. First, one mile of streetcar track and overhead wire cost about $30,000 in the early 1890s, a huge sum of money at the time. Second, having had the experience of dealing with electric companies and the unsightly, obstructionist, and occasionally dangerous mess they left in terms of overhead poles and wires, city councils were much more cautious in handing out streetcar concessions to utility entrepreneurs. Initially, this meant figuring out both the business and the technology in order to squeeze the best possible service at the lowest cost for residents. Eventually, it would lead many city councils to public ownership of the streetcar companies.

The initial establishment of streetcar operations took two basic forms. In smaller cities such as Vancouver, equipment suppliers such as Thomson-Houston or Royal Engineering could set up the streetcar operations on a turnkey basis. In larger cities experienced railway owners joined forces with local financiers and a key engineer skilled in electric streetcar system–building who was generally from the United States, including H.A. Everett from Cleveland and Dr F.S. Pearson of Boston. Everett worked extensively on constructing the Toronto, Montreal, and Winnipeg streetcar systems in partnership with railway entrepreneurs such as William Mackenzie and Donald Mann (who would eventually establish the Canadian Northern) as well as William *Van Horne and James Ross of the Canadian Pacific Railway.

Fred Stark Pearson would become even better known to Canadian utility entrepreneurs and financiers over time. A professor of engineering at the Massachusetts Institute of Technology, Pearson had worked on two of the larger streetcar construction projects then in existence in the world—the Metropolitan Street Railway in New York and the West End Street Railway in Boston. He worked with another fellow American, H.M. Whitney, to finance and construct an electric railway for Halifax. Then he began to experiment with power generated by water, rather than by thermal plants fired by coal and powered by steam, and to search out interesting utility ventures in other countries, particularly in Latin America and the Caribbean. Both developments were to have a profound impact on utilities within Canada.

By the time hydroelectric power was introduced, Canadians had developed such an expertise in financing, organizing, and running utilities that they began to look abroad for an opportunity to make a profit out of this expertise. Moreover, technical expertise grew rapidly through engineers, with experimentation and results rapidly disseminated through the Canadian Electrical Association, and many were prepared to take on larger challenges outside the country. Starting in the late 1890s these Canadian utility entrepreneurs and engineers, in association with individuals such as Pearson, set up over a dozen utility companies from Spain and England to Brazil, Mexico, and Cuba. Almost all combined electric power generation with urban lighting and streetcar systems. Most of the larger enterprises were built around new hydroelectric projects.

By 1905 these foreign utilities were worth double the nominal capital of all domestic utilities, although some discounting is in order given the extent to which their promoters engaged in stock watering. Some of these enterprises were sold after the First World War, others in the 1920s. Those that survived were part of companies with a strong engineering base in Canada, such as the Montreal Engineering Company, or part of the consolidated holdings that made up the Brazilian operations. A few of the more notable utilities that continued operating after this time were eventually nationalized after the Second World War by governments unhappy with either the level of service or the flow of profits out of their respective countries. Before its sale to the Brazilian government in 1978, Brazilian Traction was the core business of the Canadian *conglomerate known as Brascan.

Within Canada, some utility enterprises also shifted from private to *public ownership during the course of the 20th century. Initially, public ownership was spurred by a negative civic reaction to the high charges and poor services provided by some of the private street railways and power companies. Ontario Hydro was the largest and most notable of this early wave of public ownership but civic ownership of mass transportation in Canada's growing cities became the rule rather than the exception. After the Second World War both federal and provincial governments became more activist and reorganized some utilities into Crown corporations as part of their development strategies. 'Province-building', in particular, relied upon the public ownership of electric power and other utilities. Although by the 1980s these policies, as well as public ownership, began to be criticized, Crown corporations such as Hydro-Québec, Manitoba Hydro, and SaskPower continue to play a major role in their provincial economies at the beginning of the 21st century.

GREGORY P. MARCHILDON

See also INVESTMENT ABROAD.

vaccination. The introduction, orally or by injection, of a vaccine, a liquid preparation of treated disease-producing micro-organisms used to stimulate the production of antibodies, thereby procuring immunity from one or more diseases. Vaccination has been effective in the prevention of such diseases as pertussis (whooping cough), measles, mumps, rubella, hepatitis B, and meningitis. *Smallpox was the greatest success in the history of vaccination. Edward Jenner's use of cowpox vaccine (1796) launched a two-century-long campaign to eradicate smallpox. The World Health Organization's aggressive immunization campaign beginning in 1967 resulted in the eradication of smallpox in 1980.

Although primarily a medical issue, vaccination has significant social dimensions. Because compulsory vaccination is required to secure widespread compliance, civil liberties issues arise: citizens' right to determine the scope and method of their medical treatment conflicts with the state's duty to protect the public good. In Montreal, opposition to vaccination erupted in riots in 1875 and 1885. In early-20th-century Toronto, anti-vaccinationists organized petition drives, mass rallies, and demonstrations to protest the unfair application of vaccination upon poor and immigrant populations. Canada witnessed renewed opposition to vaccination in the 1980s, as the success of immunization led to claims that the side-effects of vaccines outweighed their benefits. The danger remains that when immunization rates drop, entire populations are placed at risk. In the wake of the attacks of 11 September 2001, the issue of vaccination gained renewed currency amidst fears of bio-terrorism. KATHERINE ARNUP

Vallières, Pierre (1938–98). Director of **Cité libre* in 1963–4, Vallières was forced to resign and founded the journal *Révolution québécoise* with Charles Gagnon. In 1965 he secretly joined the *Front de libération du Québec and the following year, in May, was found guilty in a bombing death. His autobiography, *Nègres blancs d'Amérique* (1968), translated as *White Niggers of America* (1971) by Joan Pinkham, was written in a New York prison before he was extradited to Canada to face the charges. In 1970 Vallières was pardoned, and subsequently urged Felquistes to end terrorist action. A journalist at *Le Devoir* and *Le Jour*, 1973–6, he supported the *Parti Québécois but nevertheless declined René *Lévesque's invitation to be a PQ candidate. He became a community worker and, eventually, a gay activist. On his deathbed he wrote that he wanted to 'die a Franciscan', perhaps a flashback to his years (1958–61) as a novice.
RAYMOND HUDON

Vancouver. Located on a mainland peninsula in the southwest corner of *British Columbia, Vancouver was incorporated in 1886 and quickly superseded *Victoria as the province's largest city. With a population of 514,008 (1996), it centres a Greater Vancouver regional district of 1,831,665 people, the third largest urban concentration in Canada. Long before English and Spanish explorers entered the waters around Vancouver in the 1790s Coast Salish peoples had located there, the Musqueam on the north arm of the Fraser River and the Squamish on the shores of Burrard Inlet. Europeans disrupted the Aboriginal way of life when drawn to the area in the mid-19th century, first as gold seekers, then as missionaries, loggers, and sawmill workers. The pace of change accelerated in the 1880s when the CPR chose Coal Harbour, near the entrance to Burrard Inlet, as its western terminus, a choice encouraged by a provincial grant to the railway of more than 25 sq km of land. Local property owners then incorporated the lumber village of Granville as a city and called it Vancouver, a name chosen by CPR executive William *Van Horne to honour the British naval explorer George *Vancouver.

For almost a century Vancouver's growth responded to the rhythm of British Columbia's mining, commercial fishing, and forest industries, with which the city was tied by railways and an excellent harbour, and it quickly emerged as BC's most important management and service centre. Significantly, apart from sawmills and salmon canneries the Vancouver area did not become a centre of factory-based manufacturing. This economic base generated a cyclical pattern of growth and recession that levelled out into a period of sustained expansion only in the 1940s. For the next thirty years, while Vancouver prospered and expanded outward through suburbanization, it remained a small provincial city, in many ways still 'a village on the edge of the rain'.

Substantial change occurred in the 1980s when Vancouver emerged as an international city linked by tourism, finance, and information and cultural networks to Pacific Rim countries in Asia. Vancouver companies extended engineering, management, architectural, and legal services to Asia while Asia-Pacific investors in Hong Kong and Taiwan pumped money into the Vancouver property market. The extraordinary success of Vancouver's 1986 international fair, Expo 86, on the railway and industrial lands along the north side of False Creek in the city's core, greatly increased the flow of Asian capital and led Kong Hong billionaire Li Ka Shing to purchase and then start to develop the False Creek lands into a distinctive neighbourhood of glass residential towers. This 'city of glass' has come to symbolize what Thomas Hutton, in a recent book, calls the transformation of Canada's Pacific metropolis.

Vancouver's reorientation from a regional service centre to a city of international status has been closely tied to immigration from Asia. From the 1880s to the 1970s Vancouver's ethnic composition remained remarkably stable, the vast majority of citizens being white and of European origin. British influence predominated, finding expression in various ways, from the Tudor Revival styles of pre–First World War mansions to the city's many parks and trees. In 1971, 60 per cent of Greater Vancouver's residents still claimed family ancestry in Britain. Until the post-war years the city's white majority expressed its identity through persistent outbursts of racial antipathy towards minorities, the largest of which were *Chinese and *Japanese. Tensions were highlighted by anti-immigration riots in Chinatown and Japantown in 1907, the turning back of South Asian immigrants on the **Komagata Maru* in 1914, and the expulsion of Japanese residents in 1942. While greater tolerance towards minorities and a more open immigration policy in Canada laid the foundation in the 1960s for a more pluralistic city, in 1971 the Asian population still equalled only 5.4 per cent of the total. Since then, Vancouver has become decidedly less British; the Asian portion, led by immigrants from Hong Hong and India, approaches 25 per cent, much more in certain neighbourhoods. Of particular note is the suburb of Richmond, where a second Chinese commercial centre rivals Vancouver's historic Chinatown.

Richly endowed with a mild climate and a magnificent setting, Vancouver is often described as a place less hurried than its eastern rivals, a city where residents take time to enjoy outdoor pleasures such as hiking, skiing, or walks around Stanley Park. Yet today, as Vancouver evolves from urban village to global city, problems of traffic congestion, pollution, and drug abuse are challenging its quality of life and its status as Canada's 'lotusland'.

ROBERT A.J. McDONALD

Vancouver, George (1757–98), British naval explorer. After accompanying Captain James *Cook on two of his epic voyages through the Pacific, Vancouver was given command of his own expedition to the northwest coast of America with orders to survey the shoreline from California to Alaska and to resolve a disagreement with Spain over the ownership of the area. He arrived off the coast in April 1792 in his ship *Discovery*, and spent the next three summer seasons mapping the entire shoreline of what would become British Columbia. His expedition effectively ended speculation about the existence of a *Northwest Passage through North America to the Atlantic and gave Europeans the missing pieces they needed to complete a realistic map of the Pacific basin. Vancouver was less successful on the diplomatic front. Although his relations with the Spanish at *Nootka Sound were cordial, he was unable to resolve the diplomatic impasse. Vancouver arrived back in England in October 1795. He had been in declining health for some time, and he spent his last years preparing an account of his voyage, which was published shortly after his death as *A Voyage of Discovery to the North Pacific Ocean and Round the World*.

DANIEL FRANCIS

Vancouver Island colony. A stroke of the imperial pen brought the colony into official existence on 13 January 1849. This administrative act formalized the changes brought about by territorial expansion and trade since the close of the 18th century. Britain delegated much of its imperial authority to the *Hudson's Bay Company, which was given a monopoly on trade in exchange for settling the island with Europeans.

Imperial visions were challenged and transformed on Vancouver Island's muddy ground. Richard Blanshard, the first governor, quickly quit his post. He was replaced in 1850 by James *Douglas, chief factor of the HBC, governor until 1864. The fur trade remained economically significant throughout the 1850s, as did agriculture, coal mining, forestry, and, most of all, foraging activities. British settlers mixed with French-Canadian, Iroquois, and *Kanaka servants, local Salishan- and Wakashan-speaking peoples, and the Haida, Nisga'a, and Tsimshian who visited the island for trade and wage work. Settlers were a distinct minority, especially outside *Victoria and its neighbouring farming communities, the coal-mining community of Nanaimo, and the British naval base at Esquimalt. In 1855, about 774 settlers, two-thirds of them male, lived among roughly 25,873 First Nations people.

The HBC grant was revoked in 1859. But it was the *Fraser River gold rush of 1858, rather than any official policies, that shifted the course of Vancouver Island's history. In 1858 alone, as many as 30,000 people passed through the colonial capital of Victoria en route to the mainland's diggings. A shifting, largely male diaspora joined the island's already mixed population. Chinatowns took root in the towns, and the African-American population numbered 500–600 in Victoria alone in the early 1860s. Agriculture, lumbering, and the service economy were fuelled by the trade in gold, and the settler population spanned out further across the island. Aboriginal people were a crucial labour force in these new industries, but they would pay dearly for these small opportunities. The *smallpox epidemic of 1862 dealt heavy blows, and, with the exception of those covered by the 14 treaties signed between Douglas and the First Nations in the 1850s, land claims remained unresolved.

The creation of the neighbouring colony of *British Columbia in 1858 indicated the impact of the gold rush, and ultimately facilitated the demise of Vancouver Island as a separate jurisdiction. By the mid-1860s, Victoria was home to fewer than 4,000 souls. The colonial legislature was locked in apparently intractable conflict, and both colonies were mired in crippling debt. In this climate of dashed expectations and dwindling prospects, the two colonies were merged in 1866. The new colony would bear British Columbia's name, much to the eternal chagrin of island loyalists. That it retained the island capital remains a quiet but persistent reminder of Vancouver Island's separate imperial history. ADELE PERRY

Van Horne, Sir William Cornelius (1843–1915). Born at Chelsea, Illinois, Van Horne began his railway career at the Illinois Central Railroad in 1857 and worked for several American railroad companies before being appointed general manager of the *Canadian Pacific Railway in 1882. The most difficult portions of the CPR's transcontinental main line were built under his supervision. While president of the company (1888–99) he expanded its operations to include telegraph, express, steamship, hotel, land development, and mining operations. The company was run efficiently and profitably, but Van Horne did not find the operations as challenging as building the railway had been. He resigned when senior shareholders failed to support his strategy of aggressive competition with rival American railroads.

Van Horne was a multi-talented man. He was an artist and a discerning collector of paintings and Chinese fine porcelain. He remained active in numerous business ventures after 1899, devoting most of his time, energy, and resources to the construction of a major new railway in Cuba. T.D. REGEHR

Vanier, Georges-Philéas (1888–1967), the first French Canadian to become *governor general. Following studies at Loyola College and Université Laval, Vanier was admitted to the Quebec bar in 1911. He enlisted in the army in 1915 and was awarded the Military Cross and the Distinguished Service Order. In 1925 he was named commander of the Royal 22nd Regiment, which he had helped to found. He was a member of the 1928 Canadian delegation to the *League of Nations. He was named secretary to the Office of the High Commissioner in London in 1931, then Canada's minister to France in 1939, and in 1943 minister to all the Allied governments in exile in London. From 1944 to 1959 he was ambassador in Paris. In the course of his mandate as governor general, 1959–1967, Vanier and his wife, Pauline, were particularly interested in the disadvantaged, young people, and the family. Even as the *indepéndantiste* movement was growing in Quebec, Vanier made himself the defender of Canadian unity. CHRISTINE HUDON

Vatican II. The Second Vatican Council, 1962–5, effected liturgical and organizational reforms in the *Roman Catholic Church, promoted ecumenism, and emphasized the role of the laity. Announced on 25 January 1959, it initially provoked more reaction from leaders of the non-Catholic Christian churches than from Canada's Catholic bishops. Obviously Pope John XXIII's initiative took Catholics by surprise.

In the preliminary stages of preparation (1959–60), 88 per cent of Canadian bishops informed Rome of their concerns; these *vota*, without any great originality, did not wish to see the council pass any new condemnations. In the preparatory phase (1960–2) several Quebec bishops undertook to inform the public about the council. With the *Quiet Revolution under way, Quebec dioceses were experiencing a certain ferment, which was relayed by the press. Of the 25 Canadian bishops who took part in the preparatory commissions, Cardinal Paul-Émile *Léger made by far the most important contribution, pleading for a veritable renewal of the Catholic Church in his letter to the pope just before the council opened. From 1962 to 1965 the Canadian bishops played an active role in Vatican II, while religious life in Canada underwent profound changes. Not without several clashes, the liturgical reform, the shift towards ecumenism, and the reform of religious congregations and clergy reshaped Canadian Catholicism. GILLES ROUTHIER

VE Day riots, 7–8 May 1945. While other Canadians celebrated Allied victory in Europe with parades and fireworks, *Halifax marked war's end with a two-day orgy of rioting and looting some called 'the biggest drunk in Canadian history'. In part, the riots were the inevitable result of six tumultuous war years. As the western terminus of the North Atlantic *convoys during the Battle of the *Atlantic, Halifax was, as one British admiral put it, the 'most important port in the world'. But it was ill equipped for its role. The city's population doubled, and people lined up for everything from restaurants to brothels. Thanks to the still-powerful *temperance movement, there were no bars or taverns for thirsty servicemen. War's usual shortages and price gouging only exacerbated tensions between locals and newcomers. When the city's stores, restaurants, movie theatres, and liquor outlets shuttered their premises as soon as the Allied victory was announced, the recriminations began. By the time it ended, 3 were dead, 363 arrested. The liquor stores were emptied, 207 other businesses looted, and 564 more damaged. A royal commission blamed the riots on the local 'Naval Command', ignominiously ending the career of Admiral Leonard *Murray and touching off a who-was-really-to-blame controversy that continues to this day. STEPHEN KIMBER

venereal diseases. The term venereal diseases (VD), and the more modern designation sexually transmitted diseases (STDs), refers to disease that spreads through sexual contact. Although there are about 20 STDs, syphilis and gonorrhea have received the most attention as social threats and are the only ones almost exclusively identified as venereal. Before widespread availability of penicillin in the 1950s, VD was as greatly feared as HIV/AIDS is today. Sufferers faced discrimination similar to that faced by the infected among the modern gay community. It is notable that HIV/AIDS is not included in STDs but is treated as a separate and more shameful illness.

Venereal disease was most probably brought to Canada by early explorers. Syphilis reached epidemic proportions in western Europe during the 1500s; gonorrhea had been endemic in the Mediterranean for centuries. By far the more prevalent, gonorrhea can cause acute local pain, arthritis, and sterility. Children of infected mothers can be born blind. Syphilis can cause skin lesions, embolisms, paralysis, insanity, and death. Children can be infected in utero.

Canada joined with other Western countries in a campaign against venereal diseases (also called social diseases) at the time of the Great War. The new art of statistics revealed that recruits were infected to a degree thought to be socially unacceptable. Feminists and imperialists, obsessed with a perceived need to reproduce the white races, read these VD rates as direct threats to population increase. Canada did indeed have high infant and maternal mortality rates at the time, but these were due more to social conditions and tuberculosis than to VD. Although the main objective of the campaign was sexual continence, treatments for both gonorrhea and syphilis were made publicly available. Gonorrhea was treated largely with salves and irrigations until sulfa drugs were developed in 1932. Syphilis was treated by systemic and extended introduction of arsenic into the body and, in the insane, by intentional infection with malaria. The major side effect of the latter was death due to high fever; the side effects of the former included extreme pain, long-term poisoning, and death from shock. All those attending clinics also risked exposure as immoral. Both diseases were reportable and treatment enforced wherever possible.

Before it could be controlled, VD wreaked terrible damage on Canadians. Yet, the fact that the VD campaign was less about disease control than social control is evident in reformers' rejection of prevention through promotion of condom use, which was seen as damaging to the social fabric. With civilian introduction of a cure, penicillin, at the end of the Second World War, public attitudes towards VD changed. Infection was still socially unacceptable, but the physical consequences became minimal.

JANICE DICKIN

Verchères, Madeleine de (1678–1747). Madeleine de Verchères is renowned for her heroic actions in organizing the defence of the ill-defended family fort at Verchères, to the east of Montreal, against an *Iroquois attack in 1692. Aged 14, she rallied the inhabitants of the fort and displayed tremendous personal courage, firing the cannon and shooting her gun. These are the details she reported in a letter to the wife of the minister of the marine in 1699, thereby securing a pension for her bravery. Later in life, as the wife of the seigneur of Ste-Anne de la Pérade, she continued to display a fierce bravado, sometimes involving herself in conflicts with neighbours and local priests. In the late 19th and early 20th centuries, she came to represent one of the key heroic figures of the country's past, a Canadian Joan of Arc, and became the subject of the first French-Canadian feature film.

COLIN M. COATES

Vertical Mosaic, The. The title of John Porter's classic tome that, in 1965, marked the coming of age of Canadian social science. Subtitled *An Analysis of Social Class and Power in Canada*, this breakthrough book impressed through its original scope, insight, and innovative data analysis. The title refers to the dominance by the two charter groups reinforced by patterns of immigration. In contrast to the image of a US 'melting pot', Porter's findings were of a 'hierarchical relationship between Canada's many cultural groups'. The British charter group dominated all elite groups, especially in the economy, and shared power with the French in the state sector. Non-charter groups were under-represented in elite positions. Ethnicity in Canada was a barrier to access to elite power positions and individual mobility in the class system. Porter challenged the wisdom of 'multicultural' policies that reinforce descent-based social practices like ethnicity, rather than those based on merit and talent. His views were developed in *The Measure of Canadian Society: Education, Equality and Opportunity*, a collection of his articles published shortly after his death in 1979. Colleagues marked an anniversary of his great volume with a collection of articles entitled *'The Vertical Mosaic' Revisited* (1998).

WALLACE CLEMENT

Veterans Charter. The name given to the program, embodied in several statutes and many regulations, of the government of Canada for the veterans of the Second World War. Remembering the bitter and divisive aftermath of the Great War, the government of Mackenzie *King began planning early for post-war re-establishment. A cabinet committee on *demobilization and rehabilitation was formed in December 1939 and PC 7633, the 'Post-Discharge Re-establishment Order', was issued on 1 October 1941. Whereas only disabled veterans and those who had enlisted as minors had been eligible for rehabilitation benefits after the earlier war, PC 7633 promised assistance to all who served in the new war. It also provided that military service would count as insurable employment under the Unemployment Insurance Act, 1940. Carrying out the promise of PC 7633 occupied veterans planners for the remainder of the war. The key officials were Ian Mackenzie, the first minister of veterans affairs (appointed 1944), and his close public service associates Walter Sainsbury Woods and Robert England. All three were born in the United Kingdom and were veterans of the Great War. Woods, perhaps the key planner on the government side, favoured a program that would give long-term support to those who could not be expected to look after themselves while providing the able-bodied with a short-term program of 'Opportunity with Security'. Given the right assistance, most veterans would soon be off the government's books, paying taxes and building families. The Canadian Legion, giving voice to the interest of a new generation of veterans, also moulded the Veterans Charter through its constructive representations and well-publicized conventions. Legislative landmarks were the Veterans' Land Act, 1942; the War Service Grants Act, 1944; the Veterans Rehabilitation Act, 1945; and the Veterans' Business and Professional Loans Act, 1946. The program was explained to serving members of the armed forces in the several editions of the pamphlet *Back to Civil Life*. 'The object of Canada's plan for the rehabilitation of her Armed forces', they were told, 'is that every man and woman discharged from the forces shall be in a position to earn a living'. A distinct failing of the charter was its lack of provision for housing, but after 1945 strong veteran pressure steered the government in this direction. Overall, the Veterans Charter helped to sustain demand in the Canadian economy following the war and to keep the country moving forward.

PETER NEARY

veterans, First World War. In 1915, when Ernest Scammell, secretary of the new Military Hospitals Committee, drafted a policy for Canada's Great War veterans, he had plenty of precedents, most of them bad. In Canada, thousands of veterans had been paid off with free frontier land, some of it worthless, little of it useful to ex-soldiers. In Britain, many old soldiers begged in the streets; in the US, reformers described generosity to Union veterans of the Civil War as 'the pension evil'. Scammell urged the MHC to retrain disabled ex-soldiers. Wages, not pensions, would be their main income. The MHC and its heir, the Department of Soldiers' Civil Re-Establishment, pioneered vocational training and placement though, like most pioneers, hopes exceeded success. In 1916, with ideas developed by Dr J.L. Todd of McGill from French and British experience, a new Board of Pension Commissioners tried to remove pensions from political influence and compensate the disabled on principles derived from workers' compensation systems—the percentage loss of function for an unskilled labourer. Re-establishment benefits provided a cash gratuity based on months of service, a clothing allowance, cheap insurance, and limited medical treatment. In place of traditional 'veterans' bounty', a *Soldier Settlement Act invited qualified and motivated soldiers to take up farming. Others had extra help to find work and qualified for short-term welfare in the winter of 1919–20.

Rational principles and a booming wartime economy satisfied mostly disabled veterans released during the war but not the hundreds of thousands of able-bodied veterans released in 1919. Members of the *Canadian Expeditionary Force returned to a Canada prosperous for all but their families; inflation devoured their gratuities, and only brief interest was showed in their welfare. About half followed Scammell's advice, found old jobs or new, and tried to forget their experiences. Others, perhaps reflecting post-traumatic stress or pre-enlistment instability, demanded more. A 'Bonus Movement' sought up to $2,000 a man as compensation for lost income. When the movement failed, veterans' political influence faded too. Leaders of the main organization, the *Great War Veterans Association, focused on raising pensions for widows and the disabled and worked closely with the government to achieve modest gains, some of which were delayed by the Senate. GVWA membership faded and split as rival organizations emerged. In 1925, Earl Haig, wartime British commander, visited Canada to urge a single organization. The GVWA dissolved into the Canadian Legion. Depressions in 1921 and 1930–7 undermined veterans and plans designed to help them. Veterans of the Second World War could benefit from both the experience of their predecessors and the much richer Canada of 1945–60.

DESMOND MORTON

Victoria. *British Columbia's capital projects a clear image: a bit of 19th-century England where snow rarely falls and the hectic pace of modern life is absent. This beguiling construction belies a harsher history, one that exhibits many of the challenges common to other North American urban centres.

Boom and bust characterized the city's early years. *The Hudson's Bay Company established Fort Victoria at the southern tip of *Vancouver Island in 1843. The hoped-for 'depot of the coast' grew slowly. Songhees Natives provided food and labour paid for by Hudson's Bay blankets and whisky. A gold rush on the mainland increased the town's population from 1,000 in 1857 to 30,000 in 1859. Retired HBC officials and the company itself profited hugely from the ensuing land rush. Local Natives contracted *smallpox and many were shipped north, spreading disease as they went. Others survived by odd jobs and prostitution. Early hospital records reveal that one-fifth of general admittances suffered from 'fungus of the testicle', syphilis, and gonorrhea.

By 1866 gold finds were few and the population plummeted to 5,000. Thanks to railroad construction and the building of a dry dock at Esquimalt, Victoria experienced the second-highest growth rate of any Canadian city in the 1880s, reaching 16,841 people in 1891. That year Victoria ranked in the top five Canadian cities in per capita value of manufacturing. Ten years later it ranked a lowly 20th, and *Vancouver, situated on the mainland, had exceeded Victoria's population.

Vancouver became the terminus for the Canadian Pacific Railroad in 1885. Unequal *freight rates further contributed to Victoria's deindustrialization: Ontario manufacturers shipped more cheaply to the West than Victoria manufacturers could to the East. By 1901 Victoria's modern economy was in place. A tourist development association was established and a booklet published by the board of trade proclaimed Victoria to be a 'bit of Old England'. In 1980 tourist-related industries employed more Victorians than any other economic sector.

The city was always more than a bit of Old England. The Songhees outnumbered the British in the 1850s, as did American gold seekers in the early 1860s—indeed, an American hired by the city invented the bit of Old England slogan! Chinese railway navvies were a third of Victoria's population in the 1880s, and at the turn of the century a babel of tongues could be heard in the outer harbour. By 1901 the Canadian-born represented 46 per cent of Victoria's population. Few, however, worried about misleading advertisements. The British were welcome: Natives, Chinese, and Blacks were not. In 1912 the local Chinese Consolidated Benevolent Association warned potential migrants that a 'sea of sorrow' awaited them. The city council contacted South African cities for advice on how to deal with its non-white population. Not until the late 1970s was the near vacant Chinatown redeveloped as a tourist site.

In two other ways events in the early 20th century informed the city's subsequent development. First, by 1930 Victoria led Canadian cities in the proportion of its population over the age of 65 and in the generation of income from pensions and investments rather than wages and salaries. The income and age profiles of many other Canadian cities would follow Victoria's lead. Second, a real estate boom that collapsed in 1913 left the city with massive debts not finally controlled until the 1950s. By then it had become too expensive for single families to own a home in the city: apartments and renters dominated in the 1960s and the surrounding municipalities, especially Saanich, outpaced Victoria in population growth.

Victoria inherited much natural splendour. Yet an official plan for playground and park development appeared only in the 1960s. The city dumped its garbage into the ocean until 1959, and continues to view the sea as a bottomless pit, a receptacle for its raw sewage. Victoria's image has always hidden more than it has revealed.

PETER BASKERVILLE

Victorian Order of Nurses. The VON was established in 1897 in response to public concerns over Canada's high rates of infant and maternal mortality. The campaign to provide improved obstetrical services, especially in working-class neighbourhoods and in remote regions of the West, was led by Lady Aberdeen, wife of Canada's governor general. Aberdeen used her patronage and political savvy to overcome medical opposition and create the national organization, named in honour of Queen Victoria. Local VO volunteer committees raised funds while staff nurses charged a minimal fee (which they waived for poor families) for home visits. The organization was so successful that in the 1910s the Metropolitan Life Assurance Company contracted their services in some cities and found that insurance claims declined as a result. VO nurses were easily recognized by their distinctive uniforms of grey dresses, blue capes, black bags, and, by the 1920s, fashionable cloche hats. Even after the advent of *medicare, the Victorian Order continued to play a key role in community health. They now provide services such as home-based palliative care and health care for community shelters. KATHRYN McPHERSON

Victoria Pioneer Rifles. Volunteer militia unit organized at Fort Victoria, Vancouver Island, with the active support of Governor James *Douglas and the Hudson's Bay Company in August 1859 by American Blacks who had emigrated from the San Francisco area in 1858. The name Pioneer Rifles was officially adopted in April 1860. Until the spring of 1861 it was the only rifle corps in the colony. The Black community provided funds for uniforms and equipment, and with one exception, the bandmaster, non-Blacks were not permitted to volunteer. Membership never exceeded 50 men, and the Rifles, often referred to as the African Rifles, were never called out on active service. In 1864, Sir Arthur E. Kennedy, Douglas's successor, recommended that the unit be disbanded. While its demise in 1866 can be attributed in part to growing racial prejudice, the Rifles were largely ineffective because of small numbers, poor equipment, and a lack of proper training. GLENN WRIGHT

Villeneuve, Gilles (1950–82), automobile racer. Born in Chambly, Quebec, he moved to Berthierville at age eight. At a time when Quebeckers were asserting their identity on the world's stage, Villeneuve established himself as one of the best in a sport dominated by European and South American racers. He won his first Grand Prix at Montreal in 1978 and added five more titles in 67 races. A crash during a qualifying race in Zolder, Belgium, brought his life to an end at age 32. Today, his son, Jacques Villeneuve, follows in his father's tracks, along with Canadians Paul Tracy, Patrick Carpentier, Alex Tagliani, and Scott Goodyear. COLIN HOWELL

Vimy Ridge. Dubbed by the press 'Canada's Easter gift to France', the Battle of Vimy Ridge began on Easter Monday, 9 April 1917, and lasted four days. The Canadian attack, and the success of the Third British Army immediately to its south, captured more prisoners, guns, and ground than any previous British offensive. For Canadians it became a symbol of success and independence as well as proof of war's enormous cost and waste.

Vimy Ridge was the only occasion on which all four Canadian divisions attacked simultaneously, and was the last battle in which a British general commanded the Canadians. General Byng's meticulous preparations included building a large replica of the battlefield so that soldiers could study routes, obstacles, and objectives. Eleven huge underground galleries were dug to protect infantry prior to the attack. More than 32 km of light railway track, 95 km of telephone wire, and 80 km of water pipeline were laid to facilitate supply and communications. Artillery preparations included a two-week, preliminary bombardment.

Attacking at 5:30 A.M. the 1st, 2nd, and 3rd Canadian Divisions were quickly on the crest of the ridge. The 4th Division, which had the most difficult tasks and the heaviest fighting, took all of its objectives by the morning of 12 April. Victory imposed a high cost: 3,598 killed (including three of the four Victoria Crosses won on 9 April) and 7,004 wounded. Near the centre of the Canadian line on Vimy Ridge stands the most impressive of all Canadian *war memorials. A.M.J. HYATT

Voice of Women. The 5,000 women who flocked to the Voice of Women/Voix des femmes banner in the months following its founding in Toronto in July 1960

sought to combat the popular impression that nothing could be done to prevent the drift towards nuclear war. VOW insisted that nuclear disarmament was possible and that Canada could pursue an independent foreign policy that rejected nuclear weapons. Buoyed by the rising tide of a worldwide 'ban the bomb' movement, VOW had some success lobbying government and educating the public about the dangers of nuclear war and the health and environmental hazards associated with nuclear weapons testing. In concert with other peace groups, VOW helped to persuade US and Soviet heads of state to sign the Partial Nuclear Test Ban Treaty in 1963. Flush with this victory, VOW sought to publicize the human cost of the Vietnam War. It also initiated a plan for a world peace year that resulted in the United Nations designating 1965 as International Co-operation Year.

At its inception, VOW served as a lightning rod for women's discontent with Cold War politics and helped to bring into debate women's marginalized civic role. Initially the group's presentation of its members as serious-minded and responsible mother-citizens secured a public hearing. But as VOW grouped women together in challenge to the male-dominant structures and values associated with militarism and war making and rapidly absorbed the militant spirit and goals of a burgeoning left-leaning social protest movement, the organization eventually lost favour in the public eye.

VOW leaders in the second half of the 1960s, notably Kay Macpherson and Muriel Duckworth, found themselves guiding a smaller but more resilient and focused group of peace activists into a new era of social protest strongly influenced by the emergence of second-wave *feminism. In the 1970s, VOW members founded or participated in a host of feminist organizations, including the *National Action Committee on the Status of Women. Although no longer an organization on the cutting edge of social change, VOW has survived into the 21st century.
FRANCES H. EARLY

voyageurs. Literally translated, the term means travellers, but its use in New France and British North America has varied. In general, it referred to men who travelled from the St Lawrence Valley into the interior of the continent seeking furs by trapping or trading with First Nations peoples. Voyageurs included explorers who mapped routes; merchants who financed expeditions, controlled the distribution of trade goods and profit, negotiated relations with First Nations, and established posts; clerks who managed accounts; and servants (**engagés*) who paddled canoes, carried goods, and manned the posts. The term has also been used to refer more specifically to small-scale independent fur traders, working alone or in small groups, with some financial backing from merchants, between the late 17th and the mid-18th centuries. By the late 18th century, the term became confined in the historic record to *engagés*. These voyageurs came primarily from parishes surrounding Montreal and Trois-Rivières.

After the end of the Seven Years' War in 1763 a fierce competition for furs between the English-chartered *Hudson's Bay Company and the various partnerships based in Montreal, which eventually merged into the *North West Company, led to a dramatic expansion of the trade. Increasing distances between trading posts and Montreal necessitated a reorganization of the NWC. In 1784 the company divided its servants into two groups. The first transported goods from Montreal to the administrative centre at the western tip of Lake Superior in canoes called *canots du maître*, which were capable of carrying about four tonnes and required eight to ten men to operate. These seasonally employed summer men were known as *mangeurs de lard* or Porkeaters. The other set of men transported goods from Lake Superior to the posts in the interior country, some as far as 5,000 km away. To navigate the smaller rivers and creeks, they used smaller canoes, *canots du nord*, requiring four to six men to operate, and carrying loads up to two tonnes. These men, who wintered in the interior, were referred to as *hommes du nord* or Northmen. Competition between the HBC and NWC led to rapid increases in numbers of servants employed to transport the mounting volume of trade goods and to work at the posts. At the height of competition, 3,000 voyageurs worked in the trade. The number rapidly declined after 1821, when the HBC merged with the NWC. This class of worker disappeared in the 1880s, when the trade declined in economic importance.

Voyageurs had a significant impact on the *fur trade and cultural landscape of the **pays d'en haut*. The *lingua franca* of the fur trade was French until the mid-19th century. A large portion of *Metis people had French ancestry. Many francophone communities exist in northwestern North America today. These patterns are rooted in the history of the French-speaking servants of fur trade companies. Voyageurs numerically dominated the Montreal fur trade, they formed kin ties with Native women, and many settled in the Northwest to raise their families. Today, voyageurs are highly visible as colourful caricatures in popular culture and history. CAROLYN PODRUCHNY

Waffle Group. In 1969 dissidents within the *New Democratic Party, many of them university based, wrote a manifesto entitled 'For an Independent Socialist Canada'. Ironically dubbed the Waffle Manifesto, it took the NDP by storm, and the group was created as a caucus of radicals and militants within the party. In 1971 Waffle leader James Laxer, a 29-year-old graduate student, ran second to David Lewis for the leadership of the federal party on a program that endorsed Quebec's right to self-determination. There was a strong women's caucus within the Waffle. Too strong to be tolerated by the established leadership and the trade unions affiliated with the party, but not strong enough to take over the party, the Waffle was ordered in 1972 to disband as an organized caucus or be expelled. The group chose to leave the NDP and try to become a party in its own right. It had disintegrated by 1974, but left a legacy of leftist nationalism that found expression in the scholarly study of Canada's political economy. MELVILLE WATKINS

Wallace, Frederick William (1886–1958). Wallace is best known as the author of *Wooden Ships and Iron Men* (1924), an account of square-rigged vessels constructed on Canada's east coast before 1920. A book less read than cited, the title became a convenient shorthand to represent a supposed golden age of Maritime prosperity. Modern scholarship has dealt severely with the romantic stereotype the book's title symbolized, with adverse consequences for the author's reputation.

This result distorts both Wallace's limited intention in writing *Wooden Ships* as well as the book's importance relative to his overall career. Born in Glasgow, the son of a captain of the Allan Line, Wallace was captivated by the masculine world of the seafarer. Shortly after the family moved to Montreal in 1904, he gave up clerking for life as a journalist specializing in the shipping industry. Seven research trips, 1911–17, aboard Nova Scotia banks schooners were formative. These voyages, along with his father's reminiscences, were the grist from which he milled innumerable articles and short stories as well as three novels, beginning with *Blue Water* in 1914. That same year he was hired as founding editor of the *Canadian Fisherman*, a position he held until his retirement in 1953. In 1955 he produced his most important work, the autobiography *Roving Fisherman*. Predominantly an account of his early schooner voyages, it is an incomparable look at Nova Scotia's banks fishery and the fishermen of the small communities of the Fundy Shore. M. BROOK TAYLOR

wampum. White and purple marine shell beads from the Atlantic coast, made into strings and woven belts. These had great spiritual and political meanings for tribes across eastern North America. Symbols woven into wampum belts made them records of events and tribal law, and visible pledges of alliances. Wampum was made before European contact but became more readily available after Europeans established wampum factories and brought metal tools that made Native production easier. Wampum was so important that eastern tribes traded for it from Europeans. It was used in ways similar to *currency, but its primary value lay in its symbolic meanings as a record of political events or pledges. Today, tribal peoples value wampum belts as heritage items and consider as valid the promises they record. LAURA PEERS

war art. A visual image in any medium or style that has war as its subject. In Canada, images of war include 19th-century newspaper illustrations of battles fought on Canadian soil, such as those of the *North-West Rebellion, or overseas, such as the *South African War. Portraits of significant figures in Canadian military history, such as General James Wolfe or Victoria Cross–winner Billy *Bishop, and portrayals of anonymous home-front workers, also constitute the war art record. Caricatures, cartoons, and propaganda, fundraising, and information posters round out the genre. 'Official' war art is more narrowly determined as art commissioned for the nation in time of conflict. Except in individual cases where a painting is a reconstruction of an event, official war art's salient characteristic is that it usually has its origins in the battlefield and is born of experience. Canada has had two official war art programs: the First World War Canadian War Memorials Fund and the Second World War Canadian War Records. The first was initiated by the Canadian expatriate businessman Lord Beaverbrook in response to a perceived lack of a permanent visual record of that war. A romantic, ambitious, and nationalist endeavour, it resulted in a collection of traditional and avant-garde art by important Canadian and international artists that has not been matched in succeeding programs, including that of the Second World War. Post-war Canadian Armed Forces Civilian Artists' Program artists such as Allan Harding MacKay, who painted in Somalia in 1993, most often depicted defence or *peacekeeping operations that reflected the military point of view. The products of these programs, with a few exceptions, are in the collection of the Canadian War Museum in Ottawa. The museum's

20,000-item collection includes First World War paintings by future *Group of Seven artists A.Y. Jackson, Fred Varley, Arthur Lismer, and Frank Johnston; Second World War compositions by Alex Colville, Molly Lamb Bobak, and Jack Nichols; and art by Second World War service personnel who were encouraged to paint, draw, and exhibit their work in special exhibitions as a recreational activity. These artworks form a uniquely clear-sighted and unencumbered record of war. LAURA BRANDON

war brides. Women who married Canadian servicemen stationed abroad during the Second World War and accepted government-assisted mass migration to Canada. The vast majority of these women were the British wives of army personnel, but many married other service personnel or came from Newfoundland, Australia, the Caribbean, Holland, Belgium, France, and other European countries. The term 'war brides' was a misnomer for those women who had been married for years, who arrived with one child or more, or who were widowed before or shortly after arrival.

The monumental task of moving most wives—and children—of Canadian servicemen began in August 1944. Many of the earliest immigrant brides arrived well in advance of their husbands. However, most were moved between February and December 1946, after their husbands had been repatriated. The Canadian government, Department of National Defence, *Canadian Red Cross, and *Salvation Army coordinated efforts to prepare the women and organize transportation. *Welcome to War Brides*, the official government pamphlet for British war wives, included information about transportation arrangements, Canadian customs, currency, weather, housing, employment, and social services. The women travelled by ship to Canada and then by train across country. Sponsored passages were one-way only and no exit permits would be issued during the war, making the trip temporarily irrevocable. Although relationships between Canadian servicemen and foreign women were officially discouraged, and many war brides were accused of economic motivations or immorality, 69,733 war wives and dependants had immigrated by January 1947.
TINA DAVIDSON AND RUTH ROACH PIERSON

war crimes. Prior to 1944, Canadians had taken little part in the movement for justice against Axis war criminals. The grim discovery near a Normandy chateau on 9 June 1944 of the remains of murdered Canadian *prisoners of war gave Canada a stake in finding the perpetrators. An Allied board of inquiry uncovered the murder of 107 prisoners, nearly all of them Canadians, in Normandy. Most of these killings had been committed by the 12th SS Panzer Division 'Hitler Youth' during the first two weeks after the D-Day invasion. In the confusion of war none of those responsible were identified. Ottawa seemed reluctant to pursue the matter, but federal officials were ultimately spurred into establishing a war crimes unit by Canadian investigating officer Lt. Col. Bruce Macdonald. This unit ferreted out many of the killers, including Nazi agents who had orchestrated the lynching of captured airmen. The most compelling figure turned over to Canadian authorities was the commander of the 12th SS, Brigadeführer Kurt Meyer. His court martial in December 1945 for his part in the brutal killing of 18 Canadians at his command post was leading news across North America and Britain. Just before his trial began, hundreds of families were formally advised that their loved ones had been killed after capture and that their names might be raised in the proceedings. While Meyer denied any culpability, it was apparent that he had either ordered or tolerated the execution of prisoners by his troops. To the sombre satisfaction of the public, Meyer was convicted and sentenced to death. When Canadian generals, perhaps conscious of their own actions towards prisoners, commuted Meyer's sentence to life imprisonment, there was a violent public reaction against the government of Mackenzie King. Further Canadian war crimes trials in Europe were curtailed and all remaining cases were turned over to British authorities. In Asia, Canadian officers under British or American jurisdiction prosecuted Japanese soldiers who had killed or maltreated prisoners taken after the fall of *Hong Kong. Canada played an active role at the Tokyo trial of major war criminals. Brigadier Henry Nolan was one of the main prosecutors and Justice E. Stuart McDougall of Quebec sat on the court that sentenced seven militarists, including premier Hidecki Tojo, to hang.

Canada's decision to create an independent war crimes unit in Europe and to prosecute those responsible for killing prisoners was a major step for the country. In many ways, it foreshadowed Canada's later participation in NATO and UN bodies in the enforcement of international law. PATRICK BRODE

War Measures Act. This statute, adopted August 1914 on the model of British legislation, gave emergency powers to the federal cabinet, allowing it to govern by decree when it declared the existence of 'war, invasion or insurrection, real or apprehended'. The act was proclaimed and remained in force during both world wars, imposing extensive limits on Canadian freedom. Its most controversial use, to detain and remove property from Canadians of German, Ukrainian, and Slavic origins in the First World War and Japanese Canadians during the Second, resulted in belated apologies and compensation in the 1980s. Interim emergency legislation derived from War Measures extended some wartime powers after the Second World War and during the *Korean War in the 1950s.

The act was applied only once during a domestic crisis, by the Trudeau government in October and November 1970, when emergency regulations led to the arrest of over 400 persons in Quebec in response to two kidnappings by the *Front de Libération du Québec. Few were charged and none convicted under the regulations. Subsequently the Liberal government promised amendments to limit use of the act in internal crises, but failed to follow through for 14 years. In 1988 the Mulroney Conservative government adopted a more precise and limited

Emergencies Act to replace the War Measures Act. In its 2001 response to the terrorist attacks in New York and Washington, the Chrétien government sponsored the adoption of anti-terrorist legislation, which widened peacetime police powers of surveillance, arrest, and detention previously possible only by exceptional use of War Measures. DENIS SMITH

war memorials. In 1915, the artist A.Y. Jackson predicted glumly that war memorials would soon 'disfigure every town and village in the country'. He was right to foresee their ubiquity but wrong in imagining that they would become blots on the landscape. In fact, war memorials are some of the most poignant and powerful testaments to the nation's history.

In the absence of a complete register of memorials, we can only guess at their number, which perhaps approaches 10,000. The War of 1812, the Crimean War, the rebellions of 1870 and 1885, and the Boer War all spawned memorials, but the First World War produced the most intense and concentrated commemorative activity that the country has ever seen. The Second World War and the Korean War, in contrast, were usually marked only by the addition of new text or design elements to an earlier memorial, while more recent efforts at commemoration have produced a spate of memorials more reminiscent of headstones than anything else.

Quite apart from the sheer number of war memorials, one is struck by their variety. They fall generally into two types: the aesthetic, those monuments whose sole purpose is to commemorate, and the utilitarian, which perform some other function beyond the commemorative. Within these categories, Canadians have been remarkably ingenious in devising meaningful forms. A cairn built of local stone allowed all members of a community to make a tangible contribution to the monument. A German artillery piece celebrated the victory of Canadian soldiers on the battlefield. A grove of trees reminded observers of the power of the regenerative process. A memorial school ensured that students were constantly reminded of those who died to preserve their way of life. Canada certainly has its share of mass-marketed marble soldiers, but there are many other inspired memorials, including neo-Gothic bell towers, stately cenotaphs (many patterned on the Whitehall cenotaph in London), scholarships, art collections, libraries, and monuments that defy both logic and description. Walter *Allward's memorial at *Vimy Ridge, Frederick Clemesha's Brooding Soldier at St Julien, Belgium, and Vernon March's National War Memorial in Ottawa are among the nation's finest, but charming and equally evocative memorials can be found across the country: a kilted Highlander in Chester, Nova Scotia; a dignified obelisk in Bengough, Saskatchewan; a marble infant at play in Chesley, Ontario.

Whatever their form, Canada's war memorials are linked by a common purpose. Their sponsors intended them as lasting tributes to the men and women who served and sacrificed in wartime, and constant reminders of the values for which those individuals fought. But they are also historical documents in their own right, for they reveal the values and aspirations of the communities that erected them. JONATHAN VANCE

War of 1812. A conflict between Great Britain and the United States, the war revolved around maritime rights as well as control of the Old Northwest. In 1806, Napoleon closed western Europe off to British goods; in return British orders in council (1807) imposed a naval blockade on France, prohibiting all ships—including American vessels—from trading with that country. Although the United States was officially not involved in the European conflict, many of its ships were boarded, and many sailors seized in the North Atlantic. American resentment also grew at the British commercial presence south of the St Lawrence, where the British retained posts as *Loyalist claims for compensation were not being met. Although *Jay's Treaty (1794) had ceded the forts to the Americans, Canadian commerce was allowed to continue south of the line. Native peoples in the area also attempted to maintain trade with Upper Canada, and to resist American settlers. Matters came to a head with the Battle of Tippecanoe (1811) in which *Tecumseh and his brother, the Prophet, fought against American forces. American expansionists sought a campaign that would resolve these issues and strengthen their position in relation to Great Britain. Americans living in the South also contributed to war effort; they wished to obtain parts of Florida that were held by the Spanish, who were British allies.

Hopes by American 'war hawks' of quickly taking Canada proved optimistic. The US Congress underestimated British power in North America and the determination of the imperial power to retain its colonies. Congress believed that American troops would be welcomed as liberators in Upper Canada, where many former Americans resided—Thomas Jefferson opined that it would be a 'mere matter of marching'. Such thinking resulted in strategic errors: American forces chose to attack east of the Detroit River first, rather than sever lines of communications between Montreal and Kingston, which could have rendered Upper Canada helpless.

Major General Isaac *Brock contributed to early Canadian successes, having trained the militia, enhanced fortifications, and maintained relations with the Native people who had been fighting American frontiersmen for generations around the Great Lakes region. Tecumseh along with hundreds of his warriors helped the British take Michilimackinac, a key fur-trading post, during the early phase of the war on 17 July 1812. Native allies also played an important role in the taking of Detroit, first by cutting off American communications with the fort, then by intimidating General William Hull, who believed that Brock had 5,000 Native warriors with him, when in fact there were only 600. This victory demonstrated that Upper Canada could be defended, and on 13 October 1812 Brock had another opportunity to prove himself at the Battle of Queenston Heights, where the American militia were crossing the Niagara River. Brock led a combined force of British regulars, Canadian militia, and 500

Iroquois. Though he was killed in action, he managed to encircle the Americans and force their surrender, taking 900 prisoners. Queenston Heights was a very significant battle for Canadians: it prevented the Americans from obtaining a key hold in the area.

In mid-1813 American forces briefly occupied York (now Toronto), and the British were forced to retreat to the Burlington Heights following a second invasion of the Niagara Peninsula. Only a surprise attack at Stoney Creek, in June 1813, removed the American threat, and may have saved Upper Canada. Gradually, British forces began to reassert themselves. A successful naval blockade along the Atlantic coast from Boston to New Orleans meant that American attacks were principally confined to the land. A battle at Beaver Dams led to an American defeat, thanks to Laura *Secord, a settler who informed the British of the Americans' whereabouts. Although Oliver Perry's naval victory over the British on Lake Erie (September 1813) resulted in American dominance on the Great Lakes, security of the Upper Canada peninsula remained in imperial hands. However, following this defeat, the British retreated from Detroit, and Tecumseh was killed at the ensuing Battle of Moraviantown along the Thames River on 5 October 1813. Tecumseh's death meant the collapse of his Confederacy as well as the close association between the British and Native peoples living south of the St Lawrence. A final notable conflict in 1813 took place on 11 November near present-day Morrisburg, Ontario. During the Battle of Crysler's Farm, an invasion force of 4,000 Americans attempting to capture Montreal was decisively defeated by Lt.-Col. Joseph Wanton Morrison, who led a combined force of 800 British regulars, Canadian militia, and Native allies. The remainder of the army was forced to leave Canada.

By 1814, American forces were faced with a lack of secure sources of supplies, and New England began openly to oppose the war. Moreover, with Napoleon constrained in Europe, Britain could devote more time and effort to the American campaign. This threat prompted peace negotiations, which began in August. On 25 July 1814, American forces led by General Brown were repulsed at *Lundy's Lane, and were forced to fall back to Fort Erie, their earlier stronghold. Another British victory at Blandensburg on 24 August paved the way for General Robert Ross to march on Washington, DC, where troops burned public buildings, including the White House (indeed, the name 'White House' derived from the paint used to cover the discolouration from the smoke). The victorious British were halted at Fort McHenry before Baltimore. By September 1814, the British had assembled a joint army-navy invasion force of 11,000 under Sir George Prevost and planned to capture Plattsburgh in upper New York State. The task seemed simple—the town had a mere 4,000 defenders—yet Prevost, upon hearing of the naval loss in Plattsburgh Bay, promptly called off the ground invasion and retreated into Lower Canada. Prevost's reputation suffered a great deal as a result; indeed, his actions forced the British peace negotiators to lower their claims. The last major battle took place at New Orleans in January 1815, 15 days after the peace treaty was signed. During this conflict, 10,000 British veterans were defeated by forces under Andrew Jackson.

The Treaty of Ghent was signed at Ghent, Belgium, on 24 December 1814. Following long discussions, both parties were to use their efforts to abolish the slave trade, and a commission was to be established to determine the boundary from St Croix to Lake of the Woods. Ironically, many of the causes of the war—the fisheries question, the impressment of American seamen, or rights of neutral commerce—were not addressed. Largely due to their failure at Plattsburgh, the British had to give up rights on the Great Lakes as well as their plans for a separate Native American state to the northwest of the Ohio River. The strains and destruction of the war created anti-American sentiment even among the non-Loyalist settlers in Upper Canada, and the seeds of nationalism were sown. Civilian soldiers came to believe that they had won the war for Canadians, despite the fact that British regulars had formed the backbone of most of the successful battles. Loyalists had become Canadian, wishing to remain in Upper Canada rather than joining the American fighting forces. Native people faced the greatest losses—that of their great leader, and later of their rights as the broken confederation was forced to sign treaties and give up land for American expansionism. BARRY M. GOUGH

Wars, The. The first major novel to address Canada's experience in the First World War since Philip Child's *God's Sparrows* in 1937, Timothy Findley's book was inspired by family photographs and the wartime correspondence of his uncle. It tells the story of Robert Ross, a 19-year-old artillery officer, and his efforts to cope with both personal loss and the larger human tragedy of the Great War. *The Wars* was published in 1977 to immediate critical acclaim; it was honoured with the Governor General's Award for Fiction, and the book's success solidified Findley's reputation as a major writer. He later adapted the novel for the screen, but the 1983 National Film Board co-production (directed by Robin Phillips and scored by Glenn *Gould) was a failure with critics, who found it disjointed and convoluted, and audiences, who stayed away from it in droves. JONATHAN VANCE

Wartime Elections Act, 1917. Robert *Borden faced an election in 1917. His Liberal opponent, Sir Wilfrid *Laurier, would no longer agree to a postponement because of dire war circumstances, as Laurier had agreed in 1916. Those circumstances, however, were worse than ever, with Russia leaving the war while the Americans armed to enter it. The final test of Allied forces seemed imminent.

Borden was convinced that he must win the election. To that end, he and his government put forward two acts that reshaped the electorate. The first, the Military Voters' Act of 1917, expanded the franchise to those who supported the war, extending the vote to female relatives of soldiers and simplifying voting by soldiers themselves.

Parliament passed the Wartime Elections Act on 20 September 1917. It disfranchised citizens of enemy alien birth (German and Austro-Hungarian) naturalized after 31 March 1902 and granted the vote to wives, mothers, and sisters of soldiers. It helped Borden to win the election of 1917 but hurt the Conservatives for many generations.

JOHN ENGLISH

wartime internment. When Canada went to war against Germany and the Austro-Hungarian Empire in 1914, unwelcome foreigners became enemy aliens. In response to public fears about these people, the federal government established a national registration system, as well as a network of internment camps for those considered a security threat. Eventually, over 8,000 individuals, including women and children, were held in two dozen stations and camps across the country, including four *national parks. Interned men were technically prisoners of war but, apart from a small minority of German nationals, the majority were unemployed or destitute *Ukrainians who had been brought to Canada in large numbers in the early 20th century to help build the railroads and other construction projects. They were put to work in isolated camps until 1917, when they were paroled to help ease a severe labour shortage; only a few were deported at war's end.

When Canada entered the Second World War in 1939, there was another round of internment—communists, fascists (mostly *Italians), and critics of the war effort (including Mayor Camillien *Houde of Montreal)—under the *Defence of Canada Regulations. The Department of National War Services allowed declared conscientious objectors to work the equivalent of basic military training in agriculture, industry, or government service on the understanding that the labour would not benefit the war effort. Several hundred *Mennonites, Hutterites, and *Doukhobors fulfilled their term of service in national park camps in western Canada. In the wake of the Japanese attack on Pearl Harbor in December 1941, the Canadian government removed roughly 23,000 *Japanese, including those who were Canadian-born, living within 100 miles of the Pacific coast. These people had committed no crime against the state, but were relocated simply because of their race. Ottawa wanted to appease the white population of British Columbia. Entire families were sent to new settlements in the British Columbia interior, while thousands of Japanese men worked on road-building projects or provided agricultural labour. Many were repatriated to Japan after the war, even though some were Canadian citizens. The last group of internees during the Second World War were German prisoners of war. Canada had reluctantly agreed to be one of the jailers for the Allied war effort, and by 1946 more than 34,000 enemy soldiers were being housed at 25 different sites across the country. Many volunteered to work on prairie farms or in wood-cutting camps in northwestern Ontario. The more dangerous prisoners were held at a special camp in Neys, Ontario.

BILL WAISER

wartime nursing. Traditionally nursing in wartime was delivered by female relatives of injured or ill soldiers, or by religious orders of nursing sisters. During the *North-West Rebellion of 1885, the Canadian government for the first time recruited hospital-trained nurses to accompany troops. Then, in 1899, eight nurses joined Canadian medical units in the *South African War. More than 3,000 nurses served in the First World War, enjoying officer status with relative-rank of lieutenant. Nurses often worked in difficult and dangerous conditions. They treated soldiers who had horrific injuries and diseases like dysentery and malaria, while battling infestations of lice and flies. They coped with limited supplies, especially in front-line hospitals that were often hastily constructed and even more hastily evacuated. Nurses themselves took ill and dodged bullets, and some were killed. The death, in June 1918, of 14 nursing sisters aboard the hospital ship *Llandovery Castle* when it was sunk by a German submarine riveted public attention on the perils nurses faced. The outbreak of the Second World War mobilized over 3,500 Canadian nurses, most working in military hospitals in Canada and England or accompanying soldiers in transit. A small number worked at the front—the only female personnel to do so—serving in field hospitals, casualty-clearing stations, and mobile surgical units, sometimes labouring for more than 24 hours straight. The circumstances of war demanded that nurses help apply innovative medical technologies, such as new surgical techniques, burn therapies, blood transfusions, and penicillin. Nurses have also participated in Canadian military and *peacekeeping missions in international conflict zones such as Korea and Bosnia.

KATHRYN McPHERSON

Wartime Prices and Trade Board. Created 3 September 1939, a week before Canada declared war, the WPTB regulated the price, supply, and distribution of food, fuel, and other commodities. With the return of full employment, the war's initial impact on consumers was positive: 1940 was a strong year for the automobile industry, 1941 the best year ever for the sales of electric stoves and refrigerators. But inflation was correspondingly high, and in October 1941 the government responded by enacting wage and price controls. Thereafter, the cost of living increased just 2.8 per cent, the lowest of any belligerent.

To discourage consumer spending, the board mounted an advertising campaign encouraging thrift, conservation, and the purchase of War Savings Bonds. A monthly publication, *Consumer's News*, kept the public abreast of the bewildering slate of regulations governing commerce. Nonetheless, Canadians did not respond to regulation as uniformly as is sometimes believed. A substantial black market arose. Advertisers devised ingenious ways of converting wartime anxieties into rationales for consumption, and retail spending continued to rise, even when most consumer durables became unavailable after 1941. Shortages and rationing, which took effect in 1942, probably did more than the board's moral exhortations in preventing retail spending from rising even further.

Of the board's three chairmen the most important was Donald Gordon, a former banker, who was at the helm from 1942 to 1947. At its peak the board employed nearly 8,000 personnel and oversaw five Crown corporations. After victory, the board gradually eased regulations, and it finally dissolved in 1951. GRAHAM BROAD

Waste Heritage. Irene Baird's grimly realistic novel about the Depression in British Columbia was published in 1939. Based on her first-hand observation of the desperate plight of the thousands of jobless young men who congregated in Vancouver and Victoria (re-named Aschelon and Gath, the cities of the Philistines) as they moved westward seeking work, Baird effectively captured their angry voices as well as their wretched accommodations and the political tension of the times. The novel's documentary quality is enhanced by her detailed depiction of the protestors who occupied the Vancouver Post Office during the Sit-Down of the Single Unemployed in the summer of 1938. The narrative follows their trek to Victoria by focusing on two transient men, the astute Matt Striker and his dependent friend, Eddy. Plot development is minimal; emphasis is placed on the depiction of realistic characters and on giving the reader an ironic awareness of the futility of their protest. Written before the Depression was ended by the outbreak of the Second World War, the book implicitly predicts no other solution to the problems it depicts. CAROLE GERSON

weather forecasting. Meteorological observations were recorded as early as 1742 at Quebec City and soon after at Hudson's Bay Company posts in the Northwest. Over the following decades observations were commenced by army and church personnel and by individuals at many locations in what became eastern Canada. It was, however, the establishment of a Magnetic and Meteorological Observatory at Toronto in 1839–40 that led to the establishment of the Meteorological Service of Canada. After Confederation the observatory obtained financial assistance from the government to organize a network of volunteer weather observers and thus build up knowledge of the country's climate. But, because the government was most interested in storm warnings along the Atlantic coast and over the Great Lakes, the observatory director recruited observers to report by telegraph and began an exchange of observations with the new weather service in the United States, where the first forecasts were made. In 1876 the first Canadian-made storm warnings were telegraphed to Canadian ports and harbours; soon daily weather forecasts were issued to the newspapers of eastern Canada. In the West, telegraph reporting stations were established in the 1880s, and by about the turn of the century weather forecasts for that region were issued daily from the Toronto observatory. At about the same time, meteorological observing stations were opened in British Columbia and an office in Victoria began to forecast weather for the southern portions of that province. Expansion of the observing network into the North began once wireless communications became available in the 1920s.

For years, meteorological science and technology made few advances; until the mid-1930s Canadian weather forecasting remained more of an empirical art than an applied science. But aviation's rapidly increasing need for weather forecasts brought the adoption of new scientific theories and additional resources for the Meteorological Service. Forecasters were trained and, when Trans-Canada Airlines (now Air Canada) commenced scheduled flights in 1937, aviation forecast offices were opened at several air terminals across the country. That same year a forecast office was opened in Newfoundland to provide aviation forecasts for experimental flights over the Atlantic Ocean. During the Second World War, the Meteorological Service provided meteorological training and forecasts for the *Royal Canadian Air Force at scores of *British Commonwealth Air Training Plan stations and at operational air bases on the Atlantic and Pacific coasts. The needs of the RCAF combined with the needs for aircraft ferrying operations and increased commercial flying were responsible for rapid expansion in the Meteorological Service; the number of meteorologists increased from 60 in 1939 to over 400 in 1945.

In peacetime, when attention turned to civilian needs, public and marine weather forecasting was decentralized and improved and the networks of surface and upper-air observing stations were extended to the arctic islands. The volunteer climatological station network was greatly expanded throughout the country to better delineate climates, and atmospheric research programs were instituted to gain more knowledge of the properties of the atmosphere. When federal and provincial governments expressed needs for services in applied meteorology and climatology, the service expanded to meet these and to give guidance to private industry and commerce in meteorological matters. The most significant advancement in meteorology has been the development of numerical models of the atmosphere and the increasing use of computers and other modern technology. Weather radar and satellites now provide timely information regarding severe weather, and computers have allowed not only a major advance in the transmission and processing of weather and climate information but also the use of numerical models to produce improved weather forecasts.

While public, aviation, and marine weather forecasting continue to be of prime importance, the Meteorological Service, now part of Environment Canada, has additional responsibilities in air quality research, water quantity monitoring, sea ice forecasting, and other environmental issues. MORLEY THOMAS

Weinzweig, John (1913–), composer and teacher, born in Toronto. After studies at the University of Toronto and the Eastman School (Rochester, New York), Weinzweig began teaching at the Royal Conservatory in Toronto in 1939. One of the first composers in Canada to write in an advanced contemporary idiom, he introduced to Canadian music the 12-tone system that had originated with Arnold Schoenberg. Weinzweig's Polish-Jewish family background placed him outside the British and French traditions and the Romantic Germanic musical influences that dominated Canada in his early years, and likely contributed to the individualistic avant-garde attitudes that distinguish his music and his life. His works for chamber ensemble, large orchestra, and solo instruments are in a style consistently clean, clear, rhythmic (often with jazz elements), and distinctively modern. As a teacher at the conservatory (1939–60) and at the University of Toronto (1952–78), Weinzweig numbered many of Canada's most important composers among his students.

CARL MOREY

welfare state. The 'welfare state'—a term coined in Great Britain during the Second World War—commonly refers to programs of social protection against the major risks to income in a market economy. Through the welfare state governments provide health care, social housing, education, public pensions, unemployment insurance, minimum wages, disability allowances, social assistance, children's benefits, and various forms of social services. From the 1940s until the 1970s—the era of Keynesian economics—the welfare state also implied some commitment to providing high and stable levels of employment.

State income-security schemes predate the Second World War. Ontario's Workmen's Compensation Act provided benefits for injured workers beginning in 1914. In 1916–20, governments in western Canada and Ontario responded to lobbying by women's organizations by enacting *mothers' allowances, paid to widows and deserted wives with children. Canada's first means-tested *old-age pension scheme dates from 1927, when two Labour members of Parliament, J.S. *Woodsworth and A.A. Heaps, agreed to support Mackenzie *King's minority Liberal government in exchange for aid to the elderly.

The *Great Depression put the need for a welfare state on the political agenda. The Depression, which hit Canada harder than any nation except the United States, pushed governments to assume wider responsibility for social welfare to prevent mass starvation after one in three workers had lost his or her job by 1933, and one in five Canadians was dependent on state support. But the relief provided was administered grudgingly and in ways calculated to humiliate the Depression's victims. Single men were sent to work camps to labour for 20¢ a day or placed on farms for an even smaller wage. Married men were forced to shovel snow, dig ditches, or rake leaves to prove their moral worthiness for relief allowances kept below minimal standards of adequacy for themselves and their families. On the eve of the 1935 federal election Conservative prime minister R.B. *Bennett promised Canadians a 'New Deal', which included an Employment and Social Insurance Act and minimum-wage legislation. Passed without provincial consent, the bills were unconstitutional. Under the British North America Act, primary responsibility for employment, health, and social welfare belonged to the provinces, even though the dominant tax revenues rested with Ottawa. Once the Second World War began, all provinces, under pressure of winning the war, agreed to transfer exclusive jurisdiction over *unemployment insurance to the federal government, a constitutional surrender unique in Canadian history. For Liberal prime minister Mackenzie King, the 1940 Unemployment Insurance Act was crucial for avoiding social unrest if depression returned upon the war's end. The wartime labour market had given organized labour the chance to double its membership. Workers, farmers, and growing numbers of middle-class Canadians demanded a 'reconstructed' Canada that would guarantee jobs and social security as a right of citizenship. In 1943 the socialist Co-operative Commonwealth Federation, briefly Canada's most popular political party, came within four seats of winning the Ontario election. That same year a parliamentary committee on reconstruction published *Social Security for Canada*, by Leonard *Marsh, which laid out a sweeping blueprint for a post-war welfare state at a cost of $1 billion annually. A year later, Saskatchewan voters chose CCF leader Tommy *Douglas as their premier. Anxious to forestall a national CCF victory, as well as to reduce union demands for higher wages, King's government passed the Family Allowance Act in 1945, creating a universal program of monthly children's benefits paid to all Canadian mothers. The cost was $250 million, almost two-thirds of Ottawa's total expenditure on relief during the Depression. Family allowances would give every child 'an equal start in the battle of life', King told Parliament. The Liberals also created the *Veterans Charter, a generous program of educational, training, land, and housing entitlements for former members of Canada's armed forces. In a sign of the new Keynesian economic thinking, a 1945 White Paper on Employment pledged Ottawa to maintaining 'high and stable levels of employment'. At the 1945 federal–provincial conference on *reconstruction, Ottawa introduced its Green Book proposals for health insurance, universal old-age pensions, social housing, unemployment assistance, and revenue transfers for 'have-not' provinces, ideas that were scrapped when Ontario and Quebec refused to surrender further taxing authority. The Liberals' sudden shift to the left staved off the political threat from the CCF and helped King win the critical 1945 election. Their enthusiasm for the welfare state quickly waned as the CCF's popularity faded and post-war prosperity became apparent. UI, family allowances, and the Veterans Charter constituted King's key wartime legacy of social reform.

In 1951 his successor, Louis *St Laurent, delivered on one further wartime promise of social reform. Widespread public dissatisfaction with the 1927 means-tested old-age pension scheme, which helped only 40 per cent of Canada's elderly, pushed Ottawa to implement a plan of universal old-age security, giving $40 a month to all Canadians reaching the age of 70. This 'citizen's wage' represented a long overdue recognition of the contribution the elderly had made to building the nation. OAS was hardly generous, but it provided a floor upon which private pensions could be built.

During the 1950s the momentum for expanding Canada's welfare state shifted from Ottawa to the provinces. In 1947 Tommy Douglas's CCF government in Saskatchewan pioneered North America's first scheme of universal hospital insurance, providing free hospital care in return for an annual premium of $5 per person. Saskatchewan's success fuelled demands in the 1950s for a national program, a campaign backed by Ontario's Conservative premier Leslie *Frost, anxious to secure Ottawa's help in dealing with soaring hospital costs. Frost's leadership pushed the St Laurent government into passing the Hospital Insurance and Diagnostic Services Act of 1957, legislation that provided 50 per cent federal funding for provinces that established universal, publicly administered hospital insurance plans. By 1961 virtually all Canadians were covered under the scheme.

The 1960s was the key decade for consolidating Canada's welfare state. In 1961 the New Democratic Party, strongly backed by organized labour, replaced the CCF in pushing an aggressive social policy agenda. This was an era of intense political competition, beginning with the startling defeat of St Laurent's government by Conservative leader John *Diefenbaker in 1957. Governing without interruption since 1935, the Liberals had grown increasingly conservative in office, a point underscored by their miserly increase of $6 a month for pensions to the elderly just before the 1957 election. Thrust unexpectedly into opposition under the new leadership of Lester B. *Pearson, the Liberals rediscovered the welfare state as a means of finding their way back into power.

Diefenbaker helped. Despite his massive victory in the 1958 election, the Tory leader's indecisiveness, combined with a stubborn recession over the next four years, resulted in confusion. Diefenbaker promised Canadians a new public pension scheme, but then refused to act. He appointed the Royal Commission on Health Services in 1962 chiefly to deflect attention from Saskatchewan's scheme of universal public medical insurance, implemented the previous year. In contrast, the Liberals, under the impetus of a reformist wing led by Maurice Lamontagne, Walter *Gordon, David Croll, and Tom Kent, drafted an ambitious social policy agenda committing the party to making possible 'retirement without worry' through a new contributory public pension plan, accompanied by a national *medicare scheme to 'wipe out the fear of heavy medical bills'. If returned to power the Liberals promised '60 Days of Decision' in which they would launch their reform program. It was enough to win Pearson a minority government in 1963.

Two years later the Liberals successfully delivered the *Canada Pension Plan, after conceding that Quebec could run its own parallel scheme. The CPP/QPP provided Canadians with a modest earnings-related pension equal to 25 per cent of the average industrial wage, which could be stacked on top of their existing OAS benefits. The retirement age was also lowered to 65, and in 1967 a Guaranteed Income Supplement was introduced for the elderly, overwhelmingly women, who could not qualify for the CPP. In 1964, through amendments to the 1944 National Housing Act, the Liberals also injected new life into a moribund social housing program by offering to pay 90 per cent of the capital costs and half the operating costs of provincial low-income housing. Over the next decade the number of units jumped more than tenfold from 10,000 to 115,000. By 1978, when the program was terminated, 164,000 new low-income units had been built. As part of their 1965 Speech from the Throne pledge to 'abolish poverty', the Liberals also introduced the *Canada Assistance Plan in 1966, a cost-shared program that provided 50 per cent federal funding and new national standards for almost all provincial social assistance programs and services.

Medicare was the Liberals' greatest social policy challenge. In 1964 the final report of the Royal Commission on Health Services, chaired by Emmett Hall, recommended the creation of a universal public medical insurance plan for all Canadians. Hall's report, along with continuing pressure from the NDP, helped to keep the Liberals committed to medicare. Two years after the report, despite internal cabinet dissension, Pearson's administration introduced the Medical Care Insurance Act. This six-page document was based on four simple principles. Ottawa would provide 50 per cent funding to any provincial medical insurance scheme on the condition that it was universal, comprehensive, portable, and publicly administered. Facing a $750 million deficit, Pearson postponed implementation until 1968. Medicare's opponents—including doctors, the insurance industry, and a number of powerful premiers—jumped on the delay in order to fight the legislation. Ontario would not participate, Conservative premier John Robarts argued, because universality was too expensive, and the idea of a 'compulsory plan' was wrong. Public medical insurance should be available only to those who could not afford to pay for private plans. By August 1968 only Saskatchewan and British Columbia had created schemes that satisfied Ottawa's four principles. A new majority Liberal government led by Pierre Elliott *Trudeau broke the impasse. Trudeau introduced a new 2 per cent tax in 1968 to finance medicare, paid by all Canadians whether or not they lived in a province covered by the scheme. Robarts denounced Trudeau's 'Machiavellian scheme', but there was little he or other reluctant premiers could do except join. Otherwise, taxpayers would be financing half the cost of public medical services in every province but their own. By 1972 all ten provinces had established health insurance plans that conformed to medicare's four principles.

The early 1970s marked the end of an era. The liberalization of UI in 1971 to encompass 96 per cent of the workforce and provide paid maternity benefits was the last example of a major new national social entitlement. Since then UI has been dramatically cut back, universality has been scrapped in both children's benefits and old-age security, the Canada Assistance Plan has been abolished, governments have stopped building social housing, provincial welfare benefits have been slashed, work tests have been reimposed on the poor, and a commitment to high employment has disappeared from the political landscape.

Universality survives only in medicare, but even there it is under attack. The child-poverty rate has jumped more than 40 per cent in the last decade. Opinion polls reveal that Canadians still believe the 'social safety net' defines their nation. If so, it is an image that bears increasingly little resemblance to the ideal of a welfare state.

JAMES STRUTHERS

Wentworth, Sir John (1737–1820), colonial governor. A scion of the most prominent family in colonial New Hampshire, John Wentworth, because of his natural abilities and family connections, became its governor at age 30. When faced with rebellion, he sought compromise and to keep New Hampshire loyal. He was the last royal governor to leave his post and would be the only one to secure another governorship. He became lieutenant-governor of Nova Scotia in 1792; a knighthood followed in 1795. Wentworth would be governor for 16 years. When he arrived the colony was paralyzed by feuding between the old inhabitants and the *Loyalists, was so far in debt it could not pay its bills, and was losing Loyalists in large numbers. Under his energetic governorship, Nova Scotians gained a sense of themselves as a people and a loyalty to their land that has remained one of their most distinguishing and enduring characteristics. Government House in Halifax remains a fine architectural testimony to his governorship and that of his fashionable wife, Frances.

BRIAN CUTHBERTSON

west coast Aboriginals. The Aboriginals of the West Coast include an array of individuals and groups who occupy the coastal region of British Columbia and trace their ancestry to those who lived in the area before the arrival of Europeans in the late 17th century. Today, most of these groups prefer to be referred to as nations or First Nations. The north coastal region includes the territories of the Haida, Haisla, Gitksan, Nisga'a, and Tsimshian. The Champagne and Aishihik have territories that extend from the Yukon into the northwest corner of British Columbia. On many maps the Kwakiutl or Kwagiulth are shown as occupying much of the central coast, but they are really only one of several nations of the larger Kwakwaka'wakw group. Also on the central coast are the Oweekeno, the Nuxalk, who used to be known as the Bella Coola, and the Heiltsuk (Bella Bella). Coast Salish has often been used to distinguish the groups of the south coastal region but it is now more common to refer to the individual ethnic groups of the area, including the Homalco, Klahoose, Sliammon, Sechelt, Straits Salish, Hul'qumi'num, Comox, Squamish, Tsleil-Waututh, Sto:lo, Musqueam, and Tsawwassen. The Aboriginal groups occupying the west coast of Vancouver Island, historically called the Nootka, are now known as the Nuu-chah-nulth. All these people have similarities with Aboriginals from the coastal regions of southern Alaska, Washington, Oregon, and northern California; when discussing Aboriginal lifeways the entire region is known as the Northwest Coast culture area.

The record of Aboriginals in the area extends at least 10,000 years into the past. Aboriginal people often claim that they have lived here since 'time immemorial', which roughly means forever, or since before memory. Although no unequivocal older physical evidence of human occupation has been found, many archaeologists believe that it is reasonable to think that people lived and travelled in the unglaciated parts of the coast 15,000 years ago or more. The first people likely came from the north during the late stages of the last ice age, venturing through a coastal migration route linking ice-free parts of what is now Alaska with the rest of the Americas south of the ice-sheets. While earlier occupation remains speculative, an estimated 12,000 recorded archaeological sites provide a substantial amount of information on activities during the last 10,000 years. People who occupied the region between 10,000 and 5,000 years ago can be characterized as generalized foragers, living in small nomadic bands and exploiting a wide range of resources from land and sea. The people occupying the north coastal region likely had their roots in populations living in what is now Alaska, while those in the southern coastal region likely had roots in what is now the coast of Washington and Oregon. Beginning about 5,000 years ago, populations increased sharply, the proportion of salmon in the diet rose substantially, cedar became a key resource, settlements became larger and more permanent, social organization became more complex, and the distinctive west coast *Aboriginal art style emerged.

West coast Aboriginals are well known for their distinctive culture, which continues to be based on salmon and cedar. Salmon has been the dominant component of the diet for 5,000 years, with the surplus catch supporting large populations, the accumulation of wealth, and craft specialization. People moved throughout their territory in small groups for much of the year but returned to large, permanent villages following major harvests of salmon in the autumn. The villages, with populations typically ranging from a few hundred to a thousand, consisted of several large cedar-plank houses facing the ocean, each accommodating several related families. Cedar, the most important non-food resource, was also used for canoes, three-dimensional masks, and totem poles, and was softened and woven to make baskets, mats, and clothing. People were recognized as belonging to specific houses and clans. A house was a group of related extended families living together in one of the houses making up the winter village, and the leader of the house was the chief, a hereditary position. The house often controlled access to specific fishing, hunting, and gathering locations as well as rights to songs, dances, and stories. Because each house had its own chief, there was no single authority for each village or nation. Clans were groups of related houses from different villages within the territory of the larger ethnic group or nation. Traditional Nisga'a society, for example, was—and still is—organized into 60 houses, which in turn belonged to one of four clans: Raven, Killer Whale, Wolf, or Eagle. As was common among peoples throughout the world, the belief systems of west coast Aboriginals included the notions that many types of phenomena could contain spirits, shamans could access the supernatural world, and many natural and cultural phenomena could be explained as a result of the actions of supernatural characters in the past. Many of the stories include individuals known as transformers, who could change themselves and others at will into other animate and inanimate forms. Because they often accomplished their feats through trickery, some transformers are also known as tricksters. The best-known trickster among west coast Aboriginals is Raven. The arts, including painting, carving, storytelling, music, and dance, remain important elements of the cultures. Villages were often adorned with a variety of carved wooden sculptures such as totem, house, and mortuary poles. Designs were regularly incorporated into baskets, clothing, jewellery, storage boxes, and tools. The designs often depicted clan identification, followed specific rules such as the use of ovoids and bold form lines, and sometimes became very abstract. Performing arts such as storytelling, music, and dance were often performed at important events such as *potlatches.

Some researchers speculate that Europeans or Asians may have visited the region earlier, but the conventional view is that the first direct contact between west coast Aboriginals and non-Aboriginals began with sailing forays into the area by Europeans in the 1770s. Over the next 150 years, the Aboriginal population likely decreased by at least 80 per cent, primarily because of smallpox epidemics. The combination of dwindling numbers, the process of colonialization, and increasing numbers of settlers led to change in many elements of traditional lifeways. Before the mid-19th century, relations between Native and newcomer were based primarily on the *fur trade and although there was some population loss through *smallpox epidemics there was relatively little conflict. With official colonial rule beginning in the mid-1800s, the nature of the relationship changed. With the backing of colonial administrators, non-Aboriginal settlers took control of much of the traditional territories and resources of the Aboriginals. As a result, many Aboriginals who were forced to abandon their traditional subsistence methods of hunting, fishing, trapping, and gathering became dependent on the settlers for wage labour. Some traditional activities, such as the potlatch, were made illegal.

Between 1851 and 1854, the governor of Vancouver Island made 14 treaties with Aboriginal groups, but despite the apparent desire of many other groups to negotiate with successive colonial, provincial, and federal governments, no further treaties were successfully negotiated until the Nisga'a treaty in the 1990s. As experienced elsewhere, beginning in the late 1800s the west coast Aboriginals were subjected to the assimilation policies of the federal government, including the use of *residential schools where children, often forcibly removed from the care of their parents, were subjected to attempts to break them of ties to their language, culture, and families. Since the late 1800s the people have asserted their rights in several ways, including protests, petitions, confrontations, litigation, and negotiation. Throughout the late 19th and early 20th centuries many assemblies were held to protest the denial of *Aboriginal rights and the lack of government willingness to negotiate treaties. Formal petitions were submitted to provincial, federal, and British governments and representatives travelled to Victoria, Ottawa, and England to seek redress. Confrontations, including the blocking of rail lines and roads, have been a common strategy used to pressure governments and corporations to negotiate outstanding issues and claims. Often successful, such tactics rarely escalated to violence. In the latter half of the 20th century many west coast groups chose to assert their rights through the Supreme Court of Canada. Three of the most significant cases include *Calder*, which in 1973 affirmed the existence of Aboriginal rights of the Nisga'a at the time of European settlement; *Sparrow*, which in 1990 affirmed the Aboriginal right of the Musqueam people to fish; and *Delgamuukw*, which in 1997 affirmed that the Gitksan and Wet'suwet'en people had *Aboriginal title. Since 1992, many groups have been negotiating treaties with the provincial and federal governments. The latter half of the 20th century witnessed substantial growth in population and a revitalization of Aboriginal culture. Many became involved in the repatriation of cultural and human remains. Potlatches once again became common, and other expressions of culture such as the raising of totem poles were openly celebrated. Highly successful economic, social, and cultural initiatives were undertaken. It became common for Aboriginal groups to implement programs in language, education, and health, and to become competitive in a number of industries, including tourism. ROBERT J. MUCKLE

west coast exploration. The first European explorers to visit the west coast of what is now British Columbia were Spanish navigators who sailed north from their bases in Mexico in the 18th century. Spain claimed the entire Pacific coast of America following a late-16th-century papal division of the world between Spain and Portugal, and the Spanish were concerned that the Russians might be expanding their influence south from Alaska. They also were interested in locating a possible entrance to the rumoured *Northwest Passage. In 1774 Juan Pérez left San Blas, Mexico, commanding the *Santiago*. On 18 July he sighted the north end of the Queen Charlotte Islands and encountered Haida people, who launched canoes from Langara Island and traded with his crew. Later Pérez anchored off Nootka Sound on the west coast of Vancouver Island, again trading with local people but neither landing nor officially claiming the area for Spain. These were the first confirmed contacts between Europeans and Aboriginal people on the northwest coast.

The Spanish sent two more expeditions north to Alaskan waters, then seemed to lose interest briefly in the area. That changed with the arrival of the British mariner, James *Cook, in Nootka Sound. Cook, on his third voyage into the Pacific, stopped at Nootka in the spring of 1778 to resupply his vessels before proceeding towards

Alaska to search for the Northwest Passage. Following this visit British fur traders became active on the coast, alarming the Spanish, who responded by establishing an outpost at the present-day village of Yuquot in Friendly Cove in Nootka Sound in 1789. In a bold, some say reckless, assertion of sovereignty, the Spanish commander Estéban José Martínez seized several British trading vessels, touching off the so-called *Nootka Sound Controversy, which was not resolved until 1795, when Spain, unwilling to risk war with Britain, gave up its claim to Nootka.

While diplomats wrangled, exploration of the coast continued. The Spanish penetrated Juan de Fuca Strait, hoping that it led to a northwest passage. In 1791 Francisco de Eliza and José María Narvaez in the tiny schooner *Santa Saturnina* became the first Europeans to enter Georgia Strait. They were followed the next year by two schooners, the *Sutil*, commanded by Dionisio Alcalá-Galiano, and the *Mexicana*, commanded by Cayetano Valdes. To their surprise, the Spanish encountered Captain George *Vancouver, who had been sent by the British with two vessels of his own, *Discovery* and *Chatham*, to conduct a thorough survey of the northwest coast. The Spanish and British in tandem explored the maze of islands separating Vancouver Island from the mainland, then made their separate ways to Nootka. This marked the end of significant Spanish activity on the coast, but it was only the beginning for Vancouver, who returned during the summers of 1793 and 1794 to complete his meticulous survey from California to the Alaskan panhandle. Vancouver developed an effective technique for conducting his explorations. Using his two large vessels as mother ships, he dispatched longboats to carry out most of the surveying. It has been estimated that his men rowed these vessels a total of 16,000 km to conduct their inlet-by-inlet survey. One of the wonders of Vancouver's expedition is that he accomplished so much with so little loss of life: only six men died during the four-year expedition, well below the average mortality rate for other voyages of the period. During Vancouver's second summer on the coast, in July 1793, he just missed meeting the fur-trade explorer Alexander *Mackenzie in Dean Channel. Mackenzie had travelled from northern Alberta, reaching the coast at what is now Bella Coola, to become the first European to cross North America overland to the Pacific.

Vancouver's voyages marked the end of the age of imperial exploration on the northwest coast. He laid to rest any possibility that an entrance to a northwest passage existed along the coast and added the last portions of the Pacific basin to the map of the world. He also made good on Britain's claim to this part of the world. By describing it in such meticulous detail on a chart, he lent credence to the notion that Europeans had 'discovered' this region and had every right to colonize it. There was still much left for outsiders to learn, but after Vancouver exploration was incidental to trade and, eventually, settlement.

DANIEL FRANCIS

West Country merchants. For over 300 years, merchants dominated the Newfoundland fishery. From the 17th century, merchants from the west of England controlled most of the capital on which the cod fishery relied. They sold the extensive supplies needed each spring—provisions, fishing gear, clothing, and alcohol—and in August they set the price to be paid locally for salt fish. After settling their accounts each autumn, many merchants returned to Devon and Dorset, where some of them were prominent members of the gentry. Merchants used webs of clientage and patronage to establish their authority over fishing communities, wielding power through a strict paternalism guided by profit. Most of them treated Newfoundland as an extension of their businesses in England, where they invested much of the wealth accrued from the fish trade.

Merchants generally opposed introducing civil government in Newfoundland, but structural changes in the cod fishery during the Napoleonic Wars altered their position. From 1793 to 1815 the fishery transformed into a largely resident operation, massive immigration dramatically boosted the local population, and a political reform movement emerged. Reformers began to campaign against the perceived tyranny of the West Country merchants. Merchants came under attack for exploiting the credit, or *'truck', system to their advantage. Each spring most fishing families borrowed from a merchant house the necessary supplies for the summer fishery; in return they were bound to sell their catch only to that merchant's firm. Since merchants influenced both the cost of provisions and the price paid for cod, families often found themselves in debt when their accounts were settled. Forced to obtain additional credit from merchants to procure winter supplies, some families fell into a cycle of debt and dependence in which fish and provisions formed the sole currency. In the 19th century, St John's became the commercial centre of the fishery, as merchants built large premises along Water Street. They became a tightly knit community and played a central role in politics well into the 20th century. Although scholars have challenged the traditional view of merchants as despots, the theme of mercantile oppression remains a salient feature of Newfoundland historiography.

JERRY BANNISTER

western alienation. The belief that the views of westerners are not given sufficient weight nationally. Pragmatically, alienation reflects the fact that the western population is a minority, outweighed by the large populations of Ontario and Quebec. If regional issues compete for national attention, those of the central Canadian provinces more often top the priority list.

The history of western alienation is far from uniform. First, 'the West' is not a single entity. The economic 'have-not' provinces of Saskatchewan and Manitoba are in a very different position than Alberta and British Columbia. So, too, it is difficult to equate the protests of Metis and Natives in the late 19th century with the hostility of late-20th-century oil executives to federal policy. It is possible, though, to discern three phases of alienation. The first came when Metis and Native populations resisted integration into the mainstream economy of Canada after 1870. Economic decline and loss of influence occurred as

Canada built an agrarian economy linked to the east–west trading system. The most violent expression of western disaffection came in the *Red River Resistance and the 1885 *North-West Rebellion. After 1885 the costs of integration continued to be felt but the power of the original inhabitants had been broken. The West had passed into new hands.

Soon the new agricultural population began to understand alienation. The notion of an agrarian hinterland feeding its products to manufacturing centres in the East was not always beneficial to the primary producers. By the turn of the century complaints arose about unfair railway practices, tariffs, and a host of other matters. A pattern of agrarian alienation emerged that rested on a combination of hard fact and folk myth. It reached its peak in the years after the First World War, when a new party, the *Progressives, captured 65 seats in the 1921 federal election. The party soon fragmented, torn apart by internal battles and intra-regional differences. Nonetheless, the Progressives were important. They demonstrated that the West would, if sufficiently unhappy, abandon the national party structure. Also, a core of Progressives survived as the United Farmers of Alberta, transforming themselves into a new regional party, *Social Credit, in 1935. Until Social Credit's demise as a western party in the 1950s, the West had significant representation by parties without a national context.

Western alienation continued in the latter half of the 20th century but changed form for several reasons. Most importantly, the western economy was becoming more complex. The discovery of oil in Alberta after the Second World War, the growth of Vancouver, Calgary, and Edmonton as major metropolitan areas, the population growth in Alberta and British Columbia, all transformed traditional agrarian politics into something more complex. Moreover, with the rise of separatism in Quebec in the 1960s, concerns about that province's place in Canada became central to federal politics; but westerners sometimes felt this to be an 'eastern quarrel'. Through much of the 1960s and 1970s westerners tended to remain at odds with national political majorities, opting instead for opposition parties. This disaffection was exacerbated after 1973, when oil prices surged and the three western-most provinces, especially Alberta, found themselves with significant new revenues. Ongoing battles between the federal government and the provinces over control of oil led to charges of greed in the East and colonialism in the West. More generally, the Western Economic Opportunities Conference of 1973 became a forum for a litany of complaints about federal treatment. With the creation of the *National Energy Program in 1980 the conflict reached a peak and even brought a short-lived western separatist party into being.

As the West has evolved so too has the nature of western alienation. The years since the NEP have contained many contradictions. A new western party, Reform, recreated the tradition of the Progressives. On the other hand, issues that many thought were West versus East—such as constitutional reform—took on different shapes. Through much of the 1980s and early 1990s the federal government had strong western support. Sheer demographics and economics have given the West a more powerful role in national affairs. Yet the sense of alienation, once rooted, becomes a part of regional identity and is hard to erase completely. DOUG OWRAM

Western Charters. Royal patents granted in 1634, 1661, and 1676 to the Devon and Dorset ports seasonally involved in the migratory, inshore cod fishery on the *English Shore; they are supposed, in Newfoundland historical mythology, to have hindered settlement. The charters formalized traditional 'Newfoundland Law', notably by prescribing how masters could claim fishing rooms and by empowering some, as *fishing admirals, to settle disputes. Controls on forestry practices, dumping ballast, destruction of fishing stages and cookrooms, sabbath observance were often ignored. The 1634 charter tacitly recognized settlement by banning taverns, normally operated by planters. A 1637 grant to Sir David *Kirke permitted settlement if over six miles inland, but the restriction was ignored. In 1653, the Council of State recognized planter rights to waterfront property and the 1661 charter explicitly recognized settlers. A 1671 amendment resuscitated the impractical six-mile rule and, in 1675, a faction of merchants convinced Whitehall to instruct inhabitants to leave Newfoundland, although the Royal Navy effectively ignored the order. The 1676 charter incorporated the six-mile rule, but Whitehall soon had doubts, in 1677 prohibiting enforcement and in 1680 rescinding the recent restriction and withdrawing the long-ignored ban on taverns. This compromise, recognizing settlement without the 'settled government' that planters sought, was the basis of *King William's Act of 1699. PETER E. POPE

western subarctic Aboriginals. Often referred to collectively as the northern Dene, these people, who speak several closely related Athapaskan languages, include in Canada the Gwich'in, Han, Hare, Tutchone, Kaska, Slave, Dogrib, Beaver, and Chipewyan peoples. The word 'Dene', or a similar term, means 'person' or 'human', and it has come to represent the culture as a whole. Their traditional territory, located principally in what is now the Northwest Territories, stretches from the northern edge of the western provinces, east to Nunavut, and north to the tree-line, which reaches nearly to the Arctic Ocean in the Mackenzie Delta, and nearly to the Bering Strait in the west.

It has been suggested, by academics and others, that Dene society was based on food production, but it is clear that socio-political factors, including the development of trade and political relations between groups, held a primary role in the manner in which they organized their social life. Their history is multifaceted, although here we largely focus on economic history and recent relations with Canada.

Human habitation in this region began at least 25,000 years ago, possibly much earlier. In any case, the people maintain that as long as they have been who they are they have lived on this land. It is a region dominated by the boreal forest and the transitional zone of boreal vegetation and tundra. In the late pre-contact period small groups of 20 to 30 related people—called 'local groups' by anthropologists—relied on local resources for food, clothing, and shelter. They hunted moose and caribou as well as smaller game such as snowshoe hare and beaver, fished for arctic char, whitefish, and salmon, and gathered plant life, including several species of berries, and wood from spruce and birch. Small animals were snared with babiche or sinew while larger game was hunted with bow and arrow, club, or spear while the prey was crossing open country or water. The capture of large game usually required co-operative labour in hunting parties, and resources were distributed on the basis of reciprocity or mutual sharing. In general, all participated equally in the good fortune of the hunters and all suffered when their luck turned bad. Thus it was the whole membership of the local group, and not each family or individual, that defined the self-sufficient unit. There was trade between groups as well as across the region, so people were not isolated.

In the early days of the *fur trade, European goods tended to flow along the existing Aboriginal trade lines, with Russian goods coming in from the west and British and French goods from the east and south. Alexander *Mackenzie, who in 1789 travelled through the heart of Dene country, down the river that now bears his name, noted that the people were already familiar with trade goods. However, direct trade with Europeans did not begin until late in the 18th century. The *North West Company arrived first and maintained a near monopoly until 1821, when it was amalgamated with the *Hudson's Bay Company. In the early days, because of poor transportation, few goods were available, although decorative and luxury items were important. The Aboriginals traded items intended mainly to sustain the traders, primarily meat and fish, with furs of secondary importance.

With the advent of steamships on the major rivers in the late 19th century, circumstances changed. Traders, provisioned from the south, could focus on the more profitable trade in furs. The HBC lost its monopoly with the sale of its territories in 1870. Competition, improved transportation, and the Yukon gold rush of 1898, all resulted in a transformation of the fur trade. The Dene continued to trade local resources, but whereas earlier either provisions or furs could be used in exchange, now both HBC and free traders could manipulate exchange rates to encourage the trade in furs. New items introduced to the region by 1900 were the repeating rifle, the steel trap, and wide varieties of European clothing. As well, the quantities of traditional exchange items such as food staples, blankets, and metal utensils increased dramatically. Although the Dene economy was still largely based in bush life, there were shifts in residency and hunting patterns because of the increased focus on the trapping of fur-bearing animals.

In the early part of the 20th century the Dene continued to make their living from the bush, but the high price of furs led to an ever increasing reliance on trade goods. Rising prices, particularly during the First World War, also led to an influx of European trappers and settlers and therefore to competition for land. The stability of the local economy became dependent both on external economic conditions, such as a high market price for furs in relation to the price of trade goods, and on the availability of a surplus in one resource, furs. With the influx of Europeans during the 1920s, the fur trade began to collapse because of the increasing shortage of furs.

Government interventions also changed the life of the people. The introduction of family allowances and old-age pensions during the late 1940s enabled most to maintain their living standards. By the 1950s, however, it became apparent that the fur economy would never return, and the government assumed incorrectly that the collapse meant the loss of a way of life. As a result, Dene were encouraged and coerced to move into towns, where their children would be educated in a Western system and be in a position to take jobs in the wage economy. The program was not successful, for jobs were few. Direct government payments continued to replace productive labour as the main resource for obtaining trade goods. During the past few decades, the Dene have also been subjected to massive political and economic intrusions from the south. Many of their traditional institutions and values have been put under tremendous strain, generating social problems such as alcoholism, poor housing, high welfare rates, health problems, and increased crime.

In the late 20th century the Dene became involved in politics at all levels. In 1970 the 'Dene Nation' was formed to represent the people in resolving outstanding land and governance issues with the government of Canada. The organization developed as a response to long-standing concerns over the written terms found in the government's version of Treaties 8 and 11, negotiated with the Dene in 1899–1900 and 1921–2 respectively. The Dene argued that these treaties established a nation-to-nation political relationship between themselves and the Canadian state, a view repeated in the wording on self-determination in the Dene Declaration (1975) and at the *Mackenzie Valley Pipeline Inquiry (1975–7). The government's position was that fundamental political issues had been resolved in the treaties and it therefore insisted on focusing on non-political matters. In 1990 the Dene national assembly declared that resolving political relations lay at the heart of the Dene Nation's motivation for entering into negotiations. In response, Ottawa suspended its dealings with the Dene Nation and reached agreements separately in three of the five Dene regions, resulting in the fragmentation of Dene political solidarity. The impasse concerning the general political relationship remains crucial, complicated by pressures on the Dene to 'develop' their lands further through expansion of the petro-chemical industry. ROBERT WISHART AND MICHAEL ASCH

West Indies trade. Trade between British North America and the West Indies played a key role in the development of the Atlantic economy. Sugar and molasses were by far the most important commodities imported from the West Indies. In addition to refining sugar for local consumption, by the 1640s North American merchants began to establish distilleries to convert molasses into rum. By 1770 merchants were importing over 27 million litres of molasses, from which approximately 140 distilleries produced about 23 million litres of rum each year. Merchants exported mainly manufactured goods to the West Indies, such as earthenware, furniture, vehicles, and wooden casks. They also exported commodities, in particular salt codfish, which was used to feed the enslaved workers on West Indian plantations. In the 19th century, the British West Indies became an important market for salt fish from Nova Scotia and Newfoundland. By the 1820s, the British West Indies was importing an average of 6,400 metric tons of Newfoundland fish each year. Encouraged by relatively low tariffs, merchants relied on the West Indies as a market for their poorest grade of saleable fish. Newfoundland salt fish was shipped directly, and indirectly via Halifax, to colonies such as Jamaica and Barbados, where it was valued as a cheap, easily preserved source of protein. This commerce helped to support the exploitation of slave labour, though it outlived the abolition of slavery. The trade began to decline in the late 19th century; by 1900 Newfoundland was exporting an average of 4,200 metric tons of salt fish to the British West Indies each year.

JERRY BANNISTER

westward expansion. From the earliest European settlement a symbiosis existed between the St Lawrence–Great Lakes region and the West. The hinterland was a source of furs, while businessmen and adventurers in the East had added to colonial wealth by mounting expeditions westward. In 1821 the British-based *Hudson's Bay Company absorbed the Montreal-based *North West Company and the connection between these regions was largely severed. Henceforth trade and corporate influence flowed from Britain directly to the vast territories known as *Rupert's Land. Upper and Lower Canadians occupied themselves with filling their own agricultural land and paid little attention to the West.

In the 1850s the relationship changed. Canada had settled its agricultural land. For a society that depended upon cheap land to attract immigrants this was no small matter. To make matters worse, the United States had successfully expanded across the continent, and this expansion contrasted with the cul-de-sac faced by the Canadas. The most ominous lesson came in the way in which Oregon, which had been run by the HBC as a fur colony, fell out of British control and into American. When a fur economy collided with an agricultural frontier, the fur trade was displaced. The implications for the vast territories north of the 49th parallel were not reassuring. In response a group of Canadians came together to raise interest in the North-West Territories. Centred in Toronto, they were a mixture of scientists, boosters, and nationalists. Key among them was George *Brown, politician and owner of the Toronto *Globe*. In 1856 Brown wrote a series of pieces extolling the West. He was supported by individuals such as Allan Macdonell, who wrote letters to the paper praising the region, and by *Clear Grit leader William McDougall. This rhetoric challenged the HBC by pitting progress, growth, and British freedoms against stereotypes of a feudal and backward mercantile empire.

Initially much of the advocacy was based more on hope than substance. Little assessment had been done of the territory's suitability for settlement. Indeed, the image in popular writings to that point had been one of a desolate wilderness. However, in 1857 both the Canadian and British governments sent out expeditions to assess the agricultural potential of the region. There were some differences in emphasis, with Henry Youle *Hind, from Canada, enthusing about a vast fertile belt stretching from Red River in an arc westward to the Rockies. British Captain John *Palliser emphasized the southern 'triangle' that he considered unsuitable for settlement and that, ever since, has borne his name. Cumulatively, however, the expeditions reinforced the argument of the expansionists. The West had vast areas that were suitable for settlement. Expansionists used the information to carry out a campaign in favour of annexation.

Confederation had to come before the Province of Canada was in a position to assume control of the vast territory. Thus, by 1867, expansion became entwined with emerging nationalist enthusiasm and became possible because a federal system provided a feasible means of governance. The idea of the West was picked up by groups like *Canada First (formed in 1868) and made an essential element of the Canadian 'destiny'. For its part, Great Britain recognized that the era when a vast portion of North America could be governed by a fur trade company was at an end.

The actual transfer was messy. The enthusiasm for annexation in Canada was not matched by many living in the territory's main settlement, Red River. Years of factionalism between transplanted Upper Canadians and local residents had left people suspicious. When William McDougall, Canada's appointment as governor, arrived he was turned away by armed residents. Subsequent months of confusion, bluster, and negotiation were settled only when an armed force was sent to assert Canadian authority. Much remained to be done before the expansionist vision of an agricultural utopia could be realized. By 1870, though, expansion was an accomplished fact and the West a part of Canada.

DOUG OWRAM

whaling. The first people to hunt whales in what is now Canada were the Nuu-chah-nulth (Nootka) on the west coast of Vancouver Island and the *Inuit in the Arctic and on *Hudson Bay. Both groups carried on a subsistence hunt, killing a small number of animals each year. The first commercial whalers in Canada were Basque mariners from Spain who began visiting the Gulf of St Lawrence in the 1520s. They were followed by ships from northern Europe, which ventured into the eastern Arctic in significant numbers after 1720. At first they confined their activities to the Greenland side of Davis Strait, but after 1820 they began crossing Baffin Bay to Lancaster Sound and the coast of Baffin Island. Between 1820 and 1840 as many as 100 wooden whaling ships visited Davis Strait annually, mainly from Britain, in some years killing more than 1,000 bowhead whales, the largest of the species that inhabit the Arctic. In the 1860s American whalers opened a new ground in the northwest corner of Hudson Bay where bowhead migrated each summer. Because the ice delayed their arrival in the area, these vessels usually overwintered in the bay. With overhunting, the population of bowhead in Hudson Bay declined rapidly and the ground was all but deserted by 1900. By this time the centre of activity had shifted to the western Arctic. Again it was American ships, mainly from San Francisco, that pushed their way around Point Barrow into the Beaufort Sea. They established a winter harbour at Herschel Island and, from 1899, pursued the hunt as far west as Amundsen Gulf.

Initially, whalers followed their prey in small, open boats armed with hand-held harpoons and lances. Once the animal was killed, it was towed back to the ship for processing. In the mid-19th century weaponry became more sophisticated with the introduction of harpoon guns that fired explosive charges. At about the same time, vessels converted from sail power to steam engines. With these innovations, whaling became progressively more destructive. Oil obtained from whale blubber was used as a lubricant and in lamps until it was replaced by petroleum products in the late 19th century, though whale oil continued to be used in the manufacture of margarine, paints, and other products. Certain whale species also produce baleen, a flexible, bone-like substance that grows in the animal's mouth; it was used to make corset stays, buggy whips, fishing rods, and a vast array of other products until its value plummeted early in the 20th century with the advent of spring steel and plastics.

Whaling in the Arctic had a profound impact on the Inuit inhabitants. Whalers introduced wage labour, epidemic diseases, and manufactured trade goods. They also placed a strain on local food resources, decimating caribou herds as well as almost eradicating whale stocks. The presence of foreign whalers prompted the Canadian government to assert its sovereignty over the *Arctic Archipelago by dispatching patrol vessels and establishing police outposts.

Commercial whaling in the Arctic was winding down by the outbreak of the First World War. On the coast of British Columbia, however, and in Newfoundland and Nova Scotia, whaling continued from shore-based stations into the 1970s. In these operations, speedy catcher boats killed the whales with bow-mounted harpoon cannon, then towed the carcasses to land for processing. Canada was a member of the International Whaling Commission, formed in 1946 to regulate the worldwide hunt, until it withdrew in 1982 because of a disagreement with IWC policy. Canada has banned commercial whaling since 1972, when the last two shore stations closed. Conservation measures have allowed the recovery of some stocks of whales in Canadian waters but others, notably the beluga in the St Lawrence River and right whales in Atlantic Canada, continue to be at risk.

DANIEL FRANCIS

White, Portia (1911–68), contralto. Born in Truro, Nova Scotia, to African-Canadian Baptist parents, White became a schoolteacher but was catapulted to international stardom as a singer after triumphant debuts in Toronto (1941) and New York (1944). Performing throughout Canada, the United States, the Caribbean, and South America, her bel canto technique, mastery of languages, and three-octave range drew accolades from audiences and critics. She was dubbed the 'New Star of the Concert Stage', and her achievement was unique in a period when race and gender defined women's place in society. Poor health and management problems sidelined her brief though unprecedented career. Based in Toronto in the 1950s she became the voice teacher of choice for aspiring Canadian theatre and television performers.

SYLVIA D. HAMILTON

white feather campaign. This campaign began in the early days of the First World War in Great Britain, where women were encouraged to pin white feathers on young men who were not in military uniform. The hope was that this mark of cowardice would shame them into 'doing their bit' in the war. The practice soon spread to Canada, where patriotic women, in response to declining voluntary recruitment figures, organized committees to issue white feathers to men in civilian clothes and publicly denounced the 'slackers' and 'shirkers'. Although male recruitment officials condemned this 'shaming' tactic and did their best to discourage it, especially since it was not effective, the notorious practice continued until *conscription was introduced in 1917.

THOMAS P. SOCKNAT

White Paper on Indian Policy. On 25 June 1969 Jean *Chrétien, minister of Indian and northern affairs, presented to Parliament 'The Statement of the Government of Canada on Indian Policy, 1969'. In this White Paper the government promised to end Canada's discriminatory Indian policy, repeal the *Indian Act, do away with the Department of Indian Affairs and any special programs or program-delivery systems for Indians, give control of Indian lands to Indian bands, terminate *Indian treaties, and create an *Indian Claims Commission to deal with any outstanding claims to which Aboriginal peoples may have been entitled by treaty. It also made clear that it would not recognize any *Aboriginal rights or *Aboriginal title.

Initially non-Native groups supported the White Paper. However, Aboriginals across the country were outraged at what they believed to be the government's betrayal of a commitment made, in a series of consultation meetings in late 1968, to honour the treaties and accept the concept of Aboriginal rights before making any changes to the Indian Act. This feeling of outrage provided the impetus for Aboriginal organization. The National Indian Brotherhood emerged as the principal Aboriginal organization after Harold Cardinal, leader of the Indian Association of Alberta, convinced the brotherhood to adopt the IAA's position paper, 'Citizens Plus', as the NIB official response to the White Paper. This response, called 'The Red Paper', stated that the government–Indian relationship must be based on government recognition of treaty and Aboriginal rights and required the establishment of a claims commissioner to deal with issues arising from those rights. Native opposition caused non-Aboriginals to reconsider support for the government's proposals, resulting in the withdrawal of the White Paper in 1973. JOHN L. TOBIAS

White Pass and Yukon Railway. This narrow-gauge line was built by a British company in 1898–1900 from Skagway, at the head of the Lynn Canal, 175 km to Whitehorse, the head of navigation on the *Yukon River, where freight and passengers were transferred to steamboats for the trip to *Dawson City and the Klondike. Thirty-five men were killed during its construction. It traverses the White Pass at 889 m, rather than the higher and more familiar *Chilkoot Pass (1,074 m). Although the gold rush was over by the time it was finished, it served the expanding hardrock mining and the tourism industries of the Yukon Territory, and provided heroic service in the construction of the *Alaska Highway during the Second World War. The line pioneered the use of containers, and also owned the steamboats that ran between Whitehorse and Dawson City, providing the territory with an efficient and integrated transportation system. The company also ran a winter passenger and sled service between the two communities. It operated the North's first regularly scheduled airline, and after a highway was opened to Dawson City in 1955 it stopped running steamboats and began a bus service.

With the coming of southern air service to the Yukon, and especially when a highway was built along the Skagway–Whitehorse route, the line lost most of its passenger traffic, and the collapse of the Yukon mining industry led to its closing in 1982. A few years later, however, it was reopened as far as the Canadian border and Lake Bennett as a tourist attraction, and it has prospered with the growth of the cruise-ship trade to Skagway. Since it is only 35 km from sea level to the summit of the pass, the line has astonishingly steep grades, a testimony to the skill of the engineers and workers who built it.

K.S. COATES AND W.R. MORRISON

Whiteway, William Vallance (1828–1908). Whiteway moved to Newfoundland from his native England to work in the fish trade but started practising law in 1852. He was elected as a Conservative in 1859, serving as speaker of the House from 1865 to 1869, when, as a pro-Confederate, he lost his seat. Re-elected in 1874, he was solicitor general until 1878, when he became premier. Whiteway favoured removing the obstacles to development of the west coast imposed by French fishing rights, and constructing a railway to develop the resources of the island. Sectarian tensions and the first railway company's failure tore apart the Conservative coalition in 1885. After a period in opposition Whiteway returned as premier in 1889, leading the Liberal Party. His government attempted to negotiate an end to the irritant of the *French Shore and reciprocity with the United States, but both failed due to British and Canadian opposition and the less-conciliatory lieutenants within his party. The opposition brought down the government through legal technicalities in 1894. While the elderly Whiteway resumed the premiership in 1895, younger cabinet members outshone him. Three years after losing the election of 1897, Whiteway was ousted as Liberal leader by Robert *Bond. JEFF WEBB

White Women's Labour Laws. Canada holds the questionable distinction of being the only country in the Anglo-American community to pass legislation prohibiting Asian men from hiring white women, under penalty of fines and imprisonment. The law was first enacted in Saskatchewan in 1912, and replicated in Manitoba in 1913, Ontario in 1914, and British Columbia in 1919. Versions remained on the books until 1969. Church leaders, women's organizations, business leaders, trade unions, and social reformers all advocated passage of the acts. Racist whites conceptualized white women as the 'guardians of the race', and enshrined their reproductive capacity as the most valuable property of white men, to be protected from encroachment by men of other races. Canada had a long history of anti-Asian discrimination of which these laws formed one piece. Racially based immigration law had made it difficult for Asian men to settle in Canada, and almost impossible for Asian women. Racist whites then expressed fears that Asian men from the overwhelmingly male immigrant community would seek social, sexual, and marital liaisons with white women. The 'White Women's Labour Laws' were designed to reduce interracial social connection in a setting where Asian men were thought to be capable of exercising power over white female employees. The acts were also intended to reduce the competitiveness of Asian restaurateurs and launderers, who were unable to benefit from the cheaper wages paid to women. *Chinese and *Japanese businessmen challenged the laws in court, arguing that the legislators had failed to define what they meant by terms such as 'white' and 'Chinaman'. Judges ignored their astute arguments over the indeterminacy of racial categories, and enforced the statutes nonetheless. In 1914, Saskatchewan restaurateurs Quong Wing and Quong Sing failed in their quest to have the Supreme Court of Canada declare the act unconstitutional.

CONSTANCE BACKHOUSE

Whitton, Charlotte (1896–1975), one of Canada's most celebrated female activists. In 1920 Whitton joined the Canadian Council for Child Welfare (now the Canadian Council on Social Development), transforming it into the focal point for child-welfare advocacy and social work professionalism. She launched investigations of welfare services in Canada's major cities, lobbied for the protection of juvenile immigrants, fought for higher standards of foster care, and developed 'Whitton's network', a cadre of female social workers she placed strategically in local welfare agencies. During the Depression she was a key adviser on unemployment relief policy for both R.B. *Bennett and Mackenzie *King. Fears of eroding the work ethic led her to argue that governments were spending too much, not too little, on relief. Such conservative views forced her resignation as council director in 1941.

In 1950 Whitton entered Ottawa municipal politics; she was elected mayor in 1951, making her the first woman mayor in Canada. She held this position almost continuously until 1964. An opponent of gender inequality in the workplace, she commented, 'Whatever women do they must do twice as well as men to be thought half as good. Luckily, it's not difficult.' Her belief in equal rights, however, was limited to single women; she opposed more liberal divorce laws and criticized married women who worked. Voted Canada's 'Woman of the Year' six times before her death, Whitton once quipped, 'Whatever my sex, I'm no lady'. JAMES STRUTHERS

Willan, (James) Healey (1880–1968), composer and organist. Born in the United Kingdom, Willan was one of the first musicians in Canada to have an international reputation as a composer. He came to Canada in 1913 to teach at the Toronto (Royal) Conservatory. An outstanding organist and choral director, he was music director first at St Paul's Anglican Church, then at St Mary Magdalene's, where he remained from 1921 to 1967. Willan's style never changed from a conservative late-19th-century Romanticism, but within this style he wrote forcefully and convincingly. He composed two operas, two symphonies, and a piano concerto, but principally his music was for organ, which is firmly established in the repertoire, and for choir, mainly for the Anglican service, where it has had great success and influence. Renewed interest in his choral works in the 1990s resulted in several fine recordings. CARL MOREY

Wilson, Alice (1881–1964). Born and educated in Ontario, Alice Wilson developed a deep love for and curiosity about nature, which led her to audit science courses while studying languages at the University of Toronto. As the first woman scientist at the *Geological Survey of Canada, this frail-looking but determined woman fought for her right to conduct fieldwork and obtain a graduate degree. While her male colleagues travelled afar, her fieldwork was restricted largely to the Ottawa–St Lawrence Valleys, and she was denied the paid study leaves granted men. After a decade of refusals, she enrolled part-time at the University of Chicago (PhD, 1929), but her advancement at the GSC remained slow because of her gender. Nevertheless, she received many honours (MOBE, 1935) and was the first Canadian woman scientist to be elected Fellow of the *Royal Society of Canada (1938). MARIANNE GOSZTONYI AINLEY

Wilson, Cairine (1884-1962). A liberal, philanthropist, humanitarian, and mother of eight, Montreal-born Wilson (née Reay Mackay) was the first woman appointed to the Canadian *Senate, in 1930, a year after the *Persons case established the right of women to become senators. Although not as prominent as some feminist crusaders, Wilson participated in many reform causes: the Red Cross, the Presbyterian Women's Missionary Society, the YWCA, the Ottawa Welfare Bureau, and the *National Council of Women. In the interwar years she embraced the internationalist principles of the *League of Nations; under her presidency in the 1930s the Canadian League of Nations Society became an active women's peace group. A senator who supported more liberal divorce laws and helped found the Canadian National Committee on Refugees in 1938, she was one of few Canadian public figures to protest the highly restrictive admission laws that prohibited *Jews fleeing Nazi Germany from entering Canada. After the Second World War she promoted a more 'open-door' immigration and refugee policy, headed the Senate Standing Committee on Immigration and Labour (1946–8), and in 1949 became Canada's first woman delegate to the *United Nations.

FRANCA IACOVETTA

Wilson, Sir Daniel (1816–92), polymath, man of letters, artist, watercolourist, antiquarian, ethnologist, anthropologist, university teacher and administrator. Wilson's scholarly reputation in his native Scotland rested on *Memorials of Edinburgh in the Olden Time* (1848), an illustrated account of picturesque buildings and architectural detail, and *The Archaeology and prehistoric annals of Scotland* (1851), a comprehensive survey of Scottish prehistory, a word he introduced into the English language. Appointed in 1853 to teach history and English literature at University College in Toronto, Wilson turned to the study of North American Indians, who he supposed resembled the inhabitants of prehistoric Europe. He believed that all peoples shared a common origin as well as the same faculties and instincts and that all were equally capable of progress. Different levels of technological development were due more to environmental circumstances than to biological differences. Wilson's *Prehistoric Man: researches into the origin of civilization in the Old and the New World* (1862) emphasized the importance of the Native cultures of North America for understanding the remote past in Europe; they conveyed in lavish detail the ways a common humanity expressed itself in technology, architecture, art, superstitions, and uses of narcotics. Wilson never accepted Darwin's contention that natural selection accounted for intellectual and spiritual as well as physical development or that the differences between people and animals were ones of degree not kind. As president of University College after 1880, and first president of the University of Toronto after 1887, Wilson resolutely defended the nondenominational principle and the university's independence from political interference in appointments, although he was forced by the government of Ontario to accept the admission of women. CARL BERGER

Winnipeg. The capital of *Manitoba, Winnipeg is located at the confluence of the Red and Assiniboine Rivers, almost at the geographic centre of North America. 'Gateway to the West', it stands where the *Canadian Shield gives way to the prairie. The city's name probably derives from the Cree word for the lake 64 km to the north, *win-nipi*, possibly meaning 'murky water'.

Frequented by Cree hunters, the area attracted the first European fur traders as early as 1738, when *La Vérendrye built Fort Rouge at the 'forks'. The first settlement was established in 1812 around a general store some distance from the future Hudson's Bay Company post of Upper *Fort Garry, built on the banks of the Red River in 1821–2. Winnipeg was incorporated as a city in 1873, though it numbered only 3,700 persons and was little more than a collection of shacks.

Over the years a small, compact, ethnically homogeneous community has become a large, sprawling, cosmopolitan city. With the exception of a sharp increase in the early 1880s and the decade 1900–11, growth was steady and primarily resulted from immigration from Britain and Ontario. These early groups established a dominance that persisted until after 1945, despite the arrival of other 'foreigners'. Growth after 1900 was phenomenal, and by 1911 Winnipeg was the third-largest city in Canada. Rapid growth created serious problems in public health and the provisions of services. But the most serious problem was the conflict of values between the 'charter groups' and other immigrants, many of whom were Slavs and *Jews who did not easily fit into the Anglo-Canadian mould and who experienced overt discrimination, ranging from residential segregation to job discrimination and destruction of property. A deeply prejudiced majority saw immigrants as a threat. Tensions eased as immigration declined between 1920 and 1960 and natural increase played a greater role in population growth. The decrease in hostilities was apparent when Stephen Juba, of Ukrainian origin, was elected mayor in 1956, soon to be joined by other non-Anglo-Saxons on city council and in other public positions. After 1960 the population of the central city declined as surrounding municipalities grew. The region was recognized as one city with the creation of Unicity in 1972.

Winnipeg dominates the economy of Manitoba, containing more than half the population and over 60 per cent of its employees, producing over 80 per cent of its manufactured goods, and accounting for over 60 per cent of its retail sales. The city is still pre-eminently a transportation centre. Secondary manufacturing has traditionally been seen as the key to expansion, and prairie settlement has given impetus to consumer industries. In recent decades, large increases in employment have been seen in the public and private service industries. The provincial and federal governments support a large public service, and Winnipeg has long been a financial and insurance centre. There is also a tradition of 'boosterism'. In 1906 the Winnipeg Development and Industrial Bureau was organized to promote manufacturing and commerce. It became the Industrial Development Board in 1925 and operated until 1979, when a new group, Winnipeg Business Development, was formed to attract high technology industry.

Winnipeg is a major cultural centre of the Prairie provinces and has long held a reputation as a thriving community of literature, music, education, and art. The city is the home to the acclaimed Royal Winnipeg Ballet, the Winnipeg Symphony Orchestra, Rainbow Stage, the Winnipeg Art Gallery, and the Manitoba Theatre Centre, one of the most important regional theatres in North America. The Assiniboine Park Zoo, the Manitoba Museum of Man and Nature, the Provincial Archives of Manitoba, the *Royal Canadian Mint, and Lower Fort Garry (a historic restoration located just north of the city) are major attractions. The Manitoba Music Festival, held each spring, is the largest in Canada. Since 1970, an annual weeklong festival called Folklorama has celebrated the city's cosmopolitan culture.

Between 1947 and 1971 Winnipeg rinks won the Canadian curling championship eight times while the Winnipeg Blue Bombers football team have won the Grey Cup eight times. In 1967 Winnipeg was host to the fifth Pan-American Games, leaving the city with many new sports facilities.

Winnipeg is the location of the University of Manitoba (1877), University of Winnipeg (1871), St Boniface College (1818), and Red River Community College, as well as numerous private schools and special facilities, such as the Manitoba School for the Deaf. A city of many ethnic and religious groups, Winnipeg has a wide variety of ethnic clubs and organizations, religious colleges and institutes, synagogues and cathedrals. ALAN F.J. ARTIBISE

Winnipeg General Strike. For six weeks, from mid-May to late June 1919, Winnipeg was gripped by the largest general strike in Canadian history. Over 30,000 workers—the bulk of the city's labour force—remained off work. Factories and stores closed, streetcars and mail delivery stopped, newspapers were closed and telephones silenced.

The immediate impetus for the strike was the attempt by workers in the metal and building trades to force employers to negotiate with their union federations. As a measure of support, the Winnipeg Trades and Labor Council, the umbrella organization of trade unions in the city, polled its affiliated members on whether to hold a general sympathetic strike of all members. The result was definitive: 11,000 in favour, 500 against. Nonetheless, the response on the first day of the strike overwhelmed even the most optimistic. Most of those who struck were not even members of unions, had little stake in the immediate issues behind the strike, and had no union to protect them from the reprisals of employers.

The massive character of the strike, and similar sentiment in cities across the country (about 20 general strikes broke out in 1919), reflected both the deep resentments over the consequences of Canadian industrialization as well as the hopes and frustrations that had accumulated during the First World War. Wartime had brought shortages, inflation, and the restriction of civil liberties, along with the promise of social improvements and an expanded democracy at its conclusion. A tight labour market had allowed workers to unionize more effectively, and socialist and labourist ideas had spread widely.

In Winnipeg, alarmed by workers' determination and unity, business and government set out to crush the strike and discredit its ideas and leadership. The city's employers formed the Citizen's Committee of One Thousand, and published an anti-strike paper, the *Citizen*, to paint the strikers as 'Bolsheviks' and 'enemy aliens' who were undermining 'British values'. Similarly, the federal government ignored the key issue of workers' rights to free collective bargaining and viewed the strike as a revolutionary challenge to 'constitutional authority'.

The strike was orderly: workers followed their leaders' advice to deprive the state of any excuse to resort to military force. Essential services were maintained, but when the police refused to sign a no-strike pledge, the city fired the entire force, replacing them with 1,800 anti-strike 'Specials'. Not surprisingly, the appearance of an untrained, hostile force on the city's streets raised tensions. At the same time, the authorities acted on several fronts. Additional armaments were sent to Fort Osborne army barracks, a new immigration act was pushed through Parliament in a matter of hours giving the government the power to deport British subjects, and the infamous section 98 of the Criminal Code was passed broadening the definition of sedition. In late-night raids in mid-June, the leaders of the strike were arrested (as well as a handful of immigrant radicals—bolstering the government's claim of an 'alien' conspiracy).

The wildcard in the city proved to be the returned *veterans from the First World War. For the most part, authorities' attempts to appeal to soldiers' loyalty against the 'foreigners' and 'reds' failed. City Hall banned the regular marches undertaken by both pro- and anti-strike veterans. On 21 June—on what came to be known as Bloody Saturday—the Mounted Police attacked a silent parade of returned solders who were attempting to demonstrate their support for the strike. The Mounties fired into the crowd: two men were killed and many others wounded. The Specials pursued the demonstrators through the streets of downtown Winnipeg. Authorities then shut down the strikers' paper, the *Western Labour News*, arresting its editors. A few days later the strike was called off.

The seven strike leaders who were jailed for up to two years came to symbolize the struggle for a democracy that would include workers' aspirations. Several of them were elected to the Manitoba legislature in the 1920 election. Only the redrawing of electoral boundaries in Winnipeg prevented labour from dominating City Hall in the following decade. The echo of the general strike died very slowly: the city remained deeply divided between a Tory south end and a sprawling working-class north end that elected socialist and communist candidates for decades to come.

JAMES NAYLOR

winter. Winters in Canada were a nasty surprise to Europeans. St Malo, the port from which Jacques *Cartier sailed, is about 48°N latitude and Stadacona (now Quebec City), where he wintered 1535–6, is about 47°N. Cartier, who certainly knew about latitude, likely anticipated that the Canadian winter would be like that of St Malo. Winters in Europe could often be dark, dank, and dreary. Canada's were at times like that too, but they could also be bright, brisk, exhilarating—and cold. In later years, when Europeans learned to adjust, winter was a time of snow and sleighs, snowshoes and toboggans, frostbite and blizzards. Canadians quickly learned that they had to prepare for the winter. Houses in the country or in villages or towns had storm windows to be put on. They also had root cellars, stocked with turnips, potatoes, cabbages, and barrels of apples. Firewood and coal, for innumerable stoves and fireplaces, were stored separately.

Outside work stopped in November with the freeze-up—*la prise des glaces*—when the 80 per cent of Canadians who lived on farms (at least up to 1900) looked forward to putting away the ploughs, the harrows, and the harvesters, giving up the long hours at seeding and weeding. The land was resting, as were the men and women who worked it. For rural folk, the winter was the time for social life, sleighing, barn dances, courting, and frolics of all sorts. There were also commercial consequences to winter. Building stopped. Winter froze the rivers and lakes; transportation by water—the only means for bulk transport—stopped. Moreover, until the development of steam engines in the 1820s, water was the only source of power; lumber mills, flour mills, whatever depended on the power of running water, ground to a halt. Commerce slowed to a trickle.

If winter could be a festive time of year, there was no denying its tyranny. T.C. *Keefer, a mid-19th-century engineer, was poetic but rueful: 'An embargo which no human power can remove is laid on all our ports . . . The animation of business is suspended, the life blood of commerce is curdled and stagnant in the St. Lawrence—the great aorta of the North . . . blockaded and imprisoned by ice and apathy.' Keefer used such imagery to argue for the necessity of railways, and, after mid-century, Canadians shared his enthusiasm. Public and politicians took to railways, as one historian remarked, 'like a cheerful child to a pot of jam'. This zeal would last for the next 70 years, until the motor car came into its own. Winter was not conquered—it could not be, except on the west coast, where it resembled the western European variety—but with railways it no longer jeopardized commerce. When the great blizzards did come, there was still a primitive joy in being at home when the winds howled and the snow swirled around the house and barns, and the fireplace was the centre of the world.

P.B. WAITE

winter sports. Because of its long winters, when much of the land is covered by ice and snow, Canada is naturally a winter sports country. From early days settlers found recreational opportunities in the outdoors, from sleighing to skating to snowshoeing. Winter amusement included riding toboggans down the run at Quebec City, sledding down the ice cones formed by spray at Montmorency Falls, skating on the Rideau Canal at Ottawa, riding in a horse-drawn sleigh while bundled in bearskin, or playing hockey on frozen fields in the Prairies.

Most winter sports were of necessity outdoor activities. However, in central Canada, indoor curling and skating rinks were constructed, their natural ice maintained by the frigid air coming through large, open windows. After the first artificial ice rink was built in 1911, increasing numbers of Canadians were able to partake in winter sports, whether as participants or spectators. By the late 19th century winter sports had been modernized, rules standardized, and competition was developing from the local to the international level. The first Winter Olympics were held in 1924—although some winter sports had been included in the Olympics as early as 1908. Over the decades the games have inspired some of Canada's greatest athletic achievements.

Curling is the oldest organized sport in Canada, its first club formed in 1807 in Montreal. The first dominion championship was held in 1927. The first women's club was organized in 1894, but the first national ladies' championship was not held until 1961. Internationally, Canadian curlers have long held prominent positions: the men's and women's teams have won more world championships than any other country. Sandra Schmirler skipped three world championship rinks and in 1998 led her team to Canada's only curling Olympic gold medal in the sport.

Skiing can trace its origins, as a means of transportation, to prehistoric times in northern Europe. Cross-country skiing is the oldest form of ski racing. In Canada, the first cross-country runs were located in Quebec, in the Laurentians; the oldest club, the Montreal Ski Club, was formed in 1904. The Canadian Ski Marathon is the longest skiing event in North America, a two-day, 160-km run from Lachute, Quebec, to Ottawa. Since the mid-1980s, two forms of racing have been recognized for national and international competition: classical, in prepared grooves, and the faster freestyle skiing. At the 2002 Olympics, Beckie Scott won Canada's first cross-country medal in the 5-km free pursuit.

Alpine skiing races were first held in the Swiss Alps in 1902. In Canada, the emphasis gradually shifted from cross-country to alpine skiing, aided by the 1932 invention of the tow-rope in Quebec. Performances dramatically improved after cable bindings were introduced in 1935. Three competitive events developed: downhill, slalom, and giant slalom. The best-known and most successful woman skier is Nancy Greene Raine, who won the women's World Cup in 1967 and 1968, and two medals (gold and silver) at the 1968 Olympics. In the late 1970s and early 1980s, the 'Crazy Canucks'—Dave Irwin, Dave Murray, Steve Podborski, and Ken Read—dominated men's downhill, winning 14 events.

While skating has had a long history as a recreational activity in Europe, figure skating as a sport originated in the 1840s; by the 1880s precision figure tests for competition had been developed. Free skating, characterized by jumps and spins, had been introduced in the 1860s. The first men's world championship, combining figures and free skating, was held in 1896, and the first women's championship in 1906. In Canada, the most important figure skater of the late 1800s was Louis Rubenstein of Montreal, who won the unofficial world championship in 1890. Barbara Ann Scott brought glory to Canada, winning world championships in 1947 and 1948 and establishing herself as 'Canada's sweetheart' by winning the Olympic title in 1948. Petra Burka (1965) and Karen Magnussen (1973) also won world titles. Kurt Browning, the first man to perform a quadruple jump in competition, was world champion four times between 1989 and 1993. Other world champions are Norris Bowden (1954, 1955), Donald Jackson (1961), Donald McPherson (1963), Brian Orser (1987), and Elvis Stojko (1994, 1995, 1997). In pairs, Barbara Wagner and Robert Paul won four world titles (1957–1960) and Olympic gold (1960). They were followed as world champions by Maria and Otto Jelinek (1962), Barbara Underhill and Paul Martini (1984), and Isabelle Brasseur and Lloyd Eisler (1993). At the 2002 Olympics, Jamie Salé and David Pelletier saw their silver medals replaced with gold following a judging controversy. In 2003 Shae-Lynn Bourne and Victor Kraatz, ten-time Canadian champions, became the first Canadian ice dancers to win the world championship. Other outstanding Canadian ice dancers include Tracy Wilson and Robert McCall, who won the Olympic bronze medal in 1988.

Speed-skating races have been staged in Canada since 1854. Jack McCulloch won the world championships in 1897. During the 1920s and 1930s, several Canadians were successful internationally, especially in the demonstration events at the 1932 Olympics. In 1976 Sylvia Burka became the women's world champion. At the 1984 Olympics, Gaétan Boucher won two gold medals and one bronze. Catriona Le May Doan won the 500-m event in both the 1998 and 2002 Olympics. Speed-skating races are now staged on 400-m ovals. By contrast, short-track speed-skating races are held on 111-m tracks. In 1988 this form of speed skating come to prominence as an Olympic demonstration sport, with Canadians taking one first place, two seconds, and two thirds. At the 1992 Olympics, the women's short-track relay team won its event and Annie Perreault won the 500-m short-track event in 1998. Canada's most successful Olympic speed skater is Marc Gagnon: between 1994 and 2002 he won more medals (five, including three golds) than any other Canadian winter Olympian.

Tobogganing, or sledding, developed in Quebec, using the type of sled employed by Natives for transportation. Toboggan racing began in the late 1890s and evolved into three competitive forms. The bobsleigh, which is operated by teams of two or four, consists of two sleds, one behind the other, each with a pair of runners. At the Olympics, Vic Emery's four-man team won the 1964 event and Pierre Lueders and Dave MacEachern won the two-man event in 1998. Luge (singles or doubles) uses a single sled with the rider on his or her back. Skeleton also uses a single sled, but the rider lies face down.

Other winter sports include the biathlon, a Nordic sport that combines cross-country skiing with rifle shooting. Canada's greatest biathlete is Myriam Bédard, who won both the 7.5-km and 15-km events at the 1994 Olympics. Freestyle skiing, which consists of three events—moguls, ballet, and aerials—became an organized sport in the 1950s and an official Olympic event in 1992. Jean-Luc Brassard won moguls in 1994. Ringette, a Canadian game, was developed in 1963 as a winter sport for girls. Teams of six play on ice *hockey surfaces using straight sticks and a rubber ring. The first national tournament was held in 1975, and international contests are regularly played with teams from the northern United States. Ski jumping, a Nordic sport, uses a specially constructed hill. Jumps are evaluated for distance and style. Snowboarding, which emerged in the 1980s, became an Olympic sport in 1998, when Ross Rebagliati won the giant slalom. BARBARA SCHRODT

witchcraft. In the second half of the 17th century, when witchcraft beliefs and trials were prevalent in Europe, New France was a small frontier community. The settlers brought with them traditional folkloric culture, in which the devil, magic, and supernatural occurrences played a strong role. While witchcraft beliefs thrived, few trials for witchcraft occurred. Three cases are documented. The accused were all men, charged for using demonic spells against their former sweethearts. In 1658, René Besnard cast a spell by knotting a string, which caused a newly married couple not to be able to consummate their marriage. He was fined and banished from Montreal. A few years later, Daniel Will, who caused a woman to be possessed by demons, was executed (he was found guilty of other offences, so it is not clear that the possession offence was capital). In 1685, Jean Campagnard, accused of causing several people to become ill through witchcraft, was acquitted on appeal. By this time, witchcraft trials had practically ceased in France, and the colonial elite reflected French practices. Local factors played a role as well. In Europe, most witchcraft accusations were directed against women. In Quebec women were in very short supply. In 1660 single men outnumbered eligible women by six to one. Even widows with children remarried easily. Isolated, older women were often those accused of witchcraft in Europe, but in New France this category did not exist. In the colony the settlers lived on separate properties along the St Lawrence. The basic social unit was the family farmstead, in which members co-operated in clearing land, growing crops, and defending against Indian attacks. These patterns of settlement and the unusual demographic structure of the colony seem to underlay the paucity of witchcraft proceedings in New France. JONATHAN PEARL

Wolseley Expedition. As events in *Red River over the winter of 1869–70 increasingly indicated that reaching an agreement with the insurgents in the settlement would be difficult, the Canadian government began to consider the possibility of armed intervention. The prospect of military action by a joint British–Canadian force was first seriously broached by cabinet on 4 February 1870. After much negotiation, the British government agreed to provide troops, on the condition that they were not used to enforce Canadian sovereignty on the inhabitants of Red River. Before the discussions began between the Canadian government and delegates from Red River in late April, Colonel Garnet Wolseley was chosen as field commander, the 60th Rifles were accepted as the British contribution, and plans for a volunteer militia from Ontario and Quebec were in motion. The first troops were sent west in mid-May. By this time the Manitoba Act had been passed, and there seemed little need for military force. Nonetheless the expedition continued to advance, overcoming many obstacles beyond *Thunder Bay in its passage by boats along the Winnipeg River system to Lake Winnipeg and the Red River. Wolseley and his troops harboured hope that the Riel government would resist them, and Wolseley certainly believed that the expedition was intended to be punitive. He sent the British regulars back east almost as soon as they had arrived, leaving the volunteer force—mainly from Ontario—in virtual occupation of Winnipeg for many months. J.M. BUMSTED

Woman's Christian Temperance Union. The WCTU began in 1874 in small-town Ontario. Local unions multiplied, provincial unions formed, and in 1885 the national WCTU was created. By 1891 it had 9,343 members; in 1914 there were 16,000. It was one of the first non-denominational national women's organizations, and from its formation to the First World War, when *prohibition was adopted, it was one of the strongest, most vocal, and farthest ranging in its involvement in Canadian society. Its members, mostly middle-class women with an evangelical Protestant outlook, blamed intemperance for many of society's problems. Their solution was total prohibition through the power of the state. In its effort to win prohibition, the WCTU came to advocate votes for women as a way of making its members heard. In supporting both prohibition and *women's suffrage, the WCTU emerged as one of the more radical reform organizations in the pre-war period. In addition, it endorsed many other reforms and charitable activities: *social purity, assistance to unwed mothers, sex education and the teaching of the science underlying temperance beliefs, industrial schools, and the work of city missions. The real work of the WCTU was done at the local level, and these unions chose their own causes.

With the end of prohibition in the 1920s, the WCTU found itself out of step with much of society. It maintained its reform orientation—*child welfare, sex hygiene, *public health—and remained active in the *temperance movement but could point to few successes. By the 1960s, even though it kept up with concerns about contemporary drug use, many of its interests seemed aligned with an 'older' type of moral reform. As well, temperance organizations lost their monopoly on the social analysis of alcohol consumption as this was taken over by medical and social science research. WCTU membership declined from 3,787 in the 1980s to about 500 today. WENDY MITCHINSON

women and medicine. Women have long had an uneasy relationship with organized medicine. Since before the 19th century, physicians have judged men's bodies the norm against which women's appeared more mysterious, complex, and prone to physical and psychological breakdown. Throughout the last two centuries, three interrelated themes impinging on medical treatment of women have dominated: the close relationship between medicine and culture, the expansion of medicine's influence in society, and medicine's increasing ability to intervene in the workings of the human body.

Over these years, Canadians have been strong believers in the adage that 'biology is destiny'. Women could give birth to children, therefore they *should* give birth to children. Doctors believed this as well. However, they also believed that women, who once gave birth with the support of *midwives and other female friends or relatives, could no longer do so. By the end of the 19th century, doctors argued that women needed medical assistance in childbirth. In particular they offered them anaesthesia to take away the pain. Many Canadian women, attracted by what they saw as the advances of 'science', believed that by seeking medical help they were ensuring the best for themselves and their unborn babies. So much so that, by the early years of the 20th century, most women had physicians with them during birth. While most births still occurred at home, throughout the 1920s and 1930s increasing numbers occurred in hospitals. By 1940 over 45 per cent took place in hospitals, by 1945 over 63 per cent, and by the end of the century 99 per cent. The maternal mortality rate remained high in Canada compared to many other industrialized nations where midwife-managed births dominated. With the introduction of antibiotics in the 1940s the rate declined from 6.4 deaths per 1,000 live births in 1925–6 to 1.64 in 1946. With hospital births came more intervention and standardization. Caesarean sections increased from 5 per cent in the late 1940s to 20 per cent by the early 1990s. Until recently, women in labour were placed in the lithotomy position, were refused the comfort of family, and underwent enemas, episiotomies, and shaving of the pubic area. The women's health movement of the late 20th century challenged the degree of intervention in childbirth and helped alter the way hospital personnel treated birthing women.

Linked to medical intervention in childbirth is the issue of contraception. Until the beginning of the 20th century, physicians in Canada were publicly opposed to contraception, arguing it was immoral, unnatural, and medically dangerous. After the First World War the profession was not as engaged with this issue, and physicians' moral arguments against it had lessened. Evidence suggests that many non-Catholic physicians, in response to patient inquiry and demand, were offering married women birth-control advice. Physicians supported contraception to control the number of children in a family but not to enable women to remain childless. As late as the 1970s, many physicians regarded women who did not want children as deviant. *Abortion was a form of *birth control that physicians strongly opposed, supporting anti-abortion legislation in the 19th century. However, non-Catholic physicians did give the life of the mother priority over that of the fetus and performed therapeutic abortions in exceptional cases, even though their legality was unclear until changes in legislation in 1969. Hospital abortion committees, which followed from this legislation, reinforced doctors' control over abortion and resulted in uneven access across the country. In 1988 the Supreme Court of Canada struck down the abortion law. Both birth control and abortion forced Canadians to acknowledge female sexuality. Still, physicians continued to downplay the significance of women's sexuality as compared to men's. Moreover, until recently they sanctioned the expression of this sexuality only within a heterosexual, marital relationship.

Doctors shared society's view of women's physical vulnerability, despite the strength women demonstrated in factories, on farms, and in giving birth. In the 19th century, although encouraging mild exercise, physicians advised women to stay away from strenuous athletic activities. They also suggested that women should not engage in taxing mental challenges—such as higher education—in order to save their limited energy for the future trials of pregnancy and childbirth. Such arguments declined after the First World War, but medical debates continued about the ability of women to engage in elite sport.

The pressures of puberty were another concern for physicians. Girls who grew up in the first half of the 20th century sometimes had their physical activities curtailed while they were menstruating. If physicians considered the menstrual cycle both emotionally and physically taxing, its termination was equally problematic. Early medical literature often depicted menopausal women as irrational; well into the late 20th century pharmaceutical advertisements, aimed at doctors, portrayed them as needy. In the late 1930s physicians began to prescribe estrogen for women with severe menopausal symptoms. By the end of the century, hormone replacement therapy had become the prescribed treatment.

Doctors viewed women as more susceptible than men to disease, and cancer rates reinforced that image. The belief that women were meant to have children was underscored by the link between breast cancer and childlessness; at the same time, doctors overlooked that cervical and uterine cancer was linked to childbearing. From the late 19th century until well after the mid-20th, the favoured treatment for breast cancer was radical mastectomy. Yet, because such procedures were challenged by women and some surgeons, less invasive surgery had become the norm by the end of the century.

Society has long viewed women as more emotional than men and more prone to mental illness. In the 19th century physicians regarded 'hysteria' as a female disease. Even in the late 20th century, doctors prescribed twice as many minor tranquilizers, especially anti-depressants, to women than to men.

In the late 19th century, gynecology became a medical specialty predicated on the assumption that the female reproductive system was problematic. With the increasing safety of surgery as a result of anaesthesia and antiseptic procedures, physicians could increasingly intervene, and they helped many women. But some physicians feared that women were being subjected to too much surgery. In the late 19th century, in some asylums, physicians such as Richard *Bucke performed surgery on women with a variety of gynecological disorders in the hopes of curing them of their insanity. In the 1920s and 1930s, sterilization procedures were performed on some women to prevent the birth of 'feeble-minded' children. In the early 1970s, tubal ligations were more frequently performed on Native women than on non-Native. Estimates were that in some provinces one half of the hysterectomies performed in the 1970s were unnecessary. If earlier in the century some physicians focused on preventing certain categories of women from reproducing, by later in the century the treatment of infertility had become a growing concern. New and sometimes invasive procedures were developed to facilitate conception, some of which sparked debate on issues of medical ethics.

Physicians' attitudes towards and treatment of women are reflections of the society in which they live. Yet women have not passively accepted the treatment offered. They acted on the medical advice they agreed with, ignored that with which they disagreed, and often looked beyond the medical profession for help. In recent years, women have become even more active as patients, raising the image of a health-care partnership between patient and doctor. WENDY MITCHINSON

women and the law. Whether Canadian *law operated visibly or invisibly, whether it aided or coerced women, regulated or frustrated them, it has been an important factor shaping their family, sexual, reproductive, work, social, and political lives. Federal statutes, for example, determined whether and how women could control their own reproduction, what was deemed 'criminal' behaviour for their sex, who qualified as a Canadian citizen, and, of course, who could vote. Provincial laws shaped many women's work lives, their welfare entitlement (or lack of it), and their responsibilities to their *children, to name only a few areas of regulation. The law's reach was immense, but it did not affect all women in a similar manner: its implementation through policing and the judicial system varied significantly by class, culture, and race. Generalization is thus a difficult task.

Historians have generally focused on a variety of approaches, stressing the way in which the law regulated women's social and more intimate lives; how women used the law, often to increase their freedom, peace, or independence; and how and why the law changed over time, shaped by factors such as politics, ideology, and power relations. While some early writing focused on the law as a gendered norm, and a very oppressive one, later works have complicated this by stressing how class shaped women's experience of the law, and also how the law was racialized and racist. Historians have also distinguished between *Quebec's civil law and English Canada's common law. In the 19th century, the civil code shaped a family regime in which widows inherited a share of their husband's estate, offering women a small measure of economic protection. Yet in some English-Canadian provinces, women had to fight for analogous 'dower' rights. Advantages under the civil code were balanced by disadvantages: married women in Quebec could not legally control their own wages until 1931, nor was the vote secured until 1940. Different legal regimes and social entitlements remain a continuing theme for Quebec women today.

Another area of difference has been Native women's experience under Canadian law, particularly the *Indian Act (1876). Nineteenth-century Canadian courts felt they had a right to interpret whether Native customary marriages were 'legal' or not; similar debates and struggles continued in the 20th century, as some Native communities protested the sections of the Indian Act that denied Native women 'Indian status' if they married a non-Native. Over the course of the 19th and 20th centuries, the law was a contested site for Native women, whose families and communities sometimes drew on their own legal procedures, while also incorporating legal traditions of the Canadian state.

Nineteenth-century Canadian law, argues Constance Backhouse, was 'an almost perfect example of a formally patriarchal institution', presuming a household in which power resided with the father/husband, with this pre-eminence extending to the broader society. Nowhere was this more evident than in family law, with children seen as the property of their father, although feminist efforts to extend mothers' rights had some success after the late 19th century. It was not simply statute law (i.e., legislated codes), but case law as interpreted by the courts that reflected the dominant (often patriarchal) ideology of the time. Similar themes hold for 20th-century studies that argue that legal protection from *'rape' or 'wife beating' could be quite hollow: the courts endorsed a double standard that scorned those women who were perceived to stand outside the rigid sexual and familial standards of the time. Protection was more likely to aid white, middle-class, monogamous women; less likely to cover women of colour, poor women, or those deemed sexually non-conformist.

While the regulatory force of the law has been the theme of many historical studies, another predominant theme has been women's use of the law, to protect themselves and their *families, and to resist oppression, individually or collectively. Indeed, a prevailing concern of 19th- and 20th-century *feminists has been law reform. During the 20th century, reformers attempted to gain admission of women to the *legal profession, equalize divorce laws, legislate equal pay, and create equality rights for lesbians and gays. While 19th-century feminists were deeply concerned with women's property rights and had little interest in *birth control, 20th-century feminists attempted to equalize employment rights and, after the

1960s, give women legal control over their own bodies and reproduction. Historians remain divided over how *possible* meaningful reform is under the law: the more liberal and optimistic see the state as a powerful potential ally in this regard; materialist, Marxist, and radical feminists are more wary of the possibility of successfully altering the law to secure economic, social, and political equality.

JOAN SANGSTER

women doctors. Before and after European conquest, diverse populations of Canadian women practised *midwifery, herbalism, and *nursing, but they could not work legally as allopathic physicians until the late 19th century. In order to practise, Canada's first woman physician, James Miranda Barry (1795–1865), disguised her sex. Emily Stowe (1831–93), usually recognized as Canada's pioneer woman doctor, Jennie Kidd Gowanlock Trout (1841–1921), the first Canadian woman to receive a medical licence, and Irma LeVasseur (1887–1964), the first French-Canadian woman to practise medicine, were denied admission to Canadian *medical schools, receiving their degrees from American institutions. Upon their return they struggled to establish practices, often specially for women. After graduation from Clemence Sophia Lozier's homeopathic New York Medical College for Women, Stowe was denied a Canadian medical licence by the Ontario College of Physicians and Surgeons. A renegade, she practised unlicensed for over ten years, used homeopathic principles and remedies and the herbalist traditions of her mother, and was tried for performing an abortion. Trout passed the provincial qualifying exams easily, but similarly struggled to established an eclectic practice that incorporated electric and galvanic treatments.

Canada's early women physicians, often from families that valued women's education, promoted the medical education of women. Stowe's parents, Quakers who immigrated to Upper Canada from Vermont, were committed to educating their six daughters. Stowe, like Trout, graduated from normal school and taught before attending medical school. She mentored other women, including Jennie Trout and her own daughter Ann Augusta Stowe-Gullen (1857–1943). Stowe's activism secured a place for her daughter at the Toronto School of Medicine, later the University of Toronto. Stowe-Gullen, the first woman to graduate from a Canadian medical school, later described her education as 'not a pathway strewn with roses'. Though she interned at the Toronto General Hospital, the doors of both universities and hospitals closed behind her. Opportunities outside Ontario were similarly limited. Dalhousie Medical College officially opened to women in 1881 but Annie Isabella Hamilton (1866–1941) became its first graduate only in 1888.

Women's struggle for medical education reflected broader Victorian debates about women, science, and education. In 1883 Stowe and Stowe-Gullen collaborated with leading male physicians to found the Toronto Women's Medical College, which promised to train women to the same scientific standard as men. Stowe-Gullen, appointed demonstrator in anatomy, became the first and only woman on the faculty. Jennie Trout had a different vision, in which women and Canadians dominated the administration, trustees, and staff. Trout's separatist ideals gave shape to a rival school in Kingston. The two institutions, merged in 1894 into the Ontario Medical College for Women, provided opportunities for classroom and clinical training until 1906, when the University of Toronto accepted women and the college dispensary evolved into the Women's College Hospital.

Women doctors faced different geographic, social, and professional barriers but shared aspirations and struggles. Many, including Annie Hamilton, worked as missionaries in India and China; others provided medical assistance to needy Canadian women. Several became political leaders and advocates for social change. Stowe, a 'scientific socialist' committed to applying science to the improvement of the human condition, was first vice-president of the Canadian Women's Suffrage Association and a leader of the *National Council of Women. Elizabeth *Smith-Shortt (1859–1949), an early graduate of Queen's, advocated women's equality and maternal and child health. These women made few scientifically significant discoveries; no diseases or procedures are named for them. Yet they paved the way for women's entry into the profession and cared for needy women at home and abroad. Their battles to open medical education to women expose the diversity of women's healing traditions, the tensions within healing professions, and the impacts of science on late-19th- and early-20th-century Canadian society.

GEORGINA FELDBERG

women in the labour movement. When industrialization led to an increased demand for workers, women and children joined men in various forms of waged work. Despite the increasingly prominent role of women workers by the last third of the 19th century, working-class culture envisioned men as the main breadwinners, and women as wives and mothers, thus discouraging or denigrating women's paid labour. As school attendance and child labour laws cut back the number of children employed, women took up the slack, filling unskilled and semi-skilled jobs as servants and as laundry, factory, and agricultural workers. At best, women were viewed as temporary and unskilled workers who sometimes threatened men's jobs and wages. Labour organizations most often ignored them, with a few exceptions: the shoemakers' Knights of St Crispin inspired the Daughters of St Crispin in the 1870s, and in the 1880s the *Knights of Labor pledged to organize all workers regardless of gender, race, creed, or skill. Although the Knights did not live up to all their promises, women were involved in at least 25 of their assemblies (locals) before their decline in the 1890s. This decade also witnessed the creation of a number of women's organizations, including Toronto's Working Women's Protective Association.

Although until 1914 the Trades and Labor Congress of Canada passed formal resolutions urging their exclusion from the labour force, women continued to work for pay, and some joined trade *unions, particularly in the *garment industry. Between 1900 and 1914 women were involved in over 100 disputes in the garment and textile trades alone. The First World War era witnessed a surge of union organization that culminated in the *Winnipeg General Strike, which involved several thousand women workers. After the Second World War, efforts in highly feminized work places, such as Quebec's textile mills, resulted in intimidation and the arrest of organizers such as Madeleine *Parent of the United Textile Workers of America.

Women's presence in the labour movement improved dramatically in the 1960s and 1970s, when public sector workers won the right to bargain collectively. The Canadian Union of Public Employees, founded in 1963, had by 1975 become the largest single union in Canada; in the early 1990s women made up over half its membership. Despite a long history of professional organization, in most provinces nurses and teachers had to wait until the 1970s before they gained the right to withdraw their labour.

The growing presence of women in labour organizations at a time when the second-wave women's movement gained prominence led to debates on issues including equal pay for work of equal value, sexual harassment, reproductive health, childcare, and racism. Women formed committees and caucuses to push for equality within the labour movement, demanding more women in positions of authority. In the last 25 years women have achieved prominence as leaders of unions (Grace Hartman, Judy Darcy, in CUPE) and within the *Canadian Labour Congress (Shirley Carr, Nancy Riche).

LINDA KEALEY

women's education. Women were originally taught by their elders. First Nations girls learned to sew or make snowshoes from their older relatives and absorbed the ways of their people from play, song, and ceremony. Girls in New France and the early British North American colonies continued in the same way, learning what they needed to know from family and community.

Formal education, when it came, had both religious and socio-economic roots. Missionary zeal and upward mobility alike drove New France's first tiny convent schools, dedicated to both indigenous and settlers' daughters. *Ursuline and *Congrégation de Notre-Dame sisters taught practical arts as well as reading, writing, and religion, and, perhaps most importantly, the discipline of the ordered school day, week, and year. By the mid-18th century these schools had grown more numerous, although their impact was limited chiefly to urban centres. Soon, Protestant English-speaking settlers were introducing other styles of schooling. Girls were taught by a governess at home or, more typically, by a *school mistress in her home, while ladies' academies, similarly domestic, were created for those with higher class aspirations. By the mid-19th century it was in such seminaries, or the burgeoning French and English convent academies, that young women learned about literature and science and had the opportunity to study modern languages or practise domestic arts. The more important, denominationally sponsored schools moved into larger premises where many girls could live and study. In the meantime, the majority of girls were learning to attend the tax-supported, chiefly co-educational government schools that were gradually created, by law, in every settler community. Some Aboriginal girls went to these schools but increasingly attended mission schools instead, although at least one girls' boarding school in British Columbia included them. All 19th-century schools emphasized discipline, but minority and poor girls probably suffered most from overly strict regimes, foreshadowing the incarceration of some in 20th-century reform or Indian *residential schools.

By Confederation, ladies' schools were entrenched, as were many older or larger government institutions, some of which belonged to city systems boasting a central school for advanced pupils. Girls were excluded from government-funded grammar schools or the religious seminaries intended to prepare boys for university and, equally, from elite colleges and universities themselves. Families with daughters began to resent their exclusion from institutions that were, in part, supported by their taxes. Nor were they appeased when, in Ontario, girls were admitted to grammar schools but counted as only half what boys were worth in calculating the government grant. By the end of the 19th century grammar schools had been replaced by *high schools and collegiate institutes, which accepted girls on more equal terms. Young women also attended teacher-training institutions in growing numbers. By the 20th century, they were additionally drawn to both publicly and privately funded schools dedicated to commercial or musical education, household science (especially in Quebec), or, in one interesting Toronto case, 'physical culture and expression', foreshadowing the idea of physical education for all girls. Hospitals had nursing schools, and a small college trained *women doctors.

Women's struggle to enter *universities began in the 1860s. Opposition was powerful, as men resisted the idea of women seeking professional or even arts and science degrees in institutions that had always been male enclaves. There were no women's washrooms, beleaguered university presidents complained. The first successes were in the 1870s: Grace Annie Lockhart's BSc from Mount Allison in 1875 was the first university degree granted to a woman in the British Empire. By 1890, most anglophone universities admitted women, although not as equals. Many women were steered into female fields such as household science, or discouraged from entering supposedly male areas of study or pursuing graduate degrees. The struggle for equity would continue into the 20th century, as women fought to get into Quebec universities, which held out longer, into schools like engineering, or to be treated equally once admitted. Universities had washrooms for women, but sometimes very unequal athletic facilities, and few women faculty. Newer universities were more welcoming to women. When, in the 1970s, women scholars developed a field dedicated to understanding the gendering of education, along with much else in Canadian life, they encountered hostility similar to that experienced a century before by the first university women. But as earlier generations did, they also found friends. Women's and gender studies continue to grow and prosper, as more Canadians, both women and men, share the goal of greater equality between the sexes in education and society. ALISON PRENTICE

Women's Institutes. Rural women's organization, founded at Stoney Creek, Ontario. In 1897 Adelaide *Hoodless, a social reformer, argued that improving the quality of life for rural women through domestic science education would help to curb *rural depopulation. Based on that logic, the Ontario Department of Agriculture supplied funding and personnel to begin establishing Women's Institutes by the turn of the century. Other provinces soon created their own versions of these popular women's organizations. By 1909, British Columbia and Alberta had WI groups; in Saskatchewan the groups were called Homemakers' Clubs, and in Manitoba, Household Science Societies. The WI was established in Quebec and New Brunswick by 1911, and in Prince Edward Island and Nova Scotia by 1913. In Newfoundland, groups known as Jubilee Guilds were established in 1935, and after entering Confederation in 1949 they too adopted the WI name. By 1919, Ontario had 899 WI branches and expansion continued across the country. In February 1919, at a meeting in Winnipeg, Emily *Murphy was elected the first national president of the new Federated Women's Institutes of Canada. Canadians introduced the idea of WI in Britain during the First World War, and by 1933 an international organization known as the Associated Country Women of the World was created; its first president, Margaret Robertson Watt, was from British Columbia. Today the ACWW represents rural women in over 70 countries and enjoys consultative status with the *United Nations.

Best known for promoting domestic science education, the WI has also provided a forum for lobbying governments at various levels. From resolutions to improve roads and schools, to provincial health reforms and national standards for consumer products, the WI became an important voice for rural women's concerns. Historians debate the nature of this activism: some regard it as very conservative and traditional, while others identify it as rural *feminism. Local WI activities include the compilation of community history books called the Tweedsmuir Books, after Lady Tweedsmuir. During both world wars the WI was active in fundraising, knitting, preserving food, and providing material aid to the overseas campaigns. The organization's popularity peaked when emphasis on domestic skill and consumer lobbying activity coincided with the return to domesticity after the Second World War. In 1953, the national membership surpassed 87,000 women.

The FWIC submitted a brief to the Royal Commission on the Status of Women, but did not share the emerging ideas of radical feminism. Recent social changes, including the rise of post-secondary education, women's participation in the paid labour force, and the demise of the family farm have transformed rural life and help to explain the WI's decline. In 1997, national membership stood at 24,000 women in 1,567 local branches. This once forceful women's organization faces significant challenges for its future. LINDA M. AMBROSE

Women's Royal Canadian Naval Service. With the creation of the WRCNS on 31 July 1942, the navy became the last of the three armed forces to admit women. At a total enlistment of 7,126 it was the smallest, and therefore most selective, of the three women's services; as such, it managed to avoid much of the gossip maligning servicewomen's morality. Most Wrens, as members were called, worked on shore stations, predominantly as clerical staff, wireless operators, and drivers. Wrens were stationed at naval bases across Canada, as well as in Newfoundland, New York, and Washington, DC. Approximately 1,000 received a coveted posting to England. The first class of enlistees trained in Ottawa in October 1942 under officers borrowed from the British Women's Royal Naval Service. Virtually all other enlistees were trained in Galt, Ontario, on the *Conestoga*, the *Royal Canadian Navy's first ship to be commanded by a woman, Lt Cdr Isabel Macneill. Advanced and trades training occurred on a variety of other WRCNS establishments. The WRCNS was disbanded by December 1946, but was restored to service in 1951, during the *Korean War. It ceased to exist in January 1955, when the RCN became the first Commonwealth navy to enrol women in the Regular Force.
TINA DAVIDSON AND RUTH ROACH PIERSON

women's suffrage movement. Canadian suffragism originated in an acute recognition that women were substantially disadvantaged by their lack of political equality. Its supporters were overwhelmingly 'suffragists', or supporters of non-violent tactics, and not 'suffragettes', as the militants of Britain's Women's Social and Political Union (WSPU) were known. As the *franchise simultaneously widened over the 19th century to include a wider range of men and shrank to eliminate some propertied women, feminists turned to the vote both as an expression of natural justice and as an instrument for bringing maternal values to bear on society. In time, too, the vote was justified as one means of controlling potential challenges to middle-class elites. From the mid-19th century on, women reformers, often inspired by religious—especially Protestant—evangelism, targeted education, the law, poverty, child welfare, employment, public health, violence, and temperance. The slow pace of reform, together with growing confidence in female moral superiority and equal rights, inspired increasing numbers of suffragists, although until the beginning of the 20th century this option was often considered radical. Foremost across Canada in pressing for the vote was the *Woman's Christian Temperance Union. Founded in Ontario in 1874 by Letitia Youmans, it became a national organization in 1883. In 1891 it endorsed female suffrage. The first group to dedicate itself exclusively to the suffrage cause was the Canadian Women's Suffrage Association (CWSA) in 1883, founded as the Toronto Women's Literary Club in 1876 by Dr Emily Howard Stowe. In 1881 Sarah Curzon of the literary club became associate editor of *Canadian Citizen*, a weekly temperance newspaper endorsing the vote.

The 1870s and 1880s seemed full of promise. A suffrage bill was introduced in the British Columbia legislature in 1872; that province's propertied women received the municipal franchise in 1873, and Ontario spinsters and widows won the same right in 1882, those in New Brunswick in 1886, Nova Scotia in 1887, and Prince Edward Island in 1888; and Prime Minister John A. *Macdonald came out as a supporter in the debates over the 1885 Franchise Act. In 1889 the CWSA was reinvigorated as the Dominion Women's Enfranchisement Association (DWEA) and initiated an active campaign that included visits from leading American suffragists such as Dr Anna Shaw and Susan B. Anthony. Although it remained Toronto-based, the DWEA hosted the first national suffrage convention.

By the 1890s, suffrage agitation faltered as a wide variety of causes, including not only temperance and prohibition but maternal health, child welfare, prison reform, and immigration, preoccupied female activists. Changes attendant on rising levels of industrialization, urbanization, and immigration, along with fears about social instability and mixing, encouraged interest in the conservative potential of female voters. More than before, some suffragists trusted that women, especially those from the middle class, would enhance the legitimacy of the state and counter the electoral potential of unruly workers and immigrants. Such justification on grounds of expediency existed side by side with the stress on equal rights and maternalism. Discussions about the vote were further complicated by the emergence of the educated, employed, and independent 'new woman', as depicted in Agnes Maule Machar's novel *Roland Graeme: Knight* (1892). Just what was the role of the new woman in Canada's increasingly complicated race and class politics? A strong current of *anti-feminism was one fearful response: women had to accept male leadership or society would collapse. Reactionary threats stifled some voices, but suffragists targeted male privilege everywhere and looked for allies in organizations like the *National Council of Women of Canada (NCWC) and its local councils (LCW). In 1906 the NCWC established a Standing Committee on Political Equality; two years later the Victoria LCW became the first to endorse the franchise. In 1910, after years of attempting to avoid offending conservatives, the NCWC embraced suffrage. Occasional victories, such as the election of three women to the Toronto School Board in 1892 and the winning of the right of women to practise law in New Brunswick in 1906, kept hearts hopeful. In 1894, the Manitoba Equal Franchise Club became the first suffrage group west of Ontario. The 1890s also produced the first 'Mock Parliaments', a fundraising strategy that turned the tables—men begged women for the vote. Into the first decade of the 20th century, the WCTU remained on the front line almost everywhere.

Suffrage groups with national aspirations almost invariably started in Toronto. In 1907 the DWEA became the Canadian Suffrage Association (CSA). Seven years later Toronto's Political Equality League claimed the title of the National Union of Woman Suffrage Societies of Canada. CSA leaders included the pioneer free-thinking physician Emily Stowe and her daughter Dr Augusta Stowe-Gullen but also relative newcomers such as the unconventional dressmaker and journalist Flora MacDonald *Denison, who admired the suffragettes. In 1911 the WSPU's Emmeline Pankhurst captivated Torontonians.

Elsewhere suffragists rarely aspired to national leadership. By the 1890s, Prairie activists were visible, often in association with the WCTU, and that region produced Canada's best-known suffragist, Nellie L. *McClung. Suffragists also emerged from Manitoba's egalitarian Icelandic community; in 1898–1910 Margret Benedictsson and her husband, Sigfus, published a woman's rights magazine, *Freyja (Woman)*. Official endorsement by the Grain Growers' Association of Manitoba in 1911 signaled the rising support that helped produce the Winnipeg Political Equality League, which included such notables as Francis Marion *Beynon, Lillian Beynon Thomas, Cora *Hind, and McClung. When Alberta and Saskatchewan became provinces in 1905, they already counted suffrage supporters among WCTU and NCWC members. An English immigrant to Saskatchewan, Violet *McNaughton, and an Ontario-born newcomer to Alberta, Emily *Murphy, became influential champions. The West Coast had a still longer history. As usual, the WCTU led the way in energizing suffrage-minded immigrants, who like their counterparts elsewhere largely ignored the political interests of indigenous women. Between 1884 and 1899 suffrage bills regularly disturbed Victoria's legislature. In 1908 the Political Equality League of Victoria became the province's pioneer suffrage group, followed almost immediately by a similar Vancouver League. In 1911 they became the provincial Political Equality League, captained by long-time temperance leader Maria Grant. On its left stood the BC Woman's Suffrage League, led by working-class British suffragette Helena *Gutteridge.

On the other coast, eastern feminists encountered more opposition, notably a well-established Catholic Church, scattered and smaller settlements, steady out-migration, and fewer allies, whether from the labour or farmer movements. The WCTU was often a lonely champion, although from the 1890s on LCWs marshalled protest. Intrepid spirits in New Brunswick inaugurated the Women's Enfranchisement Association in 1894 and nine years later the Equal Franchise League. Attention to victories elsewhere and a visit to Saint John by British suffragette Sylvia Pankhurst in 1912 heartened provincial activists such as the WEA's Ella Hatheway as they criticized recalcitrant legislatures. Nova Scotia produced six suffrage bills, 1891–7, but no independent society emerged. Suffragists such as Dr Eliza Ritchie, Edith Murray, Edith Archibald, and Agnes Dennis concentrated on the LCW. Not until 1917 were they confident enough to establish the NS Equal Franchise Association. In Prince Edward Island and Newfoundland only the WCTU was brave enough to endorse the vote. PEI never produced a suffrage group. The Newfoundland Women's Franchise League waited until 1920, although the island's suffragists, such as Armine Gosling, were consoled by ties to the International Woman Suffrage Alliance.

Nova Scotia introduced suffrage in 1918, New Brunswick in 1919, PEI in 1922, and Newfoundland in 1925. Women's contribution to the war effort and Liberals' desire for their vote brought suffrage still earlier, in 1916, to the Prairie provinces and, a year later, to Ontario and British Columbia. Ottawa also began to shift, enfranchising female relatives of servicemen in 1917 and other women in 1918. Two groups of women were notably absent from the federal franchise: status Indians and those of Asian descent. The vote led to a series of 'firsts'—woman in a provincial legislature (BC, 1916), female member of Parliament (1921), and female senator (1930).

Hobbled by conservative Catholic nationalism, Quebec resisted provincial enfranchisement throughout the 1920s and 1930s. From its founding, the Montreal LCW aspired to link French- and English-speaking feminists but the former remained a minority. In 1907 francophones such as Marie *Lacoste-Gérin-Lajoie drew on French Catholic feminism to establish the *Fédération nationale St-Jean-Baptiste, which concentrated on charity, education, and employment and avoided the suffragist question. Montreal anglophones created the Montreal Suffrage Association (1913–19). Thereafter, the Franchise Committee of the Montreal Women's Club continued the struggle. More important was the Provincial Franchise Committee (PFC), with a dual French–English leadership, established in 1922, although determined opposition restricted its efforts. In 1927 McGill professor Idola *Saint-Jean created the more distinctly French-Canadian and working-class Alliance canadienne pour le vote des femmes du Québec. In 1928 Thérèse *Casgrain became sole president of the PFC, which had become the League for Women's Rights. In the 1930s the Alliance and the League for Women's Rights organized numerous educational campaigns but suffrage bills failed. Not until 1940 did the Liberal government, pressed hard by the federal party, dare introduce a successful suffrage measure. Some Canadians had to wait even longer. Like the men in their communities, female Chinese and Indo-Canadians gained federal and provincial franchises in 1947, the Japanese a year later. Non-status Indians were enfranchised, starting with British Columbia in 1949 and finishing with Quebec in 1969. The *Inuit received the federal franchise in 1950 and status Indians in 1960. These gains, while often ignored, are also part of the history of female enfranchisement, although *feminism, owing to its early preoccupation with European Canadians, is only peripherally associated with any of them.

VERONICA STRONG-BOAG

women's work. Women's work, both informal (unpaid) and formal (paid), has been central to the production of Canadian wealth and well-being, with informal labour often less visible, performed within the household as 'domestic labour' or in the community as volunteer labour. Fundamental to women's work for wages and salaries in the 19th and 20th centuries was the 'ghettoization' of female labour: gender, race, and class structured women's work choices and experiences. For many women, work was primarily a means of survival; however, they also took pride in their skills and economic contribution and some attempted to alter women's profoundly unequal place in the labour force.

Women's paid labour was apparent in 19th-century white settler societies as girls and women laboured as maids, farm workers, or, less often, as teachers in home-based schools. Only a few were self-supporting; most contributed their meagre wages to the larger project of family survival. This pattern continued with industrialization and women's employment in *factory-based work, an extremely uneven process across the country. Young women were also likely to be engaged in home labour, sometimes unrecorded in the census, such as sewing piecework for subcontractors.

By 1901, women constituted 13.4 per cent of the labour force across Canada. They were employed in farm and domestic work, and in *manufacturing, especially textiles, garment making, boot and shoe production, food and tobacco work. While this appeared to extend women's domestic tasks into the industrial workplace, some home-based work, such as dairying, was assumed by male workers as it moved into the arena of mass production and new technology. Women's wage work was generally perceived to be unskilled, but notions of skill were shaped by gender ideology and might alter over time, as women's exclusion from printing and telegraph work in the late 19th century made clear.

In contrast, by the turn of the century teaching in English Canada was a 'feminized' profession, with a smaller cohort of male teachers located in the higher grades and management positions. Similarly, retail and clerical work 'feminized' with the advent of large *department stores and highly bureaucratized, expanding corporate enterprises that sought less costly female labour, though women's suitability was rationalized with a gender ideology of innate sexual differences. In Quebec, women professionals experienced a distinct history: jobs such as *nursing, teaching, and social service work were dominated by Catholic religious orders that provided career-minded women with a highly respected work option other than marriage and motherhood.

Despite the hopes of suffragists that the First World War would alter women's work roles, few women assumed 'men's jobs' and major changes did not materialize, although the influx of white, educated women into areas such as bank telling may have accelerated. By the 1920s, work as a temporary endeavour before marriage was accepted for working-class girls, although the ideal—

often unattainable—of the 'family wage', or male breadwinner, still prevailed. Patterns of inequality were modernized as young white women took up new forms of routinized white-collar or mass production work, while still earning about 60 per cent of men's average wages.

Patterns of low female unionization also persisted, in part because the union movement was dominated by skilled workers more interested in securing a family wage. Socialist and communist radicals who tried to organize unskilled and marginalized women had some small success in a few industries such as garment making, indicating the desire of working women to improve workplace lives that were characterized by intense supervision, little chance of upward mobility, uncertain and seasonal rhythms of work, and low wages. Although the female workforce was predominantly white, it also evidenced rigid racial boundaries, with African-Canadian women relegated to a second layer of job segregation and Native women, usually only partially integrated into the wage economy, also marginalized by racial exclusion. Immigrant women, if they were deemed 'less desirable'—such as Irish women in the 19th century or Asian in the 20th—also found work opportunities limited or training denied.

While the Great Depression of the 1930s highlighted the problems of low-paid female labour, including their relegation to domestic work, it also reinforced a male-breadwinner mentality, encoded in 1930s relief provision and in subsequent social legislation such as the Unemployment Insurance Act. Nonetheless, the emergence of large industrial *unions that were more likely to include women as part of their mandate, the temporary replacement of some skilled men during the Second World War, and changing patterns of family provision as well as economic growth after the war, did alter the female labour force. Although women were pushed out of some jobs after the war, by the 1960s a new life cycle of wage and family labour was emerging in which women's wage work was temporarily interrupted for marriage and child-bearing. By 1981, 51.6 per cent of women participated in the workforce; increasingly those numbers included mothers with small children.

After the 1960s, women's unionization rates increased, stimulated by the growth of white-collar and public sector unions. Nonetheless, studies from the 1970s to the 1990s pointed to the continued segregation of women into lower-paid service, clerical, and manufacturing 'ghettos'; the persistence of racism and a racial division of labour; and legal disadvantages for recent immigrants and 'temporary workers' doing domestic work. Women's 'caring' work in daycares or *hospitals remains undervalued, and home-based contracting out under sweatshop conditions persists. To combat such problems, union women, in conjunction with organizations seeking women's equality, have pursued unionization, women's self-organization within the labour movement, and government lobbying to secure improved labour and human rights legislation as partial solutions to continued gender inequalities at work.

JOAN SANGSTER

Wood, Henry Wise (1860–1941), farmer, politician. Born near Monroe City, Missouri, the son of a prosperous family, a Campbellite in religion, a student of agrarian reform, Wood immigrated to Alberta in 1905. Active in the Society of Equity, he joined the United Farmers of Alberta in 1909, becoming a director (1914) and president (1916–31). A charismatic and enigmatic leader, he helped define Alberta's political culture, particularly in the years after 1921, when the UFA formed the provincial government. He challenged the conventional system of partisan parliamentary government with his group government theory, and he helped define the platform of the *Progressive Party. A champion of farmer-controlled marketing systems, he helped in the development of the Alberta Wheat Pool. A powerful orator with remarkable leadership skills, he was one of the most powerful farm and political leaders on the Prairies in his time.

IAN MacPHERSON

Woodcock, George (1912–95; pseudonym Anthony Appenzell), prolific biographer, social historian, travel writer, critic, poet, radio dramatist. Born in Winnipeg, raised in Shropshire, Woodcock met George Orwell (subject of his award-winning 1966 biography, *The Crystal Spirit*) and other writers in 1930s London. A pacifist, he espoused intellectual freedom, editing the literary/anarchist journals *Now* and *War Commentary*, and publishing pamphlets analyzing social structure and policy. His utopian interests underlay subsequent books: histories of *Doukhobors and anarchism, interpretations of Canadian political figures (Amor *De Cosmos, Gabriel *Dumont), studies of Native culture, biographies of Kropotkin, Gandhi, and many more. With his wife Ingeborg (Linzer), Woodcock returned to Canada in 1949, attempting to settle in Sooke, British Columbia, as a market gardener. When that enterprise failed and he was refused entry to the United States to accept a job offer at the University of Washington, he began teaching European literature at the University of British Columbia, where he subsequently became first editor (1959–77) of the critical quarterly *Canadian Literature*. Aside from extensive travels to Latin America, Asia, and the South Pacific, Woodcock spent the rest of his life in Vancouver, where he was friends with artists and writers and where he and his wife founded the charitable organization Canada–India Village Aid.

W.H. NEW

Woodsmen of the West was written by Martin Allerdale Grainger in 1908 to raise money to enable him to marry. Based on his own experiences as a coastal hand-logger in British Columbia during the first years of the 20th century, it is less a novel than a series of dramatized observations set in the area of Knight Inlet (here called Coola Inlet), recounted by a narrator bearing the author's own name and identity. Intrigued by the individualism and initiative of the independent western logger, Mart recounts anecdotes of men who were at once enterprising and foolhardy, shrewd and naive, fearless and undisciplined.

The loose plot centres on Mart's conflicts with his boss, Carter, who personifies the raw spirit of free enterprise, a ruthless exploiter of men and the natural environment. The book opens with a brilliant description of early Vancouver from the point of view of the logger and concludes rather abruptly with Mart choosing domestic bliss in Victoria. Grainger himself went on to become a major participant in the development of the BC Forest Service, before turning to his own private lumber business.

CAROLE GERSON

Woodsworth, James Shaver (1874–1942), Christian minister and parliamentary socialist. Born near Toronto, Woodsworth grew up in Manitoba and became a Methodist minister. He suffered a crisis of faith and left the church in 1918. Until then he assuaged his doubts by alternative service in the *social gospel, after 1907 as superintendent of a mission, and then as a welfare administrator. In 1917 he was fired from his position after criticizing the federal government's wartime policy. He supported the *Winnipeg General Strike in 1919 and was arrested, although never charged. In December 1921 he was elected to Parliament in Winnipeg Centre. He was re-elected thereafter. A saintly man, he agitated tirelessly for a *democratic socialism. His consummate triumph was in 1932–3: the founding of the *Co-operative Commonwealth Federation, Canada's first, broadly based, socialist party. Although attempts to represent Woodsworth as an impractical idealist are largely mistaken, the assessment did apply to his position on global conflict. Here Woodsworth was a complete *pacifist who believed that military action was ineffective and immoral; this view led to his lonely opposition to Canada's declaration of war in September 1939. In domestic policy, however, he was pragmatic, even opportunistic, believing that every small step of social progress was desirable. Improvements such as the old-age pension program in 1927 laid the foundations of the *welfare state. Woodsworth established the Canadian left as both principled and practical. The admixture would never win it national power but, with Liberal government help, it did influence the shape of the contemporary Canadian state.

ALLEN MILLS

workers' revolt. A term used to describe a period of intense working-class disaffection, radicalization, and mobilization between 1917 and 1925, the revolt grew out of workers' frustrations with rapidly rising retail prices, disruptive practices on the job, employers' anti-unionism, and government mismanagement and indifference to workers' interests. Although these were longstanding issues, employment at better wages made it easier for workers to stand up to their bosses, as did the pervasive propaganda about democracy, which labour leaders turned into a call for industrial democracy. Labour activists wanted economic security and more power for workers in post-war Canadian society.

Union membership grew enormously. Many women and non-English-speaking immigrants got involved for the first time, as did wage earners in previously unorganized sectors, including the public sector. All-inclusive industrial *unions and councils of unions in different trades and industries, often led by radicals, reduced barriers between workers. In the same vein, the *One Big Union, founded in June 1919, united most of western Canadian labour. Some employers agreed to collective bargaining, but most refused to negotiate. Unionists launched an unprecedented number of strikes, in which the eight-hour day became an increasingly common demand. Some were sympathy strikes. In spring 1919 general strikes erupted in Amherst, Nova Scotia, briefly in Toronto, more dramatically for six weeks in Winnipeg, and then in several more cities across western Canada. The revolt also included new *independent labour parties in every province, which soon won seats in municipal councils, provincial legislatures (where in Ontario they formed a coalition government with the United Farmers of Ontario in 1919), and the House of Commons. Lively labour newspapers carried the message in many communities.

The revolt had lost its momentum by 1920. As a severe post-war depression settled in, employers aggressively broke strikes and tried to cultivate their employees' loyalty with company welfare measures. In Quebec they welcomed new Catholic unions controlled by the clergy. Governments also tried to pacify moderate labour leaders with a royal commission on industrial relations and other vague gestures, while using harsh coercion against radicals and militants. Police and military forces crushed the *Winnipeg General Strike in 1919 and major strikes of miners and steelworkers in Cape Breton in 1923 and 1925. With a criminal law amendment aimed at 'subversion' and a new RCMP spying agency, the federal government joined business in spreading a *'red scare' about the alleged threat of 'Bolshevism'. Working-class unity soon shattered into factions of anti-political unionists, parliamentary socialists, and communists. By the mid-1920s little but hard memories survived of this period of intense agitation and organization.

CRAIG HERON

Workers' Unity League (1929–36), created by the *Communist Party of Canada on Christmas Day 1929. A product of the Communist International's 1928–9 'left turn', it aimed to 'organize the unorganized' in Canada's mass-production industries into new industrial unions and offer a complete revolutionary alternative to the Trades and Labor Congress and other reformist union centrals. In the early 1930s it led a handful of sometimes impressive, sometimes violent strikes, but continually rising unemployment inhibited its organizational consolidation. In the upturn of 1933–4 it played a massively disproportionate part in leading a national strike-wave, notably in the meat-packing, textiles, furniture, shoe and leather, auto-parts, metal-mining, logging, and clothing industries. While the WUL never claimed more than 40,000 members, its strikes invariably brought some degree of economic success, and its 'red' unions began to operate on a 'real' trade union basis. Highlighting these achievements, throughout 1935 the CPC resisted growing pressure from Moscow to facilitate the new Popular Front line by dissolving the WUL into the TLC. Between November 1935 and May 1936—a year later than in the United States—the WUL was 'liquidated', leaving its veterans to carry their experiences into the emergent Congress of Industrial Organizations. JOHN MANLEY

world wars. *See* FIRST WORLD WAR; SECOND WORLD WAR.

Wright, Philemon (1760–1839), pioneer, entrepreneur. Born in Massachusetts, Wright led a party of associates in 1800 to take up a land grant in the township of Hull, Lower Canada. Despite large investments to create a self-sufficient farming community, by 1806 he needed a cash crop and winter employment for his labourers, so he initiated the timber trade in the upper Ottawa Valley. Always an innovator, he sent his son, Ruggles, to Scandinavia to study timber technology; in 1829 Ruggles built the first timber slide at the Chaudière falls. Philemon was a respectable community leader, creating the necessary social and economic institutions, yet he was also a ruthless competitor who invaded others' property to cut timber. Wright did take the initiative to bring some order to the Ottawa trade by obtaining the 'Gatineau Privilege' from the government of Lower Canada. It established geographic limits and production quotas for the major timberers on the Lower Canadian side of the Ottawa. Wright finally achieved his dream, retiring to a farm upriver from Hull, where he died. MICHAEL S. CROSS

York boat. Named for the Hudson's Bay Company post at *York Factory, this boat was the workhorse of the inland *fur trade. Flat-bottomed, over 12 m in length, and capable of carrying over 2,700 kg of cargo, the craft was developed in the mid-18th century by *Orkney boatbuilders at Albany Fort on James Bay. Superior to the *canot du nord* in terms of carrying capacity and durability, the boats were rowed by a crew of six to eight tripmen or propelled by a single-masted sail on larger bodies of water. At portages, they were manhandled over log rollers along wide 'roads' cut through the bush. Work on the York boat brigades was back-breaking for the Native tripmen, and many died or were incapacitated. By the late 19th century the boats were replaced by steamboats on many northern routes, and by 1920 the York boat had passed from service. ROBERT J. COUTTS

York Factory. Established in 1684 at the mouth of the Hayes River by English traders for the *Hudson's Bay Company, York Fort (as it was first called) quickly rose to prominence as the major fur-trading post on western *Hudson Bay. Situated astride a major river route to the interior, it became a trade destination for First Nations groups as far away as the northern plains. In the late 18th century, with expansion inland of the company's post network, York became the headquarters of the HBC's Northern Department and served as the chief transshipment point for furs, supplies, and trade goods freighted between the western interior and Europe. At the height of its influence in the late 1850s it boasted some 50 buildings as well as a large complement of European, Métis, and *Omushkego* Cree servants. With the development of railways and steamboats in the late 19th century, the HBC slowly abandoned its Hudson Bay route, and York Factory dwindled to a mere regional trading post.

ROBERT J. COUTTS

Young, John (1773–1837), merchant, agriculturalist, politician. Young moved from his native Scotland in 1814, seeking his fortune in the commercial boom at Halifax late in the Napoleonic Wars. Trapped there by the hard times that came with peace, he drew on his theoretical knowledge of Lowland Scottish farming to agitate for improved agricultural methods as the key to achieving colonial economic prosperity. Writing as 'Agricola', and with the backing of Lieutenant-Governor *Dalhousie, Young emerged as the secretary-treasurer of the newly established Central Board of Agriculture, which coordinated promotion of innovations such as crop rotation, importation of pedigree livestock, and the use of farm machinery. The board died in 1826, thanks in large measure to Young's dictatorial manner and refusal to admit that Nova Scotia's scarred terrain and difficult climate gave it only limited agricultural potential. He then turned to politics, entering the legislature to campaign for reforms ranging from lower taxes to decentralization of the public administration. Although widely regarded as an ambitious opportunist, Young did help focus debate on issues of public policy and thus contributed to Nova Scotia's early-19th-century 'intellectual awakening'. D.A. SUTHERLAND

Young Men's Christian Association. Founded in 1844 by a young Englishman, George Williams, the YMCA served the spiritual, intellectual, and physical needs of Christian males in the industrial age. After the first North American branch was founded in Montreal in 1851, other centres established YMCAs as thousands of young men flocked to Canada's growing cities. In addition to providing physical and social programming, the YMCA pioneered in the field of job training and operated as an employment agency.

In 1911 Canada's YMCAs established a separate national organization and, through membership in the World Alliance of YMCAs, gained representation on the world stage. By the late 19th century membership had been extended to younger boys, and in 1913 Taylor Statten, the YMCA's first national boys' work secretary, launched a fourfold training program that generations of Canadians followed in Trail Rangers and Tuxis squares. The YMCA also provided Canada's first classes for non-English immigrants and took the lead in the adult education field, where association efforts culminated in the founding of Sir George Williams College in Montreal. During both world wars YMCA staff and volunteers were sent abroad to serve Canada's soldiers. Over the second half of the 20th century programming continued to evolve to meet the changing needs of Canada's increasingly urbanized, multicultural population. As the YMCA celebrated 150 years in Canada in 2001, 61 branches offered a broad range of recreational, educational, and social services to men, women, and children of all ages, faiths, and ethnicities.

PATRICIA G. DIRKS

Young Women's Christian Association. Canada's first YWCA was organized in Saint John in 1870; within five years there were associations in Toronto, Montreal,

Quebec City, and Halifax. In these and other urban centres the women who ran YWCAs provided the growing population of single females, many of whom had left their family homes in search of work, with a wide variety of services, including accommodation and respectable recreational opportunities. Canada's YWCAs were brought together as a national organization in 1893; two years later the Canadian YWCA held its first annual meeting and was the fifth national association to join the world's YWCA. Ever since, at home and abroad, this charitable, voluntary association has striven for the improvement and development of the status of women and their families.

Early in the 20th century the YWCA expanded to meet the perceived needs of Canada's girls. In addition to getting domestic science taught in the nation's schools, it introduced Canadian girls to camping beginning in 1910. During the First World War it developed Canadian Girls in Training, a program designed to produce well-rounded, self-sufficient female citizens as well as homemakers. As the century progressed, YWCA programming evolved to provide women of all ages, races, and religions with opportunities to realize their full potential. By the dawn of the 21st century YWCA and YMCA–YWCAs operated in over 200 communities across Canada so as to achieve the YWCA's Mission: 'A Voice of Equality . . . A Strong Voice for Women'. PATRICIA G. DIRKS

youth. Definitions of 'youth' are as diverse as its historic experiences. Rather than any specific age-marker, adulthood has historically been signified by the establishment of an independent household, most commonly through marriage. The *Canadian Youth Commission, initiated by the federal government in 1943, encompassed young people 15 to 25. The difficulty of setting age boundaries reflects the importance of socio-historical context for understanding life stages.

In pre-industrial Canada, the labour of *children and young people contributed significantly to the family economy. Although the setting changed from farm, artisanal workshop, or family business to factory and office with industrialization, the majority of young people were working full time by the age of 14. By the end of the 19th century, laws proscribing child labour and establishing mandatory elementary schooling to age 14 defined childhood's end, just as changes in production were making self-sustaining employment for older children more difficult to find. A growing proportion of children of all classes were residing with their parents into their late teens and early twenties, as schooling gradually replaced apprenticeship, domestic service, or other wage labour for adolescents. By the 1920s, a broader public appreciation of the socio-economic benefits of secondary schooling, declining job opportunities for youth, and the effects of provincial education laws raising the age of school-leaving to 16, made for unprecedented high school enrolments, increasingly regular attendance, and rising graduation rates.

Also at this time the subject of 'problem youth' attracted public attention. Adult anxieties were reflected in such measures as the 1908 federal Juvenile Delinquency Act, which established a whole new category of youthful lawbreakers. One of the period's most striking developments, and the cause of much public concern, was the emergence of a distinctive youth culture. The abundant and varied diversions of the new day—the dance halls, cinemas, spectator sports, and automobile trips—energized an emergent youth culture that would come to signify mass culture itself, a youth-oriented, mixed-sex world of pleasure. As young people became a stronger market force after the Great War, the public perception of adolescence as a distinct life-stage with its own unique culture was enhanced.

Even the hardships of the Great Depression would not reverse this trend. During the 1930s youth unemployment reached crisis proportions. Many of those who 'rode the rails' in search of work and sustenance were single young men, sparking fears of revolution and moral degeneration. With the 1940s and the great demand for industrial, volunteer, and military recruits to prosecute the war, young people again became a valuable national resource. The immediate post-war years would see this generation compensate for the postponement of marriage and family life entailed by depression and war, fostering a renewed 'cult of domesticity' based on early marriages and the demographic explosion known as the *baby boom (1946–59).

The 1950s also witnessed the 'cult of the teenager', with the mass media—especially television, Hollywood, and advertisers—united in exploiting the lucrative teenage market. The term 'teenager' came into widespread use as the age group took on new visibility. The backdrop to these developments was an unprecedented affluence. As the baby boomers came of age during the 1960s, these 'revolutionary' years were characterized by youthful mobilization and the rise of a youth 'counterculture' premised on rock and roll, experimentation with drugs and sex, and the 'generation gap'. Unprecedented enrolments forced post-secondary institutions to expand, modernize, and democratize. Movements to remedy the historic marginality of Black and Native Canadians, of women and homosexuals, gained much support from the organized student movement. Quebec youth were galvanized by the *Quiet Revolution. Sexual liberation and women's liberation became key objectives, as the advent of the birth control pill removed the constraint of pregnancy. The Liberal governments of Lester *Pearson and Pierre *Trudeau tried to address the increasingly politicized needs of youth through initiatives such as the 1963 Canada Student Loan Fund to support post-secondary education, job-creation programs such as Opportunities for Youth, and the 1965 Company of Young Canadians, intended to channel youthful enthusiasm into projects in underprivileged communities.

The youth rebellion was short-lived, not only because of the transitory nature of youth and university attendance, but also because of global economic changes. In the insecurity of the 1970s and 1980s, the new concern of the 'Generation X' cohort, or 'Echo' generation, born between 1960 and 1977, was survival, as the upward mobility of their boomer parents was no longer guaranteed to them. A renewed sense of a 'youth crisis' prompted a dramatic revision of juvenile crime legislation with the 1982 Young Offenders Act, tightened several times since in the face of public perceptions of rising youthful crime rates, despite evidence to the contrary. A special Senate Committee on Youth was established in 1986, and an on-going National Longitudinal Survey on Children and Youth continues to investigate the current generation's problems. CYNTHIA COMACCHIO

Ypres, Second Battle of, 22 April–4 May 1915. This series of bloody battles was the first major engagement fought by the 1st Canadian Division in the Great War. The 2nd and 3rd Canadian brigades, commanded by Brigadiers A.W. *Currie and R.E.W. Turner, with the 1st (M.S. Mercer) in reserve, held the apex of a huge bulge in the Allied line above the Belgian city of Ypres. On 22 April the German 4th Army launched the first chlorine gas attack against French colonial troops on the Canadian left. This burned a large hole in the Allied line, threatening a catastrophic 'breakthrough'. Then, and for the next several days, the inexperienced Canadians withstood direct attacks of blinding, choking gas and withering machine-gun and artillery fire. In spite of conflicting communications, few reserves, and *Ross rifles that jammed, their determination blocked the German advance, first by extending their line into the gap left by the French and counterattacking at places such as Kitcheners Wood, and then by forced fighting withdrawals from Gravenstafel Ridge and St Julien until British and some French reinforcements could stabilize the line. Canadian casualties were immense: 6,038 out of 10,000. The salient was reduced by 3 km, but remained in Allied hands. Brigadier Turner's command lacked both comprehension and initiative, but Currie's was good if controversial. Yet, with four Victoria Crosses, the battle was a triumph for the ordinary soldier and his commanders. It built the confidence and spirit that later would characterize the famous *Canadian Corps. For Canadians at home it was the first of many shocks of the horror of modern war.

RONALD HAYCOCK

Yukon Consolidated Gold Corporation, 1923–66. Yukon gold mining started in the 1880s. However, Joe *Boyle's Canadian Klondyke Mining Company (1905) and Guggenheim's Yukon Gold Company (1906) introduced industrialized corporate mining to the Klondike. After post-war inflation drove out both companies, A.N.C. Treadgold, a long-time Klondike promoter, combined the surviving infrastructure into a new firm, Yukon Consolidated. Reduced labour and equipment costs and the doubling of the price of gold during the Depression rejuvenated the company. Prospecting expanded its reserves and major re-investment led to rebuilding seven large dredges. Through the late 1930s and early war years gold production was steady. After Lend-Lease in 1941, gold mining lost access to labour and strategic materials. The well-stocked warehouses and large machine shop of the isolated Yukon operation, however, allowed continued mining there. Post-war inflation again ruined prospects and in 1950 the company decided to run the dredges into the ground. The durable nature of the operation meant it was 16 years before the last dredge finally shut down. The company's camp and Dredge #4 are preserved as historic sites. DAVID NEUFELD

Yukon Field Force. In 1898, at the height of the *Klondike gold rush, there were nearly 40,000 people in the Yukon. To regulate a diverse and potentially turbulent society, to emphasize Canadian sovereignty, and to enforce the criminal and civil law, the government rushed 350 members of the *North-West Mounted Police to the region. To help them, the Yukon Field Force was also sent to the Yukon. It comprised 203 members of the cavalry, infantry, and artillery of the permanent Canadian armed forces. To avoid crossing American territory, the force travelled up the Stikine River to Telegraph Creek, British Columbia, then went north over the old telegraph trail to the Yukon. There they supported the work of the police, and helped to provide a ratio of law enforcement to population far higher than anywhere else in Canada. Half the force was withdrawn in 1899 and the rest left the next year.

K.S. COATES AND W.R. MORRISON

Yukon Order of Pioneers, mutual aid society, established at Forty Mile, Yukon, 1894. Originally limited to those newcomers in the Yukon watershed prior to 1888, membership criteria later included those committed to the development and settlement of the Yukon. The order became an important network of Yukon miners and businessmen with lodges from Nome through Seattle. By the 1920s all but the Dawson lodge had disappeared. The order survived as a Dawson community organization, retaining its original fraternal purpose and meeting periodically to reminisce and maintain the order's cemetery. The business-network function was gradually replaced as parallel organizations grew up from the 1950s, though membership retains an appeal. Community service remains its most significant legacy.

From its founding the order recognized the importance of its history; over time this record has become the story of the Yukon. The order initiated the celebration of Discovery Day, the territory's official summer holiday since 1912. This holiday reflects the broad public acceptance of the newcomers' vision of a future based on resource development and external investment. Challenges to this story are rising from both First Nations and women's organizations. A Supreme Court ruling, *Gould v. Yukon Order of Pioneers* (1996), confirmed the diminished role of the order by ruling that the group provided no service to the public. DAVID NEUFELD

Yukon River. The central element of the boreal sub-arctic ecosystem characterizing much of Yukon and central Alaska, the river rises in the southern lakes of the Yukon and northern British Columbia. It arcs northwest to the

Arctic Circle in Alaska, then southwest, draining into the Bering Sea, about 3,200 km from its origin. Major tributaries include the White and Tanana, glacier-fed rivers entering from the south, and, from the northern permafrost taiga flats, the Porcupine and Koyukuk. The river follows a serpentine course through a broad valley; in some areas it has cut its way down 250 m in the last 5 million years. The valley is thought to have been one of the corridors for intercontinental animal and plant exchanges during the time of the Beringian land bridges (37,000–17,000 BC).

The river is a central element in the Athapaskan cultural landscape. The story cycle of the Traveller, a mythic hero who travelled down the river establishing the finely balanced order of the world, is a shared legacy among indigenous river people. The regular arrival of spawning salmon in three runs through the late summer and the migration of caribou herds are regarded as a part of this established compact between the human, natural, and spiritual worlds. These relationships remain important elements in the Aboriginal civilization of the Yukon basin.

From the mid-19th century, Euro-American fur traders and prospectors entered the area. The development of trade and mining was built upon the extension of a riverboat transportation system that operated until the 1950s. The natural resources of the region and large flows of the river continued to spawn grand schemes for water diversion, power generation, and industrialization. To date only one modest hydro dam, at Whitehorse, has been built. The river is a popular canoe trip. DAVID NEUFELD

Yukon Territory. The territory, with an area of 482,00 sq km, is named after the river that drains it, the Yukon—or 'Yu-kun-ah', meaning 'great river' in the indigenous language. Mount Logan in the southwestern Yukon is, at 5,951 m, the highest point in Canada. For millennia the Yukon has been home to First Nations people, most of them Athapaskan, related to the Dene of the Mackenzie Valley, with a small population in the territory's southwest corner related to the people of the Pacific coast. There was as well an *Inuit population along the Arctic coast.

Europeans came to the region first as explorers (Sir John *Franklin, 1825) and as fur traders (Robert Campbell and John Bell of the Hudson's Bay Company in the 1840s), but the Yukon was otherwise undisturbed by newcomers until gold seekers began to prospect on the *Yukon River in the 1870s. By 1890 there were about a thousand of them, centred on the community of Forty Mile, downstream from present-day *Dawson City. The region was abruptly hauled into the modern world when, on 17 August 1896, gold was discovered on *Bonanza Creek, sparking a gold rush that saw the population of the Yukon (created a territory in 1898) reach nearly 40,000. Some claims produced as much as $1 million in gold, in an era when the metal was worth $25 an ounce; it was the chance of such wealth that lured men and women to try the difficult journey over the *Chilkoot Pass, though most found little or no gold when they arrived. The rush saw Dawson City, which did not exist in 1896, develop into a modern city by 1898, with electricity, telephone, telegraph to the 'outside', many saloons, and even a railway (abandoned in 1912) to the gold fields. The role of the *North-West Mounted Police in maintaining order in a potentially turbulent community earned them a worldwide reputation. The mystique of the era was indelibly recorded in the poetry of Robert *Service, the 'bard of the *Klondike', who worked in a Whitehorse bank after the gold rush.

The rush was over by 1898, and gold miners turned to more capital-intensive methods, which required fewer people. The population began to fall, and by 1921 had declined to just over 4,000, of whom 1,500 were First Nations. The Yukon was revived by the construction of the *Alaska Highway in 1942, which brought thousands of construction workers north. Unlike the gold rush, the highway was permanent, affecting the territory in a number of ways. Notably it resulted in 1953 in the transfer of the capital from Dawson City, which was not on the highway, to Whitehorse, which was transformed from a small transportation centre to a modern city almost overnight. Whitehorse was founded in 1898 at the head of navigation on the Yukon River; at the town travellers left the train (after 1900) and took steamboats to Dawson. Whitehorse has come to dominate the Yukon because it is the centre of tourism and government; over 24,000 of the Yukon's 30,000 residents live there, the rest in about a dozen small communities around the territory. Dawson City survives as a popular tourist attraction, with some gold mining when the world price is high enough.

Mining has continued since the gold rush days, first in precious metals, then in lead, zinc, copper, asbestos, and tungsten. It has been susceptible to world prices and the high cost of production. In some years production has been very active, in others there is virtually no commercial mining. Towns such as Faro have been heavily affected by these factors, while Whitehorse, which depends on government, has been much more stable.

The First Nations of the Yukon, who now make up a quarter of its population, remained excluded from its development for much of the 20th century. In 1973, however, they began to press a claim for their *Aboriginal rights, and since no treaty had ever been signed with them the federal government felt compelled to negotiate. In 1994 the government approved an agreement in principle that brought the Yukon First Nations into a partnership with others in the management of the territory's resources, as well as compensating them for loss of their traditional lands. K.S. COATES AND W.R. MORRISON

Yvettes. During the campaign leading in to the 1980 Quebec referendum on *sovereignty-association, Lise Payette, former journalist and broadcaster and *Parti Québécois minister of state for the status of women, undertook to forge a political alliance between feminism and nationalism. Associated with feminists who believed there could be no liberation for women without liberation for Quebec, Payette compared those women who opposed sovereignty to the good little 'Yvette' described in school readers: 'Yvette always finds a way to please her parents . . . a very obliging little girl'. She presented Claude Ryan, Quebec Liberal leader and head of the federalists, as champion of the Yvettes: 'He is just the kind of man that I hate. He wants a Quebec full of Yvettes . . . Besides, he's married to one'.

Thus was launched the 'Yvette affair'. Nearly 50,000 women, led by partisan polarization into the federalist camp and calling themselves 'Yvettes', took part in meetings across the province, helping the 'No' side to victory. The affair revealed both the new role of women in politics and the existence of different feminist viewpoints. The attempt to establish a parallel between sovereignty and the emancipation of all oppressed groups (francophones, women, Catholics) ran up against a diversity of opinions and political positions. YOLANDE COHEN

zombies. A pejorative term for soldiers conscripted during the Second World War for service in Canada only, as distinct from those who volunteered for duty overseas in the Canadian Active Service Force (CASF). To preserve national unity in Canada, the government had repeatedly pledged not to introduce compulsory overseas military service (*conscription). Under the National Resources Mobilization Act of 1940, eligible adult males were called up initially for military training and later to serve 'for the defence of Canada' until the war ended. NRMA men, with their distinctive drab uniforms, were vilified as equivalent to the living dead or 'zombies' popularized by a contemporary American horror film. About 150,000 men enrolled in the NRMA force. After the government was released from its anti-conscription pledge in April 1942, political pressure mounted to compel the 'zombies' to fight for Canada in Europe. In fact, nearly 60,000 volunteered for general service (or 'converted' to the CASF), while another 6,000 transferred to the navy or air force. Faced with a reinforcement crisis in the autumn of 1944, the government decided to send as many as 16,000 NRMA men to join the First Canadian Army. However, the defence minister admitted in January 1945 that nearly as many 'zombies' had gone absent without leave as had arrived at camps in Britain. By war's end, 13,000 NRMA men had been sent overseas, of whom 2,463 were posted to units of the army. Of that number, 69 were killed, 232 were wounded, and 13 were taken prisoner.

HECTOR MACKENZIE

Zouaves. Canadian volunteers who went to defend the papal states against the partisans of Italian unity. Most of the 388 zouaves came from various regions of Quebec, just five from Ottawa. The first contingent left Montreal on 19 February 1868. It had been preceded by three volunteers: Benjamin Testard de Montigny and Hugh Murray in 1861, Alfred LaRoque in 1867. The last detachment left in 1870.

The bishop of Montreal, Mgr *Bourget, was the main instigator of this project, which received little support in the archdiocese of Quebec, the authorities preferring to send money. Propagandists presented it as a spontaneous impulse on the part of young people springing to the defence of the pope. Historians, however, have seen in it an ultramontane strategy to influence public opinion: the movement was to serve as a counterweight to the influence of the *Institut canadien and liberal newspapers. Above all, the expedition was intended to help spread *ultramontanism and to consolidate clerical power in Quebec. The Union Allet, an association of Quebec zouaves founded on 19 February 1871, after the volunteers' return, tried to perpetuate attachment to the person of the pope, religious values, and the principles of order and discipline.

CHRISTINE HUDON

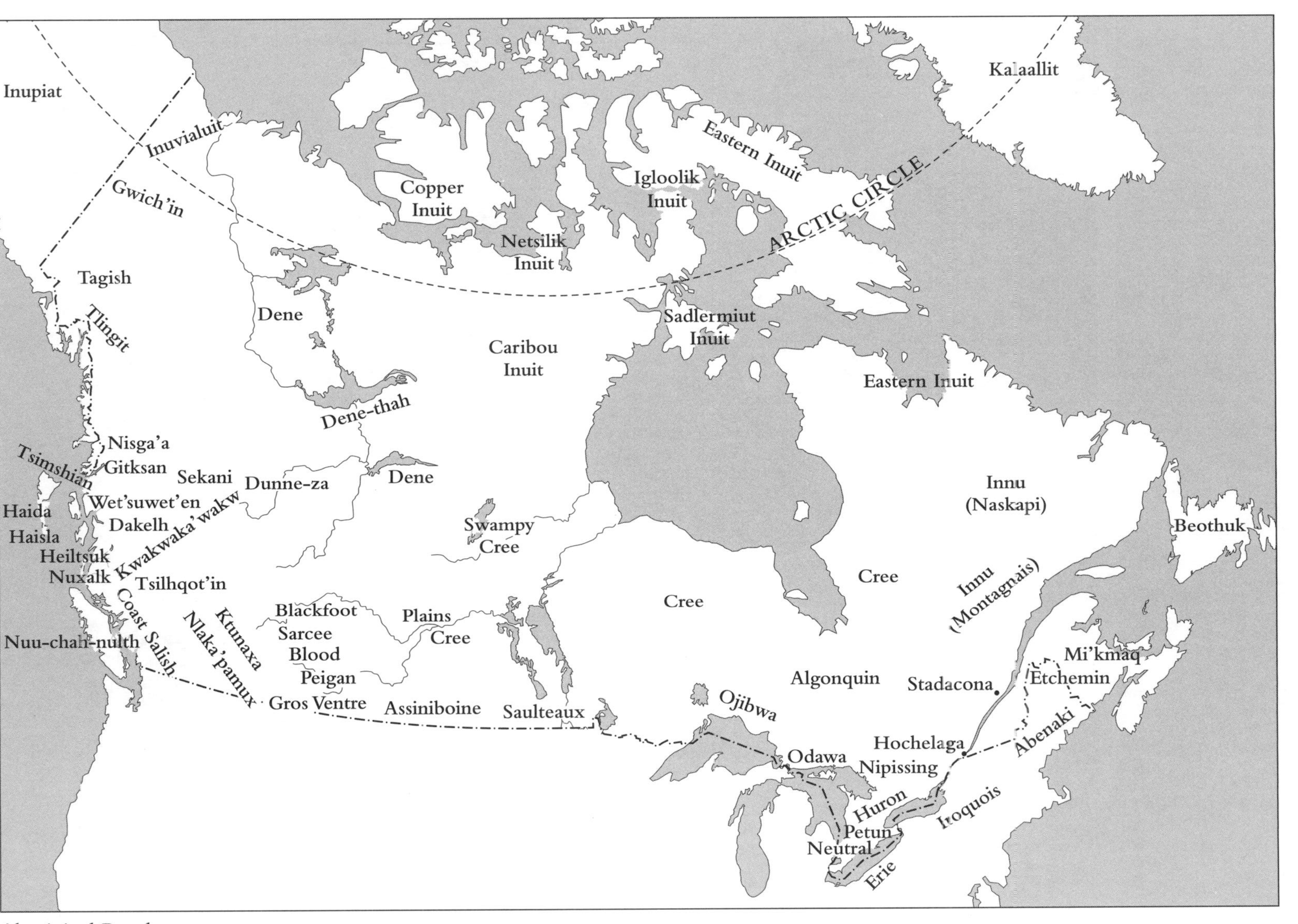

Aboriginal Peoples

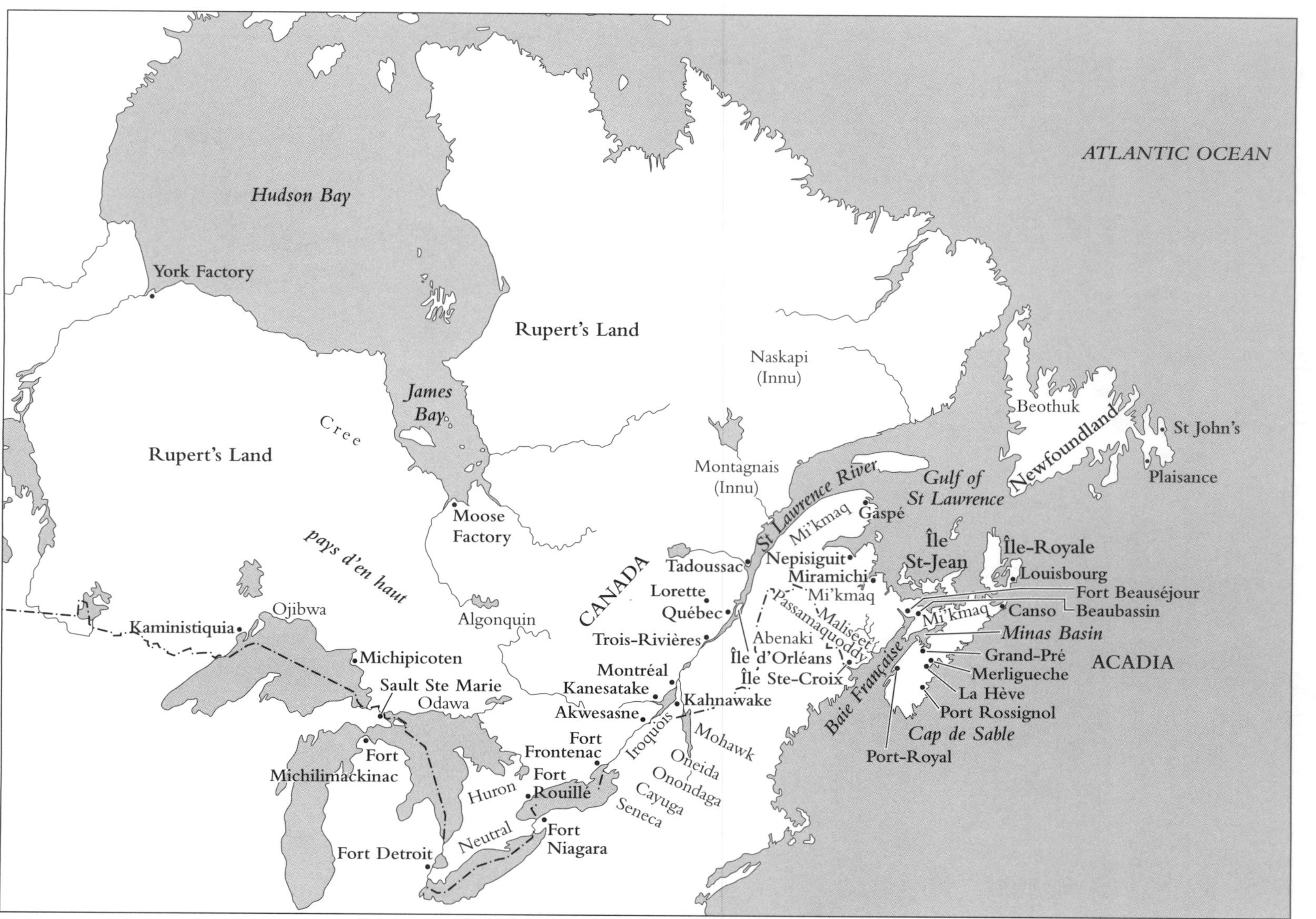
ATLANTIC OCEAN
Hudson Bay
York Factory
Rupert's Land
Rupert's Land
James Bay
Cree
Naskapi (Innu)
Montagnais (Innu)
Beothuk
Newfoundland
St John's
Plaisance
Gulf of St Lawrence
St Lawrence River
Moose Factory
pays d'en haut
Algonquin
Ojibwa
Kaministiquia
Michipicoten
Sault Ste Marie
Odawa
Fort Michilimackinac
Huron
Neutral
Fort Detroit
Fort Frontenac
Fort Rouillé
Fort Niagara
CANADA
Tadoussac
Lorette
Québec
Trois-Rivières
Montréal
Kanesatake
Akwesasne
Kahnawake
Iroquois
Mohawk
Oneida
Onondaga
Cayuga
Seneca
Mi'kmaq
Gaspé
Nepisiguit
Miramichi
Mi'kmaq
Passamaquoddy
Maliseet
Abenaki
Île d'Orléans
Île Ste-Croix
Île St-Jean
Île-Royale
Louisbourg
Fort Beauséjour
Beaubassin
Mi'kmaq
Canso
Minas Basin
ACADIA
Grand-Pré
Merligueche
La Hève
Port Rossignol
Cap de Sable
Port-Royal
Baie Française

New France

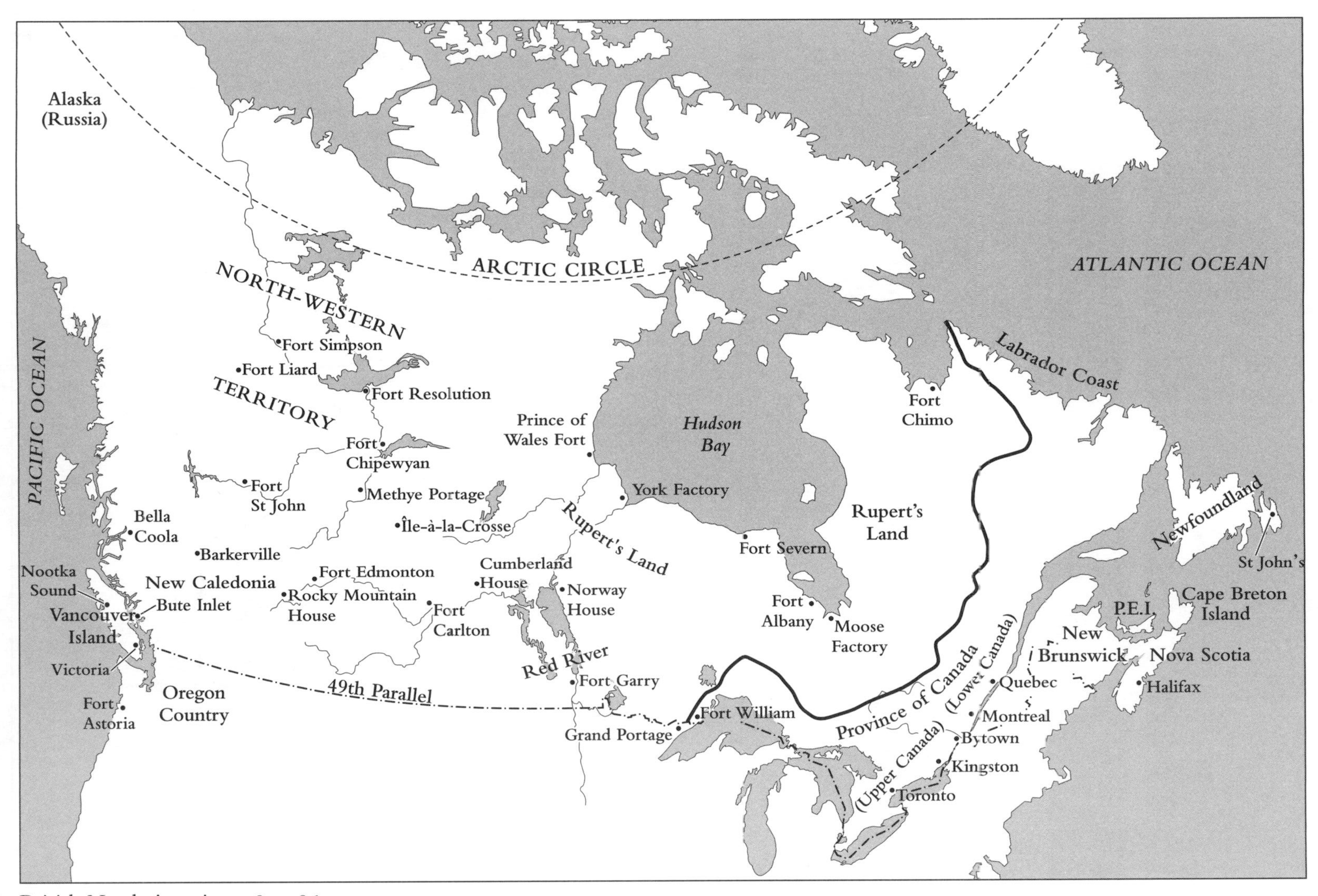

British North America 1783–1867

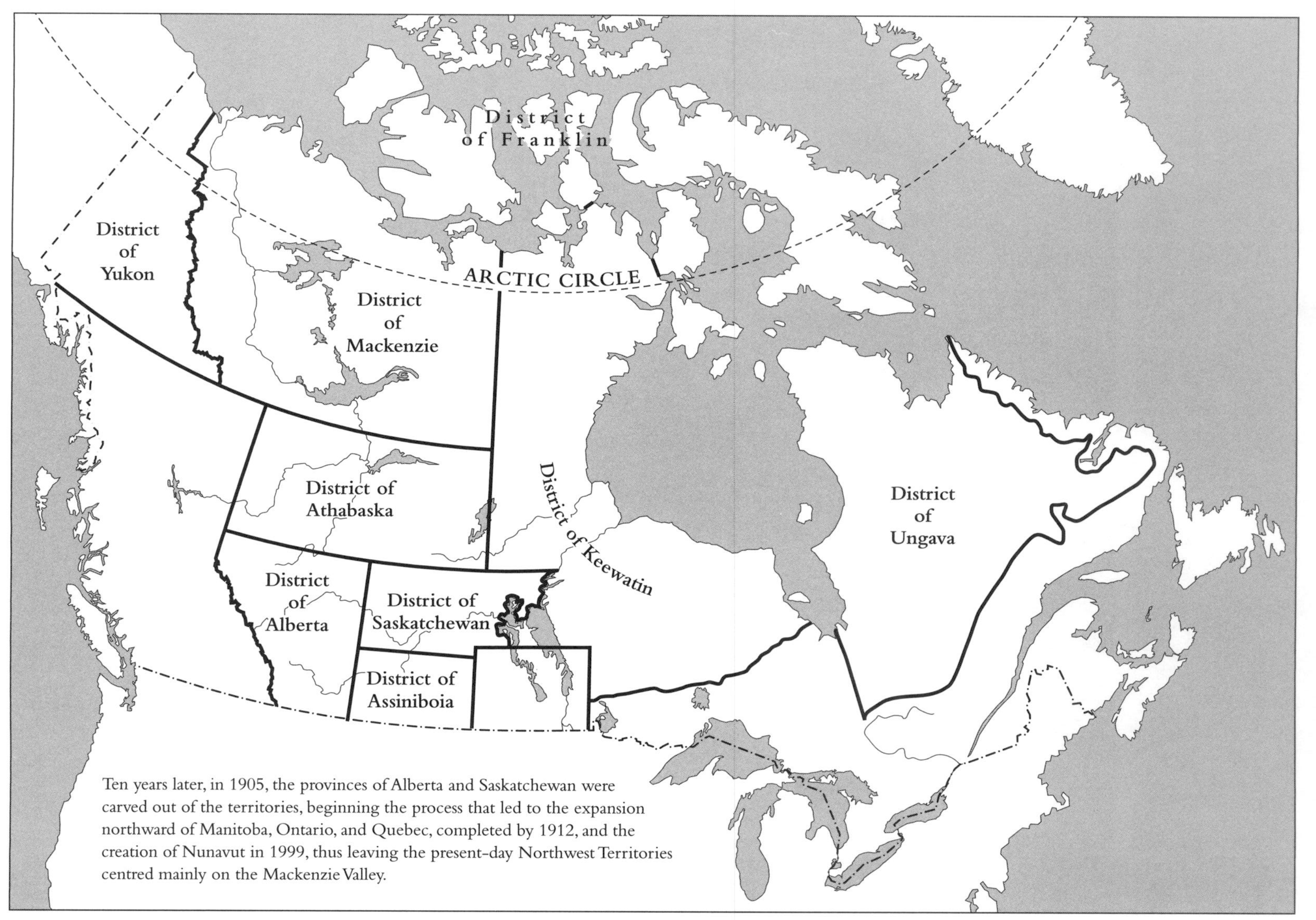

North-West Territories 1895

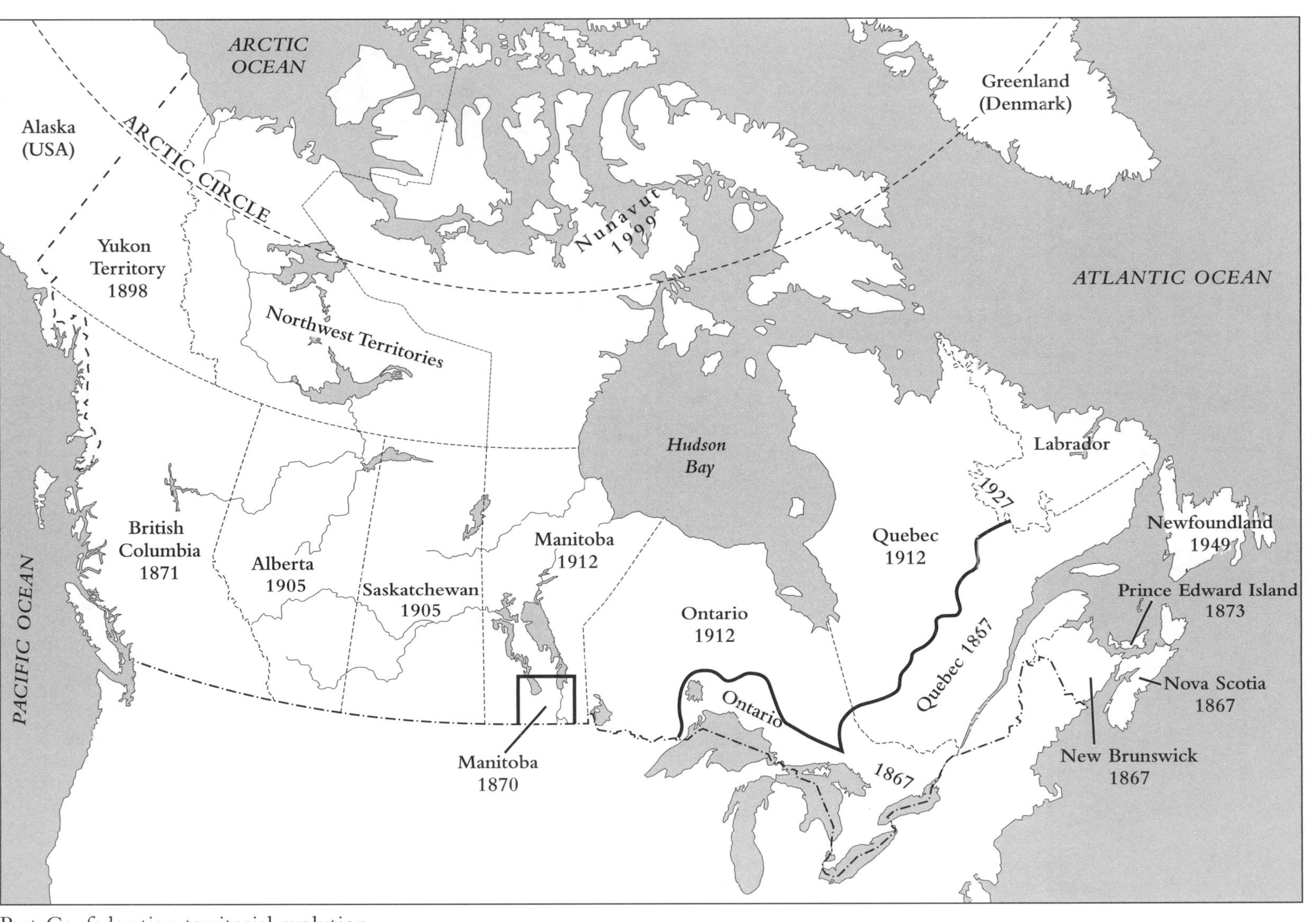

Post-Confederation territorial evolution

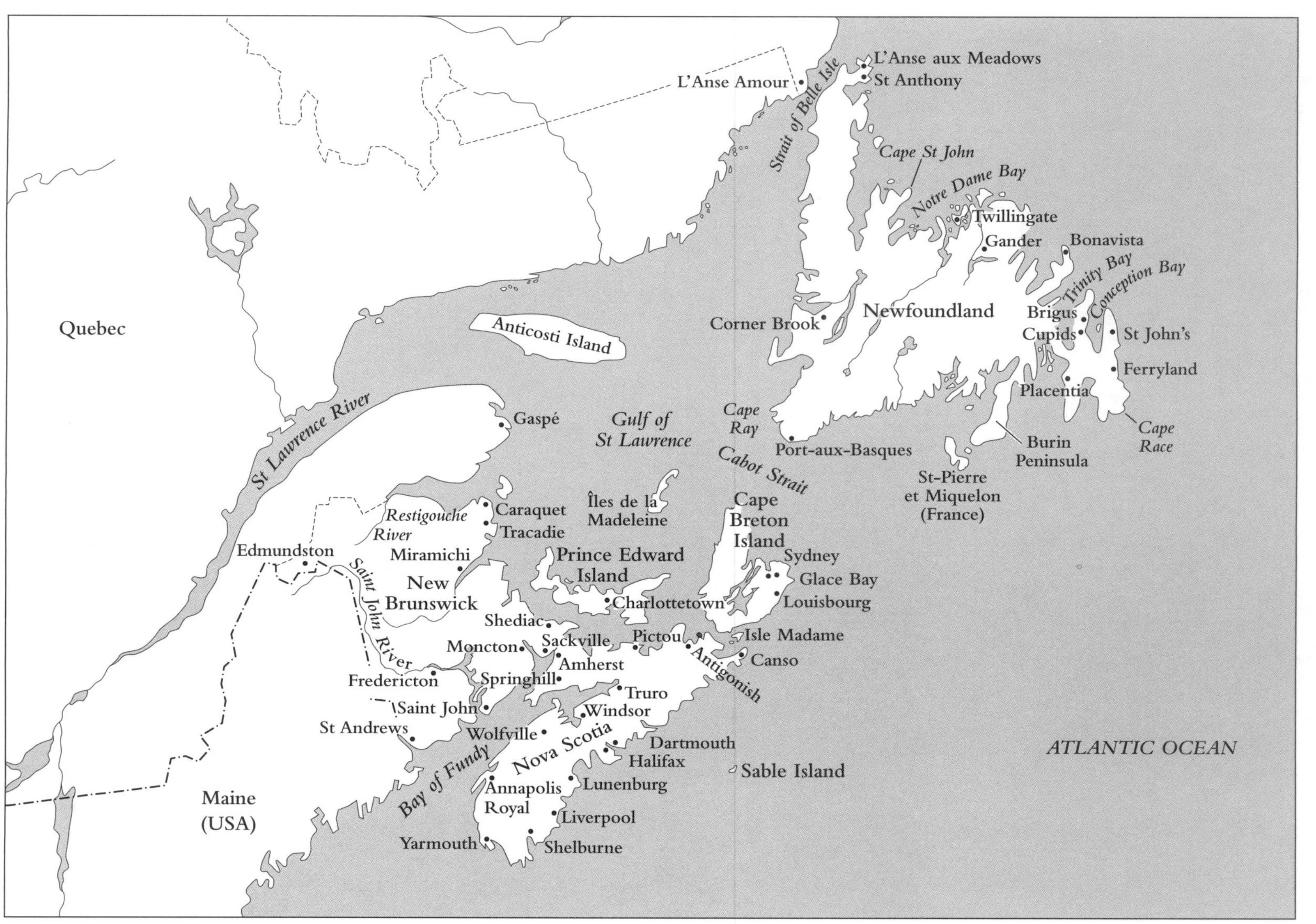

Atlantic Canada

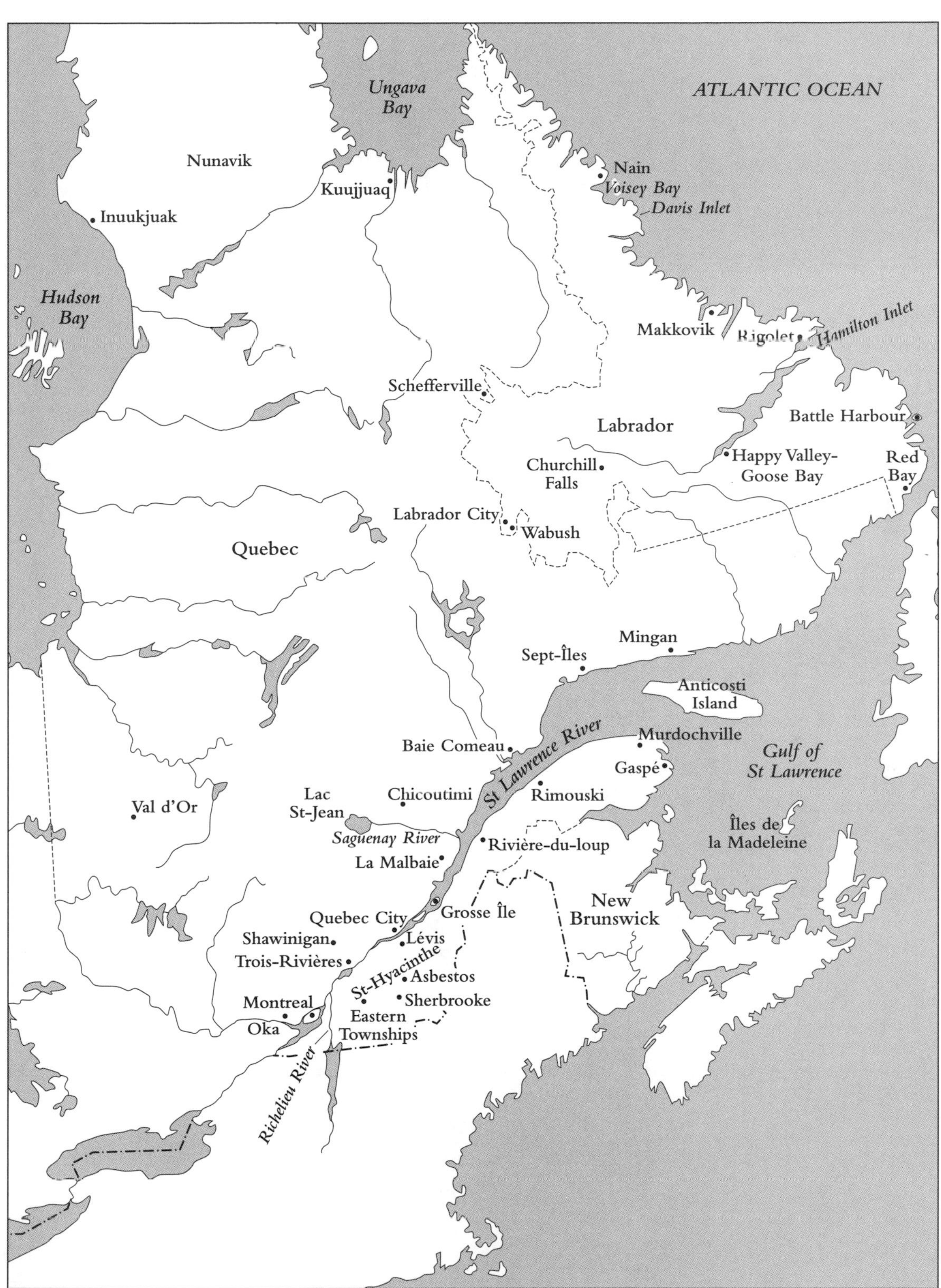

Quebec and Labrador

Hudson Bay
James Bay
Ontario
Moosonee
Moose Factory
Kenora
Lake of the Woods
Fort Frances
Thunder Bay
Kapuskasing
Cochrane
Timmins
Rouyn-Noranda
Kirkand Lake
Lake Superior
Ottawa River
Sault Ste Marie
Sudbury
Algonquin Park
Chalk River
Hull
Ottawa
Cornwall
Georgian Bay
Lake Huron
Lake Michigan
Owen Sound
Orillia
Brockville
Peterborough
Kingston
Oshawa
Port Hope
Belleville
Goderich
Toronto
Kitchener
Hamilton
Lake Ontario
Stratford
Sarnia
London
St Catharines
Niagara Falls
Windsor
Dresden
Lake Erie

Ontario

Western Canada

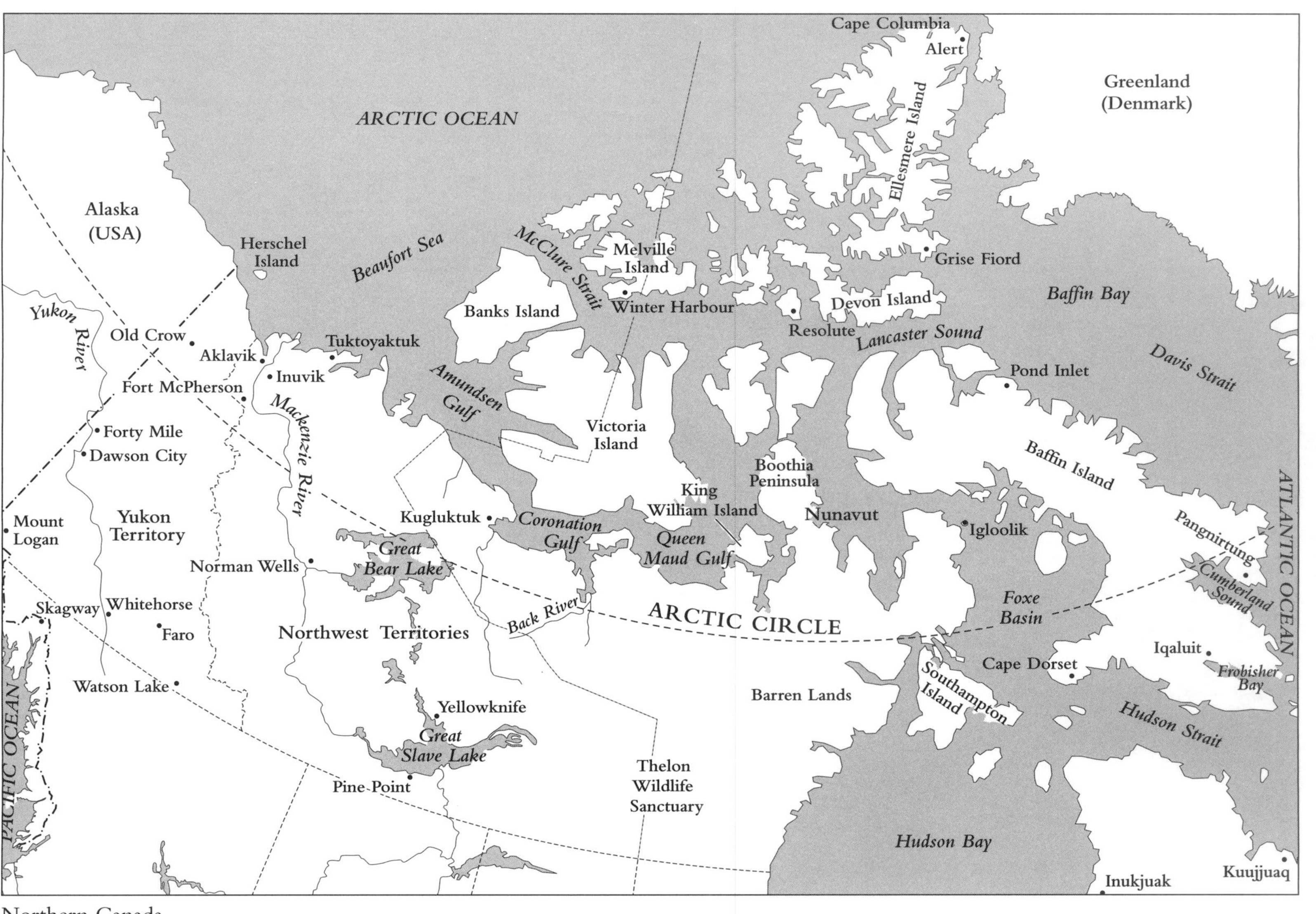

Northern Canada

Monarchs

Since John Cabot's explorations in 1497, some 32 French and British kings and queens have ruled over territory that eventually became Canada. François I was king of France when Jacques Cartier explored the Gulf of St Lawrence in 1534. Elizabeth, the Virgin Queen, was on the throne of England when Sir Humphrey Gilbert took possession of Newfoundland in 1583. Louis XIV, the Sun King, for once worried about the public purse, claimed to be able to see the towers of Louisbourg rising over the Atlantic. George III, unfairly characterized as the Mad King, was sovereign at the time of the Treaty of Paris in 1763, when New France was ceded to the British. Queen Victoria, who made the 19th century her own, ruled almost as long as Louis XIV. In the 21st century, Elizabeth II remains the Canadian head of state, though her powers and authorities in Canada have been delegated to the governor general.

French regime

François I	(1515)–1547	Charles IX	1560–74	Louis XIII	1610–43
Henri II	1547–59	Henri III	1574–89	Louis XIV	1643–1715
François II	1559–60	Henri IV	1589–1610	Louis XV	1715–(1774)

British monarchs who have ruled over what became Canada

Henry VII	(1485)–1509	Charles II	1660–85	George IV	1820–30
Henry VIII	1509–47	James II	1685–8	William IV	1830–7
Edward VI	1547–53	William III and Mary	1689–1702 1689–94	Victoria	1837–1901
Mary I	1553–8			Edward VII	1901–10
Elizabeth I	1558–1603	Anne	1702–14	George V	1910–36
James I	1603–25	George I	1714–27	Edward VIII	1936
Charles I	1625–49	George II	1727–60	George VI	1936–52
Republic	1649–60	George III	1760–1820	Elizabeth II	1952–

Governors General of Canada

Viscount Monck of Ballytrammon	1867–9
Baron Lisgar of Lisgar and Bailieborough	1869–72
The Marquess of Dufferin and Ava	1872–8
The Marquess of Lorne	1878–83
The Marquess of Lansdowne	1883–8
Baron Stanley of Preston	1888–93
The Earl of Aberdeen	1893–8
The Earl of Minto	1898–1904
Earl Grey	1904–11
HRH Prince Arthur, Duke of Connaught and Strathearn	1911–16
The Duke of Devonshire	1916–21
Viscount Byng of Vimy	1921–6
Viscount Willingdon of Ratton	1926–31
The Earl of Bessborough	1931–5
Baron Tweedsmuir of Elsfield	1935–40
The Earl of Athlone	1940–6
Earl Alexander of Tunis	1946–52
Vincent Massey	1952–9
Georges Vanier	1959–67
Roland Michener	1967–74
Jules Léger	1974–9
Edward Schreyer	1979–84
Jeanne Sauvé	1984–90
Ramon Hnatyshyn	1990–5
Roméo LeBlanc	1995–9
Adrienne Clarkson	1999–2005

PRIME MINISTERS OF CANADA

Sir John A. Macdonald	1867–73	Conservative
Alexander Mackenzie	1873–8	Liberal
Sir John A. Macdonald	1878–91	Conservative
Sir John J.C. Abbott	1891–2	Conservative
Sir John S.D. Thompson	1892–4	Conservative
Sir Mackenzie Bowell	1894–6	Conservative
Sir Charles Tupper	1896	Conservative
Sir Wilfrid Laurier	1896–1911	Liberal
Sir Robert L. Borden	1911–20	Conservative 1911–17, Union 1917–20
Arthur Meighen	1920–1	Conservative
W.L. Mackenzie King	1921–6	Liberal
Arthur Meighen	1926	Conservative
W.L. Mackenzie King	1926–30	Liberal
Richard B. Bennett	1930–5	Conservative
W.L. Mackenzie King	1935–48	Liberal
Louis S. St Laurent	1948–57	Liberal
John G. Diefenbaker	1957–63	Progressive Conservative
Lester B. Pearson	1963–8	Liberal
Pierre Elliott Trudeau	1968–79	Liberal
Joseph Clark	1979–80	Progressive Conservative
Pierre Elliott Trudeau	1980–4	Liberal
John Turner	1984	Liberal
Brian Mulroney	1984–93	Progressive Conservative
Kim Campbell	1993	Progressive Conservative
Jean Chrétien	1993–2003	Liberal
Paul Martin, Jr	2003–	Liberal

Provincial Premiers

Nova Scotia 1867–

Hiram Blanchard	1867	Liberal
William Annand	1867–75	Anti-Confederation
Philip Carteret Hill	1875–8	Liberal
Simon Hugh Holmes	1878–82	Conservative
John S.D. Thompson	1882	Conservative
William Thomas Pipes	1882–4	Liberal
William Stevens Fielding	1884–96	Liberal
George Henry Murray	1896–1923	Liberal
Ernest Howard Armstrong	1923–5	Liberal
Edgar Nelson Rhodes	1925–30	Conservative
Gordon Sidney Harrington	1930–3	Conservative
Angus L. Macdonald	1933–40	Liberal
Alexander S. Macmillan	1940–5	Liberal
Angus L. Macdonald	1945–54	Liberal
Harold Joseph Connolly	1954	Liberal
Henry Davies Hicks	1954–6	Liberal
Robert Stanfield	1956–67	Conservative
George Isaac Smith	1967–70	Conservative
Gerald A. Regan	1970–8	Liberal
John M. Buchanan	1978–90	Conservative
Roger Bacon	1990–1	Conservative
Donald W. Cameron	1991–3	Conservative
John Savage	1993–7	Liberal
Russell MacLellan	1997–9	Liberal
John F. Hamm	1999–	Conservative

New Brunswick 1867–

Peter Mitchell	1866–7	
Andrew Rainsford Wetmore	1867–70	
George Luther Hatheway	1871–2	
George Edwin King	1972–8	
John James Fraser	1878–82	
Daniel Lionel Hanington	1882–3	
Andrew George Blair	1883–96	Liberal
James Mitchell	1896–7	Liberal
Henry Robert Emmerson	1897–1900	Liberal
Lemuel John Tweedie	1900–7	Liberal
William Pugsley	1907	Liberal
Clifford William Robinson	1907–8	Liberal
John Douglas Hazen	1908–11	Conservative
James Kidd Flemming	1911–14	Conservative
George Johnson Clarke	1914–17	Conservative
James Alexander Murray	1917	Conservative
Walter Edward Foster	1917–23	Liberal
Peter John Veniot	1923–5	Liberal
John Babington Macaulay Baxter	1925–31	Conservative
Charles Dow Richards	1931–3	Conservative
Leonard Percy de Wolfe Tilley	1933–5	Conservative
A. Allison Dysart	1935–40	Liberal
John Babbitt McNair	1940–52	Liberal
Hugh John Flemming	1952–60	Conservative
Louis-J. Robichaud	1960–70	Liberal
Richard B. Hatfield	1970–87	Conservative
Frank McKenna	1987–97	Liberal
Joseph Frenette	1997–8	Liberal
Camille Thériault	1998–9	Liberal
Bernard Lord	1999–	Conservative

Quebec 1867–

Pierre-Joseph-Olivier Chauveau	1867–73	Conservative
Gédéon Ouimet	1873–4	Conservative
Charles-Eugène Boucher de Boucherville	1874–8	Conservative
Henri-Gustave Joly de Lotbinière	1878–9	Liberal
Joseph-Adolphe Chapleau	1879–82	Conservative
Joseph-Alfred Mousseau	1882–4	Conservative
John Jones Ross	1884–7	Conservative
Louis-Olivier Taillon	1887	Conservative
Honoré Mercier	1887–91	Liberal
Charles-Eugène Boucher de Boucherville	1891–2	Conservative
Louis-Olivier Taillon	1892–6	Conservative
Edmund James Flynn	1896–7	Conservative
Félix-Gabriel Marchand	1897–1900	Liberal
Simon Napoléon Parent	1900–5	Liberal
Jean-Lomer Gouin	1905–20	Liberal
Louis-Alexandre Taschereau	1920–36	Liberal
Joseph-Adélard Godbout	1936	Liberal
Maurice Duplessis	1936–9	Union nationale
Joseph-Adélard Godbout	1939–44	Liberal
Maurice Duplessis	1944-59	Union nationale
Paul Sauvé	1959–60	Union nationale
J. Antonio Barrette	1960	Union nationale
Jean Lesage	1960-6	Liberal
Daniel Johnson	1966–8	Union nationale
Jean-Jacques Bertrand	1968–70	Union nationale
Robert Bourassa	1970-6	Liberal
René Lévesque	1976–85	Parti Québécois
Pierre-Marc Johnson	1985	Parti Québécois
Robert Bourassa	1985–94	Liberal
Daniel Johnson, Jr	1994	Liberal

Jacques Parizeau	1994–6	Parti Québécois
Lucien Bouchard	1996-2001	Parti Québécois
Bernard Landry	2001–3	Parti Québécois
Jean Charest	2003-	Liberal

Ontario 1867–

John Sandfield Macdonald	1867–71	Liberal-Conservative
Edward Blake	1871–2	Liberal
Oliver Mowat	1872–96	Liberal
Arthur Sturgis Hardy	1896–9	Liberal
George William Ross	1899–1905	Liberal
James Pliny Whitney	1905–14	Conservative
William Howard Hearst	1914–19	Conservative
Ernest Charles Drury	1919–23	United Farmers of Ontario
George Howard Ferguson	1923–30	Conservative
George Stewart Henry	1930–4	Conservative
Mitchell Hepburn	1934–42	Liberal
Gordon Daniel Conant	1942–3	Liberal
Harry Corwin Nixon	1943	Liberal
George Drew	1943–8	Conservative
Thomas Laird Kennedy	1948–9	Conservative
Leslie Miscampbell Frost	1949–61	Conservative
John Robarts	1961–71	Conservative
William Grenville Davis	1971–85	Conservative
Frank Miller	1985	Conservative
David Peterson	1985–90	coalition, Liberal
Bob Rae	1990–5	New Democratic Party
Mike Harris	1995–2002	Conservative
Ernie Eves	2002–3	Conservative
Dalton McGuinty	2003–	Liberal

Manitoba 1870–

Alfred Boyd	1870–1	
Marc-A. Girard	1871–2	
Henry J. Clarke	1872–4	
Marc-A. Girard	1874	
Robert A. Davis	1874–8	
John Norquay	1878–87	
David H. Harrison	1887–8	
Thomas Greenway	1888–1900	Liberal
Hugh John Macdonald	1900	Conservative
Rodmond P. Roblin	1900–15	Conservative
Tobias C. Norris	1915–22	Liberal
John Bracken	1922–8	United Farmers of Manitoba
John Bracken	1928–42	coalition
Stuart S. Garson	1942–8	coalition
Douglas L. Campbell	1948–58	coalition
Dufferin Roblin	1958–67	Conservative
Walter C. Weir	1967–9	Conservative
Edward R. Schreyer	1969–77	New Democratic Party
Sterling Lyon	1977–81	Conservative
Howard Pawley	1981–8	New Democratic Party
Gary Filmon	1988–99	Conservative
Gary Doer	1999–	New Democratic Party

British Columbia 1871–

John Foster McCreight	1871–2	
Amor De Cosmos	1872–4	
George Anthony Walkem	1874–6	
Andrew Charles Elliott	1876–8	
George Anthony Walkem	1878–82	
Robert Beaven	1882–3	
William Smithe	1883–7	
Alexander Edmund Batson Davie	1887–9	Conservative

John Robson	1889–92	Liberal
Theodore Davie	1892–5	
John Herbert Turner	1895–8	
Charles Augustin Semlin	1898–1900	Conservative
Joseph Martin	1900	Liberal
James Dunsmuir	1900–2	Conservative
Edwar Gawler Prior	1902–3	Conservative
Sir Richard McBride	1903–15	Conservative
William John Bowser	1915–16	Conservative
Harlan Carey Brewster	1916–18	Liberal
John Oliver	1918–27	Liberal
John Duncan MacLean	1927–8	Liberal
Simon Fraser Tolmie	1928–33	Conservative
Thomas Dufferin Pattullo	1933–41	Liberal
John Hart	1941–7	coalition
Byron Ingemar Johnson	1947–52	coalition
W.A.C. Bennett	1952–72	Social Credit
David Barrett	1972–5	New Democratic Party
William Richards Bennett	1975–86	Social Credit
William Vander Zalm	1986–91	Social Credit
Rita Johnson	1991	Social Credit
Michael Harcourt	1991–6	New Democratic Party
Glen Clark	1996–9	New Democratic Party
Dan Miller	1999–2000	New Democratic Party
Ujjal Dosanjh	2000–1	New Democratic Party
Gordon Campbell	2001–	Liberal

Prince Edward Island 1873–

James Colledge Pope	1873	Conservative
L.C. Owen	1873–6	Conservative
L.H. Davies	1876–9	Liberal
W.W. Sullivan	1879–89	Conservative
N. McLeod	1889–91	Conservative

F. Peters	1891–7	Liberal
A.B. Warburton	1897–8	Liberal
D. Farquharson	1898–1901	Liberal
A. Peters	1901–8	Liberal
F.L. Haszard	1908–11	Liberal
H. James Palmer	1911	Liberal
John A. Mathieson	1911–17	Conservative
Aubin E. Arsenault	1917–19	Conservative
J.H. Bell	1919–23	Liberal
James D. Stewart	1923–7	Conservative
Albert C. Saunders	1927–30	Liberal
Walter M. Lea	1930–1	Liberal
James D. Stewart	1931–3	Conservative
William J.P. MacMillan	1933–5	Conservative
Walter M. Lea	1935–6	Liberal
Thane A. Campbell	1936–43	Liberal
J. Walter Jones	1943–53	Liberal
Alexander W. Matheson	1953–9	Liberal
Walter R. Shaw	1959–66	Conservative
Alexander B. Campbell	1966–78	Liberal
W. Bennett Campbell	1978–9	Liberal
J. Angus McLean	1979–81	Conservative
James M. Lee	1981–6	Conservative
Joseph A. Ghiz	1986–93	Liberal
Catherine S. Callbeck	1993–6	Liberal
Keith Milligan	1996	Liberal
Pat Binns	1996–	Conservative

Saskatchewan 1905–

T. Walter Scott	1905–16	Liberal
William M. Martin	1916–22	Liberal
Charles A. Dunning	1922–6	Liberal
James G. Gardiner	1926–9	Liberal

James T.M. Anderson	1929–34	Conservative
James G. Gardiner	1934–5	Liberal
William J. Patterson	1935–44	Liberal
Thomas C. Douglas	1944–61	Co-operative Commonwealth Federation
Woodrow S. Lloyd	1961–4	CCF/New Democratic Party
W. Ross Thatcher	1964–71	Liberal
Allan E. Blakeney	1971–82	New Democratic Party
D. Grant Devine	1982–91	Conservative
Roy Romanov	1991–2001	New Democratic Party
Lorne Calvert	2001–	New Democratic Party

Alberta 1905–

Alexander Cameron Rutherford	1905–10	Liberal
Arthur Lewis Sifton	1910–17	Liberal
Charles Stewart	1917–21	Liberal
Herbert Greenfield	1921–5	United Farmers of Alberta
John Edward Brownlee	1925–34	United Farmers of Alberta
Richard Gavin Reid	1934–5	United Farmers of Alberta
William Aberhart	1935–43	Social Credit
Ernest Charles Manning	1943–68	Social Credit
Harry Edwin Strom	1968–71	Social Credit
Peter Lougheed	1971–85	Conservative
Donald Getty	1985–92	Conservative
Ralph Klein	1992–	Conservative

Newfoundland 1949–

prime ministers since 1900

Sir Robert Bond	1900–9	Liberal
Sir Edward Morris	1909–17	People's Party
Sir Edward Morris	1917–18	National Government
Sir William F. Lloyd	1918–19	National Government
Sir Michael Cashin	1919	Union Party
Sir Richard Squires	1919–23	Liberal Reform Party

Provincial premiers

William Warren	1923–4	
Albert E. Hickman	1924	Liberal-Progressive Party
Walter Monroe	1924–8	Liberal-Conservative
Frederick C. Alderdice	1928	Liberal-Conservative
Sir Richard Squires	1928–32	Liberal
Frederick C. Alderdice	1932–4	United Newfoundland Party
Commission of Government	1934–49	
post-Confederation		
Joseph R. Smallwood	1949–72	Liberal
Frank D. Moores	1972–9	Conservative
Brian Peckford	1979–89	Conservative
Thomas Rideout	1989	Conservative
Clyde K. Wells	1989–96	Liberal
Brian Tobin	1996–2000	Liberal
Beaton Tulk	2000–1	Liberal
Roger Grimes	2001–3	Liberal
Danny Williams	2003–	Conservative

NATIONAL ANTHEMS

O Canada!
Our home and native land!
True patriot love in all thy sons command.

With glowing hearts we see thee rise,
The True North strong and free!

From far and wide,
O Canada, we stand on guard for thee.

God keep our land glorious and free!
O Canada, we stand on guard for thee.

O Canada, we stand on guard for thee.

O Canada! Terre de nos aïeux,
Ton front est ceint de fleurons glorieux!
Car ton bras sait porter l'épée,
Il sait porter le croix!
Ton histoire est une épopée
Des plus brillants exploits.

Et ta valeur, de foi trempée,
Protégera nos foyer et nos droits.
Protégera nos foyer et nos droits.

The music for 'O Canada!' was written by Calixa Lavallée in 1880. The French words, written by Sir Adolphe-Basile Routhier for a Société St-Jean-Baptiste festival, were first sung in Quebec City that year. Mr Justice Robert Stanley Weir's words (1908) became the most popular version in English. The song became the official national anthem on 1 July 1980. 'God Save the Queen', which had long been considered an unofficial anthem, was designated the royal anthem.

God save our gracious Queen,
Long live our noble Queen,
God save the Queen:
Send her victorious,
Happy and glorious,
Long to reign over us:
God save the Queen.

Until Newfoundland and Canada united in 1949, Newfoundland had an official national anthem called 'Ode to Newfoundland', written by Sir Cavendish Boyle (governor 1901–4), music composed by Sir Hubert Parry (1902).

When sun-rays crown thy pine-clad hills,
And summer spreads her hand,
When silvern voices tune thy rills,
We love thee, smiling land.

We love thee, we love thee,
We love thee, smiling land.

As loved our fathers, so we love,
Where once they stood we stand,
Their prayer we raise to heaven above,
God guard thee, Newfoundland.

God guard thee, God guard thee,
God guard thee, Newfoundland.

INDEX

Note: Page numbers in **boldface** indicate a major discussion of the topic.